MW01039790

To our wonderful colleagues—the health law
students and teachers who have used this
casebook over the last thirty-five years.

PREFACE

———————

This ninth edition of this casebook marks the thirty-fifth anniversary edition of this text, first published in 1987. Since that first edition, the American health care system has undergone striking changes. The system has been stressed by demographic changes, buffeted by the winds of political change, and utterly transformed by social and economic developments. The formal structure of the business of health care was a small part of the subject of health law when the first edition was published; it is now the largest industry in the country and the subject of entire graduate programs. The for-profit commercial sector of the health care economy sounded like a lamb twenty years ago; now it roars like a lion. Until a few years ago virtually no one attained elective office because of her position on issues related to health care; now, more than 10 years after the passage of the Patient Protection and Affordable Care Act (ACA), health care and health care reform is the most politically controversial issue in America.

Since the last edition of this text, the COVID-19 pandemic has inflicted devastating loss of life and health, as well as profound economic and social disruption. It has exposed and exacerbated inequities experienced by racial and ethnic minorities, people with disabilities, and other disadvantaged groups, underscoring the growing view of health law and policy as part of a broader framework that encompasses movements addressing social inequities and injustices. The ninth edition centers the broader goal of a more just and equitable health care system, and reimagines the traditional concerns of cost, quality, access and choice through this lens. We still want to know, in pursuing justice and equity, what role the law might play in promoting the quality of health care, in organizing the delivery of health care, in assuring adequate control of the cost of health care, in promoting access to necessary health care, and in protecting the human rights and the individual values of those who are provided care within the health care system.

The ninth edition of this casebook incorporates issues of equity and justice throughout the broad organization that health law teachers and students found so helpful in the prior editions. As was the case in previous editions, we employ materials from a variety of sources. This book continues to contain the most significant and useful judicial opinions dealing with the issues of health law, drawn from the federal and state courts. The book also contains statutes, legislative history, administrative regulations, excerpts from contracts, consent forms, trial transcripts and a host of other kinds of materials designed to bring the subject of health law to life in the classroom. It also contains many classroom-tested problems that should be helpful in encouraging reflections on these materials. While many of the problems and other materials have been brought forward from earlier editions of this book, every section of this casebook has been rewritten and the organization of the text reflects new developments in American health care. All cases, statutes, regulations, and other materials in the casebook have been edited to enhance their teaching value while assuring that they reflect problems faced by health lawyers coping with the health system in 2022 and beyond. The notes expose students to a range of the most subtle health law inquiries under discussion at the time of publication, including issues raised by the COVID-19 pandemic.

This casebook is divided into an introduction and four major sections. Chapter 1 provides an introduction to health law and policy as part of a broader framework that encompasses justice and equity movements, and reframes traditional concerns of cost, access, quality and choice. The next four chapters (chapters 2 through 5) address ways in which the law can contribute to the promotion of the quality of health care. This part of the casebook includes thorough treatment of governmental efforts to assure the quality of health care services, including the interaction between public and private quality initiatives, as well as analysis of both professional licensing law and medical malpractice law. In this edition, materials on the professional-patient relationship and medical malpractice have been combined into a single chapter.

The second part of the text (chapters 6 through 10) is substantially updated and the chapters reordered for this new edition. The section now begins with an expanded chapter on discrimination and unequal treatment in health care, followed by an updated chapter explaining the options available to those who want to reform the American health care system. The chapters then provide a full analysis of the consequences of ERISA, an updated chapter addressing the ACA and its subsequent legal and political challenges, and a chapter on the two largest government health care financing programs—Medicare and Medicaid.

The third part of the book (chapters 11 through 15) describes the role of the law in organizing the health care enterprise. This section of the casebook includes materials on different ways in which the business of health care delivery can be organized, materials describing the legal relationships among different players in the health care enterprise, including separate chapters on professional relationships in health care, organizational structures and corporate law, tax, health care fraud and abuse, and the application of antitrust law to health care.

Finally, the fourth major section of the text, (chapters 16 through 21) provides students with background on the role law plays in protecting the human rights of those who interact with the health care system as patients or as participants in medical research. This section of the casebook addresses the current status of laws regulating abortion, contraception, assisted conception, and human reproduction. This section of the casebook provides extensive and up-to-date discussions of the controversies over the definition of death, organ transplantation, the law of health care decision-making, and medically assisted dying. The casebook also includes a review of legal regulation of research involving human subjects, and it concludes with a chapter that addresses current developments in population health. Throughout the text, we have included materials on genetics, as well as updated and expanded materials on issues of justice and equity across many dimensions. All of these materials have been reviewed to assure that a wide range of perspectives leaven the authors' analysis of health law.

This casebook is designed to be a teachable book. We are grateful for the many comments and helpful suggestions that health law teachers across the U.S. (and from elsewhere, too) have made to help us improve this new edition. We attempt to present all sides of policy issues, not to evangelize for any political, economic or social agenda of our own. This task is made easier, undoubtedly, by the diverse views on virtually all policy issues that the several different authors of this casebook bring to this endeavor. A large number of very well-respected health law teachers have contributed a great deal to this and previous editions by making suggestions, reviewing problems, or encouraging our more thorough investigation of a wide range of health law subjects. We are especially grateful to Charles Baron, Eugene Basanta, David Bennahum, Robert Berenson, Kathleen Boozang, Kathy Cerminara, Don Chalmers, Ellen Wright Clayton, Judith Daar, Dena Davis, Arthur Derse, Kelly Dineen, Ileana Dominguez-Urban, Stewart Duban, Barbara Evans, Margaret Farrell, Rob Field, David Frankford, Michael Gerhart, Joan McIver Gibson, Susan Goldberg, Jesse Goldner, Andrew Grubb, Sarah Hooper, Art LaFrance, Diane Hoffmann, Jill Horwitz, Amy Jaeger, Eleanor Kinney, Thomasine Kushner, Pam Lambert, Theodore LeBlang, Antoinette Sedillo Lopez, Mary Pareja, Lawrence Singer, Joan Krause, Leslie Mansfield, Thomas Mayo, Maxwell Mehlman, Alan Meisel, Vicki Michel, Frances Miller, John Munich, David Orentlicher, Vernellia Randall, Ben Rich, Arnold Rosoff, Karen Rothenberg, Mark Rothstein, Sallie Sanford, Giles Scofield, Jeff Sconyers, Charity Scott, Ross Silverman, Loane Skene, George Smith, Roy Spece, Jr., Carol Suzuki, Michael Vitiello, Sidney Watson, Lois Weithorn, Ellen Wertheimer, William Winslade and Susan M. Wolf for the benefit of their wisdom and experience.

We wish to thank those remarkable research assistants who provided support for our research and the preparation of the manuscript, Joseph Allen, Debra Au, Elizabeth Bertolino, Elysia Buckley, Laura Hagen, Joshua Hasyniec, Jordan Hobbs, Menqi Rebecca Hsu, Delanie Inman, and Adella Katz. We are also very appreciative of the tremendous support and the publication assistance provided by Greg Olson, Jon Harkness and

Cathy Lundeen of West Academic Publishing. We are also indebted to our casebook shepherds—Mary Ann Jauer for the first 25 years of the casebook, and now Cheryl Cooper. We appreciate those who were there for us during the nights and weekends we spent working on this project: Roger Fuse Brown, Maripat Loftus Gatter, Victor Richardson, Ben Walker, and Cary White. Finally, we wish to thank our deans, LaVonda Reed, William Johnson, Eric Mitnick and Michael Waterstone.

It has been a splendid opportunity to work on this casebook. It has been a constant challenge to find a way to teach cutting edge issues influencing our health care system—at times before the courts or legislatures have given us much legal material for our casebook. Each new edition presents us with developments that we find difficult to assess as to whether they will become more significant during the lifespan of the edition or are simply blips. It is always difficult to delete materials that required much labor and still remain quite relevant but that have been eclipsed in importance by others, and the length of each succeeding edition attests to our challenge. The good news is that this edition retains the substantially slimmed-down size of the prior edition. We do not write this casebook for our classes alone, but for yours as well. We enjoy teaching, and we hope that comes through to the students and teachers who use this book.

Finally, this edition marks the first edition authored by this group of five authors. We are deeply grateful to the original authors who created this book and sustained it over eight editions, Barry R. Furrow, Thomas L. Greaney, Sandra J. Johnson, Timothy S. Jost, and Robert L. Schwartz, for guiding us through the last edition. We know that we stand on your shoulders and are heartened by your trust in us to carry this book forward. We also thank Jaime King, who joined us for the eighth edition, and warmly welcome Liz McCuskey to the fold.

BRIETTA CLARK
LOS ANGELES

ERIN FUSE BROWN
ATLANTA

ROBERT GATTER
ST. LOUIS

ELIZABETH MCCUSKEY
PROVIDENCE

ELIZABETH PENDO
ST. LOUIS

April 2022

ACKNOWLEDGMENTS

American College of Obstetrics and Gynecology Committee on Ethics, The Limits of Conscientious Refusal in Reproductive Medicine, 110 Obstetrics Genecology 1203 (2007, reaffirmed 2016). Reprinted with permission.

American Medical Association, AMA Principles of Medical Ethics VI (adopted June 1957, revised June 1980, revised June 2001). Used with permission of the American Medical Association. All rights reserved.

American Medical Association, CEJA Medical Ethics Opinions 1.1.2, 1.1.7, 5.5, 5.6, 5.7, 5.8, 8.5, 11.1.4 (2016). Used with permission of the American Medical Association.

Austin, C.R., Human Embryos: Debate on Assisted Reproduction (1989). Copyright 1989, Oxford University Press. Reprinted by permission of Oxford University Press.

Colorado Medical Orders for Scope of Treatment (2015 form). Reprinted with permission.

Crown copyright is produced with the permission of the Controller of Her Majesty's Stationery Office.

Devers, Kelly and Robert Berenson, Can Accountable care Organizations Improve the Value of Health Care by Solving the Cost and Quality Quandaries?, copyright 2009, The Urban Institute. Reprinted with permission.

Enthoven, Alain, Health Plan: The Only Practical Solution to the Soaring Costs of Health Care 1–12 (1980). Copyright 1980 Alain Enthoven. Reprinted with permission.

Ethics Committee of the American Society for Reproductive Medicine, Informing Offspring of Their Conception by Gamete or Embryo Donation, 109 Fertilization and Sterilization 601 (2018). Reprinted with permission from Elsevier.

Fletcher, Joseph, Indicators of Humanhood, 2 Hastings Center Report (5) 1 (November 1972). Copyright 1972, the Hastings Center. Reprinted with permission of the Hastings Center.

Froedtert Hospital—Medical College of Wisconsin, Futile Medical Care Policy (2020). Reprinted with permission.

Gostin, Lawrence O., Public Health Law: Power, Duty, Restraint. Copyright 2000, University of California Press. Reprinted with permission of the University of California Press.

Hacker, Jacob S., and Theodore R. Marmor, How Not to Think About "Managed Care," 32 University of Michigan Journal of Law Reform 661 (1999). Copyright University of Michigan Journal of Law Reform. Used with permission.

Horney, James R. and Van de Water, Paul N., House-Passed And Senate Health Bills Reduce Deficit, Slow Health Care Costs, and Include Realistic Medicare Savings, Copyright, 2009, Center on Budget and Policy Priorities (used with permission).

Leape, Lucian L., Error in Medicine, 272 JAMA 1851 (1994). Copyright 1994, American Medical Association. Reprinted with permission of the American Medical Association.

National Conference of Commissioners on Uniform State Laws, Uniform Anatomical Gift Act. Copyright 2009, National Conference of Commissioners on Uniform State Laws. Reprinted with permission of National Conference of Commissioners on Uniform State Laws.

National Conference of Commissioners on Uniform State Laws, Uniform Determination Death Act. Copyright 1980, National Conference of Commissioners on Uniform State Laws. Reprinted with permission of National Conference of Commissioners on Uniform State Laws.

National Conference of Commissioners of Uniform State Laws, Uniform Health-Care Decisions Act. Copyright 1994, National Conference of Commissioners on Uniform State Laws. Reprinted with permission of National Conference of Commissioners on Uniform State Laws.

National Conference of Commissioners on Uniform State Laws, Uniform Parentage Act. Copyright 1973, 2000, 2002, and 2017, National Conference of Commissions on Uniform State Laws. Reprinted with permission of National Conference of Commissioners on Uniform State Laws.

National Conference of Commissioners on Uniform State Laws, Uniform Probate Code. Copyright, National Conference of Commissioners on Uniform State Laws. Reprinted with permission of National Conference of Commissioners on Uniform State Laws.

Randall, Vernelia, Trusting the Health Care System Ain't Always Easy! An African-American Perspective on Bioethics, 15 St. Louis U. Public L. Rev. 191 (1996). Reprinted with permission of the St. Louis U. Public Law Review.

Schneider, Eric C., et al., Mirror Mirror 2017: International Comparison Reflects Flaws and Opportunities for Better U.S. Health Care, Commonwealth Fund (2017).

Ulrich, Lawrence P., Reproductive Rights of Genetic Disease, in J. Humber and R. Almeder, eds., Biomedical Ethics and the law. Copyright 1986. Reprinted with permission.

SUMMARY OF CONTENTS

TABLE OF CONTENTS

TABLE OF CASES

The principal cases are in bold type.

HEALTH LAW
CASES, MATERIALS AND PROBLEMS

Ninth Edition

CHAPTER 1

EVOLVING THEMES AND VALUES

■ ■ ■

I. INTRODUCTION

Since the first edition of this book was published 35 years ago, no part of the American landscape has changed more than the American health care system. The system has been stressed by demographic changes, buffeted by the winds of political change, and utterly transformed by social and economic developments. Along the way, different themes and values have emerged and evolved. Today, we are increasingly seeing health law and policy as part of a broader framework that encompasses movements addressing social inequities and injustices.

The Patient Protection and Affordable Care Act (ACA), signed into law in 2010, is seen by many as the culmination of decades of health equity reform efforts, including efforts to advance mental health, improve the health of racial minorities and other vulnerable populations, and implement universal health reforms. See Daniel E. Dawes, 150 Years of Obamacare (2016), for a comprehensive history of the health equity movement leading to the enactment of the ACA. Less than ten years later, the COVID-19 pandemic brought the need for health equity reform into devastating relief as it exposed and exacerbated the persistent inequities experienced by racial and ethnic minorities, people with disabilities, and other disadvantaged groups.

As the chapters in this book demonstrate, health law and policy can be motivated by diverse economic, political, cultural, and social justice goals. This chapter highlights concerns about justice and equity that are increasingly reflected in health care law and policy and that appear throughout this book. Section II of the chapter introduces the concepts of just allocation of health care resources and costs, discrimination and inequities in the health care system, and health equity. Section III then introduces the traditional concerns of the health care system—cost, quality, and access—and shows how they fit within the larger frame of justice and equity. Section IV briefly addresses the legal and ethical principles of equitable distribution of health risks through insurance, and it compares pre-ACA and post-ACA concepts of health insurance. It also discusses what counts as a health care "cost" and highlights issues of justice and equity that arise in distributing the cost of illness and the cost of care. Section V presents a case addressing a dispute about what counts as illness and what counts as health care. Studying that case will trigger a number of fundamental questions. How helpful are the metrics of cost, quality, and access in individual cases or when designing what will be covered under insurance? How do we equitably balance those concerns when they conflict? How do we know whether a treatment is useful or not? Who should decide?

II. JUSTICE AND EQUITY

The growing focus on justice and equity in health law and bioethics highlights three concepts: just allocation of health care resources and costs; discrimination and inequities in the health care system; and health equity. Concerning the first, the vigorous discussion and debate around the ACA shined a powerful spotlight on the values and principles underlying the allocation of health care resources and costs within the U.S. health care system. The continuing legal and political challenges to the ACA reflect competing conceptions of resource allocation. See Chapter 7. Concern for distributive justice, or the just distribution of scarce or restricted health care resources, did, of course, pre-date the ACA. For example, such concern has figured prominently in decision-making regarding the retrieval and allocation of scarce human organs for transplantation, which is examined in Chapter 17.

Traditionally, ethical and legal analysis of the distribution of health care begins with addressing one question: is health care is distinguishable from other goods and services that are governed by market transactions? Differing opinions on this question are reflected in the social solidarity and actuarial fairness models of insurance introduced in Section III of this chapter. A second question is how much of a role, if any, the market should play in the allocation of health care resources. Because the private market continues to play a large role in the distribution of health insurance and health care in the U.S., a core focus of debate is whether regulation, competition, or some combination of the two is the best strategy for improving our health care system and moving it toward the ultimate goal of providing quality health care to more people at lower cost. This central debate is highlighted in Section III and explored in detail in Chapter 7.

Addressing the second concept, discrimination has shaped our health care system, and individual and structural inequities continue to play a significant role in health care access, quality, financing, and reform. Consider that U.S. hospitals and other health care facilities were segregated by law well into the late 1960s, and by custom for some time thereafter. Consider, too, that well into the 1990s, individuals with disabilities were subject to unnecessary institutionalization, often under inhumane conditions, as a form of "treatment" for a wide range of physical and mental disabilities.

Today, there is a strong and growing literature about the health effects of discrimination for individuals and communities. The importance of equal and non-discriminatory access is reflected in the number of federal laws prohibiting discrimination in health insurance or health care. These laws prohibit discrimination in health care, health insurance, or both, on the basis of race, color and national origin, disability, genetic information, gender, and age. Section 1557 of the ACA affirmed and expanded many of these pre-existing protections. Chapter 6 examines how effectively these and related laws address the individual and structural barriers experienced by patients in health care services, programs, and activities, and in health insurance.

Civil rights laws have long attempted to address inequities across many areas of American life, but these laws have proved challenging to apply in the context of health policy. Reliance on the private market, the historic linkage of insurance with employment, and American ideas about individualism have all been identified as barriers. See, e.g., Angela P. Harris & Aysha Pamukcu, The Civil Rights of Health: A New Approach to Challenging Structural Inequality, 67 UCLA L. Rev. 758 (2020). The structure of antidiscrimination law itself also presents challenges. The typical approach of these laws is to prohibit discrimination based on an individual's specific characteristics that signify membership in a "protected class" or group that has experienced a history of discrimination and disadvantage. But some have argued instead for a universal approach, one that provides uniform protections to all without reference to specific characteristics. Supporters of this approach argue that it avoids counterproductive reliance on group identity and captures forms of unfairness not addressed under traditional anti-discrimination law.

The ACA reflects both approaches: it builds on and expands existing protections for disadvantaged groups, and it provides other protections that apply to all, regardless of membership in a protected class. For example, a law that prohibits insurers from charging higher premiums based on race reflects the traditional approach, whereas a guarantee of affordable coverage for all (defined as a percentage of household income) reflects the universal approach. These and other reforms to private and public insurance are examined in Chapters 7 and 9.

As for the third concept, achieving equity (and justice) in health care means going beyond addressing discrimination to deal with underlying health disparities. A "health disparity" is a particular type of population-level health difference that is linked to a history of social, economic, or environmental disadvantage. The term generally refers to differences in health status or health outcomes, such as a higher burden of illness, injury, or mortality. It can also refer to differences in access to health care and differences in the quality of care received. Related terms, such as health inequity, emphasize that such differences are unfair, unjust, and avoidable. However, despite decades of health equity reform efforts, health inequities across race, gender, and disability persist, even after controlling for factors such as ability to pay and medical need. These inequities raise not only ethical concerns about discrimination and social injustice in our health care system, but also pragmatic concerns for that system because they signal a pattern of lapses in quality of care and the creation of excess cost.

The ACA contains multiple provisions aimed at reducing and eliminating health inequities. For example, provisions promoting broader access to affordable and adequate care, such as those authorizing the expansion of Medicaid and requiring that new plans cover preventive services without deductibles or copayments, contribute to the reduction of health inequities by aiming to improve health overall. Other provisions address disparities specifically. They include the Section 1557 discrimination prohibition mentioned earlier in this chapter and new tools to collect, analyze, and share standardized data. These provisions are discussed throughout the book, and in more detail in Chapters 6, 9, and 10.

Ultimately, the concepts of justice and equity point to the goal of health equity. Health equity is an ambitious goal, encompassing and going beyond each of the three concepts addressed above. Consider this definition of health equity from Paula Braveman et al., What is Health Equity? And What Difference Does a Definition Make? Princeton, NJ: Robert Wood Johnson Foundation, 2017:

> Health equity means that everyone has a fair and just opportunity to be as healthy as possible. This requires removing obstacles to health such as poverty, discrimination, and their consequences, including powerlessness and lack of access to good jobs with fair pay, quality education and housing, safe environments, and health care.

Equal access to quality care is important to the health of individuals and communities, but it is not the only factor that influences health. It is well established that social and economic factors also influence health outcomes. These factors, commonly referred to as "social determinants of health," include conditions of early childhood, education, employment, income, housing, the physical environment, access to food, and discrimination and social problems. Addressing these social determinants of health is important for achieving greater and more equitable health on a population-wide level. See Chapter 21.

III. COST, QUALITY, AND ACCESS

Cost, quality, and access—what some have called the "iron triangle"—have been the traditional concerns of health policy in the U.S. Yet, given the broader aspiration that our health care system will become just and equitable, they must be reimagined. For example, in pursuing justice and equity, we want to know what role the law might play in promoting the quality of health care, in organizing the delivery of health care, in assuring adequate control of the cost of health care, in promoting access to necessary health care, and in protecting the human rights and the values of individuals and populations who are provided care within our health care system. For a discussion of the impact of this iron triangle of cost, quality, and access within emergent health justice framing, see Chapter 7. See also Lindsay F. Wiley, Elizabeth Y. McCuskey, Matthew B. Lawrence, and Erin C. Fuse Brown, Health Reform Reconstruction, 55 U.C. Davis L. Rev. 657 (2021).

The area of "cost" encompasses actual health-related expenses, such as amounts individuals pay out of pocket for medical services and products, and—for those who are insured—premiums paid for health insurance. Such expenses also include the cost to employers and taxpayers of providing tax-advantaged health insurance to employees, as well as the cost to taxpayers of funding and operating public insurance programs, Veterans Administration hospitals and clinics, state hospitals, and other public health care programs and providers. Additionally, they include the systematic cost of uncompensated care, which leads directly to higher health care prices and indirectly—through consumer bankruptcies—to higher prices generally, especially higher consumer credit interest rates. Finally, there is the cost of unnecessary care, which increases utilization of care, drives up the cost of insurance, and increases the incidence of iatrogenic injuries (unintended injuries resulting from medical treatment) that generate still more costs.

When reconceived within a health equity and justice framework, however, our understanding of cost must stretch to account for more than just actual expenses; it must encompass the cost of *health care that is not received when needed*. Sick or injured individuals who forgo needed care incur personal cost when, for example, they lose income from missed workdays, and their lost productivity imposes costs on their employers and co-workers. But the COVID-19 pandemic has underscored that the costs can be far greater than that: when untreated, contagious disease will spread to others, can create even greater disruptions to work and education, and can overwhelm the hospitals and personnel who provide life-saving care.

Injuries or illnesses that are not treated thoroughly and in a timely manner also impose non-financial costs. The ability of individuals to participate in family life, social life, and political life is diminished by under-treated illnesses and injuries and, when the incidence of under-treated ill-health becomes significant at a population level, these become significant societal costs as well. Sickness, injury, and impairments also impose costs not typically categorized as "health care costs," including uncompensated caregiving by family or friends; equipment, supports and services necessary to maintain function and independent living when possible; residential supports such as assisted living; and transportation to and from health care offices and facilities.

In short, the concept of cost as used here recognizes that, as a matter of personal and public well-being, there are both monetary and non-monetary costs for ill-health and for health care, and these costs are not distributed equitably. The issue of cost is discussed throughout the book, and in more detail in Chapters 6, 7, and 9.

Turning to reenvision the next angle of the iron triangle, a just and equitable health care system must deliver care *of at least a minimal "quality"* for *everyone*. Quality is implicated by efforts both to promote and preserve good health and, when illness or injury occurs, to restore health safely and effectively through the work of health care professionals, institutions, and integrated delivery systems. So, for example, the quality of care a patient receives is determined not only by the professionalism of her physician or other medical professional, but also by the ability of the payer network and the clinic or hospital through which her physician practices to organize all aspects of the delivery of that patient's care.

Increasingly, physicians and hospitals are parts of ever-larger delivery systems that provide thousands of individuals with all the care they might need, and many such systems include health plans that provide coverage for care received through an integrated delivery system. As those systems exert more control over their affiliated health care professionals and institutions, quality of care is determined more often by the quality of integration and management of these systems. For these reasons, quality is increasingly important as a measurable outcome that can be used by patients, policymakers, and payers to evaluate providers, institutions, and systems. These aspects of quality are explored most particularly in Chapters 2–5.

The concept of quality also has a regulatory dimension. Preventing ill-health and, when necessary, restoring health depend not only on private health care providers, but also on public systems. For example, state licensing systems and conditions imposed by Medicare and Medicaid on participating providers assure levels of provider quality. Licensure is addressed in Chapter 2, and "conditions of participation" in public insurance programs as quality levers are explored in Chapter 3. Similarly, the Food and Drug Administration assures that privately marketed drugs and devices are safe, effective, and unadulterated. State and federal public health systems that track infectious diseases, require certain food labels, inspect grocery stores and restaurants, and monitor drinking water also promote quality by preventing illness and injury and responding to health problems at a population level. The tools of public health are presented in Chapter 21.

Reimagining "access," the third concern, most clearly requires addressing inequities related to health and health care. Concern about access highlights the problem that many Americans experience: inability to obtain health care because they cannot afford to pay for it or because they cannot find qualified providers willing and able to provide it. The access problem is most clearly demonstrated by the 29.6 million Americans who remained uninsured at the end of 2019. Those without private insurance and who are not eligible for Medicare or Medicaid lack a reliable means to pay for health care services should they experience a significant injury or illness. Even absent a crisis, they tend to suffer from poor health because they are less likely to obtain preventive care or care for chronic conditions. Moreover, in another instance of inequity, the uninsured are significantly more likely to have low incomes, which means that any medical services they receive are likely to result in bills that create a financial crisis. For a thorough description of insurance and access, among other things, see Chapter 7.

A focus on access casts a wide net across health law and policy and implicates obstacles to care beyond the ability to pay. Concerns over access include issues as disparate as the absence of accessible medical and diagnostic equipment for treating patients with physical disabilities; the lack of providers in rural areas; and conscience-based refusal by health care providers regarding particular health care services when those providers dominate available services. Along with the concern about quality, raising concern about access draws attention to patterns of unequal access and treatment experienced by disadvantaged groups, as well as discrimination on the basis of race, gender, disability, and other characteristics, across the health care system. These patterns are examined in Chapter 6. Discussing access also focuses attention on inequities in social conditions that affect population health, including the fact that those in poverty are significantly less likely to enjoy clean air and drinking water, safe outdoor spaces for exercise, and reasonable proximity to a health care provider or a source for purchasing healthy food.

NOTE: THINKING CRITICALLY ABOUT CHOICE

Some have suggested an additional concern in health care law and policy: "choice." Choice acknowledges that respect for persons is uniquely important in relation to health and health care. Individuals can experience profound vulnerability because of ill-health and as a result of paying for medical care to restore and maintain health. Demonstrating respect for that experience by allowing personal choice is a common theme throughout health law, bioethics, and policy.

Most typically, choice is associated with protection for patient autonomy in health care decision-making, and it is reflected in the right to refuse unwanted medical treatment, as well as the laws of informed consent, patients' access to quality information, and confidentiality protections, among others. See Chapters 4, 18 and 19. The concept, however, has a broader reach that warrants close examination. What is meant by "choice" when it is deployed in the context of health care reform? What is the impact of employing "choice" as a concern in health care law and policy? Is the concept serving or undermining overarching goals of justice and equity?

Sometimes, choice is described as a value that advances access to, and quality of, care. For example, insurance contracts that exclude coverage for alternative therapies or expensive drugs, or that restrict coverage to a narrow network of providers, have been criticized for denying patients access to the care they need and believe is best. In response, insurance regulations have been enacted to help promote patient choice, such as benefit mandates, "freedom of choice" provisions, and network adequacy standards. Financial subsidies, such as those available to consumers through the health insurance exchanges created under the ACA, also promote choice by ensuring patients have the means to buy meaningful health coverage and to use it. These types of laws, and the regulation of insurance plans and managed care more generally, are examined in Chapters 9 and 10. Of course, sometimes a patient's treatment choices are restricted by government regulation in the name of quality, such as through laws that prohibit unproven drugs from entering the market or licensing laws that limit the types of services certain professionals can provide.

Too often, however, the concept of choice can mask structural, institutional, and interpersonal discrimination that creates and exacerbates health inequality. As discussed in Chapter 6, choice has been used to justify refusals to treat individuals because they had a disfavored form of insurance; because of their race, ethnicity, or national origin; because of their gender; or because they had a particular type of disability. Choice has also been used to promote "health care consumerism," a model in which individuals would bear full or much greater responsibility for paying for and managing their own health and health care. See discussion of consumer-driven health care in Chapter 7.

Choice also implicates population health, often with negative effects. U.S. law and policy generally allow a variety of unhealthy health-related choices by individuals—to use tobacco, to eat unhealthy foods, to live a sedentary life. As a result, as a community we experience higher rates of illness, and we pay higher insurance premiums when the cost of treating those who have made unhealthy choices is spread to others. Included later in this chapter, and again in Chapter 7 and 9, are materials examining health insurance and the regulation of premiums.

The COVID-19 pandemic has glaringly demonstrated the ill-effects individual choice can have on population health. As this book goes to print, state legislators are clawing back executive public health powers, while claiming that getting vaccinated, wearing a mask, and operating a business in an unrestricted manner are matters of individual choice—even when those choices put other individuals and entire communities at increased risk of infection and death, deplete hospital resources, and undermine our local and national economies. We explore this theme in Chapter 21, which addresses public health law.

* * *

The three traditional concerns of quality, access, and cost—as well as different conceptions of choice—operate in a dynamic and complex relationship with each other and with the larger goal of achieving health equity and justice. To appreciate their interplay, consider the seemingly logical assumption that increasing quality or access must naturally increase costs. So, for example, increasing the required staff-to-patient ratio in health care facilities in the name of improving quality might also increase the costs of care. The same assumption could be made about the cost impact of increasing the number of individuals eligible for, or the range of services covered by, Medicaid and Medicare—the public insurance programs primarily responsible for older adults, people with disabilities, and low-income individuals and families. In each of these examples, however, it is possible that total cost is actually lowered, such as by avoiding injuries or infections in understaffed facilities or by providing timely care that prevents the extraordinary costs incurred if an untreated medical condition or disease progresses to later stages. In other situations, however, enhancing one value may have the expected impact, but whether that result is a benefit or harm is itself a complex question. Preserving individual choice through maintaining the private health insurance system, for example, most likely increases costs overall—but perhaps the increase in cost is justified.

The concerns of quality, access, cost, and choice, whether examined separately or in various combinations, also have complex relationships with the larger goal of health justice and equity. First, recognizing the role of each concern is instrumental to that goal. As explained above, a health care system cannot achieve equity and justice without accounting for quality, access, cost and choice. Second, the role each concern should play ideally should be determined in large measure by the goal of health justice and equity. But inherent tensions in the system can make this evaluation complicated. Consider, for example, the earlier description of choice. A just and equitable health care system must assure that individuals have a meaningful choice to accept or refuse proposed medical care or participation in human subject research—and yet, health justice and equity are undermined when the law accommodates individual choices that obstruct public health measures taken in response to an infectious disease threat or permits discriminatory refusals to treat. The same tension arises when striking a balance between two or more concerns. So, for example, equity and justice should be the touchstones in any Medicaid expansion debates, but this approach puts concerns about cost and access in tension with each other.

Finally, when they make health policy decisions affecting quality, access, cost and choice, having a goal of achieving a just and equitable health care system requires policymakers to account for structural inequities deeply embedded in our society. For example, Medicaid expansion by itself does not assure equitable access to needed health care services if policymakers fail to account for the other barriers to care that Medicaid beneficiaries face, such as difficulty in getting needed time off if they have low-wage, hourly jobs or the challenge of finding a Medicaid provider close by who is also willing to take them. Similarly, even if federal regulations address choice by requiring investigators to obtain informed consent before enrolling people in a human subject research protocol, choice cannot be made in an equitable manner unless regulators also account for the literacy of those they seek to enroll. As shown by these and many other possible examples, quality, access, cost and choice, when informed by the goal of achieving a just and equitable health care system, force us to account as well for social and political determinants of health.

Of course, analyzing the impact of a particular legal and policy decision on cost, quality, access, and choice is not entirely a dispassionate, rational, empirically based calculation. Political strength, economic power, culture and tradition, and social justice goals all influence how we view relative advantages and disadvantages and how we ultimately design our systems. In addition, gains and losses are not shared equally, and different stakeholders may differ in their evaluations of which trade-offs are acceptable or just.

Ongoing debates about the ACA further illustrate the complex interplay of our areas of concern. Public understanding of the ACA centers on the tentative adoption of the principle that providing access to some form of basic medical care is important to the health and flourishing of society as a whole. Access to adequate care remains the banner headline for the ACA, even as that principle faces continued opposition. But means of achieving this goal rest on a concept so embedded in our culture that forward progress for the ACA was probably impossible without honoring it: individual choice. Choice is reflected in the oft-stated mantra in the campaign to gain public support for the ACA: "No one will make you change your coverage; if you like it, you can keep it." The conflict between increasing access and the question of individual choice has taken center stage in the battles over the constitutionality of the ACA. And in addition to responding to concerns about access and choice, the ACA is also attempting to do much more in refashioning health care delivery and payment systems. The goal is to develop a system that provides higher quality health care to more people at lower cost. It is ambitious.

In the end, cost, quality, access, and, in some cases, choice concerns recognize that health is a fundamental human need. Without it, economies stall, social and democratic structures are strained, and the lives of at least some individuals are upended. The COVID-19 pandemic is a prime example. As of September 2021, nearly 640,000 Americans have died as a result of infection with COVID-19. Additionally, nearly a quarter of the 40 million American survivors of the infection have sought or will seek treatment for lingering symptoms—including so-called "brain fog"—even after recovering from the acute phase of the disease. On the economic front, 60% of businesses closed for at least some portion of 2020 because of the pandemic, and most businesses reported a substantial decline in revenue in 2020 when compared to 2019. Not surprisingly, more than 9 million Americans lost their jobs in 2020 due to cutbacks forced on their employers by the pandemic. Moreover, voters in some jurisdictions faced the inhumane choice to either risk becoming infected with COVID-19 or not vote in the 2020 presidential election.

The losses of life, health, income, and political voice due to COVID-19 have not been distributed equitably. Instead, vulnerable and disenfranchised populations have borne a disproportionate share of these burdens. The poorest among us have become infected and died during the pandemic at significantly higher rates than others. The same is true of Black Americans and those people living with disability.

All in all, systems designed to maintain and restore both individual and population health are essential, as are laws designed to assure those systems are competent, affordable, accessible, and fair to all who rely on them. While these laws have roots in a wide range of other fields of law—such as administrative law, antitrust, business associations, civil rights law, constitutional law, insurance regulation, taxation, torts, and others—they take on new meaning when applied to promote individual and population health. Wendy K. Mariner identifies this phenomenon in her article Toward an Architecture of Health Law, 35 Am. J. L. & Med. 67 (2009), when she explains how health law pursues justice in the context of health:

> Most fundamentally, health law adopts and adapts principles from other legal domains to protect the value of health within a framework of justice and the rule of law. Thus, it is not simply the rote application of contract doctrine to an agreement between entities that happen to be in the health field, but an interpretation of whether and how that doctrine ought to be modified both to achieve the goal of contract law and to recognize the value of health. In this very broad sense, health law has dual normative goals: justice and protection of health.

This adopt-and-adapt phenomenon is evident throughout the materials in this book. Later in this chapter, for example, the court in Katskee v. Blue Cross/Blue Shield of Nebraska notes the interpretive principle in contract law "that an ambiguous [insurance] policy will be construed in favor of the insured," and it does so in the context of determining that an individual's health coverage includes coverage for a latent genetic condition. In short, health law involves more than public and private health systems to which any given law is merely applied; rather, law applied in this arena must be reinterpreted because health and health care are fundamental needs. Thus, health and justice uniquely combine as "Health Law."

IV. EQUITABLY SPREADING HEALTH RISKS

A. THE ROLE OF INSURANCE

Illness and injury do not visit everyone at the same point in their lives or to the same degree. As will be examined in detail in Chapter 7, insurance exists to spread the financial risk of needing medical care from individuals to all members of a group. But how can we ensure that the personal, financial, and social costs of illness are distributed equitably? Another way to ask this is: How do we ensure that the resources necessary to fight illness and maintain health are equally distributed throughout society? What can we learn from the experiences of other developed countries?

In most developed countries, it is assumed that everyone has a right to health care. While private health insurance exists in almost all nations, most countries rely on a public health insurance financing system to ensure universal access to health care. In some nations, such as England, Canada, the Scandinavian countries, and the Iberian and Mediterranean countries, the government finances health insurance directly through general revenue funds. In many of these countries, hospitals are publicly owned, and specialists are hospital employees. In many, including England, general practitioners are not public employees and contract with the health care system. Other nations, including France, Germany, Austria, Belgium, and Japan, have social insurance systems. In these systems, quasi-public social insurance funds pay for health care under contracts with providers, financed largely by employer and employee contributions. Some hospitals are publicly owned, but many are nonprofit, and some are for-profit private facilities. Specialists tend to work for hospitals, and general practitioners tend to be private practitioners.

Finally, Switzerland and the Netherlands finance care through private insurance companies. Everyone is required to be insured, however, and insurance is financed in part through public funds, for lower-income households in Switzerland, and for everyone in the Netherlands. Insurance in these countries is heavily regulated (underwriting based on health status is prohibited) and in some respects looks more like the social insurance programs in their neighboring countries than like private insurance in the U.S.

The U.S. is unique in that it does not attempt to make health care universally available. Since the middle of the twentieth century, the U.S. has cobbled together a system of private and public insurance that covers most Americans but still leaves many without health insurance. In 2019, about 56% of Americans were covered by health insurance they receive through their job. This insurance is heavily subsidized by the public, generally through tax exclusions and deductions, and it is paid for in varying proportions by employers and employees. Another 34%—primarily the elderly, disabled, and poor children—were covered through public programs. About 10% were covered by other private insurance—often policies they purchased themselves. About 8% of Americans were uninsured. See Katherine Keisler-Starkey & Lisa N. Bunch, U.S. Bureau of the Census, Health Insurance Coverage in the United States 2019 (Sept. 2020).

Uninsured individuals have a right to obtain emergency care in a hospital, regardless of ability to pay, but they do not have a right to nonemergency care, including continuing care after an emergency condition is treated. See Chapter 6. There is a great deal of evidence that the uninsured get less care and get it later (often when it is ineffective), resulting in worse health status and earlier death.

The ACA dramatically expanded access to health care even though it has not been fully implemented. Since the ACA's insurance reforms and Medicaid expansion took effect in 2014, the percentage of uninsured American residents dropped from more than 16% to the 8% mentioned above. The ACA increased access to care by expanding Medicaid for lower-income Americans in those states that chose to do so, and by offering insurance premium tax credits to help middle-income uninsured Americans purchase health insurance. Had it been implemented nationwide, by 2019 the Medicaid expansion would have increased Medicaid coverage by adding 11 million recipients to the 32 million Americans who already received Medicaid. But the Supreme Court effectively made the Medicaid expansion optional for states, and to date, there are still twelve states that have not expanded. See Chapter 10.

Originally, the ACA required Americans who could afford health insurance to purchase it or pay a penalty; however, the Tax Cuts and Jobs Act of 2017 eliminated the tax penalty as of 2019. The ACA also penalizes large employers who do not offer their employees adequate, affordable insurance and whose employees end up receiving public subsidies. Finally, it prohibits insurers from discriminating against applicants or enrollees with medical conditions requiring care.

Although proposals for universal health care have been considered in the U.S. since the 1910s, they have always faced strong opposition from some sectors of the health care industry (in the 40s, 50s, and 60s, from physicians; now primarily from insurers). Government-financed universal health care has rarely enjoyed broad political support in the U.S. The political institutions and ideological bent of the U.S. have been quite different from those of Canada and most European countries, especially in the post-World War II era when many of those nations adopted public health insurance systems. See Theodore Marmor, The Politics of Medicare (2d ed. 2000); Carolyn Hughes Tuohy, Accidental Logics (1999); Timothy S. Jost, Why Can't We Do What They Do? 32 J. L. Med. & Ethics 433 (2004); Timothy S. Jost, Disentitlement? The Threats Facing Our Public Health-Care Programs and a Rights-Based Response (2003). Racism has also played an important role in the evolution of U.S. health policy, and it continues to shape health care politics today. Jeneen Interlandi, Why Doesn't the United States have Universal Health Care? The Answer Has Everything to do with Race, N.Y. Times Magazine (Aug. 14, 2019).

A transformation may be occurring, however, as public support seems to be growing for some version of a "Medicare for all" national health insurance program that would replace private insurance. See Bradley Jones, Increasing share of Americans favor a single government program to provide health care coverage, Pew Research Center (Sep. 29, 2020).

Finally, returning to the earlier focus on justice and equity, insurance, as a general matter, suggests a vision of justice that distributes risk broadly. Indeed, social insurance, based on the principle of social solidarity, distributes risk among the broadest possible group, the entire citizenry. But insurance can also be based on an alternative vision of justice, that of actuarial fairness, under which the price that individuals pay for insurance varies based on an estimate of their individual health risks. This difference in vision is explored in Deborah Stone's classic article on this topic, The Struggle for the Soul of Health Insurance, 18 J. Health Pol., Pol'y & L. 287 (1993).

Stone asserts that "[m]utual aid among a group of people who see themselves as sharing common interests is the essence of community; a willingness to help each other is the glue that holds people together as a society." She continues:

> While in most societies sickness is widely accepted as a condition that should trigger mutual aid, the American polity has had a weak and wavering commitment to that principle. The politics of health insurance can only be understood as a struggle over the meaning of sickness and whether it should be a condition that automatically generates mutual assistance. . . . The private insurance industry, the first line of defense in the U.S. system of mutual aid for sickness, is

organized around a principle profoundly antithetical to the idea of mutual aid, and indeed, the growth and survival of the industry depends on its ability to finance health care by charging the sick and to convince the public that "each person should pay for his own risk."

Stone concludes:

Actuarial fairness—each person paying for his own risk—is more than an idea about distributive justice. It is a method of organizing mutual aid by fragmenting communities into ever-smaller, more homogeneous groups and a method that leads ultimately to the destruction of mutual aid. This fragmentation must be accomplished by fostering in people a sense of their differences, rather than their commonalities, and their responsibility for themselves only, rather than their interdependence. Moreover, insurance necessarily operates on the logic of actuarial fairness when it, in turn, is organized as a competitive market.

NOTES AND QUESTIONS

1.   *Actuarial Fairness and the ACA.* The term "actuarial fairness" implies that fairness requires individuals to pay premiums based on an estimate of their likely need for medical care. If the fairness principle can be expressed as "treating like cases alike," is the actuarial fairness approach fairer than a mutual aid approach? Is it fair for an individual in perfect health, for example, to pay the same premium as someone with a chronic illness such as multiple sclerosis? What if a person is not ill but is engaging in behaviors that increase their risk of illness or injury, such as smoking or skiing or working under hazardous conditions?

The ACA rejects the notion of actuarial fairness in most respects, although it allows premiums to reflect the individual's age, tobacco use, and geographic area of residence. For example, the ACA allows insurers to impose a premium surcharge of up to 50% for tobacco use, which may make health insurance unaffordable for many smokers. For these reasons 10 states have further limited tobacco surcharges, and several of those prohibit tobacco rating altogether. What is the basis for the above exceptions? Are they fair? Would you delete any of them? Would you add any others?

2.   *Social Solidarity and the ACA.* Although the ACA modifies the practice of health insurance by rejecting health status underwriting and expanding public coverage, it does not embrace a vision of a universal right to health care, one based on social solidarity and mutual aid. Should we move toward that right, or should we in fact be moving in the other direction? See Brietta Clark, A Moral Mandate & the Meaning of Choice: Conceiving the Affordable Care Act after NFIB, 6 St. Louis U. J. Health L. & Pol'y 267 (2013).

3.   *Defining Essential Health Benefits.* Is it possible (or desirable) to define a basic level of health care to which all are entitled but provide health care above that level only for those who can afford it? What would be included in that package? See discussion of the "essential benefits package" under the

ACA in Chapter 9 and of distributive justice in allocation of health care resources, particularly organ transplantation, in Chapter 17. See also discussion in Section B of this chapter, below.

4.   *Barriers Beyond Insurance.* Ability to pay is not the only determinant of access to health care. Even if an individual has insurance that covers the needed treatment, he or she may not be able to get that treatment or may get a substandard level of treatment. Empirical evidence proves, for example, that persons of color do not get necessary treatment or get a significantly lesser quality of care than do other people. In addition, individuals with certain types of disabilities or medical conditions, such as HIV, chronic pain, or substance use disorders, often have substantial difficulty in finding health care professionals willing to provide care. See Chapter 6 for a discussion of laws addressing these situations.

B. THE COST AND BENEFIT OF HEALTH CARE SPENDING

Health care is expensive. The U.S. spends far more on health care than any other nation in the world—whether measured by percentage of the gross domestic product or by dollars spent per capita. We also spend more on health care than we do on anything else, and health care expenditures have been growing much more rapidly than the economy generally for decades. You might expect that such spending would result in our being the world's healthiest country. That is not the case, however, as demonstrated by the following report. We must pursue a greater and more equitable return on our health care investment.

ERIC C. SCHNEIDER ET AL., MIRROR, MIRROR 2017: INTERNATIONAL COMPARISON REFLECTS FLAWS AND OPPORTUNITIES FOR BETTER U.S. HEALTH CARE
Commonwealth Fund (2017).

The United States spends far more on health care than other high-income countries, with spending levels that rose continuously over the past three decades [ ]. Yet the U.S. population has poorer health than other countries. Life expectancy, after improving for several decades, worsened in recent years for some populations, aggravated by the opioid crisis. In addition, as the baby boom population ages, more people in the U.S.—and all over the world—are living with age-related disabilities and chronic disease, placing pressure on health care systems to respond.

Timely and accessible health care could mitigate many of these challenges, but the U.S. health care system falls short, failing to deliver indicated services reliably to all who could benefit. In particular, poor access to primary care has contributed to inadequate prevention and management of chronic diseases, delayed diagnoses, incomplete adherence to treatments, wasteful overuse of drugs and technologies, and coordination and safety problems.

This report uses recent data to compare health care system performance in the U.S. with that of 10 other high-income countries [Australia, Canada, France, Germany, the Netherlands, New Zealand, Norway, Sweden, Switzerland, and the United Kingdom] and considers the different approaches to health care organization and delivery that can contribute to top performance. We based our analysis on 72 indicators that measure performance in five domains important to policymakers, providers, patients, and the public: Care Process, Access, Administrative Efficiency, Equity, and Health Care Outcomes.

Our data come from a variety of sources. One is comparative survey research. Since 1998, The Commonwealth Fund, in collaboration with international partners, has supported surveys of patients and primary care physicians in advanced countries, collecting information for a standardized set of metrics on health system performance. Other comparative data are drawn from the most recent reports of the Organization for Economic Cooperation and Development (OECD), the European Observatory on Health Systems and Policies, and the World Health Organization (WHO).

* * *

Based on a broadly inclusive set of performance metrics, we find that U.S. health care system performance ranks last among 11 high-income countries. The country's performance shortcomings cross several domains of care including Access, Administrative Efficiency, Equity, and Health Care Outcomes. Only within the domain of Care Process is U.S. performance close to the 11-country average. These results are troubling because the U.S. has the highest per capita health expenditures of any country and devotes a larger percentage of its GDP to health care than any other country.

The U.S. health care system is unique in several respects. Most striking: it is the only high-income country lacking universal health insurance coverage. The U.S. has taken an important step to expand coverage through the Affordable Care Act. . . . [T]he ACA has catalyzed widespread and historic gains in access to care across the U.S. More than 20 million Americans gained insurance coverage. Additional actions could extend insurance coverage to those who lack it. Furthermore, Americans with coverage often face far higher deductibles and out-of-pocket costs than citizens of other countries, whose systems offer more financial protection. Incomplete and fragmented insurance coverage may account for the relatively poor performance of the U.S. on health care outcomes, affordability, administrative efficiency, and equity.

* * *

The U.S. could learn important lessons from other high-income countries [ ]. For example, the U.S. performs poorly in administrative efficiency mainly because of doctors and patients reporting wasting time on billing and insurance claims. Other countries that rely on private health insurers, like the Netherlands, minimize some of these problems by standardizing basic benefit packages, which can both reduce administrative burden for providers and ensure that patients face predictable copayments.

* * *

NOTES AND QUESTIONS

1. *Cost Control Reforms.* This report illustrates that greater cost doesn't necessarily buy better health or better health care. In fact, some cost control strategies focus primarily on improving the quality of care in order to reduce the number of iatrogenic injuries; increasing the management of care to reduce duplicative testing and rightsize the level of care; and improving knowledge about the comparative effectiveness of different interventions or pharmaceuticals. Others focus on creating incentives for higher quality and lower cost care, including increasing competition over quality and cost and linking payment to quality and efficiency. See Chapter 7 for an extensive discussion of cost control efforts.

2. *Cost Shifting.* One of the challenges in analyzing the costs of care and targeting cost containment strategies is that health care costs are so easily shifted among entities within our fragmented health care system. Incentives for early discharge from hospitals, for example, intended to reduce the costs of hospital care, can shift costs to nursing homes, which then experience increased expense in caring for sicker residents. For the elderly population, the move also shifts costs from Medicare (which pays for most of that population's hospital care) to Medicaid (which pays for most of that population's nursing home care). See discussion in Chapter 3. Discharges to home can increase costs for family members who may be required to take unpaid family leave to care for the patient. In another example of complexities due to shifting costs, increasing access to Medicaid or Medicare may increase costs on one side of the ledger, but can reduce costs on another. Expanding Medicaid eligibility, for example, may reduce hospitals' costs in their emergency departments caring for safety net patients, and expanding the Medicare home health care benefit may reduce Medicaid's cost for nursing home care.

3. *Unequal Distribution of Benefits.* The Commonwealth Fund report found that the U.S. ranks last with respect to health outcomes and equity while ranking 5th in "care process," the category that takes into account the safety and coordination of clinical care as well as the degree to which episodes of care are patient-centered. These findings may explain why some individuals in the U.S. are highly satisfied with their care despite our nation's poor overall outcomes. This dichotomy highlights the difference between individual health and population health, which is explored in Chapter 21. The report's equity findings also suggest the quality of care is unevenly distributed across different

segments of our population. For an analysis of discrimination and unequal access, see Chapter 6.

4.   *A Broader Lens?* One challenge in comparing the U.S. "return on investment" for health care relative to those of other countries is that most analyses focus only on spending within the health care system, as opposed to looking more broadly at other spending that impacts health in even more significant ways. In The American Health Care Paradox: Why Spending More is Getting us Less (2013), Elizabeth Bradley and Lauren Taylor present research that sheds new light on how to understand the problem:

> [This research] shows that the central paradox faced by the US health care system—exorbitantly high spending and relatively poor health outcomes—could be explained by examining a broader set of national expenditures. We demonstrate that when both social services and health services were taken into account, the United States was *not* a high spender. The country had moderate levels of spending and moderate health outcomes. Paradox unraveled. The credo of public health schools everywhere was made manifest: the health of a nation is created by more than the money spent in the health care sector. Investments in larger systems of economic, environmental, and social support produce health and support individuals' quest for well-being.

Indeed, research demonstrates public health spending results in significant benefits. A recent meta-analysis of published research concluded there is a 4:1 return on investment for all local and national public health spending. That ratio jumps to 27:1 when only national public health spending is considered. Rebecca Masters et al., Return on Investment of Public Health Interventions: A Systematic Review, 71 J. Epidemiol. Community Health 827 (2017). For more on population health, see Chapter 21.

Given the growing pressure to control health care costs, this research has captured the attention of federal and state law makers, health plans, and providers. These traditional health system actors now recognize that social and environmental factors, such as food insecurity, housing insecurity, environmental hazards, and poor education, have a greater impact on health than medical care. And they are experimenting with non-traditional ways of improving patients' health (and thus ultimately reducing health care cost) by addressing their unmet social needs. Specifically, they are incorporating social services and other non-clinical support into health care delivery in order to attack the root causes of poor health. For example, some physicians go beyond simply counseling patients with heart disease or diabetes about the importance of eating healthy food. They can now "prescribe" healthy food that patients can get from the hospital food pantry. Some Medicaid health plans are working with providers to offer an even broader range of nutritional support for patients, including delivery of medically tailored meals, cooking and shopping classes, and nutritional counseling. Early reviews suggest that such efforts can reduce costs, but more evidence is needed about which kinds of innovations work and why. Lauren A. Taylor et al., Leveraging the Social Determinants of

Health: What Works? (2016) (analyzing peer-reviewed literature that examined the impact of investments in social services as part of health care and finding that "several interventions in the areas of housing, income support, nutrition support, and care coordination and community outreach have had positive impact in terms of health improvements or health care spending reduction").

5. *Mirror, Mirror 2021*. An updated Commonwealth Fund report, published in 2021, Eric C. Schneider et al., Mirror, Mirror 2021—Reflecting Poorly: Health Care in the U.S. Compared to Other High-Income Countries, Commonwealth Fund (Aug. 2021), found that the U.S. continues to rank last overall, despite spending far more of its gross domestic product on health care. It also found that the U.S. ranks last on four of the five key domains—access to care, administrative efficiency, equity, and health care outcomes—but second on measures of care process.

PROBLEM: WHERE IS THE COST?

Imagine that your spouse has been severely and permanently injured, your parent is suffering from dementia, or your child has serious cognitive and emotional disabilities. What kind of care do you and your family member need? Of the care you need, what will be considered "health care"?

If you quit your job to care for your spouse or parent, will health insurance pay you a wage for doing so? Should it pay for the care you provide if it would pay someone else to be there? If your spouse or parent needs help in bathing and eating, is that health care? What if they need supplies for incontinence like bed pads or diapers?

If you need to make changes to your home to accommodate assistive devices for your spouse to provide some mobility or allow communication, should this be considered medical care? Should health insurance pay for these devices?

If your child needs to attend a special summer camp to improve his skills in interacting with other children, is this health care? If you have to hire someone with special skills to provide care for your child while you take care of other obligations, is this health care?

If your child needs to submit a negative COVID-19 test result to attend the summer camp, is this health care? Are COVID-19 tests in the absence of symptoms or exposure health care? Or do they only serve public health surveillance purposes?

Our current health insurance coverage draws some lines. For example, Medicare does not cover long-term care or nursing home care, just short-term rehabilitation care. Medicaid covers long-term nursing home care, for those meeting eligibility standards, but does not contribute toward less restrictive environments like retirement communities or assisted living. Private insurance plans typically have provided very limited, if any, mental health care. The ACA requires that private insurers provide parity in their coverage of mental health care, but there are still issues in defining that care.

The ACA requires that an "essential benefits package" be defined for health insurance plans. The Secretary of Health and Human Services has allowed the states to use the typical employer-provided health plan as a benchmark. See Chapter 9. The typical private health plan, however, excludes categories of services that might be considered "social" or "educational," services where functioning cannot be restored, assistive equipment and supplies, and so on. See Sara Rosenbaum, Medicaid's Next Fifty Years: Aligning an Old Program with the New Normal, 6 St. Louis U. J. Health L. & Pol'y 329 (2013).

Does the additional stress, economic burden, and related illness experienced by family caregivers count as a health care cost associated with the cost-containment effort of early hospital discharge or extremely limited coverage for professional home care or nursing home care? Furthermore, should the concern over the quality of health care focus on health care services and outcomes for the patient, or should it reach more broadly? Is the health of family members ever relevant to whether quality care has been delivered? In the case of health care insurance access, costs associated with higher rates of bankruptcies due to medical costs (with default to other creditors as well); higher rates of more serious illnesses and deaths for lack of preventive care or early interventions; and loss of productivity at work as well as loss of jobs are usually kept on a separate "ledger" and not included in calculations of health care costs.

Finally, third-party payers can reduce their costs significantly by establishing co-pays and high deductibles. These cost reductions are shifted directly to individuals. They may, in fact, encourage individuals to forego health care they would ordinarily have used. High co-pays and deductibles, however, are seen as necessary to induce individuals to make financially responsible decisions in their use of health care services. See discussion in Chapter 7.

V. WHAT IS ILLNESS?

We all have an operational definition of health and sickness. I know when I am depressed, have a broken leg, a headache or a hangover. In these circumstances I consider myself to be in ill health because I am not functioning as well as I usually do, even though I may lack a scientific medical explanation of my malaise. But am I in poor health because my arteries are gradually becoming clogged, a process that probably began when I was a teenager? Am I sick or in poor health if I am obese, addicted to alcohol or drugs, experiencing age-related impairments, or struggling with a discrepancy between my experienced gender and the sex assigned to me at birth?

We need some definition of health in order to assess the quality of care needed to promote, restore, or, in the case of health disparities, measure it. A malpractice suit or medical quality audit depends on an ability to distinguish a bad from a good medical care outcome. An understanding of the nature of sickness and health is required to determine what health care society should provide the poor and how much society ought to spend on health care. Should Medicaid (a federal/state health care program for the poor) or a commercial insurer, for example, cover in vitro fertilization or abortions? If the state of being old becomes a state of sickness, does it mean that sickness must be "cured" at public expense? Finally, the definition of health raises questions of autonomy, responsibility, and personhood. Should health be defined by the doctor as scientist, the patient as person, or both?

The Constitution of the World Health Organization defines health as "[a] state of complete physical, mental and social well-being and not merely the absence of disease or infirmity." When did you last feel that way? Can health ever be achieved under this definition, or is everyone always in a state of ill health? How much can physicians and hospitals contribute to health under this definition? A further provision of the WHO Constitution provides that "[g]overnments have a responsibility for the health of their peoples which can be fulfilled only by the provision of adequate health and social measures." What are the political ramifications of these principles?

Health can be viewed in a more limited sense as the performance by each body part of its "natural" function. Definitions in terms of biological functioning tend to be more descriptive and less value laden. As Englehardt writes, "The notion required for an analysis of health is not that of a good man or a good shark, but that of a good specimen of a human being or shark." H. Tristam Englehardt, "The Concepts of Health and Disease," in Concepts of Health and Disease 552 (Arthur Caplan, H. Tristam Engelhardt, and James McCartney, eds. 1981) (hereafter Concepts).

Boorse compares health to the mechanical condition of a car, which can be described as good because it conforms to the designer's specifications, even though the design is flawed. Disease is then a biological malfunction, a deviation from the biological norm of natural function. Illness can be defined as a subset of disease. Boorse writes:

> An illness must be, first, a reasonably *serious* disease with incapacitating effects that make it undesirable. A shaving cut or mild athlete's foot cannot be called an illness, nor could one call in sick on the basis of a single dental cavity, though all these conditions are diseases. Secondly, to call a disease an illness is to view its owner as deserving special treatment and diminished moral accountability . . . . Where we do not make the appropriate normative judgments or

activate the social institutions, no amount of disease will lead us to use the term "ill." . . .

There are, then, two senses of "health." In one sense it is a theoretical notion, the opposite of "disease." In another sense it is a practical or mixed ethical notion, the opposite of "illness."

Christopher Boorse, "On the Distinction between Disease and Illness," in Concepts, *supra* at 553.

Illness is thus a socially constructed deviance from a socially constructed "normal." Something more than a mere biological abnormality is needed. To be ill is to have deviant characteristics for which the sick role is appropriate. The sick role, as Parsons has described it, exempts one from normal social responsibilities and removes individual responsibility. See Talcott Parsons, The Social System (1951). Our choice of words reflects this: an individual with "alcohol use disorder" is sick; a "drunkard" is not.

Illness has many ramifications. First, it may relieve the individual of certain responsibility. The sick person need not report for work that day; the post-traumatic stress syndrome or premenstrual syndrome victim may be declared not guilty of an assault. A doctor can thus decide whether a patient is culpable or not, disabled or malingering. Sickness also means loss of control. Mild pain may have disproportionate effects on the individual who sees it as the harbinger of cancer or a brain tumor.

Second, a sick person can be assisted by treatment defined by the medical model. The physician can restore control by providing a rational explanation for the experience of impairment. The sick person becomes a patient, an object of medical attention by a doctor. The doctor has the right and the ability to label someone ill, to determine whether the lump on a patient's skin is a blister, a wart, or a cancer. Perhaps more importantly, illness enjoins the physician to action to restore the patient to health.

Finally, illness costs money. It may cost the patient money in lost time and in medical expenses. And someone receives that money for trying to treat that patient's illness. But if the patient has private or public insurance, illness means the patient is entitled to have insurance cover some or all of these costs. Thus, our understanding of illness also affects society. Defining a condition as an illness to be aggressively treated, rather than as a natural condition of life to be accepted and tolerated, has significant economic effects.

Medical care is an object of economic choice, a good that many perceive to be different from other goods, with greater, sometimes immeasurable value. Some people are willing to pay far more for medical care than they would for other goods, or, more typically, to procure insurance that will deliver them from ever having to face the choice of paying for health care and abandoning all else. Society may also feel a special obligation to pay for the medical expenses of those who need treatment but lack resources to pay for it.

Katskee v. Blue Cross/Blue Shield of Nebraska

Supreme Court of Nebraska, 1994.
515 N.W.2d 645.

White, Justice.

This appeal arises from a summary judgment issued by the Douglas County District Court dismissing appellant Sindie Katskee's action for breach of contract. This action concerns the determination of what constitutes an illness within the meaning of a health insurance policy issued by appellee, Blue Cross/Blue Shield of Nebraska. We reverse the decision of the district court and remand the cause for further proceedings.

In January 1990, upon the recommendation of her gynecologist, Dr. Larry E. Roffman, appellant consulted with Dr. Henry T. Lynch regarding her family's history of breast and ovarian cancer, and particularly her health in relation to such a history. After examining appellant and investigating her family's medical history, Dr. Lynch diagnosed her as suffering from a genetic condition known as breast-ovarian carcinoma syndrome. Dr. Lynch then recommended that appellant have a total abdominal hysterectomy and bilateral salpingo-oophorectomy, which involves the removal of the uterus, the ovaries, and the fallopian tubes. Dr. Roffman concurred in Dr. Lynch's diagnosis and agreed that the recommended surgery was the most medically appropriate treatment available.

After considering the diagnosis and recommended treatment, appellant decided to have the surgery. In preparation for the surgery, appellant filed a claim with Blue Cross/Blue Shield. Both Drs. Lynch and Roffman wrote to Blue Cross/Blue Shield and explained the diagnosis and their basis for recommending the surgery. Initially, Blue Cross/Blue Shield sent a letter to appellant and indicated that it might pay for the surgery. Two weeks before the surgery, Dr. Roger Mason, the chief medical officer for Blue Cross/Blue Shield, wrote to appellant and stated that Blue Cross/Blue Shield would not cover the cost of the surgery. Nonetheless, appellant had the surgery in November 1990.

Appellant filed this action for breach of contract, seeking to recover $6,022.57 in costs associated with the surgery. Blue Cross/Blue Shield filed a motion for summary judgment. The district court granted the motion. It found that there was no genuine issue of material fact and that the policy did not cover appellant's surgery. Specifically, the court stated that (1) appellant did not suffer from cancer, and although her high-risk condition warranted the surgery, it was not covered by the policy; (2) appellant did not have a bodily illness or disease which was covered by the policy; and

(3) under the terms of the policy, Blue Cross/Blue Shield reserved the right to determine what is medically necessary. Appellant filed a notice of appeal to the Nebraska Court of Appeals, and on our motion, we removed the case to the Nebraska Supreme Court.

Appellant contends that the district court erred in finding that no genuine issue of material fact existed and granting summary judgment in favor of appellee.

* * *

Blue Cross/Blue Shield contends that appellant's costs are not covered by the insurance policy. The policy provides coverage for services which are medically necessary. The policy defines "medically necessary" as follows:

The services, procedures, drugs, supplies or Durable Medical Equipment provided by the Physician, Hospital or other health care provider, in the diagnosis or treatment of the Covered Person's Illness, Injury, or Pregnancy, which are:

1. *Appropriate for the symptoms and diagnosis of the patient's Illness*, Injury or Pregnancy; and

2. Provided in the most appropriate setting and at the most appropriate level of services[;] and

3. Consistent with the standards of good medical practice in the medical community of the State of Nebraska; and

4. Not provided primarily for the convenience of any of the following:

a. the Covered Person;

b. the Physician;

c. the Covered Person's family;

d. any other person or health care provider; and

5. Not considered to be unnecessarily repetitive when performed in combination with other diagnoses or treatment procedures.

We shall determine whether services provided are Medically Necessary. Services will not automatically be considered Medically Necessary because they have been ordered or provided by a Physician.

(Emphasis supplied.) Blue Cross/Blue Shield denied coverage because it concluded that appellant's condition does not constitute an illness, and thus the treatment she received was not medically necessary. Blue Cross/Blue Shield has not raised any other basis for its denial, and we therefore will limit our consideration to whether appellant's condition constituted an illness within the meaning of the policy.

The policy broadly defines "illness" as a "bodily disorder or disease." The policy does not provide definitions for either bodily disorder or disease.

An insurance policy is to be construed as any other contract to give effect to the parties' intentions at the time the contract was made. When the terms of the contract are clear, a court may not resort to rules of construction, and the terms are to be accorded their plain and ordinary meaning as the ordinary or reasonable person would understand them. In such a case, a court shall seek to ascertain the intention of the parties from the plain language of the policy. [ ]

Whether a policy is ambiguous is a matter of law for the court to determine. If a court finds that the policy is ambiguous, then the court may employ rules of construction and look beyond the language of the policy to ascertain the intention of the parties. A general principle of construction, which we have applied to ambiguous insurance policies, holds that an ambiguous policy will be construed in favor of the insured. However, we will not read an ambiguity into policy language which is plain and unambiguous in order to construe it against the insurer. [ ]

When interpreting the plain meaning of the terms of an insurance policy, we have stated that the " ' "natural and obvious meaning of the provisions in a policy is to be adopted in preference to a fanciful, curious, or hidden meaning." ' "[ ] We have further stated that " '[w]hile for the purpose of judicial decision dictionary definitions often are not controlling, they are at least persuasive that meanings which they do not embrace are not common.' "[ ]

Applying these principles, our interpretation of the language of the terms employed in the policy is guided by definitions found in dictionaries, and additionally by judicial opinions rendered by other courts which have considered the meaning of these terms. Webster's Third New International Dictionary, Unabridged 648 (1981), defines disease as an impairment of the normal state of the living animal or plant body or of any of its components that interrupts or modifies the performance of the vital functions, being a response to environmental factors . . . to specific infective agents . . . to inherent defects of the organism (as various genetic anomalies), or to combinations of these factors: Sickness, Illness. The same dictionary defines disorder as "a derangement of function: an abnormal physical or mental condition: Sickness, Ailment, Malady." [ ]

These lay definitions are consistent with the general definitions provided in Dorland's Illustrated Medical Dictionary (27th ed. 1988). Dorland's defines disease as

> any deviation from or interruption of the normal structure or function of any part, organ, or system . . . of the body that is manifested by a characteristic set of symptoms and signs and whose etiology [theory of

origin or cause], pathology [origin or cause], and prognosis may be known or unknown.

[ ] Dorland's defines disorder as "a derangement or abnormality of function; a morbid physical or mental state." [ ]

* * *

[The court looked at similar definitional disputes in other jurisdictions, noting that hemophilia, aneurysms, and chronic alcoholism had been held to be diseases or illnesses under insurance policies.]

We find that the language used in the policy at issue in the present case is not reasonably susceptible of differing interpretations and thus not ambiguous. The plain and ordinary meaning of the terms "bodily disorder" and "disease," as they are used in the policy to define illness, encompasses any abnormal condition of the body or its components of such a degree that in its natural progression would be expected to be problematic; a deviation from the healthy or normal state affecting the functions or tissues of the body; an inherent defect of the body; or a morbid physical or mental state which deviates from or interrupts the normal structure or function of any part, organ, or system of the body and which is manifested by a characteristic set of symptoms and signs.

The issue then becomes whether appellant's condition—breast-ovarian carcinoma syndrome—constitutes an illness.

Blue Cross/Blue Shield argues that appellant did not suffer from an illness because she did not have cancer. Blue Cross/Blue Shield characterizes appellant's condition only as a "predisposition to an illness (cancer)" and fails to address whether the condition itself constitutes an illness. This failure is traceable to Dr. Mason's denial of appellant's claim. Despite acknowledging his inexperience and lack of knowledge about this specialized area of cancer research, Dr. Mason denied appellant's claim without consulting any medical literature or research regarding breast-ovarian carcinoma syndrome. Moreover, Dr. Mason made the decision without submitting appellant's claim for consideration to a claim review committee. The only basis for the denial was the claim filed by appellant, the letters sent by Drs. Lynch and Roffman, and the insurance policy. Despite his lack of information regarding the nature and severity of appellant's condition, Dr. Mason felt qualified to decide that appellant did not suffer from an illness.

Appellant's condition was diagnosed as breast-ovarian carcinoma syndrome. To adequately determine whether the syndrome constitutes an illness, we must first understand the nature of the syndrome.

The record on summary judgment includes the depositions of Drs. Lynch, Roffman, and Mason. In his deposition, Dr. Lynch provided a thorough discussion of this syndrome. In light of Dr. Lynch's extensive research and clinical experience in this particular area of medicine, we consider his discussion extremely helpful in our understanding of the syndrome.

According to Dr. Lynch, some forms of cancer occur on a hereditary basis. Breast and ovarian cancer are such forms of cancer which may occur on a hereditary basis. It is our understanding that the hereditary occurrence of this form of cancer is related to the genetic makeup of the woman. In this regard, the genetic deviation has conferred changes which are manifest in the individual's body and at some time become capable of being diagnosed.

At the time that he gave his deposition, Dr. Lynch explained that the state of medical research was such that detecting and diagnosing the syndrome was achieved by tracing the occurrences of hereditary cancer throughout the patient's family. Dr. Lynch stated that at the time of appellant's diagnosis, no conclusive physical test existed which would demonstrate the presence of the condition. However, Dr. Lynch stated that this area of research is progressing toward the development of a more determinative method of identifying and tracing a particular gene throughout a particular family, thus providing a physical method of diagnosing the condition.

Women diagnosed with the syndrome have at least a 50-percent chance of developing breast and/or ovarian cancer, whereas unaffected women have only a 1.4-percent risk of developing breast or ovarian cancer. In addition to the genetic deviation, the family history, and the significant risks associated with this condition, the diagnosis also may encompass symptoms of anxiety and stress, which some women experience because of their knowledge of the substantial likelihood of developing cancer.

The procedures for detecting the onset of ovarian cancer are ineffective. Generally, by the time ovarian cancer is capable of being detected, it has already developed to a very advanced stage, making treatment relatively unsuccessful. Drs. Lynch and Roffman agreed that the standard of care for treating women with breast carcinoma syndrome ordinarily involves surveillance methods. However, for women at an inordinately high risk for ovarian cancer, such as appellant, the standard of care may require radical surgery which involves the removal of the uterus, ovaries, and fallopian tubes.

Dr. Lynch explained that the surgery is labeled "prophylactic" and that the surgery is prophylactic as to the prevention of the onset of cancer. Dr. Lynch also stated that appellant's condition itself is the result of a genetic deviation from the normal, healthy state and that the recommended surgery treats that condition by eliminating or significantly reducing the presence of the condition and its likely development.

Blue Cross/Blue Shield has not proffered any evidence disputing the premise that the origin of this condition is in the genetic makeup of the individual and that in its natural development it is likely to produce devastating results. Although handicapped by his limited knowledge of the syndrome, Dr. Mason did not dispute the nature of the syndrome as explained by Dr. Lynch and supported by Dr. Roffman, nor did Dr. Mason dispute the fact that the surgery falls within the standard of care for many women afflicted with this syndrome.

In light of the plain and ordinary meaning of the terms "illness," "bodily disorder," and "disease," we find that appellant's condition constitutes an illness within the meaning of the policy. Appellant's condition is a deviation from what is considered a normal, healthy physical state or structure. The abnormality or deviation from a normal state arises, in part, from the genetic makeup of the woman. The existence of this unhealthy state results in the woman's being at substantial risk of developing cancer. The recommended surgery is intended to correct that morbid state by reducing or eliminating that risk.

Although appellant's condition was not detectable by physical evidence or a physical examination, it does not necessarily follow that appellant does not suffer from an illness. The record establishes that a woman who suffers from breast-ovarian carcinoma syndrome does have a physical state which significantly deviates from the physical state of a normal, healthy woman. Specifically, appellant suffered from a different or abnormal genetic constitution which, when combined with a particular family history of hereditary cancer, significantly increases the risk of a devastating outcome.

We are mindful that not every condition which itself constitutes a predisposition to another illness is necessarily an illness within the meaning of an insurance policy. There exists a fine distinction between such conditions . . . .

* * *

The issue raised in Fuglsang [ ] was whether the disease from which the plaintiff suffered constituted a preexisting condition which was excluded from coverage by the terms of the policy. Blue Cross/Blue Shield relies on the following rule from Fuglsang as a definition of "disease": A disease, condition, or illness exists within the meaning of a health insurance policy excluding preexisting conditions only at such time as the disease, condition, or illness is manifest or active or when there is a distinct symptom or condition from which one learned in medicine can with reasonable accuracy diagnose the disease. [ ]

This statement concerns when an illness exists, not whether the condition itself is an illness. If the condition is not a disease or illness, it would be unnecessary to apply the above rule to determine whether the condition was a preexisting illness. In the present case, Blue Cross/Blue Shield maintains that the condition is not even an illness.

Even assuming arguendo that the rule announced in Fuglsang is a definition of "disease," "illness," and "condition," the inherent problems with the argument put forth by Blue Cross/Blue Shield undermine its reliance on that rule. Blue Cross/Blue Shield emphasizes the fact that appellant was never diagnosed with cancer and therefore, according to Blue Cross/Blue Shield, appellant did not have an illness because cancer was not active or manifest. Appellant concedes that she did not have cancer prior to her surgery. The issue is whether the condition she did have was an illness. Blue Cross/Blue Shield further argues that "[n]o disease or illness is 'manifest or active' and there is no 'distinct symptom or condition' from which Dr. Lynch or Dr. Roffman could diagnose a disease." We stated above that lack of a physical test to detect the presence of an illness does not necessarily indicate that the person does not have an illness.

When the condition at issue—breast-ovarian carcinoma syndrome—is inserted into the formula provided by the Fuglsang rule, the condition would constitute an "illness" as Blue Cross/Blue Shield defines the term. The formula is whether the breast-ovarian carcinoma syndrome was manifest or active, or whether there was a distinct symptom or condition from which one learned in medicine could with reasonable accuracy diagnose the disease. The record establishes that the syndrome was manifest, at least in part, from the genetic deviation, and evident from the family medical history. The condition was such that one learned in medicine, Dr. Lynch, could with a reasonable degree of accuracy diagnose it. Blue Cross/Blue Shield does not dispute the nature of the syndrome, the method of diagnosis, or the accuracy of the diagnosis.

In the present case, the medical evidence regarding the nature of breast-ovarian carcinoma syndrome persuades us that appellant suffered from a bodily disorder or disease and, thus, suffered from an illness as defined by the insurance policy. Blue Cross/Blue Shield, therefore, is not entitled to judgment as a matter of law. Moreover, we find that appellant's condition did constitute an illness within the meaning of the policy. We reverse the decision of the district court and remand the cause for further proceedings. [ ]

NOTES AND QUESTIONS

1. *Preventive vs. Curative Care.* Why did the court hold that Katskee was ill when she had no symptoms and no cancer? Can we have a variable definition of illness? For example, could Katskee be ill for purposes of payment for the surgery but not ill for purposes of pre-existing condition exclusions or excusal from work? What about treatment for high blood pressure or arteriosclerosis? The medications to prevent heart attacks are expensive and

are typically covered by health insurance plans. Why would Blue Cross resist covering this treatment for this problem?

2.   *Genetic Predispositions.* Katskee was diagnosed with breast-ovarian carcinoma syndrome, a genetically based condition. Genes for cystic fibrosis, breast cancer, colon cancer, obesity, various aspects of sexuality, violence, and many other conditions, characteristics, behaviors, and personal identities have been identified, and sometimes de-identified, since the 1990s. The explosion of knowledge in genetics is in large part the result of the Human Genome Project (HGP), a project involving 16 nations and lasting longer than a decade, through which scientists mapped the human genome and developed technologies that greatly enhance further genetic exploration.

What does it mean to have a genetically related condition or disease? Some genetically related diseases are monogenic; that is, they are associated with the presence of a single mutated gene. Even with monogenic conditions, the presence of the mutated gene may not provide a clue as to whether the individual will be severely affected, moderately affected, or will experience no symptoms of the disease at all. Furthermore, while a single gene may be associated with the disease, there may be hundreds of different mutations of that single gene that can signal quite serious manifestations of the disease or none at all.

Most conditions associated with genes are not monogenic or even polygenic (requiring the interaction of more than one gene), but rather are multifactorial. Multifactorial conditions, such as cancer, are those in which there is a genetic influence (often requiring the combined effect of several genes) but in which nongenetic elements, including environmental factors, are also essential.

Many genetic conditions require two copies of the relevant genetic material for disease to be expressed, so an individual who carries only one copy of the required material will not have the disease. Examples of such conditions, involving what are called recessive genes, include sickle cell and cystic fibrosis. If an individual with this genetic characteristic produces children with another individual with the same characteristic, those children may have one copy of the genetic material (a 50% chance for each child conceived) or two copies of the genetic material (a 25% chance for each child conceived) or none at all (a 25% chance for each child conceived). More than 10 million individuals in the U.S. carry one copy of the mutated CFTR gene responsible for cystic fibrosis, for example, and about 30,000 people have the disease itself.

While many diseases involve mutation in genes, not all mutated genes are associated with or cause disease. A mutated gene may not have any health consequences at all. Also, genetic mutations that can trigger disease may occur at any time of life, for example, from environmental toxins or radiation or a virus or aging. Nor are genes necessarily single effect. Rather, the same gene that is associated with a particular disease may also increase resistance to another.

The method used to identify a genetic connection to particular conditions may also affect the meaning of a genetic "association" with a disease or condition. Most of the genetic connections established before genome mapping advances were based on epidemiological studies of the occurrence of particular characteristics or conditions, rather than by direct identification of the gene itself. An association between genetic trait and disease established by epidemiological studies alone cannot predict the presence of the trait in any given individual and cannot conclusively rule out that other factors may be required to trigger the disease. A finding of "association" between the presence of a gene or mutation and a particular disease does not establish causation.

Despite dramatic advances in knowledge as a result of the HGP, our everyday language is often inadequate and imprecise. Does it make a difference if something is called a genetic "trait" as compared to a genetic "condition" or a genetic "disease," "defect," or "anomaly"? If Katskee were merely a carrier of a recessive gene associated with a genetically related disorder, would that qualify her as ill? What is the "normal" human genotype? Which genetic traits should be cured, corrected, removed, or, through pre-implantation screening, avoided? Who decides whether a genetic trait should be remedied? Is this a medical decision, a religious decision, a political decision, a social decision, or something else?

3.   *Rethinking "Responsibility" and "Choice."* The syndrome in *Katskee*, if it materializes, is a medical problem for which the patient bears no responsibility. A more difficult problem area in defining "disease" involves those conditions or syndromes that are or appear to be within some control of the individual. Consider, for example, alcohol use disorder a disease. What difference does such a label make? What characteristics of alcohol misuse justify the label "disease"? See The National Center on Addiction and Substance Abuse, Addiction as a Disease (2017) (noting that "like diabetes, cancer, and heart disease, addiction is caused by a combination of behavioral, environmental and biological factors," and that the "consequences of untreated addiction often include other physical and mental health disorders that require medical attention."). See also Nora D. Volkow et al., Neurobiologic Advances from the Brain Disease Model of Addiction, 374 NEJM 363 (2016) (explaining that "research has increasingly supported the view that addiction is a disease of the brain" and "[a]lthough [this] brain disease model of addiction has yielded effective preventive measures, treatment interventions, and public health policies to address substance-use disorders, the underlying concept of substance abuse as a brain disease continues to be questioned.")

Courts have also had to confront the legal significance of such conditions. See, e.g., Ledezma-Cosino v. Sessions, 857 F.3d 1042 (9th Cir. 2017) (en banc) (holding that plaintiff, who was a "habitual drunkard," did not meet the deportation exception for persons of good moral character). A concurring opinion identified the competing characteristics of alcohol use disorder that can lead to different conclusions about how the law should treat people with such conditions:

. . . In my view, Congress could rationally deem habitual drunkards to be at least partially responsible for having developed their condition. Habitual drunkards are those who have allowed themselves to become so addicted to alcohol that they can no longer control their habit of drinking to excess. That loss of control does not come about overnight; it is acquired as a result of frequent, repetitive acts of excessive drinking. [This] is conduct that Congress could rationally view as volitional, and therefore the proper subject of moral blame.

None of this is to say that Congress' decision . . . is a wise one. We know considerably more about alcohol addiction today than we did back in 1952, when Congress enacted [the statute]. Scientists tell us, for example, that some people are much more prone to becoming addicted to substances like alcohol than others, with genetic factors accounting for 40 to 70 percent of individual differences in the risk for addiction. . . . In addition, there is a high correlation between alcohol abuse and post-traumatic stress disorder (PTSD), a condition that virtually no one could be blamed for acquiring. As the Surgeon General's report notes, "[i]t is estimated that 30–60 percent of patients seeking treatment for alcohol use disorder meet criteria for PTSD, and approximately one third of individuals who have experienced PTSD have also experienced alcohol dependence at some point in their lives.

Obesity is another example of a condition whose disease classification has been contested. The AMA did not officially recognize obesity as a disease until 2013, a move that many hoped would remove the stigma associated with it, encourage health care providers to pay more attention to it, and make insurers more likely to cover treatments for it. This decision was made despite contrary recommendations by the AMA's Council on Science and Public Health. American Medical Association Resolution 115–A–12 (2013). See also Caroline M. Apovian, 374 NEJM 177 (2016) ("There is good evidence indicating that although obesity may start as a lifestyle-driven problem, it can rapidly lead to disturbed energy-balance regulation as a result of impaired hypothalamic signaling, which leads to a higher body-weight set point. Thus, obesity may be considered a disease initiated by a complex interaction of genetics and the environment.").

    4. *Does the "Disease" Label Decrease or Increase Stigma?* In the case of addiction and obesity, labeling the condition a disease or disability is generally thought to help reduce stigma and increase the opportunity for appropriate health interventions. In other cases, however, people may resist these labels based on concerns that they may encourage discrimination and even undermine health and well-being. Historically, this has been the case for mental health conditions, for example. In determining whether to classify a particular condition as a disease, or which disease category should apply, should social and legal considerations be permissible, or should only medical and scientific considerations be used? Should the answer depend on the identity of the decision maker, the reasons for the label, or how much we know about the etiology of the condition?

PROBLEM: THE COUPLE'S ILLNESS

You represent Thomas and Jill Henderson, a couple embroiled in a dispute with their health insurance plan over coverage of infertility treatments. The Hendersons have been having trouble getting pregnant. Thomas has a low sperm count and motility, while Jill has irregular ovulation. They have undergone infertility treatment successfully in the past and have one child. They sought further treatment to have a second child. A simple insemination procedure failed. The health and disability group benefit plan of Thomas's employer, Clarion, paid their health benefits for this procedure.

They were then advised to try a more complex and expensive procedure, called Protocol I, which involved treating Thomas' sperm to improve its motility. Drug therapy was prescribed for Jill to induce ovulation. Semen was then taken from Thomas and put through an albumin gradient to improve its motility. The semen was then reduced to a small pellet size and injected directly into the uterine cavity at the time of ovulation.

The Hendersons underwent Protocol I and submitted a bill to Clarion, which refused to pay it. Clarion cited a provision in its plan, Article VI, section 6.7, which provided:

> If a covered individual incurs outpatient expenses relating to injury or illness, those expenses charged, including but not limited to, office calls and for diagnostic services such as laboratory, x-ray, electrocardiography, therapy or injections, are covered expenses under the provisions of [the plan].

Under section 2.24 of the plan, "illness" was defined as "any sickness occurring to a covered individual which does not arise out of or in the course of employment for wage or profit." Clarion denied the Hendersons' claim on the grounds that the medical services were not performed because of any illness of Jill or Thomas, as required under section 6.7. No provisions in the plan specifically excluded fertilization treatments like Protocol I.

What arguments can you make on behalf of the Hendersons that their situation is an "illness"? Is it relevant that infertility can be considered a disability under federal antidiscrimination law? See Chapter 6. What arguments can you make for the insurance company that it is not?

CHAPTER 2

QUALITY CONTROL REGULATION: LICENSING HEALTH CARE PROFESSIONALS

■ ■ ■

I. INTRODUCTION

According to the Institute of Medicine:

> . . . quality of care is the degree to which health services for individuals
> and populations increase the likelihood of desired health outcomes and
> are consistent with current professional knowledge. Institute of
> Medicine, Medicare: A Strategy for Quality Assurance, Vol. I, 20 (K.
> Lohr, Ed.1990).

To promote quality of care, the law regulates the quality of health care
professionals in a wide variety of ways. It enforces the standard of care
through malpractice suits, polices relationships between professional and
institutional providers, and enforces contractual provisions that permit
insurers to refuse payment for poor quality or unproven treatments, among
others. As examined in this chapter, the law also enables and monitors
licensing systems for health care professionals in each state.

State law controls the licensure of health care professionals under the
state's police power. State licensing statutes govern entry into the licensed
professions, regulate the health care services that licensed professionals
may provide, and prohibit unlicensed persons from providing services
reserved for the licensed professions. The system also monitors the quality
of care provided by licensees and penalizes or removes incompetent
practitioners from practice.

Health professional licensure in the United States is commonly
described as a system of professional self-regulation because the entities,
often called "boards," that implement the applicable statutes are generally
dominated by members of the licensed profession and often rely on
customary practices of the professions for standards. The boards, however,
operate formally as state administrative agencies, usually include lay
members to represent a consumer perspective, are governed by procedures
and standards set in the state's licensing statute and administrative
procedures act, and are subject to judicial review in both their adjudicatory
and rulemaking decisions. The characterization of professional licensure

and discipline as professional self-regulation has become less valid over time, but the licensed professions retain significant influence over the decisions of the boards.

Although the central legal framework for licensure and discipline is a matter of state law, there is a federal overlay. Licensure is subject to federal (and state) Constitutional requirements for procedural and substantive due process and equal protection. Certain federal statutes, including antidiscrimination laws such as the Americans with Disabilities Act, apply to licensure boards as well, although there are Constitutional limits on their application.

Licensure, as noted above, is only one component of the quality control array in health care. It also includes malpractice and negligence litigation, institutional licensure, private accreditation, hospital credentialing, public information disclosure requirements, and public and private payment and reimbursement standards. Each of these is covered elsewhere in this casebook.

Core issues for this chapter are whether the prohibitions and restrictions imposed by licensure and discipline serve the public good or established professional interests, and whether the state health professions boards are the best tool for achieving the goals of patient safety and accessible care. The debate over the performance and ultimate cost and benefit of professional licensure and discipline is an old one, dating back to the emergence of the health professions boards. For an historical perspective on the dominance of licensure by allopathic physicians (traditional M.D.s), see Paul Starr, The Social Transformation of American Medicine (1982). Professional domination of licensure has long been a source of criticism of board performance. See, e.g., Carl F. Ameringer, State Medical Boards and the Politics of Public Protection (1999).

The boards' heavy reliance on the participation of their licensees advances the public interest by bringing expertise to the evaluation of professionals' competency and behavior. In this era of more intense competition among a broader range of health care professionals, however, this reliance creates substantial opportunities for anticompetitive conduct facilitated by the authority of the board. See Chapter 15, *infra*, addressing antitrust law as applied in the health care industry. For an analysis of the inefficiencies and anticompetitive risks associated with medical licensure as currently structured, see Kevin Dayaratna, Paul J. Larkin, Jr. and John O'Shea, Reforming American Medical Licensure, 42 Harv. J. L. & Pub. Pol'y 253 (2019).

The traditional rationale for health care quality regulation is the lack of information available to consumers, limiting their ability to make their own risk-benefit balance in choosing providers, as well as the limited capacity of patients to evaluate the information that is available. As health care data become cheaper and more accessible, health care quality regulation will be challenged. Kristin Madison, for example, speculates that more robust health databanks will lead to contradictory claims that greater direct consumer access to quality information reduces the need for state medical boards and that the boards should take a greater role in actively monitoring quality as data improves. See Kristin Madison, Regulating Health Care Quality in an Information Age, 40 U.C. Davis L. Rev. 1577 (2007). See also Timothy S. Jost, Oversight of the Quality of Medical Care: Regulation, Management or the Market, 37 Ariz. L. Rev. 825 (1995); William M. Sage, Regulating through Information: Disclosure Laws and American Healthcare, 99 Colum. L. Rev. 1701 (1999).

Licensure boards currently reflect the traditional way we determine what appropriate care is: relying on customary practices of the majority of practitioners with some reliance on a rather spotty and non-clinically relevant body of studies. The Affordable Care Act (ACA) pushes stronger reliance on scientific evidence of effectiveness and outcomes as the gold measure for quality. If the hopes for this shift toward scientific evidence are realized, it will have implications for enforcement and standard-setting by the health professions boards.

The ACA also fosters expanded roles for nurses and physician assistants as the health care system is reorganized to emphasize continuity of care, accessible preventive care, and management of chronic illness at a lower cost. The activities of the licensure boards in restricting the work of these professionals are coming under increased scrutiny.

This chapter begins with the standard setting and adjudicative functions of the boards in responding to claims that individual physicians have provided substandard medical care to patients. It then continues addressing the challenge of setting regulatory standards for medical care, but in the context of licensees who offer complementary and alternative medicine. Finally, the chapter examines the border-patrolling functions of the various health professions boards in two areas: the provision of services by unlicensed providers and the scope of practice of non-physician licensed health care professionals.

II. DISCIPLINE

IN RE WILLIAMS
Supreme Court of Ohio, 1991.
573 N.E.2d 638.

Syllabus by the Court

* * *

... Between 1983 and 1986, Dr. Williams prescribed Biphetamine or Obetrol for fifty patients as part of a weight control treatment regimen. [Both drugs are controlled substances.]

On November 17, 1986, appellant, the Ohio State Medical Board ("board"), promulgated Ohio Adm. Code 4731–11–03(B), which prohibited the use of [drugs such as Biphetamine and Obetrol] for purposes of weight control. Dr. Williams ceased prescribing Biphetamine and Obetrol for weight control upon becoming aware of the rule.

By letter dated March 12, 1987, the board charged Dr. Williams with violating R.C. 4731.22(B)[2] by prescribing these stimulants without "reasonable care," and thereby failing to conform to minimal standards of medical practice. The crux of the board's charge was that Dr. Williams had departed from accepted standards of care by using these drugs as a long-term, rather than a short-term, treatment.

A hearing was held before a board examiner. The parties stipulated to the accuracy of the medical records of the patients in question, which detailed the use of Biphetamine and Obetrol for periods ranging from nearly seven months to several years. The board also introduced into evidence the Physician's Desk Reference entries for Biphetamine and Obetrol, which recommend that these drugs be used for only "a few weeks" in the treatment of obesity. The board presented no testimony or other evidence of the applicable standard of care.

Dr. Williams presented expert testimony from Dr. John P. Morgan, the director of the pharmacology program at the City University of New York

---

[2] R.C. 4731.22(B) provides in pertinent part:

"The board, pursuant to an adjudicatory hearing ... shall, to the extent permitted by law, ... [discipline] the holder of a certificate [to practice medicine] for one or more of the following reasons:

. . .

"(2)   Failure to use reasonable care, discrimination in the administration of drugs, or failure to employ acceptable scientific methods in the selection of drugs or other modalities for treatment of disease;

"(3)   Selling, prescribing, giving away, or administering drugs for other than legal and legitimate therapeutic purposes ... ;

. . .

"(6)   A departure from, or the failure to conform to, minimal standards of care ... [.]"

Medical School, and Dr. Eljorn Don Nelson, an associate professor of clinical pharmacology at the University of Cincinnati College of Medicine. These experts stated that there are two schools of thought in the medical community concerning the use of stimulants for weight control. The so-called "majority" view holds that stimulants should only be used for short periods, if at all, in weight control programs. The "minority" view holds that the long-term use of stimulants is proper in the context of a supervised physician-patient relationship. Both experts testified that, though they themselves supported the "majority" view, Dr. Williams's application of the "minority" protocol was not substandard medical practice.

The hearing examiner found that Dr. Williams's practices violated R.C. 4731.22(B). The examiner recommended subjecting Dr. Williams to a three-year monitored probation period. The board modified the penalty, imposing a one-year suspension of Dr. Williams's license followed by a five-year probationary period, during which he would be unable to prescribe or dispense controlled substances.

Dr. Williams appealed to the Court of Common Pleas of Franklin County pursuant to R.C. 119.12. The court found that the board's order was ". . . not supported by reliable, probative and substantial evidence and . . . [was] not in accordance with law." The court of appeals affirmed.

HERBERT R. BROWN, JUSTICE.

In an appeal from an administrative agency, a reviewing court is bound to uphold the agency's order if it is ". . . supported by reliable, probative, and substantial evidence and is in accordance with law. . . ."[ ]. In the instant case, we must determine if the common pleas court erred by finding that the board's order was not supported by sufficient evidence. For the reasons which follow, we conclude that it did not and affirm the judgment of the court below.

In its arguments to this court, the board contends that Arlen v. Ohio State Medical Bd. (1980), 61 Ohio St.2d 168, 15 O.O.3d 190, 399 N.E.2d 1251, is dispositive. In *Arlen*, the physician was disciplined because he had written prescriptions for controlled substances to a person who the physician knew was redistributing the drugs to others, a practice prohibited by R.C. 3719.06(A). The physician appealed on the ground that the board failed to present expert testimony that such prescribing practices fell below a reasonable standard of care.

We held that the board is not required in every case to present expert testimony on the acceptable standard of medical practice before it can find that a physician's conduct falls below this standard. We noted that the usual purpose of expert testimony is to assist the trier of facts in understanding "issues that require scientific or specialized knowledge or experience beyond the scope of common occurrences. . . ."[ ] The board was then made up of ten (now twelve) persons, eight of whom are licensed physicians. [ ] Thus, a majority of board members are themselves experts in the medical field who already possess the specialized knowledge needed to determine the acceptable standard of general medical practice.

While the board need not, in every case, present expert testimony to support a charge against an accused physician, the charge must be supported by some reliable, probative and substantial evidence. It is here that the case against Dr. Williams fails, as it is very different from *Arlen.*

Arlen involved a physician who dispensed controlled substances in a manner that not only fell below the acceptable standard of medical practice, but also violated the applicable statute governing prescription and dispensing of these drugs. In contrast, Dr. Williams dispensed controlled substances in what was, at the time, a legally permitted manner, albeit one which was disfavored by many in the medical community. The only evidence in the record on this issue was the testimony of Dr. Williams's expert witnesses that his use of controlled substances in weight control programs did not fall below the acceptable standard of medical practice. While the board has broad discretion to resolve evidentiary conflicts [ ] and determine the weight to be given expert testimony [ ], it cannot convert its own disagreement with an expert's opinion into affirmative evidence of a contrary proposition where the issue is one on which medical experts are divided and there is no statute or rule governing the situation.

It should be noted, however, that where the General Assembly has prohibited a particular medical practice by statute, or where the board has done so through its rulemaking authority, the existence of a body of expert opinion supporting that practice would not excuse a violation. Thus, if Dr. Williams had continued to prescribe Biphetamine or Obetrol for weight control after the promulgation of Ohio Adm. Code 4731–11–03(B), this would be a violation of R.C. 4731.22(B)(3), and the existence of the "minority" view supporting the use of these substances for weight control would provide him no defense. Under those facts, *Arlen* would be dispositive. Here, however, there is insufficient evidence, expert or otherwise, to support the charges against Dr. Williams. Were the board's decision to be affirmed on the facts in this record, it would mean that a doctor would have no access to meaningful review of the board's decision. The board, though a majority of its members have special knowledge, is not entitled to exercise such unbridled discretion.

WRIGHT, JUSTICE, dissenting.

The message we send to the medical community's regulators with today's decision is one, I daresay, we would never countenance for their counterparts in the legal community. We are telling those charged with policing the medical profession that their expertise as to what constitutes the acceptable standard of medical practice is not enough to overcome the assertion that challenged conduct does not violate a state statute. . . .

HOOVER V. THE AGENCY FOR HEALTH CARE ADMINISTRATION

District Court of Appeal of Florida, 1996.
676 So. 2d 1380.

JORGENSON, JUDGE.

Dr. Katherine Anne Hoover, a board-certified physician in internal medicine, appeals a final order of the Board of Medicine penalizing her and restricting her license to practice medicine in the State of Florida. We reverse because the board has once again engaged in the uniformly rejected practice of overzealously supplanting a hearing officer's valid findings of fact regarding a doctor's prescription practices with its own opinion in a case founded on a woefully inadequate quantum of evidence.

In March 1994, the Department of Business and Professional Regulation (predecessor in these proceedings to the Agency for Health Care Administration) filed an administrative complaint alleging that Dr. Hoover (1) inappropriately and excessively prescribed various ... controlled substances to seven of her patients and (2) provided care of those patients that fell below that level of care, skill, and treatment which is recognized by a reasonably prudent similar physician as being acceptable under similar conditions and circumstances; in violation of sections 458.331(1)(q) and (t), Florida Statutes, respectively. All seven of the patients had been treated by Dr. Hoover for intractable pain arising from various non-cancerous diseases or ailments.

Dr. Hoover disputed the allegations of the administrative complaint and requested a formal hearing. . . .

The agency presented the testimony of two physicians as experts. Neither had examined any of the patients or their medical records. The sole basis for the opinions of the agency physicians was computer printouts from pharmacies in Key West where the doctor's patients had filled their prescriptions. These printouts indicated only the quantity of each drug filled for each patient, occasionally referring to a simplified diagnosis. Both of these physicians practiced internal medicine and neither specialized in the care of chronic pain. In fact, both doctors testified that they did not treat but referred their chronic pain patients to pain management clinics. The hearing officer found that this was a common practice among physicians—perhaps to avoid prosecutions like this case.[5] Both doctors "candidly testified that without being provided with copies of the medical records for those patients they could not evaluate Respondent's diagnoses or what alternative modalities were attempted or what testing was done to support the use of the medication chosen by Respondent to treat those patients." Despite this paucity of evidence, lack of familiarity, and seeming

---

[5] Referral to a pain management clinic was not an option for Dr. Hoover's indigent Key West resident patients.

lack of expertise, the agency's physicians testified at the hearing that the doctor had prescribed excessive, perhaps lethal amounts of narcotics, and had practiced below the standard of care.

Dr. Hoover testified in great detail concerning the condition of each of the patients, her diagnoses and courses of treatment, alternatives attempted, the patients' need for medication, the uniformly improved function of the patients with the amount of medication prescribed, and her frequency of writing prescriptions to allow her close monitoring of the patients. She presented corroborating physician testimony regarding the appropriateness of the particular medications and the amounts prescribed and her office-setting response to the patients' requests for relief from intractable pain.

Following post-hearing submissions, the hearing officer issued her recommended order finding that the agency had failed to meet its burden of proof on all charges. The hearing officer concluded, for instance, "Petitioner failed to provide its experts with adequate information to show the necessary similar conditions and circumstances upon which they could render opinions that showed clearly and convincingly that Respondent failed to meet the standard of care required of her in her treatment of the patients in question."

The agency filed exceptions to the recommended findings of fact and conclusions of law as to five of the seven patients. The board of medicine accepted all the agency's exceptions, amended the findings of fact in accordance with the agency's suggestions, and found the doctor in violation of sections 458.331(1)(q) and (t), Florida Statutes. The board imposed the penalty recommended by the agency: a reprimand, a $4,000 administrative fine, continuing medical education on prescribing abusable drugs, and two years probation. This appeal follows.

For each of the five patients, the hearing officer found the prescribing practices of Doctor Hoover to be appropriate. This was based upon (1) the doctor's testimony regarding the specific care given, (2) the corroborating testimony of her physician witness, and (3) the fact that the doctor's prescriptions did not exceed the federal guidelines for treatment of intractable pain in cancer patients, though none of the five patients were diagnosed as suffering from cancer.

The board rejected these findings as not based on competent substantial evidence. As particular reasons, the board adopted the arguments of the agency's exceptions to the recommended order that (1) the hearing officer's findings were erroneously based on irrelevant federal guidelines, and (2) the agency's physicians had testified that the doctor's prescription pattern was below the standard of care and outside the practice of medicine. . . .

First, the board mischaracterizes the hearing officer's reference to the federal guidelines. The board reasoned in its final order that "[t]he record reflects that the federal guidelines relied upon by the Hearing Officer for this finding were designed for cancer patients and [the five patients at issue were] not being treated for cancer." It is true, as the hearing officer noted, that

> Respondent presented expert evidence that there is a set of guidelines which have been issued for the use of Schedule II controlled substances to treat intractable pain and that although those guidelines were established to guide physicians in treating cancer patients, those are the only guidelines available at this time. Utilizing those guidelines, because they exist, the amount of medication prescribed by Respondent to the patients in question was not excessive or inappropriate.

[ ]. In so finding, however, the hearing officer did not, as the board suggests, rely solely upon the federal guidelines in its ruling that the doctor's prescribing practices were not excessive. Rather, the federal guidelines merely buttressed fact findings that were independently supported by the hearing officer's determination of the persuasiveness and credibility of the physician witnesses on each side. For example, though he admitted he had not even reviewed the federal guidelines, one of the agency physicians asserted that the amounts prescribed constituted a "tremendous number of pills" and that the doses involved would be lethal. That Dr. Hoover's prescriptions fell within the guidelines for chronic-pained cancer patients may properly be considered to refute this assertion. Such a use of the federal guidelines was relevant and reasonable.

Second, Dr. Hoover testified in great detail concerning her treatment of each patient, the patient's progress under the medication she prescribed, and that the treatment was within the standard of care and practice of medicine. The hearing officer, as arbiter of credibility, was entitled to believe what the doctor and her physician expert opined. [ ] The agency's witnesses' ultimate conclusions do not strip the hearing officer's reliance upon Dr. Hoover of its competence and substantiality. The hearing officer was entitled to give Dr. Hoover's testimony greater weight than that of the agency's witnesses, who did not examine these patients or regularly engage in the treatment of intractable pain.

[T]he hearing officer explicitly recognized that the 1994 [Florida] intractable pain law was not in effect at the time of Dr. Hoover's alleged infractions but cited it for a permissible purpose—to rebut any claim that there is a strong public policy mandate in favor of the board's draconian policy of policing pain prescription practice. [ ] . . .

Reversed.

NOTES AND QUESTIONS

1. *Administrative Law.* In both *Williams* and *Hoover,* the outcome of the case turns on an administrative law evidentiary standard. As noted earlier, medical boards are agencies subject to state administrative codes. Such codes commonly require that an agency's factual findings following a hearing must be based on "reliable, probative and substantial evidence" that is in the hearing record. This standard is easy to satisfy, and so it is remarkable that the board in *Williams* failed to meet it. At the same time, this explains why the court in *Hoover* readily held that the board lacked a basis in law to ignore the hearing officer's recommendations. Administrative law principles are at the heart of many of the decisions you will read in this chapter and throughout this casebook because much of health care is regulated by local, state and federal administrative agencies.

2. *Disciplinary "Chilling Effect."* The court in *Hoover* implies that disciplinary actions by a state medical board against individual physicians have an effect on other physicians' practices. Beyond penalizing or removing the "bad apple" from practice, this effect is, in fact, a core objective of professional discipline. In the case of treatment for pain, however, this deterrence has been called the "Chilling Effect" because the threat of legal sanction seems to lead doctors to avoid legitimate and effective treatments. Judge Kozinski of the Ninth Circuit, quoting an expert on this point, observes:

> Physicians are particularly easily deterred by the threat of governmental investigation and/or sanction from engaging in conduct that is entirely lawful and medically appropriate. . . . [A] physician's practice is particularly dependent upon the physician's maintaining a reputation of unimpeachable integrity. A physician's career can be effectively destroyed merely by the fact that a governmental body has investigated his or her practice. . . . Concurring Opinion in Conant v. Walters, 309 F.3d 629 (9th Cir. 2002), *cert. denied,* 540 U.S. 946 (2003).

If physicians provide inadequate care because of their fear of legal entanglement, what are the implications for medical boards that want to encourage quality care? Physicians dread being investigated and avoid occasions that might trigger investigation because of the high cost of legal representation and the emotional stress. See Sandra H. Johnson, Regulating Physician Behavior: Taking Doctors' "Bad Law" Claims Seriously, 53 St. Louis U. L.J. 973 (2009). This chilling effect has rematerialized in the current treatment of pain as licensing boards and other regulators have again become suspicious of physicians prescribing opioids in the wake of the opioid overdose crisis in the U.S. See Kelly K. Dineen, Definitions Matter: A Taxonomy of Inappropriate Prescribing to Shape Effective Opioid Policy and Reduce Patient Harm, 67 U. Kan. L. Rev. 961, 964 (2019) ("fear of legal and regulatory scrutiny is among" the reasons that physicians are again under-treating pain).

3. *Pain Control Provision.* The Florida statute referenced in *Hoover* provides:

Notwithstanding any other provision of law, a physician may prescribe or administer any controlled substance to a person for the treatment of intractable pain, provided the physician does so in accordance with the level of care, skill, and treatment recognized by a reasonably prudent physician under similar conditions and circumstances.

This statute follows a pattern that is familiar in statutes regulating a particular treatment. It is intended to allow or encourage a specific practice (through a form of safe harbor) while at the same time retaining significant authority for discipline in particular cases. How well does this statute satisfy these two goals?

4. *State Variation in Physician Discipline.* Rates of serious disciplinary action vary considerably among the states. From 2017–2019, for example, the District of Columbia had the lowest rate, at 0.29/1,000 doctors, and Kentucky had the highest, at 2.29/1,000. Public Citizen's Health Research Group, Ranking of the Rate of State Medical Boards' Serious Disciplinary Actions, 2017–2019 (2021). This is consistent with the variability found by two researchers at the University of Michigan. See John Alexander Harris and Elena Byhoff, Variations by State in Physician Disciplinary Actions by US Medical Licensure Boards, 26 BMJ Quality & Safety 200 (2017). These researchers surmise that "[f]actors such as how easy it is to make a complaint to a state board, how many resources a board has to investigate complaints, the actual makeup of the board, including how many nonphysicians are on it, and the standards for making a judgment and choosing a disciplinary action all play into the variation." Kara Gavin, For Doctors Behaving Badly, Punishments Vary by State, University of Michigan Industry Dx (March 24, 2016).

5. *Character Rather than Competence.* Although licensing boards generally have the authority to prosecute the physicians they license for malpractice, they tend not to do so unless and until a physician has amassed multiple paid malpractice claims. See David A. Hyman, Mohammad Rahmati and Bernard Black, Medical Malpractice and Physician Discipline: The Good, the Bad, and the Ugly, 18 J. Empirical Leg. Stud. 131 (2021) (based on data from 1990–2016, the likelihood that the Illinois medical licensing agency would take disciplinary action against a physician increased steadily with each paid malpractice claim amassed by a physician). State licensing agencies have limited resources, and they may choose to spend those resources on addressing a physician's substandard medical care only when one or more malpractice verdicts or settlements have not resulted in improved performance.

Evidence also shows that state licensing agencies use their resources to pursue the most egregious forms of unprofessional behavior rather than incidents of substandard medical care. As Professor Nadia Sawicki put it, physician discipline by state licensing agencies usually addresses problems of "character, not competence." Nadia N. Sawicki, Character, Competence, and the Principles of Medical Discipline, 13 J. Health Care L. & Pol'y 285, 302–306 (2010) (licensing actions against physicians for malpractice make up only about 20 percent of all disciplinary actions). Similarly, an analysis of the nearly 300 cases that came before the American Medical Association's Council for Ethical and Judicial Affairs over a 5-year period found that the majority of cases (55 percent) were related to substance abuse disorder or controlled-substance violations, while physician negligence accounted for 21 percent of cases. The remaining cases related to fraud, misrepresentation, criminal activity, and physician-patient boundary issues. See Kavita Shah Arora, Sharon Douglas and Susan Dorr, *What Brings Physicians to Disciplinary Review? A Further Subcategorization*, 5 AJOB Empirical Bioethics 53 (2014). Likewise, the Federation of State Medical Boards (FSMB) reviewed its 2019 data and identified 1638 disciplinary actions likely related to physician sexual misconduct. See Patricia A. King, Humayun J. Chaudhry, DO and Mark L. Staz, *State Medical Board Recommendations for Stronger Approaches to Sexual Misconduct by Physicians*, 325 JAMA 1609 (2021). For reference, FSMB separately reported that state boards took a total of 8,166 disciplinary actions in 2019. FSMB, *U.S. Medical Licensing and Disciplinary Data Report, 2019*, Table 5.

6.   *Interstate Licensing.* Critics of the current state-by-state medical licensing system urge expansion of interstate licensing, see, e.g., Eli Y. Adashi, I. Glenn Cohen and Winston L. McCormick, *The Interstate Medical Licensure Compact: Attending to the Underserved*, 325 JAMA 1607 (2021), or creating a federal medical license, see, e.g., Bob Kocher, *Doctors Without State Borders: Practicing Across State Lines*, Health Aff. Blog (Feb. 18, 2014). Because states traditionally regulate the practice of medicine, however, a federal licensing system is less likely to be developed than a uniform system of state reciprocity. Indeed, the Interstate Medical Licensure Compact, which became operational in 2017, has created a model interstate agreement and presented it to state legislatures. The result is a streamlined system to license physicians in several states at once.

> The Compact creates a voluntary, expedited pathway to state licensure for physicians who want to practice medicine in multiple states. Eligible physicians can qualify to practice medicine in multiple states by completing just one application within the Compact, receiving separate licenses from each state in which they intend to practice.
>
> These licenses are still issued by the individual states—just as they would be using the standard licensing process—but because the application for licensure in these states is routed through the Compact, the overall process of gaining a license is significantly streamlined. Physicians receive their licenses much faster and with fewer burdens.

Interstate Medical Licensure Compact, *General FAQs about the Compact* (visited July 22, 2021). Through the Compact, states retain legal authority over medical licensure through their existing administrative agencies based on existing state law as amended to authorize participation in the Compact. As of 2021, more than 30 jurisdictions are participating in the Compact, and legislation has been introduced in several more. See generally Interstate

Medical Licensure Compact website. The Compact was created with the cooperation of FSMB and several state licensing boards. It is operated by a Commission comprised of two medical board members or agency administrators from each participating jurisdiction.

   7.   *Telemedicine.* Telemedicine has become commonplace and offers increased access to medical care and potential cost reductions, for example, by enabling remote consultation on imaging by specialists. The practice has raised a host of issues. It tests the state-based structure of medical licensure, and a central issue is whether a physician must be licensed by the state where the patient is located. State statutes have taken a variety of approaches ranging from the very restrictive to the very open. See, e.g., Smith v. Laboratory Corp. of America, 2010 WL 5464770 (W.D. Wash. 2010) (contrasting the approaches of Washington and Idaho in case of a Washington physician providing remote review of biopsies for patients in Idaho). Internet-only pharmacies that offer one-stop service for patients who fill out an online medical questionnaire and have a prescription written by a physician working for the pharmacy have raised serious concerns, especially when controlled substances are prescribed. See Regina A. Bailey, The Legal, Financial, and Ethical Implications of Online Medical Consultations, 16 J. Tech. L. & Pol'y 53 (2011).

   By necessity, providers and patients substantially increased their use of telemedicine as the community spread of COVID-19 increased. In February 2020 telemedicine visits comprised close to zero percent of patients' office visits; this percentage increased to 14 percent in April 2020. See Ateev Mehrotra et al., The Impact of the COVID-19 Pandemic on Outpatient Visits: Changing Patterns of Care in the Newest COVID-19 Hot Spots, Commonwealth Fund Report (Aug. 13, 2020). Likewise, the number of federally funded health centers offering telemedicine visits jumped from 43 percent pre-pandemic to 95 percent during the pandemic. See Hanna B. Demeke et al., Trends in Use of Telehealth Among Health Centers During the COVID-19 Pandemic—United States, June 26–November 6, 2020, 70 MMWR 240 (Feb. 19, 2021).

   To enable medical care during the pandemic while also limiting the spread of COVID-19, the law in all jurisdictions changed temporarily to allow physicians and other licensed health professionals to practice in those jurisdictions with a temporary license or collaborative agreement or without any license if they hold a license in good standing in at least one jurisdiction. See FSMB, U.S. States and Territories Modifying Licensure Requirements for Physicians in Response to COVID-19 (July 19, 2021) (surveying the law in all U.S. jurisdictions). So, for example, through executive action, the Governor of Missouri waived licensing restrictions so that "physicians and surgeons licensed in another state can provide care to Missouri citizens, in person or using telehealth options, as long as they are actively licensed in another state and their license has not been disciplined," for the duration of the state's COVID-19 emergency declaration. Press Release, Office of the Governor, Governor Parson Continues Efforts to Eliminate Barriers, Expand Ability to Provide Health Care during COVID-19 Crisis (Mar. 30, 2020).

Proponents of telemedicine argue that our positive experience with telemedicine during the COVID-19 pandemic warrants permanent changes to relevant laws so our society can enjoy the efficiencies of telemedicine on a permanent basis. See Samyukta Mullangi, Mohit Agrawal and Kevin Schulman, The COVID-19 Pandemic—An Opportune Time to Update Medical Licensing, 181 JAMA Internal Med. 307 (2021); Anita Slomski, Telehealth Success Spurs a Call for Greater Post-COVID-19 License Portability, 324 JAMA 1021 (2021).

NOTE: THE NATIONAL PRACTITIONER DATA BANK

Congress established the National Practitioner Data Bank (NPDB)—also commonly referred to as the "data bank"—in part to create an effective system for preventing doctors with disciplinary history in one state from moving to another and practicing until detected (if ever). 42 U.S.C. §§ 11101–11152. State disciplinary and licensure boards are required to report certain disciplinary actions against physicians. Hospitals and other entities engaging in peer review processes are required to report adverse actions as well. Licensure boards have access to the NPDB to check on licensees, and hospitals must check the NPDB regarding physicians applying for staff privileges and, periodically, physicians who hold staff privileges. See discussion in Chapter 11. The ACA directed HHS to fold its collection of data concerning adverse actions for fraud and abuse (the Healthcare Integrity and Protection Data Bank (HIPDB)) into the NPDB. See HHS Final Rule, 78 Fed. Reg. 20473–01 (Apr. 5, 2013). Practitioners have access to their own records in the NPDB except for the reports made through the HIPDB, for which access could compromise ongoing criminal investigations. 76 Fed. Reg. 9295 (Feb. 17, 2011).

The public is not allowed access to information on individual practitioners in the NPDB, although access to anonymized information is permitted. For arguments for and against public access, see Kristen Baczynski, Do You Know Who Your Physician Is?: Placing Physician Information on the Internet, 87 Iowa L. Rev. 1303 (2002); Laura A. Chernitsky, Constitutional Arguments in Favor of Modifying the HCQIA to Allow the Dissemination of Information to Healthcare Consumers, 63 Wash. & Lee L. Rev. 737 (2006).

Following the lead of Massachusetts, most states have established publicly accessible websites where they post physician profiles. The Massachusetts site posts background information on the physician (such as education, specialties, insurance plans) as well as malpractice claims paid, hospital credentialing actions, criminal convictions, and board disciplinary actions. Mass. Bd. of Reg. in Med., On-Line Physician Profile Site.

A review of data from the NPDB revealed that only 45% of doctors with an NPDB report of adverse privileges actions or malpractice settlements also had a report of a disciplinary action by their state medical board. See Alan Levine et al., State Medical Boards Fail to Discipline Doctors with Hospital Actions against Them, Public Citizen (2011). Most state boards reported that they had been aware of the reports against specific physicians in all but the rarest of cases, but that their board's investigation had concluded that the circumstances did not warrant disciplinary action in the specific cases at issue. Medical boards in a couple of states, however, responded that they were not aware of the reports of adverse action against a good number of their licensees. See 20 Health Law Rptr. 1615 (2011).

The watchdog group Public Citizen has revealed HHS's failure to report paid claims of HHS's own practitioners. In a 2019 letter to key Congressional committees, it reported that HHS had failed to report at least 2100 paid malpractice claims against its practitioners over a 22-year period. See Public Citizen, Letter dated July 16, 2019 to Chairman and Ranking Member of Senate Committee on Health, Education, Labor and Pensions. The letter also noted that the Office of the Inspector General at HHS had investigated HHS's failure to make data bank reports in 2003, and the letter highlighted the fact that the FSMB had contacted the OIG during its investigation to remind the agency that such reporting is essential to the integrity of the work that state licensing agencies do to safeguard the public. Id.

NOTE: FEDERALISM AND PRESCRIBING DRUGS

Both *Williams* and *Hoover* involve disciplinary action by a state medical board based on a physician's prescribing practices. Prescribing is also regulated by the Food and Drug Administration (FDA) and the Drug Enforcement Administration (DEA), two powerful federal agencies. Public and private payers (including Medicare, Medicaid, and private insurers) also influence prescribing through coverage and payment policies.

In our federal system, the regulation of the practice of medicine traditionally has belonged to the states through the police power. Congress did not intend that either the FDA or the DEA regulatie the *legitimate* practice of medicine. The boundary between the agencies' statutory authority and the restraint on their regulation of medical practice is blurry, however, because it is nearly impossible to regulate prescribing without regulating the practice of medicine in some way.

The FDA has the authority to approve and monitor the safety of drugs and devices, and this role certainly makes the FDA an important gatekeeper of access to drugs. Once a drug is approved for prescribing, however, the FDA does not have the authority to restrict physicians in how they prescribe the drug for particular purposes. Thus, once a drug is approved for a particular purpose (e.g., for the treatment of a particular sort of cancer), a physician may prescribe the drug "off-label" for other purposes (e.g., for the treatment of another type of cancer). See Sandra H. Johnson, Polluting Medical Judgment? False Assumptions in the Pursuit of False Claims Regarding Off-Label Prescribing, 9 Minn. J. L. Sci. Tech. 61 (2008).

The DEA more directly regulates prescribing practices through its authority under the Controlled Substances Act (CSA). See 21 U.S.C. § 801. Under the CSA, the DEA governs the production and distribution of drugs that have the potential for abuse or addiction. Such drugs are categorized as controlled substances and placed on a "schedule" that rates a drug by its abuse potential from Schedule V (the lowest potential) to Schedules I and II (the highest potential). Schedule I drugs, including heroin and marijuana, are viewed as having a very high potential for abuse and no therapeutic benefit. Doctors may not prescribe Schedule I drugs.

Doctors must obtain a permit issued by the DEA to prescribe drugs on Schedules II through V. The DEA may revoke the permit or pursue criminal action against a physician whose prescription or distribution of these drugs falls outside of the DEA's view of legitimate medical practice.

The overlapping jurisdictions of federal and state government over the practice of medicine and the issuing of prescriptions can create conflict. Consider, for example, the legalization of marijuana. Many states have enacted legislation to allow physicians or patients access to marijuana for the treatment of medical conditions. See, e.g., Cal. Health & Saf. Code § 11362.5. The Supreme Court, in Gonzales v. Raich, 545 U.S. 1 (2005), ruled that the federal government has the power under the Constitution to enforce the CSA against even intrastate production, sale and distribution of marijuana that is authorized under state law. Yet, recent Presidential administrations have had little interest in spending federal prosecutorial resources to enforce the CSA against marijuana growers, dispensers, or users in states that have legalized its medicinal use. For a federalism analysis of this clash between federal and state law, see Erwin Chemerinsky et al., Cooperative Federalism and Marijuana Regulation, 62 UCLA L. Rev. 74 (2015); Symposium: Marijuana, Federal Power and the States, 65 Case W. Res. L. Rev. 505–794 (2015). See also JONATHAN ADLER, ED., OUR FEDERALISM ON DRUGS: UNCLE SAM AND MARY JANE (2020); Nicole Huberfeld, Health Equity, Federalism, and Cannabis Policy, 101 B.U. L. Rev. 897 (2021).

Pain medication prescribing practices fall into another arena in which federal and state health policy may continue to conflict. As if on a pendulum, the law swings back and forth between encouraging adequate treatment of pain by protecting physicians who prescribe opioids from administrative or criminal punishment, and then lowering those protections to discourage opioid prescribing patterns that lead to increased addiction. See Timothy Atkinson et al., The Damage Done by the War on Opioids: The Pendulum Has Swung Too Far, 7 J. Pain Res. 265 (2014); Lindsey E. Dayer et al., A Recent History of Opioid Use in the U.S.: Three Decades of Change, 54 Substance Use & Misuse 331 (2019)

At the time of the *Hoover* case, there was strong evidence that medical boards had not adjusted their standards to reflect medical evidence that supported the use of opioids for treatment over the long term and in higher doses than had been customary. As a result, doctors who treated their patients' chronic pain effectively were at risk of disciplinary action, while those doctors who provided inadequate treatment faced no legal risk at all. In an attempt to balance legal risks, nearly half of the states enacted legislation generally referred to as "intractable pain treatment acts" which limit state agencies in taking action against physicians in certain circumstances, as discussed in the notes below. The Federation of State Medical Boards (FSMB) also adopted a model policy specifically recognizing that opioids are essential to the treatment of pain and that state medical boards should be just as concerned about pain treatment neglect as they are about prescription abuse. FSMB, Model Policy for the Use of Controlled Substances for the Treatment of Pain (2004). Between 2002 and 2010, however, opioid abuse increased significantly, as did related deaths. It then decreased again between 2011 and 2013. See Richard Dart et al., Trends in Opioid Analgesic Abuse and Mortality in the United States, 372 N. Engl. J. Med. 241 (2015).

Overall, policymakers have become fearful that incompetent or even corrupt physicians are to blame for prescribing opioids for pain too freely. As a result, we are seeing shifts in the law. Tennessee legislators, for example, allowed the state's intractable pain act to lapse without renewal in 2015. See 2015 Pub. Acts, c. 26, § 1. Vermont adopted new regulations to limit the quantity of opioids. See Vermont Dept. of Health, Rule Governing the Prescribing of Opioids for Pain. Similarly, a guideline from the Centers for Disease Control and Prevention (CDC) discourages physicians from prescribing opioids for pain as a first line of treatment, and it recommends dosage limitations when opioids are used. See CDC, Guideline for Prescribing Opioids for Chronic Pain (2016). See also Deborah Dowell, Tamara Haegerich, and Roger Chou, No Shortcuts to Safer Opioid Prescribing, 380 N. Engl. J. Med. 2285 (2019) (CDC guidelines have been misunderstood and used to justify hard limits on dosages and even abrupt discontinuation of opioid-based pain treatment).

Additionally, FSMB has updated its Model Policy twice since 2004. While the current version continues to encourage opioid prescriptions when necessary to treat pain, it also encourages the use of other less addictive medications, treats acute and chronic pain differently, substantially reduces the duration of an opioid trial period, and places more responsibility on physicians to inform patients more thoroughly about opioid risks and monitor patients taking opioids more closely. See FSMB, Model Policy for the Use of Controlled Substances for the Treatment of Pain (2017).

During this period, the DEA has pursued an aggressive stance against prescribers of controlled substances for pain management. The National Association of Attorneys General expressed concern that, while state medical boards were taking steps to ensure access to pain treatment, the DEA was moving to criminalize physician prescribing. The Association commented that "state and federal policies are diverging with respect to the relative emphasis on ensuring the availability of prescription pain medications to those who need them."

Conflict between state and federal policy on this issue continues, although there is evidence that state prosecutions of physicians prescribing pain medication has increased as well. On prosecutions of physicians, see David D. Kim and Nabil Sibai, The Current State of Opioid Prescribing and Drug

Enforcement Agency (DEA) Action Against Physicians: An Analysis of DEA Database 2004–2017, 23 Pain Physician 297 (2020); Julia B. Berman & Guohua Li, Characteristics of Criminal Cases Against Physicians Charged with Opioid-Related Offenses Reported in the U.S. News Media, 1995–2019, Injury Epidemiol. 50 (2020); Diane E. Hoffmann, Treating Pain v. Reducing Drug Diversion and Abuse: Recalibrating the Balance in Our Drug Control Laws and Policies, 1 St. Louis U. J. Health & Pol'y 231 (2008). See also Kelly Dineen and James DuBois, Between a Rock and a Hard Place: Can Physicians Prescribe Opioids to Treat Pain Adequately While Avoiding Legal Sanction?, 42 Am. J. L. & Med. 7 (2016).

The ACA established an Interagency Pain Research Coordinating Committee to coordinate federal research efforts, and it directed the Secretary of HHS to provide grants and contracts with health professions schools, hospices, and other entities to improve education and practice in caring for patients in pain. In response to an ACA mandate, the IOM issued a report documenting the impact of pain on public health (over 100 million persons in America are in chronic pain and costs for medical care and lost productivity exceed $560 billion annually) and making recommendations to improve pain treatment and expand research. See IOM, Relieving Pain in America: A Blueprint for Transforming Prevention, Care, Education, and Research (2011).

PROBLEM: THREE STRIKES AND YOU'RE OUT?

In 2004, Florida voters approved by an overwhelming majority the following amendment to the state constitution:

(a) No person who has been found to have committed three or more incidents of medical malpractice shall be licensed. . . .

(b)(1)   The phrase "medical malpractice" means the failure to practice medicine . . . with that level of care, skill, and treatment recognized in general law related to health care providers' licensure. . . .

(b)(2)   The phrase "found to have committed" means that the malpractice has been found in a final judgment of a court of law, final administrative agency decision, or decision of binding arbitration.

Thereafter, the Florida legislature codified the amendment in the medical licensure statute but added the following provision:

[T]he board shall not license or continue to license a medical doctor found to have committed repeated medical malpractice [defined as three or more incidents], the finding of which was based upon clear and convincing evidence. In order to rely on an incident of medical malpractice to determine whether a license must be denied or revoked under this section, if the facts supporting the finding of the incident of medical malpractice were determined on a standard less stringent than clear and convincing evidence, the board shall review the record of the case and determine whether the finding would be supported under a standard of clear and convincing evidence.

Did the legislature significantly alter the impact of the amendment? Why might they have made this change?

Assume that your state's licensure statute provides only that disciplinary action may be taken when a physician has engaged in:

Any conduct or practice which is or might be harmful or dangerous to the mental or physical health of a patient or the public; or incompetency, gross negligence or repeated negligence in the performance of the functions or duties of any profession licensed or regulated by this chapter. For the purposes of this subdivision, "repeated negligence" means the failure, on more than one occasion, to use that degree of skill and learning ordinarily used under the same or similar circumstances by the member of the applicant's or licensee's profession.

Does the medical board have the authority under this provision to issue a rule or adopt a policy that it will sanction a doctor with final judgments of malpractice in three or more cases? A doctor with ten or more malpractice claims made? Should the board adopt such a rule? Or would you argue that there should always be hearing before discipline?

III. COMPLEMENTARY AND ALTERNATIVE MEDICINE

Complementary and alternative medicine (CAM) is the term for medical products and practices that are not part of standard medical care, which are used by patients—and recommended by some practitioners—in tandem with or as a substitute for standard medical care. CAM is often associated with theories and beliefs about health and healing that differ from those intrinsic to the dominant health system of a particular society or culture in a given historical period. Boundaries within CAM and between the CAM domain and the domain of the dominant system are not always sharp or fixed. IOM, Complementary and Alternative Medicine in the United States (2005).

The National Institutes of Health, National Center for Complementary and Alternative Medicine (NCCAM) defines CAM as health services that "are not presently considered to be part of conventional medicine," and goes on to list four domains (whole medical systems, such as homeopathy; mind-body medicine, including music; energy medicine, including therapeutic touch; and bioelectromagnetic-based therapies, such as pulsed fields).

The IOM report cited above notes that all proposed definitions of CAM are "imprecise, ambiguous, or otherwise subject to misinterpretation." Both the IOM report and the NCCAM definitions are deficient because, fundamentally, they use a negative to define CAM: it is unconventional. Furthermore, they define CAM in relation to allopathic (traditional M.D.) medicine and do not communicate the integration and coherence of CAM systems standing alone. Despite their limits, the definitions do capture the fluid sense of what is conventional and what is alternative, as well as the vastness of what might be considered complementary and alternative (or integrative) medicine. They also reflect the current legal framework for CAM, including the approaches to licensure.

State professional licensure boards become involved in CAM in three ways. First, licensed doctors (or nurses, dentists, and so on) may utilize CAM therapies, integrating them within conventional medicine. See IOM, Integrative Medicine and the Health of the Public: A Summary of the February 2009 Summit (2009) (including discussion of integrating "evidence-based interventions or practices derived from ancient folk practices, cultural-specific sources, contemporary product development, or crafted from a blend of these" with allopathic approaches). Integrating CAM approaches, however, will attract the attention of the licensure board if the practice violates licensure standards for acceptable or appropriate treatment. That issue is addressed in this section. Second, licensure boards may take action against unlicensed CAM practitioners for violating the state's prohibition against the unlicensed practice of a licensed health care profession, as discussed in Section IV. Third, where CAM providers are licensed, they will be subject to restrictions on their scope of practice, as discussed in Section V of this chapter.

The IOM adopted the following "ethical commitments" to guide its work concerning CAM: a social commitment to public welfare; a commitment to protect patients and the public; respect for patient autonomy; recognition of medical pluralism; and public accountability. As you study the materials that follow, consider whether these values work as a guide for decisions by the licensure boards. Do all of the values lead to the same conclusion in each case?

IN RE GUESS

Supreme Court of North Carolina, 1990.
393 S.E.2d 833.

MITCHELL, JUSTICE.

* * *

The facts of this case are essentially uncontested. The record evidence tends to show that Dr. George Albert Guess is a licensed physician practicing family medicine in Asheville. In his practice, Guess regularly administers homeopathic medical treatments to his patients. Homeopathy has been defined as:

A system of therapy developed by Samuel Hahnemann on the theory that large doses of a certain drug given to a healthy person will produce certain conditions which, when occurring spontaneously as symptoms of a disease, are relieved by the same drug in small doses. This [is] . . . a sort of "fighting fire with fire" therapy. [ ] [Both the NCCAM and the Society of Homeopaths provide more detailed descriptions of homeopathy on their websites.]

* * *

[T]he Board charged Dr. Guess with unprofessional conduct [ ] specifically based upon his practice of homeopathy. . . .

Following notice, a hearing was held by the Board on the charge against Dr. Guess. The hearing evidence chiefly consisted of testimony by a number of physicians. Several physicians licensed to practice in North Carolina testified that homeopathy was not an acceptable and prevailing system of medical practice in North Carolina. In fact, there was evidence indicating that Guess is the only homeopath openly practicing in the State. Guess presented evidence that homeopathy is a recognized system of practice in at least three other states and many foreign countries. There was no evidence that Guess' homeopathic treatment had ever harmed a patient, and there was anecdotal evidence that Guess' homeopathic remedies had provided relief to several patients who were apparently unable to obtain relief through allopathic medicine.

Following its hearing, the Board revoked Dr. Guess' license to practice medicine in North Carolina, based upon findings and conclusions that Guess' practice of homeopathy "departs from and does not conform to the standards of acceptable and prevailing medical practice in this State," thus constituting unprofessional conduct as defined and prohibited by N.C.G.S. § 90–14(a)(6). The Board, however, stayed the revocation of Guess' license for so long as he refrained from practicing homeopathy.

Guess appealed the Board's decision to the Superior Court. . . . After review, the Superior Court . . . reversed and vacated the Board's decision. The Superior Court found and concluded that Guess' substantial rights had been violated because the Board's findings, conclusions and decision were "not supported by competent, material and substantial evidence and [were] arbitrary and capricious."

[T]he Court of Appeals rejected the Superior Court's reasoning to the effect that the Board's findings, conclusions and decision were not supported by competent evidence. [ ] The Court of Appeals, nonetheless, affirmed the Superior Court's order reversing the Board's decision,

because the Board neither charged nor found that Dr. Guess' departures from approved and prevailing medical practice either endangered or harmed his patients or the public, and in our opinion the revocation of a physician's license to practice his profession in this state must be based upon conduct that is detrimental to the public; it cannot be based upon conduct that is merely different from that of other practitioners.

We granted the Board's Petition for Discretionary Review, and now reverse the Court of Appeals.

The statute central to the resolution of this case provides in relevant part:

§ 90–14. Revocation, suspension, annulment or denial of license.

(a) The Board shall have the power to deny, annul, suspend, or revoke a license . . . issued by the Board to any person who has been found by the Board to have committed any of the following acts or conduct, or for any of the following reasons:

. . . .

(6) Unprofessional conduct, including, but not limited to, any departure from, or the failure to conform to, the standards of acceptable and prevailing medical practice, or the ethics of the medical profession, irrespective of whether or not a patient is injured thereby. . . . [ ]

The Court of Appeals concluded that in exercising the police power, the legislature may properly act only to protect the public from harm. Therefore, the Court of Appeals reasoned that, in order to be a valid exercise of the police power, the statute must be construed as giving the Board authority to prohibit or punish the action of a physician only when it can be shown that the particular action in question poses a danger of harm to the patient or the public. Specifically, the Court of Appeals held that:

Before a physician's license to practice his profession in this state can be lawfully revoked under G.S. 90–14(a)(6) for practices contrary to acceptable and prevailing medical practice that it must also appear that the deviation complained of posed some threat of harm to either the physician's patients or the public.

The Board argues, and we agree, that the Court of Appeals erred in construing the statute to add a requirement that each particular practice prohibited by the statute must pose an actual threat of harm. Our analysis begins with a basic constitutional principle: the General Assembly, in exercising the state's police power, may legislate to protect the public health, safety and general welfare. [ ] When a statute is challenged as being beyond the scope of the police power, the statute will be upheld unless it has no rational relationship to such a legitimate public purpose. [ ]

[R]egulation of the medical profession is plainly related to the legitimate public purpose of protecting the public health and safety. [ ] State regulation of the medical profession has long been recognized as a legitimate exercise of the police power. As the Supreme Court of the United States [in Dent v. West Virginia, 129 U.S. 114, 98 S.Ct. 231, 32 L.Ed. 623 (1889)] has pointed out:

> The power of the State to provide for the general welfare of its people authorizes it to prescribe all such regulations as in its judgment will secure or tend to secure them against the consequences of ignorance and incapacity as well as of deception and fraud . . . . The nature and extent of the qualifications required must depend primarily upon the judgments of the States as to their necessity. . . .

> Few professions require more careful preparation by one who seeks to enter it than that of medicine. It has to deal with all those subtle and mysterious influences upon which health and life depend. . . . Reliance must be placed upon the assurance given by his license, issued by an authority competent to judge in that respect, that he possesses the requisite qualifications. . . . The same reasons which control in imposing conditions, upon compliance with which the physician is allowed to practice in the first instance, may call for further conditions as new modes of treating disease are discovered, or a more thorough acquaintance is obtained of the remedial properties of vegetable and mineral substances, or a more accurate knowledge is acquired of the human system and of the agencies by which it is affected.

The provision of the statute in question here is reasonably related to the public health. We conclude that the legislature reasonably believed that a general risk of endangering the public is inherent in any practices which fail to conform to the standards of "acceptable and prevailing" medical practice in North Carolina. We further conclude that the legislative intent was to prohibit any practice departing from acceptable and prevailing medical standards without regard to whether the particular practice itself could be shown to endanger the public. . . . Therefore, the statute is a valid exercise of the police power.

* * *

Certain aspects of regulating the medical profession plainly require expertise beyond that of a layman. Our legislature recognized that need for expertise when it created a Board of Medical Examiners composed of seven licensed physicians and one additional member. . . . The statutory phrase "standards of acceptable and prevailing medical practice" is sufficiently specific to provide the Board—comprised overwhelmingly of expert physicians—with the "adequate guiding standards" necessary to support the legislature's delegation of authority.

The statute in question is a valid regulation which generally tends to secure the public health, safety, and general welfare, and the legislature has permissibly delegated certain regulatory functions connected with that valid exercise of the police power to the Board. There is no requirement, however, that every action taken by the Board specifically identify or address a particular injury or danger to any individual or to the public. It is enough that the statute is a valid exercise of the police power for the public health and general welfare, so long as the Board's action is in compliance with the statute. The Court of Appeals thus erred in requiring a showing of potential harm from the particular practices engaged in by Dr. Guess as a prerequisite to Board action, and for that reason the Court of Appeals' decision is reversed.

* * *

Findings by the Board of Medical Examiners, if supported by competent evidence, may not be disturbed by a reviewing court. . . . The Board's findings leading to its decision were based upon competent, material and substantial evidence regarding what constitutes "acceptable and prevailing" standards of medical practice in North Carolina. No more was required. Guess' evidence concerning the efficacy of homeopathy and its use outside North Carolina simply was not relevant to the issue before the Board.

Dr. Guess also contends that the Board's decision was arbitrary and capricious and, therefore, must be reversed. He argues that the Board's arbitrariness is revealed in its "selective" application of the statute against him. He seems to contend that if the Board is to take valid action against him, it must also investigate and sanction every physician who is the "first" to utilize any "new" or "rediscovered" medical procedure. We disagree. The Board properly adhered to its statutory notice and hearing requirements, and its decision was amply supported by uncontroverted competent, material and substantial evidence. We detect no evidence of arbitrariness or capriciousness.

Dr. Guess strenuously argues that many countries and at least three states recognize the legitimacy of homeopathy. While some physicians may value the homeopathic system of practice, it seems that others consider homeopathy an outmoded and ineffective system of practice. This conflict, however interesting, simply is irrelevant here in light of the uncontroverted evidence and the Board's findings and conclusion that homeopathy is not currently an "acceptable and prevailing" system of medical practice in North Carolina.

While questions as to the efficacy of homeopathy and whether its practice should be allowed in North Carolina may be open to valid debate among members of the medical profession, the courts are not the proper forum for that debate. The legislature may one day choose to recognize the homeopathic system of treatment, or homeopathy may evolve by proper experimentation and research to the point of being recognized by the medical profession as an acceptable and prevailing form of medical practice in our state; such choices, however, are not for the courts to make.

... The Board argues, and we agree within our admittedly limited scope of medical knowledge, that preventing the practice of homeopathy will not restrict the development and acceptance of new and beneficial medical practices. Instead, the development and acceptance of such new practices simply must be achieved by "acceptable and prevailing" methods of medical research, experimentation, testing, and approval by the appropriate regulatory or professional bodies.

* * *

REVERSED and REMANDED.

NOTES AND QUESTIONS

1.   *Comparing CAM to Prevailing Practice.* After the *Guess* decision, the North Carolina legislature amended the grounds for discipline to limit the section under which Dr. Guess was penalized:

> The Board shall not revoke the license of or deny a license to a person solely because of that person's practice of a therapy that is experimental, nontraditional, or that departs from acceptable and prevailing medical practices unless, by competent evidence, the Board can establish that the treatment has a safety risk greater than the prevailing treatment or that the treatment is generally ineffective. N.C. Gen. Stat. 90–14(a)(6).

How would the North Carolina board prove that the alternative treatment is less safe than prevailing practice where there may be little evidence that the current practice is safe? Many argue that CAM is not amenable to scientific method in testing effectiveness. See discussion in Julie Stone & Joan Matthews, Complementary Medicine and the Law (1996), arguing that while some alternative or complementary practices have a technological base and are subject to the same type of verification as allopathic medicine, other practices are not amenable to such testing, and therefore, conventional quality-control regulation is inadequate. See also IOM Report, *supra*, recommending that "the same principles and standards of evidence of treatment effectiveness apply to all treatments" but offering "innovative" methods for testing effectiveness.

One state medical board has taken a different approach to regulating CAM practices without proven value. In response to concerns about chelation therapy being used for purposes not approved by the FDA ("off-label" uses), Missouri Board of Healing Arts in 2001 promulgated a rule "declar[ing] the use of chelation therapy to be of no medical or osteopathic value" except for FDA-approved uses. The rule also provided, however, that the board would not seek disciplinary action against a licensee based solely upon a non-approved use of chelation therapy, if the patient has signed a consent form, approved by the board, that clearly describes the therapy is non-approved and of no efficacy. See Mo. 20 CSR 2150–2.165.

2. *Statutory Accommodation of CAM.* The North Carolina statute is one example of statutory approaches adopted by a good number of state legislatures to accommodate the use of CAM by licensed physicians. Other states have taken a practice-by-practice approach, authorizing licensed physicians to provide particular CAM interventions, such as acupuncture, or requiring that physicians who practice certain forms of CAM hold a separate state license or registration to do so. This approach departs from the nearly universal form of medical licensure, which grants physicians a general medical license and does not require separate licensure for medical specialties. See, e.g., Haw. Rev. Stat. 453–1. In a third CAM-friendly approach, some state statutes now require that CAM practitioners be represented on the medical board. See, e.g., N.Y. Public Health Law § 230.

3. *CAM-Specific Licensure.* While traditional licensed health care professionals are increasingly incorporating CAM into their standard medical and nursing practices, practitioners offering only alternative health care services without conventional medical or nursing training or licensure are a very significant arm of the movement toward CAM. Some states license practitioners of particular CAM therapies. See, e.g., Ariz. Rev. Stat. § 32–1521 and Alaska Stat. § 08.45.030 (licensing naturopaths); Nev. Rev. Stat. § 630A.155 (licensing homeopaths); Cal. Bus. & Prof. Code § 4935 (licensing acupuncturists).

4. *FDA Enforcement.* Homeopathic products have also proliferated. In response, the FDA issued draft guidance in 2017 under which it announced that any product marketed as homeopathic will be subject to FDA enforcement actions as with any other drug. See Drug Products Labeled as Homeopathic; Draft Guidance for Food and Drug Administration Staff and Industry, 82 Fed. Reg. 60403 (Dec. 20, 2017). It then revised its guidance in 2019 to clarify that the agency would apply a risk-based approach to determine which products to pursue. See 85 Fed. Reg. 918 (Oct. 25, 2019). For an analysis of the FDA's approach, see Carrie Scrufari James, FDA's Homeopathic Risk-Based Enforcement: Compromised Consumer Protection or Stepped-Up Scrutiny?, 70 Syracuse L. Rev. 1115 (2020).

IV. UNLICENSED PROVIDERS

In this section, we focus on the practitioner who does not have a license. State medical boards have the primary responsibility for enforcing the prohibition against the unauthorized practice of medicine by unlicensed providers, pursuant to the given state's medical practice act. This prohibition is enforced by criminal sanctions against the unlicensed practitioner and license revocation or criminal sanctions against any physician who aids and abets the unlicensed practitioner. The board responsible for licensure and discipline for nursing has parallel authority to pursue unlicensed practitioners charged with engaging in the unauthorized practice of nursing. The issue of the scope of practice of licensed health care professionals is taken up in Section V of this chapter.

State medical practice acts that define the practice of medicine broadly can create uncertainty about when someone is engaging in the practice of medicine. For example, Indiana prohibits an unlicensed person from engaging in:

> [T]he diagnosis, treatment, correction or prevention of any disease, ailment, defect, injury, infirmity, deformity, pain or other condition of human beings; [ ] the suggestion, recommendation, or prescription or administration of any form of treatment, without limitation; [ ] the performing of any kind of surgical operation upon a human being. . . , or the penetration of the skin or body orifice by any means, for the intended palliation, relief, or cure; or [ ] the prevention of any physical, mental, or functional ailment or defect of any person.

Ind. Code 25–22.5–1–1.1

Would this prohibition extend to services offered by a health club, including fitness assessment and advice on nutrition and exercise responding to specific areas needing improvement? What if this advice was designed to address a problem with obesity that was linked to other problems, such as heart disease? Would it extend to the recommendation of over-the-counter medications for particular aches, pains, or illnesses by a cashier at a pharmacy? Your friend's recommendation to take Echinacea during flu season? How would this statute apply to midwifery? Consider the following case.

STATE BOARD OF NURSING AND STATE BOARD OF HEALING ARTS v. RUEBKE

Supreme Court of Kansas, 1996.
913 P.2d 142.

LARSON, JUSTICE:

The State Board of Healing Arts (Healing Arts) and the State Board of Nursing (Nursing) appeal the trial court's denial of a temporary injunction by which the Boards had sought to stop E. Michelle Ruebke, a practicing lay midwife, from continuing her alleged practice of medicine and nursing.

* * *

Factual Background

* * *

The hearing on the temporary injunction revealed that Ruebke acts as a lay midwife comprehensively assisting pregnant women with prenatal care, delivery, and post-partum care. She is president of the Kansas Midwives Association and follows its promulgated standards, which include a risk screening assessment based upon family medical history; establishing prenatal care plans, including monthly visitations;

examinations and assistance in birth; and post-partum care. She works with supervising physicians who are made aware of her mode of practice and who are available for consultation and perform many of the medical tests incident to pregnancy.

* * *

Dr. Debra L. Messamore, an obstetrician/gynecologist, testified she had reviewed the Kansas Midwives Association standards of care and opined those standards were similar to the assessments incident to her practice as an OB/GYN. Dr. Messamore concluded that in her judgment the prenatal assessments made by Ruebke were obstetrical diagnoses.

Dr. Messamore testified that the prescriptions Ruebke has women obtain from their physicians are used in obstetrics to produce uterine contractions. She further testified the Kansas Midwives Association standard of care relating to post-delivery conditions of the mother and baby involved obstetrical judgments. She reviewed the birth records of [one] birth and testified that obstetrical or medical judgments were reflected. [She admitted] that many procedures at issue could be performed by a nurse rather than a physician. . . . She also stated her opinion that so defined obstetrics as a branch of medicine or surgery.

Ginger Breedlove, a Kansas certified advanced registered nurse practitioner and nurse-midwife, testified on behalf of Nursing. She reviewed the records [of two births] and testified nursing functions were involved. She admitted she could not tell from the records who had engaged in certain practices and that taking notes, giving enemas, and administering oxygen is often done by people who are not nurses, although education, experience, and minimum competency are required.

. . . The court held that provisions of both acts were unconstitutionally vague, Ruebke's midwifery practices did not and were not intended to come within the healing arts act or the nursing act, and her activities fell within exceptions to the two acts even if the acts did apply and were constitutional.

The factual findings, highly summarized, were that Ruebke had not been shown to hold herself out as anything other than a lay midwife; has routinely used and consulted with supervising physicians; was not shown to administer any prescription drugs; was not shown to do any suturing or episiotomies, make cervical or vaginal lacerations, or diagnose blood type; and had engaged only in activities routinely and properly done by people who are not physicians.

Regulatory History of Midwifery

One of the specific statutory provisions we deal with, K.S.A. 65–2802(a), defines the healing arts as follows:

The healing arts include any system, treatment, operation, diagnosis, prescription, or practice for the ascertainment, cure, relief, palliation, adjustment, or correction of any human disease, ailment, deformity, or injury, and includes specifically but not by way of limitation the practice of medicine and surgery; the practice of osteopathic medicine and surgery; and the practice of chiropractic.

K.S.A. 65–2869 specifically provides that for the purpose of the healing arts act, the following persons shall be deemed to be engaged in the practice of medicine and surgery:

(a) Persons who publicly profess to be physicians or surgeons, or publicly profess to assume the duties incident to the practice of medicine or surgery or any of their branches.

(b) Persons who prescribe, recommend or furnish medicine or drugs, or perform any surgical operation of whatever nature by the use of any surgical instrument, procedure, equipment or mechanical device for the diagnosis, cure or relief of any wounds, fractures, bodily injury, infirmity, disease, physical or mental illness or psychological disorder, of human beings.

* * *

[M]idwifery belonged to women from Biblical times through the Middle Ages. However, subsequent to the Middle Ages, women healers were often barred from universities and precluded from obtaining medical training or degrees. With the rise of barber-surgeon guilds, women were banned from using surgical instruments.

When midwives immigrated to America, they occupied positions of great prestige. Some communities licensed midwives and others did not. This continued until the end of the 19th century. In the 19th and 20th centuries, medical practice became more standardized. Economically and socially well-placed doctors pressed for more restrictive licensing laws and for penalties against those who violated them. [One commentator] suggests that licensure was a market control device; midwives were depriving new obstetricians of the opportunity for training; and elimination of midwifery would allow the science of obstetrics to grow into a mature medical specialty.

There is a notable absence of anything in the history of Kansas healing arts regulation illustrating any attempt to specifically target midwives. In 1870, the Kansas Legislature adopted its first restriction on the practice of medicine. . . .

[T]here can be little doubt that in 1870 Kansas, particularly in rural areas, there were not enough educated physicians available to deliver all of the children born in the state. In fact, until 1910 approximately 50 percent of births in this country were midwife assisted. [ ]

* * *

Although obstetricians held themselves out as a medical specialty in the United States as early as 1868, midwives were not seen as engaged in the practice of obstetrics, nor was obstetrics universally viewed as being a branch of medicine. In 1901, North Carolina recognized obstetricians as engaged in the practice of medicine but women midwives, as a separate discipline, were exempted from the licensure act. [ ] . . .

Although many states in the early 1900s passed laws relating to midwifery, Kansas has never expressly addressed the legality of the practice. In 1915 [ ] this court implied that a woman with considerable midwife experience was qualified to testify as an expert witness in a malpractice case against an osteopath for allegedly negligently delivering the plaintiff's child.

* * *

The 1978 Kansas Legislature created a new classification of nurses, Advanced Registered Nurse Practitioner (ARNP). [ ] One classification of ARNP is certified nurse midwives. Although the regulations permitting the practice of certified nurse midwives might be argued to show additional legislative intent to prohibit the practice of lay midwives, this argument has been rejected elsewhere. [ ]

In 1978, Kansas Attorney General opinion No. 78–164 suggested that the practice of midwifery is a violation of the healing arts act. . . . Although potentially persuasive, such an opinion is not binding on us.

Most probably in response to the 1978 Attorney General opinion, a 1978 legislative interim committee undertook a study of a proposal to recognize and regulate the practice of lay midwifery. However, the committee reached no conclusion.

* * *

A 1986 review of the laws of every state found that lay midwifery was specifically statutorily permitted, subject to licensing or regulation, in 25 jurisdictions. Twelve states, including Kansas, had no legislation governing or prohibiting lay midwifery directly or by direct implication. Several states recognized both lay and nurse midwives. Some issued new licensing only for nurse midwives, while others regulated and recognized both, often as separate professions, subject to separate standards and restrictions. [ ]

* * *

In April 1993, the Board of Healing Arts released Policy Statement No. 93–02, in which the Board stated it reaffirmed its previous position of August 18, 1984, that

[m]idwifery is the practice of medicine and surgery and any practice thereof by individuals not regulated by the Kansas State Board of Nursing or under the supervision of or by order of or referral from a licensed medical or osteopathic doctor constitutes the unlicensed practice of medicine and surgery.

* * *

This historical background brings us to the question of whether the healing arts act is unconstitutionally vague. . . .

* * *

[A] statute "is vague and violates due process if it prohibits conduct in terms so vague that a person of common intelligence cannot understand what conduct is prohibited, and it fails to adequately guard against arbitrary and discriminatory enforcement." [ ] A statute which requires specific intent is more likely to withstand a vagueness challenge than one, like that here, which imposes strict liability. [ ]

* * *

We have held that the interpretation of a statute given by an administrative agency within its area of expertise is entitled to deference, although final construction of a statute always rests with courts. [ ] However, under the facts of this case, we owe no deference to the construction expressed by Healing Arts as to the legal question of the scope of its own jurisdiction. [ ]

We do, of course, attempt wherever possible to construe a statute as constitutional [ ]. . . .

* * *

The definition of healing arts uses terms that have an ordinary, definite, and ascertainable meaning. The trial court's conclusion that "disease, ailment, deformity or injury" are not commonly used words with settled meanings cannot be justified.

* * *

. . . Although we hold the act not to be unconstitutionally vague, we also hold the definitional provisions do not cover midwifery. In their ordinary usage the terms in K.S.A. 65–2802(a) used to define healing arts clearly and unequivocally focus exclusively on pathologies (i.e., diseases) and abnormal human conditions (i.e., ailments, deformities, or injuries). Pregnancy and childbirth are neither pathologies nor abnormalities.

* * *

Healing Arts argues that the "practice of medicine" includes the practice of obstetrics. It reasons, in turn, that obstetrics includes the practices traditionally performed by midwives. From this, it concludes midwifery is the practice of medicine.

However, equating midwifery with obstetrics, and thus with the practice of medicine, ignores the historical reality, discussed above, that midwives and obstetricians coexisted for many years quite separately. From the time of our statehood, the relationship between obstetricians and midwives changed from that of harmonious coexistence, cooperation, and collaboration, to open market competition and hostility. [ ]

* * *

To even the most casual observer of the history of assistance to childbirth, it is clear that over the course of this century the medical profession has extended its reach so deeply into the area of birthing as to almost completely occupy the field. The introduction of medical advances to the childbirth process drew women to physicians to assist during the birth of their children. Yet, this widespread preference for physicians as birth attendants hardly mandates the conclusion that only physicians may assist with births.

. . . The fact that a person with medical training provides services in competition with someone with no medical degree does not transform the latter's practices into the practice of medicine.

* * *

Although we hold the practice of midwifery is not itself the practice of the healing arts under our statutory scheme, our conclusions should not be interpreted to mean that a midwife may engage in any activity whatsoever with regard to a pregnant woman merely by virtue of her pregnancy. . . .

. . . However, we need not decide the precise boundaries of what a midwife may do without engaging in the practice of the healing arts because, in the case before us, Ruebke was found to have worked under the supervision of physicians who were familiar with her practices and authorized her actions. Any of Ruebke's actions that were established at trial, which might otherwise have been the practice of the healing arts, were exempt from the healing arts act because she had worked under the supervision of such physicians.

K.S.A. 65–2872 exempts certain activities from the licensure requirements of the healing arts act. In relevant part it provides:

The practice of the healing arts shall not be construed to include the following persons:

> (g) Persons whose professional services are performed under the supervision or by order of or referral from a practitioner who is licensed under this act.

* * *

In light of the uncontested factual findings of the trial court, which were supported by competent evidence in the record, we agree with the trial court that the exception to the healing arts act recognized by K.S.A. 65–2872(g) applies to any of Ruebke's midwifery activities which might otherwise be considered the practice of the healing arts under K.S.A. 65–2802(a) and K.S.A. 65–2869.

* * *

As we have held, the legislature has never specifically acted with the intent to restrict or regulate the traditional practice of lay midwifery. Nevertheless, Nursing argues such birth assistants must be licensed nurses before they may render aid to pregnant women. In oral argument, Nursing conceded much of its argument would be muted [sic] were we to hold, as we do above, that the practice of midwifery is not the practice of the healing arts and thus not part of a medical regimen.

* * *

The practice of nursing is defined [in the Kansas nurse practice act] by reference to the practitioner's substantial specialized knowledge in areas of the biological, physical, and behavioral sciences and educational preparation within the field of the healing arts. Ruebke claims no specialized scientific knowledge, but rather readily admits she has no formal education beyond high school. Her assistance is valued not because it is the application of a firm and rarified grasp of scientific theory, but because, like generations of midwives before, she has practical experience assisting in childbirth.

Moreover, "nursing" deals with "persons who are experiencing changes in the normal health processes." As these words are commonly understood, pregnancy and childbirth do not constitute changes in the normal health process, but the continuation of it.

. . . As we have held, the practice of lay midwifery has, throughout the history of the regulation of nursing, been separate and distinct from the practice of the healing arts, to which nursing is so closely joined. While we have no doubt of the legislature's power to place lay midwifery under the authority of the State Board of Nursing, the legislature has not done so.

We find no legislative intent manifested in the language of the nursing act clearly illustrating the purpose of including the historically separate practice of midwifery within the practice of nursing. [ ] Assistance in childbirth rendered by one whose practical experience with birthing provides comfort to the mother is not nursing under the nursing act, such that licensure is required.

Affirmed in part and reversed in part.

NOTES AND QUESTIONS

1.   *Differing Childbirth Models.* Should the Kansas Supreme Court have analyzed research on the quality and safety of services provided by nurse midwives as compared to lay (also called traditional, direct-entry, or professional) midwives? What relevance would such information have to the legal challenges brought? Would the court have been usurping the role of the legislature? The Kansas statute on certified nurse midwives describes substantial educational requirements for the provision of nurse midwife services. The court concluded, however, that formal education is unnecessary and that practical experience can be valued as highly. What factors should a legislature consider in deciding whether to adopt an obstetrical model, a nursing model, or a midwifery model for childbirth? Keep this question in mind as you read the next case, Sermchief v. Gonzales. See Sara K. Hayden, The Business of Birth: Obstacles Facing Low-Income Women in Choosing Midwifery Care after the Licensed Midwifery Practice Act of 1993, 19 Berkeley Women's L. J. 257 (2004), addressing the requirement of direct physician supervision.

2.   *The California Approach.* Compare the Kansas statute in *Ruebke* to the approach taken in California, which provides that "[A]ny person who practices or attempts to practice, or who advertises or holds himself or herself out as practicing, any system or mode of treating the sick or afflicted in this state, or who diagnoses, treats, operates for, or prescribes for any ailment, blemish, deformity, disease, disfigurement, disorder, injury, or other physical or mental condition of any person" without a license is in violation of the act. The law also provides an exception. Essentially, a person will not be considered as engaging in the unauthorized practice of medicine if two conditions are met: (1) the person is prohibited from providing certain high-risk services, and (2) the person must make certain detailed disclosures to the "client." The list of prohibited services is quite thorough and includes: surgery or any other procedure that punctures the skin or harmfully invades the body; administration or prescription of X-ray radiation, legend drugs or controlled substances; recommendation of discontinuance of legend drugs or controlled substances prescribed by an appropriately licensed practitioner; willful diagnosis and treatment of a physical or mental condition that causes or creates a risk of great bodily harm, serious physical or mental illness, or death; setting fractures; and treatment of lacerations or abrasions through electrotherapy. The disclosure requirement is also detailed, and requires the person, in plain language, to disclose that the person is not a licensed physician, that the treatment is alternative or complementary to the healing arts licensed by the state, and that the provided services are not licensed by the state, as well as the nature of the services provided, the theory of treatment upon which the services are based, and the person's education, training, experience, and other qualifications. Would this statute have provided Ruebke greater protection against board action?

3.   *Dividing Childbirth into Discrete Activities.* Although a wide variety of health care services and providers have been subject to prosecution for the

unauthorized practice of medicine, the realm of assistance at childbirth has been a particularly contentious area. Doctors, nurses, nurse-midwives, physician assistants, and lay midwives have all asserted a claim to participation in assisting in childbirth. Courts rejecting unauthorized practice of medicine claims against lay midwives have sometime done so by examining individual actions that may be performed during childbirth. See, e.g., Leigh v. Board of Reg. in Nursing, 395 Mass. 670, 481 N.E.2d 1347 (1985) (distinguishing "ordinary assistance in the normal cases of childbirth" from that in which a lay midwife used "obstetrical instruments" and "printed prescriptions or formulas," with the latter constituting the practice of medicine). See also People v. Jihan, 127 Ill. 2d 379, 130 Ill. Dec. 422, 537 N.E.2d 751 (1989) (distinguishing "assisting" at birth from "delivering" the child). Does dividing childbirth assistance into discrete activities reflect and adequately address health and safety concerns?

Some courts have gone the other way, considering lay midwifery the unauthorized practice of medicine. See e.g., Sherman v. Cryns, 203 Ill. 2d 264, 271 Ill. Dec. 881, 786 N.E.2d 139 (2003), distinguishing *Ruebke* on the basis of the broad definition of professional nursing in an Illinois statute that specifically provided for licensure for certified nurse midwives but was silent on the question of lay midwifery. See also Hunter v. State, 110 Md. App. 144, 676 A.2d 968 (Ct. Spec. App. 1996), concluding that the statute permitted only certified registered nurse midwives to provide midwifery services.

4. *Encouraging Alternative Childbirth Models.* A number of states recognize lay or direct-entry midwifery by statute. See, e.g., Minn. Stat. Ann. § 147D.03 (permitting lay midwifery but prohibiting use of any surgical instrument or assisting childbirth "by artificial or mechanical means"). See also Sarah Anne Stover, Born by the Woman, Caught by the Midwife: The Case for Legalizing Direct-Entry Midwifery in All Fifty States, 21 Health Matrix 307 (2011), reporting that 41 states permit direct-entry midwifery, most by statute, and 9 states specifically prohibit the practice by statute, regulation, or case law. Several states have incorporated certification by the North American Registry of Midwives within their standards for recognition of lay midwives. See, e.g., Minn. § 147D.01; Utah Code 1953 § 58–77–302.

Some states laws encourage the use of interdisciplinary teams of midwives and non-clinical doulas in an effort to improve pregnancy care and maternal health outcomes. Laws permitting reimbursement for such services are an important catalyst for this reform. See Commonwealth Fund, Tracking State Policies to Improve Maternal Health Outcomes (Nov. 19, 2020).

5. *Physician Supervision Exception.* The court in *Ruebke* ultimately concludes that the midwife was operating within a common exception to the prohibition against the unauthorized practice of medicine by working under the supervision of a physician. See the discussion of physician assistants and delegation in Section V, below.

6. *No Constitutional Right.* Claims of a constitutional right to choice of provider of health care services consistently fail even when made in the context

of the woman's right to privacy in reproductive decision-making and the lack of empirical evidence of better childbirth outcomes with commonly used obstetrical technology. See, e.g., Lange-Kessler v. Department of Educ., 109 F.3d 137 (2d Cir.1997); Hunter v. State, 110 Md. App. 144, 676 A.2d 968 (Ct. Spec. App. 1996). See also People v. Rogers, 249 Mich. App. 77, 641 N.W.2d 595 (Ct. App. 2001), holding that the prohibition of non-M.D.s practicing naturopathy did not violate a doctor's First Amendment rights because the penalty was for conduct, not speech.

7.   *Vagueness. Ruebke* is in the overwhelming majority in refusing to declare the medical practice or nursing practice act void for vagueness in their application to unlicensed service providers. See, e.g., Weyandt v. State, 35 S.W.3d 144 (Tex. Ct. App. 2000); Sherman v. Cryns, *supra.* But see Miller v. Medical Ass'n of Georgia, 262 Ga. 605, 423 S.E.2d 664 (Ga. 1992).

V. SCOPE OF PRACTICE REGULATION

All of the policy concerns in health reform converge at the point of scope of practice (also known as SOP) regulation. Physician-directed medical care is giving way to a team approach as a core characteristic of health care delivery and as a formal requirement for medical homes and other forms of health care delivery. A stronger emphasis on preventive care, on primary care, and on chronic disease management all point to critical and greatly expanded roles for advanced nurse practitioners (ANPs) and physician assistants (PAs). The great concern over the shortage of primary care physicians to meet these goals is also fostering a push to expand practice opportunities for these midlevel practitioners. See Tine Hansen-Turton et al., Nurse Practitioners in Primary Care, 82 Temple L. Rev. 1235 (2010); Daniel Marino, Overextended: The Role of the Independent Nurse Practitioner Practice in Addressing Problems with Affordability of U.S. Primary Care, 20 Annals Health L. Advance Directive 12 (2011); Thomas R. McLean, The Schizophrenia of Physician Extender Utilization, 20 Annals of Health Law (2011).

The ACA provides significant support for health care workforce development directed toward advanced practice nursing and other non-physician health professionals. Perhaps even more importantly, several of the health care delivery models supported by the ACA—including the medical home, the Nurse-Managed Health Clinic, and the Independence at Home Medical Practice—mandate a team approach to care with very significant practice and leadership roles for ANPs and PAs. See Chapter 11. Still, the ACA defers to state law on the permissible scope of practice of these practitioners.

Licensed non-physician health care providers cannot legally practice medicine, but practices that fall within their own licensure (for example, as a nurse or a physician assistant) are not considered the practice of medicine. A nurse who is providing services authorized under the nurse practice act would not be practicing medicine while an unlicensed practitioner providing the same services would be guilty of the unauthorized practice of medicine or nursing. If a nurse engages in practices that exceed those authorized in the nurse practice act, however, that nurse would be guilty of exceeding the authorized scope of practice of the profession of nursing as well as violating the prohibition against the unauthorized practice of medicine.

Scope of practice regulation focuses on boundary setting between professions and attempts to separate medicine from nursing from other health care disciplines. In doing so, it faces an inherent difficulty, as you saw in *Ruebke*. To the extent that SOP regulation depends on identifying discrete activities that "belong" to each profession, it applies a notion that reflects neither the overlapping competencies of health care professionals nor the nature of diagnosis and treatment.

SERMCHIEF V. GONZALES

Supreme Court of Missouri, 1983.
660 S.W.2d 683.

WELLIVER, JUDGE.

This is a petition for a declaratory judgment and injunction brought by two nurses and five physicians[1] employed by the East Missouri Action Agency (Agency) wherein the plaintiff-appellants ask the Court to declare that the practices of the Agency nurses are authorized under the nursing law of this state, § 335.016.8, RSMo 1978 and that such practices do not constitute the unauthorized practice of medicine under Chapter 334 relating to the Missouri State Board of Registration For the Healing Arts (Board). . . . The holding below was against appellants who make direct appeal to this Court alleging that the validity of the statutes is involved. [ ]. . .

I

The facts are simple and for the most part undisputed. The Agency is a federally tax exempt Missouri not-for-profit corporation that maintains offices in Cape Girardeau (main office), Flat River, Ironton, and Fredericktown. The Agency provides medical services to the general public in fields of family planning, obstetrics and gynecology. The services are provided to an area that includes the counties of Bollinger, Cape Girardeau, Perry, St. Francis, Ste. Genevieve, Madison, Iron and Washington. Some thirty-five hundred persons utilized these services during the year prior to trial. The Agency is funded from federal grants, Medicaid reimbursements and patient fees. The programs are directed

---

[1] The physicians are joined for the reason that they are charged with aiding and abetting the unauthorized practice of medicine by the nurses.

toward the lower income segment of the population. Similar programs exist both statewide and nationwide.

Appellant nurses Solari and Burgess are duly licensed professional nurses in Missouri pursuant to the provisions of Chapter 335 and are employed by the Agency. Both nurses have had post-graduate special training in the field of obstetrics and gynecology. Appellant physicians are also employees of the Agency and duly licensed to practice medicine (the healing arts) pursuant to Chapter 334. Respondents are the members and the executive secretary of the Missouri State Board of Registration for the Healing Arts (Board) . . . .

The services routinely provided by the nurses and complained of by the Board included, among others, the taking of history; breast and pelvic examinations; laboratory testing of Papanicolaou (PAP) smears, gonorrhea cultures, and blood serology; the providing of and giving of information about oral contraceptives, condoms, and intrauterine devices (IUD); the dispensing of certain designated medications; and counseling services and community education. If the nurses determined the possibility of a condition designated in the standing orders or protocols that would contraindicate the use of contraceptives until further examination and evaluation, they would refer the patients to one of the Agency physicians. No act by either nurse is alleged to have caused injury or damage to any person. All acts by the nurses were done pursuant to written standing orders and protocols signed by appellant physicians. The standing orders and protocols were directed to specifically named nurses and were not identical for all nurses.

The Board threatened to order the appellant nurses and physicians to show cause why the nurses should not be found guilty of the unauthorized practice of medicine and the physicians guilty of aiding and abetting such unauthorized practice. Appellants sought Court relief in this proceeding.

* * *

III

The statutes involved are:

It shall be unlawful for any person not now a registered physician within the meaning of the law to practice medicine or surgery in any of its departments, or to profess to cure and attempt to treat the sick and others afflicted with bodily or mental infirmities, or engage in the practice of midwifery in this state, except as herein provided.

Section 334.010.

This Chapter does not apply . . . *to nurses licensed and lawfully practicing their profession within the provisions of chapter 335, RSMo; . . .*

Section 334.155, RSMo Supp.1982 (emphasis added).

Definitions.—As used in sections 335.011 to 335.096, unless the context clearly requires otherwise, the following words and terms shall have the meanings indicated:

* * *

(8) "Professional nursing" is the performance for compensation of any act which requires substantial specialized education, judgment and skill based on knowledge and application of principles derived from the biological, physical, social and nursing sciences, including, but not limited to:

(a) Responsibility for the teaching of health care and the prevention of illness to the patient and his family; or

(b) Assessment, nursing diagnosis, nursing care, and counsel of persons who are ill, injured or experiencing alterations in normal health processes; or

(c) The administration of medications and treatments as prescribed by a person licensed in this state to prescribe such medications and treatments; or

(d) The coordination and assistance in the delivery of a plan of health care with all members of the health team; or

(e) The teaching and supervision of other persons in the performance of any of the foregoing.

Section 335.016.8(a)–(e).

At the time of enactment of the Nursing Practice Act of 1975, the following statutes were repealed:

2.   A person practices professional nursing who for compensation or personal profit performs, *under the supervision and direction of a practitioner authorized to sign birth and death certificates,* any professional services requiring the application of principles of the biological, physical or social sciences and nursing skills in the care of the sick, in the prevention of disease or in the conservation of health.

Section 335.010.2, RSMo 1969 (emphasis added).

Nothing contained in this chapter shall be construed as conferring any authority on any person to practice medicine or osteopathy or to undertake the treatment or cure of disease.

Section 335.190, RSMo 1969.

The parties on both sides request that in construing these statutes we define and draw that thin and elusive line that separates the practice of medicine and the practice of professional nursing in modern day delivery of health services. A response to this invitation, in our opinion, would result in an avalanche of both medical and nursing malpractice suits alleging infringement of that line and would hinder rather than help with the delivery of health services to the general public. Our consideration will be limited to the narrow question of whether the acts of these nurses were permissible under § 335.016.8 or were prohibited by Chapter 334.

* * *

The legislature substantially revised the law affecting the nursing profession with enactment of the Nursing Practice Act of 1975. Perhaps the most significant feature of the Act was the redefinition of the term "professional nursing," which appears in § 335.016.8. Even a facile reading of that section reveals a manifest legislative desire to expand the scope of authorized nursing practices. Every witness at trial testified that the new definition of professional nursing is a broader definition than that in the former statute. A comparison with the prior definition vividly demonstrates this fact. Most apparent is the elimination of the requirement that a physician directly supervise nursing functions. Equally significant is the legislature's formulation of an open-ended definition of professional nursing. The earlier statute limited nursing practice to "services . . . in the care of the sick, in the prevention of disease or in the conservation of health." § 335.010.2, RSMo 1969. The 1975 Act not only describes a much broader spectrum of nursing functions, it qualifies this description with the phrase "including, but not limited to." We believe this phrase evidences an intent to avoid statutory constraints on the evolution of new functions for nurses delivering health services. Under § 335.016.8, a nurse may be permitted to assume responsibilities heretofore not considered to be within the field of professional nursing so long as those responsibilities are consistent with her or his "specialized education, judgment and skill based on knowledge and application of principles derived from the biological, physical, social and nursing sciences." § 335.016.8.

The acts of the nurses herein clearly fall within this legislative standard. All acts were performed pursuant to standing orders and protocols approved by physicians. Physician prepared standing orders and protocols for nurses and other paramedical personnel were so well established and accepted at the time of the adoption of the statute that the legislature could not have been unaware of the use of such practices. We see nothing in the statute purporting to limit or restrict their continued use.

Respondents made no challenge of the nurses' level of training or the degree of their skill. They challenge only the legal right of the nurses to undertake these acts. We believe the acts of the nurses are precisely the types of acts the legislature contemplated when it granted nurses the right to make assessments and nursing diagnoses. There can be no question that a nurse undertakes only a nursing diagnosis, as opposed to a medical diagnosis, when she or he finds or fails to find symptoms described by physicians in standing orders and protocols for the purpose of administering courses of treatment prescribed by the physician in such orders and protocols.

The Court believes that it is significant that while at least forty states have modernized and expanded their nursing practice laws during the past fifteen years neither counsel nor the Court have discovered any case challenging nurses' authority to act as the nurses herein acted.

. . . The hallmark of the professional is knowing the limits of one's professional knowledge. The nurse, either upon reaching the limit of her or his knowledge or upon reaching the limits prescribed for the nurse by the physician's standing orders and protocols, should refer the patient to the physician. There is no evidence that the assessments and diagnoses made by the nurses in this case exceeded such limits.

* * *

Having found that the nurses' acts were authorized by § 335.016.8, it follows that such acts do not constitute the unlawful practice of medicine for the reason that § 334.155 makes the provisions of Chapter 334 inapplicable "to nurses licensed and lawfully practicing their profession within the provisions of Chapter 335 RSMo."

This cause is reversed and remanded with instructions to enter judgment consistent with this opinion.

NOTES AND QUESTIONS

1. *Regulatory Jurisdiction.* The nurse practice act in *Sermchief* contains an open-ended definition of the practice of nursing. If the board of nursing had issued regulations embracing the plaintiffs' practice within the authorized practice of nursing, under what standard would the court review such regulations if challenged? Would the regulation of the board of nursing prevent the board of medicine from proceeding against the nurses?

In most such disputes, the key legal question is whether the board's rule is consistent with the state statute governing the specific practice or is otherwise arbitrary. For example, the Missouri Supreme Court reviewed a letter issued by the state medical board warning doctors that permitting CRNAs to perform a particular intervention would be a delegation to an unqualified individual and would, therefore, violate the state medical practice act and result in sanctions against the doctor. The Court relied on *Sermchief* and the state nursing practice act to hold that the state board of nursing held the authority to define the SOP of nurse anesthetists and that the state medical board lacked authority to restrict physicians in working with nurses. The nursing practice act permitted the two boards to issue joint rules, however. See Mo. Assoc. of Nurse Anesthetists v. State Bd. of Registration, 343 S.W.3d

348 (Mo. 2011). See also Tex. Bd. of Chiropractic Examiners v. Tex. Med. Ass'n, 375 S.W.3d 464 (Tex. App. 2012).

2. *Physician Supervision.* Scope of practice regulation provides an arena for inter-professional conflicts, often expressed in requirements that the midlevel practitioner practice only within a defined relationship with a licensed physician. State statutes and regulations often require either physician supervision at a particular intensity or formal collaboration with a licensed physician as a condition of practice. Whether rooted in concerns over quality or preserving the competitive or economic advantage of physicians, such requirements have a significant effect on the function and impact of ANPs and PAs. See note 6 below and IOM, The Future of Nursing: Leading Change, Advancing Health (2013), criticizing restrictive SOP regulation as diminishing access to care.

3. *Collaboration.* ANPs (including nurse midwives, nurse anesthetists, and other specialist nurse practitioners) view themselves as operating from a nursing model of health care and acting as independent practitioners who collaborate with physicians. The relationship described in *Sermchief* illustrates one form of collaborative practice. Some advanced practice nursing statutes require a nurse practitioner, generally applicable to named nurse practitioner specialists, to practice under the supervision of a physician. See, e.g., Cal. Bus. & Prof. Code § 2746.5(b) (certificate authorizes nurse-midwife to practice nurse-midwifery "under the supervision of a licensed physician and surgeon who has current practice or training in obstetrics"). Others recognize advanced practice nursing in collaboration with licensed physicians. See, e.g., Mo. Ann. Stat. § 334.104, enacted after *Sermchief*, authorizing collaborative practice arrangements in the form of written agreements, protocols or standing orders, but describing the prescriptive authority of the nurse practitioner as delegated. Some describe the advanced nursing practice without reference to the participation of a supervisory or collaborative physician. For a review of state requirements, see Lauren E. Battaglia, Supervision and Collaboration Requirements: The Vulnerability of Nurse Practitioners and Its Implications for Retail Health, 87 Wash. U. L. Rev. 1127 (2010).

4. *Physician Assistants.* Physician assistants have a different self-adopted professional identity than do nurses. Rather than viewing themselves as independent practitioners, they see themselves as physician delegates. Physician assistants first practiced under general delegation exceptions included in medical practice acts. General delegation exceptions in medical practice acts tend to be quite broad, as you saw in *Ruebke*. States vary in the standards and methods they use to assure that delegation to physician assistants is appropriate and supervision is adequate. It is reasonable to assume that all general delegation statutory provisions include at least implied requirements that the physician assistant have adequate training and competency for the specific practice and that the supervising physician likewise have the competency to oversee the practice.

Some states take an individualized approach and require the physician assistant or supervising physician to submit particular details about the specific position for review by an agency. See, e.g., Md. Code Ann., Health Occ. § 15–302(d). Some limit the number of physician assistants a doctor may supervise. See, e.g., Ohio Rev. Code Ann. § 4730.21. Other states define "supervision," with great specificity. See, e.g., Mo. Ann. Stat. § 334.735(10), defining supervision as "control exercised over a physician assistant working within the same facility as the supervising physician sixty-six percent of the time a physician assistant provides patient care, except a physician assistant may make follow-up patient examinations in hospitals, nursing homes, patient homes, and correctional facilities, each such examination being reviewed, approved and signed by the supervising physician."

5. *Prescribing Authority for ANPs and PAs.* Authority to prescribe medication has been a major issue in debates over the appropriate scope of practice of nurses and physician assistants. Most states authorize prescribing by ANPs and many by PAs. Some state statutes set particular limits on prescribing. See, e.g., Cal. Bus. & Prof. Code § 2836.1(d), requiring physician supervision for the furnishing of drugs or devices by nurse practitioner; Cal. Bus. & Prof. Code § 3502.1, setting specific requirements for PAs. Some licensed health care professions, such as dentistry, commonly have prescribing authority, but others do not. Prescribing authority for licensed, doctoral-trained psychologists, for example, has been particularly controversial. See Julia Johnson, Whether States Should Create Prescription Power for Psychologists, 33 Law & Psychol. Rev. 167 (2009).

6. *Scope-of-Practice Limits and Competition.* The Federal Trade Commission has long been active in contesting what it views as anticompetitive scope-of-practice regulation by health professions boards. It has brought cease-and-desist actions against state health profession boards for engaging in unfair competition in violation of the Federal Trade Commission Act by establishing restrictive scope-of-practice standards. See, e.g., North Carolina Board of Dental Examiners v. FTC, 768 F. Supp. 2d 818 (E.D.N.C. 2011). It also has regularly sent letters of support or concern to state government agencies and legislatures acting to expand or limit scope of practice.

In a letter urging the Texas legislature to adopt legislation removing restrictions on the scope of practice of ANPs, the FTC argued:

> . . . [ANP] care is generally less expensive [and is reimbursed at lower rates by Medicaid and Medicare]. . . . [The proposed statutes could reduce that cost further because] supervision and delegation requirements create administrative costs for [ANPs], and these costs would be reduced . . . . To the extent that [both bills] would increase the deployment of [ANPs] in a variety of health care delivery settings and thereby widen the range of choices available to consumers, [they] are also likely to spur innovation in health care delivery and increase the competition to provide basic health care services. . . . For example, [ANP-staffed] clinics generally offer

weekend and evening hours, which provides greater flexibility for patients, and may provide competitive incentives for other types of clinics to offer extended hours as well. . . . [P]articular health care procedures may require specialized training or heightened supervision if they are to be safely administered. There does not appear to be any evidence, however, that the safety of care provided by [ANPs] varies according to differences in physician supervision or scope of practice requirements. . . . Available evidence suggests that [ANPs] generally are safe providers of health care services when they provide services consistent with their training. . . . [I]ncreased [ANP] care may even be associated with improved outcomes for particular disease indications or patient populations. FTC Letter to Texas State Senators (May 11, 2011).

The FTC's challenge of scope-of-practice regulations is consistent with calls for lowering scope-of-practice barriers in order to achieve greater access and efficiency in health care delivery. See William H. Shrank et al., Health Costs and Financing: Challenges and Strategies for a New Administration, 40 Health Aff. 235 (2021). See also Christopher Ogolla, Litigating Hypocrisy: Turf Wars Between Health Care Professionals Regarding Diagnosis, Evaluation, and Treatment, 50 U. Tol. L. Rev. 67 (2018).

7.   *Reimbursement as a Factor.* Payment policies have a significant effect on the de facto scope of practice of advanced practice non-physician health care providers. For example, current Medicare standards require that nurse anesthetists (CRNAs) be supervised by a physician as a condition of Medicare reimbursement for their services. States are allowed to opt out of this particular provision, however, and California recently joined over a dozen other states in opting out, paving the way for reimbursement of CRNA services pursuant to physician orders rather than under physician supervision. Two California medical associations contested the state's decision, but the appeals court held that the California statute on scope of practice for CRNAs allows for the practice. See California Society of Anesthesiologists v. Superior Court, 204 Cal. App. 4th 390, 138 Cal. Rptr. 3d 745 (Cal. App. 2012).

PROBLEM: PHYSICIANS, PHYSICIAN ASSISTANTS, AND NURSES

Drs. Allison Jones and Emily Johnson have a practice in Jerrold, which is located in south St. Louis County. Both Drs. Jones and Johnson are board-certified internists with a rather broad family practice. They would like to expand their practice to Jackson County, a primarily rural area about seventy miles south of Jerrold. They are especially interested in Tesson, a town of approximately 6,000 that is centrally located among the four or five small towns in the area. They are interested in Tesson because it has a small community hospital and is located close to the interstate highway. They also believe the town is underserved by physicians. There is no pediatrician in Tesson, although there is one thirty miles away. The town has one internist. It has no obstetricians, although Joan Mayo, a certified nurse midwife, has an office in a small town about eighteen miles distant from Tesson.

Ms. Mayo has been providing childbirth, family planning, and other women's health services. She has an agreement with an obstetrician in Jerrold through which protocols and standing orders for her practice were established and are maintained. She can consult with this OB by phone at any time, and they make it a practice to meet once a month to discuss Ms. Mayo's patients. Ms. Mayo refers patients who require special services to this OB or to the internist in Tesson. Ms. Mayo has clinical privileges for childbirth services at the community hospital, although her patients must be admitted by the internist.

Mariah Ellis works as a physician assistant in the Jones/Johnson office in Jerrold. She is not separately licensed, but the doctors are impressed with her handling of routine patients. In most cases, Ms. Ellis examines the patient, decides on a course of treatment, and prescribes medication using blank prescription slips that are signed by the doctors. In more difficult cases, she asks for advice from one of the doctors. There is high patient satisfaction with her work.

Drs. Jones and Johnson would like to open an office in Tesson and employ a physician assistant and a pediatric nurse practitioner to staff the office full-time. Either Dr. Jones or Dr. Johnson would have office hours at that office once a week. They are also interested in establishing an affiliation with Ms. Mayo because they see room for growth in that area. They hope to serve the needs of Tesson by establishing active obstetrical and pediatric practices working with the pediatric nurse practitioner and Ms. Mayo.

For their Tesson office, they would like to find a physician assistant with extensive experience in trauma so that the assistant could care for the high incidence of farming and hunting injuries expected in that area. This PA, then, would complement the doctors' own skills because the doctors have had little experience with such injuries.

A.   Drs. Jones and Johnson have come to you for advice concerning their plans for a new Tesson office. They have many questions, including whether their plans are consistent with the laws regulating practice in Allstate. Please specify how they might comply with the law while maintaining a lower cost practice. If for some reason the Board decides to take action against them, what is the likelihood of the physicians' success in challenging the Board's action?

B.   Is Ms. Mayo's current practice permitted under the Allstate statutes? If Drs. Jones and Johnson acquired her practice, how should they structure their relationship in regard to the cases she takes, when she must refer patients, and their supervision of her work? Is Ms. Ellis's work as a physician assistant permitted under the Allstate statutes?

C.   As noted in the introduction to this section, the ACA creates a number of delivery organizations that anticipate expanded practice by ANPs and PAs. Do the Allstate statutes measure up to the goals of increasing access to lower cost quality care?

Allstate Nurse Practice Act and Medical Practice Act

These two Allstate statutes are identical to the Missouri statutes in *Sermchief*, above.

Allstate Stat. § 2746.5

The practice of nurse-midwifery constitutes the furthering or undertaking by any certified person, under the supervision of a licensed physician and surgeon who has current practice or training in obstetrics, to assist a woman in childbirth so long as progress meets criteria accepted as normal. All complications shall be referred to a physician immediately. The practice of nurse-midwifery does not include the assisting of childbirth by any artificial, forcible, or mechanical means. As used in this article, "supervision" shall not be construed to require the physical presence of the supervising physician. A nurse-midwife is not authorized to practice medicine and surgery by the provisions of this chapter.

Allstate Stat. § 147A.18

(a) A supervising physician may delegate to a physician assistant who is registered with the board, certified by the National Commission on Certification of Physician Assistants, and who is under the supervising physician's supervision, the authority to prescribe, dispense, and administer prescription drugs, medical devices, and controlled substances subject to the requirements in this section.

(b) The delegation must be appropriate to the physician assistant's practice and within the scope of the physician assistant's training. Supervising physicians shall retrospectively review, on a daily basis, the prescribing, dispensing, and administering of prescription and controlled drugs and medical devices by physician assistants. During each daily review, the supervising physician shall document by signature and date that the prescriptive, administering, and dispensing practice of the physician assistant has been reviewed.

Allstate § 334.104

1. Collaborative practice arrangements shall be in the form of written agreements, jointly agreed-upon protocols, or standing orders for the delivery of health care services. Collaborative practice arrangements may delegate to an advanced practice registered nurse the authority to administer or dispense drugs and provide treatment as long as the delivery of such health care services is within the scope of practice of the nurse and is consistent with that nurse's skill, training and competence.

2. The written collaborative practice arrangement shall contain at least the following provisions:

(a) A requirement that there shall be posted at every office where the advanced practice registered nurse is authorized to prescribe, in collaboration with a physician, a prominently displayed disclosure statement informing patients that they may be seen by an advanced practice registered nurse and have the right to see the collaborating physician;

(b) The manner of collaboration between the collaborating physician and the advanced practice registered nurse, including how the collaborating physician and the advanced practice registered nurse will:

(1) Engage in collaborative practice consistent with each professional's skill, training, education, and competence;

(2) Maintain geographic proximity;

(3) Provide coverage during absence, incapacity, infirmity, or emergency by the collaborating physician;

(c) A description of the advanced practice registered nurse's controlled substance prescriptive authority in collaboration with the physician, including a list of the controlled substances the physician authorizes the nurse to prescribe and documentation that it is consistent with each professional's education, knowledge, skill, and competence;

(d) A description of the time and manner of the collaborating physician's review of the advanced practice registered nurse's delivery of health care services. The description shall include provisions that the advanced practice registered nurse shall submit a minimum of ten percent of the charts documenting the advanced practice registered nurse's delivery of health care services to the collaborating physician for review by the collaborating physician, or any other physician designated in the collaborative practice arrangement, every fourteen days.

CHAPTER 3

QUALITY CONTROL REGULATION: HEALTH CARE INSTITUTIONS

■ ■ ■

I. INTRODUCTION

Patient safety and well-being are as dependent on the quality of health care institutions as they are on the quality of doctors, nurses, or therapists. The range of institutional factors that can pose a danger to patients extends from building design, maintenance, and sanitation to health information technology and management; from fiscal soundness to the selection, training, and monitoring of the individuals directly providing care; from staffing levels to food service. The patient safety movement (see Chapter 5), in fact, focuses on the quality of systems within health care organizations rather than on the actions of individual caregivers standing alone.

For most consumer goods and services, the market plays a significant role in setting an acceptable level of quality. But in the health care area, substantial barriers, such as a persistent lack of relevant, timely, and accurate information about quality measures; an inability to evaluate available information; and a health care financing and decision-making structure that places the choice of facility in the hands of someone other than the patient, diminish the impact of consumer markets.

State and federal governments have adopted initiatives to strengthen the influence of the market over the quality of health care facilities. Most of these efforts have focused on enhancing the quality of information available to consumers through mandating the measurement of certain indicators and the posting of this data on sites available to the public. In addition to allowing consumers to select among providers, the intent is to encourage providers to improve their performance on reportable factors. See generally Kristin Madison, Health Care Quality Reporting: A Failed Form of Mandated Disclosure?, 13 Ind. Health L. Rev. 310 (2016). Yet there is good evidence that disclosures made and shared through government databases, including the federal Care Compare website, are not effective at empowering consumer choices and have been subject to charges of gaming in data reporting. See Sections II and III, below. See also Nathan Cortez, Regulation by Database, 89 U. Colo. L. Rev. 1 (2018).

This chapter focuses on the system of institutional quality regulation. In its traditional approach, the government sets quality and safety standards, monitors for compliance, and imposes sanctions for violations. State and federal governments also have quality-oriented tools other than "command and control" regulation. Perhaps the most powerful tool held by the federal government is its use of Medicare payment systems that "pay for performance" or engage in "value-based purchasing." These systems typically either withhold or reduce payment for care that does not meet certain specific outcome targets (such as hospital readmissions) or provide financial incentives or enhanced payments for providers who do. See Chapter 10. In addition, the Medicare program funds several initiatives, including the QIN-QIOs described in Section II, below, to test and foster innovations in quality.

State and federal governments are not the only players in the quality arena, of course. Private nonprofit organizations offer voluntary accreditation processes through which facilities can measure their compliance against non-governmental standards established by their own segment of the industry. The Joint Commission for the Accreditation of Healthcare Organizations (JCAHO or the "Joint Commission") and the National Committee on Quality Assurance (NCQA) are two of the leading organizations in the accreditation of health care entities. While the Joint Commission accredits about 80 percent of the hospitals in the U.S., it accredits only 5 percent of U.S. nursing homes. For more on Joint Commission accreditation of hospitals, see Section V, below.

Private tort and related litigation can also create pressure for improvement. See Chapters 4 and 5. Finally, professionals working in health care facilities have ethical and legal obligations of their own to assure the quality of the organizations in which they care for patients.

II. LEARNING FROM NURSING HOME REGULATION

Public and private quality mechanisms do not work the same way across the wide variety of health care organizations and facilities that offer services to patients. The question of the appropriate mix of quality control mechanisms, therefore, does not produce a one-size-fits-all answer.

The materials in this chapter focus primarily on nursing home care, for several reasons. First, nursing home care is a critically important segment of our nation's health care sector. As of 2020, there were approximately 15,300 nursing homes in the United States with nearly 1.29 million people residing within them. See Kaiser Family Foundation, Total Number of Certified Nursing Facilities (2020) and Total Number of Residents in Certified Nursing Facilities (2020). In a typical year, nearly 3 million people receive care in a nursing home, which reflects a combination of long-term residents covered by Medicaid and short-term residents covered under Medicare.

In addition, the Affordable Care Act's focus on coordination of care, Medicare payment restrictions on hospital readmissions, bundled payments for certain surgeries, and the Improving Medicare Post-Acute Care Transformation Act of 2014 (IMPACT) has elevated the importance of nursing homes as an integral part of improving health care quality. The federal government currently contracts with twelve regional Quality Innovation Network-Quality Improvement Organizations (QIN-QIOs) that provide technical assistance, education, and data analysis for Medicare beneficiaries and providers, with a special focus on improving care coordination for Medicare beneficiaries among the many providers (e.g., physicians and nurses, hospitals, home health agencies, and nursing homes) providing care to a single beneficiary. See CMS, 2020 NQIIC Annual Report.

This chapter also focuses on nursing homes because they are subject to a high degree of quality control regulation by both federal and state governments, especially as compared to hospitals. Consequently, they provide a good example of pursuing quality through public regulation. See, e.g., Section V, below. The contrast between nursing homes and hospitals provides a framework for understanding the factors that determine under what circumstances particular forms of quality control efforts—whether reliant on the market, on intra-institutional quality structures, or on government command and control—are likely to be more or less effective.

Hospitals and nursing homes are quite distinctive organizations even though they both provide medical and nursing care for patients (in hospitals) or residents (in nursing homes). They differ in their patient population; their scope of services; the composition of their staffing; and other internal organizational characteristics. They are also subject to different external pressures. Each of these factors helps to explain why these two institutions are treated so differently in terms of governmental quality-control regulation.

Part of what makes nursing homes unique in the health care system is their responsibility for the total living environment of their residents, typically over a very long time. Their involvement with the daily life of residents usually includes assistance in activities of daily living (ADLs), including bathing, dressing, toileting, and eating. Over a third of residents are totally dependent on toileting assistance, for example, and 98% need assistance in at least one ADL. The majority of residents typically have resided in the facility for more than a year; while approximately 20% of nursing home residents stay for 6 months or less, 30% stay for 1–3 years and 12% stay for over 5 years. Nearly half of nursing home residents are over 85 years old. With the increasing utilization of home care and assisted living for moderately needy elderly people, the average skilled nursing facility resident is much sicker than those of past decades. Their physical frailty often requires rigorous and sophisticated care.

The choice of nursing home is unlike the choice of other consumer goods or even the selection of a doctor or a hospital. The selection of a nursing home generally is made under duress, often upon discharge from an unexpected hospitalization, and with uncertainty as to the individual's prognosis; these factors in turn influence whether the admission will be a short-stay rehabilitation admission or a longer term or permanent admission. The choice is often made by a family member, guardian, or another, who sometimes using strong persuasion, familial deception, or coercion to make the placement even when the individual retains some decisional capacity. See, e.g., Deborah Stone, Shopping for Long-Term Care, 23 Health Affairs 191 (2004).

Once serious considerations (such as level of care, proximity to family due to potential lengthy stay, and whether the nursing home will accept Medicaid payments upon admission or once personal funds are exhausted) are accounted for, the remaining choices can be quite slim. Quality report cards, like the federal Nursing Home Compare, have had little effect. D.B. Mukamel et al., When Patients Customize Nursing Home Ratings, Choices and Rankings Differ from the Government's Version, 35 Health Affairs 714 (April 2016); R.T. Konetzka and M.C. Parraillon, Use of Nursing Home Compare Website Appears Limited by Lack of Awareness and Initial Mistrust of the Data, 35 Health Affairs 706 (April 2016); Daniel Brauner et al., Does Nursing Home Compare Reflect Patient Safety In Nursing Homes?, 37 Health Aff. 1770 (2018) (finding that the correlation between information available on Nursing Home Compare and quality measures such as pressure sores, infections, falls, and medication errors were "weak and somewhat inconsistent"). Finally, the physical and mental frailty of the typical resident makes the transfer from one facility to another challenging to their health.

In contrast to the hospital market, the demand for nursing home care exceeds available beds. Demand may be ebbing somewhat in the private pay market with the availability of more alternatives, such as assisted living facilities. Certificate of need programs in the majority of states restrict the number of nursing homes in a particular area on the theory that more beds will raise health care costs. Low supply and excess demand, however, have been associated with lower quality, perhaps because of weak competition or because enforcement efforts are constrained by the lack of alternatives for continuing care of the residents. John V. Jacobi, Competition Law's Role in Health Care Quality, 11 Ann. Health L. 45 (2002); Portia Y. Cornell et al., Changes in Long-Term Care Markets: Assisted Living Supply and the Prevalence of Low-Care Residents in Nursing Homes, 21 JAMADA 1161 (2020); Mary Crossley, Prisons,

Nursing Homes, and Medicaid: A Covid-19 Case Study in Health Injustice, 30 Annals Health L. & Life Sci. 101 (2021) (demand for long-term care services generally—including home and community-based services (HCBS)—exceeds supply, and insufficient HCBS supply is forcing some into nursing homes unnecessarily). See also Section IV.B.2, below.

Hospitals originally developed in the United States as charitable institutions, often under the direction of religious organizations. But nursing homes originally developed as "mom-and-pop" enterprises in which individuals boarded elderly persons in private homes. After the advent of Medicare and Medicaid, nursing homes attracted substantial activity from investors and were viewed primarily as real estate investments (as are assisted living and independent living facilities today). Even today, most nursing homes are for-profit (and the proportion is growing), while most hospitals are not-for-profit. National for-profit chains own the majority of the for-profit nursing home industry. Studies of nursing homes have found consistently that not-for-profit nursing homes offer higher quality care. See A. Bos et al., Financial Performance, Employee Well-Being, and Client Well-Being in For-Profit and Not-For-Profit Nursing Homes: A Systematic Review, 42 H. Care Management Rev. 352 (2017) (reviewing 50 studies conducted over 10 years).

Physicians are still largely absent from daily medical care in nursing homes, and R.N.s act primarily as administrators rather than direct care providers. Thus, nursing homes lack the history and embedded custom that strengthen internal professional peer review processes in hospitals. See Chapters 5 and 11. Further, hospitals have long subjected themselves to accreditation by the Joint Commission, while private accreditation of nursing homes is not as well established or influential. See Chapter 5. In addition, nursing homes, unless they are part of a multifacility organization, lack the resources (such as expert quality improvement staff, functional electronic medical records systems for data analytics including outcomes monitoring, and depth in medical and nursing staffing for clinical leadership) that hospitals routinely draw upon to meet quality expectations.

Medicaid pays for nearly one million of the 1.5 million nursing home residents. Medicare pays for very limited nursing home services, covering only shorter stays for rehabilitation. See Chapter 10. Medicaid pays skilled nursing facilities a per diem for each Medicaid resident. The per diem is to cover all direct care (including nursing); indirect care (including social services, resident activities, etc.); administration (including management, food service and other dietary needs, laundry, housekeeping, maintenance, etc.) and capital costs (including depreciation, mortgage expense, etc.). The rates can be adjusted based on the severity of the needs of the facility's population, and some states provide supplemental payments.

Because nursing home care consumes a large portion of the Medicaid dollar and Medicaid is the largest spending item in state budgets, Medicaid payment levels for nursing homes are contentious, and many argue that they are inadequate, especially in light of the increasing acuity in the medical condition of nursing home residents. Rates paid for Medicaid residents in Missouri nursing homes in 2017, for example, averaged $153 per day; and in Illinois, $149. Research on whether increases in payment levels improve the quality of nursing home care, however, has produced mixed results. See, e.g., David C. Grabowski et al., Medicaid Payment and Risk-Adjusted Nursing Home Quality Measures, 23 Health Affairs 243 (2004); John R. Bowblis and Robert Applebaum, How Does Medicaid Reimbursement Impact Nursing Home Quality? The Effects of Small Anticipatory Changes, 52 Health Serv. Res. 1729 (2017). But see Brietta Clark, Medicaid Access, Rate Setting and Payment Suits: How the Obama Administration is Undermining its Own Health Reform Goals, 55 How. L.J. 771 (2012).

Hospitals are subject to frequent and substantial lawsuits brought by patients for injuries. This phenomenon has only increased during the COVID-19 pandemic given the threat the virus has posed to congregate living communities, the elderly, and those with certain chronic illnesses. See Harris Meyer, Coronavirus-Related Deaths in Nursing Homes Prompt Lawsuits and Questions about Who's Responsible, ABA Journal (Oct. 1, 2020). In contrast, nursing home residents are generally limited in their ability to bring suit themselves for any harms suffered as a result of poor care or abuse. Mental impairment also makes many nursing home residents poor witnesses. Causation, too, may be difficult to prove. Some physical injuries in very frail elderly persons may be caused either by ordinary contact or by poor care or abuse. Damage issues also can be problematic. Limited remaining life spans and disabilities minimize legally recognizable damages. Residents do not suffer lost wages, and medical costs for treatment of injuries generally will be covered by Medicaid or Medicare.

The incidence and success of private lawsuits against these facilities have increased significantly in some regions of the country, however, particularly in Florida and Texas. Some cases have produced very large verdicts, but these are rare. Even in states where private litigation has grown, the litigation tends to be concentrated on just a few facilities or multifacility owners. See Toby S. Edelman, An Advocate's Response to Professor Sage, 9 J. Health Care L. & Pol'y 291 (2006).

Litigation against nursing homes has raised concerns that damage awards might divert resources for care, although this has not been identified as an issue with hospital liability. In a provision reflecting this attitude, a plaintiff receiving an award or settlement, including punitive damages, against a nursing home in Florida is required to pay half to the

Quality of Long-Term Care Facility Improvement Trust Fund. F.S.A. § 400.0238. Because the COVID-19 pandemic forced nursing homes to lock down, the number of short-term residents declined substantially, which has depleted financial resources further, and increased concerns about liability costs, for many nursing homes. See David C. Grabowski and Vincent Mor, Nursing Home Care in Crisis in the Wake of COVID-19, 324 JAMA 23 (2020). Some years ago, many states had enacted legislation providing enhanced damages and attorney's fees to encourage nursing home patients to pursue private remedies as a means of enforcing regulatory standards. Some states have since amended these statutes, limiting damages and attorney's fees or subjecting such claims to limitations included in general tort reform legislation. See Ellen J. Scott, Punitive Damages in Lawsuits Against Nursing Homes, 23 J. Legal Med. 115 (2002).

There is no private right of action for violation of Medicare or Medicaid nursing home quality standards. See, e.g., Kalan v. Health Ctr. Comm'n, 198 F. Supp. 3d 636 (W.D. Va. 2016). But see Grammer v. John J. Kane Regional Centers-Glen Hazel, 570 F.3d 520 (3d Cir. 2009), cert. den. 559 S. Ct. 939 (2010). Federal and state agencies (and nursing home residents and employees through *qui tam* actions), however, have stepped up actions against seriously substandard nursing homes for health care fraud, claiming that the facilities provided "worthless services" for which the government paid. See, e.g., U.S. v. Houser, 754 F.3d 1335 (11th Cir. 2014). See generally Chapter 14.

Nursing homes sued for harm because of their failure to protect residents from COVID-19 infection have tried to claim immunity under the federal Public Readiness and Emergency Preparedness (PREP) Act, which grants immunity to those who use vaccines, protective gear, and diagnostic tests in the course of addressing a public emergency. See 42 U.S.C.A. § 247d–6d. Several courts, however, have rejected this defense, holding that PREP Act immunity does not extend to plaintiffs' claims alleging that nursing homes failed to take necessary steps to prevent the introduction and spread of COVID-19 in their facilities. See, e.g., Winn v. California Post-Acute LLC, 532 F. Supp. 3d 892 (C.D. Cal. Apr. 6, 2021).

Nursing homes frequently include binding predispute arbitration clauses in admission agreements. State legislatures have attempted to severely restrict these clauses, but the Supreme Court has held that such restrictions violate the Federal Arbitration Act (FAA). Kindred Nursing Centers v. Clark, 137 S. Ct. 1421 (2017). HHS banned these clauses in a 2016 final rule, but in 2019 issued a new rule allowing them with significant limitations and transparency requirements. See 42 C.F.R. § 483.70(n).

III. DEFINING AND ASSESSING QUALITY

What constitutes quality in health care? In a classic model, Avedis Donabedian, using the management of a specific episode of illness by a physician as the model, identifies three components by which the quality of care can be measured: the technical, the interpersonal, and amenities. He defines the technical as "the application of the science and technology of medicine, and of the other health sciences, to the management" of the patient's health issue. He defines the interpersonal as "the social and psychological interaction between client and practitioner." Finally, he categorizes as amenities "the more intimate aspects of the settings in which care is provided," although he notes that these may be integral to the care itself. The Definition of Quality and Approaches to Its Assessment (Vol. 1) (1980). Donabedian adopts a wholistic view, concluding that quality care is

> that kind of care which is expected to maximize an inclusive measure of patient welfare, after one has taken account of the balance of expected gains and losses that attend the process of care in all its parts.

In what Donabedian called an "absolutist" medical view, the doctor best balances the benefits and risks of care; other factors, including "the patient's expectations and valuations" are regarded as impeding or facilitating quality care. The alternative view, called "individualized" by Donabedian, holds that if advancing the patient's welfare is paramount, then "it is inevitable that the patient must share with the practitioner" the work of defining the goals of care and the evaluation of comparative risks and benefits.

Current definitions of quality, including those used in regulation, build upon this foundation. Kristin Madison, Donabedian's Legacy: The Future of Health Care Quality Law and Policy, 10 Ind. Health L. Rev. 325 (2013); Lois Shepherd & Mark Hall, Patient-Centered Health Law and Ethics (Symposium), 45 Wake Forest L. Rev. 1427 (2010). The most influential current expression of quality joins quality, cost, and access by defining quality health care as health care that is safe, effective, patient-centered, efficient, and equitable. IOM, Crossing the Quality Chasm: A New Health System for the 21st Century (2001). The IHI Triple Aim Initiative expands the definition of quality health care to include population health along with improving the patient experience of care, including both quality and satisfaction, and reducing the per capita cost of care. See Chapter 21.

Donabedian also provides a classic analysis of quality standards used to measure whether an organization is providing quality care. He identifies three major approaches to quality assessment: "structure," "process," and "outcome," which interact dynamically. Organizational structures influence the processes of care, and both influence the actual outcomes of care.

Donabedian defines structural standards for care as "the human, physical, and financial resources that are needed to provide . . . care." Structural standards for quality are perhaps the easiest to implement, and for this reason, much of quality control regulation in the past has focused on this approach. Personnel, equipment, and buildings can be counted or described; intrainstitutional policies and staff organization measured against specific criteria; and budgets and expenditures verified. Quantifiable and concrete structural standards are particularly useful in contentious enforcement systems because there is less concern with the human factor, or variability, in the inspection process. Unfortunately, structural standards don't measure whether the care is actually any good, only that the tools required for good care are present. See Smith v. Heckler, below.

Process standards relate directly to the activities that take place in the delivery of care. For example, are orders for medication written properly; are they filled and delivered to patients accurately? Are caregivers washing their hands, and do they use a checklist for certain medical and nursing procedures? Structural standards measure only the capacity for care, so Donabedian favors process standards as they relate directly to what happens in care. Donabedian notes, however, that "the use of prevalent norms as a basis for judging quality may . . . encourage dogmatism and perpetuate error," foreshadowing the evidence-based medicine movement discussed in Chapter 4.

Outcomes standards offset this significant weakness in process standards by measuring the actual improvement or decline in the patient's health status. Outcome measures also have their problems, however: the onset, duration, and extent of desired outcomes are often hard to specify, and it is often difficult to credit a good or bad outcome solely to a specific intervention. More importantly, outcomes standards used in quality measurement and payment can often favor convenience over significance by focusing on items that are easily measurable and diverting attention and effort from processes that may be more important to quality care. Attaching outcomes to poor consequences, even if only through public disclosure, may drive organizational efforts to focus on the outcomes that will be measured, whether or not these are the most important. Furthermore, the measurement of outcomes must be sensitive to the varying factors, such as acuity of patient population and social determinants of health, that may determine outcomes. Adjusting outcomes standards for specific patient populations can be difficult and controversial, but neglecting to do so may lead providers to avoid vulnerable populations or result in financial penalties that harm providers who disproportionately serve such populations. Of course, financial penalties must be well crafted to avoid unintended consequences that contribute to poor outcomes for the elderly population with chronic illnesses. See Mary D. Naylor et al.,

Unintended Consequences of Steps to Cut Readmissions and Reform Payment May Threaten Care of Vulnerable Older Adults, 31 Health Aff. 1623 (2012)

The maturing of health informatics together with pay-for-performance programs provide rich opportunities and powerful incentives for providers to study the outcomes of care they provide and to adjust their practices to improve quality. Using pattern recognition algorithms, data mining can be set to search databases to spot specific trends (as with infection control), or it can be used in a broad search strategy to mine for hidden problems that are fixable. Data mining can direct how procedures, such as discharge checklists and prescription timelines, can be changed to improve outcomes. Professor Barry R. Furrow has published a recent trilogy of articles thoroughly examining these opportunities and pressures: Searching for Adverse Events: Big Data and Beyond, 27 Annals Health L. 149 (2018); The Limits of Current A.I. in Health Care: Patient Safety Policing in Hospitals, 12 Ne. U.L. Rev. 1 (2020); The Confused and Bewildered Hospital: Adverse Event Discovery, Pay-for-Performance, and Big Data Tools as Halfway Technologies, 46 Am. J.L. & Med. 219 (2020).

PROBLEM: SETTING STANDARDS FOR STAFFING

Staff-to-resident and nurse-to-resident ratio is a structural standard that has been viewed as a key indicator of quality in nursing homes and hospitals. A few states have established mandatory staffing ratios. See, e.g., Del. Code Ann. Tit. 16, § 1162; Cal. Health & Safety Code § 1276.5. The California statute requires a minimum of 3.2 hours of nursing (defined as care by nurses' aides and orderlies as well as registered nurses, but with a weighted rate for RNs) per resident per day. See also Theresamarie Mantese et al., Nurse Staffing, Legislative Alternatives and Health Care Policy, 9 DePaul J. Health Care L. 1171 (2006). Federal requirements for nursing homes receiving Medicare or Medicaid, however, do not specify a required staff ratio although they do establish staff training requirements. Staffing data are included in the Nursing Home Compare website.

Assume that you are an attorney working for HHS or a state licensing agency, or for the American Health Care Association (representing for-profit nursing homes), or for an advocacy group representing nursing home residents. Formulate your organization's position on staff ratio requirements.

Should the federal government require minimum nurse staffing levels for nursing homes, or do you think posting staffing ratios on Nursing Home Compare will allow the market to drive up staffing? See, e.g., H. Sharma et al., The Relationship Between Reported Staffing and Expenditures in Nursing Homes, Med. Care Res. Rev. (Nov. 2017), discussing evidence of gaming on self-reported staffing ratios.

Is it better to focus on staffing ratios or on care outcomes? For example, over the past several years, HHS has targeted the rates of use of antipsychotic medications by nursing homes as a measure of quality. Jerry Gurwitz et al., Reducing Excessive Use of Antipsychotic Agents in Nursing Homes, 318 JAMA 118 (2017) (noting success of effort but also noting that shifts to other medications with similar effects may be occurring). HHS advises facilities that consistent staff assignments, increased opportunities for exercise or time outdoors, monitoring and managing pain, and planning and providing individualized activities will reduce reliance on antipsychotic medication. This initiative uses an outcome measure, and facilities may find that they need to increase the number or training of staff to achieve that outcome. Should the standards entirely abandon staffing levels as an independent criterion and rely entirely on outcomes?

If outcomes are the better measure, does requiring public posting of staffing levels mislead the public in choosing a facility? Increased staffing is likely to raise costs, but should it also raise payment levels by Medicare and Medicaid? What data would you like to see if increased payment rates are to be considered? Are there other stakeholders who should be at the table if cost to Medicare and Medicaid becomes an issue?

Is the enforceability of the standards relevant? Consider a standard that says: "The facility shall provide a nursing staff that is appropriately trained and adequate in number to care for the residents of the facility." Inspectors (called "surveyors" in Medicare and Medicaid) may have difficulty with patient-focused survey techniques. In particular, researchers have reported that surveyors hesitate to cite facilities because they may be uneasy with the sophisticated assessment required, and the contentious dispute that often follows, for a citation on a standard like the one above. See, e.g., Michael J. Stoil, Surveyors Stymied by Survey Criteria, Researchers Find, 43 Nursing Homes 58 (1994). See also Sunshine Hayes Nursing Operations v. HHS, infra. How do standards that require that the home provide "nutritious food," or that residents' nutritional status is "optimal," or that the home employ a certified dietitian compare? The third is merely structural, under Donabedian's taxonomy. Should it be eliminated?

Federal regulations promulgated in 2016 require that each nursing home engage in a "facility assessment," at least annually. 42 C.F.R. § 483.70(e). The nursing home must "determine what resources are necessary to care for its residents competently," addressing the facility's specific resident population in terms of physical and cognitive conditions and overall acuity; staff competencies required to provide the care needed by that population; the physical environment; health information technology resources; and ethnic, cultural, and religious factors affecting care. It was anticipated that the government would assess the nursing home's compliance with federal quality standards in part against these self-identified requirements. In late 2017, however, CMS delayed imposition of penalties in enforcement of this quite controversial requirement. CMS, Memorandum on Temporary Enforcement Delays, Nov. 24, 2017. If this requirement is implemented eventually, what implications does it have for setting standards for staffing?

IV. REGULATORY PROCESS

A. NURSING HOMES: LICENSURE AND MEDICARE/MEDICAID CERTIFICATION

Nursing homes that wish to receive payment for services to Medicare or Medicaid beneficiaries must be licensed by the state and must meet federal standards in order to be certified to enter into a provider agreement with those programs. Medicare and Medicaid standards apply to every resident in the facility and not only to beneficiaries. If a nursing facility chooses to participate in neither Medicare (a rare bird indeed since Medicare's rates for post-hospital care are favorable) nor Medicaid, it is subject only to state licensure requirements. State standards for licensure of nursing homes can differ from standards set by Medicare and Medicaid (called "requirements of participation" for nursing homes as compared to the "conditions of participation" applicable to hospitals), but they are often quite similar. Because nursing homes are subject to regulation and sanction by Medicare and Medicaid administrators, state administrative action against the licenses of nursing homes are much less common than are similar state actions against the license of a physician. Nonetheless, administrative actions to suspend or revoke the institutional license of a nursing home may occur when failures by a facility result in serious harm. See, e.g., Rehab. Ctr. at Hollywood Hills, LLC v. State Agency for Health Care Admin., 250 So. 3d 737 (Fla. Dist. Ct. App. 2018) (suspension by state of nursing home license justified when 8 residents died due to failure of facility to protect residents during a hurricane).

B. STANDARD SETTING, INSPECTION, AND SANCTIONS

1. Standard Setting

IN RE THE ESTATE OF MICHAEL PATRICK SMITH V. HECKLER

United States Court of Appeals, Tenth Circuit, 1984.
747 F.2d 583.

Plaintiffs . . . alleged that the Secretary of Health and Human Services (Secretary) has a statutory duty under Title XIX of the Social Security Act, 42 U.S.C.A. §§ 1396–1396n . . . to develop and implement a system of nursing home review and enforcement designed to ensure that Medicaid recipients residing in Medicaid-certified nursing homes actually receive the optimal medical and psychosocial care that they are entitled to under the Act. The plaintiffs contended that the enforcement system developed by the Secretary is "facility-oriented," not "patient-oriented" and thereby fails to meet the statutory mandate. The district court found that although a patient care or "patient-oriented" management system is feasible, the Secretary does not have a duty to introduce and require the use of such a system. [ ]

The primary issue on appeal is whether the trial court erred in finding that the Secretary does not have a statutory duty to develop and implement a system of nursing home review and enforcement, which focuses on and ensures high quality patient care. . . .

Background

[P]laintiffs instituted the lawsuit in an effort to improve the deplorable conditions at many nursing homes. They presented evidence of the lack of adequate medical care and of the widespread knowledge that care is inadequate. Indeed, the district court concluded that care and life in some nursing homes is so bad that the homes "could be characterized as orphanages for the aged." [ ]

* * *

The Medicaid Act

An understanding of the Medicaid Act (the Act) is essential to understand plaintiffs' contentions. The purpose of the Act is to enable the federal government to assist states in providing medical assistance to "aged, blind or disabled individuals, whose income and resources are insufficient to meet the costs of necessary medical services, and . . . rehabilitation and other services to help such . . . individuals to attain or retain capabilities for independence or self care." [ ] To receive funding, a state must submit to the Secretary and have approved by the Secretary, a plan for medical assistance, which meets the requirements of [the Act].

. . . A state seeking plan approval must establish or designate a single state agency to administer or supervise administration of the state plan, [ ], and must provide reports and information as the Secretary may require. [ ] Further, the state agency is responsible for establishing and maintaining health standards for institutions where the recipients of the medical assistance under the plan receive care or services. [ ] The plan must include descriptions of the standards and methods the state will use to assure that medical or remedial care services provided to the recipients "are of high quality." [ ]

The state plan must also provide "for a regular program of medical review . . . of each patient's need for skilled nursing facility care . . . , a written plan of care, and, where applicable, a plan of rehabilitation prior to admission to a skilled nursing facility. . . . " [ ] Further, the plan must provide for periodic inspections by medical review teams of:

(i) the care being provided in such nursing facilities . . . to persons receiving assistance under the State plan; (ii) with respect to each of the patients receiving such care, the adequacy of the services available in particular nursing facilities . . . to meet the current health needs and promote the maximum physical well-being of patients receiving care in such facilities . . . ; (iii) the necessity and desirability of continued placement of such patients in such nursing facilities . . . ; and (iv) the feasibility of meeting their health care needs through alternative institutional or noninstitutional services. [ ]

The state plan must provide that any skilled nursing facility receiving payment comply with [the Act]. . . . The key requirement for purposes of this lawsuit is that a skilled nursing facility must meet "such other conditions relating to the health and safety of individuals who are furnished services in such institution or relating to the physical facilities thereof as the Secretary may find necessary. . . ." [ ]

The state plan must provide for the appropriate state agency to establish a plan, consistent with regulations prescribed by the Secretary, for professional health personnel to review the appropriateness and quality of care and services furnished to Medicaid recipients. [ ] The appropriate state agency must determine on an ongoing basis whether participating institutions meet the requirements for continued participation in the Medicaid program. [ ] While the state has the initial responsibility for determining whether institutions are meeting the [requirements] of participation, [the Act] gives the Secretary the authority to "look behind" the state's determination of facility compliance, and make an independent and binding determination of whether institutions meet the requirements for participation in the state Medicaid plan. Thus, the state is responsible for conducting the review of facilities to determine whether they comply with the state plan. In conducting the review, however, the states must use federal standards, forms, methods, and procedures. . . .

Implementing Regulations

. . . Congress gave the Secretary a general mandate to promulgate rules and regulations necessary to the efficient administration of the functions with which the Secretary is charged by the Act. [ ] Pursuant to this mandate the Secretary has promulgated standards for the care to be provided by skilled nursing facilities and intermediate care facilities. [ ] . . .

The Secretary has established a procedure for determining whether state plans comply with the standards set out in the regulations. This enforcement mechanism is known as the "survey/certification" inspection system. Under this system, the states conduct reviews of nursing homes pursuant to [the Act]. The Secretary then determines, on the basis of the survey results, whether the nursing home surveyed is eligible for certification and, thus, eligible for Medicaid funds. The states must use federal standards, forms, methods, and procedures in conducting the survey. [ ] At issue in this case is the form SSA–1569, [ ], which the

Secretary requires the states to use to show that the nursing homes participating in Medicaid under an approved state plan meet the [requirements] of participation contained in the Act and the regulations. Plaintiffs contend that the form is "facility-oriented," in that it focuses on the theoretical capability of the facility to provide high quality care, rather than "patient-oriented," which would focus on the care actually provided. . . .

The Plaintiffs' Claims

* * *

The plaintiffs do not challenge the substantive medical standards, or "[requirements] of participation," which have been adopted by the Secretary and which states must satisfy to have their plans approved. [ ] Rather, plaintiffs challenge the enforcement mechanism the Secretary has established. The plaintiffs contend that the federal forms, form SSA–1569 in particular, which states are required to use, evaluate only the physical facilities and theoretical capability to render quality care. The surveys assess the care provided almost totally on the basis of the records, documentation, and written policies of the facility being reviewed. [ ] Further, out of the 541 questions contained in the Secretary's form SSA–1569 which must be answered by state survey and certification inspection teams, only 30 are "even marginally related to patient care or might require any patient observation. . . . " [ ] Plaintiffs contend that the enforcement mechanism's focus on the facility, rather than on the care actually provided in the facility, results only in "paper compliance" with the substantive standards of the Act. Thus, plaintiffs contend, the Secretary has violated her statutory duty to assure that federal Medicaid monies are paid only to facilities, which meet the substantive standards of the Act—facilities which actually provide high quality medical, rehabilitative, and psychosocial care to resident Medicaid recipients.

The District Court's Holding

[T]he district court found the type of patient care management system advocated by plaintiffs clearly feasible and characterized the current enforcement system as "facility-oriented." [ ] However, the court concluded that the failure to implement and require the use of a "patient-oriented" system is not a violation of the Secretary's statutory duty. . . .

* * *

The Secretary's Duty

. . . The Secretary of Health and Human Services has a duty to establish a system to adequately inform herself as to whether the facilities receiving federal money are satisfying the requirements of the Act, including providing high quality patient care. This duty to be adequately informed is not only a duty to be informed at the time a facility is originally certified, but is a duty of continued supervision.

Nothing in the Medicaid Act indicates that Congress intended the physical facilities to be the end product. Rather, the purpose of the Act is to provide medical assistance and rehabilitative services. [ ] The Act repeatedly focuses on the care to be provided, with facilities being only part of that care. For example, the Act provides that health standards are to be developed and maintained [ ], and that states must inform the Secretary what methods they will use to assure high quality care. [ ] In addition to the "adequacy of the services available," the periodic inspections must address "the care being provided" in nursing facilities. [ ] State plans must provide review of the "appropriateness and quality of care and services furnished," [ ], and do so on an ongoing basis. [ ]

. . . The Secretary, not the states, determines which facilities are eligible for federal funds. [ ] While participation in the program is voluntary, states who choose to participate must comply with federal statutory requirements. [ ] The inspections may be conducted by the states, but the Secretary approves or disapproves the state's plan for review. Further, the inspections must be made with federal forms, procedures, and methods.

It would be anomalous to hold that the Secretary has a duty to determine whether a state plan meets the standards of the Act while holding that the Secretary can certify facilities without informing herself as to whether the facilities actually perform the functions required by the state plan. The Secretary has a duty to ensure more than paper compliance. . . .

* * *

. . . Congress gave the Secretary authority to promulgate regulations to achieve the functions with which she is charged. The "look-behind" provision and its legislative history clearly show that Congress intended the Secretary to be responsible for assuring that federal Medicaid money is given only to those institutions that actually comply with Medicaid requirements. The Act's requirements include providing high quality medical care and rehabilitative services. In fact, the quality of the care provided to the aged is the focus of the Act. Being charged with this function, we must conclude that a failure to promulgate regulations that allow the Secretary to remain informed, on a continuing basis, as to whether facilities receiving federal money are meeting the requirements of the Act, is an abdication of the Secretary's duty. . . .

. . . Having determined that the purpose and the focus of the Act is to provide high quality medical care, we conclude that by promulgating a facility-oriented enforcement system the Secretary has failed to follow that focus and such failure is arbitrary and capricious. [ ]

Reversed and Remanded.

NOTES AND QUESTIONS

1.   The court's opinion in *Smith* describes the allocation of authority in the federal-state Medicaid quality control program. Is the federal-state effort duplicative and inefficient or useful and necessary? Should Congress consider requiring that nursing facilities receiving Medicaid or Medicare dollars merely be licensed by the state? What factors would you consider in deciding? For further discussion of federal-state relations in this arena, see Senator Charles Grassley, The Resurrection of Nursing Home Reform: A Historical Account of the Recent Revival of the Quality of Care Standards for Long-Term Care Facilities Established in the Omnibus Reconciliation Act of 1987, 7 Elder L.J. 267 (1999); William Gromley & Christine Boccuti, HCFA and the States: Politics and Intergovernmental Leverage, 26 J. Health Pol. Pol'y & L. 557 (2001).

2.   Although the *Smith* plaintiffs characterized their claim as a challenge to the enforcement system rather than to the standards, they in effect challenged the standards as applied. But which standards? Statutory standards? Standards promulgated in the regulations? When the Secretary finally issued final regulations to implement a new survey system as ordered by the court in *Smith,* she refused to include the survey instrument itself in the regulations: "[T]he new forms and instructions are not set forth in these regulations, and any future changes will be implemented through general instructions, without further changes in these regulations. This allows flexibility to revise and improve the survey process as experience is gained." 51 Fed. Reg. 21550 (June 13, 1986). What else does this allow the agency to do? The federal district court rejected the final rules because they did not include the survey instruments or instructions and held the Secretary in contempt of court. Smith v. Bowen, 675 F. Supp. 586 (D. Colo. 1987). The forms and instructions do not have the "force of law," but they do present the agency's detailed interpretation of the statute. See excerpts from the State Operations Manual in the Problem: Residents' Rights, below.

3.   After *Smith*, Congress enacted the Nursing Home Reform Act (NHRA), commonly referred to as OBRA 1987, which still provides the core of federal regulation of nursing homes. The NHRA delivered a comprehensive and significant change in federal standards, surveillance methods, and enforcement. It shifted the standards toward focusing on the actual care received by residents and included in the inspection/survey process a requirement that the survey team interview a number of residents. The NHRA standards foreshadowed the more recent emphasis on "person-centered" care now seen across the full range of health care providers, but which is especially important when the health care facility is also the individual's home.

The current incarnation of this emphasis lies in the nursing home "culture change movement," recognized in the ACA, which established a federal grants program for innovation in that direction. See, e.g., Mary Jane Koren, Person-Centered Care for Nursing Home Residents: The Culture-Change Movement, 29 Health Affairs 312 (2010), describing the 1987 NHRA as the original source of this movement; Laci Cornelison, The Culture Change Movement in Long-Term Care: Is Person-Centered Care a Possibility for the Looming Age Wave?, 12 NAELA J. 121 (2016). Advocates of culture change emphasize resident direction and choices; homelike atmosphere; bonds between caregivers and residents; staff empowerment; and collaborative decision-making. See Emily Park, Brother's Keeper or Big Brother? Resident Safety v. Resident Rights, 9 J. Health & Life Sci. L. 116 (2016).

4. In 2010, Congress enacted the Nursing Home Transparency and Improvement Act (NHTIA) as part of the ACA. The NHTIA required that nursing homes establish some of the internal quality assurance structures (such as the requirement that the facility have a Quality Assessment and Performance Improvement (QAPI) program) that had already been required of hospitals for some time. 42 U.S.C. § 1320a–7j(b). The NHTIA also added requirements for staff training and for medication review. The Improving Medicare Post-Acute Care Transformation Act of 2014 (IMPACT) requires HHS to develop and implement quality measures across all providers of post-hospitalization care, including skilled nursing facilities. See discussion in Section II, above.

In 2016, HHS promulgated the first significant revision of nursing home regulations since OBRA. 81 Fed. Reg. 68688 (Oct. 4, 2016). These regulations implement the NHTIA and IMPACT. The regulations implementing IMPACT require extensive discharge planning beginning at the time of admission and performed continuously thereafter, as well as the transmission of very detailed documentation to be sent with the patient/resident to the receiving facility upon transfer. 42 C.F.R. § 483.21.

5. During the Trump administration, HHS reviewed some requirements in the 2016 final regulations, including the QAPI requirement, to reduce burdens on providers. 82 Fed. Reg. 21014 (May 4, 2017). In addition, CMS suspended, for a period of 18 months, penalties for violation of several significant provisions in the 2016 regulations. See CMS, Memorandum on Temporary Enforcement Delays, Nov. 24, 2017.

Among the regulations for which enforcement was curtailed were some requiring nursing homes to have someone on staff to prevent infections. See Crossley, *supra* at 124. This change was made despite the fact that, from 2013-2017, 82 percent of nursing homes had been cited at least once, and 67 percent had been cited two or more times, for infection control deficiencies. See U.S. GAO, Infection Control Deficiencies Were Widespread and Persistent in Nursing Homes Prior to COVID-19 Pandemic (May 20, 2020) (figure 1). A pandemic-era Washington Post investigation found that three facilities cited for infection control problems were fined only a combined total of $18,000 despite accounting for 380 COVID-19 infections resulting in 83 deaths. See Debbie Cenziper, Joel Jacobs and Shawn Mulcahy, As Pandemic Raged and Thousands Died, Government Regulators Cleared Most Nursing Homes of Infection-Control Violations, Wash. Post (Oct. 29, 2020). See also Nina A. Kohn, Nursing Homes, Covid-19, and the Consequences of Regulatory Failure, 110 Geo. L.J. Online 1 (2021), arguing that the disproportionate number of COVID-19 infections and deaths in nursing homes stemmed from insufficient staffing, lax regulatory enforcement, and Medicare/Medicaid funding skewed in favor of institutional rather than community-based, long-term care.

6.   For a comprehensive analysis of the history of federal nursing home regulation, see Philip Aka et al., Political Factors and Enforcement of the Nursing Home Regulatory Regime, 24 J. L. & Health 1 (2011).

PROBLEM: RESIDENTS' RIGHTS

Assume that you are the attorney for Pine Acres Nursing Home. The administrator has approached you regarding the facility's obligations under federal Medicaid standards concerning two of the Home's residents.

One patient, Francis Scott, aged 88, has been a resident of the facility for a few months. Mr. Scott's mental and physical condition has been deteriorating slowly for several years and much more rapidly in the past year. His family placed him in the nursing home because they wanted him to be safe. They were concerned because he had often left his apartment and become totally lost on the way back. Mr. Scott's family always promptly pays the facility's monthly fee. Mr. Scott is angry about the placement, tends to be rude to staff, and insists on walking through the hallways and around the fenced-in grounds of the facility on his own. He has always been an early riser and likes to take his shower at the crack of dawn. He refuses to be assisted in showering by a nurses' aide. In addition, his friends from the old neighborhood like to visit. They like to play pinochle when they come, and they usually bring a six-pack.

Another patient, Emma Kaitz, has fallen twice, apparently while trying to get out of bed. The staff is very concerned that she will be hurt. The physician who is the medical director of the facility will write an order for restraints "as needed" for any resident upon the request of the director of nursing. Mrs. Kaitz's daughter is willing to try whatever the doctor advises. The staff have begun using bedrails to keep her in bed, but Mrs. Kaitz becomes agitated and cries. She says she feels like a dog when they pen her up. When she becomes agitated, she is given a sedative to help her relax, but it also tends to make her appear confused. To avoid the agitation as much as possible during the day, they have been able to position her wheelchair so that she can't get out by herself. She stops trying after a while and becomes so relaxed she nods off.

The administrator wants to know what he can do. What would you advise this administrator? Can he restrict the visiting hours for Mr. Scott? Can he require Mr. Scott to be assisted in the shower? Can Mr. Scott be transferred or discharged? Is the facility providing quality care for Mrs. Kaitz? How should an inspector treat Mr. Scott's and Mrs. Kaitz's complaints?

The text that follows includes excerpts from the Medicaid statute (Requirements for Long Term Care Facilities); relevant regulations; and excerpts from the CMS State Operations Manual, which is provided to surveyors for the inspection of facilities receiving Medicaid payments.

42 U.S.C.A. § 1396r

(b)(1)   QUALITY OF LIFE.—

(A)(2)   SCOPE OF SERVICES AND ACTIVITIES UNDER PLAN OF CARE—A nursing facility must provide services and activities to attain or maintain the highest practicable physical, mental, and psychosocial well-being of each resident in accordance with a written plan of care . . . .

* * *

(c)   REQUIREMENTS RELATING TO RESIDENTS' RIGHTS—

(1)(A)   SPECIFIED RIGHTS.

(i)   FREE CHOICE.—The right to choose a personal attending physician, to be fully informed in advance about care and treatment that may affect the resident's well-being, and (except with respect to a resident adjudged incompetent) to participate in planning care and treatment or changes in care and treatment.

(ii)   FREE FROM RESTRAINTS.—The right to be free from physical or mental abuse, corporal punishment, involuntary seclusion, and any physical or chemical restraints imposed for purposes of discipline or convenience and not required to treat the resident's medical symptoms. Restraints may only be imposed—

(I)   to ensure the physical safety of the resident or other residents, and

(II)   only upon the written order of a physician that specifies the duration and circumstances under which the restraints are to be used . . . .

(iii) PRIVACY.—The right to privacy with regard to accommodations, medical treatment, written and telephonic communications, visits, and meetings of family and of resident groups.

* * *

(v)   ACCOMMODATION OF NEEDS.—The right . . . (I) to reside and receive services with reasonable accommodations of individual needs and preferences, except where the health or safety of the individual or other residents would be endangered . . . .

* * *

(viii) PARTICIPATION IN OTHER ACTIVITIES.—The right of the resident to participate in social, religious, and community activities that do not interfere with the rights of other residents in the facility.

* * *

(D) USE OF PSYCHOPHARMACOLOGIC DRUGS.

Psychopharmacologic drugs may be administered only on the orders of a physician and only as part of [the written plan of care] designed to eliminate or modify the symptoms for which the drugs are prescribed and only if, at least annually an independent, external consultant reviews the appropriateness of the drug plan of each resident receiving such drugs.

(2) TRANSFER AND DISCHARGE RIGHTS.—

(A) IN GENERAL.—A nursing facility must permit each resident to remain in the facility and must not transfer or discharge the resident from the facility unless—

(i) the transfer or discharge is necessary to meet the resident's welfare and the resident's welfare cannot be met in the facility;

(ii) the transfer or discharge is appropriate because the resident's health has improved sufficiently so the resident no longer needs the services provided by the facility;

(iii) the safety of individuals in the facility is endangered; or

(iv) the health of individuals in the facility would otherwise be endangered; . . .

* * *

[Before effecting a transfer or discharge of a resident, a nursing facility must provide 30 days' notice except in situations described in (A)(i, iii, or iv) if transfer is required by the resident's urgent medical needs or in (ii) if the resident's health allows more immediate action. The statute also requires the state to establish a hearing process for transfers and discharges contested by the resident or legal representative, and the facility must inform the resident or representative of those procedures.]

(3) ACCESS AND VISITATION RIGHTS.—A nursing facility must—. . .

(B) permit immediate access to a resident, subject to the resident's right to deny or withdraw consent at any time, by immediate family or other relatives of the resident;

(C) permit immediate access to a resident, subject to reasonable restrictions and the resident's right to deny or withdraw consent at any time, by others who are visiting with the consent of the resident; . . . .

(4) EQUAL ACCESS TO QUALITY CARE.—

A nursing facility must establish and maintain identical policies and practices regarding transfer, discharge and the provision of services . . . for all individuals regardless of source of payment.

42 C.F.R. § 483.10 Resident rights.

(e) Respect and dignity. The resident has a right to be treated with respect and dignity, including:

(1)   The right to be free from any physical or chemical restraints imposed for purposes of discipline or convenience, and not required to treat the resident's medical symptoms, consistent with § 483.12(a)(2) . . . .

(3)   The right to reside and receive services in the facility with reasonable accommodation of resident needs and preferences except when to do so would endanger the health or safety of the resident or other residents.

(f)   Self-determination. The resident has the right to and the facility must promote and facilitate resident self-determination through support of resident choice, including but not limited to . . . .

(1)   The resident has a right to choose activities, schedules (including sleeping and waking times), health care and providers of health care services consistent with his or her interests, assessments, plan of care and other applicable provisions of this part.

(2)   The resident has the right to make choices about aspects of his or her life in the facility that are significant to the resident. . . .

* * *

(4)   The resident has a right to receive visitors of his or her choosing at the time of his or her choosing, subject to the resident's right to deny visitation when applicable, and in a manner that does not impose on the rights of another resident.

42 C.F.R. § 483.12 Freedom from abuse, neglect, and exploitation.

(a)(2)   [The facility must] ensure that the resident is free from physical or chemical restraints imposed for purposes of discipline or convenience and that are not required to treat the resident's medical symptoms. When the use of restraints is indicated, the facility must use the least restrictive alternative for the least amount of time and document ongoing re-evaluation of the need for restraints.

42 C.F.R. § 483.25 Quality of care.

(n)   Bed rails. The facility must attempt to use appropriate alternatives prior to installing a side or bed rail. If a bed or side rail is used, the facility must ensure correct installation, use, and maintenance of bed rails, including but not limited to the following elements. . . . (2) Review the risks and benefits of bed rails with the resident or resident representative and obtain informed consent prior to installation. . . .

CMS State Operations Manual, Appendix PP (11–22–17)

[A] physical restraint is any manual method, physical or mechanical device/ equipment or material that limits a resident's freedom of movement and cannot be removed by the resident in the same manner as it was applied by staff. The resident's physical condition and his/her cognitive status may be contributing factors in determining whether the resident has the ability to remove it. . . .

Examples of facility practices that meet the definition of a physical restraint include but are not limited to: Using bed rails that keep a resident from voluntarily getting out of bed; Placing a chair or bed close enough to a wall that the resident is prevented from rising out of the chair or voluntarily getting out of bed; Placing a resident on a concave mattress so that the resident cannot independently get out of bed; Tucking in a sheet tightly so that the resident cannot get out of bed, or fastening fabric or clothing so that a resident's freedom of movement is restricted; Placing a resident in a chair, such as a beanbag or recliner, that prevents a resident from rising independently; Using devices in conjunction with a chair, such as trays, tables, cushions, bars or belts, that the resident cannot remove and prevents the resident from rising; . . . and Using a position change alarm to monitor resident movement, and the resident is afraid to move to avoid setting off the alarm.

* * *

. . . There must be documentation identifying the medical symptom being treated and an order for the use of the specific type of restraint. However, the practitioner's order alone (without supporting clinical documentation) is not sufficient to warrant the use of the restraint. The facility is accountable for . . . appropriate assessment, care planning by the interdisciplinary team, and documentation of the medical symptoms and use of the physical restraint for the least amount of time possible and provide ongoing re-evaluation. The resident or resident representative may request the use of a physical restraint; however, the nursing home is responsible for evaluating the appropriateness of the request, and must determine if the resident has a medical symptom that must be treated and must include the practitioner in the review and discussion. . . . [A] resident, or the resident representative . . . does not have the right to demand a restraint be used when it is not necessary to treat a medical symptom.

* * *

. . . Falls do not constitute self-injurious behavior or a medical symptom that warrants the use of a physical restraint. Although restraints have been traditionally used as a falls prevention approach, they have major, serious drawbacks and can contribute to serious injuries. There is no evidence that the use of physical restraints . . . will prevent or reduce falls. Additionally, falls that occur while a person is physically restrained often result in more severe injuries . . . .

* * *

Reasons for using restraints for staff convenience or discipline may include: Staff state that a resident was placed in a restraint because staff are too busy to monitor the resident . . . ; Staff believe that the resident does not exercise good judgment, including that he/she forgets about his/her physical limitations in standing, walking, or using the bathroom alone and will not wait for staff assistance; Staff state that family have requested that the resident be restrained, as they are concerned about the resident falling especially during high activity times, such as during meals, when the staff are busy with other residents; . . . Staff state that new staff and/or temporary staff do not know the resident . . . and how to address behavioral symptoms or care needs so they apply physical restraints; Lack of staff education regarding the alternatives to the use of restraints as a method for preventing falls and accidents . . . .

* * *

. . . Bed rails may have the effect of restraining one individual but not another, depending on the individual resident's conditions and circumstances. . . . In many cases, the risk of using the bed rails may be greater than the risk of not using them as the risk of restraint-related injury and death is significant. . . . The use of partial bed rails may assist an independent resident to enter and exit the bed independently and would not be considered a physical restraint. To determine if a bed rail is being used as a restraint, the resident must be able to easily and voluntarily get in and out of bed when the equipment is in use. If the resident cannot easily and voluntarily release the bed rails, the use of the bed rails may be considered a restraint.

* * *

. . . If a medication has a sedating or subduing effect on a resident, and is not administered to treat a medical symptom, the medication is acting as a chemical restraint. The sedating/subduing effects to the resident may have been caused intentionally or unintentionally by staff, and would indicate an action of discipline or convenience. In the case of an unintentional chemical restraint, the facility did not intend to sedate or subdue a resident, but a medication is being administered that has that effect, and is not the least restrictive alternative to treat the medical symptom. . . .

2. Enforcement: Inspections and Sanctions

An effective command and control regulatory system requires an effective inspection (survey) process that, with an acceptable degree of accuracy, detects and documents violations of standards. Providers tend to believe that nursing home surveyors are overly aggressive; resident advocates, that they are too lax. Several studies have concluded that state and federal surveys seriously understate deficiencies, failing to cite for deficiencies or categorizing cited deficiencies as less serious than they are. See, e.g., GAO, Continued Attention is Needed to Improve Quality of Care in Small but Significant Share of Homes (May 2007). See Edward Miller & Vincent Mor, Balancing Regulatory Controls and Incentives: Toward Smarter and More Transparent Oversight in Long-Term Care, 33 J. Health Polit. Pol'y & L. 249 (2008), for a detailed analysis of the limitations of the current inspection system. Studies also have consistently concluded that there is wide variation among the states in terms of the number of citations, but it is unclear whether this variation reflects the quality of facilities or of inspection processes. See Malcolm Harkins, The Broken

Promise of OBRA '87: The Failure to Validate the Survey Protocol, 8 St. Louis U. J. Health L. & Pol'y 89 (2014).

SUNSHINE HAVEN NURSING OPERATIONS V. U.S. DEP'T OF HEALTH & HUMAN SERVICES

United States District Court of New Mexico, 2016.
2016 WL 9777239.

Sunshine Haven Nursing Operations, a skilled nursing facility ("SNF") [dba Sunshine Haven Lordsburg], appeals the Centers for Medicare and Medicaid Services' ("CMS") imposition of remedies for noncompliance with federal regulations. On April 12 and 13, 2010, an Administrative Law Judge ("ALJ") held a hearing on Sunshine's initial appeal of the CMS decision. On August 5, 2011, the ALJ determined that Sunshine was not in substantial compliance with Medicare program participation requirements from November 5, 2008, to May 6, 2009, and upheld remedies, including Civil Monetary Penalties ("CMP"), . . . Denial of Payment for New Admissions ("DPNA"), and termination of Sunshine's provider agreement with CMS. Sunshine filed an appeal of the ALJ's decision with the United States Department of Health and Human Services ("HHS") Departmental Appeals Board ("DAB"), which affirmed the ALJ's decision on April 23, 2012. Sunshine sought review of the DAB's decision by filing a Petition for Review of Agency Decision ("Petition") with the Tenth Circuit Court of Appeals on June 20, 2012. On February 14, 2014, the Tenth Circuit issued a decision on the CMPs . . . , over which it had jurisdiction [and which it upheld], and transferred the DPNA and termination of provider agreement issues to the District Court. Those matters are presently before the Court. For the reasons explained below, the Court (1) denies Sunshine's Petition as to the DPNA and termination of provider agreement issues, (2) affirms the DAB's decision with respect to those issues, and (3), therefore, dismisses the case with prejudice.

I.   *Standard of Review*

As the Tenth Circuit summarized,

> . . . "Substantial compliance" is "a level of compliance with the requirements of participation such that any identified deficiencies pose no greater risk to resident health or safety than the potential for causing minimal harm." [ ] By contrast, "[n]oncompliance means any deficiency that causes a facility to not be in substantial compliance." [ ] A "deficiency" is a violation of a statutory or regulatory participation requirement.

Sunshine Haven Nursing Operations, LLC v. U.S. Dep't of Health & Human Servs., Centers for Medicare & Medicaid Servs., 742 F.3d 1239, 1244–45 (10th Cir. 2014). A period of noncompliance is measured from the date a survey [the inspection conducted on behalf of CMS by the state survey agency (SA)] finds noncompliance until the date a facility reaches substantial compliance. State Operations Manual ("SOM") § 7317.3. A facility found to be substantially out of compliance on a Medicare participation requirement must submit a plan of correction within ten days for approval by CMS or the SA. [ ] Furthermore, "[w]hile CMS has the burden of production to establish a prima facie case of noncompliance with a regulation, once CMS has met this burden, the provider has the ultimate burden of persuasion that it was in substantial compliance with the regulation at issue." [ ] The preponderance of the evidence standard applies to this burden of persuasion. [ ]

. . . [T]he Court must "review the [Secretary's] decision to determine whether the factual findings are supported by substantial evidence in light of the entire record, and to determine whether the correct legal standards were applied." [ ] "Substantial evidence is such relevant evidence as a reasonable mind might accept as adequate to support a conclusion. It requires more than a scintilla, but less than a preponderance." [ ] . . .

II. Background

A. Procedural History

In response to a complaint regarding a Sunshine resident, CMS contacted the New Mexico Department of Health, the SA, in 2008 to conduct surveys of Sunshine. [ ] The SA conducted surveys on November 5 and 19, 2008, as well as on January 21, 2009, February 3 and 5, 2009, and April 2 and April 20, 2009. During each survey, the SA found that Sunshine was not in substantial compliance with Medicare [requirements of participation].

After conducting the November 5, 2008, survey, the SA sent Sunshine a letter dated November 19, 2008, stating that "we are giving formal notice of imposition of statutory Denial of Payment for New Admissions (DPNA) effective February 5, 2009." A DPNA is mandatory after three continuous months of noncompliance with Medicare program participation requirements. [ ] The letter also stated that "we are recommending to the CMS Regional Office that your provider agreement be terminated on April 5, 2009, if correction has not been achieved prior to that date." Termination of a provider agreement is required after six months of continuous noncompliance with Medicare program participation requirements. [ ] . . .

As a result of finding Sunshine out of substantial compliance for three continuous months and as result of the February 3, 2009, survey, the SA sent a letter to Sunshine on March 10, 2009, confirming a DPNA, effective February 5, 2009, and reiterating that termination of the provider agreement would occur on April 5, 2009, if Sunshine did not achieve substantial compliance. [ ] In a March 16, 2009 letter, CMS again confirmed the imposition of a DPNA, effective February 5, 2009, and termination of the provider agreement by April 5, 2009, if Sunshine did not achieve substantial compliance. CMS subsequently extended the time it would terminate the provider agreement to May 6, 2009, via a letter sent to Sunshine on April 21, 2009. [ ] Later, a May 28, 2009, letter from CMS to Sunshine indicated that CMS, in fact, terminated Sunshine's Medicare provider agreement on May 6, 2009, based on a finding that Sunshine was out of substantial compliance for six continuous months. [ ]

B. *The Relevant Surveys*

1. *The November 5, 2008, Survey*

On November 5, 2008, SA Surveyor Jennifer Wadley conducted a survey of Sunshine in response to a complaint by a mother that her daughter and other residents were not receiving required baths. While Wadley does not have a medical background, she has a criminal justice background and holds the surveyor minimum qualifications test ("SMQT") certification. Wadley concluded that Sunshine failed to comply with 42 C.F.R. § 483.25(a)(3), which requires that a facility "ensure that [a] resident who is unable to carry out activities of daily living receives the necessary services to maintain good nutrition, grooming, and personal and oral hygiene." Wadley based her conclusion on a review of Sunshine's bathing policy and procedure, Sunshine's charting policy and procedure, shower schedules, bath and shower forms, a facility abbreviation list, and care plans and records for three Sunshine residents. Sunshine's bathing policy required that residents receive a shower or bath "at least two times a week and prn [as needed]." The policy also required Sunshine staff to "[d]ocument the date of the shower and any abnormalities noted" as well as to "[r]eport skin changes to nurse."

Two residents, referred to as R1 and R3 for confidentiality purposes, completely depended on Sunshine staff to perform activities of daily living, including keeping themselves clean, neat, and free of body odors. R1's care plan provided that she be bathed two times per week or more as desired. However, for thirteen days, from October 15, 2008, to October 27, 2008, there was no indication that R1 received any baths or showers. R3's care plan provided that he receive a bath or shower two to three times weekly or more as desired. During the sixteen days from October 16, 2008, through October 31, 2008, there was no evidence that R3 received a bath or shower other than on October 21, 2008.

Wadley testified before the ALJ that Sunshine's failure to bathe R1 and R3, as required, created the potential for more than minimal harm to the residents based on risk of infection, skin breakdown, and harm to psychosocial well-being. However, Wadley agreed that her surveyor notes did not indicate that the residents appeared unkempt, not bathed for long periods of time, or that any negative psychosocial symptoms arose from the infrequent bathing.

As a result of Wadley's survey, Sunshine properly submitted a plan of correction that identified a December 5, 2008, completion date. A letter from the SA dated January 8, 2009, indicates that Sunshine addressed the deficiencies noted in the November 5, 2008, survey as of December 16, 2008.

2. *The November 19, 2008, Survey*

On November 19, 2008, the SA completed a second complaint survey of Sunshine, which found that the facility failed to evaluate and monitor the use of physical restraints for two residents identified as R1 and R5. The SA determined that Sunshine violated [the statute and regulation providing] that "[t]he resident has the right to be free from any physical or chemical restraints imposed for purposes of discipline or convenience, and not required to treat the resident's medical symptoms."

* * *

The surveyor found that, while Sunshine used a lap belt to restrain R5 in his wheelchair, Sunshine did not obtain a physician's order for that restraint device. Further, the surveyor found that Sunshine violated its own policy and Medicare regulations in several ways by restraining R1 with bed rails and a lap belt . . . . R1 also sustained bruises and red marks in October 2008 as a result of being trapped in the side bed rails or between the bed rails and an air mattress.

Sunshine apparently submitted two plans of correction for the November 19, 2008, survey. . . . [T]he SA contacted Sunshine via letter on March 5, 2009, regarding the November 19, 2008, survey and stated, "Your facility was found to be in compliance with the Standards of Participation based on the health revisit conducted on January 31, 2009. Note: This notice of clearance is limited only to the survey mentioned above."

3. *The January 21, 2009, Survey*

During a January 21, 2009, survey, the SA determined that Sunshine violated 42 C.F.R. § 483.25(h), which provides that "the facility must ensure that—(1) The resident environment remains as free of accident hazards as is possible; and (2) Each resident receives adequate supervision and assistance devices to prevent accidents." The SA found that Sunshine failed to ensure that a Certified Nursing Assistant ("CNA") used proper body transfer techniques, thereby causing R5 to experience pain and bruising. . . . On September 27, 2008, after R5 complained of pain in her shoulder during a transfer, Sunshine updated R5's care plan to require transfer by a . . . lift or two persons, transfer training, and use of a gait belt. . . . On November 26, 2008, a CNA documented a bruise on R5's left arm. Assuming the bruise occurred during a transfer, Sunshine's fall committee discussed R5's bruising that same day.

... The SA interviewed R5 during the January 21, 2009, survey, and R5 complained that she received bruises on her arms during [lifts and transfers]. On that date, R5 had bruises on both arms. R5 identified a specific CNA who hurt her and stated that the CNA ignored her complaints of pain and laughed at her. Records of employee counseling indicate that on December 5, 2008, Sunshine ordered the CNA to attend neglect and abuse training. However, as of January 21, 2009, Sunshine provided no documentation that the CNA attended the ordered training. Sunshine's plan of correction identified a completion date of February 21, 2009.

4. *The February 3, 2009, Survey*

On February 3, 2009, the SA conducted a survey to evaluate Sunshine's compliance with Life Safety Code ("LSC") requirements. The SA found nine violations of 42 C.F.R. § 483.70(a), which requires that a facility "be designed, constructed, equipped, and maintained to protect the health and safety of residents, personnel and the public." The SA determined that Sunshine failed to have sufficient smoke detectors, sprinklers, audiovisual alert systems, and fire-rated walls and ceilings in various parts of the facility. Sunshine does not dispute that it violated eight of the nine LSC findings of noncompliance. The parties, however, dispute whether Sunshine substantially complied with LSC deficiencies ... prior to May 6, 2009, the date CMS terminated the provider agreement.

With respect to ... failure to locate initiator devices near smoke doors, Sunshine obtained a contract on April 29, 2009, for the installation of such devices. Sunshine's administrator ... testified ... that [the LSC surveyor], told him that Sunshine would be in substantial compliance as long as it had contracts for corrections that would place the facility in compliance. Regarding ... failure to afford one-hour fire-rated enclosures with one-hour fire-rated tiles, Sunshine purchased tiles on April 27, 2009, received the tiles two weeks later, and promptly installed them. [Sunshine's administrator] testified at the ALJ hearing that the LSC surveyor told him that a receipt for the purchase of the tiles would constitute substantial compliance. As to ... failure to have smoke detectors and audio visual devices in certain rooms and corridors at Sunshine, the facility obtained a contract on April 29, 2009, for the installation of such detectors and devices. ... [Sunshine's administrator] testified at the ALJ hearing that [the LSC surveyor] informed him that the contract itself would constitute substantial compliance, because, considering Sunshine's rural location, it would take more than a week for the appropriate approvals of the detectors and devices. With respect to ... failure to equip outdoor canopies with sprinkler protection, Sunshine secured an installation contract on April 27, 2009. [Sunshine's administrator] testified at the ALJ hearing that [the LSC surveyor] informed him that the execution of the contract constituted substantial compliance. On April 29, 2009, Sunshine also contracted with a company to design, deploy, and service a fire safety system to comply with the survey and state and city codes. According to Sunshine, design and drawings of the fire safety system were not completed and submitted to the State Fire Marshal until October 2009.

On March 10, 2009, the SA informed Sunshine that it was not in substantial compliance with respect to the February 3, 2009, survey and that it recommended imposing a DPNA, effective February 5, 2009, and terminating the provider agreement, effective April 5, 2009, if Sunshine did not achieve substantial compliance by then. [Sunshine's administrator] subsequently spoke with [the LSC surveyor] about a revisit, but [the surveyor said his] boss told him not to conduct a revisit. On May 28, 2009, CMS sent a letter to Sunshine noting LSC deficiencies and stating that the DPNA was effective February 5, 2009, and that the provider agreement terminated on May 6, 2009.

As of November 4, 2009, Sunshine still had not corrected two fire-related deficiencies from the February 3, 2009, survey, including the upgrade of the fire alarm system. Sunshine wrote a letter to the New Mexico Department of Health at that time requesting a ninety-day waiver of these deficiencies for purposes of re-licensure. The facility expected to have the corrections completed by December 31, 2009.

III. Discussion

A. Whether Sunshine was in Substantial Compliance with Respect to the November 5, 2008, Survey

* * *

Sunshine argues that substantial evidence does not support a finding that it was not in substantial compliance with Medicare regulations on November 5, 2008. Sunshine contends first that the DAB based its decision on incompetent medical opinion testimony from Wadley. Specifically, Sunshine contends that because Wadley is not a medical professional and has no medical background, training, or experience, she may not opine as to whether fewer showers and baths increases residents' risk of infection or psychosocial problems. Sunshine argues that although Wadley had the required surveyor training, there was no evidence as to what training she might have received regarding increased risk of infection or psychosocial problems. Sunshine then claims that the ALJ improperly shifted the burden of proof to Sunshine to rebut Wadley's testimony.

* * *

Sunshine also points out that the lack of showers and baths did not result in a negative outcome or actual harm to residents. Accordingly, Sunshine posits that there is no competent evidence that the two residents faced more than minimal harm as a result of a short-term departure from its bathing policy.

... The Court finds that CMS established a *prima facie* case that Sunshine violated Section 483.25(a)(3) by failing to follow bath policy and care plans, thus shifting the burden of persuasion to Sunshine to show that it was in substantial compliance.... Sunshine has failed to carry that burden of persuasion. In particular, Sunshine failed to prove by a preponderance of the evidence that the CMS training and SMQ test were insufficient to allow Wadley to competently conclude that a risk of more than minimal harm existed for R1 and R3. Rather, the DAB's decision is supported by substantial evidence such as Wadley's testimony, testimony backed by the bath/shower plans that provide for noting skin conditions, and by the fact that bathing provides a means of detecting medical issues affecting the skin.... Therefore, substantial evidence supports the DAB's decision to affirm the ALJ's finding that Sunshine was not in substantial compliance on November 5, 2008, and that Sunshine corrected the deficiency by no later than December 16, 2008.

B. *Whether Sunshine was in Substantial Compliance with Respect to the January 21, 2009, Survey*

Sunshine maintains that the DAB's findings with respect to the January 21, 2009, survey are unsupported by substantial evidence, and that the DAB ignored steps Sunshine took to assess the needs of R5 and to mitigate foreseeable risks of harm when transferring R5. Sunshine argues that the DAB improperly held it strictly liable for a CNA's failure to follow facility policy, training, and R5's care plan, each of which identified appropriate care and transfer techniques for R5.... Additionally, Sunshine contends that R5's bruising was nothing other than an unavoidable accident.

Sunshine has not persuaded the Court by a preponderance of the evidence that it substantially complied with Section 485.25(h). The Court notes that the ... lift training packet provided by Sunshine only addresses repositioning in a chair, repositioning in a bed, and transferring from a bed to a stretcher. There is no information about transferring from a bed to a chair or from a bed to a wheelchair, nor is there any information on how to operate a ... lift and to avoid injuries to the resident. Contrary to Sunshine's assertion, the training information does direct a staff person to ask one or more co-workers to assist when using a ... lift. Staff notes further indicate that there was confusion over a period of months regarding whether to use the ... lift.... Meanwhile, R5 suffered several bruises due to transfers over a several month period. Upon a review of the record, the Court is hard-pressed to find that R5 simply suffered from "unavoidable" accidents. The Court concludes that substantial evidence supports the DAB's conclusion that Sunshine was not in substantial compliance with 42 C.F.R. § 483.25(h) from January 21, 2009, through February 21, 2009.

* * *

D. Whether the DAB Improperly Relied on Deficiencies in the February 3, 2009, Survey to Support a Finding of Continued Noncompliance

* * *

With regard to a revisit prior to termination of the provider agreement, "the regulations and the SOM itself make clear that whether and when revisit surveys are performed is in the discretion of the State and CMS, not the facility." [ ] Even if the SA or CMS were required to conduct a revisit prior to termination of the provider agreement on May 6, 2009, the fact that Sunshine still had not corrected all deficiencies from the February 3, 2009, survey as of November 4, 2009, well past the May 6, 2009, deadline to come into substantial compliance, indicates that any failure to revisit the facility prior to May 6, 2009, constituted harmless error. In sum, substantial evidence supports the DAB's decision that the February 3, 2009, survey provided a portion of the six-month noncompliance period.

E. Whether Substantial Evidence Supports the DAB's Conclusion that Sunshine was not in Substantial Compliance with LSC Requirements on May 6, 2009

. . . Sunshine argues that, given the significant amount of work and approvals needed to implement the LSC plan of correction, Sunshine could reasonably rely on the surveyor's statements that having a contract in place for the corrections constituted substantial compliance. Sunshine contends that it would not be reasonable for the SA or CMS to require completion of the work by May 6, 2009, as these agencies knew that the work would require months of design, development, and procurement of approvals.

The Court observes that "[a]pproving a [plan of correction] as an acceptable statement of how the facility will address the findings is not tantamount to determining that the POC [or plan of correction] has been successfully implemented and substantial compliance achieved." [ ] "[A petitioner] may well have been informed by someone from the State survey agency that the POC was accepted. That information, however, does not affect CMS's authority to impose a [remedy] for the period when [petitioner] was not in substantial compliance."

. . . [G]iven the mandatory nature of the regulations and Sunshine's noncompliance with respect to the LSC deficiencies for over a six-month period, CMS did not err in deciding to terminate the provider agreement. Therefore, the Court concludes that the DAB's conclusion that Sunshine was not in substantial compliance with LSC requirements was not erroneous and was supported by substantial evidence.

* * *

NOTES AND QUESTIONS

1.   If a facility, like Sunshine, is cited for, but then corrects, a deficiency, should it still be penalized for that violation? What arguments would support an emphasis on correction rather than penalties? What would argue against?

One of the challenges in nursing home enforcement is the pattern, observed in this case, of cited deficiencies followed by correction followed by repeat or other deficiencies. Civil fines, or civil monetary penalties (CMPs), were adopted as a remedy in nursing home enforcement in the 1970s by the states and later by the federal Medicare and Medicaid programs to address this problem. They are designed to raise the cost of deficiencies, and thus deter violations, without levying the ultimate penalty of termination of the provider agreement or licensure. CMS's final rule on CMPs discounts a fine by 50% if the facility self-reports the violation within 10 days of the date on which the facility became aware of the situation and before inspection or citation by a government agency or complaint to an agency by any individual. In addition, the facility must have taken prompt action to correct the matter, and the facility must waive its right to a hearing. This option is not available for the most serious violations or for repeated violations. 42 C.F.R. § 488.438(c)(2)(i).

The rule is intended to encourage voluntary vigilance and reporting, as well as rapid correction. Some argue that a self-reported violation should not trigger a fine at all, while CMS argues that a self-report is an admission of violation such that no hearing should be required prior to sanction. The rule also provides for a discount of 35% if a facility has not self-reported but waives their right to a hearing. 42 C.F.R. § 488.436. For a critique of the implementation of CMPs, see Stephanie Ward, The Human Cost of Doing Business, 102 ABA J. 52 (Aug. 2016), an investigation of enforcement in Illinois.

CMS has radically altered the methodology for calculating fines, with the ultimate result being a reduction in the number of fines that can be assessed. The new policy mandates a "per instance" fine rather than a "per day" fine for several categories of violations, including a single violation that has caused actual harm or a continuing violation with actual harm but where the facility has a good compliance history. The per instance fines are one-time fines for serious violations and range from $5,000 to $20,000. Per instance fines for facilities with a history of noncompliance may be increased by $1,500 to $5,000. CMS, Revision of Civil Monitor Penalty (CMP) Policies and CMP Analytic Tool, July 7, 2017.

2.   If the ultimate penalty of termination of the provider agreement or revocation of license is justified because of substandard care, does the agency fail in protecting residents or the public purse if it foregoes that result? An OIG report on CMS's implementation of mandatory statutory sanctions found that the agency failed to terminate the provider agreement in 30 out of 55 cases in which the facility remained out of compliance (on those specific citations) past the six-month deadline for reaching compliance or had an unabated condition that presented immediate jeopardy to the health and safety of the residents for

more than 23 days. CMS also failed to deny payment for new admissions to 28% of the over 700 facilities that remained out of compliance for over 3 months after citation, as required by statute. CMS reported to the OIG that it did not intend to make any changes to its policies or practices:

> While the law requires that mandatory actions occur at specified times and under specific circumstances, it also contemplates that sanctions will be used to motivate improvements and lasting corrections. Where these expectations may be in conflict, we seek to resolve the conflict with the solution that best protects the well-being of the resident. Nursing Homes that Merit Punishment Not Terminated, Federal Review Finds, 15 Health L. Rprt. 628 (2006).

3. *Sunshine* consumed considerable state and federal agency resources for the repeated surveys and appeals. See generally Sharona Hoffman, Improving Regulatory Enforcement in the Face of Inadequate Resources, 43 J. L. Med. & Ethics 33 (2015). CMS requires more frequent surveys of facilities that are in substantial noncompliance with federal standards. The ACA codified this practice and requires surveys of "Special Focus Facilities" (SFF) at least every six months. 42 U.S.C. § 1395i–3(f)(8). A report on the SFF program showed that it produced improvement in the majority of SFF facilities. GAO, Special Focus Facilities Are Often Improving, but CMS's Program Could be Strengthened (2010). Between 2013 and 2014, however, CMS reduced the number of facilities monitored under this program from 152 to 62, citing limited resources. GAO, Nursing Home Quality: CMS Should Continue to Improve Data and Oversight (2015).

4. Note that at least two of the surveys in *Sunshine* were conducted in response to complaints filed against the nursing home by residents or their representatives. The NHTIA requires that Nursing Home Compare and the state websites include a standardized complaint form with instructions on how to file complaints and a description of the process that is used to resolve them. States are required to establish a complaint resolution process that tracks complaints, determines the severity of the complaint so as to set the priority for its investigation, and sets deadlines for notifying complainants of the outcome. 42 U.S.C. §§ 1395i–3(i) and 1320a–7j(f). Although the overall number of deficiency citations against nursing homes has declined, the number of complaints has increased. GAO, Nursing Home Quality, cited above. CMS contracts with two Beneficiary and Family Centered Care-Quality Improvement Organizations (BFCC-QIOs) to review Medicare beneficiary appeals of discharges (primarily by hospitals) and beneficiary complaints about quality of care by any Medicare provider.

5. How many years passed between the initial citations and the disposition of the *Sunshine* case? What do you think was happening at the facility during this time? Check the Nursing Home Compare website entry for this nursing home. For more on Nursing Home Compare, see Sections I and III, above.

6. As a condition of participation in Medicare and Medicaid, the ACA requires every nursing home to have a "compliance and ethics program that is effective . . . in promoting quality of care." 42 U.S.C. § 1320a–7j. The implementation deadline was extended to allow HHS additional time to promulgate necessary regulations. Among the standards imposed by the regulations are requirements that each facility put their policies and procedures in writing, assign a person to implement and operate the program, and include in the program a method for anonymous reporting of apparent violations without fear of reprisal. See 42 C.F.R. § 483.85. State surveyors began inspecting facilities for implementation of such compliance programs in late 2019.

V. PRIVATE ACCREDITATION

Private accreditation is a nongovernmental, voluntary activity typically conducted by not-for-profit associations. The Joint Commission (TJC) and the National Committee on Quality Assurance (NCQA) are two of the leading organizations in the accreditation of health care entities. TJC, for example, accredits about 80% of hospitals in the United States.

As a voluntary process, accreditation may be viewed as a private communicative device, providing the accredited health care entity with a seal of approval—a method for communicating in shorthand that it meets standards established by an external organization. See Clark C. Havighurst, Foreword: The Place of Private Accrediting Among the Instruments of Government, 57 L. & Contemp. Probs. 1 (1994). In practice, however, there is a much closer marriage between some private accreditation programs and government regulation of health care facilities. This is especially true of the Joint Commission hospital accreditation program. State governments rely to a great extent on accreditation by TJC in their hospital licensure programs. See, e.g., Tex. Health & Safety Code § 222.024, exempting hospitals accredited by TJC or certain other organizations from annual licensure inspection. The TJC website has an interactive map that provides a list of such facilities for each state.

Under the Medicare statute, hospitals, home health care agencies, and a few other types of health care organizations accredited by accreditation programs approved by CMS are "deemed" to have met the requirements for Medicare certification without further inspections by the federal government. This "deemed status" is extended to Medicaid providers as well if Medicaid requirements are identical with Medicare requirements. 42 C.F.R. § 488.6.

Originally, deemed status was designed to entice an adequate number of hospitals to participate in the then-new Medicare program. That original rationale has dissipated as hospitals have become much more dependent on Medicare payments. At the same time, the federal government's reliance on private accreditation as a substitute for direct government surveillance has expanded considerably beyond the original hospital setting and now extends to clinical laboratories, home health care agencies, and several other providers. Deemed status is not recognized, however, for nursing homes and has been vigorously opposed by consumer advocates.

How does the private accreditation process compare to public regulation? Private accreditation programs traditionally have engaged in practices that encourage voluntary subscription to the accreditation program. For example, accreditation programs traditionally perform only announced site visits and keep negative evaluations confidential, at least until the accreditation itself is reduced or not renewed. Standards established by accreditation programs, which are often dominated by professionals in the industry rather than consumer groups, may differ from those set by a process that arguably fosters broader public participation. With TJC's accrediting program for hospitals, in particular, governance and policymaking are dominated by physician and hospital leaders. TJC's accreditation survey is explicitly consultative, rather than enforcement oriented, in nature.

For decades, HHS basically deferred entirely to the Joint Commission in granting deemed status to a TJC-accredited hospital. In 2008, however, the Medicare Improvements for Patients and Providers Act removed permanent deemed status for the accreditation programs and required that accreditation organizations reapply periodically for recognition of deemed status. An accreditation organization that is seeking approval from CMS for deemed status for accredited providers must provide evidence that its accreditation standards are comparable to the Medicare conditions of participation. It must also agree to perform unannounced surveys at least as often as required by statute; must supply CMS with a provider's survey reports upon request; and must inform CMS promptly of adverse accreditation decisions. The survey reports are not available to the public, however.

CMS currently provides some oversight of the effectiveness of the accreditation process by performing validation surveys to check whether providers with deemed status are actually in compliance, as well as surveys in response to specific complaints. A provider with deemed status who is determined to be out of compliance during a CMS survey does not retain deemed status. CMS is required to engage in review of CMS-approved accreditation programs on an "ongoing basis." 42 C.F.R. §§ 488.4–488.9.

The TJC accreditation process has been criticized as ineffective in assuring compliance with government regulations. In April 2017, CMS reported that the rate of disparities between serious deficiencies identified through state surveys and those identified by accrediting organizations had increased to 39%. At the same time, CMS proposed a regulation that would require CMS-approved accrediting organizations to make public the final accreditation report and any approved plans of correction for accredited providers holding deemed status. This would mirror public access to survey results performed by the state agencies on CMS's behalf. 82 Fed. Reg. 19796 (April 28, 2017). CMS later withdrew that proposal. 82 Fed. Reg. 37990 (Aug. 14, 2017).

In late 2017, the Wall Street Journal published an investigative report detailing serious safety and quality deficiencies in a number of TJC-accredited hospitals. Stephanie Armour, Hospital Watchdog Gives Seal of Approval, Even After Problems Emerge, Wall St. J. (Sept. 8, 2017). TJC accredits over 4,000 hospitals and denies accreditation on the basis of safety or quality issues to approximately four hospitals per year. TJC maintains that it focuses on improvement rather than pulling accreditation and believes that this approach best serves the public interest.

Although deemed status is currently being contested, TJC has had a tremendous influence on the operation of hospitals. For example, TJC established the framework for staff privileges and credentialing in hospitals, as described in Chapter 12, and continues to be an important arena for change in those processes, including its recent focus on disruptive health care professionals and its requirement of continuous review of outcomes for physicians with privileges. TJC's embrace of the patient safety movement, described in Chapter 6, certainly furthered diffusion of the movement's principles into hospitals. TJC's "Sentinel Event" initiative, for example, encouraged hospitals to report errors and root cause analyses for the benefit of systemic change in areas such as wrong-site surgery and medication errors, and it has spawned a number of refinements over the years. In a survey identifying the most powerful influences on hospitals' adoption of patient safety initiatives, hospital administrators reported that TJC was the key factor and that their patient safety programs were linked specifically to TJC's patient safety standards and goals. Kelly J. Devers et al., What is Driving Hospitals' Patient-Safety Efforts?, 23 Health Affairs 103 (2004).

For a history of TJC and a broad review of legal issues related to private accreditation, see Timothy S. Jost, The Joint Commission on Accreditation of Hospitals: Private Regulation of Health Care and the Public Interest, 24 B.C. L. Rev. 835 (1983). For a discussion of the relationship between private accreditation and public regulation in health care, see Louise G. Trubek, New Governance and Soft Law in Health Care Reform, 3 Ind. Health L. Rev. 139 (2006); Harold Krent, The Private Performing the Public: Delimiting Delegations to Private Parties, 65 U. Miami L. Rev. 507 (2011).

CHAPTER 4

THE PROFESSIONAL-PATIENT RELATIONSHIP

■ ■ ■

I. INTRODUCTION

This chapter considers the formation and nature of the physician-patient relationship. The analysis of legal duties and ethics in this area begins with the individual physician, or other health care professional, who has primary responsibility for seeing the patient, diagnosing the problem, and prescribing the treatment. Health care today, however, is delivered in a variety of settings—hospitals, ambulatory care clinics, nursing homes, and doctors' offices. And the institutional framework for such care, in terms of its financing, support, and obligations, may encompass medical staffs, managed care organizations, partnerships, institutional employers, and accountable care organizations. This framework may also have an impact on legal obligations, especially as the duty of the physician to the patient may be extended to the organization (or not) and as organizational controls impact the capacity of the physician to meet his or her obligations to the patient. Therefore, the nature of the physician-patient relationship is affected by numerous factors.

To start, the formation of the relationship triggers four unique duties: (1) the duty not to abandon a patient, (2) the duty to obtain informed consent to treatment, (3) the duty to keep treatment information confidential, and (4) the duty to comply with the medical standard of care. Courts often describe the physician-patient relationship as fiduciary in nature. See, e.g., Youngs v. Peacehealth, 316 P.3d 1035, 1038 (Wash. 2014)(the doctor-patient relationship is a fiduciary one of the highest degree involving every element of trust, confidence and good faith); LeBlanc v. Acevedo, 258 So. 3d 555 (Fla. Dist. Ct. App. 2018) (the requirement of doctor-patient confidentiality creates a relation of trust and confidence between the parties giving rise to a fiduciary duty). Because of the special nature of this doctor-patient relationship, each of the duties identified above requires conduct that goes beyond what the law demands in most other common relationships.

Whether the law adequately holds physicians to the standards of a fiduciary and the extent to which the law should do so are policy questions underlying the materials in this chapter. In any case, the formation of a doctor-patient relationship is consequential as a matter of law because it gives rise to heightened duties.

This chapter begins by exploring common law standards for the formation of the doctor-patient relationship (Section II). It then addresses each of the four duties triggered by formation of that relationship and their related causes of action: abandonment (Section III), informed consent (Section IV), confidentiality (Section V), and medical malpractice (Section VI).

II.   FORMING THE PHYSICIAN-PATIENT RELATIONSHIP

A physician's duties to treat another person, to obtain informed consent prior to treatment, to hold in confidence information learned about another in the course of treatment, and to comply with medical standards of care are not triggered unless and until the physician has assented, expressly or impliedly, to act as that person's physician. Consequently, someone injured in a bicycling accident cannot successfully sue a physician who passes by without stopping to render aid. Likewise, if you were to reveal to your neighbor as part of a friendly conversation that you feel anxious and depressed, your neighbor would not have a legal duty to keep that information confidential even if your neighbor happened to be a physician. Thus, the formation of a doctor-patient relationship is necessary to trigger the unique duties owed by a physician to a patient. The materials in this section examine the legal standard for forming such a relationship.

LECTION V. DYLL
Court of Appeals of Texas, 2001.
65 S.W.3d 696.

FITZGERALD, J.

* * *

Sandra M. Lection appeals the take-nothing summary judgment rendered against her in her suit for medical malpractice against Louis Dyll, M.D. . . . Lection contends the trial court committed procedural error in reconsidering Dyll's motion for summary judgment and challenges the court's determination that no doctor-patient relationship existed between Dyll and her. . . .

FACTUAL BACKGROUND

On August 15, 1992, Lection was taken by ambulance to the emergency room of The Medical Center of Mesquite with symptoms of slurred speech, hemiparesis, severe headache, dizziness, and other neurological symptoms. Dr. Nabeel Syed, the emergency room physician on duty, examined Lection, had an EKG and CT-scan performed, and then requested a nurse to page the neurologist on call. At about 7:00 p.m., Dyll, who was the neurologist on call that day, telephoned the emergency room to speak with Syed. After Syed gave Dyll the results of Syed's examination and testing, Syed asked Dyll if anything further needed to be done. Dyll responded that "no further treatment needed to be done for this patient at the time," that "it sounded like she had a hemiplegic migraine" and that "nothing further needed to be done," which included admission into the hospital. According to both Syed and Dyll, during this telephone conversation, a nurse told Syed that Lection "was no longer in the room" and he so informed Dyll. When Syed told Dyll the patient had left the hospital and asked Dyll "is that okay," Dyll said it was all right that the patient had gone home. Syed stated that "admission would be based on what Dyll had told" him, and that he could have contacted the patient to return "if it needed to be done," but "based on her [Lection's] physical findings, what Dr. Dyll had told me [Syed], and how she was at the time she left the hospital, [Syed] didn't think she needed to come back or be admitted." Had the patient still been at the hospital, Syed would have discharged her based on what Dyll said. Dyll also told Syed to "just have her come back to my office on Monday."

A factual dispute exists whether Lection left the hospital during or after Syed's telephone conference with Dyll. According to the doctors, Lection left before being discharged and while the two doctors were speaking on the phone. However, Syed stated in his deposition that he was waiting to hear from the neurologist and the cardiologist before making a decision on the correct course of treatment, and that what he (Syed) ultimately decided to do depended upon what Dyll told him to do. Syed told Lection and her husband that he wanted to hear from the neurologist before making a decision about discharge. Lection and her husband testified by deposition that Syed told Lection to go home over their objection and that Syed said Lection only had a "hysterical migraine" or something to that effect. Lection argues that Syed must have said she had a "hemiplegic migraine," thus relating Dyll's diagnosis to her and proving she did not leave the hospital until after Syed had concluded his telephone consultation with Dyll.

* * *

In his motion for summary judgment, Dyll alleged no physician-patient relationship existed because Lection left the hospital and Dyll's telephone conference with Syed did not create any duty of care to Lection. . . .

* * *

In her sole issue on appeal, Lection asserts the trial court erred in granting Dyll's motion for summary judgment.

* * *

DUTY OF AN "ON CALL" PHYSICIAN

* * *

A physician is liable for malpractice or negligence only where there is a physician-patient relationship as a result of a contract, express or implied, that the doctor will treat the patient with proper professional skill, and there is a breach of professional duty to the patient. [ ] The creation of the physician-patient relationship does not require the formalities of a contract. [ ] A contract implied in fact "arises from the acts and conduct of the parties, it being implied from the facts and circumstances that there was a mutual intention to contract." [ ] Moreover, the fact that a physician does not deal directly with a patient does not necessarily preclude the existence of a physician-patient relationship. [ ] Likewise, physical contact between a doctor and patient is not necessary to create a physician-patient relationship. See Dougherty v. Gifford, 826 S.W.2d 668, 674 (Tex.App.—Texarkana 1992, no writ) (physician-patient relationship existed between patient from whom biopsy was taken and doctors at laboratory who examined tissue from biopsy and negligently misdiagnosed malignant cancer); see also Bovara v. St. Francis Hosp., 298 Ill.App.3d 1025, 233 Ill.Dec. 42, 700 N.E.2d 143, 147 (1998) (physicians who provided service to hospital of determining whether patients were "candidates" for angioplasty procedure had physician-patient relationship with patient even though they never examined patient); [ ]. A physician may agree in advance with a hospital to the creation of a physician-patient relationship that leaves him no discretion to decline treatment of the hospital's clients. See St. John, 901 S.W.2d at 424; Day, 961 S.W.2d at 281 [ ]; cf. Hand v. Tavera, 864 S.W.2d 678, 680 (Tex.App.-San Antonio 1993, no writ) (patient's health care plan created physician-patient relationship when physician consulted was the designated doctor for the health care plan).

A physician who is not under a contractual obligation with a hospital to provide services and who is not required to be "on call" to maintain staff privileges owes no general duty to emergency room patients. [ ] When no contractual obligation exists, the mere fact that a doctor is on call does not, in itself, create a physician-patient relationship or impose any duty on the doctor to treat the patient. [ ]

If, as in this case, no prior relationship exists between physician and patient, an on-call physician may assume a duty to the patient if he takes some affirmative action to treat the patient. [ ] An on-call physician to an emergency room consulted by telephone renders medical services by evaluating the information provided and making a medical decision. [ ]

Summary Judgment Evidence

* * *

Under the Hospital By-Laws, as a requirement of maintaining active staff privileges, Dyll was required to serve as an on-call physician to the emergency room. An active staff member has the prerogative to admit patients to the hospital and is obligated to participate in patient assessments and provide emergency medical care to a patient in the emergency room. The on-call physician makes the determination whether an emergency-room patient should be admitted to the hospital, but he is not required to provide further treatment to the patient if the patient is not admitted to the hospital. The hospital rules and regulations also provide that a consultation is required in all cases where the diagnosis is obscure and where there is doubt as to the best therapeutic measures to be taken for a patient.

Dyll's Factual Arguments

Dyll asserted in his motion for summary judgment that the summary judgment evidence proves as a matter of law that no physician-patient relationship was formed between him and Lection because: (a) no opportunity existed for the formation of the relationship due to Lection's departure from the hospital; (b) he made no affirmative acts toward treating her; and (c) the Hospital By-Laws did not create a contractual physician-patient relationship. We consider each of these assertions in turn.

Dyll first argues the evidence proves he had no opportunity to form a physician-patient relationship with Lection because she left the hospital before he uttered a word to Syed. He cites to statements in his deposition asserting that he did not have the opportunity to form any opinion of Lection's diagnosis or to "get into the decision-making process in my mind about what this patient had" because Lection had already left the hospital. Dyll's statements that he made no determination of her condition and did not participate in the decision-making process is contradicted by Syed's evidence that Dyll told him Lection had a hemiplegic migraine, that it was "all right" for Lection to have left the hospital, that no immediate treatment was necessary, and for Syed to send Lection to his office on Monday. The evidence is disputed as to whether Lection had left the hospital when Dyll spoke to Syed. The medical records show a ten-minute gap between Dyll's call to Syed and the nurse's observation that Lection was "not in bed" and had left without signing for the discharge instructions. Syed testified he would not have discharged Lection without speaking to Dyll, and Lection and her husband testified they did not leave until Syed personally told them to "go home."

The summary judgment standard requires us to resolve all factual disputes in favor of the nonmovant. Having reviewed the summary judgment evidence applying this standard, we conclude that a fact issue exists whether Lection was still an emergency room patient when the telephone consultation occurred. Although Dyll's affidavit indicates he was led to believe the patient had gone and Syed's inquiry had become moot, the affidavit of an interested witness concerning his state of mind cannot be readily controverted and is not proper summary judgment evidence. [ ] Moreover, indulging every reasonable inference in Lection's favor, as we must, we conclude there is circumstantial evidence that contradicts Dyll's affidavit. [ ] According to Syed's deposition, Dyll instructed Syed to have the patient call Dyll's office on Monday. This is "some evidence" either that Dyll believed the patient was still at the hospital or that she could be readily contacted. The hospital records note a ten-minute interval between the Dyll Syed telephone call and Lection's absence from the emergency room. The hospital record does not state that Lection left without being discharged, but only that she failed to sign for the discharge instructions. Lection and her husband's testimony that Syed told them to "go home" is some evidence that Lection was discharged, and Syed testified several times he would not have discharged Lection without having first consulted Dyll. Contrary to Dyll's assertions, the evidence does not conclusively prove no opportunity existed for the formation of a physician-patient relationship.

Dyll next asserts that the evidence conclusively establishes that he made no affirmative acts toward treating Lection. Dyll states that he never met or talked to Lection, examined Lection, performed any tests or reviewed any test results on her, or sent her a bill for his services. Dyll contends he merely discussed treatment alternatives with Syed as a professional colleague. The summary judgment evidence shows Syed contacted Dyll because he was the on-call neurologist who had an obligation to the hospital to assist, and not merely because Dyll was a colleague. Although Syed testified that he remained Lection's physician, there is evidence that Syed sought and relied upon Dyll's diagnosis and treatment plan. Syed testified he intended to rely on the on-call neurologist's determination of whether Lection needed to be admitted and that he could have called Lection and told her to return to the hospital for admission if necessary. The summary judgment record contains evidence that Dyll diagnosed Lection's condition, told Syed that no other treatment was necessary, and assured Syed that it was "all right" for her to have left the hospital. These statements constitute an evaluation of the information provided and a medical decision concerning Lection's need for treatment and admission to the hospital and thus are "affirmative acts" towards Lection's treatment. [ ] We conclude the summary judgment evidence does not conclusively establish that Dyll made no affirmative acts of treatment toward Lection.

Dyll next asserts that the Hospital By-Laws do not impose a contractual physician-patient relationship. Dyll states that the by-laws obligate an on-call physician to provide emergency care to patients in the emergency room only when (1) requested by the emergency room physician, and (2) when the medical needs of the patient fall within the scope of the on-call physician's practice, training, and abilities. Thus, Dyll concludes, the by-laws "did not contain any absolute contractual obligation by Dr. Dyll to treat Lection" but required a request from Syed. Dyll argues that because Lection left the emergency room, Syed never requested that Dyll provide treatment or admit Lection to the hospital. The summary judgment evidence does not conclusively prove Dyll's arguments. As discussed above, the record contains conflicting evidence of whether Lection had left the hospital during the Syed-Dyll telephone call. The record also contains conflicting evidence of whether Syed requested Dyll's assistance in determining Lection's diagnosis and treatment and whether to admit her. Although Dyll testified he never discussed treatment with Syed, Syed testified that he asked Dyll, "do I need to do anything further," and Dyll told him, "no, just have her come to my office on Monday." As for the issue of whether Dyll was asked whether to admit Lection to the hospital, Syed's testimony that he asked Dyll whether it was all right for Lection to have left the hospital implicitly inquires whether she should have been admitted to the hospital. Syed's testimony shows Dyll responded to this inquiry with his opinion that "it was okay that the patient had gone home." Syed also testified that Dyll "said nothing further needed to be done, then nothing further—and that includes admission." We conclude that Dyll's arguments are not supported by the uncontroverted summary judgment evidence. Construing all evidence in Lection's favor, the summary judgment record shows Syed requested from Dyll a diagnosis and treatment plan for Lection, and nothing in the summary judgment evidence shows that Dyll's diagnosis of hemiplegic migraine and recommendation of no further treatment was not within the scope of his practice, training, and abilities. Dyll's argument that the Hospital By-Laws do not impose a contractual physician-patient relationship lacks merit.

* * *

CONCLUSION

Because Dyll failed to conclusively establish that no physician-patient relationship existed between Lection and him, we conclude the trial court erred in granting summary judgment in favor of Dyll. We resolve Lection's issue in her favor.

* * *

We reverse the trial court's judgment and remand the cause for further proceedings.

NOTES AND QUESTIONS

1. *Formation as a Prerequisite. Lection* reflects the doctrine that formation of a doctor-patient relationship is a pre-requisite to a patient's maintaining any sort of professional liability claim against a physician. The plaintiff in *Lection* filed a claim for medical malpractice against Dr. Dyll, and Dyll moved for summary judgment in response on the theory that he did not assent to treating the plaintiff as a patient. Additionally, the opinion reveals that determining whether a doctor-patient relationship was formed requires a factual inquiry into the words and conduct of the patient and physician. This inquiry often precludes summary judgment, as it did in *Lection*.

2. *Limited Analogy to Contract Formation.* The physician-patient relationship can be considered initially as a contractual one. Physicians have no obligation to offer services that a patient may require that are outside their competence and training; or services outside the scope of the original physician-patient agreement, in which the physician has limited the contract to a type of procedure, to an office visit, or to consultation only.

An express written contract is rarely drafted for specific physician-patient interactions. Thus, courts often draw an analogy between the formation of a physician-patient relationship and the formation of an implied contract.

The apparent voluntariness of the physician-patient relationship and its reciprocity, i.e., a fee for a service, or consideration, make the relationship look like a traditional contract. In other ways, however, the analogy to a contract is limited. Most notably, the terms of the contract are largely fixed in advance of any bargaining by standards of care and fiduciary obligations (e.g., confidentiality) that the physician must meet at the risk of professional liability. See Norton v. Hamilton, 89 S.E.2d 809, 812 (Ga. 1955) ("[t]he duty of a physician or surgeon to bring skill and care to the amelioration of the condition of his patient arises not only from the implied contract between the physician and his patient, . . . but such duty also has its foundation in public considerations which are inseparable from the nature and exercise of his calling . . . "). The exact nature of the work to be done by the physician is usually vaguely defined at best. In the end, "[a] curious combination of tort and contract—'contorts'—guides the physician-patient relationship." E. Haavi Morreim, Consumer-Defined Health Plans: Emerging Challenges from Tort and Contract, 39 J. Health L. 307, 327 (2006). It is a contract into which we impute standard intentions and reasonable expectations. See Robert Goodin, Protecting the Vulnerable 63, 64–65 (1985).

For these reasons, courts rarely recognize breach of contract as a claim that a patient may bring against a physician when the patient alleges harm resulting from treatment. Similarly, courts often refuse to enforce exculpatory clauses in hospital admission or consent forms. See, e.g., Belshaw v. Feinstein, 65 Cal. Rptr. 788 (1968) (pre-operative waiver signed by patient releasing physician of any and all liability for risks associated with or untoward consequences resulting from surgery was void as against public policy because the waiver was the kind of contract that affects the public's interest).

3. *Informal Consultations.* When a physician treating a patient consults by telephone or otherwise with another physician, some courts are reluctant to find a doctor-patient relationship created by such a conversation. The concern is that such informal conferences will be deterred by the fear of liability. See Reynolds v. Decatur Memorial Hosp., 277 Ill. App. 3d 80, 214 Ill. Dec. 44, 49, 660 N.E.2d 235, 240 (1996). Others find a duty in such a consultation even when the consulting physician is not on-call. See, e.g., Diggs v. Arizona Cardiologists, Ltd., 198 Ariz. 198, 8 P.3d 386 (2000).

4. *Third Party Contracts with Physicians.* Through contracts with hospitals and insurers, physicians can bind themselves to treat individuals they have yet to meet. For example, in *Lection* the defendant-physician was the neurologist on call for emergencies at the hospital at the time the plaintiff was treated in the hospital's emergency department. The court relied on the hospital's "on-call" policy in its determination that material questions of fact existed as to whether the defendant physician had agreed with the hospital that, while he was the on-call neurologist, he would treat all persons who came to the hospital's emergency department in need of neurologic services.

The same issue may arise from network agreements between physicians and insurers. Most physicians are part of managed care networks and therefore have a contractual relationship with the plan that requires them to treat subscribers. In Hand v. Tavera, 864 S.W.2d 678 (Ct. App. Texas 1993), the plaintiff went to the emergency room complaining of a headache. Dr. Tavera was the doctor responsible for authorizing admissions, and he sent Hand home and recommended outpatient treatment. Hand sued Tavera for malpractice after suffering a stroke. Dr. Tavera defended on the grounds that no physician-patient relationship existed.

The court reversed the trial court's grant of summary judgment, holding that contracts between Hand and his insurer and between Hand's insurer and Dr. Tavera's employer created a treatment relationship. The court explained:

> Hand paid premiums to Humana to purchase medical care in advance of need; Humana met its obligation to Hand and its other enrollees by employing Tavera's group to treat them; and Tavera's medical group agreed to treat Humana enrollees in exchange for the fees received from Humana. In effect, Hand had paid in advance for the services of the Humana plan doctor on duty that night, who happened to be Tavera, and the physician-patient relationship existed. We hold that when the health-care plan's insured shows up at a participating hospital emergency room, and the plan's doctor on call is consulted about treatment or admission, there is a physician-patient relationship between the doctor and the insured.

5. *Duty in the Absence of a Relationship.* On occasion, courts have recognized a duty to safeguard individuals even in the absence of a treatment relationship. The duty is owed to those who are at risk of harm due to a condition diagnosed or treatment prescribed by the physician. The duty is owed most often to those with whom the patient lives, and it obligates a physician to

warn those individuals whom the physician knows or should know are at risk of being harmed by the physician's patient. For example, in Bradshaw v. Daniel, 854 S.W.2d 865 (Tenn. 1993), the state Supreme Court held that a physician owed a duty to warn the wife of the physician's patient that she was at risk of contracting Rocky Mountain Spotted Fever because the physician had diagnosed the disease in the wife's husband and because ticks carrying the disease were likely clustered in or near her home, posing a risk of infecting others in the patient's household. The court specifically held that this duty attached despite the fact that the physician and the patient's wife had not formed a treatment relationship with each other.

A physician's duty to warn such third parties has also been recognized even when the third party is not known to the patient or physician at the time of diagnosis or treatment. For example, in Duvall v. Goldin, 362 N.W.2d 275 (Mich. Ct. App. 1984), a Michigan court of appeals held that a physician could be liable to a third party injured in a car accident for failing to instruct the physician's patient—whom the physician had diagnosed with epilepsy—not to drive so as to avoid the risk that the patient could experience a seizure while driving and cause an accident.

Professor Richard Saver argues that such third-party cases evidence both legal and ethical duties of physicians to protect population health in addition to the individual medical interests of their patients. See Richard S. Saver, Physicians' Elusive Public Health Duties, 99 N.C. L. Rev. 923 (2021). He highlights the importance of such duties in addressing the COVID-19 pandemic as well as other threats to public health, and he concludes that these obligations are under-developed and poorly understood. "Law generally obscures physicians' public health duties with limited, ad hoc recognition and insufficient theorization for the source and strength of these duties." Id. at 984. This shortcoming, he says, undermines population health because "[p]hysicians occupy a unique strategic role embedded between the patient, other patients, and society and perform critical sentinel, gatekeeper, and learned intermediary functions that are indispensable to effective public health protection." Id.

III. DUTY NOT TO ABANDON A PATIENT

Among the common law duties triggered by the formation of a doctor-patient relationship is the physician's duty not to abandon a patient. As the materials in this section reveal, the common law generally does not impose a legal duty on physicians to aid individuals in need of medical care unless and until a physician forms a treatment relationship, but at that point the physician becomes obligated to continue treatment until the patient's medical need is resolved. This legal duty is subject to only a few exceptions.

Abandonment claims are often associated with allegations of discrimination by physicians against individuals based on race, disability or other immutable personal characteristics. While the materials in this chapter address doctrinal elements, we revisit the invidious discrimination that can give rise to abandonment claims in Chapter 6.

RICKS V. BUDGE

Supreme Court of Utah, 1937.
64 P.2d 208.

EPHRAIM HANSON, JUSTICE.

This is an action for malpractice against the defendants who are physicians and surgeons at Logan, Utah, and are copartners doing business under the name and style of the "Budge Clinic." . . . [P]laintiff alleges that he was suffering from an infected right hand and was in immediate need of medical and surgical care and treatment, and there was danger of his dying unless he received such treatment; that defendants for the purpose of treating plaintiff sent him to the Budge Memorial Hospital [BMH] at Logan, Utah; that while at the hospital and while he was in need of medical and surgical treatment, defendants refused to treat or care for plaintiff and abandoned his case. . . .

. . . The evidence shows that on or about March 8, 1935, plaintiff caught the middle finger of his right hand on a barbed wire. Soon thereafter the finger and hand began to swell and became reddened. In the early morning of March 11th, plaintiff went to the Budge Memorial Hospital to seek treatment from the defendants. Dr. S. M. Budge, one of the defendants, was performing an emergency operation at the hospital at the time plaintiff arrived. Immediately on finishing the operation, he made an examination of plaintiff to determine the nature and extent of plaintiff's injury and the treatment necessary therefor. Dr. Budge made two lateral incisions in the finger, waited a few hours to see the result, and then later the same morning deepened the incisions in order to reach the pus, which he believed had developed. A gauze wick was then put in each incision for the purpose of drainage.

* * *

[T]he evidence shows that when plaintiff left the hospital on March 15th, Dr. [S.M.] Budge advised him to continue the same treatment that had been given him at the hospital, and that if the finger showed any signs of getting worse at any time, plaintiff was to return at once to Dr. Budge for further treatment; that on the morning of March 17th, plaintiff telephoned Dr. Budge, and explained the condition of his hand; that he was told by the doctor to come to his office, and in pursuance of the doctor's request, plaintiff reported to the doctor's office at 2 p.m. of that day. Dr. Budge again examined the hand, and told plaintiff the hand was worse; he called in Dr. D.C. Budge, another of the defendants, who examined the hand, scraped it some, and indicated thereon where the hand should be opened. Dr. S.M. Budge said to plaintiff: "You have got to go back to the hospital." . . . Within a short time after the arrival of plaintiff, Dr. S.M. Budge arrived at the hospital. Plaintiff testified: "He [meaning Dr. S.M. Budge] came into my room and said, 'You are owing us. I am not going to touch you until that account is taken care of.' " (The account referred to was, according to plaintiff, of some years' standing and did not relate to any charge for services being then rendered.) Plaintiff testified that he did not know what to say to the doctor, but that he finally asked the doctor if he was going to take care of him, and the doctor replied: "No, I am not going to take care of you. I would not take you to the operating table and operate on you and keep you here thirty days, and then there is another $30.00 at the office, until your account is taken care of." Plaintiff replied: "If that is the idea, if you will furnish me a little help, I will try to move."

[A]fter being dressed, he left [BMH] to seek other treatment. At that time it was raining. He walked to the Cache Valley Hospital [CVH], a few blocks away, and there met Dr. Randall, who examined the hand. Dr. Randall testified that when the plaintiff arrived at [CVH], the hand was swollen with considerable fluid oozing from it; that the lower two-thirds of the forearm was red and swollen from the infection which extended up in the arm, and that there was some fluid also oozing from the back of the hand, and that plaintiff required immediate surgical attention; that immediately after the arrival of plaintiff at the hospital he made an incision through the fingers and through the palm of the hand along the tendons that led from the palm, followed those tendons as far as there was any bulging, opened it up thoroughly all the way to the base of the hand, and put drain tubes in. . . . About two weeks after the plaintiff entered [CVH], it became necessary to amputate the middle finger and remove about an inch of the metacarpal bone.

* * *

Defendants contend: (1) That there was no contract of employment between plaintiff and defendants and that defendants in the absence of a valid contract were not obligated to proceed with any treatment; and (2) that if there was such a contract, there was no evidence that the refusal of Dr. S.M. Budge to operate or take care of plaintiff resulted in any damage to plaintiff.

* * *

Under this evidence, it cannot be said that the relation of physician and patient did not exist on March 17th. It had not been terminated after its commencement on March 11th. When the plaintiff left the hospital on March 15th, he understood that he was to report to Dr. S.M. Budge if the occasion required and was so requested by the doctor. Plaintiff's return to the doctor's office was on the advice of the doctor. While at the doctor's office, both Dr. S.M. Budge and Dr. D.C. Budge examined plaintiff's hand

and they ordered that he go at once to the hospital for further medical attention. That plaintiff was told by the doctor to come to the doctor's office and was there examined by him and directed to go to the hospital for further treatment would create the relationship of physician and patient. That the relationship existed at the time the plaintiff was sent to the hospital on March 17th cannot be seriously questioned.

We believe the law is well settled that a physician or surgeon, upon undertaking an operation or other case, is under the duty, in the absence of an agreement limiting the service, of continuing his attention, after the first operation or first treatment, so long as the case requires attention. The obligation of continuing attention can be terminated only by the cessation of the necessity which gave rise to the relationship, or by the discharge of the physician by the patient, or by the withdrawal from the case by the physician after giving the patient reasonable notice so as to enable the patient to secure other medical attention. A physician has the right to withdraw from a case, but if the case is such as to still require further medical or surgical attention, he must, before withdrawing from the case, give the patient sufficient notice so the patient can procure other medical attention if he desires.[ ]

* * *

We cannot say as a matter of law that plaintiff suffered no damages by reason of the refusal of Dr. S.M. Budge to further treat him. The evidence shows that from the time plaintiff left the office of the defendants up until the time that he arrived at [CVH] his hand continued to swell; that it was very painful; that when he left [BMH] he was in such condition that he did not know whether he was going to live or die. That both his mental and physical suffering must have been most acute cannot be questioned. While the law cannot measure with exactness such suffering and cannot determine with absolute certainty what damages, if any, plaintiff may be entitled to, still those are questions which a jury under proper instructions from the court must determine.

* * *

FOLLAND, JUSTICE (concurring in part, dissenting in part).

* * *

. . . The theory of plaintiff as evidenced in his complaint is that there was no continued relationship from the first employment but that a new relationship was entered into. He visited the clinic on March 17th; the Doctors Budge examined his hand and told him an immediate operation was necessary and for him to go to the hospital. I do not think a new contract was entered into at that time. There was no consideration for any implied promise that Dr. Budge or the Budge Clinic would assume the responsibility of another operation and the costs and expenses incident thereto. As soon as Dr. Budge reached the hospital he opened negotiations with the plaintiff which might have resulted in a contract, but before any contract arrangement was made the plaintiff decided to leave the hospital and seek attention elsewhere. As soon as he could dress himself he walked away. There is conflict in the evidence as to the conversation. Plaintiff testified in effect that Dr. Budge asked for something to be done about an old account. The doctor's testimony in effect was that he asked that some arrangement be made to take care of the doctor's bill and expenses for the ensuing operation and treatment at the hospital. The result, however, was negative. No arrangement was made. The plaintiff made no attempt whatsoever to suggest to the doctor any way by which either the old account might be taken care of or the expenses of the ensuing operation provided for. . . . Dr. Budge had a right to refuse to incur the obligation and responsibility incident to one or more operations and the treatment and attention which would be necessary. If it be assumed that the contract relationship of physician and patient existed prior to this conversation, either as resulting from the first employment or that there was an implied contract entered into at the clinic, yet Dr. Budge had the right with proper notice to discontinue the relationship. While plaintiff's condition was acute and needed immediate attention, he received such immediate attention at [CVH]. There was only a delay of an hour or two, and part of that delay is accounted for by reason of the fact that the doctor at [CVH] would not operate until some paper, which plaintiff says he did not read, was signed. Plaintiff said he could not sign it but that it was signed by his brother before the operation was performed. We are justified in believing that by means of this written obligation, provision was made for the expenses and fees about to be incurred. I am satisfied from my reading of the record that no injury or damage resulted from the delay occasioned by plaintiff leaving the Budge Hospital and going to [CVH]. He was not in such desperate condition but that he was able to walk the three or four blocks between the two hospitals. . . .

NOTES AND QUESTIONS

1. *Elements of an Abandonment Claim.* While stated differently in various jurisdictions, the elements of an abandonment claim are (1) a duty to treat the plaintiff, (2) a breach of that duty by withdrawing from care or failing to provide necessary care in a timely manner, which (3) is the proximate cause of (4) compensable injury to the plaintiff. See McGulpin v. Bessmer, 43 N.W.2d 121 (Iowa 1950); Cox v. Jones, 470 N.W.2d 23 (Iowa 1991); Newman v. Sonnenberg, 81 P.3d 808 (Utah App. 2003); King v. Fisher, 918 S.W.2d 108 (Tex. App. 1996); Lee v. Dewbre, 362 S.W.2d 900 (Tex. App. 1962).

As demonstrated in *Ricks*, the first element—a duty to treat the plaintiff— is addressed generally by resolving the issue of whether the doctor and patient had formed a treatment relationship. More recently, some courts have distinguished between the moment the doctor-patient relationship is established and the moment when the physician begins providing medical services. See, e.g., Newman v. Sonnenberg, 81 P.3d 808 (Utah App. 2003) (plaintiff failed to allege an abandonment claim where her complaint alleged that she formed a treatment relationship with defendant-dentist, but failed to allege that "treatment" had commenced, when the dentist refused to begin performing a root canal after having examined plaintiff, determined that she required a root canal, and administered local anesthetic). Where a patient's condition can worsen significantly if left untreated during even a short period of time, courts recognize that the duty is breached when a physician fails to provide care in a timely manner. See, e.g., McGulpin v. Bessmer, 43 N.W.2d 121 (Iowa 1950) (defendant liable for abandonment due to allowing several days to pass without amputating plaintiff's foot and without arranging for another physician to do so).

2. *Expert Testimony.* Courts may require expert testimony to prove any element of the claim where the interpreting the facts relevant to the element requires knowledge beyond that of a lay person. See, e.g., Newman v. Sonnenberg, 81 P.3d 808 (Utah App. 2003) (expert testimony required to establish when "treatment" began in context of a root canal).

3. *No Duty to Initiate a Relationship.* Because the common law duty to treat depends on the assent of a physician to enter into a treatment relationship with another person, it does not assure individuals that a physician will render aid when needed. Absent a statute or contract obligation, the common law leaves physicians free to ignore the medical needs of those who might ask for their help. Is this consistent with medical ethics? The American Medical Association's Code of Medical Ethics states that physicians are "free to choose whom they serve," but it makes an exception for "emergencies." Principles of Medical Ethics, VI (2001 revision). What, if any, ethical foundation is there for an expectation that physicians treat those in need, whether in an emergency or otherwise? Should the law be used to enforce any such ethical obligation?

4. *Good Samaritan Statutes.* Physicians point to the risk of malpractice liability as a reason some are reluctant to assist those in need of care outside their professional practices (e.g., volunteering to stop and render aid at the scene of a car accident). To alleviate this concern, all jurisdictions have enacted so-called Good Samaritan statutes that immunize physicians from liability in such circumstances. See *infra* section VI.

5. *Claims Against Institutions.* As addressed in Chapter 6, the common law duty to treat also applies to hospitals and their emergency departments. To prevent hospital emergency departments from refusing to treat individuals who come to the ER seeking care, a federal statute—the Emergency Medical Treatment and Labor Act—requires hospitals participating in Medicare to enter into a limited treatment relationship with those individuals to assess whether they are experiencing a medical emergency and, if so, to either provide care or stabilize their conditions before transferring them to another facility willing to provide care.

IV. INFORMED CONSENT: THE PHYSICIAN'S OBLIGATION

A. ORIGINS OF THE INFORMED CONSENT DOCTRINE

Informed consent has developed out of strong judicial deference toward individual autonomy, reflecting both a belief that an individual has a right to be free from nonconsensual interference with his or her person, and a basic moral principle that it is wrong to force another to act against his or her will. Justice Cardozo articulated this principle in the medical context in Schloendorff v. Society of New York Hospital, 211 N.Y. 125, 105 N.E. 92 (1914): "Every human being of adult years and sound mind has a right to determine what shall be done with his own body . . . ."

Informed consent doctrine has guided medical decision-making by setting boundaries for the doctor-patient relationship and is one of the forces altering the attitudes of a new generation of doctors toward their patients. Informed consent is a foundation for federal regulations on human experimentation (see Chapter 20), and the touchstone for end-of-life decision-making (see Chapters 18 and 19). The consent forms that health care institutions require all patients to sign upon admission and before various procedures are the most concrete manifestations of the doctrine.

Professor Alexander Capron has argued that the doctrine can serve six salutary functions. Informed consent can:

1) protect individual autonomy;

2) protect the patient's status as a human being;

3) avoid fraud or duress;

4) encourage doctors to carefully consider their decisions;

5) foster rational decision-making by the patient; and

6) involve the public generally in medicine.

Alexander Capron, Informed Consent in Catastrophic Disease Research and Treatment, 123 U. Penn. L. Rev. 340, 365–76 (1974).

Current research suggests that patient health outcomes may in fact improve if patients are fully involved in understanding their treatments and their illness, and in managing their own treatments to a greater extent. We are therefore moving beyond informed consent to a more robust model of "patient engagement" and "activation." As one study argues, "[t]he assumption is that if individual patients made more informed health care choices, were better able to manage their own conditions, and adopted healthier lifestyles, their health care costs would be lessened." The quality of care is also expected to improve when patients are engaged in their own care. See generally Judith H. Hibbard, Jessica Greene, and Valerie Overton, Patients with Lower Activation Associated With Higher Costs: Delivery Systems Should Know Their Patients' 'Scores', 32 Health Affairs 216 (2013); Yves Longtin et. al., Patient Participation: Current Knowledge and Applicability to Patient Safety, 85 Mayo Clin. Proc. 53 (2010). This is not just a policy debate. Patient engagement and shared decision-making are two central components of new methods for health care delivery and payment under the Affordable Care Act (ACA). See discussion of "meaningful use," Medical Homes, and the Medicare Shared Savings program, Chapters 11 and 13 below.

The informed consent model, although longstanding, has been an unnatural graft onto medical practice. See Jay Katz, The Silent World of Doctor and Patient (1984). The judicial development of informed consent into a distinct doctrine can be roughly divided into three periods, according to Katz. During the first period, up to the mid-twentieth century, courts built upon the law of battery and required little more than disclosure by doctors of their proposed treatment. The second period saw an emerging judicial policy that doctors should disclose the alternatives to a proposed treatment and their risks, as well as the risks of the proposed treatment itself. The third period, from 1972 to the present, has seen legislative retrenchment and judicial inertia. See also Peter H. Schuck, Rethinking Informed Consent, 103 Yale L.J. 899, 900–05 (1994) (describing the rise of the informed-consent doctrine after 1957).

During the first period of doctrinal development, the doctrine of battery provided the theoretical underpinnings for a cause of action. The doctrine of battery protects a patient's physical integrity from harmful contacts and her personal dignity from unwanted bodily contact; it requires only a showing that the patient was not informed of the very nature of the medical touching, typically a surgical procedure. Physical injury is not necessary. When a surgeon, in the course of surgery, removes or operates upon an organ other than the one he and the patient discussed, a battery action lies.

The procedural and other advantages of a battery-based action tip the scales substantially in the favor of the patient. First, the focus is on the patient's right to be free from a non-consensual touching. The physician has few defenses to a battery. Second, the plaintiff need not prove through expert testimony what the standard of care was; the only proof needed is that the physician failed to explain to the patient the nature and character of the particular procedure. Third, to prove causation, the plaintiff need only show that a nonconsensual touching occurred.

Today, a patient treated without her consent still may bring a battery action against the treating physician in most jurisdictions. See, e.g., Allison

v. Brown, 293 Va. 617, 801 S.E.2d 761 (2017). Yet claims for treatment in the complete absence of patient consent are rare. But see Chapter 16, Section V for examples of the problem of unwanted or coerced sterilizations against vulnerable populations. More commonly, a claim for a breach of the duty to obtain informed consent to treatment alleges that a physician failed to disclose important information to the patient prior to obtaining the patient's consent. Such allegations are based in negligence.

As you read the cases in this section, ask how far the courts have gone toward permitting patients to control treatment decisions that affect them. Consider also what a plaintiff must show to make out an informed consent case in various jurisdictions. Finally, ask if any other processes are likely to serve the purposes of informed consent more efficiently, and with less adverse effect on the doctor-patient relationship. Has the law improved the doctor-patient relationship?

B. THE LEGAL FRAMEWORK OF INFORMED CONSENT

1.   Negligence as a Basis for Recovery

CANTERBURY V. SPENCE

United States Court of Appeals, District of Columbia Circuit, 1972.
464 F.2d 772.

SPOTTSWOOD W. ROBINSON, III, CIRCUIT JUDGE:

This appeal is from a judgment entered in the District Court on verdicts directed for the two appellees at the conclusion of plaintiff-appellant Canterbury's case in chief. His action sought damages for personal injuries allegedly sustained as a result of an operation negligently performed by appellee Spence, a negligent failure by Dr. Spence to disclose a risk of serious disability inherent in the operation, and negligent post-operative care by appellee Washington Hospital Center. On close examination of the record, we find evidence which required submission of these issues to the jury. We accordingly reverse the judgment as to each appellee and remand the case to the District Court for a new trial.

I

The record we review tells a depressing tale. A youth troubled only by back pain submitted to an operation without being informed of a risk of paralysis incidental thereto. A day after the operation he fell from his hospital bed after having been left without assistance while voiding. A few hours after the fall, the lower half of his body was paralyzed, and he had to be operated on again. Despite extensive medical care, he has never been what he was before. Instead of the back pain, even years later, he hobbled about on crutches, a victim of paralysis of the bowels and urinary incontinence. In a very real sense this lawsuit is an understandable search for reasons.

... In December, 1958, [Canterbury, then 19 years old,] began to experience severe pain between his shoulder blades. He consulted two general practitioners, but the medications they prescribed failed to eliminate the pain. Thereafter, appellant secured an appointment with Dr. Spence, who is a neurosurgeon.

* * *

[A diagnostic procedure] revealed a "filling defect" in the region of the fourth thoracic vertebra. . . . Dr. Spence told appellant that he would have to undergo a laminectomy—the excision of the posterior arch of the vertebra—to correct what he suspected was a ruptured disc. Appellant did not raise any objection to the proposed operation nor did he probe into its exact nature.

[Canterbury's mother also spoke by phone to Dr. Spence about the proposed surgery.] Dr. Spence told her that the surgery was occasioned by a suspected ruptured disc. Mrs. Canterbury then asked if the recommended operation was serious and Dr. Spence replied "not any more than any other operation." He added that he knew Mrs. Canterbury was not well off and that her presence in Washington would not be necessary. The testimony is contradictory as to whether during the course of the conversation Mrs. Canterbury expressed her consent to the operation. Appellant himself apparently did not converse again with Dr. Spence prior to the operation.

Dr. Spence performed the laminectomy on February 11 at the Washington Hospital Center. Mrs. Canterbury traveled to Washington, arriving on that date but after the operation was over, and signed a consent form at the hospital. The laminectomy revealed several anomalies . . . . A thin hypodermic needle was inserted into the spinal cord to aspirate any cysts which might have been present, but no fluid emerged. In suturing the wound, Dr. Spence attempted to relieve the pressure on the spinal cord by enlarging the dura—the outer protective wall of the spinal cord—at the area of swelling.

For approximately the first day after the operation appellant recuperated normally, but then suffered a fall and an almost immediate setback. Since there is some conflict as to precisely when or why appellant fell, we reconstruct the events from the evidence most favorable to him. Dr. Spence left orders that appellant was to remain in bed during the process of voiding. These orders were changed to direct that voiding be done out of bed, and the jury could find that the change was made by hospital personnel. Just prior to the fall, appellant summoned a nurse and was given a receptacle for use in voiding, but was then left unattended. Appellant testified that during the course of the endeavor he slipped off the side of the bed, and that there was no one to assist him, or side rail to prevent the fall.

Several hours later, appellant began to complain that he could not move his legs and that he was having trouble breathing; paralysis seems to have been virtually total from the waist down. Dr. Spence was notified on the night of February 12, and he rushed to the hospital. Mrs. Canterbury signed another consent form and appellant was again taken into the operating room. The surgical wound was reopened and Dr. Spence created a gusset to allow the spinal cord greater room in which to pulsate.

Appellant's control over his muscles improved somewhat after the second operation but he was unable to void properly. . . . For several years after his discharge he was under the care of several specialists, and at all times was under the care of a urologist. At the time of the trial in April, 1968, appellant required crutches to walk, still suffered from urinal incontinence and paralysis of the bowels, and wore a penile clamp.

. . . The damages appellant claims include extensive pain and suffering, medical expenses, and loss of earnings.

II

* * *

At the close of appellant's case in chief, each defendant moved for a directed verdict and the trial judge granted both motions. The basis of the ruling, he explained, was that appellant had failed to produce any medical evidence indicating negligence on Dr. Spence's part in diagnosing appellant's malady or in performing the laminectomy; that there was no proof that Dr. Spence's treatment was responsible for appellant's disabilities; and that notwithstanding some evidence to show negligent post-operative care, an absence of medical testimony to show causality precluded submission of the case against the hospital to the jury. The judge did not allude specifically to the alleged breach of duty by Dr. Spence to divulge the possible consequences of the laminectomy.

We reverse. The testimony of appellant and his mother that Dr. Spence did not reveal the risk of paralysis from the laminectomy made out a prima facie case of violation of the physician's duty to disclose which Dr. Spence's explanation did not negate as a matter of law. . . .

III

* * *

. . . True consent to what happens to one's self is the informed exercise of a choice, and that entails an opportunity to evaluate knowledgeably the options available and the risks attendant upon each. The average patient has little or no understanding of the medical arts, and ordinarily has only his physician to whom he can look for enlightenment with which to reach an intelligent decision. From these almost axiomatic considerations springs the need, and in turn the requirement, of a reasonable divulgence by physician to patient to make such a decision possible.

A physician is under a duty to treat his patient skillfully but proficiency in diagnosis and therapy is not the full measure of his responsibility. The cases demonstrate that the physician is under an obligation to communicate specific information to the patient when the exigencies of reasonable care call for it. Due care may require a physician perceiving symptoms of bodily abnormality to alert the patient to the condition. It may call upon the physician confronting an ailment which does not respond to his ministrations to inform the patient thereof. It may command the physician to instruct the patient as to any limitations to be presently observed for his own welfare, and as to any precautionary therapy he should seek in the future. It may oblige the physician to advise the patient of the need for or desirability of any alternative treatment promising greater benefit than that being pursued. Just as plainly, due care normally demands that the physician warn the patient of any risks to his well-being which contemplated therapy may involve.

The context in which the duty of risk-disclosure arises is invariably the occasion for decision as to whether a particular treatment procedure is to be undertaken. To the physician, whose training enables a self-satisfying evaluation, the answer may seem clear, but it is the prerogative of the patient, not the physician, to determine for himself the direction in which his interests seem to lie. To enable the patient to chart his course understandably, some familiarity with the therapeutic alternatives and their hazards becomes essential.

A reasonable revelation in these respects is not only a necessity but, as we see it, is as much a matter of the physician's duty. It is a duty to warn of the dangers lurking in the proposed treatment, and that is surely a facet of due care. It is, too, a duty to impart information which the patient has every right to expect. The patient's reliance upon the physician is a trust of the kind which traditionally has exacted obligations beyond those associated with arms-length transactions. His dependence upon the physician for information affecting his well-being, in terms of contemplated treatment, is well-nigh abject. As earlier noted, long before the instant litigation arose, courts had recognized that the physician had the responsibility of satisfying the vital informational needs of the patient. More recently, we ourselves have found "in the fiducial qualities of [the physician-patient] relationship the physician's duty to reveal to the patient that which in his best interests it is important that he should know." We now find, as a part of the physician's overall obligation to the patient, a similar duty of reasonable disclosure of the choices with respect to proposed therapy and the dangers inherently and potentially involved.

* * *

IV

Duty to disclose has gained recognition in a large number of American jurisdictions, but more largely on a different rationale. The majority of courts dealing with the problem have made the duty depend on whether it was the custom of physicians practicing in the community to make the particular disclosure to the patient. If so, the physician may be held liable for an unreasonable and injurious failure to divulge, but there can be no recovery unless the omission forsakes a practice prevalent in the profession. We agree that the physician's noncompliance with a professional custom to reveal, like any other departure from prevailing medical practice, may give rise to liability to the patient. We do not agree that the patient's cause of action is dependent upon the existence and nonperformance of a relevant professional tradition.

There are, in our view, formidable obstacles to acceptance of the notion that the physician's obligation to disclose is either germinated or limited by medical practice. To begin with, the reality of any discernible custom reflecting a professional concensus [sic] on communication of option and risk information to patients is open to serious doubt. We sense the danger that what in fact is no custom at all may be taken as an affirmative custom to maintain silence, and that physician-witnesses to the so-called custom may state merely their personal opinions as to what they or others would do under given conditions. We cannot gloss over the inconsistency between reliance on a general practice respecting divulgence and, on the other hand, realization that the myriad of variables among patients makes each case so different that its omission can rationally be justified only by the effect of its individual circumstances. Nor can we ignore the fact that to bind the disclosure obligation to medical usage is to arrogate the decision on revelation to the physician alone. Respect for the patient's right of self-determination on particular therapy demands a standard set by law for physicians rather than one which physicians may or may not impose upon themselves.

... The caliber of the performance exacted by the reasonable-care standard varies between the professional and non-professional worlds, and so also the role of professional custom. ...

* * *

The majority rule, moreover, is at war with our prior holdings that a showing of medical practice, however probative, does not fix the standard governing recovery for medical malpractice. Prevailing medical practice, we have maintained, has evidentiary value in determinations as to what the specific criteria measuring challenged professional conduct are and whether they have been met, but does not itself define the standard. That has been our position in treatment cases, where the physician's performance is ordinarily to be adjudicated by the special medical standard of due care. We see no logic in a different rule for nondisclosure cases, where the governing standard is much more largely divorced from professional considerations. And surely in nondisclosure cases the factfinder is not invariably functioning in an area of such technical complexity that it must be bound to medical custom as an inexorable application of the community standard of reasonable care.

Thus we distinguished, for purposes of duty to disclose, the special-and general-standard aspects of the physician-patient relationship. When medical judgment enters the picture and for that reason the special standard controls, prevailing medical practice must be given its just due. In all other instances, however, the general standard exacting ordinary care applies, and that standard is set by law. In sum, the physician's duty to disclose is governed by the same legal principles applicable to others in comparable situations, with modifications only to the extent that medical judgment enters the picture. We hold that the standard measuring performance of that duty by physicians, as by others, is conduct which is reasonable under the circumstances.

V

Once the circumstances give rise to a duty on the physician's part to inform his patient, the next inquiry is the scope of the disclosure the physician is legally obliged to make. The courts have frequently confronted this problem but no uniform standard defining the adequacy of the divulgence emerges from the decisions. Some have said "full" disclosure, a norm we are unwilling to adopt literally. It seems obviously prohibitive and unrealistic to expect physicians to discuss with their patients every risk of proposed treatment—no matter how small or remote—and generally unnecessary from the patient's viewpoint as well. Indeed, the cases speaking in terms of "full" disclosure appear to envision something less than total disclosure, leaving unanswered the question of just how much.

The larger number of courts, as might be expected, have applied tests framed with reference to prevailing fashion within the medical profession. . . . We have explored this rather considerable body of law but are unprepared to follow it. The duty to disclose, we have reasoned, arises from phenomena apart from medical custom and practice. The latter, we think, should no more establish the scope of the duty than its existence. Any definition of scope in terms purely of a professional standard is at odds with the patient's prerogative to decide on projected therapy himself. That prerogative, we have said, is at the very foundation of the duty to disclose, and both the patient's right to know and the physician's correlative obligation to tell him are diluted to the extent that its compass is dictated by the medical profession.

In our view, the patient's right of self-decision shapes the boundaries of the duty to reveal. That right can be effectively exercised only if the patient possesses enough information to enable an intelligent choice. The scope of the physician's communications to the patient, then, must be measured by the patient's need, and that need is the information material to the decision. Thus the test for determining whether a particular peril must be divulged is its materiality to the patient's decision: all risks potentially affecting the decision must be unmasked. And to safeguard the patient's interest in achieving his own determination on treatment, the law must itself set the standard for adequate disclosure.

Optimally for the patient, exposure of a risk would be mandatory whenever the patient would deem it significant to his decision, either singly or in combination with other risks. Such a requirement, however, would summon the physician to second-guess the patient, whose ideas on materiality could hardly be known to the physician. That would make an undue demand upon medical practitioners, whose conduct, like that of others, is to be measured in terms of reasonableness. Consonantly with orthodox negligence doctrine, the physician's liability for nondisclosure is to be determined on the basis of foresight, not hindsight; no less than any other aspect of negligence, the issue on nondisclosure must be approached from the viewpoint of the reasonableness of the physician's divulgence in terms of what he knows or should know to be the patient's informational needs. If, but only if, the fact-finder can say that the physician's communication was unreasonably inadequate is an imposition of liability legally or morally justified.

Of necessity, the content of the disclosure rests in the first instance with the physician. Ordinarily it is only he who is in position to identify particular dangers; always he must make a judgment, in terms of materiality, as to whether and to what extent revelation to the patient is called for. He cannot know with complete exactitude what the patient would consider important to his decision, but on the basis of his medical training and experience he can sense how the average, reasonable patient expectably would react. Indeed, with knowledge of, or ability to learn, his patient's background and current condition, he is in a position superior to that of most others—attorneys, for example—who are called upon to make judgments on pain of liability in damages for unreasonable miscalculation.

From these considerations we derive the breadth of the disclosure of risks legally to be required. The scope of the standard is not subjective as to either the physician or the patient; it remains objective with due regard for the patient's informational needs and with suitable leeway for the physician's situation. In broad outline, we agree that "[a] risk is thus material when a reasonable person, in what the physician knows or should know to be the patient's position, would be likely to attach significance to the risk or cluster of risks in deciding whether or not to forego the proposed therapy."

The topics importantly demanding a communication of information are the inherent and potential hazards of the proposed treatment, the alternatives to that treatment, if any, and the results likely if the patient remains untreated. The factors contributing significance to the dangerousness of a medical technique are, of course, the incidence of injury and the degree of the harm threatened. A very small chance of death or serious disablement may well be significant; a potential disability which dramatically outweighs the potential benefit of the therapy or the detriments of the existing malady may summon discussion with the patient.

There is no bright line separating the significant from the insignificant; the answer in any case must abide a rule of reason. Some dangers—infection, for example—are inherent in any operation; there is no obligation to communicate those of which persons of average sophistication are aware. Even more clearly, the physician bears no responsibility for discussion of hazards the patient has already discovered, or those having no apparent materiality to patients' decision on therapy. The disclosure doctrine, like others marking lines between permissible and impermissible behavior in medical practice, is in essence a requirement of conduct prudent under the circumstances. Whenever nondisclosure of particular risk information is open to debate by reasonable-minded men, the issue is for the finder of the facts.

VI

Two exceptions to the general rule of disclosure have been noted by the courts. Each is in the nature of a physician's privilege not to disclose, and the reasoning underlying them is appealing. Each, indeed, is but a recognition that, as important as is the patient's right to know, it is greatly outweighed by the magnitudinous circumstances giving rise to the privilege. The first comes into play when the patient is unconscious or otherwise incapable of consenting, and harm from a failure to treat is imminent and outweighs any harm threatened by the proposed treatment. When a genuine emergency of that sort arises, it is settled that the impracticality of conferring with the patient dispenses with need for it. Even in situations of that character the physician should, as current law requires, attempt to secure a relative's consent if possible. But if time is too short to accommodate discussion, obviously the physician should proceed with the treatment.

The second exception obtains when risk-disclosure poses such a threat of detriment to the patient as to become unfeasible or contraindicated from a medical point of view. It is recognized that patients occasionally become so ill or emotionally distraught on disclosure as to foreclose a rational decision, or complicate or hinder the treatment, or perhaps even pose psychological damage to the patient. Where that is so, the cases have generally held that the physician is armed with a privilege to keep the information from the patient, and we think it clear that portents of that type may justify the physician in action he deems medically warranted. The critical inquiry is whether the physician responded to a sound medical judgment that communication of the risk information would present a threat to the patient's well-being.

The physician's privilege to withhold information for therapeutic reasons must be carefully circumscribed, however, for otherwise it might devour the disclosure rule itself. The privilege does not accept the paternalistic notion that the physician may remain silent simply because divulgence might prompt the patient to forego therapy the physician feels the patient really needs. That attitude presumes instability or perversity for even the normal patient, and runs counter to the foundation principle that the patient should and ordinarily can make the choice for himself. Nor does the privilege contemplate operation save where the patient's reaction to risk information, as reasonable foreseen by the physician, is menacing. And even in a situation of that kind, disclosure to a close relative with a view to securing consent to the proposed treatment may be the only alternative open to the physician.

VII

No more than breach of any other legal duty does nonfulfillment of the physician's obligation to disclose alone establish liability to the patient. An unrevealed risk that should have been made known must materialize, for otherwise the omission, however unpardonable, is legally without consequence. Occurrence of the risk must be harmful to the patient, for negligence unrelated to injury is nonactionable. And, as in malpractice actions generally, there must be a causal relationship between the physician's failure to adequately divulge and damage to the patient.

A causal connection exists when, but only when, disclosure of significant risks incidental to treatment would have resulted in a decision against it. The patient obviously has no complaint if he would have submitted to the therapy notwithstanding awareness that the risk was one of its perils. On the other hand, the very purpose of the disclosure rule is to protect the patient against consequences which, if known, he would have avoided by foregoing the treatment. The more difficult question is whether the factual issue on causality calls for an objective or a subjective determination.

It has been assumed that the issue is to be resolved according to whether the factfinder believes the patient's testimony that he would not have agreed to the treatment if he had known of the danger which later ripened into injury. We think a technique which ties the factual conclusion on causation simply to the assessment of the patient's credibility is unsatisfactory. To be sure, the objective of risk-disclosure is preservation of the patient's interest in intelligent self-choice on proposed treatment, a matter the patient is free to decide for any reason that appeals to him. When, prior to commencement of therapy, the patient is sufficiently informed on risks and he exercises his choice, it may truly be said that he did exactly what he wanted to do. But when causality is explored at a postinjury trial with a professedly uninformed patient, the question whether he actually would have turned the treatment down if he had known the risks is purely hypothetical: "Viewed from the point at which he had to decide, would the patient have decided differently had he known something he did not know?" And the answer which the patient supplies hardly represents more than a guess, perhaps tinged by the circumstance that the uncommunicated hazard has in fact materialized.

In our view, this method of dealing with the issue on causation comes in second-best. It places the physician in jeopardy of the patient's hindsight and bitterness. It places the factfinder in the position of deciding whether a speculative answer to a hypothetical question is to be credited. It calls for a subjective determination solely on testimony of a patient-witness shadowed by the occurrence of the undisclosed risk.

Better it is, we believe, to resolve the causality issue on an objective basis: in terms of what a prudent person in the patient's position would have decided if suitably informed of all perils bearing significance. If adequate disclosure could reasonably be expected to have caused that person to decline the treatment because of the revelation of the kind of risk or danger that resulted in harm, causation is shown, but otherwise not. The patient's testimony is relevant on that score of course but it would not threaten to dominate the findings. And since that testimony would probably be appraised congruently with the factfinder's belief in its reasonableness, the case for a wholly objective standard for passing on causation is strengthened. Such a standard would in any event ease the fact-finding process and better assure the truth as its product.

VIII

In the context of trial of a suit claiming inadequate disclosure of risk information by a physician, the patient has the burden of going forward with evidence tending to establish prima facie the essential elements of the cause of action, and ultimately the burden of proof—the risk of nonpersuasion—on those elements. These are normal impositions upon moving litigants, and no reason why they should not attach in nondisclosure cases is apparent. The burden of going forward with evidence pertaining to a privilege not to disclose, however, rests properly upon the physician. This is not only because the patient has made out a prima facie case before an issue on privilege is reached, but also because any evidence bearing on the privilege is usually in the hands of the physician alone. Requiring him to open the proof on privilege is consistent with judicial policy laying such a burden on the party who seeks shelter from an exception to a general rule and who is more likely to have possession of the facts.

As in much malpractice litigation, recovery in nondisclosure lawsuits has hinged upon the patient's ability to prove through expert testimony that the physician's performance departed from medical custom. This is not surprising since, as we have pointed out, the majority of American jurisdictions have limited the patient's right to know to whatever boon can be found in medical practice. We have already discussed our disagreement with the majority rationale. We now delineate our view on the need for expert testimony in nondisclosure cases.

There are obviously important roles for medical testimony in such cases, and some roles which only medical evidence can fill. Experts are ordinarily indispensible to identify and elucidate for the factfinder the risks of therapy and the consequences of leaving existing maladies untreated. They are normally needed on issues as to the cause of any injury or disability suffered by the patient and, where privileges are asserted, as to the existence of any emergency claimed and the nature and seriousness of any impact upon the patient from risk-disclosure. Save for relative infrequent instances where questions of this type are resolvable wholly within the realm of ordinary human knowledge and experience, the need for the expert is clear.

The guiding consideration our decisions distill, however, is that medical facts are for medical experts and other facts are for any witnesses—expert or not—having sufficient knowledge and capacity to testify to them. It is evident that many of the issues typically involved in nondisclosure cases do not reside peculiarly within the medical domain. Lay witness testimony can competently establish a physician's failure to disclose particular risk information, the patient's lack of knowledge of the risk, and the adverse consequences following the treatment. Experts are unnecessary to a showing of the materiality of a risk to a patient's decision on treatment, or to the reasonably, expectable effect of risk disclosure on the decision. These conspicuous examples of permissible uses of nonexpert testimony illustrate the relative freedom of broad areas of the legal problem of risk nondisclosure from the demands for expert testimony that shackle plaintiffs' other types of medical malpractice litigation.

* * *

Reversed and remanded for a new trial.

NOTES AND QUESTIONS

1.   *Jurisdictional Split.* While every state requires physicians to disclose material treatment information to patients, they are split over how to test "materiality." According to a 2006 survey, twenty-five states employ the prudent-physician standard, two use a hybrid standard, and the rest adopted *Canterbury's* reasonable-patient standard. Jaime Staples King and Benjamin Moulton, Rethinking Informed Consent: The Case for Shared Medical Decisionmaking, 32 Am. J. Law & Med. 429, 493–501 (2006) (Appendix).

2.   *Pursuing Autonomy with Objective Legal Standards.* The values served by the informed consent doctrine—patient autonomy and dignity—are the values we generally associate with the tort of battery, rather than negligence. It is ironic that a doctrine developed to foster and recognize individual choice should be measured by an objective standard—the category under which both the prudent-physician and the reasonable-person tests fall. This disconnect was a primary basis for Jay Katz's 1984 critique of informed consent law in his iconic book, THE SILENT WORLD OF DOCTOR AND PATIENT, and it continues to be a target of criticism today. For example, see Maytal Gilboa & Omer Y. Pelled, The Costs of Having (Too) Many Choices: Reshaping the Doctrine of Informed Consent, 84 Brook. L. Rev. 367 (2019).

3.   *The Reasonable-Patient Standard and Expert Testimony.* The effect of a patient-oriented disclosure standard is to ease the plaintiff's burden of proof, because the trier of fact could find that a doctor acted unreasonably in failing to disclose, in spite of unrebutted expert medical testimony to the contrary. The question of whether a physician disclosed risks that a reasonable person would find material is for the trier of fact, and technical expertise is not required. Pedersen v. Vahidy, 209 Conn. 510, 552 A.2d 419 (1989). Expert testimony is still needed, however, to clarify the treatments and their probabilities of risks. Cross v. Trapp, 170 W.Va. 459, 294 S.E.2d 446, 455 (1982).

4.   *Common Categories of Disclosure.*

a.   Diagnosis and prognosis. This includes the medical steps preceding diagnosis, including tests and their alternatives. In addition to disclosing a patient's diagnosis, a physician should disclose the patient's prognosis with and without treatment. This also includes communicating to a patient that she is suffering from a fatal condition and the likelihood that treatment will prolong that patient's life. Yet, in communicating this information, a physician is not obligated to disclose mortality statistics. See Arato v. Avedon, 5 Cal. 4th 1172, 23 Cal. Rptr. 2d 131, 858 P.2d 598 (1993).

b.   Nature and purpose of the proposed treatment.

c.   Risks of the treatment. The threshold of disclosure, as the *Canterbury* court suggests, varies based on the interplay of the probability and the severity of the risk. Thus, a five percent risk of lengthened recuperation might be ignored, while a one percent risk of paralysis, as in *Canterbury*, or an even smaller risk of death, should be disclosed. See Cobbs v. Grant, 8 Cal. 3d 229,

104 Cal. Rptr. 505, 502 P.2d 1 (1972). The risk, even if small, may be significant to the particular plaintiff because of unique health considerations. See Hartke v. McKelway, 707 F.2d 1544, 1549 (D.C. Cir.1983).

d.   Treatment alternatives. Doctors should disclose those alternatives that are generally acknowledged within the medical community as feasible, see Martin v. Richards, 192 Wis. 2d 156, 531 N.W.2d 70, 78 (1995), their risks and consequences, and their probability of success. This is true even if the alternative is less hazardous or noninvasive. If the alternative is not regarded as a legitimate treatment option, it need not be disclosed to the patient. See Morris v. Ferriss, 669 So. 2d 1316 (La. App. 4 Cir. 1996).

e.   Consequences of patient refusal of tests or treatments. A physician should disclose to a patient the risk of refusing a proposed treatment or test. See Truman v. Thomas, 27 Cal. 3d 285, 165 Cal. Rptr. 308, 611 P.2d 902 (1980).

f.   Disclosing the tradeoffs of treatment versus watchful waiting. In a health care environment of cost-effective care, conservative practice is the goal—doing nothing and "watchful waiting" are desirable clinical approaches to patient care. A physician may have a duty to advise a patient of the option of choosing no treatment at all. See Wecker v. Amend, 22 Kan. App. 2d 498, 918 P.2d 658 (1996).

5.   *Exceptions to the Duty of Disclosure.* The duty to disclose does not apply in the case of threats to public health or to individual medical emergencies. A physician is permitted to presume that a patient in an emergency consents to stabilizing treatment. Additionally, disclosure is not required when a patient waives the right to disclosure or the patient already knows or should know the information. Moreover, a physician is not required to disclose information to a patient who does not have decision-making capacity, but the physician is obligated in such a case to fulfill the duty by disclosing information to the patient's decision-making surrogate.

Finally, the law recognizes that physicians have a "therapeutic privilege" to withhold information that, in the physician's estimation, would cause the patient to become ill or emotionally distraught if disclosed. Because this privilege has the potential to swallow the duty to disclose entirely—as noted by *Canterbury*—courts limit its use by requiring that the physician claiming the privilege "expressly testifies that his or her decision to withhold information was based on specific considerations in the individual patient's case and identify those considerations." Barcai v. Betwee, 98 Hawai'i 470, 50 P.3d 946 (2002).

6.   *State Legislation.* More than half of the states have enacted legislation addressing informed consent, largely in response to various "malpractice crises." The statutes take a variety of forms, from specific to general, but they all share the approach of moving the informed consent standard toward greater deference to medical judgment. A consent form, or other written documentation of the patient's verbal consent, is treated in many states as presumptively valid consent to the treatment at issue, with the

burden on the patient to rebut the presumption. See Jaime Staples King & Benjamin W. Moulton, *supra*, note 2, for a fifty-state review of the law of informed consent. Given the current state of legislative limitations on common law tort remedies, and the current national mood, it may be expected that the common law of informed consent will continue to be affected by legislative action.

7. *Disclosure as a Non-Delegable Duty.* Hospitals provide forms and develop systems to support the informed consent process, and health professionals other than physicians—such as nurses and physician assistants—routinely disclose treatment information to patients and obtain written consent from patients. Nonetheless, courts frequently hold that the duty to disclose is non-delegable, belonging solely to the treating physician. See Shinal v. Toms, 162 A.3d 429 (Pa. 2017); Dehart v. Jones, 310 So. 3d 658 (La. App. 2020). For a critique of courts' application of the non-delegation doctrine in informed consent law, see Robert Gatter, The Mysterious Survival of the Policy Against Informed Consent Liability for Hospitals, 81 Notre Dame L. Rev. 1203 (2006).

8. *The Two Steps of Causation.* Causation can only be established if there is a link between the failure of a doctor to disclose and the patient's injury. Two separate showings are required to establish causation. First, the plaintiff must establish decision-causation, i.e., that the physician's failure to disclose information caused the patient's consent. Second, the plaintiff must show injury-causation, i.e., that the consented-to procedure actually caused harm. The Wisconsin Supreme Court, interpreting *Canterbury* and its own prior rulings, delineated these two different causation steps in Prissel v. Physicians Ins. Co. of Wisconsin, Inc., 269 Wis. 2d 541, 674 N.W.2d 680 (App. 1993). In that case, the spouse and estate of a patient who died after cardiac surgery sued the surgeon for failure to obtain informed consent. Plaintiffs claimed that the surgeon had breached a duty to disclose that: a) prior to practicing in Wisconsin, he had been censured by a California hospital committee for failing to obtain needed assistance in complex surgeries; 2) the Wisconsin hospital in which the procedure took place required that he be assisted in his surgeries; and 3) he would use a physician assistant rather than another physician to assist in the decedent's surgery.

Following the plaintiffs' case, the trial court directed a verdict for the defendant-physician, ruling that plaintiffs had failed to carry their burden with respect to causation. On appeal, the state supreme court affirmed this ruling, and, in so doing, clarified the two forms of causation required for an informed consent claim.

> [T]he [trial] court [correctly] held that the second link in the causal chain required proof that the undisclosed risk must have been a substantial factor in producing the patient's injury. . . .

* * *

. . . [I]f the jury finds that a reasonable patient, suitably informed of the risks, benefits, and viable alternatives would have refused the proposed treatment, the jury must be asked whether the failure to disclose the necessary information was a cause of the patient's injury. [ ]. Accordingly, a plaintiff must prove not only that a reasonably prudent patient, adequately apprised of all material risks and viable alternatives, would have chosen a different course of treatment or care. In addition, the plaintiff must show that the undisclosed risk actually materialized and was caused by the treatment. [ ].

* * *

Here, the casual connection is missing. On the record before us, the jury would have had to speculate whether the disclosure in question would have caused a reasonable patient to decline treatment. The gravity of [the decedent]'s condition is undisputed. There is no evidence refuting his son's testimony that the cardiologist stated, in effect, that without surgery, [the decedent] was not likely to survive. There is no evidence that other more experienced or more competent doctors were available to perform the surgery. . . . Based on the record, a jury would have to speculate whether a reasonable patient, in [the decedent]'s position, would have refused surgery had [the defendant-physician] disclosed that in California he was required to use a surgeon for an assistant rather than a physician's assistant and would be using a physician's assistant during [the patient]' surgery.

Also, the second step is missing. Had the jury found that a patient in [the decedent]'s position would have declined the treatment if he had been so informed, evidence that the undisclosed risk actually caused any harm is lacking. There is no evidence that using the physician's assistant caused any harm. There is no evidence that had a surgeon assisted instead, [the defendant-physician] would have done anything differently or that the result would have been different.

Id. at ¶¶ 44–49.

9.   *Objective vs. Subjective Decision-Causation Standards.* Two tests for decision-causation have emerged: the objective reasonable patient test and the subjective particular patient test. The former asks whether a reasonable patient in the patient's position would have consented to treatment had the undisclosed information been disclosed. The subjective standard asks whether the plaintiff-patient would have consented to treatment. *Canterbury* adopted the objective test out of concern that a plaintiff's hindsight testimony would be self-serving. For the same reason, all but four jurisdictions have also adopted the objective standard for decision-causation. Evelyn M. Tenenbaum, Revitalizing Informed Consent and Protecting Patient Autonomy: An Appeal to Abandon Objective Causation, 64 Okla. L. Rev. 697 (2012). Under the objective standard, a patient's testimony is not required, but is admissible and relevant. Hartke v. McKelway, 707 F.2d 1544 (D.C. Cir.1983). Further, a subjective aspect may come into play: even if the plaintiff can establish that a

reasonable patient would not have consented if properly informed, evidence that the particular plaintiff would have consented if fully informed may be presented to the jury. Bourgeois v. McDonald, 622 So. 2d 684 (La. App. 4 Cir.1993).

10. *Duty to Disclose and the Constitution.* When a treating physician is a state actor, the informed consent doctrine takes on a constitutional dimension. Several federal circuit courts have held that the Fourteenth Amendment recognizes an individual's liberty interest to refuse unwanted medical treatment and that this liberty interest necessarily includes a right to receive from a physician all treatment information material to the decision of whether to consent to or refuse treatment. See Knight v. Grossman, 942 F.3d 336 (8th Cir. 2019); Pabon v. Wright, 459 F.3d 241 (2d Cir. 2006); Benson v. Terhune, 304 F.3d 874 (9th Cir. 2002); White v. Napoleon, 897 F.2d 103 (3d Cir. 1990). While each of these cases involved the treatment of a prisoner, the constitutional right they recognize is not limited to the prison context and is implicated whenever state action is satisfied. See Robert Gatter, A Prisoner's Constitutional Right to Medical Information: Doctrinally Flawed and A Threat to State Informed Consent Law, 45 Wake Forest L. Rev. 1025 (2010).

2.   Disclosure of Physician-Specific Risk Information

As the *Prissel* case above illustrates, patients may feel that information about the physician—especially the physician's qualifications, experience, or past performance problems—is material to their decision to consent to treatment. Courts, however, typically tread carefully in the thickets of mandated physician disclosure of experience and qualifications. If the patient asks questions specifically about these issues, a physician who equivocates may risk liability. For example, in Johnson v. Kokemoor, 199 Wis. 2d 615, 545 N.W.2d 495 (1996), the court held that evidence of a surgeon's limited experience operating on a particular kind of aneurysm was properly admitted at trial because, when "the plaintiff questioned the defendant regarding his experience, he replied that he had performed the surgery she required 'several' times; asked what he meant by 'several,' the defendant said 'dozens' and 'lots of times.' " In reality, the defendant had little experience with aneurysm surgery, having performed only thirty aneurysm surgeries during his residency, and all of them involved anterior circulation aneurysms—not the much more complex posterior circulation aneurysms suffered by the plaintiff.

Similarly, in Willis v. Bender, 596 F.3d 1244 (10th Cir. 2010), the defendant Bender, a general surgeon, perforated Marcy Willis' small bowel while performing a laparoscopic surgery to remove her gallbladder. Willis had asked Dr. Bender several questions before deciding to proceed, including whether he had ever been sued, whether he had had problems with his medical license, and the extent of his experience and track record with the laparoscopic procedure. The court observed that "Bender had in fact been sued several times, including by a family of a patient who had died after undergoing [the same procedure] performed by Bender in 2001." The court framed the issue as "not whether Bender had a duty under Wyoming's informed consent law to voluntarily disclose physician-specific information but rather whether he had a duty to truthfully answer Willis' physician-specific questions."

Courts have also recognized that, when evidence shows that clinical experience is or could be associated with greater risk, information about a physician's experience is material and thus is covered by the duty to disclose. In *Kokemoor* there was published clinical evidence that when physicians with experience as limited as the defendant's operated on a particular kind of aneurysm, it posed significantly higher surgical risks than did operations by more experienced surgeons. Consequently, the court held that this difference in risk was material in the same way a less risky alternative treatment is material. See also Andersen v. Khanna, 913 N.W.2d 526 (Iowa 2018) (inexperience may be material information subject to the duty to disclose).

Apart from these circumstances, however, courts are reluctant to find that a physician must disclose information about herself to a patient as part of the informed consent process. Instead, they generally hold that the duty to disclose extends only to the patient's condition and treatment options, not to the provider. For example, the court in Kaskie v. Wright, 403 Pa. Super. 334, 589 A.2d 213 (1990) affirmed summary judgment on an informed consent claim brought the parents of an infant patient, claiming that the physician had a duty to disclose his alcoholism and the fact that he did not have a medical license. In so holding, the court wrote: "we . . . refuse to expand the informed consent doctrine to include matters not specifically germane to surgical or operative treatment. To do so, where the absent information consists of facts personal to the treating physician, extends the doctrine into realms well beyond its original boundaries." But see Hidding v. Williams, 578 So. 2d 1192 (La. App. 1991) (recognizing a duty for a physician to disclose his chronic alcoholism).

Physician disclosure is not the only avenue for patients to get some types of physician-specific risk or quality information. As noted in Chapter 2, state medical boards discipline physicians, and individuals can look up the disciplinary history of physicians. See docinfo.org. Moreover, Section 10331 of the ACA adopts a model of disclosure linked to participation in federal insurance programs. It depends on the Centers for Medicare & Medicaid Services (CMS) to require collection and public dissemination of provider performance information. Pursuant to this section, CMS launched a *Physician Compare* Internet website based on the model of the *Hospital Compare* site. These sites have been merged into a single site called *Care Compare*. This website contains information on physician performance that allows the public to compare physician performance on quality.

Physicians are able to review their results before they are publicly reported, and the Secretary of HHS is admonished to ensure that the data is statistically valid and reliable, including risk adjustment mechanisms; that it provides "a robust and accurate portrayal of a physician's performance"; that it provides "a more accurate portrayal of physician performance"; that appropriate attribution of care can be done when multiple physicians and other providers are involved in care; that "timely statistical performance feedback" is provided; and that CMS has computer and data systems capable of supporting "valid, reliable, and accurate public reporting activities authorized under this section." Most recently, CMS has included "quality payment program" performance information on clinicians participating in the Merit-Based Incentive Payment System (MIPS). For a description of MIPS, see Chapter 10, Section II, below.

Physician Compare and *Care Compare* have yet to provide much value, however, because more than 75 percent of physicians do not have any performance information listed (neither for themselves individually nor for any group in which they practice), and more than 99 percent of physicians do not have individual-level performance information listed even when such information is available for a group in which they practice. See Jun Li, Anup Das, Lena M. Chen, Assessing the Quality of Public Reporting of US Physician Performance, 179 JAMA Intern Med. 1133 (2019). Low reporting likely results from the fact that physician reporting is voluntary, and the financial incentive to report is relatively low. Id.

Physician Compare reinforces a consumerist approach to health, giving patients information about health care risks and costs to maximize their choices. Kristen Madison defines consumerism as "individual choice within a health care marketplace characterized by the exchange of money for health care goods or services." See Kristin Madison, Patients as Regulators? Patients' Evolving Influence over Health Care Delivery, 31 J. Legal Med. 9, 15 (2010).

Consumers rely on information from many different sources, particularly websites. This consumerist approach seeks to move patients from passive recipients of medical advice to aggressive shoppers seeking information to satisfy their preferences for treatments, risks, and costs. Sources of information include existing web-based sites such as WebMD®, health care report cards issued by private and public organizations, and a range of government-run websites including *Physician Compare*, *Hospital Compare*, and *Home Health Compare*. See discussion of Nursing Home Compare in Chapter 3, above.

Does this emergent consumerism, which the ACA reinforces, have problems? Some critics argue that it turns patients into consumers and healthcare into a business, risking a more predatory "buyer beware" world. But isn't the health care marketplace already a "buyer beware" environment where more information can only help consumers control their risks? It has been argued that the mere production and publication of such data is enough to motivate providers to improve their statistics in order to improve their reputation and competitiveness.

Consumerism assumes that most patients have the ability to be active consumers. The fault in this assumption is that patients are most likely to engage the health care system when they are ill, dependent, and weak. Shopping is the last thing on their minds. For a skeptical analysis of consumers as shoppers, see Mark A. Hall and Carl E. Schneider, Patients as Consumers: Courts, Contracts, and the New Medical Marketplace, 106 Mich. L. Rev. 643 (2008).

PROBLEM: CONTENT FOR PHYSICIAN COMPARE

The Secretary has discretion to add information to the *Physician Compare* site beyond what is required in the ACA. Should the Secretary include disciplinary information provided by the state medical boards? If so, should it include complaints and investigations as well as final disciplinary actions? Should the Secretary include information on denial, limitation, or revocation of staff privileges? Should the *Physician Compare* website include malpractice filings, settlements, or judgments? In other words, should the Secretary incorporate the information that is now collected in the National Practitioner Data Bank (NPDB), which is not open to the public? See discussion of the NPDB in Chapters 2 and 11. Was the failure to mention the NPDB simply a legislative oversight? Or is the ACA quietly deemphasizing the NPDB?

As noted earlier, physician participation in the quality reporting on *Physician Compare* is voluntary. CMS says on its website that "[T]here are many reasons why health care professionals and group practices may not participate in CMS Quality Programs even though they're committed to providing high-quality health care. Participation in CMS Quality Programs shows a commitment to quality care. But, participation alone does not mean quality care has been achieved. Showing a commitment to quality is the first step in achieving quality care."

The American Medical Association and other specialty societies complain that the site is confusing and misleading, and that many physicians do not participate in the quality reporting.

Pick a physician whom you or your family know, and use the Physician Compare website to see what information is available. Does it provide useful information in helping you select a physician for the first time? What would you like to see on a website to add value to your shopping for a physician?

3. Decision Aids and Informed Consent

John Wennberg and others have long argued for the use of decision aids to help patients with conditions that have several different treatment alternatives with varied associated risks and benefits, such as prostate surgery or treatments for heart disease. See John E. Wennberg & Philip G. Peters, Unwanted Variations in the Quality of Health Care: Can the Law Help Medicine Provide a Remedy/Remedies?, 37 Wake Forest L. Rev. 925, 925–941 (2002).

Decision aids (DAs) provide patients with detailed and specific information on treatment options and outcomes, help them clarify their values, and guide them through the decision-making process. See, e.g., Elie A. Akl, et al., A Decision Aid for COPD Patients Considering Inhaled Steroid Therapy: Development and Before and After Pilot Testing, 15 BMC Med. Inform. Dec. Mak. 7 (2007). A 2017 Cochrane systematic review, which examined 105 published studies of the effectiveness of decision aids among more than 31,000 patients, found that these aids increased treatment knowledge, improved risk perception, clarified personal values, reduced patient passivity, increased congruence between patient values and treatment choices, and appeared to improve doctor-patient communication. Dawn Stacey et al., Decision Aids for People Facing Health Treatment or Screening Decisions, Cochrane Database Syst. Rev. (Apr 12, 2017).

The process by which such decision aids are used by providers and patients is called "shared medical decision-making." King and Moulton define shared decision-making as "a process in which the physician shares with the patient all relevant risk and benefit information on all treatment alternatives and the patient shares with the physician all relevant personal information that might make one treatment or side effect more or less tolerable than others. Then, both parties use this information to come to a mutual medical decision." Jaime Staples King and Benjamin Moulton, Rethinking Informed Consent: The Case for Shared Medical Decisionmaking, 32 Am. J. Law & Med. 429, 431 (2006). Numerous studies indicate that when decision aids (such as brochures, DVDs, or online tools) are available to patients, and they have the opportunity to participate in medical decision-making with their physician, the patient-physician dialogue and patient well-being both improve. See Thomas H. Wieringa et al., Decision Aids that Facilitate Elements of Shared Decision Making in Chronic Illnesses: A Systematic Review, 8 Syst. Rev. 121 (2019); Center for Informed Patient Shared Decision Making, Decision Aid Library, Dartmouth-Hitchcock,   https://www.dartmouth-hitchcock.org/decision-making-help/patient-resources.

The ACA adopts the use of decision aids for preference-sensitive care in section 3506. Preference-sensitive care is:

> medical care for which the clinical evidence does not clearly support one treatment option such that the appropriate course of treatment depends on the values of the patient or the preferences of the patient, caregivers or authorized representatives regarding the benefits,

harms and scientific evidence for each treatment option, [and] the use of such care should depend on the informed patient choice among clinically appropriate treatment options.

Section 3501 of the ACA adopts the patient decision aid concept, as described above, and develops a regulatory approach for implementing shared decision aids. The stated purpose is to facilitate collaboration between patients and caregivers in decision-making, provide information on trade-offs among treatment options, and incorporate "... patient preferences and values into the medical plan."

Section 3506 requires the Secretary of HHS to contract with an independent entity to develop consensus-based standards for such aids and to develop a certification process for such patient decision aids for use in federal health programs and by other interested parties. This entity will "... synthesize evidence and convene a broad range of experts and key stakeholders to develop and identify consensus-based standards to evaluate patient decision aids for preference sensitive care." Section 3506 also requires that such aids be endorsed by the entity through a certification process. The Secretary, in collaboration with other federal agencies, disseminates these aids and develops information and training for providers in their use. The Center for Evidence and Practice Improvement within the Agency for Healthcare Quality and Research at HHS lists among its primary purposes "advanc[ing] decision and communication sciences to facilitate informed treatment and health care decisionmaking by patients and their health care providers."

The Secretary also funds "Shared Decisionmaking Resource Centers" under the ACA "to provide technical assistance to providers and to develop and disseminate best practices and other information to support and accelerate adoption, implementation, and effective use of patient decision aids and shared decisionmaking by providers." These Centers provide current clinical evidence about the risks and benefits of treatment options in an age-appropriate way, with sensitivity to different cultural and educational backgrounds. See Thaddeus Mason Pope, Certified Patient Decision Aids: Solving Persistent Problems with Informed Consent Law, 45 J. L. Med. & Eth. 12, 23 (2017).

While sustained funding for the certification of decision aids remains a challenge, at least one state—Washington—has implemented a certification process. The Washington State Health Care Authority, as part of a demonstration project, has certified more than 15 decision aids since 2019 and has a system for the submission of additional decision aids for review and potential certification. State law requires that decision aids be used, once developed and certified through the state agency, and it creates a presumption of informed consent if a practitioner uses a certified decision aid. See Rev. Code Wash § 7.70.060. The presumption can only be rebutted by clear and convincing evidence.

HHS's effort to incentivize shared decision-making through the Medicare Shared Savings Program (MSSP) appears to be on hold. Accountable Care Organizations (ACOs) that participate in MSSP are eligible to be paid a portion of any Medicare funds it saves in comparison to a target established by the Center for Medicare and Medicaid Services. Payment of shared savings to an ACO is conditioned, however, on the ACO's meeting performance standards. HHS proposed including the use of shared decision-making as one such performance standard. See 42 Fed. Reg. 33950 (July 21, 2017). Because few ACOs elected to participate in the MSSP models utilizing this performance standard, CMS discontinued their use. See Sarah Heath, CMS Cancels Shared Decision-Making Models Due to Planning Issues, Patient Engagement HIT, Policy and Regulatory News, Feb. 6, 2018. See Chapter 10 for discussion of MSSP.

Similarly, the Medicare Access and Chip Reauthorization Act of 2015 encourages shared decision-making through its merit incentive payment system for Medicare providers. Physicians can increase their reimbursement by participating in "clinical practice improvement activities" that include better engagement with patients through the use of "shared decision making mechanisms." 42 U.S.C. sec. 1395w–4.

PROBLEM: STATE LEGISLATION

Your state legislature is considering legislation providing that any physician that uses a patient decision aid, certified through the process described in the ACA, will be immune from suit under state informed consent law. You are counsel to the Governor, and she has asked you to brief her on what she should expect should the bill reach her desk. What stakeholders or interests do you expect will be contacting the Governor, and what positions will they be taking? Would you advocate that she veto the bill? What amendments might you propose to improve the legislation?

Should Congress instead choose to preempt state informed consent law and provide the same immunity? Does it have the constitutional authority to do so? Does it make any difference to you in your role as counsel whether the immunity proceeds from federal or state law?

4.   Disclosure of Financial Conflicts of Interest

Courts generally have not found that the duty to disclose material information obligates physicians to disclose their financial conflicts of interest. For example, in Neade v. Portes, 739 N.E.2d 496 (Ill. 2000), a physician in the provider network of a patient's insurance plan twice refused to authorize an angiogram for the patient when he was experiencing symptoms of coronary artery blockage. Instead, the physician relied on a thallium stress test and concluded that the patient did not have cardiac problems. The patient died a few days later from a massive myocardial infarction caused by coronary artery blockage. The plaintiff alleged that the patient should have been informed about the Plan's Medical Incentive Fund, which set aside money that would be returned to participating physicians if not used for referrals or outside tests.

The court rejected the plaintiff's claim, quoting a recent Supreme Court decision, Pegram v. Herdrich, 530 U.S. 211, 120 S. Ct. 2143, 147 L. Ed. 2d 164 (2000):

> [T]he defense of any HMO would be that its physician did not act out of financial interest but for good medical reasons, the plausibility of which would require reference to standards of reasonable and customary medical practice in like circumstances. That, of course, is the traditional standard of the common law. [ ]. Thus, for all practical purposes, every claim of fiduciary breach by an HMO physician making a mixed decision [about a patient's eligibility for treatment under an HMO and the appropriate treatment for the patient] would boil down to a malpractice claim, and the fiduciary standard would be nothing but the malpractice standard traditionally applied in actions against physicians. [ ]

The court in *Neade* then took a similar approach to the one in *Pegram*, finding that the plaintiff's claim based on a fiduciary duty to disclose merely duplicated the plaintiff's medical malpractice claim. See, e.g. Dimmick v. United States, No. C 05-0971 PJH, 2006 U.S. Dist. LEXIS 90843, at *55 (N.D. Cal. Dec. 15, 2006) (fact that prescribing physician had a consulting relationship with the manufacturer of the prescribed medication is not material to that patient's treatment decision and thus is not subject to the duty of disclosure). See Kate Greenwood, Physician Conflicts of Interest in Court: Beyond the "Independent Physician" Litigation Heuristic, 30 Ga. State. Univ. L. Rev. 778 (2014).

Moore v. Regents of the University of California, 51 Cal. 3d 120, 793 P.2d 479 (1990), is a famous exception. In that case, a patient with leukemia sued the employer of his treating physician for failure to disclose as part of seeking consent to various treatments that the physician had a financial interest in the patient's cells. Without the patient's knowledge, the physician had collected cells from various parts of the patient's body, conducted research on them, and, from them, developed a cell line that produced valuable protein mediators. The physician and the University then patented the cell line and licensed its use to a company for commercial development. The California Supreme Court held that the patient's allegations were sufficient to state a claim for failure to obtain informed consent. The Court reasoned that a physician's financial interest in obtaining cells as part of a medical procedure is material to the decision of a reasonable person about whether to consent to such a procedure.

Moore was among the first cases to address the duty to disclose conflicts of interest, and so it was viewed as harbinger of judicial opinions to come. In the end, however, it has proven to be the exception rather than the rule. For another more recent exception, see Shapira v. Christiana Care Health Servs., Inc., 99 A.3d 217 (Del. 2014) (fact that physician had a contract with the device manufacturer to be a paid speaker was material information subject to the duty of disclosure).

NOTE: PHYSICIAN PAYMENT SUNSHINE ACT

The ACA included two provisions regarding the disclosure of physician financial interests related to treatment of patients. The first creates a publicly accessible data base on industry payments made to physicians. The second requires that physicians disclose certain ownership interests to patients.

The ACA included the Physician Payment Sunshine Act (PPSA), codified at 42 U.S.C.A. § 1320a–7h (2010). The PPSA requires that manufacturers of drugs, devices, biologics, medical supplies, or other items covered by Medicare or Medicaid must submit to the Secretary of HHS a list of physicians and teaching hospitals ("covered entities") to whom they have made payments or financial transfers. Reportable transfers include consulting fees, entertainment, travel (including the destination), food, honoraria, education, research, speaking or service as a faculty member, royalties, grants, or "any other" payment. The statute includes a list of exempt items, such as educational materials supplied for patients. See Chapter 19 for discussion of the PPSA and research.

Any benefit or transfer that is valued at more than $10 must be reported. Exceptions include items provided for use in charity care, educational materials intended for the benefit of the patient, distributions or dividends paid on stock held in a publicly traded company, and devices loaned to the provider for a trial period not to exceed 90 days, among a few others. Manufacturers must also disclose if they have made a payment or contribution to any other party at the request of a covered entity. If a reportable transfer is made in connection with a specific product, the name or other identifier of the item must be disclosed as well.

The reporting obligation is enforced through civil monetary penalties. The data included in the reports will be available to the public, including physicians' patients, in a searchable web site, listed by name of the manufacturer and the covered entity. The Act also includes reporting requirements for distribution of drug samples by manufacturers.

The ACA also requires that certain doctors who are referring patients for certain radiology tests, including MRIs, in which the doctors have an ownership interest (self-referrals) disclose that interest to the patients. The disclosure must be in writing and must inform the patients that they may choose a different provider for that service.

The Sunshine Act raises a number of interesting questions. The first is whether patient awareness of physician receipt of industry payments affects patient trust in their physicians, or how they shop for physicians generally. One study found that patients viewed doctors favorably who received payments for consulting with drug companies, while they saw physicians who had no such contacts as inexperienced. Patients also reacted significantly more negatively to a doctor who received a large payment (defined as $4153) as compared to a doctor receiving either a small payment or no payment at all. The authors concluded that ". . . assuming a good faith justification is present, patients, it appears, are likely to interpret many of these financial relationships in a positive light." The authors also noted that very few patients consulted the Open Payments website. See Joshua E. Perry, Dena Cox, and Anthony D. Cox, Trust and Transparency: Patient Perceptions of Physicians' Financial Relationships with Pharmaceutical Companies, 42 J. Law, Med. & Ethics 475, 488 (2014).

A second question is whether the assumptions of the Act are realistic. Are physician prescribing patterns in fact affected by payments from industry? If they are, even at low levels of payment, should this affect patient trust in their physicians? A study quantified the association between industry payments and physician prescribing patterns. The authors' findings were quite striking. They found that, compared to the receipt of no industry-sponsored meals, "receipt of a single industry-sponsored meal, with a mean value of less than $20, was associated with prescription of the promoted brand-name drug at significantly higher rates to Medicare beneficiaries." Furthermore, the relationship was dose-dependent: more and costlier meals led to greater increases in physician prescribing of the promoted drug. See Colette DeJong et al., Pharmaceutical Industry-Sponsored Meals and Physician Prescribing Patterns for Medicare Beneficiaries, JAMA Intern Med E7 (2016).

Is a website-based disclosure approach the best regulatory strategy for reducing physician prescribing abuses? Should we consider a new regulatory approach to physician receipt of money and meals from industry? How about a total prohibition on payments? For a critique of regulatory and common-law disclosure obligations, see Robert Gatter, Communicating Loyalty: Advocacy and Disclosure of Conflicts in Treatment and Research Relationships, in I Glenn Cohen, Allison K. Hoffman & William M. Sage, eds., The Oxford Handbook of U.S. Health Law 240 (Oxford Univ. Press 2017).

V. CONFIDENTIALITY AND DISCLOSURE IN THE PHYSICIAN-PATIENT RELATIONSHIP

One of the most important obligations owed by a professional to a patient is the protection of confidences revealed by the patient to the professional. As discussed in Section V.A, state courts have developed common law rules to protect these confidences, and most states have adopted either a comprehensive medical confidentiality statute or several statutes addressing specific types of medical information. The Federal

Medical Privacy Rules under HIPAA and the amendments provided by HITECH offer an elaborate protective framework for patient information. These state and federal obligations are discussed in Section V.B.

A. BREACHES OF CONFIDENTIALITY

HUMPHERS V. FIRST INTERSTATE BANK OF OREGON

Supreme Court of Oregon, In Banc, 1985.
696 P.2d 527.

LINDE, JUSTICE.

We are called upon to decide whether plaintiff has stated a claim for damages in alleging that her former physician revealed her identity to a daughter whom she had given up for adoption.

In 1959, according to the complaint, plaintiff, then known as Ramona Elwess or by her maiden name, Ramona Jean Peek, gave birth to a daughter in St. Charles Medical Center in Bend, Oregon. She was unmarried at the time, and her physician, Dr. Harry E. Mackey, registered her in the hospital as "Mrs. Jean Smith." The next day, Ramona consented to the child's adoption by Leslie and Shirley Swarens of Bend, who named her Leslie Dawn. The hospital's medical records concerning the birth were sealed and marked to show that they were not public. Ramona subsequently remarried and raised a family. Only Ramona's mother and husband and Dr. Mackey knew about the daughter she had given up for adoption.

Twenty-one years later the daughter, now known as Dawn Kastning, wished to establish contact with her biological mother. Unable to gain access to the confidential court file of her adoption (though apparently able to locate the attending physician), Dawn sought out Dr. Mackey, and he agreed to assist in her quest. Dr. Mackey gave Dawn a letter which stated that he had registered Ramona Jean Peek at the hospital, that although he could not locate his medical records, he remembered administering diethylstilbestrol to her, and that the possible consequences of this medication made it important for Dawn to find her biological mother. The latter statements were untrue and made only to help Dawn to breach the confidentiality of the records concerning her birth and adoption. In 1982, hospital personnel, relying on Dr. Mackey's letter, allowed Dawn to make copies of plaintiff's medical records, which enabled her to locate plaintiff, now Ramona Humphers.

Ramona Humphers was not pleased. The unexpected development upset her and caused her emotional distress, worry, sleeplessness, humiliation, embarrassment, and inability to function normally. She sought damages from the estate of Dr. Mackey, who had died, by this action against defendant as the personal representative. After alleging the facts recounted above, her complaint pleads for relief on five different theories: First, that Dr. Mackey incurred liability for "outrageous conduct"; second, that his disclosure of a professional secret fell short of the care, skill and diligence employed by other physicians in the community and commanded by statute; third, that his disclosure wrongfully breached a confidential or privileged relationship; fourth, that his disclosure of confidential information was an "invasion of privacy" in the form of an "unauthorized intrusion upon plaintiff's seclusion, solitude, and private affairs;" and fifth, that his disclosures to Dawn Kastning breached a contractual obligation of secrecy. The circuit court granted defendant's motion to dismiss the complaint on the grounds that the facts fell short of each theory of relief and ordered entry of judgment for defendant. On appeal, the Court of Appeals affirmed the dismissal of the first, second, and fifth counts but reversed on the third, breach of a confidential relationship, and the fourth, invasion of privacy. [ ] We allowed review. We hold that if plaintiff has a claim, it arose from a breach by Dr. Mackey of a professional duty to keep plaintiff's secret rather than from a violation of plaintiff's privacy.

A physician's liability for disclosing confidential information about a patient is not a new problem. In common law jurisdictions it has been more discussed than litigated throughout much of this century. There are precedents for damage actions for unauthorized disclosure of facts conveyed in confidence, although we know of none involving the disclosure of an adoption. Because such claims are made against a variety of defendants besides physicians or other professional counselors, for instance against banks [ ], and because plaintiffs understandably plead alternative theories of recovery, the decisions do not always rest on a single theory.

Sometimes, defendant may have promised confidentiality expressly or by factual implication, in this case perhaps implied by registering a patient in the hospital under an assumed name. . . . [ ] A contract claim may be adequate where the breach of confidence causes financial loss, and it may gain a longer period of limitations; but contract law may deny damages for psychic or emotional injury not within the contemplation of the contracting parties, [ ] though perhaps this is no barrier when emotional security is the very object of the promised confidentiality. A contract claim is unavailable if the defendant physician was engaged by someone other than the plaintiff [ ] and it would be an awkward fiction at best if age, mental condition, or other circumstances prevent the patient from contracting; yet such a claim might be available to someone less interested than the patient, for instance her husband [ ].

Malpractice claims, based on negligence or statute, in contrast, may offer a plaintiff professional standards of conduct independent of the defendant's assent. . . . Finally, actions for intentional infliction of severe emotional distress fail when the defendant had no such intention or . . .

when a defendant was not reckless or did not behave in a manner that a factfinder could find to transcend "the farthest reaches of socially tolerable behavior." [ ] Among these diverse precedents, we need only consider the counts of breach of confidential relationship and invasion of privacy on which the Court of Appeals allowed plaintiff to proceed. Plaintiff did not pursue her other theories . . . and we express no view whether the dismissal of those counts was correct.

Privacy

Although claims of a breach of privacy and of wrongful disclosure of confidential information may seem very similar in a case like the present, which involves the disclosure of an intimate personal secret, the two claims depend on different premises and cover different ground. Their common denominator is that both assert a right to control information, but they differ in important respects. Not every secret concerns personal or private information; commercial secrets are not personal, and governmental secrets are neither personal nor private. Secrecy involves intentional concealment. . . .

For our immediate purpose, the most important distinction is that only one who holds information in confidence can be charged with a breach of confidence. If an act qualifies as a tortious invasion of privacy, it theoretically could be committed by anyone. In the present case, Dr. Mackey's professional role is relevant to a claim that he breached a duty of confidentiality, but he could be charged with an invasion of plaintiff's privacy only if anyone else who told Dawn Kastning the facts of her birth without a special privilege to do so would be liable in tort for invading the privacy of her mother.

Whether "privacy" is a usable legal category has been much debated in other English-speaking jurisdictions as well as in this country, especially since its use in tort law, to claim the protection of government against intrusions by others, became entangled with its use in constitutional law, to claim protection against rather different intrusions by government. No concept in modern law has unleashed a comparable flood of commentary, its defenders arguing that "privacy" encompasses related interests of personality and autonomy, while its critics say that these interests are properly identified, evaluated, and protected below that exalted philosophical level. Indeed, at that level, a daughter's interest in her personal identity here confronts a mother's interest in guarding her own present identity by concealing their joint past. But recognition of an interest or value deserving protection states only half a case. Tort liability depends on the defendant's wrong as well as on the plaintiff's interest, or "right," unless some rule imposes strict liability. One's preferred seclusion or anonymity may be lost in many ways; the question remains who is legally bound to protect those interests at the risk of liability.

* * *

In this country, Dean William L. Prosser and his successors, noting that early debate was more "preoccupied with the question whether the right of privacy existed" than "what it would amount to if it did," concluded that invasion of privacy "is not one tort but a complex of four" . . . Prosser and Keeton, Torts 851, § 117 (5th ed. 1984). They identify the four kinds of claims grouped under the "privacy" tort as, first, appropriation of the plaintiff's name or likeness; second, unreasonable and offensive intrusion upon the seclusion of another; third, public disclosure of private facts; and fourth, publicity which places the plaintiff in a false light in the public eye. *Id.* at 851–66. [ ]

This court has not adopted all forms of the tort wholesale. . . .

* * *

. . . The Court of Appeals concluded that the complaint alleges a case of tortious intrusion upon plaintiff's seclusion, not by physical means such as uninvited entry, wiretapping, photography, or the like, but in the sense of an offensive prying into personal matters that plaintiff reasonably has sought to keep private. [ ] We do not believe that the theory fits this case.

Doubtless plaintiff's interest qualifies as a "privacy" interest. That does not require the judgment of a court or a jury; it is established by the statutes that close adoption records to inspection without a court order. [ ] . . . But as already stated, to identify an interest deserving protection does not suffice to collect damages from anyone who causes injury to that interest. Dr. Mackey helped Dawn Kastning find her biological mother, but we are not prepared to assume that Ms. Kastning became liable for invasion of privacy in seeking her out. Nor, we think, would anyone who knew the facts without an obligation of secrecy commit a tort simply by telling them to Ms. Kastning.

Dr. Mackey himself did not approach plaintiff or pry into any personal facts that he did not know; indeed, if he had written or spoken to his former patient to tell her that her daughter was eager to find her, it would be hard to describe such a communication alone as an invasion of privacy. The point of the claim against Dr. Mackey is not that he pried into a confidence but that he failed to keep one. If Dr. Mackey incurred liability for that, it must result from an obligation of confidentiality beyond any general duty of people at large not to invade one another's privacy. We therefore turn to plaintiff's claim that Dr. Mackey was liable for a breach of confidence, the third count of the complaint.

Breach of Confidence

It takes less judicial innovation to recognize this claim than the Court of Appeals thought. A number of decisions have held that unauthorized and unprivileged disclosure of confidential information obtained in a confidential relationship can give rise to tort damages. [ ] . . .

* * *

In the case of the medical profession, courts in fact have found sources of a nonconsensual duty of confidentiality. Some have thought such a duty toward the patient implicit in the patient's statutory privilege to exclude the doctor's testimony in litigation[ ]. More directly in point are legal duties imposed as a condition of engaging in the professional practice of medicine or other occupations.

[The court noted that medical licensing statutes and professional regulations have been used as sources of a duty.]

This strikes us as the right approach to a claim of liability outside obligations undertaken expressly or implied in fact in entering a contractual relationship. [ ] The contours of the asserted duty of confidentiality are determined by a legal source external to the tort claim itself.

* * *

Because the duty of confidentiality is determined by standards outside the tort claim for its breach, so are the defenses of privilege or justification. Physicians, like members of many ordinary confidential professions and occupations, also may be legally obliged to report medical information to others for the protection of the patient, of other individuals, or of the public. *See, e.g.,* ORS 418.750 (physician's duty to report child abuse); ORS 433.003, 434.020 (duty to report certain diseases). . . . Even without such a legal obligation, there may be a privilege to disclose information for the safety of individuals or important to the public in matters of public interest. [ ] Some cases have found a physician privileged in disclosing information to a patient's spouse, [ ] or perhaps an intended spouse, [ ]. In any event, defenses to a duty of confidentiality are determined in the same manner as the existence and scope of the duty itself. They necessarily will differ from one occupation to another and from time to time. A physician or other member of a regulated occupation is not to be held to a noncontractual duty of secrecy in a tort action when disclosure would not be a breach or would be privileged in direct enforcement of the underlying duty.

A physician's duty to keep medical and related information about a patient in confidence is beyond question. It is imposed by statute. ORS 677.190(5) provides for disqualifying or otherwise disciplining a physician for "wilfully or negligently divulging a professional secret." . . .

It is less obvious whether Dr. Mackey violated ORS 677.190(5) when he told Dawn Kastning what he knew of her birth. She was not, after all, a stranger to that proceeding. . . . If Ms. Kastning needed information about her natural mother for medical reasons, as Dr. Mackey pretended, the

State Board of Medical Examiners likely would find the disclosure privileged against a charge under ORS 677.190(5); but the statement is alleged to have been a pretext designed to give her access to the hospital records. If only ORS 677.190(5) were involved, we do not know how the Board would judge a physician who assists at the birth of a child and decades later reveals to that person his or her parentage. But as already noted, other statutes specifically mandate the secrecy of adoption records.... Given these clear legal constraints, there is no privilege to disregard the professional duty imposed by ORS 677.190(5) solely in order to satisfy the curiosity of the person who was given up for adoption.

For these reasons, we agree with the Court of Appeals that plaintiff may proceed under her claim of breach of confidentiality in a confidential relationship. The decision of the Court of Appeals is reversed with respect to plaintiff's claim of invasion of privacy and affirmed with respect to her claim of breach of confidence in a confidential relationship, and the case is remanded to the circuit court for further proceedings on that claim.

NOTES AND QUESTIONS

1. *Who Uses Medical Information?* Professional and non-professional medical staff must have access to records of patients in medical institutions for treatment purposes. Consent to access for medical staff is commonly presumed. Third party payers are the most common requestors of medical records outside the treatment setting. Access to records also is sought routinely for a variety of medical evaluation and support purposes. For example, in-house quality assurance committees, Joint Commission accreditation inspection teams, and state institutional licensure reviewers all must review medical records to assess the quality of hospital care. State public health laws require medical professionals and institutions to report a variety of medical conditions and incidents: venereal disease, contagious diseases, wounds inflicted by violence, poisonings, industrial accidents, abortions, and child abuse.

2. *Non-Medical Uses of Medical Records.* Access to medical records is also sought for secondary, nonmedical purposes. Law enforcement agencies, for example, often seek access to medical information. A moderate-size Chicago hospital reported that the FBI requested information about patients as often as twice a month. Attorneys seek medical records to establish disability, personal injury, or medical malpractice claims for their clients. Though they most commonly will ask for records of their own clients, they may also want to review records of other patients to establish a pattern of knowing medical abuse by a physician or the culpability of a hospital for failing to supervise a negligent practitioner. Life, health, disability, and liability insurers often seek medical information, as do employers and credit investigators.

Disclosure of information from medical records may occur without a formal request. Though secondary users of medical information commonly receive information pursuant to patient record releases, they have been known to seek and compile information surreptitiously. These secondary disclosures of medical information are of great import to patients, as disclosure can result in loss of employment or denial of insurance or credit, or, at least, severe embarrassment. See generally the Preamble to the Medical Privacy Rules, *infra*.

3.   *Federal and State Statutes.* Several federal and state statutes protect the confidentiality of medical information. Most notably, there are the privacy rules of the Health Insurance Portability and Accountability Act (HIPAA), discussed below. Additionally, there are amendments to the Drug Abuse and Treatment Acts and Comprehensive Alcohol Abuse and Alcoholism Prevention, Treatment, and Rehabilitation Act, 42 U.S.C.A. §§ 290dd–3, 390ee–3, and implementing regulations, 42 C.F.R. Part 2, which impose rigorous requirements on the disclosure of information from alcohol and drug abuse treatment programs. Some state statutes provide civil penalties for disclosure of confidential information. See, e.g., West's Fla. Stat. Ann. § 395.1065.

4.   *Evidentiary Weight Given to Medical Records.* Medical records often play a pivotal role in medical malpractice cases. By the time a malpractice action comes to trial memories may have dimmed as to what actually occurred at the time negligence is alleged to have taken place, leaving the medical record as the most telling evidence. Medical records, if properly authenticated, will usually be admitted under the business records exception to the hearsay rule.

PROBLEM: THE HUNT FOR PATIENT RECORDS

Two partners of a law firm, Findem and Howe, got the idea of working with a hospital to determine whether unpaid medical bills could be submitted to the Social Security Administration for payment as reimbursable disability treatment. They proposed the idea to the President of the law firm, who was also a trustee of the Warner General Hospital Health System.

The hospital agreed to search patient records and provide four pieces of patient information: name, telephone number, age, and medical condition. The patient registration forms were then furnished to the firm. The hospital agreed to pay a contingency fee to the firm for claims paid by Social Security. Patients who were possible candidates were called by the firm, on behalf of the hospital, telling them that they might be entitled to Social Security benefits that would help them pay their hospital bills. Some of the patients came in to talk with firm lawyers. A total of twelve thousand patient records were examined as part of this enterprise.

A group of angry former patients of Warner General have come to you to see what rights they have for what they feel is a violation of their privacy rights. How will you proceed? What arguments can you make on their behalf?

DOE v. MEDLANTIC HEALTH CARE GROUP, INC.

District of Columbia Court of Appeals, 2003.
814 A.2d 939.

RUIZ, ASSOCIATE JUDGE:

[A jury award to John Doe against Medlantic Health Care Group, Inc. ("Medlantic") in the amount of $250,000 for breach of confidential relationship was set aside by the trial court when it granted the defendant's motion for JNOV.]

I.

Facts

In the spring of 1996, Doe held two jobs: by day he worked for a federal agency and at night he worked as a janitor for a company that contracted to clean the Department of State. Although Doe had been diagnosed with HIV in August of 1985, he had not told anyone at his janitorial job that he was HIV positive. One of Doe's co-workers in the evenings at the State Department was Tijuana Goldring, who also held a day position at the Washington Hospital Center ("WHC") as a temporary receptionist. On April 13, 1996, Doe went to WHC's emergency room suffering from severe headaches, nausea and high fever. He was discharged on April 16, 1996, but was unable to return to work for approximately two weeks because of these health problems.

On April 23, 1996, while still absent from work, Doe returned to WHC for a follow-up clinic visit after his discharge from the hospital. Knowing that Goldring worked at WHC, Doe stopped by the receptionist's desk to pay her a "courtesy call." After a brief conversation, Goldring asked him for the correct spelling of his uncommon last name because she wanted to send him a get well card. Doe testified that he did not think Goldring's request was odd and complied with the request as it was not unusual to get such a card from co-workers after having been out sick. Doe never received a card from Goldring, but did receive a card from fellow co-workers at the State Department with $50 enclosed.

Sometime in April of 1996, before Doe returned to work, Goldring told another co-worker at the State Department, Donnell Fuell, that John Doe "had that shit," meaning HIV or AIDS. When Fuell questioned her veracity, Goldring replied that it was "for real," and told Fuell she "got it from the hospital." Fuell knew that Goldring worked at WHC during the day.

Doe stipulated that within "a couple of days" of his conversation with Goldring at WHC on April 23, he learned that his co-workers at State knew of his AIDS diagnosis. On April 25, 1996, still before he returned to work, Doe went to the State Department to collect his paycheck, and he encountered co-workers Derek Nelson and Gordon Bannister outside the building. Both were laughing as Doe approached, and Nelson said to him,

"Hey motherfucker, I hear you're dying of AIDS." Doe was "stunned" by this comment, but tried to cover his shock by laughing it off, saying, "Do I look like I'm dying?" before entering the building. Doe did not ask where Nelson had gotten this information, and Nelson did not tell him. As he left the building later that same day, Doe saw Fuell, who told him that Tijuana was "going around telling everybody you got AIDS." Fuell did not tell him how Goldring knew this information. Doe had never been teased by co-workers before that Friday about having AIDS, and that weekend he called Willie Jones, a co-worker and friend from the State Department, to ask if she had heard any rumors at work that he had AIDS. Jones stated she had. Doe did not ask Jones where she had heard the rumors or if Goldring was the source.

* * *

Doe testified that his time at work after April 25, was "like a living hell," as he was teased, ridiculed, pitied and scorned. Co-workers who had previously eaten with him now shunned him, and he was the object of snide remarks, stares, and unwanted attention. This included crass comments such as, Doe has "that faggot thing," and "[don't] eat [Doe's] food."

[Doe realized that Goldring was the source of the rumors about him, and he suspected that she might have seen his medical records.] . . .

The following day, on May 21, 1996, Doe called WHC and spoke with the vice president of personnel and human resources to ask if the hospital had a policy on employees who disseminate confidential medical information. Doe explained what had happened and gave Goldring's name. The vice-president said she would talk to Goldring and told Doe that this type of dissemination was against hospital policy and the laws of the District of Columbia. She referred him to the hospital's "risk management" department.

Doe filed a complaint against Medlantic and Goldring on May 20, 1997, alleging tort claims of invasion of privacy based on Goldring's disclosure and breach of confidential relationship based on WHC's negligence in permitting Goldring's access to confidential patient information. After Goldring was dismissed from the case, it proceeded to trial against Medlantic. The jury found Medlantic liable for breach of confidential relationship and awarded damages in the amount of $250,000. The jury found against Doe on the invasion of privacy claim because Goldring's disclosure was not within the scope of Goldring's employment with WHC. . . .

* * *

B.   Motion for Judgment—Sufficiency of the Evidence

* * *

"The tort of breach of confidential relationship is generally described as consisting of the unconsented, unprivileged disclosure to a third party of nonpublic information that the defendant has learned within a confidential relationship." [ ] The tort arises from a duty that "attaches to nonpersonal relationships [such as hospital-patient] customarily understood to carry an obligation of confidence." [ ] This duty imposes an obligation—stricter than the reasonable person test—to "scrupulously honor the trust and confidence reposed in them because of that special relationship. . . . " [ ] It is undisputed that the jury was properly instructed on the elements of this tort.

We agree with the trial court that the evidence, viewed in the light most favorable to the plaintiff, sufficed to permit the jury to find that WHC breached its duty to "observe the utmost caution," . . . , in protecting the confidentiality of Doe's medical records. First, we reject the suggestion that expert testimony was necessary to establish the applicable standard of care in this case. In the negligence context, we have "refused to require expert testimony when the issue before the jury did not involve either a subject too technical for lay jurors to understand or the exercise of sophisticated professional judgment." [ ] The jury, as instructed, could consider the protocols that the hospital had established, which had been approved by a national hospital accreditation committee, as establishing the standard of care. The jury was specifically instructed that it could take into account whether the hospital's protocol "is or is not followed in practice" and "whether it was successful historically in preventing unauthorized disclosure." That instruction, which is not challenged by appellee, was proper here, where the evidence showed that Medlantic had failed to follow protocols it had established to safeguard its patients' medical records. [ ]

Substantial evidence was presented concerning the hospital's protocols and the routine failure of employees to comply with them. Crockett, a former medical records supervisor at WHC, and Ward, a worker for thirty-five years in the medical records department, testified as to the departures in practice from the established protocols. Crockett stated that while persons requesting medical records were supposed to give certain information, including their name, where they were calling from, and the purpose of the request for the record, in practice it did not always happen. The hospital's protocols were followed less often in the Employee Health department where Goldring worked as a receptionist. Ward similarly testified about lax enforcement of the protocols. As examples, she said that if a person called from the Employee Health department and merely gave his or her first name, that person's request for records would be processed without independent verification, and that individuals wearing a badge from a known department in the hospital could request medical records "stat" for emergencies—and be given the records without further inquiry if the need was considered urgent. Moreover, although Employee Health staff did not have authority to request charts of persons who were not hospital employees, if a person with a hospital department badge asked for a record, staff at the records control desk would accept what the person requesting the record said, without independently verifying if the record requested pertained to an employee.

Evidence was also presented showing that Goldring was a receptionist at the Employee Health department in April 1996 and that, of all Doe's co-workers, she alone could have had access to his medical records at WHC. She was identified by Fuell and others as the source of the rumors about Doe's condition, and it was she who asked for the spelling of Doe's last name, allegedly for the purpose of sending a card, which she never did. Finally, neither the log books which purportedly recorded all requests for medical records nor computer entries of such requests were produced by the hospital to show if anyone had accessed Doe's records at the relevant time. Although there was no direct evidence that the hospital's protocols were deficient or that they were breached to obtain Doe's medical records, evidence that there were significant lapses in the enforcement of the hospital's protocols to safeguard medical records, and that pointed to Goldring, a hospital employee, as the source of the unauthorized disclosure, sufficed to permit the jury to conclude that the hospital breached its duty as a fiduciary to maintain the confidentiality of Doe's medical records.

* * *

IV.

For the foregoing reasons, the trial court's entry of judgment for appellee is reversed, and the case is remanded with instructions that the jury verdict be reinstated and judgment entered in favor of appellant.

So ordered.

NOTE AND QUESTION

The states have adopted a variety of legislative and administrative approaches to confidentiality and disclosure of information regarding HIV-positivity, ARC (AIDS-related complex), and AIDS status. All states now require physicians to report both HIV and AIDS cases to the state health department. Several states have adopted statutes mandating strict confidentiality of AIDS-related information. See, e.g., Cal. Health & Safety Code, § 199.21.

B. FEDERAL MEDICAL PRIVACY STANDARDS UNDER HIPAA

The most prominent legal requirements for the privacy and security of health information stem from the federal Health Insurance Portability and Accountability Act of 1996 (HIPAA).[1] The privacy and security standards implement the statute's administrative simplification requirements that address concerns about health information privacy heightened by the rise of electronic recordkeeping and the Internet. Although HIPAA also created rules for group health insurance plans (see Chapter 9), when most people refer to HIPAA, they are talking about the HIPAA Privacy Rule.

The Privacy Rule was first promulgated in 2000, and then amended in 2009 by the Health Information Technology for Economic and Clinical Health Act (HITECH Act, which was part of the American Recovery and Reinvestment Act of 2009). The HITECH amendments were implemented in the Omnibus HIPAA rulemaking in 2013. The HIPAA Privacy Rule is codified at 45 C.F.R. Parts 160 and 164 and enforced by the Office of Civil Rights (OCR) of the Department of Health and Human Services (HHS). Equally important, but not the subject of this chapter's privacy discussion, is the HIPAA Security Rule, which sets forth standards for keeping health data secure, including encryption and other technological and organizational requirements. The Security Rule is particularly relevant for health care entities to respond to growing cybersecurity threats, including ransomware attacks. The Security Rule is set forth at 45 C.F.R. Part 164, subpart C.

This section opens with the HHS's statement of the purposes behind the HIPAA Privacy Rule, taken from the preamble to the regulations first promulgated in 2000. It then presents select excerpts of the text of the Privacy Rule.

When reading the regulatory text of the HIPAA Privacy Rule, answer the following questions:

1. Who does the Privacy Rule apply to?

2. What information is protected by the Privacy Rule? What about information that is de-identified?

3. What is the general rule regarding information subject to the Privacy Rule?

4. The Privacy Rule breaks down uses and disclosures into three categories: (1) those that are required; (2) those permitted without authorization; and (3) those that require authorization. What are key examples of uses and disclosures that fall into each category?

---

[1] For health lawyers wishing to maintain their credibility, an important detail to note is that the correct acronym is HIPAA, not HIPPA.

STANDARDS FOR PRIVACY OF INDIVIDUALLY
IDENTIFIABLE HEALTH INFORMATION

Department of Health and Human Services Office of the Secretary.
65 Fed. Reg. 82462 (Dec. 28, 2000).

This regulation has three major purposes: (1) To protect and enhance the rights of consumers by providing them access to their health information and controlling the inappropriate use of that information; (2) to improve the quality of health care in the U.S. by restoring trust in the health care system among consumers, health care professionals, and the multitude of organizations and individuals committed to the delivery of care; and (3) to improve the efficiency and effectiveness of health care delivery by creating a national framework for health privacy protection that builds on efforts by states, health systems, and individual organizations and individuals.

* * *

In enacting HIPAA, Congress recognized the fact that administrative simplification cannot succeed if we do not also protect the privacy and confidentiality of personal health information. The provision of high-quality health care requires the exchange of personal, often-sensitive information between an individual and a skilled practitioner. Vital to that interaction is the patient's ability to trust that the information shared will be protected and kept confidential. Yet many patients are concerned that their information is not protected. Among the factors adding to this concern are the growth of the number of organizations involved in the provision of care and the processing of claims, the growing use of electronic information technology, increased efforts to market health care and other products to consumers, and the increasing ability to collect highly sensitive information about a person's current and future health status as a result of advances in scientific research.

Rules requiring the protection of health privacy in the United States have been enacted primarily by the states. While virtually every state has enacted one or more laws to safeguard privacy, these laws vary significantly from state to state and typically apply to only part of the health care system. Many states have adopted laws that protect the health information relating to certain health conditions such as mental illness, communicable diseases, cancer, HIV/AIDS, and other stigmatized conditions. An examination of state health privacy laws and regulations, however, found that "state laws, with a few notable exceptions, do not extend comprehensive protections to people's medical records." Many state rules fail to provide such basic protections as ensuring a patient's legal right to see a copy of his or her medical record. See Health Privacy Project, "The State of Health Privacy: An Uneven Terrain," Institute for Health

Care Research and Policy, Georgetown University (July 1999) [ ] (the "Georgetown Study").

Until now, virtually no federal rules existed to protect the privacy of health information and guarantee patient access to such information. This final rule establishes, for the first time, a set of basic national privacy standards and fair information practices that provides all Americans with a basic level of protection and peace of mind that is essential to their full participation in their care. The rule sets a floor of ground rules for health care providers, health plans, and health care clearinghouses to follow, in order to protect patients and encourage them to seek needed care. The rule seeks to balance the needs of the individual with the needs of the society. It creates a framework of protection that can be strengthened by both the federal government and by states as health information systems continue to evolve.

* * *

REGULATORY EXCERPTS

45 C.F.R. § 160.103—DEFINITIONS

Business associate: (1) Except as provided in paragraph (4) of this definition, business associate means, with respect to a covered entity, a person who:

(i) On behalf of such covered entity or of an organized health care arrangement (as defined in this section) in which the covered entity participates, but other than in the capacity of a member of the workforce of such covered entity or arrangement, creates, receives, maintains, or transmits protected health information for a function or activity regulated by this subchapter, including claims processing or administration, data analysis, processing or administration, utilization review, quality assurance, patient safety activities listed at 42 CFR 3.20, billing, benefit management, practice management, and repricing; or

(ii) Provides, other than in the capacity of a member of the workforce of such covered entity, legal, actuarial, accounting, consulting, data aggregation (as defined in § 164.501 of this subchapter), management, administrative, accreditation, or financial services to or for such covered entity, or to or for an organized health care arrangement in which the covered entity participates, where the provision of the service involves the disclosure of protected health information from such covered entity or arrangement, or from another business associate of such covered entity or arrangement, to the person.

(2) A covered entity may be a business associate of another covered entity.

(3) *Business associate* includes: . . . A subcontractor that creates, receives, maintains, or transmits protected health information on behalf of the business associate.

(4) [Excluding from the definition of *Business associate*, covered entities, health care providers, health plan sponsors, certain government agencies.]

* * *

Covered entity means:

(1) A health plan.

(2) A health care clearinghouse.

(3) A health care provider who transmits any health information in electronic form in connection with a transaction covered by this subchapter.

* * *

Protected health information means individually identifiable health information:

(1) Except as provided in paragraph (2) of this definition, that is:

    (i) Transmitted by electronic media;

    (ii) Maintained in electronic media; or

    (iii) Transmitted or maintained in any other form or medium.

(2) *Protected health information* excludes individually identifiable health information in:

    (i) Education records covered by the Family Educational Rights and Privacy Act, as amended, 20 U.S.C. 1232g;

    (ii) Records described at 20 U.S.C. 1232g(a)(4)(B)(iv); and

    (iii) Employment records held by a covered entity in its role as employer.

* * *

Individually identifiable health information is information that is a subset of health information, including demographic information collected from an individual, and:

(1) Is created or received by a health care provider, health plan, employer, or health care clearinghouse; and

(2) Relates to the past, present, or future physical or mental health or condition of an individual; the provision of health care to an individual; or the past, present, or future payment for the provision of health care to an individual; and

    (i) That identifies the individual; or

(ii) With respect to which there is a reasonable basis to believe the information can be used to identify the individual.

* * *

45 C.F.R. § 164.501—DEFINITIONS

* * *

Health care operations means any of the following activities of the covered entity to the extent that the activities are related to covered functions:

(1) Conducting quality assessment and improvement activities . . . ;

(2) Reviewing the competence or qualifications of health care professionals, evaluating practitioner and provider performance, health plan performance, conducting training programs in which students, trainees, or practitioners in areas of health care learn under supervision to practice or improve their skills as health care providers, training of non-health care professionals, accreditation, certification, licensing, or credentialing activities;

(3) Except as prohibited under § 164.502(a)(5)(i), underwriting, enrollment, premium rating, and other activities related to the creation, renewal, or replacement of a contract of health insurance or health benefits . . . ;

(4) Conducting or arranging for medical review, legal services, and auditing functions, including fraud and abuse detection and compliance programs;

(5) Business planning and development . . . ; and

(6) Business management and general administrative activities of the entity, including, but not limited to:

(i) Management activities relating to implementation of and compliance with the requirements of this subchapter;

(ii) Customer service, including the provision of data analyses for policy holders, plan sponsors, or other customers, provided that protected health information is not disclosed to such policy holder, plan sponsor, or customer;

(iii) Resolution of internal grievances;

(iv) The sale, transfer, merger, or consolidation of all or part of the covered entity with another covered entity, or an entity that following such activity will become a covered entity and due diligence related to such activity; and

(v) Consistent with the applicable requirements of § 164.514, creating de-identified health information or a limited data set, and fundraising for the benefit of the covered entity.

* * *

Marketing: (1) Except as provided in paragraph (2) of this definition, marketing means to make a communication about a product or service that encourages recipients of the communication to purchase or use the product or service.

(2) Marketing does not include a communication made:

(i) To provide refill reminders or otherwise communicate about a drug or biologic that is currently being prescribed for the individual, only if any financial remuneration received by the covered entity in exchange for making the communication is reasonably related to the covered entity's cost of making the communication.

(ii) For the following treatment and health care operations purposes, except where the covered entity receives financial remuneration in exchange for making the communication:

(A) For treatment of an individual by a health care provider, including case management or care coordination for the individual, or to direct or recommend alternative treatments, therapies, health care providers, or settings of care to the individual;

(B) To describe a health-related product or service (or payment for such product or service) that is provided by, or included in a plan of benefits of, the covered entity making the communication, including communications about: the entities participating in a health care provider network or health plan network; replacement of, or enhancements to, a health plan; and health-related products or services available only to a health plan enrollee that add value to, but are not part of, a plan of benefits; or

(C) For case management or care coordination, contacting of individuals with information about treatment alternatives, and related functions to the extent these activities do not fall within the definition of treatment.

(3) *Financial remuneration* means direct or indirect payment from or on behalf of a third party whose product or service is being described. Direct or indirect payment does not include any payment for treatment of an individual.

Payment means:

(1) The activities undertaken by:

(i) Except as prohibited under § 164.502(a)(5)(i), a health plan to obtain premiums or to determine or fulfill its responsibility for coverage and provision of benefits under the health plan; or

(ii) A health care provider or health plan to obtain or provide reimbursement for the provision of health care; and

(2) The activities in paragraph (1) of this definition relate to the individual to whom health care is provided and include, but are not limited to:

(i) Determinations of eligibility or coverage (including coordination of benefits or the determination of cost sharing amounts), and adjudication or subrogation of health benefit claims;

(ii) Risk adjusting amounts due based on enrollee health status and demographic characteristics;

(iii) Billing, claims management, collection activities, obtaining payment under a contract for reinsurance (including stop-loss insurance and excess of loss insurance), and related health care data processing;

(iv) Review of health care services with respect to medical necessity, coverage under a health plan, appropriateness of care, or justification of charges;

(v) Utilization review activities, including precertification and preauthorization of services, concurrent and retrospective review of services; and

(vi) Disclosure to consumer reporting agencies of any of the following protected health information relating to collection of premiums or reimbursement:

(A) Name and address;

(B) Date of birth;

(C) Social security number;

(D) Payment history;

(E) Account number; and

(F) Name and address of the health care provider and/or health plan.

* * *

Treatment means the provision, coordination, or management of health care and related services by one or more health care providers, including the coordination or management of health care by a health care provider with a third party; consultation between health care providers relating to a patient; or the referral of a patient for health care from one health care provider to another.

* * *

45 C.F.R. § 164.500—APPLICABILITY

(a) Except as otherwise provided herein, the standards, requirements, and implementation specifications of this subpart apply to covered entities with respect to protected health information.

(b) [Setting forth the provisions applicable to health care clearinghouses.]

(c) Where provided, the standards, requirements, and implementation specifications adopted under this subpart apply to a business associate with respect to the protected health information of a covered entity.

(d) The standards, requirements, and implementation specifications of this subpart do not apply to the Department of Defense or to any other federal agency, or non-governmental organization acting on its behalf, when providing health care to overseas foreign national beneficiaries.

* * *

45 C.F.R. § 164.502—USES AND DISCLOSURES OF PROTECTED HEALTH INFORMATION: GENERAL RULES

(a) *Standard.* A covered entity or business associate may not use or disclose protected health information, except as permitted or required by [the HIPAA Privacy Rule].

(1) *Covered entities: Permitted uses and disclosures.* A covered entity is permitted to use or disclose protected health information as follows:

(i)   To the individual;

(ii) For treatment, payment, or health care operations, as permitted by and in compliance with § 164.506;

(iii) Incident to a use or disclosure otherwise permitted or required by this subpart . . . ;

(iv) Except for uses and disclosures prohibited under § 164.502(a)(5)(i), pursuant to and in compliance with a valid authorization under § 164.508;

(v) Pursuant to an agreement under, or as otherwise permitted by, § 164.510; and

(vi) As permitted by and in compliance with this section, § 164.512, § 164.514(e), (f), or (g).

(2) *Covered entities: Required disclosures.* A covered entity is required to disclose protected health information:

(i)   To an individual, when requested under, and required by § 164.524 or § 164.528; and

(ii) When required by the Secretary under subpart C of part 160 of this subchapter to investigate or determine the covered entity's compliance with this subchapter.

(3) *Business associates: Permitted uses and disclosures.* A business associate may use or disclose protected health information only as permitted or required by its business associate contract or other arrangement pursuant to § 164.504(e) or as required by law. The business associate may not use or disclose protected health information in a manner that would violate the requirements of this subpart, if done by the covered entity, except for the purposes specified under § 164.504(e)(2)(i)(A) or (B) if such uses or disclosures are permitted by its contract or other arrangement.

(4) *Business associates: Required uses and disclosures.* A business associate is required to disclose protected health information:

(i)   When required by the Secretary . . . to investigate or determine the business associate's compliance with this subchapter.

(ii) To the covered entity, individual, or individual's designee, as necessary to satisfy a covered entity's obligations . . . with respect to an individual's request for an electronic copy of protected health information.

(5) *Prohibited uses and disclosures.*

* * *

(ii) Sale of protected health information:

(A) Except pursuant to and in compliance with § 164.508(a)(4), a covered entity or business associate may not sell protected health information.

(B) For purposes of this paragraph, "sale of protected health information" means:

(1) Except as provided in paragraph (a)(5)(ii)(B)(2) of this section, a disclosure of protected health information by a covered entity or business associate, if applicable, where the covered entity or business associate directly or indirectly receives remuneration from or on behalf of the recipient of the protected health information in exchange for the protected health information.

(2) Sale of protected health information does not include a disclosure of protected health information: [for public health purposes; research purposes; treatment and payment purposes; for the sale, merger, or consolidation of a covered entity; to or by a business associate; to an individual; as required by law; for any other purpose in accordance with the HIPAA Privacy Rule where the only remuneration received is a reasonable cost-based fee to transmit the PHI.]

(b) *Standard: Minimum necessary*—[1] *Minimum necessary applies.* When using or disclosing protected health information or when requesting protected health information from another covered entity or business associate, a covered entity or business associate must make reasonable efforts to limit protected health information to the minimum necessary to accomplish the intended purpose of the use, disclosure, or request.

(2) *Minimum necessary does not apply.* [Sets forth exceptions to the minimum necessary requirement, including disclosures for treatment, to an individual, pursuant to an authorization, to the Secretary, or as required by law.]

* * *

(d) *Standard: Uses and disclosures of de-identified protected health information—*

* * *

(2) *Uses and disclosures of de-identified information.* Health information that meets the standard and implementation specifications for de-identification under § 164.514(a) and (b) is considered not to be individually identifiable health information, *i.e.,* de-identified. The requirements of this subpart do not apply to information that has been de-identified in accordance with the applicable requirements of § 164.514, provided that:

(i) Disclosure of a code or other means of record identification designed to enable coded or otherwise de-identified information to be re-identified constitutes disclosure of protected health information; and

(ii) If de-identified information is re-identified, a covered entity may use or disclose such re-identified information only as permitted or required by this subpart.

(e)(1) *Standard: Disclosures to business associates.*

(i) A covered entity may disclose protected health information to a business associate and may allow a business associate to create, receive, maintain, or transmit protected health information on its behalf, if the covered entity obtains satisfactory assurance that the business associate will appropriately safeguard the information. A covered entity is not required to obtain such satisfactory assurances from a business associate that is a subcontractor.

(ii) A business associate may disclose protected health information to a business associate that is a subcontractor and may allow the subcontractor to create, receive, maintain, or transmit protected health information on its behalf, if the business associate obtains satisfactory assurances, in accordance with § 164.504(e)(1)(i), that the subcontractor will appropriately safeguard the information.

* * *

(f) *Standard: Deceased individuals.* A covered entity must comply with the requirements of this subpart with respect to the protected health information of a deceased individual for a period of 50 years following the death of the individual.

(g)(1) *Standard: Personal representatives.* As specified in this paragraph, a covered entity must, except as provided in paragraphs (g)(3) and (g)(5) of this section, treat a personal representative as the individual for purposes of this subchapter.

* * *

45 C.F.R. § 164.504—USES AND DISCLOSURES: ORGANIZATIONAL REQUIREMENTS

* * *

(e)(1) *Standard: Business associate contracts.* . . .

(2) *Implementation specifications: Business associate contracts.* A contract between the covered entity and a business associate must:

(i) Establish the permitted and required uses and disclosures of protected health information by the business associate. The contract may not authorize the business associate to use or further disclose the information in a manner that would violate the requirements of this subpart, if done by the covered entity, except that:

(A) The contract may permit the business associate to use and disclose protected health information for the proper management and administration of the business associate, as provided in paragraph (e)(4) of this section; and

(B) The contract may permit the business associate to provide data aggregation services relating to the health care operations of the covered entity.

(ii) Provide that the business associate will:

(A) Not use or further disclose the information other than as permitted or required by the contract or as required by law;

(B) Use appropriate safeguards and comply, where applicable, with subpart C of this part with respect to electronic protected health information, to prevent use or disclosure of the information other than as provided for by its contract;

(C) Report to the covered entity any use or disclosure of the information not provided for by its contract of which it becomes aware, including breaches of unsecured protected health information as required by § 164.410;

(D) In accordance with § 164.502(e)(1)(ii), ensure that any subcontractors that create, receive, maintain, or transmit protected health information on behalf of the business associate agree to the same restrictions and conditions that apply to the business associate with respect to such information;

(E) Make available protected health information in accordance with § 164.524;

(F) Make available protected health information for amendment and incorporate any amendments to protected health information in accordance with § 164.526;

(G) Make available the information required to provide an accounting of disclosures in accordance with § 164.528;

(H) To the extent the business associate is to carry out a covered entity's obligation under this subpart, comply with the requirements of this subpart that apply to the covered entity in the performance of such obligation;

(I) Make its internal practices, books, and records relating to the use and disclosure of protected health information received from, or created or received by the business associate on behalf of, the covered entity available to the Secretary for purposes of determining the covered entity's compliance with this subpart; and

(J) At termination of the contract, if feasible, return or destroy all protected health information received from, or created or received by the business associate on behalf of, the covered entity that the business associate still maintains in any form and retain no copies of such information or, if such return or destruction is not feasible, extend the protections of the contract to the information and limit further uses and disclosures to those purposes that make the return or destruction of the information infeasible.

(iii) Authorize termination of the contract by the covered entity, if the covered entity determines that the business associate has violated a material term of the contract.

* * *

45 C.F.R. § 164.506—USES AND DISCLOSURES TO CARRY OUT TREATMENT, PAYMENT, OR HEALTH CARE OPERATIONS

(a) *Standard: Permitted uses and disclosures.* Except with respect to uses or disclosures that require an authorization under § 164.508(a)(2) and (4), or that are prohibited under § 164.502(a)(5)(i), a covered entity may use or disclose protected health information for treatment, payment, or health care operations as set forth in paragraph (c) of this section, provided that such use or disclosure is consistent with other applicable requirements of this subpart.

* * *

(c) *Implementation specifications: Treatment, payment, or health care operations.*

(1) A covered entity may use or disclose protected health information for its own treatment, payment, or health care operations.

(2) A covered entity may disclose protected health information for treatment activities of a health care provider.

(3) A covered entity may disclose protected health information to another covered entity or a health care provider for the payment activities of the entity that receives the information.

(4) A covered entity may disclose protected health information to another covered entity for health care operations activities of the entity that receives the information, if each entity either has or had a relationship with the individual who is the subject of the protected health information being requested, the protected health information pertains to such relationship, and the disclosure is:

(i) For a purpose listed in paragraph (1) or (2) of the definition of health care operations; or

(ii) For the purpose of health care fraud and abuse detection or compliance.

(5) A covered entity that participates in an organized health care arrangement may disclose protected health information about an individual to other participants in the organized health care arrangement for any health care operations activities of the organized health care arrangement.

* * *

45 C.F.R. § 164.508—USES AND DISCLOSURES FOR
WHICH AN AUTHORIZATION IS REQUIRED

(a) *Standard: authorizations for uses and disclosures*—(1) *Authorization required: general rule.* Except as otherwise permitted or required by this subchapter, a covered entity may not use or disclose protected health information without an authorization that is valid under this section. When a covered entity obtains or receives a valid authorization for its use or disclosure of protected health information, such use or disclosure must be consistent with such authorization.

(2) *Authorization required: Psychotherapy notes.* Notwithstanding any provision of this subpart, other than the transition provisions in § 164.532, a covered entity must obtain an authorization for any use or disclosure of psychotherapy notes, except:

    (i) To carry out the following treatment, payment, or health care operations: [use by the originator of the notes, by a covered entity for training purposes, or by a covered entity to defend itself in a legal action brought by the individual]; and

    (ii) A use or disclosure that is required by § 164.502(a)(2)(ii) or permitted by § 164.512(a); § 164.512(d) with respect to the oversight of the originator of the psychotherapy notes; § 164.512(g)(1); or § 164.512(j)(1)(i).

(3) *Authorization required: Marketing.*

    (i) Notwithstanding any provision of this subpart . . . a covered entity must obtain an authorization for any use or disclosure of protected health information for marketing, except if the communication is in the form of:

        (A) A face-to-face communication made by a covered entity to an individual; or

        (B) A promotional gift of nominal value provided by the covered entity.

    (ii) If the marketing involves financial remuneration, as defined in paragraph (3) of the definition of marketing at § 164.501, to the covered entity from a third party, the authorization must state that such remuneration is involved.

(4) *Authorization required: Sale of protected health information.*

    (i) Notwithstanding any provision of this subpart . . . a covered entity must obtain an authorization for any disclosure of protected health information which is a sale of protected health information, as defined in § 164.502 of this subpart.

(ii) Such authorization must state that the disclosure will result in remuneration to the covered entity.

* * *

45 C.F.R. § 164.512—USES AND DISCLOSURES FOR WHICH AN AUTHORIZATION OR OPPORTUNITY TO AGREE OR OBJECT IS NOT REQUIRED

A covered entity may use or disclose protected health information without the written authorization of the individual, as described in § 164.508, or the opportunity for the individual to agree or object as described in § 164.510, in the situations covered by this section, subject to the applicable requirements of this section. When the covered entity is required by this section to inform the individual of, or when the individual may agree to, a use or disclosure permitted by this section, the covered entity's information and the individual's agreement may be given orally.

(a) *Standard: Uses and disclosures required by law*—(1) A covered entity may use or disclose protected health information to the extent that such use or disclosure is required by law and the use or disclosure complies with and is limited to the relevant requirements of such law. . . .

(b) *Standard: Uses and disclosures for public health activities*—(1) *Permitted disclosures.* A covered entity may disclose protected health information for the public health activities and purposes described in this paragraph to:

(i) A public health authority that is authorized by law to collect or receive such information for the purpose of preventing or controlling disease, injury, or disability, . . .

(ii) A public health authority or other appropriate government authority authorized by law to receive reports of child abuse or neglect;

(iii) A person subject to the jurisdiction of the Food and Drug Administration (FDA) with respect to an FDA-regulated product or activity for which that person has responsibility, for the purpose of activities related to the quality, safety or effectiveness of such FDA-regulated product or activity. [Providing a list of such purposes including: adverse event reports, tracking FDA-regulated products, product recalls, post-marketing surveillance].

(iv) A person who may have been exposed to a communicable disease or may otherwise be at risk of contracting or spreading a disease or condition, if the covered entity or public health authority is authorized by law to notify such person as necessary in the conduct of a public health intervention or investigation; or

(v) An employer, about an individual who is a member of the workforce of the employer, if [certain requirements are met relating to work-related illness or injury].

* * *

(c) *Standard: Disclosures about victims of abuse, neglect or domestic violence*—(1) *Permitted disclosures*. [Sets forth requirements].

(d) *Standard: Uses and disclosures for health oversight activities*—(1) *Permitted disclosures.* A covered entity may disclose protected health information to a health oversight agency for oversight activities authorized by law, including audits; civil, administrative, or criminal investigations; inspections; licensure or disciplinary actions; civil, administrative, or criminal proceedings or actions; or other activities necessary for appropriate oversight of:

(i)   The health care system;

(ii) Government benefit programs for which health information is relevant to beneficiary eligibility;

(iii) Entities subject to government regulatory programs for which health information is necessary for determining compliance with program standards; or

(iv) Entities subject to civil rights laws for which health information is necessary for determining compliance.

* * *

(e) *Standard: Disclosures for judicial and administrative proceedings*— (1) *Permitted disclosures.* A covered entity may disclose protected health information in the course of any judicial or administrative proceeding: [sets forth requirements].

(f) *Standard: Disclosures for law enforcement purposes.* A covered entity may disclose protected health information for a law enforcement purpose to a law enforcement official if the conditions in paragraphs (f)(1) through (f)(6) of this section are met, as applicable. [(f)(1) through (f)(6) set forth permitted law enforcement disclosures: (1) pursuant to process and as required by law; (2) for identification and location of missing persons or suspects; (3) about victims of a crime; (4) about decedents; (5) about evidence of a crime on the premises; and (6) to report a crime in an emergency].

* * *

(i) *Standard: Uses and disclosures for research purposes*—(1) *Permitted uses and disclosures.* A covered entity may use or disclose protected health information for research, regardless of the source of funding of the research, provided that [certain requirements are met, including the waiver of authorization by an IRB or a privacy board].

* * *

In addition to the key provisions of the HIPAA Privacy Rule excerpted above, the regulations, summarized below, provide individuals certain rights with respect to their protected health information (PHI) and enforcement for violations of the Privacy Rule. The Privacy Rule also requires covered entities to follow certain administrative requirements for maintaining privacy policies, designating privacy officers, training their workforce, and adopting mitigation and other data safeguards.

Rights of Individuals

Notice of Privacy Practices. Covered entities must provide individuals a notice of privacy practices describing the ways the covered entity may use or disclose PHI. This is the HIPAA notice you have likely received and signed when receiving health care services. The individual's signature is required to acknowledge receipt of the notice, but it does not authorize the covered entity to make any special uses or disclosures of your PHI. The notice also describes the covered entity's duties to protect individuals' privacy and how to file a complaint with HHS in the event of a privacy violation. 45 C.F.R. § 164.520.

Access to PHI. Individuals and their personal representatives have the right to access and obtain a copy of their PHI in a covered entity's "designated record set." A designated record set is all of the records maintained by a covered entity about an individual. Cost-based fees may be charged to the patient for copying. Upon request, the covered entity must provide individuals access to their information within 30 days in the format requested by the individual and must transmit information to third parties (such as other providers) as directed by the individual. There are certain exceptions to the right of access, including psychotherapy notes and records compiled for use in an administrative, civil, or criminal proceeding, and under certain other circumstances. 45 C.F.R. § 164.524. HIPAA's right of access has been a recent target of enforcement action by OCR. From September 2019 to June 2021, OCR announced nineteen settlements with covered entities who had failed to provide individuals timely access to their information in violation of the Privacy Rule.

Amendment of PHI. Individuals have a right to request amendments or corrections to their PHI. Covered entities may require such requests to be made in writing and to include support, documentation, and explanation for the request. The regulations provide requirements for processing and denying requests. 45 C.F.R. § 164.526.

Accounting of Disclosures. Individuals have a right to an accounting of disclosures of their PHI by covered entities and business associates made in the prior six years. The accounting of disclosures does not have to include disclosures made for treatment, payment, or health care operations; disclosures to the individual; incidental disclosures; disclosures authorized by the individual; and certain other exceptions. 45 C.F.R. § 164.528.

Payment in Cash to Avoid PHI Sharing with Health Plans. HHS responded to concerns about the sharing of certain health information that might lead to economic or other negative effects on patients. "When individuals pay by cash they can instruct their provider not to share information about their treatment with their health plan." HHS News Release, January 17, 2013.

This change allows patients worried about the harms they might suffer if their personal health information got back to their employers or others to avoid any sharing of such information by paying in cash. Physicians worry, however, that in the case of diseases like HIV/AIDS, this may mean that specialists will not have access to essential patient information, defeating the purpose of the electronic health record and putting the patient at risk of inadequate care.

Enforcement and Penalties for Noncompliance

The Office of Civil Rights (OCR) of the Department of Health and Human Services (HHS) is responsible for investigating and enforcing the HIPAA Privacy and Security Rules. The HITECH Act also expanded enforcement authority to state attorneys general, who can file civil actions in federal district court for HIPAA violations affecting their state's residents. 42 U.S.C. § 1320d–5.

Although individuals can file complaints with OCR alleging HIPAA violations, the Privacy Rule is enforced solely through administrative means, and there is no private right of action for individuals whose information has been used or disclosed in violation of the law.

Civil Monetary Penalties. The 2013 Omnibus HIPAA Rule substantially increased the potential civil monetary fines for violations by covered entities and business associates. It also established tiers of escalating penalty amounts based on increasing degrees of culpability of violators and other responsible parties, ranging from unknowing violations to willful neglect. Fines range from $100 to $50,000 per violation, with the minimum increasing with the degree of culpability and with an annual maximum of $1,500,000. 45 C.F.R. Part 160, Subpart D.

In circumstances where discretion is available, the Secretary of HHS, in determining the amount of penalty, is required to take into account the nature of the claims and the circumstances under which they were presented, the degree of culpability, any history of prior offenses, the financial condition of the person presenting the claims, and other matters. OCR also may consider factors such as the time period during which the violations occurred, reputational harm, and the number of individuals affected. 45 C.F.R. § 160.408.

Criminal Penalties. A person who knowingly obtains or discloses individually identifiable health information in violation of HIPAA faces a fine of $50,000 and up to a one year imprisonment. The criminal penalties increase to $100,000 and up to five years imprisonment if the wrongful conduct involves false pretenses, and to $250,000 and up to ten years imprisonment if the wrongful conduct involves the intent to sell, transfer, or use individually identifiable health information for commercial advantage, personal gain, or malicious harm. Criminal sanctions are enforced by the Department of Justice. 42 U.S.C. § 1320d–6.

Breach. Breaches are impermissible uses of, access to, or disclosures of PHI that compromise the privacy or security of the information. An impermissible use or disclosure of PHI is *presumed* to be a breach, unless it can be demonstrated that there is a *low probability* that PHI has been compromised based upon a four-part risk assessment that considers: (1) the nature and extent of the PHI involved in the breach; (2) the unauthorized person who used the PHI or to whom the disclosure was made; (3) whether the PHI was actually acquired or viewed; and (4) the extent to which the risk to PHI has been mitigated. If the risk assessment evaluation fails to demonstrate there is a low probability that any PHI has been compromised, breach notification is required. Certain exceptions to the definition of a breach continue to apply.

Breach Notification. Covered entities and business associates must notify affected individuals of a breach of their unsecured (e.g., unencrypted) PHI. If a business associate breaches, the covered entity is ultimately responsible for providing the notification, although the covered entity is free to delegate the breach response function to the business associate. Moreover, a business associate's knowledge of a breach will be imputed to the covered entity. Notifications must be provided within 60 days of the discovery of the breach, and must include descriptions of breach, the information involved, the steps the individual can take to protect himself/herself, contact information for the covered entity, and the steps the covered entity is taking to mitigate the breach. Breaches involving more than 500 residents in a given state must also be reported to prominent media outlets in the state. Breach notification rules are codified at 45 C.F.R. §§ 164.400 to 164.414.

The "Wall of Shame." In addition to notifying the individuals and the media, covered entities must notify the Secretary of HHS of breaches involving more than 500 individuals within 60 days of discovery. Breaches affecting fewer than 500 individuals are reported to the Secretary in an annual report. The Secretary must post a list of breaches of unsecured protected health information affecting 500 or more individuals. These breaches are now posted in a new, more accessible format that allows users to search and sort the posted breaches. See Breach Portal: Notice to the Secretary of HHS Breach of Unsecured Protected Health Information, on the HHS OCR web site.

NOTES AND QUESTIONS

1. *Assessing the Privacy Rule.* Review the purposes behind the HIPAA Privacy Rule articulated by HHS in its preamble to the first rulemaking in 2000. Has the Privacy Rule effectively served its purposes? Individuals often find themselves (wrongfully) denied access to their health information from health care workers who inaccurately cite HIPAA as the reason for denial. Does the Privacy Rule make individuals better off than before? In answering this broader question, consider the following:

a. How valuable are the rights and controls provided to individuals over their health information?

b. How effective are the boundaries and restrictions placed on the release of health information?

c. How strong or weak are the penalties for violations of the Privacy Rule—do they sufficiently protect individuals?

d. What are some of the main gaps in the protections offered by the Privacy Rule?

e. How effectively does the Privacy Rule balance the need for the free flow of information (for health care delivery, public health, research, etc.) with individual privacy interests?

You undoubtedly had at least a vague notion of the privacy protections offered by HIPAA as a consumer of health care. Now that you know the details of the Privacy Rule's requirements, do you feel more or less reassured? For a retrospective assessment of the Privacy Rule, see Anita L. Allen, HIPAA at 25—A Work in Progress, 384(23) NEJM 2169 (2021).

2. *Critiques.* Health care providers and other covered entities often bemoan the compliance burden imposed by HIPAA. Nevertheless, within the health care sector, the Privacy Rule has worked relatively well and has facilitated electronic health records and created in patients an expectation of privacy in their health information. Recent critiques focus on the limits of HIPAA, particularly when applied to big data, artificial intelligence, and genomics. Specifically, the Privacy Rule does not apply to technology companies that are not covered entities or business associates, and HIPAA's

methods for de-identification may be evaded through aggregation of big data. Finally, the algorithmic use of health data may exacerbate racial and social disparities that are baked into the data's creation. See W. Nicholson Price II and I. Glenn Cohen, Privacy in the Age of Medical Big Data, 25 Nature Medicine 37 (2019).

The inadequacy of HIPAA in relation to big data is highlighted in *Dinerstein v. Google*, 484 F. Supp. 3d 561 (N.D. Ill. 2020), in which a patient sued the University of Chicago Medical Center and Google for data privacy violations when the medical center shared de-identified patient information with Google for use in predictive health models. The District Court dismissed the case, noting that HIPAA did not create a private right of action or a property interest in the data and permitted the sharing of de-identified patient data even if it was potentially re-identifiable. An appeal to the Seventh Circuit is pending. See I. Glenn Cohen and Michelle M. Mello, Big Data, Big Tech, and Protecting Patient Privacy, 322 JAMA 1141 (2019).

3.   *Business Associates.* One of the key changes of the HITECH Act and the 2013 Omnibus Rule was to expand the definition and compliance obligations of business associates. Business associates and their subcontractors are now directly liable for violations of Privacy and Security Rules. Business associates also have the following responsibilities:

a.   To keep records and submit compliance reports to HHS when HHS requires such disclosure in order to investigate the business associate's compliance with HIPAA, and to cooperate with complaint investigations and compliance reviews;

b.   To disclose PHI as needed by a covered entity to respond to an individual's request for an electronic copy of his/her medical record;

c.   To notify the covered entity of a breach of unsecured PHI;

d.   To make reasonable efforts to limit use and disclosure of PHI, and requests for PHI, to the minimum necessary;

e.   To provide an accounting of disclosures; and

f.   To enter into agreements with subcontractors that comply with the Privacy and Security Rules.

One common task for health care attorneys is to evaluate whether covered entities have HIPAA-compliant business associate agreements with each business associate with whom they share PHI. Looking at the regulations above (particularly 45 C.F.R. § 164.504), what would you include in a checklist for evaluating a business associate agreement?

4.   *Incidental Disclosures.* Health care providers may worry about penalties over inadvertent or incidental releases of health care information to an unauthorized person. The Office of Civil Rights (OCR) has reassured providers that they can discuss a patient's treatment among themselves. "Disclosures for treatment purposes (including requests for disclosures)

between health care providers are explicitly exempted from the minimum necessary requirements."

Incidental uses and disclosures of individual identifiable health information are generally allowed when the covered entity has in place reasonable safeguards and "minimum necessary" policies and procedures to protect an individual's privacy. OCR confirmed that providers may have confidential conversations with other providers and patients even when there is a chance that they might be overheard. Nurses can speak over the phone with a patient or family member about the patient's condition. Providers may also discuss a patient's condition during training rounds at an academic medical institution.

5. *HIPAA and the COVID-19 Pandemic.* The global COVID-19 pandemic posed privacy questions for health care providers and public health authorities who sought to combat its spread. As excerpted above, the HIPAA Privacy Rule allows providers and other covered entities to use and disclose PHI for public health purposes. For example, public health authorities authorized by law can collect or receive PHI for the purpose of "preventing or controlling disease" without individual authorization. Covered entities can also notify persons at risk of contracting or spreading a disease to prevent or control the spread of that disease. 45 CFR § 164.512(b)(1).

The public health emergency also allowed further loosening of the HIPAA Privacy Rule's requirements to facilitate the pandemic response. The Secretary of HHS has authority to waive certain provisions of the Privacy Rule under the Project Bioshield Act of 2004 and § 1135(b)(7) of the Social Security Act. Following President Trump's declaration of a nationwide emergency concerning COVID-19 and HHS Secretary Alex M. Azar's declaration of a public health emergency, Secretary Azar issued the Limited Waiver of HIPAA Sanctions and Penalties During a Nationwide Public Health Emergency, effective March 15, 2020. Specifically, the waiver protected HIPAA-covered hospitals that instituted a disaster protocol from sanctions and penalties under the Privacy Rule by waiving (1) the requirements to obtain a patient's agreement to speak with family members or friends involved in the patient's care, (2) the requirement to honor a request to opt out of the facility directory, (3) the requirement to distribute a notice of privacy practices, (4) the patient's right to request privacy restrictions, and (5) the patient's right to request confidential communications. The HIPAA waiver expires upon the termination of either the declared national or public health emergency.

HHS also issued three Notices of Enforcement Discretion in April and May 2020, announcing it would exercise its discretion not to impose penalties on certain business associates using and disclosing PHI for public health purposes, on covered entities engaged in telehealth services, and on community-based testing sites for noncompliance with certain provisions of the Privacy Rule during the COVID-19 public health emergency. For a discussion of the Privacy Rule's application during the pandemic, see Stacey A. Tovino,

Covid-19 and the HIPAA Privacy Rule: Asked and Answered, 50 Stetson L. Rev. 365 (2021).

PROBLEM: THE PANDEMIC VS. THE HIPAA PRIVACY RULE

Analyzing a question under the HIPAA Privacy Rule follows a common analytic framework, which requires looking at the definitions and rules set forth in the regulations: (1) Is the entity that is disclosing or using the information a covered entity or business associate? If not, HIPAA does not apply; (2) Is the information PHI? If not, HIPAA does not apply; and (3) Is the required use or disclosure permitted without individual authorization or prohibited without individual authorization?

Using this analytic framework, answer the following questions:

1. The City Gazette newspaper reports that the reality show star, Chloe Cheetah, has tested positive for COVID-19. Ms. Cheetah claims she did not provide the information to the City Gazette and accuses the newspaper of violating HIPAA. Did the City Gazette violate the HIPAA Privacy Rule?

2. City Clinic is a covered entity and provides COVID-19 testing. Does the HIPAA Privacy Rule require City Clinic to report test results to public health authorities absent individual authorization? Does the Privacy Rule permit such reporting?

3. Southeast Airlines requires all its passengers to provide proof of COVID-19 vaccination or a negative PCR test result to board the airplane. The airline also requires all its employees who come in contact with passengers to be vaccinated for COVID-19 and requires proof of vaccination as a condition of employment. Setting aside employment and disability law issues, does Southeast Airline's vaccination policy for passengers or employees violate the HIPAA Privacy Rule?

4. Jason Jones is a flight attendant for Southeast Airlines. He went to Well-Mart (a large retail and pharmacy chain) for his COVID-19 vaccine. After he was fully vaccinated, he lost his paper vaccine card. He asked Well-Mart for a record documenting that he received the vaccination, but Well-Mart denied his request, citing HIPAA. Is Well-Mart in compliance with the Privacy Rule?

5. Well-Mart offers incentives to encourage people to get vaccinated at its in-store pharmacies, including a $20 credit at Well-Mart stores. In addition, Well-Mart shares the names and contact information of those it has vaccinated with its commercial partners, including restaurants, movie theaters, and theme parks, who send coupons and promotions to the vaccinated individuals. Assuming the individuals have not authorized the disclosure, is it a violation of HIPAA Privacy Rule for Well-Mart to share vaccinated individuals' information with its commercial partners?

NOTE: MARKETING RULES AND HEALTH INFORMATION EXCHANGES

Marketing Rules. The Privacy Rule requires individual authorization to use PHI for marketing purposes. 45 C.F.R. § 164.508(a)(3). The 2013 Omnibus Rule substantially modified the definition of marketing to address patient concerns about the use of their personal health information for marketing without their consent. Marketing now broadly means any communications about a product or service that encourage a recipient to purchase or use the product or service. 45 C.F.R § 164.501.

Exceptions to the definition of marketing include any communication that is made: (1) to provide refill reminders or information regarding a drug that is currently being prescribed, as long as any financial remuneration received by the covered entity is "reasonably related" to the cost related to the marketing; (2) to an individual as part of treatment, or to a larger population as part of operations, regarding case management, care coordination, or alternative treatment modalities; (3) to describe a health-related product or service, or payment for the product or service, provided by the covered entity or included in a plan of benefits. Examples of this last type include communications about network-participating providers, or value-added products or services not offered by a plan such as vision plan enhancements. 45. C.F.R. § 164.501.

When the covered entity makes the communication face-to-face or the communication consists of a promotional gift of nominal value, patient authorization is not required. If the marketing involves financial remuneration to the covered entity from a third party, the authorization must state that such remuneration is involved. The Privacy Rule also prohibits the sale of PHI without individual authorization where the covered entity or business associate receives remuneration in exchange for the PHI. 45 C.F.R. § 164.508.

Health Information Exchanges. The HITECH Act of 2009 provided federal grants to the states to establish statewide health information exchanges (HIEs) to promote quality and efficiency gains that are expected from interoperable electronic health records (EHRs). An HIE allows clinicians treating a patient to access necessary patient records made by others treating the patient through a one-stop portal rather than by contacting each of the patient's health care providers individually. With a master patient index that gives each patient and each provider a unique identifier, the HIE consolidates patient health information from the patient's many health care providers into one virtual record.

Despite the promise of HIEs and substantial resources expended, adoption has been slow. Observers often inaccurately blame legal barriers from the HIPAA Privacy Rule. Under the HITECH amendments to HIPAA, the HIE is obliged to protect patient privacy by assuring that disclosure of and access to PHI meets, at a minimum, HIPAA standards. HIPAA permits disclosure of PHI without individual authorization for treatment and payment purposes and, in itself, does not form an obstacle to HIEs or to provider participation in an HIE. Nor are providers liable for downstream breaches or misuse of data in the HIE.

A larger barrier to HIEs is that state laws may impose more restrictive standards for health information privacy and confidentiality than HIPAA, including requiring written consent to disclose health information to the HIE. These varying state laws create a "patchwork" of legal requirements that sometimes vary by who is targeted (e.g., certain providers, state health programs, or prisoners) or the type of information protected (e.g., HIV status, mental health records, or genetic information). Confusion about navigating the thicket of state and federal laws can stymie participation in HIEs. Despite efforts by states, governors, and expert work groups, harmonization of interstate laws regarding HIEs has not occurred.

The regulatory tide may be turning in favor of HIEs. To combat real and perceived barriers to HIE development, the 21st Century Cures Act of 2016 called for additional federal guidance and financial incentives to spur the establishment of HIEs. Federal agencies have relaxed patient consent requirements for sharing substance use data, and national technical standards have developed to segment sensitive information that has heightened consent requirements from the rest of the patient's medical record. Though efforts to establish a unique patient identification (UPI) number, the key link in HIE data, have remained elusive, the Cures Act lays the groundwork to solve the patient identification problem. In addition, the Cures Act prohibits EHR vendors from "information blocking" (a refusal to exchange information, usually for commercially competitive reasons). Though many legal and technical barriers to HIEs are either illusory or surmountable, providers and patients must be convinced that the benefits of participating in an HIE outweigh the costs.

For discussion of these issues, see Michelle Mello et al., Legal Barriers to the Growth of Health Information Exchanges—Boulders or Pebbles? 96(1) Milbank Quarterly 110 (2018). Extensive guidance is available on the website of the Office of the National Coordinator for Health Information Technology (ONC).

—————————

As noted in the prior section, states have a variety of medical privacy laws legislated by statute or recognized under common law, prompting the question of how these state medical privacy laws interact with the HIPAA Privacy Rule. The question is addressed in the following case.

BYRNE V. AVERY CENTER FOR OBSTETRICS AND GYNECOLOGY

Supreme Court of Connecticut, 2014.
102 A.3d 32.

OPINION

NORCOTT, JUSTICE.

Congress enacted the Health Insurance Portability and Accountability Act of 1996 (HIPAA), 42 U.S.C. § 1320d et seq., as a comprehensive legislative and regulatory scheme to, inter alia, protect the privacy of patients' health information given emerging advances in information technology. In this appeal, we determine whether HIPAA, which lacks a private right of action and preempts "contrary" state laws; 42 U.S.C. § 1320d–7 (2006); preempts state law claims for negligence and negligent infliction of emotional distress against a health care provider who is alleged to have improperly breached the confidentiality of a patient's medical records in the course of complying with a subpoena. The plaintiff, Emily Byrne, appeals from the judgment of the trial court dismissing counts two and four of the operative amended complaint [ ] filed against the defendant, the Avery Center for Obstetrics and Gynecology, P.C. On appeal, the plaintiff contends that the trial court improperly concluded that her state law claims for negligence and negligent infliction of emotional distress were preempted by HIPAA. We conclude that, to the extent that Connecticut's common law provides a remedy for a health care provider's breach of its duty of confidentiality in the course of complying with a subpoena, HIPAA does not preempt the plaintiff's state common-law causes of action for negligence or negligent infliction of emotional distress against the health care providers in this case and, further, that regulations of the Department of Health and Human Services (department) implementing HIPAA may inform the applicable standard of care in certain circumstances. Accordingly, we reverse the judgment of the trial court.

The trial court's memorandum of decision sets forth the following undisputed facts and procedural history. "Before July 12, 2005, the defendant provided the plaintiff [with] gynecological and obstetrical care and treatment. The defendant provided its patients, including the plaintiff, with notice of its privacy policy regarding protected health information and agreed, based on this policy and on law, that it would not disclose the plaintiff's health information without her authorization.

"In May, 2004, the plaintiff began a personal relationship with Andro Mendoza, which lasted until September, 2004. . . . In October, 2004, she instructed the defendant not to release her medical records to Mendoza. In March, 2005, she moved from Connecticut to Vermont where she presently lives. On May 31, 2005, Mendoza filed paternity actions against the plaintiff in Connecticut and Vermont. Thereafter, the defendant was served with a subpoena requesting its presence together with the plaintiff's medical records at the New Haven Regional Children's [Probate Court] on July 12, 2005. The defendant did not alert the plaintiff of the subpoena, file a motion to quash it or appear in court. Rather, the defendant mailed a copy of the plaintiff's medical file to the court around July 12, 2005. In September, 2005, '[Mendoza] informed [the] plaintiff by telephone that he reviewed [the] plaintiff's medical file in the court file.' On September 15, 2005, the plaintiff filed a motion to seal her medical file, which was granted. The plaintiff alleges that she suffered harassment and extortion threats from Mendoza since he viewed her medical records." . . .

The plaintiff subsequently brought this action against the defendant. Specifically, the operative complaint in the present case alleges that the defendant: (1) breached its contract with her when it violated its privacy policy by disclosing her protected health information without authorization; (2) acted negligently by failing to use proper and reasonable care in protecting her medical file, including disclosing it without authorization in violation of General Statutes § 52–146*o*[6] and the department's regulations implementing HIPAA;[7] (3) made a negligent misrepresentation, upon which the plaintiff relied to her detriment, that

---

[6]   General Statutes § 52–146*o* provides:

(a)   Except as provided in sections 52–146c to 52–146j, inclusive, and subsection (b) of this section, in any civil action or any proceeding preliminary thereto or in any probate, legislative or administrative proceeding, a physician or surgeon, as defined in subsection (b) of section 20–7b, shall not disclose (1) any communication made to him by, or any information obtained by him from, a patient or the conservator or guardian of a patient with respect to any actual or supposed physical or mental disease or disorder, or (2) any information obtained by personal examination of a patient, unless the patient or his authorized representative explicitly consents to such disclosure.

(b)   Consent of the patient or his authorized representative shall not be required for the disclosure of such communication or information (1) pursuant to any statute or regulation of any state agency or the rules of court, (2) by a physician, surgeon or other licensed health care provider against whom a claim has been made, or there is a reasonable belief will be made, in such action or proceeding, to his attorney or professional liability insurer or such insurer's agent for use in the defense of such action or proceeding, (3) to the Commissioner of Public Health for records of a patient of a physician, surgeon or health care provider in connection with an investigation of a complaint, if such records are related to the complaint, or (4) if child abuse, abuse of an elderly individual, abuse of an individual who is physically disabled or incompetent or abuse of an individual with intellectual disability is known or in good faith suspected.

[7]   Specifically, the plaintiff alleged, in paragraphs 25(f), (g), (h), (i) and (j) of the complaint, violations of the following regulations of the department: (1) 45 C.F.R. § 164.512(e)(1)(ii) by "failing to seek itself or obtain 'satisfactory assurances' from the person seeking the information in that the person seeking the information failed to provide to the defendant proof that reasonable efforts were made to either . . . [e]nsure that the plaintiff was provided sufficient notice of the request, or . . . [s]eek a qualified protective order"; (2) 45 C.F.R. § 164.512(e)(1)(iii) "in failing to determine that the plaintiff had not received satisfactory notice of the request for her records from the face of the subpoena"; (3) 45 C.F.R. §§ 164.508(b)(2) and 164.508c (1)–(3) "in that the subpoena was not a valid authorization to produce the records"; (4) 45 C.F.R. § 164.522 "in failing to follow the plaintiff's request for additional privacy protection of her protected health information from production to the party requesting it"; and (5) 45 C.F.R. § 164.502 "in failing to determine and produce only the minimum necessary data requested."

her "medical file and the privacy of her health information would be protected in accordance with the law"; and (4) engaged in conduct constituting negligent infliction of emotional distress. After discovery, the parties filed cross motions for summary judgment.

With respect to the plaintiff's negligence based claims in counts two and four of the complaint, the trial court agreed with the defendant's contention that "HIPAA preempts 'any action dealing with confidentiality/privacy of medical information,' " which prompted the court to treat the summary judgment motion as one seeking dismissal for lack of subject matter jurisdiction. In its memorandum of decision, the trial court first considered the plaintiff's negligence claims founded on the violations of the regulations implementing HIPAA. The court first observed the "well settled" proposition that HIPAA does not create a private right of action, requiring claims of violations instead to be raised through the department's administrative channels. The trial court then [ ]rejected the plaintiff's claim that she had not utilized HIPAA as the basis of her cause of action, but rather, relied on it as " 'evidence of the appropriate standard of care' for claims brought under state law, namely, negligence." Emphasizing that the courts cannot supply a private right of action that the legislature intentionally had omitted, the trial court noted that the "plaintiff has labeled her claims as negligence claims, but this does not change their essential nature. They are HIPAA claims." The trial court further determined that the plaintiff's statutory negligence claims founded on a violation of § 52–146*o* were similarly preempted because the state statute had been superseded by HIPAA, and thus the plaintiff's state statutory claim "amount[ed] to a claim for a HIPAA violation, a claim for which there is no private right of action."

* * *

On appeal, the plaintiff claims that the trial court improperly determined that HIPAA preempted her negligence based state law claims. Conceding that there is no private right of action under HIPAA, the plaintiff asserts that she is not asserting a claim for relief premised solely on a violation of HIPAA, but rather, relies heavily on *Merrell Dow Pharmaceuticals, Inc. v. Thompson,* 478 U.S. 804, 106 S.Ct. 3229, 92 L.Ed.2d 650 (1986), *Acosta v. Byrum,* 180 N.C. App. 562, 638 S.E.2d 246 (2006), and *R.K. v. St. Mary's Medical Center, Inc.,* 229 W.Va. 712, 735 S.E.2d 715 (2012), cert. denied, ___ U.S. ___, 133 S.Ct. 1738, 185 L.Ed.2d 788 (2013), in support of the proposition that common-law negligence actions, with HIPAA informing the standard of care, may complement rather than "obstruct" HIPAA for preemption purposes. [ ] The plaintiff further argues that, under HIPAA and its implementing regulation; see 42 U.S.C. § 1320d–7 (a)(1); 45 C.F.R. § 160.202; her state law claims for relief are not preempted because it is not "contrary to" HIPAA to provide for damages under state common-law claims for privacy breaches.

In response, the defendant relies on the long line of federal and state cases establishing that there is no private right of action, express or implied, under HIPAA [ ] and contends that, because there is no private right of action under HIPAA, "a plaintiff cannot use a violation of HIPAA as the standard of care for underlying claims, such as negligence." The defendant further emphasizes that the plaintiff's negligence claim relying on § 52–146*o* is preempted because HIPAA is more stringent than the state statute. Finally, the defendant also argues briefly, in what appears to be either alternative grounds for affirming the judgment of the trial court or matters likely to arise on remand, that: (1) there is no private right of action under § 52–146*o*; and (2) it was not obligated, as a matter of law, to inform the plaintiff that it had complied with a subpoena, and its compliance with the subpoena did not violate her privacy rights.

We note at the outset that whether Connecticut's common law provides a remedy for a health care provider's breach of its duty of confidentiality, including in the context of responding to a subpoena, is not an issue presented in this appeal. Thus, assuming, without deciding, that Connecticut's common law recognizes a negligence cause of action arising from health care providers' breaches of patient privacy in the context of complying with subpoenas, we agree with the plaintiff and conclude that such an action is not preempted by HIPAA and, further, that the HIPAA regulations may well inform the applicable standard of care in certain circumstances.

I

PREEMPTION CLAIMS

* * *

With respect to the preemptive effect of HIPAA, 42 U.S.C. § 1320d–7 (a)(i) provides that: "Except as provided in paragraph (2), a provision or requirement under this part, or a standard or implementation specification adopted or established under sections 1320d–1 through 1320d–3 of this title, *shall supersede any contrary provision of State law,* including a provision of State law that requires medical or health plan records (including billing information) to be maintained or transmitted in written rather than electronic form." (Emphasis added.) ... The department's regulations, namely, 45 C.F.R. § 160.202 (2004) and 45 C.F.R. § 160.203, provide additional explication of HIPAA's preemptive effect. Specifically, 45 C.F.R. § 160.203 provides as a "general rule" that a "standard, requirement, or implementation specification adopted under this subchapter that is *contrary to a provision of State law preempts the provision of State law.*" (Emphasis added.) A state law is "contrary" to HIPAA if "(1) A covered entity would find it *impossible to comply* with both the [s]tate and [f]ederal requirements; or (2) [t]he provision of [s]tate law stands as an obstacle to the accomplishment and execution of the full purposes and objectives of part C of title XI of [HIPAA], [§] 264 of [Public Law] 104–191, as applicable." (Emphasis added.) . . .

As relevant to this appeal, state laws exempted from preemption include those that "[relate] to the privacy of individually identifiable health information and [are] *more stringent* than a standard, requirement, or implementation specification adopted under subpart E of part 164 of this subchapter." (Emphasis added; footnote added.) 45 C.F.R. § 160.203(b). A state law is "[m]ore stringent" "in the context of a comparison of a provision of [s]tate law and a standard, requirement, or implementation specification adopted under subpart E of part 164 of this subchapter, [if it] meets one or more of the following criteria:

> "(4) With respect to the form, substance, or the need for express legal permission from an individual, who is the subject of the individually identifiable health information, for use or disclosure of individually identifiable health information, provides requirements that narrow the scope or duration, increase the privacy protections afforded (such as by expanding the criteria for), or reduce the coercive effect of the circumstances surrounding the express legal permission, as applicable. . . .

> "(6) With respect to any other matter, provides greater privacy protection for the individual who is the subject of the individually identifiable health information." 45 C.F.R. § 160.202 (2004) . . .

This statutory and regulatory background brings us to the question in the present appeal, namely, whether HIPAA preempts a state law claim sounding in negligence arising from a health care provider's alleged breach of physician-patient confidentiality in the course of complying with a subpoena. It is by now well settled that the "statutory structure of HIPAA . . . precludes implication of a private right of action. [Section] 1320d–6 [of title 42 of the United States Code] expressly provides a method for enforcing its prohibition upon use or disclosure of individual's health information—the punitive imposition of fines and imprisonment for violations." . . .

Nevertheless, it is similarly well established that, "[o]rdinarily, state causes of action are not [preempted] solely because they impose liability over and above that authorized by federal law." . . .

Consistent with these principles, the regulatory history of the HIPAA demonstrates that neither HIPAA nor its implementing regulations were intended to preempt tort actions under state law arising out of the unauthorized release of a plaintiff's medical records. As the plaintiff aptly notes, one commenter during the rulemaking process had "raised the issue of whether a private right of action is a greater penalty, since the proposed federal rule has no comparable remedy." Standards for Privacy of Individually Identifiable Health Information, 65 Fed. Reg. 82,462, 82,582

(December 28, 2000). In its administrative commentary to the final rule as promulgated in the Federal Register, the department responded to this question by stating, inter alia, that "the fact that a state law allows an individual to file [a civil action] to protect privacy does *not* conflict with the HIPAA penalty provisions," namely, fines and imprisonment. (Emphasis added.) Id. This agency commentary on final rules in the Federal Register is significant evidence of regulatory intent. . . . Indeed, "[w]here an agency has authoritatively interpreted its own rule, courts generally defer to that reading unless it is plainly erroneous or inconsistent with the regulation."
. . .

Consistent with this regulatory history, the parties' briefs and our independent research disclose a number of cases from the federal and sister state courts holding that HIPAA, and particularly its implementation through the Privacy Rule regulations, does not preempt causes of action, when they exist as a matter of state common or statutory law, arising from health care providers' breaches of patient confidentiality in a variety of contexts; indeed, several have determined that HIPAA may inform the relevant standard of care in such actions. [ ]

On the basis of the foregoing authorities, we conclude that, if Connecticut's common law recognizes claims arising from a health care provider's alleged breach of its duty of confidentiality in the course of complying with a subpoena, HIPAA and its implementing regulations do not preempt such claims. We further conclude that, to the extent it has become the common practice for Connecticut health care providers to follow the procedures required under HIPAA in rendering services to their patients, HIPAA and its implementing regulations may be utilized to inform the standard of care applicable to such claims arising from allegations of negligence in the disclosure of patients' medical records pursuant to a subpoena. The availability of such private rights of action in state courts, to the extent that they exist as a matter of state law, do not preclude, conflict with, or complicate health care providers' compliance with HIPAA. On the contrary, negligence claims in state courts support "at least one of HIPAA's goals by establishing another disincentive to wrongfully disclose a patient's health care record." *Yath v. Fairview Clinics, N.P.*, supra, 767 N.W.2d at 50. Accordingly, we conclude that the trial court improperly dismissed counts two and four of the plaintiff's complaint, sounding in negligence and negligent infliction of emotional distress.

* * *

The judgment is reversed and the case is remanded to the trial court for further proceedings according to law.

[The opinion of JUSTICES ZARELLA and ROGERS, concurring in part and dissenting in part, is omitted.]

NOTES AND QUESTIONS

1.   *HIPAA Non-Preemption of State Law.* *Byrne* represents the emerging judicial approach to arguments that HIPAA preempts state statutory and common law negligence claims for breaches of medical privacy. See also Yath v. Fairview Clinics, N.P., 767 N.W.2d 34 (Minn. App. 2009); R.K. v. St. Mary's Med. Center, Inc., 735 S.E.2d 715 (W. Va. 2012).

2.   *HIPAA's Lack of a Private Right of Action.* As noted in *Byrne*, the HIPAA Privacy Rule does not create a private right of action for violations, only the administrative enforcement mechanisms described above. See, e.g., Acara v. Banks, 470 F.3d 569, 571 (5th Cir. 2006), in which the Fifth Circuit held: "HIPAA does not contain any express language conferring private rights upon a specific class of individuals. . . . Because HIPAA specifically delegates enforcement, there is a strong indication that Congress intended to preclude private enforcement." An affected individual may file a written complaint with OCR, which exercises enforcement discretion whether to investigate the complaint, but an affected individual will not receive damages or injunctive relief for the violation. Given HIPAA's lack of a private right of action, do you agree with the court in *Byrne* that HIPAA does not preempt state common law and statutory causes of action for conduct that would constitute a HIPAA violation? Are these state law remedies "more stringent" than the HIPAA Privacy Rule and therefore subject to the exception from HIPAA preemption? For a critique of HIPAA's lack of a private right of action and suggestions for addressing the resulting enforcement gaps, see Stacey A. Tovino, A Timely Right to Privacy, 104 Iowa L. Rev. 1361 (2019).

3.   *HIPAA Standards and Private Actions.* In addition to the preemption question, *Byrne* addresses the separate issue of whether the standards set forth in the Privacy Rule can serve as evidence of a standard of care for medical records privacy in a common law negligence or breach of confidentiality case. Other courts have similarly held that despite the absence of a private right of action under HIPAA, it can inform the applicable standard of care in common law tort cases. See, e.g., Bonney v. Stephens Memorial Hosp., 17 A.3d 123 (Me. 2011); Fanean v. Rite Aid Corp. of Delaware, Inc., 984 A.2d 812 (Del. Super. 2009); Acosta v. Byrum, 638 S.E.2d 246 (N.C. Ct. App. 2006); Sorensen v. Barbuto, 143 P.3d 295 (Utah App. 2006). But see Haywood v. Novartis Pharmaceuticals Corp., 298 F. Supp. 3d 1180 (N.D. Ind. 2018), finding that HIPAA cannot be used as the basis for a negligence claim in Indiana.

Courts could go a step further and recognize that violation of HIPAA standards amounts to negligence per se, under which statutory or regulatory standards (rather than common law) establish the applicable standard of care. One court has allowed a plaintiff's tort complaint to proceed on a negligence per se theory. See I.S. v. The Washington University, Case No. 4:11CV235SNLJ (D. Mo. 2011), where the federal court held that the plaintiff's claim for negligence per se was valid; HIPAA was clearly implicated in the claim, which fell within the broad class of state claims based on federal regulations brought in the state court. However, other courts have declined to allow HIPAA standards to establish negligence per se. See Sheldon v. Kettering Health Network, 40 N.E.3d 661 (Ohio Ct. App. 2015); Young v. Carran, 289 S.W.3d 586 (Ky. App.2008), review denied, 2009 Ky. LEXIS 592 (August 19, 2009) (holding that Kentucky law limits negligence per se claims to Kentucky statutes, and HIPAA is a federal law).

Courts disagree over whether a HIPAA violation can support a state law breach of contract claim, particularly where compliance with the Privacy Rule is a term of a contract. Some courts have answered in the negative, see Brush v. Miami Beach Healthcare Grp. Ltd., 238 F. Supp.3d 1359 (2017), and others have answered in the affirmative, see Dinerstein v. Google, 484 F. Supp. 3d 561 (2020).

PROBLEM: LEAKING PATIENT INFORMATION

1.   Dr. Jasmine is a dentist in solo practice. He submits his bills only by mail, not electronically, and he does not email his patients or use electronic media in any part of his business. He therefore does not give patients a Notice of Privacy Practices or in any way indicate to patients what their rights are as to their dental history information. Jasmine sells his patient lists to various dental supply companies for their use in marketing. Has he violated HIPAA?

2.   Goldberg goes to a medical office for an appointment, and her physician decides to order some tests, gives her a form indicating which tests have been ordered, and tells her to take the form to the lab. When she arrives at the lab, she sees a sign-in sheet and a notice advising patients to deposit the form in the open basket that sits next to the sign-in sheet. The forms lie face-up in the basket, and they show a patient's name, address, birth date, social security number, and other demographic information, as well as the tests ordered. Is this a violation of HIPAA? If so, how can it be corrected?

3.   Dr. Newman, a psychiatrist, is having dinner out with colleagues when she is paged by her answering service with an urgent message to call one of her patients. She left her cell phone at home, so she borrows the phone of one of her dinner companions to return the patient's call. The borrowed cell phone automatically maintains a log of the outgoing phone number. Can a patient whose identity is thereby revealed file a complaint against Dr. Newman?

4.   During a routine blood test, Frent chats with the lab technician, Gosford, about a football game. Gosford responds by telling an amusing story about a well-known sports figure whose blood he had tested on the previous day. Gosford further mentions the high level of steroids that the test revealed. Can the athlete sue Gosford? The laboratory? What are his options?

5.   Gosford obtains her prescriptions for genital herpes treatment from XYZ pharmacies in her area. One day she receives a mailing from a pharmaceutical company advertising their herpes treatment product. The mail has piled up with other pieces in the lobby of her apartment building, and her

fellow tenants can easily see the description of the product and her name on the flyer. What recourse, if any, does Gosford have?

6.   Reconsider *Doe*, above, in light of HIPAA requirements and penalties. What if anything do the Medical Privacy Rules add to Doe's rights?

7.   Reconsider **Problem: The Hunt for Patient Records,** above, in light of HIPAA requirements and penalties. Did the hospital violate HIPAA? Did the law firm?

VI.   MEDICAL MALPRACTICE

Medical malpractice claims are an important, and the most publicly visible, legal mechanism for promoting health care quality. The doctrine requires a physician to compensate a patient injured as a result of an adverse event or medical error for which the physician is responsible.

According to the Institute of Medicine (IOM), "at least 44,000 Americans die each year as a result of medical errors . . . [and that] number may be as high as 98,000. Even when using the lower estimate, deaths due to medical errors exceed the number attributable to the 8th leading cause of death." Institute of Med., To Err Is Human: Building a Safer Health System 28 (Linda T. Kohn et al., eds., 2000). The IOM Report estimates that adverse events and medical errors cost the nation between $17 billion and $29 billion per year. The Report defines an adverse event as "an injury caused by medical management rather than the underlying condition of the patient," and a medical error as "the failure of a planned action to be completed as intended . . . or the use of a wrong plan to achieve an aim . . . ."

Quality improvement is central to the Affordable Care Act. Section 3501 mandates that the Director of the Center for Quality Improvement Programs, in collaboration with other federal agencies, "identify, develop, evaluate, disseminate, and provide training in innovative methodologies and strategies for quality improvement practices in the delivery of health care services that represent best practices in health care quality, safety, and value." As the federal government develops and disseminates innovative strategies for improving medical quality, those strategies will likely affect the standards of care for both professional and institutional providers.

A. THE STANDARD OF CARE

HALL V. HILBUN
Supreme Court of Mississippi, 1985.
466 So. 2d 856.

ROBERTSON, JUSTICE, for the Court:

I.

This matter is before the Court on Petition for Rehearing presenting primarily the question whether we should, as a necessary incident to a just adjudication of the case at bar, refine and elaborate upon our law regarding (a) the standard of care applicable to physicians in medical malpractice cases and (b) the matter of how expert witnesses may be qualified in such litigation.

* * *

When this matter was before the Court on direct appeal, we determined that the judgment below in favor of the surgeon, Dr. Glyn R. Hilbun, rendered following the granting of a motion for a directed verdict, had been correctly entered. . . .

For the reasons set forth below, we now regard that our original decision was incorrect. . . .

II.

Terry O. Hall was admitted to the Singing River Hospital in Jackson County, Mississippi, in the early morning hours of May 18, 1978, complaining of abdominal discomfort. Because he was of the opinion his patient had a surgical problem, Dr. R.D. Ward, her physician, requested Dr. Glyn R. Hilbun, a general surgeon, to enter the case for consultation. Examination suggested that the discomfort and illness were probably caused by an obstruction of the small bowel. Dr. Hilbun recommended an exploratory laparotomy [sic]. Consent being given, Dr. Hilbun performed the surgery about noon on May 20, 1978, with apparent success.

Following surgery Mrs. Hall was moved to a recovery room at 1:35 p.m., where Dr. Hilbun remained in attendance with her until about 2:50 p.m. At that time Mrs. Hall was alert and communicating with him. All vital signs were stable. Mrs. Hall was then moved to a private room where she expired some 14 hours later.

On May 19, 1980, Glenn Hall commenced this wrongful death action by the filing of his complaint. . . .

* * *

At trial Glenn Hall, plaintiff below and appellant here, described the fact of the surgery. He then testified that he remained with his wife in her hospital room from the time of her arrival from the recovery room at approximately 3:00 p.m. on May 20, 1978, until she ultimately expired at approximately 5:00 a.m. on the morning of May 21. Hall stated that his wife complained of pain at about 9:00 p.m. and was given morphine for relief, after which she fell asleep. Thereafter, Hall observed that his wife had difficulty in breathing which he reported to the nurses. He inquired if something was wrong and was told his wife was all right and that such breathing was not unusual following surgery. The labored breathing then subsided for an hour or more. Later, Mrs. Hall awakened and again complained of pain in her abdomen and requested a sedative, which was administered following which she fell asleep. Mrs. Hall experienced further difficulty in breathing, and her husband reported this, too. Again, a nurse told Hall that such was normal, that patients sometimes make a lot of noise after surgery.

After the nurse left the following occurred, according to Hall.

[A]t this time I followed her [the nurse] into the hall and walked in the hall a minute. Then I walked back into the room, and walked back out in the hall. Then I walked into the room again and I walked over to my wife and put my hand on her arm because she had stopped making that noise. Then I bent over and flipped the light on and got closer to her where I could see her, and it looked like she was having a real hard problem breathing and she was turning pale or a bluish color. And I went to screaming.

Dr. Hilbun was called and came to the hospital immediately only to find his patient had expired. The cause of the death of Terry O. Hall was subsequently determined to be adult respiratory distress syndrome (cardio-respiratory failure).

Dr. Hilbun was called as an adverse witness and gave testimony largely in accord with that above. . . .

Dr. Hilbun stated the surgery was performed on a Saturday. Following the patient's removal to her room, he "went home and was on call that weekend for anything that might come up." Dr. Hilbun made no follow-up contacts with his patient, nor did he make any inquiry that evening regarding Mrs. Hall's post-operative progress. Moreover, he was *not* contacted by the nursing staff or others concerning Mrs. Hall's condition during the afternoon or evening of May 20 following surgery, or the early morning hours of May 21, although the exhibits introduced at trial disclose fluctuations in the vital signs late in the evening of May 20 and more so, in the early morning hours of May 21. Dr. Hilbun's next contact with his patient came when he was called by Glenn Hall about 4:55 or 5:00 that morning. By then it was too late.

* * *

The autopsy performed upon Mrs. Hall's body revealed the cause of death and, additionally, disclosed that a laparotomy [sic] sponge had been left in the patient's abdominal cavity. The evidence, however, without contradiction establishes that the sponge did not contribute to Mrs. Hall's death. Although the sponge may ultimately have caused illness, this possibility was foreclosed by the patient's untimely death.

Plaintiff's theory of the case centered around the post-operative care provided by Dr. Hilbun. Two areas of fault suggested were Dr. Hilbun's failure to make inquiry regarding his patient's post-operative course prior to his retiring on the night of May 20 and his alleged failure to give appropriate post-operative instructions to the hospital nursing staff.

When questioned at trial, Dr. Hilbun first stated that he had practiced for 16 years in the Singing River Hospital and was familiar with the routine of making surgical notes, i.e., a history of the surgery. He explained that the post-operative orders were noted on the record out of courtesy by Dr. Judy Fabian, the anesthesiologist on the case. He stated such orders were customarily approved by his signature or he would add or subtract from the record to reflect the exact situation.

[Dr. Hilbun testified about the post-operative orders noted in the medical records as of May 20, 1978. Mrs. Hall had a nasogastric tube, an i.v., and a catheter; she was receiving medications for pain, nausea, and infections. He testified that he checked on Mrs. Hall in the recovery room and stayed with her, took her vital signs, and discharged her to the floor. He confirmed on cross-examination that he customarily followed his patient postoperatively until the patient left the hospital.]

* * *

Insofar as the record reflects, Dr. Hilbun gave the nursing staff no instructions regarding the post-operative monitoring and care of Mrs. Hall beyond those [summarized above]. Dr. Hilbun had no contact with Mrs. Hall after 3:00 p.m. on May 20. Fourteen hours later she was dead.

The plaintiff called Dr. S.O. Hoerr, a retired surgeon of Cleveland, Ohio, as an expert witness. The record reflects that Dr. Hoerr is a *cum laude* graduate of the Harvard Medical School, enjoys the respect of his peers, and has had many years of surgical practice. Through him the plaintiff sought to establish that there is a national standard of surgical practice and surgical care of patients in the United States to which all surgeons, including Dr. Hilbun, are obligated to adhere. Dr. Hoerr conceded that he did not know for a fact the standard of professional skill, including surgical skills and post-operative care, practiced by general surgeons in Pascagoula, Mississippi, but that he did know what the standard should have been.

. . . [T]he trial court ruled that Dr. Hoerr was not qualified to give an opinion as to whether Dr. Hilbun's post-operative regimen departed from the obligatory standard of care. . . .

* * *

Parts of Dr. Hoerr's testimony excluded under the trial judge's ruling follow:

A. My opinion is that she [Mrs. Hall] did not receive the type of care that she should have received from the general surgical specialist and that he [Dr. Hilbun] was negligent in not following this patient; contacting, checking on the condition of his patient sometime in the evening of May 20th. *It is important in the post-operative care of patients to remember that very serious complications can follow abdominal operations, in particular in the first few hours after a surgical procedure.* And this can be inward bleeding; it can be an explosive development in an infection; or *it can be the development of a serious pulmonary complication, as it was in this patient. As a result of her condition, it is my opinion that he lost the opportunity to diagnose a condition, which in all probability could have been diagnosed at the time by an experienced general surgeon, one with expertise in thoracic surgery. And then appropriate treatment could have been undertaken to abort the complications and save her life.*

There are different ways that a surgeon can keep track of his patient— "follow her" as the expression goes—besides a bedside visit, which is the best way and which need not be very long at all, in which the vital signs are checked over. The surgeon gets a general impression of what's going on. He can delegate this responsibility to a competent physician, who need not be a surgeon but could be a knowledgeable family practitioner. He could call in and ask to speak to the registered nurse in charge of the patient and determine through her what the vital signs are, and if she is an experienced Registered Nurse what her evaluation of the patient is. *From my review of the record, none of these things took place, and there is no effort as far as I can see that Dr. Hilbun made any effort to find out what was going on with this patient during that period of time.* I might say or add an additional belief that I felt that the nursing responsibility which should have been exercised was not exercised, particularly at the 4:00 a.m. level when the pulse rate was recorded at 140 per minute without any effort as far as I can see to have any physician see the patient or to get in touch with the operating surgeon and so on.

There is an additional thing that Dr. Hilbun could have done if he felt that the nursing services might be spotty—sometimes good, sometimes bad. This is commonly done in Columbus, Ohio, in Ashtabula, Pascagoula, etcetera. *He could put limits on the degree in which the vital signs can vary, expressing the order that he should be called if they exceeded that.* Examples would be: Call me if the pulse rate goes over 110; call me if the temperature exceeds 101; call me if the blood pressure drops below 100. There is a simple way of spelling out for the nursing services what the limits of discretion belong to them and the point at which the doctor should be called.

* * *

Dr. Hilbun did not place any orders on the chart for the nurses to call him in the event of a change in the vital signs of Mrs. Hall. He normally made afternoon rounds between 4:00 and 5:00 p.m. but didn't recall whether he went by to see her before going home. Dr. Hilbun was on call at the hospital that weekend for anything which might come up. Subsequent to the operation and previous to Mrs. Hall's death, he was called about one other person on the same ward, one door down, twice during the night. He made no inquiry concerning Mrs. Hall, nor did he see or communicate with her.

Dr. Donald Dohn, of expertise unquestioned by plaintiff and with years of practical experience, gave testimony for the defendant. He had practiced on the staff at the Cleveland Clinic Foundation in Cleveland, Ohio, beginning in 1958. Fortuitously, he had moved to Pascagoula, Mississippi, about one month before the trial. Dr. Dohn stated he had practiced in the Singing River Hospital for a short time and there was a great difference in the standard of care in medical procedures in Cleveland, Ohio, and those in Pascagoula, Mississippi. Although he had practiced three weeks in Pascagoula, he was still in the process of acquainting himself with the local conditions. He explained the differences as follows:

Well, there are personnel differences. There are equipment differences. There are diagnostic differences. There are differences in staff responsibility and so on. For example, at the Cleveland Clinic on our service we had ten residents that we were training. They worked with us as our right hands. Here we have no staff. So it is up to us to do the things that our residents would have done there. There we had a team of five or six nurses and other personnel in the operating room to help us. Here we have nurses in the operating room, but there is no assigned team. You get the luck of the draw that day. I am finding out these things myself. Up there it is a big center; a thousand beds, and it is a regional center. We have tremendous advantages with technical systems, various types of x-ray equipment that is [sic] sophisticated. Also in terms of the intensive care unit, we had a Neurosurgical Intensive Care with people who were specially trained as a team to work there. From my standpoint personally, I seldom had to do much paperwork there as compared to what I have to do now. I have to dictate everything and take all my notes. So, as you can see, there is a difference.

Finally, he again stated the standard of care in Ohio and the standard of care in the Singing River Hospital are very different, although it is obvious to the careful reader of Dr. Dohn's testimony that in so doing he had reference to the differences in equipment, personnel and resources and not differences in the standards of skill, medical knowledge and general medical competence a physician could be expected to bring to bear upon the treatment of a patient.

At the conclusion of the plaintiff's case, defendant moved for a directed verdict on the obvious grounds that, the testimony of Drs. Hoerr and Sachs having been excluded, the Plaintiff had failed to present a legally sufficient quantum of evidence to establish a prima facie case. The Circuit Court granted the motion. . . .

III.

A. *General Considerations*

Medical malpractice is legal fault by a physician or surgeon. It arises from the failure of a physician to provide the quality of care required by law. When a physician undertakes to treat a patient, he takes on an obligation enforceable at law to use minimally sound medical judgment and render minimally competent care in the course of the services he provides. A physician does not guarantee recovery. If a patient sustains injury because of the physician's failure to perform the duty he has assumed under our law, the physician may be liable in damages. A competent physician is not liable *per se* for a mere error of judgment, mistaken diagnosis or the occurrence of an undesirable result.

The twin principles undergirding our stewardship of the law regulating professional liability of physicians have always been reason and fairness. For years in medical malpractice litigation we regarded as reasonable and fair what came to be known as the "locality rule" (but which has always consisted of at least two separate rules, one a rule of substantive law, the other a rule of evidence).

* * *

C. *The Physician's Duty of Care:*
A primary rule of substantive law

1. *The Backdrop*

* * *

2.   *The Inevitable Ascendency of National Standards*

* * *

We would have to put our heads in the sand to ignore the "nationalization" of medical education and training. Medical school admission standards are similar across the country. Curricula are substantially the same. Internship and residency programs for those entering medical specialties have substantially common components. Nationally uniform standards are enforced in the case of certification of specialists. Differences and changes in these areas occur temporally, not geographically.

Physicians are far more mobile than they once were. They frequently attend medical school in one state, do a residency in another, establish a practice in a third and after a period of time relocate to a fourth. All the while, they have ready access to professional and scientific journals and seminars for continuing medical education from across the country. Common sense and experience inform us that the laws of medicine do not vary from state to state in anything like the manner our public law does.

Medicine is a science, though its practice be an art (as distinguished from a business). Regarding the basic matter of the learning, skill and competence a physician may bring to bear in the treatment of a given patient, state lines are largely irrelevant. That a patient's temperature is 105 degrees means the same in New York as in Mississippi. Bones break and heal in Washington the same as in Florida, in Minnesota the same as in Texas. . . .

* * *

3.   *The Competence-Based National Standard of Care: Herein of the Limited Role of Local Custom*

All of the above informs our understanding and articulation of the competence-based duty of care. Each physician may with reason and fairness be expected to possess or have reasonable access to such medical knowledge as is commonly possessed or reasonably available to minimally competent physicians in the same specialty or general field of practice throughout the United States, to have a realistic understanding of the limitations on his or her knowledge or competence, and, in general, to exercise minimally adequate medical judgment. Beyond that, each physician has a duty to have a practical working knowledge of the facilities, equipment, resources (including personnel in health related fields and their general level of knowledge and competence), and options (including what specialized services or facilities may be available in larger communities, e.g., Memphis, Birmingham, Jackson, New Orleans, etc.) reasonably available to him or her as well as the practical limitations on same.

In the care and treatment of each patient, each physician has a non-delegable duty to render professional services consistent with that objectively ascertained minimally acceptable level of competence he may be expected to apply given the qualifications and level of expertise he holds himself out as possessing and given the circumstances of the particular case. The professional services contemplated within this duty concern the entire caring process, including but not limited to examination, history, testing, diagnosis, course of treatment, medication, surgery, follow-up, after-care and the like.

* * *

Mention should be made in this context of the role of good medical judgment which, because medicine is not an exact science, must be brought to bear in diagnostic and treatment decisions daily. Some physicians are more reluctant to recommend radical surgery than are other equally competent physicians. There exist legitimate differences of opinion regarding medications to be employed in particular contexts. "Waiting periods" and their duration are the subject of bona fide medical controversy. . . . We repeat: a physician may incur civil liability only when the quality of care he renders (including his judgment calls) falls below minimally acceptable levels.

Different medical judgments are made by physicians whose offices are across the street from one another. Comparable differences in medical judgment or opinion exist among physicians geographically separated by much greater distances, and in this sense local custom does and must continue to play a role within our law, albeit a limited one.

We recognize that customs vary within given medical communities and from one medical community to another. Conformity with established medical custom practiced by minimally competent physicians in a given area, while evidence of performance of the duty of care, may never be conclusive of such compliance. [ ] The content of the duty of care must be objectively determined by reference to the availability of medical and practical knowledge which would be brought to bear in the treatment of like or similar patients under like or similar circumstances by minimally competent physicians in the same field, given the facilities, resources and options available. The content of the duty of care may be informed by local medical custom but never subsumed by it.

* * *

4.   The Resources-Based Caveat to the National Standard of Care

The duty of care, as it thus emerges from considerations of reason and fairness, when applied to the facts of the world of medical science and practice, takes two forms: (a) a duty to render a quality of care consonant with the level of medical and practical knowledge the physician may reasonably be expected to possess and the medical judgment he may be expected to exercise, and (b) a duty based upon the adept use of such medical facilities, services, equipment and options as are reasonably available. With respect to this second form of the duty, we regard that there remains a core of validity to the premises of the old locality rule.

* * *

A physician practicing in Noxubee County, for example, may hardly be faulted for failure to perform a CAT scan when the necessary facilities and equipment are not reasonably available. In contradistinction, objectively reasonable expectations regarding the physician's knowledge, skill, capacity for sound medical judgment and general competence are, consistent with his field of practice and the facts and circumstances in which the patient may be found, *the same everywhere.*

* * *

As a result of its resources-based component, the physician's non-delegable duty of care is this: given the circumstances of each patient, each physician has a duty to use his or her knowledge and therewith treat through maximum reasonable medical recovery, each patient, with such reasonable diligence, skill, competence, and prudence as are practiced by minimally competent physicians in the same specialty or general field of practice throughout the United States, who have available to them the same general facilities, services, equipment and options.

* * *

As we deal with general principles, gray areas necessarily exist. One involves the case where needed specialized facilities and equipment are not available locally but are reasonably accessible in major medical centers— New Orleans, Jackson, Memphis. Here as elsewhere the local physician is held to minimally acceptable standards. In determining whether the physician's actions comport with his duty of care, consideration must always be given to the time factor—is the physician confronted with what reasonably appears to be a medical emergency, or does it appear likely that the patient may be transferred to an appropriate medical center without substantial risk to the health or life of the patient? Consideration must also be given to the economic factors—are the proposed transferee facilities sufficiently superior to justify the trouble and expense of transfer? Further discussion of these factors should await proper cases.

D.   Who May Qualify As Expert Medical Witness
In Malpractice Case: A rule of evidence

As a general rule, if scientific, technical or other specialized knowledge will assist the trier of fact to understand the evidence or to determine a fact in issue, a witness qualified as an expert by knowledge, skill, experience, training or education (or a combination thereof), coupled with independence and lack of bias, may testify thereto in the form of an opinion or otherwise. Medical malpractice cases generally require expert witnesses to assist the trier of fact to understand the evidence. [ ]

Generally, where the expert lives or where he or she practices his or her profession has no relevance *per se* with respect to whether a person may be qualified and accepted by the court as an expert witness. There is no reason on principle why these factors should have *per se* relevance in medical malpractice cases.

* * *

In view of the refinements in the physician's duty of care . . . we hold that a qualified medical expert witness may without more express an opinion regarding the meaning and import of the duty of care . . . , given the peculiar circumstances of the case. Based on the information reasonably available to the physician, i.e., symptoms, history, test results, results of the doctor's own physical examination, x-rays, vital signs, etc., a qualified medical expert may express an opinion regarding the conclusions (possible diagnoses or areas for further examination and testing) minimally knowledgeable and competent physicians in the same specialty or general field of practice would draw, or actions (not tied to the availability of specialized facilities or equipment not generally available) they would take.

Before the witness may go further, he must be familiarized with the facilities, resources, services and options available. This may be done in any number of ways. The witness may prior to trial have visited the facilities, etc. He may have sat in the courtroom and listened as other witnesses described the facilities. He may have known and over the years interacted with physicians in the area. There are no doubt many other ways in which this could be done, but, significantly, we should allow the witness to be made familiar with the facilities (and customs) of the medical community in question via a properly predicated and phrased hypothetical question.

Once he has become informed of the facilities, etc. available to the defendant physician, the qualified medical expert witness may express an opinion what the care duty of the defendant physician was and whether the acts or omissions of the defendant physician were in compliance with, or fell substantially short of compliance with, that duty.

* * *

V. *Disposition of the Case at Bar*

[The court reversed and remanded for a new trial on the grounds that the testimony of Drs. Hoerr and Sachs was improperly excluded, and with their testimony, the plaintiff might have survived the defense motion for a directed verdict.]

NOTES AND QUESTIONS

1. *The Standard of Care and Expert Testimony.* The standard of care is set by the reasonable application of medical knowledge and skill to the particular clinical circumstances presented to a physician. Because the content of medical knowledge and skill and their application in a particular clinical circumstance are typically beyond the understanding of most fact-finders, the law requires expert medical evidence to establish the standard of care in most cases. While medical experts may disagree about the controlling standard of care in a given case, the law requires that the fact-finder base its determination of the standard of care on the expert evidence presented at trial, even while allowing the fact-finder to assess the credibility and persuasiveness of that expert evidence. In this way, the standard of care is set by the medical profession because members of the medical profession are the primary source of the expertise required in each case. This is one important way a professional negligence claim differs from a standard negligence cause of action.

2. *Customary vs. Reasonable Care. Hall* identifies the difference between conforming to professional custom and complying with the standard of care. "Conformity with established medical custom . . . , while evidence of performance of the duty of care, may never be conclusive of such compliance." A standard of care derives from the application of medical knowledge and skill to the particular clinical circumstances faced by the defendant-physician. Custom most often reflects a standard of care reconfirmed by the collective application of medical knowledge and skill to a clinical circumstance physicians often face. That is why the court in *Hall* holds that customary practice is relevant evidence of a standard of care.

Yet evidence that most physicians prescribe a particular drug to patients displaying a particular set of symptoms is not itself evidence that this customary practice is good medical practice. Conflating medical custom with the standard of care fails to account for the rare case in which customary practice is bad medicine. Consider, for example, a spinal surgeon who recently wrote an editorial calling out her fellow surgeons for customarily performing unnecessary surgeries and explaining that this is why she has testified against the practice as an expert witness in malpractice cases. See Nancy E. Epstein, Why I Testify for Some Patients/Plaintiffs, and Against Some Doctors/Defendants, 9 Surg. Neurol. Int'l 256 (Dec. 18, 2018). This physician speculated that unnecessary surgeries had become customary because of "relatively higher reimbursement rates for spine operations and the increased number of spinal surgeons" in her region, or perhaps "the seductive lure of new techniques and instrumentation." Id.

If what this surgeon said is true—that it has become customary for spinal surgeons to recommend and perform surgeries without a good medical reason—then this example helps explain why the law must tie a physician's duty to medical reasonableness rather than to medical custom. Otherwise, malpractice law would "immunize physicians who follow the pack." Philip G. Peters, Jr., The Quiet Demise of Deference to Custom: Malpractice Law at the

Millennium, 57 Wash. & Lee L. Rev. 163, 183 (2000). Thus, *Hall* clarifies that the "content of the duty of care may be informed by local medical custom but never subsumed by it."

Unlike the court in *Hall*, most courts have not been careful to distinguish between a medical custom and a standard of care, often conflating the two. To this day, imprecise language in the holdings of older judicial opinions finds its way into current case law and results in judges erroneously equating customary practice with the standard of care. The doctrine is correcting itself, albeit slowly. See id.

If courts properly understand the standard of care as the professionally reasonable application of medical knowledge and skill to *a particular set of clinical circumstances* and not as conformance with medical custom, there is no need for the "two schools of thought" defense, which has been slowly eroding over time. The "two schools of thought" defense has allowed physicians to avoid liability by showing they treated the plaintiff in the same way a "respectable minority" of other physicians would have treated a similarly-situated patient, even though the defendant's conduct was inconsistent with the customary practice of the majority of the profession. See, e.g., Leech v. Bralliar, 275 F. Supp. 897 (D.Ariz.1967). In jurisdictions that erroneously equate the standard of care with conforming to an established medical custom, the law must prop up this error with defenses that account for instances in which the profession is split and practice reveals the lack of a consensus custom.

By contrast, in jurisdictions where the standard of care turns on the reasonable deployment of medical knowledge and skill in a particular clinical circumstance, the majority and minority practices of other physicians—while relevant—is not dispositive. See Philip G. Peters, Jr., The Quiet Demise of Deference to Custom: Malpractice Law at the Millennium, 57 Wash. & Lee L. Rev. 163 (2000). The same is true of the so-called "clinical innovation" defense. See, e.g., Brook v. St. John's Hickey Mem. Hosp., 380 N.E.2d 72 (Ind. 1978). No such defenses is necessary if the standard of care is correctly understood as the professionally reasonable application of medical knowledge and skill to any clinical circumstance—whether a common clinical circumstance or one that requires a novel approach.

3.   *The Standard of Care and the Locality Rule*. As *Hall* explains, most states have moved from the locality rule to a similar locality or national standard due, in part, to worries about a "conspiracy of silence" that unfairly limits the pool of available experts. Doctors do not like to testify against one another. As the court noted in Mulder v. Parke Davis & Co., 288 Minn. 332, 181 N.W.2d 882 (1970), "All too frequently, and perhaps understandably, practicing physicians are reluctant to testify against one another. Unfortunately, the medical profession has been slow to fashion machinery for making impartial and objective assessments of the performance of their fellow practitioners."

Still, legislatures enacting malpractice reform statutes have often imposed modified locality rule tests in order to protect physicians from out-of-state witnesses testifying for plaintiffs. See, e.g. Henry v. Southeastern Ob-Gyn Assoc., 142 N.C. App. 561, 543 S.E.2d 911 (2001) ("similar locality" test of N.C. Gen. Stat. S. 90–21.12 was intended to avoid the adoption of a national standard for health care providers).

Many courts, like *Hall,* also allow evidence describing the practice limitations under which the defendant labors. *Hall's* "resource component" allows the trier of fact to consider the facilities, staff, and other equipment available to the practitioner in the institution, following the general rule that courts should take into account the locality, proximity of specialists, and special facilities for diagnosis and treatment. See, e.g., Primus v. Galgano, 329 F.3d 236 (1st Cir. 2003) (it is "permissible to consider the medical resources available to the physician as one circumstance in determining the skill and care required"); Restatement (Second) of Torts, § 299A, Comment g ("Allowance must be made also for the type of community in which the actor carries on his practice. A country doctor cannot be expected to have the equipment, facilities, experience, knowledge or opportunity to obtain it, afforded him by a large city.").

4. *Qualifying an Expert.* Qualifying an expert typically requires that the expert practice in the same specialty as the defendant. Courts, however, have allowed physicians in other specialties to testify so long as the alleged negligence involved matters within the knowledge of every physician. For example, a general surgeon was permitted to testify as to the standard of care of a plastic surgeon performing elective surgery where the testimony addressed a general surgical issue about whether nerves in the forehead should have been protected. Hauser v. Bhatnager, 537 A.2d 599 (Me. 1988). Experts need not be board certified in the subject of the claims on which they are testifying, so long as they have the appropriate education and experience. See, e.g., Hanson v. Baker, 534 A.2d 665 (Me. 1987). Testimony about the standard of care may be based upon the expert's own practice and education. See Wallbank v. Rothenberg, 74 P.3d 413 (Colo. App. 2003) (personal practices of medical experts may be relevant to the standard of care).

5. *Standard of Care and Clinical Literature.* Expert evidence can include clinical literature. Several sources of reliable and authoritative statements may be used either by experts in professional liability cases or by the trial judge as definitive in establishing the standard of care. These sources include clinical practice guidelines, pharmaceutical package insert instructions and warnings, the Physicians' Desk Reference (PDR), a learned treatise, and the results of published research.

Clinical practice guidelines (CPGs) are "statements that include recommendations intended to optimize patient care that are informed by a systematic review of evidence and an assessment of the benefits and harms of alternative care options." Institute of Medicine, Clinical Guidelines We Can Trust 4 (2011). CPGs emerged in part to address geographic variations in medical practice, suggesting that medical practice is not based sufficiently on scientific evidence. The fact that medical practice has developed more like an art than a science explains, in part, why we see so much variation in practice. See generally John E. Wennberg, Variation in Use of Medicare Services Among Regions and Selected Academic Medical Centers: Is More Better?, Commonwealth Fund Pub. No. 874, at 4 (Dec. 2005).

Despite the promise of CPGs, two fundamental problems undermine their reliability. "First, there is a lack of centralized authority to coordinate, vet, approve, and catalog guidelines. Second, there is an absence of a universal methodology to create guidelines . . . ." Gilbert Benavidez and Austin B. Frakt, Fixing Clinical Practice Guidelines, Health Affairs Blog (Aug. 5, 2019). Until it was defunded in 2018, the National Guidelines Clearinghouse—a program previously administered by the Agency for Healthcare Quality Research—had published all clinical practice guidelines that met the program's criteria for inclusion, graded the scientific basis of each guideline, and described their development process. No other centralized authority has taken the place of the Clearinghouse. Moreover, without a standard methodology for creating CPGs, there is substantial variation in the reliability of CPGs. See id.

Given the availability of CPGs and their uncertain reliability, courts must determine their evidentiary value in establishing the standard of care. Generally, judges have rejected arguments that a CPG conclusively establishes the standard of care in a malpractice case. Instead, most hold that a CPG is one piece of relevant evidence about the standard of care. See, e.g., Conn v. United States, 880 F. Supp. 2d 741 (S.D. Miss. 2012). Yet, parties may address the reliability of any CPG offered into evidence. See, e.g., Trowbridge v. United States, 703 F. Supp. 2d 1129 (D.C. Idaho 2010).

6. *Assessing Reliability of Scientific Evidence.* Outside of medical malpractice cases, judges assess the scientific reliability of expert evidence, including expert testimony, as a condition for the admissibility of such evidence. Yet, very few jurisdictions require judges to do this threshold assessment before an expert can testify with respect to the standard of care in medical malpractice cases. See Monica Lynne Coscia, "Trust Me, I'm A Doctor": Medical Malpractice as A Daubert-Free Zone, 108 Geo. L.J. 1761 (2020) (reporting results of a 50-state survey).

Judicial verification of the scientific merits of expert testimony as a condition of admissibility is based upon Daubert v. Merrell Dow Pharmaceuticals, Inc., 509 U.S. 579, 113 S. Ct. 2786, 125 L. Ed. 2d 469 (1993). In that case, the Court held that the Federal Rules of Evidence make the trial judge a gatekeeper for expert testimony. The judge must assess the reliability of an expert's testimony, its relevance, and the underlying reasoning or methodology. Expert testimony must have a valid scientific connection to the issues in the case and be based on "scientifically valid principles."

While state courts have adopted Daubert-style testing as a condition for the admissibility of most expert testimony, they have not done so for experts testifying as to the standard of care in medical malpractice cases. This difference likely is a vestige of older case law that continues, erroneously, to equate customary medical practice with the standard of care. See Julie L.

Campbell, A Reliability Check on Expert Witness Testimony in Medical Malpractice Litigation: Mandatory Medical Simulation, 31 Health Matrix 1 (2021). When expert medical testimony is used to establish causation rather than the standard of care in malpractice cases, however, state courts have more commonly required Daubert-style threshold testing. See id.

7. *Do Physicians Owe a Duty to Advocate for Insurance Coverage of Treatment?* A patient's insurance coverage and its limits affect the patient's access to care and thus the outcome they experience. As a result, a few courts have acknowledged that a treating physician may owe their patients a duty to help them secure coverage for needed care. Wickline v. State, 239 Cal. Rptr. 810, 192 Cal. App. 3d 1630 (1986), was the first to do so.

In *Wickline*, a patient covered under California's Medicaid program experienced complications following vascular surgery. Because the patient's insurance coverage for her hospitalization was about to expire, her treating physician filed a request with her plan to extend coverage for additional hospital days and explained why the additional days were medically necessary given the patient's complications. The plan denied the request. Without pursuing an available appeal of the plan's denial, the physician discharged the patient upon the expiration of her coverage. Following discharge, the patient suffered from an infection that eventually resulted in the amputation of her leg. The patient did not sue her treating physician; rather, she sued her insurance plan, alleging that its denial of her physician's request to extend her coverage caused her injury. Following a jury verdict for the plaintiff, the plan appealed. The intermediate appellate court reversed, holding that the plan's coverage decision did not override the physician's medical decision to discharge the patient and thus could not be said to have caused the patient's injury.

In dicta, the court acknowledged that the treating physician might have owed a duty to the patient to appeal the plan's denial of the extended coverage request. It said:

> [T]he physician who complies without protest with the limitations imposed by a third party payor, when his medical judgment dictates otherwise, cannot avoid his ultimate responsibility for his patient's care. He cannot point to the health care payor as the liability scapegoat when the consequences of his own determinative medical decisions go sour.
>
> There is little doubt that Dr. Polonsky was intimidated by the Medi-Cal program but he was not . . . rendered powerless to act appropriately if other action was required under the circumstances. If, in his medical judgment, it was in his patient's best interest that she remain in the acute care hospital setting for an additional four days beyond the extended time period originally authorized by Medi-Cal, Dr. Polansky should have made some effort to keep Wickline there.

Id., 192 Cal. App. 3d at 1645, 239 Cal. Rptr. at 819. See also Wilson v. Blue Cross of Southern California, 271 Cal. Rptr. 876, 222 Cal. App. 3d 660 (1990) (acknowledging that the decision of a treating physician to discharge a patient without pursuing an appeal of the patient's insurance plan decision to limit coverage could be actionable).

Despite these judicial observations, it is difficult to find a case in which a duty for a physician to help patients secure insurance coverage for proposed treatment is enforced. Wilson v. Chesapeake Health Plan, Inc., No. 88019032/CL76201 (Baltimore, MD Cir. Ct. 1988), may come the closest. There, a trial court denied a motion to dismiss a claim by the estate of a deceased patient against his treating physician alleging that the physician had failed to assist the patient adequately "in determining the scope of coverage provided by their HMO, other insurers, and alternative funding sources" to cover the cost of a potentially life-saving liver transplantation. In the absence of additional case law, however, it is unclear if the law recognizes such a duty.

8. *Contributory and Comparative Fault.* Tort doctrines of contributory and comparative fault apply in medical malpractice cases. Generally, however, courts do not permit a defendant to argue that a plaintiff's pre-treatment life-style choices (e.g., smoking, drinking, eating and exercise habits) caused or contributed to causing the plaintiff's injuries. Instead, most jurisdictions will take account of only post-treatment conduct by patients that was a factor in causing the injuries at issue in the lawsuit, particularly where patients have not complied with their physicians' instructions. See, e.g., Ostrowski v. Azzara, 111 N.J. 429, 545 A.2d 148 (N.J. 1988). Yet even this limited application of contributory and comparative fault doctrines might not account for factors beyond a patient's control that interfere with their ability to follow a treatment plan. For example, given growing evidence that a person's health is significantly affected by social determinants (access to medical care, healthy food, clean air and water, safe neighborhoods, income and education levels, among others), to what extent should the law hold individuals responsible for their health? See Ben Schwan, Responsibility Amid the Social Determinants of Health, 35 Bioethics 6 (2021).

9. *Loss of Chance.* The "loss of chance" doctrine is particularly relevant in medical malpractice claims. The doctrine "refer[s] to situations in which a failure on the part of a physician or hospital to appropriately treat an illness or condition had contributed to a diminished probability that the individual seeking treatment would survive the illness or recover from the condition." Lauren Guest, David Schap & Thi Tran, The "Loss of Chance" Rule as A Special Category of Damages in Medical Malpractice: A State-by-State Analysis, J. Legal Econ. 53, 54 (April 2015). It is relevant to the elements of causation and damages and most often arises in cases where the plaintiff alleges that the provider's negligence delayed proper treatment, which, in turn, diminished the patient's probability of making a full recovery. See, e.g., Herskovits v. Group Health Cooperative of Puget Sound, 99 Wash. 2d 609, 664 P.2d 474 (1983) (permitting damages to be based on loss of chance caused by defendant's negligent failure to make a timely cancer diagnosis); Estate of Frey v. Mastroianni, 146 Hawai'i 540, 463 P.3d 1197 (2020). While a plurality of jurisdictions have adopted the doctrine, according to a 50-state survey, significant variation exists among the states. As of 2015, about half of U.S.

jurisdictions have adopted the doctrine, 17 have rejected it, and the remainder have deferred or have yet to address the issue. See David Schap & Thi Tran, The "Loss of Chance" Rule as A Special Category of Damages in Medical Malpractice: A State-by-State Analysis, J. Legal Econ. 53 (April 2015).

Among the jurisdictions that have adopted the doctrine, there are three approaches:

    a.   Loss of an appreciable or substantial chance of recovery. This approach does not give proportional recovery based on the percentage of harm attributable to the defendant, but instead manipulates the burden of proof rather than acknowledging the lost chance as the real injury. See, e.g., Hicks v. United States, 368 F.2d 626 (4th Cir. 1966); Jeanes v. Milner, 428 F.2d 598 (8th Cir. 1970).

    b.   Increased risk of harm. This approach, found in the Restatement (Second) of Torts, § 323(a), lowers causation requirements to allow causes of action for those who have a less than 50% chance of survival. See Hamil v. Bashline, 481 Pa. 256, 392 A.2d 1280 (1978). Compensation is for the increased risk of harm rather than loss of a chance, and damage awards are not discounted for the percentage of harm caused by the physician. Death is typically the compensable injury. Any percentage is enough to get to the jury. See Thompson v. Sun City Community Hosp., Inc., 141 Ariz. 597, 688 P.2d 605 (1984) (linking Restatement (Second) of Torts, § 323(a) to the interest seen as "the chance itself.")

    c.   Compensation for the loss of a chance. This looks at damages that include the value of the patient's life reduced in proportion to the lost chance. This approach was developed by Joseph King in his seminal article, Causation, Valuation and Chance in Personal Injury Torts Involving Pre-existing Conditions and Future Consequences, 90 Yale L.J. 1353 (1981). The approach requires a percentage probability test, with the value of the patient's life determined and damages decreased accordingly. See Matsuyama v. Birnbaum, 452 Mass. 1, 890 N.E.2d 819 (Mass. 2008).

NOTE: OUTCOMES, PRACTICE GUIDELINES, BEST PRACTICES, AND THE AFFORDABLE CARE ACT

The ACA has several sections that affect the potential tort liability of physicians. Only one section deals explicitly with tort liability. What the ACA does, however, is to create four streams of pressure that converge toward measurable and specific standards of care in practice that are likely to impact tort liability.

Section 10303 of the ACA instructs the Secretary of HHS to develop provider-level outcome measures for both hospitals and physicians, as well as other providers. Such measures will include at least ten outcome measurements for acute and chronic diseases. Additionally, section 10303(c) requires the Secretary of HHS to identify existing and new clinical practice guidelines in light of the research on outcome measures and best practice.

Section 933 directs that outcomes, best practices, and guidelines be disseminated rapidly to practice settings. The Center for Quality Improvement and Patient Safety will support research on system improvements and the development of tools "to facilitate adoption of best practices that improve the quality, safety, and efficiency of health care delivery services. Such support may include establishing a *Quality Improvement Network Research Program* for the purpose of testing, scaling, and disseminating [ ] interventions to improve quality and efficiency in health care." Findings will be disseminated through multiple media and linked with the Office of the National Coordinator of Health Information Technology and used to "inform the activities of the health information technology extension program under Section 3012, as well as any relevant standards, certification criteria, or implementation specifications." Section 933 also adds to the Health Care Quality Improvement Programs by mandating that the Director "identify, develop, evaluate, disseminate, and provide training in innovative methodologies and strategies for quality improvement practices in the delivery of health care services that represent best practices in health care quality, safety, and value" in collaboration with other federal agencies.

A Patient-Centered Outcomes Research Institute (PCORI) is created by Section 6301, Patient-Centered Outcomes Research. This institute is to ". . . assist patients, clinicians, purchasers, and policy-makers in making informed health decisions by advancing the quality and relevance of evidence concerning the manner in which diseases, disorders, and other health conditions can effectively and appropriately be prevented, diagnosed, treated, monitored, and managed through research and evidence synthesis." The PCORI must release its findings within 90 days of receipt and make them available to clinicians, patients, and the general public.

NOTE: THE DEFENSE OF IMMUNITY UNDER GOOD SAMARITAN AND DECLARED EMERGENCY ACTS

To keep the risk of liability from causing a physician to avoid entering into a treatment relationship with an accident victim or a person otherwise in urgent need of medical attention, most states have enacted so-called "Good Samaritan" laws. These statutes immunize physicians from malpractice claims when those physicians provide treatment—outside their standard professional practices—to those who requires such care. So, for example, in Willingham v. Hudson, 617 S.E.2d 192 (Ga. App. 2005), an appellate court upheld summary judgment in favor of a family practitioner who volunteered in a hospital emergency department overwhelmed with patients injured by a tornado. The physician was neither on-call nor on backup call at the time he came to the ER to help. The court held that he was immune from a malpractice action brought by a patient who suffered injuries from an infected laceration that the physician had closed. The relevant Georgia statute, OCGA § 51–1–29, read:

> Any person, including [a licensed medical professional], who in good faith renders emergency care at the scene of an accident or emergency to

the victim or victims thereof without making any charge therefor shall not be liable for any civil damages as a result of any act or omission by such person in rendering emergency care or as a result of any act or failure to act to provide or arrange for further medical treatment or care for the injured person.

Similar statutes in other states often exclude from protection claims alleging grossly negligent, or reckless or intentional conduct. Because Good Samaritan statutes often are limited to medical care provided without the expectation of payment, they often fail to protect physicians who, as part of their paid positions, care for patients during a community-wide emergency.

To fill this gap, many states offer immunity for physicians against claims of medical malpractice for treatment provided during a publicly declared emergency. For example, § 8.01–225.02 of the Virginia Code reads:

In the absence of gross negligence or willful misconduct, any health care provider who responds to a disaster shall not be liable for any injury or wrongful death of any person arising from the delivery or withholding of health care when (i) a state or local emergency has been or is subsequently declared in response to such disaster, and (ii) the emergency and subsequent conditions caused a lack of resources, attributable to the disaster, rendering the health care provider unable to provide the level or manner of care that otherwise would have been required in the absence of the emergency and which resulted in the injury or wrongful death at issue.

The statute is not limited to cases in which physicians are unpaid for the services rendered. Additionally, the provision likely accounts both for patients allegedly injured as a result of affirmative treatment and those who are harmed as a result of withheld treatment when scarce personnel and other resources are triaged in favor of other patients.

Protections like this statute have received renewed attention during the COVID-19 pandemic, which at times has strained medical resources to near breaking point in some localities. Several jurisdictions that, prior to COVID-19, had not provided immunity during declared public emergencies passed new statutes, or their governors issued executive orders providing such immunity for the duration of the pandemic. See, e.g., State of New York, Executive Order 202.10, Continuing Temporary Suspension and Modification of Laws Relating to the Disaster Emergency (Mar. 23, 2020) (granting immunity to health care providers against malpractice claims arising from care provided in response to COVID-19). For a 50-state survey, see Benjamin J. McMichael et al., COVID-19 and State Medical Liability Immunity, Health Aff. Blog (May 14, 2020).

Separately, crisis standards of care likely also apply during a public emergency that forces physicians to triage scarce resources among a population of patients in need of medical care. Crisis standards of care are described as "triage protocols." Lance Gable, Allocation of Scarce Medical Resources and Crisis Standards of Care, in Public Health Law Watch, Assessing Legal Responses to COVID-19 (August 2020). They are created as informal guidance and can be triggered by executive order if and when a public emergency results in making medical resources scarce. As a matter of law, a crisis standard of care likely augments or refines the existing standard of care. As Robert Jerry explains:

> Because the standard of care is a flexible standard that recognizes the importance of changed circumstances, the 'applicable' standard of care essentially shifts when the practice environment changes. In a non-crisis environment without rationing, the standard of care is measured with respect to how reasonable and competent physicians exercise their skills and knowledge to meet the needs of their individual patients. This individual-focused norm does not disappear in a mass disaster when justifiably fearful individuals look to their personal physicians for support and assistance. But when scarce resources must be allocated among patients under conditions of triage, what is appropriate care for an individual cannot be determined in isolation from broader public health considerations. Under conditions of triage, 'the duty to steward resources . . . effectively override[s] individual patient preferences and instead suppl[ies] resources based on evidence-based assessments of the benefit of the treatment related to its scarcity.' [ ]. In sum, the standard of care is not different in a crisis, but the 'circumstances' are different, which changes how the standard of care is applied.

Robert H. Jerry, II, Covid-19: Responsibility and Accountability in a World of Rationing, 7 J.L. & Biosciences 1, 8 (2020).

CHAPTER 5

LIABILITY OF HEALTH
CARE INSTITUTIONS

■ ■ ■

I. INTRODUCTION

The hospital is the classic health care "institution." The U.S. has over 6,000 hospitals—about 3,000 are nonprofit, 1,200 are for-profit, and 1,200 are local-, state-, or federal-government owned. Most of the remainder are psychiatric and long-term care hospitals. See American Hospital Association, Fast Facts on U.S. Hospitals (2021). The vast majority of these hospitals are part of health systems, of which there are 637 in the U.S. Based on 2018 data, these 637 health systems accounted for at least 88 percent of all hospital beds in the nation. See Michael Furukawa et al., Consolidation and Health Systems in 2018: New Data from the AHRQ Compendium, Health Aff. Blog (Nov. 25, 2019).

Hospitals are major providers of emergency care and highly complicated surgical and other procedures. They are, therefore, the largest sources of patient harms in the U.S. Given the possibility of injury from hospital-based errors and serious adverse events, hospitals are at risk for institutional liability based on their roles in coordinating a variety of health care professionals and maintaining an array of complex equipment.

The pressure on hospitals to coordinate care and move patients safely from acute care situations to other institutions or locations—assisted living or long-term care or home—has only increased under the Affordable Care Act (ACA). Hospitals have been acquiring physician practices in response to the incentives of the ACA and the pressures for a better coordinated health care system. As presented later, in Chapter 10, the ACA authorizes and—through the Medicare Shared Savings Program (MSSP)—incentivizes institutional and professional providers to coordinate with each other through "Accountable Care Organizations" (ACOs). An ACO may take any legal form so long as it has a mechanism for shared governance that permits the participation of provider members in organizational decision-making. ACOs capable of providing all of the care needed by a population of at least 5000 Medicare beneficiaries may participate in the MSSP, under which an ACO that meets certain quality measures will receive a portion of any annual savings the ACO generates below a spending target set by Medicare. This incentive has spurred a new round of provider consolidations into very large ACOs that seek to generate savings through greater control over provider coordination and clinical efficiencies. Consequently, ACOs are poised to become a new target for institutional liability.

The high cost of the Health Information Technology for Economic and Clinical Health (HITECH) Act's mandate for electronic health records and other regulatory mandates has created an additional reason for free-standing hospitals to join systems; and these systems are merging to achieve market share and necessary economies of scale in an increasingly competitive environment. As a result, 3,000 formerly free-standing hospitals are now in systems, defined as either a multihospital or a diversified single hospital system. A multihospital system is two or more hospitals owned, leased, sponsored, or contract-managed by a central organization. Single, freestanding hospitals may be categorized as a system by bringing into membership three or more, and at least 25 percent, of their owned or leased non-hospital pre-acute or post-acute health care organizations. Hospitals in systems are likely to have more resources to devote to patient safety, and system pressures are likely to push hospitals toward the adoption of safety-based standards more rapidly.

Health care delivery also includes institutional forms such as managed care organizations that finance health care and contract with physicians and hospitals to provide care, as well as ambulatory care facilities such as surgicenters and physician offices. As medical care continually moves out of the hospital into less expensive settings, the liability of institutional providers of outpatient care emerges as a new concern. Historically, most case law originated with hospitals—the predominant deliverers of high technology, high risk care, and therefore where the most severe patient harms could occur—but the courts are now adapting to changes in the delivery system.

Because hospitals and ever-larger institutional delivery systems are playing an increasing role in delivering medical services, they must also play a greater—if not primary—role in preventing and responding to adverse events. The IOM Report on medical errors famously refocused attention on institutions to promote patient safety.

The decentralized and fragmented nature of the health care delivery system (some would say "nonsystem") also contributes to unsafe conditions for patients, and serves as an impediment to efforts to improve safety. Even within hospitals and large medical groups, there are rigidly-defined areas of specialization and influence. For example, when patients see multiple providers in different settings, none of whom have access to complete information, it is easier for something to go wrong than when care is better coordinated. At the same time, the provision of care to patients by a collection of loosely affiliated organizations and providers makes it difficult to implement improved clinical information systems capable of providing timely access to complete patient information. Unsafe care is one of the prices we pay for not having organized systems of care with clear lines of accountability.

Based on the above, and other, observations, the IOM made several recommendations, including:

- raising standards and expectations for improvements in safety through the actions of oversight organizations, group purchasers, and professional groups; and

- creating safety systems inside health care organizations through the implementation of safe practices at the delivery level. This level is the ultimate target of all the recommendations.

This chapter examines the liability of institutions for medical harms to patients, addressing hospitals, managed care organizations, and ACOs. It presents common-law principles as they have evolved and as they are affected by the ACA. Drawing also on material from Chapter 4, it explores the limitations of our medical tort system, as well as reforms of, and alternatives to, that system.

II. VICARIOUS LIABILITY OF HOSPITALS FOR NEGLIGENCE OF MEDICAL STAFF

A. ACTUAL AGENCY AND THE "CONTROL" TEST

Hospitals employ nurses, technicians, clerks, custodians, cooks, and others who are clearly employees of the hospital under agency principles. Their terms and conditions of employment are controlled by the hospital, which sets their hours, wages, and working conditions. When employees are negligent, the hospital is vicariously liable for their acts due to the master-servant relationship of agency law. It is the relationship of physicians to the hospital that raises more complicated agency problems.

The hospital-physician relationship is an unusual one by corporate standards. A typical hospital may have several categories of practicing physicians, but the largest group is comprised of private physicians with staff privileges. Staff privileges include the right of the physicians to admit and discharge their private patients to and from the hospital and the right to use the hospital's facilities. See generally Chapter 11, below.

These physicians have typically been independent contractors rather than employees of the hospital. This legal status means that the hospital is not easily targeted as a defendant in a malpractice suit. Generally, a hospital cannot be held vicariously liable for the negligence of a doctor affiliated with the hospital unless the doctor is employed by the hospital.

The hospital is independently liable only if it is negligent in its administrative or housekeeping functions, by, for example, causing a patient to slip and fall on a wet floor. Otherwise, the hospital has been immune in the past from liability. This situation has changed as the courts have confronted the evolution of the modern hospital and expanded the vicarious liability doctrine.

SCOTT v. SSM HEALTHCARE ST. LOUIS
Missouri Court of Appeals, Eastern District, 2002.
70 S.W.3d 560.

RICHARD B. TEITELMAN, JUDGE.

* * *

Background

In 1994 Matthew Scott, then seventeen, sustained serious injuries as a result of a sinus infection that spread into his brain. Matthew was involved in a car accident and was taken to Hospital, where he was treated for minor injuries and released to his father. Two days later Matthew returned to Hospital's emergency room, complaining of a severe headache. Dr. Doumit was Hospital's emergency room physician who examined Matthew that day. Soon after Matthew arrived, a CT scan of his head was conducted. Dr. Richard Koch, a partner in RIC, read the CT film and concluded that the CT scan was normal. Matthew was diagnosed as having a mild concussion from the previous auto accident, was given medication for his headache and sent home.

The next day, Matthew's headache had not improved. His parents called Hospital three times and informed Dr. Doumit that Matthew was lethargic, nauseous and vomiting. Dr. Doumit told them that he was still exhibiting signs of a minor concussion, that he would probably improve within a few days, that they should continue to observe him, but that if they became very concerned about his condition they could bring him back to the emergency room.

Early the next morning, Matthew collapsed in the kitchen, unable to use the right side of his body. He was rushed by ambulance to Barnes Hospital in St. Peters, Missouri. A spinal tap and CT scan revealed an infection at the top of his brain, and his brain was swelling inside his skull. Matthew was taken to Barnes Hospital in St. Louis, where a number of surgeries were performed to remove infected brain tissue and portions of his skull. He remained in a coma for several weeks.

Eventually, after undergoing skull reconstructive surgery and an extensive program of rehabilitation, Matthew was able to achieve a considerable recovery. He also has sustained serious permanent injuries, however, including among others a significant degree of paralysis on the right side of his body, and the requirement of a permanent ventricular drainage tube in his brain.

Matthew and his mother filed this medical malpractice action against Hospital and others, alleging, *inter alia,* that the negligence of Dr. Doumit and Dr. Koch caused Matthew's injuries. Specifically, plaintiffs alleged that Dr. Koch had acted below the accepted standard of care in misreading the initial CT scan on September 24, and that Dr. Doumit had acted below the standard of care by failing to instruct Matthew's parents, when they called with their concerns, to bring him back to the emergency room. Plaintiffs' suit further alleged that at all relevant times Dr. Koch had been acting as an agent for Hospital, notwithstanding the fact that he was formally employed by RIC, which had contracted to provide radiology services at Hospital. Plaintiffs' action also named Dr. Koch and RIC as defendants. Before trial, plaintiffs settled their claims against Dr. Koch and RIC for the sum of $624,800 (hereinafter, "the Koch settlement"). The case then proceeded to trial against Hospital.

[The court first found that the evidence at trial supported the allegations of medical negligence by the treating physicians. The jury found for the plaintiffs, having found that Dr. Koch was the Hospital's agent.]

Discussion

1. *Sufficiency of Evidence on Issue of Dr. Koch's Agency*

[The Court considered the differences between independent contractor status and employee status. It noted that the employer-employee relationship is a fact question for the jury.]

* * *

Two elements are required to establish an agency relationship: (1) the principal must consent, either expressly or impliedly, to the agent's acting on the principal's behalf, and (2) the agent must be subject to the principal's control. [ ] In the context of a hospital-physician relationship, the primary focus is on whether the hospital generally controlled, or had the right to control, the conduct of the doctor in his work performed at the hospital. [ ] Additionally, our courts have also cited with approval a list of ten factors set forth in the Restatement (Second) of Agency, § 220(2) (1958), as a helpful aid in "determining whether one acting for another is a servant or an independent contractor."[ ]

In the case at hand, Hospital cites a handful of facts from the record which, arguably, could support the conclusion that RIC and Dr. Koch were acting as independent contractors rather than as agents of Hospital. Among them are: the relationship between Dr. Koch and Hospital was based upon a written contract, in which RIC agreed to provide radiology services to Hospital; RIC was a partnership, of which Dr. Koch was a partner and signatory to the contract; Hospital did not employ or pay Dr.

Koch (RIC did); Hospital did not directly set Dr. Koch's hours at the Hospital; and Hospital did not bill patients for the services of Dr. Koch or the other RIC radiologists.

However, a jury question is presented when the evidence is sufficiently conflicting that reasonable minds could differ as to whether agency existed. [ ] The following evidence, all of it from the contract and/or testimony in the record, supports finding a principal-agent relationship between Hospital and Dr. Koch: (1) Hospital establishes the medical standards for the provision of radiological services at Hospital; (2) Hospital determines the qualifications necessary for Dr. Koch; (3) Hospital has the right to require Dr. Koch to submit reports regarding radiological services rendered according to standards established by Hospital; (4) Hospital sets the prices for Dr. Koch's services, and those prices cannot be changed without prior approval of Hospital; (5) Hospital required that Dr. Koch be "an active member" of Hospital's medical staff; (6) Hospital required that Dr. Koch maintain liability insurance in specific amounts; (7) in the event that Dr. Koch fails to procure such insurance, Hospital has the right to procure it for him at his expense; (8) Hospital has the right to terminate Dr. Koch if dissatisfied with his performance; (9) Hospital provides all nurses and technicians for the radiology department; (10) Hospital owns and provides all of the office space for the radiology department, as well as providing all of the radiology equipment, films, supplies and fixtures; (11) Hospital decides what type of film, film boxes and view jackets will be used; (12) the contract between Hospital and RIC is of infinite duration; (13) RIC has provided the only radiologists working at Hospital for over 60 years; (14) RIC exclusively provides all of the radiologists for Hospital, including even the doctor who serves as the administrative director of the radiology department; and (15) the RIC radiologist who was the director of the radiology department testified that he considered himself and the other RIC radiologists at Hospital to in effect be "employees of the hospital."

Despite these facts, Hospital argues that the evidence at trial was insufficient to establish agency because there was nothing in the record to show that Hospital controlled Dr. Koch specifically "in the performance of the act at the heart of plaintiffs' claim—his alleged negligent reading of Matthew Scott's CT scan." However, Missouri courts have long recognized that physicians must be free to exercise independent medical judgment; the mere fact that a physician retains such independent judgment will not preclude a court, in an otherwise proper case, from finding the existence of an employer-employee or principal-agent relationship between a hospital and physician. [ ] Courts in other states, as well, have strongly rejected the notion that such a relationship cannot be found merely because the hospital does not have the right to stand over the doctor's shoulder and dictate to him or her how to diagnose and treat patients. [ ]

In view of the foregoing principles of law, the evidence in this case and our standard of review, the trial court did not err in finding the evidence sufficient to present a jury question on the issue of Dr. Koch's agency. Point I is denied.

NOTES AND QUESTIONS

1. *Is a Physician the "Servant" of a Hospital?* The general definition of the term "servant" in the Restatement (Second) of Agency § 2(2) (1957) refers to a person whose work is "controlled or is subject to the right to control by the master." The Restatement's more specific definition of the term "servant" lists factors to be considered when distinguishing between servants and independent contractors, the first of which is "the extent of control" that one may exercise over the details of the work of the other. Id. The relevant factor for analyzing the hospital-physician relationship by agency tests is § 220(2)(a), which looks to "the extent of control which, by the agreement, the master may exercise over the details of the work." This becomes a fact-intensive analysis for the trier of fact.

Physicians need considerable autonomy in practice, given the complexity of their decisions and their legal and ethical duties to particular patients. As a result, determining the degree of control necessary to create an employment relationship in a medical malpractice claim poses a unique set of difficulties. See Lilly v. Fieldstone, 876 F.2d 857 (10th Cir. 1989).

2. *Hospital Employment of Physicians.* As of January 1, 2021, hospitals directly employed more than 301,000 physicians, including an increase of 18,600 physicians after the start of the COVID-19 pandemic. See Physician Advocacy Institute, COVID-19's Impact on Acquisitions of Physician Practices and Physician Employment 2019–2020 (June 2021). There were approximately 1 million physicians in active practice in the U.S. in 2000, see John Elflein, U.S. Physicians—Statistics & Facts, Statistica (Nov. 2020), meaning that about 30 percent of physicians nationwide are directly employed by hospitals. This is nearly double the percentage of physicians (17.3 percent) directly employed by hospitals in 2012. See AHA Hospital Statistics, 2012 edition. Thus, while hospitals continue to have a range of relationships with physicians on their medical staffs—including employment and independent contractual relationships—the number of physicians who are directly employed is increasing substantially.

3. *Corporate Control and Private Equity.* Increasingly, hospitals, nursing homes, and outpatient clinics are controlled by parent corporations or private equity firms that are not themselves institutional health care providers. See Michael Furukawa et al., Consolidation and Health Systems In 2018: New Data from the AHRQ Compendium, Health Aff. Blog (Nov. 25, 2019); Richard M. Scheffler, Laura M. Alexander and James R. Godwin, Soaring Private Equity Investment in the Healthcare Sector: Consolidation Accelerated, Competition Undermined, and Patients at Risk (May 18, 2021). Corporate and private equity investors recognize opportunities to improve the

monetary value of institutional health care providers by addressing inefficiencies in health care delivery.

While these owners, managers and investors focus their efforts on the business operations of the institutional providers they oversee, their drive toward lowering costs and increasing revenues affects how hospitals, nursing homes, clinics, and their associated physicians treat patients. For example, physicians who have sold controlling interest in their practices to private equity firms report that they are under pressure to increase their procedure volumes, to refer patients only to labs or other providers also controlled by their private equity owner, and to rely on physician assistants and other paraprofessionals to provide patient care without sufficient physician supervision. See S. Gondi and Z. Song, Potential Implications of Private Equity Investments in Health Care Delivery, 321 JAMA 1047 (2019). The influence of investors raises concerns addressed later in this book, including the corporate practice of medicine (Chapter 11) and fraud and abuse (Chapter 14). A recent study of nursing homes found that private equity ownership was associated with a 10 percent increase in mortality among Medicare residents in those nursing homes. See Atul Gupta et al., Does Private Equity Investment in Healthcare Benefit Patients? Evidence from Nursing Homes, NBER Working Paper No. 28474 (Feb. 2021). As investors and business managers exert more control over medical practice, can they be held vicariously liable for the professional negligence of the physicians who practice in the institutions that those investors and managers control?

B. APPARENT AGENCY

Absent evidence of indicia of control sufficient to make a physician the employee of a hospital, courts have turned to traditional agency tests that evaluate whether the health care institution is vicariously liable for the negligence of its independent contractors.

BURLESS V. WEST VIRGINIA UNIVERSITY HOSPITALS, INC.

Supreme Court of West Virginia, 2004.
601 S.E.2d 85.

DAVIS, JUSTICE:

In these two appeals from two orders of the Circuit Court of Monongalia County granting summary judgment to West Virginia University Hospitals (hereinafter referred to as "WVUH"), the Appellants ask this Court to rule that the circuit courts erred in finding that no actual or apparent agency relationship existed between physicians employed by the West Virginia University Board of Trustees (hereinafter referred to as "the BOT") and WVUH. We find no error in the circuit courts' rulings that no actual agency existed. However, we find that the courts erred in granting summary judgment on the issue of apparent agency. In reaching this conclusion, we find that for a hospital to be held liable for a physician's negligence under an apparent agency theory, a plaintiff must establish that: (1) the hospital either committed an act that would cause a reasonable person to believe that the physician in question was an agent of the hospital, or, by failing to take an action, created a circumstance that would allow a reasonable person to hold such a belief, and (2) the plaintiff relied on the apparent agency relationship.

I. Factual Procedural History

Each of the two cases consolidated for purposes of this opinion involve a woman who gave birth to her child at WVUH under circumstances that she alleges resulted in severe birth defects to her child. The relevant facts of each case, as developed in the pleadings, depositions, affidavits, and exhibits, follow.

A. Jaclyn Burless

In July of 1998 Jaclyn Burless learned she was pregnant and sought prenatal care at the Cornerstone Care Clinic (hereinafter referred to as "the Cornerstone Clinic" or simply "the clinic") located in Greensboro, Pennsylvania. The Cornerstone Clinic was where Ms. Burless had routinely sought her primary medical care. Similarly, Ms. Burless elected to receive her prenatal care at the clinic. She received her prenatal care from Dr. Douglas Glover for approximately seven months.

In November, 1998, Dr. Glover sent Ms. Burless to WVUH for an ultrasound. At that time, Ms. Burless signed a WVUH consent form that stated: "I understand that the faculty physicians and resident physicians who provide treatment in the hospital are not employees of the hospital." Thereafter, in February of 1999 when she was at approximately 37 weeks of gestation, Ms. Burless experienced an elevated blood pressure and edema. On February 15, 1999, Dr. Glover advised Ms. Burless to report to the WVU Emergency Department for an evaluation. On February 17, 1999, Ms. Burless presented herself at the WVUH Emergency Department as instructed and, after an evaluation, was instructed to return to the High Risk Clinic, which is located on the WVUH premises, in two days with a urine sample for testing. Ms. Burless was also advised that she would receive the remainder of her prenatal care at the High Risk Clinic. She followed the instructions to return to the High Risk Clinic in two days. She was then instructed to return in one week for further evaluation. When she returned, on February 26, 1999, she was induced into labor at 7:50 p.m. Her labor was permitted to continue throughout the remainder of February 26 and until 4:00 p.m. on February 27. She alleges that during this time, doctors, residents, and nurses at WVUH noted variable decelerations in the fetal heart rate of her unborn daughter, Alexis Price. At 4:00 p.m. on February 27 the decision was made to deliver the baby via cesarean section, and such delivery was accomplished at 4:16 p.m. The child was born with an APGAR[2] score of two at one minute and six at five minutes. Soon after birth the child began to experience seizures and suffered a stroke. Ms. Burless has alleged that the doctors and hospital were negligent, *inter alia,* in failing to monitor her labor and delivery, which negligence caused severe and permanent mental, neurological, and psychological injuries to the infant, Alexis Price.

Ms. Burless later filed a negligence action, claiming breaches of the standard of care in connection with the management of her labor, against the BOT as the physicians' employer, and claiming vicarious liability on the part of WVUH based upon a theory of apparent agency between WVUH and the physicians who provided the allegedly negligent care. WVUH moved for summary judgment asserting, in relevant part, that there was no apparent agency relationship between it and the doctors and residents who provided care to Ms. Burless. Finding no just cause for delay, pursuant to Rule 54(b) of the West Virginia Rules of Civil Procedure, the circuit court granted summary judgment to WVUH by final order entered December 11, 2002. The circuit court found that there was nothing in the record demonstrating the creation of an apparent agency relationship between the physicians who treated Ms. Burless and WVUH. Ms. Burless appealed the order and this Court granted her petition for appeal. For purposes of rendering our decision, we consolidated her case with a similar appeal filed by Ms. Melony Pritt.

B.   Melony Pritt

[Plaintiff Melony Pritt had an ovarian cyst and scheduled a laparotomy and left ovarian cystectomy. She signed several consent forms, all of which contained the statement "I understand that the faculty physicians and resident physicians who provide treatment in the hospital are not employees of the hospital." The surgery did not go well, and she suffered a massive abdominal infection, which infection caused premature labor. Her son was alleged therefore to have suffered severe permanent mental, neurological, and psychological injuries]

II.

[The court's discussion of the standard of review is omitted.]

III.

Discussion

Ms. Burless and Ms. Pritt assert that the circuit courts erred both in finding no actual agency relationship between the doctors who treated

---

   [2]   An APGAR Score is a newborn's first evaluation and serves as a predictive indicator of any potential problems. The infant is examined at one and five minutes after birth and ranked on a scale of zero to two on five characteristics: 1) skin color; 2) heart rate; 3) response to stimuli of inserting a catheter in the nose; 4) muscle tone; and 5) respiratory effort. Thus, the maximum score is 10 with most healthy newborns scoring an eight or nine. The five APGAR factors can be mnemonically summarized as *A*-ppearance, *P*-ulse, *G*-rimace, *A*-ctivity, *R*-espiration.[ ]

them and WVUH, and in finding no apparent agency relationship. We address each of these assignments of error in turn.

A. Actual Agency

[The court found no actual agency, since the hospital did not have "power of control" over the physicians who provided treatment to Ms. Burless and Ms. Pritt.]

B. Apparent Agency

Ms. Burless and Ms. Pritt next assert that the circuit courts erred in finding no apparent agency relationship between the doctors who treated them and WVUH. Because we have explained in the previous section that we find no *actual* agency relationship in these cases, we have concluded that the doctors were, in fact, independent contractors. Our cases have recognized that, as a general rule, "[i]f [a physician] is found to be an independent contractor, then the hospital is not liable for his [or her] negligence."[ ]

As with most general rules, there are exceptions to the independent contractor rule. We have previously recognized that

> One who by his acts or conduct has permitted another to act apparently or ostensibly as his agent, to the injury of a third person who has dealt with the apparent or ostensible agent in good faith and in the exercise of reasonable prudence, is estopped to deny the agency relationship.

[ ] In the instant cases, however, we are asked to determine the existence of an apparent agency relationship in the hospital/physician context. As explained in more detail below, modern hospitals and their relationships with the physicians who treat patients within their facilities are rather unique and complex. Thus, instead of relying on a general rule for apparent agency such as those quoted above, we believe a more particular rule is in order.

In the hospital/physician context, this Court has heretofore established that even where a physician charged with negligence is an independent contractor, the hospital may nevertheless be found vicariously liable where the complained of treatment was provided in an emergency room. [ ] Although we have addressed using a theory of apparent agency to overcome the physician/independent contractor rule in the context of emergency room treatment, we have never expressly defined such a rule for use outside of the emergency room setting. We do so now.

1. Hospital/Physician Apparent Agency Outside the Emergency Room Setting. The public's confidence in the modern hospital's portrayal of itself as a full service provider of health care appears to be at the foundation of the national trend toward adopting a rule of apparent agency to find hospitals liable, under the appropriate circumstances, for the negligence of physicians providing services within its walls.

In fact, this Court has itself observed that

"Modern hospitals have spent billions of dollars on marketing to nurture the image that they are full-care modern health facilities. Billboards, television commercials and newspaper advertisements tell the public to look to its local hospital for every manner of care, from the critical surgery and life-support required by a major accident to the minor tissue repairs resulting from a friendly game of softball. These efforts have helped bring the hospitals vastly increased revenue, a new role in daily health care and, ironically, a heightened exposure to lawsuits[ ]" [ ].

* * *

... [W]e now hold that for a hospital to be held liable for a physician's negligence under an apparent agency theory, a plaintiff must establish that: (1) the hospital either committed an act that would cause a reasonable person to believe that the physician in question was an agent of the hospital, or, by failing to take an action, created a circumstance that would allow a reasonable person to hold such a belief, and (2) the plaintiff relied on the apparent agency relationship.

2.   Hospital's Actions or Inactions. The first element of our test requires evidence that the hospital either committed an act that would cause a reasonable person to believe that the physician in question was an agent of the hospital, or, by failing to take an action, created a circumstance that would allow a reasonable person to hold such a belief. This portion of the test focuses on the acts of the hospital and is generally satisfied when "the hospital 'holds itself out' to the public as a provider of care."[ ] One court has explained that "[i]n order to prove this element, it is not necessary to show an express representation by the hospital. . . . Instead, a hospital is generally deemed to have held itself out as the provider of care, unless it gave the patient contrary notice."[ ] The "contrary notice" referred to by the *Mejia* court generally manifests itself in the form of a disclaimer. As one court has acknowledged, "[a] hospital generally will be able to avoid liability by providing *meaningful written notice* to the patient, acknowledged at the time of admission."[ ] It has been said that "[l]iability under apparent agency . . . will not attach against a hospital where the patient knows, or reasonably should have known, that the treating physician was an independent contractor."[ ] Thus, a hospital's failure to provide a meaningful written notice may constitute "failing to take an action" and thereby allowing a reasonable person to believe that a particular doctor is an agent of the hospital. Conversely, absent other overt acts by the hospital indicating an employer/employee relationship, an unambiguous disclaimer by a hospital explaining the independent contractor status of physicians will generally suffice to immunize the hospital from being vicariously liable for physician conduct.[14]

Turning to the cases before us, the circuit courts in both cases relied on the disclaimers signed by Ms. Pritt & Ms. Burless in granting summary judgment in favor of WVUH. In addition, the circuit court considering Ms. Pritt's case summarily concluded that WVUH had not "held the physicians out to be its employees." We disagree with these conclusions.

The disclaimer that WVUH required both Ms. Pritt and Ms. Burless to sign stated: "I understand that the faculty physicians and resident physicians who provide treatment in the hospital are not employees of the hospital." WVUH contends that this "disclaimer" was sufficient to unequivocally inform Ms. Pritt and Ms. Burless that the physicians treating them were not employees of the hospital. We disagree.

We do not find the disclaimer language used by WVUH, which indicated that "faculty physicians and resident physicians who provide treatment in the hospital" are independent contractors, was sufficient to support a grant of summary judgment in their favor. The WVUH disclaimer provision presupposes that all patients can distinguish between "faculty physicians," "resident physicians" and any other type of physician having privileges at the hospital. In other words, for this disclaimer to be meaningful, a patient would literally have to inquire into the employment status of everyone treating him or her. Obviously, "[i]t would be absurd to require . . . a patient . . . to inquire of each person who treated him whether he is an employee of the hospital or an independent contractor."

Consequently, it was improper for the circuit court to grant summary judgment in favor of WVUH. Ms. Burless and Ms. Pritt have established a genuine question of material fact as to whether WVUH has either committed an act that would cause a reasonable person to believe that the physician in question was an agent of the hospital, or, by failing to take an action, created a circumstance that would allow a reasonable person to hold such a belief.

3. **Reliance.** The reliance prong of the apparent agency test is a subjective molehill. "Reliance . . . is established when the plaintiff 'looks to' the hospital for services, rather than to an individual physician." [ ] It is "sometimes characterized as an inquiry as to whether 'the plaintiff acted in reliance upon the conduct of the hospital or its agent, consistent with ordinary care and prudence.' [ ] This factor 'simply focuses on the "patient's belief that the hospital or its employees were rendering health care." ' " [ ]

---

[14] Of course, "we do not hold that the existence of an [unambiguous] independent contractor disclaimer . . . is always dispositive on the issue [.]" [ ] A plaintiff may still be able to prove that, under the totality of the circumstances, an unambiguous disclaimer was insufficient to inform him or her of the employment status of a hospital's physicians.

242 of the test also requires consideration of the

However, this portion of the test also requires consideration of the "reasonableness of the patient's [subjective] belief that the hospital or its employees were rendering health care." [ ] "This . . . determination is made by considering the totality of the circumstances, including . . . any special knowledge the patient[/plaintiff] may have about the hospital's arrangements with its physicians." [ ]

Mrs. Pritt and Ms. Burless provided evidence indicating that they believed that the physicians treating them were employees of WVUH.

In the deposition testimony of Ms. Burless she stated her belief that the people treating her at the hospital were employees, as follows: "Q. Did anyone do anything to make you believe that they were employees of WVU Hospital? A. They were all wearing their coats and name tags and in the building, so, you know, you know they're—they work there, they're employees." In the affidavit submitted by Ms. Pritt in opposition to WVUH's motion for summary judgment, the following was stated:

> 2.   At the West Virginia University Hospitals, I was assigned doctors who treated me and consulted me through my prenatal care, surgery and delivery of my son Adam.

> 3.   Throughout all of my treatment and consultations, I believed that the doctors and nurses who treated me and spoke to me were employees of the West Virginia University Hospitals.

Ms. Burless and Ms. Pritt have also established a genuine question of material fact on the issue of their reliance on the apparent agency relationship between WVUH and their treating physicians. Consequently, on the issue of apparent agency, it is clear that summary judgment should not have been granted in favor of WVUH.

NOTES AND QUESTIONS

1.   *Hospital Medical Staff.* The medical staff is a self-governing body charged with overseeing the quality of care, treatment, and services delivered by practitioners who are credentialed and privileged through the medical staff process. See Chapter 11. The medical staff must credential and privilege all licensed independent practitioners. The self-governing organized medical staff creates and maintains a set of bylaws that defines its role within the context of a hospital setting and clearly delineates its responsibilities in the oversight of care, treatment, and services. It elects its own officers and appoints its own committees.

The organized medical staff is intimately involved in carrying out, and in providing leadership in, all patient care functions conducted by practitioners privileged through the medical staff process. The medical staff oversees the quality of patient care, treatment, and services provided by practitioners privileged through the medical staff process. It recommends practitioners for privileges to perform medical histories and physical examinations. The hospital governing body approves such privileges.

The organized medical staff is not simply another administrative component of the hospital, and it has typically been subject to only limited authority of the governing board of the hospital. While the hospital board must approve the staff's bylaws and can approve or disapprove particular staff actions, it cannot usually discipline individual physicians directly or appoint administrative officers to exercise direct authority. A hospital's medical staff is therefore a powerful body within the larger organization.

2. *Relying on the Hospital for Care.* In most cases, the patient relies on the reputation of the hospital, not any particular doctor, and for that reason selects that hospital. See, e.g., White v. Methodist Hosp. South, 844 S.W.2d 642 (Tenn. App.1992); Valerio v. Liberty Behav. Mgmt. Corp., 135 N.Y.S.3d 127 (2020). If the negligence results from emergency room care, most courts have held that a patient may justifiably rely on the physician as an agent unless the hospital explicitly disclaims an agency relationship. See Ballard v. Advocate Health & Hosps. Corps., 1999 WL 498702 (N.D. Ill. 1999). A promotional campaign or advertising can create such reliance. See Clark v. Southview Hosp. & Family Health Ctr., 68 Ohio St. 3d 435, 628 N.E.2d 46 (1994) (promotional and marketing campaign stressed the emergency departments).

To avoid liability, a hospital can try to avoid patient misunderstanding through its billing procedures, the letterhead used, signs, and other clues of the true nature of the relationship of the physician to the institution. See Cantrell v. Northeast Georgia Med. Ctr., 235 Ga. App. 365, 508 S.E.2d 716 (1998) (sign over registration desk stated that the physicians in the emergency room were independent contractors; consent form repeated this). The court is likely, however, to cut through these devices if the reliance on reputation by the patient is strong enough.

Explicit language in a patient consent form is the clearest way to put a patient on notice of the physician's legal status. A few states allow a clear statement in a consent form—that physicians in the hospital are independent contractors and not agents—to put a patient on notice. See Pendley v. Southern Regional Health Sys., Inc., 307 Ga. App. 82, 704 S.E.2d 198 (2010); Wicks v. Antelope Valley Healthcare Dist., 49 Cal. App. 5th 866, 263 Cal. Rptr. 3d 397 (2020) ("although a hospital may not control, direct or supervise physicians on its staff, a hospital may be liable for their negligence on an ostensible agency theory, unless (1) the hospital gave the patient actual notice that the treating physicians are not hospital employees, and (2) there is no reason to believe the patient was unable to understand or act on the information . . . ").

3. *ER Physicians.* Emergency room physicians are most often the source of vicarious liability claims against the contracting hospitals. In spite of various forms of notice as to the independent contractor status of emergency room physicians, many state courts have refused to allow hospitals to escape liability. The reasons typically given are based on the nature of patient reliance

when entering a hospital for emergency care. See Simmons v. Tuomey Regional Med. Ctr., 341 S.C. 32, 533 S.E.2d 312 (S.C. 2000); Popovich v. Allina Health Sys., 946 N.W.2d 885 (Minn. 2020).

4.   *Non-Delegable Duties.* Courts often refuse to allow hospitals to use the independent contractor defense in response to a claim that the hospital has breached a non-delegable duty. See, e.g., Payas v. Adventist Health Sys./Sunbelt, Inc., 238 So. 3d 887 (Fla. App. 2018) (hospital remains potentially liable for injuries associated with a surgical robot the hospital owned, operated, and maintained even though the robot was deployed by an independently contracted surgeon).

5.   *Hospital Parent Companies.* A parent company of a hospital in which physician malpractice is alleged to have occurred is not immune from liability simply because the hospital is a separate corporation from the parent company. Rather, vicarious liability doctrine is available to plaintiffs, including the doctrine of apparent agency. See, e.g., Kissun v. Humana, Inc., 479 S.E.2d 751 (Ga. 1997). In Scampone v. Highland Park Care Ctr., LLC, 57 A.3d 582 (Pa. 2012), the Pennsylvania Supreme Court held that the management company of a nursing home can be found vicariously liable for the malpractice of professional providers in the nursing home based on evidence that the management company controlled the day-to-day clinical operations of the nursing home.

PROBLEM: CREATING A SHIELD

You represent Bowsman Hospital, a small rural hospital in Iowa. The hospital has until now relied on Dr. Headley for radiology services. It provides him with space, equipment, and personnel for the radiology department, sends and collects bills on his behalf, and provides him with an office. It also pays him $300 a day in exchange for which Dr. Headley agrees to be at the hospital one day a week. Bowsman is one of several small hospitals in this part of Iowa that use Dr. Headley's services. Bowsman advertises in the local papers of several nearby communities. Its advertisements stress its ability to handle trauma injuries, common in farming areas. The ads say in part:

> Bowsman treats patient problems with big league medical talent. Our physicians and nurses have been trained for the special demands of farming accidents and injuries.

What advice can you give as to methods of shielding Bowsman from liability for the negligent acts of Dr. Headley? Must it insist that Dr. Headley operate his own outside laboratory? Or furnish his own equipment? Pay his own bills? Should the hospital hire its own radiologist?

The Chief Executive Officer asks you to develop guidelines to protect the hospital from liability for medical errors of the radiologist.

PROBLEM: IMPROVIA HEALTH MANAGEMENT

Improvia Health Management, Inc. provides emergency department staffing and management services to hospitals with which it contracts. Improvia has entered into a contract with Memorial Methodist Hospital to manage all aspects of the hospital's emergency department (ED), as well as to be the exclusive supplier of emergency physicians for the hospital's ED. Under the contract, Improvia promises the hospital that it will only assign shifts in the hospital's ED to emergency physicians who have first applied to, and been approved by, the hospital to have privileges to practice medicine as part of the hospital's medical staff in the ED. Each physician also has their own contract with Improvia under which they agree to work as assigned by Improvia, to abide by Improvia's management directives, and to be paid based in part on an hourly rate and based in part on the ED's financial productivity. These physicians are independent contractors and none of them is employed by either Improvia or the hospital.

Improvia seeks to improve the financial productivity of the hospital's ED by cutting in half the number of physicians that had been assigned to work any given shift in the ED prior to Improvia's takeover and increasing the number of physician assistants. Unlike the physicians, these physician assistants and nurse practitioners are employees of Improvia. Through a series of directives, Improvia instructs its physicians that they are to rely on physician assistants and nurse practitioners to provide patient care in all cases except where physician expertise is clearly required. Additionally, Improvia's policies require that each physician, in addition to seeing the patients that require their care, must also supervise the patient care provided by the several physician assistants and nurse practitioners working that same shift.

Imagine that a patient comes to the ED of Memorial Methodist Hospital and is initially seen by Dr. Veneer—the only physician assigned by Improvia to that shift—with several patients to attend to personally, and several more who are being treated by physician assistants and nurse practitioners under the doctor's supervision. Dr. Veneer misdiagnoses the patient's condition and believes that the necessary treatment is relatively simple. Based on this assessment, Dr. Veneer assigns the patient to a nurse practitioner who provides the treatment recommended by the doctor, and the patient is discharged. At home, the patient's condition worsens dramatically, and the patient dies. Assuming that Dr. Veneer's misdiagnosis amounts to malpractice, can Improvia be held vicariously liable for the doctor's negligence, and, if so, how so? Can the hospital be held vicariously liable for the doctor's negligence, and, if so, how so?

III. DIRECT LIABILITY OF INSTITUTIONAL PROVIDERS

Over time hospitals have engaged in a broad range of functions that directly affect the safety of their patients. It wasn't until the *Darling* case was decided in 1965 that the common law recognized the duty a hospital owes directly to its patients to assure that the personnel and medical care systems the hospital coordinates perform adequately. Today's institutional duty of a hospital to assure the safety and well-being of its patients is derived from this focus on the functions of a modern hospital to manage a complex institution safely.

DARLING V. CHARLESTON COMMUNITY MEMORIAL HOSPITAL

Supreme Court of Illinois, 1965.
211 N.E.2d 253.

This action was brought on behalf of Dorrence Darling II, a minor (hereafter plaintiff), by his father and next friend, to recover damages for allegedly negligent medical and hospital treatment which necessitated the amputation of his right leg below the knee. The action was commenced against the Charleston Community Memorial Hospital and Dr. John R. Alexander, but prior to trial the action was dismissed as to Dr. Alexander, pursuant to a covenant not to sue. The jury returned a verdict against the hospital in the sum of $150,000. This amount was reduced by $40,000, the amount of the settlement with the doctor. The judgment in favor of the plaintiff in the sum of $110,000 was affirmed on appeal by the Appellate Court for the Fourth District, which granted a certificate of importance. 50 Ill.App.2d 253, 200 N.E.2d 149.

On November 5, 1960, the plaintiff, who was 18 years old, broke his leg while playing in a college football game. He was taken to the emergency room at the defendant hospital where Dr. Alexander, who was on emergency call that day, treated him. Dr. Alexander, with the assistance of hospital personnel, applied traction and placed the leg in a plaster cast. A heat cradle was applied to dry the cast. Not long after the application of the cast plaintiff was in great pain and his toes, which protruded from the cast, became swollen and dark in color. They eventually became cold and insensitive. On the evening of November 6, Dr. Alexander "notched" the cast around the toes, and on the afternoon of the next day he cut the cast approximately three inches up from the foot. On November 8 he split the sides of the cast with a Stryker saw; in the course of cutting the cast the plaintiff's leg was cut on both sides. Blood and other seepage were observed by the nurses and others, and there was a stench in the room, which one witness said was the worst he had smelled since World War II. The plaintiff remained in Charleston Hospital until November 19, when he was transferred to Barnes Hospital in St. Louis and placed under the care of Dr. Fred Reynolds, head of orthopedic surgery at Washington University School of Medicine and Barnes Hospital. Dr. Reynolds found that the fractured leg contained a considerable amount of dead tissue which in his opinion resulted from interference with the circulation of blood in the limb

regard it as both desirable and feasible that a hospital assume certain responsibilities for the care of the patient.

We now turn to an application of these considerations to this case. . . . [W]e need not analyze all of the issues submitted to the jury. Two of them were that the defendant had negligently: "5. Failed to have a sufficient number of trained nurses for bedside care of all patients at all times capable of recognizing the progressive gangrenous condition of the plaintiff's right leg, and of bringing the same to the attention of the hospital administration and to the medical staff so that adequate consultation could have been secured and such conditions rectified; . . . 7. Failed to require consultation with or examination by members of the hospital surgical staff skilled in such treatment; or to review the treatment rendered to the plaintiff and to require consultants to be called in as needed."

We believe that the jury verdict is supportable on either of these grounds. On the basis of the evidence before it the jury could reasonably have concluded that the nurses did not test for circulation in the leg as frequently as necessary, that skilled nurses would have promptly recognized the conditions that signaled a dangerous impairment of circulation in the plaintiff's leg, and would have known that the condition would become irreversible in a matter of hours. At that point it became the nurses' duty to inform the attending physician, and if he failed to act, to advise the hospital authorities so that appropriate action might be taken. As to consultation, there is no dispute that the hospital failed to review Dr. Alexander's work or require a consultation; the only issue is whether its failure to do so was negligence. On the evidence before it the jury could reasonably have found that it was.

[The remainder of the opinion, discussing expert testimony and damages, is omitted.]

NOTES AND QUESTIONS

1. *Nurses.* Consider the issues submitted to the jury. It is alleged that both the nurses and the administrators were negligent in not taking steps to curtail Dr. Alexander's handling of the case. How can a nurse "blow the whistle" on a doctor without risking damage to her own career? See the section on labor law in health care institutions, Chapter 11, infra. How can a nurse exercise medical judgment in violation of Medical Practice statutes?

Nurses have independent obligations to care for patients. See, e.g., Brandon HMA, Inc. v. Bradshaw, 809 So. 2d 611 (Miss. 2001) (staff failed to monitor plaintiff and allowed her condition to deteriorate to a critical state before providing urgently needed care and life support; one nurse failed to take her vital signs on several visits to her room). Nurses, as *Darling* indicates, have obligations to advocate for patients when care is substandard in a hospital. See, e.g., Rowe v. Sisters of Pallottine Missionary Soc., 211 W. Va. 16, 560 S.E.2d 491 (2001) (17-year-old boy presented to the hospital emergency room after a motorcycle accident with severe pain in his left knee and numbness in his foot, and no pulse in his foot; held, nurses breached the standard of care by not adequately advocating for his interests when he was discharged with unexplained and unaddressed symptoms.)

2.   *Outdated Concept of Hospital's Role.* Darling disclosed the prevailing attitude of hospital administrators toward affiliated doctors, reflecting the earlier concept of the doctor as independent contractor. The hospital administrator testified:

'As the Board's representative, I did nothing to see that Dr. Alexander reviewed his operating techniques for the handling of broken bones. So far as I know, Dr. Alexander may not have reviewed his operating techniques since he was first licensed to practice in 1928. No examinations were ever given. I never asked questions of the doctor about this matter. The governing board, neither through me nor through any other designated administrative representative, ever checked up on the ability of Dr. Alexander as compared by medical text books. I had access at the hospital to some good orthopedic books . . . . Other than buying these books, I never made any effort to see that Dr. Alexander, or any other physician admitted to practice more than thirty years ago, read them.' Darling v. Charleston Community Memorial Hosp., 50 Ill. App. 2d 253, 295, 200 N.E.2d 149, 171 (1964).

How can a hospital administrator devise procedures to trigger an alarm when a physician is incompetent? Must the administrator himself be an M.D.? Can you think of methods that would have avoided the *Darling* tragedy? What systems might you implement to prevent such errors?

––––––––––

Over time, it became increasingly clear that hospitals were often responsible for errors, and not only their physicians. One study found that the proportion of errors with interactive or administrative causes in the hospital was as high as 25 percent. See Lori B. Andrews et al., An Alternative Strategy for Studying Adverse Events in Medical Care, 349 Lancet 309, 312 (1997). At about the same time, courts recognized that hospitals have an overarching duty to safeguard the well-being of the patients they serve.

THOMPSON V. NASON HOSP.
Supreme Court of Pennsylvania, 1991.
591 A.2d 703.

ZAPPALA, JUSTICE.

Allocatur was granted to examine the novel issue of whether a theory of corporate liability with respect to hospitals should be recognized in this

Commonwealth. For the reasons set forth below, we adopt today the theory of corporate liability as it relates to hospitals. . . .

* * *

Considering this predicate to our analysis, we now turn to the record which contains the facts underlying this personal injury action. At approximately 7 a.m. on March 16, 1978, Appellee, Linda A. Thompson, was involved in an automobile accident with a school bus. Mrs. Thompson was transported by ambulance from the accident scene to Nason Hospital's emergency room where she was admitted with head and leg injuries. The hospital's emergency room personnel were advised by Appellee, Donald A. Thompson, that his wife was taking the drug Coumadin, that she had a permanent pacemaker, and that she took other heart medications.

Subsequent to Mrs. Thompson's admission to Nason Hospital, Dr. Edward D. Schultz, a general practitioner who enjoyed staff privileges at Nason Hospital, entered the hospital via the emergency room to make his rounds. Although Dr. Schultz was not assigned duty in the emergency room, an on-duty hospital nurse asked him to attend Mrs. Thompson due to a prior physician-patient relationship. Dr. Schultz examined Mrs. Thompson and diagnosed her as suffering from multiple injuries including extensive lacerations over her left eye and the back of her scalp, constricted pupils, enlarged heart with a Grade III micro-systolic murmur, a brain concussion and amnesia. X-rays that were taken revealed fractures of the right tibia and right heel.

Following Dr. Schultz's examination and diagnosis, Dr. Larry Jones, an ophthalmologist, sutured the lacerations over Mrs. Thompson's left eye. It was during that time that Dr. Schultz consulted with Dr. Rao concerning orthopedic repairs. Dr. Rao advised conservative therapy until her critical medical condition improved.

Dr. Schultz knew Mrs. Thompson was suffering from rheumatic heart and mitral valve disease and was on anticoagulant therapy. Because he had no specific training in establishing dosages for such therapy, Dr. Schultz called Dr. Marvin H. Meisner, a cardiologist who was treating Mrs. Thompson with an anticoagulant therapy. Although Dr. Meisner was unavailable, Dr. Schultz did speak with Dr. Meisner's associate Dr. Steven P. Draskoczy.

Mrs. Thompson had remained in the emergency room during this time. Her condition, however, showed no sign of improvement. Due to both the multiple trauma received in the accident and her pre-existing heart disease, Dr. Schultz, as attending physician, admitted her to Nason Hospital's intensive care unit at 11:20 a.m.

The next morning at 8:30 a.m., Dr. Mark Paris, a general surgeon on staff at Nason Hospital, examined Mrs. Thompson. He found that she was unable to move her left foot and toes. It was also noted by Dr. Paris that the patient had a positive Babinski—a neurological sign of an intracerebral problem. Twelve hours later, Dr. Schultz examined Mrs. Thompson and found more bleeding in her eye. He also indicated in the progress notes that the problem with her left leg was that it was neurological.

On March 18, 1978, the third day of her hospitalization, Dr. Larry Jones, the ophthalmologist who treated her in the emergency room, examined her in the intensive care unit. He indicated in the progress notes an "increased hematuria secondary to anticoagulation. Right eye now involved." Dr. Schultz also examined Mrs. Thompson that day and noted the decreased movement of her left leg was neurologic. Dr. Paris's progress note that date approved the withholding of Coumadin and the continued use of Heparin.

The following day, Mrs. Thompson had complete paralysis of the left side. Upon examination by Dr. Schultz he questioned whether she needed to be under the care of a neurologist or needed to be watched there. At 10:30 a.m. that day, Dr. Schultz transferred her to the Hershey Medical Center because of her progressive neurological problem.

Linda Thompson underwent tests at the Hershey Medical Center. The results of the tests revealed that she had a large intracerebral hematoma in the right frontal temporal and parietal lobes of the brain. She was subsequently discharged on April 1, 1978, without regaining the motor function of her left side.

. . . The complaint alleged inter alia that Mrs. Thompson's injuries were the direct and proximate result of the negligence of Nason Hospital acting through its agents, servants and employees in failing to adequately examine and treat her, in failing to follow its rules relative to consultations and in failing to monitor her conditions during treatment. . . .

* * *

The first issue Nason Hospital raised is whether the Superior Court erred in adopting a theory of corporate liability with respect to a hospital. This issue had not heretofore been determined by the Court. Nason Hospital contends that it had no duty to observe, supervise or control the actual treatment of Linda Thompson.

Hospitals in the past enjoyed absolute immunity from tort liability. [ ] The basis of that immunity was the perception that hospitals functioned as charitable organizations. [ ] However, hospitals have evolved into highly sophisticated corporations operating primarily on a fee-for-service basis. The corporate hospital of today has assumed the role of a comprehensive health center with responsibility for arranging and coordinating the total health care of its patients. As a result of this metamorphosis, hospital immunity was eliminated. [ ]

Not surprisingly, the by-product of eliminating hospital immunity has been the filing of malpractice actions against hospitals. Courts have recognized several bases on which hospitals may be subject to liability including respondeat superior, ostensible agency and corporate negligence. [ ]

The development of hospital liability in this Commonwealth mirrored that which occurred in other jurisdictions. . . . We now turn our attention to the theory of corporate liability with respect to the hospital, which was first recognized in this Commonwealth by the court below.

Corporate negligence is a doctrine under which the hospital is liable if it fails to uphold the proper standard of care owed the patient, which is to ensure the patient's safety and well-being while at the hospital. This theory of liability creates a nondelegable duty which the hospital owes directly to a patient. Therefore, an injured party does not have to rely on and establish the negligence of a third party.

The hospital's duties have been classified into four general areas: (1) a duty to use reasonable care in the maintenance of safe and adequate facilities and equipment—Candler General Hospital Inc. v. Purvis, 123 Ga.App. 334, 181 S.E.2d 77 (1971); (2) a duty to select and retain only competent physicians—Johnson v. Misericordia Community Hospital, 99 Wis.2d 708, 301 N.W.2d 156 (1981); (3) a duty to oversee all persons who practice medicine within its walls as to patient care—Darling v. Charleston Community Memorial Hospital, supra.; and (4) a duty to formulate, adopt and enforce adequate rules and policies to ensure quality care for the patients—Wood v. Samaritan Institution, 26 Cal.2d 847, 161 P.2d 556 (Cal. Ct. App.1945). [ ]

Other jurisdictions have embraced this doctrine of corporate negligence or corporate liability such as to warrant it being called an "emerging trend." [ ]

* * *

Today, we take a step beyond the hospital's duty of care delineated in Riddle in full recognition of the corporate hospital's role in the total health care of its patients. In so doing, we adopt as a theory of hospital liability the doctrine of corporate negligence or corporate liability under which the hospital is liable if it fails to uphold the proper standard of care owed its patient. In addition, we fully embrace the aforementioned four categories of the hospital's duties. It is important to note that for a hospital to be charged with negligence, it is necessary to show that the hospital had actual or constructive knowledge of the defect or procedures which created the harm. [ ] Furthermore, the hospital's negligence must have been a substantial factor in bringing about the harm to the injured party.[ ]

The final question Nason Hospital raises is did Superior Court err in finding that there was a material issue of fact with respect to the hospital's duty to monitor and review medical services provided within its facilities. Nason Hospital contends that during Linda Thompson's hospitalization, it did not become aware of any exceptional circumstance which would require or justify its intervention into her treatment. The Hospital Association of Pennsylvania, as amicus curiae, argues that it is neither realistic nor appropriate to expect the hospital to conduct daily review and supervision of the independent medical judgment of each member of the medical staff of which it may have actual or constructive knowledge.

Conversely, Appellees argue that Nason Hospital was negligent in failing to monitor the medical services provided Mrs. Thompson. Specifically, Appellees claim that the hospital ignored its Rules and Regulations governing Medical Staff by failing to ensure the patient received adequate medical attention through physician consultations. Appellees also contend that Nason Hospital's medical staff members and personnel treating Mrs. Thompson were aware of her deteriorating condition, brought about by being over anticoagulated, yet did nothing.

It is well established that a hospital staff member or employee has a duty to recognize and report abnormalities in the treatment and condition of its patients. [ ] If the attending physician fails to act after being informed of such abnormalities, it is then incumbent upon the hospital staff member or employee to so advise the hospital authorities so that appropriate action might be taken. [ ] When there is a failure to report changes in a patient's condition and/or to question a physician's order which is not in accord with standard medical practice and the patient is injured as a result, the hospital will be liable for such negligence. [ ]

A thorough review of the record of this case convinces us that there is a sufficient question of material fact presented as to whether Nason Hospital was negligent in supervising the quality of the medical care Mrs. Thompson received, such that the trial court could not have properly granted summary judgment on the issue of corporate liability.

The order of Superior Court is affirmed. Jurisdiction is relinquished.

NOTES AND QUESTIONS

1. *Overarching Duty to Ensure Well-Being of Hospital Patients.* *Thompson* combines duties that can be found in isolation in the case law of other jurisdictions and announces a larger duty: "to ensure the patient's safety and well-being while at the hospital." Consequently, the fundamental duty of hospitals announced in *Thompson* leaves room for the derivation of other more specific duties in addition to the four that had been previously recognized.

2.   *Derivative Duties.* Thompson recognizes four specific duties that are derived from the general duty of hospitals to **ensure the safety and well-being of their patients**.

a.   Duty 1, Maintenance of Safe Facilities and Equipment, is really an extension of common law obligations of all institutions that invite the public onto their property. It encompasses slip-and-fall cases and all forms of injury that patients and visitors might suffer while in the hospital. Yet, it may also require that hospitals have minimum facility and support systems to treat the range of problems and side effects that accompany procedures they offer. In Hernandez v. Smith, 552 F.2d 142 (5th Cir. 1977), for example, an obstetrical clinic that lacked surgical facilities for cesarean sections was found liable for ". . . the failure to provide proper and safe instrumentalities for the treatment of ailments it undertakes to treat . . . ." This duty requires that a hospital adequately equip itself for the services it offers, although it need not be the state of the art. See Emory University v. Porter, 103 Ga. App. 752, 120 S.E.2d 668, 670 (1961); Lauro v. Travelers Ins. Co., 261 So. 2d 261 (La. App.1972). If a device such as an expensive CT scanner has come into common use, however, a smaller and less affluent hospital can argue that it should be judged by the standards of similar hospitals with similar resources.

b.   Duty 2, Selection and Retention of Competent Doctors, is the core obligation of hospitals, and in many jurisdictions, it defines corporate negligence. Probably the most important function of a hospital is to select high-quality physicians for its medical staff. We will discuss this duty in the next section.

c.   Duty 3, Supervision of All Who Practice Medicine in the Hospital, encompasses staff physicians and all other health professionals, acknowledging that modern medicine is a "team" operation. Courts increasingly recognize the team nature of medical practice in hospitals, and liability follows from this recognition. See Hoffman v. East Jefferson Gen. Hosp., 778 So. 2d 33 (La. App. 5th Cir. 2000). Institutional complexity requires accountability—a person in charge—often the attending physician in situations where residents are part of the care. See Lownsbury v. VanBuren, 94 Ohio St.3d 231, 762 N.E.2d 354 (2002).

d.   Duty 4, To Formulate, Adopt and Enforce Adequate Rules and Policies to Ensure Quality Care for the Patients, moves well beyond monitoring staff, drawing our scrutiny to how the institution operates as a system, and allowing plaintiffs to search for negligence in the very design of the operating framework of the hospital. For example, this duty underlies a holding that a psychiatric hospital was liable for the suicide of a patient because of the hospital's policy of discharging inpatients when they reached the limits of their insurance coverage. See Muse v. Charter Hosp. of Winston-Salem, Inc., 117 N.C. App. 468, 452 S.E.2d 589 (1995) (see case excerpt at Chapter 6, Section II). Staffing shortages can be considered negligence if based on the hospital's failure to adopt and enforce adequate staffing policies and practice. See Merritt

v. Karcioglu, 668 So. 2d 469 (La. App. 4th Cir.1996) (hospital ward understaffed in having only three critical care nurses for six patients).

3. *Nursing Homes.* The corporate negligence doctrine underlying direct institutional liability was first recognized with respect to hospitals, but its application is not limited to hospitals. For example, the doctrine has been applied to nursing homes. See Scampone v. Highland Park Care Ctr., LLC, 57 A.3d 582 (Pa. 2012) (a nursing home and its management company are subject to the corporate negligence doctrine in the case of a resident who died as a result of malnutrition and dehydration). The doctrine has also been extended to health plans, which is addressed later in this chapter.

4. *Expert Testimony.* Expert testimony is required to establish a corporate negligence claim, unless it involves simple issues such as structural defects within the common knowledge and experience of the jury. See generally Neff v. Johnson Mem. Hosp., 93 Conn. App. 534, 889 A.2d 921 (Conn. App. 2006) (noting the complexity of the staff credentialing process, and holding that plaintiff needed an expert to determine the standard of care in a suit against a hospital that allows a physician with three malpractice cases to be recredentialed).

5. *Accreditation Standards as Evidence.* The Joint Commission for the Accreditation of Healthcare Organizations (JCAHO or the "Joint Commission") is a private organization that accredits institutional health care providers based on a detailed set of operational standards. Joint Commission accreditation is a sign of institutional quality, and, by becoming accredited, most hospitals are also deemed to have met the conditions of participation in Medicare. Accredited hospitals agree to meet Joint Commission standards. As a result, those standards are evidence of the institutional standard of care. See e.g., Tavares v. Evergreen Hosp. Med. Ctr., 2010 WL 1541475 (Wash. App. Div. 1, Unpublished, 2010) (applying jury instructions for standard of care based on a Joint Commission standard requiring a hospital "to provide an adequate number of staff members whose qualifications are consistent with job responsibilities"); Carter v. Hucks-Folliss, 505 S.E.2d 177 (N.C. App. 1998) (JCAHO credentialing standards provide relevant evidence of the duty of care imposed on a hospital in ascertaining the qualifications of the physician to practice in the hospital). For more on Joint Commission accreditation, see "Note: Private Accreditation and Quality" in Chapter 3.

6. *Hospital Policies as Evidence.* An institution's own internal rules and safety regulations for medical procedures must be followed, and a failure to follow them may be offered as evidence of a breach of a standard of care for the trier of fact to consider. They are material and relevant on the issue of quality of care but are usually not sufficient by themselves to establish the degree of care owed. Jackson v. Oklahoma Mem. Hosp., 909 P.2d 765 (Okl. 1995). In Williams v. St. Claire Med. Ctr., 657 S.W.2d 590 (Ky. App. 1983), the court held that a hospital owes a duty to all patients, including the private patients of staff physicians, to enforce its published rules and regulations pertaining to patient care.

7. *National Practitioner Data Bank.* Under the Health Care Quality Improvement Act of 1986 (HCQIA), hospitals must check a national database maintained under contract with the Department of Health and Human Services before a new staff appointment is made. The National Practitioner Data Bank ("Data Bank") was designed to compile information on individual physicians who have been disciplined, had malpractice claims filed against them, or had privileges revoked or limited. The Data Bank has been criticized by the Government Accountability Office as having unreliable and incomplete data. See U.S. Government Accountability Office (GAO), National Practitioner Data Bank: Major Improvements are Needed to Enhance Data Bank's Reliability (Nov. 2000). For coverage of the HCQIA in hospital-physician relationships, see Chapter 11, and for the role of the Data Bank in the licensing of physicians, see Chapter 2.

8. *Credentialing.* Direct institutional liability of hospitals for negligent credentialing of a physician is based on the duty of the hospital's board of directors to oversee the hospital's quality of care and quality improvement mechanisms. See Office of Inspector General, U.S. Department of Health and Human Services et al., Practical Guidance for Health Care Governing Boards on Compliance Oversight (2015); Office of Inspector General, U.S. Department of Health and Human Services & American Health Lawyers Association, Corporate Responsibility and Health Care Quality: A Resource for Health Care Boards of Directors (2007). For a general discussion of the obligations of health care Boards of Directors, see Chapter 12.

9. *Peer Review.* Every hospital has a peer review committee that examines and assesses the competence of physicians who seek and who have privileges at the hospital. Although the proceedings of these committees are relevant and valuable to plaintiffs claiming that a hospital was negligent in appointing or failing to supervise a professional, those proceedings are not subject to discovery and are inadmissible in court. See Michael D. Benson et al., Hospital Quality Improvement: Are Peer Review Immunity, Privilege, and Confidentiality in the Public Interest?, 11 Nw. J. L. & Soc. Pol'y 1 (2016)(state statutes listed in appendix). For example, a Missouri statute provides that "the interviews, memoranda, proceedings, findings, deliberations, reports, and minutes of peer review committees, or the existence of the same, concerning the health care provided any patient are privileged and shall not be subject to discovery, subpoena, or other means of legal compulsion for their release to any person or entity or be admissible into evidence in any judicial or administrative action for failure to provide appropriate care." Mo. Ann. Stat. § 537.035(4).

Hospitals have argued that the policy (as expressed by these statutes) to keep confidential hospital credentialing and quality review findings, when combined with the burden on plaintiffs to prove that the hospital was negligent in assessing the competence of a staff physician, means that hospitals are immune from corporate liability claims arising from allegedly negligent credentialing. State courts have rejected this logic, holding that the statutory privilege merely obligates plaintiffs to prove their claims using evidence other than the proceedings of peer review committees. See, e.g., Larson v.

Wasemiller, 738 N.W.2d 300 (Minn. 2007); Towner v. Bernardo, 467 P.3d 17 (Or. App. 2020).

10. *Patient Safety Work Product.* The federal Patient Safety and Quality Improvement Act of 2005, 42 U.S.C. § 299b–22, also privileges "patient safety work product" against "discovery in connection with Federal, State or local civil, criminal, or administrative proceeding." The Act expressly pre-empts state law to the contrary. For an example of the application of this federal privilege together with state law, see Daley v. Teruel, 107 N.E.3d 1028 (Ill. App. 2018).

11. *Root Cause Investigations.* A root cause investigation is an institutional process for identifying factors—particularly factors related to institutional systems—that caused a bad clinical outcome. Such investigations when conducted in compliance with Joint Commission guidelines have been subject to discovery. In Reyes v. Meadowlands Hosp. Med. Ctr., 809 A.2d 875 (N.J. Super. 2001), the defendant hospital argued that its root cause analysis of a sentinel event (an unexpected death or serious physical or psychological injury) under Joint Commission guidelines should be protected from discovery. The court held that ". . . the Sentinel Event Policy invoked by defendant Meadowlands Hospital does not create a self-critical analysis privilege, insulating any and all discussions and statements made and conclusions reached by the participants therein and actions taken by the Hospital pursuant thereto not subject to the Civil Rules of Discovery."

12. *Mined Hospital Data.* Data mining by health systems in an effort to promote safety and efficiency is also a source of valuable evidence for plaintiffs pursuing corporate negligence claims. Moreover, mining for data is now the standard of care for large hospitals and health systems. This situation has resulted from a combination of trends: the continued consolidation of professional and institutional providers creates ever larger health care delivery systems, the emergence of electronic health records (EHR), and increased computing capacity. See Barry R. Furrow, Searching for Adverse Events: Big Data and Beyond, 27 Annals Health L. 149 (2018). Indeed, a group of researchers has developed a system to identify error-predictive indicators within EHRs so as to detect and potentially act on medical errors in real time. See David C. Classen et al., An Electronic Health Record-Based Real-Time Analytics Program for Patient Safety Surveillance and Improvement, 37 Health Aff. 1805 (2018).

PROBLEM: CASCADING ERRORS

Carolyn Gadner was driving her car on the highway when another car driven by Bob Sneed passed her, sideswiped her, ran her off the road, and drove off. Gadner caught up with Sneed and forced him to stop. She got out of her vehicle and started to walk to his car when he drove away. While Gadner was walking back to her car, Charles Otis struck her with his vehicle. Gadner was transported to Bay Hospital, a small rural hospital, where Dr. Dick Samson, a second-year pediatric resident, was the attending emergency room physician.

Upon arriving at Bay, Gadner's skin was cool and clammy, and her blood pressure was 95/55, indicative of shock. Gadner received 200 ccs per hour of fluid and was x-rayed. She actively requested a transfer because of vaginal bleeding. Nurse Gilbert voiced her own concerns about the need for a transfer to the other nurses in the emergency room. Dr. Samson did not order one.

Bay is a rural hospital and is not equipped to handle multiple trauma patients like Gadner. Bay had no protocol or procedure for making transfers to larger hospitals. Bay breached its own credentialing procedures in hiring a physician who lacked the necessary training, expertise, or demonstrated competence to work the ER. Dr. Bay, the hospital's chief of staff, had screened Samson, who was not properly evaluated before he was hired. A second-year pediatric resident is not normally assigned to an ER setting, given the lack of experience.

The nurses failed to notice that Gadner was in shock, and this failure was substandard. After they initially noted that she arrived with cool and clammy skin and a blood pressure of 95/55, they did not advise Dr. Samson that the patient was likely in shock; they failed to place her on IV fluids, elevate her feet above her head, and give oxygen as needed. Dr. Samson ordered the administration of 500 ccs of fluid per hour, but Gadner received only about 200 ccs per hour because the IV infiltrated, delivering the fluid to the surrounding tissue instead of the vein. The nursing staff normally would discover infiltration and correct it. Scanty nurses' notes revealed that vital signs were not taken regularly, depriving Dr. Samson of critical and ongoing information about Gadner's condition. Nurse Gilbert administered Valium and morphine to Gadner, following Dr. Samson's orders, a mixture of drugs counter-indicated for a patient with symptoms of shock. Nurse Gilbert did not notice or protest.

Three hours after arriving at Bay, Gadner "coded" and Dr. Samson tried unsuccessfully to revive her. After she coded, Dr. Samson attempted to use the laryngoscope, following standard practice, but the one provided was broken. He then ordered epinephrine, but there was none in the ER. An autopsy was performed, and Gadner died of treatable shock according to the coroner.

Consider the various theories of liability available to the plaintiff. Then develop a plan to improve the hospital from a patient safety perspective so that this kind of disaster will not happen again.

PROBLEM: PROCTORING PEERS

As the result of a negligence lawsuit, you have been asked by Hilldale Adventist Hospital to advise it on the implications of its use of proctors for assessing candidates for medical staff privileges. The hospital used Dr. Hook, a surgeon certified by the American Board of Orthopedic Surgery, as a proctor during two different operations on the plaintiff in the lawsuit at two different hospitals during the process of evaluation of Dr. Frank DiBianco for staff privileges. Dr. Hook had initially been asked to observe ten surgeries by Dr. DiBianco and then file a report. He observed an operation on the plaintiff during one of these observations. Two months later, he was again asked to proctor Dr. DiBianco at another hospital, and he again observed a procedure on the plaintiff. Prior to each procedure, Dr. Hook had reviewed the x-rays and discussed the operative plan, but he otherwise had taken no part in the care and treatment of the plaintiff. He did not participate in the operations, did not scrub in, and always observed from outside the "sterile field." He got no payment for his proctoring efforts, and he had never met the plaintiff nor had any other contact with her.

Can Hilldale be liable for its use of Dr. Hook as a proctor? Can Dr. Hook be directly liable for failing to stop negligent work by Dr. DiBianco?

IV.   LIABILITY OF HEALTH PLANS

Before the rise of managed care during the late 1980s and throughout the 1990s, health insurance plans permitted beneficiaries to see any primary care physician or specialist and to undergo any treatment without pre-approval. The plan would reimburse the patient or pay the physician based upon the physician's fee without a negotiated discount or capitated rate. Managed care, on the other hand, offered an alternative approach to insurance that was supposed to better control the cost of medical care while maintaining its quality. This approach included features so common today that it is hard to image health insurance without them: provider networks together with financial incentives for the beneficiary to visit only network providers; negotiated discounts on provider fees in exchange for the plan's listing the provider as part of its network; and utilization controls such as required plan pre-approval for many procedures and primary care referral prior to coverage for a specialist visit. See Chapters 8 and 9 for a fuller discussion of managed care. Of course, to the extent these mechanisms play a role in determining the level and quality of care patients can receive from their providers, they may expose managed care plans to potential liability as described in this chapter.

Importantly, however, a large portion of managed care plans are not subject to state tort liability, because they are employment-based plans governed by a federal law called ERISA, which preempts liability, including institutional liability, for state law claims. ERISA is discussed more fully in Chapter 8. In 2020 employment-based insurance covered 157 million members, and the vast majority relied on health plans that include managed care features. Indeed, fewer than one percent of the employees in all firms are enrolled in fee-for-service indemnity plans. Preferred Provider Plans (PPOs) now cover 47 percent of insured workers, High Deductible Plans cover 31 percent, HMO plans cover 13 percent, and Point of Service (POS) plans cover eight percent. See Kaiser Family Foundation, 2020 Employer Health Benefits Survey (Oct. 2020).

ERISA preemption only applies to employment-based plans; it does not apply to other kinds of insurance, in particular health plans sold in the individual market through the ACA exchanges, which currently cover more than 12 million Americans. Thus, the following discussions of liability are applicable to non-ERISA qualified plans.

A. VICARIOUS LIABILITY

Health plans in theory face the same vicarious and corporate liability questions as hospitals because they provide services through physicians, whether the physicians are salaried employees or independent contractors. These medical services, too, can injure patients/subscribers, leading to a malpractice suit for such injuries. Courts have been willing to impose vicarious liability against certain kinds of health plans, under the doctrines of both apparent authority and implied authority. See, e.g., Petrovich v. Share Health Plan of Illinois, Inc., 719 N.E.2d 756 (Ill. 1999).

Health plan advertising often describes plans using words such as "total care program," or "an entire health care system." Reliance by the subscriber on the managed care organization (MCO) for his or her choice of physicians, and any holding out by the MCO as a provider, can be sufficient to establish vicarious liability. See McClellan v. Health Maint. Org. of Pennsylvania, 413 Pa. Super. 128, 604 A.2d 1053 (1992) (ostensible agency based on advertisements by plan claiming that it carefully screened primary care physicians).

Health plans are also subject to corporate negligence claims.

B. DIRECT INSTITUTIONAL LIABILITY

SHANNON V. MCNULTY
Superior Court of Pennsylvania, 1998.
718 A.2d 828.

ORIE MELVIN, JUDGE:

Mario L. Shannon and his wife, Sheena Evans Shannon, in their own right and as co-administrators of the Estate of Evan Jon Shannon, appeal from an order entered in the Court of Common Pleas of Allegheny County denying their motion to remove a compulsory nonsuit. This appeal concerns the Shannons' claims of vicarious and corporate liability against HealthAmerica stemming from the premature delivery and subsequent death of their son. We reverse the order refusing to remove the compulsory nonsuit and remand for trial.

This medical malpractice action arises from the pre-natal care provided by appellees, Larry P. McNulty, M.D. and HealthAmerica, to Mrs. Shannon. The Shannons claimed Dr. McNulty was negligent for failing to timely diagnose and treat signs of pre-term labor, and HealthAmerica was vicariously liable for the negligence of its nursing staff in failing to respond to Mrs. Shannon's complaints by timely referring her to an appropriate physician or hospital for diagnosis and treatment of her pre-term labor. The Shannons also alleged HealthAmerica was corporately liable for its negligent supervision of Dr. McNulty's care and its lack of appropriate procedures and protocols when dispensing telephonic medical advice to subscribers.

[The trial court granted HealthAmerica's motion for compulsory nonsuit, and the Shannons appealed.]

* * *

[Thompson v. Nason Hospital, 527 Pa. 330, 591 A.2d 703 (1991), set out four corporate negligence duties:

(1) Use of "reasonable care in the maintenance of safe and adequate facilities and equipment;"

(2) Selection and retention of competent physicians;

(3) Oversight of "all persons who practice medicine within its walls as to patient care;" and

(4) Formulation, adoption and enforcement of "adequate rules and policies to ensure quality care for patients," including upholding "the proper standard of care owed its patient." Id. at 708.]

* * *

The evidence introduced by the Shannons may be summarized in relevant part as follows. Mrs. Shannon testified during the trial of this case that she was a subscriber of the HealthAmerica HMO when this child was conceived. It was Mrs. Shannon's first pregnancy. When she advised HealthAmerica she was pregnant in June 1992, they gave her a list of six doctors from which she could select an OB/GYN. She chose Dr. McNulty from the list. [ ] Her HealthAmerica membership card instructed her to contact either her physician or HealthAmerica in the event she had any medical questions or emergent medical conditions. The card contained the HealthAmerica emergency phone number, which was manned by registered nurses. [ ] She testified it was confusing trying to figure out when to call Dr. McNulty and when to call HealthAmerica because she was receiving treatment from both for various medical conditions related to her pregnancy, including asthma and reflux. [ ]

She saw Dr. McNulty monthly but also called the HealthAmerica phone line a number of times for advice and to schedule appointments with their in-house doctors. [ ] She called Dr. McNulty on October 2, 1992 with complaints of abdominal pain. The doctor saw her on October 5, 1992 and examined her for five minutes. He told Mrs. Shannon her abdominal pain was the result of a fibroid uterus, he prescribed rest and took her off of work for one week. He did no testing to confirm his diagnosis and did not advise her of the symptoms of pre-term labor. [ ]

She next called Dr. McNulty's office twice on October 7 and again on October 8 and October 9, 1992, because her abdominal pain was continuing, she had back pain, was constipated and she could not sleep. She asked Dr. McNulty during the October 8th call if she could be in pre-term labor because her symptoms were similar to those described in a reference book she had on labor. [ ] She told Dr. McNulty her pains were irregular and about ten minutes apart, but she had never been in labor so she did not know what it felt like. He told her he had just checked her on October 5th, and she was not in labor. [ ] The October 9th call was at least her fourth call to Dr. McNulty about her abdominal pain, and she testified that Dr. McNulty was becoming impatient with her. [ ]

On October 10th, she called HealthAmerica's emergency phone line and told them about her severe irregular abdominal pain, back pain, that her pain was worse at night, that she thought she may be in pre-term labor, and about her prior calls to Dr. McNulty. The triage nurse advised her to call Dr. McNulty again. [ ] Mrs. Shannon did not immediately call Dr. McNulty because she did not feel there was anything new she could tell him to get him to pay attention to her condition. She called the HealthAmerica triage line again on October 11, 1992, said her symptoms were getting worse and Dr. McNulty was not responding. The triage nurse again advised her to call Dr. McNulty. [ ] Mrs. Shannon called Dr. McNulty and told him about her worsening symptoms, her legs beginning to go numb, and she thought that she was in pre-term labor. He was again short with her and angry and insisted that she was not in pre-term labor. [ ]

On October 12, 1992, she again called the HealthAmerica phone service and told the nurse about her symptoms, severe back pain and back spasms, legs going numb, more regular abdominal pain, and Dr. McNulty was not responding to her complaints. One of HealthAmerica's in-house orthopedic physicians spoke with her on the phone and directed her to go to West Penn Hospital to get her back examined. [ ] She followed the doctor's advice and drove an hour from her house to West Penn, passing three hospitals on the way. At West Penn she was processed as having a back complaint because those were HealthAmerica's instructions, but she was taken to the obstetrics wing as a formality because she was over five (5) months pregnant. She delivered a one and one-half pound baby that night. He survived only two days and then died due to his severe prematurity. [ ]

The Shannons' expert, Stanley M. Warner, M.D., testified he had experience in a setting where patients would call triage nurses. Dr. Warner opined that HealthAmerica, through its triage nurses, deviated from the standard of care following the phone calls to the triage line on October 10, 11 and 12, 1992, by not immediately referring Mrs. Shannon to a physician or hospital for a cervical exam and fetal stress test. As with Dr. McNulty, these precautions would have led to her labor being detected and increased the baby's chance of survival. [ ] Dr. Warner further testified on cross examination that Mrs. Shannon turned to HealthAmerica's triage nurses for medical advice on these three occasions when she communicated her symptoms. She did not receive appropriate advice, and further, if HealthAmerica's triage nurses intended for the referrals back to Dr. McNulty to be their solution, they had a duty to follow up Mrs. Shannon's calls by calling Dr. McNulty to insure Mrs. Shannon was actually receiving the proper care from him. [ ]

Corporate Liability

[The court concludes that the third duty of *Thompson*, the duty to oversee all those who deliver care, is applicable.]

Similarly, in the present case Dr. Warner, on direct examination, offered the following opinion when asked whether or not HealthAmerica deviated from the standard of care:

> I believe they did deviate from the standard of care. I believe on each occasion of the calls on October 10th, 11th, and October 12th, that Mrs. Shannon should have been referred to the hospital, and the hospital notified that this woman was probably in preterm labor and needed to be handled immediately. They did have the alternative of calling for a physician, if they wanted to, for him to agree with it, but basically she needed to be evaluated in a placd [sic] where there was a fetal monitor and somebody to do a pelvic examination to see what was happening with her.

[ ] When asked whether this deviation increased the risk of harm Dr. Warner stated that "it did increase the risk of harm to the baby, and definitely decreased the chance of [the baby] being born healthy." [ ]

[Dr. Warner further testified, in response to a series of hypothetical questions, that severe abdominal pain should have led the triage nurse either to call the doctor so he could instruct the patient to get to the hospital, or tell the patient to get to the hospital as soon as possible, and that on each of the three days that Shannon called Health America, the standard of care dictated that she be sent to hospital to determine if she was in preterm labor.]

Viewing the evidence in the light most favorable to the Shannons as the non-moving party, our examination of the instant record leads us to the conclusion that the Shannons presented sufficient evidence to establish a prima facie case of corporate liability pursuant to the third duty set forth in Thompson, supra. However, due to the different entities involved, this determination does not end our inquiry. The Welsh case involved a suit against a hospital and thus Thompson was clearly applicable. Instantly, HealthAmerica, noting this Court's decision not to extend corporate liability under the facts in McClellan v. Health Maintenance Organization of Pennsylvania, [ ], argues that the Thompson duties are inapplicable to a health maintenance organization. We disagree.

In adopting the doctrine of corporate liability the Thompson court recognized "the corporate hospital's role in the total health care of its patients." [ ] Likewise, we recognize the central role played by HMOs in the total health care of its subscribers. A great deal of today's healthcare is channeled through HMOs with the subscribers being given little or no say so in the stewardship of their care. Specifically, while these providers do not practice medicine, they do involve themselves daily in decisions affecting their subscriber's medical care. These decisions may, among others, limit the length of hospital stays, restrict the use of specialists, prohibit or limit post hospital care, restrict access to therapy, or prevent rendering of emergency room care. While all of these efforts are for the laudatory purpose of containing health care costs, when decisions are made to limit a subscriber's access to treatment, that decision must pass the test of medical reasonableness. To hold otherwise would be to deny the true effect of the provider's actions, namely, dictating and directing the subscriber's medical care.

Where the HMO is providing health care services rather than merely providing money to pay for services their conduct should be subject to scrutiny. We see no reason why the duties applicable to hospitals should not be equally applied to an HMO when that HMO is performing the same or similar functions as a hospital. When a benefits provider, be it an insurer or a managed care organization, interjects itself into the rendering of medical decisions affecting a subscriber's care it must do so in a medically reasonable manner. Here, HealthAmerica provided a phone service for emergent care staffed by triage nurses. Hence, it was under a duty to oversee that the dispensing of advice by those nurses would be performed in a medically reasonable manner. Accordingly, we now make explicit that which was implicit in McClellan and find that HMOs may, under the right circumstances, be held corporately liable for a breach of any of the Thompson duties which causes harm to its subscribers.

[The court also held that HealthAmerica was vicariously liable for the negligent rendering of services by its triage nurses, under Section 323 of the Restatement (Second) of Torts.]

NOTES AND QUESTIONS

1. *Cascade of Failures.* Consider the underlying failures of the system in *Shannon*. The treating physician was impatient and inattentive to warning signs, but it was the triage nurses staffing the phone lines who failed to properly direct Shannon to a physician or hospital. How should the system have been designed to avoid such an error? What would you suggest to avoid a repetition of this kind of disaster?

2. *Poor Plan Design*. Many of the ERISA preemption cases involve claims of negligent design of the managed care plan, including telephone call-in services staffed by nurses, as in *Shannon*. Other claims of negligent design and administration of the delivery of health care services have been allowed. See McDonald v. Damian, 56 F. Supp. 2d 574 (E.D. Pa.1999) (claim for inadequacies in the delivery of medical services).

3. *HMO?* A health maintenance organization (HMO) was the defendant in *Shannon*. An HMO is one kind of MCO. According to healthcare.gov, an HMO plan "usually limits coverage to care from doctors who work for or contract with the HMO. It generally won't cover out-of-network care except in an emergency. . . . [And they] often provide integrated care and focus on prevention and wellness."

4. *Health Plan Credentialing*. An MCO, like a hospital, has been held to owe its subscribers a duty to properly select its panel members. Harrell v. Total Health Care, Inc., 1989 WL 153066 (Mo. App.1989), affirmed, 781 S.W.2d 58 (Mo. 1989).

The logic of a direct duty imposed on MCOs to properly select providers is even stronger for an MCO than for a hospital. In the hospital setting, the patient has often selected the physician. The patient is then admitted to the hospital because the physician has admitting privileges at that hospital. By contrast, under most health plans, the patient has chosen the plan, but not the physicians who are a part of the plan's network. Because patients must use the physicians in the plan's network, patients explicitly rely on the MCO for its selection of health care providers.

A duty of proper selection will expose an MCO to liability both for failing to properly screen its physicians' competence, and for failing to evaluate physicians for other problems. If the MCO empanels a physician who has evidenced incompetence, it risks liability. This situation is comparable to negligently granting staff privileges to a physician with alcohol or other substance abuse problems, or one with sexual pathologies that might affect patients. See McClellan v. Health Maint. Org. of Pennsylvania, 413 Pa. Super. 128, 604 A.2d 1053 (1992), in which the court allowed a suit against the HMO to proceed for negligence in selecting, retaining, and evaluating a primary care physician, misrepresenting the screening process for selecting its primary care physicians, and breach of contract.

5. *Duty to Supervise and Control Network Physicians*. MCOs have similar duties to those of hospitals to supervise and control staff. MCO liability for negligent control of its network physicians derives from the common law duty to select only competent physicians and from federal and state quality assurance regulations. As courts continue to characterize MCOs as health care providers, suits are likely to increase. Only PPOs, with their reduced level of physician control, might have an argument that liability should not be imposed for negligent supervision. However, statutes in some states require PPOs to implement quality assurance programs, and others contemplate the use of such programs by PPOs. See, e.g., Iowa Code Ann. § 514.21.

C. PHYSICIAN INCENTIVE SYSTEMS

When first introduced, many MCOs paid their network primary care physicians on a "capitated" basis. Such plans required beneficiaries to select a network primary care physician (PCP) at the start of the plan year. Beneficiaries were incentivized to visit their selected network PCP if and when they needed care during the year. A network PCP agreed to provide medical services as needed to plan beneficiaries who selected that physician as their go-to PCP, and, in return, the physician received from the plan a set monthly payment for each beneficiary that had selected the physician as their PCP. The plan made the monthly payment whether or not the plan beneficiary sought any care from the PCP, but the plan would not pay any more than this monthly fee, even if the payment failed to cover the PCP's costs for providing care to a particular beneficiary. In this way, capitation shifted some of the insurance risk from the plan to the network provider.

Capitation proved to be unpopular, and it has largely been displaced by discounted fee-for-service and less severe risk-sharing arrangements. See Mark Hall, The Death of Managed Care: a Regulatory Autopsy, 30 J. Health Polit., Pol'y & L. 427 (2005); James C. Robinson, The End of Managed Care, 285 JAMA 2622 (2001). Yet, for a time, patients injured as a result of their physician's alleged failure to provide necessary care were suspicious that capitation had incentivized their physicians to skimp on care.

The argument that physician judgment was "corrupted" by cost-conserving payment systems in managed care systems was litigated without much success. See, e.g., Maltz v. Aetna Health Plans of New York, Inc., 114 F.3d 9 (2d Cir. 1997) (health plan does not have a fiduciary obligation to pay beneficiary's physician on a fee-for-service rather than a capitated basis so as to keep the physician from leaving the plan's network); Pegram v. Herdrich, 530 U.S. 211 (2000) (plan beneficiary cannot state a claim for breach of fiduciary duty under ERISA where network physicians were paid on a capitated basis and failed to refer her outside of physician's clinic when it was medically necessary to do so; a federal statute expressly endorsed the payment mechanism used to pay the network physician).

V. LIABILITY OF ACOs

A. ACOs

Accountable Care Organizations (ACOs) are creations of the ACA. They are groups of professional, institutional, and ancillary service providers that agree to provide care to a population of insured individuals and to be accountable for both the quality and cost of care. To qualify for the Medicare Shared Savings Program (addressed in Chapter 10), an ACO must be large enough to take responsibility for all of the medical care required in a given year by at least 5000 Medicare beneficiaries. Thus, ACOs are large provider networks that include physicians of all kinds, hospitals, and clinics, as well as possibly labs and pharmacies.

While ACOs can be integrated to varying degrees, they each have a governance structure that allows for the creation of policies and practices that enable medical services to be provided in a more coordinated and efficient manner than was possible in many provider networks that predate the ACA. Through greater coordination, ACOs seek to provide care to a large population at an overall annual cost that is lower than a budgetary target set at the start of a given year. An ACO that comes in under this target will share in the savings, and increasingly ACOs are expected to share in the losses. In this way, ACOs take on some of the insurance risk. Yet, ACOs are not merely MCOs in new clothing. They are first and foremost provider networks while MCOs are fundamentally health insurers. For a thorough explanation of the differences between ACOs and MCOs, see Ezekiel J. Emanuel, Why Accountable Care Organizations Are Not 1990s Managed Care Redux, 307 JAMA 2263 (2012).

Evidence from early experience indicates that ACOs have reduced overall costs while maintaining quality. See Brystana G. Kaufman, Impact of Accountable Care Organizations on Utilization, Care, and Outcomes: A Systematic Review, 76 Med. Care Res. Rev. 255 (2017) (a review of 42 empirical studies show that ACO implementation is associated with "reduced inpatient use, reduced emergency department visits, and improved measures of preventive care and chronic disease management"). See also Michael Wilson, The Impacts of Accountable Care Organizations on Patient Experience, Health Outcomes and Costs: a Rapid Review, 25 J. Health Serv. Res. & Pol'y 130 (2020) (a review of 59 empirical studies shows that ACOs have cut costs without reducing quality). Unlike many managed care plans, ACOs are not protected by ERISA preemption. Thus, patients who are allegedly injured as a result of ACO structures, policies, or practices and try to sue under a theory of corporate negligence will not have their claim barred by federal law.

B. LIABILITY RISKS

ACOs present a range of liability risks, but the risks are mostly transitional as new systems and technologies are chosen and mastered. However, other liability risks are inherent in the ACO structure as established by federal law and regulations.

1. *Solidification of the Standard of Care.* As ACOs and their providers adapt to the new federal mandates and seek to deliver quality care at a lower cost, patients may be able to claim substandard care. ACOs

are premised on evidence-based medicine. In establishing best practices, ACOs must create clinical guidelines, presumably using evidence-based guidelines that are being developed by various federal initiatives. Any guideline selection process risks a claim that the guideline chosen is inappropriate when applied to a particular patient.

The ACO must provide documentation of its plans to promote evidence-based medicine, report on quality and cost metrics, and coordinate care. The ACO must report on quality measures, and quality of care is measured by clinical processes and outcomes; patient and, where practicable, caregiver, experience of care; and utilization. The use of evidence-based medicine criteria, reporting on quality and cost metrics, and documentation to show the coordination of care will likely create new duties for physicians and therefore for the ACO itself.

2. *Patient Engagement.* The ACO model is built on a concept of patient engagement and "patient-centeredness." ACOs must promote beneficiary engagement, since the ACA ties reimbursement to patient satisfaction. Using the Hospital Consumer Assessment of Healthcare Providers and Systems (HCAHPS) surveys, plans must poll discharged patients about their overall experience with hospital staff. Such a quality measure is part of the calculation of value-based incentive payments. This focus on patient centeredness and quality of care creates a distinctive new dimension of medical practice, since the ACO must demonstrate that it meets "patient-centeredness criteria." This patient focus will facilitate patient buy-in and presumably reduce their inclination to sue for adverse events; it will also set a high benchmark for patient engagement and disappointment.

3. *Cost Control.* Cost-containment goals and incentive-based payments present a theoretical liability exposure. The ACA is driving value-based compensation reforms, especially in Medicare, under which providers are paid based on positive outcomes rather than patient volume. Value-based compensation seeks to balance high-value care and lower cost. Meaningful quality measures must be developed to ensure the use of evidence-based quality measures. Physicians are expected to participate in the development of these quality metrics to ensure that the ACOs develop clinical protocols for population health management.

Reducing or eliminating some diagnostic tests, for example, will risk a missed diagnosis on occasion, which creates a risk of institutional liability. Cost-valuation justifications are not part of state medical malpractice analysis, and defenses will be hard to construct. Use of incentive-based compensation, therefore, risks resurrecting early managed care liability accusations of undertreatment leading to patient injury. Incentive-based arguments were, however, rarely if ever successful in suits brought against MCOs, because the courts demonstrated sympathy for the balance the provider had to strike between cost-containment and quality of care. Benjamin Harvey and Glenn Cohen, The Looming Threat of Liability for Accountable Care Organizations and What to Do About It, 310 JAMA 141 (2013).

4. *Electronic Health Records.* EHRs provide a clear record of care, both failures and successes, and ACO performance. They also provide a record of whether care was evidence-based, as well as document compliance. From a lawyer's perspective, standard of care evidence is critical to any malpractice case and the EHRs may be a gold mine of information. See Barry R. Furrow, The Limits of Current A.I. in Health Care: Patient Safety Policing in Hospitals, 12 Ne. U.L. Rev. 1 (2020).

5. *Allied Health Professional Liability.* The increase in the use of nurses and physician assistants as part of ACO teams will lead to increased liability risks for those providers and for the ACO as the "employer" of these teams. Coordination of care in an ACO requires that all providers master new skills in moving patients around the network and sharing information across providers. This learning curve for providers—realigning care, redefining measurements to track patient care and expenses, and establishing new processes and best practices—increases the risk of errors in the delivery of medical services.

Vicarious liability principles still would apply for provider errors as long as they are within the scope of employment. An ACO, particularly a hospital-based one, will be liable for the acts of its providers, since they are likely to be treated as employees and not independent contractors. See Marsh McLennan, A New Risk Management Frontier: Accountable Care Organizations (October 2012) for a discussion of the range of liability risks and the insurance products available to ACOs to insure against those risks.

6. *Corporate Structure.* Corporate negligence principles, following *Thompson*, logically apply to integrated organizations that manage care, whether a patient medical home, an ACO, or some other delivery form that the ACA creates. The courts are willing to look beyond the hospital form in deciding whether a health care entity might be liable for corporate negligence. For example, in Gianquitti v. Atwood Med. Assoc., Ltd., 973 A.2d 580 (R.I. 2009), the court held that a professional medical-group practice that provided on-call medical care to its patients if and when they were hospitalized could be liable for corporate negligence if it lacked a formal backup system. In another case, Davis v. Gish, 2007 WL 5007253 (Pa. Com. Pl. 2007), the court noted the kinds of activities that would turn a professional group or a physicians' practice group into an entity subject to corporate negligence, including taking on general responsibility "for arranging and coordinating the total health care of its patients."

PROBLEM: AXIS UNIVERSITY HOSPITAL

Axis University Hospital ("Axis") has decided that it needs to better coordinate its patient care from the moment patients enter the hospital until they leave and return to the care of their own physicians or specialists. Its CEO and CFO have scoured the ACA and have decided to adopt the following steps.

First, they have developed their own model of direct contracting with local physician groups, particularly cardiologists and oncologists, designed to promote risk-based comprehensive payments.

Second, for elderly patients with comorbidities, who often move between home or nursing home and the hospital, they propose a coordinated care model in which gerontologists will be paid by salary rather than fee-for-service.

Third, for primary care physicians in their community, they propose patient-centered medical homes that entail the use of medical monitoring technologies, along with extensive electronic medical recordkeeping. Physicians who agree to participate in such medical homes will receive bonus payments based on their adoption of a range of treatment measures.

You are the general counsel of *Axis* and have been asked to make a presentation to the Board of Directors on any negatives that such new payment models might create for *Axis*. Consider in particular the liability consequences of each of the three approaches. Are traditional tort concepts undermined by moving to these delivery forms? Who is more at risk for liability with these reforms—physicians, hospitals and systems, or other providers?

PROBLEM: GATEWAY HEALTH NETWORK

Gateway Health Network, Inc. ("Gateway") is a corporation that operates a network of independent professional and institutional health care providers. It does not own or employ the providers in its network, and it is not an insurance company or a health plan. Rather, it is merely a network of doctors and hospitals. Gateway is large, with more than 2000 physician members and 5 affiliated hospitals. Gateway enters into agreements with health plans to be the provider network for those plans.

Gateway is an ACO. It earns financial bonuses from the private health plans it serves when (a) care given by Gateway's providers to plan beneficiaries during a plan year costs less than the financial benchmarks agreed to by Gateway and each plan, and (b) Gateway's providers meet certain quality indicators. As part of Gateway's contracts with its affiliated providers, Gateway promises to pay the affiliated provider half of all shared-savings and quality bonuses Gateway receives from health plans for care provided to patients who receive care from that affiliated provider.

Laclede Internists, P.C. ("Laclede") is a professional corporation that operates a primary care medical practice of twelve internal medicine physicians. Laclede has a contract with Gateway to be part of its provider network. Dr. Leroy Levinson is an internist who practices at Laclede.

Amy Abelman receives her primary care from Dr. Levinson. In keeping with Gateway policies, Dr. Levinson created a plan of care for Amy at the start of their treatment relationship. As part of the plan, Dr. Levinson would do a standard pelvic examination as part of Amy's annual physical and, because Amy is 29 years old, Dr. Levinson would also do a pap smear test once every three years. In further compliance with Gateway policies, Dr. Levinson also identified a Gateway-affiliated OB/GYN specialist willing to provide specialty care to Amy in the future if needed. Dr. Levinson identified Dr. Donna Decker. Dr. Decker is an OB/GYN specialist employed at River City OB/GYN, P.C., which also has an affiliation agreement with Gateway.

Dr. Levinson confirmed that Dr. Decker would accept Amy as a patient when and if needed. Additionally, as required by Gateway policy, Dr. Decker agreed to Dr. Levinson's care plan for Amy that included his completing an annual pelvic exam and a pap smear once every three years. Finally, Drs. Levinson and Decker agreed that Dr. Levinson would refer Amy to Dr. Decker only if complications arose requiring an OB/GYN specialist.

A pap smear is a test of sample cells taken from a woman's cervix or vagina. It is used to look for cellular changes that show cancer or conditions that may develop into cancer. If detected early, cervical cancer often can be cured. Pap smears often detect cellular abnormalities even when cancer is not present, and these abnormalities often clear by themselves without treatment.

Gateway adopted a clinical guideline stating that affiliated primary care providers should not refer a female patient age 21–65 to a Gateway OB/GYN for a biopsy unless and until the patient had a total of 4 abnormal pap smear tests over a 6-month period of time. This guideline falls within the parameters of guidelines published by the American Society of Obstetricians and Gynecologists.

Following 4 abnormal pap smears over 6 months, Dr. Levinson referred Amy to Dr. Decker for a cervical biopsy. It showed that Amy had a rare and aggressive form of cervical cancer that was very serious. Despite all of Dr. Decker's best efforts over the next year, it was determined that Amy would not likely survive the cancer.

Assuming that Amy's odds of surviving her cancer would have significantly improved had it been diagnosed just two months earlier than it was, can she sustain an action against Gateway for her damages, and, if so, under what theories?

VI.   REFORMING THE TORT SYSTEM FOR MEDICAL INJURIES

Malpractice crises come and go in the United States, driven by an apparent insurance cycle of competitive entry into the market followed by rapid premium increases as the insurers' returns drop. Legislative reform efforts inevitably follow, spearheaded by angry physician groups facing increases in their insurance premiums and pockets of unavailability in some geographic areas and for some specialties. This repeated cycle has resulted in an outpouring of research and writings that highlight problems in the medical tort system and propose reforms and alternatives.

The ground-breaking 1990 Harvard Medical Practice Study in New York revealed both the pervasiveness of medical error and the failure of malpractice law to compensate injured patients without providing a windfall to patients who—for reasons other than medical error—experience a bad outcome. *See* Patients, Doctors, and Lawyers: Medical Injury, Malpractice Litigation, and Patient Compensation in New York: The Report of the Harvard Medical Practice Study to the State of New York (1990). The study looked at the incidence of injuries resulting from medical interventions (adverse events) beginning with a sample of more than 31,000 New York hospital records drawn from the study year 1984. The review was conducted by medical record administrators and nurses in the screening phase, and by board-certified physicians for the physician-review phase. Investigators also identified all New York malpractice claims related to alleged medical negligence occurring in 1984.

With respect to the incidence of injury due to medical error, the Study found that nearly four percent of all treatment episodes resulted in injury, and one quarter of those injuries were attributed to medical negligence. This means that one percent of all hospital treatment episodes in New York in 1984 resulted in an injury caused by medical error. This translated into approximately 27,000 malpractice victims in one state in one year, which highlighted the need for a robust system to identify and correct poor quality care and a mechanism to compensate those injured by medical error.

The same researchers conducted a similar study in Utah that resulted in findings consistent with those of the New York study. See David M. Studdert et al., Beyond Dead Reckoning: Measures of Medical Injury Burden, Malpractice Litigation, and Alternative Compensation Models from Utah and Colorado, 33 Ind. L. Rev. 1643, 1662 (2000).

More recent studies have confirmed that adverse events occur at even higher levels than the decades-old New York Study reported. The Office of the Inspector General found that 13.5% of Medicare hospital admissions resulted in an adverse event, with an equal percentage resulting in temporary harm. See U.S. Dep't of Health & Human Servs., Office of Inspector Gen., Adverse Events in Hospitals: National Incidence Among Medicare Beneficiaries, at i–ii (2010). Another study, using newer methodologies for discovering adverse events, concluded that patients suffer adverse events in one-third of all admissions. See David C. Classen et al., 'Global Trigger Tool' Shows that Adverse Events in Hospitals May Be Ten Times Greater than Previously Measured, 30 Health Affairs 581, 581 (2011).

Yet the Harvard Studies of New York and Utah also revealed that the tort system does a poor job of capturing the cases of actual malpractice while also weeding out cases involving bad outcomes that are not the result of medical error. For every seven to eight incidents of verified medical negligence, only one lawsuit for medical negligence was filed. Meanwhile, for every bona fide claim of medical negligence filed, five malpractice claims were filed that did *not* involve medical negligence. When claims that did not involve negligence are eliminated, only one claim of medical negligence was filed for every fifty verified incidents of medical negligence.

For a recent systematic review of all empirical studies measuring the effectiveness of the medical malpractice system in capturing only cases in which actual negligent error has occurred, see Michelle M. Mello et al., Malpractice Liability and Health Care Quality: A Review, 323 JAMA 352 (2020) (most of the 37 studies included in the review found no empirical association between malpractice liability risk and health care quality and outcomes).

A. EFFECTS OF MALPRACTICE LITIGATION ON PROVIDER BEHAVIOR

Malpractice litigation in theory operates as a quality control mechanism. The existence of a liability rule and the resulting threat of a lawsuit and judgment should encourage health care providers to reduce error and patient injury in circumstances where patients themselves lack the information (and ability) to monitor the quality of care they receive. By finding fault and assessing damages against a defendant, a court sends a signal to health care providers that if they wish to avoid similar damages in the future, they may need to change their behavior.

In practice, however, the deterrent effect of malpractice litigation is uncertain. See Mello et al., above (systematic review showing little, if any, association between malpractice liability risk and health care quality and outcomes and suggesting that this lack of association undermines deterrence); Zenon Zabinski and Bernard S. Black, The Deterrent Effect of Tort Law: Evidence from Medical Malpractice Reform, Northwestern University, Institute for Policy Research, Working Paper No. 13-xx (Oct. 2020) (finding higher medical error rates in states that have instituted caps on non-economic damages for medical malpractice cases); David A. Hyman, Medical Malpractice and the Tort System: What Do We Know and What (If Anything) Should We Do About It? 80 Tex. L. Rev. 1639 (2002) (noting that other studies looking at single institutions have found more favorable deterrent effects); Joanna C. Schwartz, A Dose of Reality for Medical Malpractice Reform, 88 N.Y.U. L. Rev. 1224 (2013) (study of effect of litigation on hospital patient safety efforts, concluding that lawsuits effectively promote patient safety by providing data about weaknesses in hospital policy, practices, staff, and administration).

Malpractice claims provide useful evidence for discovering problematic physicians; multiple malpractice claims are often predictive of physicians who will be subject to medical discipline. One study of problems with state medical licensing boards concluded that physicians with ten or more reported liability insurance payouts on the National Practitioners Databank were significantly more likely to have also been subject to action against their admitting privileges by hospitals and to have been excluded from Medicare/Medicaid. See Alan Levine et al., State Medical Boards Fail to Discipline Doctors with Hospital Actions Against Them, Pub. Citizen 9 (March. 2011). See also David Hyman et al., Medical Malpractice and Physician Discipline: The Good, The Bad and The Ugly, 18 J. Emp. Leg. Stud. 131 (2021) (Illinois physicians with two or more paid malpractice claims are more likely than other physicians to be targets of disciplinary action).

Malpractice litigation affects medical practice, making anxious providers either overestimate the risks of a suit or at least adjust their practice to a new assessment of the risk of suit, regardless of the incentive effects of judgments and premium increases. Physicians perceive a threat from the system, judging their risk of being sued as much higher than it actually is. See David M. Studdert et al., Defensive Medicine Among High-Risk Specialist Physicians in a Volatile Malpractice Environment, 293 JAMA 2609 (2005). The Harvard New York Study, surveying New York physicians, found that physicians who had been sued were more likely to explain risks to patients, to restrict their scope of practice, and to order more tests and procedures. See Patients, Doctors, and Lawyers: Medical Injury, Malpractice Litigation, and Patient Compensation in New York 9–29 (1990). But see Jing Liu and David A. Hyman, The Impact of Medical Malpractice Reforms, 16 Ann. Rev. L. & Soc. Sci. 405 (2020) (a review of empirical literature reveals that malpractice reforms have had only a modest effect in reducing defensive medicine).

These effects of malpractice litigation exist despite the availability of liability insurance that providers purchase to spread the risk of a large malpractice payout. Although such insurance may dilute or eliminate the financial incentives for these physicians to change their behavior, liability insurers use several mechanisms to assess physician insurance risks. Consequently, physicians are likely to feel the effects of increased malpractice litigation in terms of insurance availability and pricing. See generally Omri Ben-Shahar and Kyle D. Logue, Outsourcing Regulation: How Insurance Reduces Moral Hazard, 111 Mich. L. Rev. 197 (2012); Tom Baker, Liability Insurance as Tort Regulation: Six Ways that Liability Insurance Shapes Tort Law in Action, 12 Conn. Ins. L.J. 1, 3–4 (2005). For a general discussion of the incentive effects of litigation on both individual physicians and health care institutions, see Barry R. Furrow, The Patient

Injury Epidemic: Medical Malpractice Litigation as a Curative Tool, 4 Drexel L. Rev. 41 (2011).

B. LIABILITY INSURANCE CYCLES AND MALPRACTICE CRISES

Physicians and other providers organize to demand reforms of the tort system not in response to changes in the incidence of malpractice claims or of seven-figure payouts, but rather when those providers are hit with significant increases in premiums for their malpractice liability insurance. Providers incorrectly assume that increased premiums result from increased use or abuse of the tort system by disappointed patients and personal injury lawyers.

In fact, malpractice crises are more a product of the way the insurance industry does business than of changes in the frequency of medical malpractice litigation or the severity of judgments. The malpractice market is "lumpy," meaning that it is prone to cycles of underpricing and catchup. What doctors and hospitals see as "sudden" price increases are actually deferred costs passed on when premiums no longer cover payments plus profit. Once premiums reach actuarially sound levels, profits rise, new insurers enter the market with lower rates, competitive pressures return, and the cycle starts all over again.

The cyclical nature of interest rates, as a measure of return on investments, plays a central role in insurers' pricing decisions. The insurance industry engages in cash-flow underwriting, in which insurers invest the premiums they collect in the bond market and to a lesser extent in the stock market. When interest rates and investment returns are high, insurance companies accept riskier exposures to acquire more investable premium and loss reserves. If underwriting and investment results are combined during these periods, investment gains more than offset losses.

Malpractice insurance premiums charged by insurance companies thus do not relate to payouts, but rather rise and fall in concert with the state of the economy, reflecting gains and losses of invested reserves and the insurance industry's calculation of the rate of return on the investment "float" (the time between collecting premium dollars and paying out losses) provided by physician premiums. See generally Mimi Marchev, The Medical Malpractice Insurance Crisis: Opportunity for State Action (National Academy for State Health Policy, July 2002). See also U.S. General Accounting Office, Medical Malpractice Insurance: Multiple Factors Have Contributed to Increased Premium Rates (2003) (spike in malpractice liability insurance in the late 1990s resulted from decreased returns on investments by insurers). See also W. Kip Viscusi, Medical Malpractice Reform: What Works and What Doesn't, 96 Denver L. Rev. 775 (2019); José R. Guardado, Policy Research Perspectives: New Data Show the Highest Prevalence of Medical Liability Premium Increases in 15 Years, American Medical Association (2021).

Other factors affecting malpractice insurance premiums include the latent effects of pricing wars among insurers, increases in the medical inflation rate, statutory limitations on the authority of state insurance regulators to limit premium increases, and flaws in the malpractice insurance market that undermine efficient pricing.

C. APPROACHES TO REFORMING THE MEDICAL MALPRACTICE SYSTEM

1. Improving Insurance Availability

In response to the perceived malpractice crisis, several reforms have been implemented to improve the availability of liability insurance.

a. *New Sources of Insurance.* New sources of insurance were created in response to earlier crises, either by the states or by providers. Joint underwriting associations, reinsurance exchanges, hospital self-insurance programs, state funds, and provider-owned insurance companies have sprung into being. Physician-owned companies now write as much as 60 percent of malpractice coverage nationally. Hospitals have begun to self-insure. Some states have adopted state programs, such as patient compensation funds, to limit doctor liability to individual patients.

b. *Claims-Made Policies.* Medical malpractice insurers changed in the late seventies to writing policies on a claims-made rather than an occurrence basis. Before 1975, most policies had been occurrence policies, covering claims made at any time as long as the insured doctor was covered during the time the medical accident giving rise to the claim occurred. The increase in the frequency and severity of claims in the mid-70s revealed the long-term problems with this kind of insurance. Insurers struggled to reliably predict their future losses and set premium prices, and often failed.

Most insurers therefore have shifted to a claims-made policy, allowing them to use more recent claims experience to set premium prices and reserve requirements. The claims-made policy covers claims made during the year of the policy coverage, avoiding the predictability problem of the occurrence policy. Such policies arguably have allowed companies to continue to carry malpractice insurance lines, serving the goal of availability by keeping premium costs lower than they would otherwise have been.

c. *Selective Insurance Marketing.* Physician mutual companies, with physician-investors, have often ridden out the underwriting cycle with less distress than the commercial carriers.

d. *Hospital Complaint Profiling.* For hospitals, complaint profiling has been proposed, which is designed to spot litigation-prone staff physicians and facilitate intervention to retrain them to avoid risks. The Hickson study looked at six years' worth of hospital patient advocacy files and concluded that unsolicited patient complaints about physicians are a highly reliable predictor of litigation-prone physicians. The study found that 9 percent of the physicians produced 50 percent of the complaints, and the study showed an 86 percent success rate in predicting physicians with multiple claims. See Gerald B. Hickson et al., Patient Complaints and Malpractice Risk, 287 JAMA 2951 (2002).

2. Altering the Litigation Process

Starting in the 1970s, states enacted tort reform legislation. These measures were designed to restrict the operation of the tort system in several ways: (1) affecting the filing of malpractice claims; (2) limiting the award recoverable by the plaintiff; (3) altering the plaintiff's burden of proof through changes in evidence rules and legal doctrine; (4) reducing the plaintiff lawyer's contingency fee recovery; and (5) changing the role of the courts by substituting an alternative forum. These actions have been characterized by Eleanor Kinney as "first generation" reforms. See Eleanor D. Kinney, Learning from Experience, Malpractice Reforms in the 1990s: Past Disappointments, Future Success?, 20 J. Health Polit. Pol'y & L. 99 (1995). See also Joseph S. Kass and Rachel V. Rose, Historical Approaches, Alternative Models, and Communication and Resolution Programs, 18 AMA J. of Ethics 299 (2017).

The most powerful reform in actually reducing the size of malpractice awards has been a dollar limit, or cap, on awards. Caps may take the form of a limit on general damage recovery amounts, typically pain and suffering, or a maximum recoverable per case, including all damages. See David A. Hyman, Bernard Black, Charles Silver, and William M. Sage, Estimating the Effect of Damage Caps in Medical Malpractice Cases: Evidence from Texas, 1 J. Legal Anal. 355 (2009).

D. ALTERNATIVE APPROACHES TO COMPENSATION OF PATIENT INJURY

Second-generation reform proposals have aimed to eliminate or reduce some of the perceived flaws of the current system without impairing consumer access to compensation. Such proposals involve combining different reforms, choosing variables from a series of categories to create a single package. The categories that are available include: (1) the compensable event, (2) the measure of compensation, (3) the payment mechanism, (4) the forum used to resolve disputes, and (5) the method of implementing the new rights and responsibilities. See Kenneth Abraham,

Medical Liability Reform: A Conceptual Framework, 260 JAMA 68–72 (1988).

Abraham summarizes the categories and reform choices in the following table:

Compensable Event	Measure of Compensation	Payment Mechanism	Forum for Resolution of Disputes	Method of Implementation
Fault Cause Loss	Full tort damages Full out-of-pocket losses Partial out-of- pocket losses Scheduled damages Lump-sum payment Periodic payment	First-party insurance Third-party insurance Taxation Hybrid Funding	Jury trial Expert review panels Bench trial Binding arbitration Administrative boards Insurance company decision	Legislation Mandatory reform Elective options Private contract

1. Arbitration and Mediation

Arbitration and mediation are the two most common forms of alternative dispute resolution, and each has been used to resolve medical malpractice claims. See Lydia Nussbaum, Trial and Error: Legislating ADR for Medical Malpractice Reform, 76 Md. L. Rev. 247 (2017). State legislators authorize, but do not require, providers and patients to resolve their disputes through binding arbitration. A panel rules for one party or the other after an informal presentation of evidence. The panel typically consists of a doctor, a lawyer and a layperson or retired judge. The arbitration panel, however, uses members trained in dispute resolution and has the authority to make a final ruling as to both provider liability and damages. The process is initiated only when there is an agreement between the patient and the health care provider to arbitrate any claims. Legislators had hoped that arbitration would decrease claims, lower the value of awarded damages, and reduce the liability insurance premiums. Empirical evidence, however, suggests that arbitration has not resulted in any of these outcomes. See id. (reviewing the empirical literature).

Some states require mediation as a condition of filing a malpractice complaint. See, e.g., S.C. Code Ann. § 15–79–120. Unlike arbitration, mediation uses a neutral third party to facilitate a discussion between the parties aimed at reaching a settlement. While mediations could foster better communication between the parties, there is evidence that the process primarily focuses on the dollar figures of settlement offers and counteroffers. See id. A multi-year analysis of Florida's mandatory malpractice mediation program found that it was highly successful, with 70 percent of mediations resulting in a settlement. It cut the dispute resolution time period to about 6 months or less in most cases and reduced litigation expenses dramatically. See Randall C. Jenkins et al., Mandatory

Pre-Suit Mediation for Medical Malpractice: Eight-Year Results and Future Innovations, 35 Conflict Resolution Q. 73 (2017).

2. No-Fault Systems

a. Provider-Based Early Payment

Under this approach providers would voluntarily agree to identify and promptly compensate patients for avoidable injuries. Damages would be limited under most proposals. This approach was first proposed by Clark Havighurst and Lawrence Tancredi, and it has been recommended in Institute of Medicine, Fostering Rapid Advances in Health Care: Learning from System Demonstrations 82 (2002).

When the adverse outcome first occurs, the patient or provider would file the claim with the insurer, who would decide whether the injury was covered. If so, it would make prompt payment. Disputes would be resolved through the courts or arbitration. The plan as proposed would experience-rate insurance premiums paid by providers, in order to create incentives for the providers to improve the quality of care, thereby reducing their exposure for the adverse outcomes listed. Provider experience under the plan would also be used to strengthen peer review within hospitals. See Clark Havighurst and Laurence Tancredi, "Medical Adversity Insurance"—A No-Fault Approach to Medical Malpractice and Quality Assurance, 51 Milbank Memorial Fund Q. 125 (1973).

One example of such a model has been pioneered by the University of Michigan Health System, a self-insured system. Michigan limits compensation to cases where the institution determines that the care was inappropriate; it then tenders an offer to the injured patient. The offer may include compensation for all elements of loss that are compensable in tort cases, including medical expenses, lost income, other economic losses, and "pain and suffering." A patient can only accept the tendered money after agreeing that it is a final settlement, foreclosing a lawsuit. See Richard C. Boothman et al., A Better Approach to Medical Malpractice Claims? The University of Michigan Experience, 2 J. Health & Life Sci. L. 125, 135 (2009) (summarizing the approach); Michelle M. Mello and Thomas H. Gallagher, Malpractice Reform—Opportunities for Leadership by Health Care Institutions and Liability Insurers, 362 N. Engl. J. Med. 1353 (2010).

b. Administrative Systems

One administrative idea is the health court, a hybrid model based on "early-settlement" models around since the seventies. Another proposal offered by the Institute of Medicine has been to create by legislation a state system loosely based on the Workers' Compensation model. Under this approach, providers would receive immunity from tort claims in exchange for "mandatory participation in a state-sponsored, administrative system established to provide compensation to patients who have suffered avoidable injuries." See Institute of Medicine, Fostering Rapid Advances in Health Care: Learning from System Demonstrations 82 (2002). The AMA also developed an elaborate proposal in the late 1980s, but to date such state-administered systems have been limited to special categories of injuries, such as infants with brain injuries.

If a compensation system rewards many more claimants, particularly small ones, in an evenhanded and more rapid fashion than does the current tort system, it may well be an improvement. But it is unlikely to be a cheaper system. Indeed, a California study in the 1970s estimated that a no-fault system in California could increase malpractice premiums 300 percent higher than the tort system's insurance costs. See California Medical and Hospital Associations, Report on the Medical Insurance Feasibility Study (1977). And if it ends up offering plaintiffs considerably smaller awards that they would receive in a trial system, such a compensation system may trade speed and smaller payouts for defendants for inadequate compensation for plaintiffs.

3. Disclosure, Apology, and Resolution Systems

Some institutional providers have adopted communication-and-resolution programs (CRPs). Through such programs, providers "communicate with patients about adverse events; investigate and explain what happened; and, when appropriate, apologize, take responsibility, and proactively offer compensation." Allen Kachalia et al., Effects of A Communication-And-Resolution Program On Hospitals' Malpractice Claims And Costs, 37 Health Aff. 1836 (2018).

There is growing evidence that CRPs are effective. A 2018 study found that providers with CRPs experienced a decrease in total claims and defense costs, and total liability costs were unchanged despite communicating all errors resulting in injury to affected patients. Meanwhile, providers without CRPs, which were used as controls, did not experience the same benefits. See id. There is also evidence that disclosure and apology is desired by patients, and it may even serve to reduce patient inclinations to sue for malpractice when they experience a bad outcome. See, e.g., Thomas H. Gallagher et al., Patients' and Physicians' Attitudes Regarding the Disclosure of Medical Errors, 289 JAMA 1001 (2003) (finding that patients are troubled by the unwillingness of physicians to discuss the cause and future prevention of medical errors).

Apology strategies have a downside. From a defendant's perspective, such proposals offer a strategic tool to achieve an early and relative low settlement. There is a risk, however, that a settlement inspired by a provider's apology might be less than what the patient actually needs. See Erin Ann O'Hara and Douglas Yarn, On Apology and Consilience, 77 Wash. L. Rev. 1121, 1186 (2002). See also Lindsey Murtagh, Thomas H.

Gallagher, Penny Andrew, and Michelle M. Mello, *Disclosure-And-Resolution Programs That Include Generous Compensation Offers May Prompt a Complex Patient Response*, 31 Health Aff. 2681 (2012).

E. THE ACA AND TORT REFORM

The ACA made big changes to the Medicaid and Medicare programs and private insurance regulation. Its impact on medical liability reform has been much more modest, promoting state demonstration programs that are limited in their scope by the terms of grants to the states.

The primary liability reform provision in the ACA is Section 10607, *State Demonstration Programs to Evaluate Alternatives to Current Medical Tort Litigation*. The Secretary of the Department of Health and Human Services may award demonstration grants, for a period not to exceed five years, to the states "for the development, implementation, and evaluation of alternatives to current tort litigation for resolving disputes over injuries allegedly caused by health care providers or health care organizations." Section 10607(c)(1)(B) specifies that the models should resolve disputes over patient injuries and promote a reduction in medical errors "by encouraging the collection and analysis of patient safety data related to disputes resolved under subparagraph (A) by organizations that engage in efforts to improve patient safety and the quality of health care."

Section 10607(c)(2) requires the State grant seeker to demonstrate how its model:

(A) makes the medical liability system more reliable by increasing the availability of prompt and fair resolution of disputes;

(B) encourages the efficient resolution of disputes;

(C) encourages the disclosure of health care errors;

(D) enhances patient safety by detecting, analyzing, and helping to reduce medical errors and adverse events;

(E) improves access to liability insurance;

(F) fully informs patients about the differences in the alternative and current tort litigation;

(G) provides patients the ability to opt out of or voluntarily withdraw from participating in the alternative at any time and to pursue other options, including litigation, outside the alternative;

(H) would not conflict with State law at the time of the application in a way that would prohibit the adoption of an alternative to current tort litigation; and

(I)   would not limit or curtail a patient's existing legal rights, ability to file a claim in or access a State's legal system, or otherwise abrogate a patient's ability to file a medical malpractice claim.

During the five-year window for these grants, Congress awarded more than $19 million to fund several different projects, including those studying some of the reforms described above. "The projects conducted by the grantees included: (1) studies of communication methods, such as when and how physicians talk to families about instances of malpractice, including apologies; (2) improving medical procedures in risk-prone specialties, and then measuring for decreases in malpractice rates; and, (3) examining the efficacy of alternative claim settlements involving health courts, medical malpractice deferments, or judge-led negotiations." Jessica L. Bailey-Wheaton and Todd A. Zigrang, Tort Reform: The Impact of the ACA on Medical Malpractice, 10 Health Capital Topics 1 (Apr. 2017).

CHAPTER 6

DISCRIMINATION AND UNEQUAL TREATMENT IN HEALTH CARE

■ ■ ■

I. INTRODUCTION

Access to health care depends on finding providers who are willing and able to treat you. But some people are refused medical care or given inadequate treatment for economic and social reasons unrelated to medical need. Among the cases you will read in this chapter are cases in which patients were denied care or treated differently because they couldn't pay or had a disfavored form of insurance; because of their race, ethnicity, or national origin; because of their gender; or because they had a particular type of disability.

In addition to individual refusals of care, patients experience systemic or structural barriers to care, directly or indirectly related to the same characteristics that have motivated refusals. People with a lower socioeconomic status, and racial and ethnic minorities, are more likely to live in communities with an inadequate supply of providers. Residential segregation, in combination with public hospital closures and provider "flight" (physicians and private hospitals leaving poorer, predominantly minority neighborhoods in favor of more affluent, predominantly white ones), has deprived entire communities of essential health resources. Private and government insurers have excluded care that uniquely or disproportionately impacts certain genders, including certain types of reproductive care and gender-affirming care, as well as care for certain disabilities, such as HIV treatment and habilitative care (services that help an individual keep, learn, or improve skills and functioning of daily living). And transgender individuals and people with disabilities are at higher risk of not being able to find health professionals or facilities willing to provide the specific care they need. Imagine not being able to get a common diagnostic test, such as an X-ray or MRI, or never being weighed during pregnancy—this is the situation faced by many individuals with mobility impairments.

Although many factors can impact health access and outcomes, this chapter focuses on the role of discrimination and unequal treatment in health care access, quality, financing, and reform. We start, in Section II, by considering the common law—examining whether and to what extent doctors, hospitals and other types of providers may be legally obligated to treat patients needing medical care. We revisit the traditional legal principle of freedom of contract that governs the physician-patient relationship, which the physician may choose to enter or not. See Chapter 4. The main cases in this section reveal that the common law favors the freedom to contract, typically finding no initial duty to treat regardless of motive for the refusal or seriousness of medical need. Once a provider does undertake care, the common law is less clear about how and when a provider can terminate the relationship for non-medical reasons, such as for concerns about the patient's ability to pay.

This focus on providers' freedom to contract is consistent with a view of health care as an ordinary consumer good whose supply and demand should be subject to free market principles—a view that has dominated the U.S. approach to health care for much of its history. But a countervailing view—that health care is an essential public good to which everyone should have access as a right—has gained increasing support in recent years and was a dominant theme in the push for the Affordable Care Act (ACA). See Chapters 7 and 17.

But a meaningful "right" to health care cannot exist without creating a legal obligation to provide care or to ensure access to an adequate supply of providers. This, in turn, implicates questions about how resources should be allocated and who should bear the cost of care. In many of the cases you will read, access barriers are linked to cost concerns—the risk of being unable to collect payment or being undercompensated for service, as well as concerns about how to distribute limited health care resources, such as hospital services, across different communities. The ACA somewhat ameliorated, but has not eliminated, these concerns. See Chapters 9 and 10. Although socioeconomic and insurance status continue to be important factors influencing access to care, disparities in health care access and outcomes across race, gender, and disability persist even after controlling for factors such as ability to pay and medical need.

Although there is no universal right to health care in the U.S., a patchwork of federal laws imposes certain limits on providers' or payers' right to deny care. The remaining parts of the chapter examine this legal patchwork. Section III focuses on the Emergency Medical Treatment and Labor Act (EMTALA). Enacted to respond to the specific problem of "patient dumping" in hospital emergency departments, EMTALA creates a crucial but very limited duty to treat in certain settings. Section IV reviews a set of statutes that apply broader nondiscrimination principles to health care, with particular focus on discrimination based on race or national origin, sex, and disability. These antidiscrimination principles predate the modern health care system and apply in settings beyond health care delivery and financing. We focus here on how these laws limit providers' right to refuse to treat patients based on particular characteristics and, at times, have been used to limit policies or practices that result in broader systemic inequity.

II. COMMON LAW APPROACHES

Each of the cases below involves a patient denied care for reasons unrelated to medical need. Consider to what extent, if any, the common law addresses these various forms of discrimination. More specifically, what does the common law say about providers' right to deny care?

CHILDS V. WEIS

Court of Civil Appeals of Texas, 1969.
440 S.W.2d 104.

WILLIAMS, JUSTICE.

On or about November 27, 1966 Daisy Childs, wife of J.C. Childs, a resident of Dallas County, was approximately seven months pregnant. On that date she was visiting in Lone Oak, Texas, and about two o'clock A.M. she presented herself to the Greenville Hospital emergency room. At that time she stated she was bleeding and had labor pains. She was examined by a nurse who identified herself as H. Beckham. According to Mrs. Childs, Nurse Beckham stated that she would call the doctor. She said the nurse returned and stated "that the Dr. said that I would have to go to my doctor in Dallas. I stated to Beckham that I'm not going to make it to Dallas. Beckham replied that yes, I would make it. She stated that I was just starting into labor and that I would make it. The weather was cold that night. About an hour after leaving the Greenville Hospital Authority I had the baby while in a car on the way to medical facilities in Sulphur Springs. The baby lived about 12 hours."

[Dr. Weis] said that he had never examined or treated Daisy Childs and in fact had never seen or spoken to either Daisy Childs or her husband, J.C. Childs, at any time in his life. He further stated that he had never at any time agreed or consented to the examination or treatment of either Daisy Childs or her husband. He said that on a day in November 1966 he recalled a telephone call received by him from a nurse in the emergency room at the Greenville Surgical Hospital; that the nurse told him that there was a negro girl in the emergency room having a "bloody show" and some "labor pains." He said the nurse advised him that this woman had been visiting in Lone Oak, and that her OB doctor lived in Garland, Texas, and that she also resided in Garland. The doctor said, "I told the nurse over the telephone to have the girl call her doctor in Garland and see what he wanted her to do. I knew nothing more about this incident until I was served with the citation and a copy of the petition in this lawsuit."

* * *

Since it is unquestionably the law that the relationship of physician and patient is dependent upon contract, either express or implied, a physician is not to be held liable for arbitrarily refusing to respond to a call of a person even urgently in need of medical or surgical assistance provided that the relation of physician and patient does not exist at the time the call is made or at the time the person presents himself for treatment.

* * *

Applying these principles of law to the factual situation here presented we find an entire absence of evidence of a contract, either express or implied, which would create the relationship of patient and physician as between Dr. Weis and Mrs. Childs. Dr. Weis, under these circumstances, was under no duty whatsoever to examine or treat Mrs. Childs. When advised by telephone that the lady was in the emergency room he did what seems to be a reasonable thing and inquired as to the identity of her doctor who had been treating her. Upon being told that the doctor was in Garland he stated that the patient should call the doctor and find out what should be done. This action on the part of Dr. Weis seems to be not only reasonable but within the bounds of professional ethics.

We cannot agree with appellant that Dr. Weis' statement to the nurse over the telephone amounted to an acceptance of the case and affirmative instructions which she was bound to follow. Rather than give instructions which could be construed to be in the nature of treatment, Dr. Weis told the nurse to have the woman call her physician in Garland and secure instructions from him.

The affidavit of Mrs. Childs would indicate that Nurse Beckham may not have relayed the exact words of Dr. Weis to Mrs. Childs. Instead, it would seem that Nurse Beckham told Mrs. Childs that the doctor said that she would "have to go" to her doctor in Dallas. Assuming this statement was made by Nurse Beckham, and further assuming that it contained the meaning as placed upon it by appellant, yet it is undisputed that such words were uttered by Nurse Beckham, and not by Dr. Weis. . . .

[The court affirmed summary judgment in favor of the defendant.]

LYONS V. GRETHER
Supreme Court of Virginia, 1977.
239 S.E.2d 103.

POFF, JUSTICE.

We awarded a writ of error to a final order entered June 2, 1976 sustaining a demurrer to a motion for judgment filed by Magnolia Lyons (plaintiff) against Dr. Eugene R. Grether (defendant).

A demurrer confesses the truth of the facts alleged and accepts all reasonable inferences therefrom. Plaintiff, a blind person, accompanied by her four year old son and her guide dog, arrived at defendant's "medical office" on the morning of October 18, 1975, a Saturday, to keep an appointment "for a treatment of a vaginal infection". She was told that defendant would not treat her unless the dog was removed from the waiting room. She insisted that the dog remain because she "was not informed of any steps which would be taken to assure the safety of the guide dog, its care, or availability to her after treatment." Defendant "evicted" plaintiff, her son, and her dog, refused to treat her condition, and failed to assist her in finding other medical attention. By reason of defendant's "wrongful conduct", plaintiff was "humiliated" in the presence of other patients and her young son, and "for another two days while she sought medical assistance from other sources", her infection became "aggravated" and she endured "great pain and suffering". Alleging that defendant's waiting room "is a public place and a place to which the general public is invited and where she had a right to have her guide dog with her pursuant to Virginia Code s 63.1–171.2[1]", plaintiff demanded damages resulting from "breach of his duty to treat".

The order sustaining the demurrer was based upon two grounds. Ruling as matters of law, the trial court held that "the defendant had no duty to treat the plaintiff since he had not accepted her as a patient" and that "defendant's waiting room is not a public facility or place contemplated by" the White Cane Act. We address the first ruling in our determination whether the motion for judgment was sufficient to allege the creation of a physician-patient relationship and a duty to treat. If we determine that it was, then the trial court's second ruling bears upon the question whether defendant's withdrawal from the relationship for the reasons and under the circumstances alleged in plaintiff's motion excused non-performance of the duty to treat.

Although there is some conflict of authority, the courts are in substantial accord upon the rules concerning the creation of a physician-patient relationship and the rights and obligations arising therefrom. In the absence of a statute, a physician has no legal obligation to accept as a patient everyone who seeks his services. [ ] A physician's duty arises only

---

[1] This statute, part of the "White Cane Act" (Acts 1972, c. 156), reads as follows:

"s 63.1–171.2 Rights of blind and physically disabled persons in public places and places of public accommodation. . . .

"(b) The blind, the visually handicapped, and the otherwise physically disabled are entitled to full and equal accommodations, advantages, facilities, and privileges of all . . . places of public accommodation . . . and other places to which the general public is invited, subject only to the conditions and limitations established by law and applicable alike to all persons.

"(c) Every totally or partially blind person shall have the right to be accompanied by a dog guide, especially trained for the purpose, in any of the places listed in subsection (b) without being required to pay an extra charge for the dog guide; provided that he shall be liable for any damage done to the premises or facilities by such dog."

upon the creation of a physician-patient relationship; that relationship springs from a consensual transaction, a contract, express or implied, general or special [ ]; and a patient is entitled to damages resulting from a breach of a physician's duty. [ ] Whether a physician-patient relationship is created is a question of fact, turning upon a determination whether the patient entrusted his treatment to the physician and the physician accepted the case. [ ]

We consider first whether the facts stated in the motion for judgment, and the reasonable inferences deducible therefrom, were sufficient to allege the creation of a physician-patient relationship and a duty to treat. Standing alone, plaintiff's allegation that she "had an appointment with defendant" would be insufficient, for it connotes nothing more than that defendant had agreed to see her. But plaintiff alleged further that the appointment she had been given was "for treatment of a vaginal infection". The unmistakable implication is that plaintiff had sought and defendant had granted an appointment at a designated time and place for the performance of a specific medical service, one within defendant's professional competence, viz., treatment of a particular ailment. It is immaterial that this factual allegation might have been contradicted by evidence at trial. Upon demurrer, the test of the sufficiency of a motion for judgment is whether it states the essential elements of a cause of action, not whether evidence might be adduced to defeat it. [ ]

We are of opinion that the motion for judgment was sufficient to allege a consensual transaction giving rise to a physician-patient relationship and a duty to perform the service contemplated, and that the trial court erred in holding as a matter of law that defendant had not accepted plaintiff as a patient.

We consider next how a physician-patient relationship, once created, may be lawfully terminated.

As a general rule, unless the services to be rendered are conditioned or limited by notice or by the terms of employment, the physician-patient relationship continues until the services are no longer needed [ ]; however, the relationship may be terminated earlier by mutual consent or by the unilateral action of the patient; and under certain circumstances, the physician has a right to withdraw from a case, provided the patient is afforded a reasonable opportunity to acquire the services he needs from another physician. [ ]

Under plaintiff's construction of the White Cane Act, defendant's withdrawal from her case was not justified by the circumstances. She argues that defendant's office was a place "to which the public is invited" within the meaning of Code s 63.1–171.2(b) and that defendant's withdrawal violated the right to which she was entitled under Code s 63.1–171.2(c). Under the trial court's construction, defendant's office was not covered by the Act and plaintiff had no statutory right to take her dog there.

We are persuaded by plaintiff's argument as applied to the facts alleged in this case. It fairly appears from the face of the motion for judgment that defendant's office was a place to which certain members of the public were invited by prior appointment to receive certain treatment at certain scheduled hours. Plaintiff did not allege that defendant's office was a place to which the general public was generally invited to receive general medical services. Accordingly, while we hold that, under the facts alleged here, defendant's office was within the intendment of the White Cane Act and that the trial court erred in ruling otherwise, we believe it would be beyond the issues drawn for us to hold as a matter of law that the Act as presently written covers all physicians' offices under all circumstances.[2]

Even if the trial court had been correct in holding that plaintiff had no statutory right to take her guide dog to defendant's office, the question yet would have remained whether plaintiff's refusal to part with her dog without the assurances she sought constituted a circumstance justifying defendant's withdrawal from her case. Also remaining would have been the other question related to defendant's right to withdraw, viz., whether, as plaintiff expressly alleged, she was denied a reasonable opportunity to acquire the services she needed from another physician. Both questions were questions of fact which, even in the absence of the White Cane Act, were the subjects of proof, and we hold that the trial court erred in sustaining the demurrer.

The judgment is reversed and the case will be remanded with instructions to restore plaintiff's motion for judgment to the docket.

Reversed and remanded.

MUSE V. CHARTER HOSPITAL OF WINSTON-SALEM, INC.

Court of Appeals of North Carolina, 1995.
452 S.E.2d 589.

LEWIS, JUDGE.

This appeal arises from a judgment in favor of plaintiffs in an action for the wrongful death of Delbert Joseph Muse, III (hereinafter "Joe"). Joe was the son of Delbert Joseph Muse, Jr. (hereinafter "Mr. Muse") and Jane K. Muse (hereinafter "Mrs. Muse"), plaintiffs. The jury found that defendant Charter Hospital of Winston-Salem, Inc. (hereinafter "Charter

---

[2] Nor is it necessary for purposes of this opinion to decide what effect amendments, adopted since this case arose and addressed to other statutes, may have upon the White Cane Act. We refer to Acts 1976, c. 596, and Acts 1977, c. 608. Under Code ss 35–42.1 and 36–124 as amended by those Acts, "medical and dental offices" are expressly designated as places of public accommodation to which "it shall be lawful for a blind person accompanied by a 'seeing eye' dog to take such dog."

Hospital" or "the hospital") was negligent in that, *inter alia,* it had a policy or practice which required physicians to discharge patients when their insurance expired and that this policy interfered with the exercise of the medical judgment of Joe's treating physician, Dr. L. Jarrett Barnhill, Jr. The jury awarded plaintiffs compensatory damages of approximately $1,000,000. The jury found that Mr. and Mrs. Muse were contributorily negligent, but that Charter Hospital's conduct was willful or wanton, and awarded punitive damages of $2,000,000 against Charter Hospital. . . .

The facts on which this case arose may be summarized as follows. On 12 June 1986, Joe, who was sixteen years old at the time, was admitted to Charter Hospital for treatment related to his depression and suicidal thoughts. Joe's treatment team consisted of Dr. Barnhill, as treating physician, Fernando Garzon, as nursing therapist, and Betsey Willard, as social worker. During his hospitalization, Joe experienced auditory hallucinations, suicidal and homicidal thoughts, and major depression. Joe's insurance coverage was set to expire on 12 July 1986. As that date neared, Dr. Barnhill decided that a blood test was needed to determine the proper dosage of a drug he was administering to Joe. The blood test was scheduled for 13 July, the day after Joe's insurance was to expire. Dr. Barnhill requested that the hospital administrator allow Joe to stay at Charter Hospital two more days, until 14 July, with Mr. and Mrs. Muse signing a promissory note to pay for the two extra days. The test results did not come back from the lab until 15 July. Nevertheless, Joe was discharged on 14 July and was referred by Dr. Barnhill to the Guilford County Area Mental Health, Mental Retardation and Substance Abuse Authority (hereinafter "Mental Health Authority") for outpatient treatment. Plaintiffs' evidence tended to show that Joe's condition upon discharge was worse than when he entered the hospital. Defendants' evidence, however, tended to show that while his prognosis remained guarded, Joe's condition at discharge was improved. Upon his discharge, Joe went on a one-week family vacation. On 22 July he began outpatient treatment at the Mental Health Authority, where he was seen by Dr. David Slonaker, a clinical psychologist. Two days later, Joe again met with Dr. Slonaker. Joe failed to show up at his 30 July appointment, and the next day he took a fatal overdose of Desipramine, one of his prescribed drugs.

* * *

II.

Defendants . . . argue that the trial court submitted the case to the jury on an erroneous theory of hospital liability that does not exist under the law of North Carolina. As to the theory in question, the trial court instructed: "[A] hospital is under a duty not to have policies or practices which operate in a way that interferes with the ability of a physician to exercise his medical judgment. A violation of this duty would be negligence." The jury found that there existed "a policy or practice which required physicians to discharge patients when their insurance benefits expire and which interfered with the exercise of Dr. Barnhill's medical judgment." Defendants contend that this theory of liability does not fall within any theories previously accepted by our courts. . . .

Our Supreme Court has recognized that hospitals in this state owe a duty of care to their patients. [ ] [A] hospital has a duty to the patient to obey the instructions of a doctor, absent the instructions being obviously negligent or dangerous. [It also has a] duty to make a reasonable effort to monitor and oversee the treatment prescribed and administered by doctors practicing at the hospital. [ ] In light of these holdings, it seems axiomatic that the hospital has the duty not to institute policies or practices which interfere with the doctor's medical judgment. . . . Charter Hospital had a duty not to institute a policy or practice which required that patients be discharged when their insurance expired and which interfered with the medical judgment of Dr. Barnhill.

III.

* * *

We [next] conclude that in the case at hand, the evidence was sufficient to go to the jury.

Plaintiffs' evidence included the testimony of Charter Hospital employees and outside experts. Fernando Garzon, Joe's nursing therapist at Charter Hospital, testified that the hospital had a policy of discharging patients when their insurance expired. Specifically, when the issue of insurance came up in treatment team meetings, plans were made to discharge the patient. When Dr. Barnhill and the other psychiatrists and therapists spoke of insurance, they seemed to lack autonomy. For example, Garzon testified, they would state, "So and so is to be discharged. We must do this." Finally, Garzon testified that when he returned from a vacation, and Joe was no longer at the hospital, he asked several employees why Joe had been discharged and they all responded that he was discharged because his insurance had expired. Jane Sims, a former staff member at the hospital, testified that several employees expressed alarm about Joe's impending discharge, and that a therapist explained that Joe could no longer stay at the hospital because his insurance had expired. Sims also testified that Dr. Barnhill had misgivings about discharging Joe, and that Dr. Barnhill's frustration was apparent to everyone. One of plaintiffs' experts testified that based on a study regarding the length of patient stays at Charter Hospital, it was his opinion that patients were discharged based on insurance, regardless of their medical condition. Other experts testified that based on Joe's serious condition on the date of discharge, the expiration of insurance coverage must have caused Dr. Barnhill to discharge Joe. The experts further testified as to the relevant standard of care, and concluded that Charter Hospital's practices were below the standard of care and caused Joe's death. We hold that this evidence was sufficient to go to the jury. . . .

IV.

[The court held that the trial court did not err by denying the hospital's motion for judgment notwithstanding the verdict, which had argued that the patient's suicide was a supervening event that interrupted the chain of causation between the hospital's alleged breach and the plaintiffs' damages. The court reasoned that a patient's suicide cannot be deemed a supervening event to prevent liability on part of psychiatric hospital which had assumed care of a suicidal patient.]

ORR, JUDGE, dissenting.

[I] must respectfully dissent from the majority on the submission of the issue on wilful or wanton conduct [which is necessary to justify the award of punitive damages]. . . .

Our Supreme Court [has] defined wilful and wanton conduct as follows:

> An act is done wilfully when it is done purposely and deliberately in violation of law, or when it is done knowingly and of set purpose, or when the mere will has free play, without yielding to reason. 'The true conceptions of wilful negligence involves a deliberate purpose not to discharge some duty necessary to the safety of the person or property of another, which duty the person owing it has assumed by contract, or which is imposed on the person by operation of law.'

> An act is wanton when it is done of wicked purpose, or when done needlessly, manifesting a reckless indifference to the rights of others.

[Citations omitted]. Further,

> While "[o]rdinary negligence has as its basis that a person charged with negligent conduct should have known the probable consequences of his act," we have said "[w]anton and willful negligence rests on the assumption that he knew the probable consequences, but was recklessly, wantonly or intentionally indifferent to the results."

[Citations omitted]. [In this case, the] policy or practice of discharging patients when their insurance ran out . . . was obviously done for a business purpose; however, the evidence reveals that the policy was subject to being overridden on occasion by request of the treating physician or other financial consideration. Although . . . this policy may have affected Dr. Barnhill's decision to discharge the plaintiffs' son, such evidence, while perhaps supporting a negligence theory, does not go beyond that.

. . . No evidence was presented that could lead a jury to conclude that the policy in question involved a deliberate purpose not to discharge some duty necessary to the safety of the person in question. While it can be said that the policy to discharge was deliberate, there is no evidence that the hospital expected, anticipated or intended for the patient to be released in circumstances that put the person's safety in jeopardy. In fact, Joseph Muse, III was discharged into the custody and care of another physician and a community based mental health facility as well as the care of his parents with specific instructions for his care. . . .

. . . A policy to terminate a patient's hospitalization based upon insurance benefits ending in and of itself is not wilful or wanton conduct. . . . If the hospital had simply discharged the patient with no referral to another physician or medical facility, then a cognizable claim for wilful or wanton conduct would have been established. [A]lthough Dr. Barnhill's care in discharging the patient may well have been negligent, there is nothing to suggest that the hospital's policy or its implementation by Dr. Barnhill was done with reckless or deliberate disregard for the patient's safety. . . .

NOTES AND QUESTIONS

1.   *Motive.* Why did the providers refuse to treat Mrs. Childs? Ms. Lyons? The son of Mr. and Mrs. Muse? Was it due to a single motivating factor, or a combination of factors? In determining whether a physician or facility has a legal duty to provide care, should courts be guided by the reason for the refusal, the circumstances of the refusal, or both?

2.   *Ethical vs. Legal Obligations.* Even in the absence of a legal duty to treat, do providers have ethical obligations to provide care? Consider the following ethical prescriptions adopted by the American Medical Association (AMA):

> A physician shall, in the provision of appropriate patient care, except in emergencies, be free to choose whom to serve, with whom to associate, and the environment in which to provide medical care. AMA Principles of Medical Ethics VI (Adopted June 1957; revised June 1980; revised June 2001).

> . . . Differences in treatment that are not directly related to differences in individual patients' clinical needs or preferences constitute inappropriate variations in health care . . . . [P]hysicians . . . ethically are called on to provide the same quality of care to all patients without regard to medically irrelevant personal characteristics. . . . [P]hysicians should [p]rovide care that meets patient needs and respects patient preferences[;] [a]void stereotyping patients[;] [e]xamine their own practices to ensure that inappropriate considerations about race, gender identity, sexual orientation, sociodemographic factors, or other nonclinical factors, do not affect clinical judgment . . . . AMA, Opinion 8.5 Disparities in Health Care, Code of Medical Ethics (2016).

. . . Individual physicians should . . . promote access to care for individual patients, such as providing pro bono care in their office or through freestanding facilities or government programs that provide health care for the poor, or when permissible, waiving insurance copayments in individual cases of hardship. . . . AMA, Opinion 11.1.4 Financial Barriers to Health Care Access, Code of Medical Ethics (2009).

Creating an ethical principle that encourages caring for the poor is very different from creating a legal duty to treat that requires physicians to care for patients even if they cannot pay. Should we go this far? Or should the law merely narrow limits on when a provider can refuse treatment? If so, where would you draw the line? Even the AMA seems to draw certain lines in its ethical prescriptions. What factors seem most salient to the AMA's conceptions of physicians' ethical duty of care? What provider interests are implicated by creating a duty to treat?

3.   *Variations in State Common Law*. In *Childs*, the court says that "it is unquestionably the law that the relationship of physician and patient is dependent upon contract, either express or implied." But tort principles have been used by courts to find an implied duty to treat in emergency settings. See, e.g., Wilmington Gen. Hospital v. Manlove, 174 A.2d 135 (Del. 1961), holding that a hospital must provide emergency care to a person who relies on the presence of an emergency department in coming to the hospital. The court analogized this to the negligent termination of gratuitous services because "such a refusal might well result in worsening the condition of the injured person, because of the time lost in a useless attempt to obtain medical aid." The application of tort principles to find a duty to provide emergency care has been inconsistent and has varied by state. See Karen H. Rothenberg, Who Cares? The Evolution of the Legal Duty to Provide Emergency Care, 26 Hous. L. Rev. 21 (1989). Given the variations in state approaches and the often-devastating effects of such denials, the federal government eventually addressed the problem through federal statute. See Section III below.

4.   *Discrimination in Emergency Settings*. The professional and institutional discrimination evident in *Childs* is not an aberration. See, for example, New Biloxi Hospital, Inc. v. Frazier, 245 Miss. 185, 146 So.2d 882 (Miss. 1962), in which the court held a hospital liable for the death of a Black man who remained untreated in the emergency room for over two hours and died twenty-five minutes after transfer to a Veterans Administration hospital. The court based its holding on the hospital's breach of the duty to exercise reasonable care once treatment had been undertaken and it noted the special role of emergency professionals: "A hospital rendering emergency treatment is obligated to do that which is immediately and reasonably necessary for the preservation of the life, limb or health of the patient. It should not discharge a patient in a critical condition without furnishing or procuring suitable medical attention."

Indeed, as recently as 2015, there was a similarly shocking refusal by a hospital to treat a Black woman, who had sought help because she couldn't breathe. After initially being seen in the emergency room, the woman was discharged. She refused to leave, however, because she still felt unwell. The hospital's response was to call law enforcement to have her forcibly removed from the premises. In trying to get her to leave, the officer involved attempted to remove the patient's oxygen mask; when the patient refused to surrender it, hospital staff motioned toward the wall to let the officer know he could disconnect her oxygen hose from there. The officer disconnected the hose, and when he got the patient close to the police car, she collapsed. She lay on the ground—just feet away from the hospital entrance—for nearly 18 minutes before finally being taken back to the hospital, where she was ultimately pronounced dead. The woman had died from a blood clot in her lungs. Throughout this time the patient was begging for help and insisting she could not breathe, but the officer said he thought she was faking it and just being noncompliant, and the hospital treated her as a trespasser. See Michele Goodwin, Black Women Can't Breathe, Online Symposium: Understanding the Role of Race in Health, Bill of Health, Petrie-Flom Center at Harvard Law School, (Oct. 20, 2020). The hospital was ultimately cited for deficiencies in care. Joe Reedy, Florida Hospital Where Woman Died After Being Forcibly Removed Cited for Deficiencies, Orlando Sentinel (Feb. 12, 2016). For more on racial disparities in treatment that persist today, see Section IV.A. below.

5. *When May a Physician Withdraw?* In *Lyons*, the court acknowledged that a physician may withdraw unilaterally from the care of a patient if the patient is "afforded a reasonable opportunity to acquire the services he needs from another physician." In *Muse*, the court focused on the absence of an individualized assessment of continuing need prior to discharge. But both *Lyons* and *Muse* leave unanswered questions about when and how providers can terminate relationships with patients. Recall the elements of patient abandonment discussed in Chapter 4. Once a physician has entered into a health care relationship, must the physician continue to treat the patient until the patient finds someone else to take over the treatment? What if the patient can't find someone else or the alternative facilities are not adequate? This is not merely a theoretical question; questions about the contours of this duty are at the heart of challenges to hospital discharge practices of homeless patients. See, e.g., Joseph Serna, Hospital Agrees to Pay $450,000 to L.A. to Settle Homeless Patient Dumping Lawsuit, L.A. Times (Oct. 25, 2016).

6. *Delineating Common Law Duties.* *Lyons* illustrates the relevance of statutes in common law questions about provider duties. What role did the state's White Cane Act play in the court's decision? For more information on disability discrimination in health care, see Section IV.C. below.

7. *Intersecting Bases of Discrimination.* In *Muse,* the court affirmed liability against Charter Hospital based on an institutional policy or practice that automatically triggered discharge when insurance coverage ended, effectively disregarding individualized assessments of medical need. This reflects the intersection of two forms of discrimination that have impeded health care access and undermined quality of treatment. One involves discrimination based on insurance status or ability to pay, which has

disproportionately impacted groups historically excluded from private insurance, especially racial and ethnic minorities, people with disabilities, and the poor. Even those fortunate enough to qualify for public safety net programs, like Medicaid, may not be able to find providers willing to treat them. The other form of discrimination involves mental health care. Historically, the medical field and our health financing systems have treated care associated with mental health as less valuable than other kinds of health care. Inadequate provider supply and insurance barriers have made it difficult for patients to get appropriate mental and behavioral care support, as discussed more fully in Section IV.D.2. below.

8.   *State Statutes Requiring Emergency Care.* Some states have statutes or regulations limiting hospitals' ability to refuse care under certain circumstances. For example, regulations promulgated under the hospital licensure statute of North Carolina provide that:

> [a] patient has the right to expect emergency procedures to be implemented without unnecessary delay [and] the right to medical and nursing services without discrimination based upon race, color, religion, sex, sexual orientation, gender identity, national origin, or source of payment. 10A N.C. Admin. Code tit. 13B.3302(6) & (13).

Although the state licensing agency has authority to investigate violations of this provision, at least one court has held that the statute does not create a private right of action. See Williams v. U.S., 242 F.3d 169 (4th Cir. 2001). In contrast, see Thompson v. Sun City Community Hospital, Inc., 141 Ariz. 597, 688 P.2d 605 (1984), where the court relied on state hospital regulations and private accreditation standards to find a duty to provide emergency care enforceable through private litigation.

In addition, tax-exempt hospitals, regulated by federal and state laws, have "charitable" obligations. They must provide a community benefit and meet certain standards relating to emergency care and financial assistance plans. See Chapter 13.

PROBLEM: CHERYL HANACHEK

Cheryl Hanachek, a law student residing in Boston, learned she was pregnant during an "action" called by the city's obstetricians to protest Medicaid and discounted private insurance payment rates. Ms. Hanachek first called Dr. Cunetto, who had been the obstetrician for the birth of her first child two years earlier. Dr. Cunetto's receptionist told her that Dr. Cunetto wasn't taking any patients covered by her health plan.

About two weeks later, Ms. Hanachek called Dr. Simms, who had been recommended by her sister. Dr. Simms' receptionist told Ms. Hanachek that Dr. Simms was not taking any new patients because his malpractice premiums were so high that he was even considering discontinuing his obstetrical practice. In fact, however, Dr. Simms actually did not accept lawyers as patients. Ms. Hanachek reported to the receptionist that she was having infrequent minor cramping, and the receptionist told her that this was "nothing to worry about at this stage." Later that night Ms. Hanachek was admitted to the hospital on an emergency basis, in shock from blood loss due to a ruptured ectopic pregnancy. As a result of the rupture and other complications, Ms. Hanachek underwent a hysterectomy.

Ms. Hanachek has sued Dr. Cunetto and Dr. Simms. If you were representing Ms. Hanachek, how would you proceed in arguing and proving your case?

III. EMTALA: THE EXCEPTION FOR EMERGENCY CARE

This section and Section IV survey the federal statutory tools used to address certain barriers to health care. For each statutory tool, consider what particular barrier(s) the law is attempting to address, the scope of protection the law provides, and the limits of the statute. How effective is each statute at addressing the problem it was enacted to solve? What about as a tool for protecting health care access generally?

In 1986, the federal Emergency Medical Treatment and Labor Act (EMTALA), 42 U.S.C.A. § 1395dd, was enacted in response to "patient dumping," a practice in which patients are discharged in an unstable condition due to their inability to pay or for other non-therapeutic reasons. This would often take the form of a transfer from one hospital's emergency department to another's—typically from a private hospital to a public hospital that is legally obligated to treat indigent patients.

At the time of EMTALA's enactment, several empirical studies had documented patient dumping as a widespread practice. See, e.g., Robert L. Schiff et al., Transfers to a Public Hospital, 314 NEJM 552 (1986). Researchers determined that transferred patients tended to be uninsured or government-insured patients, with one study revealing that lack of insurance was the reason given for transfer in 87 percent of the cases. The findings suggested a dramatic increase in transfers during the 1980s— coinciding with large cuts in government funding for health care and a growth in uninsured Americans from 25 million in 1977 to 35 million in 1987. Researchers also found that significant percentages of patients transferred were medically unstable at the time of transfer and experienced an average delay of over five hours before receiving treatment. Finally, such transfers were found to disproportionately impact racial minorities. See also Robert L. Schiff & David Ansell, Federal Anti-Patient-Dumping Provisions: The First Decade, 28 Annals Emergency Med. 77 (1996).

EMTALA's focus is narrow: it creates limited duties to treat in the emergency setting. In other ways, however, EMTALA's reach is broad. Although EMTALA applies *only* to hospitals that accept payment from

Medicare *and* operate an emergency department, almost all hospitals participate in the Medicare program. And while EMTALA does not require a hospital to offer emergency department services, some state hospital licensure statutes do. In addition, federal tax law encourages tax-exempt hospitals to offer emergency services, and Medicare Conditions of Participation require that all hospitals receiving Medicare payments be capable of providing initial treatment in emergency situations and have an effective procedure for referral or transfer to more comprehensive facilities. Perhaps most importantly, EMTALA applies to *all* patients of such hospitals and not just to Medicare beneficiaries, so its protections apply to the uninsured or those with disfavored forms of insurance.

EMTALA specifically empowers patients to bring civil suits for damages against participating hospitals, but it does not provide a private right of action against a treating physician. The Office of the Inspector General (OIG) of the U.S. Dept. of Health and Human Services (HHS) enforces EMTALA against both hospitals and physicians. Private EMTALA litigation has burgeoned, while government enforcement has been much less active. Administrative enforcement actions under EMTALA are few; monetary penalties are quite small; and exclusion from Medicare is almost unheard of. Despite the passage of EMTALA, and perhaps because of its lax enforcement by the agency, patient dumping continues. See Sara Rosenbaum et al., Case Studies at Denver Health: "Patient Dumping" in the Emergency Department Despite EMTALA, the Law that Banned It, 31 Health Aff. 1749 (2012).

EMERGENCY MEDICAL TREATMENT AND LABOR ACT
42 U.S.C. § 1395dd.

(a) Medical screening requirement. In the case of a hospital that has a hospital emergency department, if any individual . . . comes to the emergency department and a request is made on the individual's behalf for examination or treatment for a medical condition, the hospital must provide for an appropriate medical screening examination within the capability of the hospital's emergency department, including ancillary services routinely available to the emergency department, to determine whether or not an emergency medical condition . . . exists.

(b) Necessary stabilizing treatment for emergency medical conditions and labor.

(1) In general. If any individual . . . comes to a hospital and the hospital determines that the individual has an emergency medical condition, the hospital must provide either—

(A) within the staff and facilities available at the hospital, for such further medical examination and such treatment as may be required to stabilize the medical condition, or

(B) for transfer of the individual to another medical facility in accordance with subsection (c).

* * *

(c) Restricting transfers until individual stabilized.

(1) Rule. If an individual at a hospital has an emergency medical condition which has not been stabilized . . . , the hospital may not transfer the individual unless—

(A)(i)   the individual (or a legally responsible person acting on the individual's behalf) after being informed of the hospital's obligations under this section and of the risk of transfer, in writing requests transfer to another medical facility, [or]

(ii) a physician . . . has signed a certification that[,] based upon the information available at the time of transfer, the medical benefits reasonably expected from the provision of appropriate medical treatment at another medical facility outweigh the increased risks to the individual and, in the case of labor, to the unborn child from effecting the transfer.

* * *

[and]

(B) the transfer is an appropriate transfer . . . to that facility . . . .

* * *

(2) Appropriate transfer. An appropriate transfer to a medical facility is a transfer—

(A) in which the transferring hospital provides the medical treatment within its capacity which minimizes the risks to the individual's health and, in the case of a woman in labor, the health of the unborn child;

(B) in which the receiving facility—

(i) has available space and qualified personnel for the treatment of the individual, and

(ii) has agreed to accept transfer of the individual and to provide appropriate medical treatment;

(C) in which the transferring hospital sends to the receiving facility all medical records . . . related to the emergency condition for which the individual has presented, available at the time of the transfer . . .; [and]

(D) in which the transfer is effected through qualified personnel and transportation equipment. . . .

(d) Enforcement.

(1) Civil monetary penalties. [Fines for negligent violations of the statute by hospitals of up to $50,000 for each violation; and for physicians, up to $50,000 for each negligent violation and exclusion from Medicare and Medicaid for gross and flagrant violations.]

(2) Civil enforcement.

(A) Personal harm. Any individual who suffers personal harm as a direct result of a participating hospital's violation of a requirement of this section may, in a civil action against the participating hospital, obtain those damages available for personal injury under the law of the State in which the hospital is located, and such equitable relief as is appropriate.

(B) Financial loss to other medical facility. Any medical facility that suffers a financial loss as a direct result of a participating hospital's violation of a requirement of this section may, in a civil action against the participating hospital, obtain those damages available for financial loss, under the law of the State in which the hospital is located, and such equitable relief as is appropriate. . . .

* * *

(e) Definitions. In this section:

(1) The term "emergency medical condition" means—

(A) a medical condition manifesting itself by acute symptoms of sufficient severity (including severe pain) such that the absence of immediate medical attention could reasonably be expected to result in—

(i) placing the health of the individual (or, with respect to a pregnant woman, the health of the woman or her unborn child) in serious jeopardy,

(ii) serious impairment to bodily functions, or

(iii) serious dysfunction of any bodily organ or part; or

(B) with respect to a pregnant woman who is having contractions—

(i) that there is inadequate time to effect a safe transfer to another hospital before delivery, or

(ii) that transfer may pose a threat to the health or safety of the woman or the unborn child . . . .

* * *

(3)(A)   The term "to stabilize" means . . . to provide such medical treatment of the condition as may be necessary to assure, within reasonable medical probability, that no material deterioration of the condition is likely to result from or occur during the transfer of the individual from a facility. . . .

(B) The term "stabilized" means . . . that no material deterioration of the condition is likely, within reasonable medical probability, to result from or occur during the transfer of the individual from a facility, or, with respect to an emergency medical condition described in paragraph (1)(B), that the woman has delivered (including the placenta) . . . .

* * *

(h) No delay in examination or treatment. A participating hospital may not delay provision of an appropriate medical screening examination required under subsection (a) . . . or further medical examination and treatment required under subsection (b) . . . in order to inquire about the individual's method of payment or insurance status.

BABER v. HOSPITAL CORPORATION OF AMERICA

United States Court of Appeals, Fourth Circuit, 1992.
977 F.2d 872.

WILLIAMS, CIRCUIT JUDGE:

Barry Baber, Administrator of the Estate of Brenda Baber, instituted this suit against . . . Raleigh General Hospital (RGH), Beckley Appalachian Regional Hospital (BARH), and the parent corporations of both hospitals. Mr. Baber alleged that the Defendants violated the Emergency Medical Treatment and Active Labor Act (EMTALA)[ ]. The Defendants moved to dismiss the EMTALA claim under Rule 12(b)(6) of the Federal Rules of Civil Procedure. Because the parties submitted affidavits and depositions, the district court treated the motion as one for summary judgment. See Fed.R.Civ.P. 12(b).

* * *

Mr. Baber's complaint charged the various defendants with violating EMTALA in several ways. Specifically, Mr. Baber contends that Dr. Kline, RGH, and its parent corporation violated EMTALA by:

(a) failing to provide his sister with an "appropriate medical screening examination;"

(b) failing to stabilize his sister's "emergency medical condition;" and

(c) transferring his sister to BARH without first providing stabilizing treatment.

* * *

After reviewing the parties' submissions, the district court granted summary judgment for the Defendants. . . . Finding no error, we affirm.

* * *

. . . Brenda Baber, accompanied by her brother, Barry, sought treatment at RGH's emergency department at 10:40 p.m. on August 5, 1987. When she entered the hospital, Ms. Baber was nauseated, agitated, and thought she might be pregnant. She was also tremulous and did not appear to have orderly thought patterns. She had stopped taking her anti-psychosis medications, . . . and had been drinking heavily. Dr. Kline, the attending physician, described her behavior and condition in the RGH Encounter Record as follows: Patient refuses to remain on stretcher and cannot be restrained verbally despite repeated requests by staff and by me. Brother has not assisted either verbally or physically in keeping patient from pacing throughout the Emergency Room. Restraints would place patient and staff at risk by increasing her agitation.

In response to Ms. Baber's initial complaints, Dr. Kline examined her central nervous system, lungs, cardiovascular system, and abdomen. He also ordered several laboratory tests, including a pregnancy test.

While awaiting the results of her laboratory tests, Ms. Baber began pacing about the emergency department. In an effort to calm Ms. Baber, Dr. Kline gave her [several medications]. The medication did not immediately control her agitation. Mr. Baber described his sister as becoming restless, "worse and more disoriented after she was given the medication," and wandering around the emergency department.

While roaming in the emergency department around midnight, Ms. Baber . . . convulsed and fell, striking her head upon a table and lacerating her scalp. [S]he quickly regained consciousness and emergency department personnel carried her by stretcher to the suturing room, [where] Dr. Kline examined her again. He obtained a blood gas study, which did not reveal any oxygen deprivation or acidosis. Ms. Baber was verbal and could move her head, eyes, and limbs without discomfort. . . . Dr. Kline closed the one-inch laceration with a couple of sutures. Although she became calmer and drowsy after the wound was sutured, Ms. Baber was easily arousable and easily disturbed. Ms. Baber experienced some anxiety, disorientation, restlessness, and some speech problems, which Dr. Kline concluded were caused by her pre-existing psychiatric problems of psychosis with paranoia and alcohol withdrawal.

Dr. Kline discussed Ms. Baber's condition with Dr. Whelan, the psychiatrist who had treated Ms. Baber for two years. . . . Dr. Whelan concluded that Ms. Baber's hyperactive and uncontrollable behavior during her evening at RGH was compatible with her behavior during a relapse of her serious psychotic and chronic mental illness. Both Dr. Whelan and Dr. Kline were concerned about the seizure she had while at RGH's emergency department because it was the first one she had experienced. . . . They also agreed Ms. Baber needed further treatment . . . and decided to transfer her to the psychiatric unit at BARH because RGH did not have a psychiatric ward, and both doctors believed it would be beneficial for her to be treated in a familiar setting. The decision to transfer Ms. Baber was further supported by the doctors' belief that any tests to diagnose the cause of her initial seizure, such as a computerized tomography scan (CT scan), could be performed at BARH once her psychiatric condition was under control. The transfer to BARH was discussed with Mr. Baber who neither expressly consented nor objected. His only request was that his sister be x-rayed because of the blow to her head when she fell.

* * *

Because Dr. Kline did not conclude Ms. Baber had a serious head injury, he believed that she could be transferred safely to BARH where she would be under the observation of the BARH psychiatric staff personnel. At 1:35 a.m. on August 6, Ms. Baber was admitted directly to the psychiatric department of BARH upon Dr. Whelan's orders. She was not processed through BARH's emergency department. Although Ms. Baber was restrained and regularly checked every fifteen minutes by the nursing staff while at BARH, no physician gave her an extensive neurological examination upon her arrival. Mr. Baber unsuccessfully repeated his request for an x-ray.

At the 3:45 a.m. check, the nurse found Ms. Baber having a grand mal seizure. At Dr. Whelan's direction, the psychiatric unit staff transported her to BARH's emergency department. Upon arrival in the emergency department, her pupils were unresponsive, and hospital personnel began CPR. The emergency department physician ordered a CT scan, which was performed around 6:30 a.m. The CT report revealed a fractured skull and a right subdural hematoma. BARH personnel immediately transferred Ms. Baber back to RGH because that hospital had a neurosurgeon on staff, and BARH did not have the facility or staff to treat serious neurological problems. When RGH received Ms. Baber for treatment around 7 a.m., she was comatose. She died later that day, apparently as a result of an intracerebrovascular rupture.

* * *

Mr. Baber . . . alleges that RGH, acting through its agent, Dr. Kline, violated several provisions of EMTALA. These allegations can be summarized into two general complaints: (1) RGH failed to provide an appropriate medical screening to discover that Ms. Baber had an emergency medical condition as required by 42 U.S.C.A. § 1395dd(a); and (2) RGH transferred Ms. Baber before her emergency medical condition had been stabilized, and the appropriate paperwork was not completed to transfer a non-stable patient as required by 42 U.S.C.A. § 1395dd(b) & (c). Because we find that RGH did not violate any of these EMTALA provisions, we affirm the district court's grant of summary judgment to RGH.

Mr. Baber first claims that RGH failed to provide his sister with an "appropriate medical screening". He makes two arguments. First, he contends that a medical screening is only "appropriate" if it satisfies a national standard of care. In other words, Mr. Baber urges that we construe EMTALA as a national medical malpractice statute, albeit limited to whether the medical screening was appropriate to identify an emergency medical condition. We conclude instead that EMTALA only requires hospitals to apply their standard screening procedure for identification of an emergency medical condition uniformly to all patients and that Mr. Baber has failed to proffer sufficient evidence showing that RGH did not do so. Second, Mr. Baber contends that EMTALA requires hospitals to provide some medical screening. We agree, but conclude that he has failed to show no screening was provided to his sister.

* * *

While [the Act] requires a hospital's emergency department to provide an "appropriate medical screening examination," it does not define that term other than to state its purpose is to identify an "emergency medical condition."

* * *

[T]he goal of "an appropriate medical screening examination" is to determine whether a patient with acute or severe symptoms has a life threatening or serious medical condition. The plain language of the statute requires a hospital to develop a screening procedure[6] designed to identify such critical conditions that exist in symptomatic patients and to apply that screening procedure uniformly to all patients with similar complaints.

[W]hile EMTALA requires a hospital emergency department to apply its standard screening examination uniformly, it does not guarantee that the emergency personnel will correctly diagnose a patient's condition as a result of this screening.[7] The statutory language clearly indicates that

---

[6] While a hospital emergency room may develop one general procedure for screening all patients, it may also tailor its screening procedure to the patient's complaints or exhibited symptoms. For example, it may have one screening procedure for a patient with a heart attack and another for women in labor. Under our interpretation of EMTALA, such varying screening procedures would not pose liability under EMTALA as long as all patients complaining of the same problem or exhibiting the same symptoms receive identical screening procedures. We also recognize that the hospital's screening procedure is not limited to personal observation and assessment but may include available ancillary services through departments such as radiology and laboratory.

[7] Some commentators have criticized defining "appropriate" in terms of the hospital's medical screening standard because hospitals could theoretically avoid liability by providing very cursory and substandard screenings to all patients, which might enable the doctor to ignore a

EMTALA does not impose on hospitals a national standard of care in screening patients. The screening requirement only requires a hospital to provide a screening examination that is "appropriate" and "within the capability of the hospital's emergency department," including "routinely available" ancillary services. 42 U.S.C.A. § 1395dd(a). This section establishes a standard, which will of necessity be individualized for each hospital, since hospital emergency departments have varying capabilities. Had Congress intended to require hospitals to provide a screening examination which comported with generally-accepted medical standards, it could have clearly specified a national standard. Nor do we believe Congress intended to create a negligence standard based on each hospital's capability. . . . EMTALA is no substitute for state law medical malpractice actions.

* * *

The Sixth Circuit has also held that an appropriate medical screening means "a screening that the hospital would have offered to any paying patient" or at least "not known by the provider to be insufficient or below their own standards."

* * *

Applying our interpretation of section (a) of EMTALA, we must next determine whether there is any genuine issue of material fact regarding whether RGH gave Ms. Baber a medical screening examination that differed from its standard screening procedure. Because Mr. Baber has offered no evidence of disparate treatment, we find that the district court did not err in granting summary judgment.

* * *

Mr. Baber does not allege that RGH's emergency department personnel treated Ms. Baber differently from its other patients. Instead, he merely claims Dr. Kline did not do enough accurately to diagnose her condition or treat her injury.[ ] The critical element of an EMTALA cause of action is not the adequacy of the screening examination but whether the screening examination that was performed deviated from the hospital's evaluation procedures that would have been performed on any patient in a similar condition.

* * *

---

medical condition. [ ] Even though we do not believe it is likely that a hospital would endanger all of its patients by establishing such a cursory standard, theoretically it is possible. Our holding, however, does not foreclose the possibility that a future court faced with such a situation may decide that the hospital's standard was so low that it amounted to no "appropriate medical screening." We do not decide that question in this case because Ms. Baber's screening was not so substandard as to amount to no screening at all.

Dr. Kline testified that he performed a medical screening on Ms. Baber in accordance with standard procedures for examining patients with head injuries. He explained that generally, a patient is not scheduled for advanced tests such as a CT scan or x-rays unless the patient's signs and symptoms so warrant. While Ms. Baber did exhibit some of the signs and symptoms of patients who have severe head injuries, in Dr. Kline's medical judgment these signs were the result of her pre-existing psychiatric condition, not the result of her fall. He, therefore, determined that Ms. Baber's head injury was not serious and did not indicate the need at that time for a CT scan or x-rays. In his medical judgment, Ms. Baber's condition would be monitored adequately by the usual nursing checks performed every fifteen minutes by the psychiatric unit staff at BARH. Although Dr. Kline's assessment and judgment may have been erroneous and not within acceptable standards of medical care in West Virginia, he did perform a screening examination that was not so substandard as to amount to no examination. No testimony indicated that his procedure deviated from that which RGH would have provided to any other patient in Ms. Baber's condition.

* * *

The essence of Mr. Baber's argument is that the extent of the examination and treatment his sister received while at RGH was deficient. While Mr. Baber's testimony might be sufficient to survive a summary judgment motion in a medical malpractice case, it is clearly insufficient to survive a motion for summary judgment in an EMTALA case because at no point does Mr. Baber present any evidence that RGH deviated from its standard screening procedure in evaluating Ms. Baber's head injury. Therefore, the district court properly granted RGH summary judgment on the medical screening issue.

Mr. Baber also asserts that RGH inappropriately transferred his sister to BARH. EMTALA's transfer requirements do not apply unless the hospital actually determines that the patient suffers from an emergency medical condition. Accordingly, to recover for violations of EMTALA's transfer provisions, the plaintiff must present evidence that (1) the patient had an emergency medical condition; (2) the hospital actually knew of that condition; (3) the patient was not stabilized before being transferred; and (4) prior to transfer of an unstable patient, the transferring hospital did not obtain the proper consent or follow the appropriate certification and transfer procedures.

* * *

Mr. Baber argues that requiring a plaintiff to prove the hospital had actual knowledge of the patient's emergency medical condition would allow hospitals to circumvent the purpose of EMTALA by simply requiring their personnel to state in all hospital records that the patient did not suffer from an emergency medical condition. Because of this concern, Mr. Baber urges us to adopt a standard that would impose liability upon a hospital if it failed to provide stabilizing treatment prior to a transfer when the hospital knew or should have known that the patient suffered from an emergency medical condition.

The statute itself implicitly rejects this proposed standard. Section 1395dd(b)(1) states the stabilization requirement exists if "any individual . . . comes to a hospital and the hospital determines that the individual has an emergency medical condition." Thus, the plain language of the statute dictates a standard requiring actual knowledge of the emergency medical condition by the hospital staff.

Mr. Baber failed to present any evidence that RGH had actual knowledge that Ms. Baber suffered from an emergency medical condition. Dr. Kline stated in his affidavit that Ms. Baber's condition was stable prior to transfer and that he did not believe she was suffering from an emergency medical condition. While Mr. Baber testified that he believed his sister suffered from an emergency medical condition at transfer, he did not present any evidence beyond his own belief that she actually had an emergency medical condition or that anyone at RGH knew that she suffered from an emergency medical condition. In addition, we note that Mr. Baber's testimony is not competent to prove his sister actually had an emergency medical condition since he is not qualified to diagnose a serious internal brain injury.

. . . [W]e hold that the district court correctly granted RGH summary judgment on Mr. Baber's claim that it transferred Ms. Baber in violation of EMTALA.

* * *

Therefore, the district court's judgment is affirmed.

NOTES AND QUESTIONS

1.   *Impact of the ACA.* The ACA leaves EMTALA intact, although it adopted other measures favorable to the provision of emergency care. Most notably, it incentivizes states to expand Medicaid coverage and subsidizes the cost of private coverage for those who cannot afford it. Significantly, the ACA also authorizes states to allow hospitals to make presumptive Medicaid eligibility determinations for individuals, which should reduce the volume of uncompensated care that is provided to individuals eligible for but not enrolled in Medicaid. See Chapter 10. The ACA also requires insurers to pay for emergency care under a prudent layperson standard, a provision welcomed by hospitals concerned about insurers refusing to pay for emergency services that they deem unnecessary but that hospitals were obligated to provide under EMTALA. 42 U.S.C. § 300gg–19a. The more significant anticipated impact of the ACA, of course, was that it would decrease patients' reliance on emergency

department care as a safety net and decrease preventable emergency conditions by providing greater access to primary care. Early evidence suggests, however, that insurance may not significantly reduce emergency department visits in the short term and that other factors, such as primary care wait times, also influence emergency department use. See Scott M. Dresden et al., Increased Emergency Department Use in Illinois After Implementation of the Patient Protection and Affordable Care Act, 69 Ann. Emerg. Med. 172 (2017). See also Kristen M.J. Azar et al., Disparities in Outcomes Among COVID-19 Patients in a Large Health Care System in California, 39 Health Aff. (May 21, 2020) (discussing research showing that African American patients were more likely to access care later in the acute setting, despite insurance coverage, and pointing to societal factors likely contributing to delayed care, such as structural barriers to timely health care access, unconscious bias of providers, and the distrust generated from patients' prior negative experiences with the health system). Discrimination based on race is discussed further below.

2.   *Subjective and Objective Standards.* In contrast to the standard for medical screening, the standard applied to the question of whether the patient was unstable when discharged or transferred is an objective professional standard and not defined by the specific hospital's policy. How should plaintiffs structure discovery to meet each of these two standards? What is the role for expert testimony, if any, in an "unstable transfer or discharge" claim? In an "inappropriate screening" claim?

3.   *Motive.* Improper motive is not required for a violation of the EMTALA requirement that the patient be *stabilized.* Roberts v. Galen of Va., Inc., 525 U.S. 249 (1999). The Court expressed no opinion as to whether proof of improper motive is essential for a claim of failure to provide an appropriate screening. The Circuits, except for the Sixth Circuit in Cleland v. Bronson Health Care Group, 917 F.2d 266 (6th Cir. 1990), uniformly have held that EMTALA reaches beyond economically motivated decisions and that proof of motive is not required for either a screening or a stabilization claim. Could proof of improper motive be useful to the plaintiff in distinguishing negligent misdiagnosis from an EMTALA claim? How might such proof assist the plaintiff in making his or her case? How would you go about proving motive once the physician and hospital claim medical judgment as the basis for discharge or transfer?

4.   *When Does a Patient "Come to" the Emergency Department?* One of the sticky issues in EMTALA is whether a patient has "come to" the hospital's emergency department. In a rather notorious case, a hospital emergency department refused to aid a teenager who had been shot and lay dying 35 feet from the ER doors. Kristine Marie Meece, The Future of Emergency Department Liability after the Ravenswood Hospital Incident: Redefining the Duty to Treat?, 3 DePaul J. Health Care L. 101 (1999). After years of court opinions with conflicting results, HHS promulgated regulations in 2003 (42 C.F.R. § 489.24(b)) under which a patient is determined to have "come to" an emergency department when the patient:

- "present[s] on hospital property";

- "is in a ground or air ambulance owned and operated by the hospital . . . even if the ambulance is not on hospital grounds [unless the ambulance is directed to another hospital by a communitywide emergency medical service or is operated at the direction of a physician unaffiliated with the hospital]"; or

- "is in a ground or air nonhospital-owned ambulance on hospital property [unless the hospital directs the ambulance elsewhere because the hospital is on 'diversionary status' and the ambulance abides by the hospital's direction]."

5.   *Do EMTALA Obligations End upon Admission?* For many years, courts reached conflicting results on the issue of whether a patient who had been admitted to the hospital would be covered by EMTALA or whether the EMTALA obligations of the hospital ceased upon admission. Finally, in 2003, HHS promulgated regulations providing that EMTALA's obligations end when an emergency department patient is admitted in good faith to the hospital as an inpatient. See 42 C.F.R. 489.24(d)(2). Most courts have deferred to this interpretation of the statute. See, e.g., Thornhill v. Jackson Parish Hospital, 184 F. Supp. 3d 392 (W.D. La. 2016). A lone circuit held, in dicta, that the regulations are contrary to the plain language of the statute, Moses v. Providence Hosp. & Med. Ctrs., 561 F.3d 573 (6th Cir. 2009). Several federal district courts, including the Court in *Thornhill*, have disagreed with that holding. In 2010, the Centers for Medicare and Medicaid Services (CMS) asked for comments on its 2003 regulations and ultimately decided not to change them. 77 Fed. Reg. 5213 (Feb. 2, 2012).

The Fourth Circuit recently ruled that a plaintiff alleging EMTALA violations after the patient was admitted as an inpatient to the hospital bears the burden to prove that that the hospital's admission was not in good faith. "[A] party claiming an admission was not in good faith must present evidence that the hospital admitted the patient solely to satisfy its EMTALA standards with no intent to treat the patient once admitted and then immediately transferred the patient. In other words, the standard requires evidence that the admission was a subterfuge or a ruse." Williams v. Dimensions Health Corp., 952 F.3d 531, 537 (4th Cir. 2020).

6.   *"Appropriate Transfer."* Under EMTALA, an "appropriate transfer" requires that "the receiving facility (i) has available space and qualified personnel for the treatment of the individual, and (ii) has agreed to accept transfer of the individual and to provide appropriate medical treatment." 42 U.S.C. § 1395dd(c)(2)(B). Yet neither the statute nor its associated regulations articulate what the transferring hospital must do to satisfy this requirement. This ambiguity recently arose in Ruloph v. Lammico, No. 2:20-CV-02053, 2021 WL 517044 (W.D. Ark. Feb. 11, 2021) where a patient with a badly injured leg was screened in the defendant hospital's emergency department, and the attending physician determined that the patient required a transfer to a hospital with a vascular surgeon. The attending physician contacted a second

hospital, confirmed that it had a vascular surgeon and would accept transfer of the patient, and processed the patient's transfer to that hospital. Only after the patient was in transit did the second hospital discover that it did not have a vascular surgeon on staff who was capable of performing the particular surgery needed by the patient. The resulting delay in surgery caused the patient to lose so much blood that her leg had to be amputated. The patient sued the transferring hospital under EMTALA alleging that, in fact, the hospital to which the defendant transferred the patient did not have qualified personnel to treat her and thus the defendant's transfer of the patient was not "appropriate." As a matter of first impression, the federal district court held that the determination of whether a transfer is appropriate "must be predicated on a [defendant] hospital's actual knowledge" at the time it initiated the transfer and that the transferring hospital has a right to rely on representations made by the receiving hospital about its ability to treatment the patient.

7. *Problems with On-Call Coverage.* Treatment in the emergency department often will require the services of an on-call specialist. Hospitals generally do not employ on-call specialists, but they may contract with individual physicians to provide on-call services or may require on-call coverage by physicians as a condition of receiving admitting privileges. The division of labor inherent in the emergency department/on-call relationship can be contentious and raise EMTALA risks. Consequently, the management of on-call services remains an intractable problem for hospitals. See Sarah Coyne et al., Using Deferred Compensation to Incent On-Call Coverage, 23 Health Law. 28/No4 (2011) and the Problem below.

8. *EMTALA During the COVID-19 Pandemic.* In response to the COVID-19 pandemic, CMS waived some EMTALA requirements. "Only two aspects of the EMTALA requirements can be waived under 1135 Waiver Authority: 1) Transfer of an individual who has not been stabilized, if the transfer arises out of an emergency or, 2) Redirection to another location (offsite alternate screening location) to receive a medical screening exam under a state emergency preparedness or pandemic plan." CMS, COVID-19 Emergency Declaration Blanket Waivers for Health Care Providers (as revised May 24, 2021). Waivers are retroactive to March 1, 2020. Despite the flexibility offered by these waivers, hospitals subject to EMTALA remain obligated to meet the requirements of EMTALA, and, even when operating under a waiver, such hospitals cannot discriminate between patients who are able to pay and those who are not.

With respect to the "appropriate transfer" requirement, the guidance advises hospitals to rely on the recommendations of public health officials about treating suspected or actual COVID patients when assessing whether they have the capability to treat those patients or to accept transfer of those patients from other hospitals. CMS will "take into account the CDC's recommendations at the time of the event in question in assessing whether a hospital had the requisite capabilities and capacity" when investigating whether a hospital has met the requirement. CMS, Emergency Medical

Treatment and Labor Act (EMTALA) Requirements and Implications Related to Coronavirus Disease 2019 (COVID-19) (Revised) (March 30, 2020).

Additionally, a hospital subject to EMTALA can meet its obligation to form a relationship with anyone who comes to its emergency department seeking care and to do so for the purpose of at least providing an appropriate medical screening even if the hospital directs patients to an alternative site for such screening, including a site that is off the hospital's campus. Id. This allows hospitals to meet physical distancing requirements while still treating those who come to their emergency departments: off-site locations may be used for the purpose of establishing a COVID-19 testing program. Id.

9.   *"Patient Dumping" Persists.* EMTALA, while helpful, has not ended the problem of "patient dumping," particularly among our most vulnerable subpopulations. Several hospitals in Los Angeles, for example, have settled claims that they improperly discharged homeless patients from their emergency departments back on to the streets. See Maria Castellucci, "Calf. Hospital Pays $1 Million to Settle Patient-Dumping Case," Modern Healthcare (June 24, 2016). At least some of these "skid row dumping" cases involved allegations that patients were discharged while in unstable conditions. See Editorial Board, "No Excuse for 'Patient-Dumping' in L.A.'s Skid Row," L.A. Times (Jan. 20, 2014).

PROBLEMS: EMTALA

Ms. Miller

On May 21, Ms. Nancy Miller, who was eight months pregnant, called her obstetrician, Dr. Jennifer Gibson, at 2:00 a.m. because she was experiencing severe pain which appeared to her to be labor contractions. Dr. Gibson advised Ms. Miller to go to the emergency department of the local hospital and promised to meet her there shortly. Ms. Miller was admitted to the emergency department of General Hospital at 2:30 a.m., and Dr. Gibson joined her there at 3:14 a.m. After examining Ms. Miller, Dr. Gibson concluded that Ms. Miller had begun labor and that, even though the pregnancy had not reached full-term, the labor should be continued to delivery. At that time, Dr. Gibson asked that the on-call anesthesiologist, Dr. Martig, see Ms. Miller to discuss anesthesia during the delivery. At the same time, the procedure to admit Ms. Miller to the hospital's maternity floor was begun. The nurse informed Ms. Miller that there would be a short wait because there was no space available at that point.

Dr. Martig saw Ms. Miller at 4:00 a.m. When asked, Dr. Martig informed Ms. Miller that he was not qualified to and would not be able to perform an epidural (a spinal nerve-block anesthesia, often used in childbirth). Instead, he gave her Demerol and left the emergency department.

At 4:30 a.m., Ms. Miller was admitted to the labor and delivery floor. At 4:45 a.m., the obstetrical nurse observed fetal distress and called Dr. Gibson. At 4:50 a.m., Dr. Gibson concluded that Ms. Miller had a prolapsed umbilical cord and ordered an emergency caesarean section. The OB nurse paged Dr. Martig, but he could not be located. (Dr. Martig later stated that his pager had malfunctioned.) Because Dr. Martig could not be located, Dr. Gibson and a resident performed the C-section without an anesthetic and delivered the child healthy and alive. (These facts are based on Miller v. Martig, 754 N.E.2d 41 (Ind. Ct. App. 2001).)

Assume that Ms. Miller has brought suit against the hospital and Dr. Martig. What federal and state claims might Ms. Miller make? Assume that Dr. Martig and the hospital have filed a motion for summary judgment on all claims. What result?

Mr. Liles

Jesse Liles has no health insurance but went to a local hospital (NMC) complaining of fever and shortness of breath. He was admitted to the hospital with a diagnosis of severe dehydration, bilateral pneumonia, and adult respiratory distress syndrome. According to Mr. Liles, the hospital attempted to transfer him on eighteen separate occasions during the course of his stay between December 28, 2009, and January 24, 2010. Mr. Liles charges that two physicians at NMC falsely certified that he was stable for transfer from the hospital. At 3:35 a.m. on January 1, 2010, emergency medical services (EMS) from the local privately owned ambulance service came at the hospital's request to transfer Mr. Liles to another hospital. Liles went into cardiac arrest in the ambulance where he was resuscitated by EMS personnel and brought back inside NMC. He was placed on a ventilator in the intensive care unit (ICU) and stayed at the hospital until he was discharged to home on January 24.

On January 26, 2010, Liles called the same ambulance company because of his acute respiratory distress. The EMS personnel called NMC en route, but NMC told them to take Mr. Liles to some other hospital because there was no pulmonologist available at NMC. The ambulance was already at the entry to the hospital grounds, and it stayed in contact with NMC to get further instructions. Staff at NMC made numerous calls to potential "receiving hospitals" to identify a facility willing to accept Mr. Liles. Ultimately, he was taken to another hospital where he was admitted to the ICU and underwent surgery for a collapsed lung. (These facts are based on Liles v. TH Healthcare, Ltd., 2012 WL 3930616 (E.D. Tex.).)

Assume that Mr. Liles has sued the hospital for EMTALA violations. You are the hospital's attorney. What arguments do you expect Mr. Liles to make? What are your best defenses to Liles' claims?

IV. FEDERAL ANTIDISCRIMINATION LAW

This section examines federal antidiscrimination laws that apply to a range of programs and activities, including health care, based on certain protected characteristics. It focuses primarily on the key federal statutes addressing health care discrimination based on (1) race, color or national origin; (2) gender; and (3) disability. Racism, sexism, and ableism have long shaped the unequal distribution of benefits and burdens in society and in health care—whether through outright denials of care, unequal treatment in how care is delivered, or inequity in the distribution of health care resources. This has resulted in health care barriers and poorer quality treatment for racial and ethnic minorities, women and LGBTQ individuals, and people with disabilities.

After a brief overview, the section is organized according to the different categories of discrimination that federal laws have been enacted to address. We also include discussions of mental health parity, the use of genetic information, and age discrimination. For each category of discrimination, we discuss relevant federal statutes, explain how preexisting civil rights laws intersect with the newer antidiscrimination prohibitions in Section 1557 of the ACA, and highlight evolving disputes over the scope of antidiscrimination protection playing out among regulators and courts. While antidiscrimination cases are increasingly being brought under Section 1557, many of the cases discussed below are noteworthy decisions under other relevant civil rights laws.

Overview of Antidiscrimination Law

Pre-ACA Civil Rights Laws. The 1964 Civil Rights Act (CRA) bans many forms of discrimination that affect health in profound ways. Title VI of the CRA prohibits discrimination based on race, color, or national origin in programs or activities that receive federal financial assistance, which has been particularly important for combatting race discrimination in hospitals and nursing homes dependent upon Medicare and Medicaid funding. Title VII prohibits employment discrimination based on race and sex, and after it was amended through the Pregnancy Discrimination Act, it became a particularly powerful tool for fighting sex-based discriminatory exclusions in employment-based insurance. Title IX of the Education Amendments of 1972 has extended this antidiscrimination protection to educational settings.

Laws prohibiting disability-based discrimination have been the broadest in scope. Together, Section 504 of the Federal Rehabilitation Act of 1973 (Rehabilitation Act or Section 504) and the Americans with Disabilities Act (ADA), enacted in 1990, require recipients of federal funding, health care entities, employers, educational institutions, state and local governments, and private businesses that serve the public to ensure equal access for people with disabilities.

Section 1557 of the ACA. The ACA, signed into law in 2010, affirmed and expanded the earlier antidiscrimination protections. Section 1557 of the ACA (42 U.S.C. § 18116) provides:

(a) ... [A]n individual shall not, on the ground prohibited under title VI of the Civil Rights Act of 1964 (42 U.S.C. 2000d et seq.), title IX of the Education Amendments of 1972 (20 U.S.C. 1681 et seq.), the Age Discrimination Act of 1975 (42 U.S.C. 6101 et seq.), or section 504 of the Rehabilitation Act of 1973 (29 U.S.C. 794) ... be excluded from participation in, be denied the benefits of, or be subjected to discrimination under, any health program or activity, any part of which is receiving Federal financial assistance, including credits, subsidies, or contracts of insurance, or under any program or activity that is administered by an Executive Agency or any entity established under this title (or amendments). The enforcement mechanisms provided for and available under title VI shall apply for purposes of violations of this subsection.

(b) ... Nothing in this title ... shall be construed to invalidate or limit the rights, remedies, procedures, or legal standards available to individuals aggrieved under title VI of the Civil Rights Act of 1964 [ ], title IX of the Education Amendments [ ], section 504 of the Rehabilitation Act [ ] or to supersede State laws that provide additional protections against discrimination on any basis described in subsection (a).

Section 1557 has reshaped antidiscrimination law in health care in important ways. First, by incorporating existing civil rights laws that prohibit race (Title VI), sex (Title IX), and disability (Section 504) discrimination, it broadens the application of those prohibitions to more health care entities. Specifically, Section 1557 applies to recipients of "federal financial assistance," which is defined to include grants, loans, credits, subsidies, and insurance contracts. It applies to health insurers that receive premium tax credits or cost-sharing reduction payments for enrollees. Section 1557 also applies to most providers, though there are some limits. For example, HHS maintains that payments for patient care under Medicare Part B (the program that pays for physician services for Medicare beneficiaries) do not count as "Federal financial assistance," and providers paid directly by covered health insurers are not deemed to have received "assistance" for purposes of Section 1557. Nonetheless, most of the physicians in these situations probably receive federal assistance in other forms, and the statute does apply to all physicians who receive Medicaid.

For gender health equity in particular, Section 1557 has been viewed as having transformative potential. The limited applicability of Title VII to employment and Title IX to education meant the problem of gender discrimination in health care was relatively invisible and neglected. Indeed, one of the most anticipated effects of Section 1557's new health-specific prohibition on sex discrimination is its role in combatting discrimination against transgender individuals—a group that has long experienced overt, pervasive, and harmful discrimination by health care providers and insurers. See Subsection B below.

The future of Section 1557 as a vehicle to challenge discrimination in health care is uncertain due to substantial shifts in implementing regulations under different presidential administrations. Initially, an expansive rule implementing Section 1557 was issued under the Obama-Biden Administration ("2016 Rule"). Nondiscrimination in Health Programs and Activities, 81 Fed. Reg. 31375 (May 18, 2016) (codified at 45 C.F.R. Pt. 92). A few years later, a revised rule issued under the Trump Administration attempted to significantly limit the scope of Section 1557 in terms of covered entities and protected groups ("2020 Rule"). Nondiscrimination in Health and Health Education Programs or Activities, 85 Fed. Reg. 37160–248 (June 19, 2020). Then, in 2021, the Biden-Harris Administration indicated that it would issue a new notice of proposed rulemaking to revise the Section 1557 regulations, and it has taken other steps to reverse Trump Administration policy and regulations that significantly narrowed the reach of Section 1557. Of course, regulators only have so much power to shape Section 1557's reach—implementing regulations must be consistent with the underlying statute, the contours of which are already being adjudicated by courts. These developments are detailed in the notes below, and developments in the interpretation and enforcement of Section 1557 should be watched closely.

Even with the important changes brought about by Section 1557, preexisting civil rights statutes will remain relevant in challenging health discrimination. There are a couple of reasons for this. First, preexisting laws may fill important regulatory gaps where particular entities are not subject to Section 1557. For example, as explained in Section IV.B. below, employment-based plans not subject to Section 1557 under the narrower 2020 Rule are still subject to Title VII's employment protections. Second, courts have often looked beyond the antidiscrimination statute implicated in a particular case to consider how similar antidiscrimination laws have been interpreted. For example, in Section 1557 and Title IX gender discrimination claims, courts have looked to Title VII cases for guidance; for Section 1557 disability claims, the ADA provides useful guidance. Finally, Section 1557's unusual approach to delineating protected categories—specifically, its incorporation by reference of existing federal civil rights statutes—means that the cases interpreting those laws are essential to understanding the scope of nondiscrimination protections under Section 1557. For antidiscrimination challenges brought under Section 1557, courts are looking to the jurisprudence of the incorporated statutes, as well as similar antidiscrimination protections, to help answer a number of questions that we explore in this Section: Who is protected? What kind of conduct is recognized or defined as illegal discrimination?

How must plaintiffs prove discrimination claims? What defenses or exceptions exist? What remedies are available?

A. RACE, COLOR, & NATIONAL ORIGIN

U.S. hospitals and other health care facilities were racially segregated by law well into the late 1960s and by custom for some time thereafter. White-only hospitals refused admission to African-American citizens, and those white-dominated hospitals that did admit African Americans segregated them into separate units. Even publicly owned hospitals and hospitals funded by the federal government were segregated by race.

A post-World War II federal health care funding program, known as Hill-Burton, invested millions of federal tax dollars in the construction of hospitals across the country. Yet the legislation specifically institutionalized race discrimination by allowing federally funded hospitals to exclude African Americans if other facilities were available. The segregated facilities available were hardly equal. For example, the ward for African Americans in the community hospital in Wilmington, North Carolina housed only twenty-five beds and two toilets in a building separated from the main building, which meant that surgery patients had to be transported across an open yard. And neither of the two hospitals (one public and one private) in Broward County, Florida admitted patients from the more than 30,000 African Americans residing in the county. Segregation even trumped ability to pay. For example, in 1950s Chicago, African-American union members with generous health insurance plans were steered almost entirely to Cook County Hospital despite closer facilities. See David Barton Smith, Health Care Divided: Race and Healing a Nation (1999). Not until 1962 did a federal Court of Appeals declare the "separate but equal" provision of the Hill-Burton Act unconstitutional. Simkins v. Moses H. Cone Mem'l Hosp., 323 F.2d 959 (4th Cir. 1963), cert. denied, 376 U.S. 938 (1964).

In 1964, Congress passed Title VI of the Civil Rights Act, expressly prohibiting discrimination on the basis of race, color, or national origin by any program receiving federal financial assistance. But it was the creation of Medicare and Medicaid in 1965 that gave the federal government the leverage it needed to desegregate hospitals and fight other forms of race discrimination by hospitals, nursing homes, and other facilities receiving federal funding. Importantly, early regulations clarified that Title VI prohibited the use of criteria or methods of administration that had the *effect* of subjecting individuals to discrimination on the basis of race, color, or national origin. 45 C.F.R. 80.3(b)(2).

For these reasons, some expected Title VI would be a powerful tool for combatting both intentional discrimination in health care and facially neutral health care polices or practices that had discriminatory effects.

Indeed, the ability to challenge such policies and practices was understood as vital to combatting more subtle forms of discrimination, especially as antidiscrimination norms made overt race discrimination unpalatable. Today, the policies and practices having discriminatory health effects tend to be facially neutral or the product of more subtle or implicit biases about the affected groups.

The case excerpts below present two examples of Title VI challenges to a facially neutral policy or decision having a racially discriminatory impact. In one case, the challenged policy resulted in the involuntary discharge of nursing home patients. In the other, an underserved community lost its public hospital. As you read the cases, consider why the courts reached different results. What do these cases suggest about the power of Title VI to combat systemic discrimination and other practices that contribute to health inequity?

LINTON V. COMMISSIONER OF HEALTH AND ENVIRONMENT

United States District Court, Middle District, Tennessee, 1990.
779 F. Supp. 925.

JOHN T. NIXON, DISTRICT JUDGE.

Plaintiffs are before the Court seeking to enjoin a Tennessee policy through which only a portion of the beds in Medicaid participating nursing homes are certified to be available for Medicaid patients. Plaintiffs allege that this policy artificially limits the accessibility of nursing home care to indigent Medicaid patients and fosters discrimination against indigent patients by nursing homes. Plaintiffs claim that, as a result of the challenged policy, they and other individuals similarly situated face delay or outright denial of needed nursing home care, as well as displacement from current residency in nursing home facilities. Plaintiffs bring this action under [ ] Title VI of the Civil Rights Act of 1964.

* * *

FINDINGS OF FACT

The present case was initiated on December 1, 1987 on behalf of Mildred Lea Linton. Ms. Linton suffers from rheumatoid arthritis and has been a patient for four years at Green Valley Health Care Center in Dickson, Tennessee [hereinafter "Green Valley"]. A Medicaid patient who had been receiving skilled nursing facility (SNF) level care throughout her stay, the plaintiff received notice from State Medicaid officials that she no longer qualified for such care. The same notice advised her that she would have to move to another nursing home, an intermediate care facility (ICF), to receive the level of care to which the State believed she should be downgraded. Green Valley provides ICF care, and in fact the bed occupied by Ms. Linton was dually certified for Medicaid purposes for provision of both SNF and ICF levels of care. However, Green Valley was unwilling to care for Ms. Linton at an ICF level of reimbursement. The nursing home, which had directed the State to certify only part of its ICF beds as available to Medicaid patients, reserved the right to decertify the plaintiff's bed for Medicaid ICF participation. This decertification would have compelled the plaintiff's involuntary transfer to another facility.

On December 11, 1989, plaintiff Belle Carney, an 89 year old black woman, requested intervention. She had been diagnosed in July 1987 as requiring nursing home treatment due to Alzheimer's disease, however, no nursing home placement was found for her. Plaintiff Carney asserts that the State's limited bed certification policy, which the State refers to as distinct part certification, creates an artificial restriction on the number of available Medicaid beds and that it fosters discrimination against Medicaid patients by nursing homes. Plaintiff Carney's health deteriorated over a period of several months as she was moved from one inadequate placement to another. Finally, Carney's condition declined to the point that she required emergency hospitalization. . . .

* * *

A. *The Tennessee Medicaid Program*

Tennessee participates in the federal Medicaid program to provide medical assistance to those recipients who are eligible to receive such assistance in accordance with the requirements of Title XIX of the Social Security Act. [ ] . . . The types of medical assistance that are provided under the Tennessee Medicaid program include, among others, services by skilled nursing home facilities [(SNFs)] and intermediate care facilities [(ICFs)]. [ ] [ICF services include institutional, health-related services above the level of room and board, but at a level of care below that of hospital or SNF care. SNF care consists of institutional care above the level of ICF services but below the level of a hospital. The Tennessee Department of Health and Environment (TDHE) is the single state agency responsible for administration of the Medicaid program. The Department is administered under the direction of the defendant Commissioner.] TDHE also acts as the State licensing agency for nursing homes or long term care facilities and certifies such facilities for Medicaid. . . .

* * *

Tennessee has previously had a "Medicaid Bed Management program" which represents an attempt to place a percentage limitation on the number of available Medicaid beds in nursing homes. Federal auditors recommended that this policy be discontinued, and Tennessee abolished this program on October 1, 1985.

Plaintiffs challenge what they refer to as an unwritten limited bed certification policy. Defendants assert that this policy is instead simply

Tennessee's version of distinct part certification. [Federal law authorizes State agencies to certify facilities for either SNF or ICF reimbursement. Such certification may be of a "distinct part of an institution." According to federal policy, the term "distinct part" denotes that the unit is organized and operated to give *a distinct type of care within a larger organization which otherwise renders other types or levels of care.* "Distinct" denotes both organizational and physical distinctness. A distinct part SNF must be physically identifiable and be operated distinguishably from the rest of the institution. *It must consist of all the beds within that unit such as a separate building, floor, wing or ward.*] The Court finds, however, that the Tennessee policy varies markedly from federal "distinct part" certification.

Perhaps the most fundamental difference between Tennessee's limited bed certification policy and federal "distinct part" certification is to be found in the different purposes served by the respective policies. Federal distinct part certification is intended to accommodate the delivery of qualitatively different types of health care within the same facility. Tennessee's policy, however, appears to serve the interests of nursing homes who wish to participate in the Medicaid program while also maintaining a separate private pay facility offering the same type of care.

* * *

Federal Medicaid law mandates that states set their Medicaid payments to nursing homes at levels which are "reasonable and adequate to meet the costs which must be incurred by efficiently and economically operated facilities in order to provide care and services in conformity with applicable State and Federal laws, regulations and quality and safety standards . . ." [ ]

By contrast, private pay rates are set by the market, a market in which there are more patients seeking care than there are beds to accommodate them. There are waiting lists to gain admission to nursing homes throughout Tennessee. As a result of this situation, unregulated private pay rates are substantially higher than Medicaid payments, and nursing home operators prefer private pay patients. Tennessee's present certification program allows nursing home operators to give preference to private pay patients by reserving for their exclusive use beds which are, due to lack of certification, unavailable to Medicaid patients.

. . . The [limited bed certification] policy leads to disruption of care and displacement of Medicaid patients after they have been admitted to a nursing home. Such displacement often occurs when a patient exhausts his or her financial resources and attempts transition from private pay to Medicaid. In this situation, a patient who already occupies a bed in a nursing home is told that his or her bed is no longer available to the patient because he or she is dependent upon Medicaid. . . . Involuntary transfers are triggered on other occasions when a patient already on Medicaid at

SNF level of reimbursement is reclassified to an ICF level of care [with lower reimbursement].

... [T]he Court finds that the limited bed certification policy has caused widespread displacement .... The Court is persuaded by the depositions, affidavits and exhibits concerning the severe impact of the limited bed certification policy. Finally, the Court is mindful of the Medicaid eligibility rules which allow eligibility for relatively more affluent patients already residing in nursing homes than those seeking initial admission. This phenomenon combined with the limited bed certification policy often renders the poorest and most medically needy Medicaid applicants unable to obtain the proper nursing home care.

B. *Disparate Impact on Minorities*

The Court finds that the plaintiff has established by a preponderance of the evidence that the Tennessee Medicaid program does have a disparate and adverse impact on minorities. Because of the higher incidence of poverty in the black population, and the concomitant increased dependence on Medicaid, a policy limiting the amount of nursing home beds available to Medicaid patients will disproportionately affect blacks.

Indeed, while blacks comprise 39.4 percent of the Medicaid population, they account for only 15.4 percent of those Medicaid patients who have been able to gain access to Medicaid-covered nursing home services. In addition, testimony indicates that the health status of blacks is generally poorer than that of whites, and their need for nursing home services is correspondingly greater. Finally, such discrimination has caused a "dual system" of long term care for the frail elderly: a statewide system of licensed nursing homes, 70 percent funded by the Medicaid program, serves whites; while blacks are relegated to substandard boarding homes which receive no Medicaid subsidies.

CONCLUSIONS OF LAW

* * *

B. *Plaintiffs' Claims Under Title VI of the Civil Rights Act of 1964*

Title VI of the Civil Rights Act of 1964 provides, in relevant part:

> No person in the United States shall on the ground of race, color or national origin ... be subjected to discrimination under any program or activity receiving Federal financial assistance.

[ ] Regulations under Title VI provide that a state in its administration of the federally funded program can not:

> ... directly or through contractual or other arrangements, utilize criteria or methods of administration which have the effect of subjecting individuals to discrimination because of their race, color, or

national origin, or have the effect of defeating or substantially impairing accomplishment of the objectives of the program as respect individuals of a particular race, color or national origin.

45 C.F.R. § 80.3(b)(2).

* * *

The plaintiffs have shown that the defendants' limited bed certification policy has a disparate impact on racial minorities in Tennessee. The burden of proof next falls upon the defendants to show that the disparate impact is not unjustifiable. The defendants state that the "self-selection preferences" of the minorities, based upon the minorities' reliance upon the extended family, lack of transportation, and fear of institutional care, adequately explain the disparate impact. [ ] This explanation, however, is not sufficient justification for minority underrepresentation in nursing homes. Therefore, the defendants have failed to meet their burden of proof . . . .

* * *

The Court recognizes that under Title VI, deference is accorded to the Title VI administrative agency to cure the discriminatory effects of the particular program. To be sure, THDE employs Ms. Beverly Bass as a director to monitor Title VI compliance. However, even Bass concedes that under the TDHE certification policy black Medicaid recipients are displaced or denied admission to nursing homes. Further, it is noteworthy that the Bed Management Program that was instituted in 1981, was not repealed as TDHE policy until October 13, 1987. Prior TDHE studies identified the status of minority citizen [sic] in Tennessee's Medicaid Program and the reasons for lack of minority participation. Yet, despite these studies, the Commissioner implemented a policy that fosters and continues the egregious status of minority Medicaid patients within the program. In these circumstances, continued deference to the administrative agencies is inappropriate. To cure the effects of this policy, judicial intervention is necessary. To accomplish this, the Court ORDERS the Commissioner, in consultation with [the federal agency overseeing Medicaid], to submit a plan for court approval that will redress the disparate impact upon eligible minority Medicaid patients' access to qualified nursing home care due to the THDE certification policy and the State's past noncompliance with Title VI.

* * *

BRYAN V. KOCH

United States Court of Appeals, Second Circuit, 1980.
627 F.2d 612.

NEWMAN, CIRCUIT JUDGE:

This litigation challenges New York City's decision to close Sydenham Hospital, one of its 17 municipal hospitals, on the ground that the City's proposed action would constitute racial discrimination in the use of federal funds in violation of Title VI of the Civil Rights Act of 1964, *42 U.S.C. § 2000d* et seq. Like most American cities, New York has struggled mightily to provide adequate municipal services with limited financial resources; its difficulties have become particularly severe since its budget crisis that began in the mid-1970's. Closing Sydenham is one of the many painful steps that the City has undertaken or proposed in an effort to maintain financial stability. The discrimination claim in this case arises from the fact that Sydenham, located in central Harlem, serves a population that is 98% minority (Black and Hispanic). Three related cases have been brought to prevent the closing of the Hospital, or at least to ameliorate the effects that the closing would have on the minority population it serves. This consolidated appeal is from the denial of a preliminary injunction. . . .

* * *

In April, 1979, Mayor Koch appointed a Health Policy Task Force to examine ways of reducing costly excess hospital capacity while maintaining access to high quality health services. The Task Force report, issued June 20, 1979, recommended a series of steps that the City's Health and Hospital Corporation (HHC) estimated would save $ 30 million in fiscal year 1981. With respect to the 17 hospitals of the municipal hospital system, the report proposed that some hospitals be replaced, that some hospitals reduce the number of beds, and that two hospitals, Sydenham and Metropolitan, both located in Harlem, be closed. The HHC approved the report on June 28, 1979. On August 12, 1979, the first of the three cases in this litigation, Bryan v. Koch, was filed on behalf of a class of low income Black and Hispanic residents of New York City who use the municipal hospital system. Defendants are the City and State of New York, the HHC, the State Health Department, and various city and state officials, including Mayor Koch. The U. S. Department of Health and Human Services (HHS) (formerly Department of Health, Education and Welfare) was joined as a defendant, though not charged with any violation of law. . . . [The] suits, which have been consolidated, allege that the City's proposed plan for the municipal hospital system violates various federal civil rights statutes, primarily Title VI. . . .

* * *

. . . [T]he findings that the City acted without discriminatory intent are fully supported by the evidence.

* * *

. . . Even under the effects standard, we conclude that the judgment of the District Court should be affirmed. Applying that standard, we agree with the plaintiffs that they have sufficiently shown a disproportionate racial impact to require justification by the defendants. Disparity appears from comparing the 98% minority proportion of the Sydenham patients with the 66% minority proportion of the patients served by the City's municipal hospital system. Whether the impact of this disparity is sufficiently adverse to create a prima facie Title VI violation is a closer question. The District Court was satisfied with the City's estimates for the care of Sydenham patients in nearby municipal and voluntary hospitals. Nevertheless, the District Court acknowledged that at least a small number of patients, those admitted to the emergency room because of gunshot or knife wounds or drug overdoses, would suffer adverse consequences if the nearest emergency room treatment available were at even slightly more distant locations. Moreover, we share the plaintiffs' concern that the City's estimates for alternative care of Sydenham's patients rests on projections about the availability of bed space without sufficient assurance that the voluntary hospitals on which the City relies will admit all of Sydenham's patients in financial need. Whether these hospitals will admit Sydenham's Medicaid patients remains an issue in some dispute, and even if Medicaid patients will be admitted, it is also unclear what will happen with those eligible for Medicaid who are unable to establish their eligibility at the time hospital admission is needed.

* * *

We therefore consider it appropriate to complete an assessment of plaintiffs' Title VI claim by examining the justification advanced by the City for closing Sydenham. As the District Court found, that justification is both the reduction of expenditures and the increase in efficiency within the municipal hospital system. Though the plaintiffs dispute the amount of savings the City claims will be achieved, they acknowledge that there is sufficient evidence to support the District Court's finding that closing Sydenham will reduce expenditures to some extent. However, saving money, while obviously a legitimate objective of any governmental plan to close a public facility, cannot be a sufficient justification in a case like this where public officials have made a choice to close one of 17 municipal hospitals. In such circumstances it is the choice of this particular hospital that must be justified.

To provide a basis for making this choice the Task Force report initially assessed each of the municipal hospitals against four sets of criteria: (a) hospital size, scope of patient services, and extent of usage; (b) patient access to comparable alternative facilities; (c) quality of plant and operations; and (d) present and predicted fiscal performance. Among the several hospitals considered deficient in this assessment, recommendations for closure were made for those hospitals with disproportionately high operating deficits and obsolete plants, located within 30 minutes of other municipal hospitals with comparable or broader services. These criteria are reasonably related to the efficient operation of the City's municipal hospital system, and the evidence abundantly justifies the selection of Sydenham based on these criteria. . . .

If any of the municipal hospitals are to be closed, plaintiffs do not dispute that Sydenham is an appropriate choice for closing. Their claim is that the closing of a federally funded facility resulting in a disproportionate racial impact violates Title VI unless the defendants establish the unavailability of alternative measures that would save equivalent money with less disproportionate impact. Proceeding from this premise, plaintiffs further contend that instead of closing any municipal hospitals, the City could save as much money or more and avoid a disparate racial impact by such alternatives as hospital mergers, regionalization of services, increasing Sydenham's services to reduce its deficit, or increasing Medicaid reimbursement.

Neither Title VI nor the HHS regulations explicitly require a federal fund recipient to consider alternatives to a proposed placement or closing of a public facility. It is unlikely that challenges to such governmental actions were even contemplated when Title VI was enacted in 1964. The focus at that time was on federally aided facilities that denied access to minorities or admitted them only to segregated portions of a facility. [ ] The argument for consideration of alternatives in placing or closing facilities stems from two sources. HHS has expressed its view as the administrator of federal medical care funds that its regulations should be interpreted to require consideration of alternatives. On March 5, 1980, the Undersecretary of what was then HEW wrote to Mayor Koch, in connection with the proposed closing of municipal hospitals, that if closings were to create a disparate racial impact, the City would have an opportunity to establish that they are "necessary to achieve legitimate objectives unrelated to race or national origin and that these objectives cannot be achieved by other measures having a less disproportionate adverse effect." . . .

. . . [H]owever, the inquiry could frequently become too open-ended. If, for example, a court were to assess alternative ways of saving funds throughout the administration of a city or even throughout the administration of the health care function, it would seriously risk substituting its own judgment for that of the city's elected officials and appointed specialists. We are skeptical of the capacity and appropriateness of courts to conduct such broad inquiries concerning alternative ways to carry out municipal functions. Once a court is drawn into such a complex inquiry, it will inevitably be assessing the wisdom of competing political and economic alternatives. Moreover, such policy choices would be made without broad public participation and without sufficient assurance that the alternative selected will ultimately provide more of a benefit to the minority population.

. . . [W]e do not believe Title VI requires consideration of alternatives beyond an assessment of all the municipal hospitals in order to select one or more for closing. . . . The alternatives plaintiffs wish to have considered are more appropriate for examination by administrative, legislative, and other political processes than by the courts.

Without expressing any views as to the wisdom of closing Sydenham Hospital, we conclude that the plaintiffs have shown no likelihood of success in establishing that its closing would violate Title VI, and the District Court therefore did not err in denying a preliminary injunction.

* * *

NOTES AND QUESTIONS

1. *The Health Care Safety Net.* These cases introduce you to two essential parts of the U.S. health care safety net. In *Linton*, the plaintiffs depended on Medicaid, known primarily as the public insurance program for the poor. Medicaid, which is jointly funded by federal and state government, is the primary source of payment for institutional and long-term care. See Chapters 3 and 10. In *Bryan*, the plaintiffs depended on a local public hospital system, which could not refuse to treat anyone based on ability to pay. Although there is no universal right to health care in the U.S., states may require local governments to ensure a minimal level of service to indigent residents. See, e.g., Cal. Welf. & Inst. Code § 17000 ("[E]very city and county shall relieve and support all incompetent, poor, indigent persons, and those incapacitated by age, disease, or accident, lawfully resident therein, when such persons are not supported and relieved by their relatives or friends, by their own means, or by state hospitals or other state or private institutions.") But even in these states, local governments typically have great discretion in how they satisfy this duty, including the extent to which they rely on private actors subsidized with public funds.

2. *Proving Disparate Impact.* As noted in the cases above, Title VI regulations reach beyond intentional discrimination. They prohibit the use of criteria or methods of program administration which have discriminatory effects. (Recall the excerpt of 45 C.F.R. § 80.3(b)(2) reproduced in *Linton* above.) In both *Bryan* and *Linton*, there was no evidence of discriminatory intent, but plaintiffs were able to establish a prima facie case based on disparate racial impact. What evidence did plaintiffs offer to prove disparate impact?

Consider that race-based residential patterns originally established as a matter of *de jure* segregation in housing have produced a legacy of *de facto* racial segregation still engraved on the U.S. health care system today: Hospitals and nursing homes continue to avoid predominantly African-American neighborhoods; only one-quarter of pharmacies in these neighborhoods carry necessary prescription medications; and health insurers market different and more limited health plans, if they market at all, in these neighborhoods than in predominantly Caucasian neighborhoods. See Sidney Watson, Section 1557 of the Affordable Care Act: Civil Rights, Health Reform, Race, and Equity, 55 How. L. J. 855 (2012); David Barton Smith, Healthcare's Hidden Civil Rights Legacy, supra; Ruqaiijah Yearby, African Americans Can't Win, Break Even, or Get Out of the System: The Persistence of "Unequal Treatment" in Nursing Home Care, 82 Temple L. Rev. 1177 (2010).

3.   *"Sufficiently Adverse" Impact.* In *Bryan*, the court found that plaintiffs showed a disproportionate *racial* impact, but it noted that "[w]hether the impact of this disparity is *sufficiently adverse* to create a prima facie Title VI violation was a closer question." Because public hospitals are required by state or local law to treat indigent patients, they have been the primary source of treatment for patients who otherwise could not afford care or find providers willing to treat them. The City claimed that, after the closure, Sydenham's patients would still be able to get the care they needed from private hospitals in neighboring areas. The plaintiffs' challenged this assumption and the court shared plaintiffs' concern: Why? What additional information would be needed to determine the impact of Sydenham's closure on non-emergency care?

4.   *Defenses to a Disparate Impact Claim.* Proving that a policy or practice has racially disparate effects is not enough to win a Title VI suit. In both *Bryan* and *Linton*, once the plaintiff made out a prima facie case for disparate impact, the burden shifted to the defendant to justify the challenged policy or practice. Compare the result in *Bryan* with that in *Linton*. Why did the court find the hospital closure in *Bryan* justifiable? What purpose does allowing a claim based on disparate effects or impact seem to serve? Is it designed merely to help root out pretext for intentional discrimination? Is the goal to eliminate health inequity more broadly? Or does the goal lie somewhere in-between: Is Title VI a vehicle for distinguishing *unjustifiable* policies that have discriminatory effects from *justifiable* policies that may have the unfortunate, but not illegal, effect of exacerbating health disparities? If so, then how do we determine what is justifiable?

5.   *Private Disparate Impact Litigation?* In 2001, in Alexander v. Sandoval, 532 U.S. 275 (2001), the Supreme Court dealt a significant blow to private Title VI litigation. The Court held that only intentional discrimination is actionable through private suit under Title VI. The five-to-four majority strictly construed the text of Title VI, holding that there was no private cause of action to enforce regulations that went beyond the scope of the statutory prohibition. The Court held that enforcement of regulations prohibiting policies or criteria with racially disparate *effects* was exclusively within the purview of the agency charged with Title VI enforcement. In the case of health

care, this would be the HHS Office for Civil Rights (OCR), discussed further in Notes 6 & 7 below. Although *Sandoval* was not a health care case, it has been widely understood as foreclosing private disparate impact claims in health care such as those in *Linton* and *Bryan*—that is, until enactment of Section 1557 of the ACA seemed to re-open this question.

An early case raised the possibility that the ACA's antidiscrimination provision would breathe new life into private disparate impact litigation. In Rumble v. Fairview Health Services, No. 14-CV-2037 SRN/FLN, 2015 WL 1197415 (D. Minn. Mar. 16, 2015), the court held that Congress intended to create a new, health-specific, anti-discrimination cause of action that is subject to a singular standard, regardless of a plaintiff's protected class status, because holding otherwise "would lead to an illogical result." The court explained that applying different standards would mean a plaintiff bringing a race discrimination claim under Section 1557 could allege only disparate treatment, but plaintiffs bringing a disability claim under the same statute could allege disparate treatment or disparate impact. *Rumble's* interpretation created the possibility that private disparate impact claims based on race may once again be available under Section 1557. It was also consistent with the 2016 Rule interpretation that "Section 1557 authoriz[ed] a private right of action *for claims of disparate impact discrimination on the basis of any of the criteria enumerated in the legislation.*" 81 Fed. Reg. at 31,439–40 (emphasis added). Subsequently, however, this interpretation was rejected in the 2020 Rule and it has not gained much traction with courts.

To date, most courts have found that although Congress created a private right of action for Section 1557 violations, it did not create a single standard for such claims. Rather, courts have held that Congress' express incorporation of the enforcement mechanisms from different federal civil rights statutes "manifests an intent to import the various different standards and burdens of proof into a Section 1557 claim." See Southeastern Penn. Transp. Auth. v. Gilead Sciences, 102 F. Supp. 3d 688 (E.D. Pa. 2015). *Southeastern Penn.* dealt specifically with a lawsuit challenging an insurer's denial of coverage for a Hepatitis C drug as a violation of Section 1557's prohibition of race discrimination, among other claims. The court dismissed the plaintiffs' Section 1557 claims for failure to state a viable cause of action. The court set out the required elements for a race discrimination claim under Section 1557 based on Title VI:

> To state a claim under Title VI of the Civil Rights Act, a plaintiff must show that he or she (1) was a member of a protected class, (2) qualified for the benefit or program at issue, (3) suffered an adverse action, and (4) the adverse action occurred under circumstances giving rise to an inference of discrimination. Private rights of action under Title VI itself are available only for allegations of intentional discrimination and not disparate impact. Plaintiffs suing under Title VI may show intentional discrimination with evidence demonstrating either discriminatory animus or deliberate indifference. Discriminatory animus requires plaintiff establish prejudice, spite, or ill will. To establish deliberate

indifference, a plaintiff must show that a defendant (1) knew that a harm to a federally protected right was substantially likely and (2) failed to act.

Id. at 701 (citations omitted). Other courts have agreed that the respective standards from each of four incorporated statutes should be applied based on the category of discrimination. See, e.g., York v. Wellmark, 2017 WL 11261026 (S.D. Iowa 2017) (applying Title IX standards to a Section 1557 sex discrimination claim); Briscoe v. Health Care Service Corp. 281 F. Supp. 3d 725 (N.D. Ill. 2017) (same).

6.   *Public Enforcement Efforts*. Although *Sandoval* eliminated private disparate impact claims under Title VI, this ruling does not preclude administrative enforcement on disparate impact grounds. OCR can pursue cases under both intentional discrimination and disparate effects theories, and, at times, has used its power to challenge a broad range of discriminatory actions. See Speech by Thomas Perez, Director, Office for Civil Rights, Discrimination and Health Disparities (Apr. 13, 1999) (describing actions targeting home health care chains engaging in medical redlining—a policy of refusing to serve people in predominantly minority neighborhoods; a hospital's policy of not giving epidurals to women who did not speak English; a hospital's segregated maternity wards; and a pharmacy's repeated failure to fill the prescription of an African-American Medicaid recipient).

OCR has also used its enforcement authority to intervene in hospital closures or relocations that could have a discriminatory impact. For example, in 2010 the OCR responded to complaints about a decision by the University of Pittsburgh Medical Center (UPMC) to close its hospital in Braddock, Pennsylvania, which was in a predominantly African-American community, and to relocate services to a new facility in a predominantly white area that was a great distance away. Although regulators did not stop the closure, they did reach an agreement with UPMC to ameliorate the effects on access by providing door-to-door transportation services from Braddock to its new outpatient facilities and expanding support for primary and urgent care services locally. See U.S. Department of Health and Human Services, Press Release, UPMC Agrees to Expand Access to Care After Closure of UPMC Braddock (Sep. 2, 2010).

Although OCR relies heavily on voluntary settlements, the above cases remain useful for understanding how a court might evaluate disparate impact claims if an OCR action proceeded to litigation.

7.   *Critique of Public Enforcement Efforts*. Even with OCR enforcement, the lack of a private cause of action for disparate impact claims has been a huge blow to efforts to combat race discrimination. OCR's enforcement priorities depend on its leadership, and persistent resource, organizational, and political challenges have made administrative enforcement of Title VI uneven at best. Indeed, a 1999 report by the United States Commission on Civil Rights confirmed many of the longstanding complaints lodged by patients' advocates about OCR's "timid and ineffectual enforcement" and concluded that the structure and operation of HHS/OCR actually fostered and

exacerbated health care discrimination, rather than combatting it. See Sara Rosenbaum & Joel Teitelbaum, Civil Rights Enforcement in the Modern Healthcare System: Reinvigorating the Role of the Federal Government in the Aftermath of Alexander v. Sandoval, 3 Yale J. Health Pol'y, L. & Ethics 215 (2003). For most of the period between Title VI enactment and *Sandoval*, it was private litigants—not the OCR—who primarily challenged public funding decisions having racially discriminatory effects, including hospital closures in and relocations from predominantly minority communities.

8. *Continuing Inequities*. Racial disparities in health care treatment and outcomes persist despite antidiscrimination efforts. As noted above, some disparities are linked to geographic segregation or socioeconomic status. During the COVID-19 pandemic, for example, some minority neighborhoods did not have equal access to COVID-19 testing, with Black and Latino communities more likely to experience longer wait times and understaffed testing centers. See Soo Rin Kim et al., Which Cities Have the Biggest Racial Gaps in COVID-19 Testing Access?, FiveThirtyEight.com (Jul. 22, 2020). And a recent study has found that the higher mortality of Black COVID-19 patients was attributable to the different hospitals to which Blacks and Whites were admitted, not only to patient characteristics. See David A. Asch et al., Patient and Hospital Factors Associated with Differences in Mortality Rates Among Black and White US Medicare Beneficiaries Hospitalized With COVID-19 Infection, 4 JAMA Network Open (Jun. 17, 2021).

These factors do not capture the full story, however. In 2003, a report by the Institute of Medicine (now the National Academy of Medicine) found serious racial and ethnic disparities, defined as "racial or ethnic differences in the quality of healthcare that are not due to access-related factors or clinical needs, preferences and appropriateness of intervention." Institute of Medicine, Unequal Treatment: Confronting Racial and Ethnic Disparities in Health Care (2003). Disparities in treatment decisions appear for a great variety of medical conditions. For example, studies show that African-American and Latino patients are categorized as needing less urgent care by emergency department personnel than whites with the same cardiac symptoms; are less likely to receive aspirin upon discharge after heart attack; and are less likely to receive appropriate pain medication in the emergency department for problems like bone fractures. See Rene Bowser, The Affordable Care Act and Beyond: Opportunities for Advancing Health Equity and Social Justice, 10 Hastings Race & Poverty L. J. 69 (2013). See also National Health Care Quality and Disparities Reports (2011), issued by the federal Agency on Healthcare Research and Quality, reporting that African Americans and Latinos receive lower quality care than do non-Hispanic whites on approximately 40 percent of quality measures.

There is also growing research that more directly investigates the role of racism in health care. See, e.g., David R. Williams, Jourdyn Lawrence, and Brigette Davis, Racism and Health: Evidence and Needed Research, 45 Annual

Review Public Health 105 (2019) (describing the growing attention of scientific researchers to the operation of racism in health at the individual, structural, and cultural levels). See also Dayna Bowen Matthew, Just Medicine: A Cure for Racial Inequality in American Health Care (2015). Matthew provides a comprehensive review of the social science literature showing how implicit bias leads to unequal treatment and entrenches racial and ethnic health disparities in access and outcomes. She then proposes structural reforms to combat implicit bias based on social scientific evidence concerning the presence, function, and malleability of implicit bias that has largely been ignored. Her proposals include reforming antidiscrimination laws, such as Title VI and 1557, so that intentional discrimination is not required for private causes of action, as well as creating a new negligence-based cause of action that would allow institutions to be held legally accountable for failing to address evidence that implicit bias is impacting treatment decisions. Under this negligence theory, institutions would be able to satisfy their duty through relevant training programs and other evidence-based anti-bias interventions.

9.   *Recognizing or Re-Creating Race?* Although civil rights laws have been important for combatting the type of exclusionary or animus-based overt discrimination that animated de jure segregation, antidiscrimination law has not eliminated the use of race in medical decision-making. Indeed, some in the medical community continue to justify the explicit use of race as medically justifiable or relevant. See, e.g., Sally Satel, I am a Racially Profiling Doctor, N.Y. Times Magazine (May 5, 2002) (physician describing why she factors in race for diagnosis and treatment decisions); Pamela Sankar and Jonathan Kahn, BiDil: Race Medicine or Race Marketing, 24 Health Aff. (2005) (describing the controversy around the FDA's first approved drug with a race-specific indication, BiDil, to treat heart failure in Black patients); Darshali A. Vyas et al., Hidden in Plain Sight—Reconsidering the Use of Race Correction in Clinical Algorithms, 383 NEJM 874 (2020) (identifying the continued use of race as a "corrective factor" in medical determinations about the safety of vaginal birth after a C-section, how best to manage heart failure, and the measurement of kidney function; and noting that these practices merit greater scrutiny because of their potential to expose Black patients to riskier interventions or delayed care). This not only contributes to race-based health inequities. Vyas, supra. Such uses of race in medicine have also been criticized as the product of, and as a tool for reinforcing, the longstanding myth of race as a genetic or biological factor that has shaped our understanding of disease and treatment. Such beliefs have been used to support notions of racial inferiority and racialized disease susceptibility, which, in turn, have impeded the recognition and targeting of structural forces, like modern forms of racism, that continue to have an outsize impact on health. See Dorothy E. Roberts, Fatal Invention: How Science, Politics, and Big Business Re-create Race in the Twenty-First Century (2011).

NOTE: NATIONAL ORIGIN DISCRIMINATION

Discussions of race discrimination tend to treat race and ethnicity as interchangeable concepts because of the commonality in the forms of discrimination and disparities experienced by groups identifying as racial and ethnic minorities. Nonetheless, discrimination based on national origin presents distinct legal issues, such as language barriers to access. According to the 2015 American Community Survey from the U.S. Census Bureau, a record 64.7 million people spoke a language other than English at home, and more than 25.9 million people were "limited English proficient" (LEP). Data from this annual survey is available at the U.S. Census Bureau's official website. LEP individuals experience linguistic barriers to care that impact both the ability to access care and the quality of care received. In 1974, the Supreme Court in Lau v. Nichols, 414 U.S. 563, interpreted Title VI regulations as prohibiting conduct that has a disproportionate effect on individuals with limited English proficiency as a form of national origin discrimination. (As noted above, however, *Sandoval* subsequently limited enforcement of such violations to agencies.) In 2000, Executive Order 13166, titled "Improving Access to Services for Persons with Limited English Proficiency," was issued, explaining that federal funding recipients were "required to take reasonable steps to ensure meaningful access" for LEP persons. 65 Fed. Reg. 50121 (Aug. 11, 2000).

This "meaningful access requirement" was reaffirmed in both the 2016 Rule and the 2020 Rule. The 2020 Rule, however, rescinded the more specific regulatory requirements that had been created under the Obama administration to ensure access, for example, by eliminating the requirement that non-discrimination notices must include the availability of language assistance services and taglines in the top 15 languages spoken by LEP individuals in the state. The 2020 Rule, instead, revived an earlier balancing test that had been used for Title VI compliance, noting that OCR would assess whether an entity took reasonable steps to ensure meaningful access for LEP individuals based on how the entity balances four factors: "(i) The number or proportion of limited English proficient individuals eligible to be served or likely to be encountered in the eligible service population; (ii) The frequency with which LEP individuals come in contact with the entity's health program, activity, or service; (iii) The nature and importance of the entity's health program, activity, or service; and (iv) The resources available to the entity and costs." 42 C.F.R. 92.101(b).

Perhaps the most challenging aspect of national origin discrimination is conduct motivated by or linked with immigration status. Since enactment of the Personal Responsibility and Work Opportunity Reconciliation Act of 1996 (PRWORA), Pub. L. No. 104–193, 110 Stat. 2105, federal law has severely curtailed public health care benefits for immigrants who are here legally or illegally, or whose legal status is uncertain. The ACA excludes all U.S. residents not "lawfully present" in the U.S. from access to the health insurance exchanges and subsidies for insurance. The ACA also continues the five-year waiting period for Medicaid applied to lawfully present immigrants. See

Health Coverage for Immigrants, The Henry J. Kaiser Family Foundation (Dec. 2017). See also Chapter 10.

Funding restrictions on immigrants' access to health care are often part of a broader package of immigration-related initiatives limiting immigrants' access to public services as a means of discouraging illegal immigration. Despite evidence to the contrary, this perceived link between benefits and illegal immigration persists in popular culture, negatively impacting the willingness of some providers to treat immigrants. See Brietta R. Clark, The Immigrant Health Care Narrative and What It Tells Us About the U.S. Health Care System, 17 Annals of Health Law 229 (2008). Such restrictions have also contributed to a climate of fear that makes some immigrants less willing to seek care, regardless of their status. See Wendy E. Parmet & Elisabeth Ryan, New Dangers for Immigrants and the Health Care System, Health Aff. Blog (Apr. 20, 2018).

Evidence of the chilling effect of benefits restrictions has long been available. But concerns about the health implications of this effect have increased in light of actions by the Trump administration to further restrict immigrants' use of public benefits under the "public charge" test. Some background: The Immigration and Nationality Act requires some categories of non-citizens seeking a visa or change in status to demonstrate they are not likely to become a public charge—that is, not likely to become dependent on government for cash assistance or long-term care. 8 U.S.C.A. § 1182(a)(4). Certain groups, such as asylees and refugees, are excluded from this public charge test. Under longstanding policy, health benefits, such as Medicaid and CHIP, have not been considered in the public charge test. This is because such support has been viewed as helping people stay healthy and productive.

In 2019, however, the Trump administration issued a rule that would allow such benefits to be considered in making a public charge determination. Many predicted that this change would likely discourage qualified immigrants from seeking Medicaid or CHIP benefits for themselves or their children out of fear that doing so would make them vulnerable to deportation, and these predictions seem to have been realized. Indeed, the chilling effect may have occurred even before the rule was finalized, as early as the beginning of President Trump's term when he signaled his intent to define public charge more broadly. According to U.S. Census data from 2016–2019, there was significant disenrollment by eligible immigrants from Medicaid, as well as from marketplace programs that were not even subject to the public charge rule. Randy Capps et al., Anticipated "Chilling Effects" of the Public-Charge Rule Are Real: Census Data Reflect Steep Decline in Benefits Use by Immigrant Families, Migration Policy Institute (Dec. 2020), at Migration Policy.org. See also Carol L. Galletly et al., Assessment of COVID-19-Related Immigration Concerns Among Latinx Immigrants in the US, JAMA Network Open (Jul. 19, 2021), describing the results of a survey of 336 adult Latinx immigrants in the U.S. The survey showed that 27 percent of the participants believed that hospital emergency departments provided the only source for COVID-19-related testing or treatment for uninsured immigrants, 32 percent agreed that using public COVID-19-related testing and treatment services could jeopardize an individual's immigration prospects, and 29 and 34 percent, respectively, would not identify an undocumented household member or coworker during contact tracing. The Trump rule was stayed temporarily by litigation, and in March 2021, the Biden administration rescinded the rule. 86 Fed. Reg. 14221 (Mar. 15, 2021). See also Chapter 10, Section III.A.3.

Finally, lack of health insurance has also been linked to the practice of medical repatriation, which occurs when a hospital sends critically injured or ill immigrant patients back to their native country without their consent. In these cases, hospitals sometimes also fail to ensure that the patient is being properly discharged to a facility that can appropriately meet the patient's post-discharge medical needs. See Center for Social Justice at Seton Hall Law School and the Health Justice Program at New York Lawyers for the Public Interest Joint Project Report, Discharge, Deportation, and Dangerous Journeys: A Study on the Practice of Medical Repatriation (2012).

B. SEX OR GENDER

The last few decades have brought increased attention to gender-based disparities in health care, with a particular focus on the insurance and treatment barriers experienced by women and transgender individuals. Title VII and Section 1557 are the main federal statutes helping to combat sex discrimination in health care, and courts and regulators have been engaged in disputes about the scope of this protection. These disputes have centered on two themes.

The first theme involves the definition of sex discrimination under the federal laws applicable to health care. Important questions that have been confronting courts include: Does a prohibition of sex discrimination include discrimination on the basis of gender identity or sexual orientation? What kind of activity does antidiscrimination law prohibit (or require) in health care? When does the refusal to provide or pay for care that is sex-linked or has a disparate impact on a particular gender constitute sex discrimination?

The second theme involves the scope of available defenses or exceptions. Religious entities, for example, have expressed concerns that antidiscrimination law may be interpreted to require health care treatment or coverage that is inconsistent with their religious mission or beliefs. This issue is especially prominent in cases involving reproductive or gender-affirming health care—insurance exclusions or denials of care are frequently characterized as an exercise of religious liberty that should be legally protected. Such conflicts raise important questions about how religious objections should be balanced against the health and equity interests advanced by nondiscrimination protections.

Both of these themes are explored in the cases and notes below.

ERICKSON V. THE BARTELL DRUG COMPANY

United States District Court, Washington, 2001.
141 F. Supp. 2d 1266.

LASNIK, DISTRICT JUDGE.

The parties' cross-motions for summary judgment in this case raise an issue of first impression[:] whether the selective exclusion of prescription contraceptives from defendant's generally comprehensive prescription plan constitutes discrimination on the basis of sex. In particular, plaintiffs assert that Bartell's decision not to cover prescription contraceptives such as birth control pills, Norplant, Depo-Provera, intra-uterine devices, and diaphragms under its Prescription Benefit Plan for non-union employees violates Title VII, 42 U.S.C. § 2000e *et seq.,* as amended by the Pregnancy Discrimination Act, 42 U.S.C. § 2000e(k).

A. APPLICATION OF TITLE VII

Title VII makes it unlawful for an employer "to fail or refuse to hire or to discharge any individual, or otherwise to discriminate against any individual with respect to his compensation, terms, conditions, or privileges of employment, because of such individual's race, color, religion, sex, or national origin." 42 U.S.C. § 2000e–2(a)(1). Unfortunately, the legislative history of the Civil Rights Act of 1964, of which Title VII is a part, is not particularly helpful in determining what Congress had in mind when it added protection from discrimination based on sex. . . .

. . . What is clear from the law itself, its legislative history, and Congress' subsequent actions, is that the goal of Title VII was to end years of discrimination in employment and to place all men and women, regardless of race, color, religion, or national origin, on equal footing in how they were treated in the workforce.

In 1978, Congress had the opportunity to expound on its view of sex discrimination by amending Title VII to make clear that discrimination because of "pregnancy, childbirth, or related medical conditions" is discrimination on the basis of sex. 42 U.S.C. § 2000e(k). The amendment, known as the Pregnancy Discrimination Act ("PDA"), was not meant to alter the contours of Title VII: rather, Congress intended to correct what it felt was an erroneous interpretation of Title VII by the United States Supreme Court in *General Elec Co. v. Gilbert,* 429 U.S. 125, 50 L. Ed. 2d 343, 97 S. Ct. 401 (1976). In Gilbert, the Supreme Court held that an otherwise comprehensive short-term disability policy that excluded pregnancy-related disabilities from coverage did not discriminate on the basis of sex. The Gilbert majority based its decision on two findings: (a) pregnancy discrimination does not adversely impact all women and therefore is not the same thing as gender discrimination; and (b) disability insurance which covers the same illnesses and conditions for both men and women is equal coverage. To the Gilbert majority, the fact that pregnancy-related disabilities were an uncovered risk unique to women did not destroy the facial parity of the coverage. The dissenting justices, Justice Brennan, Justice Marshall, and Justice Stevens, took issue with these findings, arguing that: (a) women, as the only sex at risk for pregnancy, were being subjected to unlawful discrimination; and (b) in determining whether an employment policy treats the sexes equally, the court must look at the comprehensiveness of the coverage provided to each sex. . . .

The language of the PDA was chosen in response to the factual situation presented in Gilbert, namely a case of overt discrimination toward pregnant employees. Not surprisingly, the amendment makes no reference whatsoever to prescription contraceptives. Of critical importance to this case, however, is the fact that, in enacting the PDA, Congress embraced the dissent's broader interpretation of Title VII which not only recognized that there are sex-based differences between men and women employees, but also required employers to provide women-only benefits or otherwise incur additional expenses on behalf of women in order to treat the sexes the same. . . .

Although this litigation involves an exclusion for prescription contraceptives rather than an exclusion for pregnancy-related disability costs, the legal principles established by Gilbert and its legislative reversal govern the outcome of this case. An employer has chosen to offer an employment benefit which excludes from its scope of coverage services which are available only to women. [T]he intent of Congress in enacting the PDA, even if not the exact language used in the amendment, shows that mere facial parity of coverage does not excuse or justify an exclusion which carves out benefits that are uniquely designed for women.

The fact that equality under Title VII is measured by evaluating the relative comprehensiveness of coverage offered to the sexes has been accepted and amplified by the Supreme Court. . . .

The other tenet reaffirmed by the PDA (*i.e.*, that discrimination based on any sex-based characteristic is sex discrimination) has also been considered by the courts. The Supreme Court has found that classifying employees on the basis of their childbearing capacity, regardless of whether they are, in fact, pregnant, is sex-based discrimination. *International Union v. Johnson Controls, Inc.*, 499 U.S. 187 (1991). The court's analysis turned primarily on Title VII's prohibition on sex-based classifications, using the PDA merely to bolster a conclusion that had already been reached. To the extent that a woman's ability to get pregnant may not fall within the literal language of the PDA, the court was not overly concerned. Rather, the court focused on the fact that disparate treatment based on unique, sex-based characteristics, such as the capacity to bear children, is sex discrimination prohibited by Title VII.

[T]he Court finds that Bartell's exclusion of prescription contraception from its prescription plan is inconsistent with the requirements of federal law. The PDA is not a begrudging recognition of a limited grant of rights to a strictly defined group of women who happen to be pregnant. Read in the context of Title VII as a whole, it is a broad acknowledgment of the intent of Congress to outlaw any and all discrimination against any and all women in the terms and conditions of their employment, including the benefits an employer provides to its employees. Male and female employees have different, sex-based disability and healthcare needs, and the law is no longer blind to the fact that only women can get pregnant, bear children, or use prescription contraception. The special or increased healthcare needs associated with a woman's unique sex-based characteristics must be met to the same extent, and on the same terms, as other healthcare needs. Even if one were to assume that Bartell's prescription plan was not the result of intentional discrimination,[7] the exclusion of women-only benefits from a generally comprehensive prescription plan is sex discrimination under Title VII.

Title VII does not require employers to offer any particular type or category of benefit. However, when an employer decides to offer a prescription plan covering everything except a few specifically excluded drugs and devices, it has a legal obligation to make sure that the resulting plan does not discriminate based on sex-based characteristics and that it provides equally comprehensive coverage for both sexes. . . .

B. SPECIFIC ARGUMENTS RAISED BY DEFENDANT-EMPLOYER

Bartell argues that opting not to provide coverage for prescription contraceptive devices is not a violation of Title VII because: (1) treating contraceptives differently from other prescription drugs is reasonable in that contraceptives are voluntary, preventative, do not treat or prevent an illness or disease, and are not truly a "healthcare" issue; (2) control of one's fertility is not "pregnancy, childbirth, or related medical conditions" as those terms are used in the PDA; (3) employers must be permitted to control the costs of employment benefits by limiting the scope of coverage; (4) the exclusion of all "family planning" drugs and devices is facially neutral; (5) in the thirty-seven years Title VII has been on the books, no court has found that excluding contraceptives constitutes sex

---

[7]   There is no evidence or indication that Bartell's coverage decisions were intended to hinder women in their ability to participate in the workforce or to deprive them of equal treatment in employment or benefits. The most reasonable explanation for the current state of affairs is that the exclusion of women-only benefits is merely an unquestioned holdover from a time when employment-related benefits were doled out less equitably than they are today. The lack of evidence of bad faith or malice toward women does not affect the validity of plaintiffs' Title VII claim. Where a benefit plan is discriminatory on its face, no inquiry into subjective intent is necessary.

discrimination; and (6) this issue should be determined by the legislature, rather than the courts. Each of these arguments is considered in turn.

(1)   Contraceptives as a health care need

An underlying theme in Bartell's argument is that a woman's ability to control her fertility differs from the type of illness and disease normally treated with prescription drugs in such significant respects that it is permissible to treat prescription contraceptives differently than all other prescription medicines. The evidence submitted by plaintiffs shows, however, that the availability of affordable and effective contraceptives is of great importance to the health of women and children because it can help to prevent a litany of physical, emotional, economic, and social consequences. . . .

Unintended pregnancies, the condition which prescription contraceptives are designed to prevent, are shockingly common in the United States and carry enormous costs and health consequences for the mother, the child, and society as a whole. Over half of all pregnancies in this country are unintended. A woman with an unintended pregnancy is less likely to seek prenatal care, more likely to engage in unhealthy activities, more likely to have an abortion, and more likely to deliver a low birthweight, ill, or unwanted baby. Unintended pregnancies impose significant financial burdens on the parents in the best of circumstances. If the pregnancy results in a distressed newborn, the costs increase by tens of thousands of dollars. In addition, the adverse economic and social consequences of unintended pregnancies fall most harshly on women and interfere with their choice to participate fully and equally in the "marketplace and the world of ideas." *Stanton v. Stanton,* 421 U.S. 7 (1975). See also *Planned Parenthood v. Casey,* 505 U.S. 833, 856 (1992) ("The ability of women to participate equally in the economic and social life of the nation has been facilitated by their ability to control their reproductive lives.").

. . . Although there are many factors which help explain the unusually high rate of unintended pregnancies in the United States, an important cause is the failure to use effective forms of birth control. [ ] Insurance policies and employee benefit plans which exclude coverage for effective forms of contraception contribute to the failure of at-risk women to seek a physician's assistance in avoiding unwanted pregnancies. [ ]

The fact that prescription contraceptives are preventative appears to be an irrelevant distinction in this case: Bartell covers a number of preventative drugs under its plan. The fact that pregnancy is a "natural" state and is not considered a disease or illness is also a distinction without a difference. Being pregnant, though natural, is not a state that is desired by all women or at all points in a woman's life. Prescription contraceptives, like all other preventative drugs, help the recipient avoid unwanted physical changes. . . .

(2) Pregnancy Discrimination Act

[I]t is clear that in 1978 Congress had no specific intent regarding coverage for prescription contraceptives. The relevant issue, however, is whether the decision to exclude drugs made for women from a generally comprehensive prescription plan is sex discrimination under Title VII, with or without the clarification provided by the PDA. The Court finds that, regardless of whether the prevention of pregnancy falls within the phrase "pregnancy, childbirth, or related medical conditions," Congress' decisive overruling of [*Gilbert*] evidences an interpretation of Title VII which necessarily precludes the choices Bartell has made in this case.

(3) Business Decision to Control Costs

Bartell also suggests that it should be permitted to limit the scope of its employee benefit programs in order to control costs. Cost is not, however, a defense to allegations of discrimination under Title VII. [ ]While it is undoubtedly true that employers may cut benefits, raise deductibles, or otherwise alter coverage options to comply with budgetary constraints, the method by which the employer seeks to curb costs must not be discriminatory. Bartell offers its employees an admittedly generous package of healthcare benefits [ ]. It cannot, however, penalize female employees in an effort to keep its benefit costs low. The cost savings Bartell realizes by excluding prescription contraceptives from its healthcare plans are being directly borne by only one sex in violation of Title VII. Although Bartell is permitted, under the law, to use non-discriminatory cuts in benefits to control costs, it cannot balance its benefit books at the expense of its female employees.

(4) Neutrality of Exclusions

Prescription contraceptives are not the only drugs or devices excluded from coverage under Bartell's benefit plan. Bartell argues that it has chosen to exclude from coverage all drugs for "family planning," and that this exclusion is neutral and non-discriminatory. There is no "family planning" exclusion in the benefit plan, however, and the contours of such a theoretical exclusion are not clear. On the list of excluded drugs and devices, contraceptive devices and infertility drugs are the two categories which might be considered "family planning" measures. Contrary to defendant's explanation, there appear to be some drugs which fall under the "family planning" rubric which are covered by the plan. Prenatal vitamins, for example, are frequently prescribed in anticipation of a woman becoming pregnant and are expressly covered under the plan.

* * *

Although the Court's decision is a matter of first impression for the judiciary, it is not the first tribunal to consider the lawfulness of a contraception exclusion. On December 14, 2000, the EEOC made a finding of reasonable cause on the same issue which is entitled to some deference. Although the Commission's analysis focused primarily on the PDA, it [came] to the same conclusion reached by this Court.

(6) Legislative Issue

Although this litigation involves politically charged issues with far-reaching social consequences, the parties' dispute turns on the interpretation of an existing federal statute.... The normal rules of statutory construction, not the give and take of a legislative body, will guide this determination. Contrary to defendant's suggestion, it is the role of the judiciary, not the legislature, to interpret existing laws and determine whether they apply to a particular set of facts. While it is interesting to note that Congress and some state legislatures are considering proposals to require insurance plans to cover prescription contraceptives, that fact does not alter this Court's constitutional role in interpreting Congress' legislative enactments in order to resolve private disputes.

C. CONCLUSION

... For all of the foregoing reasons, the Court finds that Bartell's prescription drug plan discriminates against Bartell's female employees by providing less complete coverage than that offered to male employees.

NOTES AND QUESTIONS

1. *Why Title VII Is Still Relevant After Section 1557.* Title VII was the earliest federal antidiscrimination statute applicable to sex discrimination in health care, though it was limited to employment-based benefit plans. Despite the broader health care discrimination provision in Section 1557, Title VII remains important for a couple of reasons. First, Title VII may serve as a crucial gap filler for a subset of employees whose health plans are not subject to Section 1557. Although the 2016 Rule interpreted Section 1557's nondiscrimination provision as applying broadly to *all operations* of an entity principally engaged in the provision of health insurance, 81 Fed. Reg. at 31467 (formerly codified at 45 C.F.R. s 92.4), the 2020 Rule narrowed 1557's application to cover *only the parts of an insurer's operations that receive federal funding.* As HHS explained: "To the extent that employer-sponsored group health plans do not receive Federal financial assistance . . . they would not be covered entities." 85 Fed. Reg. at 37173. Second, although Section 1557 expressly incorporates sex by reference using Title IX, which governs educational settings, regulators and courts frequently acknowledge the relevance of Title VII jurisprudence for defining the contours of sex discrimination in the context of health care.

2. *Discrimination "Because of Sex." Erickson* explains the evolution of Title VII to include the Pregnancy Discrimination Act, as well as Congress's express endorsement of the *Gilbert* dissent's approach to defining sex discrimination. Essentially, the court notes that "an exclusion which carves out benefits that are uniquely designed for women" is clearly sex-linked and thus a form of disparate treatment on the basis of sex. The court emphasized the importance of looking beyond facial parity to determine relative comprehensiveness of coverage, but such an inquiry requires identifying an appropriate benchmark for purposes of comparison. In *Erikson*, the court was unconvinced by the employer's attempt to characterize the contraception exclusion as one that was consistent with a gender-neutral policy. But in a different case, the employer fared better. See, e.g., In re Union Pacific Railroad Employment Practices Litigation, 479 F.3d 936 (8th Cir. 2007) (holding that an employer health plan that excluded contraception when used for purposes of contraception, but not for non-contraceptive medically necessary purposes, did not violate Title VII, because it excluded coverage of all contraception for men and women, both surgical and prescription).

3. *Discrimination "Because of Pregnancy, Childbirth, or Related Medical Conditions."* There has been some debate about what exactly is required by the PDA. Courts have consistently held that the PDA does not create a substantive health care mandate; rather, it clarifies the type of classifications that establish a prima facie case of sex discrimination for purposes of Title VII. See, e.g., Krauel v. Iowa Methodist Medical Center, 95 F.3d 674 (8th Cir. 1996) (noting that the PDA only requires employers to treat pregnancy, childbirth, or related medical conditions in a "neutral way"). What if a challenged exclusion from an otherwise comprehensive insurance policy is not "uniquely" sex-linked, but is nonetheless related to pregnancy and thus has a disparate impact on women, or is otherwise motivated by gender-based assumptions?

A few courts have confronted this question in the context of infertility treatment. Infertility causes and treatments tend to be characterized as female-specific or male-specific, or they may involve a combination of both. For this reason, many employers with blanket exclusions for infertility treatment have successfully characterized these exclusions as gender neutral when challenged under Title VII and the PDA. In *Krauel*, the Eighth Circuit rejected such a challenge even though plaintiffs offered evidence that the employer believed infertility benefits were used primarily, if not solely, by women, and that the employer had concerns about the costs attributable to a resulting pregnancy. The court's treatment of the exclusion as gender neutral meant the burden never shifted to the employer to justify the exclusion. Id.

The *Krauel* approach has been criticized in light of the individual and structural gender discrimination that has long shaped discriminatory benefit design by employers and insurers. With regard specifically to infertility treatment, there is evidence that such exclusions may disproportionately harm women by resulting in the implantation of more embryos at one time and thus increasing the health risk of pregnancy. See Brietta R. Clark, Erickson v.

Bartell Drug Co.: A Roadmap for Gender Equality in Reproductive Health Care or an Empty Promise? 23 Law & Inequality 299 (2005).

Based on the reasoning in *Erikson,* do you think the court would have found the exclusion of prescription contraception to be sex-linked if the exclusion affected both men and women? Consider that reversible prescription contraception may soon be available for men, too. NIH to Evaluate Effectiveness of Male Contraceptive Skin Gel, National Institutes of Health, Nov. 28, 2018, https://www.nih.gov/news-events/news-releases/nih-evaluate-effectiveness-male-contraceptive-skin-gel. How, if at all, should this development impact our understanding of the gender equity implications of prescription contraception exclusions? As described more fully in Note 5 below, this development may not impact most coverage because currently the ACA's preventive health mandate includes prescription contraception.

4.   *Private Disparate Impact Claims: Title VII vs. Section 1557.* Although Title VII allows private causes of action based on disparate impact, Section 1557 may not. Some courts have already held that Section 1557 does not permit private disparate impact claims, based on federal court decisions extending *Sandoval's* limit on private disparate impact claims under Title VI to Title IX challenges. See Briscoe v. Health Care Svc. Corp., 281 F. Supp. 3d 725, 738–739 (2017); York v. Wellmark Inc., 2017 WL 11261026, slip op. at 17–18.

5.   *Gender Equity and ACA Insurance Mandates.* Through Title VII and the PDA, Congress made clear that employers could not treat medical costs associated with pregnancy or childbirth differently from other medical costs covered by their health insurance plans. Regulations have elaborated on the contours of Title VII as well. For example, employers must treat maternity-related medical conditions the same as other medical conditions with respect to terms of reimbursement (including payment maximums, deductibles, copayments, coinsurance, and out-of-pocket maximums); preexisting condition limitations; extension of benefits following termination of employment; and limitations on freedom of choice. See 29 C.F.R. App. to Pt. 1604, Questions 25–29. But Title VII only applies to employment-based policies. Before the ACA, insurance companies in the individual markets were able to treat women differently from men, for example, by charging them higher rates and excluding woman-specific benefits—that is, unless there were state laws prohibiting this discrimination.

The ACA has been a crucial tool for eradicating these barriers—not only because of its formal antidiscrimination prohibition in Section 1557, but also because of its many other substantive insurance regulations: prohibitions on risk-rating based on sex; prohibitions on insurers from denying coverage or benefits based on preexisting conditions or health factors, such as a prior caesarian section or a history of domestic violence; and its mandate that preventive health care be covered without cost-sharing.

In defining the scope of services to be included in this preventive mandate, the relevant regulatory agencies adopted guidelines from the Health Resources

Services Administration, based on recommendations by the independent Institute of Medicine (IOM). The IOM recommended that preventive services include all forms of contraception approved by the FDA, which meant that most health insurance policies would cover hormonal methods of contraception (i.e., birth control pills and post-intercourse emergency contraception like Plan B and ella), as well as intrauterine devices (IUDs), sterilization, and patient education and counseling. See IOM, Clinical Preventive Services for Women: Closing the Gaps (National Academies Press 2011). In adopting these recommendations, federal regulators acknowledged the gender disparities that existed in the insurance market prior to the ACA and noted that "[t]he contraceptive coverage requirement is . . . designed to serve . . . compelling public health and gender equity goals. . . ." Group Health Plans and Health Insurance Issuers Relating to Coverage of Preventive Services Under the Patient Protection and Affordable Care Act, 77 Fed. Reg. 8725, 8727–8729 (Feb. 15, 2012). See Chapter 9 for more about ACA insurance regulations and benefit mandates generally.

6.   *Unequal Health Care Treatment.* There is evidence that, in addition to insurance discrimination, women experience discrimination in medical treatment. For example, studies in the U.S. have demonstrated that women tend to receive less intensive treatment for acute myocardial infarction, have an increased chance of misdiagnosis of stroke, and suffer higher rates of mortality from sepsis than men. See Viola Vaccarino et al., Sex and Racial Differences in the Management of Acute Myocardial Infarction, 1994–2002, 353 NEJM 671 (2005); David E. Newman-Toker et al., Missed Diagnosis of Stroke in the Emergency Department: A Cross-Sectional Analysis of a Large Population-Based Sample, 1 Diagnosis 155 (2014); Anthony P. Pietropaoli et al., Gender Differences in Mortality in Patients with Severe Sepsis and Septic Shock, 7 Gender Med. 422 (2010). Women are also more likely to be undertreated for, or inappropriately diagnosed and treated for, pain as compared to men. See Diane E. Hoffman and Anita J. Tarzian, The Girl Who Cried Pain: A Bias Against Women in the Treatment of Pain, 29 J. L. Med. & Ethics 13 (2001).

As with insurance, treatment discrimination has also been linked to pregnancy and reproductive capacity. For example, pregnant patients have been excluded from drug treatment programs. See Rebecca Stone, Pregnant Women and Substance Use: Fear, Stigma and Barriers to Care, 3 Health and Justice (2015). And the exclusion of pregnant women from early COVID-19 vaccine trials led to incomplete and conflicting guidance among providers advising pregnant patients about whether to get the vaccine. See Rita Rubin, Pregnant People's Paradox—Excluded from Vaccine Trials Despite Having a Higher Risk of COVID-19 Complications, 325 JAMA 1027 (2021). Pregnancy— more specifically, concern about potential fetal health risk—has also been used to override pregnant patients' autonomy rights and force them to undergo unwanted medical interventions, such as cesarean sections. See Chapter 16,

Section VI, discussing government and medical control of decision-making during pregnancy, including pregnancy exclusions in advanced directives. For more on the regulation of pregnancy and reproduction generally, see Chapter 16. While growing attention is being paid to the equity and health harms of these disparate practices, antidiscrimination law has yet to be used effectively to address them.

7. *Transgender Pregnancy.* Pregnancy-based discrimination is typically understood as a form of discrimination against women, as reflected in the use of terms like "maternal health care." In addition, cis-gender women—women whose gender identity conforms to their female sex assignment at birth—seem to be the primary focus of much research on pregnancy care. Nonetheless, there is growing recognition of the fact that people giving birth may not necessarily identify as female. See Margaret Besse et al., Experiences with Achieving Pregnancy and Giving Birth Among Transgender Men: A Narrative Literature Review, 93 Yale J. Biology & Med. 517–528 (2020) (describing research revealing that "transgender men face substantial obstacles to achieving pregnancy and significant challenges during pregnancy and birth, which are informed by institutionalized cisnormativity embedded within medical norms and practices"). The next case, *Flack v. Wisconsin Department of Health Services*, and the following notes more fully explore the implication of sex discrimination prohibitions for transgender individuals.

8. *Abortion Exceptionalism.* Do denials of abortion coverage or care constitute discrimination on the basis of sex? Like pregnancy, abortion has been traditionally understood as uniquely affecting women. Moreover, the gender equity and health effects of unwanted pregnancy that result from denying access to contraception, as described in *Erickson*, would be the same in the case of barriers to abortion. Indeed, a number of religious organizations have expressed concern that Section 1557's new sex discrimination prohibition would be interpreted to require abortion coverage or provision, and some have brought preemptive legal challenges. See Religious Sisters of Mercy v. Azar, 513 F. Supp. 3d 1113 (D.N.D. 2021).

While this may seem like a logical application of sex discrimination jurisprudence, numerous federal laws create special exceptions or protections for those opposed to covering or providing abortion, in light of the profound ethical issues raised by the termination of life and the deep ideological divides over abortion access. For example, the PDA expressly provides that employers are not required to pay for abortion, except when necessary to save the woman's life or when medical complications arise from an abortion. Federal funding cannot be used to pay for abortions in most instances—whether through Medicaid, other family funding, or federal subsidies for private insurance under the ACA. And HHS, under both Democratic and Republican administrations, has acknowledged extensive federal conscience protections—some specific to abortion, some grounded in religious liberty—that allow insurers to exclude abortion coverage and allow providers to refuse to perform abortions.

To date, Section 1557 has not been used to require regulated entities to provide or cover abortions, and courts agree this is unlikely. Religious Sisters of Mercy v. Azar, supra. at 1136 ("As interpreted today, Section 1557 does not proscribe refusal to perform or insure abortions."). Indeed, abortion jurisprudence has been criticized for its failure to acknowledge the role that gender discrimination and sex stereotyping continue to play in certain kinds of abortion regulation. Reva B. Siegel, The New Politics of Abortion: An Equality Analysis of Woman-Protective Abortion Restriction, 2007 U. Ill. L. Rev. 991. For further discussion of the legal and ethical issues involved in abortion regulation, see Chapter 16.

FLACK V. WIS. DEPT. OF HEALTH SERVS.

United States District Court, W.D. Wisconsin, 2018.
328 F. Supp. 3d 931.

WILLIAM M. CONLEY, DISTRICT JUDGE.

As a group, transgender individuals have been subjected to harassment and discrimination in virtually every aspect of their lives, including in housing, employment, education, and health care. Their own families, acquaintances and larger communities can be sources of harassment. For some transgender individuals, though certainly not all, the dissonance between their gender identity and their natally assigned sex can manifest itself in the form of "gender dysphoria," a serious medical condition recognized by both sides' experts and the larger medical community as a whole. [Wisconsin Medicaid categorically denies coverage for medically prescribed gender-affirming care. Plaintiffs Cody Flack and Sara Ann Makenzie both have long-term gender dysphoria and have filed suit challenging this exclusion under the Affordable Care Act. They seek to preliminarily enjoin defendants from enforcing the exclusion against their requests for insurance coverage.]

UNDISPUTED FACTS

A. Gender Dysphoria

Every person has a "gender identity." For most people, their gender identity matches the natal sex assigned at birth. For transgender individuals, however, that is not true: their gender identity differs from the sex they were assigned at birth. Specifically, a transgender woman's birth-assigned sex is male, but she has a female gender identity; a transgender man's birth-assigned sex is female, but he has a male gender identity.

Gender dysphoria is a serious medical condition, which if left untreated or inadequately treated can cause adverse symptoms.

Gender dysphoria refers to the distress that may accompany the incongruence between one's experienced or expressed gender and one's assigned gender. Although not all individuals will experience distress as a result of such incongruence, many are distressed if the desired physical interventions by means of hormones and/or surgery are not available. The current term is more descriptive than the previous DSM-IV term *gender identity disorder* and focuses on dysphoria as the clinical problem, not identity per se.

(DSM-5 [ ]).[3] It is worth emphasizing that not every transgender person has gender dysphoria. Adults with gender dysphoria "often" have "a desire to be rid of primary and/or secondary sex characteristics and/or a strong desire to acquire some primary and/or secondary sex characteristics of the other gender." [ ] Untreated, gender dysphoria can result in psychological distress: "preoccupation with cross-gender wishes often interferes with daily activities." [ ] Impairment—such as the development of substance abuse, anxiety and depression—is also a possible "consequence of gender dysphoria." [ ] Finally, gender dysphoria "is associated with high levels of stigmatization, discrimination, and victimization, leading to negative self-concept, increased rates of mental disorder comorbidity, school dropout, and economic marginalization, including unemployment, with attendant social and mental health risks. . . ." [ ]

Gender dysphoria can be alleviated through living consistently with one's gender identity, including being treated by others accordingly. Likewise, "appropriate individualized medical care as part of their gender transitions" can mitigate or prevent symptoms of gender dysphoria. [ ] In 2011, the World Professional Association of Transgender Health published the seventh version of *Standards of Care for the Health of Transsexual, Transgender, and Gender Nonconforming People* (the "WPATH Standards of Care"), which identifies psychotherapy, hormone therapy and various surgical procedures as treatment possibilities for gender dysphoria. . . .

B. Wisconsin Medicaid

. . . The Wisconsin Department of Health Services ("DHS") is the state agency charged with administering the Wisconsin Medicaid Program consistent with state and federal requirements. . . Wisconsin Medicaid provides coverage for "[p]hysician services," including "any medically necessary diagnostic, preventative, therapeutic, rehabilitative or palliative services . . . within the scope of the practice of medicine and surgery" that are "in conformity with generally accepted good medical practice" and provided by a physician or under one's direct supervision, unless otherwise excluded. [ ] Wisconsin Medicaid has a budget of approximately $9.7 billion to provide for its roughly 1.2 million enrollees. Approximately 5,000 of those enrollees are transgender, and some subset of this population suffers from gender dysphoria.

---

[3] DSM-5 is the fifth edition of the American Psychiatric Association's *Diagnostic and Statistical Manual of Mental Disorders.*

. . . Wisconsin Medicaid is [also] governed by [state law]. Included in the governing regulations is the "Challenged Exclusion," [Wis. Admin. Code] § 107.03(23)–(24), at issue in this case. [It] provides that "The following services are not covered . . . (23) Drugs, including hormone therapy, associated with transsexual surgery or medically unnecessary alteration of sexual anatomy or characteristics; [and] (24) Transsexual surgery." The Challenged Exclusion was adopted in 1996.[7] . . .

C. Plaintiffs' Medical Needs

1. Cody Flack

Cody Flack is an adult resident of Green Bay who suffers from gender dysphoria and identifies as male. He is unable to work because of cerebral palsy and other disabilities for which he receives Supplemental Security Income and Wisconsin Medicaid. At birth, Cody was assigned the sex of female and subsequently raised as a girl. He became aware of his male gender identity when he was about four or five years old. As a teenager, Cody began his gender transition by seeing a gender therapist, adopting the traditionally male name Cody, and presenting as a man. However, he was unable to complete his transition for several years because he lacked financial resources, was without emotional support, and feared isolation.

After relocating to Wisconsin in 2012, Cody found the wherewithal to resume his gender transition as he felt his gender identity was more supported, and he increasingly lived and presented as a man. . . . He also legally changed his name to Cody Jason Flack to align with his male gender identity and obtained a Wisconsin state identification card, identifying him as male. His Medicaid enrollment now matches his gender identity as well.

. . . . Since 2015, Cody has been seeing psychotherapist Daniel Bergman for his gender dysphoria and other mental health conditions. Since August 2016, Cody has also been receiving testosterone hormone therapy under the supervision of an endocrinologist [causing development of] facial and body hair, a more masculine appearance, and a deeper voice. In October 2016, Cody had his uterus, fallopian tubes, ovaries and cervix removed through a hysterectomy with bilateral salpingo-oophorectomy. This procedure was paid for by Wisconsin Medicaid to treat dysmenhorrhea (lower abdominal or pelvic pain during menstruation) and premenstrual dysphoric disorder (a severe form of premenstrual syndrome). . . .

Despite these changes, Cody still has female-appearing breasts. Plaintiffs and their experts, as well as Cody's treating physicians, contend this causes him severe gender dysphoria. . . . At minimum, it appears undisputed that Cody's breasts cause him significant, personal distress, as they are a marker of the female sex often contributing to his being

---

[7]   As its terms suggest, if inartfully, defendants contend that the Challenged Exclusion does not "prohibit[ ] all transition-related medical treatments, as hormone therapy is still provided to Flack and Makenzie for their gender dysphoria." [ ]

perceived as female. Cody is particularly ashamed of his breasts when in public and routinely avoids social situations as a result. In an effort to conceal his breasts, Cody has engaged in "binding," which flattens or reduces their appearance, but has difficulty binding his breasts himself due to his disabilities and finds the technique extremely painful. Binding has caused him sores, skin irritation and respiratory distress.

Since early 2017, therefore, Cody has sought a double mastectomy and male chest reconstruction. He consulted with . . . a plastic surgeon [and provided him] with letters of support from his primary care physician, his therapist, his endocrinologist, and the surgeon who performed his hysterectomy. [The letters] detailed that Cody has gender dysphoria, and he met the criteria for surgery. . . .

On August 2, 2017, DHS denied [the] prior authorization request [for the surgery] without reviewing the medical necessity of his requested surgery as "a non-covered service" and a "not covered benefit" based on the Challenged Exclusion. [On] appeal, DHS noted that "gender dysphoria . . . is an accepted medical indication for the surgical treatment requested." [ ] Nevertheless, an administrative law judge dismissed the appeal [based on the statutory exclusion]. . . .

2. Sara Ann Makenzie

Sara Ann Makenzie is an adult . . . and lifelong resident of Wisconsin. She also suffers from gender dysphoria after being assigned the male sex at birth and subsequently raised as a boy. [Sara Ann has] been found to be disabled and . . . has been enrolled in Wisconsin Medicaid for many years.

Despite being assigned the male sex at birth, Sara Ann first identified as female as a child, and she has been diagnosed with gender dysphoria for most of her life. She has legally changed her name to Sara Ann Makenzie, uses feminine pronouns, and wears women's clothing to conform with her female gender identity. Her birth certificate, passport, driver's license and Medicaid enrollment all reflect her name and female identity.

[Sara Ann] has been on hormone therapy since 2013, which has helped lessen her gender dysphoria. In 2014, she consulted with . . . her then primary care physician, about genital reconstruction surgery. . . .

Sara Ann Makenzie reports great distress upon seeing her male-appearing genitalia, which negatively affects her occupational functioning, sexuality and social life. She finds showering or seeing her body in a mirror painful; she lives in constant fear that someone will be able to see her male genitals through her clothing; and she is concerned that she may be attacked or mistreated by someone who recognizes her as transgender. Accordingly, she tries to minimize the appearance of her genitals by wearing multiple pairs of underwear at a time and engaging in "tucking," which is uncomfortable and very painful. She also does not have sex with her fiancée, which adds to her depression and anxiety. Sara Ann's treating physicians have recommended that she have surgery to create female-appearing external genitalia, specifically a bilateral orchiectomy and vaginoplasty. . . .

[In February 2018, Sara Ann's] primary care physician . . . referred Sara Ann to a plastic surgeon . . . for possible genital reconstruction surgery. Dr. Katherine Gast specializes in treating transgender individuals, and she informed Sara Ann of her eligibility for genital reconstruction after submitting two letters of support from mental health providers. However, she also advised that Wisconsin Medicaid would not pay for the procedure. [Sara Ann] was greatly distressed that Medicaid would not pay for the surgery because she could not afford it [and] has thoughts of removing her genitals on her own and of committing suicide. As a result, plaintiffs contend that her gender dysphoria has worsened.

Her psychotherapist, Jessica Bellard, notes that Sara Ann "continues to report symptoms of anxiety, depression, anger, and distress in response to the stressors of transitioning prior to completing gender reassignment surgery" and that she "has expressed a persistent desire for surgery since our original meeting." [ ] Sara Ann's independent evaluating therapist, Chelsea O'Neal Karcher, opined that "Sara's hope that the surgery will help lessen symptoms of anxiety and depression, increase happiness, help to increase her confidence, and align her body more fully with her identity" were "realistic expectations for the procedure" and that she "has met all the eligibility and readiness criteria outline[d] in the [WPATH Standards of Care]." [ ] Her former primary care physician opined that "genital reconstruction is a *medically necessary* treatment for Ms. Makenzie's gender dysphoria as it would treat the excessive mental distress that she experiences every day. . . ." [ ] . . .

OPINION

Plaintiffs seek a preliminary injunction enjoining defendants from enforcing the Challenged Exclusion against them. As "an extraordinary remedy," [t]he moving party must "mak[e] a threshold showing: (1) that he will suffer irreparable harm absent preliminary injunctive relief during the pendency of his action; (2) inadequate remedies at law exist; and (3) he has a reasonable likelihood of success on the merits." [ ] Once the moving party has done so, the court "determine[s] whether the balance of harm favors the moving party or whether the harm to other parties or the public sufficiently outweighs the movant's interests." [ ]

I.   Irreparable Harm & Inadequate Remedy at Law

While the moving party must show "more than a mere possibility of harm" to establish that it likely will suffer irreparable harm absent injunctive relief, this does not mean that the harm must occur or be certain to occur before the merits can be addressed. [ ] To be irreparable, the harm "cannot be prevented or fully rectified by the final judgment after trial." [ ]

As noted, plaintiffs are being denied coverage for medically necessary treatment that was prescribed by their doctors and meets the prevailing standards of care. They contend that allowing them to obtain their surgeries is necessary to protect their well-being and health because they "are at high risk of worsening mental health, exacerbated gender dysphoria, self-harm and stigma"—"none of which has an adequate remedy at law." [ ]

Importantly, [their] treating doctors agree. [Eds. Note: The Court then recounts much of the evidence presented in the Undisputed Facts and other testimony by treating physicians, respectively, demonstrating that the plaintiffs have a diagnosis of gender dysphoria, that plaintiffs meet the WPATH Standards of Care criteria for reconstructive surgery,* that such surgery is medically necessary, and that denial of surgery will increase the risk of harm.]

Accordingly, these plaintiffs have advanced more than enough evidence to establish that they face a possibility of irreparable harm at this point. [ ] Defendants' principal response to all this evidence is that "there is no proven medical benefit to the procedures for which Plaintiffs seek Medicaid coverage, and so Plaintiffs here will not face irreparable harm absent a preliminary injunction." [ ] [First, Defendants' expert Dr. Lawrence Mayer] opines that "[m]edical and surgical treatments have not been demonstrated to be safe and effective for gender dysphoria." [ ] More specifically, he opines based on a survey of published reports that there is only "minimal" evidence that these treatments are effective, safe and optimal, and further that "[t]here is even less evidence that [medical and surgical interventions] would be cost effective compared to social and psychological interventions." [ ]

Even Dr. Mayer acknowledges, however, that gender dysphoria "is a serious medical condition that deserves to be treated" and that such treatment "must be borne of medical necessity. [ ] He agrees that "reducing or eliminating" the very real distress associated with this condition is the "[o]ptimality consideration[ ]" for treating gender dysphoria.[ ] As outlined above, plaintiffs have the support of their treating physicians—to say nothing of their retained experts—who confirm that the surgeries they seek

---

* The court notes the following WPATH Standards of Care: For male chest reconstruction, the standards of care include: "1. Persistent, well-documented gender dysphoria; 2. Capacity to make a fully informed decision and to consent for treatment; 3. Age of majority in a given country . . .; 4. If significant medical or health concerns are present, they must be reasonably well controlled." For genital reconstructive surgery, patients must meet all the preceding criteria plus: "12 continuous months of hormone therapy as appropriate to the patient's gender goals (unless the patient has a medical contraindication or is otherwise unable or unwilling to take hormones)," and for vaginoplasty, "12 continuous months of living in a gender role that is congruent with their gender identity."

(1) are medically necessary and (2) will reduce their distress and gender dysphoria. Perhaps Dr. Mayer's opinions will prevail on the *general* efficacy of surgical interventions for gender dysphoria, although the apparent endorsement in DSM-5 and by the larger medical community would appear to make this a decidedly uphill battle.[17] Still, Dr. Mayer lays at most the foundation for defendants' general policy, while the only question at this point is whether Cody Flack and Sara Ann Makenzie have a medical need for these surgeries such that denial will be detrimental to *their* health. On the current record, the answer clearly is yes.

Second, Dr. Chester Schmidt opines that "there is an insufficient clinical basis to conclude that either Flack or Makenzie will suffer imminent, irreparable harm if they do not receive gender reassignment surgery prior to the conclusion of this case." [ ] Dr. Schmidt's opinion is based on what he describes as: (1) a lack of current mental status examinations for plaintiffs, creating "an insufficient basis for any clinician to conclude that either Flack or Makenzie faces an imminent risk of suicide or other self-harm"; (2) the insufficiency of plaintiffs' self-reports "to conclude that a serious risk of self-harm exists, let alone that receiving the surgical procedures . . . will reduce or eliminate that risk"; (3) Cody Flack's outpatient notes "do not indicate that he is so destabilized such that a substantial risk of imminent self-harm exists"; and (4) Flack's transition has been ongoing for several years, without any evidence of prior self-harm, indicating no substantial short-term risk of self-harm. [ ] While at least focused on the medical needs of the individual plaintiffs now before the court, Schmidt's opinion fundamentally misses the mark. . . . Plaintiffs were not required to prove "a substantial risk of imminent self-harm," but rather to show a likelihood of irreparable injury. Moreover, his opinion that a clinician could not conclude that these plaintiffs need these surgeries because of missing mental status reports misreads the record since both plaintiffs have opinions from their treatment providers supporting the proposed surgical interventions. Regardless, Dr. Schmidt's 10,000-foot review of the medical record and criticisms of the course of treatment proposed by plaintiffs' doctors, without offering a viable option to relieve their ongoing gender dysphoria, pales in comparison with the informed opinions of plaintiffs' treating physicians. To discount the opinions of plaintiffs' treating physicians as to the need for surgery to relieve plaintiffs' suffering at the preliminary injunction stage on the current, limited record would be tantamount to this court playing doctor.

---

[17] (*See* Am. Psychiatric Assoc. 3 ("[A]ppropriately evaluated transgender and gender variant individuals can benefit greatly from medical and surgical gender transition treatments"); Am. Med. Assoc. 2 ("[M]edical and surgical treatments for gender dysphoria, as determined by shared decision making between the patient and physician, are medically necessary as outlined by generally-accepted standards of medical and surgical practice"); Am. Endocrine Soc'y 3 ("Medical intervention for transgender individuals (including both hormone therapy and medically indicated surgery) is effective, relatively safe (when appropriately monitored), and has been established as the standard of care.").)

Accordingly, plaintiffs have established that they are at risk of irreparable harm, and this factor weighs strongly in favor of injunctive relief. [T]he Seventh Circuit already held in *Whitaker* that serious, ongoing impact on plaintiffs' health "demonstrate[s] that any award would be 'seriously deficient as compared to the harm suffered.' " . . .

II. Reasonable Likelihood of Success

. . . Plaintiffs claim that the Challenged Exclusion violates § 1557 of the ACA by unlawfully discriminating on the basis of sex—being transgender. . . .

There is no dispute that Wisconsin Medicaid is "a health program or activity" that "receiv[es] Federal financial assistance"; nor is there any dispute that Title IX prohibits discrimination "on the basis of sex." Instead, the parties dispute whether plaintiffs' transgender status falls under "sex." Facially, the answer would appear to be "yes," but because the Challenged Exclusion discriminates against coverage for "transsexual surgery," defendants argue that this no longer involves sex discrimination. Even though "sex" would seem to encompass "trans*sex*ual," defendants would distinguish between "gender identity"—what plaintiffs would define as an "internal sense of one's sex," which is innate—from one's "sex"—which is, according to defendants, "assigned at birth, refer[ring] to one's biological status as either male or female, and is associated primarily with physical attributes such as chromosomes, hormone prevalence, and external and internal anatomy," and is "immutable." [ ]

Even accepting defendants' definition of sex, however, the Challenged Exclusion certainly denies coverage for medically necessary surgical procedures based on a patient's *natal* sex, the same "immutable" sex the defendants claim the ACA intends to cover. Moreover, as plaintiffs' expert Dr. Loren Schechter explains, "[w]hen performing gender confirming surgery, surgeons use many of the same procedures that they use to treat other medical conditions." [ ] For example, if a natal female were born without a vagina, she could have surgery to create one, which would be covered by Wisconsin Medicaid if deemed medically necessary.[21] However, a natal male suffering from gender dysphoria would be denied the same medically necessary procedure because of her sex. Likewise, if a natal male were in a car accident and required a phalloplasty, that surgery would be covered if deemed medically necessary. However, a natal female seeking

---

[21] This is not just a hypothetical example. Approximately 1/100 people have bodies with anatomy differing from the typical male or female form, and one out of every 6,000 births involves a baby with vaginal agenesis (an undeveloped vagina). *See How Common Is Intersex?*, Intersex Society of North America, http://www.isna.org/faq/frequency (last visited July 24, 2018) ([sic]; *see also* Schechter Decl. (dkt. # 27) ¶ 38 ("[S]urgeons perform procedures to reconstruct male or female external genitalia for individuals who have certain medical conditions. . . . For the female genitalia, this would include procedures to correct conditions such as congenital absence of the vagina or reconstruction of the vagina/vulva following oncologic resection, traumatic injury, or infection.")).

that same medically necessary procedure for gender dysphoria would be denied because of his sex. In this case, if plaintiffs' natally assigned sexes had *matched* their gender identities, their requested, medically necessary surgeries to reconstruct their genitalia or breasts would be covered by Wisconsin Medicaid.[22] Here, plaintiffs have instead been denied coverage because of their natal sex, which would appear to be a straightforward case of sex discrimination.

Even if defendants' more tortured interpretation of the Challenged Exclusion prevailed, and "sex" needed to include transgender status, plaintiffs still have more than a reasonable likelihood of success on the merits under United States Supreme Court and Seventh Circuit precedent. This is because the scope of what qualifies as prohibited sex discrimination has changed over time. *See Hively v. Ivy Tech Cmty. Coll. of Ind.*, 853 F.3d 339, 345 (7th Cir. 2017) (en banc). As the *Hively* court explained, Title VII's prohibition on sex discrimination "has been understood to cover far more than the simple decision of an employer not to hire a woman for Job A, or a man for Job B"; it now "reaches sexual harassment in the work place, including same-sex workplace harassment; it reaches discrimination based on actuarial assumptions about a person's longevity; and it reaches discrimination based on a person's failure to conform to a certain set of gender stereotypes," which may "have surprised some who served in the 88th Congress."[ ] As the Seventh Circuit explained in *Whitaker*, "[b]y definition, a transgender individual does not conform to the sex-based stereotypes of the sex that he or she was assigned at birth." [ ] . . .

Indeed, the Seventh Circuit further concluded in *Whitaker* that a policy subjecting a transgender student—because he was transgender—"to different rules, sanctions, and treatment [compared to] non-transgender students" violated the prohibition against sex discrimination under Title IX. [ ] This is what the Challenged Exclusion does as well: it creates a different rule governing the medical treatment of transgender people. Specifically, Wisconsin Medicaid covers medically necessary treatment for other health conditions, yet the Challenged Exclusion expressly *singles out and bars* a medically necessary treatment solely for transgender people suffering from gender dysphoria. In fact, by excluding "transsexual surgery" from coverage, the Challenged Exclusion directly singles out a Medicaid claimant's transgender status as the basis for denying medical treatment. [ ] As defendants conceded at the preliminary injunction hearing, this means that if breast reduction surgery were deemed medically necessary due to back, neck or shoulder pain, a natal female's surgery would be covered by Wisconsin Medicaid. However, if breast

---

[22] Despite the possible implication of the opinions of one of their experts, defendants do *not* argue that the proposed surgical procedures are excluded because they remain experimental, perhaps out of recognition that they are now commonly offered and performed across the country to ease the suffering of those with gender dysphoria. In fact, during oral argument, defendants acknowledged this type of surgery was not experimental in nature.

reduction surgery were deemed medically necessary due to gender dysphoria, a natal female's surgery would *not* be covered. . . . This is textbook discrimination *based on sex.* . . .

Aside from being unsympathetic to a medical condition which they acknowledge both plaintiffs suffer from, defendants fail to grasp that not every transgender person requires, or even desires, gender-confirming surgery. [A]s in other areas of health care covered by Wisconsin Medicaid, individuals should be allowed to decide in consultation with their treatment providers what treatment is best and then ultimately whether to pursue it. If anything, the Challenged Exclusion feeds into sex stereotypes by requiring all transgender individuals . . . to keep genitalia and other prominent sex characteristics consistent with their natal sex no matter how painful and disorienting it may prove for some. [ ]

Accordingly, plaintiffs have made a persuasive evidentiary showing, albeit a preliminary one, that the Challenged Exclusion prevents them from getting medically necessary treatments on the basis of both their natal sex *and* transgender status, which surely amounts to discrimination on the basis of sex in violation of the ACA. . . .

III. Balance of Harms & Public Interest

. . . Here, the likelihood of ongoing, irreparable harm facing these two individual plaintiffs outweighs any marginal impacts on the defendants' stated concerns regarding public health or limiting costs. As addressed above, defendants' concern about protecting the public health by limiting Wisconsin Medicaid to "medically necessary purposes" is misplaced here, given the substantial likelihood that this interest would be served, rather than hindered, by covering plaintiffs' recommended surgical procedures. As to the latter concern, the court readily acknowledges the state's ongoing interest in reasonably reducing medical expenditures where appropriate, but as defendants also acknowledged the Challenged Exclusion is "expected to result in *nominal* savings for state government." . . . As such, the irreparable harm these plaintiffs face without injunctive relief substantially outweighs the harm the state will suffer by preliminarily enjoining the application of the Challenged Exclusion to their individual prior authorization requests. [ ] . . .

NOTES AND QUESTIONS

1. *Does Sex Discrimination Include Discrimination Based on Transgender Status or Gender Identity?* As noted above, perhaps the most anticipated development of Section 1557 was the protection it would provide transgender individuals. Indeed, in the 2016 Rule interpreting Section 1557 issued under the Obama-Biden administration, HHS defined sex discrimination to include "discrimination on the basis of . . . sex stereotyping[ ] and gender identity." It also spent significant time and attention discussing

how Section 1557 would address the various forms of health care discrimination experienced by transgender people, including by prohibiting the types of categorical exclusions of gender-affirming care challenged in *Flack*. Under the Trump administration's 2020 Rule, however, regulators repealed this definition and expressly rejected the notion that transgender people would be protected by Section 1557's sex discrimination prohibition. The 2020 Rule distinguished "biological sex" from "gender identity" and pointed to Title IX's legislative history focusing on equal opportunities for *women*. It interpreted the absence of an explicit reference to gender identity in either Title IX or Section 1557 as evidence that discrimination on the basis of transgender status was not intended to be prohibited as a form of sex discrimination. Ongoing litigation challenges to the 2020 Rule, and the Biden-Harris win in 2020, have created a kind of regulatory limbo as of the writing of this edition; that said, the new administration has, unsurprisingly, already signaled its embrace of the more protective antidiscrimination approach reflected in the 2016 Rule. HHS Office for Civil Rights, HHS Announces Prohibition on Sex Discrimination Includes Discrimination on the Basis of Sexual Orientation and Gender Identity, May 10, 2021.

Disputes about what constitutes sex discrimination have also been playing out in the courts, in ways that may constrain future regulatory interpretations. Although the Supreme Court has not yet faced the question of whether Section 1557 protects transgender individuals, the Court has done so in the context of Title VII. *Bostock v. Clayton County, Georgia,* involved three consolidated cases—one of them challenging the firing of a long-time employee for being transgender. 140 S. Ct. 1731 (2020). Justice Gorsuch delivered the opinion of the Court, in which Chief Justice Roberts and Justices Ginsburg, Breyer, Sotomayor, and Kagan joined. The majority conceded the distinction between sex and gender identity and assumed for the sake of argument that "sex" referred only to biological distinctions between male and female. The majority nonetheless concluded that sex discrimination included discrimination based on gender identity and sexual orientation. Justice Gorsuch explained that Title VII's language is clear in that "it prohibits employers from taking certain actions 'because of' sex," which "incorporates the 'simple' and 'traditional' standard of but-for causation." *Bostock*, 140 S. Ct. at 1739. In short, "an employer who intentionally treats a person worse because of sex—such as by firing the person for actions or attributes it would tolerate in an individual of another sex—discriminates against that person in violation of Title VII." Id. at 1740. Notably, the majority held that "it is impossible to discriminate against a person for being . . . transgender without discriminating against that individual based on sex." Id. at 1741–1742.

Given the majority's textualist approach to what it concluded was a rather straightforward meaning of "because of sex," its outcome did not depend on legislative history about which groups Congress intended to protect. Thus, it will almost certainly apply to similar sex discrimination prohibitions in other statutes, most notably Title IX and Section 1557. Indeed, lower courts have already begun acknowledging *Bostock's* relevance to Section 1557. See, e.g.,

Whitman-Walker Clinic, Inc. v. U.S. Dep't of Health & Hum. Servs., 485 F. Supp. 3d 1 (D.D.C. 2020) (enjoining the parts of the 2020 Rule that would have repealed the 2016 Rule definitions relating to discrimination based on sex stereotyping and gender identity, and requiring HHS to reconsider its repeal attempt in light of *Bostock*); Asapansa-Johnson Walker v. Azar, No. 20-CV-2834, 2020 WL 6363970 (E.D.N.Y. Oct. 29, 2020) (finding the 2020 Rule relating to sex discrimination contrary to *Bostock*, and staying repeal of the 2016 Rule definitions of "on the basis of sex," "gender identity," and "sex stereotyping" currently set forth in 45 C.F.R. § 92.4), *appeal filed* No. 20-3827 (2d Cir. Nov. 10, 2020). Even before *Bostock*, most courts agreed that Section 1557 prohibited discrimination against transgender individuals as a matter of statutory interpretation, which did not depend on the interpretation set forth in implementing rules. See, e.g., Flack v. Wisconsin Dept. of Health, 395 F. Supp. 3d 1001 (W.D. Wis. 2019); Tovar v. Essentia Health, 342 F. Supp. 3d 947 (D. Minn. 2018); Boyden v. Conlin, 341 F. Supp. 3d 979 (W.D. Wis. 2018); Prescott v. Rady, 265 F. Supp. 3d 1090 (S.D. Cal. 2017); Rumble v. Fairview Health Services, 2015 WL 1197415 (D. Minn. Mar. 16, 2015).

2.   *Theory of Sex Discrimination in* Flack. In determining the plaintiffs' likelihood of success in proving sex discrimination under Section 1557, the *Flack* decision (which predates *Bostock*) offers a few different rationales for finding that the challenged Medicaid exclusion constitutes sex discrimination. Which of these rationales seem(s) most consistent with the reasoning in *Bostock*? (Note that the *Flack* court looked to Title IX and Title VII jurisprudence for guidance.) Recall from *Erickson* and Note 2, above, the importance of identifying the right comparator for determining when benefit exclusions are discriminatory. What comparator(s) were used in *Flack* to illustrate differential treatment based on transgender status or natal assigned sex?

Flack is consistent with the approach taken in the 2016 Rule issued by the Obama administration, which prohibited categorical limits on all gender-affirming care. The 2016 Rule also clarified that if a plan ordinarily covers a particular treatment, whether medically necessary or elective, it must apply the same standards to its coverage of comparable procedures related to gender transition. 81 Fed. Reg. at 31,377. Although the *Flack* excerpt above dealt with a preliminary injunction request, the next year the court permanently enjoined defendants from enforcing the challenged exclusion, adopting the same analysis with respect to plaintiffs' Section 1557 claim. Flack v. Wis. Dept. of Health Servs, 395 F. Supp. 3d 1001, 1015 (W.D. Wis. 2019).

3.   *Categorical Exclusions vs. Individual Insurance Denials*. Even if categorical insurance exclusions of gender-affirming care constitute prohibited sex discrimination, this does not necessarily guarantee coverage for requested care. Coverage may still be denied if the particular treatment is not found to be medically necessary. For example, in a Title VII case, Baker v. Aetna Life Insurance Co., 228 F. Supp. 3d 764 (N.D. Tex. 2017), an employee alleging that she suffered from gender dysphoria brought an action against her employer for denying coverage for breast augmentation surgery. The court initially denied

the employer's motion to dismiss because the plaintiff plausibly alleged that she was denied coverage for medically necessary surgery based on her gender in violation of Title VII. Ultimately, however, the court rejected the plaintiff's discrimination claim for insufficient evidence. After noting that the plan did cover surgeries and other medically necessary care to treat gender dysphoria, the court highlighted the fact that the plan made an individualized determination that the plaintiff's request for breast augmentation surgery was not medically necessary, in light of the breast enhancement already achieved through hormone therapy. Baker v. Aetna Life Insurance Co. & L-3, No. 3:15-CV-3679-D, 2018 WL 572907 (Jan. 26, 2018).

In *Flack*, the parties' dispute about the plaintiffs' individual medical need and risk of harm for purposes of the preliminary injunction provides a glimpse of how such disputes may occur on an individualized basis. Given the pervasive discrimination against transgender individuals in health care and throughout society, how will courts be able to determine whether an individualized denial of specific care as not medically necessary is truly an application of the kind of neutral, nondiscriminatory criteria used for other types of conditions or care, or is instead the product of covert or implicit bias? How much weight should treating physicians' judgment be given?

4.   *Discrimination in Health Care Treatment.* Transgender individuals experience many forms of unequal treatment and barriers to care. In a 2010 survey on discrimination against LGBT people, nearly 27 percent of transgender respondents reported being denied medically necessary care outright because of their transgender status. See Lamba Legal, When Health Care Isn't Caring: Survey on Discrimination Against LGBT People and People Living with HIV (2010). In the same survey, 70 percent of the respondents reported being treated poorly by health care providers, in ways that created serious dignitary harms and potentially jeopardized health. Survey participants described a broad range of such treatment by physicians: refusing to touch them or using excessive precautions; using harsh or abusive language; being physically rough or abusive; or blaming the patients for their health status. Examples of poor treatment by hospital staff were also reported, including laughing, pointing, taunting, using slurs and making other negative comments; violating confidentiality; using an improper name and/or pronoun for the patient; exceptionally long waits for care; inappropriate questions or exams, including needless viewing of genitals; and failure to follow standards of care. See Lamba Legal, supra.

One of the earliest cases to interpret Section 1557 involved alleged treatment by health care staff that mirrored many of the findings from the Lamba survey above. In *Rumble v. Fairview Health Services*, supra, the plaintiff, who self-identified as a "female-to-male transgender man," alleged hostile and abusive touching by a physician, misclassification of the plaintiff's gender, unnecessary disclosures revealing his status, and subjection to unnecessary and improper exams. There was also evidence the plaintiff did not receive adequate pain treatment or a timely diagnosis, and that the delay could have been life-threatening. Based on this evidence, the court refused to grant defendants' motion to dismiss and found that the nature and degree of defendants' "unprofessional" and "assaultive" actions were sufficient to raise an inference of discriminatory intent under Section 1557.

Rumble is consistent with the approach taken in the 2016 Final Rule. Relying on Title IX's definition of sex discrimination as prohibiting harassment that creates a hostile environment, the 2016 Rule noted that "the persistent and intentional refusal to use a transgender individual's preferred name and pronoun and insistence on using those corresponding to the individual's sex assigned at birth constitutes illegal sex discrimination if such conduct is sufficiently serious to create a hostile environment." Although the rule interpreted Section 1557 as requiring covered entities to treat individuals in accordance with their gender identity or expression, it contained an important clarification: this requirement could not be used to deny medically necessary care. (See former 45 C.F.R. § 92.206.) For example, the rule explained that a covered entity could not deny treatment for ovarian cancer based on an individual's identification as a transgender male, if that treatment is medically indicated.

Individuals in need of gender-affirming care, such as hormone therapy, surgery, or counseling, have trouble accessing such care due not only to insurance exclusions and routine denials, but also to provider refusals to provide care, lack of qualified providers, and inadequate training of medical professionals generally with respect to the medical needs of transgender patients. See National Center for Transgender Equality and National Gay and Lesbian Task Force, Injustice at Every Turn: A Report of the National Transgender Discrimination Survey 5–6 (2011). As with insurance, where a provider is qualified and typically provides a certain type of care for some medical needs, such as a hysterectomy to treat fibroids, refusal to provide care to treat gender dysphoria may constitute discrimination on the basis of sex. Anti-discrimination law has been less effective at addressing other structural barriers to care, such as an inadequate supply of qualified providers.

5. *Discrimination on the Basis of Sexual Orientation.* Although discrimination on the basis of sexual orientation has received comparatively less attention, lesbian, gay, and bisexual (LGB) patients experience many of the same forms of discrimination as transgender patients. In a 2009 survey, almost 56 percent of LGB respondents reported encountering at least one of the following types of discrimination in care: being refused needed care; health care professionals refusing to touch them or using excessive precautions; health care professionals using harsh or abusive language; being blamed for their health status; or health care professionals being physically rough or abusive. Lamba Legal, When Health Care Isn't Caring: Lambda Legal's Survey on Discrimination Against LGBT People and People Living with HIV (2010).

Section 1557 likely provides important antidiscrimination protections for LGB individuals as well. In *Bostock*, supra, the Supreme Court was also confronted with the question of whether Title VII's sex discrimination provision prohibits discrimination based on sexual orientation. The other two consolidated cases involved challenges to the firing of two long-time employees for being gay, and the majority applied the same "simple" "but-for" test, finding it "impossible to discriminate against a person for being [gay] without discriminating against that individual based on sex." *Bostock*, 140 S. Ct. at 1741.

6.   *Discrimination on the Basis of Atypical Sex Characteristics.* Does discrimination "on the basis of sex" protect individuals born with atypical sex characteristics or traits? The 2016 Rule answered this question affirmatively. It explained that sex discrimination includes discrimination on the basis of "the presence of atypical sex characteristics and intersex traits (i.e., people born with variations in sex characteristics, including in chromosomal, reproductive, or anatomical sex characteristics that do not fit the typical characteristics of binary females or males)." See supra. Such individuals, who may identify as "intersex" individuals or as individuals with "disorders of sex development," can experience discrimination similar to that experienced by transgender people. For example, the rule noted that such individuals have been denied care or coverage for medical care that is classified as "sex-specific" where the treatment classification did not match the person's registered sex; this denial would be prohibited under Section 1557. (See the *Flack* court's discussion of treatment for those with atypical sex characteristics in footnote 21.)

The 2016 Rule failed to address, however, concerns that have been raised about medical interventions performed on intersex infants and children to conform their sexual or reproductive anatomy to a binary sex norm. Although the most extreme examples of these interventions have been rejected by the mainstream medical community and have largely disappeared, medically unnecessary surgical alteration of infants still occurs. See Julie A. Greenberg, Intersexuality and the Law: Why Sex Matters (N.Y.U. Press 2012), arguing that this practice should be considered a form of sex discrimination, and discussing the medical, ethical, and legal issues arising out of this practice.

7.   *Cost.* In both *Erickson* and *Flack*, defendants claimed cost was at least one reason for excluding the challenged treatment. How did the courts address that proffered justification? In *Flack,* the defendants acknowledged that any cost savings from denying care would be nominal. Should this matter?

8.   *Gender Dysphoria as a Disability.* There may be additional protection afforded to a subset of transgender individuals under the ADA, discussed below. "Gender identity disorders" are excluded from ADA protections unless the disorder results from a physical impairment. 42 U.S.C. § 12211(b)(1). However, since enactment of the ADA, "gender dysphoria" was added to the DSM-5 as a formal diagnosis. Some courts have determined that gender dysphoria is a distinct diagnosis that could be considered an ADA-protected condition. See Doe v. Triangle Doughnuts, 472 F. Supp. 3d 115 (E.D. Pa 2020); Doe v. Mass. Dep't of Corr., No. 17-12255-RGS, 2018 WL 2994403 (D. Mass. June 14, 2018); Blatt v. Cabela's Retail, Inc., No. 5:14-CV-04822, 2017 WL

2178123 (E.D. Pa. May 18, 2017). But see Doe v. Northrop Grumman Sys. Corp., 418 F. Supp. 3d 921 (N.D. Ala. 2019).

NOTE: RELIGIOUS OBJECTIONS TO ANTIDISCRIMINATION REQUIREMENTS

Religious liberty and other conscience protections have long played an important role in shaping health care access. Providers, insurers, and employers have raised religious objections to providing or covering certain kinds of care, and concerns about religious and conscience objections have motivated lawmakers and regulators to craft legislative or regulatory exemptions or accommodations to permit refusals under certain circumstances. As you will see elsewhere in the casebook, religious or conscience objections are perhaps most prominent in areas of health care that touch profound questions about the beginning and end of life. See Chapter 16, Reproduction and Birth, and Chapter 18, Life and Death Decisions. But they also impact health care relating to gender identity, sexual health, pregnancy prevention, and assisted reproduction. These areas implicate and challenge traditional norms or assumptions about sex and gender, heteronormativity, women's sexuality, and parenting.

As we have seen in this part of the chapter, when care or coverage is denied based on such norms, it can implicate sex antidiscrimination protections. But when such denials are linked to one's religious beliefs, they can also implicate religious liberty protections. Disputes arising out of religious objections to sex antidiscrimination protections are certainly not new—such conflicts have long arisen in states that had robust sex antidiscrimination protections before enactment of the ACA. These clashes have become more visible, however, with the new federal focus on gender equity in health seen in the ACA.

The Contraceptive Mandate & Gender Equity

To date, this conflict has been most visible in the context of insurance coverage for contraception. Because the contraceptive mandate was grounded in the preventive health mandate in the ACA, it was an early focus of religious objections to health reform. The Obama administration emphasized the importance of the mandate for ensuring gender equity in health care, but it attempted to resolve the conflict by crafting a regulatory accommodation. This accommodation would allow certain religious entities to refuse to pay for coverage but still ensured access to contraception by requiring such coverage to be provided by a third-party.

Rather than fending off litigation, however, this accommodation, along with subsequent regulatory action by the Trump administration dramatically expanding exemptions to the contraceptive mandate, has led to a flurry of litigation. Obama-era rules have been challenged as providing insufficient protection for religious liberty, and Trump-era rules have been challenged as going too far in the other direction and undermining the ACA's equity mandate. This litigation has resulted in an unusually large number of

Supreme Court opinions addressing the conflict in a relatively short amount of time. Given the rather complicated and unique regulatory and jurisprudential path of this conflict in the contraceptive mandate context, a more complete account of these developments and unresolved questions is presented in Chapter 16, Section IV (Contraception).

Antidiscrimination Prohibitions

More recently, litigation has centered on religious objections to federal sex antidiscrimination laws, especially Section 1557 and Title VII, insofar as such laws would be interpreted to require religious entities to cover or provide gender-affirming care for transgender individuals. To date, several Catholic organizations and their members have brought pre-enforcement challenges to prevent this interpretation on religious liberty grounds. Specifically, the plaintiffs have argued such interpretation would violate the federal Religious Freedom Restoration Act of 1993 (RFRA), which prohibits federal action that imposes a substantial burden on religious exercise, unless that action is narrowly tailored to serve a compelling government interest. So far, two courts have agreed, enjoining the challenged implementation against the religious plaintiffs. See *Religious Sisters of Mercy v. Azar*, 513 F. Supp. 3d 1113 (D.N.D. 2021) (Section 1557 and Title VI); *Franciscan Alliance v. Azar*, 414 F. Supp. 3d 928 (N.D. Tex. 2019) (Section 1557). On May 10, 2021, the HHS Office for Civil Rights announced its intent to comply with these orders.

In both cases, the courts held that the challenged implementation would impose a substantial burden on the Catholic plaintiffs' exercise of religion, because noncompliance could result in a significant loss of federal funding and/or liability, and compliance would require plaintiffs to violate their religious beliefs as they sincerely understand them. In *Religious Sisters*, for example, the court pointed to the fact that the plaintiffs "explained that their religious beliefs regarding human sexuality and procreation prevent them from facilitating gender transitions through either medical services or insurance coverage." 513 F. Supp. 3d at 1147. Defendants have not disputed the sincerity of these beliefs, and courts have made clear that it is not their domain to question them.

The courts then applied strict scrutiny to determine whether the challenged implementation was the least restrictive means to serve a compelling interest. They rejected the government's interest in ensuring nondiscriminatory access to health care as too broad, noting that the government must articulate how granting specific exemptions for the Catholic plaintiffs will harm the asserted interest in preventing discrimination. They then found that even if the government could show a compelling interest, less restrictive alternatives to accomplishing this interest exist. For example, in *Religious Sisters*, the court suggested other ways the government could ensure access, such as providing subsidies, reimbursements, tax credits or tax deductions to employees, or paying for services at community health centers, public clinics, and hospitals with income-based support. It also pointed to the possibility that the government could more directly "assist transgender individuals in finding and paying for transition procedures available from the growing number of health care providers who offer and specialize in those services." Id. at 22–23. Because the government had not shown these alternatives were unfeasible, the court held, the challenged implementation fails strict scrutiny.

Not all courts have applied strict scrutiny analysis in this way. In a state court case, *Minton v. Dignity Health Care*, 39 Cal.App.5th 1155 (2019), the court rejected a Catholic hospital's arguments that the religious freedom protections in the state constitution should protect its refusal to provide a hysterectomy to a transgender male patient, despite subjecting the state's antidiscrimination law to a strict scrutiny analysis. The patient sued Dignity Health Care for a discriminatory refusal to treat by one of its Catholic hospitals—Mercy Hospital. The complaint alleged discrimination on the basis of his gender identity in violation of California's Unruh Civil Rights Act, Cal. Civ. Code § 51, because his scheduled hysterectomy was canceled the day before when hospital staff learned the plaintiff was transgender. According to the complaint, Mercy routinely provided hysterectomies for other medical diagnoses, such as for chronic pelvic pain and uterine fibroids, but Mercy's president said the procedure would "never" be allowed to treat gender dysphoria.

One of the arguments raised by Dignity Health Care in the suit was that the discrimination claim should be barred by the guarantees of religious freedom in the California Constitution. (RFRA was not raised as a defense because it does not apply to state laws). Dignity claimed that Mercy, as a Catholic hospital, was bound to follow the Ethical and Religious Directives for Catholic Health Care Services (the Directives) issued by the United States Conference of Catholic Bishops. Dignity noted that under the Directives "[a]ll persons served by Catholic health care have the right and duty to protect and preserve their bodily and functional integrity." Id. at 1162. It also pointed to a provision prohibiting the "direct sterilization of either men or women, whether permanent or temporary," but they do permit "procedures that induce sterility . . . when their direct effect is the cure or alleviation of a present and serious pathology and a simpler treatment is not available." Id. Although Mercy Hospital was bound by these directives, the defendant, Dignity Health Care, was ultimately able to arrange for the procedure to be rescheduled at one of its non-Catholic hospitals. Plaintiffs alleged that this only occurred after the plaintiff and the plaintiffs' surgeon used the media and political channels to bring public attention to the refusal. The delay caused the plaintiff anxiety and grief, in part because the timing of the surgery was sensitive—it had to be performed three months before another surgery already scheduled.

The trial court dismissed Minton's claim, but the appellate court reversed. It found that Minton had stated a claim for discrimination, despite the fact that the defendant did ultimately reschedule the procedure at another hospital in response to publicity. Specifically, the court found that "it cannot constitute full equality under [the state antidiscrimination law] to cancel his procedure for a discriminatory purpose, wait to see if his doctor complains, and only then attempt to reschedule the procedure at a different hospital. 'Full and equal' access requires avoiding discrimination, not merely remedying it after it has occurred." Id. at 1165.

The court also rejected the religious freedom defense. It noted that "Minton's claim does not compel Dignity Health to violate its religious principles if it can provide all persons with full and equal medical care at comparable facilities not subject to the same religious restrictions." Id. To the extent there was compulsion, however, the court applied a strict scrutiny analysis to find that any burden on the exercise of religion was justified by California's compelling interest in ensuring full and equal access to medical treatment for all its residents, and that no less restrictive means existed to accomplish that goal. In applying strict scrutiny, it cited to an earlier California Supreme Court case coming to a similar conclusion in a sexual orientation discrimination claim brought by a lesbian patient who, based on religious grounds, was denied access to an artificial insemination procedure by a physician. North Coast Women's Care Medical Group, Inc. v. Superior Court, 44 Cal.4th 1145 (2008). The court in *North Coast* specifically noted that the defendant could comply with the antidiscrimination law and still avoid violating its religious beliefs by ensuring that patients receive "full and equal" access to the medical procedure through a North Coast physician who did not have defendants' religious objections.

Future Questions

There is no question that the antidiscrimination protections in both Section 1557 and Title VII are subject to the strict scrutiny test established in RFRA, but important questions remain about how future courts will resolve religiously based refusals to treat or pay for care. How should the government's interest in preventing the equity and health harms that result from discriminatory refusals be balanced against religious objections? In the *Minton* and *North Coast* cases, the courts emphasized the importance of having a policy to ensure full and equal access to care despite religious objections, noting that access could be achieved through a referral or an arrangement with a qualified and willing provider. Does this approach achieve the right balance of competing interests? What if the provider, employer, or insurer has religious objections to even making such referrals or arrangements, on the grounds that this would be a facilitation of sin? (For example, religious objections based on facilitation have been used to challenge the special accommodation process for the contraceptive mandate created under the Obama administration. See Chapter 16.IV.C.)

In terms of the least restrictive alternative test, is there any limit to the list of alternatives that a court can consider as evidence that a challenged law is not narrowly tailored? The list of alternative possibilities suggested by the courts in *Religious Sisters* and *Franciscan Alliance* was quite long. Should the fact that the government can theoretically create a different or new program to fill in gaps created by religious refusal be enough to prevent the government from prohibiting discriminatory actions by federal funding recipients as part of an existing comprehensive health care program? Or does the fact that the government was able and willing to create a special accommodation process for religious objections to insurance coverage of contraception support the result in *Religious Sisters* and *Franciscan Alliance*—if the government could do it for the prescription contraceptive mandate, why not for gender-affirming coverage? But consider whether it is as easy for the federal government to create an accommodation process that would prevent disruption in health care *treatment* due to provider denials of care, as opposed to *insurance denials*, especially in light of the local character of health care delivery organization and regulation.

Recent Supreme Court decisions on RFRA in the contraceptive mandate context provide important clues as to how such conflicts may be resolved. See Chapter 16 Section IV.C (The Clash Between Government Mandates and Religious or Moral Beliefs). In addition, the appointments of Justice Kavanaugh to replace Justice Kennedy, and Justice Barrett to replace Justice Ginsburg, have been widely perceived as cementing a shift in the Court that is increasingly protective of religious liberty claims, even in the face of compelling health and public health interests. Of course, the law merely establishes a legal floor in terms of one's obligations. Many professional organizations have established ethical guidelines for how their members should handle requests for care that violate their religious beliefs, encouraging them to take actions to minimize any disruption in care. See Chapter 16 Section IV.C (Note: The Ethics of Conscientious Refusals).

C. DISABILITY

People with disabilities have experienced a history of unequal treatment in medicine and health care, including denial of needed services; inadequate or inappropriate treatment; unnecessary institutionalization, often under unacceptable conditions; involuntary sterilization; and other harms. The legislative history of the ADA documents widespread discrimination against individuals with disabilities across society, including in medicine and health care. The treatment of individuals with disabilities is also discussed in later chapters addressing sterilization and reproductive care (Chapter 16), organ transplantation and the determination of death (Chapter 17), life and death decisions (Chapter 18), physician-assisted death (Chapter 19), and research (Chapter 20).

Despite passage of the ADA in 1990, inequities and barriers to care for individuals with disabilities persist. Fifteen years after ADA passage, in 2005, the Surgeon General's Call to Action to Improve the Health and Wellness of Persons with Disabilities highlighted inequities such as poorer reported health status and specific risk of secondary conditions, as well as barriers to health and health care including lack of transportation, provider attitudes and misconceptions, and inaccessible facilities and services. A few years later, the National Council on Disability published its evaluation of decades of research on health inequities and barriers experienced by people with disabilities. Its 2009 report, The Current State of Health Care for People with Disabilities, found that people with disabilities report poorer health status than people without disabilities, use fewer preventative services despite using health care services at a significantly higher rate overall, and face more problems accessing health care than other groups. The report identified lack of training on disability competence issues and on legal requirements for health care practitioners as among the most significant barriers. Reports from governmental agencies, advocacy organizations, academic researchers, and others continue to document inequities in health and health care. See, e.g., Gloria Krahn, Persons with Disabilities as an Unrecognized Health Disparity Population, 105 Am. J. Pub. Health S198 (2015); Jana J. Peterson-Besse et al., Clinical Preventative Service Use Disparities Among Subgroups of People with Disabilities: A Scoping Review, 7 Disability & Health J. 373 (2014).

While there are many reasons for these inequities, discrimination and unequal treatment play a role. For decades, research has shown that physicians hold negative views of people with disabilities and fail to fully appreciate the value and quality of life with a disability. More recently, a series of reports from the National Council on Disability have explored how persistent devaluation of the lives of people with disabilities by the medical community, legislators, researchers, and others have perpetuated inequities in health and access to health care, including life-saving care.

The ADA was enacted to end a history of discrimination based on disability and to ensure equal opportunities, integration in the community, and full participation across all areas of American life. Title I of the ADA (42 U.S.C. § 12111) applies to employment, including employer-sponsored health and wellness plans; Title II (42 U.S.C. § 12131) applies to state and local government services, programs, and activities, including state and local public hospitals and health programs such as Medicaid; Title III (42 U.S.C. § 12181) applies to public accommodations, including private health care facilities and offices open to the public; and Title IV (42 U.S.C. § 12201) includes miscellaneous provisions, including important provisions regarding insurance. See also Chapter 10 (discussing the integration mandate as applied to Medicaid); Chapter 11 (discussing employment protections for health care professionals); and Chapter 21 (discussing use of public health evidence in a disability discrimination case).

The ADA expanded the protections of an earlier law, Section 504 of the Rehabilitation Act of 1973 (29 U.S.C. § 749), which prohibits discrimination on the basis of disability only in federal employment and in programs and activities that are funded by federal agencies. The ADA and Section 504 are quite similar in most respects, and courts have used cases under the Rehabilitation Act, which applies only to programs and services receiving federal funding, to assist in interpreting the more widely applicable ADA. There are some significant differences, however, that are highlighted in the notes below. As also discussed below, Section 1557 of the ACA broadens the reach of Section 504 significantly.

The HHS Office for Civil Rights (OCR) is responsible for enforcing Title II of the ADA, Section 504 of the Rehabilitation Act, and Section 1557 of the ACA. The U.S. Department of Justice (DOJ) is also charged with enforcing Section 504, Title II and III of the ADA, and Section 1557 of the ACA. The DOJ and OCR have broad authority to investigate, mediate, litigate, and settle individual and class-based claims under these laws. Private individuals and groups can also bring actions under these laws. Public and private ADA enforcement actions and settlement agreements have addressed a wide range of barriers to health care services for individuals with disabilities. However, many experts claim that the ADA and Section 504 are underenforced, and research also shows lack of knowledge of, and noncompliance with, disability nondiscrimination laws in health care settings. See, e.g., Nicole D. Agaronnik et al., Knowledge of Practicing Physicians about Their Legal Obligations When Caring for Patients with Disability, 38(4) Health Aff. 545 (April 1, 2019).

The following materials explore the impact of the ADA, Section 504, and Section 1557 on health care for individuals with disabilities and the promise and challenge of using these laws to address different forms of discrimination based on disability in health care services, programs and activities, and in health insurance.

BRAGDON V. ABBOTT
Supreme Court of the United States, 1998.
524 U.S. 624.

KENNEDY, J., delivered the opinion of the Court, in which STEVENS, SOUTER, GINSBERG, and BREYER, JJ., joined. STEVENS, J., filed a concurring opinion. REHNQUIST, C.J., filed an opinion concurring in the judgment in part and dissenting in part, in which SCALIA and THOMAS, JJ., joined, and in Part II of which O'CONNOR, J., joined. O'CONNOR, J., filed an opinion concurring in the judgment in part and dissenting in part.

. . . We granted certiorari to review . . . whether the Court of Appeals, in affirming a grant of summary judgment, cited sufficient material in the record to determine, as a matter of law, that respondent's infection with HIV posed no direct threat to the health and safety of her treating dentist.

I

Respondent Sidney Abbott has been infected with HIV since 1986. When the incidents we recite occurred, her infection had not manifested its most serious symptoms. On September 16, 1994, she went to the office of petitioner Randon Bragdon in Bangor, Maine, for a dental appointment.

She disclosed her HIV infection on the patient registration form. Petitioner completed a dental examination, discovered a cavity, and informed respondent of his policy against filling cavities of HIV-infected patients. He offered to perform the work at a hospital with no added fee for his services, though respondent would be responsible for the cost of using the hospital's facilities. Respondent declined.

* * *

. . . Notwithstanding the protection given respondent by the ADA's definition of disability, petitioner could have refused to treat her if her infectious condition "posed a direct threat to the health or safety of others."[ ] The ADA defines a direct threat to be "a significant risk to the health or safety of others that cannot be eliminated by a modification of policies, practices, procedures, or by the provision of auxiliary aids or services."[ ] . . .

The ADA's direct threat provision stems from the recognition in School Bd. of Nassau Cty. v. Arline[ ] of the importance of prohibiting discrimination against individuals with disabilities while protecting others from significant health and safety risks, resulting, for instance, from a contagious disease. In *Arline,* the Court reconciled these objectives by construing the Rehabilitation Act not to require the hiring of a person who posed "a significant risk of communicating an infectious disease to others."[ ] . . . [The ADA's] direct threat provision codifies *Arline.* Because few, if any, activities in life are risk free, *Arline* and the ADA do not ask whether a risk exists, but whether it is significant.[ ]

The existence, or nonexistence, of a significant risk must be determined from the standpoint of the person who refuses the treatment or accommodation, and the risk assessment must be based on medical or other objective evidence.[ ] As a health care professional, petitioner had the duty to assess the risk of infection based on the objective, scientific information available to him and others in his profession. His belief that a significant risk existed, even if maintained in good faith, would not relieve him from liability. To use the words of the question presented, petitioner receives no special deference simply because he is a health care professional. It is true that *Arline* reserved "the question whether courts should also defer to the reasonable medical judgments of private physicians on which an employer has relied."[ ] At most, this statement reserved the possibility that employers could consult with individual physicians as objective third-party experts. It did not suggest that an individual physician's state of mind could excuse discrimination without regard to the objective reasonableness of his actions.

. . . In assessing the reasonableness of petitioner's actions, the views of public health authorities, such as the U.S. Public Health Service, CDC, and the National Institutes of Health, are of special weight and authority.[ ]

The views of these organizations are not conclusive, however. A health care professional who disagrees with the prevailing medical consensus may refute it by citing a credible scientific basis for deviating from the accepted norm.[ ]

* * *

[An] illustration of a correct application of the objective standard is the Court of Appeals' refusal to give weight to the petitioner's offer to treat respondent in a hospital.[ ] Petitioner testified that he believed hospitals had safety measures, such as air filtration, ultraviolet lights, and respirators, which would reduce the risk of HIV transmission.[ ] Petitioner made no showing, however, that any area hospital had these safeguards or even that he had hospital privileges.[ ] His expert also admitted the lack of any scientific basis for the conclusion that these measures would lower the risk of transmission.[ ] Petitioner failed to present any objective, medical evidence showing that treating respondent in a hospital would be safer or more efficient in preventing HIV transmission than treatment in a well-equipped dental office.

We are concerned, however, that the Court of Appeals might have placed mistaken reliance upon two other sources. In ruling no triable issue of fact existed on this point, the Court of Appeals relied on the CDC Dentistry Guidelines and the 1991 American Dental Association Policy on HIV.[ ] This evidence is not definitive. . . . [T]he CDC Guidelines recommended certain universal precautions which, in CDC's view, "should reduce the risk of disease transmission in the dental environment."[ ] The Court of Appeals determined that, "[w]hile the guidelines do not state explicitly that no further risk-reduction measures are desirable or that routine dental care for HIV-positive individuals is safe, those two conclusions seem to be implicit in the guidelines' detailed delineation of procedures for office treatment of HIV-positive patients."[ ] In our view, the Guidelines do not necessarily contain implicit assumptions conclusive of the point to be decided. The Guidelines set out CDC's recommendation that the universal precautions are the best way to combat the risk of HIV transmission. They do not assess the level of risk.

Nor can we be certain, on this record, whether the 1991 American Dental Association Policy on HIV carries the weight the Court of Appeals attributed to it. The Policy does provide some evidence of the medical community's objective assessment of the risks posed by treating people infected with HIV in dental offices. It indicates:

> "Current scientific and epidemiologic evidence indicates that there is little risk of transmission of infectious diseases through dental treatment if recommended infection control procedures are routinely followed. Patients with HIV infection may be safely treated in private dental offices when appropriate infection control procedures are

employed. Such infection control procedures provide protection both for patients and dental personnel."[ ]

We note, however, that the Association is a professional organization, which, although a respected source of information on the dental profession, is not a public health authority. It is not clear the extent to which the Policy was based on the Association's assessment of dentists' ethical and professional duties in addition to its scientific assessment of the risk to which the ADA refers. Efforts to clarify dentists' ethical obligations and to encourage dentists to treat patients with HIV infection with compassion may be commendable, but the question under the statute is one of statistical likelihood, not professional responsibility. Without more information on the manner in which the American Dental Association formulated this Policy, we are unable to determine the Policy's value in evaluating whether petitioner's assessment of the risks was reasonable as a matter of law.

* * *

We acknowledge the presence of other evidence in the record before the Court of Appeals which, subject to further arguments and examination, might support affirmance of the trial court's ruling. For instance, the record contains substantial testimony from numerous health experts indicating that it is safe to treat patients infected with HIV in dental offices.[ ] We are unable to determine the import of this evidence, however. The record does not disclose whether the expert testimony submitted by respondent turned on evidence available in September 1994.[ ]

There are reasons to doubt whether petitioner advanced evidence sufficient to raise a triable issue of fact on the significance of the risk. Petitioner relied on two principal points: First, he asserted that the use of high-speed drills and surface cooling with water created a risk of airborne HIV transmission. The study on which petitioner relied was inconclusive, however, determining only that "further work is required to determine whether such a risk exists."[ ] Petitioner's expert witness conceded, moreover, that no evidence suggested the spray could transmit HIV. His opinion on airborne risk was based on the absence of contrary evidence, not on positive data. Scientific evidence and expert testimony must have a traceable, analytical basis in objective fact before it may be considered on summary judgment.[ ]

[P]etitioner argues that, as of September 1994, CDC had identified seven dental workers with possible occupational transmission of HIV.[ ] These dental workers were exposed to HIV in the course of their employment, but CDC could not determine whether HIV infection had resulted.[ ] It is now known that CDC could not ascertain whether the seven dental workers contracted the disease because they did not present themselves for HIV testing at an appropriate time after their initial exposure.[ ] It is not clear on this record, however, whether this information was available to petitioner in September 1994. If not, the seven cases might have provided some, albeit not necessarily sufficient, support for petitioner's position. Standing alone, we doubt it would meet the objective, scientific basis for finding a significant risk to the petitioner.

* * *

We conclude the proper course is to give the Court of Appeals the opportunity to determine whether our analysis of some of the studies cited by the parties would change its conclusion that petitioner presented neither objective evidence nor a triable issue of fact on the question of risk.

JUSTICE STEVENS, with whom JUSTICE BREYER joins, concurring.

. . . I do not believe petitioner has sustained his burden of adducing evidence sufficient to raise a triable issue of fact on the significance of the risk posed by treating respondent in his office. . . . I join the opinion even though I would prefer an outright affirmance.[ ]

CHIEF JUSTICE REHNQUIST, with whom JUSTICE SCALIA and JUSTICE THOMAS join, and with whom JUSTICE O'CONNOR joins as to Part II, concurring in the judgment in part and dissenting in part.

* * *

II

I agree with the Court that "the existence, or nonexistence, of a significant risk must be determined from the standpoint of the person who refuses the treatment or accommodation," as of the time that the decision refusing treatment is made.[ ] I disagree with the Court, however, that "in assessing the reasonableness of petitioner's actions, the views of public health authorities . . . are of special weight and authority."[ ] Those views are, of course, entitled to a presumption of validity when the actions of those authorities themselves are challenged in court, and even in disputes between private parties where Congress has committed that dispute to adjudication by a public health authority. But in litigation between private parties originating in the federal courts, I am aware of no provision of law or judicial practice that would require or permit courts to give some scientific views more credence than others simply because they have been endorsed by a politically appointed public health authority (such as the Surgeon General). In litigation of this latter sort, which is what we face here, the credentials of the scientists employed by the public health authority, and the soundness of their studies, must stand on their own. The Court cites no authority for its limitation upon the courts' truth-finding function, except the statement in School Bd. of Nassau Cty. v. Arline,[ ] that in making findings regarding the risk of contagion under the Rehabilitation Act, "courts normally should defer to the reasonable medical judgments of public health officials." But there is appended to that dictum the following footnote, which makes it very clear that the Court was urging respect for *medical* judgment, and not necessarily respect for "official" medical judgment over "private" medical judgment: "This case does not present, and we do not address, the question whether courts should also defer to the reasonable medical judgments of private physicians on which an employer has relied."[ ]

Applying these principles here, it is clear to me that petitioner has presented more than enough evidence to avoid summary judgment on the "direct threat" question . . . . Given the "severity of the risk" involved here, i.e., near certain death, and the fact that no public health authority had outlined a protocol for *eliminating* this risk in the context of routine dental treatment, it seems likely that petitioner can establish that it was objectively reasonable for him to conclude that treating respondent in his office posed a "direct threat" to his safety.

* * *

NOTES AND QUESTIONS

1.   *Refusals to Treat.* The ADA and Section 504 prohibit refusals to treat based on disability. However, empirical studies demonstrate that a significant number of health care professionals refuse to provide care for persons with HIV/AIDS. See Brad Sears et al., HIV Discrimination in Dental Care: Results of a Testing Study in Los Angeles County, 45 Loy. L.A. L. Rev. 909 (2012), including results of studies from 2003–2008 demonstrating that 46 percent of skilled nursing facilities, 55 percent of OB/GYNs, and 26 percent of plastic surgeons in Los Angeles County refused to treat persons with HIV. See also Ronda Goldfein, From the Streets of Philadelphia: The AIDS Law Project of Pennsylvania's How-To Primer on Mitigating Health Disparities, 82 Temp. L. Rev. 1205 (2010). The DOJ and OCR have negotiated agreements with providers, some quite recently, concerning refusal to treat patients with HIV. The agreements are available on their respective websites. The agreements show that refusals to treat based on disability are not limited to persons with HIV/AIDS. See also *Lyons* in Section II; Chapter 18, discussing refusals to treat based on disability in the context of organ transplantation.

2.   *Denials of Care During the COVID-19 Pandemic.* During the COVID-19 pandemic, concerns arose regarding scarce medical resource allocation policies that explicitly or implicitly disadvantaged people with disabilities and others. The death of Michael Hickson, a forty-six-year-old Black man with a disability, exemplified these concerns for many. According to Mr. Hickson's family, his death resulted from a hospital's refusal to provide him with life-saving care for COVID-19 and its withholding of nutrition and hydration. According to Melissa Hickson, Mr. Hickson's wife, she recorded a conversation with a doctor who told her that the hospital would not provide her husband with medical treatment because of his low quality of life due to preexisting quadriplegia and head injury. See Ariana Eunjung Cha, Quadriplegic Man's

Death from COVID-19 Spotlights Questions of Disability, Race and Family, The Wash. Post, July 5, 2020. See discussion of medical futility in Chapter 18.

In March 2020, the OCR issued a bulletin affirming that federal disability nondiscrimination laws, like other civil rights laws, remained in effect during the pandemic. It provided that people with disabilities should not be denied medical care on the basis of "stereotypes, assessments of quality of life," or "judgments about a person's relative 'worth' based on the presence or absence of disabilities or age." Instead, decisions concerning whether an individual is a candidate for treatment should be "based on an individualized assessment of the patient based on the best available objective medical evidence." Dep't Health & Hum. Serv.'s, Bulletin: Civil Rights, HIPAA, and the Coronavirus Disease 2019 (COVID-19) (Mar. 28, 2020). The bulletin also emphasized the requirements of Section 1557 and the Rehabilitation Act, discussed later in this section, including the obligation to ensure effective communication with individuals who are deaf, hard of hearing, or blind, or who have low vision or speech disabilities, and to make reasonable modifications to address the needs of individuals with disabilities. See Samuel R. Bagenstos, Who Gets the Ventilator? Disability Discrimination in COVID-19 Medical-Rationing Protocols, 130 Yale L. J. F. 1 (2020).

3. *Assessment of "Direct Threat." Bragdon* established that the analysis of "direct threat" as a defense to a claim under the ADA must rely on an individualized assessment of scientific evidence rather than stereotyping or misconceptions. On remand, the First Circuit upheld the District Court's grant of summary judgment in favor of the plaintiff:

> The [American Dental] Association formulates scientific and ethical policies by separate procedures, drawing on different member groups and different staff complements. The Association's Council on Scientific Affairs, comprised of 17 dentists (most of whom hold advanced dentistry degrees), together with a staff of over 20 professional experts and consultants, drafted the Policy at issue here. By contrast, ethical policies are drafted by the Council on Ethics, a wholly separate body. Although the Association's House of Delegates must approve policies drafted by either council, we think that the origins of the Policy satisfy any doubts regarding its scientific foundation.

> For these reasons, we are confident that we appropriately relied on the Guidelines and the Policy. . . . Thus, we again conclude, after due reevaluation, that Ms. Abbott served a properly documented motion for summary judgment.

> We next reconsider whether Dr. Bragdon offered sufficient proof of direct threat to create a genuine issue of material fact and thus avoid the entry of summary judgment . . . . The Supreme Court suggested that one such piece of evidence—the seven cases that the CDC considered "possible" HIV patient-to-dental worker transmissions—should be reexamined. Since an objective standard pertains here, the existence of the list of seven "possible" cases does not create a genuine issue of material fact as to direct

threat. . . . Each piece of evidence to which [defendant directs] us is still "too speculative or too tangential (or, in some instances, both) to create a genuine issue of material fact."

Abbott v. Bragdon, 163 F.3d 87 (1st Cir. 1998), cert. denied, 526 U.S. 1131 (1999).

4.   *Risk of Transmission.* According to the CDC there has been only one confirmed case of occupational transmission of HIV to a health care worker reported since 1999. CDC, Occupational HIV Transmission and Prevention Among Health Care Workers (2015). The CDC recommends that "universal precautions" (using barriers such as gloves; handwashing; and design and use of sharps to reduce accidental needle sticks) against transmission of infectious diseases (including hepatitis, which is much more prevalent than HIV). For HIV in particular, the CDC recommends a specific protocol of post-exposure treatment following any exposure to prevent seroconversion in the exposed health care worker.

5.   *Definition of "Disability."* The ADA and Section 504 protect individuals who meet the statutory definition of "disability." An individual with a disability is one who has "a physical or mental impairment that substantially limits one or more major life activities of such individual; a record of such impairment; or [is] regarded as having such an impairment." 42 U.S.C. §§ 12101–12213. Disabilities are diverse, and can be physical, sensory, cognitive, intellectual, or developmental. Mental health conditions, substance use disorder, and chronic illness can also be disabilities. In *Bragdon*, a deeply divided Court concluded that asymptomatic HIV could be considered a disability based on the specific facts of the case. In a series of cases after *Bragdon*, however, the Court established a very narrow interpretation of the ADA statutory definition of disability. Congress amended the ADA in 2008 to clarify that the statutory definition of disability should be construed in favor of broad coverage of individuals.

HOWE V. HULL
U.S. District Court, Northern District, Ohio, 1994.
874 F. Supp.779.

JOHN W. POTTER, SENIOR DISTRICT JUDGE.

* * *

Plaintiff brought suit in the current action alleging that on April 17, 1992, defendants refused to provide Charon medical treatment because he was infected with HIV. Plaintiff claims that defendants' actions violate the Americans with Disabilities Act (ADA) [and] the Federal Rehabilitation Act of 1973 (FRA). . . . The defendants vehemently dispute these claims and allegations and have moved for summary judgment on all of plaintiff's claims.

* * *

On April 17, 1992, Charon and plaintiff Howe were travelling through Ohio, on their way to vacation in Wisconsin. Charon was HIV positive. That morning Charon took a floxin tablet for the first time. Floxin is a prescription antibiotic drug. Within two hours of taking the drug, Charon began experiencing fever, headache, nausea, joint pain, and redness of the skin.

Due to Charon's condition, Charon and plaintiff checked into a motel and, after consulting with Charon's treating physician in Maine, sought medical care at the emergency room of Fremont Memorial Hospital. Charon was examined by the emergency room physician on duty, Dr. Mark Reardon. There is some dispute over what Dr. Reardon's initial diagnosis of Charon's condition was.

Dr. Reardon testified that Charon suffered from a severe drug reaction, and that it was his diagnosis that this reaction was probably Toxic Epidermal Necrolysis (TEN).[2] This diagnosis was also recorded in Charon's medical records. Dr. Reardon also testified regarding Charon's condition that "possibly it was an early stage of toxic epidermal necrolysis, although I had never seen one." Dr. Reardon had no prior experience with TEN, other than what he had read in medical school.

Plaintiff's medical expert Calabrese, however, testified that, after reviewing the medical records and Reardon's deposition, while Charon did appear to be suffering from a severe allergic drug reaction, Calabrese "did not believe that [TEN] was the likely or even probable diagnosis. . . . "

Prior to Charon's eventual transfer to the Medical College of Ohio, Dr. Reardon called Dr. Lynn at MCO and asked Lynn if he would accept the transfer of Charon. Dr. Lynn testified that at no time did Dr. Reardon mention that plaintiff had been diagnosed with the extremely rare and deadly TEN. Dr. Reardon also did not inform the ambulance emergency medical technicians that plaintiff was suffering from TEN.

Dr. Reardon determined that Charon "definitely needed to be admitted" to Memorial Hospital. Since Charon was from out of town, procedure required that Charon be admitted to the on-call physician, Dr. Hull. Dr. Reardon spoke with Dr. Hull on the telephone and informed Dr. Hull that he wanted to admit Charon, who was HIV-positive and suffering from a non-AIDS related severe drug reaction.

While Dr. Reardon and Dr. Hull discussed Charon's situation, the primary area of their discussion appears to have been whether Charon's condition had advanced from HIV to full-blown AIDS. Dr. Hull inquired neither into Charon's physical condition nor vital signs, nor did he ask Dr. Reardon about the possibility of TEN. During this conversation, it is

---

[2] TEN is a very serious, very rare, and often lethal skin condition that causes an individual's skin to slough off the body.

undisputed that Dr. Hull told Dr. Reardon that "if you get an AIDS patient in the hospital, you will never get him out," and directed that plaintiff be sent to the "AIDS program" at MCO. When Dr. Hull arrived at the hospital after Dr. Reardon's shift but prior to Charon's transfer, he did not attempt to examine or meet with Charon.

* * *

Charon was transferred to the Medical College of Ohio some time after 8:45 P.M. on April 17. After his conversation with Dr. Hull and prior to the transfer, Dr. Reardon told Charon and plaintiff that "I'm sure you've dealt with this before. . . . " Howe asked, "What's that, discrimination?" Dr. Reardon replied, "You have to understand, this is a small community, and the admitting doctor does not feel comfortable admitting [Charon]."

* * *

Charon was admitted and treated at the Medical College of Ohio (MCO). Despite the TEN diagnosis, Charon was not diagnosed by MCO personnel as having TEN and, in fact, was never examined by a dermatologist. After several days, Charon recovered from the allergic drug reaction and was released from MCO.

* * *

Before examining the merits of defendants' contentions, the Court must look at and compare the applicable parameters of the ADA and FRA. There are three basic criteria plaintiff must meet in order to establish a prima facie case of discrimination under the ADA:

a) the plaintiff has a disability;

b) the defendants discriminated against the plaintiff; and

c) the discrimination was based on the disability.

42 U.S.C. § 12182(a); 42 U.S.C. § 12182(b). The discrimination can take the form of the denial of the opportunity to receive medical treatment, segregation unnecessary for the provision of effective medical treatment, unnecessary screening or eligibility requirements for treatment, or provision of unequal medical benefits based upon the disability. [ ] A defendant can avoid liability by establishing that it was unable to provide the medical care that a patient required. [ ]

Similarly, to establish a prima facie case under the FRA the plaintiff must show

a) the plaintiff has a disability;

b) plaintiff was otherwise qualified to participate in the program;

c) defendants discriminated against plaintiff solely on the basis of the disability; and

d)   the program received federal funding.

29 U.S.C. § 794(a).

[A] reasonable jury could conclude that the TEN diagnosis was a pretext and that Charon was denied treatment solely because of his disability. Further, there is no evidence to support the conclusion that Memorial Hospital was unable to treat a severe allergic drug reaction. In fact, the evidence indicates that Dr. Reardon initially planned to admit Charon for treatment. Therefore, Charon was "otherwise qualified" for treatment within the meaning of the FRA. . . .

The FRA states that "no otherwise qualified individual with a disability . . . shall, solely by reason of his or her disability . . . be subjected to discrimination. . . . ". 29 U.S.C. § 794(a). The equivalent portion of the ADA reads "No individual shall be discriminated against on the basis of disability. . . . " 42 U.S.C. § 12182(a). It is abundantly clear that the exclusion of the "solely by reason of . . . disability" language was a purposeful act by Congress and not a drafting error or oversight . . . .

The inquiry under the ADA, then, is whether the defendant, despite the articulated reasons for the transfer, improperly considered Charon's HIV status. More explicitly, was Charon transferred for the treatment of a non-AIDS related drug reaction because defendant unjustifiably did not wish to care for an HIV-positive patient? Viewing the evidence in the light most favorable to the plaintiff, the Court finds plaintiff has presented sufficient evidence to preclude a grant of summary judgment on these claims. Defendant Memorial Hospital's motion for summary judgment on the plaintiff's ADA and FRA claims will be denied.

NOTES AND QUESTIONS

1.   *Disability and Health Care Decision-Making. Howe* correctly notes that the ADA and Section 504 differ significantly on what the plaintiff must prove as the reason for the defendant's action. It may be difficult in a particular case to prove the reason for the refusal of treatment or other medical decision, much less meet the requirement that the disability be the "sole" reason for denial of adequate treatment. Recall the facts of *Lyons* in Section II above. Early cases brought under Section 504 suggested that disability nondiscrimination laws could not easily be applied to medical decision-making, or could only be applied where the underlying disability is *unrelated to* the medical decision at issue. See, e.g., U.S. v. Univ. Hosp., State Univ. at Stony Brook, 729 F.2d 144 (2d Cir. 1984). However, the ADA, and Supreme Court cases such as *Bragdon,* make clear that these laws do apply to medical services, programs, and activities. See also *Choate* and *Olmstead,* below.

How much should courts defer to a doctor's judgment as to the best course of treatment for a disabled patient in the context of a discriminatory denial of treatment claim? How would you go about proving or defending against a claim that a medical judgment defense is a subterfuge? What does the Court's analysis in *Bragdon* suggest? Does the requirement that individuals with disabilities be assessed individually based on the best available medical or scientific evidence, rather than based on stereotypes or perceived quality or value of life, help with this inquiry? See E. Haavi Morreim, Futilitarianism, Exoticare, and Coerced Altruism: The ADA Meets Its Limits, 25 Seton Hall L. Rev. 883 (1995); Mary A. Crossley, Of Diagnoses and Discrimination: Discriminatory Nontreatment of Infants with HIV Infection, 93 Colum. L. Rev. 1581 (1993).

2.   *ACA Section 1557 Adopts Existing Protections.* The ADA and Section 504 address a range of barriers in health care settings. These laws require: physical access to services and facilities, including the provision of accessible spaces and the removal of barriers; effective communication, including auxiliary aids and services such as the provision of sign language interpreters or materials in alternative formats; and reasonable modification of policies, practices, and procedures when necessary to accommodate individual needs. 28 C.F.R. 35.130(b)(7); 42 U.S.C. 12182(b)(2)(A), 12183(a). Section 1557 also prohibits discrimination on the basis of disability, and the final rule incorporates many of the ADA's regulatory requirements, including those for reasonable modifications, effective communication, and readily accessible buildings and information technology. 45 C.F.R. § 92.202–.205.

3.   *Effective Communication.* Provision of sign language interpreters for deaf patients has been an active issue in ADA and Section 504 litigation. See e.g., Loeffler v. Staten Island Univ. Hosp., 582 F.3d 268 (2d Cir. 2009), holding that an action for damages under Section 504 could proceed where facts alleged by plaintiff husband (the patient) and wife, both deaf, could support a conclusion that the hospital acted with deliberate indifference in refusing repeated requests for a sign language interpreter for the patient, forcing his minor children to interpret for him. The DOJ has brought a number of suits against providers for failing to provide sign language interpreters, and settlement agreements are available on the DOJ website.

The 2016 Rule implementing Section 1557 adopted the requirements applicable to Title II of the ADA, which require that covered entities ensure effective communication with people with disabilities and give "primary consideration" to that person's choice of auxiliary aid or service (such as a qualified interpreter, an assistive technology device, or materials in alternative formats). 45 C.F.R. § 92.202. The 2020 Rule requested public comment on communication requirements, but it did not adopt significant changes in that area.

4.   *Accessible Facilities and Equipment.* Access to medical care for persons with disabilities has been greatly compromised by providers' failure to choose medical diagnostic equipment, such as examination tables, dental and eye examination chairs, weight scales, and mammography equipment that is accessible for persons with mobility limitations. For a thorough discussion, see Elizabeth Pendo, Reducing Disparities Through Health Reform: Disability and

Accessible Medical Equipment, 2010 Utah L. Rev. 1057 (2010), which includes a review of litigation approaches and provisions of the ACA requiring promulgation of standards for accessible medical equipment. Class action litigation has targeted health care facilities for violation of the ADA regarding physical access. See, e.g., Settlement Agreement in United Spinal Association et al. v. Beth Israel Medical Center et al., No. 13-cv-5131 (S.D.N.Y., filed Nov. 17, 2017).

Regulations implementing Section 1557 incorporate existing requirements regarding readily accessible buildings, and, for most health care facilities, they adopt the 2010 ADA Standards for Accessible Design. 45 C.F.R. § 92.203. In accordance with other provisions of the ACA, the U.S. Access Board, an independent federal agency responsible for developing accessibility guidelines and standards under disability nondiscrimination laws, issued a final rule that delineates minimum technical criteria for the accessibility of examination tables, examination chairs, weight scales, mammography equipment, and other diagnostic imaging equipment. Architectural and Transportation Barriers Compliance Board, Standards for Accessible Medical Diagnostic Equipment. 82 Fed. Reg. 2810 (Jan. 9, 2017) (codified at 36 C.F.R. Part 1195). The standards become mandatory when adopted by a federal agency.

5. *Health Care Decision-Making for Newborns with Disabilities.* Questions about medical care for newborns with disabilities revolve around whether denying treatment could constitute discrimination based on disability, the role of parental decision-making in this analysis, and whether treatment is medically appropriate. For a discussion of medical decision-making for children, see Chapter 18.

ALEXANDER V. CHOATE
Supreme Court of the United States, 1985.
469 U.S. 287.

JUSTICE MARSHALL delivered the opinion of the Court.

In 1980, Tennessee proposed reducing the number of annual days of inpatient hospital care covered by its state Medicaid program. The question presented is whether the effect upon the handicapped that this reduction will have is cognizable under § 504 of the Rehabilitation Act of 1973 or its implementing regulations. We hold that it is not.

I

Faced in 1980–1981 with projected state Medicaid costs of $42 million more than the State's Medicaid budget of $388 million, the directors of the Tennessee Medicaid program decided to institute a variety of cost-saving measures. Among these changes was a reduction from 20 to 14 in the number of inpatient hospital days per fiscal year that Tennessee Medicaid would pay hospitals on behalf of a Medicaid recipient. Before the new measures took effect, respondents, Tennessee Medicaid recipients, brought a class action for declaratory and injunctive relief in which they alleged, *inter alia,* that the proposed 14-day limitation on inpatient coverage would have a discriminatory effect on the handicapped. Statistical evidence, which petitioners do not dispute, indicated that in the 1979–1980 fiscal year, 27.4% of all handicapped users of hospital services who received Medicaid required more than 14 days of care, while only 7.8% of nonhandicapped users required more than 14 days of inpatient care.

Based on this evidence, respondents asserted that the reduction would violate § 504 of the Rehabilitation Act of 1973, 87 Stat. 394, as amended, 29 U.S.C. § 794, and its implementing regulations. Section 504 provides:

> "No otherwise qualified handicapped individual . . . shall, solely by reason of his handicap, be excluded from the participation in, be denied the benefits of, or be subjected to discrimination under any program or activity receiving Federal financial assistance . . . ." 29 U.S.C. § 794.

Respondents' position was twofold. First, they argued that the change from 20 to 14 days of coverage would have a disproportionate effect on the handicapped and hence was discriminatory.[3] The second, and major, thrust of respondents' attack was directed at the use of *any* annual limitation on the number of inpatient days covered, for respondents acknowledged that, given the special needs of the handicapped for medical care, any such limitation was likely to disadvantage the handicapped disproportionately. Respondents noted, however, that federal law does not require States to impose any annual durational limitation on inpatient coverage, and that the Medicaid programs of only 10 States impose such restrictions.[4] Respondents therefore suggested that Tennessee follow these other States and do away with any limitation on the number of annual inpatient days covered. Instead, argued respondents, the State could limit the number of days of hospital coverage on a per-stay basis, with the number of covered days to vary depending on the recipient's illness (for example, fixing the number of days covered for an appendectomy); the period to be covered for each illness could then be set at a level that would keep Tennessee's Medicaid program as a whole within its budget. The State's refusal to adopt this plan was said to result in the imposition of gratuitous costs on the handicapped and thus to constitute discrimination under § 504.

A divided panel of the Court of Appeals for the Sixth Circuit held that respondents had indeed established a prima facie case of a § 504 violation. *Jennings v. Alexander,* 715 F.2d 1036 (1983). The majority apparently

---

[3] The evidence indicated that, if 19 days of coverage were provided, 16.9% of the handicapped, as compared to 4.2% of the nonhandicapped, would not have their needs for inpatient care met.

[4] As of 1980 the average ceiling in those States was 37.6 days. Six States also limit the number of reimbursable days per admission, per spell of illness, or per benefit period. See App. B to Brief for United States as *Amicus Curiae.*

concluded that any action by a federal grantee that disparately affects the handicapped states a cause of action under § 504 and its implementing regulations. Because both the 14-day rule and any annual limitation on inpatient coverage disparately affected the handicapped, the panel found that a prima facie case had been made out, and the case was remanded to give Tennessee an opportunity for rebuttal. According to the panel majority, the State on remand could either demonstrate the unavailability of alternative plans that would achieve the State's legitimate cost-saving goals with a less disproportionate impact on the handicapped, or the State could offer "a substantial justification for the adoption of the plan with the greater discriminatory impact." *Id.*, at 1045. We granted certiorari to consider whether the type of impact at issue in this case is cognizable under § 504 or its implementing regulations, 465 U.S. 1021, 104 S.Ct. 1271, 79 L.Ed.2d 677 (1984), and we now reverse.

II

The first question the parties urge on the Court is whether proof of discriminatory animus is always required to establish a violation of § 504 and its implementing regulations, or whether federal law also reaches action by a recipient of federal funding that discriminates against the handicapped by effect rather than by design. The State of Tennessee argues that § 504 reaches only purposeful discrimination against the handicapped. . . .

* * *

Discrimination against the handicapped was perceived by Congress to be most often the product, not of invidious animus, but rather of thoughtlessness and indifference—of benign neglect.[12] Thus, Representative Vanik, introducing the predecessor to § 504 in the House, described the treatment of the handicapped as one of the country's "shameful oversights," which caused the handicapped to live among society "shunted aside, hidden, and ignored." [ ]. Similarly, Senator Humphrey, who introduced a companion measure in the Senate, asserted that "we can no longer tolerate the invisibility of the handicapped in America . . . ." [ ] And Senator Cranston, the Acting Chairman of the Subcommittee that drafted § 504, described the Act as a response to "previous societal neglect."[ ] . . Federal agencies and commentators on the plight of the handicapped similarly have found that discrimination against the handicapped is primarily the result of apathetic attitudes rather than affirmative animus.

---

[12] To be sure, well-cataloged instances of invidious discrimination against the handicapped do exist. See, *e.g.*, United States Commission on Civil Rights, Accommodating the Spectrum of Individual Abilities, Ch. 2 (1983); Wegner, The Antidiscrimination Model Reconsidered: Ensuring Equal Opportunity Without Respect to Handicap Under Section 504 of the Rehabilitation Act of 1973, 69 Cornell L.Rev. 401, 403, n. 2 (1984).

In addition, much of the conduct that Congress sought to alter in passing the Rehabilitation Act would be difficult if not impossible to reach were the Act construed to proscribe only conduct fueled by a discriminatory intent. For example, elimination of architectural barriers was one of the central aims of the Act, [ ], yet such barriers were clearly not erected with the aim or intent of excluding the handicapped. Similarly, Senator Williams, the chairman of the Labor and Public Welfare Committee that reported out § 504, asserted that the handicapped were the victims of "[d]iscrimination in access to public transportation" and "[d]iscrimination because they do not have the simplest forms of special educational and rehabilitation services they need . . . ." [ ]. And Senator Humphrey, again in introducing the proposal that later became § 504, listed, among the instances of discrimination that the section would prohibit, the use of "transportation and architectural barriers," the "discriminatory effect of job qualification . . . procedures," and the denial of "special educational assistance" for handicapped children. [ ] These statements would ring hollow if the resulting legislation could not rectify the harms resulting from action that discriminated by effect as well as by design.

At the same time, the position urged by respondents—that we interpret § 504 to reach all action disparately affecting the handicapped— is also troubling. Because the handicapped typically are not similarly situated to the nonhandicapped, respondents' position would in essence require each recipient of federal funds first to evaluate the effect on the handicapped of every proposed action that might touch the interests of the handicapped, and then to consider alternatives for achieving the same objectives with less severe disadvantage to the handicapped. The formalization and policing of this process could lead to a wholly unwieldy administrative and adjudicative burden. [ ] Had Congress intended § 504 to be a National Environmental Policy Act for the handicapped, requiring the preparation of "Handicapped Impact Statements" before any action was taken by a grantee that affected the handicapped, we would expect some indication of that purpose in the statute or its legislative history. Yet there is nothing to suggest that such was Congress' purpose. Thus, just as there is reason to question whether Congress intended § 504 to reach only intentional discrimination, there is similarly reason to question whether Congress intended § 504 to embrace all claims of disparate-impact discrimination.

Any interpretation of § 504 must therefore be responsive to two powerful but countervailing considerations—the need to give effect to the statutory objectives and the desire to keep § 504 within manageable bounds. Given the legitimacy of both of these goals and the tension between them, we decline the parties' invitation to decide today that one of these goals so overshadows the other as to eclipse it. While we reject the boundless notion that all disparate-impact showings constitute prima facie cases under § 504, we assume without deciding that § 504 reaches at least some conduct that has an unjustifiable disparate impact upon the handicapped. On that assumption, we must then determine whether the disparate effect of which respondents complain is the sort of disparate impact that federal law might recognize.

III

To determine which disparate impacts § 504 might make actionable, the proper starting point is *Southeastern Community College v. Davis,* 442 U.S. 397, 99 S.Ct. 2361, 60 L.Ed.2d 980 (1979), our major previous attempt to define the scope of § 504. *Davis* involved a plaintiff with a major hearing disability who sought admission to a college to be trained as a registered nurse, but who would not be capable of safely performing as a registered nurse even with full-time personal supervision. We stated that, under some circumstances, a "refusal to modify an existing program might become unreasonable and discriminatory. Identification of those instances where a refusal to accommodate the needs of a disabled person amounts to discrimination against the handicapped [is] an important responsibility of HEW." *Id.,* at 413, 99 S.Ct., at 2370. We held that the college was not required to admit Davis because it appeared unlikely that she could benefit from any modifications that the relevant HEW regulations required, *id.,* at 409, 99 S.Ct., at 2368, and because the further modifications Davis sought—full-time, personal supervision whenever she attended patients and elimination of all clinical courses—would have compromised the essential nature of the college's nursing program, *id.,* at 413–414, 99 S.Ct., at 2370–2371. Such a "fundamental alteration in the nature of a program" was far more than the reasonable modifications the statute or regulations required. *Id.,* at 410, 99 S.Ct., at 2369. *Davis* thus struck a balance between the statutory rights of the handicapped to be integrated into society and the legitimate interests of federal grantees in preserving the integrity of their programs: while a grantee need not be required to make "fundamental" or "substantial" modifications to accommodate the handicapped, it may be required to make "reasonable" ones.

The balance struck in *Davis* requires that an otherwise qualified handicapped individual must be provided with meaningful access to the benefit that the grantee offers. The benefit itself, of course, cannot be defined in a way that effectively denies otherwise qualified handicapped individuals the meaningful access to which they are entitled; to assure meaningful access, reasonable accommodations in the grantee's program or benefit may have to be made.[21] In this case, respondents argue that the

---

[21] As the Government states: "Antidiscrimination legislation can obviously be emptied of meaning if every discriminatory policy is 'collapsed' into one's definition of what is the relevant benefit." Brief for United States as *Amicus Curiae* 29, n. 36. At oral argument, the Government also acknowledged that "special measures for the handicapped, as the *Lau* case shows, may sometimes be necessary . . . ." Tr. of Oral Arg. 14–15 (referring to *Lau v. Nichols,* 414 U.S. 563, 94 S.Ct. 786, 39 L.Ed.2d 1 (1974)).

14-day rule, or any annual durational limitation, denies meaningful access to Medicaid services in Tennessee. We examine each of these arguments in turn.

A

The 14-day limitation will not deny respondents meaningful access to Tennessee Medicaid services or exclude them from those services. The new limitation does not invoke criteria that have a particular exclusionary effect on the handicapped; the reduction, neutral on its face, does not distinguish between those whose coverage will be reduced and those whose coverage will not on the basis of any test, judgment, or trait that the handicapped as a class are less capable of meeting or less likely of having. Moreover, it cannot be argued that "meaningful access" to state Medicaid services will be denied by the 14-day limitation on inpatient coverage; nothing in the record suggests that the handicapped in Tennessee will be unable to benefit meaningfully from the coverage they will receive under the 14-day rule.[22] The reduction in inpatient coverage will leave both handicapped and nonhandicapped Medicaid users with identical and effective hospital services fully available for their use, with both classes of users subject to the same durational limitation. The 14-day limitation, therefore, does not exclude the handicapped from or deny them the benefits of the 14 days of care the State has chosen to provide.

To the extent respondents further suggest that their greater need for prolonged inpatient care means that, to provide meaningful access to Medicaid services, Tennessee must single out the handicapped for *more* than 14 days of coverage, the suggestion is simply unsound. At base, such a suggestion must rest on the notion that the benefit provided through state Medicaid programs is the amorphous objective of "adequate health care." But Medicaid programs do not guarantee that each recipient will receive that level of health care precisely tailored to his or her particular needs. Instead, the benefit provided through Medicaid is a particular package of health care services, such as 14 days of inpatient coverage. That

---

The regulations implementing § 504 are consistent with the view that reasonable adjustments in the nature of the benefit offered must at times be made to assure meaningful access. See, *e.g.*, 45 CFR § 84.12(a) (1984) (requiring an employer to make "reasonable accommodation to the known physical or mental limitations" of a handicapped individual); 45 CFR § 84.22 and § 84.23 (1984) (requiring that new buildings be readily accessible, building alterations be accessible "to the maximum extent feasible," and existing facilities eventually be operated so that a program or activity inside is, "when viewed in its entirety," readily accessible); 45 CFR § 84.44(a) (1984) (requiring certain modifications to the regular academic programs of secondary education institutions, such as changes in the length of time permitted for the completion of degree requirements, substitution of specific courses required for the completion of degree requirements, and adaptation of the manner in which specific courses are conducted).

[22] The record does not contain any suggestion that the illnesses uniquely associated with the handicapped or occurring with greater frequency among them cannot be effectively treated, at least in part, with fewer than 14 days' coverage. In addition, the durational limitation does not apply to only particular handicapped conditions and takes effect regardless of the particular cause of hospitalization.

package of services has the general aim of assuring that individuals will receive necessary medical care, but the benefit provided remains the individual services offered—not "adequate health care."

The federal Medicaid Act makes this point clear. The Act gives the States substantial discretion to choose the proper mix of amount, scope, and duration limitations on coverage, as long as care and services are provided in "the best interests of the recipients." 42 U.S.C. § 1396a(a)(19). The District Court found that the 14-day limitation would fully serve 95% of even handicapped individuals eligible for Tennessee Medicaid, and both lower courts concluded that Tennessee's proposed Medicaid plan would meet the "best interests" standard. That unchallenged conclusion indicates that Tennessee is free, as a matter of the Medicaid Act, to choose to define the benefit it will be providing as 14 days of inpatient coverage.

Section 504 does not require the State to alter this definition of the benefit being offered simply to meet the reality that the handicapped have greater medical needs. To conclude otherwise would be to find that the Rehabilitation Act requires States to view certain illnesses, *i.e.*, those particularly affecting the handicapped, as more important than others and more worthy of cure through government subsidization. Nothing in the legislative history of the Act supports such a conclusion. Cf. Doe v. Colautti, 592 F.2d 704 (CA3 1979) (State may limit covered-private-inpatient-psychiatric care to 60 days even though State sets no limit on duration of coverage for physical illnesses). Section 504 seeks to assure evenhanded treatment and the opportunity for handicapped individuals to participate in and benefit from programs receiving federal assistance. Southeastern Community College v. Davis, 442 U.S. 397, 99 S.Ct. 2361, 60 L.Ed.2d 980 (1979). The Act does not, however, guarantee the handicapped equal results from the provision of state Medicaid, even assuming some measure of equality of health could be constructed. *Ibid.*

Regulations promulgated by the Department of Health and Human Services (HHS) pursuant to the Act further support this conclusion. These regulations state that recipients of federal funds who provide health services cannot "provide a qualified handicapped person with benefits or services that are not as effective (as defined in § 84.4(b)) as the benefits or services provided to others." 45 CFR § 84.52(a)(3) (1984). The regulations also prohibit a recipient of federal funding from adopting "criteria or methods of administration that have the purpose or effect of defeating or substantially impairing accomplishment of the objectives of the recipient's program with respect to the handicapped." 45 CFR § 84.4(b)(4)(ii) (1984).

While these regulations, read in isolation, could be taken to suggest that a state Medicaid program must make the handicapped as healthy as the nonhandicapped, other regulations reveal that HHS does not contemplate imposing such a requirement. Title 45 CFR § 84.4(b)(2) (1984), referred to in the regulations quoted above, makes clear that

> "[f]or purposes of this part, aids, benefits, and services, to be equally effective, are not required to produce the identical result or level of achievement for handicapped and nonhandicapped persons, but must afford handicapped persons equal opportunity to obtain the same result, to gain the same benefit, or to reach the same level of achievement . . . ."

This regulation, while indicating that adjustments to existing programs are contemplated, also makes clear that Tennessee is not required to assure that its handicapped Medicaid users will be as healthy as its nonhandicapped users. Thus, to the extent respondents are seeking a distinct durational limitation for the handicapped, Tennessee is entitled to respond by asserting that the relevant benefit is 14 days of coverage. Because the handicapped have meaningful and equal access to that benefit, Tennessee is not obligated to reinstate its 20-day rule or to provide the handicapped with more than 14 days of inpatient coverage.

B

We turn next to respondents' alternative contention, a contention directed not at the 14-day rule itself but rather at Tennessee's Medicaid *plan* as a whole. Respondents argue that the inclusion of any annual durational limitation on inpatient coverage in a state Medicaid plan violates § 504. The thrust of this challenge is that all annual durational limitations discriminate against the handicapped because (1) the effect of such limitations falls most heavily on the handicapped and because (2) this harm could be avoided by the choice of other Medicaid plans that would meet the State's budgetary constraints without disproportionately disadvantaging the handicapped. Viewed in this light, Tennessee's current plan is said to inflict a gratuitous harm on the handicapped that denies them meaningful access to Medicaid services.

Whatever the merits of this conception of meaningful access, it is clear that § 504 does not require the changes respondents seek. In enacting the Rehabilitation Act and in subsequent amendments, Congress did focus on several substantive areas—employment, education, and the elimination of physical barriers to access—in which it considered the societal and personal costs of refusals to provide meaningful access to the handicapped to be particularly high. But nothing in the pre- or post-1973 legislative discussion of § 504 suggests that Congress desired to make major inroads on the States' longstanding discretion to choose the proper mix of amount, scope, and duration limitations on services covered by state Medicaid, see *Beal v. Doe,* 432 U.S. 438, 444, 97 S.Ct. 2366, 2370, 53 L.Ed.2d 464 (1977). And, more generally, we have already stated, *supra,* at 719–720, that § 504 does not impose a general NEPA-like requirement on federal grantees.

The costs of such a requirement would be far from minimal, and thus Tennessee's refusal to pursue this course does not, as respondents suggest, inflict a "gratuitous" harm on the handicapped. On the contrary, to require that the sort of broad-based distributive decision at issue in this case always be made in the way most favorable, or least disadvantageous, to the handicapped, even when the same benefit is meaningfully and equally offered to them, would be to impose a virtually unworkable requirement on state Medicaid administrators. Before taking any across-the-board action affecting Medicaid recipients, an analysis of the effect of the proposed change on the handicapped would have to be prepared. Presumably, that analysis would have to be further broken down by class of handicap—the change at issue here, for example, might be significantly less harmful to the blind, who use inpatient services only minimally, than to other subclasses of handicapped Medicaid recipients; the State would then have to balance the harms and benefits to various groups to determine, on balance, the extent to which the action disparately impacts the handicapped. In addition, respondents offer no reason that similar treatment would not have to be accorded other groups protected by statute or regulation from disparate-impact discrimination.

It should be obvious that administrative costs of implementing such a regime would be well beyond the accommodations that are required under *Davis*. As a result, Tennessee need not redefine its Medicaid program to eliminate durational limitations on inpatient coverage, even if in doing so the State could achieve its immediate fiscal objectives in a way less harmful to the handicapped.

IV

The 14-day rule challenged in this case is neutral on its face, is not alleged to rest on a discriminatory motive, and does not deny the handicapped access to or exclude them from the particular package of Medicaid services Tennessee has chosen to provide. The State has made the same benefit—14 days of coverage—equally accessible to both handicapped and nonhandicapped persons, and the State is not required to assure the handicapped "adequate health care" by providing them with more coverage than the nonhandicapped. In addition, the State is not obligated to modify its Medicaid program by abandoning reliance on annual durational limitations on inpatient coverage. Assuming, then, that § 504 or its implementing regulations reach some claims of disparate-impact discrimination, the effect of Tennessee's reduction in annual inpatient coverage is not among them. For that reason, the Court of Appeals erred in holding that respondents had established a prima facie violation of § 504. The judgment below is accordingly reversed.

It is so ordered.

NOTES AND QUESTIONS

1. *"Meaningful Access."* The Supreme Court in *Choate* rejected the idea that Section 504 prohibits only intentional discrimination and reaffirmed the availability of disparate impact claims. However, it also held that the mandate of Section 504 "to assure evenhanded treatment and the opportunity for handicapped individuals to participate in and benefit from programs receiving federal assistance" is met when people with disabilities are provided "meaningful access" to such programs. "Meaningful access" is a key concept, and courts have interpreted this standard in different ways. For a discussion of "meaningful access" in the context of health care, see Leslie Pickering Francis & Anita Silvers, Debilitating Alexander v. Choate: "Meaningful Access" to Health Care for People with Disabilities, 35 Fordham Urb. L. J. 447 (2008). See also Mark C. Weber, Meaningful Access and Disability Discrimination: The Role of Social Science and Other Empirical Evidence, 39 Cardozo L. Rev. 649 (2017). There also is uncertainty as to whether a claim of disparate impact requires a showing of intent (e.g., "deliberate indifference"). Some courts have borrowed the analysis of intent from Title VI, while others have not. For a discussion, see Mark C. Weber, Accidentally on Purpose: Intent in Disability Discrimination Law, 56 B.C. L. Rev. 1417 (2015).

2. *Distinguishing Choate.* How might you distinguish facially neutral treatment that falls more heavily on people with disabilities from treatment that "targets" people with disabilities? In the early 2000s, a class action lawsuit was filed under Title II of the ADA challenging a decision by Los Angeles County to close the Rancho Los Amigos National Rehabilitation Center, a facility dedicated primarily to providing inpatient and outpatient care to people with disabilities. Rodde v. Bonta, 357 F.3d 988 (9th Cir. 2004). In 2002, the county consolidated its services for people with certain severe disabilities at Rancho, one of six public facilities at the time. One year later, the county proposed closing Rancho as a means to save money. The plaintiffs were current and future participants in California's Medicaid program, Medi-Cal, with disabilities and conditions that required medical services offered by Rancho. In granting a preliminary injunction, the district court concluded that Rancho patients with disabilities could not easily be served elsewhere and that the county had made no transition plans to accommodate them.

The Ninth Circuit affirmed, distinguishing *Choate* on several grounds. First, unlike in *Choate*, the decision to close Rancho was not a facially neutral, "across-the-board" cut, but was instead the elimination of the one facility out of six that, due to the county's prior consolidation of services, provided services disproportionately required by people with disabilities. Second, there was evidence that closing Rancho would disproportionately harm people with disabilities because the services provided could not be provided elsewhere in the county system at that time. The parties reached a settlement in which the county agreed that Rancho would remain open for at least another three years, maintaining at least the same level of service.

3. *Private Disparate Impact Claims.* The Court in *Choate* assumed that Section 504 permits private actions challenging facially neutral policies and programs that have a disparate impact on people with disabilities. In support of such a right, the Court stated that "much of the conduct that Congress sought to alter in passing the Rehabilitation Act would be difficult if not impossible to reach were the Act construed to proscribe only conduct fueled by a discriminatory intent." It reasoned that, in enacting Section 504, Congress intended to reach discrimination that was not only the result of "invidious animus," but also of "thoughtlessness," "indifference," and "benign neglect."

Relying on *Choate*, at least four circuits have recognized a disparate impact theory based on lack of meaningful access under Section 504, and by extension, Section 1557. The Sixth Circuit, however, has held that a disparate impact theory is inconsistent with the text of the Rehabilitation Act, although it did not address the meaningful access standard in the context of the ACA. Doe v. BlueCross BlueShield of Tenn., Inc., 926 F.3d 235 (6th Cir. 2019); see also discussion of *Sandoval*, above.

In 2021, the U.S. Supreme Court granted a petition for certiorari on this question. In *Doe v. CVS Pharmacy*, the Ninth Circuit joined the Second, Seventh, and Tenth Circuits in recognizing a disparate impact claim under Section 504. Doe v. CVS Pharmacy, 982 F.3d. 1204 (9th Cir. 2020). In that case, HIV-positive class members challenged a provision of their health plan under which they were eligible for in-network prices for specialty medications, including HIV/AIDS medications, only if they accepted the medications by mail or through a specialty pick-up service at a CVS pharmacy, which did not include interaction with a pharmacist. Any prescriptions filled in-person were subject to out-of-network prices. The enrollees challenged this plan benefit under Section 1557, alleging that it denied them meaningful access to their prescription drug benefit within the meaning of the Section 504, as incorporated in Section 1557 of the ACA, because they did not receive effective treatment for HIV/AIDS, including medically appropriate dispensing of their medications and access to consultation with a pharmacist.

In holding that the enrollees had stated a claim, the Ninth Circuit held:

> Following Choate, we recognized that the unique impact of a facially-neutral policy on people with disabilities may give rise to a disparate impact claim where state "services, programs, and activities remain open and easily accessible to others." . . . Here, Does have alleged that even though the Program applies to specialty medications that may not be used to treat conditions associated with disabilities, the Program burdens HIV/AIDS patients differently because of their unique pharmaceutical needs. Specifically, they claim that changes in medication to treat the continual mutation of the virus requires pharmacists to review all of an HIV/AIDS patient's medications for side effects and adverse drug interactions, a benefit they no longer receive under the Program.

Id. at 1211. The Supreme Court granted CVS's petition for certiorari on the question of whether Section 504, and by extension the ACA, provides a disparate impact cause of action for plaintiffs alleging disability discrimination. CVS Pharmacy v. Doe, 141 S. Ct. 2882 (2021). CVS agreed to withdraw its petition in November 2021, effectively preserving existing access to private disparate impact actions. However, this issue, along with legal challenges and anticipated regulatory activity surrounding Section 1557, should be watched closely.

4. *Integration Mandate.* In the landmark 1999 case *Olmstead v. L.C*, the Supreme Court held that unnecessary segregation of persons with disability constitutes discrimination in violation of Title II of the ADA. Olmstead v. L.C. ex rel. Zimring, 527 U.S. 581, 592 (1992). The Court held that public entities, including state Medicaid programs, must provide community-based services to persons with disabilities when such services are appropriate, desired by the recipient, and can be reasonably accommodated by the public entity. The Court relied on the "integration mandate" in the Title II regulations that requires public entities to "administer services, programs, and activities in the most integrated setting appropriate to the needs of qualified individuals with disabilities." The regulations define the "most integrated setting" as one that "enables individuals with disabilities to interact with nondisabled persons to the fullest extent possible. . . ."

The *Olmstead* holding means individuals with a disability, including persons with cognitive and intellectual disabilities and persons with mental illness, cannot be required to live in institutions or group settings to obtain the health care and other services they need. See Chapter 10 (Medicaid) for a discussion of state reforms expanding home and community-based care.

NOTE: DISABILITY DISCRIMINATION IN HEALTH INSURANCE

People with disabilities face challenges obtaining adequate and affordable health insurance. The 2009 report, The Current State of Health Care for People with Disabilities, found that the complex, fragmented, and often overly restrictive U.S. health insurance system leaves some people with disabilities with no health care coverage and others with exclusions, limits, and cost-sharing obligations that prevent them from obtaining needed medications, medical equipment, specialty care, dental and vision care, long-term care, and care coordination. Nat'l Council on Disability, The Current State of Health Care for People with Disabilities (2009). See also Valarie Blake, An Opening for Civil Rights in Health Insurance After the Affordable Care Act, 36 Boston College J. of L. & Soc. Justice 235 (2016), discussing disability discrimination in public and private health insurance.

Challenges in Applying the ADA

On its face, several provisions of the ADA appear to prohibit insurers and employers administering benefit plans from imposing coverage terms and conditions that discriminate against persons with particular disabilities. Title I of the ADA prohibits discrimination "against a qualified individual with a disability because of the disability of such individual in regard to . . . [the] terms, conditions, and privileges of employment." 42 U.S.C. § 12112. The statute prohibits discrimination in nearly all aspects of work, including the receipt of "fringe benefits." 42 U.S.C. § 12112(b)(4); 29 C.F.R. § 1630.4(f). Title II similarly prohibits public entities from discriminating. 42 U.S.C. § 12132. Title III proscribes discrimination "on the basis of disability in the full and equal enjoyment of the goods, services, facilities, privileges, advantages, or accommodations of any place of public accommodation . . . ." 42 U.S.C. § 12182. "Public accommodation" is specifically defined to include an "insurance office." 42 U.S.C. § 12181(7)(F). Finally, Title V of the ADA contains a specific "safe harbor" provision that states that the ADA does not restrict insurers, HMOs, employers, plans, or administrators from "underwriting risks, classifying risks, or administering such risks that are based on or not inconsistent with State law," as long as the entity does not use this provision "as a subterfuge to evade the purposes" of the ADA. 42 U.S.C. § 12201(c).

The ADA has been applied to health insurance, but with significant limitations. Cases have been brought under the ADA challenging policies that provided less coverage for treatment of mental illnesses than for treatment of physical conditions, Rogers v. Dep't of Health & Envtl. Control, 174 F.3d 431 (4th Cir. 1999); Fletcher v. Tufts Univ., 367 F. Supp. 2d 99 (D. Mass. 2005); that capped coverage for AIDS but not for other conditions, Doe v. Mutual of Omaha Ins. Co., 179 F.3d 557 (7th Cir. 1999); or that excluded coverage for particular services, such as heart transplants, Lenox v. Healthwise of Kentucky, Ltd., 149 F.3d 453 (6th Cir. 1998), and infertility, Krauel v. Iowa Methodist Med. Ctr., 95 F.3d 674 (8th Cir. 1996). Although some of these cases have succeeded, they have encountered increasingly serious obstacles. First, most courts have held that the ADA does not require employers or insurers to offer any particular form of coverage; it merely prohibits them from offering different terms and conditions to disabled persons. See, e.g., EEOC v. Staten Island Sav. Bank, 207 F.3d 144 (2d Cir. 2000). The courts have held that the ADA does not demand all disabilities be treated similarly, but only that disabled persons not be disfavored in comparison to nondisabled persons. Providing different coverage for different conditions, moreover, is not even necessarily prohibited unless the condition itself is a disability or unless discrimination in the coverage of a particular condition disproportionately affects disabled persons. Even then, such distinctions may be permitted under the "safe harbor" provisions discussed below.

Second, whether and when the ADA applies to insurance policies has sparked much debate. Though Title III clearly covers insurance offices, several courts have held that it only applies to physical places and not to the terms and conditions of the products offered independent of these places. See, e.g., Weyer v. Twentieth Century Fox Film Corp., 198 F.3d 1104 (9th Cir. 2000). A number of other courts and the EEOC Guidelines, on the other hand, have held that Title III might extend to the contents of insurance policies. See, e.g., Doe v. Mut. Of Omaha Ins. Co., 179 F.3d 557, 558–59 (7th Cir. 1999); Fletcher v. Tufts Univ., 367 F. Supp. 2d 99, 114–115 (D. Mass. 2005). See Jeffrey S. Manning, Are Insurance Companies Liable Under the Americans With Disabilities Act?, 88 Calif. L. Rev. 607 (2000). Of course, if an employer offers insurance, Title I prohibits discrimination against an employee, even if Title III does not cover the insurer. However, several courts have limited Title I actions to current employees, contending that former employees, such as retirees, have no rights under the statute. See, e.g., EEOC v. CNA Ins. Cos., 96 F.3d 1039, 1045 (7th Cir. 1996). But see Castellano v. City of N.Y., 142 F.3d 58 (2d Cir. 1998). Title I of the ADA also limits the questions that employers can ask their employees about health issues, which affects workplace wellness programs. See Chapter 9.

Third, several courts have read Title V's insurance "safe harbor" broadly to protect insurer practices that are not designed to discriminate, following the Supreme Court's interpretation of the term "subterfuge" in the Age Discrimination in Employment Act of 1967, 29 U.S.C. §§ 621–630, ("ADEA") in the case Pub. Emps. Ret. Sys. Of Ohio v. Betts, 492 U.S. 158 (1989). See Ford v. Schering-Plough Corp., 145 F.3d 601 (3d Cir. 1998) and Krauel v. Iowa Methodist Med. Ctr., 95 F.3d 674, 678–9 (8th Cir. 1996). Other courts, however, have required actuarial support for treating different conditions differently, particularly when the insurance practice is also suspect under state law. Morgenthal v. Am. Tel. & Tel. Co., 1999 WL 187055 (S.D.N.Y. 1999); Chabner v. United of Omaha Life Ins. Co., 994 F. Supp. 1185 (N.D. Cal. 1998).

Section 1557

As a result of these limitations, prior to the ACA, many people with disabilities were denied health insurance, or charged higher prices, often with coverage limitations and exclusions. The ACA's insurance reforms, discussed in Chapter 9, address some of these problems. For example, prior to the ACA, many insurers were permitted to exclude or restrict coverage for individuals with a preexisting condition such as cancer, asthma, or other chronic conditions or disabilities under the ADA's "safe harbor" exception.

In addition to broad insurance reforms, Section 1557 was initially viewed as an important new way to challenge discriminatory benefit exclusions or denials based on disability and other protected categories. The 2016 Rule implementing Section 1557 defined health programs and activities to include health insurance and the provision of health-related services. It provides that covered entities may not deny, cancel, limit, or refuse to issue or renew a health insurance policy, deny or limit coverage of a health insurance claim, impose additional cost sharing or other limitations or restrictions on coverage, or use discriminatory marketing practices or insurance benefit designs on the basis of any protected category. The 2016 Rule also clarifies that if one part of an entity that is principally engaged in providing or administering health services or health insurance coverage receives federal financial assistance, the entire entity is forbidden to discriminate.

What constitutes discrimination in insurance benefit design? HHS declined to identify specific practices in the 2016 Rule, in favor of a fact-specific inquiry. The preamble did identify factors that OCR will consider when assessing whether a plan benefit design is discriminatory: whether a covered entity utilized, in a nondiscriminatory manner, a neutral rule or principle when deciding to adopt the design feature or take the challenged action; whether the reason for its coverage decision is a pretext for discrimination; and whether coverage for the same or a similar service or treatment is available to individuals outside of that protected class or those with different health conditions. It will also evaluate the reasons for any differences in coverage. See 81 Fed. Reg. at 31433.

Would placing all drugs used to treat a specific disability such HIV/AIDS in a plan's highest cost-sharing tier be considered discriminatory? See Jane Perkins and Wayne Turner, NHeLP and The AIDS Institute Complaint to HHS Re HIV/AIDS Discrimination by Florida Insurers (May 29, 2014), available at the NHeLP website, healthlaw.org. In separate guidance, CMS identified this practice as an example of potential discrimination, along with applying age limits to services that have been found clinically effective at all ages, and requiring prior authorization and/or step therapy for all or most medications in drug classes such as anti-HIV protease inhibitors and/or immune suppressants, regardless of medical evidence. 81 Fed. Reg. at 31434, n. 258.

The future of Section 1557 as a vehicle to challenge discriminatory benefit design is uncertain. As discussed above, the 2020 Rule significantly limits the scope of the 2016 Rule and eliminates the provisions prohibiting discrimination in plan benefit design. In light of an anticipated new notice of proposed rulemaking to revise the Section 1557 regulations, and other steps to reverse Trump Administration policy and regulations that significantly narrowed the reach of Section 1557, developments in the interpretation and enforcement of Section 1557 should be watched closely.

D. OTHER NONDISCRIMINATION REQUIREMENTS

This section identifies additional federal nondiscrimination laws that may apply to health care insurers and others. State nondiscrimination laws may also apply, as Section 1557 does not limit their application. 42 U.S.C. § 18116(b). State laws often parallel the protections of federal law but can differ in terms of entities covered, specific protections, and enforcement processes. State law can also address gaps or provide more protections than federal law.

1. Genetic Information

The ability to read (and, perhaps, change) a person's genetic characteristics has created tremendous hopes and terrible fears. There is a fear that the terrifying history of eugenics will repeat itself. In Buck v. Bell, 274 U.S. 200 (1927), for example, the Supreme Court tragically misunderstood and misused genetics and decided that the forced sterilization of a woman perceived to be intellectually disabled, whose mother and grandmother were also believed to be so, was not a violation of her constitutional rights. Justice Holmes, in a now infamous declaration, stated that it is desirable "to prevent those who are manifestly unfit from continuing their kind . . . . Three generations of imbeciles are enough." For a full history of that case and the family, see Paul Lombardo, Three Generations, No Imbeciles: New Light on Buck v. Bell, 60 N.Y.U. L. Rev. 30 (1985). About 8,000 Virginians who were low-income, uneducated, and believed to have intellectual disabilities were sterilized as part of a eugenics program in that state between 1924 and 1979. Thirty states engaged in such programs, and 65,000 individuals nationwide were involuntarily sterilized.

Similarly, government efforts targeted people with sickle cell based on mistaken genetic assumptions:

In the 1970s, large scale screening [for sickle cell] was undertaken with the goal of changing African American mating behavior. Unfortunately, the initiative promoted confusion regarding the difference between carriers and those with the disease. This confusion resulted in widespread discrimination against African Americans. Some states passed legislation requiring all African American children entering school to be screened for the sickle-cell trait, even though there was no treatment or cure for the sickle-cell disease. Some states required prisoners to be tested, even though there would be no opportunity for them to pass on the trait. Job and insurance discrimination were both real and attempted. The military considered banning all African Americans from the armed services. African American airline stewardesses were fired. Insurance rates went up for carriers. Some companies refused to insure carriers. During that period, many African Americans came to believe that the sickle-cell screening initiative was merely a disguised genocide attempt, since often the only advice given to African Americans with the trait was, "Don't have kids."

Vernellia R. Randall, Trusting the Health Care System Ain't Always Easy! An African American Perspective on Bioethics, 15 St. Louis U. Public L. Rev. 191 (1996). See also Norman-Bloodsaw v. Lawrence Berkeley Lab., 135 F.3d 1260 (9th Cir. 1998), involving employment-based testing for sickle cell.

The potential for discrimination against people based on genetic information was recognized by the passage of the Genetic Information Nondiscrimination Act of 2008 (GINA) which regulates the collection and use of genetic information by group health plans, by those marketing individual policies for health insurance, and by employers. GINA amends ERISA, HIPAA, and the Internal Revenue Code, and adds a provision to the federal employment discrimination statutes. See Chapter 4 (HIPAA), Chapter 8 (ERISA), and Chapter 9 (insurance). GINA prohibits health insurers, in both group health plans and in the individual market, from making insurance decisions based on "genetic information." Genetic information is defined broadly as genetic tests, the genetic tests of family members, and the manifestation of a disease or disorder in family members, with exceptions. See 42 U.S.C. § 2000ff. Insurers may consider genetic diseases that have manifested themselves in ways other than genetic tests. However, the ADA may apply for manifested diseases that meet the statutory definition of disability. The EEOC has promulgated regulations to enforce the statute in the employment context, while the OCR and other agencies have issued regulations to enforce the statute in other contexts.

Unlike the other federal nondiscrimination laws discussed in this chapter, GINA does not regulate the delivery of health care services. However, it addresses related concerns. The Preamble of the Act describes the rationale for its enactment:

> Deciphering the sequence of the human genome and other advances in genetics open major new opportunities for medical progress. New knowledge about the genetic basis of illness will allow for earlier detection of illnesses, often before symptoms have begun. Genetic testing can allow individuals to take steps to reduce the likelihood that they will contract a particular disorder. New knowledge about genetics may allow for the development of better therapies that are more effective against disease or have fewer side effects than current treatments. These advances give rise to the potential misuse of genetic information to discriminate in health insurance and employment.

> The early science of genetics became the basis of State laws that provided for the sterilization of persons having presumed genetic "defects" such as mental retardation, mental disease, epilepsy, blindness, and hearing loss, among other conditions. . . . [T]he current explosion in the science of genetics, and the history of sterilization laws by the States based on early genetic science, compels Congressional action in this area.

> Although genes are facially neutral markers, many genetic conditions and disorders are associated with particular racial and ethnic groups and gender. Because some genetic traits are most prevalent in particular groups, members of a particular group may be stigmatized or discriminated against as a result of that genetic information. . . . To alleviate some of this stigma, Congress in 1972 passed the National Sickle Cell Anemia Control Act, which withholds Federal funding from States unless sickle cell testing is voluntary.

NOTES AND QUESTIONS

1.   *Limitations of GINA and Genetic Privacy Laws.* GINA does not reach discrimination issues other than genetic discrimination in employment and health insurance. It generally provides no protection against discrimination in

the life, long-term care, or disability insurance markets, for example. See Ellen Wright Clayton et al., The Law of Genetic Privacy: Applications, Implications, and Limitations, 6 J. of L. and the Biosciences 1 (2019) and Jarrod O. Anderson, et al., The Problem with Patchwork: State Approaches to Regulating Insurer Use of Genetic Information, 22 DePaul J. of Health L. (2021) discussing limitations of existing genetic information privacy protections.

2. *Future of GINA.* While some of the insurance protections mandated under GINA are also included in the ACA, GINA will continue to be an additional source of support for those who face discrimination in health insurance eligibility, price, or conditions because of their genetic status. GINA also applies to workplace wellness plans, which have increasingly been used as a way to collect employees' health and genetic information. See Chapter 9 for a discussion of the application of the ADA and GINA to workplace wellness plans. GINA's protections may become more important as genetic information becomes more informative, more widely used in medicine and research, and more easily re-identified. Barbara J. Evans, The Genetic Information Nondiscrimination Act at 10: GINA's Controversial Assertion that Data Transparency Protects Privacy and Civil Rights, 60 William & Mary L. Rev. 2017 (2019).

3. *Devaluing "Imperfect" Lives?* Given our often-moralistic attitudes toward sickness and the continuing human history of exclusion and discrimination against minorities and people with disabilities, will "imperfect humans" be devalued and penalized? This is a familiar dynamic in history, but the new power of genetics may increase the potential for stigma and discrimination. See Nat'l Council on Disability, Genetic Testing and the Rush to Perfection (2019). Increased opportunities for control of genetic traits in reproductive decision making, for example, raise questions of choice and consequences. See Eric Rakowski, Who Should Pay for Bad Genes, 90 Cal. L. Rev. 1345 (2002), arguing that parents who choose to bear such a "genetically disadvantaged" child should incur a greater liability for the costs of the child's care. On the other hand, others are concerned about the drive toward "genetic enhancement" and the creation of a genetically perfect person (or society). See Maxwell Mehlman, Law of Above Averages: Leveling the New Genetic Enhancement Playing Field, 85 Iowa L. Rev. 517 (2000); Michael Malinowski, Choosing the Genetic Makeup of Our Children: Our Eugenics Past—Present, and Future, 36 Conn. L. Rev. 125 (2003). Reproductive decision-making is discussed in detail in Chapter 16.

4. *Implications for Groups.* Genetic information is likely to have implications for groups. The idea that groups may have concerns, interests, and perhaps rights is one that is hotly debated in genetic research. See, e.g., Joan L. McGregor, Population Genomics and Research Ethics, 35 J.L. Med. & Ethics 356 (2007); Laura Underkuffler, Human Genetics Studies: The Case for Group Rights, 35 J.L. Med. & Ethics 383 (2007). See also the discussion of research with the Havasupai tribe in Chapter 20.

Sometimes the distribution of genetic traits may appear to parallel what have been called "folk notions" of race or ethnicity. Pilar Ossorio, Race, Genetic Variation, and the Haplotype Mapping Project, 66 La. L. Rev. 131 (2005). For example, the sickle cell trait is more common in persons with ancestors from sub-Saharan Africa, Latin America, Saudi Arabia, India, and Mediterranean countries. Tay-Sachs is more common in Jews of Eastern European extraction (although 1 in 250 persons in the general population also carries the gene for the disease and it is found in higher-than-general rates in French Canadians and Cajuns). Each of these common claims of association of genetic traits with particular geographically based populations is extraordinarily imprecise and overgeneralized, however. Keith Wailoo & Stephen Pemberton, The Troubled Dream of Genetic Medicine: Ethnicity and Innovation in Tay-Sachs, Cystic Fibrosis, and Sickle Cell Disease (2006). See also Mark Rothstein, Legal Conceptions of Equality in a Genomic Age, 25 Law & Ineq. 429 (2007).

5. *International Views.* Genetic discrimination is of substantial concern beyond the U.S., and international human rights law has taken notice of the possibility of inappropriate genetic discrimination. In 1997, UNESCO issued a Universal Declaration on the Human Genome and Human Rights that requires that "no-one shall be subjected to discrimination based on genetic characteristics that is intended to infringe or has the effect of infringing human rights, fundamental freedoms and human dignity." United Nations Educational, Scientific, and Cultural Organization, Universal Declaration on the Human Genome and Human Rights art. 6 (Nov. 11, 1997).

UNESCO's International Declaration on Human Data notes that "every effort should be made to ensure that human genetic data are not used for purposes that are discriminatory or in any way that would lead to the stigmatization of an individual, a family, or a group." United Nations Educational, Scientific, and Cultural Organization, International Declaration on Human Data art. 7 (Oct. 16, 2003). Many other countries have laws regulating such discrimination, as do international regional organizations. For an interesting account of Australian practices with regard to employment, see M. Otlowski et al., Practices and Attitudes of Australian Employers with Regard to the Use of Genetic Information, 31 Comp. Lab. L. & Pol'y J. 637 (2010).

2. Mental Health Parity and Addiction Equity

Historically, stigmatization of, and misunderstandings about, mental illness have led to a devaluation of mental health care in society generally, and within the health care system more specifically. This longstanding neglect of mental health resulted in less financing and other structural resources essential for ensuring access to mental health care. For example, while some health insurers failed to provide any coverage for mental health treatment, others imposed greater restrictions on mental health services, such as higher co-payments or limits on the number of visits covered, than for medical/surgical services.

Over time, however, mental health has become a more important and visible priority in health law and policy. This is due, in part, to growing research demonstrating the significant individual and societal impact of untreated mental and behavioral health conditions, as well as important advancements in mental and behavioral science. Stigma has also decreased, especially as high-profile figures have increasingly shared their experiences, and patient advocacy groups have become more vocal in demanding access to care.

In 1996, the federal government took a limited step toward addressing discrimination against mental health care by enacting the Mental Health Parity Act. It requires group health plans to use the same aggregate lifetime and annual dollar limits for mental health benefits that the plans impose on medical/surgical benefits.

In 2008, Congress passed the Mental Health Parity and Addiction Equity Act (the "Parity Act"), which extended parity requirements to treatment limitations. It requires insurers and employers to treat benefits for mental health conditions and substance use disorders in the same manner as benefits for physical conditions. For example, limits on the frequency of treatment, number of visits, days of coverage, or other limits on the scope or duration of treatment cannot differ as between mental health/substance use and medical/surgical benefits. Additionally, financial requirements such as copays and coinsurance cannot be greater for mental health/substance use than for medical/surgical benefits. Finally, if a health plan allows patients to go out-of-network for medical/surgical benefits, it must also do so for mental health/substance use benefits. The Parity Act also includes a cost exemption that allows group health plans to receive a waiver exempting them from some of the law's requirements if they demonstrate that costs increased at least one percent as a result of compliance, but the exemption only lasts one year. Mental Health Parity and Addiction Equity Act, Pub. L. 110–343, 122 Stat. 3765, amending 29 U.S.C. 1185a, § 712 (ERISA); 42 U.S.C. 300gg–5, § 2705 (Public Health Service Act); and I.R.C. § 9812 (Internal Revenue Code) (2008).

In 2010, the ACA applied the Parity Act to insurers in the individual market and qualified health plans offered through the marketplaces. The ACA also helped close an important gap in mental health coverage, because the Parity Act did not require insurers to cover mental health and substance use conditions; it only required parity in the event the plan provided mental health or substance use coverage. The ACA went further, however, to require the inclusion of mental health and substance use conditions as part of the essential health benefits ("EHBs") insurers must cover. Patient Protection and Affordable Care Act § 1302(b)(1), 42 U.S.C. § 18022(b) (2010). As a result, all health insurance plans in the individual and employer market must include coverage for treatment of mental health and substance use conditions. In order to satisfy the EHB requirement, insurers must comply with the Parity Act. 78 Fed. Reg. 68,239 (2013); Centers for Medicare & Medicaid Services, The Mental Health Parity and Addiction Equity Act, www.cms.gov; Health Aff., Mental Health Parity (2014).

While the Parity Act and the ACA mandate mental health parity, they have failed to offer guidance on how to determine whether a plan achieves parity with respect to practices that do not lend themselves to quantitative measurement. It is simple to evaluate parity for quantitative limits like number of covered visits. But how does one determine parity in the case of nonquantitative limits, such as limits on certain types of treatments, restrictions on geographic location and provider specialty, and methods of determining provider reimbursement? What if a plan excludes a particular type of mental health treatment that may not have a direct medical/surgical analog for comparison? Compare Joseph F. v. Sinclair Servs. Co., 158 F. Supp. 3d 1239, 1262 (D. Utah 2016) (holding that the health plan's exclusion for residential treatment violated the Parity Act, because it imposed a treatment limit that applied only to mental health conditions and not to medical/surgical services provided at analogous skilled nursing facilities), with Roy C. v. Aetna Life Ins. Co., No. 2:17-CV-1216, 2018 WL 4511972, at *3 (D. Utah Sept. 20, 2018) (plaintiffs failed to allege facts sufficient to support a Parity Act violation based on the plan's exclusion of wilderness therapy, also known as outdoor behavioral health care, because plaintiffs failed to sufficiently identify a comparison or analogue to wilderness therapy in the medical and surgical fields of treatment). But see Michael D. v. Anthem Health Plans of Kentucky, Inc., 369 F. Supp. 3d 1159 (D. Utah 2019) (noting in dicta that Parity Act challenges to the exclusion of wilderness camps are complicated because there is no clear analog to wilderness camps in the medical or surgical field, but also arguing that plans should not be able to exclude mental health treatments only because a clear analog does not exist).

Ambiguity concerning non-quantitative coverage limits has created ample opportunity for consumers to test the contours of the Parity Act through litigation. For an in-depth study of the types of issues raising questions about what constitutes mental health parity, see Kelsey N. Berry et al., Litigation Provides Clues to Ongoing Challenges in Implementing Insurance Parity, 42 J. Health Polit., Pol'y, & L. 1065 (2017) (highlighting common areas of dispute, including limits or exclusions on certain habilitative treatments such as applied behavioral analysis for autism, credentialing standards for providers, and medical necessity determinations). The Consolidated Appropriations Act, 2021, Pub. L. No. 116–260, amends the Parity Act to require group health plans and issuers that provide both mental health and substance use benefits and medical/surgical benefits to prepare a comparative analysis of any nonquantitative treatment limits that apply to each category of benefits.

3. Age

Age discrimination in health care has received comparatively less attention than the other categories discussed in this chapter. But the COVID-19 pandemic has brought renewed attention to this problem, especially as early proposals for rationing treatment during the COVID-19 pandemic used age, either explicitly or indirectly, as a basis for determining access to ventilators and ICU beds. See Timothy W. Farrell et al., Rationing Limited Healthcare Resources in the COVID-19 Era and Beyond: Ethical Considerations Regarding Older Adults, 68 J. Am. Geriatr. Soc. 1143–1149 (2020). In March 2020, OCR issued a bulletin on medical resource allocation policies (discussed earlier in this Section in the notes after *Bragdon*), providing that people should not be denied medical care on the basis of "stereotypes, assessments of quality of life," or "judgments about a person's relative "worth" based on the presence or absence of disabilities *or age.*" (emphasis added). Dep't Health & Hum. Serv.'s, Bulletin, Civil Rights, HIPAA, and the Coronavirus Disease 2019 (COVID-19) (Mar. 28, 2020). For information on other OCR actions involving allegations of age discrimination in crisis standards of care, see Civil Rights and COVID-19, at HHS.gov. In addition, the advocacy group Justice in Aging has actively monitored states' crisis standards of care addressing the rationing of COVID-19 treatment, with the goal of identifying and fighting to remove age-based criteria.

The problem of age discrimination goes beyond COVID-19-specific issues, however. Ageism has long been used to deny other kinds of care and has been linked to poorer outcomes and increased mortality. See also Sharon K. Inouye, Creating an Anti-Ageist Healthcare System to Improve Care for Our Current and Future Selves, 1 Nature Aging 150 (2021).

A few laws address age discrimination related to health care. The Age Discrimination Act of 1975, 29 U.S.C. §§ 6101 et seq. ("Age Act") prohibits discrimination against any individual on the basis of age in programs and activities that receive federal financial assistance. The Age Act does permit the use of age distinctions in limited circumstances, however. For example, it permits the use of age distinctions in legislation designed to provide benefits or assistance to persons based on age, such as age requirements for Medicare eligibility. As described in the introductory note, Section 1557 of the ACA extends antidiscrimination protection for age by prohibiting discrimination on the grounds set forth in the Age Act.

Age discrimination in employment is also prohibited by the Age Discrimination in Employment Act of 1967, 29 U.S.C. §§ 621–630, ("ADEA"). The ADEA limits the ability of covered employers to discriminate among employees 40 years of age and older with respect to the provision of health insurance benefits. However, in April 2004, the EEOC issued a rule stating that employers could reduce or eliminate health benefits for Medicare-eligible beneficiaries without violating the ADEA. 68 Fed. Reg. 41,542 (2003). See also Am. Ass'n of Retired Persons v. EEOC, 489 F.3d 558 (3d Cir. 2007) (upholding the EEOC rule).

The approach to health equity reflected in the ACA targets health equity as both a vision for community well-being, and as a means to making a more efficient health care system. Health inequity which stems from social and political factors produces expensive but preventable health conditions, strains delivery and finance systems, and burdens the economy in myriad ways. As the U.S. Department of Health & Humans Services' Office of Disease Prevention & Health Promotion has expressed in its "Healthy People 2030" initiative, "[i]Investing to achieve the full potential for health and well-being for all provides valuable benefits to society." HHS ODPHP, Healthy People 2030 Framework (2021), https://health.gov/healthypeople/about/healthy-people-2030-framework. Health inequity's direct link to health economics and other social policies have thus linked it as a policy objective of both justice-based and market-based reforms. See, e.g., World Health Org., The Economics of Social Determinants of Health and Health Inequalities (2013); Paul Menzel and Donald W. Light, A Conservative Case for Universal Access to Health Care, 36 Hastings Ctr. Rep. 36 (2006).

B. HEALTH ECONOMICS

Historically, many policymakers pursuing health reform have assumed that the market for health care operated like most other markets for goods and services in a market-based economic system. Attempts to remedy imperfections in the market, such as inadequate coverage or excessive costs, have largely focused on promoting competition. Nonetheless, the market for health care remains highly dysfunctional. As a result, the U.S. spends more on health care than it would in a competitive market subject to less waste and inefficiency. Americans do not need to spend as much as they do to retain the amount and quality of care they receive. The excerpt that follows offers a classic explanation of the economic problems facing our health care system that remains relevant today.

CONGRESSIONAL BUDGET OFFICE, ECONOMIC IMPLICATIONS OF RISING HEALTH CARE COST
(Print, Pages 12–19, 1992).

In most circumstances, the free market provides an efficient mechanism for allocating resources in the economy. To achieve such efficiencies, however, free markets must operate under certain conditions. They work best when the consumer has good information about the characteristics of products and their prices—information that is most easily obtained if products are well defined and standardized and if prices can be readily ascertained without excessive search. In addition, market efficiency requires that a large number of sellers compete with each other over prices that reflect true resource costs. With a large number of sellers, no single vendor has the power to control prices, and price competition among sellers lowers prices to the point that they reflect the marginal costs of production.

The market for health care, however, does not meet many of these conditions. . . .

Consumers lack key information about the quality and price of medical services. Their ignorance about quality has two dimensions. First, most consumers do not have the expertise they need to evaluate the qualifications of their health care providers. Second, when consumers need medical care, they may not have information (independent of what they are told by a provider) about the full range of alternative treatments and the prospective outcomes of these alternatives.

Consumers also lack rudimentary information about the prices of the medical care they buy and have difficulty assessing what that price information means. Price information, such as that concerning physicians' charges, in many cases is not available to patients in advance of treatment. In some instances, the patient can call a doctor and obtain quotes for different services, but prices of physicians' services are not advertised and it may be embarrassing to ask. Sometimes even the doctor does not know the full costs of treatment, especially if it requires hospitalization or drugs. Although a patient can acquire some price information with repeated visits to a doctor, many reasons for seeing a doctor do not occur again.

Even if the price information is available, it can be hard to interpret. If a doctor charges a low price, he or she could be offering a bargain—or inferior—service. Without information on quality, price information has no meaning. . . .

Because consumers delegate a considerable amount of decision-making authority to their physicians, medical practitioners act both as agents for consumers and suppliers of medical services. With such power, physicians are in the position of being able to create a demand for their own services.

* * *

Physicians' training and professional standards strongly predispose them to use their power to give the best possible medical care without regard to cost. To many physicians, it is unethical to do otherwise. . . . Moreover, because physicians can earn higher incomes by providing more care, their financial self-interest may also contribute to excessive spending.

Efficient use of medical resources requires consumers and providers to weigh the costs and benefits of alternative medical treatments. Unfortunately, this is very difficult. Obviously, patients have little knowledge upon which to judge the benefits of a new technology. But even physicians cannot always be fully informed about all the new treatments and technologies, especially given the rapid pace of complex medical advances. More important, good statistical information concerning the effectiveness of many treatments—even many common treatments—is simply not available.

The lack of good information on the outcomes of many medical treatments has created an environment in which the doctors' preferences for particular procedures—rather than science—appear to determine how they are used, a situation that leads to significant variations in the patterns and costs of medical care around the country. . . .

* * *

For markets to allocate resources efficiently, sellers must actively compete. In a competitive environment, individual vendors have no control over the price of what they sell or over the number of competitors. Also, more efficient suppliers can offer lower prices than those who fail to control their costs.

Although there are obviously many providers in the health care sector, they do not always compete effectively on price. Of course, the medical market is diverse, and active competition can be found in some subsectors of that market. But too often, competition among medical care providers for consumers (and for the services of other providers) is directed toward the nonprice aspects of medical care. . . . This type of competition, however, can tend to increase costs. Moreover, once a new technology is introduced, it tends to be used regardless of cost.

The lack of price competition in the medical market reflects many factors. The presence of third-party payers dulls the incentives for consumers to pay much attention to costs at the point of service. The tax subsidy for **employment-based insurance** [discussed in Chapter 7]. . . also reduces some of the pressures on workers to pay attention to the costs of insurance. Difficulties in assessing information about the quality of doctors weaken the already weak incentives for consumers to seek out the lowest-cost providers. And last, many consumers have long-standing relationships with their physicians and may be reluctant to switch doctors to save money.

* * *

Limited entry and control over demand are the key elements that allow [physicians] to earn more than necessary to attract talented, well-trained people into the profession. . . . [T]he number of qualified applicants for medical school is far greater than the number of student slots available, so the entry limits probably matter. [S]tudies of the financial returns from education and training suggest that the private returns on an investment in medical school compare favorably with the returns on investments in general and exceed the returns in most other occupations.

In addition, physicians in the United States earn about five and one-half times the average annual compensation of other wage earners. The gap is smaller in other countries. . . .

* * *

The bulk of medical care is purchased through **third-party payers**. These payers include not only private insurance companies but federal, state, and local governments.

As new and more elaborate methods of treatment are developed, the cost of an episode of illness can become extremely high. In addition, an individual's need for major medical care occurs largely by chance and is difficult to predict. Most types of illnesses are statistically predictable, however, for groups of individuals. Health insurance enables consumers to take advantage of this group predictability by pooling their risks for serious accidents or diseases.

Insurance, however, imposes its own costs. Insurance means that the effective price that the patient faces at the time of treatment is much lower than the actual cost of treatment. Sick individuals and their doctors have every incentive to buy expensive treatments and tests as long as they do any good at all, because the patient does not bear much of the cost. . . .

* * *

The market for medical care is also different from other markets because of the large role played by government. In particular, the government subsidizes health care, which allows some consumers greater access to medical care than they would otherwise have. Although these programs provide essential—and in some cases life-saving—medical care to millions of people, the programs also dull the price signals from the health care markets, encouraging overuse of services. The major subsidies are provided in three ways: Medicare, Medicaid, and tax expenditures.

* * *

NOTES AND QUESTIONS

1.   *Today's Market.* This excerpt was written three decades ago when our health care system looked different than it does today. Does the current market for health care goods and services function more efficiently than it did in this description? Do patients have better access to information regarding the cost and quality of health care services? What roles have competition and consolidation among health care providers played in controlling costs? What role does increasing patients' out-of-pocket expenses play in controlling costs?

2.   *Improving or Rejecting the Market?* Are there aspects of the health care market that can be changed to better resemble a free market? Are there

others that are more difficult to change? How well does a market-based system function for health care goods and services? Are there better models?

3.   *Critiques from Behavioral Economics.* As noted in Section II.A., one fundamental critique of market-based approaches argues that health is a human right, and therefore a market-based approach to securing it is inappropriate. See, e.g., Anja Rudiger, Human Rights and the Political Economy of Universal Health Care: Designing Equitable Financing, 18 Health & Human Rts. J. 67 (2016). Another line of critique questions the central assumptions of economics and market-based approaches applied to health care. See, e.g., Allison K. Hoffman, Health Care's Market Bureaucracy, 66 UCLA L. Rev. 1926 (2019). Research from psychology and social science has developed the field of "behavioral economics," relying on empirical observations to challenge classic economic assumptions about humans making rational cost-benefit determinations to maximize personal utility and efficiency. Behavioral economics reveals many ways in which people systematically depart from the theoretical model of rationality—ways especially relevant to health policy and market-based approaches to health reform discussed below. See generally I. Glenn Cohen, Holly Fernandez Lynch, & Christopher T. Robertson, eds. Nudging Health (2016). Cf. John Aloysius Cogan, Jr., The Failed Economics of Consumer-Driven Health Plans, 54 U.C. Davis L. Rev. 1353 (2020).

4.   *Interaction with the Taxation System.* The "tax expenditures" noted at the end of the preceding excerpt takes several forms: preferential tax treatment of employer-sponsored health insurance benefits (detailed in Chapter 8), tax subsidies paid on behalf of individuals who purchase insurance through the ACA's marketplaces (detailed in Chapter 9), and the tax-exempt status granted to many health care organizations (detailed in Chapter 13). Thus, the notion of tax expenditure incorporates both payments accomplished through the Internal Revenue System (IRS), and potential revenues foregone.

C. HEALTH INSURANCE

Insurance involves, by definition, the transfer of risk from the **insured** (also called the beneficiary, recipient, member, or enrollee) to a financing entity (the insurer, carrier, issuer, managed care organization, or self-insured benefits plan). Each year a small proportion of all insureds account for a very high proportion of health care expenditures. Typically, 1% of the population accounts for 20% of health care spending and 5% of the population accounts for half of all health spending. In other words, 95% of the population accounts for half of health care expenditures. National Institute for Health Care Management, The Concentration of Health Care Spending (2017). Health insurance essentially spreads risk and costs from a small number of high-cost insureds, who account for most of health care expenditures, to the much larger group of low-cost insureds, who account for most of the premium payments, through the medium of the insurer.

Insurers deal with risk by pooling the risks of large numbers of insureds. Traditionally, however, the insurer had to be prudent about the risk it assumed from these insureds and ensure that it had the resources to cover the risk. When judging a particular applicant, the insurer had to first assess an applicant's risk level, then determine whether to take on that risk through a process called **underwriting**, and finally set an appropriate **premium**. Premiums are the amount of money an insurance company charges to insure a particular patient for a certain period of time, such as a month or a year.

The excerpt that follows discusses a number of concepts that are necessary to understand health insurance and health insurance law:

CONGRESSIONAL RESEARCH SERVICE, INSURING THE UNINSURED: OPTIONS AND ANALYSIS

(House Comm. on Education & Labor, Comm. Print, 1988).

II.   Principles of Health Insurance

* * *

For insurance to operate, there has to be a way to predict the likelihood or probability that a loss will occur as a result of a specific outcome. Such predictions in insurance are based upon probability theory and the law of large numbers. According to probability theory, "while some events appear to be a matter of chance, they actually occur with regularity over a large number of trials."[ ] By examining patterns of behavior over a large number of trials, it is therefore possible for the insurer to infer the likelihood of such behaviors in the future.

. . . Applied to insurance, probability allows the insurer to make predictions on the basis of historical data. In so doing, the insurer ". . . implicitly says, 'if things continue to happen in the future as they happened in the past, and if our estimate of what has happened in the past is accurate, this is what we may expect.'"[ ]

Losses seldom occur exactly as expected, so insurance companies have to make predictions about the extent to which actual experience might deviate from predicted results. For a small group of insured units, there is a high probability that losses will be much greater or smaller than was predicted. For a very large group, the range of probable error diminishes, especially if the insured group is similar in composition to the group upon which the prediction is based. Thus, to predict the probability of a loss, insurers seek to aggregate persons who are at a similar risk for that loss. . . .

In theory all probabilities of loss can be insured. Insurance could cover any risk for a price. As the probability of loss increases, however, the premium will increase to the point at which it approaches the actual potential pay-out.

To keep premiums competitive, there are in practice some risks that insurers will not accept. In general, insurable risks must meet the following criteria:

— There has to be uncertainty that the loss will occur, and that the loss must be beyond the control of the insured. Insurers will not sell hospital insurance to a person who is on his way to a hospital, nor fire insurance to someone holding a lit match. . . .

— The loss produced by the risk must be measurable. The insurer has to be able to determine that a loss has occurred and that it has a specific dollar value.

— There must be a sufficiently large number of similar insured units to make the losses predictable. . . .

— Generally, the loss must be significant, but there should be a low probability that a very high loss will occur. . . .

* * *

III. Ratemaking

Ratemaking is the "process of predicting future losses and future expenses and allocating those costs among the various classes of insureds." The outcome of the ratemaking process is a "premium" or price of policy. The premium is made up of expected claims against the insurer and the insurer's **"administrative expenses."** The term "administrative expenses" is used to mean any expense that the insurance company charges that is not for claims (including reserves for potential claims). . . . In the case of employer group coverage, a third part of the premium is set aside in a reserve held against unexpected claims. This reserve is often refundable to the employer if claims do not exceed expectations.

In the textbook descriptions of ratemaking for health insurance, insurers predict losses on the basis of predicted claims costs. This prediction involves an assessment of the likely morbidity (calculated in terms of the number of times the event insured against occurs) and severity (the average magnitude of each loss) of the policyholder or group of policyholders. . . .

* * *

There are different approaches to determining rates. In health insurance, the most frequently used approaches are **experience rating** and **community rating**.

Under experience rating, the past experience of the group to be insured is used to determine the premium. For employer groups, experience rating would take into account the company's own history of claims and other expenses. . . .

* * *

The advantage of experience rating is that it adjusts the cost of insurance for a specific group in a manner more commensurate with the expected cost of that particular group than is possible through the exclusive use of manual rates. In addition, the increasingly competitive environment among insurers demands that each one "make every effort to retain groups with favorable experience. Unless an insurer can provide coverage to such groups at a reasonable cost, it runs the risk of losing such policyholders to another insurer which more closely reflects the expected costs of their programs in its rates."[ ]

Under community rating, premium rates are based on the allocation of total costs to all the individuals or groups to be insured, without regard to the past experience of any particular subgroup. . . . Community or class rating has the advantage of allowing an insurer to apply a single rate or set of rates to a large number of people, thus simplifying the process of determining premiums.

* * *

IV. Adverse and Favorable Selection

If everyone in the society purchased health insurance, and if everyone opted for an identical health insurance plan, then insurance companies could adhere strictly to the models of prediction and rate-setting described above. However, everyone does not buy insurance, nor do all the purchasers of insurance choose identical benefits. People who expect to need health services are more likely than others to purchase insurance, and are also likely to seek coverage for the specific services they expect to need. . . .

Insurers use the term "**adverse selection**" to describe this phenomenon. Adverse selection is defined by the health insurance industry as the "tendency of persons with poorer than average health expectations to apply for, or continue, insurance to a greater extent than do persons with average or better health expectations."[ ]

* * *

Adjusting premiums for adverse selection results in further adverse selection. As the price of insurance goes up, healthier people are less likely to want to purchase insurance. Each upward rate adjustment will leave a smaller and sicker group of potential purchasers. If there were only a single insurance company, it would serve a steadily shrinking market paying steadily increasing premiums. However, because multiple insurance companies are operating in the market, each company may strive to enroll the lower cost individuals or groups, leaving the higher cost cases for its competitors. In this market, adverse selection consists (from the insurer's point of view) of drawing the least desirable cases from within the pool of insurance purchasers. **"Favorable selection"** occurs if the insurer successfully enrolls lower risk clients than its competitors.

It is thus necessary to distinguish between the more traditional use of "adverse selection," as a term to describe the differences between people who do and do not buy insurance, and the sense in which the term is often used today, to describe the differences among purchasers choosing various insurers or types of coverage. This second type of adverse selection can occur within an insured group, if the individuals in that group are permitted to select from among different insurance options.

Insurers are still concerned about the more traditional type of adverse selection. They use underwriting rules, to exclude or limit the worst risks. Some insurers may also attempt to limit adverse selection by careful selection of where they market and to whom they sell a policy. For example, a company offering a Medicare supplement (Medigap) plan might be more likely to advertise its plan in senior citizen recreation centers, where the patrons tend to be relatively young and healthy, than in nursing homes, where the residents are probably older and have chronic health conditions. Thus, from the perspective of the individual or group applying for insurance, the insurer's attempts to avoid adverse selection may result in lack of availability of coverage, denial of coverage, incomplete coverage or above-average premiums.

* * *

NOTES AND QUESTIONS

1. *Adverse Selection and Moral Hazard.* Adverse selection is one of the two major problems with which insurers must contend. The other is **moral hazard**, which is the tendency of insured persons to use more products and services than they would if they were not insured and had to pay the full price. Insurance greatly reduces the costs of covered products and services for consumers, thus increasing consumer demand. To correct for moral hazard, insurers impose **cost-sharing requirements**, which are obligations for individuals to bear some of the costs of care at the time they receive the services, i.e., at the **point of service**, in the form of **copays**, **coinsurance**, or **deductibles**. Moreover, professionals make many purchasing decisions in health care, such as deciding whether to prescribe a drug or to admit a patient to a hospital), and these professionals are even less sensitive to cost. Absent cost-sharing, insured consumers are "price-insensitive"—they have little incentive to shop around for products and services to get lower prices. Although insurers attempt to use managed care tools to assure that health care is, in fact, **"medically necessary,"** insurers still pay for many low-value products and services that their insureds receive.

Advocates of consumer-driven health care contend that moral hazard is the central problem of our health care system. Policy prescriptions for addressing moral hazard will be discussed in Section III of this chapter.

2. *Distributive Justice vs. Actuarial Fairness?* The Congressional Research Service asserts that the purpose of insurance is to spread risk from individuals to all members of a group. This suggests a vision of **distributive justice** that distributes risk broadly. Indeed, social insurance, based on the principle of social solidarity, distributes risk among the broadest possible group: the entire citizenry. But insurance can also be based on an alternative vision of justice, that of **actuarial fairness**, under which every individual pays for insurance based on his or her own risks. See Deborah Stone, The Struggle for the Soul of Health Insurance, 18 J. Health Pol., Pol'y & L. 287 (1993) and the discussion in Chapter 1.

Private health insurance in the U.S. has to date been largely based on the principle of actuarial fairness, although there has been considerable risk distribution within employment-related groups. As discussed further in Chapter 9, the ACA made a decisive choice in favor of distributive justice and mutual aid, as evidenced by its rejection of the notion that people should pay higher insurance premiums based on their health status. However, the ACA did not entirely reject the notion of actuarial fairness. Older people and tobacco users can still pay more, as well as people who live in higher-cost areas or those who have families. Also, large group coverage remains experience rated, based on the overall health care utilization of the group, although employers are not supposed to discriminate based on the health status of individuals.

3. *Employer-Based Health Coverage.* Most Americans receive their insurance through their employers. Employers can either contract with an insurance company for a **group plan** to cover their employees or **self-insure** their employees by taking on the financial risk themselves (also called **self-funding**). For employment-related group indemnity insurance, the insurer underwrites the group as a whole, meaning that it assesses the risk of insuring the entire group and sets a premium for the group as a whole, which is then evenly divided among the employees. Typically, the employer pays a portion of that premium for each employee, and the employee pays the remainder.

When an employer self-insures its employees' health benefits, the employer does not pay a premium to an insurance company. Instead, the employer agrees to pay their employees' health care expenses directly. Employees often pay a portion of those costs as a premium to the employer or cost-sharing to the provider. Further, self-insured employers typically contract with a **third-party administrator**, often an insurance company, to perform the administrative functions of providing health care benefits to their employees, without taking the financial risks associated with indemnity insurance. Self-insured employers also may obtain a **stop-loss reinsurance policy**, which insures the employer against losses for a single employee or the aggregate group that exceeds a certain amount. See Timothy Stoltzfus Jost & Mark A. Hall, Self-Insurance for Small Employers under the Affordable Care Act: Federal and State Regulatory Options, 68 N.Y.U. Ann. Surv. Am. L. 539 (2013). Chapter 7 provides a detailed discussion of employer-based health coverage.

D. MANAGED CARE

In the last fifty years, the majority of private health insurance plans shifted from being pure indemnity plans, which pay medical professionals directly for services provided to insureds at the rate charged by the practitioner, to **managed care plans**, which contract with medical professionals to manage the cost, utilization, and quality of care. Until the early 1990s, scholars and policymakers distinguished between insurance (meaning indemnity or service benefit insurance) and managed care as different approaches to financing health care. Private health insurance plans are now predominantly managed care products. Many Medicare and Medicaid plans now use managed care models, too.

But what exactly is "managed care"? Managed care is a means of governing health care delivery. Managed care organizations assume and spread risk, performing the core function of an insurer. See Rush Prudential HMO, Inc. v. Moran, 536 U.S. 355, 366–70 (2002). But managed care organizations do not just collect premiums and pay claims for health care goods and services as provided; they also attempt to control the price, utilization, and sometimes even quality of those goods and services. They do so by imposing controls, limits, and incentives on "participating" (or "**in-network**") health care providers and facilities, as well as managed care enrollees. In some versions of managed care, discussed in the excerpt below, the organization also provides the care itself by employing the doctors and owning the facilities that deliver needed services to its enrollees.

Managed care's combination of the risk-spreading and third-party payer functions of insurance with the selection of providers and delivery of care has led to a variety of different approaches to categorization and regulation. Managed care organizations occasionally have been regarded as sellers of health care services on a prepaid basis, rather than as insurers. State governments often regulate managed care entities like insurers. But some state regulatory programs continue to treat traditional commercial insurance and managed care organizations differently. California, for instance, has established entirely separate administrative agencies—the California Department of Insurance and the Department of Managed Health Care.

While health insurance has become largely synonymous with managed care, the distinction between the insurance and care management functions has legal ramifications, as well as implications for health reform policy. It therefore remains important to understand.

JACOB S. HACKER AND THEODORE R. MARMOR
HOW NOT TO THINK ABOUT "MANAGED CARE"

32 U. Mich. J.L. Reform 661 (1999).

From the beginning, "managed care" was a category with a strong ideological edge, employed to imply competence, concern, and, above all, control over a dangerously unfettered health insurance structure. "Managed care," . . . was an alternative "to the unbridled fee-for-service non-system" that sent "blank checks to hospitals, doctors, dentists, etc." and led to "referrals of dubious necessity" and "unmanaged and uncoordinated care . . . of poor or dubious quality." As these words indicate, managed care was portrayed less as a means to control patient behavior than as a way to bring doctors and hospitals in line with perceived economic realities. Moreover, managed care promised not only cost-control but also coordination and cooperation, not only better management but also better care. By imposing managerial authority on an anarchic "non-system," managed care would simultaneously restrain costs and rationalize an allegedly archaic structure of medical care finance and delivery.

* * *

Perhaps the most defensible interpretation of "managed care" is that it represents a fusion of two functions that once were regarded as largely separate: the financing of medical care and the delivery of medical services. This interpretation, at least, provides a reasonably accurate description of the most familiar organizational entity that marched under the managed care banner until the late 1980s: the health maintenance organization (HMO) . . . . Today, however, that is no longer the case. [As of] 1997, . . . between eighty and ninety-eight percent of . . . private health insurers appear to fall into the broad category of managed care. "Managed care" therefore does not offer any guidance as to how to distinguish among the vast majority of contemporary health plans.

The standard response to this problem has been to subdivide the managed care universe into a collage of competing acronyms, most coined by industry executives and marketers: HMOs, Preferred Provider Organizations (PPOs), and Exclusive Provider Organizations (EPOs). This is the approach taken by Jonathan Weiner and Gregory de Lissovoy in their frequently cited 1993 article, Razing a Tower of Babel: A Taxonomy for Managed Care and Health Insurance Plans. [18 J. Health Pol. Pol'y & L. 75 (1993).]

* * *

The central problem with Weiner and de Lissovoy's taxonomy— and, indeed, with most contemporary commentary about health insurance—is the tendency to confuse reimbursement methods, managerial techniques, and organizational forms. For example, fee-for-service, a payment method, is regularly contrasted with "managed care," presumably an organizational form.

* * *

The practice of conflating organization, technique, and incentives leads to unnecessary confusion. It means that when we contrast health plans we are often comparing them across incommensurable dimensions. . . . By conflating distinct characteristics, we also are tempted to presume necessary relationships between particular features of health plans (such as their payment method) and specific outcomes that are claimed to follow from these features (such as the degree of integration of medical finance and delivery). Finally, the desire to describe an assortment of disparate plan features with a few broad labels encourages a wild goose chase of efforts to come up with black-and-white standards for identifying plan types. . . .

* * *

In understanding the structure of health insurance, the crucial relationship is between those who deliver medical care and those who pay for it. Even a passive indemnity insurer stands between the patient and the medical provider as a financial intermediary and an underwriter of risk. . . . To characterize this trilateral relationship, we focus on three of its essential features: first, the degree of risk-sharing between providers and the primary bearer of risk (whether an insurer or a self-insured employer); second, the degree to which administrative oversight constrains clinical decisions; and, third, the degree to which enrollees in a plan are required to receive their care from a specified roster of providers. . . .

. . . Our argument is that health plans differ across at least [these] three principal dimensions . . . . Each dimension crucially affects the trilateral connections among provider, patient, and plan. We also wish to emphasize that there is no simple relationship between plan label and the placement of a plan along these axes. Staff-model HMOs may seem like the quintessence of "managed care," yet because they place financial constraints at the group level they do not necessarily concentrate as much risk on physicians as do other network-based health plans, nor do they necessarily entail as much clinical regulation at the micro-level. Microregulation may go hand in hand with restrictions on patient choice of provider, but it also may not. Indeed, management of individual clinical decisions and the creation of broad incentives for conservative practice patterns may very well be alternative mechanisms for lowering the cost of medical care. Finally, . . . greater risk-sharing can co-exist with almost any set of arrangements. It does not require a closed network, much less strict utilization review. . . .

Notice, too, that [we make] no mention of those popular buzzwords "integration" and "coordination." Movement toward a closed network, toward greater utilization control, or toward increased risk-sharing can create the conditions under which integration or coordination may occur. They do not imply, however, that such integrative activities actually take place. Getting the right care to the right patient at the right time is a managerial accomplishment, not a product of labels.

Finally, the conventional fee-for-service versus capitation dichotomy does not remain a useful means of distinguishing among different health plans. Instead, the crucial issue is what incentives medical providers actually face. The particular mix of payment methods that create those incentives is less important and will undoubtedly change as health plans experiment with new reimbursement modalities in the future.

* * *

NOTE: COMMON DEFINITIONS

Following Hacker and Marmor's lead, we focus primarily on how the states and the ACA regulate the various techniques described above for managing care: provider networks, utilization controls, and provider and patient incentives. However, because the abbreviations Hacker and Marmor disparage are used so ubiquitously in the health law and policy literature, and because many states base their regulatory schemes on these concepts, we offer definitions of them here.

Health Maintenance Organizations (HMOs) usually limit their members to an exclusive network of providers, permitting their members to go to out-of-network providers only in special circumstances, like medical emergencies. They have also historically emphasized preventive care, and usually use incentives such as capitation payments (a fixed payment per patient) to moderate the behavior of their professionals and providers. Some HMOs provide care by directly employing providers or contracting with direct employees of affiliated foundations (staff model HMOs), while others contract with independent networks of providers to deliver care.

Point of Service Plans (POSs) resemble HMOs but allow their members to obtain services outside the network with additional cost-sharing (deductibles, coinsurance, or copayments), and are often subject to gatekeeper controls.

Preferred Provider Organizations (PPOs) are organized systems of health care providers who agree to provide services on a discounted basis to subscribers. PPO subscribers are not limited to preferred, in-plan providers, but face financial disincentives, such as deductibles or larger copayment or coinsurance obligations, if they elect non-preferred providers. PPOs usually pay their providers on a **fee-for-service** basis, and often use utilization review controls for certain kinds of services, like hospital admissions or advanced imaging.

Provider Sponsored Organizations (PSOs), also known as Integrated Delivery Systems (IDSs), physician-hospital organizations (PHOs), and provider-sponsored networks (PSNs), are networks organized by providers that contract directly with employers or other purchasers of health benefits to provide services on a capitated basis. These various organizational structures are discussed further in Chapter 12.

Accountable Care Organizations (ACOs) are networks of doctors, hospitals, and other health care providers that agree to share medical and financial responsibility for the care of a patient population. ACOs were designed to help control costs and improve quality by incorporating incentives to promote provider collaboration, preventative care, and integrated treatment strategies. A patient's care in an ACO centers around one primary care provider who orchestrates the patient's treatment strategy. ACOs will be discussed in depth in Chapters 10 and 12.

III. TRADEOFFS IN HEALTH REFORM: ACCESS, COST, AND QUALITY

As we saw in Chapter 1, health care systems are frequently evaluated on their ability to provide equitable access to quality health care at a reasonable price for the population. How government entities structure the laws and regulations governing the health care system will directly affect the balance between access, cost, and quality. This section provides an overview of how these concepts function in the U.S. health care system.

The American health care system provides health care services for over 332 million people living in the United States, but it does not do so equally. For any individual, the level of access to, cost, and quality of care will depend on whether she has health insurance, the type of plan she has, and where she lives. The U.S. pays more for health care services than any other country both in absolute costs and per capita. Yet, it is the only high-income country lacking universal health care coverage, with more than 10% of the population remaining uninsured. The U.S. also lags behind other developed nations in terms of key quality indicators. The problems of high cost, mediocre quality, and limited access have given rise to substantial reform efforts over the last decade that offer an array of tools to achieve the "**triple aim**"—simultaneously improving the experience of care, improving population health, and reducing per capita costs.

As the Congressional Budget Office summarized in 2008:

Much of the health care provided in the United States confers tremendous benefits, extending and improving lives. But the high and rising costs for health care ... impose an increasing burden on individuals, businesses, states, and the federal government, and a substantial number of people may have trouble paying for that care because they do not have health insurance. Those issues are related: Rising costs for health care make health insurance policies more expensive and thus more difficult to afford. Lack of insurance can limit access to care, but having insurance can increase spending by encouraging the use of services that provide limited health benefits. . . . Indeed, evidence suggests that a substantial share of spending on health care contributes little if anything to the overall health of the nation, but finding ways to reduce such spending without also affecting services that improve health will be difficult.

U.S. Congressional Budget Office, Key Issues in Analyzing Major Health Insurance Proposals ix (2008).

Although the "triple aim" strategy strives to balance access, cost, and quality, the relationships among these concepts often force tradeoffs in reform proposals. See Lindsay F. Wiley, Elizabeth Y. McCuskey, Matthew B. Lawrence, and Erin C. Fuse Brown, Health Reform Reconstruction, 55 U.C. Davis L. Rev. ___ (forthcoming 2021). And health reform debates in the U.S. frequently invoke a fourth competing priority—the ability for individuals to have *choice* among providers and insurance plans. This section provides definition and context for these concepts.

A. ACCESS

In the U.S., most people access health care services through one of two avenues: 1) private health care coverage, obtained either through an employer or purchased on the individual market; or 2) by qualifying for a public insurance plan like Medicare or Medicaid. The reason access to health care services is often considered synonymous with health insurance coverage is because even basic services are so expensive that few can afford them without third-party financing. Those who do not purchase health insurance, whether because they choose not to, cannot afford it, lack available coverage options, or do not qualify for a public health care program, must pay for services out-of-pocket, often at a significant price increase.

Prior to the passage of the ACA in 2010, the number of uninsured reached an all-time high of 49.9 million Americans. Further, lack of insurance affects a much larger number of Americans if one looks at periods spanning several years. The ACA resulted in historic gains in access to health insurance by extending Medicaid eligibility and subsidizing the cost of individual health insurance for individuals earning less than 400% of the federal poverty level. By the third year of the ACA's implementation, the number of uninsured had dropped to 27.3 million, just 8.6% of the population. Jessica C. Barnett & Edward R. Berchick, U.S.

Bureau of the Census, Health Insurance Coverage in the United States 2016 (Sept. 2017).

Despite this improvement, access to health insurance remains a major issue in the U.S. health care system. Millions of people still lack insurance, geographic access to care, or sufficient finances to pay for deductibles, copays, and uncovered services. Many people do not have access to affordable health insurance through their employment, while others do not have access to Medicaid or subsidies because their state did not expand Medicaid. Many uninsured adults go without necessary medical care because they cannot afford it and often forego preventative care, as well. Kaiser Family Found., Key Facts about the Uninsured Population (Nov. 2020).

1. The Uninsured

Who are the uninsured? Most are adults under the age of 65, living in families with incomes of more than $25,000 a year and at least one year-round worker. The ethnic group with the largest number of uninsured members is white, non-Hispanic. However, groups with the highest risk of being uninsured include adults between the ages of 26 and 34; racial and ethnic minorities (particularly Hispanics); noncitizens; members of families with only part-time workers or no workers; workers employed in low-paying jobs; individuals in families with incomes below 200% of the federal poverty level; and children being cared for by persons other than their own parents. Coverage also differs significantly among the various states, with the proportion of a state's uninsured population in 2019 ranging from 18.4% in Texas to 3% in Massachusetts. See Katherine Keisler-Starkey & Lisa N. Bunch, U.S. Bureau of the Census, Health Insurance Coverage in the United States 2019 (Sept. 2020).

Why are these persons uninsured? Most are uninsured because they lack employment-related insurance, and they do not qualify for Medicaid for financial, age, or condition-related reasons, and their state did not adopt the Medicaid expansion. Although nearly all employers with 200 or more employees offer health insurance, a much smaller percentage of employers with 199 or fewer employees do. Overall, the average percentage of employers offering health insurance has declined over the past decade. The widespread job losses during the COVID-19 pandemic resulted in the loss of employer-provided health insurance for many, as well. A number of employees eligible for their employers' plan do not enroll because they cannot afford the premium contributions, which historically have increased more quickly than wages and inflation. Moreover, many employees who work for employers who insure their full-time employees are not eligible for coverage, either because they work part-time or are temporary or seasonal employees (e.g., they work in agriculture or construction). A significant number of workers in the "gig economy" also do not have employment-related insurance because they are formally independent contractors rather than employees. See Kaiser Family Found./Health Research and Ed. Trust, Employer Health Benefits, 2020 Annual Survey (2020).

Many Americans believe that the uninsured can get medical care from physicians and hospitals when they need it, but that is largely untrue. See Chapter 6. An overwhelming body of evidence, however, reveals a direct correlation between lack of insurance, lack of health care, and poor health. The long-term uninsured are more likely than the insured to fail to get necessary medical care for serious conditions, forego filling prescriptions or getting recommended tests, experience hospitalization for avoidable conditions like pneumonia or uncontrolled diabetes, and be diagnosed for cancer at later stages when treatment is less likely to succeed. They are also less likely than the insured to have a regular doctor or to receive cancer screening, cardiovascular risk-reduction assistance, or diabetes care. See Benjamin D. Sommers et al., Health Insurance Coverage and Health— What the Recent Evidence Tells Us, NEJM 586 (2017); Kaiser Family Found., Key Facts about the Uninsured Population (Sept. 2017). Further, the long-term uninsured face a 25% greater likelihood of premature death than do insured Americans, and uninsured Americans with breast or colorectal cancer are 30% to 50% more likely to die prematurely. See, e.g., Andrew P. Wilper et al., Health Insurance and Mortality in U.S. Adults, Am. J. Pub. Health 2289 (2009).

The uninsured also suffer financially. Lack of insurance leads to cost-related access problems (such as not filling a prescription or skipping a recommended medical test, treatment, or follow-up visit), and drives personal debts and bankruptcies. See Liz Hamel et al., The Burden of Medical Debt: Results from the Kaiser Family Foundation/New York Times Medical Bills Survey, Kaiser Family Found. (Jan. 2016).

2. The Underinsured

Like the uninsured, many Americans with insurance experience health-related financial problems. Many Americans are **underinsured**, meaning that despite having health insurance, they have high deductibles or out-of-pocket health care costs relative to their household income. In 2020, a Commonwealth Fund analysis showed that 21% of working-age adults with insurance were underinsured, including one quarter of those enrolled in employer-sponsored insurance plans. Sara R. Collins, Munira Z. Gunja, & Gabriella N. Aboulafia, Commonwealth Fund, U.S. Health Insurance Coverage in 2020: A Looming Crisis in Affordability (Aug. 19, 2020). While the uninsured rate went down during the first decade of the ACA, the *under*insured rate has gone up. Private health insurance plans' steadily increasing reliance on cost-sharing has increased enrollees' costs of care at a pace faster than inflation or wage-growth. Although the underinsured are more likely to receive preventive and necessary medical care than the uninsured, they still face formidable cost-related hurdles to accessing that care and also face medical debt and bankruptcy, despite paying for coverage. Sara R. Collins, Herman K. Bhupal, & Michelle M. Doty, The Commonwealth Fund, Health Insurance Coverage Eight Years After the ACA (Feb. 7, 2019).

3. Other Barriers to Access

Lack of insurance is not the only barrier to accessing health care. Americans' ability to access the health care system also depends on race, ethnicity, socioeconomic status, age, sex, disability status, sexual orientation, gender identity, and residential location. For instance, fully insured individuals in rural areas may have trouble finding a provider that will accept new patients or a particular specialist. Others may struggle to obtain the necessary transportation, time away from work, or childcare to receive care. Language and cultural barriers can also impede access and receipt of timely care. Further, racial, gender, and disability-related discrimination, can lead to denial of access, avoidance of care for fear of further discrimination, and compromised care delivery. These topics are discussed in more depth in Chapter 6.

B. COST

Affordability of health has been a persistently urgent problem for Americans for decades. See, e.g., Ezekiel Emanuel, Aaron Glickman, and David Johnson, Measuring the Burden of Health Care Costs on US Families: The Affordability Index, 318 JAMA 1863, 1863–64 (2017). American citizens, businesses, and governmental entities all struggle to pay for health care, and yet bending the health care cost curve remains elusive. This section examines what we spend on health care, how it compares to other nations, and what factors drive those costs.

1. Overview of Health Care Costs

By any measure, Americans—through our government, employers, and out of our own pockets—spend a great deal on health care. In 2019, the U.S. spent $3.8 trillion on health care goods and services. National Health Expenditures 2019 Highlights, Centers for Medicare and Medicaid Services. The U.S. spends more on health care than on any other sector of the economy, including defense, transportation, education, or housing. The nation also spends more than any other economically developed country on health care, both as a percentage of GDP (17.7%) and per capita. See Organization for Economic Cooperation and Development, Health Spending, OECD Data (2017).

The U.S. is also unique among modern industrialized nations in the extent of its reliance on private payment for health care services. Of the

$3.8 trillion spent on health care in 2019, 11% came from Americans' out-of-pocket payments, 33% came from private health insurance, and federal and state governments paid most of the rest, with Medicare providing 21% of the spending on the elderly and disabled, and Medicaid providing the remaining 16%. National Health Expenditures 2019 Highlights, Centers for Medicare and Medicaid Services.

Continuing growth in health care costs has significantly burdened employers and individuals alike. Due to the steady premium increases for employment-related insurance, employers have begun to pass an ever-increasing share of the cost of health insurance on to employees, either by requiring them to bear a larger share of the premiums, through increased cost-sharing, or through cutbacks in benefits. Collins, Bhupal, & Doty, *supra*; Uwe E. Reinhardt, The Culprit Behind High U.S. Health Care Prices, N.Y. Times: Economix (June 7, 2013).

Employers also shift premium increases to employees through increased cost-sharing in the form of deductibles, coinsurance, and copayments. Deductibles, which are the amounts patients must pay out-of-pocket before insurance kicks in, have been rising much faster than wages or inflation. Once coverage commences, most employees also must pay a portion of the cost of any medical good or service in the form of a copayment (a fixed dollar amount) or coinsurance (a fixed percentage of the price).

Like private expenditures, public expenditures on health have also continued to grow, although at a slower rate. Cost control strategies for Medicare and Medicaid will be discussed in more depth in Chapter 10.

2. Factors Increasing Health Care Costs

Numerous factors contribute to the cost of health care in America and help explain its deviance from per capita costs in other developed countries. We will consider the two most important drivers of cost first, and then turn to additional factors that experts frequently discuss but contribute less to the high cost of care.

a. *Overutilization*

The dominant narrative among policymakers and health services researchers has been that overuse of health care goods and services, i.e., waste, is the single largest driver of health care expenditures. According to research by John E. Wennberg, Elliot Fisher, and Jonathan Skinner, approximately 30% of all health care paid for by Medicare and private insurers in the U.S. is useless, unneeded, and a waste. This estimate now translates to more than $1 trillion each year. Wennberg and colleagues divided the country into 306 regions and compared Medicare expenditures for similar patients in these regions. They found dramatic geographic variations. For instance, in 2014 Medicare spent an average of $13,347 per recipient in Miami, but just $6,971 in Anchorage, even after controlling for income, health status and severity, and patient mix (race, age, sex, and ethnicity). The Dartmouth Atlas of Health Care, Medicare Reimbursements, The Dartmouth Inst. for Health Pol'y and Clinical Practice (2014). Wennberg argued that these variations could be categorized as either warranted or unwarranted. Warranted variations exist because of differences in patient mix and patient preferences. Unwarranted variations, on the other hand, result from provider practice patterns, incentives, and anything else unrelated to the patient's underlying illness and preferences. Studies conducted by the Dartmouth Atlas, McKinsey, Thompson Reuters, and the New England Healthcare Institute concluded that if the U.S. health care system could eliminate these unwarranted variations, such that average Medicare expenditures for patients in Miami looked similar to the average Medicare expenditures for patients in Anchorage, the system could save between 20%–30%. Elliot M. Fisher & Jonathan Skinner, Reflections on Geographic Variations in U.S. Health Care, The Dartmouth Inst. for Health Pol'y and Clinical Practice (May 12, 2010). As a result of this work, the majority of health reform efforts, including the ACA, focused on curbing unwarranted variations in utilization in an effort to control costs.

This work on practice variations by the Dartmouth Atlas researchers focused on Medicare data. Because Medicare sets its own prices for services, the variations in health spending and corresponding calculation of "waste" were largely driven by differences in utilization, that is, the volume and intensity of services used. In Medicaid, poverty and other social determinants of health drive substantial amounts of necessary utilization, which also drive cost. See Richard Cooper, Poverty and the Myths of Health Care Reform (2016). For private payers, which lack price controls, variations in health spending are a function not only of differences in utilization, but also differences in prices. In fact, for privately insured individuals, prices account for the vast majority of the geographic variations in spending, overshadowing differences in wages or utilization. See Chapin White, Amelia M. Bond & James D. Reschovsky, Ctr. for Studying Health Sys. Change, Research Brief No. 27, High and Varying Prices for Privately Insured Patients Underscore Hospital Market Power (2013); Joseph P. Newhouse & Alan M. Garber, Geographic Variation in Health Care Spending in the United States: Insights from an Institute of Medicine Report, 310 JAMA 1227 (2013).

The relationship between utilization and health care spending has become even more complex in recent years. Between 1996 and 2013, utilization in inpatient settings decreased, but utilization of ambulatory care and pharmaceutical treatments increased. Interestingly, even as inpatient utilization decreased, the prices and intensity of inpatient services increased enough to drive up inpatient spending overall. See,

Joseph L. Dieleman et al., Factors Associated with Increases in U.S. Healthcare Spending, 1996–2013, 318 JAMA 1668 (2017); Anne B. Martin et al., National Health Spending: Faster Growth in 2015 as Coverage Expands and Utilization Increases, 36 Health Aff. 166 (Jan. 2017).

b. *Prices*

Unfortunately, in the effort to control utilization, policymakers significantly overlooked the other key element in determining health care expenditures: prices. Just like everything else, overall health expenditures depend on not just how much you buy, but also the price you pay for each item. For the last two decades, researchers found that increases in price (including intensity of services) have been more strongly associated with overall increases in health care spending than any other commonly suggested factor. Joseph L. Dieleman et al. *supra*. Even though we spend more on health care than any other nation, Americans use the same amount of (or, according to some studies, fewer) health care services per capita than other countries. The average American sees a doctor 4 times a year, compared to 7.7 for the average Canadian or 10 for the average German. The average hospital stay for an American is 6.1 days, compared to 9 days for the average German and 7 for the average Englishman. OECD, Health at a Glance 2017: OECD Indicators 169, 177 (OECD Publishing 2017). On the other hand, we pay dramatically more per unit of health care consumed and, in many instances, per health care worker, than do most other nations. We also pay substantially more for drugs than do the citizens of many other nations, even for the same drugs. Controlling prescription drug prices has become a major focus of politicians in recent years as costs for on- and off-patent drugs have risen significantly. Aaron S. Kesselheim, Jerry Avorn & Ameet Sarpatwari, The High Cost of Prescription Drugs in the United States: Origins and Prospects for Reform, 316 JAMA 858–71 (Aug. 2016). In the end, these higher prices do not result in better quality care, nor do they lead to better health outcomes. See generally, Gerard F. Anderson et al., It's the Prices, Stupid: Why the United States Is So Different from Other Countries, 22 Health Aff. 89 (May/June 2003); Bruce C. Vladeck & Thomas Rice, Market Failure and the Failure of Discourse: Facing Up to the Power of Sellers, 28 Health Aff. 1305, 1305–06 (2009).

c. *Market Forces and Structure*

In the U.S., the health care pricing problem results largely from the use and abuse of market power of dominant health care providers. Robert A. Berenson et al., The Growing Power of Some Providers to Win Steep Payment Increases from Insurers Suggests Policy Remedies May Be Needed, 31 Health Aff. 973, 973 (2012). The market for certain health care services—including health insurance, hospital care, and specialty

Overall, while the changing nature of disease contributes to increased spending on health care, it is not a major driver of such increases. One recent analysis notes that while some chronic diseases have become more prevalent, others (such as respiratory conditions related to tobacco) are becoming less common, and that per patient expenditures are driving cost increases more than increasing disease prevalence. See Charles S. Roehrigh and David Rousseau, The Growth in Cost Per Case Explains Far More of US Health Spending Increases than Rising Disease Prevalence, 30 Health Aff. 1657 (2011).

The COVID-19 pandemic reflected a profound and immediate change in the scale of infectious disease, as well as a potential influence on the chronic diseases that may be exacerbated or created by infection. For some discussions about the influence of COVID-19 on health care costs, compare Richard Kronick, "How COVID-19 Will Likely Affect Spending, and Why Many Other Analyses May Be Wrong," Health Aff. Blog (May 19, 2020) and Caroline Humer, Nick Brown, Emilio Parodi, COVID-19 Long-term Toll Signals Billions in Healthcare Costs Ahead, Reuters (Aug. 3, 2020), with Laura Tollen & Elizabeth Keating, COVID-19, Market Consolidation, and Price Growth, Health Aff. Blog (Aug. 3, 2020).

g.   Technology

Most health economists believe that the widespread and rapid adoption of health care technology also contributes to increasing health care costs. As new medical technologies are developed, physicians often adopt them if they provide an improvement in care, with little thought to how much that improvement is worth. For instance, many new pharmaceutical drugs come with exorbitant price tags, but without the clinical benefits to match. Consider nivolumab, which on average extends a patient with metastatic renal cancer's life by nearly six months, and comes with a $65,000 price tag for Medicare and nearly twice that for commercial insurers. Motzer et al., Nivolumab Versus Everolimus in Advanced Renal-Cell Carcinoma, 373 NEJM 1803 (2017); Peter B. Bach, New Math on Drug Costs, 373 NEJM, 1797 (2015). Recent studies reveal, however, that the relationship between technology development and cost is highly complex and often conflicting. The impact of technology on cost often depends on a variety of factors, such as the availability of other interventions, the patient population, and the type of technology (e.g., cancer drugs vs. medical devices). Variation in these factors can cause one new technology to dramatically increase costs, while others can be cost neutral or cost saving. Corinna Sorenson, Michael Drummond, and Beena Bhuiyan Khan, Medical Technology as a Key Driver of Rising Health Expenditure: Disentangling the Relationship, 5 Clinicoeconomic Outcomes Research 223–34 (2013).

Further, existing payment models also create incentives for physicians to use more expensive medical technologies by paying them more to do so. For instance, the Resource-Based Relative Value Scale (RBRVS, discussed in Chapter 10), which is used to set Medicare payments for physicians, pays more for procedures and technology use than for services that require providers' cognitive skills. These payment models not only shift utilization toward increased use of technology, but also lead to significant increases in overall health care spending. Elisabeth Rosenthal, An American Sickness: How Healthcare Became Big Business and How You Can Take It Back, 62 (2017). See also, Snapshots: How Changes in Medical Technology Affect Health Care Costs, Kaiser Family Found. (Mar. 2, 2007); Sheila Smith, Joseph P. Newhouse & Mark S. Freeland, Income, Insurance, and Technology: Why Does Health Spending Outpace Economic Growth?, 28 Health Aff. 1276–84 (2009); Victor R. Fuchs, Who Shall Live?: Health, Economics and Social Choice, ix–xxviii (2nd ed. 2011).

h. Malpractice

Though malpractice continues to be a major source of irritation to medical professionals, it is not a major contributor to medical costs. The direct costs of malpractice premiums account for less than 1% of health care costs, though these costs tend to be borne disproportionately by physicians in particular specialties and geographic areas. Defensive medicine arguably is of greater concern, but the extent to which it contributes to health care costs is difficult to measure reliably. See U.S. Government Accountability Office, Medical Malpractice: Implications of Rising Premiums on Access to Health Care, GAO–03–836 (2003). Medical liability system costs, which include costs related to defensive medicine, likely accounts for 2.4 percent of total health care spending. Michelle M. Mello, Amitabh Chandra, Atul A. Gawande, & David M. Studdert, National Costs of The Medical Liability System, 29 Health Aff. 1569 (2010).

PROBLEM: HEALTH CARE COSTS

To assess the issues raised by health care costs, first consider your personal relationship to health spending. How much value do you place on health care? Do you think that we as a society spend too much, too little, or about the right amount on health care? Do you think that you as an individual spend too much, too little, or the right amount? Do you know how much your health insurance or employer-sponsored coverage costs? How much of this cost do you pay directly? Would you want your physician to discuss the price of a particular treatment in relation to its effectiveness with you when making medical decisions? How much did your insurer or employer plan spend on your care last year? Should cost factor into whether insurance should cover a particular treatment? Should the cost effectiveness of a particular treatment in comparison to other available treatments factor into insurance coverage? Would you be willing to try a treatment that was somewhat less effective than the best on the market, but significantly less expensive? What if your copay for both drugs was the same? Does the price your insurance company pays matter to your decision? What are the implications of reducing overall health care spending? Who will benefit? Who will lose?

C. QUALITY

While the quality of care in the U.S. has increased in recent years, it can be significantly improved. For instance, a recent study found medical error to be the third leading cause of death in the U.S., causing more than 250,000 deaths per year. Martin A. Makary and Michael Daniel, Medical Error—The Third Leading Cause of Death in the U.S., 353 British Med. J. 2139 (2016). For further discussion of medical error, see Chapter 5.

The U.S. health care system falls short not only in terms of cost and access when compared with other developed nations, but also on many measurements of quality and health outcomes overall. For instance, in a 2017 comparison with Australia, the United Kingdom, New Zealand, Canada, France, Germany, the Netherlands, Norway, Sweden, and Switzerland, the U.S. health care system ranked last on overall performance. In more specific categories, the U.S. performed below average on all categories, ranking last (11th) in access, equity, and health care outcomes; next to last (10th) in administrative efficiency; and 5th overall in care process. In a nutshell, the U.S. health care system vastly underperforms its peers while spending substantially more. The problems in our system are pervasive. The report found life expectancy in the U.S., after improving for several decades, has decreased in recent years for some populations, largely in connection with the opioid crisis. Likewise, "poor access to primary care has contributed to inadequate prevention and management of chronic diseases, delayed diagnosis, incomplete adherence to treatments, wasteful overuse of drugs and technologies, and coordination and safety problems." Eric C. Schneider, Arnav Shah, Michelle M. Doty, Roosa Tikkanen, Katharine Fields, & Reginald D. Williams II, et al., Mirror, Mirror 2021: Reflecting Poorly, Health Care in the U.S. Compared to Other High-Income Countries, Commonwealth Fund Report 4 (Aug. 2021). On the other hand, the report found that the U.S. tends to excel on measures that involve the doctor-patient relationship, such as wellness counseling, shared decision-making with primary care and specialist providers, chronic disease management, and end-of-life discussions. It also had better than average rates of preventative measures, such as mammography screening and immunization rates. Despite the gains made by the ACA in recent years, the study authors suggest that many of the U.S.'s quality-related shortfalls result from the combination of a lack of universal health coverage and barriers to access for primary care.

The COVID-19 pandemic highlighted both the capacity for the U.S. health care system to deliver high-quality care in exigent circumstances, and its failures to do so—particularly for already-vulnerable populations. See, e.g., Theresa Andrasfaya & Noreen Goldman, Reductions in 2020 US Life Expectancy due to COVID-19 and the Disproportionate Impact on the Black and Latino Populations, 118 Proc. of the Nat'l Acad. of Sciences e2014746118 (2021); Andy Slavitt, The COVID-19 Pandemic Underscores the Need to Address Structural Challenges of the US Health Care System, JAMA Forum (July 2, 2020).

D. CHOICE

Health policy debates about the triple aim often incorporate a related concern over "choice." As noted in Chapter 1, this particular invocation of "choice" in health care focuses on patients' choices among insurance plans and providers. In this context, "choice" is synonymous with "options." The emphasis on options accompanies arguments for market-based and consumer-driven reforms, which depend on the existence of competing options to optimize cost, quality, and access. See, e.g., U.S. Dep't of Health & Human Servs., Reforming America's Healthcare System Through Choice and Competition (2018); Richard G. Frank, The Commonwealth Fund, Making Choice and Competition Work in Individual Insurance in Health Reform Proposals (Jan. 30, 2019).

Many of the features of health insurance and managed care, discussed above, limit peoples' options for choosing insurers and providers. Most insurance markets are highly concentrated and regulated, leaving few choices of insurers. Further, a majority of Americans under the age of 65 receive health insurance as a benefit through their employers, which limit the number of plans offered, in some cases offering only one option. Insurance plans then limit the choice of providers significantly by either refusing to cover out-of-network providers and facilities, or imposing significant cost-sharing obligations for doing so. In many rural areas, as well as urban areas with highly concentrated markets, provider choice is limited further by a lack of competition and viable alternatives. Managed care organizations also frequently use primary care providers as gatekeepers to limit access to specialists and specialty services, further limiting patient choice. Finally, insurance companies limit treatment choices through coverage denials for certain types of providers and treatments.

Behavioral economics research demonstrates people are especially ill-equipped to make sound choices among health plans, and that neither more options nor decision-aids affect that shortcoming. Allison K. Hoffman, The ACA's Choice Problem, 45 J Health Pol. Pol'y & L. 501 (2020). This suggests that meaningful choice in health insurance is elusive, and that focusing health policy attention on preserving "choice" of insurers and providers can obfuscate—rather than support—access, cost, and quality advancements. *Id.*

NOTES AND QUESTIONS

1.   *Choices in the Marketplace.* In some ACA marketplaces, consumers had the choice of over 100 plans. How would you begin to assess your options? Which factors would matter most? Could the marketplaces highlight specific characteristics for comparison to facilitate choice? Many ACA marketplaces only have one insurer left. What are the implications of this?

2.   *Choices in a Single-Payer System.* How might a single-payer system, which restricts or eliminates options for health insurance other than the government-funded program, expand patients' choices among providers?

IV.   TOOLS OF HEALTH REFORM

Approaches to health care reform can generally be divided between those that rely on regulatory tools and those that rely on private market-based initiatives and incentives to govern behavior. All nations, including the U.S., have adopted a mixed strategy for addressing access, cost, and quality in health care. All have government-funded public programs for providing health insurance or health care to a portion of their population. Even in the U.S., where private enterprise is central, the government bears more than 60% of health care expenditures (including tax expenditures and the cost of insurance for government employees), even though government programs cover around one-third of the population. David U. Himmelstein and Steffie Woolhandler, The Current and Projected Taxpayer Shares of US Health Care Costs, 106 Am. J. Pub. Health 449 (Mar. 2016). All nations also have private insurance markets. In the United Kingdom, whose National Health Service is the quintessential example of socialized medicine, about one ninth of the population has private insurance. However, the particular blend of reform tools a government takes to control costs, promote access, improve quality, and offer choice differs significantly depending on the country, and in some instances, state or province. In this section, we will examine a range of market-based and regulatory health reform tools that policymakers can implement to achieve their desired ends.

A. MARKET-BASED APPROACHES

Market-based approaches encourage competition in an effort to promote access, lower costs, and improve quality. These market-based approaches attempt to change the behavior of different actors in the health care market through supply-side and demand-side controls, or, alternatively, they seek to improve the functioning of the market for health insurance.

1. Supply-Side Controls

Supply-side controls aim to constrain provider behavior in supplying health care services. As the ones who order and perform health care services, physicians drive demand. Moreover, the way we pay for health care generally rewards physicians for ordering more items and services, particularly more complex, highly paid services. Thus, it is often quipped that the most expensive piece of equipment in the hospital is the doctor's pen. Physician-induced demand leads to overutilization of health care services, which drives up costs at the expense of quality and access.

Perhaps the most successful supply-side strategy to reduce costs and improve quality in recent years has been **managed care**, which combines the financing and delivery of care, as discussed in Section I of this chapter. More modern forms of supply-side controls, such as **Accountable Care Organizations (ACOs)**, are designed to promote more efficient delivery of care by offering providers a share of the savings gained from improved prevention and care coordination. The remainder of this section discusses a variety of supply-side controls.

a. Managed Care

Managed Care Organizations (MCOs) typically use a variety of supply-side tools to manage costs by restricting members to limited provider networks, reviewing the utilization of services, or creating incentives for limiting the cost of care. Some MCOs also attempt to oversee the quality of care their members receive. As described in Section I of this chapter, managed care grew rapidly during the 1990s, and remains the dominant approach to financing health care in the U.S. Under managed care, health care cost growth slowed dramatically during the mid-1990s as MCOs saved money by reducing utilization of health care services and negotiating significant reimbursement discounts with providers. Further, health services research suggests that higher market penetration by HMOs, the most restrictive form of managed care, led to moderation of cost growth throughout the entire health care market. Laurence C. Baker et al., HMO Market Penetration and the Costs of Employer-Sponsored Health Plans, 19 Health Aff. 121 (Sept./Oct. 2000). However, by 2000, health care costs began increasing again as managed care controls weakened in response to backlash from providers, consumers, media, and legislators who objected to what they perceived as onerous rationing and restrictions on consumer choice and medical freedom. See Jon Gabel et al., Health Benefits in 2003: Premiums Reach Thirteen-Year High as Employers Adopt New Forms of Cost Sharing, 22 Health Aff. 117 (Sept./Oct. 2003). As health care costs have continued to rise, employers, insurers and policymakers have returned to more restrictive forms of managed care, like narrow network plans that include only a limited number of in-network providers and facilities, in hopes of curbing future cost growth. Some of the most common tools used by MCOs are discussed below.

b. Provider Networks

Virtually all MCOs either limit their members to a particular network of providers or impose financial disincentives to discourage their members from "going out-of-network." As noted earlier, imposition of these types of limitations has historically been a defining characteristic of certain MCOs, separating PPOs from HMOs from POS plans. MCOs generally have a good reason for limiting their members to particular providers. Often, providers agree to deliver services to MCO members at a discount in exchange for inclusion in the MCO's network of preferred providers. From the providers' perspective, they accept a lower reimbursement rate to gain access to the higher volume of patients enrolled in the MCO. Furthermore, MCOs prefer to contract with professionals and providers who share their vision of cost and utilization control. MCOs also use provider networks to limit participating providers to those who offer high quality care, or at least to exclude providers who exhibit clear quality problems. By creating distinct networks of providers, MCOs can both limit their costs and promote quality and value-based care.

c. Utilization Review

Utilization review (UR) refers to case-by-case evaluations that MCOs conduct to determine the necessity and appropriateness (and sometimes the quality) of medical care provided to MCO enrollees. UR aims to reduce the wide variations in the use of many medical services and minimize wasteful and unnecessary care.

UR can take several forms. The oldest form is retrospective review, under which an insurer denies payment for care already provided, normally by deeming it medically unnecessary, experimental, or cosmetic. Retrospective review is of limited value for containing costs overall since the practitioner has already performed the care by the time the review takes place. Instead, it mostly shifts costs from the insurance company onto the patient or the health care provider.

Contemporary UR programs stress prior or concurrent review and management of high-cost cases and diseases. **Evidence-based clinical guidelines** can provide significant guidance as to whether a particular treatment is appropriate. Prior and concurrent review techniques include 1) preadmission or preservice reviews, which occur prior to hospital admission or providing a particular service; 2) admission review (within 24 to 72 hours of emergency or urgent admissions); 3) continued stay review (to assess length of stay and sometimes accompanied by discharge planning); and 4) voluntary or mandatory second-opinions. High-cost case management addresses the small number (1%–7%) of very expensive cases that account for most benefit plan costs. Case managers create individualized treatment plans for high-cost beneficiaries. Similarly, disease management programs are designed to ensure appropriate care for particular chronic or recurring medical conditions and often focus on self-care, prevention, and appropriate use of pharmaceuticals.

d. Primary Care Physician Management

At the margins, UR blends into other care management strategies. Some forms of UR rely on primary care physicians (PCPs) to act as case managers and gatekeepers for access to specialists and more intensive medical services. MCOs have successfully utilized primary care case management to provide preventative services, avoid unnecessary emergency room use, manage chronic conditions, and coordinate care across settings. Medicaid has successfully used primary care case management to control costs and improve patient care. Take a Walk on the Supply Side: 10 Steps to Control Health Care Costs, The Commonwealth Fund (Apr. 2005). PCPs also act as gatekeepers to insurance coverage for a range of services. In many cases, if a patient wants to see a specialist or have a particular test or treatment, the PCP must make the referral; otherwise the insurance plan will not cover the specialized services. Improved coordination between the PCP and specialists can help reduce duplicative tests and eliminate other forms of waste. Naomi Freundlich, Better Care at Lower Cost: Is It Possible?, The Commonwealth Fund (Nov. 21, 2013). On the other hand, MCOs financially incentivize PCPs to control utilization and the MCO's liability for specialty services. These incentives can undermine the patient's trust in the PCP. Christopher B. Forrest et al., Managed Care, Primary Care, and the Patient-Practitioner Relationship, J. General Internal Medicine 270–77 (Apr. 2002).

e. Capitation

Like other supply-side controls, **capitation** payment models aim to shift the financial incentives for providers from providing more care (as in fee-for-service reimbursement) to providing only necessary care. Capitation models pay providers a lump sum for caring for MCO-enrolled patients over the course of a set period of time. Typically, payments are made per member per month. Thus, the providers assume financial risk from the MCO—if the costs of care for the members exceed the capitation payment, the providers lose money, and if the costs of care are below the capitation payment, then the providers make money. While many capitation models exist in health care, they can be divided into two groups—global and partial. **Global capitation** encompasses payment to a large, integrated health system or ACO to care for the comprehensive health needs of a patient population. Under a **partial or blended capitation** model, providers only receive payment for certain services on a capitated basis. For instance, a PCP would receive a capitated payment for providing certain identified primary care services, but fee-for-service payments for other ancillary payments. Why Incentives Matter: Capitation Models, Health Care Incentives Improvement Inst., www.hci3.org.

Capitation as a market-based approach to controlling the supply of medical services has significant advantages and disadvantages. First, capitation pays providers in a predictable manner, enabling them to save money for larger capital investments, such as electronic medical records systems, decision support systems, and property expansions. These systems can improve quality and lower the cost of care. On the other hand, capitation creates strong incentives for providers to care for patients in a manner that enables them to make money, including the risk of skimping on needed care. Capitation, Health Care Incentives Improvement Inst., www.hci3.org. In some instances, capitation can shift the financial risk of patient care to providers in ways that can threaten financial solvency and quality of care. Michael E. Porter & Robert S. Kaplan, How to Pay for Health Care, Harv. Bus. Rev. 88 (July-Aug. 2016), www.hbr.org. Newer models of global capitation, like ACOs, have been designed to reward high quality care through bonuses for meeting quality benchmarks. For a further discussion of ACOs, see Chapter 10 on Medicare.

f.   Integrated Care Delivery

Market-based approaches that promote provider collaboration and integration offer significant benefits in terms of controlling cost and quality of care. Ideally, integrated care is care that "is coordinated across entities, continuous over time, tailored to patients' and families' needs and preferences, and based on patients' and caregivers' sharing responsibility." Michaela J. Kerrissey et al., Medical Group Structural Integration May Not Ensure that Care Is Integrated, From the Patient's Perspective, 36 Health Aff. 885 (May 2017). As successful staff model HMOs, like Kaiser and Group Health, have demonstrated, efforts to integrate medical care can promote efficiency, reduce waste, lower administrative costs, permit coordination and sharing of medical records, and reduce testing, medication redundancies, and medical error. Further, **integrated delivery systems**, like ACOs, also align the financial incentives of many of the providers such that all providers share in any potential savings or penalty. However, integrated care delivery does not immediately result from structural integration of health care organizations, often effectuated through mergers and acquisitions—it takes more than co-ownership to effectively align care. See Michaela J. Kerrissey et al., above. True integration must come from leadership commitment to collaborative and coordinated care, as well as from physician champions dedicated to pursuing the endeavor. Integrated delivery system models are discussed further in Chapter 12.

g.   Value-Based Purchasing

The commitment to reducing excessive costs and waste lead many insurers and other payers to become interested in paying for health care goods and services based on their value. **Value-based purchasing** refers to a wide range of payment models that link provider performance to reimbursement. Historically, Medicare, Medicaid, and private insurers paid providers on a fee-for-service basis. This model pays providers more for committing medical errors—the fee for the initial treatment and the fee to resolve the error. In essence, the model financially incentivized poor quality care that harmed patients. Instead, in a value-based purchasing model, payers would pay providers on a fee-for-service basis with payment adjustments up or down based on reaching specific value metrics, also known as **pay-for-performance**. Providers can increase value by improving outcomes and quality, reducing costs, or both. For instance, payers can shift provider incentives by refusing to pay for services to remedy medical errors or rewarding providers that recommend cost-effective drugs.

In recent years, numerous federal laws have passed to promote value-based purchasing in Medicare, including the ACA and the Medicare Access and CHIP Reauthorization Act (MACRA). These laws implement payment reforms that refuse reimbursement for medical errors and financially penalize lower quality care, in an effort to save money and promote quality. Private insurers have also begun to follow suit. So far, research suggests that the impact of existing value-based purchasing models has been marginal with several potential causes. First, the financial incentives may not be sufficient to drive change. Second, providers may not understand the quality measures well enough to appropriately link behaviors and incentives. Third, too much time may exist between behavior and incentive payment, effectively decoupling the two. Finally, payers often roll incentive payments into overall reimbursement payments instead of acknowledging them as a separate reward, further decoupling behavior from incentive. For a more in depth evaluation of value-based purchasing programs, see Tingyin T. Chee et al., The Current State of Value-Based Purchasing Programs, 133 Circulation 2197 (2016); Cheryl Damberg et al., Measuring Success in Health Care Value-Based Purchasing Programs, RAND Research Report (2014). Value-based purchasing within Medicare is discussed in more depth in Chapter 10.

Overall, supply-side controls aim to incentivize providers to control health care utilization, while promoting high quality care.

2.   Demand-Side Controls

On the other side of the equation, **demand-side controls** aim to reduce the demand for health care services by changing the incentives for

health care consumers (i.e., patients). Demand-side controls seek to curb
costs at the point of purchase of health care products and services by
increasing the amount the patient must pay out-of-pocket. By giving
patients some "skin in the game," these demand-side approaches sensitize
patients to their health care costs, which leads the patient to exert market
pressure on providers through shopping or economizing on care. Many
proponents of **consumer-driven health care** believe that the primary
factor driving health care cost inflation is insurance, which shields
individuals from the financial consequences of their own health care
purchasing decisions. As discussed above, this phenomenon is known as
the **moral hazard of insurance**, and it can contribute to overutilization
due to excess patient-demand and health care cost inflation. The fact that
employer payments for insurance premiums are not subject to income tax
exacerbates this problem by encouraging individuals to purchase more
insurance coverage than they would if it were not subsidized by taxes.

Without insurance, consumer-driven analysts argue, excessive health
care costs would not be a problem because market forces would discipline
prices and supply. Consumers would decide whether and how much to
spend on a hip replacement in the same manner they decide to purchase a
car. If they were using their own money, so the theory goes, consumers
would reward providers who offer higher value, lower cost options. In the
real world, however, necessary medical expenses, in many situations,
outstrip the resources of all but the wealthiest. Therefore, some form of
insurance, private or public, is necessary to enable consumers to access
necessary health care services and ensure payment to providers. As a
result, the majority of the population purchases some form of health
insurance, and payers and policymakers must account for moral hazard in
designing insurance plans.

Within an insurance based system, the primary demand-side strategy
to manage consumers' behaviors are **cost-sharing tools** (deductibles, coinsurance, and copayments), so that, to the extent possible, consumers are
sensitized to costs at the point of service. Cost-sharing both encourages
consumers to avoid unnecessary care and to shop for the least expensive
providers for necessary care. For consumers to shop for health care goods
and services, however, the goods and services must be comparable and
consumers must have access to prices when making treatment decisions,
not after. A lack of price transparency in health care has limited the
functioning of many tools that rely on comparison shopping.

a. Copays and Coinsurance

Copays and **coinsurance** are two of the most common forms of cost-
sharing in health care. Plans with a copay require the patient to pay a set
amount of money for a physician visit, hospitalization, or a prescription.
For instance, a patient might have to pay a $20 copay at the physician's

office to be seen for a sore throat, but a $250 copay per hospitalization. Coinsurance is calculated as a percentage of the total fee that the patient must pay for a covered item or service. The coinsurance percentage may differ substantially for in-network and out-of-network providers and facilities.

Cost-sharing can be scaled to nudge patients toward lower-cost options. For instance, insurers often "tier" providers and prescription drugs by placing the lowest-cost entities on the preferred tier, with the lowest cost-sharing amounts. Insurers then place higher cost options on a lower tier, with higher cost-sharing amounts. Tiering creates financial incentives for efficient health care choices, as well as increasingly complex coverage rules for patients to navigate.

As a market-based approach to health reform, patient cost-sharing attempts to address moral hazard by adding an incremental cost to seeking additional care, giving patients incentives, even if small, to limit themselves to only necessary services after their deductible has been met. Research shows that even modest cost-sharing reduces patients' utilization of health care. However, studies also indicate cost-sharing has a disproportionate, negative impact on those with chronic illnesses and the poor, highlighting questions of distributive justice. Unfortunately, cost-sharing makes people cut back not just on unnecessary care, but necessary care as well. See Joseph P. Newhouse and the Insurance Experiment Group, Free for All? Lessons from the RAND Health Insurance Experiment (1993); Vicki Fung et al., Financial Barriers to Care Among Low-Income Children with Asthma: Health Care Reform Implications, 168 JAMA Pediatrics 649 (2014); Amal Trivedi et al., Increased Ambulatory Care Copayments and Hospitalizations among the Elderly, 362 NEJM 320 (2010).

b. Deductibles

Deductibles help control the demand for medical services by requiring patients to spend a certain amount of money out-of-pocket before their insurance begins to cover any medical expenses. For instance, a patient with a $1,000 deductible would have to pay the first $1,000 she spent on covered medical services herself. In 2020, 83% of covered American workers had a deductible for their employer-based coverage. The average annual deductible for single coverage in a 2020 employer-based plan was $1,644. Employer-based plans' average deductible amounts have increased 79% over the past decade and 25% over the past five years, with the percentage of covered workers with an annual deductible of $2,000 growing from 19% in 2015 to 26% in 2020. Kaiser Family Found., 2020 Employer Health Benefits Survey (2020). On the ACA's health insurance exchanges in 2020, the average deductible for an individual silver plan was $4,879. CMS, Plan Year 2021 Qualified Health Plan Choice and Premiums in HealthCare.gov States (Nov. 23, 2020). Deductible amounts have grown substantially in recent years with the rise of **High Deductible Health Plans with a Savings Option (HDHP/SO).**

c.   *High Deductible Health Plans with a Savings Option*

HDHP/SOs aim to limit health care demand by making patients more responsible for their health care spending. HDHP/SOs pair a high deductible health plan with a Health Savings Account (HSA) or a Health Reimbursement Arrangement (HRA). An HSA is a savings account that individuals can contribute to and withdraw from for qualified medical expenses on a tax-free basis. Individuals can use funds in their HSAs to cover out-of-pocket spending for medical, dental, and vision care, but they cannot use them to pay for insurance premiums. An HRA is an employer-funded employee health plan that reimburses employees tax free for out-of-pocket medical expenses and individual health insurance premiums up to a fixed dollar amount per year. HealthCare.gov, Health Reimbursement Arrangement (HRA) (2017). Unlike "flexible spending accounts" (FSAs) which require individuals to use their funds or lose them at the end of the year, the funds in HSAs and HRAs carry over from year to year. By 2020, 31% of covered workers enrolled in HDHP/SOs. Kaiser Family Found., 2020 Employer Health Benefits Survey (2020).

Congress adopted this consumer-driven strategy into federal law in the 2003 Medicare Modernization Act, which extended favorable tax treatment to deposits made into HSAs that were accompanied by **high-deductible health plans (HDHPs)**. In 2018, an insurance plan with a deductible of at least $1,350 for individual coverage and $2,700 deductible for family coverage qualified as a HDHP. Likewise, in 2018, the maximum tax-free contribution into an HSA was $3,450 for an individual account and $6,900 for a family account. HSA funds used for qualified medical expenses are not subject to taxation; however, the IRS will impose regular taxes plus a 20% excise tax for any funds withdrawn for other purposes (except on the event of the participant dying, becoming disabled, or becoming eligible for Medicare at age 65).

HRAs arose from an IRS determination that employer-funded contributions to health savings vehicles are eligible for tax subsidies. Rev. Rul. 2002–41. HRAs differ from HSAs in that only employers can contribute to an HRA, while an employer, employee or both can contribute money to an HSA. HRAs are also not subject to government out-of-pocket spending limits. Employers may favor HRAs because they can hold them as notional accounts, which do not require funding until the employee draws on the account, and because the employer can retain accumulated funds if the employee leaves employment.

As policy tools, HDHP/SOs aim to control health care costs by giving individuals more financial responsibility for their health care. Despite their increasing prevalence, however, HDHP/SOs remain controversial. A recent systemic review of research on HDHPs reveal that the plans reduce costs overall, but through a reduction of both appropriate and inappropriate health care services. The review demonstrated that patients with HDHP plans often reduced preventative services and did not adhere to prescriptions. Rajender Agarwal, Olena Mazurenko, and Nir Menchemi, High-Deductible Health Plans Reduce Health Care Costs and Utilization, including Needed Preventative Services, 10 Health Aff. 1762 (Oct. 1, 2017). Interestingly, the reduction in preventative services occurred despite no or low cost-sharing for preventative services. As a result, significant consumer outreach should accompany HDHPs to ensure knowledge of incentives designed to encourage receipt of certain types of care.

Research also demonstrates that in practice, most of the financial benefits of HSAs have accrued to earners in the top 5% who can contribute to the accounts throughout the year and reap the tax benefits. For instance, in 2013, earners with incomes above $200,000 were 10 times more likely to claim a tax deduction for HSA contributions than earners with incomes below $50,000. See JoAnn Volk & Justin Giovannelli, Who Would Gain under the Proposal to Expand Health Savings Accounts?, The Commonwealth Fund (Apr. 14, 2017).

Given the rise of consumer-driven health care and HDHP/SOs, Americans have become more interested in knowing the prices of their health care. Public Agenda, How Much Will It Cost?: How Americans Use Prices in Health Care (Mar. 9, 2015). Private entities like Castlight Health contract with employers to provide employees with price and quality information relevant to their medical needs and coverage in a particular area. A non-profit organization, ClearHealthCosts, has also begun to offer the cash price for health care goods and services in certain geographic areas. See ClearHealthCosts, www.clearhealthcosts.com. In some areas, ClearHealthCosts has created a "cash market" for health care services, where providers will offer lower prices for particular goods and services if the patient will pay in cash. These disruptive technologies may help promote and facilitate the use of consumer-driven health care initiatives like HDHP/SOs.

d. Reference Pricing

Similar to a deductible, **reference pricing** puts the consumer's own money at stake, but reverses who pays the first dollar for the services. Instead of making the patient pay for the first few thousand dollars of care, health plans agree to pay the price for a given service charged by a low priced provider (the reference price). Consumers are free to select a different provider, but the individual would be responsible for the difference between that provider's higher price and the reference price. California's Public Employee Retirement System (CalPERS) has successfully used reference pricing to lower spending on certain medical procedures. Interestingly, reference pricing led to cost savings by changing both patient and provider behavior—patients chose lower priced providers, and providers lowered their prices to retain patient volume. In the first two years after implementation, reference pricing saved CalPERS $2.8 million on joint replacement surgeries, $1.3 million on cataract surgeries, $7 million on colonoscopies, and $2.3 million on arthroscopies. Ann Boynton and James C. Robinson, Appropriate Use of Reference Pricing Can Increase Value, Health Aff. Blog (July 7, 2015). Reference pricing has also been used to encourage patients to use lower cost prescription drugs. Sarah Thomson, Laura Schang & Michael E. Chernew, Value-Based Cost Sharing in the United States and Elsewhere Can Increase Patients' Use of High-Value Goods and Services, 32 Health Aff. 704 (Apr. 1, 2013).

Reference pricing has limitations, however. As noted above, most health care spending is on services that are not "shoppable," which may make them less suited to reference pricing. Providers may also seek to make up profits lost on reference-priced services by raising prices for non-reference priced services. Some of the pitfalls of consumer-directed health care more generally, such as lack of choices, lack of available price and quality information, reliance on physician recommendations, and impaired ability to make choices based on information given, could similarly afflict reference pricing initiatives. See Chapin White & Megan Eguchi, Nat'l Institute for Health Care Reform, Reference Pricing: A Small Piece of the Health Care Prices and Quality Puzzle, Research Brief No. 18 (Oct. 2014).

e. *Shared Decision-Making*

Shared decision-making (SDM) offers an entirely different form of demand-side tool from those seeking to expose patients to financial responsibility for their health care choices. SDM in the health reform context refers to a process in which the physician shares with the patient all relevant risk and benefit information on all treatment alternatives, and the patient shares with the physician all relevant personal information that might make one treatment more or less tolerable than another. The physician and the patient then use this information to come to a joint treatment decision. Providers often offer patients information through use of a decision aid that provides highly researched, standardized accounts of the risks and benefits of treatment options for a particular condition, like breast cancer or colon cancer, presented in a manner that the average patient can comprehend. Decision aids come in numerous different forms, including pamphlets, videos, and interactive websites. See Jaime S. King and Benjamin Moulton, Rethinking Informed Consent: The Case for Shared Decision-Making, 32 Am. J.L. & Med. 429, 464 (2006). For further discussion of SDM, see Chapter 4.

Researchers from the Dartmouth Center for Evaluative Clinical Sciences found that changing medical practice to allow "treatment choices to reflect patient preferences has the potential to radically change the consumption and quality of health care." Center for the Evaluative Clinical Sciences, Dartmouth Medical School, Dartmouth Atlas Project Topic Brief: Preference Sensitive Care 5 (2005). By simply informing patients about the relative risks and benefits of treatment options, including watchful waiting, SDM reduced demand for certain types of invasive care, such as prostatectomies, by up to 40%, because given the option some patients prefer to decline or wait to receive more invasive (and expensive) care. Center for the Evaluative and Clinical Sciences, Dartmouth Medical School, The Quality of Medical Care in the United States: A Report on the Medicare Program, The Dartmouth Atlas of Health Care 1999, 226 (1999). The Cochrane Systemic Review analyzed 115 randomized control trials and found that SDM and the use of patient decision aids correlated with greater knowledge of key information on benefits and risks of the treatment options, more accurate risk perceptions, less decisional conflict, and greater patient involvement. See Dawn Stacey et al., Decision Aids for People Facing Health Treatment or Screening Decisions, Cochrane Database Syst Rev. 2017.

Overall, demand-side controls aim to limit patient demand for medical services to only necessary and wanted care. Most frequently this is done through HSAs, HRAs, and cost-sharing tools; however, improving patient information and engagement in medical decision-making through the use of SDM and decision aids can also prove effective.

PROBLEM: CONSUMER-DRIVEN HEALTH CARE

Would you enroll (or have you enrolled) in a consumer-driven health care plan (an HDHP coupled with an HSA or HRA)? How does it compare with other insurance plans you have had? How would a consumer-driven health care plan affect your health care purchasing decisions? How might it simplify or complicate your life? What information would you need to make responsible decisions? Would you spend more money than you do now on products and services (such as alternative therapies) that are not usually covered by insurance but may be tax deductible if you could use HSA funds to pay for them? Would you use more or less preventive care? Would you see your personal physician more or less often? Would you use the emergency room more or less often? If you had an accidental head injury (bicycling, for example), and the emergency room physician recommended a CT scan, how would the fact that you have a $3,000 deductible affect your treatment decisions? For an interesting discussion of HSAs, see Richard Thaler, Why So Many People Choose the Wrong Health Plans, The New York Times (Nov. 4, 2017); Ashish Jha, I've Put My Family in a Health Insurance Experiment. It's Been a Challenge, Stat (Feb. 6, 2017), www.statnews.com.

3. Market Controls

In addition to efforts to influence the behavior of purchasers or sellers of health care through supply-side and demand-side controls, other health reform initiatives aim to improve the functioning of the health care market itself. The most prevalent of these initiatives is **managed competition**.

Managed competition aims to increase competition between health insurers, managed care plans, and integrated delivery systems (collectively "health plans") for beneficiary enrollment. Historically, the health plan market suffered from a lack of competition due to heterogeneity of products, lack of comparison tools for consumers, information asymmetry, and market segmentation. In theory, managed competition promotes competition between health plans by standardizing insurance benefits and increasing access to comparative quality and price information. To compete, health plans bargain with providers for lower reimbursement rates and higher quality care. In short, managed competition aims to structure the market for health care goods and services to correct for existing market failures. The strategy of managed competition was originated by economist Alain Enthoven, pediatric neurologist Paul Ellwood, and other members of the Jackson Hole group. See Alain Enthoven, Health Plan: The Only Practical Solution to the Soaring Cost of Medical Care (1980); Alain C. Enthoven, The History and Principles of Managed Competition, 12 Health Aff. 24–48 (1993).

To facilitate competition, and thereby reduce premiums and increase access, managed competition proposals create health insurance marketplaces (previously called purchasing cooperatives or health alliances) to provide standards and rules for health plans that wish to sell plans to consumers in the marketplace. Managed competition marketplaces typically require health plans to sell a single uniform product or a manageable number of standardized products to ease price and quality comparisons for purchasers. For instance, participation in the marketplace would require a plan to include a standard set of benefits, such as the set of minimum essential benefits established by the ACA marketplaces (see Chapter 9). In addition to standardizing the benefits offered, managed competition marketplaces also frequently preclude **risk selection** based on pre-existing conditions. As a result, they often require health plans to open enrollment to all eligible participants, known as **guaranteed issue**, and to engage in **community rating or modified community rating**. Health plans, however, typically prefer to engage in risk selection so that they can avoid high-cost patients. To encourage health plans to participate in a marketplace that prohibits risk selection, managed competition marketplaces often offer to insulate participating plans from adverse selection by high-risk consumers by having all plan participants contribute money to a fund that would mitigate the losses of any particular plan in a particular year. Alternatively, plans with better than average risk enrollees can be asked to contribute to plans with worse than average risk enrollees. Reinsurance funded by plan contribution or taxes can also mitigate the risks of adverse selection or unexpected high claims costs. If these tools sound familiar, it is because managed competition has formed the basis of many attempted reforms of our health care system during the past two decades, including Medicare Advantage, Medicare Part D, and the ACA, as described in Chapters 9 and 10.

Overall, market-based approaches to reforming health care focus on changing either the behavior of market participants to improve quality or limit health care costs, or altering the functioning of the market itself to control for dysfunction in the existing market resulting from imperfect price and quality information, lack of product standardization of product, and market power. These tools have proven effective at controlling costs and improving quality in some instances, but federal and state regulation can often supplement and improve their efficacy.

There are limits, however, to the effectiveness of market-based approaches. First, market approaches founder where there is little choice or competition between providers due to market concentration and dominance. And as discussed above, concentrated health care markets are becoming the norm, not the exception. Without choices, patients cannot shop around or substitute the lower-cost or higher-value provider. Second, the demand for health care is more "inelastic" than other consumer goods, with consumers willing to go bankrupt if their own or a loved one's life depends on it. Third, information needed for patients to act as consumers (such as price, quality, in-network or out-of-network status) is still not readily available, and patients are often too stressed, ill, or frightened to act as a rational consumer. Finally, market approaches are limited because much of health care is not "shoppable." Acute or urgent health care does not lend itself to comparison or price shopping, and patients end up seeking care at the nearest hospital, the one to which the ambulance delivers them, or the one to which their physician refers them.

B. LEGISLATION AND REGULATION

While the U.S. remains generally committed to using market forces to control costs and promote quality in the health care system, federal and state legislation and regulations can help address a variety of market failures that exist. Rather than exploring the myriad of federal and state health care laws and regulations, this section highlights some of the most prevalent reform efforts to addressing systemic health care market distortions.

1. Access to Insurance

In the last decade, health reforms designed to promote access have largely focused on expanding access to insurance, whereas previously reforms like the Emergency Medical Treatment and Active Labor Act (EMTALA) had focused more on ensuring access to care directly (see Chapter 6). By 2010, the number of uninsured Americans approached 50 million, more than 16% of the population, creating significant pressure on policymakers to expand access to health insurance. Access to insurance has historically been limited in two major ways—cost and denial of coverage. Below are some of the tools policymakers can use to promote access to insurance.

a. Guaranteed Issue

While cost imposes a significant barrier for many people trying to obtain and maintain health insurance, others have been repeatedly denied the ability to purchase health insurance on the individual market due to a **pre-existing condition**. A pre-existing condition is one that the individual has already been diagnosed with or treated for prior to enrolling in a new insurance plan. A related underwriting technique would be to offer the individual coverage, excluding coverage for health care related to the pre-existing condition (i.e., selling a plan to a woman with breast cancer that does not cover breast cancer treatment). A **guaranteed issue clause** requires insurance companies to offer health insurance to all individuals regardless of their pre-existing conditions.

b. Community Rating

Guaranteed issue requirements only solve half of the access problem for people with pre-existing conditions. In isolation, a guaranteed issue clause only requires an insurance company to offer coverage to an individual, but it does not limit how much the insurer can charge for coverage. As a result, prior to the ACA, when they did offer coverage, insurance companies frequently charged exorbitant rates to individuals with pre-existing conditions, making insurance inaccessible. As noted above, **community rating** would require an insurance company to charge all members of a community the same premium within a plan. A **modified community rating** provision would enable the premium to vary according to certain characteristics, like age and smoking status, but not others, like pre-existing conditions, previous health care use, or gender. Paired together, guaranteed issue and community rating provisions spread the risk of high medical expenses evenly across individuals within a particular health plan. Even risk spreading, or community rating, will cause the insurance premiums to increase for younger and healthier individuals, while decreasing insurance premiums for older and sicker individuals when compared with actuarially fair insurance.

While guaranteed issue and community rating provisions significantly increase access to insurance for those with pre-existing conditions, they also create a disincentive for healthy individuals to enroll in insurance. If insurance companies have to offer everyone within particular age ranges a plan at the same price, then healthy individuals are less likely to enroll, because they can simply sign up if and when they get sick or injured, creating **adverse selection** against the health plan. As a result, the participants who enroll in the health plan tend to be sicker on average than the general population, which leads to an increase in the premiums. This increase then causes another set of healthier people to drop coverage, increasing the concentration of sicker individuals in the plan and driving the cost up again. This phenomenon is known as a **death spiral**, which can result in the failure of a health plan. Avoiding a death spiral typically requires spreading out the risk of above average medical expenses across a broader set of patients with the full range of medical risks. The following policy tools provide methods to increase the population enrolling in insurance.

c.   Insurance Enrollment Mandates

The most direct way of increasing the number of people enrolling in insurance is to mandate enrollment. By requiring all people to maintain health insurance coverage, the healthiest and the sickest people in the community (and everyone in between) will enroll in insurance, evenly spreading the financial risk associated with being ill across all individuals. Insurance mandates can either function as individual mandates, requiring each individual to obtain and maintain insurance, or as employer mandates, which require employers to offer insurance to their employees and set limits on premium costs and exclusions.

d.   Tax Incentives

Another method for encouraging individuals and employers to purchase insurance is to offer tax incentives for doing so. Since World War II, the government has not taxed premiums for employer-based health insurance. Most Americans receive health insurance from their employers due to these income tax exclusions. Offering tax credits in the individual market creates an opportunity to balance the playing field between individual and employer insurance. Tax credits also provide another important tool to encourage enrollment by lower-income individuals who may struggle to afford the premiums. Tax credits may prove especially effective with younger individuals who tend to make less and be healthier on average than older members of the population. Policymakers can use tax incentives in numerous creative ways to encourage enrollment in health insurance.

e.   Public Insurance

A state or the federal government could also attempt to expand access to insurance by expanding existing public insurance offerings, such as

Medicaid and Medicare, or by offering new public insurance programs. Expanding existing public programs has the benefit of building on existing structures that are already known in the patient population and the health care community, while creating a new public insurance model would allow policymakers to incorporate the successful features of existing plans without adopting their flaws and inefficiencies. For instance, after the ACA, states have had the option of expanding their Medicaid program to include adults between the ages of 19 and 65 that earn up to 138% of the federal poverty level, without regard to any other qualifying condition, like pregnancy or disability. As of August 2021, 38 states and the District of Columbia had expanded Medicaid under the ACA. Kaiser Family Found., State Health Facts, Status of Action on the State Medicaid Expansion Decision (Aug. 10, 2021).

As discussed in Chapter 10, government health care programs are limited to certain eligibility categories, such as age, income, or disability. Some policymakers have proposed expanding access to public insurance by allowing working-age individuals who are too young for Medicare and earn too much to qualify for Medicaid to buy into a Medicare or Medicaid managed care plan, as a "**public option**" to the private, commercial health plans offered on the individual insurance market, such as the ACA exchanges. Over the past decade, 38 bills have been introduced in 20 states proposing to create a public health insurance option, three of which have been enacted: Washington's (which began offering coverage on January 1, 2021), Colorado's (set to begin coverage in 2023), and Nevada (set to become effective in 2026). Jaime S. King, Katherine L. Gudiksen, & Erin C. Fuse Brown, Are State Public Option Health Plans Worth It?, 59 Harv. J. on Legis. ___ (forthcoming 2022).

States or the federal government could also decide to offer a new government-administered public insurance option. Such an offering could take numerous different forms, from a public plan designed to compete with plans on the private market to a **single-payer plan** in which the government either provides health insurance or direct health care services. In either case, the government would pay for health care directly through support from taxes. Instead of paying health insurance premiums to an insurance company or out-of-pocket, individuals and their employers will pay additional taxes to fund health care. Both models would enable the government to substantially lower costs by reducing administrative overhead and eliminating shareholder profits paid by insurance companies to lower the cost of providing care. Further, given the volume of patients in the public plan, the government would have the ability to negotiate lower reimbursement rates with provider organizations. For further discussion, see Victor Fuchs, Is Single Payer the Answer for the US Health Care System?, 319 JAMA 15 (Jan. 2, 2018).

Two single payer programs currently exist in the U.S.—the **Veterans Health Administration (VHA)** and **Medicare**. Taxpayers fund the VHA, which provides health care services to individuals who have served in the U.S. military, who were not dishonorably discharged, and who meet income or other eligibility requirements. The federal government directly contracts with the health care providers and private entities that provide this care. Rather than directly employing providers like the VHA, Medicare provides health insurance to persons older than age of 65 and certain other qualifying individuals. The popularity of Medicare and its ability to provide public insurance, while successfully coordinating with the private market, has led several politicians, most notably Senator Bernie Sanders, to advocate for Medicare for All. Medicare is discussed in depth in Chapter 10. Both the VHA and Medicare provide potential models for state and federal public plans.

2. Price Regulation

Some health economists and health services researchers who study the issue of rising health care prices are less optimistic than politicians about the ability of market strategies, such as consumer-directed health care, to discipline health care prices and curb spending. To address the pervasive market distortions in health care (such as market concentration, information asymmetry, moral hazard, and financial conflicts of interest), they advocate for supplementing market-based approaches with direct regulation of health care prices. These options range from passing laws to improve health care price transparency to instituting price caps to engaging in comprehensive health care rate regulation. Despite the central role that free market principles play in U.S. health care policy, health care rate-setting is pervasive and long-established in government health care programs, such as Medicare, Medicaid, and the VHA. In these programs, the government uses an administrative rate setting process, rather than negotiation, to set provider and supplier rates. Policymakers could implement the following tools in either the private or public health care markets.

a. Price Transparency

Americans currently know very little about the price of their health care services. In fact, most providers have little to no knowledge of how much their patients will pay for various services. Furthermore, the price for any given medical good or service can differ depending on the patient, plan, and provider involved, making it even more difficult for patients to find out what their costs will be. As Elisabeth Rosenthal noted, "[t]here is no such thing as a fixed price for a procedure or test," and "[p]rices will rise to whatever the market will bear." Elisabeth Rosenthal, An American Sickness, 8 Penguin Press (2017). Unfortunately, the market will bear more, in terms of prices, if patients do not have access to pricing information at the time they agree to treatment, physicians do not incorporate cost into their treatment recommendations, and policymakers cannot directly observe the pricing trends in their jurisdictions.

As a result, states have begun to pass a variety of price transparency laws to better inform patients, providers, and policymakers about health care prices. Some price transparency bills, like California's Drug Price Transparency Bill, require notification to health insurers and the government before a significant price increase. CA SB-17 Health Care: Prescription Drug Costs (2017–2018). Others mandate disclosure of prices to a state-run entity. For instance, state **all-payer claims databases (APCDs)**, like Colorado's Center for Improving Value in Health Care (CIVHC), collect claims data and payment information for health care services performed in the state and then provide patients access to price and quality information for commonly used services like vaginal birth and knee replacement. CIVHC also allows researchers and policymakers access to data for analysis. See Center for Improving Value in Health Care, Shop for Care, www.civhc.org. The Supreme Court's decision in Gobeille v. Liberty Mutual significantly limited the information that states can collect in APCDs by holding that the Employee Retirement Income Security Act of 1974 (ERISA) preempted a state's ability to require self-insured employers to submit their health care claims information to an APCD, as discussed in Chapter 7.

b. Price Caps

Another method of health care cost control is to establish a cap on private health care prices. Price cap proposals are typically described as a percentage of Medicare rates, such as 125% or 175% of Medicare rates. Price caps limit the extent of price variation by imposing a limit on high prices, but they still permit providers to compete below the cap. Instead of referencing Medicare rates, regulators could also calculate price caps as a function of the average private prices for the service in the area. Such a price cap would require access to private price data from an APCD or other publicly administered database. Another variation would apply price caps only to the rates charged for out-of-network providers and noncontracted payers, who do not typically have pre-negotiated rates.

Price caps offer a solid middle ground between full rate setting and market-based reforms. They can directly rein in extremely high provider prices, while still allowing for provider competition below the cap. These features make price caps particularly useful in a highly concentrated market with a dominant provider charging supracompetitive prices. On the other hand, price caps do not eliminate the inefficiencies and administrative costs of price discrimination by providers, the practice of charging different rates to different payers for the same service. Some have criticized rate caps and other forms of rate regulation as potentially reducing financial incentives for innovation or excellence. For a discussion of price cap proposals, see Jonathan Skinner, Elliot Fisher, & James Weinstein, The 125 Percent Solution: Fixing Variations in Health Care Prices, Health Aff. Blog (Aug. 26, 2014); Robert Murray, The Case for a Coordinated System of Provider Payments in the United States, 37 J. Health Pol. Pol'y & L. 679 (2012).

c. Rate Setting

A more comprehensive approach of health care price regulation is administrative rate setting. Outside of the public insurance programs, Maryland's **all-payer rate setting** model is the most well-known system of rate regulation in the U.S. Maryland regulates providers like utilities and all payers pay hospitals the same rate for a given service. Under an all-payer system, uniform prices are set either by a rate setting agency or through negotiation with representative body of payers. Although traditionally applied to hospitals, in its broadest form, rate setting could apply to a broad array of provider services (including physicians, outpatient, post-acute, lab, diagnostic, etc.). See Robert Murray & Robert A. Berenson, Urban Institute: Hospital Rate Setting Revisited: Dumb Price Fixing or a Smart Solution to Provider Pricing Power and Delivery Reform? 31 (2015).

Rate regulation can constrain dominant providers' pricing power, eliminate unwarranted price discrimination and variation, and reduce administrative costs associated with billing and negotiating with so many payers. But policymakers need to pair price setting with budgeting authority over total health care spending to curtail providers' incentive to increase volume to make up for lower prices. Even Maryland's all-payer rate setting system has moved from fee-for-service to **global budgets** that limit total hospital revenues to control both price and utilization. See Ankit Patel, Rahul Rajkumar, John M. Colmers et al., Maryland's Global Hospital Budgets—Preliminary Results from an All-Payer Model, 373 New Eng. J. Med. 1899 (2015).

3. Market Control Legislation

State governments have recently begun to pass legislation to prevent health care organizations from including provisions in their contracts with insurers that hinder competition and increase prices. For instance, **most-favored nation (MFN) clauses** in contracts between health care providers and insurers guarantee insurers that the provider organization will not offer any other insurer a better rate for health care services. MFN clauses most frequently occur in contracts between dominant providers and insurers. "Must-have" or dominant providers typically offer to include an MFN clause to induce dominant insurers to agree to a higher reimbursement rate. In these instances, MFNs not only lead to higher premiums for the plans of the contracting insurance company, but also all other plans in the market that contract with that "must have" provider. As a result, they effectively minimize the ability of other insurance companies to compete on price in that market. Legislation prohibiting MFN clauses can help improve competition between insurance companies, but policymakers should be wary of the agreements shifting from being written in the contract to being made orally. See Morgan Muir, Stephanie Alessi, and Jaime S. King, Clarifying Costs: Can Price Transparency Reduce Healthcare Spending?, 4 Wm. & Mary Pol'y Rev. 319, 332 (2013).

Nondisclosure agreements or **gag clauses** can also distort health care markets by preventing insurers and providers from disclosing the negotiated prices for health care goods and services to third parties. Part of state efforts to promote price transparency have been to prohibit gag clauses that prevent payers, consumers, and policymakers from knowing the exact price paid for the vast majority of health care goods and services. Without the ability to compare prices, providers, payers, and consumers cannot make the informed decisions required to control costs. However, disclosing negotiated rates to the public in markets with dominant providers and little competition could drive up prices overall, as other providers may simply raise their rates to match or be slightly less than those of the dominant provider, which has little incentive to lower rates. As a result, policymakers must exercise caution when deciding what information to disclose publicly and how to disclose that information. Although such disclosures should be conducted thoughtfully and with caution, improved price transparency can considerably improve the functioning of health care markets in the U.S.

Federal and state politicians have expressed interest in the **cross-border sale of health plans** in recent years. Permitting the sale of health plans to citizens of other states promises individuals the ability to purchase lower priced health plans not offered in their state. While this possibility has existed for some time, only six states have passed legislation permitting cross-border insurance sales, and few insurers have developed such an offering. Part of the issue lies in the challenge of developing a viable and competitive network of providers in an entirely different state.

The ACA permits cross-border sale of health plans through cooperatives and multistate plans so long as such plans remain subject to state licensing and other state insurance laws. The ACA also provides for interstate compacts for the sale of health insurance across state lines, which also retains in the states' authority to impose essential consumer protections. In this respect, the ACA differs from other proposals considered by the Republican Congress in recent years that would have allowed the sale of health insurance across state lines but removed some state authority to regulate insurers. See Phil Galewitz and Lexie Verdon,

FAQ: Selling Health Insurance Across State Lines, Kaiser Health News (2011). By stripping the states of some of their authority to regulate insurance coverage, these plans could quickly create a scenario where health plans all become domiciled in a state with the least restrictive insurance regulations and then sell to individuals throughout the country. See Nicholas Bagley, Federalism and the End of Obamacare, 127 Yale L.J. Forum 1, 21 (2017).

Association health plans (AHPs) have also received a great deal of recent interest. AHPs are health plans that small businesses of the same professional, trade, or interest group may offer to their members. For example, members of a state bar association could group together to purchase a health plan, even though many of the attorneys work in solo or small practices. AHPs offer individuals and small groups the opportunity to spread risk in a similar way to a large group. AHPs are a type of multiple employer welfare arrangement (MEWA) governed by ERISA. Under ERISA, states have regulatory authority over self-insured MEWAs and some regulatory authority over fully insured MEWAs to ensure solvency and require state licensure and financial reporting. The Department of Labor also has the authority to require fully insured and self-insured MEWAs to register with the Department. Congress granted this authority to both the states and the Department of Labor in response to fraud and insolvency in these arrangements.

The drafters of the ACA sought to retain the benefits of AHPs, but also limit fraudulent practices by imposing reporting requirements and criminal penalties for fraud. The ACA governs AHPs using the same rules as other plans. Therefore, the plans purchased by individuals and small employers through an association have the same requirements as other plans in the individual and small group markets, including the protections for individuals with pre-existing conditions, essential health benefits, new rating rules, etc. An exception exists for single ERISA-covered multiemployer plans; the exception treats the association as an employer sponsoring a single plan for its employees. As a result, the AHP can be regulated as a large group health plan under ERISA. While large group health plans are regulated by ERISA, the Health Insurance Portability & Accountability Act (HIPAA), and some, but not all, of the ACA's insurance reforms, they are exempt from most state regulation and many of the ACA's most important consumer protections, like the essential health benefits requirements. Historically, only "bona fide" associations with a "commonality of interest" have been able to exercise the exemption. These associations generally have members in the same industry, join for more than the purpose of health insurance, exercise control over the AHP, and have one or more employees in addition to the business owner and spouse. However, the Trump Administration's October 12th Executive Order, discussed in Chapter 9, ordered the Secretary of Labor to consider expanding eligibility for these plans. See Katie Keith, The Association Health Plan Proposed Rule: What It Says and What It Would Do, Health Aff. Blog, Jan. 5, 2018.

NOTES AND QUESTIONS

1. *Selecting Among Market-Based Reforms*. Which types of market-based reforms do you prefer—supply-side controls, demand-side controls, or market controls? Which actors have the most control over prices?

2. *Responding to Market Failures*. How well does a market-based system function for health care? Should policymakers continue to try to remedy different market failures? What barriers exist to price caps and rate regulation?

3. *Single Payer System*. Under a single payer system, taxes finance a health care system that covers the costs of essential health care for all residents. Would a single payer health care system promote or hinder choice in the U.S.? Consider this from different points of view: 1) a single mother of three with income at 100% of the federal poverty level in rural Texas; 2) a primary care physician with an established and successful practice in Boston, Massachusetts; 3) a family of four with an annual income of $400,000 in San Diego, California; and 4) an insurance company that offers coverage across fifteen states. How appealing is a single payer system? How appealing is a public option?

CHAPTER 8

EMPLOYEE RETIREMENT INCOME SECURITY ACT

• • •

Employment is the largest single source of health insurance in the U.S. Nearly half of all Americans get their health care coverage from their employer—either as an employee or as an employee's dependent. See Kaiser Family Foundation, Employer Health Benefit Survey (2020).

Although regulation of health insurance has traditionally been the responsibility of the states, since the 1970s, Congress has enacted a series of federal laws to regulate private health insurance. Before the Affordable Care Act (discussed in Chapter 9), the most important of these federal insurance reforms was the **Employee Retirement Income Security Act of 1974 (ERISA)**. As its title suggests, ERISA was primarily aimed at safeguarding employees' retirement benefit plans, such as pensions, but also reaches health benefits. The statute provides employee health plan beneficiaries with certain protections, including a right to sue to recover denied benefits, while imposing fiduciary obligations on plan fiduciaries. ERISA also was designed to provide a nationally uniform scheme of regulation to ease burdens of compliance for multi-state employers and encourage them to offer benefits to employees.

ERISA's primary effect on employer-sponsored health insurance has been deregulatory, as its preemptive provisions have repeatedly blocked state attempts at plan regulation, while replacing such preempted state laws with comparatively little substantive federal regulation. The exceptional breadth and ambiguity in the statute's preemption language has launched innumerable litigation challenges and prompted numerous Supreme Court opinions, often lamenting the difficulty of interpretation. Current Supreme Court precedent gives states some limited flexibility in regulating employer health plans. The exact limitations on state flexibility are not always clear, however, and courts often resolve ERISA preemption questions against the states. Supreme Court interpretation of ERISA's preemption of tort remedies, however, is much clearer and affords almost no flexibility for beneficiaries to pursue state remedies against their employer-sponsored plans.

This chapter on ERISA serves as a bridge between the earlier materials on health care provider duties and liability under state common law and subsequent chapters covering federal health care financing and regulation, including the Affordable Care Act (ACA). Part I of this chapter covers the basic framework for ERISA preemption under its two preemption provisions, known as Section 514 (the preemption of state laws that relate to employee benefit plans) and 502 (the complete preemption of some state remedies against plans). Part II surveys ERISA's regulation of employer plans, the ways that its regulatory preemption applies to state laws, and its preemptive impacts on state health reform efforts. It also includes a discussion of how the ACA and ERISA do, and do not, work together. Part III examines how ERISA § 502 preempts state tort claims against employee health plans and provides an exclusive set of remedies to employee health plan beneficiaries, as well as the fiduciary duties and remedies ERISA imposes.

I.   ERISA PREEMPTION: THE FRAMEWORK

ERISA's preemptive effects are extraordinarily broad and can result from express preemption under ERISA Section 514 (codified at 29 U.S.C. § 1144) or complete preemption of state remedies under ERISA Section 502 (codified at 29 U.S.C. § 1132). Section 514 of ERISA expressly preempts "any and all" state laws that "relate to" employee benefit plans. Section 514, however, also explicitly exempts state insurance regulation from preemption, while also prohibiting state regulation of self-insured plans. The Supreme Court has interpreted § 502 of ERISA as providing exclusive federal court jurisdiction over, and an exclusive federal cause of action for, cases that could be brought as ERISA claims. The text of these provisions follows:

29 U.S.C. § 1144 (Section 514 of ERISA)

(a)   Except as provided in subsection (b) of this section, the provisions of this subchapter and subchapter III of this chapter shall supersede any and all State laws insofar as they may now or hereafter relate to any employee benefit plan . . . .

(b)   Construction and application

* * *

(2)(A)   Except as provided in subparagraph (B), nothing in this subchapter shall be construed to exempt or relieve any person from any law of any State which regulates insurance, banking, or securities.

(B) Neither an employee benefit plan . . . nor any trust established under such a plan, shall be deemed to be an insurance company . . . or to be engaged in the business of insurance or banking for purposes of any law of any State purporting to regulate insurance companies, insurance contracts, banks, trust companies, or investment companies.

* * *

29 U.S.C. § 1132(a) (Section 502(a) of ERISA)

(a) A civil action may be brought—

    (1) by a participant or beneficiary—

* * *

        (B) to recover benefits due to him under the terms of his plan, to enforce his rights under the terms of the plan, or to clarify his rights to future benefits under the terms of the plan;

    (2) by the Secretary, or by a participant, beneficiary or fiduciary for appropriate relief under section 1109 of this title [which imposes on plan fiduciaries the obligation to "make good" to a plan any losses resulting from a breach of fiduciary duties, and authorizes "other equitable or remedial relief" for breaches of fiduciary obligations];

    (3) by a participant, beneficiary, or fiduciary (A) to enjoin any act or practice which violates any provision of this subchapter or the terms of the plan, or (B) to obtain other appropriate equitable relief (i) to redress such violations or (ii) to enforce any provisions of this subchapter or the terms of the plan . . .

The task of sorting out ERISA's complex preemption scheme has resulted in a tremendous volume of litigation, including, to date, over twenty Supreme Court decisions and hundreds of state and federal lower court decisions. Here, we examine the effects of § 514 preemption on state laws "relating to" employee health benefit plans and § 502 preemption of state law remedies against ERISA plans.

Part of the confusion inherent in ERISA preemption decisions is attributable to the fact that it comes in two distinct forms. First is **express preemption** based on § 514(a), 29 U.S.C. § 1144(a). Section 514(a), reproduced above, provides that ERISA "supersedes" any state law that "relates to" an employee benefit plan. Express preemption under § 514(a), however, is subject to the **"savings" clause**, which saves from preemption state insurance laws, including laws regulating health insurance. 29 U.S.C. § 1114(b)(2)(A). Because of the savings clause, state insurance laws apply to traditional, **fully insured** employee health plans, where the employer contracts with an insurance company to assume the financial risk for employees' health care costs in exchange for premiums. ERISA's savings clause is subject to its own exception, the **"deemer" clause**, stating that employee benefit plans cannot be "deemed . . . to be engaged in the business of insurance" for the purpose of being subjected to state regulation. 29 U.S.C. § 1144(b)(2)(B). In FMC Corporation v. Holliday, 498

U.S. 52 (1990), the Supreme Court interpreted the deemer clause broadly to exempt self-funded ERISA plans entirely from state insurance regulation because such plans are not in the business of insurance. **Self-funded plans** (also known as **self-insured plans**) are plans in which the employer retains the financial or insurance risk for its employees' health benefits. Self-funded employee plans cover more than 60% of all workers with employer-based health insurance, or about a third of the non-elderly U.S. population.

The second form of ERISA preemption is **complete preemption** under § 502, 29 U.S.C. § 1132. ERISA § 502(a) provides for federal court jurisdiction over claims against ERISA plans. The Supreme Court has long held that ERISA plans may remove to federal court claims that were brought in state courts but that could have been brought under § 502(a) in federal court. Removal is permitted under the complete preemption exception to the **well-pleaded complaint rule**. The well-pleaded complaint rule normally limits removal of cases from state into federal court on the basis of federal question jurisdiction (under 28 U.S.C. § 1331) to cases in which federal claims or issues are explicitly raised in the plaintiff's complaint. However, under the complete preemption exception to this rule, federal jurisdiction also exists when Congress has so completely preempted an area of law that any state law complaint is converted to a federal claim and is removable to federal court. Complete preemption is, in reality, a rule of federal jurisdiction.

Section 502(a) completely preempts state-law claims or remedies that "duplicate, supplement, or supplant" the federal claims provided in § 502. The federal courts have interpreted § 502 to indicate Congress's intent to preempt the entire "field" of judicial oversight of employee benefits plans and provide the exclusive set of remedies available under ERISA. Thus, state tort, contract, and even statutory claims that could have been brought as claims for benefits or for breaches of fiduciary duties are completely preempted by § 502(a). There are some limited exceptions: ERISA does not necessarily preempt state court malpractice cases brought against physician-owned managed care plans that provide as well as pay for health care, as discussed in Section III. Also, claims brought by persons who are not proper plaintiffs under § 502(a) or against persons who are not ERISA fiduciaries are not preempted by ERISA § 502(a). External review procedures imposed by the states prior to the onset of litigation also may be exempt from § 502 preemption.

Section 502(a) and § 514(a) preemption are not coextensive. Even when the savings clause saves a state law from § 514(a) express preemption, § 502(a) may nevertheless preempt the state law if it provides a state-based cause of action that duplicates, supplements, or supplants a § 502(a) remedy, as illustrated by *Moran* and *Davila*, below.

The Supreme Court case, *Rush Prudential v. Moran*, sets out the basic framework of ERISA preemption and the policy debates that surround it.

RUSH PRUDENTIAL, INC. V. DEBRA C. MORAN, ET AL.
Supreme Court of the United States, 2002.
536 U.S. 355.

JUSTICE SOUTER delivered the opinion of the Court.

* * *

Petitioner, Rush Prudential HMO, Inc., is a health maintenance organization (HMO) that contracts to provide medical services for employee welfare benefit plans covered by ERISA. Respondent Debra Moran is a beneficiary under one such plan, sponsored by her husband's employer. Rush's "Certificate of Group Coverage," issued to employees who participate in employer-sponsored plans, promises that Rush will provide them with "medically necessary" services. The terms of the certificate give Rush the "broadest possible discretion" to determine whether a medical service claimed by a beneficiary is covered under the certificate. . . .

As the certificate explains, Rush contracts with physicians "to arrange for or provide services and supplies for medical care and treatment" of covered persons. Each covered person selects a primary care physician from those under contract to Rush, while Rush will pay for medical services by an unaffiliated physician only if the services have been "authorized" both by the primary care physician and Rush's medical director.[ ]

In 1996, when Moran began to have pain and numbness in her right shoulder, Dr. Arthur LaMarre, her primary care physician, unsuccessfully administered "conservative" treatments such as physiotherapy. In October 1997, Dr. LaMarre recommended that Rush approve surgery by an unaffiliated specialist, Dr. Julia Terzis, who had developed an unconventional treatment for Moran's condition. Although Dr. LaMarre said that Moran would be "best served" by that procedure, Rush denied the request and, after Moran's internal appeals, affirmed the denial on the ground that the procedure was not "medically necessary." [ ] Rush instead proposed that Moran undergo standard surgery, performed by a physician affiliated with Rush.

In January 1998, Moran made a written demand for an independent medical review of her claim, as guaranteed by § 4–10 of Illinois's HMO Act, [ ] which provides:

> Each Health Maintenance Organization shall provide a mechanism for the timely review by a physician . . . who is unaffiliated with the Health Maintenance Organization, jointly selected by the patient . . . , primary care physician and the Health Maintenance Organization in the event of a dispute between the primary care physician and the

Health Maintenance Organization regarding the medical necessity of a covered service proposed by a primary care physician. In the event that the reviewing physician determines the covered service to be medically necessary, the Health Maintenance Organization shall provide the covered service. . . .

* * *

When Rush failed to provide the independent review, Moran sued in an Illinois state court to compel compliance with the state Act. Rush removed the suit to Federal District Court, arguing that the cause of action was "completely preempted" under ERISA.[ ]

While the suit was pending, Moran had surgery by Dr. Terzis at her own expense and submitted a $94,841.27 reimbursement claim to Rush. Rush treated the claim as a renewed request for benefits and began a new inquiry to determine coverage. The three doctors consulted by Rush said the surgery had been medically unnecessary.

Meanwhile, the federal court remanded the case back to state court on Moran's motion, concluding that because Moran's request for independent review under § 4–10 would not require interpretation of the terms of an ERISA plan, the claim was not "completely preempted" so as to permit removal. . . . The state court enforced the state statute and ordered Rush to submit to review by an independent physician. . . . [The reviewer] decided that Dr. Terzis's treatment had been medically necessary, based on the definition of medical necessity in Rush's Certificate of Group Coverage, as well as his own medical judgment. Rush's medical director, however, refused to concede that the surgery had been medically necessary, and denied Moran's claim in January 1999.

Moran amended her complaint in state court to seek reimbursement for the surgery as "medically necessary" under Illinois's HMO Act, and Rush again removed to federal court, arguing that Moran's amended complaint stated a claim for ERISA benefits and was thus completely preempted by ERISA's civil enforcement provisions, 29 U.S.C. § 1132(a) [§ 502], . . . The District Court treated Moran's claim as a suit under ERISA, and denied the claim on the ground that ERISA preempted Illinois's independent review statute.

The Court of Appeals for the Seventh Circuit reversed. . . .

* * *

To "safeguar[d] . . . the establishment, operation, and administration" of employee benefit plans, ERISA sets "minimum standards . . . assuring the equitable character of such plans and their financial soundness,"[ ] and contains an express preemption provision that ERISA "shall supersede any and all State laws insofar as they may now or hereafter relate to any employee benefit plan. . . ." § 1144(a)[§ 514(a)]. A saving clause then reclaims a substantial amount of ground with its provision that "nothing in this subchapter shall be construed to exempt or relieve any person from any law of any State which regulates insurance, banking, or securities." § 1144(b)(2)(A) [§ 514(b)(2)(A)]. The "unhelpful" drafting of these antiphonal clauses . . . occupies a substantial share of this Court's time. In trying to extrapolate congressional intent in a case like this, when congressional language seems simultaneously to preempt everything and hardly anything, we "have no choice" but to temper the assumption that " 'the ordinary meaning . . . accurately expresses the legislative purpose,' "[ ] with the qualification " 'that the historic police powers of the States were not [meant] to be superseded by the Federal Act unless that was the clear and manifest purpose of Congress.' "[ ]

It is beyond serious dispute that under existing precedent § 4–10 of the Illinois HMO Act "relates to" employee benefit plans within the meaning of § 1144(a). . . . As a law that "relates to" ERISA plans under § 1144(a), § 4–10 is saved from preemption only if it also "regulates insurance" under § 1144(b)(2)(A). . . .

[The Court clarified that HMOs are in the business of insurance because they assume financial risks of providing the benefits promised in return for a fixed fee per patient. It then proceeded to apply the savings clause analysis method that it had developed in earlier cases, concluding that the Illinois external review law was saved from preemption. As this analysis was superseded by the Court's decision in *Kentucky Association of Health Plans v. Miller*, described below, this discussion is omitted here. Ed.]

* * *

Given that § 4–10 regulates insurance, ERISA's mandate that "nothing in this subchapter shall be construed to exempt or relieve any person from any law of any State which regulates insurance," 29 U.S.C. § 1144(b)(2)(A), ostensibly forecloses preemption. [ ] Rush, however, does not give up. It argues for preemption anyway, emphasizing that the question is ultimately one of congressional intent, which sometimes is so clear that it overrides a statutory provision designed to save state law from being preempted. . . .

In ERISA law, we have recognized one example of this sort of overpowering federal policy in the civil enforcement provisions, 29 U.S.C. § 1132(a), . . . In *Massachusetts Mut. Life Ins. Co. v. Russell,*[ ] we said those provisions amounted to an "interlocking, interrelated, and interdependent remedial scheme,"[ ] which *Pilot Life* described as "represent[ing] a careful balancing of the need for prompt and fair claims settlement procedures against the public interest in encouraging the formation of employee benefit plans"[ ]. So, we have held, the civil enforcement provisions are of such extraordinarily preemptive power that they override even the "well-pleaded complaint" rule for establishing the conditions under which a cause of action may be removed to a federal forum. *Metropolitan Life Ins. Co. v. Taylor*[ ].

Although we have yet to encounter a forced choice between the congressional policies of exclusively federal remedies and the "reservation of the business of insurance to the States,"[ ] we have anticipated such a conflict, with the state insurance regulation losing out if it allows plan participants "to obtain remedies . . . that Congress rejected in ERISA."

In *Pilot Life*, an ERISA plan participant who had been denied benefits sued in a state court on state tort and contract claims. He sought not merely damages for breach of contract, but also damages for emotional distress and punitive damages, both of which we had held unavailable under relevant ERISA provisions.[ ] We not only rejected the notion that these common-law contract claims "regulat[ed] insurance,"[ ] but went on to say that, regardless, Congress intended a "federal common law of rights and obligations" to develop under ERISA,[ ] without embellishment by independent state remedies.

Rush says that the day has come to turn dictum into holding by declaring that the state insurance regulation, § 4–10, is preempted for creating just the kind of "alternative remedy" we disparaged in *Pilot Life*. As Rush sees it, the independent review procedure is a form of binding arbitration that allows an ERISA beneficiary to submit claims to a new decisionmaker to examine Rush's determination *de novo,* supplanting judicial review under the "arbitrary and capricious" standard ordinarily applied when discretionary plan interpretations are challenged[ ]. . . .

We think, however, that Rush overstates the rule expressed in *Pilot Life*. . . .

* * *

[T]his case addresses a state regulatory scheme that provides no new cause of action under state law and authorizes no new form of ultimate relief. While independent review under § 4–10 may well settle the fate of a benefit claim under a particular contract, the state statute does not enlarge the claim beyond the benefits available in any action brought under § 1132(a). And although the reviewer's determination would presumably replace that of the HMO as to what is "medically necessary" under this contract, the relief ultimately available would still be what ERISA authorizes in a suit for benefits under § 1132(a). . . .

Rush still argues for going beyond *Pilot Life,* making the preemption issue here one of degree, whether the state procedural imposition interferes unreasonably with Congress's intention to provide a uniform federal regime of "rights and obligations" under ERISA. However, "[s]uch disuniformities . . . are the inevitable result of the congressional decision to 'save' local insurance regulation."[ ][11] Although we have recognized a limited exception from the saving clause for alternative causes of action and alternative remedies in the sense described above, we have never indicated that there might be additional justifications for qualifying the clause's application. . . .

To be sure, a State might provide for a type of "review" that would so resemble an adjudication as to fall within *Pilot Life's* categorical bar. Rush, and the dissent,[ ] contend that § 4–10 fills that bill by imposing an alternative scheme of arbitral adjudication at odds with the manifest congressional purpose to confine adjudication of disputes to the courts. . . .

In the classic sense, arbitration occurs when "parties in dispute choose a judge to render a final and binding decision on the merits of the controversy and on the basis of proofs presented by the parties."[ ] Arbitrators typically hold hearings at which parties may submit evidence and conduct cross-examinations, . . .

Section 4–10 does resemble an arbitration provision, then, to the extent that the independent reviewer considers disputes about the meaning of the HMO contract and receives "evidence" in the form of medical records, statements from physicians, and the like. But this is as far as the resemblance to arbitration goes, for the other features of review under § 4–10 give the proceeding a different character, one not at all at odds with the policy behind § 1132(a). The Act does not give the independent reviewer a free-ranging power to construe contract terms, but instead, confines review to a single term: the phrase "medical necessity," used to define the services covered under the contract.[ ] This limitation, in turn, implicates a feature of HMO benefit determinations that we described in *Pegram v. Herdrich,*[ ] We explained that when an HMO guarantees medically necessary care, determinations of coverage "cannot be untangled from physicians' judgments about reasonable medical treatment."[ ] This is just how the Illinois Act operates; the independent examiner must be a physician with credentials similar to those of the primary care physician,[ ] and is expected to exercise independent medical judgment in deciding what medical necessity requires. . . .

Once this process is set in motion, it does not resemble either contract interpretation or evidentiary litigation before a neutral arbiter, as much as

---

11 Thus, we do not believe that the mere fact that state independent review laws are likely to entail different procedures will impose burdens on plan administration that would threaten the object of 29 U.S.C. § 1132(a); it is the HMO contracting with a plan, and not the plan itself, that will be subject to these regulations, and every HMO will have to establish procedures for conforming with the local laws, regardless of what this Court may think ERISA forbids. This means that there will be no special burden of compliance upon an ERISA plan beyond what the HMO has already provided for. And although the added compliance cost to the HMO may ultimately be passed on to the ERISA plan, we have said that such "indirect economic effect[s],"[ ], are not enough to preempt state regulation even outside of the insurance context. We recognize, of course, that a State might enact an independent review requirement with procedures so elaborate, and burdens so onerous, that they might undermine § 1132(a). No such system is before us.

it looks like a practice (having nothing to do with arbitration) of obtaining another medical opinion. . . .

The practice of obtaining a second opinion, however, is far removed from any notion of an enforcement scheme, and once § 4–10 is seen as something akin to a mandate for second-opinion practice in order to ensure sound medical judgments, the preemption argument that arbitration under § 4–10 supplants judicial enforcement runs out of steam.

Next, Rush argues that § 4–10 clashes with a substantive rule intended to be preserved by the system of uniform enforcement, stressing a feature of judicial review highly prized by benefit plans: a deferential standard for reviewing benefit denials. Whereas *Firestone Tire & Rubber Co. v. Bruch*,[ ] recognized that an ERISA plan could be designed to grant "discretion" to a plan fiduciary, deserving deference from a court reviewing a discretionary judgment, § 4–10 provides that when a plan purchases medical services and insurance from an HMO, benefit denials are subject to apparently *de novo* review. If a plan should continue to balk at providing a service the reviewer has found medically necessary, the reviewer's determination could carry great weight in a subsequent suit for benefits under § 1132(a), depriving the plan of the judicial deference a fiduciary's medical judgment might have obtained if judicial review of the plan's decision had been immediate.

Again, however, the significance of § 4–10 is not wholly captured by Rush's argument, which requires some perspective for evaluation. First, in determining whether state procedural requirements deprive plan administrators of any right to a uniform standard of review, it is worth recalling that ERISA itself provides nothing about the standard. It simply requires plans to afford a beneficiary some mechanism for internal review of a benefit denial, ...

Not only is there no ERISA provision directly providing a lenient standard for judicial review of benefit denials, but there is no requirement necessarily entailing such an effect even indirectly. When this Court dealt with the review standards on which the statute was silent, we held that a general or default rule of *de novo* review could be replaced by deferential review if the ERISA plan itself provided that the plan's benefit determinations were matters of high or unfettered discretion[ ]. Nothing in ERISA, however, requires that these kinds of decisions be so "discretionary" in the first place; whether they are is simply a matter of plan design or the drafting of an HMO contract. In this respect, then, § 4–10 prohibits designing an insurance contract so as to accord unfettered discretion to the insurer to interpret the contract's terms. As such, it does not implicate ERISA's enforcement scheme at all, and is no different from the types of substantive state regulation of insurance contracts we have in the past permitted to survive preemption, such as mandated-benefit statutes and statutes prohibiting the denial of claims solely on the ground of untimeliness. . . .

* * *

In deciding what to make of these facts and conclusions, it helps to go back to where we started and recall the ways States regulate insurance in looking out for the welfare of their citizens. Illinois has chosen to regulate insurance as one way to regulate the practice of medicine, which we have previously held to be permissible under ERISA[ ]. While the statute designed to do this undeniably eliminates whatever may have remained of a plan sponsor's option to minimize scrutiny of benefit denials, this effect of eliminating an insurer's autonomy to guarantee terms congenial to its own interests is the stuff of garden variety insurance regulation through the imposition of standard policy terms. . . . And any lingering doubt about the reasonableness of § 4–10 in affecting the application of § 1132(a) may be put to rest by recalling that regulating insurance tied to what is medically necessary is probably inseparable from enforcing the quintessentially state-law standards of reasonable medical care. See *Pegram v. Herdrich* [ ]. To the extent that benefits litigation in some federal courts may have to account for the effects of § 4–10, it would be an exaggeration to hold that the objectives of § 1132(a) are undermined. The savings clause is entitled to prevail here, and we affirm the judgment.

JUSTICE THOMAS, with whom THE CHIEF JUSTICE, JUSTICE SCALIA, and JUSTICE KENNEDY join, dissenting.

This Court has repeatedly recognized that ERISA's civil enforcement provision, § 502 of the Employee Retirement Income Security Act of 1974 (ERISA), 29 U.S.C. § 1132, provides the exclusive vehicle for actions asserting a claim for benefits under health plans governed by ERISA, and therefore that state laws that create additional remedies are pre-empted. [ ] Such exclusivity of remedies is necessary to further Congress' interest in establishing a uniform federal law of employee benefits so that employers are encouraged to provide benefits to their employees.[ ]

. . . Therefore, as the Court concedes,[ ] even a state law that "regulates insurance" may be pre-empted if it supplements the remedies provided by ERISA, despite ERISA's saving clause,[ ]. Today, however, the Court takes the unprecedented step of allowing respondent Debra Moran to short circuit ERISA's remedial scheme by allowing her claim for benefits to be determined in the first instance through an arbitral-like procedure provided under Illinois law, and by a decisionmaker other than a court.[ ] . . .

From the facts of this case one can readily understand why Moran sought recourse under § 4–10. . . .

In the course of its review, petitioner informed Moran that "there is no prevailing opinion within the appropriate specialty of the United States medical profession that the procedure proposed [by Moran] is safe and effective for its intended use and that the omission of the procedure would adversely affect [her] medical condition."[ ] Petitioner did agree to cover the standard treatment for Moran's ailment,[ ] concluding that peer-reviewed literature "demonstrates that [the standard surgery] is effective therapy in the treatment of [Moran's condition]."[ ]

Moran, however, was not satisfied with this option. . . . She invoked § 4–10 of the Illinois HMO Act, which requires HMOs to provide a mechanism for review by an independent physician when the patient's primary care physician and HMO disagree about the medical necessity of a treatment proposed by the primary care physician. . . .

Dr. A. Lee Dellon, an unaffiliated physician who served as the independent medical reviewer, concluded that the surgery for which petitioner denied coverage "was appropriate," that it was "the same type of surgery" he would have done, and that Moran "had all of the indications and therefore the medical necessity to carry out" the nonstandard surgery. . . . Under § 4–10, Dr. Dellon's determination conclusively established Moran's right to benefits under Illinois law.

* * *

Section 514(a)'s broad language provides that ERISA "shall supersede any and all State laws insofar as they . . . relate to any employee benefit plan," except as provided in § 514(b). 29 U.S.C. § 1144(a). This language demonstrates "Congress's intent to establish the regulation of employee welfare benefit plans 'as exclusively a federal concern.' "[ ] It was intended to "ensure that plans and plan sponsors would be subject to a uniform body of benefits law" so as to "minimize the administrative and financial burden of complying with conflicting directives among States or between States and the Federal Government" and to prevent "the potential for conflict in substantive law . . . requiring the tailoring of plans and employer conduct to the peculiarities of the law of each jurisdiction."[ ]

. . . [T]he Court until today had consistently held that state laws that seek to supplant or add to the exclusive remedies in § 502(a) of ERISA, 29 U.S.C. § 1132(a), are pre-empted because they conflict with Congress' objective that rights under ERISA plans are to be enforced under a uniform national system.[ ] The Court has explained that § 502(a) creates an "interlocking, interrelated, and interdependent remedial scheme," and that a beneficiary who claims that he was wrongfully denied benefits has "a panoply of remedial devices" at his disposal. . . .

* * *

Section 4–10 cannot be characterized as anything other than an alternative state-law remedy or vehicle for seeking benefits. In the first place, § 4–10 comes into play only if the HMO and the claimant dispute the claimant's entitlement to benefits; the purpose of the review is to determine whether a claimant is entitled to benefits. . . .

There is no question that arbitration constitutes an alternative remedy to litigation.[ ] Consequently, although a contractual agreement to arbitrate—which does not constitute a "State law" relating to "any employee benefit plan"—is outside § 514(a) of ERISA's pre-emptive scope, States may not circumvent ERISA preemption by mandating an alternative arbitral-like remedy as a plan term enforceable through an ERISA action.

To be sure, the majority is correct that § 4–10 does not mirror all procedural and evidentiary aspects of "common arbitration."[ ] But as a binding decision on the merits of the controversy the § 4–10 review resembles nothing so closely as arbitration. . . .

* * *

[I]t is troubling that the Court views the review under § 4–10 as nothing more than a practice "of obtaining a second [medical] opinion." . . . [W]hile a second medical opinion is nothing more than that—an opinion— a determination under § 4–10 is a conclusive determination with respect to the award of benefits. . . .

Section 4–10 constitutes an arbitral-like state remedy through which plan members may seek to resolve conclusively a disputed right to benefits. Some 40 other States have similar laws, though these vary as to applicability, procedures, standards, deadlines, and consequences of independent review. . . .

For the reasons noted by the Court, independent review provisions may sound very appealing. Efforts to expand the variety of remedies available to aggrieved beneficiaries beyond those set forth in ERISA are obviously designed to increase the chances that patients will be able to receive treatments they desire, and most of us are naturally sympathetic to those suffering from illness who seek further options. Nevertheless, the Court would do well to remember that no employer is required to provide any health benefit plan under ERISA and that the entire advent of managed care, and the genesis of HMOs, stemmed from spiraling health costs. To the extent that independent review provisions such as § 4–10 make it more likely that HMOs will have to subsidize beneficiaries' treatments of choice, they undermine the ability of HMOs to control costs, which, in turn, undermines the ability of employers to provide health care coverage for employees.

As a consequence, independent review provisions could create a disincentive to the formation of employee health benefit plans, a problem that Congress addressed by making ERISA's remedial scheme exclusive and uniform. While it may well be the case that the advantages of allowing States to implement independent review requirements as a supplement to the remedies currently provided under ERISA outweigh this drawback, this is a judgment that, pursuant to ERISA, must be made by Congress. I respectfully dissent.

NOTES AND QUESTIONS

1. *Preempting State Regulation and Remedies.* ERISA's statutory language preempts all state "law" relating to employee benefit plans and defines "state law" broadly to include "all laws, decisions, rules, regulations, or other State action having the effect of law . . . ." 29 U.S.C. § 1144(c)(1). As *Moran* illustrates, that includes state statutory requirements, and, by extension, also state remedies that would duplicate or supplement the federal remedies in of § 502. These two provisions set up ERISA's express preemption of state law as defense for employers to avoid compliance with or enforcement of state law, as well as establishing complete preemption of state-law remedies separate but related defense for plans to limit the remedies beneficiaries can pursue against them. The Illinois outside review provision at issue in *Moran* has some features of both. The majority categorized the provision as a "state regulatory scheme," while the dissent saw it as "an alternative state-law remedy." What makes this characterization dispositive of the preemption issue?

2. *Legislative Purposes.* What purpose do you suppose the Illinois legislature had in enacting the outside review provision in its HMO Act? Does that purpose seem to complement or contradict ERISA's goals? For an account of HMOs' evolving uses and mis-uses of "medical necessity" utilization review and backlash from patients, see Amy B. Monahan & Daniel Schwarcz, The Rules of Medical Necessity, 107 Iowa L. Rev. ___ (forthcoming 2022).

II.   ERISA PLAN REGULATION AND PREEMPTION

A.   FEDERAL REGULATION OF EMPLOYER PLANS

ERISA only governs **employee benefit plans**, i.e. benefit plans established and maintained by employers to provide benefits to their employees. It does not reach health insurance purchased by individuals as individuals (including self-employed individuals) or health benefits not provided through employment-related group plans, such as uninsured motorist insurance policies or workers' compensation. ERISA also does not apply to certain church and government-sponsored plans. See Macro v. Independent Health Ass'n, Inc., 180 F. Supp.2d 427 (W.D.N.Y.2001). And ERISA does not regulate group insurance offered by insurers to the employees of particular businesses without employer contributions or administrative involvement. See 29 C.F.R. § 2510.3–1(j); Taggart Corp. v. Life & Health Benefits Admin., Inc., 617 F.2d 1208 (5th Cir.1980), cert. denied, 450 U.S. 1030 (1981). Despite these exceptions, ERISA governs the vast majority of private health insurance in America, which is provided through employment-related group plans.

1. ERISA's Rules for Employer Plans

ERISA does not require employers to offer health benefits to employees. Instead, the statute provides a set of uniform federal rules that apply *if* an employer chooses to offer benefits. ERISA's major rules govern how the benefit plan operates, also known as administrative rules. ERISA's administrative rules require certain information disclosures to participants, establish complaint and claim review processes, and establish fiduciary duties over plan assets (discussed in Section III.C., below).

To a much lesser extent, ERISA supplies some federal rules about what employer plans must cover, known as substantive coverage rules. Over time, Congress has added piecemeal to ERISA's rules, requiring, for example, that employer plans cover preexisting conditions, 29 U.S.C §§ 1181, and prohibiting them from engaging in medical underwriting or health status discrimination, 29 U.S.C. § 1182. ERISA's coverage requirements often operate on the same *if-then* principle, stating that *if* an employer offers coverage for a certain condition, *then* it must cover related services. For example, *if* a plan covers hospitalization for the birth of a child, *then* it must cover stays of a certain minimum length without prior authorization. 29 U.S.C. § 1185. The Mental Health Parity and Addiction Equity Act of 2008 added a requirement that *if* an employer plan offers mental health or substance abuse coverage, *then* it must cover those services on parity with medical and surgical procedures. The Women's Health and Cancer Rights Act required that *if* an employer plan covers mastectomy, *then* it must also cover reconstructive surgery. 29 U.S.C. § 1185b.

2. The Affordable Care Act's Effects on ERISA

The ACA did not explicitly change ERISA's preemption provisions, but it did change the nature of ERISA plan regulation in three important respects.

First, the ACA altered the *if-then* calculation for many employers by enacting a mandate that employers with 50 or more full-time employees offer a level of minimum essential coverage or else pay a tax (discussed at length in Chapter 9). Second, the ACA applied a whole new group of federal requirements to group health insurance, including fully insured and self-funded ERISA plans. Prior to the ACA, ERISA had imposed only minimal requirements on employer-based plans. That changed dramatically with the addition of the ACA's insurance requirements to ERISA plans, and now federal regulation looks much more like state regulation, except more uniform. Nevertheless, self-funded ERISA plans are subject to fewer of the ACA requirements than fully-insured ERISA plans. Most of the ACA's health insurance requirements are applied to ERISA plans. See 42 U.S.C. § 300gg; 29 U.S.C. § 1185d; 26 U.S.C. § 9815.1. The following table lists which ACA insurance regulations apply to self-funded employer-based health plans and which do not. Descriptions of these ACA insurance rules are set forth in Chapter 9.

Table: Applicability of ACA Rules to Self-Funded ERISA Plans

Applies	Does not apply
Adult children up to age 26	Essential health benefits
No rescissions	Premium increase review
No preexisting condition exclusions	Risk adjustment
No lifetime/annual limits	Medical loss ratios
No waiting periods > 90 days	Community rating
Internal and external review	Guaranteed issue and renewability
Coverage of preventive services without cost-sharing	

Third, because of the increased federal regulation of health insurance under the ACA, some of the conflicts over state regulation of fully insured ERISA plans may be less salient after the ACA. As a co-equal federal law, the ACA requirements are not preempted by ERISA. The ACA has its own preemption provision: "Nothing in this title shall be construed to preempt any State law that does not prevent the application of the provisions of this title." ACA § 1321(d), codified at 42 U.S.C. § 18041(d). The implication, of course, is that where the ACA and state law are incompatible, the ACA will govern.

In some cases, the ACA also applies state law to group plans. For example, the ACA requires plans to offer external review of coverage and claims denials, according to state external review requirements, which in turn must at a minimum comply with the NAIC External Review Model Act, 42 U.S.C. § 300gg–19. The precise issue raised by *Moran* would not come up today, because the ACA would determine whether a state external review law applied to a group health plan. Where the ACA does not address a particular issue, however, the preemption rules of ERISA section 514 still apply. Moreover, ERISA does nothing to change the jurisdictional or remedial preemption rules of ERISA section 502. See, Mallory Jensen, Is ERISA Preemption Superfluous in the New Age of Health Care Reform?, 2011 Colum. Bus. L. Rev. 464 (2011).

B. PREEMPTION OF STATE REGULATIONS APPLIED TO EMPLOYER PLANS

1. Which State Laws "Relate to" ERISA Plans?

Early cases interpreting § 514(a) read it very broadly. The Supreme Court's first consideration of § 514(a), Shaw v. Delta Air Lines, Inc., 463 U.S. 85 (1983), adopted a very literal and liberal reading of "relates to" as including any provisions having a "connection with or reference to" a benefits plan. For over a decade following *Shaw*, the Court applied the § 514(a) test developed in *Shaw* expansively in a variety of contexts, almost always finding preemption when it found an ERISA plan to exist. The Court repeatedly expressed allegiance to the opinion that ERISA § 514(a) preemption had a "broad scope," Metropolitan Life v. Massachusetts, 471 U.S. 724, 739 (1985), and "an expansive sweep," Pilot Life Ins. Co. v. Dedeaux, 481 U.S. 41, 47 (1987), and that it was "conspicuous for its breadth," FMC Corp. v. Holliday, 498 U.S. 52, 58 (1990).

The Supreme Court finally recognized the limits of ERISA preemption, however, in New York State Conference of Blue Cross and Blue Shield Plans v. Travelers Ins. Co., 514 U.S. 645 (1995). *Travelers* held that a New York law requiring hospitals to charge different rates to insured, HMO, and self-insured plans was not preempted by § 514(a). Retreating from earlier expansive readings of ERISA preemption, the Court reaffirmed the principle applied in other areas of the law that Congress is generally presumed not to intend to preempt state law. The Court noted that in cases involving traditional areas of state regulation, such as health care, congressional intent to preempt state law should not be presumed unless it was "clear and manifest." Recognizing that the term "relate to" was not self-limiting, the Court turned for assistance in defining the term to the purpose of ERISA, which it defined as freeing benefit plans from conflicting state and local regulation. The Court reasoned that preemption was intended to affect state laws that operated directly on the structure or administration of ERISA plans, not laws that only indirectly raised the cost of various benefit options. Accordingly, the Court held the challenged rate-setting law was not "related to" an ERISA plan, and thus not preempted.

Thus, not all state laws that have *some* effect on ERISA plans "relate to an employee benefit plan." In *Travelers,* the Court has noted that everything can be conceived of to relate to everything else, so if "relate(s) to" was taken literally, there would be no practical limits to ERISA's express preemption. Particularly relevant to health care regulation, state laws primarily directed at health care *providers* that have only an incidental effect on ERISA *plans* would not "relate to" an employee benefit plan, and would not trigger ERISA's express preemption. *Travelers*, 514 U.S. at 668; De Buono v. NYSA-ILA Med. & Clinical Servs. Fund, 520 U.S. 806, 816 (1997).

The sweep of the Supreme Court's limitations on "relates to" remains hard to gauge, with a broad reading demonstrated by the *Gobeille* case and a more limited definition employed in *Rutledge,* excerpted below.

2.   Applying the Savings Clause

As *Moran* notes, a state law that is otherwise preempted under § 514(a) is saved from preemption if it regulates insurance under the "savings clause" found in § 514(b)(2)(A) (29 U.S.C. § 1144(b)(2)(A)). In its early cases interpreting this clause, the Court read the savings clause conservatively, applying both a "common sense" test as well as the three-part test developed in antitrust cases applying the McCarran-Ferguson Act for determining whether a law regulated "the business of insurance" to determine whether the savings clause applied. Metropolitan Life Ins. Co. v. Massachusetts, 471 U.S. 724, 740–44 (1985), Pilot Life Ins. Co. v. Dedeaux, 481 U.S. 41 (1987).

In Kentucky Association of Health Plans, Inc. v. Miller, 538 U.S. 329 (2003) the Court abandoned its earlier precedents and crafted a new approach to interpreting the savings clause. This case involved the claim of an association of managed care plans that Kentucky's "any willing provider" (AWP) law was preempted by ERISA. Designed to counteract managed care plans' cost-saving strategy of contracting with "narrow networks" of providers, an AWP law requires health insurers to allow any health care provider to become members of the health plan's provider network if the provider meets certain conditions (e.g., being licensed and in good standing and willing to accept the health plan's payment rates). The Sixth Circuit had held that the regulatory provision was saved from preemption under ERISA's savings clause. In a brief and unanimous opinion written by Justice Scalia (who had dissented in *Moran*), the Court held that the law was saved from preemption, abandoning its previous savings clause jurisprudence. The Court acknowledged that use of the McCarran-Ferguson test had "misdirected attention, failed to provide clear guidance to lower federal courts, and . . . added little to relevant analysis." The Court also admitted that the McCarran-Ferguson tests had been developed for different purposes and interpreted different statutory language.

The Court concluded:

Today we make a clean break from the McCarran-Ferguson factors and hold that for a state law to be deemed a 'law . . . which regulates insurance' under § 1144(b)(2)(A), it must satisfy two requirements. First, the state law must be specifically directed toward entities engaged in insurance.[ ] Second, . . . the state law must substantially affect the risk pooling arrangement between the insurer and the insured. Kentucky's law satisfies each of these requirements. 123 S.Ct. at 1479.

Earlier in the opinion it had interpreted the "risk pooling" requirement as follows:

> We have never held that state laws must alter or control the actual terms of insurance policies to be deemed 'laws . . . which regulat[e] insurance' under § 1144(b)(2)(A); it suffices that they substantially affect the risk pooling arrangement between insurer and insured. By expanding the number of providers from whom an insured may receive health services, AWP laws alter the scope of permissible bargains between insurers and insureds . . . . No longer may Kentucky insureds seek insurance from a closed network of health-care providers in exchange for a lower premium. The AWP prohibition substantially affects the type of risk pooling arrangements that insurers may offer. 123 S.Ct. at 1477–78.

Miller significantly clarifies, and expands, the scope of ERISA's savings clause. Virtually any state law that requires insurers to provide particular benefits would seem to be covered. See Matthew O. Gatewood, The New Map: The Supreme Court's New Guide to Curing Thirty Years of Confusion in ERISA Savings Clause Analysis, 62 Wash. & Lee U. L. Rev. 643 (2005). What effect is this green light to state regulation of managed care and health insurance likely to have on the willingness of employers to offer health insurance plans to their workers, or to offer insured rather than self-insured plans? Might Justice Thomas' prediction on this matter prove true? See Haavi Morreim, ERISA Takes a Drubbing: Rush Prudential and Its Implications for Health Care, 38 Tort Trial and Ins. Practice J. 933 (2003). Does the adoption of the ACA change the calculus, as it addressed in federal law many of the regulatory issues formerly addressed by state law?

3. The Deemer Clause and Self-Funded Plans

Although the savings clause saves state insurance regulation from preemption, the "deemer clause" creates an exception from the savings clause for state laws that relate to self-funded group health plans, which are not deemed to be in the business of insurance. Thus, even state insurance laws that would be saved by the savings clause with respect to fully insured plans are preempted by ERISA insofar as they apply to self-funded employee health plans.

The deemer clause offers a significant incentive for employers to become self-funded, as a self-funded plan can totally escape state regulation, and in particular, benefit mandates. Self-funding, however, also has disadvantages—it imposes upon the employer the burden of administering the plan as well as open-ended liability for employee benefit claims made under the plan. To mitigate these problems, self-funded employers often contract with **third-party administrators** to administer claims and with **stop-loss** insurers to limit their claims exposure. The courts have overwhelmingly held that employer plans remain self-insured even though they are reinsured through stop-loss plans, and have prohibited states from attempting to impose requirements on self-insured plans through regulation of stop-loss coverage. See, e.g., Bill Gray Enterprises, Inc. Employee Health and Welfare Plan v. Gourley, 248 F.3d 206 (3rd Cir.2001) and Lincoln Mutual Casualty v. Lectron Products, Inc. 970 F.2d 206 (6th Cir.1992). Third-party administrators that administer self-insured plans are also protected from state insurance regulation. NGS American, Inc. v. Barnes, 805 F. Supp. 462, 473 (W.D. Texas 1992). Thus, an employer who is willing to bear some risk can escape state regulation under the "deemer" clause, even though most of the risk of insuring the plan is borne by a stop-loss insurer and the burden of administering the plan is assumed by a third-party administrator.

States may, however, regulate stop-loss coverage itself as a form of insurance. Some states ban stop-loss coverage for small group plans, while others prohibit stop-loss policies that cover losses below a certain level. See, e.g. N.Y. Ins. Law § 3231(h); 4317(a). See also Edstom Indus. v. Companion Life Ins., 516 U.S. 546, 551 (7th Cir. 2008).

The calculus that an employer faces in deciding whether or not to self-insure further shifted under the Affordable Care Act (ACA). A number of the ACA requirements that apply to fully insured group health plans do not apply to self-insured plans, as described in the Table, above. Even small businesses with fewer than 50 employees that have traditionally avoided self-insuring, have incentives to self-insure. Insurance companies are increasingly marketing stop-loss insurance and administrative services to small, self-funded employers, but only to those with younger and healthier workers. This creates an adverse selection problem because healthy small groups can self-insure, while sicker small groups are pushed to fully-insured, ACA-compliant plans with community rating, which are also more expensive than self-funded plans. See Sabrina Corlette et al., Urban Institute, Small Business Health Insurance and the ACA: Views from the Market 2017 (July 2017); Robert S. Pozen & Anant Vinjamoori, Brookings Institution, Incentives for Small Firms to Self-Fund Their Health Plans (Nov. 19, 2014).

C. ERISA PREEMPTION AND STATE HEALTH REFORM

Despite the enormous energy devoted to health reform at the federal level, states have not stopped moving forward with their own visions of health reform across a range of areas: expanded coverage through employer "pay or play" requirements, single-payer proposals, improving price transparency for health care services and prescription drugs, health care consumer protections such as protections from so-called "surprise medical billing," and efforts to control spiraling health care costs. There are several reasons for states' continued role as engines of health reform and innovation: First, as detailed in Chapter 9, the federal scheme created by the ACA has been attacked legally and politically by a dedicated opposition, which has created uncertainty about the future of the ACA even as its programs and requirements have been implemented. Second, there is growing policy preference, even within the federal government, for increased state flexibility and responsibility over the states' own health care and insurance markets. See Erin C. Fuse Brown & Ameet Sarpatwari, Removing ERISA's Impediment to State Health Reform, 378 NEJM 5 (2018).

ERISA's expansive preemptive effects threaten to thwart many state efforts at health reforms and to limit the scope of state health reforms to the extent they would affect employee health benefit plans. Because employment-related health insurance is still the predominant form of health insurance in the United States, this is a significant limitation.

1. Price Transparency and Cost Control Efforts

To address rising drug prices, states have pursued policies to increase transparency of the factors that contribute to consumers' drug costs. At least 45 states have enacted regulations for pharmacy benefit managers (PBMs), the middlemen in the pharmaceutical supply chain that go between drug manufacturers, health plans, and pharmacies. PBMs frequently use confidential markups and rebates to administer prescription-drug coverage and reimbursement services to health plans. To counter these forms of opacity in drug pricing, states have attempted to require PBMs to disclose their pricing methodologies to state regulators and purchasers. However, ERISA preemption may thwart these state laws if the PBM administers drug benefits for self-funded ERISA plans. In 2017, the Eighth Circuit struck down Iowa's drug pricing transparency law as applied to PBMs acting as third-party administrators for ERISA plans. Pharm. Care Mgmt. Ass'n v. Gerhart, 852 F.3d 722 (8th Cir. 2017). The state law required PBMs to report their drug pricing methodology to the state insurance commissioner. The Eighth Circuit reasoned that ERISA preempts a state law requiring disclosure from PBMs that administer drug benefits for ERISA plans because it "intrudes upon a matter central to plan administration and interferes with nationally uniform plan administration." 852 F.3d at 730–31. The Eighth Circuit cited a 2017 Supreme Court case, *Gobeille v. Liberty Mutual Insurance*, which preempted state claims data collection efforts as applied to self-funded ERISA plans, as discussed in note 2, below.

To counter the effects of PBM pricing on independent and rural pharmacies, states have also enacted laws that regulate PBMs' reimbursement of the pharmacies that dispense covered drugs. After the Eighth Circuit invalidated Arkansas' law, relying on the *Gerhart* decision, the Supreme Court addressed ERISA's preemptive effect on state regulation of PBMs.

RUTLEDGE v. PHARMACEUTICAL CARE MANAGEMENT ASSOCIATION
Supreme Court of the United States, 2020.
141 S.Ct. 474.

JUSTICE SOTOMAYOR delivered the opinion of the Court.

Arkansas' Act 900 regulates the price at which pharmacy benefit managers reimburse pharmacies for the cost of drugs covered by prescription-drug plans. The question presented in this case is whether the Employee Retirement Income Security Act of 1974 (ERISA), [ ] pre-empts Act 900. The Court holds that the Act has neither an impermissible connection with nor reference to ERISA and is therefore not pre-empted.

I.A

Pharmacy benefit managers (PBMs) are a little-known but important part of the process by which many Americans get their prescription drugs. Generally speaking, PBMs serve as intermediaries between prescription-drug plans and the pharmacies that beneficiaries use. When a beneficiary of a prescription-drug plan goes to a pharmacy to fill a prescription, the pharmacy checks with a PBM to determine that person's coverage and copayment information. After the beneficiary leaves with his or her prescription, the PBM reimburses the pharmacy for the prescription, less the amount of the beneficiary's copayment. The prescription-drug plan, in turn, reimburses the PBM.

The amount a PBM "reimburses" a pharmacy for a drug is not necessarily tied to how much the pharmacy paid to purchase that drug from a wholesaler. Instead, PBMs' contracts with pharmacies typically set reimbursement rates according to a list specifying the maximum allowable cost (MAC) for each drug. PBMs normally develop and administer their own unique MAC lists. Likewise, the amount that prescription-drug plans reimburse PBMs is a matter of contract between a given plan and a PBM. A PBM's reimbursement from a plan often differs from and exceeds a

PBM's reimbursement to a pharmacy. That difference generates a profit for PBMs.

In 2015, Arkansas adopted Act 900 in response to concerns that the reimbursement rates set by PBMs were often too low to cover pharmacies' costs, and that many pharmacies, particularly rural and independent ones, were at risk of losing money and closing. [ ] In effect, Act 900 requires PBMs to reimburse Arkansas pharmacies at a price equal to or higher than that which the pharmacy paid to buy the drug from a wholesaler.

Act 900 accomplishes this result through three key enforcement mechanisms. First, the Act requires PBMs to tether reimbursement rates to pharmacies' acquisition costs by timely updating their MAC lists when drug wholesale prices increase. [ ] Second, PBMs must provide administrative appeal procedures for pharmacies to challenge MAC reimbursement prices that are below the pharmacies' acquisition costs. [ ] If a pharmacy could not have acquired the drug at a lower price from its typical wholesaler, a PBM must increase its reimbursement rate to cover the pharmacy's acquisition cost. [ ] PBMs must also allow pharmacies to "reverse and rebill" each reimbursement claim affected by the pharmacy's inability to procure the drug from its typical wholesaler at a price equal to or less than the MAC reimbursement price. [ ] Third, and finally, the Act permits a pharmacy to decline to sell a drug to a beneficiary if the relevant PBM will reimburse the pharmacy at less than its acquisition cost. [ ]

I.B

Respondent Pharmaceutical Care Management Association (PCMA) is a national trade association representing the 11 largest PBMs in the country. After the enactment of Act 900, PCMA filed suit in the Eastern District of Arkansas, alleging, as relevant here, that Act 900 is pre-empted by ERISA. [Opinion describes how the Eighth Circuit affirmed the District Court, holding that Act 900 was preempted by ERISA.] . . . .

II

ERISA pre-empts "any and all State laws insofar as they may now or hereafter relate to any employee benefit plan" covered by ERISA. 29 U.S.C. § 1144(a). "[A] state law relates to an ERISA plan if it has a connection with or reference to such a plan." [ ]

. . . Act 900 regulates PBMs whether or not the plans they service fall within ERISA's coverage.[1] Act 900 is therefore analogous to the law in *Travelers*, which did not refer to ERISA plans because it imposed surcharges "regardless of whether the commercial coverage [was] ultimately secured by an ERISA plan, private purchase, or otherwise." [ ]

---

[1] PBMs contract with a variety of healthcare plans and programs that are not covered by ERISA, including Medicaid, Medicare, military, and marketplace plans.

III

PCMA disagrees that Act 900 amounts to nothing more than cost regulation. It contends that Act 900 has an impermissible connection with an ERISA plan because its enforcement mechanisms both directly affect central matters of plan administration and interfere with nationally uniform plan administration. The mechanisms that PCMA identifies, however, do not require plan administrators to structure their benefit plans in any particular manner, nor do they lead to anything more than potential operational inefficiencies.[2]

PCMA first claims that Act 900 affects plan design by mandating a particular pricing methodology for pharmacy benefits. As PCMA reasons, while a plan might prefer that PBMs reimburse pharmacies using a MAC list constructed with an eye toward containing costs and ensuring predictability, Act 900 ignores that preference and instead requires PBMs to reimburse pharmacies based on acquisition costs. But that argument is just a long way of saying that Act 900 regulates reimbursement rates. Requiring PBMs to reimburse pharmacies at or above their acquisition costs does not require plans to provide any particular benefit to any particular beneficiary in any particular way. It simply establishes a floor for the cost of the benefits that plans choose to provide. The plans in *Travelers* might likewise have preferred that their insurers reimburse hospital services without paying an additional surcharge, but that did not transform New York's cost regulation into central plan administration.

Act 900's appeal procedure likewise does not govern central matters of plan administration. True, plan administrators must "comply with a particular process, subject to state-specific deadlines, and [Act 900] dictates the substantive standard governing the resolution of [an] appeal." Brief for Respondent 24. Moreover, if a pharmacy wins its appeal, a plan, depending on the terms of its contract with a PBM, may need to recalculate and reprocess how much it (and its beneficiary) owes. But any contract dispute implicating the cost of a medical benefit would involve similar demands and could lead to similar results. Taken to its logical endpoint, PCMA's argument would pre-empt any suits under state law that could affect the price or provision of benefits. Yet this Court has held that ERISA does not pre-empt "state-law mechanisms of executing judgments against ERISA welfare benefit plans, even when those mechanisms prevent plan participants from receiving their benefits." [ ]

PCMA also argues that Act 900 interferes with central matters of plan administration by allowing pharmacies to decline to dispense a prescription if the PBM's reimbursement will be less than the pharmacy's cost of acquisition. PCMA contends that such a refusal effectively denies

---

[2] PCMA does not suggest that Act 900's enforcement mechanisms overlap with "fundamental components of ERISA's regulation of plan administration." [ ]

plan beneficiaries their benefits, but that argument misunderstands the statutory scheme. Act 900 requires PBMs to compensate pharmacies at or above their acquisition costs. When a pharmacy declines to dispense a prescription, the responsibility lies first with the PBM for offering the pharmacy a below-acquisition reimbursement.

Finally, PCMA argues that Act 900's enforcement mechanisms interfere with nationally uniform plan administration by creating "operational inefficiencies." [ ] But creating inefficiencies alone is not enough to trigger ERISA pre-emption. [ ] PCMA argues that those operational inefficiencies will lead to increased costs and, potentially, decreased benefits. ERISA does not pre-empt a state law that merely increases costs, however, even if plans decide to limit benefits or charge plan members higher rates as a result. See *De Buono*, 520 U.S. at 816, 117 S.Ct. 1747 ("Any state tax, or other law, that increases the cost of providing benefits to covered employees will have some effect on the administration of ERISA plans, but that simply cannot mean that every state law with such an effect is pre-empted by the federal statute").

* * *

In sum, Act 900 amounts to cost regulation that does not bear an impermissible connection with or reference to ERISA. The judgment of the Eighth Circuit is therefore reversed, and the case is remanded for further proceedings consistent with this opinion.

It is so ordered.

JUSTICE BARRETT took no part in the consideration or decision of this case.

JUSTICE THOMAS, concurring.

I join the Court's opinion in full because it properly applies our precedents interpreting the pre-emptive effect of the Employee Retirement Income Security Act of 1974 (ERISA). [ ]

I write separately because I continue to doubt our ERISA pre-emption jurisprudence. [ ]The plain text of ERISA suggests a two-part pre-emption test: (1) do any ERISA provisions govern the same matter as the state law at issue, and (2) does that state law have a meaningful relationship to ERISA plans? Only if the answers to both are in the affirmative does ERISA displace state law. But our precedents have veered from the text, transforming § 1144 into a "vague and 'potentially boundless'. . . 'purposes and objectives' pre-emption" clause that relies on "generalized notions of congressional purposes." [ ] Although that approach may allow courts to arrive at the correct result in individual cases, it offers little guidance or predictability. We should instead apply the law as written.

I

When construing a statutory provision, we begin with the text. [ ] Section 1144(a) provides that certain of ERISA's provisions "shall supersede any and all State laws insofar as they may now or hereafter relate to any employee benefit plan" with certain exceptions not relevant in this case.

The term "supersede" precludes reading the statute as categorically pre-empting any state law related to employee benefit plans. Rather, it suggests a replacement or substitution instead of a blanket pre-emption.

Where Congress seeks to pre-empt state laws *without* replacing them, it typically uses different words. . . . Congress knows how to write sweeping pre-emption statutes. But it did not do so here. Applying the statutory text, the first step is to ask whether a provision in ERISA governs the same matter as the disputed state law, and thus could replace it.

* * *

II

Here, the parties have not pointed to any ERISA provision that governs the same matter as Act 900. That alone should resolve the case. But the parties certainly cannot be faulted for not raising this argument. Our amorphous precedents have largely ignored this step. [ ]

Instead, we have asked only if the state law " 'relate[d] to' " ERISA plans. [ ] But this has proved problematic because of "how much state law § 1144 would pre-empt if read literally." [ ] Instead of reverting to the text, however, we decided that "relate to" is so "indetermina[te]" that it cannot "give us much help drawing the line." [ ]

* * *

Our more recent efforts to further narrow the test have just yielded more confusion. A state law references ERISA only if it " 'acts immediately and exclusively upon ERISA plans. . . or where the existence of ERISA plans is essential to the law's operation.' " [ ] A connection with ERISA plans is impermissible only if it " 'governs. . . a central matter of plan administration' " or " 'interferes with nationally uniform plan administration.' " Although, at first blush, that may seem more precise than asking if a law "relates to" ERISA, it has proven just as difficult to apply consistently, leading many members of the Court to suggest still other methods. [ ] Instead of relying on this "accordion-like" test that seems to expand or contract depending on the year, [ ] perhaps we should just interpret the text as written.

* * *

But it is not enough for this Court to reach the right conclusions. We should do so in the way Congress instructed. Indeed, although we have generally arrived at the conclusions we would arrive at under a text-based approach, our capacious, nontextual test encourages departure from the text. The decision below is testament to that problem. We unanimously reverse that decision today, but we can hardly fault judges when they apply the amorphous test that we gave them. We can and should do better.

NOTES AND QUESTIONS

1.   *Implications for State Health Care Cost-Containment.* The *Rutledge* opinion brought some clarity to states' ability to regulate PBMs, as well as some additional latitude for other states' health reforms. On PBM regulation, *Rutledge* "clarifies that states may regulate plans' contractors, and that cost-control regulation is presumptively beyond ERISA's preemptive scope." Erin C. Fuse Brown & Elizabeth Y. McCuskey, The Implications of Rutledge v. PCMA For State Health Care Cost Regulation, Health Affairs Blog (Dec. 17, 2020). The *Rutledge* opinion goes further in that it "intimates that states may regulate in the vast 'vacuum' of issues on which ERISA offers no federal law," though the opinion does not go so far as to significantly alter ERISA preemption jurisprudence. The opinion's reliance on the 1995 *Travelers* case affirms that state laws with only "indirect economic influence" on employer-sponsored health plans do not trigger ERISA preemption. While *Travelers* focused on state regulation of health care providers' rates, the *Rutledge* opinion arguably extends this principle to a broader category of state health care cost regulation. For a collection of other state cost-containment laws potentially implicated by *Rutledge*'s reasoning, see id.

2.   *State Data-Collection Laws and* Gobeille. Health care providers' prices—not just prescription drug prices—are notoriously opaque and difficult to ascertain. Different plans pay the same provider different prices for the same service in the same geographic areas, and the prices are kept secret by nondisclosure agreement, trade secret claims, and highly complex billing mechanisms. But states can get around many of these barriers by requiring disclosure of the information to a state entity. Many states require disclosure of health care claims to an all-payer claims database (APCD). See APCD Council Interactive State Report Map (2021). APCDs are large-scale state-run databases that collect health care claims data and provider data from all payers it the state, including private insurers, employer-based plans, prescription drug plans, and government payers such as state employee health plans, Medicaid, and the Children's Health Insurance Program (CHIP). APCDs are used to promote consumer price transparency as well as to provide state regulators with the ability to monitor and oversee drivers of health care spending within the state.

Four years before *Rutledge*, the Supreme Court in *Gobeille* held that Vermont's APCD data-collection efforts were preempted as applied to employer self-funded plans. The majority opinion reasoned that the reporting requirement imposed on the third-party administrator (TPA) of an employer self-funded plan had an "impermissible 'connection with'" an ERISA plan by interfering with uniform administration of the plan's reporting requirements. Although the federal Secretary of Labor could require TPAs to report the same data, which the TPA already collected as a matter of course, the state's requirement "intrudes upon 'a central matter of plan administration'" by targeting claims data reporting. Justice Thomas concurred, but expressed his reservations about the constitutionality of the ERISA statute's broad preemption. Justice Breyer concurred, writing separately to emphasize that states could request the same data directly from the Secretary of Labor. Justices Ginsburg and Sotomayor dissented, arguing that the Vermont statute did not interfere with ERISA's "reporting" requirements, and that the lack of any actual burden from distributing the data to the state APCD fails to rise to the level of interference that would trigger ERISA preemption. For a discussion of the effects of *Gobeille* on state cost control efforts, see Erin C. Fuse Brown & Jaime S. King, The Consequences of *Gobeille v. Liberty Mutual* for Health Care Cost Control, Health Affairs Blog (Mar. 10, 2016).

3. *State Taxes on ERISA Plans*. While *Rutledge* offered some much-needed clarity by reviving the *Travelers* analysis, it also raises some questions for the future of state health reform: Does *Rutledge* limit the applicability of *Gobeille*? How can states determine whether their health care cost-containment laws, including taxes, will be preempted under *Gobeille* or not preempted under *Rutledge*? See Erin C. Fuse Brown & Elizabeth Y. McCuskey, The Implications of Rutledge v. PCMA For State Health Care Cost Regulation, Health Affairs Blog (Dec. 17, 2020).

2. Insurance Coverage Reforms

ERISA has long restricted the ability of states to reform health care. A quarter of a century ago, Hawaii's mandate that employers provide health insurance to their employees was struck down as impermissibly interfering with the terms of employee benefit plans in violation of ERISA, Standard Oil Co. of California v. Agsalud, 633 F.2d 760 (CA9 1980), summarily aff'd, 454 U.S. 801 (1981). In 1983, Congress amended ERISA to exempt from preemption certain provisions of the Hawaii Act in place before the enactment of ERISA, but no other state has been afforded such an exemption.

In 2006, Maryland adopted the "Fair Share Health Care Fund Act," which required employers with 10,000 or more Maryland employees to spend at least 8 percent of their total payrolls on employees' health insurance costs or pay the amount their spending fell short to the State of Maryland. The law resulted from a national campaign to force Wal-Mart to increase health insurance benefits for its employees and the Act's minimum spending provision was designed to only cover Wal-Mart. The Retail Industry Leaders Association, of which Wal-Mart is a member, sued, claiming the law was preempted by ERISA. The Fourth Circuit Court of Appeals held that ERISA preempted the law. Retail Industry Leaders Association v. Fielder, 475 F.3d 180 (4th Cir. 2007).

The court held:

. . . a state law has an impermissible "connection with" an ERISA plan if it directly regulates or effectively mandates some element of the structure or administration of employers' ERISA plans. On the other hand, a state law that creates only indirect economic incentives that affect but do not bind the choices of employers or their ERISA plans is generally not preempted.[ ] In deciding which of these principles is applicable, we assess the effect of a state law on the ability of ERISA plans to be administered uniformly nationwide.[ ] A state law is preempted also if it contains a "reference to" an ERISA plan, . . . The district court did not reach this issue because it found that preemption through the Fair Share Act's "connection with" ERISA plans. . . .

. . . At its heart, the Fair Share Act requires every employer of 10,000 or more Maryland employees to pay to the State an amount that equals the difference between what the employer spends on "health insurance costs" . . . and 8% of its payroll. . . .

In effect, the only rational choice employers have under the Fair Share Act is to structure their ERISA healthcare benefit plans so as to meet the minimum spending threshold. . . . Because the Fair Share Act effectively mandates that employers structure their employee healthcare plans to provide a certain level of benefits, the Act has an obvious "connection with" employee benefit plans and so is preempted by ERISA.

* * *

While the Secretary argues that the Fair Share Act is designed to collect funds for medical care under the Maryland Medical Assistance Program, the core provision of the Act aims at requiring covered employers to provide medical benefits to employees. The effect of this provision will force employers to structure their recordkeeping and healthcare benefit spending to comply with the Fair Share Act. Functioning in that manner, the Act would disrupt employers' uniform administration of employee benefit plans on a nationwide basis. . . .

* * *

The court rejected Maryland's argument that the Act was not mandatory because it gave the employer the option of increasing health spending in ways that did not qualify for ERISA plans, concluding that the choices offered to employers, such as on-site medical clinics or contributing to health savings accounts, were not meaningful alternatives under the law. The Court concluded:

. . . The undeniable fact is that the vast majority of any employer's healthcare spending occurs through ERISA plans. Thus, the primary subjects of the Fair Share Act are ERISA plans, and any attempt to comply with the Act would have direct effects on the employer's ERISA plans. . . .

Perhaps recognizing the insufficiency of a non-ERISA healthcare spending option, the Secretary relies most heavily on its argument that the Fair Share Act gives employers the choice of paying the State rather than altering their healthcare spending. . . . The Secretary contends that, in certain circumstances, it would be rational for an employer to choose to do so. . . . [I]ndeed, identifying the narrow conditions under which the Act would not force an employer to increase its spending on healthcare plans only reinforces the conclusion that the overwhelming effect of the Act is to mandate spending increases. This conclusion is further supported by the fact that Wal-Mart representatives averred that Wal-Mart would in fact increase healthcare spending rather than pay the State.

San Francisco's similar "pay-or-play" ordinance was, on the other hand, upheld by the Ninth Circuit Court of Appeals. The district court held that the ordinance was preempted by ERISA. Golden Gate Restaurant Ass'n v. City and County of San Francisco, 535 F. Supp. 2d 968 (N.D.Cal. 2007). The Ninth Circuit reversed, 546 F.2d 639 (9th Cir. 2008), and denied a petition for rehearing en banc, 558 F.3d 1000 (9th Cir. 2009). The Supreme Court denied certiorari.

The San Francisco ordinance mandates that covered employers spend a set rate per covered employee for providing health services to its employees or make a payment to the City to fund membership in San Francisco's Health Access Program (HAP) (the "City-payment option"). If an employer elects the City-payment option, its covered employees who satisfy age and income requirements and are "uninsured San Francisco residents" are allowed to enroll in the HAP, and its other covered employees will be eligible for medical reimbursement accounts with the City. Covered employees may enroll in the HAP free of charge or at reduced rates. The HAP provides enrollees with "medical services with an emphasis on wellness, preventive care and innovative service delivery."

The court first held that the San Francisco scheme was not itself an ERISA plan. It then held that the ordinance was not preempted by § 514:

The Ordinance does not require any employer to adopt an ERISA plan or other health plan. Nor does it require any employer to provide specific benefits through an existing ERISA plan or other health plan. Any employer covered by the Ordinance may fully discharge its expenditure obligations by making the required level of employee health care expenditures, whether those expenditures are made in whole or in part to an ERISA plan, or in whole or in part to the City. The Ordinance thus preserves ERISA's "uniform regulatory regime." The Ordinance also has no effect on "the administrative practices of a benefit plan," [ ] unless an employer voluntarily elects to change those practices.

The court then distinguished *Fielder*:

> We neither adopt nor reject the analysis of the Fourth Circuit in Fielder. . . . For purposes of argument, however, we assume that the panel majority in Fielder was correct. But even under the reasoning of the panel majority, San Francisco's Ordinance is valid.

Observing that Wal-Mart had no realistic choice in *Fielder* but to offer benefits, the court stated:

> In stark contrast to the Maryland law in Fielder, the City-payment option under the San Francisco Ordinance offers employers a meaningful alternative that allows them to preserve the existing structure of their ERISA plans. If an employer elects to pay the City, that employer's employees are eligible for free or discounted enrollment in the HAP, or for medical reimbursement accounts. In contrast to the Maryland law, the San Francisco Ordinance provides tangible benefits to employees when their employers choose to pay the City rather than to establish or alter ERISA plans. In its motion for summary judgment, the Association provided no evidence to demonstrate that San Francisco employers are, in practical fact, compelled to alter or establish ERISA plans rather than to make payments to the City.
>
> Because the City-payment option offers San Francisco employers a realistic alternative to creating or altering ERISA plans, the Ordinance does not "effectively mandate[ ] that employers structure their employee healthcare plans to provide a certain level of benefits."[ ] In the view of the *Fielder* court, Maryland legislators intended to "force Wal-Mart to increase its spending on healthcare benefits rather than to pay monies to the State." Unlike the Maryland law, the San Francisco Ordinance provides employers with a legitimate alternative to establishing or altering ERISA plans.

The City of Seattle enacted an ordinance in 2019 requiring large hotel employers to supplement their low-wage workers' compensation with "healthcare expenditures." These employers could satisfy the ordinance by paying the required amount directly to the employee, or to a third-party payer or provider on the employee's behalf. The Ninth Circuit upheld Seattle's ordinance against a preemption challenge by a national trade association representing the hotels, holding that it was not meaningfully distinguishable from the San Francisco program upheld in *Golden Gate*. ERISA Indus. Comm. v. City of Seattle, 840 F. App'x 248, 249 (9th Cir. 2021).

NOTES AND QUESTIONS

1. *Reconciling* Fielder *and* Golden Gate. The big question is whether a "pay or play" system can pass ERISA muster after *Fielder* and *Golden Gate*. State assessments imposed on employers to cover their uninsured workers might be vulnerable because they impose obligations on employers. The amount of the penalty may matter, with smaller penalties less likely to be seen as compelling employer participation. Pay-or-play laws that are not focused on a particular employer, do not refer to ERISA plans, do not impose penalties substantial enough to force an employer to provide benefits, and do not require the employer to establish any particular kind of benefit plan may pass muster, but will almost certainly be challenged, and, if other courts follow the Fourth Circuit, may be difficult to defend. State laws that impose significant record-keeping obligations on employers will also face ERISA challenges, even if they do not require employer financial contributions, because they essentially require an employer to spend money for administrative costs. See Joshua P. Booth & Larry I. Palmer, ERISA Preemption Doctrine as Health Policy, 39 Hofstra L. Rev. 59 (2011); Mary Ann Chirba-Martin, Drawing Lines in Shifting Sands: The U.S. Supreme Court's Mixed Messages on ERISA Preemption Imperil Healthcare Care Reform, 36 J. Legis. 91 (2010); Edward A. Zelinsky, The New Massachusetts Health Law: Preemption and Experimentation, 49 Wm. & Mary L. Rev. 229 (2007); Amy Monahan, Pay or Play Laws, ERISA Preemption, and Potential Lessons from Massachusetts, 55 Kansas L. Rev. 1203 (2007); Patricia A. Butler, ERISA Implications for State Health Care Access Initiatives: Impact of the Maryland "Fair Share Act" Court Decision, National Academy for State Health Policy (2006); and Patricia A. Butler, ERISA Update: Federal Court of Appeals Agrees ERISA Preempts Maryland's "Fair Share Act," National Academy for State Health Policy (2007).

2. *State Universal Coverage Options Under ERISA.* What routes are open to a state that wants to engage employers in an attempt to expand insurance coverage under ERISA after *Fielder, Golden Gate*, and the ACA? A direct mandate requiring employers to offer specified coverage to their employees is out of the question. On the other hand, ERISA should not affect state initiatives that offer tax credits to employers to expand coverage or use Medicaid or State Children's Health Insurance Program funds to subsidize employment-based insurance for low-income workers because they do not impose any requirements on employers or on ERISA plans. State delivery system reforms could also pass muster if they do not impose requirements directly on employers. State tax-financed universal insurance programs funded through a payroll tax may also survive an ERISA challenge, although self-funded employers will likely argue such a tax compels them to alter or discontinue offering their current health benefit plans. Finally, universal coverage systems based solely on an individual mandate should not implicate ERISA, because, again, they impose no obligations on employers. For a discussion on the effect of ERISA preemption on states' ability to expand coverage outside of the Affordable Care Act's sanctioned methods, See Nicholas Bagley, Federalism and the End of Obamacare, 127 Yale L. J. Forum 1 (2017).

A growing number of states have considered various proposals to adopt a "single payer" program, under which all residents in the state would be covered by a tax-funded government-run health care program, replacing private health insurers, employer-based insurance, individual insurance, and government payers with a single government program. If they build on existing government programs, such single payer proposals have been described as "Medicare for all" or "Medicaid for all." How could a state implement a single payer program that replaces employer-based (ERISA) health plans with the single payer without running afoul of ERISA preemption? For a discussion of the effect of ERISA on state-based single payer and other universal coverage options, see Erin C. Fuse Brown & Elizabeth Y. McCuskey, Federalism, ERISA, and State Single-Payer Health Care, 168 U. Pa. L. Rev. 389 (2020); Chapin White et al., The RAND Corporation, A Comprehensive Assessment of Four Options for Financing Health Care Delivery in Oregon (2017); William Hsiao, Steven Kappel, and Jonathan Gruber, Act 128, Health System Reform (2011).

3.   *ERISA and the Future of Federal and State Health Reforms.* As you read Chapter 9 on the ACA, consider the extent to which the ACA diminished ERISA preemption's impact, or preserved it. Recall that the ACA expressly disavowed any change to ERISA preemption, keeping it as a fixture of health reform in the ACA era. Forceful critiques of ERISA preemption as a frustrator of state health reform have amassed over the statute's lifetime. See, e.g., Peter D. Jacobson, The Role of ERISA Preemption in Health Reform: Opportunities and Limits, 37 J. L. Med. & Ethics 86 (2009); Brendan S. Maher, Regulating Employer-Based Anything, 100 Minn. L. Rev. 1257 (2016); Phyllis C. Borzi, There's 'Private' and Then There's 'Private': ERISA, Its Impact, and Options for Reform, 36 J. L. Med. & Ethics 660 (2008); Wendy E. Parmet, Regulation and Federalism: Legal Impediments to State Health Care Reform, 19 Am. J. L. & Med. 121 (1993). Proposals to alter ERISA's preemption provisions or to make them waivable have made their way into health reform debates, and have been introduced in Congress. See Elizabeth Y. McCuskey, ERISA Reform as Health Reform: The Case for an ERISA Preemption Waiver, 48 J. L. Med. & Ethics 450 (2020). The fragility of reliance on employer-sponsored health care coverage during the COVID-19 pandemic, and the race- and gender-inequities it perpetuates have amplified calls for reform. See, e.g., Jaime S. King, Covid-19 and the Need for Health Care Reform, 382 NEJM e104 (2020); Ruqaiijah Yearby & Seema Mohapatra, Systemic Racism, the Government's Pandemic Response, and Racial Inequities in COVID-19, 70 Emory L. J. 1419 (2021).

III.   ERISA REMEDIES AND PREEMPTION

Courts have struggled to determine the nature and extent of ERISA preemption in medical negligence cases. Managed care plans as defendants are subject to the same theories of liability as hospitals—vicarious liability, corporate negligence, and ordinary negligence. Most courts that have considered the question of vicarious liability against managed care organizations have allowed it. See Chapter 5. The Supreme Court, however, held that § 502(a) severely limits the reach of state tort actions against ERISA-qualified health plans.

A. BENEFICIARY REMEDIES IN ERISA

1. Competing Conceptions of Health Plan Beneficiary Rights: State Law, ERISA, and the Affordable Care Act

ERISA obligates employee benefit plans to fulfill their commitments to their beneficiaries, and provides a federal cause of action under § 502(a) when they fail to do so. The remedies provided under ERISA § 502(a) are the exclusive remedies available to ERISA plan beneficiaries in causes of action against their plans. Review the statutory language of § 502(a) at the outset of this chapter. The vision of health insurance that undergirds ERISA is very different from that which has traditionally undergirded state insurance regulation and, for that matter, the vision underlying the ACA.

State insurance regulation has generally been driven by a concern for access rights: e.g., the right of employees to have continued access to insurance coverage when they lose their jobs; the right of insureds to obtain mental health or mammography screening coverage; the right of chiropractors to have their services paid for by insurance; the right of "any willing provider" to participate in a PPO or pharmacy benefits plan; the right of small businesses to purchase insurance at affordable rates; the right of beneficiaries to ensure compliance with the insurance contract; and the right of beneficiaries to fair procedure. This body of state law looks to public utility regulation, and, more recently, civil rights laws, for its models. The ACA builds on this model. It requires all insurers to offer insurance regardless of pre-existing conditions and insurers in the individual and small group markets to cover "essential benefits" with limited out-of-pocket exposure and without annual or lifetime limits.

The categories of law that define ERISA, on the other hand, are trust law and classical contract law. ERISA does not compel employers to provide health insurance and prohibits the states from imposing such a requirement. If, however, employers choose voluntarily (or under collective bargaining agreements) to establish health benefit plans, any contributions made by employers (or employees) to such plans are held in trust for all of the participants (employee plan members) and beneficiaries (dependents and others covered under a participant's policy) of the plan and must be paid out according to the contract that defines its terms. If the plan fiduciary or administrator wrongfully withholds benefits, a participant or beneficiary is entitled to sue in federal or state court. Prior to the ACA, if a fiduciary or administrator exercised properly delegated discretion to withhold benefits that were not expressly granted or denied by the plan, the court had to defer to the judgment of the administrator or fiduciary. When the fiduciary or administrator wrongfully withheld benefits, moreover, no matter how egregious its conduct in doing so, the court would merely order the plan to pay the beneficiary the amount due. ERISA does not, as interpreted by the Supreme Court, authorize tort relief or punitive damages.

While the limited rights that beneficiaries enjoyed under ERISA have troubled courts and commentators, they are consistent with ERISA's underlying theory. State insurance laws—be they the common law of *contra proferentem* or statutory mandates enacted by the legislature— focus on the absolute claim of a beneficiary whose life or health is in jeopardy to the assets held by the insurer: your money or my life. They also honor the political claims of providers who demand their turn at the insurance trough. The health insurance pot is, apparently, infinitely elastic and must be expanded to fulfill the demands of many claimants, each of whom, considered individually, makes a compelling case. Although the ACA is less driven by the concerns of providers, it too is based on the belief that all lawful residents of the United States should have access to health insurance coverage for essential medical care.

ERISA, by contrast, sees a zero-sum game. The pot is only so big, and when it is empty, it is empty. To fudge the rules in favor of one beneficiary may result in the plan not being able to honor the legitimate claims of other beneficiaries. If one claimant treated egregiously by the plan is permitted to recover extracontractual damages from its administrator, these damages will ultimately come out of the pockets of the other beneficiaries, who have themselves done nothing wrong. As long as health insurance coverage was dependent on the generosity of employers, employees had to make do with what employers were willing to offer. In a world of scarce resources, not everyone can be taken care of. But the administrator, nevertheless, is also a fiduciary, and there are some limits to its discretion.

Reconciling ERISA with the ACA in this respect is not easy. As described above, the ACA amends ERISA and applies many of the ACA's requirements to ERISA plans. Employers are no longer completely unconstrained in their decision whether to provide employee benefits. The ACA does not require them to do so, but as described in Chapter 9, if employers fail to do so and their employees draw on the premium tax credits, the employer will owe a penalty. If an employer chooses to offer health benefits, it must comply with many ACA requirements, such as providing preventive care without cost-sharing (including contraceptives) or covering adult children up to age 26 (although many employer plans will remain grandfathered for some time and thus free from a number of these requirements). Most importantly, however, the ACA provides de novo, binding external review for ERISA plans. No longer will ERISA plan administrators have unbridled discretion to deny coverage. But what effect will this have in reality?

2. Judicial Review of Decisions of an ERISA Administrator and External Review

As noted above, the ACA requires ERISA plans, like all other health plans, to offer binding, de novo, external review. The reviewer can consider new evidence not considered by the plan decision maker below, and need not defer to the plan administrator's decision. The decision of the external reviewer is binding on the plan, and under the external review interim regulations, "binding on the plan or issuer, as well as the claimant, except to the extent other remedies are available under State or Federal law." 29 C.F.R. § 2590.715–2719(c)(xi). This federal requirement for external review would thus decide the issue in the *Moran* case if it were litigated today.

The ACA does not amend section 502 of ERISA, however, and judicial review of ERISA plan decisions will continue to be available. Pre-ACA ERISA cases involving external review decisions generally considered the decision of an external reviewer that confirmed a plan's determination to justify deference to the plan's original decision, as an external reviewer would clearly not face a conflict of interest. See Jon N. v. Blue Cross Blue Shield of Massachusetts, 684 F. Supp. 2d 190 (D. Mass. 2010), Ransteck v. Aetna Life Ins. Co., 2009 WL 1796999 (E.D.N.Y. 2009); Smith v. Blue Cross Blue Shield of Massachusetts, 597 F. Supp. 2d 214 (D. Mass. 2009). Other ERISA cases held that an external reviewer's rejection of a plan determination is additional evidence supporting a court's decision that the plan determination was arbitrary and capricious. Summers v. Touchpoint Health Plan, 749 N.W.2d 182 (2008). One court held, ingeniously, that the contractual possibility of external review justified de novo review by a court because the provision in the plan for external review negated the discretion of the plan administrator. Fry v. Regence Blueshield, 2008 WL 4223613 (W.D. Wash. 2008). Finally, one court has held that a claimant does not need to exhaust the external review remedy before filing a 502 action. Goldman v. BCBSM Foundation, 841 F. Supp. 2d 1021 (E.D. Mich. 2012).

Since the passage of the ACA, courts have begun to address the question of how the external review process interacts with ERISA preemption. For example, in Alexandra H. v. Oxford Health Ins. Inc., the 11th Circuit Court of Appeals held that, because the external review is not binding and thus does not replace or erase any ERISA remedy, ERISA did not preempt the insured from suing the insurer over the medical necessity of a procedure, even where the external review process agreed with the insurer, 833 F.3d 1299 (11th Cir. 2016).

NOTES AND QUESTIONS

1. *Extracontractual Damages Under ERISA.* Whether or not extracontractual damages (e.g., consequential or punitive damages) can ever be available under ERISA is a question that has provoked considerable

controversy. The answer seems to be no, though a good argument can be made that this is not the result Congress intended. George Flint, ERISA: Extracontractual Damages Mandated for Benefit Claims Actions, 36 Ariz. L. Rev. 611 (1994); Note, Available Remedies Under ERISA Section 502(a), 45 Ala. L. Rev. 631 (1994). In Massachusetts Mutual Life Insurance Co. v. Russell, 473 U.S. 134 (1985), the Supreme Court held that ERISA does not authorize recovery of extracontractual damages by plan participants for breach of fiduciary duty. In Mertens v. Hewitt Associates, 508 U.S. 248 (1993), the Court read provisions of ERISA permitting plan participants and beneficiaries "to obtain other appropriate equitable relief" in order to redress violations of the statute, to not authorize damage actions, as damages are not equitable in nature.

The effect of these cases is that an ERISA participant or beneficiary denied benefits can only recover the value of the claim itself and cannot recover damages caused by the claim denial. Punitive damages are also unavailable against plan administrators and fiduciaries under even the most egregious circumstances. What effect might the lack of this relief have on ERISA fiduciaries and administrators? To what extent might the fact that ERISA permits courts to award attorneys' fees in some cases ameliorate this effect? 29 U.S.C. § 1132(g). Would state tort cases against ERISA plan managed care organizations be necessary if more comprehensive remedies were available under ERISA? Arguing that many of the problems that the courts have encountered in dealing with state claims against ERISA plans could have been avoided had the Court interpreted ERISA's remedial provisions to include broader remedies, see John H. Langbein, What ERISA Means by "Equitable": The Supreme Court's Trail of Error in Russell, Mertens and Great-West, 103 Colum. L. Rev. 1317 (2003).

Attempts to obtain monetary relief in ERISA actions through traditional equitable remedies such as restitution or surcharge have failed. See, e.g., Knieriem v. Group Health Plan, Inc., 434 F.3d 1058 (8th Cir. 2006).

2. *Can Providers Sue ERISA Plans?* ERISA does not by its terms permit providers to sue plans to collect payments due them for providing services to beneficiaries. Courts have generally rejected the argument that providers are "beneficiaries" under ERISA plans. Pritt v. Blue Cross & Blue Shield of West Virginia, Inc., 699 F. Supp. 81 (S.D.W.Va.1988). Providers have been more successful in asserting their rights as assignees of participants or beneficiaries, City of Hope Nat. Med. Ctr. v. HealthPlus, Inc., 156 F.3d 223 (1st Cir. 1998); Hermann Hosp. v. MEBA Med. & Benefits Plan, 845 F.2d 1286 (5th Cir. 1988), though a few courts have held that assignees have no standing to sue as they are not mentioned as protected parties within the statute. Other courts have upheld anti-assignment clauses in plan contracts.

Courts have split on whether providers can recover from insurers when the insurer leads the provider to believe that the insured or the service is covered, and then subsequently refuses payment and claims ERISA protection. Several courts have held that ERISA is intended to control relationships between employers and employees and should not preempt common law or statutory misrepresentation claims brought by providers. Transitional Hospitals Corp. v. Blue Cross & Blue Shield of Texas, Inc., 164 F.3d 952 (5th Cir. 1999); Hospice of Metro Denver, Inc. v. Group Health Ins. of Okla., Inc., 944 F.2d 752 (10th Cir. 1991). Other courts have held that misrepresentation claims are claims for benefits that are preempted by ERISA. Cromwell v. Equicor-Equitable HCA Corp., 944 F.2d 1272 (6th Cir.1991). Finally, several courts have allowed a provider to sue an ERISA plan on a contract or state statutory claim, stating that the claim was not preempted by ERISA because the provider had no standing to sue under ERISA. See Medical and Chirurgical Faculty v. Aetna U.S. Healthcare, Inc., 221 F. Supp. 2d 618 (D.Md.2002), Foley v. Southwest Texas HMO, Inc., 226 F. Supp. 2d 886 (E.D.Tex.2002). See, generally, Scott C. Walton, Note, ERISA Preemption of Third-Party Provider Claims: A Coherent Misrepresentation of Coverage Exception, 88 Iowa L. Rev. 969 (2003); Kevin Wiggins, Medical Provider Claims: Standing, Assignments, and ERISA Preemption, 45 J. Marshall L. Rev. 861 (2012).

Courts also have held that ERISA does not preempt providers' breach of contract and promissory estoppel claims against a plan where the provider alleges that the plan agreed to pay for certain services and then reneged on the agreement. Plastic Surgery Ctr., P.A. v. Aetna Life Ins. Co., 967 F.3d 218, 223 (3d Cir. 2020) (breach of contract and promissory estoppel claims survive preemption, but unjust enrichment claim was preempted).

B. PREEMPTION OF TORT CLAIMS AGAINST HEALTH PLANS

ERISA gives beneficiaries some federal remedies against their health plans. But the statute also takes away their state remedies by complete preemption.

AETNA HEALTH INC. V. DAVILA

Supreme Court of the United States, 2004.
542 U.S. 200.

JUSTICE THOMAS delivered the opinion of the Court.

In these consolidated cases, two individuals sued their respective health maintenance organizations (HMOs) for alleged failures to exercise ordinary care in the handling of coverage decisions, in violation of a duty imposed by the Texas Health Care Liability Act (THCLA)[ ]. We granted certiorari to decide whether the individuals' causes of action are completely pre-empted by the "interlocking, interrelated, and interdependent remedial scheme,"[ ] found at § 502(a) of the Employee Retirement Income Security Act of 1974 (ERISA)[ ]. We hold that the causes of action are completely pre-empted and hence removable from state to federal court. The Court of Appeals, having reached a contrary conclusion, is reversed.

Respondent Juan Davila is a participant, and respondent Ruby Calad is a beneficiary, in ERISA-regulated employee benefit plans. Their respective plan sponsors had entered into agreements with petitioners, Aetna Health Inc. and CIGNA HealthCare of Texas, Inc., to administer the plans. Under Davila's plan, for instance, Aetna reviews requests for coverage and pays providers, such as doctors, hospitals, and nursing homes, which perform covered services for members; under Calad's plan sponsor's agreement, CIGNA is responsible for plan benefits and coverage decisions.

Respondents both suffered injuries allegedly arising from Aetna's and CIGNA's decisions not to provide coverage for certain treatment and services recommended by respondents' treating physicians. Davila's treating physician prescribed Vioxx to remedy Davila's arthritis pain, but Aetna refused to pay for it. Davila did not appeal or contest this decision, nor did he purchase Vioxx with his own resources and seek reimbursement. Instead, Davila began taking Naprosyn, from which he allegedly suffered a severe reaction that required extensive treatment and hospitalization. Calad underwent surgery, and although her treating physician recommended an extended hospital stay, a CIGNA discharge nurse determined that Calad did not meet the plan's criteria for a continued hospital stay. CIGNA consequently denied coverage for the extended hospital stay. Calad experienced postsurgery complications forcing her to return to the hospital. She alleges that these complications would not have occurred had CIGNA approved coverage for a longer hospital stay.

Respondents brought separate suits in Texas state court against petitioners. Invoking THCLA § 88.002(a), respondents argued that petitioners' refusal to cover the requested services violated their "duty to exercise ordinary care when making health care treatment decisions," and that these refusals "proximately caused" their injuries. [ ] Petitioners removed the cases to Federal District Courts, arguing that respondents' causes of action fit within the scope of, and were therefore completely pre-empted by, ERISA § 502(a). The respective District Courts agreed, and declined to remand the cases to state court. Because respondents refused to amend their complaints to bring explicit ERISA claims, the District Courts dismissed the complaints with prejudice.

Both Davila and Calad appealed . . . . The Court of Appeals [reversed].

* * *

"[W]hen a federal statute wholly displaces the state-law cause of action through complete pre-emption," the state claim can be removed.[ ] This is so because "[w]hen the federal statute completely pre-empts the state-law cause of action, a claim which comes within the scope of that cause of action, even if pleaded in terms of state law, is in reality based on federal law."[ ] ERISA is one of these statutes.

Congress enacted ERISA to "protect . . . the interests of participants in employee benefit plans and their beneficiaries" by setting out substantive regulatory requirements for employee benefit plans and to "provid[e] for appropriate remedies, sanctions, and ready access to the Federal courts."[ ]. The purpose of ERISA is to provide a uniform regulatory regime over employee benefit plans. To this end, ERISA includes expansive pre-emption provisions, see ERISA § 514,[ ], which are intended to ensure that employee benefit plan regulation would be "exclusively a federal concern."[ ]

ERISA's "comprehensive legislative scheme" includes "an integrated system of procedures for enforcement."[ ] This integrated enforcement mechanism, ERISA § 502(a),[ ] is a distinctive feature of ERISA, and essential to accomplish Congress' purpose of creating a comprehensive statute for the regulation of employee benefit plans. As the Court said in *Pilot Life Ins. Co. v. Dedeaux,*[ ]:

> "[T]he detailed provisions of § 502(a) set forth a comprehensive civil enforcement scheme that represents a careful balancing of the need for prompt and fair claims settlement procedures against the public interest in encouraging the formation of employee benefit plans. The policy choices reflected in the inclusion of certain remedies and the exclusion of others under the federal scheme would be completely undermined if ERISA-plan participants and beneficiaries were free to obtain remedies under state law that Congress rejected in ERISA. 'The six carefully integrated civil enforcement provisions found in § 502(a) of the statute as finally enacted . . . provide strong evidence that Congress did *not* intend to authorize other remedies that it simply forgot to incorporate expressly.' "[ ]

Therefore, any state-law cause of action that duplicates, supplements, or supplants the ERISA civil enforcement remedy conflicts with the clear congressional intent to make the ERISA remedy exclusive and is therefore pre-empted.[ ]

The pre-emptive force of ERISA § 502(a) is still stronger. In *Metropolitan Life Ins. Co. v. Taylor,*[ ] the Court determined that the similarity of the language used in the Labor Management Relations Act, 1947 (LMRA), and ERISA, combined with the "clear intention" of Congress "to make § 502(a)(1)(B) suits brought by participants or beneficiaries federal questions for the purposes of federal court jurisdiction in like manner as § 301 of the LMRA," established that ERISA § 502(a)(1)(B)'s pre-emptive force mirrored the pre-emptive force of LMRA § 301. Since LMRA § 301 converts state causes of action into federal ones for purposes of determining the propriety of removal,[ ] so too does ERISA § 502(a)(1)(B). Thus, the ERISA civil enforcement mechanism is one of those provisions with such "extraordinary pre-emptive power" that it "converts an ordinary state common law complaint into one stating a federal claim for purposes of the well-pleaded complaint rule."[ ] Hence, "causes of action within the scope of the civil enforcement provisions of § 502(a) [are] removable to federal court."[ ]

ERISA § 502(a)(1)(B) provides:

"A civil action may be brought—(1) by a participant or beneficiary— . . . (B) to recover benefits due to him under the terms of his plan, to enforce his rights under the terms of the plan, or to clarify his rights to future benefits under the terms of the plan."[ ]

This provision is relatively straightforward. If a participant or beneficiary believes that benefits promised to him under the terms of the plan are not provided, he can bring suit seeking provision of those benefits. A participant or beneficiary can also bring suit generically to "enforce his rights" under the plan, or to clarify any of his rights to future benefits. Any dispute over the precise terms of the plan is resolved by a court under a *de novo* review standard, unless the terms of the plan "giv[e] the administrator or fiduciary discretionary authority to determine eligibility for benefits or to construe the terms of the plan."[ ]

It follows that if an individual brings suit complaining of a denial of coverage for medical care, where the individual is entitled to such coverage only because of the terms of an ERISA-regulated employee benefit plan, and where no legal duty (state or federal) independent of ERISA or the plan terms is violated, then the suit falls "within the scope of" ERISA § 502(a)(1)(B)[ ]. In other words, if an individual, at some point in time, could have brought his claim under ERISA § 502(a)(1)(B), and where there is no other independent legal duty that is implicated by a defendant's actions, then the individual's cause of action is completely pre-empted by ERISA § 502(a)(1)(B).

To determine whether respondents' causes of action fall "within the scope" of ERISA § 502(a)(1)(B), we must examine respondents' complaints, the statute on which their claims are based (the THCLA), and the various plan documents. Davila alleges that Aetna provides health coverage under his employer's health benefits plan.[ ]. Davila also alleges that after his primary care physician prescribed Vioxx, Aetna refused to pay for it.[ ]. The only action complained of was Aetna's refusal to approve payment for Davila's Vioxx prescription. Further, the only relationship Aetna had with Davila was its partial administration of Davila's employer's benefit plan.[ ].

Similarly, Calad alleges that she receives, as her husband's beneficiary under an ERISA-regulated benefit plan, health coverage from CIGNA.[ ]. She alleges that she was informed by CIGNA, upon admittance into a hospital for major surgery, that she would be authorized to stay for only one day.[ ] She also alleges that CIGNA, acting through a discharge nurse, refused to authorize more than a single day despite the advice and recommendation of her treating physician.[ ] Calad contests only CIGNA's decision to refuse coverage for her hospital stay.[ ] And, as in Davila's case, the only connection between Calad and CIGNA is CIGNA's administration of portions of Calad's ERISA-regulated benefit plan.[ ].

It is clear, then, that respondents complain only about denials of coverage promised under the terms of ERISA-regulated employee benefit plans. Upon the denial of benefits, respondents could have paid for the treatment themselves and then sought reimbursement through a § 502(a)(1)(B) action, or sought a preliminary injunction,[ ].

Respondents contend, however, that the complained-of actions violate legal duties that arise independently of ERISA or the terms of the employee benefit plans at issue in these cases. Both respondents brought suit specifically under the THCLA, alleging that petitioners "controlled, influenced, participated in and made decisions which affected the quality of the diagnosis, care, and treatment provided" in a manner that violated "the duty of ordinary care set forth in §§ 88.001 and 88.002."[ ] Respondents contend that this duty of ordinary care is an independent legal duty.... Because this duty of ordinary care arises independently of any duty imposed by ERISA or the plan terms, the argument goes, any civil action to enforce this duty is not within the scope of the ERISA civil enforcement mechanism.

The duties imposed by the THCLA in the context of these cases, however, do not arise independently of ERISA or the plan terms. The THCLA does impose a duty on managed care entities to "exercise ordinary care when making health care treatment decisions," and makes them liable for damages proximately caused by failures to abide by that duty.[ ] However, if a managed care entity correctly concluded that, under the terms of the relevant plan, a particular treatment was not covered, the managed care entity's denial of coverage would not be a proximate cause of any injuries arising from the denial. Rather, the failure of the plan itself to cover the requested treatment would be the proximate cause.[3] More significantly, the THCLA clearly states that "[t]he standards in Subsections (a) and (b) create no obligation on the part of the health insurance carrier, health maintenance organization, or other managed care entity to provide to an insured or enrollee treatment which is not covered by the health care plan of the entity."[ ] Hence, a managed care entity could not be subject to liability under the THCLA if it denied coverage for any treatment not covered by the health care plan that it was administering.

Thus, interpretation of the terms of respondents' benefit plans forms an essential part of their THCLA claim, and THCLA liability would exist

---

[3] To take a clear example, if the terms of the health care plan specifically exclude from coverage the cost of an appendectomy, then any injuries caused by the refusal to cover the appendectomy are properly attributed to the terms of the plan itself, not the managed care entity that applied those terms.

here only because of petitioners' administration of ERISA-regulated benefit plans. Petitioners' potential liability under the THCLA in these cases, then, derives entirely from the particular rights and obligations established by the benefit plans. So, . . . respondents' THCLA causes of action are not entirely independent of the federally regulated contract itself.[ ].

Hence, respondents bring suit only to rectify a wrongful denial of benefits promised under ERISA-regulated plans, and do not attempt to remedy any violation of a legal duty independent of ERISA. We hold that respondents' state causes of action fall "within the scope of" ERISA § 502(a)(1)(B),[ ] and are therefore completely pre-empted by ERISA § 502 and removable to federal district court.[4]

The Court of Appeals came to a contrary conclusion for several reasons, all of them erroneous. First, the Court of Appeals found significant that respondents "assert a tort claim for tort damages" rather than "a contract claim for contract damages," and that respondents "are not seeking reimbursement for benefits denied them."[ ] But, distinguishing between pre-empted and non-pre-empted claims based on the particular label affixed to them would "elevate form over substance and allow parties to evade" the pre-emptive scope of ERISA simply "by relabeling their contract claims as claims for tortious breach of contract." . . . [ ]. Nor can the mere fact that the state cause of action attempts to authorize remedies beyond those authorized by ERISA § 502(a) put the cause of action outside the scope of the ERISA civil enforcement mechanism. In *Pilot Life, Metropolitan Life,* and *Ingersoll-Rand,* the plaintiffs all brought state claims that were labeled either tort or tort-like.[ ] And, the plaintiffs in these three cases all sought remedies beyond those authorized under ERISA.[ ] And, in all these cases, the plaintiffs' claims were pre-empted. The limited remedies available under ERISA are an inherent part of the "careful balancing" between ensuring fair and prompt enforcement of rights under a plan and the encouragement of the creation of such plans. [ ].

Second, the Court of Appeals believed that "the wording of [respondents'] plans is immaterial" to their claims, as "they invoke an external, statutorily imposed duty of 'ordinary care.' "[ ] But as we have already discussed, the wording of the plans is certainly material to their state causes of action, and the duty of "ordinary care" that the THCLA creates is not external to their rights under their respective plans.

Ultimately, the Court of Appeals rested its decision on one line from *Rush Prudential.* . . . Nowhere in *Rush Prudential* did we suggest that the

---

4 Respondents also argue that ERISA § 502(a) completely pre-empts a state cause of action only if the cause of action would be pre-empted under ERISA § 514(a); respondents then argue that their causes of action do not fall under the terms of § 514(a). But a state cause of action that provides an alternative remedy to those provided by the ERISA civil enforcement mechanism conflicts with Congress' clear intent to make the ERISA mechanism exclusive.[ ].

pre-emptive force of ERISA § 502(a) is limited to the situation in which a state cause of action precisely duplicates a cause of action under ERISA § 502(a).

Nor would it be consistent with our precedent to conclude that only strictly duplicative state causes of action are pre-empted.... Congress' intent to make the ERISA civil enforcement mechanism exclusive would be undermined if state causes of action that supplement the ERISA § 502(a) remedies were permitted, even if the elements of the state cause of action did not precisely duplicate the elements of an ERISA claim.

Respondents also argue ... that the THCLA is a law that regulates insurance, and hence that ERISA § 514(b)(2)(A) saves their causes of action from pre-emption (and thereby from complete pre-emption).[5] This argument is unavailing. The existence of a comprehensive remedial scheme can demonstrate an "overpowering federal policy" that determines the interpretation of a statutory provision designed to save state law from being pre-empted.[ ] ERISA's civil enforcement provision is one such example.[ ]

As this Court stated in *Pilot Life*, "our understanding of [§ 514(b)(2)(A)] must be informed by the legislative intent concerning the civil enforcement provisions provided by ERISA § 502(a).[ ]" The Court concluded that "[t]he policy choices reflected in the inclusion of certain remedies and the exclusion of others under the federal scheme would be completely undermined if ERISA-plan participants and beneficiaries were free to obtain remedies under state law that Congress rejected in ERISA."[ ] The Court then held, based on

"the common-sense understanding of the saving clause, the ... Act factors defining the business of insurance, and, *most importantly,* the clear expression of congressional intent that ERISA's civil enforcement scheme be exclusive, ... that [the plaintiff's] state law suit asserting improper processing of a claim for benefits under an ERISA-regulated plan is not saved by § 514(b)(2)(A)."[ ]

Pilot Life's reasoning applies here with full force. Allowing respondents to proceed with their state-law suits would "pose an obstacle to the purposes and objectives of Congress."[ ] As this Court has recognized in both *Rush Prudential* and *Pilot Life,* ERISA § 514(b)(2)(A) must be interpreted in light of the congressional intent to create an exclusive federal remedy in ERISA § 502(a). Under ordinary principles of conflict pre-emption, then, even a state law that can arguably be characterized as "regulating insurance" will be pre-empted if it provides a separate vehicle

---

[5]   ERISA § 514(b)(2)(A)[ ] reads, as relevant: "["[N]othing in this subchapter shall be construed to exempt or relieve any person from any law of any State which regulates insurance, banking, or securities."]."

to assert a claim for benefits outside of, or in addition to, ERISA's remedial scheme.

Respondents, their *amici,* and some Courts of Appeals have relied heavily upon *Pegram v. Herdrich,*[ ], in arguing that ERISA does not pre-empt or completely pre-empt state suits such as respondents'. They contend that *Pegram* makes it clear that causes of action such as respondents' do not "relate to [an] employee benefit plan," ERISA § 514(a),[ ] and hence are not pre-empted.[ ]

Pegram cannot be read so broadly. In *Pegram,* the plaintiff sued her physician-owned-and-operated HMO (which provided medical coverage through plaintiff's employer pursuant to an ERISA-regulated benefit plan) and her treating physician, both for medical malpractice and for a breach of an ERISA fiduciary duty.[ ] The plaintiff's treating physician was also the person charged with administering plaintiff's benefits; it was she who decided whether certain treatments were covered.[ ] We reasoned that the physician's "eligibility decision and the treatment decision were inextricably mixed."[ ] We concluded that "Congress did not intend [the defendant HMO] or any other HMO to be treated as a fiduciary to the extent that it makes mixed eligibility decisions acting through its physicians."[ ]

A benefit determination under ERISA, though, is generally a fiduciary act.[ ] "At common law, fiduciary duties characteristically attach to decisions about managing assets and distributing property to beneficiaries."[ ] Hence, a benefit determination is part and parcel of the ordinary fiduciary responsibilities connected to the administration of a plan.[ ] The fact that a benefits determination is infused with medical judgments does not alter this result.

Pegram itself recognized this principle. *Pegram,* in highlighting its conclusion that "mixed eligibility decisions" were not fiduciary in nature, contrasted the operation of "[t]raditional trustees administer[ing] a medical trust" and "physicians through whom HMOs act."[ ] A traditional medical trust is administered by "paying out money to buy medical care, whereas physicians making mixed eligibility decisions consume the money as well."[ ] And, significantly, the Court stated that "[p]rivate trustees do not make treatment judgments."[ ] But a trustee managing a medical trust undoubtedly must make administrative decisions that require the exercise of medical judgment. Petitioners are not the employers of respondents' treating physicians and are therefore in a somewhat analogous position to that of a trustee for a traditional medical trust.

ERISA itself and its implementing regulations confirm this interpretation. ERISA defines a fiduciary as any person "to the extent . . . he has any discretionary authority or discretionary responsibility in the administration of [an employee benefit] plan.[ ]. When administering employee benefit plans, HMOs must make discretionary decisions regarding eligibility for plan benefits, and, in this regard, must be treated as plan fiduciaries.[ ]" Also, ERISA § 503, which specifies minimum requirements for a plan's claim procedure, requires plans to "afford a reasonable opportunity to any participant whose claim for benefits has been denied for a full and fair review by the appropriate named fiduciary of the decision denying the claim."[ ] This strongly suggests that the ultimate decisionmaker in a plan regarding an award of benefits must be a fiduciary and must be acting as a fiduciary when determining a participant's or beneficiary's claim. The relevant regulations also establish extensive requirements to ensure full and fair review of benefit denials.[ ] These regulations, on their face, apply equally to health benefit plans and other plans, and do not draw distinctions between medical and nonmedical benefits determinations. Indeed, the regulations strongly imply that benefits determinations involving medical judgments are, just as much as any other benefits determinations, actions by plan fiduciaries.[ ] Classifying any entity with discretionary authority over benefits determinations as anything but a plan fiduciary would thus conflict with ERISA's statutory and regulatory scheme.

Since administrators making benefits determinations, even determinations based extensively on medical judgments, are ordinarily acting as plan fiduciaries, it was essential to *Pegram*'s conclusion that the decisions challenged there were truly "mixed eligibility and treatment decisions,"[ ], i.e., medical necessity decisions made by the plaintiff's treating physician *qua* treating physician and *qua* benefits administrator. Put another way, the reasoning of *Pegram* "only make[s] sense where the underlying negligence also plausibly constitutes medical maltreatment by a party who can be deemed to be a treating physician or such a physician's employer."[ ] Here, however, petitioners are neither respondents' treating physicians nor the employers of respondents' treating physicians. Petitioners' coverage decisions, then, are pure eligibility decisions, and *Pegram* is not implicated.

We hold that respondents' causes of action, brought to remedy only the denial of benefits under ERISA-regulated benefit plans, fall within the scope of, and are completely pre-empted by, ERISA § 502(a)(1)(B), and thus removable to federal district court. The judgment of the Court of Appeals is reversed, and the cases are remanded for further proceedings consistent with this opinion.[7]

---

[7] The United States, as *amicus,* suggests that some individuals in respondents' positions could possibly receive some form of "make-whole" relief under ERISA § 502(a)(3).[ ] However, after their respective District Courts denied their motions for remand, respondents had the opportunity to amend their complaints to bring expressly a claim under ERISA § 502(a). Respondents declined to do so; the District Courts therefore dismissed their complaints with prejudice.[ ] Respondents have thus chosen not to pursue any ERISA claim, including any claim arising under ERISA § 502(a)(3). The scope of this provision, then, is not before us, and we do not address it.

It is so ordered.

NOTES AND QUESTIONS

1.   *The ERISA Vacuum.* What state law claims are left to plaintiff employee benefit plan subscribers after *Davila*? In general, *Davila* leaves a "regulatory vacuum" in which consumers have no remedies if they are injured as the result of health care provided through ERISA plans. It would seem to allow tort actions for direct or vicarious liability only for physician-owned and operated managed care plans. And these are not the norm. The typical health plan today is an insurance vehicle that imposes coverage constraints on providers in its network, and would not be subject to tort liability. *Davila* does state that ERISA plan administrators are fiduciaries as to coverage decisions. But it does not explicitly recognize a cause of action for damages for breach of fiduciary duty, which earlier cases would seem to have foreclosed.

For more on ERISA preemption of managed care liability after *Davila*, see Timothy S. Jost, The Supreme Court Limits Lawsuits Against Managed Care Organizations, Health Affairs Web Exclusive 4–417 (11 August 2004); Theodore W. Ruger, The Supreme Court Federalizes Managed Care Liability, 32 J.L. Med. & Ethics 528, 529 (2004) (criticizing the current ERISA enforcement scheme as crabbed and penurious, failing to serve remedial goals of either tort or contract.) For a full discussion of litigation leading up to *Davila*, see generally Margaret Cyr-Provost, Aetna v. Davila: From Patient-Centered Care to Plan-Centered Care, A Signpost or the End of the Road?, 6 Hous. J. Health L. & Pol'y 171 (2005); M. Gregg Bloche and David Studdert, A Quiet Revolution: Law as an Agent of Health System Change, 23 Health Affairs 2942 (2004). See also Peter Jacobson, Strangers in the Night (New York: Oxford, 2002).

2.   *Limits of § 502 Preemption of State Tort Claims.* In the first wave of litigation, federal courts interpreted ERISA as totally preempting common law tort claims. See, e.g., Ricci v. Gooberman, 840 F. Supp. 316 (D.N.J.1993). It appeared from this caselaw that any managed care plan that was ERISA-qualified would receive virtually complete tort immunity. In the 1990s, however, the federal courts began to split as to the limits of such preemption. The result was a litigation explosion against managed care plans as theories were imported from hospital liability case law, fiduciary law, and contract law to use against managed care organizations.

Dukes v. U.S. Healthcare, Inc., 57 F.3d 350 (3d Cir.1995) was the watershed case that opened up a major crack in ERISA preemption of common law tort claims. In *Dukes*, the Third Circuit found that Congress, in passing ERISA, intended to ensure that promised benefits would be available to plan participants, and that § 502(a) was "intended to provide each individual participant with a remedy in the event that promises made by the plan were not kept." The court was unwilling, however, to stretch the remedies of § 502(a) to "control the quality of the benefits received by plan participants." The court concluded that " . . . [q]uality control of benefits, such as the health care benefits provided here, is a field traditionally occupied by state regulation and we interpret the silence of Congress as reflecting an intent that it remain such." The court developed the distinction between a right to benefits under a plan and a right to good quality care, holding that " . . . patients enjoy the right to be free from medical malpractice regardless of whether or not their medical care is provided through an ERISA plan." Quality of care could be so poor that it is essentially a denial of benefits. Or the plan could describe a benefit in terms that are quality-based, such as a commitment that all x-rays will be analyzed by radiologists with a certain level of training. But absent either of these extremes, poor medical care—malpractice—is not a benefits issue under ERISA.

3. *Tort Claims That Survive* Davila. Tort cases against managed care plans are not entirely dead after *Davila*. Consider Smelik v. Mann, Texas Dist. Ct. (224th Jud. Dist., Bexar Co. No. 03-CI-06936 2006), where a Texas jury awarded $7.4 million in actual damages to the family of an HMO participant who died from complications of acute renal failure. The jury found Humana liable for 35% of the $7.4 million in actual damages for negligence, but found no evidence that Humana committed fraud. The jury also determined that Humana's behavior was consistent with gross negligence, and the company stipulated to $1.6 million in punitive damages pursuant to an out-of-court agreement. Humana was found to be responsible for a total of $4.2 million.

The plaintiff in *Smelik* argued that Humana was liable for "mismanaged managed care," or negligence in the coordination of medical care, rather than for a denial of medical care, as in *Davila*, and thus ERISA did not apply. Plaintiffs convinced the jury that Humana failed to follow its own utilization management policies, failing to refer Smelik to a kidney specialist or to its disease management program. Plaintiffs also established that Humana negligently approved payment for a combination of drugs considered dangerous for patients with kidney problems.

Vicarious liability also remains a viable theory post-*Davila*. In Badal v. Hinsdale Memorial Hospital, 2007 WL 1424205 (N.D.Ill.2007), plaintiff's injured ankle was misdiagnosed by a plan physician as only a "sprain," causing serious injury. The court analyzed ERISA preemption arguments in light of *Davila*. The court noted that the plaintiff's claims under *Davila* were brought under the Texas Health Care Liability Act (THCLA) and asserted duties that did not arise independently of ERISA or the plan terms. *Davila* was about wrongful denial of benefits. In *Badal*, by contrast, the plaintiff alleged that "[w]hile committing the above acts and omissions, Dr. Lofthouse failed to apply, use or exercise the standard of care ordinarily exercised by reasonably well qualified or competent medical doctors." The court noted that the plaintiff was not complaining of the wrongful denial of benefits, quoting the plaintiff: "Plaintiff is asking for damages for the injuries caused, and does not give one iota if it was covered under the plan, or whether it should in the future be covered under some plan[ ]. In short, whether or not it was a violation of ERISA is of no concern to plaintiff."

PROBLEM: ERISA LITIGATION

John Mendez is in the advanced stages of a condition that results in degeneration of his nervous system. His doctor believes that a new gene therapy would help him. John is covered under his employer's self-insured employee benefits plan. The plan has denied coverage for the therapy, claiming that it is experimental. The terms of the plan give the administrator discretion to decide whether or not to cover experimental procedures, but the plan does not define "experimental." John's doctor claims that the procedure is still quite new, but has advanced beyond the experimental stage. What standard will a court apply in reviewing the administrator's decision if John sues under § 502? How does this standard differ from that which a court would have applied had John sued an insurer under an individual health insurance policy under standard state insurance contract law?

C. ERISA FIDUCIARY DUTY CLAIMS

The Supreme Court in *Davila* discusses at some length its earlier decision in Pegram v. Herdrich, 530 U.S. 211 (2000). In *Pegram*, an ERISA plan beneficiary, Louise Herdrich, sued the HMO administering her husband's employee benefit plans, claiming (among other theories) breach of fiduciary duty under ERISA when she suffered an undiagnosed ruptured appendix that caused peritonitis. She alleged:

> . . . that provision of medical services under the terms of the Carle HMO organization, rewarding its physician owners for limiting medical care, entailed an inherent or anticipatory breach of an ERISA fiduciary duty, since these terms created an incentive to make decisions in the physicians' self-interest, rather than the exclusive interests of plan participants."

She claimed:

> . . . that provision of medical services under the terms of the Carle HMO organization, rewarding its physician owners for limiting medical care, entailed an inherent or anticipatory breach of an ERISA fiduciary duty, since these terms created an incentive to make decisions in the physicians' self-interest, rather than the exclusive interests of plan participants."

The court noted that:

> Although it is true that the relationship between sparing medical treatment and physician reward is not a subtle one under the Carle scheme, no HMO organization could survive without some incentive connecting physician reward with treatment rationing. The essence of an HMO is that salaries and profits are limited by the HMO's fixed membership fees.[ ] This is not to suggest that the Carle provisions are as socially desirable as some other HMO organizational schemes; they

may not be.[ ] But whatever the HMO, there must be rationing and inducement to ration.

The Court observed, however, that Congress had not intended to outlaw HMOs when it enacted ERISA (federal legislation encouraging HMOs had been adopted three years earlier), and that the Court was not in a position to distinguish between good and bad HMOs.

The Court stated:

[ERISA] provides that fiduciaries shall discharge their duties with respect to a plan "solely in the interest of the participants and beneficiaries," § 1104(a)(1), that is, "for the exclusive purpose of (i) providing benefits to participants and their beneficiaries; and (ii) defraying reasonable expenses of administering the plan," § 1104(a)(1)(A).

The Court further compared ERISA fiduciary obligations to fiduciary obligations at the common law, but then observed:

Beyond the threshold statement of responsibility, however, the analogy between ERISA fiduciary and common law trustee becomes problematic. This is so because the trustee at common law characteristically wears only his fiduciary hat when he takes action to affect a beneficiary, whereas the trustee under ERISA may wear different hats.

. . . Under ERISA, however, a fiduciary may have financial interests adverse to beneficiaries. Employers, for example, can be ERISA fiduciaries and still take actions to the disadvantage of employee beneficiaries, when they act as employers (e.g., firing a beneficiary for reasons unrelated to the ERISA plan), or even as plan sponsors (e.g., modifying the terms of a plan as allowed by ERISA to provide less generous benefits). . . .

ERISA does require, however, that the fiduciary with two hats wear only one at a time, and wear the fiduciary hat when making fiduciary decisions. . . . In every case charging breach of ERISA fiduciary duty, then, the threshold question is not whether the actions of some person employed to provide services under a plan adversely affected a plan beneficiary's interest, but whether that person was acting as a fiduciary (that is, was performing a fiduciary function) when taking the action subject to complaint.

The Court proceeded to say:

The nub of the claim, then, is that when State Farm contracted with Carle, Carle became a fiduciary under the plan, acting through its physicians. At once, Carle as fiduciary administrator was subject to such influence from the year-end payout provision that its fiduciary capacity was necessarily compromised, and its readiness to act amounted to anticipatory breach of fiduciary obligation.

The pleadings must also be parsed very carefully to understand what acts by physician owners acting on Carle's behalf are alleged to be fiduciary in nature. It will help to keep two sorts of arguably administrative acts in mind. Cf. Dukes v. U.S. Healthcare, Inc., 57 F.3d 350, 361 (C.A.3 1995) (discussing dual medical/administrative roles of HMOs). What we will call pure "eligibility decisions" turn on the plan's coverage of a particular condition or medical procedure for its treatment. "Treatment decisions," by contrast, are choices about how to go about diagnosing and treating a patient's condition: given a patient's constellation of symptoms, what is the appropriate medical response?

These decisions are often practically inextricable from one another, as amici on both sides agree.[ ] This is so not merely because, under a scheme like Carle's, treatment and eligibility decisions are made by the same person, the treating physician. It is so because a great many and possibly most coverage questions are not simple yes-or-no questions, like whether appendicitis is a covered condition (when there is no dispute that a patient has appendicitis), or whether acupuncture is a covered procedure for pain relief (when the claim of pain is unchallenged). The more common coverage question is a when-and-how question. Although coverage for many conditions will be clear and various treatment options will be indisputably compensable, physicians still must decide what to do in particular cases. The issue may be, say, whether one treatment option is so superior to another under the circumstances, and needed so promptly, that a decision to proceed with it would meet the medical necessity requirement that conditions the HMO's obligation to provide or pay for that particular procedure at that time in that case. . . . In practical terms, these eligibility decisions cannot be untangled from physicians' judgments about reasonable medical treatment, and in the case before us, Dr. Pegram's decision was one of that sort. She decided (wrongly, as it turned out) that Herdrich's condition did not warrant immediate action; the consequence of that medical determination was that Carle would not cover immediate care, whereas it would have done so if Dr. Pegram had made the proper diagnosis and judgment to treat. The eligibility decision and the treatment decision were inextricably mixed, as they are in countless medical administrative decisions every day.

The kinds of decisions mentioned in Herdrich's ERISA count and claimed to be fiduciary in character are just such mixed eligibility and treatment decisions: physicians' conclusions about when to use diagnostic tests; about seeking consultations and making referrals to physicians and facilities other than Carle's; about proper standards of care, the experimental character of a proposed course of treatment, the reasonableness of a certain treatment, and the emergency character of a medical condition.

We do not read the ERISA count, however, as alleging fiduciary breach with reference to a different variety of administrative decisions, those we have called pure eligibility determinations, such as whether a plan covers an undisputed case of appendicitis. Nor do we read it as claiming breach by reference to discrete administrative decisions separate from medical judgments; say, rejecting a claim for no other reason than the HMO's financial condition. . . .

Based on our understanding of the matters just discussed, we think Congress did not intend Carle or any other HMO to be treated as a fiduciary to the extent that it makes mixed eligibility decisions acting through its physicians. . . .

The Court held that such mixed decisions were not fiduciary decisions, but were rather questions of reasonable medical judgment. It suggested that poor decisions were better addressed by state malpractice law, and there was nothing to be gained by challenging them through ERISA fiduciary litigation. It is this language that the plaintiffs invoked in *Davila*.

NOTES AND QUESTIONS

1.   *Remedy for Fiduciary Duty Claims.* One of the underlying puzzles of *Pegram* is the question of remedy. The law was clear at the time *Pegram* was brought that breach of the fiduciary obligations imposed by ERISA could only result in recoveries for the benefit of the plan, not for individual participants. Ms. Herdrich herself did not stand to benefit individually from her lawsuit. Massachusetts Mut. Life Ins. Co. v. Russell, 473 U.S. 134 (1985). In LaRue v. DeWolff, Boberg & Associates, Inc., 552 U.S. 248 (2008), however, the Supreme Court held that a member of a defined contribution pension plan could sue under ERISA for individual relief for a breach of fiduciary duty affecting his individual account. If employee health benefits move from a defined benefit to a defined contribution model (for example, though increased use of health reimbursement accounts), claims for individual relief for breach of ERISA fiduciary duties might become more common.

2.   *Relationship Between* Davila *and* Pegram. Does *Davila* close the door to malpractice claims against HMOs potentially opened by *Pegram*? Does it reopen the door to fiduciary duty claims?

3.   *Plan Administrators as Fiduciaries?* Should ERISA plan administrators be considered to be fiduciaries with respect to their beneficiaries, or should they rather be considered to be arms-length contractors? If plan administrators are considered to be fiduciaries, should fiduciary obligations only extend to management of trust funds, or should they

also extend to provision of medical treatment? Should employment-related plans have obligations beyond those imposed on non-group insurance plans? Should employers have fiduciary obligations to their employees in the selection of health insurers, benefit plans, and benefits, and how should these obligations be reconciled with obligations to shareholders/owners?

CHAPTER SUMMARY PROBLEM—ERISA PREEMPTION

Two years ago, as part of a comprehensive managed care reform statute, the state adopted two new regulatory provisions that apply to all health insurance plans in the state, including all employee health benefit plans.

The first provides that all health insurance plans must cover all care that is "medically necessary." It defines "medically necessary" to include any care recommended by a plan member's treating physician that is recognized as "standard" by at least a "respectable minority" of physicians.

The second provides a cause of action under state law that allows any plan member who has been denied payment for services by a plan determined by external review to be medically necessary (in accordance with the external review requirements of the ACA) to sue the plan in state court for injunctive relief, and also for any consequential damages attributable to the plan's service denial.

The National Association of Health Insurance Plans (NAHIP) has sued in federal court asking the court to declare the two provisions preempted by and unenforceable under ERISA.

1. Is the statutory provision that requires all health plans to cover all "medically necessary" care preempted by ERISA?

2. Is the statutory provision that creates a state law cause of action for damages and injunctive relief for denials of medically necessary care preempted by ERISA?

3. If Joe Smith is denied coverage by his employee health benefit plan (which is not self-insured) of services determined to be medically necessary, what are Joe's available remedies against the health plan? What are his remedies if the plan is self-funded?

CHAPTER 9

THE REGULATION OF INSURANCE

...

Private health insurance in the United States is regulated by a complex mix of federal and state laws. While state law plays a longstanding and important role, the enactment of the Patient Protection and Affordable Care Act (ACA) in 2010 marked the start of a new era of federal health insurance regulation. The ACA supplied a federal administrative infrastructure and baseline rules for insurance sold in the individual market, as well as federally subsidizing that insurance and adding to the federal regulation of employer-sponsored group plans.

As of the time of this edition, the ACA's federal insurance regulation framework has endured through three different presidential administrations, eleven Congresses, and numerous challenges in the Supreme Court. Legal and political challenges have altered some of the law's key provisions and weakened others, keeping health reform in a constant state of change and uncertainty since 2010. While this uncertainty has caused significant anxiety for individuals and frustration for insurers, the political wrangling during the ACA's first decade provides the opportunity to examine the range of health reform tools discussed in Chapter 7 and analyze their actual and potential impacts.

This chapter surveys the laws governing private health insurance and so examines the initiatives that the federal and state governments have pursued to reform this part of our health care system, as outlined in Chapter 7. The chapter begins with a description and analysis of the major features of the ACA—the most comprehensive of these reform efforts—and then examines the political and legal challenges mounted against it. Finally, the chapter considers other federal and state laws that regulate health insurance and managed care, with the exception of ERISA which is discussed in Chapter 8, and anti-discrimination laws detailed in Chapter 6. As you read these materials, consider what policy goals appear most important to the drafters of the reforms and what types of tools they are using to accomplish their goals.

I. THE PATIENT PROTECTION AND AFFORDABLE CARE ACT

President Barack Obama signed the ACA into law on March 23, 2010. At over 900 pages long, the ACA is the most comprehensive health reform legislation the U.S. has seen in over two generations. The ACA responded to cost and affordability crises in the U.S. health care system, focusing on the role of health insurance.

In the decade before the ACA, most Americans could not afford medical care without health insurance, and many who needed care the most due to pre-existing conditions could not afford insurance. Nearly 50 million people (more than 16% of the population) were uninsured—too young for Medicare, not eligible for Medicaid, not covered by an employer-sponsored health plan, and unable to afford insurance in the individual market. Among the privately-insured, 25 million had coverage that did not adequately protect them from high medical expenses, making them underinsured. By 2007, "nearly two-thirds of adults, or 116 million people, were either uninsured for a time during the year, were underinsured, reported a problem paying medical bills, and/or said they did not get needed health care because of cost." Sheila Rustgi, Michelle M. Doty, Sara R. Collins, & Jennifer L. Kriss, Losing Ground: How the Loss of Adequate Health Insurance Is Burdening Working Families—Findings from the Commonwealth Fund Biennial Health Insurance Surveys, 2001–2007 (Aug. 1, 2008). The gaps in coverage and care were particularly pronounced in communities of color, driving disparities in health outcomes and exacerbating economic inequality. See Thomas C. Buchmueller, Zachary M. Levinson, Helen G. Levy, & Barbara L. Wolfe, Effect of the Affordable Care Act on Racial and Ethnic Disparities in Health Insurance Coverage, 106 Am. J. Pub. Health 1416 (Aug. 2016).

In the decade before the ACA, medical bills grew to cause the majority of personal bankruptcy filings. David U. Himmelstein, Deborah Thorne, Elizabeth Warren, & Steffie Woolhandler, Medical Bankruptcy in the United States, 2007: Results of a National Study, 122 AM. J. MED. 741 (Aug. 2009). Beyond this toll on individuals, households, and communities, health care consumed 17% of the U.S. gross domestic product while costs rose far faster than general inflation rates or economic growth.

Although the ACA significantly changed the landscape of U.S. health policy, Congress built it on the fragmented, complex, and imperfect system that already existed. Thus, the ACA itself is fragmented, complex, and imperfect. Nevertheless, the ACA attempted to achieve the "triple aim" of health care discussed in Chapter 7: improving the health of populations (access), reducing per capita costs (cost), and improving care (quality). The ACA focused primarily on expanding access to *insurance* to pay for health care as a determining factor for access to care itself. The statute approached the goal of universal health insurance coverage by making the existing sources of public and private insurance more widely available and affordable, and creating some federal baseline regulations for private insurance. Title II of the ACA made public insurance available to new populations by expanding the Medicaid program, as detailed in Chapter

10. Title I made private insurance available to new populations by subsidizing the cost of insurance for individuals and small businesses, requiring private insurers to cover dependents up to age 26 and people with pre-existing medical conditions, prohibiting medical underwriting, and creating a federally-regulated marketplace for individual and small group insurance plans. Title I also encouraged uninsured individuals to get insured or face a tax penalty, and similarly encouraged larger businesses to offer their employees group health insurance to avoid a tax.

Together, these expansions of public and private insurance access contributed to the ACA's most tangible accomplishment: extending meaningful health insurance coverage to 20 million individuals, bringing the percentage of uninsured people in the U.S. to 9% in 2016—the lowest percentage on record. Robin E. Cohen et al., Nat'l Center for Health Statistics, Health Insurance Coverage: Early Release of Estimates from the National Health Interview Survey, 2016 (May 2017). The overall drop in the percentage uninsured belies some significant variations over time and between populations.

The uninsured rate dropped most noticeably when the ACA's insurance provisions became effective with the extension of dependent coverage starting in 2013 and the subsidies, marketplace, pre-existing condition protection, mandate, and Medicaid expansion provisions starting in 2014. Political changes gave opponents of the ACA control of the federal Executive and Legislative branches in 2017, reversing the downward trend of the uninsured rate. The arrival of the coronavirus pandemic in the U.S. in early 2020 and the change in political control of the Executive and Legislative branches at the start of 2021 further influenced the uninsured rate in ways that current future data analyses will strive to capture. As HHS's Office of Health Policy has illustrated:

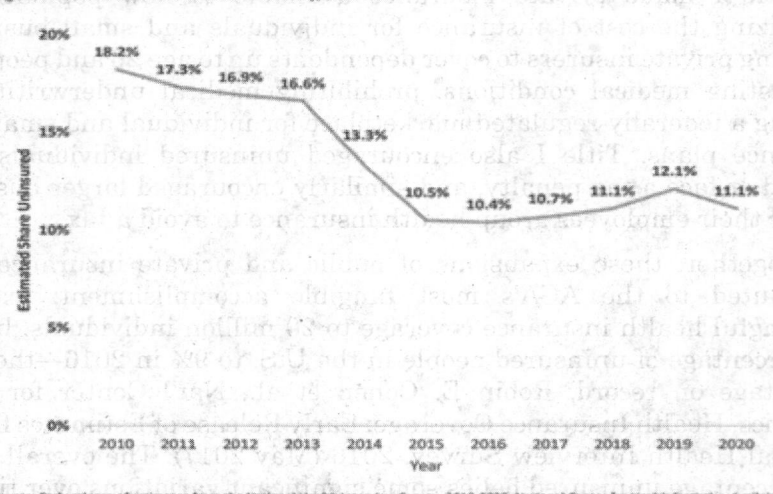

Figure 2. Uninsured Share of U.S. Nonelderly, 2010-2020

Source: Early release of estimates from the National Health Interview Survey, 2018-2020. National Center for Health Statistics. Available from https://www.cdc.gov/nchs/nhis/healthinsurancecoverage.htm. 2020 estimates are for January-June only.

Kenneth Finegold, Ann Conmy, Rose C. Chu, Arielle Bosworth, and Benjamin D. Sommers, ISSUE BRIEF: TRENDS IN THE U.S. UNINSURED POPULATION, 2010–2020 (U.S. DEP'T OF HEALTH & HUMAN SERVS., ASS'T SEC'Y FOR PLANNING & EVAL., OFC. OF HEALTH POL'Y, Feb. 11, 2021). See also Adam Gaffney, David Himmelstein, and Steffie Woolhandler, "How Much Has The Number of Uninsured Risen Since 2016—And At What Cost To Health And Life?," HEALTH AFFAIRS BLOG (Oct. 29, 2020).

Though the ACA produced particularly large coverage gains for Blacks, Latinos, Asian Americans, Native Americans, and lower-income families, it did not successfully close the racial coverage gap that has long persisted in the U.S. health care system. Feingold, et al., Trends in the U.S. Uninsured Population, at 1. As of 2021 the uninsured remain "disproportionately likely to be Black or Latino; be young adults; have low incomes; or live in states that have not expanded Medicaid." Id. at 1. See also Leonard E. Egede, & Rebekah J. Walker, Structural Racism, Social Risk Factors, and Covid-19—A Dangerous Convergence for Black Americans, New England J. Med. (Jul. 22, 2020) (connecting the disproportionate lack of insurance to elevated COVID-19 risk factors for Black Americans).

The ACA's coverage gains have come with only moderate increases in overall health spending. Unsurprisingly, total health care spending initially increased as the ACA expanded both public and private coverage, but the rate of health care cost growth decelerated in 2016 and remained steady, at least until the coronavirus pandemic in 2020. See Anne B. Martin, Micah Hartman, David Lassman, & Aaron Catlin, National Health

Care Spending In 2019: Steady Growth For The Fourth Consecutive Year, 40 HEALTH AFF. 14 (Jan. 2021).

Spending on private health insurance accounted for 31% of the total expenditures as of 2019, *id.*, with 11.3 million individuals enrolled in Marketplace plans as of February 2021, HHS OHP, ISSUE BRIEF: HEALTH COVERAGE UNDER THE AFFORDABLE CARE ACT: ENROLLMENT TRENDS AND STATE ESTIMATES (June 5, 2021). Although Marketplace premiums were initially lower than expected, they climbed steadily when Marketplace enrollees turned out to be older and sicker than insurers had hoped. Uncertainty about the future of the ACA and efforts to undermine it further destabilized the Marketplaces, causing many insurers to either raise premiums or exit the Marketplaces entirely, thereby reducing choices for Marketplace consumers. Nevertheless, the ACA has reduced individuals' medical debt and personal bankruptcies, as well as uncompensated care at hospitals in states that expanded Medicaid. See, Amy E. Cha & Robin A. Cohen, Problems Paying Medical Bills, 2018, Nat'l Center for Health Statistics, Data Brief No. 357 (Feb. 2020); Allen St. John, How the Affordable Care Act Drove Down Personal Bankruptcy, Consumer Reports (May 2, 2017); David Dranove, Craig Garthwaite & Christopher Ody, Uncompensated Care Decreased at Hospitals in Medicaid Expansion States but Not at Hospitals in Nonexpansion States, 35 Health Aff. 1471 (2016). Most consumers are satisfied with Marketplace or Medicaid coverage. Sara R. Collins et al., The Commonwealth Fund, What Do Americans Think About Their Health Coverage Ahead of the 2020 Election? (Sept. 26, 2019).

While the ACA made insurance coverage more affordable for millions of Americans, the statute did not directly address a major driver of health spending: the price of care, particularly hospital care and prescription drugs. See Erin C. Fuse Brown, The Blind Spot in the Patient Protection and Affordable Care Act's Cost-Control Policies, 163 Annals Internal Med. 871 (2015). Growth in the costs of health care has outpaced growth in household income for most Americans, see Sara R. Collins, Herman K. Bhupal, & Michelle M. Doty, Health Insurance Coverage Eight Years After the ACA, Commonwealth Fund (Feb. 7, 2019), and medical debt still burdens households, see David U. Himmelstein, Robert M. Lawless, Deborah Thorne, Pamela Foohey, Steffie Woolhandler, Medical Bankruptcy: Still Common Despite the Affordable Care Act, 109 Am. J. Pub. Health 431 (Mar. 2019), with an especially heavy burden on low-income households and those in states that refused the ACA's Medicaid expansion, Raymond Kluender, Neale Mahoney, Francis Wong, et al., Medical Debt in the US, 2009–2020, 326 JAMA 250 (Jul. 20, 2021).

Despite the ACA's progress in expanding access to insurance, deep political divisions have surrounded the statute from the time of its passage and frustrated its implementation. Not a single Republican member of

Congress voted to enact the ACA. Almost immediately, opponents mounted legal and political challenges in attempts to dismantle the law. Republican-led state governments have resisted implementing the ACA's programs, including the Marketplaces and Medicaid expansion. Republicans in Congress have tried repeatedly to repeal the legislation, although total repeal is an increasingly chimerical notion as the ACA has become deeply embedded in our health care system. Opponents have filed dozens of lawsuits challenging the ACA and its implementation. The individual mandate has borne the brunt of the controversy. The Supreme Court's first ACA opinion in 2012 upheld the mandate's constitutionality. The Republican-led Tax Cuts and Jobs Act of 2017 effectively repealed the mandate's enforceability. And the Supreme Court in 2021 declined to disturb its earlier ruling, ending yet another unsuccessful litigation challenge to the mandate. Though the ACA also divided public opinion along party lines, a majority has come to support the law overall, with its popularity strengthened by the coronavirus pandemic. Liz Hamel, et al., 5 Charts About Public Opinion on the Affordable Care Act and the Supreme Court, KFF.org (Dec. 18, 2020).

The ACA has been under constant legal attack and threat of repeal. The law's opponents have not succeeded in repealing the statute, but they have won major legal and legislative victories that limit the Medicaid expansion and eliminate the individual mandate's penalty. The Trump administration took steps to undo and reverse many rules and policies implementing the ACA. Yet the law has endured and Congress has expanded on it, providing critical infrastructure for coronavirus pandemic relief legislation in 2020 and 2021. Private insurance remains the source of medical coverage for most Americans, and the ACA remains the primary legal infrastructure governing private insurance.

A.   ACA TITLE I: OVERVIEW

The ACA's goal of affordably providing health insurance to those without access due to a preexisting condition or inability to pay is reflected in the Act's major features. The Act provides substantive protections and benefits for consumers. Unlike the pre-ACA era, insurers can no longer deny coverage or charge individuals more for health insurance based on a preexisting condition, coverage no longer has annual or lifetime limits, an insurer cannot rescind coverage after a person develops a health condition, and all plans must cover a specified set of essential health benefits, as described below. In essence, these rules ensure that individuals are no longer "uninsurable" because of their health status and less likely to be "underinsured" by exclusions and limitations in their coverage.

The ACA's key health insurance reforms are a set of interlocking requirements known as the "**three-legged stool**":

- The first leg consists of new rules for health insurance companies requiring them to adopt nondiscriminatory coverage through **guaranteed issue** (an insurer cannot deny coverage due to health status or preexisting condition) and **community rating** for health insurance premiums (premiums do not vary by health status). These new nondiscriminatory health policies cover a standardized set of **essential health benefits** and are sold in new online exchanges called **Marketplaces**.

- The second leg is the so-called **individual mandate**, which requires nearly all persons to have health insurance coverage or pay a penalty. The individual mandate was intended to prevent adverse selection in the insurance risk pool by encouraging young and healthy individuals to participate. Individuals can satisfy the individual mandate through employer coverage, purchasing individual coverage, or maintaining government coverage (e.g., Medicare, Medicaid, or veterans' benefits).

- The third leg of the stool is the **premium assistance tax credits**, or subsidies, that makes purchasing health insurance affordable for those who earn between 100%–400% of the federal poverty level (FPL). In addition to the premium subsidies, the ACA provided **cost-sharing reduction payments** to reduce cost-sharing amounts (deductibles, copays, and co-insurance) for those earning between 100%–250% FPL.

The idea behind the three-legged stool was that the ACA's approach to universal coverage would need all three requirements to function properly. The rules for health insurers would require them to sell meaningful coverage, even to those with pre-existing conditions, and would forbid them from charging sick people higher premiums. The subsidies would enable more people to afford to buy that insurance. And the individual mandate would give people the incentive to buy and maintain insurance coverage before they develop an expensive medical condition. Johnathan Gruber, Center for American Progress, Health Care Reform is a "Three-Legged Stool" (Aug. 5, 2010). As discussed in section II.A. below, repeal of the individual mandate's penalty did not immediately topple the stool, highlighting the experimental nature of many assumptions behind the ACA's original design.

The ACA created a complicated web of interdependent policies, such that changes to or repeal of any one provision are likely to affect the functioning of other provisions. The following chart highlights the major features of the ACA, discussed in more depth below.

Core Provisions of ACA Title I—Insurance Reforms

Reform	Citation	Description
Health Insurance Underwriting Rules		
1. Preexisting conditions and health status discrimination	ACA § 1201; 42 U.S.C. §§ 300gg–3, 300gg–4	Prohibits preexisting condition exclusion, and coverage denial or premium rating based on health status.
2. Guaranteed issue	ACA § 1201; 42 U.S.C. § 300gg–1	Requires insurance companies to issue a health plan to any applicant regardless of the applicant's health status or other factors.
3. Community rated premiums	ACA § 1201; 42 U.S.C. § 300gg	Prohibits health insurers from varying premiums within a geographic area based on gender, health status, or other factors. Allows premiums to vary based on age (up to 3x), geographic area, and tobacco status.
Mandates		
4. Individual mandate	ACA § 150; 26 U.S.C. § 5000A	Requires all individuals to have minimum essential coverage or else pay a penalty.
5. Employer mandate and small business tax credits	ACA § 1513; 26 U.S.C. § 4980H (employer mandate) ACA § 1421; 26 U.S.C. § 45R (small business tax credits)	Applies penalty to all businesses with 50 or more employees that fail to provide insurance. Small businesses can qualify for a tax credit if: 1) they have 24 or fewer full time employees; 2) average wages less than $50,000; and 3) they cover at least 50% of the cost of health care coverage.
Insurance Affordability		
6. Premium tax credits	ACA § 1401; 26 U.S.C. § 36B	Provides premium assistance tax credit for individuals earning between 100%–400% FPL.*
7. Cost-sharing reductions	ACA § 1402; 42 U.S.C. § 18071	Reduces cost-sharing for individuals earning between 100%–250% FPL in Marketplace plans.

Reform	Citation	Description
Insurance Marketplaces		
8. Qualified health plans (QHPs)	ACA § 1301; 42 U.S.C. § 18021	QHPs are insurance plans that provide essential health benefits, meet standardized levels of actuarial value (metal tiers), follow established limits on cost-sharing, and meet other requirements outlined within the application process.
9. Marketplaces	ACA § 1311; 42 U.S.C. § 18031	Establishes state-based Marketplaces for individual and small-group health insurance (can be run by federal gov't—HealthCare.gov).
10. Essential Health Benefits	ACA § 1302; 42 U.S.C. § 1802	10 types of services that must be covered by health plans (nongroup plans).

B. ACA's CORE INSURANCE REFORMS

1. Preexisting Conditions and Health Status Discrimination—ACA § 1201; 42 U.S.C. §§ 300gg–3, 300gg–4

The ACA prohibits group or individual health plans from excluding coverage for a person's preexisting condition. Separately, the ACA prohibits such health plans from establishing eligibility rules based on any health status factor, including health conditions, previous medical history, genetic information, or any other factor relating to health status.

42 U.S.C. § 300gg–3—PROHIBITION OF PREEXISTING CONDITION EXCLUSIONS OR OTHER DISCRIMINATION BASED ON HEALTH STATUS

(a) IN GENERAL.—A group health plan and a health insurance issuer offering group or individual health insurance coverage may not impose any preexisting condition exclusion with respect to such plan or coverage.

(b) Definitions. For purposes of this part:

(1) Preexisting condition exclusion

(A) The term "preexisting condition exclusion" means, with respect to coverage, a limitation or exclusion of benefits relating to a condition based on the fact that the condition was present before the date of enrollment for such coverage, whether or not any medical advice, diagnosis, care, or treatment was recommended or received before such date.

(B) Treatment of genetic information. Genetic information shall not be treated as a condition described in subsection (a)(1) in the absence of a diagnosis of the condition related to such information.

42 U.S.C. § 300gg–4—PROHIBITING DISCRIMINATION AGAINST INDIVIDUAL PARTICIPANTS AND BENEFICIARIES BASED ON HEALTH STATUS.

(a) IN GENERAL.—A group health plan and a health insurance issuer offering group or individual health insurance coverage may not establish rules for eligibility (including continued eligibility) of any individual to enroll under the terms of the plan or coverage based on any of the following health status-related factors in relation to the individual or a dependent of the individual:

(1) Health status.

(2) Medical condition (including both physical and mental illnesses).

(3) Claims experience.

(4) Receipt of health care.

(5) Medical history.

(6) Genetic information.

(7) Evidence of insurability (including conditions arising out of acts of domestic violence).

(8) Disability.

(9) Any other health status-related factor determined appropriate by the Secretary.

2. Guaranteed Issue—ACA § 1201; 42 U.S.C. § 300gg–1

Guaranteed issue and community rating form the foundation for the ACA's expansion of health insurance in the private market. As noted later in this chapter, these provisions expand upon the protections offered by the Health Insurance Portability and Accountability Act of 1996 (HIPAA), which prohibited group health insurance plans from considering health status in determining eligibility or premium rates for group coverage and limited group plans' use of preexisting conditions exclusions. The guaranteed issue provision ensures that no insurer can deny access to health insurance because of a preexisting condition. The following provisions establish the guaranteed issue requirements of the ACA:

42 U.S.C. § 300gg–1—GUARANTEED AVAILABILITY OF COVERAGE

(a) Guaranteed issuance of coverage in the individual and group market— Subject to subsections (b) through (e), each health insurance issuer that offers health insurance coverage in the individual or group market in a

State must accept every employer and individual in the State that applies for such coverage. [ ]

* * *

3. Modified Community Rated Premiums—ACA § 1201; 42 U.S.C. § 300gg

The modified community rating provisions of the ACA prohibit insurance plans from charging those in the individual or small group health insurance market higher rates based on their health status, health history, gender, or any other factor other than geographic location, age, and tobacco usage.

Section 2701 of the Public Health Service Act (PHSA), added by Section 1201 of the ACA, provides:

42 U.S.C. § 300gg—FAIR HEALTH INSURANCE PREMIUMS

(a) Prohibiting Discriminatory Premium Rates—(1) With respect to the premium rate charged by a health insurance issuer for health insurance coverage offered in the individual or small group market:

(A) such rate shall vary with respect to the particular plan or coverage involved only by:

(i)   whether such plan or coverage covers an individual or family;

(ii) rating area . . .;

(iii) age, except that such rate shall not vary by more than 3 to 1 for adults . . .; and

(iv) tobacco use, except that such rate shall not vary by more than 1.5 to 1; and

(B) such rate shall not vary with respect to the particular plan or coverage involved by any other factor not described in subparagraph (A).

* * *

4. The Individual Mandate—ACA § 1501; 26 U.S.C. § 5000A

Once guaranteed issue and community rating offered individuals guaranteed access to insurance at rates that did not vary according to health status, concern arose that individuals would wait until they got sick or knew they planned to have a procedure to enroll in insurance. This phenomenon, known as **adverse selection**, led the drafters of the ACA to include a **shared responsibility payment** provision, commonly referred to as the **individual mandate**. The ACA required most people to enroll in health insurance that meets minimum standards or pay a tax penalty. The individual mandate, as enacted, was designed to encourage healthier individuals from all sectors of society to sign up for health insurance, enabling insurance companies to spread the risk of insuring those with preexisting conditions across more people and offer lower rates.

The ACA permitted exemptions from the individual mandate for a variety of reasons. First, the law exempted people who cannot afford insurance, such as: 1) people whose income falls below the income tax filing limit ($12,400 for a single individual, $24,800 for a married couple filing jointly for 2020); 2) people who would have to pay more than 8.16% of their income in 2017 for insurance coverage after employer contributions and subsidies; and 3) citizens who earn less than 100% of the FPL, but do not qualify for Medicaid because they live in states that did not expand Medicaid. The ACA also exempted undocumented immigrants, individuals with religious objections (such as the Amish), incarcerated individuals, Native Americans, people uninsured for less than a three-month period, and expatriates. Finally, the statute also provided for hardship exemptions, which the Internal Revenue Service (IRS) has interpreted quite broadly. By 2018, 3 million of the 10.7 million uninsured were exempt from the mandate. Matthew Rae, Larry Levitt & Ashley Semanskee, Kaiser Family Found., How Many of the Uninsured Can Purchase a Marketplace Plan for Less Than Their Shared Responsibility Payment? (Nov. 9, 2017).

The ACA required that individuals subject to the mandate who failed to purchase insurance pay a penalty. As enacted, the statute set the penalty payment as the greater of either 1) $695 for each adult plus half that amount for each child in the household, up to $2,085 total for a family (updated for inflation); or 2) 2.5% of household income above the filing limit, but not more than the cost of a bronze-level (basic, high cost-sharing) insurance policy. By 2017, most of the uninsured could buy a Marketplace plan, using premium subsidies, for less than what they would owe under the individual mandate penalty—often with no premium contribution whatsoever. Matthew Rae, Larry Levitt & Ashley Semanskee, Kaiser Family Found., How Many of the Uninsured Can Purchase a Marketplace Plan for Less Than Their Shared Responsibility Payment? (Nov. 9, 2017). Of the 7.7 million people uninsured and not exempt from the mandate in 2017, approximately 6.3 million were eligible for at least some subsidies to purchase insurance on the Marketplace. *Id.*

In 2017, the Republican-controlled Congress passed tax reform legislation which set the individual mandate's penalty to $0 (starting in January 1, 2019) and left the IRS with effectively "no means of enforcement," though the mandate itself remains in force. *California v. Texas*, 593 U.S. ___, 141 S. Ct. 2104 (2021); Tax Cuts & Jobs Act of 2017 ("TCJA"), PL 115–97, 131 Stat. 2054 (Dec. 22, 2017). This alteration of the mandate provision is discussed in detail below in section II.A.2. But even prior to the legislative repeal, the federal government never had the full panoply of available tools to enforce the mandate, as the ACA prohibits the use of liens or levies on property or criminal sanctions to enforce the requirement. While the IRS could offset penalties against refunds owed to taxpayers, compliance has always largely been voluntary.

Initially, the mandate and penalty helped drive coverage expansion across all insurance markets. It provided some additional incentive for individuals to sign up for private insurance or Medicaid, based on their eligibility. Similarly, the mandate drove employees to demand insurance from their employers, buttressing our employer-based insurance system. Finally, it encouraged higher-income uninsured individuals who did not have access to public or employer-based coverage to buy insurance. While the subject of significant controversy, research demonstrates that the individual mandate generally succeeded in enrolling younger and healthier individuals. For instance, the uninsured rate of college-educated males 26– 34 dropped from 6.9% in 2013 to 3.8% in 2015. Sherry A. Glied & Adlan Jackson, The Commonwealth Fund, Why There's No Substitute for the Individual Mandate, To the Point (July 12, 2017); but see Chris Pope, Why Didn't Obamacare's Mandate Work?, National Review (Sept. 9, 2020). After the Congress eliminated the penalty in 2019, many predicted these enrollment trends to reverse. But the removal of the penalty did not significantly affect enrollment, as discussed in section II.A.2, below.

Despite all of this wrangling, the mandate provision remains in effect, though unenforceable.

5. Employer Mandate and Small Business Tax Credits—ACA §§ 1421, 1513; 26 U.S.C. §§ 45R, 4890

After creating the individual mandate and expanding Medicaid, to make the plan financially viable, the ACA's drafters needed to support the existing employer-based insurance system to avoid **crowd out**, which occurs when employers stop offering insurance benefits in favor of allowing employees to seek coverage from Medicaid or the individual market. As a result, the ACA includes **employer shared responsibility provisions**, which require employers to either offer **minimum essential coverage** (discussed below) that is "affordable" and provides "minimum value" to their employees and their families, or potentially make an employer shared responsibility payment to the IRS. The employer shared responsibility provisions are often referred to as the **employer mandate** or the "**pay or play provisions**."

The employer mandate only affects applicable large employers (ALEs). To qualify as an ALE in a particular year, an employer must have had an average of at least 50 full-time employees during the preceding calendar year. All types of employers, including tax exempt and government employers, can qualify as an ALE. ALEs also have significant reporting responsibilities under the ACA regarding minimum essential coverage.

An ALE will owe a shared responsibility payment in two scenarios if its employees purchase a federally-subsidized plan on the **health insurance marketplace** (Marketplace) (discussed below). First, if the ALE *does not* offer minimum essential coverage to at least 95% of its full-time employees and their dependents (including children up to the age of 26), and at least one of its full-time employees receives the premium tax credit for purchasing coverage through the Marketplace, the ALE will owe a shared responsibility payment. In 2021, employers in this situation must pay a shared responsibility payment of $2,700 for each employee, minus the first 30 employees, including those who receive minimum essential coverage from the employer.

Second, if the ALE *does* offer minimum essential coverage to at least 95% of its full-time employees and their dependents, it may still owe a shared responsibility payment for each full-time employee who receives the premium tax credit for purchasing coverage through the Marketplace if: 1) the minimum essential coverage offered by the employer is not "affordable," 2) the minimum essential coverage does not provide "minimum value;" or 3) the employer did not offer the minimum essential coverage to that employee. The ACA deems a plan affordable based on a percentage of the individual's income (as discussed below), and it deems the plan as meeting the minimum value requirement if it covers at least 60% of the total costs incurred under the plan. In this instance, the employer will pay $4,060 in 2021 per full-time employee that receives a premium subsidy tax credit. But the total payment for each month is capped to ensure an ALE that offers minimum essential coverage cannot owe more than one that does not offer it.

For smaller employers, the ACA also provides a health insurance tax credit for two consecutive years that covers up to 50% of premiums paid for small business employers and 35% of premiums paid for small tax-exempt employers. To be eligible for the credit, a small employer must have fewer than 25 full-time equivalent employees, pay an average annual wage per full-time equivalent employee that does not exceed $50,000, and pay at least 50% of the premiums for employees enrolled in qualified health plan on the Small Business Health Options Program (SHOP) Marketplace or qualify for an exemption. The amount of the credit phases out as the total number of full time employees rises from 10 to 25 and as the average annual wages of the employer rises from $26,000 to $53,000, adjusted for inflation. Tax-exempt organizations can write off the credit against their payroll tax liability or receive a refund, while taxable businesses can write off the credit against taxes they would otherwise owe. *See* Small Business Health Care Tax Credit Estimator, Healthcare.gov https://www.health care.gov/shop-calculators-taxcredit/.

PROBLEM: COMPLYING WITH THE EMPLOYER MANDATE

To envision the impact of the employer mandate, imagine that in 2013, you owned a business with 58 full-time employees. You had historically offered health insurance to all of your full-time employees, but the plan only covered catastrophic loss and preventative services and had a deductible of $5,000. The actuarial value of your plan was approximately 40%. How would you react to the employer mandate taking effect in 2014? What changes would you consider making to your business? Do those changes comport with the goals of the ACA?

6. Premium Assistance Tax Credits—ACA § 1401; 26 U.S.C. § 36B

Once the ACA expanded access through guaranteed issue, community rating, the Medicaid expansion, and the employer mandate, and promoted risk spreading through the individual mandate, Congress needed to make sure that coverage in the individual and small group markets was affordable for individuals with incomes just above Medicaid eligibility. The ACA expanded access to health insurance for middle-income Americans by using means-tested tax credits to subsidize the purchase of private health insurance. In the ACA, Democratic legislators embraced this strategy that had long been a feature of Republican health reform proposals.

Starting in 2014, Americans earning between 100% and 400% of the federal poverty level ($12,880–$51,520 for an individual and $26,500–$106,000 for a family of four in 2021) who purchased nongroup (individual) health insurance through an ACA Marketplace became eligible for a tax credit to help make the premiums more affordable. The amount of the individual's tax credit (TC) is based on the insurance premium (IP), defined as the lesser of (i) the monthly premium cost for the plan that an individual or family is enrolled in, or (ii) the monthly premium for the **benchmark plan** (the second lowest cost "silver" plan), an affordability index (AI), and the taxpayer's household income (HI). The tax credit formula is:

$$TC = IP - (AI \times HI)/12$$

The affordability index increases on a sliding scale from the initial to the final premium percentage within an income tier. The affordability index for 2021 is as follows:

2021 Affordability Index		
In the case of household income (expressed as FPL):	The initial premium percentage is:	The final premium percentage is:
Less than 133%	2.07%	2.07%
133% to <150%	3.10%	4.14%
150% to <200%	4.14%	6.52%
200% to <250%	6.52%	8.33%
250% to <300%	8.33%	9.83%
300% to <400%	9.83%	9.83%

The affordability index allows the percentage that individuals spend on health insurance to remain stable, such that if premiums significantly increase more rapidly than income, as they have in the past, the individual and the government will continue to pay roughly the same proportion of the premium. The premium tax credit amount adjusts for age, but not for any premium discount attributable to a wellness program or for a premium surcharge based on tobacco use.

Not everyone who is eligible to purchase coverage on the Marketplace qualify for premium tax credits. Individuals qualify for premium tax credits if they are U.S. citizens or are lawfully present, earn between 100% and 400% of FPL, and are ineligible for other "minimum essential coverage," which includes Medicare, Medicaid, and most employer-based coverage. Individuals who are eligible for an employer-based plan do not qualify for premium tax credits unless the employer plan does not satisfy the minimum value requirement of 60% actuarial value (defined below) or the employee's share of the premium exceeds the affordability index percentage of their household income. Although legal resident aliens with incomes below 100% of the poverty level who do not qualify for Medicaid (generally, those present in the country for fewer than 5 years) are eligible, United States citizens with incomes below 100% of the poverty level in states that reject the Medicaid expansion remain ineligible for premium tax credits. See Chapter 10, below. See also Section II.C., below, discussing a temporary change extending eligibility for tax credits above 400% of FPL as a response to the COVID-19 pandemic.

7. Cost-Sharing Reduction Payments—ACA § 1402; 42 U.S.C. § 18071

The ACA provided not only for tax credits to reduce the cost of health insurance premiums, but also for direct payments to qualified health plans to reduce eligible individuals' **cost sharing** (including deductibles, coinsurance, and copayments). The law limits cost-sharing for Marketplace plans in two different ways. First, the legislation imposes a maximum out-of-pocket expenditure limit, close to the limit imposed on high-deductible policies that accompany health savings accounts ($8,550 for an individual and $17,100 for a family in 2021). Second, qualified health plans in the individual and small group market must offer coverage of a specific **actuarial value (AV)**, the percentage of an average person's health costs that a plan will pay for covered benefits. The ACA assigned plans to four "precious metal" tiers according to their AV—Bronze (60%), Silver (70%), Gold (80%), and Platinum (90%). For example, on average, a Bronze plan with an actuarial value of 60% will pay 60% of covered health care expenses, while the enrollee will pay the remaining 40% through some combination of deductibles, copays, and coinsurance. Typically, higher AV plans offer lower cost-sharing, but will also charge higher premiums. Further, AV is determined by the overall structure of a plan and does not dictate the out-of-pocket expenses a particular individual or family will incur in a particular year.

Cost-sharing reduction (CSR) payments are payments made by the federal government directly to an insurer on behalf of an "eligible individual" to lower that individual's cost-sharing obligations. The federal government stopped making CSR payments to insurers in 2017, which was the subject of litigation discussed below in section II.C. But insurers remain required by the statute to reduce cost-sharing for some of their lower-income enrollees. Only individuals with household incomes between 100%–250% of the poverty level who enroll in individual **Silver tier plans** through an ACA Marketplace are eligible for cost-sharing reduction. People with employer-based coverage are not eligible, nor are people who enroll in Bronze, Gold, and Platinum plans.

8. The Health Insurance Marketplaces—ACA § 1311; 42 U.S.C. § 18031

At the heart of the ACA is the concept of the **health insurance Marketplace**, referred to as a **health benefit exchange** in the text of the law. A Marketplace is a consumer-friendly market for health insurance, resembling a farmer's market, stock market, or online travel service. It is a place where consumers can go, browse through the range of available insurance options, and choose the insurance plan that best suits themselves and their families.

To be eligible to purchase coverage on the ACA Marketplace, an individual must: (1) be a U.S. citizen or lawfully present; (2) be a resident of the U.S.; and (3) not be incarcerated. 45 C.F.R. § 155.305. In addition, those enrolled in Medicare cannot purchase Marketplace coverage. Note that the eligibility criteria to purchase Marketplace coverage are broader than the requirements to qualify for premium tax credits to help pay for the coverage, described above.

The ACA drafters envisioned that the ACA Marketplaces would standardize health insurance products in terms of AV and baseline benefits, and then offer consumers understandable and transparent information on those plans to simplify health insurance choices. See Troy Oechsner & Magda Schaler-Haynes, Keeping It Simple: Health Plan Benefit Standardization and Regulatory Choice under the Affordable Care Act, 74 Albany L. Rev. 241 (2010–2011). In addition, the ACA drafters planned to manage competition between the participating insurance plans to attract and maintain participating insurers. To do so, the ACA provided protections for Marketplace insurers including three **premium stabilization programs**: risk adjustment (individual and small group plans), reinsurance (individual plans), and risk corridors (qualified health plans), discussed further below. For a more detailed description of managed competition in the Marketplaces, see, John Holanhan et al., The Urban Inst., Cross-Cutting Issues: Insurer Participation and Competition in Health Insurance Exchanges: Early Indicators from Selected States (July 2013).

To establish a Marketplace, the ACA required states to create an entity that would bear responsibility for:

- certifying, recertifying, and decertifying health plans;
- operating a toll-free consumer hotline;
- maintaining an internet website providing standardized comparative information on qualified health plans;
- providing for annual open enrollment periods and for special enrollment periods under certain circumstances;
- rating plans, using a standardized format for providing health benefit information;
- assisting individuals in applying for Medicaid, Children's Health Insurance Program (CHIP), or other government programs;
- making available a calculator to assist individuals to determine the cost of coverage after the application of premium and cost-sharing subsidies;
- certifying individuals as exempt from the individual mandate;
- providing the IRS with information on individual mandate exemptions and employer mandate violations; and
- establishing a Navigator program to conduct public education, distribute information, and help qualified individuals enroll in Marketplace plans and receive premium credits and cost-sharing reduction payments.

Following these guidelines, under Section 1311, by January 1, 2014, states had the option of establishing separate Marketplaces for the nongroup market and the small group (SHOP) market or combining the two. Alternatively, states could default into using the federally facilitated Marketplace. The ACA also permitted regional Marketplaces if all participating states and the Department of Health and Human Services (HHS) approved of a regional approach.

As of 2021, 20 states and the District of Columbia operated Marketplaces in which the state is responsible for performing all or most of the functions for the individual market. Kaiser Family Found., State Health Insurance Marketplace Types, 2021 (July 2021) (15 of the 21 still rely on the federal "Healthcare.gov" platform for individual eligibility and enrollment functions). The other 30 states rely entirely on HHS to perform these functions through the federally-facilitated Marketplace on Healthcare.gov. *Id.* To date, no states have established a regional Marketplace.

While the individual Marketplaces of all types saw significant enrollment, the SHOP Marketplace fell far short of enrollment goals. In 2019, CMS shuttered the federal SHOP Marketplace on HealthCare.gov. Small businesses can still enroll in SHOP coverage, but must do so through an agent, broker, or the company. See Timothy Jost, Market Stabilization Stalls; States Step In, 37 Health Aff. (May 14, 2018). And state-based SHOP exchanges may continue exist in several states. Centers for Medicare and Medicaid Serv., The Future of the SHOP: CMS Intends to Allow Small Businesses in SHOPs Using HealthCare.gov More Flexibility when Enrolling in Healthcare Coverage (May 15, 2017).

9. Qualified Health Plans—ACA § 1301; 42 U.S.C. § 18021

The Marketplaces can only offer **qualified health plans (QHPs)**. HHS established certification standards that all QHPs must meet to be sold in a state or federal Marketplace. 45 C.F.R. § 155.1000 (2017). To be certified, QHPs must:

- be licensed and in good standing;

- cover the Essential Health Benefits package;

- ensure network adequacy and information;

- include essential community providers, where available, to serve low income, medically underserved individuals;

- be accredited by an entity recognized by HHS;

- implement a quality improvement strategy to improve health outcomes, prevent hospital readmissions, reduce medical errors, promote wellness and prevention, and reduce health and health care disparities;

- utilize a uniform enrollment form and the standard format developed for presenting health benefits options;

- provide information on cost-sharing for specific services in a timely manner on request through an internet website and otherwise for individuals without internet access;

- provide parity in mental health services;

- provide information in plain language; and

- provide information on health plan quality performance.

These standards can be found throughout the statute and associated regulations. For a detailed list of the QHP statutory requirements and the varied regulations that apply to them, see Mila Kofman, Katie Dunton & Sally McCarty, Robert Wood Johnson Found., Qualified Health Plan (QHP) Issuer Certification Checklist (Jan. 2013).

As noted above, QHPs in the individual and small group market must offer coverage of a specific AV that fits into one of four tiers—Bronze (60%), Silver (70%), Gold (80%), and Platinum (90%). 45 U.S.C. § 18022 (d) (2017). The actuarial value of services is based on the cost of providing the essential health benefits (discussed below) to a standard population, not the actual population of the plan.

To facilitate comparison of QHPs on the Marketplaces, HHS developed a Quality Rating System (QRS). 45 C.F.R. §§ 155.1400 & 155.1405. CMS calculates and assigns star ratings based on validated clinical quality and surveys that participating insurers submit for each of their plans sold on the Marketplace. The QRS star-rating accounts for data on "medical care" (how well the plans' network providers manage members' basic health services), "member experience" (enrollee satisfaction surveys), and "plan administration" (customer service, access to needed information, and network providers ordering appropriate tests and treatment). Marketplaces then post the QRS star ratings for consumers as they shop for plans.

10. Essential Health Benefits—ACA § 1302; 42 U.S.C. § 18022

Never before has federal law attempted to specify the benefits that private insurance plans must cover, beyond a handful of specific mandates. Indeed, although many states require insurers to cover specific services, states do not generally specify a comprehensive bundle of items and services that health insurance must cover.

The ACA, however, requires insurers that offer coverage in the individual and small group markets to cover an **essential benefits package** specified by the law. The essential health benefits requirement does not apply to large group or self-insured plans, nor does it apply to **grandfathered plans**, which existed as of the date of enactment of the

ACA. It does apply, however, to all non-grandfathered, individual, and small group plans, whether or not they are sold through the Marketplaces.

Section 1302 requires HHS to define **essential health benefits (EHBs)**, 42 U.S.C. § 18022 (2017), but lists ten categories of benefits that must be included, including:

- ambulatory patient services;

- emergency services;

- hospitalization;

- maternity and newborn care;

- mental health and substance use disorder services;

- prescription drugs;

- rehabilitation and habilitation services;

- laboratory services;

- preventive and wellness services including chronic disease management; and

- pediatric services, including oral and vision care.

The ACA-defined EHBs must be equal in scope to those offered under a typical employer plan. HHS must also make sure that the benefits:

- are "not unduly weighted toward any category";

- do not discriminate based on age, disability, or expected length of life;

- consider the needs of diverse segments of the population;

- ensure that essential benefits are not denied to individuals against their wishes based on age, expected length of life, present or predicted disability, dependency, or quality of life;

- provide access to emergency care without prior approval, limitation to in-network providers, or higher cost-sharing for using out-of-network providers; and

- are periodically reviewed and updated.

HHS decided to implement this provision by asking each state to designate a **benchmark plan**, the benefits of which become the standard for essential health benefits in that state. 45 C.F.R. § 156.100 (2017). The state may choose a benchmark plan from one of the following: 1) the largest plan of the three largest small group products in the state, 2) one of the three largest state employee plans in the state, 3) any of the largest three national Federal Employee Health Benefits plans, or 4) the state's largest commercial non-Medicaid HMO plan. If the plan chosen does not cover any of the ten required benefit categories, the state must add benefits from another plan. Under HHS rules, plans must cover at least two (where applicable) drugs in every United States Pharmacopeia (USP) category or class, or must offer the same number of drugs in each category and class as the EHB-benchmark plans. 45 C.F.R. § 156.122 (2017). Plans need not cover the same drugs as the benchmark plan, as long as they cover the minimum number of drugs. Insurers will have some flexibility in substituting benefits within categories as long as they are equivalent in value and none of the other requirements are violated. And states may change their designated benchmarks, but must stay within parameters set by HHS. 45 C.F.R. § 156.111 (2020).

While the ACA established a minimum set of essential benefits, state laws mandating coverage for certain treatments and conditions still apply within individual states, as discussed below in section IV. Health plans may also offer additional benefits beyond the EHBs to attract enrollees.

NOTES AND QUESTIONS

1. *A Complex Approach to a Complicated System.* What factors explain the complexity of the ACA's approach to providing access to health insurance? How will it affect consumers, insurers, providers, and employers? How could this have been done more simply? How did the complexity affect the perception of the law?

2. *Guaranteed Issue & Community Rating.* Does a guaranteed issue provision necessitate either a) a community rating provision, which requires all individuals in a plan to be charged either the same premium, or b) a modified community rating provision, which limits the variance in premiums between individuals? Why? What enrollment incentives do the guaranteed issue and community rating provisions create for individuals considering purchasing insurance? What risks does that create?

3. *Modifying Community Rating for Age and Gender.* Is the 3 to 1 ratio in rate variation based on age a surrogate for health status underwriting, as health status tends to deteriorate with age? Is it otherwise justified? Is the fact that the ACA also eliminates gender discrimination in the individual and small group market warranted? In fact, per capita spending on women typically exceeds spending on men in all age groups after the age of 15. See, Joseph L. Dieleman, US Spending on Personal Health Care and Public Health, 1996–2013, 316 JAMA 2627 (2016). In 2017, Republicans proposed a 5 to 1 premium ratio based on age. Does this seem more or less appropriate? Why?

4. *Single Risk Pool.* The ACA also included a single risk pool provision which required insurers to consider all enrollees in a particular market to be members of a single risk pool when developing rates and premiums. Each insurer can have one individual market pool and one small group market pool, and states can choose to merge these pools. Why would the ACA include such a provision?

5. *Anti-Discrimination.* In addition to the prohibitions on health status underwriting and limitations on individual rate variation based on age and gender, the ACA's Section 1557, 42 U.S.C. § 18116, directly prohibited discrimination on the basis of race, color, national origin, sex, disability, and age in any health program that receives federal funds. As discussed in detail in Chapter 6, this provided an important new vehicle by which individuals could challenge discriminatory decisions or denials by insurers that receive premium assistance tax credits or CSR payments for Marketplace enrollees. See also, e.g., Amy Post, Ashley Stephens, & Valarie K. Blake, Sex Discrimination in Healthcare: Section 1557 and LGBTQ Rights After Bostock, 11 UCLA L. Rev. Online 545 (2021); Valarie K. Blake, An Opening for Civil Rights in Health Insurance After the Affordable Care Act, 36 B.C.J.L. & Soc. Just. 235 (2016). Is Section 1557 redundant of the ACA's core coverage reforms? If not, what additional protections does it offer individuals and/or what additional obligations does it impose on insurers? May an insurer discriminate if it sells its plans to employers or directly to the enrollees outside of the ACA Marketplaces? See "Antidiscrimination Law," Section III.B., below, and Chapters 7 and 8.

6. *Reform Tools.* Recall the discussion of health reform policy in Chapter 7. What tools of health reform from do you see among these core insurance reforms enacted in the ACA? What ethos do you see reflected in their selection? How does Congress's selection of these core provisions implicate the "triple aim" concepts of expanding access, controlling costs, and improving quality? What are the implications for the related concept of "choice"? Why do you think the ACA's drafters made these choices?

7. *Comprehensive Reform?* How are the core insurance reforms of the ACA interdependent? Which provisions can function independently? Which provisions depend on other parts of the law to be effective? What implications does this have for piecemeal reform efforts?

8. *Consumer Behavior.* Did the Marketplaces succeed in reducing confusion and simplifying comparison of plans? For a detailed discussion of the challenges and cognitive biases individual consumers still face in comparing plans on the Marketplaces, see Allison K. Hoffman, The ACA's Choice Problem, 45 J. Health Pol. Pol'y & L. 501 (2020), and Erin Audrey Taylor et al., RAND Corp., Consumer Decisionmaking in the Health Care Marketplace (2016).

C. ACA's OTHER INSURANCE REFORMS

Without entirely repealing and replacing existing state and federal law, the ACA dramatically changed the scope of federal insurance regulation, largely by extending federal regulation over the nongroup (individual) market to an unprecedented extent. Previously, federal law left the nongroup market largely untouched. The ACA also applies a much larger body of federal requirements to group health insurance plans, including self-insured plans. While the ACA's major features provide the structure for accomplishing the most important goals of the Act, the legislation also enacted numerous other insurance reforms. This Section examines some of the most prominent and important.

1. Coverage Reforms—ACA § 1001; 42 U.S.C. § 300gg et seq.

Several provisions of the ACA address specific coverage reforms, including coverage requirements, limits, rescissions, and review of coverage determinations. This part includes both statutory language for some of the provisions and summaries of other provisions. Section 1001 of the ACA amended the PHSA, 42 U.S.C. § 300gg et seq., to introduce these significant insurance reforms.

ACA § 2711; 42 U.S.C. § 300gg–11. NO LIFETIME OR ANNUAL LIMITS.

(a) IN GENERAL.—A group health plan and a health insurance issuer offering group or individual health insurance coverage may not establish:

(1) lifetime limits on the dollar value of benefits for any participant or beneficiary; or

(2) . . . annual limits on the dollar value of benefits for any participant or beneficiary [except within "restricted annual limit" parameters set by the Secretary].

(b) PER BENEFICIARY LIMITS.—Subsection (a) shall not be construed to prevent a group health plan or health insurance coverage that is not required to provide essential health benefits under section 1302(b) of the Patient Protection and Affordable Care Act from placing annual or lifetime per beneficiary limits on specific covered benefits to the extent that such limits are otherwise permitted under Federal or State law.

ACA § 2712; 42 U.S.C. § 300gg–12. PROHIBITION ON RESCISSIONS.

A group health plan and a health insurance issuer offering group or individual health insurance coverage shall not rescind such plan or coverage with respect to an enrollee once the enrollee is covered under such plan or coverage involved, except that this section shall not apply to a covered individual who has performed an act or practice that constitutes fraud or makes an intentional misrepresentation of material fact as prohibited by the terms of the plan or coverage. Such plan or coverage may not be cancelled except with prior notice to the enrollee, and only as permitted under section 2702(c) or 2742(b).

ACA § 2713; 42 U.S.C. § 300gg–13. COVERAGE OF PREVENTIVE HEALTH SERVICES.

(a) IN GENERAL.—A group health plan and a health insurance issuer offering group or individual health insurance coverage shall, at a minimum provide coverage for and shall not impose any cost sharing requirements for—

(1) evidence-based items or services that have in effect a rating of 'A' or 'B' in the current recommendations of the United States Preventive Services Task Force;

(2) immunizations that have in effect a recommendation from the Advisory Committee on Immunization Practices of the Centers for Disease Control and Prevention with respect to the individual involved; and

(3) with respect to infants, children, and adolescents, evidence-informed preventive care and screenings provided for in the comprehensive guidelines supported by the Health Resources and Services Administration.

(4) with respect to women, such additional preventive care and screenings not described in paragraph (1) as provided for in comprehensive guidelines supported by the Health Resources and Services Administration for purposes of this paragraph.

(5) for the purposes of this Act, and for the purposes of any other provision of law, the current recommendations of the United States Preventive Service Task Force regarding breast cancer screening, mammography, and prevention shall be considered the most current other than those issued in or around November 2009.

Nothing in this subsection shall be construed to prohibit a plan or issuer from providing coverage for services in addition to those recommended by United States Preventive Services Task Force or to deny coverage for services that are not recommended by such Task Force.

* * *

ACA § 2714; 42 U.S.C. § 300gg–14. EXTENSION OF DEPENDENT COVERAGE.

(a) IN GENERAL.—A group health plan and a health insurance issuer offering group or individual health insurance coverage that provides dependent coverage of children shall continue to make such coverage available for an adult child (who is not married) until the child turns 26 years of age. Nothing in this section shall require a health plan or a health insurance issuer described in the preceding sentence to make coverage available for a child of a child receiving dependent coverage.

(b) REGULATIONS.—The Secretary shall promulgate regulations to define the dependents to which coverage shall be made available under subsection (a).

(c) RULE OF CONSTRUCTION.—Nothing in this section shall be construed to modify the definition of 'dependent' as used in the Internal Revenue Code of 1986 with respect to the tax treatment of the cost of coverage.

* * *

Internal and External Reviews. Section 2719 of the ACA, 42 U.S.C. § 300gg–19, requires group health plans and insurers to offer plan members both internal and external review procedures for coverage and claims determinations. An **internal appeal** is one filed by the consumer to ask the health plan to reconsider its denial of services, payment of a claim, or application for coverage. Health plans complete internal appeals themselves. Whereas, independent third-parties conduct **external reviews**.

Under the law, non-grandfathered group and individual health plans must satisfy basic standards for conducting internal appeals and external reviews. 45 CFR § 147.136. In a culturally and linguistically appropriate manner, plans and insurers must provide enrollees with notices of available internal and external appeal procedures and the availability of a state office of health insurance consumer assistance or ombudsman for assistance with appeals. They must allow enrollees to review their files and to present evidence and testimony. Group health plan internal appeals processes must comply with the Department of Labor ERISA claims and appeals regulations plus several additional requirements, while individual insurance internal review procedures must comply with state law and standards promulgated by HHS.

Group health plans and insurers must comply with either their state or the federal external review requirements. If a state has in place an external review process offering at least as much protection as the National Association of Insurance Commissions (NAIC) Model Act, an insurer must comply with the state law. Nat'l Ass'n of Ins. Comm'rs, Uniform Health Carrier External Review Model Act (Apr. 2010). For a list of requirements for state external review processes, see Dept. of the Treasury, Dept. of Labor, Dept. of Health and Human Services, Interim Final Rules for Group Health Plans and Health Insurance Issuers Relating to Internal Claims and Appeals and External Review Processes under the Patient Protection and Affordable Care Act, 75 Fed. Reg. 43335 (July 23, 2010) (codified at 26 C.F.R. §§ 54, 602; 29 C.F.R. § 2590; 45 C.F.R. § 147). Plans and insurers not subject to state law (e.g., self-insured employee benefit plans because of ERISA) or located in states without external review laws as protective as the NAIC Model Act must comply with a federal external review process. The relationship between the external review requirement and ERISA is discussed in Chapter 8.

In addition, HHS established an external review process, known as HHS-Administered Federal External Review Process, similar to the state process to govern self-insured plans and insured plans not governed by state law. For more detail, see, Dept. of Health and Human Services, Standards for Self-Insured Non-Federal Governmental Health Plans and

Health Insurance Issuers Offering Group and Individual Health Coverage Using the HHS-Administered Federal External Review Process (Jan. 11, 2017).

Discrimination. Section 1201 of the ACA added Section 2706 to the PHSA, 42 U.S.C. § 300gg–5, prohibiting group health plans and insurers from discriminating against providers acting within the scope of their license or certification under state law. This section also prohibits group health plans and insurers from discriminating against an individual who benefits from a premium tax credit or cost-sharing reduction payment.

Contraception Coverage. HHS has defined contraception as a preventive service for women that insurers must cover without cost-sharing. This ruling was met with strong resistance from Catholic and other religious organizations. HHS exempted religious employers from covering contraception, and gave nonprofit organizations sponsored by religious organizations (such as universities, hospitals, and charities) until August of 2013 to comply. HHS further proposed a compromise under which religious organizations would not need to cover contraception, but their insurers or self-insured plan administrators must offer contraception coverage to employees of the religious organizations. This issue was litigated in dozens of cases, which were brought under the First Amendment and Religious Freedom Restoration Act, including Burwell v. Hobby Lobby Stores, Inc., 573 U.S. 682 (2014). For a more detailed discussion of Hobby Lobby and subsequent administrative changes to the requirement, see Chapter 16.

Abortion Coverage. Section 1303 of the ACA, 42 U.S.C. § 18023, prohibits the use of federal subsidies to finance abortion coverage beyond coverage for rape, incest, or to protect the mother from physical life endangerment. The preexisting condition high-risk pool is also prohibited from paying for abortions. Several cases have been brought challenging the preventive service regulation's requirement that group health plans and insurers cover post-intercourse contraceptives, thought by some to be abortifacients. These provisions are also discussed further in Chapter 16.

NOTES AND QUESTIONS

1.   If plans were able to keep lifetime and annual limits on liability, how would that affect other major provisions and overarching goals of the ACA?

2.   Why would the ACA eliminate cost-sharing for preventative services recommended by the United States Preventative Services Task Force? What effects, positive or negative, might that have?

3.   What were the drafters of the ACA attempting to accomplish by allowing young adults to stay on their parents' health plans until the age of 26? Why eliminate that coverage at 26?

4.   Although most of the provisions in the ACA did not become effective until 2014, several benefit mandates established by § 1001 went into effect for plan years beginning after September 2010, including requirements for the coverage of preventative services without cost-sharing, dependent children up to age 26, and emergency services without prior authorization and without higher cost-sharing for out-of-network providers. What explains prioritizing these provisions for early effective dates?

5.   *Grandfathered Plans.* Many of the ACA's requirements do not apply to **"grandfathered" plans**. The ACA guaranteed that group and nongroup insurance plans that existed on the effective date of the statute could continue indefinitely and be renewed without having to comply with many of the statute's requirements. Employers could add new employees and enrollees could add family members to these plans. The plans could remain active so long as they did not change significantly.

In addition, the provisions relating to annual limits and prohibiting exclusion of preexisting conditions apply to grandfathered group plans, although they need not cover adult children if other non-grandfathered coverage is available. Elizabeth Weeks Leonard, Can You Really Keep Your Health Plan? The Limits of Grandfathering under the Affordable Care Act, 36 J. Corp. L. 753 (2011). Despite fears that ACA plans would cost more due to essential health benefits, premiums and cost-sharing for grandfathered plans and ACA-compliant plans in the individual and small group markets were roughly equivalent in 2014. Heidi Whitmore et al., Grandfathered, Grandmothered, and ACA-Compliant Health Plans Have Equivalent Premiums, 36 Health Aff. 306 (2017). By 2020, 14% of employees with employer-sponsored insurance were enrolled in a grandfathered plan. Kaiser Family Found., Employer Health Benefits Survey 2020 Annual Survey.

6.   *Grandmothered Plans.* President Obama promised the American public, "if you like the insurance you have, you can keep it." While enabling grandfathered plans to continue indefinitely technically supported this promise, it failed to account for the ability of insurers and employers to stop offering existing plans. The Congressional Budget Office (CBO) predicted in 2010 that up to 3 million people would lose their employer-based insurance after the ACA's passage. See, Cong. Budget Office, H.R. 4872, Reconciliation Act of 2010 (Final Health Care Legislation) (Mar. 20, 2010). Furthermore, nongroup and small group market plans had to offer essential health benefits and other requirements, which necessitated cancelling and restructuring existing plans. Many Americans believed that President Obama's statement also encompassed plans that they enrolled in after the ACA was enacted in 2010, in part due to President Obama repeating portions of this promise during the campaign. As many of the ACA's insurance reforms began to go into effect for January 1, 2014, people began to realize that they would lose coverage they had obtained since 2010. On November 14, 2013, the Obama Administration announced that states could extend this noncompliant transitional coverage, so called **"grandmothered" plans**, for plan years beginning before October 2014.

7. *Judicial Review of External Review.* Whether, and to what extent, external review decisions will be subject to judicial review remains somewhat of an open question. ACA § 2719(b)(1) provides that the external review must be binding on the health plan. The federal guidance further provides, "Upon receipt of a notice of a final external review decision reversing the adverse benefit determination or final internal adverse benefit determination, the plan immediately must provide coverage or payment (including immediately authorizing or immediately paying benefits) for the claim." It would seem, therefore, that the external review decision is effectively a final decision. The federal regulation implementing the provision, however, states that the decision of an external reviewer "is binding on the plan or issuer, as well as the claimant, except to the extent other remedies are available under State or Federal law." 75 Fed. Reg. 43330, 43335 (2010). The Departments of the Treasury, Labor, and Health and Human Services later clarified that a plan or issuer may not delay payment because the plan intends to seek judicial review. Instead it must act in accordance with the external review until there is a judicial decision otherwise. 45 C.F.R. § 147.136 (2011). This suggests that in some instances, external review decisions are reviewable in court.

Many states have adopted external review laws that explicitly make the decisions of an external reviewer binding on the insurer (but not the enrollee) or both the insurer and enrollee. See William Pitsenberger, "Sez Who?" State Constitutional Concerns with External Review Laws and the Resulting Conundrum Posed by Rush Prudential HMO v. Moran, 15 Conn. Ins. L. J. 85, 94–99 (2008). Some states, such as Iowa, included a judicial appeal option in their statutes. See, Iowa Code § 514J.110; Gjerde v. United Healthcare Plan of the River Valley, Inc., 859 N.W.2d 672 (Iowa Ct. App. Nov. 13, 2014). But plans are developing ways to evade external review and judicial review of coverage denials. Amy B. Monahan & Daniel Schwarcz, The Rules of Medical Necessity, 107 Iowa L. Rev. ___ (forthcoming 2022).

For those states without a clear option for judicial review, few reported cases address the question of whether "binding" external review decisions are reviewable. However, courts appear to be moving toward judicial reviewability. For example, a series of New York cases, interpreting the New York statute, have held that the external review is the final step of the administrative process, but remains reviewable by a court. Alexandra H. v. Oxford Health Ins. Inc., 833 F.3d 1299 (11th Cir. 2016); Mercy Flight Cent., Inc. v. Kondolf, 973 N.Y.S.2d 521 (N.Y. City Ct. 2013); Schulman v. Group Health Inc., 833 N.Y.S.2d 62 (N.Y. App. Div. 2007); Vellios v. IPRO, 765 N.Y.S.2d 222 (N.Y. Sup. Ct. 2003). In the vast majority of cases, however, the external review decisions will not be appealed and will, as a practical matter, be binding.

8. *Student Health Insurance Plans.* In early 2011, HHS issued a regulation recognizing a new category of health insurance plans: student health plans. Student health plans are health insurance plans that are only available to college and university students. They are regulated like individual

insurance coverage except that they are not subject to some of the ACA's regulatory provisions. Student health plans, for example, do not need to admit all applicants, only students; they can charge an administrative fee for the use of the student health services; and due to their size and special circumstances are not subject to a medical loss ratio, discussed below. As of 2014, student health programs may no longer impose annual limits on essential health benefits. Student health plans are not required to offer health plans keyed to specific metal levels, but cannot offer plans that have actuarial values less than 60 percent. Finally, student health plans at religious universities are subject to the same rules regarding contraception coverage that apply to employees at those institutions. See, Dept. of Health and Human Services, Student Health Insurance Coverage, 45 C.F.R. §§ 144, 147, 158 (2017). Otherwise, however, they must comply with the ACA.

9. *Prohibiting Discrimination.* The ACA enacted a new antidiscrimination provision directly applicable to private health insurance in the provision known as Section 1557, discussed in Chapter 6.

PROBLEMS: INSURANCE REFORMS

1. George McNamara purchased an insurance policy in 2020. The policy covers pharmaceuticals, but does not cover a particular drug that he is taking for his asthma. Must the plan do so? It also does not cover physical therapy, which he has been prescribed because of a recent injury. Must the plan cover physical therapy, and can it limit the number of visits to which George is entitled?

2. Valley Products has covered all its employees with health insurance since the year 2000. Since 2010, it has increased its deductibles three times, but each time the increase did not exceed the growth in the medical care component of the Consumer Price Index since the last increase. Must the plan comply with the ACA's internal and external review requirements?

2. Consumer Protections—ACA § 1001; 42 U.S.C. § 300gg–18, § 300gg–94

The ACA also included several provisions intended to protect consumers. The two highlighted here focus on preventing insurers from spending too much of premium dollars on administrative costs or increasing premiums unreasonably.

Medical Loss Ratios. Section 10101 of the ACA adds Section 2718 of the PHSA, 42 USC § 300gg–18, which requires insurers to spend a minimum proportion of their premium revenues on health care services and activities that improve health care quality, the so-called minimum **medical loss ratio** (MLR) requirement. Health insurers must report to HHS the percentage of premium revenue that they spend on clinical services, activities that improve health care quality, and on all other non-claim (administrative) costs. The MLR is the ratio of amounts that the insurer spent on clinical services and for activities that improve health care quality to adjusted premium revenue. HHS allows insurers to apply the costs of a wide range of quality improvement activities against the MLR, including activities that reduce medical errors and protect patient safety, improve outcomes of care, encourage prevention and wellness, and prevent rehospitalizations, as well as a range of health IT costs.

Health insurers must provide annual rebates to their enrollees if their MLRs are less than 85% of premium revenue in the large group market or 80% in the small group or individual market (also referred to as the "80/20 Rule"). The rebates must equal the product of the percentage by which a company's MLR falls short of the allowed percentage for its state and market and the total amount of premium revenue. In other words, if an insurer in the individual market pays 75% of its adjusted premiums for clinical services and 2% for health care quality improvement activities (such as disease management or patient education programs), it would owe a rebate of 3% for the year. Rebates are based on the average MLRs of the preceding three years and higher rebates often reflect high profitability for insurers.

In 2011, the first year of the program, insurers paid out over a billion dollars in rebates to consumers. By 2019, insurers owed a record high of nearly $2.46 billion in rebates to more than 11 million consumers. The rebates have tended to be highest in the individual market, though there is considerable variation by state and by insurer. See Katie Keith, ACA Round-Up: Record-High Medical Loss Ratio Rebates, Pass-Through Funding, Preventive Services, Health Affairs Blog (Nov. 17, 2020).

Unreasonable Premium Increases. Section 1003 of the ACA adds Section 2794 to the PHSA, 42 U.S.C. § 300gg–94, establishing an annual review process by HHS and the states of "unreasonable" increases (those 10% or higher) in health insurance premiums. Health insurers must provide justifications for unreasonable premium increases to HHS and all relevant states, and prominently post this information on their websites. Insurers also must justify any annual increases greater than 10% or whatever the state-specific standard is if the state has **effective rate review**. If a state has an effective rate review program, the state evaluates any premium increase above this level. If the state does not have such a program, HHS will review the rate increase. 45 C.F.R. § 154.215(d)(6).

The ACA, however, did not give HHS or the states the authority to disapprove proposed rate increases. Centers for Medicare and Medicaid Services, State Effective Rate Review Programs, www.cms.gov (2017). Some states have this authority under state law, others do not, but the ACA does not expand their authority. However, a Marketplace can review whether a plan has a history of excessive or unjustified premium increases in determining whether to make a particular health plan available.

3. Corporate Wellness—ACA § 2705; 42 U.S.C. § 300gg–4(j)

Section 2705 contains a general exception to the guaranteed issue and community rating provisions, discussed above, that allows employers to grant premium discounts or rebates, or reduced cost-sharing for participation in "Programs of Health Promotion or Disease Prevention," also called **wellness programs**. The ACA provides:

Programs of Health Promotion or Disease Prevention.—

(1) GENERAL PROVISIONS.—

(A) GENERAL RULE.—. . . a program of health promotion or disease prevention . . . shall be a program offered by an employer that is designed to promote health or prevent disease that meets the applicable requirements of this subsection.

(B) NO CONDITIONS BASED ON HEALTH STATUS FACTOR.—If none of the conditions for obtaining a premium discount or rebate or other reward for participation in a wellness program is based on an individual satisfying a standard that is related to a health status factor, such wellness program shall not violate this section if participation in the program is made available to all similarly situated individuals and the requirements of paragraph (2) are complied with.

(C) CONDITIONS BASED ON HEALTH STATUS FACTOR.—If any of the conditions for obtaining a premium discount or rebate or other reward for participation in a wellness program is based on an individual satisfying a standard that is related to a health status factor, such wellness program shall not violate this section if the requirements of paragraph (3) are complied with.

(2) WELLNESS PROGRAMS NOT SUBJECT TO REQUIREMENTS.—If none of the conditions for obtaining a premium discount or rebate or other reward under a wellness program as described in paragraph (1)(B) are based on an individual satisfying a standard that is related to a health status factor (or if such a wellness program does not provide such a reward), the wellness program shall not violate this section if participation in the program is made available to all similarly situated individuals. The following programs shall not have to comply with the requirements of paragraph (3) if participation in the program is made available to all similarly situated individuals:

(A) A program that reimburses all or part of the cost for memberships in a fitness center.

(B) A diagnostic testing program that provides a reward for participation and does not base any part of the reward on outcomes.

(C) A program that encourages preventive care related to a health condition through the waiver of the copayment or deductible requirement under group health plan for the costs of certain items or services related to a health condition (such as prenatal care or well-baby visits).

(D) A program that reimburses individuals for the costs of smoking cessation programs without regard to whether the individual quits smoking.

(E) A program that provides a reward to individuals for attending a periodic health education seminar.

(3) WELLNESS PROGRAMS SUBJECT TO REQUIREMENTS.—If any of the conditions for obtaining a premium discount, rebate, or reward under a wellness program as described in paragraph (1)(C) is based on an individual satisfying a standard that is related to a health status factor, the wellness program shall not violate this section if the following requirements are complied with:

(A) The reward for the wellness program, together with the reward for other wellness programs with respect to the plan that requires satisfaction of a standard related to a health status factor, shall not exceed 30 percent of the cost of employee-only coverage under the plan.... A reward may be in the form of a discount or rebate of a premium or contribution, a waiver of all or part of a cost-sharing mechanism (such as deductibles, copayments, or coinsurance), the absence of a surcharge, or the value of a benefit that would otherwise not be provided under the plan. The Secretaries of Labor, Health and Human Services, and the Treasury may increase the reward available under this subparagraph to up to 50 percent of the cost of coverage if the Secretaries determine that such an increase is appropriate.

(B) The wellness program shall be reasonably designed to promote health or prevent disease. A program complies with the preceding sentence if the program has a reasonable chance of improving the health of, or preventing disease in, participating individuals and it is not overly burdensome, is not a subterfuge for discriminating based on a health status factor, and is not highly suspect in the method chosen to promote health or prevent disease.

(C) The plan shall give individuals eligible for the program the opportunity to qualify for the reward under the program at least once each year.

(D) The full reward under the wellness program shall be made available to all similarly situated individuals. For such purpose, among other things:

(i) The reward is not available to all similarly situated individuals for a period unless the wellness program allows—

(I) for a reasonable alternative standard (or waiver of the otherwise applicable standard) for obtaining the reward for any individual for whom, for that period, it is unreasonably difficult due to a medical condition to satisfy the otherwise applicable standard; and

(II) for a reasonable alternative standard (or waiver of the otherwise applicable standard) for obtaining the reward for any individual for whom, for that period, it is medically inadvisable to attempt to satisfy the otherwise applicable standard.

(ii) If reasonable under the circumstances, the plan or issuer may seek verification, such as a statement from an individual's physician, that a health status factor makes it unreasonably difficult or medically inadvisable for the individual to satisfy or attempt to satisfy the otherwise applicable standard.

(E) The plan or issuer involved shall disclose in all plan materials describing the terms of the wellness program the availability of a reasonable alternative standard (or the possibility of waiver of the otherwise applicable standard) required under subparagraph (D). If plan materials disclose that such a program is available, without describing its terms, the disclosure under this subparagraph shall not be required.

* * *

Wellness programs are touted as improving the health of individuals who participate in them while saving employers money. These programs prove very popular with those who believe that individuals' choices and behaviors are largely responsible for their health outcomes (and accompanying health care costs), and that individuals who do not take care of themselves should bear the cost of their health care rather than impose them on society. Workplace wellness has become a $8 billion industry in the United States with 81% of large employers offering one or more wellness programs. Kaiser Family Found., Employer Health Benefits: 2020 Summary of Findings (2020).

Despite employers' enthusiasm for the programs, studies have found limited evidence of their effectiveness in promoting health and preventing disease. Karen Pollitz and Matthew Rae, Kaiser Family Found., Trends in Workplace Wellness Programs and Evolving Federal Standards (June 9, 2020). Researchers also have identified common problems throughout the wellness plan literature which into question the quality and reliability of evidence supporting these plans. See, reviewing the literature, Camila Strassle and Benjamin E. Berkman, Workplace Wellness Programs:

Empirical Doubt, Legal Ambiguity, and Conceptual Confusion, 61 Wm. & Mary L. Rev. 1663 (2020).

Under 2013 HHS regulations, wellness programs that condition incentives on meeting a health status standard, such as body mass index (BMI), blood pressure, or not smoking, must satisfy five requirements. First, all persons eligible for the program must be given an opportunity at least once a year to qualify. Second, the size of the reward cannot exceed 30% of the total cost of coverage, including both the employer and employee's contribution. The rule allows a 20% additional reward (for a total of 50% of cost) for smoking cessation to counterbalance the permissible 1.5 to 1 tobacco use surcharge in the individual and small group markets. Third, health-contingent wellness programs must provide a "reasonable alternative standard" or waiver of the health-contingent standard for individuals who find it unreasonably difficult to meet the standard because of their medical condition, or for whom it is medically inadvisable to attempt to satisfy the standard. Fourth, health-contingent wellness programs must also be reasonably designed to promote health or prevent disease, not be overly burdensome, not be a subterfuge for health status discrimination, and not use a highly suspect approach. Fifth, the program must require plans and insurers to disclose the availability of other means of qualifying for a reward or the possibility of waiver of a standard. Dept. of the Treasury, Internal Revenue Service, Dept. of Labor, Employee Benefits Sec. Admin., Dept. of Health and Human Services, Incentives for Nondiscriminatory Wellness Programs in Group Health Plans, 78 Fed. Reg. 33157 (June 3, 2013) (codified at 26 C.F.R. § 54; 29 C.F.R. § 2590; 45 C.F.R. §§ 146, 147).

NOTES AND QUESTIONS

1. To what extent do the wellness incentive provisions continue to allow health status underwriting? Are the protections built into the legislation and regulations to keep wellness programs from becoming a substitute for health status underwriting likely to be effective? Are they realistic? See, discussing these issues, Scott D. Halpern et al., Patients as Mercenaries?, 2 Circulation: Cardiovascular Quality & Outcomes 514 (2009). See also, on the appropriateness of using health insurance to encourage wellness, Wendy Mariner, The Affordable Care Act and Health Promotion: The Role of Insurance in Defining Responsibility for Health Risks and Costs, 50 Duq. L. Rev. 271 (2012).

2. Since wellness programs must comply with other federal statutes, the Equal Employment Opportunity Commission (EEOC) issued a series of guidelines to clarify compliance across statutes. For instance, the Americans with Disabilities Act (ADA) prohibits mandatory medical examinations or workplace health inquiries unless the examination or inquiry is job related and consistent with business necessity. 42 U.S.C. § 12112(d)(4). Employers,

however, may conduct voluntary medical examinations or inquiries as part of an employee health program, which includes employee wellness programs. In addition, the Genetic Information Nondiscrimination Act (GINA), 42 U.S.C. §§ 2000ff, et seq., prohibits employers with 15 or more employees from requesting, requiring, or purchasing genetic information regarding their employees unless at least one of six narrow exceptions applies. One of the exceptions applies when an employee voluntarily accepts health services from an employer, which can include wellness program services. The question thus arises under both the ADA and GINA as to when wellness programs may legally offer incentives to "voluntarily" obtain current or past health information regarding employees, their spouses, or their children.

The EEOC issued a guidance in 2000 stating that "a wellness program is 'voluntary' as long as an employer neither requires participation nor penalizes employees who do not participate." After Congress passed the ACA, the EEOC issued a new final rule clarifying its interpretation of "voluntary" to include wellness plans that offer incentives up to 30% of the employee's cost of coverage, among other requirements. Equal Employment Opportunity Commission, Regulations under the Americans With Disabilities Act, 81 Fed. Reg. 31125 (May 17, 2016) (codified at 29 C.F.R. § 1630). The rest of the EEOC regulations largely track the requirements imposed by the ACA and tri-department regulations promulgated under it, although they apply to all employer-sponsored workplace wellness programs and not just those associated with employer-sponsored health plans. The interpretation of "voluntary" in the new final rules was challenged in court, and the court vacated the challenged portions of the rule effective January 1, 2019. AARP v. United States Equal Employment Opportunity Comm'n, 267 F. Supp. 3d 14 at 16 (D.D.C. Aug. 22, 2017); AARP v. United States Equal Employment Opportunity Comm'n, 292 F. Supp. 3d 238 (D.D.C. 2017) (amended order). The EEOC proposed new rules on January 7, 2021, which were withdrawn pursuant to the Biden Administration's memorandum imposing regulatory freeze pending review. Memorandum for the Heads of Executive Departments and Agencies; Regulatory Freeze Pending Review, 82 Fed. Reg. 8346 (Jan. 24, 2017).

PROBLEM: DESIGNING A CORPORATE WELLNESS PROGRAM

As legal counsel for a corporation that expects to purchase health insurance for its employees, you have been asked to review the design of a proposed wellness program for legal issues. The corporate human resources manager would like to give employees a substantial discount on their portion of their health insurance premium if they participate in the program. In particular, the human resources manager has proposed giving each participating employee a 10% discount on that employee's health insurance premium for each one of the following "wellness opportunities" that employee undertakes during the initial pilot year:

    (1)   a smoking cessation program, with the discount available to anyone who does not smoke, or who successfully completes this program;

(2)   a "maintaining appropriate body weight" program, with the discount available to anyone who maintains a proper body weight, or who makes substantial progress toward maintaining a proper body weight, during the program;

(3)   an immunization program, with the discount available to any employee who has received every medically recommended immunization;

(4)   a basic care program, with the discount available to anyone who visits a primary care provider at least once during the year, and, finally;

(5)   a basic safety program, with the discount available to anyone who agrees not to own or ride on a motorcycle, bicycle, skidoo, or jetski, or engage in a dangerous sport (like skiing and diving).

In addition, the human resources manager wants to give another 5% discount on the premium to an employee if for six months neither the employee nor a family member uses medical care covered by the health plan.

Several of the employees have complained about the contours of the proposed program. An overweight employee has a letter from a website from which he purchased a genetic test, which says that his obesity is a consequence, at least in great part, of genetic factors. A few employees object to the immunization program because they have decided to forgo immunization (for themselves and their children) either for medical, philosophical, or religious reasons. A Christian Scientist objects to the requirement that he see a primary care provider regularly to partake in the discounts. An employee who just bought a timeshare in a ski resort argues that it would be unfair to create the basic safety program. A pregnant employee argues that she will be excluded from some discounts because of her pregnancy.

Can the employer institute these wellness programs and give premium discounts if it does? How would you structure these programs to make them consistent with the limitations of the ACA? Could the employer use its wellness program to impose premium surcharges for employees who are not vaccinated against certain transmissible diseases?

4.   Disclosure Requirements—ACA § 1001; 42 U.S.C. § 300gg–15

In addition to the disclosure requirements discussed above for QHPs, the ACA also imposes a number of additional requirements on health plans to increase the information available to plan enrollees or prospective enrollees. Disclosure enhances consumer control by allowing consumers to identify and choose plans with the features that they desire and avoid plans with characteristics they wish to avoid. Disclosure increases competition by helping consumers identify and compare differences in price and quality. It also can improve performance by making poor performance more visible, and thus more expensive.

The ACA specifies both the information to be disclosed and the method of disclosure. Part of this disclosure occurs on the official HHS website,

HealthCare.gov, through which the residents of any state can identify health insurance options, including private insurance, Medicaid, CHIP, and a state high-risk pool. HHS has developed a standard format for presenting information on this website, including information on eligibility, availability, premium rates, cost sharing, and medical loss ratios.

As required by the ACA, HHS has developed standards for disclosure of a **summary of benefits and coverage (SBC)** to applicants, enrollees, and policy or certificate-holders by insurers and self-insured plans. 42 U.S.C. § 300gg–15, 45 C.F.R. § 147.200. These HHS standards preempt state laws that allow plans to provide less information. HHS requirements for the SBC provides a uniform format that requires plans to provide information that is culturally and linguistically appropriate, in readily understandable language, and limited to four pages (doubled-sided, in fact eight pages). HHS has also developed uniform definitions of insurance and medical terms for use in the forms.

The SBC must include a description of coverage for all health benefits categories, including a description of exceptions, reductions, and limitations on coverage; cost-sharing provisions; and renewability provisions. The SBC also must include **coverage facts labels**, which illustrate coverage and cost-sharing requirements for common procedures and conditions, such as a normal delivery and type II diabetes. For example, a coverage fact label could say that if you have diabetes, you can expect coverage for the following listed products and services with specific cost-sharing obligations. Plans must also notify patients of any modifications in benefits 60 days prior to the effective date. The form also sets forth an amount the insurer is likely to pay and an amount the patient is likely to pay. Plans are required to disclose whether they cover at least 60% of allowed costs to ensure that they meet minimum coverage requirements. If any employer plan fails to do so, the employee may be able to get a premium tax credit and purchase insurance through the Marketplace. Finally, a plan must provide a contact number for consumers to call with additional questions and a web address where they can find a copy of the actual policy or certificate. 45 C.F.R. § 147.200.

NOTES AND QUESTIONS

1.   What is the legal effect of the SBC disclosure document? The SBC is supposed to use language that "accurately describes the benefits and coverage under the applicable plan or coverage," but it must also include "a statement that the outline is a summary of the policy or certificate and that the coverage document itself should be consulted to determine the governing contractual provisions." Therefore, the disclosure document, which is intended to promote comparison-shopping, would hold little value for this purpose if it has no

binding legal effect. On the other hand, most insurance contracts are likely to have provisions that are not in the four-page disclosure document.

2. Who is entitled to see SBC disclosure documents? 42 U.S.C. § 300gg–15 provides that the information should be provided to "applicants, enrollees, and policyholders or certificate holders," but the document is useless for comparison-shopping purposes unless it is also available to prospective applicants. The HHS rule requires insurers to provide the SBC information to "shoppers," but they may do so through the HealthCare.gov website rather than mailing individual copies. Insurers are permitted to disclose the SBC document by posting it on the Internet as long as consumers have notice that this is how it is being provided. 45 C.F.R. § 147.200.

5. State Flexibility—ACA §§ 1331, 1332; 42 U.S.C. §§ 18051, 18052

Two provisions of the ACA give states additional flexibility in implementing health reform. First, Section 1331, 42 U.S.C. § 18051, allows states to establish a basic health care program under which the state can offer one or more **standard health plans** that cover the essential health benefits to individuals who have (1) household incomes between 133% and 200% FPL (or up to 133% for legal aliens), (2) are not eligible for Medicaid or affordable employment-related coverage, and (3) are under age 65. Standard plans are private insurance plans that contract with the state and meet a number of requirements. Individuals eligible for the program must not be required to pay a premium higher than the premium for the benchmark plan (the second-lowest-cost Silver plan) in the Marketplace after the application of premium tax credits and cost-sharing reductions. In addition, standard plans cannot ask eligible individuals with household incomes less than 133% of FPL to pay cost-sharing more than that for a Platinum plan through the Marketplace (10%), or that of a Gold plan (20%) if they earn more than 133% of FPL. HHS must pay a state that operates a basic health program 95% of the premium tax credits and cost-sharing reductions for which enrolled individuals would have been eligible if they had received health insurance through the Marketplace.

Second, Section 1332 of the ACA, 42 U.S.C. § 18052, enables states to apply for a waiver to modify key provisions of the ACA and create a new coverage system that better suits the local context and preferences, while still fulfilling the goals of the ACA. Under this "**State Innovation Waiver**" provision, a state may apply to HHS for a waiver of the requirements in the ACA for:

- Marketplaces;
- qualified health plans;
- premium affordability credits;
- cost-sharing reduction payments;

- small employer tax credits; and

- individual and employer mandates.

HHS will approve a § 1332 waiver request if the state proposal would: 1) provide coverage at least as comprehensive as the coverage offered by QHPs through the Marketplace; 2) with at least as affordable premiums and cost-sharing; 3) to at least a comparable number of the state's residents; and 4) without increasing the federal deficit. These four requirements are often referred to as the waiver's "guardrails" because they are intended to keep waivers from going too far outside the statute's goals of expanding access to comprehensive, affordable health care coverage.

Waiver requests are subject to a number of procedural requirements to ensure public input and may last up to five years. After granting a waiver, HHS must pay the state equivalent to what the residents of the state would have received through premium tax credits, cost-sharing reductions, and small business tax credits. This waiver payment is often referred to as "pass-through" funding because the federal government passes some of the money it would have spent on individuals through to the state.

Since the § 1332 waiver program became effective in 2017, HHS has approved waivers for 16 states. Most of the approved waivers establish reinsurance programs, which lower premiums in Marketplace plans by insuring the insurers against certain high-cost claims or enrollees with certain high-cost medical conditions. See generally, Jack Pitsor & Samantha Scotti, State Roles Using 1332 Health Waivers, Nat'l Conf. of State Legislatures (July 1, 2021). Two other waivers have enabled states to operate alternatives to the Marketplaces. Hawaii secured a waiver which allows employers to use their small business tax credits to apply directly to a state fund, rather than use a SHOP Marketplace. The Trump administration granted Georgia a waiver to privatize its Marketplace operations such that, by 2023, consumers must shop for and buy ACA coverage from private web brokers or insurer's websites, instead of HealthCare.gov. In 2021, provider groups sued the federal government over Georgia's waiver and the Biden administration requested more information from Georgia, signaling its concern that the waiver does not meet statutory guardrails and opening the door to termination. See Katie Keith, CMS Requests Information To Assess Georgia's ACA Section 1332 Waiver, Health Aff. Blog (Jun. 9, 2021).

Though most of the state waivers thus far have been modest in scope, the § 1332 waiver provision has the potential to support more significant state-level reforms. A § 1332 waiver and its pass-through funding could, for example, enable a state to pursue a **public-option plan** or **single-payer system**, as long as it stays within the waiver's guardrails. For example, state public-option plans passed in Washington, Colorado, and Nevada call for § 1332 waivers to allow the states the flexibility to offer a public option on their Marketplaces and access pass-through funds from premium tax credits to help pay for it. State single-payer reforms, such as Vermont's ill-fated Green Mountain Care, would also require a 1332 waiver and pass-through funding. For a discussion of the role of waivers in state health reforms, see, Jaime S. King, Katherine L. Gudiksen, & Erin C. Fuse Brown, Are State Public Option Plans Worth It?, 59 Harv. J. on Legis. ___ (2022); Lindsay F. Wiley, Medicaid for All? State-Level Single-Payer Health Care, 79 Ohio St. L. J. 843 (2018).

But the same waiver mechanisms—the suspension of ACA requirements and the pass-through of funding to the state—have the potential to erode the ACA's protections, as well. The Trump Administration in 2018 announced a rebranding of § 1332 waivers as "State Relief and Empowerment Waivers," and a relaxing the standards for determining whether waiver proposals met the statutory guardrails. HHS offered several "waiver concepts" illustrating the kinds of waivers the administration favored. Overall, the guidance suggested that states could use waivers to enact reforms that might decrease enrollment, move those with pre-existing conditions into a separate risk pool, and apply tax-credits to plans that do not comply with ACA coverage requirements, but discouraged states from using waivers to expand public programs, create public plan options, or pursue single-payer. See Jennifer Tolbert & Karen Pollitz, New Rules for Section 1332 Waivers: Changes and Implications, Kaiser Family Found. (Dec. 10, 2018). In the final days of the Trump Administration, HHS passed its guidance into regulation. In July 2021, the Biden Administration published a proposed rule that would reverse the Trump Administration regulation, and add a guardrail that waivers must not adversely affect vulnerable populations. 86 Fed. Reg. 35156 (July 1, 2021).

6. Premium Stabilization—ACA § 1343; 42 U.S.C. § 18063

The ACA also introduced three premium stabilization programs, **risk adjustment**, **reinsurance**, and **risk corridors**, to mitigate the effects of **risk selection** on insurance premiums. The programs aimed to ensure that insurers who successfully game the system by disproportionately attracting good risks and repelling bad risks (a.k.a. **favorable selection**) are not rewarded for it, and likewise prevent insurers who attract poor risks (a.k.a. **adverse selection**) from dropping out of the market.

The reinsurance and risk corridor programs were temporary and only lasted from 2014 to 2016. The reinsurance program shielded insurers from incurring losses from high-cost patients whose costs exceeded a certain threshold up to the reinsurance cap. The reinsurance program proved so successful that states have begun to replicate it. In the risk corridor program, HHS collected funds from plans with lower than expected actual claims and made payments to plans with higher than expected actual claims.

The third program, risk adjustment, embedded a permanent **managed competition** scheme into the individual and small group markets. Under Section 1343, states can charge a fee to health plans and health insurers in the individual and small group markets (other than self-insured group health plans or grandfathered plans) whose enrollees' average actuarial risk is below average, and then make payments to plans and insurers (other than self-insured group health plans or grandfathered plans) whose enrollees' average actuarial risk is above average. This risk adjustment attempts to level the playing field between plans who have experienced both favorable and adverse selection. Tom Baker, Health Insurance, Risk, and Responsibility after the Patient Protection and Affordable Care Act, 159 U. Penn. L. Rev. 1577 (2011). After litigation challenged CMS's risk adjustment calculation as arbitrary and capricious, the agency briefly suspended risk adjustment and promulgated a new methodology, upheld in 2019. See Katie Keith, The 2021 Final Payment Notice, Part 3: Risk Adjustment and Final Letter to Issuers, Health Aff. Blog (May 10, 2020);

7. Consumer Choice—ACA §§ 1312, 1322, 1334; 42 U.S.C. §§ 18032, 18042, 18054

Section 1312 of the ACA, 42 U.S.C. § 18032, specifies that qualified individuals may enroll through the Marketplace in any QHP. A qualified individual is a resident of a state who is not otherwise insured through employment or a public program and who is neither incarcerated (other than pending the disposition of charges) nor an alien who is illegally in the United States. Qualified employers may offer their employees insurance through the Marketplace and may specify the level of coverage available to their employees. A qualified employer is a small employer that covers all of its full-time employees through the Marketplace, or, at a state's option, larger employers. In 2015, the Protecting Affordable Coverage for Employees Act (PACE Act) amended the ACA and the PHSA to define a small employer as having 50 or fewer employees, while granting states the opportunity to broaden the definition to organizations with 100 or fewer employees. 42 U.S.C. § 18024(b) (2015).

Under the statute, employees may choose any QHP offered through the Marketplace within the tier specified by their employer. The final rules also allow employers to pick a particular plan for their employees or to allow employees a wider choice between plans and tiers. Employers who purchase insurance for their employees through the SHOP Marketplace may pursue a "**defined contribution**" approach, which enables the employer to pay an amount sufficient to cover a share of the cost of a lower-cost plan and the employee must pay extra if the employee wants a higher cost plan. This approach presents some legal challenges. The Age Discrimination in Employment Act (ADEA) regulations prohibit employers with 20 or more employees from paying a lower proportion of health benefits' costs for older employees (aged 40 or older) than for younger employees. 29 C.F.R. § 1625.10(d)(4)(ii). An employer subject to the ADEA could not, therefore, pay a flat dollar amount if it meant older employees would need to pay a higher proportion of their premiums. An employer could, however, pay a fixed percentage of premiums, or pick a particular plan and require employees to pay the additional cost of a more expensive plan.

The ACA provides several other options to increase consumer choice and competition, although most of the insurance plans sold within the Marketplace are offered by private insurers that otherwise operate within the same state. First, Section 1322 provides federal grants and loans to encourage the creation of nonprofit, **consumer owned and operated plans (co-ops)** governed by majority vote. These entities cannot be government entities or preexisting insurance companies. They are tax exempt, but are also subject to a number of requirements to make sure that they do not compete unfairly with private insurers. In 2014, 23 cooperative plans received federal funding, by August 2016, 16 of those plans had shut down due to significant financial losses. Many of these plans closed in the middle of the year, leaving tens of thousands unexpectedly without coverage. Opponents of the ACA often point to these failed cooperative plans as evidence of the law's shortcomings and failures. See, Rick Cohen, Nonprofit Health Co-Ops: Designed to Compete for the Public Good, Nonprofit Quarterly (Oct. 24, 2014); Phil Galewitz, Seven Remaining Obamacare Co-Ops Prepare Survival Strategies, Kaiser Health News (July 13, 2016).

Second, under Section 1333, states may enter into interstate compacts, known as **Health Care Choice Compacts**, under which qualified health insurance plans may be offered in one state subject to the laws and regulations of another. Although the home state regulates the interstate insurer, the ACA requires these interstate plans to remain subject to the market conduct, unfair trade practices, network adequacy, consumer protection, and dispute resolution standards of any state in which the insurance is sold. The interstate insurers must also be licensed in each state, and notify consumers that it was not otherwise subject to the laws of the selling state. HHS is required to approve interstate insurance compacts. The plans sold under these compacts must be at least as comprehensive as the coverage required under the ACA. The inability to offer greater variation in coverage under the ACA may make selling these plans less desirable. To date, while five states have passed legislation to approve the sale of insurance across state lines, no Health Care Choice

Compact has been established. See Jenn Jenson and Trish Reilly, Nat'l Acad. for State Health Pol'y, Selling Insurance Across State Lines: Lessons for States and Questions for Policymakers (Feb. 2017).

Finally, the ACA also enabled multistate plans to be offered on the Marketplaces. Section 1334 of the law, 42 U.S.C. § 18054, authorizes the Office of Personnel Management (OPM) to enter into contracts with multistate insurance plans to offer individual or small group coverage through the Marketplaces. HHS deems plans that have contracts with OPM certified to participate in the Marketplaces. At least two plans must be available in each state, at least one of which must be a non-profit. OPM may negotiate with the plans a medical loss ratio, profit margin, premium levels, and other terms and conditions that are in the interests of the enrollees. Multistate plans must be licensed and comply with the requirements of each state in which they do business and with all standards that apply to the Federal Employees Health Benefit Plan (FEHBP) that are consistent with the reform law. See, on multistate plans, Sidney Watson et al., Creating Multi-State Qualified Health Plans in Health Insurance Exchanges: Lessons for Rural and Urban America From the Federal Employees Health Benefit Program, 6 St. Louis U. J. Health L. & Pol'y 103 (2011); Sarah Goodell et al., The Multi-State Plan Program, Health Aff. Blog (May 29, 2014); Robert E. Moffit & Neil R. Meredith, Multistate Health Plans: Agents for Competition or Consolidation?, INQUIRY: The J. of Health Care Org., Provision, & Financing (Sept. 7, 2015).

NOTES AND QUESTIONS

1. *Risk Pooling and Selection.* Although insurers may sell policies both through the Marketplaces and outside of them, they must consider all enrollees in all health plans (except grandfathered plans) in the individual market, whether in plans in or outside of the Marketplace, to be a single risk pool. The same is true with respect to the small group market. A state may require the merger of the individual and small group risk pools. Policies sold outside of the Marketplace to individuals and small groups must also offer the essential benefits package. Insurers must charge the same premium for QHPs purchased in and outside of the Marketplace. State benefit requirements also continue to apply outside of the Marketplace. Insurers will undoubtedly find ways to steer good risks outside of the Marketplace, and the termination of CSR payments will potentially exacerbate risk selection.

2. *Stop Loss Insurance.* One way insurers can risk select is by offering stop-loss insurance to self-insured plans outside of the Marketplace. Many of the requirements of the ACA, including the essential health benefits package, metal tiers, the risk pooling and risk adjustment programs, medical loss ratio requirements, unreasonable premium increase justification requirement, and premium taxes do not apply to self-insured plans. Self-insured plans are now common in the large group market, and are becoming more common in the

small group market. Small employers can rarely bear the risk of catastrophic medical costs, but insurers are increasingly selling "stop-loss" insurance to small employers, effectively insuring them for significant medical costs, but allowing the employer to qualify as self-insured. This strategy could destabilize the small group market both in and outside of the Marketplaces. Sabrina Corlette et al., Small Business Health Insurance and the ACA: Views from the Market 2017, Robert Wood Johnson Found. (July 2017); Sara Hansard, More Smaller Companies Are Self-Insuring Health Benefits, Bloomberg Law (Aug. 7, 2017); Mark A. Hall, Regulating Stop-Loss Coverage May be Needed to Deter Self-Insuring Small Employers from Undermining Market Reforms, 31 Health Aff. 316 (2012).

II. LEGAL AND POLITICAL CHALLENGES FOLLOWING THE ACA

Since its inception, the ACA has been embroiled in turmoil and controversy. States, organizations, and even the House of Representatives have posed numerous legal challenges to a variety of provisions in the Act that have wound their way through the courts, resulting in multiple Supreme Court cases. In addition, political opposition in Congress has resulted in over 70 attempts to repeal the ACA and its essential components. To date, the ACA still stands as the law of the land, though efforts to undermine it have hindered it substantially. This section examines the ACA's legal and political challenges, as well as the impact of these challenges on health care in America.

A. INDIVIDUAL MANDATE

1. Constitutionality of Enactment

No sooner was the ink of the president's signature dry on the ACA than the attorneys general from Florida and a dozen other states filed a lawsuit challenging the constitutionality of the legislation. After the lawsuits were filed, several other attorneys general joined in the Florida lawsuit, which eventually included 26 state plaintiffs, as well as the National Federation of Independent Business (NFIB), and two individual plaintiffs. A variety of other groups and individuals throughout the country brought about two dozen other lawsuits with most of them challenging the individual mandate, but some raising other issues as well.

The case focused on the constitutionality of the individual mandate. The plaintiffs argued that the federal government lacked the authority to require individuals to purchase health insurance. That question, along with several others, was decided by the Supreme Court, which upheld the minimum coverage requirement in June 2012.

NATIONAL FEDERATION OF INDEPENDENT
BUSINESS V. SEBELIUS

Supreme Court of the United States, 2012.
567 U.S. 519.

ROBERTS, CHIEF JUSTICE.

Today we resolve constitutional challenges to two provisions of the Patient Protection and Affordable Care Act of 2010: the individual mandate, which requires individuals to purchase a health insurance policy providing a minimum level of coverage; and the Medicaid expansion, which gives funds to the States on the condition that they provide specified health care to all citizens whose income falls below a certain threshold. We do not consider whether the Act embodies sound policies. That judgment is entrusted to the Nation's elected leaders. We ask only whether Congress has the power under the Constitution to enact the challenged provisions.

In our federal system, the National Government possesses only limited powers; the States and the people retain the remainder. . . . In this case we must again determine whether the Constitution grants Congress powers it now asserts, but which many States and individuals believe it does not possess. . . .

* * *

This case concerns two powers that the Constitution does grant the Federal Government, but which must be read carefully to avoid creating a general federal authority akin to the police power. The Constitution authorizes Congress to "regulate Commerce with foreign Nations, and among the several States, and with the Indian Tribes." [ ] Our precedents read that to mean that Congress may regulate "the channels of interstate commerce," "persons or things in interstate commerce," and "those activities that substantially affect interstate commerce." [ ] The power over activities that substantially affect interstate commerce can be expansive. That power has been held to authorize federal regulation of such seemingly local matters as a farmer's decision to grow wheat for himself and his livestock, and a loan shark's extortionate collections from a neighborhood butcher shop. [ ]

Congress may also "lay and collect Taxes, Duties, Imposts and Excises, to pay the Debts and provide for the common Defence and general Welfare of the United States." U.S. Const., Art. I, § 8, cl. 1. Put simply, Congress may tax and spend. This grant gives the Federal Government considerable influence even in areas where it cannot directly regulate. The Federal Government may enact a tax on an activity that it cannot authorize, forbid, or otherwise control. [ ]

The reach of the Federal Government's enumerated powers is broader still because the Constitution authorizes Congress to "make all Laws which shall be necessary and proper for carrying into Execution the foregoing Powers." Art. I, § 8, cl. 18. . . .

Our permissive reading of these powers is explained in part by a general reticence to invalidate the acts of the Nation's elected leaders. "Proper respect for a coordinate branch of the government" requires that we strike down an Act of Congress only if "the lack of constitutional authority to pass [the] act in question is clearly demonstrated." [ ] Members of this Court are vested with the authority to interpret the law; we possess neither the expertise nor the prerogative to make policy judgments. Those decisions are entrusted to our Nation's elected leaders, who can be thrown out of office if the people disagree with them. It is not our job to protect the people from the consequences of their political choices.

Our deference in matters of policy cannot, however, become abdication in matters of law. "The powers of the legislature are defined and limited; and that those limits may not be mistaken, or forgotten, the constitution is written." [ ] Our respect for Congress's policy judgments thus can never extend so far as to disavow restraints on federal power that the Constitution carefully constructed. . . . And there can be no question that it is the responsibility of this Court to enforce the limits on federal power by striking down acts of Congress that transgress those limits. [ ]

* * *

The Government's first argument is that the individual mandate is a valid exercise of Congress's power under the Commerce Clause and the Necessary and Proper Clause. According to the Government, the health care market is characterized by a significant cost-shifting problem. Everyone will eventually need health care at a time and to an extent they cannot predict, but if they do not have insurance, they often will not be able to pay for it. Because state and federal laws nonetheless require hospitals to provide a certain degree of care to individuals without regard to their ability to pay, [ ] hospitals end up receiving compensation for only a portion of the services they provide. To recoup the losses, hospitals pass on the cost to insurers through higher rates, and insurers, in turn, pass on the cost to policy holders in the form of higher premiums. Congress estimated that the cost of uncompensated care raises family health insurance premiums, on average, by over $1,000 per year. [ ]

In the Affordable Care Act, Congress addressed the problem of those who cannot obtain insurance coverage because of preexisting conditions or other health issues. It did so through the Act's "guaranteed-issue" and "community rating" provisions. These provisions together prohibit insurance companies from denying coverage to those with such conditions or charging unhealthy individuals higher premiums than healthy individuals. [ ]

The guaranteed-issue and community-rating reforms do not, however, address the issue of healthy individuals who choose not to purchase insurance to cover potential health care needs. In fact, the reforms sharply exacerbate that problem, by providing an incentive for individuals to delay purchasing health insurance until they become sick, relying on the promise of guaranteed and affordable coverage. The reforms also threaten to impose massive new costs on insurers, who are required to accept unhealthy individuals but prohibited from charging them rates necessary to pay for their coverage. This will lead insurers to significantly increase premiums on everyone. [ ]

The individual mandate was Congress's solution to these problems. By requiring that individuals purchase health insurance, the mandate prevents cost-shifting by those who would otherwise go without it. In addition, the mandate forces into the insurance risk pool more healthy individuals, whose premiums on average will be higher than their health care expenses. This allows insurers to subsidize the costs of covering the unhealthy individuals the reforms require them to accept. . . .

The Government contends that the individual mandate is within Congress's power because the failure to purchase insurance "has a substantial and deleterious effect on interstate commerce" by creating the cost-shifting problem. [ ] The path of our Commerce Clause decisions has not always run smooth, [ ] but it is now well established that Congress has broad authority under the Clause. We have recognized, for example, that "[t]he power of Congress over interstate commerce is not confined to the regulation of commerce among the states," but extends to activities that "have a substantial effect on interstate commerce." [ ] Congress's power, moreover, is not limited to regulation of an activity that by itself substantially affects interstate commerce, but also extends to activities that do so only when aggregated with similar activities of others. [ ]

Given its expansive scope, it is no surprise that Congress has employed the commerce power in a wide variety of ways to address the pressing needs of the time. But Congress has never attempted to rely on that power to compel individuals not engaged in commerce to purchase an unwanted product. Legislative novelty is not necessarily fatal; there is a first time for everything. But sometimes "the most telling indication of [a] severe constitutional problem . . . is the lack of historical precedent" for Congress's action. [ ]

The Constitution grants Congress the power to "*regulate* Commerce." Art. I, § 8, cl. 3 The power to *regulate* commerce presupposes the existence of commercial activity to be regulated. . . . The language of the Constitution reflects the natural understanding that the power to regulate assumes there is already something to be regulated. [ ]

Our precedent also reflects this understanding. As expansive as our cases construing the scope of the commerce power have been, they all have one thing in common: They uniformly describe the power as reaching "activity." It is nearly impossible to avoid the word when quoting them. [ ]

The individual mandate, however, does not regulate existing commercial activity. It instead compels individuals to *become* active in commerce by purchasing a product, on the ground that their failure to do so affects interstate commerce. Construing the Commerce Clause to permit Congress to regulate individuals precisely *because* they are doing nothing would open a new and potentially vast domain to congressional authority. . . . Allowing Congress to justify federal regulation by pointing to the effect of inaction on commerce would bring countless decisions an individual could *potentially* make within the scope of federal regulation, and—under the Government's theory—empower Congress to make those decisions for him.

* * *

Applying the Government's logic to the familiar case of *Wickard v. Filburn* shows how far that logic would carry us from the notion of a government of limited powers. In *Wickard,* the Court famously upheld a federal penalty imposed on a farmer for growing wheat for consumption on his own farm. [ ] That amount of wheat caused the farmer to exceed his quota under a program designed to support the price of wheat by limiting supply. The Court rejected the farmer's argument that growing wheat for home consumption was beyond the reach of the commerce power. It did so on the ground that the farmer's decision to grow wheat for his own use allowed him to avoid purchasing wheat in the market. That decision, when considered in the aggregate along with similar decisions of others, would have had a substantial effect on the interstate market for wheat. [ ]

Wickard has long been regarded as "perhaps the most far reaching example of Commerce Clause authority over intrastate activity," but the Government's theory in this case would go much further. Under *Wickard* it is within Congress's power to regulate the market for wheat by supporting its price. But price can be supported by increasing demand as well as by decreasing supply. The aggregated decisions of some consumers not to purchase wheat have a substantial effect on the price of wheat, just as decisions not to purchase health insurance have on the price of insurance. Congress can therefore command that those not buying wheat do so, just as it argues here that it may command that those not buying health insurance do so. The farmer in *Wickard* was at least actively engaged in the production of wheat, and the Government could regulate that activity because of its effect on commerce. The Government's theory here would effectively override that limitation, by establishing that individuals may be regulated under the Commerce Clause whenever enough of them are not doing something the Government would have them do.

Indeed, the Government's logic would justify a mandatory purchase to solve almost any problem. [ ] To consider a different example in the health care market, many Americans do not eat a balanced diet. That group makes up a larger percentage of the total population than those without health insurance. [ ] The failure of that group to have a healthy diet increases health care costs, to a greater extent than the failure of the uninsured to purchase insurance. [ ] Those increased costs are borne in part by other Americans who must pay more, just as the uninsured shift costs to the insured. [ ] Congress addressed the insurance problem by ordering everyone to buy insurance. Under the Government's theory, Congress could address the diet problem by ordering everyone to buy vegetables. [ ]

People, for reasons of their own, often fail to do things that would be good for them or good for society. Those failures—joined with the similar failures of others—can readily have a substantial effect on interstate commerce. Under the Government's logic, that authorizes Congress to use its commerce power to compel citizens to act as the Government would have them act.

That is not the country the Framers of our Constitution envisioned. . . . While Congress's authority under the Commerce Clause has of course expanded with the growth of the national economy, our cases have "always recognized that the power to regulate commerce, though broad indeed, has limits." [ ] The Government's theory would erode those limits, permitting Congress to reach beyond the natural extent of its authority, "everywhere extending the sphere of its activity and drawing all power into its impetuous vortex." [ ] Congress already enjoys vast power to regulate much of what we do. Accepting the Government's theory would give Congress the same license to regulate what we do not do, fundamentally changing the relation between the citizen and the Federal Government.

. . . The Framers gave Congress the power to *regulate* commerce, not to *compel* it, and for over 200 years both our decisions and Congress's actions have reflected this understanding. . . .

The Government sees things differently. It argues that because sickness and injury are unpredictable but unavoidable, "the uninsured as a class are active in the market for health care, which they regularly seek and obtain." [ ] The individual mandate "merely regulates how individuals finance and pay for that active participation—requiring that they do so through insurance, rather than through attempted self-insurance with the back-stop of shifting costs to others."[ ]

The Government repeats the phrase "active in the market for health care" throughout its brief, [ ] but that concept has no constitutional significance. An individual who bought a car two years ago and may buy another in the future is not "active in the car market" in any pertinent sense. The phrase "active in the market" cannot obscure the fact that most of those regulated by the individual mandate are not currently engaged in any commercial activity involving health care, and that fact is fatal to the Government's effort to "regulate the uninsured as a class." [ ] Our precedents recognize Congress's power to regulate "class[es] of *activities*,"[ ], not classes of *individuals,* apart from any activity in which they are engaged [ ].

The individual mandate's regulation of the uninsured as a class is, in fact, particularly divorced from any link to existing commercial activity. The mandate primarily affects healthy, often young adults who are less likely to need significant health care and have other priorities for spending their money. It is precisely because these individuals, as an actuarial class, incur relatively low health care costs that the mandate helps counter the effect of forcing insurance companies to cover others who impose greater costs than their premiums are allowed to reflect. [ ] If the individual mandate is targeted at a class, it is a class whose commercial inactivity rather than activity is its defining feature.

The Government, however, claims that this does not matter. The Government regards it as sufficient to trigger Congress's authority that almost all those who are uninsured will, at some unknown point in the future, engage in a health care transaction. . . .

The proposition that Congress may dictate the conduct of an individual today because of prophesied future activity finds no support in our precedent. We have said that Congress can anticipate the *effects* on commerce of an economic activity. [ ] But we have never permitted Congress to anticipate that activity itself in order to regulate individuals not currently engaged in commerce. . . .

Everyone will likely participate in the markets for food, clothing, transportation, shelter, or energy; that does not authorize Congress to direct them to purchase particular products in those or other markets today. The Commerce Clause is not a general license to regulate an individual from cradle to grave, simply because he will predictably engage in particular transactions. Any police power to regulate individuals as such, as opposed to their activities, remains vested in the States.

The Government argues that the individual mandate can be sustained as a sort of exception to this rule, because health insurance is a unique product. According to the Government, upholding the individual mandate would not justify mandatory purchases of items such as cars or broccoli because, as the Government puts it, "[h]ealth insurance is not purchased for its own sake like a car or broccoli; it is a means of financing health-care consumption and covering universal risks." [ ] But cars and broccoli are no more purchased for their "own sake" than health insurance. They are purchased to cover the need for transportation and food.

The Government says that health insurance and health care financing are "inherently integrated." [ ] But that does not mean the compelled purchase of the first is properly regarded as a regulation of the second. No matter how "inherently integrated" health insurance and health care consumption may be, they are not the same thing: They involve different transactions, entered into at different times, with different providers. And for most of those targeted by the mandate, significant health care needs will be years, or even decades, away. The proximity and degree of connection between the mandate and the subsequent commercial activity is too lacking to justify an exception of the sort urged by the Government. . . .

The Government next contends that Congress has the power under the Necessary and Proper Clause to enact the individual mandate because the mandate is an "integral part of a comprehensive scheme of economic regulation"—the guaranteed-issue and community-rating insurance reforms. [ ] Under this argument, it is not necessary to consider the effect that an individual's inactivity may have on interstate commerce; it is enough that Congress regulate commercial activity in a way that requires regulation of inactivity to be effective.

The power to "make all Laws which shall be necessary and proper for carrying into Execution" the powers enumerated in the Constitution, Art. I, § 8, cl. 18, vests Congress with authority to enact provisions "incidental to the [enumerated] power, and conducive to its beneficial exercise," [ ] Although the Clause gives Congress authority to "legislate on that vast mass of incidental powers which must be involved in the constitution," it does not license the exercise of any "great substantive and independent power[s]" beyond those specifically enumerated. [ ] Instead, the Clause is " 'merely a declaration, for the removal of all uncertainty, that the means of carrying into execution those [powers] otherwise granted are included in the grant.' "[ ]

As our jurisprudence under the Necessary and Proper Clause has developed, we have been very deferential to Congress's determination that a regulation is "necessary." We have thus upheld laws that are " 'convenient, or useful' or 'conducive' to the authority's 'beneficial exercise.' " [ ] But we have also carried out our responsibility to declare unconstitutional those laws that undermine the structure of government established by the Constitution. Such laws, which are not "consist[ent] with the letter and spirit of the constitution," [ ] are not "*proper* [means] for carrying into Execution" Congress's enumerated powers. Rather, they are, "in the words of The Federalist, 'merely acts of usurpation' which 'deserve to be treated as such.' " [ ]

Applying these principles, the individual mandate cannot be sustained under the Necessary and Proper Clause as an essential component of the insurance reforms. Each of our prior cases upholding laws under that Clause involved exercises of authority derivative of, and in service to, a granted power.... The individual mandate, by contrast, vests Congress with the extraordinary ability to create the necessary predicate to the exercise of an enumerated power.

This is in no way an authority that is "narrow in scope," [ ] or "incidental" to the exercise of the commerce power [ ]. Rather, such a conception of the Necessary and Proper Clause would work a substantial expansion of federal authority. No longer would Congress be limited to regulating under the Commerce Clause those who by some preexisting activity bring themselves within the sphere of federal regulation. Instead, Congress could reach beyond the natural limit of its authority and draw within its regulatory scope those who otherwise would be outside of it. Even if the individual mandate is "necessary" to the Act's insurance reforms, such an expansion of federal power is not a "proper" means for making those reforms effective.

* * *

Just as the individual mandate cannot be sustained as a law regulating the substantial effects of the failure to purchase health insurance, neither can it be upheld as a "necessary and proper" component of the insurance reforms. The commerce power thus does not authorize the mandate. [ ]

That is not the end of the matter. Because the Commerce Clause does not support the individual mandate, it is necessary to turn to the Government's second argument: that the mandate may be upheld as within Congress's enumerated power to "lay and collect Taxes." Art. I, § 8, cl. 1.

The Government's tax power argument asks us to view the statute differently than we did in considering its commerce power theory. In making its Commerce Clause argument, the Government defended the mandate as a regulation requiring individuals to purchase health insurance. The Government does not claim that the taxing power allows Congress to issue such a command. Instead, the Government asks us to read the mandate not as ordering individuals to buy insurance, but rather as imposing a tax on those who do not buy that product.

Under the mandate, if an individual does not maintain health insurance, the only consequence is that he must make an additional payment to the IRS when he pays his taxes. *See*, § 5000A(b). That, according to the Government, means the mandate can be regarded as establishing a condition—not owning health insurance—that triggers a tax—the required payment to the IRS. Under that theory, the mandate is not a legal command to buy insurance. Rather, it makes going without insurance just another thing the Government taxes, like buying gasoline or earning income. And if the mandate is in effect just a tax hike on certain taxpayers who do not have health insurance, it may be within Congress's constitutional power to tax.

* * *

The exaction the Affordable Care Act imposes on those without health insurance looks like a tax in many respects. The "[s]hared responsibility payment," as the statute entitles it, is paid into the Treasury by "taxpayer[s]" when they file their tax returns. [ ] It does not apply to individuals who do not pay federal income taxes because their household income is less than the filing threshold in the Internal Revenue Code. [ ] For taxpayers who do owe the payment, its amount is determined by such familiar factors as taxable income, number of dependents, and joint filing status. [ ]. The requirement to pay is found in the Internal Revenue Code and enforced by the IRS, which—as we previously explained—must assess and collect it "in the same manner as taxes." [ ] This process yields the essential feature of any tax: it produces at least some revenue for the Government. . . .

It is of course true that the Act describes the payment as a "penalty," not a "tax." . . .

We have similarly held that exactions not labeled taxes nonetheless were authorized by Congress's power to tax. . . . ("[M]agic words or labels" should not "disable an otherwise constitutional levy"). [ ]

Our cases confirm this functional approach. For example, in *Drexel Furniture,* we focused on three practical characteristics of the so-called tax on employing child laborers that convinced us the "tax" was actually a penalty. First, the tax imposed an exceedingly heavy burden—10 percent of a company's net income—on those who employed children, no matter how small their infraction. Second, it imposed that exaction only on those who knowingly employed underage laborers. Such scienter requirements are typical of punitive statutes, because Congress often wishes to punish only those who intentionally break the law. Third, this "tax" was enforced in part by the Department of Labor, an agency responsible for punishing violations of labor laws, not collecting revenue. [ ]

The same analysis here suggests that the shared responsibility payment may for constitutional purposes be considered a tax, not a penalty: First, for most Americans the amount due will be far less than the price of insurance, and, by statute, it can never be more. . . . Second, the individual mandate contains no scienter requirement. Third, the payment is collected solely by the IRS through the normal means of taxation—except that the

Service is *not* allowed to use those means most suggestive of a punitive sanction, such as criminal prosecution. [ ] . . .

None of this is to say that the payment is not intended to affect individual conduct. Although the payment will raise considerable revenue, it is plainly designed to expand health insurance coverage. But taxes that seek to influence conduct are nothing new. . . . Today, federal and state taxes can compose more than half the retail price of cigarettes, not just to raise more money, but to encourage people to quit smoking. And we have upheld such obviously regulatory measures as taxes on selling marijuana and sawed-off shotguns. . . .

In distinguishing penalties from taxes, this Court has explained that "if the concept of penalty means anything, it means punishment for an unlawful act or omission." [ ] While the individual mandate clearly aims to induce the purchase of health insurance, it need not be read to declare that failing to do so is unlawful. Neither the Act nor any other law attaches negative legal consequences to not buying health insurance, beyond requiring a payment to the IRS. The Government agrees with that reading, confirming that if someone chooses to pay rather than obtain health insurance, they have fully complied with the law. [ ]

* * *

The plaintiffs contend that Congress's choice of language—stating that individuals "shall" obtain insurance or pay a "penalty"—requires reading § 5000A as punishing unlawful conduct, even if that interpretation would render the law unconstitutional. We have rejected a similar argument before. . . .

The joint dissenters argue that we cannot uphold § 5000A as a tax because Congress did not "frame" it as such. [ ] In effect, they contend that even if the Constitution permits Congress to do exactly what we interpret this statute to do, the law must be struck down because Congress used the wrong labels. [L]abels should not control here. . . .

* * *

The Affordable Care Act's requirement that certain individuals pay a financial penalty for not obtaining health insurance may reasonably be characterized as a tax. Because the Constitution permits such a tax, it is not our role to forbid it, or to pass upon its wisdom or fairness.

The Federal Government does not have the power to order people to buy health insurance. Section 5000A would therefore be unconstitutional if read as a command. The Federal Government does have the power to impose a tax on those without health insurance. Section 5000A is therefore constitutional, because it can reasonably be read as a tax.

[Justice Ginsburg, in an opinion joined by Justices Breyer, Sotomayor, and Kagan, dissented from the Chief Justice's opinion on the Commerce Clause issue but concurred in the holding that the law was a constitutional tax. Justices Scalia, Kennedy, Alito, and Thomas dissented jointly against the Chief Justice's conclusion that the mandate was constitutional. They would have held the mandate and the Medicaid expansions to be unconstitutional and the entire ACA to be nonseverable and thus nullified. The Medicaid portion of the decision is reproduced in Chapter 10].

* * *

NOTES AND QUESTIONS

1.   Does reframing the penalty for failing to obtain health insurance as a tax change the likelihood that an uninsured individual, who could otherwise afford health insurance, would purchase it? Does the NFIB decision limit the ability of Congress to further address problems of access, cost, and quality in health care? What types of solutions is it most likely to discourage? Did the ACA's opponents win the battle, but lose the war, or could this be said of the ACA's supporters? The Tax Cuts and Jobs Act of 2017 repealed the tax for failing to have insurance, but not the mandate. Under NFIB, does the mandate continue to exist without the tax penalty? See *infra*, II.A.2. for a discussion of *Texas v. United States*, in which 20 states argued that the elimination of the tax penalty renders the ACA unconstitutional under *NFIB*.

2.   Chief Justice Roberts cast the deciding vote and wrote the opinion in this case. What political and legal reasons did he have for framing the mandate as a tax?

2.   Tax Reform and Litigation

NFIB v. Sebelius allowed the individual mandate and the ACA to stand as of 2012. Congressional Republicans attempted to repeal and replace the ACA after the presidential administration change in 2017, but never secured the votes to enact a law. See Section II.D, *infra*. In 2017, Republicans instead modified the ACA as part of a tax reform bill, the Tax Cuts and Jobs Act, which repealed only the tax penalty linked to the ACA's individual mandate, effective as of 2019.

Republicans had two reasons for repealing the individual mandate penalty. First, the CBO projected that eliminating the penalty would decrease federal deficits by around $338 million from 2018 to 2027, which Republicans needed to successfully pass their planned tax cuts. The CBO projected these federal savings would result from fewer people enrolling in health insurance coverage subsidized federally by the ACA, Cong. Budget Office, Repealing the Individual Health Insurance Mandate: An Updated Estimate (Nov. 2017), though these predicted effects did not materialize, Sarah Kliff, "Republicans Killed the Obamacare Mandate. New Data

Shows It Didn't Really Matter," N.Y. Times (Sept. 18, 2020). Second, removing the penalty allowed congressional Republicans to follow through on their campaign promises to repeal at least a portion of the ACA. See, Timothy Jost, Mandate Repeal Provision Ends Health Care Calm, 37 Health Aff. 13 (2018).

The elimination of the penalty prompted Republican-led states to relitigate *NFIB*'s holding that the mandate was constitutionally enacted as a tax. In February 2018, Republican state attorneys general from Texas and 19 other states filed suit against HHS and the IRS. The states argued that without the tax penalty, the individual mandate no longer functions as a valid tax, rendering it, and the rest of the ACA, unconstitutional. Two individual plaintiffs joined the suit, claiming that they bought health insurance because the federal statute commands them to do so, but that the command is unconstitutional without a tax penalty.

Although the U.S., HHS Secretary, and IRS Commissioner were nominally the defendants, the Justice Department under the Trump administration took the state plaintiffs' position and refused to defend the federal law. Nineteen Democratic state attorneys general and the District of Columbia intervened, arguing that their interests differed significantly from those of the federal government because striking down the ACA would deprive their citizens of the law's benefits and deprive states themselves of more than $650 billion in federal health care funds. On appeal, the U.S. House of Representatives joined the intervenor defendants.

The District Court held that the state plaintiffs had standing to challenge the individual mandate, that the mandate was unconstitutional without the penalty, and that the mandate could not be severed from the rest of the law, declaring the entire ACA unconstitutional. *Texas v. U.S.*, 340 F. Supp. 3d 579 (ND Tex. 2018). On appeal, the Fifth Circuit agreed that plaintiffs had standing and that the mandate was unconstitutional, but found the District Court's severability analysis "incomplete" to justify striking the entire Act. It remanded the case for further analysis. *Texas v. U.S.*, 945 F.3d 355 (5th Cir. 2019). California and the other defending intervenor states petitioned the Supreme Court for certiorari.

In a 7–2 majority opinion by Justice Breyer, the Supreme Court dismissed the case, holding that all of the plaintiffs lacked standing to challenge the now-unenforceable mandate. *California v. Texas*, 593 U.S. ___, 141 S.Ct. 2104 (2021). As the Court summarized:

> The Constitution gives federal courts the power to adjudicate only genuine "Cases" and "Controversies." Art. III, § 2. That power includes the requirement that litigants have standing. A plaintiff has standing only if he can "allege personal injury fairly traceable to the defendant's allegedly unlawful conduct and likely to be redressed by the requested relief." [ ]

Id. The individual plaintiffs lacked standing because, "while [the mandate] tells them to obtain [health] coverage," it "has no means of enforcement . . . [w]ith the penalty zeroed out . . . ." Thus, their "pocketbook injury" of paying for health insurance cannot be "causally connected" to any possible Government enforcement action because the IRS cannot take any action against them based on their health insurance status. Further, the individual plaintiffs' claimed injury is not redressable through the injunctive relief they requested because the mandate "is unenforceable," leaving "no one, and nothing, to enjoin" from enforcing it, even if the court found the provision unconstitutional.

The state plaintiffs alleged that the individual mandate caused them financial injury indirectly by encouraging state residents to enroll in insurance programs paid at least in part by the states, namely Medicaid, CHIP, and state-employee health plans. Factually, the Court found insufficient evidence that the mandate drove enrollment in these insurance plans. Logically, the Court found it "counterintuitive . . . that an unenforceable mandate will cause [state] residents to enroll in valuable benefits programs that they would otherwise forgo." *Id.* The states' Medicaid, CHIP, and employee health plan expenditures thus had insufficient causal connection to the mandate.

The state plaintiffs also alleged injury directly from a variety of increased administrative and compliance expenses that they argued the mandate and other "inextricably interwoven" provisions of the ACA required, such as the "costs of providing beneficiaries of state health plans with information about their health insurance coverage [and] the cost of furnishing the IRS with that related information," as well as the cost of satisfying the employer mandate by providing health benefits to state employees. "The problem with these claims, however, is that other provisions of Act, not the [individual mandate], impose these other requirements. Nothing in the text of these form provisions suggests that they would not operate without" the individual mandate." *Id.* The "state plaintiffs attack the constitutionality of only the [individual mandate]," not the other provisions in the ACA they allege caused the direct financial injuries. Thus, the Court held that the states had no standing because they had not alleged a "concrete, particularized injury . . . fairly traceable to'" the mandate.

Justices Thomas and Alito wrote separately, both repeating their dissenting arguments from *NFIB*. Justice Thomas concurred with the outcome and the majority's conclusions on lack of standing, but took the opportunity to reiterate his dissents from *NFIB*'s conclusion on the mandate's constitutionality as a tax. Justice Alito's dissent in *California*, joined by Justice Gorsuch, proceeded to the merits of the toothless mandate's constitutionality and severability, repeating many of the arguments made in the *NFIB* dissent and arguing that the entire law should fall.

The Tax Cuts and Jobs Act's removal of the individual mandate penalty thus did not invalidate the mandate itself, let alone the whole ACA. In effect, the removal of this third "leg" in the "three legged-stool" served as a test of the mandate's actual role in maintaining the ACA's universal coverage strategy. The removal of the mandate's penalty in 2019 did not cause significant disenrollment, adverse selection, or observable destabilization in the individual market. See Rachel Fehr, Daniel McDermott, & Cynthia Cox, Individual Insurance Market Performance in 2019, Kaiser Family Foundation (May 13, 2020). The individual market's stability on the two remaining and weakened legs defied the assumptions of the CBO, the Congress that enacted the ACA in 2009, and many of the ACA's proponents. But see John F. Shiels & Randall Haught, Without the individual mandate, the Affordable Care Act would still cover 23 million; premiums would rise less than predicted, 30 Health Affairs 2177 (2011); Molly Frean, Jonathan Gruber, & Benjamin D. Sommers, Disentangling the ACA's Coverage Effects—Lessons for Policymakers, 375 NEJM 1605 (Oct. 27, 2016).

The ACA's defenders in *NFIB* had emphasized this supposedly "essential" connection between the mandate and the other two legs, arguing for their inseverability to uphold the mandate. See Sections II.A.1, *supra*, and II.B, *infra*. But the surprising evidence from 2019 that removing the mandate's penalty had little effect on enrollment altered those assumptions, suggesting that the mandate was no longer necessary to counteract adverse selection. After the ACA's initial implementation, the subsidies to help pay for coverage that consumers found valuable may have done the work of the mandate for those eligible for subsidies. The ACA-defenders' arguments *for* severability in *California v. Texas* incorporated this new evidence and reversed position. As Justice Thomas observed in his concurrence, "times have changed" over the ACA's first decade, and "those who would preserve the Act [now] reverse course and argue that the mandate has transformed from the cornerstone of the law into a standalone provision." *California v. Texas*, 593 U.S. ___, 141 S.Ct. 2104 (2021). Though the Supreme Court did not reach the legal issue of severability, the individual mandate has, for all practical purposes, been cleaved from the overall ACA with little effect.

NOTES AND QUESTIONS

1. *Lingering Questions.* If the states and individual plaintiffs in *California v. Texas* did not have standing to challenge the mandate after Congress removed the monetary penalty, would any other plaintiff have standing to mount this challenge? If a plaintiff with standing did exist to successfully bring this litigation, what would happen in the health care system

if a court invalidated the mandate? In this hypothetical scenario, how should a court's severability analysis proceed?

2. *Congressional Intent.* What effect should Congress's subsequent expansions of ACA provisions have on the interpretation of the TCJA? In particular, Congress passed COVID relief legislation in March 2020 that expanded on the ACA's provisions to require insurance coverage for COVID-19 testing and vaccination, among many other things. See Families First Coronavirus Response Act (FFCRA); Coronavirus Aid, Relief, and Economic Security Act (CARES). Congress's extension of other core provisions in the ACA *after* zeroing out the individual mandate penalty in 2017 suggests that Congress intended for the rest of the ACA to remain in effect, even if the individual mandate were struck down. See John Aloysuis Cogan Jr., Congress Has Already Ruled in California v. Texas, 62 B.C. L. Rev. Online (Nov. 24, 2020) (discussing the FFCRA and CARES Act as "legislative overrides" relevant to severability analysis).

3. *ACA Here to Stay?* It took two and a half years for the District Court's 2018 decision invalidating the entire ACA to wind its way to reversal in the Supreme Court in 2021. During that time, there was upheaval all three branches of government and throughout society. Justice Barrett replaced Justice Ginsburg on the Supreme Court, the 2020 election replaced President Trump with President Biden and put the Democratic Party in bare majority control of the Senate, and the coronavirus pandemic ravaged the country and the world. The pendency of the litigation cast a pall of uncertainty over the ACA's future throughout this tumultuous period, despite that legal scholars considered the plaintiffs' arguments exceedingly weak. See, e.g., Jonathan H. Adler & Abbe R. Gluck, "What the Lawless Obamacare Ruling Means," N.Y. TIMES (Dec. 15, 2018); Nicholas A. Bagley, "A Case That Should Have Been Laughed Out of Court May Kill Obamacare," THE ATLANTIC (Dec. 29, 2019).

After surviving years of attacks, one of the ACA's essential "legs," the individual mandate, has been knocked out. In light of the Supreme Court's dismissal on standing grounds, how vulnerable does the ACA remain as a whole? How permanent are its protections safeguarding access to insurance? What would be required to further secure its protections? For an interesting discussion of the ACA's potential role as a "super statute" or "quasi-super statute," see, Erin C. Fuse Brown, Developing a Durable Right to Healthcare, 14 J. Minn. L. Sci. & Tech 439 (2013).

Consider the cumulative effects of these repeated challenges to the individual mandate in conjunction with the other challenges discussed in the following sections.

B. PREMIUM ASSISTANCE TAX CREDITS

In 2015, the Supreme Court resolved a series of lawsuits claiming that the ACA only authorized Congress to offer premium tax credits to individuals in state-based Marketplaces, but not in the federally-facilitated Marketplace. In the following opinion, the Supreme Court grappled with

Congress's "inartful drafting" of the ACA that could have proved fatal to the goals of the law.

KING V. BURWELL

Supreme Court of the United States, 2015.
576 U.S. 473.

ROBERTS, CHIEF JUSTICE.

The Patient Protection and Affordable Care Act adopts a series of interlocking reforms designed to expand coverage in the individual health insurance market. First, the Act bars insurers from taking a person's health into account when deciding whether to sell health insurance or how much to charge. Second, the Act generally requires each person to maintain insurance coverage or make a payment to the Internal Revenue Service. And third, the Act gives tax credits to certain people to make insurance more affordable.

In addition to those reforms, the Act requires the creation of an "Exchange" in each State—basically, a marketplace that allows people to compare and purchase insurance plans. The Act gives each State the opportunity to establish its own Exchange, but provides that the Federal Government will establish the Exchange if the State does not.

This case is about whether the Act's interlocking reforms apply equally in each State no matter who establishes the State's Exchange. Specifically, the question presented is whether the Act's tax credits are available in States that have a Federal Exchange.

* * *

The Affordable Care Act. . . requires the creation of an "Exchange" in each State where people can shop for insurance, usually online. [ ] An Exchange may be created in one of two ways. First, the Act provides that "[e]ach State shall . . . establish an American Health Benefit Exchange . . . for the State." [ ] Second, if a State nonetheless chooses not to establish its own Exchange, the Act provides that the Secretary of Health and Human Services "shall . . . establish and operate such Exchange within the State." [ ]

The issue in this case is whether the Act's tax credits are available in States that have a Federal Exchange rather than a State Exchange. The Act initially provides that tax credits "shall be allowed" for any "applicable taxpayer." [ ] The Act then provides that the amount of the tax credit depends in part on whether the taxpayer has enrolled in an insurance plan through "an Exchange established by the State under section 1311 of the Patient Protection and Affordable Care Act." [ ]

The IRS addressed the availability of tax credits by promulgating a rule that made them available on both State and Federal Exchanges. . . . At this point, 16 States and the District of Columbia have established their own Exchanges; the other 34 States have elected to have HHS do so.

Petitioners are four individuals who live in Virginia, which has a Federal Exchange. They do not wish to purchase health insurance. In their view, Virginia's Exchange does not qualify as "an Exchange established by the State under [42 U.S.C. § 18031]," so they should not receive any tax credits. That would make the cost of buying insurance more than eight percent of their income, which would exempt them from the Act's coverage requirement. [ ]

Under the IRS Rule, however, Virginia's Exchange would qualify as "an Exchange established by the State under [42 U.S.C. § 18031]," so petitioners would receive tax credits. That would make the cost of buying insurance less than eight percent of petitioners' income, which would subject them to the Act's coverage requirement. The IRS Rule therefore requires petitioners to either buy health insurance they do not want, or make a payment to the IRS.

Petitioners challenged the IRS Rule in Federal District Court. The District Court dismissed the suit, holding that the Act unambiguously made tax credits available to individuals enrolled through a Federal Exchange. [ ] The Court of Appeals for the Fourth Circuit affirmed. The Fourth Circuit viewed the Act as "ambiguous and subject to at least two different interpretations." [ ] The court therefore deferred to the IRS's interpretation. . . .

The Affordable Care Act addresses tax credits in what is now Section 36B of the Internal Revenue Code. That section provides: "In the case of an applicable taxpayer, there shall be allowed as a credit against the tax imposed by this subtitle . . . an amount equal to the premium assistance credit amount." [ ] Section 36B then defines the term "premium assistance credit amount" as "the sum of the premium assistance amounts determined under paragraph (2) with respect to all coverage months of the taxpayer occurring during the taxable year." [ ] Section 36B goes on to define the two italicized terms—"premium assistance amount" and "coverage month"—in part by referring to an insurance plan that is enrolled in through "an Exchange established by the State under [42 U.S.C. § 18031]." [ ]

* * *

[The Court initially concluded that the IRS's interpretation was not entitled to deference under administrative law principles because the question has "deep 'economic and political significance'" and potentially central importance to "health insurance policy," which is not the IRS's area of expertise.]It is instead our task to determine the correct reading of

Section 36B. If the statutory language is plain, we must enforce it according to its terms. [ ]. But oftentimes the "meaning—or ambiguity—of certain words or phrases may only become evident when placed in context." [ ] So when deciding whether the language is plain, we must read the words "in their context and with a view to their place in the overall statutory scheme." . . .

We begin with the text of Section 36B. As relevant here, Section 36B allows an individual to receive tax credits only if the individual enrolls in an insurance plan through "an Exchange established by the State under [42 U.S.C. § 18031]." In other words, three things must be true: First, the individual must enroll in an insurance plan through "an Exchange." Second, that Exchange must be "established by the State." And third, that Exchange must be established "under [42 U.S.C. § 18031]." We address each requirement in turn.

First, all parties agree that a Federal Exchange qualifies as "an Exchange" for purposes of Section 36B. [ ] Section 18031 provides that "[e]ach State shall . . . establish an American Health Benefit Exchange . . . for the State." [ ] Although phrased as a requirement, the Act gives the States "flexibility" by allowing them to "elect" whether they want to establish an Exchange. § 18041(b). If the State chooses not to do so, Section 18041 provides that the Secretary "shall . . . establish and operate such Exchange within the State." [ ]

By using the phrase "such Exchange," Section 18041 instructs the Secretary to establish and operate the same Exchange that the State was directed to establish under Section 18031. [ ] In other words, State Exchanges and Federal Exchanges are equivalent—they must meet the same requirements, perform the same functions, and serve the same purposes. . . . A Federal Exchange therefore counts as "an Exchange" under Section 36B.

Second, we must determine whether a Federal Exchange is "established by the State" for purposes of Section 36B. At the outset, it might seem that a Federal Exchange cannot fulfill this requirement. . . . But when read in context, "with a view to [its] place in the overall statutory scheme," the meaning of the phrase "established by the State" is not so clear. [ ]

After telling each State to establish an Exchange, Section 18031 provides that all Exchanges "shall make available qualified health plans to qualified individuals." [ ] Section 18032 then defines the term "qualified individual" in part as an individual who "resides in the State that established the Exchange." [ ] And that's a problem: If we give the phrase "the State that established the Exchange" its most natural meaning, there would be no "qualified individuals" on Federal Exchanges. . . . As we just mentioned, the Act requires all Exchanges to "make available qualified health plans to qualified individuals"—something an Exchange could not do if there were no such individuals. [ ] And the Act tells the Exchange, in deciding which health plans to offer, to consider "the interests of qualified individuals . . . in the State or States in which such Exchange operates"— again, something the Exchange could not do if qualified individuals did not exist. § 18031(e)(1)(B). This problem arises repeatedly throughout the Act. [ ]

These provisions suggest that the Act may not always use the phrase "established by the State" in its most natural sense. . . .

Third, we must determine whether a Federal Exchange is established "under [42 U.S.C. § 18031]." . . .

The Act defines the term "Exchange" to mean "an American Health Benefit Exchange established under section 18031." [ ] If we import that definition into Section 18041, the Act tells the Secretary to "establish and operate such 'American Health Benefit Exchange established under section 18031.'" That suggests that Section 18041 authorizes the Secretary to establish an Exchange under Section 18031, not (or not only) under Section 18041. Otherwise, the Federal Exchange, by definition, would not be an "Exchange" at all. [ ]

This interpretation of "under [42 U.S.C. § 18031]" fits best with the statutory context. All of the requirements that an Exchange must meet are in Section 18031, so it is sensible to regard all Exchanges as established under that provision. In addition, every time the Act uses the word "Exchange," the definitional provision requires that we substitute the phrase "Exchange established under section 18031." If Federal Exchanges were not established under Section 18031, therefore, literally none of the Act's requirements would apply to them. Finally, the Act repeatedly uses the phrase "established under [42 U.S.C. § 18031]" in situations where it would make no sense to distinguish between State and Federal Exchanges. [ ] A Federal Exchange may therefore be considered one established "under [42 U.S.C. § 18031]."

The upshot of all this is that the phrase "an Exchange established by the State under [42 U.S.C. § 18031]" is properly viewed as ambiguous. . . .

* * *

The Affordable Care Act contains more than a few examples of inartful drafting. . . . Anyway, we "must do our best, bearing in mind the fundamental canon of statutory construction that the words of a statute must be read in their context and with a view to their place in the overall statutory scheme." [ ] After reading Section 36B along with other related provisions in the Act, we cannot conclude that the phrase "an Exchange established by the State under [Section 18031]" is unambiguous.

Given that the text is ambiguous, we must turn to the broader structure of the Act to determine the meaning of Section 36B. " . . . Here, the statutory scheme compels us to reject petitioners' interpretation because it would destabilize the individual insurance market in any State with a Federal Exchange, and likely create the very "death spirals" that Congress designed the Act to avoid. [ ]

Under petitioners' reading, . . . the Act would operate quite differently in a State with a Federal Exchange. As they see it, one of the Act's three major reforms—the tax credits—would not apply. And a second major reform—the coverage requirement—would not apply in a meaningful way. As explained earlier, the coverage requirement applies only when the cost of buying health insurance (minus the amount of the tax credits) is less than eight percent of an individual's income. So without the tax credits, the coverage requirement would apply to fewer individuals. And it would be a lot fewer. In 2014, approximately 87 percent of people who bought insurance on a Federal Exchange did so with tax credits, and virtually all of those people would become exempt. [ ] If petitioners are right, therefore, only one of the Act's three major reforms would apply in States with a Federal Exchange.

The combination of no tax credits and an ineffective coverage requirement could well push a State's individual insurance market into a death spiral. . . . And those effects would not be limited to individuals who purchase insurance on the Exchanges. Because the Act requires insurers to treat the entire individual market as a single risk pool, premiums outside the Exchange would rise along with those inside the Exchange. [ ]

It is implausible that Congress meant the Act to operate in this manner. . . .

Petitioners respond that Congress was not worried about the effects of withholding tax credits from States with Federal Exchanges because "Congress evidently believed it was offering states a deal they would not refuse." . . .

Section 18041 refutes the argument that Congress believed it was offering the States a deal they would not refuse. That section provides that, if a State elects not to establish an Exchange, the Secretary "shall . . . establish and operate such Exchange within the State." 42 U.S.C. § 18041(c)(1)(A). The whole point of that provision is to create a federal fallback in case a State chooses not to establish its own Exchange. Contrary to petitioners' argument, Congress did not believe it was offering States a deal they would not refuse—it expressly addressed what would happen if a State did refuse the deal.

Finally, the structure of Section 36B itself suggests that tax credits are not limited to State Exchanges. Section 36B(a) initially provides that tax credits "shall be allowed" for any "applicable taxpayer." Section 36B(c)(1) then defines an "applicable taxpayer" as someone who (among other things) has a household income between 100 percent and 400 percent of the federal poverty line. Together, these two provisions appear to make anyone in the specified income range eligible to receive a tax credit.

According to petitioners, however, those provisions are an empty promise in States with a Federal Exchange. In their view, an applicable taxpayer in such a State would be eligible for a tax credit—but the amount of that tax credit would always be zero. . . .

We have held that Congress "does not alter the fundamental details of a regulatory scheme in vague terms or ancillary provisions." [ ] But in petitioners' view, Congress made the viability of the entire Affordable Care Act turn on the ultimate ancillary provision: a sub-sub-sub section of the Tax Code. We doubt that is what Congress meant to do. . . .

Petitioners' arguments about the plain meaning of Section 36B are strong. But while the meaning of the phrase "an Exchange established by the State under [42 U.S.C. § 18031]" may seem plain "when viewed in isolation," such a reading turns out to be "untenable in light of [the statute] as a whole." . . .

Reliance on context and structure in statutory interpretation is a "subtle business, calling for great wariness lest what professes to be mere rendering becomes creation and attempted interpretation of legislation becomes legislation itself." [ ] For the reasons we have given, however, such reliance is appropriate in this case, and leads us to conclude that Section 36B allows tax credits for insurance purchased on any Exchange created under the Act. Those credits are necessary for the Federal Exchanges to function like their State Exchange counterparts, and to avoid the type of calamitous result that Congress plainly meant to avoid.

In a democracy, the power to make the law rests with those chosen by the people. Our role is more confined—"to say what the law is." [ ] That is easier in some cases than in others. But in every case we must respect the role of the Legislature, and take care not to undo what it has done. A fair reading of legislation demands a fair understanding of the legislative plan.

Congress passed the Affordable Care Act to improve health insurance markets, not to destroy them. If at all possible, we must interpret the Act in a way that is consistent with the former, and avoids the latter. Section 36B can fairly be read consistent with what we see as Congress's plan, and that is the reading we adopt.

The judgment of the United States Court of Appeals for the Fourth Circuit is

Affirmed.

[Justice Scalia, joined by Justices Thomas and Alito, dissented.]

NOTES AND QUESTIONS

1. *Battling over Statutory Interpretation.* Justice Scalia's dissent emphasized the literal meaning of the statute's words, lamenting that, "[w]ords no longer have meaning if an Exchange that is not established by a State is 'established by the State.'" While the dissenters agreed that "sound interpretation requires paying attention" to context to divine congressional intent, they felt bound to "apply the presumption that lawmakers use words in 'their natural and ordinary signification.'" They did not find the contextual evidence sufficient to support what they viewed as "the implausible conclusion that Congress used 'by the State' to mean 'by the State or not by the State.'" Justice Scalia surmised that "[i]t is perfectly possible for" the guaranteed issue, community rating, and individual mandate "to operate independently of tax credits" in states that do not operate their own Exchanges. He further gave weight to what he saw as a "congressional preference" in the ACA "for state participation in the establishment of Exchanges."

Justice Scalia, Thomas, and Alito also dissented from Justice Roberts's majority approach to interpretation in *NFIB v. Sebelius.* Justice Scalia explicitly referred to those fault lines in his *King v. Burwell* dissent, expressing his view that Justice Roberts's opinions had "change[d] the usual rules of statutory interpretation for the sake of the Affordable Care Act," by "revis[ing] major components of the statute in order to save them from unconstitutionality." Justice Scalia's dissent further bemoaned that, "[w]e should start calling this law SCOTUScare." For an artful discussion of the role of the Supreme Court in interpreting Congressional intent, see, Abbe Gluck, Imperfect Statutes, Imperfect Courts: Understanding Congress' Plan in the Era of Unorthodox Lawmaking, 129 Harv. L. Rev. 62 (2015).

2. *Evolving Understanding of the ACA's Entwined Provisions.* Consider Justice Roberts's descriptions in *NFIB* and *King* of how Congress intended the ACA's core provisions to operate. Note also the alignment of the Justices in majority and dissenting opinions in those opinions. Given the changes to the individual mandate and in the composition of the Supreme Court since *King* in 2015, how would you predict the Supreme Court would have decided the constitutionality and severability questions raised in *Texas v. California* if it had the opportunity to reach them?

C. COST-SHARING REDUCTION & RISK CORRIDOR PAYMENTS

On July 30, 2014, the Republican majority in the House of Representatives voted to file a lawsuit challenging the Obama administration's implementation of the ACA. The complaint focused on two issues: the administration's 2013 decision to delay the implementation of the employer mandate for a year, and the administration's funding of the ACA's CSR payments without an explicit appropriation by Congress.

The Obama administration moved to dismiss the House's complaint, relying on well-established precedent in contending that the federal courts have no jurisdiction to hear complaints from members of Congress challenging the actions of the executive branch. The U.S. District Court for the District of Columbia dismissed the House's complaint regarding the employer mandate delay issue, but retained the House's claim that the funding of the CSRs without an explicit annual appropriation infringed on the constitutional authority of Congress to appropriate funds. U.S. House of Representatives v. Burwell, 130 F. Supp. 3d 53 (2015). As noted above, CSRs provide substantial reductions in cost-sharing (deductibles, copays, coinsurance, and out-of-pocket maximums) for individuals who enroll in a silver plan on the Marketplace. Eliminating these payments while the ACA still required insurers to limit cost-sharing could have amounted to over $130 billion in unreimbursed expenses for insurers over the next ten years.

After the Trump administration assumed control of HHS, attorneys general from 17 states and the District of Columbia were permitted to intervene in the case on the bases that (1) the states had shown a substantial risk that granting the injunction would directly lead to increased premiums in their state, which in turn would lead to an increase in the number of uninsured individuals that the state would have to provide health care, and (2) the Trump Administration did not adequately represent their interests. House of Representatives v. Hargan, 2017 WL 3271445 (2017).

Shortly afterward, HHS under the Trump administration announced that it would not continue the CSR payments to insurers. The House, the Trump administration, and the state intervenors then began negotiating a settlement to the litigation. During the years of litigation and months of negotiation, uncertainty loomed regarding whether insurers in the Marketplace would remain legally required to reduce cost-sharing without reimbursement. Burdened with these costs without reimbursement, many insurers threatened to cease offering Marketplace coverage or raise premiums significantly. Uncertainty about CSR payments, and health reform more generally, had a great destabilizing effect on the Marketplaces and health insurance more generally. See, Timothy Jost, House, Administration Oppose State Intervention in House v. Price; New Developments in the Section 1557 Case, Health Aff. Blog (July 11, 2017); Nicholas Bagley, Trump's Ominous Threat to Withhold Payment from Health Insurers, Explained, Vox (Aug. 2, 2017).

On October 12, 2017, HHS announced that it would discontinue CSR payments, leading to a chaotic Marketplace open-enrollment period that began in November 2017. See Rabah Kamal et al., Kaiser Family Found., How the Loss of Cost-Sharing Subsidy Payments Is Affecting 2018 Premiums (Oct. 27, 2017). Most enrollees were not adversely affected because the ACA required premium subsidies to increase to maintain the same level of plan affordability for enrollees. But those earning more than 400% of FPL were ineligible for premium subsidies and thus faced double-digit premium increases. The complex workarounds in many Marketplace plans, known as "silver-loading" mitigated some of these effects, as insurers increased only silver-plan premiums to account for the uncompensated CSRs. Because premium tax credits are calculated based on the cost of the second-cheapest silver plan, most enrollees were insulated from these premium increases as tax credits increased accordingly. But the Congressional Budget Office estimated that stopping CSR payments would increase federal spending and the budget deficit by $194 billion by 2026. Cong. Budget Office, The Effects of Terminating Payments for Cost Sharing Reductions (Aug. 15, 2017).

The parties to the House litigation—namely the House, the Trump Administration, and the intervenor states—reached a settlement based on the recognition that the Trump administration's decision to stop making CSR payments eliminated the need for judicial resolution to the dispute, though their disagreements about the significant standing, separation of powers, and appropriation issues implicated by the suit still remain. See Matthew B. Lawrence, Disappropriation, 120 Colum. L. Rev. 1 (2020).

The statute still requires the government to pay CSRs to insurers, despite the administrative action terminating the payments. In December 2017, insurers began filing suits—including class action suits—to enforce this statutory requirement. See, e.g., Complaint at Maine Community Health Options v. U.S., No. 1:17-cv-02057-MMS (Fed. Cl. 2017); Nicholas Bagley, Legal Limits and the Implementation of the Affordable Care Act, 164 U. Pa. L. Rev. 1715 (2016). The Federal Circuit held that the ACA unambiguously required the federal government to make CSR payments, but that the silver-loading strategy and federal tax subsidies that enabled insurers to account for CSR non-payment by charging higher premiums should offset the CSR payments due. Cmty. Health Choice, Inc. v. United States, 970 F.3d 1364 (Fed. Cir. 2020). The Supreme Court denied certiorari. ME Com. Health Options v. United States, 141 S.Ct. 2796 (2021), and United States v. ME Com. Health Options, 141 S.Ct. 2796 (2021).

Insurers also had filed suit against the government in 2016, seeking to force the administration to pay the full risk-corridor payments contemplated by the statutory language in the ACA. During the first three "phase in" years of the ACA's Marketplaces (2014–2016), HHS collected less money through the program from profitable insurers than it owed to insurers who took financial losses. But Congress included riders to CMS's budget preventing the agency from making the full risk-corridor payments. The Supreme Court held, in an 8–1 decision, that the statutory language dictated that HHS "shall pay" insurers under the risk-corridor provision and was not impliedly repealed by the lack of appropriation. Maine Cmty. Health Options v. United States, 140 S.Ct. 1308 (2020).

QUESTIONS

How does applying the premium increases that are necessary to cover the expense of CSR payments on to silver plans only mitigate the harm to consumers? How would doing so change the enrollment in other plans? How would doing increase federal expenditures?

D. EFFORTS TO EXPAND OR REPEAL AND REPLACE THE ACA

The ACA has served as the target for political maneuvering and further reforms since its enactment. Republicans have campaigned on repealing and replacing it; Democrats have campaigned on strengthening and expanding it. Despite the attacks and blows described in the preceding sections, as well as failed attempts at legislative repeal and executive actions undermining it, the ACA remained in force when the COVID-19 pandemic hit and the law supplied the critical regulatory mechanisms on which Congress built many of its responses to the pandemic. This section summarizes that legislative expansion, as well as the failed legislative repeal efforts and the impacts of Executive actions.

1. Congressional Attempts to Repeal and Replace the ACA in 2017

While critics of the ACA were trying to dismantle the law through the judicial system from 2010 to 2016, Congress repealed Titles 1, 2, and 9 in January 2016. President Obama vetoed that bill. Because Republicans were unable to acquire the votes to override the veto, prominent party members ran their election campaigns on a promise to repeal the ACA, or at least the individual mandate. See, Henry C. Jackson, 6 Promises Trump Has Made About Health Care, CNN.com (Mar. 13, 2017).

Soon after the 2016 election, with the election of President Trump and control of Congress, Republican leaders took their first opportunity to replace the ACA, introducing the **American Health Care Act (AHCA)**, H.R. 1628, 115th Cong. (2017), under the budget reconciliation process. Instead of completely repealing the ACA, the AHCA would have replaced and weakened several of the ACA's core insurance provisions. In large part, the AHCA attacked the three-legged stool of the ACA by eliminating the coverage mandates and diminishing the federal government's fiscal responsibility for health care. The final version of the AHCA included the following key features:

- Eliminating the taxes and tax increases imposed by the ACA to fund its provisions;

- Dramatically reducing Medicaid expenditures by phasing out funding for the Medicaid expansions and imposing either a block grant or per capita cap on Medicaid;

- Removing the individual and employer mandate penalties;

- Permitting states to waive the ACA's essential health benefit requirements;

- Retaining the protections for individuals with preexisting conditions (guaranteed issue and modified community rating);

- Increasing the age rating ratios from 1:3 to 1:5 in the individual and small group markets, and allowing states to increase the ratio by waiver;

- Imposing a 30% premium surcharge on individuals who do not maintain continuous coverage; or allowing states to obtain waivers to allow insurers to underwrite individuals based on health status for individuals who do not maintain continuous coverage;

- Eliminating the actuarial value tiering of health plans established by the ACA (bronze, silver, gold, and platinum), allowing plans to cover less than 60% of the cost of care, which would decrease premiums, but increase deductibles and cost sharing;

- Allocating $138 billion to assist states in covering high cost consumers, subsidizing premiums, paying for mental health care and drug addiction treatment, and other expenses;

- Terminating the ACA's premium tax credits that adjusted for income by 2020, and substituting them with age-adjusted fixed-dollar tax credits that ranged from $2,000 to $4,000 per year (credits begin to phase out at $75,000 for individuals and $150,000 for families); and

- Providing a $300 billion tax cut for high-income families over ten years.

H.R. 1628, 115th Cong. (2017). For a description of the original bill and the subsequent amendments, see, Timothy Jost, House Passes AHCA: How It Happened, What Would It Do, And Its Uncertain Senate Future, Health Aff. Blog (May 4, 2017).

The AHCA would have replaced the individual mandate, with a continuous coverage mandate, penalizing individuals who had more than a two-month gap in coverage by increasing their premiums 30% for one year if they subsequently purchased insurance. Which would be a bigger financial burden on individuals—an individual mandate penalty capped at $695 per year or the continuous coverage penalty?

Although the AHCA would have nominally retained the ACA's popular consumer protections, the AHCA and the subsequent Senate version of the bill, the Better Care Reconciliation Act (BCRA), would have allowed states to apply for waivers to opt out of many of the ACA's provisions, including the essential health benefits requirements, community ratings and preexisting conditions provisions, age rating requirements, actuarial value requirements, out-of-pocket limits, and preventive services coverage. This state loophole was generally seen as a significant erosion of the ACA's protections.

The House passed the AHCA by a thin margin in May 2017. By the time the Senate introduced its own version of the AHCA, key stakeholders, including health care providers, patient advocacy groups, many insurers, state and local governments, and health policy experts, had opposed the bill, leading to a sharp decline in popularity. Cuts to Medicaid proved especially unpopular in swing states, leading to moderate Republican Senators' disapproval. The AHCA and the BCRA also received poor scores from the CBO, which reported that the bill would lead to higher uninsured rates and higher premiums. Cong. Budget Office, H.R. 1628, American Health Care Act of 2017 (May 24, 2017); Cong. Budget Office, H.R. 1628, Better Care Reconciliation Act of 2017 (June 26, 2017). As a result, the bill failed to pass the Senate and the direct repeal and replacement of the ACA through the legislative process appeared to be dead. See, Robert Pear et al., Health Care Debate: Obamacare Repeal Fails as McCain Casts Decisive No Vote, N.Y. Times (July 27, 2017). Despite Republican control of both chambers of Congress and the presidency in 2017, the effort to repeal and replace the ACA through legislation failed, leaving litigation and executive action as the key remaining strategies to undo the ACA.

NOTES AND QUESTIONS

1. *A Difference in Ideologies.* How does the AHCA compare to the ACA? What policy tools did the drafters of the AHCA keep? Which did they change? How do the respective plans reflect the policy goals of their drafters?

2. *Budget Reconciliation.* In March 2010, Congress used the budget reconciliation process to make important changes to pass the ACA, and Republicans attempted to use the same process for their repeal and replace reform efforts. The budget reconciliation process, created by the Congressional Budget Act of 1974, allows for expedited consideration of certain tax, spending, and debt limit legislation. Under a budget reconciliation process, the Senate can pass a bill with only a simple majority and without filibusters, so long as the bill follows the Byrd Rule, 2 U.S.C. § 644. The Byrd Rule states that a budget reconciliation bill must raise or lower spending and taxes in ways that do not increase the long-term deficit, and that the bill's provisions must affect federal revenues, spending, or the federal deficit and not be "merely incidental"

to budgetary effects. The Senate Parliamentarian rules whether a bill or provision complies with the Byrd Rule.

Many parts of the AHCA and the BCRA may not have qualified under these requirements. For example, the AHCA's allowance for state waivers from some of the ACA's requirements may not have satisfied the "budget related" test. The Byrd Rule and Its Effect on Health Reform: A Short Guide, Comm. for a Responsible Federal Budget, Apr. 28, 2017. In recent years, both Democrats and Republicans have passed major legislation under the reconciliation process, and political scientists expect Congress to continue using this tool in the future in the absence of filibuster reform in the Senate. With the availability of the budget reconciliation process, what are the implications for future health care reform efforts? How will they be structured? Should this process be allowed?

2.   Executive Actions' Impact on the ACA

Upon taking office, President Trump signed an executive order establishing the administration's policy to seek complete repeal of the ACA. Exec. Order No. 13,765, 82 Fed. Reg. 8351 (Jan. 20, 2017). After the Senate failed to pass a repeal and replace bill, the Trump administration instead turned to executive actions through executive orders and administrative rulemaking to undermine the ACA.

On October 12, 2017, President Trump signed an executive order that permitted the expansion of **association health plans (AHPs)** to small businesses, the extension of the duration of **short-term health plans** to match regular insurance plans, and the expansion of employers' ability to use **health reimbursement accounts** to allow employers to pay for employees' premiums to enroll in these alternative non-ACA compliant plans. Exec. Order No. 13,813, 82 Fed. Reg. 48385 (Oct. 12, 2017). Agency rulemaking implemented the directives in the Executive Order. 83 Fed. Reg. 38,212 (Oct. 2, 2018) (short-term plans); 83 Fed. Reg. 21,982 (Aug. 20, 2018 (association health plans); 84 Fed. Reg. 28,888 (Aug. 19, 2019) (health reimbursement accounts).

These alternative plans do not have to comply with ACA insurance requirements and are generally offer less comprehensive, "skinny" benefits. Thus, expanding their availability could undermine ACA-compliant plans by siphoning off younger and healthier individuals into these plans. Observers also worried that consumers would buy these plans because of lower premiums, and then suffer financially under the plans' skimpy coverage limits. For an assessment of short-term plans, see a report by the U.S. House of Representatives, Committee and Energy and Commerce, Shortchanged: How the Trump Administration's Expansion of Junk Short-Term Health Insurance Plans is Putting Americans at Risk (June 2020). The rules expanding short-term plans and association health plans both faced litigation challenges, but only the AHP rule was invalidated. Compare Ass'n for Cmty. Affiliated Plans v. U.S. Dep't of Treasury, 966 F.3d 782, 785 (D.C. Cir. 2020) (upholding short-term plan rule); New York v. U.S. Dep't of Labor, 363 F. Supp. 3d 109 (D.D.C. 2019) (invalidating AHP final rule as "clearly an end-run around the ACA" that "exceeds the statutory authority delegated by Congress in ERISA").

In addition to expanding access to non-ACA compliant plans, the Trump administration undermined the ACA by slashing the budget for outreach to help people enroll in Marketplace plans by 90%, shortening open enrollment from 90 days to 45 days, and frequently shutting down HealthCare.gov for maintenance on weekends. See, e.g., Kim Soffen, These Are the Steps the Trump Administration is Taking to Undermine the ACA, Washington Post (Oct. 13, 2017); Phil Galewitz, Sunday Hours: Obamacare Website To Be Shut Down For Portion of Most Weekends, Kaiser Health News (Sept. 22, 2017).

When President Biden took office in 2021, one of his first actions was to rescind President Trump's 2017 Executive Order directing the agencies to expand access to non-ACA compliant plans. Executive Order No. 14,009 (Jan. 28, 2021), 86 Fed. Reg. 7793 (Feb. 2, 2021). Although executive orders can be reversed with the stroke of a pen, the agency rules that implemented the policy directives of the executive order cannot be rescinded without following proper administrative procedures, including notice-and-comment rulemaking. Thus, President Biden's executive order directs the agencies to reexamine rules, guidance, and policies that undermine the ACA Marketplaces and the ACA's protections for people with preexisting conditions and take actions to revise or rescind these prior administration rules and policies. Id.

In addition to requiring a wholesale regulatory review to undo the Trump administration's actions to undermine the ACA, President Biden's January 28, 2021 executive order opened HealthCare.gov for a **special enrollment period** and restored funding for outreach, citing the public health emergency caused by the COVID-19 pandemic. The special enrollment period (extended through August 15, 2021) and outreach efforts resulted in a record 31 million total enrollees in ACA plans. See Katie Keith, Marketplace Special Enrollment Reaches 2.5 Million; Administration Announces Health Care Reconciliation Priorities, Health Affairs Blog (Aug. 10, 2021).

3. Expanding on the ACA in the COVID-19 Pandemic and Beyond

In March 2020, Congress passed two pieces of emergency legislation to address the COVID-19 pandemic: the Families First Coronavirus Response Act (FFCRA), Pub. L. No. 116–127, 134 Stat. 178 (2020), and the Coronavirus Aid, Relief, and Economic Security Act (CARES), Pub. L. No.

116–136, 134 Stat. 281 (2020). Both statutes were passed with broad bipartisan support, and both expanded emergency access to health benefits by extending key provisions of the ACA's insurance coverage. They required Marketplace plans to cover COVID-19 testing and vaccination and set the method for determining reimbursement, as well as prohibited insurers from using COVID-19 test results for underwriting purposes. These provisions apply only to ACA-Marketplace insurance and expire when the federally-declared emergency period ends. See John Aloysius Cogan, Jr., Congress has Already Ruled in *California v. Texas*, 62 B.C. L. Rev. E. Supp. I-11 (2021).

One year later, Congress passed a more ambitious stimulus bill, the American Rescue Plan Act of 2021 (ARP), Pub. L. No. 117–2, 135 Stat. 4 (2021), on a party-line vote. The ARP made ACA Marketplace plans more accessible and affordable by expanding the ACA's premium assistance tax credits. While the ACA had made the tax credits available only to those with incomes below 400% of the federal poverty level (the so-called "subsidy cliff"), the ARP makes subsidies available to those with incomes above 400% of FPL, temporarily eliminating the subsidy cliff, and lowers the percentage of household income that must go toward premiums before the subsidy kicks in (8.5%). See CMS.gov, American Rescue Plan and the Marketplace (Mar. 12, 2021). In addition to effectively extending the tax credits to higher-income people, ARP increased the subsidy amount for everyone receiving premium assistance. Id. Under the ARP's expanded premium assistance formula, people with incomes between 100% and 150% would not pay any premium for an ACA Marketplace plan. See Zack Buck, Biden's Early Focus: Durable and Attainable Private Insurance, Bill of Health (May 13, 2021). For workers who lost their jobs and employer-sponsored insurance, the ARP also maximizes the tax credit amount for those receiving unemployment benefits, and subsidizes COBRA coverage. See Katie Keith, New ACA Subsidies Available On April 1, Health Aff. Blog (Mar. 17, 2021).

The ARP's expansion of subsidies, coupled with the COVID-19 special enrollment period opened by President Biden's Executive Order, brought over 2.5 million more people into ACA Marketplace plans. See Katie Keith, Marketplace Special Enrollment Reaches 2.5 Million; Administration Announces Health Care Reconciliation Priorities, Health Aff. Blog (Aug. 10, 2021). The ARP's provisions are set to expire in 2023, but the enrollment and affordability gains from its 2021 implementation suggest that lawmakers may consider making these expansions permanent features of the ACA. See Joan Stephenson, Making New Law's Health Insurance Subsidies Permanent Could Cut Uninsured by 4.2 Million, Study Finds, JAMA Health Forum (Apr. 20, 2021).

The ARP's extension of core features in the ACA also reflects the Biden administration's stated approach to health reform beyond the pandemic—

namely to strengthen and expand on the ACA. While the ACA will remain a prominent political target, it is likely that the Biden administration and Democratic Congress will pursue further expansions on its approach to insurance regulation. See, e.g., Katie Keith, The Affordable Care Act in the Biden Era: Identifying Federal Priorities for Administrative Action, Commonwealth Fund (May 17, 2021); Erin C. Fuse Brown, Symposium Introduction: Recommendations for a Biden/Harris Health Policy Agenda, Bill of Health (May 3, 2021).

III. OTHER FEDERAL LAWS REGULATING INSURANCE

Even prior to the adoption of the ACA, federal law offered some protection to insured individuals, and even if Congress were to repeal the ACA entirely, these laws would remain in place. The most important of these protections were the rights to insurance portability and to freedom from discrimination on the basis of health status provided by the **Health Insurance Portability and Accountability Act of 1996 (HIPAA)**, the continuation of coverage benefits available under the **Consolidated Omnibus Budget Reconciliation Act of 1985**, (commonly called "**COBRA coverage**"), and the protections against discrimination provided in federal laws such as **ACA Section 1557**, the **Mental Health Parity and Addiction Equity Act (MHPAEA)**, and the other federal statutes detailed in Chapter 6.

A. HIPAA AND COBRA COVERAGE REQUIREMENTS

HIPAA began as an attempt to enact the least controversial elements of the much more ambitious Clinton health insurance reform proposals of 1993 and 1994. In the end, it became a lengthy "Christmas tree" bill addressing a hodge-podge of topics. For example, HIPAA included major changes in the fraud and abuse laws, introduced tax subsidies for health savings accounts, provided tax incentives for the purchase of long-term care insurance, and encouraged the creation of state high-risk insurance pools. While HIPAA is predominantly known for its privacy provisions, discussed in Chapter 4, the Act was named, however, for its provisions to increase the portability and accessibility of health insurance, particularly for those with employer-based coverage. The ACA's insurance provisions largely replaced or extended these HIPAA provisions (since much of the ACA is technically an amendment to HIPAA), as described below.

First, HIPAA limited the use of preexisting conditions exclusions for plans in the group market. HIPAA provided that group health insurers could only impose a preexisting condition exclusion if it related to a physical or mental condition for which medical advice, diagnosis, care, or treatment was recommended or received in the six months prior to the enrollment date. 29 U.S.C.A. §§ 1181(a)(1), 300gg(a)(1). Under HIPAA, a preexisting condition exclusion could only last for a maximum period of twelve months (or eighteen months if an individual, without any valid excuse, enrolled in a plan later than when it was initially available). 29 U.S.C.A. §§ 1181(a)(2), 300gg(a)(2), (f)(1). Moreover, an insurer could only impose this preexisting condition exclusion for twelve months, but this period would be reduced by the amount of time the beneficiary had previously been enrolled under another private or public health plan (called "creditable coverage" under HIPAA), so long as there was no break in coverage for more than 63 days. In other words, if a person who had been insured under a group health plan at one job for at least twelve months moved directly into another job with coverage, without being uninsured for more than two months between jobs, the new plan could not impose a preexisting condition exclusion. Insurers also could not impose preexisting conditions exclusions with respect to newborns, adopted children, or pregnant women. In an expansion of this provision, the ACA banned preexisting conditions clauses for all populations in 2014 and eliminated waiting periods of more than 90 days.

Second, HIPAA prohibited group health plans from discriminating against individuals when determining enrollment eligibility and when setting premiums on the basis of an individual's (or their dependent's) health status-related characteristics. These characteristics include health status, medical conditions (including both physical and mental illnesses), claims experience, receipt of health care, medical history, genetic information, evidence of insurability (including conditions arising out of acts of domestic violence), or disability. 29 U.S.C.A § 1182(a) & (b). The ACA extended this protection to all insureds.

Third, HIPAA required individual market insurers to make coverage available to people with 18 months or more of creditable coverage who 1) had lost that coverage and exhausted COBRA coverage (see below); and 2) had not had a gap of more than 63 days between the end of their coverage and their application for extension coverage. Insurers could not impose preexisting conditions clauses on such individuals and had to guarantee renewal. 42 U.S.C. §§ 300gg–41, 300gg–32. The ACA superseded this rule in 2014.

Finally, HIPAA also required small group market insurers to guarantee availability and renewability to all employers who applied for small group coverage, and to all employees of such employers who opt for coverage on a timely basis. 42 U.S.C.A. §§ 300gg–11, 300gg–12. The legislation did not, however, regulate the rates that insurers could charge employers. The ACA continued this requirement.

HIPAA's guaranteed issue requirement supplemented COBRA's earlier requirements. COBRA applies to private employers and state and local government entities that employ 20 or more employees on a typical business day and that sponsor a group health plan. 29 U.S.C.A. § 1161. COBRA protects a "**qualified beneficiary**" whose group insurance is terminated because of a "**qualifying event.**" Qualified beneficiaries include covered employees (or, in some circumstances, formerly-covered employees), as well as their spouses and dependent children who were plan beneficiaries on the day before the qualifying event. 29 U.S.C.A. § 1167(3).

Qualifying events entitling qualified beneficiaries to continuation coverage include: loss of coverage due to the death of the covered employee, termination of the employee's employment or reduction in hours (not caused by the employee's "gross misconduct"), the covered employee's divorce or legal separation from their spouse, the employee's eligibility for Medicare, or the cessation of dependent child status under the health plan. 29 U.S.C.A. § 1163. An employer's filing of bankruptcy proceedings is a qualifying event with respect to a retired employee (and the employee's previously covered spouse, dependent child, or surviving spouse), so long as the employee retired before the elimination of coverage and the employer substantially eliminates coverage within one year of the bankruptcy filing. 29 U.S.C.A. § 1163(6).

Upon the occurrence of a qualifying event, qualified beneficiaries are entitled to purchase continuation coverage for up to either 1) 18 months for termination of work or reduction in hours, or 2) 36 months for most other qualifying events. 29 U.S.C.A. § 1162(2). Coverage of a retiree of a bankrupt employer lasts until the employee's death. The right to continuation coverage may terminate before the end of the coverage period if: the employer ceases to provide group health insurance to any employee; the qualified beneficiary fails to make a timely payment of the plan premium; the qualified beneficiary becomes covered under another group health plan that does not exclude or limit coverage for a preexisting condition; or the qualified beneficiary becomes eligible for Medicare. 29 U.S.C.A. § 1162(2)(B), (C), (D). Where the employer is self-insured, it may make a reasonable estimate of plan cost for similarly situated beneficiaries either on an actuarial basis or base the premium on the costs of the preceding determination period (adjusted for inflation). 29 U.S.C.A. § 1164(2).

In response to the coronavirus pandemic, the American Rescue Plan Act of 2021 provided a 100% COBRA premium subsidy for certain individuals who lost their employer-based health coverage due to an involuntary termination of employment or reduction in hours. The subsidy was available to from April 1 to September 30, 2021 to employer-sponsored health plans subject to COBRA under ERISA. Employers who provided the subsidized COBRA coverage were entitled to a refundable payroll tax credit. American Rescue Plan Act of 2021, Pub. L. 117–2, § 9501 (2021).

NOTES AND QUESTIONS

1.   Do HIPAA and COBRA together provide sufficient protection for Americans seeking health insurance? Who would not be covered under these plans? What populations are the most vulnerable under HIPAA and COBRA? What does the ACA account for that HIPPA and COBRA together do not?

2.   Who pays for COBRA coverage: employers, insurers, employees, or health insurance consumers? Under what circumstances would a person eligible for COBRA coverage be well-advised to decline it and seek coverage in the nongroup market instead? Final regulations implementing COBRA, promulgated in 2001, are found at 26 C.F.R. §§ 59.4980B1–B10. Depending on the state, most lower and middle-income Americans will find coverage available through the Marketplaces subsidized by premium tax credits more affordable than COBRA coverage.

B.   ANTIDISCRIMINATION LAW

In addition to the federal insurance regulations discussed in this chapter, certain aspects of health insurance are also be subject to federal antidiscrimination protections detailed in Chapter 6: the Americans with Disabilities Act (ADA), Title VII of the Civil Rights Act (Title VII), Mental Health Parity and Addiction Equity Act (MHPAEA), the Genetic Information Nondiscrimination Act of 2008 (GINA), and the Age Discrimination in Employment Act (ADEA)., and ACA Section 1557 Historically, these anti-discrimination provisions have provided rather limited protections because they apply narrowly only to a particular type of insurance, and because courts have interpreted them not to require a certain type or level of coverage.

IV.   STATE LAWS REGULATING INSURANCE

States have historically borne primary responsibility for regulating private health care insurance. Federal law has played an ever-increasing role over the past half century—a trajectory culminating in the ACA. See Elizabeth Y. McCuskey, Body of Preemption: Health Law Traditions and the. Presumption against Preemption, 89 Temple L. Rev. 95 (2017). The ACA dramatically expanded the role of the federal government in regulating health insurance, while relying on states for important aspects of its implementation. Despite the predominance of federal law, plenty of room remains for state regulation of health insurance. Yet, the Employee Retirement Income Security Act of 1974 (ERISA), discussed in Chapter 8, preempts state regulation relating to the largest single source of health insurance for the population, employer-sponsored insurance. This contributes to a complicated but important role for state health insurance regulation in the ACA era.

Prior to the passage of the ACA, states used regulation to increase access to health insurance and ensure adequate coverage. Most states had regulated underwriting practices in the individual market. For instance, prior to the implementation of the ACA, states had adopted restrictions on preexisting conditions limitations, community rating requirements, rating bands (i.e., requiring that the highest premiums charged not be more than a specified percentage higher than the lowest premiums charged) and other rate restrictions, and provisions for voluntary or mandatory participation in reinsurance pools.

Underwriting for large group insurance went largely unregulated before the ACA, but every state has adopted small group regulations limiting insurer discretion in rating. By the time the federal government had implemented HIPAA's reforms, numerous states had already enacted many of the same changes, and many states passed protections for individuals that went beyond HIPAA's minimum requirements. Prior to the ACA, all states also required insurers who sold in small group markets to offer coverage and guarantee renewal to any small group that requested it, regardless of the health status or claims experience of the group's members.

In adopting the ACA, Congress concluded that the federal government needed to intervene to reform private insurance markets to increase access and lower costs. But the vision of federalism enacted in the ACA preserves a significant role for states, offering them financial incentives to participate in implementing federal programs, deferring to their policy choices and existing rules, and funding their experiments with alternative rules. The ACA created new federal standards and subsidies for purchasing insurance, but left many enforcement functions and the responsibility establishing the Marketplaces with the state governments, as well as delegating to states the task of identifying the "benchmark plan" that defines the essential health benefits. The ACA's Section 1332 state innovation waiver provision enables HHS to suspend the majority of the ACA's core provisions: the employer and individual mandates, the qualified health plan and essential benefits provisions; the exchange rules and individual market risk pooling, the cost-sharing provisions, and the premium assistance tax credits. The pass-through funding in the 1332 waiver program thus funds states to deviate from the ACA's rules.

Some scholars have argued that it ceded more regulatory authority to the states than necessary. See, Abbe R. Gluck, Federalism from Federal Statutes: Health Reform, Medicaid, and the Old-Fashioned Federalists' Gamble, 81 Fordham L. Rev. 1749, 1752 (2013); Nicholas Bagley, Federalism and the End of Obamacare, The Yale L.J. Forum (Feb. 14, 2017).

The ACA does not affect any state regulation of insurance or managed care plans as long as the state law implements or supplements, but does not conflict, with the reform law. As a result, state law will continue to govern many aspects of insurance. All states, for example, tax the premiums of commercial insurers and most tax Blue Cross/Blue Shield plan premiums (though some at a lower rate than commercial plans). States oversee the financial solvency of insurers by imposing minimal requirements for financial reserves and for allowable investments, and by requiring annual statements and conducting periodic examinations of insurers (usually on a triennial basis). States also regulate insurance marketing and claims practices. State insurance commissions investigate consumer complaints and place insolvent companies into receivership. These issues are left largely untouched by the ACA and will remain subject to state regulation.

State law will also continue to control health insurance issues that the ACA does not directly address. For instance, to control costs after the ACA, many managed care organizations (MCOs) have increased limitations on their networks and created **"skinny" or narrow networks** that include only a select set of providers who have agreed to their terms. States can still pass and retain laws related to network limitations, such as **any willing provider** laws that limit the ability of MCOs to exclude providers that agree to take their reimbursement rate for a particular service. They can also implement **network adequacy requirements** that mandate an acceptable ratio of providers to enrollees in a geographic area. Some states require MCOs to allow members to go out-of-network if network coverage is inadequate. Other states simply require plans to disclose their provider selection criteria.

As detailed in Chapter 7, states can also continue to pass more general health reform laws in an attempt to promote access and quality while controlling costs. Legislation that increases price transparency, creates all-payer claims databases, enables provider rate oversight and rate setting, prohibits balance billing, and limits the abuse of market power can improve the market for health insurance in any given state.

As federal health reform after the ACA has sputtered, states have been called to address many of the existing challenges facing health care in America. But their ability to do so is currently handicapped in several ways. First and foremost, as described in Chapter 8, ERISA preempts state attempts to regulate employee benefit plans, including employer-sponsored health insurance. ERISA preemption limits state efforts to control health care costs, increase access, and any attempt to provide universal coverage that builds on employer-sponsored insurance. See, e.g., Erin C. Fuse Brown & Elizabeth Y. McCuskey, Federalism, ERISA, and State Single-Payer Health Care, 168 U. Penn. L. Rev. 389 (2020)

Second, unlike the federal government, states, with the exception of Vermont, are required to balance their budget every year. Yet, funding for health care coverage is countercyclical. In economic downturns, people lose their jobs and their employer-sponsored coverage, increasing the need for government-sponsored insurance at the same time tax revenues are declining. The federal government can address these countercyclical fluctuations through deficit-spending, but the states cannot. As a result, states have been reluctant to take on large spending obligations, especially countercyclical ones, like health insurance. See, David Super, Rethinking Fiscal Federalism, 118 Harv. L. Rev. 2544 (2008).

Third, both political parties may seek to offer greater flexibility to states to deviate from the ACA's key provisions, although for different reasons. President Trump's 2017 Executive Order promoting short term plans and association health plans discussed above, is an example of a policy promoting greater state flexibility to undermine the ACA's core protections and introduce greater volatility in the private health insurance market. By contrast, progressive health reformers may seek broad § 1332 state innovation waivers to allow states to pursue expansive reforms such as a state public option or single payer health care.

NOTES AND QUESTIONS

1.   While states may see the federal government relinquishing power, they have little ability to take the needed steps to reform health care at the state level. To properly empower states, Republicans and the Trump Administration should take the necessary steps to eliminate ERISA's stranglehold on state health reform efforts. Congress could do this by amending ERISA, or the Department of Labor could issue regulations clarifying the ability of states to govern certain aspects of all health insurance, including self-insured plans. See Elizabeth Y. McCuskey, ERISA Reform as Health Reform: The Case for and ERISA Preemption Waiver, 48 J. L. Med. & Ethics 450 (2020).

2.   Are 50 different state systems better than a national one? What advantages do state governments have over the federal government in terms of designing and implementing health reform? See Kristin Madison Building a Better Laboratory: The Federal Role in Promoting Health System Experimentation, 41 Pepp. L. Rev. 765 (2013)

3.   One option states may consider in light of the repeal of the ACA's individual mandate, is to pass one of their own. Since 2006, Massachusetts has mandated that all residents, for whom health insurance is affordable, obtain and maintain health insurance that meets minimum coverage requirements, which are similar to the essential health benefits established in the ACA. For a description of the mandate, see, Massachusetts Individual Mandate, The Massachusetts Health Connector, available at www.betterhealthconnector.

com. As a result of implementing this individual mandate, Massachusetts has maintained some of the highest levels of coverage in the nation.

CHAPTER 10

PUBLIC HEALTH CARE FINANCING PROGRAMS: MEDICARE AND MEDICAID

■ ■ ■

I. INTRODUCTION

Government participation in health care is pervasive and powerful. Federal and state spending account for nearly half of all health care outlays—an amount that does not include the $270 billion "tax expenditure" that results from the exclusion from individuals' income taxes permitted for employer health insurance contributions. However, it would be a mistake to think the United States has developed a coordinated or uniform way to spend its health care dollars. There are diverse programs for direct provision of care and for providing insurance, and the federal government funds a number of important programs, some targeting groups deemed particularly worthy and some providing services considered essential for promotion of population health. For example, the federal government provides or funds care to over 9 million veterans in over 1200 veterans' health care facilities and over 9 million active and retired members of the military and their dependents through the TRICARE program; to over 2.5 million Native Americans in approximately 600 Indian Health Service and tribal facilities; and to disabled coal miners through the Black Lung program. The federal government also provides block grants to the states for a variety of purposes: maternal and child health, including vaccinations; family planning and prevention of sexually transmitted diseases; addiction and mental health treatment; and other preventive health and primary care needs. As an employer, the federal government provides health insurance to over eight million civil federal employees, retirees, and their families. State and local governments have longstanding commitments to directly provide care through government-sponsored acute care, university, and mental hospitals, and to provide coverage through insurance programs for the indigent, elderly, people with disabilities, and workers' compensation.

By far the largest public health care programs, however, are the federal Medicare program and the joint state-federal Medicaid program, which respectively spent about $799.4 and $613.5 billion in 2019. This chapter focuses on these two programs and also discusses the State Children's Health Insurance Program (CHIP), which was established in 1997 to expand health insurance for poor children and is an important supplement to the Medicaid program. Today these programs are undergoing rapid change. There are many reasons why every law student should pay close attention to these programs. First, they are the subject of contentious and passionate fiscal debates about the changes wrought by the Affordable Care Act (ACA) and recurring reform proposals by the leaders of the Republican party. Together, Medicare and Medicaid consume nearly a quarter of the federal budget; Medicaid is the largest and fastest growing item in the budgets of most states; and Medicare's projected growth threatens to overwhelm the financing mechanisms that currently support it. Second, and certainly no less important, these programs provide the assurance that many of our fellow citizens—the indigent, disabled, elderly, and children—are afforded some guarantee that they will receive health care when they need it, regardless of their financial status. Finally, these programs are of immense importance to providers and commercial payers. Besides providing funding for services, the regulations and norms of these programs shape the way health care is delivered and paid for in the private sector.

This chapter is designed to introduce the complex web of regulation that has evolved around Medicare, Medicaid, and CHIP and to the alternative paths that are underway or proposed. It examines several examples of lawyers' nitty gritty work interpreting and applying legislation and regulation governing key issues of finance and access. At the same time, you will have the opportunity to consider economic, sociological, and ethical issues raised by the laws and regulations examined. To keep the big picture in focus, we suggest you consider the following issues.

First, who receives the program's benefits? Are the targeted recipients characterized by economic need, a particular disease, advanced age, disability, residence in a particular geographic jurisdiction, employment in a certain industry, or status as an enrollee and contributor to a social insurance fund? From these questions, others follow: Who in fact receives most of the program's benefits? Whom does the program leave out? Why are some groups included and others excluded? Also, should beneficiaries be entitled to some level of benefits, or should coverage be subject to governmental discretion or caps on program enrollment?

Second, what benefits will the program provide? Should the program stress institutional services such as hospitalization and nursing home care and/or non-institutional alternatives such as home health care? Should it encourage preventive care? Should the program be limited to services commonly covered by private insurance like hospital and physician care, or should it also cover services such as dental care and items such as eyeglasses that private insurance covers less often because their use is more predictable and middle-class insureds can afford to pay for them out-of-pocket? These services may be inaccessible to the poor unless the program covers them. Should the program cover medically controversial treatment, such as services or drugs for which there is a significant dispute about the asserted benefits versus potential risks? What about socially controversial services, such as abortion—what role should social norms or values play in health program design? What role should cost play? Should a program cover services that provide relatively small marginal or speculative benefit at a very high cost, such as some organ transplants or some last-ditch cancer therapies? Finally, how can the benefits package be kept up to date? In particular, how should the program evaluate new technologies as they become available?

Third, how should the program provide or pay for benefits? Should it pay private professionals and institutions to deliver the services, as do Medicare and Medicaid, or should it deliver services itself directly, as does the Veterans Administration through its hospitals? To what extent should a government program use provider payment systems to encourage changes in the health care delivery system or to improve the quality of care? Should it purchase services through "vendor payments" based on cost or charge, as Medicare used to, or through an administered price system, as Medicare does now for most services, or on a capitated basis through managed care plans, as Medicare does through parts C and D and most state Medicaid plans do for many recipients? Alternatively, should beneficiaries simply be given vouchers and be expected to purchase their own insurance in the private market? Should public health insurance programs be defined-contribution or defined-benefit programs? Should recipients be expected to share in the costs through coinsurance or deductibles?

Fourth, who should play what role in administering the program? Should the program be run by the federal, state, or local government? Should policy be set by the legislature or by an administrative agency? Should payments to providers be administered by the government or by private contractors? Should program beneficiaries (or providers) have rights enforceable in state or federal court, or should the government retain unreviewable discretion in running the program?

Fifth, how should the program be financed? Through payroll taxes, income taxes, consumption taxes, or premiums? By state or federal taxes? Should taxes be earmarked (hypothecated) for health care, or should the program be funded through general revenue funds? If premiums play a role, should they be means tested?

Sixth, what are the alternatives? Notice the fragmentation and disconnectedness discussed in earlier chapters also characterizes our public health care financing programs. Unlike some other nations, we do not have a single public system creating a safety net for all of society, but rather a patchwork of programs, creating a variety of safety nets, some higher and some lower, many fairly tattered, and none catching everyone.

Whom do the safety nets miss? What problems does this fragmented system create? What alternative approaches are feasible? Which of the myriad changes to Medicare and Medicaid under the Affordable Care Act should be continued? Improved upon? Abandoned?

II. MEDICARE

Medicare is perhaps best known as the federal health insurance program for retirees—created originally to fund hospital and physician services for individuals aged 65 or older, regardless of income and health status. But its enactment in 1965 alongside the Medicaid program, and its subsequent expansions in eligibility and coverage, have been transformational in creating an even broader, more robust health care safety net for those most vulnerable to exclusion from private insurance markets and most likely to have significant health needs. In 2018, Medicare covered over 60 million people, including people with disabilities under age 65, and enrollment is projected to grow to nearly 80 million by 2033. About 20% of Medicare beneficiaries are low-income and also covered by Medicaid, and Medicare coverage has expanded to include outpatient drugs, some skilled nursing facility care, and home health services.

Although Medicare and Medicaid are essential partners in the U.S. health care safety net, public perception of Medicare has largely been formed based on its difference from Medicaid. For example, the federal character of Medicare is often contrasted with the more complex and local character of Medicaid due to state administration. Early and enduring popular support of Medicare has been contrasted with persistent state budgetary cuts to Medicaid that have made it more vulnerable. And providers have viewed Medicare's payment system as more generous, and thus more attractive, than Medicaid. Indeed, the moniker "Medicare-for-all," used for various health reform plans proposed by democratic presidential candidates in the 2020 elections, likely had such widespread resonance because it invoked positive sentiment about the actual Medicare program, and because it reinforced the idea that there was a simple way to reduce cost and expand coverage through one program for everyone.

Yet, Medicare, as it exists today, is anything but simple. As described in this section, the Medicare program is divided into four different "parts," and each part is subject to different rules with respect to coverage, rate-setting, and financing. Medicare beneficiaries have had to rely on supplemental coverage to help pay for care, and increasingly beneficiaries get Medicare coverage through private managed care plans. Finally, as Medicare spending has increased, the federal government has implemented successive payment reforms to try to contain cost. In fact, the ACA has ushered in a vast new range of reforms that touch every part of the Medicare program. This has added even more layers of complexity to the program, as regulators experiment with various financial incentives and risk-sharing arrangements, linked to reporting of performance measures, in order to encourage greater clinical integration and drive health delivery reform. The tripartite goal of reform is improved care, better outcomes, and reduced cost; but with each new reform, questions persist about whether payment reforms are achieving the stated goals, or instead are driving changes and cuts that may undermine the very safety net that Medicare helped create. The remainder of this section describes the core elements of the Medicare program today, while also highlighting likely areas for continued reform.

A. ELIGIBILITY

Medicare eligibility is generally linked to that of the Social Security program, the other major social insurance program of the United States. Persons who are eligible for retirement benefits under Social Security are automatically eligible for Medicare upon reaching age 65. Spouses or former spouses who qualify for Social Security as dependents may also begin receiving Medicare at 65, as may former federal employees eligible for Civil Service Retirement and Railroad Retirement beneficiaries, 42 U.S.C.A. § 426(a).

Disabled persons who are eligible for Social Security or Railroad Retirement benefits may also receive Medicare, but only after they have been eligible for cash benefits for at least two years, 42 U.S.C.A. § 426(b). Persons who are eligible for Social Security (although not necessarily receiving it) and have end-stage renal (kidney) disease (ESRD) may receive Medicare benefits after a three-month waiting period, 42 U.S.C.A. § 426–1. Persons disabled with amyotophic lateral sclerosis (ALS or Lou Gehrig's disease) get Medicare Parts A and B the month their disability benefits begin. Of the more than 60 million Medicare beneficiaries, almost nine million were eligible based on disability, 51.8 million based on age, and nearly a half million because of ESRD.

CRITICAL THINKING ABOUT MEDICARE: EXERCISE 1

Consider what alternative approaches might be taken for defining the scope of Medicare eligibility. First, why is Medicare, a social insurance program, only available to older adults and people with disabilities? Why is it available to all members of these groups, regardless of their income or wealth? Historically, Medicare beneficiaries all paid the same premiums and cost-sharing regardless of wealth, but adjustments have been made for certain groups over time. For example, since 1989 low-income beneficiaries have received help with their premiums and cost-sharing through Medicaid, and since 2006 through the Medicare prescription drug low-income subsidy program. In recent years, higher income beneficiaries have faced higher premiums for the Part B (professional services) and Part D (prescription drug) programs.

Next consider the relationship between benefits and financing. Is it a good idea to charge more for program benefits to those who have higher incomes? What effect does Medicare have on the workers who support it through their payroll taxes? What effect does it have on the children of Medicare recipients? What effect might it have on the children of Medicare recipients at the death of the recipient? The idea surfaces from time to time of extending Medicare to cover all the uninsured. Why has this idea not been adopted? What about a more incremental expansion that allows adults ages 60–64 to enroll (as proposed in the Democrats' 2021 budget plan)?

PROBLEM: DESIGNING MEDICARE

Before we move on to analyze the mechanics of Medicare as it has evolved over time, consider the following demographic data. What does it suggest about the regulatory structure needed to serve the Medicare beneficiaries? For example, are market-based arrangements suitable for all? How should beneficiary cost-sharing responsibilities be structured? Is there a need for programs targeting the needs of certain groups?

Characteristics of the Medicare Population	Percent of Total Medicare Population
Income below $26,200	50%
Savings below $74,450	50%
Functional impairment	32%
Fair/poor self-reported health	25%
5+ Chronic conditions	22%
Under age 65 with permanent disabilities	15%
Age 85+	12%
Long-term care facility resident	3%

Source: *An Overview of Medicare*, Kaiser Family Found. (Feb. 2019).

B. BENEFITS

1. Coverage

Somewhat confusingly, Medicare is divided into four "parts" that signify specific benefit options. Part A, Hospital Insurance, and Part B, Supplemental Medical Insurance, comprise the original program which was enacted in 1965 along with Medicaid as part of the Great Society reforms under President Lyndon Johnson. Together, **Parts A and B are sometimes referred to as "traditional Medicare." Part C**, which is now referred to as **Medicare Advantage**, is an alternative program supplied by private managed care entities (largely health maintenance organizations (HMOs)) that beneficiaries may choose in lieu of traditional Medicare. **Part D** is the optional **pharmaceutical benefit** option added as part of the Medicare Modernization Act of 2004. Part D benefits are provided by separate contract with private companies or as part of Medicare Advantage plans.

Traditional Medicare. Part A pays for hospital, nursing home, home health, and hospice services. Part B covers physicians' services and a variety of other items and services including outpatient hospital services, home health care, physical and occupational therapy, prosthetic devices, durable medical equipment, and ambulance services. Some 70% of Medicare beneficiaries are in traditional Medicare, although the number electing to join Medicare Advantage is growing rapidly.

Owing to the fact that Medicare was modeled on the standard federal employee or Blue Cross/Blue Shield benefits package available in the mid-1960s, traditional Medicare seems quite antiquated compared to today's commercial insurance and there are significant gaps in coverage. Importantly, and in contrast to Medicare Advantage, traditional Medicare has **no out-of-pocket limits** and imposes **high deductibles** and **copayments**. It covers only 90 days of hospital services in a single benefit period ("spell of illness"*), although each beneficiary also has an extra 60 "lifetime reserve" days of hospital coverage. A sizeable deductible ($1,484 in 2021) must be paid each year before hospital coverage begins, as well as a high daily copayment after the sixtieth day of hospital care ($371 in 2021), and an even higher daily copayment after the ninetieth day ($742 in 2021). 42 U.S.C.A. § 1395e. The Medicare statute only provides for coverage up to 100 days of skilled nursing care, 42 U.S.C.A. § 1395d(a)(2), because this benefit is intended to cover those recovering from an acute illness or injury, not to cover long-term chronic care. Hospice benefits are provided on a limited basis, 42 U.S.C.A. § 1395d(a)(4). Physician services are provided subject to an annual deductible ($203 in 2021) and a 20% coinsurance amount. Medicare does not cover dental benefits, though Democrats in Congress proposed to add dental coverage to Medicare in a 2021 budget bill.

In recent years, however, Congress has sought to modify or "modernize" Medicare. For example, the ACA altered traditional Medicare to cover, with no copayment or deductible, an annual **wellness visit** and personalized prevention plan services, including a comprehensive health risk assessment, and it eliminated coinsurance for most preventive services. Furthermore, the Secretary of the Department of Health and Human Services (HHS) is authorized to modify the coverage of any currently covered preventive service in the Medicare program to the extent

---

* A spell of illness begins when a patient is hospitalized and continues until the patient has been out of a hospital or nursing home for at least 60 days. 42 U.S.C.A. § 1345x(a). Thus, a chronically ill person could remain indefinitely in a single spell of illness.

that the modification is consistent with the U.S. Preventive Services Task Force's recommendations.

To contain the significant out-of-pocket costs of traditional Medicare, most seniors purchase Medicare supplement policies (known as **"MedSupp" or "Medigap"** plans). Although these plans help fill the gaps left under traditional Medicare, they are expensive, and, as a result, low-income seniors tend to choose Medicare Advantage plans (discussed in section 4 below). For those who qualify, the so-called **"dual eligibles,"** Medicaid covers most out-of-pocket costs of traditional Medicare.

Coverage Determinations. The statutory standard for coverage under Medicare states that no payments may be made under Part A or Part B that "are not **reasonable and necessary** for the diagnosis and treatment of illness or injury or to improve the functioning of a malformed body member." 42 U.S.C.A. § 1395y(a)(1)(A). Note the absence of explicit authority to consider the cost-effectiveness of new technologies and services. This omission has established a de facto bar against weighing costs and benefits, a policy that was underscored by language in the ACA prohibiting the Patient Centered Outcomes Research Institute, a government-sponsored institute charged with evaluating comparative effectiveness, from using "incremental cost effectiveness" measures for recommending or precluding use of medical interventions. 42 U.S.C.A. § 1320e–1(e).

Decisions as to whether Medicare will finance new treatments or technologies are made at different levels. In determining whether new treatments and technologies are reasonable and necessary, CMS employs an **evidence-based process** that can involve extramural technology assessments and consultations with advisory committees. **National Coverage Determinations (NCDs)** set forth the extent to which Medicare will cover specific services, procedures or technologies on a national basis. Where an NCD does not mention, exclude, or limit an item or service, **Medicare Administrative Contractors ("MACs")** can create **Local Coverage Determinations (LCDs)** which are only applicable in the MAC's jurisdiction. MACs administer Medicare Parts A and B claims and are usually private insurers (such as Blue Cross plans) that process claims for Medicare. This means private entities are essentially deciding what products and services Medicare covers. LCDs are far more common than NCDs, as NCDs tend to be limited to more controversial and expensive technologies. Manufacturers often attempt to get a number of contractors to cover a technology through LCDs before attempting to get an NCD. See Susan Bartlett Foote, Focus on Locus: Evolution of Medicare's Local Coverage Policy, 22 Health Aff., July/Aug. 2003; at 137.

A beneficiary in need of a noncovered item or service may request an NCD. 42 U.S.C.A. § 1395ff(f)(4) & (5). CMS must act on the request within ninety days (although if CMS determines that the review will take longer than ninety days, it can simply say so and explain why). Not surprisingly, since there is a great deal of money involved, the Medicare coverage process is highly politicized, and CMS comes under tremendous pressure from the drug and device industry, professional and disease groups (which are often funded in part by industry), and Congress when it denies or threatens to deny coverage for a new technology. Medicare has taken steps to focus the process more on effectiveness review and speed up approvals in certain cases, perhaps with the intent and effect of depoliticizing it. For example, in 2014, CMS released an updated guidance document refining a process called **coverage with evidence development (CED)** which allows payment for new and innovative interventions subject to the condition of generating clinical data to demonstrate the treatment's effect on health outcomes and comparative effectiveness. CMS, Guidance for the Public, Industry and CMS Staff Coverage with Evidence Development (Nov. 20, 2014). While multiple layers of appeal are available for LCDs, MACs in fact less formally make many coverage decisions in individual cases, which are reviewable primarily through the general Medicare appeals process described below. Ultimately, whether any particular service is provided to any particular Medicare beneficiary will depend on the decision of a private Medicare contractor interpreting federal policy as mediated by Medicare regulations, manuals and manual transmittals, regional office instructions, NCDs and LCDs. This process is attended by a fair bit of inconsistency.

MEDICARE ADMINISTRATIVE APPEALS

Most Medicare disputes involve individual cases in which a **Medicare Administrative Contractor (MAC)** decides that care provided to a particular beneficiary in a particular instance is not covered. There is now a **uniform appeals process** for Part A and Part B which can involve five levels of appeal after the MAC has made its initial determination:

Level 1: The first level of appeal is a **"MAC redetermination"**—an examination of a claim by someone other than the person who made the initial claim determination. A minimum monetary threshold is not required to request a redetermination.

Level 2: The second level of appeal is a **"reconsideration"**—an independent review by a **Qualified Independent Contractor,** a private entity with which Medicare contracts for this purpose.

Level 3: If the claimant disagrees with the level 2 decision, an appeal can be taken to an **Administrative Law Judge** within the **Office of Medicare Hearings and Appeals**.

Level 4: The final internal step is a further appeal to a specialized panel called the **Medicare Appeals Council**.

Judicial review: If the claim involves $1,000 or more, it can be appealed to federal district court.

What advantages and disadvantages might accrue from having multiple levels of review by diverse entities? The law imposes **time limits** at every step of the review process, and in some cases allows for expedited review such as where a provider plans to discharge a patient or to terminate services where the failure to provide the services is likely to put the beneficiary's health at significant risk. 42 U.S.C.A. §§ 1395ff(b)(1)(F); (c)(3)(C)(iii). This may create complicated problems where no adequate record has been developed owing to the truncated procedure. See Eleanor D. Kinney, Medicare Beneficiary Appeals Processes, Guide to Medicare Coverage Decision-Making and Appeals, 65 (2002).

CRITICAL THINKING ABOUT MEDICARE: EXERCISE 2

What categories of services should Medicare cover? Should its coverage be identical to employment-related benefit packages, or should it vary in some respects? What items might be more, or less, important to its beneficiary population than to working-age Americans? Should Medicare cover nursing home care—a benefit of obvious interest to the elderly—to a greater extent? Should Medicare take cost into account in setting coverage policy for new technologies? If so, what role should cost play in coverage determinations? Though "added value" is among the criteria that CMS proposed in 2000 for evaluating technologies, CMS asserts that it does not consider cost explicitly. Does it serve the public interest to have private "contractors" make many coverage decisions with limited opportunities for appeal?

2. Part D: Prescription Drugs

At the time Medicare was created in 1965, private insurance policies did not generally cover outpatient prescription drugs. Prescription drugs were still relatively affordable and were not as important a part of the management of medical problems as they are today. Recognizing the greatly increased importance of pharmaceuticals for patient care and the rapidly rising costs, Congress, in 2004, enacted the Medicare Modernization Act, which finally added a prescription drug benefit to Medicare, called **Part D**. The law, which narrowly passed (it had a one-vote margin in the House of Representatives), has several distinct characteristics that reflect the ideological differences between Democrats and Republicans at the time.

First, the program had to be **voluntary** so that beneficiaries could choose to join or not, like Part B. To encourage voluntary membership, however, the program would have to appeal to beneficiaries who had relatively low drug costs as well as those with higher costs. Second, it had to be administered by **private "prescription drug plans" (PDPs)** rather than directly by the government. In particular, administered prices set by the Medicare program, which have been used in other parts of the Medicare program to hold down costs, were not acceptable to the drug companies or to congressional leadership. Third, the cost of the program could not exceed $400 billion over ten years. This meant that Medicare beneficiaries would have to continue to bear a considerable share of total Medicare drug costs through **cost-sharing obligations and premiums**. Finally, the legislation had to provide some relief for the poor from these cost-sharing obligations and premiums. Medicare could not continue to be a social insurance program available to all on equal terms but would become partially means tested.

Eligibility and Choice of Plans. The law entitles all persons eligible for Medicare to enroll in a plan. They may get their benefits from three sources: standalone **PDPs**; Medicare Advantage managed care plans offering drug benefits; and employers who offer drug coverage to employed or retired beneficiaries. Each beneficiary must have a choice of at least two PDPs or of one PDP and one Medicare Advantage plan.

Plan Bidding and Financing. Medicare Part D is financed from a combination of general revenues, beneficiary premiums, and state contributions. Beneficiary premiums cover 25.5% and Medicare covers the remaining 74.5% of the cost of "standard coverage," which is based on plans' annual bids to CMS. Higher income beneficiaries pay a larger share of their premiums. The U.S. is divided into 34 PDP regions, and PDPs submit bids to cover these regions. Beyond the enormous subsidy it provides for drug coverage, the federal government also makes a payment to plans called "individual reinsurance" which assumes 80% of the plan's responsibility for beneficiaries who reach the high out-of-pocket, "catastrophic" level of drug spending. Together the direct subsidy and individual reinsurance have helped prevent large increases in beneficiary premiums. See MedPAC Blog, Slow Growth in Part D Premiums Is Only Part of the Story (Sept. 1, 2015).

Beneficiary Copayments and the "Doughnut Hole." The benefits offered by PDPs vary from plan to plan in terms of specific design, coverage, and cost. But plans are required to offer either the statutorily defined standard benefit or its actuarial equivalent. "Standard prescription drug coverage" under the legislation is defined largely in terms of cost-sharing obligations. For 2021, "standard" coverage includes a $445 deductible and a 25% enrollee coinsurance obligation for the initial $4,130 in drug costs. This relatively generous coverage at the low end is intended to attract relatively healthy beneficiaries to the program. Once total drug expenditures reach $4,130, however, the beneficiary hits a phase that was originally called the **"doughnut hole"** because it resulted in a coverage gap. Under the original 2003 law, the beneficiary would receive no further coverage from the program until reaching the catastrophic level, set for 2021 at $6,550 in total costs. At this "out-of-pocket threshold" amount, stop-loss coverage would kick in, and the beneficiary would thereafter responsible for only 5% of further costs (or for a copayment of $3.70 for generics or $9.20 for brand name drugs if this is higher). The ACA has helped plug this doughnut hole, however. Now beneficiaries must only pay 25% of both brand name and generic drugs in this range, with drug manufacturers and plans covering the remainder. For brand-name drugs, drug manufacturers provide a 70% discount and plans pay the remaining 5%; for generics, plans pay the remaining 75%. Additional gap coverage, when offered, is generally limited to generic drugs only. In any event, plans must make available to the beneficiary the actual prices that they negotiate for drugs, including any discounts, concessions, rebates, or other remuneration, even in situations where no benefits are payable because of cost-sharing obligations. For a more detailed description, see Kaiser Family Foundation, An Overview of the Medicare Part D Prescription Drug Benefit (Oct. 14, 2020).

Beneficiary Protections. Medicare provides PDP beneficiaries with several protections. PDP sponsors are required to permit the participation of any pharmacy that accepts a plan's terms and conditions, although PDPs may reduce cost-sharing obligations to encourage the use of in-network pharmacies. Plans must secure participation of enough pharmacies in their networks to meet **"convenient access" requirements**, and they may not charge more for using community rather than mail-order pharmacies. PDPs may use formularies (lists of drugs covered by the plan), but a formulary must be based on scientific standards, and must include each therapeutic category and class of covered Part D drugs. Benefits may not be designed to discourage enrollment by particular categories of beneficiaries. PDPs must offer **grievance and appeal procedures** like those available in the Medicare Advantage program, including independent review. A beneficiary may gain access to drugs not included in the formulary or avoid increased cost-sharing for non-preferred drugs only if the prescribing physician determines that formulary or preferred drugs are not as effective for the beneficiary, cause adverse effects, or both. PDP sponsors must be licensed by their state or meet federal solvency requirements. For Medicaid-eligible individuals, or those with incomes below 150% of the poverty level and modest assets, the law provides additional premium and cost-sharing assistance through the Low-Income Subsidy Program.

Evaluating Part D & the Need for Reform. Has Part D been successful? Part D premiums have risen slowly and at least 25 plans are available in every region of the country. In 2020, about 46 million Medicare beneficiaries were enrolled in Medicare drug plans, including 24.8 million in PDPs and 22.7 million in Medicare Advantage plans. Their evaluations are overwhelmingly positive. Plans use their negotiating leverage to negotiate discounts and rebates from brand name pharmaceutical manufacturers in return for favorable placement on formularies. See generally AHIP, The Medicare Part D Program: A Record of Success (Sept.

2016). On the other hand, Part D spending has spiked in recent years owing largely to extreme price increases in specialty drugs, and drug prices have risen faster than inflation. Medicare Trustees project spending to increase at rates higher than Part A or Part B. See MedPAC Blog, Slow Growth in Part D Premiums Is Only Part of the Story (Sept. 1, 2015). Given the large federal subsidies and risk-sharing arrangements under Part D, taxpayers will bear the burden of increasing costs. Moreover, unlike Medicare's power to set rates for hospital or physician services, Medicare Part D contains a provision that limits the federal government's ability to dictate drug prices. This provision, commonly referred to as the "noninterference" clause, provides that HHS "may not interfere with the negotiations between drug manufacturers and pharmacies and PDP sponsors, and may not require a particular formulary or institute a price structure for the reimbursement of covered part D drugs." 42 U.S.C. § 1395w–111(i). This prohibition has long been viewed as an impediment to containing costs, and it has been an important focus of recent drug pricing reform proposals.

As of late 2021, several proposals to rein in rising drug costs in Part D and beyond are being actively considered. These include proposals to allow Medicare to negotiate the price of drugs, to require drug manufacturers to pay a rebate if drug prices increase faster than inflation, and to cap total out-of-pocket spending or shift greater responsibility for catastrophic coverage to manufacturers and PDP plans. Two other reforms—establishing U.S. prices based on the drug prices in other countries and permitting drug importation—were attempted through regulatory action late in the Trump administration's term; the status of these reform efforts is uncertain, however, because of litigation and reconsideration by the Biden administration. President Biden has signaled support for these types of reforms, but critiques of the Trump administration's approach may lead to rule revisions. Juliette Cubanski, Meredith Freed, & Tricia Neuman, A Status Report on Prescription Drug Policies and Proposals at the Start of the Biden Administration, Kaiser Family Foundation (Feb. 11, 2021).

CRITICAL THINKING ABOUT MEDICARE: EXERCISE 3

PDPs negotiate with drug manufacturers over drug prices, but HHS is prohibited from interfering in these negotiations or exercising its vastly superior bargaining power. Why might Congress choose this approach rather than an administrative price approach, as Medicare uses elsewhere? Are PDPs likely to have negotiating leverage with respect to patent-protected, high-cost pharmaceuticals for which there are no effective substitutes? Who might have more bargaining power with respect to those drugs, the federal government or PDPs? What tools might PDPs use to enhance their bargaining power, even though their market share is much less than that of the federal government? Why did Congress enact Part D with large federal subsidies without raising taxes or cutting spending when concerns about federal deficits are prominent in every political campaign?

C. PAYMENT FOR SERVICES

Most litigated cases involving the Medicare program concern neither eligibility nor benefit coverage, but rather payment for services. Medicare payment reform has been a primary focus of government efforts to reduce cost, in light of the significant Medicare spending noted earlier. A prominent example of this was Congress' 1983 overhaul of its hospital inpatient reimbursement system—from one that was cost-based to a prospective payment system intended to encourage providers to operate more efficiently. The cost adjustment methodology under this system was the subject of the *Bellevue Hospital* case below. *Bellevue Hospital* provides a detailed view of how reimbursement is determined in a prospective payment system, and the role of courts when providers challenge methodology. The dispute in the case also reflects a more fundamental challenge underlying any payment reform that is designed to influence provider behavior, and where payment depends on certain assumptions about what is required for good quality and cost-efficient care. A prominent modern example of this is the value-purchasing programs promoted heavily in the ACA. Such payment reforms inevitably implicate questions about the accuracy and fairness of underlying assumptions, as well as concerns about the potential unintended, harmful effects to providers and Medicare beneficiaries.

BELLEVUE HOSPITAL CENTER V. LEAVITT

United States Court of Appeals, Second Circuit, 2006.
443 F.3d 163.

KATZMANN, CIRCUIT JUDGE.

Seventy-six hospitals, plaintiffs-appellants here, challenge the Department of Health and Human Services' ("HHS") implementation of a statutory requirement that the agency adjust hospitals' reimbursements for the costs of administering care to Medicare recipients to reflect "differences in hospital wage levels" across "geographic area[s]." 42 U.S.C. § 1395ww(d)(3)(E)(I).

For more than two decades, HHS has divided the nation into geographic areas for these purposes by adopting the Metropolitan Statistical Areas ("MSAs") formulated by the Office of Management and Budget ("OMB"). Most recently, in 2004, it adopted the version of the MSAs released by OMB in 2003. Compared with previous iterations, the New York City MSA was slightly expanded and now includes certain additional hospitals in northern New Jersey. Because the New Jersey hospitals' wages are somewhat lower, the average wage level in the MSA dropped, along with the wage adjustment for hospitals in that MSA. Plaintiffs allege they will receive $812 million less in reimbursements over the next ten years than they would have under their former wage adjustment.

* * *

The Medicare program, established by Title XVIII of the Social Security Act, 42 U.S.C. § 1395 et seq., pays for covered medical services provided to eligible aged and disabled persons. Of relevance to this case, it reimburses hospitals for the cost of serving Medicare beneficiaries. . . .

From the inception of Medicare in 1965 until 1983, hospitals were reimbursed for their actual costs in treating beneficiaries, so long as those costs were reasonable. In 1983, Congress overhauled the reimbursement system, switching to what is known as the Inpatient Prospective Payment System ("IPPS"). [ ] Under the IPPS, hospitals are not reimbursed for their actual costs, but are instead paid fixed rates for providing specific categories of treatment, known as "diagnosis related groups," or "DRGs." [ ] Separate DRG rates are set for hospitals in urban and rural areas. [ ] The purpose of this switch was to "encourage health care providers to improve efficiency and reduce operating costs." [ ]

Of particular significance for this case, the Secretary [of Health and Human Services] must adjust DRG payment rates for the relative labor costs in each hospital's geographic area. Accordingly, the base DRG payment rate is divided into two portions: the labor-related costs, which get adjusted for these geographic differences, and the non-labor-related costs, which do not. While the relative proportions of these two cost sources formerly were "estimated by the Secretary from time to time," [ ] for discharges occurring on or after October 1, 2004, Congress has removed the Secretary's discretion and set the labor-cost proportion at sixty-two percent of the base DRG payment. . . . [T]he Secretary must, at least once annually, compute a wage factor for each hospital "reflecting" the relative wage level in that hospital's "geographic area," and then apply that factor to the sixty-two percent of the DRG base rate that is attributable to labor costs. These adjustments must be cost neutral, so that any increase in one hospital's wage factor must be offset by a decrease in another's.

From its initial implementation of this law in 1985 through the present, CMS [the Center for Medicare and Medicaid Services] has consistently grouped hospitals into geographic areas by adopting the Metropolitan Statistical Areas ("MSAs") developed by the Office of Management and Budget ("OMB") for use throughout the federal government. Since the beginning, CMS has acknowledged that MSAs, which were not designed for this specific purpose, are an imperfect proxy for labor markets, particularly with respect to hospitals in rural areas. It has promised to consider alternative methodologies that are based on "objective criteria that will provide more equitable labor market area definitions than the current MSA/non-MSA classifications." [ ]

. . . . By 1995, CMS had rejected . . . other proposed modifications. It concluded that "there is no clear 'best' labor market area option" that would be obviously superior to the MSA system. [ ] Because the industry itself could reach "no consensus" (unsurprisingly, since any modification to a cost-neutral system means much of the industry loses money), and because CMS was less than captivated by any of the alternatives, it decided to simply stay with the MSA system. . . .

Although well aware of this controversy, Congress has never directed CMS to implement any methodology for dividing core from ring or otherwise deviate in any fundamental way from the MSA system. Instead, Congress has enacted a series of exceptions by which hospitals particularly aggrieved by MSA cut-offs can get some relief by, for example, relocating into other MSAs or having dramatic changes to their wage factors phased in over a period of time.[ ]

On December 27, 2000, OMB announced various changes to its methodology for computing MSAs. . . .

On June 6, 2003, OMB published its revised list of MSAs, incorporating information from the 2000 Census and using its new methodology. * * * Most previously existing MSAs became smaller. However, the old New York City MSA, which already had included the outlying New York counties of Westchester, Putnam, and Rockland, was expanded to include the New Jersey counties of Bergen, Passaic, and Hudson. [ ] . . .

On May 18, 2004, CMS proposed to adopt OMB's new MSAs. [ ] On July 12, 2004, plaintiffs' trade association filed comments in opposition, arguing that hospitals in the New Jersey counties had much lower wages ("only" 117 percent of the national average) and should not be included in the New York City MSA, since their inclusion would trim plaintiffs' wage index from 136 percent of the national average to 133 percent, cutting into plaintiffs' reimbursements at a time when New York City hospitals were struggling financially for other reasons. . . .

On August 11, 2004, CMS adopted OMB's new MSAs for purposes of the hospital wage index. . . . CMS observed that commenters had proposed completely inconsistent alternatives, with some emphasizing "expanding existing MSAs" and others calling for "creating smaller units or at least distinguishing segments within larger MSAs." [ ] It added that, while many commenters had demonstrated that their proposals would better serve their "specific situations," it could not adopt any alternative without assessing "all of the effects that these proposed revisions might have." . . .

* * *

In 2000, Congress directed CMS to refine its survey of hospital wages in geographic areas by controlling for differences in hospitals' occupational mixes. [ ] Specifically, Congress instructed the Secretary of HHS to "provide for the collection of data every 3 years on occupational mix for employees of each [covered] hospital ... in the provision of inpatient hospital services, in order to construct an occupational mix adjustment in the hospital area wage index." As codified, CMS's instruction is to "measure the earnings and paid hours of employment by occupational category and [to] exclude data with respect to the wages and wage-related costs incurred in furnishing skilled nursing facility services." [ ] In uncodified language that is a subject of the instant controversy, Congress added:

By not later than September 30, 2003, for application beginning October 1, 2004, the Secretary shall first complete (A) the collection of data [on occupational mix]; and (B) the measurement [of earnings and paid hours of employment by occupational category]." [ ]

By the summer of 2001, CMS had promulgated a final rule as to how it would collect these data and expressed its intention to survey hospitals during the 2002 calendar year. [ ] Nonetheless, for reasons that are unclear, not until September 19, 2003 did CMS publish a final notice of intent to collect data. [ ] ....

In the final rule being challenged here, CMS stated that it lacked full confidence in its data for several reasons .... In light of its lack of confidence in its data, CMS decided to apply the occupational mix adjustment to only ten percent of the wage index for FY 2005, an action that was supported by a "majority of commenters." [ ]

The following year, rather than conduct a new survey (an action which, it noted, the statute only compels it to take once every three years), CMS used largely the same data.... [B]ecause CMS had the same concerns about the robustness of its data, it continued to apply the occupational mix adjustment to only ten percent of the wage index.

* * *

On November 1, 2004, plaintiffs filed this action in the Southern District of New York pursuant to the Administrative Procedure Act ("APA"), 5 U.S.C. § 701 et seq., as well as the judicial review provision of the Medicare Act, see 42 U.S.C. § 1395oo(f)(1), challenging CMS's adoption of the new MSAs and its decision to implement the occupational mix adjustment at only ten-percent effectiveness. ...

* * *

At the outset, we describe the scope of our review. On appeal from a grant of summary judgment in a challenge to agency action under the APA, we review the administrative record and the district court's decision de novo. [ ]

With respect to each challenged action, we begin by reviewing the agency's construction of the statute at issue. We do so by applying the familiar two-step process of statutory interpretation set forth in Chevron

U.S.A. Inc. v. Natural Resources Defense Council, Inc., 467 U.S. 837 (1984). Under Chevron, the first question is "whether Congress has directly spoken to the precise question at issue;" if so, our inquiry is at an end. [ ] If there is silence or ambiguity in the statute on the question, then the agency has discretion in its implementation, and we ask only if the construction it has given the statute is reasonable.[11] [ ]

Assuming the agency's action was authorized by statute, we then ask whether it was "arbitrary, capricious, [or] an abuse of discretion," 5 U.S.C. 706(2)(A), or "unsupported by substantial evidence," id. § 706(2)(E). Such a finding, which is required to overturn an agency action, can be made only where the agency "has relied on factors which Congress has not intended it to consider, entirely failed to consider an important aspect of the problem, offered an explanation for its decision that runs counter to the evidence before the agency, or is so implausible that it could not be ascribed to a difference in view or the product of agency expertise." [ ]

Our task, then, is limited. We have no license to substitute our policy judgment for that of the agency, but only to overturn actions that are not authorized by statute or that are arbitrary or capricious. [ ]

We first review the defendant's use of OMB's MSAs. . . .

CMS's task is unambiguous: to calculate a factor that reflects geographic-area wage-level differences, and nothing else. We reject defendant's contention that this provision, or any other in the Medicare Act, confers upon him the discretion to take into account all sorts of unrelated policy considerations, such as whether certain hospitals receive unwarranted advantages from other provisions of the Medicare reimbursement scheme.

At the same time, as plaintiffs conceded at argument, the statute leaves considerable ambiguity as to the term "geographic area," . . . . CMS's discretion in interpreting this ambiguous term is cabined by the need to fulfill two somewhat contradictory policies expressed by the text of the provision and the legislative history of the IPPS: (1) the geographic areas must be small enough to actually reflect differences in wage levels and, (2) each geographic area must include enough hospitals that their costs can be meaningfully averaged and individual hospitals do not get reimbursed for their own actual costs. In balancing these two considerations, the agency has considerable discretion. Moreover, even after determining the scale of each geographic area, lines must be drawn between areas that inevitably will be contested and may seem arbitrary; once again, the statute is silent as to how this process is to take place, leaving the agency with broad discretion.

---

[11] Defendant argues that even greater deference is required in all cases interpreting the Medicare statute, given the complex and highly technical nature of much of the statutory scheme. However, the discrete issue here is as readily reviewable as is any other administrative action.[ ]

There is no question that MSAs are, literally, "geographic areas," and thus their use complies with the language of the statute. Furthermore, their use comports with the two purposes set out above. Because MSAs are based on commuting patterns into and out of the central county, hospitals in each MSA presumably compete in the same labor market, and so it is likely that their wages bear at least rough similarity. On the other hand, each MSA provides a large enough pool of hospitals to allow cost averaging. We conclude that the use of MSAs to fill the gap left by the ambiguous term "geographic areas" is reasonable. In doing so, we express no opinion as to whether any alternative interpretation would have been "better," as we are not empowered to set aside a reasonable interpretation on that basis. [ ]

* * *

Finally, we observe that CMS has now used MSAs to fill this statutory gap for more than two decades without any action from Congress suggesting disapproval. The fact that defendant has now adopted an MSA-based wage index multiple times certainly counsels deference to its decision to do so this time. . . .

Having concluded that the Medicare statute authorizes an MSA's use as a proxy for a "geographic area," we now ask whether this policy choice was arbitrary or capricious. Before undertaking this inquiry, we pause to note that an agency's burden of supplying a "reasoned analysis" justifying its policy is lower where, as here, an agency is continuing a long-standing policy compared to where the agency is suddenly changing that policy. . . .

* * *

Finally, we would think that, despite the plaintiffs' fears that the agency favors rural hospitals, the consistent use of MSAs has dampened any such favoritism. MSAs, after all, are constructed through an objective methodology, deliberately without reference to any political considerations, by a different agency that has no involvement in this rulemaking. . . . All other things being equal, it is rational and permissible for an agency to adopt an already extant measure that uses objective criteria rather than assuming the task of creating its own measure in the face of a sharply divided regulated industry that has not proposed any clearly superior alternatives. [ ] Under these circumstances, the agency's continued use of MSAs was not arbitrary and capricious.

* * *

In an uncodified section of the 2000 Bill, Congress instructed the agency as follows: "By not later than September 30, 2003, for application beginning October 1, 2004, the Secretary shall first complete (A) the collection of data [on occupational mix]; and (B) the measurement [of earnings and paid hours of employment by occupational category]." [ ] . . . .

We think that the provision can only be fairly read to contemplate application in full on October 1, 2004. Congress need not explicitly tell an agency to implement a program "in full," any more than it need tell the agency to do the job "competently"; any reasonable reader trying to do justice to Congress's intent will infer that meaning. Nor is a call for application "beginning on" a date certain reasonably interpreted as a grant of discretion to the agency to apply the adjustment on that date at whatever limited strength the agency believes is appropriate. There is no ambiguity in the statute on this point, and so the defendant's interpretation does not receive deference under Chevron.

* * *

Not only are the agency's actions violative of the statute, but they are arbitrary and capricious. CMS simply asserts that its data justify implementation at precisely ten percent effectiveness, with no explanation given as to why ten percent was chosen instead of, e.g., twenty percent or fifty percent. In addition, the agency has not accounted for its continuing failure to comply with Congress's unambiguous mandate that the agency complete the necessary data collection and measurement by September 30, 2003. Without any explanation, the agency did not even begin its data collection until September 19, 2003, although it appeared to be ready two years earlier. When the data it then gathered in rushed fashion predictably proved inadequate to permit full implementation on schedule, the agency simply stated its intent to do better the next time it believed it was required to collect data, three years later, and until then apparently intends to continue applying the adjustment at greatly limited effectiveness. Under these circumstances, it was arbitrary and capricious for the agency not to return to data gathering immediately, or at least explain why it is not doing so, rather than proceed as if it had successfully completed the initial data gathering.

* * *

Having easily concluded that the agency's actions were in violation of law, we move to the more difficult task of formulating a remedy. Obviously, at this late date the agency cannot be ordered into compliance with the schedule set by Congress. We therefore recognize at the outset that any remedy we devise is necessarily imperfect. However, we must endeavor, to the extent possible, to honor Congress's intent as well as the language of the statute.

The district court simply granted plaintiff its requested relief and ordered CMS to immediately apply the occupational mix adjustment in full based on the data it has already collected. While this approach holds some appeal, in that it would prevent any further agency delay, we think it is not what Congress would have wanted. . . . We think immediate application of the adjustment using such flawed data not only would result in irrational policy (and almost certainly damage some of the intended beneficiaries of this adjustment, through no fault of their own) but would contravene Congress's purpose in setting up this two-step schedule.

Accordingly, we instead order the agency to immediately return to the first step and collect data that are sufficiently robust to permit full application of the occupational mix adjustment. All data collection and measurement and any other preparations necessary for full application should be complete by September 30, 2006, at which time we instruct the agency to immediately apply the adjustment in full. . . . Although we cannot undo the past and remedy the agency's failure to comply with its statutory obligations through one full round of data collection, we can order the agency to follow the schedule originally anticipated by Congress from this date forward.

* * *

NOTES AND QUESTIONS

1.   Consider first the context of Medicare payment under prospective payment. What services are the plaintiff providers supplying? How are they being paid for their services? What are they complaining about? What policy decisions does the method of payment under consideration represent? What is the stake of Medicare beneficiaries in this litigation? What is the interest of taxpayers?

2.   Next, consider the bigger picture. What does this case tell us about how Medicare is administered? What is the role of law in the administration of the program? What are the respective roles of the Centers for Medicare and Medicaid Services (a division of the Department of Health and Human Services mysteriously referred to as CMS rather than CMMS), Congress, and the courts? What practical constraints does CMS face in making determinations such as this (i.e., what trade-offs are necessary)? How much deference should the courts afford CMS in making these determinations, and does *Chevron* strike the right balance?

———

Over Medicare's history, the program has relied primarily on three payment strategies: cost or charge-based reimbursement, prospective payment, and managed competition. At the outset, it followed the then-current practice of health insurers by paying institutions on the basis of their reported costs and professionals on the basis of their charges. This proved, not surprisingly, to be wildly inflationary, and over time Medicare increasingly imposed restrictions on cost- and charge-based payment. In the end, Medicare abandoned cost- and charge-based payment in favor of administered payment systems, under which Medicare itself sets the price it pays for services. As noted above, Medicare began by implementing **prospective payment** for hospitals in the early 1980s. The next major step toward prospective payment was the **resource-based relative value scale (RBRVS)** for paying physicians, implemented in the early 1990s. Under the Balanced Budget Act of 1997, Medicare implemented prospective payment systems for home health, skilled nursing facilities, outpatient hospital care, and inpatient rehabilitation hospitals. Paying for almost one-third of the nation's hospital care and one-fifth of physician care, Medicare has been able to offer payment rates to many professionals and providers on a take-it-or-leave-it basis, and to hold rates to levels that are below those paid generally in the private market. It has been less successful, however, at controlling the volume of services it pays for, leading to continuing increases in overall costs.

The following subsections describe the evolution of payment reforms in Medicare to address rising costs. The first two sections focus on the two major administered price programs under Medicare: the diagnosis-related group prospective payment system for hospitals under Part A and the resource-based relative value scale for physicians under Part B. The next subsection examines the managed care option under Part C, Medicare Advantage. The final section describes some of the ACA's significant payment reforms intended to not only reduce cost, but also encourage new delivery methods that would improve clinical quality and health outcomes.

1. Medicare Part A: Prospective Payment to Hospitals

As noted above, Congress established the **diagnosis-related group (DRG)** prospective payment system for hospitals in 1982. A DRG is a means of categorizing patients to reflect **relative intensity of use of services**. DRG-based payment treats hospitals as coordinating services to produce particular products, such as the diagnosis and treatment of heart attacks, ulcers, or tumors. The DRG system groups patients primarily by principal (admitting) diagnoses, which, together with other factors, are used to categorize patients. The purpose of this analysis is to yield groups of hospital patients, each covered by a distinct DRG, that more or less require the same quantity of medical resources. Once DRGs were defined, Medicare arrayed DRGs by relative intensity of resource consumption, with average resource use defined as a single unit. In 2008, CMS refined DRG classification to take into account **comorbidities and complications**—where there was previously only one code for each procedure there are now three codes distinguished by levels of severity.

To determine a hospital's actual payment for caring for a Medicare patient, the relative DRG weight assigned to that patient is first multiplied by a **standardized amount** that is divided into **labor-related** and **nonlabor-related** shares. In theory, the standardized amounts represent the cost of an efficient hospital for an average case. This basic amount, however, is only the starting point for determining **Inpatient Prospective Payment System (IPPS)** hospital reimbursement. A hospital's actual IPPS payment is determined by calculating the sum of the products of the total DRG weights of all Medicare cases treated in the hospital and their respective standardized amounts; this sum is then adjusted in several respects, such as to account for geographic variation in expenses, as in *Bellevue Hospital*. IPPS payment also provides for several "add-ons" that recognize the cost of extraordinarily expensive cases, or "**outliers**." IPPS payments are also enhanced to compensate teaching hospitals for the indirect costs of operating **medical education programs**. Finally, payments are adjusted to benefit special categories of hospitals, such as **disproportionate share hospitals** (which serve large numbers of low-income patients, who presumably cost more to treat) or **sole-community hospitals** (which serve communities distant from other hospitals and are protected by federal policy). A few categories of hospital costs continue to be reimbursed on a cost basis, such as medical education programs reimbursed on a pass-through cost basis and hospital **bad debts** related to uncollectible Medicare deductible and coinsurance amounts.

Evaluations of the IPPS are mixed. The reform succeeded at its principal goal, limiting the escalation of Medicare expenditures for inpatient care. IPPS also resulted in (or at least was accompanied by) a massive shift of care within hospitals from inpatient to outpatient settings or to long-term care units, often located within or owned by the same hospitals that had previously provided inpatient care. A great deal of surgery that used to be done on an inpatient basis, such as cataract surgery, is now done outpatient. IPPS payment also encouraged hospitals to find ways to align their interests with those of their doctors, who in the end are responsible for admitting and discharging patients and ordering the tests and procedures that increase hospital costs. Although prospective payment mimics the incentives of the marketplace to the extent it encourages cost-economizing, in other ways it is quite distinct. For example, quality and outcomes are not rewarded; the best and worst hospitals receive the same base payment. As the Chairman of the Mayo Clinic put it: "It doesn't pay to be good."

Providers have tried to game the system. For example, there is considerable evidence that there has been "DRG creep" over the years, as hospitals have moved to coding cases as more complicated, and thus earned higher payment. CMS, in turn, has responded by including a rate reduction as a "behavioral offset" to acknowledge the likelihood that hospitals will inflate coding of case severity as CMS moves to severity-adjusted DRGs. As discussed in Chapter 14, the government has devoted enormous resources to prosecuting knowing violations of the coding system as illegal false claims.

Bellevue Hospital notwithstanding, IPPS does not seem to be making much business for lawyers. Most of the important issues IPPS raises are not justiciable. Issues raised by IPPS are either political questions, such as the standardized amount update level for any particular year, or technical questions, such as how a particular DRG should be weighted or which DRG should be assigned by a hospital to a particular admission. Congress has made it clear that it does not want the courts getting involved in these determinations:

> There shall be **no administrative or judicial review** under Section 1395*oo* of this title or otherwise of
>
> > (A) the determination of the requirement, or the proportional amount, of any adjustment effected pursuant to subsection (e)(1) [of this section providing for updates in the standardized amount]
> >
> > [and]
> >
> > (B) the establishment of diagnosis-related-groups, of the methodology for the classification of discharges within such groups, and of the appropriate weighting of factors thereof . . . .

42 U.S.C.A. § 1395ww(d)(7).

Congress has established a tripartite dialogue among itself, CMS, and the **Medicare Payment Advisory Commission (MedPAC)**, an independent advisory body established to advise Congress through annual and special reports. This alliance determines these questions and has left no place for the courts. See Timothy Stoltzfus Jost, Governing Medicare, 51 Admin. L. Rev. 39 (1999). Even beyond the hospital IPPS, courts have declined to hear cases challenging Medicare regulations. See Shalala v. Illinois Council of Long Term Care, Inc., 529 U.S. 1, 120 S.Ct. 1084, 146 L.Ed.2d 1 (2000) (holding that plaintiffs' challenge to Medicare regulations on nursing home participation was statutorily precluded from judicial review until they had exhausted the administrative appeals process with HHS). Not only do the courts defer to HHS procedurally by refusing to take jurisdiction over direct challenges to HHS regulations, they also tend to defer substantively by generally upholding HHS's interpretation of the Medicare statutes and its own regulations.

Insofar as IPPS generates work for lawyers, it is primarily in the area of advising clients how to take advantage of IPPS. Consider the following problem:

PROBLEM: IPPS

You are the in-house counsel for a large urban hospital that has a high percentage of Medicare patients. In recent years, your hospital has either lost money or barely broken even. At the request of the hospital's CEO, you are serving on a committee considering how to improve the hospital's financial situation, focusing particularly on your situation with respect to Medicare.

What strategies might be available for increasing your hospital's IPPS revenues? Would changing your case-mix help? How might you achieve that?

What opportunities might be available in terms of how discharges are coded? (Reconsider this question after you study Medicare fraud and abuse in Chapter 14.) What possibilities are available under Medicare prospective payment for increasing your Medicare payments that are not strictly tied to your case-mix? How does your hospital's teaching mission affect your Medicare reimbursement? How might you go about increasing your Medicare reimbursement for non-inpatient services?

Alternatively, how might you go about lowering the cost of treating Medicare patients? In particular, what strategies can you use to create incentives for your doctors to reduce costs? (Be forewarned: tax law, fraud and abuse laws, and antitrust law covered in Chapters 13–15 will limit your options.) Will cost reductions be accompanied by Medicare payment reductions?

NOTE: ACA REFORMS TO PART A & VALUE-BASED PURCHASING

After private insurance, the Medicare program received the most attention from the ACA. Among the most important factors driving reform was widespread dissatisfaction with the effects of fee-for-service provider payment. While not eliminating or even radically restructuring provider payments under Parts A and B, the ACA moves traditional Medicare away from its historic focus on payment for services. Section 3001 of the ACA creates a new **"value-based purchasing program" (VBP)**, which adjusts the IPPS payments based on quality measures, tying a percentage of hospital payments to performance on high-cost conditions, including acute myocardial infarction, surgical and health care infections, and pneumonia. In its Final Rule implementing the VBP program, CMS set out three domains within which the program measures performance: Process of Care, Experience of Care, and Outcomes. CMS, Medicare Program; Hospital Inpatient Value-Based Purchasing Program, 76 Fed. Reg. 26489 (May 6, 2011). Process of Care regulation includes several **clinical and quality measures**. For example, among the measures are assessments as to whether hospitals 1) ensure that patients who might have had a heart attack receive care within 90 minutes; 2) provide care within a 24-hour window to surgery patients to prevent blood clots; and 3) communicate discharge instructions to heart-failure patients; and ensure hospital facilities are clean and well-maintained. The ACA requires CMS to evaluate each hospital's performance using the higher of either **an achievement score or an improvement score**. It also requires CMS to establish an appeals procedure limited to the review of the calculation of a hospital's performance assessment with respect to the performance standards. See CMS, Hospital-Based Purchasing Program Results for Fiscal Year 2017 (Nov. 2016). CMS has added value-based programs for skilled nursing, home health, and end-stage renal disease payments. CMS, CMS's Value Based Programs.

CMS also **penalizes hospitals for poor performance**, such as having disproportionate amounts of hospital acquired conditions, see CMS, Hospital Acquired Conditions Program, and readmissions. With almost 18% of hospitalizations resulting in readmission within 30 days (accounting for $15 billion in Medicare spending) in the years preceding its enactment, the ACA directed HHS to establish the **Hospital Readmission Reduction Program (HRRP)**, which financially penalizes hospitals with relatively high rates of Medicare readmissions. The program now covers readmissions for a number of conditions including acute myocardial infarction, heart failure, pneumonia, elective hip and knee replacement, and CABG surgery. CMS defines readmission as an admission to a hospital within 30 days of a discharge from the same or another hospital. The program also employs an **"all cause" definition of readmission**, meaning any readmission, regardless of the reason, will be judged as a readmission, unless it is a planned hospitalization, as might be the case for a scheduled coronary angioplasty. CMS, Inpatient Prospective Payment Final Rule (2012).

As of 2017, CMS had imposed $500 million in penalties and data reflected a steady decline of readmissions since 2012, giving some evidence that hospitals have adopted new interventions in response to the HRRP. However, analyses of which hospitals have been penalized has confirmed concerns that the program could have adverse and unwarranted effects on safety net hospitals. See Cristina Boccuti & Giselle Casillas, The Henry J. Kaiser Family Foundation Issue Brief, Aiming for Fewer Hospital U-Turns: The Medicare Hospital Readmission Program (March 2017) (summarizing studies and concluding that "Medicare beneficiaries who go to certain types of hospitals— namely major teaching hospitals and hospitals with relatively greater shares of low-income beneficiaries—are more likely to stay in penalized hospitals and hospitals with higher penalties"). Although the program adjusts for risk based on demographic characteristics such as age, it initially did not adjust for **socioeconomic or community based factors**. Why might those factors be especially important with regard to a hospital's responsibility for readmission? See Section III.C.4 of this Chapter (Medicaid Delivery Reforms).

Congress responded to this issue in 2017, through a provision in the 21st Century Cures Act directing the Secretary of HHS to divide hospitals into peer groups for purposes of determining performance. 42 U.S.C. § 1395ww(q)(3)(D). But the problem persists. A recent study of the HRRP by Harvard Medical School researchers found that between 10% and 12% of hospitals were incorrectly penalized due to misclassification errors, with lower-revenue hospitals more likely to be wrongly penalized. See Changyu Shen et al., Misclassification of Hospital Performance Under the Hospital Readmissions Reduction Program: Implications for Value-Based Programs 6 JAMA Cardiology 332 (2021). Moreover, a fundamental question remains about whether a 30-day readmission is an appropriate proxy for poorer quality care. See Boccuti and Casillas supra. See also Karen E. Joynt & Ashish K. Jha, Thirty Day Readmissions—Truth and Consequences, 366 N. Eng. J. Med. 1366

(2012) (hospitals with high readmission rates arguably provide higher quality of care because they have lower mortality rates).

In addition to the targeted payment adjustments of hospital services described above, value-based purchasing reforms under the ACA also included broader changes designed to foster greater integration of care. These are discussed below in section 4, *Integrating Delivery and Payment.*

2.   Medicare Part B: Payment of Physicians

Medicare Part B payment for most services (including physician services) was based initially, at least in theory, on reimbursement of actual charges (minus deductibles and coinsurance). A number of concerns, however, including the rapid rise in the cost of physician services, increasing "balance-billing" to beneficiaries, and inequities in payments among medical specialties, led to consensus that payment reform was needed.

At the heart of the payment reform was the creation of a **physician fee schedule**. As with Part A prospective payment, fees are determined by multiplying a weighted value (in this case representing a medical procedure rather than a diagnosis) times a conversion factor, which is adjusted to consider geographic variations in cost. Relative value units (RVUs) are assigned to procedures based on the CMS Common Procedure Coding System and American Medical Association Common Procedural Terminology (CPT) codes. The **Relative Value Scale** consists of three components: a **physician work** component, a **practice expense** component, and a **malpractice** component.

The physician work component is based on estimates of the relative time and intensity of physician work involved in delivering specified services. With respect to major surgeries, physician work is defined globally to include pre-operative evaluation and consultation (inpatient or outpatient), beginning with the day before surgery, and post-operative care for a normal recovery from surgery for the ninety days following the surgery.

The practice expense component accounts for physician overhead, including rent and office expenses. The practice expense is based on resource use. Different practice expense RVUs are applied depending on whether the services are furnished in a physician's office or a facility (hospital, skilled nursing facility, or ambulatory surgery center). Malpractice expenses for particular services are separated out from other practice expenses and are based on the malpractice expense resources required to furnish the service.

The RVUs are adjusted by a **geographic practice cost index** to recognize differences in cost in various parts of the country and then multiplied by a conversion factor to reach a final fee payment amount (of which Medicare pays 80%, the other 20% representing the beneficiary coinsurance obligation). The RBRVS system also provides special bonuses for physicians working in health practitioner shortage areas and for physicians working in rural areas. Rates are also adjusted downward for physicians who are not participating providers (i.e., who do not accept assignment for the claims of all of their Medicare patients).

While the resource-based prices set by RBRVS addressed the problem of price inflation in physician payment, it failed to address rising costs due to providers **increasing the volume** of their services. Congress tried and failed to address this problem in a couple of ways. First, CMS used the Volume Performance Standard (VPS) to try to discourage physicians from overusing services by reducing per service payment levels if overall volume increases exceeded a specified threshold. This approach ignored the patent collective action problem: there was simply no reason for an individual physician to reduce the volume of services based on a net reduction in per service payment levels nationally or even regionally. A few years later, in 1997, CMS adopted the Sustainable Growth Rate (SGR) formula which imposed *cumulative* forced reductions in physician payments when total physician spending exceeded a fixed spending. But this approach failed to anticipate Congress's response to proposed reductions in physician incomes resulting from the process: each year from 2001 to 2015 (barring one year), Congress passed legislation that overrode fee reductions. After years of confusion and complaints, the SGR was finally repealed and replaced by the **Medicare Access and CHIP Reauthorization Act of 2015 (MACRA)** discussed below. At bottom, even with all these reforms, Medicare's physician fee schedule is still fundamentally a **fee-for-service** method of payment, so physicians' incentives to increase the volume and intensity of services persist.

Another critical flaw of Medicare physician payment has been its failure to satisfy an original goal of the RBRVS experiment: correcting unjustified payment variations among clinical services. Because of CMS's reliance on the American Medical Association's Relative Value Update Committee, which is dominated by specialists, it has tended to overweigh specialty procedures and undervalue primary care. See Peter Whoreskey & Dan Keating, How a Secretive Committee Uses Data that Distorts Doctors' Pay, Wash. Post (July 20, 2013). Improvements have been made through coding changes that better value the cognitive services physicians provide as part of care. See, e.g. Seymour Katz & Eileen Petrilak, Update on Relative Value Units and the Cognitive Physician Visit, 14 Gastroenterology & Hepatology 41 (2018) (describing a new code that allows primary care physicians coordinating care for chronically ill patients to bill for non-face-to-face coordination services).

PROBLEM: RELATIVE VALUE SCALE
FOR LAW SCHOOL GRADING

Most law students will agree that not all law school classes are equal. Some require more reading, some have harder exams, others require periodic written assignments or in-class exercises, some involve providing clinical services, and some are simply more challenging intellectually. Yet the grades received in each class counts the same on students' GPA. You are the student representative on a committee tasked with designing a relative value scale to level the playing field among courses for grading purposes. What factors should be used to establish the scale? How should they be measured and weighted? How should these decisions be made?

3.   Medicare Part C: Medicare Advantage

The Turbulent History of Medicare HMOs. Although Medicare began as a **fee-for-service (FFS)** program, it has offered managed care options since the early 1980s. Managed care enrollment grew slowly at first, but growth was rapid in the mid-1990s: between 1995 and 1997 enrollment doubled from three to six million. Prior to the Balanced Budget Act of 1997 (BBA), Medicare health maintenance organizations (HMOs) were paid 95% of the cost of Medicare fee-for-service costs in the same county (with crude risk adjustment). Because of biased selection (i.e., HMOs got healthier beneficiaries), HMOs did very well, particularly in counties with high fee-for-service costs. Because they were required to share their excess income with beneficiaries, Medicare managed care plans generally offered attractive benefit packages—in particular prescription drug coverage—which in turn led to rapid growth. The BBA created the Medicare+Choice program, attempting to encourage continued growth in Medicare managed care, while at the same time dealing with some of the problems of the prior program. The hope was that Medicare+Choice would give beneficiaries a choice of health plans, benefits, and cost-sharing options, and that managed competition among health plans would hold down the cost of the Medicare program. The BBA changes, however, were a disaster for Medicare managed care, leading to a rapid decline in plan participation and enrollment. This, in turn, led to the Medicare Prescription Drug, Improvement and Modernization Act (MMA), enacted in 2003 and which renamed the program **"Medicare Advantage" (MA)**. This Act added regional PPOs and private fee-for-service plans to expand the availability of plans to previously unserved or underserved areas and adopted new bidding and risk-sharing regulations.

Underlying the MMA changes was a straightforward purpose: promote MA enrollment by **overpaying** private plans. The changes achieved that goal; by 2009, MA plans were receiving payments in excess of 114% of fee-for-service and some of the newly designed MA plans (the so-called "private fee-for-service plans") were not even designed to provide integrated care.

Instead, the MA overpayments were designed to undermine traditional Medicare and draw enrollees into MA plans. See Thomas L. Greaney, Controlling Medicare Costs: Moving Beyond Inept Administered Pricing and Ersatz Competition?, 6 St. Louis U. J. Health L. & Pol'y 229 (2013).

The roller coaster for Medicare managed care continued under the ACA which instituted another series of bidding reforms, discussed below, that are designed to "**level the playing field**" between MA plans and traditional fee-for-service Medicare by moving payments to plans closer to 100% of FFS payment.

Plan Bidding Under Medicare Advantage. Medicare Advantage reimbursement to private plans is based on a **bidding system**. Although superficially designed to emulate competition in the private sector, the process falls short of replicating a competitive market even after important amendments made by the ACA. Payments to MA plans are determined by comparing each plan's bid (which must reflect the plan's estimated costs) to a benchmark. Plans bidding below the benchmark receive their bid plus a **"rebate"** equal to 75% of the difference between the bid and the benchmark. Those bidding above the benchmark—a rare occurrence— receive the benchmark but must require that each of their enrollees pay a premium equal to the difference between the bid and the benchmark. The ACA **adjusted the bidding framework** by gradually lowering plan benchmarks to levels closer to the cost of enrollees in traditional Medicare in each county, setting relatively lower benchmarks in counties with high fee-for-service Medicare costs, and relatively higher benchmarks in counties with lower fee-for-service costs. By retaining bidding against a **preset benchmark** based in part on historic private plan rates, the process does not fully encourage plans to compete on bids. Even so, Medicare Advantage plans do seem to have had some success in negotiating with hospitals. See Laurence C. Baker, Medicare Advantage Plans Pay Hospitals Less Than Fee-For-Service Pays, Health Aff. (August 2016) (Medicare Advantage plans pay 12% less for hospital services than fee-for-service).

The ACA introduced a **quality measure** that also impacts plan reimbursement. Under the **Star Rating program**, plans that perform well on quality scores can achieve bonus payments based on performance metrics designed by CMS. Bonus payments may (but are not required to) be used to help reduce cost sharing or cover supplemental benefits. The Henry J. Kaiser Family Foundation, Medicare Advantage in 2021: Star Ratings and Bonuses Payments (2021).

Beneficiary Protections in Medicare Managed Care. Medicare beneficiaries receiving care from managed care organizations may be subject to abuses which may be even more harmful because of the greater needs and lesser capacities of some beneficiaries. See Joyce Dubow,

Improving the Medicare Market: Adding Choice and Protections, National Academy of Sciences (1996). MA organizations are, therefore, subject to a host of regulatory requirements. MA organizations are responsible for providing their members with detailed **descriptions** of plan provisions, including disclosure of any coverage limitations or regulations. 42 U.S.C.A. § 1395w–22(c). MA coordinated care plans must provide **access** to providers 24 hours a day, 7 days a week; ensure services are "culturally competent" and that hours of operation of providers are convenient and non-discriminatory; provide adequate and coordinated **specialist treatment** for persons with complex or serious medical conditions; and allow women enrollees direct access to women's health specialists. 42 U.S.C.A. § 1395w–22(d), 42 C.F.R. § 422.112. MA plans must have an **ongoing quality assurance and performance improvement** program. 42 U.S.C.A. § 1395w–22(e). They must have mechanisms in place to detect both under- and over-utilization. Most types of plans must make provision for independent **quality review**. Organizations accredited by approved national accreditation agencies can be deemed to meet quality requirements. 42 U.S.C.A. § 1395w–22(e)(4).

MA organizations may not **discriminate against professionals** on the basis of their licensure or certification, and they must provide notice and a hearing to physicians whose participation rights are terminated. 42 C.F.R. §§ 422.202, .205. MA organizations may not interfere with provider advice to enrollees regarding care and treatment. 42 U.S.C.A. § 1395w–22(j)(3). Plans that fail substantially to provide **medically necessary services** where the failure adversely affects (or is substantially likely to adversely affect) health, impose unpermitted premiums, wrongly expel or refuse to reenroll a beneficiary, provide false information, interfere with practitioner's advice to enrollees, or commit other specified wrongful acts may be subject to civil money penalties up to $25,000. Plans that deny or discourage enrollment of persons on the basis of a medical condition or provide false information to CMS are subject to fines of up to $100,000. 42 U.S.C.A. 1395w–27(g)(2). CMS may also impose civil penalties of $25,000 for deficiencies that directly affect or have a substantial likelihood of adversely affecting enrollees, plus $10,000 a week penalty if the deficiency remains uncorrected. 42 U.S.C.A. § 1395w–27(g)(2).

Can Medicare Advantage and Traditional Medicare Compete on a Level Playing Field? Should They? A recurring issue is whether the managed care sector should in some sense **compete** against the traditional fee-for-service sector. The meaning of "competition" here is somewhat obscure. Various proposals, including **premium support plans**, have insisted that fee-for-service payments should be adjusted downward if total reimbursements to Medicare managed care plans are lower than under traditional Medicare. There is obviously no way in which the diffused providers delivering services under traditional Medicare can collectively "compete"; so the notion is that loss of patients to MA plans will encourage providers to accept lower administered prices without abandoning Medicare patients.

However, several regulatory issues complicate this picture. First, as noted above, traditional Medicare is required to make some payments that are not directly linked to the cost of caring for Medicare beneficiaries, such as payments for direct and indirect medical education costs and disproportionate share hospital payments, or special payments to rural providers. MA rates are reduced to exclude direct medical education costs, but otherwise are not modified to reflect payments made by traditional Medicare for non-Medicare purposes, even though MA plans do not have to cover these costs when they make payments to providers. Second, although payments to MA plans are supposed to be **risk-adjusted** to account for the fact that Medicare managed care beneficiaries are usually younger, healthier, and less expensive than beneficiaries who stay with traditional Medicare, risk adjustment is less than an exact science. See J. Michael McWilliams et al., New Risk-Adjustment System Was Associated with Reduced Favorable Selection in Medicare Advantage, Health Aff. (Dec. 2012). However, MA plans may be **coding** patients more intensively than is done under FFS because they have a strong incentive to do so. This may distort the relative payments to the two systems. See Richard Kronik, Projected Coding Intensity in Medicare Advantage Could Increase Costs by $200 Billion Over Ten Years, 36 Health Aff. (Feb. 2017). See also, Robert A. Berenson & Melissa A. Goldstein, Will Medicare Wither on the Vine? How Congress Has Advantaged Medicare Advantage—And What's a Level Playing Field Anyway?, 1 St. Louis U. J. Health L. & Pol'y 5 (2007).

As you read the following section, note how the ACA and MACRA provide strong incentives to integrate delivery under traditional Medicare, and consider whether the principles of managed care and administered pricing are converging.

4. Integrating Delivery and Payment: Bundled Payment, ACOs and MACRA

In a thought-provoking essay, Dr. Atul Gawande compared the ACA's proposed health care reforms to the revolution that occurred in American agriculture at the beginning of the last century. Atul Gawande, Testing, Testing, New Yorker (Dec. 14, 2009). Farming at that time was highly inefficient, fragmented, and disorganized, which resulted in high prices, low output, and poor quality. The U.S. Department of Agriculture instituted a series—what Gawande calls a "hodgepodge"—of experiments and demonstrations designed to develop and spread scientific methods of farming, and significantly also to foster widespread acceptance among the nation's highly independent farmers. Gawande draws an analogy to the reforms ultimately enacted in the ACA, noting that it seeks to promote experimentation and encourage greater attention to scientific evidence and the emergence of organizations capable of effecting change. The task, as Gawande sees it, is best accomplished by testing new approaches:

> Almost half of [the Senate bill] is devoted to programs that would test various ways to curb costs and increase quality. The bill is a hodgepodge. And it should be . . . . To figure out how to transform medical communities, with all their diversity and complexity, is going to involve trial and error. And this will require pilot programs—a lot of them.

Gawande, *supra*; See also Francis Crosson et al., How Can Medicare Lead Health Delivery Reform?, Commonwealth Fund Issues Brief (Nov. 2009).

Much of the change has focused on dealing with **fragmented delivery** and **financing that rewards volume**, not value. ACA reforms use financial incentives to nudge providers toward greater clinical integration for the purposes of controlling costs and improving care. To that end, the ACA gave the Secretary of HHS broad authority to establish within CMS a new Center for Medicare & Medicaid Innovation (CMMI) to research, develop, test, and expand innovative payment and delivery arrangements that improve quality of care and reduce costs. Given a wide-ranging mandate and considerable powers in this center, the CMMI undertook a variety of **pilots, demonstrations, and tests**. In addition, the ACA began several payment programs that attempted to directly move traditional Medicare to an **integrated delivery model**.

a. *Bundled Payment*

As discussed above, with a few exceptions Medicare's fee-for-service payment system reimburses providers one at a time for individual items or services provided to patients even when those services are provided for a single acute episode. With many Medicare beneficiaries having complex health conditions and multiple co-morbidities, most observers agree this system has significant cost and quality implications: it provides no incentives for **coordination of care** and it tolerates duplicative and costly provision of services. The ACA empowered the Secretary of HHS to establish, test, and evaluate a five-year pilot program "for integrated care during an **episode of care** . . . around a hospitalization in order to improve the coordination, quality, and efficiency of health care services." Under the **bundled payment** concept, a single payment is made for an "episode of care"—i.e., a defined set of services delivered by designated providers in specified health care settings, usually delivered within a certain period of time, related to treating a patient's medical condition or performing a major surgical procedure.

CMS's first bundled program, the **Comprehensive Care for Joint Replacement (CJR)** model, involved one of Medicare's most common (and costly) care episodes: hip and knee replacements. The program was mandatory for some 800 hospitals in 67 metropolitan areas. The CJR model employed a modified bundled payment arrangement. All providers (e.g., hospitals, physicians, post-acute care providers) continued to receive standard fee-for-service payments from Medicare for all claims from admission through 90 days after discharge. However, at the end of each performance year, CMS compared participating hospitals' 90-day episode payments against a "target episode price" based on historical spending for this procedure. Hospitals received additional payments if their actual 90-day episode spending (and that of their affiliated physicians and post-acute care providers) was less than the target, but they were required to pay CMS back if their episode spending exceeded this metric. What challenges does such an arrangement pose for hospitals that are not vertically integrated, i.e., that do not employ surgeons or physical therapy providers and lack post-acute facilities? Why should the program be mandatory? How should the target price be determined?

In the waning days of the Obama administration, CMS announced plans to expand mandatory bundled payment models to other episodes of care including heart attack and hip fracture. One year later, the Trump administration announced it was cancelling or reducing the number of mandatory bundled payment models; but it quickly changed course to adopt a similar but slightly revamped bundled payment model, reflecting bipartisan support for the goal of changing how the federal government pays for care.

b. Accountable Care Organizations in the Medicare Shared Savings Program

Undoubtedly, the most widely discussed (and in the opinion of some, most promising) systemic reform contained in the ACA is the **"Medicare Shared Savings Program" (MSSP)**, which is designed to test and spur the development of **Accountable Care Organizations (ACOs)**. The ACO is the latest in a long line of efforts to develop integrated delivery systems that bear financial responsibility for treatment decisions. ACOs are entities controlled by providers who work together to coordinate care, control costs, and improve quality. ACOs participating in the MSSP must provide a group of at least 5,000 Medicare beneficiaries the full range of Part A and B services and meet a host of quality and organizational requirements. While most ACOs bill Medicare on a fee-for-service basis, they share in any cost savings they achieve, and may also be responsible for excess costs they incur.

The goals of the program extend much further than provision of Part A and B services. As summarized in the preamble to Section 3022 of the ACA, the program seeks to promote accountability; encourage investment in infrastructure; coordinate provision of services under Parts A and B of

Medicare; and redesign care processes for high quality and efficient service delivery. See Donald M. Berwick, Launching Accountable Care Organizations—The Proposed Rule for the Medicare Shared Savings Program, 364 New Eng. J. Med. 1 (Apr. 21, 2011) (purpose of ACOs is to achieve a "**triple aim**": "better care for individuals, better health for populations, and slower growth in costs through improvements in care"). At bottom, the aspiration is to transform the delivery system by incentivizing diverse and fragmented providers to abandon their silos and instead offer services jointly.

Organizational Requirements. The MSSP makes groups of providers who voluntarily meet certain quality criteria eligible to share in the cost savings they achieve for the Medicare program. To qualify, an ACO must:

- be a legal entity that is recognized and authorized under applicable state law (such as a nonprofit corporation or LLC);

- agree to be accountable for the overall care of a defined group of Medicare beneficiaries;

- have sufficient participation of primary care physicians;

- have processes that promote evidence-based medicine, report on quality and costs, and be capable of coordinating care;

- have a governance structure that vests proportionate control over the ACO's decision-making process in "ACO participants" (defined as Medicare-enrolled providers of services and/or a supplier that alone or together with other participants "comprise" the ACO).

Payment Benchmarks. ACOs qualify for an annual **incentive bonus** if they achieve a threshold level of savings for total per beneficiary spending under Medicare parts A and B for those beneficiaries assigned to the ACO. To determine an ACO's qualification to receive shared savings (or its accountability for losses), each ACO's performance is measured against a "**benchmark**." The benchmark is based in part on the ACO providers' historical costs in providing Medicare FFS Parts A and B expenditures for ACO members; but under recent changes, this benchmark also includes factors that account for the ACO's performance relative to other providers in its region. See CMS, Final Medicare Shared Savings Program Rule (CMS–1644–F), 81 Fed. Reg. 112 (June 6, 2016). Finally, CMS employs over thirty **measures of attainment and improvement in quality** that are considered when calculating the sharing rate for most ACOs. For example, an ACO earning a 90% rating on the quality domains would receive 90% of the ACO's share of the potential shared savings possible under the risk model it participates in; thus if the risk model provides for 50% shared savings, it would receive 45% of savings generated.

Payment Tracks. Over time, the MSSP has offered different ACO tracks, based on varying risk arrangements and other parameters.

Originally, the MSSP offered four tracks (labeled 1, 1+, 2, 3), but these options are ending. (ACOs that began a contract under one of these prior tracks before July 2019 may complete the remainder of the contract for up to three years). As of July 2019, MSSP offers only two tracks: Basic and Enhanced.

The Basic track contains five levels (A–E), reflecting increasing levels of risk. For example, Levels A & B of the Basic Track use a one-sided risk model, in which the ACO shares in some savings up to a designated benchmark but shares no losses. (This corresponds to Track 1 under the prior system). Basic Track levels C–E and the Enhanced Track are two-sided risk models, in which ACOs share in savings and losses. ACOs in the Basic Track are generally expected to move up one level each year until they reach the highest level of risk (Level E). As of January 2020, 325 MSSP ACOs were in a one-sided risk arrangement (Basic Levels A & B, and Track 1) and 192 were in a two-sided risk arrangement (Basic Levels C, D, & E, Enhanced, & Tracks 1+, 2). Risk parameters for the Basic and Enhanced Tracks are noted below:

MSSP ACO Parameters by Track and Level

	MAXIMUM SHARED SAVINGS		MAXIMUM SHARED LOSS	
BASIC TRACK	Rate	Limit	Rate	Limit
A & B level	40%	10% of benchmark	No shared loss	
C level	50%	10% of benchmark	30%	2% of revenue, 1% of benchmark
D level	50%	10% of benchmark	30%	4% of revenue, 2% of benchmark
E level	50%	10% of benchmark	30%	8% of revenue, 4% of benchmark
ENHANCED TRACK	75%	20% of benchmark	40–75%	15% of benchmark

Source: MEDPAC, Accountable Care Organizations Payment Systems (Oct. 2020).

Beneficiary Assignment. Medicare beneficiaries will be "**attributed**" under the MSSP to the primary care doctor (and assigned to that doctor's ACO) from whom they receive a plurality of their primary care services. Beneficiaries who have not recently had primary care services provided by a primary care physician will be **assigned to an ACO** based on the specialist physician or certain non-physician providers including clinical nurse specialists and physician assistants from whom the beneficiary has received a plurality of primary care services. Each year, ACOs in all models of the Basic and Enhanced tracks are given the choice between prospective and retrospective beneficiary assignment. For ACOs using prospective assignment, CMS assigns beneficiaries at the beginning of the year, based on services provided the prior year. For ACOs using retrospective assignment, beneficiaries are only provisionally assigned initially, with a final assignment to be made at the end of the performance year based on services provided during the performance year. What are the implications of each approach for ACOs? Is one approach clearly preferable to the other or does it depend on specific ACO characteristics, such as size or specialty areas? CMS also allows beneficiaries to designate a "main doctor," which is then used to assign beneficiaries to an ACO, regardless of whether an ACO has chosen prospective or retrospective assignment. This practice, also called "voluntary alignment," is viewed by some as an important tool for enabling ACOs to better promote care and reduce costs. To date, however, few beneficiaries do this.

Most importantly, assignment to an ACO does not restrict the right of the beneficiaries assigned to an ACO to opt to receive health benefits from providers **outside the ACO** to which they are assigned. How does this differ from HMO or PPO arrangements? What strategies must an ACO employ to keep beneficiaries "in ACO"?

While beneficiaries will not receive advance notice of their ACO assignment, providers participating in ACOs will be required to post signs in their facilities indicating their participation in the program and to make available standardized written information to Medicare fee-for-service beneficiaries whom they serve. Additionally, all Medicare patients treated by participating providers must receive a standardized written notice of the provider's participation in the program and will have the option of opting out of participation.

Evaluation. Has the ACO experiment been a success? A government study of the results of the program's first three years demonstrated net spending reductions of over $1 billion, with 82% of MSSP ACOs showing improvement in quality measures over that period and overall performing better than fee-for-service providers. Office of the Inspector General (OIG) of HHS, Medicare Shared Savings Plan ACOs Have Shown Potential for Reducing Spending and Improving Quality (Aug. 2017). Studies have also revealed a divergence in performance based on type of ACO and length of participation. See id. (only 31% of MSSP ACOs earned shared savings bonuses in 2015 and the largest savings were achieved by relatively few "high performing" ACOs); J. Michael McWilliams et al., Medicare Spending after 3 Years of the Medicare Shared Savings Program, 379 N. Engl. J Med. 1139 (2018) (spending reductions were greater for physician-led ACOs than hospital-integrated ACOs, and reductions grew with longer participation in the program). Other studies have concluded that evidence for ACO performance is mixed in terms of savings and quality. Some participants are dropping out, savings is concentrated among a small number of ACOs, and quality seems to stay the same or improve only modestly for most ACOs. In some cases, evidence also points to concerning reductions in the use of appropriate care and the potential widening of health disparities. See Zirui Song, Taking Account of Accountable Care, 384 Health Services Res. (2021).

Participation in ACOs has also declined slightly, because of recent changes instituted by CMS that seems to have made the program less attractive relative to fee-for-service for some providers. As discussed further below, payment reform under MACRA is expected to be an important factor in shaping provider integration, including participation in ACOs. See Tim Gronniger et al., The (SGR) Fix Is In: How MACRA Short-Circuited Incentives for Joining Two-Sided Models, Health Aff. Blog, July 21, 2021. That said, the ACO phenomenon is not confined to Medicare. Large commercial insurers and several state Medicaid programs are also offering ACOs, and participation overall is growing rapidly. See David Muelstein et al., Spread of ACOs and Value-Based Payment Models in 2019, Health Aff. Blog, October 21, 2019.

Finally, consider what the proper measure of "success" should be. How is quality measured and how should quality improvements be weighed against cost savings? Michael Wilson et al., The impacts of accountable care organizations on patient experience, health outcomes and costs, 25 J. of Health Services, Res. & Pol'y 130 (2020) ("While evidence suggests ACOs reduce costs and may improve quality, more evidence is needed to determine whether ACOs result in better patient experience of care and population health."). Should spillover effects of ACOs on practices outside of the MSSP be counted? Consider also **regulatory spillovers**: ACO cost savings affect the benchmarks for Medicare Advantage plans, thereby improving cost effectiveness in that sector. See Michael E. Chernew and Christopher Barbey, A Framework for Evaluating "Savings" in Accountable Care Organizations, Health Aff. Blog (Oct. 17, 2017) (distinguishing program savings, societal savings, and utilization savings).

NOTES AND QUESTIONS

1. *ACOs Beyond MSSP.* CMMI has used lessons from early demonstrations to innovate and test different ACO models outside of MSSP. For example, responding in part to the initial reluctance of many of the nation's leading integrated systems to participate in the MSSP, CMS in 2012 inaugurated its Pioneer ACO model, which was designed primarily for organizations that were already highly integrated and experienced in coordinating care for patients across care settings. It began with 32 selected participants and by 2016 the number had dropped to 9, with most of the departing ACOs choosing to join the MSSP. Although most achieved some

savings, there were problems associated with the attribution of beneficiaries and savings that did not recognize that Pioneer ACOs were already cost efficient. In 2016, the Pioneer ACO demonstration was concluded, and CMS sought to address many of the problems associated with it by creating its Next Generation ACO model (NextGen). The NextGen model, which has 35 participants, offers higher levels of risk and reward than the MSSP and receive their budgets prospectively so they can plan and manage care according to these targets from the beginning of the performance year. They have also been given "benefit enhancement tools" to better manage patient care, such as additional coverage of telehealth and greater access to post-discharge home visits and skilled nursing facility services. See CMS, Next Generation ACO Model (2021 website update). The National Association of Accountable Care Organizations (NAACOS) advocated to make this model permanent, in part, because it viewed this as a nice bridge between the MSSP Enhanced Track and the full-capitation option offered through the Global and Professional Direct Contracting Model, described in the section on MACRA below. But CMS is allowing the NextGen demonstration to conclude as of December 31, 2021.

2.   *Provider Choice.* As described above, the several ACO models offer providers different levels of benefits and risks. What skills, resources, provider membership, and other factors are likely to be important in making this choice? How might other federal laws impact providers' willingness or ability to choose certain value-based arrangements? See Chapter 13 (tax-exempt organization law), Chapter 14 (fraud and abuse law), and Chapter 15 (antitrust law).

c.   *MACRA*

Enacted in 2015 with strong bi-partisan support, the **Medicare Access and CHIP Reauthorization Act of 2015 (MACRA)** has the potential to greatly accelerate provider integration and consolidation, perhaps ultimately reconfiguring the nation's delivery system. As noted above, MACRA permanently repeals the unpopular and unsuccessful Sustainable Growth Rate provisions governing reimbursement updating. It also sunsets the payment adjustments associated with the Physician Quality Reporting System, the Value-Based Payment Modifier, and the Medicare Electronic Health Record (EHR) incentive program. The new payment framework created under MACRA incorporates value-based criteria in the Medicare physician fee schedule updates and gives strong (some say irresistible) incentives for physicians to join ACOs and other forms of integrated delivery, or accept employment with hospitals. It does so by establishing a **Quality Payment Program** that includes two alternative paths for physicians to choose between: the Merit-Based Incentive Payment System **(MIPS)** and participation in certain Alternative Payment Models **(APMs)**. Beginning in 2017, most physicians were required to choose whether to be evaluated under MIPS or to participate in an APM, with payment adjustments beginning in 2019. Although physicians have been a crucial focus of the program, it applies to "eligible clinicians," defined broadly to include physicians, physician assistants, nurse practitioners, clinical nurse specialists, certified registered nurse anesthetists, clinical psychologists, physical therapists, occupational therapists, qualified speech-language pathologists, qualified audiologists, registered dietitians or nutrition professionals, and groups that include such clinicians.

Path 1: MIPS. Eligible clinicians participating in MIPS receive an upward, downward, or no payment adjustment based on their performance in four categories: **Quality; Cost** (or Resource Use); **Clinical Practice Improvement Activities; and Promoting Interoperability** (formerly referred to as Meaningful Use of Certified EHR Technology or Advancing Care Information). MIPS requires the Secretary of HHS to develop and provide clinicians with a Composite Performance Score that incorporates MIPS performance on each of these categories, but clinicians have some flexibility to choose which measures will be used from among a range of options. For example, in the Quality category, clinicians would choose six measures from a range of options that accommodate differences among specialties and practices (there were a total of 209 quality measures for the 2021 performance period). Under Clinical Performance Improvement, clinicians can be rewarded for activities in areas, such as care coordination, beneficiary engagement, patient safety, population management, and health equity. Even with this flexibility, MIPS imposes **extensive and costly reporting requirements** on providers to generate data used to measure performance.

Since 2019, physicians have faced a range of payment adjustments, starting with potential penalties of 4% and bonuses as high as 12% in 2019. These penalties and bonuses will grow to payment reductions of as much as 9% and increases of up to 27% after the first few years of the program. Notably, MACRA requires MIPS to be budget neutral. Therefore, clinicians' positive and negative MIPS scores will approximately cancel each other out. The first performance year for measurement was 2017, used to determine payment adjustments in 2019. In the first year of implementation, performance in the Quality category was weighted much higher than Cost, but their relative weights have been incrementally adjusted up to 2022, when they must be equally weighted at 30% according to statute. For performance year 2021, the weighting was: Quality 40%, Cost 20%, Promoting Interoperability 25%, and Improvement Activities 15%.

Path 2: Advanced Alternate Payment Models (APMs). To encourage physicians to move away from fee-for-service payments that do not reward value, MACRA offers **strong incentives to choose Path 2** which involves participating in qualified advanced alternative payment models. Clinicians participating to a sufficient extent in "**Advanced APMs**" would be exempt from MIPS reporting requirements and would qualify for a 5% Medicare

Part B incentive payment. To be an Advanced APM, the model generally must require participants to bear a certain amount of **financial risk**; base payments on quality measures comparable to those used in the MIPS quality performance category; and require participants to use certified EHR technology. A perhaps unintended consequence may be to add further incentives for physicians to become employed by health systems.

Criticisms and Exemptions. Physicians and health care systems pushed back against the implementation of MIPS, arguing that they could not be ready for the transition in a timely manner. Furthermore, they argued that the system was flawed: self-reporting leads to manipulation of data; the system rewards better reporting, not better medical care; the quality score allows for too much variation; and the gap between reporting and rewards (2 years) is much too long to actually implement change that will improve medical care. See Niam Yaraghi, MACRA Proposed Rule Creates More Problems than It Solves, Health Aff. Blog (Oct. 12, 2016).

In response to these criticisms, CMS undertook a number of changes and clarifications through rulemaking. First, CMS introduced options allowing physicians to delay some requirements by picking their pace of participation for the first performance period. Second, it clarified a third possibility, which is technically part of the MIPS track, the so-called **MIPS-APM tract**. This option affords flexibility to providers that participate in one-sided risk ACOs and does not punish them for low scores on MACRA performance categories. See Maria Castellucci, The Forgotten Track: Medicare ACOs Qualify for Third MACRA Option, Modern Healthcare (May 26, 2017). The rationale for this option is to allow physicians to shift to value-based systems while giving them time to prepare for the significant jump in risk associated with other forms of ACOs. These physicians can earn annual bonuses of 5% and may exempt themselves from the MIPS reporting requirements. Third, CMS also granted a MIPS exclusion for the very large number of providers who treat a "low volume" of Medicare patients ($90,000 or less in Medicare Part B allowed charges, or 200 or fewer Medicare Part B beneficiaries). CMS, Medicare Program; CY 2018 Updates to the Quality Payment Program; and Quality Payment Program: Extreme and Uncontrollable Circumstance Policy for the Transition Year, 82 Fed. Reg. 53568 (Nov. 16, 2017).

NOTES AND QUESTIONS

1. *Financial Incentives.* Note the financial incentives facing clinicians under MACRA. If a physician chooses the MIPS path, she will receive very modest annual inflationary updates (.5%) and risk significant penalties (beginning at 4% and growing to 9% by 2022), while having the opportunity to earn substantial bonuses if quality scores are high. Practices which receive over 25% of their Medicare fee schedule revenue from advanced APMs earn a 5% incentive payment, and higher updates in later years. While this payment

structure gives physicians a strong nudge to join advanced APMs, it applies the 5% incentive payment to all of the physician's Medicare fee schedule revenue, not just the revenue attributable to the APMs.

2.   *Budget Neutrality.* As explained, under MIPS total negative payment adjustments must equal total positive adjustments. Exempting two-thirds of MIPS-eligible effectively destroys the distribution curve, financially undermining the participating pool. Essentially, those who do well under the MIPS program lose. Consider MIPS-scored APMs:

> [F]or example, Track 1 ACOs have made infrastructure investments with the reasonable expectation that they would be competitive under MIPS. This problem becomes substantially worse the longer CMS excludes a significant percentage of eligible clinicians from MIPS participation because the annual payment rate adjustments . . . accumulate year over year. In addition, with such small payment adjustments, one is left to wonder whether eligible clinicians will fully engage in the program or will MIPS become largely a check-the-box compliance exercise for those required to participate. This "pick your pace" approach, as former CMS acting administrator Andy Slavitt termed it, also leaves one to question why CMS is not working harder to design and implement more incentive neutral policies to improve quality and spending efficiency.

David Introcaso, The Many Problems with Medicare's MIPS Exclusion Thresholds, Health Aff. Blog (Aug. 3, 2017).

3.   *The Future of the Quality Payment Program.* In January 2018, MedPAC voted to recommend to Congress that it repeal MIPS. It noted a number of flaws in the self-reporting mechanism used to assess quality and the significant costs for providers to track and report MIPS measures (as much as $1 billion in 2017). Concern was also expressed that large groups might not include doctors who treat high needs patients, such as dual eligibles, thus denying them the opportunity to earn bonuses. For MedPAC's preliminary analysis of the flaws in the program and possible alternative approaches, see MedPAC, Report to Congress: Medicare and the Health Care Delivery System (June 2017). In response to ongoing complaints from providers and other stakeholders about the reporting system under traditional MIPS, CMS is creating new reporting frameworks for the MIPS and APM pathways. See CMS, Calendar Year (CY) 2022 Physician Fee Schedule Notice of Proposed Rule Making: Quality Payment Program (QPP) Proposals Overview, Fact Sheet (2021). The MIPS Value Pathways (MVPs) should be available beginning the 2023 performance year, will likely be voluntary for the first few years, and is expected to eventually replace the traditional MIPS program. The goal is to improve the quality of data collected and provide more meaningful feedback to clinicians, based on more granular data for certain activities or measures. CMS has proposed MVPs for seven areas: rheumatology, stroke care and prevention, heart disease, chronic disease management, emergency medicine, lower extremity joint repair, and anesthesia. Adjustments are based on the same four categories noted above, with the addition of a population health measure

selected by the participant. CMS is also creating the APM Performance Pathway (APP) to complement the MVP. APP is available to participants in MIPS APMs, and its goal is to improve alignment of reporting across different payment models. Like MVP, APP is based on a fixed set of measures for each performance category, but the Cost category is weighted at 0 because participants are already responsible for cost containment.

D. WHITHER/WITHER MEDICARE?

Medicare Part A, like traditional social insurance programs, is funded through payroll taxes, paid by both employers and employees. These payroll taxes are paid into a **"trust fund"** which is supposed to accumulate funds for future fund imbalances as the population ages; but since the trust fund is invested in federal savings bonds, the trust fund is effectively a mechanism for funding general federal government deficit spending. The 2021 Medicare Trustees Report projects that the Trust Fund will be exhausted by 2026. In future years, Medicare expenditures, as a percentage of the federal budget and of the gross domestic product, are also certain to climb, as the cost of medical care continues to grow and the population continues to age. Moreover, funding Medicare Part A through a **payroll tax** will become less feasible, as the ratio of the population over 65 to that in the workforce continues to worsen, and as wages become a smaller part of the national income relative to other forms of income, such as rent, dividends, interest, or capital gains. However, it should be borne in mind that Medicare costs have declined sharply on a per capita basis: growth was only 1.7% between 2010 and 2018, compared to 7.4% between 2000 and 2010. The causes for this remarkable **slowdown** include reductions in payments to plans and providers and delivery system and payment reforms under the ACA. See The Henry J. Kaiser Family Foundation, The Facts on Medicare Spending and Financing (August 2019). But from 2018 to 2028, per capita spending is projected to grow at an average annual rate of 5.1%, based on rising prices, increased enrollment, and higher utilization and level of care.

The future of the Medicare program has long been the subject of contentious debate in presidential elections. While both parties routinely pledge not to cut Medicare and charge the other with intending to do so, the combination of rapid growth in the number of beneficiaries and projected shortfalls discussed above make the prospects for some reform a near certainty. With the nation facing an additional $1.5 trillion in deficits resulting from enactment of the Tax Cut and Jobs Act of 2017, attention to budget cutting is most likely to focus on entitlement spending, with Medicare and Medicaid as the top targets. At the other end of the political spectrum, there is strong sentiment among progressives, notably Senator Bernie Sanders, to go in an entirely different direction and adopt a single payer system, "Medicare for All," under which a national health insurance program would replace private insurance. Other Democrats, including President Biden, favor more moderate reforms under which everyone would be able to purchase a Medicare-type plan as a public option, or (narrower still) lowering the age of Medicare eligibility to 60. These proposals may not increase overall coverage significantly, but they could reduce the costs of care by shifting workers from more expensive employer-based coverage to Medicare.

The concept of privatizing Medicare has its roots in proposals as far back as 1995 when Congress passed legislation that would cut Medicare expenditures by 14% with the goal of prodding seniors to join HMOs. (That proposal was vetoed by President Clinton, rather dramatically using the same pen Lyndon Johnson had used to sign the original Medicare law). Subsequently, reforms under the Medicare Modernization Act heavily subsidizing Medicare Advantage plans were intended to make traditional Medicare "wither on the vine," as House Speaker Newt Gingrich put it. In 2016, congressional Republicans proposed a plan to replace the current Medicare program with a "**premium support**" plan, which would provide beneficiaries with a premium subsidy or voucher to purchase either a private health insurance plan, similar to Medicare Advantage, or traditional Medicare. The idea was originated by then-Speaker of the House Paul Ryan in his 2010 "Roadmap For America's Future."

Premium support proposals raise several thorny policy and regulatory issues. First, would the benchmark, which affects what beneficiaries ultimately pay, keep up with medical cost inflation, which is generally significantly higher than overall rates of inflation? If premium supports do not rise as quickly as medical costs, then beneficiaries could find themselves with inadequate coverage or unaffordable out-of-pocket costs, or both. Another controversial ingredient of the plan is its treatment of the scope of benefits provided by plans. Should plans have flexibility to offer a different package than traditional Medicare? Currently, all Medicare beneficiaries are entitled to the same benefits whether they are covered under Medicare Advantage or traditional Medicare, but some premium support proposals would have eliminated this requirement. Close regulatory scrutiny might be needed to assure that this flexibility does not become a means by which more cost and risk are shifted to beneficiaries and that plans do not morph into "skinny" coverage alternatives. Next, what would "competition" between traditional Medicare and plans under premium support entail? The long-term sustainability of traditional Medicare would depend on whether it continues to attract sicker beneficiaries than the private competitors. Finally, in what ways could premium support disproportionately burden low-income Medicare beneficiaries or others for whom "choice" is not a meaningful alternative, either due to their geographic location or their extensive health care needs? For an overview of these issues, see Gretchen Jacobsen & Patricia Neuman,

The Henry J. Kaiser Family Foundation Issues Brief: Turning Medicare into a Premium Support Program: Frequently Asked Questions (July 2016).

Despite Medicare's broad popularity and economic significance, its future is far from certain. What is clear is that policymakers will continue to grapple with ideas to reform, transform, expand, or erode the Medicare program.

III.   MEDICAID

In contrast to Medicare, which is a federal social insurance program, Medicaid is a welfare program for the poor. It is jointly funded by the federal government and states but is primarily administered by states. Medicaid was created almost as an afterthought during the Medicare debate in the 1960s and has always been controversial, always vulnerable. All aspects of the program—even whether it should continue to exist at all as an entitlement program—have been hotly contested since its creation. Despite this, Medicaid is the nation's largest health insurance program, covering more Americans than Medicare and playing a vital role in the health care safety net.

This section of the chapter will introduce you to Medicaid law and policy, through the core elements that define any health care program: eligibility, benefits, financing, and program administration. This introduction presents four overarching themes to help you navigate the complex web of Medicaid regulation explored in the rest of this section.

Traditional vs. New Medicaid. Enacted in 1965 through Title XIX of the Social Security Act, 42 U.S.C. § 1396 et seq. (the "Medicaid Act"), the Medicaid program was established "to furnish . . . medical assistance on behalf of families with dependent children and of aged, blind, or disabled individuals, whose income and resources are insufficient to meet the costs of necessary medical services, and . . . rehabilitation and other services to help such families and individuals attain or retain capability for independence or self-care." Medicaid's origin as a welfare program has meant that traditionally eligibility has been tied to both economic need and to being in a category of people deemed to be worthy of aid. This means that most poor persons were not eligible for Medicaid prior to the ACA; rather Medicaid covered only those considered to be the "deserving" poor, such as individuals who were unable to work due to disability and thus effectively excluded from the private insurance market. At times, utilitarian considerations also motivated Medicaid policy decisions, such as providing prenatal care or care for infants to avoid more expensive conditions later.

The Affordable Care Act transformed and simplified the original Medicaid program in a crucial respect: it expanded coverage to all individuals under a certain income level; that is to all poor citizens, rather than only a "deserving" few. But, of course, nothing about health care is simple. In fact, traditional Medicaid eligibility categories persist under current law for a couple of reasons. One is that the ACA built upon the platform of the prior law, retaining traditional categories for certain purposes, such as determining required benefits or the federal funding match. More significantly, though, not all states have expanded Medicaid under the ACA, because the Supreme Court effectively made the expansion optional.

Almost immediately after the ACA's enactment, several states brought a constitutional challenge to the Medicaid expansion, which reached the Supreme Court in National Federation of Independent Business et al. v. Sebelius, 567 U.S. 519 (2012). (See the case excerpt below.) States argued that by conditioning all Medicaid funding on states' expansion of eligibility to all people below a certain income threshold, the federal government was effectively compelling states to enact this new regulatory scheme, exceeding its power under the Spending Clause of the constitution. The Court affirmed the power of the federal government to use federal funding to "encourage" states to enact certain policies, but it found the ACA "crossed the line distinguishing encouragement from coercion." The problem, according to the Court, was that the federal government was tying funding for the "traditional" Medicaid program to a requirement that states create an entirely "new" Medicaid program—one that "is no longer a program to care for the neediest among us, but rather an element of a comprehensive national plan to provide universal health insurance coverage." The practical effect of this decision was to make the Medicaid expansion optional for states: As of August 2021, 39 states (including the District of Columbia) have expanded Medicaid; 12 states have not.

State Flexibility in Program Design. The Medicaid program is subject to basic constraints of the Medicaid Act and regulations. Nonetheless, it is a state administered program and federal law gives states great flexibility to define most elements of program design. For example, while federal law mandates certain categories of eligibility and benefits coverage, states have significant discretion in setting income eligibility limits and determining the type and scope of benefits offered. States perhaps have the most discretion over setting provider rates, and they control other program design decisions that impact health care access and quality.

In addition to the flexibility built into the Medicaid Act, the law provides opportunities for states to seek waivers from certain federal requirements for Medicaid "demonstration projects." States have long used waivers to expand coverage of certain services and to experiment with financing and delivery system reforms, creating significant variability among state Medicaid programs. Once the Supreme Court ruled the Medicaid expansion optional, states felt empowered to seek even greater flexibility in program design as a condition of expansion—submitting waiver requests testing the limits of what federal law allows.

This flexibility effectively means that there is not one Medicaid program. Rather each state's Medicaid program is different, and each state has its own state laws and regulations (in addition to the federal minimum standards) that govern state program design. Indeed, this flexibility was an important character of the program as conceived, because it allowed states to tailor Medicaid to reflect state-specific values and priorities.

Bending the Medicaid Cost Curve. Perhaps the area where we are seeing the greatest focus and tension brewing over Medicaid is its cost. Medicaid is an open-ended entitlement program, with the federal government providing a generous financial match to state spending. This means that neither states nor federal costs are fixed; as the number of enrollees and the costs of their medical needs increase, so do federal and state funding obligations.

States have always felt significant pressure to reduce Medicaid costs, from the federal government and because of their own state budgetary obligations. Even with a generous federal match, state Medicaid budgets are significant and can crowd out other state priorities. In addition, almost all states are required to balance their budgets, and Medicaid spending is a prime target for reductions. States use their flexibility to respond to cost concerns in a variety of ways: in particularly lean times, states may cut optional services or provider payments; and some states use waivers to add program restrictions. More sustainable reforms are needed, however, and the ACA promotes delivery system reform to increase accountability and yield better value in terms of individual and population health. This has catalyzed state innovation to find new delivery or financing structures that can reduce cost through improved care.

The Uncertain Future of Medicaid. Medicaid is a central focus of the enduring debate about federal health policy, with cost containment and state flexibility as recurring themes. Proponents of a robust Medicaid entitlement program view it as serving important societal goals—whether because they see it as a smart economic or political investment, as promoting health justice and anti-poverty goals, or some combination of these. Others fear that Medicaid spending is unsustainable and that it has expanded too far beyond the original vision of only providing government assistance to the most vulnerable. They seek to give states even greater flexibility by rolling back Medicaid's entitlements, and they want to curb federal spending through caps on Medicaid funding.

Although the debate about whether Medicaid should be an open-ended entitlement program will certainly continue, the policy goals and values animating these different visions of Medicaid also inform more modest program decisions: state policy decisions defining eligibility and benefit rules; federal-state cooperation to experiment with health care delivery and financing reform; and decisions by the federal government about how much additional flexibility to give states through waivers. The Medicaid program has created a fascinating laboratory of health care experimentation. While it is impossible to predict exactly what Medicaid will look like tomorrow, we know that any reform must address the fundamental elements of program design explored in this chapter.

NATIONAL FEDERATION OF INDEPENDENT BUSINESS V. SEBELIUS

Supreme Court of the United States, 2012.
567 U.S. 519.

CHIEF JUSTICE ROBERTS, JUSTICES BREYER and KAGAN.

[The first part of the decision, upholding the individual mandate as a tax, is reproduced in Chapter 9, Section III.]

The States also contend that the Medicaid expansion exceeds Congress's authority under the Spending Clause. They claim that Congress is coercing the States to adopt the changes it wants by threatening to withhold all of a State's Medicaid grants, unless the State accepts the new expanded funding and complies with the conditions that come with it. This, they argue, violates the basic principle that the "Federal Government may not compel the States to enact or administer a federal regulatory program." [ ]

There is no doubt that the Act dramatically increases state obligations under Medicaid. The current Medicaid program requires States to cover only certain discrete categories of needy individuals—pregnant women, children, needy families, the blind, the elderly, and the disabled. [ ] There is no mandatory coverage for most childless adults, and the States typically do not offer any such coverage. The States also enjoy considerable flexibility with respect to the coverage levels for parents of needy families. [ ] On average States cover only those unemployed parents who make less than 37 percent of the federal poverty level, and only those employed parents who make less than 63 percent of the poverty line. [ ]

The Medicaid provisions of the Affordable Care Act, in contrast, require States to expand their Medicaid programs by 2014 to cover *all* individuals under the age of 65 with incomes below 133 percent of the federal poverty line. [ ] The Act also establishes a new "[e]ssential health benefits" package, which States must provide to all new Medicaid recipients—a level sufficient to satisfy a recipient's obligations under the individual mandate. [ ] The Affordable Care Act provides that the Federal Government will pay 100 percent of the costs of covering these newly eligible individuals through 2016. [ ] In the following years, the federal payment level gradually decreases, to a minimum of 90 percent. . . .

The Spending Clause grants Congress the power "to pay the Debts and provide for the . . . general Welfare of the United States." [ ]. We have long recognized that Congress may use this power to grant federal funds to the States, and may condition such a grant upon the States' "taking certain actions that Congress could not require them to take." [ ] Such measures "encourage a State to regulate in a particular way, [and] influenc[e] a State's policy choices." [ ] The conditions imposed by Congress ensure that the funds are used by the States to "provide for the . . . general Welfare" in the manner Congress intended.

At the same time, our cases have recognized limits on Congress's power under the Spending Clause to secure state compliance with federal objectives. "We have repeatedly characterized . . . Spending Clause legislation as 'much in the nature of a *contract*.'" [ ] The legitimacy of Congress's exercise of the spending power "thus rests on whether the State voluntarily and knowingly accepts the terms of the 'contract.'" [ ] Respecting this limitation is critical to ensuring that Spending Clause legislation does not undermine the status of the States as independent sovereigns in our federal system. . . . For this reason, "the Constitution has never been understood to confer upon Congress the ability to require the States to govern according to Congress' instructions." [ ] Otherwise the two-government system established by the Framers would give way to a system that vests power in one central government, and individual liberty would suffer.

That insight has led this Court to strike down federal legislation that commandeers a State's legislative or administrative apparatus for federal purposes. [ ] It has also led us to scrutinize Spending Clause legislation to ensure that Congress is not using financial inducements to exert a "power akin to undue influence." [ ] Congress may use its spending power to create incentives for States to act in accordance with federal policies. But when "pressure turns into compulsion," [ ] the legislation runs contrary to our system of federalism. . . . That is true whether Congress directly commands a State to regulate or indirectly coerces a State to adopt a federal regulatory system as its own.

Permitting the Federal Government to force the States to implement a federal program would threaten the political accountability key to our federal system. "[W]here the Federal Government directs the States to regulate, it may be state officials who will bear the brunt of public disapproval, while the federal officials who devised the regulatory program may remain insulated from the electoral ramifications of their decision." [ ] Spending Clause programs do not pose this danger when a State has a legitimate choice whether to accept the federal conditions in exchange for federal funds. In such a situation, state officials can fairly be held politically accountable for choosing to accept or refuse the federal offer. But when the State has no choice, the Federal Government can achieve its objectives without accountability .... Indeed, this danger is heightened when Congress acts under the Spending Clause, because Congress can use that power to implement federal policy it could not impose directly under its enumerated powers.

* * *

... Congress may attach appropriate conditions to federal taxing and spending programs to preserve its control over the use of federal funds. In the typical case we look to the States to defend their prerogatives by adopting "the simple expedient of not yielding" to federal blandishments when they do not want to embrace the federal policies as their own. [ ] The States are separate and independent sovereigns. Sometimes they have to act like it.

The States, however, argue that the Medicaid expansion is far from the typical case. They object that Congress has "crossed the line distinguishing encouragement from coercion," [ ] in the way it has structured the funding: Instead of simply refusing to grant the new funds to States that will not accept the new conditions, Congress has also threatened to withhold those States' existing Medicaid funds. The States claim that this threat serves no purpose other than to force unwilling States to sign up for the dramatic expansion in health care coverage effected by the Act.

Given the nature of the threat and the programs at issue here, we must agree. We have upheld Congress's authority to condition the receipt of funds on the States' complying with restrictions on the use of those funds, because that is the means by which Congress ensures that the funds are spent according to its view of the "general Welfare." Conditions that do not here govern the use of the funds, however, cannot be justified on that basis. When, for example, such conditions take the form of threats to terminate other significant independent grants, the conditions are properly viewed as a means of pressuring the States to accept policy changes.

* * *

In this case, the financial "inducement" Congress has chosen is much more than "relatively mild encouragement"—it is a gun to the head. Section 1396c of the Medicaid Act provides that if a State's Medicaid plan does not comply with the Act's requirements, the Secretary of Health and Human Services may declare that "further payments will not be made to the State." [ ] A State that opts out of the Affordable Care Act's expansion in health care coverage thus stands to lose not merely "a relatively small percentage" of its existing Medicaid funding, but *all* of it. [ ] Medicaid spending accounts for over 20 percent of the average State's total budget, with federal funds covering 50 to 83 percent of those costs.... In addition, the States have developed intricate statutory and administrative regimes over the course of many decades to implement their objectives under existing Medicaid. . . . The threatened loss of over 10 percent of a State's overall budget, in contrast, is economic dragooning that leaves the States with no real option but to acquiesce in the Medicaid expansion.[12]

. . . The States contend that the expansion is in reality a new program and that Congress is forcing them to accept it by threatening the funds for the existing Medicaid program. We cannot agree that existing Medicaid and the expansion dictated by the Affordable Care Act are all one program simply because "Congress styled" them as such. [ ] If the expansion is not properly viewed as a modification of the existing Medicaid program, Congress's decision to so title it is irrelevant.

Here, the Government claims that the Medicaid expansion is properly viewed merely as a modification of the existing program because the States agreed that Congress could change the terms of Medicaid when they signed on in the first place. The Government observes that the Social Security Act, which includes the original Medicaid provisions, contains a clause expressly reserving "[t]he right to alter, amend, or repeal any provision" of that statute. 42 U.S.C. § 1304. So it does. But "if Congress intends to impose a condition on the grant of federal moneys, it must do so unambiguously." A State confronted with statutory language reserving the right to "alter" or "amend" the pertinent provisions of the Social Security Act might reasonably assume that Congress was entitled to make adjustments to the Medicaid program as it developed. Congress has in fact done so, sometimes conditioning only the new funding, other times both old and new. [ ]

The Medicaid expansion, however, accomplishes a shift in kind, not merely degree. The original program was designed to cover medical services for four particular categories of the needy: the disabled, the blind, the elderly, and needy families with dependent children. [ ] Previous amendments to Medicaid eligibility merely altered and expanded the boundaries of these categories. Under the Affordable Care Act, Medicaid is transformed into a program to meet the health care needs of the entire nonelderly population with income below 133 percent of the poverty level. It is no longer a program to care for the neediest among us, but rather an element of a comprehensive national plan to provide universal health insurance coverage.

---

[12] JUSTICE GINSBURG observes that state Medicaid spending will increase by only 0.8 percent after the expansion. [ ] That not only ignores increased state administrative expenses, but also assumes that the Federal Government will continue to fund the expansion at the current statutorily specified levels. It is not unheard of, however, for the Federal Government to increase requirements in such a manner as to impose unfunded mandates on the States. More importantly, the size of the new financial burden imposed on a State is irrelevant in analyzing whether the State has been coerced into accepting that burden. "Your money or your life" is a coercive proposition, whether you have a single dollar in your pocket or $500.

Indeed, the manner in which the expansion is structured indicates that while Congress may have styled the expansion a mere alteration of existing Medicaid, it recognized it was enlisting the States in a new health care program. Congress created a separate funding provision to cover the costs of providing services to any person made newly eligible by the expansion. . . . The conditions on use of the different funds are also distinct. Congress mandated that newly eligible persons receive a level of coverage that is less comprehensive than the traditional Medicaid benefit package. [ ]

As we have explained, "[t]hough Congress' power to legislate under the spending power is broad, it does not include surprising participating States with postacceptance or 'retroactive' conditions." [ ]

JUSTICE GINSBURG claims that in fact this expansion is no different from the previous changes to Medicaid, such that "a State would be hard put to complain that it lacked fair notice." [ ] But the prior change she discusses—presumably the most dramatic alteration she could find—does not come close to working the transformation the expansion accomplishes. She highlights an amendment requiring States to cover pregnant women and increasing the number of eligible children. [ ] But this modification can hardly be described as a major change in a program that—from its inception—provided health care for "families with dependent children." Previous Medicaid amendments simply do not fall into the same category as the one at stake here.

The Court in *Steward Machine* [an earlier Supreme Court case that had mentioned the coercion doctrine in dicta] did not attempt to "fix the outermost line" where persuasion gives way to coercion. [ ] The Court found it "[e]nough for present purposes that wherever the line may be, this statute is within it." [ ] We have no need to fix a line either. It is enough for today that wherever that line may be, this statute is surely beyond it. Congress may not simply "conscript state [agencies] into the national bureaucratic army," [ ] and that is what it is attempting to do with the Medicaid expansion.

* * *

Nothing in our opinion precludes Congress from offering funds under the Affordable Care Act to expand the availability of health care, and requiring that States accepting such funds comply with the conditions on their use. What Congress is not free to do is to penalize States that choose not to participate in that new program by taking away their existing Medicaid funding. . . . In light of the Court's holding, the Secretary cannot apply § 1396c to withdraw existing Medicaid funds for failure to comply with the requirements set out in the expansion.

That fully remedies the constitutional violation we have identified. The chapter of the United States Code that contains § 1396c includes a severability clause confirming that we need go no further. That clause specifies that "[i]f any provision of this chapter, or the application thereof to any person or circumstance, is held invalid, the remainder of the chapter, and the application of such provision to other persons or circumstances shall not be affected thereby." [ ] Today's holding does not affect the continued application of § 1396c to the existing Medicaid program. Nor does it affect the Secretary's ability to withdraw funds provided under the Affordable Care Act if a State that has chosen to participate in the expansion fails to comply with the requirements of that Act.

* * *

The question remains whether today's holding affects other provisions of the Affordable Care Act. . . . The question here is whether Congress would have wanted the rest of the Act to stand, had it known that States would have a genuine choice whether to participate in the new Medicaid expansion. Unless it is "evident" that the answer is no, we must leave the rest of the Act intact. [ ]

We are confident that Congress would have wanted to preserve the rest of the Act. It is fair to say that Congress assumed that every State would participate in the Medicaid expansion, given that States had no real choice but to do so. The States contend that Congress enacted the rest of the Act with such full participation in mind; they point out that Congress made Medicaid a means for satisfying the mandate, [ ] and enacted no other plan for providing coverage to many low-income individuals. According to the States, this means that the entire Act must fall.

We disagree. The Court today limits the financial pressure the Secretary may apply to induce States to accept the terms of the Medicaid expansion. As a practical matter, that means States may now choose to reject the expansion; that is the whole point. But that does not mean all or even any will. Some States may indeed decline to participate, either because they are unsure they will be able to afford their share of the new funding obligations, or because they are unwilling to commit the administrative resources necessary to support the expansion. Other States, however, may voluntarily sign up, finding the idea of expanding Medicaid coverage attractive, particularly given the level of federal funding the Act offers at the outset.

We have no way of knowing how many States will accept the terms of the expansion, but we do not believe Congress would have wanted the whole Act to fall, simply because some may choose not to participate. The other reforms Congress enacted, after all, will remain "fully operative as a law," [ ] and will still function in a way "consistent with Congress' basic objectives in enacting the statute," [ ]. Confident that Congress would not have intended anything different, we conclude that the rest of the Act need not fall in light of our constitutional holding.

* * *

NOTES AND QUESTIONS

As you read the material that follows, consider the following questions. Did Chief Justice Roberts understand the history and nature of the Medicaid program? Does he describe accurately the relationship between the federal and state governments that has traditionally characterized the program? How does the Court's opinion change that relationship? Does the opinion accurately characterize the changes brought about in Medicaid by the ACA? Does it affect any of the changes made in the program by the ACA other than the expansion? How does this decision limit the power of Congress to change the program in the future?

A. ELIGIBILITY

1. Traditional Medicaid Eligibility

Medicaid eligibility has traditionally been very complex and only covered certain narrow categories of the very poor. This section describes the categories of the "deserving" poor covered under traditional Medicaid—that is, prior to the Medicaid expansion in the ACA.

Mandatory "Categorically Needy." Historically the categories of **mandatory eligibles** that states had to cover included the **aged, blind, and permanently and totally disabled**, who were either eligible for assistance under the Federal Supplemental Security Income Program (SSI) or the earlier state Aid to the Aged, Blind and Disabled program (based on requirements in effect in 1972). States were also required to cover "**needy families**"—dependent children and their caretaker relatives eligible for assistance under the former federal/state Aid to Families with Dependent Children Program (AFDC). In the 1980s, **poor children and pregnant women** were added as mandatory coverage categories. Over time the link between cash assistance and Medicaid eligibility weakened, particularly after the abolition of AFDC in 1996. Nevertheless, eligibility has continued to require membership in some category of the "deserving" poor.

In the late 1980s and early 1990s, the Medicaid Act was amended to require Medicaid assistance for low-income Medicare beneficiaries (and certain other qualified groups) to pay some or all of their Medicare premiums, deductibles, and other cost-sharing requirements. Low-income seniors and people with disabilities are typically covered by both Medicaid and Medicare, and they are referred to as "**Dual Eligibles**." Most Dual Eligibles typically have incomes at or below 73% of the Federal Poverty Level (FPL), and Medicaid plays a vital role for individuals in this category, who are more likely to suffer from serious chronic and disabling conditions that are complex and expensive to treat. The **low-income subsidy program** also helps individuals who do not qualify for Medicaid eligibility, but who need help paying the high out of pocket costs they may incur under Medicare. Because these individuals are not eligible for Medicaid benefits, they are referred to as "**partial duals**" (as opposed to **full Dual Eligibles**).

Optional "Categorically Needy." The deserving poor also include a whole host of "**optional categorically needy**," a variety of groups that states can choose to cover, but who then must be provided the full scope of benefits offered the categorically needy. These groups are typically **children, parents, aged, and disabled** who have too much income to fit in the mandatory eligibility category. The eligibility limits have also been relaxed to encourage more **pregnant women** to be covered because prenatal care is considered to be highly cost effective in avoiding future health care costs. The optional categorically needy group also includes **persons who would be eligible for Medicaid if institutionalized**, but who are instead receiving services in the community.

Optional "Medically Needy." From the beginning, states have also been permitted to cover a third group, the "**medically needy**." The medically needy are **categorically-related** (aged, disabled, blind, or families with dependent children) persons whose income exceeds the financial eligibility levels established by the states, but **who incur regular medical expenses that, when deducted from their income, bring their net disposable income below the eligibility level for financial assistance**. The medically needy are generally persons in need of expensive nursing home or hospital care. The medically needy program is effectively a catastrophic health insurance program that covers many Americans who were comfortably middle-class until their need for long-term care consumed their life savings.

Income Eligibility. In addition to fitting into one of the above categories, individuals must satisfy income requirements to be eligible for Medicaid. Federal law establishes the income eligibility criteria for mandatory eligibles. For the optional categories described above, federal law sets upper income limits, but states have the flexibility to establish the eligibility threshold. For example, the chart below shows the current mandatory and optional income limits for Children and Pregnant Women based on percentage of Federal Poverty Level (FPL). In 2021, the FPL for a family of three was $21,960.

Category	Mandatory Eligible (minimum standards)	Optional for States (upper income limit)
Children	Income up to 133% FPL*	Income up to 200% FPL**
Pregnant Women	Income up to 133% FPL	Income up to 200% FPL***

Most states have used their flexibility to go beyond the minimum standards. As of January 2021, 48 states cover children with incomes up to at least 200% FPL, with more than a third of states covering children at or above 300% FPL. Thirty-five states cover pregnant women at or above 200% FPL. As noted in footnotes to the chart above, states have even greater flexibility to increase income limits beyond those shown, through another federal program called the Children's Health Insurance Program (CHIP), discussed in Note 4 below.

PROBLEM: YOUR STATE'S MEDICAID INCOME ELIGIBILITY RULES FOR PREGNANT WOMEN AND CHILDREN

Do you know what the eligibility rules are in your state? You should be able to find this information at the official government site for your state's Medicaid agency. Another helpful resource is The Henry J. Kaiser Family Foundation Webpage at KFF.org, Report: Medicaid and CHIP Eligibility and Enrollment Policies as of January 2021: Findings from a 50-State Survey [hereinafter "KFF Medicaid Eligibility Report"] (you can find your state's income eligibility levels in Tables 1 and 2 of the report).

2. ACA Medicaid Expansion: The "Newly Eligible"

The ACA expansion provides coverage for many adults who did not fit within any of the previous eligibility categories, but who likely are working in jobs that do not provide insurance coverage and whose incomes are either too low or too unstable for them to buy and maintain coverage in the private insurance market.

"Newly Eligible." For states that have expanded Medicaid, mandatory eligibility now includes adults **aged 19–64 with household incomes**

---

* Among other changes to eligibility discussed in the next section, the ACA aligned the minimum income eligibility threshold for all children. Prior to 2014, states were required to cover children under age six with family incomes below 133% FPL, but to cover children ages six to eighteen only up to 100% FPL. Now, all children up to 133% FPL must be covered. The law also allows for a five percentage point of income disregard that effectively raises the minimum to 138% FPL.

** A state is given the option of covering children up to 150% of the state's Medicaid eligibility levels, if this is higher than 200% FPL; but in this case, the additional coverage would be funded through the Children's Health Insurance Program (CHIP), described in the following notes.

*** A state is given the option of covering pregnant women at higher income levels, also through CHIP.

that do not exceed 133% of the federal poverty level and who are not pregnant, covered by Medicare, or otherwise entitled to Medicaid. Individuals who fall into this category of "**newly eligible**" are often also referred to as "**non-disabled adults**" or "the **expansion population**." If states choose to expand Medicaid, they must cover the entire expansion population if they want to take advantage of the enhanced federal match for this population.

Income Eligibility. Although the statute sets the eligibility level at 133% of poverty, **a 5% income disregard is added, raising the effective eligibility level to 138%.** If implemented nationwide, this "newly eligible" category of adults in Medicaid would have increased Medicaid coverage by 11 million recipients by 2019 over the 32 million Americans who already received Medicaid, accounting for almost a third of those newly insured under the Affordable Care Act. Most Americans with a full-time minimum-wage job would be eligible for Medicaid under the Medicaid expansion, as would poor parents whose incomes do not fall below state-established traditional Medicaid eligibility levels, which are very low in some states. See KFF Medicaid Eligibility Report, supra, Table 4 (showing eligibility levels as low as 18% FPL for Alabama and Texas).

PROBLEM: YOUR STATE'S MEDICAID INCOME ELIGIBILITY RULES FOR PARENTS

Do you live in an expansion state? If not, what is the income eligibility for parents in your state and would the expansion help them? (Refer once again to the website for your state Medicaid program). If you do live in an expansion state, review Table 4 of the KFF Medicaid Eligibility Report, supra: How significant is the difference in the income eligibility threshold between expansion and non-expansion states?

3. Immigrants & Medicaid Categorical Exclusions

Medicaid coverage is limited to U.S. citizens and lawfully present immigrants with a "qualified" immigration status. This means that undocumented immigrants do not qualify for coverage, subject to a limited exception that reimburses hospitals for emergency care provided. **"Qualified" immigrant categories** include, among others, lawful permanent residents, refugees, asylees, victims of human trafficking with valid visa, and certain victims of domestic violence. Immigrants here lawfully, but not "qualified", are not eligible for Medicaid. This includes people with a "Non-immigrant Status," such as worker visas, student visas, and other types of visas.

Even those who are "qualified" are typically barred from receiving Medicaid until they have resided in the United States for five years. This **five-year bar** applies, for example, to Legal Permanent Residents or "Green Card" holders, though there are exceptions for certain groups such as asylees or refugees. States can opt to eliminate the five-year waiting period and extend coverage to those without a qualified status. In some instances, **state law may limit a state's ability to delay coverage**. See, e.g., Finch v. Commonwealth Health Ins. Connector Auth., 959 N.E.2d 970 (Mass. 2012), holding that Massachusetts' program applying Medicaid's five-year waiting period to eligibility for state-provided insurance subsidies violated the state constitutional equal protection provision. As of January 2021, 41 states have used state funds to cover immigrants subject to the five-year bar or a broader group immigrants who cannot meet federal eligibility. See Table 3 of the KFF Medicaid Eligibility Report, supra, to compare different states' approaches. There are narrow exceptions to immigration-related restrictions in federally-funded programs: Medicaid coverage for emergency care is available and access to public health care, such as immunizations and treatment for communicable diseases is allowed for immigrants regardless of their immigration status.

Additional barriers to care for immigrants include confusion about eligibility rules and fear of becoming a "public charge." The Immigration and Nationalization Act requires some categories of non-citizens seeking a visa or change in status to demonstrate they are not likely to become a public charge—that is, not likely to become dependent on government for cash assistance or long-term care. 8 U.S.C.A. § 1182(a)(4). Certain groups, such as asylees and refugees, are excluded from this public charge test. Under longstanding policy, health benefits, such as Medicaid and CHIP, have not been considered in the public charge test. This is because such support has been viewed as helping people stay healthy and productive. In a sharp departure from this approach, the Trump administration issued a rule that would have allowed such benefits to be considered in making a public charge determination. Litigation initially halted the rule's implementation, and the Biden administration has since formally withdrawn the rule. As noted in Chapter 6, Section IV.A. however, the mere announcement of a broadening of the public charge test appeared to have a chilling effect on immigrants' willingness to access coverage or care for which they were otherwise eligible.

4. State Waivers for New Eligibility Restrictions

Since the beginning of the Medicaid program, the federal government has authorized state demonstration projects under Section 1115 of the Social Security Act, often referred to as Section **1115 Waivers**. 42 U.S.C. § 1315. This provision permits states to deviate from certain federal Medicaid requirements to conduct an "experimental, pilot or demonstration project, which in the judgment of the Secretary [of HHS] promotes the objectives" of the Medicaid program. This section gives HHS a lot of discretion, but it also creates two important requirements: the project must be **experimental** and it must further **Medicaid objectives** to "**furnish ... medical assistance** to [limited income individuals] and [ ] **rehabilitation and other services to help [such individuals] attain or retain capability for independence and self-care.**" 42 U.S.C. 1396– 1. A waiver may be successfully challenged in court if the Secretary arbitrarily approves a waiver without following the procedural requirements set out in the law, or if the Secretary fails to evaluate the waiver to determine if it meets the above substantive requirements. For example, a waiver request for a simple benefits cut, which might save money but has no research goal, would not satisfy the experimental requirement. See Newton-Nations v. Betlach, 660 F.3d 370 (9th Cir. 2013) (invalidating an HHS-approved waiver to increase cost sharing because of the Secretary's failure to consider the factors required by law).

Waivers have always been a popular tool for a variety of state demonstration projects. Prior to the ACA, states used waivers primarily to expand services and for health care delivery and financing reform, though longstanding policy has required that such demonstrations be budget neutral (federal Medicaid expenditures cannot be allowed to exceed what would have occurred without the demonstration). Since the Supreme Court made the ACA's Medicaid expansion optional, however, there has been a growing trend of states attempting to use Section 1115 waivers to implement a more restrictive form of Medicaid expansion, as well as to impose greater restrictions on some traditional eligible categories. Examples include requests to limit expansion eligibility to 100% FPL, require asset tests, impose time limits on coverage, lock people out for failure to timely renew eligibility, require drug testing, and impose work reporting requirements. In general, the federal government has tended to reject waiver proposals viewed as undermining existing eligibility protections, though such proposals were viewed more favorably by the Trump administration. During that time, CMS encouraged state waiver requests to impose work reporting requirements on Medicaid eligible individuals. For more on the legal and political fate of such waivers, see Note 5 below. For up-to-date information on Medicaid waiver status generally, consult The Henry J. Kaiser Family Foundation, Medicaid Waiver Tracker: Approved and Pending Section 1115 Waivers by State (Nov. 1, 2021).

NOTES AND QUESTIONS

1. *Rules for Determining Financial Eligibility*. Traditionally, Medicaid eligibility was conditioned not just on income but also on **assets**—previously eligible Medicaid recipients could only possess nominal assets, other than their home. In addition, rules for counting income under traditional Medicaid have varied from state to state, with some states allowing certain **income disregards** or **deductions** not allowed by others. Even in states that participate in the expansion, **pre-ACA income and asset eligibility rules**

continue to apply to some individuals who are not part of the expansion group, including individuals who are eligible for traditional Medicaid because of Supplemental Security Income or other benefits, persons who are 65 or older, the medically needy, or Dual Eligibles. Different income computation rules also apply to individuals and families who qualify based upon age or disability and those receiving nursing facility services or home-and community-based care services.

For the "newly eligible" adult category (the expansion population), as well as pregnant women and children, however, the ACA introduced a new income definition—**Modified Adjusted Gross Income (MAGI)** for purposes of determining eligibility. For most people, MAGI is the same as (or very close to) Adjusted Gross Income as calculated under federal income tax rules, plus any foreign income, tax-exempt interest, and non-taxable social security income. MAGI does not include an asset test. It also standardizes how income is counted for the relevant populations nationwide; in contrast to state rules that have allowed various income disregards, MAGI takes into account virtually all income (except for the 5% disregard mentioned above).

2. *The Role of Assets & Medicaid Planning.* The role of assets in determining eligibility is as important as the role of income. Although assets are not considered in determining eligibility for expanded Medicaid, they continue to be a factor for other categories of Medicaid recipients, including residents of nursing homes. Traditionally, Medicaid recipients could only possess nominal assets, other than their home. Eligibility requirements mandate that such persons "spend down" their assets until they reach Medicaid asset eligibility levels; thereafter, they must spend all of their income, except for a very small personal needs allowance, on their medical care, with Medicaid paying the difference between the amount the recipient can pay and the allowed nursing facility reimbursement level. Sooner or later many persons who require long-term nursing facility care become impoverished, regardless of their financial status at the time they entered a nursing facility, as nursing homes range on average from around $90,000 to $100,000 a year. A temptation exists, therefore, for persons who anticipate the need for nursing home care to transfer their assets to their children or to others in order to establish premature Medicaid eligibility. They may also be tempted (or advised by lawyers who specialize in Medicaid planning) to put their assets into a trust so that they can continue to enjoy the benefit of the assets until such time as nursing home care is required and then become impecunious. Finally, if an institutionalized individual leaves behind a spouse in the community, it is necessary to provide for the needs of the community spouse at some decent level before directing the income of the institutionalized spouse toward the cost of care.

Beginning in 1980, Congress (encouraged by the states and the long term care insurance industry) adopted a series of laws attempting to discourage asset transfers intended to create eligibility. Congress even tried to criminalize the knowing and willful disposition of assets to become eligible for Medicaid, but this "granny goes to jail" provision provoked a public outcry. The following year Congress repealed the provision, putting in its place a statute criminalizing the knowing and willful counseling or assistance of an individual to dispose of assets to become eligible for Medicaid. Then-Attorney General Reno refused to defend the constitutionality of this provision, and its enforcement was enjoined. John M. Broderick, To Transfer or Not to Transfer: Congress Failed to Stiffen Penalties for Medicaid Estate Planning, But Should the Practice Continue? 6 Elder L. J. 257 (1999). Current law provides that anyone who transfers assets for less than their market value within sixty months before entering a nursing facility and applying for Medicaid is ineligible for Medicaid for the number of months of nursing home care that the assets would have covered, beginning with the date the applicant would otherwise have been eligible for Medicaid. There are special rules affecting annuities, life estates, loans, trusts, entry fees to continuing care communities, and other approaches to reducing assets. The law also allows states to deny Medicaid to persons who have over $500,000 in home equity (which can be extended to $750,000 at a state's option). There are special rules for hardship cases and for transfers to certain individuals (such as spouses), but the law makes voluntary impoverishment quite difficult. See 42 U.S.C.A. § 1396p. What is the rationale for exempting the value of a house?

3.   *The Role of Family Support Networks.* One of the pervasive tensions in welfare programs is the conflict between familial and social responsibility. Should adult children be responsible for the medical expenses of their indigent elderly parents? Is it fair for elderly persons to expect the taxpayers to finance their medical care through Medicaid rather than look to their children for help? On the other hand, is it fair to require children of indigent parents to contribute to their support, when our society does not otherwise expect adult children to support their parents? What effect would such a requirement have on parent-child relationships? Would it perpetuate a cycle of poverty? The Medicaid Act expressly forbids holding adult children responsible for the care of their parents. Many states, however, have "filial responsibility" laws on the books (which date back to the Elizabethan poor laws), which impose criminal penalties for failing to support parents but are rarely enforced.

Should parents bear the full burden of the very expensive care required by severely disabled children in nursing facilities? Institutionalized disabled children are currently eligible regardless of the wealth of their families because SSI eligibility rules do not attribute the income or resources of parents to a child who has been institutionalized for more than 30 days. States also have the option of providing Medicaid coverage to noninstitutionalized disabled children who are being cared for in their homes, even if they do not qualify for SSI because their family's income is too high. To qualify for eligibility under this option, the child would have to be eligible for SSI if institutionalized, the child must require a level of care normally provided in an institution, and the state must determine that it is appropriate to provide care outside of an institution and that the estimated cost for providing care in the home is equal to or less than the amount that would be spent to keep the child in an institution. This is also referred to as the "Katie Beckett" option, named after a child who was ventilator-dependent and had to be institutionalized not for medical reasons, but because her parents' income made her ineligible for the Medicaid coverage that would have enabled her to be appropriately cared for at home. In states not electing this option, middle class parents may need to institutionalize their children to get Medicaid coverage.

4. *CHIP's Role in Covering Children and Pregnant Women.* Congress created CHIP, Title XXI of the Social Security Act, 42 U.S.C.A. §§ 1397aa–1397jj, as part of the 1997 Balanced Budget Act to provide coverage for uninsured children in families with income above Medicaid eligibility levels. Unlike Medicaid, CHIP was not created as an entitlement for recipients, but rather as a grant-in-aid (or "block grant") program to the states, established for ten years and affording the states even greater flexibility in program administration within broad federal guidelines. States have three options for how they use CHIP funds: expand Medicaid coverage for children; establish a new CHIP program to cover children ineligible for Medicaid or private insurance; or a combination of the two. Section 1115 waiver authority may be used to alter eligibility requirements, but the most significant CHIP expansion has been to cover pregnant women. As of January 2021, CHIP funds coverage for children with incomes at or above 200% FPL in almost all states, with 19 covering children with incomes at or above 300% FPL. Six states also extend Medicaid coverage to pregnant women through CHIP, and 17 states use CHIP to provide coverage for pregnant women regardless of immigration status through the "unborn child option," which allows states to consider a fetus a "low-income child" for purpose of CHIP coverage.

5. *Medicaid Work Requirements.* As noted above, a number of states, especially those resistant to the Medicaid expansion, have sought waivers that would allow them to impose additional restrictions on Medicaid eligibility. Section 1115 waivers seeking to impose work reporting requirements have received the greatest attention in recent years. Although both Democratic and Republican administrations have consistently rejected such requests as inconsistent with Medicaid's objectives, the Trump administration approved work reporting requirements on the Medicaid expansion population, arguing that the requirements would promote economic self-sufficiency, self-esteem, and improve health.

These claims were undermined by evidence from Arkansas, the only state to fully implement such requirements, and the demonstration was ultimately halted by litigation. Gresham v. Azar, 950 F.3d 93 (D.C. Cir. 2020), *cert. granted but withdrawn* (affirming the district court's finding that the Secretary's approval was arbitrary and capricious, and inconsistent with Medicaid's objectives). Notably, most of the coverage losses due to "noncompliance" were suffered by people who were, in fact, working or legally entitled to an exemption from the requirement. The main reasons for noncompliance appeared to be a lack of awareness of the requirements, the complexity of the compliance process, and technological and other barriers to reporting. There was also evidence that the work requirements did not actually promote work. Finally, a survey documented adverse consequences resulting from coverage loss, such as delaying care and having difficulty paying medical debt. Jennifer Wagner & Jessica Schubel, States' Experiences Confirm Harmful Effects of Medicaid Work Requirements, Center on Budget and Policy Priorities (Nov. 18, 2020). The Biden administration has signaled its opposition to work reporting requirements and similar eligibility restrictions that would undermine coverage goals.

6. *ACA Procedural Reforms.* The ACA included a number of other reforms designed to ease Medicaid eligibility determinations and enrollment. For example, it streamlined eligibility determinations, made it somewhat easier for enrollees to prove citizenship, and expanded hospitals' ability to make presumptive eligibility determinations—all of which have helped increase Medicaid enrollment for the traditional as well as newly eligible populations. Some states have sought waivers attempting to roll back some of these changes.

7. *Medicaid's Relationship to Private Insurance Reforms in the ACA.* Although the ACA has received the most attention for its private insurance reforms, the Medicaid expansion is an essential component for achieving the ACA's coverage goals. In states rejecting the Medicaid expansion, there is a significant coverage gap for low-income citizens. Recall from Chapter 9 that citizens whose household incomes fall below 100% of FPL are not eligible for premium tax credits, even if they are ineligible for Medicaid because they live in a non-expansion state. Although premium tax credits are available to individuals with household incomes between 100% and 133% of FPL, they have to pay premiums for coverage and face higher cost-sharing than they would under Medicaid. This population will likely continue to receive uncompensated care, creating serious financial consequences for hospitals and other providers. Significant job loss and other economic challenges caused by the COVID-19 pandemic have increased calls for the federal government to fill the coverage gap, by extending federal marketplace coverage to people with incomes under 100% of FPL with enhanced premium and cost-sharing subsidies.

PROBLEM: MEDICAID ELIGIBILITY

Four generations of the Sawatsky family live together in two neighboring apartments. Stanislaus Sawatsky emigrated from Poland in the 1990s, became a U.S. citizen ten years later, and has worked thirty years in construction. Work has been intermittent, however, and he has never been able to build up a nest egg. For the past year, Stanislaus, now in his late 50s, has been unable to work because of his heart condition. He was recently awarded SSI because of his disability. His son, Peter, who lives next door, is married to Maria and has three children, ages 1, 5, and 7. Peter was recently laid off from his job in a trailer factory. He is working in a fast-food restaurant, but his income is only a fraction of what it used to be. Maria is pregnant and not employed outside the home. Finally, Stanislaus' mother, Elzbieta, aged 83, has been living with Peter for a year now. She came to the U.S. from Poland last year on a tourist visa and has not returned (even though the visa has expired). She fell yesterday and is in the hospital with a broken hip. No one in the family can afford to help pay her medical bills, and the hospital is saying she will need to be discharged to a nursing home. Who in this group, if anyone, is eligible for Medicaid? What sources of law would you consult to answer this question? What additional facts would you have to know to determine eligibility?

B. BENEFITS

As with eligibility, the benefits provided by Medicaid programs have historically varied from state to state, and this variation has continued even with ACA implementation. This section first describes the benefits covered by the traditional Medicaid law, which continues to apply to the non-expansion population. It then describes an option created by the Deficit Reduction Act of 2005 that allows states to provide certain Medicaid beneficiaries, including the adult expansion population, with "benchmark" or "benchmark equivalent" coverage. It concludes with a discussion of Medicaid assistance premiums.

1. Traditional Medicaid Benefits

The Medicaid statute lists several categories of **mandatory services** that States are required to provide the traditional categorically needy, as well as about three dozen categories of **optional services** that states may cover for traditional Medicaid recipients, including a final catch-all category of "any other medical care, and any other type of remedial care recognized under State law, specified by the Secretary." At least one state has covered acupuncture under this category. Every state covers some optional services, most notably prescription drugs. The chart below lists the mandatory benefits, as well as selected optional benefits commonly covered by states. For more information about state trends and variations in benefit coverage, see Kathleen Gifford & Elizabeth Hinton, Medicaid Moving Ahead in Uncertain Times: Results from a 50-State Medicaid Budget Survey for State Fiscal Years 2017 and 2018, The Henry J. Kaiser Family Foundation (Oct. 2017).

MANDATORY BENEFITS	OPTIONAL BENEFITS (SELECTED)
Inpatient hospital services	Prescription drugs
Outpatient hospital services	Clinic services
Physician Services	Physical, occupational, and speech therapy
Rural health clinic (RHC) & federally-qualified health center (FQHC) services	Other diagnostic, screening, preventive and rehabilitative services
Nursing facility services	Prosthetic devices, dentures, eyeglasses
Home health care services (for those entitled to nursing facility care)	Home health care services (for those not entitled to nursing facility care)
Laboratory and X-ray services	Intermediate care facilities for intellectual and developmental disabilities (ICF/IDD) services
Early and periodic screening, diagnostic and treatment (EPSDT) services (for children)	Inpatient psychiatric care for individuals under 21
Family planning services and supplies	Personal care services with option to self direct
Nurse-midwife and other certified nurse practitioner services	Home health services to individuals with chronic conditions
Smoking cessation services for pregnant women	Hospice services
Transportation to and from medically necessary care	Case management

Some Medicaid services are aimed at specific population groups. The most prominent example of these is the EPSDT program (defined in the chart above), which requires not only that states provide screening to diagnose physical or mental conditions in children, but also obligates states to provide treatment for identified conditions, whether or not the services required are otherwise included in its Medicaid plan. For example, vision, dental, and hearing services must be covered.

Pregnancy care has also been considered a priority for Medicaid, though state discretion in the type and duration of coverage for women before, during and after pregnancy creates gaps in care that can impact maternal and fetal health. For example, states commonly cover substance use disorder treatment and nurse home visits, but many fail to cover doula care, which is increasingly viewed as a tool for improving pregnancy care and outcomes. In addition, states are only required to provide postpartum coverage up to sixty days after birth. But poor maternal health outcomes, especially the stark racial disparities in mortality and morbidity among Black and Native American women, have sparked calls for states to expand full Medicaid coverage during the postpartum period from sixty days to the first full year after birth. This new option has been extended to states through the American Rescue Plan of 2021, enacted in response to the COVID-19 pandemic. It is scheduled to take effect April 1, 2022, and would be available for five years.

States have had considerably more discretion in the benefits they provide to the medically needy. There are some limits to this discretion, however. States that provide institutional services for any group must also cover ambulatory services. Moreover, if a state covers institutional care for persons with mental illness or intellectual disabilities, it must also provide them with either the services it provides to the categorically needy or any seven services offered generally to Medicaid recipients. If a state covers nursing facility services, it must also pay for home health services.

In addition to the flexibility states have with respect to coverage of optional services, the law gives states flexibility with respect to determining the **amount, duration, and scope** of covered benefits, and it allows them to place "**appropriate limits** on a service based on such criteria as **medical necessity** or **utilization control**." Nonetheless, this discretion is limited somewhat. States must provide a **sufficient** amount, duration, and scope to achieve Medicaid's purpose reasonably. States **cannot arbitrarily deny or reduce** the amount, duration, or scope of a required service **solely because of the diagnosis, type of illness, or condition**. This means that even though states can refuse to cover specified optional categories of services (such as eyeglasses or dental care), once they decide to cover a service, they cannot decide to cover it for some medical diagnoses or conditions but not others.

2. Alternative Benefit Plans

The Deficit Reduction Act of 2005 created what was originally called a new benchmark or benchmark-equivalent coverage option. This allowed state Medicaid plans to ignore requirements regarding mandatory and optional service coverage (as well as other program design requirements relating to access discussed in Section D below) with respect to most children and parents and to pregnant women with incomes above 133% of FPL. This benchmark coverage, now called "Alternative Benefit Plan" (ABP), is coverage that a state can choose to peg to private insurance available in the state or, with HHS approval, to the traditional Medicaid package offered to other Medicaid-eligibles. The ACA specifically requires that Alternative Benefit Plans be used for the adult expansion population, and they must cover the ten essential health benefits required under the ACA. See Chapter 9. Most states have chosen to base the ABP on the state plan for reasons of equity and administrative convenience.

3.   Medicaid Premium Assistance

The ACA requires states to make available **premium subsidies** for Medicaid-eligible individuals covered by employer coverage rather than cover them under Medicaid directly if it is cost effective to do so. States cannot, however, require Medicaid recipients to enroll in employer coverage. This kind of premium assistance is not new. States were using Medicaid funds as premium assistance for eligible individuals to purchase private health insurance as an alternative to direct Medicaid coverage long before the ACA. Historically, these programs were not very large because few Medicaid beneficiaries had the option to purchase employment-based coverage or could afford private insurance, even with the subsidy. The creation of the marketplaces under the ACA has renewed states' interest in this option. Currently, only one state is using the Medicaid premium assistance option to purchase Marketplace coverage for their expansion adults.

One risk of using this approach is that beneficiaries may not have access to the full scope of benefits required under Medicaid. For example, many private plans will not offer the full range of EPSDT services Medicaid requires for children. States using premium assistance generally must provide wrap-around benefits and cost-sharing protections so that Medicaid beneficiaries receiving private coverage will not have access to fewer benefits or pay higher out-of-pocket costs when private coverage fails to meet Medicaid's level of coverage or is more expensive. But there is not much evidence about how well these protections work, and some states have discontinued premium assistance programs due to low enrollment or other administrative issues. See The Henry J. Kaiser Family Foundation, Using Medicaid to Wrap Around Private Insurance: Key Questions to Consider (Jul. 2017).

CRITICAL THINKING EXERCISE: HOW WOULD YOU DECIDE WHAT SERVICES TO COVER?

What explains the federal line drawing between mandatory and optional services? Why do you think all states cover prescription drugs? Should they be mandatory? Why would Medicaid require coverage of a non-medical service, like transportation? A few states have sought waivers that would allow them to exclude non-emergency medical transportation for the expansion population. Should this request be allowed? What factors are relevant to your answers to the prior questions? Do you think any of the optional services should be re-classified as mandatory, or the reverse?

NOTES AND QUESTIONS

1. *Challenging State Benefit Design Decisions Under the Medicaid Act.* Although states have discretion in defining the amount, duration, and scope of benefits provided, federal limits on this discretion, such as the requirement that states not arbitrarily deny care based on diagnosis, type of illness or condition, has spawned litigation challenging coverage exclusions and denials. For example, a state's provision covering eyeglasses for individuals suffering from eye disease, but not for individuals with refractive error, was invalidated, White v. Beal, 555 F.2d 1146 (3d Cir. 1977), as was a state's denial of medically necessary orthopedic footwear and compression stockings to patients with certain medical conditions, Davis v. Shah, 821 F.3d 231 (2d Cir. 2016). Courts have also invalidated a $50,000 cap on payment for hospital services which precluded coverage of $200,000 liver transplants, Montoya v. Johnston, 654 F. Supp. 511 (W.D.Tex. 1987), and a state's refusal to cover gender-affirming surgery (which would fall within the general mandatory categories of hospital and physician services), Smith v. Rasmussen, 57 F. Supp. 2d 736 (N.D.Iowa 1999). Beneficiaries can bring claims in federal court to enforce their rights to benefits, as discussed further in Section D on Program Administration and Rights Enforcement.

2. *The Role of Civil Rights Law.* Civil rights law may also limit state discretion in determining what benefits to provide under the Medicaid program. For example, in Olmstead v. L.C., 527 U.S. 581 (1999), patients with mental disabilities brought suit challenging the state's failure to provide a community-based placement for them. This failure resulted in the patients' prolonged confinement in a hospital psychiatric unit, despite their treating physician's determination that they could be appropriately cared for in a community-based setting. Justice Ginsburg, writing for a majority of the Court, concluded that, under Title II of the Americans with Disabilities Act of 1990 (ADA), and implementing regulations requiring public entities to administer "programs in the most integrated setting appropriate to the needs of qualified individuals with disabilities," 28 CFR § 35.130(d), the state of Georgia was obligated to care for persons with mental disabilities in community-based programs rather than state institutions under the following circumstances: such placement is determined appropriate by the state's treatment professionals; transfer to a less restrictive setting is not opposed by the affected individual; and the placement could reasonably be accommodated, taking into account the resources available to the State and other patients' needs. Notwithstanding this duty, Justice Ginsburg, joined by Justices O'Connor, Souter, and Breyer, concluded in Part III-B of the opinion that the State's responsibility in this regard was not unlimited. They approved a rationing approach to community-based placement, as long as the State could demonstrate it had a comprehensive, effectively-working plan for such placements and a waiting list that moved at a reasonable pace not controlled

by the State's endeavors to keep its institutions fully populated. *Olmstead* spawned a host of ADA Medicaid cases. See Sara Rosenbaum, Joel Teitelbaum and Alexandra Stewart, Olmstead v. L.C.: Implications for Medicaid and Other Publicly Funded Health Services, 12 Health Matrix 93 (2002). For a closer look at the role of antidiscrimination law in health coverage, see Chapter 6, Section IV.

3. *The Role of the Constitution*. Does the U.S. Constitution have any relevance to the question of whether certain items or services must be covered by public benefits programs? In Harris v. McRae, 448 U.S. 297 (1980), the Court upheld the Hyde Amendment, which prohibited federal funding for some abortions. In his majority opinion, Justice Stewart held that although the freedom to choose an abortion was protected against unwarranted government interference, this right "does not confer an entitlement to such funds as may be necessary to realize all the advantages of that freedom." In states that choose to cover non-federally funded abortions anyway, the state must pay 100% of the cost. Some states are required to cover abortions under their state constitutions. See Chapter 16, Section III.

4. *CHIP Benefits*. Recall from the discussion of CHIP in Section A that states may choose to establish separately-administered CHIP programs. In these instances, states must provide health care benefit packages equivalent to coverage provided by "benchmark equivalent plans," as discussed above. Federal law establishes other antidiscrimination and access protections, but CHIP explicitly does not create an entitlement for any particular child to receive coverage. This is an important difference between CHIP and Medicaid. See Section D below.

5. *The Shift to Non-Institutional Care*. A striking feature of the benefit packages provided by Medicaid traditionally is its emphasis on institutional care; Medicaid pays for much of the care provided in hospitals, nursing homes and intermediate care facilities (ICFs). Payors and health advocates have urged that more care be provided outside of these institutions, when appropriate, with the hope of improving patients' health and even preventing the need for institutionalization in some cases. CMS has taken steps to encourage states to do just that. As already noted, states can cover community-based personal care services as an optional category. In addition, federal law allows Medicaid agencies to request waivers under Section 1915(c) of the Social Security Act to offer home-and community-based service alternatives to institutional care provided in a nursing facility, an ICF (for individuals with intellectual disabilities), or a hospital. This is commonly referred to as a **Section 1915(c) waiver**. States have great flexibility in deciding which populations to cover under § 1915(c) waivers, though as with other waivers, reforms are supposed to be budget neutral. Covered services may include case management, homemaker services, home health aide services, personal care, adult day health care, habilitation, and respite care. The ACA continues this approach of encouraging community-based care, giving states great flexibility in determining eligibility and scope of services. For example, states may use need-based criteria for individuals with family income up to 300% of the federal

poverty level and offer home-and community-based care services that may differ in type, amount, duration, and scope based on specific need-based criteria.

6. *Medicaid's Role in the Health Care Safety Net.* Medicaid plays a central role in funding institutional and community and home-based care; births, children's health, and family planning services; and chronic health care. Medicaid does more than simply pay for services, however; it plays a vital role in supporting the nation's health care infrastructure. For example, Medicaid makes disproportionate share hospital (DSH) payments to hospitals that serve a disproportionate number of Medicaid and uninsured patients and are therefore unable to rely on private-pay patients to fully cross-subsidize the expense of caring for these patients. This includes teaching, public, and private, nonprofit hospitals, which also have charitable obligations. See Chapter 13 (Tax-Exempt Health Care Organizations).

PROBLEM: *MEDICAID BENEFITS*

Each member of the Sawatsky family needs medical services. Elzbieta is in the hospital and needs a hip replacement and a nursing home placement. Stanislaus needs to take an expensive medication for his heart, and he worries that he may need another bypass operation like the one last year. Peter badly needs dental work. Maria needs prenatal care and will soon need maternity care. The seven-year old's teacher claims he has attention deficit disorder, the five-year-old needs glasses, and the one-year-old has recurrent earaches. If the Sawatskys are entitled to Medicaid, to what services are they entitled? What hurdles might they face in getting covered services?

C. MEDICAID FINANCING & PAYMENT FOR SERVICES

Medicaid is an open-ended entitlement program, with the federal government providing a generous financial match to state spending. States receive a **Federal Medical Assistance Percentage (FMAP)** ranging from 50% to around 74% for the traditional Medicaid population. States that participate in the Medicaid expansion under the terms of the ACA receive an enhanced FMAP for the "newly eligible" category: 100% in 2014, 2015 and 2016, 95% for 2017, 94% for 2018, 93% for 2019, and 90% for 2020 and thereafter. States that already covered the expansion population receive federal assistance for the expansion population at lower percentage levels initially, but federal funding gradually increases until it reaches the levels received by expansion states. The Congressional Budget Office has estimated that the Medicaid (and CHIP) expansions, if fully implemented in all states would cost the federal government $642 billion between 2012 and 2022, while costing the states about $41 billion.

Nonetheless, Medicaid expenditures remain a significant budget item for all states. The cost of Medicaid, in both expansion and nonexpansion states, remains a major source of concern. The ACA effectively transformed the narrative around health care coverage, causing people to see it as both a right and responsibility, which, in turn, motivated millions to seek coverage. Enrollment gains were not only among the expansion populations, but in new Medicaid signups among traditional populations as well. The pressure to contain and reduce Medicaid spending has not been ameliorated. In fact, the ACA has heightened the focus on reducing cost through **health care financing and delivery reform**.

1.   Fee-for-Service Medicaid

The original vision of the Medicaid program was that it would provide mainstream care for its recipients. In line with this dream, the Medicaid statute guaranteed recipients **free choice of participating providers**. With respect to access to physician services, however, this goal has not always been realized. Physicians also have freedom of choice as to whether or not to participate in Medicaid. Medicaid physician fee schedules have been largely driven by state budget constraints, and low Medicaid fees have discouraged physician participation in the program. Historically, Medicaid has, on average, only paid physicians about 72% of Medicare rates (which is less than commercial rates), but some states have only paid 40% or less. Low payment levels, along with paperwork and billing hassles, have contributed to low physician participation in Medicaid. Physicians also overwhelmingly report difficulty in referring Medicaid and CHIP patients to specialists, compared to about a quarter of doctors referring privately insured patients. GAO, Most Physicians Serve Covered Children but have Difficulty Referring them for Specialty Care (2011). When physicians are not readily available, Medicaid recipients have often had to rely on hospital outpatient clinics and emergency rooms for primary care. Hospitals and nursing homes are more limited in their ability to refuse Medicaid patients: many hospitals are obligated to serve Medicaid patients because of their tax-exempt status or other federal funding obligations, and many nursing homes may not have enough private pay business to decline Medicaid participation. Nonetheless, Medicaid discrimination by these institutions persists. See Chapters 6 and 13.

One tool for addressing access barriers linked to low payment rates is a federal requirement that Medicaid **rates** be "**sufficient to enlist enough providers** so that care and services are available under the plan at least to the extent that such care and services are available to the general population in the geographic area." 42 U.S.C.A. § 1396a(a)(30)(A). Commonly referred to as § 30(A) or the Equal Access provision, this requirement has been used by Medicaid beneficiaries and providers to challenge state rates in court. This has yielded mixed success, however, as discussed further in section D below.

2. Medicaid Cost Sharing

As noted in Chapter 7, one strategy for controlling health care utilization and cost favored by conservative advocates is increased cost-sharing by consumers. Whatever merits this strategy may offer in the private sector, it has very limited possibilities in the Medicaid program because of the limited financial abilities of Medicaid recipients. Until 2006, the law permitted only very nominal cost-sharing for Medicaid recipients, and prohibited cost sharing altogether for children, pregnant women with respect to pregnancy-related services, terminally ill individuals in hospice, and institutionalized recipients. Perhaps most importantly, the law prohibited Medicaid providers from denying services to recipients who could not afford a copayment.

The 2006 Deficit Reduction Act dramatically changed this to allow cost-sharing for most services of up to 10% of service cost for recipients with income of 100% to 150% of FPL, and up to 20% of the service cost for recipients with incomes above 150% of the FPL, capped at 5% of total income. The DRA also allowed states to charge **premiums** for recipients with incomes above 150% of the FPL. Cost-sharing is still prohibited for the recipient groups listed above, as well as for emergency and family planning services. Updated rules provide for **copayments** of up to $4 for outpatient visits for persons with incomes up to 100% of FPL and for $8 for nonemergency use of emergency rooms, $4 for preferred prescription drugs and $8 for non-preferred drugs for recipients with incomes up to 150 percent of poverty. States may allow participating providers to refuse services to recipients with household incomes above 100% of FPL who do not pay required cost-sharing amounts.

Some states have expanded Medicaid using section 1115 waivers that have allowed them to charge premiums or impose cost sharing on some of the expansion population. Proponents suggest this is a way to promote personal responsibility, to support or "teach" enrollees how to make value-conscious health decisions, and to facilitate their transition to a private insurance plan. States also cite a need to control the costs of expansion, despite the enhanced federal match that covers almost all new spending. Opponents have raised concerns about cost sharing among low-income populations, citing research suggesting that it does not generate much savings and that even small levels of cost-sharing can be a barrier to coverage and lead to reduced access to medically necessary care. See The Henry J. Kaiser Family Foundation, The Effects of Premiums and Cost Sharing on Low-Income Populations: Updated Review of Research Findings (Jun. 2017).

3. Medicaid Managed Care

Although the original vision of Medicaid was that recipients would have the same free choice of providers then enjoyed by the general population, Medicaid has in recent years, like private health insurance, moved dramatically in the direction of managed care. While most families and children are covered by managed care, the big push in the recent past has been to move disabled recipients to managed care as well. Medicaid managed care refers to both **HMOs that receive capitated payments** and **Primary Care Case Management (PCCM) programs** in which primary care providers receive additional payments to serve as the primary care home for Medicaid enrollees who continue to receive services on a fee-for-service basis.

This move to managed care has been driven by several factors. The most important, perhaps, has been the hope of saving money. Managed care seemed to have cut costs in the private sector, and it was expected to work for Medicaid as well. Managed care advocates claimed that it might not only reduce the price of services, but that it would also reduce inappropriate use of expensive services like emergency room care. The move to managed care was also driven by the belief that it would increase Medicaid beneficiaries' access to providers and improve quality and coordination of care. A number of states, including Tennessee and Oregon, also thought savings from managed care might enable them to expand coverage to low-income uninsured not otherwise eligible for Medicaid.

Attempts to move Medicaid recipients to managed care were thwarted for a time by federal requirements that guaranteed Medicaid recipients free choice of providers. In the late 1980s and 1990s, however, it became increasingly common for states to try to get this requirement waived through § 1915(b) or § 1115 waivers. Federal law was amended in 1997 to give states more options to enroll people in managed care, subject to certain limits such as ensuring some choice of plans. The law also creates protections for managed care beneficiaries, such as enrollment termination rights and prohibitions on discrimination on the basis of health status or need for health service in enrollment, reenrollment, or disenrollment of recipients. Medicaid managed care plans are subject to many of the same consumer rights afforded private managed care members under state law. See Chapter 9. In a number of instances, recipients have brought class actions against states for operating managed care programs in violation of federal requirements. See Michelle M. Mello, Policing Medicaid and Medicare Managed Care: The Role of Courts and Administrative Agencies, 27 J. Health Pol., Pol'y & L. 465 (2002).

Medicaid managed care has, not surprisingly, a mixed record. Medicaid managed care may be very different from the commercial plans' normal lines of business. Medicaid recipients are often plagued by chronic and expensive problems. Medicaid pays parsimoniously but imposes demanding program requirements. In particular, it requires services that many commercial plans do not cover and coverage of populations that live in places where commercial plans do not have providers. Some providers that contract with commercial plans, moreover, do not want to treat Medicaid recipients. Nonprofit plans tend to have lower administrative costs and offer better quality than commercial plans. Michael McCue and Michael Balit, Assessing the Financial Health of Medicaid Managed Care Plans and the Quality of Patient Care They Provide (Commonwealth Fund, 2011).

Medicaid managed care does, however, offer states the opportunity to shift the risk of covering Medicaid recipients to private insurers, and states have increasingly embraced this opportunity. There is some evidence that managed care saves the state and federal government money, and this is a powerful motivator for the states. See John Iglehart, Desperately Seeking Savings: States Shift More Medicaid Enrollees to Managed Care, 20 Health Aff. 1627 (2011). But see Isaac D. Buck, 11 St. Louis U. J. Health L. & Pol'y 107, Managing Medicaid (2017) (describing states' challenges with Medicaid managed care).

In the end, managed care has arguably proved better at containing costs in Medicaid than in Medicare, as discussed earlier in the chapter. In most states managed care has not saved Medicaid programs a great deal of money, but neither has it added to program cost. Several studies show that it has decreased dependence of Medicaid recipients on emergency rooms, but most studies show that access to care has otherwise been unaffected. In some states, however, money has been saved and access and quality improved. The bottom line seems to be that in some states Medicaid had so many problems before managed care that improvement was not difficult and was sometimes achieved. See also, discussing Medicaid managed care, Jane McCahill & Joseph T. Van Leer, The Challenges of Reform for Medicaid Managed Care, 21 Annals Health L. 541 (2012).

In May 2016, HHS released a final rule **modernizing managed care** in Medicaid and the Children's Health Insurance Program (CHIP). Medicaid and Children's Health Insurance Program (CHIP) Programs; Medicaid Managed Care, CHIP Delivered in Managed Care, and Revisions Related to Third Party Liability, 81 Fed. Reg. 27498 (May. 6, 2016). Approximately one-half of Medicaid spending runs through capitation contracts with managed care organizations, and this will grow as states move populations with more complex and costly needs—those with disabilities and those receiving long-term-services and supports, for instance—into managed care arrangements. Thus, the rule is important because of the reforms it is spurring and the impact it will have on a growing number of beneficiaries with more complex needs.

CMS described the rule as having four major goals: (1) supporting states' efforts to advance delivery system reform and quality of care improvements; (2) strengthening the consumer experience of care and providing key consumer protections, including nondiscrimination protections, requiring assistance with enrollment, disenrollment, and the appeals process, and requiring states to establish time and distance network adequacy standards to ensure the availability and accessibility of services; (3) strengthening program integrity by improving accountability and transparency, such as requiring additional transparency in setting Medicaid rates with respect to utilization and quality data; and (4) aligning rules across health insurance coverage programs, including marketplace plans, to improve efficiency and coverage transitions. For further information on the rule see Sara Rosenbaum, Twenty-First Century Medicaid: the Final Managed Care Rule, Health Aff. Blog (May 5, 2016), and Timothy Jost, Medicaid Managed Care Final Rule: Examining The Alignment with Qualified Health Plan Requirements, Health Aff. Blog (Apr. 29, 2016). The rule's provisions were intended to be implemented in phases over the next three years, beginning on July 1, 2017, but in June of that year, under a new administration, the Center for Medicaid and CHIP Services, within CMS, issued an informational bulletin announcing that it would use its "enforcement discretion" to delay some of the July 1 compliance dates on a state-specific basis and review the regulations to determine if changes should be made.

In November 2020, CMS issued a final rule that relaxed or revised some of the standards relating to beneficiary protections, network adequacy, and quality oversight. For example, it relaxed accessibility requirements for written materials for people with disabilities and those with limited English proficiency, let states shorten the timeframe for enrollees to request a state fair hearing, and eliminated the requirement for enrollees to submit a written appeal after an oral appeal. It also repealed the requirement that states use time and distance standards to ensure network adequacy, allowing states to use other nonquantitative standards instead, and weakened requirements intended to ensure comparable measurement of quality improvements and alignment across different insurance programs. For a more detailed summary of the rule changes, see Elizabeth Hinton and MaryBeth Musumeci, CMS's 2020 Final Medicaid Managed Care Rule: A Summary of Major Changes (Nov. 23, 2020) at KFF.org.

4.   Delivery System Reform

Although the overwhelming focus of mainstream discussion about the ACA has been on insurance expansion, the ACA reflects a comprehensive endeavor to achieve multifaceted goals. As explained in the Medicare section of this chapter, the ACA encouraged reforms to achieve a **triple**

aim: better care for individuals, better health for populations, and slower growth in costs through improvements in care. Although the most widely discussed reforms relating to this triple aim have been in the area of Medicare, similar efforts are driving Medicaid reforms. The Center for Medicare and Medicaid Innovation (CMMI) is helping to catalyze reform through myriad pilots and demonstrations designed to test new approaches to paying Medicare and Medicaid providers. For up-to-date information about these innovations, visit the Innovation Models website at CMS.gov. This area is fast-moving, as more states, Medicaid managed care plans, and providers work together to experiment with different kinds of payment methodologies and delivery reforms. As discussed below, there are certain principles underlying these reforms that are common to health reform initiatives broadly, but also highlight the unique aspects of Medicaid helping to drive reforms in, perhaps, unexpected directions.

Value-Based Purchasing. CMS identifies **value-based payment** reform as essential to the government's "larger quality strategy to reform how health care is delivered and paid for." This strategy is to find alternative payment structures to **realign incentives** so that providers are paid based on the quality of care they provide, rather than the volume of services they deliver. As with most health care concepts, the idea of value-based programs is not a simple one to implement. As discussed in the prior section on Medicare reform, this is a broad concept that includes many different kinds of payment methodologies and a range of incentives, such as **shared savings**, **penalties for certain outcomes**, or more significant **shifting of risk to providers**.

But for Medicaid health plans and providers, it can be difficult to properly measure the "value" attributable to actions that the plan or provider can control. Take the example of the Hospital Readmission Reduction Program (HRRP) discussed in the Medicare section of this chapter. Penalty for readmission is only a fair and effective incentive to improve care if the readmission is likely attributable to some failure by the hospital. In that case, the hospital would be encouraged to provide better discharge planning or care coordination to improve the chances that the patient will have the necessary support to recover and maintain good health. But as explained in the Medicare section, the HRRP has failed to adequately account for socioeconomic or community-based factors, and not surprisingly, safety net hospitals that served primarily Medicaid and uninsured individuals have been hit hardest with readmission penalties.

In short, the need for this kind of adjustment reflects the growing recognition that social and behavioral factors play an outsized role in determining health, far greater than even the actual health care received. Food insecurity, unsafe and unstable, social isolation, trauma, discrimination, environmental hazards, and inadequate education are examples of the social factors that shape one's health and health care need.

Individuals with unmet social needs are more likely to suffer from certain chronic conditions, end up in the emergency room, and have difficulty keeping doctor's appointments. This is not a new discovery. In fact, the challenges created by **poverty-related determinants of health** have historically led some providers and plans to avoid the poor. But a significant shift is occurring—states, plans, and providers are beginning to use this understanding of social determinants of health to create opportunities for reform they believe will improve individual and population health, while reducing cost.

Integrating Social Services into Health Care Delivery. One type of reform with exciting potential is the **integration of social services in health care delivery**; that is, health care actors moving beyond the medical center to try to address patients' social (non-medical) needs that have a direct impact on health. An example of this is occurring in the area of nutrition. Health plans are partnering with hospitals and food delivery services to have medically-tailored meals prescribed and delivered to the homes of patients being treated for certain conditions, such as diabetes or heart disease. The goal is to help them better manage their own health and prevent the need for costly health care later. Some hospitals now "prescribe" healthy food that patients can pick up from the hospital pantry, as they would get medication from a hospital pharmacy. See, e.g., Mathew Swinburne, Katie Garfield, and Aliza R. Wasserman, Reducing Hospital Readmissions: Addressing the Impact of Food Security and Nutrition, 45 J. L. Med. & Ethics 86–89 (2017).

It is still early to determine if such innovations really can achieve the triple aim, but Medicaid plans and providers are increasingly partnering with community-based organizations and government agencies in order to help meet a broader range of social needs: medical respite housing and affordable housing placement; employment assistance and training; parenting and life skills training; and behavioral and peer support. See Addressing Social Determinants of Health via Medicaid Managed Care Contracts and Section 1115 Demonstrations, Center for Health Care Strategies (Dec. 2018). This has been accelerated by the COVID-19 pandemic, which profoundly exacerbated existing disparities in the social determinants of health, as well as health outcomes.

Medicaid ACOs. While there are various ways to achieve the reforms described above, Medicaid plans are increasingly looking to **ACOs** as a model for encouraging **greater accountability** and establishing a structure that could support **greater integration** of social services. See Section II.C.5(b) of this chapter for a discussion of ACOs. See also Center for Health Care Strategies, Medicaid Accountable Care Organizations: State Update (Feb. 2018).

Dual Eligibles. The ACA includes a number of state options and demonstration projects intended to improve the quality and coordination of care offered Medicaid recipients. These include demonstration projects for pediatric ACOs, global payment systems, integrated care around a hospitalization, and health homes for enrollees with chronic conditions. One of the options getting the most attention is care coordination for the **Dual Eligibles** through managed care. Policy makers are concerned about this population for a few reasons. First, they tend to be a high cost, high need group. In addition to the poverty-related factors mentioned above, they often have extensive health care needs, stemming from multiple illnesses and disabilities. As a group, Dual Eligibles use a much greater percentage of long-term services and supports than other beneficiaries, and they account for a disproportionate share of health spending. Second, Medicare and Medicaid have separate funding streams, different payment rates and different coverage rules, which create conflicting incentives and unnecessary or duplicative services that increase cost. Third, this fragmentation impedes coordination among different care settings, which would likely improve care and further reduce cost.

To address this misalignment of incentives, CMS launched the Financial Alignment Initiative (FAI) in 2011—the largest effort to date to test integrated payment and delivery demonstration programs, in which thirteen states participated. Preliminary results suggested mixed results in terms of care coordination goals and revealed implementation challenges. One challenge has been low enrollment according to a 2017 analysis. See David C. Grabowski et al, Passive Enrollment of Dual-Eligible Beneficiaries Into Medicare and Medicaid Managed Care Has Not Met Expectations, Health Aff. (May 2017). It showed that beneficiary enrollment was low, despite using an automatic enrollment approach that required beneficiaries to opt-out of the program. An opt-out option was necessary to comply with existing Medicare freedom of choice protections. The reasons that beneficiaries opted out of the plan were unclear but could be due in part to the tumultuous history that some Medicare beneficiaries and providers have had with managed care. Of course, as FAI study authors noted, "[i]f policy makers want to increase enrollment in integrated care programs, CMS may need to go beyond passive enrollment by making enrollment mandatory." But with lawmakers across the political spectrum touting the importance of consumer choice in health care, it may be too costly politically to eliminate it, even in service of cost and quality goals.

CRITICAL THINKING EXERCISE: CHOICE V. TRIPLE AIM

As discussed above, some Medicaid innovations have the goal of reducing cost by providing non-medical services for beneficiaries, such as care coordination and social service integration, to improve health. Yet the Financial Alignment Initiative, discussed above, demonstrates the challenge with getting large numbers of beneficiaries to enroll in these integrated plans. If the freedom of choice provision is a barrier, should this requirement be eliminated? Would this solve the problem, or might there be other barriers to meaningful beneficiary engagement that states would need to address for these reforms to be successful?

NOTES AND QUESTIONS

1. *Changes to Medicaid Provider Payment Levels Under the ACA.* The ACA contains provisions increasing payments for some Medicaid providers and cutting payments for others. It increased Medicaid payments for family and general practitioners, and pediatricians providing primary care services, to 100% of Medicare payment levels for 2013 and 2014 with a 100% federal match of increased state expenditures attributable to the requirement, but the provision was limited to two years. The law also increases to $11 billion new appropriations for community health centers, which will also serve new Medicaid recipients (as well as immigrants excluded from the exchanges). On the other hand, provider complaints of underpayment by Medicaid continue. The ACA reduces Medicaid DSH payments for the states, in part based on the assumption that the uncompensated care burden of hospitals should diminish as a higher proportion of the population is insured. Hospitals have been understandably nervous about the impact of this, especially in non-expansion states, and hospital and state officials have raised concerns that uncompensated care is not being reduced to the degree expected. Reductions have been delayed several times, and as of this writing, are expected to begin in Fiscal Year 2024. Anticipation of reductions has reinvigorated calls for reforming the DSH program, including proposals to improve transparency and more closely link allotments to direct measures of uncompensated care.

2. *CHIP Cost Sharing & Limits on Funding.* Recall that CHIP can cover children and pregnant women with incomes too high to qualify for Medicaid. CHIP also gives states greater flexibility than Medicaid to impose cost-sharing obligations, including premiums and copayments. As of January 2020, 30 states require premium or enrollment fees and 21 states require copayments for services, in part to reduce program costs, but also to make the program look less like a welfare program and to discourage "crowd out" (i.e., families dropping private insurance for CHIP coverage or staying with CHIP coverage even after an offer for private insurance becomes available). Though cost sharing might achieve these results, it also discourages participation and increases administrative complexity. See Mary Jo O'Brien, et al., State Experiences with Cost-Sharing Mechanisms in Children's Health Insurance Expansions (Commonwealth Fund, 2000). Further, although early studies seemed to show high levels of crowd-out, more recent work demonstrates that a very small proportion of CHIP enrollees—fewer than 10%—in fact had affordable private coverage that they gave up in favor of CHIP. Anna Sommers et al., Substitution of CHIP for Private Coverage: Results from a 2002 Evaluation in Ten States, 26 Health Aff. 529 (2007). See also David B. Muhlestein & Eric E. Seiber, State Variability in Children's Medicaid/CHIP

Crowd-Out Estimates, 3 Medicare & Medicaid Res. Rev. E1 (2013) (finding considerable heterogeneity in the crowd-out that occurs in each state, ranging from no crowd-out to over 18% in states with similar eligibility thresholds). Because CHIP is an important partner to Medicaid in covering children and pregnant women, it is important to understand the difference in financing and its implications for coverage. Unlike Medicaid, CHIP was not created as an entitlement for recipients, but rather as a grant-in-aid (or "block grant") program. Lack of legal entitlement, as well as the need for funding to be re-authorized periodically, creates uncertainty for those who depend on CHIP coverage.

D. PROGRAM ADMINISTRATION AND RIGHTS ENFORCEMENT: FEDERAL/STATE RELATIONSHIP

The federal-state relationship that defines the Medicaid program is dynamic and sometimes contentious. States leverage generous federal funding to achieve important state priorities with tremendous discretion and control over the structure of the health care system. But states are also subject to federal rules and oversight that states feel unduly restricts their flexibility at times. For a discussion of the federal-state relationship in quality control regulation of Medicaid providers, such as nursing homes, see Chapter 3, Section IV.

Medicaid state program design is subject to federal oversight at several levels. States must submit a **Medicaid state plan** to CMS demonstrating that their programs conform to federal law. If a state Medicaid program ceases to be in substantial compliance with federal requirements, CMS may, after a hearing, **terminate federal funding** to the state. Because this remedy is so drastic, CMS has rarely convened a hearing and has never terminated a state program. Additional statutory provisions permit HHS to **disallow reimbursement** claimed by the state where the services covered by the state are not eligible for reimbursement. These provisions are used more frequently, and occasionally result in litigation between the federal government and the states.

Particularly controversial has been the role of the federal courts in enforcing the rights that the program affords recipients and providers. As of this writing in late 2021, Medicaid is still a **federal entitlement program** in the sense that the federal Medicaid statute and regulations create at least some federal rights that are enforceable against the states. The following materials explore the contours of these rights.

WESTSIDE MOTHERS V. HAVEMAN

United States Court of Appeals, Sixth Circuit, 2002.
289 F.3d 852.

MERRITT, CIRCUIT JUDGE.

This suit filed under 42 U.S.C. § 1983 alleges that the state of Michigan has failed to provide services required by the Medicaid program. Plaintiffs, Westside Mothers, . . . allege that defendants James Haveman, director of the Michigan Department of Community Health, . . . did not provide the early and periodic screening, diagnosis, and treatment services mandated by the Medicaid Act and related laws.

* * *

At issue here is the federal requirement that participating states provide "early and periodic screening, diagnostic, and treatment services . . . for individuals who are eligible under the plan and are under the age of 21." *Id.* § 1396d(a)(4)(B)[ ]. The required services include periodic physical examinations, immunizations, laboratory tests, health education, *see* 42 U.S.C. § 1396d(r)(1), eye examinations, eyeglasses, *see id.* § 1396d(r)(2), teeth maintenance, *see id.* § 1396d(r)(3), diagnosis and treatment of hearing disorders, and hearing aids, *see id.* § 1396d(r)(4).

In 1999, plaintiffs sued the named defendants under § 1983, which creates a cause of action against any person who under color of state law deprives an individual of "any right, privileges, or immunities secured by the Constitution and laws" of the United States. 42 U.S.C. § 1983. They alleged that the defendants had refused or failed to implement the Medicaid Act, its enabling regulations and its policy requirements, by (1) refusing to provide, and not requiring [HMOs participating in the Medicaid program] to provide, the comprehensive examinations required by §§ 1396a(a)(43) and 1396d(r)(1) and 42 C.F.R. § 441.57; (2) not requiring participating HMOs to provide the necessary health care, diagnostic services, and treatment required by § 1396d(r)(5); (3) not effectively informing plaintiffs of the existence of the screening and treatment services, as required by § 1396a(a)(43); (4) failing to provide plaintiffs the transportation and scheduling help needed to take advantage of the screening and treatment services, as required by § 1396a(a)(43)(B) and 42 C.F.R. § 441.62; and (5) developing a Medicaid program which lacks the capacity to deliver to eligible children the care required by §§ 1396(a)(8), 1396a(a)(30)(A), and 1396u–2(b)(5).[ ]

Defendants moved to dismiss the plaintiffs and for dismissal of the suit. . . .

In March 2001 the district court granted defendants' motion to dismiss all remaining claims. [ ] In a detailed and far-reaching opinion, the district court held that Medicaid was only a contract between a state and the federal government, that spending-power programs such as Medicaid were not supreme law of the land, that the court lacked jurisdiction over the case because Michigan was the "real defendant and therefore possess[ed] sovereign immunity against suit," *id.*, that in this case *Ex parte Young* was unavailable to circumvent the state's sovereign immunity, and that even if it were available § 1983 does not create a cause of action available to plaintiffs to enforce the provisions in question.

This appeal followed. We reverse on all issues presented.

Analysis

A.   Medicaid Contracts and the Spending Power

Much of the district court's decision rests on its initial determinations that the Medicaid program is only a contract between the state and federal government and that laws passed by Congress pursuant to its power under the Spending Clause are not "supreme law of the land." We address these in turn.

1.   *Whether Medicaid is only a contract.*—The district court held that "the Medicaid program is a contract between Michigan and the Federal government." [ ] The program, it points out, is not mandatory; states choose whether to participate. [ ] If a state does choose to participate, Congress may then "condition receipt of federal moneys upon compliance by the recipient with federal statutory and administrative directives." [ ]

To characterize precisely the legal relationship formed between a state and the federal government when such a program is implemented, the district court turned to two Supreme Court opinions on related subjects. In *Pennhurst State School and Hosp. v. Halderman* ("*Pennhurst I*"), the Court described the Medicaid program as "much in the nature of a contract," and spoke of the " 'contract' " formed between the state and the federal government. . . .

Justice Scalia expanded on this contract analogy in his concurrence in *Blessing v. Freestone*. He maintained that the relationship was "in the nature of a contract" because:

> The state promises to provide certain services to private individuals, in exchange for which the Federal government promises to give the State funds. In contract law, when such an arrangement is made (A promises to pay B money, in exchange for which B promises to provide services to C), the person who receives the benefit of the exchange of promises between two others C is called a third-party beneficiary.

520 U.S. 329, 349, 117 S.Ct. 1353, 137 L.Ed.2d 569 (1997) (Scalia, J., concurring).

Drawing on above language, the district judge then concluded that the "Medicaid program is a contract between Michigan and the Federal government," [ ] . . . . The only significant difference between Medicaid and an ordinary contract, he asserted, is "the sovereign status of the parties," which limits the available remedies each can seek against the other. [ ]

Contrary to this narrow characterization, the Court in *Pennhurst I* makes clear that it is using the term "contract" metaphorically, to illuminate certain aspects of the relationship formed between a state and the federal government in a program such as Medicaid. It does not say that Medicaid is *only* a contract. It describes the program as "much in the nature of" a contract, and places the term "contract" in quotation marks when using it alone. [ ] It did not limit the remedies to common law contract remedies or suggest that normal federal question doctrines do not apply. . . .

Binding precedent has put the issue to rest. The Supreme Court has held that the conditions imposed by the federal government pursuant to statute upon states participating in Medicaid and similar programs are not merely contract provisions; they are federal laws. In Bennett v. Kentucky Department of Education, Kentucky argued that a federal-state grant agreement "should be viewed in the same manner as a bilateral contract." 470 U.S. 656, 669, 105 S.Ct. 1544, 84 L.Ed.2d 590 (1985). The Court rejected this approach, holding that, "[u]nlike normal contractual undertakings, federal grant programs originate in and remain governed by statutory provisions expressing the judgment of Congress concerning desirable public policy." . . . .

   2.   *Whether acts passed under the Spending Power are Supreme Law of the Land.*—After holding that Medicaid is only a contract to pay money enacted under the spending power, the district court then held that programs enacted pursuant to the Constitution's spending power are not the "supreme law of the land" and do not give rise to remedies invoked for the violation of federal statutes.[ ] Relying on its determination that Medicaid and similar programs are "contracts consensually entered into by the States with the Federal Government . . . ," the district court then reasons that they are "not statutory enactments by which States must automatically submit to federal prerogatives." [ ]. There are two ways to understand this passage. One is that the district court is merely following the logic of its previous finding, and holding that federal-state programs are not supreme law because they are only contracts. We have already rejected the line of reasoning that begins with the assumption that Medicaid is only a contract.

The district court may also be claiming that acts passed under the spending power are not supreme law because the spending power only gives Congress the power to set up these programs, not to force states to participate in them. . . . *South Dakota [v. Dole]* upholds the power of Congress to place conditions on a state's receipt of federal funds. 483 U.S.

at 211–12, 107 S.Ct. 2793. *Pennhurst I* holds that if Congress wishes to impose obligations on states that choose to participate in volitional spending power programs, it must make the obligations explicit. [ ]

* * *

The district court acknowledges that "the Supreme Court has in the past held that federal-state cooperative programs enacted under the Spending Power fall within the ambit of the Supremacy Clause." [ ] It then states that in "recent years . . . the Supreme Court has conducted a more searching analysis of the nature and extent of the Supremacy Clause," suggesting erroneously that its departure from precedent is dictated by recent Supreme Court jurisprudence. [ ] . . . The well-established principle that acts passed under Congress's spending power are supreme law has not been abandoned in recent decisions.

* * *

B.   Whether the Suit is Barred Under Sovereign Immunity

The district court next held that the plaintiffs' suit is foreclosed by doctrines of sovereign immunity because Michigan is the "real party at interest" in the suit and plaintiffs cannot invoke any of the exceptions to sovereign immunity that would allow their suit. [ ]

As explained by the Supreme Court in many cases, sovereign immunity, though partially codified in the Eleventh Amendment, is a basic feature of our federal system. [ ] . . . .

Under the doctrine developed in *Ex parte Young* and its progeny, a suit that claims that a state official's actions violate the constitution or federal law is not deemed a suit against the state, and so barred by sovereign immunity, so long as the state official is the named defendant and the relief sought is only equitable and prospective. [ ]

Of course, *Ex parte Young* is a "fiction" to the extent it sharply distinguishes between a state and an officer acting on behalf of the state, but it is a necessary fiction, required to maintain the balance of power between state and federal governments. "The availability of prospective relief of the sort awarded in *Ex parte Young* gives life to the Supremacy Clause." [ ] . . . On its surface this case fits squarely within *Ex parte Young*. Plaintiffs allege an ongoing violation of federal law, the Medicaid Act, and seek prospective equitable relief, an injunction ordering the named state officials henceforth to comply with the law.

The district court nonetheless held that *Ex parte Young* was inapplicable for four separate reasons. Two can be quickly dismissed. First, it held that plaintiffs could not invoke *Ex parte Young* because that doctrine can only be invoked to enforce federal laws that are supreme law of the land. [ ] Since we held above that spending clause enactments are supreme law of the land, they may be the basis for an *Ex parte Young* action. Second, the district court held *Ex parte Young* is unavailable because under this doctrine a court lacks "authority to compel state officers performing discretionary functions." [ ] This correctly states the holding in *Young*, but misunderstands what it means by "discretion." "An injunction to prevent [a state official] from doing that which he has no legal right to do is not an interference with the discretion of an officer." [ ] Since the plaintiffs here claim that the defendants are acting unlawfully in refusing to implement mandatory elements of Medicaid's screening and treatment program, they seek only to prevent the defendants from doing "what [they] have no legal right to do," and their suit is permitted under *Ex parte Young*.

Third, the district court asserts that *Ex parte Young* is unavailable because the state "is the real party in interest when its officers act within their lawful authority." [ ] It has two reasons for finding Michigan the real party in interest. Its first reason follows from its finding that Medicaid is a contract. If Medicaid were only a contract, then this would be a suit seeking to compel a state to specific performance of a contract. Such suits are barred under a nineteenth century Supreme Court case, *In re Ayers*, 123 U.S. 443, 8 S.Ct. 164, 31 L.Ed. 216 (1887), which held that a "claim for injunctive relief against state officials under the Contracts Clause is barred by state sovereign immunity because the state [is] the real party at interest." [ ] We have already held that Medicaid is not merely a contract, but a federal statute. This suit seeks only to compel state officials to follow federal law, and thus is not barred by *Ayers*.

The district court also says erroneously that Michigan is the real party in interest because "[t]here is no personal, unlawful behavior attributed" to the defendants that plaintiffs seek to enjoin [ ]. In their initial complaint, plaintiffs make clear that they are suing the named defendants because of "their failure to provide children in Michigan . . . with essential medical, dental, and mental health services *as required by federal law*." [ ]

Finally, the district court refused to allow plaintiffs to proceed under *Young* because of the Supreme Court's holding in *Seminole Tribe* that "[w]here Congress has prescribed a detailed remedial scheme for the enforcement against a State of a statutorily created right, a court should hesitate before casting aside those limitations and permitting an action against a state officer based upon *Ex parte Young*." [ ] The Medicaid Act allows the Secretary of Health and Human Services to reduce or cut off funding to states that do not comply with the program's requirements.[ ] This one provision, the district court held, was a detailed remedial scheme sufficient to make *Ex parte Young* unavailable. [ ]

We disagree. In *Seminole Tribe,* the Supreme Court found *Ex parte Young* was unavailable because Congress had established a "*carefully crafted and intricate* remedial scheme. . . . for the enforcement of a *particular* federal right." [ ] The scheme here, in contrast, simply allows the Secretary to reduce or cut off funds if a state's program does not meet federal requirements. *See* 42 U.S.C. § 1396c. This is not a detailed "remedial" scheme sufficient to show Congress's intent to preempt an action under *Ex parte Young.* [ ]

Plaintiffs seek only prospective injunctive relief from a federal court against state officials for those officials' alleged violations of federal law, and they may proceed under *Ex parte Young.*

C.   Whether There is a Private Right of Action Under § 1983

Section 1983 imposes liability on anyone who under color of state law deprives a person of "rights, privileges, or immunities" secured by the laws or the constitution of the United States 42 U.S.C. § 1983. The Supreme Court and this court have held that in some circumstances a provision of the Medicaid scheme can create a right privately enforceable against state officers through § 1983. *See Wilder* [ ].

In *Blessing,* the Supreme Court set down the framework for evaluating a claim that a statute creates a right privately enforceable against state officers through § 1983. [ ] A statute will be found to create an enforceable right if, after a particularized inquiry, the court concludes (1) the statutory section was intended to benefit the putative plaintiff, (2) it sets a binding obligation on a government unit, rather than merely expressing a congressional preference, and (3) the interests the plaintiff asserts are not so " 'vague and amorphous' that [their] enforcement would strain judicial competence." [ ] If these conditions are met, we presume the statute creates an enforceable right unless Congress has explicitly or implicitly foreclosed this.[ ] The district court erred when it did not apply this test to evaluate plaintiffs' claims.

We now apply this test. First, the provisions were clearly intended to benefit the putative plaintiffs, children who are eligible for the screening and treatment services. [ ] We have found no federal appellate cases to the contrary. Second, the provisions set a binding obligation on Michigan. They are couched in mandatory rather than precatory language, stating that Medicaid services "*shall* be furnished" to eligible children, 42 U.S.C. § 1396a(a)(8) (emphasis added), and that the screening and treatment provisions "*must* be provided," *id.* § 1396a(a)(10)(A). Third, the provisions are not so vague and amorphous as to defeat judicial enforcement, as the statute and regulations carefully detail the specific services to be provided. *See* 42 U.S.C. § 1396d(r). Finally, Congress did not explicitly foreclose recourse to § 1983 in this instance, nor has it established any remedial scheme sufficiently comprehensive to supplant § 1983. [ ]

Plaintiffs have a cause of action under § 1983 for alleged noncompliance with the screening and treatment provisions of the Medicaid Act.

* * *

NOTE ON GONZAGA & RIGHTS RETRENCHMENT

Since *Westside Mothers,* many battles over the nature of the Medicaid entitlement have been fought. Two important Supreme Court decisions have narrowed the scope of enforceable Medicaid rights. In 2002, the Supreme Court in Gonzaga University v. Doe, 536 U.S. 273 (2002), made it more difficult for plaintiffs to show that a right was enforceable under **§ 1983**. It held that a statute must **"be phrased in terms of the persons benefited"** with **"an unmistakable focus on the benefited class"** and that it must "confer[ ] entitlements **"sufficiently specific and definite** to qualify as enforceable rights." "Nothing short of an **unambiguously conferred right**" would permit a cause of action under § 1983.

This led courts to examine the Medicaid statute section by section to determine enforceability. Thirty-seven federal appellate court cases decided between the *Gonzaga* decision in 2002 and 2012 held thirteen provisions of the Medicaid statute enforceable under § 1983 and seven provisions unenforceable. Jane Perkins, National Health Law Program, Update on Private Enforcement of the Medicaid Act Pursuant to 42 U.S.C. § 1983 (Oct. 28, 2013). For example, several circuit courts of appeals considering the issue have held that Medicaid recipients can enforce 42 U.S.C. § 1396a(a)(8), which requires the states to provide Medicaid assistance with "reasonable promptness," and 42 U.S.C. § 1396a(a)(10)(A), which requires states to provide Medicaid to all mandatory categories. But at least one circuit has expressed skepticism about a right of private enforcement for the "reasonable promptness" provision, in light of the Supreme Court's recent decision in *Armstrong v. Exceptional Child Center, Inc.*, excerpted below. See Nasello v. Eagleson, 977 F.3d 599, 602 (7th Cir. 2020). Another example is 42 U.S.C. § 1396a(a)(23), which allows Medicaid recipients to obtain services from any "qualified" provider. Until recently, every circuit court of appeals considering the issue had held the provision to be privately enforceable. But as described further in Note 4 below, some circuits have recently disagreed.

Rights enforcement of other program design decisions have not fared as well under the *Gonzaga* test. One noteworthy example of this occurs in the context of Medicaid rate setting. As noted in the prior section, low payments create barriers to access and can result in lower quality care. Medicaid promises of coverage are not meaningful if beneficiaries have trouble finding qualified providers willing to treat them. This link between rates and access is reflected in the Equal Access provision of the Medicaid Act, 42 U.S.C.A. § 1396a(30)(A), and providers and patients have brought suits challenging state rates on the grounds that they violate federal rate-setting requirements. Plaintiffs have used different legal theories to try to **enforce these requirements**. They used § 1983 until *Gonzaga* was interpreted as foreclosing that avenue. Plaintiffs then used the Supremacy Clause, arguing that rates set using state methodology that did not comply with the Equal Access Provision of § 30(A) were preempted by federal law. The availability of private rate challenges using the Supremacy Clause had been assumed for the most part by lower federal courts for many years, which is why many were surprised when the Supreme Court decided to take up a rate-setting case that challenged this theory of rights enforcement. As you read the Court's decision below in *Armstrong v. Exceptional Child Center*, consider what it means not only for rate-setting cases, but how it may impact the enforceability of other federal Medicaid protections.

ARMSTRONG V. EXCEPTIONAL CHILD CENTER, INC.

Supreme Court of the United States, 2015.
575 U.S. 320.

JUSTICE SCALIA delivered the opinion of the Court, except as to Part IV.

We consider whether Medicaid providers can sue to enforce § (30)(A) of the Medicaid Act. 81 Stat. 911 (codified as amended at 42 U.S.C. § 1396a(a)(30)(A)).

I

Medicaid is a federal program that subsidizes the States' provision of medical services to "families with dependent children and of aged, blind, or disabled individuals, whose income and resources are insufficient to meet the costs of necessary medical services." [ ] Like other Spending Clause legislation, Medicaid offers the States a bargain: Congress provides federal funds in exchange for the States' agreement to spend them in accordance with congressionally imposed conditions.

In order to qualify for Medicaid funding, the State of Idaho adopted, and the Federal Government approved, a Medicaid "plan," [ ] which Idaho administers through its Department of Health and Welfare. Idaho's plan includes "habilitation services"—in-home care for individuals who, "but for the provision of such services . . . would require the level of care provided in a hospital or a nursing facility or intermediate care facility for the mentally retarded the cost of which could be reimbursed under the State plan," [ ]. Providers of these services are reimbursed by the Department of Health and Welfare.

Section 30(A) of the Medicaid Act requires Idaho's plan to:

"provide such methods and procedures relating to the utilization of, and the payment for, care and services available under the plan . . . as may be necessary to safeguard against unnecessary utilization of such care and services and to assure that payments are consistent with efficiency, economy, and quality of care and are sufficient to enlist enough providers so that care and services are available under the plan at least to the extent that such care and services are available to the general population in the geographic area. . . ." [ ]

Respondents are providers of habilitation services to persons covered by Idaho's Medicaid plan. They sued petitioners—two officials in Idaho's Department of Health and Welfare—in the United States District Court for the District of Idaho, claiming that Idaho violates § 30(A) by reimbursing providers of habilitation services at rates lower than § 30(A) permits. They asked the court to enjoin petitioners to increase these rates.

The District Court entered summary judgment for the providers, holding that Idaho had not set rates in a manner consistent with § 30(A). [ ] The Ninth Circuit affirmed. [ ] It said that the providers had "an implied right of action under the Supremacy Clause to seek injunctive relief against the enforcement or implementation of state legislation." [ ] We granted certiorari. [ ]

II

The Supremacy Clause, Art. VI, cl. 2, reads:

"This Constitution, and the Laws of the United States which shall be made in Pursuance thereof; and all Treaties made, or which shall be made, under the Authority of the United States, shall be the supreme Law of the Land; and the Judges in every State shall be bound thereby, any Thing in the Constitution or Laws of any State to the Contrary notwithstanding."

It is apparent that this Clause creates a rule of decision: Courts "shall" regard the "Constitution," and all laws "made in Pursuance thereof," as "the supreme Law of the Land." They must not give effect to state laws that conflict with federal laws. [ ] It is equally apparent that the Supremacy Clause is not the " 'source of any federal rights,' " [ ] and certainly does not create a cause of action. It instructs courts what to do when state and federal law clash, but is silent regarding who may enforce federal laws in court, and in what circumstances they may do so.

Hamilton wrote that the Supremacy Clause "only declares a truth, which flows immediately and necessarily from the institution of a Federal Government." [ ] And Story described the Clause as "a positive affirmance of that, which is necessarily implied." [ ] These descriptions would have been grossly inapt if the Clause were understood to give affected parties a constitutional (and hence congressionally unalterable) right to enforce federal laws against the States. And had it been understood to provide such significant private rights against the States, one would expect to find that mentioned in the preratification historical record, which contained ample discussion of the Supremacy Clause by both supporters and opponents of ratification. [ ] We are aware of no such mention, and respondents have not provided any. Its conspicuous absence militates strongly against their position.

Additionally, it is important to read the Supremacy Clause in the context of the Constitution as a whole. Article I vests Congress with broad discretion over the manner of implementing its enumerated powers, giving it authority to "make all Laws which shall be necessary and proper for carrying [them] into Execution." Art. I, § 8. . . . It is unlikely that the Constitution gave Congress such broad discretion with regard to the enactment of laws, while simultaneously limiting Congress's power over the manner of their implementation, making it impossible to leave the enforcement of federal law to federal actors. If the Supremacy Clause includes a private right of action, then the Constitution requires Congress to permit the enforcement of its laws by private actors, significantly curtailing its ability to guide the implementation of federal law. . . .

To say that the Supremacy Clause does not confer a right of action is not to diminish the significant role that courts play in assuring the supremacy of federal law. For once a case or controversy properly comes before a court, judges are bound by federal law. Thus, a court may not convict a criminal defendant of violating a state law that federal law prohibits. [ ] Similarly, a court may not hold a civil defendant liable under state law for conduct federal law requires. [ ] And, as we have long recognized, if an individual claims federal law immunizes him from state regulation, the court may issue an injunction upon finding the state regulatory actions preempted. [ ]

Respondents contend that our preemption jurisprudence—specifically, the fact that we have regularly considered whether to enjoin the enforcement of state laws that are alleged to violate federal law— demonstrates that the Supremacy Clause creates a cause of action for its violation. They are incorrect. . . . What our cases demonstrate is that, "in a proper case, relief may be given in a court of equity . . . to prevent an injurious act by a public officer." [ ] The ability to sue to enjoin unconstitutional actions by state and federal officers is the creation of courts of equity, and reflects a long history of judicial review of illegal executive action, tracing back to England. [ ] It is a judge-made remedy, and we have never held or even suggested that, in its application to state officers, it rests upon an implied right of action contained in the Supremacy Clause. That is because, as even the dissent implicitly acknowledges, [ ] it does not. The Ninth Circuit erred in holding otherwise.

III

We turn next to respondents' contention that, quite apart from any cause of action conferred by the Supremacy Clause, this suit can proceed against Idaho in equity.

The power of federal courts of equity to enjoin unlawful executive action is subject to express and implied statutory limitations. [ ] " 'Courts of equity can no more disregard statutory and constitutional requirements and provisions than can courts of law.' " [ ] In our view the Medicaid Act implicitly precludes private enforcement of § 30(A), and respondents cannot, by invoking our equitable powers, circumvent Congress's exclusion of private enforcement. [ ]

Two aspects of § 30(A) establish Congress's "intent to foreclose" equitable relief. [ ] First, the sole remedy Congress provided for a State's failure to comply with Medicaid's requirements—for the State's "breach" of the Spending Clause contract—is the withholding of Medicaid funds by the Secretary of Health and Human Services. [ ] . . . .

The provision for the Secretary's enforcement by withholding funds might not, by itself, preclude the availability of equitable relief. [ ] But it does so when combined with the judicially unadministrable nature of § 30(A)'s text. It is difficult to imagine a requirement broader and less specific than § 30(A)'s mandate that state plans provide for payments that are "consistent with efficiency, economy, and quality of care," all the while "safeguard[ing] against unnecessary utilization of . . . care and services." Explicitly conferring enforcement of this judgment-laden standard upon the Secretary alone establishes, we think, that Congress "wanted to make the agency remedy that it provided exclusive," thereby achieving "the expertise, uniformity, widespread consultation, and resulting administrative guidance that can accompany agency decisionmaking," and avoiding "the comparative risk of inconsistent interpretations and misincentives that can arise out of an occasional inappropriate application of the statute in a private action." [ ] The sheer complexity associated with enforcing § 30(A), coupled with the express provision of an administrative remedy, [ ] shows that the Medicaid Act precludes private enforcement of § 30(A) in the courts.

The dissent agrees with us that the Supremacy Clause does not provide an implied right of action, and that Congress may displace the equitable relief that is traditionally available to enforce federal law. It disagrees only with our conclusion that such displacement has occurred here.

The dissent insists that, "because Congress is undoubtedly aware of the federal courts' long-established practice of enjoining preempted state action, it should generally be presumed to contemplate such enforcement unless it affirmatively manifests a contrary intent." [ ] But a "long-established practice" does not justify a rule that denies statutory text its fairest reading. Section 30(A), fairly read in the context of the Medicaid Act, "display[s] a[n] intent to foreclose" the availability of equitable relief. [ ] We have no warrant to revise Congress's scheme simply because it did not "affirmatively" preclude the availability of a judge-made action at equity. [ ]

* * *

Finally, the dissent speaks as though we leave these plaintiffs with no resort. That is not the case. Their relief must be sought initially through the Secretary rather than through the courts. The dissent's complaint that the sanction available to the Secretary (the cut-off of funding) is too massive to be a realistic source of relief seems to us mistaken. We doubt that the Secretary's notice to a State that its compensation scheme is inadequate will be ignored.

IV

[SCALIA, J., joined by ROBERTS, C.J., and THOMAS and ALITO, J.J.]

The last possible source of a cause of action for respondents is the Medicaid Act itself. They do not claim that, and rightly so. Section 30(A) lacks the sort of rights-creating language needed to imply a private right of action. [ ] It is phrased as a directive to the federal agency charged with approving state Medicaid plans, not as a conferral of the right to sue upon the beneficiaries of the State's decision to participate in Medicaid. The Act says that the "Secretary shall approve any plan which fulfills the conditions specified in subsection (a)," the subsection that includes § 30(A). [ ] We have held that such language "reveals no congressional intent to create a private right of action." [ ] And again, the explicitly conferred means of enforcing compliance with § 30(A) by the Secretary's withholding funding, [ ] suggests that other means of enforcement are precluded [ ].

Spending Clause legislation like Medicaid "is much in the nature of a contract." The notion that respondents have a right to sue derives, perhaps, from the fact that they are beneficiaries of the federal-state Medicaid agreement, and that intended beneficiaries, in modern times at least, can sue to enforce the obligations of private contracting parties. [ ] We doubt, to begin with, that providers are intended beneficiaries (as opposed to mere incidental beneficiaries) of the Medicaid agreement, which was concluded for the benefit of the infirm whom the providers were to serve, rather than for the benefit of the providers themselves. [ ] More fundamentally, however, the modern jurisprudence permitting intended beneficiaries to sue does not generally apply to contracts between a private party and the government, [ ] much less to contracts between two governments. Our precedents establish that a private right of action under federal law is not created by mere implication, but must be "unambiguously conferred," [ ]. Nothing in the Medicaid Act suggests that Congress meant to change that for the commitments made under § 30(A).

* * *

The judgment of the Ninth Circuit Court of Appeals is reversed.

It is so ordered.

* * *

JUSTICE SOTOMAYOR, with whom JUSTICE KENNEDY, JUSTICE GINSBURG, and JUSTICE KAGAN join, dissenting.

Suits in federal court to restrain state officials from executing laws that assertedly conflict with the Constitution or with a federal statute are not novel. To the contrary, this Court has adjudicated such requests for equitable relief since the early days of the Republic. Nevertheless, today the Court holds that Congress has foreclosed private parties from invoking the equitable powers of the federal courts to require States to comply with § 30(A) of the Medicaid Act, 42 U.S.C. § 1396a(a)(30)(A). It does so without pointing to the sort of detailed remedial scheme we have previously deemed necessary to establish congressional intent to preclude resort to equity. Instead, the Court relies on Congress' provision for agency enforcement of § 30(A)—an enforcement mechanism of the sort we have already definitively determined not to foreclose private actions—and on the mere fact that § 30(A) contains relatively broad language. As I cannot agree that these statutory provisions demonstrate the requisite congressional intent to restrict the equitable authority of the federal courts, I respectfully dissent.

Most important for purposes of this case is not the mere existence of this equitable authority, but the fact that it is exceedingly well established—supported, as the Court puts it, by a "long history." [ ] Congress may, if it so chooses, either expressly or implicitly preclude Ex parte Young enforcement actions with respect to a particular statute or category of lawsuit. [ ] But because Congress is undoubtedly aware of the federal courts' long-established practice of enjoining preempted state action, it should generally be presumed to contemplate such enforcement unless it affirmatively manifests a contrary intent. "Unless a statute in so many words, or by a necessary and inescapable inference, restricts the court's jurisdiction in equity, the full scope of that jurisdiction is to be recognized and applied." [ ] In this respect, equitable preemption actions differ from suits brought by plaintiffs invoking 42 U.S.C. § 1983 or an implied right of action to enforce a federal statute. Suits for "redress designed to halt or prevent the constitutional violation rather than the award of money damages" seek "traditional forms of relief." [ ]

By contrast, a plaintiff invoking § 1983 or an implied statutory cause of action may seek a variety of remedies—including damages—from a potentially broad range of parties. Rather than simply pointing to background equitable principles authorizing the action that Congress presumably has not overridden, such a plaintiff must demonstrate specific congressional intent to create a statutory right to these remedies. . . . For these reasons, the principles that we have developed to determine whether a statute creates an implied right of action, or is enforceable through § 1983, are not transferable to the Ex parte Young context.

* * *

. . . . The Court identifies only a single prior decision—*Seminole Tribe*—in which we have ever discerned such congressional intent to foreclose equitable enforcement of a statutory mandate. [In that case, we observed that Congress had created a] carefully crafted and intricate remedial scheme . . . . and we concluded that Congress must have intended this procedural route to be the exclusive means of enforcing [the statute].

What is the equivalent "carefully crafted and intricate remedial scheme" for enforcement of § 30(A)? The Court relies on two aspects of the Medicaid Act, but, whether considered separately or in combination, neither suffices.

First, the Court cites 42 U.S.C. § 1396c, which authorizes the Secretary of Health and Human Services (HHS) to withhold federal Medicaid payments to a State in whole or in part if the Secretary determines that the State has failed to comply with the obligations set out in § 1396a, including § 30(A). [ ] But . . . § 1396c provides no specific procedure that parties actually affected by a State's violation of its statutory obligations may invoke in lieu of Ex parte Young—leaving them without any other avenue for seeking relief from the State. Nor will § 1396c always provide a particularly effective means for redressing a State's violations: If the State has violated § 30(A) by refusing to reimburse medical providers at a level "sufficient to enlist enough providers so that care and services are available" to Medicaid beneficiaries to the same extent as they are available to "the general population," agency action resulting in a reduced flow of federal funds to that State will often be self-defeating. [ ] Far from rendering § 1396c "superfluous," then, Ex parte Young actions would seem to be an anticipated and possibly necessary supplement to this limited agency-enforcement mechanism. . . .

* * *

Second, perhaps attempting to reconcile its treatment of § 1396c (2012 ed.) with this longstanding precedent, the Court focuses on the particular language of § 30(A), contending that this provision, at least, is so "judicially unadministrable" that Congress must have intended to preclude its enforcement in private suits. [ ] Admittedly, the standard set out in § 30(A) is fairly broad . . . . But mere breadth of statutory language does not require the Court to give up all hope of judicial enforcement—or, more important, to infer that Congress must have done so.

In fact, the contention that § 30(A)'s language was intended to foreclose private enforcement actions entirely is difficult to square with the provision's history. . . .

* * *

Of course, the broad scope of § 30(A)'s language is not irrelevant. But rather than compelling the conclusion that the provision is wholly unenforceable by private parties, its breadth counsels in favor of interpreting § 30(A) to provide substantial leeway to States, so that only in rare and extreme circumstances could a State actually be held to violate its mandate. The provision's scope may also often require a court to rely on HHS, which is "comparatively expert in the statute's subject matter." [ ] When the agency has made a determination with respect to what legal standard should apply, or the validity of a State's procedures for implementing its Medicaid plan, that determination should be accorded the appropriate deference. [ ] And if faced with a question that presents a special demand for agency expertise, a court might call for the views of the agency, or refer the question to the agency under the doctrine of primary jurisdiction. [ ] Finally, because the authority invoked for enforcing § 30(A) is equitable in nature, a plaintiff is not entitled to relief as of right, but only in the sound discretion of the court. [ ] Given the courts' ability to both respect States' legitimate choices and defer to the federal agency when necessary, I see no basis for presuming that Congress believed the Judiciary to be completely incapable of enforcing § 30(A).

* * *

The Court's error today has very real consequences. Previously, a State that set reimbursement rates so low that providers were unwilling to furnish a covered service for those who need it could be compelled by those affected to respect the obligation imposed by § 30(A). Now, it must suffice that a federal agency, with many programs to oversee, has authority to address such violations through the drastic and often counterproductive measure of withholding the funds that pay for such services. Because a faithful application of our precedents would have led to a contrary result, I respectfully dissent.

NOTES AND QUESTIONS

1. *Availability of Injunctive Relief.* The majority rejected the idea of a private "Supremacy Clause cause of action." Instead, it reframed the issue as whether a claim for injunctive relief from a state action that allegedly violates federal law is properly before the Court. What test did the majority establish for answering this question? On what basis do the majority and dissent disagree? After *Armstrong*, is it possible that a patient or provider could seek injunctive relief for a provision that does *not* create enforceable rights under Section 1983?

2. *Federal Regulatory Oversight of State Plan.* The majority's holding relies in part on the federal regulatory scheme established in the Medicaid Act, and particularly HHS's ability to withhold state funds as a means to enforce

state plan requirements. In a concurring opinion (not reproduced above), Justice Breyer also noted that providers can seek relief from HHS under the Administrative Procedure Act (APA), for example, by asking the agency to enforce an existing rule or promulgate a new one, and he notes that HHS can sue the State to compel compliance with federal rules. The dissent expressed concern about relying exclusively on a federal agency to enforce federal rights because of the number of programs and scope of responsibility it has. In the Medicaid rate setting context, in particular, there has been underenforcement of § 30(A) access and quality protections for decades. Regulators have been more concerned about keeping cost down, than ensuring rates were high enough to satisfy § 30(A) requirements. In 2015, CMS promulgated a final rule intended to strengthen CMS review and enforcement, by requiring more information from states to allow CMS to better monitor and ensure Medicaid access to care. Methods for Assuring Access to Covered Medicaid Services, 80 Fed. Reg. 67576 (Nov. 2, 2015). The Trump administration, however, adopted a decidedly de-regulatory stance toward health care. See Reducing Regulatory Burdens Imposed by the Patient Protection and Affordable Care Act & Improving Health Care Choices To Empower Patients, 82 Fed. Reg. 26885 (Jun. 12, 2017). Should enforcement of certain program decisions, like rate-setting, reside exclusively in HHS/CMS or should judicial oversight play an important role?

3. *APA Challenges to Federal Regulatory Approval.* The majority characterized § 30(A) requirements as "judicially unadministrable," in part, because of a concern that § 30(A) litigation would require courts to engage in rate-setting, which involves complex and competing policy judgments better suited to agency experts. In a separate concurrence, Justice Breyer emphasized this concern:

> I recognize that federal courts have long become accustomed to reviewing for reasonableness or constitutionality the rate-setting determinations made by agencies. But this is not such an action. Instead, the lower courts here . . . required the State to set rates that "approximate the cost of quality care provided efficiently and economically." [ ] To find in the law a basis for courts to engage in such direct rate-setting could set a precedent for allowing other similar actions, potentially resulting in rates set by federal judges . . . outside the ordinary channel of federal judicial review of agency decisionmaking.

While Justice Breyer's concern about courts engaging in direct rate setting is understandable, the decision by the lower court in *Armstrong* to require the state to increase its Medicaid rates is unusual. A more common scenario in § 30(A) litigation has been providers seeking to prevent states from cutting rates without *any* consideration of § 30(A) factors. In these cases, states admit to cutting provider reimbursement based solely on budgetary considerations and without any analysis of whether the new rates will satisfy federal access and quality requirements; such cases do not present the complex or judgment-laden questions the *Armstrong* majority fears. Instead, courts have viewed these as easy examples of arbitrary and capricious decisionmaking by the state officials who propose the cuts and by HHS in approving the cuts based solely on state paper assurances of compliance. In addition, the providers in these cases seek only to enjoin the proposed cuts (that is, to maintain the status quo) until the state is able to justify its proposed rate cuts according to the requisite federal factors. They are not asking courts to set and enforce new rates.

Indeed, this more common scenario appeared in another rate-setting challenge that reached the Supreme Court just three years earlier, in Douglas v. Independent Living Center of Southern California, Inc., 565 U.S. 606 (2012). At that time, the Court did not decide the question of whether private rate challenges could be brought using the Supremacy Clause; instead it reframed and remanded the case back to the Ninth Circuit. Justice Breyer wrote a brief majority opinion, joined by Justices Kennedy, Ginsburg, Sotomayor, and Kagan, suggesting that providers may not need the Supremacy Clause to challenge rates because they would likely be able to bring the challenge against the federal government under the Administrative Procedure Act (APA). 5 U.S.C. §§ 701–706. The APA requires a reviewing court to set aside agency action found to be "arbitrary, capricious, an abuse of discretion, or otherwise not in accordance with law," § 706(2)(A), but the standard of review is very deferential.

After *Armstrong*, is the APA an effective avenue for judicial relief from rates set in violation of § 30(A)? See Hoag Memorial Hospital Presbyterian v. Tom Price, Secretary of U.S. Department of Health and Human Services, 866 F.3d 1072 (2017) (finding the Secretary's approval of a 10% rate cut for outpatient services to be arbitrary and capricious under the APA because he failed to consider whether § 30(A)'s equal access requirement would be satisfied, and remanding the case back to the district court for further proceedings). Does this approach strike the appropriate balance between the important interests served by rights enforcement, on the one hand, and protection for state flexibility and deference to federal agency expertise on the other?

4. *Freedom of Choice.* The provider rate challenge cases illustrate how patients' and providers' interests in enforcing certain Medicaid provisions can overlap. Another example of this is the Medicaid's freedom of choice provision, which allows recipients to obtain services from any "qualified" provider. 42 U.S.C. § 1396a(a)(23). Based on this provision, several federal courts have struck down state laws attempting to defund Planned Parenthood clinics by prohibiting Medicaid payments to health care providers who provide abortions or are affiliated with an entity that provides abortions, even though no Medicaid funding would be used for abortions. For example, in Planned Parenthood of Indiana v. Indiana Comm'r of Health, 699 F.3d 962 (7th Cir. 2012), Planned Parenthood and two of its low-income patients challenged the state's defunding law as violating the freedom of choice provision. The Seventh Circuit held the freedom of choice provision was enforceable under § 1983:

[Section (a)(23)] mandates that all state Medicaid plans provide that "any individual eligible for medical assistance . . . may obtain such assistance from any institution, agency, community pharmacy, or person, qualified to perform the service or services required." Medicaid patients are the obvious intended beneficiaries of the statute; it states that *any* Medicaid-eligible person may obtain medical assistance from *any* institution, agency, or person qualified to perform that service. [Section (a)(23)] uses "individually focused terminology," unmistakably " 'phrased in terms of the persons benefitted,' " . . . .

Second, the right is administrable and falls comfortably within the judiciary's core interpretive competence. . . .

Finally, [Section (a)(23)] is plainly couched in mandatory terms. It says that all states "must provide" in their Medicaid plans that beneficiaries may obtain medical care from any provider qualified to perform the service. . . .

Indiana points [ ] to the HHS Secretary's authority to review state plans for compliance and withhold or curtail Medicaid funds as a means of bringing non-compliant states into line [suggesting] this feature [ ] implies that Congress foreclosed private enforcement[ ]. But the Secretary's power to shut off all or part of a state's funding is not a "comprehensive enforcement scheme," [ ] nor does the administrative-approval process for plan amendments provide an avenue for beneficiaries to vindicate their free-choice-of-provider rights.

In addition to the Seventh Circuit, the Fourth, Sixth, Ninth and Tenth Circuits have also held that the freedom of choice provision creates an enforceable right under § 1983, but the Fifth and Eighth Circuits recently went the other way. See Planned Parenthood of Greater Texas Family Planning v. Kauffman 981 F.3d 347, 364–365 (5th Cir. 2020) (describing the circuit split).

5. *Federal Regulatory Review of State Waiver Requests.* A major factor in the relationship between the federal and state governments in Medicaid has been the § 1115 demonstration project waiver program. Demonstration projects have been allowed to continue for years with little or no attempt to determine whether the project was yielding meaningful results. Section 1115 has, in effect, been used to allow states to design their own Medicaid or CHIP programs without much accountability. The ACA amended the law to address this. It requires that an application or renewal of any 1115 project that would result in an impact on eligibility, enrollment, benefits, cost-sharing, or financing with respect to a state Medicaid or CHIP program be considered through a process of public notice and comment at the State level, including public hearings, sufficient to ensure meaningful public input. The state must also submit periodic reports on the implementation of the project and HHS must periodically evaluate demonstration projects and submit an annual report to Congress regarding them. 42 U.S.C.A. § 1315(d); 42 C.F.R. § 431.408. Under the Trump administration, CMS announced steps to minimize this process, but the Biden administration is reversing course. How do we assess whether the waiver review and approval process is achieving the right balance of accountability and flexibility? See Laura Hermer, Federal/State Tensions in

Fulfilling Medicaid's Purpose, 21 Annals Health L. 615 (2012), exploring the relationship between federal and state government in Medicaid.

E. WHITHER/WITHER MEDICAID

As shown in this section, there is a great deal of variability in the Medicaid program. Indeed, it should be clear from these materials that there is not just one Medicaid program, but each state has used its flexibility to create its own Medicaid program according to its own values and priorities. The most certain prediction one can make is that states will continue to use their flexibility to innovate and adapt.

The big uncertainty confronting states, providers, and the public, however, is whether Medicaid will continue to be an open-ended, entitlement program or whether it will be scaled down to a more limited aid program, such as a block grant. In fact, a proposal to radically restructure Medicaid was introduced soon after Republicans assumed control of Congress and the presidency as a result of the November 2016 elections. In May 2017, Republicans in the House of Representatives approved the **American Health Care Act (AHCA)**, H.R. 1628, 115th Cong. (2017), as a plan to repeal and replace the ACA under the budget reconciliation process. The AHCA would have dramatically altered the Medicaid program.

First, it would have ended the ACA's Medicaid Expansion over a period of several years, increasing the number of uninsured individuals by over 20 million individuals by 2026. Congr. Budget Office, The American Health Care Act (March 13, 2017). The AHCA also proposed transitioning federal funding for Medicaid to one of two models: a per capita cap or block grant model. Under a **per capita cap model**, federal spending is limited to a set amount per Medicaid enrollee in the state, without consideration of the state's actual needs or costs. The AHCA also gave states the option to receive a block grant to fund low-income adults and children in Medicaid. Under a **block grant**, the state would receive funding equal to the per capita cost for the eligible Medicaid population times the number of enrollees in the year prior, adjusted annually by the growth in consumer price index (but not adjusted for changes in population size).

Both the block grant and per capita cap models would drastically lower the funding available for state Medicaid programs. See Loren Adler, Effects of the Medicaid Per Capita Cap included in the House-passed American Health Care Act, Center for Health Policy at Brookings (May 10, 2017). When program needs grow unexpectedly because of an economic downturn, environmental disaster, or major public health threat, a funding cap means that the state simply may not have enough money to meet these needs. Consider the short and long-term health and financial consequences of increasingly severe wildfires and storms, water crises like the one in Flint, Michigan, and of course, the COVID-19 pandemic. Although emergency

Medicaid waivers may help address some short-term needs, they do not effectively address the longer-term needs of individuals, communities, and safety net providers.

Funding caps also tend to mean that beneficiaries will not have the kind of enforceable rights to coverage they have under the current Medicaid program. For example, block grants typically have minimal federal guidelines that states must follow, and to the extent there are federal rules, they tend not to be privately enforceable. CHIP illustrates how states respond to inadequate funding in grants: by freezing enrollment or limiting services. Block grants and per capita caps have been justified on the grounds that they will give states more flexibility, but most states— even Republican-led ones—strongly oppose spending caps, because the significant funding loss would actually undermine their flexibility and power to provide care to their residents. Many states point to waivers as a better way to increase flexibility.

Any new reform proposal that emerges, no matter how significant or modest the changes, must confront fundamental questions about who should be eligible, what benefits should be covered, how care should be financed and delivered, and how the program should be administered. Such questions can be controversial because they implicate deeply held values and priorities about whom we think is deserving of help and why, how much decision-making discretion we are willing to entrust to states, what rights we believe beneficiaries should have, and what trade-offs we are willing to make to achieve a model of health care delivery and financing that can reduce cost through improved individual and population health.

CHAPTER 11

PROFESSIONAL RELATIONSHIPS IN HEALTH CARE ENTERPRISES

■ ■ ■

This chapter examines the relationships between health care providers organized in a modern health care enterprise. The first part of the chapter focuses on the hospital-physician relationship, including medical staff membership and physician employment. The legal issues stemming from efforts to limit, terminate, or deny a physician's medical staff privileges are illustrated by the collection of cases included in Section I. The first case, *Sokol,* sets out the traditional hospital staff privileges system as it begins to respond to the increased emphasis on outcomes data and individual behaviors. Next, *Mateo-Woodburn* illustrates physician-hospital contracting and delineates the interaction of contract and privileges. *Mahan* then focuses on the interaction of hospital administration and the organized medical staff, especially around issues of competition. Section II presents the challenge posed by the corporate practice of medicine doctrine for physician employment, as shown in the *Berlin* case.

The last two Sections in this chapter provide an overview of legal and policy issues that arise when health care professionals are employees. Section III addresses employment-at-will and protections for employee speech relating to quality of care, patient safety, and other policies, while Section IV addresses employment discrimination law.

I. STAFF PRIVILEGES AND HOSPITAL-PHYSICIAN CONTRACTS

Hospital Privileges and Medical Staff Membership

A physician, or other independent health care professional, may treat his or her patients in a particular hospital only if the practitioner has "privileges" at that hospital. Hospital privileges include two distinct parts: admitting privileges for the authority to admit patients to the hospital, and clinical privileges for the authority to use hospital facilities to treat patients. The scope of an individual provider's clinical privileges is often specific to the provider's specialty and qualifications, and the hospital determines the scope of services and procedures the provider may perform. The process through which privileges are awarded is called credentialing.

A separate but related concept is medical staff membership, which authorizes physicians and other types of providers to vote on medical staff issues, access the facility, and state their affiliation with the hospital. Although medical staff members often hold hospital privileges, occasionally a provider can hold one but not the other. For example, retired or emeritus providers may still be members of the medical staff, but they may no longer have clinical privileges.

If a physician is a member of the medical staff or has hospital privileges, this does *not* mean the physician is employed by the hospital. The hospital does not compensate a provider who only holds privileges or medical staff membership and who has no other relationship (such as employment, a contract for services, or a joint business venture) with the hospital. Despite the absence of remuneration between a hospital and its medical staff members, medical staff membership and hospital privileges are critically important to providers who cannot practice their profession without access to a hospital. At the same time, hospitals have growing financial incentives to manage the quality and costs of the services provided by the medical staff, with little financial or contractual leverage over medical staff members. These competing forces help explain why medical staff issues are hotly contested.

The hospital medical staff historically functioned as a relatively independent association within the hospital organization. The medical staff is subject to two separate sets of governing documents, the hospital's corporate bylaws and the medical staff bylaws. The medical staff bylaws typically set forth the rules and procedures governing the credentialing process through which physicians receive and maintain privileges, including the qualifications required and the procedural requirements to limit or terminate privileges. Only the hospital's governing board has legal authority to grant, deny, limit, or revoke privileges, but it is the hospital's medical staff that generally controls the credentialing process up to the point of the final decision. Medical staff committees review physicians applying for and holding privileges; may set substantive standards for privileges for particular services; and make a decision, reviewable by the hospital board, as to denial or granting of privileges.

There are three common scenarios under which a hospital may seek to terminate, limit, or deny hospital privileges and medical staff membership to physicians: (1) to address concerns about quality (illustrated by *Sokol*); (2) to enter into an exclusive contract to staff a department of the hospital (*Mateo-Woodburn*); and (3) to control physicians' utilization and costs or avert competition, often called "economic credentialing" (*Mahan*).

The Shift to Contract and Employment

The traditional voluntary medical staff model is undergoing significant change from two directions. First, physicians in some markets have become direct competitors with hospitals in providing certain services, such as surgery or imaging, as illustrated by the rise of physician-owned ambulatory surgery centers and freestanding imaging facilities. Second, an increasing number of physicians are becoming employed by a hospital or engaged contractually to provide hospital-based services, as described below.

Hospitals have shifted substantially toward formal contractual and employment relationships with physicians providing care within the facility. Hospitals have been rapidly acquiring physician practices, converting independent physicians to employees. As of 2020, 40% of physicians were employed by hospitals or groups owned by a hospital, up from 29% in 2012. American Medical Association, Recent Changes in Physician Practice Arrangements (2021). If contractual affiliation is added to employment, more than half of physicians are affiliated with hospitals, having grown 11 percentage points from 40% in 2016 to 51% in 2018. Michael F. Furukawa et al., Consolidation of Providers into Health Systems Increased Substantially, 2016–2018. 39(8) Health Aff. 1321 (2020).

Contracts for medical services are especially prevalent among the hospital-based practice areas, such as radiology, anesthesiology, pathology, emergency medicine, and hospitalists (who oversee or manage the in-hospital care of patients admitted to the hospital), and for some essential surgical specialties. What hospital-based specialties have in common is that these physicians do not have patients or a medical practice outside the hospital setting. Often these hospital-based providers enter into an exclusive contract with the hospital to provide all the services (e.g., radiology) that the hospital requires. Entering an exclusive contract means that clinical privileges to provide those services are no longer open to all qualified providers; thus, the process is called the "closure" of a hospital department. The termination or denial of non-contracted physicians' privileges in conjunction with the closure of a hospital department raises procedural fairness issues under state law and the medical staff bylaws, as illustrated in *Mateo-Woodburn*.

The trend toward increased physician employment by hospitals has been driven by changes in payment models, delivery system reforms, and the increased data-reporting obligations of providers and hospitals alike. Hospitals have increased management control over medical care in their facilities as changes in the payment system have put hospitals at financial risk for providing excess, wasteful, or poor-quality care. Medicare payment and delivery reforms under the ACA and MACRA (Chapter 10) increasingly link Medicare payment to hospitals and physicians to patients' health outcomes and costs. Finally, the increased requirements for data reporting on health care costs, quality, and patient satisfaction create significant administrative and technological challenges, which are more burdensome if providers are fragmented instead of centrally administered.

These forces have pushed health care systems to employ and thus manage medical staff physicians while also enticing more physicians toward employment to escape the administrative burdens of intensive data and quality reporting and increased financial risk of new payment models. As we will see in later chapters, the integration of hospitals and physicians through contract, joint venture, or employment raises a host of legal and compliance concerns, including risks to the hospital's tax-exempt status (Chapter 13), fraud and abuse liability (Chapter 14), and antitrust enforcement (Chapter 15).

SOKOL V. AKRON GENERAL MEDICAL CENTER
United States Court of Appeals for the Sixth Circuit, 1999.
173 F.3d 1026.

NORRIS, CIRCUIT JUDGE.

Plaintiff is a cardiac surgeon on staff at Akron General. The Medical Council at Akron General received information in the mid-1990's indicating that plaintiff's patients had an excessively high mortality rate. Concerned about plaintiff's performance of coronary artery bypass surgery ("CABG"), the Medical Council created the CABG Surgery Quality Task Force in 1994 to conduct a review of the entire cardiac surgery program at Akron General. The Task Force hired Michael Pine, M.D., a former practicing cardiologist who performs statistical risk assessments for evaluating the performance of hospitals. At a presentation in 1994 attended by plaintiff, Dr. Pine identified plaintiff as having a mortality rate of 12.09%, a "high risk-adjusted rate." Risk adjustment analyzes the likelihood that a particular patient or group of patients will die, as compared to another patient or group of patients. Dr. Pine stated in a summary of his findings that the predicted mortality rate for plaintiff's CABG patients was 3.65%, and plaintiff's "high mortality rate was of great concern and warrants immediate action."

James Hodsden, M.D., Chief of Staff at Akron General, requested that the Medical Council consider plaintiff for possible corrective action. Pursuant to the Medical Staff Bylaws, the Medical Council forwarded the complaint to the chairman of plaintiff's department, who appointed an Ad Hoc Investigatory Committee to review plaintiff's CABG surgery performance. The Medical Staff Bylaws require the Investigatory Committee to interview the staff member being reviewed and provide the Medical Council with a record of the interview and a report. The

Investigatory Committee met with plaintiff three times. At the first meeting, the Investigatory Committee identified the issues before it to include addressing questions raised by plaintiff about the Pine study and determining the cause of plaintiff's excessive mortality rate. At the second meeting, the Investigatory Committee examined the mortality rate of plaintiff's patients using the Society of Thoracic Surgeons ("STS") methodology. Under STS methodology, the Investigatory Committee, like Dr. Pine, determined that plaintiff's CABG risk-adjusted mortality rate was roughly three times higher than the predicted mortality rate. The Investigatory Committee discussed the results of this analysis with plaintiff at the meeting.

At the third meeting, the Investigatory Committee reviewed with plaintiff various records of his twenty-six CABG patients who died either during or around the time of surgery. The Investigatory Committee determined that one factor leading to the deaths of these patients was poor case selection, meaning plaintiff did not adequately screen out those patients for whom CABG surgery was too risky. The Investigatory Committee also found that the excessive number of deaths may have been due to insufficient myocardial protection, which led to heart attacks.

The Investigatory Committee ultimately reported to the Medical Council that plaintiff's mortality rate was excessively high and that the two principal causes for this high mortality rate were poor case selection and "improper myocardial protection." The Investigatory Committee recommended that all cases referred to plaintiff for CABG surgery undergo a separate evaluation by another cardiologist who could cancel surgery felt to be too risky. It also recommended that plaintiff not be permitted to do emergency surgery or serve on "cathlab standby" and that there be an ongoing review of his CABG patients by a committee reporting to the Medical Council. Finally, it recommended that a standardized myocardial protection protocol be developed, and that all cardiac surgeons should be required to comply with the protocol.

Plaintiff appeared before the Medical Council on November 21, 1996, and the Medical Council voted to implement the recommendations. Under the Akron General Medical Staff Bylaws, when the Medical Council makes a decision adverse to the clinical privileges of a staff member, the staff member must be given notice of the decision of the Medical Council, and the notice shall specify "what action was taken or proposed to be taken and the reasons for it." This notice allows the staff member to prepare for a hearing to review the Medical Council's decision. . . .

Plaintiff and representatives from the Medical Council appeared before an Ad Hoc Hearing Committee on March 27, 1997. Plaintiff was represented by legal counsel, submitted exhibits, and testified on his own behalf. Dr. Gardner, a member of the Investigatory Committee, testified that although the Pine study and the STS methodology tended to underestimate the actual risk in some of plaintiff's cases, the Investigatory Committee concluded that the STS risk stratification tended to corroborate the Pine analysis. When asked about the Medical Council's determination that plaintiff engaged in poor case selection, Dr. Gardner had difficulty identifying specific cases that should not have had CABG surgery, yet he stated that "in the aggregate" there was poor case selection.

The Hearing Committee recommended that the Medical Council restore all plaintiff's CABG privileges. The Medical Council rejected the recommendation of the Hearing Committee and reaffirmed its original decision. In accordance with the Bylaws, plaintiff appealed the Medical Council's determination to the Executive Committee of the Board of Trustees of Akron General. This Committee affirmed the Medical Council's decision. Plaintiff then asked the district court for injunctive relief against Akron General.

* * *

Under Ohio law, private hospitals are accorded broad discretion in determining who will enjoy medical staff privileges at their facilities, and courts should not interfere with this discretion "unless the hospital has acted in an arbitrary, capricious or unreasonable manner or, in other words, has abused its discretion." [ ] However, hospitals must provide "procedural due process ... in adopting and applying" "reasonable, nondiscriminatory criteria for the privilege of practicing" surgery in the hospital. [ ]

A.   Insufficient notice

This appeal requires us to examine the extent of the procedural protections afforded plaintiff under Ohio law. In addition to an appeals process, "[f]air procedure requires meaningful notice of adverse actions and the grounds or reasons for such actions" when a hospital makes an adverse decision regarding medical staff privileges. [ ] Akron General's Medical Staff Bylaws require that notice of an adverse decision by the Medical Council state "what action was taken or proposed to be taken and the reasons for it" and thus do not contractually provide for a quality of notice exceeding that required by Ohio law.

The President of Akron General sent plaintiff a letter notifying him of the Medical Council's initial decision. The letter refers plaintiff to the minutes of the Medical Council's meeting which set out the reasons for the Council's decision. These minutes, provided to plaintiff, indicate that the findings and recommendations of the Investigatory Committee were presented. The Investigatory Committee found that "[t]he number and percentage of deaths in Dr. Sokol's population was excessively high compared to the published national statistics and other local surgeons."

Two reasons for this high percentage were offered—poor case selection and problems with protecting against myocardial infarctions. . . .

According to the magistrate judge, the notice provided plaintiff was insufficient because [it failed] to provide Dr. Sokol with specific cases where he engaged in poor case selection and where he failed to provide appropriate myocardial protection.

The sort of notice demanded by the magistrate judge was not required by the circumstances of this case. Had Akron General restricted plaintiff's rights because the Medical Council determined that he had poor case selection or provided insufficient protections against myocardial infarctions, then perhaps specific patient charts should have been indicated, along with specific problems with each of those charts. However, Akron General had a more fundamental concern with plaintiff's performance: too many of his patients, in the aggregate, were dying, even after accounting for risk adjustment. Poor case selection and problems in preventing myocardial infarction were just two reasons suggested by the Investigatory Committee for the high mortality rate.

Plaintiff takes issue with the Pine study and the STS algorithm, claiming that they do not present an accurate picture of his performance as a surgeon because he is the "surgeon of last resort." In other words, so many of his patients die because so many of his patients are already at death's door. Perhaps plaintiff is correct about that. However, it is not for us to decide whether he has been inaccurately judged by the Investigatory Committee and the Medical Council. Instead, we are to determine whether plaintiff had sufficient notice of the charges against him to adequately present a defense before the Hearing Committee. He knew that the Medical Council's decision was based upon the results of the Pine study and the STS analysis, knew the identity of his patients and which ones had died, and had access to the autopsy reports and medical records of these patients. . . . Manifestly, he had notice and materials sufficient to demonstrate to the Hearing Committee's satisfaction that limiting his privileges was inappropriate.

It was well within Akron General's broad discretion to base its decision upon a statistical overview of a surgeon's cases. We are in no position to say that one sort of evidence of a surgeon's performance—a statistical overview—is medically or scientifically less accurate than another sort of evidence—the case-by-case study plaintiff suggests we require of Akron General.

B. Arbitrary decision

The magistrate judge also ruled that the Medical Council's decision was arbitrary. She reasoned that because Akron General did not have a fixed mortality rate by which to judge its surgeons before it limited plaintiff's privileges, it was arbitrary to take action against him based upon his mortality rate. We cannot agree. Surely, if plaintiff's mortality rate were 100%, the Medical Council would not be arbitrary in limiting his medical staff privileges, despite not having an established mortality rate. The magistrate judge's reasoning would prevent the Medical Council from instituting corrective action unless there were a preexisting standard by which to judge its staff. It is true that surgeons must be judged by "nondiscriminatory criteria." [ ] However, in this context, that means, for example, that if it came to the attention of the Medical Council that another surgeon had a mortality rate as high as plaintiff's, the latter surgeon's medical privileges would be similarly limited. . . .

On appeal, plaintiff argues that the Medical Council's decision was so wrong that it was arbitrary, capricious, or unreasonable. He points to evidence tending to show that the Medical Council's case against him was assailable. Indeed, the Hearing Committee recommended that plaintiff's full privileges be restored. But as the Ohio Supreme Court has recognized, "[t]he board of trustees of a private hospital has broad discretion in determining who shall be permitted to have staff privileges." [ ] The board of trustees will not have abused its discretion so long as its decision is supported by any evidence. Here, the Medical Council had both the Pine Study and the STS analysis. While it is conceivable that these are inaccurate measurements of plaintiff's performance, they are evidence that the hospital was entitled to rely upon, and accordingly, we are unable to say that Akron General abused its discretion in limiting plaintiff's privileges.

MERRITT, CIRCUIT JUDGE, dissenting.

* * *

The heart surgeon has been treated unfairly by his hospital. The Hearing Committee was the only group composed of experts independent of the hospital administration. . . . The Committee completely exonerated Dr. Sokol. No one has cited a single operation or a single instance in which Dr. Sokol has made a mistake, not one.

* * *

NOTES AND QUESTIONS

1. *Common Law Fundamental Fairness.* Are the public's interests well served by statutory or common law procedural protections for actions against a physician's staff privileges, or do these efforts create an obstacle to the removal of incompetent physicians? The court in *Sokol* examines the fairness of the procedures used by the hospital. The basis for this requirement is the common law doctrine of "fundamental fairness" applied to private associations generally. The common law notion of fundamental fairness should not be confused with the constitutional requirements for due process applicable to government actors, although courts often use similar language to describe

these two concepts. The requirements of fundamental fairness have been established on a case-by-case basis, and so its minimum requirements are not always clear. The majority of states supplement common law requirements by imposing specific substantive and procedural requirements by statute. See, e.g., N.Y. Public Health Law § 2801–b, which requires that the hospital provide a written statement of reasons and provides for review by the state's Public Health Council of any denial or diminution of privileges. The federal Health Care Quality Improvement Act (HCQIA), discussed below, also establishes minimum procedures for hospitals desiring HCQIA immunity.

The procedures for credentialing in public, i.e., state-run, hospitals must meet constitutional due process requirements. See, e.g., Brandner v. Providence Health & Servs., 394 P.3d 581 (Alaska 2017); Osuagwu v. Gila Reg. Med. Ctr. 850 F. Supp. 2d 1216 (D.N.M. 2012); Ripley v. Wyoming Med. Ctr., Inc. 559 F.3d 1119 (10th Cir. 2009), cert. den. 558 U.S. 879 (2009). But the physicians' property interest in their privileges at a public hospital can be waived or extinguished by the terms of the medical staff bylaws. Ramsey v. Muna, 819 F. App'x 505 (9th Cir. 2020).

2. *Substantial Evidence vs. "Any" Evidence.* In *Sokol*, the court, applying Ohio law, limited its scope of review over the merits of the hospital's decision, testing only whether the hospital's decision was arbitrary and whether there was "any evidence" supporting its decision. A few other states allow limited judicial review of the merits of staff privileges decisions, but not always using the same standard of review. For example, California allows courts to reject denial or revocation of privileges if those decisions are not supported by substantial evidence. See Ellison v. Sequoia Health Services, 183 Cal. App. 4th 1486, 108 Cal. Rptr. 3d 728 (Cal. App. 2010). But see Sadler v. Dimensions Healthcare Corp., 378 Md. 509, 836 A.2d 655 (2003) (holding that substantial evidence review is inappropriate under Maryland law). Would a substantial evidence standard change the result in *Sokol*?

3. *Compliance with Bylaws.* Only a minority of states allow substantive review of privileges decisions, whether under the arbitrariness standard applied in *Sokol* or the substantial evidence standard described in note 2. In most states, the law does not allow the courts to review the merits of privileges decisions at all. Instead, most states restrict judicial review to the question of whether the hospital followed its own bylaws; and for most of these states, the question is limited to compliance with the bylaws' procedural requirements only. See, e.g., Molleston v. River Oaks Hosp., Inc., 195 So.3d 815 (Miss. Ct. App. 2015). What policy and practical considerations support broader and narrower judicial review? Why is the staff privileges system generally considered protective of physicians when judicial review is so limited in the majority of states? Do the procedures described in *Sokol* provide any insight here?

4. *Joint Commission Standards.* The Joint Commission (a hospital accrediting body described in Chapter 3) has had extraordinary influence on credentialing procedures through its hospital accreditation standards.

Joint Commission standards for credentialing and granting of privileges include several *substantive* requirements: (1) the hospital determines it has the resources necessary to support the requested privilege; (2) the hospital collects information regarding each practitioner's current license status, training, expertise, competence and ability to perform the requested privileges; (3) the decision to grant, renew, or deny privileges is an objective, evidence-based process; (4) the organized medical staff reviews and analyzes all relevant information regarding each requesting practitioner's current licensure status, training, experience, current competence, and ability to perform the requested privilege.

The Joint Commission also prescribes *procedural* standards for credentialing decisions, including a fair hearing and appeal process for addressing adverse decisions regarding reappointment and denial, reduction, suspension, or revocation of privileges that may relate to quality of care, treatment, and services issues.

Finally, there are standards for granting temporary privileges and telemedicine privileges, including requiring the originating site of telemedicine services to be responsible for credentialing and privileging determinations for telemedicine providers. Joint Commission Standards: Medical Staff Chapter (2020).

5. *Use of Data Monitoring.* Joint Commission standards on credentialing have increased the focus on ongoing monitoring of physician quality. The standards, for example, provide for the organized medical staff to monitor and evaluate physicians' performance and address reported concerns about individual physicians. These standards accelerate the use of data such as that relied upon in *Sokol*. See also Lo v. Provena Covenant Med. Ctr., 796 N.E.2d 607 (2003), considering a privileges action based on a review of patient data revealing that a physician's mortality and return-to-surgery rates were about double the national average. Greater capacity for aggregating and analyzing patient data and an emphasis on outcomes for payment may make such actions more common. See, e.g., Barry R. Furrow, Searching for Adverse Events: Big Data and Beyond, 27 Annals Health L. 149 (2018), arguing that data mining and analytics enhance hospitals' ability to spot adverse events and patient safety issues, and that hospitals may be negligent if they fail to use available data effectively to address adverse events.

6. *Waiver.* Hospitals can reduce the risk of litigation over credentialing decisions considerably by including clauses in their physician contracts or medical staff bylaws in which physicians waive their right to sue over adverse actions. See, e.g., Sadler v. Dimensions Healthcare Corp., 378 Md. 509, 836 A.2d 655 (2003), suggesting that hospitals pursue this option, and Sternberg v. Nanticoke Mem. Hosp., 2012 WL 5830150 (Del Super.), for an example of language waiving procedural rights and obligating physicians to pay the hospital's attorney's fees. See also the discussion of "clean sweep" clauses in the notes following *Mateo-Woodburn*, below.

7. *Fundamental Fairness and Managed Care Organizations.* The common law doctrine of fundamental fairness has also been applied to the termination of physicians as participating or preferred providers by a managed care organization. In Potvin v. Metropolitan Life Ins. Co., 997 P.2d 1153 (Cal. 2000), the California Supreme Court held that managed care organizations must comply with the common law doctrine of fair procedure before removing physicians from their preferred provider lists. The court noted that the obligation to afford providers fair procedures "arises only when the insurer possesses power so substantial that the removal significantly impairs the ability of an ordinary, competent physician to practice medicine or a medical specialty in a particular geographic area, thereby affecting an important, substantial economic interest." Id. at 1071.

Accountable care organizations, described in Chapters 10 and 12, are also likely to exert control over utilization of particular medical services, very much as managed care organizations have. Should physicians or nurse practitioners who participate in an accountable care organization have any procedural or substantive rights regarding termination?

NOTE: THE HEALTH CARE QUALITY IMPROVEMENT ACT (HCQIA)

The federal Health Care Quality Improvement Act (HCQIA), 42 U.S.C. § 11101, affords hospitals immunity from damages actions over their credentialing decisions, except for civil rights claims. (See Section IV on discrimination statutes, below.) The HCQIA provides immunity to hospitals (and other entities) if their credentialing decisions meet substantive and procedural statutory standards. Several states have also enacted local variations on the HCQIA, as the Act does not override or preempt state laws which provide "incentives, immunities, or protection for those engaged in a professional review action that is in addition [to] or greater than that provided" in the federal statute. See, e.g., DeKalb Med. Ctr. v. Obekpa, 728 S.E.2d 265 (Ga. App. 2012), applying a state statute that reaches beyond the HCQIA in providing immunity from equitable relief.

The HCQIA creates a presumption that the credentialing decision (termed a "professional review action" in the Act) complies with the standards of the Act. To rebut this presumption, the plaintiff must prove by a preponderance of the evidence that the health care entity: (1) did not act in the reasonable belief that the action was in furtherance of quality health care; (2) did not make a reasonable effort to obtain the facts of the matter; (3) did not afford the physician adequate notice and hearing procedures and such other procedures required by fairness under the circumstances; or (4) did not act in the reasonable belief that the action was warranted by the facts known after such reasonable effort to determine the facts and after meeting the Act's procedural requirements. For a case that clearly lays out the plaintiff's burden, see Van v. Anderson, 199 F. Supp. 2d 550 (N.D. Tex. 2002).

In testing these "four reasonables," courts use an objective standard of reasonableness. Neither the ultimate accuracy of the hospital's conclusions nor direct evidence of improper motive or bad faith is considered relevant to the objective reasonableness of the hospital's actions. See Sherr v. HealthEast Care Sys., 416 F. Supp. 3d 823 (D. Minn. 2019), aff'd, 999 F.3d 589 (8th Cir. 2021); Austin v. McNamara, 979 F.2d 728 (9th Cir. 1992), first establishing the objective standard so that immunity would be decided at an early stage of litigation.

The courts have been generous with HCQIA immunity, ordinarily resolving cases through summary judgment in favor of the hospital. In fact, physicians only rarely succeed in overturning the rebuttable presumption of immunity. But see Granger v. Christus Health Ctr. Louisiana, 144 So. 3d 736 (La. 2013), for a notable exception resulting in a damages award of nearly $3,000,000. Although evidence of improper motive or bad faith is not relevant under the HCQIA, such evidence may be used to prove violation of civil rights or discrimination laws. See Zawislak v. Mem. Hermann Hosp. System, 2011 WL 5082422 (S.D. Tex. 2011), denying the hospital's motion to dismiss where the physician produced facts supportive of a claim of retaliation. For a critique of HCQIA's protections for participants in the hospital peer-review process, see Michael D. Benson et. al., Hospital Quality Improvement: Are Peer Review Immunity, Privilege, and Confidentiality in the Public Interest?, 11 Nw. J. L. & Soc. Pol'y 1 (2016).

The HCQIA has deterred physicians from bringing suits over credentialing decisions for two reasons. First, hospitals have generally been successful in claiming HCQIA immunity for actions based on a physician's disruptive conduct even without evidence of substandard medical treatment or specific harm to patients. See, e.g., Tshibaka v. Sernulka, 673 Fed. App'x 272 (4th Cir. 2016), in which the hospital was granted immunity after terminating a physician's privileges for alleged sexual harassment; Sternberg v. Nanticoke Mem. Hosp., 15 A.3d 1225 (Del. 2011), in which the court held that the HCQIA provided immunity for summary suspension of a physician engaging repeatedly in verbally aggressive behavior against staff, even when patients were not in imminent danger. Second, the HCQIA provides that physicians who bring frivolous or bad faith suits challenging credentialing decisions may be ordered to pay defendant's attorney's fees and costs. See, e.g., Cohlmia v. St. John Med. Ctr., 906 F. Supp. 2d 1188 (N.D. Okla. 2012), awarding over $700,000 in attorneys' fees to hospital. But see Sternberg, above, denying attorney's fees to hospital defendant.

The HCQIA also established the National Practitioner Data Bank (NPDB). 42 U.S.C. §§ 11131–11135; 45 C.F.R. §§ 60.1–60.22. (See Note on the NPDB in Chapter 2.) To earn HCQIA immunity, hospitals must report certain adverse credentialing decisions to the NPDB and must check NPDB records on the individual physician when considering an application for privileges, and every two years for physicians who hold privileges. In addition, medical malpractice payouts must be reported to the NPDB. The HCQIA provides hospitals limited immunity for their reports to the NPDB, and the physician bears the burden of proving that the hospital did not meet statutory standards in its reporting. See, e.g., In Murphy v. Goss, 103 F. Supp. 3d 1234 (D. Or. 2015), noting that HCQIA provides immunity to entities for reports to the NPDB unless the entity knew of the falsity of the information contained in the report.

Several observers have criticized the NPDB for creating a "blacklist" for practitioners with consequences so harsh that it has generated widespread underreporting and evasion rather than disclosure. Created to protect patients and institutions from negligent and unsafe providers, the NPDB also creates incentives for providers to avoid settling malpractice claims, compensating injured patients, and participating in hospitals' programs of disclosure, apology, and resolution—all to evade the NPDB. Institutions may avoid reporting to the NPDB by pressuring the physician to "voluntarily" resign or take a leave of absence. See, e.g., Hooper v. Columbus Reg'l Healthcare System, 956 So. 2d 1135 (Ala. 2006); *Sternberg*, above (describing use of leave-of-absence instead of precautionary suspension to avoid NPDB reporting). These critiques of the NPDB and questions as to its constitutionality are detailed in Haavi Morreim, Moral Hazard: The Pros and Cons of Avoiding Data Bank Reports, 4 Drexel L. Rev. 265 (2011); Katharine A. Van Tassel, Blacklisted: The Constitutionality of the Federal System for Publishing Reports of "Bad" Doctors in the National Practitioner Data Bank, 33 Cardozo L. Rev. 2031 (2012); and Gabriel H. Teninbaum, Reforming the National Practitioner Data Bank to Promote Fair Med-Mal Outcomes, 5 Wm. & Mary Pol'y Rev. 83 (2013).

MATEO-WOODBURN V. FRESNO COMMUNITY HOSPITAL

Court of Appeal, Fifth District, 1990.
221 Cal. App. 3d 1169, 270 Cal. Rptr. 894.

BROWN, J.

* * *

Prior to August 1, 1985, and as early as 1970, the FCH department of anesthesiology operated as an open staff. The department was composed of anesthesiologists who were independently competing entrepreneurs with medical staff privileges in anesthesiology. Collectively, the anesthesiologists were responsible for scheduling themselves for the coverage of regularly scheduled, urgent and emergency surgeries.

[E]ach anesthesiologist was rotated, on a daily basis, through a first-pick, second-pick, etc., sequence whereby each anesthesiologist chose a particular operating room for that particular date. Usually no work was available for one or more anesthesiologists at the end of the rotation schedule. Once an anesthesiologist rotated through first-pick, he or she went to the end of the line. In scheduling themselves, the anesthesiologists established a system that permitted each anesthesiologist on a rotating basis to have the "pick" of the cases. This usually resulted in the "first-pick" physician taking what appeared to be the most lucrative cases available for that day.

The rotation system encouraged many inherent and chronic vices. For example, even though members of the department varied in their individual abilities, interests, skills, qualifications and experience, often "first-picks" were more consistent with economic advantage than with the individual abilities of the physician exercising his or her "first-pick" option. At times, anesthesiologists refused to provide care for government subsidized patients, allegedly due to economic motivations.

The department chairman had the authority to suggest to fellow physicians that they only take cases for which they were well qualified. However, the chairman was powerless to override the rotation system in order to enforce these recommendations.

Under the open-staff rotation system, anesthesiologists rotated into an "on call" position and handled emergencies arising during off hours. This led to situations where the "on-call" anesthesiologist was not qualified to handle a particular emergency and no formal mechanism was in place to ensure that alternative qualified anesthesiologists would become promptly available when needed. . . .

* * *

These chronic defects in the system led to delays in scheduling urgent cases because the first call anesthesiologists in charge of such scheduling at times refused to speak to each other. Often, anesthesiologists, without informing the nursing staff, left the hospital or made rounds while one or more of their patients were in post-anesthesia recovery. This situation caused delays as the nurses searched for the missing anesthesiologist.

The trial court found these conditions resulted in breaches of professional efficiency, severely affected the morale of the department and support staff, and impaired the safety and health of the patients. As a result of these conditions, the medical staff (not the board of trustees) initiated action resulting ultimately in the change from an "open" to a "closed" system. We recite the highlights of the processes through which this change took place.

* * *

[Mr.] Helzer, President and Chief Executive Officer of FCH, established an "Anesthesia Task Force" to study the proposed closure. In a subsequent memo to Helzer, dated April 6, 1984, the task force indicated it had considered four alternative methods of dealing with problems in the department of anesthesiology: (1) continuation of the status quo, i.e., independent practitioners with elected department chairman, (2) competitive groups of anesthesiologists with an elected department chairman, (3) an appointed director of anesthesia with independent practitioners and (4) an appointed director with subcontracted anesthesiologists, i.e., a closed staff.

The memo noted that under the third alternative—a director with independent practitioners—the director would have no power to determine who would work in the department of anesthesiology. "Any restriction or disciplinary action recommended by the director would need to go through the usual hospital staff procedure, which can be protracted." It was also noted in the memo that a director with subcontracted practitioners "would have the ability to direct their activities without following usual hospital staff procedures." The committee recommended a director with subcontracted practitioners.

[The board accepted the committee's recommendation and formed a search committee to recruit a director for the department.]

* * *

Mateo-Woodburn was offered the position of interim director on June 13, 1984, which position she accepted. Mateo-Woodburn was interviewed for the position of director on September 25, 1984. Hass was interviewed for the position on March 7, 1985.

At a special meeting of the board of trustees held on April 10, 1985, the anesthesia search committee recommended to the board that Hass be hired as director of the department of anesthesiology, and the recommendation was accepted by the board.

At the same April 10 meeting, the board authorized its executive committee to close the department of anesthesiology. On the same day, the executive committee met and ordered the department closed.

* * *

An agreement between FCH and the Hass corporation was entered into on June 7, 1985. On June 18, 1985, Helzer sent a letter to all members of the department of anesthesiology which states in relevant part:

* * *

"The Board of Trustees has now entered into an agreement with William H. Hass, M.D., a professional corporation, to provide anesthesiology services for all hospital patients effective July 1, 1985. The corporation will operate the Department of Anesthesia under the direction of a Medical Director who will schedule and assign all medical personnel. The corporation has appointed Dr. Hass as Medical Director, and the hospital has concurred with the appointment. The agreement grants to the corporation the exclusive right to provide anesthesia services to all hospital patients at all times."

"To provide the services called for by the agreement, it is contemplated that the Hass Corporation will enter into contractual arrangements with individual physician associates who must obtain Medical Staff membership and privileges as required by the staff bylaws. The negotiations with such associates are presently ongoing, and the hospital does not participate in them."

"Effective August 1, 1985, if you have not entered into an approved contractual agreement, with the Hass Corporation, you will not be permitted to engage in direct patient anesthesia care in this hospital. However, at your option, you may retain your staff membership and may render professional evaluation and assessment of a patient's medical condition at the express request of the attending physician."

The contract between the Hass corporation and FCH provided that the corporation was the exclusive provider of clinical anesthesiology services at the hospital; the corporation was required to provide an adequate number of qualified physicians for this purpose; physicians were to meet specific qualifications of licensure, medical staff membership and clinical privileges at FCH, and to have obtained at least board eligibility in anesthesiology; and the hospital had the right to review and approve the form of any contract between the corporation and any physician-associate prior to its execution.

Subject to the terms of the master contract between the Hass corporation and FCH, the corporation had the authority to select physicians with whom it would contract on terms chosen by the corporation subject to the approval of FCH. The contract offered to the anesthesiologists, among many other details, required that a contracting physician be a member of the hospital staff and be board certified or board eligible. The Hass corporation was contractually responsible for all scheduling, billing and collections. Under the contract, the corporation was to pay the contracting physician in accordance with a standard fee arrangement. The contracting physician was required to limit his or her professional practice to FCH except as otherwise approved by the FCH board of trustees.

[The contract also provided:] ". . . Provider shall not be entitled to any of the hearing rights provided in the Medical Staff Bylaws of the Hospital and Provider hereby waives any such hearing rights that Provider may have. However, the termination of this Agreement shall not affect Provider's Medical Staff membership or clinical privileges at the Hospital other than the privilege to provide anesthesiology services at the Hospital."

Seven of the thirteen anesthesiologists on rotation during July 1985 signed the contract. Of the six plaintiffs in this case, five refused to sign the contract offered to them. The sixth plaintiff, Dr. Woodburn, was not offered a contract but testified that he would not have signed it, had one been offered.

* * *

Some of the reasons given for refusal to sign the contract were: (1) the contract required the plaintiffs to give up their vested and fundamental rights to practice at FCH; (2) the 60-day termination clause contained no provisions for due process review; (3) the contract failed to specify amounts to be taken out of pooled income for administrative costs; (4) the contract required plaintiffs to change medical malpractice carriers; (5) the contract required plaintiffs to obtain permission to practice any place other than FCH; (6) the contract imposed an unreasonable control over plaintiffs' financial and professional lives; (7) the contract failed to provide tenure of employment. The Hass corporation refused to negotiate any of the terms of the contract with plaintiffs.

* * *

. . . Numerous cases recognize that the governing body of a hospital, private or public, may make a rational policy decision or adopt a rule of general application to the effect that a department under its jurisdiction shall be operated by the hospital itself through a contractual arrangement with one or more doctors to the exclusion of all other members of the medical staff except those who may be hired by the contracting doctor or doctors. . . .

* * *

[The position] of a staff doctor in an adjudicatory one-on-one setting, wherein the doctor's professional or ethical qualifications for staff privileges is in question, take[s] on a different quality and character when considered in light of a rational, justified policy decision by a hospital to reorganize the method of delivery of certain medical services, even though the structural change results in the exclusion of certain doctors from the operating rooms. If the justification is sufficient, the doctor's vested rights must give way to public and patient interest in improving the quality of medical services.

It is also noted, where a doctor loses or does not attain staff privileges because of professional inadequacy or misconduct, the professional reputation of that doctor is at stake. In that circumstance, his or her ability to become a member of the staff at other hospitals is severely impaired. On the other hand, a doctor's elimination by reason of a departmental reorganization and his failure to sign a contract does not reflect upon the doctor's professional qualifications and should not affect his opportunities to obtain other employment. The trial court correctly found the decision to close the department of anesthesiology and contract with Hass did not reflect upon the character, competency or qualifications of any particular anesthesiologist.

* * *

[I]f the hospital's policy decision to make the change is lawful, and we hold it is, then the terms of the contracts offered to the doctors was part of the administrative decision and will not be interfered with by this court unless those terms bear no rational relationship to the objects to be accomplished, i.e., if they are substantially irrational or they illegally discriminate among the various doctors.

Given the conditions existing under the open rotation method of delivering anesthesia services, including among others the lack of control of scheduling and the absence of proper discipline, we cannot say the terms of the contract were irrational, unreasonable or failed to bear a proper relationship to the object of correcting those conditions. Considered in this light, the terms are not arbitrary, capricious or irrational.

* * *

As to the contract provision which required waiver of hearing rights set forth in the staff bylaws, . . . those rights do not exist under the circumstances of a quasi-legislative reorganization of a department by the board of trustees. This quasi-legislative situation is to be distinguished from a quasi-judicial proceeding against an individual doctor grounded on unethical or unprofessional conduct or incompetency. Accordingly, the waiver did not further detract from or diminish plaintiffs' rights.

* * *

Plaintiffs contend the department of anesthesiology could not be reorganized without amending the bylaws of the medical staff in accordance with the procedure for amendment set forth therein. Closely allied to this argument is the assertion the hospital unlawfully delegated to Hass the medical staff's authority to make staff appointments.

. . . The hospital's action did not change the manner or procedure by which the medical staff passes upon the qualifications, competency or skills of particular doctors in accordance with medical staff bylaws. . . . In fact, plaintiffs remain members of the staff and the contract requires contracting anesthesiologists to be members of the staff. Moreover, it is clear the medical staff does not appoint medical staff members—it makes recommendations to the board of trustees who then makes the final medical staff membership decision. Hass was never given authority to appoint physicians to medical staff and never did so. Hass was merely hired to provide anesthesiology services to the hospital. His decision to contract with various anesthesiologists in order to provide those services was irrelevant to medical staff appointments except that all persons contracting with Hass were required to qualify as members of the medical staff.

We conclude the trial court's determination that the defendants' "actions were proper under the circumstance and that plaintiffs' Medical Staff privileges were not unlawfully terminated, modified or curtailed" is fully supported by the evidence and is legally correct.

NOTES AND QUESTIONS

1. *Enforceability of "Clean Sweep" Provisions. Mateo-Woodburn* considers two issues related to exclusive contracting: (1) the procedural rights to terminate the privileges of the physicians who held privileges prior to the institution of the exclusive contract; and (2) the termination provision in the exclusive contract itself. Regarding the latter, exclusive contracts with physician groups often contain what is known as a "clean sweep" provision, which provides that termination of the contract will result automatically in termination of staff privileges without benefit of the procedures in the medical staff bylaws. Why is a clean sweep provision necessary in an exclusive contract? Like the court in *Mateo-Woodburn*, most jurisdictions have upheld and enforced contractual clean sweep provisions. See, e.g., Van Valkenburg v. Paracelsus Healthcare Corp., 606 N.W.2d 908 (N.D. 2000); Madsen v. Audrain Health Care, 297 F.3d 694 (8th Cir. 2002); Stears v. Sheridan County Memorial Hosp. Bd. of Trustees, 491 F.3d 1160 (10th Cir. 2007). However, a minority of jurisdictions have found clean sweep provisions unenforceable unless they are expressly permitted by the medical staff bylaws. See, e.g., Satilla Health Services, Inc. v. Bell, 280 Ga. App. 123, 633 S.E.2d 575 (2006), holding that a clean sweep provision was not enforceable because the hospital did not reserve the right to automatic termination in the medical staff bylaws or in contracts with the individual physicians.

2. *Medical Staff Membership vs. Clinical Privileges.* Some court opinions have separated medical staff membership from clinical privileges with the result that hospitals are not required to use procedures for revocation of staff membership when they have revoked or limited only the physician's clinical privileges, which allow the physician to admit or treat patients. See, e.g., Plummer v. Community Gen'l Hosp. of Thomasville, Inc., 155 N.C. App. 574, 573 S.E.2d 596 (2002); Ripley v. Wyoming Med. Ctr., Inc., 2008 WL 5875551 (D. Wyo. 2008). What is the rationale for this approach?

3. *Public Hospitals and Due Process Requirements.* Public hospitals may be required to maintain an open staff and thus be precluded from entering into an exclusive contract, because closing the staff may implicate procedural due process concerns under the 14th Amendment of the Constitution. See Shaw v. Hosp. Auth. of Cobb County, 614 F.2d 946 (5th Cir. 1980). In addition, some states have extended the same restriction on exclusive contracting to hospitals that are considered to be "quasi-public." See, e.g., Kessel v. Monongalia County Gen'l Hosp., 215 W. Va. 609, 600 S.E.2d 321 (2004). But see Gaalla v. Brown, 2012 WL 512687 (5th Cir. 2012), holding that a public hospital's entering into

an exclusive contract for cardiology services and terminating existing privileges of an excluded physician did not violate procedural due process.

4. *Economic Credentialing.* Hospitals may also seek to make credentialing decisions to control costs or for other economic reasons by limiting or denying privileges to physicians on the basis of their utilization of or referrals to the facility or their holding staff privileges at or business interests in competitors. "Economic credentialing," a term that the AMA coined to describe certain standards for determining medical staff status, occurs when a hospital makes privileging decisions based on financial factors unrelated to quality. Physicians and others may be concerned that economic credentialing may threaten patients with inadequate diagnostic or medical care or violate fraud and abuse laws like the Anti-Kickback Statute (Chapter 14).

Conflicts over financial considerations in credentialing have intensified as hospitals use their credentialing process to exclude physicians who have business interests, such as ambulatory surgical centers, which compete directly with those of the hospital itself. See *Mahan*, below. For an excellent analysis of economic credentialing, see John D. Blum, Beyond the ByLaws: Hospital-Physician Relationships, Economics, and Conflicting Agendas, 53 Buff. L. Rev. 459 (2005). Many states have enacted legislation relevant to economic credentialing, some restrictive and some permissive. See Beverly Cohen, An Examination of the Right of Hospitals to Engage in Economic Credentialing, 77 Temp. L. Rev. 705 (2004).

MAHAN V. AVERA ST. LUKE'S
Supreme Court of South Dakota, 2001.
621 N.W.2d 150.

GILBERTSON, JUSTICE.

Orthopedic Surgery Specialists (OSS), a South Dakota corporation, and its individual physicians, commenced this action against Avera St. Lukes (ASL) alleging breach of contract. The trial court granted OSS' motion for summary judgment and entered a mandatory permanent injunction against ASL. ASL then filed this appeal. We reverse.

Facts and Procedure

ASL is a private, nonprofit, general acute care hospital located in Aberdeen, South Dakota, organized under the nonprofit corporation laws of South Dakota. [OSS opened a freestanding orthopedic surgery center, unrelated to the hospital, shortly before the hospital's decisions at issue in this case.]

ASL is part of Avera Health, a regional health care system sponsored by the Sisters of the Presentation of the Blessed Virgin Mary of Aberdeen, South Dakota. Since 1901, the Presentation Sisters have been fulfilling their mission statement "to respond to God's calling for a healing ministry . . . by providing quality health services" to the Aberdeen community. ASL has expanded its mission beyond the Aberdeen community to become the only full-service hospital within a 90-mile radius of Aberdeen.

* * *

In mid-1996, ASL's neurosurgeon left Aberdeen. After his departure, the Board passed a resolution to recruit two neurosurgeons or two spine-trained orthopedic surgeons to fill the void. During the recruitment process, ASL learned that most neurosurgeon applicants would not be interested in coming to Aberdeen if there was already an orthopedic spine surgeon practicing in the area. This was due to the small size of the community and the probable need for the neurosurgeon to supplement his or her practice by performing back and spine surgeries. Back and spine surgeries are also performed by orthopedic spine surgeons and the applicants were doubtful whether Aberdeen could support the practice of both a neurosurgeon and an orthopedic spine surgeon.

ASL was successful in recruiting a neurosurgeon who arrived in December, 1996. Around this time, ASL learned that OSS, a group of Aberdeen orthopedic surgeons, had decided to build a day surgery center that would directly compete with ASL. During the first seven months that OSS' surgery center was open, ASL suffered a 1000 hour loss of operating room usage. In response to the loss of operating room income, ASL's Board passed two motions on June 26, 1997. The first motion closed ASL's medical staff with respect to physicians requesting privileges for three spinal procedures: (1) spinal fusions, (2) closed fractures of the spine and (3) laminectomies. The second motion closed ASL's medical staff to applicants for orthopedic surgery privileges except for two general orthopedic surgeons being recruited by ASL. The effect of "closing" the staff was to preclude any new physicians from applying for privileges to use hospital facilities for the named procedures. The Board's decision did not affect those physicians that had already been granted hospital privileges, including the physician-members of OSS. In making its decision, the Board specifically determined that the staff closures were in the best interests of the Aberdeen community and the surrounding area.

In the summer of 1998, OSS recruited Dr. Mahan (Mahan), a spine-fellowship trained orthopedic surgeon engaged in the practice of orthopedic surgery. While OSS was recruiting Mahan, one of the OSS physicians advised Mahan that the staff at ASL had been closed to orthopedic surgery privileges. Despite this warning, Mahan began practicing with OSS. On at least two occasions, Mahan officially requested an application for staff privileges with ASL. These requests were denied due to the Board's decision on July 26, 1997.

In September of 1998, Mahan and OSS (Plaintiffs) commenced this action against ASL, challenging the Board's decision to close the staff. Plaintiffs claimed that the action was a breach of the medical/dental staff bylaws (Staff Bylaws) and sought a writ of mandamus and permanent injunction ordering ASL to consider Mahan's application for hospital privileges. Both parties submitted cross motions for summary judgment. After a hearing, the circuit court determined that ASL had breached the Staff Bylaws by closing the staff. In making its decision, the circuit court relied exclusively on the Staff Bylaws. The circuit court determined that the Board had delegated a significant amount of its power and authority concerning staff privileges to the medical staff. The circuit court reasoned that because of this delegation, the Board no longer had the power to initiate actions that affected the privileges of the medical staff. The circuit court concluded the Board had breached its contract with the medical staff when it closed the staff to the named procedures without first consulting the staff. Plaintiffs' request for a permanent injunction was granted, requiring ASL to consider Mahan's application for privileges. ASL appeals raising the following issues:

    1.   Whether the individual OSS physicians have standing to challenge the Board's decision.

    2.   Whether the Board's decision breached its contract with the Staff.

Analysis

    1.   Whether the individual OSS physicians have standing to challenge the Board's decision.

It is well settled in South Dakota that "a hospital's bylaws constitute a binding contract between the hospital and the hospital staff members." [ ] It is also well settled that when such bylaws are approved and accepted by the governing board they become an enforceable contract between the hospital and its physicians. [ ]

* * *

In regard to whether the OSS staff doctors suffered an injury, the circuit court found:

"It is undisputed that the Board's decision resulted in an economic benefit for ASL and an economic hardship for these doctors in their private medical practice, OSS. It is also undisputed that the OSS staff doctors, through their medical corporation OSS, spent time and money to recruit Mahan, only to end up with him unable to perform certain procedures because of his inability to obtain staff privileges at ASL. As a result, the OSS staff doctors have had to support Mahan while being unable to build their practice or increase their patient base as expected. Clearly [the OSS] [d]octors . . . have standing."

The circuit court properly found that the OSS staff doctors have standing to bring a cause of action for breach of contract.

2.   Whether the Board's decision breached its contract with the Staff.

* * *

Pursuant to its authority, the Board of ASL has delegated certain powers associated with the appointment and review of medical personnel to its medical staff. These designated powers are manifested in the Staff Bylaws. Plaintiffs now claim that the Staff Bylaws trump the decision-making ability of the Board as to all decisions relating in any way to, or incidentally affecting, medical personnel issues. We do not agree.

The circuit court failed to give sufficient weight to the fact that the Staff Bylaws are derived from the Corporate Bylaws. Under Article XIV, section 14(u) of the Corporate Bylaws, any powers supposedly granted under the Staff Bylaws must originate from, and be authorized by, the Board pursuant to the Corporate Bylaws. Their legal relationship is similar to that between statutes and a constitution. They are not separate and equal sovereigns. . . .

Therefore, the medical staff has no authority over any corporate decisions unless specifically granted that power in the Corporate Bylaws or under the laws of the State of South Dakota. Plaintiffs have not alluded to any powers that arise under the statutory or common-law of South Dakota.

* * *

Under section 14(u), all that is designated to the medical staff is the responsibility to make recommendations to the Board regarding the professional competence of staff members and applicants. Article XVI, section 1(a) directs the Board to organize the staff under medical-dental bylaws, which must be approved by the Board before they become effective. Finally, article XVI, section 2(a) commands the Board to "assign to the medical-dental staff reasonable authority for ensuring appropriate professional care to the hospital's patients."

Clearly, under these explicit powers, the Board has the authority to make business decisions without first consulting the medical staff. Nowhere in the Corporate Bylaws is the staff explicitly authorized to make business decisions on behalf of the corporation. Plaintiffs instead rely on the Staff Bylaws as their source of authority to assume the Board's power. Yet, even within the Staff Bylaws, there is no explicit provision granting the medical staff control over personnel issues. Instead, the circuit court found that the actions of the Board violated "the spirit of the bylaws taken as a whole." Such reliance on the "spirit of the [Staff] bylaws" turns the corporate structure of ASL upside down, granting control over day to day hospital administration to a medical staff that is not legally accountable for the hospital's decisions, has no obligation to further the mission of the

Presentation Sisters, and has unknown experience in running a hospital or meeting the medical needs of the community. . . .

When the Board made its decision to close the medical staff to the three procedures on June 26, 1997, it was acting within the powers granted it in the Corporate Bylaws. When making these decisions, the Board specifically determined that the staff closures were in the Aberdeen community's best interests, and were necessary to insure 24-hour neurosurgical coverage for the Aberdeen area. By preserving the profitable neurosurgical services at ASL, the Board also insured that other unprofitable services would continue to be offered in the Aberdeen area. When, as here, it is clear from the Corporate Bylaws that the Board has the authority to manage the corporation, that authority "would necessarily include decisions on how to operate individual departments in order to best serve the corporation's purposes. . . . The cost of such care and promotion of community health is vitally important to the community and a legitimate concern for the board." ASL cannot continue to offer unprofitable, yet essential services including the maternity ward, emergency room, pediatrics and critical care units, without the offsetting financial benefit of more profitable areas such as neurosurgery. The Board responded to the effect the OSS hospital would have on the economic viability of ASL's hospital and the health care needs of the entire Aberdeen community. These actions were within the power of the Board. It surely has the power to attempt to insure ASL's economic survival. As such, the courts should not interfere in the internal politics and decision making of a private, nonprofit hospital corporation when those decisions are made pursuant to its Corporate Bylaws.

* * *

. . . [M]erely because a decision of the Board affects the staff does not give the staff authority to overrule a valid business decision made by the Board. Allowing the staff this amount of administrative authority would effectively cripple the governing Board of ASL. ASL would cease to function in its current corporate form if its staff were given such power.

* * *

. . . There is no logical reason why ASL could close certain areas of its facility to all but a few physicians (via an exclusive contract), yet not be allowed to close its facilities to any new orthopedic surgeons performing certain, named procedures. In a sense, ASL has entered into an implied exclusive contract with all current orthopedic spine surgeons. The same implicit authority that allows the Board to enter into exclusive contracts allows it to close ASL's staff as was done here.

* * *

The Board's decision to close the hospital's facility for certain, named procedures was a reasonable administrative decision. It had determined that the closures were necessary to insure the continued viability of the hospital. The Board must be allowed to make such reasonable, independent decisions if it is to continue to provide comprehensive medical services to the Aberdeen community. . . .Therefore, any allegations that ASL breached its implied duty of good faith must fail. * * *

* * *

Because the actions of ASL's Board were permissible under the Corporate Bylaws and done in good faith, there has been no breach of the contract between the Board and the staff. Therefore, the circuit court's judgment is reversed.

NOTES AND QUESTIONS

1. *Hospital vs. Medical Staff.* The conflict between the hospital and its medical staff in *Mahan* is not unique. For example, the administration at Lawnwood Medical Center in Florida decided to limit privileges for its new cardiovascular surgery unit to a single physician. The executive committee of the medical staff disagreed with the corporate decision and awarded privileges to another physician, following the procedures in the medical staff bylaws. The Board of Trustees promptly denied privileges to that physician. Thereafter, the Board asked that the physician leaders of the medical staff be investigated by the hospital for failure to meet their fiduciary duty to the corporation. The Board ultimately removed the medical staff's elected officers, whereupon the officers sued.

During the course of the suit, the hospital successfully sought special legislation from the state legislature to resolve the conflict in favor of the hospital, and the medical staff sued, arguing that the statute was unconstitutional. The Board also amended the hospital's corporate bylaws to give the Board unilateral authority to amend the medical staff bylaws, even though the latter bylaws required approval of the medical staff for amendment. In contrast to *Mahan*, the court upheld the authority of the medical staff as against the Board, and the Florida Supreme Court held that the special legislation violated the Florida state constitution. See Lawnwood Med. Ctr. v. Seeger, 990 So. 2d 503 (Fla. 2008), describing the course of the dispute and finding the legislation unconstitutional; Lawnwood Med. Ctr. Inc. v. Sadow, 43 So. 3d 710 (Fla. App. 2010), refusing to set aside a jury verdict in favor of the physician applicant. See also James W. Marks & Jayme R. Matchinski, Conflicts Credentialing: Hospitals and the Use of Financial Considerations to Make Medical Staffing Decisions, 31 Wm. Mitchell L. Rev. 1009 (2005), describing a notorious California dispute involving litigation and subsequent legislation on medical staff authority relative to the Board on credentialing.

2. *Drafting Bylaws.* The battle of the bylaws in *Lawnwood*, in note 1 above, may provide guidance on drafting corporate and medical staff by-laws. If you were revising the governance structure through which hospitals now operate, would you maintain the current triad of administration, governing

board, and medical staff, or would you dismantle it? The 2020 Joint Commission Standards contemplate a power-sharing arrangement between the medical staff and the hospital governing body. Though medical staff is self-governed, it is ultimately accountable to the governing body. The medical staff develops and adopts the medical staff bylaws and policies that specify its various roles, responsibilities, and governance, but these bylaws and policies must be approved by the hospital's governing body.

Despite the Joint Commission's admonition for a collaborative relationship between the medical staff and hospital governing body, the power-sharing arrangement can breed conflict. Thus, the standard also requires that there be a conflict resolution process in place for disputes between the medical staff and the governing body. For a discussion of these governance issues in two articles each offering new models, see Brian Peters & Robin Locke Nagele, Promoting Quality Care & Patient Safety: The Case for Abandoning the Joint Commission's "Self-governing" Medical Staff Paradigm, 14 Mich. St. U. J. Med. & L. 313 (2010), and John D. Blum, The Quagmire of Hospital Governance, 31 J. Legal Med. 35 (2010). See Elisabeth Belmont et al., Quality in Action: Paradigm for a Hospital Board-Driven Quality Program, 4 Health & Life Sci. L. 95 (2011), summarizing a manual for governing boards and describing legal standards for governing board accountability. See also Thomas L. Greaney, New Governance Norms and Quality of Care in Nonprofit Hospitals, 14 Annals Health L. 421 (2005).

3. *Economic Credentialing to Forestall Competition.* In a footnote, the *Mahon* court notes:

> How can a doctor who is a part owner of the for-profit OSS be expected to fulfill his or her duties towards his or her co-owners and in the same instance fulfill the duties towards the principal, ASL, who is a nonprofit hospital? This does not imply ill-will on the part of the doctor, it simply faces fundamental medical issues such as at which institution does the doctor place his or her patients, OSS or ASL? We have often stated that an agent cannot serve two masters. This rule applies to medical professionals as well.

A version of economic credentialing, "conflicts credentialing" is the practice of denying privileges because the physician is the owner or member of a competitor of the hospital. The issue has escalated the controversy over the propriety of economic motivation in credentialing. If hospitals are concerned about doctors taking unfair advantage of information gained as members of their medical staff or influencing the medical staff's decisions in a fashion that advantages their competing enterprise, would a conflict-of-interest policy that excludes such doctors from leadership positions in the hospital but allows them to retain clinical privileges provide adequate protection for the hospital? Elizabeth Weeks, The New Economic Credentialing: Protecting Hospitals from Competition by Medical Staff Members, 36 J. Health L. 247 (2003).

Not all courts have followed *Mahan*. The Arkansas Supreme Court affirmed a preliminary injunction against the exclusion of competing doctor-owners holding, in part, that the doctors were likely to succeed in their claims that the hospital intended the exclusion of the doctor-owners to interfere with their relationships with their patients and that the hospital's action violated the state deceptive trade practices statute (as an "unconscionable" act), thus making the principle of nonreview of privileges decisions in state law inapplicable. See Baptist Health v. Murphy, 365 Ark. 115, 226 S.W.3d 800 (2006). See also Pacific Radiation Oncology, LLC v. Queen's Med. Ctr., 861 F. Supp. 2d 1170 (D. Hawai'i 2012), granting a preliminary injunction in favor of a radiation oncologist who claimed that the hospital closed the unit and offered privileges only if the plaintiff physician would agree to admit all patients to the hospital rather than to a competing facility.

II. THE CORPORATE PRACTICE OF MEDICINE

BERLIN V. SARAH BUSH LINCOLN HEALTH CENTER
Supreme Court of Illinois, 1997.
688 N.E.2d 106.

JUSTICE NICKELS delivered the opinion of the court:

Plaintiff, Richard Berlin, Jr., M.D., filed a complaint for declaratory judgment and a motion for summary judgment seeking to have a restrictive covenant contained in an employment agreement with defendant, Sara [sic] Bush Lincoln Health Center (the Health Center), declared unenforceable. The circuit court of Coles County, finding the entire employment agreement unenforceable, granted summary judgment in favor of Dr. Berlin. The circuit court reasoned that the Health Center, as a nonprofit corporation employing a physician, was practicing medicine in violation of the prohibition on the corporate practice of medicine. A divided appellate court affirmed [ ], and this court granted the Health Center's petition for leave to appeal. . . .

The central issue involved in this appeal is whether the "corporate practice doctrine" prohibits corporations, which are licensed hospitals from employing physicians to provide medical services. We find the doctrine inapplicable to licensed hospitals and accordingly reverse.

Background

The facts are not in dispute. The Health Center is a nonprofit corporation duly licensed under the Hospital Licensing Act [ ] to operate a hospital. In December 1992, Dr. Berlin and the Health Center entered into a written agreement whereby the Health Center employed Dr. Berlin to practice medicine for the hospital for five years. The agreement provided that Dr. Berlin could terminate the employment relationship for any reason prior to the end of the five-year term by furnishing the Health Center with 180 days advance written notice of such termination. The agreement also contained a restrictive covenant, which prohibited Dr.

Berlin from competing with the hospital by providing health services within a 50-mile radius of the Health Center for two years after the end of the employment agreement.

On February 4, 1994, Dr. Berlin informed the Health Center by letter that he was resigning effective February 7, 1994, and accepting employment with the Carle Clinic Association. After his resignation, Dr. Berlin immediately began working at a Carle Clinic facility located approximately one mile from the Health Center. Shortly thereafter, the Health Center sought a preliminary injunction to prohibit Dr. Berlin from practicing at the Carle Clinic based on the restrictive covenant contained in the aforesaid employment agreement.

* * *

Hospital Employment of Physicians

The Health Center and its supporting *amici curiae* contend that no judicial determination exists which prohibits hospitals from employing physicians. In support of this contention, the Health Center argues that this court has acknowledged the legitimacy of such employment practices in past decisions. See, e.g., Gilbert v. Sycamore Municipal Hospital, 156 Ill.2d 511, 190 Ill. Dec. 758, 622 N.E.2d 788 (1993); Darling v. Charleston Community Memorial Hospital, 33 Ill.2d 326, 211 N.E.2d 253 (1965). In the alternative, the Health Center contends that if a judicial prohibition on hospital employment of physicians does exist, it should be overruled. In support of this contention, the Health Center argues that the public policies behind such a prohibition are inapplicable to licensed hospitals, particularly nonprofit hospitals.

The Health Center also contends that there is no statutory prohibition on the corporate employment of physicians. The Health Center notes that no statute has ever expressly stated that physicians cannot be employed by corporations. To the contrary, the Health Center argues that other legislative actions recognize that hospitals can indeed employ physicians. . . .

Dr. Berlin and supporting amici curiae contend that this court, in People ex rel. Kerner v. United Medical Service, Inc., 362 Ill. 442, 200 N.E. 157 (1936), adopted the corporate practice of medicine doctrine, which prohibits corporations from employing physicians. Dr. Berlin concludes that the Health Center, as a nonprofit corporation, is prohibited by the Kerner rule from entering into employment agreements with physicians.

Dr. Berlin also disputes the Health Center's contention that public policy supports creating an exception to the Kerner rule for hospitals. He argues that, because no legislative enactment subsequent to the Kerner case expressly grants hospitals the authority to employ physicians, the legislature has ratified the corporate practice of medicine doctrine as the public policy of Illinois. At this point, a review of the corporate practice of medicine doctrine is appropriate.

Corporate Practice of Medicine Doctrine

The corporate practice of medicine doctrine prohibits corporations from providing professional medical services. Although a few states have codified the doctrine, the prohibition is primarily inferred from state medical licensure acts, which regulate the profession of medicine and forbid its practice by unlicensed individuals. See A. Rosoff, The Business of Medicine: Problems with the Corporate Practice Doctrine, 17 Cumb. L. Rev. 485, 490 (1987). The rationale behind the doctrine is that a corporation cannot be licensed to practice medicine because only a human being can sustain the education, training, and character screening, which are prerequisites to receiving a professional license. Since a corporation cannot receive a medical license, it follows that a corporation cannot legally practice the profession. . . .

The rationale of the doctrine concludes that the employment of physicians by corporations is illegal because the acts of the physicians are attributable to the corporate employer, which cannot obtain a medical license. [ ] The prohibition on the corporate employment of physicians is invariably supported by several public policy arguments, which espouse the dangers of lay control over professional judgment, the division of the physician's loyalty between his patient and his profitmaking employer, and the commercialization of the profession. . . .

Application of Doctrine in Illinois

This court first encountered the corporate practice doctrine in Dr. Allison, Dentist, Inc. v. Allison, 360 Ill. 638, 196 N.E. 799 (1935). In Allison, the plaintiff corporation owned and operated a dental practice. When defendant, a dentist formerly employed by plaintiff, opened a dental office across the street from plaintiff's location, plaintiff brought an action to enforce a restrictive covenant contained in defendant's employment contract. Defendant's motion to dismiss the action was granted on the grounds that plaintiff was practicing dentistry in violation of . . . the Dental Practice Act [ ]. In affirming the judgment of the lower court, this court stated:

> "To practice a profession requires something more than the financial ability to hire competent persons to do the actual work. It can be done only by a duly qualified human being, and to qualify something more than mere knowledge or skill is essential. The qualifications include personal characteristics, such as honesty, guided by an upright conscience and a sense of loyalty to clients or patients, even to the extent of sacrificing pecuniary profit, if necessary. These requirements are spoken of generically as that good moral character which is a prerequisite to the licensing of any professional man. No corporation can

qualify." [The Court next discussed cases finding the corporate practice doctrine barred corporations from operating dental clinics employing dentists and prevented a medical clinic providing medical services through licensed physicians.]

* * *

Prior to the instant action, apparently no Illinois court has applied the corporate practice of medicine rule set out in People ex rel. Kerner v. United Medical Service, Inc., or specifically addressed the issue of whether licensed hospitals are prohibited from employing physicians. We therefore look to other jurisdictions with reference to the application of the corporate practice of medicine doctrine to hospitals.

Applicability of Doctrine to Hospitals in Other Jurisdictions

Although the corporate practice of medicine doctrine has long been recognized by a number of jurisdictions, the important role hospitals serve in the health care field has also been increasingly recognized. Accordingly, numerous jurisdictions have recognized either judicial or statutory exceptions to the corporate practice of medicine doctrine which allow hospitals to employ physicians and other health care professionals. See, e.g., Cal. Bus. & Prof. Code § 2400 (West 1990) (exception for charitable hospitals) [ ]. A review of this authority reveals that there are primarily three approaches utilized in determining that the corporate practice of medicine doctrine is inapplicable to hospitals.

First, some states refused to adopt the corporate practice of medicine doctrine altogether when initially interpreting their respective medical practice act. These states generally determined that a hospital corporation that employs a physician is not practicing medicine, but rather is merely making medical treatment available. See, e.g., State ex rel. Sager v. Lewin, 128 Mo. App. 149, 155, 106 S.W. 581, 583 (1907) ("[H]ospitals are maintained by private corporations, incorporated for the purpose of furnishing medical and surgical treatment to the sick and wounded. These corporations do not practice medicine but they receive patients and employ physicians and surgeons to give them treatment") [ ].

Under the second approach, the courts of some jurisdictions determined that the corporate practice doctrine is inapplicable to nonprofit hospitals and health associations. These courts reasoned that the public policy arguments supporting the corporate practice doctrine do not apply to physicians employed by charitable institutions. See, e.g., Group Health Ass'n v. Moor, 24 F. Supp. 445, 446 (D.D.C. 1938) (actions of nonprofit association which contracts with licensed physicians to provide medical treatment to its members in no way commercializes medicine and is not the practice of medicine), aff'd, 107 F.2d 239 (D.C.Cir.1939) [ ].

In the third approach, the courts of several states have determined that the corporate practice doctrine is not applicable to hospitals, which employ physicians because hospitals are authorized by other laws to provide medical treatment to patients [ ].

We find the rationale of the latter two approaches persuasive. We decline to apply the corporate practice of medicine doctrine to licensed hospitals. The instant cause is distinguishable from Kerner, Allison, and Winberry. None of those cases specifically involved the employment of physicians by a hospital. More important, none of those cases involved a corporation licensed to provide health care services to the general public. . . .

The corporate practice of medicine doctrine set forth in Kerner was not an interpretation of the plain language of the Medical Practice Act. The Medical Practice Act contains no express prohibition on the corporate employment of physicians.[1] Rather, the corporate practice of medicine doctrine was inferred from the general policies behind the Medical Practice Act. [ ] Such a prohibition is entirely appropriate to a general corporation possessing no licensed authority to offer medical services to the public, such as the appellant in Kerner. However, when a corporation has been sanctioned by the laws of this state to operate a hospital, such a prohibition is inapplicable. . . .

The legislative enactments pertaining to hospitals provide ample support for this conclusion. For example, the Hospital Licensing Act defines "hospital" as:

> "any institution, place, building, or agency, public or private, whether organized for profit or not, devoted primarily to the maintenance and operation of facilities for the diagnosis and treatment or care of * * * persons admitted for overnight stay or longer in order to obtain medical, including obstetric, psychiatric and nursing, care of illness, disease, injury, infirmity, or deformity." (Emphasis added.) 210 ILCS 85/3 (West Supp.1995).

[The Court cites other statutes that require hospitals to furnish services.]

The foregoing statutes clearly authorize, and at times mandate, licensed hospital corporations to provide medical services. We believe that the authority to employ duly-licensed physicians for that purpose is reasonably implied from these legislative enactments. . . .We further see no justification for distinguishing between nonprofit and for-profit

---

[1] In contrast, the Dental Practice Act, applied by this court in [the dental clinic and *Allison* cases], expressly prohibited a corporation from furnishing dentists and owning and operating a dental office.

hospitals in this regard. The authorities and duties of licensed hospitals are conferred equally upon both entities. . . .

In addition, we find the public policy concerns, which support the corporate practice doctrine inapplicable to a licensed hospital in the modern health care industry. The concern for lay control over professional judgment is alleviated in a licensed hospital, where generally a separate professional medical staff is responsible for the quality of medical services rendered in the facility.[5] . . .

Furthermore, we believe that extensive changes in the health care industry since the time of the Kerner decision, including the emergence of corporate health maintenance organizations. . . , have greatly altered the concern over the commercialization of health care. In addition, such concerns are relieved when a licensed hospital is the physician's employer. Hospitals have an independent duty to provide for the patient's health and welfare. [Citations to Darling and other cases omitted].

We find particularly appropriate the statement of the Kansas Supreme Court that "[i]t would be incongruous to conclude that the legislature intended a hospital to accomplish what it is licensed to do without utilizing physicians as independent contractors or employees. . . . To conclude that a hospital must do so without employing physicians is not only illogical but ignores reality." St. Francis Regional Med. Center v. Weiss, 254 Kan. 728, 745, 869 P.2d 606, 618 (1994). Accordingly, we conclude that a duly-licensed hospital possesses legislative authority to practice medicine by means of its staff of licensed physicians and is excepted from the operation of the corporate practice of medicine doctrine.

Consequently, the employment agreement between the Health Center and Dr. Berlin is not unenforceable merely because the Health Center is a corporate entity.

* * *

NOTES AND QUESTIONS

1. *Policy Rationale for the Corporate Practice Doctrine.* Consider the following rationale for the corporate practice of medicine doctrine offered by the Illinois Supreme Court:

[T]he practice of a profession is subject to licensing and regulation and is not subject to commercialization or exploitation. To practice a profession . . . requires something more than the financial ability to hire competent persons to do the actual work. It can be done only by a duly qualified human being, and to qualify something more than mere knowledge or skill

---

[5]   Moreover, in the instant case, the employment agreement expressly provided that the Health Center had no control or direction over Dr. Berlin's medical judgment and practice, other than that control exercised by the professional medical staff. Dr. Berlin has never contended that the Health Center's lay management attempted to control his practice of medicine.

is essential . . . No corporation can qualify. People v. United Medical Service, 362 Ill. 442, 200 N.E. 157, 163 (1936).

Historically, the AMA considered the corporate practice of medicine the "commercialization" of medicine and believed that it would increase physician workload, decrease the quality of patient care, and introduce lay control over the practice of medicine that would interfere with the physician-patient relationship. Are the sources of the doctrine statutory or do they emanate from general public policy principles? If the latter, what are those principles and are they still valid today? For a decidedly negative assessment of the doctrine, see Mark A. Hall, Institutional Control of Physician Behavior: Legal Barriers to Health Care Cost Containment, 137 U. Pa. L. Rev. 431, 509–518 (1988) (describing the corporate practice of medicine as a "puzzling doctrine . . . clouded with confused reasoning and . . . founded on an astounding series of logical fallacies"). See also Cassandra Burke Robertson, Private Ordering in the Market for Professional Services, 94 B.U. L. Rev. 179 (2014).

In the modern health care enterprise, which may consist of a complex organization of hospitals, physicians, post-acute providers, and health plans, the public policy concerns seem somewhat antiquated. Gabriel Scheffler observes that over time, the teeth of the corporate practice doctrine have been worn down by payment and delivery reforms. The Dynamism of Health Law: Expanded Insurance Coverage as the Engine of Regulatory Reform, 10 UC Irvine L. Rev. 729 (2020). Has the rise of physician employment borne out the concerns posed by the corporate practice prohibition or largely discredited them? In particular, the recent wave of physician acquisitions by private equity investors, spurring surprise out-of-network medical bills and other dubious revenue strategies, has raised calls to re-invigorate the corporate practice of medicine with respect to these non-health-care investors. Erin C. Fuse Brown et al., Private Equity Investment as a Divining Rod for Market Failure: Policy Responses to Harmful Physician Practice Acquisitions, USC-Brookings Schaeffer Initiative for Health Policy (Oct. 2021).

2.   *Non-Physician Providers.* Does the corporate practice of medicine doctrine apply to nonphysicians and complementary and alternative medicine (CAM) providers? The answer depends on whether the services in question implicate the policy concerns underlying the doctrine. Some professions, like dentistry, can be subject to the corporate practice prohibition because their practice requires licensure by the state. See Treiber v. Aspen Dental Mgmt., Inc., 94 F. Supp. 3d 352, 361 (N.D.N.Y. 2015), aff'd, 635 F. App'x 1 (2d Cir. 2016). If one construes the doctrine broadly to apply to other types of "healing" professions, it might reach many forms of CAM. However, courts, attorneys general, and legislatures have tended to require that the healing practice in question must involve significant training and education, and that the practitioner exercise independent professional judgment. Thus, for example, because massage therapy requires no training or licensure under Minnesota law, the Minnesota Supreme Court found the corporate practice doctrine inapplicable. Isles Wellness, Inc. v. Progressive Northern Ins., 703 N.W.2d 513 (Minn. 2005). Likewise, because physical therapy services required an order or

referral from a physician or other licensed practitioners, and in some cases periodic review of the treatment provided by the physical therapist, the court concluded that "the public policy concerns regarding a conflict of interest between the health care provider and the lay person or entity are lessened" and again declined to apply the doctrine. However, the court went on to find that the doctrine did apply to chiropractors because that profession requires extensive training and is provided without supervision by other professionals, whereas physical therapists direct patients under the order or referral or periodic review of other specified health care providers.

3.   *Professional Corporations.* In states recognizing the corporate practice of medicine doctrine, what is the relationship between that doctrine's prohibitions and other statutes permitting physicians to organize their practice under a professional corporation form? In the *Treiber* case cited in the preceding note, the court noted that New York permits dentists to form professional corporations as long as the corporations are owned, operated, and controlled by licensed dentists. 94 F. Supp. 3d at 362. In Colorado, the state supreme court held that the state's professional corporation statute carved out an exception to the corporate practice prohibition allowing professional corporations to practice medicine while prohibiting them from doing anything that violates medical standards of conduct; the court also noted that the professional corporation would be subject to liability under principles of *respondeat superior.* Pediatric Neurosurgery v. Russell, 44 P.3d 1063 (Colo. 2002).

4.   *Honored in the Breach.* Although, by some estimates, over half of the states have statutory or common law prohibitions on the corporate practice of medicine, in many states relevant precedent is quite old and, in some cases, widely ignored. How should an attorney counsel a client as to the legal risks and propriety of undertaking actions that violate old precedent of questionable current force? One commentator has observed:

> Obviously, in modern practice the rule against physician employment is honored mainly in the breach. That does not mean that these traditional prohibitions cannot again serve as a basis for hospital liability. . . . Therefore, it is usually best, whenever possible, to establish true independent contractor arrangements or retain physicians through a separate corporation.

Norman P. Jeddeloh, Physician Contract Audits: A Hospital Management Tool, 21 J. Health & Hosp. L. 105 (1988). In fact, health care attorneys do still counsel ways to avoid the dangers of this latent doctrine, typically through structuring the transaction to ensure that licensed physicians maintain medical decision-making authority in a "friendly PC," while the assets and practice management functions are controlled by an affiliated Management Services Organization for a fee. See, e.g., Melesa Freerks et al., Corporate Practice of Medicine—"A Bad Penny Always Turns Up," 20(3) J. Health Care Compliance 17 (2018).

III. LABOR AND EMPLOYMENT

General principles of labor and employment law apply to employment relationships throughout the health care enterprise. The first case below, *Turner*, introduces the employment-at-will doctrine. The common law at-will doctrine varies widely among the states, but generally provides that the employment relationship can be terminated without cause at the will of either the employer or the employee. The at-will doctrine allows a few exceptions, which in most states are relatively narrow. In contrast, as illustrated in the second case below, *New York University Med. Ctr. And Assn. of Staff Psychiatrists, Bellevue Psychiatric Hosp.*, the National Labor Relations Act (NLRA) provides a substantial degree of protection to health care workers, whether unionized or not, who act together to improve the terms and conditions of their employment.

Doctors, nurses, administrators, and in-house counsel working without an employment contract or under a contract that does not provide for a specific term of employment are subject to the doctrine of employment-at-will. By contrast, employees working under a collective bargaining agreement or under a contract with express provisions concerning length of employment or termination for just cause alone are not employees-at-will. The majority of nurses have long practiced as at-will employees. In contrast, doctors traditionally have practiced as owners of their own practices and have had the further protection of the staff privileges system for their economically necessary relationship with a hospital. Increasingly, however, doctors have become employees (often at-will employees) of group practices, HMOs, or hospitals. In addition, some courts have borrowed from the at-will doctrine in deciding cases of physician termination or delisting from health plans.

The beginning of the 21st century has seen a surge in unionization in the health care field, including unionization of doctors and nurses. Concerns related to workplace safety during the COVID-19 pandemic may further this trend. Health care workplace issues include compensation levels, benefits, mandatory overtime, and workplace safety, just as in other settings, but staffing levels for professionals has been a key issue for health care unions.

TURNER V. MEMORIAL MEDICAL CENTER

Illinois Supreme Court, 2009.
911 N.E.2d 369.

JUSTICE FREEMAN delivered the judgment of the court, with opinion.

Plaintiff, Mark Turner, brought a retaliatory discharge action * * * against defendant, Memorial Medical Center (Memorial). The circuit court dismissed plaintiff's * * * complaint. A divided panel of the appellate court upheld the dismissal. We * * * affirm the judgment of the appellate court.

* * * Plaintiff is a trained and licensed respiratory therapist. Beginning in 1983, plaintiff was employed by Memorial, which is a community hospital. During his employment, plaintiff had consistently met legitimate employment expectations, and his employment evaluations consistently indicated excellent work performance.

In September 2006, the Joint Commission * * * performed an on-site survey at Memorial. The Joint Commission is an independent, not-for-profit organization that establishes various health-care standards and evaluates an organization's compliance with those standards and other accreditation requirements. The purpose of the on-site survey was to determine whether Memorial would continue to receive Joint Commission accreditation. Memorial's failure to receive this accreditation would result in the loss of federal Medicare/Medicaid funding.

Memorial uses a computer charting program that allows medical professionals to electronically chart a patient's file. The Joint Commission standard is that such electronic charting be performed immediately after care is provided to a patient. However, Memorial's respiratory therapy department did not require immediate charting. Rather, Memorial required a respiratory therapist to chart patient care merely at some point during his or her shift.

On September 28, 2006, plaintiff was asked to speak with a Joint Commission surveyor. Also present at this meeting was Memorial's vice-president of patient care services. During this meeting, plaintiff truthfully advised the surveyor of the discrepancy between the Joint Commission standard of immediate charting and Memorial's requirement of charting at some point during the shift. Plaintiff further advised the surveyor that Memorial's deviation from the Joint Commission standard was jeopardizing patient safety. Plaintiff alleged that as a result of his truthful statements to the Joint Commission surveyor, Memorial discharged plaintiff on October 4, 2006.

* * *

In Illinois, "a noncontracted employee is one who serves at the employer's will, and the employer may discharge such an employee for any reason or no reason." [ ] * * * However, an exception to this general rule of at-will employment arises where there has been a retaliatory discharge of the employee. This court has recognized a limited and narrow cause of action for the tort of retaliatory discharge. [ ] To state a valid retaliatory discharge cause of action, an employee must allege that (1) the employer discharged the employee, (2) in retaliation for the employee's activities, and (3) that the discharge violates a clear mandate of public policy. [ ]

Surveying many cases from across the country, this court [has noted in an earlier case]:

> "There is no precise definition of the term [clear mandate of public policy]. In general, it can be said that public policy concerns what is right and just and what affects the citizens of the State collectively. It is to be found in the State's constitution and statutes and, when they are silent, in its judicial decisions. Although there is no precise line of demarcation dividing matters that are the subject of public policies from matters purely personal, a survey of cases in other States involving retaliatory discharges shows that a matter must strike at the heart of a citizen's social rights, duties, and responsibilities before [the] tort will be allowed." [ ]

* * *

At the outset, we reject plaintiff's contention that whether the failure to perform immediate charting jeopardizes the public policy of "patient safety" is a question of fact that precludes dismissal of his complaint* * *. It is widely recognized that the existence of a public policy, as well as the issue whether that policy is undermined by the employee's discharge, presents questions of law for the court to resolve* * *. Accordingly, the questions of whether "patient safety" is a clearly mandated public policy and, if so, whether plaintiff's discharge violated that policy are questions of law for the court.

Turning to the merits, plaintiff contends that Memorial, by discharging him in retaliation for reporting the alleged patient charting discrepancy, violated the clearly mandated public policy of "patient safety." Indeed, plaintiff asks us to "definitively declare that patient safety is a matter of public policy in the state of Illinois and that terminating an employee who speaks out in favor of patient safety violates that public policy." Plaintiff overlooks a basic substantive requirement of a common law retaliatory discharge action.

The tort of retaliatory discharge "seeks to achieve 'a proper balance * * * among the employer's interest in operating a business efficiently and profitably, the employee's interest in earning a livelihood, and society's interest in seeing its public policies carried out.'" * * * A broad, general statement of policy is inadequate to justify finding an exception to the general rule of at-will employment. [ ] Indeed: "Any effort to evaluate the public policy exception with generalized concepts of fairness and justice will result in an elimination of the at-will doctrine itself." [ ]

Further, generalized expressions of public policy fail to provide essential notice to employers* * *. "An employer should not be exposed to liability where a public policy standard is too general to provide any specific guidance or is so vague that it is subject to different interpretations." [ ]

[U]nless an employee at will identifies a "specific" expression of public policy, the employee may be discharged with or without cause. [ ] * * *

* * *

The [plaintiff's] complaint contains the following specific allegations concerning the Joint Commission standards* * *. Plaintiff alleged that the Joint Commission's "role is recognized by the federal government as an important component in assuring patient safety." Plaintiff then alleged that the Joint Commission "has certain standards and criteria" pertaining to electronic patient charting. "One of the standards requires that [electronic] charting be done immediately after care is provided to a patient." Plaintiff further alleged: "The rationale behind immediate [electronic] charting is to enhance patient care and safety."

The circuit court found that plaintiff "failed to establish the existence of a public policy clearly mandated by a provision of law which is violated when a concern is voiced to a [Joint Commission] surveyor about the time during a given work shift when patient care is charted. No Illinois law or administrative regulation directly requires immediate bedside charting of patient care." However, the circuit court further found that Joint Commission "standards are not Illinois law and thus cannot be said to be representative of the public policy of the State of Illinois." * * * Regardless of whether * * * the Joint Commission "is the functional equivalent of [a] government regulator," plaintiff's complaint fails to recite or even refer to a specific Joint Commission standard in support of his allegation. This allegation fails to set forth a specific public policy.

Plaintiff did identify an additional, specific source of his alleged clearly mandated public policy of "patient safety." The complaint alleged that section 3 of the Medical Patient Rights Act "recognizes Illinois public policy establishing '[t]he right of each patient to care consistent with sound nursing and medical practices.'"[ ] * * *

We do not read section 3 of the Medical Patients Rights Act to establish a clearly mandated public policy of patient safety that was violated by plaintiff's discharge. Section 3(a) of the Act establishes the following rights:

(a) The right of each patient to care consistent with sound nursing and medical practices, to be informed of the name of the physician responsible for coordinating his or her care, to receive information concerning his or her condition and proposed treatment, to refuse any treatment to the extent permitted by law, and to privacy and confidentiality of records except as otherwise provided* * *.

It is apparent that, as far as this section addresses medical record preparation at all, it is only concerned with record confidentiality, rather than record timeliness. This is understandable since the Hospital Licensing Act requires hospitals licensed in Illinois to develop a medical record for each of its patients as required by Department of Public Health rules. [ ] In turn, Department of Public Health rules require that patient medical records be "accurate, *timely* and complete." [ ]

* * *

We agree with the appellate court's view of this case* * *. The appellate court * * * reasoned that plaintiff simply told the Joint Commission surveyor that Memorial's practice was to update patients' charts before the end of the employee's shift, instead of immediately updating patients' charts as the Joint Commission allegedly recommended. The court concluded: "Such action falls short of the supreme court's public-policy threshold * * *."

[Court of Appeals] Presiding Justice Appleton wrote separately to state that "the limitations on the determination of what is 'public policy' are not only cumbersome but also so restrictive as to emasculate any common understanding of what we, as a society, expect." He further opined that it should be "the public policy of the State of Illinois for professional health-care providers to speak truthfully to State regulatory agencies concerning hospital practices involving—even tangentially—patient safety."

We agree with the appellate court special concurrence to the extent that the provision of good medical care by hospitals is in the public interest. "It does not follow, however, that all health care employees should be immune from the general at-will employment rule simply because they claim to be reporting on issues that they feel are detrimental to health care." [ ] * * * Adherence to a narrow definition of public policy, as an element of a retaliatory discharge action, maintains the balance among the recognized interests. Employees will be secure in knowing that their jobs are safe if they exercise their rights according to a clear mandate of public policy. Employers will know that they may discharge their at-will employees for any or no reason unless they act contrary to public policy. Finally, the public interest in the furtherance of its public policies, the stability of employment, and the elimination of frivolous lawsuits is maintained. [ ]

* * *

Affirmed. [By a unanimous court.]

NEW YORK UNIVERSITY MED. CTR. AND ASSN. OF STAFF PSYCHIATRISTS, BELLEVUE PSYCHIATRIC HOSP.

324 N.L.R.B. No. 139 (1997).

[T]he evidence shows that the Association [of Staff Psychiatrists, is a labor organization under the Act even though it is not a union because it] has an already defined unit, that of staff psychiatrists at Bellevue Psychiatric Hospital, [which] was formed in 1973 for the purpose of dealing with the Respondent regarding such matters as salaries, working hours and conditions, and grievances of its members, has elected officials (executive board) by elections held every 2 years, has dues paying membership, holds membership meetings, and has actually dealt with the Respondent, mainly through the director of psychiatry, Dr. Manual Trujillo, concerning issues such as wages (equalizing or improving the salary structure of the psychiatrists at Bellevue), the hours and working conditions of the psychiatrists, and grievances* * *.

* * *

The complaint alleges in substance, that the Respondent violated Section 8(a)(1) of the [National Labor Relations Act] by threatening employees with cutbacks, layoffs, and other consequences if they continued to protest a change in employee work hours, and violated Section 8(a)(1) and (3) of the Act by discharging Drs. John Graham, Ebrahim Kermani, Martin Geller, Jerome Steiner, Stanley Portnow, and Meave Mahon [all members of the executive committee of the Association] because they engaged in protected concerted activities.

* * *

Under an affiliated contract with New York City Health and Hospital Corporation (HHC), the Respondent provides psychiatrists and other health care professionals to Bellevue Hospital Center for the purpose of delivering medical and psychiatrist patient care and services. * * * HHC is a quasi public corporation responsible for operating the municipal hospital system of New York City, including Bellevue Hospital. * * *

* * *

For a number of years, HHC had expressed dissatisfaction with a practice under which certain psychiatrists employed by the Respondent at Bellevue Hospital worked from 9 a.m. to 3 p.m. HHC maintained that * * * the affiliation contract required physicians to provide at least 40 hours of service per week, inclusive of unpaid meal hours. By memorandum dated September 30, 1994, HHC Executive Director Pam Brier advised Dr. Trujillo that because of an extremely serious fiscal situation, "Effective November 1, 1994, all full-time staff must fulfill the obligation explicitly delineated in the affiliate contract to work at least 35 hours per week. As we've discussed, there really can be no exception to this policy regardless of any informal agreements."

On September 30, 1994, the Respondent conducted the first of several staff meetings to discuss the "9 to 3" issue. About 30–40 psychiatrists attended, including association executive board members Drs. Graham, Kermani, Mahon, Geller, and Portnow, among others. Dr. Trujillo announced that because of budget problems there would no longer be any "9 to 3" hours, that everybody had to increase productivity and work 9 a.m. to 4:30 p.m. or take a decrease in salary, as the only solution. Dr. Maeve Mahon testified that she suggested that clinical work be assigned to [the physician] administrators. Dr. Mahon related that it was chiefly the members of the executive board [of the Association], particularly Drs. Graham and Kermani, who spoke out against the Respondent's announced changes in working hours* * *.

* * *

Dr. Mahon also testified that she attended another meeting in which Dr. Trujillo mentioned that the "9–3" psychiatrists were going to have to work more hours, and she asked why [the physician administrators] couldn't "come downstairs from their offices and do some clinical care?" Dr. Mahon testified that she perceived animosity from Dr. Trujillo at every meeting she attended as an elected member of the Association. Dr. Trujillo appeared angry, difficult, and stated that the Association wasn't a union or labor group and represented no one.

Dr. Portnow's testimony which substantially supported that of Dr. Mahon as to what occurred at these meetings testified that after [a] meeting had ended, and while he was waiting for an elevator, Dr. Trujillo told him that "Dr. Mahon's behavior was disgraceful, disloyal, undesirable and that it would lead to trouble for the attendings." Portnow also recalled that within the same day or the next Dr. Trujillo said to him that "the Association would be punished" for its position on the "9 to 3" issue; that it was a political issue and that "we should have taken the offer of renegotiating our time to eight-tenths time."

* * *

[I]n the fall of 1994 HHC notified the Respondent that the mental health portion of the affiliation contract budget at Bellevue had to be reduced by approximately $2 million. According to the testimony of several of the Respondent's witnesses they "tried to protect the psychiatrists working at Bellevue" by arguing against the reduction and offering an alternate proposal. After prolonged negotiations, however, HHC insisted on the budget cut and determined it could only be achieved by a reduction in the staff of 10 psychiatrists.

* * * Dr. Trujillo and his senior administrators implemented plans to reorganize the psychiatric department* * *. [T]hey first determined that the reduction should be made in the in-patient rather than the out-patient units. They then decided that a unit would have to be closed and other medical units combined or reorganized. Because the new system would require the implementation of a treatment plan to rapidly stabilize and dispose of patients, the Respondent began to review the productivity and

performance, especially the management and leadership skills of psychiatrists and of the unit chiefs, to determine which would be most effective in the new structure and "enable the department to fulfill its mission with ten less psychiatrists."

[Six members of the executive committee of the Association were among the ten psychiatrists terminated in the reorganization.]

* * *

[T]he evidence clearly establishes that the Association and its member psychiatrists engaged in a series of concerted actions in protest against the Respondent's announced changes in their working hours and that the Respondent was aware of such activities.

* * *

* * * Dr. Trujillo [admitted] that he often told [a group of psychiatrists] that if they did not do something "constructive" to deal with the 9 a.m. to 3 p.m. issue, there would be further budgetary problems, that the problem would just get worse and effect everybody. Dr. Trujillo admitted that he may have [said] * * * that "it was not a good idea, in a budgeting shortness to have an open issue like the 9:00 to 3:00. It makes you very visible for the chopping block."

The record is replete with evidence of statements of animus by Dr. Trujillo toward the Association and the Association's executive board and would lend credence to the view that Dr. Trujillo would not hesitate to tell the Association that it would be "punished" for opposing a change in the 9 a.m. to 3 p.m. work schedules. The Respondent's contentions that Dr. Trujillo was simply trying to warn the psychiatrists that a failure to resolve the 9 a.m. to 3 p.m. issue would cause more budgeting problems and possibly layoffs is irrelevant. However, given Dr. Trujillo's demonstrated history of animus toward the Association and its officers, no reasonable person would have believed that Dr. Trujillo's pronouncements were anything but a threat. This remains true even if one credits Dr. Trujillo's statement that a failure to resolve the 9 to 3 issue makes the psychiatrists "very visible for the chopping block." * * *

* * *

* * * I am persuaded that * * * a motivating factor in the discharge of the six alleged discriminatees was their protected concerted activities based on the abundant evidence of animus toward the Association and its various executive board members on the part of the Respondent, their open opposition to the change in the 9 to 3 work schedule and other activities on behalf of the psychiatrists and the Respondent's knowledge thereof, the unlawful implicit threats of cutbacks, layoffs and other consequences if they continued to protest such change, and the timing of the discharges relative to their protected activity. Accordingly, the burden shifts to the Respondent to establish that it would have terminated [members of the Association] even in the absence of their protected concerted activities. [ ] The Respondent asserts that the layoff of the six alleged discriminatees was not in violation of Section 8(a)(1) and (3) of the Act because it was motivated by a reduction in budget mandated by the Health and Hospital Corporation of New York City and based on the Respondent's judgment concerning the best personnel to operate the reorganized department and not by their activity on behalf of the Association.

I do not agree.

* * *

NOTES AND QUESTIONS

1.   *Public Policy Exception.* Most courts employ a narrow concept of public policy and exclude, for example, professional codes of conduct as a legitimate basis for an exception to at-will employment. See, e.g., Lurie v. Mid-Atlantic Permanente Medical Grp., P.C., 729 F. Supp. 2d 304 (D.D.C. 2010), holding that a physician's reliance on professional standards for public policy fails both the Maryland and D.C. public policy exceptions requiring statutory or judicially established requirements; Tanay v. Encore Healthcare, LLC, 810 F. Supp. 2d 734 (E.D. Pa. 2011), detailing Pennsylvania's narrow public policy exception in the health care context but holding that the plaintiff met the exception; Scott v. Missouri Valley Physicians, P.C., 460 F.3d 968 (8th Cir. 2006), holding that a physician employee could not claim wrongful discharge under the public policy exception as he did not report his concerns about the violation of federal anti-kickback laws to anyone outside of his employer physician group, which the court viewed as reporting only to the "purported wrongdoer"; Wright v. Shriners Hosp. for Crippled Children, 589 N.E.2d 1241 (Mass. 1992), holding that a nurse's report of quality concerns to corporate leadership was not protected under common law public policy exception. Why would most states maintain such a narrow exception to employment-at-will? Aren't professional ethics and integrity important?

2.   *Whistleblower Legislation.* Should doctors and nurses working under at-will arrangements receive broader legal protection than other employees, especially for complaints and actions concerning quality of patient care or illegal financial arrangements? Many states have whistleblower statutes that protect employees who report wrongdoing to government agencies. See, e.g., Stewart-Dore v. Webber Hosp. Assn, 13 A.3d 733 (Me. 2011), interpreting Maine's general whistleblower statute. Several states have statutes that provide protection specifically for health care professionals. See, e.g., Colo. Rev. St. § 8–2–123; N.Y. Lab. Law § 741; Wis. Stat. § 146.997; Lark v. Montgomery Hospice, Inc., 994 A.2d 968 (Md. 2010) (extending a state health care whistleblower statute to cover internal as well as external reports of quality concerns). But see *Lurie*, above, which denied a claim of an at-will employee-

physician against a medical group that the termination violated a D.C. whistleblower statute. A great number of statutes include specific protections for reports of their violation, including for example, the False Claims Act and the Emergency Medical Treatment and Labor Act. Health care professionals working in public hospitals also have some very limited protection under the First Amendment for their expressed opposition to hospital policies. See, e.g., Hilden v. Hurley Med. Ctr., 831 F. Supp. 2d 1024 (E.D. Mich. 2011).

3.   *"Implied Contract"?* Most states accept a theory of "implied contract" to take a relationship out of the at-will category. Personnel manuals may be a source of an implied contract in at-will cases, but employers can avoid this effect by inserting an unambiguous and prominently displayed disclaimer stating that the manual does not constitute a contract and that employees are terminable at will. Courts have often held that medical staff bylaws are contractual in nature when the issue is whether bylaws procedures for credentialing must be followed. In the context of at-will employment, however, medical staff bylaws generally have not been accepted as implied contracts binding the hospital. See, e.g., Hrehorovich v. Harbor Hosp. Ctr., 93 Md. App. 772, 614 A.2d 1021 (1992).

4.   *Membership in Formal Union Not Required.* The NLRA's protection for employees engaged in concerted activities does not require that the employees belong to a formal union. While the Association of Staff Psychiatrists was a statutory labor organization, though it had not been "certified" as a union by the NLRB, even this level of organization was not required in order for an employee to be engaged in concerted action protected by the NLRA. See, e.g., Gaylord Hospital and Jeanine Connelly, 2012 WL 3878931 (2012), in which the ALJ found that the hospital's termination of a respiratory therapist was done in retaliation for protected concerted activity where Connelly participated in meetings where she made statements concerning staffing of the department and other issues; Family Healthcare, Inc. and Kristine McCallum, 354 NLRB No. 29 (2009), in which the Board held that termination of a physician from a practice group as retaliation for the physician's opposition to the physician compensation terms of a new employment agreement violated the NLRA.

5.   *"Supervisor."* Supervisors are excluded from the NLRA's definition of employee. The purpose of the exclusion is to assure that supervisory employees do not have a conflict as between representing management and participating with other employees in collective action. After a long period of disagreement in the federal courts over the appropriate meaning of "supervisor," the Board in Oakwood Healthcare, Inc., 348 NLRB No. 37 (2006) revisited three key statutory terms (within quotation marks in the following text) used to determine supervisory status. It found that permanent charge nurses at an acute care hospital did not "responsibly direct" other nurses because they were not held accountable for their delegation of discrete tasks to other nurses. However, the Board determined that the permanent charge nurses were supervisors because they "assigned" work using "independent judgment" to assess patients' needs, the nursing personnel's skills and expertise, and other

factors they deemed relevant. The Board's decision in *Oakwood* was a significant departure from its earlier position, and it appeared to significantly narrow the range of health care professionals who fall within the scope of the NLRA. However, it is not clear that it has had that impact. Tyler S. Gibb, A Smack on the Chin or a Nibble? Content Analysis of the Impact of The Oakwood Trilogy, 14 Mich. St. U. J. Med. & L. 93 (2010).

6.   *Employee vs. Independent Contractor.* Doctors may seek recognition as a formal union in part because recognition provides an exemption from antitrust restrictions on concerted action (Chapter 15). In order for an individual worker to be covered by the NLRA, however, he or she must work as an employee, not as an independent contractor. The NLRA relies on the traditional common law distinction between independent contractors and employees, and thus focuses on the degree of control exercised over the work of the physician. See, e.g., AmeriHealth and United Food and Commercial Workers Union, 329 NLRB No. 76 (1999), considering whether a managed care organization (MCO) exercised such a degree of control over the practices of contracting physicians that those physicians could be considered employees of the MCO and, therefore, covered by the Act. After discussing in significant detail the MCO's control over the doctors' rights to accept or refuse patients; obligations regarding office facilities, equipment, accessibility, safety practices, and record keeping as well as standards for the number of patients seen per hour; maximum wait times; and annual performance reviews, the Board concluded that the doctors were independent contractors. The NLRB has certified physician unions in HMOs that employ, rather than contract with, doctors, as well as such unions in hospitals with physician employees. See generally Micah Prieb Stoltzfus Jost, Independent Contractors, Employees, and Entrepreneurialism under the National Labor Relations Act: A Worker-by-Worker Approach, 68 Wash. & Lee L. Rev. 311 (2011).

7.   *Workplace Tensions.* A doctor or nurse who is vocal in her opposition to the organization's policies can be viewed as prophetic or disruptive or both, especially if she engages others in her activities. Such situations can strain relationships among employees; however, the NLRA protects those activities, at least to a point. The Board in St. Luke's Episcopal-Presbyterian Hosps. v. NLRB, 268 F.3d 575 (8th Cir. 2001), consistent with long-standing decisions, had held that the reaction of coworkers was irrelevant in evaluating the employer's action. However, the court disagreed and held that the discharge was appropriate, stating:

> * * * Common sense teaches that patient care is directly affected by the ability of a team of physicians and nurses to work together in the confines of an operating room; that a hospital must not risk staffing the operating room with doctors and nurses who cannot work effectively together; and that surgeons cannot be expected to tolerate operating room staff who seem to be more interested in publicizing flaws in the process than in helping protect the patient.

Does this view reach only the operating room or does it extend beyond? Does it depend on how the employee voiced his concerns? Won't conflict usually cause tension? Are protections of the NLRA consistent with Joint Commission requirements for handling disruptive health care professionals? See discussion in Section I, above.

PROBLEM: TAKING CHARGE

St. Margaret's Hospital has undertaken an initiative, called "Take Charge!," which is intended to increase volume, decrease costs, and improve quality. As part of this initiative, St. Margaret's has decided to enter into exclusive contracts for anesthesiology and radiology. The physicians who currently provide services in each of these departments hold staff privileges and are not paid a salary by the hospital, although the hospital provides all of their equipment, supplies, and nursing and technical staff. The hospital does the billing for services the doctors provide in the hospital, but the charges are payable directly to the doctors.

The departments hold regular medical staff meetings each quarter to review events at the hospital, to discuss concerns about nurse staffing and equipment, and to air any problems that might be developing. The medical staff in each department elects their own chairperson to handle these meetings. The chair has no administrative appointment with the hospital itself. At a meeting last spring, the medical staff in the department of radiology decided to send a letter to hospital administration opposing the move to exclusive contracting. Dr. Ellen Stitch and Dr. Robert Morales agreed to draft the letter and to meet with administration to discuss the physicians' concerns. They did so. Although reports of the meeting vary, the hospital CEO apparently said that he thought Dr. Stitch and Dr. Morales should focus on more constructive responses to the situation. Later, when the hospital announced that it was seeking a physician group to provide exclusive radiology services, Dr. Stitch and Dr. Morales bid for the contract. St. Margaret's granted the contract to another group. Physicians who did not have a contract with that group, including Doctors Stitch and Morales, were told that they could retain privileges, but could not provide radiology services unless by specific request of a treating physician.

Also, as part of Take Charge!, St. Margaret's changed its nurse staffing in surgery to require nurses to work on a "PRN," or as needed, basis. If no surgeries are scheduled, the nurses are assigned to other units or are released for the day without pay. Nurse Georgia Jones was particularly vocal in her concern over this change. She was concerned that nurses would be sent to work in units where they were not qualified and that emergency surgeries would not be adequately covered. Nurse Jones felt a particular accountability for the nurses as she was the head nurse in the intensive care unit. As head nurse, she monitored the performance of the nurses in that unit and dealt with conflicts as they arose. She didn't have authority to hire or discipline the nurses who worked in her unit, but the Director of Nursing and the Personnel Office usually followed her suggestions.

Roberta Farr, the hospital's Director of Nursing, met privately with Nurse Jones, and Jones communicated her concerns over staffing. Ms. Farr subtly indicated that she shared Nurse Jones' concerns but said that the system should be tried first. The Director of Nursing's comments quickly circulated along the hospital's grapevine. Ms. Farr demoted Nurse Jones who then went to the local newspaper to tell the story. One week later, the hospital discharged Ms. Farr.

Are Doctors Stitch and Morales and Nurses Jones and Farr covered by the NLRA? If they are included within the coverage of the Act, have they engaged in concerted activities of mutual aid so that the hospital's action violated the Act? Would any of these individuals have a claim under other legal doctrine you studied in this chapter? For wrongful discharge under employment-at-will? Under common law governing hospital-physician exclusive contracting? Would the doctors have an action against the hospital for termination of their privileges?

IV. EMPLOYMENT DISCRIMINATION

Discrimination cases arise in the health care setting as they do in any workplace, but there appears to be an increase in such litigation brought by health care professionals and especially by physicians. One factor that might explain the increased activity includes the movement toward formal employment relationships or significant control of practice rather than independent contractor arrangements. In addition, the HCQIA (described in Section I of this chapter) does not provide immunity for civil rights violations, so it may be funneling litigation concerning staff privileges toward discrimination or civil rights violations.

For most issues, the health care workplace does not present unique issues for the application of state and federal laws protecting individuals against employment discrimination based on age (the Age Discrimination in Employment Act, 29 U.S.C. § 621), sex, national origin, religion, or race (Title VII of the Civil Rights Act of 1964, 42 U.S.C. § 2000e), and disability (Americans with Disabilities Act, 42 U.S.C. § 12101 or the Rehabilitation Act, 29 U.S.C. § 701). However, some disability discrimination claims raise concerns over patient safety in the health care setting that must be carefully assessed. Other provisions of these laws are in Chapter 6.

ESTATE OF MAURO V. BORGESS MEDICAL CENTER

United States Court of Appeals for the Sixth Circuit, 1998.
137 F.3d 398.

GIBSON, CIRCUIT JUDGE.

William C. Mauro brought an action against his former employer, Borgess Medical Center, alleging violations of the Americans with Disabilities Act, 42 U.S.C. §§ 12101–12213 (1994), and the Rehabilitation

Act, 29 U.S.C. §§ 701–796 (1994). The district court granted Borgess's motion for summary judgment, determining that Mauro, who was infected with human immunodeficiency virus, or HIV, the virus that causes AIDS, was a direct threat to the health and safety of others that could not be eliminated by reasonable accommodation and thus concluded that Borgess took no illegal action in removing Mauro from his position as surgical technician. [ ] Mauro appeals, arguing that as a surgical technician at Borgess he did not pose a direct threat to the health and safety of others and that therefore the district court erred in granting summary judgment to Borgess. We affirm.

Borgess employed Mauro from May 1990 through August 24, 1992, as an operating room technician. In June of 1992, an undisclosed source telephoned Robert Lambert, Vice President of Human Resources for Borgess Medical Center and Borgess Health Alliance, and informed Lambert that Mauro had "full blown" AIDS. Because of Borgess's concern that Mauro might expose a patient to HIV, Georgiann Ellis, Vice President of Surgical, Orthopedic and Clinical Services at Borgess, and Sharon Hickman, Mauro's supervisor and Operating Room Department Director, created a new full-time position of case cart/instrument coordinator, a position that eliminated all risks of transmission of the HIV virus. In July of 1992, Borgess officials offered Mauro this position, which he refused.

After Mauro's refusal of the case cart/instrument coordinator position, Borgess created a task force to determine whether an HIV-positive employee could safely perform the job responsibilities of a surgical technician. Lambert and Ellis informed Mauro by a letter dated August 10, 1992, that the task force had determined that a job requiring an HIV-infected worker to place his or her hands into a patient's body cavity in the presence of sharp instrumentation represented a direct threat to patient care and safety. Because the task force had concluded that an essential function of a surgical technician was to enter a patient's wound during surgery, the task force concluded that Mauro could no longer serve as a surgical technician. Lambert and Ellis concluded by offering Mauro two choices: to accept the case cart/instrument coordinator position, or be laid off. Mauro did not respond by the deadline stated in the letter, and Borgess laid him off effective August 24, 1992. Mauro filed this suit in January 1994.

* * *

Mauro's first claim alleges that Borgess discriminated against him in violation of section 504 of the Rehabilitation Act, which provides that no otherwise qualified individual with handicaps shall, solely by reason of his or her handicap, be excluded from participation in, or be denied benefits of any program receiving federal financial assistance. Through the passage of the Rehabilitation Act, Congress intended to protect disabled individuals "from deprivations based on prejudice, stereotypes, or unfounded fear, while giving appropriate weight to such legitimate concerns * * * as avoiding exposing others to significant health and safety risks." School Board of Nassau County v. Arline, 480 U.S. 273, 107 S.Ct. 1123, 94 L.Ed.2d 307 (1987). *Arline* specifically noted:

> Few aspects of a handicap give rise to the same level of public fear and misapprehension as contagiousness* * *. The Act is carefully structured to replace such reflexive reactions to actual or perceived handicaps with actions based on reasoned and medically sound judgments* * *. The fact that some persons who have contagious diseases may pose a serious health threat to others under certain circumstances does not justify excluding from the coverage of the Act all persons with actual or perceived contagious diseases. Such exclusion would mean that those accused of being contagious would never have the opportunity to have their condition evaluated in light of medical evidence* * *. Rather, they would be vulnerable to discrimination on the basis of mythology—precisely the type of injury Congress sought to prevent.

In order to recover under the Rehabilitation Act, a plaintiff must establish that he or she is "otherwise qualified" to do the job within the meaning of the Act. An "otherwise qualified" person is one who can perform the "essential functions" of the job at issue. [ ] In a situation regarding the employment of a person with a contagious disease, the inquiry should also include a determination of whether the individual poses "a significant risk of communicating the disease to others in the workplace." [ ]

Mauro's second claim alleges that Borgess discriminated against him in violation of the Americans with Disabilities Act, which provides that no qualified individual with a disability shall, by reason of such disability, be excluded from participation in or denied the benefits of the services of public entities.

To prevail under his Americans with Disabilities Act claim, Mauro must show that he is "otherwise qualified" for the job at issue. [ ] A person is "otherwise qualified" if he or she can perform the essential functions of the job in question. [ ] A disabled individual, however, is not "qualified" for a specific employment position if he or she poses a "direct threat" to the health or safety of others which cannot be eliminated by a reasonable accommodation. [ ]

The "direct threat" standard applied in the Americans with Disabilities Act is based on the same standard as "significant risk" applied by the Rehabilitation Act. [ ]. Our analysis under both Acts thus merges into one question: Did Mauro's activities as a surgical technician at Borgess pose a direct threat or significant risk to the health or safety of others?

Arline laid down four factors to consider in this analysis: (a) the nature of the risk (how the disease is transmitted), (b) the duration of the risk (how long is the carrier infectious), (c) the severity of the risk (what is the potential harm to third parties) and (d) the probabilities the disease will be transmitted and will cause varying degrees of harm. [ ]

To show that one is "otherwise qualified," neither Act requires the elimination of all risk posed by a person with a contagious disease. In *Arline* the Supreme Court determined that a person with an infectious disease "who poses a significant risk of communicating an infectious disease to others in the workplace," is not otherwise qualified to perform his or her job. [ ] If the risk is not significant, however, the person is qualified to perform the job. The EEOC guidelines provide further insight:

> An employer, however, is not permitted to deny an employment opportunity to an individual with a disability merely because of a slightly increased risk. The risk can only be considered when it poses a significant risk, i.e. high probability, of substantial harm; a speculative or remote risk is insufficient. [ ]

* * * Thus, our analysis in the instant case must not consider the possibility of HIV transmission, but rather focus on the probability of transmission weighed with the other three factors of the *Arline* test.

The parties agree that the first three factors of the *Arline* test: the nature, duration, and severity of the risk, all indicate that Mauro posed a significant risk to others. Mauro argues, however, that because the probability of transmission, the fourth factor of *Arline*, was so slight, it overwhelmed the first three factors and created a genuine issue of material fact.

In determining whether Mauro posed a significant risk or a direct threat in the performance of the essential functions of his job as a surgical technician, *Arline*, instructs that courts should defer to the "reasonable medical judgments of public health officials." [ ] The Centers for Disease Control is such a body of public health officials. [ ] The Centers for Disease Control has released a report discussing its recommendations regarding HIV-positive health care workers. [ ]

The Report states that the risk of transmission of HIV from an infected health care worker to a patient is very small, and therefore recommends allowing most HIV-positive health care workers to continue performing most surgical procedures, provided that the workers follow safety precautions outlined in the Report. [ ] The Report, however, differentiates a limited category of invasive procedures, which it labels exposure-prone procedures, from general invasive procedures. [ ] General invasive procedures cover a wide range of procedures from insertion of an intravenous line to most types of surgery. [ ] Exposure-prone procedures, however, involve those that pose a greater risk of percutaneous (skin-piercing) injury. Though the Centers for Disease Control did not specifically identify which types of procedures were to be labeled exposure-prone, it supplies a general definition: "Characteristics of exposure-prone procedures include digital palpation of a needle tip in a body cavity or the simultaneous presence of the [health care worker's] fingers and a needle or other sharp instrument or object in a poorly visualized or highly confined anatomic site." [ ] The Report advises that individual health care institutions take measures to identify which procedures performed in their hospital should be labeled exposure-prone and recommends that HIV-infected health care workers should not perform exposure-prone procedures unless they have sought counsel from an expert review panel and have been advised under what circumstances they may continue to perform these procedures. The Report further recommends that those health care workers who engage in exposure-prone procedures notify prospective patients of their condition.

We must defer to the medical judgment expressed in the Report of the Centers for Disease Control in evaluating the district court's ruling on whether Mauro posed a direct threat in the essential functions of his job.

Mauro stated in his deposition that during surgery his work did not include assisting in surgery, but instead handing instruments to the surgeon and helping the surgeon with whatever else he or she needed. During surgery, Mauro would at times hold a retractor with one hand in the wound area, and pass instruments as needed with his other hand. When asked if he would be actually inside a wound holding a retractor, Mauro answered "Me personally, no." But when questioned further about his hands in the wound area, he stated: "Usually if I have my hands near the wound, it would be to like, on an abdominal incision, to kind of put your finger in and hold—kind of pull down on the muscle tissue and that—where the two met in like a V shape at the bottom and the top, and pull that back. But it happened very, very rarely because they had retractors to do that." The purpose of this action was to give the surgeon more room and more visibility.

The continued questioning led to a distinction between the wound and the body cavity. Mauro was asked if he ever had his hands in a body cavity, described as being past the wound area, and Mauro stated that he personally never had his hand in a body cavity because the small size of the surgical incision prevented too many hands from being placed inside the body cavity.

* * *

Mauro explained that during his training, discussion had occurred indicating that nicks and cuts were always a possibility for a surgical technician. In fact, the record included two incident reports involving Mauro. One report indicated that Mauro had sliced his right index finger while removing a knife blade from a handle on June 25, 1991, and another report indicated that he had scratched his hand with the sharp end of a dirty needle while threading it on June 8, 1990.

* * *

Sharon Hickman, a registered nurse, was the interim director of operating rooms at Borgess in June and July of 1992. While serving as interim director Hickman supervised the surgical technicians at Borgess, including Mauro. In her affidavit Hickman described a meeting of the Ad Hoc HIV Task Force for the hospital on July 23, 1992 and the statements she made at that meeting. Hickman stated that she told the task force that the duties of a surgical technician include preparing and maintaining the equipment used during surgery, but that, on an infrequent basis, the Surgical Technician is required to assist in the performance of surgery by holding back body tissue, with the use of either retractors or the Technician's hands, to assist the surgeon in visualizing the operative site. The Surgical Technician also may assist the surgeon with suturing and other duties related to the performance of the operation.

She also advised the task force that, although the need for a surgical technician's assistance in the performance of a surgical procedure arises infrequently, it is not possible to restructure the job to eliminate the surgical technician from performing such functions because this need arises on an emergency basis and cannot be planned in advance. In some cases, particularly on off-shifts, Hickman stated that the surgical technician is required to assist at the surgery because a registered nurse or surgical assistant is not available. In other surgical proceedings a nurse or surgical assistant may be present, but due to the complexity or other unexpected requirements of the procedure, another pair of hands may be needed in the operative site, and the surgical technician is then required to assist. Most often, the surgical technician is required to assist in the operative site because more hands are needed to visualize the surgical area.

* * *

We conclude that the district court did not err in determining that Mauro's continued employment as a surgical technician posed a direct threat to the health and safety of others.

* * *

BOGGS, CIRCUIT JUDGE, dissenting.

The concept of "significant risk" that emerges from the [statutes] directly mandates that patients be exposed to, and employers be required to expose their patients to, some amount of risk that is deemed "insignificant" to some determining body. As with other questions of fact and degree in a civil case, a district judge may find that the relevant risk is so small as to be insignificant as a matter of law; so large as to be significant as a matter of law (in each case because no reasonable person could differ with the court's judgment, even though the contrary is staunchly asserted by the opposing attorneys); or, somewhere in between, so that reasonable minds could differ on the degree of risk, and so a jury must be permitted to determine the question.

* * *

Mauro poses some risk. It is not ontologically impossible for him to transmit a disease of very great lethality. However, the chance that he will do so to any given patient is "small." Whether we call the risk "extremely small," "vanishingly small," "negligible," or whatever, assessing the risk remains a judgment that must be made by considering both the actual probability of harm and the degree of the consequences, just as the Supreme Court instructed us.

That is what the District Court did not do, and that is why I would reverse its decision and remand for reconsideration under the correct standard—a full assessment of both the risk and the consequence* * *. [T]he exact nature of Mauro's duties [is] a matter of considerable dispute, especially when the record is read, as we must read it, in a light most favorable to him. Whether the procedures he may perform cross the line from the merely "invasive" to the actionable "exposure-prone" is a genuine and material issue, on which reasonable minds can differ.

* * *

The CDC "has estimated that the risk to a single patient from an HIV-positive surgeon ranges from .0024% (1 in 42,000) to .00024% (1 in 417,000)." [ ] This estimate, of course, is for surgeons, who by the very nature of their work enter surgical wounds with sharp instruments during virtually every procedure they perform. Common sense—and, of course, the court's obligation to interpret the evidence in the light most favorable to the nonmovant—requires us to suppose, in the absence of contrary information, that the activities of a surgical technician such as Mauro who touched only the margin of the wound, and that only very rarely, would pose an even smaller risk. So may the resulting coefficients of risk—numbers somewhat smaller than .0024% to .00024%—still be deemed "significant?"

* * * To assess whether Mauro posed a significant risk, the decision-maker should know more about any particular hazards (physical or moral) that might have affected the likelihood that this individual would transmit HIV to others. If surgeons whom the surgical technician assisted were to testify, for instance, that the assistant had a record of impeccable reliability, technical skills, and professionalism, and that they themselves

were not concerned about risks they incurred by performing surgery with him, then a fact-finder could easily conclude that an employee with a contagious blood-borne disease did not pose a significant risk. On the other hand, if the testimony showed that the employee's co-workers found him to be inattentive, careless, and physically clumsy, then the jury might well conclude that, however small the theoretical risk of transmission, it would not be a safe bet for this particular person to continue working in surgery, and that he was not, therefore, "otherwise qualified."

It is perhaps to this end that the court notes that "the record included two incident reports involving Mauro [one of which] indicated that Mauro had sliced his right index finger while removing a knife blade from a handle on June 25, 1991, and another [of which] indicated that he had scratched his hand with the sharp end of a dirty needle while threading it on June 8, 1990." However, there is absolutely no indication in the record, other than Nurse Hickman's wholly vague assertion that one of these incidents "might have resulted in patient exposure," that either of these events occurred during surgery, in proximity to a patient or another worker, or threatened anyone other than Mauro in any way * * *. One can imagine many other important facts that could be developed at trial and influence a jury's conclusions—for instance, the employees' viral load (and therefore his degree of contagiousness) at the time of his termination, and whether the person reliably took prescribed antiviral medications, and the effectiveness thereof.

* * *

The court apparently has concluded, though without an explicit statement, that Mauro sometimes participated, or might be expected to participate, in "exposure-prone" procedures. This conclusion seems to flow from the belief that any time a health-care worker enters or touches the surgical wound with his fingers or hands, then it is an "exposure-prone" procedure. The court appears to have misunderstood the Guidelines, which clearly contemplate that, in the ordinary case, "surgical entry into tissues, cavities, or organs or repair of major traumatic injuries" should be regarded only as "invasive" procedures, not "exposure-prone" ones.

* * *

NOTES AND QUESTIONS

1. *Data on Risk of Transmission.* There have been no cases of provider-to-patient transmission of HIV worldwide since 2003. See David Henderson et al., Society for Healthcare Epidemiology of America (SHEA) Guidelines for Management of Healthcare Workers Who Are Infected with Hepatitis B Virus, Hepatitis C Virus, and/or Human Immunodeficiency Virus, 31 Inf. Control & Hosp. Epidemiology 203 (2010); David K. Henderson et al., SHEA White Paper, Management of Healthcare Personnel Living with Hepatitis B, Hepatitis C, or

Human Immunodeficiency Virus in US Healthcare Institutions, Inf. Control & Hosp. Epidemiology 1 (2020). There have been only six patients to whom HIV was transmitted by a health care worker in the U.S., and they all were patients of a single dentist reported before 1990. Studies conducted on 22,000 patients treated by 63 HIV-positive health care providers found no evidence of transmission from the providers. CDC, Guidelines for Infection Control in Dental Health-Care Services (2003). Hepatitis B is the most commonly transmitted bloodborne pathogen in the health care setting, whether provider to patient or patient to provider, and it is expected that hepatitis C, the most common bloodborne infection in the U.S., will become a more common source of infection within the health care setting in the coming years.

Current guidelines for health care workers with HIV are much more granular than in years past and relate the specific viral load of the individual health care worker to the categories of work they are able to perform in light of risks to patients. In fact, workers with the lowest viral load can safely work in "exposure prone" activities (now called Category III activities). See SHEA Guidelines, *supra*. For a discussion of the application of the ADA to the treatment of patients with HIV and data indicating only one confirmed case of patient-health care worker transmission reported since 1999, see Chapter 6.

2.   *Qualification and Reasonable Accommodation*. Health care workers with a wide variety of disabilities have brought employment discrimination claims under Section 504 and the ADA. Many of these claims raise issues of actual or perceived patient risk and reasonable accommodation similar to those in the HIV cases. See, e.g., Grosso v. UPMC, 857 F. Supp. 2d 517 (W.D. Pa. 2012)(diabetic perfusionist—operator of a heart-lung machine—who suffered repeated episodes of low blood sugar posed a direct threat to surgical patients).

Although risks to patient safety appear most explicitly in the direct threat defense, as in *Mauro*, courts may incorporate risk assessment and mitigation in analyses of whether the health care worker is qualified to perform the essential functions of the position with, or without, reasonable accommodation. See, e.g., Jakubowski v. The Christ Hospital, Inc., 627 F.3d 195 (6th Cir. 2010)(physician with autism and patterns of confusion and errors in patient care is not qualified to perform the essential functions of the position). But see Leslie Francis and Anita Silvers, The Health Care Workforce: How to Understand Accommodations, 9 St. Louis Univ. J. of Health L. & Pol'y 57 (2015), illustrating that when employers raise concerns about patient safety in disability discrimination cases, courts may defer without careful assessment. On the question of reasonable accommodation, see Robert R. Niccolini & Nina Basu, Disability and Accommodation in the Healthcare Workplace, 2 J. Health & Life Sci. L. 93 (2009).

3.   *Broad Interpretation of Disability*. Congress enacted the Americans with Disabilities Act Amendment Act (ADAAA) in 2008 with the express intent of setting aside the Supreme Court's restrictive applications of the ADA's definition of disability. The ADAAA and its regulations clarify that the definition should be construed in favor of broad coverage of individuals. The

newer EEOC regulations, for example, define disability to include episodic conditions that are disabling when active and conditions that can be ameliorated by mitigating measures (but not including corrective lenses). The regulations also apply a broad concept of "major life activity," so that conditions that limit the performance of a wider range of activities (such as immune function or neurological function) will be considered to be disabilities. See 76 Fed. Reg. 16978 (Mar. 25, 2011).

Employment cases decided under the ADAAA show an increased focus on whether the plaintiff is qualified to perform the essential functions of the position with, or without, reasonable accommodation. See Stephen Befort, An Empirical Examination of Case Outcomes under the ADAAA, 70(4) Wash. & Lee L. Rev. 2027 (2013).

4. *Sexual Harassment.* Reports of sexual harassment in the health care workplace have received increased attention in the wake of the #MeToo movement. Title VII prohibits discrimination and harassment in employment on the basis of race, color, religion, sex, or national origin. See Chapter 6. Despite these protections, a 2016 study of clinician-researchers found that 30% of women reported having experienced sexual harassment in their careers as compared with 4% of men. Reshma Jagsi et al., Sexual Harassment and Discrimination Experiences of Academic Medical Faculty, 315 JAMA 2120 (2016).

Employers have an obligation to take reasonable measures to protect employees from sexual harassment by others in the workplace. This obligation extends to claims of harassment by patients, customers, and other third-parties. See Garner v. CLC of Pascagoula, L.L.C., 915 F.3d 320 (5th Cir. 2019), permitting a harassment claim brought by a Certified Nursing Assistant at an assisted living facility against her employer based on verbal and physical harassment by an impaired patient to proceed.

5. *Accommodation of Religious Beliefs.* There has been an increased focus on religious conflicts in health care, including in the health care workplace. For discussion of statutory provisions directly addressing conscientious objection to treatment (for example in the abortion context), see Chapter 16. Title VII protects employees against religious discrimination and requires employers to reasonably accommodate employees' religious beliefs. So, for example, a hospital must take reasonable steps to accommodate an employee who objects on religious grounds to participating in specific treatments by arranging for other employees to cover the service or by reassignment. The employer, however, is not required to undertake an unduly burdensome action to accommodate the objecting employee. See Robert Wolff & Alex Frondorf, Religious Accommodation Issues for the Health Care Employer: Termination of Pregnancy and Related Issues, 21 Health Law Rptr. 586 (2012).

Religiously affiliated health care organizations may be able to claim an exemption from the application of the federal employment discrimination statutes, at least for certain positions. See, e.g., Kennedy v. St. Joseph's

Ministries, 657 F.3d 189 (4th Cir. 2011), relying on Title VII's statutory exemption in dismissing the plaintiff's claim against a Catholic nursing home that terminated an employee for wearing garb typical of the Church of the Brethren. See also Hosanna-Tabor Evangelical Lutheran Church and School v. EEOC, 565 U.S. 171 (2012), holding that the First Amendment prohibited application of the ADA to a lay teacher denominated a "minister." The ADA also includes a provision that allows religious employers to require that employees "conform to the religious tenets" of the organization. See 42 U.S.C. § 12113(d)(2).

6. *Vaccination Requirements.* The Centers for Disease Control and Prevention and many states recommend that health care employees receive numerous approved vaccines, including influenza, measles, mumps, and rubella ("MMR"); tetanus, diphtheria, and pertussis ("Tdap"). While health care institutions are generally permitted to require that employees receive vaccinations, employee objections to vaccines, some resulting in litigation, have increased in recent years. Employers must consider reasonable accommodations for disability and religious reasons under the ADA and related laws. See Brian Dean Abramson, Vaccine Law in the Health Care Workplace, 12 J. Health & Life Sci. L. 22 (2019); Y. Tony Yang et al., The Americans with Disabilities Act and Healthcare Employer-Mandated Vaccinations, 38(16) Vaccine 3179 (Apr. 3, 2020). The EEOC has issued specific guidance, available on the EEOC website, related to employer vaccination policies and COVID-19 vaccination.

7. *Definition of Employee.* Only employees are covered by the ADA, Title VII, and the Age Discrimination in Employment Act. A formal employment relationship is not required, however. If the plaintiff can prove that he or she is dependent upon the defendant for opportunities to practice or that the defendant exercises sufficient control over the plaintiff's work, the plaintiff generally will meet the requirement of an employment relationship under the statutes. Health care professionals whose only relationship with a hospital is traditional staff privileges, however, would not meet the statutory standard for employment. See, e.g., Levitin v. Northwest Comm. Hosp., 923 F.3d 499 (7th Cir. 2019).

CHAPTER 12

THE STRUCTURE OF THE HEALTH CARE ENTERPRISE

■ ■ ■

This chapter examines the organizational structures of health care enterprises and the issues of corporate governance and fiduciary duties owed by the governing bodies of health care organizations.

Section I of the chapter explores the larger structural changes in health care enterprises, particularly the trend toward increased integration of health care organizations, accelerated by health reform initiatives such as accountable care organizations (ACOs, as described in Chapter 10). The structure of health care enterprises can either impede or advance the goals of higher quality care at lower cost.

In Section II, the *Stern* and *Caremark* cases examine how board members' fiduciary duties apply to the governance and sale of health care organizations, complicated by the frequent mixing of nonprofit and for-profit corporate forms.

The chapter concludes in Section III with a brief discussion of certificate of need (CON) regulation and its impact on the supply of health care services, competition, cost, and quality.

I. HEALTH CARE ORGANIZATIONAL STRUCTURES

A. THE RISE OF HEALTH CARE INTEGRATION

Organizational arrangements for the delivery of health services have undergone dramatic changes over the last forty years. For many years, health care services were delivered primarily by doctors working in solo practices or as members of small groups, usually practicing the same specialty, and by nonprofit hospitals operating independently or as part of relatively simple systems that shared a few administrative or operational services. This began to change with the advent of managed care in the 1980s as hospitals adopted more complex organizational structures and entered into joint ventures and alliances with other hospitals and with their physicians. As payers moved from traditional indemnity insurance to managed care, providers (including physicians, hospitals, and others) began to form larger, integrated organizations of providers that had previously operated independently. The purpose of provider integration was to absorb the financial risks associated with capitated payments and to improve care management for managed care enrollees.

Providers integrate to take advantage of certain economies of scale and scope. First, larger groups of providers can better manage the financial ups and downs of accepting fixed per-member/per-month (capitated) payments when spread over a larger number of managed care members in the same way larger insurance risk pools are more predictable. Second, providers that are part of larger organizations can more readily negotiate with managed care payers within the constraints of the antitrust laws (discussed in Chapter 15). Third, integrated providers can, in theory, better coordinate care and reduce overutilization through shared financial incentives and intra-organizational communication.

Nevertheless, a consumer "backlash" against managed care occurred at the end of the 1990s based on increasing concerns about patient safety, limitations on choice of providers, and quality of care. In response, organizational structures began to change once again, ushering in a new era. Physicians and hospitals "dis-integrated," with many organizations disbanding and hospitals selling back to physicians their practices. Looser networks of physicians and alliances became more prominent, while administrators focused on means of improving the flow of information both internally and to consumers. See Cara S. Lesser et al., The End of an Era: What Became of the "Managed Care Revolution?" 38 Health Serv. Research 337 (2003). The pendulum has begun to swing back toward integration again, with the rise of Accountable Care Organizations and alternative payment models, as discussed further below and in Chapter 10, discussing Medicare and MACRA.

B. TAXONOMY OF HEALTH CARE ORGANIZATIONAL STRUCTURES

The health care organizations discussed in this section are business entities (e.g., corporations, LLCs, partnerships, or contractual joint ventures) that link providers "horizontally," "vertically," or both. **Horizontal integration** combines the same type of services in the same geographic market, such as when hospitals merge with other hospitals to form health systems or physicians combine with other physicians to form group practices or networks. **Vertical integration** refers to the combination of different types of health care services, typically hospitals and physicians and sometimes health plans, to create **integrated delivery systems** that bring together complementary provider services.

A useful way to understand the taxonomy of different organizational structures is to compare them along four dimensions:

- First is the *level of formal organizational integration and control.* Some of these organizations only loosely link hospitals and physicians through contracts or affiliation agreements and are primarily devices to facilitate joint contracting with payers. Other forms of integration more fully bind the providers under common control through formal mergers or acquisitions among entities or employment of physicians.

- Second is the *ability for the organization to take on financial risk.* The financial risk comes from payers shifting the risk of members' excess health care costs to the provider organization through capitation, bonuses, withholds, or other forms of non-fee-for-service payments. The ability to take on financial risk often varies with the level of the organizational members' financial interdependence, called **financial integration**, which indicates the degree to which providers' collective financial fortunes rise and fall together.

- Third is the *ability for the organization to engage in clinical management over a patient's entire episode of care across providers and settings,* also called **clinical integration**. Clinical integration often requires central or coordinated management of the various providers involved in a patient's care, including the ability to develop shared clinical guidelines, health information technology, communication channels, quality metrics, and financial incentives to work within the organization.

- Fourth is the *degree of exclusivity in the relationships between organizational entities.* Relationships between hospitals and affiliated physicians can be exclusive or non-exclusive. Non-exclusive physicians can provide services at hospitals outside the affiliated health system and also contract separately with health plans, whereas exclusive physicians cannot. In addition, hospitals may affiliate with an exclusive group of physicians and limit the degree to which independent physicians outside the exclusive arrangement can participate in the organization.

The following taxonomy describes several organizational models for health care entities, ordered generally from less integrated to more integrated across the four dimensions of integration.

Independent Practice Association

An **independent practice association (IPA)** is a loose organization of physicians into a contracting entity that enables them to offer a single network to payers. Typically, an IPA contracts with a payer, such as a Preferred Provider Organization (PPO), to deliver care to a defined group of patients at discounted fee-for-service rates and to submit to certain controls on utilization or membership restrictions based on quality and utilization criteria. IPAs involve only limited formal, operational, or clinical integration of physician practices through shared billing services, group purchasing, and utilization review. The degree of financial integration is also relatively low. Although IPA members sometimes assume some financial risks through withholds of a portion of their fees, neither IPAs nor PPOs typically have strong controls over physician behavior, and the percentage of each physician's revenues from the IPA is often not sufficient to cause significant changes in the way he or she provides care. IPAs are typically non-exclusive, and physicians may participate in more than one IPA, retain ownership of their own practices, and may contract separately with other payers.

Physician-Hospital Organization

A **physician-hospital organization (PHO)** is a looser form of affiliation between a hospital and its medical staff or an IPA to contract with payers on behalf of the hospital and its affiliated physicians. The PHO is in many respects the least structurally integrated and least complex form of vertical integration among hospitals and physicians.

A PHO's primary purpose is to negotiate and administer managed care contracts for its providers. Although PHOs may provide some utilization review and quality monitoring, they typically provide fewer administrative services for physician practices than do the other organizational forms and do not significantly alter the clinical practice patterns of providers. PHOs may be open to all medical staff physicians or be exclusive to certain physicians. Like IPAs, the affiliated physicians in a PHO usually retain their own practices and can contract independently with payers outside the PHO relationship. The PHO usually accounts for only a modest share of the physician's or hospital's business. As with IPAs, the PHO can move toward greater centralized control over practice management and medical practice.

Multi-Specialty Group Practice

A **multi-specialty group practice (MSGP)** is an organization of physicians of multiple specialties, which usually takes the form of a professional corporation or unincorporated entity such as an LLC. MSGPs typically entail considerable operational integration among the physicians. For example, MSGPs may provide centralized governance that controls all aspects of the group's business, formal quality control, utilization management programs, responsibility for entering into managed care contracts on behalf of group members, and income allocation systems that rely on achievements of the group rather than individual performance. In the traditional model of managed care, a Health Maintenance Organization (HMO) may have contracted with a MSGP to provide all the physician services to the HMO's members. Although MSGPs involve substantial integration among physicians, they may have only a loose affiliation with hospitals or health systems.

Management Services Organization

A **management services organization (MSO)** provides non-clinical services to physicians, notably managed care contracting services. MSOs also provide many of the "back-room" administrative functions necessary to operate physician offices, including billing, claims processing, group purchasing of supplies, ancillary services, and many of the credentialing and utilization control services needed for managed care contracting. In the more comprehensive form, MSOs may acquire physician practices outright or supply "turnkey" operations by purchasing and leasing equipment and office space and hiring staff for physicians.

An MSO may be owned by a hospital, a physician group, a health plan, a joint venture between a hospital and physicians, or non-provider investors. Although some MSOs sell practice management services to physicians via contract, other MSOs may employ the physicians whose practice assets it acquires, which may pose issues in states that prohibit the corporate practice of medicine. In some cases, hospitals use MSOs to purchase and operate physician practices in exchange for a share of the physicians' revenues. In this way, an MSO can involve greater levels of formal, clinical, and financial integration between hospitals and physicians than a PHO.

Integrated Delivery System

Integrated delivery systems (IDSs) are large, complex organizations of hospitals, physicians, ancillary providers, and even health plans linked in fully integrated and often exclusive arrangements. As described by economist Alain Enthoven, an IDS is best understood as the opposite of the traditionally fragmented system of independent health care providers, and is defined as:

> [A]n organized, coordinated, and collaborative network that: (1) links various healthcare providers, via common ownership or contract, across 3 domains of integration—economic, noneconomic, and clinical—to provide a coordinated, vertical continuum of services to a particular patient population or community and (2) is accountable, both clinically and fiscally, for the clinical outcomes and health status of the population or community served, and has systems in place to manage and improve them. Alain Enthoven, Integrated Delivery Systems: The Cure for Fragmentation, 25 Am. J. Managed Care S284 (2009).

IDSs themselves can have several organizational forms, including foundation model, staff model, and equity model IDSs where physicians contract with, are employed by, or are owners of the health system entity, respectively. Fully integrated IDSs bring together under common ownership or control a range of health care services, from hospital to physician to ancillary, and is thus able to coordinate entire episodes of patient care and manage population health.

NOTE: MANAGING RISK

Recall from earlier chapters that public and private payers have moved decisively to shift financial risk to providers. However, payment methodologies differ in the amount and nature of risk that is shifted. As organizations take on greater risk, they may require more complete integration of providers. The greater the level of integration among the providers through common ownership, shared capital, employment, or ownership of physicians' practices, the greater the ability to manage the health care services and costs of a population's health care needs. Integration makes providers more clinically interdependent (through shared clinical protocols, guidelines, etc.), which makes greater risk-sharing viable. Moreover, it is also generally true that greater risk produces greater potential rewards in the form of bonus payments, retained revenues, or cost savings. The following chart illustrates this relationship for several forms of provider integration.

Organizational Integration & Risk Management

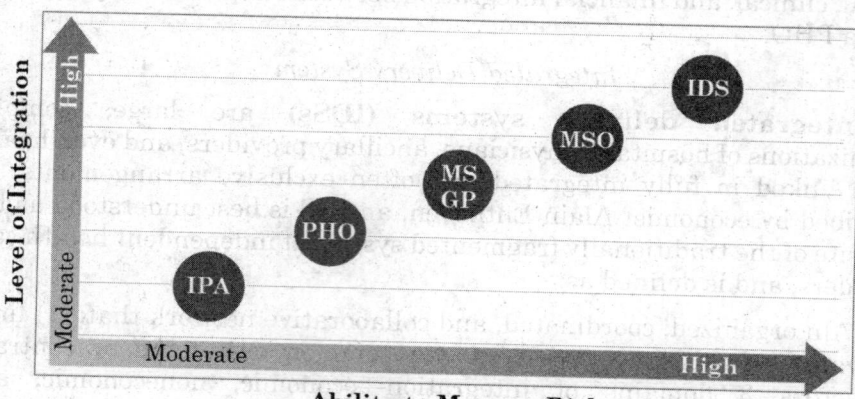

Financial risk to a health care organization increases as payment moves from fee-for-service reimbursement (low risk) to capitation (high risk). Other forms of payment such as withholds, bonuses, and shared savings payments, would fall somewhere in between. The degree of risk providers assume in their payments may influence their choice of practice arrangements. While capitation encourages the formation of multi-specialty groups and integrated delivery systems to enable providers to make cost-benefit tradeoffs, fee-for-service reimbursement creates incentives for physicians to provide more of the most profitable procedures and ancillary services. Today, as payment moves away from fee-for-service toward value-based payments, organizational arrangements may again be moving toward greater integration.

C. THE CURRENT LANDSCAPE FOR HEALTH CARE ORGANIZATIONS

The Affordable Care Act reinvigorated interest in integration. As discussed in Chapter 15, there has been a wave of mergers as hospitals have acquired other hospitals, physicians have consolidated practices, and hospitals have gone on a buying spree acquiring physician practices. Further, in response to incentives created by the ACA's reforms to Medicare and private insurance, providers have undertaken joint ventures specifically geared to providing integrated care through accountable care organizations, medical homes, and other arrangements. Medicare payment reforms contained in the ACA, such as bundled payments and value-based reimbursement, and organizational innovations, such as accountable care organizations (all described in Chapter 10), have signaled that payers will reward coordinated, efficient, and seamless delivery systems in the future. Moreover, many of these new arrangements shift financial risk to providers. Therefore, integrating organizations must take up the challenge of promoting high quality, cost-effective care while also assuring that providers with somewhat divergent economic interests cooperate.

In counseling in this area, it is critical to have a firm understanding of the different objectives of the various parties. For example, physicians typically are looking for a structure that will assist them in contracting with payers by providing capital, information systems, administrative support, patient referrals, and access to a competitively strong network. At the same time, physicians want some assurance that their incomes will not erode and that they will have a substantial voice in the governance of the new organization. Hospitals are eager to assure themselves of an adequate flow of patients to fill their beds and outpatient facilities and a cadre of physicians committed to their organization. Yet hospitals are reluctant to give up control of the organizational structure of the enterprise (after all, they usually supply the lion's share of the financial investment), although shared control is sometimes attempted.

Accountable Care Organizations

Accountable Care Organizations (ACOs) (discussed in Chapter 10) are groups of providers organized into a formal legal entity that agrees to be collectively accountable for the cost and quality of the health care for a defined population of individuals. Payers reward ACO providers for improving quality and care coordination while reducing unnecessary utilization by paying the ACO a share of the amount the ACO providers save for the payer. The model was adopted by the ACA in the form of the

Medicare Shared Savings Program, which established ACOs for Medicare with the idea that the model would spread to the private market. ACOs' shared savings payments and the incentives for coordination encourage hospitals, physicians, and ancillary providers to integrate.

Where does the ACO fit in the taxonomy of organizations described above? Any of these organizational structures can form the basis of an ACO. The ACA permits ACOs to form under a wide variety of arrangements, ranging from fully integrated delivery systems (IDSs) to organizations that link providers or entities such as PHOs and IPAs by contractual agreements. Private ACOs are also rapidly emerging to serve commercial insurance markets and are doing so in diverse organizational forms.

As of 2019, there were 995 ACOs with 1,588 contracts with public and private payers, covering more than 44 million people, or over 13% of the population. David Muhlestein, et al., Spread of ACOs and Value-Based Payment Models in 2019, Health Aff. Blog, October 21, 2019. The ACOs contract with commercial payers, Medicare, Medicaid, or some combination. Most of the contracts are with commercial payers (55%), with Medicare (38%) and Medicaid (17%) making up the rest. *Id.* Though provider participation in Medicare ACOs declined slightly after 2018, when Medicare implemented more stringent requirements for ACOs, the ones that remained have moved toward assuming greater financial risk, showing a higher level of sophistication and experience than when the program first began.

ACO performance varies depending on whether it is led by a hospital or physicians. Unlike in early years, more ACOs are physician-led than hospital-led, and data suggest physician-led ACOs are better at generating cost-savings for payers. See J. Michael McWilliams et al., Medicare Spending after 3 Years of the Medicare Shared Savings Program, 379 N. Engl. J Med. 1139 (2018). Performance overall is mixed, with some ACOs dropping out, a minority generating substantial savings, and most either offering the same or modest improvements in quality. See Zirui Song, Taking Account of Accountable Care, 384 Health Services Res. (2021).

Commercial health insurers participate in ACOs in partnership with providers and may offer PPO plans that encourage enrollees to select an ACO and obtain their care from physicians and hospitals participating the ACO. Typically, these products offer tiered levels of cost-sharing to encourage patients to choose ACO providers over non-ACO providers. See James C. Robinson, Accountable Care Organizations for PPO Patients: Challenges and Opportunities in California (2011). ACOs that serve commercial payers tend to be larger, more efficient, and take on greater financial risk than Medicare-only ACOs. See David Peiris et al., ACOs Holding Commercial Contracts are Larger and More Efficient than

Noncommercial ACOs, 35 Health Aff. 1849 (2016). Data on the performance of commercial ACOs are harder to find, but emerging studies suggest that they, too, struggle to generate significant cost-savings and have modest, positive effects on the quality of care. See Michael E. Chernew, Do Commercial ACOs Save Money? Interpreting Diverse Evidence, 57 Medical Care 843 (2019).

D. LIMITED LIABILITY AND CORPORATE FORM

The choice of organizational form for any health care entity depends on its business goals (e.g., organizational growth, access to capital) and a multiplicity of legal factors, such as limitation of liability, tax considerations (Chapter 13), fraud and abuse requirements (Chapter 14), antitrust concerns (Chapter 15), as well as the drive for integration discussed above.

An important consideration for investors or owners, whether individuals or entities, is limited liability, i.e., the guarantee that they will not be liable for the acts or debts of the business except to the extent of their investment. Limited liability is a key characteristic of corporations, limited partnerships, limited liability companies, and limited liability partnerships. By contrast, general partnerships have unlimited liability for owners.

Veil-Piercing. Although it is not a common occurrence, courts have been willing to disregard the corporate form, or "pierce the corporate veil," and hold shareholders personally liable in certain circumstances. Although piercing is rarely allowed, egregious facts, coupled with severe undercapitalization bordering on fraud, may occasionally justify disregard of the corporate entity. See, e.g., Autrey v. 22 Texas Services Inc., 79 F. Supp. 2d 735 (S.D. Tex. 2000) (triable issues found in wrongful death action against severely undercapitalized corporation that owned forty-nine nursing homes).

In cases involving hospital systems with multiple corporate entities, courts are usually reluctant to pierce the corporate veil even where the parent exercises extensive control over the subsidiary and its name is prominently displayed in the advertising, signs, and literature of the subsidiary hospital. See, e.g., Kissun v. Humana, Inc., 267 Ga. 419, 479 S.E.2d 751 (1997); see also Ritter v. BJC Barnes Jewish Christian Health Systems, 987 S.W.2d 377 (Mo. Ct. App. 1999) (refusing to hold parent entity liable on agency, veil-piercing, vicarious liability, or apparent authority theories despite extensive control over subsidiary hospital's operations).

However, where regulatory evasion is possible, piercing might be available. In United States v. Pisani, 646 F.2d 83 (3d Cir. 1981), the government sought to recover Medicare overpayments made to a corporation owned by a single physician/shareholder. The Third Circuit pierced the corporate veil, holding the physician personally liable despite the absence of fraud. In other cases, courts have pierced the corporate veil despite the absence of any traditional factors where failure to do so would allow providers to avoid the strong statutory objective of preventing abuse of the Medicare and Medicaid program. United States v. Normandy House Nursing Home, Inc., 428 F. Supp. 421 (D. Mass. 1977); see also United States v. Arrow Medical Equip. Co., 1990 WL 210601 (E.D. Pa. 1990). On the other hand, multiple corporate entities can effectively shield business operations from regulatory sanctions. See Joseph E. Casson & Julia McMillen, Protecting Nursing Home Companies: Limiting Liability Through Corporate Restructuring, 36 J. Health L. 577 (2003) (multi-corporate form enables nursing home chains to limit licensure revocation and Medicare sanctions to individual entities). The Affordable Care Act requires increased disclosure of ownership and operating control in response to studies showing multi-facility chains provided much lower quality of care and avoided regulatory scrutiny. ACA Section 6101, 42 U.S.C. § 1320a–3.

   Professional Corporations and Limitation of Liability. Many professional corporations statutes expressly limit professionals' liability, providing for example: (1) limited liability for shareholders as to the ordinary business obligations of the corporation (e.g., business debts, negligence unrelated to professional services, bankruptcy); (2) unlimited liability as to the shareholder's own professional negligence and the negligence of those under his/her direct supervision and control; and (3) limited liability (or capped joint and several liability) for the negligent acts of other shareholders or other employees not under their supervision or control. See, e.g., Kan. Stat. Ann. § 17–2715; Me. Rev. Stat. tit. 13, § 753. What policies justify these differences? Are they still valid in an era of greater integration among practitioners operating in business entities? Even as multiple entities integrate, some may separately incorporate each facility to limit liability to the larger parent organization and each other. This practice is particularly common among nursing home chains. See, e.g., Schwartzberg v. Knobloch, 98 So. 3d 173 (Fla. Dist. Ct. App. 2017). What arrangements might you advise for a professional corporation that anticipates purchasing expensive assets like an MRI or valuable interests in real estate? Are there arrangements that might also help allocate capital expenditures in a multi-specialty practice where not every physician will be using the MRI?

II. CORPORATE GOVERNANCE AND FIDUCIARY DUTIES

   The governance of corporations is shared by three groups: shareholders (or members in the case of nonprofits), the board of directors, and officers. In practice, particularly in large corporations, the officers have almost complete control over the business affairs of the corporation. This separation of ownership and control in the for-profit corporate setting may give rise to the exploitation of shareholders. It also poses problems in nonprofit corporations as boards may not faithfully or diligently pursue the entity's charitable purposes. To deal with this problem, the common law imposes fiduciary duties on those who govern the corporation, essentially obligating directors and officers to act in its best interests.

Governing boards of health care corporations, like all corporations, owe the corporation the **duty of care** and the **duty of loyalty**. The duty of care requires a board member fiduciary to act in good faith and in the manner of a reasonably prudent person in a like position and under similar circumstances, which includes the obligation to stay informed about the organization's operations. In the case of a charity, the circumstances include the charitable nature of the entity and its purposes. The duty of loyalty obligates fiduciaries to act in the best interest of the corporation, which includes the duty to avoid voting on decisions in which the director has a conflict of interest, to avoid so-called "self-dealing," and to avoid usurping a corporate opportunity. In the charitable context, the fiduciary must "act in good faith and in a manner the fiduciary reasonably believes to be in the best interests of the charity in light of its purposes." Restatement of the Law, Charitable Nonprofit Orgs. § 2.02(a). In the health care context, in which many organizations are organized as nonprofit corporations, a critical question is whether nonprofit directors owe the same duties and are held to the same standard as for-profit corporations. The *Stern* case addresses both these questions.

The American Law Institute's Restatement of the Law, Charitable Nonprofit Organizations (2021) sets forth the current view that officers and directors of nonprofit organizations owe substantially the same fiduciary duties of care and loyalty as fiduciaries of for-profit corporations. There are, however, a couple of differences. For the duty of loyalty, while for-profit fiduciary duties are owed to the *corporation*, fiduciaries of a charity have a duty to advance the entity's *purposes*. Id. § 2.02. Regarding the duty of care, the **business judgment rule (BJR)** applies, but the standard for applying the business judgment rule to nonprofits is that the fiduciary *reasonably* believed the decision was in the best interests of the organization in light of its purposes, rather than the more lenient standard of *rationality* applicable to for-profits in many states (though some states apply the reasonable standard to for-profits). Id. § 2.03.

The contours of these duties are discussed in *Stern* and *Caremark* and in the notes following these cases.

STERN V. LUCY WEBB HAYES NATIONAL TRAINING SCHOOL FOR DEACONESSES AND MISSIONARIES

United States District Court, District of Columbia, 1974.
381 F. Supp. 1003.

GESELL, DISTRICT JUDGE.

This is a class action which was tried to the Court without a jury. Plaintiffs were certified as a class under Rule 23(b)(2) of the Federal Rules of Civil Procedure and represent patients of Sibley Memorial Hospital, a District of Columbia non-profit charitable corporation organized under D.C. Code s 29–1001 et seq. They challenge various aspects of the Hospital's fiscal management. The amended complaint named as defendants nine members of the Hospital's Board of Trustees, six financial institutions, and the Hospital itself. Four trustees and one financial institution were dropped by plaintiffs prior to trial, and the Court dismissed the complaint as to the remaining financial institutions at the close of plaintiffs' case.

* * *

The two principal contentions in the complaint are that the defendant trustees conspired to enrich themselves and certain financial institutions with which they were affiliated by favoring those institutions in financial dealings with the Hospital, and that they breached their fiduciary duties of care and loyalty in the management of Sibley's funds. The defendant financial institutions are said to have joined in the alleged conspiracy and to have knowingly benefited from the alleged breaches of duty. The Hospital is named as a nominal defendant for the purpose of facilitating relief.

I. Corporate History

The Lucy Webb Hayes National Training School for Deaconesses and Missionaries was established in 1891 by the Methodist Women's Home Missionary Society for the purpose, in part, of providing health care services to the poor of the Washington area. The School was incorporated under the laws of the District of Columbia as a charitable, benevolent and educational institution by instrument dated August 8, 1894. During the following year, the School built the Sibley Memorial Hospital on North Capitol Street to facilitate its charitable work. Over the years, operation of the Hospital has become the School's principal concern, so that the two institutions have been referred to synonymously by all parties and will be so treated in this Opinion.

* * *

Under the ... by-laws, the Board was to consist of from 25 to 35 trustees, who were to meet at least twice each year. Between such meetings, an Executive Committee was to represent the Board, and was authorized, inter alia, to open checking and savings accounts, approve the

Hospital budget, renew mortgages, and enter into contracts. A Finance Committee was created to review the budget and to report regularly on the amount of cash available for investment. Management of those investments was to be supervised by an Investment Committee, which was to work closely with the Finance Committee in such matters.

In fact, management of the Hospital from the early 1950's until 1968 was handled almost exclusively by two trustee officers: Dr. Orem, the Hospital Administrator, and Mr. Ernst, the Treasurer. Unlike most of their fellow trustees, to whom membership on the Sibley Board was a charitable service incidental to their principal vocations, Orem and Ernst were continuously involved on almost a daily basis in the affairs of Sibley. They dominated the Board and its Executive Committee, which routinely accepted their recommendations and ratified their actions. Even more significantly, neither the Finance Committee nor the Investment Committee ever met or conducted business from the date of their creation until 1971, three years after the death of Dr. Orem. As a result, budgetary and investment decisions during this period, like most other management decisions affecting the Hospital's finances, were handled by Orem and Ernst, receiving only cursory supervision from the Executive Committee and the full Board.

Dr. Orem's death on April 5, 1968, obliged some of the other trustees to play a more active role in running the Hospital. The Executive Committee, and particularly defendant Stacy Reed (as Chairman of the Board, President of the Hospital, and ex officio member of the Executive (Committee), became more deeply involved in the day-to-day management of the Hospital while efforts were made to find a new Administrator. The man who was eventually selected for that office, Dr. Jarvis, had little managerial experience and his performance was not entirely satisfactory. Mr. Ernst still made most of the financial and investment decisions for Sibley, but his actions and failures to act came slowly under increasing scrutiny by several of the other trustees, particularly after a series of disagreements between Ernst and the Hospital Comptroller which led to the discharge of the latter early in 1971.

Prompted by these difficulties, Mr. Reed decided to activate the Finance and Investment Committee in the Fall of 1971. However, as Chairman of the Finance Committee and member of the Investment Committee as well as Treasurer, Mr. Ernst continued to exercise dominant control over investment decisions and, on several occasions, discouraged and flatly refused to respond to inquiries by other trustees into such matters. It has only been since the death of Mr. Ernst on October 30, 1972, that the other trustees appear to have assumed an identifiable supervisory role over investment policy and Hospital fiscal management in general.

Against this background, the basic claims will be examined.

II. Conspiracy

Plaintiffs first contend that the five defendant trustees and the five defendant financial institutions were involved in a conspiracy to enrich themselves at the expense of the Hospital. They point to the fact that each named trustee held positions of responsibility with one or more of the defendant institutions as evidence that the trustees had both motive and opportunity to carry out such a conspiracy.

* * *

Plaintiffs further contend that the defendants accomplished the alleged conspiracy by arranging to have Sibley maintain unnecessarily large amounts of money on deposit with the defendant banks and savings and loan associations, drawing inadequate or no interest . . . [T]he Hospital in fact maintained much of its liquid assets in savings and checking accounts rather than in Treasury bonds or investment securities, at least until the investment review instituted by Mr. Reed late in 1971. In that year, for example, more than one-third of the nearly four million dollars available for investment was deposited in checking accounts, as compared to only about $135,000 in securities and $311,000 in Treasury bills.

* * *

It is also undisputed that most of these funds were deposited in the defendant financial institutions. A single checking account, drawing no interest whatever and maintained alternately at Riggs National Bank and Security National Bank, usually contained more than $250,000 and on one occasion grew to nearly $1,000,000.

Defendants were able to offer no adequate justification for this utilization of the Hospital's liquid assets. By the same token, however, plaintiffs failed to establish that it was [the] result of a conscious direction on the part of the named defendants.

* * *

[The court concluded that plaintiffs failed to establish a conspiracy between the trustees and the financial institutions or among the members of each group.]

III. Breach of Duty

Plaintiffs' second contention is that, even if the facts do not establish a conspiracy, they do reveal serious breaches of duty on the part of the defendant trustees and the knowing acceptance of benefits from those breaches by the defendant banks and savings and loan associations.

A. The Trustees

Basically, the trustees are charged with mismanagement, nonmanagement and self-dealing ... [T]he modern trend is to apply corporate rather than trust principles in determining the liability of the directors of charitable corporations, because their functions are virtually indistinguishable from those of their "pure" corporate counterparts.

1. Mismanagement

Both trustees and corporate directors are liable for losses occasioned by their negligent mismanagement of investments. However, the degree of care required appears to differ in many jurisdictions. A trustee is uniformly held to a high standard of care and will be held liable for simple negligence, while a director must often have committed "gross negligence" or otherwise be guilty of more than mere mistakes of judgment. [ ]

This distinction may amount to little more than a recognition of the fact that corporate directors have many areas of responsibility, while the traditional trustee is often charged only with the management of the trust funds and can therefore be expected to devote more time and expertise to that task. Since the board members of most large charitable corporations fall within the corporate rather than the trust model, being charged with the operation of ongoing businesses, it has been said that they should only be held to the less stringent corporate standard of care. Beard v. Achenbach Mem. Hosp. Ass'n, 170 F.2d 859, 862 (10th Cir.1948). [ ] More specifically, directors of charitable corporations are required to exercise ordinary and reasonable care in the performance of their duties, exhibiting honesty and good faith. Beard v. Achenbach Mem. Hosp. Ass'n, *supra*, at 862.

2. Nonmanagement

Plaintiffs allege that the individual defendants failed to supervise the management of Hospital investments or even to attend meetings of the committees charged with such supervision. Trustees are particularly vulnerable to such a charge, because they not only have an affirmative duty to "maximize the trust income by prudent investment," Blankenship v. Boyle, 329 F. Supp. 1089, 1096 (D.D.C. 1971), but they may not delegate that duty, even to a committee of their fellow trustees. Restatement (Second) of Trusts § 171, at 375 (1959). A corporate director, on the other hand, may delegate his investment responsibility to fellow directors, corporate officers, or even outsiders, but he must continue to exercise general supervision over the activities of his delegates. [ ] Once again, the rule for charitable corporations is closer to the traditional corporate rule: directors should at least be permitted to delegate investment decisions to a committee of board members, so long as all directors assume the responsibility for supervising such committees by periodically scrutinizing their work.[ ]

Total abdication of the supervisory role, however, is improper even under traditional corporate principles. A director who fails to acquire the information necessary to supervise investment policy or consistently fails even to attend the meetings at which such policies are considered has violated his fiduciary duty to the corporation. While a director is, of course, permitted to rely upon the expertise of those to whom he has delegated investment responsibility, such reliance is a tool for interpreting the delegate's reports, not an excuse for dispensing with or ignoring such reports. [ ] A director whose failure to supervise permits negligent mismanagement by others to go unchecked has committed an independent wrong against the corporation; he is not merely an accessory under an attenuated theory of respondent [sic] superior or constructive notice. [ ]

3.   Self-dealing

Under District of Columbia Law, neither trustees nor corporate directors are absolutely barred from placing funds under their control into a bank having an interlocking directorship with their own institution. In both cases, however, such transactions will be subjected to the closest scrutiny to determine whether or not the duty of loyalty has been violated. [ ] A deliberate conspiracy among trustees or Board members to enrich the interlocking bank at the expense of the trust or corporation would, for example, constitute such a breach and render the conspirators liable for any losses. [ ] In the absence of clear evidence of wrongdoing, however, the courts appear to have used different standards to determine whether or not relief is appropriate, depending again on the legal relationship involved. Trustees may be found guilty of a breach of trust even for mere negligence in the maintenance of accounts in banks with which they are associated [ ], while corporate directors are generally only required to show "entire fairness" to the corporation and "full disclosure" of the potential conflict of interest to the Board. [ ]

Most courts apply the less stringent corporate rule to charitable corporations in this area as well. [ ] It is, however, occasionally added that a director should not only disclose his interlocking responsibilities but also refrain from voting on or otherwise influencing a corporate decision to transact business with a company in which he has a significant interest or control. [ ]

Although defendants have argued against the imposition of even these limitations on self-dealing by the Sibley trustees, the Hospital Board recently adopted a new by-law, based upon guidelines issued by the American Hospital Association, which essentially imposes the modified corporate rule.

* * *

Having surveyed the authorities as outlined above and weighed the briefs, arguments and evidence submitted by counsel, the Court holds that a director or so-called trustee of a charitable hospital organized under the Non-Profit Corporation Act of the District of Columbia . . . is in default of his fiduciary duty to manage the fiscal and investment affairs of the hospital if it has been shown by a preponderance of the evidence that:

(1) while assigned to a particular committee of the Board having general financial or investment responsibility under the by-laws of the corporation, he has failed to use due diligence in supervising the actions of those officers, employees or outside experts to whom the responsibility for making day-to-day financial or investment decisions has been delegated; or

(2) he knowingly permitted the hospital to enter into a business transaction with himself or with any corporation, partnership or association in which he then had a substantial interest or held a position as trustee, director, general manager or principal officer without having previously informed the persons charged with approving that transaction of his interest or position and of any significant reasons, unknown to or not fully appreciated by such persons, why the transaction might not be in the best interests of the hospital; or

(3) except as required by the preceding paragraph, he actively participated in or voted in favor of a decision by the Board or any committee or subcommittee thereof to transact business with himself or with any corporation, partnership or association in which he then had a substantial interest or held a position as trustee, director, general manager or principal officer; or

(4) he otherwise failed to perform his duties honestly, in good faith, and with a reasonable amount of diligence and care.

Applying these standards to the facts in the record, the Court finds that each of the defendant trustees has breached his fiduciary duty to supervise the management of Sibley's investments. All except Mr. Jones were duly and repeatedly elected to the Investment Committee without ever bothering to object when no meetings were called for more than ten years. Mr. Jones was a member of the equally inactive Finance Committee, the failure of which to report on the existence of investable funds was cited by several other defendants as a reason for not convening the Investment Committee. In addition, Reed, Jones and Smith were, for varying periods of time, also members of the Executive Committee, which was charged with acquiring at least enough information to vote intelligently on the opening of new bank accounts. By their own testimony, it is clear that they failed to do so. And all of the individual defendants ignored the investment sections of the yearly audits which were made available to them as members of the Board. In short, these men have in the past failed to exercise even the most cursory supervision over the handling of Hospital funds and failed to establish and carry out a defined policy.

The record is unclear on the degree to which full disclosure preceded the frequent self-dealing which occurred during the period under consideration. It is reasonable to assume that the Board was generally aware of the various bank affiliations of the defendant trustees, but there is no indication that these conflicting interests were brought home to the relevant committees when they voted to approve particular transactions. Similarly, while plaintiffs have shown no active misrepresentation on defendants' part, they have established instances in which an interested trustee failed to alert the responsible officials to better terms known to be available elsewhere.

It is clear that all of the defendant trustees have, at one time or another, affirmatively approved self-dealing transactions. Most of these incidents were of relatively minor significance.

* * *

That the Hospital has suffered no measurable injury from many of these transactions—including the mortgage and the investment contract— and that the excessive deposits which were the real source of harm were caused primarily by the uniform failure to supervise rather than the occasional self-dealing vote are both facts that the Court must take into account in fashioning relief, but they do not alter the principle that the trustee of a charitable hospital should always avoid active participation in a transaction in which he or a corporation with which he is associated has a significant interest.

* * *

IV. Relief

* * *

[The Court ordered by injunction (1) that the appropriate committees and officers of the Hospital present to the full Board a written policy statement governing investments and the use of idle cash in the Hospital's bank accounts and other funds, (2) the establishment of a procedure for the periodic reexamination of existing investments and other financial arrangements to insure compliance with Board policies, and (3) that each trustee fully disclose his affiliation with financial institutions doing business with the Hospital. Declining to remove defendant trustees from the Board or to impose personal liability on directors, Judge Gesell offered the following guidance.]

The management of a non-profit charitable hospital imposes a severe obligation upon its trustees. A hospital such as Sibley is not closely regulated by any public authority, it has no responsibility to file financial reports, and its Board is self-perpetuating. The interests of its patients are funneled primarily through large group insurers who pay the patients' bills, and the patients lack meaningful participation in the Hospital's affairs. It is obvious that, in due course, new trustees must come to the Board of this Hospital, some of whom will be affiliated with banks, savings and loan associations and other financial institutions. The tendency of representatives of such institutions is often to seek business in return for advice and assistance rendered as trustees. It must be made absolutely clear that Board membership carries no right to preferential treatment in the placement or handling of the Hospital's investments and business accounts. The Hospital would be well advised to restrict membership on its Board to the representatives of financial institutions which have no substantial business relationship with the Hospital. The best way to avoid potential conflicts of interest and to be assured of objective advice is to avoid the possibility of such conflicts at the time new trustees are selected.

As an additional safeguard, the Court will require that each newly-elected trustee read this Opinion and the attached Order. [The Court also required public disclosure of all business dealings between the hospital and any financial institution with which any officer or trustee of the hospital is affiliated and that the hospital make summaries of all such dealings available on request to all patients.]

IN RE CAREMARK INTERNATIONAL INC. DERIVATIVE LITIGATION
Court of Chancery of Delaware, 1996.
698 A.2d 959.

ALLEN, CHANCELLOR.

Pending is a motion . . . to approve as fair and reasonable a proposed settlement of a consolidated derivative action on behalf of Caremark International, Inc. ("Caremark"). The suit involves claims that the members of Caremark's board of directors (the "Board") breached their fiduciary duty of care to Caremark in connection with alleged violations by Caremark employees of federal and state laws and regulations applicable to health care providers. As a result of the alleged violations, Caremark was subject to an extensive four year investigation by the United States Department of Health and Human Services and the Department of Justice. In 1994 Caremark was charged in an indictment with multiple felonies. It thereafter entered into a number of agreements with the Department of Justice and others. Those agreements included a plea agreement in which Caremark pleaded guilty to a single felony of mail fraud and agreed to pay civil and criminal fines. Subsequently, Caremark agreed to make reimbursements to various private and public parties. In all, the payments that Caremark has been required to make total approximately $250 million.

[As part of its patient care business, which accounted for the majority of its revenues, Caremark provided alternative site health care services, including infusion therapy, growth hormone therapy, HIV/AIDS-related treatments and hemophilia therapy. Caremark's managed care services included prescription drug programs and the operation of multi-specialty group practices and it employed over 7,000 employees in ninety branch operations. Caremark had taken a number of steps to assure compliance with the anti-kickback provisions of the Medicare fraud and abuse law discussed in Chapter 14. As early as 1989, Caremark's predecessor issued an internal "Guide to Contractual Relationships" ("Guide"), which was reviewed and updated, annually, to govern its employees in entering into contracts with physicians and hospitals. After the federal government had commenced its investigation, Caremark announced that it would no longer pay management fees to physicians for services to Medicare and Medicaid patients and required its regional officers to approve each contractual relationship it entered into with a physician. Caremark also established an internal audit plan designed to assure compliance with its business and ethics policies. Although a report by Price Waterhouse, its outside auditor, concluded that there were no material weaknesses in Caremark's control structure, the Board's ethics committee adopted a new internal audit charter, and took various other steps throughout to assure compliance with its policies.

In August and September, 1994, two federal grand juries indicted Caremark and individuals for violations of the anti-kickback laws, charging among other things that Caremark had made payments to a physician under "the guise of research grants ... and consulting agreements" so he would prescribe Protropin, a Caremark-manufactured drug. Plaintiff shareholders filed this derivative suit claiming Caremark directors breached their duty of care by failing adequately to supervise Caremark employees or institute corrective measures thereby exposing the company to liability. In September, 1994, Caremark publicly announced that as of January 1, 1995, it would terminate all remaining financial relationships with physicians in its home infusion, hemophilia, and growth hormone lines of business.]

This suit was filed in 1994, purporting to seek on behalf of the company recovery of these losses from the individual defendants who constitute the board of directors of Caremark. The parties now propose that it be settled.

* * *

The ultimate issue then is whether the proposed settlement appears to be fair to the corporation and its absent shareholders.

* * *

Legally, evaluation of the central claim made entails consideration of the legal standard governing a board of directors' obligation to supervise or monitor corporate performance. For the reasons set forth below I conclude, in light of the discovery record, that there is a very low probability that it would be determined that the directors of Caremark breached any duty to appropriately monitor and supervise the enterprise. Indeed the record tends to show an active consideration by Caremark management and its Board of the Caremark structures and programs that ultimately led to the company's indictment and to the large financial losses incurred in the settlement of those claims. It does not tend to show knowing or intentional violation of law. Neither the fact that the Board, although advised by lawyers and accountants, did not accurately predict the severe consequences to the company that would ultimately follow from the deployment by the company of the strategies and practices that ultimately led to this liability, nor the scale of the liability, gives rise to an inference of breach of any duty imposed by corporation law upon the directors of Caremark.

B.   Directors' Duties To Monitor Corporate Operations

The complaint charges the director defendants with breach of their duty of attention or care in connection with the on-going operation of the corporation's business. The claim is that the directors allowed a situation to develop and continue which exposed the corporation to enormous legal liability and that in so doing they violated a duty to be active monitors of corporate performance. The complaint thus does not charge either director self-dealing or the more difficult loyalty-type problems arising from cases of suspect director motivation, such as entrenchment or sale of control contexts. The theory here advanced is possibly the most difficult theory in corporation law upon which a plaintiff might hope to win a judgment.

* * *

1.   *Potential liability for directorial decisions*: Director liability for a breach of the duty to exercise appropriate attention may, in theory, arise in two distinct contexts. First, such liability may be said to follow *from a board decision* that results in a loss because that decision was ill advised or "negligent". Second, liability to the corporation for a loss may be said to arise from an *unconsidered failure of the board to act* in circumstances in which due attention would, arguably, have prevented the loss. [ ] The first class of cases will typically be subject to review under the director-protective business judgment rule, assuming the decision made was the product of a process that was *either* deliberately considered in good faith or was otherwise rational. [ ] What should be understood, but may not widely be understood by courts or commentators who are not often required to face such questions, is that compliance with a director's duty of care can never appropriately be judicially determined by reference to *the content of the*

board decision that leads to a corporate loss, apart from consideration of the good faith or rationality of the process employed. That is, whether a judge or jury considering the matter after the fact, believes a decision substantively wrong, or degrees of wrong extending through "stupid" to "egregious" or "irrational", provides no ground for director liability, so long as the court determines that the process employed was either rational or employed in *a good faith* effort to advance corporate interests. To employ a different rule—one that permitted an "objective" evaluation of the decision—would expose directors to substantive second guessing by ill-equipped judges or juries, which would, in the long-run, be injurious to investor interests.[16] Thus, the business judgment rule is process oriented and informed by a deep respect for all *good faith* board decisions.

* * *

2. *Liability for failure to monitor*: The second class of cases in which director liability for inattention is theoretically possible entail circumstances in which a loss eventuates not from a decision but, from unconsidered inaction. Most of the decisions that a corporation, acting through its human agents, makes are, of course, not the subject of director attention. Legally, the board itself will be required only to authorize the most significant corporate acts or transactions: mergers, changes in capital structure, fundamental changes in business, appointment and compensation of the CEO, etc. As the facts of this case graphically demonstrate, ordinary business decisions that are made by officers and employees deeper in the interior of the organization can, however, vitally affect the welfare of the corporation and its ability to achieve its various strategic and financial goals.

* * *

Modernly this question has been given special importance by an increasing tendency, especially under federal law, to employ the criminal law to assure corporate compliance with external legal requirements, including environmental, financial, employee and product safety as well as assorted other health and safety regulations. In 1991, pursuant to the Sentencing Reform Act of 1984, the United States Sentencing Commission adopted Organizational Sentencing Guidelines which impact importantly on the prospective effect these criminal sanctions might have on business

---

[16] The vocabulary of negligence while often employed, is not well-suited to judicial review of board attentiveness, especially if one attempts to look to the substance of the decision as any evidence of possible "negligence." . . . It is doubtful that we want business men and women to be encouraged to make decisions as hypothetical persons of ordinary judgment and prudence might. The corporate form gets its utility in large part from its ability to allow diversified investors to accept greater investment risk. If those in charge of the corporation are to be adjudged personally liable for losses on the basis of a substantive judgment based upon what persons of ordinary or average judgment and average risk assessment talent regard as "prudent," "sensible" or even "rational", such persons will have a strong incentive at the margin to authorize less risky investment projects.

corporations. The Guidelines set forth a uniform sentencing structure for organizations to be sentenced for violation of federal criminal statutes and provide for penalties that equal or often massively exceed those previously imposed on corporations. The Guidelines offer powerful incentives for corporations today to have in place compliance programs to detect violations of law, promptly to report violations to appropriate public officials when discovered, and to take prompt, voluntary remedial efforts.

* * *

[I]t would, in my opinion, be a mistake to conclude that our Supreme Court's [prior statements regarding directors' duty to monitor] means that corporate boards may satisfy their obligation to be reasonably informed concerning the corporation, without assuring themselves that information and reporting systems exist in the organization that are reasonably designed to provide to senior management and to the board itself timely, accurate information sufficient to allow management and the board, each within its scope, to reach informed judgments concerning both the corporation's compliance with law and its business performance.

Obviously the level of detail that is appropriate for such an information system is a question of business judgment. And obviously too, no rationally designed information and reporting system will remove the possibility that the corporation will violate laws or regulations, or that senior officers or directors may nevertheless sometimes be misled or otherwise fail reasonably to detect acts material to the corporation's compliance with the law. But it is important that the board exercise a good faith judgment that the corporation's information and reporting system is in concept and design adequate to assure the board that appropriate information will come to its attention in a timely manner as a matter of ordinary operations, so that it may satisfy its responsibility.

Thus, I am of the view that a director's obligation includes a duty to attempt in good faith to assure that a corporate information and reporting system, which the board concludes is adequate, exists, and that failure to do so under some circumstances may, in theory at least, render a director liable for losses caused by non-compliance with applicable legal standards.

* * *

[The Court went on to find that the Caremark directors had not breached their duty of care because, first, there was no evidence they knew of the violations of the law and they reasonably relied on expert reports that their company's practices, although "contestable," were lawful. Second, applying a test of whether there was a "sustained or systematic failure . . . to exercise reasonable oversight," it found no actionable failure to monitor. The court concluded that the corporate oversight systems described above constituted a "good faith effort to be informed of relevant facts."]

NOTES AND QUESTIONS

1.   *Corporate vs. Trust Standard for Nonprofits.* The *Stern* case resolved questions about whether corporate or trust standards applied to fiduciaries of nonprofits. The Restatement of the Law for Charitable Nonprofit Organizations and nearly all states adopt a standard that is closer to the modern corporate standard for fiduciaries of a charity, rather than the traditional trust standard. What's the difference? What arguments support applying the same standard for nonprofit and for-profit corporations? For a pre-*Stern* case applying a trust standard, see Lynch v. John M. Redfield Foundation, 9 Cal. App. 3d 293, 88 Cal. Rptr. 86 (1970). Occasionally, state attorneys general still raise questions about the application of trust standards to fiduciaries of nonprofit organizations. In 2013, the South Carolina attorney general seemed to apply charitable trust law's simple negligence standard as the test for imposing liability on the directors of Tuomey Healthcare System for that organization's sizable penalties for Stark Law and False Claims Act violations (*Tuomey* is discussed in Chapter 14), suggesting that Tuomey would be unable to indemnify its directors for liability. Op. S.C. Atty. Gen., Sept. 3, 2013.

2.   *Duty of Care and the Business Judgment Rule.* Under corporate law, the **business judgment rule (BJR)** poses an almost impermeable shield protecting directors and officers charged with breaches of the **duty of care** in connection with business decisions that prove to be unwise or imprudent. As long as the director has made a business judgment that is (a) in good faith, (b) free of conflicts of interest, (c) informed, and (d) reasonably in the best interests of the organization, courts will not second-guess that judgment, even if the decision would not meet the simple negligence standard applicable to the "ordinarily prudent person." In other words, the BJR immunizes directors from liability for all decisions that do not fall below a gross negligence standard. *Caremark* establishes that the duty of care includes a duty to monitor. Does the standard for the duty of care established by the Chancellor in approving the settlement of the Caremark litigation give directors and senior officers of large, far-flung corporate enterprises sufficient incentives to ensure that their employees comply with the law? What factors militate against imposing a simple negligence standard regarding the duty to monitor? Are the interests of the Caremark shareholders advanced by this holding? What role, if any, should the public interest in compliance with the anti-kickback laws play?

Although not entirely without controversy, the BJR has also been applied to business decisions of nonprofit corporations. See Janssen v. Best & Flanagan, 662 N.W.2d 876, 883 (Minn. 2003) ("[T]he primary rationales for applying the business judgment rule in the for-profit context apply in the nonprofit context as well. . . Therefore, we conclude that the boards of nonprofit corporations may receive the protection of the business judgment rule.").

The Restatement of the Law for Charitable Nonprofit Organizations provides that a nonprofit director who makes a business decision in good faith will not be subject to further review for breach of the duty of care if, at the time the decision is made, s/he:

(a)   has no interest, direct or indirect, in the subject of the decision and is otherwise able to exercise independent judgment;

(b)   is reasonably informed with respect to the subject of the decision using material information reasonably available under the circumstances; and

(c)   reasonably believes that the decision is in the best interests of the charity in light of its purposes.

Restatement of the Law, Charitable Nonprofit Orgs., § 2.03 (2021). Looking at the Restatement's articulation of the BJR, above, in what ways did the trustees of Sibley hospital in the *Stern* case fail to satisfy the BJR?

Not everyone agrees that the BJR should apply to nonprofit directors. See Denise Ping Lee, Note, The Business Judgment Rule: Should It Protect Nonprofit Directors? 103 Colum. L. Rev. 925 (2003). Does the absence of shareholders or a public market for the stock make a difference? Are directors of nonprofit boards (who typically serve without pay) more or less likely to be vigilant and savvy businesspersons than their for-profit counterparts?

As reflected in the first item in the Restatement's articulation above, the BJR does not protect decisions of a director who has a conflict of interest. The *Stern* case illustrates how the duties of care and loyalty overlap. Where the board member approves a transaction in which s/he has a conflict of interest, both the duty of loyalty and the duty of care are implicated. Courts are more receptive to duty-of-care complaints where the transaction is tainted by duty-of-loyalty implications. See Evelyn Brody, The Limits of Charity Fiduciary Law, 57 Md. L. Rev. 1400, 1442 (1998) ("One wonders whether Judge Gesell would have found any duty-of-care breach—or, more important, even granted standing to the plaintiff patients—had the funds been deposited at banks where the hospitals' directors were not also directors.").

3.   *Duty of Loyalty and Conflicts of Interest.* The **duty of loyalty** applies to transactions in which directors or officers acting in their corporate capacity serve their own interests at the expense of those of the corporation. Conflicts of interest, self-dealing, taking of corporate opportunities, and acting in competition with the corporation may violate this duty. See, e.g. Delaware Open MRI Radiology Associates v. Kessler, 898 A.2d 290 (Del. Ch. 2006) (directors representing majority shareholders of radiology group voting to "squeeze out" minority's ownership via merger constitutes a conflict of interest and subjects transaction to judicial review of fairness of procedure and of buyout price). However, directors owe fiduciary duties only to their corporations (or to advance their organizational purposes, in case of charitable nonprofits), not to individual shareholders or employees. Hence a professional corporation's termination of the contract of a physician shareholder-employee will not implicate the duty of loyalty. Berman v. Physical Medicine Associates, 225 F.3d 429 (4th Cir. 2000).

Because nonprofit charities lack shareholders and are organized to advance a charitable purpose, state attorneys general play a critical role enforcing breaches of fiduciary duties by directors of nonprofits. State attorneys general have frequently advanced claims based on breaches of the duty of loyalty in cases involving conflicts of interest, such as a hospital entering into an emergency room contract with a physician group owned by the chairman of its board; loans from a hospital to a physician serving on the board; and the hiring of architectural firms and employment agencies in which trustees have an interest. See Michael W. Peregrine, The Nonprofit Board's Duty of Loyalty in an "Integrated" World, 29 J. Health & Hospital L. 211 (1996). See also Lifespan Corp. v. New England Medical Center, 2011 WL 2134286 (May 24, 2011) (finding conflict of interest in the desire of a parent corporation's financial officer—a fiduciary—to join a banker's wine club, which motivated him to adopt the banker's risky financial strategy for a subsidiary hospital). The *Lifespan* case also illustrates an issue raised by complicated organizational structures: a fiduciary must advance the purposes of the entity the fiduciary serves, rather than the interests of a parent or subsidiary entity.

4.   *Resolving Conflicts of Interest.* Most state statutes governing nonprofit and for-profit corporations make it relatively easy to resolve conflicts of interest. A conflict-of-interest transaction may be valid if:

(a)   All material facts about the conflict and the transaction are disclosed by the interested director (or other fiduciary);

(b)   A majority of disinterested directors approve the transaction in good faith and the conflicted director is recused from deliberation and voting; and

(c)   The disinterested directors determine that the transaction is fair to the organization.

See, e.g., Model Business Corp. Act. (MBCA) §§ 8.60 et seq.; Model Nonprofit Corporations Act (MNCA) § 8.60. In many states, conflicted transactions involving nonprofit organizations may also be shielded from liability if the transaction is approved or subsequently ratified by the state attorney general or a court, where the state attorney general is joined as a party. See Restatement of the Law, Charitable Nonprofit Orgs. § 2.02 (2021).

The obligation of fiduciaries to make full disclosures in self-dealing transactions is illustrated by Boston Children's Heart Foundation, Inc. v. Nadal-Ginard, 73 F.3d 429 (1st Cir. 1996). The case involved a physician, Dr. Nadal-Ginard, who was president and a member of the board of Boston Children's Heart Foundation ("BCHF"), a nonprofit corporation that conducted the clinical and research activities of the cardiology department at Boston Children's Hospital. Conflicting interest problems arose in connection with Dr. Nadal-Ginard's activities on behalf of the Howard Hughes Medical Institute ("Institute"), which provided him substantial compensation for directing the Institute's activities at Boston Children's Hospital. In his capacity as president of BCHF, Dr. Nadal-Ginard was empowered to set his own salary and determine other compensation-related matters. However, Dr. Nadal-Ginard failed to disclose to the BCHF board that BCHF was paying him for much of the same work for which he was receiving substantial compensation from the Institute. The First Circuit concluded that Dr. Nadal-Girard's actions setting his own compensation at BCHF constituted self-dealing and required full disclosure of all material information regarding his salary and compensation determinations. Despite the fact that the BCHF bylaws granted Dr. Nadal-Ginard exclusive authority to set his own salary, the Court found that he had not acted in good faith in failing to make full disclosures, specifically in failing to inform the BCHF board of his compensation from the Institute. 73 F.3d at 434. It further held the information regarding his compensation arrangements with the Institute was material because, had BCHF been armed with the information, it may have concluded that he was over-compensated. In so holding, the First Circuit rejected the defendant's claim that no breach occurred because the salary was fair and reasonable, as the failure to act in good faith was sufficient to establish the breach regardless of the reasonableness of the salary. Id. For an analysis of the implications of fiduciary duties and other legal obligations for physicians serving on hospital boards, see Michael Peregrine, Structuring Physician Membership on the Hospital Governing Board, 31 J. Health L. 133 (1998).

5.   *A Nonprofit Duty of Obedience?* Some commentators and courts have recognized a separate fiduciary duty for nonprofit organizations: a duty of obedience to remain faithful to the organization's stated purposes in its organizing documents. See Manhattan Eye, Ear & Throat Hospital v. Spitzer, 715 N.Y.S.2d 575 (N.Y. Sup. Ct. 1999). See also, Daniel Kurtz, Board Liability: Guide for Nonprofit Director 84–85 (1988); Linda Sugin, Resisting the Corporatization of Nonprofit Governance: Transforming Obedience into Fidelity, 76 Fordham L. Rev. 1677 (2009); Rob E. Atkinson, Obedience as a Foundation of Fiduciary Duty, 34 J. Corp. Law 43 (2008); U.S. Dept. of Health and Human Services, Office of Inspector General and American Health Lawyers Ass'n, Corporate Responsibility and Health Care Quality: A Resource for Health Care Organization Boards of Directors (June 2007) (recognizing a duty of obedience). However, the American Law Institute rejects the existence of a separate fiduciary duty of obedience for nonprofit organizations. Instead, for charities the duty of loyalty encompasses a duty to advance the charity's purposes as expressed in its organizational documents, purposes that serve the public, which is the ultimate beneficiary. Restatement of the Law, Charitable Nonprofit Orgs. § 2.02, n. 25 (2021).

Regardless of whether the jurisdiction recognizes a standalone duty of obedience or whether it is subsumed in the duty of loyalty, courts generally allow directors considerable leeway in interpreting broadly stated corporate purposes (which are usually found in the corporation's charter or bylaws). However, directors must follow clearly stated charitable objectives even if other alternatives exist that are more profitable, efficient, or needed by the community. Failure to do so would constitute a breach of their fiduciary duty of obedience or loyalty. Nor is it a simple matter for a charitable nonprofit to alter its purposes. Making fundamental changes to a charity's purposes requires a lengthy process governed by the organizational documents and applicable law or court approval via a *cy pres* proceeding, with the state attorney general as a necessary party. See id. §§ 3.01 to 3.02; Attorney General v. Hahnemann Hospital, 494 N.E.2d 1011, 1021 (1986) (applying the *cy pres* doctrine to forbid a charitable hospital from applying existing assets to its new purposes. "By simply amending its charter purposes, a charitable corporation would itself be able to exercise the power to devote funds to new charitable purposes whenever the trustees decided to do so, without any requirement that the new purposes be similar and not contradictory.")

Even when the duty of obedience is explicitly recognized, it may not fully resolve a tension facing directors of nonprofits: how to balance "mission and margin" when business interests and charitable purposes conflict. One proposal would establish a principle of "mission primacy" that recognizes the charitable purposes as the central objective of the nonprofit enterprise but allow directors presumptive deference in interpreting and determining how to advance that mission. Thomas L. Greaney & Kathleen Boozang, Mission, Margin and Trust in the Nonprofit Health Care Enterprise, 5 Yale J. Health Pol'y. L. & Ethics 1 (2005).

PROBLEM: THE CATCH-22 OF DIVIDED LOYALTY

As a result of changes in federal reimbursement policies and anti-kickback laws and because of persistently high maintenance costs, Corsica Medical Group, LLC (CMG) has concluded that it is impractical for it to continue to own the lithotripter it uses in its outpatient clinic. As part of negotiations with Pianosa Community Hospital regarding a joint venture to operate outpatient facilities, CMG has offered to sell its lithotripter to the hospital. Dr. Daneka is a member of CMG and also serves on the board of directors of Pianosa Community Hospital. What advice would you give to CMG regarding its proposed transaction? What information should the Pianosa Community Hospital board review before making its decision?

NOTE: CONVERSIONS, ASSET SALES, AND MERGERS OF NONPROFIT CORPORATIONS

Over the past several decades, but especially in the 1990s, many nonprofit health insurance companies, HMOs, and hospitals have chosen to convert to for-profit status or to merge with, be acquired by, or form joint ventures with for-profit entities. Many Blue Cross Blue Shield health insurers have undertaken steps to do so, and hundreds of hospitals have been acquired by or entered into some form of joint venture with proprietary entities. Conversions from nonprofit to for-profit status raise more concerns than transactions between nonprofits.

In a for-profit conversion, the assets of the nonprofit organization are sold to a for-profit entity. Because charitable assets must be held for public rather than private benefit, state laws typically require the proceeds of the sale of a nonprofit to a for-profit to be used to establish a charitable foundation that makes grants to advance the purposes of the nonprofit. Once the assets are distributed, the nonprofit entity dissolves. The state attorney general is responsible for ensuring that the assets of nonprofits benefit the public in accordance with the purposes specified in the organization's governing documents. Thus, many states require the attorney general be notified of significant transactions involving a charitable nonprofit's assets, particularly for-profit conversions.

The Restatement for Charitable Nonprofit Organizations provides that a charitable nonprofit entity may convert or transfer all or substantially all of its assets to a for-profit entity:

(1) pursuant to any applicable terms in its organizational documents;

(2) in accordance with any applicable laws governing the conversion or transaction, or in a state with no laws governing the conversion or transaction, with court approval; and

(3) with prior notice to the state attorney general.

Restatement of the Law, Charitable Nonprofit Orgs. § 3.04 (2021). Moreover, the nonprofit must receive fair market value for the sale of all or substantially all its assets to a for-profit entity and may not pay more than fair market value for the purchase or other transfer of assets from a for-profit entity. Id.

The majority of states have enacted statutes governing the process and setting standards for regulatory approvals of conversions of nonprofits, with some applying specific requirements to health care entities. Most states impose procedural requirements upon converting entities, such as prior notification and information reporting to the state attorney general or other reviewing authorities, who may conduct a public hearing or seek to block the transaction in court. E.g., Cal. Corp. Code §§ 5914–5930 (West 2013); Colo. Rev. Stat. § 10–16–324 (West 2013); D.C. Code Ann. §§ 31–3501 to 31–3514 (2010); Neb. Rev. Stat. §§ 71–20, 102 to 71–20,114 (2009). Some states require consent or prior approval of nonprofit conversions by the state attorney general or a court. E.g., N.Y. Not-For-Profit Corp. Law §§ 510 to 511a, 907 to 908. Some states forbid nonprofit entities from merging with for-profits, unless the resulting entity is itself a nonprofit. See e.g., N.J. Stat. Ann. § 15A:10–1; Fla. Stat. Ann. § 617.1102; Del. Code Ann. tit. 8, §§ 255, 257, 258. For a discussion of nonprofit hospital conversions, see David M. Cutler & Jill R. Horwitz, Converting Hospitals from Not-for-Profit to For-Profit Status: Why and What Effects?, in The Changing Hospital Industry 45 (David M. Cutler ed., 2000); David A. Hyman, Hospital Conversions: Fact, Fantasy, and Regulatory Follies, 23 J. Corp. L. 741 (1998); and John D. Colombo, A Proposal for An Exit Tax on Nonprofit Conversion Transactions, 23 J. Corp. L. 779 (1998). For a discussion of health insurance conversions, see Jill R. Horwitz & Marion Fremont-Smith, The Common Law Power of the Legislature: Insurer Conversion and Charitable Funds, 83 Milbank Q. 225 (2005).

PROBLEM: HOPE SPRINGS ETERNAL

Hope Springs Eternal Health System, a nonprofit hospital system headquartered in Hope Springs, Kansas, operates three acute care hospitals in Kansas and one in New Budapest, Missouri. Two of its four hospitals (one in Kansas and one in Missouri) have lost money over the last two years and both are operating as a drain on the System's overall finances. One of the hospitals losing money, Western Missouri Hope (WMH), located in rural New Budapest, is the only hospital in its small town and its emergency room there operates at a large loss. The articles of incorporation, drafted upon WMH's formation during the Great Depression, describe as its purpose "to operate a hospital and other facilities to best serve the health needs of the deserving in New Budapest."

WMH enjoys strong community support and receives substantial local donations, and volunteer services have kept it afloat for many years. The System's CEO is concerned about newspaper reports that Milo Minderbender, president and chairman of the board of WMH, has attended several expensive seminars in Las Vegas and San Francisco to learn from national experts about correcting the problems of distressed hospitals. The local newspaper in New Budapest has also gathered data showing that Minderbender's salary ranks in the top 1% of all hospital executives running comparable rural hospitals. Further, the paper has discovered that despite the considerable poverty in New Budapest, WMH Hospital provides less charity care than any other Missouri hospital located in similar economically deprived communities.

Without telling the System Board, the System's CEO hired a consultant to make recommendations regarding the future of WMH. The consultant's study confirmed the dire financial status of WMH, but explored only the option of closing the hospital. The CEO wants to put several proposals before the Board at its next meeting. She would like your advice on the legal risks associated with each.

- Close the hospital in New Budapest and form a limited liability company with a group of local physicians to own and operate an ambulatory surgery center, leasing the old hospital facility to this joint venture. The hospital system will own 51% of the joint venture. According to the consultant, the venture should be sufficiently profitable to offset the losses of the other System hospital losing money and contribute to the capital needs of its other hospitals.

- Keep the hospital running but stop accepting patients who are insured by MissouriCares, a State-run insurance program for the working poor. MissouriCares, which is not affiliated with Medicaid or CHIP, sets its reimbursement rates for hospitals at levels lower than Medicaid and fails to cover WMH's costs of service to its beneficiaries. The CEO believes this move might shake up state policy makers and get them to reconsider their rate structure for both Medicaid and MissouriCares.

- Award a large consulting contract to Dr. Homer Green, a senior board member of WMH who has just sold his medical practice in New Budapest. It is hoped that his strong professional and personal contacts in the medical community will be instrumental in obtaining the joint venture agreement with the physicians and facilitating the transition from operating a hospital to partnering with physicians to run an ambulatory surgery center.

III. CERTIFICATE OF NEED REGULATION

Many states require local facilities to obtain a certificate of need (CON) prior to undertaking construction or renovation of facilities, purchasing major equipment, or offering new health services. Operating under the mandates of state statutory schemes, health planning agencies require that health care facilities demonstrate the "need" for such improvements and meet other financial and regulatory requirements. CON regulation is often criticized for inhibiting competition and innovation by requiring that providers satisfy regulatory requirements that are often vague, subjective, and conflicting. Moreover, the process of demonstrating need, financial feasibility, and quality of service may entail lengthy and costly administrative proceedings. At the same time, CON laws provide the states one of the few mechanisms by which they can control the supply and location of health care resources.

State CON regulation was spawned by the 1974 National Health Planning and Resources Development Act (NHPRDA), 42 U.S.C. §§ 300k–300t, Pub. L. No. 93–641 (1974), which conditioned eligibility for a variety of health care funding programs on adoption of state plans for allocating health care resources and CON laws to help implement those plans. As originally conceived, it was thought that state CON laws would reduce health care costs by reducing wasteful duplication of facilities while also improving access by rationalizing the allocation of service providers. Although 49 states eventually adopted CON laws, the repeal of NHPRDA in 1987 prompted many states to alter their CON statutes, with twelve states repealing CON altogether. As a result, state CON laws vary considerably in the kinds of facilities subject to CON regulation (e.g., hospitals, skilled nursing facilities, intermediate care facilities, and ambulatory surgical facilities), the capital thresholds at which the law applies, and the standards used to determine need. Currently, 35 states plus the District of Columbia, Puerto Rico, and the U.S. Virgin Islands maintain active CON programs. See generally, National Conference of State Legislatures, Certificate of Need State Laws (Dec. 2019). Three states—Arizona, Minnesota, and Wisconsin—do not have an official CON program but regulate health care services, facilities, and operations through similar laws.

Because they burden interstate commerce, CON laws have been challenged as violative of the dormant commerce clause. A threshold issue is whether the federal NHPRDA authorizing state CON laws, though now repealed, supplies authorization for a CON statute. See, e.g., Yakima Valley Memorial Hospital v. Washington State Department of Health, 654 F. 3d 919 (9th Cir. 2011) (remanding for determination of whether state CON regulations that prevent a hospital from providing angioplasty procedures do not violate the dormant Commerce Clause). On remand, however, the district court concluded that the regulations in question placed only incidental and "highly attenuated" burdens on commerce because they "do not treat in-state and out-of-state actors differently, nor are they an even-handed law that incidentally makes it harder for out-of-state actors to do business in the state." Yakima Valley Memorial Hospital v. Washington State Dept. of Health, 2012 WL 2720874 (E.D. Wash. July 9, 2012).

Most commentary is highly critical of CON regulation, arguing that it imposes obstacles to efficient reorganization of health care markets, invites obstructionist behavior, and is incompatible with the evolution of competitive health care markets. See, e.g., Emily Whelan Parento, Certificate of Need in the Post-Affordable Care Act Era, 105 Ky. L. J. 201, 207 (2017) ("Legal and policy scholars have been fairly unrestrained in their criticism of CON programs, noting the potential for regulatory capture by entrenched incumbent providers and the increasing irrelevance of CON laws in a dramatically altered reimbursement environment for healthcare providers."); Lauretta H. Wolfson, State Regulation of Health Facility Planning: The Economic Theory and Political Realities of Certificate of Need, 4 DePaul J. Health Care L. 261, 310 (1997) ("The process of obtaining a CON has become an enterprise in itself, becoming so lucrative that it attracts many politicians and former politicians who successfully use their influence to weight the process for those who employ their services."). The growth of ambulatory, retail, and freestanding clinics could provide options for patients to receive care in lower-cost settings, but restrictive CON and facility licensing laws may limit the ability of new types of facilities to enter the market to compete with established hospitals.

A number of studies question whether CON laws have achieved their purposes of lowering costs and allocating services more equitably. To the contrary, CON laws have been shown to increase costs without improving quality. See, e.g., Martin Gaynor, Farzad Mostashari, & Paul Ginsburg. Brookings Institution, Making Markets Work: Competition Policy for Healthcare (April 2017). A longstanding justification for CON laws is to ensure adequate supply of health care services—avoiding overutilization driven by oversupply or diminished access due to undersupply of services in rural areas. But the literature on CON laws' impact on health spending, patient outcomes, and access are mixed, leading some commentators to conclude that the costs of CON laws outweigh the benefits. Christopher J.

Conover & James Bailey, Certificate of Need Laws: A Systematic Review and Cost-Effectiveness Analysis, 20 BMC Health Services Res. 1 (2020).

The efficacy of CON regulation may also be affected by national health care trends. For example, during the COVID-19 pandemic when additional medical resources were needed to confront the public health crisis, some states suspended their CON laws to allow the rapid addition of hospital beds and emergency services and authorized emergency approvals for CON applications. Other states suspended their CON laws indefinitely for projects deemed necessary to respond to COVID-19. Empirical research suggests these measures were beneficial to the pandemic response. For states with high ICU utilization, suspending CON appears to have reduced weekly deaths from COVID-19. Sriparna Ghosh, Agnitra Roy Choudhury & Alicia Plemmons, Certificate-of-Need Laws and Healthcare Utilization during COVID-19 Pandemic (SSRN preprint, July 29, 2020).

Another difficulty with CON statutes lies in their drafting. In many cases, the approach is to set forth a "laundry list" of numerous factors, many of which are vague and thus invite subjective determinations. For example, Connecticut's statute contains twelve criteria for assessing need; another provision allows regulators to consider any additional criteria they see fit in determining need. Conn. Gen. Stat. Ann. § 19A–639 (West 2021).

As noted, CON laws were widely regarded as out of step with the development of competitive health care markets. Can you make a case for maintaining or strengthening CON laws as a backstop for health reform? Some health policy experts propose repurposing and modernizing CON to encourage quality improvements and value-based payment reforms. See Parento, supra. We will revisit the role of CON regulation in several contexts such as its effect on the development of specialty hospitals and its importance in planning joint ventures and integrated systems.

CHAPTER 13

TAX-EXEMPT HEALTH CARE ORGANIZATIONS

∎ ∎ ∎

I. FEDERAL TAX-EXEMPTION UNDER SECTION 501(c)(3)

Exemption from federal income taxation plays a prominent role in the affairs of many health care organizations. As described in Chapter 12, hospitals may be nonprofit, for-profit, or government-owned— classifications that refer to the ownership type and the corporate form under state law. By contrast, an organization's tax status refers to whether the entity is exempt from federal or state taxation. Although nonprofit hospitals need not be tax-exempt, in practice, the two classifications are often used interchangeably because most nonprofit hospitals are also tax-exempt. In addition, government-owned hospitals may have "dual status" as government-run and tax-exempt. In the U.S., 57% of hospitals are organized as nonprofits, 24% of hospitals are for-profits, and 19% are government-owned. Kaiser Family Foundation, Hospitals by Ownership Type, Time Frame: 2019.

Federal tax-exemption can also be contrasted with **state tax-exemption**. Section I of this chapter discusses the federal requirements for tax-exempt health care organizations, and Section II explores state tax-exemption. Federal tax-exemption is an important legal concern for health care organizations, not necessarily because more money is at stake than with state tax-exemption, but because federal tax law reaches into many aspects of health care entities' operations, including governance, relationships with other providers, and financial assistance policies.

Federal tax-exempt status carries with it significant benefits. Besides exemption from the corporate income tax, it permits the organization to enjoy exemption from federal unemployment taxes, preferred postal rates, and various other benefits respecting pensions and special treatment under various regulatory laws. Second, only donations to charitable organizations exempt under Section 501(c)(3) are deductible to donors under Internal Revenue Code (IRC) Section 170. Third, only charitable organizations can issue tax-exempt bonds, an important source of financing for nonprofit hospitals. IRC § 145.

26 U.S.C. § 501(c)(3)

Section 501(c)(3) of the Internal Revenue Code exempts from federal income tax entities "organized and operated exclusively for religious, charitable, scientific, testing for public safety, literary, or educational purposes, or to foster . . . amateur sports competition . . . or for the prevention of cruelty to animals." An organization must meet three important requirements to qualify for tax-exempt status:

(1) no part of its net earnings may inure to the benefit of any private shareholder or individual;

(2) no substantial part of its activities may consist of certain activities aimed at influencing legislation; and

(3) it may not participate or intervene in any political campaign on behalf of any candidate for public office.

Is there an internal logic to these requirements? Does the view that foregoing taxes on charitable nonprofit and other organizations amounts to a "subsidy" help explain these provisions?

A. CHARITABLE PURPOSES

1. Community Benefit Standard

To qualify for § 501(c)(3) status, a health care facility must meet both an "**organizational test**," which requires that the hospital's constitutive documents, such as the corporate articles of incorporation, limit its activities to exempt purposes, and an "**operational test**," which requires that the hospital be operated primarily for exempt purposes, including "charitable," "educational," or "religious" purposes. Note that "health care" is *not* listed among the exempt purposes, which means that to satisfy the operational test, most hospitals must qualify as being operated primarily for **charitable purposes**. However, the definition of charitable purposes under the Code has been quite controversial, with the Internal Revenue Service (IRS) attempting to adjust the definition to meet changes in the modern health care sector while the statute remains unchanged. Unfortunately, the federal tax authorities have not been clear or consistent in explaining when provisions of health care services are charitable. As a practical matter, few hospitals have failed to satisfy the flexible—some say overly flexible—standard that has evolved. However, as you read subsequent sections in this chapter, notice that the IRS and courts have been far less lenient with other kinds of health care entities.

The confused trail of the "charitable purposes" standard for hospitals begins with a 1956 Revenue Ruling that required a tax-exempt hospital to be operated "to the extent of its financial ability for those not able to pay for the services rendered." Rev. Ruling 56–185. In 1958, the Tax Court upheld the denial of exempt status for a hospital that devoted between 2% and 5% of its revenue to care for the indigent (Lorain Avenue Clinic v. Commissioner, 31 T.C. 141). Thus, earlier in its history, the IRS identified direct link between a hospital's exempt status and the provision of a specified quantum of free care for the poor.

A pivotal turning point, however, occurred in 1969 when an IRS Revenue Ruling adopted a "**community benefit**" standard, under which the provision of charity care was no longer the *sine qua non* for charitable status, instead requiring only that the hospital promote health for the general benefit of the community. Rev. Rul. 69–545. The Ruling suggested that the existence of a governing board composed of "independent civic leaders" drawn from the community; an emergency room open to all; an open medical staff; treatment of government-insured patients, and the application of any surplus to improving facilities, equipment, patient care, and medical training, education, and research would provide adequate evidence the entity was serving charitable purposes. Notably, the 1969 Ruling concluded, "Revenue Ruling 56–185 is hereby modified to remove therefrom the requirements relating to caring for patients without charge or at rates below cost." Indeed, the example hospital that the IRS concluded would qualify for tax-exemption did not serve indigent patients who were unable to pay for care, other than in the emergency context.

Commentators have noted that Revenue Rul. 69–545 marked the IRS's shift from the older "quid-pro-quo" theory, under which tax-exemption was justified as a quid-pro-quo for the hospital relieving the government's burden to care for the poor, to the community benefit theory that renders the hospital's activity as charitable because it benefits the community, not because it relieves a government burden. See Mark Hall & John Colombo, The Charitable Hospital, 20 Wash. L. Rev. 307 (1991). The remarkable shift marked by Revenue Ruling 69–545 was not the product of an informed analysis of the benefits of nonprofit health care, nor did it involve legislative action. Instead, it appears it was the result of the erroneous assumption of IRS staff attorneys that the recently-enacted Medicaid statute would obviate the need for charity care and that a new justification was therefore needed to preserve the dominant nonprofit hospital sector. See generally, Daniel M. Fox & Daniel C. Schaffer, Tax Administration as Health Policy: Hospitals, The Internal Revenue Service and the Courts, 16 J. Health Pol. Pol'y & L. 251 (1991).

The link to the provision of free care to the indigent under federal law was further diluted by a 1983 Revenue Ruling in which a hospital qualified for tax-exempt status even though it did not operate an emergency room and usually referred indigent patients to another hospital. The illustrative hospital did not operate an ER because the state health planning agency had concluded that the emergency room was not needed in the area as other nearby hospitals had adequate emergency services. Rev. Rul. 83–157.

Thus, for almost fifty years, federal tax-exempt status has not been strictly tied to the provision of free care to the indigent, or for that matter, to doing anything terribly different than for-profit hospitals. For academic criticism of the community benefit standard for hospital-tax exemption, see John D. Colombo, The Failure of Community Benefit, 15 Health Matrix 29 (2005); Nancy Kane, Tax-Exempt Hospitals: What Is Their Charitable Responsibility and How Should It Be Defined and Reported, 51 St. Louis U. L. J. 459 (2007). For a defense nonprofit hospitals' continued tax-exemption, see, e.g., Jill Horwitz, Why We Need the Independent Sector: The Behavior, Law, and Ethics of Not-for-Profit Hospitals, 50 UCLA L. Rev. 1345 (2003).

Growing dissatisfaction with the community benefit standard led to increasing scrutiny for tax-exempt hospitals at the federal level. In the mid-2000s, Congress engaged in a flurry of activities in reaction to public outcry generated by media reports and class-action lawsuits against tax-exempt hospitals alleging that tax-exempt hospitals had violated their charitable obligations by providing minimal free or reduced-cost care to indigent patients (colloquially called "charity care") and engaging in harsh billing and collection practices against their patients. Members of Congress, particularly Senator Charles Grassley, then-chair of the Senate Finance Committee, began publicly questioning whether tax-exempt hospitals were providing sufficient community benefits to earn tax-exemption. The critique was multi-faceted, touching upon inadequate charity care, unreasonable prices, harsh collection tactics, excessive executive compensation, and the lack of transparency and accountability about the value of community benefits provided. In the years leading up to the passage of the Affordable Care Act (ACA) in 2010, both chambers of Congress pursued policies to tighten requirements for tax-exempt hospitals. There were three committee hearings, two reports each by the Government Accountability Office and Congressional Budget Office, a discussion draft, and two bills, including the Senate Finance Committee's America's Healthy Future Act, the proposals of which were incorporated into the ACA's new requirements for tax-exempt hospitals, codified in IRC § 501(r).

One of the most important outcomes of this flurry of activity was the IRS's issuance of a redesigned **Form 990**—the information return that tax-exempt organizations must file annually. Modeled to some extent on SEC disclosure forms, the new Form 990 radically changed the reporting requirements for tax-exempt entities. Of particular relevance to hospitals, the form added **Schedule H**, which requires tax-exempt hospital organizations to submit a Community Benefit Report that includes reporting for seven categories of patient financial assistance and community benefit, a description of its financial assistance policy, a statement of how it assesses community needs, and detailed information about billing and debt collection practices. See Gerald M. Griffith et al., IRS Mandates Heightened Transparency in Redesigned Form 990, 11 Health Law. News 8 (Aug. 2007). Following the passage of the ACA, the IRS amended Schedule H again to account for changes imposed by the ACA, including the new requirements for exempt status discussed in the following section.

2. Additional Requirements for Tax-Exempt Charitable Hospitals: IRC Section 501(r)

The ACA incorporated some ideas from previous reform proposals dealing with the issue of tax-exempt hospitals' uncharitable actions, but stopped short of mandating specific levels of financial assistance as advocated by some in Congress. The law added new Section 501(r) to the Internal Revenue Code, which imposes a series of specific statutory requirements that hospitals must satisfy in order to qualify for exemption under IRC Section 501(c)(3).

These provisions apply to any "hospital organization," defined as an organization that operates at least one facility that is required to be licensed or registered as a hospital under state law, as well as any organization that the Secretary of the Treasury determines provides hospital care as the principal basis for its tax exemption. Significantly, hospital organizations operating more than one hospital facility must meet the 501(r) requirements separately for each facility. The rules apply to dual-status government hospitals that are tax-exempt. Hospital-owned physician practices that are part of a hospital organization (and not separate taxable entities) are subject to both the community health needs assessment and financial assistance obligations.

On December 29, 2014, the IRS issued its Final Rule implementing section 501(r). 79 Fed. Reg. 78954 (Dec. 31, 2014), codified at 26 C.F.R. 1.501(r). For an excellent summary and analysis of the regulations, see Sara Rosenbaum, Additional Rules for Charitable Hospitals: Final Rules on Community Health Needs Assessment and Financial Assistance, Health Aff. Blog (Jan. 25, 2015).

Section 501(r), as further implemented by IRS rules, includes the following requirements:

1. Community Health Needs Assessment

Tax-exempt hospitals must conduct a **community health needs assessment (CHNA)** at least once every three years and must make that assessment widely available to the public. The ACA mandates that hospitals then adopt an implementation strategy to meet the needs identified in the assessment. In so doing, hospitals must obtain input from a broad cross-section of the community they serve. Any hospital that fails to conduct the CHNA will be subject to an excise tax of $50,000.

The IRS rules make clear that CHNAs must address not only the community's deficits in health care or access but also its health *needs*. The responsibility therefore extends to assessing social determinants of health including housing, environment, and nutrition. The IRS emphasized the need to "prevent illness" and "address social, behavioral, and environmental factors that influence health in the community." 79 Fed. Reg. 78963 (Dec. 31, 2014). The rule also stressed that CHNAs must assess the broader community that needs the hospital's care, not simply the hospital's current patients. Drawing a somewhat fuzzy line, the rule states that in defining its community, a hospital can take into account the geographic market it serves, its target populations, and its principal functions, but may not exclude various groups, such as the medically underserved and low-income populations, or take into account the uninsured or publicly insured status of the community. 26 C.F.R. § 1–501(r)–3.

2.   *Financial Assistance and Emergency Medical Care Policies*

Tax-exempt hospitals must maintain and widely publicize a written **financial assistance policy (FAP)** that sets forth eligibility criteria for free or discounted care for low-income patients as well as how charges to such patients are calculated. The hospital's emergency care policy must require it to provide, without discrimination, care for emergency medical conditions regardless of the patient's eligibility under the financial assistance policy. IRC § 501(r)(4). However, the 501(r) rules do not contain any guidelines for how hospitals must determine eligibility for financial assistance, leaving these determinations to the hospitals' complete discretion. 26 C.F.R. § 501(r)–4.

The IRS rules make clear that the FAP applies not only to emergency and medically necessary care provided by the hospital but also to such care provided by "substantially related entities," such as partnerships with other entities. For entities that do not meet the substantially related test, such as contracted organizations that are separate for tax purposes, the FAP must specify such relationships. Notably, where a hospital facility outsources the operation of its emergency room to a third party that is not covered under the hospital facility's FAP, the hospital facility may not be considered to operate an emergency room for purposes of the community benefit factors considered in Rev. Rul. 69–545. As to what constitutes medically necessary care, the rule provides some flexibility, allowing hospitals to define the extent of such care, stating "a hospital facility may but is not required to use a definition of medically necessary care applicable under the laws of the state in which it is licensed, including the Medicaid definition, a definition that refers to the generally accepted standards of medicine in the community, or to an examining physician's determination." 26 C.F.R. § 501(r)–4.

3.   Limitations on Charges

For individuals who are eligible to receive financial assistance under the hospital's policy, a hospital cannot charge more than the **"amounts generally billed" (AGB)** to insured individuals for emergency and other medically necessary care. The hospital may not charge patients who are eligible for financial assistance "gross charges," defined in the rules as the chargemaster rate, a hospital facility's full, established price for medical care that the hospital facility consistently and uniformly charges patients before applying any contractual allowances, discounts, or deductions. 26 C.F.R. § 1.501(r)–1(16).

The IRS rules provide three alternate methods of calculating AGB. The first method calculates AGB as the amount that would be paid by Medicare, including Medicare beneficiary co-insurance. The second method of calculating AGB takes into account the amounts received for patients insured by both Medicare and private insurers. The third method bases AGB on the amount paid by Medicaid, either alone or in combination with the rates paid by Medicare and private insurers. 26 C.F.R. § 1.501(r)–5. The IRS regulations do not allow AGB to be calculated solely on rates paid by private insurers.

4.   Billing and Collection

A hospital must make reasonable efforts to determine whether a patient is eligible for assistance under its financial assistance policy before taking any **"extraordinary collection actions" (ECAs)** to collect unpaid bills. The IRS defines extraordinary collection actions to include lawsuits against the patient, placing a lien or foreclosing on residences, seizing bank accounts or personal property, arrest, garnishing wages, reporting an individual to a credit agency, selling debt to a third-party collector, and requiring payment of a prior debt before providing medically necessary care. To have made "reasonable efforts," a hospital must determine whether an individual is eligible for financial assistance or notify the patient about the availability of financial assistance during a notification period that ends 120 days after the date of the first bill. 26 C.F.R. § 1.501(r)–6. The 501(r) requirements do not prohibit a hospital from using extraordinary collection actions if it follows the required procedures to notify and allow the patient to complete an application for financial assistance. Although the rules require the hospital to suspend or reverse ECAs against patients deemed eligible for financial assistance, once it has made "reasonable efforts", the hospital may use ECAs to collect unpaid medical bills from patients who are ineligible for financial assistance or who fail to complete the application within the allotted time. Tax-exempt hospitals must have a billing and collections policy or include in their financial assistance policies the actions the hospital may take if bills are not paid.

5. Audited Financial Statements

Exempt hospitals will be required to provide, along with their IRS Form 990 filing (and hence publicly disclose), copies of audited financial statements for the organization or consolidated financial statements for organizations that prepare financials on a consolidated basis.

NOTES AND QUESTIONS

1. *Failure to Satisfy § 501(r).* In the most extreme cases, a tax-exempt hospital can lose its exempt status—the "death penalty"—for failure to comply with the requirements of 501(r). The IRS rules give some guidance on when the IRS will revoke a hospital's exempt status under 501(r), outlining a ten-factor "facts and circumstances" test to evaluate the potential seriousness of violations. This test takes into account the nature and scope of the failure, past conduct, the existence of a compliance plan at the time of the failure, and actions to correct and disclose the failure. An entire hospital organization operating multiple hospital facilities could lose its tax-exempt status even if only one of its hospital facilities fails to meet the requirements of 501(r). Alternatively, the hospital organization could retain its tax-exempt status, but income from the noncompliant hospital facility could be taxed. "Minor omissions and errors" that are inadvertent or due to reasonable cause will not result in loss of exempt status or income taxation, but prompt reporting and correction are expected. However, any hospital facility that fails to meet the CHNA requirement will be subject to a $50,000 excise tax, even upon correction and disclosure. 26 C.F.R. § 1.501(r)–2.

In 2017 and 2018, the IRS announced that it had revoked the tax-exemption from two dual-status government-owned hospitals for failure to satisfy the requirements of IRC § 501(r). The IRS explained that the revocation was based upon the hospital's failures to perform an adequate CHNA and to adopt the required implementation strategy to address identified community needs The second hospital also had not posted its FAP, emergency care policy, or billing and collection policy on its website, as required by law. Neither hospital contested the IRS's assertions, remaining as government-owned hospitals and agreeing to loss of tax-exemption. IRS P.L.R. 201731014 (Feb. 14, 2017); IRS P.L.R. 201829017 (July 20, 2018).

2. *Relationship Between 501(r) and Community Benefit.* Does a hospital's compliance with 501(r) mean that the hospital has satisfied the community benefit standard for charitable purposes? The IRS regulations are not clear. On the one hand, the 501(r) requirements are characterized as "additional" requirements for hospitals to maintain their tax-exemption, suggesting they do not supplant the prior requirements of the community benefit standard. On the other hand, if a hospital satisfies all the requirements of 501(r), particularly the CHNA and offering financial assistance, it would

appear to be operating for the benefit of the community. What becomes of the factors suggested in Rev. Rul. 69–545, and does the hospital that satisfies 501(r) still need to operate an emergency room, have a community board and open medical staff, and see Medicare and Medicaid patients? See Mary Crossley, Health and Taxes: Hospitals, Community Health and the IRS, 16 Yale J. Health Pol'y, L. & Ethics 51 (2016).

3.   *Limits of Financial Assistance, Billing, and Collection Requirements.* As noted above, 501(r) does not require tax-exempt hospitals to provide charity care. Moreover, the rules give hospitals broad discretion to determine eligibility for financial assistance, which triggers the protections against billing patients gross charges and using extraordinary collection actions. Under the rules, a hospital could adopt a narrow financial assistance policy with very restrictive income requirements or make applying for financial assistance so onerous that few are able to complete the process to qualify. A great deal of variation persists among hospitals' financial assistance and billing and collection policies and practices. See Erin C. Fuse Brown, IRS rules Will Not Stop Unfair Hospital Billing and Collection Practices, 17 AMA J. of Ethics 763 (2015). Some question whether the 501(r) requirements have done enough to improve investments in community benefit by tax-exempt hospitals, especially when compared to their for-profit counterparts. See Gary Young et al., Community Benefit Spending By Tax-Exempt Hospitals Changed Little After ACA, 37 Health Aff. 121 (2019); Ge Bai et al., Analysis Suggests Government And Nonprofit Hospitals' Charity Care Is Not Aligned With Their Favorable Tax Treatment, 40 Health Aff. 629 (2021).

4.   *Enforcement and Oversight.* The IRS enforces the rules and regulations related to tax-exempt hospitals through its Tax Exempt and Government Entities (TE/GE) division. Tax-exempt hospitals are required to report community benefit expenditures and 501(r) requirements on Schedule H to Form 990 on their annual tax returns. The TE/GE division uses the information from tax disclosures during triannual Community Benefit Activity Reviews (CBARs) to determine whether a hospital has satisfied the tax-exempt requirements or, alternatively, whether to conduct an audit of the hospital's practices.

Despite new enforcement provisions provided by the ACA, the effective oversight of tax-exempt hospitals remains a challenge for the IRS. A report by the Government Accountability Office (GAO) identified certain obstacles to assessing whether tax-exempt hospitals satisfy community benefit and 501(r) requirements. See generally, United States Government Accountability Office, Opportunities Exist to Improve Oversight of Hospitals' Tax-Exempt Status (September 2020). According to the GAO, the rules and regulations designed to assess community benefit are too ambiguous to provide effective levels of enforcement. Id. at 9. For example, although the Code requires hospitals to provide a community benefit, the regulations do not provide clear or specific examples of what activities satisfy the requirement, and instead refer in the negative to activities that do not create a community benefit. Moreover, some of the factors identified by the IRS may be outdated. The GAO remarks that maintaining an open medical staff and accepting Medicare and Medicaid patients are common practices at most tax-exempt hospitals, which means that some hospitals could gain tax-exempt status despite providing minimal or no community benefit. To close these enforcement gaps, the GAO report recommended, among other things, for Congress to provide clarity with regard to activities that satisfy the community benefit standard and for the IRS impose requirements to ensure greater transparency from hospitals.

3. Charitable Purposes: Health Maintenance Organizations and Integrated Delivery Systems

As discussed in previous chapters, health maintenance organizations (HMOs) typically deliver both office-based primary care and hospital-based acute care to their subscribers who prepay a premium to the HMO to cover needed services regardless of the amount or cost of medical services actually used. In this way, HMOs combine the functions of insurance and health care delivery. In their provision of office-based primary care, HMOs resemble doctors' medical practices, which traditionally have been organized as for-profit entities and have not received tax exemption. As discussed in Chapters 10 and 12, integrated delivery systems like IHC and Geisinger combine physician, hospital and other provider services with management and support services and, sometimes, a health plan. The structures chosen for integration will have implications for the tax status of individual organizations within the system and of the integrated system itself.

The *IHC Health Plan* case and the *Geisinger* cases in the notes that follow discuss exempt status under the community benefit standard for stand-alone HMOs and those that are part of an integrated delivery system. As illustrated in these cases, courts have struggled to devise a test regarding whether an HMO warrants exemption based on its relationship to the integrated delivery system.

IHC Hᴇᴀʟᴛʜ Pʟᴀɴs, Iɴᴄ. ᴠ. Cᴏᴍᴍɪssɪᴏɴᴇʀ OF Iɴᴛᴇʀɴᴀʟ Rᴇᴠᴇɴᴜᴇ
United States Court of Appeals, Tenth Circuit, 2003.
325 F.3d 1188.

Before Tᴀᴄʜᴀ, Cʜɪᴇғ Cɪʀᴄᴜɪᴛ Jᴜᴅɢᴇ, Hᴏʟʟᴏᴡᴀʏ, and Eʙᴇʟ, Cɪʀᴄᴜɪᴛ Jᴜᴅɢᴇs.

Tᴀᴄʜᴀ, Cʜɪᴇғ Cɪʀᴄᴜɪᴛ Jᴜᴅɢᴇ.

I. Background

IHC Health Plans, Inc. ("Health Plans"), on its own behalf and as successor in interest to IHC Care, Inc. ("Care") and IHC Group, Inc. ("Group") (collectively "petitioners"), appeals the Tax Court's decision denying petitioners' request for tax exemption under 26 U.S.C. § 501(c)(3).

The sole issue presented in this appeal is whether petitioners qualify for tax-exempt status under 26 U.S.C. § 501(c)(3) as organizations operated exclusively for charitable purposes.

A.   The IHC Integrated Delivery System

* * *

[Intermountain Health Care Inc. ("IHC") formed IHC Health Services ("Health Services") in 1982 as a Utah nonprofit corporation to operate twenty-two hospitals located in Utah and Idaho, employing approximately 300 primary care physicians and 100 specialist physicians in its Physician Division and separately employing approximately 120 physicians in its Hospital Division.] Between 1997 and 1999, Health Services provided nearly $1.2 billion in health care services, without reimbursement to patients covered by Medicare, Medicaid, and other governmental programs. During the same period, Health Services furnished more than $91 million in free health-care services to indigent patients.

The Commissioner has recognized Health Services as a tax-exempt organization under section 501(c)(3).

3.   Health Plans, Care, and Group

In order to further integrate its provision of health-care services, IHC formed Health Plans, Care, and Group to operate as health maintenance organizations ("HMOs") within the IHC Integrated Delivery System. . . .

* * *

E.   The Commissioner's Decision

In 1999, the Commissioner concluded that neither Health Plans, Care, nor Group operated exclusively for exempt purposes under section 501(c)(3). . . . Accordingly, the Commissioner revoked Health Plans' tax-exempt status, retroactive to January 1, 1987, and denied exemptions to Care and Group.

Health Plans, Care, and Group brought suit in the United States Tax Court, seeking a declaratory judgment reversing the Commissioner's adverse determinations. On September 25, 2001, the Tax Court affirmed the Commissioner's conclusions in three separate opinions. [ ] This appeal followed.

II.   Discussion

A.   Standard of Review

. . . The appropriate legal standard for determining whether an organization operates for a "charitable" purpose is a legal question, which we review de novo. Whether an organization in fact operates exclusively for a charitable purpose, however, is a question of fact, which we review for clear error. [ ] As the taxpayer claiming entitlement to exemption, petitioners bear the burden of proof. [ ]

B.   *Overview of Applicable Law*

* * *

. . . In this case, the sole question we must consider is whether Health Plans, Care, and Group operated exclusively for exempt purposes within the meaning of section 501(c)(3).

C.   *Whether Health Plans, Care, and Group Operated for a Charitable Purpose*

This inquiry requires us to address two basic questions. First, we must consider whether the purpose proffered by petitioners qualifies as a "charitable" purpose under section 501(c)(3). "The term 'charitable' is used in section 501(c)(3) in its generally accepted legal sense and is . . . not to be construed as limited by the separate enumeration in section 501(c)(3)." 26 C.F.R. § 1.501(c)(3)–1(d)(2). An organization will not be considered charitable, however, "unless it serves a *public rather than a private interest*." 26 C.F.R. § 1.501(c)(3)–1(d)(1)(ii) (emphasis added).[11]

Second, we must determine whether petitioners in fact operated *primarily* for this purpose. [ ] Under the "operational test" set forth in the IRS regulations, "[a]n organization will be regarded as 'operated exclusively' for one or more exempt purposes only if it engages primarily in activities which accomplish one or more of such exempt purposes specified in section 501(c)(3). An organization will not be so regarded if more than an insubstantial part of its activities is not in furtherance of an exempt purpose."[12] 26 C.F.R. § 1.501(c)(3)–1(c)(1).

In this case, the Tax Court concluded that "the promotion of health for the benefit of the community is a charitable purpose," [ ] but found that neither Health Plans, Care, nor Group operated primarily to benefit the community. [ ] For the reasons set forth below, we agree.

1.   *The promotion of health as a charitable purpose*

In defining "charitable," our analysis must focus on whether petitioners' activities conferred a *public* benefit.[ ] The public-benefit requirement highlights the *quid pro quo* nature of tax exemptions: the public is willing to relieve an organization from the burden of taxation in exchange for the public benefit it provides. [ ] As the Supreme Court has recognized, "[c]haritable exemptions are justified on the basis that the

---

[11] Although we are not bound by IRS regulations or revenue rulings, we do accord them deference. [ ]

[12] The Supreme Court construed a similar provision under the Social Security Act in *Better Business Bureau v. United States,* concluding that "a single non-[exempt] purpose, if substantial in nature, will destroy the exemption regardless of the number or importance of truly [exempt] purposes." 326 U.S. 279, 283, 66 S. Ct. 112, 90 L. Ed. 67 (1945).

exempt entity confers a *public benefit*—a benefit which the society or the community may not itself choose or be able to provide, or which supplements and advances the work of public institutions already supported by tax revenues." *Bob Jones Univ. v. United States,* 461 U.S. 574, 591, 103 S.Ct. 2017, 76 L.Ed.2d 157 (1983) (emphasis added).

* * *

[The Court reviews the IRS and judicial interpretations of the community benefit standard]. Thus, under the IRS's interpretation of section 501(c)(3), in the context of health-care providers, we must determine whether the taxpayer operates *primarily for the benefit of the community.*[16] And while the concept of "community benefit" is somewhat amorphous, we agree with the IRS, the Tax Court, and the Third Circuit that it provides a workable standard for determining tax exemption under section 501(c)(3).

b.   Defining "community benefit"

In giving form to the community-benefit standard, we stress that "not every activity that promotes health supports tax exemption under § 501(c)(3). For example, selling prescription pharmaceuticals certainly promotes health, but pharmacies cannot qualify for . . . exemption under § 501(c)(3) on that basis alone." [ ] In other words, engaging in an activity that promotes health, *standing alone,* offers an insufficient indicium of an organization's purpose. Numerous for-profit enterprises offer products or services that promote health.

Similarly, the IRS rulings in 69–545 and 83–157 demonstrate that an organization cannot satisfy the community-benefit requirement based solely on the fact that it offers health-care services to all in the community[17] in exchange for a fee.[18] Although providing health-care products or services to all in the community is necessary under those rulings, it is insufficient,

---

[16] [C]ourt decisions have highlighted several factors relevant under the "community benefit" analysis. These factors include:

(1) size of the class eligible to benefit; (2) free or below-cost products or services; (3) treatment of persons participating in governmental programs such as Medicare or Medicaid; (4) use of surplus funds for research or educational programs; and (5) composition of the board of trustees.[ ] Douglas M. Mancino, Income Tax Exemption of the Contemporary Nonprofit Hospital, 32 ST. LOUIS U. L.J. 1015, 1037–70 (1988).

[17] We recognize that certain health-care entities provide specialized services, which are not required by "all" in the community, and we do not mean to foreclose the possibility that such entities may qualify as "charitable" under section 501(c)(3). As the IRS recognized in Rev. Rul. 83–157:

Certain specialized hospitals, such as eye hospitals and cancer hospitals, offer medical care limited to special conditions unlikely to necessitate emergency care and do not, as a practical matter, maintain emergency rooms. These organizations may also qualify under section 501(c)(3) if there are present similar, significant factors that demonstrate that the hospitals operate exclusively to benefit the community.

[18] At least where the fee is above cost. We express no opinion on whether an enterprise that sold health-promoting products or services entirely at or below cost would qualify for tax exemption under 501(c)(3).

standing alone, to qualify for tax exemption under section 501(c)(3). Rather, the organization must provide some additional "plus."

This plus is perhaps best characterized as "a benefit which the society or the community may not itself choose or be able to provide, or which supplements and advances the work of public institutions already supported by tax revenues." [ ] Concerning the former, the IRS rulings provide a number of examples: providing free or below-cost services, *see* Rev. Rul. 56–185; maintaining an emergency room open to all, regardless of ability to pay, *see* Rev. Rul. 69–545; and devoting surpluses to research, education, and medical training, *see* Rev. Rul. 83–157. These services fall under the general umbrella of "positive externalities" or "public goods."[19] Concerning the latter, the primary way in which health-care providers advance government-funded endeavors is the servicing of the Medicaid and Medicare populations.

c.   Quantifying "community benefit"

Difficulties will inevitably arise in quantifying the required community benefit. The governing statutory language, however, provides some guidance. Under section 501(c)(3), an organization is not entitled to tax exemption unless it operates for a charitable *purpose*. Thus, the existence of some incidental community benefit is insufficient. Rather, the magnitude of the community benefit conferred must be sufficient to give rise to a strong inference that the organization operates *primarily for the purpose of benefitting the community*. [ ]

Thus, our inquiry turns "not [on] the nature of the activity, but [on] the *purpose* accomplished thereby." [ ] Of course, because of the inherent difficulty in determining a corporate entity's subjective purpose, we necessarily rely on objective indicia in conducting our analysis. [ ] In determining an organization's purpose, we primarily consider the manner in which the entity carries on its activities. [ ]

d.   The resulting test

In summary, under section 501(c)(3), a health-care provider must make its services available to all in the community *plus* provide additional community or public benefits. The benefit must either further the function of government-funded institutions or provide a service that would not likely be provided within the community but for the subsidy. Further, the additional public benefit conferred must be sufficient to give rise to a strong inference that the public benefit is the *primary purpose* for which the organization operates. In conducting this inquiry, we consider the totality

---

[19]   Under the Treasury Department's view, for-profit enterprises are unlikely to provide such services since " 'market prices . . . do not reflect the benefit [these services] confer on the community as a whole.' " [ ] Thus, the provision of such "public goods"—at least when conducted on a sufficiently large scale—arguably supports an inference that the enterprise is responding to some inducement that is not market-based. *Cf. id.*

of the circumstances. With these principles in mind, we proceed to review the Tax Court's decision in the present case.

* * *

3.   *The Tax Court correctly concluded that petitioners do not operate primarily to promote health for the benefit of the community.*

Petitioners ... argue that the Tax Court erred in concluding that petitioners did not operate primarily for the benefit of the community. We disagree.

a.   Nature of the product or service and the character of the transaction

In this case, we deal with organizations that do not provide health-care services directly. Rather, petitioners furnish group insurance entitling enrollees to services of participating hospitals and physicians. Petitioners determine premiums using two methods: (1) an adjusted community rating for individuals and small employers; and (2) past-claims experience for large employers. Thus, ... petitioners "sell [ ] insurance coverage ... extend[ing] benefits in return for a premium based generally on the risk assumed." [ ] In other words, petitioners primarily perform a "risk-bearing function." In *Church of the Brethren,* as in the instant case, the commercial nature of this activity inspired doubt as to the entity's charitable purpose. 759 F.2d at 795; *cf. Federation Pharmacy Servs., Inc. v. C.I.R.,* 72 T.C. 687, 691–92, 1979 WL 3712 (1979), *aff'd* 625 F.2d 804 (8th Cir.1980) (noting that selling pharmaceuticals is "an activity that is normally carried on by a commercial profit making enterprise[ ]"). Where, as here, "[i]t is difficult to distinguish the plaintiff corporation from a mutual insurance company," we must carefully scrutinize the organization's operation.[23]

b.   Free or below-cost products or services

The fact that an activity is normally undertaken by commercial for-profit entities does not necessarily preclude tax exemption, particularly where the entity offers its services at or below-cost.[ ] But petitioners provide virtually no free or below-cost health-care services.[ ] All enrollees must pay a premium in order to receive benefits.[25] As the Eighth Circuit has recognized, "[a]n organization which does not extend some of its benefits to individuals financially unable to make the required payments [generally] reflects a commercial activity rather than a charitable one."

---

[23] We are primarily concerned with this characteristic as it bears on our determination of petitioners' purpose. However, we also note that petitioners not only resemble commercial insurance providers, petitioners in fact compete with commercial insurance providers. Thus, "granting a tax exemption to [petitioners] would necessarily disadvantage other for-profit [entities] with which [petitioners] compete[ ]."

[25] Petitioners note that Care and Group offered "risk" and "cost" Medicare health plans, and contend that Care and Group went forward with these plans "with the full knowledge that those plans might lose money." Care and Group discontinued these plans, however, based on concerns of "financial feasibility."

Federation Pharmacy Servs., Inc. v. C.I.R., 625 F.2d 804, 807 (8th Cir.1980). Further, the fact that petitioners in no way subsidize dues for those who cannot afford subscribership distinguishes this case from the HMOs in *Sound Health Ass'n v. C.I.R.,* 71 T.C. 158, 1978 WL 3393 (1979), and *Geisinger I,* 985 F.2d at 1219.

We acknowledge, as did the Tax Court, that petitioners' "adjusted community rating system[ ] likely allowed its enrollees to obtain medical care at a lower cost than might otherwise have been available." [ ] Again, however, selling services at a discount tells us little about the petitioners' *purpose.* "Many profit making organizations sell at a discount." [ ] In considering price as it relates to an organization's purpose, there is a qualitative difference between selling at a discount and selling below cost.[26]

In sum, petitioners['] sole activity is arranging for health-care services in exchange for a fee. To elevate the attendant health benefit over the character of the transaction would pervert Congress' intent in providing for charitable tax exemptions under section 501(c)(3). Contrary to petitioners' insinuation, the Tax Court did not accord dispositive weight to the absence of free care. Neither do we. Rather, it is yet another factor that belies petitioners' professions of a charitable purpose.[27]

[The court also found that nothing in the record indicates that petitioners conducted research or offered free educational programs to the public, noting that petitioners' "Core Wellness Program" was offered exclusively to enrollees.]

d.   The class eligible to benefit

(1) Health Plans

As the Tax Court noted, "[Health Plans] offered its [coverage] to a broad cross-section of the community including individuals, the employees of both large and small employers, and individuals eligible for Medicaid benefits." In fact, in 1999, Health Plans' enrollees represented twenty percent of Utah's total population and fifty percent of Utah residents eligible for Medicaid benefits.[29]

---

[26] Further, as the Tax Court noted, "the benefit associated with these cost savings is more appropriately characterized as a benefit to petitioner[s]' enrollees as opposed to the community at large."

[27] As the Eighth Circuit has noted, "a 'charitable' hospital may impose charges or fees for services rendered, and indeed its charity record may be comparatively low depending upon all the facts ... but a serious question is raised where its charitable operation is virtually inconsequential." *Federation Pharmacy,* 625 F.2d at 807 (8th Cir.1980) (quoting *Sonora Cmty. Hosp. v. C.I.R.,* 46 T.C. 519, 526, 1966 WL 1319 (1966)) (internal quotation marks omitted).

[29] We acknowledge that Health Plans' service to Utah's Medicaid community provides some community benefit. The relevant inquiry, however, is not "whether [petitioner] benefited the community at all ... [but] whether it primarily benefited the community, as an entity must in order to qualify for tax-exempt status." [ ]

Nevertheless, even though almost all Utahans were potentially eligible to enroll for Health Plans coverage, the self-imposed requirement of membership tells us something about Health Plans' operation. As the Third Circuit noted in *Geisinger I:*

> The community benefited is, in fact, limited to those who belong to [the HMO] since the requirement of subscribership remains a condition precedent to any service. Absent any additional indicia of a charitable purpose, this self-imposed precondition suggests that [the HMO] is primarily benefitting itself (and, perhaps, secondarily benefiting the community) by promoting subscribership throughout the areas it serves.

985 F.2d at 1219. Further, while the absence of a large class of potential beneficiaries may preclude tax-exempt status, its presence standing alone provides little insight into the organization's purpose. Offering products and services to a broad segment of the population is as consistent with self promotion and profit maximization as it is with any "charitable" purpose.

(2)   Care and Group

Neither Care nor Group offered their health plans to the general public. Rather, both Care and Group limited their enrollment to employees of large employers (employers with 100 or more employees). Thus, as the Tax Court found, "[Care and Group] operate[d] in a manner that substantially limit[ed] [the] universe of potential enrollees." [ ] Based on this finding, the Tax Court correctly concluded that neither Care nor Group promoted health for the benefit of the community.

e.   Community board of trustees

Finally, we consider petitioners' board composition. Prior to 1996, Health Plans' bylaws provided that "[a] plurality of Board members shall represent the buyer-employer community and an approximately equal number of physicians and hospitals representatives shall be appointed." As the IRS noted, Health Plans' pre-1996 bylaws skewed control towards subscribers, rather than the community at large. In 1996, however, Health Plans amended its bylaws to require that a majority of board members be disinterested and broadly representative of the community.

It makes little difference whether we consider petitioners' board prior to 1996 or following the amendments. Even if we were to conclude petitioners' board broadly represents the community, the dearth of any actual community benefit in this case rebuts any inference we might otherwise draw.

4. *Conclusion*

For the above reasons, we agree with the Tax Court's conclusion that petitioners, standing alone, do not qualify for tax exemption under section 501(c)(3).

* * *

D. *Whether Petitioners Qualify for Tax-Exempt Status as an "Integral Part" of Health Services*

Petitioners contend that even if they do not qualify for tax exemption standing alone, they qualify based on the fact that their activities are an "integral part" of Health Services, essential to Health Services in accomplishing its tax-exempt purpose. We disagree.

In general, "separately incorporated entities must qualify for tax exemption on their own merits." [ ] Several circuits, however, have recognized a so-called "exception" to this general rule, commonly called the integral-part doctrine. [ ] ("[The] 'integral part doctrine' . . . may best be described as an exception to the general rule that entitlement to exemption is derived solely from an entity's own characteristics."); [ ] Under the integral-part doctrine, where an organization's sole activity is an "integral part" of an exempt affiliate's activities, the organization may derive its exemption from that of its affiliate. [ ]

To the extent the integral-part doctrine rests on a derivative theory of exemption, it runs contrary to two fundamental tenets of tax law: (1) the "doctrine of corporate entity," under which a corporation is a separate and distinct taxable entity; and (2) the canon of statutory interpretation requiring strict construction of exemptions from taxation.[31] . . . IHC separately incorporated Health Services, Health Plans, Care, and Group. "It cannot now escape the tax consequences of that choice, no matter how bona fide its motives or longstanding its arrangements." [ ] Further, we reject petitioners' contention that the integral-part doctrine constitutes a "less rigorous" road to tax exemption. The rigor of the charitable-purpose requirement remains constant, regardless of the theory upon which the taxpayer bases its entitlement to tax exemption under section 501(c)(3).

Nevertheless, to the extent the integral-part doctrine recognizes that we should consider the totality of the circumstances in determining an organization's purpose, the doctrine is in accord with our section 501(c)(3) jurisprudence. One of the myriad factors we may consider in determining an organization's purpose is whether an essential nexus exists between an organization seeking tax exemption and a tax-exempt affiliate. The example cited in the Treasury Regulations aptly illustrates the point: "a

---

[31] As the Third Circuit noted in *Geisinger II*, the "integral-part doctrine" is not codified. 30 F.3d at 499. Although it finds support in 26 C.F.R. § 1.502–1(b), it must ultimately be justified under section 501(c)(3) and its charitable-purpose requirement.

subsidiary organization which is operated for the sole purpose of furnishing electric power used by its parent organization, a tax-exempt educational organization, in carrying on its educational activities."[32] 26 C.F.R. § 1.502–1(b). In other words, as we interpret the integral-part doctrine, it simply recognizes that "[t]he performance of a particular activity that is not inherently charitable may nonetheless further a charitable purpose." Rev. Rul. 69–572, 1969 WL 19169. "The overall result in any given case is dependent on *why* and *how* that activity is actually being conducted." *Id.* (emphasis added).

Using the example cited in Treasury Regulation 1.502–1(b), if we were to consider the nature of the subsidiary's activity in isolation—furnishing electricity—we would have no indication that the subsidiary serves an exempt purpose. On the other hand, when we look at the totality of the circumstances, it becomes clear that the subsidiary's activity furthers the exempt purpose of education: the product provided is essential; the subsidiary furnishes its product solely to the tax-exempt affiliate; and the tax-exempt parent exercises control over the subsidiary. These facts, considered in conjunction with the exempt purpose for which the tax-exempt parent operates, support a strong inference that the subsidiary operates for the same exempt purpose as does the parent.

In this case, we need not decide whether petitioners provide a service necessary to Health Services in conducting its exempt activities. The required nexus between the activities of petitioners and Health Services is lacking. As the Tax Court noted, "petitioner[s]' enrollees received approximately 20 percent of their physician services from physicians employed by or contracting with Health Services, while petitioner contracted for the remaining 80 percent of such physician services directly with independent physicians." *Health Plans,* 82 T.C.M. at 606. Thus, unlike the subsidiary furnishing electricity in Treasury Regulation § 1.502–1(b), petitioners do not function solely to further Health Services' performance of its exempt activities. Rather, a substantial portion (eighty percent) [ ] of petitioners' enrollees received physician services from "physicians with no direct link to [Health Services]."[35] *Health Plans,* 82 T.C.M. at 606. Thus, our consideration of petitioners' "connectedness" to Health Services in no way detracts from our earlier conclusion that

---

[32] We need not decide whether such an organization operates for an exempt purpose per se. We merely note that these facts would suggest that the subsidiary operates for an exempt purpose.

[35] We recognize that when we consider petitioners standing alone, drawing a distinction between a "staff-model HMO" (as in *Sound Health*) and a "contract HMO" (as in *Geisinger* and here) may not make sense. Colombo, *supra,* at 245. "[T]he 'community benefits' attributable to a particular [HMO] are the same whether treatment is performed by employee physicians or independent contractors pursuant to a service agreement." *Id.* at 245–46. Under the integral-part doctrine, however, the distinction is highly relevant, since we seek to determine whether an essential nexus exists between petitioners' operations and those of Health Services, the tax-exempt affiliate.

petitioners do not qualify for a charitable tax exemption under section 501(c)(3).

NOTES AND QUESTIONS

1.   *HMO Tax-Exemption.* What factors will enable an HMO to obtain 501(c)(3) status? Does the court's "plus" standard mean that the provision of health services is not a sufficient community benefit to carry the day? See also Geisinger Health Plan v. Commissioner, 985 F.2d 1210 (3d Cir. 1993) ("Geisinger I") (applying similar analysis of qualitative factors and also finding that providing subsidy to only thirty-five people constituted quantitatively an insufficient community benefit). The community benefit requirements and "plus factors" articulated by the court in *IHC Health Plan* sounds a lot like the hospital factors. How applicable are these factors to HMOs? Does the fact that the subsidized enrollees still pay a fee to become "members" of the HMO simply make it definitionally impossible for the subsidization to be counted as a "community" benefit?

Summarizing the impact of the IHC opinion's charitable purpose and integral-part analyses on 501(c)(3) for HMOs, one commentator has stated, "If other circuits follow [IHC], it pretty much sounds the death knell for 501(c)(3) status for any HMO unless it's a staff model HMO, primarily a Medicaid plan, or a captive group model where all the participating physicians are employed by a related health system." Federal Appeals Court Upholds IRS Decision Denying Nonprofit Status to Three IHC HMOs, 12 Health L. Rep. 626, (BNA), Apr. 17, 2003. See PLR 2007-14027 (Jan. 9, 2007) (finding that an HMO organized as for-profit did not qualify for tax exemption because it was not organized exclusively for exempt purposes). Recall however that HMOs may still obtain the somewhat less desirable exempt status under 501(c)(4), though the degree of community benefit required under that provision remains uncertain.

2.   *Tax-Exemption for Integrated Delivery Systems.* In "Geisinger II," the HMO discussed in note 1 also contended that it would warrant exemption if it were merged into the clinic or other part of the large Geisinger integrated system. The Third Circuit developed the "boost" test, which asks whether the HMO's "relationship to its parent somehow enhances the subsidiary's own exempt character to the point that, when the boost provided by the parent is added to the contribution made by the subsidiary itself, the subsidiary would be entitled to 501(c)(3) status." Geisinger Health Plan v. Commissioner, 30 F.3d 494 (3d Cir. 1994). The Court noted that GHP, the HMO subsidiary, failed to satisfy this test:

As our examination of the manner in which GHP interacts with other entities in the System makes clear, its association with those entities does nothing to increase the portion of the community for which GHP promotes health—it serves no more people as a part of the System than it would serve otherwise. It may contribute to the System by providing more patients than the System might otherwise have served, thus arguably allowing the System to promote health among a broader segment of the community than could be served without it, but its provision of patients to the System does not enhance its own promotion of health; the patients it provides—its subscribers—are the same patients it serves without its association with the System. To the extent it promotes health among non-GHP-subscriber patients of the System, it does so only because GHP subscribers' payments to the System help finance the provision of health care to others. An entity's mere financing of the exempt purposes of a related organization does not constitute furtherance of that organization's purpose so as to justify exemption.

Id. at 502. See Douglas M. Mancino, Tax Exemption Issues Facing Managed Care Organizations, in American Health Lawyers, Tax Issues for Healthcare Organizations (2000) (characterizing the "boost" test as "incomprehensible" and stating that it "cannot be distilled from prior decisions or Treasury regulations."). Does the IHC opinion's "essential nexus" test add any clarity to the integral part issue? Why does the provision of services by independent physicians detract from the "connectedness" to the integrated delivery system so as to bar application of the integral part doctrine?

3.   *Single-Entity Integrated Delivery Systems.* In contrast to integrated systems that create separate subsidiaries for its various entities, when parts of a system are placed in a single entity such as an integrated delivery system, the issue for exemption purposes turns on whether the system considered as a whole satisfies the community benefit standard, which appears likely based on the cases just discussed. See John D. Colombo, Health Care Reform and Federal Tax Exemption: Rethinking the Issues, 29 Wake Forest L. Rev. 215, 249 (1994) ("had the Geisinger Clinic operated the HMO, little doubt exists that it could have done so on an exempt basis"). So, if not based on organizational form, on what basis should the law draw distinctions for analyzing charitable purpose?

4.   *Tax-Exempt Status for ACOs.* A separate question from whether a tax-exempt entity can participate in an accountable care organization (ACO) as a joint venture (discussed below) is whether the ACO itself can qualify for tax-exempt status. The answer, according to the IRS, is yes, provided that the ACO meet all the requirements for tax-exemption under the § 501(c)(3), including the requirement that it engages exclusively in activities that accomplish one or more charitable purposes. This guidance applies to ACOs that participate in both the Medicare Shared Savings Program (MSSP) and non-MSSP (e.g., Medicaid or private payer) ACOs. IRS Fact Sheet on Exempt Organizations Participating in Medicare Shared Savings Program through Accountable Care Organizations (October 20, 2011).

It is clear, however, that ACOs that do not participate in the MSSP will find it difficult to qualify for tax-exemption. In a 2016 private letter ruling (PLR), the IRS denied tax-exemption to a nonprofit ACO that did not participate in the MSSP and engaged primarily in non-Medicare accountable care activities on behalf of private payers. I.R.S. Priv. Ltr. Ruling 201615022

(Jan. 15, 2016). The ACO was formed by a nonprofit tax-exempt health care system ("System") along with System physicians as well as independent physicians and groups unaffiliated with the System and collectively negotiated agreements with commercial payers.

The IRS concluded that the ACO was not operated "exclusively" for charitable purposes, finding that it did not in any way lessen the burdens of government by negotiating with third-party payers outside of the MSSP and was not engaged primarily in assisting the Medicare or Medicaid population. The IRS found that the ACO's negotiation of third-party payer agreements on behalf of independent and non-System affiliated physicians was not a charitable activity. Because the non-charitable activity comprised a substantial part of the ACO's activities and conferred an impermissible private benefit to the unaffiliated physicians and the private benefit was substantial, the IRS found that the ACO did not qualify for exemption under section 501(c)(3). Moreover, because the ACO's activities were not exclusively for the benefit of the System, the IRS found that the ACO, even if it had qualified for exemption under section 501(c)(3), would not qualify as a supporting organization and would be considered a private foundation.

The implication of the PLR is that ACO activities for private, commercial payers does not, in the IRS's view, further charitable purposes. This PLR then created uncertainty for ACOs engaged in both MSSP and non-MSSP activities for private payers and stood at odds with the 2011 IRS guidance that mixed MSSP and non-MSSP ACOs could qualify for tax-exemption. The American Hospital Association responded quickly to the PLR, stating the ruling is "in conflict with the direction that [HHS] has given to the hospital field" and asking the IRS to publish guidance affirming that "hospitals may participate in ACOs without generating a tax cost or incurring the catastrophic loss of their tax-exempt status." Letter from Melinda Reid Hatton, General Counsel, American Hospital Ass'n to Mark Mazur, Ass't Secretary, Dep't of the Treasury (May 16, 2016).

B. JOINT VENTURES BETWEEN TAX-EXEMPT AND FOR-PROFIT ORGANIZATIONS

Tax-exempt organizations may engage in some non-tax-exempt activities. Section 501(c)(3) requires that the exempt entity be organized and operated "exclusively" for exempt purposes, but the IRS regulations interpret this standard under the operational test as requiring that exempt organizations engage "primarily in activities that accomplish one or more . . . exempt purposes" and further state that the exempt organization violates this standard if "more than an insubstantial" amount of its activities are not in furtherance of exempt purposes. 26 C.F.R. § 1.501(c)(3)–1(c)(1). Thus, § 501(c)(3) organizations may engage in trade or business unrelated to their exempt purposes, although income from such unrelated business is taxable and the activity must be "insubstantial" as compared to the organization's exempt activities.

An exempt organization also may engage in business activities jointly with for-profit organizations and may own for-profit organizations. Its participation in a joint venture with a for-profit entity will not affect its tax-exempt status provided the purpose of its involvement in the venture is in furtherance of its exempt purpose. Activities of a joint venture entity that is itself tax-exempt results in nontaxable, exempt income to the tax-exempt member of the venture. If the joint venture's activities are not tax-exempt, the income will be taxable as **"unrelated business taxable income" (UBTI)** to the exempt organization; and, if not insubstantial, may jeopardize the organization's exempt status. In evaluating the permissibility of joint ventures between for-profit and exempt entities, the IRS has long used a two-prong "close scrutiny" test. That test requires (1) that the exempt organization's participation in the venture furthers a charitable purpose, and (2) that the structure of the venture permits the exempt organization to act exclusively in furtherance of its charitable purpose and does not allow private inurement or private benefit to be conferred on private investors or other for-profit persons. IRS, GCM 39005 (Dec. 17, 1982).

For an exempt organization, "unrelated trade or business" is activity carried on by the organization, "the conduct of which is not substantially related (aside from the need of such organization for income or funds or the use it makes of the profits derived)" to its exempt purpose and is taxable as UBTI. 26 CFR § 1.513–1(a). Services that contribute to patient recovery and convenience are "related" to the exempt purposes of the health care organization and income from these activities is not taxable.

Generally, services provided to non-hospital patients are taxable as UBTI unless they fall within certain narrow exceptions relating to (1) whether the services to non-patients are otherwise available in the community or (2) whether the services to non-patients contribute to the achievement of other exempt purposes, such as medical education. Thus, sales of pharmaceuticals to individuals who are not hospital patients are taxable, with limited exceptions made for situations in which there are no local alternatives. See Hi-Plains Hosp. v. U.S., 670 F.2d 528 (5th Cir. 1982). See also Private Letter Ruling 8125007 (undated), in which the IRS decided that sophisticated lab services, not otherwise available and provided by an exempt hospital to industry for employee examinations, did not produce UBTI. The PLR concluded, however, that the provision of ordinary lab services performed for non-hospital patients of private physicians may generate UBTI. This may lead to rather confusing results. A hospital's revenues from providing MRI services to patients of another hospital or to outpatients served by its staff physicians might well produce UBTI, though the revenues from the same services to admitted patients would not. Likewise, income from management or administrative services sold by a tax-exempt hospital to physicians in private practices could certainly be considered UBTI. If the hospital purchased the physician practices, would the provision of these services to the hospital-owned practices produce taxable income? On the issue of gift shops, parking facilities and cafeterias on hospital campuses, the law carves out an exception to taxable income by excluding business "carried on by the organization primarily for the convenience of its ... members, patients or employees." I.R.C. § 513(a) (2006).

The following material takes us through the several strands of law that apply to a wide variety of joint ventures between for-profit and tax-exempt entities in health care.

REVENUE RULING 98–15
1998–12 I.R.B. 6.

[In this Revenue Ruling, the IRS provides the following examples to illustrate whether an organization that operates an acute care hospital constitutes an organization whose principal purpose is providing charitable hospital care when it forms a limited liability company (LLC) with a for-profit corporation and then contributes its hospital and all of its related operating assets to the LLC, which then operates the hospital.]

Situation 1

A is a nonprofit corporation that owns and operates an acute care hospital. A has been recognized as exempt from federal income tax ... as an organization described in § 501(c)(3). ... B is a for-profit corporation that owns and operates a number of hospitals.

A concludes that it could better serve its community if it obtained additional funding. B is interested in providing financing for A's hospital, provided it earns a reasonable rate of return. A and B form a limited liability company, C. A contributes all of its operating assets, including its hospital to C. B also contributes assets to C. In return, A and B receive ownership interests in C proportional and equal in value to their respective contributions.

C's Articles of Organization and Operating Agreement ("governing documents") provide that C is to be managed by a governing board consisting of three individuals chosen by A and two individuals chosen by B. A intends to appoint community leaders who have experience with hospital matters, but who are not on the hospital staff and do not otherwise engage in business transactions with the hospital.

The governing documents further provide that they may only be amended with the approval of both owners and that a majority of three board members must approve certain major decisions relating to C's operation including decisions relating to any of the following topics:

    A.   C's annual capital and operating budgets;

    B.   Distributions of C's earnings;

    C.   Selection of key executives;

    D.   Acquisition or disposition of health care facilities;

    E.   Contracts in excess of $x per year;

    F.   Changes to the types of services offered by the hospital; and

    G.   Renewal or termination of management agreements.

The governing documents require that C operate any hospital it owns in a manner that furthers charitable purposes by promoting health for a broad cross section of its community. The governing documents explicitly provide that the duty of the members of the governing board to operate C in a manner that furthers charitable purposes by promoting health for a broad cross section of the community overrides any duty they may have to operate C for the financial benefit of its owners. Accordingly, in the event of a conflict between operation in accordance with the community benefit standard and any duty to maximize profits, the members of the governing board are to satisfy the community benefit standard without regard to the consequences for maximizing profitability.

The governing documents further provide that all returns of capital and distributions of earnings made to owners of C shall be proportional to their ownership interests in C. The terms of the governing documents are legal, binding, and enforceable under applicable state law.

C enters into a management agreement with a management company that is unrelated to A or B to provide day-to-day management services to C. The management agreement is for a five-year period, and the agreement is renewable for additional five-year periods by mutual consent. The management company will be paid a management fee for its services based on C's gross revenues. The terms and conditions of the management agreement, including the fee structure and the contract term, are reasonable and comparable to what other management firms receive for similar services at similarly situated hospitals. C may terminate the agreement for cause.

None of the officers, directors, or key employees of A who were involved in making the decision to form C were promised employment or any other inducement by C or B and their related entities if the transaction were approved. None of A's officers, directors, or key employees have any interest . . . in B or any of its related entities.

. . . C will be treated as a partnership for federal income tax purposes.

A intends to use any distributions it receives from C to fund grants to support activities that promote the health of A's community and to help the indigent obtain health care. Substantially all of A's grantmaking will be funded by distributions from C. A's projected grantmaking program and its participation as an owner of C will constitute A's only activities.

Situation 2

D is a nonprofit corporation that owns and operates an acute care hospital. D has been recognized as exempt from federal income tax . . . as an organization described in § 501(c)(3). . . . E is a for-profit hospital corporation that owns and operates a number of hospitals and provides management services to several hospitals that it does not own.

D concludes that it could better serve its community if it obtained additional funding. E is interested in providing financing for D's hospital, provided it earns a reasonable rate of return. D and E form a limited liability company, F. D contributes all of its operating assets, including its hospital to F. E also contributes assets to F. In return, D and E receive ownership interests proportional and equal in value to their respective contributions.

F's Articles of Organization and Operating Agreement ("governing documents") provide that F is to be managed by a governing board consisting of three individuals chosen by D and three individuals chosen by E. D intends to appoint community leaders who have experience with hospital matters, but who are not on the hospital staff and do not otherwise engage in business transactions with the hospital.

The governing documents further provide that they may only be amended with the approval of both owners and that a majority of board members must approve certain major decisions relating to F's operation, including decisions relating to any of the following topics:

A. F's annual capital and operating budgets;

B. Distributions of F's earnings over a required minimum level of distributions set forth in the Operating Agreement;

C. Unusually large contracts; and

D. Selection of key executives.

F's governing documents provide that F's purpose is to construct, develop, own, manage, operate, and take other action in connection with operating the health care facilities it owns and engage in other health care-related activities. The governing documents further provide that all returns of capital and distributions of earnings made to owners of F shall be proportional to their ownership interests in F.

F enters into a management agreement with a wholly-owned subsidiary of E to provide day-to-day management services to F. The management agreement is for a five-year period, and the agreement is renewable for additional five-year periods at the discretion of E's subsidiary. F may terminate the agreement only for cause. E's subsidiary will be paid a management fee for its services based on gross revenues. The terms and conditions of the management agreement, including the fee structure and the contract term other than the renewal terms, are reasonable and comparable to what other management firms receive for similar services at similarly situated hospitals.

As part of the agreement to form F, D agrees to approve the selection of two individuals to serve as F's chief executive officer and chief financial officer. These individuals have previously worked for E in hospital management and have business expertise. They will work with the management company to oversee F's day-to-day management. Their compensation is comparable to what comparable executives are paid at similarly situated hospitals.

. . . F will be treated as a partnership for federal income tax purposes.

D intends to use any distributions it receives from F to fund grants to support activities that promote the health of D's community and to help the indigent obtain health care. Substantially all of D's grantmaking will be funded by distributions from F. D's projected grantmaking program and its participation as an owner of F will constitute D's only activities.

ANALYSIS

A § 501(c)(3) organization may form and participate in a partnership, including an LLC treated as a partnership for federal income tax purposes, and meet the operational test if participation in the partnership furthers a charitable purpose, and the partnership arrangement permits the exempt organization to act exclusively in furtherance of its exempt purpose and only incidentally for the benefit of the for-profit partners. Similarly, a § 501(c)(3) organization may enter into a management contract with a private party giving that party authority to conduct activities on behalf of the organization and direct the use of the organization's assets provided that the organization retains ultimate authority over the assets and activities being managed and the terms and conditions of the contract are reasonable, including reasonable compensation and a reasonable term. However, if a private party is allowed to control or use the non-profit organization's activities or assets for the benefit of the private party, and the benefit is not incidental to the accomplishment of exempt purposes, the organization will fail to be organized and operated exclusively for exempt purposes.

Situation 1

After A and B form C, and A contributes all of its operating assets to C, A's activities will consist of the health care services it provides through C and any grantmaking activities it can conduct using income distributed to C. A will receive an interest in C equal in value to the assets it contributes to C, and A's and B's returns from C will be proportional to their respective investments in C. The governing documents of C commit C to providing health care services for the benefit of the community as a whole and to give charitable purposes priority over maximizing profits for C's owners. Furthermore, through A's appointment of members of the community familiar with the hospital to C's board, the board's structure, which gives A's appointees voting control, and the specifically enumerated powers of the board over changes in activities, disposition of assets, and renewal of the management agreement. A can ensure that the assets it owns through C and the activities it conducts through C are used primarily to further exempt purposes. Thus, A can ensure that the benefit to B and other private parties, like the management company, will be incidental to the accomplishment of charitable purposes. Additionally, the terms and conditions of the management contract, including the terms for renewal and termination are reasonable. Finally, A's grants are intended to support education and research and give resources to help provide health care to the indigent. All of these facts and circumstances establish that, when A participates in forming C and contributes all of its operating assets to C, and C operates in accordance with its governing documents, A will be furthering charitable purposes and continue to be operated exclusively for exempt purposes.

* * *

Situation 2

When D and E form F, and D contributes its assets to F, D will be engaged in activities that consist of the health care services it provides through F and any grantmaking activities it can conduct using income distributed by F. However, unlike A, D will not be engaging primarily in activities that further an exempt purpose. . . . In the absence of a binding obligation in F's governing documents for F to serve charitable purposes or otherwise provide its services to the community as a whole, F will be able to deny care to segments of the community, such as the indigent. Because D will share control of F with E, D will not be able to initiate programs within F to serve new health needs within the community without the agreement of at least one governing board member appointed by E. As a business enterprise, E will not necessarily give priority to the health needs of the community over the consequences for F's profits. The primary source of information for board members appointed by D will be the chief executives, who have a prior relationship with E and the management company, which is a subsidiary of E. The management company itself will have broad discretion over F's activities and assets that may not always be under the board's supervision. For example, the management company is permitted to enter into all but "unusually large" contracts without board approval. The management company may also unilaterally renew the management agreement. Based on all these facts and circumstances, D cannot establish that the activities it conducts through F further exempt purposes. "[I]n order for an organization to qualify for exemption under § 501(c)(3) the organization must 'establish' that it is neither organized nor operated for the 'benefit of private interests.'"[ ] Consequently, the benefit to E resulting from the activities D conducts through F will not be incidental to the furtherance of an exempt purpose. Thus, D will fail the operational test when it forms F, contributes its operating assets to F, and then serves as an owner to F.

NOTES AND QUESTIONS

1.   While Situation 1 effectively carves out a safe harbor for structuring a joint venture with a tax-exempt participant, what lessons can be drawn about the required degree of control the exempt organization must possess? For example, consider whether the following changes for the hospital in Situation 2 would enable it to retain its § 501(c)(3) status: shortening the management term to five years, requiring a 24-hour emergency room at one or more of the LLC hospitals, and adopting a list of reserved powers similar to those in Situation 1. See Gerald M. Griffith, Revenue Ruling 98–15: Dimming the Future of All Nonprofit Joint Ventures?, 31 J. Health L. 71, 88 (1998).

2.   Although eagerly awaited, the guidance offered by Revenue Ruling 98–15 was met with criticism for what it does not address. See Robert C. Louthian, III, IRS Provides Whole Hospital Joint Venture Guidance in Revenue Ruling 98–15, 7 Health L. Rep., Mar. 19, 1998, at 477. Many feel that the ruling's "polar opposite" situations do not help to clarify the many gray areas seen in joint ventures. The next case provides guidance on the requisite elements of control.

ST. DAVID'S HEALTH CARE SYSTEM V. UNITED STATES

United States Court of Appeals, Fifth Circuit, 2003.
349 F.3d 232.

GARZA, J.

St. David's Health Care System, Inc. ("St. David's") brought suit in federal court to recover taxes that it paid under protest. St. David's argued that it was a charitable hospital, and therefore tax-exempt under 26 U.S.C. § 501(c)(3). The Government responded that St. David's was not entitled to a tax exemption because it had formed a partnership with a for-profit company and ceded control over its operations to the for-profit entity. Both St. David's and the Government filed motions for summary judgment. The district court granted St. David's motion, and ordered the Government to refund the taxes paid by St. David's for the 1996 tax year. The district court also ordered the Government to pay $951,569.83 in attorney's fees and litigation costs. The Government filed the instant appeal. We conclude that this case raises genuine issues of material fact, and that the district court thus erred in granting St. David's motion for summary judgment. We therefore vacate the district court's decision, and remand for further proceedings.

I

For many years, St. David's owned and operated a hospital and other health care facilities in Austin, Texas. For most of its existence, St. David's was recognized as a charitable organization entitled to tax-exempt status under § 501(c)(3).

In the 1990s, due to financial difficulties in the health care industry, St. David's concluded that it should consolidate with another health care organization. Ultimately, in 1996, St. David's decided to form a partnership with Columbia/HCA Healthcare Corporation ("HCA"), a for-profit company that operates 180 hospitals nationwide. HCA already owned several facilities in the suburbs of Austin, and was interested in entering the central Austin market. A partnership with St. David's would allow HCA to expand into that urban market.

St. David's contributed all of its hospital facilities to the partnership. HCA, in turn, contributed its Austin-area facilities. The partnership hired Galen Health Care, Inc. ("Galen"), a subsidiary of HCA, to manage the day-to-day operations of the partnership medical facilities.

In 1998, the IRS audited St. David's and concluded that, due to its partnership with HCA, St. David's no longer qualified as a charitable (and, thus, tax-exempt) hospital. The IRS ordered St. David's to pay taxes. St. David's paid the requisite amount under protest, and subsequently filed the instant action, requesting a refund.

. . . The district court granted the motion filed by St. David's and ordered the Government to refund the taxes paid by the hospital for the 1996 tax year. . . . The Government filed this appeal.

II

. . . In order to qualify for tax-exempt status, St. David's was required to show that it was "organized and operated exclusively" for a charitable purpose. 26 C.F.R. § 1.501(c)(3)–1(a). The "organizational test" required St. David's to demonstrate that its founding documents: (1) limit its purpose to "one or more exempt purposes"; and (2) do not expressly empower St. David's to engage more than "an insubstantial part of its activities" in conduct that fails to further its charitable goals. *Id.* § 1.501(c)(3)–1(b). The parties agree that St. David's articles of incorporation satisfy the organizational test.

To pass the "operational test," St. David's was required to show: (1) that it "engage[s] primarily in activities which accomplish" its exempt purpose; (2) that its net earnings do not "inure to the benefit of private shareholders or individuals"; (3) that it does "not expend a substantial part of its resources attempting to influence legislation or political campaigns"; and (4) that it "serve[s] a valid purpose and confer[s] a public benefit." [ ] [The parties agree that the latter three elements of the operational test are not at issue in this case.]

The Government argues that St. David's cannot demonstrate the first element of the operational test. The Government asserts that, because of its partnership with HCA, St. David's cannot show that it engages "primarily" in activities that accomplish its charitable purpose. The Government does not contend that a non-profit organization should automatically lose its tax-exempt status when it forms a partnership with a for-profit entity. Instead, the Government argues that a non-profit organization must sacrifice its tax exemption if it cedes control over the partnership to the for-profit entity. The Government asserts that, when a non-profit cedes control, it can no longer ensure that its activities via the partnership primarily further its charitable purpose. In this case, the Government contends that St. David's forfeited its exemption because it ceded control over its operations to HCA.

St. David's responds in part that the central issue in determining its tax-exempt status is not which entity *controls* the partnership. Instead, St. David's appears to assert, the pivotal question is one of *function:* whether the partnership engages in activities that further its exempt purpose. St. David's argues that it passes the "operational test" because its activities via the partnership further its charitable purpose of providing health care to all persons.

St. David's relies in particular on a revenue ruling issued by the IRS, which provides guidelines for hospitals seeking a § 501(c)(3) exemption. Revenue Ruling 69–545 sets forth what has come to be known as the "community benefit standard." *See IHC Health Plans, Inc. v. Commissioner,* 325 F.3d 1188, 1197 (10th Cir.2003); *see also* Rev. Rul. 83–157, 1983–2 C.B. 94, 1983 WL 190185 (1983) (noting that hospitals can be tax-exempt if various factors demonstrate that the "hospitals operate exclusively to the benefit of the community"). The IRS generally accords tax-exempt status to independent non-profit hospitals that satisfy this standard.

Under the "community benefit standard," a non-profit hospital can qualify for a tax exemption if it: (1) provides an emergency room open to all persons, regardless of their ability to pay; (2) is willing to hire any qualified physician; (3) is run by an independent board of trustees composed of representatives of the community ("community board"); and (4) uses all excess revenues to improve facilities, provide educational services, and/or conduct medical research. *See* Rev. Rul. 69–545, 1969–2 C.B. 117, 1969 WL 19168 (1969) (outlining the community benefit standard); *see also IHC Health Plans,* 325 F.3d at 1197 n. 16 (noting several relevant factors for determining whether a hospital confers a significant community benefit, including the provision of free or below-cost care; the treatment of individuals eligible for Medicare or Medicaid; the use of extra funds for research and educational programs; and the composition of the board of trustees). A hospital need not demonstrate all of these factors in order to qualify for § 501(c)(3) tax-exempt status. *See Geisinger*, 985 F.2d at 1219; Rev. Rul. 69–545, 1969–2 C.B. 117 (1969) (stating that "[t]he absence of particular factors" will not necessarily prevent a hospital from obtaining an exemption). [ ] Instead, the hospital must show, based on the "totality of the circumstances," that it is entitled to a tax exemption. *Geisinger*, 985 F.2d at 1219.

St. David's contends that its activities via the partnership more than satisfy the community benefit standard. St. David's notes that the partnership hospitals perform a number of charitable functions in the Austin community. According to St. David's, the partnership not only provides free emergency room care, but also has opened the rest of its facilities to all persons, regardless of their ability to pay. In addition, St. David's asserts, the partnership hospitals maintain open medical staffs. Finally, St. David's states that it uses the profits that it receives from the partnership revenues to fund research grants and other health-related initiatives.

We have no doubt that St. David's via the partnership provides important medical services to the Austin community. Indeed, if the issue in this case were whether the partnership performed any charitable functions, we would be inclined to affirm the district court's grant of summary judgment in favor of St. David's.

However, we cannot agree with St. David's suggestion that the central issue in this case is whether the partnership provides some (or even an extensive amount of) charitable services. It is important to keep in mind that § 501(c)(3) confers tax-exempt status only on those organizations that operate *exclusively* in furtherance of exempt purposes. 26 C.F.R. § 1.501(c)(3)–1(a). As a result, in determining whether an organization satisfies the operational test, we do not simply consider whether the organization's activities further its charitable purposes. We must also ensure that those activities do *not* substantially further other (non-charitable) purposes. If more than an "insubstantial" amount of the partnership's activities further non-charitable interests, then St. David's can no longer be deemed to operate *exclusively* for charitable purposes. [The court notes that the requirement that an organization operate "exclusively" for exempt purposes is satisfied even if it is operated "primarily" for charitable purposes.]

Therefore, even if St. David's performs important charitable functions, St. David's cannot qualify for tax-exempt status under § 501(c)(3) if its activities via the partnership substantially further the private, profit-seeking interests of HCA. [ ] . . .

In order to ascertain whether an organization furthers non-charitable interests, we can examine the structure and management of the organization. [ ] In other words, we look to which individuals or entities *control* the organization. [ ] If private individuals or for-profit entities have either formal or effective control, we presume that the organization furthers the profit-seeking motivations of those private individuals or entities. That is true, even when the organization is a partnership between a non-profit and a for-profit entity. *See Redlands Surgical Servs. v. Commissioner,* 113 T.C. 47, 75, 1999 WL 513862 (1999) ("An organization's property may be impermissibly devoted to a private use where private interests have control, directly or indirectly, over its assets, and thereby secure nonincidental private benefits."). When the non-profit organization cedes control over the partnership to the for-profit entity, we assume that the partnership's activities substantially further the for-profit's interests. As a result, we conclude that the non-profit's activities via the partnership are not exclusively or primarily in furtherance of its charitable purposes. Thus, the non-profit is not entitled to a tax exemption. *See* Rev. Rul. 98–15 . . . .

Conversely, if the non-profit organization enters into a partnership agreement with a for-profit entity, and retains control, we presume that the non-profit's activities via the partnership primarily further exempt purposes. Therefore, we can conclude that the non-profit organization should retain its tax-exempt status. . . .

The present case illustrates why, when a non-profit organization forms a partnership with a for-profit entity, courts should be concerned about the relinquishment of control. St. David's, by its own account, entered the partnership with HCA out of financial *necessity* (to obtain the revenues needed for it to stay afloat). HCA, by contrast, entered the partnership for reasons of financial *convenience* (to enter a new market). The starkly different financial positions of these two parties at the beginning of their partnership negotiations undoubtedly affected their relative bargaining strength. Because St. David's "needed" this partnership more than HCA, St. David's may have been willing to acquiesce to many (if not most) of HCA's demands for the final Partnership Agreement. In the process, of course, St. David's may not have been able to give a high priority to its charitable objectives. As a result, St. David's may not have been able to ensure that its partnership with HCA would continually provide a "public benefit" as opposed to a private benefit for HCA. . . .

These precedents and policy concerns indicate that, when a non-profit organization forms a partnership with a for-profit entity, the non-profit should lose its tax-exempt status if it cedes control to the for-profit entity.

See Redlands, 242 F.3d at 904 (holding that a non-profit organization is no longer entitled to tax-exempt status when it "has ceded effective control . . . to private parties") (internal quotation marks omitted). Therefore, in our review of the district court's summary judgment ruling, we examine whether St. David's has shown that there is no genuine issue of material fact regarding whether St. David's ceded control to HCA.

A recent IRS revenue ruling provides a starting point for our analysis. In Revenue Ruling 98–15, the IRS indicated how a non-profit organization that forms a partnership with a for-profit entity can establish that it has retained control over the partnership's activities. [ ] The revenue ruling states that a non-profit can demonstrate control by showing some or all of the following: (1) that the founding documents of the partnership expressly state that it has a charitable purpose and that the charitable purpose will take priority over all other concerns; (2) that the partnership agreement gives the non-profit organization a majority vote in the partnership's board of directors; and (3) that the partnership is managed by an independent company (an organization that is not affiliated with the for-profit entity). *See id.*

The partnership documents in the present case, examined in light of the above factors, leave us uncertain as to whether St. David's has ceded control to HCA. St. David's did manage to secure some protections for its charitable mission. First of all, Section 3.2 of the Partnership Agreement expressly states that the manager of the partnership "shall" operate the partnership facilities in a manner that complies with the community benefit standard. This provision appears to comport with the first factor in Revenue Ruling 98–15, which indicates that the partnership's founding documents should contain a statement of the partnership's charitable purpose. . . .

According to St. David's, [certain] protections in the partnership documents (the purpose statement in the Partnership Agreement; St. David's power to terminate the Management Services Agreement and the CEO; its ability to block proposed action of the Board of Governors; and its power of dissolution) provide it with a large measure of control over partnership operations.

However, as the Government argues, there are reasons to doubt that the partnership documents provide St. David's with sufficient control. First of all, St. David's authority within the Board of Governors is limited. St. David's does not control a majority of the Board. *See* Rev. Rul. 98–15, 1998–1 C.B. 718 (1998) (indicating that a non-profit can retain control over a partnership with a for-profit if it selects a majority of the partnership's board of directors, but will have difficulty controlling the partnership if it has only an equal share of the board). As a result, although St. David's can veto board actions, it does not appear that it can initiate action without the support of HCA. Thus, at best, St. David's can prevent the partnership from taking action that might undermine its charitable goals; St. David's cannot necessarily ensure that the partnership will take new action that furthers its charitable purposes. *See Redlands,* 113 T.C. at 79–80 (finding that the non-profit did not have sufficient control in part because the non-profit could only veto partnership action; the non-profit could not initiate action without the consent of the for-profit entity).

Second, Galen, which manages the operations of the partnership on a day-to-day basis, is a for-profit subsidiary of HCA. As a result, it is not apparent that Galen would be inclined to serve charitable interests. It seems more likely that Galen would prioritize the (presumably non-charitable) interests of its parent organization, HCA. *See* Rev. Rul. 98–15, 1998–1 C.B. 718 (1998) (indicating that a charitable hospital is unlikely to be in control of a partnership with a for-profit entity when the partnership manager is a subsidiary of the for-profit entity); *see also Redlands,* 113 T.C. at 83–84 ("[T]his long-term management contract with an affiliate of [the for-profit entity] is a salient indicator of [the non-profit's] surrender of effective control over the [partnership's] operations"). [The court notes that it is concerned about Galen's "extraordinarily long term" as manager and compensation based on a percentage of the partnership's revenues increase its incentives to maximize revenues and make it less likely to prioritize St. David's charitable goals.] . . .

St. David's also asserts that it can control the management of the partnership via its position on the Board of Governors. However, the power of the Board is limited in scope. The Board of Governors is empowered to deal with only major decisions, not the day-to-day operation of the partnership hospitals. Thus, St. David's could not, via its position on the Board, overrule a management decision that fell outside the range of the Board's authority.

* * *

[The court agrees that the Management Services Agreement appears to provide St. David's with a certain degree of control over Galen. But the court expresses skepticism over the degree of control St. David's exercises over the partnership's CEO, due to lack of punitive actions taken for CEO's failing to prepare charity care reports as required in the Partnership Agreement, and questions the degree to which St. David's has the power to control the partnership by threatening dissolution because the consequences would be far worse for St. David's, which would cease to exist, compared to HCA.]

The evidence presented by the parties demonstrates that there remain genuine issues of material fact regarding whether St. David's ceded control to HCA. Therefore, we vacate the district court's grant of summary judgment in favor of St. David's.

For the above reasons, we VACATE the district court's summary judgment ruling and its award of attorney's fees and costs and REMAND for further proceedings.

NOTES AND QUESTIONS

1.   *The* St. David's *Framework.* The Fifth Circuit remanded the case to the district court to determine whether control was effectively ceded to HCA. Although on remand a jury held that St. David's should retain its exempt status, the IRS adheres to the view that the Fifth Circuit opinion "provided the proper framework for judging joint ventures between non-profits and for-profits . . . [i.e.] a non-profit must have effective control in the joint venture." Fred Sokeld, IRS Official Unfazed by Jury Decision in Joint Venture Case, 2004 Tax Notes Today 50 (May 12, 2004).

The succinct verdict of the commentators after Revenue Ruling 98–15 was that "control is king." This view was strongly reinforced by the *St. David's* decision. Why should that be so? Can you make an argument based on the language and history of the tax code that control should not be the ultimate touchstone for exemption? Can you imagine a compelling set of circumstances in which exemption is warranted even though the exempt organization lacked control over a partnership with a for-profit entity? See the discussion of tax exemption and accountable care organizations in the next section of this chapter.

2.   *Ancillary Joint Ventures.* Unlike the whole hospital joint ventures in Rev. Rul. 98–15 and *St. David's*, **ancillary joint ventures** operate less than a whole hospital, and the tax-exempt entity does not contribute all its hospital assets to the venture. Instead, the exempt hospital retains its separate existence, is subject to the community benefit standard, and often is contributing only a fraction of its assets. See Nicholas A. Mirkay, Relinquish Control! Why the IRS Should Change its Stance on Exempt Organizations in Ancillary Joint Ventures, 6 Nev. L. J. 21, 50 (2005). The implications of *St. David's* for ancillary joint ventures are somewhat uncertain. In *St. David's*, the Fifth Circuit cited the case of Redlands Surgical Services v. Comm'r of Internal Revenue, 113 T.C. 47, aff'd per curiam 242 F.3d 904 (2001), which involved an ancillary joint venture between a tax-exempt organization and for-profit partners to operate an ambulatory surgical center. In *Redlands*, the tax court concluded that the nonprofit entity did not qualify for tax exemption because it lacked requisite control over the joint venture and had instead ceded control to for-profit partners. In that case, like in *St. David's*, the tax-exempt entity only had veto power over the partnership's governing board, and the management company was a subsidiary of the for-profit partner. In addition, the partnership's organizational documents failed the organizational test because it contained no affirmative obligation for the partnership to put the tax-exempt entity's charitable purposes ahead of non-charitable objectives. The Ninth Circuit affirmed in a short per curiam opinion, stating, "we adopt the tax court's holding that [the nonprofit organization] has ceded effective

control over the operations of the partnerships and the surgery center to private parties, conferring impermissible private benefit." Id. at 904.

Nevertheless, the IRS has approved dozens of ancillary joint ventures involving medical office buildings, imaging centers, ambulatory surgical centers, treatment centers, physical therapy centers, hospital home care services, and nursing homes. And although the *Redlands* case applied the control standard to ancillary joint ventures, a notable ruling suggests that the IRS may be willing to loosen the control standard. In Revenue Ruling 2004–51, the IRS approved an LLC joint venture between a tax-exempt university offering seminars to teachers to improve their skills and a for-profit entity that conducted interactive video training programs. Membership in the LLC was divided equally between the for-profit and the university, but the latter retained "exclusive right to approve curriculum, training materials and instructors and determine standards" for the seminars. Noting that the venture did not constitute a substantial part of the University's activities, the IRS ruled that its participation in the venture would not jeopardize its exempt status. The fact that the ruling cited *St. David's* and Rev. Ruling 98–15, but did not explicitly apply those precedents or invoke the "control" standard and permitted a 50–50 venture to go forward has been interpreted by some to suggest that the test may be loosened in the future. See Mirkay, *supra*, but also quoting an IRS official reminding tax lawyers that Revenue Ruling 98–15 is "still on the books".

C. INUREMENT, PRIVATE BENEFIT, EXCESS BENEFIT TRANSACTIONS

Physicians and hospitals are highly interdependent both clinically and financially. In the language of economics, they jointly produce the services provided to patients. As you have seen in the previous sections of this chapter, hospitals may establish joint ventures with physicians for ancillary services or to provide care through freestanding entities. Hospitals are motivated by both the desire to more efficiently use these resources and to cement their relationships with the physicians and thus assure themselves a steady flow of patients. For similar reasons, hospitals and integrated delivery system also have frequently purchased physician practices or recruited physicians to establish a private practice in their geographic area, usually supplying some form of financial support provided to entice the doctor to relocate or open a practice. The creation of ACOs under the Medicare Shared Savings Program and for commercial payers further increases the incentives for hospitals and physicians to vertically integrate through contractual affiliations or formal acquisition.

These relationships between private, non-exempt physicians and tax-exempt organizations raise issues for the tax-exempt entity. Several of these have been explored in the earlier sections of this chapter: IRS limitations on control in joint ventures; standards for unrelated trade or business income; and the achievement and protection of its charitable purposes. In addition, the exempt organization must comply with three other major legal constraints on relationships between non-exempt (which includes physicians) and tax-exempt health care organizations. These are the proscriptions against **private benefit** and against **private inurement** (both of which flow from the language of Section 501(c)(3)) and the statutory sanctions against **excess benefit transactions** (codified in IRC Section 4958). The latter statute, providing "intermediate sanctions" for excess benefit transactions, discussed at the end of this section, continues to be the predominant tool for enforcement of the prohibitions on inurement or impermissible private benefit by the IRS.

1. Joint Ventures with Physicians

GENERAL COUNSEL MEMORANDUM 39862
(I.R.S. Dec. 2, 1991).

[The IRS reviews a physician-hospital agreement in which the hospital sold its future net income from certain departments to entities that were owned by physicians who admitted and treated patients at the hospital. For example, obstetricians who treated patients at the hospital could invest in the hospital's OB department with the return on investment being a proportionate share of the net income of that department. Thus, the physician practicing in the department would experience financial gain or loss depending on the department's financial performance.]

A driving force behind the new hospital operating environment was the federal Medicare Program's 1983 shift from cost-based reimbursement for covered inpatient hospital services to fixed, per-case, prospective payments. This change to a diagnosis-related prospective payment system ("PPS") dramatically altered hospital financial incentives. PPS severed the link between longer hospital stays with more services provided each patient and higher reimbursement. It substituted strong incentives to control the costs of each individual inpatient's care while attracting a greater number of admissions. Medicare policies are highly influential; the program accounts for nearly 40% of the average hospital's revenues.

The need to increase admission volume was accompanied by a perceived need to influence physician treatment decisions which, by and large, were unaffected by the change to PPS. Hospitals realized that, in addition to attracting more patients, they needed to control utilization of ancillary hospital services, discharge Medicare beneficiaries as quickly as is medically appropriate, and operate more efficiently. Traditionally, physicians treating their private patients at a hospital had enjoyed nearly complete independence of professional judgment. Since they are paid separately by Medicare and other third party payers on the basis of billed charges, they still have an incentive to render more services to each patient over a longer period in order to enhance their own earnings. Once hospital and physician economic incentives diverged, hospitals began seeking ways to stimulate loyalty among members of their medical staffs and to encourage or reward physician behaviors deemed desirable. . . .

Whenever a charitable organization engages in unusual financial transactions with private parties, the arrangements must be evaluated in light of applicable tax law and other legal standards. Like any hospital-physician joint venture, the sale of revenue stream transactions described above must be carefully scrutinized. We believe the transactions described above cannot withstand such scrutiny and should not be the subject of favorable rulings. Instead, these transactions must be viewed as jeopardizing a hospital's tax exempt status for three reasons: they allow inurement of part of a charitable organization's net earnings to the benefit of private individuals; they confer more than incidental benefits on private interests; and they may well violate federal law.

I.   Sale of the Revenue Stream From a Hospital Activity Allows Net Profits To Inure to the Benefit of Physician-Investors

* * *

Protecting charitable organizations against private inurement serves important purposes. A charitable organization is viewed under the common law and the Internal Revenue Code as a trust whose assets must irrevocably be dedicated to achieving charitable purposes. The inurement prohibition serves to prevent anyone in a position to do so from siphoning off any of a charity's income or assets for personal use.

The proscription against inurement generally applies to a distinct class of private interests—typically persons who, because of their particular relationship with an organization, have an opportunity to control or influence its activities. . . . These individuals are often referred to informally as "insiders."

[Eds. Note: At the time of this GCM, the IRS took the position that all physician members of the medical staffs of hospitals—including those not employed by the hospital—have a such a close working relationship with and a private interest in the exempt hospital so as to be considered "insiders." The GCM stressed physicians' close professional working relationship with the hospitals, that "they largely control the flow of patients to and from the hospital and patients' utilization of hospital services while there," the binding effect of the medical staff bylaws, and the fact that some may serve other roles at the hospital, such as that of part-time employee, department head, Board member, etc. As we will see later in this chapter, the Service does not take the position that staff physician are "disqualified persons" with regard to application of the Excess Benefit statute, which will govern most inurement-type questions in the future. It is therefore unlikely that it would adhere to the position taken in this GCM that staff member physicians are categorically considered "insiders" for purposes of inurement analysis.]

Even though medical staff physicians are subject to the inurement proscription, that does not mean there can be no economic dealings between them and the hospitals. The inurement proscription does not prevent the payment of reasonable compensation for goods or services. It is aimed at preventing dividend-like distributions of charitable assets or expenditures to benefit a private interest. This Office has stated "inurement is likely to arise where the financial benefit represents a transfer of the organization's financial resources to an individual solely by virtue of the individual's relationship with the organization, and without regard to the accomplishment of exempt purposes." [ ] . . .

The proper starting point for our analysis of the net revenue stream arrangements is to ask what the hospital gets in return for the benefit conferred on the physician-investors. Put another way, we ask whether and how engaging in the transaction furthers the hospital's exempt purposes. Here, there appears to be little accomplished that directly furthers the hospitals' charitable purposes of promoting health. No expansion of health care resources results; no new provider is created. No improvement in treatment modalities or reduction in cost is foreseeable. We have to look very carefully for any reason why a hospital would want to engage in this sort of arrangement. . . .

Whether admitted or not, we believe the hospitals engaged in these ventures largely as a means to retain and reward members of their medical staffs; to attract their admissions and referrals; and to pre-empt the physicians from investing in or creating a competing provider. . . . Giving (or selling) medical staff physicians a proprietary interest in the net profits of a hospital under these circumstances creates a result that is indistinguishable from paying dividends on stock. Profit distributions are made to persons having a personal and private interest in the activities of the organization and are made out of the net earnings of the organization. Thus, the arrangements confer a benefit which violates the inurement proscription of section 501(c)(3).

* * *

II.   Sale of the Revenue Stream From a Hospital Activity Benefits Private Interests More Than Incidentally

[A] key principle in the law of tax exempt organizations is that an entity is not organized and operated exclusively for exempt purposes unless it serves a public rather than a private interest. Thus, in order to be exempt, an organization must establish that it is not organized or operated for the benefit of private interests such as designated individuals, the creator or his family, shareholders of the organization, or persons controlled, directly or indirectly, by such private interests. [ ] However, this private benefit prohibition applies to all kinds of persons and groups, not just to those "insiders" subject to the more strict inurement proscription.

* * *

In our view, some private benefit is present in all typical hospital-physician relationships. Physicians generally use hospital facilities at no cost to themselves to provide services to private patients for which they earn a fee. The private benefit accruing to the physicians generally can be considered incidental to the overwhelming public benefit resulting from having the combined resources of the hospital and its professional staff available to serve the public. Though the private benefit is compounded in the case of certain specialists, such as heart transplant surgeons, who depend heavily on highly specialized hospital facilities, that fact alone will not make the private benefit more than incidental.

In contrast, the private benefits conferred on the physician-investors by the instant revenue stream joint ventures are direct and substantial, not incidental. If for any reason these benefits should be found not to constitute inurement, they nonetheless exceed the bounds of prohibited private benefit. Whether viewed as giving the physicians a substantial share in the profits of the hospital or simply as allowing them an extremely profitable investment, the arrangements confer a significant benefit on them. Against this, we must balance the public benefit achieved by the hospitals in entering into the arrangements. The public benefit expected to result from these transactions—enhanced hospital financial health or greater efficiency achieved through improved utilization of their facilities—bears only the most tenuous relationship to the hospitals' charitable purposes of promoting the health of their communities. Obtaining referrals or avoiding new competition may improve the competitive position of an individual hospital, but that is not necessarily the same as benefiting its community.

* * *

. . . In our view, there are a fixed number of individuals in a community legitimately needing hospital services at any one time. Paying doctors to steer patients to one particular hospital merely to improve its efficiency seems distant from a mission of providing needed care. We question whether the Service should ever recognize enhancing a hospital's market share vis-a-vis other providers, in and of itself, as furthering a charitable purpose. In many cases, doing so might hamper another charitable hospital's ability to promote the health of the same community.

* * *

2. Physician Recruitment

It may be surprising to learn that hospitals can expend significant resources to recruit physicians. Typically, the hospital pays certain expenses for physicians to relocate their practices to the hospital's service area and join the medical staff to provide needed services to patients. Benefits are usually conditioned upon the physician remaining in the area for a period of years. The hospital is not necessarily recruiting the physician to become an employee of the hospital, so the arrangements are more complicated than simply offering an attractive salary. The recruited physician may set up solo practice or join an independent group. Terms of such arrangements vary, but financial benefits offered to physicians may include a signing bonus, the physician's home mortgage expenses, moving expenses, an income guarantee, loan and loan forgiveness, practice expenses, or liability insurance. Transferring financial resources to the recruited physician or his or her private practice can threaten the tax-exempt status of the hospital if it constitutes inurement or an impermissible private benefit. Revenue Ruling 97–21 sets forth the IRS's guidelines for physician recruitment. Note, physician recruitment can also raise issues under fraud and abuse laws discussed in Chapter 14.

REVENUE RULING 97–21

1997–18 I.R.B. 8.

* * *

Situation 1

Hospital A is located in County V, a rural area, and is the only hospital within a 100 mile radius. County V has been designated by the U.S. Public Health Service as a Health Professional Shortage Area for primary medical care professionals (a category that includes obstetricians and gynecologists). Physician M recently completed an ob/gyn residency and is not on Hospital A's medical staff. Hospital A recruits Physician M to establish and maintain a full-time private ob/gyn practice in its service area and become a member of its medical staff. Hospital A provides Physician M a recruitment incentive package pursuant to a written agreement negotiated at arm's-length. The agreement is in accordance with guidelines for physician recruitment that Hospital A's Board of Directors establishes, monitors, and reviews regularly to ensure that recruiting practices are consistent with Hospital A's exempt purposes. The agreement was approved by the committee appointed by Hospital A's Board of Directors to approve contracts with hospital medical staff. Hospital A does not provide any recruiting incentives to Physician M other than those set forth in the written agreement.

In accordance with the agreement, Hospital A pays Physician M a signing bonus, Physician M's professional liability insurance premium for a limited period, provides office space in a building owned by Hospital A for a limited number of years at a below market rent (after which the rental will be at fair market value), and guarantees Physician M's mortgage on a residence in County V. Hospital A also lends Physician M practice start-up financial assistance pursuant to an agreement that is properly documented and bears reasonable terms.

Situation 2

Hospital B is located in an economically depressed inner-city area of City W. Hospital B has conducted a community needs assessment that indicates both a shortage of pediatricians in Hospital B's service area and difficulties Medicaid patients are having obtaining pediatric services. Physician N is a pediatrician currently practicing outside of Hospital B's service area and is not on Hospital B's medical staff. Hospital B recruits Physician N to relocate to City W, establish and maintain a full-time pediatric practice in Hospital B's service area, become a member of Hospital B's medical staff, and treat a reasonable number of Medicaid patients. Hospital B offers Physician N a recruitment incentive package pursuant to a written agreement negotiated at arm's-length and approved by Hospital B's Board of Directors. Hospital B does not provide any recruiting incentives to Physician N other than those set forth in the written agreement.

Under the agreement, Hospital B reimburses Physician N for moving expenses [], reimburses Physician N for professional liability "tail" coverage for Physician N's former practice, and guarantees Physician N's private practice income for a limited number of years. The private practice income guarantee, which is properly documented, provides that Hospital B will make up the difference to the extent Physician N practices full-time in its service area and the private practice does not generate a certain level of net income (after reasonable expenses of the practice). The amount guaranteed falls within the range reflected in regional or national surveys regarding income earned by physicians in the same specialty.

Situation 3

Hospital C is located in an economically depressed inner city area of City X. Hospital C has conducted a community needs assessment that indicates indigent patients are having difficulty getting access to care because of a shortage of obstetricians in Hospital C's service area willing to treat Medicaid and charity care patients. Hospital C recruits Physician O, an obstetrician who is currently a member of Hospital C's medical staff, to provide these services and enters into a written agreement with Physician O. The agreement is in accordance with guidelines for physician recruitment that Hospital C's Board of Directors establishes, monitors, and reviews regularly to ensure that recruiting practices are consistent with Hospital C's exempt purpose. The agreement was approved by the officer designated by Hospital C's Board of Directors to enter into contracts with hospital medical staff. Hospital C does not provide any recruiting incentives to Physician O other than those set forth in the written agreement. Pursuant to the agreement, Hospital C agrees to reimburse Physician O for the cost of one year's professional liability insurance in return for an agreement by Physician O to treat a reasonable number of Medicaid and charity care patients for that year.

Situation 4

Hospital D is located in City Y, a medium to large size metropolitan area. Hospital D requires a minimum of four diagnostic radiologists to ensure adequate coverage and a high quality of care for its radiology department. Two of the four diagnostic radiologists currently providing coverage for Hospital D are relocating to other areas. Hospital D initiates a search for diagnostic radiologists and determines that one of the two most qualified candidates is Physician P.

Physician P currently is practicing in City Y as a member of the medical staff of Hospital E (which is also located in City Y). As a diagnostic radiologist, Physician P provides services for patients receiving care at Hospital E, but does not refer patients to Hospital E or any other hospital in City Y. Physician P is not on Hospital D's medical staff. Hospital D recruits Physician P to join its medical staff and to provide coverage for its radiology department. Hospital D offers Physician P a recruitment incentive package pursuant to a written agreement, negotiated at arm's-length and approved by Hospital D's Board of Directors. Hospital D does not provide any recruiting incentives to Physician P other than those set forth in the written agreement.

Pursuant to the agreement, Hospital D guarantees Physician P's private practice income for the first few years that Physician P is a member of its medical staff and provides coverage for its radiology department. The private practice income guarantee, which is properly documented, provides that Hospital D will make up the difference to Physician P to the extent the private practice does not generate a certain level of net income (after reasonable expenses of the practice). The net income amount guaranteed falls within the range reflected in regional or national surveys regarding income earned by physicians in the same specialty.

* * *

Analysis

When a § 501(c)(3) hospital recruits a physician for its medical staff who is to perform services for or on behalf of the organization, the organization meets the operational test by showing that, taking into account all of the benefits provided the physician by the organization, the organization is paying reasonable compensation for the services the physician is providing in return. A somewhat different analysis must be applied when a § 501(c)(3) hospital recruits a physician for its medical staff to provide services to members of the surrounding community but not necessarily for or on behalf of the organization. In these cases, a violation will result from a failure to comply with the [requirements that] . . . the organization . . . not engage in substantial activities that do not further the hospital's exempt purposes or that do not bear a reasonable [or]in activities that result in inurement of the hospital's net earnings to a private shareholder or individual; [or] engage in substantial activities that cause the hospital to be operated for the benefit of a private interest rather than public; [or]engage in substantial unlawful activities.

Situation 1

. . . Hospital A has objective evidence demonstrating a need for obstetricians and gynecologists in its service area and has engaged in physician recruitment activity bearing a reasonable relationship to promoting and protecting the health of the community. . . . [The hospital's payments and loans] . . . are reasonably related to causing Physician M to become a member of Hospital A's medical staff and to establish and maintain a full-time private ob/gyn practice in Hospital A's service area. . . .

Situation 2

Like Hospital A in Situation 1, Hospital B has objective evidence demonstrating a need for pediatricians in its service area and has engaged in physician recruitment activity bearing a reasonable relationship to promoting and protecting the health of the community [and the incentives provided] are reasonably related to causing Physician N to become a member of Hospital B's medical staff and to establish and maintain a full-time private pediatric practice in Hospital B's service area. . . .

Situation 3

In accordance with the standards for exemption. . . . Hospital C admits and treats Medicaid patients on a non-discriminatory basis. Hospital C has identified a shortage of obstetricians willing to treat Medicaid patients. The payment of Physician O's professional liability insurance premiums in return for Physician O's agreement to treat a reasonable number of Medicaid and charity care patients is reasonably related to the accomplishment of Hospital C's exempt purposes. Because the amount paid by Hospital C is reasonable and any private benefit to Physician O is outweighed by the public purpose served by the agreement, the recruitment activity described is consistent with the requirements for exemption as an organization described in § 501(c)(3).

Situation 4

Hospital D has objective evidence demonstrating a need for diagnostic radiologists to provide coverage for its radiology department so that it can promote the health of the community. The provision of a reasonable private practice income guarantee as a recruitment incentive that is conditioned upon Physician P obtaining medical staff privileges and providing coverage for the radiology department is reasonably related to the accomplishment of the charitable purposes served by the hospital. A significant fact in determining that the community benefit provided by the activity outweighs the private benefit provided to Physician P is the determination by the Board of Directors of Hospital D that it needs additional diagnostic radiologists to provide adequate coverage and to ensure a high quality of medical care.

* * *

Holding

The hospitals in Situations 1, 2, 3, and 4 have not violated the requirements for exemption from federal income tax as organizations described in § 501(c)(3) as a result of the physician recruitment incentive agreements they have made because the transactions further charitable purposes, do not result in inurement, do not result in the hospitals serving a private rather than a public purpose, and are assumed to be lawful for purposes of this revenue ruling. . . .

3. Accountable Care Organizations

Tax-exempt health care organizations, such as hospitals, may enter into joint ventures with for-profit entities, such as physician organizations, to form an accountable care organization (ACO) under the Medicare Shared Savings Program (MSSP), to contract with commercial payers to operate a private ACO, or both, discussed in Chapter 11. The question arises whether a tax-exempt organization can participate in an ACO without jeopardizing its tax-exempt status. As explained in IRS Notice 2011–20, the answer is yes, but there is substantially more flexibility for tax-exempt organizations to participate in the MSSP than in private ACOs.

NOTICE 2011–20

2011–16 I.R.B. 652 (2011).

This notice addresses the application of section 501(c)(3) of the Code to tax-exempt organizations participating in the Medicare Shared Savings Program (MSSP) through an accountable care organization (ACO) as described in section 3022 of the Patient Protection and Affordable Care Act.

* * *

Participation in the MSSP Through ACOs
by Tax-Exempt Organizations

The IRS anticipates that tax-exempt organizations typically will be participating in the MSSP through an ACO along with private parties, including some that might be considered insiders with respect to the tax-exempt organization. The IRS further anticipates that a tax-exempt organization's participation may take a variety of forms, including membership in a nonprofit membership corporation, ownership of shares in a corporation, ownership of a partnership interest in a partnership (or a membership interest in an LLC), and contractual arrangements with the ACO and/or its other participants.

To avoid adverse tax consequences, the tax-exempt organization must ensure that its participation in the MSSP through an ACO is structured so as not to result in its net earnings inuring to the benefit of its insiders or in its being operated for the benefit of private parties participating in the ACO. The IRS must determine whether prohibited inurement or impermissible private benefit has occurred on a case-by-case basis, based on all the facts and circumstances. Because of CMS regulation and oversight of the MSSP, as a general matter, the IRS expects that it will not consider a tax-exempt organization's participation in the MSSP through an ACO to result in inurement or impermissible private benefit to the private party ACO participants where:

- The terms of the tax-exempt organization's participation in the MSSP through the ACO (including its share of MSSP payments or losses and expenses) are set forth in advance in a written agreement negotiated at arm's length.

- CMS has accepted the ACO into, and has not terminated the ACO from, the MSSP.

- The tax-exempt organization's share of economic benefits derived from the ACO (including its share of MSSP payments) is proportional to the benefits or contributions the tax-exempt organization provides to the ACO. If the tax-exempt organization receives an ownership interest in the ACO, the ownership interest received is proportional and equal in value to its capital contributions to the ACO and all ACO returns of capital, allocations and distributions are made in proportion to ownership interests.

- The tax-exempt organization's share of the ACO's losses (including its share of MSSP losses) does not exceed the share of ACO economic benefits to which the tax-exempt organization is entitled.

- All contracts and transactions entered into by the tax-exempt organization with the ACO and the ACO's participants, and by the ACO with the ACO's participants and any other parties, are at fair market value.

An additional issue raised by the participation of tax-exempt organizations in ACOs is whether the share of the MSSP payments received by a tax-exempt organization will be subject to unrelated business income tax (UBIT) under § 511. Whether the MSSP payments will be subject to UBIT depends on whether the activities generating the MSSP payments are substantially related to the exercise or performance of the tax-exempt organization's charitable purposes constituting the basis for its exemption under § 501.

The IRS expects that, absent inurement or impermissible private benefit, any MSSP payments received by a tax-exempt organization from an ACO would derive from activities that are substantially related to the performance of the charitable purpose of lessening the burdens of government within the meaning of Treas. Reg. § 1.501(c)(3)–1(d)(2), as long as the ACO meets all of the eligibility requirements established by CMS for participation in the MSSP. *See, e.g.*, Rev. Rul. 81–276 (recognizing that the federal government considers the provision of Medicare to be its burden). Congress established the MSSP to be conducted through ACOs in order to promote quality improvements and cost savings, thereby lessening the government's burden associated with providing Medicare benefits.

* * *

ACO's Conduct of Activities Unrelated to the MSSP

The IRS understands that some tax-exempt organizations might participate in ACOs conducting activities unrelated to the MSSP, including entering into and operating under shared savings arrangements with other types of health insurance payers (non-MSSP activities). The IRS anticipates that, in contrast to activities conducted as part of the MSSP, many non-MSSP activities conducted by or through an ACO are unlikely to lessen the burdens of government within the meaning of Treas. Reg. § 1.501(c)(3)–1(d)(2). For example, negotiating with private health insurers on behalf of unrelated parties generally is not a charitable activity, regardless of whether the agreement negotiated involves a program aimed at achieving cost savings in health care delivery. However, the IRS recognizes that certain non-MSSP activities may further or be substantially related to an exempt purpose. For example, the [Notice of Proposed Rulemaking released March 30, 2011 by the Centers for Medicare and Medicaid Services] anticipates that ACOs may also participate in shared savings arrangements with Medicaid, which may further the charitable purpose of relieving the poor and distressed or the underprivileged. *See* Treas. Reg. § 1.501(c)(3)–1(d)(2). This notice does not address whether and under what circumstances a tax-exempt organization's participation in non-MSSP activities through an ACO will be consistent with an organization's tax-exemption under § 501(c)(3) or not result in UBIT. However, the IRS requests comments regarding what guidance, if any, is necessary or appropriate regarding a tax-exempt organization's participation in non-MSSP activities through an ACO.

* * *

NOTES AND QUESTIONS

1. *Private Inurement vs. Private Benefit.* Note the key differences between private inurement and private benefit. The former is akin to a per se rule, requiring revocation or denial of exempt status, with no *de minimis* exception. Moreover, it applies only to "insiders," defined as private shareholders or individuals having a personal and private interest in or opportunity to influence the activities of the organization from the inside. Treas. Reg. § 1.50(a)–1(c). The private benefit limitation applies to transactions with "outsiders" to the exempt organization and entails a broader inquiry, weighing private benefits against community benefits. What goals of the two proscriptions explain the different approaches? What factors did the IRS take into account in evaluating each of the scenarios in Rev. Ruling 97–21? Why did the balance tip against the hospital in GCM 39862? Who is considered an insider for inurement purposes? Might a prominent donor and fundraiser for a tax-exempt hospital qualify even if she or he holds no formal office with the hospital? An influential consultant under contract to give management advice? The IRS's view that staff physicians were in a position to influence administrators of tax-exempt hospitals led the IRS to treat them as "insiders" for inurement purposes, a position that it no longer adheres to as seen in the discussion of the Excess Benefits Transactions law, below.

2. *Tax-Exempt Entity Contribution and Value Derived.* The core of the analysis of private benefit and private inurement is the relationship between what the exempt organization pays and the value of what it receives. For ACOs, the factors in Notice 2011–20 emphasize that the tax-exempt entity's share of economic gains/losses must be proportional to its contribution, its share of losses cannot exceed its share of gains, and all contracts with ACO participants must be fair-market value. The IRS clarified that a charitable organization participating in an ACO need not satisfy all five of the factors set forth in Notice 2011–20. IRS Fact Sheet on Exempt Organizations Participating in Medicare Shared Savings Program through Accountable Care Organizations, FS-2011-11 (October 20, 2011). However, the satisfaction of all five factors by an exempt organization participating in an MSSP establishes a kind of safe-harbor, and the IRS will not consider the organization's participation in the ACO to result in inurement or private benefit to the physicians and other private ACO participants.

Note as well that for ACO joint ventures, the IRS does not require the tax-exempt entity to control the joint venture, unlike in Rev. Rul. 98–15 and the

St. David's case. The IRS explained that it "expects that CMS's regulation and oversight of the ACO will be sufficient to ensure that the ACO's participation in the Shared Savings Program furthers the charitable purpose of lessening the burdens of government." IRS Fact Sheet 2011–11, *supra*. Recall that another guiding principle behind the creation of ACOs is that they would be physician-led, not hospital-led. May that further explain the differences between the five factors in Notice 2011–20 and the general factors for tax-exempt organizations participating in a joint venture with for-profit entities?

    3.   *Fair Market Value.* The requirement that the § 501(c)(3) organization pay no more than fair market value for the physician practice or for physician compensation or for services received in a joint venture is a clear and understandable goal. However, it is hard to monitor compliance with the standard in the absence of functioning markets. The valuation of physician practices in particular presents substantial problems. Appraisal of the future income potential of the practice itself is particularly difficult and subject to differences among professional appraisers. Furthermore, although the IRS wants to assure that the § 501(c)(3) organization pays for no more than it receives in value, the Medicare and Medicaid programs prohibit payment for the value of future referrals by the doctors to the hospital, which raises overlapping concerns under the fraud and abuse laws discussed in Chapter 14. Thus, the parties might lean toward inflating the value of certain intangibles or certain allowable items (such as copy expenses for patient records) to bear the value of the referrals to the hospital. Does GCM 39862 indicate that the IRS does not consider future referrals a value received? What issues arise when a system decides to divest itself of unprofitable physician practices and decides to sell the practices back to the physicians at a much lower price than it originally paid?

4.   Excess Benefit Transactions: Intermediate Sanctions Under Internal Rev. Code § 4958

    In 1996 Congress adopted the Taxpayer Bill of Rights II (26 U.S.C.A. § 4958), an important law designed to clarify the obligations of insiders in exempt organizations and to provide an **"intermediate sanction"** for violations as an alternative to the harsh "death penalty" of the revocation of an entity's tax-exemption under traditional inurement and private benefit analysis. The basic concept of the law is straightforward: it imposes an excise tax on insiders ("disqualified persons") engaged in "excess benefit transactions" and on organizational mangers who approve them. But, as we've seen, nothing in tax law is simple. In January 2002, following four years of comment and revision, the Department of the Treasury issued final regulations which supply guidance concerning the numerous new concepts contained in IRC § 4958. 26 C.F.R. §§ 53.4958–1 to 53.4958–8. Some key terminology and concepts must be mastered to apply the supposedly simple, "bright line" approach of the statute. The following material outlines the key elements of the law.

Scope. Congress intended § 4958 to be the exclusive sanction unless the conduct arises to such an extreme level (evidenced by the size and scope of the excess benefit and the organization's efforts to prevent the conduct) that the tax-exempt organization can no longer be regarded as "charitable" and hence revocation is the appropriate sanction.

Excess Benefit Transactions. The statute defines an **"excess benefit transaction" (EBT)** as any transaction in which an economic benefit is provided by a tax-exempt organization directly or indirectly to or for the use of a "disqualified person" where the value of the economic benefit provided by the organization exceeds the value of the consideration (including the performance of services) received for providing the benefit. 26 U.S.C.A. § 4958(c)(1). The core prohibited transactions are those in which the disqualified person engages in *non-fair market transactions*, such as a bargain sale or loan; *unreasonable compensation arrangements*; or proscribed *revenue sharing arrangements*. The regulations give some additional guidance, such as indicating that compensation is reasonable only if it is an amount that ordinarily would be paid for like services by like enterprises under like circumstances existing at the time the contract was made. 26 C.F.R. § 53.4958–4(b)(3). Further, compensation includes all forms of deferred income if earned and vested and fringe benefits (even if not taxable); however, payments must be intended as compensation by the tax-exempt entity. 26 C.F.R. § 53.4958–4(c).

Disqualified Persons. **"Disqualified persons" (DQPs)** include "any person who was, at any time during the 5-year period ending on the date of such transaction, in a position to exercise substantial influence over the affairs of the organization, a member of the family of [such] an individual, or a 35-percent controlled entity [an entity in which such persons own more than 35% of the combined voting power if a corporation or of the profits interest if a partnership or of the beneficial interest of a trust or estate]." I.R.C. 4958(f)(1)(A).

Among those included in the category of DQPs are: officers, directors, and their close relatives. However, the detailed regulations make clear that persons with such titles are not to be so regarded if their position is honorary or they have no powers or ability to exercise substantial influence. 26 C.F.R. § 53.4958–3(c). Conversely, those with "substantial influence" can be DQPs regardless of whether they hold a formal position with the exempt organization.

An important issue for hospitals has been whether staff physicians will automatically be considered to have substantial influence. Although the IRS had previously indicated that they would be considered "insiders" for inurement purposes, it has reversed its position for excess benefit analysis, as the following excerpts from the regulations indicate. What generalizable principles emerge from these examples that can be applied in other factual settings?

26 C.F.R. § 53.4958–3(g)—DEFINITION
OF DISQUALIFIED PERSON

* * *

Example 10. U is a large acute-care hospital that is an applicable tax-exempt organization for purposes of section 4958. U employs X as a radiologist. X gives instructions to staff with respect to the radiology work X conducts, but X does not supervise other U employees or manage any substantial part of U's operations. X's compensation is primarily in the form of a fixed salary. In addition, X is eligible to receive an incentive award based on revenues of the radiology department. X's compensation is greater than the amount referenced for a highly compensated employee in section 414(q)(1)(B)(i) in the year benefits are provided. X is not related to any other disqualified person of U. X does not serve on U's governing body or as an officer of U. Although U participates in a provider-sponsored organization [ ] X does not have a material financial interest in that organization. X does not receive compensation primarily based on revenues derived from activities of U that X controls. X does not participate in any management decisions affecting either U as a whole or a discrete segment of U that represents a substantial portion of its activities, assets, income, or expenses. Under these facts and circumstances, X does not have substantial influence over the affairs of U, and therefore X is not a disqualified person with respect to U.

Example 11. W is a cardiologist and head of the cardiology department of the same hospital U described in Example 10. The cardiology department is a major source of patients admitted to U and consequently represents a substantial portion of U's income, as compared to U as a whole. W does not serve on U's governing board or as an officer of U. W does not have a material financial interest in the provider-sponsored organization (as defined in section 1855(e) of the Social Security Act) in which U participates. W receives a salary and retirement and welfare benefits fixed by a three-year renewable employment contract with U. W's compensation is greater than the amount referenced for a highly compensated employee in section 414(q)(1)(B)(i) in the year benefits are provided. As department head, W manages the cardiology department and has authority to allocate the budget for that department, which includes authority to distribute incentive bonuses among cardiologists according to criteria that W has authority to set. W's management of a discrete segment of U that represents a substantial portion of its income and activities (as compared to U as a whole) places W in a position to exercise substantial influence over the affairs of U. Under these facts and circumstances, W is a disqualified person with respect to U.

Organization Managers. Besides imposing penalties on the individuals receiving the benefits (see below), the act also levies a separate excise tax of 10 percent on "organization managers," whose participation in the transaction was "knowing, willful and not due to reasonable cause." The regulations define organization managers to include directors, trustees or officers, and administrators with delegated or regularly exercised administrative powers, but not independent contractors such as lawyers and accountants, investment advisors or middle managers with power to make recommendations but not to implement decisions. See 26 C.F.R. § 53.4958–3(d)(2)(i). Where the organizational manager makes full disclosure of all facts to a professional advisor and relies on that advisor's reasoned, written legal opinion, no penalty will be imposed; the advisor may be a lawyer, accountant or independent valuation firm with expertise. 26 C.F.R. § 53.4958–1(d)(4)(iii).

Rebuttable Presumption of Reasonableness. A key element of the intermediate sanctions statutory scheme is a rebuttable presumption of reasonableness applicable to compensation arrangements and transfers of property with a disqualified person where specified procedural steps are followed. To qualify for the presumption, the terms of the transaction must be approved by a board of directors or committee thereof composed entirely of individuals who (1) have no conflicts of interest with respect to the transaction, (2) have obtained and relied upon appropriate comparability data prior to making their determination, and (3) have adequately documented the basis for the determination. See 26 C.F.R. § 53.4958–6. The IRS may rebut the presumption with evidence that the compensation was not reasonable or the transfer was not at fair market value, such as by contesting the validity of comparables. The regulations give detailed instructions on standards for comparability determinations and give some relief for small organizations as to the data that must be used. Id. In its first advisory on compensation, the IRS found reliance by an independent board on a five-year old consultant report and the board's failure to separately evaluate compensation to comparable CEOs rendered the record inadequate to establish the rebuttable presumption under Section 4958. Internal Revenue Service, Technical Advice Memorandum 200244028 (June 21, 2002).

Penalties and "Correction." Sanctions, in the form of an initial tax of 25 percent of the excess benefit, are imposed on any DQP who benefited from the transaction; the excess benefit is calculated as the amount by which a transaction differs from fair market value. 26 C.F.R. § 53.4958–1. In addition, DQPs are subject to an additional tax of 200 percent of the excess benefit if the transaction is not "corrected" promptly (generally meaning that the DQP must undo the transaction and compensate the exempt organization for any losses caused by the transaction). Notably, no sanctions are imposed on the exempt organization. However, as described above, organizational managers who knowingly and willfully participate are subject to a 10 percent tax of the excess benefit. Abatement of penalties is possible where the violation is due to reasonable cause and not willful neglect.

Caracci v. Commissioner. Caracci v. Commissioner, 118 T.C. 379 (2002), rev'd 456 F.3d 444 (5th Cir. 2006), the Tax Court took on for the first time the task of applying the intermediate sanctions provisions to a health care organization and, in a major setback, was reversed by the Fifth Circuit. The Caracci family had operated their tax-exempt home health businesses, known as the Sta-Home Health Agency, very much as a family business. Family members were the sole members of the board of each of the tax-exempt entities and also held all key employment positions. For these services, the Caracci family paid themselves what the tax court characterized as "executive level" compensation. After experiencing operating losses for three years, and facing the prospect that Medicare, the principal payer for Sta-Home patients, would shift from cost reimbursement to prospective payment, the Caracci's undertook to convert the entities to for-profit status by selling their assets to three closely held corporations which were controlled and operated by the Caracci family. Concluding that the corporations paid inadequate consideration for the assets of the tax-exempt entities, the Service asserted that the transaction resulted in an excess benefit transaction under § 4958. In a 71-page opinion the Tax Court upheld the IRS's assessment of excise taxes but rejected revocation of the Sta-Home entities' tax-exempt status. It also concluded that the total excess benefit to the disqualified persons was approximately $5 million.

The Fifth Circuit's reversal contained a blistering criticism of the IRS's valuation analysis. It emphasized the lack of qualifications of the IRS's appraiser and his lack of direct exposure to the specific circumstances of the home healthcare market in Mississippi. Although the Caracci's tax advisor rendered an opinion at the time of the transaction and the family later obtained an appraisal from an expert appraiser with greater experience, the Tax Court had sided with the Internal Revenue Service. Indeed, the Sta-Home entities had lost money and had a negative cash flow, but the Tax court found value in the entities' intangible assets. For an analysis of *Caracci* and its implications for future disputes over valuation, authored by the taxpayers' expert witness, see Allen D. Hahn, Caracci and the Valuation of Exempt Organizations, 40 J. Health L. 267 (2007) (valuation models and reliance on comparables must be sensitive to the characteristics of the exempt organization and the regulatory policies affecting reimbursement).

PROBLEMS: EXCESS BENEFIT TRANSACTIONS

1.   Analyze whether the excess benefit law would apply in the following situations:

- Expenditures by a tax-exempt hospital to recruit an obstetrician, currently practicing at a nearby hospital, to relocate his office nearby and obtain staff privileges. The expenditures (free rent, moving allowances, malpractice insurance subsidies) exceed payments customarily made and there is no documentation of a community shortage of obstetricians.

- Payment by a tax-exempt hospital to certain Department Chairs, a fixed percentage of all revenues of the department.

- C, a tax-exempt hospital, contracts with Y, a management company, which will provide a wide range of services for a management fee of 7% of C's adjusted gross revenues, as specifically defined in the contract. Y will also receive payments for any expenses it incurs including legal, consulting or accounting throughout the term of the contract.

2.   Larry Levy, CEO of Exempt Hospital (EH) has received an offer from a for-profit system in another state that will pay him $2.2 million per year; provide him with a loan of $1 million; and give a performance bonus of $500,000 per year if he meets revenue targets. This package amounts to 50 percent more than EH currently pays him. It is believed to be in line with compensation at for-profit systems but is about 20 percent more than comparable nonprofit hospital systems pay. What should the Board of EH do and why?

3.   EH currently pays Dr. Brady, an independent staff physician who serves as its Department Chair of Oncology (with responsibility for hiring staff, supervising credentialing, and handling administrative duties of hospital but no role in budgetary matters), a sum of $1000 per month. Dr. Brady has requested a new compensation arrangement pursuant to which EH would pay him an additional $1000 for each new patient he or any member of the staff admits to EH who incurs total bills greater than $10,000. The EH Board approved this arrangement after a short briefing from its CEO who stressed that EH would have to shut down its oncology department if they didn't accede to Dr. Brady's demand. What excess benefit tax liability and for whom? What steps should the parties take?

II.   STATE TAX EXEMPTION

In addition to federal tax exemption, entities can seek exemption from state and local taxes, particularly property taxes. From a financial standpoint, state property tax exemption can be quite valuable to health care organizations that occupy large parcels of developed land. Historically, states tended to follow federal law when defining what constitutes charitable activities to qualify for state tax exemption. Even today, many states still apply a community benefit test similar to the federal standard. But the tide may be shifting.

The Supreme Court of Utah articulated well the historic justifications for state tax exemption for charitable health care organizations in Utah County v. Intermountain Healthcare, Inc.:

> These [tax] exemptions confer an indirect subsidy and are usually justified as the *quid pro quo* for charitable entities undertaking functions and services that the state would otherwise be required to perform. A concurrent rationale, used by some courts, is the assertion that the exemptions are granted not only because charitable entities relieve government of a burden, but also because their activities enhance beneficial community values or goals. Under this theory, the benefits received by the community are believed to offset the revenue lost by reason of the exemption. . . . An entity may be granted a charitable tax exemption for its property under the Utah Constitution only if it meets the definition of a "charity" or if its property is used exclusively for "charitable" purposes. Essential to this definition is the element of gift to the community. . . A gift to the community can be identified either by a substantial imbalance in the exchange between the charity and the recipient of its services or in the lessening of a government burden through the charity's operation. 709 P.2d 265 (Utah 1985).

In the *Intermountain* case, the court questioned whether the modern health care enterprise bore any resemblance to the historic tax-exempt hospitals which were places of low-tech convalescence for the poor and infirm, funded primarily through charitable donations rather than fees. The Supreme Court of Illinois confronted similar questions in the *Provena* case below, as did the New Jersey Tax Court in the *Morristown* case in the notes that follow. A confluence of factors may explain states' increasing willingness to apply more rigorously their requirements for state tax exemption, including localities' budgetary shortfalls and an increasing proportion of insured patients following the coverage expansion of the ACA leading to a reduced burden of uncompensated care. Thus, to a greater extent than the IRS, some states have been willing to revoke state tax exemption from hospitals, insist on a clearer relationship between tax exemption and the provision of charity care to indigent patients, and question the distinctions between nonprofit and for-profit hospitals.

PROVENA COVENANT MEDICAL CENTER
v. THE DEPARTMENT OF REVENUE

Supreme Court of Illinois, 2010.
925 N.E.2d 1131.

JUSTICE KARMEIER.

The central issue in this case is whether Provena Hospitals established that it was entitled to a charitable exemption under section 15–65 of the Property Tax [ ] for the 2002 tax year for various parcels of real estate it owns in Urbana. The Director of Revenue determined that it had not and denied the exemption. . . . For the reasons that follow, we now affirm the judgment of the appellate court upholding the decision by the Department of Revenue to deny the exemption.

The appellant property owner and taxpayer in this case is Provena Hospitals. Provena Hospitals is one of four subsidiaries of Provena Health, a corporation created when the Servants of the Holy Heart and two other groups affiliated with the Roman Catholic Church merged their health-care operations. . . . Provena Hospitals owns and operates six hospitals, including Provena Covenant Medical Center (PCMC), a full-service hospital located in the City of Urbana.

* * *

Provena Hospitals is exempt from federal income tax under section 501(c)(3) of the Internal Revenue Code (26 U.S.C. § 501(c)(3) (1988)). The Illinois Department of Revenue has also determined that the corporation is exempt from this state's retailers' occupation tax [ ], service occupation tax [ ], use tax [ ], and service use tax. [ ]

* * *

PCMC was not required to participate in the Medicare and Medicaid programs, but did so because it believed participation was "consistent with its mission." Participation was also necessary in order for Provena Hospitals to qualify for tax exemption under federal law. In addition, it provided the institution with a steady revenue stream.

* * *

During 2002, the amount of aid provided by Provena Hospitals to PCMC patients under the facility's charity care program was modest. The hospital waived $1,758,940 in charges, representing an actual cost to it of only $831,724. This was equivalent to only 0.723% of PCMC's revenues for that year and was $268,276 less than the $1.1 million in tax benefits which Provena stood to receive if its claim for a property tax exemption were granted.

* * *

Under Illinois law, taxation is the rule. Tax exemption is the exception. All property is subject to taxation, unless exempt by statute, in conformity with the constitutional provisions relating thereto. . . .

The burden of establishing entitlement to a tax exemption rests upon the person seeking it. [ ] The burden is a very heavy one. The party claiming an exemption must prove by clear and convincing evidence that the property in question falls within both the constitutional authorization and the terms of the statute under which the exemption is claimed. . . .

. . . Provena Hospitals has been granted a tax exemption by the federal government. There is no dispute, however, that tax exemption under federal law is not dispositive of whether real property is exempt from property tax under Illinois law. . . .

* * *

In Methodist Old Peoples Home v. Korzen, 39 Ill.2d 149, 156–57, 233 N.E.2d 537 (1968), we identified the distinctive characteristics of a charitable institution as follows: (1) it has no capital, capital stock, or shareholders; (2) it earns no profits or dividends but rather derives its funds mainly from private and public charity and holds them in trust for the purposes expressed in the charter; (3) it dispenses charity to all who need it and apply for it; (4) it does not provide gain or profit in a private sense to any person connected with it; and (5) it does not appear to place any obstacles in the way of those who need and would avail themselves of the charitable benefits it dispenses. [ ] For purposes of applying these criteria, we defined charity as "a gift to be applied . . . for the benefit of an indefinite number of persons, persuading them to an educational or religious conviction, for their general welfare-or in some way reducing the burdens of government."[ ]

* * *

Provena Hospitals clearly satisfies the first of the factors identified by this court Methodist Old Peoples Home v. Korzen for determining whether an organization can be considered a charitable institution: it has no capital, capital stock, or shareholders. Provena Hospitals also meets the fourth Korzen factor. It does not provide gain or profit in a private sense to any person connected with it. While the record focused on PCMC rather than Provena Hospitals, it was assumed by all parties during the administrative proceedings that Provena Hospitals' policies in this regard were the same as those of PCMC, and it was stipulated that PCMC diverted no profits or funds to individuals or entities for their own interests or private benefit.

* * *

While Korzen factors one and four thus tilt in favor of characterizing Provena Hospitals as a charitable institution, application of the remaining factors demonstrates that the characterization will not hold. Provena Hospitals plainly fails to meet the second criterion: its funds are not derived mainly from private and public charity and held in trust for the purposes expressed in the charter. They are generated, overwhelmingly, by providing medical services for a fee. While the corporation's consolidated statement of operations for 2002 ascribes $25,282,000 of Provena Hospitals' $739,293,000 in total revenue to "other revenue," that sum represents a mere 3.4% of Provena's income, and no showing was made as to how much, if any, of it was derived from charitable contributions. The only charitable donations documented in this case were those made to PCMC, one of Provena Hospitals' subsidiary institutions, and they were so small, a mere $6,938, that they barely warrant mention.

Provena Hospitals likewise failed to show by clear and convincing evidence that it satisfied factors three or five, namely, that it dispensed charity to all who needed it and applied for it and did not appear to place any obstacles in the way of those who needed and would have availed themselves of the charitable benefits it dispenses. . . .

. . . [E]ligibility for a charitable exemption under section 15–65 of the Property Tax Code (35 ILCS 200/15–65 (West 2002)) requires not only charitable ownership, but charitable use. Specifically, an organization seeking an exemption under section 15–65 must establish that the subject property is "actually and exclusively used for charitable or beneficent purposes, and not leased or otherwise used with a view to profit." 35 ILCS 200/15–65 (West 2002). When the law says that property must be "exclusively used" for charitable or beneficent purposes, it means that charitable or beneficent purposes are the primary ones for which the property is utilized. Secondary or incidental charitable benefits will not suffice, nor will it be enough that the institution professes a charitable purpose or aspires to using its property to confer charity on others. . . .

In rejecting Provena Hospitals' claim for exemption, the Department determined that the corporation also failed to satisfy this charitable use requirement. As with the issue of charitable ownership, the appellate court concluded that this aspect of the Department's decision was not clearly erroneous. Again we agree.

In explaining what constitutes charity, *Methodist Old Peoples Home v. Korzen,* applied the definition adopted by our court more than a century ago. [ ] We held there that

" 'charity, in a legal sense, may be more fully defined as a gift, to be applied consistently with existing laws, for the benefit of an indefinite number of persons, either by bringing their hearts under the influence of education or religion, by relieving their bodies from disease, suffering or constraint, by assisting them to establish themselves for life, or by erecting or maintaining public buildings or works, or otherwise lessening the burdens of government.' " [ ]

* * *

Conditioning charitable status on whether an activity helps relieve the burdens on government is appropriate. After all, each tax dollar lost to a charitable exemption is one less dollar affected governmental bodies will have to meet their obligations directly. If a charitable institution wishes to avail itself of funds which would otherwise flow into a public treasury, it is only fitting that the institution provide some compensatory benefit in exchange. While Illinois law has never required that there be a direct, dollar-for-dollar correlation between the value of the tax exemption and the value of the goods or services provided by the charity, it is a *sine qua non* of charitable status that those seeking a charitable exemption be able to demonstrate that their activities will help alleviate some financial burden incurred by the affected taxing bodies in performing their governmental functions.

* * *

. . . The situation before us here stands in contrast to People ex rel. Cannon v. Southern Illinois Hospital Corp., 404 Ill. 66, 88 N.E.2d 20 (1949). In that case, the hospital seeking the charitable exemption adduced evidence showing that the county in question did undertake to provide treatment for indigent residents. The hospital charged the county deeply discounted rates to treat those patients. Moreover, because the hospital was the only one in the area, the court reasoned that its acceptance of relief patients relieved the government from having to transport and pay for the treatment of those patients elsewhere. [ ] As a result, the hospital's operations could be said to reduce a burden on the local taxing body. No such conclusion was made or could be made based on the record in this case.

Even if Provena Hospitals were able to clear this hurdle, there was ample support for the Department of Revenue's conclusion that Provena failed to meet its burden of showing that it used the parcels in the PCMC complex actually and exclusively for charitable purposes. As our review of the undisputed evidence demonstrated, both the number of uninsured patients receiving free or discounted care and the dollar value of the care they received were *de minimus*. With very limited exception, the property was devoted to the care and treatment of patients in exchange for compensation through private insurance, Medicare and Medicaid, or direct payment from the patient or the patient's family.

To be sure, Provena Hospitals did not condition the receipt of care on a patient's financial circumstances. Treatment was offered to all who requested it, and no one was turned away by PCMC based on their inability to demonstrate how the costs of their care would be covered. The record showed, however, that during the period in question here, Provena Hospitals did not advertise the availability of charitable care at PCMC. Patients were billed as a matter of course, and unpaid bills were automatically referred to collection agencies. Hospital charges were discounted or waived only after it was determined that a patient had no insurance coverage, was not eligible for Medicare or Medicaid, lacked the resources to pay the bill directly, and could document that he or she qualified for participation in the institution's charitable care program. As a practical matter, there was little to distinguish the way in which Provena Hospitals dispensed its "charity" from the way in which a for-profit institution would write off bad debt. [ ]

* * *

Provena Hospitals argues that the amount of free and discounted care it provides to self-pay patients at the PCMC complex is not an accurate reflection of the scope of its charitable use of the property. In its view, its treatment of Medicare and Medicaid patients should also be taken into account because the payments it receives for treating such patients do not cover the full costs of care. As noted earlier in this opinion, however, participation in Medicare and Medicaid is not mandatory. Accepting Medicare and Medicaid patients is optional. While it is consistent with Provena Hospitals' mission, it also serves the organization's financial interests. In exchange for agreeing to accept less than its "established" rate, the corporation receives a reliable stream of revenue and is able to generate income from hospital resources that might otherwise be underutilized. Participation in the programs also enables the institution to qualify for favorable treatment under federal tax law, which is governed by different standards.

Mindful of such considerations, our appellate court has held that discounted care provided to Medicare and Medicaid patients is not considered charity for purposes of assessing eligibility for a property tax exemption.[ ] Similarly, the Catholic Health Association of the United States, one of the signatories to a friend of the court brief filed in this case in support of Provena Hospitals, does not include shortfalls from Medicaid and Medicare payments in its definition of charity. Provena Health itself adopted this view. The consolidated financial statements and supplementary information it prepared for itself and its affiliates for 2001 and 2002 did not identify any costs or charges incurred by PCMC in connection with subsidizing Medicaid or Medicare patients in its explanation of "charity care." That being so, it can scarcely complain that such costs and charges should have been included by the Department in evaluating Provena Hospitals' charitable contributions.[12]

* * *

CONCLUSION

For the foregoing reasons, the Department of Revenue properly denied the charitable and religious property tax exemptions requested by Provena Hospitals in this case. The judgment of the appellate court reversing the circuit court and upholding the Department's decision is therefore affirmed.

JUSTICE BURKE, concurring in part and dissenting in part:

I join that portion of the plurality opinion which holds that Provena Hospitals failed to demonstrate it was entitled to a religious exemption based on the lack of sufficient evidence. . . .

I also join the plurality opinion's conclusion that Provena Hospitals failed to establish it is a charitable institution. The defining characteristics of a charitable institution include, *inter alia,* that the institution dispenses charity to all who need it and apply for it, and that it does not appear to place any obstacles in the way of those who need and would avail themselves of the charitable benefits it dispenses. *Methodist Old Peoples Home v. Korzen,* 39 Ill. 2d 149, 157, 233 N.E.2d 537 (1968). There is evidence in the record detailing Provena Covenant Medical Center's (PCMC) charity care policy, evidence that PCMC's staff engaged in outreach efforts to communicate the availability of charity care and encouraged patients to apply, and evidence that charitable care would be considered by PCMC at any time. However, there is no such evidence in connection with Provena Hospitals, the actual owner of the subject property. Accordingly, the record in the case at bar is inadequate to establish that Provena Hospitals is a charitable institution, a necessary prerequisite to receiving a charitable exemption. For this reason alone, I agree with the plurality that Provena Hospitals is not entitled to a charitable exemption in this case.

I do not join that portion of the plurality opinion which addresses the doctrine of charitable use. Without citation to authority, the plurality holds that Provena Hospital's use of the property in 2002 was not a "charitable use" because the charity care provided was *de minimus.* . . . I disagree with this rationale. By imposing a quantum of care requirement and monetary threshold, the plurality is injecting itself into matters best left to the legislature.

---

[12] It would, in fact, be anomalous to characterize services provided to Medicare and Medicaid patients as charity. That is so because, as the Department correctly points out, charity is, by definition, a type of gift and gifts, as we have explained, must, by definition, be gratuitous. Hospitals do not serve Medicare and Medicaid patients gratuitously. They are paid to do so.

The legislature did not set forth a monetary threshold for evaluating charitable use. We may not annex new provisions or add conditions to the language of a statute. . . . I do not believe this court can, under the plain language of section 15–65, impose a quantum of care or monetary requirement, nor should it invent legislative intent in this regard. Setting a monetary or quantum standard is a complex decision which should be left to our legislature, should it so choose. The plurality has set a quantum of care requirement and monetary requirement without any guidelines. This can only cause confusion, speculation, and uncertainty for everyone: institutions, taxing bodies, and the courts. Because the plurality imposes such a standard, without any authority to do so, I cannot agree with it.

* * *

NOTES AND QUESTIONS

1. *Statutory Requirements for Hospital Tax Exemption.* Following the *Provena* decision, the Illinois legislature passed a law governing hospitals' property and sales tax exemptions requiring that the value of "[s]ervices that address the health care needs of low-income or underserved individuals or relieve the burden of government" equal or exceed the estimated value of its property tax liability based on the fair market value of its property. 35 ILCS 200/15–86. The law delineates services that will be credited, including providing free and discounted care, uncompensated care to low-income and underserved patients, disease management or financial assistance to the indigent, and financial support to other hospitals or for government programs that aid the indigent. Further, a separate statute requires that Illinois hospitals must provide medically necessary free care to individuals with family incomes up to 200 percent of federal poverty guidelines in urban areas and 125 percent in rural areas. 210 ILCS 89/10. Two cases have been brought attempting to invalidate the property tax exemption statute. Oswald v. Hamer, 115 N.E.3d 181 (Ill. 2018) and Carle Found. v. Cunningham Twp., 89 N.E.3d 341 (Ill. 2017). Both cases challenged the statute under the Illinois constitution, which requires that tax exempt property be "used exclusively" for charitable purposes. Oswald, 115 N.E.3d at 185. In *Oswald* the Illinois Supreme Court upheld the law as constitutional, noting the legislature's passage of the statute in response to the *Provena* decision in support of its decision. Although a lower court found the statute unconstitutional in *Carle Foundation*, the Illinois Supreme Court vacated and remanded the decision for jurisdictional reasons. Carle Found.,89 N.E.3d at 355. Another Illinois statute also provides an income tax credit for *investor-owned* hospitals in the amount of the lesser of property tax paid or charity care provided. 35 ILCS 5/223. What policy rationale would justify giving tax credits to for-profit entities? Looking at the bigger picture, should state legislatures or taxing authorities reconsider their laws requiring minimum levels of charity care in view of the changing magnitude and characteristics of the uninsured population?

2. *Variety of State Approaches.* A few states have adopted a "prescriptive" approach, requiring hospitals to make specified minimum expenditures on community benefits. State quantitative standards vary widely however. See, e.g. 10 Pa. Cons. Stat. Ann. Sec. 375 (setting forth five statutory standards including providing uncompensated goods or services equal to at least 5% of costs or maintaining an open admissions policy and providing uncompensated goods or services equal to at least 75% of net operating income, but not less than 3% of total operating expenses; also allowing payments in lieu of taxes); Nevada Revised Statutes § 439B.320 (requiring that hospitals with at least 100 beds provide 0.6 percent of their net revenue in free care to indigent patients each year); Tex. Code Ann. § 11.1801 (a)(4) (charity care and community benefits combined must equal at least five percent of the hospital's or hospital system's net patient revenues). There is also considerable disparity among the states imposing specific requirements over the specifics of community benefit obligations. See U.S. General Accountability Office, Nonprofit Hospitals Variation in Standards and Guidance Limits Comparison of How Hospitals Meet Community Benefit Requirements (2008) (of the fifteen states having community benefit requirements in statutes or regulations, consensus does not exist to define bad debt—the amount that the patient is expected to, but does not, pay—or the unreimbursed cost of Medicare or Medicaid).

3. *Morristown Medical Center in New Jersey.* In a wide-ranging opinion, the New Jersey Tax Court stripped a hospital of most of its property tax exemption. AHS Hosp. Corp. v. Town of Morristown, 28 N.J. Tax 456 (2015). Rather than appeal, Morrison Medical Center settled the case by agreeing to pay the town $26 million in property taxes. After surveying the complicated financial relationships of the hospital and its parent company, the court noted that if all nonprofit hospitals operated like Morristown Medical Center, then "for purposes of the property tax exemption, modern nonprofit hospitals are essentially legal fictions." Id. at 536. The court interpreted New Jersey's statute authorizing property tax exemptions as requiring hospitals to serve a charitable function in contrast to Morristown Medical Center's mixture of for-profit and non-profit activities. The court found that the hospital failed the "profit test" under New Jersey law, emphasizing (1) the impossibility of determining which portions of the hospital were used by for-profit (non-employee) physicians and which were used by physicians employed by the hospital; (2) the ownership by the hospital's parent corporation of several for-profit companies (including one that was essentially an offshore bank account); and (3) the fact that trustees on the boards of the system's nonprofit entities often served as statutory officers for the for-profit companies.

The court was particularly troubled by the fact that non-employed physicians provided their services throughout the subject property and used the facility to generate bills that they charged patients directly, concluding that "by entangling its activities and operations with those of for-profit entities, the Hospital allowed its property to be used for profit." Doesn't this describe the practices of independent physicians at virtually all tax-exempt hospitals?

What policy complications flow from a requirement that exempt hospitals rely primarily or exclusively on employed physicians?

A 2021 New Jersey law took an opposing stance from the *Morristown* court on this issue. The law, Act of Feb. 22, 2021, ch. 17, 2021 N.J. Laws, was passed in response to *Morristown* and amended the statutes relied on by the court in its ruling, N.J. Stat. § 54:4–3.6. Supported by hospital groups, the new law explicitly allows for "any portion of a hospital . . . used by a profit-making medical provider for . . . delivery of health care services directly to the hospital" to be exempt from taxation. The law also dismissed ongoing lawsuits by other communities seeking tax payments under following *Morristown*. Several localities filed a lawsuit in 2021 challenging the constitutionality of the new law.

Although the legal basis for the decisions in *Provena* and *Morristown* were state-specific, the broader theme is that state courts and taxing authorities are willing to rigorously enforce the requirement that tax-exempt hospitals exclusively serve charitable purposes, the concept for which has expanded beyond simply providing adequate charity care to caring for vulnerable populations in the community, increasing affordability for all patients, and clearly separating a hospital system's nonprofit and for-profit activities, including services by independent physicians.

CHAPTER 14

FRAUD AND ABUSE

■ ■ ■

Health care providers are subject to a large body of law governing their financial arrangements with one another and with federal health care programs. These federal and state laws cover many practices that amount to fraud, bribery, or stealing. In addition, they prohibit many contractual relationships, investments, and marketing and recruitment practices that are perfectly legal in other businesses. These laws aim to save the government and taxpayers money, recoup funds paid based on false and fraudulent claims, prevent overutilization of health care services, and prevent conflicts of interest that taint physicians' clinical decisions for their patients.

Although the term "fraud and abuse" connotes intentional wrongdoing, it is used very broadly and covers a large number of activities, ranging from negligent or careless practices that result in unintentional overbilling, to outright fraudulent schemes to bill knowingly for services or goods never furnished. The term also refers to so-called "self-referral arrangements" between physicians and entities with whom they have financial ties, which are seen as improperly encouraging overutilization and waste in federal health care programs.

Fraud enforcement is "big business" for the federal government, and because of the size of federal health care programs, health care fraud enforcement plays an outsized role, dwarfing the recoveries from other industries, such as defense, mortgage, agriculture, or transportation. In 2019, the Department of Justice recovered more than $3 billion in settlements and judgments under the False Claims Act, the vast majority of which ($2.6 billion) came from the health care industry, with the pharmaceutical and life sciences sectors drawing increasing attention and some of the largest settlements, including a $2.8 billion settlement with Purdue Pharma announced in 2020 for false claims from improper kickbacks to promote its opioid drug, OxyContin. Although disruptions from the global COVID-19 pandemic caused FCA recoveries to decline in 2020 (health care recoveries fell to $1.86 billion), the 922 new FCA cases filed was the highest number in history, signaling that federal enforcement activity remains vigorous. The federal statutes under which the government may investigate, prosecute, and punish instances of systematic fraud are also bewilderingly complicated and have generated confusion and cynicism in the health care industry. Further, while some aspects of these laws may prove anachronistic under evolving payment systems, they will continue to have a profound impact on the health care industry for some time to come. These complex laws generate an enormous amount of work for health care lawyers advising organizations that must comply with their strictures.

According to some estimates, Medicare and Medicaid fraud and abuse costs federal and state governments tens of billions of dollars per year. By one estimate, approximately 25% of U.S. health care spending, or $760 to $935 billion annually, is spent on waste, fraud, and abuse. William H. Shrank, Teresa L. Rogstad, & Natasha Parekh, Waste in the US Health Care System: Estimated Costs and Potential for Savings, 322 JAMA 1501 (2019). The Government Accountability Office estimated that in 2016 improper payments for waste, fraud, and abuse cost Medicare and Medicaid $95 billion out of the $1.1 trillion of total program spending. GAO, Report to Congress: Medicare and Medicaid (Dec. 2017). Much of this problem undoubtedly can be traced to the structure and complexities of Medicare and Medicaid payment systems, which give incentives and opportunities to engage in fraud or to "game the system" to maximize reimbursement. The programs' emphasis on rapid payment to providers further exacerbates these problems by allowing perpetrators to avoid detection and prosecution. See Health Affairs, Health Policy Brief, Eliminating Fraud and Abuse (July 31, 2012).

This chapter focuses on three federal fraud and abuse statutes: Section I covers the False Claims Act, 31 U.S.C. §§ 3729 to 3733; Section II discusses the Anti-Kickback Statute, 42 U.S.C. § 1320a–7b; and Section III examines the Ethics in Patient Referrals Act, better known as the Stark Law, 42 U.S.C. § 1395nn.

While this chapter focuses on the "big three" fraud and abuse statutes, there are others. Some, like the Civil Monetary Penalties law, 42 U.S.C. § 1320a–7a, and the Physician Payments Sunshine Act, 42 U.S.C. § 1320a–7h, apply specifically to participants in federal health care programs. Other anti-fraud laws apply more generally, including statutes prohibiting mail fraud, 18 U.S.C. § 1341, wire fraud, 18 U.S.C. § 1343, and racketeering, 18 U.S.C. § 1961. In addition to federal statutes, a number of states have adopted laws that closely follow the federal False Claims Act, as well as state anti-fee splitting laws and anti-referral laws that follow the federal Anti-Kickback Statute and Stark Law, respectively.

I. FALSE CLAIMS ACT

31 U.S.C. § 3729

(a) Liability for Certain Acts. (1) In general . . . [A]ny person who—

(A) knowingly presents, or causes to be presented, a false or fraudulent claim for payment or approval;

(B) knowingly makes, uses, or causes to be made or used, a false record or statement material to a false or fraudulent claim;

(C) conspires to commit a violation of subparagraph (A), (B), (D), (E), (F), or (G);

* * *

(G) knowingly makes, uses, or causes to be made or used, a false record or statement material to an obligation to pay or transmit money or property to the Government, or knowingly conceals or knowingly and improperly avoids or decreases an obligation to pay or transmit money or property to the Government,

is liable to the United States Government for a civil penalty of not less than $5,000 and not more than $10,000, as adjusted by the Federal Civil Penalties Inflation Adjustment Act of 1990, plus 3 times the amount of damages which the Government sustains because of the act of that person.

* * *

(b)(1)   the terms "knowing" and "knowingly"—

    (A) mean that a person, with respect to information—

        (i)   has actual knowledge of the information;

        (ii) acts in deliberate ignorance of the truth or falsity of the information; or

        (iii) acts in reckless disregard of the truth or falsity of the information; and

    (B) require no proof of specific intent to defraud;

* * *

(4) the term "material" means having a natural tendency to influence, or be capable of influencing, the payment or receipt of money or property.

During the Civil War, long before the federal government got into the health care business, Congress enacted the False Claims Act in response to unscrupulous military contractors who were billing the government for faulty and poor quality equipment and weapons. The statute remains the government's primary tool for recovering property and funds under a variety of federal government programs and contracts, but it has become increasingly focused on recovering improper payments under federal health care programs like Medicare and Medicaid. COVID-19 triggered increased enforcement of fraud and abuse under the trillions spent in pandemic relief, including both health and non-health measures.

One reason False Claims Act liability is such a grave concern to health care organizations is how large the penalties can be. The civil penalties for violations of the False Claims Act have increased over time, adjusting for inflation. In 2021, the minimum penalty per-claim was $11,803 and the maximum was $23,607. 86 Fed. Reg. 2005 (Jan. 11, 2021). In addition, violations are magnified by adding "**treble damages**," which triple the total amount the government's damages, usually the amount the government paid for the claims. For health care providers that submit thousands of claims to federal health care programs, total civil liability under the False Claims Act can quickly reach tens or even hundreds of millions of dollars—enough to financially devastate even large health care organizations.

In addition to civil liability, federal law also makes it a felony to knowingly and willfully make or cause to be made a false claim or statement to receive payment under federal health care programs, including Medicare and Medicaid. 42 U.S.C. § 1320a–7b(a). Since 2015, the Department of Justice has increased its enforcement focus on the individual participants in corporate fraud cases and operated under a policy that civil and criminal investigations should be coordinated from the inception and operate in parallel proceedings. Deputy Attorney General Sally Quinlan Yates, Memorandum: Individual Accountability for Corporate Wrongdoing (Sept. 9, 2015) (the "**Yates Memo**"). In 2019, the Department of Justice updated its enforcement policy, narrowing the scope of Yates Memo to focus on senior officials and those "substantially involved" in the wrongdoing for the corporation to earn cooperation credit. Justice Manual, Section 4–3.000, Compromising and Closing. One legacy of the Yates Memo is that the Civil Division of the Justice Department will share all new qui tam complaints with the Criminal Division when they are filed, and the Criminal Division evaluates complaints for circumstances meriting concurrent criminal investigation.

Congress has expanded the applicability of the False Claims Act over the years. It amended the Act in the **Fraud Enforcement and Recovery Act of 2009 (FERA)**, which added in subsection (G) to statute above, prohibiting not just the submission of a false claim to the government, but also "**reverse false claims**." A reverse false claim involves the knowing retention of government funds erroneously paid. In the health care context, the knowing retention of overpayments may occur, for example, when a health care entity discovers Medicare paid for claims that were improperly coded or that were tainted by a Stark Law or Anti-Kickback violation. Thus, once the provider or supplier discovers an overpayment, it becomes a false claim when the entity knowingly conceals or avoids an obligation to return the overpayment to the government. The Affordable Care Act (ACA) subsequently added the "**60-day rule**" requiring claimants to return overpayments by the later of 60 days after the date on which they are "identified" or the date any corresponding cost report is due. 42 U.S.C. § 1320a–7k(d). Implementing regulations clarify that an overpayment is "identified" when the entity has, or should have through the exercise of reasonable diligence, determined that it has received, and quantified the amount of, the overpayment. 42 C.F.R. § 401.305(a)(2). The preamble to the rules suggests that providers may take up to six months to investigate with reasonable diligence before the 60-day clock begins, resulting in a rough limit of eight months to investigate, identify, quantify, and repay overpayments. The rules establish a **six-year look-back period** during which providers and suppliers are responsible for investigating and identifying overpayments subject to the False Claims Act. In addition, if the overpayment was the result of an Anti-Kickback or Stark Law violation, the 60-day clock can be tolled if the provider makes a voluntary self-disclosure to the applicable enforcement agency (HHS OIG or CMS). Self-disclosure is further discussed in Sections II and III, below.

The ACA also expanded the reach of the False Claims Act to private plans sold on ACA Exchanges by providing "payments made by, through, or in connection with an Exchange are subject to the False Claims Act if those payments include any Federal funds." 42 U.S.C. § 18033. In addition, as discussed below, the ACA codifies the holding of several courts that Anti-Kickback Statute violations are material for purposes of the False Claims Act.

A. GOVERNMENT AND *QUI TAM* ENFORCEMENT

While the Attorney General through the Department of Justice may enforce the False Claims Act, the statute also contains a provision under which private individual whistleblowers, called *qui tam* **relators**, may seek to enforce False Claims Act violations. Upon filing the action, the *qui tam* relator must notify the government, which may intervene in the case

31 U.S.C. § 3730

Civil actions for false claims

(a) Responsibilities of the Attorney General.—The Attorney General diligently shall investigate a violation under section 3729. If the Attorney General finds that a person has violated or is violating section 3729, the Attorney General may bring a civil action under this section against the person.

(b) Actions by private persons.—(1) A person may bring a civil action for a violation of [the False Claims Act] for the person and for the United States Government. The action shall be brought in the name of the Government. The action may be dismissed only if the court and the

Attorney General give written consent to the dismissal and their reasons for consenting.

(2) A copy of the complaint and written disclosure of substantially all material evidence and information the person possesses shall be served on the Government . . . The complaint shall be filed in camera, shall remain under seal for at least 60 days, and shall not be served on the defendant until the court so orders. The Government may elect to intervene and proceed with the action within 60 days after it receives both the complaint and the material evidence and information.

* * *

(4) Before the expiration of the 60-day period or any extensions obtained under paragraph (3), the Government shall—

(A) proceed with the action, in which case the action shall be conducted by the Government; or

(B) notify the court that it declines to take over the action, in which case the person bringing the action shall have the right to conduct the action.

* * *

(c) Rights of the parties to qui tam actions.—(1) If the Government proceeds with the action, it shall have the primary responsibility for prosecuting the action, and shall not be bound by an act of the person bringing the action. Such person shall have the right to continue as a party to the action, subject to the limitations set forth in paragraph (2).

* * *

(d) Award to qui tam plaintiff.—(1) If the Government proceeds with an action brought by a person under subsection (b), such person [shall receive between 15 and 25 percent of the proceeds of the action or settlement of the claim, depending on the extent to which the person contributed to the prosecution, plus attorneys' fees and costs. If the government does not proceed the person may receive between 25 and 30 percent plus attorneys' fees and costs. If the action was brought by a person who planned and initiated the violation of the statutes, the court may reduce the person's share of proceeds and if the person is convicted of a crime for his or her role that person may not share any proceeds.]

(e) Certain actions barred.

* * *

(3) In no event may a person bring an action under subsection (b) which is based upon allegations or transactions which are the subject of a civil suit or an administrative civil money penalty proceeding in which the Government is already a party.

(4)(A)   The court shall dismiss an action or claim under this section, unless opposed by the Government, if substantially the same allegations or transactions as alleged in the action or claim were publicly disclosed—(i) in a Federal criminal, civil, or administrative hearing in which the Government or its agent is a party; (ii) in a congressional, Government Accountability Office, or other Federal report, hearing, audit, or investigation; or (iii) from the news media, unless the action is brought by the Attorney General or the person bringing the action is an original source of the information.

(B) For purposes of this paragraph, "original source" means an individual who either (i) prior to a public disclosure under subsection (e)(4)(a), has voluntarily disclosed to the Government the information on which allegations or transactions in a claim are based, or (2) who has knowledge that is independent of and materially adds to the publicly disclosed allegations or transactions, and who has voluntarily provided the information to the Government before filing an action under this section.

* * *

(h) Relief from retaliatory actions.—(1) In general.—Any employee, contractor, or agent shall be entitled to all relief necessary to make that employee, contractor, or agent whole, if that employee, contractor, or agent is discharged, demoted, suspended, threatened, harassed, or in any other manner discriminated against in the terms and conditions of employment because of lawful acts done by the employee, contractor, or agent on behalf of the employee, contractor, or agent or associated others in furtherance of other efforts to stop 1 or more violations of this subchapter. (2) Relief— Relief under paragraph (1) shall include reinstatement with the same seniority status that employee, contractor, or agent would have had but for the discrimination, 2 times the amount of back pay, interest on the back pay, and compensation for any special damages sustained as a result of the discrimination, including litigation costs and reasonable attorneys' fees. An action under this subsection may be brought in the appropriate district court of the United States for the relief provided in this subsection.

Although the False Claims Act defines the statute of limitations as six years from the date of the violation for private *qui tam* relators or up to ten years for the government, in 2019 the Supreme Court ruled that the **ten-year statute of limitations** applies to both private and government plaintiffs, whether or not the government intervenes in the case. 31 U.S.C. § 3731; Cochise Consultancy, Inc. v. United States ex rel. Hunt, 139 S. Ct. 1507 (2019). The date of the violation is generally the date that the provider allegedly submitted the false claim. If the government elects to intervene in a case, the government's complaint relates back to the qui tam relator's filing date. The *Cochise* case raises questions about the six-year regulatory lookback period for investigating overpayments mentioned above. Some attorneys advise that the two timing rules remain separate and that providers may still rely on the six-year lookback period for overpayments. Nevertheless, the lengthier statute of limitations after *Cochise* will increase the value of these cases for whistleblowers and the potential liability for defendants, so an exacting compliance program may be the best defense.

A significant obstacle for *qui tam* relators is the statute's bar on actions in which there has been "**public disclosure**" of the allegations or transactions, which includes government hearings, investigations, and media reports. However, the law provides an exception (see 31 U.S.C. § 3730(e)(4)(B) *supra*) where the relator is an "**original source**" of the information, meaning that the relator either disclosed the information about the allegations to the government before it became public or has "knowledge that is independent of and materially adds to the publicly disclosed allegations or transactions." On the issue of whether a relator's information is independent of and materially adds to a public disclosure, courts have generally held the answer turns on whether the disclosure and the allegations are "substantially similar." However, case law holds that public disclosures that are highly general will not bar *qui tam* lawsuits raising particularized allegations containing genuinely new information.

Congress has repeatedly strengthened the hand of *qui tam* relators. For example, the ACA expanded the universe of potential *qui tam* relators by reversing several Supreme Court cases. The ACA provides that the public disclosure bar extends only to suits based on a disclosure "in a congressional, [GAO] or other Federal report, hearing, audit, or investigation," reversing the case of Graham County Soil & Water Conservation District v. United States ex rel. Wilson, 545 U.S. 409 (2005). Under FERA, government contractors and agents may be protected whistleblowers, and the False Claims Act applies to claims submitted to a government contractor, not just the government itself, reversing the Supreme Court's decision in Allison Engine Co. v. U.S. ex rel. Sanders, 553 U.S. 662 (2008). However, FERA narrowed protections against retaliation to whistleblowers who have taken actions to stop illegal behavior; merely pursuing a *qui tam* complaint will not be sufficient.

Qui tam actions have become the principle means by which the government uncovers fraud, as whistleblowers initiate over 80 percent of all government false claims actions. Although the Department of Justice intervenes in only about 20 percent of *qui tam* actions, about 90 percent of recoveries are from cases where the government intervened. For the view that "privatization" of public law enforcement through the qui tam statute creates incentives to over-enforce the False Claims Act, see Dana Bowen Matthew, The Moral Hazard Problem with Privatization of Public

Enforcement: The Case of Pharmaceutical Fraud, 40 Mich. J. L. Ref. 281 (2007). On the other hand, *qui tam* relators often face enormous personal and financial risk in undertaking a *qui tam* suit. See Timothy Stoltzfus Jost, Optimizing Qui Tam Litigation and Minimizing Fraud and Abuse: A Comment on Christopher Alexion's Open the Door, Not the Floodgates, 69 Wash. & Lee L. Rev. 419 (2012).

B. SCIENTER REQUIREMENT

UNITED STATES V. KRIZEK

United States District Court, District of Columbia, 1994.
859 F. Supp. 5.

SPORKIN, DISTRICT JUDGE.

Memorandum Opinion and Order

On January 11, 1993, the United States filed this civil suit against George O. Krizek, M.D. and Blanka H. Krizek under the False Claims Act, 31 U.S.C. §§ 3729–3731, and at common law. The government brought the action against the Krizeks alleging false billing for Medicare and Medicaid patients. The five counts include claims for (1) "Knowingly Presenting a False or Fraudulent Claim", 31 U.S.C. § 3729(a)(1); (2) "Knowingly Presenting a False or Fraudulent Record", 31 U.S.C. § 3729(a)(2); (3) "Conspiracy to Defraud the Government"; (4) "Payment under Mistake of Fact"; and (5) "Unjust Enrichment". In its claim for relief, the government asks for triple the alleged actual damages of $245,392 and civil penalties of $10,000 for each of the 8,002 allegedly false reimbursement claims pursuant to 31 U.S.C. § 3729.

The government alleges two types of misconduct related to the submission of bills to Medicare and Medicaid. The first category of misconduct relates to the use of billing codes found in the American Medical Association's "Current Procedural Terminology" ("CPT"), a manual that lists terms and codes for reporting procedures performed by physicians. The government alleges that Dr. Krizek "up-coded" the bills for a large percentage of his patients by submitting bills coded for a service with a higher level of reimbursement than that which Dr. Krizek provided. As a second type of misconduct, the government alleges Dr. Krizek "performed services that should not have been performed at all in that they were not medically necessary." [ ]

Given the large number of claims, and the acknowledged difficulty of determining the "medical necessity" of 8,002 reimbursement claims, it was decided that this case should initially be tried on the basis of seven patients and two hundred claims that the government believed to be representative of Dr. Krizek's improper coding and treatment practices. [ ] It was agreed by the parties that a determination of liability on Dr. Krizek's coding practices would be equally applicable to all 8,002 claims in the complaint. A three week bench trial ensued.

Findings of Fact

Dr. Krizek is a psychiatrist. Dr. Krizek's wife, Blanka Krizek was responsible for overseeing Dr. Krizek's billing operation for a part of the period in question. Dr. Krizek's Washington, D.C. psychiatric practice consists in large part in the treatment of Medicare and Medicaid patients. Much of Doctor Krizek's work involves the provision of psychotherapy and other psychiatric care to patients at the Washington Hospital Center.

Under the Medicare and Medicaid systems, claims for reimbursement are submitted on documents known as Health Care Financing Administration ("HCFA") 1500 Forms. These forms are supposed to contain the patient's identifying information, the provider's Medicaid or Medicare identification number, and a description of the provided procedures for which reimbursement is sought. These procedures are identified by a standard, uniform code number as set out in the American Medical Association's "Current Procedural Terminology" ("CPT") manual, a book that lists the terms and codes for reporting procedures performed by physicians.

* * *

The government in its complaint alleges both improper billing for services provided and the provision of medically unnecessary services. The latter of these two claims will be addressed first.

Medical Necessity

The record discloses that Dr. Krizek is a capable and competent physician.... The trial testimony of Dr. Krizek, his colleagues at the Washington Hospital Center, as well as the testimony of a former patient, established that Dr. Krizek was providing valuable medical and psychiatric care during the period covered by the complaint. The testimony was undisputed that Dr. Krizek worked long hours on behalf of his patients, most of whom were elderly and poor.

Many of Dr. Krizek's patients were afflicted with horribly severe psychiatric disorders and often suffered simultaneously from other serious medical conditions....

The government takes issue with Dr. Krizek's method of treatment of his patients, arguing that some patients should have been discharged from the hospital sooner, and that others suffered from conditions which could not be ameliorated through psychotherapy sessions, or that the length of the psychotherapy sessions should have been abbreviated. The government's expert witness's opinions on this subject came from a cold review of Dr. Krizek's notes for each patient. The government witness did not examine or interview any of the patients, or speak with any other doctors or nurses who had actually served these patients to learn whether the course of treatment prescribed by Dr. Krizek exceeded that which was medically necessary.

Dr. Krizek testified credibly and persuasively as to the basis for the course of treatment for each of the representative patients. The medical necessity of treating Dr. Krizek's patients through psychotherapy and hospitalization was confirmed via the testimony of other defense witnesses. The Court credits Dr. Krizek's testimony on this question as well as his interpretation of his own notes regarding the seriousness of each patients' condition and the medical necessity for the procedures and length of hospital stay required. The Court finds that the government was unable to prove that Dr. Krizek rendered services that were medically unnecessary.

Improper Billing

On the question of improper billing or "up-coding," the government contends that for approximately 24 percent of the bills submitted, Dr. Krizek used the CPT Code for a 45–50 minute psychotherapy session (CPT Code 90844) when he should have billed for a 20–30 minute session (CPT Code 90843). The government also contends that for at least 33 percent of his patients, Dr. Krizek billed for a full 45–50 minute psychotherapy session, again by using CPT code 90844, when he should have billed for a "minimal psychotherapy" session (CPT 90862). These two latter procedures are reimbursed at a lower level than 90844, the 45–50 minute psychotherapy session, which the government has referred to as "the Cadillac" of psychiatric reimbursement codes.

The primary thrust of the government's case revolves around the question whether Dr. Krizek's use of the 90844 CPT code was appropriate. For the most part, the government does not allege that Dr. Krizek did not see the patients for whom he submitted bills. Instead, the government posits that the services provided during his visits either did not fall within the accepted definition of "individual medical psychotherapy" *or*, if the services provided *did* fit within this definition, the reimbursable service provided was not as extensive as that which was billed for. In sum, the government claims that whenever Dr. Krizek would see a patient, regardless of whether he simply checked a chart, spoke with nurses, or merely prescribed additional medication, his wife or his employee, a Mrs. Anderson, would, on the vast majority of occasions, submit a bill for CPT code 90844—45–50 minutes of individual psychotherapy.

[Documents sent to providers by Pennsylvania Blue Shield, the Medicare carrier for Dr. Krizek's area, explained the services in the 90800 series of codes as involving "[i]ndividual medical psychotherapy by a physician, with continuing medical diagnostic evaluation, and drug management when indicated, including insight oriented, behavior modifying or supportive psychotherapy" for specified periods of time.]

* * *

The government's witnesses testified that as initially conceived, the definition of the CPT codes is designed to incorporate the extra time spent in its level of reimbursement. It was expected by the authors of the codes that for a 45–50 minute 90844 session a doctor would spend additional time away from the patient reviewing or dictating records, speaking with nurses, or prescribing medication. The government's witnesses testified that the reimbursement rate for 90844 took into account the fact that on a 45–50 minute session the doctor would likely spend twenty additional minutes away from the patient. As such, the doctor is limited to billing for time actually spent "face-to-face" with the patient.

Dr. and Mrs. Krizek freely admit that when a 90844 code bill was submitted on the doctor's behalf, it did not always reflect 45–50 minutes of face-to-face psychotherapy with the patient. Instead, the 45–50 minutes billed captured generally the total amount of time spent on the patient's case, including the "face-to-face" psychotherapy session, discussions with medical staff about the patient's treatment/progress, medication management, and other related services. Dr. Krizek referred to this as "bundling" of services, all of which, Dr. and Mrs. Krizek testified, they reasonably believed were reimbursable under the 90844 "individual medical psychotherapy" code.

Defendant's witnesses testified that it was a common and proper practice among psychiatrists nationally, and in the Washington, D.C. area, to "bundle" a variety of services, including prescription management, review of the patient file, consultations with nurses or the patients' relatives into a bill for individual psychotherapy, whether or not these services took place literally in view of the patient. Under the defense theory, if a doctor spent 20 minutes in a session with a patient and ten minutes before that in a different room discussing the patient's symptoms with a nurse, and fifteen minutes afterwards outlining a course of treatment to the medical staff, it would be entirely appropriate, under their reading and interpretation of the CPT, to bill the 45 minutes spent on that patients' care by using CPT code 90844.

The testimony of the defense witnesses on this point was credible and persuasive. . . . The CPT codes which the government insists require face-to-face rendition of services never used the term "face-to-face" in its code description during the time period covered by this litigation. The relevant language describing the code is ambiguous.

The Court finds that the government's position on this issue is not rational and has been applied in an unfair manner to the medical community, which for the most part is made up of honorable and dedicated professionals. One government witness testified that a 15 minute telephone call made to a consulting physician in the patient's presence would be reimbursable, while if the doctor needed to go outside the patient's room to use the telephone—in order to make the *same* telephone call—the time would not be reimbursable. . . .

The Court will not impose False Claims Act liability based on such a strained interpretation of the CPT codes. The government's theory of liability is plainly unfair and unjustified. Medical doctors should be appropriately reimbursed for services legitimately provided. They should be given clear guidance as to what services are reimbursable. The system should be fair. The system cannot be so arbitrary, so perverse, as to subject a doctor whose annual income during the relevant period averaged between $100,000 and $120,000, to potential liability in excess of 80 million dollars[3] because telephone calls were made in one room rather than another.

The Court finds that Doctor Krizek did not submit false claims when he submitted a bill under CPT Code 90844 after spending 45–50 minutes working on a patient's case, even though not all of that time was spent in direct face-to-face contact with the patient. . . . The Court finds that the defendants' "bundled" services interpretation of the CPT code 90844 is not inconsistent with the plain, common-sense reading of the "description of services" listed by Pennsylvania Blue Shield in its published Procedure Terminology Manual.

Billing Irregularities

While Dr. Krizek was a dedicated and competent doctor and cannot be faulted for his interpretation of the 90844 code, his billing practices, or at a minimum his oversight of his wife's and Mrs. Anderson's billing system, was seriously deficient. Dr. Krizek knew little or nothing of the details of how the bills were submitted by his wife and Mrs. Anderson. . . .

The basic method of billing by Mrs. Krizek and Mrs. Anderson was to determine which patients Dr. Krizek had seen, and then to assume what had taken place was a 50-minute psychotherapy session, unless told specifically by Dr. Krizek that the visit was for a shorter duration. Mrs. Krizek frequently made this assumption without any input from her husband. Mrs. Krizek acknowledged at trial that she never made any specific effort to determine exactly how much time was spent with each

---

[3]   The government alleges in the complaint that overbills amounted to $245,392 during the six-year period covered by the lawsuit. Trebling this damage amount, and adding the $10,000 statutory maximum penalty requested by the government for each of the 8,002 alleged false claims, results in a total potential liability under the complaint of more than $80,750,000. Dr. Krizek is not public enemy number one. He is at worst, a psychiatrist with a small practice who keeps poor records. For the government to sue for more than eighty million dollars in damages against an elderly doctor and his wife is unseemly and not justified. During this period, a psychiatrist in most instances would be reimbursed between $48 and $60 for a 45–50 minute session and $40 or less for a 20–30 minute session. This is hardly enough for any professional to get rich.

patient. Mrs. Krizek felt it was fair and appropriate to use the 90844 code as a rough approximation of the time spent, because on some days, an examination would last up to two hours and Mrs. Krizek would still bill 90844.

Mrs. Anderson also would prepare and submit claims to Medicare/Medicaid with no input from Dr. Krizek. Routinely, Mrs. Anderson would simply contact the hospital to determine what patients were admitted to various psychiatrists' services, and would then prepare and submit claims to Medicare/Medicaid without communicating with Dr. or Mrs. Krizek about the claims she was submitting and certifying on Dr. Krizek's behalf. . . .

The net result of this system, or more accurately "nonsystem," of billing was that on a number of occasions, Mrs. Krizek and Mrs. Anderson submitted bills for 45–50 minute psychotherapy sessions on Dr. Krizek's behalf when Dr. Krizek could not have spent the requisite time providing services, face-to-face, or otherwise. . . . The defendants do not deny that these unsubstantiated reimbursement claims occurred or that billing practices which led to such inaccurate billings continued through March of 1992.

While the Court does not find that Dr. Krizek submitted bills for patients he did not see, the Court does find that because of Mrs. Krizek's and Mrs. Anderson's presumption that whenever Dr. Krizek saw a patient he worked at least 45 minutes on the matter, bills were improperly submitted for time that was not spent providing patient services. Again, the defendants admit this occurred. . . .

At the conclusion of the trial, both parties agreed that an appropriate bench-mark for excessive billing would be the equivalent of twelve 90844 submissions (or nine patient-service hours) in a single service day. . . . Considering the difficulty of reviewing all Dr. Krizek's patient records over a seven-year period, Dr. Wilson's testimony as to having submitted as many as twelve 90844 submissions in a single day, and giving full credence to unrefuted testimony that Dr. Krizek worked very long hours, the Court believes this to be a fair and reasonably accurate assessment of the time Dr. Krizek actually spent providing patient services. *See Bigelow v. RKO Radio Pictures, Inc.*, 327 U.S. 251, 264, 66 S.Ct. 574, 579, 90 L. Ed. 652 (1946) (permitting factfinder to make "just and reasonable estimate of damage based on relevant data" where more precise computation is not possible). Dr. and Mrs. Krizek will therefore be presumed liable for bills submitted in excess of the equivalent of twelve 90844 submissions in a single day.

Nature of Liability

While the parties have agreed as to the presumptive number of excess submissions for which Dr. and Mrs. Krizek may be found liable, they do not

SEC. I   FALSE CLAIMS ACT   867

agree on the character of the liability. The government submits that the Krizeks should be held liable under the False Claims Act, 31 U.S.C. § 3729, *et seq.* By contrast, defendants posit that while the United States may be entitled to reimbursement for any unjust enrichment attributable to the excess billings, the Krizeks' conduct with regard to submission of excess bills to Medicare/Medicaid was at most negligent, and not "knowing" within the definition of the statute. In their defense, defendants emphasize the "Ma and Pa" nature of Dr. Krizek's medical practice, the fact that Mrs. Krizek did attend some Medicare billing seminars in an effort to educate herself, and the fact that Mrs. Krizek consulted hospital records and relied on information provided by her husband in preparing bills.

By its terms, the False Claims Act provides, *inter alia*, that: Any person who—

(1) knowingly presents, or causes to be presented, to [the Government] . . . a false or fraudulent claim for payment or approval;

(2) knowingly makes, uses, or causes to be made or used, a false record or statement to get a false or fraudulent claim paid or approved by the Government;

(3) conspires to defraud the Government by getting a false or fraudulent claim allowed or paid;

* * *

is liable to the United States Government for a civil penalty of not less than $5,000.00 and not more than $10,000.00, plus three times the amount of damages which the Government sustains because of the act of that person. . . .

31 U.S.C. § 3729(a). The mental state required to find liability under the False Claims Act is also defined by the statute:

For the purposes of this section, the terms "knowing" and "knowingly" mean that a person, with respect to information—

(1) has actual knowledge of the information;

(2) acts in deliberate ignorance of the truth or falsity of the information; or

(3) acts in reckless disregard of the truth or falsity of the information, and no proof of specific intent is required.

31 U.S.C. § 3729(b). The provision allowing for a finding of liability without proof of specific intent to defraud was a feature of the 1986 amendments to the Act.

* * *

The Court finds that, at times, Dr. Krizek was submitting claims for 90844 when he did not provide patient services for the requisite 45 minutes. The testimony makes clear that these submissions were made by Mrs. Krizek or Mrs. Anderson with little, if any, factual basis. Mrs. Krizek made no effort to establish how much time Dr. Krizek spent on a particular matter. Mrs. Krizek and Mrs. Anderson simply presumed that 45–50 minutes had been spent. There was no justification for making that assumption. In addition, Dr. Krizek failed utterly in supervising these agents in their submissions of claims on his behalf. As a result of his failure to supervise, Dr. Krizek received reimbursement for services which he did not provide.

These were not "mistakes" nor merely negligent conduct. Under the statutory definition of "knowing" conduct, the Court is compelled to conclude that the defendants acted with reckless disregard as to the truth or falsity of the submissions. As such, they will be deemed to have violated the False Claims Act.

Conclusion

Dr. Krizek must be held accountable for his billing system along with those who carried it out. Dr. Krizek was not justified in seeing patients and later not verifying the claims submitted for the services provided to these patients. Doctors must be held strictly accountable for requests filed for insurance reimbursement.

The Court believes that the Krizeks' billing practices must be corrected before they are permitted to further participate in the Medicare or Medicaid programs. Therefore an injunction will issue, enjoining the defendants from participating in these systems until such time as they can show the Court that they can abide by the relevant rules.

The Court also will hold the defendants liable under the False Claims Act on those days where claims were submitted in excess of the equivalent of twelve (12) 90844 claims (nine patient-treatment hours) in a single day and where the defendants cannot establish that Dr. Krizek legitimately devoted the claimed amount of time to patient care on the day in question. The government also will be entitled to introduce proof that the defendants submitted incorrect bills when Dr. Krizek submitted bills for less than nine (9) hours in a single day. The assessment of the amount of overpayment and penalty will await these future proceedings.

Other Observations

While the Court does not discount the seriousness of the Krizeks' conduct here, this case demonstrates several flaws in this country's government health insurance program. The government was right in bringing this action, because it could not countenance the reckless nature of the reimbursement systems in this case. While we are in an age of computers, this does not mean that we can blindly allow coding systems to determine the amount of reimbursement without the physician being accountable for honestly and correctly submitting proper information, whether by code or otherwise.

Nonetheless, the Court found rather troubling some of the government's procedures that control reimbursements paid to providers of services. Here are some of these practices:

1)   The government makes no distinction in reimbursement as to the status or professional attainment or education of the provider. Thus, a non-technical person rendering a coded service will be reimbursed the same amount as a board-certified physician.

2)   The sums that the Medicare and Medicaid systems reimburse physicians for services rendered seem to be so far below the norm for charges reimbursed by non-governmental insurance carriers. Indeed, the amount could hardly support a medical practice. As the evidence shows in this case, Board certified physicians in most instances were paid at a rate less than $60 per hour and less than $35 per 1/2 hour. The government must certainly review these charges because if providers are not adequately compensated, they may not provide the level of care that our elderly and underprivileged citizens require. What is more, the best physicians will simply not come into the system or will refuse to take on senior citizens or the poor as patients.

3)   The unrealistic billing concept of requiring doctors to bill only for face-to-face time is not consistent with effective use of a doctor's time or with the provision of good medical services. Doctors must be able to study, research, and discuss a patient's case and be reimbursed for such time.

4)   When Medicare dictates that a physician must report each service rendered as a separate code item, the physician is entitled to believe that he will be reimbursed for each of the services rendered. In actuality, the system pays for only one of the multitude of services provided. If this were done by a private sector entity, it would be considered deceitful. Because the government engages in such a deceitful practice does not make it right.

These are the lessons learned by this Court during this case. Hopefully, HCFA will reexamine its reimbursement practices to see what, if any, changes should be made.

UNITED STATES V. KRIZEK

United States Court of Appeals, District of Columbia Circuit, 1997.
111 F.3d 934.

SENTELLE, CIRCUIT JUDGE.

This appeal arises from a civil suit brought by the government against a psychiatrist and his wife under the civil False Claims Act ("FCA"), 31

U.S.C. §§ 3729–3731, and under the common law. The District Court found defendants liable for knowingly submitting false claims and entered judgment against defendants for $168,105.39. The government appealed, and the defendants filed a cross-appeal. We hold that the District Court erred and remand for further proceedings.

[The Court held that the district court erred in changing its benchmark for a presumptively false claim from 9 hours billed in any given day to 24 hours because it did not afford the government the opportunity to introduce additional evidence. It also agreed with the Krizeks cross-appeal that the District Court erroneously treated each CPT code as a separate "claim" for purposes of computing civil penalties instead of treating the government form 1500 which contained multiple codes as the "claim."

The court questioned the fairness of the government's definition of claim because it "permitted it to seek an astronomical $81 million worth of damages for alleged actual damages of $245,392."

* * *

[W]e turn now to the question whether, in considering the sample, the District Court applied the appropriate level of scienter. The FCA imposes liability on an individual who "knowingly presents" a "false or fraudulent claim." 31 U.S.C. § 3729(a). A person acts "knowingly" if he:

(1) has actual knowledge of the information;

(2) acts in deliberate ignorance of the truth or falsity of the information; or

(3) acts in reckless disregard of the truth or falsity of the information,

and no proof of specific intent to defraud is required.

31 U.S.C. § 3729(b). The Krizeks assert that the District Court impermissibly applied the FCA by permitting an aggravated form of gross negligence, "gross negligence-plus," to satisfy the Act's scienter requirement.

In Saba v. Compagnie Nationale Air France, 78 F.3d 664 (D.C. Cir. 1996), we considered whether reckless disregard was the equivalent of willful misconduct for purposes of the Warsaw Convention. We noted that reckless disregard lies on a continuum between gross negligence and intentional harm. In some cases, recklessness serves as a proxy for forbidden intent. [ ] Such cases require a showing that the defendant engaged in an act known to cause or likely to cause the injury. [ ] Use of reckless disregard as a substitute for the forbidden intent prevents the defendant from "deliberately blind[ing] himself to the consequences of his tortuous action." Id. at 668. In another category of cases, we noted, reckless disregard is "simply a linear extension of gross negligence, a palpable failure to meet the appropriate standard of care." Id. In Saba, we determined that in the context of the Warsaw Convention, a showing of willful misconduct might be made by establishing reckless disregard such that the subjective intent of the defendant could be inferred. [ ]

The question, therefore, is whether "reckless disregard" in this context is properly equated with willful misconduct or with aggravated gross negligence. In determining that gross negligence-plus was sufficient, the District Court cited legislative history equating reckless disregard with gross negligence. A sponsor of the 1986 amendments to the FCA stated,

> Subsection 3 of Section 3729(c) uses the term "reckless disregard of the truth or falsity of the information" which is no different than and has the same meaning as a gross negligence standard that has been applied in other cases. While the Act was not intended to apply to mere negligence, it is intended to apply in situations that could be considered gross negligence where the submitted claims to the Government are prepared in such a sloppy or unsupervised fashion that resulted in overcharges to the Government. The Act is also intended not to permit artful defense counsel to require some form of intent as an essential ingredient of proof. This section is intended to reach the "ostrich-with-his-head-in-the-sand" problem where government contractors hide behind the fact they were not personally aware that such overcharges may have occurred. This is not a new standard but clarifies what has always been the standard of knowledge required.

132 Cong. Rec. H9382–03 (daily ed. Oct. 7, 1986) (statement of Rep. Berman). While we are not inclined to view isolated statements in the legislative history as dispositive, we agree with the thrust of this statement that the best reading of the Act defines reckless disregard as an extension of gross negligence. Section 3729(b)(2) of the Act provides liability for false statements made with deliberate ignorance. If the reckless disregard standard of section 3729(b)(3) served merely as a substitute for willful misconduct—to prevent the defendant from "deliberately blind[ing] himself to the consequences of his tortuous action"—section (b)(3) would be redundant since section (b)(2) already covers such struthious conduct. [ ] Moreover, as the statute explicitly states that specific intent is not required, it is logical to conclude that reckless disregard in this context is not a "lesser form of intent," [ ] but an extreme version of ordinary negligence.

We are unpersuaded by the Krizeks' citation to the rule of lenity to support their reading of the Act. Even assuming that the FCA is penal, the rule of lenity is invoked only when the statutory language is ambiguous. . . . Because we find no ambiguity in the statute's scienter requirement, we hold that the rule of lenity is inapplicable.

We are also unpersuaded by the Krizeks' argument that their conduct did not rise to the level of reckless disregard. The District Court cited a number of factors supporting its conclusion: Mrs. Krizek completed the submissions with little or no factual basis; she made no effort to establish how much time Dr. Krizek spent with any particular patient; and Dr. Krizek "failed utterly" to review bills submitted on his behalf. . . . Most tellingly, there were a number of days within the seven-patient sample when even the shoddiest record keeping would have revealed that false submissions were being made—those days on which the Krizeks' billing approached twenty-four hours in a single day. On August 31, 1985, for instance, the Krizeks requested reimbursement for patient treatment using the 90844 code thirty times and the 90843 code once, indicating patient treatment of over 22 hours. Outside the seven-patient sample the Krizeks billed for more than twenty-four hours in a single day on three separate occasions. . . . These factors amply support the District Court's determination that the Krizeks acted with reckless disregard.

Finally, we note that Dr. Krizek is no less liable than his wife for these false submissions. As noted, an FCA violation may be established without reference to the subjective intent of the defendant. Dr. Krizek delegated to his wife authority to submit claims on his behalf. In failing "utterly" to review the false submissions, he acted with reckless disregard.

* * *

NOTES AND QUESTIONS

1. *Unlawful Conduct?* Exactly what conduct by Dr. Krizek did the government charge violated the False Claims Act? For what conduct and on what basis was he exonerated by the District Court? Did the court's finding of liability rest on Dr. Krizek's actions or those of his subordinates? The United States introduced expert evidence that the CPT codes 90843 and 90844 (individual psychotherapy) envisioned face-to-face therapy with the patient for the entire time for which the service was billed (either 25 or 50 minutes). The Krizeks admitted they received reimbursement for time spent other than in face-to-face therapy, and introduced evidence from other physicians that such "bundling" was common practice in obtaining reimbursement for private payers. What was the legal basis for absolving Dr. Krizek of liability for "upcoding"?

2. *Reckless Disregard.* Does the Court of Appeals' opinion in *Krizek* clarify the boundary between reckless disregard and willful misconduct? Between reckless disregard and gross negligence? What evidence did it rely upon to reach its conclusion that the Krizeks had run afoul of that standard? Can you explain at what point evidence of shoddy record keeping and submission of implausible claims would constitute "reckless disregard" under the False Claims Act?

3. *Too Much Piling On?* Following the Court of Appeals' determination that each 1500 Form constituted a "claim," the District Court faced on remand the question of how many of the multiple forms, which taken together exceeded 24 hours in a single day, constituted separate "claims." Absent proof as to which specific claims were submitted beyond the 24-hour limit, the District Court chose to count only the number of days (three) exceeding the 24-hour benchmark rather than the total number of claims exceeding that benchmark (eleven). United States v. Krizek, 7 F. Supp. 2d 56 (D.D.C. 1998). Judge Sporken voiced continued frustration with the government's case: "The Government's pursuit of Dr. Krizek is reminiscent of Inspector Javert's quest to capture Jean Valjean in Victor Hugo's Les Miserables . . . [T]here comes a point when a civilized society must say enough is enough." Id. at 60. Do Judge Sporkin's observations betray a judicial sympathy toward medical professionals that is not customarily afforded to other defendants charged with violating the law? Are they persuasive? The *Krizek* case became a *cause célèbre* for some in the provider community who felt the government was overreaching in its prosecution of false claims against providers. Mrs. Krizek testified before a congressional committee relating her views on the case and the government's conduct. Administrative Crimes and Quasi Crimes: Hearing Before the Subcomm. on Commercial and Admin. Law of the H. Comm. on the Judiciary, 105th Cong. (1998). For an account of the colorful back story of this case, see Thomas L. Greaney & Joan H. Krause, U.S. v. Krizek: Rough Justice Under the False Claims Act in Cases In Context, in Health Law and Bioethics (2009).

C. FALSITY, MEDICAL NECESSITY, AND STATISTICAL SAMPLING

The Element of Falsity in Medical Necessity Cases

As discussed in the preceding materials, a qui tam relator or the government plaintiff bringing a False Claims Act case must prove the element of knowledge. In addition, the plaintiff must prove the element of **falsity**—that the defendant presented a false or fraudulent claim to the government. It is unclear how to prove that a claim for payment is false when the evidence largely rests on the opposing opinions of experts. A circuit split has emerged over whether and what type of evidence is needed to prove falsity under the False Claims Act—whether the plaintiff must prove "**objective falsity**" based on an objectively verifiable fact or whether falsity can be proved based on an expert's subjective clinical opinion.

As illustrated in *Krizek*, above, the question of falsity has arisen most vividly in cases involving questions of **medical necessity**, where the alleged fraud is that the care provided and billed to the government was not medically necessary. Medical necessity cases are often argued via a "battle of the experts," with each side presenting an expert's opinion that the services were or were not medically necessary.

On one side of the circuit split is the Eleventh Circuit case of U.S. v. AseraCare, 938 F.3d 1278 (11th Cir. 2019). In *AseraCare*, the government filed a False Claims Act complaint against hospice provider AseraCare, alleging that AseraCare knowingly submitted $67.5 million in false claims to Medicare for hospice care for patients who were not terminally ill. In total, including treble damages, the government sought more than $200 million from AseraCare. At the district court trial, the government relied upon the testimony of its medical expert, who reviewed a sample of patients' records to provide his clinical opinion that the patients were ineligible for Medicare hospice benefits because they did not have a prognosis of fewer than six months to live. 153 F. Supp. 3d 1372 (N.D. Ala. 2015); 176 F. Supp. 3d 1282 (N.D. Ala. 2016). AseraCare presented its own clinical experts who pointed to different aspects of the patients' medical records to reach the opposite conclusion. The district court concluded that "(1) the [False Claims Act] requires 'proof of an objective falsehood'; and (2) a mere difference of opinion, without more, is not enough to show falsity." 153 F. Supp. 3d at 1381. The district court subsequently granted AseraCare's motion for summary judgment because the government failed to prove "objective evidence of falsity" by proffering only one expert's subjective clinical opinion based on medical records that the defendant's experts also reviewed and reached a different opinion. The court noted that scientific and medical opinion, "about which reasonable minds may differ— cannot be false" and concluded that "contradiction based on clinical judgment or opinion alone cannot constitute falsity under the [False Claims Act] as a matter of law." 176 F. Supp. 3d at 1286. Animating District Judge Bowdre's decision was her concern that allowing a difference of clinical opinion to prove falsity would "short-circuit" the falsity requirement and undermine the inherently subjective clinical judgments involved in these cases:

> [A]llowing a mere difference of opinion among physicians alone to prove falsity would totally eradicate the clinical judgment required of the certifying physicians. . . . If the court were to find that all the Government needed to prove falsity in a hospice provider case was one medical expert who reviewed the medical records and disagreed with the certifying physician, hospice providers would be subject to potential FCA liability any time the Government could find a medical expert who disagreed with the certifying physician's clinical judgment. The court refuses to go down that road. *Id.* at 1285.

On appeal, the Eleventh Circuit affirmed the district court's ruling in *AseraCare* that the FCA's falsity element requires proof of an objective falsehood and that a reasonable difference of opinion between physicians is insufficient to show objective falsity. 938 F.3d 1278 (11th Cir. 2019), Examples of such objective evidence of falsity include: (1) where a certifying physician fails to review a patient's medical records before asserting that the patient is terminal; (2) where there is proof a certifying physician did not, in fact, subjectively believe that the patient was terminally ill at the time of certification; or (3) when expert evidence shows that no reasonable physician could have concluded that a patient was terminally ill from the medical records. The Eleventh Circuit said, "In each of these examples, the clinical judgment on which the claim is based contains a flaw that can be demonstrated through verifiable facts. By contrast, . . [a] properly formed and sincerely held clinical judgment is not untrue even if a different physician later contends that the judgment is wrong." 938 F.3d at 1297.

The Third and Ninth Circuits have disagreed with the Eleventh Circuit's *AseraCare* decision. The case of U.S. v. Care Alternatives, 952 F.3d 89 (3d Cir. 2020), involved a similar set of facts as *AseraCare*, but the Third Circuit held that a hospice provider's claim for Medicare reimbursement could be considered false under the False Claims Act based solely on medical expert testimony asserting that some patient certifications did not support a terminal illness prognosis. The Third Circuit rejected the objective falsity test, saying that the plaintiffs were not required to show that the physicians' prognoses of terminal illness were objectively false. The Third Circuit criticized the *AseraCare* decision, saying that the Eleventh Circuit incorrectly limited the issue to factual falsity—whether the facts contained within the claim were untrue—and ignored legal falsity, which would be satisfied by a showing that a claimant falsely certified that it had complied with a statue or regulation necessary to receive government reimbursement for the claim. The court concluded that, under the legal falsity inquiry, a difference of medical opinion is enough evidence to create a triable question of fact on the issue of falsity under the False Claims Act.

The Ninth Circuit also distinguished *AseraCare* when it held that the False Claims Act does not require a plaintiff to plead objective falsity in a medical necessity case. Winter ex rel. U.S. v. Gardens Reg'l Hosp. & Med. Ctr., Inc., 953 F.3d 1108 (9th Cir. 2020). The Ninth Circuit concluded that a physician's Medicare certification that an inpatient hospitalization is medically necessary could be false within the meaning of the False Claims Act. The Ninth Circuit distinguished *AseraCare* on two grounds: First, the Eleventh Circuit only concluded that a reasonable disagreement between physicians, *without more*, was insufficient to prove falsity, not that a medical opinion could never be false or fraudulent. Second, the objective falsehood requirement did not necessarily apply to a physician's certification of medical necessity outside of the hospice eligibility context, which is more deferential to a physician's subjective judgment.

Although Care Alternatives, the hospice defendant in the Third Circuit case, petitioned the Supreme Court to resolve the circuit split over the issue of objective falsity, the Court denied the petition. Thus, the question of objective falsity and its applicability in medical necessity cases remains disputed among courts and creates ongoing uncertainty for providers and plaintiffs.

The debate over objective falsity has high stakes. On the one hand, requiring objective falsity creates a powerful defense for health care providers, who can defeat a medical necessity claim by framing the plaintiff's case as based on mere difference of clinical opinion between their expert and the plaintiff's expert. On the other hand, the government and *qui tam* relators argue that it is the jury's job to determine falsity after hearing the evidence from both sides. In this view, A*seraCare* improperly takes the determination of falsity away from the jury. Which rule do you agree with? Should the plaintiff be able to prove falsity by providing a differing clinical opinion by its own expert? Should objective falsity be limited to hospice cases, where prognostication is particularly difficult? See Isaac Buck, A Farewell to Falsity: Shifting Standards in Medicare Fraud Enforcement, 49 Seton Hall L. Rev. 1 (2018).

Statistical Sampling

In large-scale fraud and abuse cases, like *AseraCare*, the number of potential claims can reach into the tens of thousands, making it difficult and costly for the plaintiff to evaluate each claim to prove liability or damages. Thus, an emerging legal question is whether the parties may use **statistical sampling** to prove liability (not just damages) based on a sample of the larger universe of potential claims. For example, the case of U.S. ex rel Martin v. Life Care Centers involved over 150,000 claims from 55,000 patients. 114 F. Supp. 3d 549 (E.D. Tenn. 2014). Because it would be nearly impossible for the plaintiff to prove each claim is false, plaintiffs argue that it would be effective and more efficient to allow a qualified expert to analyze a smaller, representative sample upon which the court can extrapolate conclusions about the larger population from which it is drawn. Defendants argue that statistical sampling threatens their due process rights because such techniques always contain a margin of error, and the factually unique nature of health care claims makes drawing conclusions about liability from a sample improper.

Observers await clarity from appellate courts to resolve divergent district court opinions on the availability of statistical sampling to prove False Claims Act liability. District courts in Massachusetts, Texas, and South Carolina have barred the use of statistical sampling, whereas courts in Tennessee and Kentucky have allowed statistical sampling on the question of liability. Observers had hoped that the Fourth Circuit would weigh in on the issue of statistical sampling in the appeal of the *Agape* case from South Carolina, but the appellate court did not reach the issue, leaving parties in False Claims Act cases to rely on conflicting district court precedents. *Compare* United States v. Friedman, Civil Action No. 86-0610-MA, 1993 U.S. Dist. LEXIS 21496 (D. Mass. July 23, 1993) (barring use of statistical sampling), U.S. ex rel. Wall v. Vista Hospice Care, Inc., No. 3:07-cv-00604, 2016 WL 3449833 (N.D. Tex. June 20, 2016) (same), United States ex rel. Michaels v. Agape Senior Cmty., Inc., No. 0:12-3466-JFA, 2015 WL 3903675 (D.S.C. June 25, 2015), order corrected, No. CA 0:12-3466-JFA, 2015 WL 4128919 (D.S.C. July 6, 2015), and aff'd in part, appeal dismissed in part sub nom. 848 F.3d 330 (4th Cir. 2017) (same), *with* U.S. ex rel. Martin v. Life Care Centers, 114 F. Supp. 3d 549 (E.D. Tenn. 2014) (allowing statistical sampling) and United States v. Robinson, No. 13-CV-27-GFVT, 2015 WL 1479396 (E.D. Ky. Mar. 31, 2015) (same); and United States v. Rite Aid Corp., No. 2:12-CV-01699-KJM-EFB, 2020 WL 3970201 (E.D. Cal. 2020) (same).

Should plaintiffs be able to prove liability in False Claims Act involving thousands of claims based on statistical sampling? If so, what should the cutoff be to use statistical sampling—1,000 claims, 5,0000, 10,000? What safeguards can protect Defendants' due process rights and from erroneous sampling techniques?

D. MATERIALITY

UNIVERSAL HEALTH SERVICES, INC. V. UNITED STATES ET AL. EX REL. ESCOBAR ET AL.

Supreme Court of the United States, 2016.
579 U.S. 176.

THOMAS, J., delivered the opinion for a unanimous Court.

Opinion

JUSTICE THOMAS delivered the opinion of the Court.

The False Claims Act, [ ] imposes significant penalties on those who defraud the Government. This case concerns a theory of False Claims Act liability commonly referred to as "implied false certification." According to this theory, when a defendant submits a claim, it impliedly certifies compliance with all conditions of payment. But if that claim fails to disclose the defendant's violation of a material statutory, regulatory, or contractual requirement, so the theory goes, the defendant has made a misrepresentation that renders the claim "false or fraudulent" under § 3729(a)(1)(A). This case requires us to consider this theory of liability and to clarify some of the circumstances in which the False Claims Act imposes liability.

We first hold that, at least in certain circumstances, the implied false certification theory can be a basis for liability. Specifically, liability can attach when the defendant submits a claim for payment that makes specific representations about the goods or services provided, but knowingly fails to disclose the defendant's noncompliance with a statutory, regulatory, or contractual requirement. In these circumstances, liability may attach if the omission renders those representations misleading.

We further hold that False Claims Act liability for failing to disclose violations of legal requirements does not turn upon whether those requirements were expressly designated as conditions of payment. Defendants can be liable for violating requirements even if they were not expressly designated as conditions of payment. Conversely, even when a requirement is expressly designated a condition of payment, not every violation of such a requirement gives rise to liability. What matters is not the label the Government attaches to a requirement, but whether the defendant knowingly violated a requirement that the defendant knows is material to the Government's payment decision.

A misrepresentation about compliance with a statutory, regulatory, or contractual requirement must be material to the Government's payment decision in order to be actionable under the False Claims Act. We clarify below how that rigorous materiality requirement should be enforced.

Because the courts below interpreted § 3729(a)(1)(A) differently, we vacate the judgment and remand so that those courts may apply the approach set out in this opinion.

* * *

B

The alleged False Claims Act violations here arose within the Medicaid program, a joint state-federal program in which healthcare providers serve poor or disabled patients and submit claims for government reimbursement. [ ] The facts recited in the complaint, which we take as true at this stage, are as follows. For five years, Yarushka Rivera, a teenage beneficiary of Massachusetts' Medicaid program, received counseling services at Arbour Counseling Services, a satellite mental health facility in Lawrence, Massachusetts, owned and operated by a subsidiary of petitioner Universal Health Services. Beginning in 2004, when Yarushka started having behavioral problems, five medical professionals at Arbour intermittently treated her. In May 2009, Yarushka had an adverse reaction to a medication that a purported doctor at Arbour prescribed after diagnosing her with bipolar disorder. Her condition worsened; she suffered a seizure that required hospitalization. In October 2009, she suffered another seizure and died. She was 17 years old.

Thereafter, an Arbour counselor revealed to respondents Carmen Correa and Julio Escobar—Yarushka's mother and stepfather—that few Arbour employees were actually licensed to provide mental health counseling and that supervision of them was minimal. Respondents discovered that, of the five professionals who had treated Yarushka, only one was properly licensed. The practitioner who diagnosed Yarushka as bipolar identified herself as a psychologist with a Ph. D., but failed to mention that her degree came from an unaccredited Internet college and that Massachusetts had rejected her application to be licensed as a psychologist. Likewise, the practitioner who prescribed medicine to Yarushka, and who was held out as a psychiatrist, was in fact a nurse who lacked authority to prescribe medications absent supervision. Rather than ensuring supervision of unlicensed staff, the clinic's director helped to misrepresent the staff's qualifications. And the problem went beyond those who treated Yarushka. Some 23 Arbour employees lacked licenses to provide mental health services, yet—despite regulatory requirements to the contrary—they counseled patients and prescribed drugs without supervision.

When submitting reimbursement claims, Arbour used payment codes corresponding to different services that its staff provided to Yaruskha, such as "Individual Therapy" and "family therapy." [ ] Staff members also misrepresented their qualifications and licensing status to the Federal Government to obtain individual National Provider Identification numbers, which are submitted in connection with Medicaid reimbursement claims and correspond to specific job titles. For instance, one Arbour staff member who treated Yaruskha registered for a number associated with "Social Worker, Clinical," despite lacking the credentials and licensing required for social workers engaged in mental health counseling. [ ]

After researching Arbour's operations, respondents filed complaints with various Massachusetts agencies. Massachusetts investigated and ultimately issued a report detailing Arbour's violation of over a dozen Massachusetts Medicaid regulations governing the qualifications and supervision required for staff at mental health facilities. Arbour agreed to a remedial plan, and two Arbour employees also entered into consent agreements with Massachusetts.

In 2011, respondents filed a *qui tam* suit in federal court, alleging that Universal Health had violated the False Claims Act under an implied false certification theory of liability. The operative complaint asserts that Universal Health (acting through Arbour) submitted reimbursement claims that made representations about the specific services provided by specific types of professionals, but that failed to disclose serious violations of regulations pertaining to staff qualifications and licensing requirements for these services. Specifically, the Massachusetts Medicaid program requires satellite facilities to have specific types of clinicians on staff, delineates licensing requirements for particular positions (like psychiatrists, social workers, and nurses), and details supervision requirements for other staff. [ ] Universal Health allegedly flouted these regulations because Arbour employed unqualified, unlicensed, and unsupervised staff. The Massachusetts Medicaid program, unaware of these deficiencies, paid the claims. Universal Health thus allegedly defrauded the program, which would not have reimbursed the claims had it known that it was billed for mental health services that were performed by unlicensed and unsupervised staff. The United States declined to intervene.

[The District Court granted Universal Health's motion to dismiss the complaint, finding that although the First Circuit precedent had previously embraced the implied false certification theory of liability, respondents had failed to state a claim because the regulations were not a condition of payment. Reversing the District Court, the First Circuit held that a statutory, regulatory, or contractual requirement can be a condition of payment either by expressly identifying itself as such or by implication. It concluded that the Massachusetts Medicaid regulations "clearly impose conditions of payment" and held that the regulations themselves "constitute[d] dispositive evidence of materiality," because they identified adequate supervision as an "express and absolute" condition of payment and "repeated[ly] reference[d]" supervision.]

We granted certiorari to resolve the disagreement among the Courts of Appeals over the validity and scope of the implied false certification theory of liability. [ ] The Seventh Circuit has rejected this theory, reasoning that only express (or affirmative) falsehoods can render a claim "false or fraudulent" under 31 U. S. C. § 3729(a)(1)(A). [ ] Other courts have accepted the theory, but limit its application to cases where defendants fail to disclose violations of expressly designated conditions of payment. *E.g.*, *Mikes v. Straus*, 274 F. 3d 687, 700 (CA2 2011). Yet others hold that conditions of payment need not be expressly designated as such to be a basis for False Claims Act liability. [ ]

II

We first hold that the implied false certification theory can, at least in some circumstances, provide a basis for liability. By punishing defendants who submit "false or fraudulent claims," the False Claims Act encompasses claims that make fraudulent misrepresentations, which include certain misleading omissions. When, as here, a defendant makes representations in submitting a claim but omits its violations of statutory, regulatory, or contractual requirements, those omissions can be a basis for liability if they render the defendant's representations misleading with respect to the goods or services provided.

To reach this conclusion, "[w]e start, as always, with the language of the statute." [ ] The False Claims Act imposes civil liability on "any person who . . . knowingly presents, or causes to be presented, a false or fraudulent claim for payment or approval." [ ] Congress did not define what makes a claim "false" or "fraudulent." But "[i]t is a settled principle of interpretation that, absent other indication, Congress intends to incorporate the well-settled meaning of the common-law terms it uses." [ ]

Because common-law fraud has long encompassed certain misrepresentations by omission, "false or fraudulent claims" include more than just claims containing express falsehoods. The parties and the Government agree that misrepresentations by omission can give rise to liability. . . .

The parties instead dispute whether submitting a claim without disclosing violations of statutory, regulatory, or contractual requirements constitutes such an actionable misrepresentation. Respondents and the Government invoke the common-law rule that, while nondisclosure alone ordinarily is not actionable, "[a] representation stating the truth so far as it goes but which the maker knows or believes to be materially misleading because of his failure to state additional or qualifying matter" is actionable. Restatement (Second) of Torts § 529, p. 62 (1976). They contend that every submission of a claim for payment implicitly represents that the claimant is legally entitled to payment, and that failing to disclose violations of material legal requirements renders the claim misleading. Universal Health, on the other hand, argues that submitting a claim involves no representations, and that a different common-law rule thus governs: nondisclosure of legal violations is not actionable absent a special "duty . . . to exercise reasonable care to disclose the matter in question," which it says is lacking in Government contracting. [ ]

We need not resolve whether all claims for payment implicitly represent that the billing party is legally entitled to payment. The claims in this case do more than merely demand payment. They fall squarely within the rule that half-truths—representations that state the truth only so far as it goes, while omitting critical qualifying information—can be actionable misrepresentations. . . .

So too here, by submitting claims for payment using payment codes that corresponded to specific counseling services, Universal Health represented that it had provided individual therapy, family therapy, preventive medication counseling, and other types of treatment. Moreover, Arbour staff members allegedly made further representations in submitting Medicaid reimbursement claims by using National Provider Identification numbers corresponding to specific job titles. And these representations were clearly misleading in context. Anyone informed that a social worker at a Massachusetts mental health clinic provided a teenage patient with individual counseling services would probably—but wrongly—conclude that the clinic had complied with core Massachusetts Medicaid requirements (1) that a counselor "treating children [is] required to have specialized training and experience in children's services," [ ] and also (2) that, at a minimum, the social worker possesses the prescribed qualifications for the job [ ]. By using payment and other codes that conveyed this information without disclosing Arbour's many violations of basic staff and licensing requirements for mental health facilities, Universal Health's claims constituted misrepresentations.

Accordingly, we hold that the implied certification theory can be a basis for liability, at least where two conditions are satisfied: first, the claim does not merely request payment, but also makes specific representations about the goods or services provided; and second, the defendant's failure to disclose noncompliance with material statutory, regulatory, or contractual requirements makes those representations misleading half-truths.

III

The second question presented is whether, as Universal Health urges, a defendant should face False Claims Act liability only if it fails to disclose the violation of a contractual, statutory, or regulatory provision that the Government expressly designated a condition of payment. We conclude that the Act does not impose this limit on liability. But we also conclude that not every undisclosed violation of an express condition of payment automatically triggers liability. Whether a provision is labeled a condition of payment is relevant to but not dispositive of the materiality inquiry.

A

Nothing in the text of the False Claims Act supports Universal Health's proposed restriction. Section 3729(a)(1)(A) imposes liability on those who present "false or fraudulent claims" but does not limit such claims to misrepresentations about express conditions of payment. See *SAIC*, 626 F. 3d, at 1268 (rejecting any textual basis for an express-designation rule). Nor does the common-law meaning of fraud tether liability to violating an express condition of payment. A statement that misleadingly omits critical facts is a misrepresentation irrespective of whether the other party has expressly signaled the importance of the qualifying information. [ ]

The False Claims Act's materiality requirement also does not support Universal Health. Under the Act, the misrepresentation must be material to the other party's course of action. But, as discussed below, [ ], statutory, regulatory, and contractual requirements are not automatically material, even if they are labeled conditions of payment. [ ]

Nor does the Act's scienter requirement [ ] support Universal Health's position. A defendant can have "actual knowledge" that a condition is material without the Government expressly calling it a condition of payment. If the Government failed to specify that guns it orders must actually shoot, but the defendant knows that the Government routinely rescinds contracts if the guns do not shoot, the defendant has "actual knowledge." Likewise, because a reasonable person would realize the imperative of a functioning firearm, a defendant's failure to appreciate the materiality of that condition would amount to "deliberate ignorance" or "reckless disregard" of the "truth or falsity of the information" even if the Government did not spell this out.

Universal Health nonetheless contends that False Claims Act liability should be limited to undisclosed violations of expressly designated conditions of payment to provide defendants with fair notice and to cabin liability. But policy arguments cannot supersede the clear statutory text. [ ] In any event, Universal Health's approach risks undercutting these policy goals. The Government might respond by designating every legal requirement an express condition of payment. But billing parties are often subject to thousands of complex statutory and regulatory provisions. Facing False Claims Act liability for violating any of them would hardly help would-be defendants anticipate and prioritize compliance obligations. And forcing the Government to expressly designate a provision as a condition of *payment* would create further arbitrariness. Under Universal Health's view, misrepresenting compliance with a requirement that the Government expressly identified as a condition of payment could expose a defendant to liability. Yet, under this theory, misrepresenting compliance with a condition of eligibility to even participate in a federal program when submitting a claim would not.

Moreover, other parts of the False Claims Act allay Universal Health's concerns. "[I]nstead of adopting a circumscribed view of what it means for a claim to be false or fraudulent," concerns about fair notice and open-ended liability "can be effectively addressed through strict enforcement of the Act's materiality and scienter requirements." [ ] Those requirements are rigorous.

B

As noted, a misrepresentation about compliance with a statutory, regulatory, or contractual requirement must be material to the Government's payment decision in order to be actionable under the False Claims Act. We now clarify how that materiality requirement should be enforced.

Section 3729(b)(4) defines materiality using language that we have employed to define materiality in other federal fraud statutes: "[T]he term 'material' means having a natural tendency to influence, or be capable of influencing, the payment or receipt of money or property." See *Neder*, 527 U.S., at 16 (using this definition to interpret the mail, bank, and wire fraud statutes); *Kungys v. United States*, 485 U.S. 759, 770 (1988) (same for fraudulent statements to immigration officials). This materiality requirement descends from "common-law antecedents." [ ] Indeed, "the common law could not have conceived of 'fraud' without proof of materiality." [ ]

We need not decide whether § 3729(a)(1)(A)'s materiality requirement is governed by § 3729(b)(4) or derived directly from the common law. Under any understanding of the concept, materiality "look[s] to the effect on the likely or actual behavior of the recipient of the alleged misrepresentation." . . .

The materiality standard is demanding. The False Claims Act is not "an all-purpose antifraud statute," [ ] or a vehicle for punishing garden-variety breaches of contract or regulatory violations. A misrepresentation cannot be deemed material merely because the Government designates compliance with a particular statutory, regulatory, or contractual requirement as a condition of payment. Nor is it sufficient for a finding of materiality that the Government would have the option to decline to pay if it knew of the defendant's noncompliance. Materiality, in addition, cannot be found where noncompliance is minor or insubstantial. . . .

In sum, when evaluating materiality under the False Claims Act, the Government's decision to expressly identify a provision as a condition of payment is relevant, but not automatically dispositive. Likewise, proof of materiality can include, but is not necessarily limited to, evidence that the defendant knows that the Government consistently refuses to pay claims in the mine run of cases based on noncompliance with the particular statutory, regulatory, or contractual requirement. Conversely, if the Government pays a particular claim in full despite its actual knowledge that certain requirements were violated, that is very strong evidence that those requirements are not material. Or, if the Government regularly pays a particular type of claim in full despite actual knowledge that certain requirements were violated, and has signaled no change in position, that is strong evidence that the requirements are not material.[6]

These rules lead us to disagree with the Government's and First Circuit's view of materiality: that any statutory, regulatory, or contractual violation is material so long as the defendant knows that the Government would be entitled to refuse payment were it aware of the violation. [ ] If the Government contracts for health services and adds a requirement that contractors buy American-made staplers, anyone who submits a claim for those services but fails to disclose its use of foreign staplers violates the False Claims Act. To the Government, liability would attach if the defendant's use of foreign staplers would entitle the Government not to pay the claim in whole or part—irrespective of whether the Government routinely pays claims despite knowing that foreign staplers were used. [ ] Likewise, if the Government required contractors to aver their compliance

---

[6] We reject Universal Health's assertion that materiality is too fact intensive for courts to dismiss False Claims Act cases on a motion to dismiss or at summary judgment. The standard for materiality that we have outlined is a familiar and rigorous one. And False Claims Act plaintiffs must also plead their claims with plausibility and particularity under Federal Rules of Civil Procedure 8 and 9(b) by, for instance, pleading facts to support allegations of materiality.

with the entire U.S. Code and Code of Federal Regulations, then under this view, failing to mention noncompliance with any of those requirements would always be material. The False Claims Act does not adopt such an extraordinarily expansive view of liability.

* * *

Because both opinions below assessed respondents' complaint based on interpretations of § 3729(a)(1)(A) that differ from ours, we vacate the First Circuit's judgment and remand the case for reconsideration of whether respondents have sufficiently pleaded a False Claims Act violation. [ ] We emphasize, however, that the False Claims Act is not a means of imposing treble damages and other penalties for insignificant regulatory or contractual violations. This case centers on allegations of fraud, not medical malpractice. Respondents have alleged that Universal Health misrepresented its compliance with mental health facility requirements that are so central to the provision of mental health counseling that the Medicaid program would not have paid these claims had it known of these violations. Respondents may well have adequately pleaded a violation of § 3729(a)(1)(A). But we leave it to the courts below to resolve this in the first instance.

The judgment of the Court of Appeals is vacated, and the case is remanded for further proceedings consistent with this opinion.

* * *

NOTES AND QUESTIONS

1. *Materiality After* Escobar. The element of materiality is not required in all cases brought under the False Claims Act. Review the statutory language of 39 U.S.C. § 3729(a) set forth at the outset of this Chapter. Which types of actions require proving materiality? What are the factors to determine materiality under *Escobar*?

After *Escobar*, the implied certification theory can be a basis for False Claims Act liability when (1) the defendant makes a specific representation on a claim for payment to the government and (2) the defendant fails to disclose noncompliance with a material requirement. Despite a plethora of cases from nearly every circuit court citing, analyzing, and interpreting *Escobar*, the varied and inconsistent results in cases applying *Escobar* shows the materiality standard to be a highly fact-specific inquiry. For a critique of the Supreme Court's ill-defined standard of materiality, see Joan Krause, Reflections on Certification, Interpretation, and the Quest for Fraud that "Counts" Under the False Claims Act, 2017 U. Illinois L. Rev. 1811 (2017).

Following *Escobar*, practitioners have discerned some emerging trends. First, taking the Court's opinion in *Escobar* to heart, courts seem to be applying the materiality standard rigorously, which generally favors defendants. Second, a particularly strong factor for disproving materiality is where the government knew of the noncompliance, but took no adverse action—by paying the defendant anyway, renewing the defendant's contract, or declining to impose administrative sanctions. Courts remain divided about whether government knowledge of noncompliance defeats the plaintiff's claim altogether or merely shifts the burden to the plaintiff to overcome a rebuttable presumption against materiality. Third, the materiality test is more rigorous than a simple breach of contract claim, but noncompliance or breach that goes to the "essence of the bargain" may be material. Fourth, courts are split whether specific representations are necessary. Given the fact-specific nature of the inquiry, a considerable amount of effort is spent trying to apply *Escobar's* materiality standard to new and varying facts, but clarity about the standard remains elusive. What is the difference between these approaches for plaintiffs and defendants?

    2.   *Pre-Trial Motions and Materiality.* In footnote 6, the Court addressed the concern that the fact-intensive nature of the materiality standard will make it less likely that parties will be able to resolve False Claims Act cases with a motion to dismiss or a motion for summary judgment. Again, it is too soon to tell what impact *Escobar's* materiality standard will have on parties' efforts to get cases disposed of at the motion to dismiss or summary judgment phase of litigation. However, initial cases suggest that courts are continuing to grant motions to dismiss and for summary judgment, often in favor of the defendants, citing plaintiffs' failures to sufficiently plead materiality under its "demanding" and "rigorous" standard.

E. ADDITIONAL ENFORCEMENT METHODS

    The False Claims Act provides for enforcement by the Attorney General via the Justice Department and by private *qui tam* relators. Violations of the Anti-Kickback Statute and the Stark Law, while punishable with their own penalties, can also form the basis of a False Claims Act case. As we will see in the following parts of the chapter, divisions within the Department of Health and Human Services (HHS) enforce the Anti-Kickback Statute (the Office of Inspector General (OIG)) and the Stark Law (the Centers for Medicare and Medicaid Services (CMS)). Thus, False Claims Act cases involving Medicare fraud and abuse, in particular, are often enforced by both the Department of Justice and HHS or its contractors.

    RACs. An important—and controversial—enforcement innovation is the role of **Recovery Audit Contractors (RACs)**. RACs are private entities that contract with the federal government to audit payments made to providers and suppliers by the Medicare and Medicaid programs. RACs are paid for their auditing services on a contingency fee basis, receiving payments based on the amount of improper payments to providers they identify. Their mission is to identify both underpayments and overpayments and coordinate their efforts with other entities providing auditing services, such as state and federal law enforcement officials. When the RAC identifies an overpayment, the provider may either return the funds or appeal the RAC's findings through a five-stage administrative appeals process with HHS. If it decides to appeal, the provider may either pay the amount identified by the RAC audit immediately and be reimbursed by the federal government with interest if it prevails, or defer payment, but take the chance that it will owe the entire amount plus interest if it loses the appeal. With appeals taking several years to resolve, this can be a difficult financial decision for providers.

By 2013, the number of provider appeals exceeded 384,000, creating an enormous backlog of appeals before the administrative law judges who were statutorily required (but unable) to resolve each appeal within 90 days. In 2014, the American Hospital Association filed suit seeking a mandamus order to compel the Secretary of HHS (then Sylvia Burwell, later Tom Price, and eventually Alex Azar) to clear the backlog of RAC appeals and comply with the 90-day timeframe. After bouncing back and forth between the D.C. District Court and D.C. Circuit, in 2018, the D.C. District Court issued a mandamus order to the Secretary of HHS to clear the backlog of RAC appeals according to a prescribed timetable by the end of 2022. Am. Hosp. Ass'n v. Azar, No. CV 14-851, 2018 WL 5723141 (D.D.C. 2018). Although HHS had argued that mandamus was improper because compliance was impossible, the court noted that in 2017 Congress more than doubled HHS's appropriation to work through the appeals. It seems to have worked. By March 2021, HHS reported that it had complied with the order, reducing the backlog by 69%, from 426,594 to 131,961 pending appeals.

Corporate Integrity Agreements. When the Department of Justice enters a settlement agreement with a provider to resolve civil fraud and abuse actions, HHS OIG may also enter into a **Corporate Integrity Agreement (CIA)** with the providers to impose continuing oversight, compliance, and reporting obligations, lasting five to ten years. David E. Matyas et al. Legal Issues in Healthcare Fraud and Abuse: Navigating the Uncertainties 431 (2012). Providers or other entities consent to these CIA obligations in exchange for the OIG's agreement not to exclude them from participation in Medicare, Medicaid, or other federal health care programs. The OIG states that CIAs address the specific facts at issue and "attempt to accommodate many of the elements of preexisting voluntary compliance programs" but typically include requirements to:

- hire a compliance officer/appoint a compliance committee;
- develop written standards and policies;
- implement a comprehensive employee training program;
- retain an independent review organization to conduct annual reviews;

- establish a confidential disclosure program;

- restrict employment of ineligible persons;

- report overpayments, reportable events, and ongoing investigations/legal proceedings; and

- provide an implementation report and annual reports to OIG on the status of the entity's compliance activities.

Critics question whether expansive CIAs go too far by intruding into matters of corporate governance, imposing excessive costs, and burdening boards with responsibilities they are not equipped to handle. CIAs are also controversial in situations in which the government seeks to encourage "best practices" in an industry by specifying that parties agree to conform to certain internal governance or monitoring requirements. Kathleen Boozang & Simone Handler-Hutchinson, Monitoring Corporate Governance: DOJ's Use of Deferred Prosecution Agreements in Health Care, 35 Am. J. L. Med. 89 (2009). In an active era of health care mergers and acquisitions, transactional attorneys must confront how to manage the additional compliance risks and potential liability when acquiring an entity under a CIA. Although purchasers may structure the transaction to limit the amount of liability it takes on, the seller's CIA is binding on the purchaser, and the OIG may be unwilling release the purchaser organization from the seller's CIA obligations.

Medicare Fraud Strike Force. Since 2007, the government has used Strike Force teams to combine enforcement officials from Department of Justice, including U.S. Attorneys and the Federal Bureau of Investigation, HHS OIG, and state and local enforcers. Strike Force teams use data analysis to identify and bring criminal actions against providers for Medicare and Medicaid fraud in select geographic areas, including parts of California, Florida, Illinois, Louisiana, Michigan, New Jersey, New York, Pennsylvania, Texas, Washington, DC, and the Appalachian region. As of 2020, the Medicare Fraud Strike Force had brought 2,386 criminal actions, resulting in 3,075 indictments and yielding nearly $4 billion in recoveries. In 2020, for example, the Strike Force charged 345 defendants, including over 100 health care practitioners, with participating in fraudulent telehealth and opioid distribution and treatment schemes amounting to an alleged $6 billion in false billing to federal health care programs. In addition to criminal charges, 256 health care practitioners were excluded from participating in federal health care programs. See Department of Justice, Press Release: National Health Care Fraud and Opioid Takedown Results in Charges Against 345 Defendants Responsible for More than $6 Billion in Alleged Fraud Losses, September 20, 2020.

II.   THE ANTI-KICKBACK STATUTE

Sharing the profits of collective economic activity is common throughout the economy. Landlords rent commercial properties under percentage leases, agents sell goods and services produced by others on commission, merchants grant discounts to those who use their services or encourage others to do so. Such activity has, however, long been frowned upon as it relates to health care. It is widely believed that patients lack the knowledge and information (or even the legal right, in the case of prescription drugs) to make health care decisions for themselves. Thus, policymakers have attempted to protect patients from corrupt medical decision-making or steering due to financial incentives between parties in a position to make health care decisions for them, such as providers and suppliers. With the advent of government financing of health care, this concern has been supplemented by another: that financial rewards to providers for patient referrals might drive up program costs by encouraging the provision of unnecessary or inordinately expensive medical care.

For these reasons, the Anti-Kickback Statute prohibits paying or receiving any remuneration (directly or indirectly, overtly or covertly) for referring, purchasing, or ordering goods, facilities, items or services paid for by Medicare or Medicaid). Interpreted broadly, however, these provisions seem to proscribe a wide variety of transactions that might encourage competition or efficient production of health care. Query whether the statute and the judicial and administrative interpretations thereof successfully distinguish beneficial and detrimental conduct in the current market environment.

42 U.S.C. § 1320a–7b

* * *

(b)   *Illegal remunerations.*

(1)   Whoever knowingly and willfully solicits or receives any remuneration (including any kickback, bribe, or rebate) directly or indirectly, overtly or covertly, in cash or in kind—

> (A) in return for referring an individual to a person for the furnishing or arranging for the furnishing of any item or service for which payment may be made in whole or in part under a Federal health care program, or
>
> (B) in return for purchasing, leasing, ordering, or arranging for or recommending purchasing, leasing, or ordering any good, facility, service, or item for which payment may be made in whole or in part under a Federal health care program,

shall be guilty of a felony and upon conviction thereof, shall be fined not more than $100,000 or imprisoned for not more than ten years, or both.

(2) Whoever knowingly and willfully offers or pays any remuneration (including any kickback, bribe or rebate) directly or indirectly, overtly or covertly, in cash or in kind to any person to induce such person—

(A) to refer an individual to a person for the furnishing or arranging for the furnishing of any item or service for which payment may be made in whole or in part under a Federal health care program, or

(B) to purchase, lease, order, or arrange for or recommend purchasing, leasing, or ordering any good, facility, service, or item for which payment may be made in whole or in part under a Federal health care program,

shall be guilty of a felony and upon conviction thereof shall be fined not more than $100,000 or imprisoned for not more than ten years, or both.

* * *

[Subsection (b)(3) sets forth statutory exceptions from the Anti-Kickback Statute prohibitions listed in (b)(1) and (b)(2).]

(f) *"Federal health care program" defined.* For purposes of this section, the term "Federal health care program" means—

(1) any plan or program that provides health benefits, whether directly, through insurance, or otherwise, which is funded directly, in whole or in part, by the United States Government [other than the federal employees health benefit program]; or

(2) any State health care program, as defined in section 1320a–7(h) of this title.

* * *

(h) *Actual knowledge or specific intent not required.* With respect to violations of this section, a person need not have actual knowledge of this section or specific intent to commit a violation of this section.

The Anti-Kickback Statute applies broadly to *anyone* who solicits, receives, offers, or pays remuneration to induce referrals or recommendations for *any* items or services paid for by *any* federal health care program. Physicians are attractive targets of kickback schemes because they are the sources of referrals for other providers and they order tests and services and prescribe drugs. However, the Anti-Kickback Statute is not limited to physicians and health care entities, but includes any person in a position to recommend or refer federally reimbursed items and services. This includes remuneration offered to patients (e.g., routine waivers by providers or suppliers of patient co-payments could violate the statute), drug or device companies (e.g., drug company perks for physicians could violate the statute), and other types of service suppliers or providers (e.g., durable medical equipment manufacturers, laboratories, ambulance services, etc.). "Federal health care program" is also defined broadly and certainly includes Medicare and Medicaid. Although the OIG has not explicitly listed which health care programs fall under the Anti-Kickback Statute's definition of "federal health care program," the statutory text potentially includes other programs such as federally subsidized insurance from the Affordable Care Act Exchanges, Veterans Health Administration, TRICARE for military members and their families, and the Indian Health Services.

As provided in the statute above, the knowing and willful offer, payment, solicitation, or receipt of illegal remuneration under the Anti-Kickback Statute constitutes a felony, and **criminal penalties** for violations include criminal fines up to $100,000 and up to ten years in prison, or both. To be criminally liable for violations of the Anti-Kickback Statute, enforcers must prove defendant(s) possessed the requisite *mens rea* or criminal intent, as discussed in the following subsection.

Of equal concern to providers, however, are the **civil penalties** and **exclusion powers** of the **Office of Inspector General (OIG)** of the Department of Health and Human Services (HHS). Civil sanction proceedings are administrative in nature, criminal intent need not be shown, and the standard of proof is a preponderance of the evidence, rather than beyond a reasonable doubt. As of 2018, violations of the Anti-Kickback Statute are subject to civil penalties of up to $100,000 per violation plus treble damages equal to three times the amount of illegal remuneration. 42 U.S.C. § 1320a–7a(a)(7). Congress increased both the criminal and civil penalties dramatically in the Bipartisan Budget Act of 2018, which are subject to periodic inflation adjustments.

For providers dependent on Medicare and Medicaid for a large share of their business, exclusion from these programs can be effectively a death warrant, at least as serious as a felony conviction. Criminal convictions for violations of the Anti-Kickback Statute results in **mandatory exclusion** for at least five years from participation in federal health care programs. Even absent a criminal conviction, the Secretary of HHS *may* **exclude** individuals and entities that the Secretary has determined violated the Anti-Kickback Statute. 42 U.S.C. § 1320a–7. Exclusion or criminal conviction frequently results in disciplinary action by state professional licensure boards, and can thus end a provider's professional career even if the provider sees few Medicaid and Medicare patients, because private payers often require such professionals to participate in Medicare. Moreover, the OIG may exclude and impose civil penalties on any person (including health care providers, entities, health plans, and corporations) who knowingly employs or contracts with excluded individuals, even for non-clinical positions. This severely limits opportunities for such individuals to work in health care even in administrative positions, and it attaching liability to corporate entities that may acquire or employ an excluded provider. 42 U.S.C. 1320a–7a(6); 42 C.F.R. § 1003.200(b)(4).

The Anti-Kickback Statute does not provide a private right of action for civil enforcement. However, private individuals can bring *qui tam* actions under the False Claims Act for submissions of claims that were tainted by violations of the Anti-Kickback Statute. To resolve conflicting case law regarding the relationship between the Anti-Kickback Statute and the False Claims Act, the Affordable Care Act clarified that claims for items and services that were the result of unlawful remuneration under the Anti-Kickback Statute are false claims under the False Claims Act. Thus, the statute codified that an Anti-Kickback violation can establish the "falsity" of a claim under the False Claims Act, providing that "a claim that includes items or services resulting from a violation [of the Anti-Kickback Statute] constitutes a false or fraudulent claim for purposes of [the False Claims Act]." 42 U.S.C. § 1320a–7b(g). Consequently, the government or a whistleblower need only allege that the defendant violated the False Claims Act by knowingly submitting claims that were affected by an underlying Anti-Kickback Statute violation.

The OIG provides for a voluntary **self-disclosure protocol** to allow persons subject to the statute (such as providers or suppliers) to identify, report, and resolve Anti-Kickback Statute violations. The purposes of self-disclosure are to more efficiently and possibly more cheaply resolve violations than going through lengthy government investigation or False Claims Act litigation. For providers, the potential upsides for disclosure are to avoid exclusion from federal health care programs without a Corporate Integrity Agreement, to toll the 60-day rule for overpayments under the False Claims Act (discussed in Section I, above), to settle violations with lower penalties, including the potential for a smaller multiplier of damages (sometimes closer to 1.5 rather than 3 times damages). Downsides of self-disclosure include the uncertainty over the process, the likelihood that the OIG will initiate an investigation, and the certainty of having to pay at least some penalty and no guarantee that penalties will be reduced. The OIG has provided guidance on its self-disclosure protocol over the years. See OIG's Provider Self-Disclosure Protocol, April 17, 2013. As discussed in Section III of this chapter, the Centers for Medicare and Medicaid Services (CMS) maintains a separate self-referral disclosure protocol for Stark Law violations, and the OIG has advised that it will not accept disclosures involving Stark Law violations unless the arrangement also involves a colorable Anti-Kickback Statute violation.

A. MENS REA UNDER THE ANTI-KICKBACK STATUTE

UNITED STATES V. GREBER
United States Court of Appeals, Third Circuit, 1985.
760 F.2d 68, cert. denied, 474 U.S. 988.

WEIS, CIRCUIT JUDGE.

In this appeal, defendant argues that payments made to a physician for professional services in connection with tests performed by a laboratory cannot be the basis of Medicare fraud. We do not agree and hold that if one purpose of the payment was to induce future referrals, the Medicare statute has been violated. . . .

After a jury trial, defendant was convicted on 20 of 23 counts in an indictment charging violations of the mail fraud, Medicare fraud, and false statement statutes. Post-trial motions were denied, and defendant has appealed.

Defendant is an osteopathic physician who is board certified in cardiology. In addition to hospital staff and teaching positions, he was the president of Cardio-Med, Inc., an organization which he formed. The company provides physicians with diagnostic services, one of which uses a Holter-monitor. This device, worn for approximately 24 hours, records the patient's cardiac activity on a tape. A computer operated by a cardiac technician scans the tape, and the data is later correlated with an activity diary the patient maintains while wearing the monitor.

Cardio-Med billed Medicare for the monitor service and, when payment was received, forwarded a portion to the referring physician. The government charged that the referral fee was 40 percent of the Medicare payment, not to exceed $65 per patient.

Based on Cardio-Med's billing practices, counts 18–23 of the indictment charged defendant with having tendered remuneration or kickbacks to the referring physicians in violation of 42 U.S.C. § 1395nn(b)(2)(B) (1982).

* * *

The proof as to the Medicare fraud counts (18–23) was that defendant had paid a Dr. Avallone and other physicians "interpretation fees" for the doctors' initial consultation services, as well as for explaining the test results to the patients. There was evidence that physicians received "interpretation fees" even though defendant had actually evaluated the monitoring data. Moreover, the fixed percentage paid to the referring physician was more than Medicare allowed for such services.

The government also introduced testimony defendant had given in an earlier civil proceeding. In that case, he had testified that ". . . if the doctor didn't get his consulting fee, he wouldn't be using our service. So the doctor got a consulting fee." In addition, defendant told physicians at a hospital that the Board of Censors of the Philadelphia County Medical Society had said the referral fee was legitimate if the physician shared the responsibility for the report. Actually, the Society had stated that there should be separate bills because "for the monitor company to offer payment for the physicians . . . is not considered to be the method of choice."

The evidence as to mail fraud was that defendant repeatedly ordered monitors for his own patients even though use of the device was not medically indicated. As a prerequisite for payment, Medicare requires that the service be medically indicated.

The Department of Health and Human Services had promulgated a rule providing that it would pay for Holter-monitoring only if it was in operation for eight hours or more. Defendant routinely certified that the temporal condition had been met, although in fact it had not.

* * *

I. Medicare Fraud

The Medicare fraud statute was amended by P. L. 95–142, 91 Stat. 1183 (1977). Congress, concerned with the growing problem of fraud and abuse in the system, wished to strengthen the penalties to enhance the deterrent effect of the statute. To achieve this purpose, the crime was upgraded from a misdemeanor to a felony.

Another aim of the amendments was to address the complaints of the United States Attorneys who were responsible for prosecuting fraud cases. They informed Congress that the language of the predecessor statute was "unclear and needed clarification." H. Rep. No. 393, Part II, 95th Cong., 1st Sess. 53, *reprinted in* 1977 U.S. CODE CONG. & AD. NEWS 3039, 3055.

A particular concern was the practice of giving "kickbacks" to encourage the referral of work. Testimony before the Congressional committee was that "physicians often determine which laboratories would do the test work for their Medicaid patients by the amount of the kickbacks and rebates offered by the laboratory. . . . Kickbacks take a number of forms including cash, long-term credit arrangements, gifts, supplies and equipment, and the furnishing of business machines." Id. at 3048–3049.

To remedy the deficiencies in the statute and achieve more certainty, the present version of 42 U.S.C. § 1395nn(b)(2) was enacted. It provides:

"whoever knowingly and willfully offers or pays any remuneration (including any kickback, bribe or rebate) directly or indirectly, overtly or covertly in cash or in kind to induce such person—

(B) to purchase, lease, order, or arrange for or recommend purchasing . . . or ordering any . . . service or item for which payment may be made . . . under this title, shall be guilty of a felony."

The district judge instructed the jury that the government was required to prove that Cardio-Med paid to Dr. Avallone some part of the amount received from Medicare; that defendant caused Cardio-Med to make the payment; and did so knowingly and willfully as well as with the intent to induce Dr. Avallone to use Cardio-Med's services for patients covered by Medicare. The judge further charged that even if the physician interpreting the test did so as a consultant to Cardio-Med, that fact was immaterial if a purpose of the fee was to induce the ordering of services from Cardio-Med.

Defendant contends that the charge was erroneous. He insists that absent a showing that the only purpose behind the fee was to improperly induce future services, compensating a physician for services actually rendered could not be a violation of the statute.

The government argues that Congress intended to combat financial incentives to physicians for ordering particular services patients did not require.

The language and purpose of the statute support the government's view. Even if the physician performs some service for the money received, the potential for unnecessary drain on the Medicare system remains. The statute is aimed at the inducement factor.

The text refers to "any remuneration." That includes not only sums for which no actual service was performed but also those amounts for which some professional time was expended. "Remunerates" is defined as "to pay an equivalent for service." Webster Third New International Dictionary (1966). By including such items as kickbacks and bribes, the statute expands "remuneration" to cover situations where no service is performed. That a particular payment was a remuneration (which implies that a service was rendered) rather than a kickback, does not foreclose the possibility that a violation nevertheless could exist.

In United States v. Hancock, 604 F.2d 999 (7th Cir.1979), the court applied the term "kickback" found in the predecessor statute to payments made to chiropractors by laboratories which performed blood tests. The chiropractors contended that the amounts they received were legitimate handling fees for their services in obtaining, packaging, and delivering the specimens to the laboratories and then interpreting the results. The court rejected that contention and noted, "The potential for increased costs to the Medicare-Medicaid system and misapplication of federal funds is plain, where payments for the exercise of such judgments are added to the legitimate cost of the transaction. . . . [T]hese are among the evils Congress sought to prevent by enacting the kickback statutes. . . . " Id. at 1001.

Hancock strongly supports the government's position here, because the statute in that case did not contain the word "remuneration." The court nevertheless held that "kickback" sufficiently described the defendants' criminal activity. By adding "remuneration" to the statute in the 1977 amendment, Congress sought to make it clear that even if the transaction was not considered to be a "kickback" for which no service had been rendered, payment nevertheless violated the Act.

We are aware that in United States v. Porter, 591 F.2d 1048 (5th Cir.1979), the Court of Appeals for the Fifth Circuit took a more narrow view of "kickback" than did the court in *Hancock*. *Porter's* interpretation of the predecessor statute which did not include "remuneration" is neither binding nor persuasive. We agree with the Court of Appeals for the Sixth Circuit, which adopted the interpretation of "kickback" used in *Hancock* and rejected that of the *Porter* case. United States v. Tapert, 625 F.2d 111 (6th Cir. 1980).

We conclude that the more expansive reading is consistent with the impetus for the 1977 amendments and therefore hold that the district court correctly instructed the jury. If the payments were intended to induce the physician to use Cardio-Med's services, the statute was violated, even if the payments were also intended to compensate for professional services.

A review of the record also convinces us that there was sufficient evidence to sustain the jury's verdict.

* * *

Having carefully reviewed all of the defendant's allegations, we find no reversible error. Accordingly, the judgment of the district court will be affirmed.

NOTES AND QUESTIONS

1. *Agree with* Greber? What is controversial about the *Greber* decision? What kinds of salutary or benign practices might it affect? What purposes does the Anti-Kickback legislation serve? Can it be argued that the law sweeps too broadly given the dynamics of today's market?

2. *Multiple Purposes.* Other courts dealing with arrangements that have multiple purposes have generally followed *Greber's* holding that the purpose to induce referrals need not be the dominant or sole purpose of the scheme in order to fall within the Anti-Kickback Statute's prohibition. See, e.g., United States v. McClatchey, 217 F.3d 823, 834–35 (10th Cir. 2000); see also, United States v. Borrasi, 639 F.3d 774, 782 (7th Cir. 2011) (if part of the payment compensated past referrals or induced future referrals, that portion of the payment violates the [statute]). However, several decisions have introduced variations on that theme. For example, one court has required proof of a "material purpose" to obtain money for the referral of services to support a conviction under the statute. United States v. Katz, 871 F.2d 105, 108 (9th

Cir. 1989). Another, more demanding approach holds that proof that a "primary purpose" of the payment was to induce future referrals is required. United States v. Bay State Ambulance and Hosp. Rental Serv., 874 F.2d 20, 30 (1st Cir. 1989). Not surprisingly, the OIG has chosen to follow the *Greber* standard. 42 C.F.R. § 1001.951(a)(2)(i) (exclusion applies "irrespective of whether the individual or entity may be able to prove that the remuneration was also intended for some other purpose . . . ").

3. *Mens Rea and the Advice of Counsel.* With the defendant's intent to obtain referrals in exchange for remuneration as the central issue in most criminal prosecutions under the Anti-Kickback Statute, courts usually must evaluate circumstantial evidence regarding defendant's mental state. The widely-noted case United States v. McClatchey, 217 F.3d 823 (10th Cir. 2000), involved the appeal from conviction under the act by Dennis McClatchey, Chief Operating Officer of Baptist Medical Center. McClatchey oversaw negotiations with doctors Robert and Ronald LaHue who were principals in Blue Valley Medical Group, a medical practice providing care to nursing home patients. Prior contracts between Baptist and the LaHues had provided for payment of $75,000 per year to the doctors for serving as co-directors of gerontology services at Baptist; however, the LaHues performed almost no services and circumstances strongly suggested that the payments were made in return for their referring patients to Baptist. 217 F.3d at 828–30. The evidence at trial showed that McClatchy directed negotiations which resulted in a revised contract and that he sought and received legal advice throughout the process. Weighing competing inferences regarding defendant's intent, the Tenth Circuit upheld a jury verdict convicting McClatchey. The court found that his knowledge that the LaHues had not performed substantial services under prior contracts, that the hospital staff did not want the LaHues' services, and that McClatchey stressed the importance of maximizing admissions from BVMG patients constituted sufficient evidence to sustain the jury's findings. Id. at 830. Concerning McClatchey's reliance on counsel, the court held as follows:

> McClatchey also argues that his actions throughout the negotiation process cannot give rise to an inference of his criminal intent because they were entirely directed and controlled by legal counsel. McGrath [a subordinate directly involved in the negotiations with the LaHues] testified however, that he and McClatchey told the lawyers what services to include in the contracts, not *visa versa*. Thus, the jury could reasonably attribute to McClatchey and McGrath both the decision to remove a minimum hour provision from the contract after the LaHues objected to such a requirement and the inculpatory inference of intent that can be drawn therefrom. Moreover, it was not the attorneys but McClatchey, Anderson, and McGrath who made the important decision to negotiate a new contract rather than ending Baptist's relationship with BVMG. Finally, McClatchey did not always heed the attorneys' advice. . . . The evidence, therefore, permitted the jury to reasonably reject McClatchey's good faith reliance on counsel defense and instead find he harbored the specific intent to violate the Act.

Id. at 830–31. The advice of counsel "defense" in this context really amounts to a claim that the government did not establish that the defendant "knowingly and willfully" engaged in unlawful kickback activities. To avail oneself of this defense, however, the defendant must establish that he disclosed all relevant facts to his attorneys and that he relied in good faith on that advice and acted in strict accordance with it. What problems do you foresee for a defendant wanting to invoke this defense at trial? The District Court acquitted two attorneys indicted for their role in the scheme finding they did not cover up fraud with sham agreements, had "attempted to advise their clients to engage in legal transactions," and relied on clients' representations as to their conduct. See Former Hospital Executives Convicted by Kansas Jury in Bribery Scheme, 8 Health L. Rep. (Apr. 18, 1999). What implications do these holdings have for attorney-client communications? The government also named several prominent attorneys as unindicted co-conspirators, though the court subsequently held that the government had violated the due process rights of these individuals by identifying them in a pre-trial motion.

4.   *Specific Intent vs. Knowledge That Conduct Is Unlawful.* The *Greber* case dealt with the issue of whether defendant's evidence of purpose satisfied the statutory standard that remuneration be given or received "in return for" an item or service reimbursable under Medicare or Medicaid. A second and distinct *mens rea* requirement concerns whether defendant knew that their conduct was unlawful.

Before the Affordable Care Act, there was disagreement among the circuits about the requisite intent to prove an Anti-Kickback Statute violation. The Ninth Circuit, for example, interpreted the Anti-Kickback Statute's *mens rea* standard to require that the defendant (i) knows that the Anti-Kickback Statute prohibits offering or paying remuneration to induce referrals, and (ii) engages in the prohibited conduct with the specific intent to disobey the law. Hanlester Network v. Shalala, 51 F.3d 1390 (9th Cir. 1995).

By contrast, the case of U.S. v. Starks, 157 F.3d 833 (11th Cir. 1998) held that it was enough to show that the defendants knew that they were breaking the law even if they may not have known that they were specifically violating the Anti-Kickback Statute. The *Starks* court noted,

> Given that the government only had to show that they knew that they were acting unlawfully . . . [t]he government produced ample evidence, including the furtive methods by which [defendants were remunerated— in cash, in parking lots and restaurants], from which the jury could reasonably have inferred that [defendants] knew that they were breaking the law—even if they may not have known that they were specifically violating the Anti-Kickback statute.

Id. at 839. The *Starks* court applied the Supreme Court's opinion in Bryan v. United States, 524 U.S. 184 (1998), which clarified the general principles of intent applicable in criminal cases, but did not fully resolve the issue with respect to the Anti-Kickback Statute. *Bryan* held that "As a general matter, when used in the criminal context, a 'willful' act is one undertaken with a 'bad purpose.' " Id. at 191. This standard may be satisfied by showing that the defendant acted with "an evil-meaning mind," which the Court defined as acting "with knowledge that his conduct was unlawful." Id. at 193. *Bryan* lowered the standard of proof necessary to satisfy its test unless the relevant statute is "highly technical." The *Starks* court found that the Anti-Kickback Statute is "not a highly technical tax or financial regulation that poses a danger of ensnaring persons engaged in apparently innocent conduct." While this characterization may be debatable, the conclusion was endorsed by Congress.

The Affordable Care Act resolved the confusion about the intent requirement in the Anti-Kickback Statute, providing that "a person need not have actual knowledge of [the Anti-Kickback Statute] or specific intent to commit a violation of [the Anti-Kickback Statute]." 42 U.S.C. § 1320a–7b(h). Thus, after the Affordable Care Act, the *Starks* rule is the rule for all.

B. ANTI-KICKBACK STATUTE SAFE HARBORS

The Anti-Kickback Statute contains several statutory and regulatory exceptions, called "**safe-harbors**." Safe harbors protect from criminal and civil enforcement certain payment and business arrangements between parties in a position to refer or generate business for each other that would otherwise constitute illegal remuneration under the statute. For example, there are safe harbors to address personal services and rental agreements, investments in ambulatory surgery centers, discounted items or services, and payments to bona fide employees. The regulatory Anti-Kickback safe harbors are set forth at 42 C.F.R. § 1001.952. To be protected by a safe harbor, the arrangement must satisfy all the requirements of the safe harbor. However, unlike the Stark Law exceptions (discussed in Section III of this chapter), arrangements that do not meet all the requirements of an Anti-Kickback safe harbor are not necessarily illegal, and the OIG will evaluate the arrangement on a case-by-case basis under the "**totality of facts and circumstances**."

When evaluating an arrangement for compliance with the Anti-Kickback Statute or an applicable safe harbor, three sources provide helpful guidance:

- First, attorneys should review the **safe harbor regulations** as well as applicable preamble commentary explaining the agency's view of the requirements. As with all regulations, the safe harbor rules are set forth in the Code of Federal Regulations (at 42 C.F.R. § 1001.952), and the preamble commentary is published in the Federal Register when the rules are finalized. For example, in 2020, OIG promulgated several new safe harbors relating to value-based payment arrangements, cybersecurity technology, and patient engagement and support, among others. OIG issued these new rules in conjunction with CMS, which set forth parallel rules under the Stark Law. The OIG explained its thinking and addressed public comments in the preamble to the final Anti-Kickback Statute rule at 85 Fed. Reg. 77,684 (Dec. 2, 2020). Preamble commentary is not itself legally binding, but it may provide helpful insight to the agency's view of a regulation.

- Second are OIG's **Special Fraud Alerts** and **Special Advisory Bulletins**, which are guidance documents available on the OIG website that set forth the OIG's interpretation of the statute as applied in particular situations and are intended to encourage individuals to report suspected violations to the government. Topics of fraud alerts range from joint venture arrangements with referral sources (1994), provision of nursing home services (1996), rental of office space to physicians (2000), telemarketing by durable medical equipment suppliers (2003 and 2010), laboratory payments to referring physicians (2014), and physician speaker programs by pharmaceutical and medical device companies (2020). Special Advisory Bulletins have addressed a similarly broad range of topics, including gainsharing payments from hospitals to physicians to reduce unnecessary services (1999), patient assistance programs to Medicare Part D beneficiaries (2005), and pharmaceutical manufacturer copayment coupons (2014).

- Third, **OIG Advisory Opinions** provide guidance about OIG's application of the Anti-Kickback Statute (and other fraud and abuse laws) to a requesting party's existing or proposed business arrangement. OIG Advisory Opinions are available on the OIG website, and they are very useful to assess how OIG interprets the safe harbor provisions and applies the "totality of the facts and circumstances" analysis to specific arrangements. While these opinions disclaim having any binding or precedential effect on third parties, they often signal the agency's posture on arrangements that fall outside the strict requirements of a safe harbor. For the party that requested the advisory opinion, receiving a favorable advisory opinion protects the party from OIG administrative sanctions, so long as the arrangement at issue is conducted in accordance with the facts submitted to the OIG. In the absence of case law applying the Anti-Kickback Statute's safe harbors to novel and nonconforming facts, the OIG Advisory Opinions provide useful examples of what sorts of arrangements the OIG considers either low-risk or a target of enforcement.

Currently, there are thirty-four regulatory safe harbors covering a wide array of arrangements. To provide a sense of what the safe harbors require, select safe harbor regulations are excerpted below.

42 C.F.R. § 1001.952—EXCEPTIONS

* * *

(b) *Space rental.* As used in section 1128B of the Act, "remuneration" does not include any payment made by a lessee to a lessor for the use of premises, as long as all of the following six standards are met—

(1) The lease agreement is set out in writing and signed by the parties.

(2) The lease covers all of the premises leased between the parties for the term of the lease and specifies the premises covered by the lease.

(3) If the lease is intended to provide the lessee with access to the premises for periodic intervals of time, rather than on a full-time basis for the term of the lease, the lease specifies exactly the schedule of such intervals, their precise length, and the exact rent for such intervals.

(4) The term of the lease is for not less than one year.

(5) The aggregate rental charge is set in advance, is consistent with fair market value in arms-length transactions and is not determined in a manner that takes into account the volume or value of any referrals or business otherwise generated between the parties for which payment may be made in whole or in part under Medicare, Medicaid or other Federal health care programs.

(6) The aggregate space rented does not exceed that which is reasonably necessary to accomplish the commercially reasonable business purpose of the rental. Note that for purposes of paragraph (b) of this section, the term *fair market value* means the value of the rental property for general commercial purposes, but shall not be adjusted to reflect the additional value that one party (either the prospective lessee or lessor) would attribute to the property as a result of its proximity or convenience to sources of referrals or business otherwise generated for which payment may be made in whole or in part under Medicare, Medicaid and all other Federal health care programs.

* * *

(d) *Personal services and management contracts and outcomes-based arrangements.*

(1) As used in section 1128B of the Act, "remuneration" does not include any payment made by a principal to an agent as compensation for the services of the agent, as long as all of the following seven standards are met:

(i) The agency agreement is set out in writing and signed by the parties.

(ii)   The agency agreement covers all of the services the agent provides to the principal for the term of the agreement and specifies the services to be provided by the agent.

(iii)   The term of the agreement is not less than 1 year.

(iv)   The methodology for determining the compensation paid to the agent over the term of the agreement is set in advance, is consistent with fair market value in arms-length transactions and is not determined in a manner that takes into account the volume or value of any referrals or business otherwise generated between the parties for which payment may be made in whole or in part under Medicare, Medicaid or other Federal health care programs.

(v)   The services performed under the agreement do not involve the counseling or promotion of a business arrangement or other activity that violates any State or Federal law.

(vi)   The aggregate services contracted for do not exceed those which are reasonably necessary to accomplish the commercially reasonable business purpose of the services.

(2)   As used in section 1128B of the Act, "renumeration" does not include any outcomes-based payment as long as all of the standards in paragraphs (d)(2)(i) through (viii) of this section are met.

(i)   To receive an outcomes-based payment, the agent achieves one or more legitimate outcome measures that:

(A)   Are selected based on clinical evidence or credible medical support; and

(B)   Have benchmarks that are used to quantify:

(1)   Improvements in, or the maintenance of improvements in, the quality of patient care;

(2)   A material reduction in costs to or growth in expenditures of payors while maintaining or improving quality of care for patients; or

(3)   Both.

(ii)   The methodology for determining the aggregate compensation (including any outcomes based payments) paid between or among the parties over the term of the agreement is: set in advance; commercially reasonable; consistent with fair market value; and not determined in a manner that directly takes into account the volume or value of any referrals or business otherwise generated between the parties for which payment may be made in whole or in part by a Federal health care program.

(iii) The agreement between the parties is set out in writing and signed by the parties in advance of, or contemporaneous with, the commencement of the terms of the outcomes-based payment arrangement. The writing states at a minimum: a general description of the services to be performed by the parties for the term of the agreement; the outcome measure(s) the agent must achieve to receive an outcomes-based payment; the clinical evidence or credible medical support relied upon by the parties to select the outcome measure(s); and the schedule for the parties to regularly monitor and assess the outcome measure(s).

(iv) The agreement neither limits any party's ability to make decisions in their patients' best interest nor induces any party to reduce or limit medically necessary items or services.

(v)   The term of the agreement is not less than 1 year.

(vi) The services performed under the agreement do not involve the counseling or promotion of a business arrangement or other activity that violates any State or Federal law.

(vii) For each outcome measure under the agreement, the parties:

(A) Regularly monitor and assess the agent's performance, including the impact of the outcomes-based payment arrangement on patient quality of care; and

(B) Periodically assess, and as necessary revise, benchmarks and remuneration under the arrangement to ensure that the remuneration is consistent with fair market value in an arm's length transaction as required by paragraph (d)(2)(ii) of this section during the term of the agreement.

(viii)   The principal has policies and procedures to promptly address and correct identified material performance failures or material deficiencies in quality of care resulting from the outcomes-based payment arrangement.

(3)   For purposes of this paragraph (d),

(i)   An agent of a principal is any person, other than a *bona fide* employee of the principal, who has an agreement to perform services for, or on behalf of, the principal.

(ii) Outcomes-based payments are limited to payments between or among a principal and an agent that:

(A) Reward the agent for successfully achieving an outcome measure described in paragraph (d)(2)(i) of this section; or

(B) Recoup from or reduce payment to an agent for failure to achieve an outcome measure described in paragraph (d)(2)(i) of this section.

(iii) Outcomes-based payments exclude any payments:

(A) Made directly or indirectly by the following entities:

(1) A pharmaceutical manufacturer, distributor, or wholesaler;

(2) A pharmacy benefit manager;

(3) A laboratory company;

(4) A pharmacy that primarily compounds drugs or primarily dispenses compounded drugs;

(5) A manufacturer of a device or medical supply as defined in paragraph (ee)(14)(iv) of this section;

(6) A medical device distributor or wholesaler that is not otherwise a manufacturer of a device or medical supply, as defined in paragraph (ee)(14)(iv) of this section; or

(7) An entity or individual that sells or rents durable medical equipment, prosthetics, orthotics, or supplies covered by a Federal health care program (other than a pharmacy or a physician, provider, or other entity that primarily furnishes services); or

(B) Related solely to the achievement of internal cost savings for the principal; or

(C) Based solely on patient satisfaction or patient convenience measures.

* * *

(i) Employees. As used in section 1128B of the Act, "remuneration" does not include any amount paid by an employer to an employee, who has a bona fide employment relationship with the employer, for employment in the furnishing of any item or service for which payment may be made in whole or in part under Medicare, Medicaid or other Federal health care programs. For purposes of paragraph (i) of this section, the term *employee* has the same meaning as it does for purposes of 26 U.S.C. 3121(d)(2).

* * *

(r) Ambulatory surgical centers. As used in section 1128B of the Act, "remuneration" does not include any payment that is a return on an investment interest, such as a dividend or interest income, made to an investor, as long as the investment entity is a certified ambulatory surgical center (ASC) under part 416 of this title, whose operating and recovery room space is dedicated exclusively to the ASC, patients referred to the investment entity by an investor are fully informed of the investor's investment interest, and all of the applicable standards are met within one of the following four categories—

[Subparagraphs (1) and (2) set forth requirements for surgeon-owned and single-specialty ASCs, respectively.]

(3) *Multi-Specialty ASCs*—If all of the investors are physicians who are in a position to refer patients directly to the entity and perform procedures on such referred patients; group practices, as defined in this paragraph, composed exclusively of such physicians; or investors who are not employed by the entity or by any investor, are not in a position to provide items or services to the entity or any of its investors, and are not in a position to make or influence referrals directly or indirectly to the entity or any of its investors, all of the following seven standards must be met—

(i)   The terms on which an investment interest is offered to an investor must not be related to the previous or expected volume of referrals, services furnished, or the amount of business otherwise generated from that investor to the entity.

(ii) At least one-third of each physician investor's medical practice income from all sources for the previous fiscal year or previous 12-month period must be derived from the physician's performance of procedures (as defined in this paragraph).

(iii) At least one-third of the procedures (as defined in this paragraph) performed by each physician investor for the previous fiscal year or previous 12-month period must be performed at the investment entity.

(iv) The entity or any investor (or other individual or entity acting on behalf of the entity or any investor) must not loan funds to or guarantee a loan for an investor if the investor uses any part of such loan to obtain the investment interest.

(v) The amount of payment to an investor in return for the investment must be directly proportional to the amount of the capital investment (including the fair market value of any pre-operational services rendered) of that investor.

(vi) All ancillary services for Federal health care program beneficiaries performed at the entity must be directly and integrally related to primary procedures performed at the entity, and none may be separately billed to Medicare or other Federal health care programs.

(vii) The entity and any physician investors must treat patients receiving medical benefits or assistance under any Federal health care program in a nondiscriminatory manner.

(4) *Hospital/Physician ASCs*—If at least one investor is a hospital, and all of the remaining investors are physicians who meet the requirements of paragraphs (r)(1), (r)(2) or (r)(3) of this section; group practices (as defined in this paragraph) composed of such physicians; surgical group practices (as defined in this paragraph); or investors who are not employed by the entity or by any investor, are not in a position to provide items or services to the entity or any of its investors, and are not in a position to refer patients directly or indirectly to the entity or any of its investors, all of the following eight standards must be met—

(i) The terms on which an investment interest is offered to an investor must not be related to the previous or expected volume of referrals, services furnished, or the amount of business otherwise generated from that investor to the entity.

(ii) The entity or any investor (or other individual or entity acting on behalf of the entity or any investor) must not loan funds to or guarantee a loan for an investor if the investor uses any part of such loan to obtain the investment interest.

(iii) The amount of payment to an investor in return for the investment must be directly proportional to the amount of the capital investment (including the fair market value of any pre-operational services rendered) of that investor.

(iv) The entity and any hospital or physician investor must treat patients receiving medical benefits or assistance under any Federal health care program in a nondiscriminatory manner.

(v) The entity may not use space, including, but not limited to, operating and recovery room space, located in or owned by any hospital investor, unless such space is leased from the hospital in accordance with a lease that complies with all the standards of the space rental safe harbor set forth in paragraph (b) of this section; nor may it use equipment owned by or services provided by the hospital unless such equipment is leased in accordance with a lease that complies with the equipment rental safe harbor set forth in paragraph (c) of this section, and such services are provided in accordance with a contract that complies with the personal services and management contracts safe harbor set forth in paragraph (d) of this section.

(vi) All ancillary services for Federal health care program beneficiaries performed at the entity must be directly and integrally related to primary procedures performed at the entity, and none may be separately billed to Medicare or other Federal health care programs.

(vii) The hospital may not include on its cost report or any claim for payment from a Federal health care program any costs associated with the ASC (unless such costs are required to be included by a Federal health care program).

(viii) The hospital may not be in a position to make or influence referrals directly or indirectly to any investor or the entity.

(5) For purposes of paragraph (r) of this section, *procedures* means any procedure or procedures on the list of Medicare-covered procedures for ambulatory surgical centers in accordance with regulations issued by the Department and *group practice* means a group practice that meets all of the standards of paragraph (p) of this section. *Surgical group practice* means a group practice that meets all of the standards of paragraph (p) of this section and is composed exclusively of surgeons who meet the requirements of paragraph (r)(1) of this section.

In addition to the excerpted safe harbor provisions from the Code of Federal Regulations, summaries of additional safe harbors are provided below.

Investment Interests

This complex safe harbor provides that there is no violation for returns on "investment interests" including both equity and debt interests in corporations, partnerships and other entities held directly or indirectly through family members or other indirect ownership vehicles. It covers, first, investments in large, publicly-traded entities registered with the SEC and having $50 million in net tangible assets. The investment must also be obtained on terms equally available to the public, and the entity must market items and services in the same way to investors and non-investors and must comply with other requirements. Second, certain investments in small entities are permitted provided no more than 40 percent of the value of the investment interests in each class of investment is held by persons who are in a position to make or influence referrals to, furnish items or services to, or otherwise generate business for the entity. Moreover, no more than 40 percent of the gross revenue of the entity may come from referrals, items or services from investors. A number of other requirements apply including several that are different for active investors and passive investors. Amendments to this safe harbor allow for higher investment percentages in medically underserved areas. The importance of this safe harbor is limited by the fact that it does not shelter arrangements covered by the Stark Law (discussed in Section III of this chapter), which applies different standards to investments. However, for services not covered by Stark, the safe harbor has continuing importance. 42 C.F.R. § 1001.952(a).

Practitioner Recruitment

A practitioner recruitment safe harbor protects recruitment efforts by hospitals and entities located in government-specified health professional shortage areas (HPSAs). It permits payments or other exchanges to induce practitioners relocating from a different geographic area or new practitioners (in practice within their current specialty for less than one year) provided nine conditions are met. Among those conditions are that the agreement be in writing; that at least 75 percent of the business of the relocated practice come from new patients; that at least 75 percent of the new practice revenue be generated from the HPSA or other defined underserved areas; that the practitioner not be barred from establishing staff privileges with or referring to other entities; and that benefits and amendments to the contract may not be based on the value or volume of practitioners' referrals. 42 C.F.R. § 1001.952(n).

Investments in Group Practices

A safe harbor shelters payments (such as dividend or interest income) received in return for investment interests in group practices. It covers business arrangements having centralized decision-making, pooled expenses and revenues, and profit distribution systems "not based on satellite offices operating substantially as if they were separate enterprises or profit centers." Modeled on the Stark exception, it adopts that statute's definition of "group practice" and provides that income from ancillary services must meet the Stark definition of "in-office ancillary services." 42 C.F.R. § 1001.952(p).

Value Based Arrangements

The 2020 Anti-Kickback Statute rules added three new safe harbors for value based arrangements involving participants collaborating pursuant to a written arrangement to achieve certain "value-based purposes": (1) coordinating and managing the care of a target patient population; (2) improving quality of care for a target patient population; (3) appropriately reducing costs to payors while maintaining quality of patient care; or (4) transitioning from health care delivery and payment mechanisms based on the value of items and services provided to mechanisms based on the quality of care and control of costs of care for a target patient population. These safe harbors are designed to reduce regulatory barriers for payment arrangements between payers and providers designed to improve the quality of care, health outcomes, and efficiency. The three safe harbors for value-based arrangements vary the requirements according to the extent of financial risk assumed by the providers from the payer, but common requirements include: (a) the arrangement must not cause the parties to reduce or limit medically necessary items or services furnished to any patient; (b) the remuneration must not be exchanged or used for the purpose of marketing to patients; (c) the remuneration must not take into account the volume or value of or condition remuneration on referrals of patients who are not part of the target population or business covered under the value-based arrangement; and (d) for six years, participants in value-based enterprises must make available to the Secretary upon request all records and materials sufficient to establish compliance with the safe harbor requirements. The value-based arrangement safe harbors are not available to pharmaceutical or medical device manufacturers or distributors, durable medical equipment suppliers, pharmacy benefit managers, compounding pharmacies, or laboratories. 42 C.F.R. § 1001.952(ee), (ff), (gg).

Donated Electronic Health Records, Electronic Prescribing, and Cybersecurity Technology

Three safe harbors establish conditions under which hospitals and certain other entities may provide physicians with (1) interoperable electronic health records (EHR), software, information technology, and training services, and (2) hardware, software, or information technology and training services necessary and used solely for electronic prescribing, and (3) cybersecurity technology and services. CMS adopted substantially similar standards as exceptions to the Stark Law, discussed in the next section.

The electronic prescribing safe harbor covers items and services that are necessary and used solely to transmit and receive electronic prescription information and requires that donated technology comply with standards adopted by the Secretary of HHS. Protected donors and recipients are: (1) hospitals to members of their medical staffs; (2) group practices to physician members; (3) prescription drug plan sponsors and Medicare Advantage organizations to network pharmacists, pharmacies, and prescribing health care professionals. There is no limit on the value of donations but donors may not select recipients using any method that takes into account the volume or value of referrals from the recipient or other business generated between the parties. 42 C.F.R. § 1001.952(x).

The EHR safe harbor protects arrangements involving new or replacement software or information technology and training services necessary and used predominately to create, maintain, transmit, or receive electronic health records. While neither hardware nor software with a core functionality other than electronic health records is covered, software packages may include functions related to patient administration such as clinical support. Protected donors are individuals and entities that provide covered services to any federal health care program and health plans. Donors may not select recipients using any method that takes into account directly the volume or value of referrals from the recipient or other business between the parties and while there is no limit on the aggregate value of technology that may qualify for safe harbor protection, recipients must pay 15 percent of the donor's cost for the donated technology. 42 C.F.R. § 1001.952(y).

The cybersecurity safe harbor was added in 2020, allowing donations of cybersecurity technology, such as encrypted servers or malware prevention software, so long as the technology is necessary and used predominantly to implement, maintain, or reestablish cybersecurity. The arrangement must not directly take into account the volume or value of referrals nor be a condition of doing business or making referrals. The arrangement must be set forth in a written agreement and may not shift costs to federal health care programs. 42 C.F.R. § 1001.952(jj).

OIG ADVISORY OPINION NO. 03–5
(Issued February 6, 2003).

Dear [name redacted]:

We are writing in response to your request for an advisory opinion regarding an ambulatory surgery center (an "ASC") that would be jointly owned by a hospital and a multi-specialty group practice that has a substantial number of physician members who would not personally use the ASC (the "Proposed Arrangement"). Specifically, you have inquired whether the Proposed Arrangement would constitute grounds for the imposition of sanctions under the exclusion authority at section 1128(b)(7) of the Social Security Act (the "Act") or the civil monetary penalty provision at section 1128A(a)(7) of the Act, as those sections relate to the commission of acts described in section 1128B(b) of the Act.

* * *

I.   Factual Background

[Company X] (the "Surgical Center") is an [state redacted] ("State") limited liability company formed for the purpose of planning, developing, and operating an ASC that will be certified by Medicare under 42 C.F.R. section 416. [Company Y], an acute care hospital (the "Hospital"), owns 49% of the Surgical Center, and [Company Z], a multi-specialty clinic (the "Group") owns 51% of the Surgical Center.[1] For each investor, the return on the Surgical Center investment will be directly proportional to the amount of capital that the investor contributed. The Surgical Center will

---

[1]   The Surgical Center has two classes of members: the voting, Class A Members, consisting solely of the Hospital and the Group, and the non-voting, Class B Members, each of whom must be either a State-licensed physician eligible for credentialing at the Surgical Center or a State legal entity with a majority of its owners being physicians who meet the foregoing requirements. No Class B memberships have been sold.

maintain an open medical staff. It will be located on land owned by the Hospital and leased to the Surgical Center pursuant to a written lease.

The Group has fifty-two shareholders (the "Group Shareholders"), each of whom is a licensed physician and an employee of the Group. Each Group Shareholder owns one share of the Group's stock, and any dividends paid by the Group are divided equally among the Group Shareholders. In addition, the Group employs other physicians who do not own Group stock (the "Group Associates") and other health care professionals, such as physical therapists, optometrists, and licensed nurse practitioners. Group Shareholders and Group Associates are collectively referred to herein as "Group Physicians." Some Group Physicians are surgeons; however, most are not. For example, there are fourteen family practitioners, eleven internists, six pediatricians, five obstetricians/gynecologists, two general surgeons, three orthopedic surgeons, and two ophthalmologists. The Surgical Center has certified that the salaries, bonuses, and any other forms of employment-related remuneration payable to Group Physicians will not take into account the physicians' referrals of patients to the Surgical Center or the volume of surgical procedures performed by the physicians at the Surgical Center or elsewhere.

The Hospital is wholly owned by a nonprofit corporation that is also the sole owner of two other hospitals. The Hospital employs forty-two physicians, including eight family practitioners, twelve internal medicine practitioners, eight obstetricians/gynecologists, and two pediatricians. Currently, the Hospital has eight operating suites for both inpatient and outpatient surgery, and physicians employed by the Group perform approximately 25% of all surgeries performed at the Hospital.

II. Legal Analysis

A. Law

* * *

The Department of Health and Human Services has promulgated safe harbor regulations that define practices that are not subject to the anti-kickback statute because such practices would be unlikely to result in fraud or abuse. See 42 C.F.R. § 1001.952. The safe harbors set forth specific conditions that, if met, assure entities involved of not being prosecuted or sanctioned for the arrangement qualifying for the safe harbor. However, safe harbor protection is afforded only to those arrangements that precisely meet all of the conditions set forth in the safe harbor.

The safe harbor for investment interests in ambulatory surgical centers jointly owned by hospitals and physicians, 42 C.F.R. § 1001.952(r)(4), is relevant to the Proposed Arrangement.[2] One condition

---

[2] In cases, such as the instant case, where the ASC is located in space owned by the hospital, the space rental safe harbor, 42 C.F.R. § 1001.952(b), is also relevant.

of the hospital-physician ASC safe harbor is that investing physicians who are in a position to refer patients to the ASC can only invest as individuals who meet the requirements for surgeon-owned ASCs, single-specialty ASCs, or multi-specialty ASCs set forth at 42 C.F.R. § 1001.952(r)(1), (r)(2), or (r)(3), as applicable, or as group practices composed of such physicians or surgical group practices.[3] Since the Surgical Center's investing physicians are investing through a multi-specialty group practice, for safe harbor protection the group practice (*i.e.*, the Group) must meet all the requirements of the group practice safe harbor at 42 C.F.R. § 1001.952(p) and the group practice must be composed of physicians who meet both the one-third practice income test at 42 C.F.R. § 1001.952(r)(3)(ii) and the one-third practice test at 42 C.F.R. § 1001.952(r)(3)(iii).[4]

B. Analysis

Surgical center joint ventures that include physician-investors in a position to generate surgical business are susceptible to fraud and abuse. Notwithstanding, in recognition that some physician-owned ASC ventures may be beneficial to the federal programs and their beneficiaries, the Department issued a narrow safe harbor for physician-owned ASCs that meet criteria carefully tailored to mitigate the risks of fraud and abuse. With respect to physician-investors, the safe harbor is carefully circumscribed to apply only to physicians who are unlikely to use the investment as a vehicle for profiting from their referrals to other physicians using the ASC. Accordingly, safe harbor protection is limited to physician-investors who actually use the ASC on a regular basis as part of their medical practices or who practice the same specialty as other physician-investors and are therefore unlikely to refer substantial business to "competing" physician-investors when they can earn the fees themselves.

The majority of the Group Physicians fit neither category. Since the Group is a multi-specialty group, there is a substantial likelihood of cross-specialty referrals for services performed in the ASC. Moreover, few of the Group Physicians will actually use the Surgical Center on a regular basis as part of their medical practice. In other words, the Proposed Arrangement would allow those Group Physicians for whom the Surgical Center is not an extension of their office practices to profit from their referrals to the Surgical Center or to their partners who perform procedures there. In this respect, the Proposed Arrangement poses the

---

[3] The terms "group practice" and "surgical group practice" are defined at 42 C.F.R. § 1001.952(r)(5).

[4] Under the one-third practice income test, 42 C.F.R. § 1001.952(r)(3)(ii), at least one-third of each physician investor's medical practice income from all sources for the previous fiscal year or previous 12-month period must be derived from the physician's performance of procedures. Under the one-third practice test, 42 C.F.R. § 1001.952(r)(3)(iii), at least one-third of the procedures performed by each physician investor for the previous fiscal year or previous 12-month period must be performed at the investment entity. The term "procedures" is defined at 42 C.F.R. § 1001.952(r)(5).

same risks as an ASC owned directly by surgeons and primary care physicians in the same community. In these circumstances, the fact that the ownership of the ASC is held indirectly through a group practice whose membership includes both surgeons and other potential referring physicians does not reduce the risk that the venture may be used to reward referrals.

Accordingly, we cannot conclude that the Proposed Arrangement poses a minimal risk of fraud and abuse.

III. Conclusion

Based on the facts certified in your request for an advisory opinion and supplemental submissions, we conclude that the Proposed Arrangement could potentially generate prohibited remuneration under the anti-kickback statute and that the OIG could potentially impose administrative sanctions on [Company X] under sections 1128(b)(7) or 1128A(a)(7) of the Act (as those sections relate to the commission of acts described in section 1128B(b) of the Act) in connection with the Proposed Arrangement. Any definitive conclusion regarding the existence of an anti-kickback violation requires a determination of the parties' intent, which determination is beyond the scope of the advisory opinion process.

IV. Limitations

This advisory opinion has no application to, and cannot be relied upon by, any other individual or entity; may not be introduced into evidence in any matter involving an entity or individual that is not a requestor of this opinion; is applicable only to the statutory provisions specifically noted above and will not bind or obligate any agency other than the U.S. Department of Health and Human Services; is limited in scope to the specific arrangement described in this letter and has no applicability to other arrangements, even those which appear similar in nature or scope. No opinion is expressed herein regarding the liability of any party under the False Claims Act or other legal authorities for any improper billing, claims submission, cost reporting, or related conduct.

NOTES AND QUESTIONS

1. *ASC Safe Harbor.* What are the concerns for federal health care programs (and taxpayers) associated with physician ownership and operation of ASCs? How does the ASC safe harbor and the OIG attempt to strike a balance between the risks and benefits of these arrangements? The OIG's conclusions regarding any arrangement analyzed in an Advisory Opinion are limited to the specific facts presented. For example, the OIG issued an Advisory Opinion in 2021, which concluded the OIG would not pursue sanctions against a hospital-physician ASC joint venture despite the fact that not all the investor physicians would satisfy the one-third practice income test, due to certain safeguards the parties had implemented against improperly

induced referrals. Adv. Op. 21–02 (Apr. 26, 2021). If you were to compare Adv. Op. 21–02 to Adv. Op. 03–05, could you identify what safeguards contributed to the different results? How would you advise a client interested in pursuing a hospital-physician ASC joint venture?

2.   *OIG Advisory Opinions vs. Special Fraud Alerts.* Over the ten-year period from 2010 to 2020, the OIG issued a total of 165 advisory opinions, averaging over 16 per year. Advisory opinions are numbered according to the year and their numerical order within the year; thus, for example, Advisory Opinion 17–05 is the fifth opinion issued in 2017. These opinions may conclude that the proposed conduct falls outside a safe harbor but decline to impose sanctions because it poses little risk due to the use of additional safeguards. Alternatively, the opinion may conclude that the proposed arrangement constitutes illegal remuneration that would be subject to sanctions. Although most advisory opinions address whether the arrangement violates the Anti-Kickback Statute, others address violations of the Civil Monetary Penalties law, discussed below.

In contrast to Advisory Opinions, which refer to the specific facts of a proposed transaction, Special Fraud Alerts are written as general guidance to industry signaling the agency's enforcement priorities on widely observed practices that the OIG believes pose high risks of fraud and abuse. Compared to Advisory Opinions, Special Fraud Alerts are relatively rare. Prior to an alert on speaker programs in 2020, the last alert was issued in 2014 on laboratory payments to referring physicians. Thus, the publication of a Special Fraud Alert is a strong signal to industry actors that the OIG is particularly concerned with the arrangements described and will aggressively enforce the law in these areas.

3.   *Special Fraud Alert on Speaker Programs.* In 2020, OIG issued a Special Fraud Alert on "speaker programs," events sponsored by pharmaceutical or medical device companies where physicians make presentations to other health care professionals about a drug or device on behalf of the company. In return, the company generally pays the speaker an honorarium, and often pays remuneration (for example, free meals) to the attendees. The Alert stated,

> OIG is skeptical about the educational value of such programs. Our investigations have revealed that, often, [health care providers (HCPs)] receive generous compensation to speak at programs offered under circumstances that are not conducive to learning or to speak to audience members who have no legitimate reason to attend. Such cases strongly suggest that one purpose of the remuneration to the HCP speaker and attendees is to induce or reward referrals. OIG Special Fraud Alert: Speaker Programs 3 (Nov. 16, 2020).

The Alert lists nine factors that OIG believes would make a speaker program suspect under the Anti-Kickback Statute, including where the program offers little substantive information, where alcohol or expensive meals are offered to attendees, or programs are held at restaurants, entertainment, or sports venues not conducive to educational exchange.

This Special Fraud Alert was a warning shot to the pharmaceutical and medical device industries about their widespread practice of paying physicians to present at and attend so-called "educational" events about their products that are really marketing boondoggles. It also provides a good illustration of how the Anti-Kickback Statute applies to life sciences companies. As a case in point, the Alert followed Novartis's $642 million settlement with DOJ and CIA with OIG for hosting tens of thousands dubious speaker programs. While the Alert mainly describes things companies may not do, the Novartis CIA may provide a roadmap for how speaker programs might be structured and tightly circumscribed to avoid violating the Anti-Kickback Statute. See Corporate Integrity Agreement Between the Off. of Inspector Gen. of the Dep't of Health & Hum. Servs. and Novartis Corp., June. 30, 2020.

NOTE: GAINSHARING AND BENEFICIARY INDUCEMENTS UNDER CMP LAW AND ANTI-KICKBACK STATUTE

The **Civil Monetary Penalties (CMP)** law is codified in the U.S. Code section immediately preceding the Anti-Kickback Statute. 42 U.S.C. § 1320a–7a. True to its name, the CMP law imposes civil money penalties on a variety of activities believed to increase the risk of abuse to federal health care programs and harm to program beneficiaries. The CMP law contains a variety of proscriptions, including prohibiting hospitals from paying physicians inducements to reduce or limit services to beneficiaries (**the gainsharing prohibition**) and also prohibiting any person from offering an inducement to Medicare or Medicaid beneficiary that may influence the beneficiary's choice of provider (**beneficiary inducement prohibition**). These prohibitions have been criticized for limiting providers' ability to adapt to new payment and delivery models, to control costs, and to improve access for beneficiaries. As a result, both Congress and the OIG have taken steps to modernize and liberalize the CMP law's prohibitions on gainsharing and beneficiary inducements.

Gainsharing Arrangements. A "gainsharing arrangement" is broadly defined as "an arrangement in which a hospital gives physicians a share of any reduction in the hospital's costs attributable in part to the physicians' efforts." Hearing on Gainsharing Before the Subcomm. on Health of the H. Comm. on Ways and Means, 109th Cong. (2005) (testimony of Lewis Morris, Chief Counsel to the Inspector General, U.S. Dep't of Health and Hum. Servs.). In a simple example, a hospital could pay its surgeons a portion of the money saved if the surgeons wait to open packages of sterilized disposable surgical instruments until they are needed in surgery, because once opened, instruments have to be disposed of whether they are used or not. More controversially, a hospital could offer to pay physicians a bonus from the amount saved for the hospital if the physicians work together to reduce hospital patients' length of stay. Although gainsharing can align hospital and physician incentives to reduce unnecessary utilization and waste, these arrangements also pose a risk to beneficiaries by creating incentives for providers to stint on medically necessary items and services.

Previously, the CMP law prohibited hospitals from "knowingly [making] a payment, directly or indirectly, to a physician as an inducement to reduce or limit services provided to [Medicare beneficiaries]." The OIG interpreted this provision to cover gainsharing payments that involved the reduction of *any* services, not just *medically necessary* services. Despite this restrictive interpretation of the CMP law, the OIG approved over a dozen gainsharing arrangements in advisory opinions deemed to pose a low risk of abuse. See OIG Advisory Opinions 01–01, 05–02, 05–03, 05–04, 05–05, 05–06, 06–22, 07–21, 07–22, 08–09, 08–15, 08–21, and 09–06. Nevertheless, commenters advocated for changes to the CMP law to allow for broader use of gainsharing arrangements that reduce overutilization and waste while protecting beneficiaries from stinting on medically necessary care.

Congress provided the opening that providers and commenters had been hoping for when it passed the Medicare Access and CHIP Reauthorization Act in 2015 (MACRA) (See Chapter 10). MACRA amended the CMP law's gainsharing provision by inserting the words "medically necessary," so that the prohibition now applies only to payments to physicians as an inducement to reduce or limit *medically necessary* services. Now gainsharing arrangements that target reductions in unnecessary items and services are permitted under the CMP law.

MACRA also required the Secretary of HHS to submit a report to Congress containing additional options for statutory amendments or regulatory changes to further expand the availability of gainsharing arrangements. In her 2016 report, however, the then-Secretary of HHS concluded that she had no further legislative or regulatory changes to recommend, noting her continued concern that gainsharing arrangements may, under certain circumstances, violate federal fraud and abuse laws, noting the particular difficulty posed by the Stark Law's requirement that physician compensation not take into account the volume or value of referrals between the parties. Secretary of Health & Human Services, Report to Congress: Fraud and Abuse Laws Regarding Gainsharing or Similar Arrangements between Physicians and Hospitals (2016). Thus, while MACRA opened the door to gainsharing arrangements, OIG is still standing guard to monitor these arrangements for potential abuse.

Beneficiary Inducement. The CMP law also prohibits any person from offering remuneration to Medicare or Medicaid beneficiaries that could influence the beneficiaries' selection of providers or suppliers (including hospitals, clinics, physicians, or drug or device makers or sellers). However, many commenters have advocated for additional flexibility to provide discounts, cost-sharing relief, transportation, and other forms of assistance to beneficiaries to reduce financial and practical barriers to care.

In December 2016 and 2020, the OIG issued final rules amending the requirements of the beneficiary inducement prohibition, including the promulgation of several exceptions to the CMP law and amendments to Anti-

Kickback Statute safe harbors. 81 Fed. Reg. 88368 (Dec. 7, 2016) and 85 Fed. Reg. 77684 (Dec. 2, 2020). The 2016 rules amended the definition of "remuneration" in the CMP law to create several new exceptions from the beneficiary inducement prohibition. 42 C.F.R. § 1003.110. Exceptions include: copayment reductions for certain hospital outpatient departments; remuneration that promotes access to care and poses a low risk of harm; retailer coupons, rebates, or other rewards that are available to beneficiaries on equal terms to the general public; free or discounted items or services offered to financially needy individuals; and copayment waivers for the "first fill" of a generic drug prescription. In the 2020 rules, OIG amended the definition of "remuneration" in the CMP rules to add a new statutory exception to the prohibition on beneficiary inducements for telehealth technologies furnished to certain in-home dialysis patients with end-stage renal disease. 42 C.F.R. § 10003.110.

In addition to creating exceptions under the CMP law, the beneficiary inducement final rules in 2016 and 2020 modified several existing Anti-Kickback Statute safe harbors and added others. For example, the 2016 final rule added a new provision to the existing safe harbor for beneficiary cost-sharing waivers by pharmacies and emergency ambulance providers. 42 C.F.R. 1001.952(k). The 2016 rules also added a safe harbor for the provision of free or discounted local transportation services for beneficiaries to obtain medically necessary items and service, which was further expanded in the 2020 rules. 42 C.F.R. § 1001.952(bb). The 2020 rules also added new protections for certain patient engagement and support tools offered by value-based enterprises as part of the new value-based arrangements safe harbors. Such patient supports must be in-kind items valued at less than $500 annually, rather than cash or gift-cards, be recommended by the patient's health care professional, and bear a direct connection to the coordination and management of the patient's care. 42 CFR § 1001.952(hh).

Concurrently with the 2016 beneficiary inducement rules, OIG issued updated guidance on what constitutes a gift to a beneficiary of "nominal value" under the statutory exception for nominal gifts. OIG increased its standard for "nominal value" from $10–$15 to $50–$75 in aggregate value per patient.

ANTI-KICKBACK STATUTE PROBLEM: DR. LEE'S LEASE

Samaritan Hospital is a community hospital that owns a medical office building adjacent to its inpatient facility. Dr. Lisa Lee is a prominent cardiologist who refers many of her patients for cardiac surgery at Samaritan and performs tests, such as cardiac catheterization, at Samaritan. Samaritan leases Dr. Lee office space for her private practice in its medical office building. The terms of the lease are: Dr. Lee pays $25/square foot per year for 1,000 square feet of office space. The lease rate was calculated to be consistent with fair market value at the time the lease was entered into. There is an annual inflation adjustment of 2% (so in year 1, the annual rent is $25,000; in year 2 it is $25,500; in year 3 it is $26,010, etc.). The lease is for a term of 3 years, and it must be renewed in writing. A compliance audit of Samaritan's leases reveals the following: the 1,000 square feet in Dr. Lee's lease does not include the office building's common spaces, such as hallways, parking for herself or her staff, lobby, or restrooms. Second, the lease was signed on July 1, 2014. By its own terms, the lease expired on June 30, 2017, and the parties never executed a renewal lease. Dr. Lee still occupies the space and has been paying $25,000 per year every year for the office space. Samaritan has not collected the inflation-adjustment. Evaluate Samaritan Hospital's potential liability under the Anti-Kickback Statute's space lease safe harbor (excerpted above). What would you advise Samaritan Hospital?

ANTI-KICKBACK STATUTE PROBLEM: RECRUITING DR. RYAN

Anxious to develop its newly-enlarged surgical department, Community Hospital, located in Rocky Shoals, N.C. recruited Dr. Henry Ryan to relocate from Arizona and set up an independent practice in the area. Community's contract with Dr. Ryan recited the region's need for additional surgeons and specified it would provide a number of financial inducements for Dr. Ryan to relocate: a guarantee that the doctor's cash collections for professional services would not be less than an average of $40,000 per month; that Community would extend this commitment for an additional two additional one-year terms "should Physician and Hospital believe it to be necessary"; and that Community would lease medical office space on its campus to Dr. Ryan at a cost 50 percent below the market average and provide financial assistance in obtaining medical office furniture and equipment if desired. The contract goes on to provide as follows:

> You recognize that [Community] Hospital is a convenient acute care medical facility for the majority of patients likely to utilize your services for medical treatment and that the Hospital is duly accredited by the Joint Commission and is certified for participation in the Medicare and Medicaid programs, and has excellent special facilities and treatment capabilities.

> We, of course, hope that the quality and cost-effective nature of our Hospital's services will commend themselves to your patients. However, we clearly understand that the choice of services and the choice of service suppliers which you make on behalf of your patients must be, and will be, made ONLY with regard to the best interests of the patients themselves. Therefore, so there will be no misunderstanding, the compensation which you are to receive is not conditional on the use of any item or service offered by this Hospital.

Shortly after Dr. Ryan's arrival in Rocky Hills, Community Hospital was acquired by Nosh Hospital. After Nosh reneged on many of the commitments contained in the contract, Dr. Ryan sued for breach. Raising affirmative defenses including the unenforceability of the contract based on the federal Anti-Kickback Statute, the hospital has moved for summary judgment. In response, Dr. Ryan argues that the unambiguous language of the contract establishes that the parties did not have intent to induce referrals. How should the court rule?

III.   THE STARK LAW

The third of the "big three" federal fraud and abuse laws applicable to federal health care programs is **The Ethics in Patient Referrals Act**, commonly referred to as the **Stark Law** in recognition of the legislation's principal sponsor, former Rep. Fortney "Pete" Stark. 42 U.S.C. § 1395nn. The Stark Law's primary aim is to protect patients and the resources of federal health care programs from the conflicts of interest that arise when a physician stands to gain financially from referring patients to entities with which the physician (or an immediate family member) has a financial relationship.

The Stark law prohibits physicians from making "**referrals**" for the furnishing of "**designated health services**" **(DHS)** payable by Medicare to "**entities**" with whom the referring physician (or an immediate family member) has a "**financial relationship**," unless the arrangement satisfies an **exception**. In addition to making it illegal for physicians to make such referrals, the Stark Law also **prohibits entities from billing** Medicare for any services provided pursuant to illegal referrals. Key statutory provisions and defined terms are set forth below.

The **Centers for Medicare and Medicaid Services (CMS)** is the primary enforcement authority for the Stark Law. Any amounts billed in violation of the Stark Law constitute an overpayment that must be refunded to the government within 60 days of being identified (the 60-day rule is discussed in Section I, above), whether or not the improper billing was known or intentional. The imposition of civil and administrative penalties, however, does have a scienter requirement: any person who knowingly bills or fails to make a refund in violation of the Stark Law's prohibition is subject to a statutory civil fine of $15,000 per item billed, treble damages equal to three times the amount improperly billed, and exclusion from Medicare 42 U.S.C. § 1395nn(g)(3). The amount of civil fines is subject to inflation adjustment, so by 2020 the per-claim penalty has increased to $25,820. See Annual Civil Monetary Penalties Inflation Adjustment, 85 Fed. Reg. 2869 (Jan. 17, 2020). Stark Law violations frequently form the basis of False Claims Act cases, which (as discussed in Section I) are subject to *qui tam* whistleblower enforcement and significant additional damages liability.

Note that the Stark Law adopts a "bright line" or strict liability standard. Unlike the Anti-Kickback Statute, there is no mens rea or scienter required to establish a violation. Moreover, an arrangement that fails to meet all the requirements of an applicable exception has violated the law, and no facts and circumstances analysis will save it. Unlike the

Anti-Kickback Statute, which applies to any person (including pharmaceutical or medical device companies), the Stark Law is only implicated when there are financial arrangements between physicians and health care entities, such as hospitals.

Like OIG's self-disclosure protocol for Anti-Kickback Statute violations, CMS issued a voluntary **"Self-Referral Disclosure Protocol" (SRDP)** for Stark Law violations pursuant to a directive in the Affordable Care Act. The SRDP allows providers who wish to self-disclose actual or potential violations of the Stark Law to reduce their potential liability for improper billing and referrals under the Stark Law. CMS indicated that it may resolve violations for less than the maximum penalty through the SRDP, although it is not obligated to do so. While pending before CMS, participation in the SRDP suspends the 60-day deadline for returning overpayments. However, providers are responsible for returning overpayments within 60 days of the date when a settlement agreement is entered, the entity withdraws from the SRDP, or CMS removes the entity from the SRDP. Despite these benefits, the SRDP carries some risks: the Department of Justice and the Office of Inspector General may have access to the provider's disclosure and may still impose sanctions under the Anti-Kickback Statute or False Claims Act because the SRDP settlement does not release liability under those statutes; documentation requirements could lead to charges under false statement, obstruction of justice, and other laws; and no appeals are available of CMS's resolution under the SRDP. For an analysis of the shortcomings of the SRDP and proposals for improving the process, see Jean Wright Veilleux, Catching Flies with Vinegar: A Critique of the Centers for Medicare and Medicaid Self-Disclosure Program, 22 Health Matrix 169 (2011).

For a variety of reasons, the Stark Law was traditionally thought to apply only to referrals for Medicare services, but some ambiguity persisted about the relationship between Stark and Medicaid. In the past decade, *qui tam* relators, the Department of Justice, and courts have begun to apply the Stark Law to Medicaid claims, which has further heightened confusion. See U.S. ex rel. Baklid-Kunz v. Halifax Hospital Medical Center, 2012 WL 5415108 (M.D. Fla. 2012), U.S. ex rel. Parikh v. Citizens Med. Ctr., 977 F. Supp. 2d 654 (S.D. Tex. 2013); U.S. ex rel. Schubert v. All Children's Health System, 2013 WL 6054803 (M.D. Fla. 2013). These cases addressed the issue at the motion-to-dismiss phase and have not been appealed, and thus do not completely resolve the question. Nevertheless, the industry views these cases as a signal that plaintiffs may increasingly (and successfully) assert Stark Law violations based on Medicaid claims. Applying Stark to Medicaid substantially broadens the scope of compliance, auditing, and potential liability for providers and brings providers that serve more Medicaid patients than Medicare (such as children's hospitals) into the sweep of Stark Law's complex proscriptions.

A. STARK LAW: STATUTE AND REGULATIONS

42 U.S.C. § 1395nn

(a) Prohibitions of certain referrals

(1) In general. Except as provided in subsection (b), if a physician (or an immediate family member of such physician) has a financial relationship with an entity specified in paragraph (2), then—

(A) the physician may not make a referral to the entity for the furnishing of designated health services for which payment otherwise may be made under this subchapter, and

(B) the entity may not present or cause to be presented a claim under this subchapter or bill to any individual, third party payor, or other entity for designated health services furnished pursuant to a referral prohibited under subparagraph (A)

(2) Financial relationship specified. For purposes of this section, a financial relationship of a physician (or an immediate family member of such physician) with an entity specified in this paragraph is—

(A) except as provided in subsections (c) and (d) of this section, an ownership or investment interest in the entity, or

(B) except as provided in subsection (e) of this section, a compensation arrangement (as defined in subsection (h)(1) of this section) between the physician (or an immediate family member of such physician) and the entity.

An ownership or investment interest described in subparagraph (A) may be through equity, debt, or other means and includes an interest in an entity that holds an ownership or investment interest in any entity providing the designated health service.

42 C.F.R. § 411.351—DEFINITIONS

* * * *Commercially reasonable* means that the particular arrangement furthers a legitimate business purpose of the parties to the arrangement and is sensible, considering the characteristics of the parties, including their size, type, scope, and specialty. An arrangement may be commercially reasonable even if it does not result in profit for one or more of the parties.

* * *

Designated health services (DHS) means any of the following services (other than those provided as emergency physician services furnished outside of the U.S.), as they are defined in this section:

(1)(i) Clinical laboratory services.

(ii)   Physical therapy, occupational therapy, and outpatient speech-language pathology services.

(iii)   Radiology and certain other imaging services.

(iv)   Radiation therapy services and supplies.

(v)   Durable medical equipment and supplies.

(vi)   Parenteral and enteral nutrients, equipment, and supplies.

(vii)   Prosthetics, orthotics, and prosthetic devices and supplies.

(viii) Home health services.

(ix)   Outpatient prescription drugs.

(x)   Inpatient and outpatient hospital services.

(2)   Except as otherwise noted in this subpart, the term "designated health services" or DHS means only DHS payable, in whole or in part, by Medicare. [DHS do not include SNF Part A services or ASC services. DHS also excludes services furnished in hospital inpatients if the service does not increase the hospital's Medicare payment under any of the Medicare prospective payment systems.]

* * *

Entity means—(1) A physician's sole practice or a practice of multiple physicians or any other person, sole proprietorship, public or private agency or trust, corporation, partnership, limited liability company, foundation, nonprofit corporation, or unincorporated association that furnishes DHS. An entity does not include the referring physician himself or herself, but does include his or her medical practice. A person or entity is considered to be furnishing DHS if it—

(i)   Is the person or entity that has performed services that are billed as DHS; or

(ii)   Is the person or entity that has presented a claim to Medicare for the DHS . . .

* * *

Fair market value means—

(1)   *General.* The value in an arm's-length transaction, consistent with the general market value of the subject transaction.

(2)   *Rental of equipment.* With respect to the rental of equipment, the value in an arm's-length transaction of rental property for general commercial purposes (not taking into account its intended use), consistent with the general market value of the subject transaction.

(3)   *Rental of office space.* With respect to the rental of office space, the value in an arm's-length transaction of rental property for general

commercial purposes (not taking into account its intended use), without adjustment to reflect the additional value the prospective lessee or lessor would attribute to the proximity or convenience to the lessor where the lessor is a potential source of patient referrals to the lessee, and consistent with the general market value of the subject transaction.

General market value means—

(1) *Assets.* With respect to the purchase of an asset, the price that an asset would bring on the date of acquisition of the asset as the result of bona fide bargaining between a well-informed buyer and seller that are not otherwise in a position to generate business for each other.

(2) *Compensation.* With respect to compensation for services, the compensation that would be paid at the time the parties enter into the service arrangement as the result of bona fide bargaining between well-informed parties that are not otherwise in a position to generate business for each other.

(3) *Rental of equipment or office space.* With respect to the rental of equipment or the rental of office space, the price that rental property would bring at the time the parties enter into the rental arrangement as the result of bona fide bargaining between a well-informed lessor and lessee that are not otherwise in a position to generate business for each other.

* * *

Referral—(1)   Means either of the following:

(i)   Except as provided in paragraph (2) of this definition, the request by a physician for, or ordering of, or the certifying or recertifying of the need for, any designated health service for which payment may be made under Medicare Part B, including a request for a consultation with another physician and any test or procedure ordered by or to be performed by (or under the supervision of) that other physician, but not including any designated health service personally performed or provided by the referring physician. A designated health service is not personally performed or provided by the referring physician if it is performed or provided by any other person, including, but not limited to, the referring physician's employees, independent contractors, or group practice members.

(ii) Except as provided in paragraph (2) of this definition, a request by a physician that includes the provision of any designated health service for which payment may be made under Medicare, the establishment of a plan of care by a physician that includes the provision of such a designated health service, or the certifying or recertifying of the need for such a designated health service, but not including any designated health service personally performed or provided by the referring physician. A designated health service is not personally performed or provided by the referring physician if it is performed or provided by any other person including, but not limited to, the referring physician's employees, independent contractors, or group practice members.

(2) [Sets forth an exception for certain requests by pathologists, radiologists, and radiation oncologists.]

(3) Can be in any form, including, but not limited to, written, oral, or electronic.

(4) A referral is not an item or service for purposes of section 1877 of the Act and this subpart.

* * *

42 C.F.R. § 411.354—FINANCIAL RELATIONSHIP, COMPENSATION, AND OWNERSHIP OR INVESTMENT INTEREST

(a) *Financial relationships.*

(1) *Financial relationship* means—

(i) A direct or indirect ownership or investment interest (as defined in paragraph (b) of this section) in any entity that furnishes DHS; or

(ii) A direct or indirect compensation arrangement (as defined in paragraph (c) of this section) with an entity that furnishes DHS.

(2) *Types of financial relationships.*

(i) A *direct* financial relationship exists if remuneration passes between the referring physician (or a member of his or her immediate family) and the entity furnishing DHS without any intervening persons or entities between the entity furnishing DHS and the referring physician (or a member of his or her immediate family).

(ii) An *indirect* financial relationship exists under the conditions described in paragraphs (b)(5) and (c)(2) of this section.

(a) *Ownership or investment interest.* An ownership or investment interest in the entity may be through equity, debt, or other means, and includes an interest in an entity that holds an ownership or investment interest in any entity that furnishes DHS. . . .

(b) *Compensation arrangement.* A compensation arrangement is any arrangement involving remuneration, direct or indirect, between a physician (or a member of a physician's immediate family) and an entity. . . .

(1)(i) A direct compensation arrangement exists if remuneration passes between the referring physician (or a member of his or her immediate family) and the entity furnishing DHS without any intervening persons or entities.

(ii) Except as provided in paragraph (c)(3)(ii)(C) of this section, a physician is deemed to "stand in the shoes" of his or her physician organization and have a direct compensation arrangement with an entity furnishing DHS if—

(A) The only intervening entity between the physician and the entity furnishing DHS is his or her physician organization; and

(B) The physician has an ownership or investment interest in the physician organization.

(iii) A physician (other than a physician described in paragraph (c)(1)(ii)(B) of this section) is permitted to "stand in the shoes" of his or her physician organization and have a direct compensation arrangement with an entity furnishing DHS if the only intervening entity between the physician and the entity furnishing DHS is his or her physician organization.

(2) An *indirect compensation arrangement* exists if all of the conditions of paragraphs (c)(2)(i) through (iii) of this section exist:

(i) Between the referring physician (or a member of his or her immediate family) and the entity furnishing DHS there exists an unbroken chain of any number (but not fewer than one) of persons or entities that have financial relationships (as defined in paragraph (a) of this section) between them (that is, each link in the chain has either an ownership or investment interest or a compensation arrangement with the preceding link);

(ii)(A) The referring physician (or immediate family member) receives aggregate compensation from the person or entity in the chain with which the physician (or immediate family member) has a direct financial relationship that varies with the volume or value of referrals or other business generated by the referring physician for the entity furnishing the DHS, and the individual unit of compensation received by physician (or immediate family member)—

(1) Is not fair market value for items or services actually provided;

(2) Includes the physician's referrals to the entity furnishing DHS as a variable, resulting in an increase or decrease in the physician's (or immediate family member's) compensation that positively correlates with the number or value of the physician's referrals to the entity; or

(3) Includes other business generated by the physician for the entity furnishing DHS as a variable, resulting in an increase

or decrease in the physician's (or immediate family member's) compensation that positively correlates with the physician's generation of other business for the entity.

(B) For purposes of applying paragraph (c)(2)(ii)(A) of this section, a positive correlation between two variables exists when one variable decreases as the other variable decreases, or one variable increases as the other variable increases.

(C) If the financial relationship between the physician (or immediate family member) and the person or entity in the chain with which the referring physician (or immediate family member) has a direct financial relationship is an ownership or investment interest, the determination whether the aggregate compensation varies with the volume or value of referrals or other business generated by the referring physician for the entity furnishing the DHS will be measured by the nonownership or noninvestment interest closest to the referring physician (or immediate family member). (For example, if a referring physician has an ownership interest in company A, which owns company B, which has a compensation arrangement with company C, which has a compensation arrangement with entity D that furnishes DHS, we would look to the aggregate compensation between company B and company C for purposes of this paragraph (c)(2)(ii)).

(iii) The entity furnishing DHS has actual knowledge of, or acts in reckless disregard or deliberate ignorance of, the fact that the referring physician (or immediate family member) receives aggregate compensation that varies with the volume or value of referrals or other business generated by the referring physician for the entity furnishing the DHS.

(iv)(A) For purposes of paragraph (c)(2)(i) of this section, except as provided in paragraph (c)(3)(ii)(C) of this section, a physician is deemed to "stand in the shoes" of his or her physician organization if the physician has an ownership or investment interest in the physician organization.

(B) For purposes of paragraph (c)(2)(i) of this section, a physician (other than a physician described in paragraph (c)(2)(iv)(A) of this section) is permitted to "stand in the shoes" of his or her physician organization.

(3)(i) For purposes of paragraphs (c)(1)(ii) and (c)(2)(iv) of this section, a physician who "stands in the shoes" of his or her physician organization is deemed to have the same compensation arrangements (with the same parties and on the same terms) as the physician organization. . .

. . .

(d) *Special rules on compensation.* The following special rules apply only to compensation under section 1877 of the Act and subpart J of this part:

(1) *Set in advance.*

(i) Compensation is deemed to be "set in advance" if the aggregate compensation, a time-based or per-unit of service-based (whether per-use or per-service) amount, or a specific formula for calculating the compensation is set out in writing before the furnishing of the items, services, office space, or equipment for which the compensation is to be paid. The formula for determining the compensation must be set forth in sufficient detail so that it can be objectively verified.

(ii) Notwithstanding paragraph (d)(1)(i) of this section, compensation (or a formula for determining the compensation) may be modified at any time during the course of a compensation arrangement and satisfy the requirement that it is "set in advance" if all of the following conditions are met:

(A) All requirements of an applicable exception in §§ 411.355 through 411.357 are met on the effective date of the modified compensation (or the formula for determining the modified compensation).

(B) The modified compensation (or the formula for determining the modified compensation) is determined before the furnishing of the items, services, office space, or equipment for which the modified compensation is to be paid.

(C) Before the furnishing of the items, services, office space, or equipment for which the modified compensation is to be paid, the formula for the modified compensation is set forth in writing in sufficient detail so that it can be objectively verified. Paragraph (e)(4) of this section [regarding writing and signature requirements] does not apply for purposes of this paragraph (d)(1)(ii)(C).

[Paragraphs (d)(2) and (3) set forth rules for unit-based compensation, such as time-based or per-unit of service-based compensation. Paragraph (d)(4) sets forth rules for directed referrals, where physician compensation can be conditioned upon the physician's referrals to certain practitioners, providers, or suppliers.]

(5) *Compensation to a physician.*

(i) Compensation from an entity furnishing designated health services to a physician (or immediate family member of the physician) takes into account the volume or value of referrals only if the formula used to calculate the physician's (or immediate family member's) compensation includes the physician's referrals to the entity as a variable, resulting in an increase or decrease in the physician's (or immediate family member's) compensation that positively correlates with the number or value of the physician's referrals to the entity.

. . .

(iii) For purposes of applying this paragraph (d)(5), a positive correlation between two variables exists when one variable decreases as the other variable decreases, or one variable increases as the other variable increases.

[Paragraph (d)(6) discusses special rules for compensation *from* a physician to an entity for the furnishing of designated health services.]

(e) *Special rule on compensation arrangements*—

(1) *Application.* This paragraph (e) applies only to compensation arrangements as defined in section 1877 of the Act and this subpart.

(2) *Writing requirement.* In the case of any requirement in this subpart for a compensation arrangement to be in writing, such requirement may be satisfied by a collection of documents, including contemporaneous documents evidencing the course of conduct between the parties.

(3) *Signature requirement.* In the case of any signature requirement in this subpart, such requirement may be satisfied by an electronic or other signature that is valid under applicable Federal or State law.

(4) *Special rule on writing and signature requirements.* In the case of any requirement in this subpart for a compensation arrangement to be in writing and signed by the parties, the writing requirement or the signature requirement is satisfied if—

(i) The compensation arrangement between the entity and the physician fully complies with an applicable exception in this subpart except with respect to the writing or signature requirement of the exception; and

(ii) The parties obtain the required writing(s) or signature(s) within 90 consecutive calendar days immediately following the date on which the compensation arrangement became noncompliant with the requirements of the applicable exception (that is, the date on which the writing(s) or signature(s) were required under the applicable exception but the parties had not yet obtained them).

NOTES AND QUESTIONS

1. *Complexity and the Stark Law.* If the statute and regulations appear complex, you are not mistaken. And the regulations are only the beginning. Practitioners must also analyze hundreds of pages of agency commentary that

interprets and explains the law. Stark Law regulations have come in phases, starting with Phase I in 1995, 60 Fed. Reg. 41,914 (Aug. 14, 1995), Phase II in 2004, 69 Fed. Reg. 15,932 (Mar. 26, 2004), Phase III in 2007, 72 Fed. Reg. 51012 (Sept. 5, 2007). Though not called another "phase," CMS issued significant modifications and additions to the Stark rules in December 2020 as part of HHS's Regulatory Sprint to Coordinated Care. 85 Fed. Reg. 77492 (Dec. 2, 2020).

Each wave of regulations offered clarifications, new exceptions, and volumes of preamble commentary by CMS explaining its thinking about these regulations. Strong criticisms have been lodged against the Stark Law. Organized medicine argues that the law is too complex and needlessly duplicative of other laws affecting self-referrals. Moreover, to the extent that similar conduct is sanctioned under both the Stark Law and the Anti-Kickback Statute (and all of it can form the basis of a False Claims Act case), providers are rightly concerned about the regulatory and compliance burden that comes from the law's inordinate complexity, strict liability, and onerous penalties. On the other side, the law has been defended as a pragmatic legislative choice that avoids the pitfalls of case-by-case litigation over issues of intent or reasonableness while unambiguously barring the most risk-prone referrals and permitting most efficiency-enhancing arrangements. For legal practitioners, it is also a source of much sought-after legal advice and analysis.

2.   *The 2020 Stark Rules*. In 2020, CMS issued significant rule changes to the Stark Law, 85 Fed. Reg. 77492 (Dec. 2, 2020) in coordination with OIG's rulemaking on the Anti-Kickback Statute discussed in Section II, above. The 2020 Stark rules added or broadened several Stark exceptions to facilitate the move to value-based payment models. The 2020 rules also modified several of Stark's regulatory definitions to accommodate the new exceptions and provide greater flexibility and clarity to providers, reflected in the excerpts above. For instance, the rules newly define "commercially reasonable" (42 C.F.R. § 411.351), clarify the definition of "fair market value," and define a standard for the "volume or value of referrals" (Id. at § 411.354(d)(5)) to decouple the volume/value requirement from the fair market value calculation, which had been muddied by various court opinions. Thus, under the new standards, an entity's payment of a fixed salary to a physician will comply with the volume or value standard, even if the compensation is above fair market value, so long as the formula for compensation doesn't include the physician's referrals as a variable or rise or fall with the volume or value of those referrals. In addition, the 2020 rules loosen the writing and signature requirements present in several Stark exceptions, allowing additional time to comply with the requirement (Id. at § 411.354(e)).

For many years, the Stark rules have been criticized for their harshness and complexity, particularly as courts have narrowly construed the rules' strict or ambiguous requirements. The 2020 changes address (but do not eliminate) some of these criticisms, clarify ambiguous terms, and adapt to health care payment models focusing on value instead of quantity. The American Health

Lawyers Association and most major health law firm have published copious analyses and helpful redline comparisons of the new rules.

3. *Indirect Compensation Relationships and "Stand in the Shoes."* Two particularly illustrative examples of the Stark Law's regulatory complexity include the definition of an **indirect compensation arrangement** and the application of the requirement that physicians **"stand in the shoes" (SITS)** of their physician organization. Under the regulations excerpted above, an indirect compensation arrangement exists when: (i) there is an unbroken chain of financial relationships between a referring physician and the DHS entity; (ii) the referring physician receives aggregate compensation that varies with the volume or value of referrals or other business generated by the referring physician to the DHS entity and the individual unit of compensation (a) is not fair market value; or (b) includes the physician's referrals to or other business generated for the DHS entity as a variable, resulting in an increase or decrease in the physician's compensation that positively correlates with the number or value of the physician's referrals; and (iii) the DHS entity knows or is recklessly indifferent to the fact that the physician's aggregate compensation varies in this way. Note that when determining whether the physician's aggregate compensation varies with or takes into account the volume or value of referrals, you look to the compensation arrangement (non-ownership interest) closest to the referring physician. 42 C.F.R. § 411.354(c)(2). In 2020, CMS modified the definition of indirect compensation arrangement with an eye to reducing the number of arrangements subject to the Stark Law.

Significantly, if a multi-tiered arrangement does not meet this definition of an indirect compensation arrangement, then there is no financial relationship, and *the Stark Law does not apply*. In particular, an arrangement could escape Stark entirely if there were two or more links between the physician and the DHS entity, and the aggregate compensation in the compensation arrangement closest to the referring physician did not vary with the volume or value of referrals or other business generated between the referring physician and the DHS entity. This formula created a significant loophole—physicians could simply contract via their physician practices to escape Stark. For instance, if the referring physician was an owner of the medical practice that contracted with a hospital to provide medical director services for $10,000 a month, the compensation arrangement closest to the referring physician (the medical director arrangement) did not vary with or otherwise reflect the volume or value of referrals or other business generated between the parties even if it was not fair market value. In the absence of a direct or indirect financial relationship, the Stark Law simply did not apply, and the parties did not need to meet any exception.

Believing that many arrangements were structured between a physician practice and a DHS entity to take advantage of this loophole, CMS included in the 2007 Phase III Stark Law rules a requirement that physicians "stand in the shoes" (SITS) of their physician organization (i.e., a physician practice, group practice, physician sole proprietorship, or wholly-owned professional corporation) in which they have an ownership or investment interest, so that the physicians are deemed to have all the same financial relationships that their practice does. In the hypothetical arrangement above, the application of the SITS requirement creates a direct financial relationship between a physician and a DHS entity if the only intervening entity between the two is a physician organization. Thus, in the hypothetical above, the physician owner would stand in the shoes of the group, and the medical director agreement would have to satisfy the requirements of a Stark exception.

For Stark Law purposes, CMS treats an agreement between a DHS entity and a physician group practice as if the agreement were between the DHS entity and each individual physician owners of the group practice. The SITS rule is only required of physicians with an ownership or investment interest in the physician organization. A physician who is not an owner of a physician organization, such as an employed physician or an independent contractor, may but need not stand in the shoes of the physician organization. 73 Fed. Reg. 48,434 (Aug. 19, 2008).

4.   *Analytic Framework.* Owing to the Stark Law's complexity, it is helpful to identify an analytic framework for analyzing Stark Law issues. Luckily, the framework itself is fairly straightforward:

> First, is there a financial relationship between the referring physician and a DHS entity? (a) Is it an ownership or compensation arrangement? (b) Is it direct or indirect?

> Second, if there is a financial relationship, does the arrangement meet all the requirements of an applicable exception? Exceptions are codified at 42 C.F.R. §§ 411.355 to .357.

In essence, the first question asks whether the Stark Law applies to the arrangement at all. If it doesn't, then there is no need to look for an exception. However, if the Stark Law does apply, then the arrangement must meet all the requirements of an applicable exception, discussed in the next subsection.

B. STARK EXCEPTIONS

The Stark Law is an example of what is sometimes called an "exceptions bill." It sweepingly prohibits self-referrals but then legitimizes a large number of specific arrangements. Stark's exceptions are of three kinds: (1) those applicable to ownership or investment financial relationships; (2) those applicable to compensation arrangements; and (3) exceptions that apply to all financial arrangements. 42 C.F.R. §§ 411.355 to 411.357.

Unlike the Anti-Kickback Statute safe harbors (discussed in Section II, above), an arrangement must strictly satisfy all the requirements of a Stark Law exception or else it is illegal. There is no "totality of the facts and circumstances" analysis that will save a noncompliant arrangement from violating the Stark Law.

Although the exceptions vary considerably, there are common themes among them. First is the requirement that physician compensation cannot **"vary with or take into account the volume or value of referrals"** between the parties. Second are the requirements that compensation be **"fair market value"** and **"commercially reasonable."** These concepts are interrelated and often the subject of litigation, as we will see in the *Tuomey* case, discussed below.

When evaluating an arrangement for compliance with the Stark Law, practitioners should refer to the following sources:

- First, the **Stark regulations** (42 C.F.R. § 411.350 et seq.) and the voluminous **preamble commentary** that accompanied the publication of the major phases of rulemaking in the Federal Register. On its website, CMS has compiled a list of the Significant Regulatory History under the Stark Law, with links to the Federal Register publications for each rulemaking.

- Second, CMS guidance in the form of **CMS Advisory Opinions** and **Frequently Asked Questions**, also available on the CMS website. Unlike the dozens of advisory opinions issued by OIG every year on the Anti-Kickback Statute and CMP law, however, CMS issues advisory opinions much more infrequently.

- Third are **cases** interpreting the Stark Law. Frequently, these are False Claims Act cases where the false claims are bills that were illegally submitted to Medicare for services referred in violation of the Stark Law.

The 2020 rule changes under the Stark Law created new exceptions and modified several exceptions in response to industry concerns that value-based arrangements, such as quality incentives and pay-for-performance models, would not be protected by existing exceptions. Like the corresponding Anti-Kickback safe harbors, the 2020 Stark rules created a new exception for **"value-based arrangements,"** which applies to providers who offer at least one value-based activity for a target patient population that reduces costs and/or improves the quality of care for that target population. 42 C.F.R. § 411.357(aa). This exception imposes fewer requirements on providers as they assume more financial risk, and significantly, it does not require that compensation be fair market value or prohibit payment based on the volume and value of referrals. Other existing compensation exceptions were broadened to protect more arrangements. For example, the fair market value compensation exception would be expanded to include arrangements for the rental of office space or equipment for a term of less than a year.

The updated regulatory text of several of the most commonly used Stark Law compensation arrangement exceptions are excerpted below. Some of the key terms used in the exceptions, such as "fair market value," "commercially reasonable," the "volume or value" standard, or "set in advance" are defined in the excerpted regulations above.

42 C.F.R. § 411.357—EXCEPTIONS TO THE REFERRAL PROHIBITION RELATED TO COMPENSATION ARRANGEMENTS

(a) *Rental of office space.* Payments for the use of office space made by a lessee to a lessor if the arrangement meets the following requirements:

(1) The lease arrangement is set out in writing, is signed by the parties, and specifies the premises it covers.

(2) The duration of the lease arrangement is at least 1 year. To meet this requirement, if the lease arrangement is terminated with or without cause, the parties may not enter into a new lease arrangement for the same space during the first year of the original lease arrangement.

(3) The space rented or leased does not exceed that which is reasonable and necessary for the legitimate business purposes of the lease arrangement and is used exclusively by the lessee when being used by the lessee (and is not shared with or used by the lessor or any person or entity related to the lessor), except that the lessee may make payments for the use of space consisting of common areas if the payments do not exceed the lessee's pro rata share of expenses for the space based upon the ratio of the space used exclusively by the lessee to the total amount of space (other than common areas) occupied by all persons using the common areas. For purposes of this paragraph (a), exclusive use means that the lessee (and any other lessees of the same office space) uses the office space to the exclusion of the lessor (or any person or entity related to the lessor). The lessor (or any person or entity related to the lessor) may not be an invitee of the lessee to use the office space.

(4) The rental charges over the term of the lease arrangement are set in advance and are consistent with fair market value.

(5) The rental charges over the term of the lease arrangement are not determined—

   (i) In any manner that takes into account the volume or value of referrals or other business generated between the parties; or

   (ii) Using a formula based on—

      (A) A percentage of the revenue raised, earned, billed, collected, or otherwise attributable to the services performed or business generated in the office space; or

      (B) Per-unit of service rental charges, to the extent that such charges reflect services provided to patients referred by the lessor to the lessee.

(6) The lease arrangement would be commercially reasonable even if no referrals were made between the lessee and the lessor.

(7) If the lease arrangement expires after a term of at least 1 year, a holdover lease arrangement immediately following the expiration of the lease arrangement satisfies the requirements of paragraph (a) of this section if the following conditions are met:

(i) The lease arrangement met the conditions of paragraphs (a)(1) through (6) of this section when the arrangement expired;

(ii) The holdover lease arrangement is on the same terms and conditions as the immediately preceding arrangement; and

(iii) The holdover lease arrangement continues to satisfy the conditions of paragraphs (a)(1) through (6) of this section.

(b) *Rental of equipment.* Payments made by a lessee to a lessor for the use of equipment under the following conditions:

(1) The lease arrangement is set out in writing, is signed by the parties, and specifies the equipment it covers.

(2) The equipment leased does not exceed that which is reasonable and necessary for the legitimate business purposes of the lease arrangement and is used exclusively by the lessee when being used by the lessee (and is not shared with or used by the lessor or any person or entity related to the lessor). For purposes of this paragraph (b), exclusive use means that the lessee (and any other lessees of the same equipment) uses the equipment to the exclusion of the lessor (or any person or entity related to the lessor). The lessor (or any person or entity related to the lessor) may not be an invitee of the lessee to use the equipment.

(3) The duration of the lease arrangement is at least 1 year. To meet this requirement, if the lease arrangement is terminated with or without cause, the parties may not enter into a new lease arrangement for the same equipment during the first year of the original lease arrangement.

(4) The rental charges over the term of the lease arrangement are set in advance, are consistent with fair market value, and are not determined—

(i) In any manner that takes into account the volume or value of referrals or other business generated between the parties; or

(ii) Using a formula based on—

(A) A percentage of the revenue raised, earned, billed, collected, or otherwise attributable to the services performed on or business generated through the use of the equipment; or

(B) Per-unit of service rental charges, to the extent that such charges reflect services provided to patients referred by the lessor to the lessee.

(5) The lease arrangement would be commercially reasonable even if no referrals were made between the parties.

(6) If the lease arrangement expires after a term of at least 1 year, a holdover lease arrangement immediately following the expiration of the lease arrangement satisfies the requirements of this paragraph (b) if the following conditions are met:

　　(i) The lease arrangement met the conditions of paragraphs (b)(1) through (5) of this section when the arrangement expired;

　　(ii) The holdover lease arrangement is on the same terms and conditions as the immediately preceding lease arrangement; and

　　(iii) The holdover lease arrangement continues to satisfy the conditions of paragraphs (b)(1) through (5) of this section.

(c) *Bona fide employment relationships.* Any amount paid by an employer to a physician (or immediate family member) who has a *bona fide* employment relationship with the employer for the provision of services if the following conditions are met:

(1) The employment is for identifiable services.

(2) The amount of the remuneration under the employment is—

　　(i) Consistent with the fair market value of the services; and

　　(ii) Except as provided in paragraph (c)(4) of this section, is not determined in any manner that takes into account the volume or value of referrals by the referring physician.

(3) The remuneration is provided under an arrangement that would be commercially reasonable even if no referrals were made to the employer.

(4) Paragraph (c)(2)(ii) of this section does not prohibit payment of remuneration in the form of a productivity bonus based on services performed personally by the physician (or immediate family member of the physician).

(5) If remuneration to the physician is conditioned on the physician's referrals to a particular provider, practitioner, or supplier, the arrangement satisfies the conditions of § 411.354(d)(4).

(d) *Personal service arrangements.* (1) *General.* Remuneration from an entity under an arrangement or multiple arrangements to a physician or his or her immediate family member, or to a group practice, including remuneration for specific physician services furnished to a nonprofit blood center, if the following conditions are met:

　　(i) Each arrangement is set out in writing, is signed by the parties, and specifies the services covered by the arrangement.

(ii) Except for services provided under an arrangement that satisfies all of the conditions of paragraph (z) of this section, the arrangement(s) covers all of the services to be furnished by the physician (or an immediate family member of the physician) to the entity. This requirement is met if all separate arrangements between the entity and the physician and the entity and any family members incorporate each other by reference or if they cross-reference a master list of contracts that is maintained and updated centrally and is available for review by the Secretary upon request. The master list must be maintained in a manner that preserves the historical record of contracts. A physician or family member may "furnish" services through employees whom they have hired for the purpose of performing the services; through a wholly-owned entity; or through *locum tenens* physicians (as defined at § 411.351, except that the regular physician need not be a member of a group practice).

(iii) The aggregate services covered by the arrangement do not exceed those that are reasonable and necessary for the legitimate business purposes of the arrangement(s).

(iv) The duration of each arrangement is at least 1 year. To meet this requirement, if an arrangement is terminated with or without cause, the parties may not enter into the same or substantially the same arrangement during the first year of the original arrangement.

(v) The compensation to be paid over the term of each arrangement is set in advance, does not exceed fair market value, and, except in the case of a physician incentive plan (as defined at § 411.351), is not determined in any manner that takes into account the volume or value of referrals or other business generated between the parties.

(vi) The services to be furnished under each arrangement do not involve the counseling or promotion of a business arrangement or other activity that violates any Federal or State law.

(vii) If the arrangement expires after a term of at least 1 year, a holdover arrangement immediately following the expiration of the arrangement satisfies the requirements of paragraph (d) of this section if the following conditions are met:

  (A) The arrangement met the conditions of paragraphs (d)(1)(i) through (vi) of this section when the arrangement expired;

  (B) The holdover arrangement is on the same terms and conditions as the immediately preceding arrangement; and

  (C) The holdover arrangement continues to satisfy the conditions of paragraphs (d)(1)(i) through (vi) of this section.

(viii) If remuneration to the physician is conditioned on the physician's referrals to a particular provider, practitioner, or supplier, the arrangement satisfies the conditions of § 411.354(d)(4).

* * *

(*l*) *Fair market value compensation.* Compensation resulting from an arrangement between an entity and a physician (or an immediate family member) or any group of physicians (regardless of whether the group meets the definition of a group practice set forth in § 411.352) for the provision of items or services or for the lease of office space or equipment by the physician (or an immediate family member) or group of physicians to the entity, or by the entity to the physician (or an immediate family member) or a group of physicians, if the arrangement meets the following conditions:

(1) The arrangement is in writing, signed by the parties, and covers only identifiable items, services, office space, or equipment. The writing specifies—

(i) The items, services, office space, or equipment covered under the arrangement;

(ii) The compensation that will be provided under the arrangement; and

(iii) The timeframe for the arrangement.

(2) An arrangement may be for any period of time and contain a termination clause. An arrangement may be renewed any number of times if the terms of the arrangement and the compensation for the same items, services, office space, or equipment do not change. Other than an arrangement that satisfies all of the conditions of paragraph (z) of this section, the parties may not enter into more than one arrangement for the same items, services, office space, or equipment during the course of a year.

(3) The compensation must be set in advance, consistent with fair market value, and not determined in any manner that takes into account the volume or value of referrals or other business generated by the referring physician. Compensation for the rental of office space or equipment may not be determined using a formula based on—

(i) A percentage of the revenue raised, earned, billed, collected, or otherwise attributable to the services performed or business generated in the office space or to the services performed on or business generated through the use of the equipment; or

(ii) Per-unit of service rental charges, to the extent that such charges reflect services provided to patients referred by the lessor to the lessee.

(4) The arrangement would be commercially reasonable even if no referrals were made between the parties.

(5) The arrangement does not violate the anti-kickback statute (section 1128B(b) of the Act).

(6) The services to be performed under the arrangement do not involve the counseling or promotion of a business arrangement or other activity that violates a Federal or State law.

(7) The arrangement satisfies the requirements of § 411.354(d)(4) in the case of—

(i) Remuneration to the physician that is conditioned on the physician's referrals to a particular provider, practitioner, or supplier; or

(ii) Remuneration paid to the group of physicians that is conditioned on one or more of the group's physicians' referrals to a particular provider, practitioner, or supplier.

NOTES AND QUESTIONS

1. *Rules Reducing Risk for Technical "Foot Fault" Violations.* In 2015, CMS published the Medicare Physician Fee Schedule Final Rule, which included a number of provisions relaxing technical requirements of the Stark Law that have ensnared many physician arrangements. 80 Fed. Reg. 70,886, 71,300–71,341 (Nov. 16, 2015). For example, many of the compensation arrangement exceptions require that the arrangement be set forth in writing, signed by the parties, that compensation be set in advance, and the arrangement have a term of at least one-year. Thus, common instances of "technical noncompliance" included lacking a written agreement, missing or late signatures, expired agreements, or failure to include a term of at least a year in the agreement. Because of the strictness of the Stark Law, these "foot faults" meant the whole arrangement was noncompliant, tainting any referrals and bills arising between the parties to the arrangement, even though an enforceable agreement between the parties may exist under state contract law. The 2015 rules provided some relief and flexibility to certain common forms of technical noncompliance as follows:

- Clarifying that the "in writing" requirement of certain exceptions (e.g., for space leases, equipment leases, and personal services) need not be a formal contractual agreement, but can be satisfied by "a collection of documents, including contemporaneous documents evidencing the course of conduct between the parties."

- Clarifying that arrangements previously required to have a "term" of at least one year term will be satisfied if the actual duration of the arrangement is at least one year, even if there is no written agreement provision specifying a term of at least one year.

- Allows parties a 90-day grace period to obtain missing signatures (expanding from a previous 30-day grace period). The 2020 rules extended the 90-day grace period to the writing requirement and clarified that an electronic signature satisfies the signature requirement.

- Extending indefinitely (up from 6-months) the protection for "holdover" arrangements that continue to abide by the same terms (e.g., compensation) of a prior written arrangement and that continue to be compliant with all the elements of an applicable exception over time (e.g., fair market value), from a six-month holdover.

2. *Fair Market Value*. The term **"fair market value" (FMV)** is defined for Stark Law purposes at 42 C.F.R. § 411.351 (excerpted above). A consistent requirement of the Stark exceptions, the concept of FMV compensation is critical for assessing a health care arrangement's compliance with the Stark Law. The definition relies on the notion that FMV is the amount that results from well-informed parties' arm's-length negotiations when the parties are not in a position to generate business for each other.

Due to the central importance of FMV, an industry of valuation consultants, experts, and physician salary and compensation surveys has developed to assist with the weighty task of determining FMV. Of note, it is generally *not* the role of attorneys advising on a health care arrangement to calculate or determine FMV, but attorneys typically are involved in retaining valuation consultants or evaluating valuation reports, both to protect such materials within the attorney-client privilege and because valuations have such significance to the overall compliance of the arrangement. As the *Tuomey* case below illustrates, the concept of FMV is slippery; what evidence does a court evaluate to determine whether a particular compensation arrangement is FMV?

3. *The COVID-19 Pandemic and the Stark Law*. The declarations of a public health emergency on January 31, 2020 by the Secretary of HHS and a national emergency by the President on March 13, 2020 triggered § 1135 of the Social Security Act, which authorizes the Secretary of HHS to waive or modify certain requirements of Medicare, Medicaid, CHIP, and HIPAA. Pursuant to this authority, on March 30, 2020, the Secretary of HHS issued blanket waivers of the Stark Law, temporarily suspending the applicability of the Stark Law sanctions to certain arrangements that are "solely related to COVID-19 Purposes." Such purposes include the diagnosis and treatment of COVID-19 or securing practitioners to provide such services or respond to the outbreak. The waivers are retroactive to March 1, 2020, apply nationwide, and remain in effect for the duration of the public health emergency. On April 21, 2020 CMS issued further explanatory guidance on the blanket waivers.

The Stark Law blanket waivers exempted eighteen types of remuneration from sanctions. These include, for example, remuneration from an entity to a physician that is above or below the fair market value for services personally performed by the physician, or referrals by a physician in a group practice for medically necessary DHS furnished by the group practice in a location that does not qualify as a "same building" or "centralized building" under the in-office ancillary services exception. CMS stated that under the blanket waivers, it will "pay claims for designated health services that, but for satisfying the conditions of a blanket waiver, would violate the physician self-referral law." Parties may use the blanket waivers without submission of specific documentation or advance notice to CMS, although records relating to the use of the blanket waivers must be made available to the Secretary upon request. The blanket waivers do not extend to the Anti-Kickback Statute or prevent *qui tam* relators from bringing a suit under the False Claims Act.

STARK LAW PROBLEM: DR. LEE'S LEASE

The Stark Law covers much of the same conduct Anti-Kickback Statute, but Stark has its own exceptions that are worded somewhat differently. How would your analysis of the problem "Dr. Lee's Lease" in Section II, above, change applying the Stark Law exception for rentals of office space (42 C.F.R. § 411.357(a), excerpted above)? Would the provisions relaxing the Stark Law rules for technical "foot-fault" violations, noted above, help Samaritan's situation?

UNITED STATES EX REL. MICHAEL K. DRAKEFORD V. TUOMEY

United States Court of Appeals, Fourth Circuit, 2015.
792 F.3d 364.

DIAZ, CIRCUIT JUDGE:

In a qui tam action in which the government intervened, a jury determined that Tuomey Healthcare System, Inc., did not violate the False Claims Act ("FCA") [ ]. The district court, however, vacated the jury's verdict and granted the government a new trial after concluding that it had erroneously excluded excerpts of a Tuomey executive's deposition testimony. The jury in the second trial found that Tuomey knowingly submitted 21,730 false claims to Medicare for reimbursement. The district court then entered final judgment for the government and awarded damages and civil penalties totaling $237,454,195.

Tuomey contends that the district court erred in granting the government's motion for a new trial. Tuomey also lodges numerous other challenges to the judgment entered against it following the second trial. It argues that it is entitled to judgment as a matter of law (or, in the alternative, yet another new trial) because it did not violate the FCA. In the alternative, Tuomey asks for a new trial because the district court failed to properly instruct the jury. Finally, Tuomey asks us to strike the damages and civil penalties award as either improperly calculated or unconstitutional.

We conclude that the district court correctly granted the government's motion for a new trial, albeit for a reason different than that relied upon by the district court. We also reject Tuomey's claims of error following the second trial. Accordingly, we affirm the district court's judgment.

I

A

Tuomey is a nonprofit hospital located in Sumter, South Carolina, a small, largely rural community that is a federally-designated medically underserved area. At the time of the events leading up to this lawsuit, most of the physicians that practiced at Tuomey were not directly employed by the hospital, but instead were members of independent specialty practices.

Beginning around 2000, doctors who previously performed outpatient surgery at Tuomey began doing so in their own offices or at off-site surgery centers. The loss of this revenue stream was a source of grave concern for Tuomey because it collected substantial facility fees from patients who underwent surgery at the hospital's outpatient center. Tuomey estimated that it stood to lose $8 to $12 million over a thirteen-year period from the loss of fees associated with gastrointestinal procedures alone. To stem this loss, Tuomey sought to negotiate part-time employment contracts with a number of local physicians.

* * *

Beginning in 2003, Tuomey sought the advice of its longtime counsel, Nexsen Pruet, on the Stark Law implications arising from the proposed employment contracts. Nexsen Pruet in turn engaged Cejka Consulting, a national consulting firm that specialized in physician compensation, to provide an opinion concerning the commercial reasonableness and fair market value of the contracts. Tuomey also conferred with Richard Kusserow, a former Inspector General for the United States Department of Health and Human Services, and later, with Steve Pratt, an attorney at Hall Render, a prominent healthcare law firm.

The part-time employment contracts had substantially similar terms. Each physician was paid an annual guaranteed base salary. That salary was adjusted from year to year based on the amount the physician collected from all services rendered the previous year. The bulk of the physicians' compensation was earned in the form of a productivity bonus, which paid the physicians eighty percent of the amount of their collections for that year. The physicians were also eligible for an incentive bonus of up to seven percent of their earned productivity bonus. In addition, Tuomey agreed to pay for the physicians' medical malpractice liability insurance as well as their practice group's share of employment taxes. The physicians were also allowed to participate in Tuomey's health insurance plan. Finally, Tuomey agreed to absorb each practice group's billing and collections costs.

The contracts had ten-year terms, during which physicians could maintain their private practices, but were required to perform outpatient surgical procedures exclusively at the hospital. Physicians could not own any interest in a facility located in Sumter that provided ambulatory surgery services, save for a less-than-two-percent interest in a publicly traded company that provided such services. The physicians also agreed not to perform outpatient surgical procedures within a thirty-mile radius of the hospital for two years after the expiration or termination of the contracts.

Tuomey ultimately entered into part-time employment contracts with nineteen physicians. Tuomey, however, was unable to reach an agreement with Dr. Michael Drakeford, an orthopedic surgeon. Drakeford believed that the proposed contracts violated the Stark Law because the physicians were being paid in excess of their collections. He contended that the compensation package did not reflect fair market value, and thus the government would view it as an unlawful payment for the doctor's facility-fee-generating referrals.

* * *

Unable to break the stalemate in their negotiations, in May 2005, Tuomey and Drakeford sought the advice of Kevin McAnaney, an attorney in private practice with expertise in the Stark Law. McAnaney had formerly served as the Chief of the Industry Guidance Branch of the United States Department of Health and Human Services Office of Counsel to the Inspector General. In that position, McAnaney wrote a "substantial portion" of the regulations implementing the Stark Law.

McAnaney advised the parties that the proposed employment contracts raised significant "red flags" under the Stark Law.[2] [ ] In particular, Tuomey would have serious difficulty persuading the government that the contracts did not compensate the physicians in excess of fair market value. Such a contention, said McAnaney, would not pass the "red face test." [ ] McAnaney also warned Tuomey that the contracts presented "an easy case to prosecute" for the government. [ ]

Drakeford ultimately declined to enter into a contract with Tuomey. He later sued the hospital under the qui tam provisions of the FCA, alleging that because the part-time employment contracts violated the Stark Law, Tuomey had knowingly submitted false claims for payment to Medicare. As was its right, the government intervened in the action and filed additional claims seeking equitable relief for payments made under mistake of fact and unjust enrichment theories.

* * *

---

[2] According to McAnaney, the joint venture alternative raised separate concerns under the Anti-Kickback Statute [ ] which bars "the payment of remuneration for the purpose of inducing the purchase of health care covered by any federal health care insurance program." [ ]

II

A

Tuomey's appeal presents these issues: First, did the district court err in granting the government's motion for a new trial on the FCA claim? If not, did the district court err in (1) denying Tuomey's motion for judgment as a matter of law (or, in the alternative, for yet another new trial) following the second trial; and (2) awarding damages and penalties against Tuomey based on the jury's finding of an FCA violation? We address each issue in turn, but first provide a general overview of the Stark Law.

B

The Stark Law is intended to prevent "overutilization of services by physicians who [stand] to profit from referring patients to facilities or entities in which they [have] a financial interest." [ ] The statute prohibits a physician from making a referral to an entity, such as a hospital, with which he or she has a financial relationship, for the furnishing of designated health services. [ ] If the physician makes such a referral, the hospital may not submit a bill for reimbursement to Medicare. [ ] Similarly, the government may not make any payment for a designated health service provided in violation of the Stark Law. [ ] If a person collects any payment for a service billed in violation of the Stark Law, "the person shall be liable to the individual for, and shall refund on a timely basis to the individual, any amounts so collected." [ ][4]

Inpatient and outpatient hospital services are considered designated health services under the law. [ ] A referral includes "the request by a physician for the item or service." [ ] A referral does not include "any designated health service personally performed or provided by the referring physician." [ ] However, there is a referral when the hospital bills a "facility fee" (also known as a "facility component" or "technical component") "in connection with the personally performed service." [ ]

A financial relationship constitutes a prohibited "indirect compensation arrangement," if (1) "there exists an unbroken chain of any number . . . of persons or entities that have financial relationships . . . between them," (2) "[t]he referring physician . . . receives aggregate compensation . . . that varies with, or takes into account, the volume or value of referrals or other business generated by the referring physician for the entity furnishing" the designated health services, and (3) the entity has knowledge that the compensation so varies. [ ] *see also Drakeford*, 675 F.3d at 408 ("[C]ompensation arrangements that take into account anticipated referrals . . . implicate the volume or value standard."). The statute, however, does not bar indirect compensation arrangements where: (1) the

---

4   Because the Stark Law does not create its own right of action, the government in this case sought relief under the FCA, which provides a right of action with respect to false claims submitted for Medicare reimbursement.

referring physician is compensated at fair market value for "services and items actually provided"; (2) the compensation arrangement is "not determined in any manner that takes into account the volume or value of referrals"; (3) the compensation arrangement is "commercially reasonable"; and (4) the compensation arrangement does not run afoul of any other federal or state law. [ ]

Once a relator or the government has established the elements of a Stark Law violation, it becomes the defendant's burden to show that the indirect compensation arrangement exception shields it from liability. [ ]

* * *

III

We turn now to Tuomey's challenges to the judgment entered following the second trial. Tuomey asks for judgment as a matter of law because a reasonable jury could not have found that (1) the part-time employment contracts violated the Stark Law, or (2) Tuomey knowingly submitted false claims. Alternatively, Tuomey asks for a new trial because of the district court's refusal to tender certain jury instructions.

* * *

1

Tuomey argues that it is entitled to judgment as a matter of law because the contracts between it and the physicians did not run afoul of the Stark Law. As we explain, however, a reasonable jury could find that Tuomey violated the Stark Law when it paid aggregate compensation to physicians that varied with or took into account the volume or value of actual or anticipated referrals to Tuomey.

To begin with, we note that the Stark Law's "volume or value" standard can be implicated when aggregate compensation varies with the volume or value of referrals, *or* otherwise takes into account the volume or value of referrals. [ ] That is precisely what the district court directed the jury in the second trial to assess. Tuomey insists, however, that our earlier opinion in this case foreclosed the jury's consideration of whether the contracts varied with the volume or value of referrals. Instead, says Tuomey, the *only* question that should have been put to the jury was "whether the contracts, on their face, took into account the value or volume of anticipated referrals." *Drakeford,* 675 F.3d at 409.

We disagree. The district court properly understood that the jury was entitled to pass on the contracts as they were actually implemented by the parties. We said as much in our earlier opinion, where

we emphasize[d] that our holding . . . [was] limited to the issues we specifically address[ed]. On remand, a jury must determine, in light of our holding, whether the aggregate compensation received by the physicians under the contracts *varied with,* or took into account, the volume or value of the facility component referrals.

Id. at 409 n. 26 (emphasis added).

A reasonable jury could have found that Tuomey's contracts in fact compensated the physicians in a manner that varied with the volume or value of referrals. There are two different components of the physicians' compensation that we believe so varied. First, each year, the physicians were paid a base salary that was adjusted upward or downward depending on their collections from the prior year. In addition, the physicians received the bulk of their compensation in the form of a productivity bonus, pegged at eighty percent of the amount of their collections.

As Tuomey concedes, "the aggregate compensation received by the physicians under the Contracts was based solely on collections for personally performed professional services." [ ] And as we noted in our earlier opinion, there are referrals here, "consisting of the facility component of the physicians' personally performed services, and the resulting facility fee billed by Tuomey based upon that component." *Drakeford,* 675 F.3d at 407. In sum, the more procedures the physicians performed at the hospital, the more facility fees Tuomey collected, and the more compensation the physicians received in the form of increased base salaries and productivity bonuses.

The nature of this arrangement was confirmed by Tuomey's former Chief Financial Officer, William Paul Johnson, who admitted "that every time one of the 19 physicians . . . did a legitimate procedure on a Medicare patient at the hospital pursuant to the part-time agreement[,] the doctor [got] more money," and "the hospital also got more money." [ ] We thus think it plain that a reasonable jury could find that the physicians' compensation varied with the volume or value of actual referrals. The district court did not err in denying Tuomey's motion for judgment as a matter of law on this ground.[10]

---

[10] We are not persuaded by Tuomey's reliance on commentary promulgated by the Centers for Medicare & Medicaid Services as it developed implementing regulations for the Stark Law. Tuomey points to a portion of the commentary wherein the agency states that the "fact that corresponding hospital services are billed would not invalidate an employed physician's personally performed work, for which the physician may be paid a productivity bonus (subject to the fair market value requirement)." 69 Fed. Reg. at 16089. But this statement deals only with a productivity bonus based on the fair market value of the work personally performed by a physician—it says nothing about the propriety of varying a physician's base salary based on the volume or value of referrals.

In any case, the commentary regarding productivity bonuses appears under a section of the regulations that specifically addresses comments related to the exception for bona fide employment relationships. This exception covers circumstances where there is a meaningful administrative relationship between the physician and the hospital. The jury was instructed on this exception at trial, and rejected it. Tuomey does not quarrel with that aspect of the jury's verdict; rather it contends that the commentary applies irrespective of whether a bona fide employment relationship actually exists. Nothing in the statute or the regulations, however, supports this notion.

2

Tuomey next argues that the district court erred in not granting its motion for judgment as a matter of law because it did not knowingly violate the FCA. Specifically, Tuomey claims that because it reasonably relied on the advice of counsel, no reasonable jury could find that Tuomey possessed the requisite intent to violate the FCA. Because the record here is replete with evidence indicating that Tuomey shopped for legal opinions approving of the employment contracts, while ignoring negative assessments, we disagree.

The FCA imposes civil liability on any person who "knowingly presents, or causes to be presented, a false or fraudulent claim for payment or approval" to an officer or employee of the United States Government. 31 U.S.C. § 3729(a)(1)(A), (b)(2)(A)(i). Under the Act, the term "knowingly" means that a person, with respect to information contained in a claim, (1) "has actual knowledge of the information;" (2) "acts in deliberate ignorance of the truth or falsity of the information;" or (3) "acts in reckless disregard of the truth or falsity of the information." *Id.* § 3729(b)(1). The purpose of the FCA's scienter requirement is to avoid punishing "honest mistakes or incorrect claims submitted through mere negligence." [ ]

The record evidence provides ample support for the jury's verdict as to Tuomey's intent. Indeed, McAnaney's testimony, summarized above, is alone sufficient to sweep aside Tuomey's claim of error.[11] We agree with the district court's conclusion that "a reasonable jury could have found that Tuomey possessed the requisite scienter once it determined to disregard McAnaney's remarks." [ ] A reasonable jury could indeed be troubled by Tuomey's seeming inaction in the face of McAnaney's warnings, particularly given Tuomey's aggressive efforts to avoid hearing precisely what McAnaney had to say regarding the contracts.

Nonetheless, a defendant may avoid liability under the FCA if it can show that it acted in good faith on the advice of counsel. *Cf. United States v. Painter,* 314 F.2d 939, 943 (4th Cir.1963) (holding, in a case involving fraud, that "[i]f in good faith reliance upon legal advice given him by a lawyer to whom he has made full disclosure of the facts, one engages in a course of conduct later found to be illegal, the trier of fact may in appropriate circumstances conclude the conduct was innocent because 'the guilty mind' was absent"). However, "consultation with a lawyer confers no automatic immunity from the legal consequences of conscious fraud." [ ] Rather, to establish the advice-of-counsel defense, the defendant must

---

[11] We note also that the jury at the second trial considered the deposition testimony of Tuomey executive Gregg Martin. While this evidence is (for reasons we have explained) not overly compelling in isolation, it is not without some value in showing that Tuomey was aware that its proposed contracts raised Stark Law concerns.

show the "(a) full disclosure of all pertinent facts to [counsel], and (b) good faith reliance on [counsel's] advice." [ ]

Tuomey contends that it provided full and accurate information regarding the proposed employment contracts to Hewson, who in turn advised Tuomey that the contracts did not run afoul of the Stark Law. But as the government aptly notes, "[i]n determining whether Tuomey reasonably relied on the advice of its counsel, the jury was entitled to consider *all* the advice given to it by *any* source."

In denying Tuomey's post-trial motions, the district court noted—and we agree—that a reasonable jury could have concluded that Tuomey was, after September 2005, no longer acting in good faith reliance on the advice of its counsel when it refused to give full consideration to McAnaney's negative assessment of the part-time employment contracts and terminated his representation. Tuomey defends its dismissal of McAnaney's warnings by claiming that his opinion was tainted by undue influence exerted by Drakeford and his counsel. But there was evidence before the jury suggesting that Tuomey also tried to procure a favorable opinion from McAnaney. Indeed, Tuomey's counsel admitted that he was trying "to steer McAnaney towards [Tuomey's] desired outcome" and that Tuomey needed to "continue playing along and influence the outcome of the game as best we can." [ ] Thus, a reasonable jury could conclude that Tuomey ignored McAnaney because it simply did not like what he had to say.

Tuomey points to the fact that it retained Steve Pratt, a prominent healthcare lawyer, and Richard Kusserow, former Inspector General at the United States Department of Health and Human Services, as further evidence that it acted in good faith and did not ignore McAnaney's warnings. Pratt rendered two opinions that generally approved of the employment contracts. But he did so without being told of McAnaney's unfavorable assessment, even though Tuomey had that information available to it at the time. In addition, Pratt reviewed and relied on the view of Tuomey's fair-market-value consultant that the employment contracts would compensate the physicians at fair market value, but he did not consider how the consultant arrived at its opinion. Nor did he know how much the doctors earned prior to entering into the contracts, or that the hospital stood to lose $1.5–2 million a year, not taking into account facility fees, by compensating the physicians above their collections. We thus think it entirely reasonable for a jury to look skeptically on Pratt's favorable advice regarding the contracts.

The same can be said of the Kusserow's advice. Kusserow—who was called by the government to rebut Tuomey's advice-of-counsel defense—advised Tuomey regarding the employment contracts about eighteen months before the parties retained McAnaney. As was the case with Pratt, he received no information regarding the fair market value of the employment contracts, information that Kusserow considered vital "to be able to do a full Stark analysis of [the proposed contracts]." [ ] And although Kusserow did say in a letter to Tuomey's counsel that he did not believe the contracts presented "significant Stark issues," [ ], he hedged considerably on that view because of "potentially troubling issues related to the productivity and [incentive bonus provisions in the contracts] that have not been fully addressed." [ ]

As the district court observed, "the jury evidently rejected Tuomey's advice of counsel defense" as of the date that Tuomey received McAnaney's warnings, "grounded on the fact that the jury excluded damages from [before the termination of McAnaney's engagement] in making its determination" of the civil penalty and damages. [ ] Thus, while Kusserow's advice was certainly relevant to Tuomey's advice-of-counsel defense, a reasonable jury could have determined that McAnaney's warnings (and Tuomey's subsequent inaction) were far more probative on the issue.

In sum, viewing the evidence in the light most favorable to the government, we have no cause to upset the jury's reasoned verdict that Tuomey violated the FCA.

IV

Finally, Tuomey makes several challenges to the $237,454,195 judgment entered against it. First, it argues that the district court improperly calculated the civil penalty. Next, it claims that the district court used the incorrect measure of actual damages. Finally, it brings constitutional challenges to the award under the Fifth and Eighth Amendments.

A defendant found liable under the FCA must pay the government "a civil penalty of" not less than $5,500 and not more than $11,000 "plus 3 times the amount of damages which the Government sustains because of that person." [ ] In this case, the jury found that Tuomey had submitted 21,730 false claims, for which it awarded actual damages of $39,313,065, which the district court trebled. The district court then added a civil penalty of $119,515,000 to that sum, which it calculated by multiplying the number of false claims by the $5,500 statutory minimum penalty.

* * *

1

According to Tuomey, the civil penalty assessed was improperly inflated because the jury was permitted to take into account both inpatient and outpatient procedures performed by the contracting physicians. Instead, relying on our earlier opinion in this case, Tuomey claims that the only relevant claims "were those Tuomey 'presented, or caused to be presented, to Medicare and Medicaid for payment of facility fees generated *as a result of outpatient procedures performed pursuant to the contracts.'"* [ ] Tuomey is incorrect.

It is true that the contracts solely addressed compensation for outpatient procedures. That is, the physicians' collections (which form the basis for both their base salaries and their productivity bonuses) do not account for the volume or value of inpatient procedures performed. Tuomey, however, takes out of context language from our earlier opinion recognizing this fact to suggest that we commanded that the relevant claims be limited to those seeking payment for outpatient procedures. We said nothing of the sort.

If a physician has a financial relationship with a hospital, then the Stark Law prohibits the physician from making *any* referral to that hospital for the furnishing of designated health services. *E.g., United States ex rel. Bartlett v. Ashcroft*, 39 F. Supp. 3d 656, 669 (W.D. Pa. 2014) ("Because a 'compensation arrangement' existed between Physician Defendants and [the] Hospital, the Stark [Law] prohibited Physician Defendants from making *any* patient referrals to [the] Hospital for designated health services." (emphasis added)). Inpatient hospital services are designated health services. [ ] And a referral includes "the request or establishment of a plan of care by a physician which includes the provision of the designated health service." [ ] Plainly, then, inpatient services constitute a prohibited referral for the furnishing of designated health services, and the district court properly instructed the jury to factor them into the damages calculation.

* * *

Finally, we do not discount the concerns raised by our concurring colleague regarding the result in this case. But having no found no cause to upset the jury's verdict in this case and no constitutional error, it is for Congress to consider whether changes to the Stark Law's reach are in order.

AFFIRMED.

WYNN, CIRCUIT JUDGE, concurring:

Because Tuomey opened the door to the admission of Kevin McAnaney's testimony by asserting an advice of counsel defense, and because I cannot say, based on the record before me, that no rational jury could have determined that Tuomey violated both the Stark Law and the False Claims Act, I concur in the outcome today.

But I write separately to emphasize the troubling picture this case paints: An impenetrably complex set of laws and regulations that will result in a likely death sentence for a community hospital in an already medically underserved area.

* * *

The government argues, among other things, that the McAnaney evidence went to the heart of an issue wholly beyond the scope of Rule 408's limited exclusionary ambit—namely, Tuomey's advice of counsel defense. With this, I must agree.

As explained by a district court in this Circuit in the context of a False Claims Act fraud claim, "good faith reliance on the advice of counsel may contradict any suggestion that a [defendant] 'knowingly' submitted a false claim." [ ] "[I]f a [defendant] seeks the advice of counsel in good faith, provides full and accurate information, receives advice which can be reasonably relied upon, and, in turn, faithfully follows that advice, it cannot be said that the defendant 'knowingly' submitted false information or acted with deliberate ignorance or reckless disregard of its falsity, even if that advice turns out in fact to be false." [ ] *United States v. Butler,* 211 F.3d 826, 833 (4th Cir.2000) (identifying the elements of the advice of counsel defense as "(a) full disclosure of all pertinent facts to [a lawyer], and (b) good faith reliance on the [lawyer]'s advice").

When a party raises an advice of counsel defense, however, all advice on the pertinent topic becomes fair game. "It has . . . become established that if a party interjects the 'advice of counsel' as an essential element of a claim or defense," then "all advice received concerning the same subject matter" is discoverable, not subject to protection by the attorney-client privilege, and, by logical extension, admissible at trial. [ ] . . . Having put the advice it got from its lawyers squarely at issue, Tuomey should not have been permitted to cherry-pick which advice of counsel the jury was permitted to hear. Instead, the jury should have been allowed to consider all the advice of all Tuomey's counsel—including McAnaney.

The record makes clear that . . . Tuomey did not follow McAnaney's advice. McAnaney advised Tuomey that the proposed contracts raised significant "red flags" under the Stark Law. [ ] McAnaney advised that Tuomey would have difficulty persuading the government that the contracts did not compensate the physicians in excess of fair market value. And McAnaney warned Tuomey that the contracts presented "an easy case to prosecute" for the government. [ ] Rather than heed this advice and back away from the contracts, however, Tuomey told McAnaney not to put his conclusions in writing and ended his engagement.

* * *

Given this complexity and the strict liability nature of the statute, a Stark Law "compliance program can help a physician or entity prove good faith and obtain leniency in the event of a violation; however, the Stark Law's complexity and frequent revisions make it difficult for physicians and entities to develop and implement such programs." [ ] Against this problematic backdrop, the availability of an advice of counsel defense should perhaps be especially robust in Stark Law cases prosecuted under the False Claims Act.

The False Claims Act discourages fraud against the federal government by imposing liability on "any person who . . . *knowingly* presents, or causes to be presented, a false or fraudulent claim for payment or approval." 31 U.S.C. § 3729(a)(1)(A) (emphasis added). The False Claims Act is meant "to indemnify the government . . . against losses caused by a defendant's *fraud*," [ ] as opposed to a defendant's mistake.

Accordingly, a defendant may skirt False Claims Act liability by showing good faith reliance on the advice of counsel. As the majority opinion recognizes, in fraud cases, " '[i]f in good faith reliance upon legal advice given him by a lawyer to whom he has made full disclosure of the facts, one engages in a course of conduct later found to be illegal,' " the trier of fact may conclude that the conduct was innocent because " 'the guilty mind' was absent." [ ]

In the context of the Stark Law, it is easy to see how even diligent counsel could wind up giving clients incorrect advice. Between the law's being amended to have a broader scope but then narrowed with various exceptions, along with the promulgation and amendment of copious associated rules and regulations, "the Stark Law bec[ame] a classic example of a moving target. For lawyers, who must depend on the predictability of the law when they give counsel to their clients, such unpredictability [i]s an unusually heavy burden." [ ]

* * *

Nevertheless, as the majority opinion notes, "a reasonable jury could have concluded that Tuomey was . . . no longer acting in good faith reliance on the advice of its counsel when it refused to give full consideration to McAnaney's negative assessment of the" contracts. [ ] As already explained, McAnaney, the former Chief of the Industry Guidance Branch at the Department of Health and Human Services' Office of Counsel to the Inspector General, also served as Tuomey's counsel. And he advised Tuomey that the proposed arrangements raised significant red flags and may well be unlawful. Had Tuomey followed McAnaney's advice, it likely would have faced no lawsuit in which to raise an advice of counsel, or any other, defense.

This case is troubling. It seems as if, even for well-intentioned health care providers, the Stark Law has become a booby trap rigged with strict liability and potentially ruinous exposure—especially when coupled with the False Claims Act. Yet, the district court did not abuse its discretion when it granted a new trial and the jury did not act irrationally when it determined that Tuomey violated both the Stark Law and the False Claims Act. Accordingly, I must concur in the outcome reached by the majority.

NOTES AND QUESTIONS

1. *Take-Aways from* Tuomey. The *Tuomey* decision has sent shockwaves throughout the health care industry. One key take-away is that "referrals" include the facility fee component of personally performed services. How could a DHS entity structure productivity bonuses for physicians after this decision? Second, the "red flags" that took down Tuomey contributed to the overall impression that the arrangements were not commercially reasonable. These oddities included: part-time employment contracts with disproportionately rich, full-time benefits, paying physicians more than their collections, and the sense that the arrangements were motivated by a desire to forestall competition from ambulatory surgery centers.

2. *Advice of Counsel.* As in-house counsel for a health system about to undertake an arrangement with doctors that might implicate Stark, what advice would you give regarding soliciting the opinion of outside counsel? What are the dangers revealed in *Tuomey* of advice-shopping?

3. *Devastating Liability.* The $237 million verdict affirmed by the Fourth Circuit exceeded the annual revenues of the Tuomey Healthcare System. The defendant entered into a settlement to conclude its ten-year legal battle under which Tuomey would pay the government $72.4 million, would sell the system to Palmetto Health, a health system from Columbia, South Carolina, and agreed to be subject to 5-year Corporate Integrity Agreement with independent review of all physician arrangements. Dr. Drakeford, the whistleblower, received $18.1 million from the settlement. See Lisa Schenker, Tuomey Will Pay U.S. $72.4 Million to Duck $237 Million False Claims Verdict, Mod. Healthcare (Oct. 16, 2015). What is your verdict on *Tuomey*—is it an object lesson about the flaws of the Stark Law or does it send an important message to those who would flaunt the law? Would you feel differently about the application of Stark Law to Tuomey's arrangement if the penalties were not so financially ruinous to the health care system? Do you agree with the last paragraph of Judge Wynn's concurring opinion?

4. *Takes into Account the Volume or Value of Referrals.* The compensation arrangement in *Tuomey* ran afoul of the Stark Law, in part, because it "varied with" the volume or value of the physicians' referrals (the facility component of the surgeons' personally performed services). Thus, lawyers often advise their health care clients that paying physicians according to a fixed compensation formula is less risky because the payments do not so vary. Nevertheless, even fixed compensation amounts can violate Stark if they **"take into account"** referrals, including **anticipated referrals**. In United States ex rel. Singh v. Bradford Regional Medical Center, 752 F. Supp. 2d 602 (W.D. Pa. 2010), the court considered this question when evaluating an arrangement in which Bradford Regional Medical Center (BRMC) paid fixed compensation amounts to two physicians, Drs. Vaccaro and Saleh. Drs.

Vaccaro and Saleh leased their own nuclear camera and drew significant imaging business away from BRMC by doing their own imaging. To regain Vaccaro and Saleh's nuclear imaging business, BRMC agreed to sublease the nuclear camera from Vaccaro and Saleh by assuming their monthly lease payments of $6,545. In addition, BRMC paid Vaccaro and Saleh $23,655 monthly for a covenant not to compete, in which Vaccaro and Saleh agreed not to compete with BRMC in the provision of nuclear cardiology or other diagnostic imaging services. BRMC's valuation consultant justified the value of the non-compete by calculating BRMC's anticipated revenues from Vaccaro and Saleh's referrals to BRMC for nuclear cardiology and imaging services they would no longer be providing themselves due to the non-compete. BRMC then argued that the compensation paid to Vaccaro and Saleh for the sublease and non-compete was a fixed monthly amount and therefore did not vary with or take into account the volume or value of the physicians' referrals. The court disagreed, concluding that the non-compete compensation was based on the value and expectation of physicians' *anticipated referrals* to BRMC, and therefore "took into account" those referrals, even if they did not "vary with" the number of referrals. Thus, the compensation arrangement did not reflect fair market value, as required by the Stark Law. 752 F. Supp. 2d at 632–33. Like the court in *Tuomey*, the *Bradford* court may have been responding to a general sense that the arrangement was not commercially reasonable absent the expectation of referrals: after BRMC entered the agreement for the sublease and non-compete, it acknowledged it did not need the nuclear camera and in fact never moved it from Vaccaro and Saleh's offices. If the arrangement was not to obtain a camera for BRMC, the implication was it was only to avoid competition and secure Vaccaro and Saleh's referrals. The *Bradford* case indicates that paying non-employed physicians not to compete is very risky, particularly when there is an expectation that the physicians will refer to the DHS entity, because of the presumption that the non-compete compensation takes into account the value of anticipated referrals from the physicians.

STARK LAW PROBLEM: MEDICAL DIRECTORS

To improve efficiency, quality of care, and patient satisfaction, Alta Bonita Central Hospital ("Hospital") has appointed medical directors to head two departments: Cardiology and Surgery. Medical directors are typically staff physicians who perform certain administrative functions such as assisting in the development and implementation of standards of care, ensuring compliance with Joint Commission standards, providing consultations on high-risk cases, and participating in the work of various hospital committees.

Dr. Hicks is the cardiology medical director. He is an independent contractor who practices with a medical group in the community. On January 1, the Hospital entered into a one-year medical director agreement with Dr. Hicks, which delineates his duties as medical director and specifies that he is expected to work a minimum of 10 hours and a maximum of 15 hours per month, for which he will be paid $200 per hour, for a total monthly compensation not to exceed $3000. To receive his compensation, he is required to submit a time sheet every month specifying the number of hours he worked.

Dr. Russell is the surgery medical director. She is an employee of the hospital and will be eligible for extra compensation for her efforts as medical director, at amounts not to exceed $3000 per month. The hospital attaches a rider to her employment agreement specifying her duties as medical director of surgery and providing that she will be expected to devote 15 hours per month to her medical director duties.

Salary surveys show that average administrative compensation for cardiologists and surgeons in the area range from $190–$225 per hour.

In June of the same year, the Chief Operating Officer of the Hospital, Diane Chung, discovers that neither Dr. Hicks nor Dr. Russell ever signed their medical director contract. Moreover, neither has been submitting time sheets documenting the amount of time spent on medical director duties, and anecdotal reports suggest that both physicians only spent a handful of hours on medical director duties in the months of April and May. Nevertheless, accounts payable has been issuing checks of $3000 every month to both Dr. Hicks and Dr. Russell. Dr. Hicks and Dr. Russell have heard that the neighboring hospital pays its medical directors $250 per hour and have approached Ms. Chung to demand that their hourly compensation be increased to $250 per hour. Dr. Hicks said if he does not get the raise starting in July, he will "take his business elsewhere." Ms. Chung is inclined to increase their medical director compensation to $250/hour so as not to lose either Dr. Hicks or Dr. Russel. Ms. Chung has approached you if these medical director arrangements raise any problems under the Stark Law.

After reviewing the Stark exceptions for bona fide employment relationships, personal service arrangements, and fair market value compensation, please briefly answer the following questions:

1. What is your assessment of Dr. Hicks' arrangement under the Stark Law? Should the Hospital agree to increase Dr. Hicks' compensation to $250/hour? What advice do you have for Hospital with regard to Dr. Hick's arrangement?

2. What is your assessment of Dr. Russell's arrangement under the Stark Law? Should the Hospital agree to increase Dr. Russel's compensation to $250/hour? What advice do you have for Hospital with regard to Dr. Russell's arrangement?

NOTE: STATE APPROACHES TO KICKBACKS, REFERRALS AND FEE SPLITTING

Most states have enacted laws that prohibit kickbacks or deal in some way with the specific problem of referrals. These laws vary considerably in scope and detail. For example, most states prohibit Medicaid fraud, but some rely on more general statutes outlawing fraud or theft by deception or false statements to public officials; some impose both criminal and civil penalties for kickbacks;

many apply regardless of whether government or private payment plans were involved; and a few are broader than the federal Anti-Kickback Statute, e.g., by prohibiting the provision of unnecessary care.

Another source of law governing physician referral practices are the state **medical practice acts**. Such laws commonly provide that paying referral fees or **"fee-splitting"** constitutes grounds for revocation or suspension of a physician's license. See, e.g., Mass. Gen. L. Ch. 112 §§ 12AA, 23P (1991). These statutes have sometimes been construed to prohibit arrangements that go beyond simple sharing of fees in connection with referral arrangements. See, e.g., in Lieberman & Kraff v. Desnick, 614 N.E.2d 379 (1993). Florida's fee-splitting statute has called into question the legality of many physician practice management arrangements whereby a physician pays a large organization a percentage of profits in exchange for management, marketing, and networking services. See Gold, Vann & White, P.A. v. Friedenstab, 831 So.2d 692 (Fla. Dist. Ct. App. 2002) (service agreement between physicians and medical management company providing management company a percentage of revenue constituted an illegal fee splitting arrangement). See Richard O. Jacobs & Elizabeth Goodman, Splitting Fees or Splitting Hairs? Fee Splitting and Health Care—The Florida Experience, 8 Annals Health L. 239 (1999).

The states also protect the Medicaid program and beneficiaries through **Medicaid Fraud Control Units (MFCUs)**. These state agencies are typically located within the state attorney general's office and investigate and prosecute Medicaid provider fraud and patient abuse and neglect under federal and fraud and abuse laws. The establishment of state MFCUs was authorized in the Medicare-Medicaid Anti-Fraud and Abuse Amendments to the Social Security Act. Pub. L. 95–142 (1977), codified at 42 U.S.C. § 1396b. Since then, all 50 states as well as the District of Columbia have established MFCUs. The OIG, which oversees and certifies state MFCUs, issued updated regulations in 2019, including changes relating to the MFCU's organization, prosecutorial authority, staffing requirements, and relationship with the state Medicaid agency. 84 Fed. Reg. 10700 (Mar. 22, 2019).

MFCUs face the familiar problem of funding. Although the federal government typically provides 75 percent of the agency's costs, states are often strained for the resources to cover the remaining expenditures. Given that Medicaid accounts for a large percentage of a state's annual budget, MFCUs' criminal fines and civil recoveries are critical to preserving and maximizing state Medicaid resources. In 2020, MFCUs yielded 1,107 criminal convictions (down from 1,527 in 2019 due to challenges of the pandemic), 786 civil judgments and settlements, for a total of over $1 billion in recoveries. For every dollar MFCUs spent, they recovered $3.36. OIG, Medicaid Fraud Control Units Fiscal Year 2020 Annual Report (Mar. 2021). MFCUs can maximize their resources by working together in complex, interstate health care fraud cases that involve multiple state Medicaid programs through the National Association of Medicaid Fraud Control Units (NAMFCU), which coordinates efforts with the federal government to investigate and negotiate on behalf of the states. Some of the largest health care fraud settlements have involved multi-state participation through NAMFCU. See, e.g., DOJ Press Release, Justice Department Obtains $1.4 Billion from Reckitt Benckiser Group in Largest Recovery in a Case Concerning an Opioid Drug in United States History (July 11, 2019).

IV. ACOs AND FRAUD AND ABUSE LAWS

As discussed in Chapter 12, providers are integrating rapidly under a wide variety of arrangements. Providers forming **accountable care organizations (ACOs)** through contractual arrangements and joint ventures encounter obstacles under the laws discussed in this chapter. The ACA strongly encouraged these developments and sought to ease the legal burdens by empowering the Secretary of HHS to waive certain laws for Medicare ACOs.

Contemporaneously with the issuance of the notice of the Final Rule on ACOs discussed in Chapter 10, CMS and the OIG published an interim final rule establishing waivers of three federal fraud and abuse laws for ACOs participating in the Medicare Shared Savings Program (MSSP). 76 Fed. Reg. 67,992 (Nov. 2, 2011). Having waded through the material in this chapter, the need for such waivers may be fairly obvious. As one example: the ACO concept necessarily entails an exchange of payments among providers reflecting their contributions to the enterprise's goal of reducing costs. Although, in theory, distributions might come under existing exceptions requiring a showing of "fair market value," demonstrating the "costs" associated with physicians modifying their clinical practices and the value of physicians' work would be speculative and difficult to document. See Daniel H. Melvin & Webb Millsaps, The Proposed Waivers of the Fraud and Abuse Laws for ACOs: Have OIG and CMS Gone Far Enough? 15 Health Care Fraud Report (BNA) 422 (May 4, 2011).

Pursuant to the broad grant of authority to the Secretary of HHS to waive the Anti-Kickback Statute, the Stark Law, and the civil monetary penalties applicable to gainsharing (Gainsharing CMP), the interim final rule sets forth the following waivers for ACOs participating in the MSSP.

Pre-Participation Waiver. The intent of this waiver is to permit ACO participants to share resources in starting up ACOs. It waives the Anti-Kickback Statute, Stark Law, and Gainsharing CMP laws for start-up arrangements that meet various conditions, including acting in good faith with intent to develop an ACO that will participate in the MSSP; taking "diligent steps" to develop an ACO that is eligible to participate in the MSSP; and the ACO's governing board making a bona fide determination that the start-up arrangement is reasonably related to the purposes of the MSSP and contemporaneously documenting these steps.

Participation Waiver. This waiver of the Anti-Kickback Statute, Stark Law, and Gainsharing CMP laws applies broadly to ACO-related arrangements during the term of the ACO's participation in the MSSP. Conditions include, entering into and participating in the MSSP and meeting program requirements; having a duly authorized determination by the ACO's governing board that the arrangement is reasonably related to the purposes of the MSSP; and contemporaneously documenting and publicly disclosing the arrangement.

Shared Savings Distribution Waiver. This waiver, also applicable to the Anti-Kickback Statute, Stark Law, and Gainsharing CMP law, covers the actual distribution of savings to or among the ACO participants, ACO providers/suppliers, or individuals or entities that were its ACO participants or ACO providers/suppliers during the year that the shared savings were earned. The savings may also be "used" by the ACO for activities that are reasonably related to purposes of the MSSP such as paying parties outside the ACO. An additional requirement pertaining to the waiver of the Gainsharing CMP, provides that shared savings distributions that are made directly or indirectly from a hospital to a physician not be made knowingly to induce a physician to reduce or limit medically necessary items or services to patients under the direct care of the physician.

Compliance with the Stark Law Waiver. This waiver broadly waives the Anti-Kickback Statute and Gainsharing CMP with respect to any financial relationship between or among the ACO, its ACO participants, and its ACO providers/suppliers that implicates the Stark Law, provided that the financial relationship is reasonably related to the purposes of the MSSP and it fully complies with an exception to the Stark Law.

Waiver for Patient Incentives. This waiver waives the Anti-Kickback Statute and a CMP specifically applicable to beneficiary inducements. It applies to items or services provided by an ACO, its ACO participants, or its ACO providers/suppliers to beneficiaries for free or below fair-market value. The rule applies the following conditions: a reasonable connection between the items or services and medical care of the beneficiary; the items or services are in-kind and are preventive care, or advance one or more of the clinical goals of adherence to a treatment regime; adherence to a drug requirement; and, adherence to a follow-up care plan or management of a chronic disease or condition.

Note that these waivers are quite broad. For example, the participation and pre-participation waivers may allow donations by hospitals to physicians of electronic health records beyond current exceptions to the Stark Law and also allow compensation by ACOs to physicians contingent upon reductions of length of stay, substitution of lower cost devices, and improvements in operating efficiency that would be prohibited under the Gainsharing CMP without a favorable advisory opinion from the OIG.

Important questions remain regarding the implications of the CMS/ OIG waivers beyond the MSSP. CMS and OIG resisted appeals to make these waivers applicable to ACOs participating in arrangements with commercial insurers or employers. However, the interim final rule states "avenues exist to provide flexibility for ACOs participating in commercial ACOs . . . nothing precludes arrangements 'downstream' of commercial plans (for example, arrangements between hospitals and physician groups) from qualifying for the [MSSP] participation waiver."

The 2020 rule changes to the Stark Law and Anti-Kickback Statute, particularly the new provisions for value-based arrangements, may provide providers the flexibility they need to enter in financial risk-sharing arrangements as part of commercial ACOs, which are a type of value-based arrangement. Although the agencies suggested that the new rules may reduce the need to rely on the MSSP ACO waivers, the 2020 Stark and Anti-Kickback Statute rules did not make any changes to the scope or availability of the waivers. Thus, the waivers remain in effect and offer more flexibility for value-based arrangements that also participate in an MSSP ACO than the new value-based Stark Law exceptions and Anti-Kickback Statute safe harbors.

CHAPTER 15

ANTITRUST

• • •

I. INTRODUCTION

Antitrust law has played a pivotal role in the development of institutional and professional arrangements in health care. In 1975, the Supreme Court held that "learned professions"—including law and medicine—were not implicitly exempt from the antitrust laws, Goldfarb v. Virginia State Bar, 421 U.S. 773 (1975), paving the way for extensive antitrust litigation, which spurred significant changes in the health care industry. Most importantly, cases following *Goldfarb* helped remove a series of private restraints of trade that had long inhibited competition in health care.

Antitrust enforcement has come to assume a somewhat different, albeit equally important, focus in today's market. The law has emerged as a powerful check on institutional and professional arrangements and ideally helps assure the evolution of market structures that will preserve the benefits of a competitive marketplace.

Market-based approaches to health care regulation and reform (detailed in Chapter 7) depend on the competitive conditions that antitrust law aims to promote. Recall that many of the key elements of the Affordable Care Act (ACA) discussed elsewhere in this casebook are designed to improve market competition. For example, health insurance exchanges facilitate comparison shopping by standardizing insurance products. The ACA established organizational structures more conducive to effective competition, such as patient-centered medical homes and accountable care organizations. Competitive bidding and price negotiation programs feature prominently in the ACA and proposals to replace it, relying on competitive markets to control cost and improve quality. Consequently, antitrust enforcement will likely continue to play an important role governing the conduct and structure in health care markets. At the same time, however, antitrust law may not have an effective solution to the extensive concentration that has developed in many provider and health insurance markets which may undermine competition. See Thomas L. Greaney, Coping with Concentration, 36 Health Aff. 1564 (2017).

Applying antitrust law to the health care industry entails some special problems because health care markets, like the health care economics discussed in Chapter 7, do not conform to classical assumptions. In particular, the peculiarities and distortions of health care markets often necessitate a sophisticated analysis in order to reach economically sound results. A host of questions arise: What place is there for defenses related to the quality of health care in a statutory regime designed to leave such issues to the market? Does the behavior of nonprofit health care providers conform to traditional economic assumptions about competitors? If not, should they somehow be treated differently? What impact do the widespread interventions by state and federal government have on the application of federal antitrust law? Do "market failures" in health care, particularly imperfect information, suggest more restrained approaches to applying antitrust law? What role does competition policy play in health inequities, and what role could it play in health justice? Perspectives on these and other questions underlying antitrust's role in health care are found in a number of academic writings. See, e.g., Diana L. Moss, Can Competition Save Lives? The Intersection of COVID-19, Ventilators, and Antitrust Enforcement, Am. Antitrust Inst. (Mar. 31, 2020); Theodosia Stavroulaki, Mind the Gap: Antitrust, Health Disparities and Telemedicine, 45 Am. J. L. & Med. 171 (2019); Sara Rosenbaum, A Dose of Reality: Assessing the Federal Trade Commission/Department of Justice Report in an Uninsured, Underserved, and Vulnerable Population Context, 31 J. Health Pol. Pol'y & L. 657 (2006); Thomas L. Greaney, Chicago's Procrustean Bed: Applying Antitrust Law in Health Care, 71 Antitrust L.J. 857 (2004); Peter J. Hammer & William M. Sage, Antitrust, Health Care Quality, and the Courts, 102 Colum. L. Rev. 545 (2002); Thomas Rice, The Economics of Health Care Reconsidered (1998).

This introduction provides the basic statutory framework, interpretive principles, and vocabulary of antitrust law. Sections II and III which follow it illustrate common applications of antitrust law in health care contexts.

A. THE STATUTORY FRAMEWORK

The principal antitrust statutes are notable for their highly generalized proscriptions. Rather than specifying activities that it deemed harmful to competition, Congress vested the federal courts with the power to create a common law of antitrust.

This chapter will not deal with all of the antitrust laws applicable to the health care industry. Instead it summarizes portions of the three principal federal statutes: the Sherman Act, the Federal Trade Commission Act, and the Clayton Act. Most states have enacted antitrust statutes that are identical to or closely track these federal laws. Multiple entities enforce the antitrust laws. The Department of Justice, Federal Trade Commission and State Attorneys General may bring actions in federal court, the FTC also enforces the law through its administrative authorities, and State Attorneys General can bring cases in state court. By far the largest number of cases are brought by private plaintiffs who can receive treble damages and attorneys' fees for successful litigation.

1.   Sherman Act § 1: Restraints of Trade

Section One of the Sherman Act prohibits "every contract, combination . . . or conspiracy in restraint of trade." 15 U.S.C. § 1. This broad proscription establishes two substantive elements for finding a violation: an agreement and conduct that restrains trade. The concept of an agreement—the conventional shorthand for Section One's "contract, combination or conspiracy" language—limits the law's reach to concerted activities, i.e., those that are a result of a "meeting of the minds" of two or more independent persons or entities. The second requirement of Section One, that the agreement restrain trade, has generated extensive analysis by the courts. Recognizing that all commercial agreements restrain trade, the Supreme Court has narrowed the inquiry to condemn only "unreasonable restraints" and has developed presumptive ("*per se*") rules to simplify judicial inquiries in particular circumstances. Among the restraints of trade that are reached by Section One are: **price fixing** (the setting of prices or terms of sale cooperatively by two or more businesses that do not involve sharing substantial risk in a common business enterprise); **market division** (allocating product lines, customers, or territories between competitors); **exclusive dealing** (requiring that a person deal exclusively with an enterprise so that competitors are foreclosed or otherwise disadvantaged in the marketplace); **group boycotts** (competitors collectively refusing to deal, usually taking the form of denying a rival an input or something it needs to compete in the marketplace); and **tying arrangements** (a firm with market power selling one product on the condition that the buyer buy a second product from it).

2.   Sherman Act § 2: Monopolization and Attempted Monopolization

Section Two of the Sherman Act prohibits monopolization, attempted monopolization, and conspiracies to monopolize. 15 U.S.C. § 2. Unlike Section One, it is primarily directed at unilateral conduct. Monopolization entails two elements: the possession of **monopoly power**, defined as the power to control market prices or exclude competition, and the willful acquisition or maintenance of that power as distinguished from growth or development as a consequence of a superior product, business acumen, or historic accident.

3.   Clayton Act § 7: Mergers and Acquisitions

Section Seven of the Clayton Act prohibits mergers and acquisitions where the effect may be "substantially to lessen competition" or "to tend to create a monopoly." 15 U.S.C. § 18. To test the legality of a proposed merger or acquisition, courts emphasize market share and concentration data but also take other factors into consideration to determine whether a merger makes it more likely than not that the merged firm will exercise market power. **Horizontal mergers**, which are those involving actual or potential competitors, draw particular scrutiny. See U.S. Dep't of Justice & Fed. Trade Comm'n, Horizontal Merger Guidelines (2010). Courts apply two methods of analysis to horizontal mergers. Those that create or enhance the ability of firms to act cooperatively are analyzed under a **"coordinated effects" test**, which requires courts to assess the likelihood of tacit or express cooperation in the market. Mergers that enable the merged entity to raise price without regard to the actions of rivals because of strong consumer preferences for the merging parties are analyzed under a **"unilateral effects" test**, which assesses the strength of consumer preferences and possible repositioning by rivals. **Vertical mergers** combine entities that provide different services or components of the same supply chain and typically draw less scrutiny. See U.S. Dep't of Justice & Fed. Trade Comm'n, Vertical Merger Guidelines (2020).

4. Federal Trade Commission Act § 5: Unfair Methods of Competition

Section Five of the Federal Trade Commission Act prohibits "unfair methods of competition" (which the courts have interpreted to include all violations of the Sherman Act and Clayton Act), and "unfair or deceptive acts or practices." 15 U.S.C. § 45(a)(1). The Act empowers the FTC to enforce the provisions of the Sherman Act in civil suits, as well as by administrative procedures. Although the FTC Act covers only the activities of a corporation "organized to carry on business for its own profit or that of its members," courts have found that nonprofit associations whose activities provide substantial economic benefit to their members are within the FTC's jurisdiction.

5. Defenses and Exemptions

There are numerous statutory and judicially-crafted defenses to antitrust liability, several of which are of particular importance to health care antitrust litigation. The **state action doctrine** exempts from antitrust liability actions taken pursuant to a clearly-expressed state policy to restrict free competition, where the challenged conduct is under the active control and supervision of the state. The McCarran-Ferguson Act generally exempts the "business of insurance" from antitrust enforcement to the extent that the particular insurance activities are regulated by state law, 15 U.S.C. § 1011, but does not otherwise exempt "insurance companies" from antitrust scrutiny. The Noerr-Pennington doctrine protects the exercise of the First Amendment right to petition the government, shielding some lobbying efforts on and participation in administrative proceedings which may lead to an outcome that lessens competition. Health care has its own statutory defense in the Health Care Quality Improvement Act, which grants limited immunity for peer review activities, discussed in Chapter 11. 42 U.S.C. §§ 11101–11152.

B. INTERPRETIVE PRINCIPLES

1. The Law's Exclusive Focus on Competitive Concerns

Courts have long agreed that antitrust inquiries should focus exclusively on competitive effects and should not take into account purported non-economic benefits of collective activities such as advancing social policies or even protecting public safety. See National Society of Professional Engineers v. United States, 435 U.S. 679 (1978) (rejecting as a matter of law a professional society's safety justifications for its ban on competitive bidding). This self-imposed boundary is based on the judiciary's skepticism about its competence to balance disparate social policies and the judgment that such concerns are more appropriately addressed to the legislature. Importantly, then, under Section One of the Sherman Act, courts will not consider justifications other than those asserting that a practice, on balance, promotes competition. As discussed *infra*, this constraint is in obvious tension with justifications by professionals that their collective activities have the purpose of advancing the quality of patient care.

An important corollary is the often-repeated maxim that antitrust law seeks to "**protect competition, not competitors**." Brown Shoe Co. v. United States, 370 U.S. 294 (1962). This tenet emphasizes the distinction between harm to competitors who lose out in the competitive struggle due to chance or their own inadequacies, versus harm resulting from the impermissible conduct of rivals. Only the latter are cognizable under the federal antitrust laws. Courts have fashioned rules regarding standing and antitrust injury for private plaintiffs as well as substantive doctrines that serve to preserve this distinction.

2. Per Se Rules and the Rule of Reason

Traditionally, judicial analyses of conduct under Section One of the Sherman Act have employed two approaches to testing the "reasonableness" of restraints on competition. Some activities, such as price fixing, market allocations, and certain group boycotts have been considered so likely to harm competition that they are deemed illegal "*per se*." That is, if a plaintiff can prove that the defendant's conduct fits within one of these categories, the inquiry ends; the agreement itself constitutes a violation of the statute. In effect, the per se categorization establishes a conclusive presumption of illegality.

Activities not falling within the *per se* rubric are subject to broader examination under the **rule of reason**. Under this analysis, defendants escape liability if they prove the pro-competitive benefits of the challenged activity outweigh any anticompetitive effects so that competition is strengthened rather than restrained. In theory, courts undertaking a full-blown rule of reason analysis will balance competitive harms against competitive benefits. For example, if a large number of hospitals collectively assembled and shared information about the utilization practices of physicians on their staffs, a court might balance the potential collusive harm resulting from lessened inter-hospital competition against the market-wide competitive benefits of disseminating such information—assuming the information was shared with payers.

In practice, however, such fact-specific balancing is rarely done. Courts usually truncate the process in one of several ways. For example, they may find that an alleged restraint has no possibility of harming competition where the colluding parties lack "**market power**," which is defined as the ability to profitably raise price (or reduce quality or output). As a proxy for market power, courts estimate the market shares of the colluding parties and examine other market conditions. Doing this, of course, requires that the fact finder define the dimensions of the geographic and product markets—determinations that require the exercise of considerable discretion and may be more complex than they appear.

Indeed, in recent years, a series of Supreme Court decisions have shifted antitrust analyses away from a rigid per se/rule of reason dichotomy, treating the approaches instead as "complementary" and essentially establishing a continuum of levels of scrutiny. See California Dental Association v. FTC, *infra* Section II.B. Thus, the modern approach allows courts to undertake threshold examinations of purported justifications and competitive effects before characterizing the conduct as governed by the per se rule. By the same token, courts may need only a "**quick look**" to condemn conduct under the rule of reason; they may dispense with prolonged factual inquiries when the truncated review reveals that purported efficiency benefits are lacking or an anticompetitive effect is obvious.

II. CARTELS AND PROFESSIONALISM

A. CLASSIC CARTELS

IN RE MICHIGAN STATE MEDICAL SOCIETY

Federal Trade Commission, 1983.
101 F.T.C. 191.

Opinion of the Commission

BY CLANTON, COMMISSIONER:

I.   Introduction

This case involves allegations that direct competitors, acting through a professional association, conspired to restrain trade by organizing boycotts and tampering with the fees received from third party insurers of their services. Of particular antitrust significance is the fact that the competitors are medical doctors practicing in Michigan, the association is the Michigan State Medical Society ["MSMS"], and the insurers are Blue Cross and Blue Shield of Michigan ("BCBSM") and Michigan Medicaid.

[T]he complaint in this matter charges . . . that the medical society unlawfully conspired with its members to influence third-party reimbursement policies in the following ways: by seeking to negotiate collective agreements with insurers; by agreeing to use coercive measures like proxy solicitation and group boycotts; and by actually making coercive threats to third party payers. * * *

* * *

[MSMS was negotiating with BCBSM over the terms of its members participation in BCBSM plan networks. They reached a stalemate on reimbursement, claim forms, and even use of CPT codes. In frustration, MSMS urged its members to write letters to BCBSM withdrawing from participation in its plans, but asked them to mail the letters directly to MSMS to be held as "proxies," which MSMS's negotiators could use if they came to an impasse with BCBSM MSMS also mailed each of its members blank "power of attorney" forms authorizing the Negotiating Committee to withdraw them from BCBSM or Medicaid participation and urged members to protest new reimbursement policies by writing to BCBSM and threatening to withdraw from participation. MSMS's chair reminded members that BCBSM's enabling legislation required a threshold of participating physicians for it to continue operations, and urged them to resist BCBSM's "so-called cost-containment programs."

BCBSM withdrew its proposals for changing reimbursement of some specialist services. And, when Michigan's Medicaid program proposed an 11% cut in physician reimbursement, MSMS representative protested by brandishing the stack of departicipation proxies during meetings with officials.]

* * *

Conspiracy Allegations

The threshold issue here is whether MSMS' importunings with BCBSM and the Medicaid program amounted to conspiratorial conduct of the kind alleged in the complaint or simply represented nonbinding expressions of views and policy, as argued by respondent. [ ] As discussed previously, the evidence quite clearly reveals that MSMS members, acting through their House of Delegates, agreed in 1976 to establish a Division of Negotiations for the purpose of working out differences with third party payers. The Division was specifically empowered, *inter alia*, to coordinate all negotiating activities of MSMS, collect "non-participation" proxies and obtain a negotiated participation agreement with third party payers that would obviate the need for physician non-participation. [ ] It also was specifically contemplated by MSMS that the Division of Negotiations would obtain authorization of all members to serve as their "exclusive bargaining agent." The debate in the House of Delegates clearly indicated that, although the Division would not negotiate specific fees, it would have authority to negotiate the manner by which fees or reimbursement levels would be established. [ ]

Thus, at the outset we find that the very creation of the Division of Negotiations reveals a collective purpose on the part of MSMS and its members to go beyond the point of giving advice to third party payers; in fact, it reveals a purpose to organize and empower a full-fledged representative to negotiate and resolve controversies surrounding physician profiles, screens and other similar matters. [ ] [T]he Negotiating Division not only had the authority to reach understandings with third party payers but also utilized that authority (acting as agent for its members) in soliciting, collecting and threatening to exercise physician departicipation proxies, as well as in other negotiations with third party payers.

* * *

Turning to the boycott issue, the law is clear that the definition of that term is not limited to situations where the target of the concerted refusal to deal is another competitor or potential competitor. As the Supreme Court indicated, . . . a concerted refusal to deal may be characterized as an unlawful group boycott where the target is a customer or supplier of the combining parties. [ ] In the instant case, the alleged boycott involves concerted threats by MSMS and its members to refrain from participating in BCBSM and Medicaid unless the [payers] modified their reimbursement policies. Although BCBSM and Medicaid—the targets of the boycott—are not in competitive relationships with MSMS, that fact alone does not preclude a finding of a boycott.

[MSMS] however, argues that the proxies were not exercised and, in the case of the departication letter campaign, that there was no adverse effect on BCBSM. As to the latter contention, MSMS points out that more physicians signed up to participate in BCBSM during the relevant period than withdrew from the program as a result of the campaign. The success [or] failure of a group boycott or price-fixing agreement, however, is irrelevant to the question of either its existence or its legality. Whether or not the action succeeds, "[i]t is the concerted activity for a common purpose that constitutes the violation." [ ] Furthermore, an agreement among competitors affecting price does not have to be successful in order to be condemned.

It is the "contract, combination . . . or conspiracy in restraint of trade or commerce" which § 1 of the [Sherman] Act strikes down, whether the concerted activity be wholly nascent or abortive on the one hand, or successful on the other. [ ]

Moreover, even if less than all members of an organization or association agree to participate, that fact does not negate the presence of a conspiracy or combination as to those who do participate. [ ]

As for the collection of proxies that were never exercised, the law does not require that a competitor actually refuse to deal before a boycott can be found or liability established. Rather, the threat to refuse to deal may suffice to constitute the offense. [ ] The evidence indicates that the threat implicit in the collection of departication proxies and the attendant publicity can be as effective as the actual execution of the threatened action. Indeed, it may be assumed that parties to a concerted refusal to deal hope that the announcement of the intended action will be sufficient to produce the desired response. That appears to be precisely what happened here, and there are contemporaneous testimonials by MSMS officials confirming the success of that strategy. For example, Dr. Crandall suggested that MSMS' "waving the proxies in the face of the legislature" persuaded the state attorney general that if he sued MSMS the state would have "orchestrated the demise of the entire Michigan Medicaid program." [ ] Also, as noted above, the Negotiations Division credited the members' response to the proxy solicitation with the favorable outcome of the dispute between the radiologists and BCBSM. [ ] And, as further evidence, there is the fact that MSMS reached a formal agreement with BCBSM which included the implementation of a statewide screen. [ ]

* * *

B. Legality of the Concerted Action

* * *

[I]t would appear that respondent's conduct approaches the kind of behavior that previously has been classified as per se illegal. Nevertheless, since this conduct does not involve direct fee setting, we are not prepared to declare it per se illegal at this juncture and close the door on all asserted pro-competitive justifications. * * *

[MSMS] has offered the following justifications for its behavior: (1) the practices had no effect on fee levels and, in any event, BCBSM and Medicaid took independent action to correct the perceived problems; (2) MSMS simply sought to insure that physicians were treated fairly especially in view of BCBSM's bargaining power; (3) the actions were, in part, an effort to counter BCBSM's violations of its charter and Michigan law in connection with its modified participation program; and (4) MSMS was striving to correct abuses of the Medicaid system and the poor perpetrated by "Medicaid mills."

With respect to respondent's first contention, MSMS claims that the conduct never led to uniform fees or prevented individual physicians from deciding whether to participate in BCBSM or Medicaid. We believe that these arguments miss the point with respect to the likely competitive effects of the restrictive practices. Where horizontal arrangements so closely relate to prices or fees as they do here, a less elaborate analysis of competitive effects is required. [ ] The collective actions under scrutiny clearly interfere with the rights of physicians to compete independently on the terms of insurance coverage offered by BCBSM and Medicaid. Moreover, the joint arrangements directly hamper the ability of third party payers to compete freely for the patronage of individual physicians and other physician business entities. * * *

* * *

On the question of whether the proposed policies of BCBSM and Medicaid were fair to physicians, respondent would apparently have us become enmeshed in weighing the comparative equities of the different parties to these transactions. . . . For us to consider whether the terms offered by the third party payers were fair or reasonable would lead us into the kind of regulatory posture that the courts have long rejected. . . . We believe that it is undesirable and inappropriate for us to step in and attempt to determine which party had the better case in these dealings.

* * *

* * * Respondent also suggests that its activities were motivated by concern for the welfare of its members' patients, especially in the case of Medicaid where, it is alleged, reductions in reimbursement levels might

lead to lower physician participation rates and force low-income patients to seek less reputable providers (the so-called Medicaid mills). [ ]

* * * We concluded there that the relationship between such reimbursement mechanisms and health care quality was simply too tenuous, from a competitive perspective, to justify the broad restrictions imposed.

* * * While granting MSMS' laudable concerns about the effects of physician withdrawal from Medicaid, we observe that respondent clearly had public forums [ ] available to it to correct perceived mistakes made by the state legislature or the administrators of Medicaid; it could have expressed its views in ways that fell well short of organized boycott threats.

Finally, we find no suggestion among MSMS' justifications that the concerted behavior here enhanced competition in any market by injecting new elements or forms of competition, reducing entry barriers, or facilitating or broadening consumer choice. The price-related practices in question here are not ancillary to some broader pro-competitive purpose, such a joint venture, an integration of activities, or an offer of a new product or service. * * *

* * *

In fact, we believe there are less anti-competitive ways of providing such information to insurers. [Our Order] allows [MSMS] to provide information and views to insurers on behalf of its members, so long as the Society does not attempt to extract agreements, through coercion or otherwise, from third party payers on reimbursement issues. [ ] In allowing respondent to engage in non-binding, non-coercive discussions with health insurers, we have attempted to strike a proper balance between the need for insurers to have efficient access to the views of large groups of providers and the need to prevent competitors from banding together in ways that involve the unreasonable exercise of collective market power. [ ]

* * *

NOTES AND QUESTIONS

1. *Pro-Competitive Justification?* Although the FTC does not invoke the *per se* label, note that its analysis does not require proof of an actual effect on prices. How does it treat the justifications proffered by the medical society? Do any meet the requirement discussed in the introduction to this chapter that justifications must concern pro-competitive benefits arising from the restraint? On the other hand, might there be situations in which collective negotiations could be viewed as a market-improving step if they corrected market imperfections? See Thomas L. Greaney, Quality of Care and Market Failure Defenses in Antitrust Health Care Litigation, 21 Conn. L. Rev. 605, 650–52 (1989).

2. *Boycotts.* Note that the conduct at issue had elements of both a boycott (doctors collectively refusing to deal with payers) and a price fix (an agreement to contract only on agreed upon terms). This kind of boycott—one in aid of fixing prices—has been treated as illegal per se. FTC v. Superior Court Trial Lawyers Ass'n, 493 U.S. 411 (1990) (boycott of lawyers demanding higher pay for treating indigent defendants). However boycotts with some plausible efficiency justifications will be judged under the Rule of Reason (or as we will see in the following case, a "quick look" analysis) which requires the plaintiff to show actual anticompetitive effects. See e.g., Hahn v. Oregon Physicians' Service, 868 F.2d 1022 (9th Cir. 1988) (applying rule of reason analysis to alleged boycotts where providers were excluded from an IPA based on valid cost containment objectives).

3. *Other Provider Cartel Cases.* The federal agencies have successfully challenged scores of provider cartels that engaged in a wide variety of practices designed to raise prices, thwart competition from other providers, or stymie cost containment efforts of managed care organizations. See, e.g., In re Montana Associated Physicians, Inc. and Billings Physician Hospital Alliance, Inc., FTC Docket No. C-3704, 62 Fed. Reg. 11,201 (1997) (organization representing 43% of all area physicians formed to present a "united front" in dealing with MCOs and to "resist competitive pressures to discount fees"). See also United States v. Oklahoma State Chiropractic Independent Physicians Ass'n (N.D. Oklahoma, Complaint and Consent Decree filed Jan. 10, 2013) (chiropractors' agreement to specify a reimbursement floor to payers); United States v. North Dakota Hospital Association, 640 F. Supp. 1028 (D.N.D. 1986) (hospitals' joint refusal to extend discounts in bidding for contracts); American Medical Association, 94 F.T.C. 701 (1979) (final order and opinion), aff'd, 638 F.2d 443 (2d Cir. 1980), aff'd by an equally divided court, 455 U.S. 676 (1982) (ethical rules barring salaried employment, working for "inadequate compensation," and affiliating with non-physicians).

NOTE: CARTELIZING SCHEMES IN THE PHARMACEUTICAL INDUSTRY—"REVERSE PAYMENTS" BY BRAND NAME DRUG MANUFACTURERS

Prescription drugs account of a substantial share of health care spending. Some of the most significant litigation in the history of antitrust law (measured by the dollars at stake) has been brought by the FTC, private plaintiffs, and state attorneys general challenging payments made by brand-name drug manufacturers to potential-rival generic manufacturers usually accompanied by an agreement to delay entry by the generic into the market. These payments typically occur in the context of settling patent disputes. They are referred to as **"reverse payment"** cases because the flow of the monetary settlement—from patentee to alleged infringer—is in the opposite direction of that typically expected in a patent settlement case. Another nickname for these settlements is **"pay for delay"**—reflecting the net value accruing to the branded drug manufacturer by "purchasing" a later entry by the generic.

The complex interplay of patent law and prescription drug regulation has created strong financial incentives to violate the antitrust laws. Patent law gives the patent holder the legal right to exclude rivals and, practically, the ability to charge monopoly prices for its drug during the 20-year term of the patent. However, the patent process allows for the grant of patents without close review of their merits and many are overturned once challenged. See Jon Leibowitz, Comm'r, FTC, Anticompetitive Patent Settlements in the Pharmaceutical Industry: The Benefits of a Legislative Solution, Prepared Statement of the FTC Before the Committee on the Judiciary of the United States Senate 23–25 (Jan. 17, 2007). After the patent term expires, competitors can sell generic versions of the drug, driving down the market price and eating into the brand's market share. Additional generic competitors drive the price down further. See Richard G. Frank & David S. Salkever, Generic Entry and the Pricing of Pharmaceuticals, 6 J. Econ. & Mgmt. Strategy 75, 89 (1997). Recognizing the potential for substantial consumer savings, Congress enacted the Hatch-Waxman law in 1984 to encourage generic drug manufacturers to challenge questionable patents. That law provides that the first generic manufacturer to make certain certifications before the Food and Drug Administration will have 180 days of marketing exclusivity, during which the FDA may not approve another generic applicant. Though highly successful in inducing generic entry, Hatch-Waxman contained a serious flaw: it created a strong incentive for brand and generic manufacturers to conspire to delay marketing of the first generic and to divide the profits of the extended period of monopoly of the branded drug.

A manufacturer paying a rival not to compete has long been regarded as a per se violation of the Sherman Act, but extensive litigation in the reverse payment context produced widely differing interpretations in the courts. The problem in these cases was reconciling antitrust law's prohibition against anticompetitive practices with the rights of a patent holder to exclude rivals. In "reverse payment" settlements, the victim of the alleged infringement (the brand name drug maker) pays the alleged infringer (the generic manufacturer) a large payment in return for the generic agreeing to delay its entry into the market. Some courts held that such deals are not anticompetitive as long as the patent was legitimately obtained and the deal does not block generics from entering the market after the brand-name manufacturer's patent rights expire. See e.g., FTC v. Watson Pharmaceuticals, Inc., 677 F.3d 1298,1315 (11th Cir. 2012) ("deciding a patent case within an antitrust case about the settlement of the patent case [is] a turducken task.").

In 2013, the Supreme Court finally settled some of the key questions regarding antitrust enforcement of reverse payment cases. While declining to hold such settlements presumptively unlawful, it held that such claims are cognizable under antitrust law and clarified that in the rule of reason analysis, "large and unjustified" reverse payment "can bring with it the risk of anticompetitive effects." FTC v. Actavis, Inc., 570 U.S. 136, 158 (2013). While the *Actavis* decision was undoubtedly a major victory for antitrust enforcers and effectively ended cash payments in exchange for delayed entry, it did not solve the problem. Pharmaceutical companies have advanced a series of new strategies designed to circumvent the precise issue decided by the Supreme Court. For example, some have contended (with limited success) that *Actavis* only applies to cash payments and not to other arrangements such as licensing and co-promotion "side deals" involving other drugs in exchange for the generic's agreement to delay entry. Another approach has been for the brand name drug to agree to delay its own entry into the generic market (so-called "authorized generics") in exchange for delay by the generic challenger. These and other strategies are analyzed in an excellent book by Robin Feldman and Evan Frondorf, Drug Wars (2017). See also Michael Carrier, Payment After Actavis, 100 Iowa L. Rev. 7 (2014).

Another strategy that has attracted antitrust scrutiny involves efforts to extend (or "evergreen") patents on brand name drugs. In these cases, brand name drug companies whose patent protection will soon expire make minor changes typically in the dosage or delivery mode of the original drug and secures a new patent. Together with other steps, such as removing the original patented drug from regulatory lists, it may prevent generics from competing against either formulation. See Feldman and Frondorf supra, 66–79. What does all this suggest about the efficacy of litigation to deal with competition-obstructing conduct? What regulatory interventions might be tried?

B. COLLECTIVE ACTIVITIES WITH JUSTIFICATIONS

CALIFORNIA DENTAL ASSOCIATION V. FEDERAL TRADE COMMISSION

Supreme Court of the United States, 1999.
526 U.S. 756.

JUSTICE SOUTER delivered the opinion of the Court.

There are two issues in this case: whether the jurisdiction of the Federal Trade Commission extends to the California Dental Association (CDA), a nonprofit professional association, and whether a "quick look" sufficed to justify finding that certain advertising restrictions adopted by the CDA violated the antitrust laws. We hold that the Commission's jurisdiction under the Federal Trade Commission Act (FTC Act) extends to an association that, like the CDA, provides substantial economic benefit to its for-profit members, but that where, as here, any anticompetitive effects of given restraints are far from intuitively obvious, the rule of reason demands a more thorough enquiry into the consequences of those restraints than the Court of Appeals performed.

I

[Petitioner CDA, a nonprofit association of local dental societies to which about three-quarters of the State's dentists belong, provides desirable insurance and preferential financing arrangements for its members and engages in lobbying, litigation, marketing, and public relations for members' benefit. Members agree to abide by the CDA's Code of Ethics, which, *inter alia*, prohibits false or misleading advertising. The CDA has issued interpretive advisory opinions and guidelines relating to advertising. The FTC claimed that in applying its guidelines so as to restrict two types of truthful, nondeceptive advertising (price advertising, particularly discounted fees, and advertising relating to the quality of dental services), the CDA violated § 5 of the FTC Act. In its administrative proceedings, the Commission held that the advertising restrictions violated the Act under an abbreviated rule-of-reason analysis. In affirming, the Ninth Circuit sustained the Commission's jurisdiction and concluded that an abbreviated or "quick look" rule of reason analysis was proper in this case.]

The dentists who belong to the CDA . . . . agree to abide by a Code of Ethics (Code) including the following § 10:

> "Although any dentist may advertise, no dentist shall advertise or solicit patients in any form of communication in a manner that is false or misleading in any material respect. In order to properly serve the public, dentists should represent themselves in a manner that contributes to the esteem of the public. Dentists should not misrepresent their training and competence in any way that would be false or misleading in any material respect." [ ]

The CDA has issued a number of advisory opinions interpreting this section, and through separate advertising guidelines intended to help members comply with the Code and with state law the CDA has advised its dentists of disclosures they must make under state law when engaging in discount advertising.[2]

Responsibility for enforcing the Code rests in the first instance with the local dental societies, to which applicants for CDA membership must submit copies of their own advertisements and those of their employers or referral services to assure compliance with the Code. The local societies also actively seek information about potential Code violations by applicants or CDA members. Applicants who refuse to withdraw or revise objectionable advertisements may be denied membership; and members who, after a hearing, remain similarly recalcitrant are subject to censure, suspension, or expulsion from the CDA. [ ]

---

2   The disclosures include:

1. The dollar amount of the nondiscounted fee for the service[.]

2. Either the dollar amount of the discount fee or the percentage of the discount for the specific service[.]

3. The length of time that the discount will be offered[.]

4. Verifiable fees[.]

5. [The identity of] [s]pecific groups who qualify for the discount or any other terms and conditions or restrictions for qualifying for the discount. Id., at 724.

* * *

III

Because we decide that the Court of Appeals erred when it held as a matter of law that quick-look analysis was appropriate (with the consequence that the Commission's abbreviated analysis and conclusion were sustainable), we do not reach the question of the substantiality of the evidence supporting the Commission's conclusion.[8]

In National Collegiate Athletic Assn. v. Board of Regents of Univ. of Okla.[ ] we held that a "naked restraint on price and output requires some competitive justification even in the absence of a detailed market analysis." [ ]. Elsewhere, we held that "no elaborate industry analysis is required to demonstrate the anticompetitive character of" horizontal agreements among competitors to refuse to discuss prices. [ ] In each of these cases, which have formed the basis for what has come to be called abbreviated or "quick-look" analysis under the rule of reason, an observer with even a rudimentary understanding of economics could conclude that the arrangements in question would have an anticompetitive effect on customers and markets. * * * As in such cases, quick-look analysis carries the day when the great likelihood of anticompetitive effects can easily be ascertained. * * *

The case before us, however, fails to present a situation in which the likelihood of anticompetitive effects is comparably obvious. Even on Justice Breyer's view that bars on truthful and verifiable price and quality advertising are prima facie anticompetitive, and place the burden of procompetitive justification on those who agree to adopt them, the very issue at the threshold of this case is whether professional price and quality advertising is sufficiently verifiable in theory and in fact to fall within such a general rule. Ultimately our disagreement with Justice Breyer turns on our different responses to this issue. Whereas he accepts, as the Ninth Circuit seems to have done, that the restrictions here were like restrictions on advertisement of price and quality generally, [ ] it seems to us that the CDA's advertising restrictions might plausibly be thought to have a net procompetitive effect, or possibly no effect at all on competition. The restrictions on both discount and nondiscount advertising are, at least on their face, designed to avoid false or deceptive advertising[9] in a market characterized by striking disparities between the information available to the professional and the patient.[10] [ ] In a market for professional services,

---

[8]   We leave to the Court of Appeals the question whether on remand it can effectively assess the Commission's decision for substantial evidence on the record, or whether it must remand to the Commission for a more extensive rule-of-reason analysis on the basis of an enhanced record.

[9]   That false or misleading advertising has an anticompetitive effect, as that term is customarily used, has been long established. [ ]

[10]   "The fact that a restraint operates upon a profession as distinguished from a business is, of course, relevant in determining whether that particular restraint violates the Sherman Act. It

in which advertising is relatively rare and the comparability of service packages not easily established, the difficulty for customers or potential competitors to get and verify information about the price and availability of services magnifies the dangers to competition associated with misleading advertising. What is more, the quality of professional services tends to resist either calibration or monitoring by individual patients or clients, partly because of the specialized knowledge required to evaluate the services, and partly because of the difficulty in determining whether, and the degree to which, an outcome is attributable to the quality of services (like a poor job of tooth-filling) or to something else (like a very tough walnut). See Leland, Quacks, Lemons, and Licensing: A Theory of Minimum Quality Standards, 87 J. Pol. Econ. 1328, 1330 (1979); 1 B. Furrow, T. Greaney, S. Johnson, T. Jost, & R. Schwartz, Health Law § 3–1, p. 86 (1995) (describing the common view that "the lay public is incapable of adequately evaluating the quality of medical services"). Patients' attachments to particular professionals, the rationality of which is difficult to assess, complicate the picture even further. [ ] The existence of such significant challenges to informed decisionmaking by the customer for professional services immediately suggests that advertising restrictions arguably protecting patients from misleading or irrelevant advertising call for more than cursory treatment as obviously comparable to classic horizontal agreements to limit output or price competition.

* * *

[The Court of Appeals] brush[ed] over the professional context and describe[d] no anticompetitive effects. Assuming that the record in fact supports the conclusion that the CDA disclosure rules essentially bar advertisement of across-the-board discounts, it does not obviously follow that such a ban would have a net anticompetitive effect here. Whether advertisements that announced discounts for, say, first-time customers, would be less effective at conveying information relevant to competition if they listed the original and discounted prices for checkups, X-rays, and fillings, than they would be if they simply specified a percentage discount across the board, seems to us a question susceptible to empirical but not a priori analysis. * * * Put another way, the CDA's rule appears to reflect the prediction that any costs to competition associated with the elimination of across-the-board advertising will be outweighed by gains to consumer information (and hence competition) created by discount advertising that is exact, accurate, and more easily verifiable (at least by regulators). As a matter of economics this view may or may not be correct, but it is not

---

would be unrealistic to view the practice of professions as interchangeable with other business activities, and automatically to apply to the professions antitrust concepts which originated in other areas. The public service aspect, and other features of the professions, may require that a particular practice, which could properly be viewed as a violation of the Sherman Act in another context, be treated differently." Goldfarb v. Virginia State Bar, 421 U.S. 773, 788–789, n. 17, 95 S.Ct. 2004, 44 L.Ed.2d 572 (1975).

implausible, and neither a court nor the Commission may initially dismiss it as presumptively wrong.[12]

* * *

The Court of Appeals was comparably tolerant in accepting the sufficiency of abbreviated rule-of-reason analysis as to the nonprice advertising restrictions [characterizing them as "] in effect a form of output limitation, as they restrict the supply of information about individual dentists' services." . . . The question is not whether the universe of possible advertisements has been limited (as assuredly it has), but whether the limitation on advertisements obviously tends to limit the total delivery of dental services. The court . . . assert[ed] that limiting advertisements regarding quality and safety "prevents dentists from fully describing the package of services they offer," [ ] adding that "[t]he restrictions may also affect output more directly, as quality and comfort advertising may induce some customers to obtain nonemergency care when they might not otherwise do so," ibid. This suggestion about output is also puzzling. If quality advertising actually induces some patients to obtain more care than they would in its absence, then restricting such advertising would reduce the demand for dental services, not the supply; and it is of course the producers' supply of a good in relation to demand that is normally relevant in determining whether a producer-imposed output limitation has the anticompetitive effect of artificially raising prices.[13] * * *

Although the Court of Appeals acknowledged the CDA's view that "claims about quality are inherently unverifiable and therefore misleading," [ ] it responded that this concern "does not justify banning all quality claims without regard to whether they are, in fact, false or misleading," [ ]. As a result, the court said, "the restriction is a sufficiently naked restraint on output to justify quick look analysis." [ ] The court assumed, in these words, that some dental quality claims may escape

---

[12] Justice Breyer suggests that our analysis is "of limited relevance," because "the basic question is whether this . . . theoretically redeeming virtue in fact offsets the restrictions' anticompetitive effects in this case." He thinks that the Commission and the Court of Appeals "adequately answered that question," but the absence of any empirical evidence on this point indicates that the question was not answered, merely avoided by implicit burden-shifting of the kind accepted by Justice Breyer. The point is that before a theoretical claim of anticompetitive effects can justify shifting to a defendant the burden to show empirical evidence of procompetitive effects, as quick-look analysis in effect requires, there must be some indication that the court making the decision has properly identified the theoretical basis for the anticompetitive effects and considered whether the effects actually are anticompetitive. Where, as here, the circumstances of the restriction are somewhat complex, assumption alone will not do.

[13] Justice Breyer wonders if we "mea[n] this statement as an argument against the anticompetitive tendencies that flow from an agreement not to advertise service quality." But as the preceding sentence shows, we intend simply to question the logic of the Court of Appeals's suggestion that the restrictions are anticompetitive because they somehow "affect output," presumably with the intent to raise prices by limiting supply while demand remains constant. We do not mean to deny that an agreement not to advertise service quality might have anticompetitive effects. We merely mean that, absent further analysis of the kind Justice Breyer undertakes, it is not possible to conclude that the net effect of this particular restriction is anticompetitive.

justifiable censure, because they are both verifiable and true. But its implicit assumption fails to explain why it gave no weight to the countervailing, and at least equally plausible, suggestion that restricting difficult-to-verify claims about quality or patient comfort would have a procompetitive effect by preventing misleading or false claims that distort the market. It is, indeed, entirely possible to understand the CDA's restrictions on unverifiable quality and comfort advertising as nothing more than a procompetitive ban on puffery. * * *

The point is not that the CDA's restrictions necessarily have the procompetitive effect claimed by the CDA; it is possible that banning quality claims might have no effect at all on competitiveness if, for example, many dentists made very much the same sort of claims. And it is also of course possible that the restrictions might in the final analysis be anticompetitive. The point, rather, is that the plausibility of competing claims about the effects of the professional advertising restrictions rules out the indulgently abbreviated review to which the Commission's order was treated. The obvious anticompetitive effect that triggers abbreviated analysis has not been shown.

In light of our focus on the adequacy of the Court of Appeals's analysis, Justice Breyer's thorough-going, *de novo* antitrust analysis contains much to impress on its own merits but little to demonstrate the sufficiency of the Court of Appeals's review. The obligation to give a more deliberate look than a quick one does not arise at the door of this Court and should not be satisfied here in the first instance. Had the Court of Appeals engaged in a painstaking discussion in a league with Justice Breyer's (compare his 14 pages with the Ninth Circuit's 8), and had it confronted the comparability of these restrictions to bars on clearly verifiable advertising, its reasoning might have sufficed to justify its conclusion.

Saying here that the Court of Appeals' conclusion at least required a more extended examination of the possible factual underpinnings than it received is not, of course, necessarily to call for the fullest market analysis. Although we have said that a challenge to a "naked restraint on price and output" need not be supported by "a detailed market analysis" in order to "requir[e] some competitive justification," * * * [t]he truth is that our categories of analysis of anticompetitive effect are less fixed than terms like "*per se*," "quick look," and "rule of reason" tend to make them appear. We have recognized, for example, that "there is often no bright line separating *per se* from Rule of Reason analysis," since "considerable inquiry into market conditions" may be required before the application of any so-called "*per se*" condemnation is justified. * * * As the circumstances here demonstrate, there is generally no categorical line to be drawn between restraints that give rise to an intuitively obvious inference of anticompetitive effect and those that call for more detailed treatment. What is required, rather, is an enquiry meet for the case, looking to the circumstances, details, and logic of a restraint. The object is to see whether the experience of the market has been so clear, or necessarily will be, that a confident conclusion about the principal tendency of a restriction will follow from a quick (or at least quicker) look, in place of a more sedulous one. And of course what we see may vary over time, if rule-of-reason analyses in case after case reach identical conclusions. For now, at least, a less quick look was required for the initial assessment of the tendency of these professional advertising restrictions. Because the Court of Appeals did not scrutinize the assumption of relative anticompetitive tendencies, we vacate the judgment and remand the case for a fuller consideration of the issue.

It is so ordered.

JUSTICE BREYER, with whom JUSTICE STEVENS, JUSTICE KENNEDY, and JUSTICE GINSBURG join, concurring in part and dissenting in part.

I . . . agree that in a "rule of reason" antitrust case "the quality of proof required should vary with the circumstances," that "[w]hat is required . . . is an enquiry meet for the case," and that the object is a "confident conclusion about the principal tendency of a restriction." [ ] But I do not agree that the Court has properly applied those unobjectionable principles here. In my view, a traditional application of the rule of reason to the facts as found by the Commission requires affirming the Commission—just as the Court of Appeals did below.

I

The Commission's conclusion is lawful if its "factual findings," insofar as they are supported by "substantial evidence," "make out a violation of Sherman Act § 1." [ ] To determine whether that is so, I would not simply ask whether the restraints at issue are anticompetitive overall. Rather, like the Court of Appeals (and the Commission), I would break that question down into four classical, subsidiary antitrust questions: (1) What is the specific restraint at issue? (2) What are its likely anticompetitive effects? (3) Are there offsetting procompetitive justifications? (4) Do the parties have sufficient market power to make a difference?

A

The most important question is the first: What are the specific restraints at issue? [ ] Those restraints do *not* include merely the . . . promise to refrain from advertising that is " 'false or misleading in any material respect.' "[ ] Instead, the Commission found a set of restraints arising out of the way the Dental Association implemented this innocent-sounding ethical rule in practice, through advisory opinions, guidelines, enforcement policies, and review of membership applications. [ ] As implemented, the ethical rule reached beyond its nominal target, to prevent truthful and nondeceptive advertising. In particular, the Commission determined that the rule, in practice:

(1) "precluded advertising that characterized a dentist's fees as being low, reasonable, or affordable,"

(2) "precluded advertising . . . of across the board discounts," and

(3) "prohibit[ed] all quality claims."

Whether the Dental Association's basic rule as implemented actually restrained the truthful and nondeceptive advertising of low prices, across-the-board discounts, and quality service are questions of fact. . . . And the question for us—whether [The Commission's] findings are supported by substantial evidence, is not difficult.

The Court of Appeals referred explicitly to some of the evidence that it found adequate to support the Commission's conclusions. It pointed out, for example, that the Dental Association's "advisory opinions and guidelines indicate that . . . descriptions of prices as 'reasonable' or 'low' do not comply" with the Association's rule; that in "numerous cases" the Association "advised members of objections to special offers, senior citizen discounts, and new patient discounts, apparently without regard to their truth"; and that one advisory opinion "expressly states that claims as to the quality of services are inherently likely to be false or misleading," all "without any particular consideration of whether" such statements were "true or false." [ ]

The Commission itself had before it far more evidence. It referred to instances in which the Association, without regard for the truthfulness of the statements at issue, recommended denial of membership to dentists wishing to advertise, for example, "reasonable fees quoted in advance," "major savings," or "making teeth cleaning . . . inexpensive." It referred to testimony that "across-the-board discount advertising in literal compliance with the requirements 'would probably take two pages in the telephone book' and '[n]obody is going to really advertise in that fashion.'" And it pointed to many instances in which the Dental Association suppressed such advertising claims as "we guarantee all dental work for 1 year," "latest in cosmetic dentistry," and "gentle dentistry in a caring environment." [ ]

* * *

B

Do each of the three restrictions mentioned have "the potential for genuine adverse effects on competition"? [ ] I should have thought that the anticompetitive tendencies of the three restrictions were obvious. An agreement not to advertise that a fee is reasonable, that service is inexpensive, or that a customer will receive a discount makes it more difficult for a dentist to inform customers that he charges a lower price. If the customer does not know about a lower price, he will find it more difficult to buy lower price service[s]. That fact, in turn, makes it less likely that a dentist will obtain more customers by offering lower prices. And that likelihood means that dentists will prove less likely to offer lower prices. * * *

The restrictions on the advertising of service quality also have serious anticompetitive tendencies [because they inhibit[ ]] customers from learning about the quality of a dentist's service.

Nor did the Commission rely solely on the unobjectionable proposition that a restriction on the ability of dentists to advertise on quality is likely to limit their incentive to compete on quality. Rather, the Commission pointed to record evidence affirmatively establishing that quality-based competition is important to dental consumers in California. [The dissent goes on to summarize evidence that advertising concerning quality will bring in more patients and that restrictions adversely affected dentists who advertise.]

C

We must also ask whether, despite their anticompetitive tendencies, these restrictions might be justified by other procompetitive tendencies or redeeming virtues. [ ] This is a closer question—at least in theory. The Dental Association argues that the three relevant restrictions are inextricably tied to a legitimate Association effort to restrict false or misleading advertising. The Association, the argument goes, had to prevent dentists from engaging in the kind of truthful, nondeceptive advertising that it banned in order effectively to stop dentists from making unverifiable claims about price or service quality, which claims would mislead the consumer.

The problem with this or any similar argument is an empirical one. Notwithstanding its theoretical plausibility, the record does not bear out such a claim. The Commission ... characterized petitioner's efficiencies argument as rooted in the (unproved) factual assertion that its ethical rule "challenges only advertising that is false or misleading." [ ] Regardless, the Court of Appeals wrote, in respect to the price restrictions, that "the record provides no evidence that the rule has in fact led to increased disclosure and transparency of dental pricing." [ ] With respect to quality advertising, the Commission stressed that the Association "offered no convincing argument, let alone evidence, that consumers of dental services have been, or are likely to be, harmed by the broad categories of advertising it restricts."[ ] Nor did the Court of Appeals think that the Association's unsubstantiated contention that "claims about quality are inherently unverifiable and therefore misleading" could "justify banning all quality claims without regard to whether they are, in fact, false or misleading." [ ]

With one exception, my own review of the record reveals no significant evidentiary support for the proposition that the Association's members must agree to ban truthful price and quality advertising in order to stop untruthful claims. The one exception is the obvious fact that one can stop untruthful advertising if one prohibits all advertising. But since the Association made virtually no effort to sift the false from the true, [ ] that fact does not make out a valid antitrust defense. [ ]

In the usual Sherman Act § 1 case, the defendant bears the burden of establishing a procompetitive justification. [ ] And the Court of Appeals was correct when it concluded that no such justification had been established here.

* * *

NOTES AND QUESTIONS

1. *Role of Economic Evidence.* On remand, the Ninth Circuit ordered dismissal, finding the FTC had failed to show that the California Dental Association's (CDA) restrictions had a net anticompetitive effect and that the evidence of anticompetitive intent was ambiguous. 224 F.3d 942 (9th Cir. 2000). While acknowledging that the Supreme Court had not mandated a full blown rule of reason inquiry, the Ninth Circuit "opt[ed] for a particularly searching rule of reason inquiry in light of the plausibility and strength of the procompetitive justifications" supplied by expert testimony that advertising restrictions tend to protect the public from false or misleading information or unscrupulous providers.

How exacting should a court's proof requirements be when dealing with empirical economic evidence? Does the expertise of the FTC as an administrative agency charged with combating misleading advertising supply a basis for decreasing the role of the courts as arbiters of competing economic studies? For a useful survey of the evidence concerning the effects of advertising, concluding that evidence not in the record before the Supreme Court "overwhelmingly demonstrates that the fears of the *CDA* majority [were] unjustified," see Timothy J. Muris, The Rule of Reason After California Dental, 68 Antitrust L.J. 527 (2000).

2. *Quick Look.* In FTC v. Indiana Federation of Dentists, 476 U.S. 447 (1986), the FTC examined an agreement among dentists to refuse to submit x-rays used for diagnosis and treatment of patients to insurers. Insurers required x-rays to carry out review of the necessity of treatment pursuant to dental insurance plans limiting payment to the "least expensive set adequate treatment." While not employing the per se rule, the Court adopted the form of analysis described in CDA as a "quick look."

Application of the Rule of Reason to these facts is not a matter of any great difficulty. The Federation's policy takes the form of a horizontal agreement among the participating dentists to withhold from their customers a particular service that they desire—the forwarding of x-rays to insurance companies along with claim forms. "While this is not price fixing as such, no elaborate industry analysis is required to demonstrate the anti-competitive character of such an agreement." ... A refusal to compete with respect to the package of services offered to customers, no less than a refusal to compete with respect to the price term of an agreement, impairs the ability of the market to advance social welfare by ensuring the provision of desired goods and services to consumers at a price approximating the marginal cost of providing them.

Id. at 459. Is there a significant difference between the conduct in *California Dental* and *Indiana Federation of Dentists*? Didn't both cases involve actions by a sizable majority of dentists to withhold information from purchasers on the grounds that they could not adequately evaluate it? Note the absence of direct proof of the restraint's effect on consumers in either case. Has the Court changed the requirements for "quick look" evaluations? What does *California Dental* suggest about the way courts should evaluate restrictions involving professionals in the future? Are the problems associated with asymmetry of information so pronounced in health care markets that professionals should be free from antitrust scrutiny? For an insightful analysis of how antitrust might evaluate restraints of trade that improve overall welfare by overcoming market imperfections, see Peter J. Hammer, Antitrust Beyond Competition: Market Failures, Total Welfare, and the Challenge of Intramarket Second-Best Tradeoffs, 98 Mich. L. Rev. 849 (2000).

3. *Information Sharing.* Under what circumstances would competing providers sharing information on fees or other competitively sensitive topics pose a significant threat? Should it ever be deemed *per se* illegal? See United States v. Burgstiner, 1991–1 Trade Cas. (CCH) ¶ 69,422 (S.D. Ga. 1991) (consent decree) (exchange of information about fees among twenty-two OB/GYNs after local businesses announced their intention to form a PPO; fees for normal deliveries and caesarean sections increased by $500 after the exchange). However, in some circumstances, joint provision and dissemination of data may improve competitive conditions and should be evaluated under the rule of reason. The federal agencies' enforcement guidelines allow providers to collectively provide factual information concerning fees provided they adopt "reasonable safeguards" against anticompetitive activities. See U.S. Dept. of Justice & Federal Trade Commission, Statement of Antitrust Enforcement Policy in Health Care, Stmt. 5 (1996). How should antitrust law treat price surveys by business coalitions or other buyers of health services? When might buyer power (monopsony) pose competitive problems? See Clark C. Havighurst, Antitrust Issues in the Joint Purchasing of Health Care, 1995 Utah L. Rev. 409 (1995); Frances H. Miller, Health Insurance Purchasing Alliances: Monopsony Threat or Procompetitive Rx for Health Sector Ills, 79 Cornell L. Rev. 1546 (1994). The FTC and DOJ have issued numerous advisory opinions and business review letters approving such arrangements.

4. *Quality of Care Considerations.* Should courts consider defendant's potential to improve the quality of care as a defense or mitigating factor in a case involving professional restraints of trade? The Supreme Court addressed

the defendants' quality of care justifications in *Indiana Federation of Dentists*, 476 U.S. at 462–463:

> The gist of [defendant's] claim is that x-rays, standing alone, are not adequate bases for diagnosis of dental problems or for the formulation of an acceptable course of treatment. Accordingly, if insurance companies are permitted to determine whether they will pay a claim for dental treatment on the basis of x-rays as opposed to a full examination of all the diagnostic aids available to the examining dentist, there is a danger that they will erroneously decline to pay for treatment that is in fact in the interest of the patient, and that the patient will as a result be deprived of fully adequate care.

> The Federation's argument is flawed both legally and factually. The premise of the argument is that, far from having no effect on the cost of dental services chosen by patients and their insurers, the provision of x-rays will have too great an impact: it will lead to the reduction of costs through the selection of inadequate treatment. . . . The argument is, in essence, that an unrestrained market in which consumers are given access to the information they believe to be relevant to their choices will lead them to make unwise and even dangerous choices. Such an argument amounts to "nothing less than a frontal assault on the basic policy of the Sherman Act." [ ]

> Moreover, there is no particular reason to believe that the provision of information will be more harmful to consumers in the market for dental services than in other markets. Insurers deciding what level of care to pay for are not themselves the recipients of those services, but it is by no means clear that they lack incentives to consider the welfare of the patient as well as the minimization of costs. They are themselves in competition for the patronage of the patients—or, in most cases, the unions or businesses that contract on their behalf for group insurance coverage— and must satisfy their potential customers that they will not only provide coverage at a reasonable cost, but also that the coverage will be adequate to meet their customers' dental needs. . . .

The Court has ruled decisively on this issue in several cases. The leading case is National Society of Professional Engineers v. United States, 435 U.S. 679 (1978) wherein the Court refused to credit a professional association's justification for banning competitive bidding based on the assertion that some engineers would submit successful low bids by reducing quality, and as a result defective structures would be built, ultimately threatening public safety. See Thomas L. Greaney, Quality of Care and Market Failure Defenses in Antitrust Health Care Litigation, 21 Conn. L. Rev. 605 (1989). Characterizing this defense as an appeal to public interest considerations that were more properly addressed to Congress, the Court stated that the antitrust laws reflect Congress's judgment that "ultimately competition will not only produce lower prices, but also better goods and services" and concluded that antitrust scrutiny must focus exclusively on an activity's net effect on competitive conditions. *Professional Engineers, supra* at 695.

NOTE: PHYSICIAN STAFF PRIVILEGES

Hundreds of physicians who have been denied staff privileges at hospitals or had their privileges revoked, suspended, or limited have brought suit under the antitrust laws against the hospital, its medical staff or both. These cases— aptly termed the "junk food of antitrust health care litigation"—have been almost uniformly unsuccessful. See 2 John J. Miles, Health Care and Antitrust Law § 10–1; Hammer & Sage, Antitrust, Health Care Quality and the Courts, *supra*. For a rare example of a successful challenge to a staff privileges determination, see Boczar v. Manatee Hospitals & Health Systems, Inc., 993 F.2d 1514 (11th Cir. 1993).

Aggrieved physicians typically employ one of three antitrust theories. First, many assert that the denial of privileges is an anticompetitive boycott, usually instigated by rivals on the hospital's medical staff. See Oltz v. St. Peter's Community Hospital, 861 F.2d 1440 (9th Cir. 1988) (upholding nurse anesthetist's claim that a group of anesthesiologists had acquired an exclusive contract with a hospital by coercing it to terminate the anesthetist's contract; after plaintiff left the hospital each of the defendant anesthesiologists experienced a forty to fifty percent increase in earnings). Courts have dismissed or granted summary judgment in almost all such cases on one of several grounds with virtually all decisions applying the rule of reason. See e.g., Singh v. Memorial Medical Center, Inc., 536 F. Supp. 2d 1244 (D.N.M. 2008). Recall that under the Sherman Act, defendants engaged in a collective refusal to deal must advance a procompetitive justification in order to avoid per se treatment. Why is this requirement so readily met with respect to staff privileges determinations?

Under the rule of reason, plaintiff must establish that defendants have market power (unless, as in *Oltz* there is direct proof of effect), which is generally not present if there is a number of alternative hospitals at which the physician may practice. Robinson v. Magovern, 521 F. Supp. 842 (W.D. Pa. 1981), aff'd 688 F.2d 824 (3d Cir. 1982). Second, plaintiffs often cannot meet the conspiracy requirement under Section 1 of the Sherman Act because, where the hospital is the ultimate decision-maker on the grant of staff privileges, there is no plurality of actors. Under an alternative theory—the claim that the hospital has conspired with its medical staff—the courts are sharply divided. Compare Weiss v. York Hospital, 745 F.2d 786 (3d Cir. 1984) with Bolt v. Halifax Hosp. Medical Center, 891 F.2d 810 (11th Cir. 1990). For a representative case surveying many of the defenses available to hospitals in staff privileges cases, see Oksanen v. Page Memorial Hospital, 945 F.2d 696 (4th Cir. 1991) (concluding with the observation "the antitrust laws were not intended to inhibit hospitals from promoting quality patient care through peer review nor were the laws intended as a vehicle for converting business tort claims into antitrust causes of action").

Many challenges involve exclusive contracts, pursuant to which certain medical services such as radiology, pathology, and anesthesiology are provided in a hospital by a single group of physicians. Plaintiffs challenging these contracts on antitrust grounds have attempted to characterize the contracts as "tying" arrangements which are *per se* illegal. This claim requires the plaintiff to prove that a seller with market power in one product (the tying product) has forced a buyer to purchase another product (the tied product) that the buyer ordinarily would prefer to purchase separately. Plaintiff doctors have been uniformly unsuccessful in challenging exclusive contracts as illegal tying arrangements. See Jefferson Parish Hospital Dist. No. 2 v. Hyde, 466 U.S. 2 (1984); Collins v. Associated Pathologists, Ltd., 844 F.2d 473 (7th Cir. 1988). Finally, an important factor further limiting the viability of these lawsuits is the Health Care Quality Improvement Act, 42 U.S.C. §§ 11101–11152, discussed in Chapter 11, which affords immunity to individuals involved in making staff privileges determinations in certain circumstances.

PROBLEM: FAST STOP CLINICS

Drug World, a pharmacy chain operating a large number of retail pharmacies in the upper Midwest, has announced plans to open 24-Hour "Fast Stop Clinics" at all of its locations. The clinics will be staffed by RNs and PAs depending on state licensure and scope of practice laws. These providers will perform routine exams, take cultures, and prescribe medications within the scope of practice permitted under state law. Each clinic will enter into referral agreements with one or more local hospitals to assure direct access to physicians when the need presents. Good Samaritan Hospital (GSH) has entered into such an arrangement with a local Fast Stop Clinic. Under their partnership agreement, all doctors providing back up to Fast Stop RNs will have admitting privileges at GSH, and the clinics will be able to "streamline" a patient's journey to a specialist or through the emergency room at GSH, when medically appropriate.

A number of doctors holding staff privileges at GSH became quite upset when they got wind of this agreement. The group, though small (fewer than 5% of all doctors with privileges at the hospital), includes both primary care physicians who are concerned about losing current patients to the doctors to whom the clinic refers and several prominent specialists who feel they will lose established lines of referrals from primary care physicians. Some doctors believe that patients will come to them in worse shape, with missed diagnoses, and inadequate follow up. They have posted a notice at the hospital calling for an emergency meeting to discuss options to counter GSH's plan. The doctors propose three possible courses of action, asking colleagues to:

- Agree that no doctors will serve as a collaborating or supervisory physician to Fast Stop Clinic RNs or PAs or accept referrals from the Clinic;

- Sign a letter to GSH administrators insisting that all patients receiving services from the clinic be advised that they should contact their primary care physician regarding any additional referrals or services needed; or

• Send a letter to all GSH physicians supplying academic studies and historical evidence of potential risks to patients who receive care from nonphysicians under arrangements such as those proposed.

The CEO of GSH has approached you for advice on the legality of each action contemplated by the staff physicians. She says she wants to fight them vigorously and that she is willing to consider filing an antitrust lawsuit, complaining to the Department of Justice, terminating the staff privileges of the ringleaders of the group, or undertaking any other steps you recommend.

III. HEALTH CARE ENTERPRISES, INTEGRATION AND FINANCING

As discussed in Chapter 12, the integration and consolidation of the health care industry spawned a wide variety of provider networks, alliances, and new organizational arrangements. These entities and contractual relationships often entail cooperation or outright mergers between previously competing providers or health plans seeking to achieve efficiencies and improve quality of care. They also raise the full spectrum of antitrust issues. For attorneys counseling clients forming such organizations, antitrust law merits close attention because many entities are quite openly seeking to acquire the maximum leverage they can in the competitive fray.

A. PROVIDER-CONTROLLED NETWORKS AND HEALTH PLANS

ARIZONA V. MARICOPA COUNTY MEDICAL SOCIETY
Supreme Court of the United States, 1982.
457 U.S. 332.

JUSTICE STEVENS delivered the opinion of the Court.

The question presented is whether § 1 of the Sherman Act [ ] has been violated by agreements among competing physicians setting, by majority vote, the maximum fees that they may claim in full payment for health services provided to policyholders of specified insurance plans. The United States Court of Appeals for the Ninth Circuit held that the question could not be answered without evaluating the actual purpose and effect of the agreements at a full trial. [ ] Because the undisputed facts disclose a violation of the statute, we granted certiorari, and now reverse.

* * *

II

The Maricopa Foundation for Medical Care is a nonprofit Arizona corporation composed of licensed doctors of medicine, osteopathy, and podiatry engaged in private practice. Approximately 1,750 doctors, representing about 70% of the practitioners in Maricopa County, are members.

The Maricopa Foundation was organized in 1969 for the purpose of promoting fee-for-service medicine and to provide the community with a competitive alternative to existing health insurance plans. [ ] The foundation performs three primary activities. It establishes the schedule of maximum fees that participating doctors agree to accept as payment in full for services performed for patients insured under plans approved by the foundation. It reviews the medical necessity and appropriateness of treatment provided by its members to such insured persons. It is authorized to draw checks on insurance company accounts to pay doctors for services performed for covered patients. In performing these functions, the foundation is considered an "insurance administrator" by the Director of the Arizona Department of Insurance. Its participating doctors, however, have no financial interest in the operation of the foundation.

The fee schedules limit the amount that the member doctors may recover for services performed for patients insured under plans approved by the foundations. To obtain this approval the insurers—including self-insured employers as well as insurance companies—agree to pay the doctors' charges up to the scheduled amounts, and in exchange the doctors agree to accept those amounts as payment in full for their services. The doctors are free to charge higher fees to uninsured patients, and they also may charge any patient less than the scheduled maxima. A patient who is insured by a foundation-endorsed plan is guaranteed complete coverage for the full amount of his medical bills only if he is treated by a foundation member. He is free to go to a nonmember physician and is still covered for charges that do not exceed the maximum-fee schedule, but he must pay any excess that the nonmember physician may charge.

The impact of the foundation fee schedules on medical fees and on insurance premiums is a matter of dispute. The State of Arizona contends that the periodic upward revisions of the maximum-fee schedules have the effect of stabilizing and enhancing the level of actual charges by physicians, and that the increasing level of their fees in turn increases insurance premiums. The foundations, on the other hand, argue that the schedules impose a meaningful limit on physicians' charges, and that the advance agreement by the doctors to accept the maxima enables the insurance carriers to limit and to calculate more efficiently the risks they underwrite and therefore serves as an effective cost-containment mechanism that has saved patients and insurers millions of dollars. * * *

* * *

III

The respondents recognize that our decisions establish that price-fixing agreements are unlawful on their face. But they argue that the *per se* rule does not govern this case because the agreements at issue are horizontal and fix maximum prices, are among members of a profession, are in an industry with which the judiciary has little antitrust experience, and are alleged to have pro-competitive justifications. * * *

* * *

B

Our decisions foreclose the argument that the agreements at issue escape *per se* condemnation because they are horizontal and fix maximum prices. [The cases] place horizontal agreements to fix maximum prices on the same legal—even if not economic—footing as agreements to fix minimum or uniform prices. [ ] The per se rule "is grounded on faith in price competition as a market force [and not] on a policy of low selling prices at the price of eliminating competition." [ ] In this case the rule is violated by a price restraint that tends to provide the same economic rewards to all practitioners regardless of their skill, their experience, their training, or their willingness to employ innovative and difficult procedures in individual cases. Such a restraint also may discourage entry into the market and may deter experimentation and new developments by individual entrepreneurs. It may be a masquerade for an agreement to fix uniform prices, or it may in the future take on that character.

* * *

The respondents' principal argument is that the *per se* rule is inapplicable because their agreements are alleged to have pro-competitive justifications. The argument indicates a misunderstanding of the *per se* concept. The anti-competitive potential inherent in all price-fixing agreements justifies their facial invalidation even if pro-competitive justifications are offered for some. [ ] Those claims of enhanced competition are so unlikely to prove significant in any particular case that we adhere to the rule of law that is justified in its general application. Even when the respondents are given every benefit of the doubt, the limited record in this case is not inconsistent with the presumption that the respondents' agreements will not significantly enhance competition.

The respondents contend that their fee schedules are pro-competitive because they make it possible to provide consumers of health care with a uniquely desirable form of insurance coverage that could not otherwise exist. The features of the foundation-endorsed insurance plans that they stress are a choice of doctors, complete insurance coverage, and lower premiums. The first two characteristics, however, are hardly unique to these plans. Since only about 70% of the doctors in the relevant market are members of either foundation, the guarantee of complete coverage only applies when an insured chooses a physician in that 70%. If he elects to go to a nonfoundation doctor, he may be required to pay a portion of the doctor's fee. It is fair to presume, however, that at least 70% of the doctors in other markets charge no more than the "usual, customary, and reasonable" fee that typical insurers are willing to reimburse in full. [ ] Thus, in Maricopa and Pima Counties as well as in most parts of the country, if an insured asks his doctor if the insurance coverage is complete, presumably in about 70% of the cases the doctor will say "Yes" and in about 30% of the cases he will say "No."

It is true that a binding assurance of complete insurance coverage—as well as most of the respondents' potential for lower insurance premiums—can be obtained only if the insurer and the doctor agree in advance on the maximum fee that the doctor will accept as full payment for a particular service. Even if a fee schedule is therefore desirable, it is not necessary that the doctors do the price fixing. The record indicates that the Arizona Comprehensive Medical/Dental Program for Foster Children is administered by the Maricopa Foundation pursuant to a contract under which the maximum-fee schedule is prescribed by a state agency rather than by the doctors. [ ] This program and the Blue Shield plan challenged in Group Life & Health Insurance Co. v. Royal Drug Co., 440 U.S. 205 (1979), indicate that insurers are capable not only of fixing maximum reimbursable prices but also of obtaining binding agreements with providers guaranteeing the insured full reimbursement of a participating provider's fee. In light of these examples, it is not surprising that nothing in the record even arguably supports the conclusion that this type of insurance program could not function if the fee schedules were set in a different way.

The most that can be said for having doctors fix the maximum prices is that doctors may be able to do it more efficiently than insurers. The validity of that assumption is far from obvious,[28] but in any event there is no reason to believe that any savings that might accrue from this arrangement would be sufficiently great to affect the competitiveness of

---

[28] In order to create an insurance plan under which the doctor would agree to accept as full payment a fee prescribed in a fixed schedule, someone must canvass the doctors to determine what maximum prices would be high enough to attract sufficient numbers of individual doctors to sign up but low enough to make the insurance plan competitive. In this case that canvassing function is performed by the foundation; the foundation then deals with the insurer. It would seem that an insurer could simply bypass the foundation by performing the canvassing function and dealing with the doctors itself. Under the foundation plan, each doctor must look at the maximum-fee schedule fixed by his competitors and vote for or against approval of the plan (and, if the plan is approved by majority vote, he must continue or revoke his foundation membership). A similar, if to some extent more protracted, process would occur if it were each insurer that offered the maximum-fee schedule to each doctor.

these kinds of insurance plans. It is entirely possible that the potential or actual power of the foundations to dictate the terms of such insurance plans may more than offset the theoretical efficiencies upon which the respondents' defense ultimately rests.[29]

* * *

IV

Having declined the respondents' invitation to cut back on the per se rule against price fixing, we are left with the respondents' argument that their fee schedules involve price fixing in only a literal sense. For this argument, the respondents rely upon Broadcast Music, Inc. v. Columbia Broadcasting System, Inc., 441 U.S. 1 (1979).

In *Broadcast Music* we were confronted with an antitrust challenge to the marketing of the right to use copyrighted compositions derived from the entire membership of the American Society of Composers, Authors and Publishers (ASCAP). The so-called "blanket license" was entirely different from the product that any one composer was able to sell by himself. [ ] Although there was little competition among individual composers for their separate compositions, the blanket-license arrangement did not place any restraint on the right of any individual copyright owner to sell his own compositions separately to any buyer at any price. [ ] But a "necessary consequence" of the creation of the blanket license was that its price had to be established. [ ] We held that the delegation by the composers to ASCAP of the power to fix the price for the blanket license was not a species of the price-fixing agreements categorically forbidden by the Sherman Act. The record disclosed price fixing only in a "literal sense." [ ]

This case is fundamentally different. Each of the foundations is composed of individual practitioners who compete with one another for patients. Neither the foundations nor the doctors sell insurance, and they derive no profits from the sale of health insurance policies. The members of the foundations sell medical services. Their combination in the form of the foundation does not permit them to sell any different product. [ ] Their combination has merely permitted them to sell their services to certain customers at fixed prices and arguably to affect the prevailing market price of medical care.

The foundations are not analogous to partnerships or other joint arrangements in which persons who would otherwise be competitors pool their capital and share the risks of loss as well as the opportunities for profit. In such joint ventures, the partnership is regarded as a single firm

---

[29] In this case it appears that the fees are set by a group with substantial power in the market for medical services, and that there is competition among insurance companies in the sale of medical insurance. Under these circumstances the insurance companies are not likely to have significantly greater bargaining power against a monopoly or doctors than would individual consumers of medical services.

competing with other sellers in the market. The agreement under attack is an agreement among hundreds of competing doctors concerning the price at which each will offer his own services to a substantial number of consumers. It is true that some are surgeons, some anesthesiologists, and some psychiatrists, but the doctors do not sell a package of three kinds of services. If a clinic offered complete medical coverage for a flat fee, the cooperating doctors would have the type of partnership arrangement in which a price-fixing agreement among the doctors would be perfectly proper. But the fee agreements disclosed by the record in this case are among independent competing entrepreneurs. They fit squarely into the horizontal price-fixing mold.

The judgment of the Court of Appeals is reversed.

It is so ordered.

JUSTICE BLACKMUN and JUSTICE O'CONNOR took no part in the consideration or decision of this case.

JUSTICE POWELL, with whom THE CHIEF JUSTICE and JUSTICE REHNQUIST join, dissenting.

* * *

II

* * *

NOTES AND QUESTIONS

1. *The* Maricopa *Dissent.* The dissenters in *Maricopa* objected to *per se* categorization of an arrangement that "[o]n its face . . . seems to be in the public interest." The dissent observed that, "[u]nlike the classic cartel agreement," the Maricopa plan allowed participating doctors to associate with other plans, and serve patients outside the plan at other fee levels. And, the dissent noted that "there [was] no evidence of opposition to the foundation plan by . . . members of the public" or by insurers—arguably the market participants most concerned with medical costs. The dissent saw the foundation plan as analogous to the ASCAP blanket license in *Broadcast Music* because both were "prompted by the need for better service to the consumers . . . [a]nd each ma[d]e possible a new product by reaping otherwise unattainable efficiencies." Thus, the dissent would have rejected *per se* characterization as inappropriate for price agreements that "achieve[ ] for the public pro-competitive benefits that otherwise are not attainable."

2. *Revisiting Per Se Treatment of Maximum Prices. Maricopa* has been criticized for its wooden application of the *per se* rule. Can you detect, notwithstanding the opinion's more sweeping pronouncements, an attempt to evaluate the nature and necessity of the price agreements and the justifications offered? Consider how the ancillary restraints doctrine would apply in this case: what, for example, is the plurality's assessment of the

"reasonable necessity" of the price agreement? Another notable feature was the fact that the foundations adopted maximum, rather than minimum, fee schedules. Commentators contend that the dangers of maximum price fixing are not sufficiently large to justify *per se* treatment. Is it possible that the foundation may have adopted its pricing policies with an eye to limiting the risk of entry by HMOs? In that case wouldn't the arrangement be objectionable for its propensity to preserve supracompetitive prices, albeit at a lower level than existed before the foundations were formed? See Keith B. Leffler, Arizona v. Maricopa County Medical Society: Maximum-Price Agreements in Markets with Insured Buyers, 2 Sup.Ct. Econ. Rev. 187 (1983). See also Roger Blair & Jill Boylston Herndon, Physician Cooperative Bargaining Ventures: An Economic Analysis, 71 Antitrust L.J. 989 (2004) (physician bargaining power can sometimes be benign or even procompetitive under conditions of bilateral monopoly, i.e., where physicians face insurers with market power).

3. *Physician Integration. Maricopa* left open many questions about when integration among providers would be permissible, especially those involving PPOs having little financial integration. As will be discussed *infra*, the formation of networks or other joint ventures as part of accountable care organizations has focused considerable attention on degree of integration among participating physicians. The FTC/Department of Justice Policy Statements, which have been revised several times since their original promulgation in 1994, give guidance on several important issues. Compare the agencies' analysis in the following Policy Statement and Advisory Opinion with *Maricopa's* treatment of issues such as risk sharing, market power and efficiencies.

U.S. DEPARTMENT OF JUSTICE AND FEDERAL TRADE COMMISSION, STATEMENTS OF ANTITRUST ENFORCEMENT POLICY IN HEALTH CARE
4 Trade Reg. Rep. (CCH) para. 13,153.
(August 18, 1996).

8. Statement of Department of Justice and Federal Trade Commission Enforcement Policy on Physician Network Joint Ventures

* * *

A. *Antitrust Safety Zones*

This section describes those physician network joint ventures that will fall within the antitrust safety zones designated by the Agencies. The antitrust safety zones differ for "exclusive" and "non-exclusive" physician network joint ventures. In an "exclusive" venture, the network's physician participants are restricted in their ability to, or do not in practice, individually contract or affiliate with other network joint ventures or health plans. In a "non-exclusive" venture, on the other hand, the physician participants in fact do, or are available to, affiliate with other networks or contract individually with health plans. * * *

  1.   Exclusive Physician Network Joint Ventures That The Agencies Will Not Challenge, Absent Extraordinary Circumstances

The Agencies will not challenge, absent extraordinary circumstances, an exclusive physician network joint venture whose physician participants share substantial financial risk and constitute 20 percent or less of the physicians [ ] in each physician specialty with active hospital staff privileges who practice in the relevant geographic market. [ ] In relevant markets with fewer than five physicians in a particular specialty, an exclusive physician network joint venture otherwise qualifying for the antitrust safety zone may include one physician from that specialty, on a non-exclusive basis, even though the inclusion of that physician results in the venture consisting of more than 20 percent of the physicians in that specialty.

  2.   Non-Exclusive Physician Network Joint Ventures That The Agencies Will Not Challenge, Absent Extraordinary Circumstances

The Agencies will not challenge, absent extraordinary circumstances, a non-exclusive physician network joint venture whose physician participants share substantial financial risk and constitute 30 percent or less of the physicians in each physician specialty with active hospital staff privileges who practice in the relevant geographic market. In relevant markets with fewer than four physicians in a particular specialty, a non-exclusive physician network joint venture otherwise qualifying for the antitrust safety zone may include one physician from that specialty, even though the inclusion of that physician results in the venture consisting of more than 30 percent of the physicians in that specialty.

  3.   Indicia of Non-Exclusivity

  * * * [T]he Agencies caution physician participants in a non-exclusive physician network joint venture to be sure that the network is non-exclusive in fact and not just in name. The Agencies will determine whether a physician network joint venture is exclusive or non-exclusive by its physician participants' activities, and not simply by the terms of the contractual relationship. * * *

  4.   Sharing Of Substantial Financial Risk By Physicians In A Physician Network Joint Venture

  To qualify for either antitrust safety zone, the participants in a physician network joint venture must share substantial financial risk in providing all the services that are jointly priced through the network. [ ] The safety zones are limited to networks involving substantial financial risk sharing not because such risk sharing is a desired end in itself, but because it normally is a clear and reliable indicator that a physician network involves sufficient integration by its physician participants to achieve significant efficiencies. [ ] Risk sharing provides incentives for the physicians to cooperate in controlling costs and improving quality by managing the provision of services by network physicians.

The following are examples of some types of arrangements through which participants in a physician network joint venture can share substantial financial risk: [ ]

(1) agreement by the venture to provide services to a health plan at a "capitated" rate; [ ]

(2) agreement by the venture to provide designated services or classes of services to a health plan for a predetermined percentage of premium or revenue from the plan;

(3) use by the venture of significant financial incentives for its physician participants, as a group, to achieve specified cost-containment goals. Two methods by which the venture can accomplish this are:

(a) withholding from all physician participants in the network a substantial amount of the compensation due to them, with distribution of that amount to the physician participants based on group performance in meeting the cost-containment goals of the network as a whole; or

(b) establishing overall cost or utilization targets for the network as a whole, with the network's physician participants subject to subsequent substantial financial rewards or penalties based on group performance in meeting the targets; and

(4) agreement by the venture to provide a complex or extended course of treatment that requires the substantial coordination of care by physicians in different specialties offering a complementary mix of services, for a fixed, predetermined payment, where the costs of that course of treatment for any individual patient can vary greatly due to the individual patient's condition, the choice, complexity, or length of treatment, or other factors. * * *

B.   *The Agencies' Analysis Of Physician Network Joint Ventures That Fall Outside The Antitrust Safety Zones*

Physician network joint ventures that fall outside the antitrust safety zones also may have the potential to create significant efficiencies, and do not necessarily raise substantial antitrust concerns.

* * *

1.   *Determining When Agreements Among Physicians In A Physician Network Joint Venture Are Analyzed Under The Rule Of Reason*

Antitrust law treats naked agreements among competitors that fix prices or allocate markets as *per se* illegal. Where competitors economically integrate in a joint venture, however, such agreements, if reasonably necessary to accomplish the pro-competitive benefits of the integration, are analyzed under the rule of reason. [ ] In accord with general antitrust principles, physician network joint ventures will be analyzed under the rule of reason, and will not be viewed as *per se* illegal, if the physicians' integration through the network is likely to produce significant efficiencies that benefit consumers, and any price agreements (or other agreements that would otherwise be *per se* illegal) by the network physicians are reasonably necessary to realize those efficiencies. [ ]

Where the participants in a physician network joint venture have agreed to share substantial financial risk as defined in Section A.4. of this policy statement, their risk-sharing arrangement generally establishes both an overall efficiency goal for the venture and the incentives for the physicians to meet that goal. The setting of price is integral to the venture's use of such an arrangement and therefore warrants evaluation under the rule of reason.

Physician network joint ventures that do not involve the sharing of substantial financial risk may also involve sufficient integration to demonstrate that the venture is likely to produce significant efficiencies. Such integration can be evidenced by the network implementing an active and ongoing program to evaluate and modify practice patterns by the network's physician participants and create a high degree of interdependence and cooperation among the physicians to control costs and ensure quality. This program may include: (1) establishing mechanisms to monitor and control utilization of health care services that are designed to control costs and assure quality of care; (2) selectively choosing network physicians who are likely to further these efficiency objectives; and (3) the significant investment of capital, both monetary and human, in the necessary infrastructure and capability to realize the claimed efficiencies.

* * *

Determining that an arrangement is merely a vehicle to fix prices or engage in naked anti-competitive conduct is a factual inquiry that must be done on a case-by-case basis to determine the arrangement's true nature and likely competitive effects. However, a variety of factors may tend to corroborate a network's anti-competitive nature, including: statements evidencing anti-competitive purpose; a recent history of anti-competitive behavior or collusion in the market, including efforts to obstruct or undermine the development of managed care; obvious anti-competitive structure of the network (e.g., a network comprising a very high percentage of local area physicians, whose participation in the network is exclusive, without any plausible business or efficiency justification); the absence of any mechanisms with the potential for generating significant efficiencies or otherwise increasing competition through the network; the presence of anti-competitive collateral agreements; and the absence of mechanisms to prevent the network's operation from having anti-competitive spillover effects outside the network.

* * *

[The Statement sets forth the methodology for balancing anticompetitive and procompetitive effects under the rule of reason: assessing the market power of the network in each physician services relevant market; evaluating effects by considering incentives for anticompetitive conduct and whether "there are many other networks or many physicians . . . available to form competing networks;" evaluating the risks of "spillover" effects on contracts outside the networks; and weighing the offsetting efficiency benefits uniquely achievable through the networks.]

NOTES AND QUESTIONS

1.   The Statements repeatedly emphasize that merely because a physician network joint venture does not fall within a safety zone does not mean that it is unlawful under the antitrust laws. Many arrangements outside the safety zones have received favorable business review letters or advisory opinions from the agencies. See, e.g., Letter from Anne K. Bingaman, Assistant Attorney General, to John F. Fischer (Oklahoma Physicians Network, Inc.) (Jan. 17, 1996) (approving non-exclusive network with "substantially more" than 30% of several specialties, including more than 50% in one specialty). What facts might be particularly persuasive in mitigating the agencies' concerns about a network whose size exceeded safety zone thresholds?

2.   *Messenger Model Arrangements.* Another section of the 1996 Policy Statements created a relief valve for physicians wanting to form networks but unwilling to undertake financial risk sharing or clinical integration. Under so-called "messenger model" network agreements, physicians may use a common agent to convey information to and from payers about the prices and price-related terms they are willing to accept. Policy Statements, *supra,* Statement 9. However, the messenger must communicate individually with each network physician and not act as a conduit for information sharing or agreements among members. The permitted model is violated when:

> the agent coordinates the providers' responses to a particular proposal, disseminates to network providers the views or intentions of other network providers as to the proposal, expresses an opinion on the terms offered, collectively negotiates for the providers, or decides whether or not to convey an offer based on the agent's judgment about the attractiveness of the prices or price-related terms. Id.

In essence, the 1996 Policy Statements establish a presumption that physicians complying with the messenger model's parameters have not collectively agreed upon prices, but instead have determined their prices individually. Central to the concept, of course, is the integrity of the messenger—he or she must function solely as a conduit for offers and exchanges between payers and individual providers. One commentator has suggested that the messenger model operates under such unrealistic assumptions that it may be the case that the government "purposely created a gray area of enforcement" to allow physicians to share the economic rewards of networks despite restrictions imposed by the case law. Jeffrey L. Harrison, The Messenger Model: Don't Ask, Don't Tell?, 71 Antitrust L.J. 1017, 1017 (2004). Other factors underlying the government's endorsement of the messenger model may include political pressures faced by the antitrust agencies and the increasingly regulatory role the agencies have assumed. See Thomas L. Greaney, Thirty Years of Solicitude: Antitrust Law and Physician Cartels, 7 Hous. J. Health L. & Pol. 101 (2007).

In an astounding number of cases, physician networks have engaged in blatant violations of the messenger model. The FTC has brought over 60 administrative actions challenging these, typically branding them as *per se* price fixing schemes. For the most part these cases involve noncompliance with obvious prohibitions of the model, such as polling members on desired prices and using those prices to negotiate on behalf of members. Yet violations have continued apace, a practice likely attributable to the fact that the FTC typically only imposes injunctive prohibitions ("go forth and sin no more") in consent decrees. See e.g. In the Matter of Southwest Health Alliances, Inc. FTC File No. 091–0013 (July 15, 2011) (cease and desist order involving an association of 900 physicians in the Amarillo Texas area that the Commission alleged had fixed prices and terms at which it would contract with health plans).

3. *Clinical Integration.* The antitrust agencies have recognized a second relief valve for physician networks not undertaking financial risk to avoid per se treatment. A series of advisory opinions have approved networks that undertook significant "clinical integration." The opinions summarize the concept as involving "performance of one or more business functions of the participants in a way that potentially benefits consumers by expanding output, reducing price, or enhancing quality, service or innovation, and that could not reasonably be achieved by the participants individually." FTC Advisory Opinion, In re MedSouth Inc. (Feb. 12, 2002). The opinions cite a variety of factors such as the collective development and implementation of the protocols and benchmarks to guide medical decisions; the use of tools to share information about efficacy and cost such as electronic medical records; practices that integrate primary and specialty services; and rules governing the selection and where appropriate expulsion of providers who fail to adhere to network standards. At bottom, the inquiry seeks to assure that the providers are as sufficiently interdependent as they are in risk sharing arrangements so that individual physicians have incentives to pursue network rather than individual goals regarding cost and quality. It is important to note however that clinical integration is not a free pass: the network must still satisfy the standards under the rule of reason with regard to the size of the network in relevant product and geographic markets and avoid spillover harms such as agreements by providers to abide by network prices in their negotiations outside of the network.

4.   *Physician Specialties.* Do recognized areas of specialization constitute a distinct market for analysis under the Policy Statements? The answer depends on whether there is substitution across specialty areas. Compare Letter from Anne K. Bingaman, Assistant Attorney General, Antitrust Division, to Steven J. Kern and Robert J. Conroy (March 1, 1996) (concluding that family practitioners and other primary care physicians who treat children were not widely accepted substitutes for pediatricians) with Letter from Anne K. Bingaman, Assistant Attorney General, Antitrust Division to James M. Parker (Oct. 27, 1994) (board-certified pulmonologists are not exclusive providers of pulmonology-type services; merger of two pulmonology groups allowed to proceed because of significant competition from surgeons, family practitioners and other primary care physicians). What facts would you gather and what witnesses would you interview to decide whether a given specialty constitutes a relevant market? See also Statement 9 of the Policy Statements (analyzing the competitive implications of "multiprovider networks," i.e., ventures such as physician-hospital organizations (PHOs), whereby providers who offer both competing and complementary services may jointly market their services. The statement counsels against overbroad vertical exclusive arrangements that restrict providers from dealing with other networks or other providers in a network; for example a network may enlist such a large proportion of the market's general surgeons that competition from rival networks or hospitals may be inhibited. These concerns arise only where the other networks have few alternatives to which they may turn and they are unable to recruit needed providers from outside the market.

B. ACCOUNTABLE CARE ORGANIZATIONS

In accountable care organizations (ACOs), providers work together to coordinate care, control costs, and improve quality. Despite these laudable goals, the ACO model of integration implicates antitrust law because it has providers jointly contracting with payers, sharing patient information, payment, and financial risk.

Contemporaneously with CMS's Final Rule on ACOs (see Chapter 10), the FTC and DOJ ("the Agencies") released a Final Statement of antitrust enforcement policy regarding Medicare ACOs which set forth a detailed exposition of the standards they will apply to review ACOs for potential antitrust violations. FTC & U.S. Dep't. of Justice Statement of Antitrust Enforcement Policy Regarding Accountable Care Organizations Participating in the Medicare Shared Savings Program, 76 Fed. Reg. 67,026 (Oct. 28, 2011) (Final Statement). Unlike the fraud and abuse laws, the ACA does not authorize the Secretary of HHS to waive the applicability of the antitrust laws to ACO formation and operation. Hence, clarification of the Agencies' approach to analyzing ACOs under the antitrust law was important to remove uncertainty for providers considering forming these entities. (Note, however, that state attorneys general and private parties may also bring actions under federal or state antitrust laws and are not bound by the standards contained in the Final Statement or by the decision of the Agencies not to pursue a case).

The overarching objective of the Final Statement is to prevent ACOs from enhancing or entrenching market power and to encourage, to the extent possible, the development of competitive ACOs in local markets around the country. See generally Thomas L. Greaney, Accountable Care Organizations—The Fork in the Road, 364 NEJM e1 (2011); Taylor Burke & Sara Rosenbaum, Accountable Care Organizations: Implications for Antitrust Policy (Robert Wood Johnson Foundation 2010). Although the Final Statement purports to deal primarily with procedural policies that will govern their review of ACOs, it also contains or hints at a number of important substantive determinations that will apply.

Clinical Integration. The Final Statement provides that ACOs meeting CMS's standards of participation in the MSSP will be deemed sufficiently integrated so that participants contracting with commercial payers will be judged under the rule of reason and not the *per se* standard of illegality. From the standpoint of removing uncertainty and clarifying the steps that ACOs must undertake to satisfy the Agencies' analysis of horizontal restraints (see discussion of clinical integration *supra*), this is an important concession. It was probably not a difficult one, however, as the ACA contains detailed prescriptions that go a long way in assuring that physicians and other providers are truly interdependent and invested in the success of the ACO. Moreover, CMS will collect detailed cost, utilization, and quality information for ACOs, which will allow the Agencies to test whether the CMS eligibility criteria do, in fact, produce meaningful integration and quality and cost improvements. Somewhat more controversially, the Final Statement also indicates that if an ACO receives CMS approval, it will treat joint negotiations with private payers as reasonably necessary to realize the ACOs primary purpose of improving health care delivery.

Safety Zone. The Final Statement sets forth a "safety zone" stating that, absent extraordinary circumstances, the Agencies will not challenge an ACO comprised of independent ACO participants that provide a common service where the ACO's combined share of the common service is 30 percent or less in each ACO participant's primary service areas (PSAs). Note: a "common service" refers to services provided by two or more *previously independent* entities offering their services through the ACO; it does not cover services of a single entity. Several important restrictions and exceptions apply:

- *Hospitals and ASCs.* Any hospital or ambulatory surgery center participating in an ACO regardless of size must be non-exclusive to the ACO in order to qualify for the safety zone.

- *Rural Provider Exception.* ACOs may include one physician or one physician group practice per specialty from each rural area even if inclusion causes the ACO's share of any common service to exceed 30 percent, provided the physician or group participates on a non-exclusive basis. ACOs may also include rural hospitals, even if inclusion of a rural hospital causes the ACO's share of any common service to exceed 30 percent, again so long as the rural participant participates on a non-exclusive basis. For purposes of this exception, rural hospitals include "critical access hospitals" or "sole community hospitals," as defined under Medicare regulations or any other hospital with fewer than 50 beds and located in a rural area not within 35 miles from any other acute care hospital.

- *Dominant Provider Limitation.* ACOs that include a dominant provider (a participant with greater than a 50 percent share in its primary service area for any service that no other ACO participant provides) must be non-exclusive to the ACO to qualify for the safety zone. In addition, an ACO with a dominant provider cannot require a payer to contract exclusively with the ACO or otherwise restrict the payer's ability to contract with other ACOs or provider networks.

Antitrust Agency Review of ACOs. Backing away from the approach set forth in their Proposed Statement, the Agencies and CMS eliminated a requirement for *mandatory* antitrust review as prerequisite to certification for participation in the MSSP. Mandatory review had initially been contemplated for any ACO whose share exceeded 50 percent in any common service that two or more of its independent participants provided in the same primary service area. Without fully crediting any particular objection, CMS noted various criticisms it had received including claims that mandatory review conferred unreviewable authority on the antitrust agencies to disqualify entities from participating in the MSSP which is subject to the regulatory oversight of HHS alone; that the process converted antitrust review into a regulatory process; and, that review imposed entry-inhibiting costs on ACOs. CMS Medicare Shared Savings Program: Accountable Care Organizations, 76 Fed. Reg. 67, 802, 67,806–961 (Nov. 2, 2011) (CMS Final Rule). Instead of mandatory review, the Final Statement offers an expedited voluntary review process for ACOs outside the safety zone.

The Final Statement goes on to identify specific categories of conduct that it counsels may, under certain circumstances, raise competitive concerns and should be avoided. The most obvious warning, applicable to all ACOs regardless of their market power, is directed at garden-variety horizontal collusion. It states that significant antitrust concerns arise when an ACO's operation leads to price fixing or other collusion among

ACO participants in their sale of competing services outside the ACO and suggests that participants avoid improper exchanges of price or other competitively sensitive information that may facilitate such collusion. The Final Statement goes on to identify four types of conduct that "may raise competitive concerns" for an ACO with high PSA shares or other indicia of market power:

1. Discouraging private payers from directing or incentivizing patients to choose certain providers through contractual terms such as "anti-steering," "anti-tiering," "guaranteed inclusion," and "most favored nations" provisions.

2. Tying sales of the ACO's services to the private payer's purchase of other services from providers outside the ACO, and vice versa.

3. Contracting with ACO participants on an exclusive basis.

4. Restricting a private payer's ability to make available cost, quality, efficiency, and performance information to aid enrollees in evaluating and selecting providers in the health plan if it is similar to that used in the shared savings program.

Applying the Market Tests. Note that the above thresholds apply to each service provided by at least two *independent* ACO participants. Thus, an ACO combining an independent surgeon who has an 8 percent market share with a hospital that employs a surgery group with a 25 percent share would fall outside the safety zone of 30 percent. On the other hand, an ACO comprised of a single surgery group with 33 percent share would not fall outside the safety zone for that service. Thus, ACO applicants will need to calculate their shares for dozens of services. An ACO comprised solely of an integrated health system and its employed physicians would not have to submit an application to the Agencies even if the physicians or hospitals in the ACO hold a PSA share in excess of 50 percent.

The Final Statement proposes to employ primary service areas (PSAs) to calculate the foregoing shares and as a rough proxy for the markets served by ACO participants. For purposes of defining "services," a physician's "service" is the physician's primary specialty, as identified by the Medicare Specialty Code. A hospital's "services" consists of each major diagnostic category (MDC), a grouping of the diagnosis related groups (DRGs) used by Medicare for reimbursement purposes. ACOs must identify the PSA for each common service for each participant in the ACO. The Statement defines the PSA as "the lowest number of contiguous zip codes from which" the ACO participant "draws at least 75 percent" of its patients, which is a concept borrowed from the Stark Law. The ACO must calculate the ACO's PSA share for each common service in each PSA from which at least two ACO participants serve patients for that service.

NOTES AND QUESTIONS

1.   The ACO Final Statement attempts to balance the need for administrability, accuracy, and speed for antitrust reviews. Does it get the balance right? Consider some of the following criticisms.

- The Final Statement does not address the potential market power of ACOs formed through mergers and acquisitions.

- PSAs are an inadequate proxy to use for identifying antitrust markets (see FTC v. Advocate Healthcare, *infra*).

- The emphasis on non-exclusivity in the Final Statement is inconsistent with ACOs' need to get providers to invest time and capital to efficiently integrate their delivery system.

2.   In abandoning mandatory review, did CMS miss an opportunity to improve competitive conditions by leveraging its regulatory oversight in the ACO approval process? For example would it have been better positioned to insist that dominant providers not abuse their market position (a problem discussed in the following section)? See Thomas L. Greaney, Regulators as Market Makers: Accountable Care Organizations and Competition Policy, 46 Ariz. St. L. J. 1 (2014).

3.   The primary reason for concern about the competitive effects of ACOs is that most entities will be offering their services in the private insurance market at the same time they are participating in the Medicare Shared Savings Program. Indeed, the ACA encourages such participation: Section 3022 provides that the Secretary of HHS "may give preference to ACOs who [sic] are participating in similar arrangements with other payers." At the same time, extensive scholarship has shown that hospital and many specialty physician markets are highly concentrated. What can the Agencies do about this? Do the four warnings contained in the Final Statement address the conduct that might harm competition by ACOs formed by dominant providers? How will they be used in the context of applying ACOs? For suggestions on this topic see, Clark C. Havighurst and Barak D. Richman, The Provider Monopoly Problem in Health Care, 89 Or. L. Rev. 847 (2011); Thomas L. Greaney, The Affordable Care Act and Competition Policy: Antidote or Placebo?, 89 Or. L. Rev. 811 (2011); Joe Miller, The Proposed Accountable Care Organization Antitrust Guidance: A First Look, Health Aff. Blog (April 14, 2011).

PROBLEM: ORGANIZING AN ACO

Midsize Hospital is one of three hospitals in the town of Midlands. Three hundred independent physicians hold staff privileges at the hospital, with most belonging to groups of five or fewer doctors. There are two large multispecialty groups (each consisting of 40 doctors) that practice at Midsize Hospital and also practice at Dominion, the largest hospital in town. The CEO of Midsize says he would like to "get the ball rolling on this ACO thing." He hopes he can be the first in town to organize his doctors and get them to agree to participate in a Medicare MSSP ACO which he also plans to market to private insurance companies. He wants to make sure his ACO is comprised of only the most capable doctors and those willing to abide by strict guidelines, protocols, and cost containment measures. He would like to get some, but not all, of the smaller practices on board. He is also thinking of enlisting only one of the two large multispecialty groups, but realizes that this may be "politically impossible." From past experience, it is likely that some physician groups will insist that others not be included.

The CEO is open to all possibilities, including "teaming up" with the other hospitals in town or acquiring physician practices. What general guidance can you give him about antitrust issues and practical problems that may arise as he starts discussions with potential participants in the ACO? What strategy should be adopted in lining up primary care physicians and specialists in connection with the Agencies' Policy Statement, *supra*? For example: should the hospital seek to come within the Safety Zone? What problems arise if the ACO results in a dominant provider for any common service?

C. PAYERS WITH MARKET POWER

UNITED STATES V. BLUE CROSS BLUE SHIELD OF MICHIGAN

United States District Court, E.D. Michigan, 2011.
809 F. Supp. 2d 665.

DENISE PAGE HOOD, DISTRICT JUDGE.

I. BACKGROUND/FACTS

On October 18, 2010, Plaintiffs United States of America ("United States") and the State of Michigan ("Michigan") filed the instant action against Defendant Blue Cross Blue Shield of Michigan ("Blue Cross") alleging that Blue Cross' use of most favored nation ("MFN") clauses in its agreements with various hospitals violate: Section 1 of the Sherman Act, 15 U.S.C. § 1 (Count One) and Section 2 of the Michigan Antitrust Reform Act, M.C.L. § 445.772 (Count Two). The Complaint alleges that each of the provider agreements between Blue Cross and Michigan hospitals containing an MFN provision is a contract, combination and conspiracy within the meaning of Section 1 of the Sherman Act, 15 U.S.C. § 1. [ ] The Complaint further alleges that Blue Cross entered into agreements with hospitals in Michigan that unreasonably restrain trade and commerce in violation of Section 2 of the Michigan Antitrust Reform Act, M.C.L. § 445.772. [ ]

Blue Cross is a Michigan nonprofit healthcare corporation headquartered in Southfield, Michigan.[ ] Blue Cross is subject to federal taxation but is exempt from state and local taxation under Michigan law. [ ] Directly and through its subsidiaries, Blue Cross provides commercial and other health insurance products, including preferred provider organization ("PPO") health insurance products and health maintenance organization ("HMO") health insurance products.[ ] Blue Cross is the largest provider of commercial health insurance in Michigan. [ ] Blue Cross competes with for-profit and nonprofit health insurers. [ ] Blue Cross' commercial health insurance policies cover more than three million Michigan residents, more than 60% of the commercially insured population. [ ] Blue Cross insures more than nine times as many Michigan residents as its next largest commercial health insurance competitor. [ ] Blue Cross had revenues in excess of $10 billion in 2009. [ ]

* * *

Blue Cross has sought to include MFNs (sometimes called "most favored pricing," "most favored discount," or "parity" clauses) in many of its contracts with hospitals over the past several years. [ ] Blue Cross currently has agreements containing MFNs or similar clauses with at least 70 of Michigan's 131 general acute care hospitals. [ ] These 70 hospitals operate more than 40% of Michigan's acute care hospital beds. [ ]

Blue Cross generally enters into two types of MFNs, which require a hospital to provide hospital services to Blue Cross' competitors either at higher prices than Blue Cross pays or at prices no less than Blue Cross pays. [ ] Both types of MFNs inhibit competition. [ ] The first type is known as "MFN-plus." [ ] Blue Cross' existing MFNs include agreements with 22 hospitals that require the hospital to charge some or all other commercial insurers *more* than the hospital charges Blue Cross, typically by a specified percentage differential. [ ] These hospitals include major hospitals and hospital systems, and all of the major hospitals in some communities. [ ] These 22 hospitals operate approximately 45% of Michigan's tertiary care hospital beds (providing a full range of basic and sophisticated diagnostic and treatment services, including many specialized services.) [ ] Blue Cross' MFN-plus clauses require that some hospitals charge Blue Cross' competitors as much as 40% more than they charge Blue Cross. [ ] Two hospital contracts with MFN-plus clauses also prohibit giving Blue Cross' competitors better discounts than they currently receive during the life of the Blue Cross contracts. [ ] Blue Cross' MFN-plus clauses guarantee that Blue Cross' competitors cannot obtain hospital services at prices comparable to the prices Blue Cross pays, which limits other health insurers' ability to compete with Blue Cross. [ ] Blue Cross has sought and, on most occasions, obtained MFN-plus clauses when hospitals have sought significant rate increases. [ ]

The second type of MFN clause is considered as "Equal-to MFNs." [ ] Blue Cross entered into agreements containing MFNs with more than 40 small, community hospitals, which typically are the only hospitals in their communities, requiring the hospitals to charge other commercial health insurers at least as much as they charge Blue Cross. [ ] Under these agreements, Blue Cross agreed to pay more to community hospitals, which Blue Cross refers to as "Peer Group 5" hospitals, raising Blue Cross' own costs and its customers' costs, in exchange for the equal-to MFN. [ ] A community hospital that declines to enter into these agreements would be paid approximately 16% less by Blue Cross than if it accepts the MFN clause. [ ] Blue Cross also entered into equal-to MFNs with some larger hospitals as well. [ ]

Blue Cross sought and obtained MFNs in many hospital contracts in exchange for increases in the prices it pays for the hospitals' services. [ ] In these instances, Blue Cross has purchased protection from competition by causing hospitals to raise the minimum prices they can charge to Blue Cross' competitors but, in doing so, has also increased its own costs. [ ] Blue Cross has not sought or used MFNs to lower its own cost of obtaining hospital services. [ ]

The United States and Michigan argue Blue Cross' MFNs have caused many hospitals to (1) raise prices to Blue Cross' competitors by substantial amounts, or (2) demand prices that are too high to allow competitors to compete, effectively excluding them from the market. [ ] By denying Blue Cross' competitors access to competitive hospital contracts, the MFNs have deterred or prevented competitive entry and expansion in health insurance markets in Michigan. [ ] This has resulted in increased prices for health insurance sold by Blue Cross and its competitors, in addition to higher prices for hospital services paid by insureds and self-insured employers. [ ]

Michigan purchases group health insurance for approximately 52,000 employees and 180,000 retirees and dependents, including residents of each of the areas directly affected by Blue Cross' conduct. [ ] In particular, Michigan purchases health insurance for its employees from Blue Cross and others, and 60% of Michigan employees and nearly all Michigan retirees are covered by Blue Cross health plans. Michigan employees covered by Blue Cross are self-insured by Michigan, and increases in hospital costs are borne directly by Michigan and its employees. [ ] Michigan claims it has been injured, and is likely to be injured, in its business and property as a result of Blue Cross' violations. [ ]

* * *

B. Section 1 of the Sherman Act

1. Elements

In order to establish a violation of Section 1 of the Sherman Act, three elements must be met: 1) an agreement 2) affecting interstate commerce 3) that unreasonably restrains trade.[ ] * * *Blue Cross . . . moves to dismiss under the third element—whether the MFN clauses at issue unreasonably restrain trade. The parties agree that in order to assess whether the MFN clauses unreasonably restrain trade, the "rule of reason" is applied. An agreement violates the rule of reason if it "may suppress or even destroy competition," rather than promote competition. * * *In order to survive a motion to dismiss under the rule of reason test, the complaint must plausibly allege that the MFNs produced adverse anticompetitive effects within relevant product and geographic markets.

* * *

Blue Cross argues that the Complaint fails to plausibly allege relevant product markets, geographic markets, market power, [and] anticompetitive effects arising from the use of MFNs. * * *

[The Court held the complaint plausibly alleged two product markets affected by the MFN clauses alleged in the Complaint: commercial group health insurance and commercial individual health insurance. It also found the Complaint plausibly alleged 17 specific geographic markets for health insurance based on allegations that such markets are local because the purchasers of health insurance demand access to networks of hospitals and physicians close to their homes and workplaces.]

4. Market Power

[The Court finds that government's allegations as to market share (ranging from 40% to more than 80%) are plausible at this pleading stage.]

5. Anticompetitive Effects

Blue Cross asserts that the MFNs are procompetitive, therefore, the Complaint fails to state the MFNs' anticompetitive effects. The United States and Michigan respond that the Complaint alleges detailed allegations as to how Blue Cross' MFN clauses have negatively affected competition in the health insurance markets throughout Michigan. Although MFNs may be procompetitive, the United States and Michigan argue that a factual inquiry and, ultimately, a balancing of anticompetitive and procompetitive effects must be made but not at the pleading stage.

The Complaint alleges that the MFN clauses have negatively impacted competition in the health insurance markets throughout Michigan, by raising competitors' costs, likely increasing premiums, and directly increasing costs to self-insured employers. [ ] The Complaint sets forth various examples, such as the Upper Peninsula, Alpena County and the Lansing area. In the Upper Peninsula, the Complaint alleges that the MFN-plus entered into by Blue Cross with Marquette General, affects competition because the hospital is the only tertiary care hospital in the Upper Peninsula. The United States and Michigan claim the requirement that the hospital charge competing insurers at least 23% more than it charges Blue Cross affects potential competitors, such as Priority Health. [ ] Blue Cross has asserted that its contract will "keep blue lock on U.P." [ ] In Alpena County, Blue Cross offered Alpena Regional Medical Center, the only hospital in the area, a substantial rate increase in exchange for an

MFN-plus and a commitment that during the term of the contract, the hospital would not improve the discount it gave to any other health insurer. [ ] The United States and Michigan claim this has resulted in loss of competition in that Priority Health's prices have increased. [ ] Blue Cross entered into a ten-year contract with Sparrow Hospital in Lansing that requires Sparrow to charge most other insurers at least 12% more than Blue Cross pays. The Complaint alleges that this will likely result in a price increase to other insurers in Lansing and could cause other hospitals in the area to increase prices charged to Sparrow's own health plan. [ ]

Based on the allegations in the Complaint, it is plausible that the MFNs entered into by Blue Cross with various hospitals in Michigan establish anticompetitive effects as to other health insurers and the cost of health services in those areas.

NOTES AND QUESTIONS

1. *Most-Favored Nation Clauses.* What would explain hospitals' motives for acceding to BCBS Michigan's request for MFN clauses in their contracts? Note the difference between "MFN-Plus" contracts and "Equal to MFN contracts." How does each threaten to harm competition? In March 2013, the Department of Justice filed a motion to voluntarily dismiss this lawsuit after the Michigan legislature adopted a statute banning the use of MFNs by commercial insurers. Dept. of Justice Press Release (March 25, 2013). Is a legislative prohibition preferable to case-by-case antitrust review of MFNs? Should the legislature ban all MFNs? If not, how should it discriminate among insurers? The Department of Justice and State attorneys general have ongoing investigations in a number of other states in which MFNs are used.

2. *No Consensus of MFN.* Several courts have examined MFN clauses with mixed results. For example, *Ocean State Physicians Health Plan, Inc. v. Blue Cross & Blue Shield of Rhode Island*, 883 F.2d 1101 (1st Cir. 1989), involved an MFN imposed by a Blue Cross/Blue Shield plan that controlled 80% of the Rhode Island private health insurance market. When Ocean State, a new HMO, began to make significant inroads into its market, the Blue plan insisted that participating physicians grant them the same discount they granted Ocean State. Thereafter about 350 of Ocean State's 1200 participating physicians left that plan. A jury found the Blue plan guilty of violating Section 2 and of tortious interference with Ocean State's contractual relationships and awarded Ocean State $3.2 million. The First Circuit affirmed a judgment notwithstanding the verdict, finding that the "most favored nations" clause was a legitimate competitive strategy to assure that the Blue plan could get the lowest price for services rather than an attempt to monopolize the health insurance market. See also Willamette Dental Group, P.C. v. Oregon Dental Service Corp., 130 Ore. App. 487, 882 P.2d 637 (1994) (criticizing *Ocean State* and rejecting defendants' argument that an MFN can never constitute predatory pricing); Reazin v. Blue Cross and Blue Shield of Kansas, Inc., 899

F.2d 951 (10th Cir. 1990), cert. denied, 497 U.S. 1005(1990) (MFN is evidence that insurer possessed monopoly power and MFN contributed to that power).

    3.   *McCarran-Ferguson as an Antitrust Shield?* The McCarran-Ferguson Act provides a limited exemption for the "business of insurance" if the state regulates those activities and they do not constitute "boycott, coercion or intimidation." 15 U.S.C. §§ 1011–15. Two cases, Group Life and Health Insurance Co. v. Royal Drug Co., 440 U.S. 205 (1979) rehearing denied, 441 U.S. 917 (1979) and Union Labor Life Insurance Co. v. Pireno, 458 U.S. 119 (1982), have interpreted the term "business of insurance" very restrictively, limiting the meaning of that term to activities involving risk-spreading and transferring the policyholders' risk; relationships between insurers; and usually only parties in the insurance industry. This leaves many cost-containment activities of insurers subject to antitrust oversight. The Insurance Antitrust Handbook (M. Horning & R. Langsdorf, eds. 1995). At the same time, the McCarran-Ferguson Act shields a wide range of obviously anticompetitive conduct. Agreements among insurers to fix subscriber premiums or actions of a dominant insurer regarding the types of policies it will sell or the conditions attached thereto are exempt. See *Royal Drug, supra*; Klamath-Lake Pharmaceutical Ass'n v. Klamath Medical Service Bureau, 701 F.2d 1276 (9th Cir. 1983). In *Ocean State, supra*, the court found that the McCarran-Ferguson Act immunized defendants' marketing and pricing policies in its HMO coverage and the imposition of higher rates on employers that offered a competing HMO option.

PROBLEM: MOUNTAIN HEALTH CARE

    Mountain Health Care (MHC), the largest managed care company in its market, sells nearly seventy percent of all private health insurance policies there. MHC, which began as a nonprofit association of hospitals, owns hospitals that deliver 60 percent of all inpatient health care services in the same market. A group of forty-nine optometrists have filed suit against MHC claiming that it has violated Sections 1 and 2 of the Sherman Act by conspiring with ophthalmologists on its managed care panels (who also have staff privileges at MHC hospitals) to exclude optometrists from being placed on the preferred panels of MHC managed care plans. Plaintiffs claim that in exchange for MHC's agreement not to panel optometrists, the conspiring ophthalmologists agreed to refer their patients to MHC's hospitals and surgical facilities instead of those operated by MHC's competitors.

    Optometrists sell optical hardware (glasses and contact lenses) and are licensed to perform the full scope of nonsurgical eye care (NSEC) and to prescribe prescription drugs. Ophthalmologists also perform NSEC but also are licensed to perform surgical eye care, and usually have staff privileges at hospitals to perform those procedures. The ophthalmologists' trade association in the state has long sought to limit the ability of optometrists to compete, having lobbied against legislation that was adopted ten years ago allowing the latter to perform the full range of NSEC. More recently, prominent ophthalmologists on staff at MHC hospitals have repeatedly urged managers of MHC's managed care subsidiary not to panel optometrists, arguing that only those practicing under the supervision of ophthalmologists should be accepted "in order to maintain the high quality of care provided by MHC." The optometrists are prepared to prove that they provide NSEC at lower cost than do ophthalmologists and have come upon one internal MHC study showing that its managed care plans could save $400,000 per year by adding optometrists to its panels.

MHC has recently amended its plans' provider agreements to permit it to engage in economic credentialing including terminating any providers "based on business or competitive reasons" or on "under-utilization of MHC related providers and facilities." MHC has terminated at least one ophthalmologist for failure to direct his patients to MHC surgical facilities. MHC's accounting records suggest that it saves money on implementing peer review, quality control, and credentialing for its health plans when it contracts with providers who have staff privileges at its hospitals, as contrasted with optometrists who cannot have staff privileges. In addition, administrators of the MHC plans believe they save costs and improve quality by selective contracting and do not need additional providers of NSEC at this time.

What antitrust claims might be brought under Section 1 and 2 of the Sherman Act? What additional evidence would be of importance to evaluating each theory? Your preliminary legal research has uncovered the following:

> In order to present enough evidence for a jury to infer an antitrust conspiracy, something more than "mere complaints" from a distributor to a manufacturer are necessary. Other "plus factors" such as evidence that alleged conspirators were acting contrary to their independent interest when taking action can give rise to an inference of a conspiracy. See Monsanto Co. v. Spray-Rite Serv. Corp., 465 U.S. 752 at 764 (1984). See also Matsushita Elec. Indus. Co. v. Zenith Radio Corp., 475 U.S. 574, 588 (1986) ("Antitrust law limits the range of permissible inferences from ambiguous evidence in a Section 1 case.").

WEST PENN ALLEGHENY HEALTH SYSTEM, INC. v. UPMC; HIGHMARK, INC.

United States Court of Appeals, Third Circuit, 2010.
627 F.3d 85.

SMITH, CIRCUIT JUDGE.

The plaintiff in this antitrust case is Pittsburgh's second-largest hospital system. It sued Pittsburgh's dominant hospital system and health insurer under the Sherman Act and state law. The plaintiff asserts that the defendants violated Sections 1 and 2 of the Sherman Act by forming a conspiracy to protect one another from competition. The plaintiff says that pursuant to the conspiracy, the dominant hospital system used its power in the provider market to insulate the health insurer from competition, and in exchange the insurer used its power in the insurance market to strengthen the hospital system and to weaken the plaintiff. The plaintiff also asserts that the dominant hospital system violated Section 2 of the Sherman Act by attempting to monopolize the Pittsburgh-area market for specialized hospital services. * * * Because we conclude that the District Court erred in dismissing the Sherman Act claims, we will reverse in part, vacate in part, and remand for further proceedings.

I.   Facts

* * *

A.   Cast of Characters

This lawsuit involves three parties. The plaintiff, West Penn Allegheny Health System, Inc. ("West Penn"), is Pittsburgh's second-largest hospital system; it has a share of less than 23% of the market for hospital services in Allegheny County, which includes the City of Pittsburgh. The defendant University of Pittsburgh Medical Center ("UPMC") is Pittsburgh's dominant hospital system. It enjoys a 55% share of the Allegheny County market for hospital services, and its share of the market for tertiary and quaternary care services exceeds 50%.[ ] West Penn and UPMC are the two major competitors in the Allegheny County market for hospital services, and are the only competitors in the market for tertiary and quaternary care services. The defendant Highmark, Inc. is the dominant insurer in the Allegheny County market for health insurance.[ ] Highmark's market share has remained between 60% and 80% since 2000.

B.   Pre-Conspiracy Conduct

In 2000, The Western Pennsylvania Healthcare System merged with several financially distressed medical providers, including Allegheny General Hospital, to form West Penn. Highmark funded the merger with a $125 million loan. Highmark's largesse did not spring from a sense of altruism, but was intended to preserve competition in the market for hospital services. Had the financially distressed providers comprising West Penn failed, UPMC would have attained nearly unchecked dominance in the market. This would not have been good for Highmark: the more dominant UPMC becomes, the more leverage it gains to demand greater reimbursements from Highmark. * * *

After the merger, Highmark and West Penn continued to enjoy a good relationship, as Highmark recognized that preserving West Penn was in its interests. Thus, Highmark encouraged investors to purchase bonds from West Penn, touting its financial outlook and the quality of its medical services. And in early 2002, Highmark gave West Penn a $42 million grant to invest in its facilities.

In contrast to Highmark, UPMC has been hostile to West Penn since its inception. UPMC opposed the merger creating West Penn: it intervened in the merger proceedings, filed an unsuccessful lawsuit to prevent

Highmark from funding the merger, and attempted (with some success) to dissuade investors from purchasing West Penn bonds. UPMC's hostility towards West Penn continued after the merger. Since West Penn's formation, UPMC executives have repeatedly said that they want to destroy West Penn, and they have taken action to further that goal on more than a few occasions. But more on that later. See Section I.E, *infra*.

Historically, UPMC has also had a bitter relationship with Highmark. For example, when UPMC demanded purportedly excessive reimbursement rates from Highmark, Highmark responded by forming Community Blue, a low-cost insurance plan. To participate in Community Blue, a hospital had to agree to accept reduced reimbursements, but would receive a higher volume of patients. West Penn participated in Community Blue, but UPMC did not, claiming that its reimbursement rates were too low. UPMC responded to Community Blue by forming its own health insurer, UPMC Health Plan. UPMC Health Plan has been Highmark's main competitor in the Allegheny County market for health insurance since its formation.

[Highmark also sued UPMC under the Lanham act over alleged false statements in an advertisement and challenged UPMC's acquisition of a children's hospital.]

C. The Conspiracy Begins; the Dynamics Change

In 1998, UPMC offered a "truce" to Highmark. Under the terms of the truce, each entity would use its market power to protect the other from competition. Highmark initially rejected UPMC's offer, criticizing it as an illegal "attempt to form a 'super' monopoly for the provision of health care in Western Pennsylvania in which [UPMC], the leading provider of hospital services, and Highmark, the leading health insurer, would combine forces." [ ].

The complaint alleges, however, that in the summer of 2002, over the course of several meetings, Highmark reconsidered and decided to accept UPMC's offer of a truce. The complaint alleges that UPMC agreed to use its power in the provider market to prevent Highmark competitors from gaining a foothold in the Allegheny County market for health insurance, and in exchange Highmark agreed to take steps to strengthen UPMC and to weaken West Penn. The complaint offers the following factual allegations in support of the conspiracy claim.

UPMC engaged in conduct that effectively insulated Highmark from competition. First, it refused to enter into competitive provider agreements with Highmark's rivals. This prevented the rivals from entering the Allegheny County health insurance market because, given UPMC's dominance, an insurer cannot succeed in the market without being able to offer a competitively-priced plan that includes UPMC as an in-network provider.[3]

Second, UPMC shrunk UPMC Health Plan (Highmark's main competitor in the insurance market). It cut the Health Plan's advertising budget and increased its premiums, which led to a sharp drop in enrollment. It also refused to sell the Health Plan to insurers interested in buying it, which might have revived it as a Highmark competitor. UPMC acknowledged that it decided to shrink the Health Plan as a result of negotiations with Highmark, in which Highmark had agreed to take Community Blue off the market.

Meanwhile, Highmark took action that enhanced UPMC's dominance. Most significantly, it paid UPMC supracompetitive reimbursement rates. To afford UPMC's reimbursements, Highmark had to increase its insurance premiums (which, according to West Penn, it was able to do without losing business because UPMC had insulated it from competition). [Highmark also provided UPMC with a $70 million grant and $160 million low interest loan to build a new facility and supported its acquisition of another facility.] In addition, Highmark vowed not to offer a health plan that did not include UPMC as an in-network provider. Thus, in 2004, Highmark eliminated its low-cost insurance plan, Community Blue, in which UPMC had declined to participate. With the elimination of a leading low-cost insurance plan, health insurance premiums in Allegheny County rose. Furthermore, in 2006, Highmark publicly supported UPMC's acquisition of Mercy Hospital, which, other than West Penn, was UPMC's only other competitor in the market for tertiary and quaternary care services. Finally, in 2006, Highmark leaked confidential financial information regarding West Penn to UPMC, "which in turn leaked a distorted version of the information to credit-rating agencies and to the business media in an attempt to destroy investor confidence in West Penn." [ ]

In addition, Highmark essentially cut West Penn off from its financial support, thus hampering its ability to compete with UPMC. Highmark, for instance, repeatedly rejected West Penn's requests to refinance the $125 million loan that was used to fund the 2000 merger. [ ] Although Highmark believed refinancing the loan made business sense, it declined to do so out of fear that UPMC would retaliate against it for violating their agreement—an agreement that Highmark candidly admitted was "probably illegal." Highmark said that it was under a "constant barrage" from UPMC and that UPMC was "obsessed" with driving West Penn out of business. Highmark explained that if it helped West Penn financially, UPMC would allow one of Highmark's competitors to enter the Allegheny

---

[3] In fact, United Healthcare tried to enter the Allegheny County insurance market in 2005 and 2006, but it was effectively prevented from doing so because UPMC would not offer it a competitive contract.

County insurance market or would sell UPMC Health Plan to a Highmark competitor. Indeed, UPMC had sent Highmark a letter containing such a warning. [ ]

Moreover, Highmark maintained West Penn's reimbursement rates at artificially depressed levels and repeatedly refused to increase them. In 2005 and 2006, for example, West Penn asked Highmark for a general increase in its rates, which were originally set in 2002. Highmark initially acknowledged that West Penn's rates were too low and suggested that it would raise them, but it ultimately refused to follow through, explaining that it could not help West Penn because, if it did, UPMC would retaliate.

Finally, Highmark "discriminated against West Penn [ ] in the award of grants to improve the quality of medical care in" Allegheny County. * * *

D.   The Effects of the Conspiracy

The conspiracy ended in 2007, when the Antitrust Division of the Department of Justice began investigating Highmark's and UPMC's relationship. During the years covered by the conspiracy, UPMC and Highmark reaped record profits. * * * On the other hand, West Penn struggled during the years covered by the conspiracy. It was forced to scale back its services, and to abandon projects to expand and improve its services and facilities. In essence, West Penn was unable to compete with UPMC as vigorously as it otherwise would have.

E.   UPMC's Unilateral Conduct

Besides the conspiracy with Highmark, UPMC has taken a number of actions on its own to weaken West Penn. UPMC has systematically "raided" key physicians from West Penn . . . by paying them salaries that were well above market rates. Although UPMC incurred financial losses because of the hirings (that is, it paid the physicians more money than they generated), it admitted that it was willing to do so in order to injure the hospitals.

UPMC's physician "raiding" has "continued unabated" since West Penn's formation . . . As before, though, UPMC admitted that it was not trying to earn profits. It was trying to drive the hospital out of business. In the end, the anesthesiologists were lured away by UPMC's bloated salary offers. * * *

[The Court identifies other examples in the complaint of "so-called physician raiding;" pressuring community hospitals into entering joint ventures by threatening to build satellite facilities next to them; and making false statements about West Penn's financial health in order to discourage investors from purchasing West Penn bonds.]

* * *

V.   The Conspiracy Claims

* * *

A.   Agreement

* * *

West Penn's theory on the conspiracy claims is that in the summer of 2002, UPMC and Highmark formed an agreement to protect one another from competition. West Penn asserts that UPMC agreed to use its power in the provider market to exclude Highmark's rivals from the Allegheny County health insurance market, and that in exchange Highmark agreed to take steps to strengthen UPMC and to weaken its primary rival, West Penn. We conclude that the complaint contains non-conclusory allegations of direct evidence of such an agreement.

* * *

B.   Unreasonable Restraint

The defendants make a half-hearted argument that even if the complaint alleges that they formed a conspiracy to shield one another from competition, the section 1 claim is still deficient because the complaint does not allege that the conspiracy unreasonably restrained trade. We disagree. At the pleading stage, a plaintiff may satisfy the unreasonable-restraint element by alleging that the conspiracy produced anticompetitive effects in the relevant markets. [ ]

* * * In . . . concluding [that plaintiff's allegations are sufficient to suggest that the conspiracy produced anticompetitive effects] we do not reach West Penn's argument that-given the horizontal aspect of the conspiracy, *i.e.,* UPMC's agreement to shrink UPMC Health Plan-the conspiracy is subject to *per se* condemnation. Even if the more demanding rule of reason applies, the complaint adequately alleges that the conspiracy stifled competition in the relevant markets.

C.   Antitrust Injury

[T]he Supreme Court [has] held that an antitrust plaintiff must do more than show that it would have been better off absent the violation; the plaintiff must establish that it suffered an antitrust injury. An antitrust injury is an "injury of the type the antitrust laws were intended to prevent and that flows from that which makes [the] defendants' acts unlawful."
* * *

[The Court rejected West Penn's claims that the conspiracy caused it antitrust injury based on Highmark's decision to take Community Blue off the market, noting that a supplier does not suffer an antitrust injury when competition is reduced in the downstream market in which it sells goods or services. The Court also rejected West Penn's allegation that it sustained an antitrust injury based on Highmark's refusals to refinance the $125 million loan noting that because Highmark was just one of many possible sources of financing, even if it acted with anticompetitive motives, Highmark's refinancing refusals could not have been competition-*reducing* aspects of the conspiracy.]

Finally, West Penn argues that it sustained an antitrust injury in the form of artificially depressed reimbursement rates. The complaint alleges that during the conspiracy, West Penn asked Highmark to renegotiate and raise its rates. The complaint suggests that Highmark acknowledged that the rates were too low and initially agreed to raise them, but that Highmark refused to follow through, citing its agreement with UPMC, under which it was not to do anything to benefit West Penn financially. West Penn asserts that the amount of the underpayments—*i.e.*, the difference between the reimbursements it would have received in a competitive market and those it actually received—constitutes an antitrust injury. For their part, the defendants do not take issue with West Penn's suggestion that its reimbursement rates would have been greater absent the conspiracy. They argue, instead, that paying West Penn depressed reimbursement rates was not an element of the conspiracy that posed antitrust problems. They reason that low reimbursement rates translate into low premiums for subscribers, and that it would therefore be contrary to a key purpose of the antitrust laws—promoting consumer welfare—to allow West Penn to recover the amount of the underpayments. West Penn has it right.

Admittedly, had Highmark been acting alone, West Penn would have little basis for challenging the reimbursement rates. A firm that has substantial power on the buy side of the market (*i.e.*, monopsony power) is generally free to bargain aggressively when negotiating the prices it will pay for goods and services. [ ]This reflects the general hesitance of courts to condemn unilateral behavior, lest vigorous competition be chilled. [ ]

But when a firm exercises monopsony power pursuant to a conspiracy, its conduct is subject to more rigorous scrutiny, [ ] and will be condemned if it imposes an unreasonable restraint of trade. [ ] * * *

Here, the complaint suggests that Highmark has substantial monopsony power. It alleges that Highmark has a 60%–80% share of the Allegheny County market for health insurance, that there are significant entry barriers for insurers wishing to break into the market (including UPMC's unwillingness to deal competitively with non-Highmark insurers), and that medical providers have very few alternative purchasers for their services.[12] The complaint also alleges that Highmark paid West Penn

---

[12] Indeed, the complaint alleges that the only other insurer with a significant market share is UPMC Health Plan, and that UPMC Health Plan has basically been unwilling to deal with West Penn.

depressed reimbursement rates, not as a result of independent decision making, but pursuant to a conspiracy with UPMC, under which UPMC insulated Highmark from competition in return for Highmark's taking steps to hobble West Penn. In these circumstances, it is certainly plausible that paying West Penn depressed reimbursement rates unreasonably restrained trade. Such shortchanging poses competitive threats similar to those posed by conspiracies among buyers to fix prices [ ], and other restraints that result in artificially depressed payments to suppliers— namely, suboptimal output, reduced quality, allocative inefficiencies, and (given the reductions in output) higher prices for consumers in the long run.

The defendants argue, though, that Highmark's paying West Penn depressed reimbursements did not pose antitrust problems because it enabled Highmark to set low insurance premiums, and thus benefited consumers. We disagree. First, even if it were true that paying West Penn depressed rates enabled Highmark to offer lower premiums, it is far from clear that this would have benefited consumers, because the premium reductions would have been achieved only by taking action that tends to diminish the quality and availability of hospital services. [ ] Warren S. Grimes, The Sherman Act's Unintended Bias Against Lilliputians, 69 Antitrust L.J. 195, 210 (2001) ("The very nature of monopsony or oligopsony power is that it tends to suppress output and reduce quality or choice."). Second, the complaint alleges that Highmark did *not* pass the savings on to consumers. It alleges, instead, that Highmark pocketed the savings, while repeatedly ratcheting up insurance premiums. *See also* Roger D. Blair & Jeffrey L. Harrison, Antitrust Policy and Monopsony, 76 Cornell L. Rev. 297, 339 (1991) (explaining that "lower input prices resulting from the exercise of monopsony power do not ultimately translate into lower prices to the monopsonist's customers").

But most importantly, the defendants' argument reflects a basic misunderstanding of the antitrust laws. The Ninth Circuit's discussion in Knevelbaard Dairies v. Kraft Foods, Inc., 232 F.3d 979 (9th Cir.2000), illustrates the point well. There, the plaintiff milk producers established that the defendant cheese makers had conspired to depress the price they paid for milk. The cheese makers argued that the plaintiffs' injuries were not antitrust injuries—*i.e.,* were not the kind of injuries "the antitrust laws were intended to prevent," [ ] because the conspiracy enabled them to purchase milk at lower costs and thus to sell cheese to consumers at lower prices. [ ] Ninth Circuit properly rejected this argument:

The fallacy of th[e defendants'] argument becomes clear when we recall that the central purpose of the antitrust laws . . . is to preserve competition. It is competition—not the collusive fixing of prices at levels either low or high—that these statutes recognize as vital to the public interest. The Supreme Court's references to the goals of achieving "the lowest prices, the highest quality and the greatest material progress," and of "assur[ing] customers the benefits of price competition," [ ], do not mean that conspiracies among buyers to depress acquisition prices are tolerated. Every precedent in the field makes clear that the interaction of competitive forces, not price-rigging, is what will benefit consumers. [ ]

Similar reasoning applies here. Highmark's improperly motivated exercise of monopsony power, like the collusive exercise of oligopsony power by the cheese makers in *Knevelbaard,* was anticompetitive and cannot be defended on the sole ground that it enabled Highmark to set lower premiums on its insurance plans.

Having concluded that paying West Penn artificially depressed reimbursement rates was an anticompetitive aspect of the alleged conspiracy, it follows that the underpayments constitute an antitrust injury. [ ]

* * *

VI. The Attempted Monopolization Claim

In addition to the conspiracy claims, West Penn alleges that UPMC violated section 2 of the Sherman Act by attempting to monopolize the Allegheny County market for specialized hospital services. The elements of attempted monopolization are (1) that the defendant has a specific intent to monopolize, and (2) that the defendant has engaged in anticompetitive conduct that, taken as a whole, creates (3) a dangerous probability of achieving monopoly power. [ ] The District Court dismissed the attempted monopolization claim on the ground that the complaint fails to allege anticompetitive conduct, and the parties have addressed only that issue here. We limit our review accordingly.

Broadly speaking, a firm engages in anticompetitive conduct when it attempts "to exclude rivals on some basis other than efficiency." [ ] * * *

For present purposes, it is sufficient to note that anticompetitive conduct can include a conspiracy to exclude a rival [ ] * * * We previously recognized—though perhaps in overly broad terms—that making false statements about a rival, without more, rarely interferes with competition enough to violate the antitrust laws. See Santana Prods., Inc. v. Bobrick Washroom Equip., Inc., 401 F.3d 123, 132 (3d Cir.2005) (stating, in the context of a section 1 case, that " 'deception, reprehensible as it is, can be of no consequence so far as the Sherman Act is concerned' "). But in some cases, such defamation, which plainly is not competition on the merits, can give rise to antitrust liability, especially when it is combined with other anticompetitive acts. [ ]

The complaint alleges the following anticompetitive conduct. First, the defendants engaged in a conspiracy, a purpose of which was to drive West

Penn out of business. Second, UPMC hired employees away from West Penn by paying them bloated salaries. UPMC admitted to hiring some of the employees not because it needed them but in order to injure West Penn; UPMC could not absorb some of the employees and had to let them go; and UPMC incurred financial losses as a result of the hiring. These allegations are sufficient to suggest that at least some of the hirings were anticompetitive. [ ] Relatedly, UPMC tried unsuccessfully to lure a number of employees away from West Penn; UPMC could not have absorbed the additional employees, and although the employees remained with West Penn, they did so only after West Penn raised their salaries to supracompetitive levels. Third, UPMC approached community hospitals and threatened to build UPMC satellite facilities next to them unless they stopped referring oncology patients to West Penn and began referring all such patients to UPMC. Nearly all of the community hospitals caved in, which deprived West Penn of a key source of patients. Moreover, under pressure from UPMC, several of the community hospitals have stopped sending *any* of their tertiary and quaternary care referrals to West Penn and have begun sending them all to UPMC. Finally, on several occasions, UPMC made false statements about West Penn's financial health to potential investors, which caused West Penn to pay artificially inflated financing costs on its debt.

Viewed as a whole, these allegations plausibly suggest that UPMC has engaged in anticompetitive conduct, *i.e.*, that UPMC has competed with West Penn "on some basis other than the merits." [ ] The District Court erred in concluding otherwise.

* * *

For the reasons set forth above, the judgment of the District Court will be reversed in part and vacated in part, and the case will be remanded for further proceedings.

NOTES AND QUESTIONS

1. *The Saga Continues.* Pittsburgh's health care drama did not end with the Third Circuit's decision. Following an unsuccessful petition for certiorari by UPMC, Highmark and West Penn announced plans to merge and for Highmark to invest $475 million in West Penn. The merger between Highmark and West Penn fell apart and came back together again, while UPMC declared that it would no longer contract with Highmark because it was establishing a competing provider network. People with Highmark insurance had no idea whether they would be covered at UPMC facilities Eventually, UPMC and Highmark signed a consent decree brokered by Pennsylvania's Governor in June 2014, allowing for a gradual separation by June 2019. Meanwhile, Pennsylvania's Attorney General sued UPMC sued for unfair trade practices and public charities law violations, but ultimately brokered an additional 10-year settlement agreement giving many Highmark insurance members access

to UPMC doctors. See Harris Myer, UPMC, Highmark sign 10-year truce on in-network access, Modern Healthcare (Jun. 24, 2019).

Does the sequence of events described above suggest that the power of dominant payers and providers can offset each other? Did consumers benefit from the changing alliances? On countervailing power in health care see John B. Kirkwood, Buyer Power and Healthcare Prices, 91 Wash. L. Rev. 253 (2016); Thomas L. Greaney, Dubious Health Care Merger Justifications—The Sumo Wrestler and "Government Made Me Do It" Defenses, Health Affairs Blog (Feb. 24, 2015). Note that within a year of the "truce" agreement, UPMC's profits and volume of patients from Highmark had increased. See Rebecca Pifer, UPMC topline soars on Highmark truce, Healthcare Dive (Mar. 2, 2020).

2. *Sherman Act Section 1.* Does the Third Circuit's opinion suggest that agreements between dominant hospitals and dominant insurers to achieve mutually beneficial terms will necessarily run afoul of Section 1 of the Sherman Act? What factors create an inference that the agreements will restrain trade? Note also that private litigants must prove that the alleged restraint of trade or acts of monopolization do more than harm them, but actually injure competition. Why is this showing problematic in the context of an insurer exercising its power *vis-a-vis* providers?

3. *Sherman Act Section 2.* Dominant hospitals flexing their muscle may run afoul of Section 2 of the Sherman Act as well. In February, 2011, the U.S. Department of Justice and Texas Attorney General's Office announced the simultaneous filing and settlement of monopolization claims under Section 2 of the Sherman Act against United Regional Health Care System of Wichita Falls, Texas. The complaint charged that United Regional, the dominant hospital in its market, coerced health insurers to refrain from contracting with other competing hospitals in the Wichita Falls area. U.S. Dept. of Justice, Press Release (Feb. 25, 2011). The alleged coercion took place by offering steep "discounts" to insurers ranging from 15 to 27 percent if the insurers refused to contract with other providers in the market. The government focused on the "exclusionary contracts" United Regional entered into with payers that it alleged "effectively prevent insurers from contracting with United Regional's competitors." For a critical examination of the underlying economics of the government's case, see David A. Argue and John M. Gale, Reexamining DOJ's Predation Analysis in United Regional (Jan. 2012).

However, some antitrust theories impose high hurdles for plaintiffs. In Methodist Health Services Corp. v. OSF Healthcare System, 859 F.3d 408 (7th Cir. 2017) a small hospital challenged the dominant health system in the market with illegal exclusive dealing by insisting to insurers that it would be the only in-network hospital for their plans. Judge Posner asserted that competition was protected because there was "competition for the market," i.e. plaintiff hospital could try to outbid the defendant at the annual contract renewal and if necessary could make itself more competitive by offering a broader array of services, including Level 1 trauma care. Is this realistic?

D. MERGERS AND ACQUISITIONS

1. Hospital Mergers

FEDERAL TRADE COMMISSION AND STATE OF ILLINOIS V. ADVOCATE HEALTH CARE NETWORK, ET AL.
United States Court of Appeals, Seventh Circuit, 2016.
841 F.3d 460.

HAMILTON, CIRCUIT JUDGE.

This horizontal merger case under the Clayton Act depends on proper definition of geographic markets for hospitals. Defendants Advocate Health Care Network and NorthShore University HealthSystem both operate hospital networks in Chicago's northern suburbs. They propose to merge. Section 7 of the Clayton Act forbids asset acquisitions that may lessen competition in any "section of the country."[ ] The Federal Trade Commission and the State of Illinois sued in district court to enjoin the proposed Advocate-NorthShore merger while the Commission considers the issue through its ordinary but slower administrative process. [ ]

* * *

I. *The Proposed Merger and the District Court Proceedings*

In the United States today, most hospital care is bought in two stages. In the first, which is highly price-sensitive, insurers and hospitals negotiate to determine whether the hospitals will be in the insurers' networks and how much the insurers will pay them. Gregory Vistnes, Hospitals, Mergers, and Two-Stage Competition, 67 Antitrust L.J. 671, 674–75 (2000). In the second stage, hospitals compete to attract patients, based primarily on non-price factors like convenience and reputation for quality. [ ] Concerns about potential misuse of market power resulting from a merger must take into account this two-stage process.

Chicago area providers of hospital care include defendant NorthShore University HealthSystem, which has four hospitals in Chicago's north suburbs. The area surrounding NorthShore's hospitals has roughly eight other hospitals. Two of those hospitals belong to defendant Advocate Health Care Network, which has a total of nine hospitals in the Chicago area. * * *

In September 2014, Advocate and NorthShore announced that they intended to merge. The Federal Trade Commission and the State of Illinois took action in December 2015 by filing a complaint in the Northern District of Illinois seeking a preliminary injunction against the merger. The court heard six days of evidence on that motion. Executives from several major insurers testified. Some of the details of their testimony are under seal, but they testified unequivocally that it would be difficult or impossible to market a network to employers in metropolitan Chicago that excludes both NorthShore and Advocate. Additional evidence shows that no health insurance product has been successfully marketed to employers in Chicago without offering access to either NorthShore hospitals or Advocate hospitals.

[The court summarizes testimony from the FTC's economic expert Dr. Tenn who used the "hypothetical monopolist test" to identify the geographic market relevant to the case. That test asks whether a single firm controlling all output of a product within a given region would be able to raise prices profitably a bit above competitive levels. Dr. Tenn simulated the market's response to a price increase imposed by a monopolist controlling NorthShore's hospitals and the two nearby Advocate hospitals. He found that the monopolist could profitably impose the increase. He therefore concluded that the contiguous area including just those six party hospitals is a relevant geographic market.]

Dr. Tenn also tested a larger candidate market, using three criteria. First, he distinguished between local hospitals and academic medical centers, which he rather inauspiciously called "destination hospitals." Academic medical centers draw patients from across the Chicago area, including the northern suburbs, even though they are not in the northern suburbs. Dr. Tenn excluded those hospitals from his candidate market, reasoning that patients require insurers to provide them more local and convenient hospital options. Second, Dr. Tenn identified hospitals that had at least a two percent share of the admissions from the same areas the parties' hospitals drew from. Finally, he included only hospitals that drew from both Advocate's and NorthShore's service areas.

Those criteria produced an eleven-hospital candidate market: the six party hospitals and five other nearby hospitals, without any academic medical centers. Dr. Tenn simulated the response to a price increase by a hypothetical firm controlling those eleven hospitals. He again found that the price increase would be profitable. He therefore concluded that the area around the eleven hospitals is a relevant geographic market. The plaintiffs focused their arguments on the larger, eleven-hospital market both in the district court and on appeal; they and we refer to it as the North Shore Area.

* * *

As part of his simulations, Dr. Tenn calculated the percentage of patients at each of the North Shore Area hospitals who would turn to each of the other available hospitals if their first choice hospital were closed. For example, he determined that if Advocate's Lutheran General Hospital closed, 9.3 percent of its patients would likely go to NorthShore's Evanston Hospital instead. These measures are called diversion ratios. Dr. Tenn calculated that for 48 percent of patients in the North Shore Area, both their first and second choice hospitals were inside the Commission's proposed market.

* * *

The district court rejected Dr. Tenn's analysis, found that plaintiffs had not shown a likelihood of success on the merits, and denied an injunction. [ ] Its analysis focused on Dr. Tenn's candidate-market criteria and echoed [defendant's expert] Dr. McCarthy's criticisms of those criteria. [ ] There was, the court said, no economic basis for distinguishing between academic medical centers and local hospitals and no reason to think a competitor had to constrain both Advocate and NorthShore to be in the geographic market. [ ]The court also criticized Dr. Tenn's assumption that patients generally insist on access to local hospitals, calling the evidence on that point "equivocal" and pointing to the 52 percent of patients whose second-choice hospitals were outside the proposed market. [ ] At several points in the opinion, the court implied that Dr. Tenn's analysis was circular, saying that he "assume[d] the answer" to the geographic market question. [ ]

* * *

II. Relevant Antitrust Markets

* * *

A. The Product Market

* * * As in many other hospital merger cases, the parties here agree that the product market here is just such a cluster: inpatient general acute care services—specifically, those services sold to commercial health plans and their members. [ ] That market is a cluster of medical services and procedures that require admission to a hospital, such as abdominal surgeries, childbirth, treatment of serious infections, and some emergency care.

B. The Geographic Market

The dispute here is about the relevant geographic market. The relevant geographic market is "where ... the effect of the merger on competition will be direct and immediate." [ ]

1. Geographic Markets in General

Since at least 1982, the Commission has used the "hypothetical monopolist test" to identify relevant geographic markets. That test asks what would happen if a single firm became the only seller in a candidate geographic region. [ ] If that hypothetical monopolist could profitably raise prices above competitive levels, the region is a relevant geographic market. * * * But if customers would defeat the attempted price increase by buying from outside the region, it is not a relevant market; the test should be rerun using a larger candidate region. [ ] This process is iterative, meaning it should be repeated with ever-larger candidates until it identifies a relevant geographic market. [ ]

* * *

The hypothetical monopolist test focuses on "the area of *effective* competition" between firms. [ ] A geographic market does not need to include all of the firm's competitors; it needs to include the competitors that would "substantially constrain [the firm's] price-increasing ability." [ ]

* * *

2. *Geographic Markets for Hospitals*

Markets for hospital services have three notable features. First, because most patients prefer to go to nearby hospitals, there are often only a few hospitals in a geographic market. * * * This case's record reflects that preference: in the Commission's proposed market, 80 percent of patients drove to the hospital of their choice in 20 minutes or less.

Second, patients vary in their hospital preferences. Getting an appendectomy is not like buying a beer; one Pabst Blue Ribbon or Hoegaarden may be as good as another, no matter where they are bought. For surgery patients, who their surgeon will be matters, the hospital's reputation matters, and the hospital's location matters. Different patients value these and other factors differently. [ ] For example, some patients will be willing to travel to see a particular specialist. [ ] Others will not. That means that, as Dr. Elzinga himself has explained, the Elzinga-Hogarty test will often overestimate the size of hospital markets. [ ] The test assumes that if some patients presently travel for care, more would do so to avoid a price increase, making an increase unprofitable. But in fact, often a "silent majority" of patients will not travel, enabling anticompetitive price increases. *Id.* The economic literature began describing this problem—termed the "silent majority fallacy"—as early as 2001. Cory S. Capps, From Rockford to Joplin and Back Again: The Impact of Economics on Hospital Merger Enforcement, 59 Antitrust Bull. 443 (2014).

Finally, consumers do not directly pay the full cost of hospital care. Instead, insurance companies cover most hospital costs. [ ] Insurance thus splits hospital competition into two stages: one in which hospitals compete to be included in insurers' networks, and a second in which hospitals compete to attract patients. [ ] Insured patients are usually not sensitive to retail hospital prices, while insurers respond to both prices and patient preferences. FTC v. Penn State Hershey, 838 F.3d 327, 341 (3d Cir. 2016) (explaining that insurers "feel the impact of price increases" and that patient behavior "affects the relative bargaining positions of insurers and hospitals as they negotiate rates").

The geographic market question is therefore most directly about "the 'likely response of insurers,'" not patients, to a price increase. [ ] This complication is sometimes termed the "payer problem."[ ]

[The court goes on to discuss the judiciary's response "to the academy's evolving understanding of hospital markets." A number of recent cases have moved away from earlier cases that employed the Elzinga-Hogarty test which focused on "patient flow" data, i.e. the proportion of patients that come into and go out of hypothetical geographic markets. The court observed that the Elzinga-Hogarty test "produced relatively large geographic markets in hospital merger cases" which may harm consumers "because the likely anticompetitive effects of hospital mergers will be understated."]

III. *Analysis*

* * * We find that the district court made clear factual errors. Its central error was its misunderstanding of the hypothetical monopolist test: it overlooked the test's results and mistook the test's iterations for logical circularity. Even if the court's focus on the candidate market had been correct, its criticisms were mistaken in three ways. It incorrectly found that Dr. Tenn lacked a basis for distinguishing local hospitals from academic medical centers. It erroneously determined that the evidence about patient preferences for local hospitals was "equivocal." Finally, its analysis fell prey to a version of the silent majority fallacy.

A. *The Hypothetical Monopolist Test*

As explained above, the hypothetical monopolist test is an iterative analysis. The analyst proposes a candidate market, simulates a monopolization of that market, then adjusts the candidate market and reruns the simulation as necessary. The district court criticized Dr. Tenn's candidate market but did not mention his results. The court did not explain why it thought that a narrow candidate market would produce incorrect results. Nor do the hospitals. We have not found support for that assumption. The economic literature explains that if a candidate market is too narrow, the test will show as much, and further iterations will broaden the market until it is big enough. [ ]

The district court seems to have mistaken those iterations for circularity. It criticized Dr. Tenn's candidate market for "assum[ing] the answer" to the market definition question. [ ] But in fact, the candidate market offers a hypothetical answer to that question; the hypothetical monopolist analysis then tests the hypothesis and adjusts the market definition if the results require it. That is not circular reasoning.

B. *Academic Medical Centers*

When Dr. Tenn proposed a candidate market, he excluded what he called "destination hospitals," which are hospitals—primarily academic medical centers—that attract patients at long distances from throughout the Chicago metropolitan area. The district court criticized that classification, saying it had no "economic basis."[ ] The record belies that assessment: the witnesses consistently used the term "academic medical center" and recognized that demand for those few hospitals differs from demand for general acute care hospitals like these parties' hospitals, which draw patients from much smaller geographic areas.

For example, one insurance executive explained that some insured patients will "travel . . . for a higher level of care potentially at an Academic Medical Center." NorthShore's CEO also distinguished between academic medical centers and community hospitals, explaining that the former provide both "basic" and "complex" services. Other witnesses agreed. Another insurance executive explained that individual consumers want their insurance network to include "[their] physician, [their] community hospital, and maybe potential access to an academic medical center." An executive of one academic medical center differentiated between "community hospitals" and "an Academic Medical Center" in terms of the complexity of the services provided. Another insurance executive explained that NorthShore and Advocate hospitals were not academic medical centers. That testimony provides an obvious and sound basis for distinguishing between academic medical centers and other hospitals like those operated by Advocate and NorthShore.

C. *Patient Preference for Local Hospitals*

Before Dr. Tenn chose a candidate market, he determined that patients generally choose hospitals close to their homes. The district court called the evidence on that point "equivocal," citing testimony that workplace locations and outpatient relationships also influence patient choices. But most of the cited testimony addressed medical care broadly, not inpatient acute care specifically. For instance, one insurance executive testified that Chicago area consumers use "services" close to both their homes and their workplaces. Similarly, another witness explained that employees choose providers based on where they live, work, and have relationships with doctors, but that witness was speaking about "people . . . consuming benefits" generally, not about hospital choice in particular.

When it came to hospital care, the evidence was not equivocal on Dr. Tenn's central point. As one insurance executive put it: "Typically [patients] seek [hospital] care in their own communities." [ ] The evidence on that point is strong, not equivocal. For example, 73 percent of patients living in plaintiffs' proposed market receive hospital care there. Eighty percent of those patients drive less than 20 minutes or 15 miles to their chosen hospital. Ninety-five percent of those patients drive 30 miles or less—the north-to-south length of plaintiffs' proposed market—to reach a hospital. [ ]

* * *

D. *The Silent Majority Fallacy*

The insurance executives were unanimous on a second point: in the North Shore Area, an insurer's network must include either Advocate or NorthShore to offer a product marketable to employers. The record as a whole supports that testimony. There is no evidence that a network has succeeded with employers without one or the other of the merging parties in its network. (One company offers a network in the Chicago area without either of the merging parties, but that network's membership is overwhelmingly individuals rather than employers. And fewer than two percent of those individual members live near NorthShore's hospitals.) Cf. Penn State Hershey, 838 F.3d at 342 (noting that [an] antitrust defendant in theory "may be able to demonstrate that enough patients would buy a health plan . . . with no in-network hospital in the proposed geographic market," but not when an insurer that tried it "lost half of its membership").

The district court discounted that testimony, citing Dr. Tenn's diversion ratios, although it did not explain what it inferred from the ratios. [ ] We assume the court was referring to two of their features: the proportion (52 percent) of patients who, if their first choice hospital were unavailable, would seek care outside the proposed market, and the proportion (7.2–29.2 percent) of patients who, if their first choice hospital were unavailable, would divert to Northwestern Memorial Hospital, an academic medical center outside Dr. Tenn's proposed market.

If patients were the relevant buyers in this market, those numbers would be more compelling since diversion ratios indicate which hospitals patients consider substitutes. But as we have explained, insurers are the most relevant buyers. Insurers must consider both whether employers would offer their plans and whether employees would sign up for them. "[E]mployers generally try to provide all of their employees at least one attractive option," and may not offer even a broadly appealing plan if it lacks services in a particular region. [ ] As a result, measures of patient substitution like diversion ratios do not translate neatly into options for insurers. The district court erred in assuming they did.

The hospitals correctly point out that, strictly speaking, that reasoning is not the same as the silent majority fallacy. The silent majority fallacy treats present travel as a proxy for post-merger travel, while diversion ratios predict likely post-merger travel more directly. But the district court's reasoning and the silent majority fallacy share a critical flaw: they focus on the patients who leave a proposed market instead of on hospitals' market power over the patients who remain, which means that the hospitals have market power over the insurers who need them to offer commercially viable products to customers who are reluctant to travel farther for general acute hospital care.

That flaw runs through the district court's decision. The court focused on identifying hospitals that compete with those in the Commission's proposed market. But the relevant geographic market does not include every competitor. It is the "area of *effective* competition."[ ] It includes the competitors that discipline the merging hospitals' prices. [ ]The geographic market question asks in essence, how many hospitals can insurers convince most customers to drive past to save a few percent on their health insurance premiums? We should not be surprised if that number is very small. Plaintiffs have made a strong case that it is.

We REVERSE the district court's denial of a preliminary injunction and REMAND for further proceedings consistent with this opinion. The merger shall remain enjoined pending the district court's reconsideration of the preliminary injunction motion.

NOTES AND QUESTIONS

1.   *Unilateral Effects.* The underlying theory of competitive harm is based on a "unilateral effects" analysis. That is, because each of the merging hospitals are a strong second choice for the other, the combined entity would be able to raise price to payers (or reduce quality) independent of whether other hospitals raised their prices. See U.S. Department of Justice and Federal Trade Commission, Merger Guidelines § 6 (1992), 57 Fed. Reg. 41552 (Sept. 10, 1992); In the Matter of Evanston Northwestern Healthcare Corp., F.T.C. Docket No. 9315, 2007 WL 2286195 (Aug. 6, 2007); In the Matter of ProMedica Health System, Inc., 2012–1 Trade Cas. (CCH) ¶ 77840, 2012 WL 1155392 (Mar. 28, 2012). Many prior antitrust merger cases relied on a different theory of harm, i.e. "coordinated effects" analysis. Under that model, plaintiffs must prove that the merging parties are likely to raise price or reduce quality in tacit or express agreement with their rivals in the market. See Merger Guidelines § 7. In a notable case affirming the FTC's application of that theory in an early challenge to a hospital merger, Judge Posner explained the economic theory involved.

> When an economic approach is taken in a section 7 case, the ultimate issue is whether the challenged acquisition is likely to facilitate collusion. In this perspective the acquisition of a competitor has no economic significance in itself; the worry is that it may enable the acquiring firm to cooperate (or cooperate better) with other leading competitors on reducing or limiting output, thereby pushing up the market price.

Hosp. Corp. of America v. FTC, 807 F.2d 1381, 1386 (1986). Judge Posner discussed HCA's arguments that collusion is unlikely because of the heterogeneity of hospital markets, the rapid technological and economic change experienced by the hospital industry, and the size of third party payers. On the other side of the ledger were the highly concentrated structure of the market, high barriers to entry, and a history of coordinated action by hospitals. Calling the FTC's decision a "model of lucidity" the Seventh Circuit agreed that the likelihood of oligopolistic coordination was sufficient to satisfy the standard under the antitrust merger precedents.

2. *Hospital Product Markets. Advocate Health* focused on definition of the relevant *geographic* market because the parties agreed on the relevant *product* market definition as the "cluster" of "general acute care services," covering "surgeries, childbirth, treatment of serious infections, and some emergency care." But in other cases, the relevant hospital "product" or service market is contested. Consider that the antitrust agencies' Horizontal Merger Guidelines § 4.1 states that a relevant product market must "identify a set of products that are reasonably interchangeable[.]" Are knee surgeries and childbirth reasonably interchangeable or substitutable? The FTC and the Sixth Circuit in *ProMedica v. FTC* thought not. In *ProMedica*, the FTC challenged a merger of the county's dominant multi-facility health system, ProMedica, with a single high-quality hospital, St. Luke's. Though ProMedica had argued for a single "package deal" product market for all hospital services, the Court upheld the FTC's position that the anti-competitive effects of the merger should be assessed across separate product markets for the cluster of hospital primary and secondary services (such as general surgeries), a separate assessment in the market for obstetrics, noting that patients have very different preferences in choosing obstetric care and will travel different distances to act on those preferences. The proposed merger would have taken the number of facilities offering obstetric care in the geographic market from three to two and increased concentration in the market for obstetrics "in spectacular fashion," making the deal presumptively anti-competitive. ProMedica Health Sys. Inc. v. FTC, 749 F.3d 559 (6th Cir. 2014), cert. denied, 575 U.S. 996 (2015).

3. *Efficiencies.* The law on efficiencies as a defense to an otherwise anticompetitive merger is somewhat unclear. Older Supreme Court case law and the legislative history of the Clayton Act does not seem to support an efficiencies defense, see Alan A. Fisher & Robert Lande, Efficiency Considerations in Merger Enforcement, 71 Cal. L. Rev. 1580 (1983); see also FTC v. Penn St. Hershey supra at 350 (expressing skepticism that an "efficiencies defense even exists"). However, several lower courts have explicitly considered potential cost-savings and other efficiencies associated with mergers both as an absolute defense and as a factor to be considered in evaluating the merger's likely competitive effects. See, e.g., FTC v. University Health, Inc., 938 F.2d 1206 (11th Cir. 1991). The DOJ/FTC Merger Guidelines and most of the litigated cases require that the parties show that the claimed efficiencies are verifiable, cannot be realized by means short of a merger, and are "merger specific" (i.e., attributable to and causally related to the combination of the two firms). Merger Guidelines § 4. Inability to clear these hurdles is often decisive in cases in which courts reject the efficiencies defense. See Penn St. Hershey supra at 351 (finding capital cost savings not verifiable and adoption of risk-based contracting achievable without the merger).

4. *Nonprofit Status.* If the government establishes a *prima facie* case of illegality based on market share and market concentration data, defendants may overcome that presumption by showing that the merger is not likely to have anticompetitive effects. They may do this by proving that market conditions or special characteristics of the merging firms make it unlikely that they will exercise market power after the merger is consummated. Several courts have refused to find that the nonprofit status of the merging hospitals constitutes sufficient grounds to rebut the government's prima facie case, see, e.g., U.S. v. Rockford Memorial Corp., 898 F.2d 1278 (7th Cir. 1990). However, one district court has held that nonprofit hospitals do not operate in the same manner as profit-maximizing businesses, especially when their boards of directors are comprised of community business leaders who have a direct stake in maintaining high quality, low cost hospitals. FTC v. Butterworth Health Corporation and Blodgett Memorial Medical Center, 946 F. Supp. 1285 (W.D. Mich. 1996), aff'd 121 F.3d 708 (6th Cir. 1997).

Do you agree that such hospitals are, as the court in *Butterworth* suggested, more likely to behave in the interests of their consumers (akin to "consumer cooperatives") rather than acting as profit maximizers? What assumptions does this finding make about the role of board members in directing the affairs of a hospital? What limits are placed on them by their fiduciary duties as board members? In this connection, the *Butterworth* court also relied on a number of voluntary "community commitments" made by the merging hospitals, including a freeze on prices or charges, commitments to limit profit margins, and promises to serve the medically needy. Do such assurances provide a sufficient guarantee that the parties will not exercise market power? See Barak K. Richman, Antitrust and Nonprofit Hospital Mergers: A Return to Basics, 156 U. Penn L. Rev. 121 (2007) (criticizing courts' analysis of nonprofit status and arguing the issue has diverted attention from the core concerns of antitrust merger doctrine); Thomas L. Greaney, Antitrust and Hospital Mergers: Does the Nonprofit Form Affect Competitive Substance? 31 J. Health Pol. Pol'y & L. 511 (2006) (rejecting FTC/DOJ preemptive approach and suggesting that systematic differences between nonprofit and for-profit hospital behavior may warrant consideration in some cases).

5. *Cross-Market Mergers.* Historically, antitrust enforcers have rarely brought challenges to mergers of entities occupying different geographic markets because they are not direct competitors. However, developments in economic theory and empirical research now offer evidence that under some circumstances, mergers of hospitals in separate geographic markets that share common customers may increase the merged entity's market power and enable it to raise prices. Economists theorized that cross-market health care mergers could have anticompetitive effects due to the ability of the newly merged entity to bargain with employers and insurers (common customers) that serve employees and customers in different geographic markets. To the employer and insurer, the key element is the provider bundle, such that they will consider tradeoffs between providers that are in different geographic and product markets, as opposed to tradeoffs between direct competitors. Under

the theory of "cross market effects," a health system's market power increases when it adds more providers due to the ability to tie (or "pull through") the system's acquired providers to its strongest "must-have" providers when bargaining with health plans. Moreover, increasing the number of important providers in a system increases the number and significance of network "holes" the merged health system can threaten if the health plan does not accept the health system's higher prices, particularly when bargaining on an all-or-nothing basis. Leemore Dafny, Kate Ho & Robin S. Lee, The Price Effects of Cross-Market Hospital Mergers, Nat'l Bureau of Econ. Research, Working Paper No. 22106 (June 2017); Gregory S. Vistnes & Yianis F. Sarafidis, Cross-Market Hospital Mergers: A Holistic Approach, 79 Antitrust L. J. 253 (2013).

For example, large, geographically dispersed hospital systems in California have increasingly leveraged their market power by bargaining on an all-or-nothing basis and have raised prices beyond what would be expected due to local market advantages. Glenn A. Melnick & Katya Fonkych, Hospital Prices Increase in California, Especially Among Hospitals in the Largest Multi-Hospital Systems, 53 Inquiry, 1 (2016). Although antitrust enforcers have indicated interest in challenging cross-market mergers in appropriate cases, a number of evidentiary hurdles need to be addressed. See Jaime S. King & Erin Fuse Brown, The Anticompetitive Potential of Cross-Market Mergers in Healthcare, 11 St. Louis U. J. Health L. & Pol'y 43 (2017) (discussing the potential for analyzing the effects of a merger on a health plan's entire provider network and the need for limiting principles to identify cross-market mergers with the greatest risk to competition).

6. *State Action Doctrine Protection.* In a unanimous decision, the Supreme Court overturned a decision by the Eleventh Circuit that found a monopoly-granting hospital merger in Albany, Georgia was protected from federal antitrust challenge by the "state action" doctrine. FTC v. Phoebe Putney Health System, Inc., 568 U.S. 216 (2013). As noted in the introduction to this chapter, the state action doctrine immunizes private entities from antitrust law when their anticompetitive conduct is clearly contemplated and actively supervised by the State. The transaction at issue in *Phoebe Putney* involved the county Hospital Authority's acquisition of Palmyra Medical Center, combining it with the only other hospital in the area, Phoebe Putney. At issue was whether Georgia's grant of general corporate powers to hospital authorities to acquire hospitals was a "clear articulation" of an intent to displace competition as required to apply state-action immunity. The Court held that it was not, observing that a "substate governmental entity" such as a hospital authority, must "show that it has been delegated authority to act or regulate anticompetitively." Id. at 133 S.Ct. at 1009. Therefore, the hospital authority's power to acquire hospitals did not "clearly articulate" a state policy to allow anticompetitive hospital acquisitions. Ultimately, however, the FTC was unable to prevent or unwind the merger due to the application of the state's certificate of need (CON) law. The agency interpreting Georgia's CON law deemed the Albany hospital market "over-bedded" and precluded approval of any divestiture of the acquired hospital to an independent entity.

Consequently, despite its victory in the Supreme Court, the FTC abandoned its challenge to the merger and entered into a consent order under which the hospital committed to notifying the agency of future acquisitions and agreed not to challenge CON applications of any potential rivals in the future. FTC Statement In re Phoebe Putney Health Care System, Inc. (March 31, 2013). With only one monopoly provider in Albany, Georgia, health care prices have risen considerably and health insurance premiums are among the highest in the country. See Jordan Rau, In Southwest Georgia, The Affordable Care Act is Having Trouble Living Up to Its Name, Kaiser Health News (Feb. 3, 2014).

NOTE: CONCENTRATION REMEDIES

Despite decades of litigation challenging hospital mergers, the majority of local hospital markets have become highly concentrated, and many are dominated by one "must-have" hospital system. An extensive economic literature indicates that concentrated hospital and physician markets translate into higher prices for consumers with neutral or even negative effects on quality. See Martin Gaynor and Robert Town, Robert Wood Johnson Foundation, The Impact of Hospital Consolidation—Update (Jun. 2012) (summarizing studies). Indeed, some studies suggest that the pricing power of dominant providers is a leading driver of the persistently high cost of health care in America. Confronted with the dilemma of high prices driven by market dominance and the inadequacy of antitrust remedies to break up such systems, several states have turned to regulation. See Thomas L. Greaney, Coping with Concentration, 36 Health Aff. 1564 (2017); Jaime S. King and Erin C. Fuse Brown, The Double-Edged Sword of Health Care Integration: Consolidation and Cost Control, 92 Ind. L. Rev. 55 (2016).

Rather than block or break-up consolidated health care entities, some state attorneys general have entered into **consent decrees** that allow mergers to proceed, on the condition that the merging entities commit to limit price increases, assure access for indigent patients, and limit future acquisitions. See e.g. Commonwealth of Pennsylvania v. Geisinger Medical Center and Shamokin Area Community Hospital, No. 344 MD 2011, consent decree, No. 344 MD 2011 (Commw. Ct. Pa. Jul. 26, 2011) (consent decree contingent on hospital's commitment to continue contracts with certain Medicare Advantage plans at prices adjusted annually and restricting the system's ability to terminate staff privileges for physicians). But see Commonwealth v. Partners Healthcare System, SUCv201–02033–BLS2, 2015 Mass. Super. LEXIS 4, *4–5 (Mass. Sup. Ct. Jan. 29, 2015) (rejecting a proposed merger settlement as not in the public's interest, as it would "cement [the acquiring hospital system's] already strong position," finding proposed price caps and conduct remedies insufficient to offset anticompetitive effects, and questioning its own capacity to monitor and administer price and bargaining between the hospital system and payers).

Other states have sought to regulate dominant hospitals by enacting so-called **Certificate of Public Advantage (COPA)** laws. These laws allow state authorities to grant state-action immunity to merging health care entities, conditioned on continued state oversight of the consolidated entity's promises to limit price increases, maintain critical access facilities, report on quality, and invest in community- and population-health activities. As described in the discussion of *Phoebe Putney*, above, under the two-prong test for state action immunity, a merger can be immunized from federal antitrust scrutiny if it is undertaken pursuant to a "clearly articulated and affirmatively expressed state policy" and "actively supervised" by the state. Notably, the latter requirement compels states approving mergers and conferring such immunity to follow a thoroughgoing regulatory scheme that addresses the costs and benefits of the merger to consumers. COPAs satisfying these requirements empower state regulatory agencies to immunize mergers from federal antitrust challenge while retaining supervision over the merged entity's conduct for a period of time. For example, the FTC abandoned a challenge to a hospital merger to near monopoly in West Virginia after that state adopted a COPA law and ultimately approved the merger. See FTC Press Release, FTC Dismisses Complaint Challenging Merger of Cabell Huntington Hospital and St. Mary's Medical Center (Jul. 6, 2016). The FTC also participated in COPA proceedings in two states over the merger of the Ballad Health System spanning eastern Tennessee and southwest Virginia, arguing the proposed merger would lessen competition in markets in both states. Both state authorities approved the merger, finding the benefits to the community along with continued state oversight outweighed any potential harm from lost competition. See Alex Kacik, Mountain States, Wellmont Skirt Federal Regulation and Score Merger Approval, Mod. Healthcare (Nov. 3, 2017).

What are the pros and cons of such regulation? Might other regulatory interventions such as limitations on provider pricing under state insurance regulation be preferable? See Greaney supra.

PROBLEM: EVALUATING A HOSPITAL MERGER IN YOUR COMMUNITY

Suppose the largest and third largest hospitals (or hospital systems) in your community proposed to merge. What will the key issues be? What facts would you gather in seeking to defend this transaction against antitrust challenges? What testimony from payers, employers, expert witnesses, or parties to the transaction would be helpful?

2. Physician Practice Mergers

SAINT ALPHONSUS MEDICAL CENTER-NAMPA INC.; FEDERAL TRADE COMMISSION & STATE OF IDAHO v. ST. LUKE'S HEALTH SYSTEM

United States Court of Appeals, Ninth Circuit, 2015.
778 F.3d 775.

HURWITZ, CIRCUIT JUDGE:

This case arises out of the 2012 merger of two health care providers in Nampa, Idaho. The Federal Trade Commission and the State of Idaho sued, alleging that the merger violated § 7 of the Clayton Act, [ ], and state law; two local hospitals filed a similar complaint. Although the district court believed that the merger was intended to improve patient outcomes and might well do so, the judge nonetheless found that the merger violated § 7 and ordered divestiture.

As the district court recognized, the job before us is not to determine the optimal future shape of the country's health care system, but instead to determine whether this particular merger violates the Clayton Act. In light of the careful factual findings by the able district judge, we affirm the judgment below.

I. Background

A. *The Health Care Market in Nampa, Idaho*

Nampa, the second-largest city in Idaho, is some twenty miles west of Boise and has a population of approximately 85,000. Before the merger at issue, St. Luke's Health Systems, Ltd. ("St. Luke's"), an Idaho-based, not-for-profit health care system, operated an emergency clinic in the city. Saltzer Medical Group, P.A. ("Saltzer"), the largest independent multi-specialty physician group in Idaho, had thirty-four physicians practicing at its offices in Nampa. The only hospital in Nampa was operated by Saint Alphonsus Health System, Inc. ("Saint Alphonsus"), a part of the multistate Trinity Health system. Saint Alphonsus and Treasure Valley Hospital Limited Partnership ("TVH") jointly operated an outpatient surgery center.

The largest adult primary care physician ("PCP") provider in the Nampa market was Saltzer, which had sixteen PCPs. St. Luke's had eight PCPs and Saint Alphonsus nine. Several other PCPs had solo or small practices.

B. *The Challenged Acquisition*

Saltzer had long had the goal of moving toward integrated patient care and risk-based reimbursement. After unsuccessfully attempting several informal affiliations, including one with St. Luke's, Saltzer sought a formal partnership with a large health care system.

[St. Luke's acquired Saltzer's assets and entered into a five-year professional service agreement ("PSA") with the Saltzer physicians in 2012. After St. Alphonsus and TVH filed a complaint seeking to enjoin the merger, the district court denied a motion for a preliminary injunction based on a commitment in the PSA providing a process for unwinding the transaction if it were declared illegal. Subsequently, after the FTC and the State of Idaho filed a complaint in the district court to enjoin the merger, the court consolidated the two cases and after a 19-day bench trial found the merger prohibited by the Clayton Act and the Idaho Competition Act because of its anticompetitive effects on the Nampa adult PCP market.]

The district court expressly noted the troubled state of the U.S. health care system, found that St. Luke's and Saltzer genuinely intended to move toward a better health care system, and expressed its belief that the merger would "improve patient outcomes" if left intact. Nonetheless, the court found that the "huge market share" of the post-merger entity "creates a substantial risk of anticompetitive price increases" in the Nampa adult PCP market. Rejecting an argument by St. Luke's that anticipated post-merger efficiencies excused the potential anticompetitive price effects, the district court ordered divestiture. This appeal followed.

* * *

B. *The Relevant Market*

[Defendants conceded that the relevant product market was "adult PCP services which include physician services provided to commercially insured patients aged 18 and over by physicians practicing internal medicine, family practice, and general practice." The court of appeals upheld the district court's finding that the Adult PCP geographic market was local, noting testimony that Nampa residents "strongly prefer access to local PCPs" and that "commercial health plans need to include Nampa PCPs in their networks to offer a competitive product." Although one-third of Nampa residents travel to Boise for PCPs, it concluded that fact did not prove that a significant number of other residents would so travel in the event of a price increase because those who traveled generally went to PCPs near their Boise places of employment.]

* * *

[The court of appeals went on to summarize the district court's findings regarding pre- and post-merger market concentration. The court calculated post-merger HHI in the Nampa PCP market as 6,219 and the increase as 1,607, noting that these HHI numbers "are well above the thresholds for a presumptively anticompetitive merger (more than double and seven times their respective [DOJ/FTC Merger Guidelines] thresholds, respectively).")]

* * *

2. *PCP Reimbursements*

The district court also found that St. Luke's would likely use its post-merger power to negotiate higher reimbursement rates from insurers for PCP services. Recognizing that the § 7 inquiry is based on a prediction of future actions, *see Phila. Nat'l Bank,* 374 U.S. at 362, 83 S.Ct. 1715, this finding was not clearly erroneous.

Because St. Luke's and Saltzer had been each other's closest substitutes in Nampa, the district court found the acquisition limited the ability of insurers to negotiate with the merged entity. Pre-acquisition internal correspondence indicated that the merged companies would use this increased bargaining power to raise prices. An email between St. Luke's executives discussed "pressur[ing] payers for new directed agreements," and an exchange between Saltzer executives stated that "[i]f our negotiations w/ Luke's go to fruition," then "the clout of the entire network" could be used to negotiate favorable terms with insurers. The court also examined a previous acquisition by St. Luke's in Twin Falls, Idaho, and found that St. Luke's used its leverage in that instance to force insurers to "concede to their pricing proposal."

* * *

4. *The Prima Facie Case*

... [T]he district court's conclusion that a prima facie case was established is amply supported by the record. "Section 7 does not require proof that a merger or other acquisition has caused higher prices in the affected market. All that is necessary is that the merger create an appreciable danger of such consequences in the future." [ ]

The extremely high HHI on its own establishes the prima facie case. [ ] In addition, the court found that statements and past actions by the merging parties made it likely that St. Luke's would raise reimbursement rates in a highly concentrated market. [ ] And, the court's uncontested finding of high entry barriers "eliminates the possibility that the reduced competition caused by the merger will be ameliorated by new competition from outsiders and further strengthens the FTC's case."

* * *

D. *The Rebuttal Case*

Because the plaintiffs established a prima facie case, the burden shifted to St. Luke's to "cast doubt on the accuracy of the Government's evidence as predictive of future anticompetitive effects." [ ] The rebuttal evidence focused on the alleged procompetitive effects of the merger, particularly the contention that the merger would allow St. Luke's to move toward integrated care and risk-based reimbursement.

1. *The Post-Merger Efficiencies Defense*

The Supreme Court has never expressly approved an efficiencies defense to a § 7 claim. *See H.J. Heinz*, 246 F.3d at 720. Indeed, *Brown Shoe* cast doubt on the defense:

> Of course, some of the results of large integrated or chain operations are beneficial to consumers. Their expansion is not rendered unlawful by the mere fact that small independent stores may be adversely affected. It is competition, not competitors, which the Act protects. But we cannot fail to recognize Congress' desire to promote competition through the protection of viable, small, locally owned business. Congress appreciated that occasional higher costs and prices might result from the maintenance of fragmented industries and markets. It resolved these competing considerations in favor of decentralization. We must give effect to that decision.

370 U.S. at 344, 82 S.Ct. 1502. Similarly, in *FTC v. Procter & Gamble Co.*, the Court stated that "[p]ossible economies cannot be used as a defense to illegality. Congress was aware that some mergers which lessen competition may also result in economies but it struck the balance in favor of protecting competition." 386 U.S. 568, 580, 87 S.Ct. 1224, 18 L.Ed.2d 303 (1967).

Notwithstanding the Supreme Court's statements, four of our sister circuits (the Sixth, D.C., Eighth, and Eleventh) have suggested that proof of post-merger efficiencies could rebut a Clayton Act § 7 prima facie case. [ ] The FTC has also cautiously recognized the defense, noting that although competition ordinarily spurs firms to achieve efficiencies internally, "a primary benefit of mergers to the economy is their potential to generate significant efficiencies and thus enhance the merged firm's ability and incentive to compete, which may result in lower prices, improved quality, enhanced service, or new products." Merger Guidelines § 10 [ ]. However, none of the reported appellate decisions have actually held that a § 7 defendant has rebutted a prima facie case with an efficiencies defense; thus, even in those circuits that recognize it, the parameters of the defense remain imprecise.

* * *

We remain skeptical about the efficiencies defense in general and about its scope in particular. [The court cited several prominent Chicago School judges who expressed skepticism about courts' ability to weigh efficiencies in merger cases.] . . .

Nonetheless, we assume, as did the district court, that because § 7 of the Clayton Act only prohibits those mergers whose effect "may be substantially to lessen competition," 15 U.S.C. § 18, a defendant can rebut a prima facie case with evidence that the proposed merger will create a more efficient combined entity and thus increase competition. . . .

* * *

2. *The St. Luke's Efficiencies Defense*

St. Luke's argues that the merger would benefit patients by creating a team of employed physicians with access to Epic, the electronic medical records system used by St. Luke's. The district court found that, even if true, these predicted efficiencies were insufficient to carry St. Luke's' burden of rebutting the prima facie case. We agree.

It is not enough to show that the merger would allow St. Luke's to better serve patients. The Clayton Act focuses on competition, and the claimed efficiencies therefore must show that the prediction of anticompetitive effects from the prima facie case is inaccurate. [ ] Although the district court believed that the merger would eventually "improve the delivery of health care" in the Nampa market, the judge did not find that the merger would increase competition or decrease prices. Quite to the contrary, the court, even while noting the likely beneficial effect of the merger on patient care, held that reimbursement rates for PCP services likely would increase. Nor did the court find that the merger would likely lead to integrated health care or a new reimbursement system; the judge merely noted the desire of St. Luke's to move in that direction.

The district court expressly did conclude, however, that the claimed efficiencies were not merger-specific. The court found "no empirical evidence to support the theory that St. Luke's needs a core group of employed primary care physicians beyond the number it had before the Acquisition to successfully make the transition to integrated care," and that "a committed team can be assembled without employing physicians." The court also found that the shared electronic record was not a merger-specific benefit because data analytics tools are available to independent physicians.

These factual findings were not clearly erroneous. Testimony highlighted examples of independent physicians who had adopted risk-based reimbursement, even though they were not employed by a major health system. The record also revealed that independent physicians had access to a number of analytic tools, including the St. Luke's Epic system.

But even if we assume that the claimed efficiencies were merger-specific, the defense would nonetheless fail. At most, the district court concluded that St. Luke's might provide better service to patients after the merger. That is a laudable goal, but the Clayton Act does not excuse mergers that lessen competition or create monopolies simply because the merged entity can improve its operations. [ ] The district court did not clearly err in concluding that whatever else St. Luke's proved, it did not demonstrate that efficiencies resulting from the merger would have a positive effect on competition.

IV. Remedy

* * *

. . . [T]he district court did not abuse its discretion in choosing divestiture over St. Luke's' proposed "conduct remedy"—the establishment of separate bargaining groups to negotiate with insurers. Divestiture is "simple, relatively easy to administer, and sure," [ ] while conduct remedies risk excessive government entanglement in the market, *see* U.S. Dep't of Justice, *Antitrust Division Policy Guide to Merger Remedies* § II n. 12 (2011) (noting that conduct remedies need to be "tailored as precisely as possible to the competitive harms associated with the merger to avoid unnecessary entanglements with the competitive process"). The district court, moreover, found persuasive the rejection of a similar proposal in *In re ProMedica Health System, Inc.* [ ] Even assuming that the district court might have been within its discretion in opting for a conduct remedy, we find no abuse of discretion in its declining to do so. *See ProMedica,* 749 F.3d at 572–73 (holding that the FTC did not abuse its discretion in choosing divestiture over a proposed conduct remedy).

V.   Conclusion

For the reasons stated above, we AFFIRM the judgment of the district court.

NOTES AND QUESTIONS

1.   *Efficiencies?* Is the Ninth Circuit's rejections of efficiencies at odds with the strong incentives for provider integration found in the Affordable Care Act and new Medicare reimbursement policies? Can those initiatives succeed in markets dominated by dominant hospitals or physician groups?

2.   *Horizontal vs. Vertical Mergers.* Note that the district court and Ninth Circuit did not address claims made by a rival hospital that the acquisition of Saltzer also violated the Clayton Act on a vertical theory: i.e., that by acquiring the lion's share of primary care physicians, St. Luke's would effectively foreclose competition in the hospital market as the rival would not receive referrals from employed physicians. Vertical challenges of this sort have been rare and impose high hurdles for plaintiffs. See Thomas L. Greaney & Douglas Ross, Navigating Through the Fog of Vertical Merger Law: A Guide to Counselling Hospital-Physician Consolidation Under the Clayton Act, 91 Wash. L. Rev. 199 (2016).

3.   *Physician Market Consolidation.* Studies show that concentration in many local physician specialty markets has increased significantly, although much of the increase is attributable to acquisitions too small to merit challenge

and by expansion of these practices. See Cory Capps et al., Physician Practice Consolidation Driven by Small Acquisitions, So Antitrust Agencies Have Few Tools, 36 Health Aff. 1556 (Sept. 2017); Richard Scheffler and Daniel Arnold, Insurer Market Power Lowers Prices in Numerous Concentrated Provider Markets, 36 Health Affairs 1539 (2017). In a rare attempt to undo a series of acquisitions of physician practices resulting in near monopoly of orthopedic services and impose penalties for affiliations that amounted to price fixing, the Attorney General of Washington filed a civil suit under Section 7 of the Clayton Act and Section 1 of the Sherman Act. See State of Washington v. Franciscan Health System, et al., No. 3:17-cv-05690 (W.D. Wash. Aug. 31, 2017). What evidentiary issues likely arise in challenging consummated mergers? What problems are associated with unwinding a physician acquisition by a hospital?

3. Insurance Mergers

UNITED STATES V. ANTHEM, INC.

United States Court of Appeals, District of Columbia Circuit, 2016.
855 F.3d 345.

ROGERS, CIRCUIT JUDGE:

This expedited appeal arises from the government's successful challenge to "the largest proposed merger in the history of the health insurance industry, between two of the four national carriers," Anthem, Inc. and Cigna Corporation. [ ] In July 2015, Anthem, which is licensed to operate under the Blue Cross Blue Shield brand in fourteen states, reached an agreement to merge with Cigna, with which Anthem competes largely in those fourteen states. The U.S. Department of Justice, along with eleven States and the District of Columbia (together, the "government"), filed suit to permanently enjoin the merger on the ground it was likely to substantially lessen competition in at least two markets in violation of Section 7 of the Clayton Act. Following a bench trial, the district court enjoined the merger, rejecting the factual basis of the centerpiece of Anthem's defense, and focus of its current appeal, that the merger's anticompetitive effects would be outweighed by its efficiencies because the merger would yield a superior Cigna product at Anthem's lower rates. The district court found that Anthem had failed to demonstrate that its plan is achievable and that the merger will benefit consumers as claimed in the market for the sale of medical health insurance to national accounts in the fourteen Anthem states, as well as to large group employers in Richmond, Virginia.

* * *

For the following reasons, we hold that the district court did not abuse its discretion in enjoining the merger based on Anthem's failure to show the kind of extraordinary efficiencies necessary to offset the conceded anticompetitive effect of the merger in the fourteen Anthem states: the loss of Cigna, an innovative competitor in a highly concentrated market. Additionally, we hold that the district court did not abuse its discretion in enjoining the merger based on its separate and independent determination that the merger would have a substantial anticompetitive effect in the Richmond, Virginia large group employer market. Accordingly, we affirm the issuance of the permanent injunction on alternative and independent grounds.

Following a six-week bench trial, the district court permanently enjoined the merger on the basis of its likely substantial anticompetitive effect in the market for the sale of health insurance to national accounts in the Anthem states, as well as in the market for the sale of health insurance to large group employers in Richmond, Virginia. [ ]. It first defined the relevant national accounts market, accepting the government's proposed definition of "national account" as an employer purchasing health insurance for more than 5,000 employees across more than one state. It also found that the market properly included both fully insured and "administrative services only" ("ASO") plans. Under a fully-insured plan, the employer pays for claims adjudication, access to the insurer's provider network (including whatever discounted rates the insurer has negotiated), and coverage of the employees' medical costs. Under an ASO plan, the employer pays for claims adjudication and network access, but the employer self-insures and thus takes on the risk of its employees' medical costs. Finally, the district court found that the relevant geographic market for national accounts was the fourteen Anthem states, because that is where Anthem and Cigna currently compete most prominently, given the geographical restrictions imposed on Anthem under its Blue Cross license.

With the national accounts market so defined, the district court then found a presumption of anticompetitive effect based on the combined company's market share. It determined that the merger would increase HHI by 537 to 3000, while the Guidelines threshold is an increase of 200 to 2500, resulting in a highly concentrated market. [ ]

Next, the district court found that Anthem had provided sufficient evidence to rebut the government's prima facie case. It relied on evidence that Anthem's primary competitor for national accounts is United Healthcare, not Cigna; that national accounts tend to be sophisticated, well-informed customers and thus better able to thwart an attempted price increase; that new entrants to the market will constrain pricing; and that the combined company would have incentives to innovate in its collaborative care arrangements with healthcare providers.

Finally, the district court found that the merger's overall effect in the Anthem states would be anticompetitive by reducing the number of national health insurance carriers from four to three. It rejected Anthem's efficiencies defense, which posited the combined company would realize

$2.4 billion in medical cost savings through its ability to (1) "rebrand" Cigna customers as Anthem in order for them to access Anthem's existing lower rates; (2) exercise an affiliate clause in some of its provider agreements to allow Cigna customers access to Anthem rates; and (3) renegotiate lower rates with providers. [ ]

Additionally, with regard to the Richmond market for large group employers, the district court found a presumption of anticompetitive effect based on the fact that Anthem and Cigna were the city's first- and second-largest competitors, with a combined market share of between 64% and 78%. It found that Anthem rebutted the presumption by challenging the government's calculations, pointing to additional competitors outside the Richmond area and claiming that Anthem customers in the Federal Employee Program skewed its Richmond market share. Overall, however, the district court credited the testimony of the government's expert that even accepting all of Anthem's claimed efficiencies, the merger would still have a net anticompetitive effect. Because Anthem had not shown that the remaining competition (or potential market entrants) could likely constrain a price increase by the combined company, it found that the merger should be enjoined on that additional basis as well.

III.

* * *

Any claimed efficiency must be shown to be merger-specific, meaning that it "cannot be achieved by either company alone because, if [it] can, the merger's asserted benefits can be achieved without the concomitant loss of a competitor. [ ]

* * *

The crux of Anthem's argument regarding merger-specificity is the theory that the combined company will allow Anthem to create a "new product" that is "unavailable on the market today": a product that features both "Cigna's customer-facing programs" and Anthem's "generally lower . . . rates." [ ]. One way Anthem maintains the merger will result in this new product is through rebranding. According to Anthem, "rebranding means [the combined company] retain[s] the Cigna product but brand[s] it under the Anthem name with Anthem's negotiated provider rates." [ ] The record, however, refutes rather than substantiates Anthem's proposed rebranding approach.

[The court cites testimony from Anthem executives acknowledging that rebranding would simply involve Anthem "offer[ing] Cigna customers Anthem products," in a manner that is "no different" than Anthem "selling new business in the market" and would take considerable time and effort to realize.]

* * *

To the extent Anthem has failed to devote the resources needed to improve its product, it is in no position to claim that consumers will benefit from it swallowing up Cigna's superior product.

Put differently, rebranding does not create a merger-specific benefit in either the short- or long-term. Perhaps Anthem could create some brief, interim benefit in the mid-term by integrating Cigna's product faster than it could develop a comparable product of its own. [ ] But Anthem made no sufficient factual showing in the district court on this point. It has offered no evidence to show how long it would take, once the necessary resources were allocated, to develop an improved product. Nor has it shown how long it would take to roll out a hybrid Anthem-Cigna product.

* * *

As discussed, Anthem plans to achieve the claimed savings through a combination of three mechanisms: rebranding, renegotiating provider contracts, and exercising Anthem's affiliate clause. The district court found that practical business realities would undermine the execution of that plan, making achievement of the savings speculative, and therefore unverifiable. With regard to the affiliate clause, the district court focused on evidence of the potential for provider discontent if the lower Anthem rates are forced on providers that must expend extra effort and resources to deliver the Cigna product, without any corresponding increase in value for providers. This evidence included testimony by both Anthem and Cigna witnesses as well as documents from Anthem and Cigna that acknowledged the likely "abrasi[on]."[ ]. The record indicates that physician contracts can be terminated by either party with only 90 days' notice, so the affiliate clause would accomplish little if the contract is terminated or renegotiated soon after the clause is exercised. Hospital contracts tend to involve three-year commitments, so the affiliate clause may bind them to offer lower rates for a longer period. Still, when those hospital contracts expire, large delivery systems with greater leverage "could push back hard" in renegotiation. [ ] In either event, it is probable, as Cigna CEO David Cordani testified, that some providers will eventually "react [by] renegotiating . . . and putting upward pressure on rates, which has been a market force to date." [ ] That "very few" Anthem providers have preemptively sought to renegotiate proves little because the feared abrasion would not occur until Anthem invokes the affiliate clause, assuming it ever does so.

This raises another practical difficulty with the affiliate clause: although it is theoretically useful to Anthem, in reality it is unlikely to be widely exercised because it works counter to Anthem's contractual obligations. Under the "Best Efforts" clause in Anthem's licensing agreement with the Blue Cross Blue Shield Association, 80% of Anthem's revenue within the Anthem states must be Blue-branded, as must 66.67% of its revenue nationwide. The merger would immediately throw Anthem out of compliance and so Anthem intends to rebrand a "lion's share" of current Cigna customers in order to count that revenue as Blue-branded. [ ] By contrast, widespread exercise of the affiliate clause would remove any incentive for Cigna customers to convert to Anthem because those customers would then be receiving the Cigna product at Anthem prices, Dr. Israel's much-touted "best of both worlds" scenario. Anthem fails to address this reality when it maintains that 80% of the savings to Cigna customers could be achieved rapidly using the affiliate clause.[ ] Because doing so would work contrary to Anthem's own contractual obligations, its witnesses conceded that it will instead rely heavily on rebranding, which, as discussed, gives rise to no merger-specific benefits.

As for renegotiation, the short answer is that *if* Anthem cannot persuade providers to extend lower rates to Cigna under its affiliate clauses—where it has apparent contractual recourse to do so—then it is speculative that Anthem could get them to agree to do the same thing through negotiations absent compulsion. [ ] This is especially true for large hospital networks with significant bargaining power.

To the extent that some medical savings would be achieved for Cigna customers at the bargaining table due to the combined company's volume, the district court expressed concern over how long such savings would take to be realized. Anthem's CEO Swedish testified that capturing medical savings requires a "long gestation period," in part because existing hospital contracts span three to five years and would not be subject to renegotiation "for a considerable period of time." [ ] He also rejected the idea that Anthem would simply "drop[ ] the hammer" on providers by insisting on maximum discounts across-the-board because Anthem instead relies upon "customized relationship-driven contract[s]" that seek to optimize performance on a case-by-case basis, rather than focusing solely on discounts. [ ] Anthem's expert agreed that renegotiations in the ordinary course of business will take place over time. The longer it takes for an efficiency to materialize, the more speculative it can be [ ] so the district court was on solid ground to give less weight to the claimed renegotiation savings.

In sum, although renegotiation will lead to a decrease in Cigna's rates, the assumption that it will in every instance lead to the Anthem rate is farfetched. [ ] Indeed, as the district court observed, "the Department of Justice is not the only party raising questions about Anthem's characterization of the outcome of the merger" because Cigna itself had "provided compelling testimony undermining the projections of future savings." [ ]

* * *

The fact is, it is widely accepted that customers value the existing Cigna product, and that Cigna is a leading innovator in collaborative patient care. That threat to innovation is anticompetitive in its own right. [ ] And the problem is neither answered by Anthem's evidence nor offset by its purported efficiency of offering a degraded Cigna product at a lower rate.

* * *

Moreover, Anthem has not explained why these projected savings would even exist. The record is clear that Anthem, unlike Cigna, has already achieved whatever economies of scale are available. [ ]

Next, the claimed medical cost savings only improve consumer welfare to the extent that they are actually passed through to consumers, rather than simply bolstering Anthem's profit margin.[ ] After all, the merger potentially harms consumers by creating upward pricing pressure due to the loss of a competitor, and so only efficiencies that create an equivalent downward pricing pressure can be viewed as "sufficient to reverse the merger's potential to harm consumers . . . , e.g., by preventing price increases." [ ] "[A] sufficient amount of any efficiencies [must] be passed on that the post-merger price is no higher than the pre-merger price." [ ]

Because ASO customers pay their employees' medical costs directly, any reduction in medical rates would result in savings that automatically pass through to the customer, absent some corresponding ASO price increase by Anthem. This would improve the quality of one aspect of the ASO product (*i.e.*, access to more deeply discounted network rates), and it could thus be procompetitive even if it did not immediately result in an ASO price decrease. *See* Guidelines § 10. Dr. Israel's analysis rested on the assumption that rather than raising ASO prices to capture the medical cost savings, Anthem would attempt to increase its market share by providing a much superior product at only a slightly higher price, thereby maximizing its profits through increased sales. The district court highlighted internal Anthem documents that discussed ways to keep those savings for itself, in particular where Anthem listed seven alternatives with 100% pass-through to ASO customers considered last. Contrary to Dr. Israel's assumption, then, Anthem apparently concluded that total pass-through was not the profit-maximizing, "optimal solution to capture the most value from [the] deal," and that it could actually lose business if customers initially saw savings that were not sustained over the long term. [ ] Amici Professors offer another reason why Anthem might have come to this conclusion: in highly concentrated markets, already-large insurers are less constrained by competition and thus tend to find it more profitable to capture medical savings and increase premiums. [ ]([I]n highly concentrated markets "there is less competition present to ensure that the benefit of efficiencies will flow to consumers."). That corroborates rather than remediates anticompetitive concerns.

As for fully insured customers, which comprise $619.8 million of the projected savings, the estimated pass-through is even less likely given that the savings would automatically inure to Anthem's benefit absent some corresponding price decrease to its customers. [ ]

* * *

The savings projected by [defendants' experts]—uncritically relied on by the dissent, [ ]—were without a doubt enormous. The problem is, those projections fall to pieces in a stiff breeze. If merging companies could defeat a Clayton Act challenge merely by offering expert testimony of fantastical cost savings, Section 7 would be dead letter.

Having considered the totality of circumstances [ ] we hold that the district court reasonably determined Anthem failed to show the kind of "extraordinary efficiencies" that would be needed to constrain likely price increases in this highly concentrated market, and to mitigate the threatened loss of innovation.

* * *

Anthem fares no better in its challenge to the district court's independent and alternative determination that the merger should be enjoined on the basis of its anticompetitive effect in the Richmond, Virginia market for the sale of health insurance to "large group" employers with more than fifty employees. There, the government's prima facie case was even stronger than in the market for national accounts in the fourteen Anthem states. Depending on how market share was calculated (i.e., including all Blue customers as Anthem or not, including fully insured customers or just ASO), the companies' combined market share ranged from 64% to 78%. Even under the calculation most favorable to Anthem (ASO-only, disregarding non-Anthem Blue customers), the merger would raise an overwhelming presumption of anticompetitive effect: HHI would rise 1511 to a post-merger total of 4350, where the Guidelines presumption threshold is an increase of 200 to a post-merger total of 2500. As the President of Anthem Virginia acknowledged, Anthem has the biggest share of the large group employer market across all of Virginia, and in Richmond, Cigna is its strongest competitor.

* * *

In conclusion, the district court did not clearly err in its factual findings that the merger would have anticompetitive effects in the Richmond market, and importantly, Anthem does not allege any error of law with respect to that determination. Thus, the district court did not abuse its discretion in enjoining the merger on the basis of the merger's anticompetitive effects in the Richmond market. And, as previously noted, this holding provides an independent basis for the injunction, even absent a finding of anticompetitive harm in the fourteen-state national accounts market.

Accordingly, we affirm the issuance of the permanent injunction on alternative and independent grounds.

NOTES AND QUESTIONS

1. *Insurance Product Markets.* Note that the merger affected two distinct product markets. First, Anthem and Cigna competed in a national accounts market serving large employers that provide health insurance for employees located in multiple states. These employers are largely self-insured and require only **administrative services ("ASO" services)** from insurance companies, which importantly include contracts with provider networks negotiated at favorable rates and care management services. Second, the two firms offered "fully insured" services for large groups which included insurance coverage. The overlap in this product market was significant only in Richmond Virginia, where the firms had a combined market share between 64% and 78%.

2. *Efficiencies?* The nature of the ASO services supplied by Cigna and Anthem differed to an important extent. Cigna employed a strategy of "value-based purchasing" working closely with its network providers to encourage them to provide wellness programs and other health improving services. Anthem's market approach relied heavily on its ability to negotiate highly favorable reimbursement terms with its providers which it passed along to employers. The crux of the appeal in the case came down to the claim that the merger would enable the combined firm to impose its lower rates on providers and sell a "Cigna product at the Anthem price." What facts led the court to doubt that these efficiencies would be realized? What other factors undermined confidence that consumers would benefit even if such savings did occur?

3. *Merger Fever.* Simultaneous with the Anthem/Cigna merger, DOJ, the District of Columbia, and eight state attorneys general successfully challenged another merger of two large insurance companies. In United States v. Aetna, Inc., 240 F. Supp. 3d 1 (D.D.C. 2017), the district court enjoined the merger of Aetna and Humana finding it likely to substantially lessen competition in the sale of Medicare Advantage (MA) plans in 364 counties and in the sale of commercial insurance on public exchange markets. After closely examining the switching behavior of beneficiaries between MA products and traditional Medicare, extensive econometric evidence applying the hypothetical monopolist test, differences between the coverage offered by each, and pricing strategies employed by MA firms, the court concluded that the sale of MA plans is a relevant antitrust product market. In an interesting twist, the court rejected Aetna's claim that any harm to exchange markets was mooted by its decision to withdraw from those markets. The court found that Aetna withdrew from the individual public exchanges in three states to evade judicial

scrutiny of the proposed merger and that absent this strategy future competition was likely.

REVIEW PROBLEM: THE HEART SPECIALTY HOSPITAL

Heart-of-the-Midwest Orthopedic Surgical Hospital (HOTMOSH) has applied to its state health planning agency for a certificate of need (CON) to open a new acute care hospital in Bedrock, Kansas. It will offer facilities for inpatient and outpatient orthopedic surgery and related procedures and a variety of outpatient services including radiology and laboratory services. The hospital is owned by an LLC controlled by two groups of orthopedic surgeons each of which own 40 percent of the membership interest; the remaining ownership is held by other Bedrock physicians.

The three community hospitals in Bedrock are very concerned about the impact HOTMOSH will have on their revenues. Freda Fieldstone, CEO of Bedrock Community Hospital (BCH), has called a meeting with the other hospitals to discuss formulating a "joint response" to the CON application. Besides urging the other hospitals to ask the planning commission to reject the application, she hopes to enlist their support in a campaign to elicit help from managed care organizations. One idea is to have each hospital commit to contacting one managed care organization (MCO) (its "dancing partner") to urge that company not to contract with HOTMOSH and, if necessary, to "intimate" that the other hospitals in the market would probably be very unhappy if the MCO chose to include the specialty hospital in its network.

Because BCH is the largest orthopedic hospital in the area and other hospitals are not at risk for losing nearly as much business, Ms. Fieldstone believes she must come up with a strategy to ensure she will have the support of the other hospitals. Because St. Lucas Hospital has filed a CON application to add 20 new oncology beds to its campus, Ms. Fieldstone believes that if she "hints" that BCH might oppose this CON application unless St. Lucas supports her on the HOTMOSH issue, she will "get their attention." If that doesn't work, she plans to hint that BCH may also be thinking of opening a new oncology service.

Finally, Ms. Fieldstone has several "backup" plans:

- Terminate the staff privileges of every doctor at BCH who has an ownership interest or who refers more than five patients per year to HOTMOSH.

- Create a "super PHO" to bargain with MCOs on behalf of the other hospitals performing orthopedic services in town. If that is not possible, to "clinically integrate" the orthopedic surgeons on her staff who do not have an ownership in HOTMOSH so that they can negotiate as a unit with MCOs.

- If all else fails, negotiate a merger or joint venture with HOTMOSH once it establishes that it is successful in the market.

Recognizing that these ideas may raise some antitrust concerns, Ms. Fieldstone has solicited your counsel. Advise on the possible antitrust risks you see for each strategic option and what might be done to reduce legal risk.

CHAPTER 16

REPRODUCTION AND BIRTH

. . .

I. INTRODUCTION

As the other chapters in this book have demonstrated, health policy can be motivated by diverse economic, political, cultural, and social justice goals. These goals, in turn, are often shaped by deeply held beliefs about the ethical principles and moral values that should inform government's role in society. Perhaps no area of health law stimulates as much passionate debate and reveals as sharply diverging views on the appropriate role of government, as the regulation of reproduction and birth.

One reason for this is that regulation of reproduction implicates questions of personhood. The rights, obligations, privileges, and relationships previously described in this book are generally rights, obligations, privileges, and relationships of people. But who ought to be recognized as a person, subject to the legal principles that regulate our rights and obligations? When does a person, entitled to formal legal respect as such, come into existence? And how much work does this do to resolve difficult disputes involving competing fundamental interests? Can such answers be resolved through an analysis of medicine, philosophy, ethics, law, social history, anthropology, theology and other disciplines which seek to answer the basic questions of human existence?

Physicians and lawyers have necessarily been involved in these questions, as demonstrated by conflicts over government regulation of abortion and contraception, compelled medical intervention during pregnancy, and legal questions about the treatment of embryos arising out of the growing use of assisted reproductive technology. It is therefore appropriate to consider these issues in this text. The deeply contested and complex legal and philosophical questions around personhood are surveyed in the first portion of this chapter, and this issue is an important theme in the legal and ethical questions considered throughout the rest of the chapter.

The issues surveyed in this chapter also raise important gender, racial, disability, and socioeconomic justice concerns, which have motivated complaints of both too much and too little government regulation in the area of reproduction. Gender concerns are most obviously implicated, because although all people have reproductive health care needs, the ability to get pregnant has been linked to stereotypes about women's proper role in society, including presumptions of motherhood, limits on sexual liberty, exclusion from employment, and many other forms of discrimination. Socioeconomic concerns are implicated because the ability to control the timing and manner of pregnancy impacts individual and family well-being and socioeconomic opportunities. Many of the reforms combatting pregnancy-based discrimination have been driven by concerns about gender equity, as well as the particular health and social consequences of denying care that enables, prevents, or terminates pregnancy.

While reproductive *rights* advocates have traditionally focused on women's ability to prevent pregnancy and birth, a more recent movement around reproductive *justice* has shone a light on government actions that regulate and control reproduction more broadly. This includes government actions that create barriers to procreation, attempt to police behavior during pregnancy, and undermine the right to safe and dignified parenting for historically marginalized groups. For example, assumptions about who *ought* to be a parent, or who can be trusted to parent effectively, have motivated government sterilization programs targeting people with developmental disabilities, the poor, racial and ethnic minorities, and women in prison. In addition, state and federal laws have traditionally made it more difficult for some groups to realize their procreative dreams through assisted reproductive technology, especially those who do not conform to traditional gender and sexual norms.

The remaining parts of this chapter are not intended to be a comprehensive analysis of all of the legal and ethical questions raised by reproduction. The goal of this chapter is to provide structure for an analysis of issues surrounding procreation and reproduction that are likely to be of special concern to patients, the health care professionals and institutions entrusted with their care, and the attorneys helping to navigate disputes when they arise.

II. WHEN DOES HUMAN LIFE BECOME A "PERSON"?

This society has had difficulty defining who is a "person." In part, this arises out of the different and inconsistent purposes for which we seek a definition. The "person" from whom we wish to harvest a kidney for transplantation may be defined differently from the "person" who is protected by the Fourteenth Amendment, federal civil rights laws, and various other federal and state laws. Even when the purpose of the definition is settled—such as who is a person able to bring an action under state tort law—there is no consensus on when the status of "personhood" first attaches. The most obvious definition of personhood is a recursive one:

a human being (and, thus, a "person") is the reproductive product of other human beings. Even if we accept this "human stock" definition of person, however, the inquiry remains open. Does that human stock become a person, for tort law or other purposes, upon conception? Upon quickening? Upon viability? Upon birth? A year after birth? Upon physical maturity?

The definition of "person" is not limited to various stages in the development of human stock. "Personhood" could commence upon ensoulment, upon the development of self-concept, upon the development of a sense of personal history, or upon the ability to communicate through language although none of these points is easy to identify in individual cases. The resolution of the question appears to require a resort to first principles.

In the vast majority of cases, it is not difficult to distinguish a person from something else. You are easily distinguishable from your arms, your dog, your insurance company and your smart phone, as close as you may feel to each of them. The most difficult questions tend to arise at the very beginning and at the very end of human life. Just as you may be able to identify the fact that you were in love, but not be able to identify exactly when it began, or the moment when it ended, the beginnings and the endings of "personhood" are the fuzzy portions.

There are limits to what may reasonably be considered a "person," even when we limit our consideration to human stock. Few suggest that anything independent of the unified sperm and ovum, or its consequences, ought to be considered a person, although advances in cloning and cellular manipulation may challenge this assumption. A great many religious groups consider "personhood" to attach at conception. Aristotle viewed the development of the person as a three-stage process, going from vegetable (at conception) to animal (in utero), to rational (sometime after birth). For many centuries, Christian theology fixed the point of "immediate animation" when the fetus was "ensouled" as forty days after conception for males and eighty days after conception for females. St. Thomas Aquinas determined that the ensoulment took place at the time of quickening, usually fourteen to eighteen weeks after conception, and his determination had a very substantial effect on the development of the common law in England and in this country. Recently some philosophers have suggested that "personhood," at least to the extent that it includes a right to life, depends on attributes that are not likely to be developed until sometime after birth.

One thoughtful and oft-cited set of attributes of personhood has been developed by Joseph Fletcher, a bioethicist. Consider his fifteen criteria, described below, and determine whether some or all of them can be used to properly define who is your colleague in personhood and who is not. Consider whether the fact that many of these criteria disqualify fetuses, newborns, and those with serious cognitive and intellectual disabilities, including those with severe brain injuries and disorders of consciousness (discussed in Chapter 17), should or does affect their acceptability as standards. Further, does the fact that some animal or machine might eventually fulfill all of these criteria cause you to doubt their validity? What are the consequences of our failure to define as a person a clone, a highly intelligent and communicative ape, a robot, or a manufactured cell that can be brought to term in an artificial womb, with regard to our conceptions of "democracy" and "slavery," for example?

JOSEPH FLETCHER, "HUMANNESS," IN HUMANHOOD: ESSAYS IN BIOMEDICAL ETHICS
12–16 (1979).

Synthetic concepts such as human and man and person require operational terms, spelling out the which and what and when. Only in that way can we get down to cases—to normative decisions. There are always some people who prefer to be visceral and affective in their moral choices, with no desire to have any rationale for what they do. But ethics is precisely the business of rational, critical reflection (encephalic and not merely visceral) about the problems of the moral agent—in biology and medicine as much as in law, government, education, or anything else.

To that end, then, for the purposes of biomedical ethics, I now turn to a *profile of man* in concrete and discrete terms. . . . There is time only to itemize the inventory, not to enlarge upon it, but I have fifteen positive propositions. Let me set them out, in no rank order at all, and as hardly more than a list of criteria or indicators, by simple title.

1.   Minimum Intelligence

Mere biological life, before minimal intelligence is achieved or after it is lost irretrievably, is without personal status.

2.   Self-awareness
***

3.   Self-control

If an individual is not only not controllable by others (unless by force) but not controllable by the individual himself or herself, a low level of life is reached about on a par with that of a paramecium. . . .

4.   A Sense of Time
***

5.   A Sense of Futurity

How "truly human" is any man who cannot realize there is a time yet to come as well as the present? Subhuman animals do not look forward in time; they live only on what we might call visceral strivings, appetites. Philosophical anthropologies (one recalls that of William Temple, the Archbishop of Canterbury, for instance) commonly emphasize purposiveness as a key to humanness. Chesterton once remarked that we would never ask a puppy what manner of dog it wanted to be when it grows up. . . .

6.   A Sense of the Past

* * *

7.   The Capability to Relate to Others

Interpersonal relationships, of the sexual-romantic and friendship kind, are of the greatest importance for the fullness of what we idealize as being truly personal. . . .

8.   Concern for Others

Some people may be skeptical about our capacity to care about others (what in Christian ethics is often distinguished from romance and friendship as "neighbor love" or "neighbor concern"). . . . But whether concern for others is disinterested or inspired by enlightened self-interest, it seems plain that a conscious extra-ego orientation is a trait of the species . . . .

9.   Communication

Utter alienation or disconnection from others, if it is irreparable, is dehumanization. . . .

10. Control of Existence

It is of the nature of man that he is not helplessly subject to the blind workings of physical or physiological nature. He has only finite knowledge, freedom, and initiative, but what he has of it is real and effective. . . .

11. Curiosity

To be without affect, sunk in *anomie*, is to be not a person. Indifference is inhuman. Man is a learner and a knower as well as a tool maker and user. . . .

12. Change and Changeability

To the extent that an individual is unchangeable or opposed to change, he denies the creativity of personal beings. It means not only the fact of biological and physiological change, which goes on as a condition of life, but the capacity and disposition for changing one's mind and conduct as well. Biologically, human beings are developmental: birth, life, health, and death are processes, not events, and are to be understood progressively, not episodically. All human existence is on a continuum, a matter of becoming . . . .

13. Balance of Rationality and Feeling

. . . . As human beings we are not coldly rational or cerebral, nor are we merely creatures of feeling and intuition. It is a matter of being both, in different combinations from one individual to another. . . .

14. Idiosyncrasy

The human being is idiomorphous, a distinctive individual. . . . To be a person is to have an identity, to be recognizable and callable by name.

15. Neocortical Function

In a way, this is the cardinal indicator, the one all the others are hinged upon. Before cerebration is in play, or with its end, in the absence of the synthesizing function of the cerebral cortex, the person is nonexistent. Such individuals are objects but not subjects. This is so no matter how many other spontaneous or artificially supported functions persist in the heart, lungs, neurologic and vascular systems. Such noncerebral processes are not personal. . . .

NOTES AND QUESTIONS

1. *Capacity for Consciousness.* Some commentators have concluded that the real consensus requirement of personhood is the capacity for conscious experience. Do you think that this is a necessary attribute? A sufficient attribute? Does it encompass many—or all—of the attributes described by Fletcher? Capacity for conscious experience is also relevant to questions about the determination of death. See Chapter 18.

2. *A Bundle of Attributes?* Fletcher commenced a serious debate over whether the persons protected by law ought to be defined in terms of attributes we wish to protect or in terms of the human stock from which the person is created. Both forms of definition may be valuable for different purposes. We provide some rights to people because they possess many or all of the attributes that distinguish human beings. The right to make medical decisions, based on the autonomy of individuals, is not accorded to those without some "minimum intelligence." See discussion of competence in Chapter 17. On the other hand, we provide minimally adequate housing, food, medical care, and other necessities for those of human stock, even when they do not meet some of Fletcher's criteria, and even when we do not provide those same benefits to others, (e.g., animals) who fail the same criteria. In the end, the Fletcher propositions may be useful in determining some of the rights of persons and the "human stock" definition may be helpful in determining others. Just as property is often described as a bundle of rights, it may turn out that "personhood" is a bundle of attributes that need to be separated out and individually analyzed.

PROBLEM: DOES THINKING MAKE IT HUMAN?

Assume that a laboratory has learned enough about neuroscience and the operation of the brain, artificial intelligence, robotics and psychology to create a machine that acts in a way that is indistinguishable from a human being. Assume that without actually seeing the mechanical interior of this machine it would be effectively impossible for a person to distinguish the machine from any another human being. It speaks well, it "sees" accurately, and it has reactions that we would expect from one with all of the attributes, including the emotional attributes, of a human being. Further, it looks like any other human being—at least from the outside—and it has an ability to learn and change the way human beings do. It does not have the ability to reproduce the way other human beings do, but it does have the ability to reconstruct itself in the workshop, and thus can continue its line. Those of you with a background in philosophy or artificial intelligence will recognize this as a slightly updated version of the renowned "Turing test" first proposed by the brilliant computer scientist Alan Turing in one of the most influential philosophical works of the last century. A. Turing, Computing Machinery and Intelligence, 49 Mind 433 (1950). See also Stuart Russell and Peter Norving, Artificial Intelligence: A Modern Approach (2d ed. 2003).

For legal and other purposes, should this machine be treated as a human being? Should it be able to vote or otherwise be protected by the Fourteenth Amendment? If you don't think it should be treated like a human being, why is that? What attribute is it missing? What if it had that attribute, too? Is there some attribute of the human mind (or the human being more generally) that is not a part of the physical human brain? What are the consequences of treating this machine as a person? What are the consequences of failing to do so?

What if a natural human being whose brain had failed as a result of an utterly disastrous stroke had her brain replaced by an electronic version. Would that still be a person? Would it be the same person? What is the relationship between the mind, the brain, our individual histories and values, and our personhood? Is there a place for the consideration of the "soul" in this discussion? Are the questions raised here the same as the basic questions raised by the "mind vs. brain" debate over the past millennia? There has been a great deal of discussion of the issue of machine-as-human recently, with several provocative books, articles, and movies exploring both the future possibilities and ethical implications of continued evolution in AI. There has also been discussion of intellectual property issues that may grow out of nontraditional human beings. See, e.g., Eric Zylstra, Presumed Sapient: A Proposed Test for the Constitutional Personhood and Patentability of Human-Animal Chimeras and Hybrids, 46 U. S. F. L. Rev. 1075 (2012).

Is the only way out of this dilemma to define a human being as one created through human stock—that is, one who is born (in more or less the traditional way) of other human beings? Of course, as we saw earlier, even the adoption of a "human stock" definition does not answer the question of when that human stock becomes a person. What is the attribute of the human stock that makes it a person—genetic uniqueness? Responsiveness? The potential to be born? The appearance of a human being? Consider the following list of the alternative medical points of personhood.

C.R. AUSTIN, "WHEN DOES A PERSON'S LIFE REALLY BEGIN?" IN HUMAN EMBRYOS: THE DEBATE ON ASSISTED REPRODUCTION
22–31 (1989).

. . . . Probably most people who were asked this question would answer "at fertilization" (or "conception"). Certainly, several interesting and unusual things happen then—it is really the most *obvious* event to pick— but for biologists the preceding and succeeding cellular processes are *equally* important. Nevertheless, "fertilization" continues to be the cry of many religious bodies and indeed also of the august World Medical Association, who, in 1949, adopted the Geneva Convention Code of Medical Ethics, which contains the clause: "I will maintain the utmost respect for human life from the time of conception." So we do need to look more closely at this choice, for a generally acceptable "beginning" for human life would be a great help in reaching ethical and legal consensus.

In the first place human *life,* as such, obviously begins before fertilization, since the egg or oocyte is alive before sperm entry, as were innumerable antecedent cells, back through the origin of species into the mists of time. A more practical starting point would be that of the life of the human *individual,* so it is individuality that we should be looking for, at least as one of the essential criteria. Now the earliest antecedents of the eggs, as of sperm, are the primordial germ cells, which can be seen as a group of distinctive little entities migrating through the tissues of the early embryo. When they first become recognizable, they number only about a dozen or two, but they multiply fast and soon achieve large numbers, reaching a peak of 7–10 million about 6 months after conception. Then, despite continued active cell division, there is a dramatic decline in the cell population, which has tempted people to suggest that some sort of "selection of the fittest" occurs, but there is no good evidence in support of this idea; nor is there any good reason to look for individuality in that mercurial population. In due course, the primordial germ cells, while still undergoing cell divisions, settle down in the tissues of the future ovary, change subtly in their characteristics, and thus become oogonia; and then, soon after birth, *cell division ceases,* the cells develop large nuclei and are now recognizable as primary oocytes. From now on, there are steady cell losses but no further cell divisions . . . ; it is the same entity that was a primary oocyte, becomes a fertilized egg, and then develops as an embryo. The primary oocytes are very unusual cells, for they have the capacity to live for much longer than most other body cells; the *same* oocytes can be seen in the ovaries of women approaching the menopause—cells that have lived for about 40 years or longer. And it is with the emergence of the primary oocytes that we can hail the start of *individuality*. Then, in those oocytes that are about to be ovulated, the first meiotic division takes place—another important step, for the "shuffling" of genes that occurs at that point bestows *genetic uniqueness* on the oocyte. So both individuality and genetic uniqueness are established before sperm penetration and fertilization; these processes have distinctly different actions—providing the stimulus that initiates cleavage and contributing to biparental inheritance. Thus, the preferred choice for the start of the human individual should surely be the formation of the primary oocyte, but there is certainly no unanimity on this score.

Passing over now the popularity of fertilization, for many people it is instead the emergence of the embryonic disc and primitive streak that most appeals as the stage in which to identify the start of "personhood" (one or more persons, in view of the imminent possibility of twinning), and there is much to support this opinion. Here, for the first time, are structures that are designed to have a different destiny than *all the rest of the embryo*— they represent the primordium of the fetus, and the developmental patterns of embryo and fetus progressively diverge from this stage onwards. An additional point is that this new emergence is not inevitable, for in around one in two-thousand pregnancies the embryo grows, often to quite a large size, but there is no fetus . . . .

At the time of appearance of the embryonic disc, and shortly beforehand, the process of implantation is occurring, and this is considered by many to have special significance in relation to embryonic potential—so far as we know, implantation cannot occur once the development of the embryo has passed the stage when interaction with . . . the uterus normally takes place.

But despite all that has been said, there are still many folk who remain unconvinced—is the being at this stage sufficiently "human" to qualify as the start of a person? After all, the disc is just a collection of similar cells, virtually undifferentiated, poorly delineated from its surroundings, about a fifth of a millimetre long, non-sentient, and without the power of movement. It is in no way a "body" and it does not bear the faintest resemblance to a human being—*and* the soul cannot enter yet, for the disc may yet divide in the process of twinning, and the soul being unique is indivisible. Also, it is argued that we should be looking for some spark of personality, and a moral philosopher has proposed that some sort of responsiveness is an essential feature.

One of the earliest succeeding changes in the direction of humanness could be the development of the heart primordium, and soon after that the beginnings of a circulatory system; the first contractions of the heart muscle occur possibly as early as day 21, with a simple tubular heart at that stage, and in the fourth week a functional circulation begins. With the heart beats we have the first movements initiated within the embryo (?fetus) and thus in a way the first real "sign of life." The conceptus is now about 6 mm long. During the fifth and sixth weeks, nerve fibres grow out from the spinal cord and make contact with muscles, so that at this time or soon afterwards, a mechanical or electrical stimulus might elicit a muscle twitch; this is important for it would be the first indication of sentient existence—of "responsiveness." At this stage, too, the embryo could possibly feel pain. But, still, some would find cause to demur: only an expert could tell that this embryo/fetus, now 12–13 mm in length, with branchial arches (corresponding to the "gill-slits" in non-mammalian embryos), stubby limbs, and a prominent tail, is human. A marginally more acceptable applicant is the fetus at 7½ weeks, when the hands and feet can be seen to have fingers and toes, and thereafter physical resemblance steadily improves; also at this time, a special gene on the Y-chromosome (the "testis-determining factor" or TDF) is switched on, and the fetuses that have this chromosome, the males, proceed thenceforward to develop *as* males, distinguishable from females.

At about 12 weeks, electrical activity can be detected in the brain of the fetus, which could signal the dawn of consciousness. Here, we would seem to have a very logical stage marking the *start* of a person, for the cessation of electrical activity in the brain ("brain death") is accepted in both medical and legal circles as marking the *termination* of a person—as an indication that life no longer exists in victims of accidents or in patients with terminal illnesses. Around the fourth or fifth month of pregnancy, the mother first experiences movements of the fetus ("quickening"), which were regarded by St. Thomas Aquinas as the first indication of life, for he believed that life was distinguished by two features, knowledge and movement; moreover, it would seem logical that the fetus would move when the *animus* (life or soul) took up residence. . . .

At about 24 weeks, the fetus reaches a state in which it can commonly survive outside the maternal body, with assistance. . . . Just which stage marks the start of a person's life is a matter of personal opinion. Much of the foregoing argumentation may seem to some people difficult to comprehend, especially if they have not had formal training in biology, and to others may even seem irrelevant, in view of the firm line taken by many church authorities. But it really is important that we should try to reach a consensus on just when a person's life should be held to begin, for the decision does have important practical consequences—it directly affects the rights of other embryos, of fetuses, and of people.

III.   ABORTION

Abortion is the area where the most high profile and controversial debates have occurred over questions about when life begins, as well as how the answer to this question should inform government regulation of reproduction. We begin this section with the seminal case, *Roe v. Wade*, defining abortion as a privacy right. This right has been subject to several decades of legal contests. In most of these, a state has enacted legislation that regulates or restricts access to abortions, and patients or providers challenge the laws on constitutional grounds. Abortion restrictions or regulations have tested, and often narrowed the boundaries of the constitutional right to abortion established in *Roe*. As this edition goes to print near the end of 2021, *Roe* still stands, even if in a somewhat altered form. But as described further in the Notes and Questions following *Whole Woman's Health v. Hellerstedt*, recent developments have called the fate of *Roe* into question once again.

A.   ABORTION AS A PRIVACY RIGHT

ROE V. WADE

Supreme Court of the United States, 1973.
410 U.S. 113.

MR. JUSTICE BLACKMUN delivered the opinion of the Court.

* * *

We forthwith acknowledge our awareness of the sensitive and emotional nature of the abortion controversy, of the vigorous opposing views, even among physicians, and of the deep and seemingly absolute convictions that the subject inspires. One's philosophy, one's experiences, one's exposure to the raw edges of human existence, one's religious training, one's attitudes toward life and family and their values, and the moral standards one establishes and seeks to observe, are all likely to influence and to color one's thinking and conclusions about abortion.

In addition, population growth, pollution, poverty, and racial overtones tend to complicate and not to simplify the problem.

Our task, of course, is to resolve the issue by constitutional measurement, free of emotion and of predilection. We seek earnestly to do this, and, because we do, we have inquired into, and in this opinion place some emphasis upon, medical and medical-legal history and what that history reveals about man's attitudes toward the abortion procedure over the centuries. We bear in mind, too, Mr. Justice Holmes' admonition in his now-vindicated dissent in Lochner v. New York[ ]:

[The Constitution] is made for people of fundamentally differing views, and the accident of our finding certain opinions natural and familiar or novel and even shocking ought not to conclude our judgment upon the question whether statutes embodying them conflict with the Constitution of the United States.

* * *

The principal thrust of appellant's attack on the Texas statutes is that they improperly invade a right, said to be possessed by the pregnant woman, to choose to terminate her pregnancy. Appellant would discover this right in the concept of personal "liberty" embodied in the Fourteenth Amendment's Due Process Clause; or in personal, marital, familial, and sexual privacy said to be protected by the Bill of Rights or its penumbras,[ ]; or among those rights reserved to the people by the Ninth Amendment[ ]. Before addressing this claim, we feel it desirable briefly to survey, in several aspects, the history of abortion, for such insight as that history may afford us, and then to examine the state purposes and interests behind the criminal abortion laws.

VI

It perhaps is not generally appreciated that the restrictive criminal abortion laws in effect in a majority of States today are of relatively recent vintage. Those laws, generally proscribing abortion or its attempt at any time during pregnancy except when necessary to preserve the pregnant woman's life, are not of ancient or even of common-law origin. Instead, they derive from statutory changes effected, for the most part, in the latter half of the 19th century.

[The Court then reviewed, in great detail, ancient attitudes, the Hippocratic Oath, the common law, English statutory law, American Law, the position of the American Medical Association, the position of the American Public Health Association, and the position of the American Bar Association.]

VII

Three reasons have been advanced to explain historically the enactment of criminal abortion laws in the 19th century and to justify their continued existence.

It has been argued occasionally that these laws were the product of a Victorian social concern to discourage illicit sexual conduct. Texas, however, does not advance this justification in the present case, and it appears that no court or commentator has taken the argument seriously. . . .

A second reason is concerned with abortion as a medical procedure. When most criminal abortion laws were first enacted, the procedure was a hazardous one for the woman. . . . Thus, it has been argued that a State's real concern in enacting a criminal abortion law was to protect the pregnant woman, that is, to restrain her from submitting to a procedure that placed her life in serious jeopardy.

Modern medical techniques have altered this situation. Appellants and various amici refer to medical data indicating that abortion in early pregnancy, this is, prior to the end of the first trimester, although not without its risk, is now relatively safe. Mortality rates for women undergoing early abortions, where the procedure is legal, appear to be as low as or lower than the rates for normal childbirth. Consequently, any interest of the State in protecting the woman from an inherently hazardous procedure, except when it would be equally dangerous for her to forgo it, has largely disappeared. Of course, important state interests in the area of health and medical standards do remain. The State has a legitimate interest in seeing to it that abortion, like any other medical procedure, is performed under circumstances that assure maximum safety for the patient. . . .

The third reason is the State's interest—some phrase it in terms of duty—in protecting prenatal life. Some of the argument for this justification rests on the theory that a new human life is present from the moment of conception. . . . Logically, of course, a legitimate state interest in this area need not stand or fall on acceptance of the belief that life begins at conception or at some other point prior to live birth. [R]ecognition may be given to the less rigid claim that as long as at least potential life is involved, the State may assert interests beyond the protection of the pregnant woman alone.

* * *

It is with these interests, and the weight to be attached to them, that this case is concerned.

VIII

The Constitution does not explicitly mention any right of privacy. In a line of decisions, however, going back perhaps as far as[ ] 1891 the Court has recognized that a right of personal privacy, or a guarantee of certain areas or zones of privacy, does exist under the Constitution. In varying contexts, the Court or individual Justices have, indeed, found at least the roots of that right in the First Amendment,[ ] in the Fourth and Fifth Amendments,[ ] in the penumbras of the Bill of Rights, Griswold v. Connecticut,[ ] the Ninth Amendment,[ ] or in the concept of liberty guaranteed by the first section of the Fourteenth Amendment.[ ] These decisions make it clear that only personal rights that can be deemed "fundamental" or "implicit in the concept of ordered liberty,"[ ] are included in this guarantee of personal privacy. They also make it clear that the right has some extension to activities relating to marriage,[ ] family relationships,[ ] and child rearing and education[ ].

This right of privacy, whether it be founded in the Fourteenth Amendment's concept of personal liberty and restrictions upon state action, as we feel it is, or, as the District Court determined, in the Ninth Amendment's reservation of rights to the people, is broad enough to encompass a woman's decision whether or not to terminate her pregnancy. The detriment that the State would impose upon the pregnant woman by denying this choice altogether is apparent. Specific and direct harm medically diagnosable even in early pregnancy may be involved. Maternity, or additional offspring, may force upon the woman a distressful life and future. Psychological harm may be imminent. Mental and physical health may be taxed by child care. There is also the distress, for all concerned, associated with the unwanted child, and there is the problem of bringing a child into a family already unable, psychologically and otherwise, to care for it. In other cases, as in this one, the additional difficulties and continuing stigma of unwed motherhood may be involved. All these are factors the woman and her responsible physician necessarily will consider in consultation.

On the basis of elements such as these, appellant and some amici argue that the woman's right is absolute and that she is entitled to terminate her pregnancy at whatever time, in whatever way, and for whatever reason she alone chooses. With this we do not agree. . . . [A] State may properly assert important interests in safeguarding health, in maintaining medical standards, and in protecting potential life. At some point in pregnancy, these respective interests become sufficiently compelling to sustain regulation of the factors that govern the abortion decision.

* * *

IX

* * *

Appellee argues that the State's determination to recognize and protect prenatal life from and after conception constitutes a compelling state interest. [W]e do not agree fully with [this] formulation.

[ ] The appellee and certain amici argue that the fetus is a "person" within the language and meaning of the Fourteenth Amendment. In support of this, they outline at length and in detail the well-known facts of fetal development. If this suggestion of personhood is established, the appellant's case, of course, collapses, for the fetus' right to life is then guaranteed specifically by the Amendment. The appellant conceded as much on reargument. On the other hand, the appellee conceded on reargument that no case could be cited that holds that a fetus is a person within the meaning of the Fourteenth Amendment.

The Constitution does not define "person" in so many words. Section 1 of the Fourteenth Amendment contains three references to "person." The first, in defining "citizens," speaks of "persons born or naturalized in the United States." The word also appears both in the Due Process Clause and in the Equal Protection Clause. "Person" is used in other places in the Constitution: in the listing of qualifications for Representatives and Senators [ ]; in the Apportionment Clause [ ][53] in the Migration and Importation provision [ ]; in the Emolument Clause [ ]; in the Electors provisions [ ]; in the provision outlining qualifications for the office of President [ ]; in the Extradition provisions, [ ], and the superseded Fugitive Slave Clause; and in the Fifth, Twelfth, and Twenty-second Amendments, as well as in §§ 2 and 3 of the Fourteenth Amendment. But in nearly all these instances, the use of the word is such that it has application only postnatally. None indicates, with any assurance, that it has any possible prenatal application.[54]

* * *

All this, together with our observation . . . that throughout the major portion of the 19th century prevailing legal abortion practices were far freer than they are today, persuades us that the word "person," as used in the Fourteenth Amendment, does not include the unborn. . . .

* * *

Texas urges that, apart from the Fourteenth Amendment, life begins at conception and is present throughout pregnancy, and that, therefore, the State has a compelling interest in protecting that life from and after conception. We need not resolve the difficult question of when life begins. When those trained in the respective disciplines of medicine, philosophy, and theology are unable to arrive at any consensus, the judiciary, at this point in the development of man's knowledge, is not in a position to speculate as to the answer.

* * *

---

[53] We are not aware that in the taking of any census under this clause, a fetus has ever been counted.

[54] When Texas urges that a fetus is entitled to Fourteenth Amendment protection as a person, it faces a dilemma. Neither in Texas nor in any other State are all abortions prohibited. Despite broad proscription, an exception always exists. The exception contained in Art. 1196, for an abortion procured or attempted by medical advice for the purpose of saving the life of the mother, is typical. But if the fetus is a person who is not to be deprived of life without due process of law, and if the mother's condition is the sole determinant, does not the Texas exception appear to be out of line with the Amendment's command?

There are other inconsistencies between Fourteenth Amendment status and the typical abortion statute. It has already been pointed out [ ] that in Texas the woman is not a principal or an accomplice with respect to an abortion upon her. If the fetus is a person, why is the woman not a principal or an accomplice? Further, the penalty for criminal abortion specified by Art. 1195 is significantly less than the maximum penalty for murder prescribed by Art. 1257 of the Texas Penal Code. If the fetus is a person, may the penalties be different?

X

In view of all this, we do not agree that, by adopting one theory of life, Texas may override the rights of the pregnant woman that are at stake.

* * *

With respect to the State's important and legitimate interest in the health of the mother, the "compelling" point, in the light of present medical knowledge, is at approximately the end of the first trimester. This is so because of the now-established medical fact . . . that until the end of the first trimester mortality in abortion may be less than mortality in normal childbirth. It follows that, from and after this point, a State may regulate the abortion procedure to the extent that the regulation reasonably relates to the preservation and protection of maternal health. . . .

This means, on the other hand, that, for the period of pregnancy prior to this "compelling" point, the attending physician, in consultation with his patient, is free to determine, without regulation by the State, that, in his medical judgment, the patient's pregnancy should be terminated. If that decision is reached, the judgment may be effectuated by an abortion free of interference by the State.

With respect to the State's important and legitimate interest in potential life, the "compelling" point is at viability. This is so because the fetus then presumably has the capability of meaningful life outside the mother's womb. State regulation protective of fetal life after viability thus has both logical and biological justifications. If the State is interested in protecting fetal life after viability, it may go so far as to proscribe abortion during that period, except when it is necessary to preserve the life or health of the mother.

* * *

XI

To summarize and to repeat:

1. A state criminal abortion statute of the current Texas type, that excepts from criminality only a *lifesaving* procedure on behalf of the mother, without regard to pregnancy stage and without recognition of the other interests involved, is violative of the Due Process Clause of the Fourteenth Amendment.

(a) For the stage prior to approximately the end of the first trimester, the abortion decision and its effectuation must be left to the medical judgment of the pregnant woman's attending physician.

(b) For the stage subsequent to approximately the end of the first trimester, the State, in promoting its interest in the health of the mother, may, if it chooses, regulate the abortion procedure in ways that are reasonably related to maternal health.

(c) For the stage subsequent to viability, the State in promoting its interest in the potentiality of human life may, if it chooses, regulate, and even proscribe, abortion except where it is necessary, in appropriate medical judgment, for the preservation of the life or health of the mother.

* * *

NOTES AND QUESTIONS

1. *State Regulation of Abortion.* The Court rejected Texas' ability to apply its "theory of life" to "override the rights of the pregnant woman at stake," but the Court also acknowledged the state's interest in protecting prenatal life. How did the Court understand the various interests at stake and what balance did it strike?

2. *The State's "Theory of Life."* In *Roe*, the Court was confronted with the question of when personhood begins for purposes of determining rights under the Fourteenth Amendment of the Constitution, but Justice Blackmun refused to answer "the difficult question of when life begins." Indeed, the Supreme Court has never formally determined when a fetus becomes a "person" for Constitutional purposes. This has left an open question about whether the substantive provisions of the Constitution (as interpreted by the Court) put any limit on the way that states may define "person" for *other* purposes? In 1989, the Supreme Court faced this question in Webster v. Reproductive Health Services, 492 U.S. 490, 109 S.Ct. 3040, 106 L.Ed.2d 410 (1989). The Supreme Court reviewed a Missouri statute that restricted the availability of abortions in several ways. The statute also included a preamble that defined personhood:

1. The general assembly of this state finds that:

   (1) The life of each human being begins at conception;

   (2) Unborn children have protectable interests in life, health, and well-being;

   * * *

2. [T]he laws of this state shall be interpreted and construed to acknowledge on behalf of the unborn child at every stage of development, all the rights, privileges, and immunities available to other persons, citizens, and residents of this state, subject only to the Constitution of the United States, and decisional interpretations thereof . . . .

3. As used in this section, the term "unborn children" or "unborn child" shall include all unborn child or children or the offspring of human beings from the moment of conception until birth at every stage of biological development.

* * *

Vernon's Ann.Mo.Stat. § 1.205. This preamble was attacked on the grounds that it was beyond the constitutional authority of the state legislature to define personhood, at least to the extent that the definition extended personhood to pre-viable fetuses. The Supreme Court sidestepped that question by concluding that the preamble was nothing more than a state value judgment favoring childbirth over abortion, and that such a value judgment was clearly within the authority of the legislature. It noted that the preamble itself did not regulate abortions and could be interpreted to do no more than offer protections to unborn children in tort and probate law.

Questions about personhood have influenced states' decisions to expand statutory and common law rights for fetuses outside the abortion context. The debate over the common law recognition of the personhood of the fetus has been waged primarily over whether a fetus may recover under state wrongful death and survival statutes. Today, many states allow such claims as a matter of common law or through statute. See Ex Parte Ankrom, 152 So.3d 397, 425–428 (Ala. 2013) (Parker, J. concurring) (noting that forty states and D.C. allow recovery for the wrongful death of an unborn child when post-viability injuries to that child cause its death before birth, and eleven of these states allow recovery regardless of stage of pregnancy). One reason given is the perception that a live birth requirement is an arbitrary line that serves no purpose of the wrongful death and survival statutes. Others, more influenced by the arguments over abortion, have urged that such actions should be recognized because the fetus is a full human being entitled to all protections accorded to all other human beings. Indeed, debates about extending protections to fetuses in these contexts are often shaped by the fear or hope that doing so will influence abortion jurisprudence, allowing for greater restrictions on a woman's right to have an abortion.

Over the past several years, some states have made the penalties for feticide commensurate with the penalties for homicide. Typically such statutes were used to allow recovery or impose punishment on third parties who harmed a fetus. Id. at 423–424 (noting that a majority of states treat killing an unborn child as criminal homicide unless it occurs as the result of a medical abortion). Increasingly, however feticide laws are being used to punish pregnant women who want to carry a pregnancy term, but who suffer a miscarriage or stillbirth believed to be the result of harmful or risky behavior by the woman. For a discussion of how feticide and other "fetal protection" laws are used to regulate and punish women's behavior during pregnancy, see Section VI of this chapter.

3.   *The Role of Sexual Morality in Reproductive Regulation.* In exploring the reasons for the emergence of abortion bans, the Court mentions, but quickly dismisses, the argument that such laws were the product of a "Victorian social concern to discourage illicit sexual conduct." But does the Court give this short shrift? When it says no court or commentator has taken the argument seriously, is it that the Court does not believe that this is an underlying motivation of such laws? Or is it dismissing its legitimacy as a state interest for purposes of this analysis? If there is evidence that a state's desire

to regulate sexual morality motivated abortion regulation, what impact, if any, should that have on a court's constitutional analysis? For a history of the relationship between sex, religion, and reproductive regulation, see Geoffrey R. Stone, Sex and the Constitution (2017).

4.   *Bans on Use of Government Resources for Abortion.* *Roe* invalidated a criminal ban on abortion, but access to health care also depends on having the resources to access a particular service. A 2014 survey found that three-fourths of abortion patients were low income—49% living at less than the federal poverty level, and 26% living at 100–199% of the poverty level. See Jenna Jerman et al., Characteristics of U.S. Abortion Patients in 2014 and Changes Since 2008, Guttmacher Institute (May 2016). Traditionally, the poor have been less likely to be employed in jobs that offered health insurance, and they have been more likely to depend on public resources, such as public hospitals or public insurance. Pregnant women are eligible for Medicaid coverage only if their income is low enough to qualify. Immediately after *Roe*, the battle over abortion quickly moved into the realm of funding. To the extent that federal and state governments were funding or providing health care services, did the privacy right in *Roe* have anything to say about government's ability to exclude abortion from these programs?

In a series of cases, the Supreme Court has made clear that the Constitution does not prevent the government from excluding abortion from public insurance coverage or from banning abortions in government run facilities. Beal v. Doe, 432 U.S. 438 (1977); Maher v. Roe, 432 U.S. 464 (1977); Poelker v. Doe, 432 U.S. 519 (1977). In 1980, in Harris v. McRae, 448 U.S. 297 (1980), the Court addressed the constitutionality of the Hyde Amendment, which limits federal Medicaid funding for abortions. The Hyde Amendment only funds abortions in cases of life endangerment, rape or incest. It excludes funding for abortions that may not be viewed as life threatening but are otherwise medically necessary because carrying a pregnancy to term would pose a serious danger to a woman's health or may even shorten her life. Examples of cases where abortions may be deemed medically necessary, though not immediately life threatening, are where pregnancy would exacerbate medical risky conditions, such as heart conditions, diabetes, or cancer, and could lead to permanent damage to the woman's health. The Supreme Court upheld the Hyde amendment against due process and equal protection challenges, with Justice Stewart writing for the court:

. . . . [R]egardless of whether the freedom of a woman to choose to terminate her pregnancy for health reasons lies at the core or the periphery of the due process liberty recognized in Roe v. Wade, 410 U.S. 113, 93 S.Ct. 705, 35 L.Ed.2d 147 (1973), it simply does not follow that a woman's freedom of choice carries with it a constitutional entitlement to the financial resources to avail herself of the full range of protected choices. [A]lthough government may not place obstacles in the path of a woman's exercise of her freedom of choice, it need not remove those not of its own creation. Indigency falls in the latter category. The financial constraints that restrict an indigent woman's ability to enjoy the full range of constitutionally protected freedom of choice are the product not of governmental restrictions on access to abortions, but rather of her indigency. Although Congress has opted to subsidize medically necessary services generally, but not certain medically necessary abortions, the fact remains that the Hyde Amendment leaves an indigent woman with at least the same range of choice [ ] as she would have had if Congress had chosen to subsidize no health care costs at all. . . . Although the liberty protected by the Due Process Clause affords protection against unwarranted government interference with freedom of choice in the context of certain personal decisions, it does not confer an entitlement to such funds as may be necessary to realize all the advantages of that freedom. . . .

Quoting another case that upheld a similar abortion restriction by a state, the Court made clear that " 'the constitutional freedom recognized in Roe v. Wade and its progeny, did not prevent [government] from making a value judgment favoring childbirth over abortion, and . . . implement[ing] that judgment by the allocation of public funds.' " Id. (quoting Maher v. Roe, 432 U.S. 464 (1977).

5. *Impact of the ACA.* The ACA reinforced Hyde Amendment restrictions, which have been attached to Medicaid and other relevant appropriations by the U.S. Department of Health and Human Services (HHS) since the 1970s. The ACA extended federal funding limits on abortion in significant ways. It excludes abortion from the required essential health benefits, requires each health insurance exchange to offer at least one multi-state plan that does not include abortion coverage, and allows states to forbid exchange plans from covering abortion. Most state laws banning abortion coverage provide narrow exceptions for life endangerment, rape, or incest, but Louisiana and Tennessee do not provide any exceptions.

The ACA permits plans to cover abortion but establishes strict rules for how this can be done. 42 U.S.C.A. § 18023. Plans that offer abortion coverage must essentially do so by selling a separate abortion rider; that is, they must charge a separate, actuarially segregated premium for that service, which is paid separately by each insured who desires that coverage (and each insured's employer, if the employer contributes to the employee's health coverage). The actuarial value of this coverage may not count savings arising from the performance of an abortion (such as prenatal care or delivery). These restrictions have created administrative barriers to abortion coverage, as well as confusion among enrollees as to whether certain plans even cover abortion. For example, a 2019 review of marketplace plans found that eight states that did not have laws restricting abortion coverage (and thus allowed plans to cover it) nonetheless had no marketplace plans that included coverage. See Alina Salganicoff et al., Coverage for Abortion Services in Medicaid, Marketplace Plans and Private Plans, The Henry J. Kaiser Family Foundation (Jun. 2019). Before the ACA, most private health insurance plans covered abortion. Now, "as a combined result of the state laws and insurance company choices, women in 34 states . . . do not have access to insurance coverage for abortions through a Marketplace plan—the only place where consumers can qualify for tax subsidies to help pay for the cost of health insurance premiums if they are income eligible." Id.

Finally, the ACA contains a provision providing that nothing in the ACA shall be construed as preempting state law regarding the prohibition of or requirement of coverage, funding, or procedural requirements on abortion. 42 U.S.C.A. § 18023(c)(1). This has been understood to preserve state power to regulate abortion coverage, outside of the specific limits mentioned above. But see the Note on Federal Conscience Protections at the end of Section III of this chapter.

6. *State Approaches to Funding Abortion.* In the face of federal funding restrictions on abortion (pre- and post-ACA), states have responded very differently. Most states have followed the federal government's lead in restricting abortion coverage. In Medicaid, thirty-five states (including D.C.) prohibit coverage of abortions excluded by the Hyde Amendment, and one of those states is even more restrictive, only covering abortion in cases of life-endangerment. For private insurance, twenty-six states prohibit marketplace plans from offering abortion coverage, and eleven of those prohibit all insurers from providing abortion coverage. Again, most laws allow narrow exceptions similar to those in the Hyde Amendment. See Salganicoff, supra.

On the other hand, some states have responded by filling in the gaps. Sixteen states use only state funds for abortions excluded by the Hyde Amendment. Id. Some state legislatures have done this voluntarily, while others have been required to do so by the courts. See, e.g., Right to Choose v. Byrne, 450 A.2d 925 (N.J. 1982); Moe v. Secretary of Administration and Finance, 417 N.E.2d 387 (Mass. 1981); Committee to Defend Reproductive Rights v. Myers, 625 P.2d 779 (Cal. 1981). Since *Harris v. McRae*, thirteen state supreme courts have recognized a state constitutional right to have state Medicaid programs pay for abortions as it does other medical procedures. In the case of private insurance, however, only three states require nearly all insurance plans to provide abortion coverage, including marketplace plans.

7. *Beyond Abortion Funding: Attempts to Defund Planned Parenthood & the Fungibility Theory.* For decades, anti-abortion advocates have gone further than simply seeking bans on funding for abortion services; they have proposed absolute government funding bans on clinics that perform abortions or have an affiliation with such clinics. Planned Parenthood, widely recognized as a provider of abortion and advocate for access to legal abortion services, has been the primary target of such defunding attempts. It is important to distinguish this from bans on funding used for abortion: as noted above, there have long been prohibitions on the use of federal funding for abortion except in extreme cases, and many states have taken this approach with state funding as well. Funding bans targeting clinics, like Planned Parenthood, would deprive such clinics of government funding for *any* service—they would not be able to receive funding to provide the non-abortion services they typically provide, such as health checkups, cancer screenings, disease prevention, and contraception. In addition, some of the bans proposed to date would apply to

clinics that do not even perform abortions. The theory behind this more sweeping funding ban is the "fungibility" of money—the presumed interchangeability of government and private funds. The argument is that any amount of government money that funds such clinics frees up money to be used to provide abortion, thus funding it indirectly.

At the federal level, bans targeting Planned Parenthood by name have been introduced, but have not passed both houses of Congress. See, e.g., Defund Planned Parenthood Act of 2017, H.R. 354, 115th Cong. (2017) (providing that for one-year, no federal funding "may be made available for *any purpose* to Planned Parenthood Federation of America, Inc. [(PPFA)] or *any affiliate* or *clinic* of [PPFA], unless such entities certify that [PPFA and its] affiliates and clinics will not perform, and will not provide any funds to any other entity that performs, an abortion during such period.") (emphasis added). A similar provision was part of the ACA repeal and replace bill approved by the House in May 2017. See American Health Care Act, H.R. 1628, 115th Cong. (2017).

State bans have been easier to enact but have been challenged on several grounds. The most successful challenges have come in the context of exclusions from the Medicaid program. Most circuits hearing these challenges have struck down states' attempts to exclude Planned Parenthood and similar clinics from receiving Medicaid payments, as violating a provision in the Medicaid Act that guarantees patients the freedom to choose their provider; but recently two circuits have allowed the exclusion. See Chapter 10, Section III.D, Note 4. Challenges to state exclusions from other federally funded programs have yielded mixed results. See, e.g., Planned Parenthood Ass'n of Utah (PPAU) v. Herbert, 828 F.3d 1245 (10th Cir. 2016) (finding PPAU established a likelihood of success on its claim that the Governor's directive to a state health department official to stop distributing federal grant funds to PPAU violated the First and Fourteenth Amendments under the unconstitutional conditions doctrine, where the denial of funding was likely retaliation for PPAU's role in providing abortions, advocacy for abortion rights, and its affiliation with Planned Parenthood Federation of America, Inc.). But see Planned Parenthood of Greater Ohio v. Hodges, 201 F. Supp. 3d 898 (S.D. Ohio 2016), *aff'd*, 888 F.3d 224 (6th. Cir. 2018), *rehearing en banc*, 917 F.3d 908 (6th Cir. 2019) (upholding a state law prohibiting federal funds to entities that performed or promoted nontherapeutic abortions, or contracted with or became an affiliate of such an entity); Planned Parenthood Ass'n of Hidalgo County Texas, Inc. v. Suehs, 692 F.3d 343 (5th Cir. 2012) (upholding a narrower state ban on Women's Health Program (WHP) funds to entities that perform or promote elective abortions, in light of WHP's stated goal of subsidizing non-abortion family planning).

8.   *After Roe v. Wade.* The Court's decision invigorated political forces opposed to abortion, encouraging state legislatures to seek creative ways to discourage abortions without directly running afoul of the right articulated in *Roe*. Outside of the funding context, *Roe* initially proved to be a formidable check on state abortion restrictions. The "compelling interest" standard was used to strike down a number of state regulations of abortion. For example, a

requirement that all second-trimester abortions be performed in a hospital was struck down as an unreasonable health regulation in light of evidence that such abortions could be safely performed in an outpatient clinic. City of Akron v. Akron Center for Reproductive Health, Inc., 462 U.S. 416 (1983), *overruled by* Planned Parenthood v. Casey, 505 U.S. 833 (1992). In another case, the Court invalidated a state's requirement that physicians must provide certain information to women before an abortion, such as descriptions of fetal characteristics or locations of agencies providing alternatives to abortion. The Court viewed the information as medically irrelevant, emphasizing that "[s]tates are not free, under the guise of protecting maternal health or potential life, to intimidate women into continuing pregnancies." Thornburgh v. American College of Obstetricians and Gynecologists, 476 U.S. 747 (1986), *overruled by* Planned Parenthood v. Casey, 505 U.S. 833 (1992). Other state abortion restrictions repeatedly landed in court and were used to test the boundaries of this privacy right.

Gradually, however, the number of justices supporting this approach declined over time. *Roe* was reaffirmed more than a dozen times in its first decade, but by 1986 the 7–2 majority was down to 5–4, Thornburgh v. American College of Obstetricians and Gynecologists, 476 U.S. 747 (1986), and by 1989 the Court appeared to be evenly divided, with Justice O'Connor unwilling to confront the issue. Webster v. Reproductive Health Services, 492 U.S. 490 (1989). Eventually some of the same types of laws that had been invalidated by the Court under the reasoning of *Roe v. Wade*, made it back to the Supreme Court in 1992, in *Planned Parenthood v. Casey* (below). Although the Court explicitly affirmed *Roe's* "essential holding," *Casey's* reasoning and outcome signaled a significant re-shaping of abortion jurisprudence that would open the door to increased state regulation.

B. *ROE* REVISITED: THE "UNDUE BURDEN" TEST

PLANNED PARENTHOOD OF SOUTHEASTERN PENNSYLVANIA V. CASEY

Supreme Court of the United States, 1992.
505 U.S. 833.

JUSTICE O'CONNOR, JUSTICE KENNEDY, and JUSTICE SOUTER announced the judgment of the Court and delivered the opinion of the Court with respect to Parts I, II, III, V-A, V-C, and VI, an opinion with respect to Part V-E, in which JUSTICE STEVENS joins, and an opinion with respect to Parts IV, V-B, and V-D.

I.

Liberty finds no refuge in a jurisprudence of doubt. Yet 19 years after our holding that the Constitution protects a woman's right to terminate her pregnancy in its early stages,[ ] that definition of liberty is still questioned. . . .

At issue in these cases are five provisions of the Pennsylvania Abortion Control Act of 1982. . . . The Act requires that a woman seeking an abortion give her informed consent prior to the abortion procedure, and specifies that she be provided with certain information at least 24 hours before the abortion is performed.[ ] For a minor to obtain an abortion, the Act requires the informed consent of one of her parents, but provides for a judicial bypass option if the minor does not wish to or cannot obtain a parent's consent.[ ] Another provision of the Act requires that, unless certain exceptions apply, a married woman seeking an abortion must sign a statement indicating that she has notified her husband of her intended abortion.[ ] The Act exempts compliance with these three requirements in the event of a "medical emergency," which is defined in the Act.[ ] In addition to the above provisions regulating the performance of abortions, the Act imposes certain reporting requirements on facilities that provide abortion services.[ ]

* * *

After considering the fundamental constitutional questions resolved by *Roe*, principles of institutional integrity, and the rule of stare decisis, we are led to conclude this: the essential holding of Roe v. Wade should be retained and once again reaffirmed.

It must be stated at the outset and with clarity that *Roe's* essential holding, the holding we reaffirm, has three parts. First is a recognition of the right of the woman to choose to have an abortion before viability and to obtain it without undue interference from the State. Before viability, the State's interests are not strong enough to support a prohibition of abortion or the imposition of a substantial obstacle to the woman's effective right to elect the procedure. Second is a confirmation of the State's power to restrict abortions after fetal viability, if the law contains exceptions for pregnancies which endanger a woman's life or health. And third is the principle that the State has legitimate interests from the outset of the pregnancy in protecting the health of the woman and the life of the fetus that may become a child. These principles do not contradict one another; and we adhere to each.

II.

* * *

Men and women of good conscience can disagree, and we suppose some always shall disagree, about the profound moral and spiritual implications of terminating a pregnancy, even in its earliest stage. Some of us as individuals find abortion offensive to our most basic principles of morality, but that cannot control our decision. Our obligation is to define the liberty of all, not to mandate our own moral code. The underlying constitutional issue is whether the State can resolve these philosophic questions in such a definitive way that a woman lacks all choice in the matter, except perhaps in those rare circumstances in which the pregnancy is itself a danger to her own life or health, or is the result of rape or incest. . . . Abortion is a unique act. It is an act fraught with consequences for others: for the woman who must live with the implications of her decision; for the persons who perform and assist in the procedure; for the spouse, family, and society which must confront the knowledge that these procedures exist, procedures some deem nothing short of an act of violence against innocent human life; and, depending on one's beliefs, for the life or potential life that is aborted. Though abortion is conduct, it does not follow that the State is entitled to proscribe it in all instances. That is because the liberty of the woman is at stake in a sense unique to the human condition and so unique to the law. The mother who carries a child to full term is subject to anxieties, to physical constraints, to pain that only she must bear. That these sacrifices have from the beginning of the human race been endured by woman with a pride that ennobles her in the eyes of others and gives to the infant a bond of love cannot alone be grounds for the State to insist she make the sacrifice. Her suffering is too intimate and personal for the State to insist, without more, upon its own vision of the woman's role, however dominant that vision has been in the course of our history and our culture. The destiny of the woman must be shaped to a large extent on her own conception of her spiritual imperatives and her place in society.

* * *

While we appreciate the weight of the arguments made on behalf of the State in the case before us, arguments which in their ultimate formulation conclude that *Roe* should be overruled, the reservations any of us may have in reaffirming the central holding of *Roe* are outweighed by the explication of individual liberty we have given combined with the force of stare decisis. We turn now to that doctrine.

III.

A.

[In this section, the court discussed the conditions under which it is appropriate for the Court to reverse its own precedent.]

So in this case we may inquire whether *Roe's* central rule has been found unworkable; whether the rule's limitation on state power could be removed without serious inequity to those who have relied upon it or significant damage to the stability of the society governed by the rule in question; whether the law's growth in the intervening years has left *Roe's* central rule a doctrinal anachronism discounted by society; and whether *Roe's* premises of fact have so far changed in the ensuing two decades as to render its central holding somehow irrelevant or unjustifiable in dealing with the issue it addressed.

* * *

The sum of the precedential inquiry to this point shows *Roe's* underpinnings unweakened in any way affecting its central holding. While it has engendered disapproval, it has not been unworkable. An entire generation has come of age free to assume *Roe's* concept of liberty in defining the capacity of women to act in society, and to make reproductive decisions; no erosion of principle going to liberty or personal autonomy has left *Roe's* central holding a doctrinal remnant; *Roe* portends no developments at odds with other precedent for the analysis of personal liberty; and no changes of fact have rendered viability more or less appropriate as the point at which the balance of interests tips. Within the bounds of normal stare decisis analysis, then, and subject to the considerations on which it customarily turns, the stronger argument is for affirming *Roe's* central holding, with whatever degree of personal reluctance any of us may have, not for overruling it.

B.

[The Court next distinguished the rule in the abortion cases from the rules in *Lochner* and the "separate but equal" cases, two areas in which the Supreme Court did reverse its well settled precedents this century. The Court also explained that it should not expend its political capital and put the public respect for the Court and its processes at risk by reversing *Roe*.]

IV.

From what we have said so far it follows that it is a constitutional liberty of the woman to have some freedom to terminate her pregnancy. We conclude that the basic decision in *Roe* was based on a constitutional analysis which we cannot now repudiate. The woman's liberty is not so unlimited, however, that from the outset the State cannot show its concern for the life of the unborn, and at a later point in fetal development the State's interest in life has sufficient force so that the right of the woman to terminate the pregnancy can be restricted.

* * *

We conclude the line should be drawn at viability, so that before that time the woman has a right to choose to terminate her pregnancy. We adhere to this principle for two reasons. First, as we have said, is the doctrine of stare decisis. . . .

The second reason is that the concept of viability, as we noted in *Roe*, is the time at which there is a realistic possibility of maintaining and nourishing a life outside the womb, so that the independent existence of the second life can in reason and all fairness be the object of state protection that now overrides the rights of the woman. . . .

The woman's right to terminate her pregnancy before viability is the most central principle of Roe v. Wade. It is a rule of law and a component of liberty we cannot renounce.

* * *

Yet it must be remembered that Roe v. Wade speaks with clarity in establishing not only the woman's liberty but also the State's "important and legitimate interest in potential life." [ ] That portion of the decision in *Roe* has been given too little acknowledgment and implementation by the Court in its subsequent cases. Those cases decided that any regulation touching upon the abortion decision must survive strict scrutiny, to be sustained only if drawn in narrow terms to further a compelling state interest. [ ] Not all of the cases decided under that formulation can be reconciled with the holding in *Roe* itself that the State has legitimate interests in the health of the woman and in protecting the potential life within her. In resolving this tension, we choose to rely upon *Roe,* as against the later cases.

* * *

We reject the trimester framework, which we do not consider to be part of the essential holding of *Roe.* [ ] Measures aimed at ensuring that a woman's choice contemplates the consequences for the fetus do not necessarily interfere with the right recognized in *Roe*, although those measures have been found to be inconsistent with the rigid trimester framework announced in that case. A logical reading of the central holding in *Roe* itself, and a necessary reconciliation of the liberty of the woman and the interest of the State in promoting prenatal life, require, in our view, that we abandon the trimester framework as a rigid prohibition on all previability regulation aimed at the protection of fetal life.

* * *

The fact that a law which serves a valid purpose, one not designed to strike at the right itself, has the incidental effect of making it more difficult or more expensive to procure an abortion cannot be enough to invalidate it. Only where state regulation imposes an undue burden on a woman's ability to make this decision does the power of the State reach into the heart of the liberty protected by the Due Process Clause.

* * *

Not all burdens on the right to decide whether to terminate a pregnancy will be undue. In our view, the undue burden standard is the appropriate means of reconciling the State's interest with the woman's constitutionally protected liberty.

* * *

A finding of an undue burden is a shorthand for the conclusion that a state regulation has the purpose or effect of placing a substantial obstacle in the path of a woman seeking an abortion of a nonviable fetus. A statute with this purpose is invalid because the means chosen by the State to further the interest in potential life must be calculated to inform the woman's free choice, not hinder it. And a statute which, while furthering the interest in potential life or some other valid state interest, has the effect of placing a substantial obstacle in the path of a woman's choice cannot be considered a permissible means of serving its legitimate ends. . . .

Some guiding principles should emerge. What is at stake is the woman's right to make the ultimate decision, not a right to be insulated from all others in doing so. Regulations which do no more than create a structural mechanism by which the State, or the parent or guardian of a minor, may express profound respect for the life of the unborn are permitted, if they are not a substantial obstacle to the woman's exercise of the right to choose. [ ]

[The Justices then summarized their new undue burden test:]

(a) To protect the central right recognized by Roe v. Wade while at the same time accommodating the State's profound interest in potential life, we will employ the undue burden analysis as explained in this opinion. An undue burden exists, and therefore a provision of law is invalid, if its purpose or effect is to place a substantial obstacle in the path of a woman seeking an abortion before the fetus attains viability.

(b) We reject the rigid trimester framework of Roe v. Wade. To promote the State's profound interest in potential life, throughout pregnancy the State may take measures to ensure that the woman's choice is informed, and measures designed to advance this interest will not be invalidated as long as their purpose is to persuade the woman to choose childbirth over abortion. These measures must not be an undue burden on the right.

(c) As with any medical procedure, the State may enact regulations to further the health or safety of a woman seeking an abortion. Unnecessary health regulations that have the purpose or effect of presenting a substantial obstacle to a woman seeking an abortion impose an undue burden on the right.

(d) Our adoption of the undue burden analysis does not disturb the central holding of Roe v. Wade, and we reaffirm that holding. Regardless of whether exceptions are made for particular circumstances, a State may not prohibit any woman from making the ultimate decision to terminate her pregnancy before viability.

(e) We also reaffirm Roe's holding that "subsequent to viability, the State in promoting its interest in the potentiality of human life may, if it chooses, regulate, and even proscribe, abortion except where it is necessary, in appropriate medical judgment, for the preservation of the life or health of the mother." [ ]

* * *

V.

* * *

A.

Because it is central to the operation of various other requirements, we begin with the statute's definition of medical emergency. Under the statute, a medical emergency is "that condition which, on the basis of the physician's good faith clinical judgment, so complicates the medical condition of a pregnant woman as to necessitate the immediate abortion of her pregnancy to avert her death or for which a delay will create serious risk of substantial and irreversible impairment of a major bodily function." [ ]

Petitioners argue that the definition is too narrow, contending that it forecloses the possibility of an immediate abortion despite some significant health risks.

[The Justices accepted the Court of Appeals interpretation of the statute, which assured that the "abortion regulation would not in any way pose a significant threat to the life or health of a woman," and determined that the definition imposed no undue burden on a woman's right to an abortion.]

B.

We next consider the informed consent requirement. [ ] Except in a medical emergency, the statute requires that at least 24 hours before performing an abortion a physician inform the woman of the nature of the procedure, the health risks of the abortion and of childbirth, and the "probable gestational age of the unborn child." The physician or a qualified nonphysician must inform the woman of the availability of printed materials published by the State describing the fetus and providing information about medical assistance for childbirth, information about child support from the father, and a list of agencies which provide adoption and other services as alternatives to abortion. An abortion may not be performed unless the woman certifies in writing that she has been informed of the availability of these printed materials and has been provided them if she chooses to view them.

* * *

. . . If the information the State requires to be made available to the woman is truthful and not misleading, the requirement may be permissible. [The Court then rejects the argument that the physician's first amendment speech rights trump the state-mandated obligation to provide patients with identified truthful information.]

* * *

The Pennsylvania statute also requires us to reconsider the holding [ ] that the State may not require that a physician, as opposed to a qualified assistant, provide information relevant to a woman's informed consent. [ ] . . . Our cases reflect the fact that the Constitution gives the States broad latitude to decide that particular functions may be performed only by licensed professionals, even if an objective assessment might suggest that those same tasks could be performed by others. [ ] Thus, we uphold the provision as a reasonable means to insure that the woman's consent is informed.

Our analysis of Pennsylvania's 24-hour waiting period between the provision of the information deemed necessary to informed consent and the performance of an abortion under the undue burden standard requires us to reconsider the premise behind the decision in *Akron I* invalidating a parallel requirement. In *Akron I* we said: "Nor are we convinced that the State's legitimate concern that the woman's decision be informed is reasonably served by requiring a 24-hour delay as a matter of course." [ ] We consider that conclusion to be wrong. The idea that important decisions will be more informed and deliberate if they follow some period of reflection does not strike us as unreasonable, particularly where the statute directs that important information become part of the background of the decision.

* * *

C.

. . . Pennsylvania's abortion law provides, except in cases of medical emergency, that no physician shall perform an abortion on a married woman without receiving a signed statement from the woman that she has notified her spouse that she is about to undergo an abortion.

* * *

This information and the District Court's findings reinforce what common sense would suggest. In well-functioning marriages, spouses discuss important intimate decisions such as whether to bear a child. But there are millions of women in this country who are the victims of regular physical and psychological abuse at the hands of their husbands. Should these women become pregnant, they may have very good reasons for not wishing to inform their husbands of their decision to obtain an abortion. Many may have justifiable fears of physical abuse, but may be no less fearful of the consequences of reporting prior abuse to the Commonwealth of Pennsylvania. Many may have a reasonable fear that notifying their husbands will provoke further instances of child abuse; these women are not exempt from [the] notification requirement. Many may fear devastating forms of psychological abuse from their husbands, including verbal harassment, threats of future violence, the destruction of possessions, physical confinement to the home, the withdrawal of financial support, or the disclosure of the abortion to family and friends. . . .

The spousal notification requirement is thus likely to prevent a significant number of women from obtaining an abortion. It does not merely make abortions a little more difficult or expensive to obtain; for many women, it will impose a substantial obstacle. We must not blind ourselves to the fact that the significant number of women who fear for their safety and the safety of their children are likely to be deterred from procuring an abortion as surely as if the Commonwealth had outlawed abortion in all cases.

Respondents attempt to avoid the conclusion that [the spousal notification provision] is invalid by pointing out that it imposes almost no burden at all for the vast majority of women seeking abortions. . . . Respondents argue that since some of [the 20% of women who seek abortions who are married] will be able to notify their husbands without adverse consequences or will qualify for one of the exceptions, the statute affects fewer than one percent of women seeking abortions. For this reason, it is asserted, the statute cannot be invalid on its face. [ ] We disagree with respondents' basic method of analysis.

The analysis does not end with the one percent of women upon whom the statute operates; it begins there. Legislation is measured for consistency with the Constitution by its impact on those whose conduct it affects. . . . [A]s we have said, [the Act's] real target is narrower even than the class of women seeking abortions . . . : it is married women seeking abortions who do not wish to notify their husbands of their intentions and who do not qualify for one of the statutory exceptions to the notice requirement. The unfortunate yet persisting conditions . . . will mean that in a large fraction of the cases . . . , [the statute] will operate as a substantial obstacle to a woman's choice to undergo an abortion. It is an undue burden, and therefore invalid.

* * *

[The spousal notification provision] embodies a view of marriage consonant with the common-law status of married women but repugnant to our present understanding of marriage and of the nature of the rights secured by the Constitution. Women do not lose their constitutionally protected liberty when they marry. . . .

D.

* * *

Our cases establish, and we reaffirm today, that a State may require a minor seeking an abortion to obtain the consent of a parent or guardian, provided that there is an adequate judicial bypass procedure. [ ] Under these precedents, in our view, the [Pennsylvania] one-parent consent requirement and judicial bypass procedure are constitutional.

* * *

E.

[The Justices upheld all of the record keeping and reporting requirements of the statute, except for that provision requiring the reporting of a married woman's reason for failure to give notice to her husband.]

VI.

Our Constitution is a covenant running from the first generation of Americans to us and then to future generations. It is a coherent succession. Each generation must learn anew that the Constitution's written terms embody ideas and aspirations that must survive more ages than one. We accept our responsibility not to retreat from interpreting the full meaning of the covenant in light of all of our precedents. We invoke it once again to define the freedom guaranteed by the Constitution's own promise, the promise of liberty.

* * *

[In addition to those parts of the statute found unconstitutional in the three-justice opinion, Justice Stevens would find unconstitutional the requirement that the doctor deliver state-produced materials to a woman seeking an abortion, the counseling requirements, and the 24-hour-waiting requirement. His concurring and dissenting opinion is omitted. Justice Blackman's opinion, concurring in the judgment in part and dissenting in part, is also omitted.]

CHIEF JUSTICE REHNQUIST, with whom JUSTICE WHITE, JUSTICE SCALIA, and JUSTICE THOMAS join, concurring in the judgment in part and dissenting in part.

The joint opinion, following its newly-minted variation on stare decisis, retains the outer shell of Roe v. Wade, [ ] but beats a wholesale retreat from the substance of that case. We believe that *Roe* was wrongly decided, and that it can and should be overruled consistently with our traditional approach to stare decisis in constitutional cases.

* * *

The end result of the joint opinion's paeans of praise for legitimacy is the enunciation of a brand new standard for evaluating state regulation of a woman's right to abortion—the "undue burden" standard. As indicated above, Roe v. Wade adopted a "fundamental right" standard under which state regulations could survive only if they met the requirement of "strict scrutiny." While we disagree with that standard, it at least had a recognized basis in constitutional law at the time *Roe* was decided. The same cannot be said for the "undue burden" standard, which is created largely out of whole cloth by the authors of the joint opinion. It is a standard which even today does not command the support of a majority of this Court. And it will not, we believe, result in the sort of "simple limitation," easily applied, which the joint opinion anticipates. [ ] In sum, it is a standard which is not built to last.

In evaluating abortion regulations under that standard, judges will have to decide whether they place a "substantial obstacle" in the path of a woman seeking an abortion. [ ] In that this standard is based even more on a judge's subjective determinations than was the trimester framework, the standard will do nothing to prevent "judges from roaming at large in the constitutional field" guided only by their personal views. [ ]

* * *

The sum of the joint opinion's labors in the name of stare decisis and "legitimacy" is this: Roe v. Wade stands as a sort of judicial Potemkin Village, which may be pointed out to passers by as a monument to the importance of adhering to precedent. But behind the facade, an entirely new method of analysis, without any roots in constitutional law, is imported to decide the constitutionality of state laws regulating abortion. Neither stare decisis nor "legitimacy" are truly served by such an effort.

* * *

JUSTICE SCALIA, with whom the CHIEF JUSTICE, JUSTICE WHITE, and JUSTICE THOMAS join, concurring in the judgment in part and dissenting in part.

* * *

The States may, if they wish, permit abortion-on-demand, but the Constitution does not require them to do so. The permissibility of abortion, and the limitations upon it, are to be resolved like most important questions in our democracy: by citizens trying to persuade one another and then voting. As the Court acknowledges, "where reasonable people disagree the government can adopt one position or the other." [ ] The Court is correct in adding the qualification that this "assumes a state of affairs in which the choice does not intrude upon a protected liberty," [ ]—but the crucial part of that qualification is the penultimate word. A State's choice between two positions on which reasonable people can disagree is constitutional even when (as is often the case) it intrudes upon a "liberty" in the absolute sense. Laws against bigamy, for example—which entire societies of reasonable people disagree with—intrude upon men and women's liberty to marry and live with one another. But bigamy happens not to be a liberty specially "protected" by the Constitution.

That is, quite simply, the issue in this case: not whether the power of a woman to abort her unborn child is a "liberty" in the absolute sense; or even whether it is a liberty of great importance to many women. Of course it is both. The issue is whether it is a liberty protected by the Constitution of the United States. I am sure it is not. I reach that conclusion not because of anything so exalted as my views concerning the "concept of existence, of meaning, of the universe, and of the mystery of human life." [ ] I reach it for the same reason I reach the conclusion that bigamy is not constitutionally protected—because of two simple facts: (1) the Constitution says absolutely nothing about it, and (2) the longstanding traditions of American society have permitted it to be legally proscribed.

* * *

I am certainly not in a good position to dispute that the Court has saved the "central holding" of *Roe*, since to do that effectively I would have to know what the Court has saved, which in turn would require me to understand (as I do not) what the "undue burden" test means. . . . I thought I might note, however, that the following portions of *Roe* have not been saved:

• Under *Roe*, requiring that a woman seeking an abortion be provided truthful information about abortion before giving informed written consent is unconstitutional, if the information is designed to influence her choice [ ]. Under the joint opinion's "undue burden" regime (as applied today, at least) such a requirement is constitutional [ ].

• Under *Roe*, requiring that information be provided by a doctor, rather than by nonphysician counselors, is unconstitutional [ ]. Under the "undue burden" regime (as applied today, at least) it is not [ ].

• Under *Roe*, requiring a 24-hour waiting period between the time the woman gives her informed consent and the time of the abortion is unconstitutional. Under the "undue burden" regime (as applied today, at least) it is not [ ].

• Under *Roe*, requiring detailed reports that include demographic data about each woman who seeks an abortion and various information about each abortion is unconstitutional [ ]. Under the "undue burden" regime (as applied today, at least) it generally is not [ ].

* * *

NOTES AND QUESTIONS

1. Casey *vs.* Roe. At the beginning of 2018, *Casey's* holding remains the governing law with regard to abortion. Does *Casey* really affirm *Roe*? As Justice Scalia points out, several laws that had been struck down under *Roe* are being upheld under *Casey*. Which aspects of *Roe's* reasoning survived and which did not?

2. *Parental Consent and Notification Requirements.* After *Casey*, states may require minors to obtain the consent of a parent to an abortion, as long as the state permits a court to dispense with that requirement under some circumstances. As of mid-2021, thirty-eight states require some kind of parental involvement (with three states requiring both parents' consent, and one requiring notification of both parents). See Parental Involvement in Minors' Abortions, Guttmacher Institute (Jul. 2021). The Supreme Court has never determined if a two-parent consent requirement (with a proper judicial bypass provision) would pass Constitutional muster, and courts have reached different conclusions. Compare Barnes v. Mississippi, 992 F.2d 1335 (5th Cir. 1993), cert. denied, 510 U.S. 976 (1993) (upholding two-parent consent requirement because involvement of both parents will increase "reflection and deliberation" on the process, and if one parent denies consent the other will be able to go to court in support of the child) and S.H. v. D.H., 796 N.E.2d 1243 (Ind. App. 2003) (family court judge cannot require consent of both parents before an abortion is performed, even if the divorced parents have joint custody). The Supreme Court has suggested that a state requirement of mere parental notification (rather than consent) also requires a judicial bypass, and lower courts have generally assumed that it does. Ohio v. Akron Ctr. for Reproductive Health, 497 U.S. 502 (1990). But states may have more robust state constitutional protections that limit their ability to require parental notification or consent. For example, one state supreme court has found that a parental notification requirement violates the state constitution's equal protection clause when it is imposed only on those who seek abortions, not on pregnant children making other, equally medically risky, reproductive decisions. Planned Parenthood of Central New Jersey v. Farmer, 762 A.2d 620 (N.J. 2000).

3. *Judicial Bypass.* It is not clear what constitutional standard a court must apply in a "bypass" case. Under what circumstance is the court required to waive consent or notification: if it finds that the minor is sufficiently mature that she should be able to make the decision herself; if it finds that if she seeks consent from (or notifies) her parents she will be subject to abuse; if it finds that it is in her best interest to have the abortion; if it finds that it is in her best interest not to be required to notify, or get consent from, her parent; or some combination of these? See Lambert v. Wicklund, 520 U.S. 292 (1997) (per curiam).

4. *Two-Trip Requirement and Waiting Period.* Many states require patients to receive counseling before getting an abortion and impose a waiting period between the time a pregnant woman is provided information and the

time of the medical procedure. This typically requires the pregnant woman make two trips to the medical facility. In *Casey* the Court announced that a 24-hour waiting period did not constitute an unconstitutional undue burden, because it considered "[t]he idea that important decisions will be more informed and deliberate if they follow some period of reflection" to be reasonable, the statute was understood as not requiring the waiting period in a medical emergency, and "the record evidence show[ed] that in the vast majority of cases, a 24-hour delay does not create any appreciable health risk." One state supreme court had found that a three-day waiting period violated the *state* constitution's protected right of privacy, citing evidence of the burdens such a requirement could impose:

> [P]atient mortality rates for abortions increase as the length of pregnancy increases. Studies also suggest that a large majority of women who have endured waiting periods prior to obtaining an abortion have suffered increased stress, nausea and physical discomfort, but very few have reported any benefit from having to wait. [Evidence also] indicates that the waiting period increases a woman's financial and psychological burdens, since many women must travel long distances and be absent from work to obtain an abortion . . . . [which] is especially problematic for women who suffer from poverty or abusive relationships.

Planned Parenthood of Middle Tennessee v. Sundquist, 38 S.W.3d 1 (Tenn. 2000). In response, the Tennessee legislature amended the State's constitution to clarify that it does not protect the right to an abortion, and the 48-hour waiting period was restored. Bristol Regional Women's Center, P.C. v. Slatery, 7 F.4th 478 (2021).

As of early 2021, about half of the states imposed waiting periods of some sort. See Counseling and Waiting Periods for Abortion, Guttmacher Institute (Jul. 2021). What if the patient must travel a very far distance to the facility and has difficulty accessing transportation? Should this impact an undue burden analysis of a waiting period requirement? A 2014 study of the distance that patients would have to travel for an abortion revealed spatial disparities in abortion access. The median distance to the nearest clinic providing abortion services was less than 15 miles in twenty-three states, 15–29 miles in sixteen states, 30–89 miles in eight states. In three states, at least half of all women had to travel more than 90 miles (168.49 miles in Wyoming; 151.58 in North Dakota; and 92.06 miles in South Dakota). The study also found that in states with a relatively low median travel distance (like Alaska), a sizeable percentage of women still had to travel over 150 miles to reach the nearest abortion clinic. See Jonathan M. Bearak et al., Disparities and Change Over Time in Distance Women Would Need to Travel to Have an Abortion in the USA: A Spatial Analysis, 2 Lancet Public Health 493–500 (Nov. 2017).

5. *State "Informed Consent" Requirements for Abortion.* In *Casey* the Court upheld a statute requiring that a state-approved packet of material be given to the pregnant woman as a part of the informed consent process, and that the consent process be obtained by the physician, not by anyone else. The

only requirement the majority in *Casey* appears to put on the distributed material is that it is "truthful and not misleading." How should this be understood in the context of the summary of the "undue burden" test (offered in Part IV of the opinion by Justices O'Connor, Justice Kennedy, and Justice Souter), which allows the State to enact regulations that "further the health or safety of a woman seeking an abortion" but prohibits "[u]necessary health regulations that have the purpose or effect of presenting a substantial obstacle to a woman seeking an abortion." This has led to a number of conflicts as state legislatures have enacted more expansive information requirements at the behest of groups that want to discourage women from having an abortion. Consider the following examples:

- *Information About Medical Risk.* In early 1996 a couple of epidemiological studies arguably suggested a very weak relationship between having an abortion and the subsequent risk of developing breast cancer and the severity of that cancer. Subsequent reports cast doubt on this relationship. See P.A. Newcomb, et al., Pregnancy Termination in Relation to Risk of Breast Cancer, 275 JAMA 283 (1996). A handful of states require that a woman seeking an abortion be told of the purported breast cancer risk. A handful of states also require that women be told that an abortion can jeopardize a woman's future fertility and can have serious mental health consequences, despite weak or contrary scientific support.

- *Information About Fetal Pain.* Nearly a dozen states require that a woman seeking an abortion be told of the possibility that the fetus can feel pain. Should courts scrutinize the scientific basis of this assertion? (For discussion of how fetal pain theories are being used to justify previability criminal bans on abortion, see Note 5, after *Gonzales v. Carhart* below).

- *Moral Information Laws.* How far can states go in promoting their preference for pregnancy over abortion? Should a state be able to require physicians to provide materials highlighting moral objections to abortion? Five states require that a woman be told that personhood begins at conception.

- *Mandatory Ultrasound & Viewing Laws.* Several states have added requirements that before a woman can have an abortion, she must undergo an ultrasound and be required or given the opportunity to see the fetus, as well as to hear the fetal heartbeat and a description of the fetus (such as dimensions of the embryo or fetus, presence of cardiac activity, and the presence of external members and internal organs). Abortion is the only medical procedure in which the state requires a patient to undergo a particular diagnostic test even if the doctor does not believe the tests will have any diagnostic or therapeutic value and the patient does not want it. The Fourth Circuit struck down North Carolina's mandatory ultrasound law requiring the physician to display the sonogram, and describe the fetus to women seeking abortions even if the woman actively "avert[s] her eyes" and "refus[es] to hear." Stuart v. Camnitz, 774 F.3d 238 (4th Cir. 2014), *cert. denied* 576 U.S. 1028 (2015). The court found this "compelled speech" to be a violation of the First Amendment because it "interfere[d] with the physician's right to free speech beyond the extent permitted for reasonable regulation of the medical profession, while simultaneously threatening harm to the patient's psychological health, interfering with the physician's professional judgment, and compromising the doctor-patient relationship." But other courts have upheld similar statutes. See EMW Women's Surgical Center v. Behear, 920 F.3d 421 (6th Cir. 2019) (finding Kentucky's mandatory "speech-and-display" ultrasound law to be a constitutionally permissible regulation of medicine consistent with Supreme Court jurisprudence allowing mandates of "truthful, non-misleading information); see also Texas Medical Providers Performing Abortion Services v. Lakey, 667 F.3d 570 (5th Cir. 2012) (upholding a Texas law on similar reasoning).

6. *State Disclosure Requirements on Pregnancy Centers.* The battle over what information should be provided to women seeking abortions has taken a different turn recently. There is growing attention to entities often referred to as "Pregnancy Centers," "Crisis Pregnancy Centers," or "Limited-Service Pregnancy Centers." These Centers only provide support and assistance for those who want to carry a pregnancy to term. Some help women who want to keep their children but feel like they cannot afford to do so by connecting the women with resources and support, such as counseling, drug abuse treatment, and vocational training. See Michelle Oberman, The Women the Abortion War Leaves Out, N.Y. Times (Jan. 11, 2018). There is evidence, however, that some centers do not provide this kind of support and instead are focused on persuading women not to have abortions through false and misleading information about the health risks of abortion. See U.S. House of Representatives, Committee on Government Reform—Minority Staff, False and Misleading Information Provided by Federally Funded Pregnancy Resource Centers (July 2006). Findings from this report and some state investigations assert that some of these Centers intentionally "pose as full-service women's health clinics" despite their aim to discourage women from having an abortion, and then use "counseling practices that often confuse, misinform, and even intimidate women from making fully-informed, time-sensitive decisions about critical health care." See National Institute of Family & Life Advocates (NIFLA) v. Harris, 839 F.3d 823 (9th Cir. 2016).

Some states have responded to these concerns by requiring Centers to make disclosures about the limits of the services they provide as well as information about where more comprehensive family planning, including abortion, can be accessed. But the Supreme Court recently invalidated such disclosures required under California law on free speech grounds in National Institute of Family and Live Advocates, dba NIFLA v. Harris, 138 S.Ct. 2361 (2018). This surprised many legal scholars because of the deference typically given to state provider disclosure requirements for the purposes of ensuring informed patient decision-making, as well as *Casey*'s decision allowing states to mandate a broad range of information that can impact health care decision-making, including resource information about how to access alternative options. In striking down the required disclosures, Justice Thomas tried to distinguish *Casey*, reaffirming states' ability to mandate disclosures designed to discourage women from having an abortion. Although the *NIFLA* decision did not explicitly turn on religious liberty arguments, the majority was clearly sensitive to the Centers' religious objections to California's required disclosure and those objections informed their free speech challenge. For more on the First Amendment issues raised by informed consent laws in the context of abortion, see Aziza Ahmed, Informed Decision Making and Abortion: Crisis Pregnancy Centers, Informed Consent, and the First Amendment, 43 J. L. Med. & Ethics 51 (2015). For more on the tension between government regulation and religious objections, see the Note on Federal Conscience Protections at the end of Section III.

To the extent *NIFLA* limits states' ability to proactively address potential deception through disclosure requirements, what legal avenues remain available? Every state has a consumer protection law that prohibits businesses from engaging in fraud, deception, and unfair business practices. Health care consumers who encounter licensed or unlicensed health providers engaging in deceptive practices can file complaints with the state, which is then investigated by a state consumer protection agency or the State Attorney General. It is not clear how effective this will be, in part, because women most at risk for harm from delay often do not know about their rights, do not have the time or resources to file a complaint, and/or fear the stigma they believe will come from revealing their need for an abortion. Tort law also allows patients to sue providers who fail to ensure informed consent in treatment, but this may not be very effective either. First, there is the question of the appropriate standard to apply, especially where pregnancy centers are unlicensed, or licensed and expressly provide limited care. Second, harm due to delay may be difficult to prove, especially if the delay is likely one of multiple factors contributing to the woman's increased risk of harm.

GONZALES V. CARHART

Supreme Court of the United States, 2007.
550 U.S. 124.

JUSTICE KENNEDY delivered the opinion of the Court.

These cases require us to consider the validity of the Partial-Birth Abortion Ban Act of 2003 (Act), [ ] a federal statute regulating abortion procedures. . . . We conclude the Act should be sustained against the objections lodged by the broad, facial attack brought against it.

* * *

I.

A

[The Medical Procedure]

The Act proscribes a particular manner of ending fetal life, so it is necessary here [ ] to discuss abortion procedures in some detail. . . .

Abortion methods vary depending to some extent on the preferences of the physician and, of course, on the term of the pregnancy and the resulting stage of the unborn child's development. Between 85 and 90 percent of the approximately 1.3 million abortions performed each year in the United States take place in the first three months of pregnancy, which is to say in the first trimester. [ ] The most common first-trimester abortion method is vacuum aspiration (otherwise known as suction curettage) in which the physician vacuums out the embryonic tissue. Early in this trimester an alternative is to use medication, such as mifepristone (commonly known as RU-486), to terminate the pregnancy. [ ] The Act does not regulate these procedures.

Of the remaining abortions that take place each year, most occur in the second trimester. The surgical procedure referred to as "dilation and evacuation" or "D & E" is the usual abortion method in this trimester. [ ] Although individual techniques for performing D & E differ, the general steps are the same.

A doctor must first dilate the cervix at least to the extent needed to insert surgical instruments into the uterus and to maneuver them to evacuate the fetus. [ ] The steps taken to cause dilation differ by physician and gestational age of the fetus. . . .After sufficient dilation the surgical operation can commence. The woman is placed under general anesthesia or conscious sedation. The doctor, often guided by ultrasound, inserts grasping forceps through the woman's cervix and into the uterus to grab the fetus. The doctor grips a fetal part with the forceps and pulls it back through the cervix and vagina, continuing to pull even after meeting resistance from the cervix. The friction causes the fetus to tear apart. For example, a leg might be ripped off the fetus as it is pulled through the cervix and out of the woman. The process of evacuating the fetus piece by piece continues until it has been completely removed. A doctor may make 10 to 15 passes with the forceps to evacuate the fetus in its entirety, though sometimes removal is completed with fewer passes. Once the fetus has been evacuated, the placenta and any remaining fetal material are suctioned or scraped out of the uterus. The doctor examines the different parts to ensure the entire fetal body has been removed. [ ]

Some doctors, especially later in the second trimester, may kill the fetus a day or two before performing the surgical evacuation. They inject digoxin or potassium chloride into the fetus, the umbilical cord, or the amniotic fluid. Fetal demise may cause contractions and make greater dilation possible. Once dead, moreover, the fetus' body will soften, and its removal will be easier. . . .

The abortion procedure that was the impetus for the numerous bans on "partial-birth abortion," including the Act, is a variation of this standard D & E. [ ] The medical community has not reached unanimity on the appropriate name for this D & E variation. It has been referred to as "intact D & E," "dilation and extraction" (D & X), and "intact D & X." [ ] For discussion purposes this D & E variation will be referred to as intact D & E. The main difference between the two procedures is that in intact D & E a doctor extracts the fetus intact or largely intact with only a few passes. There are no comprehensive statistics indicating what percentage of all D & Es are performed in this manner.

Intact D & E, like regular D & E, begins with dilation of the cervix. Sufficient dilation is essential for the procedure. . . . In an intact D & E procedure the doctor extracts the fetus in a way conducive to pulling out its entire body, instead of ripping it apart. . . .

Intact D & E gained public notoriety when, in 1992, Dr. Martin Haskell gave a presentation describing his method of performing the operation. [ ] In the usual intact D & E the fetus' head lodges in the cervix, and dilation is insufficient to allow it to pass. [ ] Haskell explained the next step as follows:

> " 'At this point, the right-handed surgeon slides the fingers of the left [hand] along the back of the fetus and "hooks" the shoulders of the fetus with the index and ring fingers (palm down).

> " 'While maintaining this tension, lifting the cervix and applying traction to the shoulders with the fingers of the left hand, the surgeon takes a pair of blunt curved Metzenbaum scissors in the right hand. He carefully advances the tip, curved down, along the spine and under his middle finger until he feels it contact the base of the skull under the tip of his middle finger.

> " 'The surgeon then forces the scissors into the base of the skull or into the foramen magnum. Having safely entered the skull, he spreads the scissors to enlarge the opening.

> " 'The surgeon removes the scissors and introduces a suction catheter into this hole and evacuates the skull contents. With the catheter still in place, he applies traction to the fetus, removing it completely from the patient.' "[ ]

This is an abortion doctor's clinical description. Here is another description from a nurse who witnessed the same method performed on a 26-week fetus and who testified before the Senate Judiciary Committee:

" 'Dr. Haskell went in with forceps and grabbed the baby's legs and pulled them down into the birth canal. Then he delivered the baby's body and the arms—everything but the head. The doctor kept the head right inside the uterus. . . .

" 'The baby's little fingers were clasping and unclasping, and his little feet were kicking. Then the doctor stuck the scissors in the back of his head, and the baby's arms jerked out, like a startle reaction, like a flinch, like a baby does when he thinks he is going to fall.

" 'The doctor opened up the scissors, stuck a high-powered suction tube into the opening, and sucked the baby's brains out. Now the baby went completely limp. . . .

" 'He cut the umbilical cord and delivered the placenta. He threw the baby in a pan, along with the placenta and the instruments he had just used.' " [ ]

[JUSTICE KENNEDY next describes other varieties of this procedure in equally vivid terms.]

* * *

D & E and intact D & E are not the only second-trimester abortion methods. . . .

B

[The Statute]

After Dr. Haskell's procedure received public attention, with ensuing and increasing public concern, bans on " 'partial birth abortion' " proliferated. By the time of the *Stenberg* decision [finding Nebraska's statutory partial birth abortion ban to be unconstitutional in 2003], about 30 States had enacted bans designed to prohibit the procedure. [ ] In 1996, Congress also acted to ban partial-birth abortion. President Clinton vetoed the congressional legislation, and the Senate failed to override the veto. Congress approved another bill banning the procedure in 1997, but President Clinton again vetoed it. In 2003, after this Court's decision in *Stenberg,* Congress passed the Act at issue here. [ ] President Bush signed the Act into law. It was to take effect the following day. [ ]

The Act responded to *Stenberg* in two ways. First, Congress made factual findings. Congress determined that this Court in *Stenberg* "was required to accept the very questionable findings issued by the district court judge," [ ], but that Congress was "not bound to accept the same factual findings," [ ]. Congress found, among other things, that "[a] moral, medical, and ethical consensus exists that the practice of performing a partial-birth abortion . . . is a gruesome and inhumane procedure that is never medically necessary and should be prohibited." [ ]

Second, and more relevant here, the Act's language differs from that of the Nebraska statute struck down in *Stenberg*. [ ] The operative provisions of the Act provide in relevant part:

"(a) Any physician who, in or affecting interstate or foreign commerce, knowingly performs a partial-birth abortion and thereby kills a human fetus shall be fined under this title or imprisoned not more than 2 years, or both. This subsection does not apply to a partial-birth abortion that is necessary to save the life of a mother whose life is endangered by a physical disorder, physical illness, or physical injury, including a life-endangering physical condition caused by or arising from the pregnancy itself. * * *

"(b) As used in this section—

"(1) the term 'partial-birth abortion' means an abortion in which the person performing the abortion—

"(A) deliberately and intentionally vaginally delivers a living fetus until, in the case of a head-first presentation, the entire fetal head is outside the body of the mother, or, in the case of breech presentation, any part of the fetal trunk past the navel is outside the body of the mother, for the purpose of performing an overt act that the person knows will kill the partially delivered living fetus; and

"(B) performs the overt act, other than completion of delivery, that kills the partially delivered living fetus;

* * *

"(e) A woman upon whom a partial-birth abortion is performed may not be prosecuted under this section, for a conspiracy to violate this section * * *.

The Act also includes a provision authorizing civil actions [for damages following a "Partial Birth Abortion"] that is not of relevance here. [ ]

* * *

II

[The Holding in *Casey*]

The principles set forth in the joint opinion in *Casey* [ ] did not find support from all those who join the instant opinion.[ ] Whatever one's views concerning the *Casey* joint opinion, it is evident a premise central to its conclusion—that the government has a legitimate and substantial interest in preserving and promoting fetal life—would be repudiated were the Court now to affirm the judgments of the Courts of Appeals. *Casey* involved a challenge to Roe v. Wade [ ]. [One of the three essential principles of *Roe* that was upheld in Casey was] the principle that the State has legitimate interests from the outset of the pregnancy in protecting the health of the woman and the life of the fetus that may become a child. . . . [W]e must determine whether the Act furthers the legitimate interest of the Government in protecting the life of the fetus that may become a child.

To implement its holding, *Casey* rejected both *Roe*'s rigid trimester framework and the interpretation of *Roe* that considered all previability regulations of abortion unwarranted. . . .

We assume the following principles for the purposes of this opinion. Before viability, a State "may not prohibit any woman from making the ultimate decision to terminate her pregnancy." [ ] It also may not impose upon this right an undue burden, which exists if a regulation's "purpose or effect is to place a substantial obstacle in the path of a woman seeking an abortion before the fetus attains viability." [ ] On the other hand, "regulations which do no more than create a structural mechanism by which the State, or the parent or guardian of a minor, may express profound respect for the life of the unborn are permitted, if they are not a substantial obstacle to the woman's exercise of the right to choose." [ ] *Casey*, in short, struck a balance. The balance was central to its holding. We now apply its standard to the cases at bar.

III

We begin with a determination of the Act's operation and effect. A straightforward reading of the Act's text demonstrates its purpose and the scope of its provisions: It regulates and proscribes, with exceptions or qualifications to be discussed, performing the intact D & E procedure.

Respondents agree the Act encompasses intact D & E, but they contend its additional reach is both unclear and excessive. Respondents assert that, at the least, the Act is void for vagueness because its scope is indefinite. In the alternative, respondents argue the Act's text proscribes all D & Es. Because D & E is the most common second-trimester abortion method, respondents suggest the Act imposes an undue burden. In this litigation the Attorney General does not dispute that the Act would impose an undue burden if it covered standard D & E.

We conclude that the Act is not void for vagueness, does not impose an undue burden from any overbreadth, and is not invalid on its face.

A

[Interpreting the Statute]

The Act punishes "knowingly performing" a "partial-birth abortion." [ ] It defines the unlawful abortion in explicit terms. [ ]

First, the person performing the abortion must "vaginally deliver a living fetus." [ ] The Act does not restrict an abortion procedure involving the delivery of an expired fetus. The Act, furthermore, is inapplicable to abortions that do not involve vaginal delivery (for instance, hysterotomy or hysterectomy). The Act does apply both previability and postviability because, by common understanding and scientific terminology, a fetus is a living organism while within the womb, whether or not it is viable outside the womb. . . .

Second, the Act's definition of partial-birth abortion requires the fetus to be delivered "until, in the case of a head-first presentation, the entire fetal head is outside the body of the mother, or, in the case of breech presentation, any part of the fetal trunk past the navel is outside the body of the mother." . . . .

Third, to fall within the Act, a doctor must perform an "overt act, other than completion of delivery, that kills the partially delivered living fetus." [ ] For purposes of criminal liability, the overt act causing the fetus' death must be separate from delivery. And the overt act must occur after the delivery to an anatomical landmark. This is because the Act proscribes killing "the partially delivered" fetus, which, when read in context, refers to a fetus that has been delivered to an anatomical landmark. [ ]

Fourth, the Act contains scienter requirements concerning all the actions involved in the prohibited abortion. To begin with, the physician must have "deliberately and intentionally" delivered the fetus to one of the Act's anatomical landmarks. . . . In addition, the fetus must have been delivered "for the purpose of performing an overt act that the [doctor] knows will kill [it]." . . . .

B

[Vagueness]

Respondents contend the language described above is indeterminate, and they thus argue the Act is unconstitutionally vague on its face. "As generally stated, the void-for-vagueness doctrine requires that a penal statute define the criminal offense with sufficient definiteness that ordinary people can understand what conduct is prohibited and in a manner that does not encourage arbitrary and discriminatory enforcement." [ ] The Act satisfies both requirements.

. . . Unlike the statutory language in *Stenberg* that prohibited the delivery of a " 'substantial portion' " of the fetus—where a doctor might question how much of the fetus is a substantial portion—the Act defines the line between potentially criminal conduct on the one hand and lawful abortion on the other. [ ]

* * *

C

[Undue Burden]

We next determine whether the Act imposes an undue burden, as a facial matter, because its restrictions on second-trimester abortions are too broad. A review of the statutory text discloses the limits of its reach. The Act prohibits intact D & E; and, notwithstanding respondents' arguments, it does not prohibit the D & E procedure in which the fetus is removed in parts.

* * *

A comparison of the Act with the Nebraska statute struck down in *Stenberg* confirms this point. The statute in *Stenberg* prohibited " 'deliberately and intentionally delivering into the vagina a living unborn child, or a substantial portion thereof, for the purpose of performing a procedure that the person performing such procedure knows will kill the unborn child and does kill the unborn child.' " [ ]. The Court concluded that this statute encompassed D & E because "D & E will often involve a physician pulling a 'substantial portion' of a still living fetus, say, an arm or leg, into the vagina prior to the death of the fetus." . . .

Congress, it is apparent, responded to these concerns because the Act departs in material ways from the statute in *Stenberg*. It adopts the phrase "delivers a living fetus," [ ] instead of " 'delivering . . . a living unborn child, or a substantial portion thereof,' " [ ]. The Act's language, unlike the statute in *Stenberg*, expresses the usual meaning of "deliver" when used in connection with "fetus," namely, extraction of an entire fetus rather than removal of fetal pieces. . . .

The identification of specific anatomical landmarks to which the fetus must be partially delivered also differentiates the Act from the statute at issue in *Stenberg*. . . .

By adding an overt-act requirement Congress sought further to meet the Court's objections to the state statute considered in *Stenberg*. . . . The fatal overt act must occur after delivery to an anatomical landmark, and it must be something "other than [the] completion of delivery." [ ] This distinction matters because, unlike intact D & E, standard D & E does not involve a delivery followed by a fatal act.

The canon of constitutional avoidance, finally, extinguishes any lingering doubt as to whether the Act covers the prototypical D & E procedure. " 'The elementary rule is that every reasonable construction must be resorted to, in order to save a statute from unconstitutionality.' " [ ] It is true this longstanding maxim of statutory interpretation has, in the past, fallen by the wayside when the Court confronted a statute regulating abortion. . . . *Casey* put this novel statutory approach to rest. . . .

* * *

IV

[Substantial Obstacle]

Under the principles accepted as controlling here, the Act, as we have interpreted it, would be unconstitutional "if its purpose or effect is to place a substantial obstacle in the path of a woman seeking an abortion before the fetus attains viability." *Casey* [ ] The abortions affected by the Act's regulations take place both previability and postviability; so the quoted language and the undue burden analysis it relies upon are applicable. The question is whether the Act, measured by its text in this facial attack, imposes a substantial obstacle to late-term, but previability, abortions. The Act does not on its face impose a substantial obstacle, and we reject this further facial challenge to its validity.

A

[Congressional Purpose]

The Act's purposes are set forth in recitals preceding its operative provisions. A description of the prohibited abortion procedure demonstrates the rationale for the congressional enactment. The Act proscribes a method of abortion in which a fetus is killed just inches before completion of the birth process. Congress stated as follows: "Implicitly approving such a brutal and inhumane procedure by choosing not to prohibit it will further coarsen society to the humanity of not only newborns, but all vulnerable and innocent human life, making it increasingly difficult to protect such life." [ ] The Act expresses respect for the dignity of human life. Congress was concerned, furthermore, with the effects on the medical community and on its reputation caused by the practice of partial-birth abortion. . . .

There can be no doubt the government "has an interest in protecting the integrity and ethics of the medical profession." Washington v. Glucksberg, [ ] [reprinted in Chapter 19]. Under our precedents, it is clear the State has a significant role to play in regulating the medical profession.

Casey reaffirmed these governmental objectives. The government may use its voice and its regulatory authority to show its profound respect for the life within the woman. . . . The three premises of *Casey* must coexist.[ ] The third premise, that the State, from the inception of the pregnancy, maintains its own regulatory interest in protecting the life of the fetus that may become a child, cannot be set at naught by interpreting *Casey*'s requirement of a health exception so it becomes tantamount to allowing a doctor to choose the abortion method he or she might prefer. Where it has a rational basis to act, and it does not impose an undue burden, the State may use its regulatory power to bar certain procedures and substitute others, all in furtherance of its legitimate interests in regulating the medical profession in order to promote respect for life, including life of the unborn.

... The Court has in the past confirmed the validity of drawing boundaries to prevent certain practices that extinguish life and are close to actions that are condemned. *Glucksberg* found reasonable the State's "fear that permitting assisted suicide will start it down the path to voluntary and perhaps even involuntary euthanasia." [ ]

Respect for human life finds an ultimate expression in the bond of love the mother has for her child. The Act recognizes this reality as well. Whether to have an abortion requires a difficult and painful moral decision. [ ] While we find no reliable data to measure the phenomenon, it seems unexceptionable to conclude some women come to regret their choice to abort the infant life they once created and sustained. [ ] Severe depression and loss of esteem can follow. [ ]

In a decision so fraught with emotional consequence some doctors may prefer not to disclose precise details of the means that will be used, confining themselves to the required statement of risks the procedure entails. From one standpoint this ought not to be surprising. Any number of patients facing imminent surgical procedures would prefer not to hear all details, lest the usual anxiety preceding invasive medical procedures become the more intense. This is likely the case with the abortion procedures here in issue. [ ]

It is, however, precisely this lack of information concerning the way in which the fetus will be killed that is of legitimate concern to the State. [ ] The State has an interest in ensuring so grave a choice is well informed. It is self-evident that a mother who comes to regret her choice to abort must struggle with grief more anguished and sorrow more profound when she learns, only after the event, what she once did not know: that she allowed a doctor to pierce the skull and vacuum the fast-developing brain of her unborn child, a child assuming the human form.

* * *

It is objected that the standard D & E is in some respects as brutal, if not more, than the intact D & E, so that the legislation accomplishes little. ... It was reasonable for Congress to think that partial-birth abortion, more than standard D & E, "undermines the public's perception of the appropriate role of a physician during the delivery process, and perverts a process during which life is brought into the world." ... In sum, we reject the contention that the congressional purpose of the Act was "to place a substantial obstacle in the path of a woman seeking an abortion." [ ]

B

[Protecting the Health of the Mother]

The Act's furtherance of legitimate government interests bears upon, but does not resolve, the next question: whether the Act has the effect of imposing an unconstitutional burden on the abortion right because it does not allow use of the barred procedure where " 'necessary, in appropriate medical judgment, for [the] preservation of the . . . health of the mother.' " [ ] The prohibition in the Act would be unconstitutional, under precedents we here assume to be controlling, if it "subjected [women] to significant health risks." . . . Here, by contrast, whether the Act creates significant health risks for women has been a contested factual question. The evidence presented in the trial courts and before Congress demonstrates both sides have medical support for their position.

* * *

The question becomes whether the Act can stand when this medical uncertainty persists. The Court's precedents instruct that the Act can survive this facial attack. The Court has given state and federal legislatures wide discretion to pass legislation in areas where there is medical and scientific uncertainty.

* * *

In reaching the conclusion the Act does not require a health exception we reject certain arguments made by the parties on both sides of these cases. On the one hand, the Attorney General urges us to uphold the Act on the basis of the congressional findings alone. [ ] Although we review congressional factfinding under a deferential standard, we do not in the circumstances here place dispositive weight on Congress' findings. The Court retains an independent constitutional duty to review factual findings where constitutional rights are at stake. [ ]

As respondents have noted, and the District Courts recognized, some recitations in the Act are factually incorrect. . . . Uncritical deference to Congress' factual findings in these cases is inappropriate.

On the other hand, relying on the Court's opinion in *Stenberg*, respondents contend that an abortion regulation must contain a health exception "if 'substantial medical authority supports the proposition that banning a particular procedure could endanger women's health.' " . . . *Stenberg* has been interpreted to leave no margin of error for legislatures to act in the face of medical uncertainty. [ ]

A zero tolerance policy would strike down legitimate abortion regulations, like the present one, if some part of the medical community were disinclined to follow the proscription. This is too exacting a standard to impose on the legislative power, exercised in this instance under the

Commerce Clause, to regulate the medical profession. Considerations of marginal safety, including the balance of risks, are within the legislative competence when the regulation is rational and in pursuit of legitimate ends. . . . The Act is not invalid on its face where there is uncertainty over whether the barred procedure is ever necessary to preserve a woman's health, given the availability of other abortion procedures that are considered to be safe alternatives.

V

[Propriety of a Facial Attack on the Statute]

The considerations we have discussed support our further determination that these facial attacks should not have been entertained in the first instance. In these circumstances the proper means to consider exceptions is by as-applied challenge. . . . This is the proper manner to protect the health of the woman if it can be shown that in discrete and well-defined instances a particular condition has or is likely to occur in which the procedure prohibited by the Act must be used. In an as-applied challenge the nature of the medical risk can be better quantified and balanced than in a facial attack.

* * *

As the previous sections of this opinion explain, respondents have not demonstrated that the Act would be unconstitutional in a large fraction of relevant cases. . . .

The Act is open to a proper as-applied challenge in a discrete case. . . . No as-applied challenge need be brought if the prohibition in the Act threatens a woman's life because the Act already contains a life exception. []

* * *

JUSTICE THOMAS, with whom JUSTICE SCALIA joins, concurring.

I join the Court's opinion because it accurately applies current jurisprudence, including *Casey* []. I write separately to reiterate my view that the Court's abortion jurisprudence, including *Casey* and *Roe* [] has no basis in the Constitution. [] I also note that whether the Act constitutes a permissible exercise of Congress' power under the Commerce Clause is not before the Court. The parties did not raise or brief that issue; it is outside the question presented; and the lower courts did not address it. []

JUSTICE GINSBURG, with whom JUSTICE STEVENS, JUSTICE SOUTER, and JUSTICE BREYER join, dissenting.

* * *

In reaffirming *Roe*, the *Casey* Court described the centrality of "the decision whether to bear . . . a child," [] to a woman's "dignity and autonomy," her "personhood" and "destiny," her "conception of . . . her place in society." [ ] Of signal importance here, the *Casey* Court stated with unmistakable clarity that state regulation of access to abortion procedures, even after viability, must protect "the health of the woman." [ ]

Seven years ago, in *Stenberg,* [ ] the Court invalidated a Nebraska statute criminalizing the performance of a medical procedure that, in the political arena, has been dubbed "partial-birth abortion." With fidelity to the *Roe-Casey* line of precedent, the Court held the Nebraska statute unconstitutional in part because it lacked the requisite protection for the preservation of a woman's health. [ ]

Today's decision is alarming. It refuses to take *Casey* and *Stenberg* seriously. It tolerates, indeed applauds, federal intervention to ban nationwide a procedure found necessary and proper in certain cases by the American College of Obstetricians and Gynecologists (ACOG). It blurs the line, firmly drawn in *Casey*, between previability and postviability abortions. And, for the first time since *Roe*, the Court blesses a prohibition with no exception safeguarding a woman's health.

I dissent from the Court's disposition. Retreating from prior rulings that abortion restrictions cannot be imposed absent an exception safeguarding a woman's health, the Court upholds an Act that surely would not survive under the close scrutiny that previously attended state-decreed limitations on a woman's reproductive choices.

I

A

As *Casey* comprehended, at stake in cases challenging abortion restrictions is a woman's "control over her [own] destiny." . . .Women, it is now acknowledged, have the talent, capacity, and right "to participate equally in the economic and social life of the Nation." [ ] Their ability to realize their full potential, the Court recognized, is intimately connected to "their ability to control their reproductive lives." [ ] Thus, legal challenges to undue restrictions on abortion procedures do not seek to vindicate some generalized notion of privacy; rather, they center on a woman's autonomy to determine her life's course, and thus to enjoy equal citizenship stature. [ ]

In keeping with this comprehension of the right to reproductive choice, the Court has consistently required that laws regulating abortion, at any stage of pregnancy and in all cases, safeguard a woman's health. [ ]

We have thus ruled that a State must avoid subjecting women to health risks not only where the pregnancy itself creates danger, but also where state regulation forces women to resort to less safe methods of abortion. . . .

In *Stenberg*, we expressly held that a statute banning intact D & E was unconstitutional in part because it lacked a health exception. [ ] We noted that there existed a "division of medical opinion" about the relative safety of intact D & E, [ ], but we made clear that as long as "substantial medical authority supports the proposition that banning a particular abortion procedure could endanger women's health," a health exception is required. [ ] We explained:

> "The word 'necessary' in *Casey*'s phrase 'necessary, in appropriate medical judgment, for the preservation of the life or health of the [pregnant woman],' cannot refer to an absolute necessity or to absolute proof. Medical treatments and procedures are often considered appropriate (or inappropriate) in light of estimated comparative health risks (and health benefits) in particular cases. Neither can that phrase require unanimity of medical opinion. Doctors often differ in their estimation of comparative health risks and appropriate treatment. And *Casey*'s words 'appropriate medical judgment' must embody the judicial need to tolerate responsible differences of medical opinion. . . . " [ ]

Thus, we reasoned, division in medical opinion "at most means uncertainty, a factor that signals the presence of risk, not its absence." [ ] "[A] statute that altogether forbids [intact D & E] . . . consequently must contain a health exception." [ ]

B

In 2003, a few years after our ruling in *Stenberg*, Congress passed the Partial-Birth Abortion Ban Act—without an exception for women's health. [ ] The congressional findings on which the Partial-Birth Abortion Ban Act rests do not withstand inspection, as the lower courts have determined and this Court is obliged to concede.

* * *

C

* * *

During the District Court trials, "numerous" "extraordinarily accomplished" and "very experienced" medical experts explained that, in certain circumstances and for certain women, intact D & E is safer than alternative procedures and necessary to protect women's health. [ ]

According to the expert testimony plaintiffs introduced, the safety advantages of intact D & E are marked for women with certain medical conditions . . . . Further, plaintiffs' experts testified that intact D & E is significantly safer for women with certain pregnancy-related conditions, such as placenta previa and accreta, and for women carrying fetuses with certain abnormalities, such as severe hydrocephalus. [ ]

Intact D & E, plaintiffs' experts explained, provides safety benefits over D & E by dismemberment for several reasons [which Justice Ginsburg lists and describes]. . . .

* * *

Nevertheless, despite the District Courts' appraisal of the weight of the evidence, and in undisguised conflict with *Stenberg*, the Court asserts that the Partial-Birth Abortion Ban Act can survive "when . . . medical uncertainty persists." [ ] This assertion is bewildering.

* * *

II

A

The Court offers flimsy and transparent justifications for upholding a nationwide ban on intact D & E *sans* any exception to safeguard a women's health. Today's ruling, the Court declares, advances "a premise central to [*Casey*'s] conclusion"—i.e., the Government's "legitimate and substantial interest in preserving and promoting fetal life." [ ] But the Act scarcely furthers that interest: The law saves not a single fetus from destruction, for it targets only a *method* of performing abortion. [ ] And surely the statute was not designed to protect the lives or health of pregnant women. [ ]

* * *

Ultimately, the Court admits that "moral concerns" are at work, concerns that could yield prohibitions on any abortion. [ ] Notably, the concerns expressed are untethered to any ground genuinely serving the Government's interest in preserving life. By allowing such concerns to carry the day and case, overriding fundamental rights, the Court dishonors our precedent. [ ]

Revealing in this regard, the Court invokes an antiabortion shibboleth for which it concededly has no reliable evidence: Women who have abortions come to regret their choices, and consequently suffer from "severe depression and loss of esteem." [ ] Because of women's fragile emotional state and because of the "bond of love the mother has for her child," the Court worries, doctors may withhold information about the nature of the intact D & E procedure. [ ] The solution the Court approves, then, is *not* to require doctors to inform women, accurately and adequately, of the different procedures and their attendant risks. [ ] Instead, the Court deprives women of the right to make an autonomous choice, even at the expense of their safety.

This way of thinking reflects ancient notions about women's place in the family and under the Constitution—ideas that have long since been discredited. . . .

Though today's majority may regard women's feelings on the matter as "self-evident," [ ] this Court has repeatedly confirmed that "the destiny of the woman must be shaped . . . on her own conception of her spiritual imperatives and her place in society." *Casey* [ ].

B

* * *

The Court's hostility to the right *Roe* and *Casey* secured is not concealed. Throughout, the opinion refers to obstetrician-gynecologists and surgeons who perform abortions not by the titles of their medical specialties, but by the pejorative label "abortion doctor." [ ] A fetus is described as an "unborn child," and as a "baby," [ ]; second-trimester, previability abortions are referred to as "late-term," [ ]; and the reasoned medical judgments of highly trained doctors are dismissed as "preferences" motivated by "mere convenience," [ ]. Instead of the heightened scrutiny we have previously applied, the Court determines that a "rational" ground is enough to uphold the Act [ ]. And, most troubling, *Casey*'s principles, confirming the continuing vitality of "the essential holding of *Roe*," are merely "assumed" for the moment [ ], rather than "retained" or "reaffirmed," *Casey* [ ].

III

A

The Court further confuses our jurisprudence when it declares that "facial attacks" are not permissible in "these circumstances," i.e., where medical uncertainty exists. . . .

Without attempting to distinguish *Stenberg* and earlier decisions, the majority asserts that the Act survives review because respondents have not shown that the ban on intact D & E would be unconstitutional "in a large fraction of relevant cases." [ ] But *Casey* makes clear that, in determining whether any restriction poses an undue burden on a "large fraction" of women, the relevant class is *not* "all women," nor "all pregnant women," nor even all women "seeking abortions." [ ] Rather, a provision restricting access to abortion, "must be judged by reference to those [women] for whom it is an actual rather than an irrelevant restriction."[ ] Thus the absence of a health exception burdens *all* women for whom it is relevant—women who, in the judgment of their doctors, require an intact D & E because other procedures would place their health at risk. [ ] It makes no sense to conclude that this facial challenge fails because respondents have not shown that a health exception is necessary for a large fraction of second-trimester abortions, including those for which a health exception is unnecessary: The very purpose of a health *exception* is to protect women in *exceptional* cases.

B

If there is anything at all redemptive to be said of today's opinion, it is that the Court is not willing to foreclose entirely a constitutional challenge to the Act. "The Act is open," the Court states, "to a proper as-applied challenge in a discrete case." [ ] But the Court offers no clue on what a "proper" lawsuit might look like. [ ] Nor does the Court explain why the injunctions ordered by the District Courts should not remain in place, trimmed only to exclude instances in which another procedure would safeguard a woman's health at least equally well. Surely the Court cannot mean that no suit may be brought until a woman's health is immediately jeopardized by the ban on intact D & E. A woman "suffering from medical complications" [ ] needs access to the medical procedure at once and cannot wait for the judicial process to unfold. [ ]

* * *

IV

As the Court wrote in *Casey*, "overruling *Roe*'s central holding would not only reach an unjustifiable result under principles of *stare decisis*, but would seriously weaken the Court's capacity to exercise the judicial power and to function as the Supreme Court of a Nation dedicated to the rule of law." . . .

Though today's opinion does not go so far as to discard *Roe* or *Casey*, the Court, differently composed than it was when we last considered a restrictive abortion regulation, is hardly faithful to our earlier invocations of "the rule of law" and the "principles of *stare decisis*." Congress imposed a ban despite our clear prior holdings that the State cannot proscribe an abortion procedure when its use is necessary to protect a woman's health. [ ] Although Congress' findings could not withstand the crucible of trial, the Court defers to the legislative override of our Constitution-based rulings. [ ] A decision so at odds with our jurisprudence should not have staying power.

In sum, the notion that the Partial-Birth Abortion Ban Act furthers any legitimate governmental interest is, quite simply, irrational. The Court's defense of the statute provides no saving explanation. In candor, the Act, and the Court's defense of it, cannot be understood as anything other than an effort to chip away at a right declared again and again by this Court—and with increasing comprehension of its centrality to women's lives. [ ] When "a statute burdens constitutional rights and all that can be said on its behalf is that it is the vehicle that legislators have chosen for expressing their hostility to those rights, the burden is undue." [ ]

NOTES AND QUESTIONS

1.   *The Undue Burden Test.* The Court "assume[s]" for purposes of the opinion that a regulation would constitute an "undue burden" if the regulation's purpose or effect is to place a substantial obstacle in the path of a woman seeking an abortion of a nonviable fetus. How is a court expected to divine the purpose of challenged legislation? How does a court determine whether a challenged statute in "effect" creates a substantial obstacle? Is an obstacle substantial because it imposes a serious limitation on any identifiable woman, because it affects a large number of women, or because it affects a large percentage of the cases in which women would seek abortions?

2.   *Health Justifications.* One justification offered by Justice Kennedy was based on the government's interest in protecting women from a lack of information about the specific nature of the abortion procedure because of the emotional harm that could result from finding out the details after the fact. Yet, Justice Kennedy admits "there is no reliable data to measure this phenomenon." If claims about potential health risks of a procedure are being asserted to ban that procedure, should those risks have to be substantiated with scientific or medical evidence in court? Or should it be enough that such harm is "self-evident" to the Court?

3.   *The Health Exception.* Consider that, unlike the abortion regulations challenged in *Casey*, the Partial Birth Abortion Ban Act did not contain an exception for the preservation of the mother's health. (It only provided an exception for life-threatening emergencies). *Casey's* decision depended, in part, on its finding that "the abortion regulation would not in any way pose a significant threat to the life *or health* of a woman," and this was part of the reason why the partial-birth abortion ban in *Stenberg* had been struck down. Why was the absence of a "health" exception not fatal in *Carhart*? The Court notes that "there is uncertainty over whether the barred procedure is ever necessary to preserve a woman's health." As Justice Ginsburg points out in dissent, this was contradicted by numerous medical experts at trial; but even if it were true, does this type of "medical uncertainty" weigh in favor of upholding the ban without a health exception, or striking it down?

4.   Stenberg *vs.* Carhart. The Court distinguished its earlier decision striking down Nebraska's partial birth abortion ban in *Stenberg*. What were the relevant differences between the partial birth abortion ban that was rejected in *Stenberg* and the one accepted in *Carhart*? Was it the legislative findings that saved the federal statute? The more precise definition of the banned procedure? The scienter requirement? The fact that D & E abortions are still permitted? Some combination of these? Or was the change in the Court's approach due perhaps to the replacement of Justice O'Connor by Justice Alito?

5.   *Other Criminal Bans on Abortion.* Consider the ethical and legal questions raised by other state abortion bans based on *type of procedure*, *timing of procedure*, or *reason for the procedure*—laws which are currently being or have been challenged in court. For example, some states some have gone

further than the federal partial birth abortion ban, by not allowing an exception for life endangerment, and some have banned D & E (the most commonly used form of abortion) in the second trimester, with limited exceptions. Seventeen states have enacted previability bans on abortions at 20 weeks (with limited exceptions, such as life endangerment). This is often justified on the grounds the fetus may be able to feel pain at this point, despite contrary scientific evidence that the neural anatomy of a fetus is not sufficiently developed to be able to perceive pain until at least after 24 weeks of gestation. See I. Glenn Cohen & Sadath Sayeed, Fetal Pain, Abortion, Viability, and the Constitution, 39 J.L. Med. & Ethics 235 (2011). Eight states have enacted abortion previability bans for reasons of sex selection, and a few states have outlawed abortion where the fetus may have a genetic anomaly, including a recently enacted Ohio law banning abortion after prenatal tests reveal Down syndrome in a fetus.

6.   *Selective Abortion & Disability Justice.* Laws attempting to prevent abortions on the basis of genetic anomaly have been justified as anti-eugenics or anti-discrimination measures, with states citing anecdotal reports of parents feeling coerced by physicians into terminating pregnancies where prenatal diagnosis suggests Down syndrome. These justifications played a prominent role in the Sixth Circuit's decision to uphold what it characterized as a limited ban in Cleveland v. Himes, 994 F.3d 512 (6th Cir. 2021). The court denied a preliminary injunction against an Ohio law based on its interpretation that the law does not actually ban women from getting an abortion based on a Down syndrome diagnosis. Rather, the court reasoned that the law prohibits a physician from performing an abortion *only if the physician knows* the patient is seeking the abortion because the fetus has Down syndrome. But in Planned Parenthood of Ind. & Ky., Inc. v. Comm'r Ind. State Dep't of Health, the Seventh Circuit affirmed a district court opinion finding unconstitutional a law that banned previability abortions where the reason for the abortion was based on some characteristic of the fetus, such as sex, race, or Down syndrome diagnosis. 888 F.3d 300 (7th Cir. 2018), *cert. granted in part and judgment reversed in part* 139 S.Ct. 1780 (2019) (per curiam). On appeal, the Supreme Court denied certiorari on this issue, but Justice Thomas authored a concurrence highlighting the disturbing history of abortion and sterilization as eugenics tools against those deemed "unfit" due to disability. Id. at 1782 (Thomas, J. concurring).

Disability rights activists have argued that selective abortion raises moral and justice concerns, because it reinforces a view that a life with disability is not as valuable or worth living, and because such decisions seem to be driven by misinformation and pressure by health professionals. But the history of reproductive control as a tool for injustice against people with disabilities, including denying them the right to make their own reproductive choices, has led many disability rights activists to oppose abortion bans. See, e.g., Samuel Bagenstos, Disability and Reproductive Justice, 14 Harv. L. & Pol'y Rev. 273 (2020) (arguing instead for an approach informed by disability and reproductive justice frameworks that would ensure patients had the information and structural supports needed to empower the choice to have a child that may have a genetic anomaly; this would include informed consent requirements designed to counteract negative stereotypes about disability). For more on reproductive control as a eugenics tool, see Section V, below.

7. *Regulating the Abortion Procedure. Carhart* invigorated attempts to target abortion providers for stricter regulations, effectively making access more difficult. Yet, important questions remained about exactly what kind of regulation or degree of impact would constitute an undue burden under *Casey*. After *Carhart*, restrictions targeting abortion providers were easily upheld in the lower courts; but when two such restrictions reached the Supreme Court in *Whole Woman's Health* (below), it seemed that, once again, the trajectory of abortion jurisprudence may have shifted.

C. AN UNDUE BURDEN TEST WITH TEETH?

WHOLE WOMAN'S HEALTH v. HELLERSTEDT

Supreme Court of the United States, 2016.
136 S.Ct. 2292.

JUSTICE BREYER delivered the opinion of the Court.

In *Planned Parenthood of Southeastern Pa. v. Casey* [ ] a plurality of the Court concluded that there "exists" an "undue burden" on a woman's right to decide to have an abortion, and consequently a provision of law is constitutionally invalid, if the "*purpose or effect*" of the provision "*is to place a substantial obstacle* in the path of a woman seeking an abortion before the fetus attains viability." [ ] The plurality added that "[u]nnecessary health regulations that have the purpose or effect of presenting a substantial obstacle to a woman seeking an abortion impose an undue burden on the right." [ ]

We must here decide whether two provisions of Texas' House Bill 2 violate the Federal Constitution as interpreted in *Casey*. The first provision, which we shall call the "*admitting-privileges requirement*," says that

> "[a] physician performing or inducing an abortion . . . must, on the date the abortion is performed or induced, have active admitting privileges at a hospital that . . . is located not further than 30 miles from the location at which the abortion is performed or induced." [ ]

This provision amended Texas law that had previously required an abortion facility to maintain a written protocol "for managing medical emergencies and the transfer of patients requiring further emergency care to a hospital." [ ]

The second provision, which we shall call the "*surgical-center requirement*," says that "the minimum standards for an abortion facility must be equivalent to the minimum standards adopted under [the Texas Health and Safety Code section] for ambulatory surgical centers." [ ]

We conclude that neither of these provisions confers medical benefits sufficient to justify the burdens upon access that each imposes. Each places a substantial obstacle in the path of women seeking a previability abortion, each constitutes an undue burden on abortion access, [ ], and each violates the Federal Constitution. [ ]

I

A

In July 2013, the Texas Legislature enacted House Bill 2 [which is the subject of this litigation. A part of the Act, the admitting-privileges provision, was challenged on its face in *Planned Parenthood of Greater Tex. Surgical Health Servs. v. Abbott*. Ultimately, the Fifth Circuit upheld that provision, and no review was sought in the Supreme Court.]

* * *

B

[One] week after the Fifth Circuit's decision, petitioners, a group of abortion providers (many of whom were plaintiffs in the previous lawsuit), filed the present lawsuit in Federal District Court. They sought an injunction preventing enforcement of the admitting-privileges provision as applied to physicians at two abortion facilities .... They also sought an injunction prohibiting enforcement of the surgical-center provision anywhere in Texas. They claimed that the admitting-privileges provision and the surgical-center provision violated the Constitution's Fourteenth Amendment, as interpreted in *Casey*.

The District Court subsequently received stipulations from the parties and depositions from the parties' experts. The court conducted a 4-day bench trial. It heard, among other testimony, the opinions from expert witnesses for both sides. On the basis of the stipulations, depositions, and testimony, that court reached the following conclusions:

1. Of Texas' population of more than 25 million people, "approximately 5.4 million" are "women" of "reproductive age," living within a geographical area of "nearly 280,000 square miles." [ ]

2. "In recent years, the number of abortions reported in Texas has stayed fairly consistent at approximately 15–16% of the reported pregnancy rate, for a total number of approximately 60,000–72,000 legal abortions performed annually." [ ]

3. Prior to the enactment of H.B. 2, there were more than 40 licensed abortion facilities in Texas, which "number dropped by almost half leading

up to and in the wake of enforcement of the admitting-privileges requirement that went into effect in late-October 2013." [ ]

4. If the surgical-center provision were allowed to take effect, the number of abortion facilities, after September 1, 2014, would be reduced further, so that "only seven facilities and a potential eighth will exist in Texas." [ ]

* * *

7. The suggestion "that these seven or eight providers could meet the demand of the entire state stretches credulity." [ ]

8. . . . After September 2014, should the surgical-center requirement go into effect, the number of women of reproductive age living significant distances from an abortion provider will increase [substantially]. [ ]

9. The "two requirements erect a particularly high barrier for poor, rural, or disadvantaged women." [ ]

10. "The great weight of evidence demonstrates that, before the act's passage, abortion in Texas was extremely safe with particularly low rates of serious complications and virtually no deaths occurring on account of the procedure." [ ]

11. "Abortion, as regulated by the State before the enactment of House Bill 2, has been shown to be much safer, in terms of minor and serious complications, than many common medical procedures not subject to such intense regulation and scrutiny." [ ].

12. "Additionally, risks are not appreciably lowered for patients who undergo abortions at ambulatory surgical centers as compared to nonsurgical-center facilities." [ ].

13. "[W]omen will not obtain better care or experience more frequent positive outcomes at an ambulatory surgical center as compared to a previously licensed facility." [ ]

* * *

On the basis of these and other related findings, the District Court determined that the surgical-center requirement "imposes an undue burden on the right of women throughout Texas to seek a previability abortion," and that the "admitting-privileges requirement . . . in conjunction with the ambulatory-surgical-center requirement, imposes an undue burden on the right of women . . . to seek a previability abortion." [ ] The District Court concluded that the "two provisions" would cause "the closing of almost all abortion clinics in Texas that were operating legally in the fall of 2013," and thereby create a constitutionally "impermissible obstacle as applied to all women seeking a previability abortion" by "restricting access to previously available legal facilities." [ ] [T]he court enjoined the enforcement of the two provisions.

C

* * *

[T]he Court of Appeals reversed the District Court on the merits. With minor exceptions, it found both provisions constitutional and allowed them to take effect. [ ]

* * *

III

Undue Burden—Legal Standard

We begin with the standard, as described in *Casey*. We recognize that the "State has a legitimate interest in seeing to it that abortion, like any other medical procedure, is performed under circumstances that insure maximum safety for the patient." *Roe v. Wade* [ ]. But, we added, "a statute which, while furthering [a] valid state interest, has the effect of placing a substantial obstacle in the path of a woman's choice cannot be considered a permissible means of serving its legitimate ends." *Casey* [ ]. Moreover, "[u]nnecessary health regulations that have the purpose or effect of presenting a substantial obstacle to a woman seeking an abortion impose an undue burden on the right." [ ]

The Court of Appeals wrote that a state law is "constitutional if: (1) it does not have the purpose or effect of placing a substantial obstacle in the path of a woman seeking an abortion of a nonviable fetus; and (2) it is reasonably related to (or designed to further) a legitimate state interest." [ ] The Court of Appeals went on to hold that "the district court erred by substituting its own judgment for that of the legislature" when it conducted its "undue burden inquiry," in part because "medical uncertainty underlying a statute is for resolution by legislatures, not the courts." [ ]

The Court of Appeals' articulation of the relevant standard is incorrect. The first part of the Court of Appeals' test may be read to imply that a district court should not consider the existence or nonexistence of medical benefits when considering whether a regulation of abortion constitutes an undue burden. The rule announced in *Casey,* however, requires that courts consider the burdens a law imposes on abortion access together with the benefits those laws confer. [ ] And the second part of the test is wrong to equate the judicial review applicable to the regulation of a constitutionally protected personal liberty with the less strict review applicable where, for example, economic legislation is at issue. [ ] The Court of Appeals' approach simply does not match the standard that this Court laid out in *Casey,* which asks courts to consider whether any burden imposed on abortion access is "undue."

The statement that legislatures, and not courts, must resolve questions of medical uncertainty is also inconsistent with this Court's case law. Instead, the Court, when determining the constitutionality of laws regulating abortion procedures, has placed considerable weight upon evidence and argument presented in judicial proceedings. In *Casey,* for example, we relied heavily on the District Court's factual findings and the research-based submissions of *amici* in declaring a portion of the law at issue unconstitutional. [ ] (discussing evidence related to the prevalence of spousal abuse in determining that a spousal notification provision erected an undue burden to abortion access). And, in *Gonzales* the Court, while pointing out that we must review legislative "factfinding under a deferential standard," added that we must not "place dispositive weight" on those "findings." [ ] *Gonzales* went on to point out that the "*Court retains an independent constitutional duty to review factual findings where constitutional rights are at stake.*" [ ] (emphasis added). Although there we upheld a statute regulating abortion, we did not do so solely on the basis of legislative findings explicitly set forth in the statute, noting that "evidence presented in the District Courts contradicts" some of the legislative findings. [ ] In these circumstances, we said, "[u]ncritical deference to Congress' factual findings . . . is inappropriate." [ ]

Unlike in *Gonzales,* the relevant statute here does not set forth any legislative findings. Rather, one is left to infer that the legislature sought to further a constitutionally acceptable objective (namely, protecting women's health). [ ] For a district court to give significant weight to evidence in the judicial record in these circumstances is consistent with this Court's case law. As we shall describe, the District Court did so here. It did not simply substitute its own judgment for that of the legislature. It considered the evidence in the record—including expert evidence, presented in stipulations, depositions, and testimony. It then weighed the asserted benefits against the burdens. We hold that, in so doing, the District Court applied the correct legal standard.

IV

Undue Burden—Admitting-Privileges Requirement

Turning to the lower courts' evaluation of the evidence, we first consider the admitting-privileges requirement. Before the enactment of H.B. 2, doctors who provided abortions were required to "have admitting privileges *or* have a working arrangement with a physician(s) who has admitting privileges at a local hospital in order to ensure the necessary back up for medical complications." [ ] The new law changed this requirement by requiring that a "physician performing or inducing an abortion . . . must, on the date the abortion is performed or induced, have active admitting privileges at a hospital that . . . is located not further than 30 miles from the location at which the abortion is performed or induced." [ ] The District Court held that the legislative change imposed an "undue burden" on a woman's right to have an abortion. We conclude that there is adequate legal and factual support for the District Court's conclusion.

The purpose of the admitting-privileges requirement is to help ensure that women have easy access to a hospital should complications arise during an abortion procedure. [ ] But the District Court found that it brought about no such health-related benefit. The court found that "[t]he great weight of evidence demonstrates that, before the act's passage, abortion in Texas was extremely safe with particularly low rates of serious complications and virtually no deaths occurring on account of the procedure." [ ]. Thus, there was no significant health-related problem that the new law helped to cure.

[The Court then summarized the evidence that drew the trial court to that conclusion.]

* * *

At the same time, the record evidence indicates that the admitting-privileges requirement places a "substantial obstacle in the path of a woman's choice." [ ] [The Court pointed out that the evidence showed that many clinics closed when the admitting-privileges requirement went into effect.]

* * *

[There are many] common prerequisites to obtaining admitting privileges that have nothing to do with ability to perform medical procedures. See Brief for Medical Staff Professionals as *Amici Curiae* [ ] (listing, for example, requirements that an applicant has treated a high number of patients in the hospital setting in the past year, clinical data requirements, residency requirements, and other discretionary factors); see also Brief for American College of Obstetricians and Gynecologists [ ] ("[S]ome academic hospitals will only allow medical staff membership for clinicians who also . . . accept faculty appointments"). Again, returning to the District Court record, we note that Dr. Lynn of the McAllen clinic, a veteran obstetrics and gynecology doctor who estimates that he has delivered over 15,000 babies in his 38 years in practice was unable to get admitting privileges at any of the seven hospitals within 30 miles of his clinic. [ ] He was refused admitting privileges at a nearby hospital for reasons, as the hospital wrote, "not based on clinical competence considerations." [ ] The admitting-privileges requirement does not serve any relevant credentialing function.

In our view, the record contains sufficient evidence that the admitting-privileges requirement led to the closure of half of Texas' clinics, or thereabouts. Those closures meant fewer doctors, longer waiting times, and increased crowding. Record evidence also supports the finding that after the admitting-privileges provision went into effect, the "number of women of reproductive age living in a county . . . more than 150 miles from a provider increased from approximately 86,000 to 400,000 . . . and the number of women living in a county more than 200 miles from a provider from approximately 10,000 to 290,000." [ ]. We recognize that increased driving distances do not always constitute an "undue burden." [ ] But here, those increases are but one additional burden, which, when taken together with others that the closings brought about, and when viewed in light of the virtual absence of any health benefit, lead us to conclude that the record adequately supports the District Court's "undue burden" conclusion. [ ]

* * *

[T]he dissent suggests that one benefit of H.B. 2's requirements would be that they might "force unsafe facilities to shut down." [ ] To support that assertion, the dissent points to the Kermit Gosnell scandal. Gosnell, a physician in Pennsylvania, was convicted of first-degree murder and manslaughter [as a result of the operation of an abortion clinic]. . . . Gosnell's behavior was terribly wrong. But there is no reason to believe that an extra layer of regulation would have affected that behavior. Determined wrongdoers, already ignoring existing statutes and safety measures, are unlikely to be convinced to adopt safe practices by a new overlay of regulations. . . . The record contains nothing to suggest that H.B. 2 would be more effective than pre-existing Texas law at deterring wrongdoers like Gosnell from criminal behavior.

V

Undue Burden—Surgical-Center Requirement

The second challenged provision of Texas' new law sets forth the surgical-center requirement. Prior to enactment of the new requirement, Texas law required abortion facilities to meet a host of health and safety requirements [which are listed in the opinion by the court]. . . .

H.B. 2 added the requirement that an "abortion facility" meet the "minimum standards . . . for ambulatory surgical centers" under Texas law. [ ] The surgical-center regulations include, among other things, detailed specifications relating to the size of the nursing staff, building dimensions, and other building requirements. [The Court went on to list the many requirements imposed on surgical-centers.]

There is considerable evidence in the record supporting the District Court's findings indicating that the statutory provision requiring all abortion facilities to meet all surgical-center standards does not benefit patients and is not necessary. The District Court found that "risks are not appreciably lowered for patients who undergo abortions at ambulatory surgical centers as compared to nonsurgical-center facilities." [ ] The court added that women "will not obtain better care or experience more frequent positive outcomes at an ambulatory surgical center as compared to a previously licensed facility." [ ] And these findings are well supported.

The record makes clear that the surgical-center requirement provides no benefit when complications arise in the context of an abortion produced through medication. That is because, in such a case, complications would almost always arise only after the patient has left the facility. [ ] The record also contains evidence indicating that abortions taking place in an abortion facility are safe—indeed, safer than numerous procedures that take place outside hospitals and to which Texas does not apply its surgical-center requirements. . . . Nationwide, childbirth is 14 times more likely than abortion to result in death, [ ] but Texas law allows a midwife to oversee childbirth in the patient's own home. Colonoscopy, a procedure that typically takes place outside a hospital (or surgical center) setting, has a mortality rate 10 times higher than an abortion. [T]he mortality rate for liposuction, another outpatient procedure, is 28 times higher than the mortality rate for abortion. Medical treatment after an incomplete miscarriage often involves a procedure identical to that involved in a nonmedical abortion, but it often takes place outside a hospital or surgical center. And Texas partly or wholly grandfathers (or waives in whole or in part the surgical-center requirement for) about two-thirds of the facilities to which the surgical-center standards apply. But it neither grandfathers nor provides waivers for any of the facilities that perform abortions. [ ] These facts indicate that the surgical-center provision imposes "a requirement that simply is not based on differences" between abortion and other surgical procedures "that are reasonably related to" preserving women's health, the asserted "purpos[e] of the Act in which it is found." [ ]

* * *

At the same time, the record provides adequate evidentiary support for the District Court's conclusion that the surgical-center requirement places a substantial obstacle in the path of women seeking an abortion. The parties stipulated that the requirement would further reduce the number of abortion facilities available to seven or eight facilities . . . . In the District Court's view, the proposition that these "seven or eight providers could meet the demand of the entire State stretches credulity." [ ] We take this statement as a finding that these few facilities could not "meet" that "demand."

The Court of Appeals held that this finding was "clearly erroneous." . . . [W]e hold that the record provides adequate support for the District Court's finding.

* * *

More fundamentally, in the face of no threat to women's health, Texas seeks to force women to travel long distances to get abortions in crammedto-capacity superfacilities. Patients seeking these services are less likely to get the kind of individualized attention, serious conversation, and emotional support that doctors at less taxed facilities may have offered. Healthcare facilities and medical professionals are not fungible commodities. Surgical centers attempting to accommodate sudden, vastly increased demand, [ ] may find that quality of care declines. Another commonsense inference that the District Court made is that these effects would be harmful to, not supportive of, women's health. [ ].

* * *

We agree with the District Court that the surgical-center requirement, like the admitting-privileges requirement, provides few, if any, health benefits for women, poses a substantial obstacle to women seeking abortions, and constitutes an "undue burden" on their constitutional right to do so.

VI

* * *

JUSTICE GINSBURG, concurring.

The Texas law called H.B. 2 inevitably will reduce the number of clinics and doctors allowed to provide abortion services. Texas argues that H.B. 2's restrictions are constitutional because they protect the health of women who experience complications from abortions. In truth, "complications from an abortion are both rare and rarely dangerous." [ ] Many medical procedures, including childbirth, are far more dangerous to patients, yet are not subject to ambulatory-surgical-center or hospital admitting-privileges requirements. [ ] Given those realities, it is beyond rational belief that H.B. 2 could genuinely protect the health of women, and certain that the law "would simply make it more difficult for them to obtain abortions." [ ] When a State severely limits access to safe and legal procedures, women in desperate circumstances may resort to unlicensed rogue practitioners, *faute de mieux,* at great risk to their health and safety. [ ] So long as this Court adheres to *Roe v. Wade* [ ], and *Planned Parenthood of Southeastern Pa. v. Casey,* [ ] Targeted Regulation of Abortion Providers laws like H.B. 2 that "do little or nothing for health, but rather strew impediments to abortion," [ ] cannot survive judicial inspection.

JUSTICE THOMAS, dissenting.

* * *

II

Today's opinion . . . reimagines the undue-burden standard used to assess the constitutionality of abortion restrictions. Nearly 25 years ago, in *Planned Parenthood of Southeastern Pa. v. Casey* [ ] a plurality of this Court invented the "undue burden" standard as a special test for gauging the permissibility of abortion restrictions. *Casey* held that a law is unconstitutional if it imposes an "undue burden" on a woman's ability to choose to have an abortion, meaning that it "has the purpose or effect of placing a substantial obstacle in the path of a woman seeking an abortion of a nonviable fetus." [ ] *Casey* thus instructed courts to look to whether a law substantially impedes women's access to abortion, and whether it is reasonably related to legitimate state interests. As the Court explained, "[w]here it has a rational basis to act, and it does not impose an undue burden, the State may use its regulatory power" to regulate aspects of abortion procedures, "all in furtherance of its legitimate interests in regulating the medical profession in order to promote respect for life, including life of the unborn." [ ]

I remain fundamentally opposed to the Court's abortion jurisprudence. [ ] Even taking *Casey* as the baseline, however, the majority radically rewrites the undue-burden test in three ways. First, today's decision requires courts to "consider the burdens a law imposes on abortion access together with the benefits those laws confer." [ ] Second, today's opinion tells the courts that, when the law's justifications are medically uncertain, they need not defer to the legislature, and must instead assess medical justifications for abortion restrictions by scrutinizing the record themselves. [ ] Finally, even if a law imposes no "substantial obstacle" to women's access to abortions, the law now must have more than a "reasonabl[e] relat[ion] to . . . a legitimate state interest." [ ] (internal quotation marks omitted). These precepts are nowhere to be found in *Casey* or its successors, and transform the undue-burden test to something much more akin to strict scrutiny.

First, the majority's free-form balancing test is contrary to *Casey*. . . . Contrary to the majority's statements [ ] *Casey* did not balance the benefits and burdens of Pennsylvania's spousal and parental notification provisions, either. Pennsylvania's spousal notification requirement, the plurality said, imposed an undue burden because findings established that the requirement would "likely . . . prevent a significant number of women from obtaining an abortion"—not because these burdens outweighed its benefits. [ ]. And *Casey* summarily upheld parental notification provisions because even pre-*Casey* decisions had done so. [ ]

* * *

Second, by rejecting the notion that "legislatures, and not courts, must resolve questions of medical uncertainty," [ ] the majority discards another core element of the *Casey* framework. Before today, this Court had "given state and federal legislatures wide discretion to pass legislation in areas where there is medical and scientific uncertainty." . . .

Today, however, the majority refuses to leave disputed medical science to the legislature because past cases "placed considerable weight upon the evidence and argument presented in judicial proceedings." . . .

Finally, the majority overrules another central aspect of *Casey* by requiring laws to have more than a rational basis even if they do not substantially impede access to abortion. [ ] "Where [the State] *has a rational basis to act* and it does not impose an undue burden," this Court previously held, "the State may use its regulatory power" to impose regulations "in furtherance of its legitimate interests in regulating the medical profession in order to promote respect for life, including life of the unborn." [ ] No longer. Though the majority declines to say how substantial a State's interest must be, [ ] one thing is clear: The State's burden has been ratcheted to a level that has not applied for a quarter century. . . .

The majority's undue-burden test looks far less like our post-*Casey* precedents and far more like the strict-scrutiny standard that *Casey* rejected, under which only the most compelling rationales justified restrictions on abortion. [ ] One searches the majority opinion in vain for any acknowledgment of the "premise central" to *Casey*'s rejection of strict scrutiny: "that the government has a legitimate and substantial interest in preserving and promoting fetal life" from conception, not just in regulating medical procedures. . . . Moreover, by second-guessing medical evidence and making its own assessments of "quality of care" issues, [ ] the majority reappoints this Court as "the country's *ex officio* medical board with powers to disapprove medical and operative practices and standards throughout the United States." [ ] And the majority seriously burdens States, which must guess at how much more compelling their interests must be to pass muster and what "commonsense inferences" of an undue burden this Court will identify next.

III

. . . The undue-burden standard is just one variant of the Court's tiers-of-scrutiny approach to constitutional adjudication. And the label the Court affixes to its level of scrutiny in assessing whether the government can restrict a given right—be it "rational basis," intermediate, strict, or something else—is increasingly a meaningless formalism. As the Court applies whatever standard it likes to any given case, nothing but empty words separates our constitutional decisions from judicial fiat.

* * *

The Court should abandon the pretense that anything other than policy preferences underlies its balancing of constitutional rights and interests in any given case.

* * *

[Justice Alito's dissenting opinion, with whom the Chief Justice and Justice Thomas join, is omitted.]

* * *

NOTES AND QUESTIONS

1.   *The Role of Science.* Was the Texas legislature's fatal flaw its failure to make formal findings regarding the health benefits of H.B. 2 and include them in the text of the statute? If the legislature had done so, would the result have been different? Recall the question after *Carhart*: How closely should courts analyze the medical or scientific basis for state maternal or fetal health justifications? Does *Whole Women's Health* reflect the Court's willingness to scrutinize such justifications more closely than in *Carhart*?

2.   *Licensing Requirements & Scope of Practice.* Courts have had little trouble with the requirement (now in almost forty states) that only licensed physicians, not physicians' assistants or others, perform abortions, because the authority granted with professional licenses is a matter of state law. Such licensing requirements are seen as an uncontroversial way of protecting the pregnant woman, not imposing a burden on her decision to have an abortion. More recently, some states have expanded their scope of practice laws to allow non-physician certified or licensed health care professionals with the relevant specialized training to perform abortions in limited circumstances, and a growing number of professional organizations are calling for an expansion of the pool of clinicians able to provide medication abortions. Yet, significant regulatory and political barriers to doing this remain. See American Public Health Association, Policy Statement, Provision of Abortion Care by Advanced Practice Nurses and Physician Assistants (Nov. 1, 2011) (noting that the scope of primary and specialty practice of nurse practitioners, certified nurse midwives, and physician assistants includes management of conditions and procedures significantly more complex than medication or aspiration abortion; also noting evidence that with appropriate education and training, they can competently provide all components of medication abortion care). (Medication abortion is discussed further at Section IV.A., Note: The Distinction Between Contraception and Abortion).

3.   Whole Woman's Health *Revisited.* After *Whole Woman's Health*, two new appointments were made to the Supreme Court. Justice Gorsuch was appointed to fill the vacancy left by Justice Scalia's passing, and Justice Kennedy—the conservative justice whose vote was key to cementing the *Whole Women's Health* majority opinion—retired and was replaced by Justice Kavanaugh. This fueled speculation about the possibility that abortion jurisprudence would take a decisive turn toward allowing even greater state restrictions on abortion access. This was tested just four years later in *June Medical Services L.L.C. v. Russo*, 140 S.Ct. 2103 (2020), when the Court heard a constitutional challenge to a Louisiana admitting privileges law that was virtually identical to the Texas law struck down in *Whole Woman's Health*.

In a surprising development, Chief Justice Roberts, who originally sided with the dissent in *Whole Woman's Health*, voted with Justices Breyer, Ginsburg, Sotomayor, and Kagan to strike down the Louisiana law based on *Whole Woman's Health*. Justices Thomas, Alito, Gorsuch, and Kavanaugh dissented. This was not a simple application of precedent, however. There was no majority opinion affirming the underlying reasoning of *Whole Woman's Health*, but there were several opinions—a concurring opinion from Chief Justice Roberts, and several other dissenting opinions—that cast doubt on *Whole Woman's Health* legacy.

Justice Breyer wrote the plurality opinion in *June Medical*, joined by Justices Ginsburg, Sotomayor, and Kagan. It mirrored the majority's approach in *Whole Woman's Health*, reiterating the standard that "requires courts independently to review the legislative findings upon which an abortion-related statute rests and to weigh the law's 'asserted benefits against the burdens' it imposes on abortion access." Id. at 2112. Chief Justice Roberts wrote a separate opinion concurring in the judgment only, noting that his vote did not reflect a change of heart about *Whole Woman's Health*, but rather was required by *stare decisis*. Id. at 2133 (Roberts, C.J., concurring). Roberts rejected the plurality's interpretation of *Casey* as requiring courts to weigh the law's asserted benefits against the burdens it imposes on access:

> Nothing about *Casey* suggested that a weighing of costs and benefits of an abortion regulation was a job for the courts. On the contrary, we have explained that the "traditional rule" that "state and federal legislatures [have] wide discretion to pass legislation in areas where there is medical and scientific uncertainty" is "consistent with *Casey*." *Gonzales v. Carhart*, 550 U.S. 124 (2007). *Casey* instead focuses on the existence of a substantial obstacle, the sort of inquiry familiar to judges across a variety of contexts. . . .

> To be sure, the Court at times discussed the benefits of the regulations . . . . But in the context of *Casey*'s governing standard, these benefits were not placed on a scale opposite the law's burdens. Rather, *Casey* discussed benefits in considering the threshold requirement that the State have a "legitimate purpose" and that the law be "reasonably related to that goal."

> So long as that showing is made, the only question for a court is whether a law has the "effect of placing a substantial obstacle in the path of a woman seeking an abortion of a nonviable fetus." [ ]

The lack of a majority opinion as to the proper theory of the undue burden test that should be applied to regulations justified on health grounds has created uncertainty for lower courts. For example, in EMW Women's Surgical Center, P.S.C. v. Friedlander, 978 F.3d 418 (6th Cir. 2020), *rehearing en banc denied* Dec. 31, 2020, the Sixth Circuit reversed a district court ruling that found a Kentucky abortion law unconstitutional based on the *Whole Woman's Health* balancing test. In reversing and remanding this decision, a divided panel of the Sixth Circuit held that the balancing test from *Whole Woman's Health* is no longer controlling law after *June Medical*. See also Hopkins v.

Jegley, 968 F.3d 912, 915 (8th Cir. 2020) (per curiam) (combining the concurrence and dissenting opinions in *June Medical* to determine controlling law). The Seventh Circuit, however, has rejected this approach. See Planned Parenthood of Indiana and Kentucky, Inc. v. Box, 991 F.3d 740, 741 (7th Cir. 2021), *appeal filed* Mar. 29, 2021 (holding that because a majority of justices has not held otherwise, the balancing test set forth in Whole Woman's Health remains binding precedent). How, if at all, does *June Medical* change your answer to the question in Note 1?

    4.   *The Future of Abortion Jurisprudence.* The cases in this section have revealed the more significant twists and turns that abortion jurisprudence has taken since abortion was established as a constitutional right in *Roe v. Wade.* Despite the qualifications and limits that have been fleshed out since then, the Court has repeatedly affirmed the "essential" holding of *Roe* that anchors judicial scrutiny of abortion laws to a fundamental right of procreation. But how secure is this right? People on different sides of the abortion debate have long hoped or feared that a continued shift in the Supreme Court would eventually bring about *Roe's* undoing, if not through an explicit overruling of *Roe's* recognition of a fundamental right to reproductive choice, then through an equally effective evisceration of the current constitutional framework used to scrutinize laws burdening this right. Indeed, Justice Thomas has consistently expressed his disagreement with the Court's identification of abortion as a protected constitutional right and called for overruling *Roe v. Wade.*

    But a number of recent developments have revived and intensified speculation about *Roe's* fate. The first is the apparent significant shift in the Supreme Court, with Justices Gorsuch, Kavanaugh, and Barrett being appointed by President Trump, who promised as a candidate to nominate Supreme Court justices who would overturn *Roe v. Wade.* The second development is the Supreme Court's recent grant of certiorari in Dobbs v. Jackson Women's Health, 945 F.3d 265 (5th Cir. 2019), *cert. granted* 141 S.Ct. 2619 (2021). *Dobbs* is a challenge to Mississippi's Gestational Age Act, which prohibits abortions after 15 weeks' gestation—well before the viability of the fetus—except in medical emergency or in case of severe fetal abnormality. Both the District Court and Fifth Circuit found this to be a clear violation of longstanding abortion jurisprudence that prohibits bans on previability abortions, and there was no circuit court split that the Supreme Court needed to resolve. Rather, numerous scholars have observed that the only apparent reason for the Supreme Court granting certiorari on the question of whether all previability bans on abortion are unconstitutional would be to allow the state of Mississippi to present evidence challenging the viability framework used to protect abortion rights since *Roe* and *Casey.* Several states have already enacted so-called "trigger" bans—that is, laws creating previability abortion bans that are clearly prohibited under current abortion jurisprudence but will immediately take effect to the extent permitted by federal law if the Supreme Court overrules or substantially limits the constitutional right to abortion recognized in *Roe.* See State Legislation Tracker: Major

Developments in Sexual and Reproductive Health, Guttmacher Institute. Oral arguments have been scheduled for the October 2021 term, so a decision will not be issued until after the publication of this casebook. Developments in this area should be watched closely.

One final development has emerged rather suddenly as this casebook goes to print. In 2021, Texas enacted a law that would ban all abortions for pregnant patients if embryonic cardiac activity has been detected—activity that may be detectable as early as six weeks, before an embryo has a fully developed heart. Effectively, this means that abortion would be banned at six weeks, before most women know they are pregnant. Moreover, the law does not contain an exception for pregnancies that result from rape, sexual abuse, incest, or fetal defect incompatible with life after birth. Ordinarily, such a ban on previability abortions would be easily held unconstitutional under the framework established under *Roe* and *Casey,* and thus prevented from going into effect. The Texas law takes an unprecedented approach to enforcement, however, by deliberately failing to create a mechanism for state enforcement. Instead, the law effectively outsources enforcement by authorizing civil suits by private individuals against anyone who performs, aids and abets or intends to participate in a prohibited abortion. This absence of "state action" was designed to preclude those affected by the law from seeking an injunction against enforcement, and the strategy has been working so far.

The Fifth Circuit allowed the law to take effect in September 2021, and the U.S. Supreme Court initially refused to intervene at the request of providers. Whole Woman's Health v. Jackson, 141 S.Ct. 2494 (2021). Without a full argument or briefing, the Court issued a brief, late night order announcing its refusal to intervene, but Chief Justice Roberts and Justices Breyer, Sotomayor, and Kagan authored four dissenting opinions. Justice Sotomayor wrote a particularly scathing dissent that decried Texas' approach of effectively "deputizing [its] citizens as bounty hunters, offering them cash prizes for civilly prosecuting their neighbors' medical procedures" and that criticized the majority for "burying their heads in the sand" in the face of a "flagrantly unconstitutional law engineered to prohibit women from exercising their constitutional rights and evade judicial scrutiny." Id. at 2498. Not long thereafter, providers, along with the U.S. government, returned to the Supreme Court to request intervention again. This time the Court granted an expedited review with oral arguments set for November 2021—not to address the constitutionality of the Texas abortion ban, but to consider whether the design of the Texas law should be able to preclude providers, or the federal government, from enjoining enforcement of the law pending litigation. This time, the Court ruled that the providers may pursue a pre-enforcement challenge to the Texas ban against some government officials; but, once again, the Court refused to enjoin the Texas ban while the legal challenges in federal and state courts run their course. Whole Woman's Health v. Jackson, No. 21–463, slip op. (Dec. 10, 2021). Legal challenges to the Texas law are evolving quickly, but as of this writing, the Texas ban is still in effect.

NOTE: FEDERAL CONSCIENCE PROTECTIONS

Soon after *Roe v. Wade* the federal government enacted legislation known as the "Church Amendments" creating conscience protections for those objecting to providing abortion or sterilization. 42 U.S.C. § 300a–7. These Amendments apply to federal funds and grants provided pursuant to Population Research and Voluntary Family Planning Programs, and they make clear that such funds cannot be used to require individuals to perform or assist in abortions (or sterilizations), if contrary to the individual's religious or moral beliefs. Such funds also cannot be used to require entities to make their facilities available for the performance of abortions (or sterilizations), or to make personnel available for such procedures, if contrary to the moral or religious beliefs of the entity or personnel, respectively.

In 2004, Congress passed the Weldon Amendment, originally adopted as section 508(d) of the Labor-HHS Division of the 2005 Consolidated Appropriations Act, Public Law 108–447, 118 Stat. 2809, 3163 (Dec. 8, 2004), and readopted in each subsequent HHS appropriations act. The Weldon Amendment provides that "[n]one of the funds made available in this Act may be made available to a Federal agency or program, or to a state or local government, *if such agency, program, or government subjects any institutional or individual health care entity to discrimination on the basis that the health care entity does not provide, pay for, provide coverage of, or refer for abortions.*" The term "health care entity" is defined broadly to include health care professionals, hospitals and other health facilities, and health care organizations, such as health insurance plans. These statutory conscience protections remain in effect after the ACA, and the ACA extended conscience protection to providers participating in health plans offered through the exchange. The ACA language largely tracks the Weldon Amendment, prohibiting exchange plans from *discriminating against any individual health care provider or facility because of its unwillingness to provide, pay for, provide coverage of, or refer for abortions.*

When the Weldon Amendment was passed, legal challenges were brought based on concerns that it would conflict with other federal or state obligations to patients, putting funding recipients in a Catch 22: they feared that by obeying one law, they risked violating the other, and either way they risked losing funding. For example, in National Family Planning and Reproductive Health Assn. v. Gonzales, 468 F.3d 826 (D.C. Cir. 2006), the plaintiffs alleged a potential conflict between the Weldon Amendment, on the one hand, and plaintiffs' ethical and legal duties as family planning grant recipients under HHS regulations, on the other. HHS regulations required recipients to offer pregnant women the opportunity to be provided information and counseling regarding pregnancy termination. If a caregiver objected to providing this information, one way the plaintiff might respond would be to reassign that caregiver to another job; this would accommodate the worker's religious objections while ensuring patients get information that is legally and ethically required. In the lawsuit, the plaintiff expressed the concern that if the caregiver wanted to retain a pregnancy counseling job, such a reassignment may be viewed as "discrimination" under the Weldon Amendment. Without ruling on the merits, the court noted the absence of any indication that the federal government would view a reassignment or other attempts to navigate such a conflict as discrimination.

A California district court came to a similar conclusion in California v. U.S., 2008 WL 744840 (N.D. Cal. 2008). California officials claimed that the Weldon Amendment appeared to be in conflict with EMTALA, the federal law that obligates hospitals with emergency rooms to provide emergency care, as well as a state law that tried to balance provider conscience protections against duties to patients in emergency cases. California's state conscience law exempted medical personnel and facilities from participating in abortions if they objected on moral, ethical, or religious grounds, but it contained an exception for medical emergency situations and spontaneous abortions. In an unreported opinion, the court did not resolve the potential conflict. Rather, it held that California could not show an injury in fact (and thus did not have standing), because there was no clear indication from either the text of the Amendment or the federal regulator that California's emergency exception would be viewed as "discrimination" under the Weldon Amendment.

Although actual conflicts did not materialize in the above cases, during the Trump administration, HHS issued a rule that renewed concerns about how federal regulators would interpret the Weldon Amendment and other statutory conscience protections going forward. See Protecting Statutory Conscience Rights in Health Care; Delegations of Authority, 84 Fed. Reg. 23170 (May 21, 2019). The rule signaled the Trump administration's intention to interpret conscience statutes more broadly than in the past and to use its enforcement power against state laws intended to protect abortion access. But lawsuits delayed the rule's implementation, and since then the Biden Administration has signaled its intent to reverse the Trump-era approach.

For a discussion of the ethical considerations that inform conscience protections generally, see Section IV.C. below.

IV. CONTRACEPTION

Contraception, generally, has not been as controversial as abortion, and as we will in this section, the jurisprudence developed in response to contraceptive access questions has taken a somewhat different journey. This section begins with the constitutional origins of the right to procreative choice. Next, it explores how, over time, access to contraception has tended to receive broader public and private support, and even legal protection, based on health, economic, and gender equity concerns. Conflicts do arise, however, typically based on objections to certain forms of contraception as interfering with the reproductive process after "life" has begun, and often linked to religious freedom claims. The final part of this section reviews this conflict.

A. CONTRACEPTIVE USE AS A PRIVACY RIGHT

Government regulation of reproduction, in particular abortion and contraception, has ebbed and flowed throughout history. In Geoffrey Stone's book, Sex and the Constitution, he explains that during the 18th and early 19th centuries, there were no laws prohibiting either contraception or abortion before quickening. Indeed, during this time, he found that contraception and abortion were increasingly recognized as legitimate and morally acceptable practices to maintain and improve a family's economic welfare, and that advertisements for birth control products were commonplace. Social leaders concerned about overpopulation leading to poverty and social decline viewed birth control as a tool for promoting individual and societal well-being.

The increasing medicalization of the reproductive process, and a growing focus on the link between illicit sexual activity and reproductive control within powerful religious movements, brought greater public attention to reproduction, and this eventually led to greater regulation. In 1873, Congress enacted the Comstock Act, which prohibited anyone from mailing "any drug or medicine, or any article whatever, for the prevention of conception" or from mailing any information about how to obtain these articles. Anthony Comstock, the author of this act, considered contraceptive material "obscene" because it was believed to encourage immoral thoughts and behavior. According to Stone, Comstock wanted to outlaw birth control "because the availability of contraceptives reduces the risk that individuals who engage in premarital sex, extramarital sex, or prostitution will suffer the consequences of venereal disease or unwanted pregnancy."

In the next couple of decades, most states enacted similar criminal bans and some, like Connecticut went even further, criminalizing the *use* of contraception, as well as the act of helping someone to violate the law. This ban was ultimately invalidated by the Supreme Court in the seminal case Griswold v. Connecticut, 381 U.S. 479 (1965). In *Griswold,* an official of the Planned Parenthood League of Connecticut and a Yale physician were charged with aiding and abetting "the use of a drug, medicinal article, or instrument for the purpose of preventing conception," a crime under Connecticut law, by providing contraceptives to a married couple. The Supreme Court reversed their conviction. Justice Douglas, writing for the Court, concluded:

> The present case . . . concerns a relationship lying within the zone of privacy created by several fundamental constitutional guarantees. And it concerns a law which, in forbidding the *use* of contraceptives rather than regulating their manufacture or sale, seeks to achieve its goals by means having a maximum destructive impact upon that relationship. Such a law cannot stand in light of the familiar principle

so often applied by this Court, that a "governmental purpose to control or prevent activities constitutionally subject to state regulation may not be achieved by means which sweep unnecessarily broadly and thereby invade the area of protected freedoms." Would we allow the police to search the sacred precincts of marital bedrooms for telltale signs of the use of contraceptives? The very idea is repulsive to the notions of privacy surrounding the marriage relationship.

We deal with a right of privacy older than the Bill of Rights—older than our political parties, older than our school system. Marriage is a coming together for better or worse, hopefully enduring, and intimate to the degree of being sacred. It is an association that promotes a way of life, not causes; a harmony in living, not political faith; a bilateral loyalty, not commercial or social projects. Yet it is an association for as noble a purpose as any involved in our prior decisions.

381 U.S. at 484.

Griswold's articulation of the privacy right focused so heavily on preventing intrusions into the marital relationship that questions remained about the application of this right to non-married people. This was understandable in light of the moral aims of such laws to prevent pre-marital or extramarital sex. For example, three justices who concurred in *Griswold*, explained that they found the law invalid because they rejected the state's assertion of a rational relationship between the ban and the state's interest in discouraging extra-marital relations. But the justices went on to note that the Court's holding "in no way interferes with a State's proper regulation of sexual promiscuity or misconduct."

The Court was confronted with this question in 1972, in Eisenstadt v. Baird, 405 U.S. 438 (1972). The Court determined that a law that allowed married people, but not unmarried people, to have access to contraceptives violated the equal protection clause of the Fourteenth Amendment because there could be no rational basis for distinguishing between married and unmarried people in permitting access to contraceptives. The Court suggested that "if the right of privacy means anything, it is the right of the individual, married or single, to be free from unwarranted government intrusion into matters so fundamentally affecting a person as a decision whether to bear a child." In Carey v. Population Services International, 431 U.S. 678 (1977), the Court confirmed this right not only prohibits bans on the use of contraception, it prevents any *unjustified intrusion by* the State, such as a ban on the *distribution* or sale of contraceptives.

But what constitutes an unjustified intrusion? Relying on *Roe v. Wade*, the Court in *Carey v. Population Services International* made clear that recognizing a privacy right for procreative choice does not "automatically invalidate every state regulation in this area." Id. at 685-685. It noted that some regulations may not infringe on individual choice at all, and "even a burdensome regulation may be validated by a sufficiently compelling state interest." Id. at 686. As noted in Chapter 2 and discussed further below, the FDA has authority to approve and monitor the safety of drugs and devices, including prescription contraception. States also have broad power to regulate health and safety. But in *Carey*, the Court struck down a state law limiting the distribution of *nonprescription* contraceptives to licensed pharmacists, noting that the limit on these "nonhazardous" forms of contraception bore no relation to the State's interest in protecting health. A plurality opinion also invalidated a provision banning distribution of nonprescription contraceptives to those under 16.

NOTE: THE DISTINCTION BETWEEN CONTRACEPTION AND ABORTION

Early objections to the use and distribution of contraceptives tended to focus on their use for pregnancy prevention and they often applied to any type of birth control. More recently, however, objections or restrictions tend to target certain forms of contraceptives because of how and when they work. (A detailed explanation of the process of human reproduction is provided at the beginning of Section VII.A (Assisted Reproductive Technologies) of this chapter.)

Contraception is designed to work by preventing fertilization. Some forms are taken or used prior to intercourse, while others may be taken after intercourse. Two examples of medication that work after intercourse but prior to fertilization are Plan B (levonorgestrel) and ella (ulipristal acetate), also commonly referred to as "morning after pills." They are designed to avoid the development of pregnancy by inhibiting ovulation or follicle rupture. Questions have been raised, however, about whether such pills may alter the uterine lining and, possibly, make it less likely that a fertilized ovum will enter the uterus or implant in the uterine wall, though recent studies do not seem to support this theory. For those who believe that life begins at fertilization, concern that morning after pills may prevent implantation of a fertilized ovum has fueled opposition to the pills.

Plan B became available in 2006 after a long and highly political history. In 1999 an FDA advisory panel had recommended that the drug be made available over the counter for all purchasers, but objections (arguably political and arguably medical) caused the FDA to delay approval until 2003 and then require a prescription for this medication. After a threat by some members of the Senate to withhold confirmation of a newly appointed FDA Commissioner in 2006, Plan B was finally made available over the counter for persons over 18, and that age was subsequently lowered to 17. See Gardiner Harris, Morning-After Pill: Politics and the F.D.A., N.Y. Times (Aug. 28, 2015). Plan B, a two-dose regimen, was eventually replaced by Plan B One Step, which as the name suggests, is a one-dose regimen. Plan B One Step is effective at reducing the risk of pregnancy if taken within 72 hours of intercourse, and its efficacy increases if taken within 24 hours. Approved in 2010 after its own long medical and political battle, ella works in largely the same way, but can be effective within five days of having sex.

Devices and medication that prevent fertilization or implantation are considered by the medical community to be *contraceptives*, that is a form of pregnancy prevention. Use of Mifepristone (RU-486), on the other hand, is classified as a *medication abortion* because it works after pregnancy. It is designed to disrupt implantation of the fertilized embryo and to change the uterus to become less hospitable to the fertilized ovum, eventually expelling it. Mifepristone is available only through prescription and dispensed only by a certified health care provider who meets certain qualifications.

The generally accepted medical definitions used to distinguish contraception from medication abortion may not be accepted by those who believe that life begins at fertilization. People who hold this belief may have no objections to contraception that prevents fertilization; but they view medications or devices that work after fertilization as terminating life and thus would characterize them as abortifacients. This definitional disagreement can be significant in a number of contexts. As described in this Note, it can fuel political opposition to government action that would facilitate access to certain drugs. But it may also be relevant to the question of how far government can go in requiring individuals or entities to provide contraception as part of health care, a question we revisit in Section C below.

B. ACCESS TO FUNDING FOR CONTRACEPTION

As noted in Section III, the Supreme Court has made clear that a constitutional right to have one's procreative choices protected from unwarranted government intrusion does not create an entitlement to government funding or subsidization of those services. Nonetheless, other legal and policy avenues have facilitated access to funding for contraception. Antidiscrimination law has been one such avenue. For example, in Erickson v. Bartell Drug Company, 141 F. Supp. 2d 1266 (2001), plaintiff employees successfully challenged the exclusion of prescription contraception from an otherwise comprehensive employment-based insurance plan, on the grounds that such an exclusion constituted prohibited discrimination on the basis of sex. Plaintiffs brought the claim under Title VII of the 1964 Civil Rights Acts, as amended by the 1978 Pregnancy Discrimination Act.

An excerpt of *Erickson* is reproduced at Chapter 6, Section IV.B. (Gender Discrimination) of this casebook. After reading *Erickson*, consider the following Notes and Questions.

NOTES AND QUESTIONS

1. *Gender Equity and the ACA's Contraceptive Mandate.* Although the *Erickson* plaintiffs won, Title VII could provide only limited protection because it did not apply to non-employment-based health plans or to health care

providers. The ACA filled this gap, by expanding gender equity protections in several ways. One is the inclusion of a preventive health mandate, interpreted as requiring coverage for prescription contraception. Notably, federal regulators have asserted that this mandate serves compelling health and gender equity goals. For more on the limits of Title VII and the importance of the contraceptive mandate in the ACA, see Notes 2 and 5, following the *Erickson* case.

2. *Title VII's Relationship to the ACA's Sex Nondiscrimination Provision.* The ACA also created a new health-specific prohibition on sex discrimination in its Section 1557 antidiscrimination provision. For more on the relevance of Title VII to defining the scope of Section 1557's antidiscrimination protections, see Chapter 6, Section IV.B.

3. *Federal & State Family Planning Programs.* Various government health programs also provide coverage for prescription contraception for low-income individuals. For example, Medicaid plays a critical role in providing family planning services, a federally mandated benefit, to low-income populations. Although states have some discretion to determine the specific services they will cover through Medicaid, contraception is one of the primary services covered and most states offer broad coverage. See Chapter 10. Contraception is also an important service in other family planning and disease prevention programs, such as the Title X Family Planning Program.

4. *Other State Actions to Facilitate Access.* By the time of the ACA, twenty-eight states already required some form of contraceptive coverage in at least some health insurance plans sold in their states. But many states have gone further, to also require some providers to provide access to certain kinds of contraceptive care. For example, eighteen states and the District of Columbia require emergency rooms to provide information about emergency contraception to sexual assault victims, and thirteen states and DC require emergency rooms to dispense the drug to sexual assault victims on request. Four states require either pharmacies or pharmacists to fill all valid prescriptions, and eight states allow pharmacists to dispense emergency contraception without a physician's prescription under certain conditions. States have also expanded minors' authority to consent to health care generally, but in particular relating to sexual and reproductive health care. See Guttmacher Institute, Fact Sheets on Emergency Contraception and Minors' Access to Contraceptive Services (Jul. 1, 2021).

C. THE CLASH BETWEEN GOVERNMENT MANDATES AND RELIGIOUS OR MORAL BELIEFS

In response to government action to expand contraceptive access, political and legal challenges have emerged. In particular, those who object to certain medication or devices on religious or moral grounds have sought exemptions from government mandates to provide or pay for contraception. As described below, this has led to a rather dramatic back-and-forth in the regulatory space and in the courts. Indeed, several challenges involving religious objections to the mandate have reached the Supreme Court in a very short span of time, and yet the conflict continues.

1. Religious Objections to the ACA Contraceptive Mandate

Early in the process of issuing regulatory rules for coverage of preventive services under the ACA, including the prescription contraception mandate, the Obama administration included a very narrow exemption for *religious employers* that (1) have the purpose of religious inculcation of religious values, (2) employ primarily people who share its religious values, (3) primarily serve people who share its religious tenets, and (4) are non-profit organizations established to be a church, association of churches or a religious order. See Coverage of Certain Preventive Services Under the Affordable Care Act, 78 Fed. Reg. 39870 (Jul. 2, 2013). Essentially, this exemption meant *churches* and other *houses of worship* did not have to provide contraception coverage, and it applied to some religious primary and secondary schools organized to inculcate religious views and designed for attendance by coreligionists only.

The exemption did not extend to most religious colleges and universities that had students of all faiths, nor to social service organizations that provided service to people of all faiths. These religious organizations would have to provide insurance that included contraception. Because the rule was later extended to cover student health plans, the fact that religious colleges (and, in particular, Catholic universities open to students of all faiths) were not exempt proved to be very significant. Although the scope of this exemption was consistent with the kinds of religious exemptions provided in state mandates at the time, it met with strong objections from religiously affiliated organizations that the exemption was too narrow. Opposition, led by the U.S. Conference of Catholic Bishops, evangelical Christians, and conservative politicians, claimed the rule was an unconscionable intrusion on religious liberty.

Obama's Compromise: Accommodation for Religious Nonprofits

In the face of deeply held and conflicting views on the issue, the Obama administration tried to fashion a compromise that would ensure women received coverage for contraception while allowing religious employers and universities to opt out of participation in the provision of any services they found to be morally objectionable. New regulations were issued, extending protection to the *religious nonprofits* (schools and social service organizations) previously left out, if they had religious objections to providing coverage for contraceptive services required by law. See Coverage of Certain Preventive Services Under the Affordable Care Act, supra. See also Robert Pear, Birth Control Rule Altered to Allay Religious Objections, N.Y. Times (Feb. 2, 2013).

Importantly, the regulations did not *exempt* these religious nonprofits from the mandate; instead, they established an *accommodation* that would allow these religious nonprofits (classified as *"eligible organizations"* in the regulation) to "opt-out" of providing contraceptive coverage for their employees by formally announcing that they had religious objections to offering this coverage. This would not impede access, though, because it would trigger a process by which the health insurer or other third party would be required to provide the contraceptive coverage, with no cost sharing by the employee and without the employer having to pay for it or help arrange for its provision.

Legal Challenges to the Obama Era Compromise

There were two types of challenges to the Obama era rules worthy of note. The first was by for-profit companies, whose owners operated their companies in accord with religious principles, but who were not entitled to an accommodation under the Obama compromise. Numerous companies filed legal challenges to the contraceptive mandate on religious freedom grounds, and the first suit to reach the Supreme Court was Burwell v. Hobby Lobby, Inc., 573 U.S. 682 (2014). In *Hobby Lobby*, the Supreme Court determined that closely held private corporations could assert the religious liberty interests of their owners, and that the ACA's mandate to provide contraception was a violation of the federal Religious Freedom Restoration Act (RFRA), 42 U.S.C.A. § 2000bb–1(a), (b).

Justice Alito, who wrote for the 5–4 majority finding that the contraceptive mandate violated RFRA, summarized his opinion this way:

> We must decide in these cases whether the Religious Freedom Restoration Act . . . (RFRA) [ ] permits the United States Department of Health and Human Services (HHS) to demand that three closely held corporations provide health-insurance coverage for methods of contraception that violate the sincerely held religious beliefs of the companies' owners. We hold that the regulations that impose this obligation violate RFRA, which prohibits the Federal Government from taking any action that substantially burdens the exercise of religion unless that action constitutes the least restrictive means of serving a compelling government interest.

> In holding that the HHS mandate is unlawful, we reject HHS's argument that the owners of the companies forfeited all RFRA protection when they decided to organize their businesses as corporations rather than sole proprietorships or general partnerships. The plain terms of RFRA make it perfectly clear that Congress did not discriminate in this way against men and women who wish to run their businesses as for-profit corporations in the manner required by their religious beliefs.

Since RFRA applies in these cases, we must decide whether the challenged HHS regulations substantially burden the exercise of religion, and we hold that they do. The owners of the businesses have religious objections to abortion, and according to their religious beliefs the four contraceptive methods at issue are abortifacients. If the owners comply with the HHS mandate, they believe they will be facilitating abortions, and if they do not comply, they will pay a very heavy price—as much as $1.3 million per day, or about $475 million per year, in the case of one of the companies. If these consequences do not amount to a substantial burden, it is hard to see what would.

Under RFRA, a Government action that imposes a substantial burden on religious exercise must serve a compelling government interest, and we assume that the HHS regulations satisfy this requirement. But in order for the HHS mandate to be sustained, it must also constitute the least restrictive means of serving that interest, and the mandate plainly fails that test. There are other ways in which Congress or HHS could equally ensure that every woman has cost-free access to the particular contraceptives at issue here and, indeed, to all FDA-approved contraceptives.

In fact, HHS has already devised and implemented a system that seeks to respect the religious liberty of religious nonprofit corporations while ensuring that the employees of these entities have precisely the same access to all FDA-approved contraceptives as employees of companies whose owners have no religious objections to providing such coverage. [Eds. Note: This refers to the opt-out scheme, described above.] The employees of these religious nonprofit corporations still have access to insurance coverage without cost sharing for all FDA-approved contraceptives; and according to HHS, this system imposes no net economic burden on the insurance companies that are required to provide or secure the coverage.

Although HHS has made this system available to religious nonprofits that have religious objections to the contraceptive mandate, HHS has provided no reason why the same system cannot be made available when the owners of for-profit corporations have similar religious objections. We therefore conclude that this system constitutes an alternative that achieves all of the Government's aims while providing greater respect for religious liberty. And under RFRA, that conclusion means that enforcement of the HHS contraceptive mandate against the objecting parties in these cases is unlawful.

As this description of our reasoning shows, our holding is very specific. We do not hold, as the principal dissent alleges, that for-profit corporations and other commercial enterprises can "opt out of any law (saving only tax laws) they judge incompatible with their sincerely held religious beliefs." [ ] (opinion of Ginsburg, J.). Nor do we hold, as the dissent implies, that such corporations have free rein to take steps that impose "disadvantages . . . on others" or that require "the general public [to] pick up the tab." [ ] And we certainly do not hold or suggest that "RFRA demands accommodation of a for-profit corporation's religious beliefs no matter the impact that accommodation may have on . . . thousands of women employed by Hobby Lobby." [ ] The effect of the HHS-created accommodation on the women employed by Hobby Lobby and the other companies involved in these cases would be precisely zero. Under that accommodation, these women would still be entitled to all FDA-approved contraceptives without cost sharing.

Burwell v. Hobby Lobby, Inc., 573 U.S. 682, 688–693 (2014).

The second type of challenge brought against the Obama era rule was based on objections to the opt-out process itself. Numerous religious organizations and employers filed suit alleging that the requirement they submit a formal written document asking to be relieved of the mandate violated RFRA, because it constituted facilitation of a sin. The legal issues at play in the courts were whether the opt-out process itself was a substantial burden, whether the governmental interest was compelling, and whether there was a less restrictive way of serving the same interest. All but one of the courts of appeals hearing these challenges held that the accommodation adequately protected plaintiffs' religious freedom. See, e.g., Little Sisters of the Poor v. Burwell, 794 F.3d 1151 (10th Cir. 2016) (holding that the accommodation scheme does not substantially burden their religious exercise under RFRA or infringe upon their First Amendment rights). Several of these challenges were consolidated and addressed by the Supreme Court in *Zubik v. Burwell*, but the Court expressed no view on the merits of the RFRA claims. Instead, there was a unanimous decision to remand the cases to afford the parties "an opportunity to arrive at an approach going forward that accommodates petitioners' religious exercise while at the same time ensuring that women covered by petitioners' health plans 'receive full and equal health coverage, including contraceptive coverage.'" 578 U.S. 403, 403 (2016). In October 2017, however, the Trump administration issued expansive new rules (described below) which appeared to relieve these entities of the procedural obligations to which they objected. The plaintiffs entered into agreements with the government to dismiss their cases because it looked like the new rules had settled the issue in their favor.

Trump Era Rules: Expanding Exemptions & Reducing Access

On October 13, 2017, two interim final rules were issued by the regulatory agencies charged with implementation of the ACA. Religious Exemptions and Accommodations for Coverage of Certain Preventive Services Under the Affordable Care Act, 82 Fed. Reg. 47792 (Oct. 13, 2017), and Moral Exemptions and Accommodations for Coverage of Certain Preventive Services Under the Affordable Care Act, 82 Fed. Reg. 47838 (Oct. 13, 2017). These rules expanded the scope of exemptions allowed in two important ways. First, the new rules allowed any objecting religious employers or universities, even those who expressly hire and recruit people from diverse religious and ideological backgrounds, to get an exemption from the law, as opposed to requiring them to follow an opt-out process provided as an accommodation. The difference between accommodation and exemption means the difference between an employee or student getting contraceptive coverage or not. The opt-out process was created precisely to accommodate religious objections while protecting access to coverage. Granting these entities exemptions means that covered individuals would not be offered the objected-to contraception by any means.

Second, the new rules allowed those who were not previously eligible for either an exemption or accommodation to now claim an exemption, as long as they have *moral* objections to the rule. This means the exemption is no longer specifically linked to religious exercise, which is the basis of the protections in RFRA. It also increased the number of entities that could deny contraceptive coverage for employees or students. The rules did preserve the opt-out process as an option; but it would not be required.

Legal Challenges to the Trump Administration Rules

Lawsuits challenging the new rules were filed immediately. A nationwide injunction was affirmed by the Third Circuit in *Pennsylvania v. President of United States*, 930 F.3d 543 (2019), but the decision was ultimately reversed by the Supreme Court in *Little Sisters of the Poor Saints Peter and Paul Home v. Pennsylvania*, 140 S.Ct. 2367 (2020). In a 7–2 decision by Justice Thomas, the Court held that the ACA provided statutory authority for the government to promulgate exemptions to the preventive services mandate, and it rejected the claim that the rules were procedurally invalid due to the agency's failure to issue a notice of proposed rulemaking.

Although the Court permitted the rules to take effect, outstanding questions remained. First, the Supreme Court did not decide whether the scope of the exemptions were required or even permitted by RFRA. The Court also did not address the specific question of whether the rules were arbitrary and capricious in light of the federal government's failure to require an accommodation process that would also protect women's health and access to contraceptive care. At least four Justices—Ginsburg, Bryer, Kagan, and Sotomayor—seemed amendable to this as a basis for future challenge. Justices Alito and Gorsuch, on the other hand, made clear they were ready to go further than the majority to find that RFRA actually compelled the religious exemption being challenged. Id. at 287 (Alito, J., concurring). But because the Court did not go so far as to hold that the Trump exemptions were required by RFRA, this seemed to leave room for the Biden administration to reconsider the rule and return to the accommodation-based approach of the Obama administration, something Biden has signaled a willingness to do.

NOTES AND QUESTIONS

1. *RFRA Challenge: Substantial Burden on Free Exercise of Religion*. In *Hobby Lobby*, the plaintiffs objected to two forms of intrauterine devices and two forms of emergency contraception forms on religious grounds. They believed that these medications and devices worked after fertilization and thus were abortifacients. They claimed that requiring them to include these forms of contraception in their health plans substantially burdened their free exercise of religion. The Court did not engage in the debate over where the line should be drawn between abortion and contraception, for purposes of evaluating plaintiffs' claim of a substantial burden. In religious freedom cases, courts have been careful not to weigh or evaluate the relevant doctrines of faith. As long as a belief is sincere, the Court will not second-guess the underlying basis for that belief.

2. *RFRA Challenge: Does the Contraceptive Mandate Serve a Compelling Interest*? RFRA provides that government action imposing a substantial burden on religious exercise must serve a "compelling government interest." The majority did not, however, discuss whether it viewed the government's interest as compelling. It merely assumed such an interest was met for purposes of its analysis and found the mandate unconstitutional on a different basis.

Addressing potential unintended pregnancies is widely recognized as an important issue, but would a majority of the Court consider it compelling? Consider that around the time of this case, statistics showed that half of all pregnancies were unintended, a million women who do not want to become pregnant have unprotected sex each day, and 25,000 women become pregnant through sexual assault each year. See Gardiner Harris, F.D.A. Approves 5-Day Emergency Contraception, N.Y. Times (Aug. 13, 2010). Studies have also shown that cost-sharing can act as a barrier to women getting birth control, or the most effective form of birth control.

What about regulators' initial assertions that the mandate serves compelling public health and gender equity goals? How much weight should these be given in assessing the strength of the interest? Should subsequent regulators be bound by a prior administration's conclusions that the contraceptive mandate serves compelling public health and gender equity goals? Although the Obama administration had consistently asserted the mandate served a compelling interest in regulatory action and litigation, the Trump administration seemed to retreat from this position. *See Little Sisters*, 140 S.Ct. at 2392 (Alito, J., concurring) ("In *Hobby Lobby*, the Government asserted and we assumed for the sake of argument that the Government had a compelling interest in 'ensuring that all women have access to all FDA-approved contraceptives without cost sharing'. [ ] Now, the Government concedes that it lacks a compelling interest in providing such access, [ ] and this time the Government is correct.") *But see id.* at 2399 (Kagan, J., concurring) (noting that "[r]ather than dispute HRSA's prior finding that the mandate is 'necessary for women's health and well-being,' the Departments left that determination in place .... [thus] commit[ing] themselves to minimizing the impact on contraceptive coverage, even as they sought to protect employers with continuing religious objections.").

    3.   Little Sisters *vs.* Hobby Lobby. In *Hobby Lobby*, the Court's holding emphasized the fact that the government had already created an opt-out program that could accommodate religious objections without impeding access to contraception. In other words, employees would not be harmed by granting employers' relief because of the opt-out accommodation, which helped ensure prescription contraception coverage. *Little Sisters*, on the other hand, did not address the potential harm to employees from the blanket exemption created by the Trump-era rules. Is a blanket exemption that fails to try to minimize harm to those denied coverage consistent with the reasoning in *Hobby Lobby*? Should government have to require objecting entities to follow the opt-out process to preserve access, instead of simply giving them an exemption?

2.   Provider Conscientious Refusals to State Mandates

    As explained in Section IV.B. above, states have enacted their own mandates to ensure access to contraceptive care—whether through private insurance mandates or requirements that certain types of health care providers must provide contraceptive care. Just as some organizations object to funding certain forms of contraception, health care professionals and entities, including hospitals and pharmacies, have raised religious objections to dispensing or even giving information about certain forms contraception. But religious challenges to state mandates tend not to be successful. First, RFRA only applies to federal law. State law challenges are subject to the Free Exercise Clause of the federal constitution, which unlike RFRA, does not require exemptions from neutral laws of general applicability. See, e.g., Storman's, Inc. v. Selecky, 794 F.3d 1064 (9th Cir. 2015), *cert. denied* 136 S.Ct. 2433 (2016) (holding that the Free Exercise Clause provided for only rational basis review of a state's requirement that a pharmacist dispense emergency contraception). Although state mandates have also been challenged under state constitutional free exercise protections, the results tend to be the same. See, e.g., Catholic Charities v. Superior Court, 85 P.3d 67 (Cal. 2004) (rejecting a state free exercise challenge to the state's Women's Contraceptive Equity Act). Twelve states have statutory conscience protections that allow health care providers to refuse to provide contraception-related services.

NOTE: THE ETHICS OF CONSCIENTIOUS REFUSALS

The materials in the first four sections of this chapter demonstrate that questions about the regulation of access to abortion and contraception can trigger sharply divided views shaped by deeply held beliefs. Such disputes implicate ethical questions about how to balance protections for religious and moral objections to certain procedures with patients' health care needs and gender equity concerns. Claims for legal protections of providers and other entities that refuse to provide or pay for certain care on religious or moral grounds are grounded in claims about the importance of conscience. Consider how one bioethicist and physician has explained the role of conscience in such conflicts:

> Conscientious persons strive to preserve moral integrity. This requires that their external behavior be congruent with their conscience's internal dictates about what they take to be morally right and feel compelled to do. In our morally diverse world, conscientious persons may come into conflict with each other and with society's moral values. . . .

> Any society purporting to serve the good of its members is therefore obliged to protect the exercise of conscience and conscientious objection. However, this involves a serious dilemma for any pluralist, democratic, liberal, or constitutional state. On the one hand, such a society is committed to tolerance to religious diversity, freedom of individual choice, and "neutrality" with respect to religious belief. On the other hand, optimizing freedom of conscience for some individuals may often limit the legal rights, social entitlements, and moral beliefs of others.

Edmund D. Pellegrino, The Physician's Conscience, Conscience Clauses, and Religious Belief: A Catholic Perspective, 30 Fordham Urban L.J. 221, 221 (2002). In this essay, Dr. Pellegrino explored the ethical implications of religious health care professionals and institutions objecting to procedures considered standard in the medical community. He questioned whether conscience clauses can provide adequate protection for religious and moral beliefs, such as where they are written narrowly to only apply to certain kinds of providers. In addressing the conflict between patients' needs and physicians' conscience, he stated that physicians should make their positions publicly known so that patients know in advance of a crisis that what they want may not be care the physician is willing to provide. At the same time, he concluded that "[t]he only viable course for the religious physician is to maintain fidelity to moral integrity and dictates of conscience" by refusing to perform a morally objectionable procedure or treatment, even in emergencies or remote areas where the choice of physicians is limited. For some religious professionals, this would include refusing to refer a patient to another practitioner willing to perform the disputed treatment, because to do so would be cooperation in an illicit act, making the person a moral accomplice.

Compare this approach to the ethics opinion on conscientious refusals in reproductive health published by the American College of Obstetrics and Gynecology (ACOG). ACOG has offered several recommendations, which it believes "maximize respect for health care professionals' consciences without compromising the health and well-being of the women they serve":

1. In the provision of reproductive services, the patient's well-being must be paramount. Any conscientious refusal that conflicts with a patient's well-being should be accommodated only if the primary duty to the patient can be fulfilled.

2. Health care providers must impart accurate and unbiased information so that patients can make informed decisions about their health care. . . .

3. Where conscience implores physicians to deviate from standard practices, including abortion, sterilization and provision of contraceptives, they must provide potential patients with accurate and prior notice of their personal moral commitments. . . .

4. Physicians and other health care professionals have the duty to refer patients in a timely manner to other providers if they do not feel that they can in conscience provide the standard reproductive services that their patients request.

5. In an emergency in which referral is not possible or might negatively affect a patient's physical or mental health, providers have an obligation to provide medically indicated and requested care regardless of the provider's personal moral objections.

6. In resource poor areas, access to safe and legal reproductive services should be maintained. . . .

7. Lawmakers should advance policies that balance protection of providers' consciences with the critical goal of ensuring timely, effective, evidence-based, and safe access to all women seeking reproductive services.

The Limits of Conscientious Refusal in Reproductive Medicine. ACOG Committee Opinion No. 385. American College of Obstetricians and Gynecologists. Obstet Gynecol 2007; 110:1203–8 (reaffirmed 2016).

V. STERILIZATION

Voluntary sterilization, like most forms of contraception, is generally considered less controversial than abortion. Nonetheless, as with abortion and contraception, some patients have had difficulty accessing sterilization procedures because of insurance exclusions and provider refusals to treat. Recall that the Church Amendments (discussed in the Note on Federal Conscience Protections at the end of the Section III of this chapter) provided that receipt of federal funding could not be used to require recipients to provide abortions or *sterilizations*. Some consider sterilization to be a sin because it separates sexual activity from a procreative purpose. In fact, the Church Amendments were a response to an injunction initially issued by a Montana district court requiring a religiously-affiliated hospital to perform a tubal ligation despite religious objections, based in part on the fact it received federal funding. The injunction was eventually dissolved, however, based on the Church Amendments. See Taylor v. St. Vincent Hospital, 369 F. Supp. 948 (D. Mont. 1973), aff'd, 523 F. 2d 75 (9th Cir. 1975). Today, eighteen states allow health care providers to refuse to provide sterilization services. Many of the issues discussed under the sections on abortion and contraception are thus relevant to sterilization as well.

Sterilization practices also implicate reproductive justice concerns often neglected in debates over access to contraception and abortion. While much of the "reproductive rights" movement has focused on barriers to preventing or terminating pregnancy, some individuals experience *barriers to choosing procreation*. There is a long and troubling history of forced and coerced sterilization of certain groups, which complicates discussions about sterilization as a reproductive health issue.

Forced and Coerced Sterilization

Discussions about sterilization often begin with the development of the eugenics movement in the late 19th century. Among the groups targeted for sterilization were people believed to have intellectual disabilities, as well as those engaging in criminal behavior or behavior viewed as immoral, reflecting low intelligence, and/or reflecting poor character. Despite lack of evidence of a link between such characteristics and heritability, some believed society could "purify" its gene pool by sterilizing those who would "pollute" it. The aim of the eugenics movement was articulated in a now infamous decision by Justice Holmes in Buck v. Bell, 274 U.S. 200 (1927). That case dealt with an attempt by the State of Virginia to sterilize Carrie Buck, who had been committed to the State Colony for Epileptics and the Feeble Minded. This action was opposed on the grounds that the statute authorizing sterilization violated the Fourteenth Amendment by denying Ms. Buck due process of law and the equal protection of the law. Justice Holmes responded:

> Carrie Buck is a feeble minded white woman who was committed to the State Colony above mentioned in due form. She is the daughter of a feeble minded mother in the same institution and the mother of an illegitimate feeble minded child . . . .

> [The lower court found] "that Carrie Buck is the probable potential parent of socially inadequate offspring, likewise afflicted, that she may be sterilized without detriment to her general health and that her welfare and that of society will be promoted by her sterilization." . . . We have seen more than once that the public welfare may call upon the best citizens for their lives. It would be strange if it could not call upon those who already sapped the strength of the state for these

lesser sacrifices, often not felt to be such by those concerned, in order to prevent our being swamped with incompetence. It is better for all the world if instead of waiting to execute degenerate offspring for crime, or to let them starve for their imbecility, society can prevent those who are manifestly unfit from continuing their kind. The principle that sustains compulsory vaccination is broad enough to cover cutting the fallopian tubes. [ ] Three generations of imbeciles are enough.

* * *

The Supreme Court addressed eugenic sterilizations once more, in Skinner v. Oklahoma, 316 U.S. 535 (1942). The Court determined that the equal protection clause prohibited Oklahoma from enforcing a statute requiring sterilization of persons convicted of repeated criminal acts only for crimes within special categories. White collar crimes were exempted from these categories, and the Supreme Court's holding was based on the state's irrational distinction between blue collar (sterilizable) and white collar (unsterilizable) crimes. The Court was asked to, but did not, overrule Buck v. Bell.

The Supreme Court has never overturned the decision in Buck v. Bell, although it is of questionable precedential value today. Society's perception of people with disabilities has undergone significant change and, especially after the Nazi experience, for which Buck v. Bell was cited as precedent, arguments based upon eugenics are now held in low regard. In fact, when Carrie Buck was discovered in the Appalachian hills in 1980, she was found to be mentally competent and extremely disappointed that throughout her life she was unable to bear another child. Subsequent research determined that Carrie Buck's illegitimate daughter Vivian, who was conceived as the result of a rape by a relative of Carrie Buck's foster parents, was an honor roll student. At the trial that, on appeal, gave rise to Justice Holmes' regrettable opinion, Carrie Buck was poorly represented by a lawyer who did not develop the evidence or the legal arguments necessary to overcome the statute or its application to his client. For an engaging account of this case by a scholar who met Ms. Buck in the 1980s, and for pictures of Ms. Buck and her daughter, see Paul Lombardo, Facing Carrie Buck, 33 Hastings Ctr. Rep. (March–April) 14 (2003).

The Governor of Virginia apologized for the sterilization of Carrie Buck on the seventy-fifth anniversary of the Supreme Court decision in 2002. But Oklahoma and Virginia were not alone: thirty-two states have had sterilization programs, many supported with federal funding, that have targeted individuals with developmental disabilities, those of low socioeconomic status, racial and ethnic minorities, unmarried women, and prisoners. And although eugenics laws grew out of favor after WWII, forced and involuntary or coerced sterilizations have continued, targeting immigrants, people of color, and the poor.

In the 1970s, two high-profile lawsuits raised public awareness of continuing widespread sterilization abuses. One of the cases, Relf v. Weinberger, 372 F. Supp. 1196 (D.D.C. 1974), is perhaps best known because of the shocking violations committed against the Relf sister plaintiffs—the forced sterilization of two Black sisters only 12 and 14 years old by a federally-funded family planning clinic in Alabama. Id. at 1199. But the D.C. district court's findings revealed much broader abuses:

> Over the last few years, an estimated 100,000 to 150,000 low-income persons have been sterilized annually under federally funded programs. . . . Although Congress has been insistent that all family planning programs function on a purely voluntary basis, there is uncontroverted evidence in the record that minors and other incompetents have been sterilized with federal funds and that an indefinite number of poor people have been improperly coerced into accepting a sterilization operation under the threat that various federally supported welfare benefits would be withdrawn unless they submitted to irreversible sterilization. Patients receiving Medicaid assistance at childbirth are evidently the most frequent targets of this pressure, as the experience [ ] of . . . . Mrs. Waters [who] was actually refused medical assistance by her attending physician unless she submitted to a tubal ligation after the birth.

Id. Similar abuses were revealed in a complaint brought against Los Angeles County's USC Medical Center around the same time, in *Madrigal v. Quilligan*. Several women brought a lawsuit alleging systematic coerced sterilizations, including medical personnel obtaining "consent" for sterilization while the plaintiffs were in labor and, in some cases heavily medicated. Patients signed consent forms either because they thought were consenting to a cesarean section or they believed the procedure they were undergoing was reversible. The plaintiffs were Mexican-American, with limited English proficiency (LEP), and they resided in a community with inadequate medical resources. Even before the lawsuit, a young resident working in the maternity ward tried to sound the alarm to journalists, civil rights organizations and government officials about the widespread abuses he witnessed. See Maya Manian, The Story of *Madrigal v. Quilligan*: Coerced Sterilization of Mexican-American Women, in Reproductive Rights and Justice Stories (Melissa Murray, Kate Shaw, & Reva Siegel eds., 2019).

These cases revealed the disturbing paradox that "the influx of federal family planning funds in the 1960s and 1970s both increased access to reproductive health care and increased abusive sterilization practices." Id. Sterilization efforts occurred throughout the U.S. and targeted Black,

Mexican-American, Native American, Puerto Rican, and poor white women. See Lisa C. Ikemoto, Infertile by Force and Federal Complicity: The Story of *Relf v. Weinberger*, *in* Women and the Law Stories 196 (Elizabeth M. Schneider & Stephanie M. Wildman eds., 2011). Although the *Madrigal* plaintiffs ultimately lost their suit, both cases helped spur reform efforts at the state and federal levels, including requirements to ensure access to relevant bilingual medical information. For a discussion of national origin discrimination and the meaningful access requirement for LEP individuals, see Chapter 6, Section IV.A.

Since 1975, it has been a federal crime for government officials and others receiving federal financial assistance to "coerce[ ] or endeavor[ ] to coerce any person to undergo an abortion or sterilization procedure by threatening such person with the loss of, or disqualification for the receipt of, any benefit or service" under a federal program. Violation is punishable by $1000, up to one year in jail, or both. 42 U.S.C.A. § 300a–8. Nonetheless, this disturbing legacy persists. For example, California has recently come under scrutiny for coerced and unlawful sterilization of its women prisoners. See California State Auditor, Sterilization of Female Inmates: Report 2013–120 (Jun. 2014) (revealing ethical and legal lapses by corrections officials and medical personnel, including failing to follow informed consent protocols requiring a physician to certify that the required waiting period has been satisfied, that the patient appears mentally competent and understands the lasting effects of sterilization, and that the patient has been given one final opportunity to change her mind). In response, the Governor of California signed a bill increasing restrictions on sterilization in state prisons. The law prohibits "sterilization for the purpose of birth control" and prohibits sterilization by any means except when "required for the immediate preservation of the individual's life in an emergency medical situation" or when "medically necessary, as determined by contemporary standards of evidence-based medicine, to treat a diagnosed condition. . . ." Cal. Penal Code § 3440(a) & (b). Additional protections, such as heightened informed consent requirements, must also be met. If a sterilization is performed, the law requires psychological consultation and medical follow up. And the law requires the state to publish data related to the number of sterilizations it performs, disaggregated by race, age, medical justification, and method of sterilization. Id. Even more recently, there have been allegations of women in immigration detention centers being sterilized without their consent. See Caitlin Dickerson, Inquiry Ordered Into Claims Immigrants Had Unwanted Gynecology Procedures, N.Y. Times, Sep. 16, 2020.

Forced Sterilization or Right to Care?

More complex legal and ethical challenges have arisen where guardians or family members of permanently disabled individuals who lack capacity to make their own medical decisions seek permission to authorize sterilization based on the belief that it would be in that person's best interest, as in the following case below.

CONSERVATORSHIP OF VALERIE N.

Supreme Court of California, 1985.
707 P.2d 760.

GRODIN, JUSTICE.

* * *

I.

Valerie was born on July 13, 1955, apparently a victim of Downs Syndrome as a result of which she is severely retarded. Her IQ is estimated to be 30. She is now 29 years old. She lives with her mother and stepfather. Although she has no comprehension of the nature of these proceedings, she has expressed her wish to continue to have her parents care for her. Her parents' long range plan for Valerie is that she will move to a residential home should they become mentally or physically unable to care for her. She has received therapy and training for behavior modification which was not successful in eliminating her aggressive sexual advances toward men. Her parents are attempting to prepare her for the time when they can no longer care for her, and to broaden her social activities as an aspect of this preparation. They have concluded that other methods of birth control are inadequate in Valerie's case.

On September 5, 1980, appellants [Valerie's mother and stepfather] filed their petition to be named conservators of Valerie's person in the Santa Clara County Superior Court pursuant to section 1820. In the same petition they sought the additional power to authorize "a Salpingectomy or any other operation that will permanently sterilize" Valerie. The petition was supported by the declaration of Valerie's personal physician who stated that the tubal ligation procedure is "advisable and medically appropriate."

[A]ppellants submitted a declaration by a physician who had treated Valerie from the time she was 10 years old. He stated that in his opinion a tubal litigation procedure was "advisable and medically appropriate in that a potential pregnancy would cause psychiatric harm to Valerie." A second declaration [ ] by a licensed marriage, family and child counselor having a master's degree in developmental psychology, was also submitted. This declarant had worked with Valerie on a weekly basis for a year during 1977–1978. She believed that a tubal ligation was "an appropriate means of guarding against pregnancy," and had observed that Valerie acted "affectionately" toward adult men and made "inappropriate" sexual advances toward them. This declarant was of the opinion that because Valerie's parents had found it necessary to be overly restrictive in order to avoid a possible pregnancy which would have "severe psychologically damaging consequences" to Valerie, close monitoring had severely hampered Valerie's ability to form social relationships. She also believed that the level of Valerie's retardation meant that no alternative birth control methods were available that would ensure against pregnancy.

Valerie's mother testified that Valerie had not been sexually active, apart from masturbation, because she had been closely supervised. She was aggressive and affectionate toward boys. On the street she approached men, hugged and kissed them, climbed on them, and wanted to sit on their laps. Valerie had been given birth control pills in her early teens, but she rejected them and became ill. Her doctor then recommended the tubal ligation. Valerie was unable to apply other methods of birth control such as a diaphragm, and would not cooperate in a pelvic examination for an intrauterine device which the witness believed was unsafe in any event.

* * *

The parties agree that [the state statutory scheme] bars nontherapeutic sterilization of conservatees.

III. *Constitutional Rights of the Developmentally Disabled*

Our conclusion regarding the present legislative scheme requires that we confront appellants' contention that the scheme is unconstitutional. Both appellants and counsel for Valerie pose the constitutional question in terms of the right of procreative choice. Appellants argue that [the statute] deprives Valerie of that right by precluding the only means of contraception realistically available to her, while counsel for Valerie contends that the legislation furthers that right by protecting her against sterilization forced upon her by the will of others. The sad but irrefutable truth, however, is that Valerie is not now nor will she ever be competent to choose between bearing or not bearing children, or among methods of contraception. The question is whether she has a constitutional right to have these decisions made for her, in this case by her parents as conservators, in order to protect her interests in living the fullest and most rewarding life of which she is capable. At present her conservators may, on Valerie's behalf, elect that she not bear or rear children. As means of avoiding the severe psychological harm which assertedly would result from pregnancy, they may choose abortion should she become pregnant; they may arrange for any child Valerie might bear to be removed from her custody; and they may impose on her other methods of contraception, including isolation from members of the opposite sex. They are precluded from making, and Valerie from obtaining the advantage of, the one choice that may be best for her, and which is available to all women competent to choose—contraception through sterilization. We conclude that the present legislative scheme, which absolutely precludes the sterilization option, impermissibly deprives developmentally disabled persons of privacy and liberty interests protected by the Fourteenth Amendment to the United States Constitution [ ].

The right to marriage and procreation are now recognized as fundamental, constitutionally protected interests. [ ] So too, is the right of a woman to choose not to bear children, and to implement that choice by use of contraceptive devices or medication, and, subject to reasonable restrictions, to terminate a pregnancy. These rights are aspects of the right of privacy which exists within the penumbra of the First Amendment to the United States Constitution [ ]. They are also within the concept of liberty protected against arbitrary restrictions by the Fourteenth Amendment.

Although the Supreme Court has not considered the precise question of the right to contraception in the context of an assertion that the right includes sterilization, that sterilization is encompassed within the right to privacy has been acknowledged in this state. . . .

[T]he Legislature has denied incompetent women the procreative choice that is recognized as a fundamental, constitutionally protected right of all other adult women. We realize that election of the method of contraception to be utilized, or indeed whether to choose contraception at all, cannot realistically be deemed a "choice" available to an incompetent since any election must of necessity be made on behalf of the incompetent by others. The interests of the incompetent which mandate recognition of procreative choice as an aspect of the fundamental right to privacy and liberty do not differ from the interests of women able to give voluntary consent to this procedure, however. That these interests include the individual's right to personal growth and development is implicit in decisions of both the United States Supreme Court and this court.

* * *

An incompetent developmentally disabled woman has no less interest in a satisfying or fulfilling life free from the burdens of an unwanted pregnancy than does her competent sister. Her interest in maximizing her opportunities for such a life through habilitation is recognized and given statutory protection by [other state laws that have recognized that many developmentally disabled persons lead self-sufficient, fulfilling lives, and become loving, competent, and caring marriage partners and parents, as well as laws creating social supports to assist these individuals in achieving their maximum developmental potential.] If the state withholds from her the only safe and reliable method of contraception suitable to her condition, it necessarily limits her opportunity for habilitation and thereby her freedom to pursue a fulfilling life. Therefore, whether approached as an infringement of the right of privacy under the First Amendment or the privacy right that is found within the liberty protected by the Fourteenth Amendment, and whether analyzed under due process or equal protection principles, the issue is whether withholding the option of sterilization as a method of contraception to this class of women is constitutionally permissible. Because the rights involved are fundamental the permissibility of the restriction must be justified by a "compelling state interest," and may be no broader than necessary to protect that interest. [ ]

* * *

The state interest [ ] must be in precluding the option of sterilization because it is in most cases an irreversible procedure. Necessarily implicit in the interest asserted by the state is an assumption that the conservatee may at some future time elect to bear children. While the prohibition of sterilization may be a reasonable means by which to protect some conservatees' right to procreative choice, here it sweeps too broadly for it extends to individuals who cannot make that choice and will not be able to do so in the future. [ ]

Respondent argues that the ban is, nonetheless, necessary because past experience demonstrates that when the power to authorize sterilization of incompetents has been conferred on the judiciary it has been subject to abuse. Again, however, the rationale fails since less restrictive alternatives to total prohibition are available in statutory and procedural safeguards as yet untried in this state. [ ]

NOTES AND QUESTIONS

1. *Lessons of the Past.* One justice in the *Valerie N.* case wrote a particularly strong dissent:

> Today's holding will permit the state, through the legal fiction of substituted consent, to deprive many women permanently of the right to conceive and bear children. The majority run roughshod over this fundamental constitutional right in a misguided attempt to guarantee a procreative choice for one they assume has never been capable of choice and never will be. . . .

> The majority opinion opens the door to abusive sterilization practices which will serve the convenience of conservators, parents, and service providers rather than incompetent conservatees. The ugly history of sterilization abuse against developmentally disabled persons in the name of seemingly enlightened social policies counsels a different choice.

Do you share the dissent's concern? Is there a process we could use to ensure that decisions are truly being made in the person's best interest, as opposed to what is more convenient for parents or conservators? How do we ensure that discriminatory or uninformed assumptions about people with developmental disabilities are not seeping into the decision-making process and leading to decisions that devalue their autonomy and right to equal treatment?

Despite finding the sterilization ban unconstitutional, the majority ultimately affirmed the trial court's denial of the parents' request to authorize sterilization, based on insufficient evidence that sterilization was necessary and that no less intrusive means were available. The affirmance was without prejudice, though, which meant the plaintiffs could renew their application for the power to consent to Valerie's sterilization once they had supporting evidence.

2. *Judicial Safeguards Against Abuse.* The majority opinion went on to discuss the kind of procedural safeguards that have been used in other states to avoid abuse in these circumstances. The framework it referenced (and commonly used by other states) was established by the case In re Guardianship of Hayes, 608 P.2d 635 (Wash. 1980):

The decision [to authorize sterilization] can only be made in a superior court proceeding in which (1) the incompetent individual is represented by a disinterested guardian ad litem, (2) the court has received independent advice based upon a comprehensive medical, psychological, and social evaluation of the individual, and (3) to the greatest extent possible, the court has elicited and taken into account the view of the incompetent individual.

Within this framework, the judge must first find [ ] the individual is (1) incapable of making his or her own decision about sterilization, and (2) unlikely to develop sufficiently to make an informed judgment about sterilization in the foreseeable future.

Next it must be proved [ ] that there is a need for contraception. The judge must find that the individual is (1) physically capable of procreation, and (2) likely to engage in sexual activity at the present or in the near future under circumstances likely to result in pregnancy, and must find in addition that (3) the nature and extent of the individual's disability, as determined by empirical evidence and not solely on the basis of standardized tests, renders him or her permanently incapable of caring for a child, even with reasonable assistance.

Finally, there must be no alternatives to sterilization. The judge must find that (1) all less drastic contraceptive methods, including supervision, education and training, have been proved unworkable or inapplicable, and (2) the proposed method of sterilization entails the least invasion of the body of the individual. In addition, it must be shown [ ] that (3) the current state of scientific and medical knowledge does not suggest either (a) that a reversible sterilization procedure or other less drastic contraceptive method will shortly be available or (b) that science is on the threshold of an advance in the treatment of the individual's disability.

The court also noted that the standard of proof for the above requirements was "clear, cogent and convincing evidence." Do you think this framework adequately safeguards against abuse? Some have read the *Hayes* requirements as effectively removing the possibility of the sterilization of the developmentally disabled. Can you imagine a case that would meet these requirements?

VI. DECISION-MAKING DURING PREGNANCY

The topics covered so far in this chapter have dealt with either government restrictions on women's right to prevent or terminate pregnancy, or government's interference with one's ability to procreate. But when a woman is pregnant and wants to carry the fetus to term, can the government compel medical intervention when the woman either does not or cannot consent, on the grounds that such intervention is necessary to protect fetal life? Traditionally, such situations have been framed as maternal-fetal conflicts, and the *In re A.C.* excerpt below presents a particularly extreme example—where the mother is incapacitated and both the mother's and fetus's lives appear to be at stake. Such disputes are more accurately understood, however, as reflecting a physician-patient conflict over medical decision-making during pregnancy. During pregnancy, physicians perceive dual duties to care for both the fetus and the pregnant patient. Where physicians believe that certain behavior by a patient could endanger fetal health, some physicians may view the patient's failure to follow medical advice as "noncompliance" that must be overridden, including through legal action, if necessary. Consider whether the majority and dissent's contrasting approaches in *In re A.C.* are helpful for resolving the more commonly occurring physician-patient conflicts described in the following notes.

IN RE A.C.

District of Columbia Court of Appeals, 1990.
573 A.2d 1235.

TERRY, ASSOCIATE JUDGE.

* * *

We are confronted here with two profoundly difficult and complex issues. First, we must determine who has the right to decide the course of medical treatment for a patient who, although near death, is pregnant with a viable fetus. Second, we must establish how that decision should be made if the patient cannot make it for herself—more specifically, how a court should proceed when faced with a pregnant patient, *in extremis,* who is apparently incapable of making an informed decision regarding medical care for herself and her fetus. We hold that in virtually all cases the question of what is to be done is to be decided by the patient—the pregnant woman—on behalf of herself and the fetus. If the patient is incompetent or otherwise unable to give an informed consent to a proposed course of medical treatment, then her decision must be ascertained through the procedure known as substituted judgment. . . .

I

This case came before the trial court when George Washington University Hospital petitioned the emergency judge in chambers for declaratory relief as to how it should treat its patient, A.C., who was close to death from cancer and was twenty-six and one-half weeks pregnant with a viable fetus. After a hearing lasting approximately three hours, which was held at the hospital (though not in A.C.'s room), the court ordered that a caesarean section be performed on A.C. to deliver the fetus. . . . The caesarean was performed, and a baby girl, L.M.C., was delivered. Tragically, the child died within two and one-half hours, and the mother died two days later.

* * *

II

A.C. was first diagnosed as suffering from cancer at the age of thirteen. In the ensuing years she underwent major surgery several times, together with multiple radiation treatments and chemotherapy. A.C. married when she was twenty-seven, during a period of remission, and soon thereafter she became pregnant. She was excited about her pregnancy and very much wanted the child. Because of her medical history, she was referred in her fifteenth week of pregnancy to the high-risk pregnancy clinic at George Washington University Hospital.

On Tuesday, June 9, 1987, when A.C. was approximately twenty-five weeks pregnant, she went to the hospital for a scheduled check-up. Because she was experiencing pain in her back and shortness of breath, an x-ray was taken, revealing an apparently inoperable tumor which nearly filled her right lung. On Thursday, June 11, A.C. was admitted to the hospital as a patient. By Friday her condition had temporarily improved, and when asked if she really wanted to have her baby, she replied that she did.

Over the weekend, A.C.'s condition worsened considerably. Accordingly, on Monday, June 15, members of the medical staff treating A.C. assembled, along with her family, in A.C.'s room. The doctors then informed her that her illness was terminal, and A.C. agreed to palliative treatment designed to extend her life until at least her twenty-eighth week of pregnancy. The "potential outcome [for] the fetus," according to the doctors, would be much better at twenty-eight weeks than at twenty-six weeks if it were necessary to "intervene." A.C. knew that the palliative treatment she had chosen presented some increased risk to the fetus, but she opted for this course both to prolong her life for at least another two weeks and to maintain her own comfort. When asked if she still wanted to have the baby, A.C. was somewhat equivocal, saying "something to the effect of 'I don't know, I think so.'" As the day moved toward evening, A.C.'s condition grew still worse, and at about 7:00 or 8:00 p.m. she consented to intubation to facilitate her breathing.

The next morning, June 16, the trial court convened a hearing at the hospital in response to the hospital's request for a declaratory judgment. The court appointed counsel for both A.C. and the fetus, and the District of Columbia was permitted to intervene for the fetus as *parens patriae*. . . .

* * *

There was no evidence before the court showing that A.C. consented to, or even contemplated, a caesarean section before her twenty-eighth week of pregnancy. There was, in fact, considerable dispute as to whether she would have consented to an immediate caesarean delivery at the time the hearing was held. A.C.'s mother opposed surgical intervention, testifying that A.C. wanted "to live long enough to hold that baby" and that she expected to do so, "even though she knew she was terminal." Dr. Hamner [a treating obstetrician] testified that, given A.C.'s medical problems, he did not think she would have chosen to deliver a child with a substantial degree of impairment. . . .

After hearing this testimony and the arguments of counsel, the trial court made oral findings of fact. It found, first, that A.C. would probably die, according to uncontroverted medical testimony, "within the next twenty-four to forty-eight hours;" second, that A.C. was "pregnant with a twenty-six and a half week viable fetus who, based upon uncontroverted medical testimony, has approximately a fifty to sixty percent chance to survive if a caesarean section is performed as soon as possible;" third, that because the fetus was viable, "the state has [an] important and legitimate interest in protecting the potentiality of human life;" and fourth, that there had been some testimony that the operation "may very well hasten the death of [A.C.]," but that there had also been testimony that delay would greatly increase the risk to the fetus and that "the prognosis is not great for the fetus to be delivered post-mortem . . . ." Most significantly, the court found:

> The court is of the view that it does not clearly know what [A.C.'s] present views are with respect to the issue of whether or not the child should live or die. She's presently unconscious. As late as Friday of last week, she wanted the baby to live. As late as yesterday, she did not know for sure.

Having made these findings of fact and conclusions of law, . . . the court ordered that a caesarean section be performed to deliver A.C.'s child.

The court's decision was then relayed to A.C., who had regained consciousness. [When the court reconvened later in the day, Dr. Hamner testified that A.C. then consented to the procedure.] When the court suggested moving the hearing to A.C.'s bedside, Dr. Hamner discouraged the court from doing so, but he and Dr. Weingold, together with A.C.'s mother and husband, went to A.C.'s room to confirm her consent to the procedure. What happened then was recounted to the court a few minutes later:

* * *

Dr. Weingold: She does not make sounds because of the tube in her windpipe. She nods and she mouths words. One can see what she's saying rather readily. She asked whether she would survive the operation. She asked [Dr.] Hamner if he would perform the operation. He told her he would only perform it if she authorized it but it would be done in any case. She understood that. She then seemed to pause for a few moments and then very clearly mouthed words several times, *I don't want it done, I don't want it done.* Quite clear to me.

I would obviously state the obvious and that is this is an environment in which, from my perspective as a physician, this would not be an informed consent one way or the other. She's under tremendous stress with the family on both sides, but I'm satisfied that I heard clearly what she said. . . .

Dr. Weingold later qualified his opinion as to A.C.'s ability to give an informed consent, stating that he thought the environment for an informed consent was non-existent because A.C. was in intensive care, flanked by a weeping husband and mother. He added:

I think she's in contact with reality, clearly understood who Dr. Hamner was. Because of her attachment to him [she] wanted him to perform the surgery. Understood he would not unless she consented and did not consent.

That is, in my mind, very clear evidence that she is responding, understanding, and is capable of making such decisions. . . .

After hearing this new evidence, the court found that it was "still not clear what her intent is" and again ordered that a caesarean section be performed. . . . The operation took place, but the baby lived for only a few hours, and A.C. succumbed to cancer two days later.

* * *

IV

* * *

A. *Informed Consent and Bodily Integrity*

* * *

. . . [O]ur analysis of this case begins with the tenet common to all medical treatment cases: that any person has the right to make an informed choice, if competent to do so, to accept or forgo medical treatment. . . .

In the same vein, courts do not compel one person to permit a significant intrusion upon his or her bodily integrity for the benefit of another person's health. See, e.g., *McFall v. Shimp*, 10 Pa.D. & C.3d 90 (Allegheny County Ct.1978). In *McFall* the court refused to order Shimp to donate bone marrow which was necessary to save the life of his cousin, McFall:

> The common law has consistently held to a rule which provides that one human being is under no legal compulsion to give aid or to take action to save another human being or to rescue. . . .

. . . Even though Shimp's refusal would mean death for McFall, the court would not order Shimp to allow his body to be invaded. It has been suggested that fetal cases are different because a woman who "has chosen to lend her body to bring [a] child into the world" has an enhanced duty to assure the welfare of the fetus, sufficient even to require her to undergo caesarean surgery. [ ] Surely, however, a fetus cannot have rights in this respect superior to those of a person who has already been born.[8]

* * *

There are two additional arguments against overriding A.C.'s objections to caesarean surgery. First, as the American Public Health Association cogently states in its *amicus curiae* brief:

> Rather than protecting the health of women and children, court-ordered caesareans erode the element of trust that permits a pregnant woman to communicate to her physician—without fear of reprisal—all information relevant to her proper diagnosis and treatment. An even more serious consequence of court-ordered intervention is that it drives women at high risk of complications during pregnancy and childbirth out of the health care system to avoid coerced treatment.

Second, and even more compellingly, any judicial proceeding in a case such as this will ordinarily take place—like the one before us here—under time constraints so pressing that it is difficult or impossible for the mother to communicate adequately with counsel, or for counsel to organize an effective factual and legal presentation in defense of her liberty and privacy interests and bodily integrity. . . .

* * *

---

8. There are also practical consequences to consider. What if A.C. had refused to comply with a court order that she submit to a caesarean? Enforcement could be accomplished only through physical force or its equivalent. A.C. would have to be fastened with restraints to the operating table, or perhaps involuntarily rendered unconscious by forcibly injecting her with an anesthetic, and then subjected to unwanted major surgery. Such actions would surely give one pause in a civilized society, especially when A.C. had done no wrong.

B. Substituted Judgment

. . . Sometimes, however, as our analysis presupposes here, a once competent patient will be unable to render an informed decision. In such a case, we hold that the court must make a substituted judgment on behalf of the patient, based on all the evidence. This means that the duty of the court, "as surrogate for the incompetent, is to determine as best it can what choice that individual, if competent, would make with respect to medical procedures." [ ]

* * *

We have found no reported opinion applying the substituted judgment procedure to the case of an incompetent pregnant patient whose own life may be shortened by a caesarean section, and whose unborn child's chances of survival may hang on the court's decision. Despite this precedential void, we conclude that substituted judgment is the best procedure to follow in such a case because it most clearly respects the right of the patient to bodily integrity. . . .

* * *

Because it is the patient's decisional rights which the substituted judgment inquiry seeks to protect, courts are in accord that the greatest weight should be given to the previously expressed wishes of the patient. This includes prior statements, either written or oral, even though the treatment alternatives at hand may not have been addressed. . . .

Courts in substituted judgment cases have also acknowledged the importance of probing the patient's value system as an aid in discerning what the patient would choose. We agree with this approach. [Eds. Note: The court then discussed the ways in which it could determine the substituted judgment of the patient. For a fuller discussion of this issue, see Chapter 18, Section IV.]

C. The Trial Court's Ruling

. . . . The [trial] court did not . . . make a finding as to what A.C. would have chosen to do if she were competent. Instead, the court undertook to balance the state's and [the fetus's] interests in surgical intervention against A.C.'s perceived interest in not having the caesarean performed.

* * *

What a trial court must do in a case such as this is to determine, if possible, whether the patient is capable of making an informed decision about the course of her medical treatment. If she is, and if she makes such a decision, her wishes will control in virtually all cases. If the court finds that the patient is incapable of making an informed consent (and thus incompetent), then the court must make a substituted judgment. . . .

Having said that, we go no further. We need not decide whether, or in what circumstances, the state's interests can ever prevail over the interests of a pregnant patient. . . . Indeed, some may doubt that there could ever be a situation extraordinary or compelling enough to justify a massive intrusion into a person's body, such as a caesarean section, against that person's will. Whether such a situation may someday present itself is a question that we need not strive to answer here. . . .

* * *

BELSON, ASSOCIATE JUDGE, concurring in part and dissenting in part:

* * *

I think it appropriate . . . to state my disagreement with the very limited view the majority opinion takes of the circumstances in which the interests of a viable unborn child can afford such compelling reasons. The state's interest in preserving human life and the viable unborn child's interest in survival are entitled, I think, to more weight than I find them assigned by the majority when it states that "in virtually all cases the decision of the patient . . . will control." I would hold that in those instances, fortunately rare, in which the viable unborn child's interest in living and the state's parallel interest in protecting human life come into conflict with the mother's decision to forgo a procedure such as a caesarean section, a balancing should be struck in which the unborn child's and the state's interest are entitled to substantial weight.

* * *

The balancing test should be applied in instances in which women become pregnant and carry an unborn child to the point of viability. This is not an unreasonable classification because, I submit, a woman who carries a child to viability is in fact a member of a unique category of persons. Her circumstances differ fundamentally from those of other potential patients for medical procedures that will aid another person, for example, a potential donor of bone marrow for transplant. This is so because she has undertaken to bear another human being, and has carried an unborn child to viability. Another unique feature of the situation we address arises from the singular nature of the dependency of the unborn child upon the mother. A woman carrying a viable unborn child is not in the same category as a relative, friend, or stranger called upon to donate bone marrow or an organ for transplant. Rather, the expectant mother has placed herself in a special class of persons who are bringing another person into existence, and upon whom that other person's life is totally dependent. Also, uniquely, the viable unborn child is literally captive within the mother's body. No other potential beneficiary of a surgical procedure on another is in that position.

* * *

I next address the sensitive question of how to balance the competing rights and interests of the viable unborn child and the state against those of the rare expectant mother who elects not to have a caesarean section necessary to save the life of her child. The indisputable view that a woman carrying a viable child has an extremely strong interest in her own life, health, bodily integrity, privacy, and religious beliefs necessarily requires that her election be given correspondingly great weight in the balancing process. In a case, however, where the court in an exercise of a substituted judgment has concluded that the patient would probably opt against a caesarean section, the court should vary the weight to be given this factor in proportion to the confidence the court has in the accuracy of its conclusion. Thus, in a case where the indicia of the incompetent patient's judgment are equivocal, the court should accord this factor correspondingly less weight. The appropriate weight to be given other factors will have to be worked out by the development of law in this area, and cannot be prescribed in a single court opinion. Some considerations obviously merit special attention in the balancing process. One such consideration is any danger to the mother's life or health, physical or mental, including the relatively small but still significant danger that necessarily inheres in any caesarean delivery, and including especially any danger that exceeds that level. The mother's religious beliefs as they relate to the operation would appear to deserve inclusion in the balancing process.

On the other side of the analysis, it is appropriate to look to the relative likelihood of the unborn child's survival. . . . The child's interest in being born with as little impairment as possible should also be considered. This may weigh in favor of a delivery sooner rather than later. The most important factor on this side of the scale, however, is life itself, because the viable unborn child that dies because of the mother's refusal to have a caesarean delivery is deprived, entirely and irrevocably, of the life on which the child was about to embark.

* * *

NOTES AND QUESTIONS

1. *Balancing of Interests?* As the opinions in *A.C.* suggest, decisions made by or on behalf of the mother to best serve her health or other interests may conflict with what a doctor believes is important for protection of the fetus; this conflict forces courts to answer two questions. First, should the court balance the interests of the fetus (or the interests of the state in protecting the fetus) with the interests of the mother? If the answer to that question is "no," as it was for the majority in *A.C.*, the issue becomes the comparatively simple one of determining the wishes of the mother. See In re Baby Boy Doe, 632 N.E.2d 326 (Ill. App. 1994), where the court refused to balance the interests of a fetus (or the interests of the state in protecting a fetus) against the interests

of a competent pregnant woman who refused a caesarean section, even though doctors believed her decision put the life of her fetus at risk.

If there is a decision to balance the interests, however, as the dissenting opinion suggests, the court must also face the question of what standards to apply. Are the interests of the fetus or the state as strong as the interests of the mother? Can the relative strengths of these different interests vary from case to case, depending upon the stage of development of the fetus, the consequences of the decision to be made, or other factors? How might those interests be balanced if the woman objects to recommended medical care on religious grounds? See, e.g., Raleigh Fitkin-Paul Morgan Memorial Hospital v. Anderson, 201 A.2d 537 (N.J. 1964) (ordering blood transfusions to save an "unborn child" over the objections of a woman who refused the transfusion due to her religious convictions as a Jehovah's Witness); In re Application of Jamaica Hospital, 491 N.Y.S.2d 898 (Sup.Ct. 1985) (ordering blood transfusion to save fetus prior to viability); Jefferson v. Griffin Spalding County Hospital Authority, 274 S.E.2d 457 (Ga. 1981) (ordering a caesarean section against the religiously motivated wishes of the mother when physicians argued that failure to do so would result in the death of both the mother and the fetus, noting the "duty of the state to protect a living, unborn human being from meeting [ ] death before being given the opportunity to live.").

2.   *Living Wills & Pregnancy. In re A.C.* illustrates how courts use the process of substituted judgment to try to determine what a patient would have wanted, when that patient is no longer capable of making an informed decision about care. (This is discussed further in Chapter 18). Living wills and advance directives are important tools that allow patients to make their health care wishes known in the event of incapacity, and they are expressly permitted by almost every state. Yet, in most states, the law may not allow a living will to be used to refuse treatment during pregnancy, and in some states a living will is not available to pregnant patients at all. Such pregnancy exemptions have been getting increased attention since the 2014 report about a pregnant woman in Texas, Marlise Munoz, who was kept alive using life support for two months after being declared brain dead, against her family's wishes. For a critique of such exemptions and a discussion of how living wills can be used to better capture patients' preferences in the event of pregnancy, see Elizabeth Villarreal, Pregnancy and Living Wills: A Behavioral Economic Analysis, 128 Yale L. J. (2019), online form at https://www.yalelawjournal.org/forum/.

3.   *Assessing Risk to Fetal Health.* One reason that many commentators have opposed judicial intervention to require pregnant women to undergo medical care for the presumed benefit of their fetuses is the fact that medical diagnosis in this area can be wrong. Doctors seem willing to testify that intervention is necessary to save the fetus even when the prognosis following nonintervention is quite uncertain. There is a series of cases suggesting that when doctors testify that a caesarean is necessary for the health of the fetus, if the mother "escapes" and attempts a normal vaginal birth, there is a good chance the child will be born without complication. J. Fletcher, Drawing Moral

Lines in Fetal Therapy, 29 Clin. Obstetrics & Gynecology 595 (1986). Fletcher summarizes his review of six cases:

> First, inaccuracies and possible misdiagnosis appear to be involved in half of the cases . . . since babies were born healthy after vaginal delivery. If precedents flow from examples flawed by faulty assumptions or mistaken evaluations, errors may be replicated. These outcomes also should remind all concerned of the possibility of misdiagnosis before fetal therapy. Forced fetal therapy on the basis of misdiagnosis would constitute an ethical megadisaster.

29 Clin. Obstetrics and Gynecology at 599. See also In re Baby Boy Doe, supra (mother delivered a "normal and healthy" baby despite predictions of disaster). In fact, using legal action to override a pregnant patient's refusal to undergo a cesarean section or other medical intervention not only implicates autonomy principles, but also seems contrary to evolving evidence of the overuse of cesarean sections as increasing the risk of poor outcomes. See Stephanie Teleki, Birthing a Movement to Reduce Unnecessary C-Sections: An Update from California, Health Aff. Blog (Oct. 31, 2017). How closely should the court scrutinize medical assertions about the risks and benefits of procedures for fetal and maternal health?

4.   *Using the Criminal System to Compel Medical Treatment.* Medical treatment has also been coerced by threatening criminal punishment or confinement. In 1989, the Medical University of South Carolina, along with other state and local law enforcement and social service agencies, hatched a plan to deal with what they saw as the pernicious effects of drug use by pregnant women. The program targeted women who met certain guidelines, for example, those with little or incomplete prenatal care. This meant the women who were targeted were also low-income and dependent on public health care providers, such as the Medical University of South Carolina. The women were also predominantly African American.

The women were tested for cocaine use when they arrived at the hospital to deliver their babies. Those who tested positive were given a "choice" between enrolling in a substance abuse program and being arrested for their drug use. Those who chose the treatment option were not prosecuted unless they failed to adhere to the treatment plan or failed a subsequent drug test; the others were reported to, and subsequently arrested by, the police. No other hospital in Charleston chose to participate in the program.

Ten of the arrested mothers brought suit against the hospital and others. In 2001 the Supreme Court, in a 6–3 opinion, determined that the Charleston process constituted an illegal warrantless search and seizure prohibited by the Fourth Amendment. Ferguson v. City of Charleston, 532 U.S. 67 (2001). Justice Stevens, for the Court, pointed out that the "direct and primary purpose" of the test was to aid the police in enforcing a criminal law, and that the Fourth Amendment was implicated even if the ultimate goal of the hospital was to encourage women to get treatment. Justice Kennedy, concurring, pointed out that the case did not prohibit a state from punishing women who put their fetuses at risk, and Justice Scalia, dissenting, said that the majority "proves once again that no good deed goes unpunished."

Indeed, criminal prosecutions for maternal substance use, based on asserted harm to the fetus, have persisted. For example, two years after the *Ferguson* decision, a woman in South Carolina was convicted of homicide by child abuse for using cocaine during pregnancy after she suffered a stillbirth, and she was sentenced to 20 years imprisonment. State v. McKnight, 576 S.E.2d 168 (S.C. 2003). See also Ex Parte Ankrom, 152 So.3d 397 (Ala. 2013) (upholding convictions of two women for chemical endangerment of child because they ingested illegal substances during pregnancy). Most state courts have rejected the use of traditional child endangerment or abuse laws for such prosecutions. See, e.g., State v. Wade, 232 S.W.3d 663 (Mo. App. 2007); State v. Martinez, 137 P.3d 1195 (N.M. App. 2006); State v. Aiwohi, 123 P.3d 1210 (Haw. 2005); Reinesto v. Superior Court, 894 P.2d 733 (Ariz. App. 1995); Johnson v. State, 602 So.2d 1288 (Fla. 1992) (reversing a conviction for delivery of a controlled substance from a mother to her child after birth, but before the umbilical cord was severed). Nonetheless, thirty-eight states have enacted statutes specifically prohibiting feticide or harm to unborn children, and some of these have been used as authority for arresting pregnant women. Prosecutors have brought cases and secured convictions despite weak or no evidence that the pregnant woman's behavior *actually* caused harm. See Lynn M. Paltrow and Jeanne Flavin, Arrests of and Forced Interventions on Pregnant Women in the United States, 1973–2005: Implications for Women's Legal Status and Public Health, 38 J. of Health Pol., Pol'y, & L. 299 (2013). Even states that reject such criminal prosecutions may be willing to allow other government action against women who ingest drugs or alcohol during pregnancy. For example, in State v. Louk, 786 S.E.2d 219 (W. Va. 2016), the Supreme Court of Appeals of West Virginia held that an unborn fetus was not a "child" within the meaning of a statute imposing criminal penalty for child neglect resulting in death. But just one year later, the same court found that the presence of illegal drugs in a child's system at birth, in light of mother's admitted use of illegal drugs during pregnancy, was sufficient evidence that the child was abused and/or neglected for purposes of a civil petition by the state Department of Health and Human Resources. In re ALCM, 801 S.E.2d 260 (W. Va. 2017).

5.   *Civil Confinement.* The remedy of civil commitment or court ordered protective custody may be used as an alternative to criminal law to prevent pregnant mothers from engaging in certain behavior. Some states have promulgated statutes that provide explicitly that women who put their fetuses at risk may be restrained from doing so by the court. Is the use of the civil commitment or protective custody remedy any less of an infringement on women's liberty than the use of the criminal sanction?

6.   *Connection Between the State's Action and Fetal Health.* A balancing test to determine whether the state can compel intervention depends upon the state's ability to show that its action is justified by its interest in protecting fetal health. In the case of patients' drug use, however, this assertion has been

challenged by health care providers and public health officials. They agree that fetal exposure to drugs and alcohol is an important public health concern because of the risk it poses to the child's development, but they argue that a treatment-focused approach that is supportive and respects patient autonomy, rather than a punitive approach, is more effective for the health of the child and woman. See American Society of Addiction Medicine, Substance Use, Misuse, and Use Disorders During and Following Pregnancy, with an Emphasis on Opioids (Jan. 18, 2017) (noting "the importance of working with a pregnant woman to facilitate her quitting or at least reducing substance use during pregnancy, and engaging in addiction-related treatment if necessary," but "oppos[ing] criminalizing and other punitive approaches to substance use during pregnancy as they turn women away from prenatal care, thus compromising maternal and fetal well-being;" also asserting that "[p]unishing pregnant women impedes proper medical care and the promotion of public health"); American College of Obstetricians and Gynecologists Committee on Health Care for Underserved Women, Substance Abuse Reporting and Pregnancy: The Role of Obstetrician-Gynecologist, 117 Obstetrics Gynecology 200 (2011) (reaffirmed 2014) ("incarceration and the threat of incarceration have proved to be ineffective in reducing the incidence of alcohol or drug abuse" and providers are "encouraged to work with state legislators to retract legislation that punishes women for substance abuse during pregnancy"); American Academy of Pediatrics (AAP), Policy Statement: A Public Health Response to Opioid Use in Pregnancy, 139 Pediatrics 1 (Mar. 2017) (noting that punitive measures "are not in the best interest of the health of the mother-infant dyad," and recommending treatment programs that provide "nonjudgmental, trauma-informed services").

A study of drug treatment programs has shown that many pregnant women have trouble accessing them voluntarily, either because the programs will not take them or because of limited slots. See Rebecca Stone, Pregnant Women and Substance Use: Fear, Stigma, and Barriers to Care, 3 Health and Justice (2015). From a public health perspective, it seems counterproductive for states to use threats of criminal enforcement or civil confinement to force women into treatment, given the dearth of resources for women who want to access such programs voluntarily. In addition, some have argued that the state's poor treatment of pregnant women once confined actually undermines the state's purported interests in maternal and fetal health. See Paltrow & Flavin, supra. Examples of this include shackling women during childbirth and preventing incarcerated women from caring for their newborns in ways that are important for child health. See Priscilla Ocen, Punishing Pregnancy: Race, Incarceration and the Shackling of Pregnant Prisoners, 100 Cal. L. Rev. 1239 (2012).

Forced medical interventions, in combination with criminal or civil confinement, have even been used in cases where there was no evidence of conduct that created a risk of harm to the fetus. Consider an example described in a recent news article: A women who was 14 weeks pregnant voluntarily disclosed at a prenatal checkup that she had been addicted to Percocet the year before. She was not still using drugs and only mentioned it to her doctor because she thought her doctor should know. A urine test confirmed that she was not using drugs, but her doctor and a social worker insisted that she start an anti-addiction drug anyway. The patient refused, and some weeks later county sheriffs came to her home and took her to court, where her doctor accused her of endangering her fetus and she was ordered to attend a mandatory 78-day stay at a drug treatment facility or risk going to jail. Erik Eckholm, Case Explores Rights of Fetus Versus Mother, N.Y. Times (Oct. 23, 2013).

7.   *Punishing Pregnancy and Other Status?* Criminal and civil actions against pregnant women in the name of protecting fetal health have led some scholars to suggest such programs constitute a status-based system of punishment implicating reproductive justice concerns. See, e.g., Priscilla A. Ocen, Birthing Injustice: Pregnancy as a Status Offense, 85 Geo. Wash. L. Rev. 1163 (2017). If a mother is imprisoned for the term of her pregnancy *in order to protect her fetus,* is she being punished for the crime she committed, or for her pregnancy? What if the behavior the woman is punished for would otherwise be lawful if she weren't pregnant? Recall the discussion of what constitutes an illness in Chapter 1, and the tension between the various characteristics of addiction that simultaneously cause society to classify it as behavior deserving of punishment and as an illness deserving treatment. Much has been made about the growing understanding of, and empathy for, people who struggle with substance use disorder (SUD), especially with the national spotlight on opioid addiction. How are the pregnant women who suffer from SUD treated in this public discourse?

Consider also that the testing and surveillance of pregnant women for drug use effectively targets *poor* pregnant women who depend on public resources, as well as those living in disproportionately minority communities that tend to be over policed by the criminal justice system. South Carolina did not have a similar program targeting mothers who delivered their babies at private hospitals in affluent communities. The study by Lynn Paltrow and Jeanne Flavin, supra, documented over four hundred cases of medical and criminal interventions targeting pregnant women, finding that arrests or deprivations of physical liberty disproportionately impacted minorities and low-income individuals. This is despite evidence that drug use is comparable among whites and non-whites. Some scholars have argued that uneven criminal enforcement against certain groups reflects troubling assumptions that parenting by these women—namely poor women and racial or ethnic minorities—is "inherently risky"—a view that harkens back to earlier sterilization programs targeting these same groups. See, e.g., Khiara Bridges, The Poverty of Privacy Rights (2017); Michele Goodwin, Fetal Protection Laws: Moral Panic and the New Constitutional Battlefront, 102 Calif. L. Rev. 781 (2014).

The role of poverty in these cases presents another complicating factor. There is growing recognition of the outsized role of social determinants of health: food insecurity, housing insecurity, exposure to violence, trauma, environmental hazards, discrimination, and other poverty-related factors can contribute to poor physical and mental health, which in turn pose risks to maternal and fetal health. See, e.g., Z. Mahmoodi et al., Association of Maternal Working Condition with Low Birth Weight: The Social Determinants of Health Approach, 5 Ann. Med. Health Sci. Res. 385 (2015); N.N. Sarkar et al., The Impact of Intimate Partner Violence on Women's Reproductive Health and Pregnancy Outcome, 28 J. of Obstetrics and Gynaecology 266 (2008). How do we determine whether poor fetal outcomes are due to a specific act like drug or alcohol use, to some other behavioral, social, or environmental factor, or to some combination of factors? If causation cannot be proved, is it fair to use criminal or civil sanctions against pregnant women to prevent certain behavior? Consider the case of McKnight v. State, 661 S.E.2d 354, 358 n.10 (S.C. 2008). The state of South Carolina charged Regina McKnight, a twenty-one-year-old Black woman, with homicide by child abuse based on the theory that her use of cocaine caused her stillbirth. After only fifteen minutes of deliberation, the jury found her guilty and she was sentenced to twelve years in prison. Her conviction was eventually overturned due to ineffective assistance counsel because the state relied on outdated research as to the effect of drugs on pregnancy, and her own counsel failed to present "recent studies showing that cocaine is no more harmful to a fetus than nicotine use, poor nutrition, or other conditions commonly associated with the urban poor." Id. at 358 n.2. How effective will such government action be as health policy, if it only addresses substance use and only does so temporarily with confinement or imprisonment, but does not address the other social factors shaping fetal and child health?

8. *Pregnancy, Employment & Sex Discrimination.* As noted above, environmental hazards may pose a risk to fetal health, and some employment environments that are safe for workers may not be safe for workers' fetuses. Even in cases where there may be some risk to fetal health, the question of whether such employment is "good" or "bad" for the fetus may not be simple to answer. For example, employees may not have a choice of where to work, and the job may provide financial resources essential for securing basic needs for the child's well-being. Even if one has a choice, certain jobs may provide greater financial security, independence, and personal fulfillment to the parent, promoting greater psychological health and enhancing the family's resources in ways that may have a significant positive effect on pregnancy outcomes and long-term well-being.

Employers have sought to exclude pregnant women (or even women who may become pregnant) from jobs that could put fetuses at risk—either because the employers wanted to protect the fetuses, or because the employers wanted to protect themselves from adverse publicity, increased health insurance costs and potential tort liability. Should an employer be able to refuse to assign people to certain jobs based on their capacity to get pregnant because of the possible risk of future harm? This issue has received attention almost exclusively where the employee is a woman (i.e., a potential mother) rather than a man (i.e., a potential father) even though occupational hazards to men may affect the health of the fetus as well.

The U.S. Supreme Court considered this issue under Title VII of the Civil Rights Act of 1964 in International Union, United Automobile Workers v. Johnson Controls, Inc., 499 U.S. 187 (1991). Johnson Controls excluded women of child-bearing age from its battery manufacturing operation unless they had been sterilized, because workers in that process sometimes developed very high levels of lead in their blood. The Supreme Court determined that this policy constituted disparate treatment by sex, under Title VII as amended by the Pregnancy Discrimination Act, which could be justified only if sex was a bona fide occupational qualification. The Court concluded:

> It is no more appropriate for the courts than it is for individual employers to decide whether a woman's reproductive role is more important to herself and her family than her economic role. Congress has left this choice to the woman as hers to make.

VII. ASSISTED REPRODUCTIVE TECHNOLOGIES (ART)

A. INTRODUCTION

1. The Process of Human Reproduction

Those seeking medical help in facilitating reproduction do so because they want a child. The birth of a child requires the growth of a fetus in a uterus. This, in turn, requires the implantation of a fertilized ovum (also called an egg or an oocyte) in the uterine wall. At least until the cloning of human beings is perfected, the ovum can implant in the uterine wall only if it has been fertilized by a sperm, a process which generally takes place in the fallopian tube.

Within a day of an ovum being fertilized by a sperm, it has divided twice, into a two- and then a four-celled "embryo" (sometimes called a "preembryo") and it is here that we must pause to consider the impact that our language has on our conceptualization and therefore our law. The terminology of early pregnancy is rife with alternative phraseology. For example, a fertilized ovum/egg/oocyte is also called a "zygote," or a cluster of dividing "blastomeres" which eventually divide into a "blastocyst" or hollow cellular ball. Some will argue that because there is no differentiated living matter generated in forming the blastocyst (i.e., there are no fetal or placental cells yet), this division of cell material is not a constructive development of living substance. It is a process which does nothing to distribute particular developmental qualities to particular parts of a resulting fetus. On the other hand, it is the preliminary stage which makes it possible for the blastocyst cell ball to implant and use materials from the uterine wall to grow and develop into a fetus. Obviously, the fertilization of the ovum by the sperm begins the embryonic process, although some use the term "embryo" only to apply to later stages of development.

At any rate, whether it is called an embryo, a preembryo or something else, the fertilized ovum continues its migration through the fallopian tube toward the uterus. The fertilized and subdividing ovum arrives at the lower end of the fallopian tube, hesitating for about two days before being expelled into the uterus. This delay allows the uterine lining to build up for successful implantation. The implantation of this cell cluster is a complicated biological process that takes several days.

Even when all other conditions are met, not all fertilized ova actually do implant and not all implanted ova survive until birth. About 50% of fertilized ova are expelled from the body before pregnancy is discovered. Some of these spontaneous expulsions occur before implantation, and some occur during the first few days after the commencement of the implantation process.

There are several reasons that those who wish to raise children may not conceive them through this process. First, some are unable to participate in coital sexual relations, or choose not to participate in such relations. Others are infertile—that is, normal coitus does not result in a fertilized ovum that implants in the uterine wall and grows into a fetus and then a child. Although estimates vary, about twelve to fifteen percent of American couples are unable to conceive after a year of having unprotected sex. There are a variety of reasons for infertility. One may not be able to produce sperm capable of fertilizing the ovum. Others may be unable to produce ova, or they may have fallopian tubes that cannot adequately accept ova to be fertilized or do not permit the travel of fertilized ova to the uterus. In some cases, the "shell" around the ovum may not admit any sperm at all. In other cases, the ovum is successfully fertilized but the uterus is incapable of allowing for implantation of the fertilized ovum or of maintaining the implanted embryo through the pregnancy. In all of these cases, some form of intervention may allow those who could not become parents through unassisted coitus to achieve parenthood nonetheless.

2.   ART Interventions

The range of problems that prevent conception and childbearing give rise to a wide variety of alternative interventions to facilitate reproduction:

- AIH (artificial insemination-homologous): artificial insemination with the sperm of the person who is intended to be a biological and nurturing co-parent, often the husband/spouse;

- AID (artificial insemination-donor): artificial insemination with the sperm of someone who is presumed to have no continuing relationship with the child;

- IVF (*in vitro* fertilization): fertilizing an ovum outside of the uterus and then implanting it;

- embryo or egg transfer;

- genetic surrogacy: a person who is not an intended parent agrees to become pregnant through assisted reproduction using that person's own gamete; and

- gestational surrogacy: a person who is not an intended parent agrees to become pregnant through assisted reproduction using a different person's gametes.

In many cases ART requires the involvement of a host of other people. A sperm source (who is not necessarily a sperm donor—but is usually a sperm vendor) is necessary to address the inability to produce physiologically adequate sperm; an ovum source is necessary where the problem is the inability to provide a potentially fertile ovum; and a uterus source (originally called a "surrogate," now more generally described as a "gestational surrogate") is necessary where the intended parent(s) is(are) unable or unwilling to carry the fertilized ovum through the pregnancy. The interventions may also vary in complexity, depending on the specific infertility program. Medical treatment of an ovum may allow it to be fertilized, and treatment of a fertilized ovum may allow it to be implanted. And sometimes a combination of these needs requires that there be a series of interventions to produce a pregnancy and a child.

3.   The Role of the Law

The law is often required to help parties sort out the formal relationships of those who undertake processes designed to facilitate reproduction. Legal rights and responsibilities arising out of ART may include obligations of support, decision-making authority, inheritance, contractual duties, and so on. There has been an increase in the variety of non-traditional legal relationships that have developed as a consequence of medical and non-medical reproductive techniques. It is possible to have a child who is the product of sperm from one source (whose sperm may be mixed with sperm from several sources), an ovum extracted from one source, implanted in another, and carried for the benefit of yet another set of parents who intend to nurture the child from the time of its birth.

This implicates social and cultural norms about family, which have changed over time, due in part to the ability of ARTs to facilitate nontraditional family structures. In the face of this change, the law has consistently been forced to answer questions about who *ought* to be treated as the legal parents. What rights, if any, should others involved in the process have? In addition, certain forms of ART result in the production of embryos that may never be used for procreative purposes. For what other purposes can they be used? What legal principles should guide our regulation of these embryos? And how might different theories of personhood or definitions of the beginning of life be relevant to these legal principles? The remainder of this section considers these questions.

B. ART & PARENTAGE LAW

IN THE INTEREST OF K.M.H.

Supreme Court of Kansas, 2007.
169 P.3d 1025.

BEIER, J. This appeal from a consolidated child in need of care (CINC) case and a paternity action arises out of an artificial insemination leading to the birth of twins K.M.H. and K.C.H. We are called upon to decide the existence and extent of the parental rights of the known sperm donor, who alleges he had an agreement with the children's mother to act as the twins' father.

The twins' mother filed a CINC petition to establish that the donor had no parental rights under Kansas law. The donor sued for determination of his paternity. The district court sustained the mother's motion to dismiss, ruling that [the Kansas Parentage Act] was controlling and constitutional. That statute provides:

> "The donor of semen provided to a licensed physician for use in artificial insemination of a woman other than the donor's wife is treated in law as if he were not the birth father of a child thereby conceived, unless agreed to in writing by the donor and the woman." K.S.A. 38–1114(f).

Factual and Procedural Background

... The mother, S.H., is an unmarried female lawyer who wanted to become a parent through artificial insemination from a known donor. She was a friend of the donor, D.H., an unmarried male nonlawyer, who agreed to provide sperm for the insemination. Both S.H. and D.H. are Kansas residents, and their oral arrangements for the donation occurred in Kansas, but S.H. underwent two inseminations with D.H.'s sperm in Missouri. [After the second, she became pregnant and ultimately gave birth to twins.]

* * *

There was no formal written contract between S.H. and D.H. concerning the donation of sperm, the artificial insemination, or the expectations of the parties with regard to D.H.'s parental rights or lack thereof.

* * *

The district judge ruled that Kansas law governed, that K.S.A. 38–1114(f) was constitutional and applicable . . . . The [trial court judge concluded] as a matter of law that D.H. had no legal rights or responsibilities regarding K.M.H. and K.C.H.

Constitutionality of K.S.A. 38–1114(f)

In his brief, D.H. makes a general allegation that K.S.A. 38–1114(f) offends the [equal protection and due process clauses of the] Constitution. [At oral argument D.H.] acknowledged that he no longer challenges the statute as unconstitutional on its face; rather, he argues it cannot be constitutionally applied to him, as a known sperm donor who alleges he had an oral agreement with the twins' mother that granted him parental rights. . . .

* * *

Given the relative newness of the medical procedure of artificial insemination, and thus the newness of K.S.A. 38–1114(f)'s attempt to regulate the relationships arising from it, it is not surprising that the issue raised by D.H. is one of first impression, not only in Kansas but nationally. We therefore begin our discussion of the constitutionality of the statute by surveying the landscape of various states' laws governing the rights of sperm donors for artificial insemination. This landscape and its ongoing evolution provide helpful context for our analysis of K.S.A. 38–1114(f).

The majority of states that have enacted statutes concerning artificial insemination state that the husband of a married woman bears all rights and obligations of paternity as to any child conceived by artificial insemination, whether the sperm used was his own or a donor's.[ ] The 1973 Uniform Parentage Act . . . provided the model for many of the state artificial insemination statutes . . . . Section 5 of the original uniform Act provided:

> (a) If, under the supervision of a licensed physician and with the consent of her husband, a wife is inseminated artificially with semen donated by a man not her husband, the husband is treated in law as if he were the natural father of a child thereby conceived. The husband's consent must be in writing and signed by him and his wife. The physician shall certify their signatures and the date of the insemination, and file the husband's consent with the [State Department of Health], where it shall be kept confidential and in a sealed file. However, the physician's failure to do so does not affect the father and child relationship. All papers and records pertaining to the insemination, whether part of the permanent record of a court or of a file held by the supervising physician or elsewhere, are subject to inspection only upon an order of the court for good cause shown.

(b) The donor of semen provided to a licensed physician for use in artificial insemination of a *married* woman other than the donor's wife is treated in law as if he were not the natural father of a child thereby conceived." (Emphasis added.) Uniform Parentage Act (1973) § 5; 9B U.L.A. at 407–08.

The wording of this original Act and statutes that imitated it did not address the determination of a sperm donor's paternity when an *unmarried* woman conceived a child through artificial insemination. . . .

* * *

Certain states [ ] either anticipated the need for their original statutes to govern the relationship of a sperm donor to the child of an unmarried recipient as well as a married recipient or modified their original Uniform Act-patterned statutes to remove the word "married" from the § 5 (b) language. This meant these states' statutes contained complete bars to paternity for any sperm donor not married to the recipient, regardless of whether the recipient was married to someone else and regardless of whether the donor was known or anonymous. An example of such a provision reads: "The donor of semen provided to a licensed physician for use in artificial insemination of a woman other than the donor's wife is treated in law as if he were not the natural father of a child thereby conceived." See, e.g., Cal. Fam. Code § 7613(b) (West 2004) [ ].

* * *

In 1985, Kansas became one of the states that adopted portions of the Uniform Parentage Act of 1973 regarding presumptions of paternity, but it did not adopt any provision relating to artificial insemination. [ ]

In 1994, Kansas amended its statute to incorporate the 1973 Uniform Act's § 5(b) . . . . [ ] It did not differentiate between known and unknown or anonymous donors, but it did make two notable changes in the uniform language.

As discussed above, although the 1973 Uniform Act governed the paternity of children born only to married women as a result of artificial insemination with donor sperm, the version adopted by Kansas omitted the word "married." [ ] This drafting decision demonstrates the legislature's intent that the bar to donor paternity apply regardless of whether the recipient was married or unmarried.

The other alteration in the 1973 Uniform Act's language is directly at issue here. The Kansas Legislature provided that a sperm donor and recipient could choose to opt out of the donor paternity bar by written agreement. [ ] . . . .

This second drafting decision is critical and sets this case apart from [the approach taken by other states]. . . .

Ultimately, in view of the requirement that we accept as true D.H.'s evidence supporting existence of an oral agreement, we are faced with a very precise question: Does our statute's requirement that any opt-out agreement between an unmarried mother and a known sperm donor be "in writing" result in an equal protection or due process violation? . . . .

Equal Protection

K.S.A. 38–1114(f) draws a gender-based line between a necessarily female sperm recipient and a necessarily male sperm donor for an artificial insemination. By operation of the statute, the female is a potential parent or actual parent under all circumstances; by operation of the same statute, the male will never be a potential parent or actual parent unless there is a written agreement to that effect with the female. [T]he male's ability to insist on father status effectively disappears once he donates sperm. Until that point, he can unilaterally refuse to participate unless a written agreement on his terms exists. After donation, the male cannot force the fatherhood issue. The female can unilaterally decide if and when to use the donation for artificial insemination and can unilaterally deny any wish of the male for parental rights by refusing to enter into a written agreement.

The guiding principle of equal protection analysis is that similarly situated individuals should be treated alike. . . . . In order to pass muster under the federal and state equal protection provisions, a classification that treats otherwise similarly situated individuals differently based solely on the individuals' genders must substantially further a legitimate legislative purpose; the government's objective must be important, and the classification substantially related to achievement of it. [ ]

Given the biological differences between females and males and the immutable role those differences play in conceiving and bearing a child, regardless of whether conception is achieved through sexual intercourse or artificial insemination, we are skeptical that S.H. and D.H. are truly similarly situated. However, assuming for purposes of argument that they are, we perceive several legitimate legislative purposes or important governmental objectives underlying K.S.A. 38–1114(f).

. . . . K.S.A. 38–1114(f) envisions that both married and unmarried women may become parents without engaging in sexual intercourse, either because of personal choice or because a husband or partner is infertile, impotent, or ill. It encourages men who are able and willing to donate sperm to such women by protecting the men from later unwanted claims for support from the mothers or the children. It protects women recipients as well, preventing potential claims of donors to parental rights and responsibilities, in the absence of an agreement. Its requirement that any such agreement be in writing enhances predictability, clarity, and enforceability. Although the timing of entry into a written agreement is not set out explicitly, the design of the statute implicitly encourages early resolution of the elemental question of whether a donor will have parental rights. Effectively, the parties must decide whether they will enter into a written agreement before any donation is made, while there is still balanced bargaining power on both sides of the parenting equation.

In our view, the statute's gender classification substantially furthers and is thus substantially related to these legitimate legislative purposes and important governmental objectives. K.S.A. 38–1114(f) establishes the clear default positions of parties to artificial insemination. If these parties desire an arrangement different from the statutory norm, they are free to provide for it, as long as they do so in writing. . . .

Due Process

* * *

We simply are not persuaded that the requirement of a writing transforms what is an otherwise constitutional statute into one that violates D.H.'s substantive due process rights. Although we agree . . . that one goal of the Kansas Parentage Act as a whole is to encourage fathers to voluntarily acknowledge paternity and child support obligations, the obvious impact of the plain language of this particular provision in the Act is to prevent the creation of parental status where it is not desired or expected. To a certain extent, D.H. . . . evidently misunderstand[s] the statute's mechanism. It ensures no *attachment* of parental rights to sperm donors in the absence of a written agreement to the contrary; it does not *cut off* rights that have already arisen and attached.

* * *

We also reject the argument from D.H. . . . that the statute inevitably makes the female the sole arbiter of whether a male can be a father to a child his sperm helps to conceive. This may be true, as we discussed above, once a donation is made, a recipient who becomes pregnant through artificial insemination using that donation can refuse to enter into an agreement to provide for donor paternity. This does not make the requirement of written agreement unconstitutional. Indeed, it is consistent with United States Supreme Court precedent making even a married pregnant woman the sole arbiter, regardless of her husband's wishes, of whether she continues a pregnancy to term. . . .

All of this being said, we cannot close our discussion of the constitutionality of K.S.A. 38–1114(f) without observing that all that is constitutional is not necessarily wise. We are mindful of, and moved by, the Center's advocacy for public policy to maximize the chance of the availability of two parents—and two parents' resources—to Kansas children. We are also aware of continued evolution in regulation of artificial insemination in this and other countries. In particular, Britain and The Netherlands now ban anonymous sperm donations, near-perfect analogs to donations from known donors who will have no role beyond facilitating artificial insemination. These shifts formally recognize the understandable desires of at least some children conceived through artificial insemination to know the males from whom they have received half of their genes. The Human Fertilisation and Embryology Authority Act of 1990, as amended by Disclosure of Donor Information, Regulations 2004 No. 1511 (requiring, effective April 2005, British donors' identities to be made available to donor-conceived children when children become 18); Netherlands Embryos Bill, Article 3 Dutch Ministry of Health, Welfare, and Sport (2004) www. minvws.nl/en (effective June 2004, child born using donated sperm has right to obtain information about biological father at age 16). As one such child recently wrote,

> "[t]hose of us created with donated sperm won't stay bubbly babies forever. We're all going to grow into adults, and form opinions about the decision to bring us into the world in a way that deprives us of the basic right to know where we came from, what our history is and who both our parents are."

[ ] We sympathize. However, weighing of the interests of all involved in these procedures as well as the public policies that are furthered by favoring one or another in certain circumstances, is the charge of the Kansas Legislature, not of this court.

* * *

Equity

[D.H.] asserts that the district court must be reversed because S.H. has "unclean hands." In essence, he argues that he, a nonlawyer, was tricked by lawyer S.H., who failed to inform him of the statute and failed to explain how the absence of independent legal advice or a written agreement could affect his legal rights. He asserts that he asked S.H. about whether he needed a lawyer or whether they should put their arrangement in writing and was told neither was necessary. This behavior, he alleges, may have constituted a violation of S.H.'s ethical duties as a licensed lawyer.

* * *

Generally speaking, mere ignorance of the law is no excuse for failing to abide by it. [ ] There may be a case in the future in which a donor can prove that the existence of K.S.A. 38–1114(f) was concealed, or that he was fraudulently induced *not* to obtain independent legal advice or *not* to enter into a written agreement to ensure creation and preservation of his parental rights to a child conceived through artificial insemination. This is not such a case.

Affirmed.

CAPLINGER, J., dissenting: I respectfully disagree with the majority's analysis of the constitutionality of K.S.A. 38–1114(f) as applied to D.H. I would hold the statute unconstitutional as applied to D.H. for the reason that it violates his fundamental right to parent his children without due process of law.

* * *

Requirement that donor take affirmative action to protect his parental rights

In concluding that the opt-out provision in K.S.A. 38–1114(f) satisfies due process requirements, the majority states that D.H.'s "own *inaction* before donating his sperm" left him unable to meet the statute's requirements of a written agreement. [ ] Therein lies the constitutional problem with the statute. Fundamental rights must be actively waived, rather than passively lost due to inaction.

Initially, before analyzing this issue, I would note that the terminology employed by the majority, i.e., that D.H. failed to "opt out" of the statute, is a misnomer. In effect, the statute requires a known sperm donor, regardless of any agreement or understanding the donor may have as to his role in parenting a child conceived from his sperm, to *opt in* to parenthood or forever waive his right to parent. . . .

* * *

Effect of "ignorance of the law" on an individual's fundamental right to parent

Nor can I agree with the majority's conclusion that D.H.'s ignorance of the statute's writing requirement has no effect on the statute's application. . . .

* * *

I would urge the majority to consider the *complete* rationale of *Lehr*: "When an unwed father demonstrates a full commitment to the responsibilities of parenthood by 'com[ing] forward to participate in the rearing of his child,' his interest in personal contact with his child acquires substantial protection under the Due Process Clause." [ ]

That is the scenario with which this court is faced. A putative father has come forward to participate in the rearing of his children, emotionally and financially; consequently, his interest in doing so is entitled to full protection under the Due Process Clause. Instead of being given this protection and an opportunity to prove that he intended to actively parent his children, D.H. has been subjected to the workings of a statute of which he was unaware, that required him to "opt in" to fatherhood before ever donating his sperm, or be forever barred from parenting his children.

. . . Because the rights to parent are fundamental, those rights may be waived only through an intentional, free, and meaningful choice. Here, the record indicates D.H. was not even aware of K.S.A. 38–1114(f), much less its requirement that he must enter into a written agreement formalizing his intent to parent his child before he provided his sperm to S.H. . . .

* * *

HILL, J., dissenting: I must respectfully join with Judge Caplinger in her dissent. I too agree that as applied in this case, K.S.A. 38–1114(f) is unconstitutional when applied to a known donor.

But I raise my hand and ask a different question. Who speaks for the children in these proceedings? As applied by the majority in this case, this generative statute of frauds slices away half of their heritage. A man who was once considered a "putative father" in the initial child in need of care proceeding is now branded a mere "semen donor." The majority offers the children sympathy. But is this in their best interests? The trial court never got to the point of deciding the best interests of the children because it was convinced that such a consideration was barred by the operation of K.S.A. 38–1114(f) to a known donor.

None of the elaborate and meticulous safeguards our Kansas laws afford parents *and children* in proceedings before our courts when confronted with questions of parentage have been extended to these children. . . .

I agree with the Ohio Court of Common Pleas when it said:

"A father's voluntary assumption of fiscal responsibility for his child should be endorsed as a socially responsible action. A statute which absolutely extinguishes a father's efforts to assert the rights and responsibility of being a father, in a case with such facts as those *sub judice,* runs contrary to due process safeguards. [ ]" [ ]

I think the same can be said about our statute.

NOTE: THE 2017 UNIFORM PARENTAGE ACT

Most states adopted some version of the 1973 Uniform Parentage Act (UPA). In 2000, the original (1973) UPA and the Uniform Status of Children of Assisted Conception Act were combined and rewritten in the form of a new (2000) UPA, which was amended in 2002. The 2002 UPA was designed to address some of the uncertainty around parentage in assisted conception cases, but those portions of the statute proved controversial and were not embraced by many states. In addition, the 2002 statute continued to reflect certain gendered assumptions about parentage, such as the assumption that children would be born to couples with one man and one woman, which impacted legal presumptions and rights determining parentage.

The Uniform Law Commission (ULC) determined that the UPA needed updating in light of the growth of non-traditional family structures facilitated by ART, as well as the equity implications of the Supreme Court case *Obergefell v. Hodges*, 576 U.S. 644 (2015), which held laws barring marriage of same sex couples unconstitutional. This ruling was widely understood as rendering vulnerable parentage laws' differential treatment of same-sex couples versus different-sex couples, and raising questions about the constitutionality of gendered provisions of prior versions of the UPA. See also, *Pavan v. Smith*, 137 S.Ct. 2075 (2017) (invalidating an Arkansas law denying married same-sex couples the same recognition on their children's birth certificates granted to married different-sex couples). To address these inequities, and to modernize parentage laws in other ways, the Uniform Parentage Act was updated in 2017. Select provisions are reproduced below.

UNIFORM PARENTAGE ACT (2017)

* * *

[ARTICLE 1—GENERAL PROVISIONS]

§ 102.   DEFINITIONS.

(4) "Assisted reproduction" means a method of causing pregnancy other than sexual intercourse. The term includes:

   (A) intrauterine or intracervical insemination;

   (B) donation of gametes;

   (C) donation of embryos;

   (D) in-vitro fertilization and transfer of embryos; and

   (E) intracytoplasmic sperm injection.

* * *

(9) "Donor" means an individual who provides gametes intended for use in assisted reproduction, whether or not for consideration. The term does not include:

   (A) a woman who gives birth to a child by means of assisted reproduction[, except as otherwise provided in [Article] 8]; or

   (B) a parent under Article 7 [or an intended parent under Article 8].

* * *

(10) "Gamete" means sperm, egg, or any part of a sperm or egg.

* * *

(13) "Intended parent" means an individual, married or unmarried, who manifests an intent to be legally bound as a parent of a child conceived by assisted reproduction.

***

[ARTICLE 2—PARENT-CHILD RELATIONSHIP]
§ 201.   ESTABLISHMENT OF PARENT-CHILD RELATIONSHIP.

A parent-child relationship is established between an individual and a child if:

(1) the individual gives birth to the child[, except as otherwise provided in [Article] 8, concerning surrogacy agreements];

(2) there is a presumption under Section 204 of the individual's parentage of the child, unless the presumption is overcome in a judicial proceeding or a valid denial of parentage is made [pursuant to the rules established elsewhere in this Act];

(3) the individual is adjudicated a parent of the child . . . ;

(4) the individual adopts the child;

(5) the individual acknowledges parentage of the child under [the section of the Act establishing the process for voluntary acknowledgment of parentage], unless [such] acknowledgment is rescinded [ ] or successfully challenged [under other provisions of this Act];

(6) the individual's parentage of the child is established under [Article] 7 [concerning assisted reproduction] [;or

(7) the individual's parentage of the child is established under [Article] 8]

***

§ 202.   NO DISCRIMINATION BASED ON MARITAL STATUS. A parent-child relationship extends equally to every child and parent, regardless of the marital status of the parent.

***

§ 204.   PRESUMPTION OF PARENTAGE.

(a) An individual is presumed to be a parent of a child if:

(1) except as otherwise provided [in this act]:

(A) the individual and the woman who gave birth to the child are married to each other and the child is born during the marriage . . . ;

(B) the individual and the woman who gave birth to the child were married to each other and the child is born not later than 300 days after the marriage is terminated by death, [divorce, dissolution, annulment, or declaration of invalidity, or after a decree of separation or separate maintenance] . . . ; or

(C) the individual and the woman who gave birth to the child married each other after the birth of the child . . . , the individual at any time asserted parentage of the child, and [the assertion is in a [state birth] record or on the child's birth certificate]; or

(2) the individual resided in the same household with the child for the first two years of the life of the child, including any period of temporary absence, and openly held out the child as the individual's child. . . .

* * *

[ARTICLE 7—ASSISTED REPRODUCTION]

§ 701.   SCOPE OF [ARTICLE].

This [article] does not apply to the birth of a child conceived by means of sexual intercourse[, or assisted reproduction under a surrogacy agreement under [Article] 8. [Eds. Note: For a discussion of article 8, see the Note on Gestational Surrogacy and the UPA after *Johnson v. Calvert* below.]

§ 702.   PARENTAL STATUS OF DONOR.

A donor is not a parent of a child conceived by means of assisted reproduction.

§ 703.   PARENTAGE OF CHILD OF ASSISTED REPRODUCTION.

An individual who consents under Section 704 to assisted reproduction by a woman with the intent to be a parent of a child conceived by the assisted reproduction is a parent of the child.

§ 704.   CONSENT TO ASSISTED REPRODUCTION.

(a) Except as otherwise provided in subsection (b), the consent described in Section 703 must be in a record signed by a woman giving birth to a child conceived by assisted reproduction and an individual who intends to be a parent of the child.

(b) Failure to consent in a record as required by subsection (a), before, on, or after birth of the child, does not preclude the court from finding consent to parentage if: (1) the woman or the individual proves by clear-and-convincing evidence the existence of an express agreement entered into before conception that the individual and the woman intended they both would be parents of the child; or (2) the woman and the individual for the first two years of the child's life, including any period of temporary absence, resided together in the same household with the child and both openly held out the child as the individual's child . . . .

* * *

NOTES AND QUESTIONS

1.   *UPA 1973 vs. UPA 2017.* *K.M.H.* applied the Kansas version of the UPA. Would the outcome have been different under the 1973 UPA (excerpts cited in *K.M.H.*)? What about the 2017 UPA? Are there children who would have no fathers under the 1973 Act or the Kansas statute but who would have a father under the 2017 UPA? If we reject genetic essentialism (i.e., that the source of the genetic contribution is the parent), where should we look to decide if a sperm source ought to be the legal parent? Should we look to the intent of the parties? Should we look to the best interest of the child, as the dissent in *K.M.H.* suggests?

2.   *Parentage Under Common Law.* The 1973 version of the UPA applies only if the woman who is inseminated is a wife (i.e., is married), if she proceeds with the consent of her husband and the procedure is carried out under the supervision of a licensed physician. If any of these conditions is not met, the statute is inapplicable. See, e.g., Marriage of Witbeck-Wildhagen, 667 N.E.2d 122 (Ill. App. Ct. 1996) (lack of husband's consent to wife's insemination precluded statutory or equitable basis for recognition of paternity); Patton v. Vanterpool, 806 S.E.2d 493 (Ga. 2017) (statute creating an irrebuttable presumption of paternity with respect to children born during marriage who were conceived through artificial insemination did not apply to children conceived by IVF therapy). The third requirement may not be met because artificial insemination need not be done as a medical procedure by a physician. A syringe can be used to place "fresh" semen in the cervical canal or uterus directly into the person who intends to become pregnant, which can be done successfully at home by anyone who understands the underlying biological principles. Why should the involvement of a health care professional matter? When the statute does not apply, the common law has had to define the rights and interests of all of the parties. In a part of the opinion not reproduced in this casebook, the *K.M.H.* case noted that some common law cases have treated the source of the sperm to be the father, with all of the rights (including visitation) and obligations (including child support) that come with such a designation; others have not.

3.   *State Statutes & Donor Parentage.* The *K.M.H.* opinion noted that in adopting their own versions of the 1973 UPA, some states added explicit bars to donor paternity, regardless of whether the recipient was married to someone else and regardless of whether the donor was known or anonymous. Some courts have found that such a bar, while constitutional on its face, could be an unconstitutional violation of a donor's due process rights under certain conditions. See, e.g., McIntyre v. Crouch, 780 P.2d 239 (Or. Ct. App. 1989) (statute unconstitutional as applied if the donor can prove that he had an agreement with the mother to share the rights and responsibilities of parenthood); accord C.O. v. W.S., 64 Ohio Misc.2d 9 (1994). See also, L.F. v. Breit, 736 S.E. 2d. 711 (Va. 2013) (noting that the assisted conception statute

did not contemplate situations where unmarried donors have long-term relationships, as well as biological ties, where the donor and birth mother have entered into a written agreement of paternity, and where the donor has voluntarily assumed parental responsibilities; and finding that a bar to donor paternity in this case would violate the donor's due process rights). Other courts have found that a man subject to a donor paternity bar may be able to prove parentage under a different statutory provision. See Jason P. v. Danielle S. 226 Cal.App.4th 167, 796–797 (2014) (holding that the donor paternity bar in Cal. Fam. Code § 7613(b)(West 2004) does not prevent donor from attempting to qualify as a presumed parent under § 7611(d) based on evidence the donor received the child into the donor's home and held out the child out as the donor's natural child).

Although earlier versions of the UPA focused on donor *paternity*, the 2017 Act focuses more broadly on donors' *parentage* rights, in ways that eschew earlier gender assumptions. For example, Section 703 in the 2017 UPA (reproduced above) is titled "*Parentage* of Child of Assisted Reproduction" and addresses the rights of "an individual" who intends to parent; but in the 2002 version, this section was titled "*Paternity* of Child Assisted Reproduction." Section 705 in the 2002 UPA addresses limitations on *husband's dispute of paternity*, while the corresponding section in the 2017 UPA refers to limitations on *spouse's dispute of parentage*. Such changes reflect an acknowledgement that children are not necessarily born to couples with one man and one woman, as well as the increased use of egg donations by those not intending to parent. As of this writing, a number of states have enacted reforms that provide greater legal protection for children's relationship to their unmarried and LGBTQ parents, and recognize legal parentage for children born through various forms of assisted reproduction. This includes eliminating much gendered terminology, as well as eliminating stigmatizing terms, like "illegitimate", that have long been used to classify and determine the rights of children born to unmarried parents. A growing number of states are adopting or considering reforms consistent with the 2017 UPA. See the Note on ART & Changing Norms later in this chapter.

4.   *Objections to Artificial Insemination.* Virtually no legal questions have arisen surrounding the use of the sperm of a husband to inseminate his wife. Such a process may be used within a marriage to allow for processing of the semen to overcome low sperm count. In these cases, there is no question about the identity of the mother and the father of the child. While religious objections have been raised to masturbation (which is required) and to any process that alters the "natural" procreative process, artificial insemination-homologous (AIH) of a married woman with sperm from her husband has been well accepted as a social and medical matter. Artificial insemination by a donor (AID), however, has generated greater objections based on religious beliefs for some and more general social mores for others. For example, in the case of married couples who need to use a donor, some believe that AID constitutes adultery. Some have also expressed concern that the availability of AID will undermine traditional assumptions about appropriate family structure. For

others, however, the possibility that ART facilitates new and different family combinations is viewed as empowering for individuals who want to have children and as reshaping society's assumptions about what constitutes a strong and moral family unit in positive ways.

Other objections are focused on the anonymity of the process, in light of the fact that donation of sperm often occurs anonymously in the U.S. Some are concerned that the uncertainty of the screening of the sperm source in AID can provide for uncertainty in the health of the child, and that anonymity of the sperm source may have unforeseen emotional consequences. There is also an argument that AID is inappropriate because if there is no limit on the number of times one person may donate sperm there may be a genetically unacceptably large number of children who unknowingly have the same genetic parent, which may lead to the dilution of the genetic pool of some communities.

5. *Donor Anonymity.* The debate over whether donor anonymity should be protected has historically centered around sperm donation. The question of whether a prospective mother (and, ultimately, the child) should know the identity of the sperm source was seen as having important legal and practical implications for donation. An anonymous (or, at least, unknown) sperm source would have a more difficult time establishing parentage than one who is known or identifiable, which may encourage prospective mothers to choose unknown sperm sources. That, in turn, may encourage women seeking artificial insemination to seek the help of cryobanks, run as medical institutions with medical control over the processing of the gametes. In the case of both sperm and egg donations, those who seek anonymous donors typically still want to know something about those donors. Gamete banks provide profiles of their various donors, and some issue catalogs of these profiles allowing their consumers to choose the profile that seems most appropriate. A "donor catalog" may provide information on race/ethnicity, hair color and texture, eye color, height, weight, blood type, skin tone, years of education, and occupation (or major in college). In addition to relevant health information, what kind of information, if any, about the gamete source ought to be provided to the intended parents?

6. *Obligations Concerning Donor Identity.* UPA 2017 requires gamete banks and fertility clinics ("ART clinics") to collect and store certain identifying information and medical history of donors. UPA 2017 also allows donors to maintain anonymity by signing a declaration stating that the donor does not agree to have the donor's identity disclosed. Even in these cases, though, upon request from the child, the ART clinics must make a good-faith effort to notify the donor, who may then elect to withdraw the earlier nondisclosure declaration. The clinic must also make a good-faith effort to provide nonidentifying medical history if requested. The American legal preference for unknown or anonymous donors is not reflected elsewhere in the world, and, especially in Europe, the trend is toward a legal requirement that the source be made known to the child when the child becomes an adult. Which approach is better—the American protection for anonymity, or the preference elsewhere for release of this information? In the United States there has been an increase

in the number of "directed donations" of gametes—i.e., donations made by identifiable persons for use by identified persons.

At the very least, should a child be informed about being the product of ART, and that there may be a gamete source other than the parents? The most recent recommendations by the American Society of Reproductive Medicine (ASRM) encourage disclosure:

- Disclosure to donor-conceived persons of the use of donor gametes or embryos in their conception is strongly encouraged, while ultimately the choice of recipient parents.

- Counseling and informed consent about disclosure and information sharing are essential for donors and recipients.

- [ART and donation programs and facilities] should expect inquiries from donor-conceived persons about their genetic background and should develop written policies to respond to these inquiries.

- [ART and donation programs and facilities] should gather, maintain, and permanently store medical and genetic information about donors.

- Donors and recipient parents should be informed in advance about how and when ART programs; sperm, oocyte, and embryo banks; and oocyte and embryo donation programs will release donor information to recipients and offspring. Donors and recipients also should be counseled that later changes in the law may affect any agreements.

Informing Offspring of Their Conception by Gamete or Embryo Donation: An Ethics Committee Opinion. American Society for Reproductive Medicine, Fertil. Steril. 2018; 109:601–5.

7. *Timing.* Cryopreservation—the ability to freeze and thaw with viability retention—is beneficial for many reasons. For example, cryopreservation permits testing for the presence of any latent contaminant (such as HIV), and it provides greater flexibility in family planning. This flexibility can have legal and ethical implications, however, because it gives rise to the possibility that the parent of a child conceived through ART could have died years before that child's birth. The Social Security Administration faced this issue in a number of cases where claimants have sought survivor's benefits from fathers who had died before they were born (or even conceived). Their eligibility depends on whether they are recognized as heirs by the states where they reside. In some states a child may be an heir to a parent who died pre-conception; in some states a child may not be. The Uniform Status of Children of Assisted Conception Act explicitly provided that one who died before implantation of the genetic contribution was not a parent of the "resulting child." In the 2017 version of the Uniform Parentage Act, Section 708 provides that "if an individual who consented . . . to assisted reproduction by a woman who agreed to give birth to a child dies before a transfer of gametes or embryos, the deceased individual is only a parent if: (1) either[ ] the individual consented in a record that if assisted reproduction were to occur

after the death of the individual, the individual would be a parent of the child [or such intent is proved by clear-and-convincing evidence]; and (2) either [ ] the embryo is in utero not later [36] months after the individual's death or [ ] the child is born not later than [45] months after the individual's death." See also Section C below, discussing the legal and ethical implications of IVF and the disposition of frozen gametes.

JOHNSON V. CALVERT
Supreme Court of California, 1993.
851 P.2d 776.

PANELLI, J.

* * *

Mark and Crispina Calvert are a married couple who desired to have a child. Crispina was forced to undergo a hysterectomy in 1984. Her ovaries remained capable of producing eggs, however, and the couple eventually considered surrogacy. In 1989 Anna Johnson heard about Crispina's plight from a coworker and offered to serve as a surrogate for the Calverts.

On January 15, 1990, Mark, Crispina, and Anna signed a contract providing that an embryo created by the sperm of Mark and the egg of Crispina would be implanted in Anna and the child born would be taken into Mark and Crispina's home "as their child." Anna agreed she would relinquish "all parental rights" to the child in favor of Mark and Crispina. In return, Mark and Crispina would pay Anna $10,000 in a series of installments, the last to be paid six weeks after the child's birth. Mark and Crispina were also to pay for a $200,000 life insurance policy on Anna's life.

The zygote was implanted on January 19, 1990. Less than a month later, an ultrasound test confirmed Anna was pregnant.

Unfortunately, relations deteriorated between the two sides. Mark learned that Anna had not disclosed she had suffered several stillbirths and miscarriages. Anna felt Mark and Crispina did not do enough to obtain the required insurance policy. She also felt abandoned during an onset of premature labor in June.

In July 1990, Anna sent Mark and Crispina a letter demanding the balance of the payments due her or else she would refuse to give up the child. The following month, Mark and Crispina responded with a lawsuit, seeking a declaration they were the legal parents of the unborn child. Anna filed her own action to be declared the mother of the child, and the two cases were eventually consolidated. The parties agreed to an independent guardian ad litem for the purposes of the suit.

The child was born on September 19, 1990, and blood samples were obtained from both Anna and the child for analysis. The blood test results excluded Anna as the genetic mother. The parties agreed to a court order providing that the child would remain with Mark and Crispina on a temporary basis with visits by Anna.

Discussion

Determining Maternity Under the Uniform
Parentage Act [of 1973]

. . . . [W]e are left with the undisputed evidence that Anna, not Crispina, gave birth to the child and that Crispina, not Anna, is genetically related to him. Both women thus have adduced evidence of a mother and child relationship as contemplated by the [Uniform Parentage] Act [1973].[ ] Yet for any child California law recognizes only one natural mother, despite advances in reproductive technology rendering a different outcome biologically possible.

We decline to accept the contention of amicus curiae . . . that we should find the child has two mothers. Even though rising divorce rates have made multiple parent arrangements common in our society, we see no compelling reason to recognize such a situation here. The Calverts are the genetic and intending parents of their son and have provided him, by all accounts, with a stable, intact, and nurturing home. To recognize parental rights in a third party with whom the Calvert family has had little contact since shortly after the child's birth would diminish Crispina's role as mother.

We see no clear legislative preference in [the statutory law] as between blood testing evidence and proof of having given birth.

* * *

Because two women each have presented acceptable proof of maternity, we do not believe this case can be decided without enquiring into the parties' intentions as manifested in the surrogacy agreement. Mark and Crispina are a couple who desired to have a child of their own genes but are physically unable to do so without the help of reproductive technology. They affirmatively intended the birth of the child, and took the steps necessary to effect in vitro fertilization. But for their acted-on intention, the child would not exist. Anna agreed to facilitate the procreation of Mark's and Crispina's child. The parties' aim was to bring Mark's and Crispina's child into the world, not for Mark and Crispina to donate a zygote to Anna. Crispina from the outset intended to be the child's mother. Although the gestative function Anna performed was necessary to bring about the child's birth, it is safe to say that Anna would not have been given the opportunity to gestate or deliver the child had she, prior to implantation of the zygote, manifested her own intent to be the child's mother. No reason appears why Anna's later change of heart should vitiate the determination that Crispina is the child's natural mother.

We conclude that although the Act recognizes both genetic consanguinity and giving birth as means of establishing a mother and child relationship, when the two means do not coincide in one woman, she who intended to procreate the child—that is, she who intended to bring about the birth of a child that she intended to raise as her own—is the natural mother under California law.[10]

* * *

Anna urges that surrogacy contracts violate several social policies. Relying on her contention that she is the child's legal, natural mother, she cites the public policy embodied in [the] Penal Code [ ], prohibiting the payment for consent to adoption of a child. She argues further that the policies underlying the adoption laws of this state are violated by the surrogacy contract because it in effect constitutes a prebirth waiver of her parental rights.

We disagree. Gestational surrogacy differs in crucial respects from adoption and so is not subject to the adoption statutes. The parties voluntarily agreed to participate in in vitro fertilization and related medical procedures before the child was conceived; at the time when Anna entered into the contract, therefore, she was not vulnerable to financial inducements to part with her own expected offspring. As discussed above, Anna was not the genetic mother of the child. The payments to Anna under the contract were meant to compensate her for her services in gestating the fetus and undergoing labor, rather than for giving up "parental" rights to the child. Payments were due both during the pregnancy and after the child's birth.

* * *

Finally, Anna and some commentators have expressed concern that surrogacy contracts tend to exploit or dehumanize women, especially women of lower economic status. Anna's objections center around the psychological harm she asserts may result from the gestator's relinquishing the child to whom she has given birth. Some have also

---

[10] Thus, under our analysis, in a true "egg donation" situation, where a woman gestates and gives birth to a child formed from the egg of another woman with the intent to raise the child as her own, the birth mother is the natural mother under California law.

The dissent would decide parentage based on the best interests of the child. Such an approach raises the repugnant specter of governmental interference in matters implicating our most fundamental notions of privacy, and confuses concepts of parentage and custody. Logically, the determination of parentage must precede, and should not be dictated by, eventual custody decisions. The implicit assumption of the dissent is that a recognition of the genetic intending mother as the natural mother may sometimes harm the child. This assumption overlooks California's dependency laws, which are designed to protect all children irrespective of the manner of birth or conception. Moreover, the best interests standard poorly serves the child in the present situation: it fosters instability during litigation and, if applied to recognize the gestator as the natural mother, results in a split of custody between the natural father and the gestator, an outcome not likely to benefit the child. Further, it may be argued that, by voluntarily contracting away any rights to the child, the gestator has, in effect, conceded the best interests of the child are not with her.

cautioned that the practice of surrogacy may encourage society to view children as commodities, subject to trade at their parents' will.

We are unpersuaded that gestational surrogacy arrangements are so likely to cause the untoward results Anna cites as to demand their invalidation on public policy grounds. Although common sense suggests that women of lesser means serve as surrogate mothers more often than do wealthy women, there has been no proof that surrogacy contracts exploit poor women to any greater degree than economic necessity in general exploits them by inducing them to accept lower-paid or otherwise undesirable employment. We are likewise unpersuaded by the claim that surrogacy will foster the attitude that children are mere commodities; no evidence is offered to support it.

The argument that a woman cannot knowingly and intelligently agree to gestate and deliver a baby for intending parents carries overtones of the reasoning that for centuries prevented women from attaining equal economic rights and professional status under the law. To resurrect this view is both to foreclose a personal and economic choice on the part of the surrogate mother, and to deny intending parents what may be their only means of procreating a child of their own genes.

* * *

The judgment of the Court of Appeal is affirmed.

[ARABIAN, J., concurred with the majority's Uniform Parentage Act analysis, but would leave the issue of whether surrogacy contracts could be consistent with public policy to the legislature.]

KENNARD, J., dissenting.

When a woman who wants to have a child provides her fertilized ovum to another woman who carries it through pregnancy and gives birth to a child, who is the child's legal mother? Unlike the majority, I do not agree that the determinative consideration should be the intent to have the child that originated with the woman who contributed the ovum. In my view, the woman who provided the fertilized ovum and the woman who gave birth to the child both have substantial claims to legal motherhood. Pregnancy entails a unique commitment, both psychological and emotional, to an unborn child. No less substantial, however, is the contribution of the woman from whose egg the child developed and without whose desire the child would not exist.

For each child, California law accords the legal rights and responsibilities of parenthood to only one "natural mother." When, as here, the female reproductive role is divided between two women, California law requires courts to make a decision as to which woman is the child's natural mother, but provides no standards by which to make that decision. The majority's resort to "intent" to break the "tie" between the genetic and gestational mothers is unsupported by statute, and, in the absence of appropriate protections in the law to guard against abuse of surrogacy arrangements, it is ill-advised. To determine who is the legal mother of a child born of a gestational surrogacy arrangement, I would apply the standard most protective of child welfare—the best interests of the child.

* * *

Analysis of the Majority's "Intent" Test

* * *

The majority offers four arguments in support of its conclusion to rely on the intent of the genetic mother as the exclusive determinant for deciding who is the natural mother of a child born of gestational surrogacy. Careful examination, however, demonstrates that none of the arguments mandates the majority's conclusion.

The first argument that the majority uses in support of its conclusion that the intent of the genetic mother to bear a child should be dispositive of the question of motherhood is "but-for" causation. Specifically, the majority relies on a commentator who writes that in a gestational surrogacy arrangement, " 'the child would not have been born but for the efforts of the intended parents.' " [ ] [But the resort to the "but-for" test derived from tort law is unprecedented and unjustified here.]

* * *

Behind the majority's reliance on "but-for" causation as justification for its intent test is a second, closely related argument. The majority draws its second rationale from a student note: " 'The mental concept of the child is a controlling factor of its creation, and the originators of that concept merit full credit as conceivers.' " [ ]

* * *

[This concept is taken from the law of intellectual property.] The problem with this argument, of course, is that children are not property. Unlike songs or inventions, rights in children cannot be sold for consideration, or made freely available to the general public.

Next, the majority offers as its third rationale the notion that bargained-for expectations support its conclusion regarding the dispositive significance of the genetic mother's intent. Specifically, the majority states that " 'intentions that are voluntarily chosen, deliberate, express and bargained-for ought presumptively to determine legal parenthood.' "

* * * But the courts will not compel performance of all contract obligations. [ ] The unsuitability of applying the notion that, because contract intentions are "voluntarily chosen, deliberate, express and bargained-for," their performance ought to be compelled by the courts is even more clear when the concept of specific performance is used to determine the course of the life of a child. Just as children are not the intellectual property of their parents, neither are they the personal property of anyone, and their delivery cannot be ordered as a contract remedy on the same terms that a court would, for example, order a breaching party to deliver a truckload of nuts and bolts.

* * *

The majority's final argument in support of using the intent of the genetic mother as the exclusive determinant of the outcome in gestational surrogacy cases is that preferring the intending mother serves the child's interests, which are " '[u]nlikely to run contrary to those of adults who choose to bring [the child] into being.' " [ ]

I agree with the majority that the best interests of the child is an important goal . . . . The problem with the majority's rule of intent is that application of this inflexible rule will not serve the child's best interests in every case.

* * *

The Best Interests of the Child

* * *

In the absence of legislation that is designed to address the unique problems of gestational surrogacy, this court should look not to tort, property or contract law, but to family law, as the governing paradigm and source of a rule of decision. The allocation of parental rights and responsibilities necessarily impacts the welfare of a minor child. And in issues of child welfare, the standard that courts frequently apply is the best interests of the child. [ ] This "best interests" standard serves to assure that in the judicial resolution of disputes affecting a child's well-being, protection of the minor child is the foremost consideration. Consequently, I would apply "the best interests of the child" standard to determine who can best assume the social and legal responsibilities of motherhood for a child born of a gestational surrogacy arrangement.

* * *

Factors that are pertinent to good parenting, and thus that are in a child's best interests, include the ability to nurture the child physically and psychologically [ ] and to provide ethical and intellectual guidance. [ ] Also crucial to a child's best interests is the "well recognized right" of every child "to stability and continuity." [ ] The intent of the genetic mother to procreate a child is certainly relevant to the question of the child's best interests; alone, however, it should not be dispositive.

* * *

In this opinion, I do not purport to offer a perfect solution to the difficult questions posed by gestational surrogacy; perhaps there can be no perfect solution. But in the absence of legislation specifically designed to address the complex issues of gestational surrogacy and to protect against potential abuses, I cannot join the majority's uncritical validation of gestational surrogacy.

I would reverse the judgment of the Court of Appeal, and remand the case to the trial court for a determination of disputed parentage on the basis of the best interests of the child.

NOTES AND QUESTIONS

1. *Objections to Surrogacy.* Five years earlier, in In the Matter of Baby M, 109 N.J. 396 (1988), the Supreme Court of New Jersey invalidated a surrogacy contract under facts similar to *Johnson v. Calvert*. In both cases, the surrogate and the commissioning parents developed palpable animosity for each other and the surrogate sought to invalidate the surrogacy contract. The court in *Baby M* invalidated the contract as inconsistent with the prohibition on the use of money in adoption, requirements concerning parental fitness in custody determinations, and public policy. The *Baby M* decision reflected many of the objections raised to surrogacy agreements at that time. These objections generally fall into three categories—those related to the contracting parties; those related to the child; and those related to the effect of the process on society as a whole.

The first argument generally advanced against surrogacy is that it exploits women who are willing to give or rent their bodies as vessels to carry other people's children. Could the inducement of payment for pregnancy cause a woman to consent to something that otherwise would be an unthinkable intrusion upon her body? Will the development of commercial surrogacy lead to a class of poor women who will become child-bearers for wealthy women who do not want to undergo pregnancy? Does the relationship between ethnicity and the distribution of wealth in this society mean it is likely that we will develop separate childbearing races and child-raising races? For an interesting discussion of American women who "outsource" pregnancy to women in India, where the service is far cheaper than it is in the United States, see Judith Warner, Outsourced Wombs (Domestic Disturbances), N.Y. Times (Jan. 3, 2008).

Feminists have been divided on this issue. Some are deeply offended by the use of the woman's body in this way; others believe this is misguided paternalism that leads courts (and others) to conclude that women are incapable of deciding for themselves whether they should enter surrogacy contracts. There are echoes of this paternalism concern in *Johnson*, when Justice Panelli points out that "there is no proof that surrogacy contracts exploit poor women to any greater degree than economic necessity in general exploits them by inducing them to accept lower-paid or otherwise undesirable employment." Some economists argue that making surrogacy contracts unenforceable will merely lower the amount that is paid to surrogates. Thus, they suggest, making surrogacy contracts unenforceable is just another in a long history of allegedly protectionist regulations that restrict what a woman may choose to do with her body. See Debra Satz, Feminist Perspectives on Reproduction and the Family, Stanford Encyclopedia of Philosophy (rev. 2013).

Another argument is that surrogacy contracts ought to be prohibited or discouraged because they advance only the best interests of the contracting parties, not the best interest of the child. Normally in a custody dispute between those with claims as parents, the court will look to the best interest of the child in determining the appropriate placement. Enforcing a surrogacy contract seems inconsistent with this principle. How does Justice Kennard say this concern should be addressed in the dissent? In addition, some believe that children who find out that they were carried by a surrogate will be injured by that discovery; others argue that surrogacy contracts render children instruments for the use of parents, not ends in themselves, and that this is necessarily harmful for children.

Finally, some believe that the fabric of society as a whole is weakened by surrogacy arrangements, at least commercial ones. In *Baby M*, Chief Justice Wilentz compared the surrogacy contract to the sale of a child and noted that "[a]lmost every evil that prompted the prohibition of the payment of money in connection with adoptions exists here." Surrogacy contracts are often condemned on the ground that they constitute baby selling, which is illegal in every state. There is confusion over the purpose of statutes that prohibit baby selling, though: they may be intended to protect parents from financial inducements to give up their children, or they may be intended to protect children from being reduced to the status of an ordinary commodity. Should surrogacy arrangements be governed by baby selling statutes? For exploration of the debate on baby selling and its logical consequences, see E. Landes & R. Posner, The Economics of the Baby Shortage, 7 J. Legal. Stud. 323 (1978); J.R.S. Prichard, A Market for Babies?, 34 U. Toronto L.J. 341 (1984); and Michele Goodwin, The Free-Market Approach to Adoption: The Value of a Baby, 26 B.C. Third World L.J. 61 (2006).

Although surrogacy remains hotly debated in parts of the U.S., there is increased acceptance. This is likely due, in part, to growing public awareness of the benefits of surrogacy in overcoming infertility or other reproductive barriers for those who want children. This may also be due to the increased visibility of surrogates willing to publicly share their experiences and explain their choices in their own voice. In New York, for example, the Protecting Modern Families Coalition, which describes itself as "a coalition of advocates from LGBTQ+, women's, religious, and infertility organizations" worked with state lawmakers to overhaul New York's parentage law through the Child-Parent Security Act enacted in 2020. This Act legalized surrogacy and modernized rules establishing parentage for children conceived through ART. A number of surrogates wrote a letter supporting the Act, challenging what they characterized as inaccurate assumptions about surrogacy based on outdated practices or troubling but unrepresentative examples of unethical practices in some developing countries, as well as assumptions about women's lack of knowledge or agency. In describing their reason for choosing surrogacy, they explain:

> All of us are lucky to have families of our own. We know the incomparable joy that comes from raising children, and also know—from our experiences with intended parents—the deep pain that comes when you are told that parenthood isn't possible for you.

> The decision to serve as a surrogate is not one that any of us entered into lightly. We each researched the science and the legal guidelines, learned about the experiences of other surrogates, and thought deeply about the commitment and process involved. For us, it came down to giving the gift of life to people who want nothing more than to raise children of their own.

Surrogates Issue Letter in Support of Parent-Child Security Act, Jan. 23, 2020, at familyequality.org/press-releases/.

2.   *The Role of Parentage Law*. Compare the different approaches taken by the majority and dissent in *Johnson*. What do they reveal about the judges' understanding of the role of parentage law and the interests it should advance? As the *Johnson* and *Baby M* cases illustrate, courts have taken different approaches to these questions. Compare McDonald v. McDonald, 196 A.D.2d 7 (N.Y. App. Div. 1994) (a "true 'egg donation' " case, in which the court determined that a woman who gestated a child produced through the fertilization of another woman's ovum with her husband's sperm was to be considered the mother of the child that resulted, relying heavily on the reasoning of *Johnson v. Calvert*) with Belsito v. Clark, 67 Ohio Misc.2d 54 (1994) (rejecting *Johnson's* reasoning and holding that parentage was to be determined by genetic contribution, not by the intent-to-procreate of the parties to the original surrogacy agreement). But see S.N. v. M.B., 935 N.E.2d 463 (Ohio Ct. App. 2010), *rev. dismissed* 931 N.E.2d 126 (Ohio 2010) (relying on intent to enforce a surrogacy contract).

Uncertainty about the enforceability of surrogacy arrangements have motivated amendments to the original UPA. The 2002 UPA included an article recognizing and regulating surrogacy contracts, but these provisions were not popular with states. Almost half of the states had not addressed surrogacy by statute, and states that did tended to craft different approaches. In response, further updates were made in the 2017 UPA, with the goal of making them more consistent with current surrogacy practice and recently adopted statutes. Consider how the 2017 UPA addresses surrogacy in the excerpts below.

UNIFORM PARENTAGE ACT (2017)
[ARTICLE 8—SURROGACY AGREEMENT]

§ 801.   **DEFINITIONS.** In this [article]:

(1) "Genetic surrogate" means a woman who is not an intended parent and who agrees to become pregnant through assisted reproduction

using her own gamete, under a genetic surrogacy agreement as provided in this [article].

(2) "Gestational surrogate" means a woman who is not an intended parent and who agrees to become pregnant through assisted reproduction using gametes that are not her own, under a gestational surrogacy agreement as provided in this [article].

(3) "Surrogacy agreement" means an agreement between one or more intended parents and a woman who is not an intended parent in which the woman agrees to become pregnant through assisted reproduction and which provides that each intended parent is a parent of a child conceived under the agreement. Unless otherwise specified, the term refers to both a gestational surrogacy agreement and a genetic surrogacy agreement.

§ 802. ELIGIBILITY TO ENTER GESTATIONAL OR GENETIC SURROGACY AGREEMENT.

(a) To execute an agreement to act as a gestational or genetic surrogate, a woman must: (1) have attained 21 years of age; (2) previously have given birth to at least one child; (3) complete a medical evaluation related to the surrogacy arrangement by a licensed medical doctor; (4) complete a mental-health consultation by a licensed mental-health professional; and (5) have independent legal representation of her choice throughout the surrogacy arrangement regarding the terms of the surrogacy agreement and the potential legal consequences of the agreement.

(b) To execute a surrogacy agreement, each intended parent, whether or not genetically related to the child, must: (1) have attained 21 years of age; (2) complete a medical evaluation related to the surrogacy arrangement by a licensed medical doctor; (3) complete a mental-health consultation by a licensed mental health professional; and (4) have independent legal representation of the intended parent's choice throughout the surrogacy arrangement regarding the terms of the surrogacy agreement and the potential legal consequences of the agreement.

* * *

§ 804. REQUIREMENTS OF GESTATIONAL OR GENETIC SURROGACY AGREEMENT: CONTENT.

(a) A surrogacy agreement must comply with the following requirements:

(1) A surrogate agrees to attempt to become pregnant by means of assisted reproduction.

(2) Except as otherwise provided [in this Act], the surrogate and the surrogate's spouse or former spouse, if any, have no claim to parentage of a child conceived by assisted reproduction under the agreement.

(3) The surrogate's spouse, if any, must acknowledge and agree to comply with the obligations imposed on the surrogate by the agreement.

(4) Except as otherwise provided [in this Act], the intended parent or, if there are two intended parents, each one [ ] will be the exclusive parent or parents of the child, regardless of number of children born or gender or mental or physical condition of each child.

(5) Except as otherwise provided [in this Act], [the intended parents] immediately on birth will assume responsibility for the financial support of the child, regardless of number of children born or gender or mental or physical condition of each child.

* * *

(7) The agreement must permit the surrogate to make all health and welfare decisions regarding herself and her pregnancy. This [Act] does not enlarge or diminish the surrogate's right to terminate her pregnancy.

(8) The agreement must include information about each party's right under this [article] to terminate the surrogacy agreement.

(b) A surrogacy agreement may provide for: (1) payment of consideration and reasonable expenses; and (2) reimbursement of specific expenses if the agreement is terminated under this [Article]. . . .

* * *

§ 808. TERMINATION OF GESTATIONAL SURROGACY AGREEMENT.

(a) A party to a gestational surrogacy agreement may terminate the agreement, at any time before an embryo transfer, by giving notice of termination in a record to all other parties. If an embryo transfer does not result in a pregnancy, a party may terminate the agreement at any time before a subsequent embryo transfer.

(b) Unless a gestational surrogacy agreement provides otherwise, on termination of the agreement under subsection (a), the parties are released from the agreement, except that each intended parent remains responsible for expenses that are reimbursable under the agreement and incurred by the gestational surrogate through the date of termination.

(c) Except in a case involving fraud, neither a gestational surrogate nor the surrogate's spouse or former spouse, if any, is liable to the intended parent or parents for a penalty or liquidated damages, for terminating a gestational surrogacy agreement under this section.

§ 809. PARENTAGE UNDER GESTATIONAL SURROGACY AGREEMENT.

(a)   Except as otherwise provided in [this Act], on birth of a child conceived by assisted reproduction under a gestational surrogacy agreement, each intended parent is, by operation of law, a parent of the child.

(b)   Except as otherwise provided in [this Act], neither a gestational surrogate nor the surrogate's spouse or former spouse, if any, is a parent of the child.

* * *

(d)   Except as otherwise provided in [this Act], if, due to a clinical or laboratory error, a child conceived by assisted reproduction under a gestational surrogacy agreement is not genetically related to an intended parent or a donor who donated to the intended parent or parents, each intended parent, and not the gestational surrogate and the surrogate's spouse or former spouse, if any, is a parent of the child, subject to any other claim of parentage.

* * *

§ 812. EFFECT OF GESTATIONAL SURROGACY AGREEMENT.

(a)   A gestational surrogacy agreement that [complies with §§ 802–804] is enforceable.

(b)   If a child was conceived by assisted reproduction under a gestational surrogacy agreement that does not comply [with the above requirements], the court shall determine the rights and duties of the parties to the agreement consistent with the intent of the parties at the time of execution of the agreement. . . .

* * *

§ 813. REQUIREMENT TO VALIDATE GENETIC SURROGACY AGREEMENT.

(a)   Except as otherwise provided in Section 816, to be enforceable, a genetic surrogacy agreement must be validated by [designate court] [prior to commencement of the assisted reproduction].

§ 814. TERMINATION OF GENETIC SURROGACY AGREEMENT.

(a) A party to a genetic surrogacy agreement may terminate the agreement as follows:

* * *

(2) A genetic surrogate . . . may withdraw consent to the agreement any time before 72 hours after the birth of a child conceived by assisted reproduction under the agreement. . . .

[Eds. Note: The other provisions of this section follow the rules for termination of gestational surrogacy in § 808.]

§ 815. PARENTAGE UNDER VALIDATED GENETIC SURROGACY.

(a) Unless a genetic surrogate exercises the right under Section 814 to terminate a genetic surrogacy agreement, each intended parent is a parent of a child conceived by assisted reproduction under an agreement validated under Section 813.

* * *

§ 816. EFFECT OF NONVALIDATED GENETIC SURROGACY AGREEMENT.

* * *

(b) If all parties agree, a court may validate a genetic surrogacy agreement after assisted reproduction has occurred but before the birth of a child conceived by assisted reproduction. . . .

(d) If . . . a genetic surrogate [withdraws] her consent to the agreement [after 72 hours after the birth of child], the court shall adjudicate parentage of the child based on the best interest of the child, taking into account . . . the intent of the parties . . . .

* * *

NOTES AND QUESTIONS

1.   *Relaxing Surrogacy Rules.* Is the legal standard in Article 8 of the Uniform Parentage Act (2017) different from the test applied by the court in *Johnson v. Calvert*? Would the case have been decided differently under the 2017 UPA? As noted above, one of the goals of the drafters of the 2017 UPA was to update the surrogacy provisions to make them more consistent with current practice and law, including liberalizing the rules governing gestational surrogacy agreements. For example, the 2002 UPA requires procedures similar to those for adoption: parties to a surrogacy agreement must obtain court approval of the agreement before seeking medical procedures relating to the agreement, and the court's approval must be based, in part, on a home study by the relevant child-welfare agency (unless waived by the court). The 2017 version eliminates the requirement of pre-pregnancy court validation for gestational surrogacy agreements, but retains this requirement for genetic surrogacy contracts. The 2017 UPA also eliminates the home study requirement. The 2017 version contains other procedural protections for surrogacy agreements, such as requiring the intended legal parents to pay for independent legal representation for the surrogate, requiring the surrogate's spouse to be a party to the agreement, and requiring execution of the agreement before any medical procedure is performed. Importantly, the 2017

UPA provides guidance for how parentage may be determined in cases where the surrogacy agreement does not comply with the law.

2.   *Gestational vs. Genetic Surrogacy.* Another difference between the 2017 UPA and the prior version is how it regulates genetic versus gestational surrogacy agreements. The 2017 UPA permits both, but it imposes additional safeguards or requirements on genetic surrogacy agreements. As noted above, court approval is required for genetic surrogacy contracts only. In addition, while gestational surrogacy agreements are binding once successful transfer has occurred, genetic surrogates are allowed to withdraw their consent any time up to 72 hours after birth. The comments explain that "[t]his differentiation . . . is intended to reflect both the factual differences between the two types of surrogacy as well as the reality that policy makers view these two forms of surrogacy as being quite different." What are those differences?

3.   *Healthcare Decision-Making by Surrogates.* Recall the earlier discussion about decision-making during pregnancy in Section VI. What are the implications of this for intended parents who may want to require or prohibit certain behavior by surrogates? Modern surrogacy laws may address this potential conflict in various ways. How does the UPA 2017 address health care decision-making during a surrogate's pregnancy? Compare this to the approach in the Connecticut Parentage Act:

(8)   The surrogacy agreement shall not infringe on the rights of the person acting as surrogate to make all health and welfare decisions regarding the person, the person's body and the person's pregnancy throughout the duration of the surrogacy arrangement, including during attempts to become pregnant, pregnancy, delivery and post-partum. The surrogacy agreement shall not infringe upon the right of the person acting as surrogate to autonomy in medical decision making by, including, but not limited to, requiring the person acting as surrogate to undergo a scheduled, nonmedically indicated caesarean section or to undergo multiple embryo transfer. Except as otherwise provided by law, any written or oral agreement purporting to waive or limit the rights described in this subdivision are void as against public policy.

NOTE: ART & CHANGING NORMS

As noted above, the technology for facilitating reproduction has challenged social and legal decisions based on traditional assumptions of family models. It has also highlighted justice concerns arising out of the disparate treatment of certain groups under parentage laws and when trying to access to fertility care.

1.   *Application of Parentage Laws to Same Sex Couples.* Same sex couples have had difficulty establishing parentage for a couple of reasons. First, as the previous cases demonstrate, parentage laws have reflected certain heteronormative assumptions about who could be considered parents. Recall that in *Johnson v. Calvert*, the court noted that "for any child California law recognizes only one natural mother, despite advances in reproductive

technology rendering a different outcome biologically possible." Consider the implications for a same sex lesbian couple in which one person contributes the ovum and the other carries the child to term. A Florida court confronted this issue in T.M.H. v. D.M.T., 79 So.3d 787 (Fla. App. 2011). In *T.M.H.*, the ovum source and the birth mother planned to raise the child together, paid for the infertility treatment together, and did raise the child together after the child's birth. When the relationship went bad, though, the birth mother absconded with the child to Australia. The genetic mother sought an order that she was a parent of the child and entitled to parental rights. The birth mother disagreed and argued that under the relevant Florida statute an egg donor could not be mother at all:

> The donor of any egg, sperm, or preembryo, other than the commissioning couple or a father who has executed a preplanned adoption agreement [ ], shall relinquish all maternal or paternal rights and obligations with respect to the donation or the resulting children. . . .

Fla. Stat. sec. 742.14. The trial court judge reluctantly agreed that the ovum source could not be a parent under the statute, but the decision was appealed. The State Supreme Court ultimately held the application of the statute to preclude assertion of parental rights unconstitutional for two reasons. First, it deprived the biological mother of parental rights where she was an intended parent and actually established a parental relationship with the child. Second, to the extent the statutory exception to relinquishment of rights provided for a "commissioning couple" was applied to opposite sex, but not same sex, couples, this violated state and federal equal protection law. D.M.T. v. T.M.H., 129 So.3d 320 (Fla. 2013). Same sex couples have also faced barriers as a result of parentage assumptions that rely on marriage status, in states where same sex couples have been denied the right to marry. See, e.g., Miller-Jenkins v. Miller-Jenkins, 912 A.2d 951 (Vt. 2006).

Such discrimination appears to be unconstitutional after Obergefell v. Hodges, 576 U.S. 644 (2015). In a five-to-four decision, the Court held that denying the right to marry to same sex couples violated the Fourteenth Amendment, and that a state cannot treat married couples differently because of the sexual identity or preference of the spouses. The Court also expressly noted that the right to marry protects not only romantic relationships, but "safeguards children and families" as well. *Obergefell* is understood as establishing the parenting rights of same sex couples. For example, before *Obergefell* a dozen states limited the opportunity of same sex couples to adopt or foster children. In 2016, Mississippi, the last state to maintain such a statutory or regulatory limitation, saw it overturned by judicial decision in Campaign for S. Equal. v. Mississippi Dep't. of Human Servs., 175 F. Supp. 3d 691 (S.D. Miss. 2016):

> In sum, the majority opinion [in Obergefell] foreclosed litigation over laws interfering with the right to marry and "rights and responsibilities intertwined with marriage." [ ] It also seems highly unlikely that the same court that held a state cannot ban gay marriage because it would deny

benefits—expressly including the right to adopt—would then conclude that married gay couples can be denied that very same benefit.

Nonetheless, according to one scholar's comprehensive survey of contemporary regulation of parental recognition in the context of ART, even after *Obergefell* those departing from traditional norms of gender and sexuality have continued to have their parent-child relationships discounted. See Douglas NeJaime, The Nature of Parenthood, 126 Yale L.J. 2260 (2017). Indeed, the 2017 revisions to the UPA were in part an attempt to remedy apparent constitutional deficiencies of state parentage laws in light of *Obergefell*.

2.   *State Recognition of Multiple Parents*. Parentage law has undergone a significant shift since the court's observation in *Johnson v. Calvert* that a child could not have two mothers under California law. Since 2014, California law has allowed legal recognition that a child has more than two parents, but only where such a finding "is necessary to protect the child from the detriment of being separated from one of his or her parents." Cal. Fam. Code § 7612(c) provides:

> In determining detriment to the child, the court shall consider all relevant factors, including, but not limited to, the harm of removing the child from a stable placement with a parent who has fulfilled the child's physical needs and the child's psychological needs for care and affection, and who has assumed that role for a substantial period of time. A finding of detriment to the child does not require a finding of unfitness of any of the parents or persons with a claim to parentage.

Families with more than two parents are permitted but not preferred, it seems, under the judicial considerations required by the statute. A handful of other states have also recognized more-than-two-parent families, either by statute or by judicial determination. See, e.g., Nevada Assembly Bill 115 (enacted Jun. 8, 2021.

3.   *Refusal to Provide Fertility Treatment*. Despite greater social and legal recognition of non-traditional family structures, some physicians and hospitals refuse to provide the full range of infertility services to single people or those who may not conform to traditional norms of gender and sexuality. See, e.g., North Coast Women's Care Medical Group v. Superior Court, 44 Cal. 4th 1145, 189 P.3d 959 (2008) (plaintiff who was a lesbian alleged that a health care provider refused to provide her with necessary infertility treatment because of her sexual orientation in violation of state antidiscrimination law). Some states have laws that prohibit such discrimination, such as California's Unruh Civil Rights Act, which prohibits discrimination on the basis of sex, marital status, and sexual orientation, among other categories, by public accommodations. Cal. Civ. Code § 51. Although not all states contain similar antidiscrimination protections, recall from Chapter 6, Section IV.B. that the ACA's Section 1557 prohibition against sex discrimination likely includes discrimination on the basis of sexual orientation and gender identity.

Provider refusal to treat raises a broader question about the gatekeeping role of physicians generally in the area of ART. May physicians refuse to help someone have a child because that person is unmarried (and with no partner), considered psychologically immature, welfare dependent, has a history of a serious genetic disorder, or is HIV positive? Historically, such rejections were commonplace. Office of Technology Assessment, Artificial Insemination Practice in the United States (1988). A 2005 survey of assisted reproductive technology programs revealed that ART providers screened out people for a whole host of reasons. For example, among those surveyed: 81% were very or extremely likely to turn away a couple where the man had been physically abusive to his existing child; 59%—a woman who was HIV+; 55%—a woman who had severe diabetes with a 10% chance that pregnancy would lead to her death; 48%—a gay couple wanting to use a surrogate (yet only 17% were likely to turn away a lesbian couple wanting to use a sperm donor); 38%—a couple dependent on welfare; 20%—a woman with no partner. Andrea D. Gurmankin et al., Screening Practices and Beliefs of Assisted Reproductive Technology Programs, 83 Fertility and Sterility 61 (2005). Are some of these categories of refusals more troubling than others on ethical grounds? Do the underlying reasons for refusal matter? Should ART practitioners be able to consider parental fitness at all? If so, how would fitness be determined and might this trigger the kind of reproductive justice concerns identified earlier in this chapter. For example, there is evidence that some providers assume unfitness among people with certain kinds of disabilities. See Kimberly M. Mitcherson, Disabling Dreams of Parenthood: The Fertility Industry, Anti-discrimination, and Parents with Disabilities, 27 Law & Ineq. 311 (2009). Would any of the above refusals implicate antidiscrimination law, such as the Americans with Disabilities Act or Section 1557 of the ACA? (See Chapter 6).

The Ethics Committee of the American Society of Reproductive Medicine (ASRM) has issued several relevant ethics opinions concerning provider refusals to treat. See Ethics Committee Opinions and Webinars at the ASRM website at ASRM.org. In one opinion, the Committee explains that "fertility programs may withhold services from prospective patients on the basis of well-grounded reasons that those patients will be unable to provide minimally adequate or safe care for offspring." ASRM, Child-Rearing Ability and the Provision of Fertility Services, 108 Fertil. & Steril., 944 (Dec. 2017). But it goes on to advise programs to develop written policies and procedures for making such determinations, and cautions that "[b]ecause of the importance of reproduction, judgments to deny treatment should be made only when there is a strong and substantial basis for doing so." In addition to reproductive interests, this Opinion identifies important antidiscrimination principles codified in federal and state laws that limit providers' ability to refuse treatment. This opinion, and a series of others, advise that providers should not deny care solely on the basis of disability, HIV status, sexual orientation, marital status, or gender identity. See, e.g., Human Immunodeficiency Virus (HIV) and Infertility Treatment 104 Fertil. & Steril. e1 (Jul. 2015) (emphasizing that HIV is a manageable disease, and that certain ART and other medical treatments have proven highly effective in avoiding newborn infection in the case of HIV+ parents); Access to Fertility Treatment by Gays, Lesbians, and Unmarried Persons, 100 Fertil. & Steril. 1514 (Dec. 2013) (finding that no reasonable claim can be made that children reproduced outside of heterosexual marriage are harmed and taking the position that "[m]oral objection . . . itself is not an acceptable basis for limiting childrearing or reproduction" by single individuals or same-sex couples); Access to fertility services by transgender persons: an Ethics Committee opinion, 104 Fertil Steril 1111 (Nov. 2015) (providing similar guidance).

C. *IN VITRO* FERTILIZATION, EGG TRANSFER, AND EMBRYO TRANSFER

In vitro (literally, "in glass") fertilization is a highly technical medical intervention. In the normal *in vitro* case, an ovum that is ready to be released from the ovary is identified through laparoscopy or ultrasound and removed from the ovary by surgery or aspiration through a hollow needle. The ovum is placed in a container with the appropriate amount of semen containing fertile sperm. The fertilized ovum is then placed in the woman's uterus, where it is permitted to implant and develop. But in the course of this process, circumstances may change that affect the parties' intent to use the embryos for their original procreative purposes. How do courts decide what happens to the embryos in these instances?

DAVIS V. DAVIS
Supreme Court of Tennessee, 1992.
842 S.W.2d 588.

DAUGHTREY, J.

This appeal presents a question of first impression, involving the disposition of the cryogenically-preserved product of in vitro fertilization (IVF), commonly referred to in the popular press and the legal journals as "frozen embryos." The case began as a divorce action, filed by the appellee, Junior Lewis Davis, against his then wife, appellant Mary Sue Davis. The parties were able to agree upon all terms of dissolution, except one: who was to have "custody" of the seven "frozen embryos" stored in a Knoxville fertility clinic that had attempted to assist the Davises in achieving a much-wanted pregnancy during a happier period in their relationship.

I.   Introduction

Mary Sue Davis originally asked for control of the "frozen embryos" with the intent to have them transferred to her own uterus, in a post-divorce effort to become pregnant. Junior Davis objected, saying that he preferred to leave the embryos in their frozen state until he decided whether or not he wanted to become a parent outside the bounds of marriage.

Based on its determination that the embryos were "human beings" from the moment of fertilization, the trial court awarded "custody" to Mary Sue Davis and directed that she "be permitted the opportunity to bring these children to term through implantation." The Court of Appeals reversed, finding that Junior Davis has a "constitutionally protected right not to beget a child where no pregnancy has taken place" and holding that "there is no compelling state interest to justify[ ] ordering implantation against the will of either party." The Court of Appeals further held that "the parties share an interest in the seven fertilized ova" and remanded the case to the trial court for entry of an order vesting them with "joint control . . . and equal voice over their disposition."

Mary Sue Davis then sought review in this Court, contesting the validity of the constitutional basis for the Court of Appeals decision. We granted review, not because we disagree with the basic legal analysis utilized by the intermediate court, but because of the obvious importance of the case in terms of the development of law regarding the new reproductive technologies, and because the decision of the Court of Appeals does not give adequate guidance to the trial court in the event the parties cannot agree.

We note, in this latter regard, that their positions have already shifted: both have remarried and Mary Sue Davis (now Mary Sue Stowe) has moved out of state. She no longer wishes to utilize the "frozen embryos" herself, but wants authority to donate them to a childless couple. Junior Davis is adamantly opposed to such donation and would prefer to see the "frozen embryos" discarded. The result is, once again, an impasse, but the parties' current legal position does have an effect on the probable outcome of the case, as discussed below.

If we have no statutory authority or common law precedents to guide us [in this case], we do have the benefit of extensive comment and analysis in the legal journals. In those articles, medical-legal scholars and ethicists have proposed various models for the disposition of "frozen embryos" when unanticipated contingencies arise, such as divorce, death of one or both of the parties, financial reversals, or simple disenchantment with the IVF process. Those models range from a rule requiring, at one extreme, that all embryos be used by the gamete-providers or donated for uterine transfer, and, at the other extreme, that any unused embryos be automatically discarded. Other formulations would vest control in the female gamete-provider—in every case, because of her greater physical and emotional contribution to the IVF process, or perhaps only in the event that she wishes to use them herself. There are also two "implied contract" models: one would infer from enrollment in an IVF program that the IVF clinic has authority to decide in the event of an impasse whether to donate, discard, or use the "frozen embryos" for research; the other would infer from the parties' participation in the creation of the embryos that they had made an irrevocable commitment to reproduction and would require transfer either to the female provider or to a donee. There are also the so-called "equity models": one would avoid the conflict altogether by dividing the "frozen embryos" equally between the parties, to do with as they wish; the other would award veto power to the party wishing to avoid parenthood, whether it be the female or the male progenitor.

Each of these possible models has the virtue of ease of application. Adoption of any of them would establish a bright-line test that would dispose of disputes like the one we have before us in a clear and predictable manner. As appealing as that possibility might seem, we conclude that given the relevant principles of constitutional law, the existing public policy of Tennessee with regard to unborn life, the current state of scientific knowledge giving rise to the emerging reproductive technologies, and the ethical considerations that have developed in response to that scientific knowledge, there can be no easy answer to the question we now face. We conclude, instead, that we must weigh the interests of each party to the dispute, in terms of the facts and analysis set out below, in order to resolve that dispute in a fair and responsible manner.

* * *

IV. The "Person" vs. "Property" Dichotomy

One of the fundamental issues the inquiry poses is whether the preembryos in this case should be considered "persons" or "property" in the contemplation of the law. The Court of Appeals held, correctly, that they cannot be considered "persons" under Tennessee law . . . .

Nor do preembryos enjoy protection as "persons" under federal law. . . .

Left undisturbed, the trial court's ruling would have afforded preembryos the legal status of "persons" and vested them with legally cognizable interests separate from those of their progenitors. Such a decision would doubtless have had the effect of outlawing IVF programs in the state of Tennessee. But in setting aside the trial court's judgment, the Court of Appeals, at least by implication, may have swung too far in the opposite direction.

To our way of thinking, the most helpful discussion on this point is found not in the minuscule number of legal opinions that have involved "frozen embryos," but in the ethical standards set by The American Fertility Society, as follows:

Three major ethical positions have been articulated in the debate over preembryo status. At one extreme is the view of the preembryo as a human subject after fertilization, which requires that it be accorded the rights of a person. This position entails an obligation to provide an opportunity for implantation to occur and tends to ban any action before transfer that might harm the preembryo or that is not immediately therapeutic, such as freezing and some preembryo research.

At the opposite extreme is the view that the preembryo has a status no different from any other human tissue. With the consent of those who have decision-making authority over the preembryo, no limits should be imposed on actions taken with preembryos.

A third view—one that is most widely held—takes an intermediate position between the other two. It holds that the preembryo deserves respect greater than that accorded to human tissue but not the respect accorded to actual persons. The preembryo is due greater respect than other human tissue because of its potential to become a person and because of its symbolic meaning for many people. Yet, it should not be treated as a person, because it has not yet developed the features of personhood, is not yet established as developmentally individual, and may never realize its biologic potential.

* * *

In its report, the Ethics Committee then calls upon those in charge of IVF programs to establish policies in keeping with the "special respect" due preembryos and suggests:

Within the limits set by institutional policies, decision-making authority regarding preembryos should reside with the persons who have provided the gametes. . . . As a matter of law, it is reasonable to assume that the gamete providers have primary decision-making authority regarding preembryos in the absence of specific legislation on the subject. A person's liberty to procreate or to avoid procreation is directly involved in most decisions involving preembryos.[ ]

We conclude that preembryos are not, strictly speaking, either "persons" or "property," but occupy an interim category that entitles them to special respect because of their potential for human life. It follows that any interest that Mary Sue Davis and Junior Davis have in the preembryos in this case is not a true property interest. However, they do have an interest in the nature of ownership, to the extent that they have decision-making authority concerning disposition of the preembryos, within the scope of policy set by law.

V.   The Enforceability of Contract

* * *

We believe, as a starting point, that an agreement regarding disposition of any untransferred preembryos in the event of contingencies (such as the death of one or more of the parties, divorce, financial reversals, or abandonment of the program) should be presumed valid and should be enforced as between the progenitors. This conclusion is in keeping with the proposition that the progenitors, having provided the gametic material giving rise to the preembryos, retain decision-making authority as to their disposition.

At the same time, we recognize that life is not static, and that human emotions run particularly high when a married couple is attempting to overcome infertility problems. It follows that the parties' initial "informed consent" to IVF procedures will often not be truly informed because of the near impossibility of anticipating, emotionally and psychologically, all the turns that events may take as the IVF process unfolds. Providing that the initial agreements may later be modified by agreement will, we think, protect the parties against some of the risks they face in this regard. But, in the absence of such agreed modification, we conclude that their prior agreements should be considered binding.

* * *

[In this case,] we are . . . left with this situation: there was initially no agreement between the parties concerning disposition of the preembryos under the circumstances of this case; there has been no agreement since; and there is no formula in the Court of Appeals opinion for determining the outcome if the parties cannot reach an agreement in the future.

* * *

VI. The Right of Procreational Autonomy

Although an understanding of the legal status of preembryos is necessary in order to determine the enforceability of agreements about their disposition, asking whether or not they constitute "property" is not an altogether helpful question. As the appellee points out in his brief, "[as] two or eight cell tiny lumps of complex protein, the embryos have no [intrinsic] value to either party." Their value lies in the "potential to become, after implantation, growth and birth, children." Thus, the essential dispute here is not where or how or how long to store the preembryos, but whether the parties will become parents. The Court of Appeals held in effect that they will become parents if they both agree to become parents. The Court did not say what will happen if they fail to agree. We conclude that the answer to this dilemma turns on the parties' exercise of their constitutional right to privacy.

* * *

[The Court found there was a right to individual privacy in both Federal and Tennessee State law, and that this right to individual privacy encompassed the right of procreational autonomy.]

For the purposes of this litigation it is sufficient to note that, whatever its ultimate constitutional boundaries, the right of procreational autonomy is composed of two rights of equal significance—the right to procreate and the right to avoid procreation. Undoubtedly, both are subject to protections and limitations.

The equivalence of and inherent tension between these two interests are nowhere more evident than in the context of in vitro fertilization. None of the concerns about a woman's bodily integrity that have previously precluded men from controlling abortion decisions is applicable here. We are not unmindful of the fact that the trauma (including both emotional stress and physical discomfort) to which women are subjected in the IVF process is more severe than is the impact of the procedure on men. In this sense, it is fair to say that women contribute more to the IVF process than men. Their experience, however, must be viewed in light of the joys of parenthood that is desired or the relative anguish of a lifetime of unwanted parenthood. As they stand on the brink of potential parenthood, Mary Sue Davis and Junior Lewis Davis must be seen as entirely equivalent gamete-providers.

It is further evident that, however far the protection of procreational autonomy extends, the existence of the right itself dictates that decisional authority rests in the gamete-providers alone, at least to the extent that their decisions have an impact upon their individual reproductive status. . . . [N]o other person or entity has an interest sufficient to permit interference with the gamete-providers' decision to continue or terminate the IVF process, because no one else bears the consequences of these decisions in the way that the gamete-providers do.

Further, at least with respect to Tennessee's public policy and its constitutional right of privacy, the state's interest in potential human life is insufficient to justify an infringement on the gamete-providers' procreational autonomy.

Certainly, if the state's interests do not become sufficiently compelling in the abortion context until the end of the first trimester, after very significant developmental stages have passed, then surely there is no state interest in these preembryos which could suffice to overcome the interests of the gamete-providers. The [Tennessee] abortion statute reveals that the increase in the state's interest is marked by each successive developmental stage such that, toward the end of a pregnancy, this interest is so compelling that abortion is almost strictly forbidden. This scheme supports the conclusion that the state's interest in the potential life embodied by these four-to eight-cell preembryos (which may or may not be able to achieve implantation in a uterine wall and which, if implanted, may or may not begin to develop into fetuses, subject to possible miscarriage) is at best slight. When weighed against the interests of the individuals and the burdens inherent in parenthood, the state's interest in the potential life of these preembryos is not sufficient to justify any infringement upon the freedom of these individuals to make their own decisions as to whether to allow a process to continue that may result in such a dramatic change in their lives as becoming parents. The unique nature of this case requires us to note that the interests of these parties in parenthood are different in scope than the parental interests considered in other cases. Previously, courts have dealt with the childbearing and child-rearing aspects of parenthood. Abortion cases have dealt with gestational parenthood. In this case, the Court must deal with the question of genetic parenthood. We conclude, moreover, that an interest in avoiding genetic parenthood can be significant enough to trigger the protections afforded to all other aspects of parenthood. The technological fact that someone unknown to these parties could gestate these preembryos does not alter the fact that these parties, the gamete-providers, would become parents in that event, at least in the genetic sense. The profound impact this would have on them supports their right to sole decisional authority as to whether the process of attempting to gestate these preembryos should continue. This brings us directly to the question of how to resolve the dispute that arises when one party wishes to continue the IVF process and the other does not.

VII.   Balancing the Parties' Interests

Resolving disputes over conflicting interests of constitutional import is a task familiar to the courts. One way of resolving these disputes is to consider the positions of the parties, the significance of their interests, and the relative burdens that will be imposed by differing resolutions. In this case, the issue centers on the two aspects of procreational autonomy—the right to procreate and the right to avoid procreation. We start by considering the burdens imposed on the parties by solutions that would have the effect of disallowing the exercise of individual procreational autonomy with respect to these particular preembryos.

Beginning with the burden imposed on Junior Davis, we note that the consequences are obvious. Any disposition which results in the gestation of the preembryos would impose unwanted parenthood on him, with all of its possible financial and psychological consequences. The impact that this unwanted parenthood would have on Junior Davis can only be understood by considering his particular circumstances, as revealed in the record.

Junior Davis testified that he was the fifth youngest of six children. When he was five years old, his parents divorced, his mother had a nervous break-down, and he and three of his brothers went to live at a home for boys run by the Lutheran Church. Another brother was taken in by an aunt, and his sister stayed with their mother. From that day forward, he had monthly visits with his mother but saw his father only three more times before he died in 1976. Junior Davis testified that, as a boy, he had severe problems caused by separation from his parents. He said that it was especially hard to leave his mother after each monthly visit. He clearly feels that he has suffered because of his lack of opportunity to establish a relationship with his parents and particularly because of the absence of his father.

In light of his boyhood experiences, Junior Davis is vehemently opposed to fathering a child that would not live with both parents. Regardless of whether he or Mary Sue had custody, he feels that the child's bond with the non-custodial parent would not be satisfactory. He testified very clearly that his concern was for the psychological obstacles a child in such a situation would face, as well as the burdens it would impose on him. Likewise, he is opposed to donation because the recipient couple might divorce, leaving the child (which he definitely would consider his own) in a single-parent setting.

Balanced against Junior Davis's interest in avoiding parenthood is Mary Sue Davis's interest in donating the preembryos to another couple for implantation. Refusal to permit donation of the preembryos would impose on her the burden of knowing that the lengthy IVF procedures she underwent were futile, and that the preembryos to which she contributed genetic material would never become children. While this is not an insubstantial emotional burden, we can only conclude that Mary Sue Davis's interest in donation is not as significant as the interest Junior Davis has in avoiding parenthood. If she were allowed to donate these preembryos, he would face a lifetime of either wondering about his parental status or knowing about his parental status but having no control over it. He testified quite clearly that if these preembryos were brought to term he would fight for custody of his child or children. Donation, if a child came of it, would rob him twice—his procreational autonomy would be defeated and his relationship with his offspring would be prohibited.

The case would be closer if Mary Sue Davis were seeking to use the preembryos herself, but only if she could not achieve parenthood by any other reasonable means. We recognize the trauma that Mary Sue has already experienced and the additional discomfort to which she would be subjected if she opts to attempt IVF again. Still, she would have a reasonable opportunity, through IVF, to try once again to achieve parenthood in all its aspects—genetic, gestational, bearing, and rearing.

Further, we note that if Mary Sue Davis were unable to undergo another round of IVF, or opted not to try, she could still achieve the child-rearing aspects of parenthood through adoption. The fact that she and Junior Davis pursued adoption indicates that, at least at one time, she was willing to forego genetic parenthood and would have been satisfied by the child-rearing aspects of parenthood alone.

VIII.   Conclusion

In summary, we hold that disputes involving the disposition of preembryos produced by in vitro fertilization should be resolved, first, by looking to the preferences of the progenitors. If their wishes cannot be ascertained, or if there is dispute, then their prior agreement concerning disposition should be carried out. If no prior agreement exists, then the relative interests of the parties in using or not using the preembryos must be weighed. Ordinarily, the party wishing to avoid procreation should prevail, assuming that the other party has a reasonable possibility of achieving parenthood by means other than use of the preembryos in question. If no other reasonable alternatives exist, then the argument in favor of using the preembryos to achieve pregnancy should be considered. However, if the party seeking control of the preembryos intends merely to donate them to another couple, the objecting party obviously has the greater interest and should prevail.

But the rule does not contemplate the creation of an automatic veto, and in affirming the judgment of the Court of Appeals, we would not wish to be interpreted as so holding.

For the reasons set out above, the judgment of the Court of Appeals is affirmed, in the appellee's favor. This ruling means that the Knoxville Fertility Clinic is free to follow its normal procedure in dealing with unused preembryos, as long as that procedure is not in conflict with this opinion.

NOTES AND QUESTIONS

1.   Davis *Aftermath*. The Knoxville Fertility Clinic could not "follow its normal procedure in dealing with unused pre-embryos" because its normal procedure was to provide those pre-embryos to infertile couples—a procedure that would have been in conflict with the opinion. On rehearing directed to this issue, the Tennessee court looked to the report of the American Fertility Society's Ethics Committee, which authorizes the pre-embryos to be donated for research purposes (which would require the consent of both of the Davises) or to be discarded. See Davis v. Davis, Order on Petitions to Rehear (Sup.Ct.Tenn., Nov. 23, 1992).

2.   *The Relevance of Abortion Law*. The court suggests that the state interest in assuring that the embryo is implanted and allowed to develop cannot be sufficiently compelling to overcome a gamete-provider's right to avoid parenthood because, by analogy, "the state's interest does not become sufficiently compelling in the abortion context until the end of the first trimester, after very significant developmental stages have passed . . . ." Is the analogy to the abortion context a persuasive one? In the same year in which this case was decided, the U.S. Supreme Court reconsidered the value of drawing trimester lines and pointed out that the "State has legitimate interests from the outset of the pregnancy in protecting . . . the life of a fetus that may become a child." Planned Parenthood of Southeastern Pennsylvania v. Casey, *supra* Section III.B. Could the interest of the state in protecting the fetus extend back to before a fertilized ovum is even introduced into the mother's body, back to the pre-embryo in the laboratory? As a constitutional matter, could a state have an interest in protecting fertilized ova that would

be sufficiently compelling to overcome the interests of one or both of the gamete providers?

3.   *Property vs. Custody Theories.* The court describes several different rules that could be applied in disputes over the status and control of extracorporeal fertilized ova or pre-embryos. One of the alternatives is to treat the pre-embryos as personal property and apply the common law of property to them; another would be to treat those pre-embryos as if they were children entitled to protection of the state law. Each view has some legal support. See *York v. Jones,* 717 F. Supp. 421 (E.D. Va. 1989) (treating frozen embryos prepared in the course of infertility treatment as property that would be subject to the ordinary law of bailment). See also La. Rev. Stat. § 9:131 (applying the "best interest of the in vitro fertilized ovum" standard).

4.   *Enforceability of Contract.* Several courts have followed a path close to that taken in *Davis.* See *Kass v. Kass,* 696 N.E.2d 174 (N.Y. 1998) (enforcing informed consent document declaring that the clinic would use any frozen pre-embryos for research in the event that the progenitors could not agree on their disposition); *Roman v. Roman,* 193 S.W.3d 40 (Tex. Civ. App. 2006, rev. den. 2007) (enforcing the prior agreement allowing the clinic to destroy the embryos); *Dahl v. Angle,* 194 P.3d 834 (Or. Ct. App. 2008) (enforcing prior agreement).

Two courts to confront this issue expressly rejected the notion that the prior agreement of the progenitors should always govern the disposition of frozen embryos. See *A.Z. v. B.Z.,* 725 N.E.2d 1051 (Mass. 2000) (refusing to enforce agreement that provided that if the intended parents were to become separated, the frozen embryos then available would be given to one of the parents for implantation, because it forced the former husband to become a parent against his will and was thus contrary to public policy); *J.B. v. M.B.,* 783 A.2d 707 (N.J. 2001) (holding the parties would not normally be bound by a prior IVF agreement that would now require one of those parties to become a parent against that person's will).

Notably, in *Davis, Kass, Roman,* and *Dahl,* the enforceable prior agreements provided for the destruction of frozen embryos rather than their implantation; but in *A.Z.* and *J.B.,* the agreements would have resulted in the creation of a child (and, of course, parents) against one of the parties' wishes. How important might that distinction have been to explain the different outcomes? Compare *A.Z.* and *J.B.,* supra, with *Szafranski v. Dunston,* 34 N.E.3d 1132 (Ill. App. Ct. 2015) (enforcing prior agreement allowing woman to use cryopreserved pre-embryos created with ex-boyfriend, despite his desire to avoid becoming a parent). See also, Judith Daar, Litowitz v. Litowitz: Feuding over Frozen Embryos and Forecasting the Future of Reproductive Medicine in Sandra Johnson, et al. (eds), Health Law and Bioethics Cases in Context (2009), describing the backstory of an embryo disposition case that involved a battle over which of several agreements signed by the parties should prevail and providing a catalog of frozen embryo cases.

5.   *Other Relevant Factors?* In the United States, clinics conducting *in vitro* fertilization generally try to remove several eggs so that at least a few will be fertilized *in vitro* and can be replaced in the uterus. In some cases there is no fertilization or inadequate fertilization *in vitro,* and, thus, no return to the uterus, although fertilization occurs in most of the ova in which it is attempted. ART success rates can vary based on treatment factors, such as number of embryos transferred and type of ART procedure, as well as patient characteristics, such as age, infertility diagnosis, and history of prior births or miscarriages. For recent data on ART success rates, see CDC, 2018 Assisted Reproductive Technology: Fertility Clinic Success Rates Report 24 (2020).

Because the chances of success are substantially increased if several fertilized ova are returned to the uterus, and because of the high cost and physical burden of repeating the egg retrieval procedure, women undergoing *in vitro* fertilization are generally given drugs to increase the number of ova that become ripe and ready for release and fertilization in one cycle. While this "superovulation" increases the chances of successful fertilization and implantation, inducing ovulation itself may have adverse side effects. In addition, the simultaneous placement of multiple fertilized ova results in a higher rate of multiple births than in the rest of the population, increasing health risks for the woman and child. Given the difference in the burden of retrieval processes, should the ovum source (who went through an invasive surgical procedure, following sometimes debilitating hormone therapy) have greater say in the disposition of the frozen embryo than the sperm source (who went into the next room with a cup)? Would this approach violate principles of equal protection?

Most of the cases suggest that the result in a frozen embryo disposition case might be different if the party who wished to bring the frozen embryo to life were otherwise infertile, and would have no other way to become a parent. In fact, this seemed to be an important factor in the court's decision in Szafranski v. Dunston, supra Note 4. Justice Verniero, concurring in the *J.B.* case, also described in Note 4, pointed out that "the same principles that compel the outcome in this case would permit an infertile party to assert his or her right to use a preembryo against the objections of the other party, if such use were the only means of procreation. In that instance, the balance arguably would weigh in favor of the infertile party absent countervailing factors of greater weight." What might count as "countervailing factors of greater weight"? The *J.B.* majority didn't seem convinced the result would be different if the one seeking to use the embryo were otherwise infertile, saying, "[w]e express no opinion in respect of a case in which a party who has become infertile seeks use of stored preembryos against the wishes of his or her partner, noting only that the possibility of adoption also may be a consideration, among others, in the court's assessment." J.B., supra, at 720.

6.   *Poor Quality Care & Other Harms.* Reproductive technologies, such as *in vitro* fertilization and embryo cryopreservation, can give rise to a host of different kinds of liability. Of course, the physician and medical institution would be liable as in an ordinary medical malpractice case for negligently

performing the medical procedure. Would the duty of due care extend to the fetus as well as the parents? Negligently freezing an ovum or embryo, or negligently thawing it and thus destroying or damaging it, would also subject the appropriate professionals to malpractice liability. For an example of a case based on both intentional and negligent infliction of emotional distress against a provider who destroyed tissue that was cryogenically frozen to allow for later conception, see Witt v. Yale-New Haven Hosp, 977 A.2d 779 (Conn. Super. Ct. 2008). But see Miller v. American Fertility Group of Illinois, 897 N.E.2d 837 (Ill. App. Ct. 2009) (no wrongful death action allowed on behalf of mistakenly destroyed pre-embryo before its implantation in the mother).

The value of cryogenically preserved fertilized pre-embryos (or ova) may also make them targets for theft; clinic employees (or others) may be tempted to provide excess genetic material to those who need it without seeking consent from the original progenitors. Indeed, during the late 1990s that kind of redirection of ova apparently became fairly common at the University of California-Irvine's fertility clinic, where at least fifteen children were born as a result of the use of ova from women who had not consented to their transfer. It also creates the opportunity for mistakes to occur. Consider the case of Prato-Morrison v. Doe, 103 Cal.App.4th 222 (2002). Donna Prato-Morrison and Robert Morrison engaged the services of a fertility clinic without success. When the clinic later became the target of an investigation into its widespread misuse of genetic materials, the Morrisons questioned whether another family who used the fertility clinic (Judith and Jacob Doe) innocently received Donna Morrison's genetic material. The Morrisons filed a complaint in which they asked the court to determine whether they were the genetic parents of the Does' twin daughters (at the time, almost 14 years old); they sought to compel blood tests and obtain the right to visit the twins (who knew nothing about the claim). In rejecting the Morrisons' claims, the court held that plaintiffs failed to introduce admissible evidence that defendant wife had received eggs supplied by plaintiff wife, and that plaintiffs' rights as alleged biological parents did not overcome defendants' rights as presumed parents, so as to entitle plaintiffs to discover whether the twins were born as a result of the theft of their genetic materials. Finally, the court went even further to hold that even had plaintiffs presented proof of a genetic link to the twins sufficient to establish their standing to pursue a parentage action, it would not be in the best interests of the twins to have plaintiffs intrude into their lives, or to be subjected to the blood tests and mental health evaluation suggested by plaintiffs.

But in Robert B. v. Susan B., 109 Cal.App.4th 1109 (2003), the husband of a couple subject to an unintentional mix-up was able to establish parentage. In that case, a husband and wife brought a parentage action against a single woman who had given birth to the genetic brother of a child born to the couple, as the result of the placement of the wrong embryo in the single woman's uterus by a fertility clinic. The husband and wife had sought ova from an anonymous donor for fertilization with the husband's sperm, and the single woman had sought an embryo created from anonymously donated ova and sperm; but after receiving the results of genetic testing of the husband, the single woman learned that she had received ova from an anonymous donor fertilized by the husband's sperm. The Court of Appeal affirmed the trial court's determination that the husband was the child's father, but that the single woman was the child's mother. The husband's wife had no standing because she was biologically unrelated to the child.

7.   *Selective Reduction.* One consequence of the implantation of several embryos fertilized *in vitro* is that many of the embryos may continue to develop *in vivo*. While most multiple births pose no substantial problems to the mother or the neonatal siblings, sometimes the life or health of the mother (or some of the developing fetuses) can be preserved only if the number of fetuses that the mother is carrying is reduced. Is the case of such selective reduction governed by the more general law applying to abortion, described earlier in the chapter? Are there any ethical or legal concerns present in cases of selective reduction that are not present in other situations that might give rise to abortion? What legal or ethical considerations, if any, should guide the choice of which of two or more fetuses should be aborted to save the life or health of the mother or the well-being of the potential siblings?

8.   *Genetic Screening.* One consequence of the ability to freeze an embryo is that it permits evaluation of the genetic structure of the embryo before it is thawed and implanted. This allows for pre-implantation genetic screening or diagnosis (PIGD), which allows for a determination of several genetic attributes of the pre-embryo. This screening (for a wide range of conditions or attributes) or diagnosis (for a particular genetic disease) is increasingly available, as a practical matter, for more conditions, and for a lower cost. For an exploration of the social and ethical questions raised by such advances, see Jaime S. King, And Genetic Testing for All . . . The Coming Revolution in Non-Invasive Prenatal Genetic Testing, 42 Rutgers L.J. 599 (2011), and Erik Parens & Adrienne Asch, The Disability Rights Critique of Prenatal Genetic Testing: Reflections and Recommendations, 29 The Hastings Ctr Rpt S1 (1999).

9.   *ART Regulation.* Other than questions of parentage, ART is still relatively unregulated. Why are state legislatures, many of which have been active in restricting access to abortion, not banning IVF, especially to the extent that it may involve selective reduction? Why might state legislatures and the federal government be less interested in setting standards for care in this area as compared to other areas, such as nursing home care?

D. REPRODUCTIVE CLONING AND STEM CELL RESEARCH

1. Reproductive Cloning

In 1997 the world was stunned by the revelation that a Scottish laboratory had cloned a mammal—to be precise, a Finn Dorset sheep. Scientists achieved this by removing the nucleus from a sheep ovum, replacing it with the genetic material from the sheep to be cloned, and then reimplanting the genetically changed ovum back into the surrogate mother sheep. In fact, the one cloned sheep was the only success in almost 300 attempts. Other mammals were cloned using the same process, but scientists warned that the likelihood that this technology would be available for human beings remained years away. Despite this, the bioethics community began a world-wide discussion on the consequences of cloning as a form of human reproduction.

Is it possible to talk about the creation of human beings through cloning in the same terms as we talk about the creation of human beings through other processes of assisted reproduction? How are the questions raised by the existence of cloned human beings truly different from the questions raised by human beings created by other technically driven medical processes? Cloning requires in vitro manipulation (like in vitro fertilization) and then implantation in a womb (like surrogacy). Is it different from either of those two forms of assisted reproduction? Is cloning really a form of reproduction at all, or is it something different—perhaps, merely replication? Who counts as the parents of the cloned individual? Does it make sense to speak of a "parent" or must we limit ourselves to speaking of the cloned person's "antecedent" or "precursor" or "genetic source"?

For generations, science fiction has raised fears of totalitarian regimes that can clone human beings for enslavement for the benefit of the regime. Should this present a genuine worry to this society? Could cloning be appropriated by the state in support of a totalitarian eugenics policy? A related worry is that a society could treat a newly cloned person as nothing more than the continuation of the source of its genetic material—or as a body parts source for the person who provided the genetic material. But wouldn't a cloned person have all of the rights of any other person? As some bioethicists argue, if our society were to treat cloned human beings as enslaved persons or spare parts warehouses, the existence of cloning would be the least of our problems.

Would cloned people have the same relationship to each other that identical twins maintain? Identical twins have a common genetic make-up, as a clone and his source would, yet we treat those twins as separate human beings with separate lives and we have identified no social dislocation that arises out of their existence. Why should we be more worried about cloned human beings than about identical twins? In fact, because a cloned person and his source would be different ages, they would be likely to be raised in different environments, and thus to be less similar than identical twins. On the other hand, the number of identical twins is naturally limited, and there are very few identical triplets. We could, through cloning, create a much larger number of identical "siblings."

In any case, is there any justifiable reason for cloning a full human being? A few have been suggested. Suppose a child were dying of a disease that could be treated with a bone marrow transplant from a genetically identical donor, but such a donor could not be found. Might it be acceptable to clone the patient, and then, independently, determine if the newly replicated person ought to be a donor for his "brother"? (See the discussion of "savior siblings" in Note on Organ Transplantation from Living Donors at Chapter 17, Section I.C.1.) Alternatively, suppose a couple has an infertility problem which makes it impossible for either of them to become a parent in the ordinary course of events. Should they be able to opt for cloning so that their child will be related to one of them? What if only one of the parents is infertile, and they want a child that does not require the potentially interfering involvement of a third party?

The issue has become more complicated because human reproduction is not the only goal of cloning. Cloning of human stem cells may also be useful in developing therapies for medical conditions that are now untreatable. Many view cloning with the intent of creating a new human being—*reproductive cloning*—as posing far more ethical and legal difficulty than cloning human stem cells with the intent to research or create a medical treatment—*therapeutic cloning*.

Both forms of cloning generally require somatic cell nuclear transfer, a process in which the nucleus of an unfertilized human ovum is removed and replaced with the nucleus from an adult cell. The resulting ovum cell, which has the full complement of human genetic material, is then stimulated so that it will divide and form a pre-embryo. In *therapeutic cloning*, some cells from the pre-embryo are removed for purposes of medical research or treatment. These stem cells have the potential to develop into almost any human cells, and they may be useful in repairing almost any human tissue, but once those cells are removed, the pre-embryo cannot develop into a human being. In *reproductive cloning*, the pre-embryo would be placed in a uterus to develop into a human being.

The National Bioethics Advisory Commission published a comprehensive and thoughtful report on the cloning of human beings within months of the revelation that it had been successfully performed on sheep. The report includes a useful description of the relevant scientific procedures as well as a fully annotated analysis of the ethical, theological, legal and policy issues, and it was careful to distinguish between reproductive cloning (which it considered medically risky) and therapeutic cloning (which, it thought, held great scientific promise).

RECOMMENDATIONS OF THE NATIONAL BIOETHICS ADVISORY COMMISSION (NBAC) WITH REGARD TO CLONING

(1997).

* * *

As somatic cell nuclear transfer cloning could represent a means of human reproduction for some people, limitations on that choice must be made only when the societal benefits of prohibition clearly outweigh the value of maintaining the private nature of such highly personal decisions. Especially in light of some arguably compelling cases for attempting to clone a human being using somatic cell nuclear transfer, the ethics of policy making must strike a balance between the values society wishes to reflect and issues of privacy and the freedom of individual choice.

* * *

. . . . At present, the use of this technique to create a child would be a premature experiment that exposes the developing child to unacceptable risks. This in itself is sufficient to justify a prohibition on cloning human beings at this time, even if such efforts were to be characterized as the exercise of a fundamental right to attempt to procreate. More speculative psychological harms to the child, and effects on the moral, religious, and cultural values of society may be enough to justify continued prohibitions in the future, but more time is needed for discussion and evaluation of these concerns.

* * *

Within this overall framework the Commission came to the following conclusions and recommendations:

I.   The Commission concludes that at this time it is morally unacceptable for anyone in the public or private sector, whether in a research or clinical setting, to attempt to create a child using somatic cell nuclear transfer cloning. We have reached a consensus on this point because current scientific information indicates that this technique is not safe to use in humans at this time. . . .

II.   Federal legislation should be enacted to prohibit anyone from attempting, whether in a research or clinical setting, to create a child through somatic cell nuclear transfer cloning. It is critical, however, that such legislation include a sunset clause to ensure that Congress will review the issue after a specified time period (three to five years) in order to decide whether the prohibition continues to be needed. . . .

III. Any regulatory or legislative actions undertaken to effect the foregoing prohibition on creating a child by somatic cell nuclear transfer should be carefully written so as not to interfere with other important areas of scientific research. In particular, no new regulations are required regarding the cloning of human DNA sequences and cell lines, since neither activity raises the scientific and ethical issues that arise from the attempt to create children through somatic cell nuclear transfer, and these fields of research have already provided important scientific and biomedical advances.

* * *

This was not the last federal bioethics panel to consider the issue. The President's Council on Bioethics (which effectively replaced NBAC, and then itself was subsequently replaced by the Presidential Commission for the Study of Bioethical Issues) issued a series of reports, including Human Cloning and Human Dignity (2002), Monitoring Stem Cell Research (2004), and Reproduction and Responsibility (2004), which supported a ban on reproductive cloning and both a moratorium and then careful regulation of all other cloning. Although disagreements between those who opposed reproductive cloning and those who supported therapeutic cloning (and disagreements among those on each side, too) made it difficult for Congress to legislate with regard to reproductive cloning, many state legislatures have done so. Several have outlawed reproductive cloning, some have outlawed cloning of any kind, and some have outlawed reproductive cloning while at the same time authorizing state funding for stem cell research (which is thought to be both scientifically and economically promising as described further below). See National Conference of State Legislatures (NCSL), Embryonic and Fetal Research Laws, at ncsl.org (last updated Jan. 1, 2016).

2.   Stem Cell Research

Because of the scientific promise shown by stem cell research, many people who support legislation banning reproductive cloning vigorously oppose placing any limitation upon therapeutic cloning believed necessary for effective stem cell research. The ethical issues which have given rise to the legal argument are a bit more subtle than one might expect.

JUDITH JOHNSON AND ERIN WILLIAMS, CRS REPORT FOR CONGRESS: STEM CELL RESEARCH (2006)

* * *

Stem cell research is controversial not because of its goals, but rather because of the means of obtaining some of the cells. Research involving most types of stem cells, such as those derived from adult tissues and umbilical cord blood, is uncontroversial, except when its effectiveness as an alternative to embryonic stem cells is debated. The crux of the debate centers around embryonic stem cells, which enable research that may facilitate the development of medical treatments and cures, but which require the destruction of an embryo to derive. In addition, because cloning is one method of producing embryos for research, the ethical issues surrounding cloning are also relevant.

* * *

Most positions on embryonic stem cell research rest at least in part on the relative moral weight accorded to embryos and that accorded to the prospect of saving, prolonging, or improving others' lives. . . .

Some groups explore the moral standing of human embryos, and also consider the "duty to relieve the pain and suffering of others." Others take the position that embryos do not have the same moral status as persons. They acknowledge that embryos are genetically human, but hold that they do not have the same moral relevance because they lack specific capacities, including consciousness, reasoning and sentience. They also argue that viewing embryos as persons would "rule out all fertility treatments that involve the creation and discarding of excess embryos," and further assert that we do not have the same "moral or religious" response to the natural loss of embryos (through miscarriage) that we do to the death of infants. . . . They conclude that performing research to benefit persons justifies the destruction of embryos. Acceptance of the notion that the destruction of embryos can be justified in some circumstances forms the basis of pro-stem cell research opinions, and is usually modified with some combination of the distinctions and limitations that follow.

* * *

Some proponents of embryonic stem cell research base their support on the question of whether an embryo is viable. The relevance of the viability distinction rests on the premise that it is morally preferable for embryos that will not grow or develop beyond a certain stage and/or those that would otherwise be discarded to be used for the purpose of alleviating human suffering.

* * *

A separate distinction that often leads to the same conclusions as viability is the purpose for which embryos are created. This distinction draws an ethical line based upon the intent of the people creating embryos. In the view of some, it is permissible to create an embryo for reproductive purposes (such as IVF), but impermissible to create one with the intention of destroying it for research.

* * *

A further distinction has been drawn based upon the timing of the creation of embryonic stem cell lines. Here, the premise is that it is unacceptable to induce the destruction of embryos for the creation of new lines. However, in cases in which embryos have already been destroyed and the lines already exist, it is morally preferable to use those lines for research to improve the human condition. This was one central distinction drawn in the 2001 Bush policy, which limited the use of federal funding to research on lines derived on or before the date of the policy. Supporters of the Bush policy on both sides of the issue favor this distinction as a compromise.

* * *

One factual distinction that has been used to support competing ethical viewpoints is the efficacy of alternatives to embryonic stem cell research. The promise of stem cell therapies derived from adult tissue and umbilical cord blood have buttressed opposition to embryonic stem cell research. . . . These opponents argue that therapies and cures can be developed without the morally undesirable destruction of embryos. However, not all scientists agree that adult stem cells hold as much potential as embryonic stem cells. Most supporters of embryonic stem cell research believe that it is the quickest and, perhaps in some cases, the only path that will yield results. . . .

* * *

Some division over the support for and opposition to embryonic stem cell research focuses on the question of whether the use of federal funding is appropriate. Those who oppose federal funding argue that the government should not be associated with embryo destruction. They point out that embryo destruction violates the "deeply held moral beliefs of some citizens," and suggest that "funding alternative research is morally preferable." Proponents of federal funding argue that it is immoral to discourage life-saving research by withholding federal funding. They point out that consensus support is not required for many federal spending policies, as it "does not violate democratic principles or infringe on the rights of dissent of those in the minority." They argue that the efforts of both federally supported and privately supported researchers are necessary to keep the United States at the forefront of what they believe is a very important, cutting edge area of science. Furthermore, supporters believe that the oversight that comes with federal dollars will result in better and more ethically controlled research in the field.

* * *

42 U.S.C. § 289g

(Dickey-Wicker Amendment, 2006).

(a) None of the funds made available [in appropriations for the Departments of Labor, Education, and Health and Human Services] may be used for—

(1) the creation of a human embryo or embryos for research purposes; or

(2) research in which a human embryo or embryos are destroyed, discarded, or knowingly subjected to risk of injury or death greater than that allowed for research on fetuses in utero . . . .

(b) For purposes of this section, the term "human embryo or embryos" includes any organism, not protected as a human subject . . . that is derived by fertilization, parthenogenesis, cloning, or any other means from one or more human gametes or human diploid cells.

———————

When the first Dickey-Wicker Amendment was passed, scientists had no access to stem cells derived from fertilized ova ("embryonic stem cells"), but in 1998 a laboratory at the University of Wisconsin stabilized such stem cells so that they could be used in research. In 1999 the Department of Health and Human Services determined that the Dickey-Wicker Amendment did not apply to embryonic stem cell research because the stem cells were not embryos under the statute. Despite this, no federal research grants were made for stem cell research during the Clinton administration. In 2001, President Bush issued an executive order providing that federal funding could be made available for research involving embryonic stem cell lines that were already available for research, but that no new stem cell lines could be used in federally-funded research. He reasoned that the damage had already been done to the embryos that were destroyed to create the stem cell lines that were already available, but that federal funding agencies should act to assure that no new embryos would be destroyed for use in federally funded research.

In 2009, President Obama greatly expanded the class of embryonic stem cells that could be used in federally-funded research. He determined that the Dickey-Wicker Amendment permitted the use of embryonic stem cells in federally funded research, but that it did not permit federal funds to be used in deriving the stem cell from the embryo. That is, private resources would have to be expended to obtain the embryonic stem cells, an act which requires destroying the embryo, but federal funds could be used for the subsequent research upon the stem cells derived from the embryo. The Obama regulations provided that the stem cells used in federally funded research could only come from leftover fertilized ova created by infertility laboratories for patients engaged in infertility treatment, and only when the progenitors approved of the use of their cells for this purpose in writing. See 74 Fed.Reg. 32, 170–32, 175 (July 7, 2009). Two scientists tried, unsuccessfully, to challenge these regulations as a violation of the Dickey-Wicker Amendment. Sherley v. Sebelius, 689 F.3d 776 (D.C. Cir. 2012), cert. den. 568 U.S. 1087 (2013). Near the end of the Obama administration, the 21st Century Cures Act was signed into law, authorizing $30 million for regenerative medicine research but limiting its application to research with adult stem cells. Since then, the federal approach to stem cell research has continued to shift with the political tides: the Trump administration undertook several steps to undermine much of the progress made during the Obama administration, and the election of President Biden has renewed hope for a return to a more supportive approach.

State legislatures have produced far more legislation on the use of stem cells than has Congress. Some states have sought to outlaw all cloning, and thus most stem cell research, while others have encouraged stem cell research, including embryonic stem cell research, subject to certain safeguards. For example, California, which is one of a dozen states to outlaw reproductive cloning, is also one of several states enacting laws to facilitate stem cell research for therapeutic purposes. Through a ballot initiative formally called the Stem Cell Research and Cures Act, California established the California Institute of Regenerative Medicine (CIRM), originally funded by the authorization of $3 billion in state bonds, to stimulate the scientific and economic benefits many believe will follow in the wake of this research. CIRM is a state agency authorized to make grants and loans for stem cell research and facilities, and to establish related regulatory standards and oversight bodies. States encouraging stem cell research have included important protections against abuses, such as opposing reproductive cloning and the sale of embryos, and ensuring fully informed consent for the donation of gametes or embryos. States have also created an additional layer of specialized oversight, on top of the normal oversight required under federal human research subject regulation. (See Chapter 20 for more on research regulation generally). For a thoughtful overview of the various state approaches to stem cell research and important lessons to be gleaned, see Nefi D. Acosta & Sidney H. Golub, The New Federalism: State Policies Regarding Embryonic Stem Cell Research, 44 J. L. Med. & Ethics 419 (2016).

CHAPTER 17

ORGAN TRANSPLANTATION AND THE DETERMINATION OF DEATH

▪ ▪ ▪

I. ORGAN TRANSPLANTATION

A. RATIONING SCARCE ORGANS

As with other limited or shared health care resources, decision-making regarding the retrieval and allocation of scarce human organs brings issues of equity and justice to the forefront. The COVID-19 pandemic brought renewed attention to the equitable allocation of limited medical resources such as ventilators and hospital beds, as well as the potential for allocation decisions to exacerbate pre-existing health inequities. Questions about equitable access to health care resources also figure prominently in debates over the Affordable Care Act (ACA). How can these decisions be made fairly and equitably? Is it ethical, or good public policy, to ration medical care by ability to pay? And, in the case of scarce resources such as human organs or certain technologies, if not by ability to pay, then how?

Many argue that health care is distinct from ordinary consumer goods—such as iPads and cars—that we distribute entirely by ability to pay. The argument that health care is distinct rests on the dignity of persons (and what is required for human flourishing); the moral duty to relieve human suffering; and the communal benefits of fostering good health (in terms of public health and a robust economy). Counterarguments in favor of treating health care, even life-saving medical treatment, as an ordinary consumer good have been prominent during the debates over the ACA. Some argue that placing responsibility on the individual to pay for medical care incentivizes work, savings, and fitness, whereas guaranteeing health care rewards irresponsibility. See Chapter 7 as to distributive justice vs. actuarial fairness approaches.

Most arguments in favor of providing health care to those who cannot pay reference a "basic" package of health care services. See Chapter 9 discussion of "essential benefits" in the ACA. What are the relevant considerations in deciding whether particular medical treatments, such as organ transplants, fit within the basic package? Short-term or long-term survival rates? Quality of life post-transplant? And if so, how should quality be measured? Global budgets that trade off some health care interventions (e.g., transplants vs. preventive care) in order to spread limited funds most effectively? Compare Gil Siegal & Richard Bonnie, Closing the Organ Gap: A Reciprocity-based Social Contract Approach, 34 J. L. Med. & Ethics 415 (2006), calling organ transplantation a "remarkable achievement" that saves lives, improves quality of life, and reduces costs (for kidney transplants as compared to hemodialysis, for example) with Albert R. Jonsen, The God Squad and the Origins of Transplantation Ethics and Policy, 35 J. L. Med. & Ethics 238 (2007), arguing that the looming problem behind transplantation policy is the "incessant . . . demand that life must be salvaged at all costs."

What other factors should be considered? The supply of transplantable organs simply does not satisfy the need, and rationing follows. A rather famous example of explicit rationing occurred in the 1960s when the Admissions and Policy Committee (sometimes known as the "God Squad") of the Seattle Artificial Kidney Center decided which patients would receive the lifesaving "artificial kidney" (i.e., hemodialysis). The God Squad was reported to have selected patients partly on the basis of age, gender, marital status, number of dependents, emotional stability, education, and occupation, among other characteristics. Media exposure of the work of the God Squad contributed to the decision to have Medicare cover dialysis for all individuals with end-stage renal disease (ESRD), even those not otherwise eligible for Medicare; this decision was followed by one to have Medicare cover kidney transplants as well. Richard A. Rettig, Special Treatment—The Story of Medicare's ESRD Entitlement, 364 NEJM 596 (2011).

Of course, efforts have been made to increase the supply of transplantable organs, within limits. The use of brain death as the medical and legal standard for determination of death originally emerged in part in response to the need for transplantable human organs. More recent developments, i.e., donation after cardiac or circulatory death, discussed at Section II.C, further illustrate how policy decisions and legal norms can produce direct consequences for the availability and distribution of health resources, even where those norms appear unrelated to such concerns.

Ability to pay actually is one factor that determines who gets an organ transplant. A candidate generally is not placed on the active waiting list unless there is a source of payment for the transplant and the expensive lifelong post-transplant care. Even after the ACA, private insurance, Medicaid, and Medicare will not cover all medically possible transplants or necessary aftercare.

While ability to pay is the gateway to being listed for a transplant, one cannot buy an organ from a willing seller. Instead, we use other criteria to ration scarce organs. Consider the following problem.

PROBLEM: SELECTING AN ORGAN TRANSPLANT RECIPIENT

For the last few weeks, two patients have been under treatment at General Hospital for acute liver failure. One, James Patterson, is a 65-year-old retired CEO of a major computer software company. He has two children, a 40-year-old daughter with a child of her own and a 24-year-old son. Patterson is active in his church and is a financial supporter of the local university athletics department. He was exposed to hepatitis B, which has destroyed most of his liver. The second patient is Antonia Friedman, a 30-year-old attorney with two children, ages 2 and 4. She is an active member of the local city council and has contributed generously in the past year to the hospital's building fund. Friedman is in recovery from alcohol use disorder and has been through rehabilitation programs several times. This time, though, she has abstained from alcohol for six months and so meets common minimum criteria for liver transplant applied to individuals with alcohol use disorder. Within the last week, both patients have taken a turn for the worse, and both will die within the next few weeks if they do not receive a liver transplant.

A few hours ago, a patient was admitted to the hospital with massive head trauma caused by an automobile accident. The patient is brain dead but is being kept on support systems to preserve his organs for transplantation. The liver is undamaged. Tissue matching shows that it is an equally acceptable organ for either Patterson or Friedman. Circumstances make it impossible for the liver to be divided between the two patients. Patterson's physician was the first to list his patient on the transplant list, which he did three days earlier than did Friedman's physician. Who should receive the single available organ?

Is this decision essentially a medical decision to be made by the physician? Would you prefer that a committee decide? Who should be on the committee? Should your hospital establish a procedure in which patients are notified that listing is being considered and given an opportunity to advocate for themselves? Should the hospital keep a record documenting the reasons a patient wasn't listed or selected? Should the government set the criteria for deciding who gets the organ? See Section I.B, below.

Would you prefer to use a lottery system in which a recipient is selected from among all qualified candidates by drawing lots? What advantages and disadvantages would a pure "first come-first served" policy present? Should time on the waiting list make any difference? What if you knew that Patterson's doctor was more aggressive in listing patients than was Friedman's? What if you knew that other doctors at that hospital simply refuse to list individuals in recovery from alcohol use disorder for a transplant? Is considering Friedman's alcohol use disorder inappropriate or is it morally required? See, e.g., Robert S. Brown, Transplantation for Alcoholic Hepatitis—Time to Rethink the 6-Month "Rule," 365 NEJM 1836 (2011), discussing a study demonstrating the effectiveness of transplantation, in terms of survival and post-transplant abstinence from alcohol, even without a 6-month pre-transplant abstinence period; Erin Minelli & Bryan Liang, Transplant

Candidates and Substance Use: Adopting Rational Health Policy for Resource Allocation, 44 U. Mich. J. L. Reform 667 (2011).

How important is the risk of graft failure, i.e., that the organ itself will fail due to rejection? Will that consideration always outweigh other concerns? Consider that under current national kidney allocation policies, patients who have previously received a kidney that failed within a short time after transplant receive priority even though the presensitization caused by the earlier transplant increases the risk of graft failure. In addition, a person who has donated specific organs as a living donor receives priority in receiving an organ should the need arise in the future.

Projected lifespan of the patient is not the same as the risk of graft failure. Should younger patients always have precedence over older patients in the same medical situation? See Alan B. Leichtman et al., Improving the Allocation System for Deceased-Donor Kidneys, 364 NEJM 1287 (2011); Benjamin E. Hippen et al., Risk, Prognosis, and Unintended Consequences in Kidney Allocation, 364 NEJM 1285 (2011). Aside from age, are there any characteristics that are more important than others? Or more suspect? Should the post-transplant coverage provided by each patient's insurance or, alternatively, the net worth of each patient be considered?

B. REGULATING ORGAN DISTRIBUTION

The National Organ Transplant Act of 1984 (NOTA) requires the Department of Health and Human Services (HHS) to establish an Organ Procurement and Transplantation Network (OPTN) to organize the retrieval, distribution, and transplantation of human organs. OPTN is the primary vehicle for federal regulation of the organ transplant system in the U.S. (42 C.F.R. § 121). The Centers for Medicare & Medicaid Services also sets quality and policy standards as conditions for federal payments to transplant hospitals and other facilities involved in organ retrieval and transplantation.

HHS contracts with the United Network for Organ Sharing (UNOS), a private nonprofit organization, for management of the federal OPTN. OPTN/UNOS manages procedures and standards for listing patients, retrieval and testing of organs, distribution to transplant hospitals, and selection of recipients, among other issues. OPTN/UNOS policies are being constantly revised and can be found on the OPTN and UNOS websites.

Access to the Transplant Waiting List

Individual doctors and hospitals decide who gets on the transplant waiting list and when. Patient listing practices vary substantially among transplant centers around the country. Psychosocial factors, including anticipated compliance with medical recommendations, absence of a reliable support system, availability of alternative therapies, and the cause of the original organ failure influence physician listing decisions. See

Denise M. Dudzinski, Shifting to Other Justice Issues: Examining Listing Practices, 4 Am. J. Bioethics 35 (2004) (reviewing studies of listing practices that conclude that standards and procedures tend to be informal and disadvantage racial minorities and women); Geert Verleden et al., Recipient Selection Processes and Listing for Lung Transplantation, 9 J. Thoracic Disease 3372 (2017); C.K. Argo et al., Regional Variability in Symptom-Based MELD Exceptions: A Response to Organ Shortage? 11 Am J. Transplantation 2353 (2011). For a compelling narrative of the effect of race on listing decisions, see Vanessa Grubbs, Good for Harvest, Bad for Planting, 26 Health Aff. 232 (2007).

Assumptions, biases, or lack of knowledge about living with disability compromise access to the transplant waiting list for people with disabilities. A 2019 report found that disabilities unrelated to a person's need for an organ transplant generally have little or no impact on the likelihood that the transplant will be successful. However, many organ transplant centers maintain policies that categorially exclude or disfavor placing people with HIV, psychiatric disabilities, or intellectual or developmental disabilities on the organ transplant waiting list. Nat'l Council on Disability, Organ Transplant Discrimination Against People with Disabilities (2019). Assumptions that the lives of people with disabilities are of poorer quality than those of people without disabilities, or that people with certain disabilities may be unable to comply with post-operative care, also compromise evaluation of psychosocial factors. Id. Recent federal enforcement activity may suggest an increased focus on disability antidiscrimination laws in this context. See, e.g., Dept. of Justice, Massachusetts General Hospital Enters Agreement with U.S. Attorney's Office to Better Ensure Equal Access for Individuals with Disabilities (Aug. 7, 2020); Office of Civil Rights, U.S. Dept. of Health and Human Servs., OCR Resolved Disability Complaint of Individual Who Was Denied the Opportunity for Health Transplant List Placement (Feb. 12, 2019). See also Chapter 6 for discussion of federal laws that prohibit discrimination based on disability.

Hospitals doing transplants have an incentive to engage in listing practices that increase volume. Federal investigations revealed that physicians at some transplant hospitals exaggerated their patients' medical condition to move them up higher on the list so the hospital would be able to perform more transplants. The charged hospitals settled with the government without admitting guilt, with one facility paying $1 million. Nara Schoenberg, A Man of Principle, Chicago Trib. (Jan. 25, 2004). Several studies have found that transplant centers located in high-competition areas listed a higher percentage of patients for transplant than areas with less competition. See, e.g., P.S. Cho et al., Competitive Market Analysis of Transplant Centers and Discrepancy of Wait-Listing of Recipients for Kidney Transplantation, 6 Int'l J. Organ Transplant Med.

141 (2015); E. Haavi Morreim, Another Kind of End-run: Status Upgrades, 5 Am. J. Bioethics 11 (2005).

Patients seeking transplants have an incentive to seek out the list with the shortest waiting time. In fact, median waiting times for particular organs have varied significantly among geographic regions despite a federal regulation requiring that organs be distributed "over as broad a geographic region as feasible" consistent with assuring that organs are not damaged. The reasons for these variations are many: all organs are limited as to the distance they can safely be transported, so distribution favors closer organs over more distant organs, and some organs (such as hearts) are particularly vulnerable in transport; some regions have higher rates of organ donation while others have higher rates of medical need; and some localities have hospitals with more aggressive listing practices, thereby drawing in a higher share of available organs. David L. Weimer, Public and Private Regulation of Organ Transplantation: Liver Allocation and the Final Rule, 32 J. Health Polit. Pol'y & L. 9 (2007). Another potential cause of persisting regional variation may be that transplant centers in different regions vary in their assessment of and requests for symptom-based exceptions (SBE) to move patients up in line. See Argo et al., above, pointing out that Medicaid patients are least likely to receive SBEs. It is not surprising that efforts to reduce geographic disparities have provoked debate. See Lara C. Pullen, Lawsuits Drive Transplant Community Debate Over Liver Allocation, 19(5) Am. J. Transplantation 1251 (Apr. 24, 2019).

The persistent difference in regional wait times for organs encourages the practice of "multiple listing," in which patients with the means to travel at a moment's notice get listed in more than one region. Several websites provide transplant candidates with the wait time for specific organs in specific localities, along with the travel time required to get there from their home. OPTN policy allows multiple listing, but the AMA holds that physicians should "refrain" from multiple listing and instead place candidates on a "single waiting list for each type of organ." AMA Code of Medical Ethics Opinion E–6.2.1(g).

Selecting the Recipient

Federal regulations require that OPTN organ allocation policies be "equitable," "seek to achieve the best use of donated organs," "avoid wasting organs," and rely on "objective and measurable medical criteria." 42 C.F.R. § 121.8. Indeed, OPTN policies governing selection of a recipient from among listed patients use "objective and measurable medical criteria," quantifying medical urgency, measuring how good a match the organ and recipient are, and so on. But these apparently scientific criteria have measurable effects on access to organs for specific populations (minority, ethnic, age) and most obviously for specific individuals. Kidney allocation policies provide an illustration of apparently neutral criteria that have had an adverse racial impact. For years, UNOS kidney allocation policies used very granular levels of "antigen matching" to select recipients from the transplant list even though the difference in graft failure was miniscule as between each level. Before UNOS revised these criteria, whites received double the number of kidney transplants as compared to African Americans. The two populations were equally represented on the transplant waiting list (even though African Americans suffer a higher rate of total kidney failure) but in raw numbers more whites donated organs. OPTN, Annual Report 2003. Revised matching criteria have significantly increased the proportion of organs allocated to African Americans. A. Hart et al., OPTN/SRTR 2015 Annual Data Report: Early Effects of the New Kidney Allocation System, 17 Am. J. Transplantation 543 (2017).

Outside claims of discrimination, should courts get involved in deciding whether an individual patient receives an available organ? In Murnaghan v. HHS, Civ. Action No. 13-3083 (E.D. Pa. Jan. 5 and 13, 2013), the judge enjoined application of the OPTN "Under 12 Rule," so that Sarah Murnaghan, a 10-year-old girl facing imminent death, could have access to an adult lung rather than waiting for a pediatric lung. OPTN policy at the time allocated pediatric lungs to children and adult lungs to individuals over the age of 12 unless no appropriate adult recipient was on the list, in which case the lungs would be allocated to a younger child. The judge's order called the policy discriminatory, arbitrary, and capricious. The order required OPTN to consider Sarah as a candidate without applying the "Under 12 Rule."

The Secretary of HHS refused to set aside the policy on her own for Sarah's case, commenting that making a decision on "who lives and who dies" without following policies that applied to all was inappropriate. She noted that 40 other children in Pennsylvania were awaiting lung transplants at that time. Paige Cunningham, Sibelius Won't Intervene on Transplant, Politico (June 5, 2013). See also Daniel Bruggebrew, The Administrative Law Implications of Quasi-Governmental Organ Allocation, 41 Seton Hall Legis. J. 1 (2016). Sarah's first lung transplant, received within several days of the judge's order, failed, but a second transplant has sustained her since that time.

C. LEGAL FRAMEWORK FOR THE PROCUREMENT OF ORGANS AND TISSUE

NOTA defers to state law on most questions related to organ donation, and most states have adopted the Uniform Anatomical Gift Act (UAGA), with some few variations, to govern donation of organs that will be retrieved post-mortem. Donation of non-life-sustaining organs by living donors is governed by familiar informed-consent principles and by policies issued by OPTN. Legal restraints on the collection of human organs for transplantation contribute to the current shortage because they require that there be consent for organ retrieval and that organs be donated instead of purchased. Some provisions of the UAGA are excerpted below.

1.   The Uniform Anatomical Gift Act (2009) (UAGA)

§ 4. Who May Make Anatomical Gift Before Donor's Death.

(1) [T]he donor, if the donor is an adult or if the donor is a minor and is:

    (A) emancipated; or

    (B) authorized under state law to apply for a driver's license . . . :

(2) an agent of the donor, unless the power or attorney for health care or other record prohibits the agent from making an anatomical gift;

(3) a parent of the donor, if the donor is an unemancipated minor; or

(4) the donor's guardian.

§ 5. Manner of Making Anatomical Gift Before Donor's Death.

[This section provides that a donor may make an anatomical gift by indicating so on the driver's license, in a will, on a donor card, through a donor registry, or by any means of communication if terminally ill or fatally injured.]

§ 8. Preclusive Effect of Anatomical Gift, Amendment, or Revocation.

(a) Except as otherwise provided in subsection (g) . . . , in the absence of an express, contrary indication by the donor, a person other than the donor is barred from making, amending, or revoking an anatomical gift of a donor's body or part if the donor made an anatomical gift of the donor's body or part under Section 5. . . .

(g) If a donor who is an unemancipated minor dies, a parent of the donor who is reasonably available may revoke or amend an anatomical gift of the donor's body or part.

(h) If an unemancipated minor who signed a refusal dies, a parent of the minor who is reasonably available may revoke the minor's refusal.

§ 9. Who May Make Anatomical Gift of Decedent's Body or Part.

(a) [A]n anatomical gift of a decedent's body or part for purpose of transplantation, therapy, research, or education may be made by any member of the following classes of persons who is reasonably available, in the order of priority listed:

    (1) an agent [appointed by the decedent prior to death];

    (2) the spouse of the decedent;

    (3) adult children of the decedent;

(4) parents of the decedent;

(5) adult siblings of the decedent;

(6) adult grandchildren of the decedent;

(7) grandparents of the decedent;

(8) an adult who exhibited special care and concern for the decedent;

(9) the persons who were acting as the [guardians] of the person of the decedent at the time of death; and

(10) any other person having the authority to dispose of the decedent's body.

§ 14. Rights and Duties of Procurement Organization and Others.

(a) When a hospital refers an individual at or near death to a procurement organization, the organization shall make a reasonable search of the records of the [state department of motor vehicles] and any donor registry . . . to ascertain whether the individual has made an anatomical gift.

* * *

(c) When a hospital refers an individual at or near death to a procurement organization, the organization may conduct any reasonable examination necessary to ensure the medical suitability of a part that is or could be the subject of an anatomical gift . . . from a donor or a prospective donor. During the examination period, measures necessary to ensure the medical suitability of the part may not be withdrawn unless the hospital or procurement organization knows that the individual expressed a contrary intent.

* * *

(f) Upon the death of a minor who was a donor or had signed a refusal, unless a procurement organization knows the minor is emancipated, the procurement organization shall conduct a reasonable search for the parents of the minor and provide the parents with an opportunity to revoke or amend the anatomical gift or revoke the refusal.

(g) Upon referral by a hospital . . . , a procurement organization shall make a reasonable search for any person listed in Section 9 having priority to make an anatomical gift on behalf of a prospective donor. . . .

* * *

(i) Neither the physician who attends the decedent at death nor the physician who determines the time of the decedent's death may participate in the procedures for removing or transplanting a part from the decedent.

§ 18. Immunity.

(a) A person that acts in accordance with this [act] or with the applicable anatomical gift law of another state, or attempts in good faith to do so, is not liable for the act in a civil action, criminal prosecution, or administrative proceeding.

* * *

PROBLEM: ORGAN DONATION AND THE UAGA

Laurel Singer, age 16, her sister Rebecca, age 22, and Rebecca's friend Peter Klaus, also age 22, were brought to General Hospital after an extremely serious car accident. Although they were alive when treated by the emergency medical technicians at the scene, Laurel, Rebecca, and Peter have died. Physicians have initiated standard procedures to maintain respiration and circulation in their bodies and preserve their organs for transplantation, including administering certain drugs and inserting a catheter into an artery to provide perfusion (delivery of blood to the organs). Time is critical as organs deteriorate quickly. The Singer sisters' parents have arrived at the hospital, but Peter's parents are on vacation somewhere in Asia. Peter's friends and the hospital are continuing efforts to contact his parents but without success.

Laurel and Rebecca each signed the organ donor card on the back of their driver's licenses; however, their parents told the hospital to discontinue the organ maintenance procedures and objected to removal of their organs. Peter didn't have a driver's license, but his friends all agree that he was clear about his intentions to be an organ donor.

May surgeons remove Laurel's, Rebecca's, and Peter's transplantable organs? Under the UAGA, what must the hospital do in order to proceed? Do the Singer parents have the right to stop the removal of their daughters' organs? Should the hospital abide by their wishes? If Peter's parents arrive after the surgery has been completed and object to the removal of their son's organs, would they have any action against the physicians or the hospital? Why would Peter not have signed a donor card or signed up with his state's online donor registry?

NOTES AND QUESTIONS

1. *Consent Not Required.* The UAGA speaks in terms of a "gift" made by the decedent prior to death or by authorized decision-makers after the death. It does not require that there be informed consent for organ donation. What information would be required for the donor or surrogate to give informed consent for the retrieval of organs? Should they be informed of the exact medical procedures that will be performed to preserve the organs prior to death, as they would be if they were consenting to medical treatment; the criteria that will be used to determine that the patient has died; or the nature of the procedures that will be used to remove the organs (or bones or skin)? Why is informed consent not required? See Ana Iltis, Organ Donation, Brain

Death and the Family: Valid Informed Consent, 43 J.L. Med. & Ethics 369 (2015); Leili Monfared & Lois Shepherd, Organ Procurement Now: Does the U.S. Still "Opt In?", 2017 U. Ill. L. Rev. 1003. See Section I.C.2, below, as to whether the donor's permission ought to be required at all.

2. *Immunity Provision.* Although the UAGA provides immunity for "good faith" attempts at compliance (§ 18, above), courts have interpreted good faith as a question of fact, which allows the case to go to the jury. See, for example, Cooper v. Louisiana Organ Procurement, 146 So. 3d 908 (La. Ct. App. 2014); Siegel v. LifeCenter Organ Donor Network, 969 N.E.2d 1271 (Ohio Ct. App. 2011); Schembre v. Mid-America Transplant Assn., 135 S.W.3d 527 (Mo. Ct. App. 2004) (plaintiff claimed nurse was negligent in describing procedures used to harvest bones).

3. *Medicare and Medicaid Requirements.* Hospitals receiving Medicare or Medicaid are required to contact the appropriate organ procurement organization whenever they have a patient whose death is imminent or who has died. The procurement organization is then to evaluate the viability of organs and tissue and speak with the family about the option of donation. 42 C.F.R. § 482.45. Under the UAGA, interventions to preserve the organs are continued without permission unless the patient had earlier expressed a "contrary intent." See UAGA § 14, above, and Section II.C, below.

NOTE: ORGAN TRANSPLANTATION FROM LIVING DONORS

Individuals who have decisional capacity may donate non-life-sustaining organs for transplantation; such donors have supplied over 5,000 donations annually. Most frequently, the recipients are family members or friends but, increasingly, strangers in need. The possibility of donation from a stranger has led patients and families to campaign publicly to recruit a donor. Several organizations offer matching services as well.

A willing donor's organ may not be a match for the intended recipient, however. Transplant centers have overcome the problem of incompatibility by arranging for kidney paired donations (KPD). In KPD, a mismatched donor and recipient are matched with another pair in the same situation and the kidneys are exchanged, with the surgeries occurring simultaneously. Some transplant centers arrange kidney chains that result in a long series of transplantation surgeries as kidneys incompatible with a designated recipient proceed down a chain of possibly dozens of persons. Evelyn Tenenbaum, Bartering for a Compatible Kidney Using Your Incompatible, Live Kidney Donor: Legal and Ethical Issues Related to Kidney Chains, 42 Am. J.L. & Med. 129 (2016); Kimberly Krawiec et al., Contract Development in a Matching Market: The Case of Kidney Exchange, 80 L. & Contemp. Probs. 11 (2017).

Concerns over safety and outcomes for living donors are significant. The Renal and Lung Living Donors Evaluation Study (RELIVE), a multiyear study of long-term outcomes for living lung and kidney donors, produced data on several measures including long-term health effects, emotional well-being, and satisfaction. See, e.g., C.R. Gross et al., Health Related Quality of Life in

Kidney Donors from the Last Five Decades: Results from the RELIVE Study, 13 Am. J. Transplantation 2924 (Nov. 2013), reporting health status roughly equivalent to that of the general population but identifying pre-surgical conditions that predict negative health outcomes for donors.

Legal issues relating to consent can arise in any intervivos transplant (see Green v. Buell, 215 So. 3d 715 (La. Ct. App. 2017), but they are more common when the donor is legally incapacitated. The principles relied on in such cases are the same as those that govern other medical treatment decisions for incompetent patients: they rely on either the donor's best interests or substituted judgment criterion for decision-making. See Chapter 18. See also Macey Henderson and Jed Gross, Living Organ Donation and Informed Consent in the United States: Strategies to Improve the Process, 45 J.L. Med. & Ethics 66 (2017); Michael T. Morley, Proxy Consent to Organ Donation by Incompetents, 111 Yale L.J. 1215 (2002). Ethical concerns relating to coercion of living donors are not easily accounted for in a legal framework, however. See, e.g., Nat'l Council on Disability, Organ Transplant Discrimination Against People with Disabilities (2019) (examining impact of organ procurement policies and practices on people with disabilities).

Advances in reproductive technologies, particularly preimplantation genetic diagnosis (see Chapter 16), create the capacity for parents of a child in need of a transplant to conceive and birth a child (a so-called "savior sibling") who is certain to be a match for the older sibling. The practice raises serious ethical and legal concerns at the intersection of reproductive rights and organ transplants. See, e.g., Zachary E. Shapiro, Savior Siblings in the United States: Ethical Conundrums, Legal and Regulatory Void, 24 Wash. & Lee Civil Rts. & Soc. Just. 419 (2018).

2.   Presumed Consent and Property Rights

NEWMAN V. SATHYAVAGLSWARAN
United States Court of Appeals, Ninth Circuit, 2002.
287 F.3d 786.

FISHER, CIRCUIT JUDGE.

Parents, whose deceased children's corneas were removed by the Los Angeles County Coroner's office without notice or consent, brought this 42 U.S.C. § 1983 action alleging a taking of their property without due process of law. The complaint was dismissed by the district court for a failure to state a claim upon which relief could be granted. We must decide whether the longstanding recognition in the law of California, paralleled by our national common law, that next of kin have the exclusive right to possess the bodies of their deceased family members creates a property interest, the deprivation of which must be accorded due process of law under the Fourteenth Amendment of the United States Constitution. We hold that it does. . . .

* * *

Robert Newman and Barbara Obarski (the parents) each had children, Richard Newman and Kenneth Obarski respectively, who died in Los Angeles County in October 1997. Following their deaths, the Office of the Coroner for the County of Los Angeles (the coroner) obtained possession of the bodies of the children and, under procedures adopted pursuant to California Government Code § 27492.47 as it then existed, removed the corneas from those bodies without the knowledge of the parents and without an attempt to notify them and request consent. The parents became aware of the coroner's actions in September 1999 and subsequently filed this § 1983 action alleging a deprivation of their property without due process of law in violation of the Fourteenth Amendment.

II.   Property Interests in Dead Bodies

[T]he Supreme Court repeatedly has affirmed that "the right of every individual to the possession and control of his own person, free from all restraint or interference of others," [ ] is "so rooted in the traditions and conscience of our people," [ ] as to be ranked as one of the fundamental liberties protected by the "substantive" component of the Due Process Clause. [ ] This liberty, the Court has "strongly suggested," extends to the personal decisions about "how to best protect dignity and independence at the end of life." [ ] The Court has not had occasion to address whether the rights of possession and control of one's own body, the most "sacred" and "carefully guarded" of all rights in the common law, [ ] are property interests protected by the Due Process Clause. Nor has it addressed what Due Process protections are applicable to the rights of next of kin to possess and control the bodies of their deceased relatives.

A.   *History of Common Law Interests in Dead Bodies*

* * *

Many early American courts adopted Blackstone's description of the common law, holding that "a dead body is not the subject of property right." [ ] The duty to protect the body by providing a burial was often described as flowing from the "universal . . . right of sepulture," rather than from a concept of property law. [ ] As cases involving unauthorized mutilation and disposition of bodies increased toward the end of the 19th century, paralleling the rise in demand for human cadavers in medical science and use of cremation as an alternative to burial, [ ] courts began to recognize an exclusive right of the next of kin to possess and control the disposition of the bodies of their dead relatives, the violation of which was actionable at law. Thus, in holding that a city council could not "seize upon existing private burial grounds, make them public, and exclude the proprietors from their management," the Supreme Court of Indiana commented that "the burial of the dead can [not] . . . be taken out of the hands of the relatives thereof" because "we lay down the proposition, that the bodies of the dead belong to the surviving relations, in the order of inheritance, as property, and that they have the right to dispose of them as such, within restrictions analogous to those by which the disposition of other property may be regulated." [ ] . . .

B.   Interests in Dead Bodies in California Law

[The court traces the history of California law concerning the disposition of dead bodies. California courts referred to "quasi-property" rights in cases disputing the handling of cadavers, including cases in which the courts held that civil litigants had no right to demand an autopsy; held that next-of-kin could exclude the decedent's friends from the funeral; and permitted an action for retaining organs after autopsy.]

C.   The Right to Transfer Body Parts

The first successful transplantation of a kidney in 1954 led to an expansion of the rights of next of kin to the bodies of the dead. In 1968, the National Conference of Commissioners on Uniform State Laws approved the Uniform Anatomical Gift Act (UAGA), adopted by California the same year, which grants next of kin the right to transfer the parts of bodies in their possession to others for medical or research purposes. [ ] The right to transfer is limited. . . .

In the 1970s and 1980s, medical science improvements and the related demand for transplant organs prompted governments to search for new ways to increase the supply of organs for donation. [ ] Many perceived as a hindrance to the supply of needed organs the rule implicit in the UAGA that donations could be effected only if consent was received from the decedent or next of kin. [ ] In response, some states passed "presumed consent" laws that allow the taking and transfer of body parts by a coroner without the consent of next of kin as long as no objection to the removal is known. [ ] California Government Code § 27491.47, enacted in 1983, was such a law.

III. Due Process Analysis

"[T]o provide California non-profit eye banks with an adequate supply of corneal tissue," S. Com. Rep. SB 21 (Cal. 1983), § 27491.47(a) authorized the coroner to "remove and release or authorize the removal and release of corneal eye tissue from a body within the coroner's custody" without any effort to notify and obtain the consent of next of kin "if . . . [t]he coroner has no knowledge of objection to the removal." The law also provided that the coroner or any person acting upon his or her request "shall [not] incur civil liability for such removal in an action brought by any person who did not

object prior to the removal . . . nor be subject to criminal prosecution."
§ 27491.47(b).[11]

* * *

In two decisions the Sixth Circuit, the only federal circuit to address
the issue until now, held that the interests of next of kin in dead bodies
recognized in Michigan and Ohio allowed next of kin to bring § 1983 actions
challenging implementation of cornea removal statutes similar to
California's. [ ] . . .

The supreme courts of Florida and Georgia, however, have held that
similar legal interests of next of kin in the possession of the body of a
deceased family member, recognized as "quasi property" rights in each
state, are "not . . . of constitutional dimension." *Georgia Lions Eye Bank,
Inc. v. Lavant,* 255 Ga. 60, 335 S.E.2d 127, 128 (1985); *State v. Powell,* 497
So.2d 1188, 1191 (Fla. 1986) (commenting that "[a]ll authorities generally
agree that the next of kin have no property right in the remains of a
decedent"). The Florida Supreme Court recently rejected the broad
implications of the reasoning in *Powell* distinguishing that decision as
turning on a balance between the public health interest in cornea donation
and the " 'infinitesimally small intrusion' " of their removal. *Crocker v.
Pleasant,* 778 So.2d 978, 985, 988 (Fla. 2001) (allowing a § 1983 action to
go forward for interference with the right of next of kin to possess the body
of their son because "in Florida there is a legitimate claim of entitlement
by the next of kin to possession of the remains of a decedent for burial or
other lawful disposition").

We agree with the reasoning of the Sixth Circuit and believe that
reasoning is applicable here. Under traditional common law principles,
serving a duty to protect the dignity of the human body in its final
disposition that is deeply rooted in our legal history and social traditions,
the parents had exclusive and legitimate claims of entitlement to possess,
control, dispose and prevent the violation of the corneas and other parts of
the bodies of their deceased children. With California's adoption of the
UAGA, [ ], it statutorily recognized other important rights of the parents
in relation to the bodies of their deceased children—the right to transfer
body parts and refuse to allow their transfer. These are all important
components of the group of rights by which property is defined, each of
which carried with it the power to exclude others from its exercise,
"traditionally . . . one of the most treasured strands in an owner's bundle
of property rights." [ ]

* * *

---

[11] For body parts other than corneas, California adopted the 1987 version of the UAGA
authorizing transfer when no knowledge of objection is known and after "[a] reasonable effort has
been made to locate and inform [next of kin] of their option to make, or object to making, an
anatomical gift." Cal. Health & Safety Code § 7151.5(a)(2).

Nor does the fact that California forbids the trade of body parts for profit mean that next of kin lack a property interest in them. The Supreme Court has "never held that a physical item is not 'property' simply because it lacks a positive economic or market value." [ ]

We need not . . . decide whether California has transgressed basic property principles [ ] because that statute did not extinguish California's legal recognition of the property interests of the parents to the corneas of their deceased children. It allowed the removal of corneas only if "the coroner has no knowledge of objection," a provision that implicitly acknowledges the ongoing property interests of next of kin.

* * *

. . . The property rights that California affords to next of kin to the body of their deceased relatives serve the premium value our society has historically placed on protecting the dignity of the human body in its final disposition. California infringed the dignity of the bodies of the children when it extracted the corneas from those bodies without the consent of the parents. The process of law was due the parents for this deprivation of their rights.

* * *

The scope of the process of law that was due the parents is not a question that we can answer based on the pleadings alone. This question must be addressed in future proceedings.

* * *

We do not hold that California lacks significant interests in obtaining corneas or other organs of the deceased in order to contribute to the lives of the living. Courts are required to evaluate carefully the state's interests in deciding what process must be due the holders of property interests for their deprivation. [ ] An interest so central to the state's core police powers as improving the health of its citizens is certainly one that must be considered seriously in determining what process the parents were due. [ ] But our Constitution requires the government to assert its interests and subject them to scrutiny when it invades the rights of its subjects. Accordingly, we reverse the district court's dismissal of the parents' complaint and remand for proceedings in which the government's justification for its deprivation of parents' interests may be fully aired and appropriately scrutinized.

NOTES AND QUESTIONS

1. *Satisfying Due Process Requirements.* As noted in *Newman*, the California statute departed from the UAGA provision of the time, which required a "reasonable effort" to contact persons authorized to permit donation

before tissue or organs could be removed by the coroner. The Ninth Circuit leaves open the possibility that the State could structure the coroner's removal of tissue in a way that would satisfy due process concerns. Would requiring that there be a reasonable attempt to contact next-of-kin satisfy due process requirements? Would the existence of an easily accessible system for registering objections (an opt-out system) satisfy the court? The UAGA provision was removed in 2006 in response to this litigation and now provides that no tissue or organ can be removed unless there is an anatomical gift (although in an uncommon scenario, the coroner can gift a decedent's tissue under the authority provided for in the UAGA § 9(a)(10), above).

2.   *"Presumed Consent."* The California statute may be seen as relying on "presumed consent," long advocated as a tool for increasing the supply of organs and tissue for transplant. Presumed consent relies on the assumption, grounded in repeated surveys, that most people intend to donate when the opportunity arises but simply fail to do so. Presumed consent shifts the responsibility for objecting to the individual. Before the decision in *Newman*, a series of news articles demonstrated that the practice had a disproportionate impact on individuals from disadvantaged racial and ethnic groups. At the time, 80% of coroner autopsies were performed on African American or Latino individuals and only 16% on whites.

Is the assumption that the individual would consent if asked a persuasive claim in this situation? See Michele Goodwin, *Newman v. Sathyavaglswaran: Unbundling Property in the Dead*, in Health Law and Bioethics Cases in Context (Sandra Johnson et al., eds. 2009); Gil Siegel & Richard Bonnie, Closing the Organ Gap: A Reciprocity-Based Social Contract Approach, 34 J.L. Med. & Ethics 415 (2006). Almost all states have followed the lead of the 2006 UAGA in repealing presumed consent provisions. But see, e.g., Mo. Stat. § 58–770, which allows for the removal of the pituitary gland without attempting to notify the family when there is no known objection. See also David Orentlicher, Presumed Consent to Organ Donation: Its Rise and Fall in the United States, 61 Rutgers L. Rev. 295 (2009).

3.   *Commercial Market.* Several cases have focused attention on the robust commercial market for human cadaveric tissue. In Adams v. King County, 192 P.3d 891 (Wash. 2008), for example, the Washington Supreme Court held that the adult decedent's parents might have a cause of action under Washington law where their son's brain was removed by the medical examiner and given to the Stanley Medical Research Institute (SMRI). SMRI funded a position in the examiner's office in exchange for the examiner providing brains to SMRI for research. The decedent had signed a donor card donating "any organ," but the court held that Washington's anatomical gift statute provided that only hospitals could receive undesignated gifts; the pre-mortem donation document did not apply. See also Geary v. Stanley Med. Res. Inst., 939 A.2d 86 (Me. 2008), in which multiple plaintiffs alleged that an agent who was paid $1,000 per brain falsified consent forms; Commonwealth v. Mastromarino, 2 A.3d 581 (Pa. Super. Ct. 2010), reviewing a prison sentence of 25–58 years for a tissue procurer who had taken cadaver tissue and bones

without consent, earning over $1 million from tissue banks. See also Michele Goodwin, Empires of the Flesh: Tissue and Organ Taboos, 60 Ala. L. Rev. 1219 (2009).

4. *Beyond Gifts.* When claims relating to the bodies of deceased family members are raised outside the context of anatomical gifts, the cases are decided differently. See, e.g., Shelley v. County of San Joaquin, 996 F. Supp. 2d 921 (E.D. Cal. 2014) (distinguishing *Newman* as applying only to anatomical gifts and holding that loss of decedent's remains by the sheriff's office did not violate family's procedural constitutional rights). See also Chapter 20 on the ownership of tissue in research.

3. Paying "Donors" for Organs and Tissue

FLYNN V. HOLDER

United States Court of Appeals, Ninth Circuit, 2012.
684 F.3d 852.

KLEINFELD, SENIOR CIRCUIT JUDGE.

* * *

The complaint challenges the constitutionality of the ban on compensation for human organs in the National Organ Transplant Act, as applied to bone marrow transplants. . . .

Some plaintiffs are parents of sick children who have diseases such as leukemia and a rare type of anemia, which can be fatal without bone marrow transplants. Another plaintiff is a physician and medical school professor, and an expert in bone marrow transplantation. He says that at least one out of five of his patients dies because no matching bone marrow donor can be found, and many others have complications when scarcity of matching donors compels him to use imperfectly matched donors. One plaintiff is a parent of mixed race children, for whom sufficiently matched donors are especially scarce, because mixed race persons typically have the rarest marrow cell types. . . .

Another plaintiff is a California nonprofit corporation that seeks to operate a program incentivizing bone marrow donations. The corporation proposes to offer $3,000 awards in the form of scholarships, housing allowances, or gifts to charities selected by donors, initially to minority and mixed race donors of bone marrow cells, who are likely to have the rarest marrow cell type. The corporation, MoreMarrowDonors.org, alleges that it cannot launch this program because the National Organ Transplant Act criminalizes payment of compensation for organs, and classifies bone marrow as an organ.

* * *

Until about twenty years ago, bone marrow was extracted from donors' bones by "aspiration." Long needles, thick enough to suck out the soft, fatty marrow, were inserted into the cavities of the anesthetized donor's hip bones. These are large bones with big central cavities full of marrow. Aspiration is a painful, unpleasant procedure for the donor. It requires hospitalization and general or local anesthesia, and involves commensurate risks.

. . . With [a] new technique, now used for at least two-thirds of bone marrow transplants, none of the soft, fatty marrow is actually donated. Patients who need bone marrow transplants do not need everything that the soft, fatty substance from bone cavities contains, just some of the marrow's "hematopoietic stem cells." These stem cells are seeds from which white blood cells, red blood cells, and platelets grow.

These are not the embryonic stem cells often the subject of controversy. Those stem cells, taken from human embryos, are "pluripotent," that is, they can turn into any kind of cell—brain, blood, retina, toenail, whatever. The stem cells at issue in this case are "hematopoietic stem cells." . . . Hematopoietic stem cells turn into blood cells and nothing else. Humans and other large mammals produce these blood stem cells constantly in vast numbers, because our blood cells die within a few months and need continual replacement. . . . [N]ew ones are made in the bone marrow, as long as we live.

[S]ome blood stem cells flow into and circulate in the bloodstream before they mature [into blood cells]. These are called "peripheral" blood stem cells. . . . The new bone marrow donation technique, developed during the past twenty years, is called "peripheral blood stem cell apheresis." . . . This procedure begins with five days of injections of a medication called a "granulocyte colony-stimulating factor" into the donor's blood. The medication accelerates blood stem cell production in the marrow, so that more stem cells go into the bloodstream. . . .

The main difference between an ordinary blood donation and apheresis is that instead of just filling up a plastic bag with whole blood, the donor sits for some hours in a recliner while the blood passes through the apheresis machine. This same apheresis technique is sometimes used for purposes other than bone marrow donations, such as when the machine is set up to collect plasma or platelets, rather than stem cells, from a donor's blood. When it is used for these other purposes, the identical technique is called a "blood donation" or "blood plasma donation." When used to separate out and collect hematopoietic stem cells from the donor's bloodstream, apheresis is called "peripheral blood stem cell apheresis" or a "bone marrow donation."

* * *

[E]ven with [the National Marrow Donor Program registry, funded by the federal government], good [marrow] matches often cannot be found. And even when a good match is found in the registry, tracking down the potential donor from what may be an outdated address may be impossible to accomplish in time to save the patient's life—assuming the potential donor is willing to go through with the process when found.

The plaintiff nonprofit proposes to mitigate this matching problem by using a financial incentive [which plaintiff concedes constitutes "valuable consideration" under NOTA]. The idea is that the financial incentive will induce more potential donors to sign up, stay in touch so that they can be located when necessary, and go through with the donations. . . .

Plaintiffs argue that the National Organ Transplant Act, as applied to MoreMarrowDonors.org's planned pilot program, violates the Equal Protection Clause. They claim that blood stem cell harvesting is not materially different from blood, sperm, and egg harvesting, which are not included under the statutory or regulatory definitions of "human organ." Like donors of blood and sperm, a bone marrow donor undergoing apheresis suffers no permanent harm, experiences no significant risk, and quickly regenerates what is donated. Plaintiffs also argue that any rational basis that Congress had when it passed the statute no longer exists with respect to the pilot program, because of the subsequent development of the apheresis method. Plaintiffs seek declaratory and injunctive relief so that MoreMarrowDonors.org can proceed with the initiative.

* * *

. . . [NOTA] makes it a felony "to knowingly acquire, receive, or otherwise transfer any human organ for valuable consideration for use in human transplantation." And it defines the term "human organ" to include "bone marrow." Ergo, the statute expressly prohibits compensating bone marrow donors. According to the government's brief, Congress took the view that "human body parts should not be viewed as commodities," [citing a Senate Report] and had several policy reasons for disallowing compensation to donors, which suffice to serve as a rational basis for the prohibition.

[T]he government argues that because it is much harder to find a match for patients who need bone marrow transplants than for patients who need blood transfusions, exploitative market forces could be triggered if bone marrow could be bought. The government also asserts that peripheral blood stem cell apheresis poses greater health risks for the donor than blood donations do, because of the side effects of the medicine used to increase stem cell secretion. [The court holds that the question of risk is one for trial or summary judgment rather than a motion to dismiss, but notes that "there are significant risks from egg donations, but the government concedes that the statute allows them."]

. . . To the extent that plaintiffs challenge the constitutionality of the compensation ban on bone marrow donation by the old aspiration method . . . the challenge must fail.

. . . It is irrelevant that the legislative history indicates that Congress viewed certain types of regenerable tissue, such as blood, as falling outside the statutory definition of "human organ." It may be that senators themselves, their staffs, or lobbyists for blood banks argued for an exception for body substances that can regenerate, and persuaded committee staffers to put that reason in the legislative history. But the statute does not say that compensation is permitted for organs or body parts that regenerate and prohibited for those that do not. Nor is the statute consistent with such a construction. The statute defines the liver "or any subpart thereof" as an organ for which compensation is prohibited. The drafters doubtless knew that a partial resection of a liver can yield a donation that will save the recipient's life, and that the donor's liver will grow back. So the statute does expressly prohibit compensation for at least one explicitly denoted "human organ" that will regenerate.

. . . Congress may have been concerned that if donors could be paid, rich patients or the medical industry might induce poor people to sell their organs, even when the transplant would create excessive medical risk, pain, or disability for the donor. Or, looking from the other end, Congress might have been concerned that every last cent could be extracted from sick patients needful of transplants, by well-matched potential donors making "your money or your life" offers. The existing commerce in organs extracted by force or fraud by organ thieves might be stimulated by paying for donations. Compensation to donors might also degrade the quality of the organ supply, by inducing potential donors to lie about their medical histories in order to make their organs marketable. Plaintiffs argue that a $3,000 housing subsidy, scholarship, or charitable donation is too small an amount to create a risk of any of these evils, but for a lot of people that could amount to three to six months' rent.

Congress may have had philosophical as well as policy reasons for prohibiting compensation. People tend to have an instinctive revulsion at denial of bodily integrity, particularly removal of flesh from a human being for use by another, and most particularly "commodification" of such conduct, that is, the sale of one's bodily tissue. While there is reportedly a large international market for the buying and selling of human organs, in the United States, such a market is criminal and the commerce is generally seen as revolting. Leon Kass [observes]:

> [A]lthough we allow no commerce in organs, transplant surgeons and hospitals are making handsome profits from the organ-trading business, and even the not-for-profit transplant registries and procurement agencies glean for their employees a middleman's

livelihood. Why . . . should everyone be making money from this business except the person whose organ makes it possible? Could it be that [the] real uneasiness [lies] with organ donation or with transplantation itself, for if not, what would be objectionable about its turning a profit? [Leon R. Kass, *Life, Liberty and the Defense of Dignity: The Challenge for Bioethics* 177 (2002).]

. . . Kass points to the idea of "psychophysical unity, a position that regards a human being as largely, if not wholly, self-identical with his enlivened body," so that, as [Immanuel] Kant put it, to " 'dispose of oneself as a mere means to some end of one's own liking is to degrade the humanity in one's person.' " . . .

[T]here are strong arguments for contrary views. But these policy and philosophical choices are for Congress to make, not us. The distinctions made by Congress must have a rational basis, but do not need to fit perfectly with that rational basis, and the basis need merely be rational, not persuasive to all. Here, Congress made a distinction between body material that is compensable and body material that is not. The distinction has a rational basis, so the prohibition on compensation for bone marrow donations by the aspiration method does not violate the Equal Protection Clause.

The focus, though, of plaintiffs' arguments is compensation for "bone marrow donations" by the peripheral blood stem cell apheresis method. For this, we need not answer any constitutional question, because the statute contains no prohibition. Such donations of cells drawn from blood flowing through the veins may sometimes anachronistically be called "bone marrow donations," but none of the soft, fatty marrow is donated, just cells found outside the marrow, outside the bones, flowing through the veins.

Congress could not have had an intent to address the apheresis method when it passed the statute, because the method did not exist at that time. We must construe the words of the statute to see what they imply about extraction of hematopoietic stem cells by this method. . . .

Since payment for blood donations has long been common, the silence in [NOTA] on compensating blood donors is loud. . . . The government concedes that the common practice of compensating blood donors is not prohibited by the statute.

The government argues that hematopoietic stem cells in the veins should be treated as "bone marrow" because "bone marrow" is a statutory organ, and the statute prohibits compensation not only for donation of an organ, but also "any subpart thereof." . . .

We reject this argument. . . . If the government's argument that what comes from the marrow is a subpart of the marrow were correct, then the statute would prohibit compensating blood donors. . . .

[E]very blood draw includes some hematopoietic stem cells. . . . Once the stem cells are in the bloodstream, they are a "subpart" of the blood, not the bone marrow. The word "subpart" refers to the organ from which the material is taken, not the organ in which it was created. . . .

* * *

We construe "bone marrow" to mean the soft, fatty substance in bone cavities, as opposed to blood, which means the red liquid that flows through the blood vessels. The statute does not prohibit compensation for donations of blood and the substances in it, which include peripheral blood stem cells. The Secretary of Health and Human Services has not exercised regulatory authority to define blood or peripheral blood stem cells as organs. We therefore need not decide whether prohibiting compensation for such donations would be unconstitutional.

NOTES AND QUESTIONS

1.   *Tissue vs. Organs.* Flynn relies on the specific type of tissue involved (as well as the method for removing it from the body) to hold that payment is not prohibited under NOTA. Should tissue, such as corneas, be treated differently than solid organs for purposes of payment? For purposes of consent? See *Newman* and notes following, above. See also Emily Largent, NOTA: Not a Good Act for Tissues to Follow, 19 Quinnipiac Health L.J. 179 (2016), arguing that tissue generally should be subject to a different regulatory regime than are organs but that the post-retrieval market should be regulated.

2.   *Payment for Organs?* The AMA recommends that payment for organs be studied with the following limitations: incentives are modest and set at the lowest level that can reasonably be expected to increase donations, and payment should be limited to "voluntary donation" of cadaveric organs only with "an explicit prohibition against the selling of organs." AMA Code of Medical Ethics Opinion E–6.1.3. Do these limits respond persuasively to objections to payment for human body parts or not? How would you separate the act of payment from the act of selling? See, e.g., Glenn Cohen, Regulating the Organ Market: Normative Foundations for Market Regulation, 77 L. & Contemp. Probs. 71 (2014); Radhika Rao, A Small Price to Pay: Incentivizing Cadaveric Organ Donation with Posthumous Payments, 18 Minn. J.L. Sci. & Tech. 273 (2017); Jake Linford, The Kidney Donor Scholarship Act: How College Scholarships Can Provide Financial Incentives for Kidney Donation While Preserving Altruistic Meaning, 2 St. Louis U.J. Health L. & Pol'y 265 (2009); Michele Goodwin, Black Markets: The Supply and Demand of Body Parts (2006) (arguing in favor of payment). But see Institute of Medicine, Organ Donation: Opportunities for Action (2006) (rejecting market exchanges).

3.   *Other Financial Incentives.* The incentives proposed in *Flynn* did not include payments of cash to the donor. Does the form the financial transfer takes make a difference to legal, ethical, or public policy issues in providing financial incentives for donors? NOTA provides that "valuable consideration"

does not include "reasonable payments associated with the removal, transportation, implantation, processing, preservation, quality control, and storage of a human organ or the expenses of travel, housing, and lost wages incurred by the donor of a human organ in connection with the donation . . . ". 42 U.S.C.A. § 274e(c)(2). (The UAGA, which unlike NOTA applies only to cadaveric organs and tissue, has a similar provision. § 16.) "Reasonable payments" allows profit for the firms involved in transplantation. See discussion following *Newman*, above.

Some states compensate donors within these restrictions. Pennsylvania, for example, has established a public trust fund for families of decedents who donate organs. The statute limits payments to $3,000 per donor (although the program currently pays only $300) to be used to cover funeral expenses and incidental expenses (lodging, food) borne by the family in relation to the donation. 20 Pa. Cons. Stat. § 8622. Other states have state income tax incentives allowing living donors to deduct expenses related to donation, including lost wages. Wis. Stat. Ann. § 71.05(10)(i). The federal Organ Donation and Recovery Improvement Act of 2004 provides grants to procurement organizations (and other groups) for reimbursing living donors for travel and certain living expenses. 42 U.S.C. § 274f. NOTA was amended in 2007 (42 U.S.C. § 274e) to specifically exclude paired exchanges from the Act's prohibition of the payment of "valuable consideration" for organ donation even though each organ is donated for the purpose of procuring another organ for a designated recipient. See Note on Living Donors, above.

4.   *Transplant Tourism.* Organ procurement and transplantation operate on a global scale. Persons of means in need of transplants can go where the organs are. While there had once been significant concern that transplant tourism was bringing foreign nationals to the U.S. to receive one of "our" scarce organs, the situation has shifted dramatically. Now a primary concern is U.S. citizens who avoid the waiting list here by travelling abroad to receive transplants. There are concerns for public safety and quality as these patients return to the U.S. for post-transplant care. See, e.g., Anthony J. Polcari et al., Transplant Tourism—A Dangerous Journey?, 25 Clinical Transplantation 633 (2011).

The most dramatic concern, however, is that transplant tourism may have created a global black market in which organs are bought and sold or retrieved from persons under even more extreme circumstances. See, e.g., Robert Ainley, Organ Transploitation: A Model Law Approach to Combat Human Trafficking and Transplant Tourism, 13 Or. R. Int'l L. 427 (2011). But see F. Ambagtsheer et al., On Patients Who Purchase Organ Transplants Abroad, 10 Am J. Transplantation 2800 (2016), arguing that data do not support claims of this abuse.

II. THE DETERMINATION OF DEATH

A. THE UNIFORM DETERMINATION OF DEATH ACT

Determining that a person has died used to be simple. If the heart and lungs had stopped functioning, eventually other less observable processes stopped as well. The cessation of cardiopulmonary function signaled death without the need for testing whether other processes, such as neurological activity, continued.

The first well-accepted definition of death to include what has become known as "brain death" came in 1968 from the Ad Hoc Committee of the Harvard Medical School to Examine the Definition of Brain Death. The Committee identified two developments that required an expansion of the traditional heart-lung definition of death. First, the Committee pointed out that "resuscitative and support measures" had improved and were being used more frequently, though often unsuccessfully, leaving patients with serious brain injuries and burdening patients, families, and society in unacceptable ways. These technological advances could "restore 'life' as judged by the ancient standards of persistent respiration and continuing heart beat" even when "there is not the remotest possibility of an individual recovering consciousness following massive brain damage." Second, the Committee explained that the uncertainty that "brain death" was real death was hindering the ability to recover life-sustaining organs that would be used for transplantation. The full report of the Committee is available at A Definition of Irreversible Coma: Report of the Ad Hoc Committee of the Harvard Medical School to Examine the Definition of Brain Death, 205 JAMA 337 (1968).

The Committee listed characteristics of brain death (which the Committee called "irreversible coma") as unreceptivity and unresponsitivity, no autonomous movements or breathing, no reflexes, and flat electroencephalogram. The Committee recommended that death be declared before the respirator is turned off ("in our judgment it will provide a greater degree of legal protection to those involved"); that the physician in charge consult with others before the declaration of death is made; that the physician (rather than the family) determine death; and that the decision to declare death be made by physicians who are not involved "in any later effort to transplant organs or tissue from the deceased individual."

The Ad Hoc Committee suggested that "no statutory change in the law should be necessary [to accommodate brain death] since the law treats this question essentially as one of fact to be determined by physicians." Nevertheless, brain death statutes began appearing shortly after the publication of the Committee's report. In 1980, the Uniform Determination of Death Act (UDDA) ultimately was developed with the cooperation of both the AMA and the ABA.

UNIFORM DETERMINATION OF DEATH ACT (1980)

§ 1. An individual who has sustained either (1) irreversible cessation of circulatory and respiratory functions, or (2) irreversible cessation of all functions of the entire brain, including the brain stem, is dead. A determination of death must be made in accordance with accepted medical standards.

PROBLEM: WHEN DOES DEATH OCCUR?

Alberto Arcturus was found lying face down by the side of the road, apparently after being run down by a hit-and-run driver. A passing motorist called the local emergency medical services, and an ambulance arrived on the scene about 15 minutes after the call. The two paramedics found that Mr. Arcturus was not breathing and had no pulse. They also discovered that a substantial portion of his head (including his forehead and forebrain) was crushed. One paramedic looked at the other and said, "He's dead; let's call the morgue." The second, less experienced paramedic insisted on trying to resuscitate Mr. Arcturus, as was required by the emergency medical services manual for paramedics. They placed him in the ambulance and administered cardiopulmonary resuscitation throughout the fifteen-minute ride to the nearest hospital emergency room.

At the emergency room, physicians confirmed that Mr. Arcturus did not breathe spontaneously and had no spontaneous cardiac activity. One doctor told the charge nurse that he was dead and that "dead on arrival" should be marked on his chart. A young intern balked at this, however, because the hospital emergency room protocol required more before a brain-injured patient could be declared dead. The physicians then administered drugs and used paddles that sent an electric current through Mr. Arcturus's chest in an effort to start his heart. After some time, they managed to get a weak pulse, and they placed Mr. Arcturus on a ventilator and moved him to the intensive care unit. A neurology consult revealed that Mr. Arcturus's neocortex was completely and irreversibly destroyed—most of it was literally gone, left on the highway— although his brain stem remained intact. With the help of a ventilator, Mr. Arcturus's body could continue functioning indefinitely. If the ventilator were to be removed, Mr. Arcturus's heart and lung function would cease within some minutes as repeated trials proved that he could not breathe on his own.

After considerable investigation, police have captured the hit-and-run driver. They want to know whether to charge him with vehicular homicide or something else. The doctors and Mr. Arcturus's family want to know whether he is dead or alive. Further, if he is dead, the family wants to know when he died—at the roadside, in the hospital emergency room, in the intensive care unit, or somewhere else. Mr. Arcturus's health insurer is involved because insurance ordinarily won't cover medical services to a dead patient. Finally, the regional Organ Procurement Organization has been notified that there is a potential donor, and the transplant team at the hospital wants to know if Mr. Arcturus's healthy organs (including his kidneys and liver) are available for transplantation to save the life of patients on the transplant waiting list.

Is Mr. Arcturus dead? If so, when did he die?

B. VARIATION IN MEDICAL AND LEGAL STANDARDS

Although the Ad Hoc Committee advocated the adoption of neurological determination of death over 50 years ago and "brain death" has been adopted as a legal standard for death by all of the states for several decades, controversy has persisted. Cases in which families refuse to accept that their loved one is dead garner headlines because they touch a nerve. These cases are often dismissed as instances where laypersons are in denial, do not trust physicians and hospitals, are incapable of understanding that the condition of the body supported by mechanical ventilation is not evidence of life, or are relying on religious exceptionalism.

However, a deeper look reveals more. There are fissures in the medical community itself in terms of the standards and procedures used to determine brain death and, for some, even whether the legal standard requiring the cessation of *all* brain activity aligns with current medical practice in determining death. See Robert D. Truog et al., Understanding Brain Death, 323(21) JAMA 2139 (May 1, 2020); Thaddeus Pope, Brain Death Forsaken: Growing Conflict and New Legal Challenges, 37 J. Leg. Med. 265 (2017). See also Rachel Aviv, The Death Debate, New Yorker 30 (Feb. 5, 2018), describing the complexities arising in the dispute over the status of Jahi McMath, a 13-year-old girl declared brain dead by the hospital after surgery. The Nevada Supreme Court considered a similar situation in *Hailu*, below.

IN RE GUARDIANSHIP OF HAILU
Supreme Court of Nevada, 2015.
361 P.3d 524.

PICKERING, J.:

"For legal and medical purposes, a person is dead if the person has sustained an irreversible cessation of . . . [a]ll functions of the person's entire brain, including his or her brain stem." NRS 451.007(1). The determination of death "must be made in accordance with accepted medical standards." NRS 451.007(2). Here, we are asked to decide whether the American Association of Neurology [AAN] guidelines are considered "accepted medical standards" that satisfy the definition of brain death in NRS 451.007. We conclude that the district court failed to properly consider whether the [AAN] guidelines adequately measure all functions of the entire brain, including the brain stem, . . . and are considered accepted medical standards by states that have adopted the Uniform Determination of Death Act. Accordingly, we reverse the district court's order denying a petition for temporary restraining order and remand.

FACTS

Medical history

On April 1, 2015, 20-year-old university student Aden Hailu went to St. Mary's Regional Medical Center (St. Mary's) after experiencing abdominal pain. Medical staff could not determine the cause of her pain and decided to perform an exploratory laparotomy and remove her appendix. During the laparotomy, Hailu's blood pressure was low and she suffered "severe, catastrophic anoxic, or lack of brain oxygen damage," and she never woke up. After her surgery, Hailu was transferred to the St. Mary's Intensive Care Unit (ICU), under the care of Dr. Anthony Floreani. Within the first two weeks of April, three different electroencephalogram (EEG) tests were conducted, all of which showed brain functioning.

On April 13, 2015, Dr. Aaron Heide, the Director of Neurology and Stroke at St. Mary's, first examined Hailu. Dr. Heide concluded that Hailu was not brain dead at that time but was "rapidly declining." To make that determination, Dr. Heide conducted an examination of Hailu's neurological functions; her left eye was minimally responsive, she was chewing on the ventilator tube, and she moved her arms with stimulation. The next day, April 14, 2015, Hailu did not exhibit these same indicia of neurological functioning.

On May 28, 2015, St. Mary's performed an apnea test, which involved taking Hailu off ventilation support for ten minutes to see if she could breathe on her own; Hailu failed the apnea test, leading St. Mary's to conclude that "[t]his test result confirms Brain Death unequivocally." Based on Hailu's condition, Dr. Jeffrey Bacon wrote the following in his notes: "Awaiting administration and hospital lawyers for direction re care—withdrawal of Ventilator support indicated NOW in my opinion as brain death unequivocally confirmed." On June 2, 2015, St. Mary's notified Hailu's father and guardian, Fanuel Gebreyes, that it intended to discontinue Hailu's ventilator and other life support. Gebreyes opposed taking Hailu off life support and sought judicial relief.

Procedural history

Gebreyes filed an emergency motion for [a] temporary restraining order to enjoin St. Mary's from removing Hailu from life-sustaining services. On June 18, 2015, the district court held a hearing on the matter. The parties stipulated that St. Mary's would continue life-sustaining services until July 2, 2015, at 5:00 p.m. to allow Gebreyes to have an independent neurologist examine Hailu. They further stipulated that if, after the independent examination, Gebreyes wished St. Mary's to continue life support, he would need to request it through guardianship court. However, "if on July 2, 2015, it is determined that Aden Hailu is legally and clinically deceased, the hospital shall proceed as they see fit." Based on the stipulation, the district court dismissed the complaint for a temporary restraining order.

For reasons unknown, Gebreyes was unable to obtain the services of a neurologist before the stipulated July 2, 2015, deadline. Consequently, on July 1, 2015, Gebreyes filed an "Emergency Petition for Order Authorizing Medical Care, Restraining Order and Permanent Injunction." In the petition, he alleged that the doctors at St. Mary's had prematurely determined that Hailu had experienced brain death and sought to prevent the hospital from removing Hailu from the ventilator. St. Mary's opposed the emergency petition on July 2, 2015, and the district court held a hearing that same day.

At the July 2, 2015, hearing, the district court heard from four witnesses. First, Gebreyes testified that he wanted Hailu to get a tracheostomy and feeding tube to prepare her for transport; he hoped to take her home or relocate her to Las Vegas, where he resides. When asked why he did not obtain the services of another doctor to perform the tracheostomy, he stated that it was something he thought St. Mary's had to do because Hailu is at St. Mary's. Second, Gebreyes obtained the services of Dr. Paul Byrne—a known opponent of brain-death declarations who is unlicensed in Nevada—to testify that Hailu is still alive. Dr. Byrne complained that Hailu was never treated for thyroid problems and testified that this treatment will help her improve.

Third, Dr. Aaron Heide testified on behalf of St. Mary's. Dr. Heide applied the [AAN] guidelines to Hailu to determine if she was brain dead. He testified that the AAN guidelines are the accepted medical standard in Nevada. The AAN guidelines call for three determinations: (1) whether there is a coma and unresponsiveness; (2) whether there is brainstem activity (determined by conducting a clinical examination of reflexes, eyes, ears, etc.); and (3) whether the patient can breathe on her own (determined by conducting an apnea test). Although another doctor conducted the apnea test one month after Dr. Heide's last examination of Hailu, Dr. Heide believed that Hailu "had zero percent chance of any form of functional neurological outcome." Further, Dr. Heide also administered a Transcranial Doppler test, which is a test that measures blood flow to the brain. While there was still some blood flow to Hailu's brain, the lack of blood flow was consistent with brain death.

Last, Helen Lidholm, the CEO of St. Mary's, testified that the hospital is in favor of allowing Hailu to be transported to Las Vegas, where her father lives. Lidholm stated that St. Mary's "could make that happen" as long as Gebreyes arranges the proper medical equipment and transportation for Hailu and ensures a transfer location that can care for her. St. Mary's would allow the family to retain the services of any neurologist to come in and test Hailu as long as the physician is licensed in the State of Nevada; St. Mary's also offered to pay for the physician's examination fee. On cross-examination, Lidholm clarified that if the family has a licensed neurologist examine Hailu and determine that she is still alive, the physician can then order treatment for Hailu. Gebreyes said that he never received this offer before the hearing.

After Gebreyes said that he wanted to take advantage of the opportunity to bring in his own neurologist, the parties stipulated to extend the hearing until July 21, 2015, to give Gebreyes time to retain the services of a neurologist.... [T]he district court stated that Gebreyes needs a neurological expert because the matter involves "primarily neurological issues." . . .

On July 21, 2015, Gebreyes presented a plan to transport Hailu to Las Vegas based on the testimony of two physicians. First, Gebreyes called Dr. Brian Callister to testify. Dr. Callister is not a neurologist, but specializes in internal medicine and hospitalist medicine. He examined Hailu the day of his testimony and reviewed her medical records. Based on his examination of Hailu and review of her records, Dr. Callister testified: "I believe that her status is quite grim. I think that her chance of survival, her chance of awakening from her current state is a long shot. However, I do not think that the chance is zero." Dr. Callister stated that all three EEG tests did show brainwaves, albeit abnormal and slow. In Dr. Callister's opinion, the EEG tests are "something that should give you just enough pause to say you can't say with certainty that her chances are zero." Although Dr. Callister admitted that under the AAN guidelines Hailu's condition looks irreversible, Dr. Callister pointed to other factors that demonstrate improvement is a possibility. As examples, Dr. Callister cites Hailu's young age, her health, her skin, her ability to make urine and pass bowel movements, and the fact that the general functioning of the rest of her body is good. . . .

. . . [O]n cross-examination, Dr. Callister conceded that under "a strict definition" of the AAN guidelines, Hailu "would meet their category [of brain death]." On redirect, Dr. Callister concluded that "there's enough variables and enough questions based on the condition of her physical body, the EEG's and the fact that no further neurological testing has been done in several months, and the fact that no outside third party neurologist has looked at her that I would have pause."

[Gebreyes also called a doctor who was willing to perform the tracheostomy but not to take Hailu into his care for other purposes.]

* * *

Next, St. Mary's called Dr. Anthony Floreani to testify. Dr. Floreani took care of Hailu in the ICU since the night following her surgery. Dr. Floreani is a pulmonary doctor, not a neurologist. Dr. Floreani agreed with the conclusions of Dr. Heide that Hailu is brain dead. . . . Dr. Floreani testified that the St. Mary's doctors did the tests "by the book exactly how you should do it." Based on all of the evidence from the July 2 hearing and the July 21 hearing, the district court ruled in favor of St. Mary's. The district court stated that a restraining order should not be granted because the medical evidence from Dr. Heide and Dr. Floreani suggested that the AAN guidelines were followed, and thus, "medical standards were met, the outcome and criteria were satisfied in terms of the statute, the [AAN] protocol was followed, the outcome of the various three step tests under the [AAN] protocol all direct certification of death, and I agree." . . .

DISCUSSION

* * *

The district court focused exclusively on whether St. Mary's physicians satisfied the AAN guidelines, without discussing whether the AAN guidelines satisfy NRS 451.007. Although St. Mary's presented testimony that the AAN guidelines are the accepted medical standard in Nevada— albeit a simple "yes" to the question of whether the AAN guidelines are the accepted medical standard in Nevada—the district court and St. Mary's failed to demonstrate that the AAN guidelines are considered "accepted medical standards" that are applied uniformly throughout states that have enacted the UDDA . . . . The district court did not reach this issue at all, while St. Mary's has only cited one source to support its argument that the AAN guidelines are the nationally accepted medical standard.

St. Mary's cites the New Jersey Law Revision Commission's Report relating to the Declaration of Death Act. However, the report actually supports the opposite conclusion for which St. Mary's argues. . . . *See* N.J. Law Revision Comm'n, Final Report Relating to New Jersey Declaration of Death Act, at 14 (Jan. 18, 2013). [T]he report cited to multiple studies suggesting that "the AAN guidelines need more research" and "there is still a great variety of practice in U.S. hospitals" even though the AAN guidelines were published in 1995. Despite recognizing the AAN as guidelines "upon which most hospitals and physicians rely," the report concluded that the AAN guidelines were not so broadly adopted and utilized as to have become *the* accepted medical standard for determining brain death. Based on the foregoing, and the record before us, we are not convinced that the AAN guidelines are considered the accepted medical standard that can be applied in a way to make Nevada's Determination of Death Act uniform with states that have adopted it, as the UDDA requires. . . .

* * *

It appears from a layperson's review of the Harvard criteria versus the AAN guidelines that the AAN guidelines incorporated many of the clinical tests used in the Harvard criteria. [ ] However, the AAN guidelines do not require confirmatory/ancillary testing, such as EEGs. Although the AAN guidelines state that ancillary testing should be ordered "only if clinical examination cannot be fully performed due to patient factors, or if apnea testing is inconclusive or aborted," the AAN's own study recognized that a decade after publication of the guidelines, 84 percent of brain death determinations still included EEG testing. [ ]

* * *

[T]he briefing and record before us do not answer two key questions. First, the briefing and testimony do not establish whether the AAN guidelines are considered accepted medical standards among states that have enacted the UDDA. . . . Second, whatever their medical acceptance generally, the briefing and testimony do not establish whether the AAN guidelines adequately measure the extraordinarily broad standard laid out by NRS 451.007, which requires, before brain death can be declared under the UDDA, an "irreversible cessation" of "[a]ll functions of the person's entire brain, including his or her brain stem." [ ] Emphasis added. Though courts defer to the medical community to determine the applicable criteria to measure brain functioning, it is the duty of the law to establish the applicable standard that said criteria must meet. . . .

* * *

We concur: HARDESTY, C.J., and PARRAGUIRRE, DOUGLAS, CHERRY, SAITTA, and GIBBONS, JJ.

NOTES AND QUESTIONS

1.   *Appearances Are Deceiving?* The position that dead is dead (whether measured by the irreversible cessation of cardiopulmonary function or total brain function) forms the foundation for legal standards and medical practice determining whether death has occurred. It certainly can be difficult for laypersons to accept that someone who has been declared brain dead, currently often referred to as "neurological determination of death," is dead. The person who is being supported by a ventilator but who is declared dead by neurological criteria still looks so alive—warm to the touch and with a steady rhythm of breath due to the ventilator. Even health care professionals may experience cognitive dissonance in "caring for" persons who are brain dead while preparing the body for retrieval of organs for transplantation or maintaining the body on support while family matters are settled. Robert D. Truog, Brain Death—Too Flawed to Endure, Too Ingrained to Abandon, 35 J.L. Med. & Ethics 273 (2007). It should not be surprising, then, that conflicts between families and hospitals regarding the determination of death by neurological criteria occur and sometimes reach the courts.

2. *Avoiding Conflicts.* Cases like Hailu always raise questions about whether there were steps that could have been taken to avoid the conflict and lead to acceptance of the determination of death. Do you see any opportunities in Hailu? Both Aden Hailu and Jahi McMath, the subject of the New Yorker piece cited above, were young women of color. What impact might the gender and race of the patients or their next of kin make in this context? See Chapter 6. Both Ms. Hailu and Ms. McMath suffered severe injuries during surgery. As is routine, the declaration of death in each case was made by physicians affiliated with that hospital. Should hospitals establish different default procedures when the patient has been injured during the course of treatment in the hospital? If a patient is not declared to be dead, life-sustaining treatment may still be withdrawn. See Chapter 18. Is it possible that approaching the situation from that direction could produce a different result in some cases? The Ad Hoc Committee (see Section II.A, above) rejected involving the family in the determination of death and allocated the process entirely to the physician. Does a hard-edge boundary protect families or does it create alienation in the process?

3. *Defining Accepted Medical Standards.* The court is careful to note that it is not concluding that the AAN criteria are not the generally accepted medical standard for determining death, but only that the issue was not addressed in the court below. In fact, there is significant variability in the protocols doctors and hospitals use to determine whether brain death has occurred. See David M. Greer et al., Variability of Brain Death Policies in the U.S., 73 JAMA Neurology 213 (2016); David M. Greer et al., Determination of Brain Death/Death by Neurologic Criteria, The World Brain Death Project, 324(11) JAMA 1078 (Aug. 3, 2020).

After the Law Revision Commission's report cited in the court's opinion, the New Jersey legislature amended the state's determination of death statute to require that the determination of brain death be "based upon the exercise of the physician's best medical judgment and in accordance with currently accepted medical standards that are based upon nationally recognized sources of practice guidelines, including, but not limited to, those adopted by the [AAN]." After *Hailu*, the Nevada legislature went even further by requiring that the determination of brain death in adults "must be made" in compliance with the 2010 AAN Guidelines and subsequent revisions adopted by the AAN. Nev. Rev. Stat. § 451.007(2)(b)(1). See also AAN standards at James A. Russell et al., Brain Death, The Determination of Brain Death, and Member Guidance for Brain Death Accommodation Requests: AAN Position Statement, 92(5) Neurology 228 (Jan 2019). Should legislatures select the specific medical protocol to be used, or is that a question for medicine? Should the determination of death be treated differently than other medical decisions in that regard? See Chapter 4.

4. *Do Medical Standards Align with Legal Requirements?* The court implies that the brain death statute requires that it must be determined that there is absolutely no function in the brain at all. In fact, some extremely minimal activity continues in the brain (such as the secretion of hormones

regulating salts and fluids) that can continue certain bodily functions in some patients who are determined to be brain dead under current medical standards. See, e.g., Seema K. Shah, Piercing the Veil: The Limits of Brain Death as a Legal Fiction, 48 Mich. J.L. Reform 301 (2015). See also President's Council on Bioethics, Controversies in the Determination of Death (2008), recognizing the persistence of some activity but recommending continuation of the current standards as applied, although shifting the term to "total brain failure." Must state statutes be revised to account for the persistence of some brain activity if the whole brain death standard is to be retained? See *T.A.C.P.*, below. Or should the statutes remain the same, and the interpretation of "all functions of the entire brain" be understood to tolerate the incidental activity that remains?

5.   *Accommodating Objections.* Should state statutes provide for individual choice as between cardiopulmonary or neurological determination of death? New Jersey formally adopted an exemption from the application of the brain death standard for determination of death for patients who reject brain death on specific grounds:

> The death of an individual shall not be declared upon the basis of neurological criteria . . . when the licensed physician authorized to declare death, has reason to believe, on the basis of information in the individual's available medical records, or information provided by a member of the individual's family or any other person knowledgeable about the individual's personal religious beliefs that such a declaration would violate the personal religious beliefs of the individual. In these cases, death shall be declared, and the time of death fixed, solely upon the basis of cardio-respiratory criteria. . . . N.J. Stat. § 26:6A–5.

A few other states require reasonable accommodation, rather than an exemption, for families that object to the brain death standard for determination of death. The New York State Department of Health requires that hospitals provide reasonable accommodations for those with "religious or moral objections" to brain death, but explicitly does not require accommodation for persons with objections based "solely on the psychological denial that death has occurred or on an alleged inadequacy of the brain death determination." The Department's guidelines advise sensitivity in the latter case. N.Y. State Dept. of Health, Guidelines for Determining Brain Death (2011). Would either the New Jersey or New York provisions apply to the situation in *Hailu*? Compare Cal. Health & Safety Code § 1254.4, encompassing a broader range of objections but providing only for a reasonable time to allow the family to adjust to the diagnosis and, in the case of cultural or religious objections, some reasonable efforts to accommodate those "religious or cultural practices or concerns."

6.   *Consent Required?* After remand in *Hailu*, the hospital asked the trial court for permission to perform additional testing, including an electroencephalogram (EEG), over the father's objection, and the court allowed two EEGs to be performed. It's not clear whether that testing took place.

Shortly before the date of the hearing on the issue of the remand, Aden Hailu suffered cardiopulmonary arrest. The death certificate listed the date of death as January 4, 2016, the date of the arrest. Siobhan McAndres, The Contested Death of Aden Hailu, Reno-Gazette-Journal (Mar. 25, 2016). Should surrogate consent be required before a physician performs brain death diagnostic tests? One practical consequence of requiring consent (or honoring family objections) is to enable families to avoid determination of death using the brain death standard. See Pope, Brain Death and the Law: Hard Cases and Legal Challenges, above.

7.   *Revising the UDDA.* There have been many suggestions for revisions to the UDDA, often centered on the issues raised by *Hailu* and the notes above. See, e.g., Ariane Lewis et al., Determination of Death by Neurologic Criteria in the United States: The Case for Revising the Uniform Determination of Death Act, 47(4 supp.) J. Law Med. Ethics 9 (Dec. 2019); D. Alan Shewmon, Statement in Support of Revising the Uniform Determination of Death Act and in Opposition to a Proposed Reform, J. Med. & Phil. (2021) (advance article). In 2021, the Uniform Law Commission convened a committee to amend or revise the UDDA. What revisions, if any, would you suggest and why?

IN RE T.A.C.P.
Supreme Court of Florida, 1992.
609 So. 2d 588.

KOGAN, JUSTICE.

We have for review an order of the trial court certified by the Fourth District Court of Appeal as touching on a matter of great public importance requiring immediate resolution by this Court. We frame the issue as follows:

Is an anencephalic newborn considered "dead" for purposes of organ donation solely by reason of its congenital deformity?

* * *

I.   Facts

At or about the eighth month of pregnancy, the parents of the child T.A.C.P. were informed that she would be born with anencephaly. . . .

In this case, T.A.C.P. actually survived only a few days after birth. The medical evidence in the record shows that the child T.A.C.P. was incapable of developing any sort of cognitive process, may have been unable to feel pain or experience sensation due to the absence of the upper brain, and at least for part of the time was placed on a mechanical ventilator to assist her breathing. . . .

On the advice of physicians, the parents continued the pregnancy to term and agreed that the mother would undergo caesarean section during birth. The parents agreed to the caesarean procedure with the express hope that the infant's organs would be less damaged and could be used for transplant in other sick children. Although T.A.C.P. had no hope of life herself, the parents both testified in court that they wanted to use this opportunity to give life to others. However, when the parents requested that T.A.C.P. be declared legally dead for this purpose, her health care providers refused out of concern that they thereby might incur civil or criminal liability. . . .

II.   The Medical Nature of Anencephaly

Although appellate courts appear never to have confronted the issue, there already is an impressive body of published medical scholarship on anencephaly. From our review of this material, we find that anencephaly is a variable but fairly well defined medical condition. Experts in the field have written that anencephaly is the most common severe birth defect of the central nervous system seen in the United States, although it apparently has existed throughout human history.

A statement by the Medical Task Force on Anencephaly ("Task Force") printed in the New England Journal of Medicine generally described "anencephaly" as "a congenital absence of major portions of the brain, skull, and scalp, with its genesis in the first month of gestation." David A. Stumpf et al., *The Infant with Anencephaly*, 322 New Eng.J.Med. 669, 669 (1990). The large opening in the skull accompanied by the absence or severe congenital disruption of the cerebral hemispheres is the characteristic feature of the condition. *Id.*

The Task Force defined anencephaly as diagnosable only when all of the following four criteria are present:

(1) A large portion of the skull is absent. (2) The scalp, which extends to the margin of the bone, is absent over the skull defect. (3) Hemorrhagic, fibrotic tissue is exposed because of defects in the skull and scalp. (4) Recognizable cerebral hemispheres are absent.

* * *

Thus, it is clear that anencephaly is distinguishable from some other congenital conditions because its extremity renders it uniformly lethal. . . .

The Task Force stated that most reported anencephalic children die within the first few days after birth, with survival any longer being rare. . . . The Task Force reported, however, that these survival rates are confounded somewhat by the variable degrees of medical care afforded to anencephalics. Some such infants may be given considerable life support while others may be given much less care.

The Task Force reported that the medical consequences of anencephaly can be established with some certainty. All anencephalics by definition are permanently unconscious because they lack the cerebral cortex necessary for conscious thought. Their condition thus is quite similar to that of persons in a persistent vegetative state. Where the brain stem is functioning, as it was here, spontaneous breathing and heartbeat can occur. In addition, such infants may show spontaneous movements of the extremities, "startle" reflexes, and pupils that respond to light. Some may show feeding reflexes, may cough, hiccup, or exhibit eye movements, and may produce facial expressions.

* * *

There appears to be general agreement that anencephalics usually have ceased to be suitable organ donors by the time they meet all the criteria for "whole brain death," i.e., the complete absence of brainstem function. . . . There also is no doubt that a need exists for infant organs for transplantation. Nationally, between thirty and fifty percent of children under two years of age who need transplants die while waiting for organs to become available. . . .

III. Legal Definitions of "Death" & "Life"

[The court considers Florida's statute:]

> For legal and medical purposes, *where respiratory and circulatory functions are maintained by artificial means of support* so as to preclude a determination that these functions have ceased, the occurrence of death *may* be determined where there is the irreversible cessation of the functioning of the entire brain, including the brain stem, determined in accordance with this section.

§ 382.009(1), Fla.Stat. (1991) (emphasis added). A later subsection goes on to declare:

> Except for a diagnosis of brain death, the standard set forth in this section is not the exclusive standard for determining death or for the withdrawal of life-support systems.

§ 382.009(4), Fla.Stat. (1991). This language is highly significant for two reasons.

First, the statute does not purport to codify the common law standard applied in some other jurisdictions, as does the uniform act. The use of the permissive word "may" in the statute in tandem with the savings clause of section 382.009(4) buttresses the conclusion that the legislature envisioned other ways of defining "death." Second, the statutory framers clearly did not intend to apply the statute's language to the anencephalic infant not being kept alive by life support. To the contrary, the framers expressly limited the statute to that situation in which "respiratory and circulatory functions are maintained by artificial means of support."

* * *

IV. Common Law & Policy

* * *

The question remaining is whether there is good reason in public policy for this Court to create an additional common law standard applicable [only] to anencephalics. Alterations of the common law, while rarely entertained or allowed, are within this Court's prerogative. . . . We believe, for example, that our adoption of the cardiopulmonary definition of death today is required by public necessity and, in any event, merely formalizes what has been the common practice in this state for well over a century.

Such is not the case with petitioners' request. Our review of the medical, ethical, and legal literature on anencephaly discloses absolutely no consensus that public necessity or fundamental rights will be better served by granting this request.

We are not persuaded that a public necessity exists to justify this action, in light of the other factors in this case—although we acknowledge much ambivalence about this particular question. We have been deeply touched by the altruism and unquestioned motives of the parents of T.A.C.P. The parents have shown great humanity, compassion, and concern for others. The problem we as a Court must face, however, is that the medical literature shows unresolved controversy over the extent to which anencephalic organs can or should be used in transplants.

* * *

We express no opinion today about who is right and who is wrong on these issues—if any "right" or "wrong" can be found here. The salient point is that no consensus exists as to: (a) the utility of organ transplants of the type at issue here; (b) the ethical issues involved; or (c) the legal and constitutional problems implicated.

V. Conclusions

Accordingly, we find no basis to expand the common law to equate anencephaly with death. We acknowledge the possibility that some infants' lives might be saved by using organs from anencephalics who do not meet the traditional definition of "death" we reaffirm today. But weighed against this is the utter lack of consensus, and the questions about the overall utility of such organ donations. The scales clearly tip in favor of not extending the common law in this instance.

To summarize: We hold that Florida common law recognizes the cardiopulmonary definition of death as stated above; and Florida statutes create a "whole-brain death" exception applicable whenever cardiopulmonary function is being maintained artificially. There are no other legal standards for determining death under present Florida law.

Because no Florida statute applies to the present case, the determination of death in this instance must be judged against the common law cardiopulmonary standard. The evidence shows that T.A.C.P.'s heart was beating and she was breathing at the times in question. Accordingly, she was not dead under Florida law, and no donation of her organs would have been legal.

NOTES AND QUESTIONS

1. *Variation Among the States*. Despite the UDDA, there is significant variation among state statutes recognizing irreversible cessation of all brain function as a legal standard for the determination of death. These differences can be significant, as illustrated in the court's discussion of the Florida statute in *T.A.C.P.* Several states have accepted brain death for the determination of death by case law rather than by statute. In departing from the UDDA, some states adopted definitions for "irreversible," which the UDDA leaves undefined; some provide that brain function is relevant for the determination of death *only* where cardiopulmonary function is maintained by mechanical means. Some statutes provide that a person *may* (instead of *shall*) be considered dead in the presence of irreversible cessation of cardiopulmonary or all brain function. Jason Goldsmith, Wanted! Dead and/or Alive: Choosing Among the Not-So-Uniform Statutory Definitions of Death, 61 U. Miami L. Rev. 871 (2007).

2. *Implications for Others*. If the Florida court had declared that anencephaly was acceptable as a legal standard for the determination of death, what implications would that have for medical treatment of individuals with the same medical condition? Shortly after the *T.A.C.P.* opinion was issued, a mother successfully fought a hospital refusal to repeatedly resuscitate her infant who had anencephaly, with the court ultimately holding that a federal statute requiring that hospitals provide emergency care covered the child. In re Baby K, 16 F. 3d 590 (4th Cir. 1994). The hospital in *Baby K* claimed that continued treatment was futile, not that Baby K met a legal standard for death. See Chapter 18. Some states already allow individual choice in the application of the neurological determination of death. See discussion after *Hailu*, above. What are the implications of allowing individualized standards for the determination of death?

3. *"Whole" vs. "Higher" Brain Death*. Some have argued that the legal standard for death should be expanded to embrace the irreversible cessation of so-called "higher brain" functions related to cognition, identity, and personality. Proponents argue that neocortical function is essential to being human; that without it, humans cannot function as a whole; and that counting brain function in the absence of neocortical function as life is a base and animalistic view of the nature of being human. Ben Sarbey, Definition of Death: Brain Death and What Matters in a Person, 3 J. L. & Biosciences 745 (2016). Objections to this expansion range from practical to metaphysical concerns, including that death would be pronounced while the body is

breathing on its own; diagnosis of the condition continues to be challenging; newer knowledge about higher brain injuries continues to emerge; declaring a person to be dead when there is still brain function violates the sanctity of human life; and reliance on cognitive function as a measure of personhood leads inevitably to a slippery slope and devaluation of persons with cognitive disabilities. See, e.g., James Bernat et al., Defining Death in Theory and Practice, 12 Hastings Ctr. Rep. 5 (1982).

C. CARDIOPULMONARY DEATH REVIVED IN ORGAN RETRIEVAL

The adoption of the neurological determination of death, or brain death, was designed in part to increase the retrieval of life-sustaining organs for transplant. In the face of continuing shortages of organs for transplant, an Institute of Medicine report (Organ Donation: Opportunities for Action 2006) advocated the widespread adoption of the then-emerging practice of donation after cardiopulmonary (or circulatory or cardiac) death (DCD), also known as donation after circulatory determination of death (DCDD). (The literature and hospital policies have used a variety of terms over time to describe this process, including "non-heart-beating donors," "donors without a heartbeat," or "asystolic donors.") The volume of organs retrieved through DCD has increased dramatically. In 2020, there were 3,223 donors through DCD, representing 25.6% of donated cadaveric organs, a 18.6% increase over the 2019 total.

In a way, DCD appears to return to the older, common law standard as it relies on the cessation of cardiopulmonary function as the indicator that death has occurred. Although DCD at first glance appears to bring us full circle, the procedures differ quite substantially from the procedures used to determine cardiopulmonary death in earlier times and in contexts other than organ donation. The practice of DCD is now a mainstream practice, but it continues to raise significant ethical and legal controversies, including challenges to legal standards for the determination of death and the continued viability of the "dead donor rule," i.e., the rule that a person's life-sustaining organs may be removed only after death. See, e.g., Robert D. Truog, Defining Death: Getting it Wrong for All the Right Reasons, 93 Tex. L. Rev. 1885 (2015).

PROBLEM: CENTRAL CITY HOSPITAL'S PROPOSAL FOR DONATION AFTER CIRCULATORY DEATH

Central City Hospital (CCH) is a large teaching hospital. The hospital has decided to increase the volume of its organ procurement and transplant program in an effort to develop programs that produce a substantial net revenue stream, to meet the need of desperate patients, to realize the improved outcomes that a higher volume of transplants produces, and to develop a source of pride for hospital staff. CCH hired a new medical director for its transplant program, Dr. Joshua Niblet, who had been directing a very successful program at a hospital in another state.

Until now, all cadaveric organs donated at CCH have come from patients who have been declared brain dead while they are on mechanical cardiopulmonary support. Dr. Niblet is recommending that the hospital engage in organ recovery in controlled DCD. "Controlled DCD" occurs when "death is anticipated and occurs after medical supportive therapy is withdrawn [at the request of the patient, the patient's surrogate, or as directed by an advance directive], usually in an operating room, or hospital intensive care unit, or within a closely monitored time frame." IOM Report (2006). "Uncontrolled DCD" (or unexpected, unplanned, or unanticipated cardiac death) occurs when cardiopulmonary function has stopped spontaneously and usually unexpectedly. The IOM report recognizes that organ retrieval in uncontrolled cardiac death presents special challenges. Dr. Niblet is not seeking implementation of uncontrolled DCD at this time.

As a newly minted health lawyer and newly appointed assistant hospital counsel, you have been assigned to work with Dr. Niblet to help him institute the new program. You are being asked to assist in drafting the substance of the hospital's policies for DCD. Identify the issues you see in the following plan and how you would resolve them. Assume that your state has adopted the UDDA without revision. As a guide for your work, use the following federal regulation, as well as the materials that follow the regulation:

42 C.F.R. § 486.344(f)

If an [Organ Procurement Organization] recovers organs from donors after cardiac death, the OPO must have protocols that address the following: (1) Criteria for evaluating patients for donation after cardiac death; (2) Withdrawal of support, including the relationship between the time of consent to donation and the withdrawal of support; (3) Use of medications and interventions not related to withdrawal of support; (4) Involvement of family members prior to organ recovery; (5) Criteria for declaration of death and the time period that must elapse prior to organ recovery.

Potential DCD Donors

The federal policy governing organ transplantation currently provides that potential DCD donors include "patients who have died, or whose death is imminent, whose medical treatment no longer offers medical benefit to the patient as determined by the patient, the patient's authorized surrogate, or the patient's advance directive, if applicable." OPTN Policy 2.15. See Chapter 18 on treatment decision-making at the end of life. OPTN policy specifies that the decision to withdraw life-sustaining treatment be made before organ donation is discussed. If the patient who is the potential donor is making the donation decision, the patient's capacity to make that decision must be assessed. If the patient is incompetent but had earlier executed a document indicating intent to donate organs, that document (which typically does not include specific directions concerning DCD) controls. Failing those first two options, the individual identified in state law decides whether to donate organs. See Section I.C., above.

Declaration of Death

The determination of death must be made in compliance with state law. Once the decision to withdraw treatment is made, medical interventions to preserve the organs are begun, and the patient is taken to the operating room. Mechanical support sustaining cardiac function is removed, and the patient is observed to see whether the heart will begin to function on its own, before death is declared and the surgeon makes the incision and removes the organs. Although an uncommon occurrence, the hospital must be ready to treat the patient if the heart begins beating spontaneously.

Hospital protocols concerning how long to watch for spontaneous breathing vary significantly, but typically range from two to five minutes. The OPTN policy does not adopt a specific wait time. It is generally recognized that measurable brain activity continues for a significant time, perhaps up to 15 minutes after cessation of cardiopulmonary function. See Sam David Shemie and Dale Gardner, Circulatory Arrest, Brain Arrest and Death Determination, 5(15) Frontiers in Cardiovascular Med. 1 (2018); James DuBois, Is Organ Procurement Causing the Death of Patients?, 18 Issues L. & Med. 21 (2002); Jerry Menikoff, The Importance of Being Dead: Non-Heart-Beating Organ Donation, 18 Issues L. & Med. 3 (2002).

Dr. Niblet wants to set the shortest time possible, as the organs begin to deteriorate quickly once circulation stops.

Medical Interventions Prior to DCD

Medications to thin the blood, expand the blood vessels, cool down the body, and preserve the organs are administered before the patient is declared dead. Where the patient does not have decisional capacity, the decision to withdraw treatment is made by a surrogate or pursuant to the patient's advance directive (such as a living will or durable power of attorney). Most advance directives do not include instructions concerning medical treatment provided for pre-mortem organ preservation in DCD and instead only specify that medical treatment is to be stopped if certain medical conditions are met.

The Uniform Anatomical Gift Act provides that during the time in which a potential donor is being evaluated, "measures necessary to ensure the medical suitability of the [organs] may not be withdrawn unless the hospital . . . knows that the individual expressed a contrary intent." § 14(c). As to whether the typical advance directive evidences contrary intent, the Act provides that interventions required for successful organ recovery continue until the apparent conflict between the two instructions (the advance directive and the document for organ donation) is resolved, unless the interventions to preserve the organs are contraindicated for end-of-life care. § 21. See Richard Bonnie, Stephanie Wright, & Kelly Dineen, Legal Authority to Preserve

Organs in Cases of Uncontrolled Cardiac Death, 36 J.L. Med. & Ethics 741 (2008).

Some protocols use extracorporeal membrane oxygenation (ECMO) to provide oxygenated blood to preserve organs after the death. Because there is a concern that oxygenated blood flowing through the heart after mechanical support has been withdrawn would be evidence of spontaneous cardiac function, physicians may block blood flow above the diaphragm so that only the abdominal organs receive oxygenated blood. See A.L. Dalle Ave et al., Ethical Issues in the Use of ECMO in Controlled Donation after Circulatory Determination of Death, 16 Am J. Transplantation 2293 (Aug. 2016). The demand for heart transplantation, however, is driving increasing retrievals from DCD donors. Aravinda Page et al., Heart Transplantation from Donation after Circulatory Determined Death, 7 Annals of Cardiothoracic Surgery 75 (2018).

Dr. Niblet wants full discretion to employ the most effective organ preservation interventions as needed.

Questions for Hospital Policy Development

When patients or families are considering decisions relating to treatment at the end of life, when should the possibility of organ donation be raised? Who should present the option?

If the patient no longer has the capacity to make decisions but has executed a document for donation of organs upon death by signing up with the state's donor registry, as signified on the driver's license, or by signing a donor card, does that indicate consent to donation after DCD? These documents ordinarily do not provide information concerning DCD or measures that must be taken to preserve the organs. If the patient lacks decisional capacity, would you treat the organ donation document as determinative, or would you require that the consent of the surviving next-of-kin be secured?

Under the UAGA, pre-mortem documents of gift are binding on family members and others (see Section I.C, above). Would you recommend that the hospital secure informed consent from the surrogate for the specific interventions required to preserve organs, or would you structure the consent to donate organs to include permission to perform "all procedures necessary to retrieve the organs"? If the patient left an advance directive declining all medical treatment, would that preclude donation upon DCD?

What would you recommend as to wait time for the CCH policy? How does the wait time relate to whether the donor is dead under the UDDA? Could the precise language of your state's determination of death statute make a difference to your legal analysis? See *T.A.C.P.* and the notes following, above. Would you prefer that the state legislature amend its statute to specifically allow DCD, or are you satisfied that it falls within the UDDA?

CHAPTER 18

LIFE AND DEATH DECISIONS

• • •

I. INTRODUCTION

Concerns about the ethical, legal, and medical propriety of discontinuing what is now generally referred to as "life-sustaining treatment" have played a leading role in the development of law and bioethics over the last few decades. These concerns continue to capture our attention due to several factors: medical advances that have increased our ability to prolong life, debates over the "brain death" standard for determination of death (discussed in Chapter 17), increased access to medical aid in dying (discussed in Chapter 19), and attention to the consequences of individual and structural inequities in health care.

While the law is regularly invoked to resolve disputes in this area, a number of the questions brought before courts and legislatures arguably are outside the competence of the law. For example, consider what might constitute a "terminal illness," a concept that some have considered relevant in bioethical decision-making. While there surely is an element of medical judgment in a determination that a patient is "terminally ill," more than that is involved. Classifying a patient as "terminally ill" considers a combination of the patient's medical condition and anticipated life expectancy, as well as the social, ethical, and legal consequences of the classification. If such a classification triggers a provision in an advance directive, or if it allows a physician to participate in aid in dying, for example, the classification might be treated differently than if it triggers the patient's relocation from one room to another within a hospital.

If a determination of terminal illness is not solely a medical decision, but rather a hybrid of medical, ethical, social, political, and legal decisions, where is the locus of appropriate decision-making? Should the decision be made by health care professionals alone? By a patient and the patient's family? By a hospital committee? By some external committee? By a court-appointed guardian? By the court itself? By the state legislature? By Congress? Should the decision be based upon principles and rules that emerge from medicine, ethics, religion, litigation, or legislative social policy making? Finally, what substantive principles ought to govern the decision-maker? And what safeguards should be present?

The difficulties in allocating decision-making authority and developing appropriate substantive principles are not limited to the "terminal illness" classification. They extend to such defining terms as "life-sustaining treatment," "death prolonging," "extraordinary means," "heroic efforts," "intractable pain," "suffering," "persistent vegetative state," "futile," and even breathing and feeding.

For almost every question that arises within bioethics, we must make two determinations: (1) a procedural determination—who should be authorized to resolve the problem, and (2) a substantive determination— what substantive principles should apply. As one might expect, the substantive questions are often hidden in apparently procedural inquiries.

As these issues have come before the courts over the past few decades, the courts have looked to both the traditions of the common law and the traditions of ethics and medicine to discover principles for decision-making. In turn, judicial decisions have often formed the basis for new ethical and medical approaches. In fact, the debate over appropriate ethical policy in determining when life-sustaining treatment should be initiated or discontinued now involves lawyers as much as bioethics scholars, and the public debates on these issues have centered on the judicial resolution of cases and the promulgation of statutes as much as on any other source of formal principles. The law is not merely looking to ethics for potential methods of analysis, it is supplanting (some would say usurping) ethics in debate on these issues.

The law is not developed only through rationally justified and formally articulated judicial opinions. The law also comes out of political compromises in legislative action and public perceptions of well-publicized bioethical cases. The increasingly overt political nature of some questions—such as questions about the definition, meaning, and quality of life—are both profoundly personal and deeply related to larger concerns of equity and justice. Medical advances have increased our ability to prolong life. Is society spending too much to extend the life of people who are very ill or at the end of their lives? Forty years ago, Governor Lamm of Colorado was considered outrageous when he suggested that the elderly may have an obligation to die; today the social consequences of health care decisions have become a matter of real concern to those who realize that all of a family's assets easily could be consumed by a final illness.

While some are concerned that they will receive too much care at the end of life, others are concerned that they will receive too little. Many disability advocates, for example, have expressed well-founded concerns that life and death decisions by and for people perceived as ill or impaired reflect long-standing assumptions and negative beliefs about the value of life with a disability, sometimes with life-ending results (discussed in Chapter 6). If end-of-life care is a limited health care resource, how can we ensure that it is distributed equitably, regardless of age, disability, race or ethnicity, gender, or other characteristic?

The starting point for case law concerning health care decision-making is generally the law of informed consent, which is discussed in Chapter 4. The law of informed consent is bolstered by state administrative regulations (often from the state health department or its equivalent), state statutes (for example, patients' rights provisions in some states), state constitutional provisions (including the sometimes state-protected rights of privacy and dignity), federal statutes and regulations (like HIPAA and those assuring the privacy and security of medical records, and those governing research involving human subjects), and the U.S. Constitution. But another starting point for end-of-life treatment decisions is drawn from cases involving persons who are incapacitated and cannot make decisions for themselves. In such cases, the courts have often referenced the traditional law of guardianship in which the state assumes a parens patriae role to protect the incompetent person. While at times the two approaches work in harmony, at other times they lead to conflicting results.

This chapter begins with a discussion of the constitutional foundation upon which health care decision-making is based. This chapter addresses life and death decisions, but the principles that arise out of these cases are extended to other health care contexts. In the *Cruzan* case, which you will be reading in this chapter, and in the *Glucksberg* case, which you will be reading in the next chapter, the U.S. Supreme Court was called upon to apply the U.S. Constitution to end-of-life care, but the principles established in those cases have ramifications throughout the health care system. The Constitution may set the basic ground rules for recognizing health care decision-making authority, but it leaves a great deal of room for state regulation.

After examining the constitutional framework, this chapter examines the authority of an adult who has decisional capacity—a competent adult—to make his or her own health care decisions. We then move on to review the decision-making rules for adults who lack that capacity. We review advance directives such as individual instructions (previously called living wills) and durable powers of attorney, tools used for decision-making for a now-incapacitated individual. The chapter concludes with a discussion of decision-making surrounding treatment deemed futile.

In reading this chapter, consider what role individuals, families, hospitals, institutional ethics committees, health care professionals, courts, legislatures, advocacy organizations, and others ought to play in dealing with the ethical, medical, legal, social, and political questions that often arise out of our new-found technical ability to maintain life. Also consider what safeguards should be available to ensure that bias, unequal treatment, and discrimination do not find their way into decisions by each of these actors regarding withholding or withdrawing life-sustaining care.

As you review the way courts and others have considered individual cases, attempt to distill reasoned principles from their judgments. Is your analysis a procedural or substantive one? Who ought to be involved in the decision-making at each point? What principles are relevant to your analysis at each point?

II. MAKING HEALTH CARE DECISIONS ABOUT DEATH AND DYING: THE CONSTITUTIONAL FOUNDATION

CRUZAN V. DIRECTOR, MISSOURI DEPARTMENT OF HEALTH

Supreme Court of the United States, 1990.
497 U.S. 261.

CHIEF JUSTICE REHNQUIST delivered the opinion of the Court.

Petitioner Nancy Beth Cruzan was rendered incompetent as a result of severe injuries sustained during an automobile accident. Co-petitioners Lester and Joyce Cruzan, Nancy's parents and co-guardians, sought a court order directing the withdrawal of their daughter's artificial feeding and hydration equipment after it became apparent that she had virtually no chance of recovering her cognitive faculties. The Supreme Court of Missouri held that because there was no clear and convincing evidence of Nancy's desire to have life-sustaining treatment withdrawn under such circumstances, her parents lacked authority to effectuate such a request. We granted certiorari and now affirm.

On the night of January 11, 1983, Nancy Cruzan lost control of her car as she traveled down Elm Road in Jasper County, Missouri. The vehicle overturned, and Cruzan was discovered lying face down in a ditch without detectable respiratory or cardiac function. Paramedics were able to restore her breathing and heartbeat at the accident site, and she was transported to a hospital in an unconscious state. An attending neurosurgeon diagnosed her as having sustained probable cerebral contusions compounded by significant anoxia (lack of oxygen). The Missouri trial court in this case found that permanent brain damage generally results after 6 minutes in an anoxic state; it was estimated that Cruzan was deprived of oxygen from 12 to 14 minutes. She remained in a coma for approximately three weeks and then progressed to an unconscious state in which she was able to orally ingest some nutrition. In order to ease feeding and further the recovery, surgeons implanted a gastrostomy feeding and hydration tube in Cruzan with the consent of her then husband. Subsequent rehabilitative efforts proved unavailing. She now lies in a Missouri state hospital in what is commonly referred to as a persistent vegetative state: generally, a condition in which a person exhibits motor reflexes but evinces no indications of significant cognitive function. The State of Missouri is bearing the cost of her care.

After it had become apparent that Nancy Cruzan had virtually no chance of regaining her mental faculties her parents asked hospital employees to terminate the artificial nutrition and hydration procedures. All agree that such a removal would cause her death. The employees refused to honor the request without court approval. The parents then sought and received authorization from the state trial court for termination. The court found that a person in Nancy's condition had a fundamental right under the State and Federal Constitutions to refuse or direct the withdrawal of "death prolonging procedures." The court also found that Nancy's "expressed thoughts at age twenty-five in somewhat serious conversation with a housemate friend that if sick or injured she would not wish to continue her life unless she could live at least halfway normally suggests that given her present condition she would not wish to continue on with her nutrition and hydration."

The Supreme Court of Missouri reversed by a divided vote. . . .

We granted certiorari to consider the question of whether Cruzan has a right under the United States Constitution which would require the hospital to withdraw life-sustaining treatment from her under these circumstances.

* * *

State courts have available to them for decision a number of sources— state constitutions, statutes, and common law—which are not available to us. In this Court, the question is simply and starkly whether the United States Constitution prohibits Missouri from choosing the rule of decision which it did. This is the first case in which we have been squarely presented with the issue of whether the United States Constitution grants what is in common parlance referred to as a "right to die."

* * *

The Fourteenth Amendment provides that no State shall "deprive any person of life, liberty, or property, without due process of law." The principle that a competent person has a constitutionally protected liberty interest in refusing unwanted medical treatment may be inferred from our prior decisions. . . .

But determining that a person has a "liberty interest" under the Due Process Clause does not end the inquiry;[7] "whether respondent's

---

[7] Although many state courts have held that a right to refuse treatment is encompassed by a generalized constitutional right of privacy, we have never so held. We believe this issue is more

constitutional rights have been violated must be determined by balancing his liberty interests against the relevant state interests." [ ]

Petitioners insist that under the general holdings of our cases, the forced administration of life-sustaining medical treatment, and even of artificially-delivered food and water essential to life, would implicate a competent person's liberty interest. Although we think the logic of the cases discussed above would embrace such a liberty interest, the dramatic consequences involved in refusal of such treatment would inform the inquiry as to whether the deprivation of that interest is constitutionally permissible. But for purposes of this case, we assume that the United States Constitution would grant a competent person a constitutionally protected right to refuse lifesaving hydration and nutrition.

Petitioners go on to assert that an incompetent person should possess the same right in this respect as is possessed by a competent person. . . .

The difficulty with petitioners' claim is that in a sense it begs the question: an incompetent person is not able to make an informed and voluntary choice to exercise a hypothetical right to refuse treatment or any other right. Such a "right" must be exercised for her, if at all, by some sort of surrogate. Here, Missouri has in effect recognized that under certain circumstances a surrogate may act for the patient in electing to have hydration and nutrition withdrawn in such a way as to cause death, but it has established a procedural safeguard to assure that the action of the surrogate conforms as best it may to the wishes expressed by the patient while competent. Missouri requires that evidence of the incompetent's wishes as to the withdrawal of treatment be proved by clear and convincing evidence. The question, then, is whether the United States Constitution forbids the establishment of this procedural requirement by the State. We hold that it does not.

Whether or not Missouri's clear and convincing evidence requirement comports with the United States Constitution depends in part on what interests the State may properly seek to protect in this situation. Missouri relies on its interest in the protection and preservation of human life, and there can be no gainsaying this interest. As a general matter, the States—indeed, all civilized nations—demonstrate their commitment to life by treating homicide as serious crime. Moreover, the majority of States in this country have laws imposing criminal penalties on one who assists another to commit suicide. We do not think a State is required to remain neutral in the face of an informed and voluntary decision by a physically-able adult to starve to death.

But in the context presented here, a State has more particular interests at stake. The choice between life and death is a deeply personal

properly analyzed in terms of a Fourteenth Amendment liberty interest. See *Bowers v. Hardwick,* 478 U.S. 186, 194–195 (1986).

decision of obvious and overwhelming finality. We believe Missouri may legitimately seek to safeguard the personal element of this choice through the imposition of heightened evidentiary requirements. It cannot be disputed that the Due Process Clause protects an interest in life as well as an interest in refusing life-sustaining medical treatment. Not all incompetent patients will have loved ones available to serve as surrogate decisionmakers. . . . A State is entitled to guard against potential abuses in such situations. Similarly, a State is entitled to consider that a judicial proceeding to make a determination regarding an incompetent's wishes may very well not be an adversarial one, with the added guarantee of accurate factfinding that the adversary process brings with it. [ ] Finally, we think a State may properly decline to make judgments about the "quality" of life that a particular individual may enjoy, and simply assert an unqualified interest in the preservation of human life to be weighed against the constitutionally protected interests of the individual.

In our view, Missouri has permissibly sought to advance these interests through the adoption of a "clear and convincing" standard of proof to govern such proceedings.

* * *

We think it self-evident that the interests at stake in the instant proceedings are more substantial, both on an individual and societal level, than those involved in a run-of-the-mine civil dispute. But not only does the standard of proof reflect the importance of a particular adjudication, it also serves as "a societal judgment about how the risk of error should be distributed between the litigants." [ ] The more stringent the burden of proof a party must bear, the more that party bears the risk of an erroneous decision. We believe that Missouri may permissibly place an increased risk of an erroneous decision on those seeking to terminate an incompetent individual's life-sustaining treatment. An erroneous decision not to terminate results in a maintenance of the status quo; the possibility of subsequent developments such as advancements in medical science, the discovery of new evidence regarding the patient's intent, changes in the law, or simply the unexpected death of the patient despite the administration of life-sustaining treatment, at least create the potential that a wrong decision will eventually be corrected or its impact mitigated. An erroneous decision to withdraw life-sustaining treatment, however, is not susceptible of correction.

* * *

In sum, we conclude that a State may apply a clear and convincing evidence standard in proceedings where a guardian seeks to discontinue nutrition and hydration of a person diagnosed to be in a persistent vegetative state. . . .

The Supreme Court of Missouri held that in this case the testimony adduced at trial did not amount to clear and convincing proof of the patient's desire to have hydration and nutrition withdrawn. . . . The testimony adduced at trial consisted primarily of Nancy Cruzan's statements made to a housemate about a year before her accident that she would not want to live should she face life as a "vegetable," and other observations to the same effect. The observations did not deal in terms with withdrawal of medical treatment or of hydration and nutrition. We cannot say that the Supreme Court of Missouri committed constitutional error in reaching the conclusion that it did.

* * *

JUSTICE O'CONNOR, concurring.

I agree that a protected liberty interest in refusing unwanted medical treatment may be inferred from our prior decisions, and that the refusal of artificially delivered food and water is encompassed within that liberty interest. I write separately to clarify why I believe this to be so.

As the Court notes, the liberty interest in refusing medical treatment flows from decisions involving the State's invasions into the body. Because our notions of liberty are inextricably entwined with our idea of physical freedom and self-determination, the Court has often deemed state incursions into the body repugnant to the interests protected by the Due Process Clause. [ ] The State's imposition of medical treatment on an unwilling competent adult necessarily involves some form of restraint and intrusion. A seriously ill or dying patient whose wishes are not honored may feel a captive of the machinery required for life-sustaining measures or other medical interventions. Such forced treatment may burden that individual's liberty interests as much as any state coercion. [ ]

The State's artificial provision of nutrition and hydration implicates identical concerns. Artificial feeding cannot readily be distinguished from other forms of medical treatment. . . . Whether or not the techniques used to pass food and water into the patient's alimentary tract are termed "medical treatment," it is clear they all involve some degree of intrusion and restraint. Feeding a patient by means of a nasogastric tube requires a physician to pass a long flexible tube through the patient's nose, throat and esophagus and into the stomach. Because of the discomfort such a tube causes, "[m]any patients need to be restrained forcibly and their hands put into large mittens to prevent them from removing the tube." . . . A gastrostomy tube (as was used to provide food and water to Nancy Cruzan), or jejunostomy tube must be surgically implanted into the stomach or small intestine. . . . Requiring a competent adult to endure such procedures against her will burdens the patient's liberty, dignity, and freedom to determine the course of her own treatment. Accordingly, the liberty guaranteed by the Due Process Clause must protect, if it protects anything, an individual's deeply personal decision to reject medical treatment, including the artificial delivery of food and water.

I also write separately to emphasize that the Court does not today decide the issue whether a State must also give effect to the decisions of a surrogate decisionmaker. In my view, such a duty may well be constitutionally required to protect the patient's liberty interest in refusing medical treatment. Few individuals provide explicit oral or written instructions regarding their intent to refuse medical treatment should they become incompetent. States which decline to consider any evidence other than such instructions may frequently fail to honor a patient's intent. Such failures might be avoided if the State considered an equally probative source of evidence: the patient's appointment of a proxy to make health care decisions on her behalf.

* * *

Today's decision, holding only that the Constitution permits a State to require clear and convincing evidence of Nancy Cruzan's desire to have artificial hydration and nutrition withdrawn, does not preclude a future determination that the Constitution requires the States to implement the decisions of a patient's duly appointed surrogate. Nor does it prevent States from developing other approaches for protecting an incompetent individual's liberty interest in refusing medical treatment. . . . Today we decide only that one State's practice does not violate the Constitution; the more challenging task of crafting appropriate procedures for safeguarding incompetents' liberty interests is entrusted to the "laboratory" of the States, in the first instance.

JUSTICE SCALIA, concurring.

* * *

While I agree with the Court's analysis today, and therefore join in its opinion, I would have preferred that we announce, clearly and promptly, that the federal courts have no business in this field; that American law has always accorded the State the power to prevent, by force if necessary, suicide—including suicide by refusing to take appropriate measures necessary to preserve one's life; that the point at which life becomes "worthless," and the point at which the means necessary to preserve it become "extraordinary" or "inappropriate," are neither set forth in the Constitution nor known to the nine Justices of this Court any better than they are known to nine people picked at random from the Kansas City telephone directory; and hence, that even when it *is* demonstrated by clear and convincing evidence that a patient no longer wishes certain measures to be taken to preserve her life, it is up to the citizens of Missouri to decide, through their elected representatives, whether that wish will be honored. It is quite impossible (because the Constitution says nothing about the matter) that those citizens will decide upon a line less lawful than the one we would choose; and it is unlikely (because we know no more about "life-and-death" than they do) that they will decide upon a line less reasonable.

The text of the Due Process Clause does not protect individuals against deprivations of liberty *simpliciter*. It protects them against deprivations of liberty "without due process of law." To determine that such a deprivation would not occur if Nancy Cruzan were forced to take nourishment against her will, it is unnecessary to reopen the historically recurrent debate over whether "due process" includes substantive restrictions. [ ] It is at least true that no "substantive due process" claim can be maintained unless the claimant demonstrates that the State has deprived him of a right historically and traditionally protected against State interference. [ ] That cannot possibly be established here.

. . . "[T]here is no significant support for the claim that a right to suicide is so rooted in our tradition that it may be deemed 'fundamental' or 'implicit in the concept of ordered liberty.' "[ ]

Petitioners rely on three distinctions to separate Nancy Cruzan's case from ordinary suicide: (1) that she is permanently incapacitated and in pain; (2) that she would bring on her death not by any affirmative act but by merely declining treatment that provides nourishment; and (3) that preventing her from effectuating her presumed wish to die requires violation of her bodily integrity. None of these suffices.

[Scalia points out (1) that pain and incapacity have never constituted legal defenses to a charge of suicide, (2) that the distinction between "action" and "inaction" is logically and legally meaningless, and (3) that preventing suicide often (or always) requires the violation of bodily integrity, and it begs the question of whether the refusal of treatment is itself suicide.]

* * *

Are there, then, no reasonable and humane limits that ought not to be exceeded in requiring an individual to preserve his own life? There obviously are, but they are not set forth in the Due Process Clause. What assures us that those limits will not be exceeded is the same constitutional guarantee that is the source of most of our protection—what protects us, for example, from being assessed a tax of 100% of our income above the subsistence level, from being forbidden to drive cars, or from being required to send our children to school for 10 hours a day, none of which horribles is categorically prohibited by the Constitution. Our salvation is the Equal Protection Clause, which requires the democratic majority to accept for themselves and their loved ones what they impose on you and me. This Court need not, and has no authority to, inject itself into every field of human activity where irrationality and oppression may theoretically occur, and if it tries to do so it will destroy itself.

JUSTICE BRENNAN, with whom JUSTICE MARSHALL and JUSTICE BLACKMUN join, dissenting.

* * *

Today the Court, while tentatively accepting that there is some degree of constitutionally protected liberty interest in avoiding unwanted medical treatment, including life-sustaining medical treatment such as artificial nutrition and hydration, affirms the decision of the Missouri Supreme Court. The majority opinion, as I read it, would affirm that decision on the ground that a State may require "clear and convincing" evidence of Nancy Cruzan's prior decision to forgo life-sustaining treatment under circumstances such as hers in order to ensure that her actual wishes are honored. Because I believe that Nancy Cruzan has a fundamental right to be free of unwanted artificial nutrition and hydration, which right is not outweighed by any interests of the State, and because I find that the improperly biased procedural obstacles imposed by the Missouri Supreme Court impermissibly burden that right, I respectfully dissent. Nancy Cruzan is entitled to choose to die with dignity.

* * *

The right to be free from unwanted medical attention is a right to evaluate the potential benefit of treatment and its possible consequences according to one's own values and to make a personal decision whether to subject oneself to the intrusion. For a patient like Nancy Cruzan, the sole benefit of medical treatment is being kept metabolically alive. Neither artificial nutrition nor any other form of medical treatment available today can cure or in any way ameliorate her condition. Irreversibly vegetative patients are devoid of thought, emotion and sensation; they are permanently and completely unconscious. As the President's Commission concluded in approving the withdrawal of life support equipment from irreversibly vegetative patients:

> "[T]reatment ordinarily aims to benefit a patient through preserving life, relieving pain and suffering, protecting against disability, and returning maximally effective functioning. If a prognosis of permanent unconsciousness is correct, however, continued treatment cannot confer such benefits. Pain and suffering are absent, as are joy, satisfaction, and pleasure. Disability is total and no return to an even minimal level of social or human functioning is possible." [ ]

There are also affirmative reasons why someone like Nancy might choose to forgo artificial nutrition and hydration under these circumstances. Dying is personal. And it is profound. For many, the thought of an ignoble end, steeped in decay, is abhorrent. A quiet, proud death, bodily integrity intact, is a matter of extreme consequence. "In certain, thankfully rare, circumstances the burden of maintaining the corporeal existence degrades the very humanity it was meant to serve." . . .

Such conditions are, for many, humiliating to contemplate, as is visiting a prolonged and anguished vigil on one's parents, spouse, and children. A long, drawn-out death can have a debilitating effect on family members. [ ] For some, the idea of being remembered in their persistent vegetative states rather than as they were before their illness or accident may be very disturbing.

* * *

The only state interest asserted here is a general interest in the preservation of life. But the State has no legitimate general interest in someone's life, completely abstracted from the interest of the person living that life, that could outweigh the person's choice to avoid medical treatment. . . . [T]he State's general interest in life must accede to Nancy Cruzan's particularized and intense interest in self-determination in her choice of medical treatment. There is simply nothing legitimately within the State's purview to be gained by superseding her decision.

* * *

As the majority recognizes Missouri has a *parens patriae* interest in providing Nancy Cruzan, now incompetent, with as accurate as possible a determination of how she would exercise her rights under these circumstances. . . .

Accuracy, therefore, must be our touchstone. Missouri may constitutionally impose only those procedural requirements that serve to enhance the accuracy of a determination of Nancy Cruzan's wishes or are at least consistent with an accurate determination. The Missouri "safeguard" that the Court upholds today does not meet that standard. The determination needed in this context is whether the incompetent person would choose to live in a persistent vegetative state on life-support or to avoid this medical treatment. Missouri's rule of decision imposes a markedly asymmetrical evidentiary burden. Only evidence of specific statements of treatment choice made by the patient when competent is admissible to support a finding that the patient, now in a persistent vegetative state, would wish to avoid further medical treatment. Moreover, this evidence must be clear and convincing. No proof is required to support a finding that the incompetent person would wish to continue treatment.

Even more than its heightened evidentiary standard, the Missouri court's categorical exclusion of relevant evidence dispenses with any semblance of accurate factfinding. The court adverted to no evidence supporting its decision, but held that no clear and convincing, inherently reliable evidence had been presented to show that Nancy would want to avoid further treatment. . . . The court did not specifically define what kind of evidence it would consider clear and convincing, but its general discussion suggests that only a living will or equivalently formal directive from the patient when competent would meet this standard.

* * *

Finally, I cannot agree with the majority that where it is not possible to determine what choice an incompetent patient would make, a State's role as *parens patriae* permits the State automatically to make that choice itself. [ ] Under fair rules of evidence, it is improbable that a court could not determine what the patient's choice would be. Under the rule of decision adopted by Missouri and upheld today by this Court, such occasions might be numerous. But in neither case does it follow that it is constitutionally acceptable for the State invariably to assume the role of deciding for the patient. A State's legitimate interest in safeguarding a patient's choice cannot be furthered by simply appropriating it.

* * *

JUSTICE STEVENS, dissenting.

* * *

Choices about death touch the core of liberty. Our duty, and the concomitant freedom, to come to terms with the conditions of our own mortality are undoubtedly "so rooted in the traditions and conscience of our people as to be ranked as fundamental," [ ] and indeed are essential incidents of the unalienable rights to life and liberty endowed us by our Creator. [ ]

The more precise constitutional significance of death is difficult to describe; not much may be said with confidence about death unless it is said from faith, and that alone is reason enough to protect the freedom to conform choices about death to individual conscience. We may also, however, justly assume that death is not life's simple opposite, or its necessary terminus, but rather its completion. Our ethical tradition has long regarded an appreciation of mortality as essential to understanding life's significance. It may, in fact, be impossible to live for anything without being prepared to die for something. . . .

These considerations cast into stark relief the injustice, and unconstitutionality, of Missouri's treatment of Nancy Beth Cruzan. Nancy Cruzan's death, when it comes, cannot be an historic act of heroism; it will inevitably be the consequence of her tragic accident. But Nancy Cruzan's interest in life, no less than that of any other person, includes an interest in how she will be thought of after her death by those whose opinions mattered to her. There can be no doubt that her life made her dear to her family, and to others. How she dies will affect how that life is remembered.

The trial court's order authorizing Nancy's parents to cease their daughter's treatment would have permitted the family that cares for Nancy to bring to a close her tragedy and her death. Missouri's objection to that order subordinates Nancy's body, her family, and the lasting significance of her life to the State's own interests. The decision we review thereby interferes with constitutional interests of the highest order.

To be constitutionally permissible, Missouri's intrusion upon these fundamental liberties must, at a minimum, bear a reasonable relationship to a legitimate state end. [ ] Missouri asserts that its policy is related to a state interest in the protection of life. In my view, however, it is an effort to define life, rather than to protect it, that is the heart of Missouri's policy.

* * *

Life, particularly human life, is not commonly thought of as a merely physiological condition or function. Its sanctity is often thought to derive from the impossibility of any such reduction. When people speak of life, they often mean to describe the experiences that comprise a person's history, as when it is said that somebody "led a good life."[20] They may also mean to refer to the practical manifestation of the human spirit, a meaning captured by the familiar observation that somebody "added life" to an assembly. If there is a shared thread among the various opinions on this subject, it may be that life is an activity which is at once the matrix for and an integration of a person's interests. In any event, absent some theological abstraction, the idea of life is not conceived separately from the idea of a living person. Yet, it is by precisely such a separation that Missouri asserts an interest in Nancy Cruzan's life in opposition to Nancy Cruzan's own interests.

* * *

Only because Missouri has arrogated to itself the power to define life, and only because the Court permits this usurpation, are Nancy Cruzan's life and liberty put into disquieting conflict. If Nancy Cruzan's life were defined by reference to her own interests, so that her life expired when her biological existence ceased serving *any* of her own interests, then her constitutionally protected interest in freedom from unwanted treatment would not come into conflict with her constitutionally protected interest in life. Conversely, if there were *any* evidence that Nancy Cruzan herself defined life to encompass every form of biological persistence by a human being, so that the continuation of treatment would serve Nancy's own liberty, then once again there would be no conflict between life and liberty. The opposition of life and liberty in this case are thus not the result of Nancy Cruzan's tragic accident, but are instead the artificial consequence

---

[20] It is this sense of the word that explains its use to describe a biography: for example, Boswell's Life of Johnson or Beveridge's The Life of John Marshall. The reader of a book so titled would be surprised to find that it contained a compilation of biological data.

of Missouri's effort, and this Court's willingness, to abstract Nancy Cruzan's life from Nancy Cruzan's person.

* * *

The Cruzan family's continuing concern provides a concrete reminder that Nancy Cruzan's interests did not disappear with her vitality or her consciousness. However commendable may be the State's interest in human life, it cannot pursue that interest by appropriating Nancy Cruzan's life as a symbol for its own purposes. Lives do not exist in abstraction from persons, and to pretend otherwise is not to honor but to desecrate the State's responsibility for protecting life. A State that seeks to demonstrate its commitment to life may do so by aiding those who are actively struggling for life and health. In this endeavor, unfortunately, no State can lack for opportunities: there can be no need to make an example of tragic cases like that of Nancy Cruzan.

NOTES AND QUESTIONS

1.   *Subsequent Proceedings.* Subsequent to this judgment the Missouri trial court heard additional evidence, provided by Nancy Cruzan's friends and colleagues, that she had made explicit and unambiguous statements that demonstrated, clearly and convincingly, that she would not want to continue the treatment that she was receiving. Without opposition from the Attorney General of Missouri, the trial court authorized Ms. Cruzan's guardians to terminate her nutrition and hydration. See Sandra H. Johnson, Quinlan and Cruzan: Beyond the Symbols, in Health Law: Cases in Context (Sandra H. Johnson et al., eds. 2009).

2.   *Ethical Principles of Autonomy, Beneficence, and Social Justice.* There are many ethical approaches to health care decision-making. The approach that has most influenced judicial decision-making is one that relies on the identification and application of particular principles, often called the "principlist approach." Tom Beauchamp and James Childress, Principles of Biomedical Ethics (7th ed. 2013). There are three primary substantive principles that operate here: autonomy, beneficence, and social justice. Autonomy and beneficence have been the principles most often relied upon in bioethics case law, which has largely ignored questions of cost (and allocation and rationing) and health disparities that implicate social justice. The principle of autonomy declares that each person is in control of his own person, including his body and mind. This principle, in its purest form, presumes that no other person or social institution ought to overrule a person's choice, whether or not that choice is "right" from an external perspective. Essentially, it is a libertarian principle.

The principle of beneficence declares that what is best for each person should be done. The principle incorporates both the negative obligation of nonmaleficence ("primum non nocere"—"first of all, do no harm"—the foundation of the Hippocratic Oath) and the positive obligation to do that which is good. Thus, a physician is obliged to provide the highest quality of medical care for her patients. Similarly, a physician ought to treat a seriously ill newborn, or incapacitated adult, in a way that best serves that patient, whatever she may think her patient "wants" and whatever the parents of the patient may desire.

When a person does not desire what others determine to be in her best interests, the principles of autonomy and beneficence conflict. For example, if we consider the continued life of a healthy person to be in that person's interest, the values of autonomy and beneficence conflict when a healthy competent adult decides to take his own life. You can see that there can be serious conflict over what is in any individual's self-interest and that values other than autonomy and beneficence will come into play in some of these cases. Did the *Cruzan* opinions address autonomy and beneficence? Did they imply any other values?

3. *A "Right to Die"?* Does the opinion of the Court recognize a constitutional right to die? Many authoritative sources presumed that the opinion did recognize a constitutionally protected liberty interest in a competent person to refuse unwanted medical treatment. Indeed, the syllabus prepared for the Court says just that, and the case was hailed by the New York Times as the first to recognize a right to die. On the other hand, the Chief Justice's language does not support such a conclusion. While the majority agrees that "[t]he principle that a competent person has a constitutionally protected liberty interest in refusing unwanted medical treatment *may* be inferred from our prior decisions," (emphasis added) the Court never makes the inference itself. In fact, the opinion says explicitly that "*for purposes of this case,* we assume that the United States Constitution would grant a competent person a Constitutionally protected right to refuse life saving nutrition and hydration." (emphasis added).

Why is this assumption limited to the "purposes of this case"? Does the Court question (1) whether there is a constitutionally protected liberty interest in refusing unwanted medical treatment, (2) whether the right extends to life-sustaining treatment, or (3) whether it covers hydration and nutrition? It must have been difficult for the Chief Justice to craft an opinion that would be joined by a majority of the court. Justice Scalia clearly did not believe that there was any constitutional right implicated. If the Chief Justice were to formally recognize a constitutional right, he might have lost Justice Scalia's signature—and thus lost an opportunity for there to be any majority opinion. The dissents filed in this case are long and obviously heartfelt. Do the dissenters, all of whom would recognize a constitutionally protected right to refuse life-sustaining treatment, and Justice O'Connor, who would also do so, create a majority in support of this constitutional position?

4. *Heeding the Patient or Surrogate?* The majority opinion permits a state to limit its consideration to those wishes previously expressed by the patient and to ignore the decisions of another person acting on behalf of the patient. In fact, the Court explicitly does not address the question of whether

a state must defer to an appropriately nominated surrogate acting on behalf of the patient. On the other hand, the dissenting justices would recognize the decisions of a surrogate under appropriate circumstances, and Justice O'Connor suggests that the duty to give effect to those decisions "may well be constitutionally required." What is the constitutional status of surrogate decision-making after *Cruzan*?

5. *Liberty, Not Privacy.* Note that none of the opinions refers to the "right of privacy," a term which had caused the Court such tremendous grief in the abortion context. The Chief Justice analyzes this issue in the more general terms of a Fourteenth Amendment liberty interest, and none of the counsel argued the case in terms of the right to privacy. Apparently, the Court just did not wish to entangle itself any further with the "P" word. See Chapter 16.

6. *Characterizing* Cruzan. Seven years after *Cruzan* was decided, the Supreme Court again considered end-of-life medical decision-making in Washington v. Glucksberg (discussed in Chapter 19), which addressed the constitutional status of medically assisted dying. Chief Justice Rehnquist, writing for the Court, announced in *Glucksberg* that "We have . . . assumed, and strongly suggested, that the Due Process Clause protects the traditional right to refuse unwanted lifesaving medical treatment." Is that an accurate description of the holding in *Cruzan*? A few pages later, in the same opinion, Chief Justice Rehnquist describes the *Cruzan* case slightly differently: "[A]lthough Cruzan is often described as a 'right to die' case [ ], we were, in fact, more precise: we assumed that the Constitution granted competent persons a 'constitutionally protected right to refuse lifesaving hydration and nutrition.'" Is that a more accurate account of what the Court decided in *Cruzan*?

Justice O'Connor, concurring in *Glucksberg*, says that "there is no need to address the question whether suffering patients have a constitutionally cognizable interest in obtaining relief from the suffering that they may experience in the last days of their lives." This issue, according to Justice O'Connor, was decided by *Cruzan*. Is she right? Justice Stevens also commented on the *Cruzan* case in the course of his concurring opinion in *Glucksberg*. He explained that "Cruzan did give recognition . . . to the more specific interest in making decisions about how to confront an imminent death. . . . Cruzan makes it clear that some individuals who no longer have the option of deciding whether to live or to die because they are already on the threshold of death have a constitutionally protected interest [in deciding how they will die] that may outweigh the State's interest in preserving life at all costs." Is this an accurate description of *Cruzan*? If the Justices who participated in both the *Cruzan* and *Glucksberg* cases cannot agree on just what the case really means, how can your health law teacher expect you to do so?

7. *Right to Try.* Constitutional arguments are not limited to those who want to forgo treatment; they can be asserted by seriously ill patients who want

access to treatment, too. In Abigail Alliance v. von Eschenbach, 495 F.3d 695 (D.C. Cir. 2007), the D.C. Circuit, *en banc*, addressed the argument that a terminally ill patient had a constitutional right to access drugs that had not yet been approved by the FDA. The Abigail Alliance, named for a 21-year-old student who died of cancer after being denied drugs in the earliest stages of testing, argued that *Cruzan* and *Glucksberg* paved the way for the recognition of a constitutional right to access these not-yet-approved treatments, at least when those treatments provided the only hope of survival for the patient. The Court found, 8–2, that there was no such right, reversing the decision of the original three judge panel, Abigail Alliance v. von Eschenbach, 445 F.3d 470 (D.C. Cir. 2006), in part because of the longstanding tradition of governmental drug safety efforts in our legal system. The majority and the spirited dissenters disagreed about the way to articulate the right that the Abigail Alliance sought to have recognized in this case. Was the right asserted the right "to access experimental and unproven drugs," as the majority suggested, or the right to "try to save one's life," as the dissent argued?

As you have seen in *Cruzan*, and as you will recognize in *Glucksberg*, below, the due process arguments often depend upon the precise articulation of the right sought to be protected. Do you think the *Cruzan* case provides support for the position that an otherwise terminally ill cancer patient has the right to access to drugs that have not yet been found to be safe or effective through the government's required administrative process? From a constitutional perspective, is the argument that a patient is entitled to forgo treatment any different from the argument that a patient is entitled to have access to treatment?

In any case, the notion that a terminally ill person for whom no established treatment is effective should be able to try other, unapproved, treatments is a powerful one. After *Abigail Alliance*, several states passed "Right to Try" laws to permit such otherwise unauthorized experimentation with unproven treatment. In 2018, the federal Right to Try Act created a process through which terminally ill persons may seek quicker access to certain investigational treatment. Trickett Wendler, Frank Mongiello, Jodan McLinn, and Matthew Bellina, Right to Try Act of 2017, Pub. L. No. 115–176, 132 Stat. 1372 (2018). For a discussion of the federal Act, see Jordan Paradise, Three Framings of "Faster" at the FDA and the Federal Right to Try, 11 Wake Forest J. of L. & Pol'y 53 (2020).

8.   *Should Cost Be Considered?* Except for a glancing reference by Justice Stevens in his dissent, the opinions do not consider the cost of providing care to Nancy Cruzan. Should the cost be relevant? Should the constitutional right (to liberty or to life) vary depending on who bears the cost, or how great the cost actually is to keep a patient alive under particular circumstances? Would your analysis of this case be any different if the costs were being paid by an insurance company, by Ms. Cruzan's parents, by a gofundme.com account, or by community fund-raising in Nancy Cruzan's neighborhood, rather than by the state of Missouri? Should the one who pays the bills get to do the health care decision-making?

Judge Blackmar's dissent to the Missouri Supreme Court's opinion in *Cruzan* addressed the inconsistency of requiring some patients to be kept alive, at great expense, while the state is unable (or unwilling) to provide adequate care to others who actually want that care. He pointed out:

> The absolutist position is also infirm because the state does not stand prepared to finance the preservation of life, without regard to the cost, in very many cases. In this particular case the state has Nancy in its possession, and is litigating its right to keep her. Yet, several years ago, a respected judge needed extraordinary treatment which the hospital in which he was a patient was not willing to furnish without a huge advance deposit and the state apparently had no desire to help out. Many people die because of the unavailability of heroic medical treatment. It simply cannot be said that the state's interest in preserving and prolonging life is absolute.

760 S.W.2d at 429. Judge Blackmar also pointed out, in a footnote, that "an absolutist would undoubtedly be offended by an inquiry as to whether the state, by prolonging Nancy's life at its own expense, is disabling itself from [providing] needed treatment to others who do not have such dire prognosis." 760 S.W.2d at 429 n. 4.

9. *Different State, Different Outcome?* The result of the *Cruzan* case (confirmed in *Glucksberg*) is that most law regarding health care decision-making has continued to be established on a state-by-state basis. Consider a patient who would have a right to forgo life-sustaining treatment that could be exercised by his family in California or New Jersey, but would not have that right (or would not have a right that could be exercised by his family) in Missouri or Michigan. Indeed, the conditions and extent of, and the restrictions and exceptions to, any right to forgo life-sustaining treatment might be different in each state. State policies will thus require different results in factually identical cases. Is there anything wrong with this?

What would happen if Nancy Cruzan's family had decided to move her to the Yale Medical Center "because of the more favorable medical facilities" there? Could they have moved her from Missouri to Connecticut, where removal of the gastrostomy tube clearly would be legally permitted, just for the purpose of removing the gastrostomy tube? If they could not, then Nancy Cruzan could have become a prisoner of a state that rejects her family's values—values that have been incorporated into official state policies in other jurisdictions. If they could move her, however, Missouri would have allowed the family to undercut the important policy objectives of the state law and imperil the very life the law was designed to protect. Would it violate any criminal statute to move someone across state lines for the purpose of avoiding the laws governing termination of life support in the first state? Could a state make such an action a crime?

In early 1991 the father and guardian of Christine Busalacchi sought to have his daughter moved from Missouri to Minnesota for medical consultation with a nationally known neurologist who had consulted on several leading cases that resulted in the withdrawal of life-sustaining treatment. Ms. Busalacchi, who had been living in the same nursing home that had housed Nancy Cruzan, was arguably in a persistent vegetative state. The State of Missouri sought (and obtained) an order forbidding the move because of the fear that her father wanted only to find some place where his daughter could die. A divided Missouri Court of Appeals determined that the trial court was required to commence a new hearing on whether the move could be justified by other medical objectives. In deciding the case, the majority made it clear that " . . . we will not permit [the] guardian to forum shop in an effort to control whether Christine lives or dies." The dissent argued that "Minnesota is not a medical or ethical wasteland . . . . There is a parochial arrogance in suggesting, as the state does, that only in Missouri can Christine's medical, physical, and legal well being be protected and only here will her best interests be considered." Matter of Busalacchi, 1991 WL 26851 (Mo. App.1991). Ultimately, the State decided not to pursue the case, and Busalacchi died in Missouri. See also Mack v. Mack, 329 Md. 188, 618 A.2d 744 (1993) (Maryland Court denies full faith and credit to Florida judgment appointing the Florida-resident wife of a Maryland patient in persistent vegetative state as guardian so that patient could be moved to Florida, where life-sustaining treatment could be withdrawn).

10. *Adoption of Heightened Standard.* Missouri is not the only state to adopt the strict standard approved by the majority and decried by the dissenters. See, e.g., In re Martin, 450 Mich. 204, 538 N.W.2d 399 (1995); Couture v. Couture, 549 N.E.2d 571 (Ohio Ct. App. 1989). Arguably, the same standard has also been adopted in California, Conservatorship of Wendland, 26 Cal. 4th 519, 110 Cal. Rptr. 2d 412, 28 P.3d 151 (2001), at least when a patient is in a minimally conscious state. The strict Missouri "clear and convincing evidence" rule was also applied in New York, see In re Westchester County Med. Ctr. on Behalf of O'Connor, 72 N.Y.2d 517, 534 N.Y.S.2d 886, 531 N.E.2d 607 (1988), until the Legislature adopted the Family Health Care Decisions Act, N.Y. Pub. Health Sec. 2994–d, in 2010.

NOTE: STATE LAW BASES FOR A "RIGHT TO DIE"

Although some courts have found the right to forgo life-sustaining treatment in the U.S. Constitution, *Cruzan*'s interpretation of the Fourteenth Amendment has encouraged state courts to look for other bases for this right, too. State courts find this right in state common law, state statutes, or state constitutions.

The vast majority of state courts recognizing a right to refuse life-sustaining treatment have found that right in state common law, usually in the law of informed consent, often applied even after the patient has lost the capacity to make decisions. As the Chief Justice recognized in *Cruzan*, the informed consent doctrine has become firmly entrenched in American tort law and " . . . the logical corollary of the doctrine of informed consent is that the patient generally possesses the right not to consent, that is, to refuse treatment. . . ." Once a court finds a common law right, it is not necessary to determine whether the right is also conferred by statute or by the U.S. or a state constitution. See, e.g., In re Storar, 52 N.Y.2d 363, 438 N.Y.S.2d 266, 420 N.E.2d 64 (1981).

Some courts, however, bolster their common law basis for a "right to die" with references to the state and federal Constitutions. See In the Matter of Tavel, 661 A.2d 1061 (Del. 1995). While the New Jersey court initially recognized a constitutional "right to die" in In re Quinlan, 70 N.J. 10, 355 A.2d 647, 664 (N.J. 1976), it later recognized that the constitutional determination was unnecessary and retrenched:

> While the right of privacy might apply in a case such as this, we need not decide that since the right to decline medical treatment is, in any event, embraced within the common law right to self determination. In re Conroy, 98 N.J. 321, 486 A.2d 1209, 1223 (1985).

Some courts have found the right to refuse life-sustaining treatment in state statutes. Generally, courts that rely on a statutory "right to die" also find a consistent common law right. See, e.g., McConnell v. Beverly Enterprises-Connecticut, 209 Conn. 692, 553 A.2d 596, 601–602 (1989). The Illinois Supreme Court, for example, explicitly rejected state and federal constitutional justifications for a "right to die" because of the existence of both state common law and state statutory remedies. In re Estate of Longeway, 133 Ill. 2d 33, 139 Ill. Dec. 780, 549 N.E.2d 292, 297 (1989).

Several state courts have found the "right to die" in their state constitutions. A decision based on the state constitution may be the strongest kind of support such a right can ever find, because it is not subject to review by the U.S. Supreme Court (absent an improbable argument that a state-created right would itself violate the U.S. Constitution) and it is not subject to change by the state legislature (except through the generally cumbersome state constitutional amendment process). Relevant state constitutional provisions take different forms. For example, the Florida Constitution provides that "[e]very natural person has the right to be let alone and free from governmental intrusion into his private life except as otherwise provided herein. . . . " Fla. Const., art. 1, section 23. The Arizona Constitution provides that "[n]o person shall be disturbed in his private affairs or his home invaded, without authority of law." Arizona Const., art. 2, section 8. Both of these constitutional provisions have given rise to state-court-recognized rights to forgo life-sustaining treatment. See In re Guardianship of Barry, 445 So. 2d 365 (Fla. App.1984) and Rasmussen v. Fleming, 154 Ariz. 207, 741 P.2d 674 (1987). See also DeGrella v. Elston, 858 S.W.2d 698 (Ky. 1993) and Lenz v. L.E. Phillips Career Dev. Ctr., 167 Wis. 2d 53, 482 N.W.2d 60 (1992). The California Court of Appeal also found that such a right for competent patients could be found in the California Constitution. See Bouvia v. Superior Court, 179 Cal. App. 3d 1127, 225 Cal. Rptr. 297 (1986), reprinted below following the next problem. In 2009 the Montana Supreme Court hinted that the Montana Constitution's "dignity" clause might be interpreted to give competent terminally ill individuals a right to seek and receive a prescription for a lethal dose in some circumstances. It seems likely that the same substantive constitutional source of law would guarantee the right to remove life-sustaining medical care. See Baxter v. Montana, 354 Mont. 234, 224 P.3d 1211 (2009).

III. HEALTH CARE DECISION-MAKING BY ADULTS WITH DECISIONAL CAPACITY

PROBLEM: THE CHRISTIAN SCIENTIST IN THE EMERGENCY ROOM

Shortly after Ms. Elizabeth Boroff was hit by a drunk driver who went through a red light and directly into her Volkswagen bus, she found herself being attended by paramedics and loaded into an ambulance for a trip to the Big County General Hospital emergency room. Although she was briefly unconscious at the scene of the accident, and although she suffered a very substantial blood loss, several broken bones and a partially crushed skull, she had regained consciousness by her arrival at the hospital. The doctors explained to her that her life was at risk and that she needed a blood transfusion and brain surgery immediately. She explained that she was a Christian Scientist, that she believed in the healing power of prayer, that she rejected medical care, and that she wished to be discharged immediately so that she could consult a Christian Science healer.

A quick conference of emergency room staff revealed a consensus that failure to relieve the pressure caused by her intracranial bleed would result in loss of consciousness within a few hours, and, possibly, her death. When this information was provided to her, she remained unmoved. The hospital staff asked her to identify her next of kin, and she explained that she was a widow with no living relatives except for her seven minor children, ages 1 through 9. Further inquiries revealed that she was the sole support for these children, that she had no life insurance, that she had an elementary school education, and that she had been employed as a clerk since her husband, a self-employed maintenance man, was himself killed in an automobile accident a year ago.

Uncertain of what to do, the emergency room staff called you, the hospital legal counsel, for advice. What advice should you give? Should they discharge Ms. Boroff, as she requests? Should you commence a legal action to keep her in the hospital and institute treatment? If you were to file a legal action, what relief would you seek, and what would be the substantive basis of your claim?

BOUVIA V. SUPERIOR COURT

California Court of Appeal, Second District, 1986.
179 Cal.App.3d 1127, 225 Cal.Rptr. 297.

BEACH, ASSOCIATE JUSTICE.

Petitioner, Elizabeth Bouvia, a patient in a public hospital, seeks the removal from her body of a nasogastric tube inserted and maintained against her will and without her consent by physicians who so placed it for the purpose of keeping her alive through involuntary forced feeding.

* * *

Petitioner is a 28-year-old woman. Since birth she has been afflicted with and suffered from severe cerebral palsy. She is quadriplegic. She is now a patient at a public hospital maintained by one of the real parties in interest, the County of Los Angeles. Other parties are physicians, nurses and the medical and support staff employed by the County of Los Angeles. Petitioner's physical handicaps of palsy and quadriplegia have progressed to the point where she is completely bedridden. Except for a few fingers of one hand and some slight head and facial movements, she is immobile. She is physically helpless and wholly unable to care for herself. . . . She suffers also from degenerative and severely crippling arthritis. She is in continual pain. . . .

She is intelligent, very mentally competent. She earned a college degree. She was married but her husband has left her. She suffered a miscarriage. She lived with her parents until her father told her that they could no longer care for her. She has stayed intermittently with friends and at public facilities. A search for a permanent place to live where she might receive the constant care which she needs has been unsuccessful. She is without financial means to support herself and, therefore, must accept public assistance for medical and other care.

She has on several occasions expressed the desire to die. In 1983 she sought the right to be cared for in a public hospital in Riverside County while she intentionally "starved herself to death." A court in that county denied her judicial assistance to accomplish that goal. . . . Thereafter, friends took her to several different facilities, both public and private, arriving finally at her present location. Efforts by . . . social workers to find her an apartment of her own with publicly paid live-in help or regular visiting nurses to care for her, or some other suitable facility have proved fruitless.

Petitioner must be spoon fed in order to eat. Her present medical and dietary staff have determined that she is not consuming a sufficient amount of nutrients. Petitioner stops eating when she feels she cannot orally swallow more, without nausea and vomiting. As she cannot now retain solids, she is fed soft liquid-like food. Because of her previously announced resolve to starve herself, the medical staff feared her weight loss might reach a life-threatening level. Her weight since admission to real parties' facility seems to hover between 65 and 70 pounds. Accordingly, they inserted the subject tube against her will and contrary to her express written instructions.[2]

Petitioner's counsel argue that her weight loss was not such as to be life threatening and therefore the tube is unnecessary. However, the trial court found to the contrary as a matter of fact, a finding which we must accept. Nonetheless, the point is immaterial, for, as we will explain, a patient has the right to refuse any medical treatment or medical service, even when such treatment is labeled "furnishing nourishment and hydration." This right exists even if its exercise creates a "life threatening condition."

The Right to Refuse Medical Treatment

"[A] person of adult years and in sound mind has the right, in the exercise of control over his own body, to determine whether or not to submit to lawful medical treatment." [ ] It follows that such a patient has the right to refuse *any* medical treatment, even that which may save or prolong her life. [ ]

* * *

A recent Presidential Commission for the Study of Ethical Problems in Medicine and Biomedical and Behavioral Research concluded in part: "The voluntary choice of a competent and informed patient should determine whether or not life-sustaining therapy will be undertaken, just as such choices provide the basis for other decisions about medical treatment. Health care institutions and professionals should try to enhance patients' abilities to make decisions on their own behalf and to promote understanding of the available treatment options .... Health care professionals serve patients best by maintaining a presumption in favor of sustaining life, while recognizing that competent patients are entitled to choose to forgo any treatments, including those that sustain life."

* * *

The American Hospital Association Policy and Statement of Patients' Choices of Treatment Options, approved by the American Hospital Association in February of 1985 discusses the value of a collaborative relationship between the patient and the physician and states in pertinent part: "Whenever possible, however, the authority to determine the course of treatment, if any, should rest with the patient" and "the right to choose

---

[2] Her instructions were dictated to her lawyers, written by them and signed by her by means of her making a feeble "x" on the paper with a pen which she held in her mouth.

treatment includes the right to refuse a specific treatment *or all treatment
. . . ."*

* * *

Significant also is the statement adopted on March 15, 1986, by the
Council on Ethical and Judicial Affairs of the American Medical
Association. It is entitled "Withholding or Withdrawing Life Prolonging
Medical Treatment." In pertinent part, it declares: "The social commitment
of the physician is to sustain life and relieve suffering. Where the
performance of one duty conflicts with the other, the choice of the patient,
or his family or legal representative if the patient is incompetent to act in
his own behalf, should prevail."

* * *

It is indisputable that petitioner is mentally competent. She is not
comatose. She is quite intelligent, alert and understands the risks involved.

The Claimed Exceptions to the Patient's
Right to Choose Are Inapplicable

. . . The real parties in interest, a county hospital, its physicians and
administrators, urge that the interests of the State should prevail over the
rights of Elizabeth Bouvia to refuse treatment. Advanced by real parties
under this argument are the State's interests in (1) preserving life, (2)
preventing suicide, (3) protecting innocent third parties, and (4)
maintaining the ethical standards of the medical profession, including the
right of physicians to effectively render necessary and appropriate medical
service and to refuse treatment to an uncooperative and disruptive patient.
Included, whether as part of the above or as separate and additional
arguments, are what real parties assert as distinctive facts not present in
other cases, i.e., (1) petitioner is a patient in a public facility, thereby
making the State a party to the result of her conduct, (2) she is not
comatose, nor incurably, nor terminally ill, nor in a vegetative state, all
conditions which have justified the termination of life-support system in
other instances, (3) she has asked for medical treatment, therefore, she
cannot accept a part of it while cutting off the part that would be effective,
and (4) she is, in truth, trying to starve herself to death and the State will
not be a party to a suicide.

* * *

At bench the trial court concluded that with sufficient feeding
petitioner could live an additional 15 to 20 years; therefore, the
preservation of petitioner's life for that period outweighed her right to
decide. In so holding the trial court mistakenly attached undue importance
to the *amount of time* possibly available to petitioner, and failed to give

equal weight and consideration for the *quality* of that life; an equal, if not more significant, consideration.

All decisions permitting cessation of medical treatment or life-support procedures to some degree hastened the arrival of death. In part, at least, this was permitted because the quality of life during the time remaining in those cases had been terribly diminished. In Elizabeth Bouvia's view, the quality of her life has been diminished to the point of hopelessness, uselessness, unenjoyability and frustration. She, as the patient, lying helplessly in bed, unable to care for herself, may consider her existence meaningless. She cannot be faulted for so concluding. If her right to choose may not be exercised because there remains to her, in the opinion of a court, a physician or some committee, a certain arbitrary number of years, months, or days, her right will have lost its value and meaning.

Who shall say what the minimum amount of available life must be? Does it matter if it be 15 to 20 years, 15 to 20 months, or 15 to 20 days, if such life has been physically destroyed and its quality, dignity and purpose gone? As in all matters lines must be drawn at some point, somewhere, but that decision must ultimately belong to the one whose life is in issue.

Here Elizabeth Bouvia's decision to forgo medical treatment or life-support through a mechanical means belongs to her. It is not a medical decision for her physicians to make. Neither is it a legal question whose soundness is to be resolved by lawyers or judges. It is not a conditional right subject to approval by ethics committees or courts of law. It is a moral and philosophical decision that, being a competent adult, is hers alone.

* * *

Here, if force fed, petitioner faces 15 to 20 years of a painful existence, endurable only by the constant administrations of morphine. Her condition is irreversible. There is no cure for her palsy or arthritis. Petitioner would have to be fed, cleaned, turned, bedded, toileted by others for 15 to 20 years! Although alert, bright, sensitive, perhaps even brave and feisty, she must lie immobile, unable to exist except through physical acts of others. Her mind and spirit may be free to take great flights but she herself is imprisoned and must lie physically helpless subject to the ignominy, embarrassment, humiliation and dehumanizing aspects created by her helplessness. We do not believe it is the policy of this State that all and every life must be preserved against the will of the sufferer. It is incongruous, if not monstrous, for medical practitioners to assert their right to preserve a life that someone else must live, or, more accurately, endure, for "15 to 20 years." We cannot conceive it to be the policy of this State to inflict such an ordeal upon anyone.

. . . Being competent she has the right to live out the remainder of her natural life in dignity and peace. It is precisely the aim and purpose of the many decisions upholding the withdrawal of life-support systems to accord and provide as large a measure of dignity, respect and comfort as possible to every patient for the remainder of his days, whatever be their number. This goal is not to hasten death, though its earlier arrival may be an expected and understood likelihood.

* * *

Moreover, the trial court seriously erred by basing its decision on the "motives" behind Elizabeth Bouvia's decision to exercise her rights. If a right exists, it matters not what "motivates" its exercise. We find nothing in the law to suggest the right to refuse medical treatment may be exercised only if the patient's *motives* meet someone else's approval. It certainly is not illegal or immoral to prefer a natural, albeit sooner, death than a drugged life attached to a mechanical device.

* * *

We do not purport to establish what will constitute proper medical practice in all other cases or even other aspects of the care to be provided petitioner. We hold only that her right to refuse medical treatment even of the life-sustaining variety, entitles her to the immediate removal of the nasogastric tube that has been involuntarily inserted into her body. The hospital and medical staff are still free to perform a substantial, if not the greater part of their duty, i.e., that of trying to alleviate Bouvia's pain and suffering.

Petitioner is without means to go to a private hospital and, apparently, real parties' hospital as a public facility was required to accept her. Having done so it may not deny her relief from pain and suffering merely because she has chosen to exercise her fundamental right to protect what little privacy remains to her.

Personal dignity is a part of one's right of privacy. . . .

NOTES AND QUESTIONS

1. *Reliance on Earlier Case.* The *Bouvia* court depended, in large part, upon Bartling v. Superior Court, 163 Cal. App. 3d 186, 209 Cal. Rptr. 220 (1984), the first case to confirm a competent patient's right to make decisions to forgo life-sustaining treatment. Mr. Bartling was a competent adult suffering from depression (the original reason for his hospitalization), a tumor on his lung, and emphysema. He had a living will, a separate declaration asking that treatment be discontinued, and a durable power of attorney appointing his wife to make his health care decisions. He and his wife continuously asked that the ventilator that was preserving his life be removed, and he, his wife, and his daughter all executed documents releasing the hospital from any liability claims arising out of honoring Mr. Bartling's request. Still, the hospital, which was a Christian hospital established and

operated on pro-life principles, opposed discontinuation of Mr. Bartling's ventilator on ethical grounds. The California Court of Appeal found that the trial court should have granted Mr. Bartling's request for an injunction against the hospital, concluding that, "if the right to patient self-determination as to his own medical treatment means anything at all, it must be paramount to the interests of the patient's hospital and doctors. The right of a competent adult to refuse medical treatment is a constitutionally guaranteed right which must not be abridged."

2. *The Disability Critique.* The court describes the quality of Elizabeth Bouvia's life in startling terms. Are they also offensive terms? Does the court describe her life as useless, meaningless, and embarrassing solely because that was her view of her own life, or does it reflect the court's assumptions? Many disability rights advocates have critized *Bouvia* as a case which denigrated the quality and value of life with disability, and in which a disabled person was driven to desperate measures for lack of needed opportunities and supports to continue to live in the community. See, e.g., Paul K. Longmore, Elizabeth Bouvia, Assisted Suicide and Social Prejudice, 3 Issues L. & Med. 141 (1987).

Disability rights advocates have become key players in controversies over end-of-life decision-making, generally seeking to assure that those who seek to justify ending life by terminating life-sustaining treatment or by medically assisted dying have not equated the worth or dignity of an individual with the absence of disability or need for support. See Nat'l Council on Disability, Medical Futility and Disability Bias (2019); Mary Crossley, Ending-Life Decisions: Some Disability Perspectives, 33 Ga. S. Univ. L. Rev. 893 (2017). For a wonderful attempt to reconcile the principles of bioethics (and especially the principle of autonomy) with the principles of protection (and beneficence) that underlie the disability rights movement, see Alicia Ouellette, Bioethics and Disability: Toward a Disability-Conscious Bioethics (2011). For a discussion of racial disparities in end-of-life care, see Barbara Noah, The Role of Race in End-of-Life Care, 15 J. Health Care L. & Pol'y 349 (2012).

3. *Conscience-Based Objections.* Do you agree that the hospital had an obligation to accept Ms. Bouvia and provide her with medical relief from her pain and suffering, even though the physicians and hospital found her conduct immoral and her request an abuse of the medical profession? Is the obligation anything more than to provide adequate end-of-life care, even when the patient refuses a particular course of treatment? Compare Brophy v. New England Sinai Hospital, Inc., 398 Mass. 417, 497 N.E.2d 626 (1986), where the Massachusetts Supreme Judicial Court found that a patient in a persistent vegetative state could, through his family, deny consent to feeding through a gastric tube, but that the hospital need not remove or clamp the tube if it found it to be contrary to the ethical dictates of the medical profession. The *Brophy* decision required that the family move the patient to another medical institution more receptive to his apparent desire for his feeding tube to be removed.

The New Jersey Supreme Court took a middle ground in In re Jobes, 108 N.J. 394, 529 A.2d 434, 450 (1987):

> The trial court held that the nursing home could refuse to participate in the withdrawal of the j-tube by keeping Mrs. Jobes connected to it until she is transferred out of that facility. Under the circumstances of this case, we disagree, and we reverse that portion of the trial court's order.
>
> Mrs. Jobes' family had no reason to believe that they were surrendering the right to choose among medical alternatives when they placed her in the nursing home. [ ] The nursing home apparently did not inform Mrs. Jobes' family about its policy toward artificial feeding until May of 1985 when they requested that the j-tube be withdrawn. In fact there is no indication that this policy has ever been formalized. Under these circumstances Mrs. Jobes and her family were entitled to rely on the nursing home's willingness to defer to their choice among courses of medical treatment. . . .
>
> We do not decide the case in which a nursing home gave notice of its policy not to participate in the withdrawal or withholding of artificial feeding at the time of a patient's admission. Thus, we do not hold that such a policy is never enforceable. But we are confident in this case that it would be wrong to allow the nursing home to discharge Mrs. Jobes. The evidence indicates that at this point it would be extremely difficult, perhaps impossible, to find another facility that would accept Mrs. Jobes as a patient. Therefore, to allow the nursing home to discharge Mrs. Jobes if her family does not consent to continued artificial feeding would essentially frustrate Mrs. Jobes' right of self-determination.

Some state statutes governing end-of-life decision-making include specific provisions for situations in which health care professionals or facilities object to the decisions of patients (or their surrogates). See, e.g., Uniform Health-Care Decisions Act, below. The option to inform patients in advance of particular policies and then seek transfer is the most common compromise. Many states also have enacted statutes allowing such conscience-based actions by health care professionals in particular contexts, such as medically assisted dying. For a discussion of the employment issues that could arise out of a decision by a health care professional to refrain from providing legal but morally objectionable care, see Chapter 11. Might such a decision also constitute abandonment? See Chapter 4.

4. *What Information Must Be Provided?* If we take seriously the *Bouvia* suggestion that hospitals have an obligation to provide comfort to patients who choose to forgo treatment and thus die, do physicians have an obligation to inform patients of the various ways of dying that are available to them, and the consequences of choosing any one of them? See Margaret Battin, The Least Worst Death, 13 Hastings Ctr. Rep. 13–16 (April 1983).

5. *Concerns Regarding Overtreatment.* Growing concerns that patients are provided more treatment at the end of life than they really want gave rise

to the promulgation of the Right to Know End of Life Options Act in California in 2009 and the stronger Palliative Care Information Act in New York in 2010. Both statutes are designed to assure that patients are given all of the information they request (in California) or need (in New York) once they have been diagnosed as terminally ill. In California the Right to Know End of Life Options Act was opposed by Right to Life organizations and medical professional groups, which generally object to all statutory intrusion on the doctor-patient relationship. The stronger New York statute was opposed only by medical professional organizations, and it passed by large margins in both houses of the legislature. The New York statute is a simple statement of principle, more hortatory than enforceable:

Palliative Care Patient Information
New York Pub. Health Law § 2997–c

1. Definitions. . . .

(a) "Appropriate" means consistent with applicable legal, health and professional standards; the patient's clinical and other circumstances; and the patient's reasonably known wishes and beliefs.

* * *

(c) "Palliative care" means health care treatment, including interdisciplinary end-of-life care, and consultation with patients and family members, to prevent or relieve pain and suffering and to enhance the patient's quality of life, including hospice care . . . .

(d) "Terminal illness or condition" means an illness or condition which can reasonably be expected to cause death within six months, whether or not treatment is provided.

2. If a patient is diagnosed with a terminal illness or condition, the patient's attending health care practitioner shall offer to provide the patient with information and counseling regarding palliative care and end-of-life options appropriate to the patient, including but not limited to: the range of options appropriate to the patient; the prognosis, risks and benefits of the various options; and the patient's legal rights to comprehensive pain and symptom management at the end of life. The information and counseling may be provided orally or in writing. Where the patient lacks capacity to reasonably understand and make informed choices relating to palliative care, the attending health care practitioner shall provide information and counseling under this section to a person with authority to make health care decisions for the patient. The attending health care practitioner may arrange for information and counseling under this section to be provided by another professionally qualified individual.

Is this kind of a statute a good idea? Should other states follow the lead of California and New York? See, e.g., M.G.L.A. 111 § 227 (2012) (Massachusetts); O.R.S. § 413.273 (2015) (Oregon). Writing in The New

England Journal of Medicine just three months after the New York statute became effective, two New York physicians argue that barriers to respectful conversations at the end of life are better addressed through professional standards of care than legislation.

Alan Astrow and Beth Propp, Perspective: The Palliative Care Information Act in Real Life (Topics: Public Health, NEJM, May 18, 2011). Are they right? Should the underlying question be one about patients' and families' experiences, physicians' experiences, or both? The original Right to Know End of Life Options bill introduced in California explicitly mentioned some alternatives about which patients should be informed in appropriate circumstances—for example, palliative sedation (described in the *Cruzan* case) and the voluntary stopping of eating and drinking (often referred to as "VSED") (discussed in Chapter 19). Political compromise required that mention of those specific alternatives be deleted from the bill. Would general language, like that in the New York statute, require that a patient be told of those end-of-life alternatives? Under what circumstances?

6. *Ms. Bouvia's Decision.* After the California Supreme Court confirmed Ms. Bouvia's right to choose to die, she decided to accept the medical care necessary to treat her pain and to keep her alive. She appeared on television (on "60 Minutes") in 1998, where she expressed the hope that she would die soon. Why would someone seek judicial confirmation of a "right to die" and then not act upon it? Does it indicate that people waver on this issue? Does it suggest that knowing that one has the choice—when it becomes necessary— contributes to that person's well-being? Are those who seek a judicially confirmed "right to die" really seeking control over their destiny, not their death? Ironically, the existence of a right to die may be the reason that some people choose to live, just as the existence of medically assisted dying may be a reason that many people choose not to ingest the lethal dose of medication they have been legally prescribed. See Chapter 19.

7. *Few State Statutes.* Is it surprising that the fundamental principle that competent adults can make all of their own health care decisions has made it into the statutes of only a very few states? For an exception to this general rule, see N.M. Stat. Ann. Section 24–7A–2. Especially after the concern shown for this issue in *Bouvia*, one might expect more legislatures to have confirmed this right. Have they failed to do so because the law is so clear that legislative confirmation is unnecessary, or because there is a real dispute about the substance of the principle?

NOTE: COUNTERVAILING STATE INTERESTS

The right to choose to forgo life-sustaining treatment is not absolute, even for competent adults. In Superintendent of Belchertown State School v. Saikewicz, 373 Mass. 728, 370 N.E.2d 417 (1977), the Massachusetts Supreme Judicial Court first identified the four "countervailing State interests" that could overcome a patient's choice: (1) preservation of life; (2) protection of the interests of innocent third parties; (3) prevention of suicide; and (4) maintenance of the ethical integrity of the medical profession.

Although *Saikewicz* involved an incompetent patient who was born with significant intellectual and developmental disabilities and had never been competent, the mantra of those four interests has also been applied in later cases involving competent patients—including *Bouvia*—but they have never been found to be sufficient to overcome the choice of a *competent* patient. You will see the state's interests discussed in almost every case in this chapter.

In *Saikewicz* the Massachusetts Supreme Judicial Court explored the significance of these four state interests and their limitations:

> It is clear that the most significant of the asserted State interests is that of the preservation of human life. Recognition of such an interest, however, does not necessarily resolve the problem where the affliction or disease clearly indicates that life will end soon, and inevitably be extinguished. The interest of the State in prolonging a life must be reconciled with the interest of an individual to reject the traumatic cost of that prolongation. There is a substantial distinction in the State's insistence that human life be saved where the affliction is curable, as opposed to the State interest where, as here, the issue is not whether but when, for how long, and at what cost to the individual that life may be briefly extended. Even if we assume that the State has an additional interest in seeing to it that individual decisions on the prolongation of life do not in any way tend to "cheapen" the value which is placed on the concept of living, we believe it is not inconsistent to recognize a right to decline medical treatment in a situation of incurable illness. The constitutional right to privacy, as we conceive it, is an expression of the sanctity of individual free choice and self-determination as fundamental constituents of life. The value of life as so perceived is lessened not by a decision to refuse treatment, but by the failure to allow a competent human being the right of a choice.

> A second interest of considerable magnitude, which the State may have some interest in asserting, is that of protecting third parties, particularly minor children, from the emotional and financial damage which may occur as a result of the decision of a competent adult to refuse life-saving or life-prolonging treatment. Thus, even when the State's interest in preserving an individual's life was not sufficient, by itself, to outweigh the individual's interest in the exercise of free choice, the possible impact on minor children would be a factor which might have a critical effect on the outcome of the balancing process.

* * *

The last State interest requiring discussion[11] is that of the maintenance of the ethical integrity of the medical profession as well as allowing

---

[11] The interest in protecting against suicide seems to require little if any discussion. In the case of the competent adult's refusing medical treatment such an act does not necessarily

hospitals the full opportunity to care for people under their control. The force and impact of this interest is lessened by the prevailing medical ethical standards. Prevailing medical ethical practice does not, without exception, demand that all efforts toward life prolongation be made in all circumstances. Rather, the prevailing ethical practice seems to be to recognize that the dying are more often in need of comfort than treatment. Recognition of the right to refuse necessary treatment in appropriate circumstances is consistent with existing medical mores; such a doctrine does not threaten either the integrity of the medical profession, the proper role of hospitals in caring for such patients or the State's interest in protecting the same. It is not necessary to deny a right of self-determination to a patient in order to recognize the interest of doctors, hospitals, and medical personnel in attendance on the patient. Also, if the doctrines of informed consent and right of privacy have as their foundations in the right to bodily integrity, and control of one's own fate, then those rights are superior to the institutional considerations. 370 N.E.2d at 425–427.

In fact, these four interests raise issues beyond those discussed in *Saikewicz*:

(1)   *Preservation of life.* If the value of the preservation of life is the very question faced by the court in right-to-die cases, does it make sense to define it, *a priori,* as a value that is countervailing to the patient's desire to discontinue treatment?

The nature of the state's interest in the preservation of life was discussed in the *Cruzan* case, in which it was the only interest advanced by the state of Missouri. The Chief Justice said that

> a state may properly decline to make judgments about the 'quality' of life that a particular individual may enjoy, and simply assert an unqualified interest in the preservation of human life to be weighed against the constitutionally protected interests of the individual.

Not surprisingly, the dissenters viewed the state's interest in the preservation of life very differently. Justice Stevens objected to Missouri's policy of "equating [Cruzan's] life with the biological persistence of her bodily functions." He pointed out that,

> [l]ife, particularly human life, is not commonly thought of as a merely physiological condition or function. Its sanctity is often thought to derive from the impossibility of any such reduction. When people speak of life,

---

constitute suicide since (1) in refusing treatment the patient may not have the specific intent to die, and (2) even if he did, to the extent that the cause of death was from natural causes, the patient did not set the death producing agent in motion with the intent of causing his own death. Furthermore, the underlying State interest in this area lies in the prevention of irrational self-destruction. What we consider here is a competent, rational decision to refuse treatment when death is inevitable, and the treatment offers no hope of cure or preservation of life. There is no connection between the conduct here in issue and any State concern to prevent suicide.

they often mean to describe the experiences that comprise a person's history. . . .

Justice Brennan was especially offended by the notion that the generalized state interest in life could overcome the liberty interest to forgo life-sustaining treatment. One's rights, he argued, may not be sacrificed just to make society feel good:

> If Missouri were correct that its interests outweigh Nancy's interests in avoiding medical procedures as long as she is free of pain and physical discomfort, [ ] it is not apparent why a state could not choose to remove one of her kidneys without consent on the ground that society would be better off if the recipient of that kidney were saved from renal poisoning . . . , patches of her skin could also be removed to provide grafts for burn victims, and scrapings of bone marrow to provide grafts for someone with leukemia. . . . Indeed, why could the state not perform medical experiments on her body, experiments that might save countless lives, and would cause her no greater burden than she already bears by being fed through her gastrostomy tube? This would be too brave a new world for me and, I submit, for our constitution.

497 U.S. 261, 312–14 n. 13, 110 S. Ct. 2841, 2869–70 n. 13, 111 L. Ed. 2d 224. Chief Justice Rehnquist stated in *Glucksberg*, discussed in Chapter 19, that *Cruzan* had decided that states may choose to act to protect the sanctity of all life, independent of any inquiry into quality of life, and independent of the value of that life to the one living it.

(2) *Protection of innocent third parties.* Does the protection of the interests of innocent third parties have any meaning if courts are not willing to force people to stop pursuing their own interests and to serve some undefined communal goal? Is it merely a make-weight argument in a society as individualistic as ours? On the other hand, might children, for example, have a claim on the lives of their parents? Under what circumstances would such a claim be strongest?

(3) *Prevention of suicide.* Although *Glucksberg* confirmed that a state could make assisting suicide a crime, committing suicide is no longer a crime in any state. Is there still a consensus behind Justice Nolan's position, dissenting in Brophy v. New England Sinai Hosp., 398 Mass. 417, 497 N.E.2d 626, 640 (1986), that "suicide is direct self-destruction and is intrinsically evil. No set of circumstances can make it moral . . . ."?

(4) *Protecting the ethical integrity of the medical profession.* Finally, there is no longer any reason to believe that the ethics of the medical profession do not permit discontinuation of medical treatment to a competent patient who refuses it. See AMA Code of Medical Ethics Opinion 5.3, Withholding or Withdrawing Life-Prolonging Medical Treatment (2016). Even if there were, though, should the protection of the "ethical integrity of the medical profession" overcome an otherwise proper decision to forgo some form of treatment? If all other analyses point to allowing a patient to deny consent to some form of

treatment, in what cases, if any, should the medical profession be able to require the treatment in the interest of its own self-defined integrity?

Are there special circumstances in which the interest of the patient ought not to be recognized or the interest of the state is especially important? Can the state require a criminal defendant to submit to medical treatment to make him competent to stand trial? See Sell v. United States, 539 U.S. 166, 123 S. Ct. 2174, 156 L. Ed. 2d 197 (2003), holding that forced medication may violate Due Process rights. Does the national interest allow the military to require its soldiers to undergo life-saving (or other) medical care so that they can be returned to the front? Can a prisoner refuse kidney dialysis that is necessary to save his life unless the prison administration moves him from a medium to minimum security prison? See Commissioner of Correction v. Myers, 379 Mass. 255, 399 N.E.2d 452 (1979) (interest in "orderly prison administration" outweighs any privacy right of the prisoner to refuse dialysis unless he were moved to another site); People ex rel. Illinois Dep't of Corrections v. Millard, 335 Ill. App. 3d 1066, 270 Ill. Dec. 407, 782 N.E.2d 966 (2003) (force feeding of prisoner allowed). For a general discussion of several courts' approaches to balancing a patient's right to refuse treatment with these countervailing state interests, see Alan Meisel, Kathy L. Cerminara and Thaddeus Mason Pope, The Right to Die, 3rd ed. (2004, and 2017 Supplement).

APPLICATION OF THE PRESIDENT AND DIRECTORS OF GEORGETOWN COLLEGE

United States Court of Appeals, District of Columbia Circuit, 1964.
331 F.2d 1000.

J. SKELLY WRIGHT, CIRCUIT JUDGE.

Mrs. Jones was brought to the hospital by her husband for emergency care, having lost two thirds of her body's blood supply from a ruptured ulcer. She had no personal physician, and relied solely on the hospital staff. She was a total hospital responsibility. It appeared that the patient, age 25, mother of a seven-month-old child, and her husband were both Jehovah's Witnesses, the teachings of which sect, according to their interpretation, prohibited the injection of blood into the body. When death without blood became imminent, the hospital sought the advice of counsel, who applied to the District Court in the name of the hospital for permission to administer blood. Judge Tamm of the District Court denied the application, and counsel immediately applied to me, as a member of the Court of Appeals, for an appropriate writ.

* * *

Mr. Jones, the husband of the patient . . . [s]aid, that if the court ordered the transfusion, the responsibility was not his.

* * *

I tried to communicate with her, advising her again as to what the doctors had said. The only audible reply I could hear was "Against my will." It was obvious that the woman was not in a mental condition to make a decision. I was reluctant [t]o press her because of the seriousness of her condition and because I felt that to suggest repeatedly the imminence of death without blood might place a strain on her religious convictions. I asked her whether she would oppose the blood transfusion if the court allowed it. She indicated, as best I could make out, that it would not then be her responsibility.

* * *

I thereupon signed the order allowing the hospital to administer such transfusions as the doctors should determine were necessary to save her life.

It has been firmly established that the courts can order compulsory medical treatment of children for any serious illness or injury, and that adults, sick or well, can be required to submit to compulsory treatment or prophylaxis, at least for contagious diseases, *e.g.,* Jacobson v. Massachusetts. [ ] And there are no religious exemptions from these orders . . . .

The right to practice religion freely does not include liberty to expose the community or the child to communicable disease or the latter to ill health or death. [ ]

Of course, there is here no sick child or contagious disease. However, the sick child cases may provide persuasive analogies because she was as little able competently to decide for herself as any child would be. Under the circumstances, it may well be the duty of a court of general jurisdiction, such as the United States District Court for the District of Columbia, to assume the responsibility of guardianship for her, as for a child, at least to the extent of authorizing treatment to save her life. And if, as shown above, a parent has no power to forbid the saving of his child's life, *a fortiori* the husband of the patient here had no right to order the doctors to treat his wife in a way so that she would die. . . .

[Another] set of considerations involved the position of the doctors and the hospital. Mrs. Jones was their responsibility to treat. The hospital doctors had the choice of administering the proper treatment or letting Mrs. Jones die in the hospital bed, thus exposing themselves, and the hospital, to the risk of civil and criminal liability in either case. . . .

[N]either the principle that life and liberty are inalienable rights, nor the principle of liberty of religion, provides an easy answer to the question whether the state can prevent martyrdom. Moreover, Mrs. Jones had no wish to be a martyr. And her religion merely prevented her consent to a transfusion. If the law undertook the responsibility of authorizing the transfusion without her consent, no problem would be raised with respect to her religious practice. Thus, the effect of the order was to preserve for Mrs. Jones the life she wanted without sacrifice of her religious beliefs.

The final, and compelling, reason for granting the emergency writ was that a life hung in the balance. There was no time for research and reflection. Death could have mooted the cause in a matter of minutes, if action were not taken to preserve the *status quo*. To refuse to act, only to find later that the law required action, was a risk I was unwilling to accept. I determined to act on the side of life.

NOTES AND QUESTIONS

1. *State Action.* Unlike *Cruzan, Bouvia,* and *Wons,* below, *Georgetown College* did not involve a state facility. However, for purposes of federal constitutional analysis, state action can be found where a private person or entity takes control over a traditionally state function. The court in *Matter of Welfare of Colyer* explains:

> The existence of 'state action' for constitutional purposes depends on 'whether there is a sufficiently close nexus between the State and the challenged action of the regulated entity so that the action of the latter may be fairly treated as that of the State itself.' [ ]. Here, the presence of the state is manifested by its capability of imposing criminal sanctions on the hospital and its staff [ ], by its licensing of physicians [ ], by the required involvement of the judiciary in the guardianship appointment process [ ], and by the State's parens patriae responsibility to supervise the affairs of incompetents. [ ]. Taken together, these factors show a sufficient nexus between the state and the prohibitions against withholding or discontinuance of life sustaining treatment to call into play the constitutional right of privacy.

660 P.2d 738, 742 (1983). See also TL v. Cook Children's Med Ctr, cited in Section VI (discussing existence of state action despite the private nature of the hospital that sought to terminate life-sustaining treatment unilaterally).

2. *Justification for Judicial Review.* The right to choose to forgo life-sustaining treatment is usually based upon the premise that a person rationally may decide that death is preferable to the pain, expense, and inconvenience of life. Given that the process of weighing the value of life and death is necessarily based in personal history, religious and moral values, and individual sensitivity to a number of different factors, and given that it finds its philosophical basis in the principle of autonomy, is there any justification for independent judicial evaluation of whether the balancing was properly, or even rationally, performed by the patient?

3. *Religious Beliefs.* Most difficult cases have arisen over decisions based upon the dictates of religious principles. For example, Christian Scientists generally accept the healing power of prayer to the exclusion of medical assistance, so most Christian Scientists refuse most traditional

medical care. Christian Scientists may be less likely than Jehovah's Witnesses to find themselves in litigation over their refusal of medical treatment, however, because they are less likely to be at the hospital seeking medical care. For an account of the Christian Science position, see Mary Baker Eddy, Manual of the Mother Church 17–19 (1935) (first edition published in 1895). Given the ability of medicine at the time, it was likely that in its early days the Christian Science faith saved more lives than it cost by discouraging its adherents from seeing doctors. Research suggests that today Christian Scientists do not live quite as long as others. See W. Simpson, Comparative Longevity in a College Cohort of Christian Scientists, 262 JAMA 1657 (1989).

Jehovah's Witnesses, on the other hand, accept most medical care, but they do not accept blood transfusions, which they perceive to be a violation of the biblical prohibition on the ingestion of blood. The Jehovah's Witness belief that the ingestion of blood is prohibited finds its source in a number of Biblical passages. See Leviticus 17:10 ("As for any man . . . who eats any sort of blood, I shall certainly set my face against the soul that is eating the blood . . ."); Leviticus 17:14 ("You must not eat the blood of any sort of flesh . . ."); Acts 15:10; Genesis 9:4. These passages cause Witnesses to believe that receiving blood products will render them unable to obtain resurrection and eternal life.

Other sects also believe that God will provide any cure that is appropriate for each sick person, and their actions pose the same legal and ethical problems as do those of the Christian Scientists and the Jehovah's Witnesses. In England, for example, the "Peculiar People" presented the British courts with this issue long before the first case arose on this side of the Atlantic. See R v. Senior, All ER 511 (1895–9).

Should the courts ever attempt to decide whether an interpretation of the Bible is correct, or even just reasonable? Is it relevant that others consider the religious ban on the ingestion of blood or the rejection of all medical treatment to be irrational? Because courts were less able to empathize with patients who had unusual religious beliefs than with others, for many years courts were less willing to entertain the right to forgo life-sustaining treatment on religious grounds than on other grounds. Should a court treat a Christian Scientist or Jehovah's Witness who chooses for religious reasons to forgo necessary care any differently than it treats Elizabeth Bouvia?

4. *Judicial Rationalization?* In *Georgetown College*, Judge Wright concluded that Jehovah's Witnesses were not required by their religious code to forgo blood transfusions; they were merely required to refuse consent to those transfusions. Thus, a weak denial was taken as a plea for medical intervention against the patient's stated, but misleading, request to be left without adequate care. Would the decision, based on this reasoning, vindicate the principle of autonomy? Is it appropriate for Judge Wright, in his role as a federal judge, to determine that the Jehovah's Witness faith requires only that an adherent deny consent to a transfusion, not that she avoid actually having one? Is it relevant that Jehovah's Witness religious authorities reject this position?

The other reasons for the court's decision in *Georgetown College* seem equally fragile. The hospital could hardly claim that the risk of civil or criminal liability would require the transfusion after the hospital went to court to determine its legal responsibility. This claim is better understood as one asking for resolution of the liability issues should the hospital follow or override refusals of transfusions in future cases. Finally, the presumption that anyone so ill as to need a blood transfusion to save her life is likely to be incompetent is simply unsupported by fact. The need for a blood transfusion is hardly sufficient to justify the literal infantalization of a patient like Mrs. Jones. These bases for the decision demonstrate why this opinion by one of the great federal judges of the last century has come to be seen as one of the most painful examples of judicial rationalization.

5. *Most Courts Recognize the Right to Refuse Treatment.* Most of the cases that have considered this issue have concluded that competent adult Jehovah's Witnesses may choose to forgo medical treatment, whatever the results of those decisions may be, because the patient bears the consequences of choosing to forgo life-sustaining treatment. See, e.g., Norwood Hosp. v. Munoz, 409 Mass. 116, 564 N.E.2d 1017 (1991); In re Brooks' Estate, 32 Ill. 2d 361, 205 N.E.2d 435 (1965); In re Osborne, 294 A.2d 372 (D.C. App.1972). Compare Fosmire v. Nicoleau, 75 N.Y.2d 218, 551 N.Y.S.2d 876, 551 N.E.2d 77 (1990) (Jehovah's Witness mother permitted to forgo a blood transfusion during child birth even though her life was thus put at risk) with Raleigh Fitkin-Paul Morgan Mem. Hosp v. Anderson, 42 N.J. 421, 201 A.2d 537 (1964), cert. denied, 377 U.S. 985, 84 S. Ct. 1894, 12 L. Ed. 2d 1032 (1964) (pregnant Jehovah's Witness not permitted to refuse a necessary transfusion).

Courts may be more disposed to recognize religious beliefs that prohibit forms of medical treatment when the courts are familiar with the beliefs (as in the case of Jehovah's Witnesses) and where there are a large number of believers who share the limitation. In In the Matter of J.M., 416 N.J. Super. 222, 3 A.3d 651 (Super. Ct. 2010) the Chancery Division of the New Jersey Superior Court was faced with an arguably incompetent patient who decided, inconsistently with the medical advice she received, that she did not need dialysis because "Jesus would save her." The psychiatrists split on her competence, but the court decided that her views were not based on her religion because there was no tenet of her religion that explicitly rejected dialysis and her evangelical pastor had attempted to talk her into accepting the dialysis. Her dependence on her view that Jesus would save her was thus not a religious view upon which a competent person could base a decision; rather, it was part of her delusional thought process. The court thus found her incompetent, transferred decision-making authority to a special medical guardian, and ordered that she undergo dialysis. Was that the proper analysis of that case?

Even when others (such as children) are indirectly affected, the courts now tend to recognize the competent adult's right to forgo treatment:

PUBLIC HEALTH TRUST OF DADE COUNTY V. WONS

Supreme Court of Florida, 1989.
541 So.2d 96.

KOGAN, JUSTICE.

* * *

The Court of Appeal has certified the following question as one of great public importance:

WHETHER A COMPETENT ADULT HAS A LAWFUL RIGHT TO REFUSE A BLOOD TRANSFUSION WITHOUT WHICH SHE MAY WELL DIE.

* * *

The issues presented by this difficult case challenge us to balance the right of an individual to practice her religion and protect her right of privacy against the state's interest in maintaining life and protecting innocent third parties.

Norma Wons entered . . . a medical facility operated by the Public Health Trust of Dade County, with a condition known as dysfunctional uterine bleeding. Doctors informed Mrs. Wons that she would require treatment in the form of a blood transfusion or she would, in all probability, die. Mrs. Wons, a practicing Jehovah's Witness and mother of two minor children, declined the treatment on ground that it violated her religious principles to receive blood from outside her own body. At the time she refused consent Mrs. Wons was conscious and able to reach an informed decision concerning her treatment.

The Health Trust petitioned the Circuit Court to force Mrs. Wons to undergo a blood transfusion. . . . [T]he court granted the petition, ordering the hospital doctors to administer the blood transfusion, which was done while Mrs. Wons was unconscious. The trial judge reasoned that minor children have a right to be reared by two loving parents, a right which overrides the mother's rights of free religious exercise and privacy. Upon regaining consciousness, Mrs. Wons appealed to the Third District which reversed the order. After holding that the case was not moot due to the recurring nature of Mrs. Wons condition . . . , the district court held that Mrs. Wons' constitutional rights of religion and privacy could not be overridden by the state's purported interests.

* * *

The Health Trust asserts that the children's right to be reared by two loving parents is sufficient to trigger the compelling state interest [in protection of innocent third parties]. While we agree that the nurturing and support by two parents is important in the development of any child, it is not sufficient to override fundamental constitutional rights. . . . As the district court noted in its highly articulate opinion below:

> Surely nothing, in the last analysis, is more private or more sacred than one's religion or view of life, and here the courts, quite properly, have given great deference to the individual's right to make decisions vitally affecting his private life according to his own conscience. It is difficult to overstate this right because it is, without exaggeration, the very bedrock upon which this country was founded.

NOTES AND QUESTIONS

1. *Determining the Best Interests of the Children.* A concurring opinion in *Wons* depends in part upon the fact that the children would be cared for by relatives even if Mrs. Wons were to die. In that opinion the Chief Justice points out:

> The medical profession may consider a blood transfusion a rather ordinary or routine procedure, but, given Mrs. Wons' religious beliefs, that procedure for her is extraordinary. . . . [W]e must not assume from her choice that Mrs. Wons was not considering the best interests of her children. She knows they will be well cared for by her family. As a parent, however, she also must consider the example she sets for her children, how to teach them to follow what she believes is God's law if she herself does not. The choice for her can not be an easy one, but it is hers to make. It is not for this court to judge the reasonableness or validity of her beliefs. Absent a truly compelling state interest to the contrary, the law must protect her right to make that choice.

2. *Parental Abandonment Rationale.* The dissent in *Wons* depended in part upon another portion of *Georgetown College,* above, where Judge Wright concluded that

> [t]he state, as parens patriae, will not allow a parent to abandon a child, and so it should not allow this most ultimate of voluntary abandonments. The patient had a responsibility to the community to care for her infant. Thus the people had an interest in preserving the life of this mother.

Would this rationale support state intervention and an injunction to stop a mother (or a father) who had decided to take up hang-gliding, bronco-riding, working as a firefighter, or some other dangerous occupation? Why do you think it is applied in the case of a Jehovah's Witness, and not in any of these other cases?

3. *Refusing Treatment for Children.* The rule allowing patients to adhere to their religious faiths, even if that means that they choose to forgo life-sustaining treatment, is different for children. The courts have always held that children are not permitted to become martyrs to their parents' (or their own) religious beliefs. Where the refused treatment is not highly invasive, and where it is likely to return the child to full health—as in the case of a blood transfusion for a Jehovah's Witnesses child—courts universally order the

treatment. On the other hand, where the chance of success is lower—as in the case of certain kinds of chemotherapy for some childhood cancers—the courts are less likely to overrule the parents and the child. See Section V of this chapter, below.

IV. HEALTH CARE DECISIONS FOR ADULTS WITHOUT DECISION-MAKING CAPACITY

A. DECISIONAL CAPACITY

PROBLEM: DETERMINING THE DECISIONAL CAPACITY OF A DYING PATIENT

Theodore Flores is a 27-year-old who has been quadriplegic since a serious auto accident (in which he was driving while intoxicated) about a year ago. His spinal injury was so high and so substantial that he requires intermittent ventilator support, and he is fed through a gastrostomy tube that has been inserted through his abdominal wall and directly into his stomach. Although he has not worked since his accident, he had been employed as a pharmacist. He now communicates with others by winking his eyes or blowing through a straw connected to an alphabet board. The accident appears to have had no effect on his intellectual abilities, although he is now unable to concentrate for more than a few minutes, and he sometimes refuses to communicate to outsiders for days at a time.

Mr. Flores has now informed his physician that he wishes to have the ventilator disconnected and the feeding tube removed. His physician has informed him of the certainty that death will follow from either of these acts. Mr. Flores refuses to respond to such information, except to repeat his request. Mr. Flores has read most of the important recent medical journal articles about his condition, and his physician believes that Mr. Flores understands the risks, benefits, and alternatives more thoroughly than most similarly situated patients. Despite this, though, the physician is concerned about whether Mr. Flores has the capacity to decide to forgo ventilator support and nutrition and hydration. His concern grows out of several circumstances, including Mr. Flores's limited concentration span, his occasional unwillingness to communicate with anyone, and the following three factors:

(1) A psychiatrist who has been seeing Mr. Flores regularly has informed his physician that Mr. Flores became seriously depressed about three weeks ago, when he began to realize that there would never be any improvement in his physical condition. As the psychiatrist pointed out, of course, most reasonable people would become depressed upon such a realization. The psychiatrist has recommended antidepressants for Mr. Flores, but he refuses to take them.

(2) Since the accident, Mr. Flores has become a devoted follower of August Marsh, a religious leader who preaches that self-abnegation (and, particularly, self-abnegation leading to death) is the only way to gain

salvation. In particular, Rev. Marsh believes that the self-discipline of starvation (he usually recommends a period of a week) can bring substantial and, perhaps, eternal joy.

(3) Mr. Flores has always desperately wanted to father a child. His ability to contribute gametes to create a fertilized ovum is not precluded by his current condition. While the doctors have explained to Mr. Flores that his reproductive system is intact and unaffected by the accident, he insists that there is no way that he will be able to have children. No matter what the medical staff does, and despite Mr. Flores's generally sophisticated understanding of his medical condition, he does not understand how he will be able to become a father.

Does Mr. Flores possess sufficient decisional capacity to make the choice to forgo nutrition and hydration and ventilator support? What other information would you want to have before you make this determination? Remember, you are looking only for information relevant to a determination of decisional capacity, you are not looking for information that is relevant to the substantive decision. What process should be employed to make this capacity determination? Is a court order required to confirm Mr. Flores's capacity? Incapacity? What kind of evidence should be introduced in the hearing that would lead to an appropriate court order?

To determine whether a patient can choose to undergo (or forgo) medical care, someone must determine whether the patient has the capacity to make that choice. Because the theory behind decisional capacity serves the social principle of autonomy, capacity determinations should not be entirely medical; social, philosophical, and political factors should also be considered.

Until recently, most courts that addressed this issue referred to the "competency" of the patient. In other areas of law, such as those concerned with guardianships and conservatorships, "competency" was often employed as a term with all-or-nothing consequences. A person was either competent for all purposes and at all times, or incompetent for all purposes and at all times. When we evaluate the ability of a patient to make a health care decision, though, we are dealing with something far more subtle. A patient may have the capacity to make some simple health care decisions, and not to make other more complex decisions. Similarly, a patient may be able to make certain decisions at some times but not at others. To recognize these potential variabilities in competency, many courts and legislatures use the term "decisional capacity"—a term which focuses on the actual decision to be made—rather than "competency"—a term which focuses on the status of the patient. The change has been recognized in the law of guardianship and conservatorship in many states, too. In this text, the terms "decisional capacity" and "competency" are used interchangeably.

Courts have been reluctant to articulate a standard for decisional capacity. There are few reported opinions in which courts state and apply any formal principle. Courts have been much more likely to finesse the issue out of the law and back into medicine by inviting physicians, especially psychiatrists, to testify about the mental state and, thus, capacity of a patient. Ironically, medical textbooks point out that the standard for capacity is a legal, not a medical, one.

For many years, physicians were likely to find that a patient had decisional capacity to make a serious medical decision whenever that patient agreed with the physician. When the patient disagreed with the physician—especially if that the patient's choice would lead to the death of the patient—the physician, and subsequently the court, would be likely to find that the patient lacked capacity and then seek out some surrogate decision-maker more likely to agree with the physician. In reaction to this, and as a consequence of the frustration of attempting to develop any consistent and practical definition of competence, consumerist attorneys and physicians in the 1970s suggested that any patient who could indicate an affirmative or negative ought to be considered to have decisional capacity. Of course, this reactionary view is no more satisfactory than the previously prevailing view. Neither serves the purpose of protecting the individual personality of the patient and the authority of the patient to control his own life in a way that is consistent with his own values.

Despite the extremes described above, some scholars have attempted to categorize the possible tests for decisional capacity (or competency) that could be applied to patients of questionable capacity. Five different kinds competency tests were described in an early and influential article prepared by a psychiatrist, a lawyer, and a sociologist with extensive expertise in psychiatry. In Loren H. Roth, Alan Meisel, and Charles W. Lidz, Tests of Competency to Consent to Treatment, 134 Am. J. Psychiatry 279 (1977), the authors reviewed the legal and medical literature and concluded that there are five different tests applied to determine if a patient is competent:

(1) Does the patient evidence a choice? This test sets the lowest standard for competency. If the patient can communicate a choice, the patient is competent.

(2) Is the outcome of the patient's choice reasonable (or "right" or "responsible")?

(3) Whether or not the outcome is "reasonable," was the choice based on "rational" reasons?

(4) Does the patient have the ability to understand the information that must be communicated as a matter of informed consent—the risks, benefits, and alternatives of treatment?

(5) Does the patient actually understand that information?

Would you find any one of these tests for competency to be satisfactory? Which one? Might you apply different tests under different circumstances?

Roth, Meisel, and Lidz suggested that each test is influenced by the evaluator's analysis of whether the treatment would succeed—that is, whether the evaluator would consent for herself under the same circumstances. The authors concluded that where the benefit of treatment is likely to far outweigh the risk (i.e., the evaluator would choose to undergo it), there is likely to be a low standard for competency when the patient consents and a high standard for competency when the patient refuses. Analogously, where the risk greatly outweighs the benefit (again, of course, in the evaluator's mind), a low standard for competency will be applied if the patient refuses treatment, but a high standard will be applied when the patient consents.

In what might have been the most successful endeavor to unpack the theoretical basis of decision-making capacity, in 1980 the President's Commission for the Study of Ethical Problems in Medicine and Biomedical and Behavioral Research articulated the three elements of capacity:

(1) Possession of a set of values and goals,

(2) The ability to communicate and to understand information, and

(3) The ability to reason and to deliberate about one's choices.

President's Commission, 1 Making Health Care Decisions 57–60 (1980). Is this a complete list of the elements of capacity? Does the President's Commission approach serve the purposes that we require a patient to have capacity before we allow that patient to make health care decisions? As a practical matter, how easy is it to apply the President's Commission's test?

One case that squarely faced the question of whether a patient had the capacity to refuse life-sustaining treatment involved Robert Quackenbush, a 72-year-old recluse whose gangrenous leg would have to be amputated to avoid a certain, quick death. He was rambunctious, belligerent, and "a conscientious objector to medical therapy" who had shunned medical care for 40 years. In deciding that the patient was competent, the court depended on the testimony of two psychiatrists and the judge's own visit with Mr. Quackenbush.

> The testimony concerning Quackenbush's mental condition was elicited from two psychiatrists. The first, appearing for the hospital, was Dr. Michael Giuliano. Dr. Giuliano . . . saw Quackenbush once on January 6. The doctor's conclusions are that Quackenbush is suffering from an organic brain syndrome with psychotic elements. He asserts that the organic brain syndrome is acute—i.e., subject to change—and could be induced by the septicemia . . . . [Dr. Giuliano] concluded that

Quackenbush's mental condition was not sufficient to make an informed decision concerning the operation.

* * *

Dr. [Abraham] Lenzner [a specialist in geriatric psychiatry testifying at the request of the court] is of the opinion, based upon reasonable medical certainty, that Quackenbush has the mental capacity to make decisions, to understand the nature and extent of his physical condition, to understand the nature and extent of the operations, to understand the risks involved if he consents to the operation, and to understand the risks involved if he refuses the operation . . . .

I visited with Quackenbush for about ten minutes on January 12. During that period he did not hallucinate, his answers to my questions were responsive and he seemed reasonably alert. His conversation did wander occasionally but to no greater extent than would be expected of a 72-year-old man in his circumstances. He spoke somewhat philosophically about his circumstances and desires. He hopes for a miracle but realizes there is no great likelihood of its occurrence. He indicates a desire—plebian [sic], as he described it—to return to his trailer and live out his life. He is not experiencing any pain and indicates that if he does, he could change his mind about having the operation.

* * *

. . . My findings . . . are that Robert Quackenbush is competent and capable of exercising informed consent on whether or not to have the operation. I do not question the events and conditions described by Dr. Giuliano but find they were of a temporary, curative, fluctuating nature, and whatever their cause the patient's lucidity is sufficient for him to make an informed choice.

* * *

In re Quackenbush, 156 N.J. Super. 282, 383 A.2d 785, 788 (1978).

Did the court merely choose the more credible of the two psychiatrists, or did the court depend upon some intuitive conclusions that followed the judge's ten-minute visit with the patient? Which would be the more satisfying basis for the court's determination of competency?

To what extent do value judgments and prejudices enter into decisions regarding competency? Would the *Quackenbush* case have been a simpler one if Mr. Quackenbush were a retired lawyer leading a middle-class life rather than a belligerent hermit? One fascinating review of "right to die" cases suggests that gender may be an important factor, and that the legal system takes the expressed wishes of men more seriously than those of women. Steven Miles & Allison August, Courts, Gender, and "The Right to

Die," 18 L. Med. & Health Care 85 (1990). Stereotypes about the elderly and about dementia may also have an effect on evaluations of capacity by family members and doctors. For a discussion of evaluating capacity for individuals in these groups, see Jennifer Moye, Evaluating the Capacity of Older Adults: Psychological Models and Tools, 17 Nat'l Acad. Elder L. Attys 3 (2004).

How significant is it that terminally ill patients who seek a right to die are often depressed, or perceived to be so? Isn't it natural for someone dying of an incurable disease to be depressed? Two psychiatrists have suggested that physicians should attempt to treat depression in the seriously ill and those facing imminent death, but that psychiatrists also should recognize that some depression in terminally ill patients is not treatable. They also acknowledge that seriously ill patients do not lose their right to refuse medical treatment simply because they are experiencing depression. Mark Sullivan & Stuart Youngner, Depression, Competence, and the Right to Refuse Lifesaving Medical Treatment, 151 Am. J. Psych. 971, 977 (1994). See also Candice T. Player, Death with Dignity and Mental Disorder, 60 Ariz. L. Rev. 115 (2018). Do any of the suggested tests help you decide when depression renders a person incapable of making a health care decision?

B. ADVANCE DIRECTIVES

It is very difficult to serve the underlying goal of autonomy, if that goal is defined as personal choice, in patients who no longer have decisional capacity. One way to serve this principle is through the application of the doctrine of substituted judgment. Under this doctrine, a person, committee, institution, or other substitute decision-maker attempts to determine what the patient would do if the patient had decisional capacity. It may be possible to review the values of a formerly competent patient to determine whether that patient would choose to undergo or forgo proposed medical care. This can be done through a thoughtful analysis of the patient's values during life or through review of formal statements made by the patient when the patient had capacity. The most relevant considerations may be statements made by the patient about the proposed treatment itself. Indeed, such statements may provide the only *constitutionally* relevant information about an incompetent patient's wishes with regard to life-sustaining medical treatment after *Cruzan.*

Of course, there is no way to know with certainty what the now-incompetent patient would do under the precise circumstances at the time the decision must be made. Some have argued that the doctrine of substituted judgment is too speculative to be applied reliably and that there is simply no way to protect the autonomy of a patient without decisional capacity. Where there is no possible method for establishing what the autonomous patient would do, bioethicists (and increasingly, courts) move to another principle of bioethical decision-making, beneficence. In these circumstances, the alternative to serving autonomy is serving beneficence, and the alternative to the doctrine of substituted judgment is the doctrine of the "best interest" of the patient. As we shall see, the more difficult it becomes to decide what the patient would do if that patient had decisional capacity, the more likely it is that the court will apply the principle of beneficence rather than the principle of autonomy.

Although there are several kinds of statutes that allow competent individual patients to control some element of their health care when they lose decisional capacity, the most influential model statute within the U.S. is probably the Uniform Health-Care Decisions Act, which was adopted by the Uniform Law Commissioners in the early 1990s. Although it has not been fully adopted by most states, it forms the basis of several states' laws with regard to advance directives.

UNIFORM HEALTH-CARE DECISIONS ACT
Uniform Law Commissioners, 1993.

SECTION 1.　DEFINITIONS. In this [Act]:

(1) "Advance health-care directive" means an individual instruction or a power of attorney for health care.

(2) "Agent" means an individual designated in a power of attorney for health care to make a health-care decision for the individual granting the power.

(3) "Capacity" means an individual's ability to understand the significant benefits, risks, and alternatives to proposed health care and to make and communicate a health-care decision.

* * *

(5) "Health care" means any care, treatment, service, or procedure to maintain, diagnose, or otherwise affect an individual's physical or mental condition.

(6) "Health-care decision" means a decision made by an individual or the individual's agent, guardian, or surrogate, regarding the individual's health care, including:

(i)   selection and discharge of health-care providers and institutions;

(ii) approval or disapproval of diagnostic tests, surgical procedures, programs of medication, and orders not to resuscitate; and

(iii) directions to provide, withhold, or withdraw artificial nutrition and hydration and all other forms of health care.

* * *

(9) "Individual instruction" means an individual's direction concerning a health-care decision for the individual.

* * *

(12) "Power of attorney for health care" means the designation of an agent to make health-care decisions for the individual granting the power.

* * *

(16) "Supervising health-care provider" means the primary physician or, if there is no primary physician or the primary physician is not reasonably available, the health-care provider who has undertaken primary responsibility for an individual's health care.

(17) "Surrogate" means an individual, other than a patient's agent or guardian, authorized under this [Act] to make a health-care decision for the patient.

SECTION 2.   ADVANCE HEALTH-CARE DIRECTIVES.

(a)   An adult or emancipated minor may give an individual instruction. The instruction may be oral or written. The instruction may be limited to take effect only if a specified condition arises.

(b)   An adult or emancipated minor may execute a power of attorney for health care, which may authorize the agent to make any health-care decision the principal could have made while having capacity. The power must be in writing and signed by the principal. The power remains in effect notwithstanding the principal's later incapacity and may include individual instructions. . . .

(c)   Unless otherwise specified in a power of attorney for health care, the authority of an agent becomes effective only upon a determination that the principal lacks capacity, and ceases to be effective upon a determination that the principal has recovered capacity.

(d)   Unless otherwise specified in a written advance health-care directive, a determination that an individual lacks or has recovered capacity, or that another condition exists that affects an individual instruction or the authority of an agent, must be made by the primary physician.

(e)   An agent shall make a health-care decision in accordance with the principal's individual instructions, if any, and other wishes to the extent known to the agent. Otherwise, the agent shall make the decision in accordance with the agent's determination of the principal's best interest. In determining the principal's best interest, the agent shall consider the principal's personal values to the extent known to the agent.

* * *

SECTION 4.   OPTIONAL FORM. The [form included in this Act] may, but need not, be used to create an advance health-care directive.

* * *

SECTION 5.   DECISIONS BY SURROGATE.

(a)   A surrogate may make a health-care decision for a patient who is an adult or emancipated minor if the patient has been determined by the primary physician to lack capacity and no agent or guardian has been appointed or the agent or guardian is not reasonably available.

(b)   An adult or emancipated minor may designate any individual to act as surrogate by personally informing the supervising health-care provider. In the absence of a designation, or if the designee is not reasonably available, any member of the following classes of the patient's family who is reasonably available, in descending order of priority, may act as surrogate:

  (1)   the spouse, unless legally separated;

  (2)   an adult child;

  (3)   a parent; or

  (4)   an adult brother or sister.

(c)   If none of the individuals eligible to act as surrogate under subsection (b) is reasonably available, an adult who has exhibited special care and concern for the patient, who is familiar with the patient's personal values, and who is reasonably available may act as surrogate.

* * *

(e)   If more than one member of a class assumes authority to act as surrogate, and they do not agree on a health-care decision and the supervising health-care provider is so informed, the supervising health-care provider shall comply with the decision of a majority of the members of that class who have communicated their views to the provider. If the class is evenly divided concerning the health-care decision and the supervising health-care provider is so informed, that class and all individuals having lower priority are disqualified from making the decision.

(f)   A surrogate shall make a health-care decision in accordance with the patient's individual instructions, if any, and other wishes to the extent known to the surrogate. Otherwise, the surrogate shall make the decision in accordance with the surrogate's determination of the patient's best interest. In determining the patient's best interest, the surrogate shall consider the patient's personal values to the extent known to the surrogate.

* * *

SECTION 7.   OBLIGATIONS OF HEALTH-CARE PROVIDER.

* * *

(e) A health-care provider may decline to comply with an individual instruction or health-care decision for reasons of conscience. A health-care institution may decline to comply with an individual instruction or health-care decision if the instruction or decision is contrary to a policy of the institution which is expressly based on reasons of conscience and if the policy was timely communicated to the patient or to a person then authorized to make health-care decisions for the patient.

(f) A health-care provider or institution may decline to comply with an individual instruction or health-care decision that requires medically ineffective health care or health care contrary to generally accepted health-care standards applicable to the health-care provider or institution.

(g) A health-care provider or institution that declines to comply with an individual instruction or health-care decision shall:

(1) promptly so inform the patient, if possible, and any person then authorized to make health-care decisions for the patient;

(2) provide continuing care to the patient until a transfer can be effected; and

(3) unless the patient or person then authorized to make health-care decisions for the patient refuses assistance, immediately make all reasonable efforts to assist in the transfer of the patient to another health-care provider or institution that is willing to comply with the instruction or decision.

(h) A health-care provider or institution may not require or prohibit the execution or revocation of an advance health-care directive as a condition for providing health care.

* * *

SECTION 11.   CAPACITY.

(a) This [Act] does not affect the right of an individual to make health-care decisions while having capacity to do so.

(b) An individual is presumed to have capacity to make a health-care decision, to give or revoke an advance health-care directive, and to designate or disqualify a surrogate.

* * *

SECTION 14.   JUDICIAL RELIEF. On petition of a patient, the patient's agent, guardian, or surrogate, a health-care provider or institution involved with the patient's care, or an individual described in

Section 5(b) or (c), the [appropriate] court may enjoin or direct a health-care decision or order other equitable relief.

NOTES AND QUESTIONS

1.   *Should Decisions Regarding Life-Sustaining Treatment Be Treated Differently?* Should decisions to terminate life-sustaining medical treatment be treated differently from other kinds of health care decisions? The Uniform Health-Care Decisions Act does not distinguish between life-sustaining medical treatment and other forms of treatment. Should it make that distinction and treat decisions that may lead to the patient's death differently from decisions that will not?

2.   *Role of Institutional Ethics Committees.* The Uniform Health-Care Decisions Act does not defer to institutional ethics committees under any circumstances. Should it have been written to recognize and defer to an "ethics review committee," as the more recent New York statute does, at least in the most serious of cases? See Family Health Care Decisions Act, NY Pub. Health sec. 2994–d. Might the fact that these committees now have formal statutory authority enhance the status of hospital and nursing home ethics committees? Does it make sense to look to the courts as an alternative to a determination of institutional ethics committees?

3.   *Revising the Uniform Health-Care Decisions Act.* In 2021, the Uniform Law Commission convened a committee to amend or revise the Uniform Health-Care Decisions Act. Key issues for consideration include: whether the Act should include procedures for determining whether an individual lacks capacity to make their own decisions, and, if so, what those procedures should be; requirements for execution and revocation of advanced directives, especially when in electronic format; review of the default surrogate priority list; the relationship between advanced directives and a Physician Order for Life Sustaining Treatment (POLST), discussed below; psychiatric advanced directives; the authority of an agent or surrogate to apply for health benefits; the grounds for disqualification of an agent or default surrogate; whether additional qualifications should be required to make mental health decisions; the benefits and costs of statutory forms; and whether oral designation of surrogates should be honored. What revisions, if any, would you suggest and why?

NOTE: THE DEVELOPMENT OF ADVANCE DIRECTIVES AND SURROGATE CONSENT LAWS

The Uniform Health-Care Decisions Act, excerpted above, takes a comprehensive approach to the issue by combining several elements of existing state laws into a single legal document, as well as adding new provisions. Because the Uniform Act has not been fully adopted by most states, it remains important to understand the variations in state law among states that have not adopted the Act. This note provides an overview of the development of advance directive and surrogate consent laws, noting areas of variation among the states.

The Starting Point: Family Consent Policies and Laws. Over the past century, it became standard medical practice to seek consent to any medical procedure from close family members of an incompetent patient. There is no common law authority for this practice; it is an example of medical practice (and good common sense) being subtly absorbed by the law. The President's Commission suggests five reasons for this deference to family members:

(1) The family is generally most concerned about the good of the patient.

(2) The family will also usually be most knowledgeable about the patient's goals, preferences, and values.

(3) The family deserves recognition as an important social unit that ought to be treated, within limits, as a responsible decision-maker in matters that intimately affect its members.

(4) Especially in a society in which many other traditional forms of community have eroded, participation in a family is often an important dimension of personal fulfillment.

(5) Since a protected sphere of privacy and autonomy is required for the flourishing of this interpersonal union, institutions and the state should be reluctant to intrude, particularly regarding matters that are personal and on which there is a wide range of opinion in society.

President's Commission, Deciding to Forego Life-Sustaining Treatment, 128 (1983). It is difficult to determine whether the resort to close relatives to give consent is merely a procedural device to discover what the patient, if competent, would choose, or whether it is based in an independent substantive doctrine. Although it seems essentially procedural—the family is most likely to know what the patient would choose—many courts are willing to accept most decisions of family members even when there is little support for the position that these family members are actually choosing what the patient would choose. Of course, the assumptions about family relationships are quite optimistic. Consulting with family members also neutralizes potential malpractice plaintiffs; this factor accounts for part of the longstanding popularity of this decision-making process among health care providers.

Over the past several decades some states have enacted formal family consent laws that authorize statutorily designated family members to make health care decisions for their relatives in circumscribed situations. These statutes often apply to a wide range of health care decisions (including, in most cases, decisions to forgo life-sustaining treatment), although sometimes they apply only when there has been a physician's certification of the patient's inability to make the health care decision. Sometimes they are limited to particular kinds of treatment (e.g., cardiopulmonary resuscitation) or exclude particular decisions (like discontinuing nutrition and hydration). In addition, family consent laws often provide immunity from liability for family members and physicians acting in good faith, as well as judicial authority to resolve disputes about the authority of the family members under the statutes.

The definition of "family member" and the position of each family member in the hierarchy vary from state to state. In some states those in a long-term spouse-like relationship with the patient are included in the list of family members who can make decisions for the incompetent patient; in some states they are not. Some lists include a residuary class of anyone who knows the values, interests, and wishes of the patient; some states list the physician as the residuary decision-maker; some provide for no residuary decision-maker. Some states give a general guardian top priority; some states place surrogates actually appointed by the patient (whether family members or not) ahead of the general guardian.

The Rise of Living Wills. Nearly two decades before the Uniform Health-Care Decisions Act was proposed, many people first became concerned about the potential abuses of powerful new forms of life-sustaining medical treatment. In the wake of the *Quinlan* case, several states had adopted statutes that formally recognized certain forms of written statements requesting that some kinds of medical care be discontinued. These statutes, generally referred to as "living will" statutes, "right to die" legislation, or "natural death" acts, provided a political outlet for the frustration that accompanied the empathy for Ms. Quinlan.

The statutes, which still provide the only statutory advance directive in some jurisdictions, vary among the states in several respects. In some states living wills may be executed by any person, at any time (and in some states they may be executed on behalf of minors), while in other states they require a waiting period, and may not be executed during a terminal illness. In most states they are of indefinite duration, although in some states they expire after a determined number of years.

Some statutes address only the terminally ill, others include those in "irreversible coma" or persistent vegetative state, and still others provide for different conditions to trigger the substantive provisions of the document. In many states, living wills are not effective while the patient is pregnant. See Chapter 16, Section VI. Some states require the formalities of a will for the living will to be recognized by statute, while other states require different formalities. Living will statutes that do not apply to those in persistent vegetative state, irreversible coma, or any other medical condition that may not be considered "terminal" are of no assistance to people in the position of Nancy Cruzan. Is there a reason to limit legislation to terminal conditions, or should such statutes be extended to other conditions where there is broad social consensus that patients should have the right to forgo life-sustaining treatment?

The statutes generally relieve physicians and other health care providers of any civil or criminal liability for withdrawal of treatment if they properly follow the requirements of the statute. A living will is always relevant as evidence of a patient's intent, although immunity does not apply unless the statute is followed.

Some of the statutes require any physician who cannot in good conscience carry out those provisions to transfer the patient to a physician who can. The statutes also provide that carrying out the provisions of a properly executed living will does not constitute homicide or suicide for any legal purpose. It is hard to know whether the absence of litigation over the terms of living wills means that these documents are working well or that they are not working at all. Because health care providers were not used to seeing these documents and were used to making these decisions on their own, many were reluctant to accept and follow the instructions in living wills. Some health care professionals are still reluctant to carry out advance directives, even when they are clearly legally authorized.

Many living will statutes specifically exclude "the performance of any procedure to provide nutrition or hydration" from the definition of death-prolonging or life-sustaining procedures, and thus do not extend any statutory protection to those who remove nutrition or hydration from a patient. For the most famous example, see Vernon's Ann. Mo. Stat. § 459.010(3). After the U.S. Supreme Court decision in *Cruzan,* are such exceptions legally meaningful? Are they constitutional? For an example of judicial avoidance of the unwelcome consequences of a nutrition and hydration exception to a living will statute, see McConnell v. Beverly Enterprises-Connecticut, 209 Conn. 692, 553 A.2d 596 (1989). See also In re Guardianship of Browning, 568 So. 2d 4 (Fla. 1990).

The Next Step: Durable Powers of Attorney for Health Care. Another means of identifying who should speak for the patient when the patient is incompetent is to allow competent individuals to designate a spokesperson or agent to act should the individual become incompetent. This designation may be accomplished through the individual's execution of a durable power of attorney, the most common form of advance directive available today.

Powers of attorney have been available over the past several centuries to allow for financial transactions to be consummated by agents of a principal. A power of attorney may be executed by any competent person. It provides that the agent designated shall have the right to act on behalf of the principal for purposes that are described and limited in the document itself. Thus, a principal may give an agent a power of attorney to enter into a particular contract, a particular kind of contract, or all contracts. The power may be limited by time, by geographic area, or in any other way. It may be granted to any person, who, upon appointment, becomes the agent and "attorney-in-fact" for the principal.

At common law, a power of attorney expired upon the "incapacity" of the principal. This was necessary to assure that the principal could maintain adequate authority over his agent. As long as a power of attorney expired upon the incapacity of the principal, the power of attorney had no value in making medical decisions. After all, a competent patient could decide for himself; there was no reason for him to delegate authority to an agent.

In the mid-1970s, it became clear that the value of the power of attorney could be increased if it could extend beyond the incapacity of the principal. For example, as an increasing number of very elderly people depended upon their children and others to handle their financial affairs, it became important that there be some device by which they could delegate their authority to these agents. For such principals, it was most important that the authority remain with their agents when they did become incapacitated. The Uniform Probate Code was therefore amended to provide for a durable power of attorney; that is, a power of attorney that would remain in effect (or even only become effective) upon the incapacity of the principal if the document clearly stated that direction.

There is no reported judicial opinion formally holding that the authority of a durable power of attorney executed under the Uniform Probate Code extends to health care decision-making. The President's Commission assumed, without any discussion, that it could be used for this purpose. See President's Commission, Deciding to Forego Life-Sustaining Treatment 145–149 (1983). The vast majority of states have now adopted statutes that formally authorize the execution of durable powers of attorney for health care decisions.

Health care providers, who were uncertain about how to deal with living wills that were often ambiguous and rarely written with knowledge of the patient's eventual diagnosis and prognosis, were more accepting of the durable power of attorney for health care, at least in theory. Providers need a sure decision by a clear decision-maker when they cannot get informed consent from a patient, and the durable powers allowed clearly identified decision-makers to make exactly the decision that confronted the patient at any given moment. Durable powers, then, protected patients, who could appoint trusted family members and friends to make decisions, and physicians, who needed someone they could rely upon to be present and actually make the decisions.

Some state statutes now allow an agent authorized by a durable power of attorney to make health care decisions for a principal even if the principal has capacity—as long as that is the explicit desire of the principal. Why should an agent make a decision for a principal *with* capacity? Doesn't that undermine the principle of autonomy? Such a provision gives health care providers a surrogate decision-maker to turn to in the case of a patient with capacity that is highly variable. Some argue that, in such cases, health care providers ought to be able to depend upon the consent of a patient-designated surrogate without doing a full competency analysis each time a health care decision is to be made. Of course, the decision of the surrogate can always be overruled by the patient herself if she has capacity.

The legal significance of a durable power of attorney for health care is defined by each state's durable power statute. Recall that in her concurring opinion in *Cruzan*, though, Justice O'Connor suggested that there may also be constitutional significance to a properly executed durable power of attorney.

The Development of the Uniform Health-Care Decisions Act. The Uniform Health-Care Decisions Act, excerpted above, takes a comprehensive approach to the issue by combining the living will (which is retitled the "individual instruction"), the durable power of attorney (now called the "power of attorney for health care"), a family consent law, and some provisions concerning organ donation together in one statute. Further, the statute integrates the current living will and durable power (and statement of desire to donate organs) into a single document. The Uniform Act provides a statutory form, but it also explicitly declares that the form is not a mandatory one, and that individuals may draft their own form that includes only some of the kinds of instructions permitted in the unified form. The new "individual instruction" can apply to virtually any health care decision, not just the end-of-life decisions to which living wills are typically applicable. Further, "health care decision" is defined very broadly.

The Uniform Health-Care Decisions Act also makes the execution of the unified document very easy. It has no witness requirement, and it does not require that the document be notarized. The drafters of the proposed act concluded that the formalities often associated with living wills and durable powers served to discourage their execution more than to deter fraud. Despite this approach of the Uniform Act, most adopting states have added some execution formalities. Do you think that executing these documents ought to require witnesses, an oath, a seal, a notary, or some other formalizing act?

The residual decision-making portion of the Uniform Act is very much like the family consent statutes that have now been adopted in some states, and this section of the Act applies only if there is no applicable individual instruction or appointed agent. While it provides for a common family hierarchy of decision-makers for decisionally incapacitated patients, it also provides that the family can be trumped by an "orally designated surrogate," who may be appointed by a patient informing her "supervising physician" that the surrogate is entitled to make health care decisions on her behalf. Thus, patients can effectively orally appoint decision-making agents who previously could only be appointed in a writing signed pursuant to a rigorous process.

Thus, under the Uniform Act, a health care decision will be made by the first available in this hierarchy:

(1) the patient, if the patient has decisional capacity,

(2) the patient, through an individual instruction,

(3) an agent appointed by the patient in a written power of attorney for health care, unless a court has given this authority explicitly to a guardian,

(4) a guardian appointed by the court,

(5) a surrogate appointed orally by the patient,

(6) a surrogate selected from the list of family members and others who can make health care decisions on behalf of the patient.

The Uniform Act explicitly provides that the decision-maker (whether an agent, guardian, or surrogate) should decide based on the principle of substituted judgment rather than the best interest principle. If it is impossible to apply the substituted judgment principle, the statute would allow the substitute decision-maker to apply the best interest principle.

The Uniform Act includes the normal raft of recordkeeping provisions, limitations on the reach of the criminal law, assurances regarding the insurance rights of those who execute the documents, and restrictions on the liability of those who act under the statute in good faith. A provision for $500 in liquidated damages in actions for breach of the Act may not encourage litigation when the statute is ignored, but the provision for attorney's fees in those cases might provide an incentive for lawyers to bring those cases. The Act applies only to adults.

Physicians' Orders Regarding End-of-Life Care. Health care providers have been inconsistent in their recognition and implementation of advance directives, even when there is no doubt about the authenticity or legality of the advance directive under local law. By custom, health care institutions and health care workers caring for patients rely on orders given by the health care professional responsible for the patient's treatment, not on documents signed outside of the health care system. Recognizing the strength of this custom, some patient advocates argue that the best way to protect a patient's interests at the end of life is to incorporate the patient's health care decisions into a physician's order.

One particularly effective way of achieving this protection is to incorporate the decisions into a Physician Order for Life Sustaining Treatment (POLST). A POLST (which goes by a variety of other names with other acronyms in other states—MOST, MOLST, SMOST, TPOP, or, in the Veteran's Administration hospitals, SAPO) may include information about a patient's decisions with regard to resuscitation orders, the extent of appropriate medical intervention, the use of antibiotics and other pharmaceuticals, the provision of nutrition and hydration, the desired place of treatment (home, hospital or nursing home), the identity of the authorized health care decision-maker, and other relevant issues likely to arise in each case.

Modeled on emergency medical services' DNR or DNAR ("do not resuscitate," or, more recently, "do not attempt resuscitation") orders, the POLST is a real medical order, signed by a health care provider—in some states it must be a physician, but in others it can be signed by other providers—with authority to issue that order. As a result, it is more likely to be implemented across health care settings: in the emergency room, at the rehabilitation hospital, in the nursing home, and in the field. It is designed to travel with the patient as the patient moves among these health care settings. An example of a POLST—this one called a "MOST" ("Medical Orders for Scope of Treatment") and used by providers in Colorado—is reprinted below. For discussion of the development of this MOST and a useful discussion of the utility of the document, see http://coloradoadvancedirectives.com/most-in-colorado/.

SEND ORIGINAL FORM WITH PERSON WHENEVER TRANSFERRED OR DISCHARGED

Colorado Medical Orders
for Scope of Treatment (MOST)

- **FIRST** follow these orders, **THEN** contact Physician, Advanced Practice Nurse (APN), or Physician Assistant (PA) for further orders if indicated.
- These Medical Orders are based on the person's medical condition & wishes.
- If Section A or B is not completed, full treatment for that section is implied.
- May only be completed by, or on behalf of, a person 18 years of age or older.
- Everyone shall be treated with dignity and respect.

Legal Last Name	
Legal First Name/Middle Name	
Date of Birth	Sex
Hair Color	Eye Color	Race/Ethnicity

In preparing these orders, please inquire whether patient has executed a living will or other advance directive.
If yes and available, review for consistency with these orders and update as needed. (See additional instructions on page 2.)

A Check one box only	**CARDIOPULMONARY RESUSCITATION (CPR)** ***Person has no pulse and is not breathing.*** ☐ **Yes CPR:** Attempt Resuscitation ☐ **No CPR:** Do Not Attempt Resuscitation *NOTE: Selecting 'Yes CPR' requires choosing "Full Treatment" in Section B.* *When not in cardiopulmonary arrest, follow orders in Section B.*

B
Check one
box only
	MEDICAL INTERVENTIONS ***Person has pulse and/or is breathing.***
	☐ **Full Treatment**—primary goal to prolong life by all medically effective means:
	   In addition to treatment described in Selective Treatment and Comfort-focused Treatment, use intubation, advanced airway interventions, mechanical ventilation, and cardioversion as indicated. Transfer to hospital if indicated. Includes intensive care.
	☐ **Selective Treatment**—goal to treat medical conditions while avoiding burdensome measures:
	   In addition to treatment described in Comfort-focused Treatment below, use IV antibiotics and IV fluids as indicated. <u>Do not intubate.</u> May use noninvasive positive airway pressure. Transfer to hospital if indicated. <u>Avoid intensive care.</u>
	☐ **Comfort-focused Treatment**—primary goal to maximize comfort:
	   Relieve pain and suffering with medication by any route as needed; use oxygen, suctioning, and manual treatment of airway obstruction. Do not use treatments listed in Full and Selective Treatment unless consistent with comfort goal. <u>Do not transfer to hospital for life-sustaining treatment. Transfer only if comfort needs cannot be met in current location.</u>
	Additional Orders: _____

C Check one box only	**ARTIFICIALLY ADMINISTERED NUTRITION** *Always offer food & water by mouth if feasible.* Any surrogate legal decision maker (Medical Durable Power of Attorney [MDPOA], Proxy-by-Statute, guardian, or other) must follow directions in the patient's living will, if any. Not completing this section *does not* imply any one of the choices—further discussion is required. *NOTE: <u>Special rules for Proxy-by-Statute apply;</u> see reverse side ("Completing the MOST form") for details.* ☐ Artificial nutrition by tube long term/permanent if indicated. ☐ Artificial nutrition by tube short term/temporary only. (May state term & goal in "Additional Orders") ☐ No artificial nutrition by tube. *Additional Orders:* _____
D	**DISCUSSED WITH** (check all that apply): ☐ Patient ☐ Agent under Medical Durable Power of Attorney ☐ Proxy-by-Statute (per C.R.S. 15-18.5-103(6)) ☐ Legal guardian ☐ Other: _____

SIGNATURES OF PROVIDER AND PATIENT, AGENT, GUARDIAN, OR PROXY-BY-STATUTE AND DATE (*MANDATORY*)

Significant thought has been given to these instructions. Preferences have been discussed and expressed to a healthcare professional. This document reflects those treatment preferences, which may also be documented in a Medical Durable Power OA, CPR Directive, living will, or other advance directive (attached if available). To the extent that previously completed advance directives do not conflict with these *Medical Orders for Scope of Treatment*, they shall remain in full force and effect.

If signed by surrogate legal decision maker, preferences expressed must reflect patient's wishes as best understood by surrogate.

Patient/Legal Decision Maker Signature (Mandatory)	Name (Print)	Relationship/Decision maker status (Write "self" if patient)	Date Signed (Mandatory; Revokes all previous MOST forms)
Physician / APN / PA Signature (Mandatory) Colorado License #:	Print Physician / APN / PA Name, Address, and Phone Number		Date Signed (Mandatory)

HIPAA PERMITS DISCLOSURE OF THIS INFORMATION TO OTHER HEALTHCARE PROFESSIONALS AS NECESSARY

Authority for this form and process is granted by C.R.S. 15-18.7: Directives Concerning Medical Orders for Scope of Treatment, enacted 2010.

SEND ORIGINAL FORM WITH PERSON WHENEVER TRANSFERRED OR DISCHARGED

ADDITIONAL INFORMATION: *Please provide contact information below, in case follow up or more information needed.*

Patient Legal Last Name	Patient Legal First Name	Patient Middle Name (if any)	Patient Date of Birth
Primary Contact Person for the Patient	Relationship and/or MDPOA, Proxy, Guardian	Phone Number/email/Other contact information	
Healthcare Professional Preparing Form	Preparer Title	Phone Number/Email	Date Prepared
Patient Primary Diagnosis	Hospice Program (if applicable) /Address		Hospice Phone Number

DIRECTIONS FOR HEALTH CARE PROFESSIONALS

For more information, please refer to the "Getting the MOST Out of the Medical Orders for Scope of Treatment: Guidelines for Healthcare Professionals," www.ColoradoMOST.com

Completing the MOST form:

- MOST form master may be downloaded from www.ColoradoMOST.com and photocopied onto **Astrobrights® "Vulcan Green"** or **"Terra Green"** 60lb paper. This special paper is strongly encouraged but not required. Visit www.ColoradoMOST.com for a link to paper suppliers.
- The form must be signed by a physician, advanced practice nurse, or physician assistant to be valid as medical orders. Physician assistants must include physician name and contact information. In the absence of a provider signature, however, the patient selections should be considered as valid, documented patient preferences for treatment.
- Verbal orders are acceptable with follow-up signature by physician, advanced practice nurse, or physician assistant in accordance with facility policy, but not to exceed 30 days.
- **Completion of the MOST form is _not_ mandatory.** "A healthcare facility shall not require a person to have executed a MOST form as a condition of being admitted to, or receiving medical treatment from, the healthcare facility" per C.R.S. 15-18.7-108.
- Patient preferences and medical indications shall guide the healthcare professional in completing the MOST form.
- Patients with capacity should participate in the discussion and sign these orders; a healthcare agent, Proxy-by-Statute, or guardian may complete these orders on behalf of an incapacitated patient, *making selections according to patient preferences, if known.*
- "Proxy-by-Statute" is a decision maker selected through a proxy process, per C.R.S. 15-18.5-103(6). Such a decision maker may not decline artificial nutrition or hydration (ANH) for an incapacitated patient without an attending physician and a second physician trained in neurology certifying that "the provision of ANH is merely prolonging the act of dying and is unlikely to result in the restoration of the patient to independent neurological functioning."
- **Photocopy, fax, and electronic images of signed MOST forms are legal and valid.**

Following the Medical Orders:

- Per C.R.S. 15-18.7-104: Emergency medical personnel, a healthcare provider, or healthcare facility _shall_ comply with an adult's properly executed MOST form that has been executed in this state or another state and is apparent and immediately available. The fact that the signing physician, advanced practice nurse, or physician assistant does not have admitting privileges in the facility where the adult is receiving care does not remove the duty to comply with these orders. Providers who comply with the orders are immune from civil and criminal prosecution in connection with any outcome of complying with the orders.
- If a healthcare provider considers these orders *medically* inappropriate, she or he should discuss concerns with the patient or surrogate legal decision maker and revise orders only after obtaining the patient or surrogate consent.
- If Section A or B is not completed, full treatment is implied for that section.
- **Comfort care is never optional.** Among other comfort measures, oral fluids and nutrition must be offered if tolerated.
- When "Comfort-focused Treatment" is checked in Section B, hospice or palliative care referral is strongly recommended.
- If a healthcare provider or facility cannot comply with these orders due to policy or ethical/religious objections, the provider or facility must arrange to transfer the patient to another provider or facility and provide appropriate care until transfer.

Reviewing the Medical Orders:

- These medical orders should be reviewed
  - regularly by the person's attending physician or facility staff with the patient and/or patient's legal decision maker;
  - on admission to or discharge from any facility or on transfer between care settings or levels;
  - at any substantial change in the person's health status or treatment preferences; and
  - when legal decision maker or contact information changes.
- If substantive changes are made, please complete a new form and void the replaced one.
- **To void the form, draw a line across Sections A through C and write "VOID" in large letters. Sign and date.**

REVIEW OF THIS COLORADO MOST FORM

Review Date	Reviewer	Location of Review	Review Outcome
			☐ No Change ☐ New Form Completed
			☐ No Change ☐ New Form Completed
			☐ No Change ☐ New Form Completed
			☐ No Change ☐ New Form Completed

HIPAA PERMITS DISCLOSURE OF THIS INFORMATION TO OTHER HEALTHCARE PROFESSIONALS AS NECESSARY

Colorado Advance Directives Consortium, www.ColoradoMOST.com   2015

POLST forms are generally entered in the patient's medical record after the provider has discussed all of the relevant issues with the patient, the patient's family, the agent or surrogate authorized to make health care decisions, and others. The POLST form may include a summary of the values and goals of the patient that form the basis of the order, and the nature of the discussions that gave rise to the order. The patient or the patient's decision-maker is often asked to countersign the order, so it is clear that it represents the agreed view of the patient and the provider. Sometimes the patient's (or the patient's representative's) signature is required; sometimes it is not. In some jurisdictions there is no place for the countersignature at all. In order to assure that these forms are not lost in the patient's chart, they are often printed on distinctively colored (usually bright pink or bright green) paper. Such orders can be recognized by state law (as they are in a many states), or by institutional or community policy.

The process of entering a POLST requires discussion among all of the relevant parties, and it provides a way of integrating a patient's advance directive and the physician's order. It does not override a legally authorized advance directive, but it may make it easier for succeeding health care providers to be aware of advance directives made earlier by the patient; and it eliminates a provider's concern over the obligation to carry out an advance directive that appears to be inconsistent with an order of a physician. The POLST is usually filled out by those familiar with the current medical needs of the patient when the need for end-of-life care is imminent, and those factors may also account for the very high level of implementation of these documents.

Some people are concerned that the development of the POLST paradigm marks a return to the days of paternalistic medicine when it was the physician, not the patient, who decided the treatment to be applied in each case. Here, the provider's signature on the POLST effectively supplants the patient's signature on an advance directive, although the effect is ameliorated by the fact that the entry of a POLST requires a discussion with the patient or the substitute decision-maker, and, often, that person's signature as well. Does the POLST require a patient to give up some level of autonomy that the patient might have had when making decisions through other forms of advance directives? Is the fact that the POLST really will be honored enough to justify giving up that autonomy? For a good account of the state of POLSTs in the U.S. (and Canada and Australia, where similar concepts have developed), see Thaddeus Mason Pope and Melinda Hexum, Legal Briefing: POLST: Physicians Order for Life-Sustaining Treatment, 36 J. Clinical Ethics 353 (2012). See also Keith Sonderling, POLST: A Cure for the Common Advance Directive—It's Just What the Doctor Ordered, 33 Nova L. Rev. 451 (2009) and Susan Hickman et al., Hope for the Future: Achieving the Original Intent of Advance Directives, 35 Hastings Ctr. Rep. (6) Supp. 26–30 (2005).

Religious Objections to Some Provisions of Advance Directives. Some religious denominations have principled objections to facilitating certain decisions that might be made in advance directives. These objections are reflected in a range of state statutes, often because those statutes are products of political compromise. For example, as this note suggests, many states limit the applicability of advance directives when the patient is pregnant or when the patient wishes to reject some forms of nutrition or hydration. These limitations are consistent with the tenets of particular religious groups (although there are secular arguments to support them as well). Advance directive laws without these explicit limitations often include other "conscience" provisions, which serve to relieve health care institutions and individual providers from taking actions that violate their own values. See section 7(e) of the Uniform Health-Care Decisions Act, above.

What should happen when a patient with particular values makes a decision that is protected by law in that jurisdiction but is inconsistent with the religious values of a health care institution? What if the legally authorized decision-maker (through a durable power of attorney) or the patient (through an individual instruction) requests that all artificial nutrition and hydration be terminated if the patient is in a persistent vegetative state, but the patient finds himself in a religious hospital that refuses to honor that decision? What if a patient seeking palliative sedation finds himself at a religious hospital that, as a matter of religious and ethical principle, will not provide that form of treatment? What if the family of a religious person seeks the continuation of nutrition and hydration as long as the patient remains in a persistent vegetative state, treatment arguably required by the patient's faith, in an institution that considers it to be a medically useless and futile form of treatment?

Several advocacy groups now provide sample language that individuals can include in their advance directives to request that, if the patient must be hospitalized, the hospitalization take place—for example—in a Catholic hospital bound by the Ethical and Religious Directives (ERDs) of the Catholic Church, or alternatively, that the patient *not* be hospitalized in a Catholic hospital bound by the ERDs. Should providers be bound by that kind of request, on either side? Under the California Right to Know End of Life Options Act and the New York Palliative Care Information Act, must hospitalized patients be told of legal alternatives that might not be available at the hospital because they are not permitted by religious doctrine? Is it a violation of the First Amendment to require that those institutions provide care (or information about care) to which they have strong moral objection?

The Patient Self-Determination Act and Advance Directives. The federal Patient Self-Determination Act applies to hospitals, skilled nursing facilities, home health agencies, hospice programs, and HMOs that receive Medicaid or Medicare funding. It requires each of those covered by the Act to provide each patient with written information concerning:

(i)   an individual's rights under State law (whether statutory or as recognized by the courts of the State) to make decisions concerning ... medical care, including the right to accept or refuse medical or surgical treatment and the right to formulate advance directives ... and

(ii)   the written policies of the provider or organization respecting the implementation of such rights.

42 U.S.C.A. § 1395cc(a)(1)(f)(1)(A). In addition, those covered must document in each patient's record whether that patient has signed an advance directive, assure that the state law is followed in the institution, and provide for education of both the staff and the public concerning living wills and durable powers of attorney.

A few states have also taken action to increase the utility of advance directives. For example, some states have central registries of advance directives, and a handful of states provide for drivers' licenses to show if a patient has an advance directive. At least one statute requires managed health care providers to discuss advance directives with their patients/enrollees. There has also been some attention given to how to make advance directives of various stripes enforced across state and provincial borders.

NOTES AND QUESTIONS

1.   *The Values History and the "Five Wishes" Form.* Because it is almost impossible to predict exactly what kinds of medical care one might need and what kinds of medical conditions one will suffer, some courts and scholars have suggested that the most helpful kind of advance directive would be one that appoints a substitute decision-maker (through a durable power of attorney) and then describes generally the principal's interests and values that are likely to be significant in subsequent decision-making over medical treatment.

One particularly good device for encouraging such discussion (and for recording the results) is the "Values History Form," which asks prospective patients about their general values; their medical values; their relationships with family members, friends, and health care providers; their wishes in particular cases; and a host of other issues likely to become relevant if they become incompetent and health care decisions must be made on their behalf. There is no doubt that the existence of such a document would be of great value to a substitute decision-maker and to any court called upon to confirm that substitute's decision even though it doesn't carry the immunity provision or requirement of compliance that a living will does. See Joan McIver Gibson, Reflecting on Values, 51 Ohio St. L.J. 451 (1990).

In addition, over the past several years the "Five Wishes" document, a simple and easy-to-use advance directive that is arguably legally effective under the laws of most states, has become popular. The Five Wishes document, developed by the advocacy group Aging with Dignity, tells your family and doctors: (1) which person you want to make health care decisions for you when you can't make them; (2) the kind of medical treatment you want or don't want; (3) how comfortable you want to be; (4) how you want people to treat you; and (5) what you want your loved ones to know.

2.   *Prior Preferences or Current Interests?* There has been considerable research on the efficacy of advanced directives generally and their value in particular circumstances—for example, when a patient is experiencing, or is likely to experience, dementia. Several research and advocacy groups now offer particular advance directive language that might be useful to those dementia

patients, as long as that language is also consistent with other state statutory requirements. See Paula Span, The New Old Age: One Day Your Mind May Fade. But You Can Plan Ahead, NY Times, January 23, 2018. While the law generally requires that the patient's prior preferences and values be used to guide decision-making, some have argued that the patient's current interests should be used instead. See, e.g., Rebecca Dresser, Precommitment: A Misguided Strategy for Securing Death with Dignity, 81 Tex. L. Rev. 1823 (2003) (describing problems with precommitment).

3. *Supported Decision-Making.* Scholars have noted that the law of health care decision-making in the U.S. reflects a model of decision-making that is personal, private, and independent. Is this how most people make decisions? Or do they turn to trusted friends, family members, and others for advice and support? Supported decision-making, developed to allow people with disabilities to retain decision-making capacity as an alternative to surrogate decision-making or guardianship, reflects the latter approach. People using supported decision-making rely on trusted friends, family members, professionals, and others, to make their own decisions. An increasing number of states have adopted laws related to supported decision-making for people with disabilities. Peter Blanck & Jonathan G. Martinis, "The Right to Make Choices": The National Resource Center for Supported Decision-Making, 3 Inclusion 24 (2015). See also Megan S. Wright, Dementia, Autonomy, and Supported Healthcare Decisionmaking, 79 Md. L. Rev. 257 (2020); Megan S. Wright, End of Life and Autonomy: The Case for Relational Nudges in End-of-Life Decision-Making Law and Policy, 77 Md. L. Rev. 1062 (2018).

4. *Outmoded Distinctions as to Treatment.* Distinctions between "active" and "passive" conduct and between "withholding" and "withdrawing" treatment are anachronistic distinctions which have not found a safe harbor in the law, just as they have been increasingly recognized as meaningless in ethics. An early New Jersey case, *In re Conroy*, 98 N.J. 321, 486 A.2d 1209 (N.J. 1985), considered each of these distinctions and summarized the ethical and legal literature and the reasons for rejecting the distinctions. As to the distinction between active and passive conduct, the *Conroy* court announced:

> We emphasize that in making decisions whether to administer life-sustaining treatment to patients such as Claire Conroy, the primary focus should be the patient's desires and experience of pain and enjoyment—not the type of treatment involved. Thus, we reject the distinction that some have made between actively hastening death by terminating treatment and passively allowing a person to die of a disease as one of limited use in a legal analysis of such a decision-making situation.

> Characterizing conduct as active or passive is often an elusive notion, even outside the context of medical decision-making .... The distinction is particularly nebulous, however, in the context of decisions whether to withhold or withdraw life-sustaining treatment. In a case like that of Claire Conroy, for example, would a physician who discontinued

nasogastric feeding be actively causing her death by removing her primary source of nutrients; or would he merely be omitting to continue the artificial form of treatment, thus passively allowing her medical condition, which includes her inability to swallow, to take its natural course? [ ] The ambiguity inherent in this distinction is further heightened when one performs an act within an over-all plan of non-intervention, such as when a doctor writes an order not to resuscitate a patient. . . .

For a similar reason, we also reject any distinction between withholding and withdrawing life-sustaining treatment. Some commentators have suggested that discontinuing life-sustaining treatment once it has been commenced is morally more problematic than merely failing to begin the treatment. Discontinuing life-sustaining treatment, to some, is an "active" taking of life, as opposed to the more "passive" act of omitting the treatment in the first instance.

This distinction is more psychologically compelling than logically sound. As mentioned above, the line between active and passive conduct in the context of medical decisions is far too nebulous to constitute a principled basis for decision-making. Whether necessary treatment is withheld at the outset or withdrawn later on, the consequence—the patient's death— is the same. Moreover, from a policy standpoint, it might well be unwise to forbid persons from discontinuing a treatment under circumstances in which the treatment could permissibly be withheld. Such a rule could discourage families and doctors from even attempting certain types of care and could thereby force them into hasty and premature decisions to allow a patient to die. [ ]

486 A.2d at 1233–1234.

As to the distinction between "ordinary" and "extraordinary" treatment, *Conroy* pointed out:

We also find unpersuasive the distinction relied upon by some courts, commentators, and theologians between "ordinary" treatment, which they would always require, and "extraordinary" treatment, which they deem optional. . . . The terms "ordinary" and "extraordinary" have assumed too many conflicting meanings to remain useful. To draw a line on this basis for determining whether treatment should be given leads to a semantical milieu that does not advance the analysis.

The distinction between ordinary and extraordinary treatment is frequently phrased as one between common and unusual, or simple and complex, treatment [ ]; "extraordinary" treatment also has been equated with elaborate, artificial, heroic, aggressive, expensive, or highly involved or invasive forms of medical intervention [ ]. Depending on the definitions applied, a particular treatment for a given patient may be considered both ordinary and extraordinary. [ ] Further, since the common/unusual and simple/complex distinctions among medical treatments "exist on continuums with no precise dividing line," [ ] and the continuum is constantly shifting due to progress in medical care, disagreement will often exist about whether a particular treatment is ordinary or extraordinary. In addition, the competent patient generally could refuse even ordinary treatment; therefore, an incompetent patient theoretically should also be able to make such a choice when the surrogate decision-making is effectuating the patient's subjective intent. In such cases, the ordinary/extraordinary distinction is irrelevant except insofar as the particular patient would have made the distinction.

The ordinary/extraordinary distinction has also been discussed in terms of the benefits and burdens of treatment for the patient. If the benefits of the treatment outweigh the burdens it imposes on the patient, it is characterized as ordinary and therefore ethically required; if not, it is characterized as extraordinary and therefore optional. [ ] This formulation is extremely fact-sensitive and would lead to different classifications of the same treatment in different situations.

. . . Moreover, while the analysis may be useful in weighing the implications of the specific treatment for the patient, essentially it merely restates the question: whether the burdens of a treatment so clearly outweigh its benefits to the patient that continued treatment would be inhumane.

468 A.2d at 1234–1235. See also Brophy v. New England Sinai Hosp., Inc., 398 Mass. 417, 497 N.E.2d 626 (1986) ("while we believe that the distinction between extraordinary and ordinary care is a factor to be considered, the use of such a distinction as the sole, or major, factor of decision tends . . . to create a distinction without meaning.")

DOCTORS HOSPITAL OF AUGUSTA V. ALICEA
Supreme Court of Georgia, 2016.
788 S.E.2d 392.

NAHMIAS, JUSTICE.

In March 2012, Jacqueline Alicea's 91-year-old grandmother, Bucilla Stephenson, died at the end of a two-week stay at Doctors Hospital of Augusta, LLC . . . . In May 2013, Alicea, acting as the administratix of her grandmother's estate, sued the Hospital and Dr. Phillip Catalano . . . . Alicea alleged among other things that they intubated her grandmother and put her on a mechanical ventilator, which prolonged her life when she was in a terminal condition and caused her unnecessary pain and suffering, contrary to her advance directive for health care and the specific directions of Alicea, her designated health care agent. The Defendants filed a motion for summary judgment, arguing among other things that the Georgia Advance Directive for Health Care Act ("Advance Directive Act" or "Act") [ ] provided them immunity from liability.

* * *

On November 12, 2009, Stephenson, who was then 89 years old, executed an advance directive for health care ("Advance Directive"), designating as her health care agent Alicea, the granddaughter with whom she lived. The Advance Directive specified that Alicea was "authorized to make all health-care decisions for me, including decisions to provide, withhold, or withdraw artificial nutrition and hydration, and all other forms of health care to keep me alive." The Advance Directive also said:

> My agent shall make health-care decisions for me in accordance with this power of attorney for health care, any instructions I give in this form, and my other wishes to the extent known to my agent. . . .

Stephenson repeatedly told her family members that "she was ready to go when the good Lord called her," and said "when it's my time, it's my time, don't prolong it." She told Alicea specifically that "[s]he did not want . . . to rely on a machine to have to live," including a ventilator to breathe for her. In 2007, Alicea's 80-year-old father had died at the Hospital after entering it with pneumonia and without an advance directive or other document concerning end-of-life decisions. Because Alicea's mother had Alzheimer's disease, Alicea ultimately had to make the decision to take her father off a ventilator. Stephenson did not want Alicea to have to make that kind of decision about her. In the paragraph of the Advance Directive addressing "end-of-life decisions," Stephenson initialed the option that said:

> Choice NOT to Prolong Life.

> I do not want my life to be prolonged if (1) I have an incurable[ ] and irreversible condition that will result in my death within a relatively short time, (2) I become unconscious and, to a reasonable degree of medical certainty, I will not regain consciousness, or (3) the likely risks and burdens of treatment would outweigh the expected benefits.

[] Two years passed. Then, around February 28, 2012, Stephenson developed a persistent cough. On Saturday, March 3, she woke up lethargic; she was minimally responsive and had urinated on herself. After Alicea and her husband assisted Stephenson in sitting up, she became more aware, and they helped her to the bathroom to clean up. As Alicea was bathing her, Stephenson lost control of her bowels, and her eyes rolled toward the back of her head. Alicea and her husband feared that Stephenson was having a stroke and drove her to the Hospital's emergency room; Alicea brought the Advance Directive with her.

Blood tests and a chest x-ray showed that Stephenson was suffering from pneumonia, sepsis, and acute renal failure, and she was admitted to the Hospital. Alicea gave the Hospital the Advance Directive, which was placed in Stephenson's medical record, but not in the front behind the admission tab as required by hospital policy to ensure its ready availability to all doctors and hospital staff. Alicea also gave the Hospital her contact information, including her home, work, and cell phone numbers and her husband's cell phone number, so that she could be reached whenever she was away from the Hospital. Alicea has presented evidence showing that from the time Stephenson arrived at the Hospital, she was unable or chose not to make significant health care decisions for herself, triggering Alicea's authority to make those decisions pursuant to the Advance Directive.

Around 9:00 a.m. the next day, Dr. Catalano, a surgeon with staff privileges at the Hospital, called Alicea to tell her that he was taking care of Stephenson and that she was being moved to the intensive care unit ("ICU"). Dr. Catalano said that he planned to perform a computed tomography ("CT") scan to better assess her condition. Alicea did not object to the CT scan, but she told Dr. Catalano about Stephenson's Advance Directive and specifically instructed that "by no means was CPR [cardio-pulmonary resuscitation] to ever be administered" and that "no heroic measures were to be used" to prolong Stephenson's life.

[Another physician at the hospital] asked Alicea about ventilation specifically, and Alicea directed him to call her before intubating Stephenson and putting her on a ventilator. [That physician] wrote twice in his progress note that Stephenson was "no CPR" and that Alicea had to be called "before patient is intubated."

On Monday morning, March 5, Dr. Catalano called Alicea and requested her verbal consent for a "surgical" thoracentesis to drain more fluid from Stephenson's lung cavity. . . . Dr. Catalano had not read the Advance Directive or the progress notes in Stephenson's medical chart; he did not tell Alicea, and she did not know, that this procedure would require intubation and the use of a ventilator. Had Alicea known that intubation was required, she would not have consented to the surgery. During the surgery, Dr. Catalano found that much of Stephenson's right lung was necrotic (dead tissue), and he removed two-thirds of the lung. Stephenson was extubated in the recovery room, and Alicea was not told that she had been intubated and put on a ventilator.

Two days later, on March 7, Stephenson was experiencing respiratory distress in the early morning hours . . . . Around 4:00 a.m., the nursing staff called Dr. Catalano at home. Dr. Catalano decided to have Stephenson intubated and put on a ventilator to prevent her from going into respiratory or cardiac arrest. A nurse asked Dr. Catalano if he wanted to call Alicea before ordering the life-prolonging intubation, but he rebuffed her, saying, "I'm not going to call her at six o'clock in the morning and scare the hell out of her. I'll wait till, you know, she wakes up and then I'm going to call her and tell her what happened." Dr. Catalano then spoke to the on-duty doctor and directed him to intubate Stephenson, telling the doctor, "I don't want her to die."[3] The on-duty doctor arrived at Stephenson's bedside . . . ,

---

[3]   In his deposition, Dr. Catalano explained his thought process at the time as follows:

performed the intubation, and hooked Stephenson up to a ventilator. No effort was made to contact Alicea before or after Stephenson was intubated.

When Alicea's husband stopped by the Hospital that morning around 8:00 a.m. to check on Stephenson, he was surprised to see her on a ventilator. He called Alicea, who was shocked by the news, and told her that the nursing staff could not find the Advance Directive. . . . It took the nursing staff 15 to 20 minutes of searching to locate the Hospital's copy of the Advance Directive, and one nurse remarked to Alicea's husband, "Boy, somebody has really messed up. I found it."

When Alicea got to the Hospital, she . . . held up the Advance Directive and told the doctor that her grandmother had expressed her wishes, which were contrary to what had happened, and that Alicea had specifically said to call her before putting Stephenson on a ventilator. . . .

Alicea asked [the director of the ICU] about possible next steps. He told her that she could decide to have Stephenson taken off the ventilator and extubated, which would cause her grandmother to suffocate and die (as had happened with Alicea's father), and that the only other option was to perform another surgery to clean out Stephenson's lung cavity more. Had Stephenson been allowed to die that morning, Alicea "would have understood that it was her time and God took her." Having been deprived of the opportunity to let nature take its course, Alicea consented to the surgical procedure and others recommended by Dr. Catalano and the Hospital staff over the next week, including the placement of a feeding tube, a bronchoscopy to remove pus from Stephenson's airway, and a tracheostomy to provide an alternate airway and to remove secretions.

On March 14, Alicea was informed that Stephenson's kidneys were shutting down and that she needed dialysis, and Alicea gathered the family at the Hospital to discuss the situation. . . . Alicea then authorized the removal of the ventilator and the provision of comfort measures only, and three days later, on March 17, 2012, Stephenson died.

[ ] On May 14, 2013, Alicea, acting as the administratrix of Stephenson's estate, filed a complaint against the Hospital and Dr. Catalano, raising claims of breach of agreement, professional and ordinary negligence, medical battery, intentional infliction of emotional distress, and breach of fiduciary duty. The Hospital's alleged liability was based on respondeat superior for the actions of its agents and employees. The

---

I'm thinking, well, I mean what's the worst. If the family does not want her on the respirator, well, we can just pull the tube out. And, you know, we've wasted an hour or two of her staying in the hospital ICU but, on the other hand, if we try to make calls she'd be dead. I mean I can't call the family. . . . I said, well, let's just do what's right for the patient. My God, we can always undo it. But . . . if the patient dies, you know, that's my ultimate loss. There's no way I can get her back. So when this happened I really didn't go into any of the code/no code/do not intubate/resuscitate. Save the patient's life first and then we'll do whatever it takes to make the family and that patient whatever, but we can't undo death. So that's what I was thinking.

complaint alleged that Dr. Catalano and other medical personnel associated with the Hospital had subjected the terminally ill Stephenson to unnecessary medical procedures, in particular her intubation and placement on a ventilator on . . . in violation of her Advance Directive and the directions of Alicea as her designated health care agent.

In support of her claims, Alicea relied on an expert on gerontology, geriatrics, and palliative care. The expert concluded that when Stephenson arrived at the Hospital on March 4, she already "had an incurable and irreversible condition that was likely to result in her death within a relatively short period of time thereafter," and that "her condition was such that the likely risk and burdens of any invasive procedures and treatment outweighed any expected benefits." Consequently, the expert opined that the Defendants were required under the standard of care to refrain from taking steps to prolong her life in accordance with her Advance Directive as well as the instructions of Alicea, her designated health care agent. According to Alicea's expert, Dr. Catalano breached the standard of care by, among other things, failing to review Stephenson's Advance Directive and the progress notes in her medical chart to determine if Alicea had given any directions for Stephenson's care and by failing to obtain basic consent from Alicea before the March 7 intubation. The expert further opined that the nurses employed by the Hospital had violated the standard of care by failing to contact Alicea before the March 7 intubation and failing to call Dr. Catalano's attention to Stephenson's Advance Directive and the notation in the progress notes regarding intubation.

[T]he Defendants filed a motion for summary judgment, contending among other things that they were immune from liability based on the March 7 surgical procedure under [the provisions of the Georgia Advance Directive Act].

* * *

[ ] The Defendants argue that the Court of Appeals misconstrued the Advance Directive Act as requiring health care providers to act in "good faith reliance" on the designated health care agent's directions and decisions in order to qualify for the immunity from civil liability [ ]. Our rejection of this argument depends in part on our understanding of the Act's overall purpose and operation, so we will [first] outline those features before turning to a detailed examination of [the statute].

(a) In 2007, the General Assembly enacted the statute . . . . As the uncodified first section of the 2007 statute explained:

> The General Assembly has long recognized the right of the individual to control all aspects of his or her personal care and medical treatment, including the right to insist upon medical treatment, decline medical treatment, or direct that medical treatment be withdrawn.

[ ] Thus,

the clear expression of an individual's decisions regarding health care, whether made by the individual or an agent appointed by the individual, is of critical importance not only to citizens but also to the health care and legal communities, third parties, and families.

. . . Thus, a clear objective of the Act is to ensure that in making decisions about a patient's health care, it is the will of the patient or her designated agent, and not the will of the health care provider, that controls.

* * *

The Act . . . sets forth several rules for how decisions are to be made in caring for a patient with an advance directive. If the patient's attending physician determines in good faith that the patient is able to understand the general nature of the health care procedure being consented to or refused, the patient's own decision about that procedure prevails over contrary instructions by a health care agent. . . . However,

[w]henever a health care provider believes a declarant is unable to understand the general nature of the health care procedure which the provider deems necessary, the health care provider shall consult with any available health care agent known to the health care provider who then has power to act for the declarant under an advance directive for health care.

* * *

The health care decision now at issue in this case is the decision that needed to be made on March 7, 2012, about whether Stephenson should be intubated and put on a ventilator to prolong her life. Stephenson was unable to, and clearly did not, make that decision for herself, so Alicea had the authority to make that decision for Stephenson under her Advance Directive, which Alicea had given to the Hospital's staff and had discussed with them and with Dr. Catalano. With respect to the duties of "[e]ach health care provider and each other person with whom a health care agent interacts under an advance directive for health care" in this situation, the Act says the following [ ]:

A health care decision made by a health care agent in accordance with the terms of an advance directive for health care shall be complied with by every health care provider to whom the decision is communicated, subject to the health care provider's right to administer treatment for the [patient's] comfort or alleviation of pain; provided, however, that if the health care provider is unwilling to comply with the health care agent's decision, the health care provider shall promptly inform the health care agent who shall then be responsible for arranging for the [patient's] transfer to another health care provider. A health care provider who is unwilling to comply with the health care agent's decision shall provide reasonably necessary consultation and care in connection with the pending transfer.

Thus, a health care provider in this situation generally must comply with the health care agent's decision, with two exceptions. The first, not pertinent here, is as to pain treatment. The second recognizes that the provider may be "unwilling" to comply with the agent's decision, on medical, moral, or other grounds. But the unwilling provider is not entitled to then make the health care decision for the patient himself, or to just walk away. The Act requires such a provider to "promptly inform" the agent of his unwillingness to comply and also to "provide reasonably necessary consultation and care" in connection with the transfer of the patient to another care-giver as arranged by the agent—presumably a transfer to a provider (who may be in the same facility) who will comply with the agent's decision.

The Advance Directive Act then includes a series of immunity provisions [ ]. The Defendants seek to rely [first, on] a general release of liability for

[e]ach health care provider, health care facility, and any other person who acts in good faith reliance on any direction or decision by the health care agent . . . to the same extent as though such person had interacted directly with the declarant as a fully competent person.

The Act then says:

Without limiting the generality of the foregoing, the following specific provisions shall also govern, protect, and validate the acts of the health care agent and each such health care provider, health care facility, and any other person acting in good faith reliance on such direction or decision: . . . .

After the colon come five specific immunity provisions.[ ]

The first three of these statutory immunity provisions, it is important to recognize, mirror the statutory duties imposed on health care providers by [the statute]. Corresponding to the first clause [ ] which requires that "[a] health care decision made by a health care agent in accordance with the terms of an advance directive for health care shall be complied with by every health care provider to whom the decision is communicated," [the statute] grants providers immunity from civil or criminal liability or professional discipline "solely for complying with any direction or decision by the health care agent, even if death or injury to the declarant ensues." And corresponding to the proviso [ ] for health care providers who are "unwilling to comply with the health care agent's decision," [the statute] give such providers similarly broad immunity—so long as they promptly inform the agent of the "refusal or failure" to comply with the agent's direction or decision and assist with the patient's continued care to the extent of continuing to provide reasonably necessary consultation and care in connection with a pending transfer of the patient, acting substantially in accord with reasonable medical standards, and cooperating in any transfer of the patient as authorized by [the statute itself].

* * *

[O]nly health care providers who act in good faith reliance on the agent's directions are entitled to immunity [ ], the introductory clause speaks of "each such health care provider . . . acting in good faith reliance on such direction or decision"—the "such" referring back to the providers discussed in the preceding general-release sentence, that is, "[e]ach health care provider who acts in good faith reliance on any direction or decision by the health care agent."

* * *

The [statute] plainly authorizes a health care provider to make no effort to comply with an agent's direction—to refuse or fail entirely to comply—so long as the provider promptly informs the agent of that choice and takes the other steps of care and cooperation that the Act requires. . . . What is critical, in our view, is that a provider claiming to have acted in "good faith reliance" on the agent's direction or decision can show that he acted in dependence on that direction or decision, not without reference to the agent's wishes. . . .

Recall that a primary purpose of the Advance Directive Act is to ensure that in making decisions about a patient's health care, it is the will of the patient or her designated agent, rather than the will of the health care provider, that controls. OCGA § 31–32–8 (1) enforces this purpose by declaring that a health care provider who

> believes a declarant is unable to understand the general nature of the health care procedure which the provider deems necessary . . . shall consult with any available health care agent known to the health care provider who then has power to act for the declarant under an advance directive for health care.

If a provider is aware of what the agent has decided, and then proceeds as the statute mandates [ ]—either by complying with that decision or by taking the steps required when he is unwilling to comply with the decision—then he may look to the immunity provisions [ ] for protection. But a provider cannot claim this immunity when his action was not based in good faith on the agent's direction, just because the decision he made for the patient happens to be one that arguably complied or failed to comply with what the agent would have decided. . . .

. . . The health care decision in question is the decision to intubate Stephenson and put her on a ventilator as a life-prolonging measure around 4:00 a.m. on the morning of March 7, 2012. Although there is evidence to the contrary, there is ample evidence that in ordering that procedure, Dr. Catalano was not acting in good faith reliance—in honest dependence—on any decision Alicea had made as Stephenson's health care agent, either to comply with it or to refuse or fail to comply with it and then promptly inform Alicea of his unwillingness. Instead, the evidence would support a finding that Dr. Catalano made the health care decision himself, in the exercise of his own medical and personal judgment. . . .

[T]he Advance Directive Act is all about letting patients and their health care agents, rather than the health care provider, control such decisions. . . .

Because there is at least a disputed issue of fact as to whether Dr. Catalano acted with good faith reliance on any decision made by his patient's health care agent, Dr. Catalano cannot on motion for summary judgment claim the immunity that [is available] to providers who honestly depend on such a decision to either comply with it or promptly inform the patient that they are unwilling to comply with it. Likewise, the Hospital points to no evidence that its staff acted based on a decision by Alicea with respect to the March 7 intubation; when Dr. Catalano made the decision himself, the staff simply proceeded based on his directive.

NOTES AND QUESTIONS

1. *Subsequent Settlement.* In this case, the matter was settled just before the trial was scheduled to begin in 2017. One report suggests the plaintiff originally sought $200,000 to compensate for additional medical expenses, as well as punitive damages and attorneys' fees. In fact, the case settled for about $1,000,000. While normally the settlement figure itself would be kept confidential by agreement of the parties, in this case the plaintiffs insisted that the amount be made public so that it would serve as a warning to other physicians and institutions in Georgia who might be tempted to ignore agents and advance directives. See S. Hodson, Hospital Settles Lawsuit Failing to Honor Patient's Wishes on Extending Life, Augusta Chronicle, May 25, 2017. See also Paula Span, Filing Suit for "Wrongful Life," New York Times (Jan. 26. 2021) (noting other cases that have recognized wrongful prolongation of life claims).

2. *Calculating Damages.* Should damages that are accrued because physicians ignore agents be assessed in the same way as damages that are accrued because physicians ignore patients themselves? Should damages that accrue from the failure of a hospital to follow a POLST be treated just like damages that accrue because physicians ignore agents and patients? The Georgia statute authorizing agents to make decisions for incompetent patients in this case is based on the Uniform Health-Care Decisions Act, excerpted earlier in this chapter. Would you expect the same rule on damages to apply in other states that have adopted this form of that Uniform Act? Should the

Uniform Act be amended to explicitly provide that damages are available under these circumstances?

3. *Hospital Liability?* The Georgia Supreme Court suggests that the hospital is liable in this case because it is vicariously liable for the acts of the physicians. Is that always true? Were the physicians here agents of the hospital? Apparent or ostensible agents of the hospital? Might the hospital be directly liable for not enforcing its policy on the placement of advance directives at the front of the patient chart? Might the hospital be liable for not having an adequate policy recognizing the decision-making authority of agents and surrogate? See Chapter 5.

4. *Failure of Informed Consent?* When a physician or an institution ignores the request of a patient, agent, or surrogate, does that automatically create an informed consent action on behalf of the patient? Are informed consent damages different from other damages (like ordinary tort damages or medical malpractice damages) that might be awarded to a patient under these circumstances? See Chapter 4.

5. *Immunity Provision.* This case focused on the meaning of the immunity provision in the statute. Is that provision necessary? Why do you think it was included in the statute? If there is no liability in any case, why would a provider have to worry about immunity?

C. DECISION-MAKING IN THE ABSENCE OF ADVANCE DIRECTIVES OR STATUTORILY DESIGNATED SURROGATES

IN RE EICHNER
New York Court of Appeals, 1981.
420 N.E.2d 64.

WACHTLER, JUDGE.

For over 66 years Brother Joseph Fox was a member of the Society of Mary, a Catholic religious order which, among other things, operates Chaminade High School in Mineola. . . .

While [an] operation was being performed . . . he suffered cardiac arrest, with resulting loss of oxygen to the brain and substantial brain damage. He lost the ability to breathe spontaneously and was placed on a respirator which maintained him in a vegetative state. The attending physicians informed Father Philip Eichner, who was the president of Chaminade and the director of the society at the school, that there was no reasonable chance of recovery and that Brother Fox would die in that state.

After retaining two neurosurgeons who confirmed the diagnosis, Father Eichner requested the hospital to remove the respirator. The hospital, however, refused to do so without court authorization. Father Eichner then applied . . . to be appointed committee of the person and property of Brother Fox, with authority to direct removal of the respirator. The application was supported by the patient's 10 nieces and nephews, his only surviving relatives. The court appointed a guardian ad litem and directed that notice be served on various parties, including the District Attorney.

At the hearing the District Attorney opposed the application and called medical experts to show that there might be some improvement in the patient's condition. All the experts agreed, however, that there was no reasonable likelihood that Brother Fox would ever emerge from the vegetative coma or recover his cognitive powers.

There was also evidence, submitted by the petitioner, that before the operation rendered him incompetent the patient had made it known that under these circumstances he would want a respirator removed. Brother Fox had first expressed this view in 1976 when the Chaminade community discussed the moral implications of the celebrated *Karen Ann Quinlan* case, in which the parents of a 19-year-old New Jersey girl who was in a vegetative coma requested the hospital to remove the respirator [ ]. These were formal discussions prompted by Chaminade's mission to teach and promulgate Catholic moral principles. At that time it was noted that the Pope had stated that Catholic principles permitted the termination of extraordinary life support systems when there is no reasonable hope for the patient's recovery and that church officials in New Jersey had concluded that use of the respirator in the *Quinlan* case constituted an extraordinary measure under the circumstances. Brother Fox expressed agreement with those views and stated that he would not want any of this "extraordinary business" done for him under those circumstances. Several years later, and only a couple of months before his final hospitalization, Brother Fox again stated that he would not want his life prolonged by such measures if his condition were hopeless.

[A trial court had held that Father Eichner could refuse ongoing life-sustaining treatment as a surrogate on behalf of Brother Fox because there was evidence that Brother Fox, when competent, had expressed his opposition to such treatment for himself if he was ever in a persistent vegetative state, and the trial court found this evidence to be "unchallenged at every turn and unimpeachable in its sincerity." The District Attorney appealed, questioning—among other things—the standard of proof required of a surrogate refusing life-sustaining treatment on behalf of an incompetent patient on the grounds that the patient had previously expressed a wish not to receive such treatment. The Court ruled that Father Eichner was required to present "clear and convincing" evidence of Brother Fox's wishes, and then the Court considered the evidence that had been presented at trial.]

* * *

In this case the proof was compelling. There was no suggestion that the witnesses who testified for the petitioner had any motive other than to see that Brother Fox' stated wishes were respected. The finding that he carefully reflected on the subject, expressed his views and concluded not to have his life prolonged by medical means if there were no hope of recovery is supported by his religious beliefs and is not inconsistent with his life of unselfish religious devotion. These were obviously solemn pronouncements and not casual remarks made at some social gathering, nor can it be said that he was too young to realize or feel the consequences of his statements [ ]. That this was a persistent commitment is evidenced by the fact that he reiterated the decision but two months before his final hospitalization. There was, of course, no need to speculate as to whether he would want this particular medical procedure to be discontinued under these circumstances. What occurred to him was identical to what happened in the *Karen Ann Quinlan* case, which had originally prompted his decision. In sum, the evidence clearly and convincingly shows that Brother Fox did not want to be maintained in a vegetative coma by use of a respirator.

* * *

NOTES AND QUESTIONS

1. *Substituted Judgment.* The Illinois Supreme Court has described the principle of substituted judgment clearly and simply:

> Under substituted judgment, a surrogate decisionmaker attempts to establish, with as much accuracy as possible, what decision the patient would make if he were competent to do so. Employing this theory, the surrogate first tries to determine if the patient had expressed explicit intent regarding this type of medical treatment prior to becoming incompetent. [ ] Where no clear intent exists, the patient's personal value system must guide the surrogate. . . .

In re Estate of Longeway, 133 Ill. 2d 33, 139 Ill. Dec. 780, 549 N.E.2d 292, 299 (1989).

2. *Evidence of Patient Wishes.* In applying the principle of substituted judgment, most courts look wherever they can to determine the patient's wishes. In Brophy v. New England Sinai Hosp., Inc., 398 Mass. 417, 497 N.E.2d 626 (1986), the Massachusetts Supreme Court based its conclusion that food and hydration could be withheld from a comatose adult on the substituted judgment analysis done by the lower court.

> [After a full hearing] the judge found on the basis of ample evidence which no one disputes, that Brophy's judgment would be to decline the provision of food and water and to terminate his life. In reaching that conclusion, the judge considered various factors including the following: (1) Brophy's expressed preferences; (2) his religious convictions and their relation to refusal of treatment; (3) the impact on his family; (4) the probability of

adverse side effects; and (5) the prognosis, both with and without treatment. The judge also considered present and future incompetency as an element which Brophy would consider in his decision-making process. The judge relied on several statements made by Brophy prior to the onset of his illness. Although he never had discussed specifically whether a G-tube or feeding tube should be withdrawn in the event that he was diagnosed as being in a persistent vegetative state following his surgery, the judge inferred that, if presently competent, Brophy would choose to forgo artificial nutrition and hydration by means of a G-tube. The judge found that Brophy would not likely view his own religion as a barrier to that choice.

3.   *Other Factors That Have Been Considered.* Other factors that have been considered include the patient's diagnosis, life history, ability to knowingly participate in treatment, potential quality of life, and, more generally, the patient's values and attitude toward health care. See, e.g., Mack v. Mack, 329 Md. 188, 618 A.2d 744 (1993) (focusing on the "moral views, life goals, and values" of the patient, and her "attitudes toward sickness, medical procedures, suffering and death."); DeGrella v. Elston, 858 S.W.2d 698 (Ky. 1993). For a thorough and well-annotated list of relevant factors that have been considered by the courts see Alan Meisel, Kathy L. Cerminara, and Thaddeus Mason Pope, The Right to Die, 3rd ed. (2004, and 2017 Supplement).

4.   *Decision-Making for Adults Who Have Never Been Competent.* Where the patient has never been competent—where the patient has been severely intellectually and developmentally disabled from birth, for example—the courts still make an attempt to determine what the patient's choice would be when deciding what treatment would be legally appropriate. Of course, it is exceptionally difficult to imagine what a person who has never been competent would want to do if that person were suddenly competent. Are you concerned that our society might be more willing to err on the side of removing life-sustaining treatment when the patient has a severe disability? Perhaps the courts should review all decisions to remove life-sustaining medical treatment from patients in this class, even if the courts need not be involved in similar cases with previously competent patients. See Protection and Advocacy Sys., Inc. v. Presbyterian Healthcare Servs., 128 N.M. 73, 989 P.2d 890 (1999). See also Kathy Cerminara, Critical Essay: Musings on the Need to Convince Some People With Disabilities that End-of-Life Decision Making Advocates Are Not Out to Get Them, 37 Loy. U. Chi. L.J. 343 (2006); Adrienne Asch, Recognizing Death While Affirming Life: Can End of Life Reform Uphold a Disabled Person's Interest in Continued Life?, Hastings Ctr. Spec. Rep. on Improving End of Life Care (Jennings et al., eds. 2005).

5.   *Distinguishing the Two Standards.* How difficult is it for a surrogate decision-maker to distinguish what the patient would really want from what that decision-maker would want if she were in the position of that patient? Is it really possible to clearly distinguish the subjective "substituted judgment" standard from an objective standard that asks what a reasonable person would do under the circumstances? Courts do struggle to distinguish the "substituted

judgment" and "best interest" principles, and even those that appear to adopt the "best interest" approach may qualify it by requiring that the best interest of the patient be defined in terms of the wishes, values, and desires of the patient. Some state courts appear to adopt the best interest test, but they actually take the "substituted judgment" approach. See Conservatorship of Drabick, 200 Cal. App. 3d 185, 245 Cal. Rptr. 840 (1988); In re Gordy, 658 A.2d 613 (Del. Ch. 1994).

NOTE: THE SPECIAL STATUS OF NUTRITION AND HYDRATION

The issue of withdrawing nutrition and hydration has become an especially contentious one. Recall, for example, that the living will statutes of some states treat procedures to provide nutrition and hydration differently from other forms of life-sustaining medical care. Medical sources generally recognize the irrelevancy of distinguishing between nutrition and hydration and other forms of medical treatment. Generally, courts also have concluded that the termination of nutrition and hydration is no different from the termination of other forms of mechanical support. For example, *Conroy* suggested:

> Some commentators, . . . have made yet [another] distinction, between the termination of artificial feedings and the termination of other forms of life-sustaining medical treatment. . . . According to the Appellate Division:
>
>> If, as here, the patient is not comatose and does not face imminent and inevitable death, nourishment accomplishes the substantial benefit of sustaining life until the illness takes its natural course. Under such circumstances nourishment always will be an essential element of ordinary care which physicians are ethically obligated to provide. [ ]
>
> Certainly, feeding has an emotional significance. As infants we could breathe without assistance, but we were dependent on others for our lifeline of nourishment. Even more, feeding is an expression of nurturing and caring, certainly for infants and children, and in many cases for adults as well.
>
> Once one enters the realm of complex, high-technology medical care, it is hard to shed the "emotional symbolism" of food. . . . Analytically, artificial feeding by means of a nasogastric tube or intravenous infusion can be seen as equivalent to artificial breathing by means of a respirator. Both prolong life through mechanical means when the body is no longer able to perform a vital bodily function on its own.
>
> Furthermore, while nasogastric feeding and other medical procedures to ensure nutrition and hydration are usually well tolerated, they are not free from risks or burdens; they have complications that are sometimes serious and distressing to the patient.
>
> Finally, dehydration may well not be distressing or painful to a dying patient. For patients who are unable to sense hunger and thirst,

withholding of feeding devices such as nasogastric tubes may not result in more pain than the termination of any other medical treatment. . . . Thus, it cannot be assumed that it will always be beneficial for an incompetent patient to receive artificial feeding or harmful for him not to receive it. . . .

Under the analysis articulated above, withdrawal or withholding of artificial feeding, like any other medical treatment, would be permissible [under some circumstances]. A competent patient has the right to decline any medical treatment, including artificial feeding, and should retain that right when and if he becomes incompetent. In addition, in the case of an incompetent patient who has given little or no trustworthy indication of an intent to decline treatment . . . the pain and invasiveness of an artificial feeding device, and the pain of withdrawing that device, should be treated just like the results of administering or withholding any other medical treatment.

98 N.J. 321, 486 A.2d 1209, 1235–1237.

In McConnell v. Beverly Enterprises-Connecticut, 209 Conn. 692, 553 A.2d 596 (1989), the court authorized the withdrawal of feeding by a gastrostomy tube despite a statute that appeared to say that under such circumstances "nutrition and hydration must be provided." The court reasoned that the nutrition and hydration that was implicated in the statute was that provided by "a spoon or a straw," and that feeding by gastrostomy tube was no different than any other mechanical or electronic medical intervention.

In 1990, at least, a majority of the Supreme Court (the four dissenters and concurring Justice O'Connor in *Cruzan*) viewed nutrition and hydration as another form of medical care. As Justice O'Connor pointed out, "artificial feeding cannot readily be distinguished from other forms of medical treatment. Whether or not the techniques used to pass food and water into the patient's alimentary tract are termed 'medical treatment,' it is clear they all involve some degree of intrusion and restraint." She concluded that "the liberty guaranteed by the due process clause must protect, if it protects anything, an individual's deeply personal decision to reject medical treatment, including the artificial delivery of food and water."

In his dissent, Justice Brennan reached the same conclusion, vividly describing the medical processes involved:

The artificial delivery of nutrition and hydration is undoubtedly medical treatment. The technique to which Nancy Cruzan is subject—artificial feeding through a gastrostomy tube—involves a tube implanted surgically into her stomach through incisions in her abdominal wall. It may obstruct the intestinal tract, erode and pierce the stomach wall, or cause leakage of the stomach's contents into the abdominal cavity. [ ] The tube can cause pneumonia from reflux of the stomach's contents into the lung. [ ] Typically, and in this case, commercially prepared formulas are used, rather than fresh food. [ ] The type of formula and method of administration must be experimented with to avoid gastrointestinal problems. [ ] The patient must be monitored daily by medical personnel as to weight, fluid intake and fluid output; blood tests must be done weekly.

Artificial delivery of food and water is regarded as medical treatment by the medical profession and the federal government. . . . The federal government permits the cost of the medical devices and formulas used in enteral feeding to be reimbursed under Medicare. [ ] The formulas are regulated by the Federal Drug Administration as "medical foods," [ ] and the feeding tubes are regulated as medical devices [ ].

497 U.S. at 306–308, 110 S. Ct. at 2866–67.

To many, nutrition and hydration remain symbols of the bonds between human beings; the care we provide to the ones we love includes, at the very least, food and water. For others, the provision of artificial nutrition and hydration has religious and moral significance. Consider the following documents defining the Catholic position on this issue.

UNITED STATES CONFERENCE OF CATHOLIC BISHOPS, ETHICAL AND RELIGIOUS DIRECTIVES FOR CATHOLIC HEALTH CARE SERVICES
(6th ed. 2018).

* * *

The Church's teaching authority has addressed the moral issues concerning medically assisted nutrition and hydration. We are guided on this issue by Catholic teaching against euthanasia, which is "an action or an omission which of itself or by intention causes death, in order that all suffering may in this way be eliminated."[ ] While medically assisted nutrition and hydration are not morally obligatory in certain cases, these forms of basic care should in principle be provided to all patients who need them, including patients diagnosed as being in a "persistent vegetative state" (PVS), because even the most severely debilitated and helpless patient retains the full dignity of a human person and must receive ordinary and proportionate care.

* * *

[DIRECTIVE 58] In principle, there is an obligation to provide patients with food and water, including medically assisted nutrition and hydration for those who cannot take food orally. This obligation extends to patients in chronic and presumably irreversible conditions (e.g., the "persistent vegetative state") who can reasonably be expected to live indefinitely if given such care. [ ] Medically assisted nutrition and hydration become morally optional when they cannot reasonably be expected to prolong life or when they would be "excessively burdensome for the patient or [would] cause significant physical discomfort, for example resulting from complications in the use of the means employed."[ ] For instance, as a patient draws close to inevitable death from an underlying progressive and fatal condition, certain measures to provide nutrition and hydration may become excessively burdensome and therefore not obligatory in light of their very limited ability to prolong life or provide comfort.

* * *

CONGREGATION FOR THE DOCTRINE OF THE FAITH, RESPONSES TO CERTAIN QUESTIONS OF THE UNITED STATES CONFERENCE OF CATHOLIC BISHOPS CONCERNING ARTIFICIAL NUTRITION AND HYDRATION
(2007)

First question: Is the administration of food and water (whether by natural or artificial means) to a patient in a "vegetative state" morally obligatory except when they cannot be assimilated by the patient's body or cannot be administered to the patient without causing significant physical discomfort?

Response: Yes. The administration of food and water even by artificial means is, in principle, an ordinary and proportionate means of preserving life. It is therefore obligatory to the extent to which, and for as long as, it is shown to accomplish its proper finality, which is the hydration and nourishment of the patient. In this way suffering and death by starvation and dehydration are prevented.

Second question: When nutrition and hydration are being supplied by artificial means to a patient in a "permanent vegetative state", may they be discontinued when competent physicians judge with moral certainty that the patient will never recover consciousness?

Response: No. A patient in a "permanent vegetative state" is a person with fundamental human dignity and must, therefore, receive ordinary and proportionate care which includes, in principle, the administration of water and food even by artificial means.

For interpretations of the content and application of this statement within the Roman Catholic tradition, see John Hardt & Kevin O'Rourke, Nutrition and Hydration: The [Congregation for the Doctrine of Faith], In Perspective, 88 Health Progress 1 (2007), arguing, inter alia, that Catholic Canon Law requires that the statement be interpreted strictly as it restricts rights; that the form of the statement has less force than other vehicles for establishing directives; that the use of the term "in principle" indicates that there are exceptions. In particular, in contrast to earlier statements on nutrition and hydration, this statement is specifically confined to circumstances of confirmed diagnosis of PVS and addresses only nutrition and hydration and not other medical interventions. See also Daniel Sulmasy, Preserving Life? The Vatican and PVS, 134 Commonweal (No. 21) 16 (Dec. 7, 2007).

PROBLEM: NOT QUITE PERSISTENT VEGETATIVE STATE

When unhelmeted 57-year-old Tad Gonzales ran his motorcycle into a bridge support post on an interstate highway, he was revived at the scene and rushed to Big Central Hospital. There he underwent several hours of emergency surgery designed to preserve his life and repair the very substantial head injuries he sustained. A few days after the surgery, he began to regain consciousness, and a week later he was able to be removed from the ventilator which was supporting his breathing, although he still needs ventilator assistance from time to time. During his first two weeks in the hospital, Tad showed little improvement. He was not in a coma, but he was only occasionally responsive, and he demonstrated no awareness of Ralph, his partner of twenty-two years, or his two brothers and his parents, even though Tad had always shared a close relationship with all of them.

After two weeks, Big City Hospital transferred Tad to Commercial Affiliated Nursing Home, where he began receiving physical and occupational therapy. After a year of care there, he has shown little improvement. He still does not seem to recognize Ralph, who visits daily, or anyone else. He is able to sit up and his eyes sometimes seem to be following images on a screen. He grunts when he is hungry or uncomfortable. He cannot eat or drink, and he is fed through a feeding tube in his abdomen. He cannot control his bowels or bladder. He has regularly suffered from urinary tract infections and asthma during his nursing home stay, although his need for the ventilator is becoming rarer. On a few, increasingly rare, occasions, his heart stopped beating, but he was resuscitated immediately. Doctors believe that there is little chance of substantial improvement in his condition (although, in the words of one doctor, "Who knows? Anything can happen.") Tad's doctors estimate that his life expectancy could be another twenty years or more.

Tad's doctor and Ralph have developed a good working relationship, and the doctor has called upon Ralph to approve any change in Tad's treatment regimen even though Tad never signed any kind of advance directive. Ralph has now informed the doctor that he believes that Tad would want the use of the feeding tube (and the occasional use of the ventilator) discontinued, and that he would not want to be resuscitated (i.e., if his heart were to stop beating, he would not want health care providers to try to start it again). When the doctor challenged him on this, Ralph respectfully ordered the doctor to terminate feeding, and to note that Tad was not to be mechanically ventilated or resuscitated. Ralph explained that he had spoken with Tad often about "this kind of thing," and that Tad had said that the indignity of being fed, or wearing diapers, or being bed-bound, was not worth the value of life to him. In particular, Ralph remembers Tad describing one of their friends, another motorcyclist who became a quadriplegic and suffered some intellectual impairment after an accident, as "better off dead." Tad and Ralph promised each other that neither would ever let that happen to the other.

Tad's parents and one of his brothers agree that there is no doubt that Tad would want all treatment terminated under these circumstances. Tad's other brother disagrees. As he has articulated it, "How can we know what he would want? He could never have imagined himself in this situation, and we shouldn't read anything into what he said about other people. Maybe he thought those other people could feel more pain than he can."

Tad's doctor has approached you, the hospital counsel, to ask you what she should do. Should she discontinue feeding? The use of the ventilator? Should the hospital pursue an action in court? What position should the hospital take if Ralph, or Tad's dissenting brother, pursues an action in court? How should that action be resolved?

NOTE: THE ROLE OF THE COURT IN RESOLVING DISPUTES ABOUT THE PROVISION OF LIFE-SUSTAINING MEDICAL CARE

The drafters of the Uniform Health-Care Decisions Act make it clear in their comments that one purpose of the statute is to assure that these intimate health care decisions remain within the realm of the patient, the patient's family and close friends, and the health care providers, and that others not be permitted to disrupt that process. The court would very rarely have a role in any decision-making under the Unform Act, and outsiders (including outside organizations) who do not think a patient is adequately protected have no standing to seek judicial intervention. See Protection and Advocacy Sys., Inc. v. Presbyterian Healthcare Servs., 128 N.M. 73, 989 P.2d 890 (1999).

Should courts have a role in resolving disputes about the provision of life-sustaining medical care? On the one hand, there is a fear that the absence of judicial oversight will lead to arbitrary, biased, or discriminatory decisions that end the lives of already vulnerable people. On the other hand, any attempt to bring every case that could result in the termination of life-sustaining treatment to the courts would result in an intolerable caseload and delay the deaths of many patients who desperately seek that relief. In addition, there is little reason to believe that courts have any wisdom that will make them better (or less susceptible to bias) than a patient's family at making these decisions.

Should judicial review of all decisions to terminate life-sustaining treatment be required? Should such judicial review be required in some cases, for example, in cases involving allegations of bias or discrimination? In cases in which there is no written advance directive? In which there is no agreement among family members? In which the patients disagree with the health care providers? In which the health care providers disagree among themselves? In which the decision-maker is self-interested? In which there is an ambiguity in the previous statements of the patient? Is there any way to adequately categorize those cases in which judicial review ought to be required? If judicial review is not required, should some other form of review—by an ethics committee or an independent board, for example—be required in its stead?

When resort to a court is required, what procedure ought to be employed by the court? Should the court's involvement be limited to the appointment of a decision-maker, should the court make the decision itself, or should the court review every decision (or some decisions) made by an appointed decision-maker? Should the action be a special statutory action, an injunction action, or a guardianship? Does the form of the action really make much difference? Should the court always appoint a guardian ad litem for the patient? What would the role of such a guardian be? Every state has a nursing home ombudsman. Should the ombudsman be notified whenever discontinuation of treatment of a nursing home patient is requested? Should the ombudsman participate in every such case?

In In re Guardianship of Hamlin, 102 Wash. 2d 810, 689 P.2d 1372 (1984), the Washington Supreme Court announced two entirely separate processes—one to be followed where there is "total agreement among the patient's family, treating physicians and prognosis committee as to the course of medical treatment," and one to be followed where there is "an incompetent with no known family, who has never made his wishes known." No judicial process or formal guardianship is required in the first case where "the incompetent patient is in . . . a persistent vegetative state with no reasonable chance of recovery and . . . the patient's life is being maintained by life support systems." In the second situation a guardian must be appointed by the court, but that guardian need not obtain judicial confirmation of any particular decision "if the treating physicians and prognosis committee are unanimous that life-sustaining efforts should be withheld or withdrawn and the guardian concurs." Of course, most cases fall between the two extremes discussed in Hamlin.

Who should have standing to commence a judicial action seeking to review a decision to terminate life-sustaining medical treatment? All relatives? Health care providers? Health care institutions? Patient advocacy groups? Right-to-Life or Right-to-Die or disability advocacy groups? Who should be able to join such litigation as a party? Is the Uniform Health-Care Decisions Act approach to this issue—that there will be no judicial hearing unless a relative or health care provider is willing to file an action—the best way of dealing with this issue? See Protection and Advocacy Sys., Inc. v. Presbyterian Healthcare Servs., 128 N.M. 73, 989 P.2d 890 (1999) (no standing in advocacy group to challenge unanimous decision of family members and health care providers).

If there is to be a judicial process, should it be an adversary process? While Chief Justice Rehnquist appeared to think that the adversary process would be helpful in these cases (see Cruzan, above), that part of the opinion gave Justice Stevens pause:

> The Court recognizes that "the state has been involved as an adversary from the beginning" in this case only because Nancy Cruzan "was a patient at a state hospital when this litigation commenced." . . . It seems to me, however, that the Court draws precisely the wrong conclusion from this insight. The Court apparently believes that the absence of the state from the litigation would have created a problem, because agreement

among the family and the independent guardian *ad litem* as to Nancy Cruzan's best interests might have prevented her treatment from becoming the focus of a "truly adversarial" proceeding. [ ] It may reasonably be debated whether some judicial process should be required before life-sustaining treatment is discontinued; this issue has divided the state courts. [ ] . . . I tend, however, to agree . . . that the intervention of the state in these proceedings as an *adversary* is not so much a cure as it is part of the disease.

Cruzan v. Director, Missouri Dept. of Health, 497 U.S. 261, 341, n.13, 110 S. Ct. 2841, 2884, n.13, 111 L. Ed. 2d 224 (1990) (Stevens, J., dissenting).

A decade earlier, the Florida Supreme Court had expressed the same reservations:

Because the issue with its ramifications is fraught with complexity and encompasses the interests of the law, both civil and criminal, medical ethics and social morality, it is not one which is well suited for a solution in an adversary judicial proceeding.

Satz v. Perlmutter, 379 So. 2d 359, 360 (Fla. 1980). See also *Protection and Advocacy System*, cited at the beginning of this note. Are the "advantages" of an adversary proceeding truly advantageous in these agonizing cases? See Nancy Dubler, Conflict and Consensus at the End of Life, in Hastings Ctr. Spec. Rep. on Improving End of Life Care (Jennings et al., eds. 2005); Alan Meisel, The Role of Litigation in End of Life Care: A Reappraisal, in Hastings Ctr. Spec. Rep. on Improving End of Life Care (Jennings et al., eds. 2005).

V. HEALTH CARE DECISION-MAKING FOR CHILDREN

PROBLEM: CHOOSING TO FORGO CANCER TREATMENT

Michael Armstrong was a healthy, socially well-adjusted, intelligent 14-year-old when he discovered that he had testicular cancer that had also produced a mass in his liver. The prognosis was not terribly optimistic: with intensive intervention he would have about a 50% chance of surviving for two years, and a 25% chance of a "cure" (i.e., of surviving five years). "Intensive intervention" would include several months of painful and debilitating chemotherapy, surgery to remove part of his liver and his testes, and a substantial amount of radiation therapy. Without treatment, Michael would probably die within six months.

Michael has informed his oncologist that he has decided to forgo the proposed surgery, even though he recognizes that this will result in his death. He explained that he reached this conclusion after reading everything accessible to him about his cancer and the proposed treatment, after praying with his religious advisor and mentor, and after discussing the issue with his family, friends, and two patients (names provided by the oncologist with the consent of those patients) who had previously undergone the same surgery and chemotherapy. He also admits that the teasing he has taken over the primary location of his disease, and his consequent extreme embarrassment, were not irrelevant factors in his decision.

Michael's parents, who are divorced and have joint legal and physical custody, are split on this issue. His father believes that it is Michael's decision to make, and he supports Michael's decision. His mother insists that the oncologist and the hospital provide the proposed treatment. In addition, a social worker in the local child protective services office (which was informed about the case by one of Michael's teachers) has informed all of the parties that, in her opinion, Michael would be a neglected child if the treatment were not administered.

Michael's parents have now filed cross petitions seeking to vindicate their positions. Michael has filed a petition as well. The oncologist and the hospital have filed a declaratory judgment action seeking an order of the court before taking any action, and the child protective services agency has filed a neglect petition against the father. All of these actions have been consolidated and all assigned to the same trial court judge to resolve. How should the judge proceed? What kind of hearing, if any, should the judge hold? How should she rule?

NEWMARK V. WILLIAMS
Supreme Court of Delaware, 1991.
588 A.2d 1108.

MOORE, JUSTICE.

Colin Newmark, a three year old child, faced death from a deadly aggressive and advanced form of pediatric cancer known as Burkitt's Lymphoma. We were presented with a clash of interests between medical science, Colin's tragic plight, the unquestioned sincerity of his parents' religious beliefs as Christian Scientists, and the legal right of the State to protect dependent children from perceived neglect when medical treatment is withheld on religious grounds. The Delaware Division of Child Protective Services ("DCPS") petitioned the Family Court for temporary custody of Colin to authorize the Alfred I. DuPont Institute ("DuPont Institute"), a nationally recognized children's hospital, to treat Colin's condition with chemotherapy. His parents, Morris and Kara Newmark, are well educated and economically prosperous. As members of the First Church of Christ, Scientist ("Christian Science") they rejected medical treatment proposed for Colin, preferring instead a course of spiritual aid and prayer. The parents rely upon provisions of Delaware law, which exempt those who treat their children's illnesses "solely by spiritual means" from the abuse and neglect statutes. Thus, they opposed the State's petition. [ ] The Newmarks also claimed that removing Colin from their custody would violate their First Amendment right, guaranteed under the United States Constitution, to freely exercise their religion.

* * *

[The Court explained how the Newmarks discovered that Colin suffered from Burkitt's Lymphoma, an extremely fast growing and dangerous form of pediatric cancer, when they took him to the doctor "out of concern for their potential criminal liability . . . ."]

We have concluded that Colin was not an abused or neglected child under Delaware law. Parents enjoy a well established legal right to make important decisions for their children. Although this right is not absolute, the State has the burden of proving by clear and convincing evidence that intervening in the parent-child relationship is necessary to ensure the safety or health of the child, or to protect the public at large. DCPS did not meet this heavy burden. This is especially true where the purpose of the custody petition was to administer, over the objections of Colin's parents, an extremely risky, toxic and dangerously life threatening medical treatment offering less than a 40% chance for "success".

* * *

Dr. Meek [an attending physician and board-certified pediatric hematologist-oncologist] opined that chemotherapy offered a 40% chance of "curing" Colin's illness. She concluded that he would die within six to eight months without treatment. The Newmarks . . . advised Dr. Meek that they would place him under the care of a Christian Science practitioner and reject all medical treatment for their son. Accordingly, they refused to authorize the chemotherapy. There was no doubt that the Newmarks sincerely believed, as part of their religious beliefs, that the tenets of their faith provided an effective treatment.

II.

We start with an overview of the relevant Delaware statutory provisions. Delaware law defines a neglected child as:

[A] child whose physical, mental or emotional health and well-being is threatened or impaired because of inadequate care and protection by the child's custodian, who has the ability and financial means to provide for the care but does not or will not provide adequate care; or a child who has been abused or neglected . . .

[The statute] further defines abuse and neglect as:

Physical injury by other than accidental means, injury resulting in a mental or emotional condition which is a result of abuse or neglect, negligent treatment, sexual abuse, maltreatment, mistreatment, nontreatment, exploitation or abandonment, of a child under the age of 18. (Emphasis added).

Sections of the Delaware Code, however, contain spiritual treatment exemptions which directly affect Christian Scientists. Specifically, the exemptions state:

No child who in good faith is under treatment solely by spiritual means through prayer in accordance with the tenets and practices of a recognized church or religious denomination by a duly accredited practitioner thereof shall for that reason alone be considered a neglected child for purposes of this chapter.

[ ] These exceptions reflect the intention of the Delaware General Assembly to provide a "safe harbor" for parents, like the Newmarks, to pursue their own religious beliefs. [We recognize] that the spiritual treatment exemptions reflect, in part, "the policy of this State with respect to the quality of life" a desperately ill child might have in the caring and loving atmosphere of his or her family, versus the sterile hospital environment demanded by physicians seeking to prescribe excruciating, and life threatening, treatments of doubtful efficacy.

. . . [W]e recognize the possibility that the spiritual treatment exemptions may violate the ban against the establishment of an official State religion guaranteed under both the Federal and Delaware Constitutions. Clearly, in both reality and practical effect, the language providing an exemption only to those individuals practicing "in accordance" with the "practices of a recognized church or religious denomination by a duly accredited practitioner thereof" is intended for the principal benefit of Christian Scientists. Our concern is that it possibly forces us to impermissibly determine the validity of an individual's own religious beliefs.

Neither party challenged the constitutionality of the spiritual treatment exemptions in either the Family Court or on appeal. Thus, except to recognize that the issue is far more complicated than was originally presented to us, we must leave such questions for another day.

III.

Addressing the facts of this case, we turn to the novel legal question whether, under any circumstances, Colin was a neglected child when his parents refused to accede to medical demands that he receive a radical form of chemotherapy having only a forty percent chance of success. [The court then explained that it would apply a balancing test to answer this question.]

* * *

A.

Any balancing test must begin with the parental interest. The primacy of the familial unit is a bedrock principle of law. [ ] We have repeatedly emphasized that the parental right is sacred which can be invaded for only the most compelling reasons.

* * *

Courts have also recognized that the essential element of preserving the integrity of the family is maintaining the autonomy of the parent-child relationship. [ ] In Prince v. Commonwealth of Massachusetts, [ ] the United States Supreme Court announced:

> It is cardinal with us that the custody, care and nurture of the child reside first in the parents, whose primary function and freedom include preparation for obligations the state can neither supply nor hinder. [ ]

Parental autonomy to care for children free from government interference therefore satisfies a child's need for continuity and thus ensures his or her psychological and physical well-being. [ ]

Parental authority to make fundamental decisions for minor children is also a recognized common law principle. A doctor commits the tort of battery if he or she performs an operation under normal circumstances without the informed consent of the patient. [ ] Tort law also assumes that a child does not have the capacity to consent to an operation in most situations. [ ] Thus, the common law recognizes that the only party capable of authorizing medical treatment for a minor in "normal" circumstances is usually his parent or guardian. [ ]

Courts, therefore, give great deference to parental decisions involving minor children. In many circumstances the State simply is not an adequate surrogate for the judgment of a loving, nurturing parent. [ ] As one commentator aptly recognized, the "law does not have the capacity to supervise the delicately complex interpersonal bonds between parent and child." [ ]

B.

We also recognize that parental autonomy over minor children is not an absolute right. Clearly, the State can intervene in the parent-child relationship where the health and safety of the child and the public at large are in jeopardy. [ ] Accordingly, the State, under the doctrine of parens patriae, has a special duty to protect its youngest and most helpless citizens.

The parens patriae doctrine is a derivation of the common law giving the State the right to act on behalf of minor children in certain property and marital disputes. [ ] More recently, courts have accepted the doctrine of parens patriae to justify State intervention in cases of parental religious objections to medical treatment of minor children's life threatening conditions. [ ] The Supreme Court of the United States [pointed out] that parental autonomy, under the guise of the parents' religious freedom, was not unlimited. [ ] Rather, the Court held:

> Parents may be free to become martyrs themselves. But it does not follow they are free, in identical circumstances, to make martyrs of their children before they have reached the age of full and legal discretion when they can make that choice for themselves. [ ]

The basic principle underlying the parens patriae doctrine is the State's interest in preserving human life. [ ] Yet this interest and the parens patriae doctrine are not unlimited. In its recent Cruzan opinion, the Supreme Court of the United States announced that the state's interest in preserving life must "be weighed against the constitutionally protected interests of the individual." [ ]

The individual interests at stake here include both the Newmarks' right to decide what is best for Colin and Colin's own right to life. We have already considered the Newmarks' stake in this case and its relationship to the parens patriae doctrine. The resolution of the issues here, however, is incomplete without a discussion of Colin's interests.

C.

All children indisputably have the right to enjoy a full and healthy life. Colin, a three year old boy, unfortunately lacked the ability to reach a detached, informed decision regarding his own medical care. This Court must therefore substitute its own objective judgment to determine what is in Colin's "best interests." [ ]

There are two basic inquiries when a dispute involves chemotherapy treatment over parents' religious objections. The court must first consider the effectiveness of the treatment and determine the child's chances of survival with and without medical care. [ ] The court must then consider the nature of the treatments and their effect on the child. [ ]

The "best interests" analysis is hardly unique or novel. Federal and State courts have unhesitatingly authorized medical treatment over a parent's religious objection when the treatment is relatively innocuous in comparison to the dangers of withholding medical care. [ ] Accordingly, courts are reluctant to authorize medical care over parental objection when the child is not suffering a life threatening or potential life threatening illness. [ ]

The linchpin in all cases discussing the "best interests of a child," when a parent refuses to authorize medical care, is an evaluation of the risk of the procedure compared to its potential success. This analysis is consistent with the principle that State intervention in the parent-child relationship is only justifiable under compelling conditions. [ ] The State's interest in forcing a minor to undergo medical care diminishes as the risks of treatment increase and its benefits decrease.

* * *

Applying the foregoing considerations to the "best interests standard" here, the State's petition must be denied. The egregious facts of this case indicate that Colin's proposed medical treatment was highly invasive, painful, involved terrible temporary and potentially permanent side effects, posed an unacceptably low chance of success, and a high risk that the treatment itself would cause his death. The State's authority to intervene in this case, therefore, cannot outweigh the Newmarks' parental prerogative and Colin's inherent right to enjoy at least a modicum of human dignity in the short time that was left to him.

IV.

Dr. Meek originally diagnosed Colin's condition as Burkitt's Lymphoma. She testified that the cancer was "a very bad tumor" in an advanced disseminated state and not localized to only one section of the body. She accordingly recommended that the hospital begin an "extremely intensive" chemotherapy program scheduled to extend for at least six months.

[The court then explained how intensive such a chemotherapy program would be, and how such a treatment program would itself threaten Colin's life.]

Dr. Meek prescribed "maximum" doses of at least six different types of cancer-fighting drugs during Colin's chemotherapy. This proposed "maximum" treatment represented the most aggressive form of cancer therapy short of a bone marrow transplant. The side effects would include hair loss, reduced immunological function creating a high risk of infection in the patient, and certain neurological problems. The drugs also are toxic to bone marrow.

The record demonstrates that this form of chemotherapy also would adversely affect other parts of Colin's body.

* * *

The physicians planned to administer the chemotherapy in cycles, each of which would bring Colin near death. Then they would wait until Colin's body recovered sufficiently before introducing more drugs.

* * *

Dr. Meek also wanted the State to place Colin in a foster home after the initial phases of hospital treatment. Children require intensive home monitoring during chemotherapy. For example, Dr. Meek testified that a usually low grade fever for a healthy child could indicate the presence of a potentially deadly infection in a child cancer patient. She believed that the Newmarks, although well educated and financially responsible, were incapable of providing this intensive care because of their firm religious objections to medical treatment.

Dr. Meek ultimately admitted that there was a real possibility that the chemotherapy could kill Colin. In fact, assuming the treatment did not itself prove fatal, she offered Colin at "best" a 40% chance that he would "survive."[12] Dr. Meek additionally could not accurately predict whether, if Colin completed the therapy, he would subsequently suffer additional tumors.

A.

No American court, even in the most egregious case, has ever authorized the State to remove a child from the loving, nurturing care of his parents and subject him, over parental objection, to an invasive regimen of treatment which offered, as Dr. Meek defined the term, only a forty percent chance of "survival."

* * *

B.

The aggressive form of chemotherapy that Dr. Meek prescribed for Colin was more likely to fail than succeed. The proposed treatment was also highly invasive and could have independently caused Colin's death. Dr. Meek also wanted to take Colin away from his parents and family during the treatment phase and place the boy in a foster home. This certainly would have caused Colin severe emotional difficulties given his medical condition, tender age, and the unquestioned close bond between Colin and his family.

In sum, Colin's best interests were served by permitting the Newmarks to retain custody of their child. Parents must have the right at some point to reject medical treatment for their child. Under all of the circumstances here, this clearly is such a case. The State's important and legitimate role in safeguarding the interests of minor children diminishes in the face of this egregious record.

Parents undertake an awesome responsibility in raising and caring for their children. No doubt a parent's decision to withhold medical care is both deeply personal and soul wrenching. It need not be made worse by the invasions which both the State and medical profession sought on this record. Colin's ultimate fate therefore rested with his parents and their faith.

---

[12] Dr. Meek testified that there was no available medical data to conclude that Colin could survive to adulthood. Rather, she stated that the term "survival", as applied to victims of leukemia or lymphoma, refers only to the probability that the patient will live two years after chemotherapy without a recurrence of cancer.

NOTES AND QUESTIONS

1.　*Majority Approach.* Most judicial encounters with parents' rights to refuse medical treatment for their children follow the pattern established in *Newmark.* The court first announces the legal presumption that parents can make important decisions, including health care decisions, for their children. This is a common law right in every state, and it is protected by the U.S. Constitution as well. See Troxel v. Granville, 528 U.S. 1151, 120 S. Ct. 1225, 145 L. Ed. 2d 1068 (2000), Parham v. J.R., 442 U.S. 584, 99 S. Ct. 2493, 61 L. Ed. 2d 101 (1979); Santosky v. Kramer, 455 U.S. 745, 102 S. Ct. 1388, 71 L. Ed. 2d 599 (1982). However, this presumption can be overcome if the conditions of the state's child protective services statute are met.

Most state child abuse and neglect statutes are similar to the Delaware statute discussed in *Newmark,* and they provide—with greater or lesser specificity—that the parents' failure to provide adequate health care for their children constitutes neglect. If parents neglect their children, the state may commence a legal process (as the state did in *Newmark*) to obtain legal custody of the child to assure that the child is no longer medically neglected. The state need not take physical custody of the child, and the child can (as a technical legal matter) remain in the physical custody of the parents even while receiving the medical care to which the parents object.

2.　*What Standard Did the Court Apply?* What is the legal test that the court applied to determine that Colin Newmark should not be ordered to undergo the proposed chemotherapy? Did the court determine that it was in Colin's best interests not to undergo this treatment, or did the court apply a balancing test and determine that the parents' interest in maintaining custody of their child (and in making health care decisions for their child) outweighed the state's interest in providing Colin with potentially life-saving treatment? The choice between these two alternative forms of analysis may make no difference in this particular case, but can you think of a case in which the choice between these two legal positions would be dispositive?

3.　*Age of the Child.* As a general matter, courts reviewing young children's decisions to forgo life-sustaining treatment apply the "best interests" test (with a substantial bow to the articulated desires of the parents, who are deemed to have the best interests of their children in mind). While the application of the "substituted judgment" standard seems appropriate as the children approach majority, a few states attempt to apply the "substituted judgment" theory to very young children, too. Compare, e.g., Care and Protection of Beth, 412 Mass. 188, 587 N.E.2d 1377 (1992) and Custody of a Minor, 385 Mass. 697, 434 N.E.2d 601 (1982) (applying the substituted judgment test) with In re K.I., B.I. and D.M., 735 A.2d 448 (D.C. 1999) (applying the best interests test). See In re Christopher I., 106 Cal. App. 4th 533, 131 Cal. Rptr. 2d 122 (2003) (applying the best interests test to a child in the custody of the state).

Does the "substituted judgment" standard make any sense when it is applied to infants or very young children? Although it may be absurd to search for the values, interests, desires, and expectancies of a newborn or a three-month old, or even a four-year old, might not a seven- or eight-year-old child's parents be able to talk about all of those attributes? Of course, it is hard to imagine anyone other than the parents (or their legal substitutes) being able to evaluate such factors. Does that mean that a court's decision to apply a substituted judgment standard to small children amounts to a *de facto* decision to defer to the parent's wishes?

In Matter of AB, 196 Misc. 2d 940, 768 N.Y.S.2d 256 (Sup. Ct. 2003), a New York trial court confirmed the right of a mother of a child in persistent vegetative state to discontinue life-sustaining medical treatment—but only because the best interests test had been met:

> Thus, this Court holds that it is [the mother's] right, as a parent and natural guardian of AB, to exercise her responsibility and prerogative to make this decision to withhold extraordinary life-prolonging measures, with the assistance of treating physicians. CD's parental choice, made in the best interest of her child, to allow her daughter to pass away peacefully and with dignity are to be honored. This decision respects the values of family privacy without compromising a patient's rights or overstepping the State's legitimate interests.

> Having sought judicial intervention, CD has proven by clear and convincing evidence that it is in the best interest of her child to remove the mechanical ventilator. As CD sought intervention, this Court has employed the best interest standard, weighing whether the burdens of prolonged life outweigh any physical pleasure, emotional enjoyment, or intellectual satisfaction that the child may still be able to derive from life.

768 N.Y.S.2d at 271–272. In the *Matter of AB* case, AB's mother had sought a court order only because the hospital refused to permit the removal of treatment unless a court order supported that decision. Is the mother free to make health care decisions for her child—but only if the court agrees that the decisions are in the best interest of the child? Who is the real decision-maker in this case?

In a subsequent case, ethics consultants, a guardian ad litem appointed for the child by the court, the institution's ethics committee, and the parents all agreed that the termination of treatment was proper. Because one board eligible doctor and one nurse at the institution thought that the treatment would not constitute an "extraordinary burden" on the patient, though, the trial judge determined that the consensus determination of all other interested parties did not rise to the level of clear and convincing evidence that removal of the treatment was in the best interest of the teenager. See In re D.H., 15 Misc. 3d 565, 834 N.Y.S.2d 623 (Sup. 2007).

4.   *Determining the Best Interest of a Child.* How is a court to determine what is in the best interest of a child? Does the court look to its own values, to values derived from community sources, to values held by the child's family, or elsewhere? For example, in the case of a neurologically devastated child with

no cognitive facilities and no hope of regaining any—a child who is entirely insensate and cannot feel pleasure or pain—is the terminal removal of a feeding tube or a ventilator *always* in the child's best interest, *never* in the child's best interest, or *sometimes* in the child's best interest? If you chose "sometimes," what other factors are relevant?

In *Matter of AB*, the court depended on standards provided by the New York Health Care Decisions for Mentally Retarded Persons Act and AMA guidelines. The AMA best interests guidelines, which are designed to address decision-making for newborns, are available at American Medical Association, Code of Medical Ethics, Opinion 2.2.4, Treatment Decisions for Seriously Ill Newborns (2016). In In re Christopher I., 106 Cal. App. 4th 533, 131 Cal. Rptr. 2d 122 (Cal. App. 2003), the court announced an exhaustive list of factors, drawn from local and national state court guidelines:

> We conclude that a court making the decision of whether to withhold or withdraw life-sustaining medical treatment from a dependent child should consider the following factors: (1) the child's present levels of physical, sensory, emotional and cognitive functioning; (2) the quality of life, life expectancy and prognosis for recovery with and without treatment, including the futility of continued treatment; (3) the various treatment options, and the risks, side effects, and benefits of each; (4) the nature and degree of physical pain or suffering resulting from the medical condition; (5) whether the medical treatment being provided is causing or may cause pain, suffering, or serious complications; (6) the pain or suffering to the child if the medical treatment is withdrawn; (7) whether any particular treatment would be proportionate or disproportionate in terms of the benefits to be gained by the child versus the burdens caused to the child; (8) the likelihood that pain or suffering resulting from withholding or withdrawal of treatment could be avoided or minimized; (9) the degree of humiliation, dependence and loss of dignity resulting from the condition and treatment; (10) the opinions of the family, the reasons behind those opinions, and the reasons why the family either has no opinion or cannot agree on a course of treatment; (11) the motivations of the family in advocating a particular course of treatment; and (12) the child's preference, if it can be ascertained, for treatment.

131 Cal. Rptr. at 551, 552. How helpful are these lists of factors? What factors do you believe a court should employ in determining if the removal of life-sustaining medical care is in the best interest of a child?

5.   *Mature Minor Doctrine*. Parental rights to make health care decisions for their children are terminated when the child reaches majority. Those rights may be diminished or terminated earlier if the child is a "mature minor," a condition governed by statute (in some states) or the common law (in other states) or both. At the very least, a child is a mature minor when he can "present clear and convincing evidence that he [is] mature enough to exercise an adult's judgment and [understand] the consequences of his decision." *Newmark*, at 1116 n. 9. See In re E.G., 133 Ill. 2d 98, 139 Ill. Dec. 810, 549

N.E.2d 322 (1989), where a Jehovah's Witness child "just months shy of her eighteenth birthday" was found to be sufficiently mature to choose to forgo a blood transfusion in a case with a rather slim chance of long-term survival. See also Belcher v. Charleston Area Med. Ctr., 188 W. Va. 105, 422 S.E.2d 827 (1992) (17-year-old may have been mature enough to demand a DNR order; the issue was for the jury in a subsequent informed consent action). For a discussion of the propriety of statutory recognition of the decision-making authority of teenagers, see Molly J. Walker Wilson, "Legal and Psychological Considerations in Adolescents' End-Of-Life Choices" 109 Nw. U. L. Rev. Online 203 (2015); Rhonda Hartman, Coming of Age: Devising Legislation for Adolescent Medical Decision-Making, 28 Am. J.L. & Med. 409 (2002).

Courts may give some weight to the statements of older children even if those courts are reluctant to declare those children "emancipated" or "mature minors." Although children under 16 typically are not found sufficiently mature to independently choose to forgo life-sustaining treatment, many courts have given considerable weight to the statements made by children considerably younger than that. See, e.g., In re Guardianship of Crum, 61 Ohio Misc. 2d 596, 580 N.E.2d 876 (Prob.Ct., Franklin Co. 1991). See also the discussion of children's assent to participation in research in Chapter 20.

At least one state explicitly authorizes children who understand the relevant health care factors to make their own decisions with regard to end-of-life care, even if they have not been emancipated and are not authorized to make other health care decisions. See N.M. Stat. Ann. § 24–7A–6.1(C), providing:

> [I]f an unemancipated minor has capacity sufficient to understand the nature of that unemancipated minor's medical condition, the risks and benefits of treatment and the contemplated decision to withhold or withdraw life-sustaining treatment, that unemancipated minor shall have the authority to withhold or withdraw life-sustaining treatment.

Should a child who cannot consent to an appendectomy under state law have the authority to consent to removal of life-sustaining treatment? Are children who are most likely to meet the statutory standard—those teenagers who have spent years suffering from a degenerative disease, for example—more likely than others to be able to recognize and apply their own life values to these important decisions? For a particularly interesting account of the roles of parents and children in consenting to body-reshaping medical care, see Alicia Ouellette, Shaping Parental Authority over Children's Bodies, 85 Ind. L.J. 955 (2010).

6. *Overriding Parental Religious Objections.* As the *Newmark* court explained, courts have "unhesitatingly authorized medical treatment over a parent's religious objection when the treatment is relatively innocuous in comparison with the dangers of withholding medical care." Of course, what constitutes an innocuous treatment for most of us might constitute a very serious intrusion for others. Most people are not terribly concerned by the prospect of a blood transfusion; for others, it may eliminate a possibility of

eternal salvation. Despite this, courts have not flinched when they have been presented with requests for treatment that is "medically necessary"—i.e., when the child will surely die if the treatment is not provided, and just as surely will live if the treatment is provided. Courts routinely and consistently order blood transfusions for children of objecting Jehovah's Witness parents, at least when they meet this requirement of medical necessity. In this sense, the courts treat Jehovah's Witness children very differently from Jehovah's Witness adults. On the other hand, courts generally do not order treatment for children who do not face life-threatening conditions. The hardest cases, like the *Newmark* case, are those cases in which the proposed treatment is highly invasive, but the child faces a life-threatening condition. As the chance of temporary remission and long-term cure increases, the courts are more likely to order the treatment. Is this consistent with evaluation under the factors listed in note 4, above?

7. *When Parents Seek Treatment for Children.* While courts regularly face parental decisions that their children not receive treatment, they are sometimes confronted with the reverse situation. In In re K.I., B.I. and D.M., 735 A.2d 448 (D.C. 1999) the District of Columbia Court of Appeals approved a DNR order for a neglected, comatose two-year-old child who was born "neurologically devastated." The child was taken from his intoxicated mother after he had been left alone for days without his necessary heart and lung medication. The mother opposed the hospital's request that the child be given DNR status. Applying the best interests (rather than the substituted judgment) standard, the court recognized that the mother might be criminally liable for homicide if the child were to die, and it thus disregarded her request that there be aggressive attempts at resuscitation. See also Care and Protection of Sharlene, 445 Mass. 756, 840 N.E.2d 915 (2006).

Can you imagine other circumstances in which a parent might inappropriately demand treatment for a child? Should these cases be treated any differently from those in which the parent denies consent for (rather than demands) the recommended care? See also *In re Christopher I*, above, in which the father, whose abuse had resulted in the child's serious neurological injury, argued that the child's life should be maintained, and J.N. v. Superior Court, 156 Cal. App. 4th 523, 67 Cal. Rptr. 3d 384 (Cal. App. 2007), where the court ultimately permitted the withdrawal of a breathing tube but not the entry of a "do not attempt resuscitation" order in an abuse and neglect case involving an arguably criminally "shaken baby." A family court also allowed for the de-escalation of treatment of a child placed in the custody of the state due to abuse and neglect in Hunt v. Div. of Family Servs., 146 A.3d 1051 (Del. 2015). See also Division of Family Services v. Truselo, 846 A.2d 256 (Del. Fam. Ct. 2000).

8. *"Spiritual Healing."* Like Delaware, most states have promulgated statutes that provide that "spiritual healing" *per se* cannot constitute child abuse or neglect for purposes of the state's criminal or child protective services statutes. In fact, for some time the existence of such protections was required as a condition of receiving some forms of federal funding. These spiritual healing statutes were the consequence of lobbying by the Christian Science

church, and they were written using terms (e.g., "accredited practitioner") that have well defined meanings within that church. Are such statutes constitutional? Might they violate the Establishment Clause of the First Amendment because they give a preference to Christian Scientists and protect them in ways that they do not protect others? Is it relevant that the statute only protects members of "recognized" religions, and that the state is called upon to determine which religions it will "recognize"? Might they violate the Establishment Clause because they disfavor children within certain religious communities?

Most commentators who have considered the issue have determined that these statutes are not constitutional (at least as they are applied to civil abuse and neglect proceedings) because they violate either the Establishment Clause or the Equal Protection Clause of the Fourteenth Amendment. For good accounts of the best arguments on this issue, see Shaakirrah R. Sanders, Religious Healing Exemptions and the Jurisprudential Gap Between Substantive Due Process and Free Exercise Rights, 8 U.C. Irvine L. Rev. 633 (2018); Ann MacLean Massie, The Religion Clauses and Parental Health Care Decision-making for Children: Suggestions for a New Approach, 21 Hastings Const. L. Q. 725 (1994). See also State v. Miskimens, 22 Ohio Misc. 2d 43, 490 N.E.2d 931 (Com. Pl. 1984); Walker v. Superior Court, 222 Cal. Rptr. 87 (Cal. App. 1986), aff'd 47 Cal. 3d 112, 253 Cal. Rptr. 1, 763 P.2d 852 (1988).

9.   *Decision-Making for Newborns.* The law generally views decision-making for newborns as a separate inquiry from decision-making for other children. Questions about the propriety of discontinuing treatment for newborns and infants often revolve around whether denying treatment would constitute discrimination based on the newborn's medical condition. During the 1980s, the case of Baby Doe focused attention on denial of care to seriously ill newborns based on disability. In 1983, Baby Doe was born with Down syndrome and a tracheoesophageal fistula that would require repair to allow him to consume nutrition orally. The parents decided not to authorize the necessary surgery because of the Down syndrome, and the baby was given phenobarbital and morphine until he died, six days after birth. A lawsuit by the hospital in the local children's court was rendered moot by Baby Doe's death.

Several political groups, including right-to-life groups and disability advocacy groups, were outraged by the circumstances of Baby Doe's death. The Secretary of HHS issued emergency regulations pursuant to Section 504 of the federal Rehabilitation Act, discussed in Chapter 6, to assure that no hospital would deny treatment to seriously ill newborns based on disability. After a furious political battle, a compromise was reached in the form of the Child Abuse Amendments of 1984, 42 U.S.C.A. § 5102, that conditions each state's receipt of some federal funding on the maintenance of procedures for dealing with reports of the medical neglect of newborns. Regulations issued under the Child Abuse Amendments interpret "medical neglect" to include "the withholding of medically indicated treatment from a disabled infant with a life threatening condition." 45 C.F.R. § 1340.15(b)(1). Further, the regulations provide that the " 'withholding of medically indicated treatment' means the failure to respond to the infant's life threatening conditions by providing treatment (including appropriate nutrition, hydration, and medication) which in the treating physicians' . . . reasonable medical judgment will be most likely to be effective in ameliorating or correcting all such conditions." 45 C.F.R. § 1340.15(b)(2). There is no obligation to provide care to an infant who is "chronically and irreversibly comatose," when the treatment would "merely prolong the dying process" of the infant and not ameliorate or correct the underlying medical problem (and thus be futile), or when the treatment would be "virtually futile" and "inhumane." *Id.*

PROBLEM: CONJOINED TWINS

After a woman was diagnosed as carrying conjoined twins, she left her home village of Xaghra on the Mediterranean island of Gozo to seek medical care at a hospital in the United Kingdom well known for its care of such birth anomalies. At birth, it was clear that one baby's heart and lungs were providing for the circulation in both babies. That baby, Jodie, was generally healthy, while her conjoined sibling, Mary, suffered from severe brain damage as well as other substantial disabilities. The doctors concluded that Jodie could lead a fairly normal life if she were separated from her sister and provided a series of reconstructive surgeries. Of course, the separation would result in Mary's immediate death. Alternatively, the failure to separate the twins would result in both of their deaths within the next several months.

The devout Catholic parents denied consent for the surgery, saying "[w]e cannot begin to accept or contemplate that one of our children should die to enable the other one to survive." Others also pointed out that the decision to allow Mary to die during the separation surgery could be met with horror in Xaghra and make it very difficult for the family to return home. The physicians, however, were distressed that both children would be allowed to die when one could be saved, and they sought an order from the court to authorize the separation surgery.

Would it be homicide to do the surgery with the certain knowledge that it would result in Mary's death? Is it medical neglect to deny consent to surgery that will save one child but result in the death of the second? Should the decision be left to the parents, or should the state intervene and exercise its *parens patriae* authority? What would you do if you were (1) a parent of these children? (2) the primary care physician for these children? (3) the judge before whom the case was presented?

The court was well briefed in this case. In addition to counsel retained by the parents and the public health service, a guardian ad litem was appointed for each child. What position should each of those guardians ad litem have taken? For description of this case (and how it came out), see Jacob Appel, Recent Developments in Health Law, 28 J.L. Med. & Ethics 312 (2000); Alexander MacLeod, Medical, Religious Values Clash Over Conjoined Twins, Christian Science Monitor, September 29, 2000, p. 7.

VI.   "FUTILE" TREATMENT

BETANCOURT V. TRINITAS HOSPITAL
Superior Court of New Jersey, Appellate Division, 2010.
1 A.3d 823.

PER CURIAM.

* * *

. . . On January 22, 2008, Rueben [Betancourt] underwent surgery at defendant to remove a malignant tumor from his thymus gland. . . . [T]he surgery went well, but while Rueben was recovering in the post-operative intensive care unit, the ventilation tube that was supplying him with oxygen somehow became dislodged. As a result, his brain was deprived of oxygen, and he developed anoxic encephalopathy, a condition that left him in a persistent vegetative state.

Rueben was subsequently discharged from defendant and admitted to other facilities that attempted rehabilitative treatments. He was readmitted to defendant on July 3, 2008, however, with a diagnosis of renal failure. Further attempts at placement in another facility proved fruitless, and he remained at defendant until his death on May 29, 2009.

At the time of his death, Rueben had not executed an advanced directive under the New Jersey Advanced Directives for Health Care Act. [] He had neither designated a health care representative nor memorialized "specific wishes regarding the provision, withholding or withdrawal of any form of health care, including life-sustaining treatment." []

Witnesses for both parties to the dispute presented disparate views of Rueben's condition, the impact of treatment and prognosis. At the hearing, Rueben's attending physician, Dr. Arthur E. Millman, indicated that Rueben was a seventy-three-year-old man who was suffering from multi-system organ failure; his kidneys had failed, his lungs had failed, he was intermittently septic, he had hypertensive heart disease and congestive heart disease, and his skin was breaking down. He had "truly horrific decubitus ulcers" that had progressed to the bone, developing into osteomyelitis. Rueben was on a ventilator and received renal dialysis three times per week; he was fed through a tube into his stomach, given antibiotics and was turned frequently in his bed.

Millman stated that Rueben's most overwhelming problem was his permanent anoxic encephalopathy. He described Rueben's neurological state as "non-cognitive" with no higher mental functioning. He did believe, however, that Rueben was responsive to pain because he had personally witnessed Rueben's reactions to it. There had been no change in Rueben's neurological condition since he was admitted in July 2008, and Millman believed that the likelihood of his return to cognizant function was "virtually zero."

Dr. Bernard Schanzer, Chief of Neurology at defendant, corroborated most of Millman's views concerning Rueben's neurological condition. He explained that the cortical part of Rueben's brain had been irreversibly damaged. As a result, Rueben was in a permanent vegetative state, unable to speak or respond to verbal cues, and although Rueben's eyes were open and he appeared awake, he was not alert or aware of his environment. Schanzer disagreed with Millman, however, concerning Rueben's ability to experience pain. He believed that Rueben did not feel pain, and Rueben's responses to stimuli were due to basic reflexes of the brain stem and spinal cord. He opined that there was no chance that Rueben would ever regain a cognitive state.

Dr. Maria Silva Khazaei, a nephrologist, concluded that Rueben was suffering from end-stage renal disease, and there was no likelihood of improvement. She opined that it was contrary to accepted standards of medical care to continue dialysis treatments because they only prolonged Rueben's dying process.

Not surprisingly, plaintiff's consulting nephrologist had a different opinion. Dr. Carl Goldstein, a nephrologist retained by plaintiff, stated that Rueben's current plan of dialysis "comports in every way with the prevailing standards of care." He explained that the dialysis had been effective in removing excess fluid and waste products from Rueben's body. Rueben was tolerating the treatment well, and it was not harmful or dangerous to him.

Dr. William J. McHugh, Medical Director at defendant, was a member of the hospital's prognosis committee. The committee had been consulted concerning the efficacy of continuing Rueben's treatment; as a result, McHugh reviewed many, but not all, of the relevant medical records. He concluded that Rueben had "no outlook" because no affirmative treatment would improve his condition. As opposed to Millman, who believed that Rueben would probably die within a matter of months regardless of continued treatment, McHugh stated that Rueben's death "may take some time." In fact, he opined that if treatment were continued at the present level, Rueben "could go on for quite a while." On cross-examination, McHugh admitted that Rueben's present medical treatment was harmful only in the sense that the doctors were continuing to treat a hopeless situation.

Other members of the hospital's prognosis committee weighed in as well. Dr. Paul Veiana, president of the defendant's medical staff, examined Rueben the day before the hearing while Rueben was "wheeling" down to dialysis. Based on his review, he concluded that the doctors were not treating Rueben—they were just treating a body. He stated that the everyday drawing of blood and injections violated Rueben's body, and as a Christian, he believed that a body should not be so desecrated.

On several occasions, the hospital administration sought agreement from Rueben's family to place a DNR order and cease dialysis treatment, but they staunchly refused. It also made "exhaustive efforts" to transfer Rueben to another facility, but no other facility was willing to accept him. Ultimately, defendant acted unilaterally, placing the DNR order in Rueben's chart as well as surgically removing a dialysis port from Rueben's body.

At the hearing [on a motion to appoint plaintiff, Rueben's daughter Jacqueline Betancourt, as Rueben's guardian and for a temporary restraining order enjoining the hospital from withholding treatment], plaintiff provided information about Rueben. Before his illness, Rueben lived with his wife and his two adult sons. Plaintiff resided next door and saw her father every day. The family had always been very close, and Rueben was "dedicated" to his wife and children.

Plaintiff described Rueben's history of medical treatment at the hospital, asserting that it was the hospital's fault that he suffered a brain injury. She visited her father in the hospital almost daily and saw him make movements and gestures that led her to believe that he was awake and alert. She did not, however, believe that he was suffering. The family determined that they did not want a DNR order placed in Rueben's chart and did not want the dialysis treatment to be stopped. Rather, they wanted to make the decision as to whether Rueben was "ready to go." Plaintiff explained: "[M]y father is a fighter. He will not give up."

Robin, Rueben's thirty-six-year-old son, offered that his father was his "only . . . real friend" and that he loved him very much. He recalled, anecdotally, that he and his father had discussed the Terri Schiavo case when it was in the news, and his father had said that it was the right of Schiavo's parents—not her doctors—to decide what to do. Robin stated that his father reacted to him during hospital visits, and that those reactions were not simply reflexes. He described how his father had different facial expressions depending on what was happening around him and how his father's pulse would slow down when family members spoke to him or played music. He said the family did not trust the doctors to make the decision as to when to terminate his father's life.

Maria, Rueben's wife of thirty-seven years, was convinced that her husband reacted positively when she spoke to him or touched him. She believed that he would want "to continue living until God wished."

Nonetheless, the trial judge acknowledged that the temporary restraining order procedure should rarely be used to direct affirmative relief, but he found that the matter presented an "extreme situation" in which he needed to move quickly in order to maintain the status quo. The judge ordered defendant to re-establish the level of treatment that had been provided to Rueben prior to the discontinuation of dialysis and also to remove a DNR order that had been placed in his chart. He then ordered a hearing, which was held approximately two weeks later.

Following the hearing, Judge Malone issued a written opinion in which he concluded that decisions concerning the proper course of treatment for Rueben could not be made by the hospital; rather, such decisions should be made by a surrogate who could take Rueben's personal value systems into account when determining what medical treatment was appropriate. He granted plaintiff's application, appointed plaintiff as her father's guardian and permanently restrained the hospital from discontinuing treatment to Rueben. This was memorialized in a March 20, 2009 order. This appeal followed.

On May 29, 2009, Rueben died. Plaintiff filed a motion to dismiss the appeal as moot, and we reserved decision on the motion pending consideration of the merits of the appeal. We now grant the motion and dismiss the appeal.

[The portion of the opinion discussing mootness is omitted. The court determined that the sparse record and the unique circumstances of the case—the plaintiff thought that Reuben's death was caused by the defendant's negligence, and they thought that the hospital's conduct was generated by the fact that they owed so much for the care provided by defendant—made it appropriate to dismiss on mootness grounds even though the case presented a matter of substantial public importance that would likely to arise again and could easily evade judicial review. The Supreme Court of New Jersey denied review.]

TEX. HEALTH & SAFETY CODE § 166.046; § 166.052; § 166.053 [THE "TEXAS FUTILITY STATUTE," A PART OF THE TEXAS ADVANCE DIRECTIVES ACT]

* * *

§ 166.046—Procedure if Not Effectuating a Directive or Treatment Decision

(a) If an attending physician refuses to honor a patient's advance directive or a health care or treatment decision made by or on behalf of a patient, the physician's refusal shall be reviewed by an ethics or medical committee. The attending physician may not be a member of that committee. The patient shall be given life-sustaining treatment during the review.

(b) The patient or the person responsible for the health care decisions of the individual who has made the decision regarding the directive or treatment decision:

(1) may be given a written description of the ethics or medical committee review process and any other policies and procedures related to this section adopted by the health care facility;

(2) shall be informed of the committee review process not less than 48 hours before the meeting called to discuss the patient's directive, unless the time period is waived by mutual agreement;

(3) at the time of being so informed, shall be provided:

(A) a copy of the appropriate statement [describing this process]; and

(B) a copy of the registry list of health care providers and referral groups that have volunteered their readiness to consider accepting transfer or to assist in locating a provider willing to accept transfer . . .; and

(4) is entitled to:

(A) attend the meeting;

(B) receive a written explanation of the decision reached during the review process;

(C) receive a copy of the portion of the patient's medical record related to the treatment received by the patient in the facility for the lesser of:

(i) the period of the patient's current admission to the facility; or

(ii) the preceding 30 calendar days; and

(D) receive a copy of all of the patient's reasonably available diagnostic results and reports related to the medical record provided under Paragraph (C).

(c) The written explanation . . . must be included in the patient's medical record.

(d) If the attending physician, the patient, or the person responsible for the health care decisions of the individual does not agree with the decision reached during the review process under Subsection (b), the physician shall make a reasonable effort to transfer the patient to a physician who is willing to comply with the directive. If the patient is a patient in a health care facility, the facility's personnel shall assist the physician in arranging the patient's transfer to:

(1) another physician;

(2) an alternative care setting within that facility; or

(3) another facility.

(e)   If the patient or the person responsible for the health care decisions of the patient is requesting life-sustaining treatment that the attending physician has decided and the ethics or medical committee has affirmed is medically inappropriate treatment, the patient shall be given available life-sustaining treatment pending transfer under Subsection (d). This subsection does not authorize withholding or withdrawing pain management medication, medical procedures necessary to provide comfort, or any other health care provided to alleviate a patient's pain. The patient is responsible for any costs incurred in transferring the patient to another facility. The attending physician, any other physician responsible for the care of the patient, and the health care facility are not obligated to provide life-sustaining treatment after the 10th day after both the written decision and the patient's medical record required under Subsection (b) are provided to the patient or the person responsible for the health care decisions of the patient unless ordered to do so under Subsection (g), except that artificially administered nutrition and hydration must be provided unless, based on reasonable medical judgment, providing artificially administered nutrition and hydration would:

(1)   hasten the patient's death;

(2)   be medically contraindicated such that the provision of the treatment seriously exacerbates life-threatening medical problems not outweighed by the benefits of the provision of the treatment;

(3)   result in substantial irremediable physical pain not outweighed by the benefit of the provision of the treatment;

(4)   be medically ineffective in prolonging life; or

(5)   be contrary to the patient's or surrogate's clearly documented desire not to receive artificially administered nutrition or hydration.

(e–1)   If during a previous admission to a facility a patient's attending physician and the review process . . . have determined that life-sustaining treatment is inappropriate, and the patient is readmitted to the same facility within six months from the date of the decision reached during the review process conducted upon the previous admission, Subsections (b) through (e) need not be followed if the patient's attending physician and a consulting physician who is a member of the ethics or medical committee of the facility document on the patient's readmission that the patient's condition either has not improved or has deteriorated since the review process was conducted.

(f)   Life-sustaining treatment under this section may not be entered in the patient's medical record as medically unnecessary treatment until the time period provided under Subsection (e) has expired.

(g)   At the request of the patient or the person responsible for the health care decisions of the patient, the appropriate district or county court shall extend the time period provided under Subsection (e) only if the court finds, by a preponderance of the evidence, that there is a reasonable expectation that a physician or health care facility that will honor the patient's directive will be found if the time extension is granted.

(h) . . . This section does not apply to hospice services provided by a home and community support services agency . . . .

* * *

§ 166.052—Statements Explaining Patient's Right to Transfer

(a) In cases in which the attending physician refuses to honor an advance directive or health care or treatment decision requesting the provision of life-sustaining treatment, the statement required . . . shall be in substantially the following form:

When There Is A Disagreement About Medical Treatment: The Physician Recommends Against Certain Life-Sustaining Treatment That You Wish To Continue

You have been given this information because you have requested life-sustaining treatment* for yourself as the patient or on behalf of the patient, as applicable, which the attending physician believes is not medically appropriate. This information is being provided to help you understand state law, your rights, and the resources available to you in such circumstances. It outlines the process for resolving disagreements about treatment among patients, families, and physicians. It is based upon [this section].

When an attending physician refuses to comply with an advance directive or other request for life-sustaining treatment because of the physician's judgment that the treatment would be medically inappropriate, the case will be reviewed by an ethics or medical committee. Life-sustaining treatment will be provided through the review.

You will receive notification of this review at least 48 hours before a meeting of the committee related to your case. You are entitled to attend the meeting. With your agreement, the meeting may be held sooner than 48 hours, if possible.

You are entitled to receive a written explanation of the decision reached during the review process.

---

* "Life-sustaining treatment" means treatment that, based on reasonable medical judgment, sustains the life of a patient and without which the patient will die. The term includes both life-sustaining medications and artificial life support, such as mechanical breathing machines, kidney dialysis treatment, and artificially administered nutrition and hydration. The term does not include the administration of pain management medication or the performance of a medical procedure considered to be necessary to provide comfort care, or any other medical care provided to alleviate a patient's pain.

If after this review process both the attending physician and the ethics or medical committee conclude that life-sustaining treatment is medically inappropriate and yet you continue to request such treatment, then the following procedure will occur:

1.   The physician, with the help of the health care facility, will assist you in trying to find a physician and facility willing to provide the requested treatment.

2.   You are being given a list of health care providers, licensed physicians, health care facilities, and referral groups that have volunteered their readiness to consider accepting transfer, or to assist in locating a provider willing to accept transfer. . . . You may wish to contact providers, facilities, or referral groups on the list or others of your choice to get help in arranging a transfer.

3.   The patient will continue to be given life-sustaining treatment until the patient can be transferred to a willing provider for up to 10 days from the time you were given both the committee's written decision that life-sustaining treatment is not appropriate and the patient's medical record. The patient will continue to be given after the 10-day period treatment to enhance pain management and reduce suffering, including artificially administered nutrition and hydration, unless, based on reasonable medical judgment, providing artificially administered nutrition and hydration would hasten the patient's death, be medically contraindicated such that the provision of the treatment seriously exacerbates life-threatening medical problems not outweighed by the benefit of the provision of the treatment, result in substantial irremediable physical pain not outweighed by the benefit of the provision of the treatment, be medically ineffective in prolonging life, or be contrary to the patient's or surrogate's clearly documented desires.

4.   If a transfer can be arranged, the patient will be responsible for the costs of the transfer.

5.   If a provider cannot be found willing to give the requested treatment within 10 days, life-sustaining treatment may be withdrawn unless a court of law has granted an extension.

6.   You may ask the appropriate district or county court to extend the 10-day period if the court finds that there is a reasonable expectation that you may find a physician or health care facility willing to provide life-sustaining treatment if the extension is granted. Patient medical records will be provided to the patient or surrogate in accordance with [the] Texas Health and Safety Code.

* * *

(c) An attending physician or health care facility may, if it chooses, include any additional information concerning the physician's or facility's policy, perspective, experience, or review procedure.

§ 166.053—Registry to Assist Transfers

(a) The [Texas Department of State Health Services] shall maintain a registry listing the identity of and contact information for health care providers and referral groups . . . that have voluntarily notified the department they may consider accepting or may assist in locating a provider willing to accept transfer of a patient under [this statute].

(b) The listing of a provider or referral group in the registry described in this section does not obligate the provider or group to accept transfer of or provide services to any particular patient.

* * *

FROEDTERT HOSPITAL—MEDICAL COLLEGE OF WISCONSIN, FUTILE MEDICAL CARE POLICY
(revised, 2020 version).

* * *

A. If, in the judgment of the Attending Physician and a staff physician consultant, life-sustaining medical treatment would be futile, the Attending Physician may write an order withholding or withdrawing the treatment after notifying the patient or patient's Surrogate(s). Appropriate palliative care measures should be instituted.

B. A life-sustaining medical intervention should be considered "futile" if it cannot be expected to restore or maintain vital organ function or to achieve the expressed goals of the patient when decisional.

C. Life-sustaining medical treatment includes cardiopulmonary resuscitation ("CPR"), mechanical ventilation, artificial nutrition and hydration, blood products, renal dialysis, vasopressors, or any other treatment that prolongs dying.

D. Consultation with Palliative Medicine, Social Services, and Chaplaincy, as appropriate, is strongly encouraged. If there are remaining questions, the physician should consult the Ethics Committee. If the patient (or Surrogate) disagrees, the Attending Physician should consider whether transfer to another attending physician, or another health care facility willing to accept the patient, is feasible. If transfer to a physician or facility willing to accept the patient is not feasible, further life-sustaining medical treatment may be withdrawn.

* * *

F. The Attending Physician must contact the Office of the Chief Medical Officer ("CMO") verbally when this policy is invoked and document in the patient's legal health record ("LHR") a progress note . . . .

NOTES AND QUESTIONS

1. *How Would You Resolve the Case?* The *Betancourt* case was never resolved on its merits. Should the court have decided it on the merits even though it was moot? How should it have been decided? You have been presented with the factual portion of the opinion; how would you write the substantive legal analysis? How would this issue have been resolved if the hospital had a policy like the Froedtert policy?

2. *Who Decides?* Who has the final authority to make that decision under the Texas statute and the hospital policy? Who would you allow to be the final arbiter of whether a proposed treatment is futile? For a discussion of the advantages and disadvantages of different decision-making bodies in resolving futility disputes, see Janet L. Dolgin, Medical Disputes and Conflicting Values: Is There a "Right to Die" Later?, 2020 B.Y.U. L. Rev. 95 (2020).

3. *The Limits of Autonomy?* As noted in Section II, the law of health care decision-making has relied heavily on the principle of autonomy. The right of a patient to make his or her own informed decisions to accept or refuse medical care, the substituted judgment standard, and access to medically assisted death (covered in Chapter 19) all reflect this principle. Medical futility disputes, however, raise questions about the limits of patient autonomy. How would you explain this apparent departure? Is it a conflict between autonomy and beneficence? Or between autonomy and other values? Is it similar to the specific provisions for situations in which health care professionals or facilities object to the health care decisions of patients (or their surrogates) covered earlier in this chapter? Why or why not?

4. *Defining "Futility."* When is requested care truly "futile"? Under the hospital policy, how is futility defined? Who has the authority to make that decision? Under the Texas statute, how is futility defined? Which definition makes the most sense, given the purposes of futility laws and policies? How would you define futility? See Janet L. Dolgin, Remaking the 'Right to Die': Give Me Liberty but Do Not Give Me Death, 73 S.M.U. L. Rev. 47 (2020); Meir Katz, When Is Medical Care Futile? The Institutional Competence of the Medical Profession Regarding the Provision of Life-Sustaining Medical Care, 90 Neb. L. Rev.1 (2011).

5. *Medical vs. Ethical Futility.* The term futility is subject to a variety of interpretations. Treatment is *scientifically futile* (or *medically futile*) when it cannot achieve the medical result that is expected by the patient (or by the family) making the request. As a general matter, scientifically futile treatment need not be offered or provided to a patient. A seriously ill cancer patient need not be provided with laetrile, a useless drug that has been popularized by those who would prey upon desperate patients and their families, even if that

treatment is requested. A child with a viral illness need not be prescribed an antibiotic, even if the child's parents request one, because, as a matter of science, the antibiotic will not be effective in treating that illness. Doctors need not do a CAT scan on a patient with a cold, even if that is what the patient wants, because there is no reason to believe that there will be any connection between what can be discovered on the scan and the appropriate treatment of the cold. As a general matter, health care providers, who are trained in the science of medicine, are entitled to determine which treatments are scientifically futile.

A harder question arises when a patient requests treatment that is not scientifically futile, but that is, in the opinion of the health care provider, *ethically futile*. Treatment is ethically futile if it will not serve the underlying interests of the patient. For example, some providers believe that it is ethically futile to keep a patient's body aerated and nourished when that patient is in a persistent vegetative state. These health care providers believe that it is beyond the scope of medicine to sustain mere corporeal existence. Some health care providers believe that it would be ethically futile to engage in CPR under circumstances in which the most that can be accomplished through that intervention would be to prolong the patient's life by a few hours. Families may disagree with physicians over what constitutes ethically futile treatment. Is there any reason to adopt the provider's perspective, rather than the family's, as the ethically "correct" one?

The Council on Ethical and Judicial Affairs of the AMA has determined that:

> Physicians are not required to offer or provide interventions that, in their best medical judgment, cannot reasonably be expected to yield the intended clinical benefit or achieve agreed-on goals for care. Respecting patient autonomy does not mean that patients should receive specific interventions simply because they (or their surrogates) request them.

Code of Medical Ethics Opinion 5.5, *Medically Ineffective Interventions* (2016).

Is the Council's position a convincing one, or is it merely a device to transfer the authority to make ethically charged decisions from patients to physicians? See Patrick Moore, An End-of-Life Quandary in Need of a Statutory Response: When Patients Demand Life-Sustaining Treatment That Physicians Are Unwilling to Provide, 48 B.C. L. Rev. 433 (2007).

6. *Risk of Bias and Discrimination.* How can we ensure that unexamined assumptions and value judgments do not find their way into medical decisions to withhold or withdraw care deemed futile? A 2019 report by the National Council on Disability found that such decisions are compromised by negative biases and lack of knowledge about the quality of life of people with disabilities, and they often lack objectivity and procedural safeguards. Nat'l Council on Disability, Medical Futility and Disability Bias (2019).

The death of Michael Hickson in 2020 focused attention on these concerns. Mr. Hickson, a 46-year-old Black man and father of five, sought treatment for serious COVID-19 disease. The hospital refused to provide life-saving care over the objection of his wife, Melissa Hickson. News coverage included reports of a recording of a conversation between Melissa Hickson and a physician at the hospital who informed her that the hospital would not provide medical treatment because it deemed Mr. Hickson to have a poor quality of life due to his pre-existing quadriplegia and head injury. Joseph Shapiro, One Man's COVID-19 Death Raises the Worst Fears of Many People with Disabilities, Nat'l Public Radio, July 31, 2020. In June 2021, Melissa Hickson filed a complaint raising claims under federal laws prohibiting discrimination based on disability and under state laws. Complaint, Hickson v. St. David's Healthcare Partnership, No. 1:21-cv-514 (W.D. Tex., Austin Div. 2021).

Federal disability antidiscrimination laws apply to medical futility decisions, but they have received little attention in this context to date. See also Chapter 6 for discussion of federal laws that prohibit discrimination based on disability.

7.   *Procedural Requirements*. Under the Texas statute, what process must be followed before a patient seeking futile care is discharged from the hospital? You might prepare a flow chart including all of the steps required by the statute. Do these requirements seem reasonable? Is ten days enough to find an alternative placement for one who is about to have futile treatment removed?

8.   *Challenges to Texas Statute*. The Texas statute has given rise to litigation. In one celebrated case, the mother of Sun Hudson, an infant, sought judicial intervention to avoid the discontinuation of treatment that physicians believed to be futile. In another case involving an adult, Spiro Nikolouzos had been transferred once after ventilator support was found to be futile. When the receiving institution reached the same conclusion and began to prepare for his discharge, his family sought more time to arrange for yet a second transfer. Both cases were decided on procedural grounds largely unrelated to the substantive provisions of the statute, but each ultimately recognized the authority of the health care provider to make futility determinations. See Hudson v. Texas Children's Hosp., 177 S.W.3d 232 (Tex. Ct. App. 2005); Nikolouzos v. St. Luke's Episcopal Hosp., 162 S.W.3d 678 (Tex. Ct. App. 2005).

Several other litigated cases have resulted in a great deal of press coverage. In the recent case of Tinslee Lewis, an infant patient and her mother sought injunctive relief from a hospital's unilateral discontinuation of life-sustaining treatment, alleging that the statutory committee review process did not provide adequate procedural due process protections. In July 2020, the court of appeals directed the trial court to render an order granting the temporary injunction pending a decision on the merits. T.L. v. Cook Children's Med. Ctr., 607 S.W.3d 9 (2020), cert. denied 141 S. Ct. 1069 (2021).

9.   *Uniform Health-Care Decisions Act Model*. Some states with statutes modeled on the Uniform Health-Care Decisions Act, reprinted above, provide

that physicians need not give futile care. Recall that section 7(f) of that Uniform Act provides that "[a] health-care provider or institution may decline to comply with an individual instruction or health-care decision that requires medically ineffective health care or health care contrary to generally accepted health-care standards applicable to the health-care provider or institution." See also Md. Code Ann., Health-Gen. section 5–611 and Va. Code Ann. section 54.1–2990. The Texas statute differs from these earlier statutes by providing an authoritative and conclusive endpoint for disputes. See Thaddeus Mason Pope, Procedural Due Process and Intramural Hospital Dispute Resolution Mechanisms: The Texas Advance Directives Act, 10 St. Louis U.J. of Health L. & Pol'y 93 (2016) (closely analyzing Texas statute and suggesting amendments to better comport with fundamental notions of procedural due process).

10. *Notice Requirements.* In 2012 Froedtert Hospital was cited by a CMS inspector for not telling a patient about the existence of the hospital's futility policy. In that case a dying patient had been hospitalized 21 times in the past year and was in such failing health that the physicians concluded that any further life-sustaining treatment would be futile under the hospital policy. The family objected and continued to insist that all available treatment, including near daily blood transfusions, be continued. The patient was given DNR status without the agreement of the family. The CMS inspector did not find that the Froedtert futility policy violated any law, but, rather, that the hospital violated the Patient Self Determination Act, described earlier in this chapter, by not telling the patient and his family of the existence of the futility policy. Ultimately the patient's family requested the transfer of the patient to another facility, and Froedtert cooperated in arranging for that transfer.

11. *Mediation?* Robert Truog, a thoughtful physician and bioethicist, writes that medical futility issues are based in "power, trust, hope, money, and suffering." Robert Truog, Medical Futility, 25 Ga. St. U.L. Rev. 985, 986 (2009). Is he right? If he is right, is this fact helpful in figuring out how to resolve disputes over medical futility? Mediation is often employed to help resolve these disputes in health care institutions. How helpful is mediation in dealing with conflict based in power, trust, hope, money, and suffering?

CHAPTER 19

MEDICALLY ASSISTED DYING

• • •

I. INTRODUCTION

There has been a significant debate in the U.S. and elsewhere over the past quarter of a century over the propriety of medically assisted death, that is, medical care designed to help a patient die how and when the patient wants to die. As the last chapter established, every state allows a physician to assist a competent adult patient who wishes to refuse or discontinue life-sustaining medical care, at least under most circumstances. But may a health care provider also provide affirmative intervention to a patient who wishes to hasten death? If so, under what circumstances?

The language we use to discuss these questions has become especially divisive over the past few years, and we must be careful how we use words that have become laden with political and philosophical meaning. "Euthanasia," for example, generally refers to an affirmative act that directly and immediately causes the death of a patient for the benefit of that patient. "Involuntary euthanasia" is sometimes used to describe euthanasia against the will of the patient, although sometimes it means euthanasia without the formal and expressed consent of the patient. "Voluntary euthanasia" is sometimes used to refer to euthanasia upon request of the patient, although most careful thinkers avoid using that term altogether. "Active euthanasia" sometimes refers to some affirmative act of euthanasia, while "passive euthanasia" generally refers, technically incorrectly, to withholding or withdrawing life-sustaining treatment.

"Suicide" can refer to any act taken by a person to intentionally end his own life (including the act of a patient taking a prescribed lethal dose of medication), but sometimes it refers only to an act taken by someone acting irrationally, or under the influence of extraordinary emotional distress or mental disease (and not, for example, to the act of a terminally ill, competent patient who knowingly takes a prescribed lethal dose to end his suffering). Both "euthanasia" and "suicide" have highly negative connotations, and the people who use those terms generally oppose the propriety of the act. The words "death" and "killing" in this context also have strong negative connotations, and those terms are used to describe medically assisted dying primarily by those who oppose its legality.

On the other hand, "death with dignity," "patient choice," or "end-of-life option," which often refer to these same acts, have positive connotations for many. That is why advocates of the practice use similar language on state initiatives. Similarly, "Right to Die" is generally a popular concept, and that term is used almost exclusively by those who approve of the use of this practice. For years, however, the phrase was used to describe the withdrawal of life-sustaining treatment. Using the same phrase in this context implicitly argues that there is no difference between the two.

Opponents of medically assisted dying often use the terms "assisted suicide" or "physician assisted suicide," and they have raised a range of concerns about the practice.

As with life and death decision-making addressed in Chapter 18, advocates for disability rights have brought attention to the impact of individual and structural biases that may distort decision-making by and for people with disabilities and other marginalized populations in this context. What safeguards are needed to address these concerns? How does medically assisted death intersect with issues of equity and justice in health care, more generally?

As you read the materials that follow, make sure that you identify with specificity exactly what practice is being considered. While there are a few countries that permit euthanasia under certain limited circumstances, that has never been a legally available option in the U.S., and it is rarely part of the legal debate. In this country, the debate has centered on the propriety (and legality) of a medically prescribed lethal dose of medication designed to be ingested by the competent, fully informed patient who originally requested a prescription for it from a physician. It is that practice that forms the core of the discussion in this chapter. While, increasingly, physicians, judges and scholars are calling this assistance "Aid in Dying," the authors have chosen to call it "Medically Assisted Dying" because this term is not used in advocacy either for or against these actions.

II.   THE CONSTITUTIONAL FRAMEWORK

WASHINGTON V. GLUCKSBERG
Supreme Court of the United States, 1997.
521 U.S. 702.

REHNQUIST, C. J., delivered the opinion of the Court, in which O'CONNOR, SCALIA, KENNEDY, and THOMAS, JJ., joined. O'CONNOR, J., filed a concurring opinion, in which GINSBURG and BREYER, JJ., joined in part. STEVENS, J., SOUTER, J., GINSBURG, J., and BREYER, J., filed opinions concurring in the judgment.

CHIEF JUSTICE REHNQUIST delivered the opinion of the Court.

The question presented in this case is whether Washington's prohibition against "causing" or "aiding" a suicide offends the Fourteenth Amendment to the United States Constitution. We hold that it does not.

* * *

The plaintiffs assert [ ] "the existence of a liberty interest protected by the Fourteenth Amendment which extends to a personal choice by a mentally competent, terminally ill adult to commit physician-assisted suicide." [ ] Relying primarily on Planned Parenthood v. Casey, [ ] and Cruzan v. Director, Missouri Dept. of Health, [ ] the District Court agreed, [ ] and concluded that Washington's assisted-suicide ban is unconstitutional because it "places an undue burden on the exercise of [that] constitutionally protected liberty interest." [ ] The District Court also decided that the Washington statute violated the Equal Protection Clause's requirement that " 'all persons similarly situated . . . be treated alike.' "[ ]

A panel of the Court of Appeals for the Ninth Circuit reversed, emphasizing that "in the two hundred and five years of our existence no constitutional right to aid in killing oneself has ever been asserted and upheld by a court of final jurisdiction." [ ] The Ninth Circuit reheard the case en banc, reversed the panel's decision, and affirmed the District Court. [ ] Like the District Court, the en banc Court of Appeals emphasized our Casey and Cruzan decisions. [ ] The court also discussed what it described as "historical" and "current societal attitudes" toward suicide and assisted suicide, [ ] and concluded that "the Constitution encompasses a due process liberty interest in controlling the time and manner of one's death—that there is, in short, a constitutionally-recognized 'right to die.' "[ ] After "weighing and then balancing" this interest against Washington's various interests, the court held that the State's assisted-suicide ban was unconstitutional "as applied to terminally ill competent [ ] adults who wish to hasten their deaths with medication prescribed by their physicians." [ ] We granted certiorari [ ] and now reverse.

I

We begin, as we do in all due-process cases, by examining our Nation's history, legal traditions, and practices. [ ] In almost every State—indeed, in almost every western democracy—it is a crime to assist a suicide. The States' assisted-suicide bans are not innovations. Rather, they are longstanding expressions of the States' commitment to the protection and preservation of all human life. [ ] Indeed, opposition to and condemnation of suicide—and, therefore, of assisting suicide—are consistent and enduring themes of our philosophical, legal, and cultural heritages. [ ]

More specifically, for over 700 years, the Anglo-American common-law tradition has punished or otherwise disapproved of both suicide and assisting suicide. . . . [The Chief Justice then reviews the common law of England, the American colonies, and U.S. states, from the 13th century to the present, with regard to suicide.]

* * *

Attitudes toward suicide itself have changed since [the 13th Century prohibitions on suicide] . . . but our laws have consistently condemned, and continue to prohibit, assisting suicide. Despite changes in medical technology and notwithstanding an increased emphasis on the importance of end-of-life decisionmaking, we have not retreated from this prohibition. Against this backdrop of history, tradition, and practice, we now turn to respondents' constitutional claim.

II

The Due Process Clause guarantees more than fair process, and the "liberty" it protects includes more than the absence of physical restraint. [ ] The Clause also provides heightened protection against government interference with certain fundamental rights and liberty interests. [ ] In a long line of cases, we have held that, in addition to the specific freedoms protected by the Bill of Rights, the "liberty" specially protected by the Due Process Clause includes the rights to marry, [ ]; to have children, [ ]; to direct the education and upbringing of one's children, [ ]; to marital privacy, [ ]; to use contraception, [ ]; to bodily integrity, [ ] and to abortion, [ ]. We have also assumed, and strongly suggested, that the Due Process Clause protects the traditional right to refuse unwanted lifesaving medical treatment. [ ]

But we "have always been reluctant to expand the concept of substantive due process because guideposts for responsible decisionmaking in this unchartered area are scarce and open-ended." [ ] By extending constitutional protection to an asserted right or liberty interest, we, to a great extent, place the matter outside the arena of public debate and legislative action. We must therefore "exercise the utmost care whenever we are asked to break new ground in this field" [ ] lest the liberty protected by the Due Process Clause be subtly transformed into the policy preferences of the members of this Court [ ].

Our established method of substantive-due-process analysis has two primary features: First, we have regularly observed that the Due Process Clause specially protects those fundamental rights and liberties which are, objectively, "deeply rooted in this Nation's history and tradition" [ ] and "implicit in the concept of ordered liberty," such that "neither liberty nor justice would exist if they were sacrificed" [ ]. Second, we have required in substantive-due-process cases a "careful description" of the asserted fundamental liberty interest. [ ] Cruzan, supra, at 277–278. Our Nation's history, legal traditions, and practices thus provide the crucial "guideposts for responsible decisionmaking" [ ] that direct and restrain our exposition of the Due Process Clause. As we stated recently in Flores, the Fourteenth Amendment "forbids the government to infringe . . . 'fundamental' liberty interests at all, no matter what process is provided, unless the infringement is narrowly tailored to serve a compelling state interest." [ ]

* * *

Turning to the claim at issue here, the Court of Appeals stated that "properly analyzed, the first issue to be resolved is whether there is a liberty interest in determining the time and manner of one's death" [ ] or, in other words, "is there a right to die?" [ ]. Similarly, respondents assert a "liberty to choose how to die" and a right to "control of one's final days," [ ] and describe the asserted liberty as "the right to choose a humane, dignified death" [ ] and "the liberty to shape death" [ ]. As noted above, we have a tradition of carefully formulating the interest at stake in substantive-due-process cases. For example, although Cruzan is often described as a "right to die" case [ ] we were, in fact, more precise: we assumed that the Constitution granted competent persons a "constitutionally protected right to refuse lifesaving hydration and nutrition." [ ] The Washington statute at issue in this case prohibits "aiding another person to attempt suicide," [ ] and, thus, the question before us is whether the "liberty" specially protected by the Due Process Clause includes a right to commit suicide which itself includes a right to assistance in doing so.

. . . With this "careful description" of respondents' claim in mind, we turn to Casey and Cruzan.

[The Chief Justice next discusses the Cruzan case, where, he says,] "we assumed that the United States Constitution would grant a competent person a constitutionally protected right to refuse lifesaving hydration and nutrition."

* * *

The right assumed in Cruzan, however, was not simply deduced from abstract concepts of personal autonomy. Given the common-law rule that forced medication was a battery, and the long legal tradition protecting the decision to refuse unwanted medical treatment, our assumption was entirely consistent with this Nation's history and constitutional traditions. The decision to commit suicide with the assistance of another may be just as personal and profound as the decision to refuse unwanted medical treatment, but it has never enjoyed similar legal protection. Indeed, the two acts are widely and reasonably regarded as quite distinct. [ ] In Cruzan itself, we recognized that most States outlawed assisted suicide—and even more do today—and we certainly gave no intimation that the right to refuse unwanted medical treatment could be somehow transmuted into a right to assistance in committing suicide. [ ]

Respondents also rely on Casey. There, the Court's opinion concluded that "the essential holding of Roe v. Wade should be retained and once again reaffirmed." [ ] We held, first, that a woman has a right, before her fetus is viable, to an abortion "without undue interference from the State"; second, that States may restrict post-viability abortions, so long as exceptions are made to protect a woman's life and health; and third, that the State has legitimate interests throughout a pregnancy in protecting the health of the woman and the life of the unborn child. [ ] In reaching this conclusion, the opinion discussed in some detail this Court's substantive-due-process tradition of interpreting the Due Process Clause to protect certain fundamental rights and "personal decisions relating to marriage, procreation, contraception, family relationships, child rearing, and education," and noted that many of those rights and liberties "involve the most intimate and personal choices a person may make in a lifetime." [ ]

* * *

That many of the rights and liberties protected by the Due Process Clause sound in personal autonomy does not warrant the sweeping conclusion that any and all important, intimate, and personal decisions are so protected, [ ] and Casey did not suggest otherwise.

The history of the law's treatment of assisted suicide in this country has been and continues to be one of the rejection of nearly all efforts to permit it. That being the case, our decisions lead us to conclude that the asserted "right" to assistance in committing suicide is not a fundamental liberty interest protected by the Due Process Clause. The Constitution also requires, however, that Washington's assisted-suicide ban be rationally related to legitimate government interests. [ ] This requirement is unquestionably met here. As the court below recognized, [ ] Washington's assisted-suicide ban implicates a number of state interests. [ ]

First, Washington has an "unqualified interest in the preservation of human life."

* * *

Relatedly, all admit that suicide is a serious public-health problem, especially among persons in otherwise vulnerable groups. [ ] The State has an interest in preventing suicide, and in studying, identifying, and treating its causes. [ ]

* * *

The State also has an interest in protecting the integrity and ethics of the medical profession. . . . [T]he American Medical Association, like many other medical and physicians' groups, has concluded that "physician-assisted suicide is fundamentally incompatible with the physician's role as healer." [ ] And physician-assisted suicide could, it is argued, undermine the trust that is essential to the doctor-patient relationship by blurring the time-honored line between healing and harming. [ ]

Next, the State has an interest in protecting vulnerable groups— including the poor, the elderly, and disabled persons—from abuse, neglect, and mistakes. . . . [One respected state task force] warned that "legalizing physician-assisted suicide would pose profound risks to many individuals who are ill and vulnerable. . . . The risk of harm is greatest for the many individuals in our society whose autonomy and well-being are already compromised by poverty, lack of access to good medical care, advanced age, or membership in a stigmatized social group." [ ] If physician-assisted suicide were permitted, many might resort to it to spare their families the substantial financial burden of end-of-life health-care costs.

. . . The State's assisted-suicide ban reflects and reinforces its policy that the lives of terminally ill, disabled, and elderly people must be no less valued than the lives of the young and healthy, and that a seriously disabled person's suicidal impulses should be interpreted and treated the same way as anyone else's. [ ]

Finally, the State may fear that permitting assisted suicide will start it down the path to voluntary and perhaps even involuntary euthanasia. . . . [Justice Rehnquist then discussed how this fear could arise out of the practice in the Netherlands.]

We need not weigh exactly the relative strengths of these various interests. They are unquestionably important and legitimate, and Washington's ban on assisted suicide is at least reasonably related to their promotion and protection. We therefore hold that [the Washington ban on assisting suicide] does not violate the Fourteenth Amendment, either on its face or "as applied to competent, terminally ill adults who wish to hasten their deaths by obtaining medication prescribed by their doctors."[24] [ ]

* * *

Throughout the Nation, Americans are engaged in an earnest and profound debate about the morality, legality, and practicality of physician-assisted suicide. Our holding permits this debate to continue, as it should in a democratic society. The decision of the en banc Court of Appeals is

---

[24] Justice Stevens states that "the Court does conceive of respondents' claim as a facial challenge—addressing not the application of the statute to a particular set of plaintiffs before it, but the constitutionality of the statute's categorical prohibition. . . . "[ ] We emphasize that we today reject the Court of Appeals' specific holding that the statute is unconstitutional "as applied" to a particular class. [ ] Justice Stevens agrees with this holding, [ ] but would not "foreclose the possibility that an individual plaintiff seeking to hasten her death, or a doctor whose assistance was sought, could prevail in a more particularized challenge," ibid. Our opinion does not absolutely foreclose such a claim. However, given our holding that the Due Process Clause of the Fourteenth Amendment does not provide heightened protection to the asserted liberty interest in ending one's life with a physician's assistance, such a claim would have to be quite different from the ones advanced by respondents here.

reversed, and the case is remanded for further proceedings consistent with this opinion.

It is so ordered.

JUSTICE O'CONNOR, concurring [in both this case, Glucksberg, and Vacco, the case excerpted after this one in this book].*

Death will be different for each of us. For many, the last days will be spent in physical pain and perhaps the despair that accompanies physical deterioration and a loss of control of basic bodily and mental functions. Some will seek medication to alleviate that pain and other symptoms.

The Court frames the issue in this case as whether the Due Process Clause of the Constitution protects a "right to commit suicide which itself includes a right to assistance in doing so," [ ] and concludes that our Nation's history, legal traditions, and practices do not support the existence of such a right. I join the Court's opinions because I agree that there is no generalized right to "commit suicide." But respondents urge us to address the narrower question whether a mentally competent person who is experiencing great suffering has a constitutionally cognizable interest in controlling the circumstances of his or her imminent death. I see no need to reach that question in the context of the facial challenges to the New York and Washington laws at issue here. [ ] The parties and amici agree that in these States a patient who is suffering from a terminal illness and who is experiencing great pain has no legal barriers to obtaining medication, from qualified physicians, to alleviate that suffering, even to the point of causing unconsciousness and hastening death. [ ] In this light, even assuming that we would recognize such an interest, I agree that the State's interests in protecting those who are not truly competent or facing imminent death, or those whose decisions to hasten death would not truly be voluntary, are sufficiently weighty to justify a prohibition against physician-assisted suicide. [ ]

Every one of us at some point may be affected by our own or a family member's terminal illness. There is no reason to think the democratic process will not strike the proper balance between the interests of terminally ill, mentally competent individuals who would seek to end their suffering and the State's interests in protecting those who might seek to end life mistakenly or under pressure. As the Court recognizes, States are presently undertaking extensive and serious evaluation of physician-assisted suicide and other related issues. [ ] In such circumstances, "the . . . challenging task of crafting appropriate procedures for safeguarding . . . liberty interests is entrusted to the 'laboratory' of the States . . . in the first instance." [ ]

---

*   Justice Ginsburg concurs in the Court's judgments substantially for the reasons stated in this opinion. Justice Breyer joins this opinion except insofar as it joins the opinions of the Court.

In sum, there is no need to address the question whether suffering patients have a constitutionally cognizable interest in obtaining relief from the suffering that they may experience in the last days of their lives. There is no dispute that dying patients in Washington and New York can obtain palliative care, even when doing so would hasten their deaths. The difficulty in defining terminal illness and the risk that a dying patient's request for assistance in ending his or her life might not be truly voluntary justifies the prohibitions on assisted suicide we uphold here.

JUSTICE STEVENS, concurring in the judgments [in both Glucksberg and Vacco].

The Court ends its opinion with the important observation that our holding today is fully consistent with a continuation of the vigorous debate about the "morality, legality, and practicality of physician-assisted suicide" in a democratic society. [ ] I write separately to make it clear that there is also room for further debate about the limits that the Constitution places on the power of the States to punish the practice.

I

The morality, legality, and practicality of capital punishment have been the subject of debate for many years. In 1976, this Court upheld the constitutionality of the practice in cases coming to us from Georgia, Florida, and Texas. In those cases we concluded that a State does have the power to place a lesser value on some lives than on others; there is no absolute requirement that a State treat all human life as having an equal right to preservation. Because the state legislatures had sufficiently narrowed the category of lives that the State could terminate, and had enacted special procedures to ensure that the defendant belonged in that limited category, we concluded that the statutes were not unconstitutional on their face. In later cases coming to us from each of those States, however, we found that some applications of the statutes were unconstitutional.

Today, the Court decides that Washington's statute prohibiting assisted suicide is not invalid "on its face," that is to say, in all or most cases in which it might be applied. That holding, however, does not foreclose the possibility that some applications of the statute might well be invalid.

* * *

History and tradition provide ample support for refusing to recognize an open-ended constitutional right to commit suicide. Much more than the State's paternalistic interest in protecting the individual from the irrevocable consequences of an ill-advised decision motivated by temporary concerns is at stake. There is truth in John Donne's observation that "No man is an island." The State has an interest in preserving and fostering the benefits that every human being may provide to the community—a community that thrives on the exchange of ideas, expressions of affection, shared memories and humorous incidents as well as on the material contributions that its members create and support. The value to others of a person's life is far too precious to allow the individual to claim a constitutional entitlement to complete autonomy in making a decision to end that life. Thus, I fully agree with the Court that the "liberty" protected by the Due Process Clause does not include a categorical "right to commit suicide which itself includes a right to assistance in doing so." [ ]

But just as our conclusion that capital punishment is not always unconstitutional did not preclude later decisions holding that it is sometimes impermissibly cruel, so is it equally clear that a decision upholding a general statutory prohibition of assisted suicide does not mean that every possible application of the statute would be valid. A State, like Washington, that has authorized the death penalty and thereby has concluded that the sanctity of human life does not require that it always be preserved, must acknowledge that there are situations in which an interest in hastening death is legitimate. Indeed, not only is that interest sometimes legitimate, I am also convinced that there are times when it is entitled to constitutional protection.

II

In Cruzan [ ] the Court assumed that the interest in liberty protected by the Fourteenth Amendment encompassed the right of a terminally ill patient to direct the withdrawal of life-sustaining treatment. As the Court correctly observes today, that assumption "was not simply deduced from abstract concepts of personal autonomy." [ ] Instead, it was supported by the common-law tradition protecting the individual's general right to refuse unwanted medical treatment. [ ] We have recognized, however, that this common-law right to refuse treatment is neither absolute nor always sufficiently weighty to overcome valid countervailing state interests. . . .

Cruzan, however, was not the normal case. Given the irreversible nature of her illness and the progressive character of her suffering, Nancy Cruzan's interest in refusing medical care was incidental to her more basic interest in controlling the manner and timing of her death. In finding that her best interests would be served by cutting off the nourishment that kept her alive, the trial court did more than simply vindicate Cruzan's interest in refusing medical treatment; the court, in essence, authorized affirmative conduct that would hasten her death. When this Court reviewed the case and upheld Missouri's requirement that there be clear and convincing evidence establishing Nancy Cruzan's intent to have life-sustaining nourishment withdrawn, it made two important assumptions: (1) that there was a "liberty interest" in refusing unwanted treatment protected by the Due Process Clause; and (2) that this liberty interest did not "end the inquiry" because it might be outweighed by relevant state interests. [ ] I agree with both of those assumptions, but I insist that the source of Nancy Cruzan's right to refuse treatment was not just a common-law rule. Rather, this right is an aspect of a far broader and more basic concept of freedom that is even older than the common law. This freedom embraces, not merely a person's right to refuse a particular kind of unwanted treatment, but also her interest in dignity, and in determining the character of the memories that will survive long after her death. In recognizing that the State's interests did not outweigh Nancy Cruzan's liberty interest in refusing medical treatment, Cruzan rested not simply on the common-law right to refuse medical treatment, but—at least implicitly—on the even more fundamental right to make this "deeply personal decision," [ ].

* * *

While I agree with the Court that Cruzan does not decide the issue presented by these cases, Cruzan did give recognition, not just to vague, unbridled notions of autonomy, but to the more specific interest in making decisions about how to confront an imminent death. Although there is no absolute right to physician-assisted suicide, Cruzan makes it clear that some individuals who no longer have the option of deciding whether to live or to die because they are already on the threshold of death have a constitutionally protected interest that may outweigh the State's interest in preserving life at all costs. The liberty interest at stake in a case like this differs from, and is stronger than, both the common-law right to refuse medical treatment and the unbridled interest in deciding whether to live or die. It is an interest in deciding how, rather than whether, a critical threshold shall be crossed.

III

The state interests supporting a general rule banning the practice of physician-assisted suicide do not have the same force in all cases. First and foremost of these interests is the " 'unqualified interest in the preservation of human life' "[ ].

. . . Although as a general matter the State's interest in the contributions each person may make to society outweighs the person's interest in ending her life, this interest does not have the same force for a terminally ill patient faced not with the choice of whether to live, only of how to die. . . .

Similarly, the State's legitimate interests in preventing suicide, protecting the vulnerable from coercion and abuse, and preventing euthanasia are less significant in this context. I agree that the State has a compelling interest in preventing persons from committing suicide because of depression, or coercion by third parties. But the State's legitimate interest in preventing abuse does not apply to an individual who is not victimized by abuse, who is not suffering from depression, and who makes a rational and voluntary decision to seek assistance in dying.

* * *

The final major interest asserted by the State is its interest in preserving the traditional integrity of the medical profession. The fear is that a rule permitting physicians to assist in suicide is inconsistent with the perception that they serve their patients solely as healers. But for some patients, it would be a physician's refusal to dispense medication to ease their suffering and make their death tolerable and dignified that would be inconsistent with the healing role . . . .

. . . I do not . . . foreclose the possibility that an individual plaintiff seeking to hasten her death, or a doctor whose assistance was sought, could prevail in a more particularized challenge. Future cases will determine whether such a challenge may succeed.

IV

* * *

There may be little distinction between the intent of a terminally-ill patient who decides to remove her life-support and one who seeks the assistance of a doctor in ending her life; in both situations, the patient is seeking to hasten a certain, impending death. The doctor's intent might also be the same in prescribing lethal medication as it is in terminating life support. . . .

Thus, although the differences the majority notes in causation and intent between terminating life-support and assisting in suicide support the Court's rejection of the respondents' facial challenge, these distinctions may be inapplicable to particular terminally ill patients and their doctors. Our holding today in Vacco v. Quill that the Equal Protection Clause is not violated by New York's classification, just like our holding in Washington v. Glucksberg that the Washington statute is not invalid on its face, does not foreclose the possibility that some applications of the New York statute may impose an intolerable intrusion on the patient's freedom.

There remains room for vigorous debate about the outcome of particular cases that are not necessarily resolved by the opinions announced today. How such cases may be decided will depend on their specific facts. In my judgment, however, it is clear that the so-called "unqualified interest in the preservation of human life," [ ] is not itself sufficient to outweigh the interest in liberty that may justify the only possible means of preserving a dying patient's dignity and alleviating her intolerable suffering.

JUSTICE SOUTER, concurring in the judgment.

* * *

When the physicians claim that the Washington law deprives them of a right falling within the scope of liberty that the Fourteenth Amendment guarantees against denial without due process of law, they are not claiming some sort of procedural defect in the process through which the statute has been enacted or is administered. Their claim, rather, is that the State has no substantively adequate justification for barring the assistance sought by the patient and sought to be offered by the physician. Thus, we are dealing with a claim to one of those rights sometimes described as rights of substantive due process and sometimes as unenumerated rights, in view of the breadth and indeterminacy of the "due process" serving as the claim's textual basis. The doctors accordingly arouse the skepticism of those who find the Due Process Clause an unduly vague or oxymoronic warrant for judicial review of substantive state law, just as they also invoke two centuries of American constitutional practice in recognizing unenumerated, substantive limits on governmental action. . . .

* * *

[Justice Souter explains that he is adopting Justice Harlan's approach to the Constitutional evaluation and protection of unenumerated rights under the Due Process Clause, as articulated in his dissent in Poe v. Ullman.] My understanding of unenumerated rights in the wake of the Poe dissent and subsequent cases avoids the absolutist failing of many older cases without embracing the opposite pole of equating reasonableness with past practice described at a very specific level. [ ] That understanding begins with a concept of "ordered liberty," [ ] comprising a continuum of rights to be free from "arbitrary impositions and purposeless restraints" [ ].

* * *

This approach calls for a court to assess the relative "weights" or dignities of the contending interests, and to this extent the judicial method is familiar to the common law. Common law method is subject, however, to two important constraints in the hands of a court engaged in substantive due process review. First, such a court is bound to confine the values that it recognizes to those truly deserving constitutional stature, either to those expressed in constitutional text, or those exemplified by "the traditions from which [the Nation] developed," or revealed by contrast with "the traditions from which it broke." [ ]

The second constraint, again, simply reflects the fact that constitutional review, not judicial lawmaking, is a court's business here. The weighing or valuing of contending interests in this sphere is only the first step, forming the basis for determining whether the statute in question falls inside or outside the zone of what is reasonable in the way it resolves the conflict between the interests of state and individual.

* * *

The State has put forward several interests to justify the Washington law as applied to physicians treating terminally ill patients, even those competent to make responsible choices: protecting life generally [ ], discouraging suicide even if knowing and voluntary [ ], and protecting terminally ill patients from involuntary suicide and euthanasia, both voluntary and nonvoluntary [ ].

It is not necessary to discuss the exact strengths of the first two claims of justification in the present circumstances, for the third is dispositive for me. . . . [Justice Souter explains why the Washington State Legislature, on the basis of information now available, could have reasonably decided that a statute forbidding assisting suicide might protect terminally ill patients.]

* * *

The Court should accordingly stay its hand to allow reasonable legislative consideration. While I do not decide for all time that respondents' claim should not be recognized, I acknowledge the legislative institutional competence as the better one to deal with that claim at this time.

JUSTICE BREYER, concurring in the judgments [in both Glucksberg and Vacco].

I believe that Justice O'Connor's views, which I share, have greater legal significance than the Court's opinion suggests. I join her separate opinion, except insofar as it joins the majority. . . .

I agree with the Court in Vacco v. Quill [ ] that the articulated state interests justify the distinction drawn between physician assisted suicide and withdrawal of life-support. I also agree with the Court that the critical question in both of the cases before us is whether "the 'liberty' specially protected by the Due Process Clause includes a right" of the sort that the respondents assert. [ ] I do not agree, however, with the Court's formulation of that claimed "liberty" interest. The Court describes it as a "right to commit suicide with another's assistance." [ ] But I would not reject the respondents' claim without considering a different formulation, for which our legal tradition may provide greater support. That formulation would use words roughly like a "right to die with dignity." But irrespective of the exact words used, at its core would lie personal control over the manner of death, professional medical assistance, and the avoidance of unnecessary and severe physical suffering—combined.

* * *

I do not believe, however, that this Court need or now should decide whether or a not . . . [a right to die with dignity] is "fundamental." That is because, in my view, the avoidance of severe physical pain (connected with death) would have to comprise an essential part of any successful claim and because . . . the laws before us do not force a dying person to undergo that kind of pain. [ ] Rather, the laws of New York and of Washington do not prohibit doctors from providing patients with drugs sufficient to control pain despite the risk that those drugs themselves will kill. [ ] And under these circumstances the laws of New York and Washington would overcome any remaining significant interests and would be justified, regardless.

* * *

Were the legal circumstances different—for example, were state law to prevent the provision of palliative care, including the administration of drugs as needed to avoid pain at the end of life—then the law's impact upon serious and otherwise unavoidable physical pain (and accompanying death) would be more directly at issue. And as JUSTICE O'CONNOR suggests, the Court might have to revisit its conclusions in these cases.

* * *

VACCO V. QUILL
Supreme Court of the United States, 1997.
521 U.S. 793.

CHIEF JUSTICE REHNQUIST delivered the opinion of the Court.

In New York, as in most States, it is a crime to aid another to commit or attempt suicide, but patients may refuse even lifesaving medical treatment. The question presented by this case is whether New York's prohibition on assisting suicide therefore violates the Equal Protection Clause of the Fourteenth Amendment. We hold that it does not.

. . . Respondents, and three gravely ill patients who have since died, sued the State's Attorney General in the United States District Court. They urged that because New York permits a competent person to refuse life-sustaining medical treatment, and because the refusal of such treatment is "essentially the same thing" as physician-assisted suicide, New York's assisted-suicide ban violates the Equal Protection Clause. [ ]

The District Court disagreed . . . .

The Court of Appeals for the Second Circuit reversed. [ ] The court determined that, despite the assisted-suicide ban's apparent general applicability, "New York law does not treat equally all competent persons who are in the final stages of fatal illness and wish to hasten their deaths," because "those in the final stages of terminal illness who are on life-support systems are allowed to hasten their deaths by directing the removal of such systems; but those who are similarly situated, except for the previous attachment of life-sustaining equipment, are not allowed to hasten death by self-administering prescribed drugs." [ ] The Court of Appeals then examined whether this supposed unequal treatment was rationally related to any legitimate state interests, and concluded that "to the extent that [New York's statutes] prohibit a physician from prescribing medications to be self-administered by a mentally competent, terminally-ill person in the final stages of his terminal illness, they are not rationally related to any legitimate state interest." [ ] We granted certiorari [ ] and now reverse.

The Equal Protection Clause commands that no State shall "deny to any person within its jurisdiction the equal protection of the laws." This provision creates no substantive rights. [ ] Instead, it embodies a general rule that States must treat like cases alike but may treat unlike cases accordingly. [ ] If a legislative classification or distinction "neither burdens a fundamental right nor targets a suspect class, we will uphold [it] so long as it bears a rational relation to some legitimate end." [ ]

New York's statutes outlawing assisting suicide affect and address matters of profound significance to all New Yorkers alike. They neither infringe fundamental rights nor involve suspect classifications. [ ] These laws are therefore entitled to a "strong presumption of validity." [ ]

On their faces, neither New York's ban on assisting suicide nor its statutes permitting patients to refuse medical treatment treat anyone differently than anyone else or draw any distinctions between persons. Everyone, regardless of physical condition, is entitled, if competent, to refuse unwanted lifesaving medical treatment; no one is permitted to assist a suicide. Generally speaking, laws that apply evenhandedly to all "unquestionably comply" with the Equal Protection Clause. [ ]

The Court of Appeals, however, concluded that some terminally ill people—those who are on life-support systems—are treated differently than those who are not, in that the former may "hasten death" by ending treatment, but the latter may not "hasten death" through physician-assisted suicide. [ ] This conclusion depends on the submission that ending or refusing lifesaving medical treatment "is nothing more nor less than assisted suicide." [ ] Unlike the Court of Appeals, we think the distinction between assisting suicide and withdrawing life-sustaining treatment, a distinction widely recognized and endorsed in the medical profession and in our legal traditions, is both important and logical; it is certainly rational. [ ]

The distinction comports with fundamental legal principles of causation and intent. First, when a patient refuses life-sustaining medical treatment, he dies from an underlying fatal disease or pathology; but if a patient ingests lethal medication prescribed by a physician, he is killed by that medication. [ ]

Furthermore, a physician who withdraws, or honors a patient's refusal to begin, life-sustaining medical treatment purposefully intends, or may so intend, only to respect his patient's wishes and "to cease doing useless and futile or degrading things to the patient when [the patient] no longer stands to benefit from them." [ ] The same is true when a doctor provides aggressive palliative care; in some cases, painkilling drugs may hasten a patient's death, but the physician's purpose and intent is, or may be, only to ease his patient's pain. A doctor who assists a suicide, however, "must, necessarily and indubitably, intend primarily that the patient be made dead." [ ] Similarly, a patient who commits suicide with a doctor's aid necessarily has the specific intent to end his or her own life, while a patient who refuses or discontinues treatment might not. [ ]

The law has long used actors' intent or purpose to distinguish between two acts that may have the same result. [ ] Put differently, the law distinguishes actions taken "because of" a given end from actions taken "in spite of" their unintended but foreseen consequences. [ ]

Given these general principles, it is not surprising that many courts, including New York courts, have carefully distinguished refusing life-sustaining treatment from suicide. . . .

Similarly, the overwhelming majority of state legislatures have drawn a clear line between assisting suicide and withdrawing or permitting the refusal of unwanted lifesaving medical treatment by prohibiting the former and permitting the latter. [ ] And "nearly all states expressly disapprove of suicide and assisted suicide either in statutes dealing with durable powers of attorney in health-care situations, or in 'living will' statutes." [ ] Thus, even as the States move to protect and promote patients' dignity at the end of life, they remain opposed to physician-assisted suicide.

* * *

This Court has also recognized, at least implicitly, the distinction between letting a patient die and making that patient die. In Cruzan [ ] we concluded that "the principle that a competent person has a constitutionally protected liberty interest in refusing unwanted medical treatment may be inferred from our prior decisions," and we assumed the existence of such a right for purposes of that case [ ]. But our assumption of a right to refuse treatment was grounded not, as the Court of Appeals supposed, on the proposition that patients have a general and abstract "right to hasten death," [ ] but on well established, traditional rights to bodily integrity and freedom from unwanted touching [ ]. In fact, we observed that "the majority of States in this country have laws imposing criminal penalties on one who assists another to commit suicide." [ ]

Cruzan therefore provides no support for the notion that refusing life-sustaining medical treatment is "nothing more nor less than suicide."

For all these reasons, we disagree with respondents' claim that the distinction between refusing lifesaving medical treatment and assisted suicide is "arbitrary" and "irrational.[11] Granted, in some cases, the line between the two may not be clear, but certainty is not required, even were it possible. Logic and contemporary practice support New York's judgment that the two acts are different, and New York may therefore, consistent with the Constitution, treat them differently. By permitting everyone to refuse unwanted medical treatment while prohibiting anyone from assisting a suicide, New York law follows a longstanding and rational distinction.

New York's reasons for recognizing and acting on this distinction—including prohibiting intentional killing and preserving life; preventing suicide; maintaining physicians' role as their patients' healers; protecting vulnerable people from indifference, prejudice, and psychological and financial pressure to end their lives; and avoiding a possible slide towards euthanasia—are discussed in greater detail in our opinion in Glucksberg, ante. These valid and important public interests easily satisfy the constitutional requirement that a legislative classification bear a rational relation to some legitimate end.

The judgment of the Court of Appeals is reversed.

* * *

JUSTICE SOUTER, concurring in the judgment.

Even though I do not conclude that assisted suicide is a fundamental right entitled to recognition at this time, I accord the claims raised by the patients and physicians in this case and Washington v. Glucksberg a high degree of importance, requiring a commensurate justification. [ ] The reasons that lead me to conclude in Glucksberg that the prohibition on assisted suicide is not arbitrary under the due process standard also support the distinction between assistance to suicide, which is banned, and practices such as termination of artificial life support and death-hastening pain medication, which are permitted. I accordingly concur in the judgment of the Court.

---

[11] Respondents also argue that the State irrationally distinguishes between physician-assisted suicide and "terminal sedation," a process respondents characterize as "inducing barbiturate coma and then starving the person to death." [ ] Petitioners insist, however, that " 'although proponents of physician-assisted suicide and euthanasia contend that terminal sedation is covert physician-assisted suicide or euthanasia, the concept of sedating pharmacotherapy is based on informed consent and the principle of double effect.' "[ ] Just as a State may prohibit assisting suicide while permitting patients to refuse unwanted lifesaving treatment, it may permit palliative care related to that refusal, which may have the foreseen but unintended "double effect" of hastening the patient's death. [ ]

* * *

NOTES AND QUESTIONS

1.   *Defining the Interest at Stake.* In *Glucksberg*, proponents of the right to medically assisted death asserted a constitutionally protected liberty interest that extended to a personal choice by a competent, terminally ill adult to choose the time and manner of their death with the aid of a physician. Writing for the Court, Justice Rehnquist reframed the asserted interest as a more generalized right to assisted suicide. In her concurrence, Justice O'Connor agreed that there is no generalized right to commit suicide but stated that there was no need to address "the narrower question of whether a mentally competent person who is experiencing great suffering has a constitutionally cognizable interest in controlling the circumstances of his or her imminent death." What is the legal and ethical significance of these different framings of the interest at issue?

2.   *Discerning "Legal Tradition."* In *Glucksberg*, the Court held that the asserted right was not a fundamental liberty interest protected by the Due Process Clause because it was not a right deeply rooted in U.S. history, legal traditions, and practices. To what extent have states (like Oregon) changed their laws with respect to medically assisted death such that the "legal tradition" may have changed since *Glucksberg*? What kind of change would be required to conclude that the liberty interest has become fundamental? In other cases, the Court has been willing to recognize constitutionally protected interests in the absence of a tradition of legal protection. For a discussion of such cases before and after *Glucksberg*, see Kenji Yoshino, A New Birth of Freedom? Obergefell v. Hodges, 129 Harv. L. Rev. 147 (2015); Erwin Chemerinsky, Washington v. Glucksberg Was Tragically Wrong, 106 Mich. L. Rev. 1501 (2008).

3.   *Contentious Debate.* These cases generated many highly emotional responses. Although the Supreme Court's unanimous decision brought a semblance of propriety back to the discussion of these issues, supporters and opponents of medically assisted dying continue to attack the arguments of their opponents—and, as in the case of the abortion debate—they continue to attack their opponents, too. Some of the commentary on the Ninth Circuit opinions was especially personal. Judge Reinhardt (who wrote the primary decision finding the Washington law to be unconstitutional) was roundly criticized for his ACLU connections, which, some said, made it impossible for him to fairly decide the case. On the other hand, Judge Noonan (who would have upheld the statute for the first panel) had been criticized for his Right to Life connections and his Catholic faith which, others argued, made it impossible for him to be impartial.

Should judges recuse themselves from cases involving these difficult and controversial bioethics issues if they have deeply held personal beliefs about the underlying practice—here, medically assisted dying? Does it make a difference if they were members (or officers, or high-ranking employees) of organizations which have taken explicit positions on the underlying issues? On the particular case in litigation? Should they recuse themselves if the issue is one on which the religion to which they subscribe has taken a formal position? Should Catholic judges recuse themselves from abortion and medically assisted dying cases? Should judges who belong to the United Church of Christ (which has been strongly pro-choice for decades) recuse themselves from abortion cases? Should the member of a congregation whose rabbi helped organize a march to support access to contraception through the ACA recuse herself from all contraception rights cases? Is their obligation any different from the obligation of a judge who is a dedicated ACLU (or American Family Association or Republican Party) member and who confronts a case upon which the ACLU (or the American Family Association, or the Republican Party) has taken a firm position?

4.   *Determining Legislative Intent of Old Laws.* Judge Calabresi concurred in the Second Circuit decision in *Vacco* but on entirely different grounds. Depending on the theory of statutory construction that he had explained 15 years earlier in his text, A Common Law for the Age of Statutes (1982), he concluded that the history of the New York manslaughter statute suggested that there was no reason to believe that its framers ever intended it to apply to cases of competent terminally ill patients seeking aid in dying from physicians. Still, as he pointed out, "neither *Cruzan*, nor *Casey*, nor the language of our Constitution, nor our constitutional tradition clearly makes these laws invalid."

So, what should the court do with a "highly suspect" but "not clearly invalid" statute that may no longer serve the purposes for which it was originally promulgated? The answer, according to Judge Calabresi, is the "constitutional remand." Under this approach, a court would not determine the validity of the state law in the absence of clear and current statements by the people or elected officials of the state, or, if the court made a determination, it would leave open the possibility of reconsideration. Thus, Judge Calabresi finds the New York statute unconstitutional, but he "takes no position" on whether verbatim identical statutes would be constitutional "were New York to reenact them while articulating the reasons for the distinctions it makes. . . . " Is this a reasonable way to deal with ancient statutes effectively criminalizing medically assisted dying? Is this argument still available to those challenging state statutes that forbid assisting suicide? For a history of criminal laws related to medically assisted dying, see Alan Meisel, A History of the Law of Assisted Dying in the United States, 73(1) SMU L. Rev. 119 (2020).

5.   *Intersection with Criminal Law.* Medically assisted dying may constitute murder, manslaughter, some other form of homicide, or no crime at all, depending on the language of the state statute and the nature of the physician's act. While most states criminalize assisting suicide, it is not always easy to determine what conduct is prohibited by those statutes. Consider one representative statute:

Every person who deliberately aids, or advises, or encourages another to commit suicide, is guilty of a felony. Cal. Pen. Code § 401.

Would this statute apply to a physician who clamps a feeding tube? To a physician who withholds antibiotics? To a physician who prescribes morphine to a patient in persistent pain, provides enough morphine to constitute a lethal dose? To a physician who prescribes that same morphine and tells the patient what would constitute a lethal dose? To those who publish instructions on how to hasten death for the use of those who are terminally ill or in excruciating pain? To those who make generally available information about how to commit suicide at home? See, e.g., State v. Melchert-Dinkel, 844 N.W.2d 13 (Minn. 2014) (rejecting application of statute prohibiting "encouraging" or "advising"—but not "assisting"—another in committing suicide on free speech grounds); Final Exit Network v. State, 290 Ga. 508, 722 S.E.2d 722 (2012) (rejecting application of statute prohibiting offers of assistance of another in committing suicide on free speech grounds); McCollum v. CBS, Inc., 202 Cal. App. 3d 989, 249 Cal. Rptr. 187 (1988) (rejecting on free speech grounds application of the statute to those who play rock music with lyrics that suggest that suicide is acceptable).

6. *Disability Critiques.* As discussed in Chapter 18, the disability rights movement has become a key player in controversies over medically assisted death and other health care decisions with life and death consequences. A 2019 report by the National Council on Disability documented a host of concerns with the legalization of medically assisted death, asserting that "some people's lives, particularly those of people with disabilities, will be ended without their fully informed and free consent, through mistakes, abuse, insufficient knowledge, and the unjust lack of better options." See Nat'l Council on Disability, Medical Futility and Disability Bias (2019) at p. 14–15. The report describes a lack of adequate safeguards and oversight, as well as the impact of individual and structural biases that distort decision-making by and for people with disabilities in this context.

The report also notes concerns that people of color are particularly at risk of being harmed by these laws. See also Mary Crossley, Ending-Life Decisions: Some Disability Perspectives, 33 Ga. St. Univ. L. Rev. 893 (2017) (drawing parallels with concerns about racial justice and policing that have been expressed by the African-American community). Of course, we should not assume that all people with disabilities, or people who are members of any other group, hold the same views on a given issue, including medically assisted death.

7. *Gender Considerations.* Might women, specifically, be put at risk in a society that permits medically assisted dying? That argument is made by Susan Wolf, who regularly has argued that women's requests should be better respected by the health care system and that requests to remove life-sustaining treatment should be heeded.

As I have argued, there is a strong right to be free of unwanted bodily invasion. Indeed, for women, a long history of being harmed specifically through unwanted bodily invasion such as rape presents particularly compelling reasons for honoring a woman's refusal of invasion and effort to maintain bodily intactness. When it comes to the question of whether women's suicides should be aided, however, or whether women should be actively killed, there is no right to command physician assistance, the dangers of permitting assistance are immense, and the history of women's subordination cuts the other way. Women have historically been seen as fit objects for bodily invasion, self-sacrifice, and death at the hands of others. The task before us is to challenge all three.

Certainly some women, including some feminists, will see this problem differently. That may be especially true of women who feel in control of their lives, are less subject to subordination by age or race or wealth, and seek yet another option to add to their many. I am not arguing that women should lose control of their lives and selves. Instead, I am arguing that when women request to be put to death or ask help in taking their own lives, they become part of a broader social dynamic of which we have properly learned to be extremely wary. These are fatal practices. We can no longer ignore questions of gender or insights of feminist argument.

Susan Wolf, Gender, Feminism and Death: Physician Assisted Suicide and Euthanasia, in S. Wolf, Feminism and Bioethics: Beyond Reproduction 308 (1996). For an account of Professor Wolf's thoughtful approach to death and dying, see Daniel Bergner, Death in the Family, N.Y. Times Magazine (December 2, 2007) (reporting that 72% of the 75 individuals assisted by euthanasia advocate Kevorkian were women).

Susan Wolf also wrote a moving account of her own father's death, including her own response when he inquired whether it could be "accelerated" beyond withdrawing treatment. Her answer to her father was no, and she explains why in her essay; but she doesn't romanticize his dying and the great difficulties he and his family faced in getting the end-of-life care he needed. Confronting Physician-Assisted Suicide and Euthanasia: My Father's Death, 38 Hastings Ctr. Rept. 23 (2008).

8. *Medical Organizations.* Organized medical groups generally oppose any medical participation in euthanasia or assisted death. As to euthanasia, the AMA Council on Ethical and Judicial Affairs provides:

Code of Medical Ethics Opinion 5.8, Euthanasia (2013)

Euthanasia is the administration of a lethal agent by another person to a patient for the purpose of relieving the patient's intolerable and incurable suffering.

It is understandable, though tragic, that some patients in extreme duress—such as those suffering from a terminal, painful, debilitating illness—may come to decide that death is preferable to life.

However, permitting physicians to engage in euthanasia would ultimately cause more harm than good.

Euthanasia is fundamentally incompatible with the physician's role as healer, would be difficult or impossible to control, and would pose serious societal risks. Euthanasia could readily be extended to incompetent patients and other vulnerable populations.

The involvement of physicians in euthanasia heightens the significance of its ethical prohibition. The physician who performs euthanasia assumes unique responsibility for the act of ending the patient's life.

Instead of engaging in euthanasia, physicians must aggressively respond to the needs of patients at the end of life. Physicians:

(a) Should not abandon a patient once it is determined that cure is impossible.

(b) Must respect patient autonomy.

(c) Must provide good communication and emotional support.

(d) Must provide appropriate comfort care and adequate pain control.

As to Physician Assisted Suicide, the Council has adopted this position:

Code of Medical Ethics Opinion 5.7, Physician Assisted Suicide (2016)

Physician-assisted suicide occurs when a physician facilitates a patient's death by providing the necessary means and/or information to enable the patient to perform the life-ending act (eg, the physician provides sleeping pills and information about the lethal dose, while aware that the patient may commit suicide).

It is understandable, though tragic, that some patients in extreme duress—such as those suffering from a terminal, painful, debilitating illness—may come to decide that death is preferable to life. However, allowing physicians to participate in assisted suicide would cause more harm than good.

Physician-assisted suicide is fundamentally incompatible with the physician's role as healer, would be difficult or impossible to control, and would pose serious societal risks.

Instead of engaging in assisted suicide, physicians must aggressively respond to the needs of patients at the end of life. Physicians:

(a) Should not abandon a patient once it is determined that cure is impossible.

(b) Must respect patient autonomy.

(c) Must provide good communication and emotional support.

(d) Must provide appropriate comfort care and adequate pain control.

Does the AMA oppose both of these kinds of medically assisted dying because they are equally morally reprehensible, or because they are too morally complicated? See Christine Cassel and Diane Meier, Morals and Moralism in the Debate Over Euthanasia and Assisted Suicide, 323 NEJM 750, 751 (1990) (opining that a strong prohibition against medically assisted death may limit ethical consideration of complex individual cases).

9.   *Palliative Sedation.* In a footnote in *Vacco*, Justice Rehnquist raises the issue of the legal status of "terminal sedation," which is sometimes described as "palliative sedation" because it is employed to provide palliation both in patients who are quickly approaching death and in those who are suffering but not yet otherwise terminal. Patients whose suffering cannot be ameliorated in any other way can be sedated with enough medication so that they are put into a medication-induced coma. This sedation may be accompanied by the withdrawal of other forms of treatment, including artificial nutrition and hydration. This withdrawal may (and, with the withdrawal of nutrition and hydration, will) lead to the patient's death. Justice Rehnquist suggests that terminal sedation, which has not given rise to the ethical objections that have come with medically assisted dying, is distinguishable from an affirmative act intended to bring about death, applying the principle of "double effect." Do you agree?

Under *Vacco*, whether palliative sedation is treated like the withdrawal of life-sustaining treatment or like an affirmative act causing death makes all the legal difference. As an ethical and legal matter, should terminal sedation be treated like the withdrawal of treatment or like medically assisted dying? For differing views on this question, see Thomas D. Riisfeldt, Weakening the Ethical Distinction between Euthanasia, Palliative Opioid Use and Palliative Sedation, 45 J. Med. Ethics 125 (2019) and responses. See also Paulo Rodrigues et al., Palliative Sedation for Existential Suffering: A Systematic Review of Argument-Based Ethics Literature, 55(6) J. Pain & Symptom Mgmt. 1577 (2018).

In 2008, over a decade after *Glucksberg* was decided, the AMA adopted a policy providing that it is ethically appropriate for physicians to offer palliative sedation, which the AMA called "sedation to unconsciousness in end-of-life care" at least to some terminally ill patients. The relevant opinion was amended in 2016:

> **Code of Medical Ethics Opinion 5.6, Sedation to Unconsciousness in End-of-Life Care (2016)**
>
> The duty to relieve pain and suffering is central to the physician's role as healer and is an obligation physicians have to their patients. When a terminally ill patient experiences severe pain or other distressing clinical symptoms that do not respond to aggressive, symptom-specific palliation it can be appropriate to offer sedation to unconsciousness as an intervention of last resort.
>
> Sedation to unconsciousness must never be used to intentionally cause a patient's death.
>
> When considering whether to offer palliative sedation to unconsciousness, physicians should:

(a) Restrict palliative sedation to unconsciousness to patients in the final stages of terminal illness.

(b) Consult with a multi-disciplinary team (if available), including an expert in the field of palliative care, to ensure that symptom-specific treatments have been sufficiently employed and that palliative sedation to unconsciousness is now the most appropriate course of treatment.

(c) Document the rationale for all symptom management interventions in the medical record.

(d) Obtain the informed consent of the patient (or the authorized surrogate when the patient lacks decision-making capacity).

(e) Discuss with the patient (or surrogate) the plan of care relative to:

(1) Degree and length of sedation

(2) Specific expectations for continuing, withdrawing, or withholding future life-sustaining treatments

(f) Monitor care once palliative sedation to unconsciousness is initiated.

The 2016 revision of this Ethical Opinion made a couple of notable changes to the earlier version of the opinion. First, the following paragraph, part of the 2008 version of the Ethical Opinion, was omitted from the more recent version:

> Palliative sedation is not an appropriate response to suffering that is primarily existential, defined as the experience of agony and distress that may arise from such issues as death anxiety, isolation and loss of control. Existential suffering is better addressed by other interventions. For example, palliative sedation is not the way to address suffering created by social isolation and loneliness; such suffering should be addressed by providing the patient with needed social support.

Does the omission suggest that sedation to unconsciousness is appropriate for existential suffering under some circumstances? Is it? Can all suffering (except physical pain) be treated through the provision of social support? Should palliative sedation be reserved for those with physical, not psychic, pain? See A. de Graeff and M. Dean, Palliative Sedation Therapy in the Last Weeks of Life: A Literature Review and Recommendations for Standards, 10 J. Palliative Med. 67 (2007); Allysa L. Ciancio et al., The Use of Palliative Sedation to Treat Existential Suffering: A Scoping Review on Practices, Ethical Considerations, and Guidelines, 35 J. Palliative Care 13 (2020). Some studies suggest that palliative sedation does not actually shorten the lives of cancer patients. M. Maltoni et al., Palliative Sedation in End-of-Life Care and Survival: A Systematic Review, 30 J. Clin. Oncology 1378 (2012); So-Jung Park, et al., Association between Continuous Deep Sedation and Survival Time in Terminally Ill Cancer Patients, 29 Supportive Care in Cancer 525 (2020).

Second, in 2016 the following portion of the Ethical Opinion was removed:

> When symptoms cannot be diminished through all other means of palliation, including symptom-specific treatments, it is the ethical obligation of a physician to offer palliative sedation to unconsciousness as an option for the relief of intractable symptoms.

Why was this sentence removed? Is it no longer an ethical obligation to offer palliative sedation to a patient? Should there be such an obligation if the physician believes that it is unethical to provide that form of care?

10. *Voluntary Stopping of Eating and Drinking*. Voluntary stopping of eating and drinking (VSED) has attracted increasing attention as a widely accessible alternative to medically assisted dying. As Chapter 18 established, every state allows a competent adult patient to refuse or discontinue life-sustaining medical care, and a physician to assist in implementing that decision, at least under most circumstances. Further, courts generally have concluded that the termination of artificial nutrition and hydration procedures is no different from the termination of other forms of mechanical support. But what if the patient is not receiving *artificial* nutrition and hydration or other life-sustaining care? Many assert a competent adult patient may opt for VSED as a method of hastening the patient's own death, and a health care provider may provide support to the patient, under such circumstances. For a discussion of clinical, ethical and legal issues surrounding VSED, see Timothy E. Quill et al, Voluntarily Stopping Eating and Drinking: A Compassionate, Widely Available Option for Hastening Death (2021).

III. STATE LEGISLATION AND LITIGATION TO SUPPORT MEDICALLY ASSISTED DYING

The debate over the proper role of physicians in assisting their patients in death has been carried on through legislative and citizen initiative processes as well as through litigation. "Death with Dignity" initiatives were narrowly defeated in California in 1991 and in Washington in 1992. However, Oregon's "Death with Dignity" initiative was approved by voters in the November 1994 election, and it thus became part of the statutory law of Oregon.

DEATH WITH DIGNITY ACT
Or. Rev. Stat. §§ 127.800–.897.

127.800. Definitions.

The following words and phrases, whenever used in ORS 127.800 to 127.897, have the following meanings:

(1) "Adult" means an individual who is 18 years of age or older.

(2) "Attending physician" means the physician who has primary responsibility for the care of the patient and treatment of the patient's terminal disease.

(3) "Capable" means that in the opinion of a court or in the opinion of the patient's attending physician or consulting physician, psychiatrist or psychologist, a patient has the ability to make and communicate health care decisions to health care providers, including communication through persons familiar with the patient's manner of communicating if those persons are available.

(4) "Consulting physician" means a physician who is qualified by specialty or experience to make a professional diagnosis and prognosis regarding the patient's disease.

(5) "Counseling" means one or more consultations as necessary between a state licensed psychiatrist or psychologist and a patient for the purpose of determining that the patient is capable and not suffering from a psychiatric or psychological disorder or depression causing impaired judgment.

(6) "Health care provider" means a person licensed, certified or otherwise authorized or permitted by the law of this state to administer health care or dispense medication in the ordinary course of business or practice of a profession, and includes a health care facility.

(7) "Informed decision" means a decision by a qualified patient, to request and obtain a prescription to end his or her life in a humane and dignified manner, that is based on an appreciation of the relevant facts and after being fully informed by the attending physician of:

(a) His or her medical diagnosis;

(b) His or her prognosis;

(c) The potential risks associated with taking the medication to be prescribed;

(d) The probable result of taking the medication to be prescribed; and

(e) The feasible alternatives, including, but not limited to, comfort care, hospice care and pain control.

(8) "Medically confirmed" means the medical opinion of the attending physician has been confirmed by a consulting physician who has examined the patient and the patient's relevant medical records.

(9) "Patient" means a person who is under the care of a physician.

(10) "Physician" means a doctor licensed to practice medicine * * *

(11) "Qualified patient" means a capable adult who is a resident of Oregon and has satisfied the requirements of ORS 127.800 to 127.897 in

order to obtain a prescription for medication to end his or her life in a humane and dignified manner.

(12) "Terminal disease" means an incurable and irreversible disease that has been medically confirmed and will, within reasonable medical judgment, produce death within six months.

127.805. Who may initiate a written request for medication.

(1) An adult who is capable, is a resident of Oregon, and has been determined by the attending physician and consulting physician to be suffering from a terminal disease, and who has voluntarily expressed his or her wish to die, may make a written request for medication for the purpose of ending his or her life in a humane and dignified manner in accordance with ORS 127.800 to 127.897.

(2) No person shall qualify under the provisions of ORS 127.800 to 127.897 solely because of age or disability.

127.810. Form of the written request.

(1) A valid request for medication under ORS 127.800 to 127.897 shall be in substantially the form described in ORS 127.897, signed and dated by the patient and witnessed by at least two individuals who, in the presence of the patient, attest that to the best of their knowledge and belief the patient is capable, acting voluntarily, and is not being coerced to sign the request.

(2) One of the witnesses shall be a person who is not:

(a) A relative of the patient by blood, marriage or adoption;

(b) A person who at the time the request is signed would be entitled to any portion of the estate of the qualified patient upon death under any will or by operation of law; or

(c) An owner, operator or employee of a health care facility where the qualified patient is receiving medical treatment or is a resident.

(3) The patient's attending physician at the time the request is signed shall not be a witness.

(4) If the patient is a patient in a long term care facility at the time the written request is made, one of the witnesses shall be an individual designated by the facility and having the qualifications specified by the Department of Human Services by rule.

127.815. Attending physician responsibilities.

(1) The attending physician shall:

(a) Make the initial determination of whether a patient has a terminal disease, is capable, and has made the request voluntarily;

(b) Request that the patient demonstrate Oregon residency pursuant to ORS 127.860;

(c) To ensure that the patient is making an informed decision, inform the patient of:

(A) His or her medical diagnosis;

(B) His or her prognosis;

(C) The potential risks associated with taking the medication to be prescribed;

(D) The probable result of taking the medication to be prescribed; and

(E) The feasible alternatives, including, but not limited to, comfort care, hospice care and pain control;

(d) Refer the patient to a consulting physician for medical confirmation of the diagnosis, and for a determination that the patient is capable and acting voluntarily;

(e) Refer the patient for counseling if appropriate pursuant to ORS 127.825;

(f) Recommend that the patient notify next of kin;

(g) Counsel the patient about the importance of having another person present when the patient takes the medication prescribed pursuant to ORS 127.800 to 127.897 and of not taking the medication in a public place;

(h) Inform the patient that he or she has an opportunity to rescind the request at any time and in any manner, and offer the patient an opportunity to rescind at the time the patient makes the patient's second oral request pursuant to ORS 127.840;

(i) Verify, immediately prior to writing the prescription for medication under ORS 127.800 to 127.897, that the patient is making an informed decision;

(j) Fulfill the medical record documentation requirements of ORS 127.855;

(k) Ensure that all appropriate steps are carried out in accordance with ORS 127.800 to 127.897 prior to writing a prescription for medication to enable a qualified patient to end his or her life in a humane and dignified manner; and

(A) Dispense medications directly . . . or [(B) through a pharmacist].

(2) Notwithstanding any other provision of law, the attending physician may sign the patient's report of death.

127.820. Consulting physician confirmation.

Before a patient is qualified under ORS 127.800 to 127.897, a consulting physician shall examine the patient and his or her relevant medical records and confirm, in writing, the attending physician's diagnosis that the patient is suffering from a terminal disease, and verify that the patient is capable, is acting voluntarily and has made an informed decision.

127.825. Counseling referral.

If in the opinion of the attending physician or the consulting physician a patient may be suffering from a psychiatric or psychological disorder or depression causing impaired judgment, either physician shall refer the patient for counseling. No medication to end a patient's life in a humane and dignified manner shall be prescribed until the person performing the counseling determines that the patient is not suffering from a psychiatric or psychological disorder or depression causing impaired judgment.

127.830. Informed decision.

No person shall receive a prescription for medication to end his or her life in a humane and dignified manner unless he or she has made an informed decision as defined in ORS 127.800 (7). Immediately prior to writing a prescription for medication under ORS 127.800 to 127.897, the attending physician shall verify that the patient is making an informed decision.

127.835. Family notification.

The attending physician shall recommend that the patient notify the next of kin of his or her request for medication pursuant to ORS 127.800 to 127.897. A patient who declines or is unable to notify next of kin shall not have his or her request denied for that reason.

127.840. Written and oral requests.

(1) In order to receive a prescription for medication to end his or her life in a humane and dignified manner, a qualified patient shall have made an oral request and a written request, and reiterate the oral request to his or her attending physician no less than 15 days after making the initial oral request.

(2) Notwithstanding subsection (1) of this section, if the qualified patient's attending physician has medically confirmed that the qualified patient will, within reasonable medical judgment, die within 15 days after making the initial oral request under this section, the qualified patient may reiterate the oral request to his or her attending physician at any time after making the initial oral request.

(3) At the time the qualified patient makes his or her second oral request, the attending physician shall offer the patient an opportunity to rescind the request.

127.845. Right to rescind request.

A patient may rescind his or her request at any time and in any manner without regard to his or her mental state. No prescription for medication under ORS 127.800 to 127.897 may be written without the attending physician offering the qualified patient an opportunity to rescind the request.

127.850. Waiting periods.

(1) No less than 15 days shall elapse between the patient's initial oral request and the writing of a prescription under ORS 127.800 to 127.897. No less than 48 hours shall elapse between the patient's written request and the writing of a prescription under ORS 127.800 to 127.897.

(2) Notwithstanding subsection (1) of this section, if the qualified patient's attending physician has medically confirmed that the qualified patient will, within reasonable medical judgment, die before the expiration of at least one of the waiting periods described in subsection (1) of this section, the prescription for medication under ORS 127.800 to 127.897 may be written at any time following the later of the qualified patient's written request or second oral request under ORS 127.840.

* * *

127.860. Residency requirement.

Only requests made by Oregon residents under ORS 127.800 to 127.897 shall be granted. Factors demonstrating Oregon residency include but are not limited to [being licensed to drive, registering to vote, owning property, and paying taxes in Oregon.]

* * *

127.880. Construction of Act.

Nothing in ORS 127.800 to 127.897 shall be construed to authorize a physician or any other person to end a patient's life by lethal injection, mercy killing or active euthanasia. Actions taken in accordance with ORS 127.800 to 127.897 shall not, for any purpose, constitute suicide, assisted suicide, mercy killing or homicide, under the law.

* * *

127.897. Form of the request.

A request for a medication as authorized by ORS 127.800 to 127.897 shall be in substantially the following form:

REQUEST FOR MEDICATION TO END MY LIFE IN A HUMANE AND DIGNIFIED MANNER

I, _____, am an adult of sound mind.

I am suffering from _____, which my attending physician has determined is a terminal disease and which has been medically confirmed by a consulting physician.

I have been fully informed of my diagnosis, prognosis, the nature of medication to be prescribed and potential associated risks, the expected result, and the feasible alternatives, including comfort care, hospice care and pain control.

I request that my attending physician prescribe medication that will end my life in a humane and dignified manner.

INITIAL ONE:

_____ I have informed my family of my decision and taken their opinions into consideration.

_____ I have decided not to inform my family of my decision.

_____ I have no family to inform of my decision.

I understand that I have the right to rescind this request at any time.

I understand the full import of this request and I expect to die when I take the medication to be prescribed. I further understand that although most deaths occur within three hours, my death may take longer and my physician has counseled me about this possibility.

I make this request voluntarily and without reservation, and I accept full moral responsibility for my actions.

[SIGNATURE LINE; WITNESS LINES]

* * *

NOTE: OREGON DEATH WITH DIGNITY ACT, 2020 ANNUAL REPORT

Under Oregon's Death with Dignity Act (DWDA), the Oregon Public Health Division is required to collect information on compliance and to issue an annual report. All of the annual reports are available at the Oregon Department of Health website. The key findings from the 2020 report, released February 2021, are summarized below.

- Since the law was passed in 1997, a total of 2,895 people have had DWDA prescriptions written and 1,905 people have died from ingesting medications prescribed under the DWDA. Both the number of prescriptions and the number of deaths have risen nearly every year since 1998.

- In 2020, 370 people received DWDA prescriptions, a 25% increase over the prior year. Of the 370 people, 223 (60%) died as a result of ingesting the medication. Sixty-seven (67) people (18%) did not take the medications and later died of other causes.

- An additional 22 people died in 2020 as a result of ingesting medication prescribed in 2019.

- Ingestion status is unknown for 80 people who were prescribed DWDA medications in 2020. Thirty-six of these patients died, but ingestion status is unknown. For the remaining 44 patients, both death and ingestion status are unknown.

- Of the 245 DWDA deaths during 2020, most (81%) were aged 65 years or older; the median age was 74 years. As in previous years, most were white (97%), well-educated (42% had a least a baccalaureate degree), and had cancer (66%). Three people were referred for formal psychiatric or psychological evaluation.

- Most (92%) patients died at home; and most (95%) were enrolled in hospice care either at the time the DWDA prescription was written or at the time of death. Excluding unknown cases, all (100%) had some form of health care insurance, although the number of patients who had private insurance (26%) continued to decline from previous years, and the number of patients who had only Medicare or Medicaid insurance (74%) continued to increase from previous years.

- As in previous years, the three most frequent concerns (as reported by physicians or family members of patients) were: decreasing ability to participate in activities that made life enjoyable (94%), loss of autonomy (93%), and loss of dignity (72%).

- Prescribing physicians were present at the time of death for 29 patients (12%), and 55 patients (22%) had other health care providers present.

- Data on time from ingestion to death is available for 138 DWDA deaths (56%) in 2020. Among those patients, time from ingestion until death ranged from six minutes to eight hours, with a median time of 50 minutes. Time from ingestion to death is influenced by the specific medications prescribed under the DWDA, which have changed over time.

- A total of 142 physicians wrote the 370 prescriptions in 2020 (range of 1–31 prescriptions per physician).

- During 2020, no referrals were made to the Oregon Medical Board for failure to comply with DWDA requirements.

NOTES AND QUESTIONS

1. *Other Provisions.* The Oregon Death with Dignity Act provides that no contract or statute can affect a person's request for medically assisted death, and that no insurance policy can be conditioned upon, or affected by, a patient's decision to choose (or reject) medically assisted death. The measure includes a section providing immunity for those who follow the requirements of the statute, and imposing liability on those who violate it.

2. *Minor Amendments.* The Oregon statute has been amended, but the changes are not substantial. The legislature added the definition of "capable," added some new language designed to encourage patients to discuss the matter with their families, and provided some factors to be considered in determining residency. The amendments also made clear the broad extent of the institutional conscience exception to the statute, which permits health care institutions to limit physicians from engaging in assisted death on their premises or in their organizations. It also changed the written consent form to assure that patients recognize that death will probably, but not always, take place about three hours after taking the medication.

3. *Legal Challenges.* The Oregon initiative was immediately challenged for a wide range of reasons. Some argued that it discriminated against the disabled, for example, by coercing them into choosing medically assisted dying, and others argued it discriminated against the disabled because those with physical disabilities that made it impossible to take oral medications would not be able to use the statute. The U.S. District Court in Oregon issued a preliminary injunction against enforcing the initiative shortly after its passage and issued a permanent injunction several months later. Ultimately, the Ninth Circuit reversed the District Court, finding that those challenging the Oregon initiative had no standing to raise the issue in federal court. Lee v. Oregon, 107 F.3d 1382 (9th Cir.1997).

4. *Federalism Concerns.* The federal government has not ignored medically assisted dying, either. Even before the Oregon statute became effective, Congress passed the Assisted Suicide Prevention Restriction Act of 1997, which outlawed the use of federal money to aid medically assisted dying, directly or indirectly.

Shortly after the Oregon Death with Dignity Act became effective, some suggested that any physician who prescribed a lethal drug under that statute would be prescribing that drug without a "legitimate medical purpose," and thus would be acting inconsistently with the federal Controlled Substances Act (CSA). A physician's violation of the Act could lead to both the loss of prescribing authority and criminal indictment. In 1998, after the matter had been pending for some time, the U.S. States Department of Justice published a report concluding that use of controlled substances under the Oregon statute would satisfy the "legitimate medical purpose" requirement of the federal Act.

Members of the House and Senate then introduced the Lethal Drug Abuse Prevention Act of 1998, which would have expanded the authority of the Drug

Enforcement Agency to investigate the lethal use of controlled substances, which the Act provided could not be used with the intent of causing death. Supporters of medically assisted dying joined many of their staunchest opponents and mainstream medical organizations (including the AMA) in opposing the bill because, they said, it would be likely to chill physicians from providing adequate pain relief at the end of life.

Although the bill failed, it was resurrected in slightly milder form in 2000 as the Pain Relief Promotion Act (PRPA), which included a well-publicized section announcing that the provision of medication with the intent to manage pain (and not the intent to cause death) was protected. The 2000 version of the bill also provided for the education of health care professionals on issues related to pain management, and it was supported by the AMA (but opposed by the American Bar Association, the American Cancer Society, and most groups advocating for improved pain management). Although the stated purpose of PRPA was to promote adequate pain relief practices, its effect would be (and, some say, its real purpose was) to render it impossible for physicians in Oregon to carry out the provisions of the Death with Dignity Act. The PRPA died when Congress adjourned in late 2000.

In 2001, the Attorney General, John Ashcroft, issued an interpretive rule that reversed the 1998 Department of Justice position on the issue of the application of the CSA and implemented an enforcement action. Within a day of the announcement of this change in the federal position, Oregon sought relief from the Attorney General's decision in the federal court. A private action seeking an injunction against the Ashcroft position was filed shortly thereafter on behalf of an Oregon oncologist. The District Court immediately restrained the U.S. from enforcing the new interpretation of the CSA, and in 2006 the Supreme Court determined that the Attorney General's interpretive rule was beyond the scope of his authority and was improperly promulgated. Gonzales v. Oregon, 546 U.S. 243, 126 S. Ct. 904, 163 L. Ed. 2d 748 (2006). The Court left open the possibility that the Attorney General could properly promulgate a substantive rule that would bar the operation of the Oregon Death with Dignity Act, and that Congress could amend the Controlled Substances Act to achieve this end. Neither has happened to date.

5. *Adequate Oversight?* Does the Annual Report address whether the requirements of Section 127.815, or any other section of the DWDA, actually were followed in practice? How would the Department determine the answer to that question? Those who are skeptical about whether the Annual Report accurately presents the impact of the Act point out that the report can describe only those cases that are reported to the state. They argue that cases that do not comply with the specific requirements of the statute will not be reported. It is in this potential body of unreported cases that evidence for concerns over the effectiveness of the statute's boundaries would be found. See, e.g., Nat'l Council on Disability, Medical Futility and Disability Bias (2019); Margaret K. Dore, "Death with Dignity"; A Recipe for Elder Abuse and Homicide (Albeit Not by Name), 11(2) Marquette Elder's Advisor 387 (Spring 2010) (noting

possibility that someone other than the patient could administer the prescribed medications).

6.   *Reported Reasons.* As the Annual Report published in 2020 indicates, according to patient physicians and families, most Oregonians who have sought medically assisted dying have done so because of decreasing ability to participate in activities that made life enjoyable (94%) and loss of autonomy (93%), as well as perceived loss of dignity (72%), not because of physical pain. An excerpt from Oregon's Second Annual Report, published in 2000, explains this:

> Responses from both physician and family interviews indicate that patient's decisions to request PAS were motivated by multiple interrelated concerns. Physical suffering was discussed by several families as a cause of loss of autonomy, inability to participate in activities that made life enjoyable, or a "non-existent" quality of life. For example, "She would have stuck it out through the pain if she thought she'd get better . . . [but she believed that] when quality of life has no meaning, it's no use hanging around." For another participant, a feeling of being trapped because of ALS contributed to concern about loss of autonomy. Family members frequently commented on loss of control of bodily functions when discussing loss of autonomy. Those reporting patient concern about being a burden on friends and family also reported concern about loss of autonomy and control of bodily functions. Reasons for requesting a prescription were sometimes so interrelated they were difficult to categorize. According to one family member being asked to distinguish reasons for the patient's decision, "It was everything; it was nothing; [he was suffering terribly]."

> Difficulty categorizing and differences in interpreting the nature of the concerns made physician and family member responses hard to compare quantitatively. Nonetheless, family interviews corroborate physician reports from both years that patients are greatly concerned about issues of autonomy and control. In addition, responses of both physicians and family consistently pointed to patient concerns about quality of life and the wish to have a means of controlling the end of life should it become unbearable. As one family member said, "She always thought that if something was terminal, she would [want to] control the end . . . It was not the dying that she dreaded, it was getting to that death."

Might physicians and family members, or both, be mistaken about what motivated a relative's decisions? In any case, could the expressed concerns have been relieved by better medical and nursing care, or by patient-directed supports and services that allowed for participation in enjoyable activities to the extent possible? Should we be concerned that decisions may be influenced by a belief that "dignity" is not possible for people who rely on caregivers or other supports to live their lives? Or are these decisions that, even if influenced by social and political factors, should be left to individuals?

7. *Requirement of Contemporaneous Competence.* The Oregon statute requires that the requesting adult be "capable" at the time of the request. The requirement of contemporaneous competence excludes individuals who are no longer competent from exercising the option for medically assisted death through an advance directive. Some have argued that advance directives opting for medically assisted death, where legally permitted, should be permitted. Do you agree? For a discussion of the application of advance directives in this context, focusing on individuals with dementia, see Paul T. Menzel & Bonnie Steinbock, Advance Directives, Dementia, and Physician-Assisted Death, 41 J.L. Med. & Ethics 484 (2013). See also Megan S. Wright, Equality of Autonomy?: Physician Aid in Dying and Supported Decision-Making, 63 Ariz. L. Rev. 157 (2021) (examining whether terminally ill people with cognitive impairments such as dementia should be able to access medically assisted death through supported decision-making).

8. *Legislation in Other States.* Advocates for medically assisted dying in Washington made that state the second to use the initiative process to provide for medically assisted dying with the passage of the Washington Death with Dignity Act, again through the initiative process and a statewide vote, in 2008. Former Washington Governor Booth Gardner, who had Parkinson's disease, became the leading advocate for an Oregon-like statute. For the story of Governor Gardner's "last campaign" from the perspective of someone who opposes medically assisted dying, see Daniel Bergner, Death in the Family, N.Y. Times Magazine (December 2, 2007). The Washington Death with Dignity statute, R.C.W. section 70.245, became effective in 2009.

In 2013 Vermont became the first state to adopt a statute permitting aid in dying through the regular legislative process (rather than through an initiative) in the Patient Choice and Control at the End of Life Act, Vt. Stat. Ann. tit. 18, §§ 5281–93. California followed with the End of Life Option Act in 2015, Cal. Health & Safety Code § 443, and the District of Columbia City Council promulgated a Death with Dignity Act in 2016, D.C. Law 21–182. Although there were threats of a Congressional veto of that legislation—a remedy available to Congress only with regard to the District, and not with regard to states—attempts to do so failed. Congress could still effectively repeal the D.C. statute through separate legislation, but it has not done so.

Voters passed the Colorado End of Life Options Act in 2016, Colo. Rev. Stat. §§ 25–48–101–23, and it became effective at the end of that year. The Hawai'i Legislature passed an Oregon-like statute in 2018. Our Care, Our Choice Act, Haw. Rev. Stat. § 327L–1. In 2019, New Jersey enacted the Medical Aid in Dying for the Terminally Ill Act, N.J. State Ann. §§ 26:16–1 et seq., and Maine enacted the Maine Death with Dignity Act, Me. Stat. tit. 22, § 2140. Finally, New Mexico passed the Elizabeth Whitefield End of Life Options Act, H.B. 46, in 2021.

In all, 11 jurisdictions in the U.S. now formally permit medically assisted dying, at least under some circumstances—Oregon, Washington, and Colorado by initiative; Vermont, California, Hawai'i, the District of Columbia, New

Jersey, Maine and New Mexico by ordinary legislative action; and, as we shall see in the Note below, Montana by judicial interpretation of current statutory law. For a discussion of variation among these laws in terms of eligibility requirements, procedural conditions, and other mandates see Thaddeus Mason Pope, Medical Aid in Dying: Key Variations Among U.S. State Laws, 14(1) J. Health & Life Sci. L. 25–59 (2020).

Legislatures in several other states are currently considering legislation that would permit medically assisted dying. Of course, not all efforts to pass such legislation will be effective. Many states have rejected such legislation, and some have rejected multiple proposals. A complete listing of proposals in the U.S. is maintained by the Patients Rights Council at their website.

9. *Adequate Pain Treatment.* Is there some common ground available between those, on the one hand, who believe that permitting medically assisted dying is necessary for patients to be properly treated at the end of life, and those, on the other hand, who believe that medically assisted dying must be outlawed for patients to be properly treated? Both groups agree that pain is often inadequately treated at the end of life, in part because physicians fear legal action for homicide (if pain relief results in the death of the patient) or for distribution of drugs (if the condition of a patient requires a larger dose of narcotic medication than is standard).

In some states advocates on both sides of the medically assisted dying issue have joined together to support intractable pain relief statutes, which are designed to protect health care providers who deliver adequate pain relief from adverse licensing and criminal actions. These statutes generally provide that a health care provider will not be liable in a state disciplinary proceeding or a criminal action for the aggressive prescription of pain medication as long as the use of that medication is in accord with accepted guidelines for pain management. Several states have promulgated intractable pain relief acts, and several more are considering them. For a model pain relief act, see 24 J.L., Med. Ethics 317 (1996). See also Ann Alpers, Criminal Act or Palliative Care? Prosecutions Involving the Care of the Dying, 26 J.L. Med. Ethics 308 (1998) (identifying factors that create a risk of prosecution); Kelly K. Dineen & James M. DuBois, Between a Rock and a Hard Place: Can Physicians Prescribe Opioids to Treat Pain Adequately While Avoiding Legal Sanction?, 42 Am. J. L. & Med. 7 (2016) (proposing a model for characterizing misprescribers).

For a series of articles on the relationship between pain relief and medically assisted dying, with the conclusion that we ought to create a system that both provides excellent palliative care in every case and allows for medically assisted dying in the rare cases in which it is necessary, see Timothy Quill and Margaret Battin, eds., Physician-Assisted Dying: The Right to Excellent End-of-Life Care and Patient Choice (2004). See also Kathleen Foley, The Case Against Assisted Suicide: For the Right to End of Life Care (2002) (written by a leading palliative care physician). For an account of the meaning of euthanasia and suicide in our society and others, and a description of how these arguments are likely to be discussed in the future, see Margaret Battin, *Ending Life: Ethics and the Way We Die* (2005).

10. *Palliative Care and Cannabis.* Federal and state policy may conflict on one kind of palliative care—the use of marijuana and cannabis products. Some cancer patients, patients with glaucoma, AIDS patients, patients with multiple sclerosis, those with migraine headaches, and others find that they can obtain relief from some of the symptoms of their condition—or from some of the side effects of the treatments for their condition—through the use of marijuana. In particular, some cancer patients find that marijuana helps them overcome the nausea that follows the use of many chemotherapeutic agents.

As of May 2021, 36 states and four territories allow for the medical use of cannabis products (under highly varying state standards). A complete listing of medical marijuana laws is maintained by the National Conference of State Legislatures at their website. However, the manufacture and distribution of cannabis is still a felony under the Federal Controlled Substances Act (CSA). In 2001, the Supreme Court determined that there was no medical necessity defense available to those who manufactured or distributed marijuana to patients in violation of the federal law. *U.S. v. Oakland Cannabis Buyers' Cooperative*, 532 U.S. 483, 121 S. Ct. 1711, 149 L. Ed. 2d 722 (2001). Four years later the Supreme Court confirmed that the CSA marijuana prohibition fell within Congress's commerce power. *Gonzales v. Raich*, 545 U.S. 1, 125 S. Ct. 2195, 162 L. Ed. 2d 1 (2005).

Wavering federal approaches toward enforcement of the federal law have added complexity to the increasing conflict between state reforms and federal laws. See Robert A. Mikos, *The Evolving Federal Response to State Marijuana Reforms*, 26 Widener L. Rev. 1 (2020). Public opinion is also shifting, increasing pressure on the federal government to act. According to a 2021 poll conducted by the Pew Research Center, an overwhelming majority of U.S. adults (91%) say either that marijuana should be legal for medical *and* recreational use (60%) or that it should be legal for medical use only (31%). Three major bills were introduced in Congress in 2019, each taking a different approach to cannabis decriminalization, legalization, and reform. For a discussion of those bills through a health equity lens, see Nicole Huberfeld, *Health Equity, Federalism, and Cannabis Policy*, 101 B.U. L. Rev. 897 (2021). See also Rebecca Haffajee and Amanda Mauri, *Cannabis Liberalization in the U.S.: The Policy Landscape*, Health Aff. Health Policy Brief (July 1, 2021).

11. *International Views.* The public interest in this issue is not limited to the U.S. Medically assisted dying has been tolerated in the Netherlands, as a legal matter, since 1969, and it was formally legalized by the Parliament in 2001 in cases of intractable suffering (not just pain), where the patient has been informed of all of the alternative treatments available, has consulted two physicians, and has followed other requirements established by the national medical association. Belgium joined the Netherlands in legalizing medically assisted dying through the legislative process, and the practice is now officially tolerated under some circumstances in Switzerland and Spain. The

Constitutional Court of Colombia has approved legislation that provides for medically assisted dying, and there has been an active debate in France, Venezuela and Australia over the propriety of permitting medically assisted dying.

Australia's Northern Territory's Parliament passed The Rights of the Terminally Ill Act (1995), which permitted what some have called "voluntary euthanasia" under some circumstances; however, the national Parliament effectively overturned that territorial statute. The national Parliament has no such control over legislation coming from the states (rather than territories) in Australia, and voluntary assisted death is permitted in the states of Victoria and Western Australia. The states of Tasmania and South Australia also have passed bills which, upon their effective dates, will authorize voluntary assisted death, also in limited circumstances. Voluntary assisted death is not lawful in other Australian States and Territories, though this may change as Australian jurisdictions consider legal reform in this area.

Canada has allowed for medically assisted dying since the Parliament permitted it, encouraged (or, perhaps, compelled) by a 2015 decision of the Supreme Court of Canada. The governing statute has many of the requirements of the Oregon and Washington statutes, although it is generally more liberal in permitting the practice, and it allows a patient to choose euthanasia (where the final dose is actually delivered by a health care provider) rather than taking the medication himself, if that is his desire. The vast majority of Canadian patients given the option to choose medical delivery of the lethal dose (rather than self-administration) have done so. The Canadian statute was encouraged by the 2015 decision in Carter v. Canada (AG), 2015 SCC 5, which found that not allowing a competent adult access to relief from suffering at the end of life by outlawing medically assisted dying violated the Canadian Charter of Rights and Freedoms.

The European Court of Human Rights considered a challenge to the laws of the United Kingdom that outlawed medically assisted dying in Pretty v. United Kingdom, 35 Eur. H. R. Rep. 1 (2002). Applying an analysis similar, in many respects, to that in *Glucksberg* and *Vacco*, the Court found that the United Kingdom had the authority to enforce its law. An English court again confirmed the legal prohibition against medically assisted dying in 2012. For a brief description of the current state of the law in other countries, see Alan Meisel, Kathy Cerminara, and Thaddeus Mason Pope, The Right to Die (3d ed. 2005, Supplement 2020).

PROBLEM: DRAFTING LEGISLATION

You are the nonpolitical legislative counsel to a state legislature. Currently that state has a statute prohibiting assisting suicide which, it is assumed, would outlaw any conduct intended to result in the death of another person. You have been asked by several members of the legislature to draft bills relating to medically assisted dying. One member has asked you to draft a bill that would outlaw all medically assisted dying, under all circumstances.

A second member wants you to draft a bill that would put as few limitations on medically assisted dying as possible; this libertarian member believes that the decision should be left to individual doctors and patients. Another member has asked you to draft a statute that would protect health care providers from potential liability for participating in medically assisted dying, and that would give providers an option to avoid participating in medically assisted dying if they chose not to do so. Yet another member has asked you to draft a statute that would prohibit managed care organizations from directly or indirectly giving any incentives to their members to choose medically assisted dying. Finally, one long-time incumbent has asked you to draft a consensus statute— one with enough political support across the spectrum that it has a reasonable chance of passing. Presumably, this would be a statute that would permit some narrow form of medically assisted dying under carefully controlled and narrowly defined circumstances.

How would you go about drafting these statutes? How would they be different? What facts (about the legal landscape in this state, about the politics of the current officeholders, about the religious backgrounds of those within the state, about other issues) would you want to have before you started drafting these statutes?

NOTE: ESTABLISHING A STATE RIGHT TO MEDICALLY ASSISTED DYING THROUGH LITIGATION

As it becomes clear that each state is going to determine the legal status of medically assisted dying within its borders, advocates of legal medically assisted dying have looked to state judiciaries as well as state legislatures to establish such a right. While the issue of the legalization of medically assisted dying has been litigated in a host of different forms over the last few decades, the highest courts of only five states—Florida, Alaska, Montana, New Mexico, and New York—have had a chance to directly address the issue in the last few years. State constitutional claims were raised in all five states, and they were rejected in all five cases. One of these courts, in Montana, also did a statutory analysis and found that there was no violation of any statute when a provider wrote a lethal prescription under circumstances similar to those permitted by statute in Oregon. Thus, the Supreme Court of Montana found that current Montana law did not outlaw medically assisted dying, even if the Montana Constitution did not independently protect a person who was seeking that form of treatment.

The other state courts to consider the issue—the Florida, Alaska, and New Mexico Supreme Courts and the New York Court of Appeals—found no state constitutional right to medically assisted dying, and, unlike the court in Montana, also found that there was no statutory right to medically assisted dying within their states because any exercise of medically assisted dying would constitute the crime of aiding or abetting (or assisting) suicide under state statute.

The Montana case, Baxter v. Montana, 354 Mont. 234, 224 P.3d 1211 (2009), rejected the argument (which had been accepted at the trial court) that outlawing medically assisted dying would violate the protection of individual dignity guaranteed by Article II, section 4 of the Montana Constitution, which provides that "[t]he dignity of the human being is inviolable." While at least one judge would have found that the individual dignity clause was sufficient to protect medically assisted dying, the majority decided the case on statutory grounds. The court determined that under Montana law consent is a defense, even to homicide crimes, as long as the defendant's conduct is not "against public policy." Here, the court determined, medically assisted dying was not contrary to public policy; indeed, the Montana Legislature had never spoken about it in a way that approved or disapproved of it. Thus, while the Montana Legislature could outlaw medically assisted dying, it had not done so as a matter of statutory law, and no state constitutional analysis was necessary.

At the next plenary Montana legislative session following *Baxter*, in 2011, the Legislature was squarely confronted both with bills that would outlaw medically assisted dying, and with a bill that would formally legalize it and impose the same kinds of restrictions that are imposed in Washington and Oregon. The bills were carefully followed by the press, and there was a good deal of advocacy by partisans on both sides of the issue. Ultimately, the Legislature rejected all of the bills on both sides of the issue and left the law as it stood the day that *Baxter* was decided.

In 2013 the Montana Legislature again faced bills to both institutionalize (on one side) and prohibit (on the other side) aid in dying. Other legislative proposals have been introduced since, without success. It seems like the default position will always be the legislative winner in Montana; whatever the law is today will remain the law indefinitely because there is inadequate legislative support either to make medically assisted death legal (if it is not) or illegal (if it is now legal).

In fact, given the difficulty of pushing legislation through a state legislature and across a Governor's desk, the state "default" position—the law in the absence of any legislation dealing directly with medically assisted dying—will determine whether medically assisted dying is permitted. This "default" position, of course, must be determined by the courts. The Montana Supreme Court described the "default" position as one in which there was no statutory provision outlawing medically assisted dying—so medically assisted dying is permitted in Montana. Other state judiciaries to consider the issue found the "default" position to be that medically assisted dying is outlawed by state statutes criminalizing assisting suicide. Thus, medically assisted dying is not permitted in Florida, Alaska, New Mexico or New York. Because neither side on this issue has the political strength to change the current statutory law on medically assisted dying—whatever that law may be—the status of the state law is really determined by the state courts in determining the "default" position in that state.

Those opposed to medically assisted dying also sought to use the administrative process to reinstate the ban in Montana. An attempt to have the Montana Board of Medical Examiners declare that they would impose professional sanctions against any Montana physician who provided medically assisted dying in accord with the *Baxter* opinion was met with this response in 2012:

Physician Aid in Dying

The Montana Board of Medical Examiners has been asked if it will discipline physicians for participating in such aid-in-dying. This statement reflects the Board's position on this controversial question.

The Board recognizes that its mission is to protect the citizens of Montana against the unprofessional, improper, unauthorized and unqualified practice of medicine by ensuring that its licensees are competent professionals. [ ] In all matters of medical practice, including end-of-life matters, physicians are held to professional standards. If the Board receives a complaint related to physician aid-in-dying, it will evaluate the complaint on its individual merits and will consider, as it would any other medical procedure or intervention, whether the physician engaged in unprofessional conduct as defined by the laws and rules pertinent to the Board.

Mont. Bd. Of Med. Examiners, Position Statement No. 20 (2012). This statement was applauded by those who support aid-in-dying and who believe that it should be treated like any other medical procedure. Montanans Against Assisted Suicide (MAAS) and for Living with Dignity, an advocacy group opposed to aid-in-dying, asked the Board to withdraw the statement, which, those advocates said, was issued without proper notice, without statutory authority, and in violation of the principle of separation of powers. They argued that the Position Statement put doctors and the public at risk. MAAS then sought a declaratory ruling that the Position Statement was invalid, but the action was dismissed after the Board rescinded the statement. See Montanans Against Assisted Suicide v. Bd. Of Med. Examiners, 379 Mont. 11, 347 P.3d 1244 (2015).

Litigation to establish the kind of right recognized in *Baxter* has not been successful outside of Montana. In Krischer v. McIver, 697 So. 2d 97 (Fla. 1997), a terminally ill AIDS patient and his physician sought an injunction against the prosecution of the physician for assisting in his patient's suicide. The Florida Supreme Court rejected a claim that the privacy provision of the Florida Constitution included the right to have a physician assist in one's death. The court announced that a properly drawn statute authorizing physician-assisted suicide would be constitutionally permissible, but that principles of separation of powers left the decision about whether it should be made legal to the legislature. The Chief Justice filed a vigorous dissent, arguing that, " . . . the right of privacy attaches with unusual force at the death bed. . . . What possible interest does society have in saving life when there is nothing of life to save but a final convulsion of agony? The state has no business in this arena." 697 So. 2d at 111. See also Sampson v. State, 31 P.3d 88 (Alaska 2001).

The New Mexico Supreme Court faced an argument that its assisting suicide statute was a violation of state constitutional law in Morris v. Brandenburg, 376 P.3d 836, 2016-NMSC-027 (2016). In that case, a patient and her physicians brought a declaratory judgment action against state officials alleging that the statute criminalizing assisting suicide was unconstitutional. Judgment was entered for the plaintiffs after a multi-day trial, and the Court of Appeals reversed. The New Mexico Supreme Court determined that medically assisted dying would constitute "assisting suicide," a crime in New Mexico, and thus it was illegal unless that criminal statute itself violated a federal or state constitutional provision. The court rejected due process arguments based on both the U.S. and state constitutions by deferring to the U.S. Supreme Court's analysis in *Glucksberg*, above. The court separately rejected the application of the New Mexico constitution's provision which assures that the state will protect such "natural, inherent and inalienable" rights as those of "seeking and obtaining safety and happiness." The court concluded that any right to medically assisted dying would have to come from its legislature.

The New York Court of Appeals faced the same issue in Myers v. Schneiderman, 85 N.E.3d 57, 30 N.Y.3d 1 (N.Y. 2017). Like the New Mexico court, the New York Court of Appeals deferred to the *Glucksberg* analysis of the due process and equal protection issues and, in addition, found that there was a rational basis for applying the law prohibiting assisted suicide. Like the New Mexico court, the New York Court of Appeals determined that the application of the criminal assisted suicide statute to those offering medically assisted dying is a matter for the New York Legislature, at least given the current state of the record. Although that application of the criminal law is not required by state constitutional law, it is not prohibited by state constitutional law either.

PROBLEM: MEDICALLY ASSISTED DYING, A LEGAL ISSUE OR A MEDICAL ISSUE?

Our country's conflict over medically assisted dying has been fought in the legal arena. Is there a right to engage in medically assisted dying? Do homicide and suicide statutes prohibit the practice of medically assisted dying? Those with more libertarian views tend to support finding such a right; those with strongly developed religious views or a more expansive view of criminal law are less likely to find such a right. The battles over legislation and most of the reported litigation reflect the rights-oriented legal battle over this issue.

Instead, should we be asking whether medically assisted dying is within the medical standard of care? If we were to take this approach, we would treat medically assisted dying as one of many end-of-life care possibilities, and we would let providers determine if it is appropriate on a case-by-case basis. Instead of arguing about the issue in the courts, we would leave it to health care professionals, who could offer to their patients whatever came within the standard of care.

Do you think the issue is best analyzed as one of legal rights and obligations, ultimately to be decided by courts, or as one of good medicine, ultimately to be determined by the physician and her patient in each case?

For an account of an early effort by physicians to establish a standard of care in this area, see T.E. Quill, C.K. Cassel and D.E. Meier, Care of the Hopelessly Ill: Proposed Clinical Criteria for Physician-Assisted Suicide, 327 NEJM 1380 (1992). For a more recent legal suggestion that physicians should be developing standards of practice in this area, written by an advocate of medically assisted death, see Kathryn Tucker, Aid in Dying: Guidance for an Emerging End-of-Life Practice, 142 Chest 218 (2012).

CHAPTER 20

REGULATION OF RESEARCH INVOLVING HUMAN SUBJECTS

• • •

I. INTRODUCTION

Medical research has contributed to relieving great human suffering. It also has been the cause of injustice and misery to individuals and groups who have been treated as grist for the research mill or as conscripts in the war against disease.

The ethical framework for the relationship between researcher and subject differs from that for physician and patient. While the goal of improving the well-being of the individual patient is held as the essential goal in the physician-patient relationship, that is simply not the case in medical research. Instead, research has as a primary goal the production of new knowledge for the good of society and typically requires risk to the individual, although formal ethical principles for medical research require respect for the autonomy and well-being of the individual subject as well. This balance rests on the fulcrum of the prohibition against research without the voluntary consent of the subject, but distrusts that consent alone is up to the task of protecting individuals while benefiting the common good.

Problems are especially likely to arise when subjects are also patients, and their physicians are also researchers. In this context, the goals of research and the goals of treatment may become incompatible in ways that are not readily apparent. Research studies, for example, adopt strict protocols to assure validity of results that may differ from the more flexible approach taken in a treatment context. In addition, claims of trust as a basis for the relationship of patient to physician rely on the primacy of the physician's duty to act in the patient's best interest, an underlying assumption that is inapt for the researcher-subject relationship. As a result, modeling the consent process for medical research upon the informed consent process for treatment creates an ill-fitting foundation for judging adequacy of consent. Similarly, applying the legal framework for rights and duties in medical treatment to the context of medical research can produce unsatisfying results.

The regulatory framework for research in the U.S. reflects that same tension between the gains in knowledge and health promised by research and the value of protecting the individual subject from harm. Research regulation constantly confronts competing claims about the nature of the research enterprise: Is medical research such a privileged endeavor for the common good that restraints should be minimal; or is competition for accomplishment, reputation, and new products so strong that robust oversight is required?

II.   STANDARDS GOVERNING PROTECTION OF HUMAN SUBJECTS

A.   THE NUREMBERG CODE

The Nuremberg Code is the foundational document for the legal and moral principles that govern research with human subjects. This Code was born of tragedy on an enormous scale. The shocking horrors that could be perpetrated in the name of medical experimentation became apparent to the world through the Nazi war crimes trials. The Medical Trial detailed experiments in which "volunteers," usually concentration camp inmates, were exposed to extremely low atmospheric pressure until they died; were forced to drink seawater or breathe mustard gas; were intentionally infected with malaria and typhus; were placed in ice water until they froze; underwent macabre surgeries, often without anesthesia; or were subjected to other tortures. Perpetrators justified their actions as legitimate medical research. Most of the twenty physicians accused of participating in or directing this experimentation were convicted, and some were hanged. A few were acquitted and one, the infamous Dr. Mengele, escaped.

In one of the tribunal's most significant actions, the court sitting in Nuremberg promulgated principles for legal and ethical medical research. Perhaps surprisingly, prosecutors at Nuremberg had struggled to find an authoritative formal legal canon governing medical research in either the U.S. or Germany, and Nuremberg code emerged from that experience. See Sandra Johnson, Nazi Experiments, the Nuremberg Code, and the United States, in Nazi Law: From Nuremberg to Nuremberg (John Michalczyk (ed.), 2018).

NUREMBERG CODE: PERMISSIBLE MEDICAL EXPERIMENTS

The great weight of the evidence before us is to the effect that certain types of medical experiments on human beings, when kept within reasonably well-defined bounds, conform to the ethics of the medical profession generally. The protagonists of the practice of human experimentation justify their views on the basis that such experiments yield results for the good of society that are unprocurable by other methods or means of study. All agree, however, that certain basic principles must be observed in order to satisfy moral, ethical, and legal concepts:

1. The voluntary consent of the human subject is absolutely essential.

This means that the person involved should have legal capacity to give consent; should be so situated as to be able to exercise free power of choice, without the intervention of any element of force, fraud, deceit, duress, over-reaching, or other ulterior form of constraint or coercion; and should have sufficient knowledge and comprehension of the elements of the subject matter involved as to enable him to make an understanding and enlightened decision. This latter element requires that before the acceptance of an affirmative decision by the experimental subject there should be made known to him the nature, duration, and purpose of the experiment; the method and means by which it is to be conducted; all inconveniences and hazards reasonably to be expected; and the effects upon his health or person which may possibly come from his participation in the experiment.

The duty and responsibility for ascertaining the quality of the consent rests upon each individual who initiates, directs, or engages in the experiment. It is a personal duty and responsibility which may not be delegated to another with impunity.

2. The experiment should be such as to yield fruitful results for the good of society, unprocurable by other methods or means of study, and not random and unnecessary in nature.

3. The experiment should be so designed and based on the results of animal experimentation and a knowledge of the natural history of the disease or other problem under study that the anticipated results will justify the performance of the experiment.

4. The experiment should be so conducted as to avoid all unnecessary physical and mental suffering and injury.

5. No experiment should be conducted where there is an *a priori* reason to believe that death or disabling injury will occur; except, perhaps, in those experiments where the experimental physicians also serve as subjects.

6. The degree of risk to be taken should never exceed that determined by the humanitarian importance of the problem to be solved by the experiment.

7. Proper preparations should be made and adequate facilities provided to protect the experimental subject against even remote possibilities of injury, disability, or death.

8. The experiment should be conducted only by scientifically qualified persons. The highest degree of skill and care should be required

through all stages of the experiment by those who conduct or engage in the experiment.

9.   During the course of the experiment the human subject should be at liberty to bring the experiment to an end if he has reached the physical or mental state where continuation of the experiment seems to him to be impossible.

10.   During the course of the experiment the scientist in charge must be prepared to terminate the experiment at any stage, if he has probable cause to believe, in the exercise of the good faith, superior skill, and careful judgment required of him, that a continuation of the experiment is likely to result in injury, disability, or death to the experimental subject.

B.   LEGAL STANDARDS IN THE U.S.

The Nuremberg Code did not have an immediate impact in the U.S., perhaps because the Nazi doctors were viewed as monsters working far outside the tradition of medical ethics in this country. See George Annas, Mengele's Birthmark: The Nuremberg Code in United States Courts, 7 J. Contemp. Health L. & Pol'y 17 (1991). In fact, the U.S. government was conducting research at the same time that would violate the principles of the Nuremberg Code. In just one example, the government tested the human response to radiation by injecting patients (many of whom were inaccurately described as terminally ill) with plutonium or uranium to observe its physical effect. These subjects were never informed of the nature of the experiments. See Advisory Committee on Human Radiation Experiments, The Human Radiation Experiments (1996); Susan Smith, Mustard Gas and American Race-Based Human Experimentation in World War II, 36 J. L. Med. & Ethics 517 (2008).

It wasn't until the publication of a landmark article detailing abuses of human subjects in the U.S. that it was recognized that medical research abuse was possible, if not common, in this country. Henry K. Beecher, Ethics and Clinical Research, 274 NEJM 1354 (1966). Just a few years later, in 1972, the most infamous violation of research ethics in twentieth-century America came to light. In the Tuskegee Syphilis Study, begun in 1932, the U.S. Public Health Service (USPHS) studied the natural course of untreated syphilis in 399 impoverished African American men. Even when penicillin, the first effective treatment for syphilis, became available, the USPHS physicians refused to offer that treatment to most of their subjects; and many of these men were expressly and regularly discouraged from seeking treatment. For nearly 40 years, the USPHS condemned these men and their wives, partners, and families to the ravages of untreated syphilis. See James H. Jones, Bad Blood: The Tuskegee Syphilis Experiment (1981); Ruquaiija Yearby, Exploitation in Medical Research:

The Enduring Legacy of the Tuskegee Syphilis Study, 67 Case W. Res. L. Rev. 1171 (2017).

The Tuskegee experiment is iconic, but it is only one episode in a long history of exploitation of African Americans in medical research. See Harriet A. Washington, Medical Apartheid: The Dark History of Medical Experimentation on Black Americans from Colonial Times to the Present (2007). Much experimentation with African-American subjects was motivated more by a voyeuristic fascination rather than a scientific research design, and it routinely relied on the disadvantages produced first by slavery and then by poverty and segregation. See also Camille A. Nelson, American Husbandry: Legal Norms Impacting the Production of (Re)productivity, 19 Yale J. L. & Fem. 1 (2007), detailing the work of Dr. Marion Sims, the "father of modern gynecology," who developed his surgical techniques through repeated unanesthetized vaginal surgeries on slave women; Section IV.E, below for a description of the case of Henrietta Lacks. Racialized medicine in the U.S. permeated these experiments and influenced pre-War Nazi health laws, which in turn laid the foundation for the Nazi experiments. See Johnson, above.

These stories do not stand alone as examples of exploitation in medical research in the U.S. Other publicized cases include a study at the Jewish Chronic Disease Hospital, in which live cancer cells were injected into patients without their knowledge, and the Willowbrook State Hospital hepatitis study, in which parents seeking hospital admission for their children were required to allow researchers to infect their child with the disease. See David Rothman, Strangers at the Bedside: A History of How Law and Bioethics Transformed Medical Decisionmaking (1991). These and other episodes, and the patterns of vulnerability and advantage-taking they reveal, influenced the regulatory framework ultimately adopted in the U.S. to govern research. For a comprehensive treatment of the history of legal standards for research in the U.S., see Carl H. Coleman et al., The Ethics and Regulation of Research with Human Subjects (2d ed. 2015).

1. Federal Regulation of Research

Congress enacted the National Research Act in 1974, shortly after Congressional hearings on the Tuskegee study. The Act established the National Commission for Protection of Human Subjects of Biomedical and Behavioral Research to identify "basic ethical principles" that should guide the conduct of research on human subjects; to develop procedures to assure that the research would be consistent with those principles; and to recommend guidelines for human subject research funded by the precursor to HHS. The Commission issued several reports between 1975 and 1978, the most significant of which is the Belmont Report, Ethical Principles and Guidelines for the Protection of Human Subjects of Research (1979). This document established an analytical framework that guided subsequent federal regulations; continues to influence research regulation today; and became the primary approach for decision making in bioethics far beyond questions relating to research.

The main federal regulations governing research with human subjects, first adopted jointly by a number of federal agencies in 1991, traditionally have been called the "Common Rule." While the Common Rule forms the core of federal regulation of medical research, other federal statutes, such as HIPAA (see Chapter 4), apply to a variety of issues that can arise in the research enterprise.

2. State Law

State law also plays an important role in controls on medical research: the Common Rule does not preempt state law that provides additional protections for individuals participating as subjects. A good number of individual states have enacted legislation to govern the conduct of research within their boundaries. Some states, for example, have enacted statutes requiring that all medical research performed in that state be subject to the standards of the federal regulations even if the research is not federally funded. See, e.g., Md. Code, Health-General § 13–2001. A good number of states have enacted legislation setting limits on the use of some types of tissue in research. See, e.g., Mo. Const. Art. 3 § 38d, regarding stem cell research. Most have statutes governing the release of state-held data or tissue for research. See, e.g., 410 Ill. Comp. Stat. § 525/9; N.D. Admin. Code § 33–06–16–05. Some states also regulate research performed on persons with cognitive disabilities. See, e.g., Ala. Code § 22–56–4.

The most influential impact of state law on medical research, however, comes in litigation under state common law. Plaintiffs claiming violation of standards for medical research most often rely on negligence, informed consent, breach of contract, or other state law claims. See Sections IV.C, D, and E, below.

III. THE COMMON RULE

The 1991 Common Rule saw no substantial revision for decades. After nearly six years of notice and comment, however, seventeen federal agencies jointly promulgated revised regulations in 2017. Significant revisions included changes in the required elements of consent, expanded categories of exempt research, and requirements for research with biospecimens and health information, among others. Jerry Menikoff et al., The Common Rule Updated, 376 NEJM 613 (2017). The revised Common Rule went into effect on January 21, 2019.

The Food and Drug Administration (FDA), in the most significant exception among federal agencies, abides by regulations on research that continue to depart significantly from the Common Rule in a few respects.

21 CFR § 50.1. All studies funded by or submitted to the FDA for its approval of drugs, devices, or other substances must meet the FDA's standards for research. Where a study is subject to both the FDA and another federal agency (e.g., pharmaceutical research funded by the National Institutes of Health (NIH)) and the regulations of the two agencies differ, the stricter of the two standards (in terms of protection of subjects) applies.

The FDA is working toward harmonizing its requirements with the Common Rule, as required by the 21st Century Cures Act, P.L. 114–255, § 3023 (2016). For example, the FDA issued guidance permitting Institutional Review Boards (IRBs) to waive or alter informed consent requirements for certain minimal risk clinical investigations. See FDA, Institutional Review Board Waiver or Alteration of Informed Consent for Clinical Investigations Involving No More Than Minimal Risk to Human Subjects; Guidance for Sponsors, Investigators, and Institutional Review Boards, 82 Fed. Reg. 34535–01 (July 25, 2017).

What follows is an edited version of the revised Common Rule. It includes the regulations needed to resolve the Problems presented in the rest of this chapter. (The numbers indicated by the underline are unique to each agency, so for example, the HHS regulations are found at 45 C.F.R. § 46.101 et seq. The regulations presented below include revisions promulgated in 2017. Where the 2017 revisions depart substantially and substantively from the earlier regulations, however, this difference is noted in the text of Notes and Problems in the rest of this chapter.) In addition to these regulations, federal agencies that regulate research issue informal guidance, policy statements, enforcement letters, and other materials that provide the agency's interpretation of the requirements of the regulations. These documents are accessible on the agencies' websites. See, e.g., www. hhs.gov/ohrp.

§ ___.101   To what does this policy apply?

(a) Except as detailed in § ___.104, this policy applies to all research involving human subjects conducted, supported, or otherwise subject to regulation by any Federal department or agency . . . . It also includes research conducted, supported, or otherwise subject to regulation by the Federal Government outside the United States. . . .

* * *

(e) Compliance with this policy requires compliance with pertinent federal laws or regulations that provide additional protections for human subjects.

(f) This policy does not affect any state or local laws or regulations (including tribal law . . .) that may otherwise be applicable and that provide additional protections for human subjects.

(g) This policy does not affect any foreign laws or regulations that may otherwise be applicable and that provide additional protections to human subjects of research.

(h) When research covered by this policy takes place in foreign countries, procedures normally followed in the foreign countries to protect human subjects may differ from those set forth in this policy. In these circumstances, if a department or agency head determines that the procedures prescribed by the institution afford protections that are at least equivalent to those provided in this policy, the department or agency head may approve the substitution of the foreign procedures in lieu of the procedural requirements provided in this policy. . . .

(i) Unless otherwise required by law, department or agency heads may waive the applicability of some or all of the provisions of this policy to specific research activities or classes of research activities otherwise covered by this policy, provided the alternative procedures to be followed are consistent with the principles of the Belmont Report. . . .

* * *

§ ___.102 Definitions for purposes of this policy.
* * *

(e) (1) Human subject means a living individual about whom an investigator ... conducting research: (i) Obtains information or biospecimens through intervention or interaction with the individual, and uses, studies, or analyzes the information or biospecimens; or (ii) Obtains, uses, studies, analyzes, or generates identifiable private information or identifiable biospecimens.

(2) Intervention includes both physical procedures by which information or biospecimens are gathered (e.g., venipuncture) and manipulations of the subject or the subject's environment that are performed for research purposes.

(3) Interaction includes communication or interpersonal contact between investigator and subject.

(4) Private information includes information about behavior that occurs in a context in which an individual can reasonably expect that no observation or recording is taking place, and information that has been provided for specific purposes by an individual and that the individual can reasonably expect will not be made public (e.g., a medical record).

(5) Identifiable private information is private information for which the identity of the subject is or may readily be ascertained by the investigator or associated with the information.

(6) An identifiable biospecimen is a biospecimen for which the identity of the subject is or may readily be ascertained by the investigator or associated with the biospecimen.

* * *

(j) Minimal risk means that the probability and magnitude of harm or discomfort anticipated in the research are not greater in and of themselves than those ordinarily encountered in daily life or during the performance of routine physical or psychological examinations or tests.

* * *

(*l*) Research means a systematic investigation, including research development, testing, and evaluation, designed to develop or contribute to generalizable knowledge. . . [T]he following activities are deemed not to be research:

* * *

(2) Public health surveillance activities, including the collection and testing of information or biospecimens, conducted, supported, requested, ordered, required, or authorized by a public health authority. Such activities are limited to those necessary to allow a public health authority to identify, monitor, assess, or investigate potential public health signals, onsets of disease outbreaks, or conditions of public health importance (including trends, signals, risk factors, patterns in diseases, or increases in injuries from using consumer products). Such activities include those associated with providing timely situational awareness and priority setting during the course of an event or crisis that threatens public health (including natural or man-made disasters).

* * *

§ ___.104   **Exempt research.**

(d)   [T]he following categories of human subjects research are exempt from this policy:

* * *

(2)   Research that only includes interactions involving educational tests . . . , survey procedures, interview procedures, or observation of public behavior . . . [under certain conditions relating to identifiability of the subject, risk of liability, financial or reputational harm to the subject, and protection of confidentiality and privacy. This category of exemption is further limited in the case of child subjects].

* * *

(4) Secondary research for which consent is not required: Secondary research uses of identifiable private information or identifiable biospecimens, if at least one of the following criteria is met:

(i) The identifiable private information or identifiable biospecimens are publicly available;

(ii) Information, which may include information about biospecimens, is recorded by the investigator in such a manner that the identity of the human subjects cannot readily be ascertained directly or through identifiers linked to the subjects, the investigator does not contact the subjects, and the investigator will not re-identify subjects;

(iii) The research involves only information collection and analysis involving the investigator's use of identifiable health information when that use is regulated under [HIPAA], for the purposes of "health care operations" or "research" . . . or for "public health activities and purposes" [as defined in HIPAA]; or

(iv) The research is conducted by, or on behalf of, a Federal department or agency using government-generated or government-collected information obtained for nonresearch activities, if [the data meets certain federal statutory standards for collection and security of identifiable private data.]

* * *

(7) Storage or maintenance for secondary research for which broad consent is required: Storage or maintenance of identifiable private information or identifiable biospecimens for potential secondary research use if an IRB conducts a limited IRB review [an expedited review by the Chair or a designated member of the IRB] and makes the determinations required by § ___.111(a)(8).

(8) Secondary research for which broad consent is required: Research involving the use of identifiable private information or identifiable biospecimens for secondary research use, if the following criteria are met:

(i) Broad consent for the storage, maintenance, and secondary research use of the identifiable private information or identifiable biospecimens was obtained in accordance with § ___.116(a)(1) through (4), (a)(6), and (d);

(ii) Documentation of informed consent or waiver of documentation of consent was obtained . . . ;

(iii) An IRB conducts a limited IRB review [an expedited review by the Chair or a designated member of the IRB] and makes the determination required by § ___.111(a)(7) and makes the determination that the research to be conducted is within the scope of the broad consent . . . ; and

(iv) The investigator does not include returning individual research results to subjects as part of the study plan. This provision does not prevent an investigator from abiding by any legal requirements to return individual research results.

* * *

§ ___.107   IRB membership.

(a) Each IRB shall have at least five members, with varying backgrounds to promote complete and adequate review of research activities commonly conducted by the institution. The IRB shall be sufficiently qualified through the experience and expertise of its members (professional competence), and the diversity of its members, including race, gender, and cultural backgrounds and sensitivity to such issues as community attitudes, to promote respect for its advice and counsel in safeguarding the rights and welfare of human subjects. The IRB shall be able to ascertain the acceptability of proposed research in terms of institutional commitments (including policies and resources) and regulations, applicable law, and standards of professional conduct and practice. The IRB shall therefore include persons knowledgeable in these areas. If an IRB regularly reviews research that involves a category of subjects that is vulnerable to coercion or undue influence, such as children, prisoners, individuals with impaired decision-making capacity, or economically or educationally disadvantaged persons, consideration shall be given to the inclusion of one or more individuals who are knowledgeable about and experienced in working with these categories of subjects.

(b) Each IRB shall include at least one member whose primary concerns are in scientific areas and at least one member whose primary concerns are in nonscientific areas.

(c) Each IRB shall include at least one member who is not otherwise affiliated with the institution and who is not part of the immediate family of a person who is affiliated with the institution.

(d) No IRB may have a member participate in the IRB's initial or continuing review of any project in which the member has a conflicting interest, except to provide information requested by the IRB.

(e) An IRB may, in its discretion, invite individuals with competence in special areas to assist in the review of issues that require expertise beyond or in addition to that available on the IRB. These individuals may not vote with the IRB.

* * *

§ ___.109 IRB review of research.

(a) An IRB shall review and have authority to approve, require modifications in (to secure approval), or disapprove all research activities covered by this policy. . . .

* * *

(e) An IRB shall conduct continuing review of research . . . at intervals appropriate to the degree of risk, not less than once per year, except [for studies eligible for expedited or limited review or studies that involve only data analysis or "accessing follow-up clinical data from procedures that subjects would undergo as part of clinical care"].

* * *

(g) An IRB shall have authority to observe or have a third party observe the consent process and the research.

* * *

§ ___.111 Criteria for IRB approval of research.

(a) [T]he IRB shall determine that all of the following requirements are satisfied:

(1) Risks to subjects are minimized: (i) By using procedures that are consistent with sound research design and that do not unnecessarily expose subjects to risk, and (ii) Whenever appropriate, by using procedures already being performed on the subjects for diagnostic or treatment purposes.

(2) Risks to subjects are reasonable in relation to anticipated benefits, if any, to subjects, and the importance of the knowledge that may reasonably be expected to result. In evaluating risks and benefits, the IRB should consider only those risks and benefits that may result from the research (as distinguished from risks and benefits of therapies subjects would receive even if not participating in the research). . . .

(3) Selection of subjects is equitable. In making this assessment the IRB should take into account the purposes of the research and the setting in which the research will be conducted. The IRB should be particularly cognizant of the special problems of research that involves a category of subjects who are vulnerable to coercion or undue influence, such as children, prisoners, individuals with impaired decision-making capacity, or economically or educationally disadvantaged persons.

(4) Informed consent will be sought from each prospective subject, or the subject's legally authorized representative, in accordance with, and to the extent required by, § ___.116.

* * *

(6) When appropriate, the research plan makes adequate provision for monitoring the data collected to ensure the safety of subjects.

(7) When appropriate, there are adequate provisions to protect the privacy of subjects and to maintain the confidentiality of data.

(8) For purposes of conducting the limited IRB review required by § ___.104(d)(7)), the IRB need not make the determinations at paragraphs (a)(1) through (7) of this section, and shall make the following determinations: (i) Broad consent for storage, maintenance, and secondary research use of identifiable private information is obtained in accordance with the requirements of § ___.116(a)(1)–(4), (a)(6), and (d); (ii) [consent is documented]; and (iii) [if there is a change in the way information or biospecimens are stored, there are adequate provisions for confidentiality and privacy.]

* * *

(b) When some or all of the subjects are likely to be vulnerable to coercion or undue influence, such as children, prisoners, individuals with impaired decision-making capacity, or economically or educationally disadvantaged persons, additional safeguards have been included in the study to protect the rights and welfare of these subjects.

§ ___.112   Review by institution.

Research covered by this policy that has been approved by an IRB may be subject to further appropriate review and approval or disapproval by officials of the institution. However, those officials may not approve the research if it has not been approved by an IRB.

§ ___.113   Suspension or termination of IRB approval of research.

An IRB shall have authority to suspend or terminate approval of research that is not being conducted in accordance with the IRB's requirements or that has been associated with unexpected serious harm to subjects. . . .

* * *

§ ___.116   General requirements for informed consent.

(a) . . . Except as provided elsewhere in this policy:

(1) Before involving a human subject in research covered by this policy, an investigator shall obtain the legally effective informed consent of the subject or the subject's legally authorized representative.

(2) An investigator shall seek informed consent only under circumstances that provide the prospective subject . . . sufficient opportunity to discuss and consider whether or not to participate and that minimize the possibility of coercion or undue influence.

(3) The information that is given to the subject ... shall be in language understandable to the subject . . . .

(4) The prospective subject . . . must be provided with the information that a reasonable person would want to have in order to make an informed decision about whether to participate, and an opportunity to discuss that information.

(5) Except for broad consent obtained in accordance with paragraph (d) of this section:

(i) Informed consent must begin with a concise and focused presentation of the key information that is most likely to assist a prospective subject . . . in understanding the reasons why one might or might not want to participate in the research. . . .

(ii) Informed consent as a whole must present information in sufficient detail relating to the research, and must be organized and presented in a way that does not merely provide lists of isolated facts, but rather facilitates the prospective subject's . . . understanding of the reasons why one might or might not want to participate.

(6) No informed consent may include any exculpatory language through which the subject . . . is made to waive or appear to waive any of the subject's legal rights, or releases or appears to release the investigator, the sponsor, the institution, or its agents from liability for negligence.

(b) Basic elements of informed consent. Except as provided in paragraph (d), (e), or (f) of this section, in seeking informed consent the following information shall be provided to each subject . . . :

(1) A statement that the study involves research, an explanation of the purposes of the research and the expected duration of the subject's participation, a description of the procedures to be followed, and identification of any procedures that are experimental;

(2) A description of any reasonably foreseeable risks or discomforts to the subject;

(3) A description of any benefits to the subject or to others that may reasonably be expected from the research;

(4) A disclosure of appropriate alternative procedures or courses of treatment, if any, that might be advantageous to the subject;

(5) A statement describing the extent, if any, to which confidentiality of records identifying the subject will be maintained;

(6) For research involving more than minimal risk, an explanation as to whether any compensation and an explanation as to whether any medical treatments are available if injury occurs and, if so, what they consist of, or where further information may be obtained; . . .

* * *

(8) A statement that participation is voluntary, refusal to participate will involve no penalty or loss of benefits to which the subject is otherwise entitled, and the subject may discontinue participation at any time without penalty or loss of benefits to which the subject is otherwise entitled; and

(9) One of the following statements about any research that involves the collection of identifiable private information or identifiable biospecimens:

(i) A statement that identifiers might be removed from the identifiable private information or identifiable biospecimens and that, after such removal, the information or biospecimens could be used for future research studies or distributed to another investigator for future research studies without additional informed consent from the subject . . . , if this might be a possibility; or

(ii) A statement that the subject's information or biospecimens collected as part of the research, even if identifiers are removed, will not be used or distributed for future research studies.

(c) Additional elements of informed consent. Except as provided in paragraph (d) . . . or (f) of this section, one or more of the following elements of information, when appropriate, shall also be provided to each subject . . . .

(1) A statement that the particular treatment or procedure may involve risks to the subject (or to the embryo or fetus, if the subject is or may become pregnant) that are currently unforeseeable;

(2) Anticipated circumstances under which the subject's participation may be terminated by the investigator without regard to the subject's . . . consent;

* * *

(4) The consequences of a subject's decision to withdraw from the research and procedures for orderly termination of participation by the subject;

(5) A statement that significant new findings developed during the course of the research that may relate to the subject's willingness to continue participation will be provided to the subject;

(6) The approximate number of subjects involved in the study;

(7) A statement that the subject's biospecimens (even if identifiers are removed) may be used for commercial profit and whether the subject will or will not share in this commercial profit;

(8) A statement regarding whether clinically relevant research results, including individual research results, will be disclosed to subjects, and if so, under what conditions; and

(9) For research involving biospecimens, whether the research will (if known) or might include whole genome sequencing.

(d) Elements of broad consent for the storage, maintenance, and secondary research use of identifiable private information or identifiable biospecimens (collected for either research studies other than the proposed research or nonresearch purposes) is permitted as an alternative to the informed consent requirements in paragraphs (b) and (c) of this section. If the subject . . . is asked to provide broad consent, the following shall be provided to each subject . . . :

(1) The information required in paragraphs (b)(2), (b)(3), (b)(5), and (b)(8) and, when appropriate, (c)(7) and (9) of this section;

(2) A general description of the types of research that may be conducted . . . . This description must include sufficient information such that a reasonable person would expect that the broad consent would permit the types of research conducted;

(3) A description of the identifiable private information or identifiable biospecimens that might be used in research, whether sharing of [this material] might occur, and the types of institutions or researchers that might conduct research with [this material];

(4) A description of the period of time that [this material] may be stored and maintained (which period of time could be indefinite), and a description of the period of time that [this material] may be used for research purposes (which period of time could be indefinite);

(5) Unless the subject . . . will be provided details about specific research studies, a statement that they will not be informed of the details of any specific research studies that might be conducted using [this material], including the purposes of the research, and that they might have chosen not to consent to some of those specific research studies; [and]

(6) Unless it is known that clinically relevant research results, including individual research results, will be disclosed to the subject in all circumstances, a statement that such results may not be disclosed to the subject. . . .

* * *

(f) (1) [A]n IRB may waive the requirement to obtain informed consent for research under paragraphs (a) through (c) of this section, provided the IRB satisfies the requirements of paragraph (f)(3) of this section. If an individual was asked to provide broad consent . . . in accordance with the requirements at paragraph (d) of this section, and refused to consent, an IRB cannot waive consent [for those activities].

(2) Alteration. An IRB may approve a consent procedure that omits some, or alters some or all, of the elements of informed consent set forth in paragraphs (b) and (c) of this section provided the IRB satisfies the requirements of paragraph (f)(3) of this section. An IRB may not omit or alter any of the requirements described in paragraph (a) of this section. If a broad consent procedure is used, an IRB may not omit or alter any of the elements required under paragraph (d) of this section.

(3) Requirements for waiver and alteration. In order for an IRB to waive or alter consent as described in this subsection, the IRB must find and document that:

(i)   The research involves no more than minimal risk to the subjects;

(ii) The research could not practicably be carried out without the requested waiver or alteration;

(iii) If the research involves using identifiable private information or identifiable biospecimens, the research could not practicably be carried out without using such information or biospecimens in an identifiable format;

(iv) The waiver or alteration will not adversely affect the rights and welfare of the subjects; and

(v)   Whenever appropriate, the subjects . . . will be provided with additional pertinent information after participation.

* * *

(i) Preemption. The informed consent requirements in this policy are not intended to preempt any applicable Federal, state, or local laws (including tribal laws . . .) that require additional information to be disclosed in order for informed consent to be legally effective.

* * *

IV. APPLYING THE COMMON RULE

A. INSTITUTIONAL REVIEW BOARDS

The Common Rule delegates the frontline enforcement of the federal regulations to institutional review boards (IRBs), which most commonly are committees of the research institution, appointed and managed by the institution itself. What is the rationale for delegating oversight to the research entity itself?

Criticisms of the efficiency and effectiveness of IRB review contributed significantly to momentum for revision of the Common Rule. For a debate over the role of IRBs, see Symposium, Censorship and Institutional Review Boards, 101 Nw. U. L. Rev. 399 (2007); see also *Grimes* in Section IV.D. The revised Common Rule generally left the structure of IRBs unchanged, but for one exception. For studies conducted at more than one institution after January 20, 2020, the revised regulations require approval by a single IRB rather than the IRBs of each institution involved in the multisite study (called "cooperative research" in the regulations). § ___.114. In addition, the revision expands the range of studies that are exempt from the Rule, and therefore from full IRB review. See § ___.104(d)(4), (7) and (8), above.

The Office for Human Research Protections (OHRP) enforces the HHS regulations through investigation of complaints and episodic audits of the human subject protection programs (including the IRBs) of organizations conducting research subject to the regulations. The FDA uses similar processes to enforce its regulations. The biggest stick that OHRP carries is the authority to suspend or terminate all HHS funding of research. It suspended funding for twenty universities during 1999–2000. This extreme remedy is still used, but only rarely. The Office of Inspector General of HHS also enforces the federal regulations on research through its prosecution of fraud and false claims. See Chapter 14. Even with this oversight, the reviews performed by an IRB are the most significant tool in assuring compliance with the federal regulations.

PROBLEM: FORMING AN IRB

Assume that you have been charged with forming the first IRB for a community hospital that has begun to apply for small federal research grants and contracts with pharmaceutical firms to conduct clinical trials. Consider §§ ___.107, .109, .111, .112, and .113, above, in forming your recommendations to these questions:

1.   What is the ideal size for your IRB to incorporate the competencies and perspectives described in the regulations? Should hospital counsel be a member? Should nonscientific members of the IRB defer to the scientific members on the questions of risk assessment, research design, or continuing review of the results being produced by the research protocol? Can they do otherwise? What sort of competency should the nonscientific member have?

2.   Assume that your hospital serves a large proportion of economically disadvantaged patients and that research subjects are likely to be recruited from among that population. Does that influence the composition of your IRB?

3.   Assume that your new IRB has already ruffled some feathers with its review process. In particular, it has asked for more information, several times, on research proposed by a prominent physician on the hospital's medical staff. This researcher has approached the hospital's CEO for assistance. What can the CEO do?

4. Instead of establishing its own IRB, the hospital could contract with and pay a free-standing independent IRB for review of protocols. See Janet Lis and Melinda Murray, The Ins and Outs of Independent IRBs, 2 J. Health & Life Sci. L. 73 (2008). See also Colleen Zern, Is the Customer Always Right? HHS Proposed Regulation Allows IRBs to Place Customer Service Ahead of the Welfare of Research Participants, 32 St. Louis U. Pub. L. Rev. 411 (2013), criticizing independent IRBs. What are the advantages and disadvantages of this approach for the hospital? For researchers? For patients who will be participating in research?

B. DEFINING "RESEARCH"

The Common Rule applies only to activities that meet its definition of research. Furthermore, the Common Rule does not apply to research that is not conducted by or funded by a federal agency; and the FDA regulations only apply to research that is funded by the FDA or submitted to the FDA for action regarding drugs or devices requiring FDA approval. An organization that conducts research subject to the Common Rule must file a Federalwide Assurance (FWA) every five years. In the FWA, the organization represents that it complies with applicable federal regulations on research covered by the Rule and maps essential components of that compliance. Most academic institutions filing an FWA voluntarily commit to compliance for all their research studies, whether federally funded or not.

PROBLEM: IS IT RESEARCH?

Use the Common Rule §§ ___.101(a), .102(e) and (l), and .104, above, to resolve whether each scenario constitutes research subject to the regulations.

1. An oncologist treating a patient with colon cancer for whom customary chemotherapy drugs have proven ineffective offers his patient the option of trying another drug. The drug is currently used for other cancers and is being tested for colon cancer, but the research is not yet complete. Although the oncologist is not participating in any of the clinical trials of this drug, preliminary unpublished reports and informal discussions with researchers testing the drug show promise. Once a drug is approved for one purpose, physicians may prescribe it for other purposes, a practice known as off-label prescribing. If the doctor gives his patient this drug, is it research as defined in the Common Rule? See Nancy Kass et al., The Research-Treatment Distinction: A Problematic Approach for Determining Which Activities Should Have Ethical Oversight, 43 Hastings Ctr. Rep. S4 (2013). See also Section IV.C, below, and Chapter 4.

2. It can be difficult to intubate seriously overweight adult patients, especially in an emergency. Assume that an experienced nurse anesthetist suggested that physicians use a pediatric tube for a particular patient, with great success. Because of their experience with this approach, the hospital decides to adopt this as a regular practice if a first attempt at intubation fails.

The nurse who developed this approach has decided to present the hospital's experience with this practice at a regional anesthesiology conference and has published an article in a professional journal. Is this research? Scenario based on Atul Gawande, "When Doctors Make Mistakes" in Complications: A Surgeon's Notes on an Imperfect Science (2002).

3.   A large multispecialty physician practice group is considering adding medical scribes to their offices. These individuals would be present as the physician works with the patient and would input findings, prescriptions, and directions into the patient's electronic medical record. This should allow physicians to focus on the patient rather than the keyboard. Because of the size of the financial investment required, the practice wants to make sure that adding scribes would be efficient and would improve accuracy and thoroughness of medical records in their particular practice setting. They have hired a small number of scribes and have established a number of variables, requiring examination of patient records and observing physician-patient interaction, which will be analyzed to judge whether further investment will add value. The group will use the results only within their own practice. They have no interest in sharing their findings. Who are the subjects of this study? Is this research subject to the Common Rule?

4.   A large university medical center shared redacted medical records of all patients treated over a multi-year period with Google as part of a project to develop a predictive health model designed to help hospitals reduce their rates of readmission. Is this research under the Common Rule? See Dinerstein v. Google, LLC, 484 F. Supp. 3d 561 (N.D. Ill. 2020). For analyses of the failure of law to account adequately for the interests of individuals whose personal data is used for research and development, see Michael Froomkin, Big Data: Destroyer of Informed Consent, 21 Yale J. L. & Tech. 27 (2019); Tara Sklar & Mabel Crescioni, Research Participants' Rights to Data Protection in the Era of Open Science, 69 DePaul L. Rev. 699 (2020); David M. Parker et. al., Privacy and Informed Consent for Research in the Age of Big Data, 123 Penn St. L. Rev. 703 (2019). See also Joshua Rolnick et al., Ethical Oversight of Quality Improvement and the Research-QI Boundary: A New Common Rule Changes Little, IRB: Ethics and Human Research 39/3 (May-June 2017).

5.   Starting in 2018, the Seattle Flu Study (SFS) routinely enrolled research subjects and collected and stored nasal swabs to improve the detection of and response to local flu outbreaks. When Seattle experienced its first COVID case in early 2020, SFS used recently collected nasal swabs to test for COVID-19 and notified those research participants whose COVID-19 tests were positive. Is this research under the Common Rule?

C. RISK AND CONSENT

The Common Rule sets standards for consent to research in §§ ____.111 and 116, above. Standardization in consent forms, to improve efficiency and effectiveness, was considered during the revision of the regulations, but that didn't occur. Instead, the regulations add a new requirement that consent forms be posted on a public website once enrollment in the study has closed. § ___.116(h). The regulations also significantly altered the consent requirements for "secondary use" of "identifiable private information" and "identifiable biospecimens." See Section IV.F, below.

The issue of risk is intertwined with consent in several ways. First, the federal regulations do not permit research, even with consenting adults, if the risks to the subject are not reasonable. See § ___.111(a)(2), above. Assuming a competent adult is acting voluntarily and without coercion, what, if anything, justifies the restrictive federal regulations concerning risk? See Richard A Epstein, Defanging IRBs: Replacing Coercion with Information, 101 Nw. U. L. Rev. 735 (2007), arguing that IRBs should assure only that information to the subject about the risks is accurate and understandable, leaving to the individual the decision to enroll or not. What criteria would you use to decide whether risk is excessive, either for yourself personally or as a matter of applying the regulation? Are these two different questions?

The consent process must communicate the nature and degree of risk (and benefit) presented in the study in an accurate and understandable manner. See *Looney*, below. In some circumstances, however, natural optimism on the part of patients, and even researchers, influences how the information is heard. The term "therapeutic misconception" was coined over thirty years ago to describe the observation that patients tend to believe that clinical trials testing only the safety of a new drug (called Phase I trials) will benefit them directly by providing treatment for their condition despite clear statements to the contrary. See Paul Appelbaum et al., The Therapeutic Misconception: Informed Consent to Psychiatric Research, 5 Int'l J.L. & Psych. 319 (1982); Lynn Jansen, Two Concepts of Therapeutic Optimism, 37 J. Med. Ethics 563 (2011). One IRB chair observed that, during an emergency, IRB members also can fall prey to therapeutic misconception. See Walter Dehority, Therapeutic Misconception, Misestimation and COVID-19, 11 Narrative Inq. in Bioeth. 61 (2021).

The calculus of risk can change over the life of a study. IRBs must perform ongoing risk assessments for certain approved studies (§ ___.109(e), above, with exceptions adopted in the 2017 revision) and must suspend research that is "associated with unexpected serious harm to subjects" (§ ___.113, above). This monitoring should assure that a study is halted when unanticipated levels of risk or unexpectedly early and strong positive results occur. How does the latter present a risk of harm?

Some research studies include medical tests that will produce results that are "clinically relevant" to individual subjects. In the context of medical treatment, a patient expects that her physician would inform her of significant test results. If this common expectation is carried to the research context, individuals may assume, to their detriment, that if the tests reveal a serious threat to their health, they would be informed. The revised Common Rule addresses this situation as an element of informed consent but does not require disclosure of results. See § ___.116(c)(8) and (d)(6), above. See Susan Wolf et al., Returning a Research Participant's Genomic Results to Relatives: Analysis and Recommendations, 43 J. L. Med. & Ethics 440 (2015).

Research on vaccines or therapeutics for COVID-19 demonstrates the difficulty of keeping research subjects informed about risks and alternatives given how quickly new information emerged about the virus, its variants, the resulting disease, and the effectiveness of masks and vaccines. For a discussion of how best to interpret and apply the Common Rule in such circumstances, see Holly Fernandez Lynch et. al., Regulatory Flexibility for Covid-19 Research, 7 J.L. & Biosciences (Jan.–June, 2020). For an ethical analysis of "challenge trials"—human experiments in which subjects are deliberately exposed to a disease—see Daniel P. Sulmasy, Are SARS-CoV-2 Human Challenge Trials Ethical?, 181 JAMA Intern Med. 1031 (2021).

PROBLEM: HOW INFORMED? HOW VOLUNTARY?

Consider the following scenarios under § ___.116, above.

1. *Taking Advantage of Medicaid Beneficiaries?* A teaching hospital is likely to enroll a large proportion of Medicaid beneficiaries and uninsured individuals in a particular study. The medication being tested has been approved for one use, but not for the one being tested in this study. Sales of the medication overall currently exceed $300 million annually even though Medicaid does not pay for the drug for the use being studied. Does the fact that Medicaid does not cover the medication make the enrollment of Medicaid beneficiaries coercive? If the protocol promises subjects hospital care that some otherwise would not receive due to inability to pay, is that coercive? See generally Ruqaiijah Yearby, Involuntary Consent: Conditioning Access to Health Care on Participation in Clinical Trials, 44 J. L. Med. & Ethics 445 (2016).

2. *When Is Payment to a Subject Too Much?* To recruit adequate numbers of subjects, an investigator at the same hospital plans on paying subjects $50 per hour for the time the subject spends traveling to and from the office as well as the time spent in undergoing tests and evaluation. How does payment relate to consent? Is the $50 excessive? Adequate? Fair? Emily Largent and Holly Lynch, Paying Research Participants: Regulatory Uncertainty, Conceptual Confusion, and a Path Forward, 17 Yale J. Health Pol'y & Ethics 61 (2017).

3. *Access to Investigational Therapies.* A terminally ill cancer patient is told by her oncologist that "nothing more can be done" to treat the disease in her case. When she contacts a cancer center at a teaching hospital, she is

invited to participate in a Phase I trial to test the safety of a new drug. The investigators have some reason to believe that the drug holds promise because of its performance in animal studies, but the drug has not been tested in humans. They plan to randomly assign subjects to receive either the drug or a placebo, and neither the physicians nor the subjects will know which arm of the study they are participating in. What issues do you see in securing informed consent under § ___.116? What if the patient tells the researcher that her willingness to continue in the trial depends on whether she is in the placebo arm? On access to investigational drugs, see Abigail Alliance for Better Access to Developmental Drugs v. von Eschenbach, 495 F.3d 695 (D.C. Cir. 2007), cert. denied, 552 U.S. 1159 (2008), rejecting plaintiff's claim of a Constitutional right to receive drugs that are in Phase I clinical trials without enrolling in the trial. After *Abigail Alliance*, the FDA increased access to experimental drugs outside of clinical trials. The 21st Century Cures Act, P.L. 114–255 (2016) adopted a number of policies to accelerate drug approval and relax standards for data required in the approval process. See also Rebecca Dresser, The "Right to Try" Investigational Drugs: Science and Stories in the Access Debate, 93 Tex. L. Rev. 1631 (2015).

4.   *Disclosing Off-Label Availability*. An individual has read about some promising results in a clinical trial of a new treatment being tested for her serious medical condition and has inquired about enrolling in the study. The medication is not new, but it has not been approved for her particular medical condition. Does the Common Rule require that she be told that her own treating physician could prescribe the medication for her off-label? See, e.g., Jerry Menikoff and Edward Richards, What the Doctor Didn't Say: The Hidden Truth About Medical Research (2006).

LOONEY V. MOORE
Court of Appeals for the 11th Circuit, 2017.
861 F.3d 1303.

Through their parents, Plaintiffs DreShan Collins, Christian Lewis, and Jaylen Malone, brought claims against Defendants for harms allegedly visited on Plaintiffs when the latter were enrolled in a clinical study while being treated for health issues accompanying their premature births. . . .

Plaintiffs brought claims against the various Defendants for negligence, negligence per se, breach of fiduciary duty, products liability, and lack of informed consent. The district court granted summary judgment on all claims. Like the district court, we conclude that Plaintiffs have failed to establish that participation in the clinical study caused any injuries, which means that the negligence, negligence per se, breach of fiduciary duty, and products liability claims were properly dismissed.

The viability of the claim alleging lack of informed consent, however, is less clear. . . .

I. BACKGROUND

The University of Alabama at Birmingham was the lead study site for a national clinical research trial known as the Surfactant, Positive Pressure, and Oxygenation Randomized Trial ("SUPPORT"). Designed by Dr. [Waldemar] Carlo and approved by the IRB Defendants, the SUPPORT study was created to analyze the effects of differing oxygen saturation levels on premature infants. At the time of the study, it was nationally accepted (and neither party contests) that the recognized standard of care was to keep the oxygen saturation levels of low-birth-weight infants at between 85% and 95%. This standard notwithstanding, it was also known that a prolonged period of high oxygen saturation can result in oxygen toxicity which leads to an increased risk of "retinopathy of prematurity". On the other hand, a prolonged period of low oxygen saturation can result in neuro-developmental impairment and death. Given the difficulties of calibrating the optimal oxygen range, the SUPPORT study sought to determine whether, within the accepted standard of care, there was a more precise range of oxygen saturation that would better reduce the risk of exposing an infant to either too much or too little oxygen.

The SUPPORT study randomly divided eligible and enrolled premature infants into two groups. One group was to be kept at an oxygen saturation level between 85–89%, which is the low end of the standard-of-care range, while the other would be kept at an oxygen saturation level between 90–95%, which is the high end of that range. Further, to ensure double-blind data collection, the study would employ specialized oximeters . . . that would "mask" to an onlooker the true oxygen saturation levels of the infants. The oximeters would, however, signal an alarm whenever an infant's oxygen level strayed below 85% or above 95%.

Publishing the results of the study in the New England Journal of Medicine, the study authors concluded that infants in the high-oxygen group were more likely to be diagnosed with retinopathy while infants in the low-oxygen group were more likely to die. There was no statistically significant difference in the incidence of neuro-developmental impairments between the high and low groups.

To enroll in the study, Plaintiffs' guardians had to execute informed consent documents that were drafted and approved by Defendants. After the study's completion, however, the Department of Health and Human Services authored a letter questioning whether these informed consent documents had properly disclosed all of the risks associated with enrollment in the SUPPORT study.

. . . Plaintiffs allege that they suffered serious injuries as a result of their participation in the study. Specifically, Plaintiffs Lewis and Malone were assigned to the low-oxygen group, with prolonged periods of low oxygen saturation being associated with neuro-developmental impairment and death. Fortunately, neither infant died, but they did develop neurological issues. Plaintiff Collins was assigned to the high-oxygen group, with prolonged high-oxygen saturation being associated with retinopathy, which can lead to blindness. Plaintiff Collins did develop retinopathy, but fortunately he did not suffer permanent vision loss. Following discovery, Defendants moved for summary judgment asserting that, based on the undisputed material facts, Plaintiffs had failed to demonstrate that participation in the SUPPORT study had caused the injuries alleged in the Complaint. The district court agreed that Plaintiffs had failed to prove that their injuries were caused by participation in the SUPPORT study, as opposed to being a consequence of their premature births.

II. ANALYSIS

We agree that under applicable Alabama law and taking all inferences in the light most favorable to Plaintiffs, Plaintiffs have failed to show that enrollment in the SUPPORT study caused their injuries. What is not clear is whether the absence of an actual physical injury caused by the SUPPORT study dooms Plaintiffs' argument that Defendants are nonetheless liable because they failed to obtain Plaintiffs' informed consent to participate in that study. . . .

. . . As far as we can tell . . . Alabama law has yet to explicitly address the question whether proof of a medical injury is also required before a plaintiff can claim that his consent to a medical procedure was not informed. Specifically, if a plaintiff cannot prove that he suffered any injury as a result of a particular medical procedure, can he still potentially prevail if he shows that the doctor failed to obtain his informed consent to that procedure? In other words, is there a free-standing tort arising from a lack of informed consent, even if there is no injury resulting from the procedure at issue? Assuming that injury is required to sustain an informed consent claim arising out of medical treatment, does that rule still apply if the medical treatment is provided as part of a clinical study?

The answer to the above questions will depend on how an informed consent claim is characterized. If an informed consent claim is considered to be a type of medical malpractice claim [under the Alabama malpractice statute] . . . then it is clear that a plaintiff must show the existence of an actual injury resulting from the procedure before he can raise a viable informed consent claim. If an informed consent claim is not classified as a malpractice type of claim—or if it exits [in] the malpractice arena when the uninformed consent pertains to participation in a medical study administered as part of the medical treatment—then we must search for an answer in Alabama common law. And if, as Plaintiffs argue, an informed consent claim arising out of a medical study is neither a malpractice nor a negligence claim, then we must identify precisely what type of claim it is and determine what Alabama law would prescribe as its elements.

* * *

. . . Because substantial doubt exists here about the answer to a material state law question, we respectfully certify the following question [to the Alabama Supreme Court] for a determination of state law:

> Must a patient whose particular medical treatment is dictated by the parameters of a clinical study, and who has not received adequate warnings of the risks of that particular protocol, prove that an injury actually resulted from the medical treatment in order to succeed on a claim that his consent to the procedure was not informed?

NOTES AND QUESTIONS

1. *The Question Remains Unanswered.* The Eleventh Circuit certified an intriguing question to the Alabama Supreme Court, but that court declined to answer it. In its subsequent opinion in the case, the Eleventh Circuit makes only a glancing reference to the distinction between medical treatment and medical experimentation, referring to plaintiffs' claim as "an informed consent claim arising out of participation in a medical study administered as part of the medical treatment" provided plaintiffs. There is no other discussion of the issue. The court concludes that, in its interpretation of Alabama law, informed consent claims are a form of negligence claim and require proof of physical injury. 2018 WL 1547260. See also the discussion of the litigation involving Jesse Gelsinger and John Moore in Section IV.E, below.

2. *Private Right of Action.* Should the federal regulations be enforceable in litigation by research participants, such as those in *Looney*, or should the government hold exclusive enforcement authority? Almost all of the cases considering the question have held that the federal regulations do not create an implied private right of action. Compare *Grimes*, below. See Valerie Koch, A Private Right of Action for Informed Consent in Research, 45 Seton Hall L. Rev. 173 (2015); Richard S. Saver, Medical Research and Intangible Harm, 74 U. Cinn. L. Rev. 941 (2006). If a private right of action is desirable, should Congress or the state legislature enact legislation providing for statutory damages in the absence of physical harm? See Cal. Health & Safety Code § 24176, providing for fines for violation of state standards for consent for research but only for research not subject to the federal regulations. Actions brought for failure of consent under the FDA's regulations on research may be barred by federal preemption of state products liability law. See Day v. Howmedica Osteonics Corp., 2015 WL 13469348 (D. Colo. 2015); but see Mink v. Smith & Nephew, Inc., 860 F.3d 1319 (11th Cir. 2017), overturning dismissal of a claim of misrepresentation.

3. *Assessing the Disclosure.* The written consent for SUPPORT stated that "[s]ometimes higher ranges [of oxygen] are used and sometimes lower ranges are used. All of them are acceptable ranges." Is this statement accurate?

Complete? The federal Office for Human Research Protections determined that consent in SUPPORT failed to meet regulatory standards as it did not clearly identify risks and how the study might impact treatment decisions. OHRP noted that, while the entire range of oxygenation was within the current standard of care, treating physicians, including those at some of the research sites, often avoid the extreme poles of the acceptable range to reduce risks. OHRP Determination Letter (June 6, 2013). See also Robert Morse and Robin Wilson, Realizing Informed Consent in Times of Controversy: Lessons from the SUPPORT Study, 44 J. L. Med. & Ethics 402 (2016). The OHRP letter states:

> Doctors are required . . . to do what they view as being best for their individual patients. Researchers do not have the same obligation: Our society relaxes that requirement because of the need to conduct research, the results of which are important to us all. As a modest but crucial trade-off . . . society requires that researchers tell subjects how participating in the study might alter the risks to which they are exposed.

OHRP, however, took no compliance action against research institutions participating in SUPPORT and stated that they would not take any action against studies with a similar design until OHRP developed and posted formal guidance. OHRP has posted Draft Guidance on Disclosing Reasonably Foreseeable Risks in Research Evaluating Standards of Care, 79 Fed. Reg. 63629 (Oct. 24, 2014).

4.   *Research Design.* The SUPPORT study is an example of comparative effectiveness research (see Chapter 4), as the study tested the outcomes of different treatment approaches in common practice at the time. D. Magnus, The SUPPORT Controversy and the Debate over Research within the Standard of Care, 13 Am. J. Bioethics 1 (2013), part of a symposium issue on SUPPORT. The June 2013 OHRP determination letter stated that OHRP "does not and has never questioned whether the design of the SUPPORT study was ethical," but only that consent was inadequate.

5.   *Research Injury Compensation.* Research participants may be injured in the course of research, just as patients may be injured in the course of treatment either through unavoidable adverse effects or through negligence. The Common Rule does not require that institutions compensate subjects injured as a result of their research participation. If, however, a research protocol provides for compensation in the event of an injury, the Common Rule requires that this be disclosed to potential subjects as part of the informed consent process. See § ___.116(b)(6), above. See also Leslie Henry, Moral Gridlock: Conceptual Barriers to No-Fault Compensation for Injured Research Subjects, 41 J. L. Med. & Ethics 411 (2013).

D. EQUITABLE SELECTION OF SUBJECTS AND VULNERABLE POPULATIONS

The Common Rule requires that IRBs assure that the selection of subjects for research be "equitable," and that special attention be paid when subjects are selected from "vulnerable populations," including but not limited to those listed in the regulation. § ___.111(a)(3), above. In addition, if research subjects are selected from populations vulnerable to undue influence or coercion, the IRB must assure that "additional safeguards" are put in place to protect these subjects. § ___.111(b), above. If an IRB regularly reviews research with vulnerable populations, it is to "give consideration" to the composition of its own membership. See Section IV.A, above.

Review these regulations before reading *Grimes*. Develop your own working definition of "equitable" and "vulnerability" to apply to the case. See Ana Iltis, Introduction: Vulnerability in Biomedical Research (Symposium), 37 J. L. Med. & Ethics 6 (2009); Ruqaiijah Yearby, Missing the "Target:" Preventing the Unjust Inclusion of Vulnerable Children for Medical Research Studies, 42 Am. J. Law & Med. 797 (2016).

GRIMES V. KENNEDY KRIEGER INSTITUTE, INC.
Court of Appeals of Maryland, 2001.
782 A.2d 807.

CATHELL, JUDGE.

* * *

[According to the record before the Court on the motion for summary judgment in] these present cases, [the Kennedy Krieger Institute,] a prestigious research institute associated with Johns Hopkins University . . . created a nontherapeutic research program[2] whereby it required certain classes of homes to have only partial lead paint abatement modifications performed, and in at least some instances, including at least one of the cases at bar, arranged for the landlords to receive public funding by way of grants or loans to aid in the modifications. The research institute then encouraged, and in at least one of the cases at bar, required, the landlords to rent the premises to families with young children. In the event young children already resided in one of the study houses, it was contemplated that a child would remain in the premises, and the child was encouraged to remain, in order for his or her blood to be periodically analyzed. In other words, the continuing presence of the children that were the subjects of the study was required in order for the study to be complete. Apparently, the children and their parents involved in the cases *sub judice*

---

[2] At least to the extent that commercial profit motives are not implicated, therapeutic research's purpose is to directly help or aid a patient who is suffering from a health condition the objectives of the research are designed to address—hopefully by the alleviation, or potential alleviation, of the health condition. Nontherapeutic research generally utilizes subjects who are not known to have the condition the objectives of the research are designed to address, and/or is not designed to directly benefit the subjects utilized in the research, but, rather, is designed to achieve beneficial results for the public at large (or, under some circumstances, for profit).

were from a lower economic strata and were, at least in one case, minorities.

The purpose of the research was to determine how effective varying degrees of lead paint abatement procedures were. Success was to be determined by periodically, over a two-year period of time, measuring the extent to which lead dust remained in, or returned to, the premises after the varying levels of abatement modifications, and, as most important to our decision, by measuring the extent to which the theretofore healthy children's blood became contaminated with lead, and comparing that contamination with levels of lead dust in the houses over the same periods of time. . . .

* * *

. . . There was no complete and clear explanation in the consent agreements signed by the parents of the children that the research to be conducted was designed, at least in significant part, to measure the success of the abatement procedures by measuring the extent to which the children's blood was being contaminated. It can be argued that the researchers intended that the children be the canaries in the mines but never clearly told the parents. . . .

. . . Institutional Review Boards (IRB) are oversight entities within the institutional family to which an entity conducting research belongs. In research experiments, an IRB can be required in some instances by either federal or state regulation, or sometimes by the conditions attached to governmental grants that are used to fund research projects. Generally, their primary functions are to assess the protocols of the project to determine whether the project itself is appropriate, whether the consent procedures are adequate, whether the methods to be employed meet proper standards, whether reporting requirements are sufficient, and the assessment of various other aspects of a research project. One of the most important objectives of such review is the review of the potential safety and the health hazard impact of a research project on the human subjects of the experiment, especially on vulnerable subjects such as children. Their function is *not* to help researchers seek funding for research projects.

. . . In a letter dated May 11, 1992, [the IRB sent a message to the researcher of this project stating, in part]:

* * *

2. *Federal guidelines are really quite specific regarding using children as controls in projects in which there is no potential benefit* [to those children]. To call a subject a normal control is to indicate that there is no real benefit to be received [by the child]. . . . So we think it would be much more acceptable to indicate that the "control group" is being studied to determine what exposure outside the home may play

in a total lead exposure; thereby, indicating that these control individuals are gaining some benefit, namely learning whether safe housing alone is sufficient to keep the blood-lead levels in acceptable bounds. We suggest that you modify ... the consent form[s] ... accordingly. [Emphasis added [by the court].]

[T]his statement shows two things: (1) that the IRB had a partial misperception of the difference between therapeutic and nontherapeutic research and the IRB's role in the process and (2) that the IRB was willing to aid researchers in getting around federal regulations designed to protect children used as subjects in nontherapeutic research. . . .

* * *

While the validity of the consent agreement and its nature as a contract, the existence or nonexistence of a special relationship, and whether the researchers performed their functions under that agreement pursuant to any special relationships are important issues in these cases that we will address, the very inappropriateness of the research itself cannot be overlooked. It is apparent that the protocols of research are even more important than the method of obtaining parental consent and the extent to which the parents were, or were not, informed. If the research methods, the protocols, are inappropriate then, especially when the IRB is willing to help researchers avoid compliance with applicable safety requirements for using children in nontherapeutic research, the consent of the parents, or of any consent surrogates, in our view, cannot make the research appropriate or the actions of the researchers and the Institutional Review Board proper.

. . . The experiment was simply a "for the greater good" project. The specific children's health was put at risk, in order to develop low-cost abatement measures that would help all children, the landlords, and the general public as well.

* * *

It is clear to this Court that the scientific and medical communities cannot be permitted to assume sole authority to determine ultimately what is right and appropriate in respect to research projects involving young children free of the limitations and consequences of the application of Maryland law. The Institutional Review Boards, IRBs, are, primarily, in-house organs. In our view, they are not designed, generally, to be sufficiently objective in the sense that they are as sufficiently concerned with the ethicality of the experiments they review as they are with the success of the experiments. . . .

The conflicts are inherent. This would be especially so when science and private industry collaborate in search of material gains. Moreover, the special relationship between research entities and human subjects used in the research will almost always impose duties.

. . . It may well be that in the end, the trial courts will determine that no damages have been incurred in the instant cases and thus the actions will fail for that reason. In that regard, we note that there are substantial factual differences [among the] cases. But the actions, themselves, are not defective on the ground that no legal duty can, according to the trial courts, possibly exist. . . .

I.   The Cases

. . . [Plaintiffs] allege that KKI [Kennedy Krieger Institute] discovered lead hazards in their respective homes and, having a duty to notify them, failed to warn in a timely manner or otherwise act to prevent the children's exposure to the known presence of lead. Additionally, plaintiffs alleged that they were not fully informed of the risks of the research.

[The trial court granted summary judgment on the basis that KKI had no legal duty to warn the subjects of their exposure to lead.]

The trial court was incorrect. Such research programs normally create special relationships and/or can be of a contractual nature that create duties. The breaches of such duties may ultimately result in viable negligence actions. Because, at the very least, there are viable and genuine disputes of material fact concerning whether a special relationship, or other relationships arising out of agreements, giving rise to duties existed between KKI and both sets of appellants, we hold that the Circuit Court erred in granting KKI's motions for summary judgment in both cases before this Court. . . .

II.   Facts & Procedural Background

In summary, KKI conducted a study of five test groups of twenty-five houses each. The first three groups consisted of houses known to have lead present. The amount of repair and maintenance conducted increased from Group 1 to Group 2 to Group 3. The fourth group consisted of houses, which had at one time lead present but had since allegedly received a complete abatement of lead dust. The fifth group consisted of modern houses, which had never had the presence of lead dust. The twenty-five homes in each of the first three testing levels were then to be compared to the two control groups: the twenty-five homes in Group 4 that had previously been abated and the 25 modern homes in Group 5. The research study was specifically designed to do less than full lead dust abatement in some of the categories of houses in order to study the potential effectiveness, if any, of lesser levels of repair and maintenance.

If the children were to leave the houses upon the first manifestation of lead dust, it would be difficult, if not impossible, to test, over time, the rate of the level of lead accumulation in the blood of the children attributable to the manifestation. . . . Thus, it would benefit the accuracy of the test, and thus KKI, the compensated researcher, if children remained in the houses over the period of the study even after the presence of lead dust in the houses became evident.

* * *

B.   Case No. 128 [Ms. Viola Hughes and Daughter Ericka Grimes]

* * *

Nowhere in the consent form was it clearly disclosed to the mother that the researchers contemplated that, as a result of the experiment, the child might accumulate lead in her blood, and that in order for the experiment to succeed it was necessary that the child remain in the house as the lead in the child's blood increased or decreased, so that it could be measured. The Consent Form states in relevant part:

"PURPOSE OF STUDY:

As you may know, lead poisoning in children is a problem in Baltimore City and other communities across the country. Lead in paint, house dust and outside soil are major sources of lead exposure for children. Children can also be exposed to lead in drinking water and other sources. We understand that your house is going to have special repairs done in order to reduce exposure to lead in paint and dust. On a random basis, homes will receive one of two levels of repair. We are interested in finding out how well the two levels of repair work. The repairs are not intended, or expected, to completely remove exposure to lead.

We are now doing a study to learn about how well different practices work for reducing exposure to lead in paint and dust. We are asking you and over one hundred other families to allow us to test for lead in and around your homes up to 8 to 9 times over the next two years provided that your house qualifies for the full two years of study. Final eligibility will be determined after the initial testing of your home. We are also doing free blood lead testing of children aged 6 months to 7 years, up to 8 to 9 times over the next two years. We would also like you to respond to a short questionnaire every 6 months. This study is intended to monitor the effects of the repairs and is not intended to replace the regular medical care your family obtains.

* * *

BENEFITS

To compensate you for your time answering questions and allowing us to sketch your home we will mail you a check in the amount of $5.00. In the future we would mail you a check in the amount of $15 each time the full questionnaire is completed. The dust, soil, water, and blood samples would be tested for lead at [KKI] at no charge to you. *We would provide you with specific blood-lead results. We would contact you to discuss a summary of house test results and steps that you could take to reduce any risks of exposure.* [Emphasis added [by the court].]"

Pursuant to the plans of the research study, KKI collected dust samples [from the Grimes' house] on March 9, 1993, August 23, 1993, March 9, 1994, September 19, 1994, April 18, 1995, and November 13, 1995.[22] The March 9, 1993 dust testing revealed what the researchers referred to as "hot spots" where the level of lead was "higher than might be found in a completely renovated [abated] house." This information about the "hot spots" was not furnished to Ms. Hughes until December 16, 1993, more than nine months after the samples had been collected and, as we discuss, *infra,* not until after Ericka Grimes's blood was found to contain elevated levels of lead.

KKI drew blood from Ericka Grimes for lead content analysis on April, 9, 1993, September 15, 1993, and March 25, 1994. Unlike the lead concentration analysis in dust testing, the results of the blood testing were typically available to KKI in a matter of days. KKI notified Ms. Hughes of the results of the blood tests by letters dated April 9, 1993, September 29, 1993, and March 28, 1994, respectively. The results of the April 9, 1993 test found Ericka Grimes blood to be [within normal range]. * * * However, on two subsequent retests, long after KKI had identified "hot spots," but before KKI informed Ms. Hughes of the "hot spots," Ericka Grimes's blood lead level registered [highly elevated] on March 25, 1994. Ms. Hughes and her daughter vacated the Monroe Street property in the Summer of 1994, and, therefore, no further blood samples were obtained by KKI after March 25, 1994.

* * *

III. Discussion

* * *

Because of the way the cases *sub judice* have arrived, as appeals from the granting of summary judgments, there is no complete record of the specific compensation of the researchers involved. . . . Neither is there in the record any development of what pressures, if any, were exerted in respect to the researchers obtaining the consents of the parents and conducting the experiment. Nor, for the same reason, is there a sufficient indication as to the extent to which the Institute has joined with

---

[22] For some unexplained reason, processing the dust samples typically took several months. KKI notified Ms. Hughes of the dust sample results via letters dated December 16, 1993, December 17, 1993, May 19, 1994, October 28, 1994, July 19, 1995, and January 18, 1996, respectively.

commercial interests, if it has, for the purposes of profit, that might potentially impact upon the researcher's motivations and potential conflicts of interest—motivations that generally are assumed, in the cases of prestigious entities such as John Hopkins University, to be for the public good rather than a search for profit.

We do note that the institution involved . . . is a highly respected entity, considered to be a leader in the development of treatments, and treatment itself, for children infected with lead poisoning. With reasonable assurance, we can note that its reputation alone might normally suggest that there was no realization or understanding on the Institute's part that the protocols of the experiment were questionable, except for the letter from the IRB requesting that the researchers mischaracterize the study.

* * *

C.   Negligence

* * *

The relationship that existed between KKI and both sets of appellants in the case at bar was that of medical researcher and research study subject. Though not expressly recognized in the Maryland Code or in our prior cases as a type of relationship which creates a duty of care, evidence in the record suggests that such a relationship involving a duty or duties would ordinarily exist, and certainly could exist, based on the facts and circumstances of each of these individual cases. . . .

IV.   The Special Relationships

A.   The Consent Agreement

* * *

By having appellants sign the Consent Form, both KKI and appellants expressly made representations, which, in our view, created a bilateral contract between the parties. At the very least, it suggests that appellants were agreeing with KKI to participate in the research study with the expectation that they would be compensated, albeit, more or less, minimally, be informed of all the information necessary for the subject to freely choose whether to participate, and continue to participate, and receive promptly any information that might bear on their willingness to continue to participate in the study. This includes full, detailed, prompt, and continuing warnings as to all the potential risks and hazards inherent in the research or that arise during the research. KKI, in return, was getting the children to move into the houses and/or to remain there over time, and was given the right to test the children's blood for lead. As consideration to KKI, it got access to the houses and to the blood of children that had been encouraged to live in a "risk" environment. In other words, KKI received a measuring tool—the children's blood. Considerations existed, mainly money, food coupons, trinkets, bilateral promises, blood to be tested in order to measure success. "Informed consent" of the type used here, which imposes obligation and confers consideration on both researcher and subject (in these cases, the parents of the subjects) may differ from the more one-sided "informed consent" normally used in actual medical practice. . . .

B. The Sufficiency of the Consent Form

* * *

A reasonable parent would expect to be clearly informed that it was at least contemplated that her child would ingest lead dust particles, and that the degree to which lead dust contaminated the child's blood would be used as one of the ways in which the success of the experiment would be measured. The fact that if such information was furnished, it might be difficult to obtain human subjects for the research, does not affect the need to supply the information, or alter the ethics of failing to provide such information. A human subject is entitled to *all* material information. . . . The "informed" consent was not valid because full material information was not furnished to the subjects or their parents.

* * *

D. The Federal Regulations

A duty may be prescribed by a statute, or a special relationship creating duties may arise from the requirement for compliance with statutory provisions. [F]ederal regulations have been enacted that impose standards of care that attach to federally funded or sponsored research projects that use human subjects. [ ] . . . [The court excerpts the Common Rule, 45 C.F.R. § 46.116, which is reproduced, above.]

* * *

. . . [T]he risks associated with exposing children to lead-based paint were not only foreseeable, but were well known by KKI . . . . Moreover, in the present cases, the consent forms did not directly inform the parents that it was possible, even contemplated, that some level of lead, a harmful substance depending upon accumulation, might contaminate the blood of the children.

Clearly, KKI, as a research institution, is required to obtain a human participant's fully informed consent, using sound ethical principles. It is clear from the wording of the applicable federal regulations that this requirement of informed consent continues during the duration of the research study and applies to new or changing risks. . . .

* * *

V.   The Ethical Appropriateness of the Research

* * *

Researchers cannot ever be permitted to completely immunize themselves by reliance on consents, especially when the information furnished to the subject, or the party consenting, is incomplete in a material respect. A researcher's duty is not created by, or extinguished by, the consent of a research subject or by IRB approval. The duty to a vulnerable research subject is independent of consent, although the obtaining of consent is one of the duties a researcher must perform. All of this is especially so when the subjects of research are children. Such legal duties, and legal protections, might additionally be warranted because of the likely conflict of interest between the goal of the research experimenter and the health of the human subject, especially, but not exclusively, when such research is commercialized. There is always a potential substantial conflict of interest on the part of researchers as between them and the human subjects used in their research. If participants in the study withdraw from the research study prior to its completion, then the results of the study could be rendered meaningless. There is thus an inherent reason for not conveying information to subjects as it arises, that might cause the subjects to leave the research project. That conflict dictates a stronger reason for full and continuous disclosure.

* * *

. . . Practical inequalities exist between researchers, who have superior knowledge, and participants "who are often poorly placed to protect themselves from risk." [ ] "[G]iven the gap in knowledge between investigators and participants and the inherent conflict of interest faced by investigators, participants cannot and should not be solely responsible for their own protection." [ ]

VI.   Parental Consent for Children to Be Subjects of Potentially Hazardous Nontherapeutic Research

The issue of whether a parent can consent to the participation of her or his child in a nontherapeutic health-related study that is known to be potentially hazardous to the health of the child raises serious questions with profound moral and ethical implications. What right does a parent have to knowingly expose a child not in need of therapy to health risks or otherwise knowingly place a child in danger, even if it can be argued it is for the greater good? . . . We have long stressed that the "best interests of the child" is the overriding concern of this Court in matters relating to children. . . .

To think otherwise, to turn over human and legal ethical concerns solely to the scientific community, is to risk embarking on slippery slopes, that all too often in the past, here and elsewhere, have resulted in practices we, or any community, should be ever unwilling to accept.

* * *

[The court describes several judicial opinions involving the donation of organs or tissue from a minor child or incompetent person to a family member.]

What is of primary importance to be gleaned in [these transplantation] cases is not that the parents or guardians consented to the procedures, but that they first sought permission of the courts, and received that permission, before consenting to a nontherapeutic procedure in respect to some of their minor children, but that was therapeutic to other of their children.

In the case sub judice, no impartial judicial review or oversight was sought by the researchers or by the parents. [Emphasis in original.] . . .

* * *

VII. Conclusion

We hold that in Maryland a parent, appropriate relative, or other applicable surrogate, cannot consent to the participation of a child or other person under legal disability in nontherapeutic research or studies in which there is any risk of injury or damage to the health of the subject.

We hold that informed consent agreements in nontherapeutic research projects, under certain circumstances can constitute contracts; and that, under certain circumstances, such research agreements can, as a matter of law, constitute "special relationships" giving rise to duties, out of the breach of which negligence actions may arise. We also hold that, normally, such special relationships are created between researchers and the human subjects used by the researchers. Additionally, we hold that governmental regulations can create duties on the part of researchers towards human subjects out of which "special relationships" can arise. Likewise, such duties and relationships are consistent with the provisions of the Nuremberg Code.

The determination as to whether a "special relationship" actually exists is to be done on a case by case basis. [ ] The determination as to whether a special relationship exists, if properly pled, lies with the trier of fact. We hold that there was ample evidence in the cases at bar to support a fact finder's determination of the existence of duties arising out of contract, or out of a special relationship, or out of regulations and codes, or out of all of them, in each of the cases.

* * *

RAKER, JUDGE, concurring in result only:

* * *

I cannot join in the majority's sweeping factual determinations that the risks associated with exposing children to lead-based paint were foreseeable and well known to appellees and that appellees contemplated lead contamination in participants' blood; that the children's health was put at risk; that there was no complete and clear explanation in the consent agreements that the research to be conducted was designed to measure the success of the abatement procedures by measuring the extent to which the children's blood was being contaminated and that a certain level of lead accumulation was anticipated; that the parental consent was ineffective; that the consent form was insufficient because it lacked certain specific warnings; that the consent agreements did not provide that appellees would provide repairs in the event of lead dust contamination subsequent to the original abatement measures; that the Institutional Review Board involved in these cases abdicated its responsibility to protect the safety of the research subjects by misconstruing the difference between therapeutic and nontherapeutic research and aiding researchers in circumventing federal regulations; that Institutional Review Boards are not sufficiently objective to regulate the ethics of experimental research; that it is never in the best interest of any child to be placed in a nontherapeutic research study that might be hazardous to the child's health; that there was no therapeutic value in the research for the child subjects involved; that the research did not comply with applicable regulations; or that there was more than a minimal risk involved in this study. I do not here condone the conduct of appellee, and it may well be that the majority's conclusions are warranted by the facts of these cases, but the record before us is limited. Indeed, the majority recognizes that the record is "sparse." The critical point is that these are questions for the jury on remand and are not properly before this Court at this time.

. . . I cannot join the majority in holding that, in Maryland, a parent or guardian cannot consent to the participation of a minor child in a nontherapeutic research study in which there is *any* risk of injury or damage to the health of the child without prior judicial approval and oversight. Nor can I join in the majority's holding that the research conducted in these cases was *per se* inappropriate, unethical, and illegal. Such sweeping holdings are far beyond the question presented in these appeals, and their resolution by the Court, at this time, is inappropriate. I also do not join in what I perceive as the majority's wholesale adoption of the Nuremberg Code into Maryland state tort law. . . .

Accordingly, I join the majority only in the judgment to reverse the Circuit Courts' granting of summary judgments to appellees.

NOTES AND QUESTIONS

1.   *Categorizing Research with Children.* HHS regulations on research with children divide that research into three categories based on the level of risk presented: (1) "research not involving greater than the minimal risk;" (2) "research involving greater than minimal risk but presenting the prospect of direct benefit to the individual subjects;" and (3) "research involving greater than minimal risk and no prospect of direct benefit to individual subjects, but likely to yield generalizable knowledge about the subject's disorder or condition." 45 C.F.R. §§ 46.401–46.409. "Minimal risk" is defined in § ___.102(j), above.

Where there is more than minimal risk but the research will also benefit the child, the risk must be justified "by the anticipated benefit to the subjects," and "[t]he relation of the anticipated benefit to the risk [must be] at least as favorable to the subjects as that presented by available alternative approaches."

Research providing no direct benefit to the individual child subject and involving more than minimal risk is not allowed unless: there is only a "minor" increase over minimal risk; the "experiences" that accompany the research are those that the child-subjects are likely to undergo anyway; and the research is aimed at a disorder or condition actually suffered by the subject. On this point, see Ana Iltis, Justice, Fairness, and Membership in a Class: Conceptual Confusions and Moral Puzzles in the Regulation of Human Subjects Research, 39 J. L. Med. & Ethics 488 (2011).

2.   *Risk and Public Health Research.* Was the *Grimes* court correct in its conclusion that federal regulations on research with children prohibited the lead study? See Loretta Kopelman, Pediatric Research Regulations Under Legal Scrutiny: Grimes Narrows Their Interpretation, 30 J.L. Med. & Ethics 38 (2002), arguing that the key issue in *Grimes* is the interpretation of "risk" as used in the regulations and that *Grimes* was correct in its application to the particular protocol. But see Lainie F. Ross, In Defense of the Hopkins Lead Abatement Studies, 30 J.L. Med. & Ethics 50 (2002), arguing that the court misinterpreted the regulations, making important research impossible. See also Diane Hoffmann and Karen Rothenberg, Whose Duty is it Anyway? The Kennedy Krieger Opinion and Its Implications for Public Health Research, 6 J. Health Care L. & Pol'y 109 (2003), criticizing the case for misunderstanding the nature of public health research. How would the regulations on research with children have applied in the SUPPORT study in *Looney*, above?

3.   *Clarifying "Any Risk"?* The Court denied the University's motion for reconsideration, but in doing so, it issued a *per curiam* opinion noting that "the only conclusion we reached as a matter of law was that . . . summary judgment was improperly granted." It went on to state:

In the Opinion, we said at one point that a parent "cannot consent to the participation of a child . . . in nontherapeutic research or studies in which there is any risk of injury or damage to the health of the subject." [W]e think is clear [that] by "any risk," we meant any articulable risk beyond the minimal kind of risk that is inherent in any endeavor. The context of the statement was a nontherapeutic study that promises no medical benefit to the child whatever, so that any balance between risk and benefit is necessarily negative. As we indicated, the determination of whether the study in question offered some benefit, and therefore could be regarded as therapeutic in nature, or involved more than that minimal risk is open for further factual development on remand.

Does this statement clarify or confuse the Court's position? Subsequent Maryland cases considered the application of *Grimes*. See, e.g., Kennedy Krieger Inst., Inc. v. Partlow, 460 Md. 607, 191 A.3d 425 (2018) (research institute owes a duty of care to a sibling of research participant who lived in the same house as the research participant); Partlow v. Kennedy Krieger Inst., 2017 WL 4772626 (Md. Ct. Spec. App. 2017) (duty of researcher to subject identified in *Grimes* extended to the sibling who lived in the same house as a child enrolled as a subject); Smith v. Kennedy Krieger Inst., 2017 WL 1076481 (Md. Ct. Spec. App. 2017) (upholding refusal to instruct jury that consent form was a contract and upholding admission of testimony of mayor as to seriousness of lead paint hazards in Baltimore); White v. Kennedy Krieger Inst., 110 A.3d 724 (Md. Ct. Spec. App. 2015) (distinguishing therapeutic trial of treatment for children with moderate lead blood levels from nontherapeutic research in *Grimes* but holding that a duty existed as between researcher and subject).

4.   *Nuremberg Code as Evidence of Legal Standard.* The *Grimes* majority noted that the "breach of obligations imposed on researchers by the Nuremberg Code, might well support actions sounding in negligence in cases such as those at issue here." Compare Washington Univ. v. Catalona, 437 F. Supp. 2d 985 (E.D. Mo. 2006), aff'd on other grounds, 490 F.3d 667 (8th Cir. 2007), in which the trial court concluded that the Nuremberg Code and the Declaration of Helsinki (see Section V, below) were irrelevant to legal standards for research in the U.S.

5.   *Protection or Exclusion?* Does the protection of particular groups always work for good, or can it have undesirable consequences? For example, pregnant women may participate as subjects in research only if the research is therapeutic and the risk to the fetus is minimized, or if the risk to the fetus is minimal. 45 C.F.R. § 46.204–207. Fetal protection practices which raise the cost or inconvenience of including women in research contribute to the exclusion of all women who could be pregnant or become pregnant during the course of a study presenting any fetal risk. As a result, nearly all women, from early adolescence through post-menopause, were excluded from most drug studies.

Fetal protection policies were not the only reason women have been excluded from research studies, but these practices contributed to the absence of research examining how life-threatening conditions behave in the female body as compared to the male body and on the effectiveness and safety of pharmaceuticals on other than the male body. See Cynthia Hathaway, *A Patent Extension Proposal to End the Underrepresentation of Women in Clinical Trials and Secure Meaningful Drug Guidance for Women*, 67 Food & Drug L. J. 143 (2012); Barbara Noah, *The Inclusion of Pregnant Women in Clinical Research*, 7 St. Louis U. J. Health L. & Pol'y 353 (2014).

In this context, can "equitable" selection of subjects be read to require inclusion of certain groups? Several federal statutes, for example, have encouraged and provided significant incentives for pharmaceutical research with children. See, e.g., Best Pharmaceuticals for Children Act and the Pediatric Research Equity Act.

People with disabilities have also been excluded from human subjects research. See Dianne Rios et al., *Conducting Accessible Research: Including People with Disabilities in Public Health, Epidemiological, and Outcomes Studies*, 106 Am. J. Publ. Health 2137–2144 (2016); A. S. Williams and S. M. Moore, *Universal Design of Research: Inclusion of Persons with Disabilities in Mainstream Biomedical Studies*, 3(82) Science Translational Medicine 82cm12 (2011).

E. COMMERCIAL INTERESTS IN RESEARCH

Several developments have worked a revolution in the financial infrastructure for research in the U.S. In 1980, Congress enacted the Bayh-Dole Act, 35 U.S.C. § 200, and unleashed the entrepreneurial spirit in academic research, transferring property rights in the products of federally funded research to the researchers and their institutions. The Act encouraged researchers to form for-profit companies for the development and marketing of the products of research for quicker translation into clinical use. Universities developed "tech transfer" offices to capitalize on this opportunity, and the number of patents issued to universities increased more than tenfold in the early years after Bayh-Dole.

Direct financial support for research also has shifted significantly, with much more research on pharmaceuticals, biologics, testing materials, and devices being supported directly by industry rather than public funds. In fact, industry support for pharmaceutical research dwarfs that available from government sources. See Marc Rodwin, *Independent Clinical Trials to Test Drugs: The Neglected Reform*, 6 St. Louis U. J. Health L. & Pol'y 113 (2012). The advent of entrepreneurial incentives and a profit-oriented infrastructure has raised serious concerns, however.

Critics of financial incentives in research argue that they can compromise research design; lead to overreaching in enrollment and retention of subjects; and lead to censoring of research results that are adverse to the sponsor. Because these financial interests are viewed as conflicting with goals of validity and credibility in research, as well as protection of human subjects, they are often called "conflicts of interest." To the extent that a conflict of interest generally requires that there be a fiduciary relationship between the parties—as between a treating physician and patient—using that term to embrace this situation may not be entirely accurate. See, e.g., William M. Sage, Some Principles Require Principals: Why Banning "Conflicts of Interest" Won't Solve Incentive Problems in Biomedical Research, 85 Tex. L. Rev. 1413 (2007). By short-handing "financial relationships" to "conflicts of interest," the latter term can be misunderstood to represent an individualized judgment about the personal integrity of the researcher. A financial conflict of interest, however, is identified at the point when the financial relationship is established and the research proposed, without an assessment of the researcher's personal character and before there is even opportunity for bad conduct. Robert Gatter, Walking the Talk of Trust in Human Subjects Research: The Challenge of Regulating Financial Conflicts of Interest, 52 Emory L.J. 327 (2003); Greg Koski, Research, Regulations, and Responsibility: Confronting the Compliance Myth: A Reaction to Professor Gatter, 52 Emory L.J. 403 (2003); Jesse Goldner, Regulating Conflicts of Interest in Research: The Paper Tiger Needs Real Teeth, 53 St. Louis U. L. J. 1211 (2009).

Financial payments and ownership interests of researchers and research institutions are not the only incentives in research, and so are not the only source of conflicts of interest. This narrow focus on financial interests alone fails to account for the broader range of incentives (reputational, competitive, etc.) that can influence researcher behavior in directions that may harm research subjects or compromise the validity of results. These incentives are often apparent in scientific misconduct cases where researchers have falsified results, rather than under the financial conflicts of interest regulations. See generally Gary Marx, An Overview of the Research Misconduct Process and an Analysis of the Appropriate Burden of Proof, 42 J.C. & U.L. 311 (2016).

The revised Common Rule addresses the issue of commercial exploitation of research results and products as a matter of consent. See § ___.116(c)(7) as to biospecimens. See also Section IV.F, below. Consider the following case:

GREENBERG V. MIAMI CHILDREN'S HOSPITAL RESEARCH INSTITUTE

United States District Court, S.D. Florida, 2003.
264 F. Supp. 2d 1064.

[Eds. Note: Canavan disease is a progressive, neurological genetic condition for which there is no cure. Symptoms usually appear in infancy, and most children with the disease do not live past the age of 10. It is genetic and primarily affects children of eastern and central European Jewish (Ashkenazi) or Saudi Arabian descent.]

* * *

The Complaint alleges a tale of a successful research collaboration gone sour. In 1987, Canavan disease still remained a mystery—there was no way to identify who was a carrier of the disease, nor was there a way to identify a fetus with Canavan disease. Plaintiff Greenberg approached Dr. Matalon, a research physician who was then affiliated with the University of Illinois at Chicago, for assistance. Greenberg requested Matalon's involvement in discovering the genes that were ostensibly responsible for this fatal disease, so that tests could be administered to determine carriers and allow for prenatal testing for the disease.

At the outset of the collaboration, Greenberg and the Chicago Chapter of the National Tay-Sachs and Allied Disease Association, Inc. ("NTSAD") located other Canavan families and convinced them to provide tissue (such as blood, urine, and autopsy samples), financial support, and aid in identifying the location of Canavan families internationally. The other individual Plaintiffs began supplying Matalon with the same types of information and samples beginning in the late 1980s. Greenberg and NTSAD also created a confidential database and compilation—the Canavan registry—with epidemiological, medical and other information about the families.

Defendant Matalon became associated in 1990 with Defendants Miami Children's Hospital Research Institute, Inc. and Variety Children's Hospital d/b/a Miami Children's Hospital. Defendant Matalon continued his relationship with the Plaintiffs after his move, accepting more tissue and blood samples as well as financial support.

The individual Plaintiffs allege that they provided Matalon with these samples and confidential information "with the understanding and expectations that such samples and information would be used for the specific purpose of researching Canavan disease and identifying mutations in the Canavan disease which could lead to carrier detection within their families and benefit the population at large." Plaintiffs further allege that it was their "understanding that any carrier and prenatal testing developed in connection with the research for which they were providing essential support would be provided on an affordable and accessible basis, and that Matalon's research would remain in the public domain to promote the discovery of more effective prevention techniques and treatments and, eventually, to effectuate a cure for Canavan disease." . . .

There was a breakthrough in the research in 1993. Using Plaintiffs' blood and tissue samples, familial pedigree information, contacts, and financial support, Matalon and his research team successfully isolated the gene responsible for Canavan disease. After this key advancement, Plaintiffs allege that they continued to provide Matalon with more tissue and blood in order to learn more about the disease and its precursor gene.

In September 1994, unbeknownst to Plaintiffs, a patent application was submitted for the genetic sequence that Defendants had identified. This application was granted in October 1997, and Dr. Matalon was listed as an inventor on the gene patent and related applications for the Canavan disease. Through patenting, Defendants acquired the ability to restrict any activity related to the Canavan disease gene, including without limitation: carrier and prenatal testing, gene therapy and other treatments for Canavan disease and research involving the gene and its mutations.

Although the Patent was issued in October 1997, Plaintiffs allege that they did not learn of it until November 1998, when MCH revealed their intention to limit Canavan disease testing through a campaign of restrictive licensing of the Patent. Specifically, on November 12, 1998, Plaintiffs allege that Defendants MCH and MCHRI began to "threaten" the centers that offered Canavan testing with possible enforcement actions regarding the recently-issued patent. Defendant MCH also began restricting public accessibility through negotiating exclusive licensing agreements and charging royalty fees.

Plaintiffs allege that at no time were they informed that Defendants intended to seek a patent on the research. Nor were they told of Defendants' intentions to commercialize the fruits of the research and to restrict access to Canavan disease testing.

... Plaintiffs generally seek a permanent injunction restraining Defendants from enforcing their patent rights, damages in the form of all royalties Defendants have received on the Patent as well as all financial contributions Plaintiffs made to benefit Defendants' research. Plaintiffs allege that Defendants have earned significant royalties from Canavan disease testing in excess of $75,000 through enforcement of their gene patent, and that Dr. Matalon has personally profited by receiving a recent substantial federal grant to undertake further research on the gene patent.

Informed Consent

... Plaintiffs, who served as research subjects, ... claim that Defendants owed a duty of informed consent. ... Defendants breached this duty, Plaintiffs claim, when they did not disclose the intent to patent and enforce for their own economic benefit the Canavan disease gene. ... Finally, the Plaintiffs allege that if they had known that the Defendants would "commercialize" the results of their contributions, they would not have made the contributions.

* * *

Defendants assert that extending a possible informed consent duty to disclosing economic interests ... would have pernicious effects over medical research, as it would give each donor complete control over how medical research is used and who benefits from that research. The Court agrees and declines to extend the duty of informed consent to cover a researcher's economic interests in this case.

Plaintiffs cite a variety of authorities in support of their contention that the duty of informed consent mandates that research subjects must be informed of the financial interests of the researcher. They first rely on *Moore v. Regents of the University of California,* where the court held that a physician/researcher had a duty of informed consent to disclose that he was both undertaking research and commercializing it. [] . . . Defendants correctly contest Plaintiffs' interpretation of *Moore.* . . . *Moore* involved a physician breaching his duty when he asked his patient to return for follow-up tests after the removal of the patient's spleen because he had research and economic interests. . . . The allegations in the Complaint are clearly distinguishable as Defendants here are solely medical researchers and there was no therapeutic relationship as in *Moore.*

In declining to extend the duty of informed consent to cover economic interests, the Court takes note of the practical implications of retroactively imposing a duty of this nature. First, imposing a duty of the character that Plaintiffs seek would be unworkable and would chill medical research as it would mandate that researchers constantly evaluate whether a discloseable event has occurred. Second, this extra duty would give rise to a type of dead-hand control that research subjects could hold because they would be able to dictate how medical research progresses. Finally, these Plaintiffs are more accurately portrayed as donors rather than objects of human experimentation, and thus the voluntary nature of their submissions warrants different treatment. . . .

* * *

Unjust Enrichment

. . . Plaintiffs allege that the [researchers' profit from the patent] violates the fundamental principles of justice, equity, and good conscience [as they would not have contributed to the research had they known that this would happen]. While Defendants claim that they have invested significant amounts of time and money in research, with no guarantee of success and are thus entitled to seek reimbursement, the same can be said of Plaintiffs. . . . The Complaint has alleged more than just a donor-donee relationship for the purposes of an unjust enrichment claim. Rather, the facts paint a picture of a continuing research collaboration that involved Plaintiffs also investing time and significant resources in the race to isolate the Canavan gene. Therefore, given the facts as alleged, the Court finds that Plaintiffs have sufficiently pled the requisite elements of an unjust enrichment claim and the motion to dismiss for failure to state a claim is DENIED as to this count.

* * *

NOTES AND QUESTIONS

1. *The* Gelsinger *Case.* The issue of financial interests in research rose to public attention with the death of Jesse Gelsinger and the subsequent lawsuit filed by his father against the University of Pennsylvania, the research physician, and the bioethicist who had consulted with the IRB in its approval of the protocol. Jesse was 18 years old and had a liver disorder that was under control. Under a research protocol and with a signed consent form, physicians inserted, into Jesse and other subjects, a virus based on the cold virus, to deliver genetic material with the hope that this genetic therapy would cure the disease. An FDA investigation after Jesse's death revealed a number of violations of federal regulations including continuing with the protocol after four patients had suffered serious reactions; failing to notify the FDA of the adverse events, contrary to a specific agreement between the University and the FDA; and altering consent forms to eliminate information that monkeys subjected to the intervention had died.

Because the protocol involved genetic therapy it had been subjected to heightened review at the FDA itself as a condition of approval. Financial conflicts of interest on the part of both the researcher and the University attracted the most public attention, however. Although reports vary in detail, it appears that the University gave Genovo, a private corporation, the exclusive rights to patent the results from the researcher's laboratory. The University also allowed the researcher to control up to 30% of Genovo stock, a company he founded, in an exception to the University's conflicts of interest guidelines. The University would receive $21 million to support research, and it also owned stock in Genovo. The University had received legal advice, covering research regulation issues, from an outside law firm in arranging the tripartite financial relationship. Gelsinger's lawsuit was resolved by a confidential settlement. Informal reports indicate that the settlement was about $5 to $10 million.

For a detailed history of the case, see Robin Fretwell Wilson, Estate of Gelsinger v. Trustees of University of Pennsylvania: Money, Prestige, and Conflicts of Interest in Human Subject Research, in Health Law & Bioethics: Cases in Context (Sandra Johnson et al., eds. 2009). See also Steven Raper, An Artless Tale: Challenges Faced in Clinical Research, 71 Food & Drug L. J. 59 (2016), written by the principal investigator in the *Gelsinger* protocol. For a description of similar cases, see Gabriela Weigel, Unresolved Conflicts of Interests in University Human Subject Research, 43 J. C. & U. L. 77 (2017).

2. *Moore v. Regents and Henrietta Lacks.* The *Moore* case involved a treating physician who removed tissue, under allegedly false pretenses, and used that tissue to develop a profitable cell line. The court in *Moore* held that the patient stated a claim for informed consent, subject to the elements required for that claim (see Section IV.C, above), because the actions occurred in a therapeutic relationship. The court rejected plaintiff's claim for conversion, however, which would have allowed the plaintiff to claim some of the profit

because the court believed that would significantly harm the research enterprise.

Henrietta Lacks was an African-American woman being treated for cancer when tissue removed in the course of treatment was used to produce one of the most widely used and lucrative cell lines in the U.S. without her knowledge or consent. Neither she nor her family or descendants received an acknowledgement, much less compensation, for decades. See Rebecca Skoot, The Immortal Life of Henrietta Lacks (2010), placing the episode in the larger context of race and human experimentation. In 2013 the surviving Lacks family reached an agreement with the National Institutes of Health to have some control over the use of the "HeLa" cell line in future research. See Carl Zimmer, A Family Consents to a Medical Gift, 62 Years Later, N.Y. Times, Aug. 7, 2013. More recently, the family hired a civil rights attorney to pursue damages from pharmaceutical companies that profited from research using the "HeLa" cell line, and possibly from Johns Hopkins University where Henrietta Lacks' cells were sampled by a physician nearly 70 years ago while treating her. See Tim Prudente, Family of Henrietta Lacks Hires Civil Rights Attorney to Seek Funds Over Famous Cells, Wash. Post, July 31, 2021.

Both the "Mo" and "HeLa" cell lines survive and continue to be used to this day. On the differences between property claims and informed consent liability, see Jorge Contreras, Genetic Property, 105 Geo. L. J. 1 (2016).

3. Greenberg *Settlement*. The *Greenberg* parties ultimately settled by agreeing that the defendants would retain their patents but that they would allow the gene to be used without fee in any research relating to Canavan disease. Kevin L. J. Oberdorfer, The Lessons of Greenberg: Informed Consent and the Protection of Tissue Sources' Research Interests, 93 Geo. L.J. 365, 376 (2004).

4. *Further Reading*. Conflicts of interest affect human subjects research conducted abroad, further exposing gaps in regulatory protections for human subjects. See Robert Gatter, Conflicts of Interest in International Human Drug Research and the Insufficiency of International Protections, 32 Am. J.L. & Med. 351 (2006); Marc A. Rodwin, Conflicts of Interest in Human Subject Research: The Insufficiency of U.S. and International Standards, 45 Am. J.L. & Med. 303, 320 (2019).

PROBLEM: MANAGING FINANCIAL INTERESTS

Several federal agencies have promulgated regulations or policies to address financial interests of researchers. These rules generally do not prohibit researchers from patenting and licensing their work, investing in research companies, or receiving financial support from industry. Instead, they place obligations on research institutions to manage these relationships.

The HHS regulation, for example, requires that organizations receiving Public Health Service grants have a written policy that defines what financial interests must be reported to the organization and identifies the procedures used by the organization to review and manage those interests. 42 C.F.R. § 50.601 et seq. Financial transactions or relationships that must be reported include intellectual property rights; sponsored travel; "any remuneration" in excess of $5,000 (except from the research institution itself); and equity interests in a publicly traded entity in excess of $5,000. The regulation requires the organization to maintain a publicly accessible website with its policies and procedures posted, as well as specifics on financial relationships that the organization has identified as a conflict of interest on the part of a researcher. The regulation provides many options, beyond terminating the financial relationship or prohibiting the researcher from conducting the study, for managing financial conflicts of interest. These include, for example, public disclosure of the financial relationship, disclosure to prospective subjects, modifying the research plan, or appointing an independent monitor for the study. See F. Lisa Murtha et al., Conflicts of Interest in Research: Assessing the Effectiveness of COI Disclosure Program, 18 J. Health Care Comp. 5 (July/August 2016).

1.   If you decide to require disclosure of a conflict of interest to subjects participating in a study, is the following statement, used in the *Gelsinger* protocol (see Note 1 following *Greenberg*, above) adequate? If not, how would you change it?

> Please be aware that the University of Pennsylvania, Dr. James M. Wilson, (the Director of the Institute for Human Gene Therapy) and Genovo, Inc. (a gene therapy company in which Dr. Wilson holds an interest) have a financial interest in a successful outcome from the research involved in this study.

Would clearer language resolve the issue? See Kevin Weinfurt et al., Disclosure of Financial Relationships to Participants in Clinical Research, 361 NEJM 916 (2009), describing an empirical study of patients' decision making.

2.   Should the following protocols be approved by your IRB or should your conflicts policy prohibit the research? If you believe it can go forward but with specific requirements, what would they be?

a.   A protocol covers a clinical trial of a new medication. The principal investigator for the protocol is on the speakers' bureau for the pharmaceutical firm that is funding the protocol and receives a fee of $1500 for every presentation she gives at any conference in relation to any research she does. The firm does not require that she submit any information regarding the content of her presentations. Last year, she received $24,000 for such presentations.

b.   A university is courting a biotech firm for a major donation for a new research building. The university's development office has asked researchers whose research is financially supported by the firm to make a presentation on the importance of the new building at the meeting at which the firm will be asked for a donation. The associate provost for research is a member of the fundraising committee and a member of the university's IRB.

c.   An untenured faculty member is in his last year before tenure. He has had difficulty in getting publishable results from his research because he has had problems in enrolling and retaining subjects for his research on early signs of dementia. This research involves a "vulnerable population" and presents significant challenges, including assessment of the subject's capacity to consent. See Section IV.D and §§ ___.111(a)(3) and (b) and 109(g), above.

F.   RESEARCH AND BIOBANKS

The use of human specimens and private health information in research is included within the definition of "human subject" (§ ___.102(e), above), whether the research protocol involves the actual removal or collection of tissue or data or whether the research merely uses material that is already stored in some sort of repository. The question of how this "secondary use" of stored specimens and data should be handled was one of the most controversial issues in the revision of the Common Rule and remains so.

There are over 600 biobanks (repositories of human specimens and related data) in the U.S. alone. The number of biobanks continues to grow explosively. The organizational structure of biobanks varies: some are associated with academic institutions or networks, others are industry created and controlled, and still others are held by federal and state governments. See Kara Swanson, Body Banking from the Bench to the Bedside (2014). 23andMe, a firm that sells popular DNA screening tests directly to consumers, has built a significant biobank with the information and specimens provided by its customers. The firm's website includes its policies on privacy and consent for research access to this material, which it sells to researchers.

Claims over ownership of biobanked material and resulting products have been litigated among researchers, research organizations, biobanks, and patients whose tissue has been used in research and product development. For example, approximately 6,000 former patients of a surgeon-researcher signed forms, at his request, directing that their tissue, stored by a university hospital, be released to the custody of the surgeon-researcher for his move to another university. Washington Univ. v. Catalona, 490 F.3d 667 (8th Cir. 2007), cert. denied, 552 U.S. 1166 (2008). The court ultimately concluded that the earlier consent forms that the patients had signed when their tissue was removed and stored governed and that their later request to remove them did not constitute withdrawal from a research protocol and would not be enforced. See § ___.116(b)(8), above. The court held that the university, and not the researcher, owned the specimens. See also Section IV.E, above, and Chapter 17 concerning property rights in tissue removed from cadavers.

Other legal protections for privacy and confidentiality of data have a significant effect on research using human biospecimens and health information. These restrictions emerge from a great number of statutory and common law provisions. See Heather Harrell and Mark Rothstein, Biobanking Research and Privacy Laws in the United States, 44 J.L. Med. & Ethics 106 (2016).

The critical issues facing regulators in the revision of the Common Rule were whether research on stored tissue and data ("secondary use") would continue to be embraced within the definition of "human subject;" and, if yes, whether use of such material requires the consent of the individual from whom the specimen or information was collected. The core value of biobanks is that they create a pool of raw material to be used in research many years down the line, much of which research cannot be anticipated when the tissue or data is collected. See Arti K. Rai, Risk Regulation and Innovation: The Case of Rights-Encumbered Biomedical Data Silos, 92 Notre Dame L. Rev. 1641 (2017).

Many argue that this material should be treated as a commons from which researchers can draw material without consent. Others argue that individual dignity and respect for persons are at risk when something as intimate as health records and body parts are used without the consent of the individual. See, e.g., Institute of Medicine, Beyond the HIPAA Privacy Rule: Enhancing Privacy, Improving Health through Research (2009), recommending that consent not be required for research on health information; Mark Rothstein, Improve Privacy in Research by Eliminating Informed Consent? IOM Report Misses the Mark, 37 J.L. Med. & Ethics 507 (2009); Sharona Hoffman & Andy Podgurski, Balancing Privacy, Autonomy, and Scientific Needs in Electronic Health Records Research, 65 S.M.U. L. Rev. 85 (2012); Ken Gatter, Biobanks as a Tissue and Information Semicommons: Balancing Interests for Personalized Medicine, Tissue Donors and the Public Health, 15 J. Health Care L. & Pol'y, 303 (2012); Chao-Tien Chang, Bank on We the People: Why and How Public Engagement Is Relevant to Biobanking, 25 Mich. Tech. L. Rev. 239, 301 (2019).

Before the revision of the Common Rule in 2017, guidance from OHRP provided researchers using repositories of data or biospecimens with only two options. They could secure consent for their specific research project from each individual whose health information or tissue they wanted to use, or they could follow a mandatory detailed procedure for "deidentifying" the material (which could result in removing relevant health data in an effort to assure that the individual could not be identified and which still presented the risk that the material could be "reidentified").

In its final form, the 2017 revision of the Common Rule appears to have landed on a compromise that retains this research within the definition of human subjects research (§ ___.102(e)(1)(ii), above) but places a good deal of research on stored tissue and data within the category of exempt research. Under the revised Rule, consent is not required for studies using identifiable private information or identifiable biospecimens that have been deidentified (as was the case before the revision) or are publicly available or are the subject of a study by or for federal agencies using information generated or collected by the government for nonresearch purposes, if the information is maintained in a fashion that meets other federal statutes regarding privacy and security. Research in these categories is considered exempt. § ___.104(d)(4), above.

For research that does not fit those categories, the Rule adopts a new concept of "broad consent" that applies to the "storage, maintenance, and secondary use of identifiable private information or identifiable biospecimens." The advantage of broad consent over the prior regime is that it accepts a one-time consent for any research that may be done in the future. For broad consent to be effective, the individual must be provided with the information listed in the regulation, and IRBs are prohibited from waiving those elements. §§ ___.116(d) and (f), above. Broad consent allows studies to use identifiable information and biospecimens, without deidentification, for many studies over many years and requires only a limited IRB review to assure merely that broad consent has been secured and documented and that, if there is a change in the way the material is stored, there have been adequate protections for privacy and confidentiality. §§ ___.104(d)(7) and (8) and ___.116(d), above.

The revised Common Rule adopted an additional significant change regarding use of medical records within organizations governed by HIPAA privacy rules for research consistent with HIPAA. Such studies are considered exempt. § ___.104(d)(4)(iii). For an analysis of "broad consent" and "secondary use" research, see Holly Fernandez Lynch, Leslie E. Wolf & Mark Barnes, Implementing Regulatory Broad Consent Under the Revised Common Rule: Clarifying Key Points and the Need for Evidence, 47 J.L. Med. & Ethics 213 (2019).

PROBLEM: DRAFTING STATE LEGISLATION

The Common Rule does not preempt state laws or tribal laws that provide additional protections for human subjects or that "require additional information to be disclosed in order for informed consent to be legally effective." §§ ___.101(f) and ___.116(i), above. States, for example, have regulated research uses of state-held biobanks such as those created by storing bloodspots collected as part of mandated screening of newborns for specific genetic conditions. See, e.g., Tufik Shayeb, Informed Consent for the Use and

Storage of Residual Dried Blood Samples from State-Mandated Newborn Genetic Screening Programs, 64 Buff. L. Rev. 1017 (2016).

Assume that you are legislative counsel to the state legislature charged with developing proposed legislation for your state. A state senator wants to propose legislation to require consent for research studies on biospecimens or health records that may offend an individual's religious or cultural values or that might stigmatize a particular group. She is also concerned that individuals might object to certain products that may be produced using their stored tissue.

The state senator has brought a particular controversy to your attention. A research team from Arizona State University collected blood samples from members of the Havasupai tribe with a consent form stating that the research would study "the causes of behavioral/medical disorders." After discussions with the researchers, those who provided blood samples thought that they would be used in diabetes and related public health research. The stored blood samples were actually used in subsequent research studies of schizophrenia, inbreeding, and migration genetics. Tribal members objected when the research turned toward areas that brought unwanted notice to the tribe; that might mark the tribe members as having a propensity toward mental illness; and that would undermine core tribal beliefs about the origins of the tribe. The tribe sued and the University settled the case. See Michelle Mello & Leslie Wolf, The Havasupai Indian Tribe Case: Lessons for Research Involving Stored Biologic Samples, 363 NEJM 204 (2010).

An earlier version of the revisions to the Common Rule proposed that consent to future unspecified research with biospecimens be allowed (as does the "broad consent" in the final Rule) but that individuals be offered the opportunity to refuse consent for use of their health records or tissue for specific categories of research that presented "unique concerns." 76 Fed. Reg. 44512 (July 26, 2011). That option was eliminated in the final version, however. Would you draw on this model for the state legislation the senator desires? Would you restrict certain uses without specific consent, or would you allow the individual to specify what uses would be prohibited? What public policy concerns arise in these proposals, and what stakeholders would be interested in the result? What enforcement tools would you use if you do adopt such a restriction?

V. INTERNATIONAL RESEARCH

The modern medical research enterprise is a global venture conducted through international academic collaborations and by multinational corporations. In 2010, an OIG report determined that over 80% of applications for FDA approval for drugs and biologics contained information generated abroad. OIG, Challenges to FDA's Ability to Monitor and Inspect Foreign Clinical Trials (June 2010). See also Darby Hall, Reining in the Commercialized Foreign Clinical Trial, 36 J. Leg. Med. 367 (2015).

International research in developing countries, in particular, presents several distinctive ethical challenges and has engendered considerable controversy. Clinical trials of pharmaceuticals in developing countries often test medications that the country will never be able to afford to provide to the very population from whom the research subjects are drawn. Ruqaiijah Yearby, Good Enough to Use for Research, But Not Good Enough to Benefit from the Results of that Research: Are the Clinical HIV Vaccine Trials in Africa Unjust?, 53 DePaul L. Rev. 1127 (2004). Limits on access to needed care may also influence research design in ethically challenging ways. In African trials of AZT, for example, U.S. agencies and pharmaceutical firms conducted a trial of low-dose AZT for pregnant women with HIV to prevent transmission of the virus to the newborn. The cost of the standard dose of AZT used for this purpose in the U.S. made its use in impoverished countries impossible without manufacturer discounts. The goal of the AIDS trials in Africa was to test whether a dose of AZT that was very significantly lower and cheaper than that used in the U.S. would be equally effective. As a control arm, however, the studies used a placebo rather than the higher, and more expensive dose used in the U.S. Jerry Menikoff and Edward Richards, What the Doctor Didn't Say: The Hidden Truth About Medical Research 67 (2006); Claire Wendland, Research, Therapy and Bioethical Hegemony, The Controversy over Perinatal AZT Trials in Africa, 51 African Studies Rev. 1 (2008); Sheryl Stolberg, U.S. AIDS Research Abroad Sets Off Outcry Over Ethics, N.Y. Times (Sept. 18, 1997).

In addition to the serious ethical issues involved in studies conducted in developing countries outside of the U.S., there are scientific concerns relating to whether specific populations (defined by race, genetics, gender, or age) and specific clinical environments might influence results in a way that would make outcomes in the U.S. less predictable. See, e.g., FDA, Draft Guidance, Acceptance of Medical Device Clinical Data from Studies Conducted Outside the United States (April 22, 2015), withdrawn as Guidance but still useful for illustrations. See also Blake Wilson, Clinical Studies Conducted Outside the United States and their Role in the FDA's Drug Marketing Approval Process, 34 U. Pa. J. Int'l L. 641 (2013).

Most nations have established standards and procedures governing medical research conducted within their own boundaries. See, e.g., Obiajulu Nnamuchi, Biobank/Genomic Research in Nigeria: Examining Relevant Privacy and Confidentiality Frameworks, 43 J.L. Med. & Ethics 776 (2015), part of a special issue on comparative approaches to research regulation; Jacob Kolman et al., Conflicts Among Multinational Ethical and Scientific Standards for Clinical Trials of Therapeutic Interventions, 40 J.L. Med. & Ethics 99 (2012).

The Common Rule governs research within the scope of the Rule even if it is performed abroad. The Rule requires that its criteria apply to that research unless the agency head determines that the country's policies provide protections for human subjects that are "at least equivalent" to those in the Common Rule. See § ___.101(h), above. This would include provisions related to vulnerable populations. See Section IV.D, above.

The FDA accepts certain investigational drug studies conducted abroad if the study was conducted "in accordance with good clinical practice (GCP)" 21 C.F.R. § 312.120. GCP is defined as a standard that assures that studies are designed, conducted, and reported in a manner that assures that the results are "credible and accurate" and that "the rights, safety and well-being of trial subjects are protected." The regulation specifies that GCP includes review and approval by an independent ethics committee and voluntary consent from the research subject as well as other protections and procedures. GCP is a concept proffered by the International Conference on Harmonisation of Technical Requirements for Registration of Pharmaceuticals for Human Use (ICH), an international organization of the pharmaceutical regulatory agencies and pharmaceutical industry in the U.S., Europe, and Japan. Earlier FDA regulations had accepted foreign clinical trials if they followed the laws of the host country or the principles of the Declaration of Helsinki, "whichever represents the greater protection of the individual." The FDA substituted compliance with GCP for drug studies in 2008 (73 Fed. Reg. 22800 (April 28, 2008)) and for device studies in 2018 (83 Fed. Reg. 7366 (Feb. 21, 2018)).

The Declaration of Helsinki, Ethical Principles for Medical Research Involving Human Subjects, is promulgated by the World Medical Association (WMA), an organization consisting of representatives from most of the world's national medical associations. Revisions of the Declaration over the past several years have struggled with issues relating to vulnerable populations. For example, the Declaration states that:

> Medical research involving a disadvantaged or vulnerable population or community is only justified if the research is responsive to the health needs or priorities of this population or community and if there is a reasonable likelihood that this population or community stands to benefit from the results of the research.

A 2000 revision of the Declaration included a statement that "every patient entered into the study should be assured of access to the best proven prophylactic, diagnostic and therapeutic methods identified by the study." This provision attracted strong opposition and may have influenced the action of the FDA to adopt GCP. The most recent revision of the Declaration (2013) modifies that article to provide:

> In advance of a clinical trial, sponsors, researchers and host country governments should make provisions for post-trial access for all participants who still need an intervention identified as beneficial in the trial.

In contrast, the Common Rule does not require that research subjects, in the U.S. or elsewhere, continue to receive medication after the clinical trial has ended. See Abney v. Amgen, 443 F.3d 540 (6th Cir. 2006), holding that the company had no fiduciary duty to subjects to provide the drug tested after a study was terminated. See also Michelle M. Mello et al., Compact v. Contract: Industry Sponsors' Obligations to their Research Subjects, 356 NEJM 2738 (2007).

International law may form a basis for claims in U.S. courts by persons injured in clinical trials conducted in foreign countries. In 1996, for example, Pfizer conducted clinical trials of the antibiotic Trovan on children in Kano, Nigeria, during an epidemic of bacterial meningitis. According to news reports, only one child had received Trovan prior to these trials, and animal testing had indicated significant potential for serious adverse effects on children. Parents consenting to administration of the drug reported that they had not been informed that the medication was experimental or that conventional treatment was available to them at no charge at the same site. Parents sued Pfizer in the U.S. under the Alien Tort Statute (ATS) alleging that the medication caused the deaths of 11 children and paralysis, deafness, and blindness in many others.

The Court of Appeals, reversing the trial court, held that nonconsensual medical research violated universal norms of customary international law and, therefore, supported a claim under the ATS. Abdullahi v. Pfizer, 562 F.3d 163 (2d Cir. 2009). Pfizer settled the case through an agreement with the Nigerian government to establish a trust fund of up to $35 million to compensate injured parties; to underwrite several health care initiatives ($30 million over two years) in Nigeria; and to reimburse Nigeria for $10 million in litigation costs. In 2011, Pfizer also settled with the private plaintiffs in an agreement that included them in the compensation trust fund. See Pfizer Settles Lawsuits Over Drug Trials on Children in Nigeria, Corp. Counsel (Feb. 23, 2011). See also Fazal Khan, The Human Factor: Globalizing Ethical Standards in Drug Trials through Market Exclusion, 57 DePaul L. Rev. 877 (2008).

A medical historian investigating archives relating to the Tuskegee syphilis study (See Section II.B., above) discovered documents revealing that the U.S. government had conducted similar research in Guatemala in the 1940s. See Kayte Spector-Bagdady & Paul Lombardo, "Something of an Adventure:" Postwar NIH Research Ethos and the Guatemala STD Experiments, 41 J. Law, Med. & Ethics 697 (2013). The Presidential Commission for the Study of Bioethical Issues conducted an investigation of the matter, and subsequently issued a report: Ethically Impossible: STD Research in Guatemala from 1946–1948. Over 5,000 prison inmates, sex workers, soldiers, children, and psychiatric patients were included in the study, and over 1,300 adults were intentionally infected with STDs. The report concluded that the study was unethical and would have been viewed as unethical even under the standards of the mid-1940s.

President Obama issued a formal apology for the research, but the federal government claimed sovereign immunity in the suit filed by those who were subjects in the study. The federal district court agreed and dismissed the suit. Garcia v. Sebelius, 867 F. Supp. 2d 125 (D.D.C., 2012), vacated in part 919 F. Supp. 2d 43 (D.D.C. 2013). In a related case (Estate of Alvarez v. Johns Hopkins Univ., 275 F. Supp. 3d 670 (D. Md. 2017)), a federal district court considered claims against a number of private parties, including the university and the pharmaceutical company, and refused to dismiss the suit as barred by the statute of limitations, stating that:

> The experimenters allegedly targeted the subjects of the Guatemala Experiments because of their inability to understand, discover, and control what was happening to them. Many of the subjects were young schoolchildren, patients in an asylum, or prisoners without access to proper medical care, education, or resources. These types of persons would have been unlikely to discover his or her exact injury and its cause.

CHAPTER 21

POPULATION HEALTH AND PUBLIC HEALTH LAW

. . .

I. INTRODUCTION

Between 1900 and 2000, life expectancy in the U.S. increased by 30 years. Five of those 30 years are attributable to the individualized health care that is the subject of most of this casebook and the basis of most of our health care industry. Twenty-five of those additional years of life, however, are a result of public health interventions. The primary goal of those interventions is population health. The Centers for Disease Control and Prevention (CDC) lists the following as the "Ten Great Public Health Achievements" of the 20th Century (48 MMWR 241):

- Vaccination
- Motor-vehicle safety
- Safer workplaces
- Control of infectious diseases
- Decline in deaths from coronary heart disease and stroke
- Safer and healthier foods
- Healthier mothers and babies
- Family planning
- Fluoridation of drinking water
- Recognition of tobacco use as a health hazard

Public health, then, is what a community, generally through its government, does to establish the conditions that allow members of that community to lead long and healthy lives. As the National Academy of Medicine has pointed out, public health generally involves collective action. Because the principle of autonomy and the value of individualism are so important in the United States, and because we tend to be suspect of government and collective action, we are called upon to weigh the benefit of public health interventions against the cost of government-imposed requirements more often than is the case in similar countries. While we do not often think about the way public health interventions protect us, we do when we need public health resources and help—when a pandemic sweeps across the nation, for example.

Because public health generally requires collective and sometimes coercive action, law is implicated in most public health interventions. The law may set standards for purity of food and water, for example, or at least designate those with appropriate expertise who will. The law may encourage or require immunization, as we will see, and it may require medical testing for diseases or conditions—either among the general population or subgroups such as teachers, students, pilots, food workers, or prisoners. Public health law may also protect the public by placing exceptions on limitations imposed by other laws, for example, by allowing needle exchanges or treatment with medication to avoid communicable diseases among individuals with substance use disorders even though drug laws may otherwise prohibit those actions. Additionally, the law may require the reporting of medical status to government agencies to allow those agencies to determine if there is a public health problem, and then how to protect the public health.

The application of public health law sometimes breaches some notions of individual privacy. Indeed, the collection of huge amounts of health information, some of it identifiable and some not, is one of the most important tools, and one of the greatest risks, of public health operations. When individually identifiable data is collected, particular follow-up measures—including, for example, tracing the contacts of those who could be transmitting communicable diseases—heighten privacy concerns. In rare circumstances, the law can require patients to receive treatment (or be placed in isolation or quarantine). For an explanation of federal and state confidentiality law as it relates to public health, see Chapter 4, Section IV.

What makes an issue a "public health" issue? Is the quality of the gene pool a public health issue? The widespread use of alternative medicines? of tobacco? Gun violence? The availability and use of video games (or just violent video games)? Domestic violence? Restrictive licensure for midwives? What difference does it make whether an issue is characterized as a public health issue? Are we more likely to defer to governmental decisions, and more likely to accept governmental intrusions on individual liberties, where the public health is involved? Article 25 of the Universal Declaration of Human Rights says:

> Everyone has a right to a standard of living adequate for the health and well-being of [oneself] and [one's] family, including food, clothing, housing and medical care and necessary social services, and the right to security in the event of unemployment, sickness, disability, widowhood, old age or other lack of livelihood in circumstances beyond one's control.

Is this a principle of public health?

Public health can endeavor to encourage healthy individual behavior just as it can act to prohibit or discourage risky behavior. For example, while the Affordable Care Act (ACA) was designed to support a private health care system, it also recognizes the value of public health approaches to many issues. The Act provides subsidies for small employers who wish to establish employee wellness programs, and it allows employers of all sizes to give premium discounts to those employees who participate in some kinds of wellness programs. (There is only limited evidence, however, that wellness programs are effective; see Chapter 9.) In addition, the ACA eliminates copays, deductibles, and other payments for some preventive care provided by private health plans, Medicare, or Medicaid, and it uses public relations strategies to increase national rates of immunization and other forms of preventive care. The ACA also requires the collection of data, including health disparity data, that will make the creation of public health approaches easier in the future.

In addition to supporting these traditional public health strategies, the ACA moves the health care system toward a greater concern for population health. The ACA, for example, encourages the formation of accountable care organizations (ACOs) as a system for delivering care. See Chapter 12. An ACO's performance is measured against its impact on outcomes relating to population health and wellness. See Susan DeVore and R. Wesley Champion, Driving Population Health through Accountable Care Organizations, 30 Health Aff. 41 (2011).

The ACA also institutes some more focused public health changes. It requires chain restaurants (those with more than 20 outlets serving essentially standardized products) to provide nutritional information on those products by posting calorie information on the menu or menu board and making additional nutritional information available to customers. It imposes the same obligations on those who sell products through vending machines, at least where customers cannot read the nutritional information already on the packaged food. The ACA also requires that employers with more than 50 employees (and others where it would not cause hardship) allow employees to express milk whenever that is necessary during the year following the birth of their children; employers must provide a clean and private space for this need and allow adequate break time, although it may be unpaid time. The law also provides for public education on a host of lifestyle and preventive care issues.

As we move toward government programs that encourage wellness, is public health entering a new era in the United States—one that depends more on incentives and price regulation than on statutory mandates? Are these new efforts—encouraging Americans to exercise, eat healthy food, stop smoking, and breastfeed their children—appropriately within the realm of government?

For a discussion of the ACA and public health, see Elizabeth Weeks Leonard, ed., Public Health Reform: Patient Protection and Affordable Care Act Implications for the Public's Health (Symposium), 39 J.L. Med. & Ethics 312 et seq. (2011). For a very thoughtful summary of the overlap of law and public health, see Barry Levy, Twenty-First Century Challenges for Law and Public Health, 32 Ind. L. Rev. 1149 (1999). For a comprehensive account of the law of public health, see Lawrence Gostin and Lindsay Wiley, Public Health Law: Power, Duty, Restraint (3d ed. 2016). See also Lawrence Gostin et al., The Law and the Public's Health: A Study of Infectious Disease Law in the United States, 99 Colum. L. Rev. 59 (1999). For an interesting historical and constitutional approach to these issues, see Wendy Parmet, Populations, Public Health, and the Law (2009). For a good account of the international public health issues, see Roger Detels et al., eds., Oxford Textbook of Public Health (4th ed. 2004).

II.   POPULATION HEALTH AND (IN)EQUITY

The inequities of our society are laid bare by population health statistics, revealing that the U.S. does not have one population with a roughly uniform, shared health status. Instead, we are an amalgam of sub-populations—white and non-white, wealthy and impoverished, able-bodied and disabled, educated and uneducated, socially connected and unconnected—that are associated with significantly different levels of population health.

- Black Americans have an average life expectancy of 72 years as compared to 78 years for white Americans. See Elizabeth Arias et al., Provisional Life Expectancy Estimates for January through June, 2020, Vital Statistics Rapid Release (Feb. 2021).

- The wealthiest Americans live, on average, 14.6 years longer than the poorest Americans. Raj Chetty et al., The Association Between Income and Life Expectancy in the United States, 2001–2014, 315(16) JAMA 1750 (2016).

- In 2017 Americans with a 4-year college degree had a life expectancy 7–10 years longer than those with only a primary education and 5–6 years longer than those with only a secondary education. Isaac Sasson and Mark D. Hayward, Association Between Educational Attainment and Causes of Death Among White and Black U.S. Adults, 2010–2017, 322(8) JAMA 756 (2019).

These statistics highlight the fact that social determinants play a substantial role in health. According to the Healthy People 2030 project,

Social determinants of health (SDOH) are the conditions in the environments where people are born, live, learn, work, play, worship, and age that affect a wide range of health, functioning, and quality-of-life outcomes and risks.

* * *

. . . Examples of SDOH include:

- Safe housing, transportation, and neighborhoods
- Racism, discrimination, and violence
- Education, job opportunities, and income
- Access to nutritious foods and physical activity opportunities
- Polluted air and water
- Language and literacy skills

SDOH also contribute to wide health disparities and inequities. For example, people who don't have access to grocery stores with healthy foods are less likely to have good nutrition. That raises their risk of health conditions like heart disease, diabetes, and obesity—and even lowers life expectancy relative to people who do have access to healthy foods.

Just promoting healthy choices won't eliminate these and other health disparities. Instead, public health organizations and their partners in sectors like education, transportation, and housing need to take action to improve the conditions in people's environments.

HHS, Office of Disease Prevention and Health Promotion, Healthy People 2030.

While public health policy recommendations often reflect the association between key social factors and health, case law about public health issues rarely addresses the social determinants of health. Perhaps this is because cases focus closely on specific parties rather than on populations where relationships between social factors and health are clear.

The following opinion is an exception. In a lawsuit challenging the constitutionality of voting procedures implemented by Alabama for the November 2020 election, which took place during the COVID-19 pandemic, the court dove deeply into the health of the sub-populations represented by the plaintiffs. In so doing, the court accounted for many of the social determinants of health and demonstrated the link between those social factors, health, and the risk of disenfranchisement of plaintiffs through voting regulation.

PEOPLE FIRST OF ALABAMA V. MERRILL

United States District Court, N.D. Alabama, 2020.
491 F. Supp. 3d 1076.

ABDUL K. KALLON, JUDGE.

I.   FINDINGS OF FACT

A.   The COVID-19 Pandemic

1.   Our nation is now in the midst of a public health emergency due to the spread of COVID-19, the respiratory disease caused by the novel coronavirus SARS-CoV-2. Since April, the United States has led the world in the total number of COVID-19 cases. [ ]. As of September 29, 2020, the United States has confirmed 7,129,383 cases of COVID-19 and reported 204,598 deaths and counting due to COVID-19. [ ]. The COVID-19 pandemic has deeply affected Alabama, and as of September 29, Alabama reported 137,564 confirmed COVID-19 cases and 2,399 confirmed COVID-19 deaths, including family members and a friend of some of the individual plaintiffs.[ ].

2.   The most common symptoms of COVID-19 are fever, cough, and shortness of breath, and other symptoms include chest pain, muscle pain, vomiting, anorexia, confusion, and lack of senses of taste and smell. [ ]. Even mild cases of COVID-19 can be more severe than the flu and involve about two weeks of fevers and dry coughs. [ ]. Severe cases of COVID-19 cause acute respiratory distress syndrome ("ARDS") in which fluid displaces air in the lungs, leaving patients to "essentially drown[ ] in their own blood and fluids because their lungs are so full." [ ]. Due to the respiratory impacts of the disease, individuals with severe cases may need supplemental oxygen or to be intubated and put on a ventilator, or suffer a permanent loss of respiratory capacity. [ ]. Along with damaging lung tissue, severe cases of COVID-19 can damage the kidneys, or lead to strokes and heart attacks. [ ].

3.   In Alabama, as of September 3, approximately 11.5 percent of those infected by COVID-19 have been hospitalized. [ ]. Thus, surges of COVID-19 cases can strain healthcare systems, leading to critical shortages of doctors, nurses, hospital beds, medical equipment, and personal protective equipment. [ ]. For that reason and others, health officials recommend that all individuals take steps to prevent the spread of the disease, not just for their own health but for the health of the community. [ ]. As the CDC put it, "[e]veryone has a role to play in slowing the spread and protecting themselves, their family, and their community." [ ].

4.   COVID-19 is highly infectious and spreads through respiratory droplets from infected individuals. [ ]. Strong evidence now suggests that SARS-CoV-2 is aerosolized, such that tiny droplets containing the virus

remain in the air for a period of time, and the virus can be transmitted to others who inhale that air. []. Further evidence indicates that aerosolized droplets with SARS-CoV-2 can linger in closed, stagnant air environments for up to fourteen minutes. []. Consequently, transmission of the virus is more likely to occur indoors when people share space in a room for an extended period of time. []. COVID-19 may also spread through contaminated surfaces, i.e., "when an infected individual touches a surface with a hand they have coughed into and then another person touches that same surface before it has been disinfected and then touches their face." []. Finally, COVID-19 is particularly dangerous because it can be spread by individuals who are a- or pre-symptomatic, and who may not know they have the disease and can spread it to others. [].

5.   No vaccine for COVID-19 currently exists, and it is unlikely a vaccine will become widely available until well into 2021. []. Accordingly, to slow the spread of COVID-19, public health officials have been left to urge the public to practice "social distancing," i.e., avoidance of close contact with others. []. For purposes of social distancing, the CDC recommends that individuals stay at least six feet away from others who do not live in their households and avoid crowded places. []. Following that recommendation, Governor Kay Ivey recognizes that "[m]aintaining a 6-foot distance between one another is paramount," and the Alabama Department of Public Health ("ADPH") has instructed the public to "spend as much time as possible at home to prevent an increase in new infections." []. The CDC and ADPH also recommend that all individuals wear masks or face coverings, which decrease the spread of COVID-19 by helping to prevent an infected individual from spreading droplets containing the virus that can infect others. []

6.   Though people of all ages have contracted COVID-19 and suffered severe manifestations of the disease, the illness poses special risks for older people, and the risk of COVID-19 increases steadily with age. []. As of September 1, 77.3 percent of COVID-19 related deaths in Alabama have been people 65 or older, and 80 percent of deaths in the United States have been people over 65. []. Thus, the CDC warns that older people should avoid interacting with people outside of their households and people who have been exposed to the virus. [].

7.   COVID-19 also presents special risks for people with disabilities. "The CDC [] warns that people with disabilities may be at increased risk of becoming infected with COVID-19 to the extent that they "(1) 'have limited mobility or cannot avoid coming into close contact with others who may be infected;' (2) 'have trouble understanding information or practicing preventative measures;' or (3) are 'not able to communicate symptoms of illness.'" []. As Susan Ellis, the Executive Director of People First of Alabama, explained, people with intellectual disabilities are not able to identify risky behavior in the same way as other people can. []. For

example, they may pick up and throw away a tissue on the floor without wearing gloves in an effort to be helpful to others without thinking of the germs on the tissue. [ ]. In addition, adults with disabilities are three times more likely than adults without disabilities to have underlying chronic medical conditions that put them at higher risk from COVID-19. [ ].

8. People with certain preexisting medical conditions, including immunological conditions, hypertension, certain heart conditions, lung diseases (asthma and chronic obstructive pulmonary disease), diabetes mellitus, obesity, chronic kidney disease, and sickle cell anemia also have an elevated risk of severe complications or death from COVID-19. [ ]. In fact, statistics from the ADPH reveal that approximately 96.2 percent of Alabamians who have died from COVID-19 had underlying health conditions. [ ]. Due to their heightened risk from COVID-19, the CDC advises people with underlying conditions to limit interactions with people outside of their households as much as possible and to avoid others who are not wearing masks. [ ].

9. Alabamians suffer from high rates of the underlying health conditions that increase their risk for COVID-19 complications: more than 14 percent have diabetes, 41.9 percent have high blood pressure, 10.4 percent have asthma, approximately 33 percent are obese, and about 1 in 11 have kidney disease. [ ]. As Alabama State Health Officer Dr. Scott Harris stated, "[c]hronic disease factors are a real risk for dying from this disease, and chronic diseases are found in about a third of our citizens." [ ]. The prevalence of underlying diseases is even more profound for older Alabamians, who are already at a higher risk from COVID-19. For example, the COVID-impact survey revealed that in the Birmingham metro region, 76.1 percent of White people and 80.3 percent of Black people over the age of 60 had at least one underlying condition that put them at an increased risk from COVID-19. [ ].

10. Racial minorities, particularly Black people, are more likely to suffer from underlying conditions that increase the risks from COVID-19, such as diabetes, heart disease, and lung disease. [ ]. That trend is reflected in Mobile, Alabama, where areas of the city with the highest percentage of Black residents have markedly higher prevalence of asthma, high blood pressure, kidney disease, COPD, and diabetes, than predominately White areas of the city. [ ]. Moreover, about 42.2 percent of Black people over the age of 65 have a disability, compared to 38.1 percent of their White cohorts. [ ].

11. People who are Black, Latinx, or Native American suffer higher rates of COVID-19 infections than non-Hispanic White individuals, and they are more likely to suffer severe outcomes and be hospitalized or die if they are infected with COVID-19. [ ]. Indeed, a CDC report published April 8, 2020, which included data from patients hospitalized across 14 states,

found that Black COVID-19 patients made up 33 percent of those for whom race or ethnicity information was available, despite representing only 18 percent of the states' populations. [ ]. This disparity has continued. As of September 21, the CDC reports that Black people represent 18.5 percent of COVID-19 cases and 21 percent of COVID-19 deaths in individuals for whom race or ethnicity is known, despite representing only 12.5 percent of the U.S. population. [ ]. And, Latinx people represent 29.5 percent of COVID-19 cases, though they represent only 18.4 percent of the population. [ ].

12. Like the rest of the country, Alabama has reported alarming racial disparities in serious illness and mortality due to COVID-19. [ ]. As of August 13, the ADPH reported that Black people in Alabama account for 41.1 percent of COVID-19 related deaths, despite making up just 27 percent of the population. [ ]. And, in Mobile County, as of August 13, Black people accounted for 51.1 percent of COVID-19 deaths, despite representing only 36 percent of the population. [ ]. In addition, counties in the Black Belt[28] in Alabama that are predominately African American, including Lowndes and Wilcox, have higher COVID-19 related death rates compared to predominantly White counties, and Lowndes County has the State's highest case fatality rate. [ ]. Dr. Latesha Elopre, the plaintiffs' expert on internal medicine, infectious diseases, and disparities in access to health care and health outcomes in Alabama, explained, "there is strong data that supports . . . looking [across] age groups, that Black people, regardless of health conditions, have higher rates of death compared to Whites." [ ].

13. The higher risk of COVID-19 infection for African Americans is tied to pre-existing and evolving inequities in structural systems and social conditions. [ ]. To begin, people who are Black, Latinx, or Native American are more likely to hold jobs that do not provide paid leave, cannot be performed remotely, and require more exposure to the public and, therefore, to COVID-19. [ ]. Also, due to patterns resulting from a history of housing discrimination, Black and Latinx individuals are more likely to live in areas impacted by environmental pollutants, or in densely populated areas, making it harder for those individuals to practice social distancing. [ ]. In addition, evidence reveals that testing resources for COVID-19 are scarcer in Black communities and that Black people are less likely to be referred for testing than White people when presenting comparable signs of infection. [ ]. Indeed, for these and other reasons, the CDC identified discrimination in housing, education, finance, and health care as a factor that puts racial and ethnic minorities at increased risk of getting sick and dying from COVID-19. [ ].

---

[28] The Black Belt is named for the region's fertile black soil. [ ].

14. The discrimination and systemic racism that contribute to elevated COVID-19 risk for Black people and other minorities nationally are evident in Alabama. [ ]. For example, in Alabama's Black Belt counties, residents face multiple stressors that lead to a relatively poor quality of life: high levels of poverty and unemployment, inadequate education, high rates of illiteracy, lack of jobs, many single-parent households, and food insecurity. [ ]. On top of that, Black Belt counties have fewer primary care physicians per resident than other counties, and, despite the high rates of infection, people living in these counties receive fewer COVID-19 tests than elsewhere in Alabama. [ ]. Disparities in access to transportation exacerbate those obstacles and make COVID-19 testing and health care even less accessible for Black people in those counties, which in turn makes it even more difficult for communities in the Black Belt to manage and slow the spread of the disease. [ ].

B. Alabama's Response to the Pandemic

[The court summarized a variety of orders by the Governor of Alabama and the state's public health agency, including orders that closed schools, prohibited gatherings of more than 25 persons, and prohibited bars and restaurants from allowing patrons to consume food or drink on site. Additionally, the court described later orders that required every person to stay at home except to perform "essential activities," that closed entertainment venues and businesses providing close-contact services, and that set standards for how "essential retailers" would operate so as to mitigate the risk of disease transmission. Finally, the court outlined the state's Safer-at-Home order, which required people to wear masks outside the home and to practice social distancing. Importantly, this order especially encouraged vulnerable populations to remain at home.]

C. Voting and Alabama's Elections in the Pandemic

* * *

21. With respect to voting in the pandemic, Dr. Anthony Fauci, head of the National Institute of Allergy and Infectious Diseases and a member of the White House's coronavirus taskforce, stated:

I don't see any reason why, if people maintain [six-foot] distancing, wearing a mask and washing hands—why you cannot, at least where I vote, go to a place and vote.

And you can do that, if you go and wear a mask, if you observe the physical distancing, and don't have a crowded situation, there's no reason why you shouldn't be able to do that. I mean, obviously if you're a person who is compromised physically or otherwise, you don't want to take the chance. There's the situation of mail-in voting that has been done for years in many places. So there's no reason why we shouldn't be able to vote in person or otherwise.

[ ]. Still, according to Dr. Reingold, traditional in-person voting exposes voters to a risk of contracting COVID-19 due to the proximity of a large number of individuals in a limited space and the large number of common surfaces that many people may touch. [ ]. And, the risk of infections increases for people who have to use public transportation or ride in a car with people outside of their household to get to the polls. [ ]. Moreover, Dr. Reingold indicated that, in Alabama, the risk of in-person voting is compounded because the State's mask order does not apply to "[a]ny person who is voting," which means that not everyone voting will wear a mask in polling places, leading to greater risk of COVID-19 transmission. [ ]. Similarly, in part because of the chance that people at polling sites will not be wearing masks, Dr. Elopre recommends that people at-risk from COVID-19 vote absentee rather than in-person. [ ].

22. Evidence exists of transmission of COVID-19 from in-person voting. Indeed, after the April 7 primary election in Wisconsin, that state's contact tracing efforts identified 71 individuals who had COVID-19 cases linked to working at the polls or voting in person at the polls. [ ]. The plaintiffs' expert, Dr. Chad Cotti, . . . concluded that counties that had higher numbers of in-person votes per polling location in the Wisconsin primary had a higher rate of COVID-19 spread at a community level after the election than counties with relatively fewer in-person votes. [ ]. In particular, he found that a 10 percent increase in in-person voter density, i.e., in-person votes per polling location, corresponds to about a 17–18 percent increase in the positive test rate. [ ]. Ultimately, Dr. Cotti concluded from his analysis that approximately 700 cases of COVID-19 in the five-week period after the April 7 Wisconsin primary were associated with in-person voting. [ ]. Based on his conclusion, Dr. Cotti opined that to reduce COVID-19 risk, "it would be prudent for election officials and state leaders to engage in as many practices to 'de-densify'[ ] polling locations as possible," including by offering more hours at the polls, early voting, and curbside voting, and by encouraging absentee voting. [ ].

23. In contrast to Dr. Cotti, the State defendants' expert, Dr. Quentin Kidd, . . . found that there was no increase in COVID-19 infection rates in the 14-day period following elections in Wisconsin, Virginia, West Virginia, Georgia, and Kentucky, based on his review of data from Johns Hopkins University. [ ]. Dr. Kidd's review, however, analyzed only the 7-day moving average for COVID-19 cases reported in databases for the 14 days after the elections. [ ]. Noticeably, he admitted he did not account for the acknowledged lag times between exposure, the onset of symptoms, testing, and results. [ ]. And, on cross examination, Dr. Kidd admitted that during the time-period between 15 and 30 days after the elections, which accounted for the lag time, a noticeable increase in COVID-19 cases could be seen in all of those jurisdictions, except Virginia. [ ]. Virginia, however, allows curbside voting for individuals over 65 and for individuals with a

disability, and only 57,500 people voted in person. [ ]. Thus, Dr. Kidd's analysis, even if the court were to accept it, does not refute Dr. Cotti's testimony that there is a link between higher numbers of in-person votes per polling location and increased COVID-19 spread in communities.

24. The CDC has issued specific guidelines to address concerns about voting during the COVID-19 pandemic. [ ]. Among other things, the CDC recommends that states "offer alternative voting methods that minimize direct contact and reduce crowd size at polling locations," including early voting, and it asked states to consider "drive-up voting for eligible voters if allowed in the jurisdiction" as a means of complying with social distancing rules and limiting personal contact during in-person voting. [ ]. The plaintiffs' experts, Dr. Reingold and Dr. Elopre, agree with the CDC's recommendations, including the recommendation for curbside or drive-up voting, though Dr. Reingold admits that curbside voting is not necessarily safer than absentee voting. [ ].

25. Alabama does not offer early, traditional in-person voting or curbside voting. [ ]. Still, Alabama has taken specific steps to make voting safer during the COVID-19 pandemic. To begin, on March 13, Secretary Merrill sent a letter to probate judges to suggest that they should sanitize polling machines and equipment frequently during voting, provide hand sanitizer to voters, and provide gloves to poll workers. [ ]. Then, on March 18, Governor Ivey rescheduled the March 31 primary runoff election to July 14. [ ]. That same day, Secretary Merrill promulgated an emergency rule titled "Absentee Voting During State of Emergency," providing in part as follows:

> [A]ny qualified voter who determines it is impossible or unreasonable to vote at their voting place for the Primary Runoff Election of 2020 due to the declared states of emergency, shall be eligible to check the box on the absentee ballot application which reads as follows: "I have a physical illness or infirmity which prevents my attendance at the polls. [ID REQUIRED]."

[ ]. In effect, this rule meant that any voter concerned about potential exposure to COVID-19 at a polling place could vote absentee in the July 14 primary runoff election. [ ]. Secretary Merrill issued a press release in March informing voters about the emergency absentee voting rule for the July election. [ ].

26. In April, Congress appropriated funds for Alabama to prepare for voting during the pandemic in the July and November elections, and the Secretary of State's office also dedicated increased funding to this effort. [ ]. The Secretary of State will use some of those funds to reimburse counties for masks, gloves, and cleaning supplies for polling places. [ ]. And, Secretary Merrill testified that his office will provide a mask to any voter at a polling place who would like one. [ ]. Still, Secretary Merrill's office

received letters from some probate judges expressing concern about their ability to comply with CDC recommendations and State and Federal election laws during the July runoff election. [ ]. And, the Secretary received a report that in Mobile County, the polling sites that would have the biggest issues complying with CDC guidelines serve predominately minority communities. [ ].

27. Alabama saw a record turnout of voters for a runoff election on July 14, with 17.6 percent of eligible voters voting. [ ]. During and after the July 14 election, Secretary Merrill received complaints that poll workers and voters did not wear masks at polling sites. [ ]. When he learned that voters in certain precincts were not wearing masks, Secretary Merrill took steps to ensure those voters were still allowed to vote in the runoff. [ ]. According to Secretary Merrill, "[n]o voter can be turned away [from a polling site] for any reason if they are a qualified elector[,]" even if they are visibly ill or have a known case of COVID-19. [ ].

28. Secretary Merrill extended the emergency absentee voting rule to apply to the November 3, 2020 general election. [ ]. Thus, any voter in Alabama who wishes to vote absentee in the November election due to concerns about COVID-19 may do so, subject to the witness and photo ID requirements. Secretary Merrill expects voter turnout in November to exceed the 2016 presidential election, and although most Alabama voters have traditionally voted in person on Election Day, he expects voters to cast a record number of absentee ballots in the November election. [ ]. On at least 14 occasions, Secretary Merrill's office issued a press release encouraging voters concerned about exposure to COVID-19 to vote absentee and providing information on how to apply for an absentee ballot and the applicable deadlines. [ ].

29. Absentee voting for the general election began on September 9, and as of September 11, more than 30,000 people had applied for absentee ballots across the State. [ ]. In addition, several hundred people have completed absentee ballots in person in their county AEM's office. [ ]. To cast an absentee ballot, a voter must complete an absentee ballot application, and return the application to the AEM by mail or in person with a copy of her photo ID at least five days before the election. [ ]. Then, after the voter receives the absentee ballot packet, she must seal the completed ballot inside an affidavit envelope, and sign the affidavit in the presence of two witnesses or a notary. [ ]. Finally, the voter must return the completed ballot and affidavit to the AEM in person up until the day before Election Day, or by mail in time to be received by noon on Election Day. [ ].

30. Voters may go in person to an AEM's office to vote before the election, and they can complete the absentee voting process in a single trip. [ ]. Alleen Barnett, the Absentee Election Coordinator for Mobile County,

estimates that her office has been serving between 40–50 voters a day since absentee voting began on September 9, and she anticipates that the number will increase. [ ], In addition to serving voters at the AEM's office, Secretary Merrill encourages AEMs and Circuit Clerks to hold events outside of their offices, such as outdoors on college campuses, in parking lots, or in nursing homes, to allow voters additional opportunities to cast absentee ballots in person before the election. [ ].

31. In the Mobile County AEM's office, Ms. Barnett and her staff wear masks, have hand sanitizer and rubber gloves available, and wipe their work areas and the voter areas with disinfectant spray. [ ]. They also practice social distancing in the office and have spaced chairs for voters at least six-feet apart. [ ]. But, Ms. Barnett's office cannot turn away a voter who does not wear a mask. [ ]. At least in part for that reason, Mr. Howard Porter, Jr., one of the individual plaintiffs from Mobile County, testified that he would not consider voting in person in the AEM's office. [ ]. Mr. Porter explained his decision for not voting in person: "I don't want any vote that I cast to be my last vote. And in Alabama, a person can vote even if they don't have on a face mask. And that's just too much for me. [ ] [A]s important as the right to vote is, I just can't endure that." [ ]. Mr. Porter, a Black man in his seventies, further explained: "[S]o many of my [ancestors] even died to vote. And while I don't mind dying to vote, I think we're past that—we're past that time. And that should not be a requirement . . . . Because voting is the only day that rich, the poor, sick, the healthy, all should be counted as one and just as easy. And any obstacle placed in the way of the opportunity to vote places an effect on the process itself." [ ].

D. Alabama's History of Disenfranchisement of Black Voters

32. For the individual plaintiffs who are Black and the organizations who advocate for the voting rights of Blacks, voting is fundamental and sacred in light of the many thousands who died to secure the right. They view any restrictions to voting as part of the centuries-old effort to deprive Blacks from accessing the ballot. As the plaintiffs testified, Black Alabamians have consistently overcome barriers to exercising their fundamental right to vote, only to later have that right curtailed. [ ]. The relevant historical facts are largely undisputed. . . .

[The Court summarized the history of changes to the law that ended slavery and promised the right to vote, and it described the many ways white Alabamians circumvented these laws to deny or otherwise undermine the ability of black Alabamians to exercise that right.]

45. Alabama's history of voter discrimination interacts with systemic disparities that currently affect Black residents' education, employment, and healthcare outcomes to negatively impact Black political participation. [ ].

46. For example, in addition to voting discrimination, racial discrimination in Alabama's public schools is also well-documented. [ ]. State and local officials fought to maintain segregation in Alabama schools long after the Supreme Court ruled the practice unconstitutional in Brown v. Board of Education, [ ]. Efforts to desegregate school systems in Alabama have continued, with dozens remaining under desegregation orders today. [ ].

47. To no surprise, consistent with CitiBank's study released last week that found that the U.S. Economy has lost $16 trillion since 2000 because of discrimination against Blacks,[38] educational discrimination has had a lasting effect in Alabama. [ ]. Of adults aged 25 years and over, 16.6 percent of Black Alabamians have not completed high school compared to 11.4 percent of their White counterparts. [ ]. For the same age range, only 17.3 percent of African Americans in the State earned a bachelor's degree or higher compared to 28.3 percent of White adults. [ ].

48. Complementing Alabama's historical racial disparities in education are entrenched disparities in employment and economic opportunities. [ ]. Over the past half-century, litigation has uncovered many examples of state entities adopting racially discriminatory employment practices. [ ]. And private employers too have faced countless allegations of racial discrimination. In 2019, for example Alabama had a higher percentage of racially-based employment discrimination claims than any other state. [ ]. Alabama was also overrepresented nationally in racially-based employment discrimination claims based on its population. [ ].

49. Relatedly, Black communities in Alabama suffer from higher concentrations of unemployment and under-employment. [ ]. The unemployment rate among Black Alabamians over age 16 is more than double the rate among White residents of the same age. [ ]. Those Black Alabamians who are employed are more likely to work lower paying jobs than White workers. Of employed Black adults in the State, 20.7 percent work in service occupations compared to just 14.8 percent of Whites. [ ]. Only 26.2 percent of employed Black Alabamians hold management or professional roles; 39.1 percent of White Alabamians hold such positions. [ ].

50. In Alabama, Black households also have fewer economic resources. The median household income for Black Alabamians is $33,503 compared to $58,257 for White households. [ ]. More than one quarter of Black Alabamians live in poverty compared to only 11.3 percent of White Alabamians. [ ]. This economic inequality has consequences. Roughly 13 percent of Black families in Alabama lack access to a vehicle compared to only 3.9 percent of White families. [ ]. Black households are eight percent

---

[38] NPR, *Cost of Racism*, [ ].

less likely than White households to own a computer, smartphone, or tablet. [ ]. Black households are also less likely to have broadband internet access—29.6 percent compared to 17.2 percent of White households. [ ].

51. These economic conditions intersect with other legacies of racial discrimination in Alabama to make the State's Black residents more likely to suffer negative health outcomes. [ ]. Historic racial residential segregation is a principal driver. [ ]. State and federal laws and practices "produced and maintained" racial residential segregation in Alabama by incentivizing discriminatory zoning, redlining, and predatory lending. [ ]. Racial residential segregation has devalued neighborhoods, reduced access to quality and affordable food, and produced disproportionately high concentrations of poverty in Black communities. [ ]. It is "one of the strongest indicators of chronic illness patterns in the Black community." [ ]. Because of racial residential segregation, Black individuals are more likely than White individuals to suffer from chronic conditions such as obesity, cancer, and asthma. [ ].

52. This is particularly true in Alabama's Black Belt counties, where "a shortage of infrastructure to support economic stability and growth compounds the inability of [residents] to move upward economically, contributing to generational poverty, especially among rural Black people who are less likely to be able to mobilize out of rural areas." [ ]. Health outcomes for Black Alabamians in rural counties are much worse than for White Alabamians in those counties. [ ]. Although impoverished people of all races face structural obstacles that adversely impact their health, a Black person living in poverty "typically [ ] would have a worse outcome compared to their counterparts." [ ].

53. These health disparities reflect, in part, callousness among elected officials in Alabama to the needs of Black residents. For example, Alabama's legislature has rejected requests to expand Medicaid under the Affordable Care Act notwithstanding the urging of Black leaders and a racial gap in insurance coverage. [ ]. Expanding Medicaid would have insured an additional 220,000 Alabamians, particularly benefiting Black residents. [ ]. This healthcare and insurance inequality helped to make Black Alabamians especially vulnerable when a novel coronavirus surfaced in early 2020. [ ].

E.   The Parties in this Lawsuit

(1)   Individual Plaintiffs

(a)   *Howard Porter, Jr.*

54. Mr. Porter is a Black man in his seventies, and a registered voter in Mobile County, Alabama who lives with his wife and adult son. [ ]. Mr. Porter has asthma and Parkinson's Disease, which causes him to have difficulty walking, and he uses a cane to walk. [ ]. Mr. Porter is at higher

risk for complications or death from COVID-19 because of his age and underlying medical conditions. [ ]. He takes the COVID-19 pandemic seriously and follows the CDC's guidance closely. [ ]. Sadly, his sister and uncle both died from COVID-19, and Mr. Porter is very fearful about becoming infected. [ ].

* * *

57. Mr. Porter has always voted in-person, but now he does not want to risk a COVID-19 infection. [ ]. Mr. Porter chose not to vote in the July 14 primary runoff election when he did not receive his absentee ballot. [ ]. He did not vote in-person in the election because he did not want to risk being infected with COVID-19. [ ]. When Mr. Porter votes in person at his polling place, he is required to walk 100 to 150 feet from his disabled parking space to the entrance. [ ]. Walking this distance is challenging for Mr. Porter due to his Parkinson's. [ ]. Mr. Porter would prefer to vote curbside as opposed to voting absentee or in-person. [ ]. He believes it would be "less strenuous" given his disability, provide less contact than going inside the polling place, and reduce the time he spends now to vote. [ ].

* * *

(c) *Annie Carolyn Thompson*

63. Ms. Thompson is a 68-year-old retiree who lives alone at her home in Mobile, Alabama. [ ]. She is Black, a U.S. citizen, has never lost her right to vote by reason of a felony conviction or court order, and is a lawfully registered voter in Alabama. [ ]. Ms. Thompson is at higher risk of contracting and having severe complications from COVID-19 because of her age and preexisting conditions, including diabetes and high blood pressure. [ ]. Ms. Thompson takes medication for both conditions. [ ].

* * *

66. Ms. Thompson testified that she would have difficulty meeting the photo ID requirement to vote absentee because she does not have the necessary technology or equipment to make a copy of her photo ID at home and would, therefore, have to venture out of her home to obtain the copy. [ ]. She also indicated that she would have difficulty meeting the witness requirement because she does not regularly interact with two people at the same time. [ ]. She further testified, however, that, having learned about the Mobile Public Library's curbside notary services in this litigation, she would use them to notarize her absentee ballot for the November election. [ ].

67. Ms. Thompson requested an absentee ballot for the July runoff election because of COVID-19, but her ballot did not arrive until the day of the election. [ ]. Accordingly, because Ms. Thompson could not vote absentee, she called a friend who works at her polling site to find out a time

when few people would be at the site. [ ]. She felt safe voting in person on that occasion because all of the poll workers wore masks and gloves, there were sanitizing stations all over, they had sneeze guards, and people practiced social distancing. [ ]. Ms. Thompson testified that she would not feel safe voting in person in November because her polling site, which is not a large facility, will be very crowded since it is a major election that will have a larger turnout. [ ]. Ms. Thompson also would not be comfortable voting in person in November because people are not required to wear masks when voting. [ ].

* * *

CONCLUSIONS OF LAW

[The court held that Alabama laws requiring that either a notary public or two adults witness an absentee ballot, requiring that a copy of the voter's photo ID accompany a mailed absentee ballot, and banning curbside voting violated the constitutionally protected liberty interest in voting when applied to the plaintiffs, who were vulnerable voters because they could not safely vote in person or satisfy the requirements for absentee voting during COVID-19 pandemic given their heightened risk of severe COVID-19 complications due to their ages, disabilities, pre-existing conditions, and race.]

NOTES AND QUESTIONS

1.   *Social Determinants of Health.* What specific social determinants of health did the court recognize as playing a role in the inequitable incidence of COVID-19 infections, hospitalizations, and deaths? How, according to the court's findings, did that inequitable incidence contribute to the burden imposed by the challenged state voting laws on the plaintiffs' right to vote?

2.   *Snowball Effect.* When two or more social factors combine to undermine the health of a sub-population, that combination can have a snowball effect by increasing the risk that members of that sub-population experience ever-worsening health outcomes. See Silvia Yee et al., Compounded Disparities: Health Equity at the Intersection of Disability, Race, and Ethnicity (2019). This phenomenon was evident during the COVID-19 pandemic:

> . . . The lower a person's socioeconomic status, the more limited their resources and ability to access essential goods and services, and the greater their chance of suffering from chronic disease, including conditions like heart disease, lung disease, and diabetes that may increase the mortality risk of COVID-19. Individuals and families in poverty have less control over their environment and few to no alternatives to substandard housing. These effects are exacerbated for people of color who are subjected to the consequences of discrimination and segregation in housing, on top of affordability challenges.

Many low-income individuals and families face significant challenges that prevent them from protecting themselves and others from COVID-19. Many lack the disposable income, flexible work schedules, and ability to do paid work from home. Nor do they have paid leave required to take care of children whose schools are closed and whose educational attainment and social development may be set back for months.

Emily A. Benfer and Lindsay F. Wiley, Health Justice Strategies to Combat COVID-19: Protecting Vulnerable Communities During A Pandemic, Health Aff. Blog, Mar. 19, 2020.

3.   *Perpetuating Inequity Through Law. People First of Alabama* does more than highlight certain social determinants of health. It also identifies how the law—in this case voting laws that unduly burden the rights of those already burdened inequitably by COVID-19—can perpetuate and exacerbate existing inequity by extending it into yet another activity, in this case, voting. Of course, laws that make voting during a pandemic more difficult or risky for those most heavily burdened by the pandemic undermine the ability of that sub-population to be heard at the polls and thus adequately represented in government in the future. In this way, *People First of Alabama* also provides an example of what Daniel E. Dawes calls the "political determinants of health." Daniel E. Dawes, The Political Determinants of Health (2020).

4.   *Additional Reading.* For additional reading on health equity, law and the social determinants of health during the pandemic, see Emily A. Benfer et al., Health Justice Strategies to Combat the Pandemic: Eliminating Discrimination, Poverty, and Health Disparities During and After COVID-19, 19 Yale J. Health Pol'y L. & Ethics 122 (2020); Ruqaiijah Yearby and Seema Mohapatra, Law, Structural Racism, and the COVID-19 Pandemic, 7 J.L. & Bioscien. 1 (2020).

III.   PUBLIC HEALTH LAW AND THE POLICE POWER

JACOBSON V. MASSACHUSETTS
Supreme Court of the United States, 1905.
197 U.S. 11.

[Eds. Note: The following two-paragraph description is reprinted from the syllabus of the Court.]

The Revised Laws of that Commonwealth [Massachusetts], c. 75, § 137, provide that "the board of health of a city or town if, in its opinion, it is necessary for the public health or safety shall require and enforce the vaccination and revaccination of all the inhabitants thereof and shall provide them with the means of free vaccination. Whoever, being over twenty-one years of age and not under guardianship, refuses or neglects to comply with such requirement shall forfeit five dollars."

* * *

Proceeding under the above statutes, the Board of Health of the city of Cambridge, Massachusetts, on the twenty-seventh day of February, 1902, adopted the following regulation: "Whereas, smallpox has been prevalent to some extent in the city of Cambridge and still continues to increase; and whereas, it is necessary for the speedy extermination of the disease, that all persons not protected by vaccination should be vaccinated; and whereas, in the opinion of the board, the public health and safety require the vaccination or revaccination of all the inhabitants of Cambridge; be it ordered, that all the inhabitants of the city who have not been successfully vaccinated since March, 1, 1897, be vaccinated or revaccinated."

MR. JUSTICE HARLAN, after making the foregoing statement, delivered the opinion of the court.

We pass without extended discussion the suggestion that the particular section of the statute of Massachusetts now in question [ ] is in derogation of rights secured by the Preamble of the Constitution of the United States. Although that Preamble indicates the general purposes for which the people ordained and established the Constitution, it has never been regarded as the source of any substantive power conferred on the Government of the United States or on any of its Departments. Such powers embrace only those expressly granted in the body of the Constitution and such as may be implied from those so granted. Although, therefore, one of the declared objects of the Constitution was to secure the blessings of liberty to all under the sovereign jurisdiction and authority of the United States, no power can be exerted to that end by the United States unless, apart from the Preamble, it be found in some express delegation of power or in some power to be properly implied therefrom. [ ]

We also pass without discussion the suggestion that the above section of the statute is opposed to the spirit of the Constitution. . . . We have no need in this case to go beyond the plain, obvious meaning of the words in those provisions of the Constitution which, it is contended, must control our decision.

What, according to the judgment of the state court, is the scope and effect of the statute? What results were intended to be accomplished by it? These questions must be answered.

* * *

The authority of the State to enact this statute is to be referred to what is commonly called the police power—a power which the State did not surrender when becoming a member of the Union under the Constitution. Although this court has refrained from any attempt to define the limits of that power, yet it has distinctly recognized the authority of a State to enact quarantine laws and "health laws of every description;" indeed, all laws that relate to matters completely within its territory and which do not by their necessary operation affect the people of other States. According to settled principles the police power of a State must be held to embrace, at least, such reasonable regulations established directly by legislative enactment as will protect the public health and the public safety. [ ]. It is equally true that the State may invest local bodies called into existence for purposes of local administration with authority in some appropriate way to safeguard the public health and the public safety. The mode or manner in which those results are to be accomplished is within the discretion of the State, subject, of course, so far as Federal power is concerned, only to the condition that no rule prescribed by a State, nor any regulation adopted by a local governmental agency acting under the sanction of state legislation, shall contravene the Constitution of the United States or infringe any right granted or secured by that instrument. . . .

We come, then, to inquire whether any right given, or secured by the Constitution, is invaded by the statute as interpreted by the state court. The defendant insists that his liberty is invaded when the State subjects him to fine or imprisonment for neglecting or refusing to submit to vaccination; that a compulsory vaccination law is unreasonable, arbitrary and oppressive, and, therefore, hostile to the inherent right of every freeman to care for his own body and health in such way as to him seems best; and that the execution of such a law against one who objects to vaccination, no matter for what reason, is nothing short of an assault upon his person. But the liberty secured by the Constitution of the United States to every person within its jurisdiction does not import an absolute right in each person to be, at all times and in all circumstances, wholly freed from restraint. There are manifold restraints to which every person is necessarily subject for the common good. On any other basis organized society could not exist with safety to its members. Society based on the rule that each one is a law unto himself would soon be confronted with disorder and anarchy. Real liberty for all could not exist under the operation of a principle which recognizes the right of each individual person to use his own, whether in respect of his person or his property, regardless of the injury that may be done to others. . . . The good and welfare of the Commonwealth, of which the legislature is primarily the judge, is the basis on which the police power rests in Massachusetts. [ ]

Applying these principles to the present case, it is to be observed that the legislature of Massachusetts required the inhabitants of a city or town to be vaccinated only when, in the opinion of the Board of Health, that was necessary for the public health or the public safety. The authority to determine for all what ought to be done in such an emergency must have been lodged somewhere or in some body; and surely it was appropriate for the legislature to refer that question, in the first instance, to a Board of Health, composed of persons residing in the locality affected and appointed, presumably, because of their fitness to determine such questions. To invest such a body with authority over such matters was not an unusual nor an unreasonable or arbitrary requirement. Upon the principle of self-defense, of paramount necessity, a community has the right to protect itself against an epidemic of disease which threatens the safety of its members. . . . Smallpox being prevalent and increasing at Cambridge, the court would usurp the functions of another branch of government if it adjudged, as matter of law, that the mode adopted under the sanction of the State, to protect the people at large, was arbitrary and not justified by the necessities of the case. We say necessities of the case, because it might be that an acknowledged power of a local community to protect itself against an epidemic threatening the safety of all, might be exercised in particular circumstances and in reference to particular persons in such an arbitrary, unreasonable manner, or might go so far beyond what was reasonably required for the safety of the public, as to authorize or compel the courts to interfere for the protection of such persons. . . . There is, of course, a sphere within which the individual may assert the supremacy of his own will and rightfully dispute the authority of any human government, especially of any free government existing under a written constitution, to interfere with the exercise of that will. But it is equally true that in every well-ordered society charged with the duty of conserving the safety of its members the rights of the individual in respect of his liberty may at times, under the pressure of great dangers, be subjected to such restraint, to be enforced by reasonable regulations, as the safety of the general public may demand.

* * *

Looking at the propositions embodied in the defendant's rejected offers of proof it is clear that they are more formidable by their number than by their inherent value. Those offers in the main seem to have had no purpose except to state the general theory of those of the medical profession who attach little or no value to vaccination as a means of preventing the spread of smallpox or who think that vaccination causes other diseases of the body. What everybody knows the court must know, and therefore the state court judicially knew, as this court knows, that an opposite theory accords with the common belief and is maintained by high medical authority. We must assume that when the statute in question was passed, the legislature of Massachusetts was not unaware of these opposing theories, and was compelled, of necessity, to choose between them. It was not compelled to commit a matter involving the public health and safety to the final decision of a court or jury. It is no part of the function of a court or a jury to determine which one of two modes was likely to be the most effective for the protection of the public against disease. That was for the legislative department to determine in the light of all the information it had or could obtain. . . . Upon what sound principles as to the relations existing between the different departments of government can the court review this action of the legislature? If there is any such power in the judiciary to review legislative action in respect of a matter affecting the general welfare, it can only be when that which the legislature has done comes within the rule that if a statute purporting to have been enacted to protect the public health, the public morals or the public safety, has no real or substantial relation to those objects, or is, beyond all question, a plain, palpable invasion of rights secured by the fundamental law, it is the duty of the courts to so adjudge, and thereby give effect to the Constitution." [ ]

Whatever may be thought of the expediency of this statute, it cannot be affirmed to be, beyond question, in palpable conflict with the Constitution. Nor, in view of the methods employed to stamp out the disease of smallpox, can anyone confidently assert that the means prescribed by the State to that end has no real or substantial relation to the protection of the public health and the public safety. Such an assertion would not be consistent with the experience of this and other countries whose authorities have dealt with the disease of smallpox. [The Court then summarizes the history of vaccination in Europe and America.]

* * *

Since then vaccination, as a means of protecting a community against smallpox, finds strong support in the experience of this and other countries, no court, much less a jury, is justified in disregarding the action of the legislature simply because in its or their opinion that particular method was—perhaps or possibly—not the best either for children or adults.

* * *

We are not prepared to hold that a minority, residing or remaining in any city or town where smallpox is prevalent, and enjoying the general protection afforded by an organized local government, may thus defy the will of its constituted authorities, acting in good faith for all, under the legislative sanction of the State [by refusing to be vaccinated]. If such be the privilege of a minority then a like privilege would belong to each individual of the community, and the spectacle would be presented of the welfare and safety of an entire population being subordinated to the notions of a single individual who chooses to remain a part of that population. . . . The safety and the health of the people of Massachusetts are, in the first instance, for that Commonwealth to guard and protect. They are matters that do not ordinarily concern the National Government. So far as they can be reached by any government, they depend, primarily, upon such action as the State in its wisdom may take; and we do not perceive that this legislation has invaded by right secured by the Federal Constitution.

Before closing this opinion we deem it appropriate, in order to prevent misapprehension as to our views, to observe . . . that the police power of a

State . . . may be exerted in such circumstances or by regulations so arbitrary and oppressive in particular cases as to justify the interference of the courts to prevent wrong and oppression. Extreme cases can be readily suggested. Ordinarily such cases are not safe guides in the administration of the law. It is easy, for instance, to suppose the case of an adult who is embraced by the mere words of the act, but yet to subject whom to vaccination in a particular condition of his health or body, would be cruel and inhuman in the last degree. We are not to be understood as holding that the statute was intended to be applied to such a case, or, if it was so intended, that the judiciary would not be competent to interfere and protect the health and life of the individual concerned.

MR. JUSTICE BREWER and MR. JUSTICE PECKHAM dissent [without opinion].

NOTES AND QUESTIONS

1.   *State Police Powers.* This oft-cited case established the foundation for the public health regulation that came during the ensuing century. Its holding plainly recognizes the authority of the state to exercise its police powers by imposing public health restrictions on willing and unwilling citizens (and others). Moreover, it clarifies that states may delegate their public health powers, whether to state agencies or to local governments. *Jacobson* also recognizes that a state's power to act in the name of public health is limited by the Constitution's protection of individuals against governmental interference. The following diagram depicts the police power, its delegation, and its constitutional limitations:

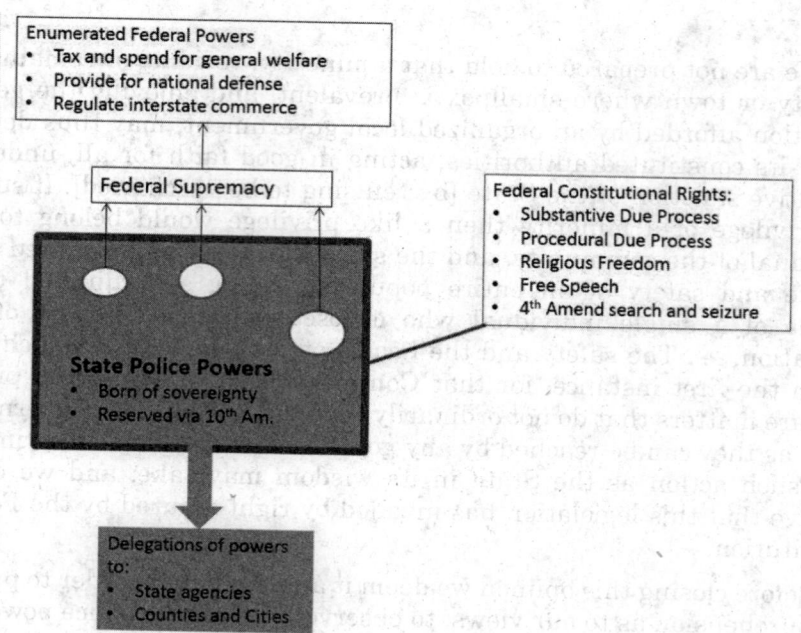

2. *Federal vs. State Public Health Powers.* The federal government does not have the police power because it is a government of only limited powers, and the police power enjoyed by each of the states is not among the powers delegated to the federal government by the states under the federal Constitution. Moreover, the 10th Amendment clarifies that "powers not delegated to the United States by the Constitution, nor prohibited by it to the States, are reserved to the States respectively, or to the people." Thus, federal legislation designed to promote population health must find its constitutional authority under an enumerated power (e.g., power to regulate interstate commerce), while similar state legislation can be based on the state's police power.

3. *"Arbitrary and Oppressive"?* Jacobson acknowledges that the Due Process Clause in the 14th Amendment to the federal Constitution restricts the state's power to act in the name of public health. Specifically, it held that the state may not act "by regulations so arbitrary and oppressive in particular cases as to justify the interference of the courts to prevent wrong and oppression." When might a state cross this line? The Court says that "[e]xtreme cases can readily be suggested," but it does not actually suggest them. Can you identify these cases?

4. *Evolution of Substantive Due Process.* Substantive due process jurisprudence has developed considerably since *Jacobson*, and, as a result, several courts have imposed standards that are more rigorous than the "non-arbitrary" test articulated in *Jacobson*. For example, three courts reviewing state orders confining individuals with tuberculosis held that state officials must prove "substantial risk" or meet a strict scrutiny standard. See City of Newark v. J.S., 279 N.J. Super. 178, 652 A.2d 265 (1993) (state must prove by clear and convincing evidence that the individual poses a substantial risk of dangerous conduct); Greene v. Edwards, 164 W. Va. 326, 263 S.E.2d 661 (1980) (same); Best v. St. Vincents Hosp., 2003 WL 21518829 (S.D.N.Y.) (confinement must be necessary to serve a substantial governmental interest). During the 2014 Ebola scare, however, two federal courts reviewing quarantine orders employed a "reasonableness" test, citing to *Jacobson*. See Hickox v. Christie, 205 F. Supp. 3d 579 (D.N.J. 2016); Liberian Community Assoc. v. Malloy, 2017 WL 4897048 (D. Conn.), aff'd, Liberian Community Assoc. v. Lamont, 970 F.3d 174 (2d Cir. 2020). What, if any, substantive due process standard is required by *Jacobson* remains unsettled, and this uncertainty has resulted in inconsistent use of *Jacobson* in the many lawsuits brought to challenge the constitutionality of COVID-19 restrictions. See Part IV in this Chapter.

5. *Wong Wai v. Williamson.* Jacobson was not the first vaccination case to be litigated in the federal courts. In Wong Wai v. Williamson, 103 F. 1 (N.D. Cal. 1900), the Circuit Court faced an action by Wong Wai, "a subject of the emperor of China, residing in the city and county of San Francisco," seeking to enjoin the city from enforcing a resolution of the board of health that prohibited Chinese residents from traveling outside of the city without proof that they had been inoculated with the "Haffkine Prophylactic," which was thought to provide immunization against bubonic plague. The resolution applied only to

those of Chinese extraction, although there was no evidence that they were any more likely than others to be subject to the plague. The Circuit Court recognized the public health authority of the city, but also recognized that there were limits to the exercise of this police power.

> The conditions of a great city frequently present unexpected emergencies affecting the public health, comfort, and convenience. Under such circumstances, officers charged with the duties pertaining to this department of the municipal government should be clothed with sufficient authority to deal with the conditions in a prompt and effective manner. Measures of this character, having a uniform operation, and reasonably adapted to the purpose of protecting the health and preserving the welfare of the inhabitants of a city, are constantly upheld by the courts as valid acts of legislation, however inconvenient they may prove to be, and a wide discretion has also been sanctioned in their execution. But when the municipal authority has neglected to provide suitable rules and regulations upon the subject, and the officers are left to adopt such methods as they may deem proper for the occasion, their acts are open to judicial review, and may be examined in every detail to determine whether individual rights have been respected in accordance with constitutional requirements.

* * *

> In the light of these well-established principles [that public health measures must have an appropriate relationship with the ends they seek to serve], the action of the defendants as described in the bill of complaint cannot be justified. They are not based upon any established distinction in the conditions that are supposed to attend this plague, or the persons exposed to its contagion, but they are boldly directed against the Asiatic or Mongolian race as a class, without regard to the previous condition, habits, exposure to disease, or residence of the individual; and the only justification offered for this discrimination was a suggestion made by counsel for the defendants in the course of the argument, that this particular race is more liable to the plague than any other. No evidence has, however, been offered to support this claim, and it is not known to be a fact. This explanation must therefore be dismissed as unsatisfactory.

103 F. at 12–15. The Court went on to find that the actions of the board of health violated not only "the express provisions of the constitution of the United States, in several particulars, but also of the express provisions of our several treaties with China and of the statutes of the United States." Id. at 23.

6.   *Vaccine Mandate Medical Exception.* The Court in *Jacobson* suggests that it may be improper to apply the Massachusetts statute and the Cambridge order to an adult whose health would be placed at risk by vaccination, even though the only exception in the statute is for children whose health would be at risk. Could an adult with some legitimate health concerns about vaccination forgo it? Would this be a matter to be determined by the Board of Health, by the courts, or by an employer or school?

7.   *School Vaccination Mandates and Religious and Moral Exemptions.* In a long historical footnote, the *Jacobson* Court traces the history of vaccination from the "first compulsory act" in England in 1853. In fact, as early as 1827 the city of Boston required vaccination for school attendance, and in 1855 Massachusetts became the first state with required childhood vaccination laws associated with school attendance. Such laws were common by the end of the nineteenth century, but, for political and other reasons, they were not regularly enforced. Some were triggered only when there was a public health threat in the community, and some courts recognized religious defenses to the obligation to be vaccinated. See Rhea v. Board of Education, 171 N.W. 103 (N.D. 1919).

Today all states provide for exemptions when the vaccination would threaten the health of the child; almost all allow for religious exemption (although the nature of those exemptions varies from state to state); and many states allow for an exemption on "moral" or other grounds. Are states required to have religious exemptions under the First Amendment or other federal law designed to protect religious freedom? If a state has a religious exemption, should that legislation also permit a "moral" exemption? Is it constitutionally required to do so under the Establishment Clause of the First Amendment or the Equal Protection Clause of the Fourteenth Amendment?

8.   *Advisory Committee on Immunization Practices.* Requiring immunizations for children to be enrolled in school is a matter of state law, but, as a general matter, states adopt the CDC list of recommended immunization developed by the Advisory Committee on Immunization Practices. In order to keep some kinds of federal funding, the states now must make an effort to enforce their own immunization laws. This issue is not entirely a scientific one, though, and vaccine manufacturers do lobby state legislatures to have their own products included on the mandatory list.

9.   *Anti-Vax Fears and Misinformation.* While the health value of continued required immunization is now well established, those who fear government overreach have often had special concerns about vaccinations. It is unclear just why this issue has become a political one as well as a public health one, but it is not hard to find those who oppose vaccination with great zeal. The CDC, the World Health Organization (WHO), and other organizations have joined together to refute several myths about vaccination that sometimes scare parents into seeking exemptions.

For a full list of the most common arguments against vaccination and the refutation of each, see the WHO publication, 6 Common Misconceptions about Vaccinations and How to Respond to Them (2010). For an excellent account of this issue, and the basis for much of the material in these notes, see James Hodge, Jr., School Vaccination Requirements: Legal and Social Perspectives, 27 NCSL State Legislative Report, No. 14 (August 2002). See also S. Omer et al., Nonmedical Exemptions to School Immunization Requirements, 296 JAMA 1757 (2006); S. Omer, Correspondence: Vaccination Polices and Rates of Exemption from Immunization, 2005–2011, 367 NEJM 1170 (2012). For an excellent overview of the issue and a clever proposal to finesse the opposition to immunization while respecting individuals' liberties, see Ross Silverman, No More Kidding Around: Restructuring Childhood Immunization Exceptions, in Insure Public Health Protection, 12 Ann. Health L. 277 (2003).

The pattern of spreading false vaccine information and conspiracy theories has continued with respect to the COVID-19 vaccines. See I. Ullah et al., Myths and Conspiracy Theories on Vaccines and COVID-19: Potential Effect on Global Vaccine Refusals, 22(2) Vacunas 93 (2021); Ana Santos Rutschman, Social Media Self-Regulation and the Rise of Vaccine Misinformation, 4 U. Pa. J. Law & Innovation 25 (2021).

10. *Side Effects.* Of course, there are side effects to vaccination, and some are very serious, although a recent comprehensive study review found "no evidence of major safety concerns" associated with childhood vaccination, including current scheduling that requires delivery of multiple vaccines at one time. Institute of Medicine, Childhood Immunization Schedule and Safety: Stakeholder Concerns, Scientific Evidence, and Future Studies (2013).

11. *Vaccine Injury Compensation Program.* Compensation for injuries that arise out of immunization is specifically addressed in the National Vaccine Injury Compensation Program, 42 U.S.C. § 300aa–10 et seq. This statute provides scheduled (and thus limited) compensation for those who can prove that their injury has been caused by a covered vaccine. It does not require proof of negligence or products liability for compensation. The payment is made by a government agency and the compensation payments and administration of the program are financed by an excise tax on the vaccines. Thus, the manufacturers pay the cost of the program, but they can pass that cost on and spread it out among those who are vaccinated—virtually everyone. This statute may be unique in providing that attorneys must inform potential plaintiffs in vaccine injury cases of the existence of the law and the remedy it provides:

> It shall be the ethical obligation of any attorney who is consulted by an individual with respect to a vaccine-related injury or death to advise such individual that compensation may be available under the program for such injury or death.

42 U.S.C. § 300aa–10(b).

For an excellent history of vaccine shortages induced by manufacturers' fears of liability that gave rise to this no-fault compensation scheme and its predecessors, see Elizabeth Scott, The National Childhood Vaccine Injury Act Turns Fifteen, 56 Food & Drug L.J. 351 (2001). See also L. Rutkow et al., Balancing Consumer and Industry Interests in Public Health: The National Vaccine Injury Compensation Program and Its Influence During the Last Two Decades, 111 Penn. St. L. Rev. 681 (2007).

IV. INDIVIDUAL RIGHTS AND CONSTITUTIONAL STANDARDS OF REVIEW FOR PUBLIC HEALTH MEASURES

As noted in *Jacobson*, the police power is not absolute. Among other things, it is limited by individual rights recognized under the federal Constitution, including the rights to substantive and procedural due process and to the free exercise of religion. The COVID-19 pandemic has forced many courts to identify the relevant standard for reviewing the constitutionality of public health actions taken by state and local officials. As excerpted above, *Jacobson* asked only whether the City's smallpox vaccination requirement had some "real or substantial relation" to protecting population health and whether it was "beyond all question, a plain, palpable invasion of rights secured by the fundamental law." Of course, *Jacobson* was decided well before the development of today's standards for constitutional review. So, courts must now confront whether the standard applied in *Jacobson* remains good law, and if so, how to reconcile it with modern substantive due process jurisprudence. The following opinion addresses that very issue.

KLAASSEN V. TRUSTEES OF INDIANA UNIVERSITY

United States District Court, N.D. Indiana, 2021.
___ F. Supp.3d ___, 2021 WL 3073926.

DAMON R. LEICHTY, UNITED STATES DISTRICT JUDGE.

* * *

This case presents . . . [the following] question: whether Indiana University has acted constitutionally in mandating the COVID-19 vaccine for its students . . . . [T]his case does so only in the context of a preliminary injunction motion, not for a final decision on the merits.

* * *

Eight students sued Indiana University because of its vaccination mandate and because of the extra requirements of masking, testing, and social distancing that apply to those who receive an exemption. They ask the court to enter a preliminary injunction . . . .

* * *

FACTS

A. Parties.

Indiana University is a world-renowned public research university, . . . providing education to over 90,000 undergraduate and graduate students and employment for over 40,000 employees [ ]. . . .

The eight students here have varied backgrounds. [They include undergraduate, graduate and professional students, ranging in age from 18 to 39. They each object to the University's policy. Seven of the eight have received or are eligible to receive a religious exemption from the mandate, but each remains subject to the University's masking and testing requirements for unvaccinated, exempt individuals. One of the eight cannot qualify for an exemption. Most of the eight are unsure if they will remain students at the University if the policy remains in effect, but one will return regardless of the outcome of the case and one will not.]

* * *

B.   COVID-19.

COVID-19 is an infectious disease caused by the novel coronavirus. It primarily spreads through respiratory droplets, viral particles suspended in the air, and touching mucosal membranes with contaminated hands [ ]. The initial presentation of an infection ranges from no symptoms at all (asymptomatic) to severe illness and death; and even after recovery, various long-term health problems may linger [ ].

Individuals with longstanding systemic health inequities or preexisting or immunocompromising conditions, and elderly individuals prove at greater risk of severe illness or hospitalization following an infection [ ]. Children and young adults are less likely to experience serious illness or death from infection [ ]. Though data from the Centers for Disease Control and Prevention (CDC) suggest that more young adults are becoming infected with the virus than other age groups [ ], these individuals are less likely to require hospitalization or die [ ].

Worldwide COVID-19 has infected almost 189 million people and caused 4 million deaths, with these numbers still changing daily. In the United States, the novel coronavirus has infected over 33.5 million citizens, losing to death over 600,000 [ ]. Since March 6, 2020, Indiana has had over 750,000 confirmed COVID-19 cases and over 13,000 deaths [ ]. The COVID winter of 2020–2021 was particularly rough, until vaccines became options first in December 2020 and then in the early months of 2021.

As vaccination now increases, data gathered by the CDC point toward the waning of new COVID infections across the country—down from a peak of 312,325 new cases reported on January 8, 2021, with a seven-day average positive test rate of 13.85 percent, to 39,719 new cases reported on July 16, 2021, with a seven-day average positive test rate of 5.01 percent. The rate of new cases today is akin, if not greater, to the rate of new cases reported during the peak of the pandemic's first wave in the spring 2020, through the relative rate of positive tests thankfully remains much lower.

* * *

In Indiana, 561 new cases were reported on July 15, 2021; and the most recent data suggest a seven-day average positive test rate of 4.3 percent for unique individuals from July 3, 2021 to July 9, 2021, lower than the national average. Of all positive cases, 18.4 percent, the highest proportion of all age populations, comes from young adults aged 20–29. In Indiana, approximately 67.3 percent of all cases came from the Delta variant. Our country and our state have vastly improved, but challenges remain.

* * *

F.   Indiana University's Vaccine Mandate.

[The University created a "Restart Committee" to study and recommend to the University policies that would permit the resumption of face-to-face education. The committee consisted of experts from a variety of relevant fields, and it made a thorough study of relevant materials before making its recommendations.]

* * *

. . . The Board of Trustees adopted the restart committee's recommendations for the 2021 fall semester [ ].

The aim was short and strategic—vaccinate everyone, subject to certain exemptions [ ]. . . . The policy today requires all students, faculty, and staff to be fully vaccinated . . . before returning to campus between August 1 to August 15 for the fall 2021 semester [ ].

The choice of foregoing vaccination is not inconsequential. If not vaccinated, students are not permitted on campus, their emails and university accounts are suspended, and their access cards are deactivated [ ]. Although it seems from argument that the university will not create an informant culture, it reserves the right to pursue disciplinary action should a student deceive the process. Faculty and staff who refuse vaccination face termination. . . .

The university's COVID-19 vaccine policy has exemptions. A student may request an exemption for religious reasons [or for medical reasons]. Students who are enrolled in an online program, with no on-campus component, don't need to receive the vaccine [ ].

For those who receive exemption from vaccination, the policy imposes additional safety requirements. These requirements apply to six of the eight students here who have received exemptions and potentially a seventh who qualifies for an exemption. Such students must participate in more frequent mitigation testing, quarantine if exposed to someone who has tested positive for COVID-19, wear a mask in public spaces, and return to their permanent address or quarantine if there is a serious outbreak of COVID-19 [ ].

H.   Emergency Use Authorization of Vaccines.

* * *

Despite creating an expedited pathway to distribute new medical products during emergencies, products that receive [emergency use authorization (EUA)] . . . still must adhere to specified safety, efficacy, and manufacturing criteria, and HHS must ensure medical providers and individuals are informed of the product's EUA status, the "significant known and potential benefits and risks of such use, and of the extent to which such benefits and risks are unknown;" and for individuals, of the option to refuse and the consequences of such a decision. [ ]. An EUA generally allows a manufacturer to apply for EUA approval using interim clinical trial data, and the data need only demonstrate the product "may be effective" and that the known and potential benefits outweigh the known and potential risks. . . .

* * *

Not all EUAs are created equally. Because of the widespread use of a COVID-19 vaccine, the FDA informed manufacturers that it expected the same level of endpoint efficacy data as required for full approval, enough safety data to justify by clear and compelling evidence the vaccine's safety, and confirmation of the technical procedures and verification steps necessary to support full approval. In short, and as described in more detail below in this opinion's analysis, the FDA promulgated guidance that enhanced the basis on which any COVID-19 vaccine would meet EUA approval. In setting these more stringent standards, the FDA invited EUA applications only for vaccines positioned well to receive full approval.

I.   COVID-19 Vaccines.

[The court summarizes the development and testing of each of the three leading COVID vaccines, and the EUA each received from the FDA.]

With these vaccines, an emerging light appeared at the end of the tunnel. As of July 17, 2021, 337,239,448 doses of vaccine have been administered, and 161 million Americans, or 48.5 percent of the total population, is fully vaccinated. Of adults over the age of eighteen, 59.4 percent are fully vaccinated. In Indiana, 5,749,173 doses have been administered, and 2,888,239 Hoosiers, or 49.6 percent of those over the age of twelve, are fully vaccinated. Of ages 18–24, who account for 9.2 percent of the U.S. population, 11,720,847, or 42.2 percent, are fully vaccinated. In Indiana, 164,098 individuals aged 20–24, or 34.7 percent, are fully vaccinated.

J.   Risks of Vaccines.

Though the vaccines show remarkable effectiveness against infection and severe cases of COVID-19, and "have undergone and will continue to undergo the most intensive safety monitoring in U.S. history," they are not without risks, heretofore rare for serious risks [ ]. Many recipients experience mild local and systemic reactions, including fever, headache, muscle pain, chills, and tiredness. In very rare cases, more serious side effects seem to emerge such as allergic reactions or blood clots with low platelets [ ]. For young men specifically, experts are studying a temporal correlation between vaccines and myocarditis, an inflammation of the heart muscle, or pericarditis, inflammation of tissue around the heart [ ]. However, the risk of myocarditis appears to be exceptionally small [ ].

The medical community closely tracks adverse events from the vaccine in a national database called VAERS, or the Vaccine Adverse Event Reporting System. . . . Based on this surveillance, reports of anaphylaxis [appear] to be rare, blood clotting concerns are rare but higher in women under the age of 50, myocarditis is rare but more common in young people, and reports of death are rare.

The FDA has issued revisions to the patient and provider fact sheets about the risk of myocarditis and pericarditis acknowledging data about this risk. Furthermore, the FDA and CDC recommended a pause on the use of Johnson & Johnson's vaccine in light of reports of clotting in young women (a pause subsequently lifted). Recent changes last week occurred because of reported neurological impacts of the Johnson & Johnson vaccine, based on VAERS data. These refinements indicate that the ongoing safety of these vaccines are rigorously monitored by agency professionals.

* * *

PRELIMINARY INJUNCTION STANDARD

. . . To obtain an injunction, the students "must make a threshold showing that: (1) absent preliminary injunctive relief, [they] will suffer irreparable harm in the interim prior to a final resolution; (2) there is no adequate remedy at law; and (3) [they have] a reasonable likelihood of success on the merits." [ ] If they make these threshold showings, the court "consider[s] the balance of harms between the parties and the effect of granting or denying a preliminary injunction on the public interest." [ ]

ANALYSIS

A. *These Students Aren't Likely to Succeed on the Merits.*

* * *

1. *The Fourteenth Amendment.*

* * *

. . . [T]he Fourteenth Amendment says no "State [may] deprive any person of life, liberty, or property, without due process of law." [ ]. . . .

Indiana University is a state actor, [ ], so the Fourteenth Amendment also applies to it.

. . . The Fourteenth Amendment protects a person's substantive rights in life, liberty, and property. [ ] Certain rights or liberties have been deemed "fundamental," so they receive greater protection. [ ]

Bearing that in mind, the court initially approaches this case in a two-fold manner. First, the law requires a "careful description" of the asserted right or liberty. [ ] Second, the court must determine whether the so-defined right or liberty is fundamental under the Constitution. [ ] The Fourteenth Amendment's due process clause specially protects fundamental rights and liberties—those that objectively are "deeply rooted in this Nation's history and tradition" and so "implicit in the concept of ordered liberty" that "neither liberty nor justice would exist if they were sacrificed." . . .

* * *

The students and university disagree on the constitutional analysis. Declaring a right or liberty fundamental has important implications. Modern constitutional jurisprudence employs a different analysis when a person's fundamental right is at stake. If the government infringes on a fundamental right, the court often applies strict scrutiny. [ ] In such circumstances, the Fourteenth Amendment "forbids the government to infringe . . . fundamental liberty interests *at all*, no matter what process is provided, unless the infringement is narrowly tailored to serve a compelling state interest." [ ] This is the most rigorous form of constitutional scrutiny of government action.

Whereas infringements on other rights or liberties, though still constitutionally scrutinized, must meet what courts call rational basis review. [ ] . . . It is less stringent than strict scrutiny. Under rational basis review, "legislation is presumed to be valid and will be sustained if the classification drawn by the statute is rationally related to a legitimate state interest." [ ] The students argue for strict scrutiny, and the university argues for rational basis review.

2.   *The Constitution in a Public Health Crisis.*

We live in the era of the COVID-19 virus—worldwide seeing to nearly 189 million cases and 4 million deaths, with these numbers changing daily. The United States hasn't been immune. Our citizens have recovered or struggled to recover from over 33 million cases of this novel coronavirus when over 606,000 tragically have passed. A public health crisis of this magnitude begs the question: how should the law respond to state action that infringes on the People's liberties during such times?

To be sure, the Constitution isn't put on the shelf. Indeed, in times of crisis, perhaps constitutional adherence proves the very anchor we all need against irrational and overweening government intrusion that would otherwise scuttle the ship. As the arbiters of the Constitution's checks and balances, [ ], the courts play an important role in ensuring that the government doesn't simply declare a never-ending public emergency and expand its powers *ad libitum* to the People's detriment.

Under our country's federalist system, state and federal governments share regulatory authority over public health matters. States traditionally exercise most authority under their inherent police power—and reasonably so when public health may flux and evolve by locale. States thus have the power, within constitutional limits, to pass laws that "provide for the public health, safety, and morals[.]" [ ]

To answer the question today, the court travels back in time to 1905: a time before the modern tiers of constitutional analysis (strict scrutiny and rational basis) and one rampaged by the smallpox epidemic. In that year, the United States Supreme Court issued a leading decision in answer to this question.

[Eds. Note: The court summarizes *Jacobson* and its relevant holdings. An excerpted version of *Jacobson* is presented in section III of this Chapter, above.]

* * *

The students want *Jacobson* confined to its time, whereas the university believes it applies with full force. In the years since, the high court has leaned on *Jacobson* to uphold government measures intended for the public welfare under effectively rational basis review, finding the measures reasonably advancing a legitimate state interest. For example, *Zucht [v. King]*, 260 U.S. [174 (1922)] . . . , relied on *Jacobson* to uphold a city ordinance excluding from its public schools children not having a certificate of vaccination, holding that it was within the state's police powers reasonably to so act. . . . This was not authorization of "arbitrary power," but only that broad discretion required for the protection of the public health." [ ] In doing so, "state and federal legislatures [enjoy] wide discretion to pass legislation in areas where there is medical and scientific uncertainty." [ ]

Based on this power, states and their authorized arms have historically adopted vaccination mandates. For instance, all fifty states and the District of Columbia have laws requiring students to receive certain vaccines before they may attend school. Many align their vaccine requirements with CDC's immunization recommendations, and all laws provide exemptions for medical reasons and nearly all religious exemptions. Adult vaccination mandates often have been limited to the private employment sector, though not always. For instance, the State of Indiana requires all public university students to receive vaccinations for diphtheria, tetanus, measles, mumps, rubella, and meningococcal disease, save for religious and medical exemptions. [ ]

* * *

. . . In this century . . . courts have returned again to [*Jacobson*'s] guidance during the COVID-19 pandemic. . . .

* * *

One such decision—and one heavily briefed by the parties—is *Roman Catholic Diocese of Brooklyn v. Cuomo*, ___ U.S. ___, 141 S. Ct. 63 [ ] (2020). In *Cuomo*, the State of New York adopted capacity restrictions on religious institutions that treated them less favorably than so-called "essential" businesses, [ ], including liquor and hardware stores, [ ]. *Cuomo* applied strict scrutiny because the law targeted religious practice contrary to the First Amendment, as incorporated against the states by the Fourteenth Amendment, and enjoined the limitations, saying they were not narrowly tailored to fulfill the state's compelling interest in controlling the spread of COVID-19. [ ]

Cuomo enhanced the law's focus under the First Amendment. [ ] So this begs another question: to what extent has *Cuomo*—if any—impacted the broad deference the court would seemingly afford a state during a pandemic under *Jacobson* to act in the interest of public health? *Cuomo*'s majority opinion never referenced *Jacobson*.

The students read *Cuomo* as implicitly overruling *Jacobson*, or at least as abrogating it. Though the Supreme Court may overrule a case without explicitly saying so, [ ], this is a tall task. Before a federal court concludes that the Supreme Court has implicitly overruled a prior decision, it must be "certain or almost certain that the decision or doctrine would be rejected by the higher court if a case presenting the issue came before it." [ ] This high bar is rarely met. [ ] It isn't met here. *Cuomo* and *Jacobson* involved entirely different modes of analysis, entirely different rights, and entirely different kinds of restriction. [ ] "*Jacobson* applied what would become the traditional legal test associated with the right at issue"—exactly what *Cuomo* did. [ ] The cases walk hand-in-hand.

* * *

Considering the modern tiers of constitutional scrutiny, the court reads *Jacobson* and *Cuomo* harmoniously, appreciating their respective spheres. Though *Jacobson* was decided before tiers of scrutiny, it effectively endorsed—as a considered precursor—rational basis review of a government's mandate during a health crisis. [ ] In its words, if a law purporting to be enacted to protect public health "has no real or substantial relation to [that legitimate aim]" or if the law proves "a plain, palpable invasion of rights secured by the fundamental law," the court's job is to give effect to the Constitution. [ ] Should the court have this melding of history and modernity wrong in faithfully adhering to the Fourteenth Amendment's plain original meaning of "life" and "liberty," comfort should come in knowing that *Jacobson*, whether rational basis review by any other name, leads to the same result today.

This view remains consistent with the right at stake in *Jacobson*: though a true "liberty" proved at stake—the right to refuse a vaccine during a smallpox epidemic—this interest in bodily autonomy, though protected by the Constitution, wasn't fundamental under the Constitution to require greater scrutiny than rational basis review. [ ] At the same time, *Jacobson* didn't hold that the government's authority in a pandemic balloons for it do whatever it wants in the name of public safety.

Jacobson instead counseled that federal courts should require a rational relation to a legitimate interest in public health. [ ] That *Cuomo* imposed heightened scrutiny of the government's interference with the free exercise of religion—a fundamental right under the First Amendment— was presciently contemplated a century beforehand by *Jacobson*: a court should intervene if a state imposes a regulation that is "beyond all question, a plain, palpable invasion of rights secured by the *fundamental law*." [ ] Because *Cuomo* involved a fundamental right, a "right[ ] secured by the fundamental law" under today's jurisprudence, the court intervened. [ ] The Constitution's original meaning should be so enduring.

The university seems to argue that *Jacobson* gave even more deference than rational basis review during a public health crisis, but not fairly so; and, even then, *Jacobson* cannot be taken once more too far. [ ]

Jacobson doesn't justify blind deference to the government when it acts in the name of public health or in a pandemic. For instance, the decision left the door open for people with legitimate medical concerns to challenge the vaccine mandate. [ ] And the deference owed to the States during a pandemic or public health crisis under *Jacobson* doesn't extend indefinitely. [ ]

> [A]t the outset of an emergency, it may be appropriate for courts to tolerate very blunt rules. . . . [B]ut a public health emergency does not give . . . public officials *carte blanche* to disregard the Constitution for as long as the medical problem persists. As more medical and scientific evidence becomes available, and as States have time to craft policies in light of that evidence, courts should expect policies that more carefully account for constitutional rights.

[ ]

In short, the Constitution doesn't permit the government to declare a never-ending public emergency and expand its powers arbitrarily. [ ] Instead, as our country and communities progress through a pandemic, the government must continually update its practices in light of the most recent medical and scientific developments. And a law or policy should be written with a mindset that medicine and science, and the circumstances that they create, will evolve, and so must the law or policy evolve or be revisited in amendment.

In sum, the law today recognizes *Jacobson* as a precursor to rational basis review. This is consistent with statements of many justices who continue to acknowledge *Jacobson* as good law, albeit with constitutional restraint. Government action that infringes on the liberty interest here, as in *Jacobson*, is subject to rational basis review. [ ]

3.   *Defining the Right & Constitutional Analysis.*

The students assert a right to refuse the vaccine, saying the mandate infringes on their bodily autonomy and medical privacy. Indiana University throws a challenge flag here. To it, these students are merely saying they have a right to refuse a vaccine *so that* they may attend college. The university says the right being infringed then isn't the right to refuse a vaccine, but the right to attend college. Indeed, if they choose to forego college at Indiana University, there is no vaccine requirement. To the university, the students aren't being forced to take the vaccination against their will; they can go to college elsewhere or forego college altogether. If this case were merely that, merely the right to attend university, this state action wouldn't trample on their rights. There is no fundamental or constitutional right to a college education, [ ], much less one at a particular institution.

But that's not what this case concerns, and that's not the liberty at stake. The "unconstitutional conditions doctrine" forbids the university from pulling the rug out from under the students in a roundabout way. Under this doctrine, argued by the students as "coercion," "the government may not deny a benefit to a person because he exercises a constitutional right." [ ] This doctrine protects constitutional rights "by preventing the government from coercing people into giving them up." [ ] It "aims to prevent the government from achieving indirectly what the Constitution prevents it from achieving directly." [ ] The students say this state actor is denying a benefit—a public university education—because they are exercising a constitutional right to refuse a vaccine.

The first step in an unconstitutional condition claim "is to identify the nature and scope of the constitutional right arguably imperiled by the denial of a public benefit." [ ] Here, the Fourteenth Amendment "liberty" at stake is a college student's right to refuse a vaccine, today at this stage of the pandemic [ ]. The Supreme Court has assumed (using its word) and strongly suggested that individuals have a constitutional right to refuse unwanted medical treatment, [ ]. *Cruzan*[*v. Director, Missouri Dep't of Health*, 497 U.S. 261 (1990)] held that a competent individual had a constitutional right to refuse unwanted lifesaving hydration and nutrition; and [*Washington v.*] *Glucksberg*[, 521 U.S. 702 (1997),] recognized that an individual had a liberty interest in refusing unwanted lifesaving medical treatment, though not any fundamental right to assisted suicide. [ ]

* * *

The rights recognized (or assumed) in these cases weren't "simply deduced from abstract concepts of personal autonomy." [ ] They were rooted in longstanding common law rules or legal traditions consistent with this Nation's history. [ ] The students, quite skillfully represented in this emergency setting, offer no preliminary record of such historic rules, laws, or traditions that would facilitate the court's announcement, now in mere days from receiving this case, that a right to refuse a vaccine is anything more than a significant liberty under the Fourteenth Amendment.

The dearth of this record isn't a passing point. Indeed, both *Cruzan* and *Glucksberg* were limited to an individual's choice related to the refusal of lifesaving subsistence or medical treatment—with no ramifications to the physical health of others. Vaccines address a collective enemy, not just an individual one. Indeed, "the elimination of communicable diseases through vaccination [is] one of the greatest achievements of public health in the 20th century," [ ], and it continues to be so now in this century. A vaccine is implemented as a matter of public health, and historically hasn't been constitutionally deterred from state mandate. [ ]

In the backdrop of the Fourteenth Amendment's ratification in 1868, for instance, England had already passed its first compulsory vaccination act for smallpox in 1853 (and so had many countries). [ ] Science wasn't absolute or infallible at that time—nor is it today. But the "possibility that the belief may be wrong, and that science may yet show it to be wrong, is not conclusive; for the legislature has the right to pass laws which, according to the common belief of the people, are adapted to prevent the spread of contagious diseases." [ ] Appreciating the relative risks of vaccines, they nonetheless "are effective in preventing outbreaks of disease only if a large percentage of the population is vaccinated." [ ]

Added comfort comes from the consistent use of rational basis review to assess mandatory vaccination measures.[ ]

Given over a century's worth of rulings saying there is no greater right to refuse a vaccination than what the Constitution recognizes as a significant liberty, the court declines the students' invitation to extend substantive due process to recognize more than what already and historically exists. [ ]

* * *

The university is presenting the students with a difficult choice—get the vaccine or else apply for an exemption or deferral, transfer to a different school, or forego school for the semester or altogether. But this hard choice doesn't amount to coercion. The students taking the vaccine are choosing it among other options, and before the shot reaches their arms, they are made aware of the risks and the option to refuse.

* * *

4. *On This Preliminary Record, Non-Exempt Students Haven't Shown a Likelihood of Success on their Claim that Indiana University Lacks a Rational Basis for Its Vaccine Mandate.*

Determining that the students have a liberty interest under the Fourteenth Amendment's due process clause doesn't end the analysis. [ ] To decide whether the students' constitutional rights have been violated, . . . the court must balance their liberty against the relevant state interests in accord with the Constitution. [ ] . . .

"Stemming the spread of COVID-19 is unquestionably a compelling interest." [ ] According to the federal government and the State of Indiana, a state of emergency persists related to COVID-19, all the while restrictions are being scaled back gradually. Recognizing today's status of this pandemic, neither health professionals, government representatives, nor this court may say public health *vis-à-vis* COVID-19 has waned from being a legitimate state interest. Improved it undoubtedly has—today seems a world altogether different from last year—but public health remains a legitimate interest of the state to pursue. Indiana University too has a legitimate interest in promoting the health of its campus communities—students, and not least the faculty and staff who come daily in contact with them.

The students argue that the pandemic is basically over, but this goes against current proclamations from the Secretary of Health and Human Services, the Indiana State Department of Health, Governor Eric Holcomb, and the CDC, all then supported for institutions of higher learning by the U.S. Department of Education and the American College Health Association. . . . Vastly improved, yes; out of the woods we aren't, not on this preliminary record.

* * *

Let's not forget why we are here at this more promising stage of the pandemic, July 18, 2021. Antibody resistance developed naturally from prior cases has been a contributor to be sure; but, materially, improvement has come because of vaccinations—nationally over 161 million complete (over 337 million doses) and statewide nearly 3 million complete (and over 5.7 million doses). The vaccination campaign has markedly curbed the pandemic. In fact, certain age-stratified, agent-based modeling of COVID-19 has concluded that another 279,000 deaths and nearly 1.25 million more hospitalizations would have occurred by the end of June 2021 but for the vaccines. . . .

It isn't a foregone conclusion that this is overkill. This pandemic continues to evolve, and medicine and science with it. Science is a process in search of fact. One such moving target is the Delta variant (B.1.617.2). A mere four days ago Indiana reported 612 COVID cases—the highest count in more than six weeks (since May 27, 2021)—that health officials attributed largely to the Delta variant and the unvaccinated population. . . . The CDC labeled Delta a "variant of concern" in mid-June. Current science shows it more virulent and transmissible. A peer-reviewed study from scientists . . . found that the Delta variant has mutations that allow it to evade certain natural antibodies, with vaccination proving the best protection [ ]. Reports of surges of Delta cases among the 12–29 age group have occurred. . . .

* * *

For the impact of this vaccine mandate, the students focus only on the student body; and that is certainly an important part of the analysis here. The students argue that the fatality rate for healthy individuals age 20–49 is far less than older individuals [ ]. . . . The students point out that the university's student body had one death last year [ ]. Indiana University reasonably views a 0.15 percent death rate as unacceptable for its communities, particularly given the safe preventative measure of a vaccine [ ]. . . .

In addition, the student's position overlooks the larger Indiana University community. . . . The university analyzed the number of individuals within its campus population known to have increased risk factors for COVID-19 and determined that over 8,500 faculty and staff remained at increased risk of complications if they contracted the disease [ ], with the ongoing risk of asymptomatic spread that vaccines help address [ ]. Faculty and staff at Indiana University who have daily contact with students represent an even broader demographic than just the student body, and this policy was intended to protect them too. . . .

* * *

Focusing on just mortality risk from COVID-19 leaves out much of the debate. . . .

Without vaccination, college-aged students remain at risk for serious long-term complication from COVID-19, including prolonged debilitating symptoms that interfere with normal life such as myocarditis, reduced aerobic capacity, and brain damage [ ]. Long COVID remains a studied phenomenon. With Indiana reporting that individuals aged 20–29 have had more positive cases than any other age demographic [ ], and with more than 260,000 cases linked to American college and universities since January 1, 2021 [ ], this proves still a legitimate risk. . . .

The students say the risks of the vaccine, especially at this stage and to their age group, outweigh any benefits a vaccine might confer. These argued risks include myocarditis, clotting, death, and others [ ]. Some of these concerns are easier to assuage based on current science than others—and the court isn't the final arbiter of an evolving science, only of the law. The court must base today's decision on the snapshot of this preliminary record alone. It answers the question only whether the students have made a strong showing that Indiana University failed to act reasonably in achieving campus health to warrant the extraordinary remedy of a preliminary injunction.

* * *

. . . [R]eports have shown the risk of myocarditis (heart inflammation), while present and something worthy of continued investigation, to be seemingly rare—one study suggesting the risk is about eight in one million and the other study suggesting the risk is about twenty in one million. This issue has garnered increasing attention. . . . [A] CDC safety panel reported a "likely association" in young adults from mRNA COVID-19 vaccines and myocarditis and pericarditis, though it emphasized that it remained rare and typically mild, with the benefits of the vaccine still outweighing the risks [ ]. This assessment of heart inflammation's rarity and the overarching benefits of the vaccines has a bench of current medical support on this record, again giving Indiana University a rational connection between its mandate and its aim of campus health. . . .

* * *

The students return to VAERS to discuss the risk of death from the vaccines. . . .

The CDC has explored this issue as well and seems to have marshaled data, at this time, that any risk of death is rarer than the risk of death from a young adult COVID-19 infection. According to the CDC, 25,038,458 individuals aged 18–29 have been given their first dose of the vaccine as of July 18, 2021, with VAERS reporting a total of 68 deaths, or approximately 0.00027 percent, if in fact any are related. Alternatively, of the 6,174,415 cases of COVID-19 in this age group, 2,732 died, or approximately a 0.04 percent. In balancing the risks, Indiana University wasn't irrational in favoring the route that promoted greater safety for its students.

* * *

To be sure, EUA of the COVID-19 vaccines occurred on a tighter timetable and has existed only since December 2020 and February 2021. The students thus voice concerns about the experimental nature of the vaccines, though their counsel assures that their suit will persist even if the FDA grants the vaccine manufacturers full approval. Not all EUAs are equal, and the one required for COVID-19 vaccines was more robust than usual.

* * *

In October 2020, the FDA released industry guidance detailing the benchmark criteria for a COVID-19 vaccine to receive an EUA. . . . Because the virus would only be overcome through the sweeping immunity of the American public, the FDA informed manufacturers that approval would be given to those EUA applications that went beyond the safety and efficacy requirements prescribed by statute, and also expected manufacturers to consult with the FDA on the various non-clinical components of vaccine development and distribution as the clinical trial progressed. The FDA wanted the same level of efficacy data as for full approval, enough safety data to justify providing the vaccine to healthy individuals, and confirmation of the technical procedures and verification steps necessary to support full approval.

* * *

Indiana University closely considered the FDA's EUA requirements when adopting its policy. The specialists on the university restart committee appreciated that all three COVID-19 vaccines had been "studied in robust multi-centered, international, randomized-controlled trials and proven both effective and safe in millions of people" [ ]. These specialists explained that the EUA vaccines had been based on technology that has been studied for decades [ ]. Though even "small differences in chemical structure can sometimes make very large differences in the type of toxic response that is produced," [ ], much like the FDA, the university concluded that campus safety reasonably outweighed any lingering risks with the vaccines. This wasn't just any ordinary EUA process, but EUA on proverbial steroids. The university reasonably concluded that the "benefit dwarfs the potential rare risks" [ ].

* * *

Today, Indiana University has a rational basis to conclude that the COVID-19 vaccine is safe and efficacious for its students. The vaccine has been used on about 157 million Americans; and data now about eight months later, though it will grow more robust in years to come, is considerable and shows major side effects are rare. Much like over 500 universities and colleges in the United States that have done the same, Indiana University reasonably relies on the vaccine as a measure to return to normal school functioning. The students say the mandate is unreasonable because no other Indiana government agency mandates the vaccine. But just because it has gone above what others have done doesn't make it unreasonable. Indeed, universities are unique places, with lots of people gathered and living together in close quarters for months at a time. That Indiana University's mandate goes beyond what other public universities in Indiana have done doesn't compel a finding that this policy is unreasonable; indeed, other universities in the state have mandated the vaccine, and many others around the country have too.

Indiana University is following the recommendations of other well-established agencies, including the Centers for Disease Control, U.S. Department of Education, and the Indiana State Department of Health. These are reliable sources to assess the reasonableness of measures implemented, though the court must be cautious not to expand the guidance beyond what it says. [ ] To be sure, the CDC doesn't recommend that schools "mandate" the vaccine—a point the students make—but such a recommendation isn't consistent with the CDC's purview, which is to act as an informative agency. At the same time, the university's policy isn't inconsistent with the CDC's recommendations. The CDC says institutions of higher learning "can return to full capacity in-person learning, without requiring or recommending masking or physical distancing for people who are fully vaccinated" [ ]. The CDC's guidance to universities is that "[v]accination is the leading prevention strategy to protect individual from COVID-19 disease and end the COVID-19 pandemic." This will enhance the student body's opportunities, allowing them to have a more fulfilling college experience.

* * *

Overall, the students' arguments amount to disputes over the most reliable science. But when reasonable minds can differ as to the best course of action—for instance, addressing symptomatic versus asymptomatic virus spread or any number of issues here—the court doesn't intervene so long as the university's process is rational in trying to achieve public health. [ ] There is a rational basis for making distinctions here. No student, including those not yet exempt, have shown that Indiana University's vaccine mandate as applied to them violates rational basis review. The court thus denies their request to enjoin it preliminarily.

NOTES AND QUESTIONS

1.   *Subsequent History of* Klaassen. The Seventh Circuit affirmed the district court's decision with a very short opinion. See Klaassen v. Trustees of Indiana University, 7 F.4th 592 (7th Cir. 2021). The appellate court agreed that *Jacobson* had applied a rational-basis test to assess the constitutionality of the smallpox vaccine mandate at issue in that case. The court also held that Indiana University's vaccine mandate does not infringe on a fundamental liberty interest because our history does not reveal laws prohibiting such mandates. The court observed, "[t]o the contrary, vaccination requirements, like other public-health measures, have been common in this nation." Id. at

593. The Supreme Court summarily denied the plaintiffs' emergency petition for injunctive relief. See Klaassen v. Trustees of Indiana University, No. 21A15 (Aug. 13, 2021) (Barrett, J.).

2. *Supreme Court on* Jacobson. While the Supreme Court has not ruled directly on the precedential value of *Jacobson*, at least two Justices have signaled their views. In *Cuomo*—a decision analyzed by the district court in *Klaassen*—Justice Gorsuch, in a concurring opinion, expressed the interpretation of *Jacobson* that was adopted by the court in *Klaassen*. "*Jacobson* didn't seek to depart from normal legal rules during a pandemic, and it supplies no precedent for doing so. Instead, *Jacobson* applied what would become the traditional legal test associated with the right at issue—exactly what the Court does today." Cuomo, 141 S. Ct. at 70. Additionally, in *South Bay United Pentecostal Church v. Newsom*, 140 S. Ct. 1613 (2020) (mem.), the Court denied an emergency request to enjoin California's enforcement of an executive order limiting the number of worshippers at in-person religious services. Chief Justice Roberts, in a concurrence, relied on and quoted from *Jacobson*: "Our Constitution principally entrusts '[t]he safety and the health of the people' to the politically accountable officials of the States 'to guard and protect.' " Id. at 1613.

3. *Other Interpretations of* Jacobson. The Fifth Circuit gave *Jacobson* an entirely different interpretation, holding that it created a special constitutional standard to be used in the judicial review of all public health measures imposed by state actors during an emergency. In *In re Abbott*, 954 F.3d 772 (5th Cir. 2020), *vacated by* Planned Parenthood v. Abbott, 141 S. Ct. 1261 (2021), the appellate court granted a writ of mandamus vacating a district court's preliminary injunction that prevented Texas from enforcing an executive order prohibiting all medical procedures not necessary to save the life of or prevent serious harm to patients. The executive order was designed to preserve medical resources during the COVID-19 pandemic. Abortion providers in Texas sued, claiming that the executive order effectively bans abortions for the duration of the order. The district court granted a preliminary injunction banning enforcement of the order against abortion providers and did so relying on the "undue burden" test conventionally applied in constitutional challenges to abortion restrictions.

The Fifth Circuit held that the district court's analysis was so flawed as to justify mandamus because the lower court had not relied on *Jacobson*, which the appellate court interpreted as creating a lower standard of review applicable during public health emergencies.

> when faced with a society-threatening epidemic, a state may implement emergency measures that curtail constitutional rights so long as the measures have at least some "real or substantial relation" to the public health crisis and are not "beyond all question, a plain, palpable invasion of rights secured by the fundamental law." [quoting *Jacobson*] . . .

* * *

Jacobson remains good law. [ ] And, most importantly for the present case, nothing in the Supreme Court's abortion cases suggests that abortion rights are somehow exempt from the *Jacobson* framework.

954 F.3d at 784–85.

This approach has been called the "suspension" interpretation of *Jacobson* because it suspends during an emergency the application of conventional constitutional standards of review in favor of the "reasonableness" standard articulated in *Jacobson*. See Lindsay F. Wiley and Stephen I. Vladeck, Coronavirus, Civil Liberties, and the Courts: The Case Against "Suspending" Judicial Review, 133 Harv. L. Rev. Forum 179 (2020) (critiquing the doctrine). As noted above, the Supreme Court vacated *In re Abbott*. Since then, district courts in the Fifth Circuit have not deployed the suspension interpretation of *Jacobson*. See, e.g., New Orleans Catering, Inc. v. Cantrell, 523 F. Supp. 3d 902 (E.D. La. 2021) (applying conventional substantive due process standards to review constitutional challenges to executive orders restricting certain business operations in New Orleans, where the authority for such executive orders was derived from a statute granting emergency powers to the governor that are triggered during a declared state of emergency, and where the COVID-19 pandemic justified the governor in declaring a state of emergency).

In contrast to the "suspension" interpretation, some courts have applied *Jacobson* as if it creates a special constitutional standard for the review of public health measures, whether or not an emergency has been declared. For example, during the 2014 Ebola scare, federal courts reviewing quarantine orders employed a "reasonableness" test, citing to *Jacobson*. See Hickox v. Christie, 205 F. Supp. 3d 579 (D.N.J. 2016); Liberian Community Assoc. v. Malloy, 2017 WL 4897048 (D. Conn), aff'd, Liberian Community Assoc. v. Lamont, 970 F.3d 174 (2d Cir. 2020). To understand how to apply *Jacobson* in the case of a quarantine order, judges relied on federal quarantine cases regardless of whether those cases involved declared disease emergencies. Is this interpretation of *Jacobson* viable given later case law?

4.   *Should Strict Scrutiny Apply?* The district and appellate courts in *Klaassen* each held that individuals have a significant, but not a "fundamental," liberty interest. As a result, the university's vaccine mandate was subject to rational basis testing only, and not strict scrutiny. The students had argued that individuals have a fundamental liberty interest to avoid unwanted violations of their bodily integrity. They relied on Supreme Court precedent acknowledging that informed consent law widely and historically adopted by states is evidence of a fundamental liberty interest to avoid a medical battery. For presentation and discussion of *Glucksberg*, see Chapter 19. *Klaassen* acknowledged that there is a liberty interest in refusing unwanted medical treatment, but the opinions distinguish infectious disease vaccination from standard medical treatment because the decision to receive or refuse such a vaccine has implications for others, and not just the person making the decision. As the district court noted, "[v]accines address a collective

enemy, not just an individual one." Id. at *24. The opinions also cited to other vaccine cases to which only rational basis testing has been applied.

Is the liberty interest at stake properly understood as a non-consensual bodily invasion because the vaccine pierces the skin and introduces medicine to the body? If so, was the court right that the liberty interest is not fundamental? When reviewing the constitutionality of a vaccine mandate, should the fundamental/non-fundamental determination take into account whether population health is being actively threatened by an infectious disease? If so, does that mean a chickenpox vaccination requirement to attend school implicates a fundamental liberty interest in the absence of an epidemic and a non-fundamental liberty interest during a chickenpox epidemic? If the university's vaccine mandate had been found to implicate a fundamental liberty interest, would it have survived strict scrutiny because it is necessary to achieve a compelling state interest?

5. *University Vaccine Mandates*. More than 1,000 of the nation's nearly 4,000 degree-granting public and private colleges and universities required at least some students or employees to receive a COVID vaccination prior to the fall 2021 semester. See Andy Thomason and Brian O'Leary, Here's a List of Colleges That Require Students or Employees to Be Vaccinated Against Covid-19, Chron. Higher Ed. (Sept. 2, 2021). The schools include the University of Massachusetts and Western Michigan University, each of which was subject to a lawsuit alleging that the universities' vaccine requirements violated the constitutional rights of students. In each suit, the students moved for a preliminary injunction. In one case, the court denied the motion, following the same analysis as in *Klaassen*. See Harris v. Univ. of Massachusetts, No. 21-CV-11244-DJC, 2021 WL 3848012 (D. Mass. Aug. 27, 2021) (students are unlikely to prevail on the merits of their substantive due process claim that the university's COVID vaccination mandate, together with the mandate's religious exemption, violates the students' protected liberty interests). In the other case, the court granted the motion, holding that strict scrutiny would apply if, as alleged, the university's vaccine mandate did not permit religious exemptions. See Dahl v. Bd. of Trustees of W. Michigan Univ., No. 1:21-CV-757, 2021 WL 3891620 (W.D. Mich. Aug. 31, 2021) (granting an *ex parte* motion for preliminary injunction to prevent the university's enforcement of its COVID vaccine mandate against members of the women's soccer team).

NOTE: PUBLIC HEALTH AND RELIGIOUS FREEDOM

The First Amendment to the federal Constitution, among other things, protects the right of individuals to exercise their religious beliefs free of governmental prohibitions (the "free exercise" clause). Public health measures occasionally burden an individual's religious freedom. For example, during the COVID-19 pandemic, orders limiting the size of gatherings or closing places where individuals gather disrupted conventional, in-person worship services. Worshippers challenged some of these orders as unconstitutional.

In "free exercise" cases, federal courts apply a rational-basis test to the allegedly unconstitutional law if that law is generally applicable to both secular and non-secular activity and if it is neutral toward religion. The burden is on the challenger, under that standard, to establish that the law in question lacks any rational basis. If, however, the challenged law is aimed at religious activity or is not neutral toward religion, then federal courts apply strict scrutiny. Under this much higher standard, the government bears the burden of establishing that the challenged law is necessary to serve a compelling state interest. See Roman Cath. Diocese of Brooklyn v. Cuomo, 141 S. Ct. 63 (2020). Thus, a court's determination of the applicable constitutional standard of review often decides the outcome of "free exercise" cases.

When assessing whether a law is neutral as to religion, courts will not only look to the law's language, but also to its application to comparable secular and non-secular activities. If, as a result of such a comparison, a court determines that the law burdens religious activities in a way it does not burden secular activities, the court will rule that the law is not neutral and that strict scrutiny applies. See id.

In *Tandon v. Newsom*, 141 S. Ct. 1294 (2021), plaintiffs were individuals seeking to gather for at-home religious services, and they challenged California's COVID-19 restriction that prohibited members of more than three different households from gathering together for any purpose in any one person's home. The plaintiffs argued that the restriction violated the Free Exercise clause. The trial court denied the plaintiffs' motion for preliminary injunction. Plaintiffs appealed and sought an emergency injunction from the Ninth Circuit pending the appeal, which emergency injunction was denied. The plaintiffs then sought from the Supreme Court—and were granted—an emergency injunction for the duration of the Ninth Circuit's appellate process.

A five-justice majority of the Supreme Court approved the application, ruling that California's uniform restriction on the size in-home gatherings for both secular and non-secular purposes was *not* a neutral law with respect to religious activities. Rather than compare secular and non-secular in-home activities under the challenged restriction, the majority opinion compared at-home religious activity with secular activities occurring outside of anyone's home. "California treats some comparable secular activities more favorably than at-home religious exercise, permitting hair salons, retail stores, personal care services, movie theaters, private suites at sporting events and concerts, and indoor restaurants to bring together more than three households at a time." Id. at 1297. Because of these differences, the majority determined that strict scrutiny applies and that the Ninth Circuit had failed to find that the restrictions were necessary to confront the comparable risk of COVID-19 transmission associated with secular activity outside of the home and religious activity inside a home.

PROBLEM: EXEMPTIONS FROM IMMUNIZATION REQUIREMENTS

You are the legal counsel to the school district in Gadsden, Alabama. The Code of Alabama, § 16–30–1 et seq., requires certain immunizations as a condition of school attendance. Exemptions to this provision are found in § 16–30–3:

The provisions of this chapter shall not apply if:

(1) In the absence of an epidemic or immediate threat thereof, the parent or guardian of the child shall object thereto in writing on grounds that such immunization or testing conflicts with his religious tenets and practices; or

(2) Certification by a competent medical authority providing individual exemption from the required immunization or testing is presented the admissions officer of the school.

First grader Miranda Black's parents, who resent the heavy burden of government, have decided that they will not submit to any immunization requirement. They reason that Miranda should not have to shoulder the public health value of immunization by risking the side effects of the immunizations. Her doctor will not provide the "certification" that the school authorities want because there is no medical reason for her to avoid immunization, and thus her parents have submitted to the school authorities a statement that "compulsory immunization violates our Christian view that the government cannot make us do anything."

School health officials are concerned because there were four cases of whooping cough in Gadsden during the last year—up from two the year before, and one the year before that. They attribute the increase to the increasing number of people who have obtained exemptions. The school officials have asked you how they should react to the request that Miranda be exempt. How will you advise them to proceed and why?

NOTE: PUBLIC HEALTH EVIDENCE AND THE LAW

Regardless of the standard applied, courts hearing constitutional challenges to public health measures should account for public health evidence, as recognized by the Supreme Court in a 1987 disability discrimination case. In School Board of Nassau County, Fla. v. Arline, 480 U.S. 273 (1987), the Court was asked to apply Section 504 of the Rehabilitation Act, a federal disability discrimination statute, in the case of a teacher with latent tuberculosis who was discharged by a public school district. School officials were concerned that the teacher might infect students or others at school if her disease became active while she was employed. The Rehabilitation Act prohibits discrimination against any person who is disabled or perceived as disabled, which includes someone who has or is perceived to have a dangerous infectious disease. The statute protected the teacher from dismissal based on disability only if the teacher was "otherwise qualified" for her position. The

Court opined that, in the context of a person with or perceived to have an infectious disease, a trial court cannot determine whether the person is "otherwise qualified" unless the court makes:

> '[findings of] facts, based on reasonable medical judgments given the state of medical knowledge, about (a) the nature of the risk (how the disease is transmitted), (b) the duration of the risk (how long is the carrier infectious), (c) the severity of the risk (what is the potential harm to third parties) and (d) the probabilities the disease will be transmitted and will cause varying degrees of harm.' In making these findings, courts normally should defer to the reasonable medical judgments of public health officials.

Id. at 288 (internal citation omitted). See also Chapter 6 (discussing federal laws prohibiting discrimination based on disability) and Chapter 11 (discussing the protections of these laws in the workplace). Thus, the Supreme Court has recognized the need to account for the scientific facts and public health risks associated with governmental action designed to safeguard population health.

Although *Arline* did not involve a constitutional challenge, its underlying principle of holding courts accountable to public health evidence should apply to any case in which the judiciary reviews measures taken in the name of public health. See Scott Burris, Rationality Review and the Politics of Public Health, 34 Vill. L. Rev. 933 (1989) (arguing for a medical rationality test that focuses judicial scrutiny on the relevant scientific facts concerning a dangerous infectious disease); Robert Gatter, Reviving Focused Scrutiny in the Constitutional Review of Public Health Measures, 64 Wash. U. J. L. & Pol'y 151 (2021).

V. SEPARATION OF POWERS AND ADMINISTRATIVE LAW AS LIMITATIONS ON PUBLIC HEALTH AUTHORITY

Constitutionally protected individual rights are not the only limitations on public health authority. Because executive agencies take action during a crisis to protect public health actions, they are also subject to federal or state administrative procedural codes and to constitutional doctrines deriving from the separation of powers. As exemplified in the materials in this section, public health officials who fail to comply with administrative procedure when implementing a public health measure may find that their measure is legally void. Likewise, public health actions taken by executive agencies or officials can be declared void if they are found to usurp policy-making authority assigned exclusively by a state constitution to the legislative branch. Opponents of ongoing business and social restrictions imposed by health officials during the COVID-19 pandemic have used both of these avenues to challenge those restrictions.

BESHEAR V. ACREE

Supreme Court of Kentucky, 2020.
615 S.W.3d 780.

* * *

FACTS AND PROCEDURAL HISTORY

. . . On January 31, 2020, the United States Department of Health and Human Services declared a national public health emergency, effective January 27, 2020, based on the rising number of confirmed COVID-19 cases in the United States. . . .

On March 6, 2020, Governor Andy Beshear, under the authority vested in him pursuant to KRS Chapter 39A, declared a state of emergency in Kentucky. [ ]. . . . After the statewide declaration, Kentucky's Cabinet for Health and Family Services (the Cabinet) began issuing orders designed to reduce and slow the spread of COVID-19 and thereby promote public health and safety. Those orders included directives such as prohibiting on-site consumption of food and drink at restaurants, closing businesses that encourage congregation, and prohibiting mass gatherings. As knowledge regarding the heretofore unknown novel coronavirus (COVID-19) grew, the Governor and the Cabinet modified their orders accordingly.

On March 17, 2020, the Cabinet issued an order requiring all public-facing businesses that encourage public congregation to close, including gyms, entertainment and recreational facilities, and theaters. These emergency measures worked to reduce COVID-19 cases by limiting gatherings where the virus could be transmitted. The Governor announced on April 21, 2020, the "Healthy at Work" initiative, a phased reopening plan based on criteria set by public health and industry experts to help Kentucky businesses reopen safely. On May 11, 2020, the Commonwealth began reopening its economy and the Cabinet issued minimum requirements that all public and private entities were required to follow, such as maintaining social distance between persons, requiring employees to wash hands regularly, and routinely cleaning and sanitizing commonly touched surfaces.

[The Court described legal actions taken by various business owners and the state Attorney General in two counties in the spring and summer of 2020. Each sought to enjoin both temporarily and permanently the enforcement of the Governor's COVID-19 orders. One trial court temporarily enjoined enforcement of some of the Governor's orders. The Governor filed for a writ of mandamus, and the Kentucky Supreme Court issued a stay of all lower court orders so as to consolidate the actions and hear them at once. Among the issues before the Court was whether (1) the Governor's orders were an exercise of legislative authority that had not been properly delegated to the executive branch and thus violated the separation of powers doctrine, and (2) the Governor was obligated to act through the promulgation of administrative regulations rather than through a series of blanket executive orders.]

* * *

ANALYSIS

Before turning to the specific issues presented, we briefly address the history of emergency powers legislation, which has existed in Kentucky since 1952. On March 5, 1952, the General Assembly enacted Chapter 39 of the Kentucky Revised Statutes, relating to civil defense. . . .

Recognizing that the Commonwealth is always subject to both contained and widespread threatening occurrences, in 1998 the General Assembly replaced KRS Chapter 39 with KRS Chapter 39A, which establishes a statewide comprehensive emergency management system. In enacting the Chapter, the General Assembly expressly noted that "response to these occurrences is a fundamental responsibility of elected government in the Commonwealth." [ ]. KRS Chapter 39A further expanded the scope of disasters and emergencies which necessitate the Governor's response and, notably, added biological and etiological hazards to the list of threats to public safety. The General Assembly recognized that the purpose of Kentucky's emergency management response had evolved from responding only to security and defense needs to responding to all types of natural and man-made hazards in order to address the contemporary needs of Kentucky citizens. [ ]. . . .KRS Chapter 39A powers have been invoked by every Governor who has served since the law's adoption in 1998. The emergencies have ranged from widespread events such as destructive storms to more localized concerns such as bridges and water supply. Since 1996, an emergency of some magnitude has been declared on approximately 115 occasions, leaving aside the accompanying orders in the face of those occurrences which prohibit price gouging or allow pharmacists to address prescription needs. As we address the issues in this case, we are cognizant of the Commonwealth's history and experience with emergency response.

* * *

II. During the Emergency, the Governor Has Exercised Executive Powers But to the Extent, If Any, KRS Chapter 39A Grants Him Legislative Authority, No Violation of the Separation of Powers Provisions of the Kentucky Constitution Has Occurred, the General Assembly Having Properly Delegated that Authority.

The Kentucky Constitution directs the separation of powers among the legislative, executive and judicial branches [ ] and prohibits any one branch from exercising "any power properly belonging to either of the others, except in the instances hereinafter expressly directed or permitted," [ ]. The

Governor maintains that in responding to the COVID-19 pandemic he has exercised executive powers derived from the Kentucky Constitution and that KRS Chapter 39A simply "recognizes, defines, and constrains" executive authority to direct an emergency response. To the extent any of his actions could be characterized as legislative, he notes that he is exercising authority lawfully delegated to him by the General Assembly in KRS Chapter 39A.

The Attorney General seemingly acknowledges some role for the Governor in the event of an emergency such as COVID-19 but generally insists that the Governor's response these last months via executive orders and emergency regulations is an unconstitutional encroachment on legislative authority. In advocating the striking of those portions of KRS Chapter 39A that permit the Governor to exercise legislative authority, . . . the Attorney General asks us to "use this case to restore the original meaning of the Constitution's separation of powers." To the extent we decline that invitation, he argues that the legislative authority in KRS Chapter 39A has been improperly delegated to the Governor. As we consider this argument, we do so guided by the presumption that the challenged statutes were enacted by the legislature in accordance with constitutional requirements. [ ]. "A constitutional infringement must be 'clear, complete and unmistakable' in order to render the statute unconstitutional." [ ]. Ultimately, we conclude that the Governor is largely exercising emergency executive power but to the extent legislative authority is involved it has been validly delegated by the General Assembly consistent with decades of Kentucky precedent, which we will not overturn.

The current Kentucky Constitution . . . does not address emergency occurrences or events directly except as to military matters which are firmly assigned to the Governor as the "commander-in-chief" of military affairs. [ ]. Generally, Section 69 vests the Governor with the "supreme executive power of the Commonwealth" and Section 81 mandates the Governor "take care that the laws be faithfully executed." Also instructive for the present case, Section 80 provides that the Governor "may, on extraordinary occasions, convene the General Assembly at the seat of government, or at a different place, if that should have become dangerous from an enemy or from contagious diseases. . . . When he shall convene the General Assembly it shall be by proclamation, stating the subjects to be considered, and no other shall be considered."

Although "extraordinary occasions" has been construed customarily to allow special legislative sessions for reasons of immediate import relating to funding and other matters, it plainly extends to those events or occurrences that qualify as a natural or man-made emergency, underscored by the "clue" regarding the convening of the legislature somewhere other than Frankfort in the event of an enemy or contagious diseases. Notably, Section 80 contains the permissive "may . . . convene" as opposed to the mandatory "shall . . . convene." Even in times when the Commonwealth is confronted with something extraordinary, to include enemies and contagious diseases, the decision to convene the General Assembly in a special session is solely the Governor's.

The implied tilt of the Kentucky Constitution toward executive powers in times of emergency is not surprising, given our government's tripartite structure with a legislature that is not in continuous session. . . .

* * *

Having a citizen legislature that meets part-time as opposed to a full-time legislative body that meets year-round, as some states have, generally leaves our General Assembly without the ability to legislate quickly in the event of emergency unless the emergency arises during a regular legislative session. The COVID-19 pandemic arose during the latter part of the 2020 legislative session, after the deadline for introducing a new bill, resulting in fourteen proposed COVID-19 related amendments to existing bills, five of which eventually passed. Most notably, Senate Bill 150, "AN ACT relating to the state of emergency in response to COVID-19 and declaring an emergency," acknowledged the Governor's declared emergency and provided:

> Notwithstanding any state law to the contrary, the Governor shall declare, in writing, the date upon which the state of emergency in response to COVID-19, declared on March 6, 2020, by Executive Order 2020-215, has ceased. In the event no such declaration is made by the Governor on or before the first day of the next regular session of the General Assembly, the General Assembly may make the determination.

. . . .

The Attorney General invites the Court to adopt a strict separation of powers stance by identifying the Governor's issuance of any rules, regulations or orders in an emergency as exercises of non-delegable legislative power (excepting only the Governor's initial declaration of an emergency perhaps) and then holding those emergency responses constitutionally invalid . . . . We decline. First, our reading of the Kentucky Constitution leaves us with no evidence that the powers at issue must be deemed legislative. The "extraordinary occasion," [ ], of a global pandemic gives rise to an obvious emergency and, as noted, the Constitution impliedly tilts to authority in the full-time executive branch to act in such circumstances. Indeed, the Governor's "commander-in-chief" status . . . reinforces the concept. Second, the structure of Kentucky government as discussed renders it impractical, if not impossible, for the legislature, in session for only a limited period each year, to have the primary role in steering the Commonwealth through an emergency.

On this latter point, the Attorney General argues that Section 80 [of the state Constitution] allows the Governor to call an extraordinary session and thus "envisions that the Governor will not go it alone during a crisis, but instead will work hand in hand with the People's representatives." Again, the language of the section is permissive not mandatory, leaving it to the Governor—also duly elected by the People—whether the General Assembly should be convened. Moreover, the view advocated by the Attorney General creates an obvious dilemma: if the Governor is not empowered to adopt emergency measures because that constitutes "legislation," the Commonwealth is left with no means for an immediate, comprehensive response because either the General Assembly is not in session and cannot convene itself or even if in session it will have limited time to deal with the matter under constitutionally mandated constraints on the length of the session. So, our examination of the Kentucky Constitution causes us to conclude the emergency powers the Governor has exercised are executive in nature, never raising a separation of powers issue in the first instance.

Fortunately, the need to definitively label the powers necessary to steer the Commonwealth through an emergency as either solely executive or solely legislative is largely obviated by KRS Chapter 39A, "Statewide Emergency Management Programs," which reflects a cooperative approach between the two branches. Plaintiffs and the Attorney General insist that the statute is in large part unconstitutional, however, because it grants the Governor legislative authority in violation of the nondelegation doctrine. We disagree.

We acknowledge, of course, that making laws for the Commonwealth is the prerogative of the legislature. Addressing a statute that authorizes the Governor to reorganize governmental bodies during the period between annual legislative sessions, we recently observed, "[t]he legislative power we understand to be the authority under the constitution to make the laws, and to alter and repeal them." Beshear v. Bevin, 575 S.W.3d 673, 682 (Ky. 2019) [ ]. "The nondelegation doctrine recognizes that the Constitution vests the powers of government in three separate branches and, under the doctrine of separation of powers, each branch must exercise its own power rather than delegating it to another branch." Id. at 681 [ ]. Nevertheless, we found KRS 12.028, at issue in that case, to be a valid delegation of legislative power, recognizing that legislative power can be delegated "if the law delegating that authority provides 'safeguards, procedural and otherwise, which prevent an abuse of discretion'" thereby " 'protecting against unnecessary and uncontrolled discretionary power.' " Id. at 683 (citations omitted). Our holding was but one in a series of Kentucky cases over several decades addressing the proper delegation of legislative power.

The United States Supreme Court [ ] held that "[i]f Congress shall lay down by legislative act an intelligible principle to which the person or body authorized to [act] . . . is directed to conform, such legislative action is not a forbidden delegation of legislative power." [ ]. Recognition of the delegation of legislative powers in Kentucky largely began with Commonwealth v. Associated Industries of Kentucky, 370 S.W.2d 584, 586 (Ky. 1963): "We find nothing in our State Constitution that declares explicitly: 'Legislative power may not be delegated.' " . . . More recently, [ ], we recognized "given the realities of modern rule-making" a legislative body "has neither the time nor the expertise to do it all; it must have help." [ ]. Examining the nondelegation doctrine generally and finding the "intelligible-principle rule" instructive if somewhat "toothless" in application by the federal courts, [ ], the Court reviewed several Kentucky cases wherein a delegation of legislative authority was deemed unlawful because the "powers were granted without 'legislative criteria,' " [ ], or the delegation lacked "standards controlling the exercise of administrative discretion," [ ]. The "unintelligible" legislative pension statute at issue in [that case] failed for those reasons—lack of "an intelligible principle" and the absence of any "standards controlling the exercise of administrative discretion." [ ].

In the case before us, the intelligible principle enunciated by the General Assembly and the legislative criteria pertinent to the use of emergency powers are set forth in KRS 39A.010 quoted above. In the event of any of those multitude of threats, the Governor (and the Division of Emergency Management and local emergency agencies) are authorized to take action "to protect life and property of the people of the Commonwealth, and to protect public peace, health, safety and welfare . . . and in order to ensure the continuity and effectiveness of government in time of emergency, disaster or catastrophe. . . ." In KRS 39A.100(1), the Governor is granted twelve enumerated "emergency powers" including in subsection (j) the following: "Except as prohibited by this section or other law, to perform and exercise other functions, powers, and duties deemed necessary to promote and secure the safety and protection of the civilian population." Given the wide variance of occurrences that can constitute an emergency, disaster or catastrophe, the criteria are necessarily broad and result-oriented, "protect life and property . . . and . . . public . . . health," KRS 39A.010, allowing the Governor working with the executive branch and emergency management agencies to determine what is necessary for the specific crisis at hand. Floods, tornadoes and ice storms require different responses than threats from nuclear, chemical or biological agents or biological, etiological, or radiological hazards but the emergency powers are always limited by the legislative criteria, i.e., they must be exercised in the context of a declared state of emergency, KRS 39A.100(1); designed to protect life, property, health and safety and to secure the continuity and effectiveness of government, KRS 39A.010; and exercised "to promote and secure the safety and protection of the civilian population." KRS 39A.100(1)(j).

In addition, KRS Chapter 39A contains procedural safeguards to prevent abuses. All written orders and administrative regulations promulgated by the Governor "shall have the full force of law" upon the filing of a copy with the Legislative Research Commission. [ ]. This provides the requisite public notice. The duration of the state of emergency, at least the one at issue in this case, is also limited by the aforementioned 2020 Senate Bill 150, Section 3, which requires the Governor to state when the emergency has ceased but, in any event, allows the General Assembly to make the determination itself if the Governor has not declared an end to the emergency "before the first day of the next regular session of the General Assembly." The enunciation of criteria for use of the emergency powers, the timely, public notice provided for all orders and regulations promulgated by the Governor and the time limit on the duration of the emergency and accompanying powers all combine to render KRS Chapter 39A constitutional to the extent legislative powers are delegated.

Recently the Michigan Supreme Court, in a sharply divided opinion, addressed two certified questions posed by the federal district court regarding the Michigan Governor's exercise of emergency powers under that state's Emergency Management Act of 1976 (EMA) and Emergency Powers of the Governor Act of 1945 (EPGA). [ ]. The EPGA gave the Governor power, indefinite in duration, to declare an emergency and issue "reasonable orders, rules, and regulations as he or she considers necessary to protect life and property or to bring the emergency situation within the affected area under control." [ ]. The majority concluded the "reasonable" and "necessary" standard failed to provide sufficient guidance to the Governor regarding the exercise of her powers and failed to constrain her actions "in any meaningful manner." [ ].

Finding the power delegated to be "of immense breadth and . . . devoid of all temporal limitations," [ ], the majority struck the statute as an unlawful delegation of legislative power to the executive branch violative of the Michigan Constitution's separation of powers provision. Chief Justice McCormack, writing for the three-justice minority, observed that the majority departed from one part of their longstanding test for delegation of legislative power, namely that "the standard must be as reasonably precise as the subject matter requires or permits." [ ]. Citing Gundy v. United States, ___ U.S. ___, 139 S. Ct. 2116, 2130, 204 L.Ed.2d 522 (2019), for the proposition that delegations of such authority must give the delegee "the flexibility to deal with real-world constraints," she noted that "given the unpredictability and range of emergencies the Legislature identified in the statute, it is difficult to see how it could have been more specific." [ ].

Our case differs from the Michigan case in several important ways but most notably our Governor does not have emergency powers of indefinite duration, 2020 S.B. 150, § 3, and our legislature is not continuously in session, ready to accept the handoff of responsibility for providing the government's response to an emergency such as the current global pandemic. Moreover, with the breadth of potential emergencies identified in KRS 39A.010, the standards of protection of life, property, peace, health, safety and welfare (along with the "necessary" qualifier in KRS 39A.100(j)) are sufficiently specific to guide discretion while appropriately flexible to address a myriad of real-world events. While the authority exercised by the Governor in accordance with KRS Chapter 39A is necessarily broad, the checks on that authority are the same as those identified in Chief Justice McCormack's dissenting opinion: judicial challenges to the existence of an emergency or to the content of a particular order or regulation; legislative amendment or revocation of the emergency powers granted the Governor; and finally the "ultimate check" of citizens holding the Governor accountable at the ballot box. [ ].

Whatever import the principle of properly delegated legislative authority has in the ordinary workings of government, its import increases dramatically in the event of a statewide emergency in our Commonwealth. A legislature that is not in continuous session and without constitutional authority to convene itself cannot realistically manage a crisis on a day-to-day basis by the adoption and amendment of laws. In any event, we decline to abandon approximately sixty years of precedent that appropriately channels and limits the delegation of legislative power in Kentucky. Applying that delegation precedent, KRS Chapter 39A passes muster as a constitutional delegation of power to the extent any of the powers accorded to and exercised by the Governor are in fact legislative.

In sum, the powers exercised by a Kentucky Governor in an emergency are likely executive powers in the first instance given provisions of our Kentucky Constitution, but to the extent those powers are seen as impinging on the legislative domain, our General Assembly has wisely addressed the situation in KRS Chapter 39A. That vital and often-used statutory scheme validly delegates any legislative authority at issue to the Governor with safeguards and criteria sufficient to pass constitutional muster.

III. KRS Chapter 13A Does Not Limit the Governor's Authority to Act Under the Constitution and KRS Chapter 39A in the Event of an Emergency.

KRS Chapter 13A, "Administrative Regulations," provides for the promulgation of administrative regulations—defined in relevant part as a "statement of general applicability . . . that implements, interprets, or prescribes law or policy," [ ]—both in the ordinary course of state government . . . and in the event of an emergency, [ ]. Plaintiffs and the Attorney General challenge the executive orders and regulations issued by the Governor as violative of KRS Chapter 13A. The Governor maintains that KRS Chapter 39A by its plain terms controls in a declared emergency, granting him the authority he has exercised but that if any conflict is perceived then the more specific statutory enactment pertaining to emergencies prevails. The plain language of the statutes supports the Governor's position. [ ].

KRS 39A.100 recognizes the authority of the Governor to declare an emergency and exercise the enumerated emergency powers. In furtherance of that authority, KRS 39A.090 provides that "[t]he Governor may make, amend, and rescind any executive orders as deemed necessary to carry out the provisions of KRS Chapters 39A to 39F." Nothing in the plain words used requires consideration of KRS Chapter 13A or even requires promulgation of regulations; the Governor can choose to act solely through executive orders. The Governor may also promulgate regulations, however, as authorized by KRS 39A.180:

> (2) All written orders and administrative regulations promulgated by the Governor, the director, or by any political subdivision or other agency authorized by KRS Chapters 39A to 39F to make orders and promulgate administrative regulations, shall have the full force of law, when, if issued by the Governor, the director, or any state agency, a copy is filed with the Legislative Research Commission .... All existing laws, ordinances, and administrative regulations inconsistent with the provisions of KRS Chapters 39A to 39F, or of any order or administrative regulation issued under the authority of KRS Chapters 39A to 39F, shall be suspended during the period of time and to the extent that the conflict exists.

[ ]. This statute plainly provides that the orders and regulations issued pursuant to the emergency authority granted the Governor in KRS Chapter 39A "shall have full force of law" upon filing with the Legislative Research Commission (LRC), the same entity that compiles, publishes and distributes administrative regulations generally. [ ]. To the extent KRS Chapter 13A contains anything "inconsistent" with either Chapter 39A or an order or regulation issued under the authority of that chapter then the General Assembly has expressly directed that it "shall be suspended during the period of time and to the extent that the conflict exists." [ ]. In short, while a state of emergency prevails the Governor can issue executive orders he or she "deem[s] necessary," . . .

* * *

In insisting that the Governor must use the regulatory process to affect private rights, the Attorney General emphasizes our statement in Bowling v. Department of Corrections, [ ]: "Regulation is . . . mandated by KRS 13A.100, which requires regulation if, as here, the regulation will prescribe statements of general applicability which implement laws . . . or affect private rights." Missing from this argument is any recognition that no state of emergency existed in Bowling, but, more importantly, any acknowledgement of the General Assembly's specific directive in KRS 39A.180(2) that inconsistent laws, ordinances and regulations are suspended by KRS Chapter 39A and the executive orders and regulations issued pursuant thereto. We find nothing strange about the legislature giving the Governor flexibility in the event of an emergency to act through either executive orders or regulations, the former being more suited to immediate response in the acute state of an emergency. . . .

In short, the General Assembly has answered this argument for us. KRS 39A.180(2) suspends any inconsistent laws. To the extent KRS Chapter 13A requires more than KRS Chapter 39A, the regular process applicable to administrative regulations has been displaced.

[Temporary injunction issued by the trial court is reversed and the matter is remanded.]

NOTES AND QUESTIONS

1. *Judicial Review of Administrative Actions.* Several lawsuits have challenged COVID-19 restrictions issued through executive branch orders on the same grounds as those used by the plaintiffs in *Beshear*, and—while most of the public health measures at issue in those lawsuits survived—some did not. For example, in *Wisconsin Legislature v. Palm*, 942 N.W.2d 900 (Wis. 2020), the Wisconsin legislature challenged a statewide "Safer at Home" order issued by the state's chief health officer in response to the population health risks posed by the COVID-19 pandemic. The legislature pursued two claims. First, the legislature alleged that the order was, in fact, a "rule" under the state's administrative procedures act and was void because it was issued without following "rulemaking" procedures. A majority of the Wisconsin Supreme Court was persuaded. The Court held that, because the executive order required individuals statewide to stay at home except to conduct certain essential tasks and close all non-essential businesses statewide, it was an agency action of "general applicability" and thus was a rule subject to standard or emergency rulemaking procedures. A dissenting opinion argued that the majority failed to account adequately for language in the public health agency's authorizing statute that empowers the agency to promulgate rules and issue "orders" necessary to protect population health. Additionally, the dissent highlighted the absurdity of relying on emergency rulemaking to respond to a fast-moving infectious disease threat because even emergency rules require between 18 and 49 days to be implemented.

Second, the legislature argued that the statute authorizing the Wisconsin Department of Health Services to all actions "necessary" to protect public health against an infectious disease threat lacked the substantive specificity and procedural safeguards required to delegate legislative authority to an executive agency. Again, a majority of the Court agreed. Rather than rely on a constitutional non-delegation doctrine, the Court based its holding on a state statute that required all agency actions to be based on an explicit, statutory delegation of authority. The majority ruled that this statute eliminated the state's public health agency's ability to rely on its broadly worded authority in its enabling statute (to take all actions necessary to prevent the spread of communicable diseases) as the basis for its Safer at Home order.

2.   *Non-Delegation Doctrine.* The non-delegation doctrine prohibits the legislative branch from generally delegating its legislative authority to any other branch of government, but it permits such delegations where the legislature has provided an "intelligible principle" that will guide and constrain those exercising the delegated powers. A key issue is whether statutes broadly authorizing executive agencies and officials to take any and all actions "necessary to protect the public health" from disease threats constitute an "intelligible principle."

In *Beshear*, the Kentucky Supreme Court held that such broad language provided an intelligible principle because the statute attempted to account for a wide variety of emergencies that could arise, which justified the use of broadly worded language designed to direct its use, and because the state legislature is often not in session. Several other courts have addressed the same issue. In Casey v. Lamont, 258 A.3d 647 (Conn. 2021), for example, a state statute granted emergency power to the governor to achieve "the efficient and expeditious execution of civil preparedness functions or the protection of the public health" and to take "such other steps as are reasonably necessary in the light of the emergency to protect the health, safety and welfare of the people of the state." The court held that the statute provides an "intelligible principle" limiting that power and thus was not an unconstitutional delegation of legislative authority to the executive branch. Similarly, in Newsom v. Superior Ct. of Sutter Cty., 278 Cal. Rptr. 3d 397 (Cal. App. 2021), the statement in an emergency management statute that its purpose is "to ensure that 'all emergency services functions' of the State and local governments, the federal government, and 'private agencies of every type,' 'be coordinated . . . to the end that the most effective use be made of all manpower, resources, and facilities for dealing with any emergency that may occur' " was held sufficient "to direct implementation of legislative policy" and thus was not an unconstitutional delegation of legislative authority to the executive branch. But see, e.g., In re Certified Questions From United States Dist. Ct., W. Dist. of Michigan, S. Div., 958 N.W.2d 1 (2020) (delegation of power to governor under expansive emergency powers statute to "promulgate reasonable orders, rules, and regulations as he or she considers necessary to protect life and property" lacked sufficient legislative guidance and thus was an unconstitutional delegation of legislative authority to the executive branch).

3.   *Rules vs. Orders.* During the COVID-19 pandemic, several courts in addition to those in *Beshear* and *Wisconsin Legislature* have addressed the distinction between administrative "rules" and "orders" as those are defined in a state administrative procedure act (APA). See, e.g., Grisham v. Romero, 483 P.3d 545 (N. Mex. 1021) (suggesting that emergency public health orders are not rules because they do not create standards for the future but, instead, respond temporarily to current emergency circumstances, and holding that the

state statute authorizing health officials to close businesses so as to protect population health creates a power to issue orders in addition to the power to promulgate rules). The Model State APA defines an order as "an agency decision that determines or declares the rights, duties, privileges, immunities, or other interests of a specific person," and it defines a rule as "an agency statement of general applicability that implements, interprets, or prescribes law or policy . . . and has the force of law." Because state and local mask orders, stay-at-home orders, and other social distancing orders issued during the pandemic apply to populations rather than specifically named individuals, they arguably fit the definition of being an administrative "rule." Rules—unlike orders—are subject to time-consuming procedures such as publishing notice of the proposed rule and providing time for public comment.

The Model State APA recognizes an exception for emergency rules designed to protect, among other things, public health. Yet such emergency rules expire after six months and, in some jurisdictions, cannot be renewed. See, e.g., Grisham v. Romero, cited above, which describes such limitations to emergency rulemaking. How does the distinction between administrative rules and orders affect legal preparedness for infectious disease threats?

4. *Legislative Claw-Back of Executive Public Health Powers.* State legislators unhappy with executive orders designed to prevent the spread of COVID-19 and unsatisfied with judicial application of doctrines related to the separation of powers have used their legislative powers to claw back public health powers from governors and executive branch public health agencies and officials. For example, new legislation in Ohio authorizes the state legislature to rescind any order or rule issued by the state's department of health or its director. Ohio Rev. Code Ann. § 101.36. Montana has enacted legislation that authorizes local legislative bodies to override emergency public health orders of local public health officials and that prohibits local public health officials from taking any action during an emergency that would interfere in any way with a person's attending a religious service in person or with the operation of a place of worship. Mont. Code Ann. § 50–2–118. For additional examples and an analysis of the risk associated with such legislative claw-backs, see NACCHO & Network for Public Health Law, Proposed Limits on Public Health Authority: Dangerous for Public Health (May 2021).

PROBLEM: EBOLA AND RETURNING AID WORKER

Chris is a nurse who volunteers with the organization "Nurses Without Borders" (NWB) to provide international medical aid. He spent the last 4 weeks treating Ebola patients in Liberia. While there, Chris wore head-to-toe protective gear (including gloves and enclosed headgear) whenever he was treating patients. He never experienced a needle prick, and neither his skin nor any other part of his body ever came into direct contact with the bodily fluids of, or any object that had come into contact with, any patient. The CDC's Ebola factsheet states:

Ebola . . . is a rare and deadly disease caused by infection with one of the Ebola virus species. . . .

Ebola is spread through direct contact (through broken skin or unprotected mucous membranes in, for example, the eyes, nose, or mouth) with:

- blood or body fluids (including but not limited to feces, saliva, sweat, urine, vomit, breast milk, and semen) of a person who is sick with Ebola,

- objects (like needles and syringes) that have been contaminated with the virus, . . .

- and . . . possibly from contact with semen from a man who has recovered from Ebola (for example, by having oral, vaginal, or anal sex).

Ebola is not spread through the air or by water, or in general, by food. . . . There is no evidence that mosquitos or other insects can transmit Ebola virus. . . .

A person infected with Ebola virus is not contagious until symptoms appear. Signs and symptoms of Ebola include: fever, severe headache, fatigue, muscle pain, weakness, diarrhea, vomiting, stomach pain, unexplained bleeding or bruising. Symptoms may appear anywhere from 2 to 21 days after exposure to the virus, but the average is 8 to 10 days.

There is a 24- to 48-hour time period after a person infected with Ebola first experiences a fever, headache or fatigue before he exhibits the "wet symptoms" (diarrhea, vomiting, bleeding) that pose a significant risk of transmission to others. Thus, of the roughly 30,000 Ebola cases recorded over 42 years, all have resulted from an uninfected person coming into contact with the wet symptoms of an infected person. There are no recorded cases of an infected person transmitting Ebola to another while experiencing only fever, headache or fatigue.

Throughout his deployment in Liberia, Chris felt fine. A day after his last shift, he took a series of flights until he re-entered the U.S. at Newark International Airport in New Jersey. Again, Chris felt fine throughout his return trip, and he did not display any symptoms.

When Chris de-planed in New Jersey, a U.S. Department of Homeland Security (DHS) officer asked him whether he had traveled to any west African countries, and Chris replied, "Yes, I was stationed with NWB in Liberia." The DHS officer asked if Chris had had any contact with any person sick with Ebola, and Chris said he had been treating Ebola patients as part of his deployment. The officer asked Chris additional questions about his exposure to Ebola patients and his health. Chris explained that he had worn protective gear whenever he treated a patient, that he had never come into direct contact with any patient, and that he had no other exposure to Ebola other than while treating his patients. Chris also reported that his health was fine. The officer noted that Chris did not report or appear to be suffering from any symptoms of any illness. Additionally, the officer took Chris's temperature three times, and each time it was normal.

The DHS officer asked Chris to wait while he informed New Jersey public health officials about Chris's status and the fact that DHS was about to permit him to enter New Jersey. An hour later, a New Jersey public health official visited Chris and told him that, "in an abundance of caution," the state would quarantine him at a nearby hospital until the incubation period for Ebola lapsed in about 19 days.

Is the proposed quarantine of Chris constitutional? If so, why? If not, what, if any, public health action may the state of New Jersey take without violating the federal Constitution?

VI.   NON-COMMUNICABLE DISEASE AND PUBLIC HEALTH

Public health has focused primarily on infectious disease. Yet, several non-communicable diseases pose greater threats. The CDC has identified heart disease, cancer, chronic lower respiratory disease, stroke, and diabetes as among the ten leading causes of death in the U.S. Actions by public health agencies designed to reduce the incidence of these diseases— restrictions on tobacco use, warnings on cigarette boxes, disclosure of fast-food nutritional information—often face legal challenge because those actions seek to change individual lifestyles and because those actions are opposed by entrenched business interests.

BOREALI V. AXELROD
Court of Appeals of New York, 1987.
517 N.E.2d 1350.

TITONE, J.

We hold that the Public Health Council overstepped the boundaries of its lawfully delegated authority when it promulgated a comprehensive code to govern tobacco smoking in areas that are open to the public. While the Legislature has given the Council broad authority to promulgate regulations on matters concerning the public health, the scope of the Council's authority under its enabling statute must be deemed limited by its role as an administrative, rather than a legislative, body. In this instance, the Council usurped the latter role and thereby exceeded its legislative mandate, when, following the Legislature's inability to reach an acceptable balance, the Council weighed the concerns of nonsmokers, smokers, affected businesses and the general public and, without any legislative guidance, reached its own conclusions about the proper accommodation among those competing interests. In view of the political, social and economic, rather than technical, focus of the resulting regulatory scheme, we conclude that the Council's actions were ultra vires and that the order and judgment of the courts below, which declared the Council's regulations invalid, should be affirmed.

I. LEGISLATIVE BACKGROUND
AND REGULATORY SCHEME

More than two decades ago, the Surgeon General of the United States began warning the American public that tobacco smoking poses a serious health hazard. Within the past five years, there has been mounting evidence that even nonsmokers face a risk of lung cancer as a result of their exposure to tobacco smoke in the environment. As a consequence, smoking in the workplace and other indoor settings has become a cause for serious concern among health professionals [ ].

This growing concern about the deleterious effects of tobacco smoking led our State Legislature to enact a bill in 1975 restricting smoking in certain designated areas, specifically, libraries, museums, theaters and public transportation facilities [ ]. Efforts during the same year to adopt more expansive restrictions on smoking in public places were, however, unsuccessful. . . .

In late 1986 the Public Health Council (PHC) took action of its own. Purportedly acting pursuant to the broad grant of authority contained in its enabling statute [ ], the PHC published proposed rules, held public hearings and, in February of 1987, promulgated the final set of regulations prohibiting smoking in a wide variety of indoor areas that are open to the public, including schools, hospitals, auditoriums, food markets, stores, banks, taxicabs and limousines. Under these rules, restaurants with seating capacities of more than 50 people are required to provide contiguous nonsmoking areas sufficient to meet customer demand. Further, employers are required to provide smoke-free work areas for nonsmoking employees and to keep common areas free of smoke, with certain limited exceptions for cafeterias and lounges. Affected businesses are permitted to prohibit all smoking on the premises if they so choose. Expressly excluded from the regulations' coverage are restaurants with seating capacities of less than 50, conventions, trade shows, bars, private homes, private automobiles, private social functions, hotel and motel rooms and retail tobacco stores. . . .

II. PROCEDURAL HISTORY

[Several parties affected by the PHC's antismoking regulations sued, and a trial court set aside the regulations, holding that they exceeded PHC's statutory authority. An intermediate appellate court affirmed, and this appeal followed.]

III. ANALYSIS

Preliminarily, we stress that this case presents no question concerning the wisdom of the challenged regulations, the propriety of the procedures by which they were adopted or the right of government in general to promulgate restrictions on the use of tobacco in public places. The degree of scientific support for the regulations and their unquestionable value in protecting those who choose not to smoke are, likewise, not pertinent except as background information. Finally, there has been no argument made concerning the personal freedoms of smokers or their "right" to pursue in public a habit that may inflict serious harm on others who must breathe the same air. The only dispute is whether the challenged restrictions were properly adopted by an administrative agency acting under a general grant of authority and in the face of the Legislature's apparent inability to establish its own broad policy on the controversial problem of passive smoking. Accordingly, we address no other issue in this appeal.

A.   The Delegation/Separation of Powers Issue

Section 225(5)(a) of the Public Health Law authorizes the PHC to "deal with any matters affecting the . . . public health". At the heart of the present case is the question whether this broad grant of authority contravened the oft-recited principle that the legislative branch of government cannot cede its fundamental policymaking responsibility to an administrative agency. As a related matter, we must also inquire whether, assuming the propriety of the Legislature's grant of authority, the agency exceeded the permissible scope of its mandate by using it as a basis for engaging in inherently legislative activities. . . .

However facially broad, a legislative grant of authority must be construed, whenever possible, so that it is no broader than that which the separation of powers doctrine permits [ ]. Even under the broadest and most open-ended of statutory mandates, an administrative agency may not use its authority as a license to correct whatever societal evils it perceives [ ]. Here, we cannot say that the broad enabling statute in issue is itself an unconstitutional delegation of legislative authority. However, we do conclude that the agency stretched that statute beyond its constitutionally valid reach when it used the statute as a basis for drafting a code embodying its own assessment of what public policy ought to be. Our reasons follow.

Derived from the separation of powers doctrine, the principle that the legislative branch may not delegate all of its law-making powers to the executive branch has been applied with the utmost reluctance—even in the early case law. . . .

The modern view is reflected in this court's statement in *Matter of Levine v. Whalen* [ ]: "Because of the constitutional provision that '[t]he legislative power of this State shall be vested in the Senate and the Assembly' (NY Const, art III, § 1), the Legislature cannot pass on its law-making functions to other bodies ... but there is no constitutional prohibition against the delegation of power, with reasonable safeguards and standards, to an agency or commission to administer the law as enacted by the Legislature"....

* * *

A number of coalescing circumstances that are present in this case persuade us that the difficult-to-define line between administrative rule-making and legislative policymaking has been transgressed. While none of these circumstances, standing alone, is sufficient to warrant the conclusion that the PHC has usurped the Legislature's prerogative, all of these circumstances, when viewed in combination, paint a portrait of an agency that has improperly assumed for itself "[t]he open-ended discretion to choose ends" [ ], which characterizes the elected Legislature's role in our system of government.

First, while generally acting to further the laudable goal of protecting nonsmokers from the harmful effects of "passive smoking," the PHC has, in reality, constructed a regulatory scheme laden with exceptions based solely upon economic and social concerns. The exemptions the PHC has carved out for bars, convention centers, small restaurants, and the like, as well as the provision it has made for "waivers" based on financial hardship, have no foundation in considerations of public health. Rather, they demonstrate the agency's own effort to weigh the goal of promoting health against its social cost and to reach a suitable compromise....

Striking the proper balance among health concerns, cost and privacy interests, however, is a uniquely legislative function. While it is true that many regulatory decisions involve weighing economic and social concerns against the specific values that the regulatory agency is mandated to promote, the agency in this case has not been authorized to structure its decision making in a "cost-benefit" model [ ] and, in fact, has not been given any legislative guidelines at all for determining how the competing concerns of public health and economic cost are to be weighed. Thus, to the extent that the agency has built a regulatory scheme on its own conclusions about the appropriate balance of trade-offs between health and cost to particular industries in the private sector, it was "acting solely on [its] own ideas of sound public policy" and was therefore operating outside of its proper sphere of authority [ ]. This conclusion is particularly compelling here, where the focus is on administratively created exemptions rather than on rules that promote the legislatively expressed goals, since exemptions ordinarily run counter to such goals and, consequently, cannot be justified as simple implementations of legislative values [ ]....

The second, and related, consideration is that in adopting the antismoking regulations challenged here the PHC did not merely fill in the details of broad legislation describing the over-all policies to be implemented. Instead, the PHC wrote on a clean slate, creating its own comprehensive set of rules without benefit of legislative guidance. Viewed in that light, the agency's actions were a far cry from the "interstitial" rule making that typifies administrative regulatory activity [ ].

A third indicator that the PHC exceeded the scope of the authority properly delegated to it by the Legislature is the fact that the agency acted in an area in which the Legislature had repeatedly tried—and failed—to reach agreement in the face of substantial public debate and vigorous lobbying by a variety of interested factions. While we have often been reluctant to ascribe persuasive significance to legislative inaction [ ], our usual hesitancy in this area has no place here. Unlike the cases in which we have been asked to consider the Legislature's failure to act as some indirect proof of its actual intentions [ ], in this case it is appropriate for us to consider the significance of legislative inaction as evidence that the Legislature has so far been unable to reach agreement on the goals and methods that should govern in resolving a society-wide health problem. Here, the repeated failures by the Legislature to arrive at such an agreement do not automatically entitle an administrative agency to take it upon itself to fill the vacuum and impose a solution of its own. Manifestly, it is the province of the people's elected representatives, rather than appointed administrators, to resolve difficult social problems by making choices among competing ends.

Finally, although indoor smoking is unquestionably a health issue, no special expertise or technical competence in the field of health was involved in the development of the antismoking regulations challenged here. Faced with mounting evidence about the hazards to bystanders of indoor smoking, the PHC drafted a simple code describing the locales in which smoking would be prohibited and providing exemptions for various special interest groups. . . .

In summary, we conclude that while Public Health Law § 225 (5) (a) is a valid delegation of regulatory authority, it cannot be construed to encompass the policy-making activity at issue here without running afoul of the constitutional separation of powers doctrine. . . .

* * *

Accordingly, the order of the Appellate Division should be affirmed.

NOTES AND QUESTIONS

1. *Administrative Law. Boreali* is representative of constitutional and administrative law challenges to public health actions aimed at non-communicable diseases. Because public health measures are commonly taken

by local, state, and federal agencies, doctrines such as separation-of-powers, non-delegation, and *ultra vires* can curtail public health powers. For example, the same court that decided *Boreali* later set aside a "soda ban" that prohibited many businesses from selling sugary drinks in sizes larger than 16 ounces—a measure designed to help fight obesity. See New York Statewide Coalition of Hispanic Chambers of Commerce v. New York City Dept. of Health & Mental Hygiene, 16 N.E.3d 538, 992 N.Y.S.2d 480, 23 N.Y.3d 681 (2014); c.f. NYC C.L.A.S.H., Inc. v. New York State Office of Parks, Recreation and Historic Preservation, 27 N.Y.3d 174, 51 N.E.3d 512, 32 N.Y.S.3d 1 (2016) (using the *Boreali* factors to uphold agency's outdoor smoking ban in parts of New York City's parks, historic places, and recreational facilities).

2.   *Free Speech and Public Health.* The First Amendment, through the commercial speech doctrine, has also been interpreted so as to limit public health authority and expand the rights of tobacco, food, and drug manufacturers. For example, in Sorrell v. IMS Health, 564 U.S. 552 (2011), the Supreme Court struck down a Vermont statute restricting the collection and disclosure of pharmacy prescribing records of individual physicians. The Court held that the restriction suppressed protected speech under the First Amendment. It then applied heightened scrutiny, requiring the State to show that the statute "directly advanced" a "substantial governmental interest" and that it was "drawn to achieve" that interest, meaning that there must be "a fit between the legislature's ends and the means chosen to accomplish those ends." Under this standard, the Court held that Vermont's interests in protecting physician privacy, preventing harassing sales behavior by manufacturers, and preserving the doctor-patient relationship were not sufficient justifications for the restriction. Additionally, it ruled that the State failed to establish a fit between the restrictions and the State's goals of promoting public health and lowering medical costs.

By giving little weight to the State's interest in protecting public health, *Sorrel* undermines the stability of laws restricting language used to market food, tobacco, and prescription drugs, as well as laws mandating certain disclosures. For example, the Second Circuit subsequently ruled that off-label promotion of a pharmaceutical was protected commercial speech subject to at least heightened scrutiny. See U.S. v. Caronia, 703 F.3d 149 (2d Cir. 2012). Meanwhile, the D.C. Circuit flip-flopped on whether regulators may justify disclosure mandates based on interests other than correcting prior deception. In R.J. Reynolds Tobacco Co. v. FDA, 696 F.3d 1205 (D.C. Cir. 2012), the court set aside FDA regulations requiring cigarette manufacturers to place graphic warnings on packaging, holding that the First Amendment requires the government to first establish that existing cigarette packaging is misleading to consumers, which it did not show. But two years later, in American Meat Inst. v. U.S. Dept. of Agriculture, 760 F.3d 18 (D.C. Cir. 2014), the same court overruled its decision in *R.J. Reynolds*.

By broadening commercial speech protection and narrowing the discretion of public health officials, First Amendment doctrine poses a significant challenge to improving population health. See Joshua Sharfstein, Public Health and the First Amendment, 93 Milbank Q. 459 (2015).

PROBLEM: OBESITY AS A PUBLIC HEALTH PROBLEM

As a legislator in your state, you have become very concerned about obesity in the population, and you are worried about the long-range consequences of this condition on the vitality of the public. In particular, you have become concerned about the proliferation of fast-food sites that offer primarily economical but very high fat foods. You are concerned about "food deserts" in your state—areas where there are no supermarkets and limited public transportation. You are also disturbed by the relatively unhealthy foods available at the public schools throughout the state, many of which have contracts with beverage companies to run their vending machines and snack bars, and by the disappearance of mandatory physical education requirements at the high school level. There is also evidence that a comparatively sedentary lifestyle that includes watching television and playing video games contributes to what some have called the "epidemic" of obesity. Furthermore, studies have repeatedly shown that obesity alone is not a predictor for shortened lifespans or significantly greater health risks. Rather, a lack of exercise or fitness is more closely associated with health risks than is obesity. A person can be obese and healthy.

Is the problem of obesity a "public health" problem, or simply a problem for some individuals? What qualifies as "obesity" for public health purposes? Is it a matter of personal responsibility that should be unrelated to the obligations of the law? Would it make any difference if you classified obesity as a "public health" problem? What legal responses might be available to the state legislature to address this problem? Are there ways to use school law, tax law, criminal law, tort law, food and drug law, insurance rate-setting, public program eligibility standards or general public health regulatory law to address this problem? What evidence is there that pulling any of these legal levers would be effective at lowering the incidence of obesity? What are the legal, political and social consequences of doing so? Are there civil liberty interests of persons who are obese (or others) that are at stake in using the law in this way? Do you feel the same way about tobacco, gun violence, bullying, or "extreme sports" as public health problems?

INDEX

References are to Pages